Jocelyn Taeger

P9-EDY-546

UNDER THE GENERAL EDITORSHIP OF

# Perry Miller
*Late of Harvard University*


THE EDITORS

NEWTON ARVIN
*Late of Smith College*

MARIUS BEWLEY
*Fordham University*

LOUISE BOGAN

WILLIAM CHARVAT
*Ohio State University*

RICHARD CHASE
*Late of Columbia University*

EDWARD H. DAVIDSON
*University of Illinois*

F. W. DUPEE
*Columbia University*

NORTHROP FRYE
*Victoria College, University of Toronto*

WILLIAM L. HEDGES
*Goucher College*

IRVING HOWE
*Stanford University*

ALVIN B. KERNAN
*Yale University*

J. C. LEVENSON
*University of Minnesota*

R. W. B. LEWIS
*Yale University*

KENNETH S. LYNN
*Harvard University*

PERRY MILLER
*Late of Harvard University*

MARK SCHORER
*University of California, Berkeley*

HENRY NASH SMITH
*University of California, Berkeley*

RICHARD WILBUR
*Wesleyan University*

This edition of *Major Writers of America*
was prepared under the editorship of
JEAN C. SISK
*Baltimore County Board of Education*

# MAJOR WRITERS OF AMERICA

**SHORTER EDITION**

Franklin · Edwards · Irving · Cooper
Bryant · Poe · Emerson · Thoreau
Hawthorne · Longfellow · Lowell
Melville · Whitman · Dickinson
Mark Twain · James · Crane · O'Neill
Frost · Anderson · Fitzgerald
Hemingway · Faulkner

HARCOURT, BRACE & WORLD, INC.

NEW YORK    CHICAGO    SAN FRANCISCO    ATLANTA    DALLAS

COPYRIGHTS AND ACKNOWLEDGMENTS

SHERWOOD ANDERSON. "The Corn-Planting" by Sherwood Anderson from *American Magazine* of November 1934, copyright 1934, renewed © 1962 by Eleanor Anderson; "The Egg" from *The Triumph of the Egg* by Sherwood Anderson, copyright 1920, renewed 1948 by Eleanor Anderson; selection from *A Story Teller's Story* by Sherwood Anderson, copyright 1924 by B. W. Huebsch, Inc., renewed 1951 by Eleanor Copenhaver Anderson. Reprinted by permission of Harold Ober Associates Incorporated. Selections from *Letters of Sherwood Anderson,* edited by H. M. Jones and Walter Rideout, copyright 1953 by Eleanor Anderson. Reprinted by permission of Little, Brown and Company.

STEPHEN CRANE. "A Man Adrift on a Slim Spar" from *The Collected Poems of Stephen Crane,* edited by Wilson Follett, copyright 1930 by Alfred A. Knopf, Inc. Reprinted by permission of the publishers. "Tell me not in joyous numbers" from *The Poetry of Stephen Crane,* edited by Daniel G. Hoffman, © 1957 by Columbia University Press. Reprinted by permission of the publishers and the Columbia University Libraries.

EMILY DICKINSON. Selections from *The Poems of Emily Dickinson,* edited by Thomas H. Johnson, copyright 1951, 1955 by The President and Fellows of Harvard College; selections from *The Letters of Emily Dickinson,* edited by Thomas H. Johnson and Theodora V. W. Ward, copyright 1958 by The President and Fellows of Harvard College. Reprinted by permission of Houghton Mifflin Company, the Trustees of Amherst College, and the publishers, The Belknap Press of Harvard University Press, Cambridge, Mass. Selections from *The Complete Poems of Emily Dickinson,* edited by Thomas H. Johnson, copyright 1914, 1924, 1935, 1942 by Martha Dickinson Bianchi, copyright 1929, © 1957 by Mary L. Hampson. Reprinted by permission of Little, Brown and Company. Selection from *The Life and Letters of Emily Dickinson* by Martha Dickinson Bianchi. Reprinted by permission of Houghton Mifflin Company.

WILLIAM FAULKNER. "The Bear" by William Faulkner, copyright 1942 by The Curtis Publishing Company. Reprinted by permission of Random House, Inc. An enlarged version of this story appears in *Go Down, Moses* by William Faulkner.

F. SCOTT FITZGERALD. "The Crack-Up" from *The Crack-Up* by F. Scott Fitzgerald, edited by Edmund Wilson, copyright 1945 by New Directions. Reprinted by permission of the publishers. "The Ice Palace" from *Flappers and Philosophers* by F. Scott Fitzgerald, copyright 1920 by The Curtis Publishing Company, renewed 1948 by Zelda Fitzgerald. Reprinted by permission of Charles Scribner's Sons.

ROBERT FROST. Introduction by Robert Frost to *The Arts Anthology: Dartmouth Verse 1925,* all rights reserved. Reprinted by permission of the Trustees of Dartmouth College, the Estate of Robert Frost, and Holt, Rinehart and Winston, Inc. Selections from *Complete Poems of Robert Frost,* copyright 1916, 1921, 1923, 1928, 1930, 1934, 1939, 1947, 1949 by Holt, Rinehart and Winston, Inc.; copyright 1936, 1942, 1944, 1951, © 1956, 1958, 1962 by Robert Frost. Reprinted by permission of the publishers.

NATHANIEL HAWTHORNE. Selections from *The English Notebooks of Nathaniel Hawthorne,* edited by Randall Stewart. Reprinted by permission of the Modern Language Association. Selections from *The American Notebooks of Nathaniel Hawthorne,* edited by Randall Stewart. Reprinted by permission of the Ohio State University Press.

ERNEST HEMINGWAY. "Could Man Be Drunk For Ever" from *The Collected Poems of A. E. Housman,* copyright 1922 by Holt, Rinehart and Winston, Inc., renewed 1950 by Barclays Bank Ltd. Reprinted by permission of Holt, Rinehart and Winston, Inc., The Society of Authors as the literary representative of the Estate of the late A. E. Housman, and Messrs. Jonathan Cape Ltd., publishers of A. E. Housman's *Collected Poems.* Selections from *The Green Hills of Africa,* pp. 2–9, 18–28, by Ernest Hemingway, copyright 1935 by Charles Scribner's Sons, renewed © 1963 by Mary Hemingway. Reprinted by permission of the publishers. "Big Two-Hearted River" from *In Our Time* by Ernest Hemingway, copyright 1925 by Charles Scribner's Sons, renewed 1953 by Ernest Hemingway. Reprinted by permission of the publishers.

HENRY JAMES. "The Real Thing" from *The Real Thing and Other Tales* by Henry James; 'Europe' from *The Soft Side* by Henry James. Reprinted by permission of John Farquharson Ltd. Selections from *The Notebooks of Henry James,* edited by F. O. Matthiessen and Kenneth B. Murdock, copyright 1947 by Oxford University Press, Inc. Reprinted by permission of the publishers.

HERMAN MELVILLE. *Billy Budd* from *Melville's Billy Budd,* edited by Frederick Barron Freeman and corrected by Elizabeth Treeman, copyright 1948, 1956 by The President and Fellows of Harvard College. Reprinted by permission of the publishers, Harvard University Press, Cambridge, Mass.

EUGENE O'NEILL. "Beyond the Horizon" from *The Plays of Eugene O'Neill,* copyright 1920, renewed 1947 by Eugene O'Neill. Reprinted by permission of Random House, Inc.

HENRY DAVID THOREAU. "Manhood" from *Collected Poems of Henry Thoreau,* edited by Carl Bode. Reprinted by permission of Hendricks House, Inc.

MARK TWAIN. "The Quarles Farm" from *Mark Twain's Autobiography,* copyright 1924 by Clara Gabrilowitsch. Reprinted by permission of Harper & Brothers. "Platform Readings" from *Mark Twain in Eruption,* edited by Bernard DeVoto, copyright 1922 by Harper & Brothers; "The War Prayer" from *Europe and Elsewhere* by Mark Twain, copyright 1923 by The Mark Twain Company; "Fenimore Cooper's Further Literary Offenses" by Mark Twain, copyright 1946 by The Mark Twain Company; "The Boys' Ambition" from *Life on the Mississippi* by Mark Twain; "Lost in a Snowstorm," "The Case of Hyde vs. Morgan," "The Story of the Old Ram," "The Coyote," and "Tom Quartz, the Cat" from *Roughing It* by Mark Twain; selection from "Jim Baker's Bluejay Yarn" from *A Tramp Abroad* by Mark Twain; "The Man That Corrupted Hadleyburg" by Mark Twain; "How to Tell a Story" by Mark Twain; "Colonel Sellers" from *The Gilded Age* by Mark Twain. Reprinted by permission of Harper & Row, Publishers, Incorporated. "Whittier Birthday Dinner Speech" by Samuel Clemens from *Harvard Library Bulletin,* Spring issue, 1955. Reprinted by permission of the Harvard College Library, Thomas G. Chamberlain, and Manufacturers Hanover Trust Company, Trustees of the Estate of Samuel L. Clemens. "Cruelty to Animals: The Histrionic Pig" from *Mark Twain's Travels with Mr. Brown,* edited by Franklin Walker and G. Ezra Dane, copyright 1940 by Alfred A. Knopf, Inc. Reprinted by permission of Thomas G. Chamberlain and Manufacturers Hanover Trust Company, Trustees of the Estate of Samuel L. Clemens.

*Library of Congress Catalog Card Number:* 66–14590

PRINTED IN THE UNITED STATES OF AMERICA

*HERE we find a vast stock of proper materials for the art and ingenuity of man to work on, — treasures of immense worth, concealed from the poor, ignorant, aboriginal natives. . . . As the celestial light of the gospel was directed here by the finger of God, it will doubtless finally drive the long, long night of heathenish darkness from America. . . . So arts and sciences will change the face of nature in their tour from hence over the Appalachian Mountains to the Western Ocean; and as they march through the vast desert, the residence of wild beasts will be broken up, and their obscene howl cease forever. Instead of which, the stones and trees will dance together at the music of Orpheus, the rocks will disclose their hidden gems, and the inestimable treasures of gold and silver be broken up. Huge mountains of iron ore are already discovered; and vast stores are reserved for future generations. This metal, more useful than gold and silver, will employ millions of hands, not only to form the martial sword and peaceful share alternately, but an infinity of utensils improved in the exercise of art and handicraft amongst men. . . . Shall not then these vast quarries that teem with mechanic stone, — those for structure be piled into great cities, and those for sculpture into statues, to perpetuate the honor of renowned heroes — even those who shall now save their country? O ye unborn inhabitants of America! should this page escape its destined conflagration at the year's end, and these alphabetical letters remain legible when your eyes behold the sun after he has rolled the seasons round for two or three centuries more, you will know that in Anno Domini, 1758, we dreamed of your times.*

NATHANIEL AMES

*from* Almanac (1758)

# Contents

[vii]

## JAMES FENIMORE COOPER WILLIAM CULLEN BRYANT

EDITED BY
Marius Bewley

## EDGAR ALLAN POE

EDITED BY
Richard Wilbur

# RALPH WALDO EMERSON
### EDITED BY
### Newton Arvin

# HENRY DAVID THOREAU
### EDITED BY
### Kenneth S. Lynn

# NATHANIEL HAWTHORNE
### EDITED BY
### Edward H. Davidson

# HENRY WADSWORTH LONGFELLOW JAMES RUSSELL LOWELL
### EDITED BY
### William Charvat

# HERMAN MELVILLE
### EDITED BY
### Richard Chase

# WALT WHITMAN

### EDITED BY
## R. W. B. Lewis

# EMILY DICKINSON

### EDITED BY
## Northrop Frye

# MARK TWAIN

### EDITED BY
Henry Nash Smith

# HENRY JAMES

### EDITED BY
F. W. Dupee

# SHERWOOD ANDERSON
# F. SCOTT FITZGERALD
# ERNEST HEMINGWAY

EDITED BY
## Mark Schorer

# WILLIAM FAULKNER

EDITED BY
## Irving Howe

# A Preface

MAJOR WRITERS OF AMERICA is made possible at this point in time not so much because the energies of its editors have been prodigious but because the study of American literature—inside and outside the universities—is now systematic and mature. This happy state of affairs is relatively recent. In fact, like the professional study of English literature, it is only about seventy-five years old. Of the two literatures, however, the American remained largely terra incognita for several decades after its discovery. History repeated itself: the Old World was settled first. Yet the New did not lack for those who could rise to the challenge of its promise. The essential landmarks were discerned. The terrain was mapped. In the perspective of these seventy-five years of discovery and exploration then, the present work acknowledges many profound debts: to the pioneer adventurers, such as Moses Coit Tyler, William Peterfield Trent, and Barrett Wendell; to subsequent masters who are represented herein by entries in the bibliographies as well as by their students; and, further, to a host of scholars contemporary with the editors, often younger than they, who attest the vitality of the vocation.

It was altogether natural that in the initial stages of this American "Great Instauration," claimants to academic dignity should strive to impress their colleagues in departments devoted to the magnificent literatures of England or of the Continent or of antiquity by heaping up as mountainous a bulk of American expression as research could excavate. While it was indisputably evident that American literary history was of painfully short duration—commencing with the seventeenth century and even then for a hundred years or more offering only "colonial" documents —still there were unearthed such permanently significant minorities as Philip Freneau, Joel Barlow, Charles Brockden Brown, and the authors of *The Contrast* and *Modern Chivalry*.

These beginnings made, the advance continued into the wilderness. New recruits expended tremendous energy in "rediscovering" forgotten authors—or sometimes in actually discovering those who had never been known at all. Among the former the pre-eminent names are Herman Melville and Emily Dickinson; among the latter, Edward Taylor. The great object in view was to establish the canon of American literature on as broad a basis as possible. Nothing canonizes literature more quickly than print. It followed that anthologies of constantly increasing poundage were compiled, and with an ever lengthening array of persons deserving inclusion, if only because they had written in America or about American things. The tacit assumption of almost all these productions was that they had to silence professional rivals who would constantly inquire, with eyebrows raised in elaborately simulated ignorance, "American literature? Oh, is there any?"

Today, after seven or eight decades of skirmishing, the battle for American literature is won. It is established as a reputable and incontestable subdivision of the English department. Courses in it proliferate. Outside the academies it has triumphed even more conclusively: hundreds of "popular" surveys, biographies, interpretations—most of them eschewing the stigmata of scholarship—are sold annually. In fact, among conscientious practitioners a dreadful anxiety now arises for fear the victory has been too overwhelming. No doubt, Philip Freneau—to take him as a test case—is a fascinating figure; but is it really a healthy curriculum which requires that he be read by a student who is utterly ignorant of Racine?

The premise of *Major Writers of America* is by no means intended as a hostile comment on those compilations which exhibit the now vast accumulation of American writings. A serious student of American civilization must come to terms with Philip Freneau, as with a multitude of his stature. Yet, while the canon is at long last becoming established, a realization gradually forces itself upon us that, as the age of discovery and of elementary mapping closes, the era of evaluation opens. Not that any piece of terrain, however minute, should be forgotten once more; nor should any possible open territory be foreclosed. Yet it is incumbent upon us to make clear which are the few peaks and which the many low-lying hills. We must, if we can, suppress an undiscriminating pedantry by distinguishing just wherein the great are truly great. We must set apart those who belong to world literature rather than merely to local (or, to what is worse, regional) patriotism. We must vindicate the study of American literature primarily because the matter is literature, and only secondarily because it is American. For this end *Major Writers of America* has been designed.

The first requirement of the design, therefore, was inevitably that the authors so nominated be represented fully enough to testify to their superiority. This meant that exclusions had to be perpetrated with surgical ruthlessness. There can be no question that Edwards, Emerson, Hawthorne, Melville, James, and Twain belong. When the problem arises of, say, Longfellow or Whittier, decision necessarily becomes arbitrary. And, as the list extends into the twentieth century, determinations are bound to appear, even to those who make them, not much more than arbitrary or even capricious indulgences of taste. However, the editors stake their credibility upon the choices they have made; moreover they have endeavored in lengthy Introductions to make plain their particular sense of the writers from whose works they have made coherent selections.

An immediately apparent corollary of this policy was a recognition that for most writers of fiction no portions of long novels could be included. Spacious as these pages be, they are not copious enough to include all of *The Scarlet Letter, Moby-Dick, The Adventures of Huckleberry Finn, The Ambassadors*. Certain set-pieces, separable from the narrative in Cooper's romances, or the chapters reproduced from the autobiographies of Twain and Franklin that have an independence vigorous enough to sustain the separation, may legitimately be taken out of context. But no segments of more closely knit works of art can be so excised. The editors feel consoled for these omissions because by now inexpensive paperback reprints of all the formidable titles are available. Wherever possible we have exhibited the techniques of master storytellers in long short stories, with what Henry James liked to call the "blest *nouvelle*."

An anthology designed to give a generous sample of the record in all its representative particulars is obliged to include too many writers. The result inevitably distorts the literary stature of the more important writers. For the purposes of a historical survey, such even-handed continuity is necessary. When, however, attention is turned from the record itself to the delicate task of evaluation, no one editor, nor partnership of editors, is capable of supplying the essential discrimination. There still remains, of course, the need for respecting continuity, of remembering the historical forces, and, above all, for reverencing chronology. Also there persists an obligation to relate, in some degree, the works to the authors' biographies, especially when, as with Franklin, the historical biography is parallel to but far from identical with the literary rendition. Still, fully granting these considerations, the second requirement of our design demanded that each major author, or each grouping of major figures — where two or three writers obviously belong together — be dealt with by an editor solely responsible for the selection, the criticism, the annotations, and the bibliographies. Not only has there been no "party line" to which individual editors were obliged to cleave, there has been no substantive line whatsoever. Certain minor editorial uniformities have been maintained — e.g., minimum standards for what in the texts required footnoting and what did not — but these were kept to a reasonable minimum. There was also an implicit rule that each contributor should be dedicated to the highest standards of excellence and clarity he could conceive, but it never had to be explicitly promulgated.

In matters of spelling, punctuation, and capitalization editors have exercised their discretion. After the early decades of the nineteenth century, the standard printed texts have generally been followed. When two dates appear at the end of a selection, the earlier one is that of composition, the later ones, that of publication. Omissions within texts, when they constitute more than a paragraph, are indicated by the insertion of ellipses at the end of one paragraph and at the beginning of the next or by a full line of dots. Unless otherwise indicated, footnotes are those of the editor of the section. The bibliographies in the Teacher's Manual have been kept to an essential minimum for obvious reasons. The reader who wishes to pursue a writer further should turn to the third volume (*Bibliography*) of the Robert E. Spiller *et al. Literary History of the United States* (1948) and to the *Bibliographical Supplement* (1959) of the same work, edited by Richard M. Ludwig.

The General Editor thinks it fair to say that while this volume has been composed with the student chiefly in mind, yet the editors have striven to make *Major Writers of America* something more than a textbook. The concerted aim of the enterprise has been to construct a book which anyone might read with pleasure. We have thought of students as those who help to constitute the noble company of "general readers," not merely as students earning course credits. We have, in short, endeavored to pay both the student and the general reader the compliment of treating them as interchangeable designations.

The Publisher and the General Editor take pleasure in thanking the several editors for their patience and their readiness to heed suggestions and to conform their presentations to spatial formats dictated by practical necessities. In one sense, this thanks should also mention their cooperation, for cooperate in myriad ways they did. In a more basic sense, however, the thanks must recognize their healthy lack of cooperation. The finished achievement is in no strict sense a collaboration, the report of a committee of certified experts. Beyond agreement among contributors to cultivate their own gardens intensely and to raid the plots and seedbeds of others solely under the decorous excuse of enriching comparative judgments, no demands were made by Publisher or General Editor. But this is not to say that the American *writers* represented in the pages which follow left their editors alone. Quite the contrary. In fact, *Major Writers of America* may best be taken as a varied testimony to the force that the literature continues to exert over and against time. Such attraction at such a distance is what signalizes a major writer.

PERRY MILLER

*Cambridge, Massachusetts*
*December 15, 1961*

# MAJOR WRITERS OF AMERICA

PERRY MILLER
*Editor*

# Benjamin Franklin

### 1706–1790

# Jonathan Edwards

### 1703–1758

THE INTELLECTUAL history—or, if you will, the spiritual history—of the United States has been dramatized by a series of pairs of personalities, contemporaneous and contrasting, which have become avatars of the contradictory thrusts within our effort to find or to create a national identity.

To begin with, there is in primordial Virginia a swashbuckling adventurer, Captain John Smith, frankly announcing that only the search for wealth will found a commonwealth and that the wilderness will become a theater of gigantic economic exploitation: whereas, on the rock-bound and unfertile coast of New England there is William Bradford directing an energy no less Elizabethan toward the realization of a holy society. After the Revolution emerge the exemplary figures of Jefferson and Hamilton, who form the division between the political convictions that have since contended for mastery. In the Civil War the sectional strife finds its perfect symbolism in the opposition of Robert E. Lee and Abraham Lincoln. But of all these, and of several lesser pairs, the pre-eminently eloquent linked antagonists in American culture will always be Jonathan Edwards and Benjamin Franklin.

This duel is all the more eloquent, not because the two met in open debate, as did Jefferson and Hamilton in the 1790's—they showed little or no awareness of each other's existence—but because they started in their contrary directions from the same parent stock, the Puritanism of New England.

Puritans originally got their name from their enemies, because their avowed purpose in England was to "purify" the Church of England from what they considered the remnants of medieval Catholicism that still adhered to it—the hierarchy, vestments, prescribed prayers, and stated forms of traditional ritual. Puritans wanted life to be regulated precisely by the rules of the supreme legal code of Christendom, the whole Bible, which in their comprehension provided precepts for all departments of life—for family, economic activity, and political policy as well as for ecclesiastical polity. In theology the Puritans were at one with the other branches of international Calvinism—Swiss,

[3]

French, German, Dutch, and Scottish. But in this vast communion, the English Puritans were distinguished by the zeal with which they pressed theological considerations into the secular realms of human behavior.

A few of them, generally of the simpler and less prosperous sort, were so impelled by this temper that they became "Separatists." Wherefore, they were harried out of the land. One band eventually became the Pilgrims of Plymouth in Massachusetts Bay. However, the majority of Puritans refused to "separate" because they wanted to fight within the Church for ultimate conquest. They did not want even toleration, let alone liberty: they intended to rule. In 1630 that hope had become remote; hence a compact company, having somehow secured a charter from Charles I which bestowed legality upon the venture, arrived at the site of Boston. In the next decade some ten thousand followed; they expanded across Massachusetts and into Connecticut; from them comes everything that has been praised or cursed in America under the name of "Puritanism." From their ranks come the two most distinguished intellects and prose artists of the tradition, who in these selections pose for us the paradox of Puritan materialism and immateriality.

Franklin in the life of the world and Edwards in the life of the spirit both strove for, and each in his widely differing manner attained, a clarity, simplicity, directness—a suppression of all showy and "literary" embellishments—which is the lasting impress of the Puritan spirit upon American expression. Not, of course, that many writers have not revolted against it, including several lineal descendants of the Puritan founders; but on the whole, one is safe in saying that the literature of America is marked by its concern, often neurotic rather than sanative, that literature be not regarded as an end in itself, but that expression be put to work in the service of a creed, a career, a philosophy, a disgruntlement, or a rage.

This rule of efficiency as the governing purpose of the spoken or written word was part and parcel of the conception Puritans brought into the control of all areas of their behavior, most strenuously into that of their pecuniary labor. The whole complex of that code has been summarized by modern sociologists as "the Protestant ethic." Though elements of it may be found in all the emerging business cultures of the time, the English Puritans perfected it more highly than others in Europe, and the New England Puritans brought it to an even higher degree of articulation. Edwards in his pulpit and in his study, Franklin in his printing shop and in the diplomatic chambers of Versailles were both assiduously practicing the ethic of their fathers.

Fundamentally, this mentality was a revulsion against what Protestants held to be the unprofitable monasticism of the Medieval Church, which centered holiness upon withdrawal from the economy of production and distribution, which consigned these crass functions to the inferior orders of peasants or merchants. Instead, the Puritans declared, every "calling"—whether it be ditch-digging, fishing, sailing a vessel, managing a bank, governing a colony, or preaching a sermon—was as much a religious exercise as any other. In this view the clergy, though of course commisioned to instruct the yeomen in faith and morals, were no whit superior to their pupils. The great sin in their society was to endeavor to live without a calling, without being industrious at *something*, as did both the Catholic monk and the European nobleman. The Rev. John Cotton, in the classic New England formulation (printed in 1641, but spoken earlier), said, "If thou beest a man that lives without a calling, though thou hast two thousands to spend, yet if thou has no calling tending to public good, thou art an unclean beast." Yet the ethic was more subtle than merely an injunction to find a job and to work in it as a holy duty: it insisted that energy expended in a calling be regarded as a service for God, and not as a means of profit or of social betterment. Wherefore the Puritan exerts himself the more vigorously in proportion to the more—again in the language of Cotton—"he depends upon God for the quickening and sharpening of his gifts in that calling." That is, he applies himself stoutly, but he attributes success not to his efforts but only to the favor, the complaisance, of God. Likewise, if despite his most energetic performance he encounters disaster—a shipwreck, a plague of locusts, a military defeat—he perceives in the reversal a chastisement of the Lord, rained upon him for his sins. Thereupon he renews with increased vigor his assault upon prosperity.

Therefore, let us be clear that for the Puritan founders the same rationale served in either ditch-digging or manufacturing as in the physical act of putting words on paper: nobody was doing it to amuse himself or others, and not directly with the intention of making money or winning converts. He was doing the job in obedience to the commands of God, or of conscience, or of probity; but he did not, if he was sanctified, bank upon his own talents for success. He cultivated and improved them assiduously, day and night, in order to make an acceptable sacrifice of them to the Puritan Jehovah, who might then be graciously inclined to bestow the desired results, but who might also be inclined, with every right on His side, to reward the desperate effort with complete devastation. Although Franklin blithely put aside the theology out of which this peculiar code arose, he as much as Edwards exemplified it every day of his life. And Edwards, even while refashioning the Jehovah of early Puritanism into a highly impersonalized design of the Newtonian universe, went on offering himself a willing victim to the whims of a Divinity bound by no such rules of justice as were supposed to prevail in human intercourse.

For Edwards, the endeavor resulted in ghastly failure, in the abject humiliation of his dismissal from the Northampton pulpit in 1750, and in his eight years of penurious exile in Stockbridge. For Franklin, the application produced wealth, fame, and the universal approbation of his contemporaries and of posterity. Both of them, in the center of their beings, were indifferent to the consequences, ill or bountiful; both were so caught up, with or without theology, in a vision of ultimate disinterestedness in relation to which either personal triumph or defeat was inconse-

quential, that the most ethereal writings of Edwards can be easily translated into the most mundane of Franklin's frivolities. Yet the division is not superficial: it is profound, irreconcilable. It also provides a theme, probably the basic and sundering theme, of American literature.

II

# Benjamin Franklin

COMMENCING his *Autobiography* at the age of sixty-five in 1771, Franklin recollects that his father's small library contained books on polemic divinity which he read—always he would read anything that came to hand—and then serenely announces how he subsequently had regretted that "more proper" books had not fallen in his way. The revolutionary violence of Franklin's development is concealed in the casualness of this remark, which is, however, like everything he ever wrote, extremely calculated. This child of New England Puritanism simply dumped the whole theological preoccupation overboard; but, not in the slightest ceasing to be a Puritan, he went about his business.

And a very busy business it turned out to be. The mind of Jonathan Edwards is difficult for modern Americans to comprehend because it is so detached from the physical world: the mind of Franklin is equally a mystery because it is so utterly immersed in the world. The life of Edwards can be recounted in a few paragraphs, but the life of Franklin requires volumes. It is possible here to recite only a few of his infinite activities. A journalist of matchless skill, a dabbler in scientific research, where he made important contributions to experimental wisdom (most notably with the kite and key apparatus which won him the admiration of Europe), founder of a university and of the American Philosophical Society, organizer of the first police department in America and of the first fire department in the modern world, inventor of a stove, of bifocal lenses, and of a harmonica—one runs out of breath trying to enumerate his performances. Postmaster general of the colonies, he developed the most efficient delivery system the world had yet beheld. Starting with nothing, he accumulated a solid fortune before he was fifty. He matched his wits with the best brains of Europe, and never lost a trick. Everything he touched he made a success, gained a profit either for himself or for mankind, and always made the doing a delight.

In between times, he improved his leisure—thus in effect depriving himself of any!—by cultivating the convivial arts, by learning French, Spanish, Latin, and Greek, by writing skits and fantasies that rank with the most sophisticated productions of the age, and by producing one indisputable literary classic which, significantly, is about himself.

His birth itself furnishes the first of the myriad differences from Edwards. Where Edwards was born to the clerical elite, Franklin arose out of the yeoman laboring class, out of what Samuel Stone, a pioneer expounder of the New England church polity, had said should be a "silent democracy" in the face of a "speaking aristocracy." His father was a member of the old South Church; this means that he had made a profession of faith and was allowed to participate in the Lord's Supper, but we may be sure he bowed low and yielded the wall to Judge Sewall, also a member, whenever he encountered that worthy. As a worker in a shop Franklin wore the then customary garb, and later, even amid the splendors of Versailles, took care to remind courtiers that he was "a leather aproned man."

The *Autobiography* tells us how he first appeared as an author by working a deception upon his brother. Though he was but sixteen, he already possessed in full the powers of wit, a genial tolerance for all manifestations of humanity, and a resolute will to rise in the world by making fun of whatever stood in his way. By the time he organized his business in Philadelphia he could exhibit the breadth of his tolerance for the minutiae of existence by vending, in addition to his printing, a staggering variety of items, ranging from soap and ballads to quills, sherry, cheese, lottery tickets, linen rags, plus a

salve concocted by his mother-in-law, according to a secret formula, which was guaranteed to cure the itch.

All this was laboring in a calling with a vengeance! We may rest assured that Franklin spent as many hours a day at his occupation as did Edwards. It is important to insist that Franklin's pursuit was as much an abnegation of self as was Edwards'. But Edwards subjected himself to the unremitting discipline in the solitude of his study and let the results appear to his fellow men only in the terrible or serene moments of utterance from his exalted pulpit. Franklin found it not incompatible with a pure devotion to his function to allow his neighbors to behold the process.

There are those who sneer at the *Autobiography* as a vulgar book, brazenly narrating the cheapest piece of social climbing this democracy has ever known. Obviously, it is a success story, and one that often is maddeningly smug. But today we are apt not to notice how it modestly insinuates that Franklin did not proceed only upon an ulterior motive, not even when he pushed his newsprint conspicuously through the streets by wheelbarrow in order to impress the Quaker burghers of Philadelphia. His philosophy and his interest always coincided. We can readily see the splendid coherence of his "Apology for Printers," which is assuredly a brave manifesto for freedom of the press, for the independence of editors, and hence a document of prime importance in the growth of liberty in America. Yet it does include, as being on the same level of respectability with any of the resounding declarations, "I got five shillings by it."

This combination of disinterested devotion to a noble cause, for which Franklin repeatedly held himself as expendable as he did when he risked life and fortune in the Revolution in 1776, with a knack of making it pay in the long run, is his way of perpetuating the Protestant ethic. He is not an exploiter or a gambler; he is not even, in the modern sense of the word, an entrepreneur. He did not so much seek the profit as he let the profit accrue to him because of his virtues.

As soon as he had accumulated what he thought would be a competence, in 1748, he wrote to a friend:

Thus you see I am in a fair way of having no other tasks than such as I shall like to give myself, and of enjoying what I look upon as a great happiness, leisure to read, study, make experiments, and converse at large with such ingenious and worthy men as are pleased to honour me with their friendship or acquaintance, on such points as may produce something for the common benefit of mankind, uninterrupted by the little cares and fatigues of business.

This is a far remove from the schemes of the normal aspirant for success in the American system, who works at his calling in order eventually to make some sort of splurge, on a mansion, yacht, collection of paintings or of race horses. Franklin put the benefit of mankind in the place of the Puritan's glory of God. Hence he could be a bit more candid about counting the fee in shillings as well as in self-congratulation. But he still saw the utility of an occupation as no more than an adjunct to its other merits. It was not as a means for enhancing his material prestige but rather a demonstration of his probity.

This un-puritanized Puritanism is what gives a special quality not only to what Franklin says but to the method in which he says it. His prose works for an effect: to instruct, to persuade, or to satirize. The style follows afterwards, so to speak, and surrounds the meaning as an additional dividend; thus in return it renders the meaning twenty times more effective. In his writing as in his business, prosperity pursued virtue, not the other way around. Purity, which was fully content to be merely its own reward, thereupon was bountifully reimbursed for its unselfishness.

Franklin tells how he wrote a pamphlet in favor of paper money; this was a cause of the people against the colony's proprietors and money-men, and here the political issue was the concrete subject of his argument. At the same time, the piece was so well written and so warmed the hearts of the populace that they brought all their printing jobs to him;

once more he made money. "This," he modestly remarks, "was another advantage gain'd by my being able to write." But a writing which was not manufactured for communication, such as the poetry of Edward Taylor—had he known about it—would have seemed to Franklin no writing at all. "In matters of general concern to the people, and especially where burthens are to be laid upon them, it is of use to consider, as well what they will be apt to think and say, as what they ought to think." His epic of success—as politician and statesman no less than as writer—consists in his never forgetting his audience. What is astounding about his epic is that he found no substantial difference between the audiences of dissolute London or sophisticated Paris, and those of provincial Philadelphia. Or at least, while there may have been wide divergencies, the technique he had perfected in the province proved equally efficacious in the capitals.

Because Franklin has been enshrined, as one historian phrases it, as the "perfect civic leader," the youth of today may understandably find him a bore. We have to exercise a vigorous historical imagination in order to comprehend how brutal was the fight through which Franklin ascended, and how ruthlessly he made his ability to manage words a weapon in that march to victory.

When he started his business in Philadelphia, and saw that he would need an Almanac were he to count on a steady income, he found the small town occupied by a printer named Titan Leeds. Franklin had to get Leeds out of the way. He resorted to a trick which he borrowed from Jonathan Swift, but he never told the Philadelphians where he got it. He predicted the death of Leeds for October 17, 1733. The more Leeds denounced him, the more publicity Franklin received, the affair climaxing in the total destruction of Franklin's victim after the seventeenth when Leeds, foolishly insisting that he still lived, was described by Franklin as an imposter. Even in sober Philadelphia Leeds could not endure the guffaws; he had to migrate to New York. Franklin then had the field to himself, and as he smugly mentions in the *Autobiography* (not relating his discomfiture of Leeds), he made *Poor Richard's Almanack* a highly remunerative enterprise.

In the shop, then, surrounded by the dizzy array of vendible articles, Franklin perfected what he had already displayed to his astonished and envious brother, the art of writing. Simple country boys from Boston to Charleston shouted with self-approving glee once they deciphered the point of such a prognostication as this, for 1734:

There will be but two eclipses: The first, April 22; the second, October 15. Both of the sun: and both, like Mrs. ——'s modesty, and old neighbor Scrape-all's money, invisible.

What it means for a literary genius to appear in a congregation of mediocrity—if, that is, the genius elects to devote himself to public relations rather than to court ostracism into Stockbridge—is displayed in the use Franklin made of the truisms of his hapless rival. Leeds had written, "Necessity is a mighty weapon." Franklin, in his always piratical manner, stole this and rephrased it, "Necessity never made a good bargain." Leeds pontificated, "Be careful of the main chance, or it will never take care of you." Franklin brought the idea to earth with "Keep thy shop, and thy shop will keep thee." Where Leeds wrote, "'Tis best to make a good use of another's folly," Franklin drove the moral home with, "Fools make feasts, and wise men eat them." Leeds endeavored to preach that "Bad hours and ill company have ruined many fine young people." Franklin put the message so that the veriest bumpkin could not miss it: "The rotten apple spoils his companions."

Thus he made his *Poor Richard*, as he was delighted to relate, "both entertaining and useful." When he summarized his accumulated sagacity in *The Way to Wealth* (1757), he spoke to the emerging mentality of business enterprise throughout the globe; the declamation was soon translated into all civilized languages, including, once-upon-a-time, the Chinese. There are no better words to describe Franklin's prose style than his own injunction:

The words used should be the most expressive that the language affords, provided that they are the most generally understood. Nothing should be expressed in two words that can as well be expressed in one; that is, no synonyms should be used, or very rarely, but the whole should be as short as possible, consistent with clearness; the words should be so placed as to be agreeable to the ear in reading; summarily, it should be smooth, clear, and short, for the contrary qualities are displeasing.

Indeed, the contrary qualities are displeasing. Franklin sought to ingratiate himself with his listeners, even when they were bound to be his adversaries. Recent investigation[1] has shown that he did not make quite so amicable a conquest of Philadelphia as the *Autobiography* intimates; in the election of 1764, when he was defeated for representative to the Assembly, he was severely traduced in the public press. Franklin could take rebuffs in stride, as Edwards never could. His writings are a constant witness, from the beginning to the end, of his fabulous equanimity. The would-be destroyer ends by wrecking himself, while Franklin remains, as he did in his lifetime, unscathed. He is what he was. Coming out of the Puritan calculation of motives and expenditures, Franklin figured that the arithmetic could be done in this world as well as in relation to the spiritual considerations outside it. Even from his deathbed in 1790 he was able to balance and to close his ledgers, as he did in the blandly heroic letter to Ezra Stiles. In this mode he wrote, and, accordingly, his writings are an imperishable treasure of the race as well as of the nation.

III

# Jonathan Edwards

JONATHAN EDWARDS, son of the majestic pastor of East Windsor, Connecticut, was born (1703) to command. But, being a child of New England and of its most cherished

[1] See J. Philip Gleason, "A Scurrilous Colonial Election and Franklin's Reputation," *William and Mary Quarterly*, XVII (January 1961), 68–84.

class, he was required from the dawn of consciousness to search his soul, to ask of himself interminably the question of whether he was actually qualified to assume the perquisites of the station to which he had been elevated.

By comparison with the living conditions in—shall we say—an apartment in a modern American city, or indeed any oil-heated house in the present New England countryside, the circumstances of mere physical survival in the parsonage of the Rev. Timothy Edwards during the early years of the eighteenth century presented hazards. Young Jonathan survived these, leaving no reference to such mundane business as stoking the fireplace in the freezing winters—though from his later allusions it is evident that he knew the full horrors of a New England winter and the anguish of its spring. Nor is there any overt recognition of the surely basically formative fact that he was the one boy in a family which otherwise consisted of ten daughters, all of them, as far as we can gather, adoring him. Evidently, he did not have to kindle the fires. Even in Connecticut, the land of steady habits, ministers of the stature of Timothy could employ servants. Jonathan was raised for the life of the mind, as that sort of life was conceived in this virtually frontier community, and to such a life he was dedicated with what proved to be ferocious intensity.

His mother's father was Solomon Stoddard of Northampton. Known as "Pope Stoddard," he dominated the Connecticut Valley from Deerfield to the Sound, an ecclesiastical empire which he defended successfully against the attacks of Boston rivals and of Harvard College. When this principality finally raised up its own college, Edwards inevitably went to Yale, entering at the age of thirteen in 1716. There could never be the slightest question about his "calling": he was predestined to the pulpit. So, after his graduation in 1720, he studied theology in New Haven, served briefly as minister in New York, and then returned for three years as tutor at Yale during an interregnum in the presidency, so that in effect he governed the institution. In 1726 Stoddard was nearing the

end of his reign in Northampton (he had come there when it was a frontier outpost, in 1669), and decided that of all his grandsons and his many pupils Jonathan was the one to succeed him. Edwards was ordained early in 1727 and in July married Sarah Pierrepont, then seventeen, about whom he had written his amazing prose poem before he had ever seen her. Stoddard died in 1729, leaving Edwards seated on the nearest thing to a pontifical throne that New England could devise.

Lofty as was that eminence, the mind of Edwards had already climbed intellectual heights far, far above it. While still an undergraduate he read John Locke and Sir Isaac Newton; he saw in a flash of profound insight that these two minds had put mankind into a new and terrifying universe. In their formulation the human organism was irresistibly conditioned by its environment and the physical order would henceforth be a vast impersonal mechanism, following cosmic laws which made no accommodations whatever to the feeble aspirations of the race. Edwards understood at once that in this awful perspective everything that Christian theology supposed it had achieved before the advent of a psychology based upon physical sensation and the mechanistic cosmos was made hopelessly obsolete. If religion was to survive, and especially if the Calvinism of New England was to be retained, then every doctrine would have to be restated in the radically altered philosophical context. He set himself, at that early age, to work out his answer, and thus wrote the "Notes on the Mind"—which he never had the opportunity to systematize into a finished work—and which were printed long after his death. Yet they are the basis, however concealed—and deliberately concealed—of all his thought and extensive expression.

For our purpose it is of primary importance to note that to Edwards the intellectual revolution produced by Locke and Newton not only made imperative a complete restatement of such ideas as predestination, religious emotion, freedom of the will and benevolence, but a still more rigorous reformulation of the plain style. He drew up rules for himself as a writer to which he subjected himself unmercifully and from which his prose derives its distinctive qualities of calmness and lucidity, its unique combination of consuming passion and flawless restraint:

When I would prove any thing, to take special care that the matter be so stated, that it shall be seen, mostly clearly and distinctly, by everyone, just how much I would prove, and to extricate all questions from the least confusion or ambiguity of words, so that the ideas shall be left naked.

The founders had insisted upon the plain style as a way of communicating with ordinary congregations; but their aesthetic permitted considerable elocution which, by contrast with that of Edwards, seems a riot of metaphor, exclamation, and rhetorical flourish. By "naked ideas" Edwards intended no less than these, in and of themselves, to communicate. In his more notorious utterances, such as "Sinners in the Hands of an Angry God," or as in the one I give as an example of this vein, "The Future Punishment of the Wicked," posterity has often concluded that he communicated only too well. He drove his listeners into paroxysms of terror which became so spectacular a legend as to create the popular image of a monster who did nothing but hail down fire and brimstone. Today it requires an extraordinary effort of the scholar to win a hearing for the more prevailing tone of Edwards' preaching, such as "A Divine and Supernatural Light," in which the technique of stripping ideas of all extraneous or ambiguous wrappings is quietly and beautifully evident.

Another of his youthful admonitions to himself runs: "To be very moderate in the use of terms of art. Let it not look as if I was much read, or was conversant with books, or with the world." He succeeded in this direction so drastically that the mass of his hearers, and most of those who read him—either in admiration or from enmity—never grasped the elaborate metaphysical depths out of which the sermons or tracts arose. His aim was to present vast ideas clean and whole, pure and crystal clear. His paragraphs move slowly, smoothly unfold, are kept under strict control. He uses few metaphors, and when he does employ one, he dwells exclu-

sively on it for as long as possible, extracting bit by bit all the value it can be compelled to provide. He employs few adjectives to distract attention; curiously, they are usually not specific and they blend with the noun to form a bare extraction which is more shattering than the admired concreteness of Franklin: "fine appearances," "rough places," "worldly possessions," "flowery meadows." The result can be called monotonous, but the intentional and studied character of the monotony becomes a strange allurement. Edwards did not depart from it in even the most horrendous of the revival sermons. One of the Northampton townsmen, referring to the physical structure of the crude churches of the time, in which the rope for the bell by which the deacon summoned them to the church hung limply down at the opposite end from the pulpit, recollected: "Mr. Edwards in preaching used no gestures, but looked straight forward: Gideon Clark said 'he looked on the bell rope until he looked it off.'"

The primitive polity of the Puritans had not been what we would call "revivalist" or even "evangelical." The founders came from an England in which there had existed stable communities, centered around a common and a church, in the pulpit of which there was a regular succession of pastors. They never had any intention of going up and down the land like the Methodists of the eighteenth century, preaching in the fields and arousing the populace to intemperate exhibitions of zeal, or of upsetting the parish structure of the society. The only complaint of the Puritans was that they should control this structure and so purify the parish churches into the Biblical pattern of worship. When they were defeated, or thought they were, and therefore migrated in companies to the wilderness, they strove in Massachusetts and Connecticut to realize the English ideal. They settled not as individuals on the frontier, but in towns—Boston, Malden, Hartford—each a close community with a common and a church. The essential difference from England was that this church was Congregational instead of Episcopal. That is, the membership consisted only of those who had given evidence of their conversion and so presumably—the founders never said absolutely—of their election. These "visible saints" would choose the minister and govern the "church," while the rest of the town, which constituted the "congregation," would be required by law to attend services and to pay for the support of the minister. Thus the assumption ran that in the ordinary year-to-year conduct of the community a certain number would, in the providence of God, undergo the experience of regeneration, make a public profession of faith, and regularly fill up the ranks of the saints. Preaching and ecclesiastical administration would be a "means" of this recruiting, but only as they were conduits through which the waters of divine grace flowed. Never, it was held, would the words of the preacher be themselves the cause of the saving emotion. Hence, we have once more the aesthetic of the plain style, which, like pious labor, depended for its effect not on its own skill but upon divine blessing.

The experience of a century showed, to the bafflement of Puritan theorists, that once the first blush of excitement wore off, the children and grandchildren of the founders failed to encounter the cataclysm of conversion. They continued earnest and pious, and worked strenuously in their callings, but fewer and fewer of them could honestly make the profession. Several devices were tried, such as the "Half-Way Covenant" (1662) by which the children of members might have their own children baptized even though they themselves could demonstrate no right to the Lord's Supper. It was Solomon Stoddard who roughly decided that the original theory was both impractical and unscriptural. He renounced the entire church covenant and the exclusive membership; he boldly took the entire town into the "church" and to the Lord's Supper. He declared the communion a "converting ordinance," and directed his preaching to the direct stimulation of fear, guilt, and emotion among his people. He demonstrated that once the concept of religious government was thus centralized there would come moments in which the ever-smoldering anxiety of the people could be fanned by a powerful preacher into

a communal flame. Stoddard called these outbursts his "harvests," and he managed to instigate five of them, in 1679, 1683, 1696, 1712, and 1718, in each of which, as he boasted, "the bigger Part of the Young People in the Town, seemed mainly concerned for their eternal salvation." Increase and Cotton Mather attacked these unseemly measures, they seeking to preserve at least the skeleton of the old Puritan conception. Stoddard stood them off; secure in his effrontery, he lead the Connecticut Valley into the perilous but exhilarating era of the "revival." When Edwards succeeded to his grandfather's office, it was incumbent upon him that he prove his princely descent by producing another "harvest," or engineering one even more spectacular than those of his predecessors, one so earthshaking that the world would have to acknowledge it a genuine outpouring of God's spirit upon the land.

In 1735 he succeeded, although of course Edwards attributed the efficient provocation to divine agency and took no credit unto himself or his "naked ideas." This flare-up soon died down, but not until Edwards had written an account of it, significantly entitled *A Faithful Narrative of the Surprising Work of God in the Conversion of Many Hundred Souls in Northampton, and the Neighboring Towns and Villages.* This became a guidebook to revivalism, but more importantly it prescribed the model for the truly colossal revival which he led, with some assistance from an English Methodist, George Whitfield, and from other divines both within New England and from the other colonies, in 1740. For several months Edwards was the most powerful mortal on the North American continent; in the full flood of this overwhelming success he delivered the "terror" sermons by which he kept the crowd in a state of religious panic.

While the Great Awakening, as it soon was termed, burned at white heat, nobody in New England dared speak out against him. Still, a number were appalled by its noise, its violence, the convulsions of those stricken with guilt, and by the dissensions erupting inside the churches. When even this mighty upheaval began to subside, as had the "surprising" work of 1735, and as would every subsequent "revival" in American history, the opponents launched a counterattack. What the critics principally charged was that the Awakening was an artificial incitation, manufactured by such sensational preaching as these riotously calm sermons of Edwards, and that it was thus an exercise in psychological malpractice. They said it was not an authentic outpouring of the divine spirit but merely an exciting of animal passions by material stimulants. From a religious point of view, they said it was simply a substitute for New England's already redoubtable rum.

As the Awakening subsided, as it turned toward embittered disillusionment, not only among those who had resisted it from the beginning but more nastily among those who had surrendered themselves to it, a rage against Edwards mounted in the Connecticut Valley as well as at Harvard College. Indeed, in the Valley it became a frenzy more intense than the exultation of the revival had been, especially because it was fomented by several blood relatives of Edwards, who resented his succession to the mantle of Stoddard. These, in the now established pattern of New England families, were resolved upon destroying the cousin who had, no matter his merit, arrogantly undertaken to become the dominant member of the tribe.

Edwards had no other course left to him, therefore, but to apply his vast energies and his judicious mind to defending the thesis that the Awakening had been, despite its subsiding, a veritable "work" of God upon New England and the other colonies. The culmination of this endeavor to vindicate the reality of the Awakening is *A Treatise Concerning Religious Affections.*

So far as Northampton was concerned, Edwards failed. At the end of a long and bitter struggle, the details of which are horrifying but need not be related here, he was expelled from his superb pulpit. Upon leaving it, Edwards delivered his "Farewell Sermon"—"a long farewell" to all his greatness—though it was spoken in 1750, and though his major writings were yet to follow. We are hard put to conceive how his congregation, most of whom had by then worked

day and night to get rid of him, sat through the delivery of this superhuman adjudication, but they held their precarious ground. Edwards and his family marched over the mountains to the then frontier outpost of Stockbridge. There, in conditions of virtual poverty, Edwards wrote the massive philosophical works that constitute the grounds for his being rated one of the few original intellects of modern Christianity.

The hinge of his dispute with the townspeople in Northampton was that, while he did not propose to revive the church covenant within the formal theory of the founders, he did nevertheless endeavor to restrict admission to the "church" only to those who could show the overt signs of a certifiable spiritual encounter. Edwards, thinking of experience in the abstruse terms of Lockean psychology and inside the frame of a Newtonian physics, set a standard of disinterested spirituality to which few countrymen could possibly come up. We may justifiably surmise, therefore, that once he was cast out, once he was exiled into the wilderness, he should in the 1750's devote his last terrible energies to setting forth in two companion pieces the dual aspect of the problem of actual holiness, the psychological and the cosmic. These treatises were not published until after his death, in 1765, but in the parade of American literature *The Nature of True Virtue* and *Dissertation Concerning the End for Which God Created the World* are his masterpieces. Though inevitably more elaborate than his anticipation of Sarah Pierrepont, they utter their implacable thoughts with the same poetic serenity; they constitute, quite apart from the theological sense, a music which sounds its own self-sufficing melody.

Both the cadences of the prose and the cleanliness of the argument make these works a triumph of the plain style, which was, we have seen, an ethic not only of ordering words but also of conducting life and earning a living. And in them, at what seems on the surface an extreme divergence from Franklin, Edwards shows himself, upon any critical analysis, Franklin's brother. Carl Becker said, in the most perceptive sentence yet written about Franklin, that it was no wonder he sought for his ultimate satisfaction in natural science, because only in the physical universe could he find a "disinterestedness" equal to his own.[2] For most readers of Franklin this observation requires second thoughts, for at first sight Franklin seems a man excessively occupied in self-seeking and self-advancement. Yet after one has reread him, and read him yet again, one learns to appreciate that the actual charm of his writing is his disengagement from all the multifarious activities of his career. He could never have described them, or written about them when in the midst of the drama, in exactly the quizzical spirit he unfailingly maintains, unless he had somewhere in his intricate constitution an ultimate sense that all these local aims were subordinate to a larger one, in relation to which they were indeed trivial.

In Edwards' two final statements he strove to define this larger, this ultimate aim, in such a manner that nothing particular, selfish, patriotic, or charitable would stand for a moment against the vastness of perfection. In *True Virtue* he defines the subjection of the temporal to the eternal from the standpoint of finite humanity, showing how every "secondary" virtue—love of self, of family, of country, of mankind itself—must be merged into the all-effacing love for "Being in general."

Franklin on his part gingerly avoided all such speculation; the older he grew, the more he let such considerations alone. Yet the older he grew, the more by his very geniality, in his weary games with the ladies of the French Court, he demonstrated the Edwardsean thesis that the universe is its own excuse for being. Both Edwards and Franklin, the former the archspiritualist of American history and the second its master worldly-wiseman, assert that he who labors in whichever of the callings, if he push either to its extreme, finds himself a negligible finite in the face of a glorious incomprehensi-

bility. To put Edwards' *Farewell Sermon* alongside Franklin's letter to Ezra Stiles is to perceive the vastness of their divergence, yet also to sense the mysterious identity of their underlying mood.

## IV

FOR a large part of our national existence, Franklin has figured as a culture hero, while Edwards, if known as anything other than the lurid preacher of hell-fire, has been widely held a fanatical reactionary. In 1926, for instance, the great Vernon Parrington, in his pioneer history of thought in America, dismissed Edwards as an "anachronism." To the nineteenth century Franklin appeared the prophet of technology, the apostle of rationality, and the surpreme vindication of the American ideal of the "self-made man."

By the middle of the twentieth century there has arisen a strong dissent from this view. No doubt thousands of practical Americans still find Franklin congenial and Edwards repulsive. Yet several hundreds discover increasingly a fascination in the mind and style of Edwards that surprises them as much as it delights them. To some of these Franklin now appears as the mummified example of the insensitive businessman, deaf to poetry and passion, translating all ideals into dollars and cents. After Sinclair Lewis made the name "Babbitt" stand for everything that many critics considered reprehensible in American civilization, Franklin was widely termed the first Babbitt, and the most contemptible of the lot. To others likewise put off by him, Franklin is the one who started the nation toward a "gadgeteers' paradise," which in their view leads to the supreme gadget, an instrument for mass destruction. Hence there has recently occurred a marked revival of interest in Jonathan Edwards. Those who bring themselves to reject Franklin flee to Edwards, as though he could offer them salvation—or at least peace of mind.

Both approaches will mislead us, give us images that are sadly mangled. Franklin was indeed a self-made triumph, but he was not a Babbitt: he strove to be a *philosophe* in the

---

[2] See Carl Becker's now classic piece on Franklin in the *Dictionary of American Biography*.

grand manner of the eighteenth century. As a matter of fact, despite his lightning experiment, he never quite made the stiff grade. He was hailed by a theater crowded with sentimental rationalists when he, in a box, embraced Voltaire. Yet he was no Voltaire, not at all a Diderot; he was an ingenious Yankee who promoted a knack for tinkering and for employing the written word to gain his usually homely ends into a reputation which, actually, he never had sufficient intellect to sustain—though he never allowed the world to realize his deficiency!

Even so, it may be that exactly in their limitations, their narrowness, these two figures are most American; herein they may be of greatest value as well as most perplexing to all who would endeavor to comprehend the baffling intellect of this Republic. Again we must be cautious not to insist that their New England consanguinity should be so presented as to minimize the chasm between them. Yet even while we have appreciated how permanently they are irreconcilable, we return to a fresh, and exhilarating, sense of their complementary natures.

In the fatigued mood of his communications to Priestly in 1782, Franklin, still harping on his boredom with humanity, continued thus:

I should rejoice much, if I could once more recover the leisure to search with you into the works of nature; I mean the inanimate not the animate or moral part of them: the more I discovered of the former the more I admired them: the more I know of the latter the more I am disgusted with them.

In the dread isolation of Stockbridge—which could not conceivably have been more opposite to Passy—Edwards, writing of *True Virtue* and stripping all human pretensions to moral worth from any title to merit, centered his definition of that which is incontestably worthy upon this conception of the Godhead:

Because God is not only infinitely greater and more excellent than all other being, but he is the head of the universal system of existence; the foundation and fountain of all being and all beauty; from whom all is perfectly derived, and on whom all is most absolutely and perfectly dependent; of whom, and through whom, and to whom is all being and all perfection; and whose being and beauty are, as it were, the sum and comprehension of all existence and excellence: much more than the sun is the fountain and summary comprehension of all the light and brightness of the day.

Franklin's "works of nature" should not be cheaply made into an interchangeable term with Edwards' "sum and comprehension of all existence and excellence." Yet, the phrases have affinities. In relation to finite human experience, they can signify essentially the same disregard of personal convenience. So we come back to our opening reflection, though I hope with a more enlightened concern. While individual predilections are not to be scorned, and each reader may prize the one more than the other, still the serious student of America, seeking accurate knowledge of the intellectual heritage, must learn fully to understand, in their own terms, *both* these massively symbolic characters.

NOTE

Wherever four dots appear in the selections that follow, the first is the author's punctuation, the other three are the editor's ellipses. A full line of space has been inserted within the text in the case of an omission of a paragraph or more.

# Benjamin Franklin

## FROM

## AUTOBIOGRAPHY

◇

⟦ FRANKLIN commenced the story of his life, as he took pains to indicate, while staying as a guest for a week in June, 1771, with Bishop Jonathan Shipley at Twyford, near Winchester. In that brief time he wrote, with matchless precision, his report up to the year 1730 of his existence, reading aloud in the evenings to the Shipley family what he had composed during the days. Obliged then to break off, and hindered by a multitude of events from continuing, he was able to resume his tale thirteen years later, 1784, in Passy, outside of Paris. He endeavored to add two more chapters in the last year of his life, 1789, in Philadelphia. The history of the partial and inaccurate publication is a bibliographical nightmare. Not until 1868 was a "first" complete edition of the four sections printed. It is, of course, one of the great "unfinished" masterpieces, since even in his last exertions Franklin was able to bring the narrative up to only his fiftieth year. The most spectacular decades of his career he had no chance to recount.

◇

Twyford, *at the Bishop of St. Asaph's,* 1771.
DEAR SON: [1] I have ever had the pleasure in obtaining any little anecdotes of my ancestors. You may remember the inquiries I made among the remains of my relations when you were with me in England, and the journey I undertook for that purpose. Imagining it may be equally agreeable to you to know the circumstances of my life, many of which you are yet unacquainted with, and expecting the enjoyment of a week's uninterrupted leisure in my present country retirement, I sit down to write them for you. To which I have besides some other inducements. Having emerged from the poverty and obscurity in which I was born and bred, to a state of affluence and some degree of reputation in the world, and having gone so far through life with a considerable share of felicity, the conducing means I made use of, which with the blessing of God so well succeeded, my posterity may like to know, as they may find some of them suitable to their own situations, and therefore fit to be imitated.

AUTOBIOGRAPHY.    1. **Son:** William Franklin (1731–1813), the last royal governor of New Jersey (1763–76), who was arrested and imprisoned during the Revolution for his Tory sympathies.

That felicity, when I reflected on it, has induced me sometimes to say, that were it offered to my choice, I should have no objection to a repetition of the same life from its beginning, only asking the advantages authors have in a second edition to correct some faults of the first. So I might, besides correcting the faults, change some sinister accidents and events of it for others more favorable. But though this were denied, I should still accept the offer. Since such a repetition is not to be expected, the next thing most like living one's life over again seems to be a recollection of that life, and to make that recollection as durable as possible by putting it down in writing.

Hereby, too, I shall indulge the inclination so natural in old men, to be talking of themselves and their own past actions; and I shall indulge it without being tiresome to others, who, through respect to age, might conceive themselves obliged to give me a hearing, since this may be read or not as one pleases. And, lastly (I may as well confess it, since my denial of it will be believed by nobody), perhaps I shall a good deal gratify my own *vanity.* Indeed, I scarce ever heard or saw the introductory words, *"Without vanity I may say,"* &c., but some vain thing immediately followed. Most people dislike vanity in others, whatever share they have of it themselves; but I give it fair quarter wherever I meet with it, being persuaded that it is often productive of good to the possessor, and to others that are within his sphere of action; and therefore, in many cases, it would not be altogether absurd if a man were to thank God for his vanity among the other comforts of life.

And now I speak of thanking God. I desire with all humility to acknowledge that I owe the mentioned happiness of my past life to His kind providence, which led me to the means I used and gave them success. My belief of this induces me to *hope,* though I must not *presume,* that the same goodness will still be exercised toward me, in continuing that happiness, or enabling me to bear a fatal reverse, which I may experience as others have done; the complexion of my future fortune being known to Him only in whose power it is to bless to us even our afflictions.

The notes one of my uncles (who had the same kind of curiosity in collecting family anecdotes) once put into my hands, furnished me with several particulars relating to our ancestors. From these notes I learned that the family had lived in the same village, Ecton, in Northamptonshire, for three hundred years, and how much longer he knew not (perhaps from the time when the name of Franklin, that before was the name of an order of people, was assumed by them as a surname when others took surnames all over the kingdom), on a freehold of about thirty acres, aided by the smith's business, which had continued in the family till his time, the eldest son being always bred to that business; a custom which he and my father followed as to their eldest sons. When I searched the registers at Ecton, I found an account of their births, marriages and burials from the year 1555 only, there being no registers kept in that parish at any time preceding. By that register I perceived that I was the youngest son of the youngest son for five generations back. My grandfather Thomas, who was born in 1598, lived at Ecton till he grew too old to follow business longer, when he went to live with his son John, a dyer at Banbury, in Oxfordshire, with whom my father served an apprenticeship. There my grandfather died and lies buried. We saw his gravestone in 1758. His eldest son Thomas lived in the house at Ecton, and left it with the land to his only child, a daughter, who, with her husband, one Fisher, of Wellingborough, sold it to Mr. Isted, now lord of the manor there. My grandfather had four sons that grew up, viz.: Thomas, John, Benjamin and Josiah. I will give you what account I can of them, at this distance from my papers, and if these are not lost in my absence, you will among them find many more particulars.

Thomas was bred a smith under his father; but, being ingenious, and encouraged in learning (as all my brothers were) by an Esquire Palmer, then the principal gentleman in that parish, he qualified himself for the business of scrivener; became a considerable man in the county; was a chief mover of all public-spirited undertakings for the county or town of Northampton, and his own village, of which many instances were related of him; and much taken notice of and patronized by the then Lord Halifax. He died in 1702, January 6, old style, just four years to a day before I was born. The account we received of his life and character from some old people at Ecton, I remember, struck you as something extraordinary, from its similarity to what you knew of mine. "Had he died on the same day," you said, "one might have supposed a transmigration."

John was bred a dyer, I believe of woolens. Benjamin was bred a silk dyer, serving an apprenticeship at London. He was an ingenious man. I remember him well, for when I was a boy he came over to my father in Boston, and lived in the house with us some years. He lived to a great

age. His grandson, Samuel Franklin, now lives in Boston. He left behind him two quarto volumes, MS., of his own poetry, consisting of little occasional pieces addressed to his friends and relations, of which the following, sent to me, is a specimen.[2] He had formed a short-hand of his own, which he taught me, but, never practicing it, I have now forgot it. I was named after this uncle, there being a particular affection between him and my father. He was very pious, a great attender of sermons of the best preachers, which he took down in his short-hand, and had with him many volumes of them. He was also much of a politician; too much, perhaps, for his station. There fell lately into my hands, in London, a collection he had made of all the principal pamphlets relating to public affairs, from 1641 to 1717; many of the volumes are wanting as appears by the numbering, but there still remain eight volumes in folio, and twenty-four in quarto and in octavo. A dealer in old books met with them, and knowing me by sometimes buying of him, he brought them to me. It seems my uncle must have left them here when he went to America, which was above fifty years since. There are many of his notes in the margins.

This obscure family of ours was early in the Reformation, and continued Protestants through the reign of Queen Mary, when they were sometimes in danger of trouble on account of their zeal against popery. They had got an English Bible, and to conceal and secure it, it was fastened open with tapes under and within the cover of a joint-stool. When my great-great grandfather read it to his family, he turned up the joint-stool upon his knees, turning over the leaves then under the tapes. One of the children stood at the door to give notice if he saw the apparitor coming, who was an officer of the spiritual court. In that case the stool was turned down again upon its feet, when the Bible remained concealed under it as before. This anecdote I had from my uncle Benjamin. The family continued all of the Church of England till about the end of Charles the Second's reign, when some of the ministers that had been outed for non-conformity holding conventicles in Northamptonshire, Benjamin and Josiah adhered to them, as so continued all their lives: the rest of the family remained with the Episcopal Church.

Josiah, my father, married young, and carried his wife with three children into New England, about 1682. The conventicles having been forbidden by law, and frequently disturbed, induced

2. **a specimen:** on the margin of the manuscript Franklin wrote, "Here insert it," but he never found time to do so, and his uncle's verse is thus lost to posterity.

some considerable men of his acquaintance to remove to that country, and he was prevailed with to accompany them thither, where they expected to enjoy their mode of religion with freedom. By the same wife he had four children more born there, and by a second wife ten more, in all seventeen; of which I remember thirteen sitting at one time at his table, who all grew up to be men and women, and married; I was the youngest son, and the youngest child but two, and was born in Boston, New England. My mother, the second wife, was Abiah Folger, daughter of Peter Folger, one of the first settlers of New England, of whom honorable mention is made by Cotton Mather, in his church history of that country, entitled Magnalia Christi Americana, as *"a godly, learned Englishman,"* if I remember the words rightly. I have heard that he wrote sundry small occasional pieces, but only one of them was printed, which I saw now many years since. It was written in 1675, in the home-spun verse of that time and people, and addressed to those then concerned in the government there. It was in favor of liberty of conscience, and in behalf of the Baptists, Quakers, and other sectaries that had been under persecution, ascribing the Indian wars, and other distresses that had befallen the country, to that persecution, as so many judgments of God to punish so heinous an offense, and exhorting a repeal of those uncharitable laws. The whole appeared to me as written with a good deal of decent plainness and manly freedom. The six concluding lines I remember, though I have forgotten the two first of the stanza; but the purport of them was, that his censures proceeded from good will, and, therefore he would be known to be the author.

> "Because to be a libeller (says he)
>   I hate it with my heart;
> From Sherburne town, where now I dwell
>   My name I do put here;
> Without offense your real friend,
>   It is Peter Folgier."

My elder brothers were all put apprentices to different trades. I was put to the grammar-school at eight years of age, my father intending to devote me, as the tithe of his sons, to the service of the Church. My early readiness in learning to read (which must have been very early, as I do not remember when I could not read), and the opinion of all his friends, that I should certainly make a good scholar, encouraged him in this purpose of his. My uncle Benjamin, too, approved of it, and proposed to give me all his short-hand volumes of sermons, I suppose as a stock to set up with, if I would learn his character. I continued, however, at the grammar-school not quite

one year, though in that time I had risen gradually from the middle of the class of that year to be the head of it, and farther was removed into the next class above it, in order to go with that into the third at the end of the year. But my father, in the mean time, from a view of the expense of a college education, which having so large a family he could not well afford, and the mean living many so educated were afterwards able to obtain —reasons that he gave to his friends in my hearing—altered his first intention, took me from the grammar-school, and sent me to a school for writing and arithmetic, kept by a then famous man, Mr. George Brownell, very successful in his profession, generally, and that by mild, encouraging methods. Under him I acquired fair writing pretty soon, but I failed in the arithmetic, and made no progress in it. At ten years old I was taken home to assist my father in his business, which was that of a tallow-chandler and sopeboiler;[3] a business he was not bred to, but had assumed on his arrival in New England, and on finding his dying trade would not maintain his family, being in little request. Accordingly, I was employed in cutting wick for the candles, filling the dipping mold and the molds for cast candles, attending the shop, going of errands, etc. . . .

I continued thus employed in my father's business for two years, that is, till I was twelve years old; and my brother John, who was bred to that business, having left my father, married, and set up for himself at Rhode Island, there was all appearance that I was destined to supply his place, and become a tallow-chandler. But my dislike to the trade continuing, my father was under apprehensions that if he did not find one for me more agreeable, I should break away and get to sea, as his son Josiah had done, to his great vexation. He therefore sometimes took me to walk with him, and see joiners, bricklayers, turners, braziers, etc., at their work, that he might observe my inclination, and endeavor to fix it on some trade or other on land. It has ever since been a pleasure to me to see good workmen handle their tools; and it has been useful to me, having learnt so much by it as to be able to do little jobs myself in my house when a workman could not readily be got, and to construct little machines for my experiments, while the intention of making the experiment was fresh and warm in my mind. My father at last fixed upon the cutler's trade, and my uncle Benjamin's son Samuel, who was bred to that business in London, being about that time estab-

---

3. sopeboiler: soap boiler.

lished in Boston, I was sent to be with him on liking. But his expectations of a fee with me displeasing my father, I was taken home again.

From a child I was fond of reading, and all the little money that came into my hands was ever laid out in books. Pleased with the Pilgrim's Progress, my first collection was of John Bunyan's works in separate little volumes. I afterwards sold them to enable me to buy R. Burton's Historical Collections; they were small chapmen's books, and cheap, 40 or 50 in all. My father's little library consisted chiefly of books in polemic divinity, most of which I read, and have since often regretted that, at a time when I had such a thirst for knowledge, more proper books had not fallen in my way, since it was now resolved I should not be a clergyman. Plutarch's Lives there was in which I read abundantly, and I still think that time spent to great advantage. There was also a book of De Foe's, called an Essay on Projects,[4] and another of Dr. Mather's, called Essays to do Good,[5] which perhaps gave me a turn of thinking that had an influence on some of the principal future events of my life.

This bookish inclination at length determined my father to make me a printer, though he had already one son (James) of that profession. In 1717 my brother James returned from England with a press and letters to set up his business in Boston. I liked it much better than that of my father, but still had a hankering for the sea. To prevent the apprehended effect of such an inclina-

tion, my father was impatient to have me bound to my brother. I stood out some time, but at last was persuaded, and signed the indentures when I was yet but twelve years old. I was to serve as an apprentice till I was twenty-one years of age, only I was to be allowed journeyman's wages during the last year. In a little time I made great proficiency in the business, and became a useful hand to my brother. I now had access to better books. An acquaintance with the apprentices of booksellers enabled me sometimes to borrow a small one, which I was careful to return soon and clean. Often I sat up in my room reading the greatest part of the night, when the book was borrowed in the evening and to be returned early in the morning, lest it should be missed or wanted. . . .

About this time I met with an odd volume of the *Spectator*. It was the third. I had never before seen any of them. I bought it, read it over and over, and was much delighted with it. I thought the writing excellent, and wished, if possible, to imitate it. With this view I took some of the papers, and, making short hints of the sentiment in each sentence, laid them by a few days, and then, without looking at the book, try'd to compleat the papers again, by expressing each hinted sentiment at length, and as fully as it had been expressed before, in any suitable words that should come to hand. Then I compared my *Spectator* with the original, discovered some of my faults, and corrected them. But I found I wanted a stock of words, or a readiness in recollecting and using them, which I thought I should have acquired before that time if I had gone on making verses; since the continual occasion for words of the same import, but of different length, to suit the measure, or of different sound for the rhyme, would have laid me under a constant necessity of searching for variety, and also have tended to fix that variety in my mind, and make me master of it. Therefore I took some of the tales and turned them into verse; and, after a time, when I had pretty well forgotten the prose, turned them back again. I also sometimes jumbled my collections of hints into confusion, and after some weeks endeavored to reduce them into the best order, before I began to form the full sentences and compleat the paper. This was to teach me method in the arrangement of thoughts. By comparing my work afterwards with the original, I discovered many faults and amended them; but I sometimes had the pleasure of fancying that, in certain particulars of small import, I had been lucky enough to improve the method or the language, and this

4. an Essay on Projects: This, the first complete book by Daniel Defoe (1660–1731) was published in 1697 as *An Essay upon Projects*. It is universally considered as beginning, in a genuinely homely and practical spirit hitherto unprecedented in English literature, the idea of a planned system of governmental benevolence. It proposed simplifications in legal procedure, construction of highways at public expense, insane asylums, an academy for the regularization of the English language, and a collegiate school for women. Considering Franklin's career, we can see how readily his youthful temperament would have jibed with that of Defoe.  5. Essays to do Good: Franklin refers to a book by Cotton Mather, published in 1710, the accurate title of which (even when abbreviated) is: *Bonifacius, an Essay upon the Good Which Is to Be Devised and Designed by Those Who Desire . . . to Do Good While They Live.* Known by its running title, *Essays to Do Good*, it was widely read in the colonies and even in England, and is a milestone in the development of New England Calvinism from a "theocracy" to a social conscience. By it and other efforts Cotton Mather was striving to mobilize the churches into a program of moral supervision that would replace the political control lost by the abrogation of the original charter and by the defection (as he conceived it) of Solomon Stoddard in the Connecticut Valley. The young Franklin bespoke the irritation of the unelected against Mather's scheme by inventing the name of "Silence Dogood" for his satirical forays, especially because Mather was the least silent of men. The old Franklin, we should note, always spoke reverently of the book—possibly because of this youthful arrogance—and insisted that it guided him into his lifelong devotion to the public welfare.

encouraged me to think I might possibly in time come to be a tolerable English writer, of which I was extreamly ambitious. My time for these exercises and for reading was at night, after work or before it began in the morning, or on Sundays, when I contrived to be in the printing-house alone, evading as much as I could the common attendance on public worship which my father used to exact of me when I was under his care, and which indeed I still thought a duty, though I could not, as it seemed to me, afford time to practise it. . . .

My brother had, in 1720 or 1721, begun to print a newspaper. It was the second that appeared in America, and was called the New England Courant.[6] The only one before it was the Boston News-Letter. I remember his being dissuaded by some of his friends from the undertaking, as not likely to succeed, one newspaper being, in their judgment, enough for America. At this time (1771) there are not less than five-and-twenty. He went on, however, with the undertaking, and after having worked in composing the types and printing off the sheets, I was employed to carry the papers thro' the streets to the customers.

He had some ingenious men among his friends, who amus'd themselves by writing little pieces for this paper, which gain'd it credit and made it more in demand, and these gentlemen often visited us. Hearing their conversations, and their accounts of the approbation their papers were received with, I was excited to try my hand among them; but being still a boy, and suspecting that my brother would object to printing anything of mine in his paper if he knew it to be mine, I contrived to disguise my hand, and, writing an anonymous paper, I put it in at night under the door of the printing-house. It was found in the morning, and communicated to his writing friends when they call'd in as usual. They read it, commented on it in my hearing, and I had the exquisite pleasure of finding it met with their approbation, and that, in their different guesses at the author, none were named but men of some character among us for learning and ingenuity. I suppose now that I was rather lucky in my judges, and that perhaps they were not really so very good ones as I then esteem'd them.

Encourag'd, however, by this, I wrote and convey'd in the same way to the press several more

papers which were equally approv'd; and I kept my secret till my small fund of sense for such performances was pretty well exhausted, and then I discovered it, when I began to be considered a little more by my brother's acquaintance, and in a manner that did not quite please him, as he thought, probably with reason, that it tended to make me too vain. And, perhaps, this might be one occasion of the differences that we began to have about this time. Though a brother, he considered himself as my master, and me as his apprentice, and, accordingly, expected the same services from me as he would from another, while I thought he demean'd me too much in some he requir'd of me, who from a brother expected more indulgence. Our disputes were often brought before our father, and I fancy I was either generally in the right, or else a better pleader, because the judgment was generally in my favor. But my brother was passionate, and had often beaten me, which I took extreamly amiss; and, thinking my apprenticeship very tedious, I was continually wishing for some opportunity of shortening it, which at length offered in a manner unexpected.[7]

One of the pieces in our newspaper on some political point, which I have now forgotten,[8] gave offense to the Assembly. He was taken up, censur'd, and imprison'd for a month, by the speaker's warrant, I suppose, because he would not discover his author. I too was taken up and examin'd before the council; but, tho' I did not give them any satisfaction, they content'd themselves with admonishing me, and dismissed me, considering me, perhaps, as an apprentice, who was bound to keep his master's secrets.

During my brother's confinement, which I resented a good deal, notwithstanding our private differences, I had management of the paper; and I made bold to give our rulers some rubs in it, which my brother took very kindly, while others began to consider me in an unfavorable light, as a young genius that had a turn for libelling and satyr. My brother's discharge was accompany'd with an order of the House (a very odd one), that *"James Franklin should no longer print the paper called the New England Courant."*

There was a consultation held in our printing-house among his friends, what he should do in this case. Some proposed to evade the order by

6. **New England Courant:** In point of fact, the *Courant* was the third newspaper in Boston and the fourth in the colonies (following one in Philadelphia), but the predecessors were merely collections of reports from Europe and attempted nothing of the literary character with which James Franklin strove, to his ultimate destruction, to invest his foredoomed venture.

7. **manner unexpected:** On the margin of the manuscript Franklin notes, "I fancy his harsh and tyrannical treatment of me might be a means of impressing me with that aversion to arbitrary power that has stuck to me through my whole life."
8. **on . . . forgotten:** Franklin had, either through failure of memory or because of convenience, elected to forget that the offending article was not "political" but a satire upon the clergy, aimed primarily against Cotton Mather.

changing the name of the paper; but my brother, seeing inconveniences in that, it was finally concluded on as a better way, to let it be printed for the future under the name of BENJAMIN FRANKLIN; and to avoid the censure of the Assembly, that might fall on him still printing it by his apprentice, the contrivance was that my old indenture should be return'd to me, with a full discharge on the back of it, to be shown on occasion: but to secure him the benefit of my service, I was to sign new indentures for the remainder of the term, which were to be kept private. A very flimsy scheme it was; however, it was immediately executed, and the paper went on accordingly, under my name for several months.

At length, a fresh difference arising between my brother and me, I took upon me to assert my freedom, presuming that he would not venture to produce the new indentures. It was not fair in me to take this advantage, and this I therefore reckon one of the first errata of my life; but the unfairness of it weighed little with me, when under the impressions of resentment for the blows his passion too often urged him to bestow upon me, though he was otherwise not an ill-natur'd man: perhaps I was too saucy and provoking.

When he found I would leave him, he took care to prevent my getting employment in any other printing-house of the town, by going round and speaking to every master, who accordingly refus'd to give me work. I then thought of going to New York, as the nearest place where there was a printer; and I was rather inclin'd to leave Boston when I reflected that I had already made myself a little obnoxious to the governing party, and, from the arbitrary proceedings of the Assembly in my brother's case, it was likely I might, if I stay'd, soon bring myself into scrapes; and farther, that my indiscrete disputations about religion began to make me pointed at with horror by good people as an infidel or atheist. I determin'd on the point, but my father now siding with my brother, I was sensible that, if I attempted to go openly, means would be used to prevent me. My friend Collins, therefore, undertook to manage a little for me. He agreed with the captain of a New York sloop for my passage, under the notion of my being a young acquaintance of his, that had got a naughty girl with child, whose friends would compel me to marry her, and therefore I could not appear or come away publicly. So I sold some of my books to raise a little money, was taken on board privately, and as we had a fair wind, in three days I found myself in New York, near 300 miles from home, a boy of but 17, without the least recommendation to, or knowledge of any person in the place, and with very little money in my pocket. . . .

. . . . . . . . . . . . . . . . . . . . . . . . . . . . . . . .

MY INCLINATIONS for the sea were by this time worne out, or I might now have gratify'd them. But, having a trade, and supposing myself a pretty good workman, I offer'd my service to the printer in the place, old Mr. William Bradford, who had been the first printer in Pennsylvania, but removed from thence upon the quarrel of George Keith. He could give me no employment, having little to do, and help enough already; but says he, "My son at Philadelphia has lately lost his principal hand, Aquila Rose, by death; if you go thither, I believe he may employ you." Philadelphia was a hundred miles further; I set out, however, in a boat for Amboy, leaving my chest and things to follow me round by sea.

In crossing the bay, we met with a squall that tore our rotten sails to pieces, prevented our getting into the Kill, and drove us upon Long Island. In our way, a drunken Dutchman, who was a passenger too, fell overboard; when he was sinking, I reached through the water to his shock pate, and drew him up, so that we got him in again. His ducking sobered him a little, and he went to sleep, taking first out of his pocket a book, which he desir'd I would dry for him. It proved to be my old favorite author, Bunyan's Pilgrim's Progress, in Dutch, finely printed on good paper, with copper cuts, a dress better than I had ever seen it wear in its own language. I have since found that it has been translated into most of the languages of Europe, and suppose it has been more generally read than any other book, except perhaps the Bible. Honest John was the first that I know of who mix'd narration and dialogue; a method of writing very engaging to the reader, who in the most interesting parts finds himself, as it were, brought into the company and present at the discourse. De Foe in his Cruso, his Moll Flanders, Religious Courtship, Family Instructor, and other pieces, has imitated it with success; and Richardson has done the same in his Pamela, etc.[9]

When we drew near the island, we found it was a place where there could be no landing,

9. **in his Pamela, etc.:** Franklin here advertises the range, and the limitations, of his aesthetic sensibility. By "Cruso" he obviously means Defoe's *Robinson Crusoe* (1719). *Moll Flanders,* also by Defoe, was published in 1722, as was his dehumanized *Religious Courtship.* His still more ceremonial *Family Instructor* was first printed in 1715 and was constantly reprinted during the century. There can hardly elsewhere be found a more stuffy monument to the dehydrated manners of the polite era. To this body of ritualistic literature, Franklin joined Samuel Richardson's (1689–1761) *Pamela* (1740), which—oddly enough—was the one work of fiction that Jonathan Edwards would approve.

there being a great surff on the stony beach. So we dropt anchor, and swung round towards the shore. Some people came down to the water edge and hallow'd to us, as we did to them; but the wind was so high, and the surff so loud, that we could not hear so as to understand each other. There were canoes on the shore, and we made signs, and hallow'd that they should fetch us; but they either did not understand us, or thought it impracticable, so they went away, and night coming on, we had no remedy but to wait till the wind should abate; and, in the mean time, the boatman and I concluded to sleep, if we could; and so crowded into the scuttle, with the Dutchman, who was still wet, and the spray beating over the head of our boat, leak'd thro' to us, so that we were soon almost as wet as he. In this manner we lay all night, with very little rest; but, the wind abating the next day, we made a shift to reach Amboy before night, having been thirty hours on the water, without victuals, or any drink but a bottle of filthy rum, the water we sail'd on being salt.

In the evening I found myself very feverish, and went into bed; but, having read somewhere that cold water drank plentifully was good for a fever, I follow'd the prescription, sweat plentifully most of the night, my fever left me, and in the morning, crossing the ferry, I proceeded on my journey on foot, having fifty miles to Burlington, where I was told I should find boats that would carry me the rest of the way to Philadelphia.

It rained very hard all the day; I was thoroughly soak'd, and by noon a good deal tired; so I stopt at a poor inn, where I staid all night, beginning now to wish that I had never left home. I cut so miserable a figure, too, that I found, by the questions ask'd me, I was suspected to be some runaway servant, and in danger of being taken up on that suspicion. However, I proceeded the next day, and got in the evening to an inn, within eight or ten miles of Burlington, kept by one Dr. Brown. He entered into conversation with me while I took some refreshment, and, finding I had read a little, became very sociable and friendly. Our acquaintance continu'd as long as he liv'd. He had been, I imagine, an itinerant doctor, for there was no town in England, or country in Europe, of which he could not give a very particular account. He had some letters, and was ingenious, but much of an unbeliever, and wickedly undertook, some years after, to travestie the Bible in doggrel verse, as Cotton had done Virgil. By this means he set many of the facts in a very ridiculous light, and might have hurt weak minds if his work had been published; but it never was.

At his house I lay that night, and the next morning reach'd Burlington, but had the mortification to find that the regular boats were gone a little before my coming, and no other expected to go before Tuesday, this being Saturday; wherefore I returned to an old woman in the town, of whom I had bought gingerbread to eat on the water, and ask'd her advice. She invited me to lodge at her house till a passage by water should offer; and being tired with my foot travelling, I accepted the invitation. She understanding I was a printer, would have had me stay at that town and follow my business, being ignorant of the stock necessary to begin with. She was very hospitable, gave me a dinner of ox-cheek with great good will, accepting only a pot of ale in return; and I thought myself fixed till Tuesday should come. However, walking in the evening by the side of the river, a boat came by, which I found was going towards Philadelphia, with several people in her. They took me in, and as there was no wind, we row'd all the way; and about midnight, not having yet seen the city, some of the company were confident we must have passed it, and would row no farther; the others knew not where we were; so we put toward the shore, got into a creek, landed near an old fence, with the rails of which we made a fire, the night being cold, in October, and there we remained till daylight. Then one of the company knew the place to be Cooper's Creek, a little above Philadelphia, which we saw as soon as we got out of the creek, and arriv'd there about eight or nine o'clock on the Sunday morning, and landed at the Market-street wharf.

I have been the more particular in this description of my journey, and shall be so of my first entry into that city, that you may in your mind compare such unlikely beginnings with the figure I have since made there. I was in my working dress, my best cloaths being to come round by sea. I was dirty from my journey; my pockets were stuff'd out with shirts and stockings, and I knew no soul nor where to look for lodging. I was fatigued with travelling, rowing and want of rest, I was very hungry; and my whole stock of cash consisted of a Dutch dollar, and about a shilling in copper. The latter I gave the people of the boat for my passage, who at first refus'd it, on account of my rowing; but I insisted on their taking it. A man being sometimes more generous when he has but a little money than when he has plenty, perhaps thro' fear of being thought to have but little.

Then I walked up the street, gazing about till near the market-house I met a boy with bread. I had made many a meal on bread, and, inquiring where he got it, I went immediately to the baker's he directed me to, in Second-street, and ask'd for bisket, intending such as we had in Boston; but they, it seems, were not made in Philadelphia. Then I asked for a three-penny loaf, and was told they had none such. So not considering or knowing the difference of money, and the greater cheapness nor the names of the bread, I bad him give me three-penny worth of any sort. He gave me, accordingly, three great puffy rolls. I was surpriz'd at the quantity, but took it, and, having no room in my pockets, walk'd off with a roll under each arm, and eating the other. Thus I went up Market-street as far as Fourth-street, passing by the door of Mr. Read, my future wife's father; when she, standing at the door, saw me, and thought I made, as I certainly did, a most awkward, ridiculous appearance. Then I turned and went down Chestnut-street and part of Walnut-street, eating my roll all the way, and coming round, found myself again at Market-street wharf, near the boat I came in, to which I went for a draught of river water; and, being filled with one of my rolls, gave the other two to a woman and her child that came down the river in the boat with us, and were waiting to go farther.

Thus refreshed, I walked again up the street, which by this time had many clean-dressed people in it, who were all walking the same way. I joined them, and thereby was led into the great meeting-house of the Quakers near the market. I sat down among them, and, after looking round awhile and hearing nothing said, being very drowsy thro' labor and want of rest the preceding night, I fell fast asleep, and continu'd so till the meeting broke up, when one was kind enough to rouse me. This was, therefore, the first house I was in, or slept in, in Philadelphia. . . .

Before I enter upon my public appearance in business, it may be well to let you know the then state of my mind with regard to my principles and morals, that you may see how far those influenc'd the future events of my life. My parents had early given me religious impressions, and brought me through my childhood piously in the Dissenting way. But I was scarce fifteen, when, after doubting by turns of several points, as I found them disputed in the different books I read, I began to doubt of Revelation itself. Some books against Deism fell into my hands; they were said to be the substance of sermons preached at Boyle's Lectures. It happened that they wrought an effect on me quite contrary to what was intended by them; for the arguments of the Deists, which were quoted to be refuted, appeared to

me much stronger than the refutations; in short, I soon became a thorough Deist. My arguments perverted some others, particularly Collins and Ralph;[10] but, each of them having afterwards wrong'd me greatly without the least compunction, and recollecting Keith's conduct towards me[11] (who was another freethinker), and my own towards Vernon[12] and Miss Read,[13] which at times gave me great trouble, I began to suspect that this doctrine, tho' it might be true, was not very useful. My London pamphlet,[14] which had for its motto these lines of Dryden:

> "Whatever is, is right. Though purblind man
> Sees but a part o' the chain, the nearest link:
> His eyes not carrying to the equal beam,
> That poises all above;"

and from the attributes of God, his infinite wisdom, goodness and power, concluded that nothing could possibly be wrong in the world, and that vice and virtue were empty distinctions, no such things existing, appear'd now not so clever a performance as I once thought it; and I doubted whether some error had not insinuated itself unperceiv'd into my argument, so as to infect all that follow'd, as is common in metaphysical reasonings.

I grew convinc'd that *truth, sincerity* and *integrity* in dealings between man and man were of the utmost importance to the felicity of life; and I form'd written resolutions, which still remain in my journal book, to practice them ever while I lived. Revelation had indeed no weight with me, as such; but I entertain'd an opinion that, though certain actions might not be bad *because* they were forbidden by it, or good *because* it commanded them, yet probably those actions might be forbidden *because* they were bad for us, or commanded *because* they were beneficial to us,

---

10. **Collins and Ralph:** John Collins was a boyhood friend of Franklin in Boston and later a companion in Philadelphia; he borrowed money from Franklin and disappeared into Barbados without repaying it. James Ralph, a Philadelphia clerk with poetic aspirations, went with Franklin to London and remained there, dying in 1762.     11. **Keith's conduct towards me:** Sir William Keith (1680–1749), governor of Pennsylvania (1717–49), promised to help Franklin to a position of profit in London, but neglected to write the requisite letters and so left the boy destitute in the metropolis. 12. **towards Vernon:** Samuel Vernon, a silversmith in Newport, R.I., commissioned Franklin to recover a debt of thirty-five pounds in Pennsylvania; Franklin secured the money, but lost most of it by lending to Collins.     13. **and Miss Read:** Franklin had "made some courtship" to Deborah ("Debby") before going to England, but gave every appearance of deserting her. She made an unfortunate marriage, which was dissolved by the time he returned. He made amends by marrying her in 1730.     14. **My London pamphlet:** *A Dissertation on Liberty and Necessity, Pleasure and Pain* (1725), printed by himself. He later strove to destroy all copies.

in their own natures, all the circumstances of things considered. And this persuasion, with the kind hand of Providence, or some guardian angel, or accidental favourable circumstances and situations, or all together, preserved me, thro' this dangerous time of youth, and the hazardous situations I was sometimes in among strangers, remote from the eye and advice of my father, without any willful gross immorality or injustice, that might have been expected from my want of religion. [Some foolish intrigues with low women excepted, which from the expense were rather more prejudicial to me than to them.]15 I say willful, because the instances I have mentioned had something of *necessity* in them, from my youth, inexperience, and the knavery of others. I had therefore a tolerable character to begin the world with; I valued it properly, and determin'd to preserve it. . . .

I began now gradually to pay off the debt I was under for the printing-house. In order to secure my credit and character as a tradesman, I took care not only to be in *reality* industrious and frugal, but to avoid all appearances to the contrary. I drest plainly; I was seen at no places of idle diversion. I never went out a fishing or shooting; a book, indeed, sometimes debauch'd me from my work, but that was seldom, snug, and gave no scandal; and, to show that I was not above my business, I sometimes brought home the paper I purchas'd at the stores thro' the streets on a wheelbarrow. Thus being esteem'd an industrious, thriving young man, and paying duly for what I bought, the merchants who imported stationery solicited my custom; others proposed supplying me with books, and I went on swimmingly. In the mean time, Keimer's credit16 and business declining daily, he was at last forc'd to sell his printing-house to satisfy his creditors. He went to Barbadoes, and there lived some years in very poor circumstances. . . .

I had been religiously educated as a Presbyterian;17 and tho' some of the dogmas of that per-

suasion, such as *the eternal decrees of God, election, reprobation, etc.,* appeared to me unintelligible, others doubtful, and I early absented myself from the public assemblies of the sect, Sunday being my studying day, I never was without some religious principles. I never doubted, for instance, the existence of the Deity; that he made the world, and govern'd it by his Providence; that the most acceptable service of God was the doing good to man; that our souls are immortal; and that all crime will be punished, and virtue rewarded, either here or hereafter. These I esteem'd the essentials of every religion; and, being to be found in all the religions we had in our country, I respected them all, tho' with different degrees of respect, as I found them more or less mix'd with other articles, which, without any tendency to inspire, promote, or confirm morality, serv'd principally to divide us, and make us unfriendly to one another. This respect to all, with an opinion that the worst had some good effects, induc'd me to avoid all discourse that might tend to lessen the good opinion another might have of his own religion; and as our province increas'd in people, and new places of worship were continually wanted, and generally erected by voluntary contribution, my mite for such purpose, whatever might be the sect, was never refused.

Tho' I seldom attended any public worship, I had still an opinion of its propriety, and of its utility when rightly conducted, and I regularly paid my annual subscription for the support of the only Presbyterian minister or meeting we had in Philadelphia. He us'd to visit me sometimes as a friend, and admonish me to attend his administrations, and I was now and then prevail'd on to do so, once for five Sundays successively. Had he been in my opinion a good preacher, perhaps I might have continued, notwithstanding the occasion I had for the Sunday's leisure in my course of study; but his discourses were chiefly either polemic arguments, or explications of the peculiar doctrines of our sect, and were all to me very dry, uninteresting, and unedifying, since not a single moral principle was inculcated or enforc'd, their aim seeming to be rather to make us Presbyterians than good citizens.

At length he took for his text that verse of the fourth chapter of Philippians, *"Finally, brethren, whatsoever things are true, honest, just, pure, lovely, or of good report, if there be any virtue, or any praise, think on these things."* And I imagin'd, in a sermon on such a text, we could not miss of having some morality. But he confin'd himself to five points only, as meant by the apos-

15. **Some . . . them:** In the manuscript, the words within brackets are struck out, but are still legible.    16. **Keimer's credit:** Samuel Keimer employed Franklin in his printing shop in 1723, rehired him in 1728, and by 1729 was driven out of Philadelphia by Franklin's brilliance and his own inefficiency.    17. **Presbyterian:** This selection comes from the portion written at Passy in 1784; though it has the Franklinian consistency of tone, it displays the immense amount of experience he had undergone since 1771. Franklin was brought up as what we call a Congregationalist, but since his father's church, the Third of Boston, formally accepted the Westminster Confession, he was content to call the creed Presbyterian. His nonchalance about the term advertises his indifference to denomination niceties.

tle, viz.: 1. Keeping holy the Sabbath day. 2. Being diligent in reading the holy Scriptures. 3. Attending duly the publick worship. 4. Partaking of the Sacrament. 5. Paying a due respect to God's ministers. These might be all good things; but, as they were not the kind of good things that I expected from that text, I despaired of ever meeting with them from any other, was disgusted, and attended his preaching no more. I had some years before compos'd a little Liturgy, or form of prayer, for my own private use (viz., in 1728), entitled, *Articles of Belief and Acts of Religion.* I return'd to the use of this, and went no more to the public assemblies. My conduct might be blameable, but I leave it, without attempting further to excuse it; my present purpose being to relate facts, and not to make apologies for them.

It was about this time I conceiv'd the bold and arduous project of arriving at moral perfection. I wish'd to live without committing any fault at any time; I would conquer all that either natural inclination, custom, or company might lead me into. As I knew, or thought I knew, what was right and wrong, I did not see why I might not always do the one and avoid the other. But I soon found I had undertaken a task of more difficulty than I had imagined. While my care was employ'd in guarding against one fault, I was often surprised by another; habit took the advantage of inattention; inclination was sometimes too strong for reason. I concluded, at length, that the mere speculative conviction that it was our interest to be completely virtuous, was not sufficient to prevent our slipping; and that the contrary habits must be broken, and good ones acquired and established, before we can have any dependence on a steady, uniform rectitude of conduct. For this purpose I therefore contrived the following method.

In the various enumerations of the moral virtues I had met with in my reading, I found the catalogue more or less numerous, as different writers included more or fewer ideas under the same name. Temperance, for example, was by some confined to eating and drinking, while by others it was extended to mean the moderating every other pleasure, appetite, inclination, or passion, bodily or mental, even to our avarice and ambition. I propos'd to myself, for the sake of clearness, to use rather more names, with fewer ideas annex'd to each, than a few names with more ideas; and I included under thirteen names of virtues all that at that time occur'd to me as necessary or desirable, and annexed to each a short precept, which fully express'd the extent I gave to its meaning.

These names of virtues, with their precepts were:

1. TEMPERANCE. Eat not to dullness; drink not to elevation.

2. SILENCE. Speak not but what may benefit others or yourself; avoid trifling conversation.

3. ORDER. Let all your things have their places; let each part of your business have its time.

4. RESOLUTION. Resolve to perform what you ought; perform without fail what you resolve.

5. FRUGALITY. Make no expense but to do good to others or yourself; i.e., waste nothing.

6. INDUSTRY. Lose no time; be always employ'd in something useful; cut off all unnecessary actions.

7. SINCERITY. Use no hurtful deceit; think innocently and justly; and, if you speak, speak accordingly.

8. JUSTICE. Wrong none by doing injuries, or omitting the benefits that are your duty.

9. MODERATION. Avoid extreams; forbear resenting injuries so much as you think they deserve.

10. CLEANLINESS. Tolerate no uncleanliness in body, cloaths, or habitation.

11. TRANQUILLITY. Be not disturbed at trifles, or at accidents common or unavoidable.

12. CHASTITY. Rarely use venery but for health or offspring, never to dullness, weakness, or the injury of your own or another's peace or reputation.

13. HUMILITY. Imitate Jesus and Socrates.

My intention being to acquire the *habitude* of all these virtues, I judg'd it would be well not to distract my attention by attempting the whole at once, but to fix it on one of them at a time; and, when I should be master of that, then to proceed to another, and so on, till I should have gone thro' the thirteen; and, as the previous acquisition of some might facilitate the acquisition of certain others, I arrang'd them with that view, as they stand above. *Temperance* first, as it tends to procure that coolness and clearness of head, which is so necessary where constant vigilance was to be kept up, and guard maintained against the unremitting attraction of ancient habits, and the force of perpetual temptations. This being acquir'd and establish'd, *Silence* would be more easy; and my desire being to gain knowledge at the same time that I improv'd in virtue, and considering that in conversation it was obtain'd rather by the use of ears than of the tongue, and therefore wishing to break a habit I was getting into of prattling, punning, and joking, which only made me acceptable to a trifling company, I gave *Silence* the second place. This and the next, *Order,*

I expected would allow me more time for attending to my project and my studies. *Resolution,* once become habitual, would keep me firm in my endeavours to obtain all the subsequent virtues; *Frugality* and *Industry* freeing me from my remaining debt, and producing affluence and independence, would make more easy the practice of *Sincerity* and *Justice,* etc., etc. Conceiving then, that, agreeably to the advice of Pythagoras in his Golden Verses, daily examination would be necessary, I contrived the following method for conducting that examination.

I made a little book, in which I allotted a page for each of the virtues. I rul'd each page with red ink, so as to have seven columns, one for each day of the week, marking each column with a letter for the day. I cross'd these columns with thirteen red lines, marking the beginning of each line with the first letter of one of the virtues, on which line, and in its proper column, I might mark, by a little black spot, every fault I found upon examination to have been committed respecting that virtue upon that day.

I determined to give a week's strict attention to each of the virtues successively. Thus, in the

FORM OF THE PAGES.

| TEMPERANCE. | | | | | | |
|---|---|---|---|---|---|---|
| EAT NOT TO DULLNESS; DRINK NOT TO ELEVATION. | | | | | | |
| | S. | M. | T. | W. | T. | F. | S. |
| T. | | | | | | | |
| S. | * | * | | * | | * | |
| O. | * * | * | * | | * | * | * |
| R. | | | · * | | | * | |
| F. | | * | | | * | | |
| I. | | | * | | | | |
| S. | | | | | | | |
| J. | | | | | | | |
| M. | | | | | | | |
| C. | | | | | | | |
| T. | | | | | | | |
| C. | | | | | | | |
| H. | | | | | | | |

first week, my great guard was to avoid even the least offence against *Temperance,* leaving the other virtues to their ordinary chance, only marking every evening the faults of the day. Thus, if in the first week I could keep my first line, marked T, clear of spots, I suppos'd the habit of that virtue so much strengthen'd, and its opposite weaken'd, that I might venture extending my attention to include the next, and for the following week keep both lines clear of spots. Proceeding thus to the last, I could go thro' a course compleat in thirteen weeks, and four courses in a year. And like him who, having a garden to weed, does not attempt to eradicate all the bad herbs at once, which would exceed his reach and his strength, but works on one of the beds at a time, and, having accomplish'd the first, proceeds to a second, so I should have, I hoped, the encouraging pleasure of seeing on my pages the progress I made in virtue, by clearing sucessively my lines of their spots, till in the end, by a number of courses, I should be happy in viewing a clean book, after a thirteen weeks' daily examination.

This my little book had for its motto these lines from Addison's *Cato:*

"Here will I hold. If there's a power above us
(And that there is, all nature cries aloud
Thro' all her works), He must delight in virtue;
And that which he delights in must be happy."

Another from Cicero,

*"O vitae Philosophia dux! O virtutum indagatrix expultrixque vitiorum! Unus dies, bene et ex praeceptis tuis actus, peccanti immortalitati est anteponendus."* [18]

Another from the Proverbs of Solomon, speaking of wisdom or virtue:

"Length of days is in her right hand, and in her left hand riches and honour. Her ways are ways of pleasantness, and all her paths are peace." iii.16, 17.

And conceiving God to be the fountain of wisdom, I thought it right and necessary to solicit his assistance for obtaining it; to this end I formed the following little prayer, which was prefix'd to my tables of examination, for daily use.

*"O powerful Goodness! bountiful Father! merciful Guide! Increase in me that wisdom which discovers*

18. *"O . . . anteponendus":* "O philosophy, guide of life! O explorer of virtue and expeller of vice! A single day, spent well and in accordance with your precepts, is to be preferred to an eternity of wrong-doing" (Cicero, *Tusculans,* 5.5).

*my truest interest. Strengthen my resolutions to per-
form what that wisdom dictates. Accept my kind
offices to thy other children as the only return in my
power for thy continual favours to me."*

I used also sometimes a little prayer which I
took from Thomson's Poems, viz.:

"Father of light and life, thou Good Supreme!
O teach me what is good; teach me Thyself!
Save me from folly, vanity, and vice,
From every low pursuit; and fill my soul
With knowledge, conscious peace, and virtue pure;
Sacred, substantial, never-fading bliss!"

The precept of *Order* requiring that *every part
of my business should have its allotted time*, one
page of my little book contain'd the following
scheme of employment for the twenty-four hours
of a natural day.

THE MORNING.
 *Question.* What
good shall I do this
day?

 5 — Rise, wash, and ad-
 6 — dress *Powerful Good-
 7 — ness!* Contrive day's
business, and take the
resolution of the day;
prosecute the present
study, and breakfast.

 8
 9 — Work.
 10
 11

NOON.
 12 — Read, or overlook
 1 — my accounts, and dine.

 2
 3
 4 — Work.
 5

EVENING.
 *Question.* What
good have I done to-
day?

 6 — Put things in their
 7 — places. Supper. Music
 8 — or diversion, or con-
 9 — versation. Examination
of the day.

NIGHT.
 10
 11
 12
 1 — Sleep.
 2
 3
 4

I enter'd upon the execution of this plan for
self-examination, and continu'd it with occasional
intermissions for some time. I was surpris'd to
find myself so much fuller of faults than I had

imagined; but I had the satisfaction of seeing
them diminish. To avoid the trouble of renewing
now and then my little book, which, by scraping
out the marks on the paper of old faults to make
room for new ones in a new course, became full
of holes, I transferr'd my tables and precepts to
the ivory leaves of a memorandum book, on
which the lines were drawn with red ink, that
made a durable stain, and on those lines I mark'd
my faults with a black-lead pencil, which marks
I could easily wipe out with a wet sponge. After
a while I went thro' one course only in a year,
and afterward only one in several years, till at
length I omitted them entirely, being employ'd in
voyages and business abroad, with a multiplicity
of affairs that interfered; but I always carried my
little book with me.

My scheme of *Order* gave me the most trouble;
and I found that, tho' it might be practicable
where a man's business was such as to leave him
the disposition of his time, that of a journeyman
printer, for instance, it was not possible to be
exactly observed by a master, who must mix with
the world, and often receive people of business
at their own hours. *Order,* too, with regard to
places for things, papers, etc., I found extreamly
difficult to acquire. I had not been early accustomed to it, and, having an exceeding good
memory, I was not so sensible of the inconvenience attending want of method. This article,
therefore, cost me so much painful attention, and
my faults in it vexed me so much, and I made so
little progress in amendment, and had such frequent relapses, that I was almost ready to give
up the attempt, and content myself with a faulty
character in that respect, like the man who, in
buying an ax of a smith, my neighbor, desired to
have the whole of its surface as bright as the edge.
The smith consented to grind it bright for him if
he would turn the wheel; he turn'd, while the
smith press'd the broad face of the ax hard and
heavily on the stone, which made the turning of
it very fatiguing. The man came every now and
then from the wheel to see how the work went on,
and at length would take his ax as it was, without
farther grinding. "No," said the smith, "turn on,
turn on; we shall have it bright by-and-by; as yet
it is only speckled." "Yes," says the man, *"but I
think I like a speckled ax best."* And I believe this
may have been the case with many, who, having,
for want of some such means as I employ'd,
found the difficulty of obtaining good and breaking bad habits in other points of vice and virtue,
have given up the struggle, and concluded that
*"a speckled ax was best;"* for something, that pretended to reason, was every now and then suggesting to me that such extream nicety as I ex-

acted of myself might be a kind of foppery in morals, which, if it were known, would make me ridiculous; that a perfect character might be attended with the inconvenience of being envied and hated; and that a benevolent man should allow a few faults in himself, to keep his friends in countenance.

In truth, I found myself incorrigible with respect to *Order;* and now I am grown old, and my memory bad, I feel very sensibly the want of it. But, on the whole, tho' I never arrived at the perfection I had been so ambitious of obtaining, but fell far short of it, yet I was, by the endeavour, a better and a happier man than I otherwise should have been if I had not attempted it; as those who aim at perfect writing by imitating the engraved copies, tho' they never reach the wish'd-for excellence of those copies, their hand is mended by the endeavour, and is tolerable while it continues fair and legible.

It may be well my posterity should be informed that to this little artifice, with the blessing of God, their ancestor ow'd the constant felicity of his life, down to his 79th year, in which this is written. What reverses may attend the remainder is in the hand of Providence; but, if they arrive, the reflection on past happiness enjoy'd ought to help his bearing them with more resignation. To *Temperance* he ascribes his long-continued health, and what is still left to him of a good constitution; to *Industry* and *Frugality,* the early easiness of his circumstances and acquisition of his fortune, with all that knowledge that enabled him to be a useful citizen, and obtained for him some degree of reputation among the learned; to *Sincerity* and *Justice,* the confidence of his country, and the honourable employs it conferred upon him; and to the joint influence of the whole mass of the virtues, even in the imperfect state he was able to acquire them, all that evenness of temper, and that cheerfulness in conversation, which makes his company still sought for, and agreeable even to his younger acquaintance. I hope, therefore, that some of my descendants may follow the example and reap the benefit.

It will be remark'd that, tho' my scheme was not wholly without religion, there was in it no mark of any of the distinguishing tenets of any particular sect. I had purposely avoided them; for, being fully persuaded of the utility and excellency of my method, and that it might be serviceable to people in all religions, and intending some time or other to publish it, I would not have any thing in it that should prejudice any one of any sect, against it. I purposed writing a little comment on each virtue, in which I would have shown the advantages of possessing it, and the mischiefs at-

tending its opposite vice; and I should have called my book THE ART OF VIRTUE, because it would have shown the means and manner of obtaining virtue, which would have distinguished it from the mere exhortation to be good, that does not instruct and indicate the means, but is like the apostle's man of verbal charity, who only without showing to the naked and hungry how or where they might get clothes or victuals, exhorted them to be fed and clothed.—James ii. 15, 16.

But it so happened that my intention of writing and publishing this comment was never fulfilled. I did, indeed, from time to time, put down short hints of the sentiments, reasonings, etc., to be made use of in it, some of which I have still by me; but the necessary close attention to private business in the earlier part of my life, and public business since, have occasioned my postponing it; for, it being connected in my mind with *a great and extensive project,* that required the whole man to execute, and which an unforeseen succession of employs prevented my attending to, it has hitherto remain'd unfinish'd.

In this piece it was my design to explain and enforce this doctrine, that vicious actions are not hurtful because they are forbidden, but forbidden because they are hurtful, the nature of man alone considered; that it was, therefore, every one's interest to be virtuous who wish'd to be happy even in this world; and I should, from this circumstance (there being always in the world a number of rich merchants, nobility, states, and princes, who have need of honest instruments for the management of their affairs, and such being so rare), have endeavoured to convince young persons that no qualities were so likely to make a poor man's fortune as those of probity and integrity.

My list of virtues contain'd at first but twelve; but a Quaker friend having kindly informed me that I was generally thought proud; that my pride show'd itself frequently in conversation; that I was not content with being in the right when discussing any point, but was overbearing, and rather insolent, of which he convinc'd me by mentioning several instances; I determined endeavouring to cure myself, if I could, of this vice or folly among the rest, and I added *Humility* to my list, giving an extensive meaning to the word.

I cannot boast of much success in acquiring the *reality* of this virtue, but I had a good deal with regard to the *appearance* of it. I made it a rule to forbear all direct contradiction to the sentiments of others, and all positive assertion of my own. I even forbid myself, agreeably to the laws of our Junto, the use of every word or expression in the language that imported a fix'd opinion, such as *certainly, undoubtedly,* etc., and I adopted, instead of them, *I conceive, I apprehend,* or *I imagine* a thing to be so or so; or *it so appears to me at present.* When another asserted something that I thought an error, I deny'd myself the pleasure of contradicting him abruptly, and of showing immediately some absurdity in his proposition; and in answering I began by observing that in certain cases or circumstances his opinion would be right, but in the present case there *appear'd* or *seem'd* to me some differences, etc. I soon found the advantage of this change in my manner; the conversations I engag'd in went on more pleasantly. The modest way in which I propos'd my opinions procur'd them a readier reception and less contradiction; I had less mortification when I was found to be in the wrong, and I more easily prevail'd with others to give up their mistakes and join with me when I happened to be in the right.

And this mode, which I at first put on with some violence to natural inclination, became at length so easy, and so habitual to me, that perhaps for these fifty years past no one has ever heard a dogmatical expression escape me. And to this habit (after my character of integrity) I think it principally owing that I had early so much weight with my fellow citizens when I proposed new institutions, or alterations in the old, and so much influence in public councils when I became a member; for I was but a bad speaker, never eloquent, subject to much hesitation in my choice of words, hardly correct in language, and yet I generally carried my points.

In reality, there is, perhaps, no one of our natural passions so hard to subdue as *pride.* Disguise it, struggle with it, beat it down, stifle it, mortify it as much as one pleases, it is still alive, and will every now and then peep out and show itself; you will see it, perhaps, often in this history; for, even if I could conceive that I had compleatly overcome it, I should probably be proud of my humility.

# A WITCH TRIAL AT MOUNT-HOLLY

◊

⟨ THIS joke was printed in the *Pennsylvania Gazette* for October 22, 1730. There is no direct evidence that

Franklin wrote it, and he seems never to have claimed it, but it has long been assigned to him, is clearly in his literary character, and is too precious to be given to anybody else. In studying it the student must recollect that only thirty-eight years before, not much more than a generation earlier, had occurred the infamous witch hysteria at Salem in Franklin's native Massachusetts.

◊

BURLINGTON, Oct. 12. Saturday last at Mount-Holly, about 8 miles from this Place, near 300 People were gathered together to see an Experiment or two tried on some Persons accused of Witchcraft. It seems the Accused had been charged with making their Neighbors Sheep dance in an uncommon Manner, and with causing Hogs to speak, and sing Psalms, &c. to the great Terror and Amazement of the King's good and peaceful Subjects in this Province; and the Accusers being very positive that if the Accused were weighted in Scales against a Bible, the Bible would prove too heavy for them; or that, if they were bound and put into the River, they would swim; the said Accused desirous to make their Innocence appear, voluntarily offered to undergo the said Trials, if 2 of the most violent of their Accusers would be tried with them. Accordingly the Time and Place was agreed on, and advertised about the Country; The Accusers were 1 Man and 1 Woman; and the Accused the same. The Parties being met, and the People got together, a grand Consultation was held, before they proceeded to Trial; in which it was agreed to use the Scales first; and a Committee of Men were appointed to search the Men, and a Committee of Women to search the Women, to see if they had any Thing of Weight about them, particularly Pins. After the Scrutiny was over, a huge great Bible belonging to the Justice of the Place was provided, and a Lane through the Populace was made from the Justices House to the Scales, which were fixed on a Gallows erected for that Purpose opposite to the House, that the Justice's Wife and the rest of the Ladies might see the Trial, without coming amongst the Mob; and after the Manner of Moorfields, a large Ring was also made. Then came out of the House a grave tall Man carrying the Holy Writ before the supposed Wizard, &c. (as solemnly as the Sword-bearer of London before the Lord Mayor), the Wizard was first put in the Scale, and over him was read a Chapter out of the Books of Moses, and then the Bible was put in the other Scale, (which being kept down before) was immediately let go; but to the great Surprize of the Spectators, Flesh and Bones came down plump, and outweighed that great good Book by abundance. After that same Manner, the others were served, and their Lumps of Mortality severally were too heavy for Moses and all the Prophets and Apostles. This being over, the Accusers and the rest of the Mob, not satisfied with this Experiment, would have the Trial by Water; accordingly a most solemn Procession was made to the Mill-pond; where both Accused and Accusers being stripp'd (saving only to the Women their Shifts) were bound Hand and Foot, and severally placed in the Water, lengthways, from the Side of a Barge or Flat, having for Security only a Rope about the Middle of each, which was held by some in the Flat. The Accuser Man being thin and spare, with some Difficulty began to sink at last; but the rest every one of them swam very light upon the Water. A Sailor in the Flat jump'd out upon the Back of the Man accused, thinking to drive him down to the Bottom, but the Person bound, without any Help came up some time before the other. The Woman Accuser, being told that she did not sink, would be duck'd a second Time; when she swam again as light as before. Upon which she declared, That she believed the Accused had bewitched her to make her so light, and that she would duck the Devil out of her. The accused Man, being surpriz'd at his own Swimming, was not so confident of his Innocence as before, but said, *If I am a Witch, it is more than I know.* The more thinking Part of the Spectators were of Opinion, that any Person so bound and plac'd in the Water (unless they were mere Skin and Bones) would swim till their Breath was gone, and their Lungs fill'd with Water. But it being the general Belief of the Populace, that the Womens Shifts, and the Garters with which they were bound help'd to support them; it is said they are to be tried again the next warm Weather, naked.

# APOLOGY FOR PRINTERS

❖

❬ THIS, by now, classic statement was printed casually in the *Pennsylvania Gazette,* for June 10, 1731. Apparently Franklin had accepted and printed a routine announcement of the sailing of a ship, but the skipper was one who believed that the clergy, in their black cloaks, were Jonahs. We assume that Franklin printed a handbill expressing the Captain's prejudice, since there is no text of the full advertisement in the *Gazette.* At any rate, the background is clear: Franklin was at-

tacked in Philadelphia for lending himself as a commercial printer to anticlerical superstition. The chance to vindicate his rooted convictions about freedom of the press was to him irresistible.

❖

BEING frequently censur'd and condemn'd by different Persons for printing Things which they say ought not to be printed, I have sometimes thought it might be necessary to make a standing Apology for my self, and publish it once a Year, to be read upon all Occasions of that Nature. Much Business has hitherto hindered the execution of this Design; but having very lately given extraordinary Offence by printing an Advertisement with a certain N.B. at the End of it, I find an Apology more particularly requisite at this Juncture, tho' it happens when I have not yet Leisure to write such a thing in the proper Form, and only in a loose manner throw those Considerations together which should have been the Substance of it.

I request all who are angry with me on the Account of printing things they don't like, calmly to consider these following Particulars

1. That the Opinions of Men are almost as various as their Faces; an Observation general enough to become a common Proverb, *So many Men so many Minds.*

2. That the Business of Printing has chiefly to do with Men's Opinions; most things that are printed tending to promote some, or oppose others.

3. That hence arises the peculiar Unhappiness of that Business, which other Callings are no way liable to; they who follow Printing being scarce able to do any thing in their way of getting a Living, which shall not probably give Offence to some, and perhaps to many; whereas the Smith, the Shoemaker, the Carpenter, or the Man of any other Trade, may work indifferently for People of all Persuasions, without offending any of them: and the Merchant may buy and sell with Jews, Turks, Hereticks, and Infidels of all sorts, and get Money by every one of them, without giving Offence to the most orthodox, of any sort; or suffering the least Censure or Ill-will on the Account from any Man whatever.

4. That it is as unreasonable in any one Man or Set of Men to expect to be pleas'd with every thing that is printed, as to think that nobody ought to be pleas'd but themselves.

5. Printers are educated in the Belief, that when Men differ in Opinion, both Sides ought equally to have the Advantage of being heard by the Publick; and that when Truth and Error have

fair Play, the former is always an overmatch for the latter: Hence they chearfully serve all contending Writers that pay them well, without regarding on which side they are of the Question in Dispute.

6. Being thus continually employ'd in serving all Parties, Printers naturally acquire a vast Unconcernedness as to the right or wrong Opinions contain'd in what they print; regarding it only as the Matter of their daily labour: They print things full of Spleen and Animosity, with the utmost Calmness and Indifference, and without the least Ill-will to the Persons reflected on; who nevertheless unjustly think the Printer as much their Enemy as the Author, and join both together in their Resentment.

7. That it is unreasonable to imagine Printers approve of every thing they print, and to censure them on any particular thing accordingly; since in the way of their Business they print such great variety of things opposite and contradictory. It is likewise as unreasonable what some assert, *That Printers ought not to print any Thing but what they approve;* since if all of that Business should make such a Resolution, and abide by it, an End would thereby be put to Free Writing, and the World would afterwards have nothing to read but what happen'd to be the Opinions of Printers.

8. That if all Printers were determin'd not to print any thing till they were sure it would offend no body, there would be very little printed.

9. That if they sometimes print vicious or silly things not worth reading, it may not be because they approve such things themselves, but because the People are so viciously and corruptly educated that good things are not encouraged. I have known a very numerous Impression of *Robin Hood's Songs* go off in this Province at 2/ per Book, in less than a Twelvemonth; when a small Quantity of *David's Psalms* (an excellent version) have lain upon my Hands above twice the Time.

10. That notwithstanding what might be urg'd in behalf of a Man's being allow'd to do in the Way of his Business whatever he is paid for, yet Printers do continually discourage the Printing of great Numbers of bad things, and stifle them in the Birth. I my self have constantly refused to print any thing that might countenance Vice, or promote Immorality; tho' by complying in such Cases with the corrupt Taste of the Majority, I might have got much Money. I have also always refus'd to print such things as might do real Injury to any Person, how much soever I have been solicited, and tempted with Offers of great Pay; and how much soever I have by refusing got the Ill-will of those who would have employ'd me.

I have heretofore fallen under the Resentment of large Bodies of Men, for refusing absolutely to print any of their Party or Personal Reflections. In this Manner I have made my self many Enemies, and the constant Fatigue of denying is almost insupportable. But the Publick being unacquainted with all this, whenever the poor Printer happens either through Ignorance or much Persuasion, to do any thing that is generally thought worthy of Blame, he meets with no more Friendship or Favour on the above Account, than if there were no Merit in't at all. Thus, as Waller says,

*Poets lose half the Praise they would have got*
*Were it but known what they discreetly blot;*

yet are censur'd for every bad Line found in their Works with the utmost Severity.

I come now to the particular Case of the N.B. above-mention'd, about which there has been more Clamour against me, than ever before on any other Account. In the Hurry of other Business an Advertisement was brought to me to be printed; it signified that such a Ship lying at such a Wharff, would sail for Barbadoes in such a Time, and that Freighters and Passengers might agree with the Captain at such a Place; so far is what's common; But at the Bottom this odd Thing was added, N.B. *No Sea Hens nor Black Gowns will be admitted on any Terms.* I printed it, and receiv'd my Money; and the Advertisement was stuck up around the Town as usual. I had not so much Curiosity at that time as to enquire the Meaning of it, nor did I in the least imagine it would give so much Offence. Several good Men are very angry with me on this Occasion; they are pleas'd to say I have too much Sense to do such things ignorantly; that if they were Printers they would not have done such a thing on any consideration; that it could proceed from nothing but my abundant Malice against Religion and the Clergy: They therefore declare they will not take any more of my Papers, nor have any farther Dealings with me; but will hinder me of all the Custom they can. All this is very hard!

I believe it had been better if I had refused to print the said Advertisement. However, 'tis done and cannot be revok'd. I have only the following few Particulars to offer, some of them in my behalf, by way of Mitigation, and some not much to the Purpose; but I desire none of them may be read when the Reader is not in a very good Humour.

1. That I really did it without the least Malice, and imagin'd the N.B. was plac'd there only to

make the Advertisement star'd at, and more generally read.

2. That I never saw the Word *Sea-Hens* before in my Life; nor have I yet ask'd the meaning of it; and tho' I had certainly known that *Black Gowns* in that Place signified the Clergy of the Church of England, yet I have the confidence in the generous good Temper of such of them as I know, as to be well satisfied such a trifling mention of their Habit gives them no Disturbance.

3. That most of the Clergy in this and the neighbouring Provinces, are my Customers, and some of them my very good Friends; and I must be very malicious indeed, or very stupid, to print this thing for a small Profit, if I had thought it would have given them just Cause of Offence.

4. That if I have much Malice against the Clergy, and withal such Sense; 'tis strange I never write or talk against the Clergy my self. Some have observed that 'tis a fruitful Topic, and the easiest to be witty upon of all others. I can print any thing I write at less Charge than others; yet I appeal to the Publick that I am never guilty this way, and to all my Acquaintance as to my Conversation.

5. That if a Man of Sense had Malice enough to desire to injure the Clergy, this is the foolishest Thing he could possibly contrive for that Purpose.

6. That I got Five Shillings by it.

7. That none who are angry with me would have given me so much to let it alone.

8. That if all People of different Opinions in this Province would engage to give me as much for not printing things they don't like, as I can get by printing them, I should probably live a very easy Life; and if all Printers were every where so dealt by, there would be very little printed.

9. That I am oblig'd to all who take my Paper, and am willing to think they do it out of meer Friendship. I only desire they would think the same when I deal with them. I think those who leave off, that they have taken it so long. But I beg they would not endeavour to dissuade others, for that will look like Malice.

10. That 'tis impossible any Man should know what he would do if he was a Printer.

11. That notwithstanding the Rashness and Inexperience of Youth, which is most likely to be prevail'd with to do things that ought not to be done; yet I have avoided printing such Things as usually give Offence either to Church or State, more than any Printer that has followed the Business in this Province before.

12. And lastly, That I have printed above a Thousand Advertisements which made not the least mention of *Sea-Hens* or *Black Gowns;* and this being the first Offence, I have the more Reason to expect Forgiveness.

I take leave to conclude with an old Fable, which some of my Readers have heard before, and some have not.

"A certain well-meaning Man and his Son, were travelling towards a Market Town, with an Ass which they had to sell. The Road was bad; and the old Man therefore rid, but the Son went a-foot. The first Passenger they met, asked the Father if he was not ashamed to ride by himself, and suffer the poor Lad to wade along thro' the Mire; this induced him to take up his Son behind him: He had not travelled far, when he met others, who said, they were two unmerciful Lubbers to get both on the Back of that poor Ass, in such a deep Road. Upon this the old Man gets off, and let his Son ride alone. The next they met called the Lad a graceless, rascally young Jackanapes, to ride in that Manner thro' the Dirt, while his aged Father trudged along on Foot; and they said the old Man was a Fool, for suffering it. He then bid his Son come down, and walk with him, and they travell'd on leading the Ass by the Halter; 'till they met another Company, who called them a Couple of sensless Blockheads, for going both on Foot in such a dirty Way, when they had an empty Ass with them, which they might ride upon. The old Man could bear no longer; My Son, said he, it grieves me much that we cannot please all these People: Let us throw the Ass over the next Bridge, and be no farther troubled with him."

Had the old Man been seen acting this last Resolution, he would probably have been call'd a Fool for troubling himself about the different Opinions of all that were pleas'd to find Fault with him: Therefore, tho' I have a Temper almost as complying as his, I intend not to imitate him in this last Particular. I consider the Variety of Humours among Men, and despair of pleasing every Body; yet I shall not therefore leave off Printing. I shall continue my Business. I shall not burn my Press and melt my Letters.

---

# THE WAY TO WEALTH
## PREFACE TO
## *Poor Richard Improved*

---

◇

❨ ON THE long voyage to England during June and July of 1757, Franklin employed his enforced leisure by composing what he at first supposed would be a conventional Preface to his next almanac. He must have had with him a file of the twenty-five numbers he had already issued, though he could possibly have depended on his fabulous memory.

During these twenty-five years he had, as he tells us, been contriving homely aphorisms out of whatever source he could tap and improving most of them with his gift for pungency and imagery. They had become the staple of his successful enterprise. On this voyage he endeavored to assemble all of them he had written, or could remember, and some which he then invented. These he put into the mouth of a no doubt fictional creation, a projection by his middle-aged self into the dream of his old-aged self (which he eventually became), and so wove a tapestry of his adages.

Franklin's nephew, Benjamin Mecom, published the compilation in Boston in 1758 as *Father Abraham's Speech.* Under the more accepted title of *The Way to Wealth* it has been republished more times than bibliographers can count, translated into all Western languages and many Oriental ones, and become, in short, the handbook of creative industry in all countries where wealth is sought.

❖

COURTEOUS READER,

I have heard that nothing gives an Author so great pleasure, as to find his Works respectfully quoted by other learned Authors. This Pleasure I have seldom enjoyed; for tho' I have been, if I may say it without Vanity, an *eminent Author* of Almanacks annually now a full Quarter of a Century, my Brother Authors in the same Way, for what Reason I know not, have ever been sparing in their Applauses; and no other Author has taken the least Notice of me, so that did not my Writings produce me some solid *Pudding,* the great Deficiency of *Praise* would have quite discouraged me.

I concluded at length, that the People were the best Judges of my Merit; for they buy my Works; and besides, in my Rambles, where I am not personally known, I have frequently heard one or other of my Adages repeated, with, *as Poor Richard says,* at the End on't; this gave me some Satisfaction, as it showed not only that my Instructions were regarded, but discovered likewise some Respect for my Authority; and I own, that to encourage the Practice of remembering and repeating those wise Sentences, I have sometimes *quoted myself* with great Gravity.

Judge then how much I must have been gratified by an Incident I am going to relate to you. I stopt my Horse lately where a great Number of People were collected at a Vendue of Merchant Goods. The Hour of Sale not being come, they were conversing on the Badness of the Times, and one of the Company call'd to a plain clean old Man, with white Locks, *Pray, Father* Abraham, *what think you of the Times? Won't these heavy Taxes quite ruin the Country? How shall we ever be able to pay them? What would you advise us to?*——Father *Abraham* stood up, and reply'd, If you'd have my Advice, I'll give it you in short, for a *Word to the Wise is enough,* and *Many Words won't fill a Bushel,* as *Poor Richard* says. They join'd in desiring him to speak his Mind, and gathering round him, he proceeded as follows:

"Friends, says he, and Neighbours, the Taxes are indeed very heavy, and if those laid on by the Government were the only Ones we had to pay, we might more easily discharge them; but we have many others, and much more grievous to some of us. We are taxed twice as much by our *Idleness,* three times as much by our *Pride,* and four times as much by our *Folly,* and from these Taxes the Commissioners cannot ease or deliver us by allowing an Abatement. However let us hearken to good Advice, and something may be done for us; *God helps them that help themselves,* as *Poor Richard* says, in his Almanack of 1733.

It would be thought a hard Government that should tax its People one tenth Part of their *Time,* to be employed in its Service. But *Idleness* taxes many of us much more, if we reckon all that is spent in absolute *Sloth,* or doing of nothing, with that which is spent in idle Employments or Amusements, that amount to nothing. *Sloth,* by bringing on Diseases, absolutely shortens Life. *Sloth, like Rust, consumes faster than Labour wears, while the used Key is always bright,* as *Poor Richard* says. But *dost thou love Life, then do not squander Time, for that's the Stuff Life is made of,* as *Poor Richard* says.—How much more than is necessary do we spend in *sleep!* forgetting that *The sleeping Fox catches no Poultry,* and that *there will be sleeping enough in the Grave,* as *Poor Richard* says. If Time be of all Things the most precious, *wasting Time* must be, as *Poor Richard* says, *the greatest Prodigality,* since, as he elsewhere tells us, *Lost Time is never found again;* and what we call *Time-enough, always proves little enough:* Let us then up and be doing, and doing to the Purpose; so by Diligence shall we do more with less Perplexity. *Sloth makes all Things difficult, but Industry all easy,* as *Poor Richard* says; and *He that riseth late, must trot all Day, and shall scarce overtake his Business at Night.* While *Laziness travels so slowly, that Poverty soon overtakes him,* as we read in *Poor Richard,* who adds, *Drive thy Business, let not that drive thee;* and *Early to Bed, and early to rise, makes a Man healthy, wealthy and wise.*

So what signifies *wishing* and *hoping* for better Times [?] We may make these Times better if we bestir ourselves. *Industry need not wish,* as *Poor Richard* says, and *He that lives upon Hope will die fasting. There are no Gains, without Pains;* then *Help Hands, for I have no Lands,* or if I have, they are smartly taxed. And as *Poor Richard* likewise observes, *He that hath a Trade hath an Estate,* and *He that hath a Calling, hath an Office of Profit and Honour;* but then the *Trade* must be worked at, and the *Calling* well followed, or neither the *Estate,* nor the *Office,* will enable us to pay our Taxes.—If we are industrious we shall never starve; for, as *Poor Richard* says, *At the working Man's House* Hunger *looks in, but dares not enter.* Nor will the Bailiff or the Constable enter, for *Industry pays Debts, while Despair encreaseth them,* says *Poor Richard.*—What though you have found no Treasure, nor has any rich Relation left you a Legacy, *Diligence is the Mother of Good luck,* as *Poor Richard* says, *and God gives all Things to Industry.* Then *plough deep, while Sluggards sleep, and you shall have Corn to sell and to keep,* says *Poor Dick.* Work while it is called To-day, for you know not how much you may be hindered To-morrow, which makes *Poor Richard* say, *One To-day is worth two To-morrows;* and farther, *Have you somewhat to do To-morrow, do it To-day.* If you were a Servant, would you not be ashamed that a good Master should catch you idle? Are you then your own Master, *be ashamed to catch yourself idle,* as *Poor Dick* says. When there is so much to be done for yourself, your Family, your Country, and your gracious King, be up by Peep of Day; *Let not the Sun look down and say, Inglorious here he lies.* Handle your Tools without Mittens; remember that *the Cat in Gloves catches no Mice,* as *Poor Richard* says. 'Tis true there is much to be done, and perhaps you are weak handed, but stick to it steadily, and you will see great Effects, for *constant Drooping wears away Stones,* and by *Diligence and Patience the Mouse ate in two the Cable;* and *little Strokes fell great Oaks,* as *Poor Richard* says in his Almanack, the Year I cannot just now remember.

Methinks I hear some of you say, *Must a Man afford himself no Leisure?*—I will tell thee, my Friend, what *Poor Richard* says, *Employ thy Time well if thou meanest to gain Leisure; and since thou art not sure of a Minute, throw not away an Hour.* Leisure, is Time for doing something useful; this Leisure the diligent Man will obtain, but the lazy Man never; so that, as *Poor Richard* says, *a Life of Leisure and a Life of Laziness are two things.* Do you imagine that Sloth will afford you more Comfort than Labour? No, for as *Poor Richard* says, *Trouble springs from Idleness, and grievous Toil from needless Ease. Many without Labour, would live by their* WITS *only, but they break for want of Stock.* Whereas Industry gives Comfort and Plenty, and Respect: *Fly Pleasures, and they'll follow you. The diligent Spinner has a large Shift;* and *now I have a Sheep and a Cow, every Body bids me Good morrow;* all which is well said by *Poor Richard.*

But with our Industry, we must likewise be *steady, settled* and *careful,* and oversee our own Affairs *with our own Eyes,* and not trust too much to others; for, as *Poor Richard* says,

*I never saw an oft removed Tree,*
*Nor yet an oft removed Family,*
*That throve so well as those that settled be.*

And again, *Three Removes is as bad as a Fire;* and again, *Keep thy Shop, and thy Shop will keep thee;* and again, *If you would have your Business done, go; If not, send.* And again,

*He that by the plough would thrive,*
*Himself must either hold or drive.*

And again, *The Eye of a Master will do more Work than both his Hands;* and again, *Want of Care does us more Damage than Want of Knowledge;* and again, *Not to oversee Workmen, is to leave them your Purse open.* Trusting too much to others' Care is the Ruin of many; for, as the *Almanack* says, *In the Affairs of this World, Men are saved, not by Faith, but by the Want of it;* but a Man's own Care is profitable; for, saith *Poor Dick, Learning is to the Studious, and Riches to the Careful,* as well as *Power to the Bold,* and *Heaven to the Virtuous.* And farther, *If you would have a faithful Servant, and one that you like, serve yourself.* And again, he adviseth to Circumspection and Care, even in the smallest Matters, because sometimes *a little Neglect may breed great Mischief;* adding, *For want of a Nail the Shoe was lost; for want of a Shoe the Horse was lost; and for want of a Horse the Rider was lost,* being overtaken and slain by the Enemy, all for want of Care about a Horse shoe Nail.

So much for *Industry,* my Friends, and Attention to one's own Business; but to these we must add *Frugality,* if we would make our *Industry* more certainly successful. A Man may, if he knows not how to save as he gets, *keep his Nose all his Life to the Grindstone,* and die not worth a *Groat* at last. *A fat Kitchen makes a lean Will,* as *Poor Richard* says; and,

*Many Estates are spent in the Getting,*
*Since Women for Tea forsook Spinning and*
*    Knitting,*
*And Men for Punch forsook Hewing and Splitting.*

*If you would be wealthy,* says he, in another Almanack, *think of Saving as well as of Getting: The* Indies *have not made* Spain *rich, because her* Outgoes *are greater than her* Incomes. Away then with your expensive Follies, and you will not have so much Cause to complain of hard Times, heavy Taxes, and chargeable Families; for, as *Poor Dick* says,

*Women and Wine, Game and Deceit,*
*Make the Wealth small, and the Wants great.*

And farther, *What maintains one Vice, would bring up two Children.* You may think perhaps, That a *little* Tea, or a *little* Punch now and then, Diet a *little* more costly, Clothes a *little* finer, and a *little* Entertainment now and then, can be no *great* Matter; but remember what *Poor Richard* says, *Many a Little makes a Mickle;* and farther, *Beware of* little *Expenses; a small Leak will sink a great Ship;* and again, *Who Dainties love, shall Beggars prove;* and moreover, *Fools make Feasts, and wise Men eat them.*

Here you are all got together at this Vendue of *Fineries* and *Knicknacks.* You call them *Goods,* but if you do not take Care, they will prove *Evils* to some of you. You expect they will be sold *cheap,* and perhaps they may for less than they cost; but if you have no Occasion for them, they must be *dear* to you. Remember what *Poor Richard* says, *Buy what thou hast no Need of, and ere long thou shalt sell thy Necessaries.* And again, *At a great Pennyworth pause a while:* He means, that perhaps the Cheapness is *apparent* only, and not *real;* or the Bargain, by straitning thee in thy Business, may do thee more Harm than Good. For in another Place he says, *Many have been ruined by buying good Pennyworth.* Again, *Poor Richard* says, *'Tis foolish to lay out Money in a Purchase of Repentance;* and yet this Folly is practised every Day at Vendues, for want of minding the Almanack. *Wise Men,* as *Poor Dick* says, *learn by others' Harms, Fools scarcely by their own;* but *Felix quem faciunt aliena Pericula cautum.* Many a one, for the Sake of Finery on the Back, have gone with a hungry Belly, and half starved their Families; *Silks and Sattins, Scarlet and Velvets,* as *Poor Richard* says, *put out the Kitchen Fire.* These are not the *Necessaries* of Life; they can scarcely be called the *Conveniences,* and yet only because they look

pretty, how many *want* to *have* them. The *artificial* Wants of Mankind thus become more numerous than the *natural;* and, as *Poor Dick* says, *For one* poor *Person, there are an hundred* indigent. By these, and other Extravagancies, the Genteel are reduced and forced to borrow of those whom they formerly despised, but who through *Industry* and *Frugality* have maintained their Standing in which Case it appears plainly, that a *Ploughman on his Legs is higher than a Gentleman on his Knees,* as *Poor Richard* says. Perhaps they have had a small Estate left them which they knew not the Getting of; they think *'tis Day, and will never be Night;* that a little to be spent out of *so much,* is not worth minding; (*a Child and a Fool,* as *Poor Richard* says, *imagine* Twenty Shillings *and Twenty Years can never be spent*) but, *always taking out of, the Meal-tub, and never putting in, soon comes to the Bottom;* then, as *Poor Dick* says, *When the Well's dry, they know the Worth of Water.* But this they might have known before, if they had taken his Advice; *If you would know the Value of Money, go and try to borrow some;* for, *he that goes a borrowing gets a sorrowing;* and indeed so does he that lends to such People, when he goes *to get it in again.—Poor Dick* farther advises, and says,

*Fond* Pride of Dress *is sure a very Curse;*
*E'er* Fancy *you consult, consult your Purse.*

And again, *Pride is as loud a Beggar as Want, and a great deal more saucy.* When you have bought one fine Thing you must buy ten more, that your Appearance may be all of a Piece; but *Poor Dick* says, *'Tis easier to* suppress *the first Desire, than to* satisfy all that follow it. And 'tis as truly Folly for the Poor to ape the Rich, as for the Frog to swell, in order to equal the Ox.

*Great Estates may venture more,*
*But little Boats should keep near Shore.*

'Tis however a Folly soon punished; for *Pride that dines on Vanity sups on Contempt,* as *Poor Richard* says. And in another Place, *Pride breakfasted with Plenty, dined with Poverty, and supped with Infamy.* And after all, of what Use is this *Pride of Appearance,* for which so much is risked, so much is suffered? It cannot promote Health, or ease Pain; it makes no Increase of Merit in the Person, it creates Envy, it hastens Misfortune.

*What is a Butterfly? At best*
*He's but a Caterpiller drest.*
*The gaudy Fop's his Picture just,*

as *Poor Richard* says.

But what Madness must it be to *run in Debt* for these Superfluities! We are offered by the Terms of this Vendue, *Six Months Credit;* and that perhaps has induced some of us to attend it, because we cannot spare the ready Money, and hope now to be fine without it. But, ah, think what you do when you run in Debt; *You give to another, Power over your Liberty*. If you cannot pay at the Time, you will be ashamed to see your Creditor; you will be in Fear when you speak to him; you will make poor pitiful sneaking Excuses, and by Degrees come to lose your Veracity, and sink into base downright lying; for, as *Poor Richard* says, *The second Vice is Lying, the first is running in Debt*. And again, to the same Purpose, *Lying rides upon Debt's Back*. Whereas a free-born *Englishman* ought not to be ashamed or afraid to see or speak to any Man living. But Poverty often deprives a Man of all Spirit and Virtue: *'Tis hard for an empty Bag to stand upright*, as *Poor Richard* truly says. What would you think of that Prince, or that Government, who should issue an Edict forbidding you to dress like a Gentleman or a Gentlewoman, on Pain of Imprisonment or Servitude? Would you not say, that you are free, and have a Right to dress as you please, and that such an Edict would be a Breach of your Privileges, and such a Government tyrannical? And yet you are about to put yourself under that Tyranny when you run in Debt for such Dress! Your Creditor has Authority at his pleasure to deprive you of your Liberty, by confining you in Gaol for Life, or to sell you for a Servant, if you should not be able to pay him! When you have got your Bargain, you may, perhaps, think little of Payment; but *Creditors, Poor Richard* tells us, *have better Memories than Debtors;* and in another Place says, *Creditors are a superstitious Sect, great Observers of set Days and Times*. The Day comes round before you are aware, and the Demand is made before you are prepared to satisfy it. Or if you bear your Debt in Mind, the Term which at first seemed so long, will as it lessens, appear extreamly short. *Time* will seem to have added Wings to his Heels as well as Shoulders. *Those have a short Lent,* saith *Poor Richard, who owe Money to be paid at Easter.* Then since, as he says, *The Borrower is a Slave to the Lender, and the Debtor to the Creditor,* disdain the Chain, preserve your Freedom; and maintain your Independency: Be *industrious* and *free;* be *frugal* and *free*. At present, perhaps, you may think yourself in thriving Circumstances, and that you can bear a little Extravagance without Injury; but,

> *For Age and Want, save while you may;*
> *No Morning Sun lasts a whole Day,*

as *Poor Richard* says—Gain may be temporary and uncertain, but ever while you live, Expence is constant and certain; and *'tis easier to build two Chimnies than to keep one in Fuel,* as *Poor Richard* says. So *rather go to Bed supperless than rise in Debt.*

> *Get what you can, and what you get hold;*
> *'Tis the Stone that will turn all your Lead into*
>     *Gold,*

as *Poor Richard* says. And when you have got the Philosopher's Stone, sure you will no longer complain of bad Times, or the Difficulty of paying Taxes.

This Doctrine, my Friends, is *Reason* and *Wisdom;* but after all, do not depend too much upon your own *Industry*, and *Frugality*, and *Prudence*, though excellent Things, for they may all be blasted without the Blessing of Heaven; and therefore ask that Blessing humbly, and be not uncharitable to those that at the present seem to want it, but comfort and help them. Remember *Job* suffered, and was afterwards prosperous.

And now to conclude, *Experience keeps a dear School, but Fools will learn in no other, and scarce in that;* for it is true, *we may give Advice, but we cannot give Conduct,* as *Poor Richard* says: However, remember this, *They that won't be counselled, can't be helped,* as *Poor Richard* says: And farther, That *if you will not hear Reason, she'll surely rap your Knuckles*.["]

Thus the old Gentleman ended his Harangue. The People heard it, and approved the Doctrine and immediately practised the contrary, just as if it had been a common Sermon; for the Vendue opened, and they began to buy extravagantly, notwithstanding all his Cautions, and their own Fear of Taxes.—I found the good Man had thoroughly studied my Almanacks, and digested all I had dropt on those Topicks during the Course of Five-and-twenty Years. The frequent Mention he made of me must have tired any one else, but my Vanity was wonderfully delighted with it, though I was conscious that not a tenth Part of the Wisdom was my own which he ascribed to me, but rather the *Gleanings* I had made of the Sense of all Ages and Nations. However, I resolved to be the better for the Echo of it; and though I had at first determined to buy Stuff for a new Coat, I went away resolved to wear my old One a little longer. *Reader,* if thou wilt do the same, thy Profit will be as great as mine.

*July 7, 1757*

> *I am, as ever,*
> *Thine to serve thee,*
> RICHARD SAUNDERS.

# THE SALE OF THE HESSIANS

◇

([ THIS skit, which barely disguises the fury of Franklin's contempt for Britain's hiring of German mercenaries, was first published in French. Though he gives it a date in February of 1777, Franklin must have written it later, when he had learned, in March, of the capture of the Hessians at Trenton the day after Christmas. There was a real Count Schaumburg who served as agent for George III in purchasing soldiers in Germany; so Franklin pilloried him forever by giving his name to the Hessian ruler.

◇

FROM THE COUNT DE SCHAUMBERGH TO THE BARON HOHENDORF, COMMANDING THE HESSIAN TROOPS IN AMERICA

Rome, February 18, 1777.

MONSIEUR LE BARON:—

On my return from Naples, I received at Rome your letter of the 27th December of last year. I have learned with unspeakable pleasure the courage our troops exhibited at Trenton, and you cannot imagine my joy on being told that of the 1,950 Hessians engaged in the fight, but 345 escaped. There were just 1,605 men killed, and I cannot sufficiently commend your prudence in sending an exact list of the dead to my minister in London. This precaution was the more necessary, as the report sent to the English ministry does not give but 1,455 dead. This would make 483,450 florins instead of 645,500 which I am entitled to demand under our convention. You will comprehend the prejudice which such an error would work in my finances, and I do not doubt you will take the necessary pains to prove that Lord North's list is false and yours correct.

The court of London objects that there were a hundred wounded who ought not to be included in the list, nor paid for as dead; but I trust you will not overlook my instructions to you on quitting Cassel, and that you will not have tried by human succor to recall the life of the unfortunates whose days could not be lengthened but by the loss of a leg or an arm. That would be making them a pernicious present, and I am sure they would rather die than live in a condition no longer fit for my service. I do not mean by this that you should assassinate them; we should be humane, my dear Baron, but you may insinuate to the surgeons with entire propriety that a crippled man is a reproach to their profession, and that there is no wiser course than to let every one of them die when he ceases to be fit to fight.

I am about to send to you some new recruits. Don't economize them. Remember glory before all things. Glory is true wealth. There is nothing degrades the soldier like the love of money. He must care only for honour and reputation, but this reputation must be acquired in the midst of dangers. A battle gained without costing the conqueror any blood is an inglorious success, while the conquered cover themselves with glory by perishing with their arms in their hands. Do you remember that of the 300 Lacedaemonians who defended the defile of Thermopylae, not one returned? How happy should I be could I say the same of my brave Hessians!

It is true that their king, Leonidas, perished with them: but things have changed, and it is no longer the custom for princes of the empire to go and fight in America for a cause with which they have no concern. And besides, to whom should they pay the thirty guineas per man if I did not stay in Europe to receive them? Then, it is necessary also that I be ready to send recruits to replace the men you lose. For this purpose I must return to Hesse. It is true, grown men are becoming scarce there, but I will send you boys. Besides, the scarcer the commodity the higher the price. I am assured that the women and little girls have begun to till our lands, and they get on not badly. You did right to send back to Europe that Dr. Crumerus who was so successful in curing dysentery. Don't bother with a man who is subject to looseness of the bowels. That disease makes bad soldiers. One coward will do more mischief in an engagement than ten brave men will do good. Better that they burst in their barracks than fly in battle, and tarnish the glory of our arms. Besides, you know that they pay me as killed for all who die from disease, and I don't get a farthing for runaways. My trip to Italy, which has cost me enormously, makes it desirable that there should be a great mortality among them. You will therefore promise promotion to all who expose themselves; you will exhort them to seek glory in the midst of dangers; you will say to Major Maundorff that I am not at all content with his saving the 345 men who escaped the massacre of Trenton. Through the whole campaign he has not had ten men killed in consequence of his orders. Finally, let it be your principal object to prolong the war and avoid a decisive engagement on either side, for I have made arrangements for a grand Italian opera, and I do not wish to be obliged to give it up. Meantime I pray God, my dear Baron de Hohendorf, to have you in his holy and gracious keeping.

# THE WHISTLE

◊

❡ MADAME BRILLON evidently had written to Franklin, in that semisolemn vein which Franklin subtly cultivated among his female entourage at Passy, on the joys of paradise and how therefore men and women ought to make the best of this present existence. Presumably, Franklin sent his answer in French. A manuscript draft, in his own handwriting, does exist; it is in many details different from the text here reprinted, which has long stood as the standard. Whether Franklin or some editor translated the French back into this English redaction remains a mystery.

◊

TO MADAME BRILLON

Passy, November 10, 1779.

I RECEIVED my dear friend's two letters, one for Wednesday and one for Saturday. This is again Wednesday. I do not deserve one for to-day, because I have not answered the former. But, indolent as I am, and averse to writing, the fear of having no more of your pleasing epistles, if I do not contribute to the correspondence, obliges me to take up my pen; and as Mr. B has kindly sent me word, that he sets out to-morrow to see you, instead of spending this Wednesday evening as I have done its namesakes, in your delightful company, I sit down to spend it in thinking of you, in writing to you, and in reading over and over again your letters.

I am charmed with your description of Paradise, and with your plan of living there; and I approve much of your conclusion, that, in the meantime, we should draw all the good we can from this world. In my opinion, we might all draw more good from it than we do, and suffer less evil, if we would take care not to give too much for *whistles*. For to me it seems, that most of the unhappy people we meet with, are become so by neglect of that caution.

You ask what I mean? You love stories, and will excuse my telling one of myself.

When I was a child of seven years old, my friends, on a holiday, filled my pocket with coppers. I went directly to a shop where they sold toys for children; and, being charmed with the sound of a *whistle,* that I met by the way in the hands of another boy, I voluntarily offered and gave all my money for one. I then came home, and went whistling all over the house, much pleased with my *whistle,* but disturbing all the family. My brothers, and sisters, and cousins, understanding the bargain I had made, told me I had given four times as much for it as it was worth; put me in mind what good things I might have bought with the rest of the money; and laughed at me so much for my folly, that I cried with vexation; and the reflection gave me more chagrin than the *whistle* gave me pleasure.

This however was afterwards of use to me, the impression continuing on my mind; so that often, when I was tempted to buy some unnecessary thing, I said to myself, *Don't give too much for the whistle;* and I saved my money.

As I grew up, came into the world, and observed the actions of men, I thought I met with many, very many, who *gave too much for the whistle.*

When I saw one too ambitious of court favour, sacrificing his time in attendance on levees, his repose, his liberty, his virtue, and perhaps his friends, to attain it, I have said to myself, *This man gives too much for his whistle.*

When I saw another fond of popularity, constantly employing himself in political bustles, neglecting his own affairs, and ruining them by that neglect, *He pays, indeed,* said I, *too much for his whistle.*

If I knew a miser, who gave up every kind of comfortable living, all the pleasure of doing good to others, all the esteem of his fellow-citizens, and the joys of benevolent friendship, for the sake of accumulating wealth, *Poor man,* said I, *you pay too much for your whistle.*

When I met with a man of pleasure, sacrificing every laudable improvement of the mind, or of his fortune, to mere corporeal sensations, and ruining his health in their pursuit, *Mistaken man,* said I, *you are providing pain for yourself, instead of pleasure; you give too much for your whistle.*

If I see one fond of appearance, or fine clothes, fine houses, fine furniture, fine equipages, all above his fortune, for which he contracts debts, and ends his career in a prison, *Alas!* say I, *he has paid dear, very dear, for his whistle.*

When I see a beautiful, sweet-tempered girl married to an ill-natured brute of a husband, *What a pity,* say I, *that she should pay so much for a whistle!*

In short, I conceive that great part of the miseries of mankind are brought upon them by the false estimates they have made of the value of things, and by their *giving too much for their whistles.*

Yet I ought to have charity for these unhappy people, when I consider, that, with all this wisdom of which I am boasting, there are certain things in the world so tempting, for example, the apples of King John, which happily are not to be bought; for if they were put to sale by auction, I might very easily be led to ruin myself in the purchase, and find that I had once more given too much for my *whistle.*

Adieu, my dear friend, and believe me ever yours very sincerely and with unalterable affection,

B. FRANKLIN.

# DIALOGUE BETWEEN FRANKLIN AND THE GOUT

❖

❪ DESPITE all the rules and regulations of his program for achieving perfection, Franklin proved unable to control his diet. He enjoyed his wine. In October 1780, he was brought down with a spell of gout which kept him in his house for six painful weeks. In the midst of it he wrote this piece of self-accusation.

It, like the two preceding selections, was composed for the delight of his friends, and in French. The manuscript contains marginal notations by Madame Brillon. She had sent him a verse dialogue, *Le Sage et la Goutte,* in which the Sage admits to having mistresses, enjoying wine, and insists he does not always win at chess. This English version first appeared in an edition of Franklin's then known *Works,* in London, 1806.

❖

Midnight, October 22, 1780.

FRANKLIN. Eh! Oh! Eh! What have I done to merit these cruel sufferings?

GOUT. Many things; you have ate and drank too freely, and too much indulged those legs of yours in their indolence.

FRANKLIN. Who is it that accuses me?

GOUT. It is I, even I, the Gout.

FRANKLIN. What! my enemy in person?

GOUT. No, not your enemy.

FRANKLIN. I repeat it; my enemy; for you would not only torment my body to death, but ruin my good name; you reproach me as a glutton and a tippler; now all the world, that

knows me, will allow that I am neither the one nor the other.

GOUT. The world may think as it pleases; it is always very complaisant to itself, and sometimes to its friends; but I very well know that the quantity of meat and drink proper for a man, who takes a reasonable degree of exercise, would be too much for another, who never takes any.

FRANKLIN. I take—Eh! Oh!—as much exercise —Eh!—as I can, Madam Gout. You know my sedentary state, and on that account, it would seem, Madam Gout, as if you might spare me a little, seeing it is not altogether my own fault.

GOUT. Not a jot; your rhetoric and your politeness are thrown away; your apology avails nothing. If your situation in life is a sedentary one, your amusements, your recreations, at least, should be active. You ought to walk or ride; or, if the weather prevents that play at billiards. But let us examine your course of life. While the mornings are long, and you have leisure to go abroad, what do you do? Why, instead of gaining an appetite for breakfast, by salutary exercise, you amuse yourself, with books, pamphlets, or newspapers, which commonly are not worth the reading. Yet you eat an inordinate breakfast, four dishes of tea, with cream, and one or two buttered toasts, with slices of hung beef, which I fancy are not things the most easily digested. Immediately afterward you sit down to write at your desk, or converse with persons who apply to you on business. Thus the time passes till one, without any kind of bodily exercise. But all this I could pardon, in regard, as you say, to your sedentary condition. But what is your practice after dinner? Walking in the beautiful gardens of those friends, with whom you have dined, would be the choice of men of sense; yours is to be fixed down to chess, where you are found engaged for two or three hours! This is your perpetual recreation, which is the least eligible of any for a sedentary man, because, instead of accelerating the motion of the fluids, the rigid attention it requires helps to retard the circulation and obstruct internal secretions. Wrapt in the speculations of this wretched game, you destroy your constitution. What can be expected from such a course of living but a body replete with stagnant humours, ready to fall a prey to all kinds of dangerous maladies, if I, the Gout, did not occasionally bring you relief by agitating those humours, and so purifying or dissipating them? If it was in some nook or alley in Paris, deprived of walks, that you played awhile at chess after dinner, this might be excusable; but the same taste prevails with you in Passy, Auteuil, Montmartre, or Sanoy, places where there are the finest gardens and walks, a pure air, beautiful women, and the most agreeable and instructive conversation; all of which you might enjoy by frequenting the walks. But these are rejected for this abominable game of chess. Fie, then Mr. Franklin! But amidst my instructions, I had almost forgot to administer my wholesome corrections; so take that twinge,—and that.

FRANKLIN. Oh! Eh! Oh! Ohhh! As much instruction as you please, Madam Gout, and as many reproaches; but pray, Madam, a truce with your corrections!

GOUT. No, Sir, no,—I will not abate a particle of what is so much for your good,—therefore—

FRANKLIN. Oh! Ehhh!—It is not fair to say I take no exercise, when I do very often, going out to dine and returning in my carriage.

GOUT. That, of all imaginable exercises, is the most slight and insignificant, if you allude to the motion of a carriage suspended on springs. By observing the degree of heat obtained by different kinds of motion, we may form an estimate of the quantity of exercise given by each. Thus, for example, if you turn out to walk in winter with cold feet, in an hour's time you will be in a glow all over; ride on horseback, the same effect will scarcely be perceived by four hours' round trotting; but if you loll in a carriage, such as you have mentioned, you may travel all day, and gladly enter the last inn to warm your feet by a fire. Flatter yourself then no longer, that half an hour's airing in your carriage deserves the name of exercise. Providence has appointed few to roll in carriages, while he has given to all a pair of legs, which are machines infinitely more commodious and serviceable. Be grateful, then, and make a proper use of yours. Would you know how they forward the circulation of your fluids, in the very action of transporting you from place to place; observe when you walk, that all your weight is alternately thrown from one leg to the other; this occasions a great pressure on the vessels of the foot, and repels their contents; when relieved, by the weight being thrown on the other foot, the vessels of the first are allowed to replenish, and, by a return of this weight, this repulsion again succeeds; thus accelerating the circulation of the blood. The heat produced in any given time, depends on the degree of this acceleration; the fluids are shaken, the humours attenuated, the secretions facilitated, and all goes well; the cheeks are ruddy, and health is established. Behold your fair friend at Auteuil; a lady who received from bounteous nature more really useful science, than half a dozen such pretenders to philosophy as you have been able to extract from all your books. When she honours you with a visit, it is on foot. She walks all hours of the day, and leaves indolence, and its

concomitant maladies, to be endured by her horses. In this see at once the preservative of her health and personal charms. But when you go to Auteuil, you must have your carriage, though it is no further from Passy to Auteuil than from Auteuil to Passy.

FRANKLIN. Your reasonings grow very tiresome.

GOUT. I stand corrected. I will be silent and continue my office, take that, and that.

FRANKLIN. Oh! Ohh! Talk on, I pray you!

GOUT. No, no; I have a good number of twinges for you to-night, and you may be sure of some more to-morrow.

FRANKLIN. What, with such a fever! I shall go distracted. Oh! Eh! Can no one bear it for me?

GOUT. Ask that of your horses; they have served you faithfully.

FRANKLIN. How can you so cruelly sport with my torments?

GOUT. Sport! I am very serious. I have here a list of offences against your own health distinctly written, and can justify every stroke inflicted on you.

FRANKLIN. Read it then.

GOUT. It is too long a detail; but I will briefly mention some particulars.

FRANKLIN. Proceed. I am all attention.

GOUT. Do you remember how often you have promised yourself, the following morning, a walk in the grove of Boulogne, in the garden de la Muette, or in your own garden, and have violated your promise, alleging, at one time, it was too cold, at another too warm, too windy, too moist, or what else you pleased; when in truth it was too nothing, but your insuperable love of ease?

FRANKLIN. That I confess may have happened occasionally, probably ten times in a year.

GOUT. Your confession is very far short of the truth; the gross amount is one hundred and ninety-nine times.

FRANKLIN. Is it possible?

GOUT. So possible, that it is fact; you may rely on the accuracy of my statement. You know M. Brillon's gardens, and what fine walks they contain; you know the handsome flight of an hundred steps, which lead from the terrace above to the lawn below. You have been in the practice of visiting this amiable family twice a week, after dinner, and it is a maxim of your own, that "a man may take as much exercise in walking a mile, up and down stairs, as in ten on level ground." What an opportunity was here for you to have had exercise in both these ways! Did you embrace it, and how often?

FRANKLIN. I cannot immediately answer that question.

GOUT. I will do it for you; not once.

FRANKLIN. Not once?

GOUT. Even so. During the summer you went there at six o'clock. You found the charming lady, with her lovely children and friends, eager to walk with you, and entertain you with their agreeable conversation; and what has been your choice? Why to sit on the terrace, satisfying yourself with the fine prospect, and passing your eye over the beauties of the garden below, without taking one step to descend and walk about in them. On the contrary, you call for tea and the chessboard; and lo! you are occupied in your seat till nine o'clock, and that besides two hours' play after dinner; and then, instead of walking home, which would have bestirred you a little, you step into your carriage. How absurd to suppose that all this carelessness can be reconcilable with health, without my interposition!

FRANKLIN. I am convinced now of the justness of poor Richard's remark, that "Our debts and our sins are always greater than we think for."

GOUT. So it is. You philosophers are sages in your maxims, and fools in your conduct.

FRANKLIN. But do you charge among my crimes, that I return in a carriage from Mr. Brillon's?

GOUT. Certainly; for, having been seated all the while, you cannot object the fatigue of the day, and cannot want therefore the relief of a carriage.

FRANKLIN. What then would you have me do with my carriage?

GOUT. Burn it if you choose; you would at least get heat out of it once in this way; or, if you dislike that proposal, here's another for you; observe the poor peasants, who work in the vineyards and grounds about the villages of Passy, Auteuil, Chaillot, &c.; you may find every day, among these deserving creatures, four or five old men and women, bent and perhaps crippled by weight of years, and too long and too great labour. After a most fatiguing day, these people have to trudge a mile or two to their smoky huts. Order your coachman to set them down. This is an act that will be good for your soul; and, at the same time, after your visit to the Brillons, if you return on foot, that will be good for your body.

FRANKLIN. Ah! how tiresome you are!

GOUT. Well, then, to my office; it should not be forgotten that I am your physician. There.

FRANKLIN. Ohhh! what a devil of a physician!

GOUT. How ungrateful you are to say so! Is it not I who, in the character of your physician, have saved you from the palsy, dropsy, and apoplexy? one or other of which would have done for you long ago, but for me.

FRANKLIN. I submit, and thank you for the past, but entreat the discontinuance of your visits for the future; for, in my mind, one had better die than be cured so dolefully. Permit me just to hint, that I have also not been unfriendly to *you*. I never feed physician or quack of any kind, to enter the list against you; if then you do not leave me to my repose, it may be said you are ungrateful too.

GOUT. I can scarcely acknowledge that as any objection. As to quacks, I despise them; they may kill you indeed, but cannot injure me. And, as to regular physicians, they are at last convinced that the gout, in such a subject as you are, is no disease, but a remedy; and wherefore cure a remedy? —but to our business,—there.

FRANKLIN. Oh! oh!—for Heaven's sake leave me! and I promise faithfully never more to play at chess, but to take exercise daily, and live temperately.

GOUT. I know you too well. You promise fair; but, after a few months of good health, you will return to your own habits; your fine promises will be forgotten like the forms of last year's clouds. Let us then finish the account, and I will go. But I leave you with an assurance of visiting you again at a proper time and place; for my object is your good, and you are sensible now that I am your *real friend.*

---

# TO EZRA STILES

---

◊

⟨ EZRA STILES (1727–95), president of Yale College since 1778, felt he had a right to demand of America's Sage, even though he knew that Franklin was in the last gasps, "the opinion of my venerable friend concerning Jesus of Nazareth." Stiles had been brought up in the severe Calvinism of Connecticut, and graduated from Yale in 1746. Although licensed by the Consociation to preach, he underwent a long period of doubt, and in despair turned to the study of law, being admitted to the bar in 1753. While in the throes of this crisis, he delivered the complimentary oration upon the visit of Franklin to New Haven in 1755. Thence onward, he and Franklin were fast friends, the tie strengthened by Stiles's great interest in science.

Stiles emerged from his struggle with skepticism to become a firm believer in divine revelation, and to serve for twenty years as minister to the Second Church of Newport, Rhode Island. He continued to correspond with Franklin; his friend persuaded the University of Edinburgh to bestow upon Stiles an honorary Doctorate of Divinity. Stiles was an ardent patriot, supported the Revolution, and carried Yale College through the crisis.

In 1790 he knew that Franklin could not live long, and that Franklin would reply, as he did, from his deathbed. Yet he had to ask, and Franklin contrived to answer. This letter was written on March 9, 1790. Franklin expired on April 17.

◊

Philad, March 9, 1790.

REVEREND AND DEAR SIR,

I received your kind Letter of Jan'y 28, and am glad you have at length received the portrait of Gov'r Yale from his Family, and deposited it in the College Library. He was a great and good Man, and had the Merit of doing infinite Service to your Country by his Munificence to that Institution. The Honour you propose doing me by placing mine in the same Room with his, is much too great for my Deserts; but you always had a Partiality for me, and to that it must be ascribed. I am however too much obliged to Yale College, the first learned Society that took Notice of me and adorned me with its Honours, to refuse a Request that comes from it thro' so esteemed a Friend. But I do not think any one of the Portraits you mention, as in my Possession, worthy of the Place and Company you propose to place it in. You have an excellent Artist lately arrived. If he will undertake to make one for you, I shall cheerfully pay the Expense; but he must not delay setting about it, or I may slip thro' his fingers, for I am now in my eighty-fifth year, and very infirm.

I send with this a very learned Work, as it seems to me, on the antient Samaritan Coins, lately printed in Spain, and at least curious for the Beauty of the Impression. Please to accept it for your College Library. I have subscribed for the Encyclopaedia now printing here, with the Intention of presenting it to the College. I shall probably depart before the Work is finished, but shall leave Directions for its Continuance to the End. With this you will receive some of the first numbers.

You desire to know something of my Religion. It is the first time I have been questioned upon it. But I cannot take your Curiosity amiss, and shall endeavour in a few Words to gratify it. Here is my Creed. I believe in one God, Creator of the Universe. That he governs it by his Providence. That he ought to be worshipped. That the most acceptable Service we render to him is doing good to his other Children. That the soul of Man is immortal, and will be treated with Justice in another Life respecting its Conduct in this. These I take to be the fundamental Principles of all sound Religion, and I regard them as you do in whatever Sect I meet with them.

As to Jesus of Nazareth, my Opinion of whom you particularly desire, I think the System of Morals and his Religion, as he left them to us, the best the World ever saw or is likely to see; but I apprehend it has received various corrupting Changes, and I have, with most of the present Dissenters in England, some Doubts as to his Divinity; tho' it is a question I do not dogmatize upon, having never studied it, and think it needless to busy myself with it now, when I expect soon an Opportunity of knowing the Truth with less Trouble. I see no harm, however, in its being believed, if that Belief has the good Consequence, as probably it has, of making his Doctrines more respected and better observed; especially as I do not perceive, that the Supreme takes it amiss, by distinguishing the Unbelievers in his Government of the World with any peculiar Marks of his Displeasure.

I shall only add, respecting myself, that, having experienced the Goodness of that Being in conducting me prosperously thro' a long life, I have no doubt of its Continuance in the next, though without the smallest Conceit of meriting such Goodness. My Sentiments on this Head you will see in the Copy of an old Letter enclosed, which I wrote in answer to one from a zealous Religionist, whom I had relieved in a paralytic case by electricity, and who, being afraid I should grow proud upon it, sent me his serious though rather impertinent Caution. I send you also the Copy of another Letter, which will shew something of my Disposition relating to Religion. With great and sincere Esteem and Affection, I am, Your obliged old Friend and most obedient humble Servant

B. FRANKLIN.

P.S. Had not your College some Present of Books from the King of France? Please to let me know, if you had an Expectation given you of more, and the Nature of the Expectation? I have a Reason for the Enquiry.

I confide, that you will not expose me to Criticism and censure by publishing any part of this Communication to you. I have ever let others enjoy their religious Sentiments, without reflecting on them for those that appeared to me unsupportable and even absurd. All Sects here, and we have a great Variety, have experienced my good will in assisting them with Subscriptions for building their new Places of Worship; and, as I have never opposed any of their Doctrines, I hope to go out of the World in Peace with them all.

# Jonathan Edwards

FROM THE

## PERSONAL NARRATIVE

◇

❡THE "Personal Narrative" of Jonathan Edwards was revealed to the world only fifty years after his death in an edition of his *Works* published in 1808. So far as we now know, the original manuscript does not survive. We remain therefore at the mercy of his transcribers.

Had he ever completed his own story, the result would surely have been a masterpiece of self-exposition which could be the perfect obverse to the reverse of Franklin's *Autobiography*. In one sense, his motives for talking about himself were widely different from Franklin's: he did not yet want to prove any success; he merely wished to leave a factual record of his spiritual (*not* his clerical) experience, so that any surgical examination of his pretensions could be diagnosed. Yet in another sense, and a happily congenial sense, he must have entertained an aspiration to do exactly what Franklin more largely did achieve. He sought to establish the criterion of success within the terms of his standards of authentic experience.

Edwards was never allowed the leisure, once he became his grandfather's heir, to find the time for further recounting of himself. Hence he had only the opportunity for a fragment of autobiography—as ultimately Franklin had only a scrap of time. Both of them, ironically, were obliged to leave unfinished statements of themselves to a posterity called to evaluate their comparative merits. The final judgment has not yet been recorded.

◇

I HAD a variety of concerns and exercises about my soul from my childhood; but had two more remarkable seasons of awakening, before I met with that change by which I was brought to those new dispositions, and that new sense of things, that I have since had. The first time was when I was a boy, some years before I went to college, at a time of remarkable awakening in my father's congregation. I was then very much affected for many months, and concerned about the things of religion, and my soul's salvation; and was abundant in duties. I used to pray five times a day in secret, and to spend much time in religious talk with other boys; and used to meet with them to pray together. I experienced I know not what kind of delight in religion. My mind was much engaged in it, and had much selfrighteous pleasure; and it was my delight to abound in religious duties. I with some of my schoolmates joined together, and built a booth in a swamp, in a very retired spot, for a place of prayer. And besides, I had particular secret places of my own in the woods, where I used to retire by myself; and was from time to time much affected. My affections seemed to be lively and easily moved, and I seemed to be in my element when engaged in religious duties. And I am ready to think, many are deceived with such affections, and such a kind of delight as I then had in religion, and mistake it for grace.

But in process of time, my convictions and affections wore off; and I entirely lost all those affections and delights and left off secret prayer, at least as to any constant performance of it; and returned like a dog to his vomit, and went on in the ways of sin. Indeed I was at times very uneasy, especially towards the latter part of my time at college; when it pleased God, to seize me with a pleurisy; in which he brought me nigh to the grave, and shook me over the pit of hell. And yet, it was not long after my recovery, before I fell again into my old ways of sin. But God would not suffer me to go on with any quietness; I had great and violent inward struggles, till, after many conflicts with wicked inclinations, repeated resolutions, and bonds that I laid myself under by a kind of vows to God, I was brought wholly to break off all former wicked ways, and all ways of known outward sin; and to apply myself to seek salvation, and practise many religious duties; but without that kind of affection and delight which I had formerly experienced. My concern now wrought more by inward struggles and conflicts, and selfreflections. I made seeking my salvation the main business of my life. But yet, it seems to me, I sought after a miserable manner; which has made me sometimes since to question, whether ever it issued in that which was saving; being ready to doubt, whether such miserable seeking ever succeeded. I was indeed brought to seek salvation in a manner that I never was before; I felt a spirit to part with all things in the world, for an interest in Christ. My concern continued and prevailed, with many exercising thoughts and inward struggles; but yet it never seemed to be proper to express that concern by the name of terror.

From my childhood up, my mind had been full of objections against the doctrine of God's sovereignty, in choosing whom he would to eternal life, and rejecting whom he pleased; leaving them eternally to perish, and be everlastingly tormented in hell. It used to appear like a horrible doctrine to me. But I remember the time very well, when I seemed to be convinced, and fully satisfied, as to this sovereignty of God, and his justice in thus eternally disposing of men, according to his sovereign pleasure. But never could give an account, how, or by what means, I was thus convinced, not in the least imagining at the time, nor a long time after, that there was any extraordinary influence of God's Spirit in it; but only that now I saw further, and my reason apprehended the justice and reasonableness of it. However, my mind rested in it; and it put an end to all those cavils and objections. And there has been a wonderful alteration in my mind in respect to the doctrine of God's sovereignty, from that day to this; so that I scarce ever have found so much as the rising of an objection against it, in the most absolute sense, in God's shewing mercy to whom he will shew mercy, and hardening whom he will. God's absolute sovereignty and justice, with respect to salvation and damnation, is what my mind seems to rest assured of, as much as of any thing that I see with my eyes; at least it is so at times. But I have often, since that first conviction, had quite another kind of sense of God's sovereignty than I had then. I have often since had not only a conviction, but a delightful conviction. The doctrine has very often appeared exceeding pleasant, bright, and sweet. Absolute sovereignty is what I love to ascribe to God. But my first conviction was not so.

The first instance that I remember of that sort of inward, sweet delight in God and divine things that I have lived much in since, was on reading those words, I Tim. i. 17. *Now unto the King eternal, immortal, invisible, the only wise God, be honour and glory for ever and ever, Amen.* As I read the words, there came into my soul, and was as it were diffused through it, a sense of the glory of the Divine Being; a new sense, quite different from any thing I ever experienced before. Never any words of scripture seemed to me as these words did. I thought with myself, how excellent a Being that was, and how happy I should be, if I might enjoy that God, and be rapt up to him in heaven, and be as it were swallowed up in him for ever! I kept saying, and as it were

singing over these words of scripture to myself; and went to pray to God that I might enjoy him, and prayed in a manner quite different from what I used to do; with a new sort of affection. But it never came into my thought, that there was any thing spiritual, or of a saving nature in this.

From about that time, I began to have a new kind of apprehensions and ideas of Christ, and the work of redemption, and the glorious way of salvation by him. An inward, sweet sense of these things, at times, came into my heart; and my soul was led away in pleasant views and contemplations of them. And my mind was greatly engaged to spend my time in reading and meditating on Christ, on the beauty and excellency of person, and the lovely way of salvation by free grace in him. I found no books so delightful to me, as those that treated of these subjects. Those words Cant. ii. I, used to be abundantly with me, *I am the Rose of Sharon, and the Lily of the valleys.* The words seemed to me, sweetly to represent the loveliness and beauty of Jesus Christ. The whole book of Canticles used to be pleasant to me, and I used to be much in reading it, about that time; and found, from time to time, an inward sweetness, that would carry me away, in my contemplations. This I know not how to express otherwise, than by a calm, sweet abstraction of soul from all the concerns of this world; and sometimes a kind of vision, or fixed ideas and imaginations, of being alone in the mountains, or some solitary wilderness, far from all mankind, sweetly conversing with Christ, and wrapt and swallowed up in God. The sense I had of divine things, would often of a sudden kindle up, as it were, a sweet burning in my heart; an ardor of soul, that I know not how to express.

Not long after I first began to experience these things, I gave an account to my father of some things that had passed in my mind. I was pretty much affected by the discourse we had together; and when the discourse was ended, I walked abroad alone, in a solitary place in my father's pasture, for contemplation. And as I was walking there, and looking up on the sky and clouds, there came into my mind so sweet a sense of the glorious *majesty* and *grace* of God, that I know not how to express. I seemed to see them both in a sweet conjunction; majesty and meekness joined together; it was a sweet, and gentle, and holy majesty; and also a majestic meekness; an awful sweetness; a high, and great, and holy gentleness.

After this my sense of divine things gradually increased, and became more and more lively, and had more of that inward sweetness. The appearance of every thing was altered; there seemed to be, as it were, a calm, sweet cast, or appearance of divine glory, in almost every thing. God's excellency, his wisdom, his purity and love, seemed to appear in every thing: in the sun, moon, and stars; in the clouds, and blue sky; in the grass, flowers, trees; in the water, and all nature; which used greatly to fix my mind. I often used to sit and view the moon for continuance; and in the day, spent much time in viewing the clouds and sky, to behold the sweet glory of God in these things; in the mean time, singing forth, with a low voice my contemplations of the Creator and Redeemer. And scarce any thing, among all the works of nature, was so sweet to me as thunder and lightning; formerly, nothing had been so terrible to me. Before, I used to be uncommonly terrified with thunder, and to be struck with terror when I saw a thunder storm rising; but now, on the contrary, it rejoiced me. I felt God, so to speak, at the first appearance of a thunder storm; and used to take the opportunity, at such times, to fix myself in order to view the clouds, and see the lightnings play, and hear the majestic and awful voice of God's thunder, which oftentimes was exceedingly entertaining, leading me to sweet contemplations of my great and glorious God. While thus engaged, it always seemed natural to me to sing, or chant for my meditations; or, to speak my thoughts in soliloquies with a singing voice.

I felt then great satisfaction, as to my good state; but that did not content me. I had vehement longings of soul after God and Christ, and after more holiness, wherewith my heart seemed to be full, and ready to break; which often brought to my mind the words of the Psalmist, Psal. cxix. 28. *My soul breaketh for the longing it hath.* I often felt a mourning and lamenting in my heart, that I had not turned to God sooner, that I might have had more time to grow in grace. My mind was greatly fixed on divine things; almost perpetually in the contemplation of them. I spent most of my time in thinking of divine things, year after year; often walking alone in the woods, and solitary places, for meditation, soliloquy, and prayer, and converse with God; and it was always my manner, at such times, to sing forth my contemplations. I was almost constantly in ejaculatory prayer, wherever I was. Prayer seemed to be natural to me, as the breath by which the inward burnings of my heart had vent. The delights which I now felt in the things of religion, were of an exceeding different kind from those before mentioned, that I had when a boy; and what I then had no more notion of, than one born blind has of pleasant and beautiful colors. They were of a more in-

ward, pure, soul animating and refreshing nature. Those former delights never reached the heart; and did not arise from any sight of the divine excellency of the things of God; or any taste of the soul satisfying and life-giving good there is in them.

My sense of divine things seemed gradually to increase, until I went to preach at New York,[1] which was about a year and a half after they began; and while I was there, I felt them, very sensibly, in a much higher degree than I had done before. . . . My heart panted after this, to lie low before God, as in the dust; that I might be nothing, and that God might be ALL, that I might become as a little child.

While at New York, I was sometimes much affected with reflections of my past life, considering how late it was before I began to be truly religious; and how wickedly I had lived till then; and once so as to weep abundantly, and for a considerable time together.

On January 12, 1723, I made a solemn dedication of myself to God, and wrote it down; giving up myself, and all that I had to God; to be for the future, in no respect, my own; to act as one that had no right to himself, in any respect. And solemnly vowed, to take God for my whole portion and felicity; looking on nothing else, as any part of my happiness, nor acting as if it were; and his law for the constant rule of my obedience: engaging to fight, with all my might, against the world, the flesh, and the devil, to the end of my life. But I have reason to be infinitely humbled, when I consider, how much I have failed, of answering my obligation.

I had, then, abundance of sweet, religious conversation, in the family where I lived, with Mr. John Smith, and his pious mother. My heart was knit in affection, to those, in whom were appearances of true piety; and I could bear the thoughts of no other companions, but such as were holy, and the disciples of the blessed Jesus. . . .

I very frequently used to retire into a solitary place, on the banks of Hudson's River, at some distance from the city, for contemplation on divine things and secret converse with God: and had many sweet hours there. Sometimes Mr. Smith and I walked there together, to converse on the things of God; and our conversation used to turn much on the advancement of Christ's kingdom in the world, and the glorious things that God would accomplish for his church in the

PERSONAL NARRATIVE.    1. **New York:** Edwards served as minister to a Scotch-Presbyterian church which met in a building at William Street, between Liberty and Wall, in New York City, from August 1722, to May 1723.

latter days. I had then, and at other times, the greatest delight in the holy scriptures, of any book whatsoever. Oftentimes in reading it, every word seemed to touch my heart. I felt a harmony between something in my heart, and those sweet and powerful words. I seemed often to see so much light exhibited by every sentence, and such a refreshing food communicated, that I could not get along in reading; often dwelling long on one sentence, to see the wonders contained in it; and yet almost every sentence seemed to be full of wonders.

I came away from New York in the month of April, 1723, and had a most bitter parting with Madam Smith and her son. My heart seemed to sink within me, at leaving the family and city, where I had enjoyed so many sweet and pleasant days. I went from New York to Wethersfield, by water; and as I sailed away, I kept sight of the city as long as I could. However, that night after this sorrowful parting, I was greatly comforted in God at Westchester, where we went ashore to lodge: and had a pleasant time of it all the voyage to Saybrook. It was sweet to me to think of meeting dear Christians in heaven, where we should never part more. At Saybrook we went ashore to lodge on Saturday, and there kept the Sabbath; where I had a sweet and refreshing season, walking alone in the fields.

After I came home to Windsor, I remained much in a like frame of mind . . . till I went to New Haven, as Tutor of the College[2] . . . [after which time] I sunk in religion; my mind being diverted from my eager pursuits after holiness, by some affairs, that greatly perplexed and distracted my thoughts.

In September, 1725, I was taken ill at New Haven, and while endeavouring to go home to Windsor, was so ill at the North Village, that I could go no farther; where I lay sick, for about a quarter of a year. In this sickness, God was pleased to visit me again, with the sweet influences of his Spirit. My mind was greatly engaged there, on divine and pleasant contemplations, and longings of soul. I observed, that those who watched with me,[3] would often be looking out wishfully for the morning; which brought to my mind those words of the Psalmist, and which my soul with delight made its own language, *My soul waiteth for the Lord, more than they that watch for the morning; I say, more than they that watch for the*

*morning*; and when the light of day came in at the window, it refreshed my soul, from one morning to another. It seemed to be some image of the light of God's glory. . . .

I have loved the doctrines of the gospel; they have been to my soul like green pastures. The gospel has seemed to me the richest treasure; the treasure that I have most desired, and longed that it might dwell richly in me. The way of salvation by Christ has appeared, in a general way, glorious and excellent, most pleasant and most beautiful. It has often seemed to me, that it would in a great measure spoil heaven, to receive it in any other way. That text has often been affecting and delightful to me, Isa. xxxii. 2. *A man shall be an hiding place from the wind, and a covert from the tempest, &c. . . .*

Sometimes, only mentioning a single word caused my heart to burn within me; or only seeing the name of Christ, or the name of some attribute of God. And God has appeared glorious to me, on account of the Trinity. It has made me have exalting thoughts of God, that he subsists in three persons; Father, Son and Holy Ghost. The sweetest joys and delights I have experienced, have not been those that have arisen from a hope of my own good estate; but in a direct view of the glorious things of the gospel. When I enjoy this sweetness, it seems to carry me above the thoughts of my own estate; it seems at such times a loss that I cannot bear, to take off my eye from the glorious, pleasant object I behold without me, to turn my eye in upon myself, and my own good estate.

My heart has been much on the advancement of Christ's kingdom in the world. The histories of the past advancement of Christ's kingdom have been sweet to me. When I have read histories of past ages, the pleasantest thing in all my reading has been, to read of the kingdom of Christ being promoted. And when I have expected, in my reading, to come to any such thing, I have rejoiced in the prospect, all the way as I read. And my mind has been much entertained and delighted with the scripture promises and prophecies, which relate to the future glorious advancement of Christ's kingdom upon earth.

I have sometimes had a sense of the excellent fulness of Christ, and his meetness and suitableness as a Saviour; whereby he has appeared to me, far above all, the chief of ten thousands. His blood and atonement have appeared sweet, and his righteousness sweet; which was always accompanied with ardency of spirit; and inward strugglings and breathings, and groanings that cannot be uttered, to be emptied of myself, and swallowed up in Christ.

---

2. as Tutor of the College: Edwards was the senior tutor at Yale, 1724–26. There was then no president, so that he was effectively in charge of a student body of sixty youths.    3. watched with me: Edwards, thus characteristically reticent, means his mother, who came to North Haven to nurse him through this dangerous illness.

Once, as I rode out into the woods for my health, in 1737, having alighted from my horse in a retired place, as my manner commonly has been, to walk for divine contemplation and prayer, I had a view that for me was extraordinary, of the glory of the Son of God, as Mediator between God and man, and his wonderful, great, full, pure and sweet grace and love, and meek and gentle condescension. This grace that appeared so calm and sweet, appeared also great above the heavens. The person of Christ appeared ineffably excellent with an excellency great enough to swallow up all thought and conception . . . which continued as near as I can judge, about an hour; which kept me the greater part of the time in a flood of tears, and weeping aloud. I felt an ardency of soul to be, what I know not otherwise how to express, emptied and annihilated; to lie in the dust, and to be full of Christ alone; to love him with a holy and pure love; to trust in him; to live upon him; to serve and follow him; and to be perfectly sanctified and made pure, with a divine and heavenly purity. I have, several other times, had views very much of the same nature, and which have had the same effects.

I have many times had a sense of the glory of the third person in the Trinity, in his office of Sanctifier; in his holy operations, communicating divine light and life to the soul. God, in the communications of his Holy Spirit, has appeared as an infinite fountain of divine glory and sweetness; being full, and sufficient to fill and satisfy the soul; pouring forth itself in sweet communications; like the sun in its glory, sweetly and pleasantly diffusing light and life. And I have sometimes had an affecting sense of the excellency of the word of God, as a word of life; as the light of life; a sweet, excellent lifegiving word; accompanied with a thirsting after that word, that it might dwell richly in my heart.

Often, since I lived in this town, I have had very affecting views of my own sinfulness and vileness; very frequently to such a degree as to hold me in a kind of loud weeping, sometimes for a considerable time together; so that I have often been forced to shut myself up. I have had a vastly greater sense of my own wickedness, and the badness of my heart, than ever I had before my conversion. It has often appeared to me, that if God should mark iniquity against me, I should appear the very worst of all mankind; of all that have been, since the beginning of the world to this time; and that I should have by far the lowest place in hell. When others, that have come to talk with me about their soul concerns, have expressed the sense they have had of their own wickedness, by saying that it seemed to them, that they were as bad as the devil himself; I thought their expressions seemed exceeding faint and feeble, to represent my wickedness.

My wickedness, as I am in myself, has long appeared to me perfectly ineffable, and swallowing up all thought and imagination; like an infinite deluge, or mountain over my head. I know not how to express better what my sins appear to me to be, than by heaping infinite upon infinite, and multiplying infinite by infinite. Very often, for these many years, these expressions are in my mind, and in my mouth, "Infinite upon infinite . . . Infinite upon infinite!" When I look into my heart, and take a view of my wickedness, it looks like an abyss infinitely deeper than hell. And it appears to me, that were it not for free grace, exalted and raised up to the infinite height of all the fulness and glory of the great Jehovah, and the arm of his power and grace stretched forth in all the majesty of his power, and in all the glory of his sovereignty, I should appear sunk down in my sins below hell itself; far beyond the sight of every thing, but the eye of sovereign grace, that can pierce even down to such a depth. And yet it seems to me, that my conviction of sin is exceeding small, and faint; it is enough to amaze me, that I have no more sense of my sin. I know certainly, that I have very little sense of my sinfulness. When I have had turns of weeping and crying for my sins I thought I knew at the time, that my repentance was nothing to my sin.

I have greatly longed of late, for a broken heart, and to lie low before God; and, when I ask for humility, I cannot bear the thoughts of being no more humble than other Christians. It seems to me, that though their degrees of humility may be suitable for them, yet it would be a vile selfexaltation in me, not to be the lowest in humility of all mankind. Others speak of their longing to be "humbled to the dust;" that may be a proper expression for them, but I always think of myself, that I ought, and it is an expression that has long been natural for me to use in prayer, "to lie infinitely low before God." And it is affecting to think, how ignorant I was, when a young Christian, of the bottomless, infinite depths of wickedness, pride, hypocrisy and deceit, left in my heart.

I have a much greater sense of my universal, exceeding dependence on God's grace and strength, and mere good pleasure, of late, than I used formerly to have: and have experienced more of an abhorrence of my own righteousness. The very thought of any joy arising in me, on any consideration of my own amiableness, performances, or experiences, or any goodness of heart or life, is nauseous and detestable to me. And yet I am greatly afflicted with a proud and selfrighteous spirit, much more sensibly than I used to be formerly. I see that serpent rising and putting forth its head continually, every where, all around me.

Though it seems to me, that, in some respects, I was a far better Christian, for two or three years after my first conversion, than I am now; and lived in a more constant delight and pleasure; yet, of late years, I have had a more full and constant sense of the absolute sovereignty of God, and a delight in that sovereignty; and have had more of a sense of the glory of Christ, as a Mediator revealed in the gospel. On one Saturday night, in particular, I had such a discovery of the excellency of the gospel above all other doctrines, that I could not but say to myself, "That is my chosen light, my chosen doctrine;" and of Christ, "This is my chosen Prophet." It appeared sweet, beyond all expression, to follow Christ, and to be taught, and enlightened, and instructed by him; to learn of him, and live to him. Another Saturday night, (January, 1739)[4] I had such a sense, how sweet and blessed a thing it was to walk in the way of duty: to do that which was right and meet to be done, and agreeable to the holy mind of God; that it caused me to break forth into a kind of loud weeping, which held me some time, so that I was forced to shut myself up, and fasten the doors. I could not but, as it were, cry out, "How happy are they which do that which is right in the sight of God! They are blessed indeed, they are the happy ones!" I had, at the same time, a very affecting sense, how meet and suitable it was that God should govern the world, and order all things according to his own pleasure; and I rejoiced in it, that God reigned, and that his will was done.

---

4. **Another Saturday night, (January, 1739):** The insertion indicates that the "Personal Narrative," in so far as written, was abandoned after the ebbing of the first revival Edwards had supervised at Northampton, at a moment of doubt as to whether another one would be given him. At this hour he was striving with might and main how he might get a second one under way, all the time depending upon the unpredictable assistance of divine mediation. When in 1740, with the mediation of George Whitefield, Edwards had his Great Awakening, he could find no further time for the "Personal Narrative," nor did he ever discover, after the tragic collapse of that endeavor, the heart to finish his own story.

# SARAH PIERREPONT

⋄

❨ THIS amazing address to the "young lady" in New Haven was written, according to legend, on the blank leaf of a book, evidently when Edwards let his attention wander from the printed page. It is traditionally dated 1723. If that is correct, she was then thirteen and he twenty.

⋄

THEY say there is a young lady in [New Haven] who is beloved of that Great Being who made and rules the world, and that there are certain seasons in which this Great Being, in some way or other invisible, comes to her and fills her mind with exceeding sweet delight, and that she hardly cares for any thing, except to meditate on him— that she expects after a while to be received up where he is, to be raised up out of the world and caught up into heaven; being assured that he loves her too well to let her remain at a distance from him always. There she is to dwell with him, and to be ravished with his love and delight forever. Therefore, if you present all the world before her, with the richest of its treasures, she disregards it and cares not for it, and is unmindful of any pain or affliction. She has a strange sweetness in her mind, and singular purity in her affections; is most just and conscientious in all her conduct; and you could not persuade her to do any thing wrong or sinful, if you would give her all the world, lest she should offend this Great Being. She is of a wonderful sweetness, calmness and universal benevolence of mind; especially after this Great God has manifested himself to her mind. She will sometimes go about from place to place, singing sweetly; and seems to be always full of joy and pleasure; and no one knows for what. She loves to be alone, walking in the fields and groves, and seems to have some one invisible always conversing with her.

---

# A DIVINE AND SUPER-
# NATURAL LIGHT

⋄

❨ THIS sermon was preached at Northampton in 1734, and published at the willing expense of his then admiring congregation. It was the second of Edwards' works to appear in print. It is his classic in the serene, calm manner in which he preached many more sermons than he ever did in the vein of terror. The doctrine is not properly to be termed a "mysticism," for Edwards does not permit a direct communication to the mind of truths or propositions; it is rather a translation of the old Puritan theology of regeneration into the language of the "new" psychology, in which the experience of regeneration, being received by sensation, works more upon the "heart" than upon the speculative reasoning of theologians. So while he is emphatically not moving in an "Antinomian" direction, he is taking up what his critics would call a dangerous position by inviting the emotions to assume a larger part in the process of conversion than seventeenth-century Puritans would have allowed.

◇

MATTHEW xvi. 17.—And Jesus answered and said unto him, "Blessed art thou, Simon Barjona: for flesh and blood hath not revealed it unto thee, but my Father which is in heaven."

DOCTRINE

THAT there is such a thing as a Spiritual and Divine Light, immediately imparted to the soul by God, of a different nature from any that is obtained by natural means.

In what I say on this subject, at this time, I would,

I. Show what this divine light is.

II. How it is given immediately by God, and not obtained by natural means.

III. Show the truth of the doctrine.

And then conclude with a brief improvement.

I. I would show what this spiritual and divine light is. And in order to do it, would show,

First, In a few things what it is not. And here,

1. Those convictions that natural men may have of their sin and misery, is not this spiritual and divine light. Men in a natural condition may have convictions of the guilt that lies upon them, and of the anger of God, and their danger of divine vengeance. Such convictions are from light or sensibleness of truth. That some sinners have a greater conviction of their guilt and misery than others, is because some have more light or more of an apprehension of truth than others. And this light and conviction may be from the Spirit of God; the Spirit convinces men of sin: but yet nature is much more concerned in it than in the communication of that spiritual and divine light that is spoken of in the doctrine; it is from the

Spirit of God only as assisting natural principles, and not as infusing any new principles. Common grace differs from special, in that it influences only by assisting of nature; and not by imparting grace, or bestowing any thing above nature. The light that is obtained is wholly natural, or of no superior kind to what mere nature attains to, though more of that kind be obtained than would be obtained if men were left wholly to themselves: or, in other words, common grace only assists the faculties of the soul to do that more fully which they do by nature, as natural conscience or reason will, by mere nature, make a man sensible of guilt, and will accuse and condemn him when he has done amiss. Conscience is a principle natural to men; and the work that it doth naturally, or of itself, is to give an apprehension of right and wrong, and to suggest to the mind the relation that there is between right and wrong, and a retribution. The Spirit of God, in those convictions which unregenerate men sometimes have, assists conscience to do this work in a further degree than it would do if they were left to themselves: he helps it against those things that tend to stupify it, and obstruct its exercise. But in the renewing and sanctifying work of the Holy Ghost, those things are wrought in the soul that are above nature, and of which there is nothing of the like kind in the soul by nature; and they are caused to exist in the soul habitually, and according to such a stated constitution or law that lays such a foundation for exercises in a continued course, as is called a principle of nature. Not only are remaining principles assisted to do their work more freely and fully, but those principles are restored that were utterly destroyed by the fall; and the mind thenceforward habitually exerts those acts that the dominion of sin had made it as wholly destitute of, as a dead body is of vital acts.

The Spirit of God acts in a very different manner in the one case, from what he doth in the other. He may indeed act upon the mind of a natural man, but he acts in the mind of a saint as an indwelling vital principle. He acts upon the mind of an unregenerate person as an extrinsic, occasional agent; for in acting upon them, he doth not unite himself to them; for notwithstanding all his influences that they may be the subjects of, they are still sensual, having not the Spirit, Jude 19. But he unites himself with the mind of a saint, takes him for his temple, actuates and influences him as a new supernatural principle of life and action. There is this difference, that the Spirit of God, in acting in the soul of a godly man, exerts and communicates himself there in his own proper nature. Holiness is the proper nature of the Spirit of God. The Holy Spirit operates in the minds of the godly, by uniting himself to them, and living in them, and exerting his own nature in the exercise of their faculties. The Spirit of God may act upon a creature, and yet not in acting communicate himself. The Spirit of God may act upon inanimate creatures; as, the *Spirit moved upon the face of the waters,* in the beginning of the creation; so the Spirit of God may act upon the minds of men many ways, and communicate himself no more than when he acts upon an inanimate creature. For instance, he may excite thoughts in them, may assist their natural reason and understanding, or may assist other natural principles, and this without any union with the soul, but may act, as it were, as upon an external object. But as he acts in his holy influences and spiritual operations, he acts in a way of peculiar communication of himself; so that the subject is thence denominated spiritual.

2. This spiritual and divine light does not consist in any impression made upon the imagination. It is no impression upon the mind, as though one saw any thing with the bodily eyes: it is no imagination or idea of an outward light or glory, or any beauty of form or countenance, or a visible lustre or brightness of any object. The imagination may be strongly impressed with such things; but this is not spiritual light. Indeed when the mind has a lively discovery of spiritual things, and is greatly affected by the power of divine light, it may, and probably very commonly doth, much affect the imagination; so that impressions of an outward beauty or brightness may accompany those spiritual discoveries. But spiritual light is not that impression upon the imagination, but an exceeding different thing from it. Natural men may have lively impressions on their imaginations; and we cannot determine but the devil, who transforms himself into an angel of light, may cause imaginations of an outward beauty, or visible glory, and of sounds and speeches, and other such things; but these are things of a vastly inferior nature to spiritual light.

3. This spiritual light is not the suggesting of any new truths or propositions not contained in the word of God. This suggesting of new truths or doctrines to the mind, independent of any antecedent revelation of those propositions, either in word or writing, is inspiration; such as the prophets and apostles had, and such as some enthusiasts pretend to. But this spiritual light that I am speaking of, is quite a different thing from inspiration: it reveals no new doctrine, it suggests no new proposition to the mind, it teaches no new

thing of God, or Christ, or another world, not taught in the Bible, but only gives a due apprehension of those things that are taught in the word of God.

4. It is not every affecting view that men have of the things of religion that is this spiritual and divine light. Men by mere principles of nature are capable of being affected with things that have a special relation to religion as well as other things. A person by mere nature, for instance, may be liable to be affected with the story of Jesus Christ, and the sufferings he underwent, as well as by any other tragical story: he may be the more affected with it from the interest he conceives mankind to have in it: yea, he may be affected with it without believing it; as well as a man may be affected with what he reads in a romance, or sees acted in a stage play. He may be affected with a lively and eloquent description of many pleasant things that attend the state of the blessed in heaven, as well as his imagination be entertained by a romantic description of the pleasantness of fairy land, or the like. And that common belief of the truth of the things of religion, that persons may have from education or otherwise, may help forward their affection. We read in Scripture of many that were greatly affected with things of a religious nature, who yet are there represented as wholly graceless, and many of them very ill men. A person therefore may have affecting views of the things of religion, and yet be very destitute of spiritual light. Flesh and blood may be the author of this: one man may give another an affecting view of divine things with but common assistance: but God alone can give a spiritual discovery of them.

But I proceed to show,

Secondly, Positively what this spiritual and divine light is.

And it may be thus described: a true sense of the divine excellency of the things revealed in the word of God, and a conviction of the truth and reality of them thence arising.

This spiritual light primarily consists in the former of these, viz., a real sense and apprehension of the divine excellency of things revealed in the word of God. A spiritual and saving conviction of the truth and reality of these things, arises from such a sight of their divine excellency and glory; so that this conviction of their truth is an effect and natural consequence of this sight of their divine glory. There is therefore in this spiritual light[:]

1. A true sense of the divine and superlative excellency of the things of religion; a real sense of the excellency of God and Jesus Christ, and of

the work of redemption, and the ways and works of God revealed in the gospel. There is a divine and superlative glory in these things; an excellency that is of a vastly higher kind, and more sublime nature than in other things; a glory greatly distinguishing them from all that is earthly and temporal. He that is spiritually enlightened truly apprehends and sees it, or has a sense of it. He does not merely rationally believe that God is glorious, but he has a sense of the gloriousness of God in his heart. There is not only a rational belief that God is holy, and that holiness is a good thing, but there is a sense of the loveliness of God's holiness. There is not only a speculatively judging that God is gracious, but a sense how amiable God is upon that account, or a sense of the beauty of this divine attribute.

There is a twofold understanding or knowledge of good that God has made the mind of man capable of. The first, that which is merely speculative and notional; as when a person only speculatively judges that any thing is, which, by the agreement of mankind, is called good or excellent, viz., that which is most to general advantage, and between which and a reward there is a suitableness, and the like. And the other is, that which consists in the sense of the heart: as when there is a sense of the beauty, amiableness, or sweetness of a thing; so that the heart is sensible of pleasure and delight in the presence of the idea of it. In the former is exercised merely the speculative faculty, or the understanding, strictly so called, or as spoken of in distinction from the will or disposition of the soul. In the latter, the will, or inclination, or heart, is mainly concerned.

Thus there is a difference between having an opinion, that God is holy and gracious, and having a sense of the loveliness and beauty of that holiness and grace. There is a difference between having a rational judgment that honey is sweet, and having a sense of its sweetness. A man may have the former, that knows not how honey tastes; but a man cannot have the latter unless he has an idea of the taste of honey in his mind. So there is a difference between believing that a person is beautiful, and having a sense of his beauty. The former may be obtained by hearsay, but the latter only by seeing the countenance. There is a wide difference between mere speculative rational judging any thing to be excellent, and having a sense of its sweetness and beauty. The former rests only in the head, speculation only is concerned in it; but the heart is concerned in the latter. When the heart is sensible of the beauty and amiableness of a thing, it necessarily

feels pleasure in the apprehension. It is implied in a person's being heartily sensible of the loveliness of a thing, that the idea of it is sweet and pleasant to his soul; which is a far different thing from having a rational opinion that it is excellent.

2. There arises from this sense of divine excellency of things contained in the word of God, a conviction of the truth and reality of them; and that either directly or indirectly.

First, Indirectly, and that two ways.

1. As the prejudices that are in the heart, against the truth of divine things, are hereby removed; so that the mind becomes susceptive of the due force of rational arguments for their truth. The mind of man is naturally full of prejudices against the truth of divine things: it is full of enmity against the doctrines of the gospel; which is a disadvantage to those arguments that prove their truth, and causes them to lose their force upon the mind. But when a person has discovered to him the divine excellency of Christian doctrines, this destroys the enmity, removes those prejudices, and sanctifies the reason, and causes it to lie open to the force of arguments for their truth.

Hence was the different effect that Christ's miracles had to convince the Scribes and Pharisees. Not that they had a stronger reason, or had their reason more improved; but their reason was sanctified, and those blinding prejudices, that the Scribes and Pharisees were under, were removed by the sense they had of the excellency of Christ and his doctrine.

2. It not only removes the hinderances of reason, but positively helps reason. It makes even the speculative notions the more lively. It engages the attention of the mind, with the more fixedness and intenseness to that kind of objects; which causes it to have a clearer view of them, and enables it more clearly to see their mutual relations, and occasions it to take more notice of them. The ideas themselves that otherwise are dim and obscure, are by this means impressed with the greater strength, and have a light cast upon them; so that the mind can better judge of them. As he that beholds the objects on the face of the earth, when the light of the sun is cast upon them, is under greater advantage to discern them in their true forms and mutual relations, than he that sees them in a dim starlight or twilight.

The mind having a sensibleness of the excellency of divine objects, dwells upon them with delight; and the powers of the soul are more awakened and enlivened to employ themselves in the contemplation of them, and exert themselves more fully and much more to the purpose. The beauty and sweetness of the objects draws on the faculties, and draws forth their exercises: so that reason itself is under far greater advantages for its proper and free exercises, and to attain its proper end, free of darkness and delusion.

But,

Secondly. A true sense of the divine excellency of the things of God's word doth more directly and immediately convince of the truth of them; and that because the excellency of these things is so superlative. There is a beauty in them that is so divine and godlike, that is greatly and evidently distinguishing of them from things merely human, or that men are the inventors and authors of; a glory that is so high and great, that when clearly seen, commands assent to their divinity and reality. When there is an actual and lively discovery of this beauty and excellency, it will not allow of any such thought as that it is a human work, or the fruit of men's invention. This evidence that they that are spiritually enlightened have of the truth of the things of religion, is a kind of intuitive and immediate evidence. They believe the doctrines of God's word to be divine, because they see divinity in them; i.e., they see a divine, and transcendent, and most evidently distinguishing glory in them; such a glory as, if clearly seen, does not leave room to doubt of their being of God, and not of men.

Such a conviction of the truth of religion as this, arising, these ways, from a sense of the divine excellency of them, is that true spiritual conviction that there is in saving faith. And this original of it, is that by which it is most essentially distinguished from that common assent, which unregenerate men are capable of.

II. I proceed now to the second thing proposed, viz., to show how this light is immediately given by God, and not obtained by natural means. And here,

1. It is not intended that the natural faculties are not made use of in it. The natural faculties are the subject of this light: and they are the subject in such a manner, that they are not merely passive, but active in it; the acts and exercises of man's understanding are concerned and made use of in it. God, in letting in this light into the soul, deals with man according to his nature, or as a rational creature; and makes use of his human faculties. But yet this light is not the less immediately from God for that; though the faculties are made use of, it is as the subject and not as the cause; and that acting of the faculties in it, is not the cause, but is either implied in the thing itself (in the light that is imparted) or is the consequence of it. As the use that we make of our eyes in beholding various objects, when the sun arises, is not the cause of the light that discovers those objects to us.

2. It is not intended that outward means have no concern in this affair. As I have observed already, it is not in this affair, as it is in inspiration, where new truths are suggested: for here is by this light only given a due apprehension of the same truths that are revealed in the word of God; and therefore it is not given without the word. The gospel is made use of in this affair: this light is the light of the glorious gospel of Christ, 2 Cor. iv. 4. The gospel is as glass, by which this light is conveyed to us 1 Cor. xiii. 12. Now we see through a glass.—But,

3. When it is said that this light is given immediately by God, and not obtained by natural means, hereby is intended, that it is given by God without making use of any means that operate by their own power, or a natural force. God makes use of means; but it is not as mediate causes to produce this effect. There are not truly any second causes of it; but it is produced by God immediately. The word of God is no proper cause of this effect: it does not operate by any natural force in it. The word of God is only made use of to convey to the mind the subject matter of this saving instruction; and this indeed it doth convey to us by natural force or influence. It conveys to our minds these and those doctrines; it is the cause of the notion of them in our heads, but not of the sense of the divine excellency of them in our hearts. Indeed a person cannot have spiritual light without the word. But that does not argue, that the word properly causes that light. The mind cannot see the excellency of any doctrine, unless that doctrine be first in the mind; but the seeing of the excellency of the doctrine may be immediately from the Spirit of God; though the conveying of the doctrine or proposition itself may be by the word. So that the notions that are the subject matter of this light, are conveyed to the mind by the word of God; but that due sense of the heart, wherein this light formally consists, is immediately by the Spirit of God. As for instance, that notion that there is a Christ, and that Christ is holy and gracious, is conveyed to the mind by the word of God: but the sense of the excellency of Christ by reason of that holiness and grace, is nevertheless immediately the work of the Holy Spirit.

# THE FUTURE PUNISH-MENT OF THE WICKED UNAVOIDABLE AND INTOLERABLE

◇

⟨ THIS "Terror" sermon was delivered in April 1741, three months before the more famous (or rather, more notorious!) "Sinners in the Hands of an Angry God." Though the latter is indubitably the masterpiece in this sort of literature, and therefore has been widely reprinted, this one is perhaps a better example of the usual devices of rhetoric Edwards employed in order to make language (which according to John Locke was an arbitrary construction and so could bear no organic relation to the objects it described) serve as a "sensational" experience. The carefully constructed paragraph leading the imagination of his trembling audience from fifteen minutes through an hour, a day, a year, into eternity is a fine example of his implacable artistry.

◇

EZEKIEL xxii. 14.—Can thine heart endure, or can thine hands be strong in the days that I shall deal with thee? I the Lord have spoken it, and will do it. . . .

### DOCTRINE

SINCE God hath undertaken to deal with impenitent sinners, they shall neither shun the threatened misery, nor deliver themselves out of it, nor can they bear it. . . .

I shall show what is implied in God's undertaking to deal with impenitent sinners. Others are not able to deal with them. They baffle all the means used with them by those that are appointed to teach and to rule over them. They will not yield to parents, or to the counsels, warnings, or reproofs of ministers: they prove obstinate and stiff-hearted. Therefore God undertakes to deal with them. This implies the following things:

1. That God will reckon with them, and take of them satisfaction to his justice. In this world God puts forth his authority to command them; and to require subjection to him. In his commands he is very positive, strictly requiring of them the performance of such and such duties, and as positively forbidding such and such things which were contrary to their duty. But they have no regard to these commands. God continues com-

manding, and they continue rebelling. They make nothing of God's authority. God threatens, but they despise his threatening. They make nothing of dishonoring God; they care not how much their behavior is to the dishonor of God. He offers them mercy, if they will repent and return. Thus they are continually plunging themselves deeper and deeper in debt, and at the same time imagine they shall escape the payment of the debt, and design entirely to rob God of his due.

But God hath undertaken to right himself. He will reckon with them; he hath undertaken to see that the debts due to him are paid. All their sins are written in his book; not one of them is forgotten, and every one must must be paid. . . .

4. God hath undertaken to rectify their judgments. Now they will not be convinced of those things which God tells them in his word. Ministers take much pains to convince them, but all is in vain. Therefore God will undertake to convince them, and he will do it effectually. Now they will not be convinced of the truth of divine things. They have indeed convincing arguments set before them; they hear and see enough to convince them; yet so prone are they to unbelief and atheism, that divine things never seem to them to be real. But God will hereafter make them seem real. . . .

Impenitent sinners, while in this world, hear how dreadful hell is. But they will not believe that it is so dreadful as ministers represent. They cannot think that they shall to all eternity suffer such exquisite and horrible torments. But they shall be taught and convinced to purpose, that the representations ministers give of those torments, agreeable to the word of God, are no bugbears; and that the wrath of God is indeed as dreadful as they declare. Since God hath undertaken to deal with sinners, and to rectify their judgments in these matters, he will do it thoroughly; for his work is perfect; when he undertakes to do things, he doth not do them by halves; therefore before he shall have done with sinners, he will convince them effectually, so that they shall never be in danger of relapsing into their former errors any more. He will convince them of their folly and stupidity in entertaining such notions as they now entertain. . . .

I come now,

To show, that therefore impenitent sinners shall not avoid their due punishment. God hath undertaken to inflict it; he hath engaged to do it; he takes it as his work, as what properly belongs to him, and we may expect it of him. If he hath sworn by his life, that he will do it; and if he hath power sufficient; if he is the living God, doubtless we shall see it done. . . .

No; let no impenitent sinner flatter himself so vainly and foolishly. If it were indeed only a man, a being of like impotency and mutability with themselves, who had undertaken to deal with them, they might perhaps with some reason flatter themselves, that they should find some means to avoid the threatened punishment. But since an omniscient, omnipotent, immutable God hath undertaken, vain are all such hopes.

There is no hope that possibly they may steal away to heaven, though they die unconverted. There is no hope that they can deceive God by any false show of repentance and faith, and so be taken to heaven through mistake; for the eyes of God are as a flame of fire; they perfectly see through every man; the inmost closet of the heart is all open to him.

There is no hope of escaping the threatened punishment by sinking into nothing at death, like brute creatures. Indeed, many wicked men upon their deathbeds wish for this. If it were so, death would be nothing to them in comparison with what it now is. But all such wishes are vain.

There is no hope of their escaping without notice, when they leave the body. There is no hope that God, by reason of the multiplicity of affairs which he hath to mind, will happen to overlook them, and not take notice of them, when they come to die; and so that their souls will slip away privately, and hide themselves in some secret corner, and so escape divine vengeance.

There is no hope that they shall be missed in a crowd at the day of judgment, and that they can have opportunity to hide themselves in some cave or den of the mountains, or in any secret hole of the earth; and that while so doing, they will not be minded, by reason of the many things which will be the objects of attention on that day. Neither is there any hope that they will be able to crowd themselves in among the multitude of the saints at the right hand of the Judge, and so go to heaven undiscovered. Nor is there any hope that God will alter his mind, or that he will repent of what he hath said; for he is not the son of man that he should repent. Hath he said, and shall he not do it? Hath he spoken, and shall he not make it good? When did God ever undertake to do any thing and fail? . . .

I come now,

To show, that neither will they be able to bear it. Neither will their hands be strong to deliver themselves from it, nor will their hearts be able to endure it. It is common with men, when they meet with calamities in this world, in the first place to endeavor to shun them. But if they find, that they cannot shun them, then after they are come, they endeavor to deliver themselves from them as soon as they can; or at least, to order things so, as to deliver themselves in some degree. But if they find that they can by no means deliver themselves, and see that the case is so that they must bear them; then they set themselves to bear them: they fortify their spirits, and take up a resolution, that they will support themselves under them as well as they can. They clothe themselves with all the resolution and courage they are masters of, to keep their spirits from sinking under their calamities.

But it will be utterly in vain for impenitent sinners to think to do thus with respect to the torments of hell. They will not be able to endure them, or at all to support themselves under them: the torment will be immensely beyond their strength. What will it signify for a worm, which is about to be pressed under the weight of some great rock, to be let fall with its whole weight upon it, to collect its strength, to set itself to bear up the weight of the rock, and to preserve itself from being crushed by it? Much more in vain will it be for a poor damned soul, to endeavor to support itself under the weight of the wrath of Almighty God. What is the strength of man, who is but a worm, to support himself against the power of Jehovah, and against the fierceness of his wrath? What is man's strength, when set to bear up against the exertions of infinite power? Matt. xxi. 44: "Whosoever shall fall on this stone shall be broken; but on whomsoever it shall fall, it will grind him to powder." . . .

I come now as was proposed,

To answer an inquiry which may naturally be raised concerning these things.

INQUIRY. Some may be ready to say, "If this be the case, if impenitent sinners can neither shun future punishment, nor deliver themselves from it, nor bear it; then what will become of them?"

ANSWER. They will wholly sink down into eternal death. There will be that sinking of heart, of which we now cannot conceive. We see how it is with the body in extreme pain. The nature of the body will support itself for a considerable time under very great pain, so as to keep from wholly sinking. There will be great struggles, lamentable groans and panting, and it may be convulsions. These are the strugglings of nature to support itself under the extremity of the pain. There is, as it were, a great lothness in nature to yield to it; it cannot bear wholly to sink.

But yet sometimes pain of body is so very extreme and exquisite, that the nature of the body cannot support itself under it; however loth it may be to sink, yet it cannot bear the pain; there are a few struggles, and throes, and pantings, and it may be a shriek or two, and then nature yields to the violence of the torments, sinks down, and the body dies. This is the death of the body. So it will be with the soul in hell; it will have no strength or power to deliver itself; and its torment and horror will be so great, so mighty, so vastly disproportioned to its strength, that having no strength in the least to support itself, although it be infinitely contrary to the nature and inclination of the soul utterly to sink; yet it will sink, it will utterly and totally sink, without the least degree of remaining comfort, or strength, or courage, or hope. And though it will never be annihilated, its being and perception will never be abolished; yet such will be the infinite depth of gloominess that it will sink into, that it will be a state of death, eternal death.

The nature of man desires happiness; it is the nature of the soul to crave and thirst after well-being; and if it be under misery, it eagerly pants after relief; and the greater the misery is, the more eagerly doth it struggle for help. But if all relief be withholden, all strength overborne, all support utterly gone; then it sinks into the darkness of death.

We can conceive but little of the matter; we cannot conceive what that sinking of the soul in such a case is. But to help your conception, imagine yourself to be cast into a fiery oven, all of a glowing heat, or into the midst of a glowing brick-kiln, or of a great furnace, where your pain would be as much greater than that occasioned by accidentally touching a coal of fire, as the heat is greater. Imagine also that your body were to lie there for a quarter of an hour, full of fire, as full within and without as a bright coal of fire, all the while full of quick sense. What horror would you feel at the entrance of such a furnace! And how long would that quarter of an hour seem to you! If it were to be measured by a glass, how long would the glass seem to be running! And after you had endured it for one minute, how over-bearing would it be to you to think that you had it to endure the other fourteen!

But what would be the effect on your soul, if you knew you must lie there enduring that torment to the full for twenty-four hours! And how much greater would be the effect, if you knew you must endure it for a whole year; and how vastly greater still, if you knew you must endure it for a thousand years! O then, how would your heart sink, if you thought, if you knew, that you must bear it forever and ever! That there would be no end! That after millions of millions of ages, your torment would be no nearer to an end, than ever it was; and that you never, never should be delivered!

But your torment in hell will be immensely greater than this illustration represents. How then will the heart of a poor creature sink under it! How utterly inexpressible and inconceivable must the sinking of the soul be in such a case!

This is the death threatened in the law. This is dying in the highest sense of the word. This is to die sensibly; to die and know it; to be sensible of the gloom of death. This is to be undone; this is worthy of the name of destruction. This sinking of the soul under an infinite weight, which it cannot bear, is the gloom of hell. We read in Scripture of sinners being lost, and of their losing their souls: this is the thing intended; this is to lose the soul: they that are the subjects of this are truly lost.

APPLICATION.

THIS subject may be applied in a use of *awakening* to impenitent sinners. What hath been said under this doctrine is for thee, O impenitent sinner, O poor wretch, who art in the same miserable state in which thou camest into the world, excepting that thou art loaded with vastly greater guilt by thine actual sins. These dreadful things which thou hast heard are for thee, who art yet unconverted, and still remainest an alien and stranger, without Christ and without God in the world. They are for thee, who to this day remainest an enemy to God, and a child of the devil, even in this remarkable season, when others both here and elsewhere, far and near, are flocking to Christ; for thee who hearest the noise, the fame of these things, but knowest nothing of the power of godliness in thine own heart.

Whoever thou art, whether young or old, little or great, if thou art in a Christless, unconverted state, this is the wrath, this is the death to which thou art condemned. This is the wrath that abideth on thee; this is the hell over which thou hangest, and into which thou art ready to drop every day and every night. . . .

Doth it seem to thee incredible, that God should be so utterly regardless of the sinner's welfare, as so to sink him into an infinite abyss of misery? Is this shocking to thee? And is it not at all shocking to thee, that thou shouldst be so utterly regardless as thou hast been of the honor and glory of the infinite God?

It arises from thy foolish stupidity and senselessness, and is because thou hast a heart of stone, that thou art so senseless of thine own wickedness as to think thou hast not deserved such a punishment, and that it is to thee incredible that it will be inflicted upon thee.—But if, when all is said and done thou be not convinced, wait but a little while, and thou wilt be convinced: God will undertake to do the work which ministers cannot do. Though judgment against thine evil works be not yet executed, and God now let thee alone, yet he will soon come upon thee with his great power, and then thou shalt know what God is, and what thou art.

Flatter not thyself, that if these things shall prove true, and the worst shall come, thou wilt set thyself to bear it as well as thou canst. What will it signify to set thyself to bear, and to collect thy strength to support thyself, when thou shalt fall into the hands of that omnipotent King, Jehovah? He that made thee, can make his sword approach unto thee. His sword is not the sword of man, nor is his wrath the wrath of man. If it were, possibly stoutness might be maintained under it. But it is the fierceness of the wrath of the great God, who is able to baffle and dissipate all thy strength in a moment. He can fill thy poor soul with an ocean of wrath, a deluge of fire and brimstone; or he can make it ten thousand times fuller of torment then ever an oven was full of fire; and at the same time, can fill it with despair of ever seeing any end to its torment, or any rest from its misery: and then where will be thy strength? What will become of thy courage then? What will signify thine attempts to bear? . . .

If the strength of all the wicked men on earth, and of all the devils in hell, were united in one, and thou wert possessed of it all; and if the courage, greatness, and stoutness of all their hearts were united in thy single heart, thou wouldst be nothing in the hands of Jehovah. If it were all collected, and thou shouldst set thyself to bear as well as thou couldst, all would sink under his great wrath in an instant, and would be utterly abolished: thine hands would drop down at once and thine heart would melt as wax.— The great mountains, the firm rocks, cannot stand before the power of God; as fast as they stand, they are tossed hither and thither, and skip like lambs, when God appears in his anger. He can tear the earth in pieces in a moment; yea, he can shatter the whole universe, and dash it to pieces at one blow. How then will thine hands be strong, or thine heart endure? . . .

Some of you have seen buildings on fire; imagine therefore with yourselves, what a poor hand you would make at fighting with the flames, if you were in the midst of so great and fierce a fire. You have often seen a spider, or some other noisome insect, when thrown into the midst of a fierce fire, and have observed how immediately it yields to the force of the flames. There is no long struggle, no fighting against the fire, no strength exerted to oppose the heat, or to fly from it; but it immediately stretches forth itself and yields; and the fire takes possession of it, and at once it becomes full of fire; and is burned into a bright coal.—Here is a little image of what you will be the subjects of in hell, except you repent and fly to Christ. However you may think that you will fortify yourselves, and bear as well as you can; the first moment you shall be cast into hell, all your strength will sink and be utterly abolished. To encourage yourselves, that you will set yourself to bear hell torments as well as you can, is just as if a worm, that is about to be thrown into a glowing furnace, should swell and fortify itself, and prepare itself to fight the flames. . . .

It is probable that here are some, who hear me this day, who at this very moment are unawakened, and are in a great degree careless about their souls. I fear there are some among us who are most fearfully hardened: their hearts are harder than the very rocks. It is easier to make impressions upon an adamant than upon their hearts. I suppose some of you have heard all that I have said with ease and quietness: it appears to you as great big sounding words, but doth not reach your hearts. You have heard such things many times: you are old soldiers, and have been too much used to the roaring of heaven's cannon, to be frighted at it. It will therefore probably be in vain for me to say any thing further to you; I will only put you in mind that erelong God will deal with you. I cannot deal with you, you despise what I say; I have no power to make you sensible of your danger and misery, and of the dreadfulness of the wrath of God. The attempts of men in this way have often proved vain.

However, God hath undertaken to deal with such men as you are. It is his manner commonly first to let men try their utmost strength: particularly to let ministers try, that thus he may show ministers their own weakness and impotency; and when they have done what they can, and all fails, then God takes the matter into his own hands. So it seems by your obstinacy, as if God intended to undertake to deal with you. He will undertake to subdue you; he will see if he cannot cure you of your senselessness and regardlessness of his threatenings. And you will be convinced; you will be subdued effectually; your hearts will be broken with a witness; your strength will be utterly broken, your courage and hope will sink. God will surely break those who will not bow. God having girded himself with his power and wrath, hath heretofore undertaken to deal with many hard, stubborn, senseless, obstinate hearts; and he never failed, he always did his work thoroughly.

It will not be long before you will be wonderfully changed. You who now hear of hell and the wrath of the great God, and sit here in these seats so easy and quiet and go away so careless; by and by will shake, and tremble, and cry out, and shriek, and gnash your teeth, and will be thoroughly convinced of the vast weight and importance of these great things, which you now despise. You will not then need to hear sermons in order to make you sensible; you will be at a sufficient distance from slighting that wrath and power of God, of which you now hear with so much quietness and indifference.

---

FROM

# THOUGHTS ON THE REVIVAL OF RELIGION IN NEW ENGLAND

---

❖

❨ WHEN the full fury of the Great Awakening broke upon the land, Edwards was supremely confident that he knew the difference between an authentic experience of divine grace and a simulated one. By the second summer of the outburst, 1741, as it was producing more and more extravagant and noisy demonstrations, those who objected to the violent methods (and in 1740 had not dared speak out) gathered courage and commenced to denounce the whole affair as a hysteria cunningly fomented by such preaching as Edwards' use of terror. Edwards delivered his first defense of the Awakening in a long sermon at Yale on September 10, 1741, which was published as *The Distinguishing Marks of A Work of the Spirit of God.* His confidence was not yet even shaken, and he could enumerate the signs and manifestations of a true work of the spirit so readily as to appear almost (for him) glib. By the next year he was beginning to wonder, and the attacks of the opponents were pressing him hard. He undertook a longer and more carefully considered exposition, from which this section, pleading that the division be not allowed to become irrevocable, is taken. The horrible prospect was opening before him: despite his dialectical ingenuity in uniting heart and head, the impact of the Awakening was threatening to sunder New England piety so deeply (into an emotionalism on the one hand and a

rationalism on the other) that the solidity of the faith would be forever lost. Charles Chauncy's *Seasonable Thoughts on the State of Religion* was a direct and snarling reply of the rationalists (in Edwards' terminology, the "Arminians") which widened the separation, left Edwards isolated between them and the extreme revivalists, and insured that eventually he should be deserted even by his own people, as came about in 1750.

❖

. . . Upon the whole it appears manifest to me, that things have as yet never been set a going in their right channel; if they had, and means had been blessed in proportion as they have been now, this work would so have prevailed, as before this time to have carried all before it, and have triumphed over New England as its conquest.

The devil, in driving things to these extremes, besides the present hinderance of the work of God, has, I believe, had in view a twofold mischief hereafter, in the issue of things; one with respect to those that are more cold in religion; to carry things to such an extreme, that people in general, at length, having their eyes opened, by the great excesses, and seeing that things must needs be wrong, he might take the advantage to tempt them entirely to reject the whole work, as being all nothing but delusion and distraction. And another is with respect to those that have been very warm and zealous, of God's own children, that have been out of the way, to sink them down in unbelief and darkness. The time is coming, I doubt not, when the bigger part of them will be convinced of their errors; and then probably the devil will take advantage to lead them into a dreadful wilderness, and to puzzle and confound them about their own experiences, and the experiences of others; and to make them to doubt of many things that they ought not to doubt of, and even to tempt them with atheistical thoughts. I believe if all true Christians all over the land, should now at once have their eyes opened, fully to see all their errors, it would seem for the present to damp religion; the dark thoughts, that it would at first be an occasion of, and, the inward doubts, difficulties, and conflicts that would rise in their souls, would deaden their lively affections and joys, and would cause an appearance of a present decay of religion. But yet it would do God's saints great good in their latter end; it would fit them for more spiritual joys, and would greatly tend to a more powerful, extensive, and durable prevalence of vital piety.

I do not know but we shall be in danger by and by, after our eyes are fully opened to see our errors, to go to contrary extremes. The devil has driven the pendulum far beyond its proper point of rest; and when he has carried it to the utmost length that he can, and it begins by its own weight to swing back, he probably will set in, and drive it with the utmost fury the other way; and so give us no rest: and if possible prevent our settling in a proper medium. What poor, blind, weak, and miserable creature is man, at his estate! We are like poor helpless sheep; the devil is too subtle for us; what is our strength! What is our wisdom! How ready are we to go astray! How easily are we drawn aside, into innumerable snares, while we in the meantime are bold and confident, and doubt not that we are right and safe! We are foolish sheep, in the midst of subtle serpents and cruel wolves, and do not know it. Oh! how unfit are we to be left to ourselves! and how much do we stand in need of the wisdom, the power, the condescension, patience, forgiveness, and gentleness of our good Shepherd! . . .

And in order to this, there must be a great deal done at confessing of faults on both sides: for undoubtedly many and great faults that have been committed, in the jangling and confusions, and mixtures of light and darkness, that have been of late. There is hardly any duty more contrary to our corrupt dispositions, and mortifying to the pride of man; but it must be done. . . .

Contrary to this mutual meekness, is each party's stigmatizing one another with odious names; as is done in many parts of New England: which tends greatly to widen and perpetuate the breach. Such distinguishing names of reproach, do as it were divide us into two armies, separated, and drawn up in battle array, ready to fight one with another; which greatly hinders the work of God. . . .

Thus I have (I hope, by the help of God) finished what I proposed. I have taken the more pains in it, because it appears to me, that God is giving us the most happy season to attempt a universal reformation, that ever was given in New England. And it is a thousand pities, that we should fail of that which would be so glorious, for want of being sensible of our opportunity, or being aware of those things that tend to hinder it, or our taking improper courses to obtain it, or not being sensible in what way God expects we should seek it. It should please God to bless any means for the convincing the country of His hand in this work, and bringing them fully and freely to acknowledge His glorious power and grace in it, and engage with one heart and soul, by due methods, to endeavor to promote it, it would be a dispensation of divine providence, that would have a most glorious aspect, happily

signifying the approach of great and glorious things to the church of God, and justly causing us to hope that Christ would speedily come, to set up his kingdom of light, holiness, peace and joy on earth, as is foretold in His word. Amen: even so come LORD JESUS!

---

# FAREWELL SERMON

---

◇

❪ EDWARDS delivered this sermon in Northampton on July 2, 1750, after his people had formally and furiously repudiated him. The text is from II Cor. 1:14: "As also ye have acknowledged us in part, that we are your rejoicing, even as ye also are ours, in the day of the Lord Jesus." It is the most personal expression in all the published works, though at the same time the most thorough example of Edwards' strict obedience to the canons of the selfless plain style. The "doctrine" is that ministers and people must eventually meet before the throne of judgment; at conventional length he argues the proposition abstractly, and then in the "application" comes to this tremendous address to those who were driving him into the wilderness.

◇

BUT NOW I have reason to think, my work is finished which I had to do as your minister: you have publicly rejected me, and my opportunities cease.

How highly therefore does it now become us, to consider of that time when we must meet one another before the chief Shepherd? When I must give an account of my stewardship, of the service I have done *for,* and the reception and treatment I have had *among,* the people he sent me to: and you must give an account of your own conduct towards me, and the improvement you have made of these *three and twenty years* of my ministry. For then both you and I must appear together, and we both must give an account in order to an infallible, righteous and eternal sentence to be passed upon us, by him who will judge us, with respect to all that we have said or done in our meetings here, all our conduct one towards another, in the house of God and elsewhere, on sabbath-days and on other days; who will try our hearts, and manifest our thoughts, and the principles and frames of our minds, will judge us with respect to all the controversies: there is nothing covered, that shall not be revealed, nor hid, which shall not be known; all will be examined in the searching, penetrating light of God's omniscience and glory, and by him whose eyes are as a flame of fire; and truth and right shall be made plainly to appear, being stripped of every veil; and all error, falsehood, unrighteousness and injury, shall be laid open, stripped of every disguise; every specious pretence, every cavil, and all false reasoning, shall vanish in a moment, as not being able to bear the light of that day. And then our hearts will be turned inside out, and the secrets of them will be made more plainly to appear than our outward actions do now. Then it shall appear what the ends are, which we have aimed at, what have been the governing principles which we have acted from, and what have been the dispositions, we have exercised in our ecclesiastical disputes and contests. Then it will appear, whether I acted uprightly, and from a truly conscientious, careful regard to my duty to my great Lord and Master, in some former ecclesiastical controversies, which have been attended with exceeding unhappy circumstances and consequences: it will appear, whether there was any just cause for the resentment which was manifested on those occasions. And then our late grand controversy, concerning the Qualifications necessary for admission to the privileges of members, in complete standing, in the Visible Church of Christ, will be examined and judged, in all its parts and circumstances, and the whole set forth in a clear, certain and perfect light. Then it will appear, whether the doctrine, which I have preached and published, concerning this matter, be Christ's own doctrine, whether he will not own it as one of the precious truths which have proceeded from his own mouth, and vindicate and honour, as such, before the whole universe. Then it will appear, what was meant by *the man that comes without the wedding garment;* for that is the day spoken of, Matt. xxii. 13., wherein such an one *shall be bound hand and foot, and cast into outer darkness, where shall be weeping and gnashing of teeth.* And then it will appear, whether, in declaring this doctrine, and acting agreeably to it, and in my general conduct in this affair, I have been influenced from any regard to my own temporal interest, or honour, or any desire to appear wiser than others; or have acted from any sinister, secular views whatsoever; and whether what I have done has not been from a careful, strict and tender regard to the will of my Lord and Master, and because I dare not offend him, being satisfied what his will was, after a long, diligent, impartial and prayerful enquiry; having this constantly in view and prospect, to engage me to great solicitude, not rashly to determine truth to be on this

side of the question, where I am now persuaded it is, that such a determination would not be for my temporal interest, but every way against it, bringing a long series of extreme difficulties, and plunging me into an abyss of trouble and sorrow. And then it will appear, whether my people have done their duty to their pastor, with respect to this matter; whether they have shown a right temper and spirit on this occasion; whether they have done me justice in hearing, attending to, and considering, what I had to say in evidence of what I believed and taught, as part of the counsel of God; whether I have been treated with that impartiality, candour and regard, which the just Judge esteemed due; and whether, in the many steps which have been taken, and the many things that have been said and done, in the course of this controversy, righteousness and charity and Christian decorum have been maintained: or, if otherwise, to how great a degree these things have been violated. Then every step of the conduct of each of us, in this affair, from first to last, and the spirit we have exercised in all, shall be examined and manifested, and our own consciences will speak plain and loud, and each of us shall be convinced, and the world shall know; and never shall there be any more mistake, misrepresentation or misapprehension of the affair, to eternity. . . .

# THE BEAUTY OF THE WORLD

◊

❪ THIS fragment survives among Edwards' papers. To what place in his projected great synthesis of Christian doctrine it was designed to appertain is unknown. The theme is similar to that suggested in some passages of *True Virtue.* The dwelling on visual effects comes from his close study of Newton's *Opticks.* The concluding corollary, that men so love the beauty of this physical world they will prefer to live in it though in pain and anguish, reveals the passion with which Edwards had to contend against his own powerfully sensuous impulses.

◊

THE BEAUTY of the world consists wholly of sweet mutual consents, either within itself or with the supreme being. As to the corporeal world, though there are many other sorts of consents, yet the sweetest and most charming beauty of it is its resemblance of spiritual beauties. The reason is that spiritual beauties are infinitely the greatest, and bodies being but the shadows of beings, they must be so much the more charming as they shadow forth spiritual beauties. This beauty is peculiar to natural things, it surpassing the art of man.

Thus there is the resemblance of a decent trust, dependence and acknowledgment in the planets continually moving round the sun, receiving his influences by which they are made happy, bright and beautiful: a decent attendance in the secondary planets, an image of majesty, power, glory, and beneficence in the sun in the midst of all, and so in terrestrial things, as I have shown in another place.

It is very probable that that wonderful suitableness of green for the grass and plants, the blues of the skie, the white of the clouds, the colours of flowers, consists in a complicated proportion that these colours make one with another, either in their magnitude of the rays, the number of vibrations that are caused in the atmosphere, or some other way. So there is a great suitableness between the objects of different senses, as between sounds, colours, and smells; as between colours of the woods and flowers and the smells and the singing of birds, which it is probable consist in a certain proportion of the vibrations that are made in the different organs. So there are innumerable other agreeablenesses of motions, figures, etc. The gentle motions of waves, of [the] lily, etc., as it is agreeable to other things that represent calmness, gentleness, and benevolence, etc., the fields and woods seem to rejoice, and how joyfull do the birds seem to be in it. How much a resemblance is there of every grace in the field covered with plants and flowers when the sun shines serenely and undisturbedly upon them, how a resemblance, I say, of every grace and beautifull disposition of mind, of an inferiour towards a superiour cause, preserver, benevolent benefactor, and a fountain of happiness.

How great a resemblance of a holy and virtuous soul is a calm, serene day. What an infinite number of such like beauties is there in that one thing, the light, and how complicated an harmony and proportion is it probable belongs to it.

There are beauties that are more palpable and explicable, and there are hidden and secret beauties. The former pleases, and we can tell why; we can explain the particular point for the agreement that renders the thing pleasing. Such are all artificial regularities; we can tell wherein the regularity lies that affects us. [The] latter sort are those beauties that delight us and we cannot tell why. Thus, we find ourselves pleased in beholding the colour of the violets, but we know not what secret regularity or harmony it is that creates that pleasure in our minds. These hidden beauties are commonly by far the greatest, because the more complex a beauty is, the more hidden is it. In this latter fact consists principally the beauty of the world, and very much in light and colours. Thus mere light is pleasing to the mind. If it be to the degree of effulgence, it is very sensible, and mankind have agreed in it: they all represent glory and extraordinary beauty by brightness. The reason of it is either that light or our organ of seeing is so contrived that an harmonious motion is excited in the animal spirits and propagated to the brain. That mixture we call white is a proportionate mixture that is harmonious, as Sir Isaac Newton has shown, to each particular simple colour, and contains in it some harmony or other that is delightfull. And each sort of rays play a distinct tune to the soul, besides those lovely mixtures that are found in nature. Those beauties, how lovely is the green of the face of the earth in all manner of colours, in flowers, the colour of the skies, and lovely tinctures of the morning and evening.

Corollary: Hence the reason why almost all men, and those that seem to be very miserable, love life, because they cannot bear to lose sight of such a beautiful and lovely world. The ideas, that every moment whilst we live have a beauty that we take not distant notice of, brings a pleasure that, when we come to the trial, we had rather live in much pain and misery than lose.

## WILLIAM L. HEDGES
*Editor*

# Washington Irving

1783–1859

THE YOUNGEST child in the large family of a New York tradesman who had emigrated from Scotland a few years before the American Revolution, Washington Irving grew up in the expectation of making a career in law or business. The elder Irving's firm, which gradually expanded and passed into the hands of the several sons, traded in a variety of importations including dry goods, sugar, wine, and hardware. Two of the sons, Peter and John Treat, educated at Columbia College, became respectively doctor and lawyer. Washington was apprenticed to a lawyer at sixteen; three years later he transferred to the office of the prominent Federalist judge, Josiah Ogden Hoffman.

Outwardly, as one peruses it, the biography reads like a version of the American success story: from inconspicuous middle-class beginnings Irving rose to become his nation's first esteemed professional man of letters. His career often reveals a capacity, similar to that observable in the Irvings generally, for adapting to practical situations and making the most of business, social, and political opportunities. But his success was by no means guaranteed in advance. With the winning of political independence Americans had begun demanding a literature expressive of their distinctiveness as a nation. There was now, at least in theory, a place in American society for the creative writer. But the writer who deliberately set out to make a

living at his calling faced stiff competition from British authors, whose work, in the absence of international copyright laws, was blithely reprinted in the United States without recompense to them. Many American readers remained hesitant about accepting native books lest the response be taken as a sign of bad taste. And while little patronage was to be looked for in a bourgeois republic, American Grubstreets, in New York, Philadelphia, or Boston, were not likely to provide young writers with the kind of stimulation that would help them finally to escape from hack work or routine journalism.

True, it was the gentlemanly thing for a man in business or one of the professions to take an interest in the arts, and New York in the first decade of the nineteenth century had something of the appearance of a boom town in fashion and culture. Literary societies flourished, and Irving's brothers participated in them. Peter and William Irving became minor writers, the former a newspaper editor as well, and though his New York *Morning Chronicle* served chiefly as a noisy conveyance for the Irvings' political views, which were at the time Burrite Republican, Peter did print Washington's early venture in theatrical criticism, *The Letters of Jonathan Oldstyle* (1802–03). The family thus recognized and encouraged the youngest son's talent. Sent abroad in 1804 on a cure for a mild consumptive tendency, Irving was expected to make his journey a kind of grand tour, improving his time in the galleries and museums. But when he returned in 1806, it was with the prospect of finally taking the bar examination. Literature was to be an avocation. For years he tried to accommodate himself to what his father and brothers considered their better judgment, that he should not altogether abandon the security of the law office or a business connection. And it was only in finally shaking off this affectionate but persistent solicitude at the age of thirty-six, long after he had achieved a minor literary triumph with *Knickerbocker's History of New York* (1809), that he made a career for himself as a writer.

Meanwhile, however, as an amateur, not dependent for his livelihood on selling his wares, Irving had been able to afford the luxury of brashness and irreverence. An element of practical joking, of hiding behind pen names and momentarily hoodwinking an audience, characterizes his youthful performances, culminating in the well-known spurious advertisements in the New York *Evening Post* in 1809 which explained that an eccentric antiquarian named Diedrich Knickerbocker had disappeared from a New York lodging-house leaving behind a manuscript history which was to be published to compensate the landlord for back rent. And in not going to college, Irving, whatever the disadvantage, at least escaped the ponderous indoctrination in religion, ethics, and the classics which American higher education in his day tended to promote. He read haphazardly but voraciously, as the breadth of allusion in *Knickerbocker* attests. He toured Europe in the same informal but enthusiastic way.

He was always an adept, though not an aggressive, socializer, and while he passed the bar examination in 1806—only, he later claimed, because "the examiners were prepossessed in my favour"—and entered a partnership with his brother John Treat, he preferred attending dances or indulging his taste for champagne, cigars, and good talk. Out of his mild carousing with other young business and professional men came the inspiration for *Salmagundi*, a periodical paper or magazine of burlesque humor and social satire with which Irving, his brother William, and James Kirke Paulding dazzled New York for a season in 1807—08.

Soon afterwards, as he worked with Peter Irving on the project which evolved into *Knickerbocker*, his realization that he had fallen in love with Judge Hoffman's daughter Matilda brought him to a crisis. For if he was to marry, he would have to earn a regular living. His prospects not being very bright, the sympathetic Hoffman offered to take him into his law firm. Irving agreed, though he dreaded the drudgery to which he felt he was condemning himself. Marriage would mean a drastic curtailment of his literary activities. But in February, 1809, Matilda fell ill of consumption and in April she died. There was a grievous irony in this catastrophe. Overwhelmed with sorrow at Matilda's death, he was yet freed from his bargain with Judge Hoffman. The complex shock suffered at this time is undoubtedly reflected in the sometimes frenzied and grotesque humor of *Knickerbocker*.

Going somewhat aimlessly to England in 1815, he found the Liverpool branch of the family enterprise on the verge of failure and Peter, who was in charge there, seriously ill. For more than two years Irving nursed the pair of invalids, until the Liverpool firm expired in bankruptcy. This exhausting and demoralizing experience, daily renewing his loathing for what he had earlier called a "sordid, dusty, soul killing way of life," removed any remaining doubts he had about trying to earn his living as a writer. By 1817 he was at work in his spare time on what was to become *The Sketch Book*, filling his notebooks with rough drafts and ideas for essays and tales, with descriptions of scenes and events encountered during holiday excursions in England, Wales, and Scotland. He made a pilgrimage to Abbotsford to see Sir Walter Scott, an admirer of *Knickerbocker*, and on Scott's advice began reading widely in German romantic literature.

As he wrote, he exercised a more restrained, studied style than that of his early period. He had an eye to immediate sales and could no longer afford to write for a purely local audience. Paying close attention to current literary vogues, he began to experiment with legendary, picturesque, sentimental, and Gothic elements in his work. When he was finally ready to publish, he carefully launched *The Sketch Book* piecemeal, watching the public's reaction to the early installments before risking others; in 1819 and 1820 he sent the material for seven separate booklets back to New York, where one of his brothers saw it through the press.

*The Sketch Book* had a good initial sale in the United States; even more important for his future reputation, the English edition, appearing almost simultaneously, won the warm approval of English critics, who praised it as the first readable piece of imaginative literature by an American. Furthermore, by retaining control of both the English and American editions, Irving prevented the book's being widely pirated and thus earned royalties in both countries at once, a stratagem which other American writers were quick to adopt.

Success kept him in Europe, following up one literary opportunity or another, for twelve more years. He was a literary celebrity now. Having won his reputation by presenting himself in *The Sketch Book* as "Geoffrey Crayon, Gent.," an American exploring England and the English past, he went on to build *Bracebridge Hall* (1822) around Crayon's extended visit to an old English manor house. His next book, *Tales of a Traveller* (1824), published after an extended stay in Germany and France, was poorly received, but the setback to his reputation was only temporary. Early in 1826 he went to Spain at the behest of Alexander Everett, head of the American legation in Madrid, whose idea it was that Irving should translate Martín Fernández de Navarrete's recently published collection of documents relevant to the voyages of Columbus. Sensing instead the need for a full-scale biography based on unused sources, Irving was soon at work in Spanish libraries and archives. He stayed the better part of four years in Spain, long enough not only to publish both *The Life and Voyages of Christopher Columbus* (1828) and a second history, *A Chronicle of the Conquest of Granada* (1829), but also to find in his visit to Granada in 1828, during which he resided in the old

Moorish palace of the Alhambra, inspiration for a Spanish "sketch book."

*The Alhambra* was published in 1832, the year in which Irving at last returned to the United States, to be greeted as a conquering hero. The year before, he had been given an honorary degree by Oxford. Henceforth he was increasingly to function as a kind of elder statesman of American literature. As early as 1826, while working on *Columbus*, he had been officially a member of the American legation. His legal training and knowledge of documents, his reputation as a writer, his social charm made him diplomatically negotiable. He had returned to London in 1829 as secretary to the legation there. Twelve years later, after having been courted for public office by both political parties, he was to accept appointment under President Tyler and Secretary of State Daniel Webster as minister to Spain.

Irving lived until 1859, enshrined after 1836 (except for the four-year mission to Spain) at Sunnyside, the old Dutch farmhouse at Tarrytown which he had converted into a studiedly picturesque country house, thereby lending his prestige to what soon became the rage for antique frills in American architecture. The last twenty-five years of his life reveal less the writer of fiction than the man of letters, deemed capable of handling almost any topic with grace and distinction. John Jacob Astor furnished him with the documentary materials for a history of the noted fur-trading venture at the mouth of the Columbia River; these Irving developed into *Astoria* (1836). *The Crayon Miscellany* (1835) contained an account of his own trans-Mississippi trip in 1832. After a book on James Bonneville's trapping and exploring expedition in the Rock Mountains, Irving produced biographies of Oliver Goldsmith and Mahomet, and terminated his career with the five-volume tribute to his namesake, *The Life of George Washington* (1855–59).

II

THE ENDURING reputation of Irving throughout the nineteenth century is an important aspect of the history of American taste. He gave the nation its first example of how to succeed at "culture," perhaps its first popular image of what it is to be cultured. He was, at least in his later years, that "dear and good Washington Irving" whom Thackeray knew: "gentle, generous, good-humored, affectionate, self-denying . . . a delightful example of complete gentlemanhood"—all the more remarkable because, as Thackeray recalled, he was "born in no very high sphere." He had developed a smooth, "correct" prose style, which served as a model for generations of students of English composition. He was a lover of soft, picturesque landscapes. Like countless other American tourists, whose attitudes he had helped to mold, he could go giddy at the sight of a Gothic cathedral or an ivy-mantled tower. He was, as Thackeray said, "the first Ambassador from the New World of Letters . . . to the Old." As one who respected European taste, he tended to identify culture with a benign sense of the past. In short, the later Irving seemed a living demonstration of the primacy in art of the qualities which the Victorian era took for beauty: polish, ornamentation, and prettiness.

Modern criticism has on the whole been too ready to accept this view, with the result that in the revolution in literary taste which this century has undergone, Irving's reputation has steadily declined. Some attention has been called to the merits of his early satire, which is apt to attract the modern reader more than the sentiment. But the legendary Irving, the genial gentleman at Sunnyside, the old-bachelor uncle playing father to a bevy of nieces and encouraging young writers, still gets in the way of a real understanding and appreciation of the more significant and complex Irving of the years before the homecoming. Too often his earlier works are misread through a compulsion to fit him as nearly as possible, from beginning to end, into the mold of the Federalist gentleman of the old school, the softspoken romantic escapist, or the gentle, warm-hearted humorist.

Humor is at the root of almost everything that is important in Irving, but one needs to ask what he was laughing at, why he needed to laugh at all. It is a myth that his humor is always affectionate and well-meaning. Some of the laughter of the early period is closer to indignation than amusement. From the time of Addison, the British, and later the American, essayist had spoken in the authoritative voice of a mature, if not elderly, gentleman of considerable experience, sense, and good taste. But New York, in 1800, was not Augustan London. American newspapers, depending heavily on a broad, explosive humor and sarcasm, had vulgarized the periodical-essay tradition. Irving's humor, in *Salmagundi* and *Knickerbocker*, substitutes frequently for the grace, wit, and restrained irony of the *Spectator* a humor of hyperbole, grotesque caricature, flagrant puns, and thunderous invective—the literary equivalent of theatrical slapstick.

Irving belonged to a young society which was as suspicious of England and the Continent as it was eager for Old World approval. While Americans acknowledged their comparative backwardness and barrenness in the arts, the realization was irksome. It is not surprising to find an undercurrent of outright philistinism, of middle-class distrust of genuine cultivation in *Salmagundi*. The satire, however, cuts several ways at once. As a whole the papers give the impression of a society intensely busy with purely local affairs but apprehensive of the existence somewhere of a more cosmopolitan point of view, a society starved for culture but hardly willing to admit it. *Salmagundi* and *Knickerbocker*, appropriating most of the basic devices of eighteenth-century English and American satire, generate an impression of a world turned topsy-turvy. Mock-heroic and mock-epic styles are so used to make both the present and past look out of joint.

The key to the *History of New York* is Diedrich Knickerbocker, a narrator so thoroughly confused as to keep the reader guessing whether Irving ever intends anything seriously. Knickerbocker is more than a pedantic antiquarian, more than another device—like the lumber of cryptic footnotes and citations of learned authorities—for satirizing dry-as-dust or overpretentious scholarship. He is a scholar whose wits seem to have been turned by the momentous burden laid upon him by his profession, the responsibility of ascertaining the true facts about the past, interpreting them reliably, and making them seem significant to the reader.

A caricature, of course, not a realistic portrayal, the eccentric Knickerbocker in his sad plight is hardly intended to compel the reader's sympathy. He is a metaphor to suggest the failure of the world as he sees it to make complete sense. Knickerbocker's wildest statements are referable not so much to a real state of mind as, in some accidental and yet half-meaningful way, to the general state of human affairs. Irving's skill is in keeping his narrator consistently inconsistent so that the reader can accept flat contradictions, irrelevant garrulity, and abrupt shifts of tone and style as all in keeping with Knickerbocker's character. Plausibly juxtaposing shrewd insight and arrant nonsense, *Knickerbocker* constantly teases the reader into the suspicion that it may be impossible to distinguish between the two.

If Irving, in spite of the irony of Knickerbocker's insistence on Peter Stuyvesant's greatness, succeeds in arousing the reader's sympathies for the Dutch governor, it is for qualities of courage, honesty, and loyalty which are constantly threatened with extinction, even by forces within the man himself. Perhaps the alarming thing about *Knickerbocker* is that it asks in effect whether *common* sense isn't simply a myth, whether human beings can in fact ever for very long overcome private prejudices and temperamental distractions so that they see things objectively. The effect of *Knickerbocker* is a combination of sheer delight in a comic world and occasional anxiety over the possibility that what can so easily be made comic may at bottom be meaningless. It is a distortion to ignore either part of the composite impression.

Irving makes the Dutch settlers of the New Netherlands the primary symbol of the stolid middle-class materialism which, like ballast, weighs down and sometimes virtually sinks American life, in spite of the lofty pull of professed ideals. In *Knickerbocker*, self-government sometimes seems no more than the petty wrangling of "meddlesome" burghers in New Amsterdam. The mock-historian compares the intolerance of partisan politicians and editors in contemporary New York with the persecution of Quakers and Anabaptists and the hanging of witches in seventeenth-century Massachusetts. In effect the book denies the newness of the New World, sees Americans through their susceptibility to human weakness and error as belonging to the world that is as old as Adam. Northerner or Southerner, Yankee or New Yorker, they are a nation of farmers and tradesmen, who are apt to drive a hard bargain, take advantage of Indians and Negroes, and show more interest in political banquets, horse races, cocktails, and bundling than in things of the mind or spirit.

### III

This curious division in allegiance—an uneasy suspension between eighteenth-century irony on the one hand and nineteenth-century sentiment on the other—became sharper in Irving's next book, *The Sketch Book.* His early work had been mocking and irreverent. Now, however, as he tested the wind before launching *The Sketch Book*, he found it no longer fashionable to mock. He found also—perhaps to his secret consternation—the springs of irony drying up within himself. A proper ironist, Swift, for example, stands upon bedrock. Human foibles magnify themselves grotesquely under his gaze because the gaze is clear and untroubled. Irving was not so situated. His intellectual and moral foundations were on sand. He would be sentimental—he would brood upon "mutability," would rhapsodize, would conjure up eerie "Gothic" mysteries—but the impulse was not native and would soon exhaust itself. Thereupon, the old satire would reassert itself. In "The Author's Account Of Himself," a panegyric upon American scenery, for example, is oddly undercut by a closely following adversion to the "gigantic race" in England from which Americans are "degenerated." Then again, cheek by jowl with Rip Van Winkle's shrewish wife, stands a paragon of selfless devotion, the brave little suburban housewife in "The Wife," a story which "Rip Van Winkle" follows. Who is this Irving then, one asks, perplexed, whose gaze at one moment is level and pitiless, the next moment filmed over with sentiment?

What saves the disparate pieces of *The Sketch Book* from incoherence is the device of the pseudonym "Geoffrey Crayon." This device of a fictitious author-editor converts Irving's intellectual and temperamental indecisiveness into a positive asset. An inscription on the title page establishes Crayon as a "mere spectator of other men's fortunes and adventures," an observer, that is, at a psychic distance. From behind this pseudonym, one can sense the actual Irving ambuscaded behind a mask. Like his fictitious editor, Irving too has become almost an old bachelor by now, his life still unsettled, drifting into middle age, the genial exterior masking an inner anxiety. In a word, he is vulnerable and unsure.

The great utility of the mask is the impunity it lends him. Behind its impassive surface, Irving may experiment with novel and often antithetical modes of feeling. He may dramatize his interest in the antique, the picturesque, and the sentimental—the whole complex of emotions characterized by the epithet "Romanticism"—and all the while be indifferent if early admirers of the Knickerbocker *History* think him ridiculous therefore. He may also get to the important business of reappraising the Old World. From this reappraisal issued an early formulation of that artifact of the search for American identity, the concept of "Europe." For Irving, as for later American writers, the concept has peculiar intensity. Europe is old, America is new. Is Europe's age—its "hoary usage and reverend custom"—a boon and source of strength, or is it on the contrary a trap for the spirit, a subtle and insidious invitation to inertia? Or, conversely, is America the brave new world, or has it cut itself off so violently from the past that its present scene constitutes a famine of effect—a radical irrelevance to lasting human concerns? All such ruminations, unseemly in Irving himself, were proper to "Geoffrey Crayon."

Irving might also—and the impulse is never long absent from his work—resurrect the broad humor of his youth. And all of this could be done without inconsistency, or at least without the *psychic* inconsistency implicit in the commitment of himself and the use of his own voice.

*The Sketch Book* accordingly gives the first important display in American literature of affection for England, for what Hawthorne was to call "our old home," for English landscape and village life, for English character and the forms and ceremonies that regulate English behavior, for architectural landmarks and monuments crusted over with associations of a memorable past.

Ironically, however, Irving's best work in *The Sketch Book* is in the American stories. These stories have absolutely nothing to do with hedgerows, Yorkshire pudding, or Robin Goodfellow. As the introductory descriptions, which avoid the inflated rhetoric of "The Author's Account of Himself," make clear, "Rip Van Winkle" and "The Legend of Sleepy Hollow" are, in spite of being adaptations of German folk tales, tributes to the natural beauty of the American countryside, an opulent, amenable terrain which the author had known in the summers of his boyhood and which remained clear in his mind even as he began to find himself a figure in an ordered, park-like English landscape.

Only gradually, as he learned what his readers would tolerate and to what extent he could square his own interests with those of his public, did Irving's Romanticism jell into the set of stock responses with which his position in American literature finally became associated. In *Bracebridge Hall* his affection for the quainter aspects of the English scene proved harder to sustain, though his audience may not have been aware of the fact. Unable to take his manor-house characters, their attitudes, ideals, and eccentricities as seriously as so extensive a work demanded, he began to make them appear more ridiculous than in his moods of Anglophilia he must originally have tended. Ironically it is a few brawling satirical scenes reminiscent of the subversive humor of his early period, together with one or two interpolated stories, that come close to saving the book today.

In *Tales of a Traveller* he cut down on mere sentiment and worked toward a curious yoking of broad humor and Gothic sensationalism. Poe was later to speak approvingly of the book in his review of Hawthorne's *Twice-Told Tales,* but the failure of Irving's *Tales* with the public helped turn him toward the safer ground of nonfiction. He worked hard at making himself a historian, learning Spanish, and taking particular pains in *Columbus* to achieve factual accuracy. But Irving's effectiveness as a historian was limited by his refusal to concern himself deeply with political, economic, and social problems. What finally interested him in Columbus was the mythic quality of the man's life; he worked instinctively to present him as an example of the archetypal romantic, quixotic visionary, by no means consistently practical, doomed to endless searching and long suffering by the combined brilliance and blindness of his imagination.

In the *Conquest of Granada* he showed his fictionalist's hand openly by reverting to the use of a pen name. An account, full of exotic costuming and pageantry, of the final expulsion of the Moors from Spain, the book is essentially true in fact, but Irving, eschewing scholarly objectivity, pretends that his narrative is a translation of a medieval chronicle written by a bigoted old ecclesiastic, Fray Antonio Agapida. The result is a legendary, romance-like quality, the book symbolically suggesting and reiterating the axiom of the inevitable doom of even the most heroic of man's attempts to reestablish a paradise on earth.

Irving was, of course, still working variations on the theme of mutability. This one had already been to a considerable extent prefigured in *Tales of a Traveller's* emphasis on the vanity of "golden dreams"—Tom Walker's, for instance. *The Alhambra* intensifies and makes more personal the same quixotic element by unifying various tales, scraps of history, and scenic sketches around Irving's own situation as a temporary occupant of the ancient palace.

When the American exile returned to his native land, he found a home at last, and conflicts ceased. Unlike Cooper, who, two years later, in 1834, after a stay in Europe, angrily discovered an America menaced by Jacksonian vulgarity and conformism, Irving, for all his love of old things, largely accepted the affluent and expanding, hard-working and self-satisfied mid-century America which had so eagerly accepted him. He left to younger writers the job of finding meanings in American life. He was getting old and had scrambled too hard simply to become a writer. Assured of an audience, he did not scruple now to write in the Romantic idiom in which they and he were fully conversant.

Looking at the wild West, he was apt to see knights and squires, noble savages, picturesque groupings around a campfire, landscapes suggesting the "golden tone" of Claude Lorrain, and light filtering through forest trees like "sunshine among the stained windows and clustering columns of a Gothic cathedral." Often he abandoned such language in favor of a more nearly objective kind of reporting which stressed ludicrous detail. The inconsistencies were less apparent and less important to an age that had not, like ours, been bred to realism. As long as he confined himself, as he usually did, to externals, he was helping Americans to *see* the West.

Inevitably the Oliver Goldsmith of his biography turned out rather like the popular image of Washington Irving, both as a man and as a writer. And in the biography of Washington (1855–59) he tried to animate the conventional metaphor of "the father of his country." Increasingly the dry ring of mid-Victorian eloquence sounded in his later prose; he was capable of complaining of the "stupid, commonplace, and often ribald" place names, like "Big River," which the settlers in the West had substituted for more picturesque Indian names. Only occasionally in these years does one come across such satirical outcroppings as when, in the late thirties, the spectacle "of that eagerness for gain, and rage for improvement, which keep our people continually on the move" ("The Creole Village"), prompted him to coin the phrase "the almighty dollar."

IV

IRVING'S literary significance begins with his instinctive realization, important in his day in a nation as puritanical in background as the United States, that literature's first function is to engage and entertain the reader. He had a healthy respect for the priority of style, the way a thing is said, to message or moral. His exuberant early style, through the popularity of *Knickerbocker*, helped establish a tradition of verbal extravagance combined with bluntness of tone which still persists at a certain level of American journalistic prose. The youthful style is itself something of a salmagundi, a conglomeration in which elegant phrases and imagery, literary echoes (used either soberly or in mockery), technical jargon, and homely idiom ironically jostle one another.

Irving's delight in language seems to begin as a response to sounds, to the brazenness, for instance, of colloquial invective—"slang-whangers," Salmagundese for newspaper editors—or to the harsh pedantry of a coinage like "logocracy"—a government by words. He is willing to go out of his way for special effects in making words jingle and clatter against one another, the most obvious instance coming in *Knickerbocker* when at the battle of Fort Christina he marshals the awkward-sounding Dutch names in a long, rhyming, rhythmic list. Above all he likes the solid, unadorned sounds of the words for the objects and activities by which most of the every day business of the world is transacted—"market-baskets, butchers' blocks, and wheelbarrows"; a "cit" who "rattles away" "in a buggy or tim-whiskey."

The mature style strives on the whole for smoother, softer sounds, for an over-all sense of grace. It relies heavily on medium to longish sentences, balanced phrasing, and a judicious mixing of latinate abstractions and concrete English nouns, adjectives, and verbs. While derived from the English eighteenth century, from Addison and Goldsmith, this style is a flexible one, on the whole more informal, less bookish than Cooper's, Hawthorne's, or Poe's. Under the polished surface there still lurks a fondness for the ordinary. It was only later, as he settled into the role of national celebrity, that his attitude in favor of the picturesque and against the commonplace hardened. In the works of the 1820's much of his concern is with commonplace material.

Numerous passages, for example, of commonplace diction and metaphor starkly and ludicrously mire Ichabod Crane in his backwater rural neighborhood, for all his "gentlemanlike" pretensions: on horseback "his sharp elbows [stick] out like grasshoppers'" and "the motion of his arms [is] not unlike the flapping of a pair of wings": on foot, he is like a "scarecrow," has a "spindle neck," a "snipe nose," a head like a "weathercock," and feet like "shovels." Again, connection with proverbial wisdom gives vitality to Rip Van Winkle, who likes to "take the world easy, eat white bread or brown, . . . and would rather starve on a penny than work for a pound": as for his wife—"a tart temper never mellows with age, and a sharp tongue is the only edged tool that grows keener with constant use."

Elsewhere, mundane and erudite connotations clash comically. Rip's dog, threatened with a "broomstick or ladle," makes for the door with "yelping precipitation." "Sleepy Hollow" begins in the mild, perhaps unconscious, whimsy of an extensively latinate diction brought to bear on the homely scene of Tarry Town, and in the euphemistic discussion of Rip's plain, ordinary laziness the exploitation of the incongruity between refined style and commonplace subject becomes quite deliberate: "The great error in Rip's composition was an insuperable aversion to all kinds of profitable labor."

At its best then Irving's mature style, though in a much more restrained way than in *Knickerbocker*, still plays off the elegant and the commonplace, the narrative voice never fully identifying with either. The peculiar sensibility of Geoffrey Crayon, the American as "Gent.," is a product of the tension. Having risen above vulgar origins, Crayon (or Irving) can contemplate the ordinary with amused fondness. At the same time he can see the humorous side of his claim to cultivation and make fun of the tendency toward inflated language which often accompanies a fashionable style.

Beyond style, though not unrelated to it, lies Irving's contribution to the development of the short story. In part this came through the invention of Crayon. For out of Crayon's situation comes Irving's most distinctive type of sketch, not a flat description of scene or character or an unrelieved evocation of mood or atmosphere, but a first-person narrative in which Crayon, as he speaks, inadvertently reveals almost as much about himself as about his surroundings. Often he appears partially alienated from the world at large, able to see it or hear it only imperfectly, at a distance or through a shadow or distraction.

Implicit in the Crayonesque sketch is the irony of the limited viewpoint, which American fiction from Irving through Melville half-consciously utilized before Henry James began to exploit it systematically. Such a viewpoint throws the emphasis from the spectacle back to the spectator. It asks what the situation may mean to him and interprets what he sees as at least partially a function of his character. Irving was no psychologist, but in finding a place in his sketches for a figure embodying some of the salient features of his own personality, he helped introduce into American fiction a potentially subtle, subjective element. It is a narrative voice whose sensibility looms in the story, becoming insistent enough finally to divert attention from the main complication of the story it is supposed to be telling to the observer himself. What precisely *is* his relation to the story, to the characters, to the complexion of events?

In his short stories Irving usually starts with stock characters—the shiftless husband, for instance, and the termagant wife. Yet he manages in his better work to set them in homely situations and surroundings which give them a kind of vitality. And his choice of incidents and descriptive details that offset, echo, or otherwise interact with one another touches off patterns of imagery which symbolically amplify basic themes. "Rip Van Winkle" and "The Legend of Sleepy Hollow" also have a mock-Gothic quality about them. Rip gets lost in an enchanted wood, but the ghosts he encounters prove merely silent and indifferent. And the only ghost in Sleepy Hollow is Brom Bones with his pumpkin. Yet these stories are more than burlesques. "The Legend of Sleepy Hollow" is a fable about American affluence. Lacking all the commonplace American virtues—physical prowess, business sense, a cheery appetite for hard work—Ichabod Crane, who enjoys frightening himself with ghost stories, is a sorry misfit doomed from the start to defeat at the hands of Brom Bones. Though he lusts after the plump Katrina and her father's fat estate from afar, the lean and hungry schoolmaster is too diffident to win his wife and fortune in the ordinary straightforward American way. He is a potential old-bachelor recluse and pedant, the likes of which Irving (or Crayon) may be half-inclined to deny in himself. Not until he has been nearly scared out of his wits does the doleful Ichabod learn to settle down to enjoying the good things of this life, which, the story seems to say, are there for anyone who is not simply afraid to reach for them. Though much of the strength of "Sleepy Hollow" stems from the fact that the author's sympathy for its quixotic mock-hero is maintained almost to the end, Irving now looks more fondly than in *Knickerbocker* on his fat, pipe-smoking Dutchmen and on a land which seems to sprout prosperity as an annual crop, a reward for American good humor.

As for the overly aggressive tendencies, the blustering and hard-bargaining that had upset Knickerbocker, "Rip Van Winkle" suggests that they may be quietly lived down. "Rip" is a justifiably famous story, though its richness of implication has until recently been largely obscured by its reputation as a children's story and by the memory of the sentimentalized play version, which the actor Joseph Jefferson made into a great nineteenth-century hit. Beneath the obvious humor and pathos, signs of decay, sterility, and impotence point to the fact that the story, like Hawthorne's "Wakefield," deals with the loss or surrender of manhood. An exchange is made of what ought to be the best twenty years of Rip's life, the years of his active maturity, for a peaceful old age. He sleeps, dreaming at first only of the silent little men playing at bowls, then of nothing. Meanwhile, back home men fight a war and establish a new nation. In the end Rip becomes, in effect, a benign old bachelor. Irving does not blink the grave difficulties involved in accommodating such a fate. They are felt in a few fearful passages, in Rip's first glance into the deep glen, in his bewilderment on waking up, in his re-entry into his deserted house.

But Rip is resilient enough to slough off his misfortune and turn it to advantage. For he has slept out a fate worse than the loss of twenty years; he has, after all, escaped that nagging, insistent spirit of American industry, his wife. And now he makes a big success of failure, as Irving's humor continues to deflate American myths. Rip gets by famously as an idler, a gossip, a dreamer, as someone who helps his neighbors and gets on well with children, not as a man who minds his own business and zealously guards his reputation for keeping his nose to the grindstone.

Irving could not work inside character (except with someone like Crayon) sufficiently well to give his more dramatic stories the psychological authenticity they demand. His best efforts come through the lighter, more relaxed, half-humorous approach. "The Devil and Tom Walker," for instance, spares the reader an obvious moral, yet in its somewhat harum-scarum, folktalish way it begins to bring certain aspects of Puritanism into dramatic focus. Irving uses a comic-Yankee stereotype and a relatively stock conception of Puritanism; as in his satiric broadsides against Puritan bigotry and superstition in *Knickerbocker*, he is still the more or less unsympathetic outsider looking on. It was to take a Hawthorne in "Young Goodman Brown" (see pp. 371) to get inside the individual Puritan's dilemma. But the two stories are worth comparing in detail. For Irving, in relating Yankee shrewdness to Puritan respectability, is already developing an imagery of darkness, rottenness, and

emptiness to contrast with the seemingly shining solidity of proper and pious professions; he sees the traditional encounter with the devil in forest and swamp as a function of attitudes visible in pulpit and counting-house.

He had not learned, as Hawthorne and, particularly, Poe were to learn, the full value of compactness in the short story. He builds toward the series of tales rather than toward the single story. But the rich profusion of Romantic props manipulated for symbolic effect—mirrors, portraits, masquerades, gardens, fountains, astrologers, buried treasure —conventional though much of it is and often extended as a not entirely satisfactory substitute for more compact action, makes Irving's work a <u>kind of seedbed of imagery in early American fiction</u>. He points to the possibility of going beyond the contemporary journalistic tale, beyond the *Blackwood's* "intensities," which Poe was to satirize, to a short fiction, which, while still using Gothic devices, can begin to suggest real intricacies of character and motive.

# A HISTORY OF NEW YORK

### FROM THE
### BEGINNING OF THE WORLD TO THE END
### OF THE DUTCH DYNASTY
### BY DIEDRICH KNICKERBOCKER

❖

❡ IRVING substantially changed *Knickerbocker*, first in 1812, then in 1848. Grown more skilled in narrative, he made structural improvements, sometimes inventing wholly new episodes. At the same time, particularly in 1848, he toned down the style, pruning it of certain awkward excesses but also eliminating some of the youthful vigor (and in spots frenzy) of the original. The 1848 edition, the only one commonly read today, represents the older Irving, more sensitive to Victorian notions of delicacy—though still by no means prudish.

Book I of *Knickerbocker* covers the history of the world from its creation through the early explorations of America. The founding of New Amsterdam occurs in Book II. Books III and IV give an account of the governorships of Van Twiller and Kieft, and V to VII of that of Peter Stuyvesant. Following his difficulties with New England in Book V, Stuyvesant becomes involved in a border dispute with the colony of New Sweden, founded by Peter Minuit in the region of the Delaware River in 1638. The dispute culminates in the Battle of Fort Christina, the climax (or grand anticlimax) of the book.

*Knickerbocker's* learned allusions, partly designed to lampoon pedantry, continue to mock the modern scholar who tries to decipher them. Most appear to have some basis in actuality, but Irving, frequently citing writers and works he has not himself consulted, is often cryptic and ambiguous in his references.

❖

## FROM BOOK VI [1809]

### CHAPTER 7

CONTAINING THE MOST HORRIBLE BATTLE
EVER RECORDED IN POETRY OR PROSE;
WITH THE ADMIRABLE EXPLOITS OF
PETER THE HEADSTRONG

"Now HAD the Dutchmen snatch'd a huge repast," and finding themselves wonderfully encouraged and animated thereby, prepared to take the field. Expectation, says a faithful matter of fact dutch poet, whose works were unfortunately destroyed in the conflagration of the Alexandrian library [1]—Expectation now stood on stilts.[2] The world forgot to turn round, or rather stood still, that it might witness the affray; like a fat round bellied alderman, watching the combat of two chivalric flies upon his jerkin. The eyes of all mankind, as usual in such cases, were turned upon Fort Christina.[3] The sun, like a little man in a crowd, at a puppet shew, scampered about the heavens, popping his head here and there, and endeavouring to get a peep between the unmannerly clouds, that obtruded themselves in his way. The historians filled their ink-horns—the poets went without their dinners, either that they might buy paper and goose-quills, or because they could not get any thing to eat—antiquity scowled sulkily out of its grave, to see itself outdone—while even

posterity stood mute, gazing in gaping extacy of retrospection, on the eventful field!

The immortal deities, who whilome had seen service at the "affair" of Troy——now mounted their feather-bed clouds, and sailed over the plain, or mingled among the combatants in different disguises, all itching to have a finger in the pie. Jupiter sent off his thunderbolt to a noted copper-smith, to have it furbished up for the direful occasion. Venus, swore by her chastity she'd patronize the Swedes, and in semblance of a blear eyed trull, paraded the battlements of Fort Christina, accompanied by Diana, as a serjeant's widow, of cracked reputation—The noted bully Mars, stuck two horse pistols into his belt, shouldered a rusty firelock, and gallantly swaggered at their elbow, as a drunken corporal— while Apollo trudged in their rear, as a bandy-legged fifer, playing most villainously out of tune.

On the other side, the ox-eyed Juno, who had won a pair of black eyes over night, in one of her curtain lectures with old Jupiter, displayed her haughty beauties on a baggage waggon——Minerva, as a brawny gin suttler, tucked up her skirts, brandished her fists, and swore most heroically, in exceeding bad dutch (having but lately studied the language), by way of keeping up the spirits of the soldiers; while Vulcan halted as a club-footed blacksmith, lately promoted to be a captain of militia. All was silent horror, or bustling preparation; war reared his horrid front, gnashed loud his iron fangs, and shook his direful crest of bristling bayonets.

And now the mighty chieftains marshalled out their hosts. Here stood stout Risingh,[4] firm as a thousand rocks——encrusted with stockades, and entrenched to the chin in mud batteries—His artillery consisting of two swivels and a carronade, loaded to the muzzle, the touch holes primed, and a whiskered bombardier stationed at each, with lighted match in hand, waiting the word. His valiant infantry, that had never turned back upon an enemy (having never seen any before)——lined the breast work in grim array, each having his mustachios fiercely greased, and his hair pomatumed back, and queued so stiffly, that he grinned above the ramparts like a grizly death's head.

There came on the intrepid Hard-koppig Piet,— a second Bayard, without fear or reproach—his brows knit, his teeth clenched, his breath held hard, rushing on like ten thousand bellowing bulls of Bashan.[5] His faithful squire Van Corlear, trudging valiantly at his heels, with his trumpet gorgeously bedecked with red and yellow ribbands,

A HISTORY OF NEW YORK. See Williams and McDowell's Introduction to *Knickerbocker* (1927), and H. M. Lydenberg's "Irving's *Knickerbocker* and Some of Its Sources," *Bulletin of the New York Public Library* LVI (1952), pp. 544-53, 596–619.

Book VI. 1. conflagration . . . library: The great library of ancient learning at Alexandria, Egypt was largely destroyed by fire in 391 A. D. 2. Expectation . . . stilts: Cf. *Henry V*, II, Prologue, 1. 8. 3. Fort Christina: chief fort of New Sweden, located between what are now Baltimore and Philadelphia.

4. Risingh: Johan Classon Rising, governor of New Sweden. 5. bulls of Bashan: Cf. Ps. 22:12.

the remembrances of his fair mistresses at the Manhattoes. Then came waddling on his sturdy comrades, swarming like the myrmidons of Achilles. There were the Van Wycks and the Van Dycks and the Ten Eycks—the Van Nesses, the Van Tassels, the Van Grolls; the Van Hœsens, the Van Giesons, and the Van Blarcoms—The Van Warts, the Van Winkles, the Van Dams; the Van Pelts, the Van Rippers, and the Van Brunts.— There were the Van Horns, the Van Borsums, the Van Bunschotens; the Van Gelders, the Van Arsdales, and the Van Bummels—The Vander Belts, the Vander Hoofs, the Vander Voorts, the Vander Lyns, the Vander Pools and the Vander Spiegels.— There came the Hoffmans, the Hooglands, the Hoppers, the Cloppers, the Oothouts, the Quackenbosses, the Roerbacks, the Garrebrantzes, the Onderdonks, the Varra Vangers, the Schermerhorns, the Brinkerhoffs, the Bontecous, the Knickerbockers, the Hockstrassers, the Ten Breecheses and the Tough Breecheses, with a host more of valiant worthies, whose names are too crabbed to be written, or if they could be written, it would be impossible for man to utter—all fortified with a mighty dinner, and to use the words of a great Dutch poet

—"Brimful of wrath and cabbage!"

For an instant the mighty Peter paused in the midst of his career, and mounting on a rotten stump addressed his troops in eloquent low dutch, exhorting them to fight like *duyvels,* and assuring them that if they conquered, they should get plenty of booty—if they fell they should be allowed the unparalleled satisfaction, while dying, of reflecting that it was in the service of their country—and after they were dead, of seeing their names inscribed in the temple of renown and handed down, in company with all the other great men of the year, for the admiration of posterity. —Finally he swore to them, on the word of a governor (and they knew him too well to doubt it for a moment) that if he caught any mother's son of them looking pale, or playing craven, he'd curry his hide till he made him run out of it like a snake in spring time.—Then lugging out his direful snickersnee, he brandished it three times over his head, ordered Van Corlear to sound a tremendous charge, and shouting the words "St. Nicholas and the Manhattoes!" courageously dashed forwards. His warlike followers, who had employed the interval in lighting their pipes, instantly stuck them in their mouths, gave a furious puff, and charged gallantly, under cover of the smoke.

The Swedish garrison, ordered by the cunning Risingh not to fire until they could distinguish the whites of their assailants' eyes, stood in horrid silence on the covert-way; until the eager dutchmen had half ascended the glacis. Then did they pour into them such a tremendous volley, that the very hills quaked around, and were terrified even unto an incontinence of water, insomuch that certain springs burst forth from their sides, which continue to run unto the present day. Not a dutchman but would have bit the dust, beneath that dreadful fire, had not the protecting Minerva kindly taken care, that the Swedes should one and all, observe their usual custom of shutting their eyes and turning away their heads, at the moment of discharge.

But were not the muskets levelled in vain, for the balls, winged with unerring fate, went point blank into a flock of wild geese, which, like geese as they were, happened at that moment to be flying past——and brought down seventy dozen of them—which furnished a luxurious supper to the conquerors, being well seasoned and stuffed with onions.

Neither was the volley useless to the musqueteers, for the hostile wind, commissioned by the implacable Juno, carried the smoke and dust full in the faces of the dutchmen, and would inevitably have blinded them, had their eyes been open. The Swedes followed up their fire, by leaping the counterscarp, and falling tooth and nail upon the foe, with furious outcries. And now might be seen prodigies of valour, of which neither history nor song have ever recorded a parallel. Here was beheld the sturdy Stoffel Brinkerhoff brandishing his lusty quarter staff, like the terrible giant Blanderon his oak tree (for he scorned to carry any other weapon), and drumming a horrific tune upon the heads of whole squadrons of Swedes. There were the crafty Van Courtlandts, posted at a distance, like the little Locrian archers [6] of yore, and plying it most potently with the long bow, for which they were so justly renowned. At another place were collected on a rising knoll the valiant men of Sing-Sing, who assisted marvellously in the fight, by chaunting forth the great song of St. Nicholas. In a different part of the field might be seen the Van Grolls of Anthony's Nose; but they were horribly perplexed in a defile between two little hills, by reason of the length of their noses. There were the Van Bunschotens of Nyack and Kakiat, so renowned for kicking with the left foot, but their skill availed them little at present, being short of wind in consequence of the hearty dinner they had eaten—and they would irretrievably have been put to rout, had they not

6. Locrian archers: ancient Greeks renowned for their ferocity.

been reinforced by a gallant corps of *Voltigeurs* [7] composed of the Hoppers, who advanced to their assistance nimbly on one foot. At another place might you see the Van Arsdales, and the Van Bummels, who ever went together, gallantly pressing forward to bombard the fortress—but as to the Gardeniers of Hudson, they were absent from the battle, having been sent out on a marauding party, to lay waste the neighbouring water-melon patches. Nor must I omit to mention the incomparable atchievement of Antony Van Corlear, who, for a good quarter of an hour waged horrid fight with a little pursy Swedish drummer, whose hide he drummed most magnificently; and had he not come into the battle with no other weapon but his trumpet, would infallibly have put him to an untimely end.

But now the combat thickened—on came the mighty Jacobus Varra Vanger and the fighting men of the Wael Bogtig; after them thundered the Van Pelts of Esopus, together with the Van Rippers and the Van Brunts, bearing down all before them—then the Suy Dams and the Van Dams, pressing forward with many a blustering oath, at the head of the warriors of Hell-gate, clad in their thunder and lightning gaberdines; and lastly the standard bearers and body guards of Peter Stuyvesant, bearing the great beaver of the Manhattoes.

And now commenced the horrid din, the desperate struggle, the maddening ferocity, the frantic desperation, the confusion and self abandonment of war. Dutchman and Swede commingled, tugged, panted and blowed. The heavens were darkened with a tempest of missives.[8] Carcasses, fire balls, smoke balls, stink balls and hand grenades, jostling each other, in the air. Bang! went the guns—whack! struck the broad swords— thump! went the cudgels—crash! went the musket stocks—blows—kicks—cuffs——scratches— —black eyes and bloody noses swelling the horrors of the scene! Thick-thwack, cut and hack, helter-skelter, higgledy-piggledy, hurley-burley, head over heels, klip-klap, slag op slag, hob over bol, rough and tumble!——Dunder and blixum! swore the dutchmen, splitter and splutter! cried the Swedes—Storm the works! shouted Hard-koppig Piet—fire the mine! roared stout Risingh—Tantara-ra-ra! twang'd the trumpet of Antony Van Corlear—until all voice and sound became unintelligible—grunts of pain, yells of fury, and shouts of triumph commingling in one hideous clamour. The earth shook as if struck with a paralytic stroke—the trees shrunk aghast, and

wilted at the sight—the rocks burrowed in the ground like rabbits, and even Christina creek turned from its course, and ran up a mountain in breathless terror!

Nothing, save the dullness of their weapons, the damaged condition of their powder, and the singular accident of one and all striking with the flat instead of the edge of their swords, could have prevented a most horrible carnage—As it was, the sweat prodigiously streaming, ran in rivers on the field, fortunately without drowning a soul, the combatants being to a man, expert swimmers, and furnished with cork jackets for the occasion —but many a valiant head was broken, many a stubborn rib belaboured, and many a broken winded hero drew short breath that day!

Long hung the contest doubtful, for though a heavy shower of rain, sent by the "cloud compelling Jove," in some measure cooled their ardour, as doth a bucket of water thrown on a group of fighting mastiffs, yet did they but pause for a moment, to return with tenfold fury to the charge, belabouring each other with black and bloody bruises. Just at this juncture was seen a vast and dense column of smoke, slowly rolling towards the scene of battle, which for a while made even the furious combatants to stay their arms in mute astonishment—but the wind for a moment dispersing the murky cloud, from the midst thereof emerged the flaunting banner of the immortal Michael Paw. This noble chieftain came fearlessly on, leading a solid phalanx of oyster-fed Pavonians,[9] who had remained behind, partly as a *corps de reserve,* and partly to digest the enormous dinner they had eaten. These sturdy yeomen, nothing daunted, did trudge manfully forward, smoking their pipes with outrageous vigour, so as to raise the awful cloud that has been mentioned; but marching exceedingly slow, being short of leg and of great rotundity in the belt.

And now the protecting deities of the army of New Amsterdam, having unthinkingly left the field and stept into a neighbouring tavern to refresh themselves with a pot of beer, a direful catastrophe had well nigh chanced to befall the Nederlanders. Scarcely had the myrmidons of the puissant Paw attained the front of battle, before the Swedes, instructed by the cunning Risingh, levelled a shower of blows, full at their tobacco pipes. Astounded at this unexpected assault, and totally discomfited at seeing their pipes broken by this "d——d nonsense," the valiant dutchmen fall in vast confusion——already they begin to fly——like a frightened drove of un-

7. *Voltigeurs:* picked French riflemen.    8. missives: missiles.

9. Pavonians: "Pavonia" was the early name for the coastal section of New Jersey below New York City.

wieldy Elephants they throw their own army in an uproar——bearing down a whole legion of little Hoppers——the sacred banner on which is blazoned the gigantic oyster of Communipaw is trampled in the dirt——The Swedes pluck up new spirits and pressing on their rear, apply their feet *a parte poste* [10] with a vigour that prodigiously accelerates their motions—nor doth the renowned Paw himself, fail to receive divers grievous and intolerable visitations of shoe leather!

But what, Oh muse! was the rage of the gallant Peter, when from afar he saw his army yield? With a voice of thunder did he roar after his recreant warriors, putting up such a war whoop, as did the stern Achilles, when the Trojan troops were on the point of burning all his gunboats. The dreadful shout rung in long echoes through the woods— trees toppled at the noise; bears, wolves and panthers jumped out of their skins, in pure af- fright; several wild looking hills bounced clear over the Delaware; and all the small beer in Fort Christina, turned sour at the sound! [11]

The men of the Manhattoes plucked up new courage when they heard their leader——or rather they dreaded his fierce displeasure, of which they stood in more awe than of all the Swedes in Christendom—but the daring Peter, not waiting for their aid, plunged sword in hand, into the thickest of the foe. Then did he display some such incredible atchievements, as have never been known since the miraculous days of the giants. Wherever he went the enemy shrunk before him— with fierce impetuosity he pushed forward, driving the Swedes, like dogs, into their own ditch—but as he fearlessly advanced, the foe, like rushing waves which close upon the scudding bark, thronged in his rear, and hung upon his flank with fearful peril. One desperate Swede, who had a mighty heart, almost as large as a pepper-corn, drove his dastard sword full at the hero's heart. But the protecting power that watches over the safety of all great and good men turned aside the hostile blade, and directed it to a large side pocket, where reposed an enormous Iron Tobacco Box, endowed like the shield of Achilles with supernatural powers——no doubt in consequence of its being piously decorated with a portrait of the blessed St. Nicholas. Thus was the dreadful blow repelled, but not without occasioning to the great Peter a fearful loss of wind.

Like as a furious bear, when gored by worrying curs, turns fiercely round, shews his dread teeth, and springs upon the foe, so did our hero turn

upon the treacherous Swede.[12] The miserable var- let sought in flight, for safety——but the active Peter, seizing him by an immeasurable queue, that dangled from his head—"Ah Whoreson Caterpillar!" roared he, "here is what shall make dog's meat of thee!" [13] So saying he whirled his trusty sword, and made a blow, that would have decapitated him, had he, like Briareus, half a hundred heads, but that the pitying steel struck short and shaved the queue forever from his crown. At this very moment a cunning arque- busier, perched on the summit of a neighbouring mound, levelled his deadly instrument, and would have sent the gallant Stuyvesant, a wailing ghost to haunt the Stygian shore——had not the watch- ful Minerva, who had just stopped to tie up her garter, seen the great peril of her favourite chief, and dispatched old Boreas with his bellows; who in the very nick of time, just as the direful match descended to the pan, gave such a lucky blast, as blew all the priming from the touch hole!

Thus waged the horrid fight——when the stout Risingh, surveying the battle from the top of a little ravelin, perceived his faithful troops, banged, beaten and kicked by the invincible Peter. Language cannot describe the choler with which he was seized at the sight——he only stopped for a moment to disburthen himself of five thousand anathemas; and then drawing his immeasurable cheese toaster,[14] straddled down to the field of combat, with some such thundering strides, as Jupiter is said by old Hesiod to have taken, when he strode down the spheres, to play off his sky rockets at the Titans.

No sooner did these two rival heroes come face to face, than they each made a prodigious start of fifty feet (flemish measure), such as is made by your most experienced stage champions. Then did they regard each other for a moment, with bitter aspect, like two furious ram cats, on the very point of a clapper clawing. Then did they throw themselves in one attitude, then in another, strik- ing their swords on the ground, first on the right side, then on the left, at last at it they went, like five hundred houses on fire! Words cannot tell the prodigies of strength and valour, displayed in this direful encounter—an encounter, compared to which the far famed battles of Ajax with Hector, of Eneas with Turnus, Orlando with Rodomont,[15]

---

10. *a parte poste:* a scholastic phrase meaning posteriorly or from behind.  11. With . . . sound!: This entire passage is omitted in the revision.

12. Like . . . Swede: The hyperbole of the epic simile is dropped in the revision.  13. "Ah . . . thee!": Cf. Falstaff in *I Henry IV*, II.ii.88, and Mercutio in *Romeo and Juliet*, III.i.112. Irving later changed "dog's" to Mercutio's "worms'."  14. cheese toaster: humorous designation for a sword.  15. Ajax . . . Rodomont: allusions to the *Iliad*, VII, and the *Aeneid*, XII, and an apparently confused reference to Ariosto's *Orlando Furioso*(1532).

Guy of Warwick with Colbrand the Dane, or of that renowned Welsh Knight Sir Owen [16] of the mountains with the giant Guylon, were all gentle sports and holliday recreations. At length the valiant Peter watching his opportunity, aimed a fearful blow with the full intention of cleaving his adversary to the very chine; but Risingh nimbly raising his sword, warded it off so narrowly, that glancing on one side, it shaved away a huge canteen full of fourth proof brandy, that he always carried swung on one side; thence pursuing its tranchant [17] course, it severed off a deep coat pocket, stored with bread and cheese—all which dainties rolling among the armies, occasioned a fearful scrambling between the Swedes and Dutchmen, and made the general battle to wax ten times more furious than ever.

Enraged to see his military stores thus wofully laid waste, the stout Risingh collecting all his forces, aimed a mighty blow, full at the hero's crest. In vain did his fierce little cocked hat oppose its course; the biting steel clove through the stubborn ram beaver, and would infallibly have cracked his gallant crown, but that the scull was of such adamantine hardness that the brittle weapon shivered into five and twenty pieces, shedding a thousand sparks, like beams of glory, round his grizly visage.

Stunned with the blow the valiant Peter reeled, turned up his eyes and beheld fifty thousand suns, besides moons and stars, dancing Scotch reels about the firmament [18]—at length, missing his footing, by reason of his wooden leg, down he came, on his seat of honour, with a crash that shook the surrounding hills, and would infallibly have wracked his anatomical system, had he not been received into a cushion softer than velvet, which providence, or Minerva, or St. Nicholas, or some kindly cow, had benevolently prepared for his reception.

The furious Risingh, in despight of that noble maxim, cherished by all true knights, that "fair play is a jewel," hastened to take advantage of the hero's fall; but just as he was stooping to give the fatal blow, the ever vigilant Peter bestowed him a sturdy thwack over the sconce, with his wooden leg, that set some dozen chimes of bells ringing triple bob-majors [19] in his cerebellum. The bewildered Swede staggered with the blow, and in the mean time the wary Peter, espying a pocket

pistol lying hard by (which had dropped from the wallet of his faithful squire and trumpeter Van Corlear during his furious encounter with the drummer) discharged it full at the head of the reeling Risingh—Let not my reader mistake—it was not a murderous weapon loaded with powder and ball, but a little sturdy stone pottle, charged to the muzzle with a double dram of true dutch courage, which the knowing Van Corlear always carried about him by way of replenishing his valour. The hideous missive sung through the air, and true to its course, as was the mighty fragment of a rock, discharged at Hector by bully Ajax, encountered the huge head of the gigantic Swede with matchless violence.

This heaven directed blow decided the eventful battle. The ponderous pericranium of general Jan Risingh sunk upon his breast; his knees tottered under him; a deathlike torpor seized upon his Titan frame, and he tumbled to the earth with such tremendous violence, that old Pluto started with affright, lest he should have broken through the roof of his infernal palace.

His fall, like that of Goliath, was the signal for defeat and victory——The Swedes gave way—the Dutch pressed forward; the former took to their heels, the latter hotly pursued—Some entered with them, pell mell, through the sally port—others stormed the bastion, and others scrambled over the curtain. Thus in a little while the impregnable fortress of Fort Christina, which like another Troy had stood a siege of full ten *hours,* was finally carried by assault, without the loss of a single man on either side. Victory in the likeness of a gigantic ox fly, sat perched upon the little cocked hat of the gallant Stuyvesant, and it was universally declared, by all the writers, whom he hired to write the history of his expedition, that on this memorable day he gained a sufficient quantity of glory to immortalize a dozen of the greatest heroes in Christendom!

## CHAPTER 8

IN WHICH THE AUTHOR AND THE READER, WHILE REPOSING AFTER THE BATTLE, FALL INTO A VERY GRAVE AND IN- STRUCTIVE DISCOURSE——AFTER WHICH IS RECORDED THE CON- DUCT OF PETER STUYVESANT IN RESPECT TO HIS VICTORY.

THANKS to St. Nicholas! I have fairly got through this tremendous battle: let us sit down, my worthy reader, and cool ourselves, for truly I am in a pro-

16. Guy . . . Owen: Guy and Owen were heroes of medieval romances. 17. tranchant: cutting; an early form of "trenchant." 18. beheld . . . firmament: In the revision this passage reads simply, "beheld a thousand suns, besides moons and stars, dancing about the firmament." 19. set . . . bob-majors: A bob-major is a change rung upon eight bells. In revising, Irving reduced the "dozen chimes" to one.

digious sweat and agitation—Body o' me, but this fighting of battles is hot work! and if your great commanders, did but know what trouble they give their historians, they would not have the conscience to atchieve so many horrible victories. I already hear my reader complaining, that throughout all this boasted battle, there is not the least slaughter, nor a single individual maimed, if we except the unhappy Swede, who was shorn of his queue by the tranchant blade of Peter Stuyvesant——all which is a manifest outrage on probability, and highly injurious to the interest of the narrative.

For once I candidly confess my captious reader has some grounds for his murmuring—But though I could give a variety of substantial reasons for not having deluged my whole page with blood, and swelled the cadence of every sentence with dying groans, yet I will content myself with barely mentioning one; which if it be not sufficient to satisfy every reasonable man on the face of the earth, I will consent that my book shall be cast into the flames—The simple truth then is this, that on consulting every history, manuscript and tradition, which relates to this memorable, though long forgotten battle, I cannot find that a single man was killed, or even wounded, throughout the whole affair!

My readers, if they have any bowels, must easily feel the distressing situation in which I was placed. I had already promised to furnish them with a hideous and unparalleled battle——I had made incredible preparations for the same——and had moreover worked myself up into a most warlike and blood-thirsty state of mind——my honour, as a historian, and my feelings, as a man of spirit, were both too deeply engaged in the business, to back out. Beside, I had transported a great and powerful force of warriors from the Nederlandts, at vast trouble and expense, and I could not reconcile it to my own conscience, or to that reverence which I entertain for them, and their illustrious descendants, to have suffered them to return home, like a renowned British expedition—with a flea in their ears.

How to extract myself from this dilemma was truly perplexing. Had the inexorable fates only allowed me half a dozen dead men, I should have been contented, for I would have made them such heroes as abounded in the olden time, but whose race is now unfortunately extinct. Men, who, if we may believe those authentic writers, the poets, could drive great armies like sheep before them, and conquer and desolate whole cities by their single arm. I'd have given every mother's son of

them as many lives as a cat, and made them die hard, I warrant you.

But seeing that I had not a single carcass at my disposal, all that was left for me, was to make the most I could of my battle, by means of kicks and cuffs, and bruises—black eyes, and bloody noses, and such like ignoble wounds. My greatest difficulty however, was, when I had once put my warriors in a passion, and let them loose into the midst of the enemy; to keep them from doing mischief. Many a time had I to restrain the sturdy Peter, from cleaving a gigantic Swede, to the very waist-band, or spitting half a dozen little fellows on his sword, like so many sparrows—And when I had set some hundreds of missives flying in the air, I did not dare to suffer one of them to reach the ground, lest it should have put an end to some unlucky Dutchman.

The reader cannot conceive how much I suffered from thus in a manner having my hands tied, and how many tempting opportunities I had to wink at, where I might have made as fine a death blow, as any recorded in history or song.

From my own experience, I begin to doubt most potently of the authenticity of many of Dan Homer's stories. I verily believe, that when he had once launched one of his hearty blades among a crowd of the enemy, he cut down many an honest fellow, without any authority for so doing, excepting that he presented a fair mark—and that often a poor devil was sent to grim Pluto's domains, merely because he had a name that would give a sounding turn to a period. But I disclaim all such unprincipled liberties—let me but have truth and the law on my side, and no man would fight harder than myself—but since the various records I consulted did not warrant it, I had too much conscience to kill a single soldier.—By St. Nicholas, but it would have been a pretty piece of business! My enemies the critics, who I foresee will be ready enough to lay any crime they can discover, at my door, might have charged me with murder outright—and I should have esteemed myself lucky to escape, with no harsher verdict than manslaughter!

And now gentle reader that we are tranquilly sitting down here, smoking our pipes, permit me to indulge in a melancholy reflection which at this moment passes across my mind.—How vain, how fleeting, how uncertain are all those gaudy bubbles after which we are panting and toiling in this world of fair delusions. The wealthy store which the hoary miser has painfully amassed with so many weary days, so many sleepless nights, a spendthrift heir shall squander away in joyless prodigality—The noblest monuments which pride has ever reared to perpetuate a name, the hand of time shall shortly tumble into promiscuous ruins ——and even the brightest laurels, gained by hardiest feats of arms, may wither and be forever blighted by the chilling neglect of mankind. —"How many illustrious heroes," says the good Boëtius, "who were once the pride and glory of the age, hath the silence of historians buried in eternal oblivion!" And this it was, that made the Spartans when they went to battle, solemnly to sacrifice to the muses, supplicating that their atchievements should be worthily recorded. Had not Homer tuned his lofty lyre, observes the elegant Cicero, the valour of Achilles had remained unsung.—And such too, after all the toils and perils he had braved, after all the gallant actions he had achieved, such too had nearly been the fate of the chivalric Peter Stuyvesant, but that I fortunately stepped in and engraved his name on the indelible tablet of history, just as the caitiff Time was silently brushing it away forever!

The more I reflect, the more am I astonished to think, what important beings are we historians! We are the sovereign censors who decide upon the renown or infamy of our fellow mortals—We are the public almoners of fame, dealing out her favours according to our judgment or caprice— we are the benefactors of kings—we are the guardians of truth—we are the scourgers of guilt —we are the instructors of the world—we are— in short, what are we not!—And yet how often does the lofty patrician or lordly Burgomaster stalk contemptuously by the little, plodding, dusty historian like myself, little thinking that this humble mortal is the arbiter of his fate, on whom it shall depend whether he shall live in future ages, or be forgotten in the dirt, as were his ancestors before him. "Insult not the dervise" [20] said a wise caliph to his son, "lest thou offend thine historian;" and many a mighty man of the olden time, had he observed so obvious a maxim, would have escaped divers cruel wipes of the pen, which have been drawn across his character.

But let not my readers think I am indulging in vain glorious boasting, from the consciousness of my own power and importance. On the contrary I shudder to think what direful commotions, what heart rending calamities we historians occasion in the world—I swear to thee, honest reader, as I am a man, I weep at the very idea!—Why, let me ask, are so many illustrious men daily tearing themselves away from the embraces of their dis-

tracted families——slighting the smiles of beauty —despising the allurements of fortune, and exposing themselves to all the miseries of war?—— Why are renowned generals cutting the throats of thousands who never injured them in their lives? —Why are kings desolating empires and depopulating whole countries? In short, what induces all great men, of all ages and countries to commit so many horrible victories and misdeeds, and inflict so many miseries upon mankind and on themselves; but the mere hope that we historians will kindly take them into notice, and admit them into a corner of our volumes. So that the mighty object of all their toils, their hardships and privations is nothing but *immortal fame*——and what is immortal fame?—why, half a page of dirty paper! ——alas! alas! how humiliating the idea—that the renown of so great a man as Peter Stuyvesant, should depend upon the pen of so little a man, as Diedrich Knickerbocker!

And now, having refreshed ourselves after the fatigues and perils of the field, it behoves us to return once more to the scene of conflict, and inquire what were the results of this renowned conquest. The Fortress of Christina being the fair metropolis and in a manner the Key to New Sweden, its capture was speedily followed by the entire subjugation of the province. This was not a little promoted by the gallant and courteous deportment of the chivalric Peter. Though a man terrible in battle, yet in the hour of victory was he endued with a spirit generous, merciful and humane—He vaunted not over his enemies, nor did he make defeat more galling by unmanly insults; for like that mirror of Knightly virtue, the renowned Paladin Orlando, he was more anxious to do great actions, than to talk of them after they were done. He put no man to death; ordered no houses to be burnt down; permitted no ravages to be perpetrated on the property of the vanquished, and even gave one of his bravest staff officers a severe rib-roasting, who was detected in the act of sacking a hen roost.

He moreover issued a proclamation inviting the inhabitants to submit to the authority of their high mightinesses; but declaring, with unexampled clemency, that whoever refused, should be lodged at the public expense, in a goodly castle provided for the purpose, and have an armed retinue to wait on them in the bargain. In consequence of these beneficent terms, about thirty Swedes stepped manfully forward and took the oath of allegiance; in reward for which they were graciously permitted to remain on the banks of the Delaware, where their descendants reside at this very day. But I

20. **dervise:** dervish.

am told by sundry observant travellers, that they have never been able to get over the chap-fallen looks of their ancestors, and do still unaccountably transmit from father to son, manifest marks of the sound drubbing given them by the sturdy Amsterdammers.

The whole country of New Sweden, having thus yielded to the arms of the triumphant Peter, was reduced to a colony called South River, and placed under the superintendance of a lieutenant governor; subject to the controul of the supreme government at New Amsterdam. This great dignitary was called Mynheer William Beekman, or rather *Beck*man, who derived his surname, as did Ovidius Naso [21] of yore, from the lordly dimensions of his nose, which projected from the centre of his countenance, like the beak of a parrot. Indeed, it is furthermore insinuated by various ancient records, that this was not only the origin of his name, but likewise the foundation of his fortune, for, as the city was as yet unprovided with a clock, the public made use of Mynheer Beckman's face, as a sundial. Thus did this romantic, and truly picturesque feature, first thrust itself into public notice, dragging its possessor along with it, who in his turn dragged after him the whole Beckman family—These, as the story further adds, were for a long time among the most ancient and honourable families of the province, and gratefully commemorated the origin of their dignity, not as your noble families in England would do, by having a glowing proboscis emblazoned in their escutcheon, but by one and all, wearing a right goodly nose, stuck in the very middle of their faces.

Thus was this perilous enterprise gloriously terminated, with the loss of only two men; Wolfert Van Horne, a tall spare man, who was knocked overboard by the boom of a sloop, in a flaw of wind, and fat Brom Van Bummel, who was suddenly carried off by a villainous indigestion; both, however, were immortalized, as having bravely fallen in the service of their country. True it is, Peter Stuyvesant had one of his limbs terribly fractured, being shattered to pieces in the act of storming the fortress; but as it was fortunately his wooden leg the wound was promptly and effectually healed.

And now nothing remains to this branch of my history, but to mention, that this immaculate hero, and his victorious army, returned joyously to the Manhattoes, marching under the shade of their laurels, as did the followers of young Malcolm, under the moving forest of Dunsinane.[22] Thus did

they make a solemn and triumphant entry into New Amsterdam, bearing with them the conquered Risingh, and the remnant of his battered crew, who had refused allegiance. For it appears that the gigantic Swede, had only fallen into a swound, at the end of the battle, from whence he was speedily restored by a wholesome tweak of the nose.

These captive heroes were lodged, according to the promise of the governor, at the public expense, in a fair and spacious castle; being the prison of state, of which Stoffel Brinkerhoff, the immortal conqueror of Oyster Bay, was appointed Lord Lieutenant; and which has ever since remained in the possession of his descendants.[23]

It was a pleasant and goodly sight to witness the joy of the people of New Amsterdam, at beholding their warriors once more returned, from this war in the wilderness. The old women thronged round Antony Van Corlear, who gave the whole history of the campaign with matchless accuracy; saving that he took the credit of fighting the whole battle himself, and especially of vanquishing the stout Risingh, which he considered himself as clearly entitled to, seeing that it was effected by his own stone pottle. The schoolmasters throughout the town gave holliday to their little urchins, who followed in droves after the drums, with paper caps on their heads and sticks in their breeches, thus taking the first lesson in vagabondizing. As to the sturdy rabble they thronged at the heels of Peter Stuyvesant wherever he went, waving their greasy hats in the air, and shouting "Hard-koppig Piet forever!"

It was indeed a day of roaring rout and jubilee. A huge dinner was prepared at the Stadt-house in honour of the conquerors, where were assembled in one glorious constellation, the great and the little luminaries of New Amsterdam. There were the lordly Schout and his obsequious deputy—the Burgomasters with their officious Schepens at their elbows—the subaltern officers at the elbows of the Schepens, and so on to the lowest grade of illustrious hangers-on of police; every Tag having his Rag at his side, to finish his pipe, drink off his heel-taps, and laugh at his flights of immortal dulness. In short—for a city feast is a city feast all the world over, and has been a city feast ever since the creation—the dinner went off much the same as do our great corporation junkettings and fourth of July banquets. Loads of fish, flesh and fowl were devoured, oceans of liquor drank, thousands

---

21. **Ovidius Naso:** the Latin poet Ovid (43 B.C.–17 A.D.).  22. **followers . . . Dunsinane:** See *Macbeth*, V.iv.

23. **These . . . descendants:** "This castle though very much altered and modernized is still in being. And stands at the corner of Pearl Street, facing Coentie's slip" [I].

of pipes smoked, and many a dull joke honoured with much obstreperous fat sided laughter.

I must not omit to mention that to this far-famed victory Peter Stuyvesant was indebted for another of his many titles—for so hugely delighted were the honest burghers with his atchievements, that they unanimously honoured him with the name of *Pieter ede Groodt,* that is to say Peter the Great, or as it was translated by the people of New Amsterdam, *Piet de Pig*—an appellation which he maintained even unto the day of his death.

*1809*

FROM

# THE SKETCH BOOK
OF GEOFFREY CRAYON, GENT.

## THE AUTHOR'S ACCOUNT OF HIMSELF

"I am of this mind with Homer, that as the snaile that crept out of her shel was turned eftsoons into a toad, and thereby was forced to make a stoole to sit on; so the traveller that stragleth from his owne country is in a short time transformed into so monstrous a shape, that he is faine to alter his mansion with his manners, and to live where he can, not where he would."

LYLY'S *Euphues.*[1]

I WAS always fond of visiting new scenes, and observing strange characters and manners. Even when a mere child I began my travels, and made many tours of discovery into foreign parts and unknown regions of my native city, to the frequent alarm of my parents, and the emolument of the town-crier. As I grew into boyhood, I extended the range of my observations. My holiday afternoons were spent in rambles about the surrounding country. I made myself familiar with all its places famous in history or fable. I knew every spot where a murder or robbery had been committed, or a ghost seen. I visited the neighboring villages, and added greatly to my stock of knowledge, by noting their habits and customs, and conversing with their sages and great men. I even journeyed one long summer's day to the summit of the most distant hill, whence I stretched my eye

over many a mile of terra incognita, and was astonished to find how vast a globe I inhabited.

This rambling propensity strengthened with my years. Books of voyages and travels became my passion, and in devouring their contents, I neglected the regular exercises of the school. How wistfully would I wander about the pier-heads in fine weather, and watch the parting ships, bound to distant climes—with what longing eyes would I gaze after their lessening sails, and waft myself in imagination to the ends of the earth!

Further reading and thinking, though they brought this vague inclination into more reasonable bounds, only served to make it more decided. I visited various parts of my own country; and had I been merely a lover of fine scenery, I should have felt little desire to seek elsewhere its gratification, for on no country have the charms of nature been more prodigally lavished. Her mighty lakes, like oceans of liquid silver; her mountains, with their bright aerial tints; her valleys, teeming with wild fertility; her tremendous cataracts, thundering in their solitudes; her boundless plains, waving with spontaneous verdure; her broad deep rivers, rolling in solemn silence to the ocean; her trackless forests, where vegetation puts forth all its magnificence; her skies, kindling with the magic of summer clouds and glorious sunshine;—no, never need an American look beyond his own country for the sublime and beautiful of natural scenery.

But Europe held forth the charms of storied and poetical association. There were to be seen the masterpieces of art, the refinements of highly-cultivated society, the quaint peculiarities of ancient and local custom. My native country was full of youthful promise: Europe was rich in the accumulated treasures of age. Her very ruins told the history of times gone by, and every mouldering stone was a chronicle. I longed to wander over the scenes of renowned achievement—to tread, as it were, in the footsteps of antiquity—to loiter about the ruined castle—to meditate on the falling tower—to escape, in short, from the commonplace realities of the present, and lose myself among the shadowy grandeurs of the past.

I had, beside all this, an earnest desire to see the great men of the earth. We have, it is true, our great men in America: not a city but has an ample share of them. I have mingled among them in my time, and been almost withered by the shade into which they cast me; for there is nothing so baleful to a small man as the shade of a great one, particularly the great man of a city. But I was anxious to see the great men of Europe; for I had read in the works of various philosophers, that all animals

THE SKETCH BOOK. **The Author's Account of Himself.** 1. John Lyly, *Euphues and His England* (1580).

degenerated in America, and man among the number.[2] A great man of Europe, thought I, must therefore be as superior to a great man of America, as a peak of the Alps to a highland of the Hudson; and in this idea I was confirmed, by observing the comparative importance and swelling magnitude of many English travellers among us, who, I was assured, were very little people in their own country. I will visit this land of wonders, thought I, and see the gigantic race from which I am degenerated.

It has been either my good or evil lot to have my roving passion gratified. I have wandered through different countries, and witnessed many of the shifting scenes of life. I cannot say that I have studied them with the eye of a philosopher; but rather with the sauntering gaze with which humble lovers of the picturesque stroll from the window of one print-shop to another; caught sometimes by the delineations of beauty, sometimes by the distortions of caricature, and sometimes by the loveliness of landscape. As it is the fashion for modern tourists to travel pencil in hand, and bring home their portfolios filled with sketches, I am disposed to get up a few for the entertainment of my friends. When, however, I look over the hints and memorandums I have taken down for the purpose, my heart almost fails me at finding how my idle humor has led me aside from the great objects studied by every regular traveller who would make a book. I fear I shall give equal disappointment with an unlucky landscape painter, who had travelled on the continent, but, following the bent of his vagrant inclination, had sketched in nooks, and corners, and by-places. His sketch book was accordingly crowded with cottages, and landscapes, and obscure ruins; but he had neglected to paint St. Peter's, or the Coliseum; the cascade of Terni,[3] or the bay of Naples; and had not a single glacier or volcano in his whole collection.

*1819, 1848*

# RIP VAN WINKLE
## A POSTHUMOUS WRITING OF DIEDRICH KNICKERBOCKER

❖

⟨ ALTHOUGH "Rip Van Winkle," like most of Irving's American stories, is attributed to Knickerbocker, its style is essentially Crayon's. Holding the "truthful" Knickerbocker responsible is a warning against a literal-minded reading.

By the time of *The Sketch Book* Irving had developed great admiration for writers, like Shakespeare, who utilize and imaginatively supplement local folk materials in such a way as to give expression to distinctive national or regional qualities. He tried himself to incorporate native folklore elements in his American stories, but, as his concluding note suggests, when they did not suffice he did not hesitate to use importations from abroad.

❖

By Woden,[1] God of Saxons,
From whence comes Wensday, that is Wodensday.
Truth is a thing that ever I will keep
Unto thylke day in which I creep into
My sepulchre—

CARTWRIGHT [2]

[The following Tale was found among the papers of the late Diedrich Knickerbocker, an old gentleman of New York, who was very curious in the Dutch history of the province, and the manners of the descendants from its primitive settlers. His historical researches, however, did not lie so much among books as among men; for the former are lamentably scanty on his favorite topics; whereas he found the old burghers, and still more their wives, rich in that legendary lore so invaluable to true history. Whenever, therefore, he happened upon a genuine Dutch family, snugly shut up in its low-roofed farmhouse, under a spreading sycamore, he looked upon it as a little clasped volume of black-letter, and studied it with the zeal of a bookworm.

The result of all these researches was a history of the province during the reign of the Dutch governors, which he published some years since. There have been various opinions as to the literary character of his work, and, to tell the truth, it is not a whit better than it should be. Its chief merit is its scrupulous accuracy, which indeed was a little questioned on its first appearance, but has since been com-

---

2. **for . . . number:** Dr. Samuel Johnson, for instance, had spoken of Americans as "a race of convicts," destined for "ages of barbarism." 3. **cascade of Terni:** artificial waterfalls in Perugia, Italy.

**Rip Van Winkle.** 1. **Woden:** Germanic god of war and storms. 2. **Cartwright:** The lines are spoken by Moth, the pedantic antiquarian in William Cartwright's *The Ordinary* (1651), III.i.1050–54.

pletely established; it is now admitted into historical collections as a book of unquestionable authority.

The old gentleman died shortly after the publication of his work; and now that he is dead and gone, it cannot do much harm to his memory to say that his time might have been much better employed in weightier labors. He, however, was apt to ride his hobby his own way; and though it did now and then kick up the dust a little in the eyes of his neighbors, and grieve the spirit of some friends, for whom he felt the truest deference and affection, yet his errors and follies are remembered "more in sorrow than in anger," and it begins to be suspected that he never intended to injure or offend. But however his memory may be appreciated by critics, it is still held dear by many folk whose good opinion is well worth having; particularly by certain biscuit-bakers, who have gone so far as to imprint his likeness on their New-Year cakes; and have thus given him a chance for immortality, almost equal to the being stamped on a Waterloo Medal, or a Queen Anne's Farthing.]

WHOEVER has made a voyage up the Hudson must remember the Kaatskill mountains. They are a dismembered branch of the great Appalachian family, and are seen away to the west of the river, swelling up to a noble height, and lording it over the surrounding country. Every change of season, every change of weather, indeed, every hour of the day, produces some change in the magical hues and shapes of these mountains, and they are regarded by all the good wives, far and near, as perfect barometers. When the weather is fair and settled, they are clothed in blue and purple, and print their bold outlines on the clear evening sky; but sometimes, when the rest of the landscape is cloudless, they will gather a hood of gray vapors about their summits, which, in the last rays of the setting sun, will glow and light up like a crown of glory.

At the foot of these fairy mountains, the voyager may have descried the light smoke curling up from a village, whose shingle-roofs gleam among the trees, just where the blue tints of the upland melt away into the fresh green of the nearer landscape. It is a little village, of great antiquity, having been founded by some of the Dutch colonists in the early times of the province, just about the beginning of the government of the good Peter Stuyvesant (may he rest in peace!), and there were some of the houses of the original settlers standing within a few years, built of small yellow bricks brought from Holland, having latticed windows and gable fronts, surmounted with weathercocks.

In that same village, and in one of these very houses (which, to tell the precise truth, was sadly time-worn and weather-beaten), there lived, many years since, while the country was yet a province of Great Britain, a simple, good-natured fellow, of the name of Rip Van Winkle. He was a descendant of the Van Winkles who figured so gallantly in the chivalrous days of Peter Stuyvesant, and accompanied him to the siege of Fort Christina. He inherited, however, but little of the martial character of his ancestors. I have observed that he was a simple, good-natured man; he was, moreover, a kind neighbor, and an obedient, hen-pecked husband. Indeed, to the latter circumstance might be owing that meekness of spirit which gained him such universal popularity; for those men are most apt to be obsequious and conciliating abroad, who are under the discipline of shrews at home. Their tempers, doubtless, are rendered pliant and malleable in the fiery furnace of domestic tribulation; and a curtain-lecture is worth all the sermons in the world for teaching the virtues of patience and long-suffering. A termagant wife may, therefore, in some respects be considered a tolerable blessing; and if so, Rip Van Winkle was thrice blessed.

Certain it is, that he was a great favorite among all the good wives of the village, who, as usual with the amiable sex, took his part in all family squabbles; and never failed, whenever they talked those matters over in their evening gossipings, to lay all the blame on Dame Van Winkle. The children of the village, too, would shout with joy whenever he approached. He assisted at their sports, made their playthings, taught them to fly kites and shoot marbles, and told them long stories of ghosts, witches and Indians. Whenever he went dodging about the village, he was surrounded by a troop of them, hanging on his skirts, clambering on his back, and playing a thousand tricks on him with impunity; and not a dog would bark at him throughout the neighborhood.

The great error in Rip's composition was an insuperable aversion to all kinds of profitable labor. It could not be from the want of assiduity or perseverance; for he would sit on a wet rock, with a rod as long and heavy as a Tartar's lance, and fish all day without a murmur, even though he should not be encouraged by a single nibble. He would carry a fowling-piece on his shoulder for hours together, trudging through woods and swamps, and up hill and down dale, to shoot a few squirrels or wild pigeons. He would never refuse to assist a neighbor even in the roughest toil, and was a foremost man at all country frolics for husking Indian corn, or building stone fences; the women of the village, too, used to employ him to run their errands, and to do such little odd jobs as their less obliging husbands would not do for them. In a word, Rip was ready to attend to anybody's business but his own; but as to doing family duty, and keeping his farm in order, he found it impossible.

In fact, he declared it was of no use to work on his farm; it was the most pestilent little piece of ground in the whole country; everything about it went wrong, and would go wrong, in spite of him. His fences were continually falling to pieces; his cow would either go astray, or get among the cabbages; weeds were sure to grow quicker in his fields than anywhere else; the rain always made a point of setting in just as he had some out-door work to do; so that though his patrimonial estate had dwindled away under his management, acre by acre, until there was little more left than a mere patch of Indian corn and potatoes, yet it was the worst conditioned farm in the neighborhood.

His children, too, were as ragged and wild as if they belonged to nobody. His son Rip, an urchin begotten in his own likeness, promised to inherit the habits, with the old clothes, of his father. He was generally seen trooping like a colt at his mother's heels, equipped in a pair of his father's cast-off galligaskins, which he had much ado to hold up with one hand, as a fine lady does her train in bad weather.

Rip Van Winkle, however, was one of those happy mortals, of foolish, well-oiled dispositions, who take the world easy, eat white bread or brown, whichever can be got with least thought or trouble, and would rather starve on a penny than work for a pound. If left to himself, he would have whistled life away in perfect contentment; but his wife kept continually dinning in his ears about his idleness, his carelessness, and the ruin he was bringing on his family. Morning, noon, and night, her tongue was incessantly going, and everything he said or did was sure to produce a torrent of household eloquence. Rip had but one way of replying to all lectures of the kind, and that, by frequent use, had grown into a habit. He shrugged his shoulders, shook his head, cast up his eyes, but said nothing. This, however, always provoked a fresh volley from his wife; so that he was fain to draw off his forces, and take to the outside of the house—the only side which, in truth, belongs to a hen-pecked husband.

Rip's sole domestic adherent was his dog Wolf, who was as much hen-pecked as his master; for Dame Van Winkle regarded them as companions in idleness, and even looked upon Wolf with an evil eye, as the cause of his master's going so often astray. True it is, in all points of spirit befitting an honorable dog, he was as courageous an animal as ever scoured the woods; but what courage can withstand the ever-during and all-besetting terrors of a woman's tongue? The moment Wolf entered the house his crest fell, his tail drooped to the ground, or curled between his legs, he sneaked about with a gallows air, casting many a sidelong glance at Dame Van Winkle, and at the least flourish of a broomstick or ladle he would fly to the door with yelping precipitation.

Times grew worse and worse with Rip Van Winkle as years of matrimony rolled on; a tart temper never mellows with age, and a sharp tongue is the only edged tool that grows keener with constant use. For a long while he used to console himself, when driven from home, by frequenting a kind of perpetual club of the sages, philosophers, and other idle personages of the village, which held its sessions on a bench before a small inn, designated by a rubicund portrait of His Majesty George the Third. Here they used to sit in the shade through a long, lazy summer's day, talking listlessly over village gossip, or telling endless sleepy stories about nothing. But it would have been worth any statesman's money to have heard the profound discussions that sometimes took place, when by chance an old newspaper fell into their hands from some passing traveller. How solemnly they would listen to the contents, as drawled out by Derrick Van Bummel, the schoolmaster, a dapper learned little man, who was not to be daunted by the most gigantic word in the dictionary; and how sagely they would deliberate upon public events some months after they had taken place.

The opinions of this junto were completely controlled by Nicholas Vedder, a patriarch of the village, and landlord of the inn, at the door of which he took his seat from morning till night, just moving sufficiently to avoid the sun and keep in the shade of a large tree; so that the neighbors could tell the hour by his movements as accurately as by a sun-dial. It is true he was rarely heard to speak, but smoked his pipe incessantly. His adherents, however (for every great man has his adherents), perfectly understood him, and knew how to gather his opinions. When anything that was read or related displeased him, he was observed to smoke his pipe vehemently, and to send forth short, frequent, and angry puffs; but when pleased, he would inhale the smoke slowly and tranquilly, and emit it in light and placid clouds; and sometimes, taking the pipe from his mouth, and letting the fragrant vapor curl about his nose, would gravely nod his head in token of perfect approbation.

From even this stronghold the unlucky Rip was at length routed by his termagant wife, who would suddenly break in upon the tranquillity of the assemblage and call the members all to naught; nor was that august personage, Nicholas Vedder himself, sacred from the daring tongue of this terrible virago, who charged him outright with encouraging her husband in habits of idleness.

Poor Rip was at last reduced almost to despair; and his only alternative, to escape from the labor of the farm and clamor of his wife, was to take gun in hand and stroll away into the woods. Here he would sometimes seat himself at the foot of a tree, and share the contents of his wallet with Wolf, with whom he sympathized as a fellow-sufferer in persecution. "Poor Wolf," he would say, "thy mistress leads thee a dog's life of it; but never mind, my lad, whilst I live thou shalt never want a friend to stand by thee!" Wolf would wag his tail, look wistfully in his master's face; and if dogs can feel pity, I verily believe he reciprocated the sentiment with all his heart.

In a long ramble of the kind on a fine autumnal day, Rip had unconsciously scrambled to one of the highest parts of the Kaatskill mountains. He was after his favorite sport of squirrel-shooting, and the still solitudes had echoed and re-echoed with the reports of his gun. Panting and fatigued, he threw himself, late in the afternoon, on a green knoll, covered with mountain herbage, that crowned the brow of a precipice. From an opening between the trees he could overlook all the lower country for many a mile of rich woodland. He saw at a distance the lordly Hudson, far, far below him, moving on its silent but majestic course, with the reflection of a purple cloud, or the sail of a lagging bark, here and there sleeping on its glassy bosom, and at last losing itself in the blue highlands.

On the other side he looked down into a deep mountain glen, wild, lonely, and shagged, the bottom filled with fragments from the impending cliffs, and scarcely lighted by the reflected rays of the setting sun. For some time Rip lay musing on this scene; evening was gradually advancing; the mountains began to throw their long blue shadows over the valleys; he saw that it would be dark long before he could reach the village, and he heaved a heavy sigh when he thought of encountering the terrors of Dame Van Winkle.

As he was about to descend, he heard a voice from a distance, hallooing, "Rip Van Winkle, Rip Van Winkle!" He looked round, but could see nothing but a crow winging its solitary flight across the mountain. He thought his fancy must have deceived him, and turned again to descend, when he heard the same cry ring through the still evening air: "Rip Van Winkle! Rip Van Winkle!" —at the same time Wolf bristled up his back, and giving a low growl, skulked to his master's side, looking fearfully down into the glen. Rip now felt a vague apprehension stealing over him; he looked anxiously in the same direction, and perceived a strange figure slowly toiling up the rocks, and bending under the weight of something he carried on his back. He was suprised to see any human being in this lonely and unfrequented place; but supposing it to be some one of the neighborhood in need of his assistance, he hastened down to yield it.

On nearer approach he was still more surprised at the singularity of the stranger's appearance. He was a short, square-built old fellow, with thick bushy hair, and a grizzled beard. His dress was of the antique Dutch fashion,—a cloth jerkin strapped round the waist—several pair of breeches, the outer one of ample volume, decorated with rows of buttons down the sides, and bunches at the knees. He bore on his shoulder a stout keg, that seemed full of liquor, and made signs for Rip to approach and assist him with the load. Though rather shy and distrustful of this new acquaintance, Rip complied with his usual alacrity; and mutually relieving one another, they clambered up a narrow gully, apparently the dry bed of a mountain torrent. As they ascended, Rip every now and then heard long, rolling peals, like distant thunder, that seemed to issue out of a deep ravine, or rather cleft, between lofty rocks, toward which their rugged path conducted. He paused for an instant, but supposing it to be the muttering of one of those transient thunder-showers which often take place in mountain heights, he proceeded. Passing through the ravine, they came to a hollow, like a small amphitheatre, surrounded by perpendicular precipices, over the brinks of which impending trees shot their branches, so that you only caught glimpses of the azure sky and the bright evening cloud. During the whole time Rip and his companion had labored on in silence; for though the former marvelled greatly what could be the object of carrying a keg of liquor up this wild mountain, yet there was something strange and incomprehensible about the unknown, that inspired awe and checked familiarity.

On entering the amphitheatre, new objects of wonder presented themselves. On a level spot in the centre was a company of odd-looking personages playing at ninepins. They were dressed in a quaint, outlandish fashion; some wore short doublets, others jerkins, with long knives in their belts, and most of them had enormous breeches, of similar style with that of the guide's. Their visages, too, were peculiar: one had a large beard, broad face, and small piggish eyes; the face of another seemed to consist entirely of nose, and was surmounted by a white sugar-loaf hat, set off with a little red cock's tail. They all had beards, of various shapes and colors. There was one who seemed to be the commander. He was a stout old gentleman, with a weather-beaten countenance; he wore a laced doublet, broad belt and hanger, high crowned hat and feather, red stockings, and high-heeled shoes, with roses in them. The whole group reminded Rip of the figures in an old Flemish painting, in the parlor of Dominie Van Shaick, the village parson, and which had been brought over from Holland at the time of the settlement.

What seemed particularly odd to Rip was, that, though these folks were evidently amusing themselves, yet they maintained the gravest faces, the most mysterious silence, and were, withal, the most melancholy party of pleasure he had ever witnessed. Nothing interrupted the stillness of the scene but the noise of the balls, which, whenever they were rolled, echoed along the mountains like rumbling peals of thunder.

As Rip and his companion approached them, they suddenly desisted from their play, and stared at him with such fixed, statue-like gaze, and such strange, uncouth, lack-lustre countenances, that his heart turned within him, and his knees smote together. His companion now emptied the contents of the keg into large flagons, and made signs to him to wait upon the company. He obeyed with fear and trembling; they quaffed the liquor in profound silence, and then returned to their game.

By degrees Rip's awe and apprehension subsided. He even ventured, when no eye was fixed upon him, to taste the beverage, which he found had much of the flavor of excellent Hollands. He was naturally a thirsty soul, and was soon tempted to repeat the draught. One taste provoked another; and he reiterated his visits to the flagon so often that at length his senses were overpowered, his eyes swam in his head, his head gradually declined, and he fell into a deep sleep.

On waking, he found himself on the green knoll whence he had first seen the old man of the glen. He rubbed his eyes—it was a bright sunny morning. The birds were hopping and twittering among the bushes, and the eagle was wheeling aloft, and breasting the pure mountain breeze. "Surely," thought Rip, "I have not slept here all night." He recalled the occurrences before he fell asleep. The strange man with a keg of liquor—the mountain ravine—the wild retreat among the rocks—the woe-begone party at ninepins—the flagon—"Oh! that flagon! that wicked flagon!" thought Rip,— "what excuse shall I make to Dame Van Winkle?"

He looked round for his gun, but in place of the clean, well-oiled fowling-piece, he found an old firelock lying by him, the barrel incrusted with rust, the lock falling off, and the stock worm-eaten. He now suspected that the grave roisters of the mountain had put a trick upon him, and, having dosed him with liquor, had robbed him of his gun. Wolf, too, had disappeared, but he might have strayed away after a squirrel or partridge. He whistled after him, and shouted his name, but all in vain; the echoes repeated his whistle and shout, but no dog was to be seen.

He determined to revisit the scene of the last evening's gambol, and if he met with any of the party, to demand his dog and gun. As he rose to walk, he found himself stiff in the joints, and wanting in his usual activity. "These mountain beds do not agree with me," thought Rip, "and if this frolic should lay me up with a fit of the rheumatism, I shall have a blessed time with Dame Van Winkle." With some difficulty he got down into the glen: he found the gully up which he and his companion had ascended the preceding evening; but to his astonishment a mountain stream was now foaming down it, leaping from rock to rock, and filling the glen with babbling murmurs. He, however, made shift to scramble up its sides, working his toilsome way through thickets of birch, sassafras, and witch-hazel, and sometimes tripped up or entangled by the wild grape-vines that twisted their coils or tendrils from tree to tree, and spread a kind of network in his path.

At length he reached to where the ravine had opened through the cliffs to the amphitheatre; but no traces of such opening remained. The rocks presented a high, impenetrable wall, over which the torrent came tumbling in a sheet of feathery foam, and fell into a broad deep basin, black from the shadows of the surrounding forest. Here, then, poor Rip was brought to a stand. He again called and whistled after his dog; he was only answered by the cawing of a flock of idle crows, sporting high in air about a dry tree that overhung a sunny precipice; and who, secure in their elevation, seemed to look down and scoff at the poor man's perplexities. What was to be done? the morning was passing away, and Rip felt famished for want of his breakfast. He grieved to give up his dog and gun; he dreaded to meet his wife; but it would not do to starve among the mountains. He shook his head, shouldered the rusty firelock, and, with a heart full of trouble and anxiety, turned his steps homeward.

As he approached the village he met a number of people, but none whom he knew, which somewhat surprised him, for he had thought himself acquainted with every one in the country round. Their dress, too, was of a different fashion from that to which he was accustomed. They all stared at him with equal marks of surprise, and whenever they cast their eyes upon him, invariably stroked their chins. The constant recurrence of this gesture induced Rip, involuntarily, to do the same, when, to his astonishment, he found his beard had grown a foot long!

He had now entered the skirts of the village. A troop of strange children ran at his heels, hooting after him, and pointing at his gray beard. The dogs, too, not one of which he recognized for an old acquaintance, barked at him as he passed. The very village was altered; it was larger and more populous. There were rows of houses which he had never seen before, and those which had been his familiar haunts had disappeared. Strange names were over the doors—strange faces at the windows— everything was strange. His mind now misgave him; he began to doubt whether both he and the world around him were not bewitched. Surely this was his native village, which he had left but the day before. There stood the Kaatskill mountains— there ran the silver Hudson at a distance—there was every hill and dale precisely as it had always been. Rip was sorely perplexed. "That flagon last night," thought he, "has addled my poor head sadly!"

It was with some difficulty that he found the way to his own house, which he approached with silent awe, expecting every moment to hear the shrill voice of Dame Van Winkle. He found the house gone to decay—the roof fallen in, the windows shattered, and the doors off the hinges. A half-starved dog that looked like Wolf was skulking about it. Rip called him by name, but the cur snarled, showed his teeth, and passed on. This was an unkind cut indeed. "My very dog," sighed poor Rip, "has forgotten me!"

He entered the house, which, to tell the truth, Dame Van Winkle had always kept in neat order. It was empty, forlorn, and apparently abandoned. This desolateness overcame all his connubial fears —he called loudly for his wife and children—the lonely chambers rang for a moment with his voice, and then all again was silence.

He now hurried forth, and hastened to his old resort, the village inn—but it too was gone. A large rickety wooden building stood in its place, with great gaping windows, some of them broken and mended with old hats and petticoats, and over the door was painted, "The Union Hotel, by Jonathan Doolittle." Instead of the great tree that used to shelter the quiet little Dutch inn of yore, there

now was reared a tall naked pole, with something on the top that looked like a red nightcap,[3] and from it was fluttering a flag, on which was a singular assemblage of stars and stripes;—all this was strange and incomprehensible. He recognized on the sign, however, the ruby face of King George, under which he had smoked so many a peaceful pipe; but even this was singularly metamorphosed. The red coat was changed for one of blue and buff, a sword was held in the hand instead of a sceptre, the head was decorated with a cocked hat, and underneath was painted in large characters, GENERAL WASHINGTON.

There was, as usual, a crowd of folk about the door, but none that Rip recollected. The very character of the people seemed changed. There was a busy, bustling, disputatious tone about it, instead of the accustomed phlegm and drowsy tranquillity. He looked in vain for the sage Nicholas Vedder, with his broad face, double chin, and fair long pipe, uttering clouds of tobacco-smoke instead of idle speeches; or Van Bummel, the schoolmaster, doling forth the contents of an ancient newspaper. In place of these, a lean, bilious-looking fellow, with his pockets full of hand-bills, was haranguing vehemently about rights of citizens—elections— members of congress—liberty—Bunker's Hill— heroes of seventy-six—and other words, which were a perfect Babylonish [4] jargon to the bewildered Van Winkle.

The appearance of Rip, with his long, grizzled beard, his rusty fowling-piece, his uncouth dress, and an army of women and children at his heels, soon attracted the attention of the tavern-politicians. They crowded round him, eying him from head to foot with great curiosity. The orator bustled up to him, and, drawing him partly aside, inquired "On which side he voted?" Rip stared in vacant stupidity. Another short but busy little fellow pulled him by the arm, and, rising on tiptoe, inquired in his ear, "Whether he was Federal or Democrat?" Rip was equally at a loss to comprehend the question; when a knowing, self-important old gentleman, in a sharp cocked hat, made his way through the crowd, putting them to the right and left with his elbows as he passed, and planting himself before Van Winkle, with one arm akimbo, the other resting on his cane, his keen eyes and sharp hat penetrating, as it were, into his very soul, demanded, in an austere tone, "What brought him to the election with a gun on his shoulder, and a mob at his heels; and whether he meant to breed a

3. **tall . . . nightcap:** liberty pole and liberty cap, symbols used in the American and French Revolutions. 4. **Babylonish:** Babel-like.

riot in the village?"—"Alas! gentlemen," cried Rip, somewhat dismayed, "I am a poor quiet man, a native of the place, and a loyal subject of the King, God bless him!"

Here a general shout burst from the by-standers —"A tory! a tory! a spy! a refugee! hustle him! away with him!" It was with great difficulty that the self-important man in the cocked hat restored order; and, having assumed a tenfold austerity of brow, demanded again of the unknown culprit, what he came there for, and whom he was seeking? The poor man humbly assured him that he meant no harm, but merely came there in search of some of his neighbors, who used to keep about the tavern.

"Well—who are they?—name them."

Rip bethought himself a moment, and inquired, "Where's Nicholas Vedder?"

There was a silence for a little while, when an old man replied, in a thin piping voice, "Nicholas Vedder! why, he is dead and gone these eighteen years! There was a wooden tombstone in the churchyard that used to tell all about him, but that's rotten and gone too."

"Where's Brom Dutcher?"

"Oh, he went off to the army in the beginning of the war; some say he was killed at the storming of Stony Point—others say he was drowned in a squall at the foot of Antony's Nose. I don't know —he never came back again."

"Where's Van Bummel, the schoolmaster?"

"He went off to the wars too, was a great militia general, and is now in congress."

Rip's heart died away at hearing of these sad changes in his home and friends, and finding himself thus alone in the world. Every answer puzzled him too, by treating of such enormous lapses of time, and of matters which he could not understand: war—congress—Stony Point;—he had no courage to ask after any more friends, but cried out in despair, "Does nobody here know Rip Van Winkle?"

"Oh, Rip Van Winkle!" exclaimed two or three, "oh, to be sure! that's Rip Van Winkle yonder, leaning against the tree."

Rip looked, and beheld a precise counterpart of himself, as he went up the mountain; apparently as lazy, and certainly as ragged. The poor fellow was now completely confounded. He doubted his own identity, and whether he was himself or another man. In the midst of his bewilderment, the man in the cocked hat demanded who he was, and what was his name.

"God knows," exclaimed he, at his wit's end; "I'm not myself—I'm somebody else—that's me yonder—no—that's somebody else got into my shoes—I was myself last night, but I fell asleep on the mountain, and they've changed my gun, and everything's changed, and I'm changed, and I can't tell what's my name, or who I am!"

The by-standers began now to look at each other, nod, wink significantly, and tap their fingers against their foreheads. There was a whisper, also, about securing the gun, and keeping the old fellow from doing mischief, at the very suggestion of which the self-important man in the cocked hat retired with some precipitation. At this critical moment a fresh, comely woman pressed through the throng to get a peep at the gray-bearded man. She had a chubby child in her arms, which, frightened at his looks, began to cry. "Hush, Rip," cried she, "hush, you little fool; the old man won't hurt you." The name of the child, the air of the mother, the tone of her voice, all awakened a train of recollections in his mind. "What is your name, my good woman?" asked he.

"Judith Gardenier."

"And your father's name?"

"Ah, poor man, Rip Van Winkle was his name, but it's twenty years since he went away from home with his gun, and never has been heard of since,—his dog came home without him; but whether he shot himself, or was carried away by the Indians, nobody can tell. I was then but a little girl."

Rip had but one question more to ask; but he put it with a faltering voice:

"Where's your mother?"

"Oh, she too had died but a short time since; she broke a bloodvessel in a fit of passion at a New-England peddler."

There was a drop of comfort, at least, in this intelligence. The honest man could contain himself no longer. He caught his daughter and her child in his arms. "I am your father!" cried he—"Young Rip Van Winkle once—old Rip Van Winkle now! —Does nobody know poor Rip Van Winkle?"

All stood amazed, until an old woman, tottering out from among the crowd, put her hand to her brow, and peering under it in his face for a moment, exclaimed, "Sure enough! it is Rip Van Winkle—it is himself! Welcome home again, old neighbor. Why, where have you been these twenty long years?"

Rip's story was soon told, for the whole twenty years had been to him but as one night. The neighbors stared when they heard it; some were seen to wink at each other, and put their tongues in their cheeks: and the self-important man in the cocked hat, who, when the alarm was over, had returned to the field, screwed down the corners of his mouth, and shook his head—upon which there was a general shaking of the head throughout the assemblage.

It was determined, however, to take the opinion of old Peter Vanderdonk, who was seen slowly advancing up the road. He was a descendant of the historian of that name, who wrote one of the earliest accounts of the province. Peter was the most ancient inhabitant of the village, and well versed in all the wonderful events and traditions of the neighborhood. He recollected Rip at once, and corroborated his story in the most satisfactory manner. He assured the company that it was a fact, handed down from his ancestor the historian, that the Kaatskill mountains had always been haunted by strange beings. That it was affirmed that the great Hendrick Hudson, the first discoverer of the river and country, kept a kind of vigil there every twenty years, with his crew of the Half-moon; being permitted in this way to revisit the scenes of his enterprise, and keep a guardian eye upon the river and the great city called by his name. That his father had once seen them in their old Dutch dresses playing at ninepins in a hollow of the mountain; and that he himself had heard, one summer afternoon, the sound of their balls, like distant peals of thunder.

To make a long story short, the company broke up and returned to the more important concerns of the election. Rip's daughter took him home to live with her; she had a snug, well-furnished house, and a stout, cheery farmer for a husband, whom Rip recollected for one of the urchins that used to climb upon his back. As to Rip's son and heir, who was the ditto of himself, seen leaning against the tree, he was employed to work on the farm; but evinced an hereditary disposition to attend to anything else but his business.

Rip now resumed his old walks and habits; he soon found many of his former cronies, though all rather the worse for the wear and tear of time; and preferred making friends among the rising generation, with whom he soon grew into great favor.

Having nothing to do at home, and being arrived at that happy age when a man can be idle with impunity, he took his place once more on the bench at the inn-door, and was reverenced as one of the patriarchs of the village, and a chronicle of the old times "before the war." It was some time before he could get into the regular track of gossip, or could be made to comprehend the strange events that had taken place during his torpor. How that there had been a revolutionary war,—that the country had thrown off the yoke of old England,—and that, instead of being a subject of his Majesty George the Third, he was now a free citizen of the United States. Rip, in fact, was no politician; the

changes of states and empires made but little impression on him; but there was one species of despotism under which he had long groaned, and that was—petticoat government. Happily that was at an end; he had got his neck out of the yoke of matrimony, and could go in and out whenever he pleased, without dreading the tyranny of Dame Van Winkle. Whenever her name was mentioned, however, he shook his head, shrugged his shoulders, and cast up his eyes; which might pass either for an expression of resignation to his fate, or joy at his deliverance.

He used to tell his story to every stranger that arrived at Mr. Doolittle's hotel. He was observed, at first, to vary on some points every time he told it, which was, doubtless, owing to his having so recently awaked. It at last settled down precisely to the tale I have related, and not a man, woman, or child in the neighborhood but knew it by heart. Some always pretended to doubt the reality of it, and insisted that Rip had been out of his head, and that this was one point on which he always remained flighty. The old Dutch inhabitants, however, almost universally gave it full credit. Even to this day they never hear a thunder-storm of a summer afternoon about the Kaatskill, but they say Hendrick Hudson and his crew are at their game of ninepins; and it is a common wish of all henpecked husbands in the neighborhood, when life hangs heavy on their hands, that they might have a quieting draught out of Rip Van Winkle's flagon.

### NOTE

The foregoing Tale, one would suspect, had been suggested to Mr. Knickerbocker by a little German superstition about the Emperor Frederick *der Rothbart,* and the Kypphäuser mountain: [5] the subjoined note, however, which he had appended to the tale, shows that it is an absolute fact, narrated with his usual fidelity.

"The story of Rip Van Winkle may seem incredible to many, but nevertheless I give it my full belief, for I know the vicinity of our old Dutch settlements to have been very subject to marvellous events and appearances. Indeed, I have heard many stranger stories than this, in the villages along the Hudson; all of which were too well authenticated to admit of a doubt. I have even talked with Rip Van Winkle myself, who, when last I saw him, was a very venerable old man, and so perfectly rational and consistent on every other point, that I think no conscientious person could refuse to take this into the bargain; nay, I have seen a certificate on the subject

5. The . . . mountain: For a full account of Irving's indebtedness, see Pochmann's "Irving's German Sources in *The Sketch Book.*"

taken before a country justice and signed with a cross, in the justice's own handwriting. The story, therefore, is beyond the possibility of doubt."

"D. K."

### POSTSCRIPT

The following are travelling notes from a memorandum-book of Mr. Knickerbocker.

The Kaatsberg, or Catskill Mountains, have always been a region full of fable. The Indians considered them the abode of spirits, who influenced the weather, spreading sunshine or clouds over the landscape, and sending good or bad hunting-seasons. They were ruled by an old squaw spirit, said to be their mother. She dwelt on the highest peak of the Catskills, and had charge of the doors of day and night to open and shut them at the proper hour. She hung up the new moons in the skies, and cut up the old ones into stars. In times of drought, if properly propitiated, she would spin light summer clouds out of cobwebs and morning dew, and send them off from the crest of the mountain, flake after flake, like flakes of carded cotton, to float in the air; until, dissolved by the heat of the sun, they would fall in gentle showers, causing the grass to spring, the fruits to ripen, and the corn to grow an inch an hour. If displeased, however, she would brew up clouds black as ink, sitting in the midst of them like a bottle-bellied spider in the midst of its web; and when these clouds broke, woe betide the valleys!

In old times, say the Indian traditions, there was a kind of Manitou or Spirit, who kept about the wildest recesses of the Catskill Mountains, and took a mischievous pleasure in wreaking all kinds of evils and vexations upon the red men. Sometimes he would assume the form of a bear, a panther, or a deer, lead the bewildered hunter a weary chase through tangled forests and among ragged rocks; and then spring off with a loud ho! ho! leaving him aghast on the brink of a beetling precipice or raging torrent.

The favorite abode of this Manitou is still shown. It is a great rock or cliff on the loneliest part of the mountains, and, from the flowering vines which clamber about it, and the wild flowers which abound in its neighborhood, is known by the name of the Garden Rock. Near the foot of it is a small lake, the haunt of the solitary bittern, with water-snakes basking in the sun on the leaves of the pond-lilies which lie on the surface. This place was held in great awe by the Indians, insomuch that the boldest hunter would not pursue his game within its precincts. Once upon a time, however, a hunter who had lost his way, penetrated to the Garden Rock, where he beheld a number of gourds placed in the crotches of trees. One of these he seized and made off with it, but in the hurry of his retreat he let it fall among the rocks, when a great stream gushed forth, which washed him away and swept him down precipices, where he was dashed to pieces, and the stream made its way to the Hudson, and continues

to flow to the present day; being the identical stream known by the name of the Kaaters-kill.

*1819, 1848*

---

# THE LEGEND OF SLEEPY HOLLOW
## FOUND AMONG THE PAPERS OF THE LATE DIEDRICH KNICKERBOCKER

---

◊

⟨ ORIGINALLY Irving juxtaposed this story with an excessively sentimental piece, "The Pride of the Village," at the end of the sixth installment of *The Sketch Book.* Subsequently, however, he made "Sleepy Hollow" the final story in the entire book.

Irving's use of German sources here, though less significant than in "Rip Van Winkle," has been carefully documented by Henry A. Pochmann.

◊

A pleasing land of drowsy head it was,
   Of dreams that wave before the half-shut eye;
And of gay castles in the clouds that pass,
   For ever flushing round a summer sky.
                                    *Castle of Indolence* [1]

IN THE bosom of one of those spacious coves which indent the eastern shore of the Hudson, at that broad expansion of the river denominated by the ancient Dutch navigators the Tappan Zee, and where they always prudently shortened sail, and implored the protection of St. Nicholas when they crossed, there lies a small market-town or rural port, which by some is called Greensburgh, but which is more generally and properly known by the name of Tarry Town. This name was given, we are told, in former days, by the good housewives of the adjacent country, from the inveterate propensity of their husbands to linger about the village tavern on market-days. Be that as it may, I do not vouch for the fact, but merely advert to it for the sake of being precise and authentic. Not far from this village, perhaps about two miles, there is a little valley, or rather lap of land, among high hills, which is one of the quietest places in the whole world. A small brook glides through it, with just murmur enough to lull one to repose;

The Legend of Sleepy Hollow.   1. *Castle of Indolence:* poem by James Thomson (1748), I.vi.1–4.

and the occasional whistle of a quail, or tapping of a woodpecker, is almost the only sound that ever breaks in upon the uniform tranquillity.

I recollect that, when a stripling, my first exploit in squirrel-shooting was in a grove of tall walnut-trees that shades one side of the valley. I had wandered into it at noon-time, when all nature is peculiarly quiet, and was startled by the roar of my own gun, as it broke the Sabbath stillness around, and was prolonged and reverberated by the angry echoes. If ever I should wish for a retreat, whither I might steal from the world and its distractions, and dream quietly away the remnant of a troubled life, I know of none more promising than this little valley.

From the listless repose of the place, and the peculiar character of its inhabitants, who are descendants from the original Dutch settlers, this sequestered glen has long been known by the name of SLEEPY HOLLOW, and its rustic lads are called the Sleepy Hollow Boys throughout all the neighboring country. A drowsy, dreamy influence seems to hang over the land, and to pervade the very atmosphere. Some say that the place was bewitched by a high German doctor, during the early days of the settlement; others, that an old Indian chief, the prophet or wizard of his tribe, held his pow-wows there before the country was discovered by Master Hendrick Hudson. Certain it is, the place still continues under the sway of some witching power, that holds a spell over the minds of the good people, causing them to walk in a continual reverie. They are given to all kinds of marvellous beliefs; are subject to trances and visions; and frequently see strange sights, and hear music and voices in the air. The whole neighborhood abounds with local tales, haunted spots, and twilight superstitions; stars shoot and meteors glare oftener across the valley than in any other part of the country, and the nightmare, with her whole nine fold [2] seems to make it the favorite scene of her gambols.

The dominant spirit, however, that haunts this enchanted region, and seems to be commander-in-chief of all the powers of the air, is the apparition of a figure on horseback without a head. It is said by some to be the ghost of a Hessian trooper, whose head had been carried away by a cannon-ball, in some nameless battle during the Revolutionary War, and who is ever and anon seen by the country folk, hurrying along in the gloom of night, as if on the wings of the wind. His haunts are not confined to the valley, but extend at times to the adjacent roads, and especially to the vicinity of a church at no great distance. Indeed certain of the most authentic historians of those parts, who have been careful in collecting and collating the floating facts concerning this spectre, allege that the body of the trooper, having been buried in the churchyard, the ghost rides forth to the scene of battle in nightly quest of his head; and that the rushing speed with which he sometimes passes along the Hollow, like a midnight blast, is owing to his being belated, and in a hurry to get back to the churchyard before daybreak.

Such is the general purport of this legendary superstition, which has furnished materials for many a wild story in that region of shadows; and the spectre is known, at all the country firesides, by the name of the Headless Horseman of Sleepy Hollow.

It is remarkable that the visionary propensity I have mentioned is not confined to the native inhabitants of the valley, but is unconsciously imbibed by every one who resides there for a time. However wide awake they may have been before they entered that sleepy region, they are sure, in a little time, to inhale the witching influence of the air, and begin to grow imaginative, to dream dreams, and see apparitions.

I mention this peaceful spot with all possible laud; for it is in such little retired Dutch valleys, found here and there embosomed in the great State of New York, that population, manners, and customs remain fixed; while the great torrent of migration and improvement, which is making such incessant changes in other parts of this restless country, sweeps by them unobserved. They are like those little nooks of still water which border a rapid stream; where we may see the straw and bubble riding quietly at anchor, or slowly revolving in their mimic harbor, undisturbed by the rush of the passing current. Though many years have elapsed since I trod the drowsy shades of Sleepy Hollow, yet I question whether I should not still find the same trees and the same families vegetating in its sheltered bosom.

In this by-place of nature, there abode, in a remote period of American history, that is to say, some thirty years since, a worthy wight of the name of Ichabod Crane; who sojourned, or, as he expressed it, "tarried," in Sleepy Hollow, for the purpose of instructing the children of the vicinity. He was a native of Connecticut, a State which supplies the Union with pioneers for the mind as well as for the forest, and sends forth yearly its legions of frontier woodsmen and country schoolmasters. The cognomen of Crane was not inapplicable to his person. He was tall, but exceedingly lank, with narrow shoulders, long arms and legs,

---

2. **nightmare . . . fold:** Cf. *King Lear*, III.iv.126.

hands that dangled a mile out of his sleeves, feet that might have served for shovels, and his whole frame most loosely hung together. His head was small, and flat at top, with huge ears, large green glassy eyes, and a long snipe nose, so that it looked like a weathercock perched upon his spindle neck, to tell which way the wind blew. To see him striding along the profile of a hill on a windy day, with his clothes bagging and fluttering about him, one might have mistaken him for the genius of famine descending upon the earth, or some scarecrow eloped from a cornfield.

His school-house was a low building of one large room, rudely constructed of logs; the windows partly glazed, and partly patched with leaves of old copy-books. It was most ingeniously secured at vacant hours by a withe twisted in the handle of the door, and stakes set against the window-shutters; so that, though a thief might get in with perfect ease, he would find some embarrassment in getting out: an idea most probably borrowed by the architect, Yost Van Houten, from the mystery of an eel-pot. The school-house stood in a rather lonely but pleasant situation, just at the foot of a woody hill, with a brook running close by, and a formidable birch-tree growing at one end of it. From hence the low murmur of his pupils' voices, conning over their lessons, might be heard in a drowsy summer's day, like the hum of a bee-hive; interrupted now and then by the authoritative voice of the master, in the tone of menace or command; or, peradventure, by the appalling sound of the birch, as he urged some tardy loiterer along the flowery path of knowledge. Truth to say, he was a conscientious man, and ever bore in mind the golden maxim, "Spare the rod and spoil the child."—Ichabod Crane's scholars certainly were not spoiled.

I would not have it imagined, however, that he was one of those cruel potentates of the school, who joy in the smart of their subjects; on the contrary, he administered justice with discrimination rather than severity, taking the burden off the backs of the weak, and laying it on those of the strong. Your mere puny stripling, that winced at the least flourish of the rod, was passed by with indulgence; but the claims of justice were satisfied by inflicting a double portion on some little, tough, wrong-headed, broad-skirted Dutch urchin, who sulked and swelled and grew dogged and sullen beneath the birch. All this he called "doing his duty" by their parents; and he never inflicted a chastisement without following it by the assurance, so consolatory to the smarting urchin, that "he would remember it, and thank him for it the longest day he had to live."

When school-hours were over, he was even the companion and playmate of the larger boys; and on holiday afternoons would convoy some of the smaller ones home, who happened to have pretty sisters, or good housewives for mothers, noted for the comforts of the cupboard. Indeed it behooved him to keep on good terms with his pupils. The revenue arising from his school was small, and would have been scarcely sufficient to furnish him with daily bread, for he was a huge feeder,[3] and, though lank, had the dilating powers of an anaconda; but to help out his maintenance, he was, according to country custom in those parts, boarded and lodged at the houses of the farmers, whose children he instructed. With these he lived successively a week at a time; thus going the rounds of the neighborhood, with all his worldly effects tied up in a cotton handkerchief.

That all this might not be too onerous on the purses of his rustic patrons, who are apt to consider the costs of schooling a grievous burden, and schoolmasters as mere drones, he had various ways of rendering himself both useful and agreeable. He assisted the farmers occasionally in the lighter labors of their farms; helped to make hay; mended the fences; took the horses to water; drove the cows from pasture; and cut wood for the winter fire. He laid aside, too, all the dominant dignity and absolute sway with which he lorded it in his little empire, the school, and became wonderfully gentle and ingratiating. He found favor in the eyes of the mothers, by petting the children, particularly the youngest; and like the lion bold, which whilom so magnanimously the lamb did hold,[4] he would sit with a child on one knee, and rock a cradle with his foot for whole hours together.

In addition to his other vocations, he was the singing-master of the neighborhood, and picked up many bright shillings by instructing the young folks in psalmody. It was a matter of no little vanity to him, on Sundays, to take his station in front of the church-gallery, with a band of chosen singers; where, in his own mind, he completely carried away the palm from the parson. Certain it is, his voice resounded far above all the rest of the congregation; and there are peculiar quavers still to be heard in that church, and which may even be heard half a mile off, quite to the opposite side of the mill-pond, on a still Sunday morning, which are said to be legitimately descended from the nose of Ichabod Crane. Thus, by divers little makeshifts in that ingenious way which is commonly denomi-

3. **huge feeder:** Cf. *Merchant of Venice*, II.v.46.   4. **lion . . . hold:** an allusion to the couplet under the letter *L* in the *New England Primer:* "The lion bold/The lamb doth hold."

nated "by hook and by crook," the worthy pedagogue got on tolerably enough, and was thought, by all who understood nothing of the labor of headwork, to have a wonderfully easy life of it.

The schoolmaster is generally a man of some importance in the female circle of a rural neighborhood; being considered a kind of idle, gentleman-like personage, of vastly superior taste and accomplishments to the rough country swains, and, indeed, inferior in learning only to the parson. His appearance, therefore, is apt to occasion some little stir at the tea-table of a farm-house, and the addition of a supernumerary dish of cakes or sweetmeats, or, peradventure, the parade of a silver teapot. Our man of letters, therefore, was peculiarly happy in the smiles of all the country damsels. How he would figure among them in the churchyard, between services on Sundays! gathering grapes for them from the wild vines that overrun the surrounding trees; reciting for their amusement all the epitaphs on the tombstones; or sauntering, with a whole bevy of them, along the banks of the adjacent mill-pond; while the more bashful country bumpkins hung sheepishly back, envying his superior elegance and address.

From his half-itinerant life, also, he was a kind of travelling gazette, carrying the whole budget of local gossip from house to house: so that his appearance was always greeted with satisfaction. He was, moreover, esteemed by the women as a man of great erudition, for he had read several books quite through, and was a perfect master of Cotton Mather's "History of New England Witchcraft,"[5] in which, by the way, he most firmly and potently believed.

He was, in fact, an odd mixture of small shrewdness and simple credulity. His appetite for the marvellous, and his powers of digesting it, were equally extraordinary; and both had been increased by his residence in this spellbound region. No tale was too gross or monstrous for his capacious swallow. It was often his delight, after his school was dismissed in the afternoon, to stretch himself on the rich bed of clover bordering the little brook that whimpered by his school-house, and there con over old Mather's direful tales, until the gathering dusk of the evening made the printed page a mere mist before his eyes. Then, as he wended his way, by swamp and stream, and awful woodland, to the farm-house where he happened to be quartered, every sound of nature, at that witching hour, fluttered his excited imagination;

the moan of the whippoorwill[6] from the hill-side; the boding cry of the tree-toad, that harbinger of storm; the dreary hooting of the screech-owl, or the sudden rustling in the thicket of birds frightened from their roost. The fire-flies, too, which sparkled most vividly in the darkest places, now and then startled him, as one of uncommon brightness would stream across his path; and if, by chance, a huge blockhead of a beetle came winging his blundering flight against him, the poor varlet was ready to give up the ghost, with the idea that he was struck with a witch's token. His only resource on such occasions, either to drown thought or drive away evil spirits, was to sing psalm-tunes; and the good people of Sleepy Hollow, as they sat by their doors of an evening, were often filled with awe, at hearing his nasal melody, "in linked sweetness long drawn out,"[7] floating from the distant hill, or along the dusky road.

Another of his sources of fearful pleasure was, to pass long winter evenings with the old Dutch wives, as they sat spinning by the fire, with a row of apples roasting and spluttering along the hearth, and listen to their marvellous tales of ghosts and goblins, and haunted fields, and haunted brooks, and haunted bridges, and haunted houses, and particularly of the headless horseman, or Galloping Hessian of the Hollow, as they sometimes called him. He would delight them equally by his anecdotes of witchcraft, and of the direful omens and portentous sights and sounds in the air, which prevailed in the earlier times of Connecticut; and would frighten them wofully with speculations upon comets and shooting stars, and with the alarming fact that the world did absolutely turn round, and that they were half the time topsy-turvy!

But if there was a pleasure in all this, while snugly cuddling in the chimney-corner of a chamber that was all of a ruddy glow from the crackling wood-fire, and where, of course, no spectre dared to show his face, it was dearly purchased by the terrors of his subsequent walk homewards. What fearful shapes and shadows beset his path amidst the dim and ghastly glare of a snowy night!—With what wistful look did he eye every trembling ray of light streaming across the waste fields from some distant window!—How often was he appalled by some shrub covered with snow, which, like a sheeted spectre, beset his very path!—How often did he shrink with curdling awe at the sound of his own steps on the frosty crust beneath

5. **"History . . . Witchcraft":** This is not an actual title. Mather wrote on the subject in *Wonders of the Invisible World* (1693), *Memorable Providences, Relating to Witchcraft* (1689), and in the *Magnalia*, Book VI, Chap. 7.

6. **Whippoorwill:** "The whippoorwill is a bird which is only heard at night. It receives its name from its note, which is thought to resemble these words" [I].   7. **"in . . . out":** Milton, "L'Allegro," l. 140.

his feet; and dread to look over his shoulder, lest he should behold some uncouth being tramping close behind him!—and how often was he thrown into complete dismay by some rushing blast, howling among the trees, in the idea that it was the Galloping Hessian on one of his nightly scourings!

All these, however, were mere terrors of the night, phantoms of the mind that walk in darkness; and though he had seen many spectres in his time, and been more than once beset by Satan in divers shapes, in his lonely perambulations, yet daylight put an end to all these evils; and he would have passed a pleasant life of it, in despite of the devil and all his works, if his path had not been crossed by a being that causes more perplexity to mortal man than ghosts, goblins, and the whole race of witches put together, and that was—a woman.

Among the musical disciples who assembled, one evening in each week, to receive his instructions in psalmody, was Katrina Van Tassel, the daughter and only child of a substantial Dutch farmer. She was a blooming lass of fresh eighteen; plump as a partridge; ripe and melting and rosy-cheeked as one of her father's peaches, and universally famed, not merely for her beauty, but her vast expectations. She was withal a little of a coquette, as might be perceived even in her dress, which was a mixture of ancient and modern fashions, as most suited to set off her charms. She wore the ornaments of pure yellow gold, which her great-great-grandmother had brought over from Saardam; the tempting stomacher of the olden time; and withal a provokingly short petticoat, to display the prettiest foot and ankle in the country round.

Ichabod Crane had a soft and foolish heart towards the sex; and it is not to be wondered at that so tempting a morsel soon found favor in his eyes; more especially after he had visited her in her paternal mansion. Old Baltus Van Tassel was a perfect picture of a thriving, contented, liberal-hearted farmer. He seldom, it is true, sent either his eyes or his thoughts beyond the boundaries of his own farm; but within those everything was snug, happy, and well-conditioned. He was satisfied with his wealth, but not proud of it; and piqued himself upon the hearty abundance rather than the style in which he lived. His stronghold was situated on the banks of the Hudson, in one of those green, sheltered, fertile nooks in which the Dutch farmers are so fond of nestling. A great elm-tree spread its broad branches over it; at the foot of which bubbled up a spring of the softest and sweetest water, in a little well, formed of a barrel; and then stole sparkling away through the grass, to a neighboring brook, that bubbled along among alders and dwarf willows. Hard by the farm-house was a vast barn, that might have served for a church; every window and crevice of which seemed bursting forth with the treasures of the farm; the flail was busily resounding within it from morning till night; swallows and martins skimmed twittering about the eaves; and rows of pigeons, some with one eye turned up, as if watching the weather, some with their heads under their wings, or buried in their bosoms, and others swelling, and cooing, and bowing about their dames, were enjoying the sunshine on the roof. Sleek unwieldy porkers were grunting in the repose and abundance of their pens; whence sallied forth, now and then, troops of sucking pigs, as if to snuff the air. A stately squadron of snowy geese were riding in an adjoining pond, convoying whole fleets of ducks; regiments of turkeys were gobbling through the farm-yard, and guinea fowls fretting about it, like ill-tempered housewives, with their peevish discontented cry. Before the barn-door strutted the gallant cock, that pattern of a husband, a warrior, and a fine gentleman, clapping his burnished wings, and crowing in the pride and gladness of his heart—sometimes tearing up the earth with his feet, and then generously calling his ever-hungry family of wives and children to enjoy the rich morsel which he had discovered.

The pedagogue's mouth watered, as he looked upon this sumptuous promise of luxurious winter fare. In his devouring mind's eye he pictured to himself every roasting-pig running about with a pudding in his belly,[8] and an apple in his mouth; the pigeons were snugly put to bed in a comfortable pie, and tucked in with a coverlet of crust; the geese were swimming in their own gravy; and the ducks pairing cosily in dishes, like snug married couples, with a decent competency of onion-sauce. In the porkers he saw carved out the future sleek side of bacon, and juicy relishing ham; not a turkey but he beheld daintily trussed up, with its gizzard under its wing, and, peradventure, a necklace of savory sausages; and even bright chanticleer himself lay sprawling on his back, in a side-dish, with uplifted claws, as if craving that quarter which his chivalrous spirit disdained to ask while living.

As the enraptured Ichabod fancied all this, and as he rolled his great green eyes over the fat meadow-lands, the rich fields of wheat, of rye, of buckwheat, and Indian corn, and the orchard burdened with ruddy fruit, which surrounded the warm tenement of Van Tassel, his heart yearned

---

8. roasting-pig . . . belly: Cf. *I Henry IV*, II.iv.498.

after the damsel who was to inherit these domains, and his imagination expanded with the idea how they might be readily turned into cash, and the money invested in immense tracts of wild land, and shingle palaces in the wilderness. Nay, his busy fancy already realized his hopes, and presented to him the blooming Katrina, with a whole family of children, mounted on the top of a wagon loaded with household trumpery, with pots and kettles dangling beneath; and he beheld himself bestriding a pacing mare, with a colt at her heels, setting out for Kentucky, Tennessee, or the Lord knows where.

When he entered the house, the conquest of his heart was complete. It was one of those spacious farm-houses, with high-ridged, but lowly-sloping roofs, built in the style handed down from the first Dutch settlers; the low projecting eaves forming a piazza along the front, capable of being closed up in bad weather. Under this were hung flails, harness, various utensils of husbandry, and nets for fishing in the neighboring river. Benches were built along the sides for summer use; and a great spinning-wheel at one end, and a churn at the other, showed the various uses to which this important porch might be devoted. From this piazza the wondering Ichabod entered the hall, which formed the centre of the mansion and the place of usual residence. Here, rows of resplendent pewter, ranged on a long dresser, dazzled his eyes. In one corner stood a huge bag of wool ready to be spun; in another a quantity of linsey-woolsey just from the loom; ears of Indian corn, and strings of dried apples and peaches, hung in gay festoons along the walls, mingled with the gaud of red peppers; and a door left ajar gave him a peep into the best parlor, where the claw-footed chairs and dark mahogany tables shone like mirrors; and irons, with their accompanying shovel and tongs, glistened from their covert of asparagus tops; mockoranges and conch-shells decorated the mantelpiece; strings of various colored birds' eggs were suspended above it; a great ostrich egg was hung from the centre of the room, and a corner-cupboard, knowingly left open, displayed immense treasures of old silver and well-mended china.

From the moment Ichabod laid his eyes upon these regions of delight, the peace of his mind was at an end, and his only study was how to gain the affections of the peerless daughter of Van Tassel. In this enterprise, however, he had more real difficulties than generally fell to the lot of a knight-errant of yore, who seldom had anything but giants, enchanters, fiery dragons, and such like easily conquered adversaries, to contend with; and had to make his way merely through gates of iron and brass, and walls of adamant, to the castle-keep, where the lady of his heart was confined; all which he achieved as easily as a man would carve his way to the centre of a Christmas pie; and then the lady gave him her hand as a matter of course. Ichabod, on the contrary, had to win his way to the heart of a country coquette, beset with a labyrinth of whims and caprices, which were forever presenting new difficulties and impediments; and he had to encounter a host of fearful adversaries of real flesh and blood, the numerous rustic admirers, who beset every portal to her heart; keeping a watchful and angry eye upon each other, but ready to fly out in the common cause against any new competitor.

Among these the most formidable was a burly, roaring, roistering blade, of the name of Abraham, or, according to the Dutch abbreviation, Brom Van Brunt, the hero of the country round, which rang with his feats of strength and hardihood. He was broad-shouldered, and double-jointed, with short curly black hair, and a bluff but not unpleasant countenance, having a mingled air of fun and arrogance. From his Herculean frame and great powers of limb, he had received the nickname of BROM BONES, by which he was universally known. He was famed for great knowledge and skill in horsemanship, being as dexterous on horseback as a Tartar. He was foremost at all races and cockfights; and, with the ascendancy which bodily strength acquires in rustic life, was the umpire in all disputes, setting his hat on one side, and giving his decisions with an air and tone admitting of no gainsay or appeal. He was always ready for either a fight or a frolic; but had more mischief than ill-will in his composition; and, with all his overbearing roughness, there was a strong dash of waggish good-humor at bottom. He had three or four boon companions, who regarded him as their model, and at the head of whom he scoured the country, attending every scene of feud or merriment for miles round. In cold weather he was distinguished by a fur cap, surmounted with a flaunting fox's tail; and when the folks at a country gathering descried this well-known crest at a distance, whisking about among a squad of hard riders, they always stood by for a squall. Sometimes his crew would be heard dashing along past the farm-houses at midnight, with whoop and halloo, like a troop of Don Cossacks; and the old dames, startled out of their sleep, would listen for a moment till the hurry-scurry had clattered by, and then exclaim, "Ay, there goes Brom Bones and his gang!" The neighbors looked upon him with a mixture of awe, admiration, and good-will; and when any madcap prank, or rustic brawl, occurred in the vicinity, always shook their heads, and warranted Brom Bones was at the bottom of it.

This rantipole [9] hero had for some time singled out the blooming Katrina for the object of his uncouth gallantries; and though his amorous toyings were something like the gentle caresses and endearments of a bear, yet it was whispered that she did not altogether discourage his hopes. Certain it is, his advances were signals for rival candidates to retire, who felt no inclination to cross a lion in his amours; insomuch, that, when his horse was seen tied to Van Tassel's paling, on a Sunday night, a sure sign that his master was courting, or, as it is termed, "sparking," within, all other suitors passed by in despair, and carried the war into other quarters.

Such was the formidable rival with whom Ichabod Crane had to contend, and, considering all things, a stouter man than he would have shrunk from the competition, and a wiser man would have despaired. He had, however, a happy mixture of pliability and perseverance in his nature; he was in form and spirit like a supplejack—yielding, but tough; though he bent, he never broke; and though he bowed beneath the slightest pressure, yet, the moment it was away—jerk! he was as erect, and carried his head as high as ever.

To have taken the field openly against his rival would have been madness; for he was not a man to be thwarted in his amours, any more than that stormy lover, Achilles. Ichabod, therefore, made his advances in a quiet and gently insinuating manner. Under cover of his character of singing-master, he had made frequent visits at the farmhouse; not that he had anything to apprehend from the meddlesome interference of parents, which is so often a stumbling-block in the path of lovers. Balt Van Tassel was an easy, indulgent soul; he loved his daughter better even than his pipe, and, like a reasonable man and an excellent father, let her have her way in everything. His notable little wife, too, had enough to do to attend to her housekeeping and manage her poultry; for, as she sagely observed, ducks and geese are foolish things, and must be looked after, but girls can take care of themselves. Thus while the busy dame bustled about the house, or plied her spinning-wheel at one end of the piazza, honest Balt would sit smoking his evening pipe at the other, watching the achievements of a little wooden warrior, who, armed with a sword in each hand, was most valiantly fighting the wind on the pinnacle of the barn. In the mean time, Ichabod

9. **rantipole:** wild, reckless.

would carry on his suit with the daughter by the side of the spring under the great elm, or sauntering along in the twilight,—that hour so favorable to the lover's eloquence.

I profess not to know how women's hearts are wooed and won. To me they have always been matters of riddle and admiration. Some seem to have but one vulnerable point, or door of access; while others have a thousand avenues, and may be captured in a thousand different ways. It is a great triumph of skill to gain the former, but a still greater proof of generalship to maintain possession of the latter, for the man must battle for his fortress at every door and window. He who wins a thousand common hearts is therefore entitled to some renown; but he who keeps undisputed sway over the heart of a coquette, is indeed a hero. Certain it is, this was not the case with the redoubtable Brom Bones; and from the moment Ichabod Crane made his advances, the interests of the former evidently declined; his horse was no longer seen tied at the palings on Sunday nights, and a deadly feud gradually arose between him and the preceptor of Sleepy Hollow.

Brom, who had a degree of rough chivalry in his nature, would fain have carried matters to open warfare, and have settled their pretensions to the lady according to the mode of those most concise and simple reasoners, the knights-errant of yore —by single combat; but Ichabod was too conscious of the superior might of his adversary to enter the lists against him: he had overheard a boast of Bones, that he would "double the schoolmaster up, and lay him on a shelf of his own school-house;" and he was too wary to give him an opportunity. There was something extremely provoking in this obstinately pacific system; it left Brom no alternative but to draw upon the funds of rustic waggery in his disposition, and to play off boorish practical jokes upon his rival. Ichabod became the object of whimsical persecution to Bones and his gang of rough riders. They harried his hitherto peaceful domains; smoked out his singing-school, by stopping up the chimney; broke into the school-house at night, in spite of its formidable fastenings of withe and window-stakes, and turned everything topsy-turvy: so that the poor schoolmaster began to think all the witches in the country held their meetings there. But what was still more annoying, Brom took opportunities of turning him into ridicule in presence of his mistress, and had a scoundrel dog whom he taught to whine in the most ludicrous manner, and introduced as a rival of Ichabod's to instruct her in psalmody.

In this way matters went on for some time,

without producing any material effect on the relative situation of the contending powers. On a fine autumnal afternoon, Ichabod, in pensive mood, sat enthroned on the lofty stool whence he usually watched all the concerns of his little literary realm. In his hand he swayed a ferule, that sceptre of despotic power; the birch of justice reposed on three nails, behind the throne, a constant terror to evil-doers; while on the desk before him might be seen sundry contraband articles and prohibited weapons, detected upon the persons of idle urchins; such as half-munched apples, popguns, whirligigs, fly-cages, and whole legions of rampant little paper game-cocks. Apparently there had been some appalling act of justice recently inflicted, for his scholars were all busily intent upon their books, or slyly whispering behind them with one eye kept upon the master; and a kind of buzzing stillness reigned throughout the school-room. It was suddenly interrupted by the appearance of a Negro, in tow-cloth jacket and trousers, a round-crowned fragment of a hat, like the cap of Mercury, and mounted on the back of a ragged, wild, half-broken colt, which he managed with a rope by way of halter. He came clattering up to the school-door with an invitation to Ichabod to attend a merry-making or "quilting frolic," to be held that evening at Mynheer Van Tassel's; and having delivered his message with that air of importance, and effort at fine language, which a Negro is apt to display on petty embassies of the kind, he dashed over the brook, and was seen scampering away up the Hollow, full of the importance and hurry of his mission.

All was now bustle and hubbub in the late quiet school-room. The scholars were hurried through their lessons, without stopping at trifles; those who were nimble skipped over half with impunity, and those who were tardy had a smart application now and then in the rear, to quicken their speed, or help them over a tall word. Books were flung aside without being put away on the shelves, inkstands were overturned, benches thrown down, and the whole school was turned loose an hour before the usual time, bursting forth like a legion of young imps, yelping and racketing about the green, in joy at their early emancipation.

The gallant Ichabod now spent at least an extra half-hour at his toilet, brushing and furbishing up his best and indeed only suit of rusty black, and arranging his looks by a bit of broken looking-glass, that hung up in the school-house. That he might make his appearance before his mistress in the true style of a cavalier, he borrowed a horse from the farmer with whom he was domiciliated, a choleric old Dutchman, of the name of Hans Van

Ripper, and, thus gallantly mounted, issued forth, like a knight-errant in quest of adventures. But it is meet I should, in the true spirit of romantic story, give some account of the looks and equipments of my hero and his steed. The animal he bestrode was a broken-down plough-horse, that had outlived almost everything but his viciousness. He was gaunt and shagged, with a ewe neck and a head like a hammer; his rusty mane and tail were tangled and knotted with burrs; one eye had lost its pupil, and was glaring and spectral; but the other had the gleam of a genuine devil in it. Still he must have had fire and mettle in his day, if we may judge from the name he bore of Gunpowder. He had, in fact, been a favorite steed of his master's, the choleric Van Ripper, who was a furious rider, and had infused, very probably, some of his own spirit into the animal; for, old and broken-down as he looked, there was more of the lurking devil in him than in any young filly in the country.

Ichabod was a suitable figure for such a steed. He rode with short stirrups, which brought his knees nearly up to the pommel of the saddle; his sharp elbows stuck out like grasshoppers'; he carried his whip perpendicularly in his hand, like a sceptre, and, as his horse jogged on, the motion of his arms was not unlike the flapping of a pair of wings. A small wool hat rested on the top of his nose, for so his scanty strip of forehead might be called; and the skirts of his black coat fluttered out almost to the horse's tail. Such was the appearance of Ichabod and his steed, as they shambled out of the gate of Hans Van Ripper, and it was altogether such an apparition as is seldom to be met with in broad daylight.

It was, as I have said, a fine autumnal day, the sky was clear and serene, and nature wore that rich and golden livery which we always associate with the idea of abundance. The forests had put on their sober brown and yellow, while some trees of the tenderer kind had been nipped by the frosts into brilliant dyes of orange, purple, and scarlet. Streaming files of wild ducks began to make their appearance high in the air; the bark of the squirrel might be heard from the groves of beech and hickory nuts, and the pensive whistle of the quail at intervals from the neighboring stubble-field.

The small birds were taking their farewell banquets. In the fulness of their revelry, they fluttered, chirping and frolicking, from bush to bush, and tree to tree, capricious from the very profusion and variety around them. There was the honest cockrobin, the favorite game of stripling sportsmen, with its loud querulous notes; and the twittering blackbirds flying in sable clouds; and the golden-winged woodpecker, with his crimson crest, his broad black gorget, and splendid plumage; and the cedar-bird, with its red-tipt wings and yellow-tipt tail, and its little montero cap of feathers; and the blue jay, that noisy coxcomb, in his gay light-blue coat and white under-clothes, screaming and chattering, nodding and bobbing and bowing, and pretending to be on good terms with every songster of the grove.

As Ichabod jogged slowly on his way, his eye, ever open to every symptom of culinary abundance, ranged with delight over the treasures of jolly autumn. On all sides he beheld vast store of apples; some hanging in oppressive opulence on the trees; some gathered into baskets and barrels for the market; others heaped up in rich piles for the cider-press. Farther on he beheld great fields of Indian corn, with its golden ears peeping from their leafy coverts, and holding out the promise of cakes and hasty-pudding; and the yellow pumpkins lying beneath them, turning up their fair round bellies [10] to the sun, and giving ample prospects of the most luxurious of pies; and anon he passed the fragrant buckwheat fields, breathing the odor of the bee-hive, and as he beheld them, soft anticipations stole over his mind of dainty slapjacks, well buttered, and garnished with honey or treacle, by the delicate little dimpled hand of Katrina Van Tassel.

Thus feeding his mind with many sweet thoughts and "sugared suppositions," he journeyed along the sides of a range of hills which look out upon some of the goodliest scenes of the mighty Hudson. The sun gradually wheeled his broad disk down into the west. The wide bosom of the Tappan Zee lay motionless and glassy, excepting that here and there a gentle undulation waved and prolonged the blue shadow of the distant mountain. A few amber clouds floated in the sky, without a breath of air to move them. The horizon was of a fine golden tint, changing gradually into a pure apple-green, and from that into the deep blue of the mid-heaven. A slanting ray lingered on the woody crests of the precipices that overhung some parts of the river, giving greater depth to the dark-gray and purple of their rocky sides. A sloop was loitering in the distance, dropping slowly down with the tide, her sail hanging uselessly against the mast; and as the reflection of the sky gleamed along the still water, it seemed as if the vessel was suspended in the air.

It was toward evening that Ichabod arrived at the castle of the Heer Van Tassel, which he found thronged with the pride and flower of the adjacent country. Old farmers, a spare leathern-faced race,

10. fair round bellies: Cf. *As You Like It*, II.vii.154.

in homespun coats and breeches, blue stockings, huge shoes, and magnificent pewter buckles. Their brisk withered little dames, in close crimped caps, long-waisted shortgowns, homespun petticoats, with scissors and pincushions, and gay calico pockets hanging on the outside. Buxom lasses, almost as antiquated as their mothers, excepting where a straw hat, a fine ribbon, or perhaps a white frock, gave symptoms of city innovation. The sons, in short square-skirted coats with rows of stupendous brass buttons, and their hair generally queued in the fashion of the times, especially if they could procure an eel-skin for the purpose, it being esteemed, throughout the country, as a potent nourisher and strengthener of the hair.

Brom Bones, however, was the hero of the scene, having come to the gathering on his favorite steed, Daredevil, a creature, like himself, full of mettle and mischief, and which no one but himself could manage. He was, in fact, noted for preferring vicious animals, given to all kinds of tricks, which kept the rider in constant risk of his neck, for he held a tractable well-broken horse as unworthy of a lad of spirit.

Fain would I pause to dwell upon the world of charms that burst upon the enraptured gaze of my hero, as he entered the state parlor of Van Tassel's mansion. Not those of the bevy of buxom lasses, with their luxurious display of red and white; but the ample charms of a genuine Dutch country tea-table, in the sumptuous time of autumn. Such heaped-up platters of cakes of various and almost indescribable kinds, known only to experienced Dutch housewives! There was the doughty doughnut, the tenderer oly koek, and the crisp and crumbling cruller; sweet cakes and short cakes, ginger-cakes and honey-cakes, and the whole family of cakes. And then there were apple-pies and peach-pies and pumpkin-pies; besides slices of ham and smoked beef; and moreover delectable dishes of preserved plums, and peaches, and pears, and quinces; not to mention broiled shad and roasted chickens; together with bowls of milk and cream, all mingled higgledy-piggledy, pretty much as I have enumerated them, with the motherly tea-pot sending up its clouds of vapor from the midst—Heaven bless the mark! I want breath and time to discuss this banquet as it deserves, and am too eager to get on with my story. Happily, Ichabod Crane was not in so great a hurry as his historian, but did ample justice to every dainty.

He was a kind and thankful creature, whose heart dilated in proportion as his skin was filled with good cheer; and whose spirits rose with eating as some men's do with drink. He could not help, too, rolling his large eyes round him as he ate, and chuckling with the possibility that he might one day be lord of all this scene of almost unimaginable luxury and splendor. Then, he thought, how soon he'd turn his back upon the old school-house; snap his fingers in the face of Hans Van Ripper, and every other niggardly patron, and kick any itinerant pedagogue out-of-doors that should dare to call him comrade!

Old Baltus Van Tassel moved about among his guests with a face dilated with content and good-humor, round and jolly as the harvest-moon. His hospitable attentions were brief, but expressive, being confined to a shake of the hand, a slap on the shoulder, a loud laugh, and a pressing invitation to "fall to, and help themselves."

And now the sound of the music from the common room, or hall, summoned to the dance. The musician was an old gray-headed Negro, who had been the itinerant orchestra of the neighborhood for more than half a century. His instrument was as old and battered as himself. The greater part of the time he scraped on two or three strings accompanying every movement of the bow with a motion of the head; bowing almost to the ground and stamping with his foot whenever a fresh couple were to start.

Ichabod prided himself upon his dancing as much as upon his vocal powers. Not a limb, not a fibre about him was idle; and to have seen his loosely hung frame in full motion, and clattering about the room, you would have thought Saint Vitus himself, that blessed patron of the dance, was figuring before you in person. He was the admiration of all the Negroes; who, having gathered, of all ages and sizes, from the farm and the neighborhood, stood forming a pyramid of shining black faces at every door and window, gazing with delight at the scene, rolling their white eyeballs, and showing grinning rows of ivory from ear to ear. How could the flogger of urchins be otherwise than animated and joyous? The lady of his heart was his partner in the dance, and smiling graciously in reply to all his amorous oglings; while Brom Bones, sorely smitten with love and jealousy, sat brooding by himself in one corner.

When the dance was at an end, Ichabod was attracted to a knot of the sager folks, who, with old Van Tassel, sat smoking at one end of the piazza, gossiping over former times, and drawing out long stories about the war.

This neighborhood, at the time of which I am speaking, was one of those highly favored places which abound with chronicle and great men. The British and American line had run near it during the war; it had, therefore, been the scene of ma-

rauding, and infested with refugees, cow-boys,[11] and all kinds of border chivalry. Just sufficient time had elapsed to enable each story-teller to dress up his tale with a little becoming fiction, and, in the indistinctness of his recollection, to make himself the hero of every exploit.

There was the story of Doffue Martling, a large blue-bearded Dutchman, who had nearly taken a British frigate with an old iron nine-pounder from a mud breastwork, only that his gun burst at the sixth discharge. And there was an old gentleman who shall be nameless, being too rich a mynheer to be lightly mentioned, who, in the battle of Whiteplains, being an excellent master of defence, parried a musket-ball with a small sword, insomuch that he absolutely felt it whiz round the blade, and glance off at the hilt; in proof of which he was ready at any time to show the sword, with the hilt a little bent. There were several more that had been equally great in the field, not one of whom but was persuaded that he had a considerable hand in bringing the war to a happy termination.

But all these were nothing to the tales of ghosts and apparitions that succeeded. The neighborhood is rich in legendary treasures of the kind. Local tales and superstitions thrive best in these sheltered long-settled retreats; but are trampled underfoot by the shifting throng that forms the population of most of our country places. Besides, there is no encouragement for ghosts in most of our villages, for they have scarcely had time to finish their first nap, and turn themselves in their graves, before their surviving friends have travelled away from the neighborhood; so that when they turn out at night to walk their rounds, they have no acquaintance left to call upon. This is perhaps the reason why we so seldom hear of ghosts, except in our long-established Dutch communities.

The immediate cause, however, of the prevalence of supernatural stories in these parts was doubtless owing to the vicinity of Sleepy Hollow. There was a contagion in the very air that blew from that haunted region; it breathed forth an atmosphere of dreams and fancies infecting all the land. Several of the Sleepy Hollow people were present at Van Tassel's, and, as usual, were doling out their wild and wonderful legends. Many dismal tales were told about funeral trains, and mourning cries and wailings heard and seen about the great tree where the unfortunate Major André[12] was taken, and which stood in the neighborhood. Some mention was made also of the woman in white, that haunted the dark glen at Raven

11. **cow-boys:** guerilla troops in the region during the American Revolution. 12. **André:** British officer executed as a spy in the Revolution.

Rock, and was often heard to shriek on winter nights before a storm, having perished there in the snow. The chief part of the stories, however, turned upon the favorite spectre of Sleepy Hollow, the headless horseman, who had been heard several times of late, patrolling the country; and, it was said, tethered his horse nightly among the graves in the churchyard.

The sequestered situation of this church seems always to have made it a favorite haunt of troubled spirits. It stands on a knoll, surrounded by locust-trees and lofty elms, from among which its decent whitewashed walls shine modestly forth, like Christian purity beaming through the shades of retirement. A gentle slope descends from it to a silver sheet of water, bordered by high trees, between which, peeps may be caught at the blue hills of the Hudson. To look upon its grass-grown yard, where the sunbeams seem to sleep so quietly, one would think that there at least the dead might rest in peace. On one side of the church extends a wide woody dell, along which raves a large brook among broken rocks and trunks of fallen trees. Over a deep black part of the stream, not far from the church, was formerly thrown a wooden bridge; the road that led to it, and the bridge itself, were thickly shaded by overhanging trees, which cast a gloom about it, even in the daytime, but occasioned a fearful darkness at night. This was one of the favorite haunts of the headless horseman; and the place where he was most frequently encountered. The tale was told of old Brouwer, a most heretical disbeliever in ghosts, how he met the horseman returning from his foray into Sleepy Hollow, and was obliged to get up behind him; how they galloped over bush and brake, over hill and swamp, until they reached the bridge; when the horseman suddenly turned into a skeleton, threw old Brouwer into the brook, and sprang away over the tree-tops with a clap of thunder.

This story was immediately matched by a thrice marvellous adventure of Brom Bones, who made light of the galloping Hessian as an arrant jockey. He affirmed that, on returning one night from the neighboring village of Sing Sing, he had been overtaken by this midnight trooper; that he had offered to race with him for a bowl of punch, and should have won it too, for Daredevil beat the goblin horse all hollow, but, just as they came to the church-bridge, the Hessian bolted, and vanished in a flash of fire.

All these tales, told in that drowsy undertone with which men talk in the dark, the countenances of the listeners only now and then receiving a casual gleam from the glare of a pipe, sank deep in the mind of Ichabod. He repaid them in kind with large extracts from his invaluable author, Cotton Mather, and added many marvellous events that had taken place in his native State of Connecticut, and fearful sights which he had seen in his nightly walks about the Sleepy Hollow.

The revel now gradually broke up. The old farmers gathered together their families in their wagons, and were heard for some time rattling along the hollow roads, and over the distant hills. Some of the damsels mounted on pillions behind their favorite swains, and their light-hearted laughter, mingling with the clatter of hoofs, echoed along the silent woodlands, sounding fainter and fainter until they gradually died away—and the late scene of noise and frolic was all silent and deserted. Ichabod only lingered behind, according to the custom of country lovers, to have a *tête-à-tête* with the heiress, fully convinced that he was now on the high road to success. What passed at this interview I will not pretend to say, for in fact I do not know. Something, however, I fear me, must have gone wrong, for he certainly sallied forth, after no very great interval, with an air quite desolate and chopfallen.—Oh, these women! these women! Could that girl have been playing off any of her coquettish tricks?—Was her encouragement of the poor pedagogue all a mere sham to secure her conquest of his rival?—Heaven only knows, not I!—Let it suffice to say, Ichabod stole forth with the air of one who had been sacking a henroost, rather than a fair lady's heart. Without looking to the right or left to notice the scene of rural wealth on which he had so often gloated, he went straight to the stable, and with several hearty cuffs and kicks, roused his steed most uncourteously from the comfortable quarters in which he was soundly sleeping, dreaming of mountains of corn and oats, and whole valleys of timothy and clover.

It was the very witching time of night [13] that Ichabod, heavy-hearted and crestfallen, pursued his travel homewards, along the sides of the lofty hills which rise above Tarry Town, and which he had traversed so cheerily in the afternoon. The hour was as dismal as himself. Far below him, the Tappan Zee spread its dusky and indistinct waste of waters, with here and there the tall mast of a sloop riding quietly at anchor under the land. In the dead hush of midnight he could even hear the barking of the watch-dog from the opposite shore of the Hudson; but it was so vague and faint as only to give an idea of his distance from this faithful companion of man. Now and then, too, the

13. very . . . night: from *Hamlet*, III.ii.406.

long-drawn crowing of a cock, accidentally awakened, would sound far, far off, from some farmhouse away among the hills—but it was like a dreaming sound in his ear. No signs of life occurred near him, but occasionally the melancholy chirp of a cricket, or perhaps the guttural twang of a bull-frog, from a neighboring marsh, as if sleeping uncomfortably, and turning suddenly in his bed.

All the stories of ghosts and goblins that he had heard in the afternoon, now came crowding upon his recollection. The night grew darker and darker; the stars seemed to sink deeper in the sky, and driving clouds occasionally hid them from his sight. He had never felt so lonely and dismal. He was, moreover, approaching the very place where many of the scenes of the ghost-stories had been laid. In the centre of the road stood an enormous tulip-tree, which towered like a giant above all the other trees of the neighborhood, and formed a kind of landmark. Its limbs were gnarled, and fantastic, large enough to form trunks for ordinary trees, twisting down almost to the earth, and rising again into the air. It was connected with the tragical story of the unfortunate André, who had been taken prisoner hard by; and was universally known by the name of Major André's tree. The common people regarded it with a mixture of respect and superstition, partly out of sympathy for the fate of its ill-starred namesake, and partly from the tales of strange sights and doleful lamentations told concerning it.

As Ichabod approached this fearful tree, he began to whistle: he thought his whistle was answered,—it was but a blast sweeping sharply through the dry branches. As he approached a little nearer, he thought he saw something white, hanging in the midst of the tree,—he paused and ceased whistling; but on looking more narrowly, perceived that it was a place where the tree had been scathed by lightning, and the white wood laid bare. Suddenly he heard a groan,—his teeth chattered and his knees smote against the saddle: it was but the rubbing of one huge bough upon another, as they were swayed about by the breeze. He passed the tree in safety; but new perils lay before him.

About two hundred yards from the tree a small brook crossed the road, and ran into a marshy and thickly wooded glen, known by the name of Wiley's swamp. A few rough logs, laid side by side, served for a bridge over this stream. On that side of the road where the brook entered the wood, a group of oaks and chestnuts, matted thick with wild grape-vines, threw a cavernous gloom over it. To pass this bridge was the severest trial. It was at this identical spot that the unfortunate André was captured, and under the covert of those chestnuts and vines were the sturdy yeomen concealed who surprised him. This has ever since been considered a haunted stream, and fearful are the feelings of the school boy who has to pass it alone after dark.

As he approached the stream, his heart began to thump; he summoned up, however, all his resolution, gave his horse half a score of kicks in the ribs, and attempted to dash briskly across the bridge; but instead of starting forward, the perverse old animal made a lateral movement, and ran broadside against the fence. Ichabod, whose fears increased with the delay, jerked the reins on the other side, and kicked lustily with the contrary foot: it was all in vain; his steed started, it is true, but it was only to plunge to the opposite side of the road into a thicket of brambles and alder bushes. The schoolmaster now bestowed both whip and heel upon the starveling ribs of old Gunpowder, who dashed forward, snuffling and snorting, but came to a stand just by the bridge, with a suddenness that had nearly sent his rider sprawling over his head. Just at this moment a plashy tramp by the side of the bridge caught the sensitive ear of Ichabod. In the dark shadow of the grove, on the margin of the brook, he beheld something huge, misshapen, black, and towering. It stirred not, but seemed gathered up in the gloom, like some gigantic monster ready to spring upon the traveller.

The hair of the affrighted pedagogue rose upon his head with terror. What was to be done? To turn and fly was now too late; and besides, what chance was there of escaping ghost or goblin, if such it was, which could ride upon the wings of the wind? Summoning up, therefore, a show of courage, he demanded in stammering accents—"Who are you?" He received no reply. He repeated his demand in a still more agitated voice. Still there was no answer. Once more he cudgelled the sides of the inflexible Gunpowder, and, shutting his eyes, broke forth with involuntary fervor into a psalm-tune. Just then the shadowy object of alarm put itself in motion, and, with a scramble and a bound, stood at once in the middle of the road. Though the night was dark and dismal, yet the form of the unknown might now in some degree be ascertained. He appeared to be a horseman of large dimensions, and mounted on a black horse of powerful frame. He made no offer of molestation or sociability, but kept aloof on one side of the road, jogging along on the blind side of old Gunpowder, who had now got over his fright and waywardness.

Ichabod, who had no relish for this strange midnight companion, and bethought himself of the adventure of Brom Bones with the Galloping Hessian, now quickened his steed, in hopes of leaving him behind. The stranger, however, quickened his horse to an equal pace. Ichabod pulled up, and fell into a walk, thinking to lag behind,—the other did the same. His heart began to sink within him; he endeavored to resume his psalm-tune, but his parched tongue clove to the roof of his mouth, and he could not utter a stave. There was something in the moody and dogged silence of this pertinacious companion, that was mysterious and appalling. It was soon fearfully accounted for. On mounting a rising ground, which brought the figure of his fellow-traveller in relief against the sky, gigantic in height, and muffled in a cloak, Ichabod was horror-struck, on perceiving that he was headless!—but his horror was still more increased, on observing that the head, which should have rested on his shoulders, was carried before him on the pommel of the saddle: his terror rose to desperation; he rained a shower of kicks and blows upon Gunpowder, hoping, by a sudden movement, to give his companion the slip,—but the spectre started full jump with him. Away then they dashed, through thick and thin; stones flying, and sparks flashing at every bound. Ichabod's flimsy garments fluttered in the air, as he stretched his long lank body away over his horse's head, in the eagerness of his flight.

They had now reached the road which turns off to Sleepy Hollow; but Gunpowder, who seemed possessed with a demon, instead of keeping up it, made an opposite turn, and plunged headlong downhill to the left. This road leads through a sandy hollow, shaded by trees for about a quarter of a mile, where it crosses the bridge famous in goblin story, and just beyond swells the green knoll on which stands the whitewashed church.

As yet the panic of the steed had given his unskilful rider an apparent advantage in the chase; but just as he had got half-way through the hollow, the girths of the saddle gave way, and he felt it slipping from under him. He seized it by the pommel, and endeavored to hold it firm, but in vain; and had just time to save himself by clasping old Gunpowder round the neck, when the saddle fell to the earth, and he heard it trampled underfoot by his pursuer. For a moment the terror of Hans Van Ripper's wrath passed across his mind —for it was his Sunday saddle; but this was no time for petty fears; the goblin was hard on his haunches; and (unskilful rider that he was!) he had much ado to maintain his seat; sometimes slipping on one side, sometimes on another, and sometimes jolted on the high ridge of his horse's

backbone, with a violence that he verily feared would cleave him asunder.

An opening in the trees now cheered him with the hopes that the church-bridge was at hand. The wavering reflection of a silver star in the bosom of the brook told him that he was not mistaken. He saw the walls of the church dimly glaring under the trees beyond. He recollected the place where Brom Bones's ghostly competitor had disappeared. "If I can but reach that bridge," thought Ichabod, "I am safe." Just then he heard the black steed panting and blowing close behind him; he even fancied that he felt his hot breath. Another convulsive kick in the ribs, and old Gunpowder sprang upon the bridge; he thundered over the resounding planks; he gained the opposite side; and now Ichabod cast a look behind to see if his pursuer should vanish, according to rule, in a flash of fire and brimstone. Just then he saw the goblin rising in his stirrups, and in the very act of hurling his head at him. Ichabod endeavored to dodge the horrible missile, but too late. It encountered his cranium with a tremendous crash,—he was tumbled headlong into the dust, and Gunpowder, the black steed, and the goblin rider, passed by like a whirlwind.

The next morning the old horse was found without his saddle, and with the bridle under his feet, soberly cropping the grass at his master's gate. Ichabod did not make his appearance at breakfast;—dinner-hour came, but no Ichabod. The boys assembled at the school-house, and strolled idly about the banks of the brook; but no schoolmaster. Hans Van Ripper now began to feel some uneasiness about the fate of poor Ichabod, and his saddle. An inquiry was set on foot, and after diligent investigation they came upon his traces. In one part of the road leading to the church was found the saddle trampled in the dirt; the tracks of horses' hoofs deeply dented in the road, and evidently at furious speed, were traced to the bridge, beyond which, on the bank of a broad part of the brook, where the water ran deep and black, was found the hat of the unfortunate Ichabod, and close beside it a shattered pumpkin.

The brook was searched, but the body of the schoolmaster was not to be discovered. Hans Van Ripper, as executor of his estate, examined the bundle which contained all his worldly effects. They consisted of two shirts and a half; two stocks for the neck; a pair or two of worsted stockings; an old pair of corduroy small-clothes; a rusty razor; a book of psalm-tunes, full of dogs' ears, and a broken pitchpipe. As to the books and furniture of the school-house, they belonged to the community, excepting Cotton Mather's *His-*

*tory of Witchcraft,* a *New England Almanac,* and a book of dreams and fortune-telling; in which last was a sheet of foolscap much scribbled and blotted in several fruitless attempts to make a copy of verses in honor of the heiress of Van Tassel. These magic books and the poetic scrawl were forthwith consigned to the flames by Hans Van Ripper; who from that time forward determined to send his children no more to school; observing, that he never knew any good come of this same reading and writing. Whatever money the schoolmaster possessed, and he had received his quarter's pay but a day or two before, he must have had about his person at the time of his disappearance.

The mysterious event caused much speculation at the church on the following Sunday. Knots of gazers and gossips were collected in the churchyard, at the bridge, and at the spot where the hat and pumpkin had been found. The stories of Brouwer, of Bones, and a whole budget of others, were called to mind; and when they had diligently considered them all, and compared them with the symptoms of the present case, they shook their heads, and came to the conclusion that Ichabod had been carried off by the Galloping Hessian. As he was a bachelor, and in nobody's debt, nobody troubled his head any more about him. The school was removed to a different quarter of the Hollow, and another pedagogue reigned in his stead.

It is true, an old farmer, who had been down to New York on a visit several years after, and from whom this account of the ghostly adventure was received, brought home the intelligence that Ichabod Crane was still alive; that he had left the neighborhood, partly through fear of the goblin and Hans Van Ripper, and partly in mortification at having been suddenly dismissed by the heiress; that he had changed his quarters to a distant part of the country; had kept school and studied law at the same time, had been admitted to the bar, turned politician, electioneered, written for the newspapers, and finally had been made a justice of the Ten Pound Court. Brom Bones too, who shortly after his rival's disappearance conducted the blooming Katrina in triumph to the altar, was observed to look exceeding knowing whenever the story of Ichabod was related, and always burst into a hearty laugh at the mention of the pumpkin; which led some to suspect that he knew more about the matter than he chose to tell.

The old country wives, however, who are the best judges of these matters, maintain to this day that Ichabod was spirited away by supernatural means; and it is a favorite story often told about the neighborhood round the winter evening fire.

The bridge became more than ever an object of superstitious awe, and that may be the reason why the road has been altered of late years, so as to approach the church by the border of the mill-pond. The school-house, being deserted, soon fell to decay, and was reported to be haunted by the ghost of the unfortunate pedagogue; and the ploughboy, loitering homeward of a still summer evening, has often fancied his voice at a distance, chanting a melancholy psalm-tune among the tranquil solitudes of Sleepy Hollow.

### POSTSCRIPT

*Found in the Handwriting of Mr. Knickerbocker*

The preceding Tale is given, almost in the precise words in which I heard it related at a Corporation meeting of the ancient city of Manhattoes, at which were present many of its sagest and most illustrious burghers. The narrator was a pleasant, shabby, gentlemanly old fellow, in pepper-and-salt clothes, with a sadly humorous face; and one whom I strongly suspected of being poor,—he made such efforts to be entertaining. When his story was concluded, there was much laughter and approbation, particularly from two or three deputy aldermen, who had been asleep the greater part of the time. There was, however, one tall, dry-looking old gentleman, with beetling eyebrows, who maintained a grave and rather severe face throughout: now and then folding his arms, inclining his head, and looking down upon the floor, as if turning a doubt over in his mind. He was one of your wary men, who never laugh, but upon good grounds—when they have reason and the law on their side. When the mirth of the rest of the company had subsided and silence was restored, he leaned one arm on the elbow of his chair, and, sticking the other akimbo, demanded, with a slight but exceedingly sage motion of the head, and contraction of the brow, what was the moral of the story, and what it went to prove?

The story-teller, who was just putting a glass of wine to his lips, as a refreshment after his toils, paused for a moment, looked at his inquirer with an air of infinite deference, and, lowering the glass slowly to the table, observed, that the story was intended most logically to prove:—

"That there is no situation in life but has its advantages and pleasures—provided we will but take a joke as we find it:

"That, therefore, he that runs races with goblin troopers is likely to have rough riding of it.

"Ergo, for a country schoolmaster to be refused the hand of a Dutch heiress, is a certain step to high preferment in the state."

The cautious old gentleman knit his brows tenfold closer after this explanation, being sorely puzzled by the ratiocination of the syllogism; while, methought, the one in pepper-and-salt eyed him with something of a triumphant leer. At length he observed, that all this was very well, but still he thought the story a little on the extravagant—there were one or two points on which he had his doubts.

"Faith, sir," replied the story-teller, "as to that matter, I don't believe one half of it myself."

D. K.

*1820, 1848*

# THE DEVIL AND TOM WALKER

❖

❮ "The Devil and Tom Walker" is one of "The Money-Diggers" series, Part IV, of *Tales of a Traveller*. All of Part IV is said by Crayon to "have been found among the papers of the late Diedrich Knickerbocker."

❖

A FEW miles from Boston in Massachusetts, there is a deep inlet, winding several miles into the interior of the country from Charles Bay, and terminating in a thickly-wooded swamp or morass. On one side of this inlet is a beautiful dark grove; on the opposite side the land rises abruptly from the water's edge into a high ridge, on which grow a few scattered oaks of great age and immense size. Under one of these gigantic trees, according to old stories, there was a great amount of treasure buried by Kidd the pirate. The inlet allowed a facility to bring the money in a boat secretly and at night to the very foot of the hill; the elevation of the place permitted a good lookout to be kept that no one was at hand; while the remarkable trees formed good landmarks by which the place might easily be found again. The old stories add, moreover, that the devil presided at the hiding of the money, and took it under his guardianship; but this, it is well known, he always does with buried treasure, particularly when it has been ill-gotten. Be that as it may, Kidd never returned to recover his wealth; being shortly after seized at Boston, sent out to England, and there hanged for a pirate.

About the year 1727, just at the time that earthquakes were prevalent in New England, and shook many tall sinners down upon their knees, there lived near this place a meagre, miserly fellow, of the name of Tom Walker. He had a wife as miserly as himself: they were so miserly that they even conspired to cheat each other. Whatever the woman could lay hands on, she hid away; a hen could not cackle but she was on the alert to secure the new-laid egg. Her husband was continually prying about to detect her secret hoards, and many and fierce were the conflicts that took place about what ought to have been common property. They lived in a forlorn-looking house that stood alone, and had an air of starvation. A few straggling savin-trees, emblems of sterility, grew near it; no smoke ever curled from its chimney; no traveller stopped at its door. A miserable horse, whose ribs were as articulate as the bars of a gridiron, stalked about a field, where a thin carpet of moss, scarcely covering the ragged beds of puddingstone, tantalized and balked his hunger; and sometimes he would lean his head over the fence, look piteously at the passer-by, and seem to petition deliverance from this land of famine.

The house and its inmates had altogether a bad name. Tom's wife was a tall termagant, fierce of temper, loud of tongue, and strong of arm. Her voice was often heard in wordy warfare with her husband; and his face sometimes showed signs that their conflicts were not confined to words. No one ventured, however, to interfere between them. The lonely wayfarer shrunk within himself at the horrid clamor and clapper-clawing; eyed the den of discord askance; and hurried on his way, rejoicing, if a bachelor, in his celibacy.

One day that Tom Walker had been to a distant part of the neighborhood, he took what he considered a short cut homeward, through the swamp. Like most short cuts, it was an ill-chosen route. The swamp was thickly grown with great gloomy pines and hemlocks, some of them ninety feet high, which made it dark at noonday, and a retreat for all the owls of the neighborhood. It was full of pits and quagmires, partly covered with weeds and mosses, where the green surface often betrayed the traveller into a gulf of black, smothering mud: there were also dark and stagnant pools, the abodes of the tadpole, the bull-frog, and the water-snake; where the trunks of pines and hemlocks lay half-drowned, half-rotting, looking like alligators sleeping in the mire.

Tom had long been picking his way cautiously through this treacherous forest; stepping from tuft to tuft of rushes and roots, which afforded precarious footholds among deep sloughs; or pacing carefully, like a cat, along the prostrate trunks of trees; startled now and then by the sudden screaming of the bittern, or the quacking of a wild duck rising on the wing from some solitary pool. At length he arrived at a firm piece of ground, which ran out like a peninsula into the deep bosom of the swamp. It had been one of the strongholds of the Indians during their wars with the first colonists.

Here they had thrown up a kind of fort, which they had looked upon as almost impregnable, and had used as a place of refuge for their squaws and children. Nothing remained of the old Indian fort but a few embankments, gradually sinking to the level of the surrounding earth, and already overgrown in part by oaks and other forest trees, the foliage of which formed a contrast to the dark pines and hemlocks of the swamp.

It was late in the dusk of evening when Tom Walker reached the old fort, and he paused there awhile to rest himself. Any one but he would have felt unwilling to linger in this lonely, melancholy place, for the common people had a bad opinion of it, from the stories handed down from the time of the Indian wars; when it was asserted that the savages held incantations here, and made sacrifices to the evil spirit.

Tom Walker, however, was not a man to be troubled with any fears of the kind. He reposed himself for some time on the trunk of a fallen hemlock, listening to the boding cry of the tree-toad, and delving with his walking-staff into a mound of black mould at his feet. As he turned up the soil unconsciously, his staff struck against something hard. He raked it out of the vegetable mould, and lo! a cloven skull, with an Indian tomahawk buried deep in it, lay before him. The rust on the weapon showed the time that had elapsed since this death-blow had been given. It was a dreary memento of the fierce struggle that had taken place in this last foothold of the Indian warriors.

"Humph!" said Tom Walker, as he gave it a kick to shake the dirt from it.

"Let that skull alone!" said a gruff voice. Tom lifted up his eyes, and beheld a great black man seated directly opposite him, on the stump of a tree. He was exceedingly surprised, having neither heard nor seen any one approach; and he was still more perplexed on observing, as well as the gathering gloom would permit, that the stranger was neither Negro nor Indian. It is true he was dressed in a rude half Indian garb, and had a red belt or sash swathed round his body; but his face was neither black nor copper-color, but swarthy and dingy, and begrimed with soot, as if he had been accustomed to toil among fires and forges. He had a shock of coarse black hair, that stood out from his head in all directions, and bore an axe on his shoulder.

He scowled for a moment at Tom with a pair of great red eyes.

"What are you doing on my grounds?" said the black man, with a hoarse growling voice.

"Your grounds!" said Tom with a sneer, "no more your grounds than mine; they belong to Deacon Peabody."

"Deacon Peabody be d——d," said the stranger, "as I flatter myself he will be, if he does not look more to his own sins and less to those of his neighbors. Look yonder, and see how Deacon Peabody is faring."

Tom looked in the direction that the stranger pointed, and beheld one of the great trees, fair and flourishing without, but rotten at the core, and saw that it had been nearly hewn through, so that the first high wind was likely to blow it down. On the bark of the tree was scored the name of Deacon Peabody, an eminent man, who had waxed wealthy by driving shrewd bargains with the Indians. He now looked around, and found most of the tall trees marked with the name of some great man of the colony, and all more or less scored by the axe. The one on which he had been seated, and which had evidently just been hewn down, bore the name of Crowninshield; and he recollected a mighty rich man of that name, who made a vulgar display of wealth, which it was whispered he had acquired by buccaneering.

"He's just ready for burning!" said the black man, with a growl of triumph. "You see I am likely to have a good stock of firewood for winter."

"But what right have you," said Tom, "to cut down Deacon Peabody's timber?"

"The right of a prior claim," said the other. "This woodland belonged to me long before one of your white-faced race put foot upon the soil."

"And pray, who are you, if I may be so bold?" said Tom.

"Oh, I go by various names. I am the wild huntsman in some countries; the black miner in others. In this neighborhood I am known by the name of the black woodman. I am he to whom the red men consecrated this spot, and in honor of whom they now and then roasted a white man, by way of sweet-smelling sacrifice. Since the red men have been exterminated by you white savages, I amuse myself by presiding at the persecutions of Quakers and Anabaptists; I am the great patron and prompter of slave-dealers, and the grandmaster of the Salem witches."

"The upshot of all which is, that, if I mistake not," said Tom, sturdily, "you are he commonly called Old Scratch."

"The same, at your service!" replied the black man, with a half civil nod.

Such was the opening of this interview, according to the old story; though it has almost too familiar an air to be credited. One would think that to meet with such a singular personage, in this wild, lonely place, would have shaken any man's nerves;

but Tom was a hard-minded fellow, not easily daunted, and he had lived so long with a termagant wife, that he did not even fear the devil.

It is said that after this commencement they had a long and earnest conversation together, as Tom returned homeward. The black man told him of great sums of money buried by Kidd the pirate, under the oak-trees on the high ridge, not far from the morass. All these were under his command, and protected by his power, so that none could find them but such as propitiated his favor. These he offered to place within Tom Walker's reach, having conceived an especial kindness for him; but they were to be had only on certain conditions. What these conditions were may be easily surmised, though Tom never disclosed them publicly. They must have been very hard, for he required time to think of them, and he was not a man to stick at trifles when money was in view. When they had reached the edge of the swamp, the stranger paused—"What proof have I that all you have been telling me is true?" said Tom. "There's my signature," said the black man, pressing his finger on Tom's forehead. So saying, he turned off among the thickets of the swamp, and seemed, as Tom said, to go down, down, down, into the earth, until nothing but his head and shoulders could be seen, and so on, until he totally disappeared.

When Tom reached home, he found the black print of a finger burnt, as it were, into his forehead, which nothing could obliterate.

The first news his wife had to tell him was the sudden death of Absalom Crowninshield, the rich buccaneer. It was announced in the papers with the usual flourish, that "A great man had fallen in Israel." [1]

Tom recollected the tree which his black friend had just hewn down, and which was ready for burning. "Let the freebooter roast," said Tom, "who cares!" He now felt convinced that all he had heard and seen was no illusion.

He was not prone to let his wife into his confidence; but as this was an uneasy secret, he willingly shared it with her. All her avarice was awakened at the mention of hidden gold, and she urged her husband to comply with the black man's terms, and secure what would make them wealthy for life. However Tom might have felt disposed to sell himself to the devil, he was determined not to do so to oblige his wife; so he flatly refused, out of the mere spirit of contradiction. Many and bitter were the quarrels they had on the subject; but the more she talked, the more resolute was Tom not to be damned to please her.

At length she determined to drive the bargain on her own account, and if she succeeded, to keep all the gain to herself. Being of the same fearless temper as her husband, she set off for the old Indian fort towards the close of a summer's day. She was many hours absent. When she came back, she was reserved and sullen in her replies. She spoke something of a black man, whom she had met about twilight, hewing at the root of a tall tree. He was sulky, however, and would not come to terms: she was to go again with a propitiatory offering, but what it was she forbore to say.

The next evening she set off again for the swamp, with her apron heavily laden. Tom waited and waited for her, but in vain; midnight came, but she did not make her appearance: morning, noon, night returned, but still she did not come. Tom now grew uneasy for her safety, especially as he found she had carried off in her apron the silver teapot and spoons, and every portable article of value. Another night elapsed, another morning came; but no wife. In a word, she was never heard of more.

What was her real fate nobody knows, in consequence of so many pretending to know. It is one of those facts which have become confounded by a variety of historians. Some asserted that she lost her way among the tangled mazes of the swamp, and sank into some pit or slough; others, more uncharitable, hinted that she had eloped with the household booty, and made off to some other province; while others surmised that the tempter had decoyed her into a dismal quagmire, on the top of which her hat was found lying. In confirmation of this, it was said a great black man, with an axe on his shoulder, was seen late that very evening coming out of the swamp, carrying a bundle tied in a check apron, with an air of surly triumph.

The most current and probable story, however, observes, that Tom Walker grew so anxious about the fate of his wife and his property, that he set out at length to seek them both at the Indian fort. During a long summer's afternoon he searched about the gloomy place, but no wife was to be seen. He called her name repeatedly, but she was nowhere to be heard. The bittern alone responded to his voice, as he flew screaming by; or the bull-frog croaked dolefully from a neighboring pool. At length, it is said, just in the brown hour of twilight, when the owls began to hoot, and the bats to flit about, his attention was attracted by the clamor of carrion crows hovering about a cypress-tree. He looked up, and beheld a bundle tied in a check apron, and hanging in the branches of the tree, with a great vulture perched hard by, as if keeping watch upon it. He leaped with joy; for he recog-

---

THE DEVIL AND TOM WALKER. 1. "A . . . Israel": II Sam. 3:38.

nized his wife's apron, and supposed it to contain the household valuables.

"Let us get hold of the property," said he, consolingly to himself, "and we will endeavor to do without the woman."

As he scrambled up the tree, the vulture spread its wide wings, and sailed off screaming into the deep shadows of the forest. Tom seized the checked apron, but woeful sight! found nothing but a heart and liver tied up in it!

Such, according to this most authentic old story, was all that was to be found of Tom's wife. She had probably attempted to deal with the black man as she had been accustomed to deal with her husband; but though a female scold is generally considered a match for the devil, yet in this instance she appears to have had the worst of it. She must have died game, however; for it is said Tom noticed many prints of cloven feet deeply stamped about the tree, and found handfuls of hair, that looked as if they had been plucked from the coarse black shock of the woodman. Tom knew his wife's prowess by experience. He shrugged his shoulders, as he looked at the signs of a fierce clapper-clawing. "Egad," said he to himself, "Old Scratch must have had a tough time of it!"

Tom consoled himself for the loss of his property, with the loss of his wife, for he was a man of fortitude. He even felt something like gratitude towards the black woodman, who, he considered, had done him a kindness. He sought, therefore, to cultivate a further acquaintance with him, but for some time without success; the old black-legs played shy, for whatever people may think, he is not always to be had for calling for: he knows how to play his cards when pretty sure of his game.

At length, it is said, when delay had whetted Tom's eagerness to the quick, and prepared him to agree to any thing rather than not gain the promised treasure, he met the black man one evening in his usual woodman's dress, with his axe on his shoulder, sauntering along the swamp, and humming a tune. He affected to receive Tom's advances with great indifference, made brief replies, and went on humming his tune.

By degrees, however, Tom brought him to business, and they began to haggle about the terms on which the former was to have the pirate's treasure. There was one condition which need not be mentioned, being generally understood in all cases where the devil grants favors; but there were others about which, though of less importance, he was inflexibly obstinate. He insisted that the money found through his means should be employed in his service. He proposed, therefore, that Tom should employ it in the black traffick; that is

to say, that he should fit out a slave-ship. This, however, Tom resolutely refused: he was bad enough in all conscience; but the devil himself could not tempt him to turn slave-trader.

Finding Tom so squeamish on this point, he did not insist upon it, but proposed, instead, that he should turn usurer; the devil being extremely anxious for the increase of usurers, looking upon them as his peculiar people.

To this no objections were made, for it was just to Tom's taste.

"You shall open a broker's shop in Boston next month," said the black man.

"I'll do it to-morrow, if you wish," said Tom Walker.

"You shall lend money at two per cent. a month."

"Egad, I'll charge four!" replied Tom Walker.

"You shall extort bonds, foreclose mortgages, drive the merchants to bankruptcy——"

"I'll drive them to the d——l," cried Tom Walker.

"You are the usurer for my money!" said black-legs with delight. "When will you want the rhino?"

"This very night."

"Done!" said the devil.

"Done!" said Tom Walker.—So they shook hands and struck a bargain.

A few days' time saw Tom Walker seated behind his desk in a counting-house in Boston.

His reputation for a ready-moneyed man, who would lend money out for a good consideration, soon spread abroad. Everybody remembers the time of Governor Belcher,[2] when money was particularly scarce. It was a time of paper credit. The country had been deluged with government bills; the famous Land Bank[3] had been established; there had been a rage for speculating; the people had run mad with schemes for new settlements; for building cities in the wilderness; land-jobbers went about with maps of grants, and townships, and Eldorados, lying nobody knew where, but which everybody was ready to purchase. In a word, the great speculating fever which breaks out every now and then in the country, had raged to an alarming degree, and everybody was dreaming of making sudden fortunes from nothing. As usual the fever had subsided; the dream had gone off, and the imaginary fortunes with it; the patients were left in doleful plight, and the whole country resounded with the consequent cry of "hard times."

2. **Governor Belcher:** Jonathan Belcher, governor of Massachusetts, 1730–41.   3. **Land Bank:** a bank of credit issuing notes against land security.

At this propitious time of public distress did Tom Walker set up as usurer in Boston. His door was soon thronged by customers. The needy and adventurous; the gambling speculator; the dreaming land-jobber; the thriftless tradesman; the merchant with cracked credit; in short, every one driven to raise money by desperate means and desperate sacrifices, hurried to Tom Walker.

Thus Tom was the universal friend of the needy, and acted like a "friend in need;" that is to say, he always exacted good pay and good security. In proportion to the distress of the applicant was the hardness of his terms. He accumulated bonds and mortgages; gradually squeezed his customers closer and closer: and sent them at length, dry as a sponge, from his door.

In this way he made money hand over hand; became a rich and mighty man, and exalted his cocked hat upon 'Change. He built himself, as usual, a vast house, out of ostentation; but left the greater part of it unfinished and unfurnished, out of parsimony. He even set up a carriage in the fulness of his vainglory, though he nearly starved the horses which drew it; and as the ungreased wheels groaned and screeched on the axle-trees, you would have thought you heard the souls of the poor debtors he was squeezing.

As Tom waxed old, however, he grew thoughtful. Having secured the good things of this world, he began to feel anxious about those of the next. He thought with regret on the bargain he had made with his black friend, and set his wits to work to cheat him out of the conditions. He became, therefore, all of a sudden, a violent churchgoer. He prayed loudly and strenuously, as if heaven were to be taken by force of lungs. Indeed, one might always tell when he had sinned most during the week, by the clamor of his Sunday devotion. The quiet Christians who had been modestly and steadfastly travelling Zionward, were struck with self-reproach at seeing themselves so suddenly outstripped in their career by this new-made convert. Tom was as rigid in religious as in money matters; he was a stern supervisor and censurer of his neighbors, and seemed to think every sin entered up to their account became a credit on his own side of the page. He even talked of the expediency of reviving the persecution of Quakers and Anabaptists. In a word, Tom's zeal become as notorious as his riches.

Still, in spite of all this strenuous attention to forms, Tom had a lurking dread that the devil, after all, would have his due. That he might not be taken unawares, therefore, it is said he always carried a small Bible in his coat-pocket. He had also a great folio Bible on his counting-house desk, and would frequently be found reading it when people called on business; on such occasions he would lay his green spectacles in the book, to mark the place, while he turned round to drive some usurious bargain.

Some say that Tom grew a little crack-brained in his old days, and that fancying his end approaching, he had his horse new shod, saddled and bridled, and buried with his feet uppermost; because he supposed that at the last day the world would be turned upside down; in which case he should find his horse standing ready for mounting, and he was determined at the worst to give his old friend a run for it. This, however, is probably a mere old wives' fable. If he really did take such a precaution, it was totally superfluous; at least so says the authentic old legend; which closes his story in the following manner.

One hot summer afternoon in the dog-days, just as a terrible black thundergust was coming up, Tom sat in his counting-house in his white linen cap and India silk morning-gown. He was on the point of foreclosing a mortgage, by which he would complete the ruin of an unlucky land speculator for whom he had professed the greatest friendship. The poor land-jobber begged him to grant a few months' indulgence. Tom had grown testy and irritated, and refused another day.

"My family will be ruined, and brought upon the parish," said the land-jobber. "Charity begins at home," replied Tom; "I must take care of myself in these hard times."

"You have made so much money out of me," said the speculator.

Tom lost his patience and his piety—"The devil take me," said he, "if I have made a farthing!"

Just then there were three loud knocks at the street door. He stepped out to see who was there. A black man was holding a black horse, which neighed and stamped with impatience.

"Tom, you're come for," said the black fellow, gruffly. Tom shrank back, but too late. He had left his little Bible at the bottom of his coat-pocket, and his big Bible on the desk buried under the mortgage he was about to foreclose: never was sinner taken more unawares. The black man whisked him like a child into the saddle, gave the horse the lash, and away he galloped, with Tom on his back, in the midst of the thunderstorm. The clerks stuck their pens behind their ears, and stared after him from the windows. Away went Tom Walker, dashing down the streets; his white cap bobbing up and down; his morning-gown fluttering in the wind, and his steed striking fire out of the pavement at every bound. When the clerks turned to look for the black man he had disappeared.

Tom Walker never returned to foreclose the mortgage. A countryman who lived on the border of the swamp, reported that in the height of the thundergust he had heard a great clattering of hoofs and a howling along the road, and running to the window caught sight of a figure, such as I have described, on a horse that galloped like mad across the fields, over the hills, and down into the black hemlock swamp towards the old Indian fort; and that shortly after a thunder-bolt falling in that direction seemed to set the whole forest in a blaze.

The good people of Boston shook their heads and shrugged their shoulders, but had been so much accustomed to witches and goblins, and tricks of the devil, in all kinds of shapes, from the first settlement of the colony, that they were not so much horror-struck as might have been expected. Trustees were appointed to take charge of Tom's effects. There was nothing, however, to administer upon. On searching his coffers all his bonds and mortgages were found reduced to cinders. In place of gold and silver his iron chest was filled with chips and shavings; two skeletons lay in his stable instead of his half-starved horses, and the very next day his great house took fire and was burnt to the ground.

Such was the end of Tom Walker and his ill-gotten wealth. Let all griping money-brokers lay this story to heart. The truth of it is not to be doubted. The very hole under the oak-trees, whence he dug Kidd's money, is to be seen to this day; and the neighboring swamp and old Indian fort are often haunted in stormy nights by a figure on horseback, in morning-gown and white cap, which is doubtless the troubled spirit of the usurer. In fact, the story has resolved itself into a proverb, and is the origin of that popular saying, so prevalent throughout New England, of "The Devil and Tom Walker."

*1825, 1849*

FROM

# A TOUR ON THE PRAIRIES

◊

❲ IRVING's one-month trip west of Fort Gibson, on the Neosho River in what is now Oklahoma, was made possible by Henry L. Ellsworth, newly appointed Indian Commissioner in the region, who invited the author and his two traveling companions, Charles Joseph La-

trobe and the Count de Pourtalès, to accompany him on an official tour of the Pawnee country in the fall of 1832. Ellsworth's party had as escort a contingent of United States Army Rangers.

The interval between Chapters 5 and 10 is two days.

◊

## CHAPTER 5

FRONTIER SCENES—A LYCURGUS OF THE BORDER—LYNCH'S LAW—THE DANGER OF FINDING A HORSE—THE YOUNG OSAGE

ON THE following morning (Oct. 11), we were on the march by half-past seven o'clock, and rode through deep rich bottoms of alluvial soil, overgrown with redundant vegetation, and trees of an enormous size. Our route lay parallel to the west bank of the Arkansas, on the borders of which river, near the confluence of the Red Fork, we expected to overtake the main body of rangers. For some miles the country was sprinkled with Creek villages and farm-houses; the inhabitants of which appeared to have adopted, with considerable facility, the rudiments of civilization, and to have thriven in consequence. Their farms were well stocked, and their houses had a look of comfort and abundance.

We met with numbers of them returning from one of their grand games of ball, for which their nation is celebrated. Some were on foot, some on horseback; the latter, occasionally, with gayly-dressed females behind them. They are a well-made race, muscular and closely knit, with well-turned thighs and legs. They have a Gipsy fondness for brilliant colors and gay decorations, and are bright and fanciful objects when seen at a distance on the prairies. One had a scarlet handkerchief bound round his head, surmounted with a tuft of black feathers like a cock's tail. Another had a white handkerchief, with red feathers; while a third, for want of a plume, had stuck in his turban a brilliant bunch of sumach.

On the verge of the wilderness we paused to inquire our way at a log house, owned by a white settler or squatter, a tall raw-boned old fellow, with red hair, a lank lantern visage, and an inveterate habit of winking with one eye, as if every thing he said was of knowing import. He was in a towering passion. One of his horses was missing; he was sure it had been stolen in the night by a straggling party of Osages encamped in a neighboring swamp; but he would have satisfaction! He would make an example of the villains. He had accordingly caught down his rifle from the wall, that invariable enforcer of right or wrong upon the frontiers, and, having saddled his steed, was about to sally forth on a foray into the swamp; while a brother squatter, with rifle in hand, stood ready to accompany him.

We endeavored to calm the old campaigner of the prairies, by suggesting that his horse might have strayed into the neighboring woods; but he had the frontier propensity to charge every thing to the Indians, and nothing could dissuade him from carrying fire and sword into the swamp.

After riding a few miles further we lost the trail of the main body of rangers, and became perplexed by a variety of tracks made by the Indians and settlers. At length coming to a log house, inhabited by a white man, the very last on the frontier, we found that we had wandered from our true course. Taking us back for some distance, he again brought us to the right trail; putting ourselves upon which, we took our final departure, and launched into the broad wilderness.

The trail kept on like a straggling footpath, over hill and dale, through brush and brake, and tangled thicket, and open prairie. In traversing the wilds it is customary for a party either of horse or foot to follow each other in single file like the Indians; so that the leaders break the way for those who follow, and lessen their labor and fatigue. In this way, also, the number of a party is concealed, the whole leaving but one narrow well trampled track to mark their course.

We had not long regained the trail, when, on emerging from a forest, we beheld our raw-boned, hard-winking, hard-riding knight-errant of the frontier, descending the slope of a hill, followed by his companion in arms. As he drew near to us, the gauntness of his figure and ruefulness of his aspect reminded me of the description of the hero of La Mancha,[1] and he was equally bent on affairs of doughty enterprise, being about to penetrate the thickets of the perilous swamp, within which the enemy lay ensconced.

While we were holding a parley with him on the slope of the hill, we descried an Osage on horseback issuing out of a skirt of wood about half a mile off, and leading a horse by a halter. The latter was immediately recognized by our hard-winking friend as the steed of which he was in quest. As the Osage drew near, I was struck with his appearance. He was about nineteen or twenty years of age, but well grown, with the fine Roman coun-

tenance common to his tribe, and as he rode with his blanket wrapped round his loins, his naked bust would have furnished a model for a statuary. He was mounted on a beautiful piebald horse, a mottled white and brown, of the wild breed of the prairies, decorated with a broad collar, from which hung in front a tuft of horse-hair dyed of a bright scarlet.

The youth rode slowly up to us with a frank open air, and signified by means of our interpreter Beatte,[2] that the horse he was leading had wandered to their camp, and he was now on his way to conduct him back to his owner.

I had expected to witness an expression of gratitude on the part of our hard-favored cavalier, but to my surprise the old fellow broke out into a furious passion. He declared that the Indians had carried off his horse in the night, with the intention of bringing him home in the morning, and claiming a reward for finding him; a common practice, as he affirmed, among the Indians. He was, therefore, for tying the young Indian to a tree and giving him a sound lashing; and was quite surprised at the burst of indignation which this novel mode of requiting a service drew from us. Such, however, is too often the administration of law on the frontier, "Lynch's law," as it is technically termed, in which the plaintiff is apt to be witness, jury, judge, and executioner, and the defendant to be convicted and punished on mere presumption; and in this way, I am convinced, are occasioned many of those heart-burnings and resentments among the Indians, which lead to retaliation, and end in Indian wars. When I compared the open, noble countenance and frank demeanor of the young Osage, with the sinister visage and high-handed conduct of the frontiersman, I felt little doubt on whose back a lash would be most meritoriously bestowed.

Being thus obliged to content himself with the recovery of his horse, without the pleasure of flogging the finder into the bargain, the old Lycurgus, or rather Draco, of the frontier, set off growling on his return homeward, followed by his brother squatter.

As for the youthful Osage, we were all prepossessed in his favor; the young Count[3] especially, with the sympathies proper to his age and incident to his character, had taken quite a fancy to him. Nothing would suit but he must have the young Osage as a companion and squire in his expedition into the wilderness. The youth was easily

---

A TOUR ON THE PRAIRIES. **Chapter 5.**  1. hero of La Mancha: Don Quixote.

2. **Beatte:** Pierre Beatte, half-breed hunter and guide to the party.  3. **Count:** Albert-Alexandre de Pourtales (1812–61), a Swiss, one of Irving's traveling companions. They had met on board ship on Irving's trip home in 1832.

tempted, and, with the prospect of a safe range over the buffalo prairies and the promise of a new blanket, he turned his bridle, left the swamp and the encampment of his friends behind him, and set off to follow the Count in his wanderings in quest of the Osage hunters.

Such is the glorious independence of man in a savage state. This youth, with his rifle, his blanket, and his horse, was ready at a moment's warning to rove the world; he carried all his worldly effects with him, and in the absence of artificial wants, possessed the great secret of personal freedom. We of society are slaves, not so much to others as to ourselves; our superfluities are the chains that bind us, impeding every movement of our bodies and thwarting every impulse of our souls. Such, at least, were my speculations at the time, though I am not sure but that they took their tone from the enthusiasm of the young Count, who seemed more enchanted than ever with the wild chivalry of the prairies, and talked of putting on the Indian dress and adopting the Indian habits during the time he hoped to pass with the Osages.

## CHAPTER 10

AMUSEMENTS IN THE CAMP—CONSULTA-TIONS—HUNTERS' FARE AND FEASTING —EVENING SCENES—CAMP MELODY —THE FATE OF AN AMATEUR OWL

ON RETURNING to the camp, we found it a scene of the greatest hilarity. Some of the rangers were shooting at a mark, others were leaping, wrestling, and playing at prison-bars.[1] They were mostly young men, on their first expedition, in high health and vigor, and buoyant with anticipations; and I can conceive nothing more likely to set the youthful blood into a flow than a wild wood-life of the kind, and the range of a magnificent wilderness, abounding with game, and fruitful of adventure. We send our youth abroad to grow luxurious and effeminate in Europe; it appears to me that a previous tour on the prairies would be more likely to produce that manliness, simplicity, and self-dependence most in unison with our political institutions.[2]

While the young men were engaged in these boisterous amusements, a graver set, composed of

the Captain,[3] the Doctor,[4] and other sages and leaders of the camp, were seated or stretched out on the grass, round a frontier map, holding a consultation about our position, and the course we were to pursue.

Our plan was to cross the Arkansas just above where the Red Fork falls into it, then to keep westerly, until we should pass through a grand belt of open forest, called the Cross Timber, which ranges nearly north and south from the Arkansas to Red River; after which we were to keep a southerly course towards the latter river.

Our half-breed, Beatte, being an experienced Osage hunter, was called into the consultation. "Have you ever hunted in this direction?" said the Captain. "Yes," was the laconic reply.

"Perhaps, then, you can tell us in which direction lies the Red Fork?"

"If you keep along yonder, by the edge of the prairie, you will come to a bald hill, with a pile of stones upon it."

"I have noticed that hill as I was hunting," said the Captain.

"Well! those stones were set up by the Osages as a landmark: from that spot you may have a sight of the Red Fork."

"In that case," cried the Captain, "we shall reach the Red Fork to-morrow; then cross the Arkansas above it, into the Pawnee country, and then in two days we shall crack buffalo bones!"

The idea of arriving at the adventurous hunting-grounds of the Pawnees, and of coming upon the traces of the buffaloes, made every eye sparkle with animation. Our further conversation was interrupted by the sharp report of a rifle at no great distance from the camp.

"That's old Ryan's rifle," exclaimed the Captain; "there's a buck down, I'll warrant!" nor was he mistaken; for, before long, the veteran made his appearance, calling upon one of the younger rangers to return with him, and aid in bringing home the carcass.

The surrounding country, in fact, abounded with game, so that the camp was overstocked with provisions, and, as no less than twenty bee-trees had been cut down in the vicinity, every one revelled in luxury. With the wasteful prodigality of hunters, there was a continual feasting, and scarce any one put by provision for the morrow. The cooking was conducted in hunters' style: the meat was stuck upon tapering spits of dogwood, which were thrust perpendicularly into the ground, so as to sustain the joint before the fire, where it was

Chapter 10.   1. prison-bars: the game of prisoner's base. 2. We . . . institutions: Irving's capacity for responding to the impressions of the moment makes him here begin to sound like Emerson in "The American Scholar" two years later.

3. Captain: Captain Jesse Bean, commander of the company of Rangers.   4. Doctor: Dr. David Holt, surgeon hired by the Army.

roasted or broiled with all its juices retained in it in a manner that would have tickled the palate of the most experienced gourmand. As much could not be said in favor of the bread. It was little more than a paste made of flour and water, and fried like fritters, in lard: though some adopted a ruder style, twisting it round the ends of sticks, and thus roasting it before the fire. In either way, I have found it extremely palatable on the prairies. No one knows the true relish of food until he has a hunter's appetite.

Before sunset, we were summoned by little Tonish [5] to a sumptuous repast. Blankets had been spread on the ground near to the fire, upon which we took our seats. A large dish, or bowl, made from the root of a maple-tree, and which we had purchased at the Indian village, was placed on the ground before us, and into it were emptied the contents of one of the camp-kettles, consisting of a wild turkey hashed, together with slices of bacon and lumps of dough. Beside it was placed another bowl of similar ware, containing an ample supply of fritters. After we had discussed [6] the hash, two wooden spits, on which the ribs of a fat buck were broiling before the fire, were removed and planted in the ground before us, with a triumphant air, by little Tonish. Having no dishes, we had to proceed in hunters' style, cutting off strips and slices with our hunting knives, and dipping them in salt and pepper. To do justice to Tonish's cookery, however, and to the keen sauce of the prairies, never have I tasted venison so delicious. With all this, our beverage was coffee, boiled in a camp-kettle, sweetened with brown sugar, and drunk out of tin cups: and such was the style of our banqueting throughout this expedition, whenever provisions were plenty, and as long as flour and coffee and sugar held out.

As the twilight thickened into night, the sentinels were marched forth to their stations around the camp: an indispensable precaution in a country infested by Indians. The encampment now presented a picturesque appearance. Camp-fires were blazing and smouldering here and there among the trees, with groups of rangers round them; some seated or lying on the ground, others standing in the ruddy glare of the flames, or in shadowy relief. At some of the fires there was much boisterous mirth, where peals of laughter were mingled with loud ribald jokes and uncouth exclamations; for the troop was evidently a raw, undisciplined band, levied among the wild youngsters of the frontier, who had enlisted, some for the sake of roving adventure, and some for the purpose of getting a knowledge of the country. Many of them were the neighbors of their officers, and accustomed to regard them with the familiarity of equals and companions. None of them had any idea of the restraint and decorum of a camp, or ambition to acquire a name for exactness in a profession in which they had no intention of continuing.

While this boisterous merriment prevailed at some of the fires, there suddenly rose a strain of nasal melody from another, at which a choir of "vocalists" were uniting their voices in a most lugubrious psalm-tune. This was led by one of the lieutenants; a tall, spare man, who we were informed had officiated as school-master, singing-master, and occasionally as Methodist preacher, in one of the villages of the frontier. The chant rose solemnly and sadly in the night air, and reminded me of the description of similar canticles in the camps of the Covenanters; and, indeed, the strange medley of figures and faces and uncouth garbs congregated together in our troop would not have disgraced the banners of Praise-God Barebones.[7]

In one of the intervals of this nasal psalmody an amateur owl, as if in competition, began his dreary hooting. Immediately there was a cry throughout the camp of "Charley's owl! Charley's owl!" It seems this "obscure bird" had visited the camp every night, and had been fired at by one of the sentinels, a half-witted lad named Charley; who, on being called up for firing when on duty, excused himself by saying, that he understood that owls made uncommonly good soup.

One of the young rangers mimicked the cry of this bird of wisdom, who, with a simplicity little consonant with his character, came hovering within sight, and alighted on the naked branch of a tree lit up by the blaze of our fire. The young Count immediately seized his fowling-piece, took fatal aim, and in a twinkling the poor bird of ill omen came fluttering to the ground. Charley was now called upon to make and eat his dish of owl-soup, but declined, as he had not shot the bird.

In the course of the evening I paid a visit to the Captain's fire. It was composed of huge trunks of trees, and of sufficient magnitude to roast a buffalo whole. Here were a number of the prime hunters and leaders of the camp, some sitting, some standing, and others lying on skins or blankets before

---

5. **Tonish:** Antoine Deshetres, Creole cook and general factotum, counterpart of Mateo in *The Alhambra*.  6. **discussed:** an ironic usage: investigated or tried the quality of; consumed.

7. **Praise-God Barebones:** Praisegod Barbon, or Barebone, a London leather-seller and Anabaptist preacher, noted for his long sermons. Cromwell's parliament of 1653, in which Barebone served, was named after him.

the fire, telling old frontier stories about hunting and Indian warfare.

As the night advanced, we perceived above the trees, to the west, a ruddy glow flushing up the sky.

"That must be a prairie set on fire by the Osage hunters," said the Captain.

"It is at the Red Fork," said Beatte, regarding the sky. "It seems but three miles distant, yet it perhaps is twenty."

About half-past eight o'clock, a beautiful pale light gradually sprang up in the east, a precursor of the rising moon. Drawing off from the Captain's lodge, I now prepared for the night's repose. I had determined to abandon the shelter of the tent, and henceforth to bivouac like the rangers. A bear-skin spread at the foot of a tree was my bed, with a pair of saddle-bags for a pillow. Wrapping myself in blankets, I stretched myself on this hunter's couch, and soon fell into a sound and sweet sleep, from which I did not awake until the bugle sounded at daybreak.

*1835, 1849*

MARIUS BEWLEY
*Editor*

---

# James Fenimore Cooper

1789–1851

# William Cullen Bryant

1794–1878

---

## James Fenimore Cooper

IT IS A commonplace of literary history that the 1850's represent the most brilliant period of achievement in American literature. *The Scarlet Letter, Moby-Dick, Walden,* and *Leaves of Grass,* to mention only the most obvious books, were produced during the first five years of the decade. The nineteenth century had seen nothing like it before, nor would it again as the nation moved through the Civil War into the genteel vulgarity of the Gilded Age. As we look back on the 1850's from the present time, the very magnitude of those achievements, which have given a characteristic stamp to the American literary sensibility, acts as a kind of watershed—dividing us from a remoter American past which one may be more inclined to visit from motives of historical interest than from any compelling sense of kinship. But in the case of James Fenimore Cooper, a kinship does exist.

Cooper died at the beginning of the 1850's, but there are aspects of his mind and writings that place him in a more direct relation-

ship with the great writers who came after him than with his strict contemporaries. Today he is commonly regarded as a writer of boys' books. As a recent American critic has pointed out, most of the great American classics may be regarded as boys' books. But this is only one way, and a very narrow way, of looking at them: and there is more than one way of looking at Cooper. Quantitatively, a good deal has been written about him in the past, but contemporary criticism, which has had so much to say about Melville and James, has tended to shy away from him. This is unfortunate, for there is a great deal in Cooper to repay scrutiny. With the exception of Hugh Henry Brackenridge, whose satirical novel on early American politics, *Modern Chivalry,* also goes unread, Cooper was the first American writer to use the novel form seriously as a vehicle of social and political criticism. He wished to argue and to communicate his ideas about society and American manners, politics, and economics. This new note of seriousness that he brought to his role as a novelist (even when he tried to disclaim it) was in itself a new recognition of the possibilities of fiction.

One of the functions and responsibilities of literature is to define nationality in the act of describing or dramatizing it. Without Shakespeare, Milton, Jane Austen, and Dickens, it is difficult to imagine that the English would know how to think and act like Englishmen. The novels of Cooper are an exercise in national definition. He sets out to tell his countrymen what it should be to think and act like an American, and if he is often too self-conscious in his mission, he nevertheless extends the range of our self-knowledge. In the great figure of Natty Bumppo he has given us a symbolic character who seems in ways almost mysterious to embody the very genius of America itself: at any rate, of that America stretching backward in time toward that early moment when, as Scott Fitzgerald said, "a fresh, green breast of the new world" presented man "for the last time in history with something commensurate to his capacity for wonder." It is essential that in an age of concrete and chrome the lines of imaginative communication with that earlier world should not be destroyed.

The American writer during the first half of the nineteenth century was in a vulnerable position. He was exposed to two dangers. He might be tempted to consider the whole idea of an American literature invalid and content himself with a servile imitation of English models. On the other hand, he might react in the opposite direction and think the United States culturally independent of the Old World, and so abandon himself to a suffocating literary provincialism. As the Connecticut poet, John Trumbull, put it much earlier in *An Essay on the Use and Advantages of the Fine Arts* (1770):

This land her Steele and Addison shall view,
The former glories equalled by the new;
Some future Shakespeare charm this rising age,
And hold in magic charm the listening page.

In either case there would have been little truth involved in the literature that resulted, and America would not have discovered her true image in such distorting mirrors.

It is a tribute to Cooper's intelligence that he successfully avoided these two pitfalls. His novels usually show a deep sympathy with his country, and a strong faith in its possibilities: but this is always accompanied by an insight into the limitations surrounding the conditions of life in America that prevents him from falling into the kind of inflationary writing that marred the work of many of his contemporaries. One of the characters in the late novel, *The Redskins*, makes a measured assessment of the American cultural scene that clarifies Cooper's lifelong attitude:

"Will New York ever be a capital? Yes—out of all question, yes. But the day will not come until after the sudden changes of condition which immediately and so naturally succeeded the revolution, have ceased to influence ordinary society, and those above again impart to those below more than they receive. This restoration to the natural state of things must take place as soon as society gets settled; and there will be nothing to prevent a town living under our own institutions—spirit, *tendencies*, and all—from obtaining the highest tone that ever yet prevailed in a capital. The folly is in anticipating the natural course of events. Nothing will more hasten these events, however, than a literature that is controlled, not by the lower, but by the higher opinion of the country; which literature is yet, in a great degree, to be created." [CHAP. 1]

This was written in 1846, shortly before the 1850's that were to go far toward creating such a literature as Cooper envisages here. The literature of that decade was no accident. More than a half-century of national history leads up to it, during which the foundations of a literary tradition were established. Without the substantial beginnings of such a tradition the later accomplishments would have been impossible, and it was Cooper who did more than any other writer to give it scope and dignity. He enlarged the function and range of the novel by making it an organ of serious intellectual criticism; he gave it a peculiarly national flavor by his celebration of American scenery and by his treatment of distinctively American problems. In some ways what Henry James was to say of Hawthorne might even more truthfully be said of Cooper: that he showed "to what a use

American matter could be put by an American hand: a consummation involving, it appeared, the happiest moral. For the moral was that an American could be an artist, one of the finest, without going 'outside' about it. . . ." Above all, the international reputation Cooper achieved as an artist lent a sense of security to a new literature that was both brash and unsure of itself.

The central preoccupation, seen under a variety of aspects, that troubles Cooper in his most representative novels is the threat to democracy in action as it exists in a country where traditional values are in the process of being supplanted by economic motives; where manners and cultural standards are in the process of being reduced to the lowest common denominator, and where the intolerant tyranny of the majority threatens the liberalism of the few. In an age vitiated by concepts of conformity, Cooper's better novels demonstrate the healthfulness of a patriotic subversiveness that does not regard flank-rubbing with the herd the most satisfactory form of social contact. Our age. has been described as one of mass civilization and minority culture. In *The American Democrat* (1838) Cooper had explained why democracies are especially prone to this cultural affliction:

The tendency of democracies is, in all things, to mediocrity, since the tastes, knowledge and principles of the majority form the tribunal of appeal. This circumstance, while it certainly serves to elevate the average qualities of a nation, renders the introduction of a high standard difficult. Thus do we find in literature, the arts, architecture and all acquired knowledge, a tendency in America to gravitate towards the common centre in this, as in other things; lending a value and estimation to mediocrity that are not elsewhere given. It is fair to expect, however, that a foundation so broad, may in time sustain a superstructure of commensurate proportions, and that the influence of masses will in this, as in other interests, have a generally beneficial effect. Still . . . the mass of no community is qualified to decide the most correctly on anything, which, in its nature, is above its reach. ["On the Disadvantages of Democracy"]

This recognition is pervasive throughout Cooper's books. It is an attitude that is easy to misinterpret unless it is focused in the full context of his political credo, and the Americans of his day did misinterpret it. "The most intense lover of his country," wrote Thomas R. Lounsbury, his first biographer, "he became the most unpopular man of letters to whom it has ever given birth." Cooper believed in the ascendency of the uncommon man, and today it would be unwise for us to forget our first major novelist who was centrally concerned in his work with a truth that has become even more urgent with the passage of time.

But it must be confessed that certain qualities in Cooper's prose militate against a widespread revival of interest in his work. At his best, Cooper is a great writer. When he describes the wilderness or the sea, few can surpass him. As Joseph Conrad said of him:

His descriptions have the magistral ampleness of a gesture indicating the sweep of a vast horizon. They embrace the colours of sunset, the peace of starlight, the aspects of storm and calm, the great loneliness of the waters, the stillness of watchful coasts. . . .[1]

But in local passages the prose is sometimes archaic and stilted, the dialogue wooden, the humor debatable. In the beginning, the reader must have patience and generous sympathy if he is to realize that Mark Twain's insulting essay, "The Literary Offenses of Fenimore Cooper," tells more about Twain's critical incapacity than it does about Cooper's limitations. In the end, one can do nothing better than remember Conrad's words: "He wrote before the great American language was born, and he wrote as well as any novelist of his time."

## II

A YEAR before he died, Cooper is reported to have said that "it takes a first class aristocrat to make a first class democrat." This might be taken as the motto of his life. It not only affected his practical political thinking to the end, but it left its mark on most of his writing, which was always a reflection of his deepest political and social convictions. It was to argue and further the cause of these

[1]Joseph Conrad, "Tales of the Sea," *Notes on Life and Letters* (1921).

convictions that it seemed worthwhile to him to write at all. There has sometimes been confusion about Cooper's politics because it has appeared to many literary historians that a man of his aristocratic predilections had no business being a Jacksonian Democrat, especially when his father had been one of the New York state partisan leaders of the Federalists—that party out of which the Whig party grew. One Cooper scholar put it this way a number of years ago:

Cooper was a country gentleman, a Whig squire. . . . He wanted to be and was loyal to the United States and its form of government, but his social ideals were in conflict with the "levelling" and "majority" tendencies present in Jacksonian America—a most uncomfortable time for a traditionalist!

But Cooper was never a Whig. He was, though perhaps with qualifications toward the end of his life, an ardent supporter of Jackson's policies, seeing in the Whig party a powerful oligarchy of vested interests based on business and financial speculation. In a political pamphlet attacking the Whigs, *A Letter to His Countrymen* (1834), Cooper described in general terms the political tendencies of his time, but he meant the application to be made to the Whigs in particular:

I had had abundant occasion to observe that the great political contest of the age was not, as is usually pretended, between the antagonist principles of monarchy and democracy, but in reality between those who, under the shallow pretence of limiting power to the *elite* of society, were contending for exclusive advantage at the expense of their fellow creatures.

In other words, Cooper in 1834 was very much in the position of the liberal of today who may well believe that standards must be maintained by a minority of informed and disciplined leaders, but who refuses to accept as an adequate substitute an "aristocracy" of intrenched capitalists intent on augmenting their own power and resources. Perhaps it would really be more accurate to describe Cooper as a Jeffersonian Demo-

crat, for his faith was in the land, and like Jefferson he envisaged America as a republic whose wealth consisted in farms and landed estates rather than in business and finance. It was natural that landed wealth should appear the best kind of wealth to him—in his boyhood he had lived with it under almost idyllic circumstances, or so it seemed when he looked back on those years from mature manhood. It seemed to him that the most precious human values attached themselves, in the course of time, to inherited property, and so were transmitted from one generation to the next. Land was the basis of social solidarity and the guarantee of social and cultural continuity. As opposed to wealth accumulated through business and financial speculation (the principal sources of Whig prosperity), landed property supported character, encouraged responsibility, and fostered tradition. Cooper knew this from the example of his father.

Judge William Cooper had been one of the most successful land agents of the Revolutionary years. By 1786 he had acquired 40,000 acres of land in western New York near Otsego Lake, and here, in 1790, he brought his family from New Jersey. The child James (Cooper took his mother's family name, Fenimore, only later in life) was then only thirteen months old. The mansion house which Judge Cooper soon built is described in a history of Cooperstown as "a great rectangular stone house with castellated roof and gothic windows, surrounded by box hedges and wide lawns trimmed precisely by black gardeners, far surpassing any other home in the far west." Growing up between the frontier freedom of the woods and the lake—the Glimmerglass of *The Deerslayer*—and the spacious ease of Otsego Hall with its retinue of slaves and servants, it is not remarkable that Cooper found his democratic and aristocratic propensities at mutual ease in later life.

Cooper's education was suitable for the son of a Congressman and the wealthiest man in his county. It culminated at Yale, from which he was expelled in his third year for an undistinguished undergraduate performance involving gunpowder in a keyhole and a donkey in the classroom. At home again, young Cooper had thoughts of the sea which his father, at this point, was willing to encourage. He sailed at first before the mast of a merchant vessel, and in 1808 entered the United States Navy as a midshipman. During these years he acquired that love of the sea and detailed knowledge of ships and sailing that enabled him to become the first great sea novelist before Conrad. By the time he resigned from the Navy in 1810 his father was dead, having been struck over the head by a political opponent, and Cooper himself was about to be married. He had chosen Miss Susan Augusta De Lancey, whose ancestors had distinguished themselves in the service of the king, and whose grandfather had been royal lieutenant governor of New York. The marriage was a happy one, and almost certainly his wife's upper-class Tory background confirmed those tendencies in Cooper's character that we have already noted.

At his father's death Cooper was very well off financially, but, for whatever reasons, within a few years his circumstances were considerably reduced. "Accident first made me a writer," Cooper once wrote, but the fact that it held out promise of financial reward undoubtedly encouraged him to continue on a course so casually begun. His first novel, *Precaution* (1820), was written as the result of a bet with his wife. Apparently he intended it to be an imitation of Jane Austen's *Persuasion*. It is not surprising that the future master of the American wilderness showed limited command of the English drawing room. His second novel, *The Spy* (1821), is one of the earliest of the American classics, and its success—8000 copies in four months—must have persuaded Cooper to continue in his new role. It is the story of a colonial family, the Whartons, living in Westchester during the Revolution, and the plot becomes a kind of debate in action between the American and the British points of view.

Cooper's third novel, *The Pioneers* (1823), sold 3500 copies on the day of publication. Natty Bumppo, who has been called the most memorable character in American fic-

tion, was first introduced in this novel. Cooper was to pursue Natty's career in the wilderness and on the prairies through four more books, but these must be discussed as a unit later. The same year saw *The Pilot*, the first of a series of sea stories in which Cooper drew on his naval experience. By this time he had become, with the possible exception of Irving, the best-known writer in America, both at home and abroad, and his income had been greatly augmented. He was now ready to fullfill an old ambition by taking his family to Europe. The extended visit lasted over seven years during which time Cooper, with characteristic but scarcely credible energy, published seven novels, a long book of American social criticism, *The Travelling Bachelor: or Notions of the Americans*, and collected the material for five travel books which he published shortly after his return in 1833. Cooper moved through Europe, not as an obscure American, but as a literary lion who was everywhere considered to be the peer of Sir Walter Scott. Lafayette was his friend, and through the American minister in Paris he secured entry into the most influential governing circles and fashionable coteries. He was an indefatigable observer of foreign manners and attitudes, and always a tireless champion of America. Yet it is probable that in subtle ways these splendid years in Europe disqualified him from ever happily settling down in the United States when he came home again.

Cooper returned to America with a more detached attitude than ever, determined to instruct his countrymen in the basic rudiments of what makes a *good* American. It is not altogether surprising that the Americans objected. The period of Cooper's popularity came to an end.

After the publication of *Homeward Bound*, a review of it appeared in the *North American Review* which indicates the new response:

Professing to be a sturdy republican, he has exhausted his powers of invective upon the manners and characters of his countrymen, who are, taking his own descriptions for truth, ignorant of the first principles of social refinement, and no better than a nation of brutes and savages. If such are the friends of Republicanism, she may well pray heaven to save her from them.

Cooper's admiration for aristocratic values came to a patriotic focus in his concept of the American gentleman. The American gentleman, so far as outward manners, spiritual refinement, and cultivated tastes went, ought not be distinguished from the finest flower of European nobility.

Alas, however, this was scarcely the breed of American Cooper found most in evidence when he returned home, and the two Effingham novels are filled with satiric portraits, often scathing and penetrating, of less admirable national types who will ring as painfully true as Sinclair Lewis' gallery. Cooper was always better when he attacked than when he praised. Here is a description of Mr. Steadfast Dodge:

Mr. Dodge came from that part of the country in which men were accustomed to think, act, almost to eat and drink and sleep, in common; or, in any other words, from one of those regions as in America, in which there was so much community, that few had the moral courage, even when they possessed the knowledge, and all the other necessary means, to cause their individuality to be respected. When the usual process of conventions, sub-conventions, caucuses, and public meetings did not supply the means of a "concentrated action," he and his neighbors had long been in the habit of having recourse to societies, by way of obtaining "energetic means," as it was termed; and from his tenth year up to his twenty-fifth, this gentleman had been either a president, vice-president, manager, or committee-man, of some philosophical, political, or religious expedient to fortify human wisdom, make men better, and resist error and despotism. His experience had rendered him expert in what may well enough be termed the language of association. No man of his years, in the twenty-six States, could more readily, apply the terms of "taking up"—"excitement"—"unqualified hostility"—"public opinion"—"spreading before the public"—or any other of those generic phrases that imply the privileges of all, and the rights of none.

[*Homeward Bound*, CHAP. 4]

After the long years abroad, Cooper was equipped to look at his countrymen with a sharper, more critical vision than he had possessed before. For Cooper a great protection against vulgar domination had been a landed gentry. From Colonial days New York had been dotted with large manorial estates of which the largest, Renesselaerwyck on the Hudson, comprised a million acres. Vast numbers of farmers rented small holdings on long leases from these great landlords for which, in addition to their yearly rent, they often performed services that were feudal in character. During the 1840's agitation became widespread in the state to force the large landowners to sell the farms outright to their tenants, and Anti-Rent societies that were formed had recourse to violence to prevent foreclosures and the collection of rents that had fallen in arrears.

Cooper wrote the Littlepage trilogy in defense of the landed gentry among whom he had grown up. After the Leatherstocking Tales, it is one of Cooper's most interesting achievements. These three novels, *Satanstoe, The Chainbearer,* and *The Redskins,* were all published in 1845 and 1846. They carry the story of the Littlepage family from colonial times through three generations, living on their landed estates or sometimes in Europe, down to Cooper's own day when such holdings were threatened by mob violence and by state law. For once Cooper had misjudged the situation. Whatever abuses the Anti-Rent agitators may have been guilty of, the land laws against which they were rebelling established wealth and poverty on a permanent basis. If the old system guaranteed that the great estates and the incomes deriving from them should be handed on from father to son, they guaranteed no less the continuity of poverty on the small, often stony and infertile holdings. Tenants frequently were able to escape from the terms of their leases only into absolute and hopeless poverty. Nor were the great landowners whom Cooper supported so bravely any longer the chivalric natural aristocracy which he seemed to remember from his youth. A fusion had already taken place between the great speculators and businessmen among the Whigs and the landed gentry of an earlier period. But Cooper was desperate in the middle forties to hold back that tidal wave of leveling influences which he saw sweeping everything before it. "The secret of this change among ourselves," he wrote in *The Redskins*, "is the innate dislike which is growing up in the country to see any man distinguished from the mass around him in anything, even though it should be in merit." Property appeared to be the last defense, and Cooper was ready to champion it, even on the most feudal of terms. "It is pretended the durable leases are feudal in their nature," he wrote. "We do not conceive this to be true; but, admitting it to be so, it would only prove that feudality, to this extent, is a part of the institutions of the state." It was an unfortunate position for a man of Cooper's liberal instincts and intelligence to find himself in, but in the total context of his thought it was understandable and forgivable. In any event, he was championing a lost cause. Nevertheless, the Littlepage trilogy remains a solid achievement.

Cooper died in 1851 on the eve of his sixty-second birthday. His life, so energetically lived, had been all of a piece, dedicated passionately to certain principles and ideals from which he never deviated for a moment in the face of that public opinion which he held in such contempt as the source of American weakness. It has been impossible to relate here the long history of Cooper's successful libel suits against the Whig newspaper editors of his day, who liked nothing more than to slander an important and articulate Jacksonian Democrat. He reduced them to glowering silence in the end. Cooper is a major artist in the American literary tradition, but not the least of his importance to us today is that he possessed, in a high degree, that beautiful attribute of being, in whatever he did, a seriously controversial figure.

### III

THE LEATHERSTOCKING TALES were written over a period of eighteen years, from 1823 when *The Pioneers* was published, to 1841 when *The Deerslayer* appeared. Nevertheless, an unusual consistency of tone and intention informs these five novels. This arises mainly from the character of Natty Bumppo, who also goes under the names of Deerslayer, Hawkeye, Pathfinder, and Leatherstocking. The creation of Leatherstocking is probably the most significant thing that happened in American literature during the first half-century of its national history. Leatherstocking belongs to that small group of fictional characters which includes Melville's Ishmael and Ahab, Huckleberry Finn, and perhaps Jay Gatsby, who seem to be related in some special way to the deepest meaning of the American experience itself. Critics have sometimes described these characters as "mythic," and for Leatherstocking they have often added the word "epic." D. H. Lawrence was among them when he said that the Leatherstocking books formed "a sort of American Odyssey, with Natty Bumppo for Odysseus." The "epic" quality of these novels is almost too obvious for comment. They create for us the primeval American wilderness as no art will ever be able to create it again. It is not, certainly, the wilderness as it ever existed, but a wilderness heroically imagined, belonging to a kind of American Golden Age. There is something undeniably Homeric about this faraway world of forest solitudes and more than life-size figures engaged in mortal combat: of Indians who have the bearing of ancient kings and can speak in poetry that would do no discredit to J. M. Synge's Irish peasants. It is a world of great but uncomplicated contrasts between cruelty and nobility, between the silence of endless woods and the sudden tumult of Indian ambuscade. All but one of the Leatherstocking Tales, *The Pioneers*, is concerned with bloody conflict, yet the fighting is always interpolated with passages of quiet beauty when that yet unspoiled American world glows on Cooper's pages like an earthly paradise.

By counterpointing his pattern of conflict and violence with scenes of forest loveliness, Cooper is not merely taking time out from action for descriptive detail. He is a master of pace and timing, and he disposes these blocks of prose in such way as to achieve the maximum of effect. The bloodcurdling cries of his savages are the more terrifying because he first creates with great artistry the awful stillness of the woods. Scenes of violence and bloodshed in Cooper are regularly followed by interludes in which the calmness of the natural world is reasserted, when the claims of battle and death give way for a time before the regenerative forces of life. It is Cooper's wonderful ability to handle these shifts of tone and viewpoint that is responsible for the sustained intensity of his actions through many chapters, and for the sense of universality he imparts so often to his incidents of forest warfare.

Cooper has a splendidly pictorial imagination that was fostered by his interest in painting. He has a habit of framing his scenes as if they were enclosed in a picture space, circumscribing the action on a visually composed stage with concentrated effect, and intensifying emotion by accents of color and skillfully deployed areas of light and shadow. Here is a night scene of an Indian encampment from *The Deerslayer* (1841) that Natty views from the safety of an offshore canoe which is concealed by darkness from the Indians themselves:

The canoe lay in front of a natural vista, not only through the bushes that lined the shore but of the trees also, that afforded a clear view of the camp. . . . In consequence of their recent change of ground, the Indians had not yet retired to their huts, but had been delayed by their preparations, which included lodging as well as food. A large fire had been made, as much to answer the purposes of torches, as for the use of their simple cookery, and at this precise moment it was blazing high and bright, having recently received a large supply of dried brush. The effect was to illuminate the arches of the forest, and to render the whole area occupied by the camp as light as if hundreds of tapers were burning. . . .

Deerslayer saw at a glance that many of the warriors were absent. His acquaintance, Rivenoak, however, was present, being seated in the foreground of a picture that Salvator Rosa would have delighted to draw, his swarthy features illuminated as much by pleasure as by the torch-like flame . . . A boy was looking over his shoulder, in dull curiosity, completing the group. More in the background, eight or ten warriors lay half re-

cumbent on the ground, or sat with their backs inclining against trees, so many types of indolent repose. Their arms were near them, sometimes leaning against the same tree as themselves, or were lying across their bodies, in indolent preparation.                                        [CHAP. 16]

Cooper handles this kind of composition almost plastically, and the result is not static, as one might fear. It confers on the action that occurs in such carefully composed scenes both tightness of form and an unforgettable theatricality. These novels are not meant to be realistic. Consider Chapter 30 from *The Deerslayer* in which the ex-pirate's beautiful daughter, Judith Hutter, attempts to rescue Deerslayer from the torture stake by emerging from the surrounding forests into the Indian encampment dressed in a magnificently regal brocade gown, which Cooper has gone to great pains in the plot to place at her disposal. The Indians are almost, but not quite, awed into submission by this glittering vision of majestic beauty. It makes no difference that the whole incident could scarcely have happened, at least in the way Cooper describes it. It has an imaginative quality that is like some ballet of the American wilderness. The scene is composed in the grand manner, and the accents of color are exactly right:

Objects became visible among the trees of the background, and a body of troops was seen advancing with measured tread. They came upon the charge, the scarlet of the king's livery shining among the bright green foliage of the forest.

But the mastery with which Cooper controls the rapid action of the Leatherstocking Tales would not in itself be enough to insure their preeminent status in American literature before the 1850's. The real source of their appeal and power lies in Natty Bumppo's character. It is as uncomplicated as the solitudes in which he dwells, as heroic as the actions he performs. Yet there is nothing primitive in his nature. Natty cannot read, but in contrast with this philosopher of the woods, the Effinghams themselves appear a little unsophisticated. Natty is never at a loss, for his wisdom seems as old as the continent, as enduring as the hills. At twenty-three in *The Deerslayer* (1841) he is as wise as he is in *The Prairie* (1827) when he is in his eighties. In his extraordinary death scene from that novel we feel that we are in the presence of some hero of the ancient world about to be raised to the status of an immortal.

Deerslayer can catch a tomahawk in mid-air and return it to the sender, and his feats of marksmanship with Killdeer, his rifle, have never been equaled. But it is not on these feats that Cooper builds up Natty's stature. Natty is a living incarnation of the natural moral law. One of the characters in *The Prairie* describes him in these words:

"The man I speak of was of great simplicity of mind, but of sterling worth. Unlike most of those who live a border life, he united the better, instead of the worst, qualities of the two people. He was a man endowed with the choicest and perhaps rarest gift of nature; that of distinguishing good from evil." [CHAP. 10]

It is not the least remarkable thing about the Leatherstocking Tales that, in the end, the reader actively and warmly shares this opinion of Natty. In attempting to present such a man, Cooper might have given us a prig and a bore; but, as D. H. Lawrence has said, Natty is a saint with a gun. His moralizing, without which he would not be Natty, is never offensive and rarely tedious. There is nothing righteous about Leatherstocking, but—and this is something quite different —an aura of goodness seems to invest this aloof but talkative celibate of the wilderness. It has seemed ironical to some that Natty, who shows more concern for the sanctity of life than any other great character in our literature, should be responsible, as hunter and fighter, for so many deaths. But the irony is in the facts of existence, not in Leatherstocking, and Chapter 7, in which Natty kills his first Indian, is an astonishing depiction of conscience struggling with brutal necessity. Natty's reverence for life is preserved through seas of blood, and the life-long effort involved renders it for us in the concrete. We observe it as an integral part

of Natty's character and behavior, even in the act of killing.

Related to this reverence for life is Leatherstocking's greatest gift, which is uniquely his among our fictional characters: a profound understanding, which goes deeper than generosity and tolerance, of the genius of race. Natty is always proud of his white "gifts," but by these he means nothing racist. The friendship between Natty and Chingachgook that runs through the five Leatherstocking Tales is symbolic of this deep understanding of "differences." Like Ishmael and Queequeg, like Huck and Jim, it is one of the great friendships of literature, and it exists because of, not in spite of, their contrasting "gifts."

Natty is a kind of tutelary spirit of the American land. It is essential to his conception that he should stand aloof and detached, with no closer, more enduring relation than his friendship for Chingachgook, who himself symbolizes the aboriginal life and culture of America. But if Cooper has created Natty in an almost mythic dimension, he has also succeeded in imparting great warmth to him, and a capacity for emotion without which his virtues might seem a little forbidding. It would have done violence to Cooper's conception of Leatherstocking to have given him a wife. There is something priestly about his role that domestic ties would have violated and rendered absurd. But in *The Pathfinder* (1840) Natty falls deeply and hopelessly in love. Cooper shows a sure control over his material here, for so far from appearing out of character, Natty's moral nature grows in stature. The final effect is to add still greater weight to the wisdom he embodies by showing as its human source a nature that is no less passionately than nobly alive.

Poised between love of America and disillusionment with her course, Cooper was able to create in Leatherstocking a symbolic character who resolved artistically the tension he had come to feel in himself between patriotic devotion and disaffection. In his old age, Leatherstocking flees to the western prairies to escape the advance of a civilization he distrusts as much as Cooper. In words that sound like Cooper's own, the old man says:

What the world of America is coming to, and where the machinations of its people are to end, the Lord, He only knows. . . . towns and villages, farms and highways, churches and schools, in short all the inventions and deviltries of man, are spread across the region.

Cooper had become deeply discouraged, but with the creation of Leatherstocking—particularly as presented in the last three novels—he expressed his ultimate, his only hope: that the wisdom of natural virtue and a purifying love of the land and forests and water might yet redeem the American from the selfishness of the settlements: by which he meant the greed for money and power that he felt was corrupting the Republic. Unlike the Effingham novels, the Leatherstocking Tales are not polemical. It is rather through poetry and discreetly symbolic action that they embody the complex tensions we have spoken of. And it is because they exist as art that they remain, both below and above the levels of conscious argument, the best vindication we have in his work of Cooper's deepest convictions.

Leatherstocking is a richly original creation, but the originality resides in the fact that Cooper was able to realize his conception with such mastery, creating him from the inside out. Leatherstocking is no lay figure dressed in a fringed green hunting shirt and a fur cap, but, as we have already said, he gives tangible form to Cooper's most searching quest for the meaning of American experience. He does not illustrate any set conclusions at which Cooper had already arrived when he began these novels. It would be more correct to say that Natty *is* Cooper's conclusion about the American world, its limitations and its possibilities, and that he arrived at it *in the process* of writing. All of Cooper's hopes and fears about America, his love and his disgust, are realized in this one symbolic character whose "great simplicity" is of that superlative kind that represents the resolution of opposed tensions in the transcendant unity of art.

# William Cullen Bryant

Bryant has been called the father of American poetry, and he probably deserves the title as much as such preposterous labels can ever be deserved. In 1821, when Bryant was twenty-seven years old, a small volume of eight of his poems was published in Cambridge. It contains some of his best work: "To a Waterfowl," "Inscription for the Entrance to a Wood," "The Yellow Violet," "Green River," and "Thanatopsis."

The attitudes toward nature in both Cooper and William Cullen Bryant appear nearly identical. Nature is the symbol of the Creator, the mighty Cause, the infinite Source. Nature, for Bryant, is a temple, and the metaphor is carried out in some detail, especially in the first stanza of "A Forest Hymn" (see p. 174): the forest trees are venerable columns, the forest paths are winding aisles, the overarching branches are dim vaults. In this solemn cathedral atmosphere the heart is filled with awe of the "Maker." Bryant uses the term advisedly, for nature is an artifact whose purpose is to keep man's mind directed to the Supreme Craftsman. Nature should impart moral instruction, and it should elevate; but it should also be able to keep man suitably depressed, on occasion, with its lessons of decay and death:

Written on thy works I read
The lesson of thy own eternity.
Lo! all grow old and die. . . .

To communicate this moral lesson, which he never substantially enlarged in his poetry after composing the first version of "Thanatopsis" at the age of seventeen, Bryant developed a sonorous blank verse that, for short passages, can be remarkably effective. But its effect depends too much on sound alone, which cannot in the end compensate for the usual commonplaceness of its imagery. Bryant is orotund without magniloquence, and if we read "Thanatopsis" with a subdued and valid pleasure, to follow this by, say, "Hymn to Death," "The Antiquity of Freedom," "An Evening Revery," "A Forest

Hymn," and "The Flood of Years," becomes a little like listening to a harmonium with the pedal stuck.

Natty also looks upon the woods as a temple which everywhere bears the impress "of the divine hand of their Creator." In a passage from *The Deerslayer* in which Natty is speaking to Judith Hutter, we find a concentration of themes which both Cooper and Bryant share with their time:

"As for farms, they have their uses, and there's them that like to pass their lives on 'em; but what comfort can a man look for in a clearin', that he can't find in double quantities in the forest? If air, and room, and light, are a little craved, the windrows and the streams will furnish 'em, or here are the lakes for such as have bigger longings in that way; but where are you to find your shades and laughing springs, and leaping brooks, and vinerable trees, a thousand years old, in a clearin'? You don't find *them*, but you find their disabled trunks, marking the 'arth like headstones in a graveyard. It seems to me that the people who live in such places must be always thinkin' of their own inds, and of universal decay that is brought about by time and natur', but the decay that follows waste and violence. They call 'em the temples of the Lord; but, Judith, the whole 'arth is a temple of the Lord to such as have the right mind." [CHAP. 15]

The decay of nature—the mutability theme —is a favorite one with Bryant. His sonnet, "Mutation," is inferior to Wordsworth's "mutability" sonnet, but not greatly so:

They talk of short-lived pleasure—be it so—
  Pain dies as quickly: stern, hard-featured pain
Expires, and lets her weary prisoner go.
  The fiercest agonies have shortest reign;
  And after dreams of horror, comes again
The welcome morning with its rays of peace.
  Oblivion, softly wiping out the stain,
Makes the strong secret pangs of shame to cease.
Remorse is virtue's root; its fair increase
  Are fruits of innocence and blessedness:
Thus joy, o'erborne and bound, doth still release
  His young limbs from the chains that round
    him press.
Weep not that the world changes—did it keep
A stable, changeless state, 'twere cause indeed to
  weep.

Generations and civilizations are born, flourish, decay, and die. This endlessly repeated cycle should teach us to look behind the passing show for that which alone is immutable and eternal, and which reverberates through Bryant's poetry as a kind of Supreme Abstraction personified. Bryant repeatedly, like many other writers and painters of his generation, invoked the vanished Indian civilization as an example of the transitoriness of earthly things, and he liked nothing better than to point out, as in the concluding stanzas of "An Indian at the Burial-Place of His Fathers" (see p. 173), that as they are now, so we shall be. Mutability is a universal theme in literature, and to see what magnificent things American poets would do with it later, one should consider Whitman's "Song of Myself," or "When Lilacs Last in the Dooryard Bloom'd," or Wallace Stevens' "Sunday Morning," or even Emily Dickinson's "The Chariot." Why then does Bryant's treatment of the theme seem so thin to us? For one thing, he characteristically approaches it under the aspect of death, and Bryant's attitude to death was a little morbid, immature, and imaginatively delimiting. Frail health in his youth, combined with an enthusiasm for the graveyard school of poetry, did a good deal of damage. But more important is the fact that Bryant's poetry rarely seems to be in touch with his vital interest in life. Poetry often seems for Bryant something hallowed and set apart, like a best parlor filled with marmoreal statuary that is only opened up on Sundays. It is a little difficult to speak naturally or breathe very deeply in it.

This is sad because Bryant was one of the most worthwhile men of his generation, intelligent and beautifully generous, and courageous enough physically to thrash William Leete Stone, the editor of the New York *Commercial Advertiser*, with a cowhide whip on Broadway for some insulting anti-Jackson statements he had published. Bryant was the editor of the New York *Evening Post* for half a century, from 1829 until his death in 1878, and his editorial record is one of distinguished liberalism. He was an ardent Jacksonian Democrat until the slavery question drove him temporarily into the ranks of the

Republicans, and in 1860 his editorials, by influencing New York opinion, greatly assisted the nomination of Lincoln. Parrington, in his excellent sketch of Bryant in *Main Currents in American Thought* (1927–30), says that a serious injustice has been done to him because critics have neglected the liberal journalist for "the youthful versifier who described American scenery." This may be true, but unfortunately we must contribute to that injustice here.

From several of our quotations it is clear that Bryant and Cooper shared certain central attitudes in common beyond the fact that they were both Democrats. Nevertheless, there were differences. Cooper, with no editorial outlet to express his political convictions or assuage the intensity of his feelings about America, poured them creatively into his novels. Even when Leatherstocking is expressing conventionally held views about nature and mutability and the infinite Source which are indistinguishable in substance from Bryant's, we never confuse them. If Natty as a symbolic character is partly forged from certain current attitudes, those attitudes are metamorphosed by Cooper in the process of creatively imagining Natty into something original and new and closely related to life. The Leatherstocking Tales grow directly out of Cooper's passionate concern with life; and where could he express that concern, being neither an active politician nor a newspaper editor, except in his art? On the other hand, Bryant tends to withdraw in his poems from the real field of his later interest, which is politics and journalism, into a genteel heaven of moral sublimity that is as unrelated to life as Bryant's daily editorial tasks were intimately a part of it. The result is that Cooper gives us major art, at least in the Leatherstocking novels, and Bryant gives us conventional, rather bloodless verse.

Bryant's was a limited genius. "To a Waterfowl" is a superb poem, and there are others as well. But something went wrong somewhere. Many of his poems are combinations of highly successful passages with sandy tracts.

It is easy to denigrate Bryant's poetry, as Poe confessed as long ago as 1846 in a criticism that is still pertinent:

But although it may be said, in general, that Mr. Bryant's position is *comparatively* well settled, still for some time past there has been a growing tendency to underestimate him. . . .

It will never do to claim for Bryant a genius of the loftiest order, but there has been latterly. . . . a growing disposition to deny him genius in any respect. He is now commonly spoken of as "a man of high poetical *talent*, very 'correct,' with a warm appreciation of the beauty of nature and great descriptive powers, but rather too much of the old-school manner of Cowper, Goldsmith, and Young." This is the truth, but not the whole truth. Mr. Bryant has genius, and that of a marked character, but it has been overlooked by modern schools, because deficient in those externals which have become in a measure symbolical of those schools.

Nevertheless, to appreciate Bryant's achievement, one has only to consider American poetry up to that point. The early Puritans, when they wrote poetry at all, wrote in an older European tradition. If we make a large exception of Philip Freneau, the American neoclassic poets (by whom we mean chiefly the Connecticut Wits) wrote competent but uninspired imitations of Pope and the later English eighteenth-century poets. In such a tradition, Bryant's poetry represented the most solid and refreshing work that had so far been produced by an American poet. The reverberations of his more solemn music, in those interminable forest aisles of his, tend to drown out his better poems, but if we listen long and hard, some sweet, distinguished notes come through.

# James Fenimore Cooper

FROM

## THE LEATHERSTOCKING TALES

❖

❲ IT IS NOT commonly a satisfactory procedure to offer excerpts from novels in an anthology. But aside from the fact that Cooper leaves us no alternative if he is to be presented at all in the role of artist, the Leatherstocking Tales are primarily concerned with the presentation of a character, Natty Bumppo, whose essential meaning may be grasped by considering a number of episodes and scenes from his life detached from the specific plot or sequence of events in which they occur. In Section III of the Introduction we have tried to suggest what this meaning is. Perhaps we might go so far as to say that Cooper's conception of Leatherstocking anticipates in practice Matthew Arnold's description of poetry as a criticism of life, for that is really Leatherstocking's final effect on us. We have chosen most of the selections from *The Deerslayer*, and in this one instance some attempt has been made to convey an idea of the total action by means of interpolated synopses of omitted chapters.

The dates of the Leatherstocking Tales are: 1823, *The Pioneers*; 1826, *The Last of the Mohicans*; 1827, *The Prairie*; 1840, *The Pathfinder*; and 1841, *The Deerslayer*. Our excerpts are presented in the chronological order of Leatherstocking's life, not in the chronological order in which Cooper wrote them. It is the last of these novels that shows Natty to us for the first time as a young man. This is probably the best of the Leatherstocking Tales, and Cooper's conception of Natty is here brought to its most rounded statement. As James Grossman says in his life of Cooper: "Time has mercifully run backward for Natty Bumppo and Chingachgook, and they are half a century younger than when we met them on this very spot in *The Pioneers*." Cooper's order of composition leaves us with a sense of Natty's immortal youth, and this is the way it ought to be.

❖

FROM

## THE DEERSLAYER

### CHAPTER 1

ON the human imagination events produce the effects of time. Thus, he who has travelled far and seen much is apt to fancy that he has lived long and the history that most abounds in important incidents soonest assumes the aspect of antiquity. In no other way can we account for the venerable air that is already gathering around American annals. When the mind reverts to the earliest days of colonial history, the period seems remote and obscure, the thousand changes that thicken along the links of recollections, throwing back the origin of the nation to a day so distant as seemingly to reach the mists of time; and yet four lives of ordinary duration would suffice to transmit, from mouth to mouth, in the form of tradition, all that civilized man has achieved within the limits of the republic. Although New York alone possesses a population materially exceeding that of either of the four smallest kingdoms of Europe, or materially exceeding that of the entire Swiss Confederation, it is little more than two centuries since the Dutch commenced their settlement, rescuing the region from the savage state. Thus, what seems venerable by an accumulation of changes is reduced to familiarity when we come seriously to consider it solely in connection with time.

This glance into the perspective of the past will prepare the reader to look at the pictures we are about to sketch, with less surprise than he might otherwise feel; and a few additional explanations may carry him back in imagination to the precise condition of society that we desire to delineate. It is matter of history that the settlements on the eastern shores of the Hudson, such as Claverack, Kinderhook, and even Poughkeepsie, were not regarded as safe from Indian incursions a century since; and there is still standing on the banks of the same river, and within musket-shot of the wharves of Albany, a residence of a younger branch [1] of the Van Rensselaers, that has loopholes constructed for defence against the same crafty enemy, although it dates from a period scarcely so distant. Other similar memorials of the infancy of the country are to be found, scattered through what is now deemed the very centre of American civilization, affording the plainest proofs that all we possess of security from invasion and hostile violence is the growth of but little more than the time that is frequently filled by a single human life.

THE DEERSLAYER.   1. "It is no more than justice to say that the Greenbush Van Rensselaers claim to be the oldest branch of that ancient and respectable family" [Cooper's note].

The incidents of this tale occurred between the years 1740 and 1745, when the settled portions of the colony of New York were confined to the four Atlantic counties, a narrow belt of country on each side of the Hudson, extending from its mouth to the falls near its head, and to a few advanced "neighborhoods" on the Mohawk and the Schoharie. Broad belts of the virgin wilderness not only reached the shores of the first river, but they even crossed it, stretching away into New England, and affording forest covers to the noise-less moccasin of the native warrior, as he trod the secret and bloody war-path. A bird's-eye view of the whole region east of the Mississippi must then have offered one vast expanse of woods, relieved by a comparatively narrow fringe of cultivation along the sea, dotted by the glittering surfaces of lakes, and intersected by the waving lines of river. In such a vast picture of solemn solitude, the district of country we design to paint sinks into insignificance, though we feel encouraged to proceed by the conviction that, with slight and immaterial distinctions, he who succeeds in giving an accurate idea of any portion of this wild region must necessarily convey a tolerably correct notion of the whole.

Whatever may be the changes produced by man, the eternal round of the seasons is unbroken. Summer and winter, seed-time and harvest, return in their stated order with a sublime precision, affording to man one of the noblest of all the occasions he enjoys of proving the high powers of his far-reaching mind, in compassing the laws that control their exact uniformity, and in calculating their never-ending revolutions. Centuries of summer suns had warmed the tops of the same noble oaks and pines, sending their heats even to the tenacious roots, when voices were heard calling to each other, in the depths of a forest, of which the leafy surface lay bathed in the brilliant light of a cloudless day in June, while the trunks of the trees rose in gloomy grandeur in the shades beneath. The calls were in different tones, evidently proceeding from two men who had lost their way, and were searching in different directions for their path. At length a shout proclaimed success, and presently a man of gigantic mould broke out of the tangled labyrinth of a small swamp, emerging into an opening that appeared to have been formed partly by the ravages of the wind, and partly by those of fire. This little area, which afforded a good view of the sky, although it was pretty well filled with dead trees, lay on the side of one of the high hills, or low mountains, into which nearly the whole surface of the adjacent country was broken.

"Here is room to breathe in!" exclaimed the liberated forester, as soon as he found himself under a clear sky, shaking his huge frame like a mastiff that has just escaped from a snowbank. "Hurrah! Deerslayer; here is daylight, at last, and yonder is the lake."

These words were scarcely uttered when the second forester dashed aside the bushes of the swamp, and appeared in the area. After making a hurried adjustment of his arms and disordered dress, he joined his companion, who had already begun his disposition for a halt.

"Do you know this spot?" demanded the one called Deerslayer, "or do you shout at the sight of the sun?"

"Both, lad, both; I know the spot, and am not sorry to see so useful a fri'nd as the sun. Now we have got the p'ints of the compass in our minds once more, and 't will be our own faults if we let anything turn them topsy-turvy ag'in, as has just happened. My name is not Hurry Harry, if this be not the very spot where the land-hunters 'camped the last summer, and passed a week. See! yonder are the dead bushes of their bower, and here is the spring. Much as I like the sun, boy, I've no occasion for it to tell me it is noon; this stomach of mine is as good a time-piece as is to be found in the colony, and it already p'ints to half-past twelve. So open the wallet, and let us wind up for another six hours' run."

At this suggestion, both set themselves about making the preparations necessary for their usual frugal but hearty meal. We will profit by this pause in the discourse to give the reader some idea of the appearance of the men, each of whom is destined to enact no insignificant part in our legend. It would not have been easy to find a more noble specimen of vigorous manhood than was offered in the person of him who called himself Hurry Harry. His real name was Henry March; but the frontiermen having caught the practice of giving *sobriquets* from the Indians, the appellation of Hurry was far oftener applied to him than his proper designation, and not unfrequently he was termed Hurry Skurry, a nickname he had obtained from a dashing, reckless, off-hand manner, and a physical restlessness that kept him so constantly on the move, as to cause him to be known along the whole line of scattered habitations that lay between the province and the Canadas. The stature of Hurry Harry exceeded six feet four, and being unusually well proportioned, his strength fully realized the idea created by his gigantic frame. The face did no discredit to the rest of the man, for it was both good-humored and handsome. His air was free, and though his manner necessarily partook of the rudeness of a border life, the grandeur that pervaded so noble a physique prevented it from becoming altogether vulgar.

Deerslayer, as Hurry called his companion, was a very different person in appearance, as well as in character. In stature he stood about six feet in his moccasins, but his frame was comparatively light and slender, showing muscles, however, that promised unusual agility, if not unusual strength. His face would have had little to recommend it except youth, were it not for an expression that seldom failed to win upon those who had leisure to examine it, and to yield to the feeling of confidence it created. This expression was simply that of guileless truth, sustained by an earnestness of purpose, and a sincerity of feeling, that rendered it remarkable. At times this air of integrity seemed to be so simple as to awaken the suspicion of a want of the usual means to discriminate between artifice and truth; but few came in serious contact with the man, without losing this distrust in respect for his opinions and motives.

Both these frontiermen were still young, Hurry having reached the age of six or eight and twenty, while Deerslayer was several years his junior. Their attire needs no particular description, though it may be well to add that it was composed in no small degree of dressed deer-skins, and had the usual signs of belonging to those who pass their time between the skirts of civilized society and the boundless forests. There was, notwithstanding, some attention to smartness and the picturesque in the arrangements of Deerslayer's dress, more particularly in the part connected with his arms and accoutrements. His rifle was in perfect condition, the handle of his hunting-knife was neatly carved, his powder-horn was ornamented with suitable devices lightly cut into the material, and his shot-pouch was decorated with wampum. On the other hand, Hurry Harry, either from constitutional recklessness, or from a secret consciousness how little his appearance required artificial aids, wore everything in a careless, slovenly manner, as if he felt a noble scorn for the trifling accessories of dress and ornaments. Perhaps the peculiar effect of his fine form and great stature was increased rather than lessened, by this unstudied and disdainful air of indifference.

"Come, Deerslayer, fall to, and prove that you have a Delaware stomach, as you say you have had a Delaware edication," cried Hurry, setting the example by opening his mouth to receive a slice of cold venison steak that would have made an entire meal for a European peasant; "fall to, lad, and prove your manhood on this poor devil of a doe with your teeth, as you've already done with your rifle."

"Nay, nay, Hurry, there's little manhood in killing a doe, and that too out of season; though there might be some in bringing down a painter or a catamount," returned the other, disposing himself to comply. "The Delawares have given me my name, not so much on account of a bold heart, as on account of a quick eye, and an actyve foot. There may not be any cowardyce in overcoming a deer, but sartain it is, there's no great valor."

"The Delawares themselves are no heroes," muttered Hurry through his teeth, the mouth being too full to permit it to be fairly opened, "or they would never have allowed them loping vagabonds, the Mingos, to make them women."

"That matter is not rightly understood—has never been rightly explained," said Deerslayer earnestly, for he was as zealous a friend as his companion was dangerous as an enemy; "the Mengwe fill the woods with their lies, and misconstruct words and treaties. I have now lived ten years with the Delawares, and know them to be as manful as any other nation, when the proper time to strike comes."

"Harkee, Master Deerslayer, since we are on the subject, we may as well open our minds to each other in a man-to-man way; answer me one question; you have had so much luck among the game as to have gotten a title, it would seem, but did you ever hit anything human or intelligible: did you ever pull trigger on an inimy that was capable of pulling one upon you?"

This question produced a singular collision between mortification and correct feeling, in the bosom of the youth, that was easily to be traced in the workings of his ingenuous countenance. The struggle was short, however; uprightness of heart soon getting the better of false pride and frontier boastfulness.

"To own the truth, I never did," answered Deerslayer; "seeing that a fitting occasion never offered. The Delawares have been peaceable since my sojourn with 'em, and I hold it to be onlawful to take the life of man, except in open and generous warfare."

"What! did you never find a fellow thieving among your traps and skins, and do the law on him with your own hands, by way of saving the magistrates trouble in the settlements, and the rogue himself the cost of the suit?"

"I am no trapper, Hurry," returned the young man proudly: "I live by the rifle, a we'pon at which I will not turn my back on any man of my years, atween the Hudson and the St. Lawrence. I never offer a skin that has not a hole in its head besides them which natur' made to see with or to breathe through."

"Ay, ay, this is all very well, in the animal way, though it makes but a poor figure alongside of scalps and ambushes. Shooting an Indian from an ambush is acting up to his own principles, and now we have what you call a lawful war on our hands, the sooner you wipe that disgrace off your character, the sounder will be your sleep; if it only come from knowing there is one inimy the less prowling in the woods. I shall not frequent your society long, friend Natty, unless you look higher than four-footed beasts to practyse your rifle on."

"Our journey is nearly ended, you say, Master March, and we can part to-night, if you see occasion. I have a fri'nd waiting for me, who will think it no disgrace to consort with a fellow-creatur' that has never yet slain his kind."

"I wish I knew what has brought that skulking Delaware into this part of the country so early in the season," muttered Hurry to himself, in a way to show equally distrust and a recklessness of its betrayal. "Where did you say the young chief was to give you the meeting?"

"At a small round rock, near the foot of the lake, where, they tell me, the tribes are given to resorting to make their treaties, and to bury their hatchets. This rock have I often heard the Delawares mention, though lake and rock are equally strangers to me. The country is claimed by both Mingos and Mohicans, and is a sort of common territory to fish and hunt through, in time of peace, though what it may become in war-time, the Lord only knows!"

"Common territory!" exclaimed Hurry, laughing aloud. "I should like to know what Floating Tom Hutter would say to that? He claims the lake as his own property, in vartue of fifteen years' possession, and will not be likely to give it up to either Mingo or Delaware without a battle for it."

"And what will the colony say to such a quarrel? All this country must have some owner, the gentry pushing their cravings into the wilderness, even where they never dare to ventur', in their own persons, to look at the land they own."

"That may do in other quarters of the colony, Deerslayer, but it will not do here. Not a human being, the Lord excepted, owns a foot of sile in this part of the country. Pen was never put to paper consarning either hill or valley hereaway, as I've heard old Tom say time and ag'in, and so he claims the best right to it of any man breath-

ing; and what Tom claims, he'll be very like to maintain."

"By what I've heard you say, Hurry, this Floating Tom must be an oncommon mortal; neither Mingo, Delaware, nor pale-face. His possession, too, has been long, by your tell, and altogether beyond frontier endurance. What's the man's history and natur'?"

"Why, as to old Tom's human natur', it is not much like other men's human natur', but more like a muskrat's human natur', seeing that he takes more to the ways of that animal than to the ways of any other fellow-creatur'. Some think he was a free liver on the salt water, in his youth, and a companion of a sartain Kidd, who was hanged for piracy, long afore you and I were born or acquainted, and that he came up into these regions, thinking that the king's cruisers could never cross the mountains, and that he might enjoy the plunder peaceably in the woods."

"Then he was wrong, Hurry; very wrong. A man can enjoy plunder *peaceably* nowhere."

"That's much as his turn of mind may happen to be. I've known them that never could enjoy it at all, unless it was in the midst of a jollification, and them ag'in that enjoyed it best in a corner. Some men have no peace if they don't find plunder, and some if they do. Human natur' is crooked in these matters. Old Tom seems to belong to neither set, as he enjoys his, if plunder he has really got, with his darters, in a very quiet and comfortably way, and wishes for no more."

"Ay, he has darters, too; I've heard the Delawares who've hunted this a way, tell their histories of these young women. Is there no mother, Hurry?"

"There was *once,* as in reason; but she has now been dead and sunk these two good years."

"Anan?" said Deerslayer, looking up at his companion in a little surprise.

"Dead and sunk, I say, and I hope that's good English. The old fellow lowered his wife into the lake, by way of seeing the last of her, as I can testify, being an eye-witness of the ceremony; but whether Tom did it to save digging, which is no easy job among roots, or out of a consait that water washes away sin sooner than 'arth, is more than I can say."

"Was the poor woman oncommon wicked, that her husband should take so much pains with her body?"

"Not onreasonable; though she had her faults. I consider Judith Hutter to have been as graceful, and about as likely to make a good ind as any woman who had lived so long beyond the sound of church bells; and I conclude old Tom sunk her as much by way of *saving* pains, as by way of *taking* it. There was a little steel in her temper, it's true, and, as old Hutter is pretty much flint, they struck out sparks once-and-a-while; but, on the whole, they might be said to live amicable like. When they did kindle, the listeners got some such insights into their past lives, as one gets into the darker parts of the woods, when a stray gleam of sunshine finds its way down to the roots of the trees. But Judith I shall always esteem, as it's recommend enough to one woman to be the mother of such a creatur' as her darter, Judith Hutter!"

"Ay, Judith was the name the Delawares mentioned, though it was pronounced after a fashion of their own. From their discourse, I do not think the girl would much please my fancy."

"Thy fancy!" exclaimed March, taking fire equally at the indifference and at the presumption of his companion, "what the devil have you to do with a fancy, and that, too, consarning one like Judith? You are but a boy—a sapling, that has scarce got root. Judith has had *men* among her suitors, ever since she was fifteen; which is now near five years; and will not be apt even to cast a look upon a half-grown creatur' like you!"

"It is June, and there is not a cloud atween us and the sun, Hurry, so all this heat is not wanted," answered the other, altogether undisturbed; "any one may have a fancy, and a squirrel has a right to make up his mind touching a catamount."

"Ay, but it might not be wise, always, to let the catamount know it," growled March. "But you're young and thoughtless, and I'll overlook your ignorance. Come, Deerslayer," he added, with a good-natured laugh, after pausing a moment to reflect, "come, Deerslayer, we are sworn fri'nds, and will not quarrel about a light-minded, jilting jade, just because she happens to be handsome; more especially as you have never seen her. Judith is only for a man whose teeth show the full marks, and it's foolish to be afeard of a boy. What *did* the Delawares say of the hussy? for an Indian, after all, has his notions of womankind, as well as a white man."

"They said she was fair to look on, and pleasant of speech; but over-given to admirers, and light-minded."

"They are devils incarnate! After all, what schoolmaster is a match for an Indian, in looking into natur'? Some people think they are only good on a trail or the war-path, but I say that they are philosophers, and understand a man as well as they understand a beaver, and a woman as well as they understand either. Now that's Judith's character to a ribbon! To own the truth to you,

Deerslayer, I should have married the gal two years since, if it had not been for two particular things, one of which was this very light-mindedness."

"And what may have been the other?" demanded the hunter, who continued to eat like one that took very little interest in the subject.

"T'other was an insartainty about her having *me*. The hussy is handsome, and she knows it. Boy, not a tree that is growing in these hills is straighter, or waves in the wind with an easier bend, nor did you ever see the doe that bounded with a more nat'ral motion. If that was all, every tongue would sound her praises; but she has such failings that I find it hard to overlook them, and sometimes I swear I'll never visit the lake ag'in."

"Which is the reason that you always come back? Nothing is ever made more sure by swearing about it."

"Ah, Deerslayer, you are a novelty in these partic'lars; keeping as true to edication as if you had never left the settlements. With me the case is different, and I never want to clinch an idee, that I do not feel a wish to swear about it. If you know'd all that I know consarning Judith, you'd find a justification for a little cussing. Now, the officers sometimes stray over to the lake, from the forts on the Mohawk, to fish and hunt, and then the creatur' seems beside herself! You can see in the manner which she wears her finery, and the airs she gives herself with the gallants."

"That is unseemly in a poor man's darter," returned Deerslayer gravely, "the officers are all gentry, and can only look on such as Judith with evil intentions."

"There's the unsartainty, and the damper! I have my misgivings about a particular captain, and Jude has no one to blame but her own folly, if I'm right. On the whole, I wish to look upon her as modest and becoming, and yet the clouds that drive among these hills are not more unsartain. Not a dozen white men have ever laid eyes upon her since she was a child, and yet her airs, with two or three of these officers, are extinguishers!"

"I would think no more of such a woman, but turn my mind altogether to the forest; *that* will not deceive you, being ordered and ruled by a hand that never wavers."

"If you know'd Judith, you would see how much easier it is to say this than it would be to do it. Could I bring my mind to be easy about the officers, I would carry the gal off to the Mohawk by force, make her marry me in spite of her whiffling, and leave old Tom to the care of Hetty, his other child, who, if she be not as handsome or as quick-witted as her sister, is much the most dutiful."

"Is there another bird in the same nest?" asked Deerslayer, raising his eyes with a species of half-awakened curiosity—"the Delawares spoke to me only of one."

"That's nat'ral enough, when Judith Hutter and Hetty Hutter are in question. Hetty is only comely, while her sister, I tell thee, boy, is such another as is not to be found atween this and the sea: Judith is as full of wit, and talk, and cunning, as an old Indian orator, while poor Hetty is at the best but 'compass meant us.'"

"Anan?" inquired, again, the Deerslayer.

"Why, what the officers call 'compass meant us,' which I understand to signify that she means always to go in the right direction, but sometimes doesn't know how. 'Compass' for the p'int, and 'meant us' for the intention. No, poor Hetty is what I call on the varge of ignorance, and sometimes she stumbles on one side of the line, and sometimes on t'other."

"Them are beings that the Lord has in his 'special care," said Deerslayer, solemnly; "for he looks carefully to all who fall short of their proper share of reason. The redskins honor and respect them who are so gifted, knowing that the Evil Spirit delights more to dwell in an artful body, than in one that has no cunning to work upon."

"I'll answer for it, then, that he will not remain long with poor Hetty; for the child is just 'compass meant us,' as I have told you. Old Tom has a feeling for the gal, and so has Judith, quick-witted and glorious as she is herself; else would I not answer for her being altogether safe among the sort of men that sometimes meet on the lake shore."

"I thought this water an onknown and little-frequented sheet," observed the Deerslayer, evidently uneasy at the idea of being too near the world.

"It's all that, lad, the eyes of twenty white men never having been laid on it; still, twenty true-bred frontiermen—hunters and trappers, and scouts, and the like,—can do a deal of mischief if they try. 'Twould be an awful thing to me, Deerslayer, did I find Judith married, after an absence of six months!"

"Have you the gal's faith, to encourage you to hope otherwise?"

"Not at all. I know not how it is: I'm good-looking, boy,—that much I can see in any spring on which the sun shines,—and yet I could not get the hussy to a promise, or even a cordial willing smile, though she will laugh by the hour. If she

*has* dared to marry in my absence, she'll be like to know the pleasures of widowhood afore she is twenty!"

"You would not harm the man she has chosen, Hurry, simply because she found him more to her liking than yourself?"

"Why not? If an inimy crosses my path, will I not beat him out of it! Look at me! am I a man like to let any sneaking, crawling, skin-trader get the better of me in a matter that touches me as near as the kindness of Judith Hutter? Besides, when we live beyond law, we must be our own judges and executioners. And if a man *should* be found dead in the woods, who is there to say who slew him, even admitting that the colony took the matter in hand and made a stir about it?"

"If that man should be Judith Hutter's husband, after what has passed, I might tell enough, at least, to put the colony on the trail."

"You!—half-grown, venison-hunting bantling! You dare to think of informing against Hurry Harry in so much as a matter touching a mink or a woodchuck!"

"I would dare to speak truth, Hurry, consarning you or any man that ever lived."

March looked at his companion, for a moment, in silent amazement; then seizing him by the throat with both hands, he shook his comparatively slight frame with a violence that menaced the dislocation of some of the bones. Nor was this done jocularly, for anger flashed from the giant's eyes, and there were certain signs that seemed to threaten much more earnestness than the occasion would appear to call for. Whatever might be the real intention of March, and it is probable there was none settled in his mind, it is certain that he was unusually aroused; and most men who found themselves throttled by one of a mould so gigantic, in such a mood, and in a solitude so deep and helpless, would have felt intimidated, and tempted to yield even the right. Not so, however, with Deerslayer. His countenance remained unmoved; his hand did not shake, and his answer was given in a voice that did not resort to the artifice of louder tones, even by way of proving its owner's resolution.

"You may shake, Hurry, until you bring down the mountain," he said quietly, "but nothing beside truth will you shake from me. It is probable that Judith Hutter has no husband to slay, and you may never have a chance to waylay one, else would I tell her of your threat, in the first conversation I held with the gal."

March released his grip, and sat regarding the other in silent astonishment.

"I thought we had been friends," he at length

added; "but you've got the last secret of mine that will ever enter your ears."

"I want none, if they are to be like this. I know we live in the woods, Hurry, and are thought to be beyond human laws,—and perhaps we are so, in fact, whatever it may be in right,—but there is a law and a law-maker, that rule across the whole continent. He that flies in the face of either need not call me a friend."

"Damme, Deerslayer, if I do not believe you are at heart a Moravian, and no fair-minded, plain-dealing hunter, as you've pretended to be!"

"Fair-minded or not, Hurry, you will find me as plain-dealing in deeds as I am in words. But this giving way to sudden anger is foolish, and proves how little you have sojourned with the redman. Judith Hutter no doubt is still single, and you spoke but as the tongue ran, and not as the heart felt. There's my hand, and we will say and think no more about it."

Hurry seemed more surprised than ever; then he burst forth in a loud, good-natured laugh, which brought tears to his eyes. After this he accepted the offered hand, and the parties became friends.

" 'Twould have been foolish to quarrel about an idee," March cried, as he resumed his meal, "and more like lawyers in the towns than like sensible men in the woods. They tell me, Deerslayer, much ill-blood grows out of idees among the people in the lower counties, and that they sometimes get to extremities upon them."

"That do they,—that do they; and about other matters that might better be left to take care of themselves. I have heard the Moravians say that there are lands in which men quarrel even consarning their religion; and if they can get their tempers up on such a subject, Hurry, the Lord have marcy on 'em. Howsever, there is no occasion for our following their example, and more especially about a husband that this Judith Hutter may never see, or never wish to see. For my part, I feel more cur'osity about the feeble-witted sister than about your beauty. There's something that comes close to a man's feelin's, when he meets with a fellow-creatur' that has all the outward show of an accountable mortal, and who fails of being what he seems, only through a lack of reason. This is bad enough in a man, but when it comes to a woman, and she a young, and maybe a winning creatur' it touches all the pitiful thoughts his natur' has. God knows, Hurry, that such poor things be defenceless enough with all their wits about 'em; but it's a cruel fortun' when that great protector and guide fails 'em."

"Harkee, Deerslayer,—you know what the hunters, and trappers, and peltry-men in general

be; and their best friends will not deny that they are headstrong and given to having their own way, without much bethinking 'em of other people's rights or feelin's,—and yet I don't think the man is to be found, in all this region, who would harm Hetty Hutter, if he could; no, not even a redskin."

"Therein, fri'nd Hurry, you do the Delawares, at least, and all their allied tribes, only justice, for a redskin looks upon a being thus struck by God's power as especially under his care. I rejoice to hear what you say, however, I rejoice to hear it; but as the sun is beginning to turn towards the a'ternoon's sky, had we not better strike the trail ag'in, and make forward, that we may get an opportunity of seeing these wonderful sisters?"

Harry March giving a cheerful assent, the remnants of the meal were soon collected; then the travellers shouldered their packs, resumed their arms, and, quitting the little area of light, they again plunged into the deep shadows of the forest.

## CHAPTER 2

OUR TWO adventurers had not far to go. Hurry knew the direction, as soon as he had found the open spot and the spring, and he now led on with the confident step of a man assured of his object. The forest was dark, as a matter of course, but it was no longer obstructed by underbrush, and the footing was firm and dry. After proceeding near a mile, March stopped, and began to cast about him with an inquiring look, examining the different objects with care, and occasionally turning his eyes on the trunks of the fallen trees, with which the ground was well sprinkled, as is usually the case in an American wood, especially in those parts of the country where timber has not yet become valuable.

"*This* must be the place, Deerslayer," March at length observed; "here is a beech by the side of a hemlock, with three pines at hand, and yonder is a white birch with a broken top; and yet I see no rock, nor any of the branches bent down, as I told you would be the case."

"Broken branches are onskilful landmarks, as the least exper'enced know that branches don't often break of themselves," returned the other; "and they also lead to suspicion and discoveries. The Delawares never trust to broken branches, unless it is in friendly times, and on an open trail. As for the beeches, and pines, and hemlocks, why, they are to be seen on all sides of us, not only by twos and threes, but by forties, and fifties, and hundreds."

"Very true, Deerslayer, but you never calculate

on position. Here is a beech and a hemlock—"

"Yes, and there is another beech and a hemlock, as loving as two brothers, or, for that matter, more loving than some brothers; and yonder are others, for neither tree is a rarity in these woods. I fear me, Hurry, you are better at trapping beaver and shooting bears, than at leading on a blindish sort of a trail. Ha! there's what you wish to find, a'ter all!"

"Now, Deerslayer, this is one of your Delaware pretensions, for hang me if I see anything but these trees, which do seem to start up around us in a most onaccountable and perplexing manner."

"Look this a way, Hurry—here, in a line with the black oak—don't you see the crooked sapling that is hooked up in the branches of the basswood, near it? Now, that sapling was once snow-ridden, and got the bend by its weight; but it never straightened itself, and fastened itself in among the bass-wood branches in the way you see. The hand of man did that act of kindness for it."

"That hand was mine!" exclaimed Hurry; "I found the slender young thing bent to the airth, like an unfortunate creatur' borne down by misfortune, and stuck it up where you see it. After all, Deerslayer, I must allow, you're getting to have an oncommon good eye for the woods!"

"'Tis improving, Hurry—'tis improving, I will acknowledge; but 'tis only a child's eye, compared to some I know. There's Tamenund, now, though a man so old that few remember when he was in his prime, Tamenund lets nothing escape his look, which is more like the scent of a hound than the sight of an eye. Then Uncas,[2] the father of Chingachgook, and the lawful chief of the Mohicans, is another that it is almost hopeless to pass unseen. I'm improving, I will allow—I'm improving, but far from being perfect, as yet."

"And who is this Chingachgook, of whom you talk so much, Deerslayer?" asked Hurry, as he moved off in the direction of the righted sapling; "a loping redskin, at the best, I make no question."

"Not so, Hurry, but the best of loping redskins, as you call 'em. If he had his rights, he would be a great chief; but, as it is, he is only a brave and just-minded Delaware; respected, and even obeyed in some things, 'tis true, but of a fallen race, and belonging to a fallen people. Ah! Harry March, 'twould warm the heart within you to sit in their lodges of a winter's night, and listen to

the traditions of the ancient greatness and power of the Mohicans!"

"Harkee, fri'nd Nathaniel," said Hurry, stopping short to face his companion, in order that his words might carry greater weight with them, "if a man believed all that other people choose to say in their own favor, he might get an oversized opinion of them, and an undersized opinion of himself. These redskins are notable boasters, and I set down more than half of their traditions as pure talk."

"There is truth in what you say, Hurry, I'll not deny it, for I've seen it, and believe it. They *do* boast, but then that is a gift from natur'; and it's sinful to withstand nat'ral gifts. See; this is the spot you come to find!"

This remark cut short the discourse, and both the men now gave all their attention to the object immediately before them. Deerslayer pointed out to his companion the trunk of a huge linden, or bass-wood, as it is termed in the language of the country, which had filled its time, and fallen by its own weight. This tree, like so many millions of its brethren, lay where it had fallen, and was mouldering under the slow but certain influence of the seasons. The decay, however, had attacked its centre, even while it stood erect in the pride of vegetation, hollowing out its heart, as disease sometimes destroys the vitals of animal life, even while a fair exterior is presented to the observer. As the trunk lay stretched for near a hundred feet along the earth, the quick eye of the hunter detected this peculiarity, and, from this and other circumstances, he knew it to be the tree of which March was in search.

"Ay, here we have what we want," cried Hurry, looking in at the larger end of the linden; "everything is as snug as if it had been left in an old woman's cupboard. Come, lend me a hand, Deerslayer, and we'll be afloat in half an hour."

At this call the hunter joined his companion, and the two went to work deliberately and regularly, like men accustomed to the sort of thing in which they were employed. In the first place, Hurry removed some pieces of bark that lay before the large opening in the tree, and which the other declared to be disposed in a way that would have been more likely to attract attention than to conceal the cover, had any straggler passed that way. The two then drew out a bark canoe, containing its seats, paddles, and other appliances, even to fishing-lines and rods. This vessel was by no means small; but such was its comparative lightness, and so gigantic was the strength of Hurry, that the latter shouldered it with seeming ease, declining all assistance, even in the act of

2. "Lest the similarity of the names should produce confusion, it may be well to say that the Uncas here mentioned is the grandfather of him who plays so conspicuous a part in *The Last of the Mohicans*" [C].

raising it to the awkward position in which he was obliged to hold it.

"Lead ahead, Deerslayer," said March, "and open the bushes; the rest I can do for myself."

The other obeyed, and the men left the spot, Deerslayer clearing the way for his companion, and inclining to the right or to the left, as the latter directed. In about ten minutes they both broke suddenly into the brilliant light of the sun, on a low gravelly point, that was washed by water on quite half its outline.

An exclamation of surprise broke from the lips of Deerslayer, an exclamation that was low and guardedly made, however, for his habits were much more thoughtful and regulated than those of the reckless Hurry, when, on reaching the margin of the lake, he beheld the view that unexpectedly met his gaze. It was, in truth, sufficiently striking to merit a brief description. On a level with the point lay a broad sheet of water, so placid and limpid that it resembled a bed of the pure mountain atmosphere, compressed into a setting of hills and woods. Its length was about three leagues, while its breadth was irregular, expanding to half a league, or even more, opposite to the point, and contracting to less than half that distance, more to the southward. Of course, its margin was irregular, being indented by bays, and broken by many projecting, low points. At its northern, or nearest end, it was bounded by an isolated mountain, lower land falling off east and west, gracefully relieving the sweep of the outline. Still the character of the country was mountainous; high hills, or low mountains, rising abruptly from the water, on quite nine tenths of its circuit. The exceptions, indeed, only served a little to vary the scene; and even beyond the parts of the shore that were comparatively low, the background was high, though more distant.

But the most striking peculiarities of this scene were its solemn solitude and sweet repose. On all sides, wherever the eye turned, nothing met it but the mirror-like surface of the lake, the placid view of heaven, and the dense setting of woods. So rich and fleecy were the outlines of the forest, that scarce an opening could be seen, the whole visible earth, from the rounded mountain-top to the water's edge, presenting one unvaried hue of unbroken verdure. As if vegetation were not satisfied with a triumph so complete, the trees overhung the lake itself, shooting out towards the light; and there were miles along its eastern shore, where a boat might have pulled beneath the branches of dark Rembrandt-looking hemlocks, "quivering aspens," and melancholy pines.

In a word, the hand of man had never yet defaced or deformed any part of this native scene, which lay bathed in the sunlight, a glorious picture of affluent forest-grandeur, softened by the balminess of June, and relieved by the beautiful variety afforded by the presence of so broad an expanse of water.

"This is grand!—'tis solemn!—'tis an edication of itself, to look upon!" exclaimed Deerslayer, as he stood leaning on his rifle, and gazing to the right and left, north and south, above and beneath, in whichever direction his eye could wander; "not a tree disturbed even by redskin hand, as I can discover, but everything left in the ordering of the Lord, to live and die according to his own designs and laws! Hurry, your Judith ought to be a moral and well-disposed young woman, if she has passed half the time you mention in the centre of a spot so favored."

"That's naked truth; and yet the gal has the vagaries. *All* her time has not been passed here, howsever, old Tom having the custom, afore I know'd him, of going to spend the winters in the neighborhood of the settlers, or under the guns of the forts. No, no, Jude has caught more than is for her good from the settlers, and especially from the gallantifying officers."

"If she has—if she has, Hurry, this is a school to set her mind right ag'in. But what is this I see off here, abreast of us, that seems too small for an island, and too large for a boat, though it stands in the midst of the water?"

"Why, that is what these gallanting gentry from the forts call Muskrat Castle; and old Tom himself will grin at the name, though it bears so hard on his own natur' and character. 'Tis the stationary house, there being two; this, which never moves, and the other, that floats, being sometimes in one part of the lake and sometimes in another. The last goes by the name of the ark, though what may be the meaning of the word is more than I can tell you."

"It must come from the missionaries, Hurry, whom I have heard speak and read of such a thing. They say that the 'arth was once covered with water, and that Noah, with his children, was saved from drowning by building a vessel called an ark, in which he embarked in season. Some of the Delawares believe this tradition, and some deny it; but it behooves you and me, as white men born, to put our faith in its truth. Do you see anything of this ark?"

"'Tis down south, no doubt, or anchored in some of the bays. But the canoe is ready, and fifteen minutes will carry two such paddles as your'n and mine to the castle."

At this suggestion, Deerslayer helped his companion to place the different articles in the canoe, which was already afloat. This was no sooner done than the two frontiersmen embarked, and by a vigorous push sent the light bark some eight or ten rods from the shore. Hurry now took the seat in the stern, while Deerslayer placed himself forward, and by leisurely but steady strokes of the paddles, the canoe glided across the placid sheet, towards the extraordinary-looking structure that the former had styled Muskrat Castle. Several times the men ceased paddling, and looked about them at the scene, as new glimpses opened from behind points, enabling them to see farther down the lake, or to get broader views of the wooded mountains. The only changes, however, were in the new forms of the hills, the varying curvature of the bays, and the wider reaches of the valley south; the whole earth apparently being clothed in a gala-dress of leaves.

"This *is* a sight to warm the heart!" exclaimed Deerslayer, when they had thus stopped for the fourth or fifth time; "the lake seems made to let us get an insight into the noble forests; and land and water alike stand in the beauty of God's providence! Do you say, Hurry, that there is no man who calls himself lawful owner of all these glories?"

"None but the King, lad. He may pretend to some right of that natur', but he is so far away that his claim will never trouble old Tom Hutter, who has got possession, and is like to keep it as long as his life lasts. Tom is no squatter, not being on land; I call him a floater."

"I invy that man! I know it's wrong, and I strive ag'in the feelin', but I invy that man! Don't think, Hurry, that I'm consarting any plan to put myself in his moccasins, for such a thought doesn't harbor in my mind; but I can't help a little invy? 'Tis a nat'ral feelin', and the best of us are but nat'ral a'ter all and give way to such feelin's at times."

"You've only to marry Hetty to inherit half the estate," cried Hurry, laughing; "the gal is comely; nay, if it wasn't for her sister's beauty she would be even handsome; and then her wits are so small that you may easily convart her into one of your own way of thinking, in all things. Do *you* take Hetty off the old fellow's hands, and *I'll* engage he'll give you an interest in every deer you can knock over within five miles of his lake."

"Does game abound?" suddenly demanded the other, who paid but little attention to March's raillery.

"It has the country to itself. Scarce a trigger is pulled on it; and as for the trappers, this is not a region they greatly frequent. I ought not to be so much here myself, but Jude pulls one way, while the beaver pulls another. More than a hundred Spanish dollars has that creatur' cost me the last two seasons, and yet I could not forego the wish to look upon her face once more."

"Do the redmen often visit this lake, Hurry?" continued Deerslayer, pursuing his own train of thought.

"Why, they come and go; sometimes in parties, and sometimes singly. The country seems to belong to no native tribe in particular; and so it has fallen into the hands of the Hutter tribe. The old man tells me that some sharp ones have been wheedling the Mohawks for an Indian deed, in order to get a title out of the colony; but nothing has come of it, seeing that no one heavy enough for such a trade has yet meddled with the matter. The hunters have a good life-lease still of this wilderness."

"So much the better, so much the better, Hurry. If I was King of England, the man that felled one of these trees without good occasion for the timber, should be banished to a desarted and forlorn region, in which no four-footed animal ever trod. Right glad am I that Chingachgook app'inted our meeting on this lake, for hitherto eye of mine never looked on such a glorious spectacle."

"That's because you've kept so much among the Delawares, in whose country there are no lakes. Now, farther north and farther west these bits of water abound; and you're young, and may yet live to see 'em. But though there be other lakes, Deerslayer, there's no other Judith Hutter!"

At this remark his companion smiled, and then he dropped his paddle into the water, as if in consideration of a lover's haste. Both now pulled vigorously until they got within a hundred yards of the "castle," as Hurry familiarly called the house of Hutter, when they again ceased paddling; the admirer of Judith restraining his impatience the more readily, as he perceived that the building was untenanted, at the moment. This new pause was to enable Deerslayer to survey the singular edifice, which was of a construction so novel as to merit a particular description.

Muskrat Castle, as the house had been facetiously named by some waggish officer, stood in the open lake, at a distance of fully a quarter of a mile from the nearest shore. On every other side the water extended much farther, the precise position being distant about two miles from the northern end of the sheet, and near, if not quite, a mile from its eastern shore. As there was not the smallest appearance of any island, but the house stood on piles, with the water flowing beneath it, and Deerslayer had already discovered that the lake was of a great depth, he was fain to ask an explanation of this singular circumstance. Hurry solved the difficulty by telling him that on this spot alone, a long, narrow shoal, which extended for a few hundred yards in a north and south direction, rose within six or eight feet of the surface of the lake, and that Hutter had driven piles into it, and placed his habitation on them, for the purpose of security.

"The old fellow was burnt out three times, atween the Indians and the hunters; and in one affray with the redskins he lost his only son, since which time he has taken to the water for safety. No one can attack him here, without coming in a boat, and the plunder and scalps would scarce be worth the trouble of digging out canoes. Then it's by no means sartain which would whip in such a scrimmage, for old Tom is well supplied with arms and ammunition, and the castle, as you may see, is a tight breastwork ag'in light shot."

Deerslayer had some theoretical knowledge of frontier warfare, though he had never yet been called on to raise his hand in anger against a fellow-creature. He saw that Hurry did not overrate the strength of this position in a military point of view, since it would not be easy to attack it without exposing the assailants to the fire of the besieged. A good deal of art had also been manifested in the disposition of the timber of which the building was constructed and which afforded a protection much greater than was usual to the ordinary log-cabins of the frontier. The sides and ends were composed of the trunks of large pines, cut about nine feet long, and placed upright, instead of being laid horizontally, as was the practice of the country. These logs were squared on three sides, and had large tenons on each end. Massive sills were secured on the heads of the piles, with suitable grooves dug out of their upper surfaces, which had been squared for the purpose, and the lower tenons of the upright pieces were placed in these grooves, giving them a secure fastening below. Plates had been laid on the upper ends of the upright logs, and were kept in their places by a similar contrivance; the several corners of the structure being well fastened by scarfing and pinning the sills and plates. The floors were made of smaller logs, similarly squared, and the roof was composed of light poles, firmly united, and well covered with bark. The effect of this ingenious arrangement was to give its owner a house that could be approached only by water, the sides of which were composed of logs closely wedged together, which were two

feet thick in their thinnest parts, and which could be separated only by a deliberate and laborious use of human hands, or by the slow operation of time. The outer surface of the building was rude and uneven, the logs being of unequal sizes; but the squared surfaces within gave both the sides and floor as uniform an appearance as was desired, either for use or show. The chimney was not the least singular portion of the castle, as Hurry made his companion observe, while he explained the process by which it had been made. The material was a stiff clay, properly worked, which had been put together in a mould of sticks, and suffered to harden, a foot or two at a time, commencing at the bottom. When the entire chimney had thus been raised, and had been properly bound in with outward props, a brisk fire was kindled, and kept going until it was burned to something like a brick-red. This had not been an easy operation, nor had it succeeded entirely; but by dint of filling the cracks with fresh clay, a safe fireplace and chimney had been obtained in the end. This part of the work stood on the log-floor, secured beneath by an extra pile. There were a few other peculiarities about this dwelling, which will better appear in the course of the narrative.

"Old Tom is full of contrivances," added Hurry, "and he set his heart on the success of his chimney, which threatened more than once to give out altogether; but parseverance will even overcome smoke; and now he has a comfortable cabin of it, though it did promise, at one time, to be a chinky sort of a flue to carry flames and fire."

"You seem to know the whole history of the castle, Hurry, chimney and sides," said Deerslayer, smiling; "is love so overcoming that it causes a man to study the story of his sweetheart's habitation?"

"Partly that, lad, and partly eyesight," returned the good-natured giant, laughing; "there was a large gang of us in the lake, the summer the old fellow built, and we helped him along with the job. I raised no small part of the weight of them uprights with my own shoulders, and the axes flew, I can inform you, Master Natty, while we were bee-ing it among the trees ashore. The old devil is no way stingy about food, and as we had often eat at his hearth, we thought we would just house him comfortably, afore we went to Albany with our skins. Yes, many is the meal I've swallowed in Tom Hutter's cabins; and Hetty, though so weak in the way of wits, has a wonderful particular way about a frying-pan or a gridiron!"

While the parties were thus discoursing, the

canoe had been gradually drawing nearer to the "castle," and was now so close as to require but a single stroke of a paddle to reach the landing. This was at a floored platform in front of the entrance, that might have been some twenty feet square.

"Old Tom calls this sort of a wharf his door-yard," observed Hurry, as he fastened the canoe, after he and his companion had left it; "and the gallants from the forts have named it the 'castle court,' though what a 'court' can have to do here is more than I can tell you, seeing that there is no law. 'Tis as I supposed; not a soul within, but the whole family is off on a v'y'age of discovery!"

While Hurry was bustling about the "door-yard," examining the fishing-spears, rods, nets, and other similar appliances of a frontier cabin, Deerslayer, whose manner was altogether more rebuked and quiet, entered the building with a curiosity that was not usually exhibited by one so long trained in Indian habits. The interior of the "castle" was as faultlessly neat as its exterior was novel. The entire space, some twenty feet by forty, was subdivided into several small sleeping-rooms; the apartment into which he first entered, serving equally for the ordinary uses of its in-mates, and a kitchen. The furniture was of the strange mixture that it is not uncommon to find in the remotely situated log-tenements of the in-terior. Most of it was rude, and to the last degree rustic; but there was a clock, with a handsome case of dark wood, in a corner, and two or three chairs, with a table and bureau, that had evidently come from some dwelling of more than usual pretension. The clock was industriously ticking, but its leaden-looking hands did no discredit to their dull aspect, for they pointed to the hour of eleven, though the sun plainly showed it was some time past the turn of the day. There was also a dark, massive chest. The kitchen utensils were of the simplest kind, and far from numerous, but every article was in its place, and showed the nicest care in its condition.

After Deerslayer had cast a look about him in the outer room, he raised a wooden latch, and entered a narrow passage that divided the inner end of the house into two equal parts. Frontier usages being no way scrupulous, and his curiosity being strongly excited, the young man now opened a door, and found himself in a bedroom. A single glance sufficed to show that the apart-ment belonged to females. The bed was of the feathers of wild geese, and filled nearly to over-flowing; but it lay in a rude bunk, raised only a foot from the floor. On one side of it were ar-ranged, on pegs, various dresses, of a quality much superior to what one would expect to meet

in such a place, with ribbons and other similar articles to correspond. Pretty shoes, with hand-some silver buckles, such as were then worn by females in easy circumstances, were not wanting; and no less than six fans, of gay colors, were placed half open, in a way to catch the eye by their conceits and hues. Even the pillow, on this side of the bed, was covered with finer linen than its companion, and it was ornamented with a small ruffle. A cap, coquettishly decorated with ribbons, hung above it, and a pair of long gloves, such as were rarely used in those days by persons of the laboring classes, were pinned ostentatiously to it, as if with an intention to exhibit them there, if they could not be shown on the owner's arms.

All this Deerslayer saw, and noted with a de-gree of minuteness that would have done credit to the habitual observation of his friends, the Delawares. Nor did he fail to perceive the distinc-tion that existed between the appearances on the different sides of the bed, the head of which stood against the wall. On that opposite to the one just described, everything was homely and uninvit-ing, except through its perfect neatness. The few garments that were hanging from the pegs were of the coarsest materials and of the commonest forms, while nothing seemed made for show. Of ribbons there was not one; nor was there either cap or kerchief beyond those which Hutter's daughters might be fairly entitled to wear.

It was now several years since Deerslayer had been in a spot especially devoted to the uses of females of his own color and race. The sight brought back to his mind a rush of childish recollections; and he lingered in the room with a tenderness of feeling to which he had long been a stranger. He bethought him of his mother, whose homely vestments he remembered to have been hanging on pegs like those which he felt must belong to Hetty Hutter; and he bethought himself of a sister, whose incipient and native taste for finery had exhibited itself somewhat in the manner of that of Judith, though necessarily in a less degree. These little resemblances opened a long hidden vein of sensations; and as he quitted the room, it was with a saddened mien. He looked no further, but returned slowly and thoughtfully towards the "door-yard."

"Old Tom has taken to a new calling, and has been trying his hand at the traps," cried Hurry, who had been coolly examining the borderer's implements; "if that is his humor, and you're dis-posed to remain in these parts, we can make an oncommon comfortable season of it; for, while the old man and I out-knowledge the beaver, you can fish, and knock down the deer, to keep body and soul together. We always give the poorest hunters half a share, but one as actyve and sartain as yourself might expect a full one."

"Thank'ee, Hurry; thank'ee, with all my heart —but I do a little beavering for myself as occasions offer. 'Tis true, the Delawares call me Deerslayer, but it's not so much because I'm pretty fatal with the venison as because that while I kill so many bucks and does, I've never yet taken the life of a fellow-creatur'. They say their traditions do not tell of another who had shed so much blood of animals that had not shed the blood of man."

"I hope they don't account you chicken-hearted, lad? A faint-hearted man is like a no-tailed beaver."

"I don't believe, Hurry, that they account me as out-of-the way timorsome, even though they may not account me as out-of-the-way brave. But I'm not quarrelsome; and that goes a great way towards keeping blood off the hands, among the hunters and redskins; and then, Harry March, it keeps blood off the conscience, too."

"Well, for my part I account game, a redskin, and a Frenchman as pretty much the same thing; though I'm as onquarrelsome a man, too, as there is in all the colonies. I despise a quarreller as I do a cur-dog; but one has no need to be over-scrupulsome when it's the right time to show the flint."

"I look upon him as the most of a man who acts nearest the right, Hurry. But this is a glorious spot, and my eyes never a-weary looking at it!"

"'Tis your first acquaintance with a lake; and these idees come over us all at such times. Lakes have a general character, as I say, being pretty much water and land, and points and bays."

As this definition by no means met the feelings that were uppermost in the mind of the young hunter, he made no immediate answer, but stood gazing at the dark hills and the glassy water in silent enjoyment.

"Have the Governor's or the King's people given this lake a name?" he suddenly asked, as if struck with a new idea. "If they've not begun to blaze their trees, and set up their compasses, and line off their maps, it's likely they've not be-thought them to disturb natur' with a name."

"They've not got to that, yet; and the last time I went in with skins, one of the King's surveyors was questioning me consarning all the region hereabouts. He had heard that there was a lake in this quarter, and had got some general notions about it, such as that there was water and hills; but how much of either, he know'd no more than you know of the Mohawk tongue. I didn't open

the trap any wider than was necessary, giving him but poor encouragement in the way of farms and clearings. In short, I left on his mind some such opinion of this country as a man gets of a spring of dirty water, with a path to it that is so muddy that one mires afore he sets out. He told me they hadn't got the spot down yet, on their maps; though I conclude that is a mistake, for he showed me his parchment, and there is a lake down on it where there is no lake in fact, and which is about fifty miles from the place where it ought to be, if they meant it for this. I don't think my account will encourage him to mark down another, by way of improvement."

Here Hurry laughed heartily, such tricks being particularly grateful to a set of men who dreaded the approaches of civilization as a curtailment of their own lawless empire. The egregious errors that existed in the maps of the day, all of which were made in Europe, were, moreover, a standing topic of ridicule among them; for, if they had not science enough to make any better themselves, they had sufficient local information to detect the gross blunders contained in those that existed. Any one who will take the trouble to compare these unanswerable evidences of the topographical skill of our fathers a century since, with the more accurate sketches of our own time, will at once perceive that the men of the woods had a sufficient justification for all their criticism on this branch of the skill of the colonial governments, which did not at all hesitate to place a river or a lake a degree or two out of the way, even though they lay within a day's march of the inhabited parts of the country.

"I'm glad it has no name," resumed Deerslayer, "or, at least, no pale-face name; for their christenings always foretell waste and destruction. No doubt, howsever, the redskins have their modes of knowing it, and the hunters and trappers, too; they are likely to call the place by something reasonable and resembling."

"As for the tribes, each has its own tongue, and its own way of calling things; and they treat this part of the world just as they treat all others. Among ourselves, we've got to calling the place the 'Glimmerglass,' seeing that its whole basin is so often fringed with pines, cast upward from its face; as if it would throw back the hills that hang over it."

"There is an outlet, I know, for all lakes have outlets, and the rock at which I am to meet Chingachgook stands near an outlet. Has *that* no colony-name yet?"

"In that particular they've got the advantage of us, having one end, and that the biggest, in their own keeping: they've given it a name which has found its way up to its source; names nat'rally working up stream. No doubt, Deerslayer, you've seen the Susquehannah, down in the Delaware country?"

"That have I, and hunted along its banks a hundred times."

"That and this are the same in fact, and, I suppose, the same in sound. I am glad they've been compelled to keep the redmen's name, for it would be too hard to rob them of both land and name!"

Deerslayer made no answer; but he stood leaning on his rifle, gazing at the view which so much delighted him. The reader is not to suppose, however, that it was the picturesque alone which so strongly attracted his attention. The spot was very lovely, of a truth, and it was then seen in one of its most favorable moments, the surface of the lake being as smooth as glass and as limpid as pure air, throwing back the mountains, clothed in dark pines, along the whole of its eastern boundary, the points thrusting forward their trees even to nearly horizontal lines, while the bays were seen glittering through an occasional arch beneath, left by a vault fretted with branches and leaves. It was the air of deep repose—the solitudes, that spoke of scenes and forests untouched by the hands of man—the reign of nature, in a word, that gave so much pure delight to one of his habits and turn of mind. Still, he felt, though it was unconsciously, like a poet also. If he found a pleasure in studying this large, and to him unusual opening into the mysteries and forms of the woods, as one is gratified in getting broader views of any subject that has long occupied his thoughts, he was not insensible to the innate loveliness of such a landscape neither, but felt a portion of that soothing of the spirit which is a common attendant of a scene so thoroughly pervaded by the holy calm of nature.

[HURRY HARRY and Deerslayer find old Tom Hutter's ark concealed in a stream opening from the far end of the lake where he has gone trapping. Judith proves to be as beautiful and gracious as Hurry has described her, and she soon shows a strong preference for Deerslayer over his companion. It is the beginning of King George's War and a band of Hurons or Mingos, allies of the French, who have been hunting on the Glimmerglass, have already received word of the new hostilities between the French and the English. They determine not to leave the territory without some white enemy scalps for trophies, and they make an attack on the ark which is unsuccessful. In the face of the common danger, Deerslayer and Hurry join forces with Hutter. The colony offers a bounty for each Indian scalp, and as there is an encampment of Hurons on the lake, including many women and children, Hutter and Hurry decide to go on a scalping expedition, against which Deerslayer strongly protests:

"My gifts are not scalpers' gifts, but such as belong to my religion and color. I'll stand by you, old man, in the ark or in the castle, but I'll not unhumanize my natur' by falling into ways that God intended for another race. If you and Hurry have got any thoughts that lean towards the colony's gold, go by yourselves in s'arch of it, and leave the females to my care."

But Deerslayer consents to help Hutter and Hurry recover two canoes that are concealed on the shores of the Glimmerglass. "The great object for people posted like ourselves," says Hutter, "is to command the water." Under cover of darkness, the three paddle to shore; but unknown to Deerslayer, the other two plan a side excursion into the Huron camp for scalps while he awaits their return in the canoe offshore. During their expedition, Hutter and Hurry are taken prisoners by the Huron warriors, and Deerslayer, unable to help them, sleeps that night on the lake in the bottom of the canoe.]

## CHAPTER 7

DAY HAD fairly dawned before the young man . . . again opened his eyes. This was no sooner done, than he started up, and looked about him with the eagerness of one who suddenly felt the importance of accurately ascertaining his precise position. His rest had been deep and undisturbed; and when he awoke, it was with a clearness of intellect and a readiness of resources that were very much needed at that particular moment. The sun had not risen, it is true, but the vault of heaven was rich with the winning softness that "brings and shuts the day," while the whole air was filled with the carols of birds, the hymns of the feathered tribe. These sounds first told Deerslayer the risks he ran. The air, for wind it could scarce be called, was still light, it is true, but it had increased a little in the course of the night, and as the canoes were mere feathers on the water, they had drifted twice the expected distance; and, what was still more dangerous, had approached so near the base of the mountain that here rose precipitously from the eastern shore, as to render the carols of the birds plainly audible. This was not the worst. The third canoe had taken the same direction, and was slowly drifting towards a point where it must inevitably touch, unless turned aside by a shift of wind, or human hands. In other respects, nothing presented itself to attract attention, or to awaken alarm. The castle stood on its shoal, nearly abreast of the canoes, for the drift had amounted to miles in the course of the night, and the ark lay fastened to its piles, as both had been left so many hours before.

As a matter of course, Deerslayer's attention was first given to the canoe ahead. It was already quite near the point, and a very few strokes of the paddle sufficed to tell him that it must touch before he could possibly overtake it. Just at this moment, too, the wind inopportunely freshened, rendering the drift of the light craft much more rapid than certain. Feeling the impossibility of preventing a contact with the land, the young man wisely determined not to heat himself with unnecessary exertions; but first looking to the priming of his piece, he proceeded slowly and warily towards the point, taking care to make a little circuit, that he might be exposed on only one side, as he approached.

The canoe adrift being directed by no such intelligence, pursued its proper way, and grounded on a small sunken rock, at the distance of three or four yards from the shore. Just at that moment, Deerslayer had got abreast of the point, and turned the bows of his own boat to the land; first casting loose his tow, that his movements might be unencumbered. The canoe hung an instant on the rock; then it rose a hair's breadth on an almost imperceptible swell of the water, swung round, floated clear, and reached the strand. All this the young man noted, but it neither quickened his pulses, nor hastened his hand. If any one had been lying in wait for the arrival of the waif, he must be seen, and the utmost caution in approaching the shore became indispensable; if no one was in ambush, hurry was unnecessary. The point being nearly diagonally opposite to the Indian encampment, he hoped the last, though the former was not only possible, but probable; for the savages were prompt in adopting all the expedients of their particular modes of warfare, and quite likely had many scouts searching the shores for craft to carry them off to the castle. As a glance at the lake from any height or projection would expose the smallest object on its surface, there was little hope that either of the canoes would pass unseen; and Indian sagacity needed no instruction to tell which way a boat or a log would drift, when the direction of the wind was known. As Deerslayer drew nearer and nearer to the land, the stroke of his paddle grew slower, his eye became more watchful, and his ears and nostrils almost dilated with the effort to detect any lurking danger. 'Twas a trying moment for a novice, nor was there the encouragement which even the timid sometimes feel, when conscious of being observed and commended. He was entirely

alone, thrown on his own resources, and was cheered by no friendly eye, emboldened by no encouraging voice. Notwithstanding all these circumstances, the most experienced veteran in forest warfare could not have behaved better. Equally free from recklessness and hesitation, his advance was marked by a sort of philosophical prudence, that appeared to render him superior to all motives but those which were best calculated to effect his purpose. Such was the commencement of a career in forest exploits, that afterwards rendered this man, in his way, and under the limits of his habits and opportunities, as renowned as many a hero whose name has adorned the pages of works more celebrated than legends simple as ours can ever become.

When about a hundred yards from the shore, Deerslayer rose in the canoe, gave three or four vigorous strokes with the paddle, sufficient of themselves to impel the bark to land, and then quickly laying aside the instrument of labor, he seized that of war. He was in the very act of raising the rifle, when a sharp report was followed by the buzz of a bullet that passed so near his body as to cause him involuntarily to start. The next instant Deerslayer staggered, and fell his whole length in the bottom of the canoe. A yell— it came from a single voice—followed, and an Indian leaped from the bushes upon the open area of the point, bounding towards the canoe. This was the moment the young man desired. He rose on the instant, and levelled his own rifle at his uncovered foe; but his finger hesitated about pulling the trigger on one whom he held at such a disadvantage. This little delay, probably, saved the life of the Indian, who bounded back into the cover as swiftly as he had broken out of it. In the meantime Deerslayer had been swiftly approaching the land, and his own canoe reached the point just as his enemy disappeared. As its movements had not been directed, it touched the shore a few yards from the other boat; and though the rifle of his foe had to be loaded, there was not time to secure his prize, and carry it beyond danger, before he would be exposed to another shot. Under the circumstances, therefore, he did not pause an instant, but dashed into the woods and sought a cover.

On the immediate point there was a small open area, partly in native grass, and partly beach, but a dense fringe of bushes lined its upper side. This narrow belt of dwarf vegetation passed, one issued immediately into the high and gloomy vaults of the forest. The land was tolerably level for a few hundred feet, and then it rose precipitously in a mountain-side. The trees were tall, large, and so free from underbrush, that they resembled vast columns, irregularly scattered, upholding a dome of leaves. Although they stood tolerably close together, for their ages and size, the eye could penetrate to considerable distances; and bodies of men, even, might have engaged beneath their cover, with concert and intelligence.

Deerslayer knew that his adversary must be employed in reloading, unless he had fled. The former proved to be the case, for the young man had no sooner placed himself behind a tree, than he caught a glimpse of the arm of the Indian, his body being concealed by an oak, in the very act of forcing the leathered bullet home. Nothing would have been easier than to spring forward, and decide the affair by a close assault on his unprepared foe; but every feeling of Deerslayer revolted at such a step, although his own life had just been attempted from a cover. He was yet unpractised in the ruthless expedients of savage warfare, of which he knew nothing except by tradition and theory, and it struck him as an unfair advantage to assail an unarmed foe. His color had heightened, his eye frowned, his lips were compressed, and all his energies were collected and ready; but, instead of advancing to fire, he dropped his rifle to the usual position of a sportsman in readiness to catch his aim, and muttered to himself, unconscious that he was speaking—

"No, no—that may be redskin warfare, but it's not a Christian's gifts. Let the miscreant charge, and then we'll take it out like men; for the canoe he *must* not, and *shall* not have. No, no; let him have time to load, and God will take care of the right!"

All this time the Indian had been so intent on his own movements, that he was even ignorant that his enemy was in the woods. His only apprehension was, that the canoe would be recovered and carried away before he might be in readiness to prevent it. He had sought the cover from habit, but was within a few feet of the fringe of bushes, and could be at the margin of the forest in readiness to fire in a moment. The distance between him and his enemy was about fifty yards, and the trees were so arranged by nature that the line of sight was not interrupted, except by the particular trees behind which each party stood.

His rifle was no sooner loaded, than the savage glanced around him, and advanced incautiously as regarded the real, but stealthily as respected the fancied position of his enemy, until he was fairly exposed. Then Deerslayer stepped from behind his own cover, and hailed him.

"This a way, redskin; this a way, if you're looking for me," he called out. "I'm young in war, but not so young as to stand on an open beach to be shot down like an owl, by daylight. It rests on yourself whether it's peace or war atween us; for my gifts are white gifts, and I'm not one of them that thinks it valiant to slay human mortals, singly, in the woods."

The savage was a good deal startled by this sudden discovery of the danger he ran. He had a little knowledge of English, however, and caught the drift of the other's meaning. He was also too well schooled to betray alarm, but, dropping the butt of his rifle to the earth, with an air of confidence, he made a gesture of lofty courtesy. All this was done with the ease and self-possession of one accustomed to consider no man his superior. In the midst of this consummate acting, however, the volcano that raged within caused his eyes to glare, and his nostrils to dilate, like those of some wild beast that is suddenly prevented from taking the fatal leap.

"Two canoes," he said, in the deep guttural tones of his race, holding up the number of fingers he mentioned, by way of preventing mistakes; "one for you—one for me."

"No, no, Mingo, that will never do. You own neither; and neither shall you have, as long as I can prevent it. I know it's war atween your people and mine, but that's no reason why human mortals should slay each other, like savage creatur's that meet in the woods; go your way, then, and leave me to go mine. The world is large enough for us both; and when we meet fairly in battle, why, the Lord will order the fate of each of us."

"Good!" exclaimed the Indian; "my brother missionary—great talk; all about Manitou."

"Not so—not so, warrior. I'm not good enough for the Moravians, and am too good for most of the other vagabonds that preach about in the woods. No, no; I'm only a hunter, as yet, though afore the peace is made, 'tis like enough there'll be occasion to strike a blow at some of your people. Still, I wish it to be done in fair fight, and not in a quarrel about the ownership of a miserable canoe."

"Good! My brother very young—but he is very wise. Little warrior—great talker. Chief, sometimes, in council."

"I don't know this, nor do I say it, Injin," returned Deerslayer, coloring a little at the ill-concealed sarcasm of the other's manner; "I look forward to a life in the woods, and I only hope it may be a peaceable one. All young men must go on the war-path, when there's occasion, but war isn't needfully massacre. I've seen enough of the last, this very night, to know that Providence frowns on it; and I now invite you to go your own way, while I go mine; and hope that we may part fri'nds."

"Good! My brother has two scalp—gray hair under t'other. Old wisdom—young tongue."

Here the savage advanced with confidence, his hand extended, his face smiling, and his whole bearing denoting amity and respect. Deerslayer met his offered friendship in a proper spirit, and they shook hands cordially, each endeavoring to assure the other of his sincerity and desire to be at peace.

"All have his own," said the Indian; "my canoe, mine; your canoe, your'n. Go look; if your'n, you keep; if mine, I keep."

"That's just, redskin; thought you must be wrong in thinking the canoe your property. Hows'ever, seein' is believin', and we'll go down to the shore, where you may look with your own eyes; for it's likely you'll object to trustin' altogether to mine."

The Indian uttered his favorite exclamation of "Good!" and then they walked side by side, towards the shore. There was no apparent distrust in the manner of either, the Indian moving in advance, as if he wished to show his companion that he did not fear turning his back to him. As they reached the open ground, the former pointed towards Deerslayer's boat, and said emphatically—

"No mine—pale-face canoe. *This* redman's. No want other man's canoe—want his own."

"You're wrong, redskin, you're altogether wrong. This canoe was left in old Hutter's keeping, and is his'n according to law, red or white, till its owner comes to claim it. Here's the seats and the stitching of the bark to speak for themselves. No man ever know'd an Injin to turn off such work."

"Good! My brother little old—big wisdom. Injin no make him. White man's work."

"I'm glad you think so, for holding out to the contrary might have made ill blood atween us, every one having a right to take possession of his own. I'll just shove the canoe out of reach of dispute at once, as the quickest way of settling difficulties."

While Deerslayer was speaking, he put a foot against the end of the light boat, and giving a vigorous shove, he sent it out into the lake a hundred feet or more, where, taking the true current, it would necessarily float past the point, and be in no further danger of coming ashore. The savage started at this ready and decided expedient, and his companion saw that he cast a

hurried and fierce glance at his own canoe, or that which contained the paddles. The change of manner, however, was but momentary, and then the Iroquois resumed his air of friendliness, and a smile of satisfaction.

"Good!" he repeated, with stronger emphasis than ever. "Young head, old mind. Know how to settle quarrel. Farewell, brother. He go to house in water—muskrat house—Injin go to camp; tell chiefs no find canoe."

Deerslayer was not sorry to hear this proposal, for he felt anxious to join the females, and he took the offered hand of the Indian very willingly. The parting words were friendly, and while the redman walked calmly towards the wood, with the rifle in the hollow of his arm, without once looking back in uneasiness or distrust, the white man moved towards the remaining canoe, carrying his piece in the same pacific manner, it is true, but keeping his eye fastened on the movements of the other. This distrust, however, seemed to be altogether uncalled for, and as if ashamed to have entertained it, the young man averted his look, and stepped carelessly up to his boat. Here he began to push the canoe from the shore, and to make his other preparations for departing. He might have been thus employed a minute, when, happening to turn his face towards the land, his quick and certain eye told him, at a glance, the imminent jeopardy in which his life was placed. The black, ferocious eyes of the savage were glancing on him, like those of the crouching tiger, through a small opening in the bushes, and the muzzle of his rifle seemed already to be opening in a line with his own body.

Then, indeed, the long practice of Deerslayer, as a hunter, did him good service. Accustomed to fire with the deer on the bound, and often when the precise position of the animal's body had in a manner to be guessed at, he used the same expedients here. To cock and poise his rifle were the acts of a single moment and at single motion; then aiming almost without sighting, he fired into the bushes where he knew a body ought to be, in order to sustain the appalling countenance which alone was visible. There was not time to raise the piece any higher, or to take a more deliberate aim. So rapid were his movements that both parties discharged their pieces at the same instant, the concussions mingling in one report. The mountains, indeed, gave back but a single echo. Deerslayer dropped his piece, and stood with head erect, steady as one of the pines in the calm of a June morning, watching the result; while the savage gave the yell that has become historical for its appalling influence, leaped through the bushes, and came bounding across the open ground, flourishing a tomahawk. Still Deerslayer moved not, but stood with his unloaded rifle fallen against his shoulders, while, with a hunter's habits, his hands were mechanically feeling for the powder-horn and charger. When about forty feet from his enemy, the savage hurled his keen weapon; but it was with an eye so vacant, and a hand so unsteady and feeble, that the young man caught it by the handle as it was flying past him. At that instant the Indian staggered and fell his whole length on the ground.

"I know'd it—I know'd it!" exclaimed Deerslayer, who was already preparing to force a fresh bullet into his rifle; "I know'd it must come to this, as soon as I had got the range from the creatur's eyes. A man sights suddenly, and fires quick when his own life's in danger; yes, I know'd it would come to this. I was about the hundredth part of a second too quick for him, or it might have been bad for me! The riptyle's bullet has just grazed my side—but say what you will for or ag'in 'em, a redskin is by no means as sartain with powder and ball as a white man. Their gifts don't seem to lie that a way. Even Chingachgook, great as he is in other matters, isn't downright deadly with the rifle."

By this time the piece was reloaded, and Deerslayer, after tossing the tomahawk into the canoe, advanced to his victim, and stood over him, leaning on his rifle, in melancholy attention. It was the first instance in which he had seen a man fall in battle—it was the first fellow-creature against whom he had ever seriously raised his own hand. The sensations were novel; and regret, with the freshness of our better feelings, mingled with his triumph. The Indian was not dead, though shot directly through the body. He lay on his back motionless, but his eyes, now full of consciousness, watched each action of his victor—as the fallen bird regards the fowler—jealous of every movement. The man probably expected the fatal blow which was to precede the loss of his scalp; or perhaps he anticipated that this latter act of cruelty would precede his death. Deerslayer read his thoughts; and he found a melancholy satisfaction in relieving the apprehensions of the helpless savage.

"No, no, redskin," he said; "you've nothing more to fear from me. I am of a Christian stock, and scalping is not of my gifts. I'll just make sartain of your rifle, and then come back and do you what sarvice I can. Though here I can't stay much longer, as the crack of three rifles will be apt to bring some of your devils down upon me."

The close of this was said in a sort of a soliloquy, as the young man went in quest of the fallen rifle. The piece was found where its owner had dropped it, and was immediately put into the canoe. Laying his own rifle at its side, Deerslayer then returned and stood over the Indian again.

"All inmity atween you and me's at an ind, redskin," he said; "and you may set your heart at rest on the score of the scalp, or any further injury. My gifts are white, as I've told you; and I hope my conduct will be white also!"

Could looks have conveyed all they meant, it is probable Deerslayer's innocent vanity on the subject of color would have been rebuked a little; but he comprehended the gratitude that was expressed in the eyes of the dying savage, without in the least detecting the bitter sarcasm that struggled with the better feeling.

"Water!" ejaculated the thirsty and unfortunate creature; "give poor Injin water."

"Ay, water you shall have, if you drink the lake dry. I'll just carry you down to it, that you may take your fill. This is the way, they tell me, with all wounded people—water is their greatest comfort and delight."

So saying, Deerslayer raised the Indian in his arms, and carried him to the lake. Here he first helped him to take an attitude in which he could appease his burning thirst; after which he seated himself on a stone, and took the head of his wounded adversary in his own lap, and endeavored to soothe his anguish in the best manner he could.

"It would be sinful in me to tell you your time hadn't come, warror," he commenced, "and therefore I'll not say it. You've passed the middle age already, and, considerin' the sort of lives ye lead, your days have been pretty well filled. The principal thing now, is to look forward to what comes next. Neither redskin nor paleface, on the whole, calculates much on sleepin' forever; but both expect to live in another world. Each has his gifts, and will be judged by 'em, and I suppose you've thought these matters over enough not to stand in need of sarmons when the trial comes. You'll find your happy hunting-grounds, if you've been a just Injin; if an onjust, you'll meet your desarts in another way. I've my own idees about these things; but you're too old and exper'enced to need any explanations from one as young as I."

"Good!" ejaculated the Indian, whose voice retained its depth even as life ebbed away; "young head—old wisdom!"

"It's sometimes a consolation, when the ind

comes, to know that them we've harmed, or *tried* to harm, forgive us. I suppose natur' seeks this relief, by way of getting a pardon on 'arth; as we never can know whether He pardons, who is all in all, till judgment itself comes. It's soothing to know that *any* pardon at such times; and that, I conclude, is the secret. Now, as for myself, I overlook altogether your designs ag'in my life; first, because no harm came of 'em; next, because it's your gifts, and natur', and trainin', and I ought not to have trusted you at all; and, finally and chiefly, because I can bear no ill-will to a dying man, whether heathen or Christian. So put your heart at ease, so far as I'm consarned; you know best what other matters ought to trouble you, or what ought to give you satisfaction in so trying a moment."

It is probable that the Indian had some of the fearful glimpses of the unknown state of being which God, in mercy, seems at times to afford to all the human race; but they were necessarily in conformity with his habits and prejudices. Like most of his people, and like too many of our own, he thought more of dying in a way to gain applause among those he left than to secure a better state of existence hereafter. While Deerslayer was speaking, his mind was a little bewildered, though he felt that the intention was good; and when he had done, a regret passed over his spirit that none of his own tribe were present to witness his stoicism, under extreme bodily suffering, and the firmness with which he met his end. With the high innate courtesy that so often distinguishes the Indian warrior before he becomes corrupted by too much intercourse with the worst class of the white men, he endeavored to express his thankfulness for the other's good intentions, and to let him understand that they were appreciated.

"Good!" he repeated, for this was an English word much used by the savages, "good! young head; young *heart,* too. *Old* heart tough; no shed tear. Hear Indian when he die, and no want to lie—what he call him?"

"Deerslayer is the name I bear now, though the Delawares have said that when I get back from this war-path, I shall have a more manly title, provided I can 'arn one."

"That good name for boy—poor name for warrior. He get better quick. No fear *there,"*— the savage had strength sufficient, under the strong excitement he felt, to raise a hand and tap the young man on his breast,—"eye sartain— finger lightning—aim, death—great warrior soon. No Deerslayer—Hawkeye—Hawkeye—Hawkeye. Shake hand."

Deerslayer—or Hawkeye, as the youth was then first named, for in after years he bore the appellation throughout all that region—Deerslayer took the hand of the savage, whose last breath was drawn in that attitude, gazing in admiration at the countenance of a stranger, who had shown so much readiness, skill, and firmness, in a scene that was equally trying and novel. When the reader remembers it is the highest gratification an Indian can receive to see his enemy betray weakness, he will be better able to appreciate the conduct which had extorted so great a concession at such a moment.

"His spirit has fled!" said Deerslayer, in a suppressed, melancholy voice. "Ah's me! Well, to this we must all come, sooner or later; and he is happiest, let his skin be what color it may, who is best fitted to meet it. Here lies the body of no doubt a brave warrior, and the soul is already flying towards its heaven or hell, whether that be a happy hunting-ground, a place scant of game, regions of glory, according to Moravian doctrine, or flames of fire! So it happens, too, as regards other matters! Here have old Hutter and Hurry Harry got themselves into difficulty, if they haven't got themselves into torment and death, and all for a bounty that luck offers to me in what many would think a lawful and suitable manner. But not a farthing of such money shall cross my hand. White I was born, and white will I die; clinging to color to the last, even though the King's majesty, his governors, and all his councils, both at home and in the colonies, forget from what they come, and where they hope to go, and all for a little advantage in warfare. No, no, warrior, hand of mine shall never molest your scalp, and so your soul may rest in peace on the p'int of making a decent appearance when the body comes to join it, in your own land of spirits."

Deerslayer arose as soon as he had spoken. Then he placed the body of the dead man in a sitting posture, with its back against the little rock, taking the necessary care to prevent it from falling or in any way settling into an attitude that might be thought unseemly by the sensitive, though wild notions of a savage. When this duty was performed, the young man stood gazing at the grim countenance of his fallen foe, in a sort of melancholy abstraction. As was his practice, however, a habit gained by living so much alone in the forest, he then began again to give utterance to his thoughts and feelings aloud.

"I didn't wish your life, redskin," he said, "but you left me no choice atween killing or being killed. Each party acted according to his gifts, I suppose, and blame can light on neither. You were treacherous, according to your natur' in war, and I was a little oversightful, as I'm apt to be in trusting others. Well, this is my first battle with a human mortal, though it's not likely to be the last. I have fou't most of the creatur's of the forest, such as bears, wolves, painters, and catamounts, but this is the beginning with the redskins. If I was Injin born, now, I might tell of this, or carry in the scalp, and boast of the expl'ite afore the whole tribe; or, if my inimy had only been even a bear, 'twould have been nat'ral and proper to let everybody know what had happened; but I don't well see how I'm to let even Chingachgook into this secret, so long as it can be done only by boasting with a white tongue. And why should I wish to boast of it a'ter all? It's slaying a human, although he was a savage; and how do I know that he was a just Injin; and that he has not been taken away suddenly to anything but happy hunting-grounds. When it's onsartain whether good or evil has been done, the wisest way is not to be boastful—still, I *should* like Chingachgook to know that I haven't discredited the Delawares, or my training!"

Part of this was uttered aloud, while part was merely muttered between the speaker's teeth; his more confident opinions enjoying the first advantage, while his doubts were expressed in the latter mode. Soliloquy and reflection received a startling interruption, however, by the sudden appearance of a second Indian on the lake shore, a few hundred yards from the point. This man, evidently another scout, who had probably been drawn to the place by the reports of the rifles, broke out of the forest with so little caution that Deerslayer caught a view of his person before he was himself discovered. When the latter event did occur, as was the case a moment later, the savage gave a loud yell, which was answered by a dozen voices from different parts of the mountain-side. There was no longer any time for delay; in another minute the boat was quitting the shore under long and steady sweeps of the paddle.

As soon as Deerslayer believed himself to be at a safe distance, he ceased his efforts, permitting the little bark to drift, while he leisurely took a survey of the state of things. The canoe first sent adrift was floating before the air, quite a quarter of a mile above him, and a little nearer to the shore than he wished, now that he knew more of the savages were so near at hand. The canoe shoved from the point was within a few yards of him, he having directed his own course towards it on quitting the land. The dead Indian lay in grim quiet where he had left him, the warrior who had shown himself from the forest had already

vanished, and the woods themselves were as silent and seemingly deserted as the day they came fresh from the hands of their great Creator. This profound stillness, however, lasted but a moment. When time had been given to the scouts of the enemy to reconnoitre, they burst out of the thicket upon the naked point, filling the air with yells of fury at discovering the death of their companion. These cries were immediately succeeded by shouts of delight when they reached the body and clustered eagerly around it. Deerslayer was a sufficient adept in the usages of the natives to understand the reason of the change. The yell was the customary lamentation at the loss of a warrior, the shout a sign of rejoicing that the conqueror had not been able to secure the scalp; the trophy, without which a victory is never considered complete. The distance at which the canoes lay probably prevented any attempts to injure the conqueror, the American Indian, like the panther of his own woods, seldom making any effort against his foe unless tolerably certain it is under circumstances that may be expected to prove effective.

As the young man had no longer any motive to remain near the point, he prepared to collect his canoes, in order to tow them off to the castle. That nearest was soon in tow, when he proceeded in quest of the other, which was all this time floating up the lake. The eye of Deerslayer was no sooner fastened on this last boat, than it struck him that it was nearer to the shore than it would have been had it merely followed the course of the gentle current of air. He began to suspect the influence of some unseen current in the water, and he quickened his exertions, in order to regain possession of it before it could drift into a dangerous proximity to the woods. On getting nearer, he thought that the canoe had a perceptible motion through the water, and, as it lay broadside to the air, that this motion was taking it towards the land. A few vigorous strokes of the paddle carried him still nearer, when the mystery was explained. Something was evidently in motion on the off-side of the canoe, or that which was farthest from himself, and closer scrutiny showed that it was a naked human arm. An Indian was lying in the bottom of the canoe, and was propelling it slowly but certainly to the shore, using his hand as a paddle. Deerslayer understood the whole artifice at a glance. A savage had swum off to the boat while he was occupied with his enemy on the point, got possession, and was using these means to urge it to the shore.

Satisfied that the man in the canoe could have no arms, Deerslayer did not hesitate to dash close alongside of the retiring boat, without deeming it necessary to raise his own rifle. As soon as the wash of the water, which he made in approaching, became audible to the prostrate savage, the latter sprang to his feet, and uttered an exclamation that proved how completely he was taken by surprise.

"If you've enj'yed yourself enough in that canoe, redskin," Deerslayer coolly observed, stopping his own career in sufficient time to prevent an absolute collision between the two boats,— "if you've enj'yed yourself enough in that canoe, you'll do a prudent act by taking to the lake ag'in. I'm reasonable in these matters, and don't crave your blood, though there's them about that would look upon you more as a due-bill for the bounty than a human mortal. Take to the lake this minute, afore we get to hot words."

The savage was one of those who did not understand a word of English, and he was indebted to the gestures of Deerslayer, and to the expression of an eye that did not often deceive, for an imperfect comprehension of his meaning. Perhaps, too, the sight of the rifle that lay so near the hand of the white man quickened his decision. At all events, he crouched like a tiger about to take his leap, uttered a yell, and the next instant his naked body disappeared in the water. When he rose to take breath, it was at the distance of several yards from the canoe, and the hasty glance he threw behind him denoted how much he feared the arrival of a fatal messenger from the rifle of his foe. But the young man made no indication of any hostile intention. Deliberately securing the canoe to the others, he began to paddle from the shore; and by the time the Indian reached the land, and had shaken himself, like a spaniel, on quitting the water, his dreaded enemy was already beyond rifleshot on his way to the castle. As was so much his practice, Deerslayer did not fail to soliloquize on what had just occurred, while steadily pursuing his course towards the point of destination.

"Well, well,"—he commenced,—"'twould have been wrong to kill a human mortal without an object. Scalps are of no account with me, and life is sweet, and ought not to be taken marcilessly by them that have white gifts. The savage was a Mingo, it's true; and I make no doubt he is, and will be as long as he lives, a ra'al riptyle and vagabond; but that's no reason I should forget my gifts and color. No, no,—let him go; if ever we meet ag'in, rifle in hand, why then 'twill be seen which has the stoutest heart and the quickest eye. Hawkeye! That's not a bad name for a warrior, sounding much more manful and valiant than Deerslayer! 'Twouldn't be a bad title to begin with, and it has been fairly 'arned. If 'twas Chingachgook, now, he might go home and boast

of his deeds, and the chiefs would name him Hawkeye in a minute; but it don't become white blood to brag, and 'tisn't easy to see how the matter can be known unless I do. Well, well— everything is in the hands of Providence; this affair as well as another; I'll trust to that for getting my desarts in all things."

Having thus betrayed what might be termed his weak spot, the young man continued to paddle in silence, making his way diligently, and as fast as his tows would allow him, towards the castle. By this time the sun had not only risen, but it had appeared over the eastern mountains, and was shedding a flood of glorious light on this as yet unchristened sheet of water. The whole scene was radiant with beauty; and no one unaccustomed to the ordinary history of the woods would fancy it had so lately witnessed incidents so ruthless and barbarous. As he approached the building of old Hutter, Deerslayer thought, or rather *felt*, that its appearance was in singular harmony with all the rest of the scene. Although nothing had been consulted but strength and security, the rude, massive logs, covered with their rough bark, the projecting roof, and the form, would contribute to render the building picturesque in almost any situation, while its actual position added novelty and piquancy to its other points of interest.

When Deerslayer drew nearer to the castle, however, objects of interest presented themselves that at once eclipsed any beauties that might have distinguished the scenery of the lake, and the site of the singular edifice. Judith and Hetty stood on the platform before the door, Hurry's door-yard, awaiting his approach with manifest anxiety; the former, from time to time, taking a survey of his person and of the canoes through the old ship's spy-glass that has been already mentioned. Never probably did this girl seem more brilliantly beautiful than at that moment; the flush of anxiety and alarm increasing her color to its richest tints, while the softness of her eyes, a charm that even poor Hetty shared with her, was deepened by intense concern. Such, at least, without pausing or pretending to analyze motives, or to draw any other very nice distinction between cause and effect, were the opinions of the young man, as his canoes reached the side of the ark, where he carefully fastened all three before he put his foot on the platform.

[CHINGACHGOOK, according to plan, now joins Deerslayer. We learn that his trip to the Glimmerglass is principally motivated by his desire to rescue the Indian maiden, Wah-ta-Wah, whom he loves. She has been abducted by Briarthorne, a renegade Delaware, and evidence suggests she has been brought among the Hurons on the lake shore. In the meantime plans are laid to gain the freedom of Hurry and Hutter. An old locked chest that had once belonged to Judith's mother is part of the furniture of Muskrat Castle. In the hope of finding suitable ransom, Judith and Deerslayer now open it. Among its contents are found letters which prove that the two girls are not the children of old Hutter; a rich brocade dress which will play a significant part in Chapter 30, and a handsome set of ivory chessmen. The castles stand on the backs of elephants, and these small carvings of an animal (which the Indians have never seen) prove the ideal ransom. After negotiations with the Indians, Hurry and Hutter are returned, but later the two men, through Mingo treachery, are ambushed in the castle. Hurry again escapes, but Hutter is scalped while still alive, and later dies.

It has been ascertained by this time that Wah-ta-Wah, or Hist, is indeed a prisoner in the Huron camp, and, during the night, Deerslayer accompanies Chingachgook to the shore to recover the girl. When Judith tries to dissuade him from so dangerous a mission, he pleads his deep friendship for Chingachgook, or the Great Serpent. In the episode that follows, Chingachgook with Natty's help brings Hist safely off, but Deerslayer himself is now captured. However, the Hurons wish desperately to secure the return of Hist, with whom one of their young braves has fallen in love, and they release Deerslayer on a furlough to carry certain peace terms to those gathered in the castle, with the understanding that he is to return to captivity voluntarily when he has accomplished the mission. In taking this risk, the Mingos have interpreted Deerslayer's character correctly, as the following exchange between Hurry and Deerslayer proves:

"What's an Injin, or a word passed, or a furlough taken from creatur's like them, that have neither souls nor names?"

"If they've got neither souls nor names, you and I have both, Harry March, and one is accountable for the other. This furlough is not, as you seem to think, a matter 'atween me and the Mingos, seeing it is a solemn bargain 'atween me and God. He who thinks he can say what he pleases, in his distress, and that 'twill all pass for nothing, because 'tis uttered in the forest, and into red men's ears, knows little of his situation, and hopes, and wants. The words are said to the ears of the Almighty. The air is his breath, and the light of the sun is little more than a glance of his eye."

Deerslayer returns to the Huron camp on the lake shore at the appointed hour. "The canoe now glided ahead, holding its way towards the point, where Deerslayer well knew that his enemies expected him, and where he now began to be afraid he might not arrive in season to redeem his plighted faith."]

# CHAPTER 27

ONE EXPERIENCED in the signs of the heavens would have seen that the sun wanted but two or three minutes of the zenith, when Deerslayer landed on the point where the Hurons were now encamped, nearly abreast of the castle. This spot was similar to the one already described, with the exception that the surface of the land was less broken and less crowded with trees. Owing to these two circumstances, it was all the better suited to the purpose for which it had been selected, the space beneath the branches bearing some resemblance to a densely wooded lawn. Favored by its position and its spring, it had been much resorted to by savages and hunters, and the natural grasses had succeeded their fires, leaving an appearance of sward in places, a very unusual accompaniment of the virgin forest. Nor was the margin of water fringed with bushes as on so much of its shore, but the eye penetrated the woods immediately on reaching the strand, commanding nearly the whole area of the projection.

If it was a point of honor with the Indian warrior to redeem his word, when pledged to return and meet his death at a given hour, so was it a point of characteristic pride to show no womanish impatience, but to reappear as nearly as possible at the appointed moment. It was well not to exceed the grace accorded by the generosity of the enemy, but it was better to meet it to a minute. Something of this dramatic effect mingles with most of the graver usages of the American aborigines, and no doubt, like the prevalence of a similar feeling among people more sophisticated and refined, may be referred to a principle of nature. We all love the wonderful, and when it comes attended by chivalrous self-devotion and a rigid regard to honor, it presents itself to our admiration in a shape doubly attractive. As respects Deerslayer, though he took a pride in showing his white blood, by often deviating from the usages of the redmen, he frequently dropped into their customs, and oftener into their feelings, unconsciously to himself, in consequence of having no other arbiters to appeal to, than their judgments and tastes. On the present occasion, he would have abstained from betraying a feverish haste by a too speedy return, since it would have contained a tacit admission that the time asked for was more than had been wanted; but, on the other hand, had the idea occurred to him, he would have quickened his movements a little in order to avoid the dramatic appearance of returning at the precise instant set as the utmost limit of his absence. Still, accident had interfered to defeat the last intention, for when the young man put his foot on the point, and advanced with a steady tread towards the group of chiefs that was seated in grave array on a fallen tree, the oldest of their number cast his eye upward at an opening in the trees, and pointed out to his companions the startling fact that the sun was just entering a space that was known to mark the zenith. A common, but low exclamation of surprise and admiration escaped every mouth, and the grim warriors looked at each other; some with envy and disappointment, some with astonishment, at the precise accuracy of their victim, and others with a more generous and liberal feeling. The American Indian always deemed his moral victories the noblest, prizing the groans and yielding of his victim under torture more than the trophy of his scalp; and the trophy itself more than his life. To slay, and not to bring off the proof of victory, indeed, was scarcely deemed honorable; even these rude and fierce tenants of the forest, like their more nurtured brethren of the court and the camp, having set up for themselves imaginary and arbitrary points of honor, to supplant the conclusions of the right, and the decisions of reason.

The Hurons had been divided in their opinions concerning the probability of their captive's return. Most among them, indeed, had not expected it possible for a pale-face to come back voluntarily, and meet the known penalties of an Indian torture; but a few of the seniors expected better things from one who had already shown himself so singularly cool, brave, and upright. The party had come to its decision, however, less in the expectation of finding the pledge redeemed, than in the hope of disgracing the Delawares by casting into their teeth the delinquency of one bred in their villages. They would have greatly preferred that Chingachgook should be their prisoner, and prove the traitor; but the pale-face scion of the hated stock was no bad substitute for their purposes, failing in their designs against the ancient stem. With a view to render the triumph as signal as possible, in the event of the hour's passing without the reappearance of the hunter, all the warriors and scouts of the party had been called in; and the whole band, men, women, and children, was now assembled at this single point, to be a witness of the expected scene. As the castle was in plain view, and by no means distant, it was easily watched by daylight; and it being thought that its inmates were now limited to Hurry, the Delaware, and the two girls, no apprehensions were felt of their being able to escape unseen. A large raft, having a breast-work of logs, had been prepared, and was in actual readiness to be used against either ark or castle, as occasion might require, as soon as the fate of Deerslayer was determined; the seniors of the party having come to the opinion that it was getting to be hazardous to delay their departure for Canada beyond the coming night. In short, the band awaited merely to dispose of this single affair, ere it brought matters to a crisis, and prepared to commence its retreat towards the distant waters of Ontario.

It was an imposing scene, into which Deerslayer now found himself advancing. All the older warriors were seated on the trunk of the fallen tree, waiting his approach with grave decorum. On the right stood the young men, armed, while the left was occupied by the women and children. In the centre was an open space of considerable extent, always canopied by leaves, but from which the underbrush, dead wood, and other obstacles had been carefully removed. The more open area had probably been much used by former parties, for this was the place where the appearance of a sward was the most decided. The arches of the woods, even at high noon, cast their sombre shadows on the spot, which the brilliant rays of the sun that struggled through the leaves contributed to mellow, and, if such an expression can be used, to illuminate. It was probably from a similar scene that the mind of man first got its idea of the effects of Gothic tracery and churchly hues; this temple of nature producing some such effect, so far as light and shadows were concerned, as the well-known offspring of human invention.

As was not unusual among the tribes and wandering bands of the aborigines, two chiefs shared, in nearly equal degrees, the principal and primitive authority that was wielded over these children of the forest. There were several who might claim the distinction of being chief men, but the two in question were so much superior to all the rest in influence, that when they agreed, no one disputed their mandates; and when they were divided, the band hesitated, like men who had lost their governing principle of action. It was also in conformity with practice—perhaps we might add, in conformity with nature, that one of the chiefs was indebted to his mind for his influence, whereas the other owed his distinction altogether to qualities that were physical. One was a senior, well known for eloquence in debate, wisdom in council, and prudence in measures; while his competitor, if not his rival, was a brave, distinguished in war, notorious for ferocity, and remarkable, in the way of intellect, for nothing but the cunning and expedients of the war-path. The first was Rivenoak, who has already been introduced to the reader, while the last was called Le Panthère, in the language of the Canadas; or the Panther, to resort to the vernacular of the English colonies. The appellation of the fighting chief was supposed to indicate the qualities of the warrior, agreeably to a practice of the redman's nomenclature; ferocity, cunning, and treachery being, perhaps, the distinctive features of his character. The title had been received from the French, and was prized so much the more from that circumstance, the Indian submitting profoundly to the greater intelligence of his pale-face allies, in most things of this nature. How well the *sobriquet* was merited, will be seen in the sequel.

Rivenoak and the Panther sat side by side, awaiting the approach of their prisoner, as Deerslayer put his moccasined foot on the strand; nor did either move or utter a syllable until the young man had advanced into the centre of the area, and proclaimed his presence with his voice. This was done firmly, though in a simple manner that marked the character of the individual.

"Here I am, Mingos," he said, in the dialect of the Delawares, a language that most present understood; "here I am, and there is the sun. One is not more true to the laws of natur', than the other has proved true to his word. I am your prisoner; do with me what you please. My business with man and 'arth is settled; nothing remains now but to meet the white man's God, accordin' to a white man's duties and gifts."

A murmur of approbation escaped even the women at this address, and, for an instant, there was a strong and pretty general desire to adopt into the tribe one who owned so brave a spirit. Still there were dissenters from this wish, among the principal of whom might be classed the Panther, and his sister, Le Sumach, so called from the number of her children, who was the widow of Le Loup Cervier, now known to have fallen by the hand of the captive. Native ferocity held one in subjection, while the corroding passion of revenge prevented the other from admitting any gentler feeling at the moment. Not so with Rivenoak. This chief arose, stretched his arm before him, in a gesture of courtesy, and paid his compliments with an ease and dignity that a prince might have envied. As, in that band, his wisdom and eloquence were confessedly without rivals, he knew that on himself would properly fall the duty of first replying to the speech of the pale-face.

"Pale-face, you are honest," said the Huron orator. "My people are happy in having captured a man, and not a skulking fox. We now know you; we shall treat you like a brave. If you have slain one of our warriors, and helped to kill others, you have a life of your own ready to give away in return. Some of my young men thought that the blood of a pale-face was too thin; that it would refuse to run under the Huron knife. You will show them it is not so; your heart is stout as well as your body. It is a pleasure to make such a prisoner; should my warriors say that the death of Le Loup Cervier ought not to be forgotten, and that he cannot travel towards the land of spirits

alone, that his enemy must be sent to overtake him, they will remember that he fell by the hand of a brave, and send you after him with such signs of our friendship as shall not make him ashamed to keep your company. I have spoken; you know what I have said."

"True enough, Mingo, all true as the Gospel," returned the simple-minded hunter; "you *have* spoken, and I *do* know not only what you have *said*, but, what is still more important, what you *mean*. I dare say your warrior, the Lynx, was a stout-hearted brave, and worthy of your fri'ndship and respect, but I do not feel unworthy to keep his company, without any passport from your hands. Nevertheless, I am ready to receive judgment from your council, if, indeed, the matter was not determined among you, afore I got back."

"My old men would not sit in council over a pale-face until they saw him among them," answered Rivenoak, looking around him a little ironically; "they said it would be like sitting in council over the winds; they go where they will, and come back as they see fit, and not otherwise. There was one voice that spoke in your favor, Deerslayer, but it was alone, like the wren whose mate has been struck by the hawk."

"I thank that voice, whosoever it may have been, Mingo, and will say it was as true a voice, as the rest were lying voices. A furlough is as binding on a pale-face, if he be honest, as it is on a redskin; and was it not so, I would never bring disgrace on the Delawares, among whom I may be said to have received my edication. But words are useless, and lead to braggin' feelin's; here I am; act your will on me."

Rivenoak made a sign of acquiescence, and then a short conference was privately held among the chiefs. As soon as the latter ended, three or four young men fell back from among the armed group, and disappeared. Then it was signified to the prisoner that he was at liberty to go at large on the point, until a council was held concerning his fate. There was more of seeming, than of real confidence, however, in this apparent liberality, inasmuch as the young men mentioned already formed a line of sentinels across the breadth of the point, inland, and escape from any other part was out of the question. Even the canoe was removed beyond this line of sentinels, to a spot where it was considered safe from any sudden attempt. These precautions did not proceed from a failure of confidence, but from the circumstance that the prisoner had now complied with all the required conditions of his parole, and it would have been considered a commendable and honorable exploit to escape from his foes. So nice, indeed, were the distinctions drawn by the savages, in cases of this nature, that they often gave their victims a chance to evade the torture, deeming it as creditable to the captors to overtake, or to outwit a fugitive, when his exertions were supposed to be quickened by the extreme jeopardy of his situation, as it was for him to get clear from so much extraordinary vigilance.

Nor was Deerslayer unconscious of, or forgetful of, his rights, and of his opportunities. Could he now have seen any probable opening for an escape, the attempt would not have been delayed a minute. But the case seemed desperate. He was aware of the line of sentinels, and felt the difficulty of breaking through it, unharmed. The lake offered no advantages, as the canoe would have given his foes the greatest facilities for overtaking him; else would he have found it no difficult task to swim as far as the castle. As he walked about the point, he even examined the spot to ascertain if it offered no place of concealment; but its openness, its size, and the hundred watchful glances that were turned towards him, even while those who made them affected not to see him, prevented any such expedient from succeeding. The dread and disgrace of failure had no influence on Deerslayer, who deemed it ever a point of honor to reason and feel like white men, rather than as an Indian, and who felt it as a sort of duty to do all he could, that did not involve a dereliction from principle, in order to save his life. Still he hesitated about making the effort, for he also felt that he ought to see the chance of success before he committed himself.

In the meantime the business of the camp appeared to proceed in its regular train. The chiefs consulted apart, admitting no one but the Sumach to their councils; for she, the widow of the fallen warrior, had an exclusive right to be heard on such an occasion. The young men strolled about in indolent listlessness, awaiting the result with Indian impatience, while the females prepared the feast that was to celebrate the termination of the affair, whether it proved fortunate or otherwise for our hero. No one betrayed feeling; and an indifferent observer, beyond the extreme watchfulness of the sentinels, would have detected no extraordinary movement or sensation to denote the real state of things. Two or three old women put their heads together, and it appeared unfavorably to the prospect of Deerslayer, by their scowling looks and angry gestures; but a group of Indian girls were evidently animated by a different impulse, as was apparent by stolen glances that expressed pity and regret. In this condition of the camp, an hour soon glided away.

Suspense is, perhaps, the feeling of all others, that is most difficult to be supported. When Deer-

slayer landed, he fully expected in the course of a few minutes to undergo the tortures of an Indian revenge, and he was prepared to meet his fate manfully; but the delay proved far more trying than the nearer approach of suffering, and the intended victim began seriously to meditate some desperate effort at escape, as it might be from sheer anxiety to terminate the scene, when he was suddenly summoned to appear, once more, in front of his judges, who had already arranged the band in its former order, in readiness to receive him.

"Killer of the Deer," commenced Rivenoak, as soon as his captive stood before him, "my aged men have listened to wise words; they are ready to speak. You are a man whose fathers came from beyond the rising sun; we are children of the setting sun; we turn our faces towards the Great Sweet Lakes when we look towards our villages. It may be a wise country and full of riches towards the morning, but it is very pleasant towards the evening. We love most to look in that direction. When we gaze at the east we feel afraid, canoe after canoe bringing more and more of your people in the track of the sun, as if their land was so full as to run over. The redmen are few already; they have need of help. One of our best lodges has lately been emptied by the death of its master; it will be a long time before his son can grow big enough to sit in his place. There is his widow! she will want venison to feed her and her children, for her sons are yet like the young of the robin before they quit the nest. By your hand has this great calamity befallen her. She has two duties; one to Le Loup Cervier, and one to his children. Scalp for scalp, life for life, blood for blood, is one law; to feed her young another. We know you, Killer of the Deer. You are honest; when you say a thing it is so. You have but one tongue and that is not forked like a snake's. Your head is never hid in the grass; all can see it. What you say that will you do. You are just. When you have done wrong, it is your wish to do right again as soon as you can. Here is the Sumach; she is alone in her wigwam, with children crying around her for food; yonder is a rifle, it is loaded and ready to be fired. Take the gun; go forth and shoot a deer; bring the venison and lay it before the widow of Le Loup Cervier; feed her children; call yourself her husband. After which, your heart will no longer be Delaware but Huron; Le Sumach's ears will not hear the cries of her children; my people will count the proper number of warriors."

"I feared this, Rivenoak," answered Deerslayer, when the other had ceased speaking; "yes, I did dread that it would come to this. Howsever, the truth is soon told, and that will put an end to all expectations on this head. Mingo, I'm white, and Christian-born; 'twould ill become me to take a wife, under redskin forms, from among heathen. That which I wouldn't do in peaceable times, and under a bright sun, still less would I do behind clouds, in order to save my life. I may never marry; most likely Providence, in putting me up here in the woods, has intended I should live single, and without a lodge of my own; but should such a thing come to pass, none but a woman of my own color and gifts shall darken the door of my wigwam. As for feeding the young of your dead warrior, I would do that cheerfully, could it be done without discredit; but it cannot, seeing that I can never live in a Huron village. Your own young men must find the Sumach venison, and the next time she marries, let her take a husband whose legs are not long enough to overrun territory that don't belong to him. We fou't a fair battle, and he fell; in this there is nothin' but what a brave expects, and should be ready to meet. As for getting a Mingo heart, as well might you expect to see gray hairs on a boy, or the blackberry growing on the pine. No, no, Huron; my gifts are white, so far as wives are consarned; it is Delaware in all things touchin' Injins."

These words were scarcely out of the mouth of Deerslayer, before a common murmur betrayed the dissatisfaction with which they had been heard. The aged women, in particular, were loud in their expressions of disgust; and the gentle Sumach herself, a woman quite old enough to be our hero's mother, was not the least pacific in her denunciations. But all the other manifestations of disappointment and discontent were thrown into the background, by the fierce resentment of the Panther. This grim chief had thought it a degradation to permit his sister to become the wife of a paleface of the Yengeese, at all, and had only given a reluctant consent to the arrangement—one by no means unusual among the Indians, however—at the earnest solicitations of the bereaved widow; and it goaded him to the quick to find his condescension slighted, the honor he had with so much regret been persuaded to accord, contemned. The animal from which he got his name does not glare on his intended prey with more frightful ferocity, than his eyes gleamed on the captive; nor was his arm backward in seconding the fierce resentment that almost consumed his breast.

"Dog of the pale-faces!" he exclaimed, in Iroquois, "go yell among the curs of your own evil hunting-grounds!"

The denunciation was accompanied by an appropriate action. Even while speaking his arm was lifted and the tomahawk hurled. Luckily the loud tones of the speaker had drawn the eye of Deerslayer towards him, else would that moment have probably closed his career. So great was the dexterity with which this dangerous weapon was thrown, and so deadly the intent, that it would have riven the skull of the prisoner, had he not stretched forth an arm, and caught the handle in one of its turns, with a readiness quite as remarkable as the skill with which the missile had been hurled. The projectile force was so great, notwithstanding, that when Deerslayer's arm was arrested, his hand was raised above and behind his own head, and in the very attitude necessary to return the attack. It is not certain whether the circumstance of finding himself unexpectedly in this menacing posture and armed, tempted the young man to retaliate, or whether sudden resentment overcame his forbearance and prudence. His eye kindled, however, and a small red spot appeared on each cheek, while he cast all his energy into the effort of his arm, and threw back the weapon at his assailant. The unexpectedness of this blow contributed to its success; the Panther neither raising an arm nor bending his head to avoid it. The keen little axe struck the victim in a perpendicular line with the nose, directly between the eyes, literally braining him on the spot. Sallying forward, as the serpent darts at its enemy even while receiving its own death-wound, this man of powerful frame fell his length into the open area formed by the circle, quivering in death. A common rush to his relief left the captive, for a single instant, quite without the crowd; and, willing to make one desperate effort for life, he bounded off with the activity of a deer. There was but a breathless instant, when the whole band, old and young, women and children, abandoning the lifeless body of the Panther where it lay, raised the yell of alarm, and followed in pursuit.

Sudden as had been the event which induced Deerslayer to make this desperate trial of speed, his mind was not wholly unprepared for the fearful emergency. In the course of the past hour, he had pondered well on the chances of such an experiment, and had shrewdly calculated all the details of success and failure. At the first leap, therefore, his body was completely under the direction of an intelligence that turned all its efforts to the best account, and prevented everything like hesitation or indecision, at the important instant of the start. To this alone was he indebted for the first great advantage, that of getting through the line of sentinels unharmed. The manner in which this was done, though sufficiently simple, merits a description.

Although the shores of the point were not fringed with bushes, as was the case with most of the others on the lake, it was owing altogether to the circumstance that the spot had been so much used by hunters and fishermen. This fringe commenced on what might be termed the mainland, and was dense as usual, extending in long lines both north and south. In the latter direction, then, Deerslayer held his way; and, as the sentinels were a little without the commencement of this thicket before the alarm was clearly communicated to them, the fugitive had gained its cover. To run among the bushes, however, was out of the question, and Deerslayer held his way for some forty or fifty yards in the water, which was barely knee deep, offering as great an obstacle to the speed of his pursuers as it did to his own. As soon as a favorable spot presented, he darted through the line of bushes, and issued into the open woods.

Several rifles were discharged at Deerslayer while in the water, and more followed as he came out into the comparative exposure of the clear forest. But the direction of his line of flight which partially crossed that of the fire, the haste with which the weapons had been aimed, and the general confusion that prevailed in the camp, prevented any harm from being done. Bullets whistled past him, and many cut twigs from the branches at his side, but not one touched even his dress. The delay caused by these fruitless attempts was of great service to the fugitive, who had gained more than a hundred yards on even the leading men of the Hurons, ere something like concert and order had entered into the chase. To think of following with rifle in hand was out of the question; and after emptying their pieces in vague hope of wounding their captive, the best runners of the Indians threw them aside, calling out to the women and boys to recover and load them again, as soon as possible.

Deerslayer knew too well the desperate nature of the struggle in which he was engaged, to lose one of the precious moments. He also knew that his only hope was to run in a straight line, for as soon as he began to turn, or double, the greater number of his pursuers would put escape out of the question. He held his way, therefore, in a diagonal direction up the acclivity, which was neither very high nor very steep, in this part of the mountain, but which was sufficiently toilsome for one contending for life, to render it painfully oppressive. There, however, he slackened his speed, to recover breath, proceeding even at a quick walk, or a slow trot, along the more difficult parts of the way. The Hurons were whooping and leaping behind him; but this he disregarded, well knowing they must overcome the difficulties he had surmounted, ere they could reach the elevation to which he had attained. The summit of the first hill was now quite near him, and he saw,

by the formation of the land, that a deep glen intervened, before the base of a second hill could be reached. Walking deliberately to the summit, he glanced eagerly about him, in every direction, in quest of a cover. None offered in the ground; but a fallen tree lay near him, and desperate circumstances required desperate remedies. This tree lay in a line parallel to the glen, at the brow of the hill; to leap on it, and then to force his person as close as possible under its lower side, took but a moment. Previously to disappearing from his pursuers, however, Deerslayer stood on the height, and gave a cry of triumph, as if exulting at the sight of the descent that lay before him. In the next instant he was stretched beneath the tree.

No sooner was this expedient adopted, than the young man ascertained how desperate had been his own efforts, by the violence of the pulsation in his frame. He could hear his heart beat, and his breathing was like the action of a bellows in quick motion. Breath was gained, however, and the heart soon ceased to throb as if about to break through its confinement. The footsteps of those who toiled up the opposite side of the acclivity were now audible, and presently voices and treads announced the arrival of the pursuers. The foremost shouted as they reached the height; then, fearful that their enemy would escape under favor of the descent, each leaped upon the fallen tree, and plunged into the ravine, trusting to get a sight of the pursued, ere he reached the bottom. In this manner, Huron followed Huron, until Natty began to hope the whole had passed. Others succeeded, however, until quite forty had leaped over the tree; and then he counted them, as the surest mode of ascertaining how many could be behind. Presently all were in the bottom of the glen, quite a hundred feet below him, and some had even ascended part of the opposite hill, when it became evident an inquiry was making, as to the direction he had taken. This was the critical moment; and one of nerves less steady, or of a training that had been neglected, would have seized it to rise and fly. Not so with Deerslayer. He still lay quiet, watching with jealous vigilance every movement below, and fast regaining his breath.

The Hurons now resembled a pack of hounds at fault. Little was said, but each man ran about, examining the dead leaves, as the hound hunts for the lost scent. The great number of moccasins that had passed made the examination difficult, though the in-toe of an Indian was easily to be distinguished from the freer and wider step of a white man. Believing that no more pursuers remained behind, and hoping to steal away unseen, Deerslayer suddenly threw himself over the tree, and fell on the upper side. This achievement appeared to be effected successfully, and hope beat high in the bosom of the fugitive. Rising to his hands and feet, after a moment lost in listening to the sounds in the glen, in order to ascertain if he had been seen, the young man next scrambled to the top of the hill, a distance of only ten yards, in the expectation of getting its brow between him and his pursuers, and himself so far under cover. Even this was effected, and he rose to his feet, walking swiftly but steadily along the summit, in a direction opposite to that in which he had first fled. The nature of the calls in the glen, however, soon made him uneasy, and he sprang upon the summit, again, in order to reconnoitre. No sooner did he reach the height than he was seen, and the chase renewed. As it was better footing on the level ground, Deerslayer now avoided the side-hill, holding his flight along the ridge; while the Hurons, judging from the general formation of the land, saw that the ridge would soon melt into the hollow, and kept to the latter, as the easiest mode of heading the fugitive. A few, at the same time, turned south, with a view to prevent his escaping in that direction; while some crossed his trail towards the water, in order to prevent his retreat by the lake, running southerly.

The situation of Deerslayer was now more critical than it ever had been. He was virtually surrounded on three sides, having the lake on the fourth. But he had pondered well on all the chances, and took his measures with coolness, even while at the top of his speed. As is generally the case with the vigorous border-men, he could outrun any single Indian among his pursuers, who were principally formidable to him on account of their numbers, and the advantages they possessed in position; and he would not have hesitated to break off, in a straight line, at any spot, could he have got the whole band again fairly behind him. But no such chance did, or indeed could now offer; and when he found that he was descending towards the glen, by the melting away of the ridge, he turned short at right angles to his previous course, and went down the declivity with tremendous velocity, holding his way towards the shore. Some of his pursuers came panting up the hill, in direct chase, while most still kept on, in the ravine, intending to head him at its termination. Deerslayer had now a different, though a desperate project in view. Abandoning all thoughts of escape by the woods, he made the best of his way towards the canoe. He knew where it lay: could it be reached, he had only to run the gauntlet of a few rifles, and success would be certain. None of the warriors had kept their weapons, which would have retarded their speed, and the risk would come either from the uncertain hands of the women, or from those

of some well-grown boy; though most of the latter were already out in hot pursuit. Everything seemed propitious to the execution of this plan, and the course being a continued descent, the young man went over the ground at a rate that promised a speedy termination to his toil.

As Deerslayer approached the point, several women and children were passed, but, though the former endeavored to cast dried branches between his legs, the terror inspired by his bold retaliation on the redoubted Panther was so great, that none dared come near enough seriously to molest him. He went by all triumphantly, and reached the fringe of bushes. Plunging through these, our hero found himself once more in the lake and within fifty feet of the canoe. Here he ceased to run, for he well understood that his breath was now all-important to him. He even stooped, as he advanced, and cooled his parched mouth, by scooping up water in his hand to drink. Still the moments pressed, and he soon stood at the side of the canoe. The first glance told him that the paddles had been removed! This was a sore disappointment after all his efforts, and, for a single moment, he thought of turning and of facing his foes by walking with dignity into the centre of the camp again. But an infernal yell, such as the American savage alone can raise, proclaimed the quick approach of the nearest of his pursuers, and the instinct of life triumphed. Preparing himself duly, and giving a right direction to its bows, he ran off into the water bearing the canoe before him, threw all his strength and skill into a last effort, and cast himself forward so as to fall into the bottom of the light craft, without materially impeding its way. Here he remained on his back, both to regain his breath and to cover his person from the deadly rifle. The lightness, which was such an advantage in paddling the canoe, now operated unfavorably. The material was so like a feather that the boat had no momentum; else would the impulse in that smooth and placid sheet have impelled it to a distance from the shore, that would have rendered paddling with the hands safe. Could such a point once be reached, Deerslayer thought he might get far enough out to attract the attention of Chingachgook and Judith, who would not fail to come to his relief with other canoes, a circumstance that promised everything. As the young man lay in the bottom of the canoe he watched its movements, by studying the tops of the trees on the mountain-side, and judged of his distance by the time and the motion. Voices on the shore were now numerous, and he heard something said about manning the raft, which fortunately for the fugitive lay at a considerable distance on the other side of the point.

Perhaps the situation of Deerslayer had not been

more critical that day than it was at this moment. It certainly had not been one half as tantalizing. He lay perfectly quiet for two or three minutes, trusting to the single sense of hearing, confident that the noise on the lake would reach his ears, did any one approach by swimming. Once or twice he fancied that the element was stirred by the cautious movement of an arm, and then he perceived it was the wash of the water on the pebbles of the strand; for in mimicry of the ocean, it is seldom that those little lakes are so totally tranquil, as not to possess a slight heaving and setting on their shores. Suddenly all the voices ceased, and a death-like stillness pervaded the spot; a quietness as profound as if all lay in the repose of inanimate life. By this time the canoe had drifted so far as to render nothing visible to Deerslayer, as he lay on his back, except the blue void of space, and a few of those brighter rays that proceed from the effulgence of the sun, marking his proximity. It was not possible to endure this uncertainty long. The young man well knew that the profound stillness foreboded evil, the savages never being so silent as when about to strike a blow; resembling the stealthy foot of the panther ere he takes his leap. He took out a knife, and was about to cut a hole through the bark in order to get a view of the shore, when he paused from a dread of being seen in the operation, which would direct the enemy where to aim their bullets. At this instant a rifle *was* fired, and the ball pierced both sides of the canoe, within eighteen inches of the spot where his head lay. This was close work, but our hero had too lately gone through that which was closer, to be appalled. He lay still half a minute longer, and then he saw the summit of an oak coming slowly within his narrow horizon.

Unable to account for this change, Deerslayer could restrain his impatience no longer. Hitching his body along, with the utmost caution, he got his eye at the bullet-hole, and fortunately commanded a very tolerable view of the point. The canoe, by one of those imperceptible impulses that so often decide the fate of men, as well as the course of things, had inclined southerly, and was slowly drifting down the lake. It was lucky that Deerslayer had given it a shove sufficiently vigorous to send it past the end of the point ere it took this inclination, or it must have gone ashore again. As it was, it drifted so near it as to bring the tops of two or three of the trees within the range of the young man's view, as has been mentioned, and, indeed, to come in quite as close proximity with the extremity of the point as was at all safe. The distance could not much have exceeded a hundred feet, though fortunately a light current of air from the southwest began to set it slowly off shore.

Deerslayer now felt the urgent necessity of resorting to some expedient to get farther from his foes, and, if possible, to apprise his friends of his situation. The distance rendered the last difficult, while the proximity to the point rendered the first indispensable. As was usual in such a craft, a large, round, smooth stone was in each end of the canoe, for the double purpose of seats and ballast; one of these was within reach of his feet. The stone he contrived to get so far between his legs as to reach it with his hands, and then he managed to roll it to the side of its fellow in the bows, where the two served to keep the trim of the light boat, while he worked his own body as far aft as possible. Before quitting the shore, and as soon as he perceived that the paddles were gone, Deerslayer had thrown a bit of dead branch into the canoe, and this was within the reach of his arm. Removing the cap he wore, he put it on the end of this stick, and just let it appear over the edge of the canoe, as far as possible from his own person. This *ruse* was scarcely adopted, before the young man had proof how much he had underrated the intelligence of his enemies. In contempt of an artifice so shallow and commonplace, a bullet was fired directly through another part of the canoe, which actually razed his skin. He dropped the cap, and instantly raised it immediately over his head, as a safeguard. It would seem that this second artifice was unseen, or what was more probable, the Hurons, feeling certain of recovering their captive, wished to take him alive.

Deerslayer lay passive a few minutes longer, his eye at the bullet-hole, however, and much did he rejoice at seeing that he was drifting gradually farther and farther from the shore. When he looked upwards, the tree-tops had disappeared, but he soon found that the canoe was slowly turning, so as to prevent his getting a view of anything at his peep-hole, but of the two extremities of the lake. He now bethought him of the stick, which was crooked, and offered some facilities for rowing, without the necessity of rising. The experiment succeeded, on trial, better even than he had hoped, though his great embarrassment was to keep the canoe straight. That his present manœuvre was seen soon became apparent by the clamor on the shore, and a bullet entering the stern of the canoe, traversed its length, whistling between the arms of our hero, and passed out at the head. This satisfied the fugitive that he was getting away with tolerable speed, and induced him to increase his efforts. He was making a stronger push than common, when another messenger from the point broke the stick out-board, and at once deprived him of his oar. As the sound of voices seemed to grow more and more distant, however, Deerslayer determined to leave all to the drift, until he believed himself beyond the reach of bullets. This was nervous work, but it was the wisest of all the expedients that offered; and the young man was encouraged to persevere in it, by the circumstance that he felt his face fanned by the air, a proof that there was a little more wind.

### *from* CHAPTER 28

BY THIS TIME, Deerslayer had been twenty minutes in the canoe, and he began to grow a little impatient for some signs of relief from his friends. The position of the boat still prevented his seeing in any direction, unless it were up or down the lake; and, though he knew that this line of sight must pass within a hundred yards of the castle, it, in fact, passed that distance to the westward of the buildings. The profound stillness troubled him also, for he knew not whether to ascribe it to the increasing space between him and the Indians, or to some new artifice. At length, wearied with fruitless watchfulness, the young man turned himself on his back, closed his eyes, and awaited the result in determined acquiescence. If the savages could so completely control their thirst for revenge, he was resolved to be as calm as themselves, and to trust his fate to the interposition of the currents and air.

Some additional ten minutes may have passed in this quiescent manner, on both sides, when Deerslayer thought he heard a slight noise, like a low rubbing against the bottom of his canoe. He opened his eyes of course, in expectation of seeing the face or arm of an Indian rising from the water, and found that a canopy of leaves was impending directly over his head. Starting to his feet, the first object that met his eyes was Rivenoak, who had so far aided the slow progress of the boat, as to draw it on the point, the grating on the strand being the sound that had first given our hero the alarm. The change in the drift of the canoe had been altogether owing to the baffling nature of the light currents of air, aided by some eddies in the water. . . .

"Come," said the Huron, with a quiet gesture of authority to order his prisoner to land; "my young friend has sailed about till he is tired; he will forget how to run again, unless he uses his legs.". . .

### CHAPTER 29

IT WAS one of the common expedients of the savages, on such occasions, to put the nerves of their victims to the severest proofs. On the other hand, it was a matter of Indian pride to betray no yielding to terror or pain; but for the prisoner to provoke his enemies to such acts of violence as would soonest produce death. Many a warrior had been known to bring his own sufferings to a

more speedy termination, by taunting reproaches and reviling language, when he found that his physical system was giving way under the agony of sufferings, produced by a hellish ingenuity, that might well eclipse all that has been said of the infernal devices of religious persecution. This happy expedient of taking refuge from the ferocity of his foes in their passions, was denied Deerslayer, however, by his peculiar notions of the duty of a white man; and he had stoutly made up his mind to endure everything, in preference to disgracing his color.

No sooner did the young men understand that they were at liberty to commence, than some of the boldest and most forward among them sprang into the arena, tomahawk in hand. Here they prepared to throw that dangerous weapon, the object being to strike the tree as near as possible to the victim's head, without absolutely hitting him. This was so hazardous an experiment, that none but those who were known to be exceedingly expert with the weapon were allowed to enter the lists at all, lest an early death might interfere with the expected entertainment. In the truest hands, it was seldom that the captive escaped injury in these trials; and it often happened that death followed even when the blow was not premeditated. In the particular case of our hero, Rivenoak and the older warriors were apprehensive that the example of the Panther's fate might prove a motive with some fiery spirit, suddenly to sacrifice his conqueror, when the temptation of effecting it in precisely the same manner, and possibly with the identical weapon with which the warrior had fallen, offered. This circumstance, of itself, rendered the ordeal of the tomahawk doubly critical for the Deerslayer.

It would seem, however, that all who now entered what we shall call the lists, were more disposed to exhibit their own dexterity than to resent the deaths of their comrades. Each prepared himself for the trial, with the feelings of rivalry, rather than with the desire for vengeance; and for the first few minutes, the prisoner had little more connection with the result, than grew out of the interest that necessarily attached itself to a living target. The young men were eager, instead of being fierce, and Rivenoak thought he still saw signs of being able to save the life of the captive, when the vanity of the young men had been gratified; always admitting, that it was not sacrificed to the delicate experiments that were about to be made.

The first youth who presented himself for the trial, was called the Raven, having as yet had no opportunity of obtaining a more warlike *sobriquet*. He was remarkable for high pretension rather than for skill or exploits; and those who knew his character, thought the captive in imminent danger, when he took his stand, and poised the tomahawk. Nevertheless, the young man was good-natured, and no thought was uppermost in his mind, other than the desire to make a better cast than any of his fellows. Deerslayer got an inkling of this warrior's want of reputation, by the injunctions that he had received from the seniors; who, indeed, would have objected to his appearing in the arena at all, but for an influence derived from his father, an aged warrior of great merit, who was then in the lodges of the tribe. Still, our hero maintained an appearance of self-possession. He had made up his mind that his hour was come, and it would have been a mercy, instead of a calamity, to fall by the unsteadiness of the first hand that was raised against him. After a suitable number of flourishes and gesticulations, that promised much more than he could perform, the Raven let the tomahawk quit his hand. The weapon whirled through the air, with the usual evolutions, cut a chip from the sapling to which the prisoner was bound, within a few inches of his cheek, and stuck in a large oak that grew several yards behind him. This was decidedly a bad effort, and a common sneer proclaimed as much, to the great mortification of the young man. On the other hand, there was a general, but suppressed murmur of admiration, at the steadiness with which the captive stood the trial. The head was the only part he could move, and this had been purposely left free, that the tormentors might have the amusement, and the tormented endure the shame, of dodging, and otherwise attempting to avoid the blows. Deerslayer disappointed these hopes, by a command of nerve that rendered his whole body as immovable as the tree to which he was bound. Nor did he even adopt the natural and usual expedient of shutting his eyes: the firmest and oldest warrior of the redmen never having more disdainfully denied himself this advantage, under similar circumstances.

The Raven had no sooner made his unsuccessful and puerile effort than he was succeeded by Le Daim-Mose, or the Moose; a middle-aged warrior, who was particularly skilful in the use of the tomahawk, and from whose attempt the spectators confidently looked for gratification. This man had none of the good-nature of the Raven, but he would gladly have sacrificed the captive to his hatred of the pale-faces generally, were it not for the greater interest he felt in his own success as one particularly skilful in the use of this weapon. He took his stand quietly, but with an air of confidence, poised his little axe but a single instant, advanced a foot with a quick motion, and threw. Deerslayer saw the keen instrument whirling towards him, and be-

lieved all was over; still he was not touched. The tomahawk had actually bound the head of the captive to the tree, by carrying before it some of his hair; having buried itself deep beneath the soft bark. A general yell expressed the delight of the spectators, and the Moose felt his heart soften a little towards the prisoner, whose steadiness of nerve alone enabled him to give this evidence of his consummate skill.

Le Daim-Mose was succeeded by the Bounding Boy, or Le Garçon qui Bondi, who came leaping into the circle, like a hound or a goat at play. This was one of those elastic youths, whose muscles seemed always in motion, and who either affected, or who from habit was actually unable to move in any other manner, than by showing the antics just mentioned. Nevertheless, he was both brave and skilful, and had gained the respect of his people by deeds in war as well as success in the hunts. A far nobler name would long since have fallen to his share, had not a Frenchman of rank inadvertently given him this *sobriquet,* which he religiously preserved as coming from his great father, who lived beyond the wide salt lake. The Bounding Boy skipped about in front of the captive, menacing him with his tomahawk, now on one side and now on another, and then again in front, in the vain hope of being able to extort some sign of fear, by this parade of danger. At length Deerslayer's patience became exhausted by all this mummery, and he spoke for the first time since the trial had actually commenced.

"Throw away, Huron!" he cried, "or your tomahawk will forget its arr'nd. Why do you keep loping about like a fa'an that's showing its dam how well it can skip, when you're a warrior grown, yourself, and a warrior grown defies you and all your silly antics? Throw, or the Huron gals will laugh in your face."

Although not intended to produce such an effect, the last words aroused the "Bounding" warrior to fury. The same nervous excitability which rendered him so active in his person, made it difficult to repress his feelings, and the words were scarcely past the lips of the speaker, than the tomahawk left the hand of the Indian. Nor was it cast without goodwill, and a fierce determination to slay. Had the intention been less deadly, the danger might have been greater. The aim was uncertain, and the weapon glanced near the cheek of the captive, slightly cutting the shoulder in its evolutions. This was the first instance in which any other object than that of terrifying the prisoner, and of displaying skill, had been manifested; and the Bounding Boy was immediately led from the arena, and was warmly rebuked for his intemperate haste, which had come so near defeating all the hopes of the band.

To this irritable person succeeded several other young warriors, who not only hurled the tomahawk but who cast the knife, a far more dangerous experiment, with reckless indifference; yet they always manifested a skill that prevented any injury to the captive. Several times Deerslayer was grazed, but in no instance did he receive what might be termed a wound. The unflinching firmness with which he faced his assailants, more especially in the sort of rally with which this trial terminated, excited a profound respect in the spectators; and when the chiefs announced that the prisoner had well withstood the trials of the knife and the tomahawk, there was not a single individual in the band who really felt any hostility towards him, with the exception of Sumach and the Bounding Boy. These two discontented spirits got together, it is true, feeding each other's ire; but, as yet, their malignant feelings were confined very much to themselves, though there existed the danger that the others, ere long, could not fail to be excited by their own efforts into that demoniacal state which usually accompanied all similar scenes among the redmen.

Rivenoak now told his people that the pale-face had proved himself to be a man. He might live with the Delawares, but he had not been made woman with that tribe. He wished to know whether it was the desire of the Hurons to proceed any further. Even the gentlest of the females, however, had received too much satisfaction in the late trials to forego their expectations of a gratifying exhibition; and there was but one voice in the request to proceed. The politic chief, who had some such desire to receive so celebrated a hunter into his tribe as a European minister has to devise a new and available means of taxation, sought every plausible means of arresting the trial in season; for he well knew, if permitted to go far enough to arouse the more ferocious passions of the tormentors, it would be as easy to dam the waters of the great lakes of his own region, as to attempt to arrest them in their bloody career. He therefore called four or five of the best marksmen to him, and bid them put the captive to the proof of the rifle, while, at the same time, he cautioned them touching the necessity of their maintaining their own credit, by the closest attention to the manner of exhibiting their skill.

When Deerslayer saw the chosen warriors step into the circle, with their arms prepared for service, he felt some such relief as the miserable sufferer, who had long endured the agonies of disease, feels at the certain approach of death. Any trifling variance in the aim of this formidable weapon would

prove fatal; since, the head being the target, or rather the point it was desired to graze without injury, an inch or two of difference in the line of projection must at once determine the question of life or death.

In the torture by the rifle there was none of the latitude permitted that appeared in the case of even Gesler's apple, a hair'sbreadth being, in fact, the utmost limits that an expert marksman would allow himself on an occasion like this. Victims were frequently shot through the head by too eager or unskilful hands; and it often occurred that, exasperated by the fortitude and taunts of the prisoner, death was dealt intentionally in a moment of ungovernable irritation. All this Deerslayer well knew, for it was in relating the traditions of such scenes, as well as of the battles and victories of their people, that the old men beguiled the long winter evenings in their cabins. He now fully expected the end of his career, and experienced a sort of melancholy pleasure in the idea that he was to fall by a weapon as much beloved as the rifle. A slight interruption, however, took place before the business was allowed to proceed. . . .

The warriors, as soon as this interruption had ceased, resumed their places, and again prepared to exhibit their skill, as there was a double object in view, that of putting the constancy of the captive to the proof, and that of showing how steady were the hands of the marksmen under circumstances of excitement. The distance was small, and, in one sense, safe. But in diminishing the distance taken by the tormentors, the trial to the nerves of the captive was essentially increased. The face of Deerslayer, indeed, was just removed sufficiently from the ends of the guns to escape the effects of the flash, and his steady eye was enabled to look directly into their muzzles, as it might be, in anticipation of the fatal messenger that was to issue from each. The cunning Hurons well knew this fact; and scarce one levelled his piece without first causing it to point as near as possible at the forehead of the prisoner, in the hope that his fortitude would fail him, and that the band would enjoy the triumph of seeing a victim quail under their ingenious cruelty. Nevertheless, each of the competitors was still careful not to injure; the disgrace of striking prematurely being second only to that of failing altogether in attaining the object. Shot after shot was made; all the bullets coming in close proximity to the Deerslayer's head, without touching it. Still, no one could detect even the twitching of a muscle on the part of the captive, or the slightest winking of an eye. This indomitable resolution, which so much exceeded everything of its kind that any present had before witnessed, might be referred to three distinct causes. The first was resignation to his fate, blended with natural steadiness of deportment; for our hero had calmly made up his mind that he must die, and preferred this mode to any other; the second was his great familiarity with this particular weapon, which deprived it of all the terror that is usually connected with the mere form of the danger; and the third was this familiarity carried out in practice, to a degree so nice as to enable the intended victim to tell, within an inch, the precise spot where each bullet must strike, for he calculated its range by looking in at the bore of the piece. So exact was Deerslayer's estimation of the line of fire, that his pride of feeling finally got the better of his resignation, and, when five or six had discharged their bullets into the trees, he could not refrain from expressing his contempt at their want of hand and eye.

"You may call this shooting, Mingos," he exclaimed, "but we've squaws among the Delawares, and I have known Dutch gals on the Mohawk, that could outdo your greatest indivors. Ondo these arms of mine, put a rifle into my hands, and I'll pin the thinnest warlock in your party to any tree you can show me; and this at a hundred yards: ay, or at two hundred, if the object can be seen, nineteen shots in twenty: or, for that matter, twenty in twenty if the piece is creditable and trusty!"

A low, menacing murmur followed this cool taunt; the ire of the warriors kindled at listening to such a reproach from one who so far disdained their efforts as to refuse even to wink, when a rifle was discharged as near his face as could be done without burning it. Rivenoak perceived that the moment was critical, and, still retaining his hope of adopting so noted a hunter into his tribe, the politic old chief interposed in time, probably, to prevent an immediate resort to that portion of the torture which must necessarily have produced death, through extreme bodily suffering, if in no other manner. Moving into the centre of the irritated group, he addressed them with his usual wily logic and plausible manner, at once suppressing the fierce movement that had commenced.

"I see how it is," he said. "We have been like the pale-faces when they fasten their doors at night, out of fear of the redman. They use so many bars, that the fire comes and burns them before they can get out. We have bound the Deerslayer too tight; the thongs keep his limbs from shaking, and his eyes from shutting. Loosen him; let us see what his own body is really made of."

It is often the case when we are thwarted in a cherished scheme, that any expedient, however unlikely to succeed, is gladly resorted to, in preference to a total abandonment of the project. So it

was with the Hurons. The proposal of the chief found instant favor; and several hands were immediately at work cutting and tearing the ropes of bark from the body of our hero. In half a minute, Deerslayer stood as free from bonds, as when, an hour before, he had commenced his flight on the side of the mountain. Some little time was necessary that he should recover the use of his limbs, the circulation of the blood having been checked by the tightness of the ligatures; and this was accorded to him by the politic Rivenoak, under the pretence that his body would be more likely to submit to apprehension, if his true tone were restored; though really with a view to give time to the fierce passions which had been awakened in the bosoms of his young men, to subside. This *ruse* succeeded; and Deerslayer, by rubbing his limbs, stamping his feet, and moving about, soon regained the circulation; recovering all his physical powers as effectually as if nothing had occurred to disturb them.

It is seldom men think of death in the pride of their health and strength. So it was with Deerslayer. Having been helplessly bound, and, as he had every reason to suppose, so lately on the very verge of the other world, to find himself so unexpectedly liberated, in possession of his strength, and with a full command of limb, acted on him like a sudden restoration to life, re-animating hopes that he had once absolutely abandoned. From that instant all his plans changed. In this he simply obeyed a law of nature; for while we have wished to represent our hero as being resigned to his fate, it has been far from our intention to represent him as anxious to die. From the instant that his buoyancy of feeling revived, his thoughts were keenly bent on the various projects that presented themselves as modes of evading the designs of his enemies; and he again became the quick-witted, ingenious, and determined woodsman, alive to all his own powers and resources. The change was so great, that his mind resumed its elasticity; and, no longer thinking of submission, it dwelt only on the devices of the sort of warfare in which he was engaged.

As soon as Deerslayer was released, the band divided itself in a circle around him, in order to hedge him in; and the desire to break down his spirit grew in them, precisely as they saw proofs of the difficulty there would be in subduing it. The honor of the band was now involved in the issue; and even the sex lost all its sympathy with suffering, in the desire to save the reputation of the tribe. The voices of the girls, soft and melodious as nature had made them, were heard mingling with the menaces of the men; and the wrongs of Sumach suddenly assumed the character of injuries inflicted on every Huron female. Yielding to this rising tumult, the men drew back a little, signifying to the females that they left the captive, for a time, in their hands; it being a common practice, on such occasions, for the women to endeavor to throw the victim into a rage, by their taunts and revilings, and then to turn him suddenly over to the men, in a state of mind that was little favorable to resisting the agony of bodily suffering. Nor was this party without the proper instruments for effecting such a purpose. Sumach had a notoriety as a scold; and one or two crones, like the Shebear, had come out with the party, most probably as the conservators of its decency and moral discipline; such things occurring in savage as well as civilized life. It is unnecessary to repeat all that ferocity and ignorance could invent for such a purpose; the only difference between this outbreaking of feminine anger, and a similar scene among ourselves, consisting in the figures of speech and the epithets; the Huron women calling their prisoner by the names of the lower and least respected animals that were known to themselves.

But Deerslayer's mind was too much occupied to permit him to be disturbed by the abuse of excited hags; and their rage necessarily increasing with his indifference, as his indifference increased with their rage, the furies soon rendered themselves impotent by their own excesses. Perceiving that the attempt was a complete failure, the warriors interfered to put a stop to this scene; and this so much the more, because preparations were now seriously making for the commencement of the real tortures, or that which would put the fortitude of the sufferer to the test of severe bodily pain. A sudden and unlooked-for announcement that proceeded from one of the look-outs, a boy ten or twelve years old, however, put a momentary check to the whole proceedings. As this interruption has a close connection with the *dénouement* of our story, it shall be given in a separate chapter.

## CHAPTER 30

It exceeded Deerslayer's power to ascertain what had produced the sudden pause in the movements of his enemies, until the fact was revealed in the due course of events. He perceived that much agitation prevailed among the women in particular, while the warriors rested on their arms, in a sort of dignified expectation. It was plain no alarm was excited, though it was not equally apparent that a friendly occurrence produced the delay. Rivenoak was evidently apprised of all, and by a gesture of his arm he appeared to direct the circle to remain unbroken, and for each person to await the issue in the situation he or she then occupied. It required but a minute or two to bring an explanation of this singular and mysterious pause, which was soon terminated by the appearance of Judith, on the exterior of the line of bodies, and her ready admission within its circle.

If Deerslayer was startled by this unexpected arrival, well knowing that the quick-witted girl would claim none of that exemption from the penalties of captivity that was so cheerfully accorded to her feeble-minded sister, he was equally astonished at the guise in which she came. All her ordinary forest attire, neat and becoming as this usually was, had been laid aside for the brocade that has been already mentioned, and which had once before wrought so great and magical an effect in her appearance. Nor was this all. Accustomed to see the ladies of the garrison, in the formal gala attire of the day, and familiar with the more critical niceties of these matters, the girl had managed to complete her dress, in a way to leave nothing strikingly defective in its details, or even to betray an incongruity that would have been detected by one practised in the mysteries of the toilet. Head, feet, arms, hands, bust, and drapery, were all in harmony, as female attire was then deemed attractive and harmonious: and the end she aimed at, that of imposing on the uninstructed senses of the savages, by causing them to believe their guest was a woman of rank and importance, might well have succeeded with those whose habits had taught them to discriminate between persons. Judith, in addition to her rare native beauty, had a singular grace of person, and her mother had imparted enough of her own deportment to prevent any striking or offensive vulgarity of manner; so that, sooth to say, the gorgeous dress might have been worse bestowed in nearly every particular. Had it been displayed in a capital, a thousand might have worn it before one could have been found to do more credit to its gay colors, glossy satins, and rich laces, than the beautiful creature whose person it now aided to adorn.

The effect of such an apparition had not been miscalculated. The instant Judith found herself within the circle, she was, in a degree, compensated for the fearful personal risk she ran, by the unequivocal sensation of surprise and admiration produced by her appearance. The grim old warriors uttered their favorite exclamation, "Hugh!" The younger men were still more sensibly overcome, and even the women were not backward in letting open manifestations of pleasure escape them. It was seldom that these untutored children of the forest had ever seen any white female above the commonest sort, and as to dress, never before had so much splendor shone before their eyes. The gayest uniforms of both French and English seemed dull compared with the lustre of the brocade; and while the rare personal beauty of the wearer added to the effect produced by its hues, the attire did not fail to adorn that beauty in a way which surpassed even the hopes of its wearer. Deerslayer himself was astounded, and this quite as much by the brilliant picture the girl presented, as at the indifference to consequences with which she had braved the danger of the step she had taken. Under such circumstances, all waited for the visitor to explain her object, which to most of the spectators seemed as inexplicable as her appearance.

"Which of these warriors is the principal chief?" demanded Judith of Deerslayer, as soon as she found it was expected that she should open the communication; "my errand is too important to be delivered to any of inferior rank. First explain to the Hurons what I say; then give an answer to the question I have put."

Deerslayer quietly complied, his auditors greedily listening to the interpretation of the first words that fell from so extraordinary a vision. The demand seemed perfectly in character for one who had every appearance of an exalted rank herself. Rivenoak gave an appropriate reply, by presenting himself before his fair visitor in a way to leave no doubt that he was entitled to all the consideration he claimed.

"I can believe this, Huron," resumed Judith, enacting her assumed part with a steadiness and dignity that did credit to her powers of imitation, for she strove to impart to her manner the condescending courtesy she had once observed in the wife of a general officer, at a similar though a more amicable scene: "I can believe you to be the principal person of this party; I see in your countenance the marks of thought and reflection. To you, then, I must make my communication."

"Let the Flower of the Woods speak," returned the old chief, courteously, as soon as her address had been translated so that all might understand it. "If her words are as pleasant as her looks, they will never quit my ears; I shall hear them long after the winter in Canada has killed the flowers, and frozen all the speeches of summer."

This admiration was grateful to one constituted like Judith, and contributed to aid her self-possession, quite as much as it fed her vanity. Smiling involuntarily, or in spite of her wish to seem reserved, she proceeded in her plot.

"Now, Huron," she continued, "listen to my words. Your eyes tell you that I am no common woman. I will not say I am queen of this country; *she* is afar off, in a distant land; but under our gracious monarchs there are many degrees of rank; one of these I fill. What that rank is precisely it is unnecessary for me to say, since you would not understand it. For that information you must trust your eyes. You *see* what I am; you must *feel* that in listening to my words, you listen to one who can be your friend or your enemy, as you treat her."

This was well uttered, with a due attention to manner and a steadiness of tone that was really surprising, considering all the circumstances of the case. It was well, though simply rendered into the Indian dialect, too, and it was received with a respect and gravity that augured favorably for the girl's success. But Indian thought is not easily traced to its sources. Judith waited with anxiety to hear the answer, filled with hope even while she doubted. Rivenoak was a ready speaker, and he answered as promptly as comported with the notions of Indian decorum; that peculiar people seeming to think a short delay respectful, inasmuch as it manifests that the words already heard have been duly weighed.

"My daughter is handsomer than the wild roses of Ontario; her voice as pleasant to the ear as the song of the wren," answered the cautious and wily chief, who of all the band stood alone in not being being fully imposed on by the magnificent and unusual appearance of Judith, but who distrusted even while he wondered; "the humming-bird is not much larger than the bee; yet its feathers are as gay as the tail of the peacock. The Great Spirit sometimes puts very bright clothes on very little animals. Still, he covers the moose with coarse hair. These things are beyond the understanding of poor Indians, who can only comprehend what they see and hear. No doubt my daughter has a very large wigwam somewhere about the lake: the Hurons have not found it on account of their ignorance?"

"I have told you, chief, that it would be useless to state my rank and residence, inasmuch as you would not comprehend them. You must trust to your eyes for this knowledge; what redman is there that cannot see? This blanket that I wear is not the blanket of a common squaw; these ornaments are such as the wives and daughters of chiefs only appear in. Now listen and hear why I have come alone among your people, and hearken to the errand that has brought me here. The Yengeese have young men as well as the Hurons; and plenty of them, too; this you well know."

"The Yengeese are as plenty as the leaves on the trees! This every Huron knows and feels."

"I understand you, chief. Had I brought a party with me it might have caused trouble. My young men and your young men would have looked angrily at each other; especially had my young men seen that pale-face bound for the tortures. He is a great hunter, and is much loved by all the garrisons, far and near. There would have been blows about him, and the trail of the Iroquois back to the Canadas would have been marked with blood."

"There is so much blood on it now," returned the chief, gloomily, "that it blinds our eyes. My young men see that it is all Huron."

"No doubt; and more Huron blood would be spilt, had I come surrounded with pale-faces. I have heard of Rivenoak, and have thought it would be better to send him back in peace to his village, that he might leave his women and children behind him; if he then wished to come for our scalps, we would meet him. He loves animals made of ivory, and little rifles. See; I have brought some with me to show him I am his friend. When he has packed up these things among his goods, he will start for his village, before any of my young men can overtake him; and then he will show his people in Canada what riches they can come to seek, now that our great fathers, across the salt lake, have sent each other the warhatchet. I will lead back with me, this great hunter, of whom I have need to keep my house in venison."

Judith, who was sufficiently familiar with Indian phraseology, endeavored to express her ideas in the sententious manner common to those people; and she succeeded even beyond her own expectations. Deerslayer did her full justice in the translation, and this so much the more readily, since the girl carefully abstained from uttering any direct untruth; a homage she paid to the young man's known aversion to falsehood, which he deemed a meanness altogether unworthy of a white man's gifts. The offering of the two remaining elephants, and of the pistols already mentioned, one of which was all the worse for the recent accident, produced a lively sensation among the Hurons generally, though Rivenoak received it coldly, notwithstanding the delight with which he had first discovered the probable existence of a creature with two tails. In a word, this cool and sagacious savage was not so easily imposed on as his followers; and with a sentiment of honor, that half the civilized world would have deemed supererogatory, he declined the acceptance of a bribe that he felt no disposition to earn by a compliance with the donor's wishes.

"Let my daughter keep her two-tailed hog, to eat when venison is scarce," he dryly answered; "and the little gun, which has two muzzles. The Hurons will kill deer when they are hungry; and they have long rifles to fight with. This hunter cannot quit my young men now; they wish to know if he is as stout-hearted as he boasts himself to be."

"That I deny, Huron," interrupted Deerslayer, with warmth; "yes, that I downright deny, as ag'in

truth and reason. No man has heard me *boast,* and no man shall, though ye flay me alive, and then roast the quivering flesh, with your own infarnal devices and cruelties! I may be humble, and misfortunate, and your prisoner; but I'm no boaster, by my very gifts."

"My young pale-face *boasts* he is *no* boaster," returned the crafty chief; "he *must* be right. I hear a strange bird singing. It has very rich feathers. No Huron ever before saw such feathers. They will be ashamed to go back to their village and tell their people that they let their prisoner go on account of the song of this strange bird, and not be able to give the *name* of the bird. They do not know how to say whether it is a wren or a catbird. This would be a great disgrace; my young men would not be allowed to travel in the woods, without taking their mothers with them to tell them the names of the birds."

"You can ask my name of your prisoner," returned the girl. "It is Judith; and there is a great deal of the history of Judith in the pale-faces' best book, the Bible. If I am a bird of fine feathers, I have also my name."

"No," answered the wily Huron, betraying the artifice he had so long practised, by speaking in English, with tolerable accuracy; "I not ask prisoner. He tired; he want rest. I ask my daughter, with feeble-mind. She speak truth. Come here, daughter; you answer. *Your* name, Hetty?"

"Yes, that's what they call me," returned the girl, "though it's written Esther, in the Bible."

"He write *him* in Bible, too? All write in Bible. No matter—what *her* name?"

"That's Judith, and it's so written in the Bible, though father sometimes called her Jude. That's my sister Judith, Thomas Hutter's daughter—Thomas Hutter, whom you called the Muskrat; though he was *no* muskrat, but a man, like yourselves—he lived in a house on the water, and that was enough for *you.*"

A smile of triumph gleamed on the hard wrinkled countenance of the chief, when he found how completely his appeal to the truth-loving Hetty had succeeded. As for Judith herself, the moment her sister was questioned, she saw that all was lost; for no sign, or even treaty, could have induced the right-feeling girl to utter a falsehood. To attempt to impose a daughter of the Muskrat on the savages, as a princess or a great lady, she knew would be idle; and she saw her bold and ingenious expedient for liberating the captive fail, through one of the simplest and most natural causes that could be imagined. She turned her eye on Deerslayer, therefore, as if imploring him to interfere, to save them both.

"It will not do, Judith," said the young man, in

answer to this appeal, which he understood, though he saw its uselessness; "it will not do. 'Twas a bold idee, and fit for a general's lady; but yonder Mingo"—Rivenoak had withdrawn to a little distance, and was out of ear-shot—"but yonder Mingo is an oncommon man, and not to be deceived by any unnat'ral sarcumventions. Things must come afore him in their right order to draw a cloud afore *his* eyes! 'Twas too much to attempt making him fancy that a queen or a great lady lived in these mountains, and no doubt he thinks the fine clothes you wear are some of the plunder of your own father—or, at least, of him who once passed for your father; as quite likely it was, if all they say is true."

"At all events, Deerslayer, my presence here will save you for a time. They will hardly attempt torturing you before my face!"

"Why not, Judith? Do you think they will treat a woman of the pale-faces more tenderly than they treat their own? It's true that your sex will most likely save you from the torments, but it will not save your liberty, and may not save your scalp. I wish you hadn't come, my good Judith; it can do no good to me, while it may do great harm to yourself."

"I can share your fate," the girl answered, with generous enthusiasm. "That shall not injure you while I stand by, if in my power to prevent it—besides—"

"Besides what, Judith? What means have you to stop Injin cruelties, or to avart Injin deviltries?"

"None, perhaps, Deerslayer," answered the girl, with firmness; "but I can suffer with my friends—die with them, if necessary."

"Ah! Judith—suffer you may; but die you will not until the Lord's time shall come. It's little likely that one of your sex and beauty will meet with a harder fate than to become the wife of a chief, if indeed your white inclinations can stoop to match with an Injin. 'Twould have been better had you stayed in the ark or the castle; but what has been done, is done. You was about to say something, when you stopped at 'besides?' "

"It might not be safe to mention it here, Deerslayer," the girl hurriedly answered, moving past him carelessly that she might speak in a low tone; "half an hour is all in all to us. None of your friends are idle."

The hunter replied merely by a grateful look. Then he turned towards his enemies, as if ready again to face the torments. A short consultation had passed among the elders of the band, and by this time they also were prepared with their decision. The merciful purpose of Rivenoak had been much weakened by the artifice of Judith, which, failing of its real object, was likely to produce re-

sults the very opposite of those she had anticipated. This was natural; the feeling being aided by the resentment of an Indian, who found how near he had been to becoming the dupe of an inexperienced girl. By this time Judith's real character was fully understood—the widespread reputation of her beauty contributed to the exposure. As for the unusual attire, it was confounded with the profound mystery of the animals with two tails, and, for the moment, lost its influence.

When Rivenoak, therefore, faced the captive again, it was with an altered countenance. He had abandoned the wish of saving him, and was no longer disposed to retard the more serious part of the torture. This change of sentiment was, in effect, communicated to the young men, who were already eagerly engaged in making their preparations for the contemplated scene. Fragments of dried wood were rapidly collected near the sapling, the splinters which it was intended to thrust into the flesh of the victim, previously to lighting, were all collected, and the thongs were already produced that were again to bind him to the tree. All this was done in profound silence, Judith watching every movement with breathless expectation, while Deerslayer himself stood seemingly as unmoved as one of the pines of the hills. When the warriors advanced to bind him, however, the young man glanced at Judith, as if to inquire whether resistance or submission were most advisable. By a significant gesture she counselled the last; and, in a minute he was once more fastened to the tree, a helpless object of any insult or wrong that might be offered. So eagerly did every one now act, that nothing was said. The fire was immediately lighted in the pile, and the end of all was anxiously expected.

It was not the intention of the Hurons absolutely to destroy the life of their victim by means of fire. They designed merely to put his physical fortitude to the severest proofs it could endure, short of that extremity. In the end, they fully intended to carry his scalp with them into their village, but it was their wish first to break down his resolution, and to reduce him to the level of a complaining sufferer. With this view, the pile of brush and branches had been placed at a proper distance, or one at which it was thought the heat would soon become intolerable, though it might not be immediately dangerous. As often happened, however, on these occasions, this distance had been miscalculated, and the flames began to wave their forked tongues in a proximity to the face of the victim that would have proved fatal in another instant, had not Hetty rushed through the crowd, armed with a stick, and scattered the blazing pile in a dozen directions. More than one hand was raised to strike the presumptuous intruder to the earth; but the chiefs prevented the blows, by reminding their irritated followers of the state of her mind. Hetty, herself, was insensible to the risk she ran; but, as soon as she had performed this bold act, she stood looking about her in frowning resentment, as if to rebuke the crowd of attentive savages for their cruelty.

"God bless you, dearest sister, for that brave and ready act," murmured Judith, herself unnerved so much as to be incapable of exertion; "Heaven itself has sent you on its holy errand."

" 'Twas well meant, Judith," rejoined the victim; " 'twas excellently meant, and 'twas timely, though it may prove ontimely in the ind! What is to come to pass must come to pass soon, or 'twill quickly be too late. Had I drawn in one mouthful of that flame in breathing, the power of man couldn't save my life; and you see that this time they've so bound my forehead as not to leave my head the smallest chance. 'Twas well-meant; but it might have been more marciful to let the flames act their part."

"Cruel, heartless Hurons!" exclaimed the still indignant Hetty; "would you burn a man and a Christian as you would burn a log of wood! Do you never read your Bibles? or do you think God will forget such things?"

A gesture from Rivenoak caused the scattered brands to be collected; fresh wood was brought, even the women and children busying themselves eagerly in the gathering of dried sticks. The flame was just kindling a second time, when an *Indian* female pushed through the circle, advanced to the heap, and with her foot dashed aside the lighted twigs in time to prevent the conflagration. A yell followed this second disappointment; but when the offender turned towards the circle, and presented the countenance of Hist, it was succeeded by a common exclamation of pleasure and surprise. For a minute, all thought of pursuing the business in hand was forgotten, and young and old crowded around the girl, in haste to demand an explanation of her sudden and unlooked-for return. It was at this critical instant that Hist spoke to Judith in a low voice, placed some small object, unseen, in her hand, and then turned to meet the salutations of the Huron girls, with whom she was personally a great favorite. Judith recovered her self-possession and acted promptly. The small, keen-edged knife, that Hist had given to the other, was passed by the latter into the hands of Hetty, as the safest and least-suspected medium of transferring it to Deerslayer. But the feeble intellect of the last defeated the well-grounded hopes of all three. Instead of first cutting loose the hands of the victim, and then concealing the knife in his clothes, in readiness for action at the most available instant, she went to work herself, with earnestness and simplicity, to cut the thongs that bound his head, that he might not again be in danger of inhaling flames. Of course this deliberate procedure was seen, and the hands of Hetty were arrested ere she had more than liberated the upper portion of the captive's body, not including his arms, below the elbows. This discovery at once pointed distrust towards Hist; and, to Judith's surprise, when questioned on the subject, that spirited girl was not disposed to deny her agency in what had passed.

"Why should I not help the Deerslayer?" the girl demanded, in the tones of a firm-minded woman. "He is the brother of a Delaware chief; my heart is all Delaware. Come forth, miserable Briarthorn, and wash the Iroquois paint from your face; stand before the Hurons, the crow that you are; you would eat the carrion of your own dead rather than starve. Put him face to face with Deerslayer, chiefs and warriors; I will show you how great a knave you have been keeping in your tribe."

This bold language, uttered in their own dialect, and with a manner full of confidence, produced a deep sensation among the Hurons. Treachery is always liable to distrust; and though the recreant Briarthorn had endeavored to serve the enemy well, his exertions and assiduities had gained for him little more than toleration. His wish to obtain Hist for a wife had first induced him to betray her and his own people; but serious rivals to his first project had risen up among his new friends, weakening still more their sympathies with treason. In a word, Briarthorn had been barely permitted to remain in the Huron encampment, where he was as closely and as jealously watched as Hist herself; seldom appearing before the chiefs, and sedulously keeping out of view of Deerslayer, who, until this moment, was ignorant even of his presence. Thus summoned, however, it was impossible to remain in the background. "Wash the Iroquois paint from his face," he did not; for when he stood in the centre of the circle, he was so disguised in these new colors, that, at first, the hunter did not recognize him. He assumed an air of defiance, notwithstanding, and haughtily demanded what any could say against Briarthorn.

"Ask yourself that," continued Hist, with spirit, though her manner grew less concentrated; and there was a slight air of abstraction that became observable to Deerslayer and Judith, if to no others. "Ask that of your own heart, sneaking woodchuck of the Delawares; come not here with the face of an innocent man. Go look in the spring; see the colors of your enemies on your lying skin; and then come back and boast how you ran from your tribe, and took the blanket of the French for your covering. Paint yourself as bright as a humming-bird, you will still be black as the crow."

Hist had been so uniformly gentle while living with the Hurons, that they now listened to her language with surprise. As for the delinquent, his blood boiled in his veins; and it was well for the pretty speaker that it was not in his power to execute the revenge he burned to inflict on her, in spite of his pretended love.

"Who wishes Briarthorn?" he sternly asked. "If this pale-face is tired of life; if afraid of Indian torments, speak, Rivenoak; I will send him after the warriors we have lost."

"No, chief,—no, Rivenoak," eagerly interrupted Hist. "The Deerslayer fears nothing; least of all a crow! Unbind him—cut his withes—place him face to face with this cawing bird; then let us see which is tired of life."

Hist made a forward movement, as if to take a knife from a young man, and perform the office she had mentioned in person; but an aged warrior interposed, at a sign from Rivenoak. The chief watched all the girl did, with distrust; for, even while speaking in her most boastful language and in the steadiest manner, there was an air of uncertainty and expectation about her, that could not escape so close an observer. She acted well; but two or three of the old men were equally satisfied that it was merely acting. Her proposal to release Deerslayer, therefore, was rejected; and the disappointed Hist found herself driven back from the sapling at the very moment she fancied herself about to be successful. At the same time the circle, which had got to be crowded and confused, was enlarged, and brought once more into order. Rivenoak now announced the intention of the old men again to proceed; the delay having been continued long enough, and leading to no result.

"Stop, Huron; stay, chiefs!" exclaimed Judith, scarce knowing what she said, or why she interposed, unless to obtain time; "for God's sake, a single minute longer—"

The words were cut short by another and a still more extraordinary interruption. A young Indian came bounding through the Huron ranks, leaping into the very centre of the circle, in a way to denote the utmost confidence, or a temerity bordering on foolhardiness. Five or six sentinels were still watching the lake at different and distant points; and it was the first impression of Rivenoak that one of these had come in with tidings of import. Still, the movements of the stranger were so rapid, and his war-dress, which scarcely left him more drapery than an antique statue, had so little distinguishing about it, that, at the first moment, it was impossible to ascertain whether he were friend or foe. Three leaps carried this warrior to the side of Deerslayer, whose withes were cut in the twinkling of an eye, with a quickness and precision that left the prisoner perfect master of his limbs. Not till this was effected did the stranger bestow a glance on any other object; then he turned and showed the astonished Hurons the noble brow, fine person, and eagle eye of a young warrior, in the paint and panoply of a Delaware. He held a rifle in each hand, the butts of both resting on the earth, while from one dangled its proper pouch and horn. This was Killdeer, which even as he looked boldly and in defiance on the crowd around him, he suffered to fall back into the hands of the proper owner. The presence of two armed men, though it was in their midst, startled the Hurons. Their rifles were scattered about against the different trees, and their only weapons were their knives and tomahawks. Still, they had too much self-possession to betray fear. It was little likely that so small a force would assail so strong a band; and each man expected some extraordinary proposition to succeed so decisive a step. The stranger did not seem disposed to disappoint them; he prepared to speak.

"Hurons," he said, "this earth is very big. The great lakes are big, too; there is room beyond them for the Iroquois; there is room for the Delawares on this side. I am Chingachgook, the son of Uncas; the kinsman of Tamenund. This is my betrothed; that pale-face is my friend. My heart was heavy when I missed him. All the Delaware girls are waiting for Wah; they wonder that she stays away so long. Come, let us say farewell, and go on our path."

"Hurons, this is your mortal enemy, the Great Serpent of them you hate!" cried Briarthorn. "If he escape, blood will be in your moccasin prints from this spot to the Canadas. *I* am *all* Huron."

As the last words were uttered, the traitor cast his knife at the naked breast of the Delaware. A quick movement of the arm, on the part of Hist, who stood near, turned aside the blow, the dangerous weapon burying its point in a pine. At the next instant, a similar weapon glanced from the hand of the Serpent, and quivered in the recreant's heart. A minute had scarcely elapsed from the moment in which Chingachgook bounded into the circle, and that in which Briarthorn fell, like a dog, dead in his tracks. The rapidity of events prevented the Hurons from acting; but this catastrophe permitted no further delay. A common exclamation followed, and the whole party was in motion. At this instant, a sound unusual to the woods was heard, and every Huron, male and female, paused to listen, with ears erect and faces filled with expectation. The sound was regular and heavy, as if the earth were struck with beetles. Objects became visible among the trees of the background, and a body of troops was seen advancing with measured tread. They came upon the charge, the scarlet of the king's livery shining among the bright green foliage of the forest.

The scene that followed is not easily described. It was one in which wild confusion, despair, and frenzied efforts were so blended as to destroy the unity and distinctness of the action. A general yell burst from the inclosed Hurons; it was succeeded by the hearty cheers of England. Still, not a musket or rifle was fired, though that steady, measured tramp continued, and the bayonet was seen gleaming in advance of a line that counted nearly sixty men. The Hurons were taken at a fearful disadvantage. On three sides was the water, while their formidable and trained foes cut them off from flight on the fourth. Each warrior rushed for his arms, and then all on the point, man, woman, and child, eagerly sought the covers. In this scene of confusion and dismay, however, nothing could surpass the discretion and coolness of Deerslayer. His first care was to place Judith and Hist behind trees, and he looked for Hetty; but she had been hurried away in the crowd of Huron women. This effected, he threw himself on a flank of the retiring Hurons, who were inclining off towards the southern margin of the point, in the hope of escaping through the water. Deerslayer watched his opportunity, and finding two of his recent tormentors in a range, his rifle first broke the silence of the terrific scene. The bullet brought down both at one discharge. This drew a general fire from the Hurons, and the rifle and warcry of the Serpent were heard in the clamor. Still, the trained men returned no answering volley, the whoop and piece of Hurry alone being heard on their side, if we except the short, prompt word of authority, and that heavy, measured, and menacing tread. Presently, however, the shrieks, groans, and denunciations that usually accompany the use of the bayonet, followed. That terrible and deadly weapon was glutted in vengeance. The scene that succeeded was one of those, of which so many have occurred in our own times, in which neither age nor sex forms an exemption to the lot of a savage warfare.

---

FROM

# THE AMERICAN DEMOCRAT

---

❖

❨ THERE is a long line of distinguished books that have attempted to analyze and define the political and social genius of this country at various points in its history. The list includes the early *Letters from an American Farmer* (1782) by St. Jean de Crèvecoeur, Alexis de Tocqueville's *Democracy in America* (1835), and Henry James's *The American Scene* (1907). Among these *The American Democrat*, published in 1838, should hold an honored place. It is as relevant to contemporary America as to Cooper's own day. It is a short book of forty-six chapters (probably intended by Cooper originally as an elementary school text) in which he analyzes the form of the American government and points out political dangers and social illusions which attend it. Although a Jacksonian Democrat, Cooper often sounds here very much like the Federalist John Adams, a man whose political philosophy in the end resembled Jeffersonian agrarianism more closely than it did the brand of capitalism sponsored by his own party under Hamilton. Cooper's Introduction makes his intention clear:

> The writer believes himself to be as good a democrat as there is in America. But his democracy is not of the impracticable school. He prefers a democracy to any other system, on account of its comparative advantages, and not on account of its perfection. He knows it has evils; great and increasing evils, and evils peculiar to itself; but he believes that monarchy and aristocracy have more. It will be very apparent to all who read this book, that he is not a believer in the scheme of raising men very far above their natural propensities.

❖

## ADVANTAGES OF A DEMOCRACY

THE PRINCIPAL advantage of a democracy, is a general elevation in the character of the people. If few are raised to a very great height, few are depressed very low. As a consequence, the average of society is much more respectable than under any other form of government. The vulgar charge that the tendency of democracies is to levelling, meaning to drag all down to the level of the lowest, is singularly untrue, its real tendency being to elevate the depressed to a condition not unworthy of their manhood. In the absence of privileged orders, entails and distinctions, devised permanently to separate men into social castes, it is true none are great but those who become so by their acts, but, confining the remark to the upper classes of society, it would be much more true to say that democracy refuses to lend itself to unnatural and arbitrary distinctions, than to accuse it of a tendency to level those who have a just claim to be elevated. A denial of a favor, is not an invasion of a right.

Democracies are exempt from the military charges, both pecuniary and personal, that become necessary in governments in which the majority are subjects, since no force is required to repress those who, under other systems, are dangerous to the state, by their greater physical power.

As the success of democracies is mainly dependant on the intelligence of the people, the means of preserving the government are precisely those which most conduce to the happiness and social progress of man. Hence we find the state endeavoring to raise its citizens in the scale of being, the certain means of laying the broadest foundation of national prosperity. If the arts are advanced in aristocracies, through the taste of patrons, in democracies, though of slower growth, they will prosper as a consequence of general information; or as a superstructure reared on a wider and more solid foundation.

Democracies being, as nearly as possible, founded in natural justice, little violence is done to the sense of right by the institutions, and men have less occasion than usual, to resort to fallacies and false principles in cultivating the faculties. As a consequence, common sense is more encouraged, and the community is apt to entertain juster notions of all moral truths, than under systems that are necessarily sophisticated. Society is thus a gainer in the greatest element of happiness, or in the right perception of the different relations between men and things.

Democracies being established for the common interests, and the publick agents being held in constant check by the people, their general tendency is to serve the whole community, and not small portions of it, as is the case in narrow governments. It is as rational to suppose that a hungry man will first help his neighbor to bread, when master of his own acts, as to suppose that any but those who feel themselves to be truly public servants, will first bethink themselves of the publick, when in situations of publick trust. In a government of one, that one and his parasites will be the first and best served; in a government of a few, the few; and in a government of many, the many. Thus the general tendency of democratical institutions is to equalize advantages, and to spread its blessings over the entire surface of society.

Democracies, other things being equal, are the cheapest form of government, since little money is lavished in representation, and they who have to pay the taxes, have also, directly or indirectly, a voice in imposing them.

Democracies are less liable to popular tumults than any other polities, because the people, having legal means in their power to redress wrongs, have little inducement to employ any other. The man who can right himself by a vote, will seldom resort to a musket. Grievances, moreover, are less frequent, the most corrupt representatives of a democratick constituency generally standing in awe of its censure.

As men in bodies usually defer to the right, unless acting under erroneous impressions, or excited by sudden resentments, democracies pay more respect to abstract justice, in the management of their foreign concerns, than either aristocracies or monarchies, an appeal always lying against abuses, or violations of principle, to a popular sentiment, that, in the end, seldom fails to decide in favor of truth.

In democracies, with a due allowance for the workings of personal selfishness, it is usually a motive with those in places of trust, to consult the interests of the mass, there being little doubt, that in this system, the entire community has more regard paid to its wants and wishes, than in either of the two others.

## ON THE DISADVANTAGES OF DEMOCRACY

DEMOCRACIES are liable to popular impulses, which, necessarily arising from imperfect information, often work injustice from good motives. Tumults of the people are less apt to occur in democracies than under any other form of government, for, possessing the legal means of redressing themselves, there is less necessity to resort to force, but, public opinion constituting, virtually, the power of the state, measures are more apt to be influenced by sudden mutations of sentiment, than under systems where the rulers have better opportunities and more leisure for examination. There is more feeling and less design in the movements of masses than in those of small bodies, except as design emanates from demagogues and political managers.

The efforts of the masses that are struggling to obtain their rights, in monarchies and aristocracies, however, are not to be imputed to democracy; in such cases, the people use their natural weapon, force, merely because they are denied any participation in the legal authority.

When democracies are small, these impulses frequently do great injury to the public service, but in large states they are seldom of sufficient extent to produce results before there is time to feel the influence of reason. It is, therefore, one of the errors of politicians to imagine democracies more practicable in small than in large communities, an error that has probably arisen from the fact that, the ignorance of masses having hitherto put men at the mercy of the combinations of the affluent and intelligent, democracies have been permitted to exist only in countries insignificant by their wealth and numbers.

Large democracies, on the other hand, while less exposed to the principal evil of this form of government, than smaller, are unable to scrutinize and understand character with the severity and intelligence that are of so much importance in all representative governments, and consequently the people are peculiarly exposed to become the dupes of demagogues and political schemers, most of the crimes of democracies arising from the faults and designs of men of this character, rather than from the propensities of the people, who, having little temptation to do wrong, are seldom guilty of crimes except through ignorance.

Democracies are necessarily controlled by publick opinion, and failing of the means of obtaining power more honestly, the fraudulent and ambitious find a motive to mislead, and even to corrupt the common sentiment, to attain their ends. This is the greatest and most pervading danger of all large democracies, since it is sapping the foundations of society, by undermining its virtue. We see the effects of this baneful influence, in the openness and audacity with which men avow improper motives and improper acts, trusting to find support in a popular feeling, for while vicious influences are perhaps more admitted in other countries, than in America, in none are they so openly avowed.

It may also be urged against democracies, that, nothing being more corrupting than the management of human affairs, which are constantly demanding sacrifices of permanent principles to interests that are as constantly fluctuating, their people are exposed to assaults on their morals from this quarter, that the masses of other nations escape. It is probable, however, that this evil, while it ought properly to be enumerated as one of the disadvantages of the system, is more than counterbalanced by the main results, even on the score of morals.

The constant appeals to public opinion in a de-mocracy, though excellent as a corrective of public vices, induce private hypocrisy, causing men to conceal their own convictions when opposed to those of the mass, the latter being seldom wholly right, or wholly wrong. A want of national manliness is a vice to be guarded against, for the man who would dare to resist a monarch, shrinks from opposing an entire community. That the latter is quite often wrong, however, is abundantly proved by the fact, that its own judgments fluctuate, as it reasons and thinks differently this year, or this month even, from what it reasoned and thought the last.

The tendency of democracies is, in all things, to mediocrity, since the tastes, knowledge and principles of the majority form the tribunal of appeal. This circumstance, while it certainly serves to elevate the average qualities of a nation, renders the introduction of a high standard difficult. Thus do we find in literature, the arts, architecture and in all acquired knowledge, a tendency in America to gravitate towards the common center in this, as in other things; lending a value and estimation to mediocrity that are not elsewhere given. It is fair to expect, however, that a foundation so broad, may in time sustain a superstructure of commensurate proportions, and that the influence of masses will in this, as in the other interests, have a generally beneficial effect. Still it should not be forgotten that, with the exception of those works, of which, as they appeal to human sympathies or the practices of men, an intelligent public is the best judge, the mass of no community is qualified to decide the most correctly on any thing, which, in its nature, is above its reach.

It is a besetting vice of democracies to substitute publick opinion for law. This is the usual form in which masses of men exhibit their tyranny. When the majority of the entire community commits this fault it is a sore grievance, but when local bodies, influenced by local interests, pretend to style themselves the publick, they are assuming powers that properly belong to the whole body of the people, and to them only under constitutional limitations. No tyranny of one, nor any tyranny of the few, is worse than this. All attempts in the publick, therefore, to do that which the publick has no right to do, should be frowned upon as the precise form in which tyranny is the most apt to be displayed in a democracy.

Democracies, depending so much on popular opinion are more liable to be influenced to their injury, through the management of foreign and hostile nations, than other governments. It is generally known that, in Europe, secret means are resorted to, to influence sentiment in this way, and we have witnessed in this country open appeals to the people, against the acts of their servants, in matters of foreign relations, made by foreign, not to say, hostile agents. Perhaps no stronger case can be cited of this weakness on the part of democracies, than is shown in this fact, for here we find men sufficiently audacious to build the hope of so far abusing opinion, as to persuade a people to act directly against their own dignity and interests.

The misleading of publick opinion in one way or another, is the parent of the principal disadvantages of a democracy, for in most instances it is first corrupting a community in order that it may be otherwise injured. Were it not for the counteracting influence of reason, which, in the end, seldom, perhaps never fails to assert its power, this defect would of itself, be sufficient to induce all discreet men to decide against this form of government. The greater the danger, the greater the necessity that all well-intentioned and right-minded citizens should be on their guard against its influence.

It would be hazardous, however, to impute all the peculiar faults of American character, to the institutions, the country existing under so many unusual influences. If the latter were overlooked, one might be induced to think frankness and sincerity of character were less encouraged by popular institutions than was formerly supposed, close observers affirming that these qualities are less frequent here, than in most other countries. When the general ease of society is remembered, there is unquestionably more deception of opinion practised than one would naturally expect, but this failing is properly to be imputed to causes that have no necessary connection with democratical institutions, though men defer to publick opinion, right or wrong, quite as submissively as they defer to princes. Although truths are not smothered altogether in democracies, they are often temporarily abandoned under this malign influence, unless there is a powerful motive to sustain them at the moment. While we see in our own democracy this manifest disposition to defer to the wrong, in matters that are not properly subject to the common sentiment, in deference to the popular will of the hour, there is a singular boldness in the use of personalities, as if men avenged themselves for the restraints of the one case by a licentiousness that is without hazard.

The base feelings of detraction and envy have more room for exhibition, and perhaps a stronger incentive in a democracy, than in other forms of government, in which the people get accustomed to personal deference by the artificial distinctions of the institutions. This is the reason that men become impatient of all superiority in a democracy, and manifest a wish to prefer those who affect a deference to the publick, rather than those who are worthy.

## ON LANGUAGE

LANGUAGE being the medium of thought, its use enters into our most familiar practices. A just, clear and simple expression of our ideas is a necessary accomplishment for all who aspire to be classed with gentlemen and ladies. It renders all more respectable, besides making intercourse more intelligible, safer and more agreeable.

The common faults of American language are an ambition of effect, a want of simplicity, and a turgid abuse of terms. To these may be added ambiguity of expression. Many perversions of significations also exist, and a formality of speech, which, while it renders conversation ungraceful, and destroys its playfulness, seriously weakens the power of the language, by applying to ordinary ideas, words that are suited only to themes of gravity and dignity.

While it is true that the great body of the American people use their language more correctly than the mass of any other considerable nation, it is equally true that a smaller proportion than common attain to elegance in this accomplishment, especially in speech. Contrary to the general law in such matters, the women of the country have a less agreeable utterance than the men, a defect that great care should be taken to remedy, as the nursery is the birthplace of so many of our habits.

The limits of this work will not permit an enumeration of the popular abuses of significations, but a few shall be mentioned, in order that the student may possess a general clue to the faults. "Creek," a word that signifies an *inlet* of the sea, or of a lake, is misapplied to running streams, and frequently to the *outlets* of lakes. A "square," is called a "park;" "lakes," are often called "ponds;" and "arms of the sea," are sometimes termed "rivers."

In pronunciation, the faults are still more numerous, partaking decidedly of provincialisms. The letter *u*, sounded like double *o*, or *oo*, or like *i*, as in vir*too*, for*tin*, for*tinate;* and *ew*, pronounced also like *oo*, are common errors. This is an exceedingly vicious pronunciation, rendering the language mean and vulgar. "New," pronounced as *"noo,"* is an example, and "few," as *"foo;"* the true sounds are *"nu"* and *"fu,"* the *u* retaining its proper soft sound, and not that of *"oo."*

The attempt to reduce the pronunciation of the

English language to a common rule, produces much confusion, and taking the usages of polite life as the standard, many uncouth innovations. All know the pronunciation of p l o u g h ; but it will scarcely do to take this sound as the only power of the same combination of final letters, for we should be compelled to call t h o u g h, thou; t h r o u g h, throu; and t o u g h, tou.

False accentuation is a common American fault. Ensign (insin,) is called en*syne,* and engine (injin,) en*gyne.* Indeed, it is a common fault of narrow associations, to suppose that words are to be pronounced as they are spelled.

Many words are in a state of mutation, the pronunciation being unsettled even in the best society, a result that must often arise where language is as variable and undetermined as the English. To this class belong "clerk," "cucumber" and "gold," which are often pronounced as spelt, though it were better and more in conformity with polite usage to say "clark," "*cow*cumber," (not cow-*cumb*er,) and "goold." For *looten*ant (lieutenant) there is not sufficient authority, the true pronunciation being *"levten*ant." By making a familiar compound of this word, we see the uselessness of attempting to reduce the language to any other laws than those of the usages of polite life, for they who affect to say *looten*ant, do not say *"looten*ant-co-lo-nel," but *"looten*ant-kurnel."

The polite pronunciation of "either" and "neither," is "i-ther" and "ni-ther," and not "eether" and "neether." This is a case in which the better usage of the language has respected derivations, for *"ei,"* in German are pronounced as in "height" and "sleight," *"ie"* making the sound of *"ee."* We see the arbitrary usages of the English, however, by comparing these legitimate sounds with those of the words "lieutenant colonel," which are derived from the French, in which language the latter word is called *"co-lo-nel."*

Some changes of the language are to be regretted, as they lead to false inferences, and society is always a loser by mistaking names for things. Life is a fact, and it is seldom any good arises from a misapprehension of the real circumstances under which we exist. The word "gentleman" has a positive and limited signification. It means one elevated above the mass of society by his birth, manners, attainments, character and social condition. As no civilized society can exist without these social differences, nothing is gained by denying the use of the term. If blackguards were to be *called* "gentlemen," and "gentlemen," "blackguards," the difference between them would be as obvious as it is today.

The word "gentleman," is derived from the French *gentilhomme,* which originally signified one of noble birth. This was at a time when the characteristics of the condition were never found beyond a caste. As society advanced, ordinary men attained the qualifications of nobility, without that of birth, and the meaning of the word was extended. It is now possible to be a gentleman without birth, though, even in America, where such distinctions are purely conditional, they who have birth, except in extraordinary instances, are classed with gentlemen. To call a laborer, one who has neither education, manners, accomplishments, tastes, associations, nor any one of the ordinary requisites, a gentleman, is just as absurd as to call one who is thus qualified, a fellow. The word must have some especial signification, or it would be synonymous with man. One may have gentleman-like feelings, principles and appearance, without possessing the liberal attainments that distinguish the gentleman. Least of all does money alone make a gentleman, though, as it becomes a means of obtaining the other requisites, it is usual to give it a place in the claims of the class. Men may be, and often are, very rich, without having the smallest title to be deemed gentlemen. A man may be a distinguished gentleman, and not possess as much money as his own footman.

This word, however, is sometimes used instead of the old terms, "sirs," "my masters," &c. &c., as in addressing bodies of men. Thus we say "gentlemen," in addressing a publick meeting, in complaisance, and as, by possibility, some gentlemen may be present. This is a license that may be tolerated, though he who should insist that all present were, as individuals, gentlemen, would hardly escape ridicule.

What has just been said of the word gentleman, is equally true with that of lady. The standard of these two classes, rises as society becomes more civilized and refined; the man who might pass for a gentleman in one nation, or community, not being able to maintain the same position in another.

The inefficiency of the effort to subvert things by names, is shown in the fact that, in all civilized communities, there is a class of men, who silently and quietly recognize each other, as gentlemen; who associate together freely and without reserve, and who admit each other's claims without scruple or distrust. This class may be limited by prejudice and arbitrary enactments, as in Europe, or it may have no other rules than those of taste, sentiment and the silent laws of usage, as in America.

The same observations may be made in relation to the words master and servant. He who employs laborers, with the right to command, is a master, and he who lets himself to work, with an obligation to obey, a servant. Thus there are house, or domestic servants, farm servants, shop servants, and various other servants; the term master being in all these cases the correlative.

In consequence of the domestic servants of America having once been Negro slaves, a prejudice has arisen among the laboring classes of the whites, who not only dislike the term servant, but have also rejected that of master. So far has this prejudice gone, that in lieu of the latter, they have resorted to the use of the word *boss,* which has precisely the same meaning in Dutch! How far a subterfuge of this nature is worthy of a manly and common sense people, will admit of question.

A similar objection may be made to the use of the word "help," which is not only an innovation on a just and established term, but which does not properly convey the meaning intended. They who aid their masters in the toil may be deemed "helps," but they who perform all the labor do not assist, or help to do the thing, but they do it themselves. A man does not usually hire his cook to *help* him cook his dinner, but to cook it herself. Nothing is therefore gained, while something is lost in simplicity and clearness by the substitution of new and imperfect terms, for the long established words of the language. In all cases in which the people of America have retained the *things* of their ancestors, they should not be ashamed to keep the *names.*

The love of turgid expressions is gaining ground, and ought to be corrected. One of the most certain evidences of a man of high breeding, is his simplicity of speech; a simplicity that is equally removed from vulgarity and exaggeration. He calls a spade, a "spade." His enunciation, while clear, deliberate and dignified, is totally without strut, showing his familiarity with the world, and, in some degree, reflecting the qualities of his mind, which is polished without being addicted to sentimentalism, or any other bloated feeling. He never calls his wife, "his lady," but "his wife," and he is not afraid of lessening the dignity of the human race, by styling the most elevated and refined of his fellow creatures, "men and women." He does not say, in speaking of a dance, that "the attire of the ladies was exceedingly elegant and peculiarly becoming at the late assembly," but that "the women were well dressed at the last ball;" nor is he apt to remark, "that the Rev. Mr. G——gave us an elegant and searching discourse the past sabbath," but, that "the parson preached a good sermon last sunday."

The utterance of a gentleman ought to be de-liberate and clear, without being measured. All idea of effort should be banished, though nothing lost for want of distinctness. His emphasis ought to be almost imperceptible; never halting, or abrupt; and least of all, so placed as to give an idea of his own sense of cleverness; but regulated by those slight intonations that give point to wit, and force to reason. His language should rise with the subject, and, as he must be an educated and accomplished man, he cannot but know that the highest quality of eloquence, and all sublimity, is in the thought, rather than in the words, though there must be an adaptation of the one to the other.

This is still more true of women than of men, since the former are the natural agents in maintaining the refinement of a people.

All cannot reach the highest standard in such matters, for it depends on early habit, and particularly on early associations. The children of gentlemen are as readily distinguished from other children by these peculiarities, as by the greater delicacy of their minds, and higher tact in breeding. But we are not to abandon all improvement, because perfection is reached but by few. Simplicity should be the first aim, after one is removed from vulgarity, and let the finer shades of accomplishment be acquired as they can be attained. In no case, however, can one who aims at turgid language, exaggerated sentiment, or pedantic utterance, lay claim to be either a man or a woman of the world.

# William Cullen Bryant

## THE YELLOW VIOLET

◊

❨ THE CULTURAL time lag between America and England prevented any widespread enthusiasm for the English romantic poets, or, indeed, any considerable knowledge of them, during the first quarter of the century, and for some time later. Nevertheless, several of Bryant's poems are indebted to Wordsworth. Among these is "The Yellow Violet," written when Bryant was twenty years old. It is one of his best poems.

◊

When beechen buds begin to swell,
    And woods the blue-bird's warble know,
The yellow violet's modest bell
    Peeps from the last year's leaves below.

Ere russet fields their green resume,
    Sweet flower, I love, in forest bare,
To meet thee, when thy faint perfume
    Alone is in the virgin air.

Of all her train, the hands of Spring
    First plant thee in the watery mould,     10
And I have seen thee blossoming
    Beside the snow-bank's edges cold.

Thy parent sun, who bade thee view
    Pale skies, and chilling moisture sip,
Has bathed thee in his own bright hue,
    And streaked with jet thy glowing lip.

Yet slight thy form, and low thy seat,
    And earthward bent thy gentle eye,
Unapt the passing view to meet
    When loftier flowers are flaunting nigh.

Oft, in the sunless April day,     21
    Thy early smile has stayed my walk;
But midst the gorgeous blooms of May,
    I passed thee on thy humble stalk.

So they, who climb to wealth, forget
    The friends in darker fortunes tried.
I copied them—but I regret
    That I should ape the ways of pride.

And when again the genial hour
    Awakes the painted tribes of light,     30
I'll not o'erlook the modest flower
    That made the woods of April bright.

*1821*                *1814*

## TO A WATERFOWL

◊

❨ IN DECEMBER 1815, Bryant was walking toward the village of Plainfield, Massachusetts, where he intended to set up a law practice. Parke Godwin in his early life (1883) described what happened on that walk:

> He walked up the hills, very forlorn and desolate indeed, not knowing what was to become of him in the big world which grew bigger as he ascended and yet darker with the coming on of night. The sun had already set, leaving behind it one of those brilliant seas of chrysolite and opal which often flood the New England skies. While he was looking on the rosy splendor with rapt admiration, a solitary bird made wing along the illuminated horizon. He watched the lone wanderer until it was lost in the distance, asking himself whither it had come and to what far home it was flying. When he went to the house where he was to stop for the night, his mind was still full of what he had seen and felt, and he wrote those lines . . . "To a Waterfowl."

◊

    Whither, midst falling dew,
While glow the heavens with the last steps of day,
Far, through their rosy depths, dost thou pursue
    Thy solitary way?

    Vainly the fowler's eye
Might mark thy distant flight to do thee wrong,
As, darkly seen against the crimson sky,
    Thy figure floats along.

    Seek'st thou the plashy brink
Of weedy lake, or marge of river wide,     10
Or where the rocking billows rise and sink
    On the chafed ocean-side?

There is a Power whose care
Teaches thy way along that pathless coast—
The desert and illimitable air—
 Lone wandering, but not lost.

All day thy wings have fanned,
At that far height, the cold, thin atmosphere,
Yet stoop not, weary, to the welcome land,
 Though the dark night is near.  20

And soon that toil shall end;
Soon shalt thou find a summer home, and rest,
And scream among thy fellows; reeds shall bend,
 Soon, o'er thy sheltered nest.

Thou'rt gone, the abyss of heaven
Hath swallowed up thy form; yet, on my heart
Deeply hath sunk the lesson thou hast given,
 And shall not soon depart.

He who, from zone to zone,
Guides through the boundless sky thy certain
  flight,  30
In the long way that I must tread alone
 Will lead my steps aright.

*1818*         *1815*

# THANATOPSIS

◇

[ THE FOLLOWING letter was written by Bryant in 1855 in reply to an enquiry concerning "Thanatopsis":

I cannot give you any information of the occasion which suggested to my mind the idea of my poem Thanatopsis. It was written when I was seventeen or eighteen years old—I have not now at hand the memorandums which would enable me to be precise—and I believe it was composed in my solitary rambles in the woods. As it was first committed to paper, it began with the half-line—"Yet a few days, and thee"—and ended with the beginning of another line with the words—"And make their bed with thee." The rest of the poem—the introduction and the close—was added some years afterward, in 1821, when I published a little collection of my poems at Cambridge.

◇

To him who in the love of Nature holds
Communion with her visible forms, she speaks
A various language: for his gayer hours
She has a voice of gladness, and a smile

And eloquence of beauty; and she glides
Into his darker musings with a mild
And healing sympathy that steals away
Their sharpness ere he is aware. When thoughts
Of the last bitter hour come like a blight
Over thy spirit, and sad images  10
Of the stern agony and shroud and pall
And breathless darkness and the narrow house
Make thee to shudder and grow sick at heart,
Go forth under the open sky and list
To Nature's teachings, while from all around—
Earth and her waters and the depths of air—
Comes a still voice—Yet a few days, and thee
The all-beholding sun shall see no more
In all his course; nor yet in the cold ground,
Where thy pale form was laid with many tears,
Nor in the embrace of ocean, shall exist  21
Thy image. Earth, that nourished thee, shall claim
Thy growth, to be resolved to earth again,
And, lost each human trace, surrendering up
Thine individual being, shalt thou go
To mix for ever with the elements,
To be a brother to the insensible rock
And to the sluggish clod, which the rude swain
Turns with his share and treads upon; the oak
Shall send his roots abroad and pierce thy mould.

  Yet not to thine eternal resting-place  31
Shalt thou retire alone, nor couldst thou wish
Couch more magnificent. Thou shalt lie down
With patriarchs of the infant world, with kings,
The powerful of the earth, the wise, the good,
Fair forms, and hoary seers of ages past,
All in one mighty sepulchre. The hills
Rock-ribbed and ancient as the sun; the vales
Stretching in pensive quietness between;
The venerable woods, rivers that move  40
In majesty, and the complaining brooks
That make the meadows green; and, poured round
  all,
Old Ocean's gray and melancholy waste,—
Are but the solemn decorations all
Of the great tomb of man. The golden sun,
The planets, all the infinite host of heaven,
Are shining on the sad abodes of death,
Through the still lapse of ages. All that tread
The globe are but a handful to the tribes
That slumber in its bosom. Take the wings  50
Of morning, pierce the Barcan wilderness,
Or lose thyself in the continuous woods
Where rolls the Oregon, and hears no sound
Save his own dashings; yet the dead are there,
And millions in those solitudes, since first

THANATOPSIS. **12. narrow house:** the grave.
**51. Barcan wilderness:** dark, North African forest.

The flight of years began, have laid them down
In their last sleep: the dead reign there alone.
So shalt thou rest; and what if thou withdraw
In silence from the living, and no friend
Take note of thy departure? All that breathe   60
Will share thy destiny. The gay will laugh
When thou art gone, the solemn brood of care
Plod on, and each one as before will chase
His favorite phantom; yet all these shall leave
Their mirth and their employments, and shall come
And make their bed with thee. As the long train
Of ages glide away, the sons of men—
The youth in life's green spring, and he who goes
In the full strength of years, matron and maid,
The speechless babe, and the gray-headed man—
Shall one by one be gathered to thy side   71
By those who in their turn shall follow them.

So live that when thy summons comes to join
The innumerable caravan which moves
To that mysterious realm where each shall take
His chamber in the silent halls of death,
Thou go not, like the quarry-slave at night,
Scourged to his dungeon, but, sustained and
    soothed
By an unfaltering trust, approach thy grave
Like one who wraps the drapery of his couch   80
About him and lies down to pleasant dreams.

*1817, 1821*                         *1811*

Of green and stirring branches is alive
And musical with birds, that sing and sport
In wantonness of spirit; while below
The squirrel, with raised paws and form erect,
Chirps merrily. Throngs of insects in the shade   20
Try their thin wings and dance in the warm beam
That waked them into life. Even the green trees
Partake the deep contentment; as they bend
To the soft winds, the sun from the blue sky
Looks in and sheds a blessing on the scene.
Scarce less the cleft-born wild-flower seems to en-
    joy
Existence, than the wingèd plunderer
That sucks its sweets. The mossy rocks themselves
And the old and ponderous trunks of prostrate
    trees
That lead from knoll to knoll a causey rude   30
Or bridge the sunken brook, and their dark roots,
With all their earth upon them, twisting high,
Breathe fixed tranquillity. The rivulet
Sends forth glad sounds, and tripping o'er its bed
Of pebbly sands, or leaping down the rocks,
Seems, with continuous laughter, to rejoice
In its own being. Softly tread the marge,
Lest from her midway perch thou scare the wren
That dips her bill in water. The cool wind,
That stirs the stream in play, shall come to thee,
Like one that loves thee nor will let thee pass   41
Ungreeted, and shall give its light embrace.

*1817*                               *1816*

# INSCRIPTION FOR THE ENTRANCE TO A WOOD

Stranger, if thou has learned a truth which
    needs
No school of long experience, that the world
Is full of guilt and misery, and hast seen
Enough of all its sorrows, crimes, and cares,
To tire thee of it, enter this wild wood
And view the haunts of Nature. The calm shade
Shall bring a kindred calm, and the sweet breeze
That makes the green leaves dance, shall waft a
    balm
To thy sick heart. Thou will find nothing here
Of all that pained thee in the haunts of men,   10
And made thee loathe thy life. The primal curse
Fell, it is true, upon the unsinning earth,
But not in vengeance. God hath yoked to guilt
Her pale tormentor, misery. Hence, these shades
Are still the abodes of gladness; the thick roof

# OH FAIREST OF THE RURAL MAIDS

◊

❲ POE SAID of these stanzas that they "will strike every poet as the truest *poem* ever written by Bryant." The "rural maid" of the poem is Frances Fairchild, whom Bryant met in the spring of 1820 while unhappily practicing law at Great Barrington, Massachusetts. They were married the following year. The obvious literary influence is Wordsworth's "Lucy" poems.

◊

Oh fairest of the rural maids!
Thy birth was in the forest shades;
Green boughs, and glimpses of the sky,
Were all that met thine infant eye.

INSCRIPTION FOR THE ENTRANCE TO A WOOD.   **30. causey:** a raised road over a marsh.

Thy sports, thy wanderings, when a child,
Were ever in the sylvan wild;
And all the beauty of the place
Is in thy heart and on thy face.

The twilight of the trees and rocks
Is in the light shade of thy locks;                    10
Thy step is as the wind that weaves
Its playful way among the leaves.

Thine eyes are springs, in whose serene
And silent waters heaven is seen;
Their lashes are the herbs that look
On their young figures in the brook.

The forest depths, by foot unpressed,
Are not more sinless than thy breast;
The holy peace, that fills the air
Of those calm solitudes, is there.                    20

*1832*                                              *1820*

---

# AN INDIAN AT
# THE BURIAL-PLACE
# OF HIS FATHERS

---

It is the spot I came to seek—
    My father's ancient burial-place,
Ere from these vales, ashamed and weak,
    Withdrew our wasted race.
It is the spot—I know it well—
Of which our old traditions tell.

For here the upland bank sends out
    A ridge toward the riverside;
I know the shaggy hills about,
    The meadows smooth and wide,              10
The plains, that, toward the southern sky,
Fenced east and west by mountains lie.

A white man, gazing on the scene,
    Would say a lovely spot was here,
And praise the lawns, so fresh and green,
    Between the hills so sheer.
I like it not—I would the plain
Lay in its tall old groves again.

The sheep are on the slopes around,
    The cattle in the meadows feed,
And laborers turn the crumbling ground,        20

Or drop the yellow seed,
And prancing steeds, in trappings gay,
Whirl the bright chariot o'er the way.

Methinks it were a nobler sight
    To see these vales in woods arrayed,
Their summits in the golden light,
    Their trunks in grateful shade,
And herds of deer that bounding go
O'er hills and prostrate trees below.          30

And then to mark the lord of all,
    The forest hero, trained to wars,
Quivered and plumed, and lithe and tall,
    And seamed with glorious scars,
Walk forth, amid his reign, to dare
The wolf, and grapple with the bear.

This bank, in which the dead were laid,
    Was sacred when its soil was ours;
Hither the silent Indian maid
    Brought wreaths of beads and flowers,      40
And the gray chief and gifted seer
Worshipped the god of thunders here.

But now the wheat is green and high
    On clods that hid the warrior's breast,
And scattered in the furrows lie
    The weapons of his rest;
And there, in the loose sand, is thrown
Of his large arm the mouldering bone.

Ah, little thought the strong and brave
    Who bore their lifeless chieftain forth—   50
Or the young wife that weeping gave
    Her first-born to the earth,
That the pale race who waste us now
Among their bones should guide the plough.

They waste us—ay—like April snow
    In the warm noon, we shrink away;
And fast they follow, as we go
    Toward the setting day—
Till they shall fill the land, and we
Are driven into the Western sea.               60

But I behold a fearful sign,
    To which the white men's eyes are blind;
Their race may vanish hence, like mine,
    And leave no trace behind,
Save ruins o'er the region spread,
And the white stones above the dead.

AN INDIAN AT THE BURIAL-PLACE OF HIS FATHERS.     **46. his rest:**
burial place.

Before these fields were shorn and tilled,
  Full to the brim our rivers flowed;
The melody of waters filled
  The fresh and boundless wood;               70
And torrents dashed and rivulets played,
And fountains spouted in the shade.

Those grateful sounds are heard no more,
  The springs are silent in the sun;
The rivers, by the blackened shore,
  With lessening current run;
The realm our tribes are crushed to get
May be a barren desert yet.

*1824*

---

# A FOREST HYMN

---

The groves were God's first temples. Ere man
    learned
To hew the shaft, and lay the architrave,
And spread the roof above them—ere he framed
The lofty vault, to gather and roll back
The sound of anthems; in the darkling wood,
Amid the cool and silence, he knelt down,
And offered to the Mightiest solemn thanks
And supplication. For his simple heart
Might not resist the sacred influence
Which, from the stilly twilight of the place,    10
And from the gray old trunks that high in heaven
Mingled their mossy boughs, and from the sound
Of the invisible breath that swayed at once
All their green tops, stole over him, and bowed
His spirit with the thought of boundless power
And inaccessible majesty. Ah, why
Should we, in the world's riper years, neglect
God's ancient sanctuaries, and adore
Only among the crowd, and under roofs
That our frail hands have raised? Let me, at least,
Here, in the shadow of this aged wood,           21
Offer one hymn—thrice happy, if it find
Acceptance in His ear.

        Father, thy hand
Hath reared these venerable columns, thou
Didst weave this verdant roof. Thou didst look
    down
Upon the naked earth, and, forthwith, rose
All these fair ranks of trees. They, in thy sun,

Budded, and shook their green leaves in thy breeze,
And shot toward heaven. The century-living crow
Whose birth was in their tops, grew old and died
Among their branches, till, at last, they stood,   32
As now they stand, massy, and tall, and dark,
Fit shrine for humble worshiper to hold
Communion with his Maker. These dim vaults,
These winding aisles, of human pomp or pride
Report not. No fantastic carvings show
The boast of our vain race to change the form
Of thy fair works. But thou art here—thou fill'st
The solitude. Thou art in the soft winds          40
That run along the summit of these trees
In music; thou art in the cooler breath
That from the inmost darkness of the place
Comes, scarcely felt; the barky trunks, the
    ground,
The fresh moist ground, are all instinct with thee.
Here is continual worship;—Nature, here,
In the tranquillity that thou dost love,
Enjoys thy presence. Noiselessly, around,
From perch to perch, the solitary bird
Passes; and yon clear spring, that, midst its herbs, 50
Wells softly forth and wandering steeps the roots
Of half the mighty forest, tells no tale
Of all the good it does. Thou hast not left
Thyself without a witness, in the shades,
Of thy perfections. Grandeur, strength, and grace
Are here to speak of thee. This mighty oak—
By whose immovable stem I stand and seem
Almost annihilated—not a prince,
In all that proud old world beyond the deep,
E'er wore his crown as loftily as he              60
Wears the green coronal of leaves with which
Thy hand has graced him. Nestled at his root
Is beauty, such as blooms not in the glare
Of the broad sun. That delicate forest flower,
With scented breath and look so like a smile,
Seems, as it issues from the shapeless mold,
An emanation of the indwelling Life,
A visible token of the upholding Love,
That are the soul of this great universe.

    My heart is awed within me when I think       70
Of the great miracle that still goes on,
In silence, round me—the perpetual work
Of thy creation, finished, yet renewed
Forever. Written on thy works I read
The lesson of thy own eternity.
Lo! all grow old and die—but see again,
How on the faltering footsteps of decay
Youth presses—ever gay and beautiful youth
In all its beautiful forms. These lofty trees
Wave not less proudly that their ancestors        80

A FOREST HYMN.   **2. architrave:** base of
a column.

30. **century-living crow:** ravens were thought to live a hundred
years.

Molder beneath them. Oh, there is not lost
One of earth's charms: upon her bosom yet,
After the flight of untold centuries,
The freshness of her far beginning lies
And yet shall lie. Life mocks the idle hate
Of his arch-enemy Death—yea, seats himself
Upon the tyrant's throne—the sepulcher,
And of the triumphs of his ghastly foe
Makes his own nourishment. For he came forth
From thine own bosom, and shall have no end.     90

There have been holy men who hid themselves
Deep in the woody wilderness, and gave
Their lives to thought and prayer, till they outlived
The generation born with them, nor seemed
Less aged than the hoary trees and rocks
Around them;—and there have been holy men
Who deemed it were not well to pass life thus.
But let me often to these solitudes
Retire, and in thy presence reassure
My feeble virtue. Here its enemies,               100
The passions, at thy plainer footsteps shrink
And tremble and are still. O God! when thou
Dost scare the world with tempests, set on fire
The heavens with falling thunderbolts, or fill,
With all the waters of the firmament,
The swift dark whirlwind that uproots the woods
And drowns the villages; when, at thy call,
Uprises the great deep and throws himself

Upon the continent, and overwhelms
Its cities—who forgets not, at the sight          110
Of these tremendous tokens of thy power,
His pride, and lays his strifes and follies by?
Oh, from these sterner aspects of thy face
Spare me and mine, nor let us need the wrath
Of the mad unchained elements to teach
Who rules them. Be it ours to meditate,
In these calm shades, thy milder majesty,
And to the beautiful order of thy works
Learn to conform the order of our lives.

*1825*                                    *1825*

# TO COLE, THE PAINTER DEPARTING FOR EUROPE

❖

⟨ THOMAS COLE (1801–48) founded the Hudson River
school of painting. He was a friend of Cooper and a
close friend of Bryant, with whom he took walking
tours in the Catskills, and whose attitude toward nature he shared. The Hudson River school, which included such painters as Thomas Doughty and Asher
Brown Durand, developed a moral philosophy of landscape that corresponds closely to that expressed, for example, in "A Forest Hymn." These painters had a contemplative and religious vision of American scenery.
Their fondness for dead, decaying trees was intended
to proclaim the mutability of all things. They used
sweeping effects of storm cloud and streaming light to
suggest the brooding presence of the Eternal, and they
liked introducing tiny human figures into panoramic
vistas to suggest the smallness of man before his Creator.
At the same time they endeavored to make their landscapes distinctively American, for the American earth
was new, and uncontaminated by the guilty European
past. It is easy to trace parallels between the landscape
vision of these painters and American scenery as described by Bryant and Cooper. Cooper's ability to describe vast panoramic tracts of forest, prairie, or river
valley, as seen from some lofty peak, is indebted to the
paintings of this school. One of its best known pictures,
"Kindred Spirits" by Durand, shows Bryant and Cole
as two small frock-coated figures standing above a Catskill gorge, with mountains, forest trees, a waterfall and
a turbulent stream, in the background. The two correct
little figures, who are soberly enjoying these wild but
solemn aspects of nature, provide a commentary on the
whole school.

❖

Thine eyes shall see the light of distant skies;
    Yet, COLE! thy heart shall bear to Europe's
        strand
    A living image of our own bright land,
Such as upon thy glorious canvas lies;
Lone lakes—savannas where the bison roves—
    Rocks rich with summer garlands—solemn
        streams—
    Skies, where the desert eagle wheels and
        screams—
Spring bloom and autumn blaze of boundless
        groves.
Fair scenes shall greet thee where thou goest—
        fair,
    But different—everywhere    the    trace    of
        men,                                          10
Paths, homes, graves, ruins, from the lowest glen
To where life shrinks from the fierce Alpine air.
    Gaze on them, till the tears shall dim thy sight,
    But keep that earlier, wilder image bright.

*1830*                                    *1829*

RICHARD WILBUR
*Editor*

# Edgar Allan Poe

## 1 8 0 9 – 1 8 4 9

EDGAR POE was born in Boston, Massachusetts on January 19, 1809. His mother, Elizabeth Arnold Poe, was an actress of some talent and much charm, who in the year of Edgar's birth was to reach the peak of her career, playing Ophelia to the Hamlet of John Howard Payne. Her husband David, an indifferent actor often humiliated by the critics, began in the same year to render himself unemployable through drink; at last, in July of 1810, he abandoned his family and vanished utterly from record. Soon after, Elizabeth Poe's fortunes and health declined, and in December of 1811, at the age of twenty-four, she died of consumption in a theatrical rooming house in Richmond, Virginia.

She left three children to the world. William Henry, the elder son, had long since been adopted by his grandfather, General David Poe of Baltimore: gifted and unbalanced, he was to become a sailor, a poet, and a drunkard, and then to die at twenty-four of the disease which had carried off his mother. Rosalie, the youngest child, about whom there were rumors of illegitimacy, was taken into the charitable Richmond household of William MacKenzie: she would live into her sixties as a markedly eccentric spinster. Three-year-old Edgar, whose life was to be both better and worse than these, was also taken from his mother's death chamber into a charitable Richmond family.

The charity seems to have been chiefly Frances Allan's; she was a soft-natured woman, and had no children of her own to love. John Allan, her husband, was a shrewd, handsome, ambitious merchant given to choler and selfrighteousness, whose reception of Edgar must have been at best a matter of cold principle. But whatever the motives and intentions of his foster-parents, the orphan boy found himself living, as a son, in the fine house of a family fast rising in Virginia's commercial aristocracy. When John Allan's business took him to England in 1815, Edgar was placed in the Manor House School at Stoke Newington, near London, where, as "Master Allan," he studied until his eleventh year. On the family's return to Richmond, John Allan continued to provide his ward with the education of a young Virginia gentleman; moreover, the Allans gave polite parties for Edgar, to which the children of Richmond's best families were invited. The boy was also encouraged to learn the rudiments of the family business, so that, although his name had now reverted to "Master Poe," it became his and Richmond's presumption that he was, or would become, John Allan's adopted son and heir.

Nevertheless, there are indications that Richmond's acceptance of Edgar Poe was frankly provisional, and that the boy could never have felt a comfortable assurance as to his place in the world. In discussing Poe's

[177]

school days, a Colonel Preston recalled that

of Edgar Poe it was known that his parents had been players, and that he was dependent upon the bounty that is bestowed upon an adopted son. All this had the effect of making the boys decline his leadership; and on looking backward on it since, I fancy it gave him a fierceness he would otherwise not have had.

It doubtless moved him to such feats as his Byronic seven-mile swim in the James River; insecurity may also have prompted, in some measure, his intense attachment to Mrs. Jane Stith Stanard, the mother of a schoolmate; and perhaps it was one cause of that growing moodiness which John Allan noted and disapproved.

As Edgar entered young manhood, there was a progressive collapse of sympathy between him and his guardian, who often accused him of idleness and a surly ingratitude. Too little is known of the substance of their differences to permit of any present adjudication, but certain things seem clear: John Allan was contemptuous of Edgar's developing literary ambition; he was disappointed by Edgar's want of interest in a mercantile career; and he was, for these and other reasons, impatient of supporting a troublesome ward with whom he had no temperamental affinity. This impatience was soon translated into action. When the respectable Royster family, in 1826, put an end to Edgar's courtship of their daughter Sarah Elmira, it was undoubtedly done on the basis of authoritative information that Edgar Poe was not to be John Allan's heir. And when Edgar, in that same year, entered the newly opened University of Virginia, it was with an allowance inadequate to his minimum needs. In an effort to escape the embarrassments which such malevolent parsimony made inevitable, he took to gambling, and in eight months lost some two thousand dollars. Since Allan then refused to pay both his legitimate debts and his "debts of honor," Edgar could not return to the university. After a violent quarrel with Allan, he left home and Richmond in March, 1827, with the vague project of "finding some place in the wide world."

In later years, Poe sometimes improved upon his life between 1827 and 1830 by tall tales of fighting in Greece, writing in Paris, or dueling in Spain. The truth is that the eighteen-year-old adventurer worked his way to Boston on a coal barge, under the alias of Henri le Rennet, found no employment there, and so enlisted in the U.S. Army as Edgar A. Perry. During the early months of his enlistment, he published at Boston a small volume entitled *Tamerlane and Other Poems*. The poems were few, the edition extremely small, and the public impact negligible.

Poe had always done honorably as a scholar; he now did honorably as a soldier, and by January of 1829 reached the highest noncommissioned grade, that of sergeant major. However, the thought of completing a five-year hitch had already become intolerable to him ("the prime of my life would be wasted"), and he now sought to secure his discharge. This was finally effected, through the kind concern of his officers and the grudging consent of his guardian, on the understanding that Sergeant Major Perry would seek appointment to the U.S. Military Academy at West Point.

While waiting for his appointment to come through, Poe shared for a time the poverty of his Grandmother Poe's household in Baltimore. Under that roof were his tubercular and dissipated brother William Henry, his aunt Maria Clemm, and a seven-year-old cousin, Virginia, who six years thereafter was to become his "child-bride." In December Poe rejoiced in the publication of *Al Aaraaf, Tamerlane and Minor Poems* by the Baltimore house of Hatch and Dunning, and in its immediate favorable notice by the novelist and critic John Neal. This literary recognition, together with his ward's obedient intention of becoming a West Point officer, moved John Allan to permit him a visit to Richmond, and there Poe remained until yet another quarrel forced his return to Baltimore in May of 1830.

The appointment, however, had at last been wangled, and in June he went on to West Point. It is plain that Poe, who was overage for a cadet and had no relish for a military future, entered the academy in the desperate hope of recovering John Allan's favor and patronage. As always, he proceeded to distinguish himself in his studies; but Allan's refusal to write, or to send him any expense money, gave reason to doubt that diligence would be rewarded. Indeed, Poe was not even notified when his guardian—then nineteen months a widower—was married in October to a woman quite young enough to give him an heir. On learning of this fatal development, Poe relinquished his hopes of an inheritance and, lacking his guardian's permission to resign from the academy, sought and gained a prompt dismissal for "gross neglect of duty" and "disobedience of orders."

During his last days at West Point, Poe wrote Allan a letter which was full, as usual, of half-truth and self-pity, of alternate accusation and entreaty. "My future life," he said, "(Which thank God will not endure long) must be passed in indigence and sickness." The prophecy was correct, and the remaining eighteen years of his existence were—despite his more romantic biographers—a Sahara of dreariness, pain, and drudgery. To be sure, Poe's marriage in 1836 to his girl-cousin Virginia secured him an oasis of affection and solicitude, and Virginia's mother, Mrs. Clemm, who ran the always impoverished household until the end, was, as one lady visitor put it, "a sort of Universal Providence for her strange children." There was also the satisfaction of winning an occasional prize—fifty dollars for "Ms. Found in a Bottle," one hundred for "The Gold Bug"—and of publishing an occasional collection of poems or tales.

But Poe was never able to support his small family by his poetry and fiction—"Ligeia" sold for ten dollars—and it was not until the celebrity of "The Raven," in 1845, that he enjoyed any real reputation as an artist. Prior to that time he was known for, and subsisted by means of, his editorial and critical labors for a series of periodicals in Richmond, Philadelphia, and New York. He was a good editor. Among other achievements, he quintupled the circulation of the *Southern Literary Messenger*, and in six

months built up the subscription list of *Graham's Magazine* from five thousand to twenty thousand—thus enriching his employers, but never, unfortunately, quite freeing his family from the necessity for supplemental begging. As a critic, Poe produced a great quantity of conscientious work, and in a period of puffery, chauvinism, and literary gang-warfare, was outstanding for his insistence on definite, high, and specifically aesthetic criteria. Because, as an editor of periodicals, he was obliged to review the books which came to his desk, Poe inevitably wasted much thought on unworthy subjects; it is lamentable that so fine a critical intellect had to concern itself, not only with Hawthorne and Bryant, but also, and mostly, with such titles as *The Canons of Good Breeding* and *Poetical Remains of the Late Lucretia Maria Davidson*.

The romantic legend of Poe minimizes the hard-plugging professional writer and editor in favor of the drunkard whose excesses cost him the editorship of the *Messenger*, and later, of *Burton's*. What should be compassionately remembered is that Poe was always unstable, and often underfed and exhausted; his usual frame of mind, as his depressing correspondence shows, was never very far from panic. Whenever his perilous balance was disturbed—as by the first signs of Virginia's fatal consumption, in 1842—he fell into a distraction of mind which, when it became insufferable, he blacked out by means of drink. It is doubtful that Poe consumed any great amount of alcohol in his lifetime, since his constitution would not tolerate it, even in modest quantities: and it seems best, as Poe himself advised, to refer the drink to the insanity, rather than the insanity to the drink.

Poe's last years were not without stable periods and literary achievements; out of them came "Ulalume," "The Domain of Arnheim," and the remarkable cosmological prose poem *Eureka*. But Virginia's decline and death robbed him of his one refuge from a world with which he could not steadily cope. It was not, as some have supposed, a burning-eyed libertine who conducted overlapping "affairs" with Mrs. Osgood, Mrs. Whitman, Mrs. Richmond, and his widowed childhood sweetheart, Elmira Royster Shelton. As W. H. Auden bluntly puts it, Poe was "an unmanly sort of man whose love-life seems to have been largely confined to crying in laps and playing house." What he sought from all these women, with the frantic anxiety of a lost child, was the equivalent of adoption.

A series of paranoid articles on Longfellow's "plagiarism," which Poe published in the *Broadway Journal* during 1845, would from a fully sane man have been dishonest, and Longfellow's decent and perceptive response was to say that the articles must have arisen from "the irritation of a sensitive nature, chafed by some indefinite sense of wrong." Thereafter the symptoms became clearer and more frequent: brain fever, fugue, persecutory hallucinations. . . . The circumstances which led to Poe's death are not fully known, and most scholars mistrust the story—eloquently evoked by Hart Crane in "The Bridge"—that Poe had been dragged, sick and drunk, from one polling place to another as a "repeater." But if his end, in October of 1849, was the result of foul play, those who left him dying in torn clothing, on a rainy Baltimore sidewalk, had only abetted an inevitable process of disintegration.

## II

POE'S fiction is full of allusions to his own history, some of them relatively open, as when he assigns his birthday to William Wilson, and some of them—as when he borrows the name of Usher from an early benefactor of his mother—obscure both in reference and in point. Such personal allusions cannot well be ignored, but the reader should be warned against concluding from their frequency that Poe's fiction is nothing but murky autobiography or psychodrama. To say that Virginia Poe equals Ligeia, or that Ligeia equals Virginia Poe, is to shed little light on either. We shall not go wrong, however, if we take Poe's autobiographical references as indicative of a taste for covert significance, and approach him with the hypothesis that his meaning lies where he said

it should, in an "under current." It would also be safe to suppose, on the basis of so many private allusions, that Poe's vision of the world was personally come by.

While detailed analogies between Poe's life and work are not of much use, there were constants in his life which, together with the prevalent literary influences, may be thought to have determined his themes and attitudes. For one thing, Poe at no time enjoyed a definite social identity. In childhood and youth, he was an orphan of "low" parentage half-assimilated to the Virginia aristocracy. In manhood, despite his gentleman's training, he found himself doomed to a life of shabbiness, loan-begging, and hack work. One consequence was that he came to think of himself as a fallen aristocrat among "low ruffians and boobies, . . . men . . . without a shadow . . . of caste." In politics, he grew aristocratic *à outrance*, hating the tyrant "Mob" and laying it down that "democracy is a very admirable form of government —for dogs." To a sense of fallen greatness we may also ascribe his continual fabrications about his family origins and European travels, his pretensions to more linguistic knowledge than he possessed. (The knowledge of languages was still, in Poe's day, one mark of a gentleman; the Prince Regent had once asked regarding a stranger, "Is he a gentleman? Has he any Greek?")

But Poe's radical solution to the problem of his place in the world was, quite simply, to secede from it. "The sole unquestionable aristocracy," he announced, was that of the intellect, and by this he intended the poetic intellect only. Scientists, in his view, were mere "diggers and pedlars of minute facts" who belonged in the "sculleries" rather than the "parlors" of Mind. And since Poe thought of poetry as concerned, not with earthly and human things, but with the pursuit of unearthly beauty, the superiority of the poet, like that of the mystic, consisted in a rapt disrelation to other men. He was monarch of the domain of his own visions, Crusoe of his desert island; his aristocracy was not social and comparative, but spiritual and absolute.

It was this Poe who told James Russell

Lowell, in answer to a request for biographical data:

I live continually in a reverie of the future. . . . You speak of "an estimate of my life," — and, from what I have already said, you will see that I have none to give. . . . My life has been *whim* — impulse — passion — a longing for solitude — a scorn of all things present, in an earnest longing for the future.

It was this Poe who wrote to a lady admirer, "My existence has been the merest Romance — in the sense of the most utter unworldliness." And it was this Poe who embodied his isolate "real self," his poetic or visionary faculty, in such high-born, rich, solitary, and visionary figures as Egaeus and Roderick Usher.

If Poe's galling sense of social anomaly inclined him toward a species of *contemptus mundi*, so also did his outrageous hunger to be loved and cared for. "The want of parental affection," he wrote, "has been the heaviest of my trials," and his letters exhibit a lifelong effort to secure too late, and from almost any quarter, the various psychic benefits of a happy childhood. The world could not answer his exorbitant emotional demands, and he was therefore, one suspects, the more disposed to look for happiness beyond it — in the shadows of memory, in the valleys of dream, in glimpses of a past or future heavenly existence.

Another constant in Poe's life was extreme emotional conflict. This was manifested in the helpless ambivalence of his letters, and also, at times, of his criticism. Elizabeth Barrett noted how Poe, in a review of her poems, oscillated between "the two extremes of laudation and reprehension." "You would have thought," she told her husband-to-be, "that it had been written by a friend and foe, each stark mad with love and hate and writing the alternate paragraphs . . ." In his conduct, as every biographer has observed, Poe was at all times his own worst enemy; he had a genius for self-defeat, and the imminence of any success, whether professional or amatory, led him to frustrate his apparent desires by doing or saying the fatal thing. He might have cried out with St. Paul, "I do not

understand my own actions. For I do not do what I want, but I do the very thing I hate." In his fiction, the theater of which was the individual soul, Poe sought to understand, and succeeded at least in portraying, that conflict and perversity from which all men have suffered, but few more fearfully than he.

That Poe was socially dislocated, emotionally starved, and torn in spirit, does not explain his art. Yet these facts may help us to understand why, as a continuator of English and European romanticism, he could carry some of its tendencies to unprecedented extremes, demanding of poetry that it totally repudiate this earthly life and making, in his psychological fiction, a vast and original contribution to that movement which Erich Heller has called "the discovery and colonization of inwardness."[1]

### III

FROM first to last, from "Al Aaraaf" to *Eureka*, Poe's vision of things was cosmic in extent, and any approach to his work must be prefaced by a brief synthetic account of that vision. The universe, as Poe conceived it, is a poetic or artistic creation, a "plot of God." It has come about through God's breaking-up of His original unity, and His self-radiation into space; it is presently at the point of maximum diffusion, and will soon begin to contract toward a final reassembly in — and as — God. Since God, in creating the universe, fragmented Himself into His creatures, and now exists only in those "infinite individualizations of Himself," it is they who must, by some counterimpulse, restore the original oneness of things.

What must this counterimpulse be? Since "the source of all motion is thought," it must be intellectual or spiritual in character. And since the creation is a work of art, the counter-impulse which can reunify it must be imaginative. In short, the duty of God's creatures is to think God together again by discovering, through the fusing power of poetic imagination, the primal unity in the present diversity.

[1]Erich Heller, *The Hazard of Modern Poetry* (1953), p. 18.

The one true response to the creation, then, is to take an imaginative delight in its beauty and harmony, seen and unseen. To deny the validity and holiness of poetic intuition, to prefer some other mode of knowledge, would be to deny God and fall away from Him. Unfortunately, the planet Earth has done just that, by succumbing to the spirit of scientific rationalism, and by preferring material "fact" to visionary truth. As a result, the souls of men have grown dark, diseased, and insensitive, and even physical nature has by contagion "fallen" from its original divine beauty and order. Before the earth can rejoin the cosmic process, and assist the other stars in reconstituting God, it will have to be redeemed from rationalism and materialism by that purifying fire which the Bible foretells.

Meanwhile, our fallen planet is not a happy environment for a poet. In him alone, of all the inhabitants of Earth, the divine spark of imagination still burns brightly; his soul alone vaguely remembers, from a previous existence, a divine harmony and beauty, and yearns to return thither. Yet everything around him conspires to reduce him to its own degraded level: the scientist and "utilitarian" discredit and abuse him, their corrupt and prosaic thought invades his consciousness, and nowhere in the human or natural environment can he find suitable objects for contemplation. His only means of escape is the suspension of outward consciousness, and a deliberate retreat from the temporal, rational, physical world into the visionary depths of his mind. There, in the immaterial regions of dream, he can purge himself of all earthly taint, and deliver himself to visions of that heavenly beauty which is the thought of God.

Poe's poet is thus at war with the external world. But he is also, unfortunately, at war within himself. As a pre-existent soul, or as a happy child, he once enjoyed a perfect psychic harmony; his consciousness was purely imaginative, and he knew the universe for the poem that it is. However, as he grew older on this corrupted Earth and entered the society of men, it was unavoidable that his integrity of being should be compromised and destroyed. His intellect learned a respect for logic and prosaic fact; his awakening passions drew him toward the merely physical; conscience began its contests with desire; and there arose in him a mysterious spirit of perversity. Like Poe's universe, the poet's soul has lost its original unity; and like that universe, it will not regain that unity save in death. Till then, the poet's imagination must struggle not only against the mundane and physical world around him, but also against the mundane and physical aspects of his divided nature; he will not now find it easy to disengage his spirit from earthly things, and commune with that heavenly harmony which is symbolized, in Poe's fiction, by such figures as the Lady Ligeia.

IV

THE *Oxford Companion to American Literature* summarizes "Ligeia" as follows:

An aristocratic young man marries Ligeia, a woman of strange, dark beauty and great learning. They are deeply in love, and share an interest in the occult, until a wasting illness triumphs over Ligeia's passionate will to live, and she dies. In melancholy grief, her husband leaves his lonely home on the Rhine to purchase an English abbey, where he grows mentally deranged under the influence of opium. He marries fair-haired Lady Rowena Trevanion, although they are not in love, and Rowena soon dies in a strange manner. Her husband watches by the bier, and sees signs of returning life in the body, but considers these to be hallucinations. At last she rises to her feet and looses the cerements from her head, so that masses of long black hair stream forth. When she opens her eyes, he realizes that the lost Ligeia's will to live has triumphed, for she has assumed what was formerly the body of Rowena.

Considering its purpose and the difficulties involved, this summary is admirable, and yet it seems ludicrously unrelated to the actual experience of reading "Ligeia." An examination of the disparities between summary and story may serve to set in relief some of Poe's characteristics as a writer of fiction.

In the first place, the summary necessarily exaggerates the prominence of plot in Poe's story, the first two-thirds of which consists mainly of rumination and brooding description. Only with the onset of Rowena's illness does narrative predominate, and the effect of the whole is not to leave us with any secure sense of fact or of causal sequence. Again, the summary confers on the persons of the story a credibility of character, motive, and feeling which they do not possess. We do not experience the narrator as "an aristocratic young man," but as a monstrous and unclassifiable sensibility. Ligeia does not strike us as a strangely beautiful and learned woman, but as an omniscient goddess. It does not seem adequate to say that the characters are "deeply in love" or "not in love," because their emotional frequencies are simply not ours: we cannot attune ourselves to a man who, looking into his beloved's eyes, is both "delighted and appalled," nor can we accept "mental alienation" as sufficient explanation of a perfectly motiveless remarriage. The fact is that Poe's characters escape our everyday understanding, and are meant to.

The main thing ignored in the summary is, of course, that "Ligeia" is not objectively told, but narrated—as so often in Poe—by a hero not quite in his ordinary mind. Such a narrative strategy has various effects, the chief one being this: that it encourages the reader to doubt that the ostensible story is the real or only one. Having come to doubt the ostensible story, the reader will perhaps decide to take it as a mad-man's misconstruction of doubtless prosaic events: but if he is familiar with Poe's criticism, he may more fruitfully decide to treat it as a cunning allegory, and look for some "mystic or secondary" meaning beneath it. Imaginative literature, Poe said, is "that class of composition in which there lies beneath the transparent upper current of meaning, an under or *suggestive* one." Since Poe thought "Ligeia" his best story, we may confidently sound it for an undercurrent.

The story begins with the narrator's confession that he "cannot remember how, when, or even precisely where" he first met Ligeia; moreover, he has never learned his beloved's surname, and cannot remember why not. Such a paroxysm of noninformativeness is potentially comic, but the inten-

tion here is serious. Vagueness and indefinitiveness were, in Poe's aesthetic theory, indispensable to the highest art, because they estrange the reader from mundane fact and meaning, and presumably set him adrift toward the spiritual and dim. This process of estrangement begins early and emphatically in "Ligeia," and is sustained throughout by the narrator's uncertainties, as well as by his repeated assertions that "words are impotent to convey" his subject matter.

But the more immediate effect of the opening paragraph is to detach Ligeia from the realm of actualities—from "when" and "where," from time and place—and thus, to suggest that she is really an idea. The hero speculates that he may have forgotten his first meeting with Ligeia "because, in truth, the character of my beloved, her rare learning, her singular yet placid cast of beauty, and the thrilling and enthralling eloquence of her low musical language, made their way into my heart by paces so steadily and stealthily progressive, that they have been unnoticed and unknown." It is true that people may "grow on us," but so sourceless and insensible a process as the hero describes would better characterize the development of some taste, or faculty, or idea within the soul. Let us see what idea is embodied in Ligeia.

Poe borrowed her name—as so much else—from Milton: in *Comus*, when the Attendant Spirit summons the nymph Sabrina to free the chaste Lady from Comus' spell, he adjures her in the name of the siren Ligeia (1.880 ff.) and other sea-immortals. Poe first used the borrowed name in his cosmic poem "Al Aaraaf," where Ligeia is one of the two presiding spirits of a wandering star, the function of which is to mediate between Heaven and the scattered worlds of the universe, conveying to the latter a redemptive awareness of divine beauty and harmony. Like Milton's siren, she is associated with song; she governs, in fact, "the music of things" (II.127), and has properly been described as "the personified harmony of nature."

If one tries the experiment of identifying the heroine of "Ligeia" with her namesake in "Al Aaraaf," one finds that the story begins at once to make sense, and that all its apparent hyperbole becomes sober statement. If Ligeia is not a woman, but a mediatory spirit embodying the Platonic idea of harmony, she quite naturally has "the beauty of beings either above or apart from the earth," and speaks with "a melody more than mortal." Being immaterial, she might be expected to come and go "as a shadow," with a step of "incomprehensible lightness." And since she is the principle of harmony which pervades all things, it is understandable that the hero should discover "in the commonest objects of the universe, a circle of analogies" to the expression of her eyes.

Ligeia's eyes are her major feature, and hidden within them, the hero says, is a "something more profound than the well of Democritus." The nature of this mystery is readily discovered, since Poe was here quoting a passage which he attributed to Joseph Glanvill, and later used as the epigraph of "A Descent into the Maelström":

The ways of God in Nature, as in Providence, are not as our ways; nor are the models that we frame in any way commensurate to the vastness, profundity, and unsearchableness of His works, which have a depth in them greater than the well of Democritus.

It is now understandable why the narrator, looking into Ligeia's eyes, should be "delighted and appalled"; what he dimly glimpses there is nothing less than "the ways of God."

In short, Ligeia is not distinguishable from what Poe called, in his review of R. H. Horne's *Orion*, "the sentiment of the beautiful—that divine sixth sense which is yet so faintly understood . . . that sense which speaks of GOD through his purest, if not his *sole* attribute—which proves, and which alone proves his existence." Because the principle of harmony belongs to all those arts through which the spirit intuits supernal beauty, Ligeia's attributes are not merely musical: her hand is marble; her skin is ivory; she resembles the Venus de' Medici; her hair interprets the Homeric epithet "hyacinthine," and she herself is a poet. She evokes Greek, Graeco-Roman, or Hebrew art

because such art was produced before the "fall" of Earth, in a golden time when man's soul was attuned to universal beauty.

The "gigantic" learning of Ligeia, which encompasses "*all* the wide areas of moral, physical, and mathematical science," must be understood in some mystic sense, because heavenly spirits cannot be supposed to study books.

We may now interpret Ligeia's universal "learning" in this way: she is the inspirer and heavenly goal of a kind of knowledge, purely aesthetic and superior to the rational, which soars intuitively toward the Forms of things, and assimilates the soul to transcendental Beauty. Such knowledge is "all sufficient" and all-inclusive, because it proceeds, by direct visionary means, toward those great answers which the trammeled reason will never reach. Such knowledge is also infallible because, the universe being an infinitely harmonious work of art, any perception of beauty or harmony must be true. The Keatsian idea that Beauty guarantees Truth was most boldly expressed by Poe in *Eureka*, where he argued that

symmetry and consistency are convertible terms:—thus Poetry and Truth are one. A thing is consistent in the ratio of its truth—true in the ratio of its consistency. *A perfect consistency, I repeat, can be nothing but an absolute truth.*

So long as Ligeia is with him as his "wife," the hero's harmonious soul is untouched by his diseased Earthly environment, and devotes itself to unbroken poetic visions of ultramundane harmony and beauty. In the superficial story, this happy period belongs to his adult life, but there are strong hints of another chronology: as Ligeia bends over the hero at his studies, he "resigns himself, with a childlike confidence, to her guidance"; when she falls ill, he is "but as a child groping benighted"; and her death leaves him with "feelings of utter abandonment." It is, in fact, as a child that the hero dwells with Ligeia and the heavenly harmony she confers; he is Wordsworth's "Mighty prophet! Seer blest!" and the passing of Ligeia is the passing of childhood and its "visionary gleam." As Poe put it in his juvenile poem "Tamerlane,"

> . . . boyhood is a summer sun
> Whose waning is the dreariest one.
> For all we live to know is known,
> And all we seek to keep hath flown.

The remainder of the story is an allegory of the efforts of the poetic soul, once compromised and disrupted by exposure to the world, to overcome the world and itself, and recover the imaginative absolutism of childhood. The poet-hero's retreat into a "remote and unsocial" English abbey, his addiction to opium, and his "incipient madness" symbolize the retreat from waking consciousness—from bodily, moral, and intellectual consciousness—into the imaginative freedom of reverie and dream. Like "The Haunted Palace," the House of Usher, and all such edifices in Poe, the abbey represents the hero's isolated and self-absorbed mind. Its decay, like that of the Usher mansion, signifies that the consciousness within is disengaging itself from the material world and the material self, and will soon (in a subjective sense) destroy them. As for the interior, which the hero has decorated in a spirit of "child-like perversity," it is, like the apartment of the hero of "The Assignation," quite literally "a bower of dreams."

The abbey's bridal chamber—the one room fully described—is pentagonal in shape, but the angles are hidden by sarcophagi, and the walls are hung with a figured material continually agitated by an artificial current of wind. The effect, therefore, is generally circular, but there is a perpetual ambiguity of form. The room thus avoids—as all Poe's dream-rooms do—that "rectangular obscenity" which Poe associated with the "harsh mathematical reason" now prevalent on Earth. The furnishings, like those of "The Assignation," reflect a scorn for "proprieties of place, and of time": the juxtaposition of Venetian, Saracenic, Druidical, and Egyptian objects exhibits the richness and daring of the hero's imagination and very concretely expresses one idea of Poe's poem "Dream-Land," that in dreams we are "out of SPACE —out of TIME."

Entering dream, one escapes not only from local and temporal limitations, but also from external sensation. "It is as if," Poe says, "the five senses were supplanted by five others alien to mortality." Therefore Poe's dreamers lead a strictly indoor or sheltered existence, and their perceptions are wholly intramural. "Ligeia's" bridal chamber has a window of "leaden hue," which denatures the daylight to a "ghastly lustre": the wind which rushes behind the draperies is "artificial": and the changeable figures of the agitated draperies suggest those vivid and ever-shifting images of the hypnagogic state which Poe took to be "glimpses of the spirit's outer world."

The bridal chamber is not only a dreaming mind, but a mind obsessed with a mournful longing for Ligeia. A vine—first in the hero's catalogue of natural objects reminiscent of his beloved—shadows the gray window: the walls, like Ligeia's intellect, are "gigantic": the fires of the pendant censer "writhe" like Ligeia's fierce spirit; and the gold-and-black decor recalls her radiant eyes and jet-black hair. Plainly, the chamber does not contain a consciousness hospitable to Rowena.

What, on the allegorical plane, does the fairhaired Rowena stand for? She is beautiful, but unlike Ligeia she is earthly, temporal, material. She is, in fact, what Poe elsewhere calls "the type of physical beauty," and she stands also for that part of the hero's compromised nature which adheres to such beauty. The progressive wasting-away of Rowena enacts, therefore, a Platonic version of the art process, in which beauty is imaginatively extricated from the temporal and physical, and may at last be glimpsed in its bodiless essence. Rowena's decomposition is a progress toward the immateriality of Ligeia; her rigor mortis is an approach to the timeless and ideal condition of statuary; and when Rowena becomes Ligeia, and the hero is "chilled into stone" by the transformation, we perceive that he has momentarily purified his consciousness of everything earthly, attained once more to the Beautiful, and "assimilated his own condition with it."

Ostensibly, the transformation is effected by the "gigantic volition" of Ligeia, but the narrator is, in truth, the sole agent in the tale; the waning of Rowena and the waxing of Ligeia are governed by his mind's gradual movement from reverie to the visionary brink of sleep. "The night waned," he tells us, "and still, with a bosom full of bitter thoughts of the one only and supremely beloved, I remained gazing upon the body of Rowena." It is this remorseless and dematerializing gaze which alters Rowena.

Ligeia appears in proportion as Rowena fades, and we first see her as "a faint, indefinite shadow of angelic aspect" in the pool of light beneath the censer. Of this censer, which hangs on its golden chain in the center of the chamber, something must be said. It derives ultimately from the *Iliad* (VIII. 18–26), but Poe plainly found it in *Paradise Lost* (II. 1004 ff., 1051 ff.), where the created universe depends from Heaven by a golden chain which serves also as the pathway of angels. In Poe's "Al Aaraaf" (II. 20 ff.), Milton's chain is incorporated into the description of the palace of Nesace, spirit of Beauty:

A dome, by linkèd light from Heaven let down,
Sat gently on these columns as a crown—
A window of one circular diamond, there,
Looked out above into the purple air,
And rays from God shot down that meteor chain
And hallowed all the beauty twice again,
Save when, between th' Empyrean and that ring,
Some eager spirit flapped his dusky wing.

The golden chain reappears, as a chandelier, in a number of Poe's interiors, signifying always the linkage between poetic imagination and the divine mind. The particolored flames of the censer in "Ligeia" are the purifying fire of imagination and consist of diffracted "rays from God." Because the golden chain is the pathway of angels, it is beneath the censer that we first spy Ligeia's "dusky wing"; and it is there, again, "in the middle of the apartment," that she at last reopens her profound eyes.

The foregoing discussion of "Ligeia" would be disproportionate were the story not so central to Poe's thought, so characteristic of his method, and so much an index of his

symbolism that it opens up the fiction in general. The typical Poe story is, in its action, an allegory of dream-experience: it occurs within the mind of a poet; the characters are not distinct personalities, but principles or faculties of the poet's divided nature; the steps of the action correspond to the successive states of a mind moving into sleep; and the end of the action is the end of a dream. Sometimes, as in "William Wilson," the narrative will have a strong admixture of realism and of credible psychology; elsewhere, as in "The Fall of the House of Usher," there will be no such admixture, and the one available coherence will be allegorical.

Generally, Poe offers the reader some suggestion that his characters are but aspects of a single personality: they will be bound together by marriage, or kinship, or old and intimate acquaintance; or perhaps they will share a common height, eye color, or birthday; or perhaps their names will have some obvious or sly similarity. In "Usher," which is essentially a retelling of "Ligeia," the narrator has been a boyhood companion of Roderick Usher and is now "his only personal friend," while Lady Madeline, the third character of the story, is Usher's twin sister and "sole companion for long years." The narrator's journey to Usher's domain is a dream-journey into his own mind, in the depths of which, and on the brink of sleep, he encounters in Roderick Usher his visionary soul. Usher embodies, in his tremulousness and in his variations of voice and mood, the incertitude of the hypnagogic state, that borderline condition wherein "the confines of the waking world blend with those of the world of dreams." Like the hero of "Ligeia," Usher is struggling to purge himself of waking and wordly consciousness, and Lady Madeline's "wasting-away," like Rowena's, enacts this process of purgation. Once dead and encoffined—once "death-refined"—Lady Madeline can rise again as a Ligeia-figure, climb to the turret room where Roderick awaits her, and "in her violent and now final death-agonies, bear him to the floor a corpse." Grisly as their death-embrace may seem, it actually symbolizes the momentary reunion of a divided soul; and, since "by sleep and its world alone is *Death* imaged," it also symbolizes the final restoration and purification of that soul in the life to come.

The dematerialization of Usher's whirl-wind-shaken house, and its collapse into its reflection in the tarn, express these same ideas; and they express as well the descent of the dreaming mind into unconscious sleep. "Ligeia" similarly ends, if not with a fall, at least with the vertigo which precedes and accompanies a fall. Its narrator's mind becomes "a helpless prey to a whirl of vi-olent emotions," and the wind-current which circles the vast room, agitating the lofty dra-peries, intensifies at the close, so that Li-geia's unbound hair "streams forth into the rushing atmosphere of the chamber."

## V

OF ALL Poe's stories, those of detection seem most complete in their "upper current" and least in need of allegorical interpretation. They have on the face of it a clear point: the superiority of intuition to reason. It is the Prefect of Police, in the three Dupin stories, who stands for that methodical reason which "creeps and crawls" and blinds itself with the "Scotch snuff of *detail*." Dupin, although Poe describes his mental operations as "analytic" and as based on a psychological calculus of probabilities, is actually repre-sentative of a pure poetic intuition bordering on omniscience. He *dreams* his solutions, and it sometimes appears that in solving a prob-lem he can dispense, not only with reason, but with the problem itself.

In "The Mystery of Marie Roget," Dupin sleeps in his armchair for seven or eight hours during the Prefect's recital of the evidence, his eyes hidden by green-glassed spectacles reminiscent of the tinted windows of Poe's dream-chambers. In "The Purloined Letter," Dupin invites the Prefect to give him the facts of the case—"or not"; just as he likes. The implication is that Dupin can somehow do without the mere facts; and indeed, within his first six speeches—well before the Prefect has told him anything—Dupin has intuitively solved the problem in all but its details. So

confident is he of his principle of solution that he teases the Prefect by repeating it thrice.

It may be objected that Poe does also present Dupin as a reasoner, who offers his conclusions logically and at length. There are several answers to that objection, one being that a flat ascription of preterhuman powers, as in *Superman Comics*, makes for dull fiction. It is characteristic of Dupin that he first arrives at some conclusion, and then explains it logically to the narrator. In so doing, he is not reproducing his original mode of thought any more than Poe, in his "Philosophy of Composition," gives a true account of the writing of "The Raven." Rather, he is translating an ineffable process into lay terms; or demonstrating that intui-tion includes and obviates reason; or—like some Kepler—investigating the possibility that there was an implicit logic in his intui-tive leap. This we know because, while Du-pin's conclusions are always correct, the logic by which he claims to have reached them is generally faulty. Readers would be more critical of Dupin's reasoning were they not disarmed by the correctness of his con-clusions.

Insofar as Dupin has any method, it con-sists in identifying his intellect with that of another and thereby divining what that per-son must think or do. Everyone has this power, in some degree, but with Dupin it is so strong that he can infallibly read the thoughts of a hypothetical Maltese sailor. In short, Dupin's power of divination is unlim-ited, and quite outflies the capabilities of his method: we are to see him not as a psychol-ogist but as a seer. Poe said in his "Margi-nalia" that "poetic genius . . . in its su-preme development, embodies all orders of intellectual capacity," and the statement applies to Dupin. He is a godlike genius who, possessing the highest and most comprehen-sive order of mind, includes in himself all possible lesser minds, and can therefore fathom any man—indeed, any primate—by mere introspection. How this omniscient sol-ipsism is related to Poe's thought in general may be seen by a footnote to *Eureka*, in which Poe is remarking on his theory that the universe, through its own imaginative efforts, is to be reabsorbed in God:

The pain of the reflection that we shall lose our individual identity, ceases at once when we further reflect that the process, as above described, is neither more nor less than that of the absorption, by each individual intelligence, of all other intelligences (that is, of the Universe) into its own. That God may be all in all, each must become God.

The poet-detective Dupin is in the vanguard of that movement.

"The Purloined Letter," despite its adequacy as a detective tale and as a vindication of pure intuition, is also an allegory of conflict within a single soul. As allegory, it belongs to a class of tales—"The Man of the Crowd," "Murders in the Rue Morgue"—in which the soul of a poet "detects" and confronts the evil or brutal principle in itself. By hint upon hint, Poe invites the reader to play detective himself, and to discover that the Minister D—— is the worldly, unprincipled "brother" or double of Auguste Dupin. And who is the queen, whom Dupin liberates from the Minister's power? Like Ligeia, she is that sense of beauty which must not be the captive of our lower natures.

## VI

THE BODY of Poe's poetry is very small in proportion to his total work, partly because he had to neglect poetry in favor of better-paid literary labors and partly because his conception of poetry, as it evolved, was so exclusive and extreme as to preclude any great productivity. Here are some random snippets from his criticism:

The phrase, "A long poem," is simply a flat contradiction in terms . . . didactic subjects are utterly *beyond*, or rather beneath, the province of true poesy . . . A satire is, of course, *no* poem . . . we agree with Coleridge, that poetry and *passion* are discordant . . . Poetry, in elevating, tranquillizes the soul. With the *heart* it has nothing to do . . . With the Intellect or with the Conscience it has only collateral relations. Unless

incidentally, it has no concern whatever with Duty or Truth . . . Give it any undue decision—imbue it with any very determinate tone—and you deprive it, at once, of its ethereal, its ideal, its intrinsic and essential character. You dispel its luxury of dream.

To the short story, which Poe regarded as a lower form than poetry, "and more appreciable by the mass of mankind," he permitted some measure of verisimilitude and a logical clarity of plot and idea. But the function of poetry being not to organize and interpret earthly experience, but to induce a mood in which the soul soars toward supernal beauty, Poe excluded from poetry everything which might detain the soul on Earth. Thus, poetry must be disembarrassed of that moral sense which involves us with humanity; it must throw overboard that factuality and that narrative or logical clarity which would render it compassable by the mundane intellect; and it must eschew all human emotions since, when compared to the sense of beauty, they are—as Poe said in reviewing Horne's *Orion*—"vapid and insignificant" and "trammel the soul in its flight to an ideal Helusion."

In practice, these principles resulted in a remorseless elaboration of those techniques of "estrangement" which we have already noted in "Ligeia." We must not, Poe warns us in a review of Macaulay, "confound obscurity of expression with the expression of obscurity," and surely the best of his tales may be defended as illuminations of a subject matter essentially obscure. But the poems, with few exceptions, do not truly illuminate, and what brilliance they have is like that of a Fourth-of-July rocket destroying itself in the void.

When one of Poe's poems has a narrative basis, the reader will often struggle in vain to derive it from the poem proper and will arrive at a plot, if at all, by interpolation from related prose works. "The Haunted Palace" and "The Raven" are, among Poe's verse-narratives, relatively clear, yet even they have a tantalizing incompleteness which one does not find in the better tales. Although the "plots" of Poe's poems always bear on his inveterate concerns, they mostly seem to be there not for plot's sake or for meaning's sake, but to furnish a substance which the poem may "waste away" and etherealize.

The celebrated vagueness of Milton's *Paradise Lost,* whereby he conveys the impression of shadowing-forth things unknowable in themselves, was appropriated by Poe for purposes fundamentally opposed to Milton's. Poe was not interested in giving a qualified concreteness to divine things, but rather in verbally destroying the concreteness of earthly things. From Milton's description of Chaos as a "dark Illimitable ocean without bound," Poe learned how to write of "seas without a shore" and "boundless floods": likewise, Milton's "dark unbottomed infinite Abyss" begot the "bottomless vales" of Poe's "Dream-Land." In Poe, the effect of such paradoxes is quite simply to annihilate the words "seas," "floods," and "vales," as we understand them, and so magically to deprive the reader of a part of the world he knows. In so doing, Poe's paradoxes support his continual explicit stress on disappearance, silence, oblivion, and all ideas which suggest nonbeing. It was the notion of approximating nothingness which most excited him in his own poetry, and in that of others. As a critic, he quoted approvingly almost any use of such words as "dim" and "unseen," and in reviewing Joseph Rodman Drake's *Culprit Fay* he characteristically observed that "in the expression 'glimmers and dies' . . . the imagination is exalted by the moral sentiment of beauty heightened in dissolution."

In an 1843 review of Rufus Griswold's *Poets and Poetry of America*, Poe scanned the first line of his "Haunted Palace" as follows:

In the/ greenest/ of our/ valleys

This supports a considerable body of contemporary testimony to the effect that Poe's reading of his poems was metronomic. There are several explanations for this feature of his poetry, aside from the relative indelicacy of Poe's ear. Expressive rhythm in poetry derives either from the things and movements described, or from the emotions embodied. The first source of rhythm was not altogether denied to Poe: we have, for instance, the line, "Down, down that town shall settle hence." But the second was precluded by Poe's having banished from his poetry all emotion save that "tremulous delight" which attends an imaginary destruction of the physical world. Poe's rhythmic regularity is not, however, wholly the result of such exclusion. He thought of the poem not as an object for contemplation but as a means of engendering "sensations which bewilder while they enthrall—and which would *not* so enthrall if they did not so bewilder." In short, he thought of the poem as casting a spell and accordingly endowed it with the brevity, repetitiveness, sonority, and the impressive rhythmic monotony of a charm or incantation. In a charm we are far less concerned with the sense than with the effect—nonsense will do, if it only works— and therefore Poe's incantatory techniques further the general effort of his poetry to nullify—in a logical and denotative sense— the words with which it is made.

Poe's poetry is pure negation: it does not and cannot acquaint us with supernal beauty, and the reader may well question whether there is anything very spiritual about a program of estranging us from the known by subverting the words through which we know it. A number of Poe's poems are enchanting in much the way they mean to be, but the present writer reserves his respect for the major tales, which, for all the secretiveness of their allegory, are great and trail-blazing realizations of inner experience.

NOTE

The editor wishes to thank Professor T. O. Mabbott for his great kindness in reading the Introduction and notes to this section, correcting several errors of fact, and supplying a number of data which the editor did not possess.

# POEMS

## EVENING STAR

❲ IN "Evening Star" the poet rejects a "lowly" and relatively earthly Beauty (the moon) in favor of a "distant" and heavenly Beauty (Venus). Note that the enshrouding of the moon increases the visibility of Venus, as the death of Rowena makes possible a vision of Ligeia. This early poem embodies Poe's basic formula of destructive transcendence.

'T was noontide of summer,
  And mid-time of night;
  And stars, in their orbits,
    Shone pale, thro' the light
Of the brighter, cold moon,
  'Mid planets her slaves,
Herself in the Heavens,
  Her beam on the waves.
  I gaz'd a while
  On her cold smile;           10
Too cold—too cold for me.
  There pass'd as a shroud,
  A fleecy cloud,
And I turn'd away to thee,
  Proud Evening Star,
  In thy glory afar,
And dearer thy beam shall be;
  For joy to my heart
  Is the proud part
Thou bearest in Heav'n at night,     20
  And more I admire
  Thy distant fire
Than that colder, lowly light.

*1827*

## THE LAKE: TO ———

❲ THIS lake anticipates all the gulfs, tarns and whirlpools through which Poe's dreaming heroes plunge into eternity. The "tremulous delight" which attends the idea of annihilation is the primary feeling—or sensation —which Poe's poetry seeks to produce.

Some scholars think that the model for Poe's lake may have been the Lake of the Dismal Swamp, near Norfolk. Its waters are believed to be poisonous, and it is said to be haunted by the ghost of a lover who, maddened by the death of his sweetheart, ran into the swamp and was lost. Thomas Moore wrote a poem on the subject in 1803.

In spring of youth it was my lot
To haunt of the wide world a spot
The which I could not love the less—
So lovely was the loneliness
Of a wild lake, with black rock bound,
And the tall pines that towered around.

But when the Night had thrown her pall
Upon that spot, as upon all,
And the mystic wind went by
Murmuring in melody,         10
Then—ah, then—I would awake
To the terror of the lone lake.

Yet that terror was not fright,
But a tremulous delight—
A feeling not the jewelled mine
Could teach or bribe me to define—
Nor Love—although the Love were thine.

Death was in that poisonous wave,
And in its gulf a fitting grave
For him who thence could solace bring   20
To his lone imagining,
Whose solitary soul could make
An Eden of that dim lake.

*1827*

## SONNET—TO SCIENCE

❲ AN INDUBITABLE source for the sestet of this sonnet has lately been discovered. In the Hunter translation of Bernadin de St. Pierre's *Studies in Nature* (1808) the following sentence appears: "It is Science which has dragged down the chaste Diana from her nocturnal car; she has banished the Hamadryads from the antique forests, and the gentle Naiads from the fountains."

Poe's sonnet sees the Earth as so corrupted by rationalism that the poet can discover beauty only in visions of "some happier star."

Science! true daughter of Old Time thou art!
  Who alterest all things with thy peering eyes.
Why preyest thou thus upon the poet's heart,
  Vulture, whose wings are dull realities?
How should he love thee? or how deem thee wise,
  Who wouldst not leave him in his wandering
To seek for treasure in the jewelled skies,
  Albeit he soared with an undaunted wing?
Hast thou not dragged Diana from her car?
  And driven the Hamadryad from the wood   10

SONNET—TO SCIENCE.   **3–4. Why . . . realities?:** The poet is likened here to Prometheus and in the second quatrain to Icarus.

To seek a shelter in some happier star?
    Hast thou not torn the Naiad from her flood,
The Elfin from the green grass, and from me
The summer dream beneath the tamarind tree?

*1829*

## ALONE

❡ THOUGH never published by Poe, this poem has lately
been proven authentic.

    From childhood's hour I have not been
    As others were—I have not seen
    As others saw—I could not bring
    My passions from a common spring—
    From the same source I have not taken
    My sorrow—I could not awaken
    My heart to joy at the same tone—
    And all I lov'd—*I* lov'd alone.
    *Then*—in my childhood—in the dawn
    Of a most stormy life—was drawn    10
    From ev'ry depth of good and ill
    The mystery which binds me still—
    From the torrent, or the fountain—
    From the red cliff of the mountain—
    From the sun that round me roll'd
    In its autumn tint of gold—
    From the lightning in the sky
    As it pass'd me flying by—
    From the thunder, and the storm—
    And the cloud that took the form    20
    (When the rest of Heaven was blue)
    Of a demon in my view.

## ISRAFEL

❡ "ISRAFEL" expresses Poe's aspiration toward a supernal
beauty which should mediate—like the gardens of Arnheim—between the earthly and the divine.

    *And the angel Israfel, whose*
    *heart-strings are a lute, and*
    *who has the sweetest voice*
    *of all God's creatures.*
                KORAN

    In Heaven a spirit doth dwell
      "Whose heart-strings are a lute;"
    None sing so wildly well
    As the angel Israfel,
    And the giddy stars (so legends tell),
    Ceasing their hymns, attend the spell
      Of his voice, all mute.

    Tottering above
      In her highest noon,
      The enamoured moon    10
    Blushes with love,
      While, to listen, the red levin
      (With the rapid Pleiads, even,
      Which were seven,)
    Pauses in Heaven.

    And they say (the starry choir
      And the other listening things)
    That Israfeli's fire
    Is owing to that lyre
      By which he sits and sings—    20
    The trembling living wire
      Of those unusual strings.

    But the skies that angel trod,
      Where deep thoughts are a duty—
    Where Love's a grown-up God—
      Where the Houri glances are
    Imbued with all the beauty
      Which we worship in a star.

    Therefore, thou are not wrong,
      Israfeli, who despisest    30
    An unimpassioned song;
    To thee the laurels belong,
      Best bard, because the wisest!
    Merrily live, and long!

    The ecstasies above
      With thy burning measures suit—
    Thy grief, thy joy, thy hate, thy love,
      With the fervour of thy lute—
      Well may the stars be mute!

    Yes, Heaven is thine; but this    40
      Is a world of sweets and sours;
      Our flowers are merely—flowers,
    And the shadow of thy perfect bliss
      Is the sunshine of ours.

    If I could dwell
    Where Israfel
      Hath dwelt, and he where I,
    He might not sing so wildly well
      A mortal melody,
    While a bolder note than this might swell    50
      From my lyre within the sky.

*1831*

ISRAFEL.  **5-7. And . . . mute:** Keats's Lamia, who is likened
in l.265 to a "descended Pleiad," sings "A song of love, too sweet
for earthly lyres,/While, like held breath, the stars drew in their
panting fires (ll. 299–300).

**12. levin:** lightning.  **13-14. With . . . seven:** Thomas Holley
Chivers and several other nineteenth-century poets wrote poems
based on a story of "the lost Pleiad."  **23. skies:** the object of
*trod.*

## TO HELEN

❮ THE ADDRESSEE of this famous poem may or may not be a mortal woman; but she is, in any case, ideally perceived, and endowed with all the attributes of a Ligeia. As Psyche, the goddess of the soul, she carries the poet back to the visionary integrity which characterized his youth (l. 5) and that of the Earth (ll. 9–10).

Helen, thy beauty is to me
  Like those Nicéan barks of yore,
That gently, o'er a perfumed sea,
  The weary, way-worn wanderer bore
  To his own native shore.

On desperate seas long wont to roam,
  Thy hyacinth hair, thy classic face,
Thy Naiad airs have brought me home
  To the glory that was Greece,
And the grandeur that was Rome.    10

Lo! in yon brilliant window-niche
  How statue-like I see thee stand,
  The agate lamp within thy hand!
Ah, Psyche, from the regions which
  Are Holy-Land!

*1831*

## THE CITY IN THE SEA

❮ THE sleeping inhabitants of the city are not, as line 4 makes plain, the wicked dead alone. Perhaps they are the dead in general, awaiting Judgment and the destruction of the symbolic Babylon. More likely still, they may be that race of dreamers described in "Al Aaraaf," who in life and after-life prefer their dreams of beauty to any "truth," human or divine, and must therefore pay the price of final annihilation.

Lo! Death has reared himself a throne
In a strange city lying alone
Far down within the dim West,
Where the good and the bad and the worst and the
  best
Have gone to their eternal rest.
There shrines and palaces and towers
(Time-eaten towers that tremble not!)
Resemble nothing that is ours.
Around, by lifting winds forgot,
Resignedly beneath the sky    10
The melancholy waters lie.

No rays from the holy heaven come down
On the long night-time of that town;
But light from out the lurid sea
Streams up the turrets silently—
Gleams up the pinnacles far and free—
Up domes—up spires—up kingly halls—
Up fanes—up Babylon-like walls—
Up shadowy long-forgotten bowers
Of sculptured ivy and stone flowers—    20
Up many and many a marvellous shrine
Whose wreathèd friezes intertwine
The viol, the violet, and the vine.

Resignedly beneath the sky
The melancholy waters lie.
So blend the turrets and shadows there
That all seem pendulous in air,
While from a proud tower in the town
Death looks gigantically down.

There open fanes and gaping graves    30
Yawn level with the luminous waves;
But not the riches there that lie
In each idol's diamond eye—
Not the gaily-jewelled dead
Tempt the waters from their bed;
For no ripples curl, alas!
Along that wilderness of glass—
No swellings tell that winds may be
Upon some far-off happier sea—
No heavings hint that winds have been    40
On seas less hideously serene.

But lo, a stir is in the air!
The wave—there is a movement there!
As if the towers had thrust aside,
In slightly sinking, the dull tide—
As if their tops had feebly given
A void within the filmy Heaven.

TO HELEN.    **2. Nicéan:** What Poe intended by this word is not clear. An interesting recent discovery is the use of "Nicéan" – signifying "victorious" – in the Langhorne translation of Plutarch (1770). The source of ll. 2–5 may be a vague recollection of Book XIII of the *Odyssey*, in which a Phaeacian bark carries the sleeping Odysseus to his native Ithaca. This supposition is supported by the fact that Homer (in VI.231 and elsewhere) likens Odysseus' hair to the hyacinth. However, the word "Nicéan" may well derive from the "Nyseian isle" mentioned by Milton in a catalogue of Edenic places (*Paradise Lost*, IV.275). This supposition is supported by the fact that, twenty-six lines thereafter, Milton is describing the "hyacinthine locks" of Adam.    **7. Thy . . . face:** The hair of the Marchesa Aphrodite, in "The Assignation," clusters "round and round her classical head, in curls like those of the young hyacinth." And Ligeia has "raven-black . . . glossy . . . luxuriant, and naturally curling tresses, setting forth the full force of the Homeric epithet, 'hyacinthine!' "    **14. Ah . . . which:** Poe's conception of Psyche, and of her relationship to visionary poetry, accords with that of Keats's "Ode to Psyche."

THE CITY IN THE SEA.    **7. Time-eaten . . . not!:** The city is a whole community of those ornate and decomposing structures in which the dreamer-heroes of Poe's fiction dwell. It especially resembles the Usher mansion, to which it corresponds in all details of atmosphere and lighting and in its final descent into the waters.

The waves have now a redder glow—
The hours are breathing faint and low—
And when, amid no earthly moans,50
Down, down that town shall settle hence,
Hell, rising from a thousand thrones,
Shall do it reverence.

*1831*

## THE SLEEPER

⟨ IN HIS "Philosophy of Composition," Poe declared "the death of a beautiful woman" to be "the most poetical topic in the world." The dead and enshrouded lady of this poem is described as sleeping, because Poe imagined death as a "conscious slumber."

At midnight, in the month of June,
I stand beneath the mystic moon.
An opiate vapour, dewy, dim,
Exhales from out her golden rim,
And, softly dripping, drop by drop,
Upon the quiet mountain top,
Steals drowsily and musically
Into the universal valley.
The rosemary nods upon the grave;
The lily lolls upon the wave;10
Wrapping the fog about its breast,
The ruin moulders into rest;
Looking like Lethe, see! the lake
A conscious slumber seems to take,
And would not, for the world, awake.
All Beauty sleeps!—and lo! where lies
Irene, with her Destinies!

Oh, lady bright! can it be right—
This window open to the night?
The wanton airs, from the tree-top,20
Laughingly through the lattice drop—
The bodiless airs, a wizard rout,
Flit through thy chamber in and out,
And wave the curtain canopy
So fitfully—so fearfully—
Above the closed and fringèd lid
'Neath which thy slumb'ring soul lies hid,
That, o'er the floor and down the wall,
Like ghosts the shadows rise and fall!

Oh, lady dear, hast thou no fear?30
Why and what art thou dreaming here?
Sure thou art come o'er far-off seas,
A wonder to these garden trees!
Strange is thy pallor! strange thy dress!
Strange, above all, thy length of tress,
And this all solemn silentness!

The lady sleeps! Oh, may her sleep,
Which is enduring, so be deep!
Heaven have her in its sacred keep!
This chamber changed for one more holy,40
This bed for one more melancholy,
I pray to God that she may lie
Forever with unopened eye,
While the pale sheeted ghosts go by!

My love, she sleeps! Oh, may her sleep,
As it is lasting, so be deep!
Soft may the worms about her creep!
Far in the forest, dim and old,
For her may some tall vault unfold—
Some vault that oft hath flung its black50
And wingèd panels fluttering back,
Triumphant, o'er the crested palls
Of her grand family funerals—

Some sepulchre, remote, alone,
Against whose portal she hath thrown,
In childhood, many an idle stone—
Some tomb from out whose sounding door
She ne'er shall force an echo more,
Thrilling to think, poor child of sin!
It was the dead who groaned within.60

*1831*

## LENORE

⟨ THE FIRST and third stanzas are spoken by the family priest, or by some false friend of the dead Lenore; her lover, Guy de Vere, speaks the second and last stanzas.

Ah, broken is the golden bowl!—the spirit flown
forever!
Let the bell toll!—a saintly soul floats on the
Stygian river:—
And, Guy de Vere, hast *thou* no tear?—weep now
or never more!
See! on yon drear and rigid bier low lies thy love,
Lenore!
Come, let the burial rite be read—the funeral song
be sung!—

---

52-53. **Hell . . . reverence:** Isaiah says, in his prophecy of the fall of Babylon (14:9), "Hell from beneath is moved for thee to meet thee at thy coming: it stirreth up the dead for thee, even all the chief ones of the earth; it hath raised up from their thrones all the kings of the nations." See also Rev. 20:14-15. THE SLEEPER. 9-10. **The . . . wave:** The rosemary and lily conventionally symbolize remembrance and purity. 18-36. **Oh . . . silentness!:** This verse-paragraph was, in an earlier version of the poem, hummed into the lady's ear by the moon. So assigned, the lines made better dramatic sense.

LENORE. 1. **Ah . . . forever!:** See Eccles. 12:6.

An anthem for the queenliest dead that ever died
    so young—
A dirge for her the doubly dead in that she died so
    young.

"Wretches! ye loved her for her wealth, and ye
    hated her for her pride;
And, when she fell in feeble health, ye blessed her
    —that she died:—
How *shall* the ritual, then, be read—the requiem
    how be sung          10
By you—by yours, the evil eye,—by yours, the
    slanderous tongue
That did to death the innocence that died, and died
    so young?"

*Peccavimus;* yet rave not thus! but let a Sabbath
    song
Go up to God so solemnly the dead may feel no
    wrong!
The sweet Lenore hath gone before, with Hope
    that flew beside,
Leaving thee wild for the dear child that should
    have been thy bride—
For her, the fair and debonair, that now so lowly
    lies,
The life upon her yellow hair, but not within her
    eyes—
The life still there upon her hair, the death upon
    her eyes.

"Avaunt!—avaunt! to friends from fiends the in-
    dignant ghost is riven—        20
From Hell unto a high estate within the utmost
    Heaven—
From moan and groan to a golden throne beside
    the king of Heaven:—
Let *no* bell toll, then, lest her soul, amid its hal-
    lowed mirth,
Should catch the note as it doth float up from the
    damnèd Earth!
And I—tonight my heart is light:—no dirge will
    I upraise,
But waft the angel on her flight with a Paean of old
    days!"

*1831*

## TO ONE IN PARADISE

Thou wast that all to me, love,
    For which my soul did pine—
A green isle in the sea, love,
    A fountain and a shrine,

13. Peccavimus:    "We have sinned."

---

All wreathed with fairy fruits and flowers,
    And all the flowers were mine.

Ah, dream too bright to last!
    Ah, starry Hope! that didst arise
But to be overcast!
    A voice from out the Future cries,    10
"On! on!"—but o'er the Past
    (Dim gulf!) my spirit hovering lies
Mute, motionless, aghast!

For, alas! alas! with me
    The light of Life is o'er!
No more—no more—no more—
    (Such language holds the solemn sea
To the sands upon the shore)
    Shall bloom the thunder-blasted tree,
Or the stricken eagle soar!    20

And all my days are trances,
    And all my nightly dreams
Are where thy grey eye glances,
    And where thy footstep gleams—
In what ethereal dances,
    By what eternal streams.

*1834*

## THE RAVEN

❡ "THE RAVEN" is the clearest and most developed of
Poe's verse-narratives, and one of a very few Poe poems
which possess any dramatic variation of tone: it progresses from mournfulness to trepidation, thence to jocularity and finally, by way of hysterical self-torture, to
despair. It has therefore been much declaimed in the
schoolrooms of America. Despite the completeness of
"The Raven" as narrative, the reader is left with a feeling that certain meanings—perhaps because of the difficulties of the chosen stanza form—have not been adequately suggested. Considering what symbolic force
sculpture usually has for Poe, it is hard to believe that
the bust of Pallas signifies merely the scholarship of
the lover; yet no other supposition is encouraged. Similarly, one does not know how much, if anything, to
make of the resemblance between the final tableaux of
"The Raven" and "The Black Cat."

Once upon a midnight dreary, while I pondered,
    weak and weary,
Over many a quaint and curious volume of for-
    gotten lore—
While I nodded, nearly napping, suddenly there
    came a tapping,
As of some one gently rapping, rapping at my
    chamber door.

" 'Tis some visitor," I muttered, "tapping at my
 chamber door—
    Only this and nothing more."

Ah, distinctly I remember it was in the bleak December;
And each separate dying ember wrought its ghost
 upon the floor.
Eagerly I wished the morrow;—vainly I had
 sought to borrow
From my books surcease of sorrow—sorrow for
 the lost Lenore—        10
For the rare and radiant maiden whom the angels
 name Lenore—
    Nameless *here* for evermore.

And the silken, sad, uncertain rustling of each
 purple curtain
Thrilled me—filled me with fantastic terrors never
 felt before;
So that now, to still the beating of my heart, I
 stood repeating,
" 'Tis some visitor entreating entrance at my
 chamber door—
Some late visitor entreating entrance at my chamber door;—
    This it is and nothing more."

Presently my soul grew stronger; hesitating then
 no longer,
"Sir," said I, "or Madam, truly your forgiveness
 I implore;          20
But the fact is I was napping, and so gently you
 came rapping,
And so faintly you came tapping, tapping at my
 chamber door,
That I scarce was sure I heard you"—here I
 opened wide the door;—
    Darkness there and nothing more.

Deep into that darkness peering, long I stood there
 wondering, fearing,
Doubting, dreaming dreams no mortal ever dared
 to dream before;
But the silence was unbroken, and the stillness
 gave no token,
And the only word there spoken was the whispered
 word, "Lenore?"
This I whispered, and an echo murmured back the
 word "Lenore!"
    Merely this and nothing more. 30

THE RAVEN.  **12. Nameless . . . evermore:** The beloved's
earthly name no longer applies to her, since she has left the earth
for Aidenn (heaven), and is there known by the angelic name of
Lenore.

Back into the chamber turning, all my soul within
 me burning,
Soon again I heard a tapping somewhat louder
 than before.
"Surely," said I, "surely that is something at my
 window lattice;
Let me see, then, what thereat is, and this mystery
 explore—
Let my heart be still a moment and this mystery
 explore;—
    'Tis the wind and nothing more!"

Open here I flung the shutter, when, with many a
 flirt and flutter,
In there stepped a stately Raven of the saintly days
 of yore;
Not the least obeisance made he; not a minute
 stopped or stayed he;
But, with mien of lord or lady, perched above my
 chamber door—       40
Perched upon a bust of Pallas just above my chamber door—
    Perched, and sat, and nothing more.

Then this ebony bird beguiling my sad fancy into
 smiling,
By the grave and stern decorum of the counte-
 nance it wore,
"Though thy crest be shorn and shaven, thou," I
 said, "art sure no craven,
Ghastly grim and ancient Raven wandering from
 the Nightly shore—
Tell me what thy lordly name is on the Night's
 Plutonian shore!"
    Quoth the Raven, "Nevermore."

Much I marvelled this ungainly fowl to hear discourse so plainly,
Though its answer little meaning—little relevancy
 bore;           50
For we cannot help agreeing that no living human
 being
Ever yet was blessed with seeing bird above his
 chamber door—
Bird or beast upon the sculptured bust above his
 chamber door,
    With such name as "Nevermore."

But the Raven, sitting lonely on the placid bust,
 spoke only
That one word, as if his soul in that one word he
 did outpour.
Nothing farther then he uttered—not a feather
 then he fluttered—
Till I scarcely more than muttered, "Other friends
 have flown before—

On the morrow *he* will leave me, as my Hopes
    have flown before."
        Then the bird said, "Nevermore."   60

Startled at the stillness broken by reply so aptly
    spoken,
"Doubtless," said I, "what it utters is its only
    stock and store
Caught from some unhappy master whom un-
    merciful Disaster
Followed fast and followed faster till his songs one
    burden bore—
Till the dirges of his Hope that melancholy burden
    bore
        Of 'Never—nevermore.' "

But the Raven still beguiling all my fancy into
    smiling,
Straight I wheeled a cushioned seat in front of
    bird, and bust and door;
Then, upon the velvet sinking, I betook myself to
    linking
Fancy unto fancy, thinking what this ominous bird
    of yore—                    70
What this grim, ungainly, ghastly, gaunt, and
    ominous bird of yore
        Meant in croaking "Nevermore."

This I sat engaged in guessing, but no syllable ex-
    pressing
To the fowl whose fiery eyes now burned into my
    bosom's core;
This and more I sat divining, with my head at
    ease reclining
On the cushion's velvet lining that the lamp-light
    gloated o'er,
But whose velvet-violet lining with the lamp-light
    gloating o'er,
        *She* shall press, ah, nevermore!

Then, methought, the air grew denser, perfumed
    from an unseen censer
Swung by Seraphim whose foot-falls tinkled on
    The tufted floor.             80
"Wretch," I cried, "thy God hath lent thee—by
    these angels he hath sent thee
Respite—respite and nepenthe from thy memories
    of Lenore;
Quaff, oh, quaff this kind nepenthe and forget this
    lost Lenore!"
        Quoth the Raven, "Nevermore."

"Prophet!" said I, "thing of evil!—prophet still, if
    bird or devil!—
Whether Tempter sent, or whether tempest tossed
    thee here ashore,
Desolate yet all undaunted, on this desert land en-
    chanted—
On this home by Horror haunted—tell me truly, I
    implore—
Is there—*is* there balm in Gilead?—tell me—tell
    me, I implore!"
        Quoth the Raven, "Nevermore."   90

"Prophet!" said I, "thing of evil!—prophet still,
    if bird or devil!
By that Heaven that bends above us—by that
    God we both adore—
Tell this soul with sorrow laden if, within the dis-
    tant Aidenn,
It shall clasp a sainted maiden whom the angels
    name Lenore—
Clasp a rare and radiant maiden whom the angels
    name Lenore."
        Quoth the Raven, "Nevermore."

"Be that word our sign of parting, bird or fiend!"
    I shrieked, upstarting—
"Get thee back into the tempest and the Night's
    Plutonian shore!
Leave no black plume as a token of that lie thy
    soul hath spoken!
Leave my loneliness unbroken!—quit the bust
    above my door!           100
Take thy beak from out my heart, and take thy
    form from off my door!"
        Quoth the Raven, "Nevermore."

And the Raven, never flitting, still is sitting, *still* is
    sitting
On the pallid bust of Pallas just above my chamber
    door;
And his eyes have all the seeming of a demon's
    that is dreaming,
And the lamp-light o'er him streaming throws his
    shadow on the floor;
And my soul from out that shadow that lies float-
    ing on the floor
        Shall be lifted—nevermore!

*1845*

---

**74. To . . . core:** See "Sonnet—to Science," ll. 2–4. "The Black Cat" also had an "eye of fire." **79–80. Then . . . floor:** Compare the censer and the "gentle foot-fall upon the carpet" in "Ligeia."

**87–88. Desolate . . . haunted:** As in "The Haunted Palace" or "The Fall of the House of Usher," the environs of the lover's house have become wasteland. **89. Is . . . implore:** See Jer. 8:22. **101. Take . . . door!:** See "Sonnet—to Science," l. 3.

## ULALUME—A BALLAD

⟨ THIS poem represents a conflict and reconciliation between the poet's self and his "Psyche," or soul. The poet owes eternal fidelity to Ulalume, his dead beloved, but in stanzas 4–7 he is forgetfully attracted to a new love and seeks to persuade his soul that the new love is redemptive and ideal. The soul then forcibly reminds the poet of his Ulalume, and prevails. In the final stanza of the poem, which has taken the form of a dream-allegory, self and soul are united in rejecting the new love as "sinful," and in supposing that the powers of dream have deluded them with false hope out of pity for their sorrow.

The skies they were ashen and sober;
    The leaves they were crispèd and sere—
    The leaves they were withering and sere:
It was night, in the lonesome October
    Of my most immemorial year:
It was hard by the dim lake of Auber,
    In the misty mid region of Weir—
It was down by the dank tarn of Auber,
    In the ghoul-haunted woodland of Weir.

Here once, through an alley Titanic,     10
    Of cypress, I roamed with my Soul—
    Of cypress, with Psyche, my Soul.
These were days when my heart was volcanic
    As the scoriac rivers that roll—
    As the lavas that restlessly roll
Their sulphurous currents down Yaanek
    In the ultimate climes of the Pole—
That groan as they roll down Mount Yaanek
    In the realms of the Boreal Pole.

Our talk had been serious and sober,     20
    But our thoughts they were palsied and
        sere—
    Our memories were treacherous and sere—
For we knew not the month was October,
    And we marked not the night of the year
    (Ah, night of all nights in the year!)—
We noted not the dim lake of Auber
    (Though once we had journeyed down
        here)—
We remembered not the dank tarn of Auber,
    Nor the ghoul-haunted woodland of Weir.

And now, as the night was senescent     30
    And star-dials pointed to morn—
    As the star-dials hinted of morn—

At the end of our path a liquescent
    And nebulous lustre was born,
Out of which a miraculous crescent
    Arose with a duplicate horn—
Astarte's bediamonded crescent
    Distinct with its duplicate horn.

And I said: "She is warmer than Dian;
    She rolls through an ether of sighs—     40
    She revels in a region of sighs.
She has seen that the tears are not dry on
    These cheeks, where the worm never dies,
And has come past the stars of the Lion,
    To point us the path to the skies—
    To the Lethean peace of the skies—
Come up, in despite of the Lion,
    To shine on us with her bright eyes—
Come up through the lair of the Lion,
    With love in her luminous eyes."     50

But Psyche, uplifting her finger,
    Said: "Sadly this star I mistrust—
    Her pallor I strangely mistrust:
Ah, hasten!—ah, let us not linger!
    Ah, fly!—let us fly!—for we must."
In terror she spoke, letting sink her
    Wings until they trailed in the dust—
In agony sobbed, letting sink her
    Plumes till they trailed in the dust—
    Till they sorrowfully trailed in the dust.     60

I replied: "This is nothing but dreaming:
    Let us on by this tremulous light!
    Let us bathe in this crystalline light!
Its Sibyllic splendor is beaming
    With Hope and in Beauty to-night:—
    See!—it flickers up the sky through the night!
Ah, we safely may trust to its gleaming,
    And be sure it will lead us aright—
We surely may trust to a gleaming
    That cannot but guide us aright,     70
    Since it flickers up to Heaven through the
        night."

Thus I pacified Psyche and kissed her,
    And tempted her out of her gloom—
    And conquered her scruples and gloom;
And we passed to the end of the vista,
    But were stopped by the door of a tomb—
    By the door of a legended tomb;
And I said—"What is written, sweet sister,
    On the door of this legended tomb?"

---

ULALUME.   **6–7. It . . . Weir:** Critics suggest that Poe may have borrowed "Auber" from Jean François Auber, composer of the "Lac des Fées," and "Weir" from Robert Walter Weir, a painter of the Hudson River school.   **14. scoriac:** scoria are volcanic cinders.

**39. Dian:** Diana, the moon. Compare Poe's contrast of moon and Venus in "Evening Star."   **43. These . . . dies:** See Isa. 66:2–4.

She replied: "Ulalume—Ulalume!— 80
'Tis the vault of thy lost Ulalume!"

Then my heart it grew ashen and sober
   As the leaves that were crispèd and sere—
   As the leaves that were withering and sere;
And I cried: "It was surely October
   On *this* very night of last year
That I journeyed—I journeyed down here!—
That I brought a dread burden down here—
   On this night of all nights in the year,
   Ah, what demon has tempted me here? 90
Well I know, now, this dim lake of Auber—
   This misty mid region of Weir—
Well I know, now, this dank tarn of Auber,
   This ghoul-haunted woodland of Weir."

Said we, then,—the two, then: "Ah, can it
   Have been that the woodlandish ghouls—
   The pitiful, the merciful ghouls—
To bar up our way and to ban it
   From the secret that lies in these wolds—
   From the thing that lies hidden in these
      wolds— 100
Have drawn up the spectre of a planet
   From the limbo of lunary souls—
This sinfully scintillant planet
   From the Hell of the planetary souls?"

*1847*


# FOR ANNIE

⟮ THE ADDRESSEE of this poem was Mrs. Richmond of Lowell, Massachusetts, with whom Poe had a fervent platonic relationship in 1848–49. In a letter of November 7, 1848, Poe reminded her of "that last holy promise . . . the promise that, under all circumstances, you would come to me on my bed of death . . ."

Thank Heaven! the crisis,
   The danger, is past,
And the lingering illness
   Is over at last—
And the fever called "Living"
   Is conquered at last.

Sadly, I know
   I am shorn of my strength,
And no muscle I move
   As I lie at full length— 10
But no matter!—I feel
   I am better at length.

And I rest so composedly,
   Now, in my bed,

That any beholder
   Might fancy me dead—
Might start at beholding me,
   Thinking me dead.

The moaning and groaning,
   The sighing and sobbing, 20
Are quieted now,
   With that horrible throbbing
At heart:—ah, that horrible,
   Horrible throbbing!

The sickness—the nausea—
   The pitiless pain—
Have ceased, with the fever
   That maddened my brain—
With the fever called "Living"
   That burned in my brain. 30

And oh! of all tortures
   *That* torture the worst
Has abated—the terrible
   Torture of thirst
For the naphthaline river
   Of Passion accurst:—
I have drank of a water
   That quenches all thirst:—

Of a water that flows,
   With a lullaby sound, 40
From a spring but a very few
   Feet under ground—
From a cavern not very far
   Down under ground.

And ah! let it never
   Be foolishly said
That my room it is gloomy
   And narrow my bed;
For man never slept
   In a different bed— 50
And, to *sleep,* you must slumber
   In just such a bed.

My tantalized spirit
   Here blandly reposes,

FOR ANNIE. **22. With . . . throbbing:** This "horrible throbbing" is the normal heartbeat, just as the madness of l. 28 is normal consciousness. They are described here as aspects of illness, because in this poem life itself is a tormenting "fever." **35–36. For . . . accurst:** Naphtha is an inflammable fluid, and Poe is thinking here of Phlegethon, a flaming river in Hades. In "The Poetic Principle" Poe wrote that "in regard to Passion, alas! its tendency is to degrade rather than to elevate the Soul." **39–44. Of . . . ground:** This suggests Lethe, the river of purification and forgetfulness in Hades. See "The Sleeper," ll. 13–15, and "Ulalume," l. 46. **53. My . . . spirit:** The word "tantalized" derives from Tantalus, who was punished in Hades by thirst, and by his hunger for the unreachable fruit.

Forgetting, or never
 Regretting, its roses—
Its old agitations
 Of myrtles and roses:

For now, while so quietly
 Lying, it fancies    60
A holier odor
 About it, of pansies—
A rosemary odor,
 Commingled with pansies—
With rue and the beautiful
 Puritan pansies.

And so it lies happily,
 Bathing in many
A dream of the truth
 And the beauty of Annie—  70
Drowned in a bath
 Of the tresses of Annie.

She tenderly kissed me,
 She fondly caressed,
And then I fell gently
 To sleep on her breast—
Deeply to sleep
 From the heaven of her breast.

When the light was extinguished,
 She covered me warm,   80
And she prayed to the angels
 To keep me from harm—
To the queen of the angels
 To shield me from harm.

And I lie so composedly,
 Now, in my bed,
(Knowing her love),
 That you fancy me dead—
And I rest so contentedly,
 Now, in my bed    90
(With her love at my breast),
 That you fancy me dead—
That you shudder to look at me,
 Thinking me dead:—

But my heart it is brighter
 Than all of the many
Stars of the sky,
 For it sparkles with Annie—
It glows with the light
 Of the love of my Annie—  100

With the thought of the light
 Of the eyes of my Annie.

*1849*

# ANNABEL LEE

❨ THE ARTFUL and incantatory use of repetition, which steadily increased in Poe's later poetry—"Eldorado," "For Annie"—reached an extreme in "Annabel Lee." Here there is not only repetition of word and line, but sustained recapitulation, as in ll. 21–26.

It was many and many a year ago,
 In a kingdom by the sea,
That a maiden there lived whom you may know
 By the name of ANNABEL LEE;
And this maiden she lived with no other thought
 Than to love and be loved by me.

*I* was a child and *she* was a child,
 In this kingdom by the sea,
But we loved with a love that was more than love—
 I and my ANNABEL LEE—  10
With a love that the wingèd seraphs of Heaven
 Coveted her and me.

And this was the reason that, long ago,
 In this kingdom by the sea,
A wind blew out of a cloud, chilling
 My beautiful ANNABEL LEE;
So that her highborn kinsmen came
 And bore her away from me,
To shut her up in a sepulchre
 In this kingdom by the sea.  20

The angels, not half so happy in Heaven,
 Went envying her and me:—
Yes!—that was the reason (as all men know,
 In this kingdom by the sea)
That the wind came out of the cloud by night,
 Chilling and killing my ANNABEL LEE.

But our love it was stronger by far than the love
 Of those who were older than we—
 Of many far wiser than we—
And neither the angels in Heaven above,  30
 Nor the demons down under the sea,
Can ever dissever my soul from the soul
 Of the beautiful ANNABEL LEE:—

---

55–58. **Forgetting . . . roses:** In the "language of flowers" myrtle and rose symbolize love and beauty. **61–66. A . . . pansies:** Pansies mean "thoughts" or "think of me"; rosemary means "remembrance"; rue means "grace," or "purification."

ANNABEL LEE. 3–4. **That . . . Lee:** The poet is withholding her heavenly name, and perhaps her earthly name as well. See "The Raven," ll. 11–12. 17. **So . . . came:** Annabel Lee's "highborn kinsmen" are "the wingèd seraphs of Heaven," in line 11. For Poe's association of spirituality with aristocracy, see Part II of the Introduction.

For the moon never beams, without bringing me
    dreams
    Of the beautiful ANNABEL LEE;
And the stars never rise, but I feel the bright eyes
    Of the beautiful ANNABEL LEE:
And so, all the night-tide, I lie down by the side
Of my darling—my darling—my life and my
    bride,
    In the sepulchre there by the sea—    40
    In her tomb by the sounding sea.

*1849*

---

# LIGEIA

---

◇

❮ "LIGEIA" was first published in the Baltimore *American Museum* of September 18, 1838. For an interpretation of the story, see the Introduction, Part IV. The reader should notice how the story is knit together by the ideas of remembering and of transmutation; also how, during the description of Rowena's illness, the reappearance of Ligeia is suggestively anticipated by the recurrence of certain words—such as "shadow," "low," "gentle," "marble," and "utterly"—which have early been associated with her.

◇

And the will therein lieth, which dieth not. Who knoweth the mysteries of the will, with its vigor? For God is but a great will pervading all things by nature of its intentness. Man doth not yield himself to the angels, nor unto death utterly, save only through the weakness of his feeble will.

                     JOSEPH GLANVILL[1]

I CANNOT, for my soul, remember how, when, even precisely where, I first became acquainted with the lady Ligeia. Long years have since elapsed, and my memory is feeble through much suffering. Or, perhaps, I cannot *now* bring these points to mind, because, in truth, the character of my beloved, her rare learning, her singular yet placid cast of beauty, and the thrilling and enthralling eloquence of her low musical language, made their way into my heart by paces so steadily and stealthily progressive that they have been unnoticed and unknown. Yet I believe that I met her first and most frequently in some large, old, de-

caying city near the Rhine. Of her family—I have surely heard her speak. That it is of a remotely ancient date cannot be doubted. Ligeia! Ligeia! Buried in studies of a nature more than all else adapted to deaden impressions of the outward world, it is by that sweet word alone—by Ligeia—that I bring before mine eyes in fancy the image of her who is no more. And now, while I write, a recollection flashes upon me that I have *never known* the paternal name of her who was my friend and my betrothed, and who became the partner of my studies, and finally the wife of my bosom. Was it a playful charge on the part of my Ligeia? or was it a test of my strength of affection, that I should institute no inquiries upon this point? or was it rather a caprice of my own—a wildly romantic offering on the shrine of the most passionate devotion? I but indistinctly recall the fact itself—what wonder that I have utterly forgotten the circumstances which originated or attended it? And, indeed, if ever that spirit which is entitled *Romance*—if ever she, the wan and the misty-winged *Ashtophet*[2] of idolatrous Egypt, presided, as they tell, over marriages ill-omened, then most surely she presided over mine.

There is one dear topic, however, on which my memory fails me not. It is the *person* of Ligeia. In stature she was tall, somewhat slender, and, in her latter days, even emaciated. I would in vain attempt to portray the majesty, the quiet ease of her demeanor, or the incomprehensible lightness and elasticity of her footfall. She came and departed as a shadow. I was never made aware of her entrance into my closed study save by the dear music of her low sweet voice, as she placed her marble hand upon my shoulder. In beauty of face no maiden ever equalled her. It was the radiance of an opium-dream—an airy and spirit-lifting vision more wildly divine than the phantasies which hovered about the slumbering souls of the daughters of Delos.[3] Yet her features were not of that regular mould which we have been falsely taught to worship in the classical labors of the heathen. "There is no exquisite beauty," says Bacon, Lord Verulam, speaking truly of all the forms and *genera* of beauty, "without some *strangeness* in the proportion."[4] Yet, although I saw that the features of Ligeia were not of a classic regularity—although I perceived that her loveliness was indeed "exquisite," and felt that there was much of

---

LIGEIA.   1. **Glanvill:** English ecclesiastic (1636–80) believer in witchcraft and the pre-existence of souls, author of *The Vanity of Dogmatizing.* The epigraph has not yet been found in Glanvill's works.

2. *Ashtophet:* doubtless refers to an Egyptian version of the Syrian love goddess Ashtoreth, identified with Astarte. Milton speaks of her in *Paradise Lost,* I.438 ff.   3. **Delos:** an Aegean island, birthplace and shrine of Apollo, god of music and poetry. 4. **"There . . . proportion":** slightly misquoted from Francis Bacon's essay "On Beauty." Bacon wrote not "exquisite" but "excellent."

"strangeness" pervading it, yet I have tried in vain to detect the irregularity and to trace home my own perception of "the strange." I examined the contour of the lofty and pale forehead—it was faultless—how cold indeed that word when applied to a majesty so divine!—the skin rivalling the purest ivory, the commanding extent and repose, the gentle prominence of the regions above the temples;[5] and then the raven-black, the glossy, the luxuriant and naturally-curling tresses, setting forth the full force of the Homeric epithet, "hyacinthine!"[6] I looked at the delicate outlines of the nose—and nowhere but in the graceful medallions of the Hebrews had I beheld a similar perfection. There were the same luxurious smoothness of surface, the same scarcely perceptible tendency to the aquiline, the same harmoniously curved nostrils speaking the free spirit. I regarded the sweet mouth. Here was indeed the triumph of all things heavenly—the magnificent turn of the short upper lip—the soft, voluptuous slumber of the under—the dimples which sported, and the color which spoke—the teeth glancing back, with a brilliancy almost startling, every ray of the holy light which fell upon them in her serene and placid yet most exultingly radiant of all smiles. I scrutinized the formation of the chin—and, here too, I found the gentleness of breadth, the softness and the majesty, the fullness and the spirituality, of the Greek —the contour which the god Apollo revealed but in a dream, to Cleomenes,[7] the son of the Athenian. And then I peered into the large eyes of Ligeia.

For eyes we have no models in the remotely antique. It might have been, too, that in these eyes of my beloved lay the secret to which Lord Verulam alludes. They were, I must believe, far larger than the ordinary eyes of our own race. They were even fuller than the fullest of the gazelle eyes of the tribe of the valley of Nourjahad.[8] Yet it was only at intervals—in moments of intense excitement—that this peculiarity became more than slightly noticeable in Ligeia. And at such moments was her beauty—in my heated fancy thus it appeared perhaps—the beauty of beings either above or apart from the earth—the beauty of the fabulous Houri of the Turk. The hue of the orbs was the most brilliant of black, and, far over them, hung jetty lashes of great length. The brows, slightly irregular in outline, had the same tint. The "strangeness," however, which I found in the eyes, was of a nature distinct from the formation, or the color, or the brilliancy of the features, and must, after all, be referred to the *expression*. Ah, word of no meaning! behind whose vast latitude of mere sound we intrench our ignorance of so much of the spiritual. The expression of the eyes of Ligeia! How for long hours have I pondered upon it! How have I, through the whole of a midsummer night, struggled to fathom it! What was it—that something more profound than the well of Democritus[9]—which lay far within the pupils of my beloved? What *was* it? I was possessed with a passion to discover. Those eyes! those large, those shining, those divine orbs! they became to me twin stars of Leda, and I to them devoutest of astrologers.

There is no point, among the many incomprehensible anomalies of the science of mind, more thrillingly exciting than the fact—never, I believe, noticed in the schools—that in our endeavors to recall to memory something long forgotten, we often find ourselves *upon the very verge* of remembrance, without being able, in the end, to remember. And thus how frequently, in my intense scrutiny of Ligeia's eyes, have I felt approaching the full knowledge of their expression—felt it approaching—yet not quite be mine—and so at length entirely depart! And (strange, oh strangest mystery of all!) I found, in the commonest objects of the universe, a circle of analogies to that expression. I mean to say that, subsequently to the period when Ligeia's beauty passed into my spirit, there dwelling as in a shrine, I derived, from many existences in the material world, a sentiment such as I felt always aroused, within me, by her large and luminous orbs. Yet not the more could I define that sentiment, or analyze, or even steadily view it. I recognized it, let me repeat, sometimes in the survey of a rapidly growing vine —in the contemplation of a moth, a butterfly, a chrysalis, a stream of running water. I have felt it in the ocean; in the falling of a meteor. I have felt it in the glances of unusually aged people. And there are one or two stars in heaven—(one especially, a star of the sixth magnitude, double and changeable, to be found near the large star in Lyra) in a telescopic scrutiny of which I have been made aware of the feeling. I have been filled with it by certain sounds from stringed instruments, and not unfrequently by passages from books. Among innumerable other instances, I well remember something in a volume of Joseph Glan-

---

5. the . . . temples: In phrenology, a science which much interested Poe, such a protuberance would argue "ideality" or imagination.   6. "hyacinthine!": See "To Helen," 7 n. The *curliness* of the hyacinth is the basis of comparison.   7. Cleomenes: Athenian sculptor of the Venus de' Medici.   8. Nourjahad: The name is taken from Mrs. Frances Sheridan's oriental tale, *The History of Nourjahad* (1767).

9. In *The Advancement of Learning* (III.iii) Bacon writes, "It was well said by Democritus that 'the truth of nature lies hid in certain deep mines and caves.'"

vill, which (perhaps from its quaintness—who shall say?) never failed to inspire me with the sentiment;—"And the will therein lieth, which dieth not. Who knoweth the mysteries of the will, with its vigor? For God is but a great will pervading all things by nature of its intentness. Man doth not yield him to the angels, nor unto death utterly, save only through the weakness of his feeble will."

Length of years and subsequent reflection, have enabled me to trace, indeed, some remote connection between this passage in the English moralist and a portion of the character of Ligeia. An *intensity* in thought, action, or speech, was possibly, in her, a result, or at least an index, of that gigantic volition which, during our long intercourse, failed to give other and more immediate evidence of its existence. Of all the women whom I have even known, she, the outwardly calm, the ever-placid Ligeia, was the most violently a prey to the tumultuous vultures of stern passion. And of such passion I could form no estimate, save by the miraculous expansion of those eyes which at once so delighted and appalled me—by the almost magical melody, modulation, distinctness, and placidity of her very low voice—and by the fierce energy (rendered doubly effective by contrast with her manner of utterance) of the wild words which she habitually uttered.

I have spoken of the learning of Ligeia; it was immense—such as I have never known, in woman. In the classical tongues was she deeply proficient, and as far as my own acquaintance extended in regard to the modern dialects of Europe, I have never known her at fault. Indeed upon any theme of the most admired, because simply the most abstruse of the boasted erudition of the academy, have I *ever* found Ligeia at fault? How singularly —how thrillingly, this one point in the nature of my wife has forced itself, at this late period only, upon my attention! I said her knowledge was such as I have never known in woman—but where breathes the man who has traversed, and successfully, *all* the wide areas of moral, physical, and mathematical science? I saw not then what I now clearly perceive, that the acquisitions of Ligeia were gigantic, were astounding; yet I was sufficiently aware of her infinite supremacy to resign myself, with a child-like confidence, to her guidance through the chaotic world of metaphysical investigation at which I was most busily occupied during the earlier years of our marriage. With how vast a triumph—with how vivid a delight— with how much of all that is ethereal in hope— did I *feel,* as she bent over me in studies but little sought—but less known—that delicious vista by slow degrees expanding before me, down whose

long, gorgeous, and all untrodden path, I might at length pass onward to the goal of a wisdom too divinely precious not to be forbidden!

How poignant, then, must have been the grief with which, after some years, I beheld my well-grounded expectations take wings to themselves and fly away! Without Ligeia I was but as a child groping benighted. Her presence, her readings alone, rendered vividly luminous the many mysteries of the transcendentalism in which we were immersed. Wanting the radiant lustre of her eyes, letters, lambent and golden, grew duller than Saturnian lead.[10] And now those eyes shone less and less frequently upon the pages over which I pored. Ligeia grew ill. The wild eyes blazed with a too—too glorious effulgence; the pale fingers became of the transparent waxen hue of the grave; and the blue veins upon the lofty forehead swelled and sank impetuously with the tides of the most gentle emotion. I saw that she must die—and I struggled desperately in spirit with the grim Azrael. And the struggles of the passionate wife were, to my astonishment, even more energetic than my own. There had been much in her stern nature to impress me with the belief that, to her, death would have come without its terrors; but not so. Words are impotent to convey any just idea of the fierceness of resistance with which she wrestled with the Shadow. I groaned in anguish at the pitiable spectacle. I would have soothed— I would have reasoned; but, in the intensity of her wild desire for life,—for life—*but* for life— solace and reason were alike the uttermost folly. Yet not until the last instance, amid the most convulsive writhings of her fierce spirit, was shaken the external placidity of her demeanor. Her voice grew more gentle—grew more low—yet I would not wish to dwell upon the wild meaning of the quietly uttered words. My brain reeled as I hearkened entranced, to a melody more than mortal—to assumptions and aspirations which mortality had never before known.

That she loved me I should not have doubted; and I might have been easily aware that, in a bosom such as hers, love would have reigned no ordinary passion. But in death only was I fully impressed with the strength of her affection. For long hours, detaining my hand, would she pour out before me the overflowing of a heart whose more than passionate devotion amounted to idolatry.

10. **Wanting . . . lead:** In medieval alchemy, which sought to transmute the baser metals into gold, *Saturnus* or Saturn was the technical term for lead. Poe is comparing the hero's loss of Ligeia's enlightening presence to a reversal of the alchemical process. Lead and gold will reappear in the leaden-hued window and golden draperies of Rowena's bridal chamber.

How had I deserved to be so blessed by such confessions?—how had I deserved to be so cursed with the removal of my beloved in the hour of her making them? But upon this subject I cannot bear to dilate. Let me say only, that in Ligeia's more than womanly abandonment to a love, alas! all unmerited, all unworthily bestowed, I at length recognized the principle of her longing with so wildly earnest a desire for the life which was now fleeing so rapidly away. It is this wild longing—it is this eager vehemence of desire for life—*but for* life—that I have no power to portray—no utterance capable of expressing.

At high noon of the night in which she departed, beckoning me, peremptorily, to her side, she bade me repeat certain verses composed by herself not many days before. I obeyed her.—They were these:

Lo! 'tis a gala night
  Within the lonesome latter years!
An angel throng, bewinged, bedight
  In veils, and drowned in tears,
Sit in a theatre, to see
  A play of hopes and fears,
While the orchestra breathes fitfully
  The music of the spheres.

Mimes, in the form of God on high,
  Mutter and mumble low,      10
And hither and thither fly—
  Mere puppets they, who come and go
At bidding of vast formless things
  That shift the scenery to and fro,
Flapping from out their Condor wings
  Invisible Wo!

That motley drama!—oh, be sure
  It shall not be forgot!
With its Phantom chased forever more,
  By a crowd that seize it not,      20
Through a circle that ever returneth in
  To the self-same spot,
And much of Madness and more of Sin
  And Horror the soul of the plot.
But see, amid the mimic rout,
  A crawling shape intrude!
A blood-red thing that writhes from out
  The scenic solitude!
It writhes!—it writhes!—with mortal pangs
  The mimes become its food,      30

And the seraphs sob at vermin fangs
  In human gore imbued.

Out—out are the lights—out all!
  And over each quivering form,
The curtain, a funeral pall,
  Comes down with the rush of a storm,
And the angels, all pallid and wan,
  Uprising, unveiling, affirm
That the play is the tragedy, "Man,"
  And its hero the Conqueror Worm.[11]   40

"O God!" half shrieked Ligeia, leaping to her feet and extending her arms aloft with a spasmodic movement, as I made an end of these lines—"O God! O Divine Father!—shall these things be undeviatingly so?—shall this Conqueror be not once conquered? Are we not part and parcel in Thee? Who—who knoweth the mysteries of the will with its vigor? Man doth not yield him to the angels, *nor unto death utterly,* save only through the weakness of his feeble will."

And now, as if exhausted with emotion, she suffered her white arms to fall, and returned solemnly to her bed of death. And as she breathed her last sighs, there came mingled with them a low murmur from her lips. I bent to them my ear, and distinguished, again, the concluding words of the passage in Glanvill—*"Man doth not yield him to the angels, nor unto death utterly, save only through the weakness of his feeble will."*

She died;—and I, crushed into the very dust with sorrow, could no longer endure the lonely desolation of my dwelling in the dim and decaying city by the Rhine. I had no lack of what the world calls wealth. Ligeia had brought me far more, very far more than ordinarily falls to the lot of mortals. After a few months, therefore, of weary and aimless wandering, I purchased, and put in some repair, an abbey, which I shall not name, in one of the wildest and least frequented portions of fair England. The gloomy and dreary grandeur of the building, the almost savage aspect of the domain, the many melancholy and time-honored memories connected with both, had much in unison with the feelings of utter abandonment which had driven me into that remote and unsocial region of the country. Yet although the ex-

---

THE CONQUEROR WORM. Line 2. **Within . . . years!:** An addendum to *Eureka* states that the reassembly and annihilation of the Universe "may take place not until the planets have become flaming suns—*from an accumulation of their own Sun's caloric, reaching from centre to surface, which shall in the lonesome latter days melt all the 'elements' and dissipate the solid foundations out as a scroll."*

11. the **Conqueror Worm:** The compassionate angel audience of this poem contemplates the madness and horror of human life, at that point in cosmic history where the Universe has reached maximum diffusion and the "lonesome" Earth is at its remotest from God's original harmony. Earthly life has become "formless," the music of the spheres is but "fitfully" heard, and mankind—though made "in the form of God on high"—must perish before the Universe can regather toward its primal unity. The conclusion of *Eureka* (see p. 241) takes an optimistic view of what is here considered tragic.

ternal abbey, with its verdant decay hanging about it, suffered but little alteration, I gave way, with a child-like perversity, and perchance with a faint hope of alleviating my sorrows, to a display of more than regal magnificence within.—For such follies, even in childhood, I had imbibed a taste, and now they came back to me as if in the dotage of grief. Alas, I feel how much even of incipient madness might have been discovered in the gorgeous and fantastic draperies, in the solemn carvings of Egypt, in the wild cornices and furniture, in the Bedlam patterns of the carpets of tufted gold! I had become a bounden slave in the trammels of opium, and my labors and orders had taken a coloring from my dreams. But these absurdities I must not pause to detail. Let me speak only of that one chamber, ever accursed, whither, in a moment of mental alienation, I led from the altar as my bride—as the successor of the unforgotten Ligeia—the fair-haired and blue-eyed Lady Rowena Trevanion, of Tremaine.

There is no individual portion of the architecture and decoration of that bridal chamber which is not now visibly before me. Where were the souls of the haughty family of the bride, when, through thirst of gold, they permitted to pass the threshold of an apartment *so* bedecked, a maiden and a daughter so beloved? I have said that I minutely remember the details of the chamber—yet I am sadly forgetful on topics of deep moment—and here there was no system, no keeping, in the fantastic display, to take hold upon the memory. The room lay in a high turret of the castellated abbey, was pentagonal in shape, and of capacious size. Occupying the whole southern face of the pentagon was the sole window—an immense sheet of unbroken glass from Venice—a single pane, and tinted of a leaden hue, so that the rays of either the sun or moon, passing through it, fell with a ghastly lustre on the objects within. Over the upper portion of this huge window, extended the trellis-work of an aged vine, which clambered up the massy walls of the turret. The ceiling, of gloomy-looking oak, was excessively lofty, vaulted, and elaborately fretted with the wildest and most grotesque specimens of a semi-Gothic, semi-Druidical device. From out the most central recess of this melancholy vaulting, depended, by a single chain of gold with long links, a huge censer of the same metal, Saracenic in pattern, and with many perforations so contrived that there writhed in and out of them, as if endued with a serpent vitality, a continual succession of parti-colored fires.

Some few ottomans and golden candelabra, of Eastern figure, were in various stations about—and there was the couch, too—the bridal couch—of an Indian model, and low, and sculptured of solid ebony, with a pall-like canopy above. In each of the angles of the chamber stood on end a gigantic sarcophagus of black granite, from the tombs of the kings over against Luxor, with their aged lids full of immemorial sculpture. But in the draping of the apartment lay, alas! the chief phantasy of all. The lofty walls, gigantic in height—even unproportionably so—were hung from summit to foot, in vast folds, with a heavy and massive-looking tapestry—tapestry of a material which was found alike as a carpet on the floor, as a covering for the ottomans and the ebony bed, as a canopy for the bed and as the gorgeous volutes of the curtains which partially shaded the window. The material was the richest cloth of gold. It was spotted all over, at irregular intervals, with arabesque figures, about a foot in diameter, and wrought upon the cloth in patterns of the most jetty black. But these figures partook of the true character of the arabesque only when regarded from a single point of view. By a contrivance now common, and indeed traceable to a very remote period of antiquity, they were made changeable in aspect. To one entering the room, they bore the appearance of simple monstrosities; but upon a farther advance, this appearance gradually departed; and step by step, as the visiter moved his station in the chamber, he saw himself surrounded by an endless succession of the ghastly forms which belong to the superstition of the Norman, or arise in the guilty slumbers of the monk.[12] The phantasmagoric effect was vastly heightened by the artificial introduction of a strong continual current of wind behind the draperies—giving a hideous and uneasy animation to the whole.

In halls such as these—in a bridal chamber such as this—I passed, with the Lady of Tremaine, the unhallowed hours of the first month of our marriage—passed them with but little disquietude. That my wife dreaded the fierce moodiness of my temper—that she shunned me and loved me but little—I could not help perceiving; but it gave me rather pleasure than otherwise. I loathed her with a hatred belonging more to demon than to man. My memory flew back, (oh, with what intensity of regret!) to Ligeia, the beloved, the august, the beautiful, the entombed. I revelled in recollections of her purity, of her widom, of her lofty, her ethereal nature, of her passionate, her

---

12. The walls of the torture chamber in "The Pit and the Pendulum" are "daubed in all the hideous and repulsive devices to which the charnel superstition of the monks has given rise." The tapestry figures of "Ligeia," like the painted devices of "The Pit and the Pendulum," represent hypnagogic images. Their changeable character anticipates the transmutation of Rowena.

idolatrous love. Now, then, did my spirit fully and freely burn with more than all the fires of her own. In the excitement of my opium dreams (for I was habitually fettered in the shackles of the drug) I would call aloud upon her name, during the silence of the night, or among the sheltered recesses of the glens by day, as if, through the wild eagerness, the solemn passion, the consuming ardor of my longing for the departed, I could restore her to the pathways she had abandoned—ah, *could* it be forever?—upon the earth.

About the commencement of the second month of the marriage, the Lady Rowena was attacked with sudden illness, from which her recovery was slow. The fever which consumed her rendered her nights uneasy; and in her perturbed state of half-slumber, she spoke of sounds, and of motions, in and above the chamber of the turret, which I concluded had no origin save in the distemper of her fancy, or perhaps in the phantasmagoric influences of the chamber itself. She became at length convalescent—finally well. Yet but a brief period elapsed, ere a second more violent disorder again threw her upon a bed of suffering; and from this attack her frame, at all times feeble, never altogether recovered. Her illnesses were, after this epoch, of alarming character, and of more alarming recurrence, defying alike the knowledge and the great exertions of her physicians. With the increase of the chronic disease which had thus, apparently, taken too sure hold upon her constitution to be eradicated by human means, I could not fail to observe a similar increase in the nervous irritation of her temperament, and in her excitability by trivial causes of fear. She spoke again, and now more frequently and pertinaciously, of the sounds—of the slight sounds—and of the unusual motions among the tapestries, to which she had formerly alluded.

One night, near the closing in of September, she pressed this distressing subject with more than usual emphasis upon my attention. She had just awakened from an unquiet slumber, and I had been watching, with feelings half of anxiety, half of vague terror, the workings of her emaciated countenance. I sat by the side of her ebony bed, upon one of the ottomans of India. She partly arose, and spoke, in an earnest low whisper, of sounds which she *then* heard, but which I could not hear—of motions which she *then* saw, but which I could not perceive. The wind was rushing hurriedly behind the tapestries, and I wished to show her (what, let me confess it, I could not *all* believe) that those almost inarticulate breathings, and those very gentle variations of the figures upon the wall, were but the natural effects of that cus-

tomary rushing of the wind. But a deadly pallor, overspreading her face, had proved to me that my exertions to reassure her would be fruitless. She appeared to be fainting, and no attendants were within call. I remembered where was deposited a decanter of light wine which had been ordered by her physicians, and hastened across the chamber to procure it. But, as I stepped beneath the light of the censer, two circumstances of a startling nature attracted my attention. I had felt that some palpable although invisible object had passed lightly by my person; and I saw that there lay upon the golden carpet, in the very middle of the rich lustre thrown from the censer, a shadow—a faint, indefinite shadow of angelic aspect—such as might be fancied for the shadow of a shade. But I was wild with the excitement of an immoderate dose of opium, and heeded these things but little, nor spoke of them to Rowena. Having found the wine, I recrossed the chamber, and poured out a gobletful, which I held to the lips of the fainting lady. She had now partially recovered, however, and took the vessel herself, while I sank upon an ottoman near me, with my eyes fastened upon her person. It was then that I became distinctly aware of a gentle foot-fall upon the carpet, and near the couch; and in a second thereafter, as Rowena was in the act of raising the wine to her lips, I saw, or may have dreamed that I saw, fall within the goblet, as if from some invisible spring in the atmosphere of the room, three or four large drops of a brilliant and ruby colored fluid. If this I saw—not so Rowena. She swallowed the wine unhesitatingly, and I forbore to speak to her of a circumstance which must, after all, I considered, have been but the suggestion of a vivid imagination, rendered morbidly active by the terror of the lady, by the opium, and by the hour.

Yet I cannot conceal it from my own perception that, immediately subsequent to the fall of the ruby-drops, a rapid change for the worse took place in the disorder of my wife; so that, on the third subsequent night, the hands of her menials prepared her for the tomb, and on the fourth, I sat alone, with her shrouded body, in that fantastic chamber which had received her as my bride.—Wild visions, opium-engendered, flitted, shadow-like, before me. I gazed with unquiet eye upon the sarcophagi in the angles of the room, upon the varying figures of the drapery, and upon the writhing of the parti-colored fires in the censer overhead. My eyes then fell, as I called to mind the circumstances of a former night, to the spot beneath the glare of the censer where I had seen the faint traces of the shadow. It was there, however, no longer; and breathing with greater freedom, I turned my glances to the pallid and rigid figure upon the bed. Then rushed upon me a thousand memories of Ligeia—and then came back upon my heart, with the turbulent violence of a flood, the whole of that unutterable wo with which I had regarded *her* thus enshrouded. The night waned; and still, with a bosom full of bitter thoughts of the one only and supremely beloved, I remained gazing upon the body of Rowena.

It might have been midnight, or perhaps earlier, or later, for I had taken no note of time, when a sob, low, gentle, but very distinct, startled me from my revery.—I *felt* that it came from the bed of ebony—the bed of death. I listened in an agony of superstitious terror—but there was no repetition of the sound. I strained my vision to detect any motion in the corpse—but there was not the slightest perceptible. Yet I could not have been deceived. I *had* heard the noise, however faint, and my soul was awakened within me. I resolutely and perseveringly kept my attention riveted upon the body. Many minutes elapsed before any circumstance occurred tending to throw light upon the mystery. At length it became evident that a slight, a very feeble, and barely noticeable tinge of color had flushed up within the cheeks, and along the sunken small veins of the eyelids. Through a species of unutterable horror and awe, for which the language of mortality has no sufficiently energetic expression, I felt my heart cease to beat, my limbs grow rigid where I sat. Yet a sense of duty finally operated to restore my self-possession. I could no longer doubt that we had been precipitate in our preparations—that Rowena still lived. It was necessary that some immediate exertion be made; yet the turret was altogether apart from the portion of the abbey tenanted by the servants—there were none within call—I had no means of summoning them to my aid without leaving the room for many minutes—and this I could not venture to do. I therefore struggled alone in my endeavors to call back the spirit still hovering. In a short period it was certain, however, that a relapse had taken place; the color disappeared from both eyelid and cheek, leaving a wanness even more than that of marble; the lips became doubly shrivelled and pinched up in the ghastly expression of death; a repulsive clamminess and coldness overspread rapidly the surface of the body; and all the usual rigorous stiffness immediately supervened. I fell back with a shudder upon the couch from which I had been so startlingly aroused, and again gave myself up to passionate waking visions of Ligeia.

An hour thus elapsed when (could it be possible?) I was a second time aware of some vague sound issuing from the region of the bed. I listened—in extremity of horror. The sound came again—it was a sigh. Rushing to the corpse, I saw—distinctly saw—a tremor upon the lips. In a minute afterward they relaxed, disclosing a bright line of the pearly teeth. Amazement now struggled in my bosom with the profound awe which had hitherto reigned there alone. I felt that my vision grew dim, that my reason wandered; and it was only by a violent effort that I at length succeeded in nerving myself to the task which duty thus once more had pointed out. There was now a partial glow upon the forehead and upon the cheek and throat; a perceptible warmth pervaded the whole frame; there was even a slight pulsation at the heart. The lady *lived;* and with redoubled ardor I betook myself to the task of restoration. I chafed and bathed the temples and the hands, and used every exertion which experience, and no little medical reading, could suggest. But in vain. Suddenly, the color fled, the pulsation ceased, the lips resumed the expression of the dead, and, in an instant afterward, the whole body took upon itself the icy chilliness, the livid hue, the intense rigidity, the sunken outline, and all the loathsome peculiarities of that which has been, for many days, a tenant of the tomb.

And again I sunk into visions of Ligeia—and again, (what marvel that I shudder while I write?) *again* there reached my ears a low sob from the region of the ebony bed. But why shall I minutely detail the unspeakable horrors of that night? Why shall I pause to relate how, time after time, until near the period of the gray dawn, this hideous drama of revivification was repeated; how each terrific relapse was only into a sterner and apparently more irredeemable death; how each agony wore the aspect of a struggle with some invisible foe; and how each struggle was succeeded by I know not what of wild change in the personal appearance of the corpse? Let me hurry to a conclusion.

The greater part of the fearful night had worn away, and she who had been dead once again stirred—and now more vigorously than hitherto, although arousing from a dissolution more appalling in its utter hopelessness than any. I had long ceased to struggle or to move, and remained sitting rigidly upon the ottoman, a helpless prey to a whirl of violent emotions, of which extreme awe was perhaps the least terrible, the least consuming. The corpse, I repeat, stirred, and now more vigorously than before. The hues of life flushed up with unwonted energy into the countenance—the limbs relaxed—and, save that the eyelids were yet pressed heavily together, and that the bandages and draperies of the grave still imparted their charnel character to the figure, I might have dreamed that Rowena had indeed shaken off, utterly, the fetters of Death. But if this idea was not, even then, altogether adopted, I could at least doubt no longer, when, arising from the bed, tottering, with feeble steps, with closed eyes, and with the manner of one bewildered in a dream, the thing that was enshrouded advanced boldly and palpably into the middle of the apartment.

I trembled not—I stirred not—for a crowd of unutterable fancies connected with the air, the stature, the demeanor of the figure, rushing hurriedly through my brain, had paralyzed—had chilled me into stone.[13] I stirred not—but gazed upon the apparition. There was a mad disorder in my thoughts —a tumult unappeasable. Could it, indeed, be the *living* Rowena who confronted me? Could it, indeed, be Rowena *at all*—the fair-haired, the blue-eyed Lady Rowena Trevanion of Tremaine? Why, *why* should I doubt it? The bandage lay heavily about the mouth—but then might it not be the mouth of the breathing Lady of Tremaine? And the cheeks—there were the roses as in her noon of life—yes, these might indeed be the fair cheeks of the living Lady of Tremaine. And the chin, with its dimples, as in health, might it not be hers?—but *had she then grown taller since her malady?* What inexpressible madness seized me with that thought? One bound, and I had reached her feet! Shrinking from my touch, she let fall from her head, unloosened, the ghastly cerements which had confined it, and there streamed forth into the rushing atmosphere of the chamber huge masses of long and dishevelled hair; *it was blacker than the raven wings of midnight!* And now slowly opened *the eyes* of the figure which stood before me. "Here then, at least," I shrieked aloud, "can I never—can I never be mistaken—these are the full, and the black, and the wild eyes—of my lost love—of the Lady—of the LADY LIGEIA."

# THE FALL OF THE HOUSE OF USHER

❖

⟨ "THE FALL OF THE HOUSE OF USHER" was first published in *Burton's Gentleman's Magazine* (September 18, 1839). For comment on this story, see the Introduction, Part IV.

---

13. chilled . . . stone: Compare Poe's use of sculpture-symbolism to that of Keats in "The Eve of St. Agnes." Especially relevant are ll. 289–324, in which Porphyro becomes first like "sculptured stone" and then like a "throbbing star," thus passing into an ideal reality and assimilating himself to Madeline's dream.

❖

*Son cœur est un luth suspendu;*
*Sitôt qu'on le touche il résonne.*
DE BÉRANGER [1]

DURING the whole of a dull, dark, and soundless day in the autumn of the year, when the clouds hung oppressively low in the heavens, I had been passing alone, on horseback, through a singularly dreary tract of country, and at length found myself, as the shades of the evening drew on, within view of the melancholy House of Usher.[2] I know not how it was—but, with the first glimpse of the building, a sense of insufferable gloom pervaded my spirit. I say insufferable; for the feeling was unrelieved by any of that half-pleasurable, because poetic, sentiment with which the mind usually receives even the sternest natural images of the desolate or terrible. I looked upon the scene before me—upon the mere house, and the simple landscape features of the domain—upon the bleak walls—upon the vacant eye-like windows—upon a few rank sedges—and upon a few white trunks of decayed trees—with an utter depression of soul which I can compare to no earthly sensation more properly than to the after-dream of the reveller upon opium—the bitter lapse into everyday life—the hideous dropping off of the veil. There was an iciness, a sinking, a sickening of the heart—an unredeemed dreariness of thought which no goading of the imagination could torture into aught of the sublime. What was it—I paused to think—what was it that so unnerved me in the contemplation of the House of Usher? It was a mystery all insoluble; nor could I grapple with the shadowy fancies that crowded upon me as I pondered. I was forced to fall back upon the unsatisfactory conclusion, that while, beyond doubt, there *are* combinations of very simple natural objects which have the power of thus affecting us, still the analysis of this power lies among considerations beyond our depth. It was possible, I reflected, that a mere different arrangement of the particulars of the scene, of the details of the picture, would be sufficient to modify, or perhaps to annihilate its capacity for sorrowful impression; and, acting upon this idea, I reined my horse to the precipitous brink of a black and lurid tarn that lay in unruffled lustre by the dwelling, and gazed down—but with a shudder even more thrilling than before—upon the remodelled and in-

THE FALL OF THE HOUSE OF USHER.    1. De Béranger: The verses are taken from "Le Refus," a poem by Pierre Jean de Beranger (1780–1857), and might be translated: "His heart is a hanging lute;/If it be but touched, it resounds." See "Israfel," l. 2.   2. Usher: Mr. and Mrs. Luke Usher, a theatrical couple, were unofficial guardians of Elizabeth Arnold, Poe's mother, when the latter was an orphaned child-actress.

verted images of the gray sedge, and the ghastly tree-stems, and the vacant and eye-like windows.

Nevertheless, in this mansion of gloom I now proposed to myself a sojourn of some weeks. Its proprietor, Roderick Usher, had been one of my boon companions in boyhood; but many years had elapsed since our last meeting. A letter, however, had lately reached me in a distant part of the country—a letter from him—which, in its wildly importunate nature, had admitted of no other than a personal reply. The MS. gave evidence of nervous agitation. The writer spoke of acute bodily illness—of a mental disorder which oppressed him—and of an earnest desire to see me, as his best and indeed his only personal friend, with a view of attempting, by the cheerfulness of my society, some alleviation of his malady. It was the manner in which all this, and much more, was said—it was the apparent *heart* that went with his request—which allowed me no room for hesitation; and I accordingly obeyed forthwith what I still considered a very singular summons.

Although, as boys, we had been even intimate associates, yet I really knew little of my friend. His reserve had been always excessive and habitual. I was aware, however, that his very ancient family had been noted, time out of mind, for a peculiar sensibility of temperament, displaying itself, through long ages, in many works of exalted art, and manifested, of late, in repeated deeds of munificent yet unobtrusive charity, as well as in a passionate devotion to the intricacies, perhaps even more than to the orthodox and easily recognizable beauties, of musical science. I had learned, too, the very remarkable fact, that the stem of the Usher race, all time-honoured as it was, had put forth, at no period, any enduring branch; in other words, that the entire family lay in the direct line of descent, and had always, with very trifling and very temporary variation, so lain. It was this deficiency, I considered, while running over in thought the perfect keeping of the character of the premises with the accredited character of the people, and while speculating upon the possible influence which the one, in the long lapse of centuries, might have exercised upon the other—it was this deficiency, perhaps, of collateral issue, and the consequent undeviating transmission, from sire to son, of the patrimony with the name, which had, at length, so identified the two as to merge the original title of the estate in the quaint and equivocal appellation of the "House of Usher"—an appellation which seemed to include, in the minds of the peasantry who used it, both the family and the family mansion.

I have said that the sole effect of my somewhat childish experiment—that of looking down within the tarn—had been to deepen the first singular im-

pression. There can be no doubt that the consciousness of the rapid increase of my superstition—for why should I not so term it?—served mainly to accelerate the increase itself. Such, I have long known, is the paradoxical law of all sentiments having terror as a basis. And it might have been for this reason only, that, when I again uplifted my eyes to the house itself, from its image in the pool, there grew in my mind a strange fancy—a fancy so ridiculous, indeed, that I but mention it to show the vivid force of the sensations which oppressed me. I had so worked upon my imagination as really to believe that about the whole mansion and domain there hung an atmosphere peculiar to themselves and their immediate vicinity—an atmosphere which had no affinity with the air of heaven, but which had reeked up from the decayed trees, and the gray wall, and the silent tarn—a pestilent and mystic vapour, dull, sluggish, faintly discernible, and leaden-hued.

Shaking off from my spirit what *must* have been a dream, I scanned more narrowly the real aspect of the building. Its principal feature seemed to be that of an excessive antiquity. The discoloration of ages had been great. Minute fungi overspread the whole exterior, hanging in a fine tangled web-work from the eaves. Yet all this was apart from any extraordinary dilapidation. No portion of the masonry had fallen; and there appeared to be a wild inconsistency between its still perfect adaptation of parts, and the crumbling condition of the individual stones. In this there was much that reminded me of the specious totality of old wood-work which has rotted for long years in some neglected vault, with no disturbance from the breath of the external air.[3] Beyond this indication of extensive decay, however, the fabric gave little token of instability. Perhaps the eye of a scrutinizing observer might have discovered a barely perceptible fissure, which, extending from the roof of the building in front, made its way down the wall in a zigzag direction, until it became lost in the sullen waters of the tarn.

Noticing these things, I rode over a short causeway to the house. A servant in waiting took my horse, and I entered the Gothic archway of the hall. A valet, of stealthy step, thence conducted me, in silence, through many dark and intricate passages in my progress to the *studio* of his master. Much that I encountered on the way contributed, I know not how, to heighten the vague sentiments of which I have already spoken. While the objects around me—while the carvings of the ceilings, the sombre tapestries of the walls, the ebon blackness of the floors, and the phantasmagoric armorial trophies which rattled as I strode, were but matters to

3. In . . . air: Compare the "rottenness" and "worm-eaten condition" of the phantom ship in "Ms. Found in a Bottle."

which, or to such as which, I had been accustomed from my infancy—while I hesitated not to acknowledge how familiar was all this—I still wondered to find how unfamiliar were the fancies which ordinary images were stirring up. On one of the staircases, I met the physician of the family. His countenance, I thought, wore a mingled expression of low cunning and perplexity. He accosted me with trepidation and passed on. The valet now threw open a door and ushered me into the presence of his master.

The room in which I found myself was very large and lofty. The windows were long, narrow, and pointed, and at so vast a distance from the black oaken floor as to be altogether inaccessible from within. Feeble gleams of encrimsoned light made their way through the trellised panes, and served to render sufficiently distinct the more prominent objects around; the eye, however, struggled in vain to reach the remoter angles of the chamber, or the recesses of the vaulted and fretted ceiling. Dark draperies hung upon the walls. The general furniture was profuse, comfortless, antique, and tattered. Many books and musical instruments lay scattered about, but failed to give any vitality to the scene. I felt that I breathed an atmosphere of sorrow. An air of stern, deep, and irredeemable gloom hung over and pervaded all.

Upon my entrance, Usher arose from a sofa on which he had been lying at full length, and greeted me with a vivacious warmth which had much in it, I at first thought, of an overdone cordiality—of the constrained effort of the *ennuyé* man of the world. A glance, however, at his countenance convinced me of his perfect sincerity. We sat down; and for some moments, while he spoke not, I gazed upon him with a feeling half of pity, half of awe. Surely, man had never before so terribly altered, in so brief a period, as had Roderick Usher! It was with difficulty that I could bring myself to admit the identity of the wan being before me with the companion of my early boyhood. Yet the character of his face had been at all times remarkable. A cadaverousness of complexion; an eye large, liquid, and luminous beyond comparison; lips somewhat thin and very pallid, but of a surpassingly beautiful curve; a nose of a delicate Hebrew model, but with a breadth of nostril unusual in similar formations; a finely moulded chin, speaking, in its want of prominence, of a want of moral energy; hair of a more than web-like softness and tenuity; these features, with an inordinate expansion above the regions of the temple,[4] made up altogether a countenance not easily to be forgotten. And now in the mere exaggeration of the pre-

vailing character of these features, and of the expression they were wont to convey, lay so much of change that I doubted to whom I spoke. The now ghastly pallor of the skin, and the now miraculous lustre of the eye, above all things startled and even awed me. The silken hair, too, had been suffered to grow all unheeded, and as, in its wild gossamer texture, it floated rather than fell about the face. I could not, even with effort, connect its Arabesque expression with any idea of simple humanity.

In the manner of my friend I was at once struck with an incoherence—an inconsistency; and I soon found this to arise from a series of feeble and futile struggles to overcome an habitual trepidancy—an excessive nervous agitation. For something of this nature I had indeed been prepared, no less by his letter, than by reminiscences of certain boyish traits, and by conclusions deduced from his peculiar physical conformation and temperament. His action was alternately vivacious and sullen. His voice varied rapidly from a tremulous indecision (when the animal spirits seemed utterly in abeyance) to that species of energetic concision—that abrupt, weighty, unhurried, and hollow-sounding enunciation—that leaden, self-balanced, and perfectly modulated guttural utterance, which may be observed in the lost drunkard, or the irreclaimable eater of opium, during the periods of his most intense excitement.

It was thus that he spoke of the object of my visit, of his earnest desire to see me, and of the solace he expected me to afford him. He entered, at some length, into what he conceived to be the nature of his malady. It was, he said, a constitutional and a family evil, and one for which he despaired to find a remedy—a mere nervous affection, he immediately added, which would undoubtedly soon pass off. It displayed itself in a host of unnatural sensations. Some of these, as he detailed them, interested and bewildered me; although, perhaps, the terms and the general manner of their narration had their weight. He suffered much from a morbid acuteness of the senses; the most insipid food was alone endurable; he could wear only garments of certain texture; the odours of all flowers were oppressive; his eyes were tortured by even a faint light; and there were but peculiar sounds, and these from stringed instruments, which did not inspire him with horror.[5]

To an anomalous species of terror I found him a bounden slave. "I shall perish," said he, "I *must*

---

4. with . . . temple: See "Ligeia," 5 n. Usher also resembles Ligeia in his large, luminous eyes and Hebrew nose.

5. He . . . horror: Usher has almost wholly dispensed with the bodily or "rudimentary" senses which perceive the external world.

perish in this deplorable folly. Thus, thus, and not otherwise, shall I be lost. I dread the events of the future, not in themselves, but in their results. I shudder at the thought of any, even the most trivial, incident, which may operate upon this intolerable agitation of soul. I have, indeed, no abhorrence of danger, except in its absolute effect—in terror. In this unnerved—in this pitiable condition—I feel that the period will sooner or later arrive when I must abandon life and reason together, in some struggle with the grim phantasm, FEAR."

I learned, moreover, at intervals, and through broken and equivocal hints, another singular feature of his mental condition. He was enchained by certain superstitious impressions in regard to the dwelling which he tenanted, and whence, for many years, he had never ventured forth—in regard to an influence whose supposititious force was conveyed in terms too shadowy here to be re-stated—an influence which some peculiarities in the mere form and substance of his family mansion had, by dint of long sufferance, he said, obtained over his spirit—an effect which the *physique* of the gray walls and turrets, and of the dim tarn into which they all looked down, had, at length, brought about upon the *morale* of his existence.

He admitted, however, although with hesitation, that much of the peculiar gloom which thus afflicted him could be traced to a more natural and far more palpable origin—to the severe and long-continued illness—indeed to the evidently approaching dissolution—of a tenderly beloved sister, his sole companion for long years, his last and only relative on earth. "Her decease," he said, with a bitterness which I can never forget, "would leave him (him, the hopeless and the frail) the last of the ancient race of the Ushers." While he spoke, the lady Madeline (for so was she called) passed slowly through a remote portion of the apartment, and, without having noticed my presence, disappeared. I regarded her with an utter astonishment not unmingled with dread; and yet I found it impossible to account for such feelings. A sensation of stupor oppressed me, as my eyes followed her retreating steps. When a door, at length, closed upon her, my glance sought instinctively and eagerly the countenance of the brother—but he had buried his face in his hands, and I could only perceive that a far more than ordinary wanness had overspread the emaciated fingers through which trickled many passionate tears.

The disease of the lady Madeline had long baffled the skill of her physicians. A settled apathy, a gradual wasting away of the person, and frequent although transient affections of a partially cataleptical character were the unusual diagnosis. Hither-

to she had steadily borne up against the pressure of her malady, and had not betaken herself finally to bed; but on the closing in of the evening of my arrival at the house, she succumbed (as her brother told me at night with inexpressible agitation) to the prostrating power of the destroyer; and I learned that the glimpse I had obtained of her person would thus probably be the last I should obtain—that the lady, at least while living, would be seen by me no more.

For several days ensuing, her name was unmentioned by either Usher or myself: and during this period I was busied in earnest endeavours to alleviate the melancholy of my friend. We painted and read together, or I listened, as if in a dream, to the wild improvisations of his speaking guitar. And thus, as a closer and still closer intimacy admitted me more unreservedly into the recesses of his spirit, the more bitterly did I perceive the futility of all attempt at cheering a mind from which darkness, as if an inherent positive quality, poured forth upon all objects of the moral and physical universe in one unceasing radiation of gloom.

I shall ever bear about me a memory of the many solemn hours I thus spent alone with the master of the House of Usher. Yet I should fail in any attempt to convey an idea of the exact character of the studies, or of the occupations, in which he involved me, or led me the way. An excited and highly distempered ideality threw a sulphureous lustre over all. His long improvised dirges will ring forever in my ears. Among other things, I hold painfully in mind a certain singular perversion and amplification of the wild air of the last waltz of Von Weber.[6] From the paintings over which his elaborate fancy brooded, and which grew, touch by touch, into vaguenesses at which I shuddered the more thrillingly, because I shuddered knowing not why;—from these paintings (vivid as their images now are before me) I would in vain endeavour to educe more than a small portion which should lie within the compass of merely written words.[7] By the utter simplicity, by the nakedness of his designs, he arrested and overawed attention. If ever mortal painted an idea, that mortal was Roderick Usher. For me at least, in the circumstances then surrounding me, there arose out of the pure abstractions which the hypochondriac contrived to throw upon his canvas, an intensity of intolerable awe, no shadow of which felt I ever yet in the contemplation of the certainly

6. **Von Weber:** German Romantic composer (1786–1826).
7. **From . . . words:** In one of his "Marginalia" (see p. 239), Poe asserts that, whereas "no thought, properly so called" is "beyond the compass of words," he has found it "absolutely impossible to adapt language" to the description of hypnagogic images.

glowing yet too concrete reveries of Fuseli.[8]

One of the phantasmagoric conceptions of my friend, partaking not so rigidly of the spirit of abstraction, may be shadowed forth, although feebly, in words. A small picture presented the interior of an immensely long and rectangular vault or tunnel, with low walls, smooth, white, and without interruption or device. Certain accessory points of the design served well to convey the idea that this excavation lay at an exceeding depth below the surface of the earth. No outlet was observed in any portion of its vast extent, and no torch or other artificial source of light was discernible; yet a flood of intense rays rolled throughout, and bathed the whole in a ghastly and inappropriate splendour.[9]

I have just spoken of that morbid condition of the auditory nerve which rendered all music intolerable to the sufferer, with the exception of certain effects of stringed instruments. It was, perhaps, the narrow limits to which he thus confined himself upon the guitar which gave birth, in great measure, to the fantastic character of his performances. But the fervid *facility* of his *impromptus* could not be so accounted for. They must have been, and were, in the notes, as well as in the words of his wild fantasias (for he not unfrequently accompanied himself with rhymed verbal improvisations), the result of that intense mental collectedness and concentration to which I have previously alluded as observable only in particular moments of the highest artificial excitement. The words of one of these rhapsodies I have easily remembered. I was, perhaps, the more forcibly impressed with it as he gave it, because, in the under or mystic current of its meaning, I fancied that I perceived, and for the first time, a full consciousness on the part of Usher of the tottering of his lofty reason upon her throne. The verses, which were entitled "The Haunted Palace,"[10] ran very nearly, if not accurately, thus:

I

In the greenest of our valleys,
    By good angels tenanted,

8. **Fuseli:** Henry Fuseli (1741–1825), Swiss-born professor at the Royal Academy in London, was a great painter of the fantastic and terrible.   9. **One . . . splendour:** "A grave? Oh, no, a lantern, slaughtered youth;/For here lies Juliet, and her beauty makes/This vault a feasting presence full of light" (*Romeo and Juliet*, V.iii.84–86).   10. **The Haunted Palace:** a key to Poe's architectural symbolism. "By 'The Haunted Palace,'" Poe wrote Rufus Griswold in 1841, "I mean to imply a mind haunted by phantoms—a disordered brain." The reader will readily see that the palace is a head, that its windows are eyes, its banners golden hair, its pearl and ruby door teeth and lips. Within the palace-head is a harmonious and imaginative consciousness, which expresses itself in "wit and wisdom." The corruption of that consciousness, which blights the palace and its valley, is not explained in the poem, but Poe is obviously retelling his basic story, as outlined in Part III of the Introduction.

Once a fair and stately palace—
    Radiant palace—reared its head.
In the monarch Thought's dominion—
    It stood there!
Never seraph spread a pinion
    Over fabric half so fair.

II

Banners yellow, glorious, golden,
    On its roof did float and flow     10
(This—all this—was in the olden
    Time long ago)
And every gentle air that dallied,
    In that sweet day,
Along the ramparts plumed and pallid,
    A winged odour went away.

III

Wanderers in that happy valley
    Through two luminous windows saw
Spirits moving musically
    To a lute's well-tunèd law,     20
Round about a throne, where sitting
    (Porphyrogene!)
In state his glory well befitting,
    The ruler of the realm was seen.

IV

And all with pearl and ruby glowing
    Was the fair palace door,
Through which came flowing, flowing, flowing
    And sparkling evermore,
A troop of Echoes whose sweet duty
    Was but to sing,     30
In voices of surpassing beauty,
    The wit and wisdom of their king.

V

But evil things, in robes of sorrow,
    Assailed the monarch's high estate;
(Ah, let us mourn, for never morrow
    Shall dawn upon him, desolate!)
And, round about his home, the glory
    That blushed and bloomed
Is but a dim-remembered story
    Of the old time entombed.     40

VI

And travellers now within that valley,
    Through the red-litten windows see
Vast forms that move fantastically
    To a discordant melody;
While, like a rapid ghastly river,

THE HAUNTED PALACE. Line 8. **fabric:** building. 15. **pallid:** yellow (Latin *pallidus*). 22. **Porphyrogene:** Poe's invented form of "porphyrogenite," meaning "born in the purple."

Through the pale door,
A hideous throng rush out forever,
And laugh—but smile no more.

I well remember that suggestions arising from this ballad, led us into a train of thought, wherein there became manifest an opinion of Usher's which I mention not so much on account of its novelty, (for other men have thought thus,) as on account of the pertinacity with which he maintained it. This opinion, in its general form, was that of the sentience of all vegetable things. But, in his disordered fancy, the idea had assumed a more daring character, and trespassed, under certain conditions, upon the kingdom of inorganization.[11] I lack words to express the full extent, or the earnest *abandon* of his persuasion. The belief, however, was connected (as I have previously hinted) with the gray stones of the home of his forefathers. The conditions of the sentience had been here, he imagined, fulfilled in the method of collocation of these stones—in the order of their arrangement, as well as in that of the many *fungi* which overspread them, and of the decayed trees which stood around —above all, in the long undisturbed endurance of this arrangement, and in its reduplication in the still waters of the tarn. Its evidence—the evidence of the sentience—was to be seen, he said (and I here started as he spoke), in the gradual yet certain condensation of an atmosphere of their own about the waters and the walls. The result was discoverable, he added, in that silent yet importunate and terrible influence which for centuries had moulded the destinies of his family, and which made *him* what I now saw him—what he was. Such opinions need no comment, and I will make none.

Our books—the books which, for years, had formed no small portion of the mental existence of the invalid—were, as might be supposed, in strict keeping with this character of phantasm. We pored together over such works as the *Ververt et Chartreuse* of Gresset; the *Belphegor* of Machiavelli; the *Heaven and Hell* of Swedenborg; the *Subterranean Voyage of Nicholas Klimm* of Holberg; the *Chiromancy* of Robert Fludd, of Jean D'Indaginé, and of De la Chambre; the *Journey into the Blue Distance* of Tieck; and the *City of the Sun* of Campanella. One favourite volume was a small octavo edition of the *Directorium Inquisitorum,* by the Dominican Eymeric de Gironne; and there were passages in Pomponius Mela, about the old African Satyrs and Œgipans, over which Usher would sit dreaming for hours. His chief delight, however, was found in the perusal of an exceed-

11. **kingdom of inorganization:** the realm of inorganic matter.

ingly rare and curious book in quarto Gothic —the manual of a forgotten church—the *Vigiliæ Mortuorum secundum Chorum Ecclesiæ Maguntinæ.*[12]

I could not help thinking of the wild ritual of this work, and of its probable influence upon the hypochondriac, when, one evening, having informed me abruptly that the lady Madeline was no more, he stated his intention of preserving her corpse for a fortnight, (previously to its final interment,) in one of the numerous vaults within the main walls of the building. The worldly reason, however, assigned for this singular proceeding, was one which I did not feel at liberty to dispute. The brother had been led to his resolution (so he told me) by consideration of the unusual character of the malady of the deceased, of certain obtrusive and eager inquiries on the part of her medical men, and of the remote and exposed situation of the burial-ground of the family. I will not deny that when I called to mind the sinister countenance of the person whom I met upon the staircase, on the day of my arrival at the house, I had no desire to oppose what I regarded as at best but a harmless, and by no means an unnatural, precaution.

At the request of Usher, I personally aided him in the arrangements for the temporary entombment. The body having been encoffined, we two alone bore it to its rest. The vault in which we placed it (and which had been so long unopened that our torches, half smothered in its oppressive atmosphere, gave us little opportunity for investigation) was small, damp, and entirely without means of admission for light; lying, at great depth,

12. **Our . . . *Maguntinæ*:** Jean Baptiste Louis Gresset wrote the two poems *Vert-Vert* (1734) and *La Chartreuse* (1735). Nicolló Machiavelli's novel *Belfagor* appeared in 1545. Emanuel Swedenborg, Swedish philosopher, scientist, and mystic, published *De Coelo . . . et de Inferno* in 1758. The Danish historian and dramatist Ludwig Holberg was the author of *Nicolai Klimii Iter Subterraneum* (1741), an imaginary-voyage tale. Robert Fludd (1574-1637) was an English physician and cabalist. D'Indaginé's *Chiromantia* (1522) and De la Chambre's *Discours sur les Principes de la Chiromancie* (1653) were studies of palmistry. Johann Ludwig Tieck (1773-1853) was a celebrated German novelist and critic: the book referred to is an English translation of Tieck's volume, *Das Alte Buch.* Tommaso Campanella, who shared Usher's belief in the sentience of all things, was the author of *Civitas Solis,* a Utopian work (1643). Eymeric, fourteenth-century Spanish Inquisitor-General, left a record of his Inquisitorial proceedings, which became the guide of Torquemada. Pomponius Mela was the author of *De Situ Orbis,* a geographical treatise of the first century A.D.: Poe pretends to quote from the work in his "Island of the Fay," but is actually quoting from Hugh Murray's *Encyclopaedia of Geography.* The manual of *Vigiliae Mortuorum,* or rites of the dead, was printed at Basel, *c.* 1500. The collective effect of this catalogue of Usher's books is to certify that their owner, like Ligeia, has "gigantic" learning, that his consciousness is not limited by place or time, and that his thoughts dwell upon imaginary worlds and the afterlife. Such thoughts are the direct cause of Lady Madeline's dissolution.

immediately beneath that portion of the building in which was my own sleeping apartment. It had been used, apparently, in remote feudal times, for the worst purposes of a donjon-keep, and, in later days, as a place of deposit for powder, or some other highly combustible substance, as a portion of its floor, and the whole interior of a long archway through which we reached it, were carefully sheathed with copper. The door, of massive iron, had been, also, similarly protected. Its immense weight caused an unusually sharp grating sound, as it moved upon its hinges.

Having deposited our mournful burden upon tressels within this region of horror, we partially turned aside the yet unscrewed lid of the coffin, and looked upon the face of the tenant. A striking similitude between the brother and sister now first arrested my attention; and Usher, divining, perhaps, my thoughts, murmured out some few words from which I learned that the deceased and himself had been twins, and that sympathies of a scarcely intelligible nature had always existed between them. Our glances, however, rested not long upon the dead—for we could not regard her unawed. The disease which had thus entombed the lady in the maturity of youth, had left, as usual in all maladies of a strictly cataleptical character, the mockery of a faint blush upon the bosom and the face, and that suspiciously lingering smile upon the lip which is so terrible in death. We replaced and screwed down the lid, and, having secured the door of iron, made our way, with toil, into the scarcely less gloomy apartments of the upper portion of the house.

And now, some days of bitter grief having elapsed, an observable change came over the features of the mental disorder of my friend. His ordinary manner had vanished. His ordinary occupations were neglected or forgotten. He roamed from chamber to chamber with hurried, unequal, and objectless step. The pallor of his countenance had assumed, if possible, a more ghastly hue—but the luminousness of his eye had utterly gone out. The once occasional huskiness of his tone was heard no more; and a tremulous quaver, as if of extreme terror, habitually characterized his utterance. There were times, indeed, when I thought his unceasingly agitated mind was labouring with some oppressive secret, to divulge which he struggled for the necessary courage. At times, again, I was obliged to resolve all into the mere inexplicable vagaries of madness, for I beheld him gazing upon vacancy for long hours, in an attitude of the profoundest attention, as if listening to some imaginary sound. It was no wonder that his condition terrified—that it infected me. I felt creeping upon

me, by slow yet certain degrees, the wild influences of his own fantastic yet impressive superstitions.

It was, especially, upon retiring to bed late in the night of the seventh or eighth day after the placing of the lady Madeline within the donjon, that I experienced the full power of such feelings. Sleep came not near my couch—while the hours waned and waned away. I struggled to reason off the nervousness which had dominion over me. I endeavoured to believe that much, if not all of what I felt, was due to the bewildering influence of the gloomy furniture of the room—of the dark and tattered draperies, which, tortured into motion by the breath of a rising tempest, swayed fitfully to and fro upon the walls, and rustled uneasily about the decorations of the bed. But my efforts were fruitless. An irrepressible tremour gradually pervaded my frame; and, at length, there sat upon my very heart an incubus of utterly causeless alarm. Shaking this off with a gasp and a struggle, I uplifted myself upon the pillows, and, peering earnestly within the intense darkness of the chamber, hearkened—I know not why, except that an instinctive spirit prompted me—to certain low and indefinite sounds[13] which came, through the pauses of the storm, at long intervals, I knew not whence. Overpowered by an intense sentiment of horror, unaccountable yet unendurable, I threw on my clothes with haste (for I felt that I should sleep no more during the night), and endeavoured to arouse myself from the pitiable condition into which I had fallen, by pacing rapidly to and fro through the apartment.

I had taken but few turns in this manner, when a light step on an adjoining staircase arrested my attention. I presently recognized it as that of Usher. In an instant afterward he rapped, with a gentle touch, at my door, and entered, bearing a lamp. His countenance was, as usual, cadaverously wan —but, moreover, there was a species of mad hilarity in his eyes—an evidently restrained *hysteria* in his whole demeanour. His air appalled me—but anything was preferable to the solitude which I had so long endured, and I even welcomed his presence as a relief.

"And you have not seen it?" he said abruptly, after having stared about him for some moments in silence—"you have not then seen it?—but, stay! you shall." Thus speaking, and having carefully shaded his lamp, he hurried to one of the casements, and threw it freely open to the storm.

The impetuous fury of the entering gust nearly lifted us from our feet. It was, indeed, a tempestu-

---

13. **certain . . . sounds:** These sounds correspond to the "slight sounds" and "unusual motions" which trouble Rowena in the first stages of her illness.

ous yet sternly beautiful night, and one wildly singular in its terror and its beauty. A whirlwind had apparently collected its force in our vicinity; for there were frequent and violent alterations in the direction of the wind; and the exceeding density of the clouds (which hung so low as to press upon the turrets of the house) did not prevent our perceiving the life-like velocity with which they flew careering from all points against each other, without passing away into the distance. I say that even their exceeding density did not prevent our perceiving this—yet we had no glimpse of the moon or stars —nor was there any flashing forth of the lightning. But the under surfaces of the huge masses of agitated vapour, as well as all terrestrial objects immediately around us, were glowing in the unnatural light of a faintly luminous and distinctly visible gaseous exhalation which hung about and enshrouded the mansion.

"You must not—you shall not behold this!" said I, shuddering, to Usher, as I led him, with a gentle violence, from the window to a seat. "These appearances, which bewilder you, are merely electrical phenomena not uncommon—or it may be that they have their ghastly origin in the rank miasma of the tarn. Let us close this casement;—the air is chilling and dangerous to your frame. Here is one of your favourite romances. I will read, and you shall listen;—and so we will pass away this terrible night together."

The antique volume which I had taken up was the *Mad Trist*[14] of Sir Launcelot Canning; but I had called it a favourite of Usher's more in sad jest than in earnest; for, in truth, there is little in its uncouth and unimaginative prolixity which could have had interest for the lofty and spiritual ideality of my friend. It was, however, the only book immediately at hand; and I indulged a vague hope that the excitement which now agitated the hypochondriac, might find relief (for the history of mental disorder is full of similar anomalies) even in the extremeness of the folly which I should read. Could I have judged, indeed, by the wild overstrained air of vivacity with which he hearkened, or apparently hearkened, to the words of the tale, I might well have congratulated myself upon the success of my design.

I had arrived at that well-known portion of the story where Ethelred, the hero of the Trist, having sought in vain for peaceable admission into the dwelling of the hermit, proceeds to make good an entrance by force. Here, it will be remembered, the words of the narrative run thus:

14. *Mad Trist:* The book has not been found and is surely of Poe's invention.

"And Ethelred, who was by nature of a doughty heart, and who was now mighty withal, on account of the powerfulness of the wine which he had drunken, waited no longer to hold parley with the hermit, who, in sooth, was of an obstinate and maliceful turn, but, feeling the rain upon his shoulders, and fearing the rising of the tempest, uplifted his mace outright, and, with blows, made quickly room in the plankings of the door for his gauntleted hand; and now pulling therewith sturdily, he so cracked, and ripped, and tore all asunder, that the noise of the dry and hollow-sounding wood alarumed and reverberated throughout the forest."

At the termination of this sentence I started and, for a moment, paused; for it appeared to me (although I at once concluded that my excited fancy had deceived me)—it appeared to me that, from some very remote portion of the mansion, there came, indistinctly, to my ears, what might have been, in its exact similarity of character, the echo (but a stifled and dull one certainly) of the very cracking and ripping sound which Sir Launcelot had so particularly described. It was, beyond doubt, the coincidence alone which had arrested my attention; for, amid the rattling of the sashes of the casements, and the ordinary commingled noises of the still increasing storm, the sound, in itself, had nothing, surely, which should have interested or disturbed me. I continued the story:

"But the good champion Ethelred, now entering within the door, was sore enraged and amazed to perceive no signal of the maliceful hermit; but, in the stead thereof, a dragon of a scaly and prodigious demeanour, and of a fiery tongue, which sate in guard before a palace of gold, with a floor of silver; and upon the wall there hung a shield of shining brass with this legend enwritten—

Who entereth herein, a conqueror hath bin;
Who slayeth the dragon, the shield he shall win.

And Ethelred uplifted his mace, and struck upon the head of the dragon, which fell before him, and gave up his pesty breath, with a shriek so horrid and harsh, and withal so piercing, that Ethelred had fain to close his ears with his hands against the dreadful noise of it, the like whereof was never before heard."

Here again I paused abruptly, and now with a feeling of wild amazement—for there could be no doubt whatever that, in this instance, I did actually hear (although from what direction it proceeded I found it impossible to say) a low and apparently distant, but harsh, protracted, and most unusual screaming or grating sound—the exact counterpart of what my fancy had already conjured up for the dragon's unnatural shriek as described by the romancer.

Oppressed, as I certainly was, upon the occurrence of this second and most extraordinary coincidence, by a thousand conflicting sensations, in which wonder and extreme terror were predominant, I still retained sufficient presence of mind to avoid exciting, by any observation, the sensitive nervousness of my companion. I was by no means certain that he had noticed the sounds in question; although, assuredly, a strange alteration had, during the last few minutes, taken place in his demeanour. From a position fronting my own, he had gradually brought round his chair, so as to sit with his face to the door of the chamber; and thus I could but partially perceive his features, although I saw that his lips trembled as if he were murmuring inaudibly. His head had dropped upon his breast— yet I knew that he was not asleep, from the wide and rigid opening of the eye as I caught a glance of it in profile. The motion of his body, too, was at variance with this idea—for he rocked from side to side with a gentle yet constant and uniform sway. Having rapidly taken notice of all this, I resumed the narrative of Sir Launcelot, which thus proceeded:

"And now, the champion, having escaped from the terrible fury of the dragon, bethinking himself of the brazen shield, and of the breaking up of the enchantment which was upon it, removed the carcass from out of the way before him, and approached valorously over the silver pavement of the castle to where the shield was upon the wall; which in sooth tarried not for his full coming, but fell down at his feet upon the silver floor, with a mighty great and terrible ringing sound."

No sooner had these syllables passed my lips, than—as if a shield of brass had indeed, at the moment, fallen heavily upon a floor of silver—I became aware of a distinct, hollow, metallic, and clangorous, yet apparently muffled, reverberation. Completely unnerved, I leaped to my feet; but the measured rocking movement of Usher was undisturbed. I rushed to the chair in which he sat. His eyes were bent fixedly before him, and throughout his whole countenance there reigned a stony rigidity. But, as I placed my hand upon his shoulder, there came a strong shudder over his whole person; a sickly smile quivered about his lips; and I saw that he spoke in a low, hurried, and gibbering murmur, as if unconscious of my presence. Bending closely over him, I at length drank in the hideous import of his words.

"Not hear it?—yes, I hear it, and *have* heard it. Long—long—long—many minutes, many hours, many days, have I heard it—yet I dared not—oh, pity me, miserable wretch that I am!—I dared not —I *dared* not speak! *We have put her living in the tomb!* Said I not that my senses were acute? I *now* tell you that I heard her first feeble movements in the hollow coffin. I heard them—many, many days ago—yet I dared not—I *dared not speak!* And now—to-night—Ethelred—ha! ha!—the breaking of the hermit's door, and the death-cry of the dragon, and the clangour of the shield!—say, rather, the rending of her coffin, and the grating of the iron hinges of her prison, and her struggles within the coppered archway of the vault! Oh whither shall I fly?[15] Will she not be here anon? Is she not hurrying to upbraid me for my haste? Have I not heard her footstep on the stair? Do I not distinguish that heavy and horrible beating of her heart? MADMAN!"—here he sprang furiously to his feet, and shrieked out his syllables, as if in the effort he were giving up his soul—"MADMAN! I TELL YOU THAT SHE NOW STANDS WITHOUT THE DOOR!"

As if in the superhuman energy of his utterance there had been found the potency of a spell, the huge antique panels to which the speaker pointed threw slowly back, upon the instant, their ponderous and ebony jaws.[16] It was the work of the rushing gust—but then without those doors there DID stand the lofty and enshrouded figure of the lady Madeline of Usher. There was blood upon her white robes, and the evidence of some bitter struggle upon every portion of her emaciated frame. For a moment she remained trembling and reeling to and fro upon the threshold, then, with a low moaning cry, fell heavily inward upon the person of her brother, and in her violent and now final death-agonies, bore him to the floor a corpse, and a victim to the terrors he had anticipated.

From that chamber, and from that mansion, I fled aghast. The storm was still abroad in all its wrath as I found myself crossing the old causeway. Suddenly there shot along the path a wild light, and I turned to see whence a gleam so unusual could have issued; for the vast house and its shadows were alone behind me. The radiance was that of the full, setting, and blood-red moon, which now shone vividly through that once barely discernible fissure, of which I have before spoken as extending from the roof of the building, in a zigzag direction, to the base. While I gazed, this fissure rapidly widened—there came a fierce breath of the whirlwind —the entire orb of the satellite burst at once upon my sight—my brain reeled as I saw the mighty

15. Oh . . . fly?: "Whither shall I go from thy spirit? Or whither shall I flee from thy presence?" (Ps. 139:7). 16. huge . . . jaws: This echoes "The Sleeper," ll. 50–51: "Some vault that oft hath flung its black/And winged panels fluttering back."

walls rushing asunder—there was a long tumultuous shouting sound like the voice of a thousand waters[17]—and the deep and dank tarn at my feet closed sullenly and silently over the fragments of the "HOUSE OF USHER."

# WILLIAM WILSON

◊

❮ THIS story was first published in *Burton's Gentleman's Magazine* for October 1839. It represents Poe's most open use of the theme of the "double," and describes the conflict, within a single personality, of soul, or conscience, and worldly passion. The name "William Wilson" suggests *will* and *wilfulness*, and the rival "wills" of Wilson and his double are frequently mentioned in the narrative.

◊

What say of it? what say [of] CONSCIENCE grim,
That spectre in my path?
　　　　　　CHAMBERLAYNE'S *"Pharronida"* 1

LET ME call myself, for the present, William Wilson. The fair page now lying before me need not be sullied with my real appellation. This has been already too much an object for the scorn—for the horror—for the detestation of my race. To the uttermost regions of the globe have not the indignant winds bruited its unparalleled infamy? Oh, outcast of all outcasts most abandoned! —to the earth art thou not for ever dead? to its honors, to its flowers, to its golden aspirations?— and a cloud, dense, dismal, and limitless, does it not hang eternally between thy hopes and heaven?

I would not, if I could, here or to-day, embody a record of my later years of unspeakable misery, and unpardonable crime. This epoch—these later years—took unto themselves a sudden elevation in turpitude, whose origin alone it is my present purpose to assign. Men usually grow base by degrees. From me, in an instant, all virtue dropped bodily as a mantle. From comparatively trivial wickedness I passed, with the stride of a giant, into more than the enormities of an Elah-Gabalus.[2] What chance—what one event brought this evil thing to pass, bear with me while I relate. Death approaches; and the shadow which foreruns him has thrown a softening influence over my spirit. I long, in passing through the dim valley, for the sympathy—I had nearly said for the pity—of my fellow men. I would fain have them believe that I have been, in some measure, the slave of circumstances beyond human control.[3] I would wish them to seek out for me, in the details I am about to give, some little oasis of *fatality* amid a wilderness of error. I would have them allow—what they cannot refrain from allowing—that, although temptation may have erewhile existed as great, man was never *thus*, at least, tempted before—certainly, never *thus* fell. And is it therefore that he has never thus suffered? Have I not indeed been living in a dream? And am I not now dying a victim to the horror and the mystery of the wildest of all sublunary visions?

I am the descendant of a race whose imaginative and easily excitable temperament has at all times rendered them remarkable; and, in my earliest infancy, I gave evidence of having fully inherited the family character. As I advanced in years it was more strongly developed; becoming, for many reasons, a cause of serious disquietude to my friends, and of positive injury to myself. I grew self-willed, addicted to the wildest caprices, and a prey to the most ungovernable passions. Weak-minded, and beset with constitutional infirmities akin to my own, my parents could do but little to check the evil propensities which distinguished me. Some feeble and ill-directed efforts resulted in complete failure on their part, and, of course, in total triumph on mine. Thenceforward my voice was a household law; and at an age when few children have abandoned their leading-strings, I was left to the guidance of my own will, and became, in all but name, the master of my own actions.

My earliest recollections of a school-life,[4] are

---

17. the voice . . . waters: This alludes to the "voice from heaven, as the voice of many waters" (Rev. 14), which precedes the fall of Babylon. Poe's myths of the cosmos and of the human soul have the same pattern, the former being an analogical extension of the latter: both cosmos and soul proceed from unity to diversity and then, through purification, back to the original unity. By comparing the fall of the Usher mansion to the symbolic fall of Babylon, Poe is indicating the destined role of the poetic soul in the purification of Earth. WILLIAM WILSON. 1. *Pharronida:* The epigraph, ascribed to William Chamberlayne's heroic poem of 1659, has not been found there.

2. Elah-Gabalus: Elagabalus, or Heliogabalus, was a profligate Roman emperor who reigned during 218–22 A.D. 3. I . . . control: Reviewing Mrs. L. Miles's *Phrenology* in 1836, Poe wrote: "We must not consider the possession of particular and instinctive propensities, as acquitting us of responsibility in the indulgence of culpable actions. On the contrary, it is the perversion of our faculties which causes the greatest misery we endure, and for which (having the free exercise of *reason*) we are accountable to God." 4. school-life: The following description is based upon Poe's recollections of the Manor House School in Stoke Newington, now a part of London.

connected with a large, rambling, Elizabethan house, in a misty-looking village of England, where were a vast number of gigantic and gnarled trees, and where all the houses were excessively ancient. In truth, it was a dream-like and spirit-soothing place, that venerable old town. At this moment, in fancy, I feel the refreshing chilliness of its deeply-shadowed avenues, inhale the fragrance of its thousand shrubberies, and thrill anew with undefinable delight, at the deep hollow note of the church-bell, breaking, each hour, with sullen and sudden roar, upon the stillness of the dusky atmosphere in which the fretted Gothic steeple lay imbedded and asleep.

It gives me, perhaps, as much of pleasure as I can now in any manner experience, to dwell upon minute recollections of the school and its concerns. Steeped in misery as I am—misery, alas! only too real—I shall be pardoned for seeking relief, however slight and temporary, in the weakness of a few rambling details. These, moreover, utterly trivial, and even ridiculous in themselves, assume, to my fancy, adventitious importance, as connected with a period and a locality when and where I recognize the first ambiguous monitions of the destiny which afterward so fully overshadowed me. Let me then remember.

The house, I have said, was old and irregular. The grounds were extensive, and a high and solid brick wall, topped with a bed of mortar and broken glass, encompassed the whole. This prison-like rampart formed the limit of our domain; beyond it we saw but thrice a week—once every Saturday afternoon, when, attended by two ushers, we were permitted to take brief walks in a body through some of the neighbouring fields—and twice during Sunday, when we were paraded in the same formal manner to the morning and evening service in the one church of the village. Of this church the principal of our school was pastor. With how deep a spirit of wonder and perplexity was I wont to regard him from our remote pew in the gallery, as, with step solemn and slow, he ascended the pulpit! This reverend man, with countenance so demurely benign, with robes so glossy and so clerically flowing, with wig so minutely powdered, so rigid and so vast,—could this be he who, of late, with sour visage, and in snuffy habiliments, administered, ferule in hand, the Draconian Laws of the academy? Oh, gigantic paradox, too utterly monstrous for solution!

At an angle of the ponderous wall frowned a more ponderous gate. It was riveted and studded with iron bolts, and surmounted with jagged iron spikes. What impressions of deep awe did it inspire! It was never opened save for the three periodical egressions and ingressions already mentioned; then, in every creak of its mighty hinges, we found a plenitude of mystery—a world of matter for solemn remark, or for more solemn meditation.

The extensive enclosure was irregular in form, having many capacious recesses. Of these, three or four of the largest constituted the play-ground. It was level, and covered with fine hard gravel. I well remember it had no trees, nor benches, nor any thing similar within it. Of course it was in the rear of the house. In front lay a small parterre, planted with box and other shrubs, but through this sacred division we passed only upon rare occasions indeed —such as a first advent to school or final departure thence, or perhaps, when a parent or friend having called for us, we joyfully took our way home for the Christmas or Midsummer holidays.

But the house!—how quaint an old building was this!—to me how veritably a palace of enchantment! There was really no end to its windings—to its incomprehensible subdivisions. It was difficult, at any given time, to say with certainty upon which of its two stories one happened to be. From each room to every other there were sure to be found three or four steps either in ascent or descent. Then the lateral branches were innumerable—inconceivable—and so returning in upon themselves, that our most exact ideas in regard to the whole mansion were not very far different from those with which we pondered upon infinity. During the five years of my residence here, I was never able to ascertain with precision, in what remote locality lay the little sleeping apartment assigned to myself and some eighteen or twenty other scholars.

The school-room was the largest in the house—I could not help thinking, in the world. It was very long, narrow, and dismally low, with pointed Gothic windows and a ceiling of oak. In a remote and terror-inspiring angle was a square enclosure of eight or ten feet, comprising the *sanctum,* "during hours," of our principal, the Reverend Dr. Bransby.[5] It was a solid structure, with massy door, sooner than open which in the absence of the "Dominie," we would all have willingly perished by the *peine forte et dure.*[6] In other angles were two other similar boxes, far less reverenced, indeed, but still greatly matters of awe. One of these was the pulpit of the "classical" usher, one of the "English and mathematical." Interspersed about the room, crossing and recrossing in endless irregularity, were innumerable benches and desks, black, ancient, and time-worn, piled desperately with

5. **Bransby:** the actual name of Poe's principal at the Manor House School.    6. *peine . . . dure:* a punishment in which the victim was pressed to death.

much-bethumbed books, and so beseamed with initial letters, names at full length, grotesque figures, and other multiplied efforts of the knife, as to have entirely lost what little of original form might have been their portion in days long departed. A huge bucket with water stood at one extremity of the room, and a clock of stupendous dimensions at the other.

Encompassed by the massy walls of this venerable academy, I passed, yet not in tedium or disgust, the years of the third lustrum of my life. The teeming brain of childhood requires no external world of incident to occupy or amuse it; and the apparently dismal monotony of a school was replete with more intense excitement than my riper youth has derived from luxury, or my full manhood from crime. Yet I must believe that my first mental development had in it much of the uncommon—even much of the *outré*. Upon mankind at large the events of very early existence rarely leave in mature age any definite impression. All is gray shadow—a weak and irregular remembrance—an indistinct regathering of feeble pleasures and phantasmagoric pains. With me this is not so. In childhood I must have felt with the energy of a man what I now find stamped upon memory in lines as vivid, as deep, and as durable as the *exergues* of the Carthaginian medals.

Yet in fact—in the fact of the world's view—how little was there to remember! The morning's awakening, the nightly summons to bed; the connings, the recitations; the periodical half-holidays, and perambulations; the play-ground, with its broils, its pastimes, its intrigues;—these, by a mental sorcery long forgotten, were made to involve a wilderness of sensation, a world of rich incident, an universe of varied emotion, of excitement the most passionate and spirit-stirring. *"Oh, le bon temps, que ce siècle de fer!"* [7]

In truth, the ardor, the enthusiasm, and the imperiousness of my disposition, soon rendered me a marked character among my schoolmates, and by slow, but natural gradations, gave me an ascendancy over all not greatly older than myself;—over all with a single exception. This exception was found in the person of a scholar, who, although no relation, bore the same Christian and surname as myself;—a circumstance, in fact, little remarkable; for, notwithstanding a noble descent, mine was one of those everyday appellations which seem, by prescriptive right, to have been, time out of mind, the

common property of the mob. In this narrative I have therefore designated myself as William Wilson,—a fictitious title not very dissimilar to the real. My namesake alone, of those who in school phraseology constituted "our set," presumed to compete with me in the studies of the class—in the sports and broils of the play-ground—to refuse implicit belief in my assertions, and submission to my will —indeed, to interfere with my arbitrary dictation in any respect whatsoever. If there is on earth a supreme and unqualified despotism, it is the despotism of a mastermind in boyhood over the less energetic spirits of its companions.

Wilson's rebellion was to me a source of the greatest embarrassment;—the more so as, in spite of the bravado with which in public I made a point of treating him and his pretensions, I secretly felt that I feared him, and could not help thinking the equality which he maintained so easily with myself, a proof of his true superiority; since not to be overcome, cost me a perpetual struggle. Yet this superiority—even this equality—was in truth acknowledged by no one but myself; our associates, by some unaccountable blindness, seemed not even to suspect it. Indeed, his competition, his resistance, and especially his impertinent and dogged interference with my purposes, were not more pointed than private. He appeared to be destitute alike of the ambition which urged, and of the passionate energy of the mind which enabled me to excel. In his rivalry he might have been supposed actuated solely by a whimsical desire to thwart, astonish, or mortify myself; although there were times when I could not help observing, with a feeling made up of wonder, abasement, and pique, that he mingled with his injuries, his insults, or his contradictions, a certain most inappropriate, and assuredly most unwelcome affectionateness of manner.[8] I could only conceive this singular behavior to arise from a consummate self-conceit assuming the vulgar airs of patronage and protection.

Perhaps it was this latter trait in Wilson's conduct, conjoined with our identity of name, and the mere accident of our having entered the school upon the same day, which set afloat the notion that we were brothers, among the senior classes in the academy.[9] These do not usually inquire with much strictness into the affairs of their juniors. I have before said, or should have said, that Wilson was

7. *"Oh . . . fer!":* The quotation, from Voltaire's "Le Mondain," might be rendered, "Oh, what a good time it is, this iron age!" The iron age, according to the Greek and Roman poets, succeeded those of gold, silver, and bronze, and brought in wickedness and war.

8. In . . . manner: Wilson's namesake has the same paradoxical mixture of benevolence and repressiveness which earlier characterized the principal. 9. Perhaps . . . academy: Brothers have been known to bear identical names; however, as P. F. Quinn observes, "identity of name" would argue *against* the notion that the two Wilsons are brothers. This faulty logic casts doubt on the narrator's claim that his double was known to others.

not, in a most remote degree, connected with my family. But assuredly if we *had* been brothers we must have been twins; for, after leaving Dr. Bransby's, I casually learned that my namesake was born on the nineteenth of January, 1813 [10]—and this is a somewhat remarkable coincidence; for the day is precisely that of my own nativity.

It may seem strange that in spite of the continual anxiety occasioned me by the rivalry of Wilson, and his intolerable spirit of contradiction, I could not bring myself to hate him altogether. We had, to be sure, nearly every day a quarrel in which, yielding me publicly the palm of victory, he, in some manner, contrived to make me feel that it was he who had deserved it; yet a sense of pride on my part, and a veritable dignity on his own, kept us always upon what are called "speaking terms," while there were many points of strong congeniality in our tempers, operating to awake in me a sentiment which our position alone, perhaps, prevented from ripening into friendship. It is difficult, indeed, to define, or even to describe, my real feelings toward him. They formed a motley and heterogeneous admixture;—some petulant animosity, which was not yet hatred, some esteem, more respect, much fear, with a world of uneasy curiosity. To the moralist it will be unnecessary to say, in addition, that Wilson and myself were the most inseparable of companions.

It was no doubt the anomalous state of affairs existing between us, which turned all my attacks upon him (and there were many, either open or covert), into the channel of banter or practical joke (giving pain while assuming the aspect of mere fun) rather than into a more serious and determined hostility. But my endeavours on this head were by no means uniformly successful, even when my plans were the most wittily concocted; for my namesake had much about him, in character, of that unassuming and quiet austerity which, while enjoying the poignancy of its own jokes, has no heel of Achilles in itself, and absolutely refuses to be laughed at. I could find, indeed, but one vulnerable point, and that, lying in a personal peculiarity, arising, perhaps, from constitutional disease, would have been spared by any antagonist less at his wit's end than myself;—my rival had a weakness in the faucial or guttural organs, which precluded him from raising his voice at any time *above a very low whisper.*[11] Of this defect I did not fail to take what poor advantage lay in my power.

Wilson's retaliations in kind were many; and there was one form of his practical wit that disturbed me beyond measure. How his sagacity first discovered at all that so petty a thing would vex me, is a question I never could solve; but having discovered, he habitually practised the annoyance. I had always felt aversion to my uncourtly patronymic, and its very common, if not plebeian prænomen. The words were venom in my ears; and when, upon the day of my arrival, a second William Wilson came also to the academy, I felt angry with him for bearing the name, and doubly disgusted with the name because a stranger bore it, who would be the cause of its twofold repetition, who would be constantly in my presence, and whose concerns, in the ordinary routine of the school business, must inevitably, on account of the detestable coincidence, be often confounded with my own.

The feeling of vexation thus engendered grew stronger with every circumstance tending to show resemblance, moral or physical, between my rival and myself. I had not then discovered the remarkable fact that we were of the same age; but I saw that we were of the same height, and I perceived that we were even singularly alike in general contour of person and outline of feature. I was galled, too, by the rumor touching a relationship, which had grown current in the upper forms. In a word, nothing could more seriously disturb me, (although I scrupulously concealed such disturbance,) than any allusions to a similarity of mind, person, or condition existing between us. But, in truth, I had no reason to believe that (with the exception of the matter of relationship, and in the case of Wilson himself) this similarity had ever been made a subject of comment, or even observed at all by our schoolfellows. That *he* observed it in all its bearings, and as fixedly as I, was apparent; but that he could discover in such circumstances so fruitful a field of annoyance, can only be attributed, as I said before, to his more than ordinary penetration.

His cue, which was to perfect an imitation of myself, lay both in words and in actions; and most admirably did he play his part. My dress it was an easy matter to copy; my gait and general manner were, without difficulty, appropriated; in spite of his constitutional defect, even my voice did not escape him. My louder tones were, of course, unattempted, but then the key, it was identical; *and his singular whisper, it grew the very echo of my own.*[12]

---

10. Poe's birthday was January 19, 1809. In different printings of the story, the year appeared as 1809, 1811, and 1813.    11. I . . . *whisper:* Poe is alluding to the "still small voice" of I Kings 19:12. The expression has come to be a synonym of "conscience."

12. Both Roderick Usher and C. Auguste Dupin are double-voiced, the higher voice being spiritual and the lower, physical.

How greatly this most exquisite portraiture harassed me, (for it could not justly be termed a caricature,) I will not now venture to describe. I had but one consolation—in the fact that the imitation, apparently, was noticed by myself alone, and that I had to endure only the knowing and strangely sarcastic smiles of my namesake himself. Satisfied with having produced in my bosom the intended effect, he seemed to chuckle in secret over the sting he had inflicted, and was characteristically disregardful of the public applause which the success of his witty endeavours might have so easily elicited. That the school, indeed, did not feel his design, perceive its accomplishment, and participate in his sneer, was, for many anxious months, a riddle I could not resolve. Perhaps the *gradation* of his copy rendered it not so readily perceptible; or, more possibly, I owed my security to the masterly air of the copyist, who, disdaining the letter, (which in a painting is all the obtuse can see,) gave but the full spirit of his original for my individual contemplation and chagrin.

I have already more than once spoken of the disgusting air of patronage which he assumed toward me, and of his frequent officious interference with my will. This interference often took the ungracious character of advice; advice not openly given, but hinted or insinuated. I received it with a repugnance which gained strength as I grew in years. Yet, at this distant day, let me do him the simple justice to acknowledge that I can recall no occasion when the suggestions of my rival were on the side of those errors or follies so usual to his immature age and seeming inexperience; that his moral sense, at least, if not his general talents and worldly wisdom, was far keener than my own; and that I might, to-day, have been a better and thus a happier man, had I less frequently rejected the counsels embodied in those meaning whispers which I then but too cordially hated and too bitterly despised.

As it was, I at length grew restive in the extreme under his distasteful supervision, and daily resented more and more openly what I considered his intolerable arrogance. I have said that, in the first years of our connection as schoolmates, my feelings in regard to him might have been easily ripened into friendship: but, in the latter months of my residence at the academy, although the intrusion of his ordinary manner had, beyond doubt, in some measure, abated, my sentiments, in nearly similar proportion, partook very much of positive hatred. Upon one occasion he saw this, I think, and afterward avoided, or made a show of avoiding me.

It was about the same period, if I remember aright, that, in an altercation of violence with him, in which he was more than usually thrown off his guard, and spoke and acted with an openness of demeanor rather foreign to his nature, I discovered, or fancied I discovered, in his accent, in his air, and general appearance, a something which first startled, and then deeply interested me, by bringing to mind dim visions of my earliest infancy—wild, confused and thronging memories of a time when memory herself was yet unborn. I cannot better describe the sensation which oppressed me than by saying that I could with difficulty shake off the belief of my having been acquainted with the being who stood before me, at some epoch very long ago—some point of the past even infinitely remote.[13] The delusion, however, faded rapidly as it came; and I mention it at all but to define the day of the last conversation I there held with my singular namesake.

The huge old house, with its countless subdivisions, had several large chambers communicating with each other, where slept the greater number of the students. There were, however (as must necessarily happen in a building so awkwardly planned), many little nooks or recesses, the odds and ends of the structure; and these the economic ingenuity of Dr. Bransby had also fitted up as dormitories; although, being the merest closets, they were capable of accommodating but a single individual. One of these small apartments was occupied by Wilson.

One night, about the close of my fifth year at the school, and immediately after the altercation just mentioned, finding every one wrapped in sleep, I arose from bed, and, lamp in hand, stole through a wilderness of narrow passages, from my own bedroom to that of my rival. I had long been plotting one of those ill-natured pieces of practical wit at his expense in which I had hitherto been so uniformly unsuccessful. It was my intention, now, to put my scheme in operation, and I resolved to make him feel the whole extent of the malice with which I was imbued. Having reached his closet, I noiselessly entered, leaving the lamp, with a shade over it, on the outside. I advanced a step and listened to the sound of his tranquil breathing. Assured of his being asleep, I returned, took the light, and with it again approached the bed. Close curtains were around it, which, in the prosecution of my plan, I slowly and quietly withdrew, when the bright rays fell vividly upon the sleeper, and my eyes, at the same moment, upon his countenance. I looked;—and a numbness, an iciness of feeling in-

13. **It . . . remote:** In infancy, and perhaps in a prior existence, Wilson's soul was undivided; the passions were either unawakened or under spiritual control, and conscience was not distinguishable from the aesthetic sense.

stantly pervaded my frame. My breast heaved, my knees tottered, my whole spirit became possessed with an objectless yet intolerable horror. Gasping for breath, I lowered the lamp in still nearer proximity to the face. Were these—*these* the lineaments of William Wilson? I saw, indeed, that they were his, but I shook as if with a fit of the ague in fancying they were not. What *was* there about them to confound me in this manner? I gazed;— while my brain reeled with a multitude of incoherent thoughts. Not thus he appeared—assuredly not *thus*—in the vivacity of his waking hours. The same name! the same contour of person! the same day of arrival at the academy! And then his dogged and meaningless imitation of my gait, my voice, my habits, and my manner! Was it, in truth, within the bounds of human possibility, that *what I now saw* was the result, merely, of the habitual practice of this sarcastic imitation? Awe-stricken, and with a creeping shudder, I extinguished the lamp, passed silently from the chamber, and left, at once, the halls of that old academy, never to enter them again.

After a lapse of some months, spent at home in mere idleness, I found myself a student at Eton. The brief interval had been sufficient to enfeeble my remembrance of the events at Dr. Bransby's, or at least to effect a material change in the nature of the feelings with which I remembered them. The truth—the tragedy—of the drama was no more. I could now find room to doubt the evidence of my senses; and seldom called up the subject at all but with wonder at the extent of human credulity, and a smile at the vivid force of the imagination which I hereditarily possessed. Neither was this species of skepticism likely to be diminished by the character of the life I led at Eton. The vortex of thoughtless folly into which I there so immediately and so recklessly plunged, washed away all but the froth of my past hours, engulfed at once every solid or serious impression, and left to memory only the veriest levities of a former existence.

I do not wish, however, to trace the course of my miserable profligacy here—a profligacy which set at defiance the laws, while it eluded the vigilance of the institution. Three years of folly, passed without profit, had but given me rooted habits of vice, and added, in a somewhat unusual degree, to my bodily stature, when, after a week of soulless dissipation, I invited a small party of the most dissolute students to a secret carousal in my chambers. We met at a late hour of the night; for our debaucheries were to be faithfully protracted until morning. The wine flowed freely, and there were not wanting other and perhaps more

dangerous seductions; so that the grey dawn had already faintly appeared in the east while our delirious extravagance was at its height. Madly flushed with cards and intoxication, I was in the act of insisting upon a toast of more than wonted profanity, when my attention was suddenly diverted by the violent, although partial, unclosing of the door of the apartment, and by the eager voice of a servant from without. He said that some person, apparently in great haste, demanded to speak with me in the hall.

Wildly excited with wine, the unexpected interruption rather delighted than surprised me. I staggered forward at once, and a few steps brought me to the vestibule of the building. In this low and small room there hung no lamp; and now no light at all was admitted, save that of the exceedingly feeble dawn which made its way through the semi-circular window. As I put my foot over the threshold, I became aware of the figure of a youth about my own height, and habited in a white kerseymere morning frock, cut in the novel fashion of the one I myself wore at the moment. This the faint light enabled me to perceive; but the features of his face I could not distinguish. Upon my entering he strode hurriedly up to me, and, seizing me by the arm with a gesture of petulant impatience, whispered the words "William Wilson!" in my ear.

I grew perfectly sober in an instant.

There was that in the manner of the stranger, and in the tremulous shake of his uplifted finger,[14] as he held it between my eyes and the light, which filled me with unqualified amazement; but it was not this which had so violently moved me. It was the pregnancy of solemn admonition in the singular, low, hissing utterance; and, above all, it was the character, the tone, *the key,* of those few, simple, and familiar, yet *whispered* syllables, which came with a thousand thronging memories of bygone days, and struck upon my soul with the shock of a galvanic battery. Ere I could recover the use of my senses he was gone.

Although this event failed not of a vivid effect upon my disordered imagination, yet was it evanescent as vivid. For some weeks, indeed, I busied myself in earnest enquiry, or was wrapped in a cloud of morbid speculation. I did not pretend to disguise from my perception the identity of the singular individual who thus perseveringly interfered with my affairs, and harassed me with his insinuated counsel. But who and what was this

14. tremulous . . . finger: Compare the fingers of the spirit-crew of "Ms. Found in a Bottle," which the narrator perceives, against "the wild glare of the battle-lanterns." They are tremulous and translucent because spectral.

Wilson?—and whence came he?—and what were his purposes? Upon neither of these points could I be satisfied; merely ascertaining, in regard to him, that a sudden accident in his family had caused his removal from Dr. Bransby's academy on the afternoon of the day in which I myself had eloped. But in a brief period I ceased to think upon the subject; my attention being all absorbed in a contemplated departure for Oxford. Thither I soon went, the uncalculating vanity of my parents furnishing me with an outfit and annual establishment, which would enable me to indulge at will in the luxury already so dear to my heart,—to vie in profuseness of expenditure with the haughtiest heirs of the wealthiest earldoms in Great Britain.

Excited by such appliances to vice, my constitutional temperament broke forth with redoubled ardor, and I spurned even the common restraints of decency in the mad infatuation of my revels. But it were absurd to pause in the detail of my extravagance. Let it suffice, that among spendthrifts I out-Heroded Herod, and that, giving name to a multitude of novel follies, I added no brief appendix to the long catalogue of vices then usual in the most dissolute university of Europe.

It could hardly be credited, however, that I had, even here, so utterly fallen from the gentlemanly estate, as to seek acquaintance with the vilest arts of the gambler by profession, and, having become an adept in his despicable science, to practice it habitually as a means of increasing my already enormous income at the expense of the weak-minded among my fellow-collegians. Such, nevertheless, was the fact. And the very enormity of this offence against all manly and honourable sentiment proved, beyond doubt, the main if not the sole reason of the impunity with which it was committed. Who, indeed, among my most abandoned associates, would not rather have disputed the clearest evidence of his senses, than have suspected of such courses, the gay, the frank, the generous William Wilson—the noblest and most liberal commoner at Oxford—him whose follies (said his parasites) were but the follies of youth and unbridled fancy—whose errors but inimitable whim —whose darkest vice but a careless and dashing extravagance?

I had been now two years successfully busied in this way, when there came to the university a young *parvenu* nobleman, Glendinning—rich, said report, as Herodes Atticus [15]—his riches, too, as easily acquired. I soon found him of weak intellect, and, of course, marked him as a fitting sub-

ject for my skill. I frequently engaged him in play, and contrived, with the gambler's usual art, to let him win considerable sums, the more effectually to entangle him in my snares. At length, my schemes being ripe, I met him (with the full intention that this meeting should be final and decisive) at the chambers of a fellow-commoner (Mr. Preston),[16] equally intimate with both, but who, to do him justice, entertained not even a remote suspicion of my design. To give to this a better colouring, I had contrived to have assembled a party of some eight or ten, and was solicitously careful that the introduction of cards should appear accidental, and originate in the proposal of my contemplated dupe himself. To be brief upon a vile topic, none of the low finesse was omitted, so customary upon similar occasions, that it is a just matter for wonder how any are still found so besotted as to fall its victim.

We had protracted our sitting far into the night, and I had at length effected the manœuvre of getting Glendinning as my sole antagonist. The game, too, was my favourite *écarté*. The rest of the company, interested in the extent of our play, had abandoned their own cards, and were standing around us as spectators. The *parvenu*, who had been induced by my artifices in the early part of the evening, to drink deeply, now shuffled, dealt, or played, with a wild nervousness of manner for which his intoxication, I thought, might partially, but could not altogether account. In a very short period he had become my debtor to a large amount, when, having taken a long draught of port, he did precisely what I had been coolly anticipating—he proposed to double our already extravagant stakes. With a well-feigned show of reluctance, and not until after my repeated refusal had seduced him into some angry words which gave a color of *pique* to my compliance, did I finally comply. The result, of course, did but prove how entirely the prey was in my toils; in less than an hour he had quadrupled his debt. For some time his countenance had been losing the florid tinge lent it by the wine; but now, to my astonishment, I perceived that it had grown to a pallor truly fearful. I say, to my astonishment. Glendinning had been represented to my eager inquiries as immeasurably wealthy; and the sums which he had as yet lost, although in themselves vast, could not, I supposed, very seriously annoy, much less so violently affect him. That he was overcome by the wine just swallowed, was the idea which most readily presented itself; and, rather with a view to

15. **Herodes Atticus:** Greek rhetorician of the second century A.D. A teacher of Marcus Aurelius, a consul, and a man of vast wealth.

16. **Preston:** John Preston was a friend and fellow student of Poe's at the University of Virginia, where Poe lost large sums by gambling.

the preservation of my own character in the eyes of my associates, than from any less interested motive, I was about to insist, peremptorily, upon a discontinuance of the play, when some expressions at my elbow from among the company, and an ejaculation evincing utter despair on the part of Glendinning, gave me to understand that I had effected his total ruin under circumstances which, rendering him an object for the pity of all, should have protected him from the ill offices even of a fiend.

What now might have been my conduct it is difficult to say. The pitiable condition of my dupe had thrown an air of embarrassed gloom over all; and, for some moments, a profound silence was maintained, during which I could not help feeling my cheeks tingle with the many burning glances of scorn or reproach cast upon me by the less abandoned of the party. I will even own that an intolerable weight of anxiety was for a brief instant lifted from my bosom by the sudden and extraordinary interruption which ensued. The wide, heavy folding doors of the apartment were all at once thrown open, to their full extent, with a vigorous and rushing impetuosity that extinguished, as if by magic, every candle in the room. Their light, in dying, enabled us just to perceive that a stranger had entered, about my own height, and closely muffled in a cloak. The darkness, however, was not total; and we could only *feel* that he was standing in our midst. Before any one of us could recover from the extreme astonishment into which this rudeness had thrown all, we heard the voice of the intruder.

"Gentlemen," he said, in a low, distinct, and never-to-be-forgotten *whisper* which thrilled to the very marrow of my bones, "Gentlemen, I make no apology for this behaviour, because in thus behaving, I am fulfilling a duty. You are, beyond doubt, uninformed of the true character of the person who has to-night won at *écarté* a large sum of money from Lord Glendinning. I will therefore put you upon an expeditious and decisive plan of obtaining this very necessary information. Please to examine, at your leisure, the inner linings of the cuff of his left sleeve, and the several little packages which may be found in the somewhat capacious pockets of his embroidered morning wrapper."

While he spoke, so profound was the stillness that one might have heard a pin drop upon the floor. In ceasing, he departed at once, and as abruptly as he had entered. Can I—shall I describe my sensations?—must I say that I felt all the horrors of the damned? Most assuredly I had little time given for reflection. Many hands roughly seized me upon the spot, and lights were imme-

diately reprocured. A search ensued. In the lining of my sleeve were found all the court cards essential in *écarté,* and, in the pockets of my wrapper, a number of packs, fac-similes of those used at our sittings, with the single exception that mine were of the species called, technically, *arrondées;* the honors being slightly convex at the ends, the lower cards slightly convex at the sides. In this disposition, the dupe who cuts, as customary, at the length of the pack, will invariably find that he cuts his antagonist an honor; while the gambler, cutting at the breadth, will, as certainly, cut nothing for his victim which may count in the records of the game.

Any burst of indignation upon this discovery would have affected me less than the silent contempt, or the sarcastic composure, with which it was received.

"Mr. Wilson," said our host, stooping to remove from beneath his feet an exceedingly luxurious cloak of rare furs, "Mr. Wilson, this is your property." (The weather was cold; and, upon quitting my own room, I had thrown a cloak over my dressing wrapper, putting it off upon reaching the scene of play.) "I presume it is supererogatory to seek here (eyeing the folds of the garment with a bitter smile) for any farther evidence of your skill. Indeed, we have had enough. You will see the necessity, I hope, of quitting Oxford— at all events, of quitting instantly my chambers."

Abased, humbled to the dust as I then was, it is probable that I should have resented this galling language by immediate personal violence, had not my whole attention been at the moment arrested by a fact of the most startling character. The cloak which I had worn was of a rare description of fur; how rare, how extravagantly costly, I shall not venture to say. Its fashion, too, was of my own fantastic invention; for I was fastidious to an absurd degree of coxcombry, in matters of this frivolous nature. When, therefore, Mr. Preston reached me that which he had picked up upon the floor, and near the folding doors of the apartment, it was with an astonishment nearly bordering upon terror, that I perceived my own already hanging on my arm (where I had no doubt unwittingly placed it), and that the one presented me was but its exact counterpart in every, in even the minutest possible particular. The singular being who had so disastrously exposed me, had been muffled, I remembered, in a cloak; and none had been worn at all by any of the members of our party with the exception of myself. Retaining some presence of mind, I took the one offered me by Preston; placed it, unnoticed, over my own; left the apartment with a resolute scowl of defiance; and, next morning ere dawn of day, commenced a hurried journey from Oxford to the continent, in a perfect agony of horror and of shame.

*I fled in vain.* My evil destiny pursued me as if in exultation, and proved, indeed, that the exercise of its mysterious dominion had as yet only begun. Scarcely had I set foot in Paris, ere I had fresh evidence of the detestable interest taken by this Wilson in my concerns. Years flew, while I experienced no relief. Villain!—at Rome, with how untimely, yet with how spectral an officiousness, stepped he in between me and my ambition! at Vienna, too—at Berlin—and at Moscow! Where, in truth, had I *not* bitter cause to curse him within my heart? From his inscrutable tyranny did I at length flee, panic-stricken, as from a pestilence; and to the very ends of the earth [17] *I fled in vain.*

And again, and again, in secret communion with my own spirit, would I demand the questions "Who is he?—whence came he?—and what are his objects?" But no answer was there found. And then I scrutinized, with a minute scrutiny, the forms, and the methods, and the leading traits of his impertinent supervision. But even here there was very little upon which to base a conjecture. It was noticeable, indeed, that, in no one of the multiplied instances in which he had of late crossed my path, had he so crossed it except to frustrate those schemes, or to disturb those actions, which, if fully carried out, might have resulted in bitter mischief. Poor justification this, in truth, for an authority so imperiously assumed! Poor indemnity for natural rights of self-agency so pertinaciously, so insultingly denied!

I had also been forced to notice that my tormentor, for a very long period of time (while scrupulously and with miraculous dexterity maintaining his whim of an identity of apparel with myself), had so contrived it, in the execution of his varied interference with my will, that I saw not, at any moment, the features of his face. Be Wilson what he might, *this,* at least, was but the veriest of affectation, or of folly. Could he, for an instant, have supposed that, in my admonisher at Eton—in the destroyer of my honor at Oxford,—in him who thwarted my ambition at Rome, my revenge at Paris, my passionate love at Naples, or what he falsely termed my avarice in Egypt,—that in this, my arch-enemy and evil genius, I could fail to recognize the William Wilson of my schoolboy days, —the namesake, the companion, the rival,—the

hated and dreaded rival at Dr. Bransby's? Impossible!—But let me hasten to the last eventful scene of the drama.

Thus far I had succumbed supinely to this imperious domination. The sentiment of deep awe with which I habitually regarded the elevated character, the majestic wisdom, the apparent omnipresence and omnipotence of Wilson, added to a feeling of even terror, with which certain other traits in his nature and assumptions inspired me, had operated, hitherto, to impress me with an idea of my own utter weakness and helplessness, and to suggest an implicit, although bitterly reluctant submission to his arbitrary will. But, of late days, I had given myself up entirely to wine; and its maddening influence upon my hereditary temper rendered me more and more impatient of control. I began to murmur,—to hesitate,—to resist. And was it only fancy which induced me to believe that, with the increase of my own firmness, that of my tormentor underwent a proportional diminution? Be this as it may, I now began to feel the inspiration of a burning hope, and at length nurtured in my secret thoughts a stern and desperate resolution that I would submit no longer to be enslaved.

It was at Rome, during the Carnival of 18—, that I attended a masquerade in the palazzo of the Neapolitan Duke Di Broglio. I had indulged more freely than usual in the excesses of the wine-table; and now the suffocating atmosphere of the crowded rooms irritated me beyond endurance. The difficulty, too, of forcing my way through the mazes of the company contributed not a little to the ruffling of my temper; for I was anxiously seeking (let me not say with what unworthy motive) the young, the gay, the beautiful wife of the aged and doting Di Broglio.[18] With a too unscrupulous confidence she had previously communicated to me the secret of the costume in which she would be habited and now, having caught a glimpse of her person, I was hurrying to make my way into her presence.—At this moment I felt a light hand placed upon my shoulder, and that ever-remembered, low, damnable *whisper* within my ear.

In an absolute frenzy of wrath, I turned at once upon him who had thus interrupted me, and seized him violently by the collar. He was attired, as I had expected, in a costume altogether similar to

17. **ends of the earth:** echoes many Biblical passages concerning the omnipotence and omnipresence of God. These qualities are later attributed to Wilson's double, who as "conscience" is God's agent.

18. **the . . . Di Broglio:** The Marchesa Aphrodite, in "The Assignation," is described as "the gayest of the gay—the most lovely where all were beautiful—but still the young wife of the old and intriguing Mentoni." Similarity of language, in Poe, generally indicates similarity of substance, and Di Broglio's wife is doubtless, like the Marchesa, "the type of spiritual beauty." Wilson's passionate designs upon her therefore create a crescendo of conflict between him and his conscience.

my own; wearing a Spanish cloak of blue velvet, begirt about the waist with a crimson belt sustaining a rapier. A mask of black silk entirely covered his face.

"Scoundrel!" I said, in a voice husky with rage, while every syllable I uttered seemed as new fuel to my fury, "scoundrel! impostor! accursed villain! you shall not—you *shall not* dog me unto death! Follow me, or I stab you where you stand!" —and I broke my way from the ballroom into a small antechamber adjoining, dragging him unresistingly with me as I went.

Upon entering, I thrust him furiously from me. He staggered against the wall, while I closed the door with an oath, and commanded him to draw. He hesitated but for an instant; then, with a slight sigh, drew in silence, and put himself upon his defence.

The contest was brief indeed. I was frantic with every species of wild excitement, and felt within my single arm the energy and power of a multitude. In a few seconds I forced him by sheer strength against the wainscotting, and thus, getting him at mercy, plunged my sword, with brute ferocity, repeatedly through and through his bosom.

At that instant some person tried the latch of the door. I hastened to prevent an intrusion, and then immediately returned to my dying antagonist. But what human language can adequately portray *that* astonishment, *that* horror which possessed me at the spectacle then presented to view? The brief moment in which I averted my eyes had been sufficient to produce, apparently, a material change in the arrangements at the upper or farther end of the room. A large mirror,—so at first it seemed to me in my confusion—now stood where none had been perceptible before; and as I stepped up to it in extremity of terror, mine own image, but with features all pale and dabbled in blood, advanced to meet me with a feeble and tottering gait.

Thus it appeared, I say, but was not. It was my antagonist—it was Wilson, who then stood before me in the agonies of his dissolution. His mask and cloak lay, where he had thrown them, upon the floor. Not a thread in all his raiment—not a line in all the marked and singular lineaments of his face which was not, even in the most absolute identity, *mine own!*

It was Wilson; but he spoke no longer in a whisper,[19] and I could have fancied that I myself was speaking while he said:

*"You have conquered, and I yield. Yet, henceforward art thou also dead—dead to the World, to Heaven, and to Hope! In me didst thou exist [20]— and, in my death, see by this image, which is thine own, how utterly thou hast murdered thyself."*

---

# THE PURLOINED LETTER

---

◊

❮ FIRST published in *The Gift* (January 1845), "The Purloined Letter" was Poe's third story about his detective-hero Dupin. For comment, see the Introduction, Part V.

◊

*Nil sapientiæ odiosius acumine nimio.*
SENECA [1]

AT PARIS, just after dark one gusty evening in the autumn of 18—, I was enjoying the twofold luxury of meditation and a meerschaum, in company with my friend C. Auguste Dupin, in his little back library, or book-closet, *au troisième, No. 33 Rue Dunôt, Faubourg St. Germain.*[2] For one hour at least we had maintained a profound silence; while each, to any casual observer, might have seemed intently and exclusively occupied with the curling eddies of smoke that oppressed the atmosphere of the chamber. For myself, however, I was mentally discussing certain topics which had formed matter for conversation between us at an earlier period of the evening; I mean the affair of the Rue Morgue, and the mystery attending the murder of Marie Rogêt. I looked upon it, therefore, as something of a coincidence, when the door of our apartment was thrown open and admitted our old acquaintance, Monsieur G——, the Prefect of the Parisian police.

We gave him a hearty welcome; for there was nearly half as much of the entertaining as of the

---

19. **no . . . whisper:** Wilson's voice earlier grew "husky with rage" (thus approximating the double's "whisper") in anticipation of the latter's adoption, here, of Wilson's stronger voice. The effect is to demonstrate their identity and common fate.

20. **In . . . exist:** The words recall St. Paul's words to the Athenians: "For in him we live, and move, and have our being" (Acts 18:28). The irrevocable deadness of Wilson is perhaps explained by Matt. 12:32. THE PURLOINED LETTER. **1. Seneca:** The epigraph, not located in Seneca, means, "Nothing is more repugnant to learning than too much insight." **2. At . . . St. Germain:** As established in "The Murders in the Rue Morgue" (1841), Dupin and the narrator live in a "time-eaten and grotesque mansion . . . tottering to its fall in a retired and desolate portion of the Faubourg St. Germain." They occupy the fourth floor only and go out only at night; during the day, they shutter the windows and in feeble candlelight, "busy their souls in dreams." Dupin is, in short, a Roderick Usher.

contemptible about the man, and we had not seen him for several years. We had been sitting in the dark, and Dupin now arose for the purpose of lighting a lamp, but sat down again, without doing so, upon G.'s saying that he had called to consult us, or rather to ask the opinion of my friend, about some official business which had occasioned a great deal of trouble.

"If it is any point requiring reflection," observed Dupin, as he forbore to enkindle the wick, "we shall examine it to better purpose in the dark."

"That is another of your odd notions," said the Prefect, who had a fashion of calling every thing "odd" that was beyond his comprehension, and thus lived amid an absolute legion of "oddities."

"Very true," said Dupin, as he supplied his visiter with a pipe, and rolled towards him a comfortable chair.

"And what is the difficulty now?" I asked. "Nothing more in the assassination way, I hope?"

"Oh no; nothing of that nature. The fact is, the business is *very* simple indeed, and I make no doubt that we can manage it sufficiently well ourselves; but then I thought Dupin would like to hear the details of it, because it is so excessively *odd.*"

"Simple and odd," said Dupin.

"Why, yes; and not exactly that either. The fact is, we have all been a good deal puzzled because the affair *is* so simple, and yet baffles us altogether."

"Perhaps it is the very simplicity of the thing which puts you at fault," said my friend.

"What nonsense you *do* talk!" replied the Prefect, laughing heartily.

"Perhaps the mystery is a little *too* plain," said Dupin.

"Oh, good heavens! who ever heard of such an idea?"

"A little *too* self-evident."

"Ha! ha! ha!—ha! ha! ha!—ho! ho! ho!"—roared our visiter, profoundly amused, "oh, Dupin, you will be the death of me yet!"

"And what, after all, *is* the matter on hand?" I asked.

"Why, I will tell you," replied the Prefect, as he gave a long, steady, and contemplative puff, and settled himself in his chair. "I will tell you in a few words; but, before I begin, let me caution you that this is an affair demanding the greatest secrecy, and that I should most probably lose the position I now hold, were it known that I confided it to any one."

"Proceed," said I.

"Or not," said Dupin.

"Well, then; I have received personal informa-

tion, from a very high quarter, that a certain document of the last importance, has been purloined from the royal apartments. The individual who purloined it is known; this beyond a doubt; he was seen to take it. It is known, also, that it still remains in his possession."

"How is this known?" asked Dupin.

"It is clearly inferred," replied the Prefect, "from the nature of the document, and from the non-appearance of certain results which would at once arise from its passing *out* of the robber's possession;—that is to say, from his employing it as he must design in the end to employ it."

"Be a little more explicit," I said.

"Well, I may venture so far as to say that the paper gives its holder a certain power in a certain quarter where such power is immensely valuable." The Prefect was fond of the cant of diplomacy.

"Still I do not quite understand," said Dupin.

"No? Well; the disclosure of the document to a third person, who shall be nameless, would bring in question the honor of a personage of most exalted station; and this fact gives the holder of the document an ascendancy over the illustrious personage whose honor and peace are so jeopardized."

"But this ascendancy," I interposed, "would depend upon the robber's knowledge of the loser's knowledge of the robber. Who would dare—"

"The thief," said G., "is the Minister D——, who dares all things, those unbecoming as well as those becoming a man. The method of the theft was not less ingenious than bold. The document in question—a letter, to be frank—had been received by the personage robbed while alone in the royal *boudoir.* During its perusal she was suddenly interrupted by the entrance of the other exalted personage from whom especially it was her wish to conceal it. After a hurried and vain endeavor to thrust it in a drawer, she was forced to place it, open it was, upon a table. The address, however was uppermost, and, the contents thus unexposed, the letter escaped notice. At this juncture enters the Minister D——. His lynx eye immediately perceives the paper, recognizes the handwriting of the address, observes the confusion of the personage addressed, and fathoms her secret.[3] After some business transactions, hurried through in his ordinary manner, he produces a letter somewhat similar to the one in question, opens it, pretends to read it, and then places it in close juxtaposition to the other. Again he converses, for some fifteen

3. At . . . secret: The Minister D—— here gives a demonstration of the instant and intuitive penetration which characterizes Dupin.

minutes, upon the public affairs. At length, in taking leave, he takes also from the table the letter to which he had no claim. Its rightful owner saw, but, of course, dared not call attention to the act, in the presence of the third personage who stood at her elbow. The minister decamped; leaving his own letter—one of no importance—upon the table."

"Here, then," said Dupin to me, "you have precisely what you demand to make the ascendancy complete—the robber's knowledge of the loser's knowledge of the robber."

"Yes," replied the Prefect; "and the power thus attained has, for some months past, been wielded, for political purposes, to a very dangerous extent. The personage robbed is more thoroughly convinced, every day, of the necessity of reclaiming her letter. But this, of course, cannot be done openly. In fine, driven to despair, she has committed the matter to me."

"Than whom," said Dupin, amid a perfect whirlwind of smoke, "no more sagacious agent could, I suppose, be desired, or even imagined."

"You flatter me," replied the Prefect; "but it is possible that some such opinion may have been entertained."

"It is clear," said I, "as you observe, that the letter is still in the possession of the Minister; since it is this possession, and not any employment of the letter, which bestows the power. With the employment the power departs."

"True," said G.; "and upon this conviction I proceeded. My first care was to make thorough search of the Minister's hotel; and here my chief embarrassment lay in the necessity of searching without his knowledge. Beyond all things, I have been warned of the danger which would result from giving him reason to suspect our design."

"But," said I, "you are quite *au fait* in these investigations. The Parisian police have done this thing often before."

"O yes; and for this reason I did not despair. The habits of the Minister gave me, too, a great advantage. He is frequently absent from home all night. His servants are by no means numerous. They sleep at a distance from their master's apartment, and, being chiefly Neapolitans, are readily made drunk. I have keys, as you know, with which I can open any chamber or cabinet in Paris. For three months a night has not passed, during the greater part of which I have not been engaged, personally, in ransacking the D—— Hôtel. My honor is interested, and, to mention a great secret, the reward is enormous. So I did not abandon the search until I had become fully satisfied that the thief is a more astute man than myself. I fancy that I have investigated every nook and corner of the premises in which it is possible that the paper can be concealed."

"But is it not possible," I suggested, "that although the letter may be in possession of the Minister, as it unquestionably is, he may have concealed it elsewhere than upon his own premises?"

"This is barely possible," said Dupin. "The present peculiar condition of affairs at court, and especially of those intrigues in which D—— is known to be involved, would render the instant availability of the document—its susceptibility of being produced at a moment's notice—a point of nearly equal importance with its possession."

"Its susceptibility of being produced?" said I.

"That is to say, of being *destroyed*," said Dupin.

"True," I observed; "the paper is clearly then upon the premises. As for its being upon the person of the Minister, we may consider that as out of the question."

"Entirely," said the Prefect. "He has been twice waylaid, as if by foot-pads, and his person rigorously searched under my own inspection."

"You might have spared yourself this trouble," said Dupin. "D——, I presume, is not altogether a fool, and, if not, must have anticipated these waylayings, as a matter of course."

"Not *altogether* a fool," said G., "but then he is a poet, which I take to be only one remove from a fool."

"True," said Dupin, after a long and thoughtful whiff from his meerschaum, "although I have been guilty of certain doggerel myself."

"Suppose you detail," said I, "the particulars of your search."

"Why the fact is, we took our time, and we searched *everywhere*. I have had long experience in these affairs. I took the entire building, room by room; devoting the nights of a whole week to each. We examined, first, the furniture of each apartment. We opened every possible drawer; and I presume you know that, to a properly trained police agent, such a thing as a *secret* drawer is impossible. Any man is a dolt who permits a 'secret' drawer to escape him in a search of this kind. The thing is *so* plain. There is a certain amount of bulk —of space—to be accounted for in every cabinet. Then we have accurate rules. The fiftieth part of a line could not escape us. After the cabinets we took the chairs. The cushions we probed with the fine long needles you have seen me employ. From the tables we removed the tops."

"Why so?"

"Sometimes the top of a table, or other similarly arranged piece of furniture, is removed by the person wishing to conceal an article; then the leg is excavated, the article deposited within the cavity, and the top replaced. The bottoms and tops of bed-posts are employed in the same way."

"But could not the cavity be detected by sounding?" I asked.

"By no means, if, when the article is deposited, a sufficient wadding of cotton be placed around it. Besides, in our case, we were obliged to proceed without noise."

"But you could not have removed—you could not have taken to pieces *all* articles of furniture in which it would have been possible to make a deposit in the manner you mention. A letter may be compressed into a thin spiral roll, not differing much in shape or bulk from a large knitting-needle, and in this form it might be inserted into the rung of a chair, for example. You did not take to pieces all the chairs?"

"Certainly not; but we did better—we examined the rungs of every chair in the hotel, and, indeed the jointings of every description of furniture, by the aid of a most powerful microscope. Had there been any traces of recent disturbance we should not have failed to detect it instantly. A single grain of gimlet-dust, for example, would have been as obvious as an apple. Any disorder in the glueing—any unusual gaping in the joints—would have sufficed to insure detection."

"I presume you looked to the mirrors, between the boards and the plates, and you probed the beds and the bed-clothes, as well as the curtains and carpets."

"That of course; and when we had absolutely completed every particle of the furniture in this way, then we examined the house itself. We divided its entire surface into compartments, which we numbered, so that none might be missed; then we scrutinized each individual square inch throughout the premises, including the two houses immediately adjoining, with the microscope as before."

"The two houses adjoining!" I exclaimed; "you must have had a great deal of trouble."

"We had; but the reward offered is prodigious."

"You include the *grounds* about the houses?"

"All the grounds are paved with brick. They gave us comparatively little trouble. We examined the moss between the bricks, and found it undisturbed."

"You looked among D——'s papers, of course, and into the books of the library?"

"Certainly; we opened every package and parcel; we not only opened every book, but we turned over every leaf in each volume, not contenting ourselves with a mere shake, according to the fashion of some of our police officers. We also measured the thickness of every book-*cover,* with the most accurate admeasurement, and applied to each the most jealous scrutiny of the microscope. Had any of the bindings been recently meddled with, it would have been utterly impossible that the fact should have escaped observation. Some five or six volumes, just from the hands of the binder, we carefully probed, longitudinally, with the needles."

"You explored the floors beneath the carpets?"

"Beyond doubt. We removed every carpet, and examined the boards with the microscope."

"And the paper on the walls?"

"Yes."

"You looked into the cellars?"

"We did."

"Then," I said; "you have been making a miscalculation, and the letter is *not* upon the premises, as you suppose."

"I fear you are right there," said the Prefect. "And now, Dupin, what would you advise me to do?"

"To make a thorough re-search of the premises."

"That is absolutely needless," replied G——. "I am not more sure that I breathe than I am that the letter is not at the hotel."

"I have no better advice to give you," said Dupin. "You have, of course, an accurate description of the letter?"

"Oh, yes!"—And here the Prefect, producing a memorandum-book, proceeded to read aloud a minute account of the internal, and especially of the external, appearance of the missing document. Soon after finishing the perusal of this description, he took his departure, more entirely depressed in spirits than I had ever known the good gentleman before.

In about a month afterward he paid us another visit, and found us occupied very nearly as before. He took a pipe and a chair and entered into some ordinary conversation. At length I said;—

"Well, but G——, what of the purloined letter? I presume you have at last made up your mind that there is no such thing as overreaching the Minister?"

"Confound him, say I—yes; I made the re-examination, however, as Dupin suggested—but it was all labor lost, as I knew it would be."

"How much was the reward offered, did you say?" asked Dupin.

"Why, a very great deal—a *very* liberal reward—I don't like to say how much, precisely; but one thing I *will* say, that I wouldn't mind giving my individual check for fifty-thousand francs to any one who could obtain me that letter. The fact is, it is becoming of more and more importance every day; and the reward has been lately doubled. If it were trebled, however, I could do no more than I have done."

"Why, yes," said Dupin, drawlingly, between the whiffs of his meerschaum, "I really—think, G——, you have not exerted yourself—to the utmost in this matter. You might—do a little more, I think, eh?"

"How?—in what way?"

"Why—puff, puff—you might—puff, puff— employ counsel in the matter, eh?—puff, puff, puff. Do you remember the story they tell of Abernethy?" [4]

"No; hang Abernethy!"

"To be sure! hang him and welcome. But, once upon a time, a certain rich miser conceived the design of spunging upon this Abernethy for a medical opinion. Getting up, for this purpose, an ordinary conversation in a private company, he insinuated his case to the physician, as that of an imaginary individual.

" 'We will suppose,' said the miser, 'that his symptoms are such and such; now, doctor, what would *you* have directed him to take?'

" 'Take!' said Abernethy, 'why, take *advice*, to be sure.' "

"But," said the Prefect, a little discomposed, "*I* am *perfectly* willing to take advice, and to pay for it. I would *really* give fifty-thousand francs to any one who would aid me in the matter."

"In that case," replied Dupin, opening a drawer, and producing a check-book, "you may as well fill me up a check for the amount mentioned. When you have signed it, I will hand you the letter."

I was astounded. The Prefect appeared absolutely thunder-stricken. For some minutes he remained speechless and motionless, looking incredulously at my friend with open mouth, and eyes that seemed starting from their sockets; then, apparently recovering himself in some measure, he seized a pen, and after several pauses and vacant stares, finally filled up and signed a check for fifty-thousand francs, and handed it across the table to Dupin. The latter examined it carefully and deposited it in his pocket-book; then, unlocking an *escritoire,* took thence a letter and gave it to the Prefect. This functionary grasped it in a perfect agony of joy, opened it with a trembling hand, cast a rapid glance at its contents, and then, scrambling and struggling to the door, rushed at length

unceremoniously from the room and from the house, without having uttered a syllable since Dupin had requested him to fill up the check.

When he had gone, my friend entered into some explanations.

"The Parisian police," he said, "are exceedingly able in their way. They are persevering, ingenious, cunning, and thoroughly versed in the knowledge which their duties seem chiefly to demand. Thus, when G—— detailed to us his mode of searching the premises at the Hôtel D——, I felt entire confidence in his having made a satisfactory investigation—so far as his labors extended."

"So far as his labors extended?" said I.

"Yes," said Dupin. "The measures adopted were not only the best of their kind, but carried out to absolute perfection. Had the letter been deposited within the range of their search, these fellows would, beyond a question, have found it."

I merely laughed—but he seemed quite serious in all that he said.

"The measures, then," he continued, "were good in their kind, and well executed; their defect lay in their being inapplicable to the case, and to the man. A certain set of highly ingenious resources are, with the Prefect, a sort of Proscrustean bed, to which he forcibly adapts his designs. But he perpetually errs by being too deep or too shallow, for the matter in hand; and many a schoolboy is a better reasoner than he. I knew one about eight years of age, whose success at guessing in the game of 'even and odd' attracted universal admiration. This game is simple, and is played with marbles. One player holds in his hand a number of these toys, and demands of another whether that number is even or odd. If the guess is right, the guesser wins one; if wrong, he loses one. The boy to whom I allude won all the marbles of the school. Of course he had some principle of guessing; and this lay in mere observation and admeasurement of the astuteness of his opponents. For example, an arrant simpleton is his opponent, and, holding up his closed hand, asks, 'Are they even or odd?' Our schoolboy replies, 'Odd,' and loses; but upon the second trial he wins, for he then says to himself, 'The simpleton had them even upon the first trial, and his amount of cunning is just sufficient to make him have them odd upon the second; I will therefore guess odd;'—he guesses odd, and wins. Now, with a simpleton a degree above the first, he would have reasoned thus: 'This fellow finds that in the first instance I guessed odd, and, in the second, he will propose to himself upon the first impulse, a simple variation from even to odd, as did the first simpleton; but then a second thought will suggest that

4. **Abernethy:** John Abernethy, celebrated English surgeon (1764–1831).

this is too simple a variation, and finally he will decide upon putting it even as before. I will therefore guess even;'—he guesses even, and wins. Now this mode of reasoning in the schoolboy, whom his fellows termed 'lucky,'—what, in its last analysis, is it?"

"It is merely," I said, "an identification of the reasoner's intellect with that of his opponent."

"It is," said Dupin; "and, upon inquiring of the boy by what means he effected the *thorough* identification in which his success consisted, I received answer as follows: 'When I wish to find out how wise, or how stupid, or how good, or how wicked is any one, or what are his thoughts at the moment, I fashion the expression of my face, as accurately as possible, in accordance with the expression of his, and then wait to see what thoughts or sentiments arise in my mind or heart, as if to match or correspond with the expression.' This response of the schoolboy lies at the bottom of all the spurious profundity which has been attributed to Rochefoucauld, to La Bougive, to Machiavelli, and to Campanella." [5]

"And the identification," I said, "of the reasoner's intellect with that of his opponent, depends, if I understand you aright, upon the accuracy with which the opponent's intellect is admeasured."

"For its practical value it depends upon this," replied Dupin; "and the Prefect and his cohort fail so frequently, first, by default of this identification, and, secondly, by ill-admeasurement, or rather through non-admeasurement, of the intellect with which they are engaged. They consider only their *own* ideas of ingenuity; and, in searching for anything hidden, advert only to the modes in which *they* would have hidden it. They are right in this much—that their own ingenuity is a faithful representative of that of *the mass;* but when the cunning of the individual felon is diverse in character from their own, the felon foils them, of course. This always happens when it is above their own, and very usually when it is below. They have no variation of principle in their investigations; at best, when urged by some unusual emergency—by some extraordinary reward—they extend or exaggerate their old modes of *practice,* without touching their principles. What, for example, in this case of D——, has been done to vary

the principle of action? What is all this boring, and probing, and sounding, and scrutinizing with the microscope, and dividing the surface of the building into registered square inches—what is it all but an exaggeration *of the application* of the one principle or set of principles of search, which are based upon the one set of notions regarding human ingenuity, to which the Prefect, in the long routine of his duty, has been accustomed? Do you not see he has taken it for granted that *all* men proceed to conceal a letter,—not exactly in a gimlet-hole bored in a chair-leg—but, at least, in *some* out-of-the-way hole or corner suggested by the same tenor of thought which would urge a man to secrete a letter in a gimlet-hole bored in a chair-leg? And do you not see also, that such *recherchés* nooks for concealment are adapted only for ordinary occasions, and would be adopted only by ordinary intellects; for, in all cases of concealment, a disposal of the article concealed—a disposal of it in this *recherché* manner,—is, in the very first instance, presumable and presumed; and thus its discovery depends, not at all upon the acumen, but altogether upon the mere care, patience, and determination of the seekers; and where the case is of importance—or, what amounts to the same thing in the policial eyes, when the reward is of magnitude,—the qualities in question have *never* been known to fail. You will now understand what I meant in suggesting that, had the purloined letter been hidden anywhere within the limits of the Prefect's examination—in other words, had the principle of its concealment been comprehended within the principles of the Prefect—its discovery would have been a matter altogether beyond question. This functionary, however, has been thoroughly mystified; and the remote source of his defeat lies in the supposition that the Minister is a fool, because he has acquired renown as a poet. All fools are poets; this the Prefect *feels;* and he is merely guilty of a *non distributio medii* [6] in thence inferring that all poets are fools."

"But is this really the poet?" I asked. "There are two brothers, I know; and both have attained reputation in letters. The Minister I believe has written learnedly on the Differential Calculus. He is a mathematician, and no poet."

"You are mistaken; I know him well; he is both. As poet *and* mathematician, he would reason well; as mere mathematician, he could not have reasoned at all, and thus would have been at the mercy of the Prefect."

"You surprise me," I said, "by these opinions, which have been contradicted by the voice of the

---

5. spurious . . . Campanella: The Duc de La Rochefoucauld (1613–80) was the author of *Moral Maxims and Reflections.* The name "La Bougive" is probably an error of transcription for "La Bruyère." Jean de la Bruyère (1645–96) was a brilliant depicter of manners and character. Niccoló Machiavelli wrote his study of statecraft, *The Prince,* in 1513. Tommaso Campanella wrote *The City of the Sun* (1643). What these authors represent to Poe is "psychological insight."

6. *non . . . medii:* an undistributed middle; a failure of logic.

world. You do not mean to set at naught the well-digested idea of centuries. The mathematical reason has long been regarded as *the* reason *par excellence.*"

" '*Il y a à parier,*' " replied Dupin, quoting from Chamfort,[7] " '*que toute idée publique, toute convention reçue, est une sottise, car elle a convenue au plus grand nombre.*' The mathematicians, I grant you, have done their best to promulgate the popular error to which you allude, and which is none the less an error for its promulgation as truth. With an art worthy a better cause, for example, they have insinuated the term 'analysis' into application to algebra. The French are the originators of this particular deception; but if a term is of any importance—if words derive any value from applicability—then 'analysis' conveys 'algebra' about as much as, in Latin, '*ambitus*' implies 'ambition,' '*religio*' 'religion,' or '*homines honesti,*' a set of *honorable* men."

"You have a quarrel on hand, I see," said I, "with some of the algebraists of Paris; but proceed."

"I dispute the availability, and thus the value, of that reason which is cultivated in any especial form other than the abstractly logical. I dispute, in particular, the reason educed by mathematical study. The mathematics are the science of form and quantity; mathematical reasoning is merely logic applied to observation upon form and quantity. The great error lies in supposing that even the truths of what is called *pure* algebra, are abstract or general truths. And this error is so egregious that I am confounded at the universality with which it has been received. Mathematical axioms are *not* axioms of general truth. What is true of *relation*— of form and quantity—is often grossly false in regard to morals, for example. In this latter science it is very usually *un*true that the aggregated parts are equal to the whole. In chemistry also the axiom fails. In the consideration of motive it fails; for two motives, each of a given value, have not, necessarily, a value when united, equal to the sum of their values apart. There are numerous other mathematical truths which are only truths within the limits of *relation*. But the mathematician argues from his *finite truths,* through habit, as if they were of an absolutely general applicability—as the world indeed imagines them to be. Bryant, in his very learned 'Mythology,' mentions an analogous source of error, when he says that 'although the Pagan fables are

not believed, yet we forget ourselves continually, and make inferences from them as existing realities.' With the algebraists, however, who are Pagans themselves, the 'Pagan fables' *are* believed, and the inferences are made, not so much through lapse of memory as through an unaccountable addling of the brains. In short, I never yet encountered the mere mathematician who would be trusted out of equal roots, or one who did not clandestinely hold it as a point of his faith that $x^2 + px$ was absolutely and unconditionally equal to $q$. Say to one of these gentlemen, by way of experiment, if you please, that you believe occasions may occur where $x^2 + px$ is *not* altogether equal to $q$, and, having made him understand what you mean, get out of his reach as speedily as convenient, for, beyond doubt, he will endeavor to knock you down.

"I mean to say," continued Dupin, while I merely laughed at his last observations, "that if the Minister had been no more than a mathematician, the Prefect would have been under no necessity of giving me this check. I knew him, however, as both mathematician and poet, and my measures were adapted to his capacity, with reference to the circumstances by which he was surrounded. I knew him as a courtier, too, and as a bold *intriguant.* Such a man, I considered, could not fail to be aware of the ordinary policial modes of action. He could not have failed to anticipate—and events have proved that he did not fail to anticipate—the waylayings to which he was subjected. He must have foreseen, I reflected, the secret investigations of his premises. His frequent absences from home at night, which were hailed by the Prefect as certain aids to his success, I regarded only as *ruses,* to afford opportunity for thorough search to the police, and thus the sooner to impress them with the conviction to which G——, in fact, did finally arrive—the conviction that the letter was not upon the premises. I felt, also, that the whole train of thought, which I was at some pains in detailing to you just now, concerning the invariable principle of policial action in searches for articles concealed—I felt that this whole train of thought would necessarily pass through the mind of the Minister. It would imperatively lead him to despise all the ordinary *nooks* of concealment. *He* could not, I reflected, be so weak as not to see that the most intricate and remote recess of his hotel would be as open as his commonest closets to the eyes, to the probes, to the gimlets, and to the microscopes of the Prefect. I saw, in fine, that he would be driven, as a matter of course, to *simplicity,* if not deliberately induced to it as a matter of choice. You will remember, perhaps, how desperately the

---

**7. Chamfort:** Nicolas Chamfort (1741–94). The quotation means, "The chances are that any popular idea, any accepted notion, is foolishness, since it has proved agreeable to the mass of mankind."

Prefect laughed when I suggested, upon our first interview, that it was just possible this mystery troubled him so much on account of its being so *very* self-evident."

"Yes," said I, "I remember his merriment well. I really thought he would have fallen into convulsions."

"The material world," continued Dupin, "abounds with very strict analogies to the immaterial; and thus some color of truth has been given to the rhetorical dogma, that metaphor, or simile, may be made to strengthen an argument as well as to embellish a description. The principle of the *vis inertiæ,* for example, seems to be identical in physics and metaphysics. It is not more true in the former, that a large body is with more difficulty set in motion than a smaller one, and that its subsequent *momentum* is commensurate with this difficulty, than it is, in the latter, that intellects of the vaster capacity, while more forcible, more constant, and more eventful in their movements than those of inferior grade, are yet the less readily moved, and more embarrassed and full of hesitation in the first few steps of their progress. Again: have you ever noticed which of the street signs, over the shop doors, are the most attractive of attention?"

"I have never given the matter a thought," I said.

"There is a game of puzzles," he resumed, "which is played upon a map. One party playing requires another to find a given word—the name of town, river, state or empire—any word, in short, upon the motley and perplexed surface of the chart. A novice in the game generally seeks to embarrass his opponents by giving them the most minutely lettered names; but the adept selects such words as stretch, in large characters, from one end of the chart to the other. These, like the over-largely lettered signs and placards of the street, escape observation by dint of being excessively obvious; and here the physical oversight is precisely analogous with the moral inapprehension by which the intellect suffers to pass unnoticed those considerations which are too obtrusively and too palpably self-evident. But this is a point, it appears, somewhat above or beneath the understanding of the Prefect. He never once thought it probable, or possible, that the Minister had deposited the letter immediately beneath the nose of the whole world, by way of best preventing any portion of that world from perceiving it.

"But the more I reflected upon the daring, dashing, and discriminating ingenuity of D——; upon the fact that the document must always have been *at hand,* if he intended to use it to good purpose; and upon the decisive evidence, obtained by the Prefect, that it was not hidden within the limits of that dignitary's ordinary search—the more satisfied I became that, to conceal this letter, the Minister had resorted to the comprehensive and sagacious expedient of not attempting to conceal it at all.

"Full of these ideas, I prepared myself with a pair of green spectacles,[8] and called one fine morning, quite by accident, at the Ministerial hotel. I found D—— at home, yawning, lounging, and dawdling, as usual, and pretending to be in the last extremity of *ennui.* He is, perhaps, the most really energetic human being now alive—but that is only when nobody sees him.

"To be even with him, I complained of my weak eyes, and lamented the necessity of the spectacles, under cover of which I cautiously and thoroughly surveyed the whole apartment, while seemingly intent only upon the conversation of my host.

"I paid especial attention to a large writing-table near which he sat, and upon which lay confusedly, some miscellaneous letters and other papers, with one or two musical instruments and a few books. Here, however, after a long and a very deliberate scrutiny, I saw nothing to excite particular suspicion.

"At length my eyes, in going the circuit of the room, fell upon a trumpery filigree card-rack of pasteboard, that hung dangling by a dirty blue ribbon, from a little brass knob just beneath the middle of the mantel-piece. In this rack, which had three or four compartments, were five or six visiting cards and a solitary letter. This last was much soiled and crumpled. It was torn nearly in two, across the middle—as if a design, in the first instance, to tear it entirely up as worthless, had been altered, or stayed, in the second. It had a large black seal, bearing the D—— cipher *very* conspicuously, and was addressed, in a diminutive female hand, to D——, the Minister, himself. It was thrust carelessly, and even, as it seemed, contemptuously, into one of the upper divisions of the rack.

"No sooner had I glanced at this letter than I concluded it to be that of which I was in search. To be sure, it was, to all appearance, radically different from the one of which the Prefect had read us so minute a description. Here the seal was large and black, with the D—— cipher; there it was small and red, with the ducal arms of the S—— family. Here, the address, to the Minister, was diminutive and feminine; there the superscription, to a certain royal personage, was markedly

8. **green spectacles:** Such spectacles are also worn by Dupin in "The Mystery of Marie Roget," and by the Devil in "Bon-Bon." The implication is that Dupin's visit to the Minister is an act of introspection.

bold and decided; the size alone formed a point of correspondence. But, then, the *radicalness* of these differences, which was excessive; the dirt; the soiled and torn condition of the paper, so inconsistent with the *true* methodical habits of D——, and so suggestive of a design to delude the beholder into an idea of the worthlessness of the document;—these things, together with the hyperobtrusive situation of this document, full in the view of every visiter, and thus exactly in accordance with the conclusions to which I had previously arrived; these things, I say, were strongly corroborative of suspicion, in one who came with the intention to suspect.

"I protracted my visit as long as possible, and, while I maintained a most animated discussion with the Minister, upon a topic which I knew well had never failed to interest and excite him, I kept my attention really riveted upon the letter. In this examination, I committed to memory its external appearance and arrangement in the rack; and also fell, at length, upon a discovery which set at rest whatever trivial doubt I might have entertained. In scrutinizing the edges of the paper, I observed them to be more *chafed* than seemed necessary. They presented the *broken* appearance which is manifested when a stiff paper, having been once folded and pressed with a folder, is refolded in a reversed direction, in the same creases or edges which had formed the original fold. This discovery was sufficient. It was clear to me that the letter had been turned, as a glove, inside out, redirected, and re-sealed. I bade the Minister good morning, and took my departure at once, leaving a gold snuff-box upon the table.

"The next morning I called for the snuff-box, when we resumed, quite eagerly, the conversation of the preceding day. While thus engaged, however, a loud report, as if of a pistol, was heard immediately beneath the windows of the hotel, and was succeeded by a series of fearful screams, and the shoutings of a mob. D—— rushed to a casement, threw it open, and looked out. In the meantime I stepped to the card-rack, took the letter, put it in my pocket, and replaced it by a *fac-simile,* (so far as regards externals) which I had carefully prepared at my lodgings; imitating the D—— cipher, very readily, by means of a seal formed of bread.

"The disturbance in the street had been occasioned by the frantic behavior of a man with a musket. He had fired it among a crowd of women and children. It proved, however, to have been without ball, and the fellow was suffered to go his way as a lunatic or a drunkard. When he had gone, D—— came from the window, whither I had followed him immediately upon securing the object in view. Soon afterward I bade him farewell. The pretended lunatic was a man in my own pay."

"But what purpose had you," I asked, "in replacing the letter by a *fac-simile?* Would it not have been better, at the first visit, to have seized it openly, and departed?"

"D——," replied Dupin, "is a desperate man, and a man of nerve. His hotel, too, is not without attendants devoted to his interests. Had I made the wild attempt you suggest, I might never have left the Ministerial presence alive. The good people of Paris might have heard of me no more. But I had an object apart from these considerations. You know my political prepossessions. In this matter, I act as a partisan of the lady concerned. For eighteen months the Minister has had her in his power. She has now him in hers; since, being unaware that the letter is not in his possession, he will proceed with his exactions as if it was. Thus will he inevitably commit himself, at once, to his political destruction. His downfall, too, will not be more precipitate than awkward. It is all very well to talk about the *facilis descensus Averni;* [9] but in all kinds of climbing, as Catalani [10] said of singing, it is far more easy to get up than to come down. In the present instance I have no sympathy—at least no pity—for him who descends. He is that *monstrum horrendum,* [11] an unprincipled man of genius. I confess, however, that I should like very well to know the precise character of his thoughts, when, being defied by her whom the Prefect terms 'a certain personage,' he is reduced to opening the letter which I left for him in the card-rack."

"How? did you put any thing particular in it?"

"Why—it did not seem altogether right to leave the interior blank—that would have been insulting. D——, at Vienna once, did me an evil turn, which I told him, quite good-humoredly, that I should remember. So, as I knew he would feel some curiosity in regard to the identity of the person who had outwitted him, I thought it a pity not to give him a clew. He is well acquainted with my MS., and I just copied into the middle of the blank sheet the words—

——Un dessein si funeste,
S'il n'est digne d'Atrée, est digne de Thyeste. [12]
They are to be found in Crébillon's *Atrée.*"

9. *facilis . . . Averni:* a quotation from Virgil, meaning "the descent to the infernal regions is easy" (*Aeneid,* VI.126). 10. **Catalani:** Angelica Catalani, Italian singer (1780–1849). 11. *monstrum horrendum:* "fearful monster." Also Vergilian. 12. Un . . . Thyeste: The quotation is taken from Prosper Jolyot de Crébillon's tragedy of 1707, *Atrée et Thyeste,* V.iv. It may be translated, "So dreadful a plot, / If unworthy of Atreus, is quite worthy of Thyestes." Crébillon's play is based upon the bloody rivalry of King Atreus of Mycenae and his brother Thyestes, and Poe's citation of it is a final hint that Dupin and the Minister are "brothers" or doubles.

# REVIEW OF NATHANIEL HAWTHORNE'S TWICE-TOLD TALES

❖

[IN THIS review (*Graham's Magazine*, May 1842), Poe proves his discernment by recognizing the merits of his contemporary. The review also offers a theory of the short story, a distinction between the provinces of poem and tale, and some observations on Hawthorne's use of "suggestion" which throw light on Poe's own intentions as a writer of fiction.

❖

THE PIECES in the volumes entitled *Twice-Told Tales,* are now in their third republication, and, of course, are thrice-told. Moreover, they are by no means *all* tales, either in the ordinary or in the legitimate understanding of the term. Many of them are pure essays; for example, "Sights from a Steeple," "Sunday at Home," "Little Annie's Ramble," "A Rill from the Town Pump," "The Toll-Gatherer's Day," "The Haunted Mind," "The Sister Years," "Snow-Flakes," "Night Sketches," and "Foot-Prints on the Sea-Shore." I mention these matters chiefly on account of their discrepancy with that marked precision and finish by which the body of the work is distinguished.

Of the Essays just named, I must be content to speak in brief. They are each and all beautiful, without being characterized by the polish and adaptation so visible in the tales proper. A painter would at once note their leading or predominant feature, and style it *repose*. There is no attempt at effect. All is quiet, thoughtful, subdued. Yet this repose may exist simultaneously with high originality of thought; and Mr. Hawthorne has demonstrated the fact. At every turn we meet with novel combination; yet these combinations never surpass the limits of the quiet. We are soothed as we read; and with all is a calm astonishment that ideas so apparently obvious have never occurred or been presented to us before. Herein our author differs materially from Lamb or Hunt or Hazlitt—who, with vivid originality of manner and expression, have less of the true novelty of thought than is generally supposed, and whose originality, at best, has an uneasy and meretricious quaintness, replete with startling effects unfounded in nature, and inducing trains of reflection which lead to no satisfactory result. The Essays of Hawthorne have much of the

character of Irving, with more of originality, and less of finish; while, compared with the *Spectator,*[1] they have a vast superiority at all points. The *Spectator,* Mr. Irving, and Hawthorne have in common that tranquil and subdued manner which I have chosen to denominate *repose;* but, in the case of the two former, this repose is attained rather by the absence of novel combination, or of originality, than otherwise, and consists chiefly in the calm, quiet, unostentatious expression of commonplace thoughts, in an unambitious, unadulterated Saxon. In them, by strong effort, we are made to conceive the absence of all. In the essays before me the absence of effort is too obvious to be mistaken, and a strong undercurrent of *suggestion* runs continuously beneath the upper stream of the tranquil thesis.[2] In short, these effusions of Mr. Hawthorne are the product of a truly imaginative intellect, restrained, and in some measure repressed, by fastidiousness of taste, by constitutional melancholy, and by indolence.

But it is of his tales that I desire principally to speak. The tale proper, in my opinion, affords unquestionably the fairest field for the exercise of the loftiest talent, which can be afforded by the wide domains of mere prose. Were I bidden to say how the highest genius could be most advantageously employed for the best display of its own powers, I should answer, without hesitation—in the composition of a rhymed poem, not to exceed in length what might be perused in an hour. Within this limit alone can the highest order of true poetry exist. I need only here say, upon this topic, that, in almost all classes of composition, the unity of effect or impression is a point of the greatest importance. It is clear, moreover, that this unity cannot be thoroughly preserved in productions whose perusal cannot be completed at one sitting. We may continue the reading of a prose composition, from the very nature of prose itself, much longer than we can persevere, to any good purpose, in the perusal of a poem. This latter, if truly fulfilling the demands of the poetic sentiment, induces an exaltation of the soul which cannot be long sustained. All high excitements are necessarily transient. Thus a long poem is a paradox. And, without unity of impression, the deepest effects cannot be brought about. Epics were the offspring of an imperfect sense of Art, and their reign is no more. A poem *too* brief may produce a vivid, but never an intense or enduring impression. Without a certain continuity of effort—without a certain duration of repeti-

REVIEW OF HAWTHORNE. 1. the *Spectator:* The *Spectator* was written and published, during 1711–14, by Joseph Addison and Richard Steele. 2. strong . . . thesis: See the latter paragraphs of Poe's review of Moore's *Alciphron*.

tion or purpose—the soul is never deeply moved. There must be the dropping of the water upon the rock. De Béranger has wrought brilliant things— pungent and spirit-stirring—but, like all immassive bodies, they lack *momentum,* and thus fail to satisfy the poetic Sentiment. They sparkle and excite, but, from want of continuity, fail deeply to impress. Extreme brevity will degenerate into epigrammatism; but the sin of extreme length is more unpardonable. *In medio tutissimus ibis.*[3]

Were I called upon, however, to designate that class of composition which, next to such a poem as I have suggested, should best fulfil the demands of high genius—should offer it the most advantageous field of exertion—I should unhesitatingly speak of the prose tale as Mr. Hawthorne has here exemplified it. I allude to the short prose narrative, requiring from a half-hour to one or two hours in its perusal. The ordinary novel is objectionable, from its length, for reasons already stated in substance. As it cannot be read at one sitting, it deprives itself, of course, of the immense force derivable from *totality.* Worldly interests intervening during the pauses of perusal, modify, annul, or counteract, in a greater or less degree, the impressions of the book. But simple cessation in reading would, of itself, be sufficient to destroy the true unity. In the brief tale, however, the author is enabled to carry out the fulness of his intention, be it what it may. During the hour of perusal the soul of the reader is at the writer's control. There are no external or extrinsic influences—resulting from weariness or interruption.

A skilful literary artist has constructed a tale. If wise, he has not fashioned his thoughts to accommodate his incidents; but having conceived, with deliberate care, a certain unique or single *effect* to be wrought out, he then invents such incidents— he then combines such events as may best aid him in establishing this preconceived effect. If his very initial sentence tend not to the outbringing of this effect, then he has failed in his first step. In the whole composition there should be no word written, of which the tendency, direct or indirect, is not to the one pre-established design. And by such means, with such care and skill, a picture is at length painted which leaves in the mind of him who contemplates it with a kindred art, a sense of the fullest satisfaction. The idea of the tale has been presented unblemished, because undisturbed; and this is an end unattainable by the novel. Undue brevity is just as exceptionable here as in the poem; but undue length is yet more to be avoided.

We have said that the tale has a point of superiority even over the poem. In fact, while the *rhythm* of this latter is an essential aid in the development of the poem's highest idea—the idea of the Beautiful—the artificialities of this rhythm are an inseparable bar to the development of all points of thought or expression which have their basis in *Truth.* But Truth is often, and in very great degree, the aim of the tale. Some of the finest tales are tales of ratiocination. Thus the field of this species of composition, if not in so elevated a region on the mountain of Mind, is a table-land of far vaster extent than the domain of the mere poem. Its products are never so rich, but infinitely more numerous, and more appreciable by the mass of mankind. The writer of the prose tale, in short, may bring to his theme a vast variety of modes or inflections of thought and expression—(the ratiocinative, for example, the sarcastic or the humorous) which are not only antagonistical to the nature of the poem, but absolutely forbidden by one of its most peculiar and indispensable adjuncts; we allude, of course, to rhythm. It may be added, here, *par parenthèse,* that the author who aims at the purely beautiful in a prose tale is laboring at a great disadvantage. For Beauty can be better treated in the poem. Not so with terror, or passion, or horror, or a multitude of such other points. And here it will be seen how full of prejudice are the usual animadversions against those *tales of effect,* many fine examples of which were found in the earlier numbers of Blackwood. The impressions produced were wrought in a legitimate sphere of action, and constituted a legitimate although sometimes an exaggerated interest. They were relished by every man of genius: although there were found many men of genius who condemned them without just ground. The true critic will but demand that the design intended be accomplished, to the fullest extent, by means most advantageously applicable.

We have very few American tales of real merit —we may say, indeed, none, with the exception of *The Tales of a Traveller* of Washington Irving, and these *Twice-Told Tales* of Mr. Hawthorne. Some of the pieces of Mr. John Neal[4] abound in vigor and originality; but in general, his compositions of this class are excessively diffuse, extravagant, and indicative of an imperfect sentiment of Art. Articles at random are, now and then, met with in our periodicals which might be advantageously compared with the best effusions of the British Magazines; but, upon the whole, we are far behind our progenitors in this department of literature.

3. *In medio . . . ibis:* "It is safest to keep to the middle way."

4. **John Neal:** novelist, poet, and critic (1793–1876), who in December 1829, wrote an appreciative notice of Poe's "Al Aaraaf" in his literary periodical the *Yankee.*

Of Mr. Hawthorne's Tales we would say, emphatically, that they belong to the highest region of Art—an Art subservient to genius of a very lofty order. We had supposed, with good reason for so supposing, that he had been thrust into his present position by one of the impudent *cliques* which beset our literature, and whose pretensions it is our full purpose to expose at the earliest opportunity; but we have been most agreeably mistaken. We know of few compositions which the critic can more honestly commend than these *Twice-Told Tales*. As Americans, we feel proud of the book.

Mr. Hawthorne's distinctive trait is invention, creation, imagination, originality—a trait which, in the literature of fiction, is positively worth all the rest. But the nature of the originality, so far as regards its manifestation in letters, is but imperfectly understood. The inventive or original mind as frequently displays itself in novelty of *tone* as in novelty of matter. Mr. Hawthorne is original in *all* points.

It would be a matter of some difficulty to designate the best of these tales; we repeat that, without exception, they are beautiful. "Wakefield" is remarkable for the skill with which an old idea—a well-known incident—is worked up or discussed. A man of whims conceives the purpose of quitting his wife and residing *incognito,* for twenty years in her immediate neighborhood. Something of this kind actually happened in London. The force of Mr. Hawthorne's tale lies in the analysis of the motives which must or might have impelled the husband to such folly, in the first instance, with the possible causes of his perseverance. Upon this thesis a sketch of singular power has been constructed. "The Wedding Knell" is full of the boldest imagination—an imagination fully controlled by taste. The most captious critic could find no flaw in this production. "The Minister's Black Veil" is a masterly composition of which the sole defect is that to the rabble its exquisite skill will be *caviare.* The *obvious* meaning of this article will be found to smother its insinuated one.[5] The *moral* put into the mouth of the dying minister will be supposed to convey the *true* import of the narrative; and that a crime of dark dye (having reference to the "young lady") has been committed is a point which only minds congenial with that of the author will perceive. "Mr. Higginbotham's Catastrophe" is vividly original and managed most dexterously.

5. The . . . one: On the other hand, the insinuated meaning must not be too clear: in "The Philosophy of Composition," Poe wrote, "It is the *excess* of the suggested meaning—it is the rendering this the upper instead of the under current of the theme—which turns into prose (and that of the very flattest kind) the so-called poetry of the so-called transcendentalists."

"Dr. Heidegger's Experiment" is exceedingly well imagined, and executed with surpassing ability. The artist breathes in every line of it. "The White Old Maid" is objectionable, even more than the "Minister's Black Veil," on the score of its mysticism. Even with the thoughtful and analytic, there will be much trouble in penetrating its entire import.

"The Hollow of the Three Hills" we would quote in full, had we space;—not as evincing higher talent than any of the other pieces, but as affording an excellent example of the author's peculiar ability. The subject is commonplace. A witch subjects the Distant and the Past to the view of a mourner. It has been the fashion to describe, in such cases, a mirror in which the images of the absent appear; or a cloud of smoke is made to arise, and thence the figures are gradually unfolded. Mr. Hawthorne has wonderfully heightened his effect by making the ear, in place of the eye, the medium by which the fantasy is conveyed. The head of the mourner is enveloped in the cloak of the witch, and within its magic folds there arise sounds which have an all-sufficient intelligence. Throughout this article also, the artist is conspicuous—not more in positive than in negative merits. Not only is all done that should be done, but (what perhaps is an end with more difficulty attained) there is nothing done which should not be. Every word *tells,* and there is not a word which does *not* tell.

In "Howe's Masquerade" we observe something which resembles a plagiarism—but which *may* be a very flattering coincidence of thought. We quote the passage in question.

*With a dark flush of wrath* upon his brow they saw the general *draw his sword* and *advance to meet* the figure *in the cloak* before the latter had stepped one pace upon the floor. *"Villain, unmuffle yourself,"* cried he, "you pass no farther!" The figure, without blenching a hair's breadth from the sword which was pointed at his breast, made a solemn pause, and *lowered the cape of the cloak* from his face, yet not sufficiently for the spectators to catch a glimpse of it. But Sir William Howe had evidently seen enough. The sternness of his countenance gave place to a look of wild amazement, if not horror, while he recoiled several steps from the figure, *and let fall his sword upon the floor.*—See vol. 2, p. 20.

The idea here is, that the figure in the cloak is the phantom or reduplication of Sir William Howe; but in an article called "William Wilson," one of the "Tales of the Grotesque and Arabesque," we have not only the same idea, but the same idea similarly presented in several respects. We quote two paragraphs, which our readers may compare with what has been already given. We have italicized, above, the immediate particulars of resemblance.

The brief moment in which I averted my eyes had been sufficient to produce, apparently, a material change in the arrangement at the upper or farther end of the room. A large mirror, it appeared to me, now stood where none had been perceptible before; and as I stepped up to it in extremity of terror, mine own image, but with features all pale and dabbled in blood, *advanced* with a feeble and tottering gait to meet me. Thus it appeared I say, but was not. It was Wilson, who then stood before me in the agonies of dissolution. Not a line in all the marked and singular lineaments of that face which was not even identically mine own. *His mask and cloak lay where he had thrown them, upon the floor.* Vol. 2, p. 336.

Here, it will be observed that, not only are the two general conceptions identical, but there are various *points* of similarity. In each case the figure seen is the wraith or duplication of the beholder. In each case the scene is a masquerade. In each case the figure is cloaked. In each, there is a quarrel—that is to say, angry words pass between the parties. In each the beholder is enraged. In each the cloak and sword fall upon the floor. The "villain, unmuffle yourself," of Mr. H. is precisely paralleled [6] by a passage at page 56, of "William Wilson."

I must hasten to conclude this paper with a summary of Mr. Hawthorne's merits and demerits.

He is peculiar and *not* original—unless in those detailed fancies and detached thoughts which his want of general originality will deprive of the appreciation due to them, in preventing them from ever reaching the *public* eye. He is infinitely too fond of allegory, and can never hope for popularity so long as he persists in it. This he will not do, for allegory is at war with the whole tone of his nature, which disports itself never so well as when escaping from the mysticism of his Goodman Browns and White Old Maids into the hearty, genial, but still Indian-summer sunshine of his Wakefields and Little Annie's Rambles. Indeed, *his* spirit of "metaphor run-mad" is clearly imbibed from the phalanx and phalanstery [7] atmosphere in which he has been so long struggling for breath. He has not half the material for the exclusiveness of authorship that he possesses for its universality. He has the purest style, the finest taste, the most

available scholarship, the most delicate humor, the most touching pathos, the most radiant imagination, the most consummate ingenuity; and with these varied good qualities he has done *well* as a mystic. But is there any one of these qualities which should prevent his doing doubly as well in a career of honest, upright, sensible, prehensible and comprehensible things? Let him mend his pen, get a bottle of visible ink, come out from the Old Manse, cut Mr. Alcott, hang (if possible) the editor of the *Dial,* and throw out of the window to the pigs all his odd numbers of the *North American Review.*[8]

FROM

# THE POETIC PRINCIPLE

❖

❨ POE gave this lecture a number of times toward the end of his life, in Providence, Richmond, and elsewhere. It was published after his death in the New York *Home Journal* for August 31, 1850. The text derives, in great part, from Poe's review of Longfellow's *Ballads* in *Graham's Magazine* for April 1842.

❖

WHILE the epic mania—while the idea that, to merit in poetry, prolixity is indispensable—has, for some years past, been gradually dying out of the public mind, by mere dint of its own absurdity, we find it succeeded by a heresy too palpably false to be long tolerated, but one which, in the brief period it has already endured, may be said to have accomplished more in the corruption of our Poetical Literature than all its other enemies combined. I allude to the heresy of *The Didactic.* It has been assumed, tacitly and avowedly, directly and indirectly, that the ultimate object of all Poetry is Truth. Every poem, it is said, should inculcate a moral; and by this moral is the poetical merit of the work to be adjudged. We Americans especially have patronised this happy idea; and we Bostonians, very especially, have developed it in full. We have taken it into our heads that to write a poem simply for the poem's sake, and to acknowledge such to have been our design, would be to confess ourselves radically wanting in the true Poetic dignity and force:—but the simple fact is,

---

6. **precisely paralleled:** Hawthorne could not have plagiarized, since his story appeared in the *Democratic Review* of May 1838, and "William Wilson" in *Burton's* for October 1839.   7. **phalanx and phalanstery:** The communal experiment at Brook Farm had begun in 1841.

8. **Let . . . *Review:*** Poe refers to Bronson Alcott (1799–1888), Transcendentalist philosopher, and to Margaret Fuller (1810–50), editor of the *Dial.* The *North American Review*, while not a Transcendentalist organ, did publish some members of the group.

that, would we but permit ourselves to look into our own souls, we should immediately there discover that under the sun there neither exists nor *can* exist any work more thoroughly dignified— more supremely noble—than this very poem— this poem *per se*—this poem which is a poem and nothing more—this poem written solely for the poem's sake.

With as deep a reverence for the True as ever inspired the bosom of man, I would, nevertheless, limit, in some measure, its modes of inculcation. I would limit to enforce them. I would not enfeeble them by dissipation. The demands of Truth are severe. She has no sympathy with the myrtles. All *that* which is so indispensable in Song, is precisely all *that* with which *she* has nothing whatever to do. It is but making her a flaunting paradox, to wreathe her in gems and flowers. In enforcing a truth, we need severity rather than efflorescence of language. We must be simple, precise, terse. We must be cool, calm, unimpassioned. In a word, we must be in that mood which, as nearly as possible, is the exact converse of the poetical. *He* must be blind indeed who does not perceive the radical and chasmal differences between the truthful and the poetical modes of inculcation. He must be theory-mad beyond redemption who, in spite of these differences, shall still persist in attempting to reconcile the obstinate oils and waters of Poetry and Truth.

Dividing the world of mind into its three most immediately obvious distinctions, we have the Pure Intellect, Taste, and the Moral Sense. I place Taste in the middle, because it is just this position which, in the mind, it occupies. It holds intimate relations with either extreme; but from the Moral Sense is separated by so faint a difference that Aristotle has not hesitated to place some of its operations among the virtues themselves. Nevertheless, we find the offices of the trio marked with a sufficient distinction. Just as the Intellect concerns itself with Truth, so Taste informs us of the Beautiful while the Moral Sense is regardful of Duty. Of this latter, while Conscience teaches the obligation, and Reason the expediency, Taste contents herself with displaying the charms:—waging war upon Vice solely on the ground of her deformity—her disproportion—her animosity to the fitting, to the appropriate, to the harmonious—in a word, to Beauty.

An immortal instinct, deep within the spirit of man, is thus, plainly, a sense of the Beautiful. This it is which administers to his delight in the manifold forms, and sounds, and odours, and sentiments amid which he exists. And just as the lily is repeated in the lake, or the eyes of Amaryllis in the mirror, so is the mere oral or written repetition of these forms, and sounds, and colours, and odours, and sentiments, a duplicate source of delight. But this mere repetition is not poetry. He who shall simply sing, with however glowing enthusiasm, or with however vivid a truth of description, of the sights, and sounds, and odours, and colours, and sentiments, which greet *him* in common with all mankind—he, I say, has yet failed to prove his divine title. There is still a something in the distance which he has been unable to attain. We have still a thirst unquenchable, to allay which he has not shown us the crystal springs. This thirst belongs to the immortality of Man. It is at once a consequence and an indication of his perennial existence. It is the desire of the moth for the star.[1] It is no mere appreciation of the Beauty before us—but a wild effort to reach the Beauty above. Inspired by an ecstatic prescience of the glories beyond the grave, we struggle, by multiform combinations among the things and thoughts of Time, to attain a portion of that Loveliness whose very elements, perhaps, appertain to eternity alone. And thus when by Poetry—or when by Music, the most entrancing of the Poetic moods—we find ourselves melted into tears—we weep then—not as the Abbate Gravina[2] supposes—through excess of pleasure, but through a certain petulant, impatient sorrow at our inability to grasp *now* wholly, here on earth, at once and for ever, those divine and rapturous joys, of which *through* the poem, or *through* the music, we attain to but brief and indeterminate glimpses.

The struggle to apprehend the supernal Loveliness—this struggle, on the part of souls fittingly constituted—has given to the world all *that* which it (the world) has ever been enabled at once to understand and to *feel* as poetic.

The Poetic Sentiment, of course, may develop itself in various modes—in Painting, in Sculpture, in Architecture, in the Dance—very especially in Music,—and very peculiarly, and with a wide field, in the composition of the Landscape Garden. Our present theme, however, has regard only to its manifestation in words. And here let me speak briefly on the topic of rhythm. Contenting myself with the certainty that Music, in its various modes of metre, rhythm, and rhyme, is of so vast a moment in Poetry as never to be wisely rejected—is so vitally important an adjunct, that he is simply silly who declines its assistance, I will not now pause to maintain its absolute essentiality. It is in Music, perhaps, that the soul most nearly attains the great end for which, when inspired by the Po-

THE POETIC PRINCIPLE. 1. desire . . . star: echoes Shelley's poem, "One word is too often profaned." 2. Gravina: Gian Vincenzo Gravina, author of *Della Ragion Poetica* (1708).

etic Sentiment, it struggles—the creation of supernal Beauty. It *may* be, indeed, that here this sublime end is, now and then, attained *in fact*. We are often made to feel, with a shivering delight, that from an earthly harp are stricken notes which *cannot* have been unfamiliar to the angels.[3] And thus there can be little doubt that in the union of Poetry with Music in its popular sense, we shall find the widest field for the Poetic development. The old Bards and Minnesingers had advantages which we do not possess—and Thomas Moore, singing his own songs, was, in the most legitimate manner, perfecting them as poems.

To recapitulate, then:—I would define, in brief, the Poetry of words as *The Rhythmical Creation of Beauty*. Its sole arbiter is Taste. With the Intellect or with the Conscience, it has only collateral relations. Unless incidentally, it has no concern whatever either with Duty or with Truth.

A few words, however, in explanation. *That* pleasure which is at once the most pure, the most elevating, and the most intense, is derived, I maintain, from the contemplation of the Beautiful. In the contemplation of Beauty we alone find it possible to attain that pleasurable elevation, or excitement, *of the soul,* which we recognize as the Poetic Sentiment, and which is so easily distinguished from Truth, which is the satisfaction of the Reason, or from Passion, which is the excitement of the heart. I make Beauty, therefore—using the word as inclusive of the sublime—I make Beauty the province of the poem, simply because it is an obvious rule of Art that effects should be made to spring as directly as possible from their causes—no one as yet having been weak enough to deny that the peculiar elevation in question is at least *most readily* attainable in the poem. It by no means follows, however, that the incitements of Passion, or the precepts of Duty, or even the lessons of Truth, may not be introduced into a poem, and with advantage; for they may subserve, incidentally, in various ways, the general purposes of the work:—but the true artist will always contrive to tone them down in proper subjection to that *Beauty* which is the atmosphere and the real essence of the poem. . . .

. . . While this [the poetic] Principle itself is, strictly and simply, the Human Aspiration for Supernal Beauty, the manifestation of the Principle is always found in *an elevating excitement of the Soul*—quite independent of that passion which is the intoxication of the Heart—or of that Truth which is the satisfaction of the Reason. For, in regard to Passion, alas! its tendency is to degrade rather than elevate the Soul. Love, on the contrary—Love—the true, the divine Eros—the Uranian, as distinguished from the Dionaean Venus[4]—is unquestionably the purest and truest of all poetical themes. And in regard to Truth—if, to be sure, through the attainment of a truth, we are led to perceive a harmony where none was apparent before, we experience, at once, the true poetical effect—but this effect is referable to the harmony alone, and not in the least degree to the truth which merely served to render the harmony manifest.

---

F R O M

# MARGINALIA

---

◇

⟨ THE "Marginalia" were published in various magazines during the period 1844–49. Often they were culled from Poe's earlier reviews, but more often they were fresh observations. The first selection below is most important to an understanding of Poe, dealing as it does with what W. B. Yeats called "that marchland between waking and dreaming where our thoughts begin to have a life of their own—the region where art is nurtured and inspiration born."

◇

How very commonly we hear it remarked, that such and such thoughts are beyond the compass of words! I do not believe that any thought, properly so called, is out of the reach of language. I fancy, rather, that where difficulty in expression is experienced, there is, in the intellect which experiences it, a want either of deliberateness or of method. For my own part, I have never had a thought which I could not set down in words, with even more distinctness than that with which I conceived it:—as I have before observed, the thought is logicalized by the effort at (written) expression.

There is, however, a class of fancies, of exquisite delicacy, which are *not* thoughts, and to which, *as yet,* I have found it absolutely impossible to adapt language. I use the word *fancies* at random, and

---

3. **We . . . angels:** recalls Poe's poem "Israfel," p. 191.

4. **Uranian . . . Venus:** The Uranian Aphrodite represents heavenly or spiritual love and beauty; Aphrodite, regarded as the offspring of Zeus and the Titaness Dione, is a lower or earthly principle. Milton invokes Urania, in preference to the Muses of Helicon, in his *Paradise Lost*, I and VII. Compare the opposition of moon and Venus in Poe's poem "Evening Star," p. 190.

merely because I must use *some* word; but the idea commonly attached to the term is not even remotely applicable to the shadows of shadows in question. They seem to me rather psychal than intellectual. They arise in the soul (alas, how rarely!) only at its epochs of most intense tranquillity—when the bodily and mental health are in perfection—and at those mere points of time where the confines of the waking world blend with those of the world of dreams. I am aware of these "fancies" only when I am upon the very brink of sleep, with the consciousness that I am so. I have satisfied myself that this condition exists but for an inappreciable *point* of time—yet it is crowded with these "shadows of shadows"; and for absolute *thought* there is demanded time's *endurance*. These "fancies" have in them a pleasurable ecstasy, as far beyond the most pleasurable of the world of wakefulness, or of dreams, as the Heaven of the Northman theology is beyond its Hell. I regard the visions, even as they arise, with an awe which, in some measure, moderates or tranquillizes the ecstasy—I so regard them, through a conviction (which seems a portion of the ecstasy itself) that this ecstasy, in itself, is of a character supernal to the Human Nature—is a glimpse of the spirit's outer world; and I arrive at this conclusion—if this term is at all applicable to instantaneous intuition—by a perception that the delight experienced has, as its element, but *the absoluteness of novelty*. I say the absoluteness—for in these fancies—let me now term them psychal impressions —there is really nothing even approximate in character to impressions ordinarily received. It is as if the five senses were supplanted by five myriad others alien to mortality.

Now, so entire is my faith in the *power of words,* that, at times, I have believed it possible to embody even the evanescence of fancies such as I have attempted to describe. In experiments with this end in view, I have proceeded so far as, first, to control (when the bodily and mental health are good) the existence of the condition:—that is to say, I can now (unless when ill) be sure that the condition will supervene, if I so wish it, at the point of time already described: of its supervention, until lately, I could never be certain, even under the most favorable circumstances. I mean to say, merely, that now I can be sure, when all circumstances are favorable, of the supervention of the condition, and feel even the capacity of inducing or compelling it:—the favorable circumstances, however, are not the less rare—else had I compelled, already, the Heaven into the earth.

I have proceeded so far, secondly, as to prevent the lapse from *the point* of which I speak—the point of blending between wakefulness and sleep

—as to prevent at will, I say, the lapse from this border-ground into the dominion of sleep. Not that I can *continue* the condition—not that I can render the point more than a point—but that I can startle myself from the point into wakefulness— and *thus transfer the point itself into the realm of Memory*—convey its impressions, or more properly their recollections, to a situation where (although still for a brief period) I can survey them with the eye of analysis.

For these reasons—that is to say, because I have been enabled to accomplish thus much—I do not altogether despair of embodying in words at least enough of the fancies in question to convey, to certain classes of intellect, a shadowy conception of their character.

In saying this I am not to be understood as supposing that the fancies, or psychal impressions, to which I allude, are confined to my individual self —are not, in a word, common to all mankind—for on this point it is quite impossible that I should form an opinion—but nothing can be more certain than that even a partial record of the impressions would startle the universal intellect of mankind, by the *supremeness of the novelty* of the material employed, and of its consequent suggestions. In a word—should I ever write a paper on this topic, the world will be compelled to acknowledge that, at last, I have done an original thing.

THERE are moments when, even to the sober eye of Reason, the world of our sad humanity must assume the aspect of Hell; but the Imagination of Man is no Carathis,[1] to explore with impunity its every cavern. Alas! the grim legion of sepulchral terrors can*not* be regarded as altogether fanciful; but like the Demons in whose company Afrasiab[2] made his voyage down the Oxus, they must sleep, or they will devour us— they must be suffered to slumber, or we perish. IF any ambitious man have a fancy to revolutionize, at one effort, the universal world of human thought, human opinion, and human sentiment, the opportunity is his own—the road to immortal renown lies straight, open, and unencumbered before him. All that he has to do is write and publish a very little book. Its title should be simple—a few plain words—*My Heart Laid Bare*. But—this little book must be *true to its title*.

Now, is it not very singular that, with the rabid thirst for notoriety which distinguishes so many of

MARGINALIA.   1. Carathis: mother of the Caliph Vathek, in William Beckford's oriental tale, *Vathek* (1786).   2. Afrasiab: the King of Turan, defeated by Rustum in the *Shahnameh*, an epic composed by the Persian poet Firdusi (950–1020).

mankind—so many, too, who care not a fig what is thought of them after death, there should not be found one man having sufficient hardihood to write this little book? To *write,* I say. There are ten thousand men who, if the book were once written, would laugh at the notion of being disturbed by its publication during their life, and who could not even conceive *why* they should object to its being published after their death. But to write it—*there* is the rub. No man dare write it. No man ever will dare write it. No man *could* write it, even if he dared. The paper would shrivel and blaze at every touch of the fiery pen.

I HAVE sometimes amused myself by endeavoring to fancy what would be the fate of any individual gifted, or rather accursed, with an intellect *very* far superior to that of his race. Of course, he would be conscious of his superiority; nor could he (if otherwise constituted as man is) help manifesting his consciousness. Thus he would make himself enemies at all points. And since his opinions and speculations would widely differ from those of *all* mankind—that he would be considered a madman, is evident. How horribly painful such a condition! Hell could invent no greater torture than that of being charged with abnormal weakness on account of being abnormally strong.

In like manner, nothing can be clearer than that a *very* generous spirit—*truly* feeling what all merely profess—must inevitably find itself misconceived in every direction—its motives misinterpreted. Just as extremeness of intelligence would be thought fatuity, so excess of chivalry could not fail of being looked upon as meanness in its last degree:—and so on with other virtues. This subject is a painful one indeed. That individuals *have* so soared above the plane of their race, is scarcely to be questioned; but, in looking back through history for traces of their existence, we should pass over all biographies of "the good and the great," while we search carefully the slight records of wretches who died in prison, in Bedlam, or upon the gallows.

---

FROM

# EUREKA

---

❖

⟨ THE FOLLOWING are the concluding paragraphs of Poe's cosmological prose poem of 1848, the general outlines of which are sketched in Part III of the Introduction. This closing passage is particularly valuable for its account of the soul's history: its previous existence, dur-

ing which it was cognizant of divine harmony; its dreamy youth on Earth; its corruption by the "conventional World-Reason"; its occasional glimpses or memories, during manhood, of its cosmic destiny; its preordained escape from material diversity into the spiritual oneness of God. All of Poe's fiction is in some measure based on this myth of the soul.

❖

I REPEAT then—Let us endeavor to comprehend that the final globe of globes will instantaneously disappear, and that God will remain all in all.

But are we here to pause? Not so. On the Universal agglomeration and dissolution, we can readily conceive that a new and perhaps totally different series of conditions may ensue—another creation and irradiation, returning into itself—another action and reaction of the Divine Will. Guiding our imaginations by that omniprevalent law of laws, the law of periodicity, are we not, indeed, more than justified in entertaining a belief—let us say, rather, in indulging a hope—that the processes we have here ventured to contemplate will be renewed forever, and forever, and forever; a novel Universe swelling into existence, and then subsiding into nothingness, at every throb of the Heart Divine?

And now—this Heart Divine—what is it? *It is our own.*

Let not the merely seeming irreverence of this idea frighten our souls from that cool exercise of consciousness—from that deep tranquillity of self-inspection—through which alone we can hope to attain the presence of this, the most sublime of truths, and look it leisurely in the face.

The *phaenomena* on which our conclusions must at this point depend, are merely spiritual shadows, but not the less thoroughly substantial.

We walk about, amid the destinies of our world-existence, encompassed by dim but ever present *Memories* of a Destiny more vast—very distant in the bygone time, and infinitely awful.

We live out a Youth peculiarly haunted by such dreams; yet never mistaking them for dreams. As Memories we *know* them. *During our Youth* the distinction is too clear to deceive us even for a moment.

So long as this Youth endures, the feeling *that we exist,* is the most natural of all feelings. We understand it *thoroughly.* That there was a period at which we did *not* exist—or, that it might so have happened that we never had existed at all—are the considerations, indeed, which *during this youth,* we find difficulty in understanding. Why we should *not* exist, is, *up to the epoch of our Manhood,* of all queries the most unanswerable. Existence—self-existence—existence from all Time and to all Eternity—seems, up to the epoch of Manhood, a normal and unquestionable condition:—*seems, because it is.*

But now comes the period at which a conventional World-Reason awakens us from the truth of our dream. Doubt, Surprise and Incomprehensibility arrive at the same moment. They say:—"You live and the time was when you lived not. You have been created. An Intelligence exists greater than your own; and it is only through this Intelligence you live at all." These things we struggle to comprehend and cannot:—*cannot,* because these things, being untrue, are thus, of necessity, incomprehensible.

No thinking being lives who, at some luminous point of his life of thought, has not felt himself lost amid the surges of futile efforts at understanding, or believing, that anything exists *greater than his own soul.* The utter impossibility of any one's soul feeling itself inferior to another; the intense, overwhelming dissatisfaction and rebellion at the thought;—these, with the omniprevalent aspirations at perfection, are but the spiritual, coincident with the material, struggles towards the original Unity—are, to my mind at least, a species of proof far surpassing what Man terms demonstration, that no one soul *is* inferior to another—that nothing is, or can be, superior to any one soul—that each soul is, in part, its own God—its own Creator:—in a word, that God—the material *and* spiritual God—*now* exists solely in the diffused Matter and Spirit of the Universe; and that the regathering of this diffused Matter and Spirit will be but the reconstitution of the *purely* Spiritual and Individual God.

In this view, and in this view alone, we comprehend the riddles of Divine Injustice—of Inexorable Fate. In this view alone the existence of Evil becomes intelligible; but in this view it becomes more—it becomes endurable. Our souls no longer rebel at a *Sorrow* which we ourselves have imposed upon ourselves, in furtherance of our own purposes—with a view—if even with a futile view —to the extension of our own *Joy.*

I have spoken of *Memories* that haunt us during our youth. They sometimes pursue us even in our Manhood:—assume gradually less and less indefinite shapes:—now and then speak to us with low voices, saying:

"There was an epoch in the Night of Time, when a still-existent Being existed—one of an absolutely infinite number of similar Beings that people the absolutely infinite domains of the absolutely infinite space. It was not and is not in the power of this Being—any more than it is in your own—to extend, by actual increase, the joy of his Existence; but just as it *is* in your power to expand or to concentrate your pleasures (the absolute amount of happiness remaining always the same) so did and does a similar capability appertain to this Divine Being, who thus passes his Eternity in perpetual variation of Concentrated Self and almost Infinite Self-Diffusion. What you call The Universe is but his present expansive existence. He now feels his life through an infinity of imperfect pleasures—the partial and pain-entangled pleasures of those inconceivably numerous things which you designate as his creatures, but which are really but infinite individualizations of Himself. All these creatures—*all*—those which you term animate, as well as those to whom you deny life for no better reason than that you do not behold it in operation—*all* these creatures have, in a greater or less degree, a capacity for pleasure and for pain:—*but the general sum of their sensations is precisely that amount of Happiness which appertains by right to the Divine Being when concentrated within Himself.* These creatures are all too, more or less conscious Intelligences; conscious, first, of a proper identity; conscious, secondly and by faint indeterminate glimpses, of an identity with the Divine Being of whom we speak—of an identity with God. Of the two classes of consciousness, fancy that the former will grow weaker, the latter stronger, during the long succession of ages which must elapse before these myriads of individual Intelligences become blended—when the bright stars become blended— into One. Think that the sense of individual identity will be gradually merged in the general consciousness—that Man, for example, ceasing imperceptibly to feel himself Man, will at length attain that awfully triumphant epoch when he shall recognize his existence as that of Jehovah. In the meantime bear in mind that all is Life—Life—Life within Life—the less within the greater, and all within the *Spirit Divine.*

## NEWTON ARVIN
*Editor*

# Ralph Waldo Emerson

## 1803–1882

EMERSON has had a curious fate, though by no means a unique one. To the older generation, at the beginning of his career, he seemed a propagator of dangerous and probably subversive ideas—"the latest form of infidelity," as a famous attack had it. The old ex-President, John Quincy Adams, wagging his head sadly over the heresies preached by this son of an old friend, could only describe them as "wild and visionary phantasies," clearly destructive of "the most important and solemn duties of the Christian faith." To the younger generation, on the contrary, he spoke as a liberator and a spurrer-on—a liberator from the handcuffs of convention and timidity, a spurrer-on to a life of rebellion, experiment, discovery, and heroic action. For younger men and women—and this over a period of decades—he played the roles both of a Socrates and of a Taillefer; of an emancipator and a warrior-bard, a questioner and an instigator to valor. He did more than any other man, said John Jay Chapman, "to rescue the youth of the next generation and fit them for the fierce times to follow. It will not be denied that he sent ten thousand sons to the war."

Time passed, however, and though this tonicity of Emerson's has probably never ceased to exercise, behind the scenes, its invigorating effect on responsive minds, a public process of dilution and vulgarization got under way: the inflammatory strains in his thought were conveniently banked over and damped down; his affirmations were translated into complacencies, his ardor into "strenuousness," and his philosophical optimism into Positive Thinking. The vulgarizers, to tell the truth, could always cite chapter and verse for their deformations of Emerson's teaching: their version is a caricature, but it is a caricature of something that is really there. In any case, his name gradually became synonymous with a shallow cheerfulness or a kind of Boy Scout gospel of essentially adolescent virility. The best minds of a later generation found less and less to make use of in Emerson, more and more to reject; and Yvor Winters was only, in his turn, caricaturing a serious and widespread view when he called Emerson "a fraud and a sentimentalist." It was quite as wrongheaded a judgment as John Quincy Adams' had been, and it will not stand up under questioning. But it can be seen through and set aside only if we return to what Emerson actually thought and wrote.

### II

UNLIKE the lives of some other American writers—Melville, for example, or Mark Twain or Hemingway—Emerson's life was externally wanting in the stuff of vivid narrative: outwardly it was not very eventful or dramatic. His real life was, for the most part, an inward one, and in that sense his biography can be quickly summarized. "Great geniuses," he once said, "have the shortest biographies. Their cousins can tell you nothing about them." There may be some striking exceptions to this rule, but Emerson himself is not one of them. He was born in Boston in 1803, during Jefferson's first administration, to a highly respectable family of strongly anti-Jeffersonian and conservatively Federalist opinions. His father was a Unitarian minister, and indeed Emerson was the scion of an ancient ministerial stock: he was to be the eighth consecutive clergyman in a line reaching back to the seventeenth century—a line, to put it otherwise, stretching down from the pristine Calvinism of the first emigrants through the evangelical fervors of Edwards' generation to what Emerson called "the pale negations of Boston Unitarianism" as they were expounded by his father from the pulpit of the First Church. Emerson came by his priestly office as naturally as any young Levite or Brahmin, and, given his genius, it was equally natural that, when the time came, he should recoil upon this paternal heritage and cast it from him.

"My recollections of early life," he once wrote, "are not very pleasant." What he had in mind in saying this was at least partly the fact that his father, the Reverend William Emerson, died when he himself was only eight, and that the family life from then on was bound in by what he calls "the iron band of poverty, of necessity, of austerity." Emerson and his brothers were early inured to the rigors of something very like penury. But this did not mean that their education was neglected. Pinched as the family life was materially, Emerson was sent to the Boston Latin School and then, at the age of fourteen, to Harvard, where he graduated in the class of 1821. A few years of rather disconsolate schoolteaching followed and in 1825, after a good deal of troubled uncertainty over the choice of a vocation, Emerson entered the Harvard Divinity School. The years that followed were made difficult not only by uncertain health but by much painful self-distrust and recurrent moods of dejection. In 1826, however, he obtained his "approbation" to preach in Unitarian churches, and

three years later he became the pastor of the Second Church in Boston.

His career as a minister was to be a short one. The young Emerson was far too sensitive to the intellectual and literary changes that were taking place in Europe and, less conspicuously, in this country, to be long contented with the essentially eighteenth-century outlook of even the "liberal Christians." "From their orthodox kind of dissent he dissented," as Lowell said of another preacher, and in 1832, despite the protests of his affectionate congregation, he resigned his pastorate. The immediate occasion for Emerson's withdrawal from the ministry was his inability to continue conscientiously to administer the Lord's Supper, but his difficulties covered more ground than that. Both his reading and his independent thinking had driven Emerson farther and farther from *any* version of institutional religion, and though he continued for a few years to preach occasionally as a substitute for other ministers, it was with less and less conviction or satisfaction, and in 1839 he gave up the pulpit once and for all.

His resignation had confronted him again with the question of a vocation, both in the sternly practical and in the ideal sense. The answer had presented itself almost providentially: the age of the lecture platform—the lyceum system—had been ushered in only a few years earlier; and in 1833, after traveling for some months in Europe, Emerson gave his first lecture from a public platform to the Natural History Society in Boston. It was only the first of scores of lectures that were to follow over a period of nearly forty years. Oratory, public speech, had from an early age been one of Emerson's abiding preoccupations (in college he is said to have been "especially happy . . . in declamation"). Despite his need of solitude and solitary meditation, he felt also the need of direct communication with a living audience, and in the long run he was to prove a deeply impressive and widely influential lecturer. Most of his essays were originally presented as lectures, though usually not in their final form, and for many years he was a familiar figure to audiences not only in New England but in the Middle States and later in "the West"—in Cleveland and Cincinnati, in Chicago and St. Louis, in Madison and Milwaukee.

Meanwhile, to return to the thirties, Emerson's life, after the discontents, the indecisions, and the false starts of his youth, had gradually taken on an outward form that, in spite of practical anxieties and a series of personal bereavements, was to harmonize more and more with the inward serenity he had somehow attained, however precariously. In 1834 he had settled for good in Concord, the village that had been the home of his ancestors; in the following year he made a second marriage—his young and lovely first wife had died before his resignation—and bought the spacious house that was to be his permanent home; and in 1836, with the publication of his first book, *Nature*, he began to gather about him those like-minded contemporaries and then, as time went on, those younger admirers and even disciples who were to demonstrate to him that, in "thinking alone" and in "speaking his own mind," he was thinking and speaking for a whole age.

Despite the physical and material strenuousness of American society at the time, or because of it, a canopy of conventionality, of oppressive stuffiness, hung over its intellectual and spiritual life; and all the dissatisfied minds that were longing to see the canopy lifted were on the alert to recognize any voice that would speak out against the prevailing grayness. *Nature* did this; and the result was that Emerson was invited, almost at once, to deliver the annual Phi Beta Kappa oration at Harvard the following summer. "The American Scholar," as he called this oration, exhilarated his hearers, especially the younger men, with the eager sense that they were listening to a manifesto of intellectual independence; and when a year later in 1838, he was invited by the graduating class at the Harvard Divinity School to deliver an address to *them*, he responded with a discourse that identified him permanently with the forces that were making for moral and spiritual renovation.

Utterances such as these, and the orations at Dartmouth and Waterville that soon followed, made Emerson for a time a kind of storm center of the "Newness," as the movement of revolt came to be called. Controversy for its own sake, however, had no charms for Emerson; he was prepared to bear witness to the truths he saw, but he had no love of dispute, of hot-tempered argument, of the jangle of debate; and though he never merely retreated to the rear of the battle, he insisted quietly on his right to withdraw, for repose and restoration, to what his "admirable gossip," Montaigne, had called the back shop of his mind. His life in Concord, as time went on, came to resemble that of a forest philosopher or a Stoic sage or even a very unorthodox anchorite. No substance so magnetic as that of Emerson's mind, however, could fail to pull other minds toward itself, and he had perhaps more than his quota of visitors and votaries—some of them bores, some of them gentle lunatics, some of them (like Thoreau and Whitman) men of independent genius.

Much of his time was spent sauntering in the woods and fields, along the riverside or pondsides of Concord, the low-pitched beauty of which he loved and which he found an inexhaustible restorer. Much of his time, too, was spent writing in the journal that he had begun at the age of sixteen, while he was a junior in college, and that he kept steadily, year after year, until his old age. One of the purposes of this journal was to serve as a kind of literary bank from the deposits in which he drew much of the material for his lectures and later his essays. But it had an independent value of its own for him. The private notebook or journal was a peculiarly natural form of literary expression for a writer who was both so sharply observant and so delicately introspective as Emerson was, and the ten volumes of his published *Journals* are an organic and indispensable part of his total literary achievement.

Morally speaking, he never retreated an inch from the advanced positions he had taken in the thirties, though he enriched and deepened and tempered them intellectually. But the rest of the country, or much of it, caught up with him as time went on; his great distinction as a speaker and writer was not to be denied, nor the force and wisdom of his exhortations; and Emerson came to be recognized, in middle and later life, as one of the two or three most eminent men of letters in America. Predictable and proper honors, even of an official sort, came to him. Though he was not invited back to Harvard for almost thirty years after the talk at the Divinity School, he was at last in 1866 given an honorary degree by the college, and in 1867 the alumni elected him an "overseer." In the same year, with a pleasant symbolic fitness, he was invited once again to deliver an address ("Progress of Culture") to the Phi Beta Kappa society. He lived for another decade and a half, trimming himself, as he said "to the storm of time," but determined to "obey the voice at eve obeyed at prime," and died peacefully in 1882.

### III

THE immense value Emerson's teaching had for his own generation was due, on the level of ideas, partly to what he rejected and partly to what he affirmed. Earlier writers—Irving, Bryant, Cooper—had given expression in their work to one impulse or another of the romantic *sensibility;* Emerson, for the first time in this country, gave full and eloquent expression to the *philosophy* of romantic idealism—of what was soon known, though Emerson came to dislike the word, as "Transcendentalism." Fortunately he was never described as "the American Coleridge" or "the American Carlyle," though the service he performed for the American mind was not dissimilar to that which Coleridge and Carlyle had performed for the English. Like them, and partly under their spell, he had come to detest the whole system of ideas that held sway over men's minds in Europe—and, somewhat less tyrannically, in America—for almost two centuries before his time, and to resolve that he would think and act in the light of truer insights and a profounder knowledge. One way to put this, though not a wholly just one, is to say that Emerson felt the world had had enough of Benjamin Franklin.

At any rate, he felt that the spiritual and intellectual biases of the seventeenth and eighteenth centuries, of the Age of Reason, however creative they might have been in their prime, had ended in sterility and denudation, and that the time had come for the reassertion of older wisdoms—still more, for the utterance of fresher ones. On the deepest level he was persuaded that the religious life had been impoverished and all but destroyed, partly by the empty traditionalism of the churches, partly by the dehydrated rationality of the Deists. He had ceased to believe, moreover, in that conception of knowledge and role of the mind formulated by Lockean empiricism, which was still the basis of philosophical teaching when he was an undergraduate and the underpinning of Unitarian doctrine when he studied at the Divinity School. The image of the world, of nature, that had been so dear to the imagination of the older materialists and mechanists—the image of a World Machine as beautifully, as delicately, constructed as a watch or an orrery, but quite as mechanical—had come to seem to Emerson, as to Goethe and Wordsworth, intolerable. In the sphere of morals, too, he was in full rebellion against the eighteenth century—against that calculus of pleasures and pains which it had made the test of right and wrong—against the tenet of what Carlyle called "the monster UTILITARIA" according to which the only criterion of good and evil in human life is the criterion of Utility. And finally, like the great European romantics, Emerson was ready to throw into the discard all those older views of beauty, of the arts, of poetry, of the role of the poet, that had been so congenial to the rationalistic mind and that have come to be known in literary history as the principles of neoclassicism.

The rationalistic mind seemed to him to have chilled and rigidified the whole of human existence, beginning with the life of the spirit on its profoundest levels. His own religious experience, like that of his grandfather in the days of Edwards and Whitefield, had taught him that religion has far less to do with the "understanding" than with what Edwards called "an affected fervent heart," and that without "a certain enthusiasm," as Emerson himself said, it is nothing. The cool, reasonable, philosophical beliefs of the Deists and of many Unitarians seemed to him a spiritless substitute for religion, not religion itself: thus for him was "an influx of the Divine mind into our mind" an ecstasy, not an induction. With institutions, with churches, with creeds and liturgies, it has at best only secondary relations. Essentially it is a superrational communication between the individual soul and what Emerson came to call the Over-Soul; its truth, as he said to the young men at the Divinity School, "is guarded by one stern condition; this, namely; it is an intuition. It cannot be received at second hand." The religion of the sects, like the religion of the Deists, had ceased, for Emerson, to be a vehicle of spiritual experience.

His *own* experience again had carried him well beyond the frontiers of even a liberalized Christianity: in that sense John Quincy Adams was right enough. The Emersonian faith is a faith that, without indeed repudiating the whole Judaeo-Christian tradition, is no longer specifically either Judaic or Christian. It is a purely idealistic belief in an ultimate spiritual reality, an impersonal and timeless Absolute, a transcendent ONE. In its true nature this One is not to be described or defined; it eludes all attempts to confine it in a net of language system; it is simply essential Being—"that Unity, that Over-Soul, within which every man's particular being is contained and made one with all other"—and in its presence all else is only relatively real, is transitional and somehow illusory. Yet this central Unity is not, as in some absolutist systems, destructive of all diversity or individuality: the reality of these may be only relative and in some ultimate sense illusory, but it is not a mere empty delusion. A mysterious contradiction is involved, but Emerson "knows" that the individual soul exists and that, without its ceasing to exist, it and the divine Soul are one. Divinity, as he says, is within as well as above: "God in us worships God." It is this divine principle that is the true self, not "the biographical Ego."

What follows from such convictions is that the physical world, real as it is empirically, is dependent for its reality on Spirit, and that the ultimate nature of things is not to be found, as materialists have always held, in matter, but in mind. In the strictest metaphysical sense, Emerson's thought probably does not hold together with perfect coherence on these levels, but he made no claim to being a system-builder, and the spirit of his teaching, its intrinsic direction, is plain enough. The philosophy that had given to the mind a dependent and secondary status in its relation to the external world, that had seen it as essentially passive in the process of knowing, that had denied to it an active, a creative role—this philosophy Emerson, like his European precursors, repudiated. What took its place for him was the conviction that the physical world is the *creation* of mind, not its formative context, and that, since mind has somehow brought that world into existence, our knowledge of it is the knowledge the artist has of his own handiwork: "the Intellect builds the universe and is the key to all it contains." As time went on, Emerson was to grow more and more doubtful about the certainty of our knowledge of particulars, of details, of "accidents"; but of the trustworthiness of the mind as the key to the Whole he felt no final skepticism.

Nor did he doubt for a moment that the whole mechanistic conception of Nature was a fallacious one. The World Machine had simply broken down, like so many machines, and what had taken its place, for the imagination, was the World Tree—or at any rate some metaphor of growth, of organic productivity, of creative burgeoning and fertility. Nature was no longer an ingenious and essentially lifeless contrivance: it was an animated and dynamic Life. "We can point nowhere," says Emerson, "to anything final; but tendency appears on all hands: planet, system, constellation, total nature is growing like a field of maize in July; is becoming somewhat else; is in rapid metamorphosis." So swift, indeed, so incessant is its movement that in order to express it in language we must avail ourselves of such metaphors not only as that of a tree but as that of a rushing stream or a series of circles rapidly expanding outward from an unchanging center.

Not only so: there is another aspect in which nature must be viewed—an aspect that follows from its dependence on mind. If, as Emerson says, "intellect is primary; nature, secondary; it is the memory of the mind," then it must follow that what are called the laws of nature are not merely objective and independent uniformities; properly conceived, they are laws of the intellect itself; they are, so to say, intellectual, not material laws, and a perfect correspondence will be discoverable between them and the laws of the human mind. What are called scientific facts will turn out to "correspond," as Swedenborg held, to spiritual facts, and indeed to be symbolic of them. "Everything transitory," said Goethe, "is only a symbol"; and for Emerson, too, the whole of physical nature, the cosmos itself, is one vast symbol of Spirit. Mere literalness, prosaic factuality, disappears from the cosmic scene; all things are metaphors, and symbolism, far from being a mere device of the poets or the theologians, is the clue to all immaterial reality. "We are symbols and inhabit symbols," says Emerson; "workman, work, and tools, words and things, birth and death, all are emblems": our knowledge of the world is inherently a symbolic knowledge, and language itself is essentially and necessarily a system of metaphors.

In all this Emerson was not only drawing upon his predecessors—Swedenborg and Goethe, Coleridge and Carlyle—but giving a turn to the doctrine of symbols that entitles him to be seen as himself a predecessor of more recent thinkers; of Ernest Cassirer, for one, with his view that "the special symbolic forms are not imitations, but *organs* of reality." In any case, by teaching that objects in nature are not merely measurable, weighable, mathematically describable facts, but emblems of the intangible, Emerson was making a complete break with the metaphysics of materialism. He made an equally complete break with its ethics. The older school of moralists—the hedonists and utilitarians—had sought to find a sanction for ethical distinctions in the experiences of pleasure and pain, and for ethical behavior

in the criterion of utility. The result was, of course, not only a materialistic but a relativistic theory of good and evil. To Emerson this theory was anathema; he described it once as "the stinking philosophy of the utilitarian." For him the distinction between virtue and vice is *relative* to nothing: it is an absolute distinction. Goodness is by no means merely that which conduces to the multiplication of pleasures or satisfactions: it is "the adherence in action to the nature of things." It is, in short, a purely ideal or transcendental conception, and what Emerson repeatedly calls the Moral Law is for him the eternal law of Being itself. As such, it is not simply a guide to conduct but an object of adoration; Emerson conceives of the Good indeed as identical with the One, and of religion as essentially its worship. "The progress of religion," he says, "is steadily to its identity with morals."

It might be supposed that, entertaining as he did so austerely ideal a conception of the good, Emerson's practical morality would be not *only* a very austere but a very safe and law-abiding one. And in fact it does make stern demands on the conscience and on personal conduct at every turn. Yet it is very far, in spirit and intention, from being an inculcation of cautious and conventional virtues; it is an inculcation, rather, of risky, unconventional, and heroic virtues—the virtues of the man who acts not in the light of received codes but in the light of the Moral Law itself. From the point of view of ordinary morality such a man is by no means sure to be "good." "I hate goodies," Emerson indeed wrote in his journal. "I hate goodness that preaches . . . Goodies make us very bad . . . We will almost sin to spite them." To the conformists who toe the harmless line of inherited morals, the Hero, the Great Man, is not always distinguishable from the law-breaker, and in practice he does often, in the merely legal sense, break the law. "The men who evince the force of the moral sentiment and of genius," says Emerson, "are not normal, canonical people, but wild and Ishmaelitish"; and his admiration went, again and again, though often with essential reservations, to men like Caesar and Cromwell and Napoleon rather than to more manageable characters.

Traditional systems of ethics have ordinarily found the sanctions of right and wrong in some appeal to the needs or demands of a group—of a race, a class, a state, a people—in short, of society. Emerson is an "immoralist" chiefly because he finds those sanctions, or seems to find them, solely in the moral sense of the individual. Here, as elsewhere in Emerson, a contradiction is involved that could lead, and has led, to much misunderstanding. But there can be no doubt that, at one pole of his teaching, Emerson intended to disseminate a new and quite radical respect for the sacredness of individuality, for the incommensurable uniqueness of the "single man," and for the virtues of moral and intellectual independence. "Nature," he says, "never rhymes her children, nor makes two men alike"; and what follows from this, in his belief, is that a man's duty consists, first of all, in resisting all pressures from without, in refusing to measure his conduct by the accepted values of society, and in thinking and acting in the light of self-derived and self-warranted standards. Through all Emerson's early addresses and essays runs like a burden this "lesson of self-help": it was the principal secret of his immense effect as an ethical teacher, and it is quite true that the lesson could be interpreted not only as a call to heroic action but also as a kind of august authorization for various forms of "immoralism."

It could do so for the very good reason that one strain in Emerson's thought is in fact a love of the spectacle not only of Heroism but of Power. The fact of personal force, of superior vitality, of great individual energy, aroused such enthusiasm in him that he was willing to make many allowances for the irregularities to which these qualities might conduce. "Power first," he says, "or no leading class. In politics and in trade, bruisers and pirates are of better promise than talkers and clerks"; and elsewhere he lays it down that "We must fetch the pump with dirty water, if clean cannot be had." Pronouncements such as this might well be expected to give aid and comfort to forms of immoralism that even the unconventional and nonconforming will dread. And indeed the step from Emerson's cult of the strong man to Nietzsche's "Will to Power" would not seem to be a very great one: Nietzsche himself, on whom Emerson had a profound effect, did not find it so.

There is a genuinely hazardous quality in all this that cannot be cheerfully whistled away, just as there is in Whitman's comparable cult of strength—of what he calls "the power of personality, just or unjust." Yet we turn from these passages in Emerson in which a doubtfully scrupulous individualism is celebrated, to other passages, apparently in baffling contradiction to them, in which the very reality of individuals, in any ultimate sense, is denied. "The study of many individuals," says one of these, "leads us to an elemental region wherein the individual is lost, or wherein all touch by their summits . . . All that respects the individual is temporary and prospective, like the individual himself, who is ascending out of his limits into a catholic existence." In short, and though real contradictions in Emerson's teaching remain, he himself was able to preach his gospel of self-trust so urgently, and sometimes so carelessly, only because his profoundest faith was not, after all, in "selfism," as he calls it scornfully, but in "the ever-blessed ONE." Whether the individual soul is really "lost" in the ONE or retains a mysterious independence is not wholly clear, but whatever its reality it is one that yields to the supreme reality of the Over-Soul, and, rightly understood, the man who relies on himself is not relying merely on his empirical self but on "the aboriginal Self, on which a universal reliance may be grounded."[1] From Emerson's point of view, this neither negates his defiant individualism nor furnishes any real ethical sanction for immoral conduct.

On the highest level the contradiction here is not at all a willful inconsistency but a special case of what holds for Emerson's thinking generally. He will never be understood by readers who fail to take it in that he is a

[1] See "Self-Reliance," p. 268.

consciously "dialectical" thinker—one, that is, who holds that contradiction is inherent in experience itself, that the natural order is through and through paradoxical, and that we shall never comprehend it truly until we have learned to "keep the diagonal line." This truth is what he calls Polarity: "The fact of two poles," he says, "of two forces, centripetal and centrifugal, is universal, and each force by its own activity develops the other." It was the great lesson he felt that he had learned from Plato, of whom he says with humorous reverence, "a man who could see two sides of a thing was born"; though if Plato had in a sense taught him this, it was because the lesson was already lurking in the grain of his own mind. In any case, the most comprehensive and abstract manifestation of the principle of Polarity was for Emerson, as for Plato, the antithesis of Unity and Variety, the One and the Many, Oneness and Otherness. It is in the light of this true paradox that the reality and the right of the individual can be asserted without our forgetting that the One also exists, and indeed, unlike the individual, has an absolute existence. For the principle of Polarity is not itself an ultimate truth; it is only an empirical one. A metaphysical choice is forced upon us, and in the end we see that Unity is a deeper fact than Variety. "We unite all things," says Emerson, "by perceiving the law which pervades them; by perceiving both the differences and the profound resemblances." It is his capacity for perceiving both the differences and the resemblances that, as much as anything, makes Emerson a permanently impressive as well as a bracing writer.

### IV

TOO MUCH can hardly be made of Emerson's role as an awakener, an agitating and fermentative force in his own time and potentially today; but it must not be forgotten that he was also a great writer, a great artist. As an artist in prose he did not quite invent a new form or mode, but he possessed himself of an inherited form, and shaped it so boldly and freely as an expressive medium for his own needs that the product has all the fresh-

ness of originality in the true sense. As a matter of fact, the derivation of Emerson's form is not perfectly simple. It was not until the appearance of his second published volume, *Essays: First Series*, in 1841, that Emerson had placed himself before his readers explicitly in the role of essayist. His earliest compositions had been sermons; he had turned from the sermon to the lecture, but in the order of publication, to ignore *Nature* for the moment, what he had begun with had been "discourses" (an "Historical Discourse at Concord" in 1835), or "orations" ("The American Scholar: An Oration . . ."), or "addresses" ("An Address Delivered Before the Senior Class in Divinity College"). In short, what he called the essay was the offspring, on one side, of some form or other of public speech—in the pulpit, on the lecture-platform, on the special occasion—and rather few of his "essays" fail to betray that their ancestry was partly in the spoken word. It was partly, too, in the written word, and his models here were such favorite authors of his from early youth as the Plutarch not only of the *Lives* but of the *Moralia* (or *Essays and Miscellanies*, as they were known in one translation), the beloved Montaigne of the *Essais*, and the Bacon of the English *Essays* (of which he said in an early lecture that "Few books ever written contain so much wisdom and will bear to be read so many times"). To the later Addisonian tradition, that of the "periodical" essay, in which Franklin had worked, Emerson owed little or nothing.

It has often been made a reproach to him that, brilliant as his sentences may be, Emerson had little feeling for the larger units of structure, and that his essays are perhaps glittering heaps of *sententiae* but not artistically ordered wholes. This criticism has been reinforced by the knowledge that both the lectures and the essays were "pieced together," like quilt-covers of variegated prose, from the journals—as though the sense of composition, if strong enough, could not produce an effect of beautiful coherence even by this process. Emerson himself, at any rate, certainly intended that his essays should have a structural firmness of their own, though not perhaps an easily obvious or rigidly logical one. Rhetoric for him, indeed, was a "species of architecture": he called it "the Building of Discourse," and was convinced that "Profoundest thoughts, sublime images, dazzling figures are squandered and lost in an immethodical harangue." Of the dangers of the "aphoristic style" he was fully conscious: he did not wish to frustrate his readers, as he felt that his friend Alcott sometimes did, with "a cord of chips for a cord of wood." Nor does he—with some exceptions—do this.

His feeling for compositional wholeness was in fact much stronger than it has usually been said to be, but if the impression remains, even in the minds of some intelligent readers, that he is a writer of aphorisms rather than of sustained discourses, the reasons are understandable. It is true that he is one of the most *quotable* of modern writers: again and again his sentences, and even his phrases, can be detached from their context, like jewels from a disregarded setting, and quoted with a delight that seems to set at naught their relation to other sentences. It is true, too, that the transition from one sentence, or even one paragraph, to another is not always explicitly made, and this produces an effect of apparent discontinuity. "It is not the masters," he said, however, "who spin the ostentatious continuity"—and if he habitually omitted the familiar connectives of logical discourse it was partly because he wished to leave some of the work of thinking to his readers, and partly because what he meant by continuity was not a logical but a superlogical principle.

It remains true that Emerson was a skilled and studious rhetorician, and that his sense of the architecture of an essay normally and beautifully triumphed over the tendency to dispersion or looseness. He had begun, after all, as a preacher in the tradition, however relaxed, of the Puritan homily, and his own early sermons are sometimes models of orderly discourse. The habit survived at least in his earliest publications: in *Nature*, in "The American Scholar," in "Self-Reliance," he is still, in certain sections, numbering his topics, and though he later abandoned this

formality, he rarely abandoned the "building" principle it was based on. A careful scrutiny of almost any one of his characteristic essays will reveal, beneath the undulating surface, the actual firmness of the design.

The excitation his prose begets depends not only on his design but on the wonderful resourcefulness of his rhetoric in the narrower sense, on his practiced command over the whole range of expressive and captivating devices of style. It is true that he is a master of the aphorism—of the terse single sentence that seems to be saying, in the briefest and wittiest way, a particular thing so that it need never be said again. But to suppose that Emerson's powers are limited to the aphorism would be to ignore a dozen other aspects of his art—his mastery of the cumulative and ascending paragraph, his powerful uses of parallelism, reiteration, and antithesis, his love of even such "artificial" devices as anaphora and the tricolon, his frank resort to apostrophe and interrogation, and, what deserves much fuller treatment than is possible here, his feeling, both strong and delicate, for the rhythms of English prose.

A careful look at such a passage as the peroration of "The American Scholar" will reveal how much of its enkindling power, to speak only stylistically and not morally, depends on the brilliance with which a whole series of such "figures" are pressed into the service of Emerson's meaning. It will also reveal—but so indeed will a look at almost any page of Emerson—how much of his power and charm as a prose writer depends on the all but Shakespearean exhaustlessness of his metaphors. This is of course because he thought in metaphors, when he thought at all intensely, as he himself recognized: "All thinking," he said, "is analogizing," and certainly this holds for the kind of thinking that lies at the base of most of his writing. Abstraction was, for him, too likely to be falsification: only the living image, the seeable and touchable metaphor, could, in the usual course, do justice to the vigor and the suppleness of his thought.

What strikes one about Emerson's metaphors is not only their freshness, their lesser dependence on literature than on experience, but their imaginative range—the fact that they stretch out over the whole space from the celestial to the common, from the lofty to the low, from "the thrones of angels" and "the whole garden of God" to "a wood-pile in the yard" or "the rats in the wall." But indeed it is not easy, beyond a certain point, to distinguish between Emerson's metaphorical language and his language generally; of *that* the catholicity, the all-inclusive hospitality, the elasticity in moving from the elevated or the learned to the colloquial and even the "vulgar" have long been recognized. It is what Lowell had in mind when he said that Emerson's diction is like "homespun cloth-of-gold." Only Melville and Whitman, among his contemporaries, have a comparable linguistic scope, and perhaps neither of them bestrews his pages with quite so generous or so various a shower of locutions as Emerson—locutions which can be erudite and even pedantic ("hodiernal," "pudency," "pleniloquence"), or familiar ("all stir and no go," "deny it up and down," "a drop too much"), or sometimes brutally plain ("this filthy enactment," "cathartic virtue," "snores and gastric noises," "all blab").

"Speak with the vulgar," he says, "think with the wise." It is a vivid way of expressing his love for actual speech, with its energy and its picturesqueness, but the witty form of the sentence is only half faithful to the truth of his practice. For him "the wise," it is true, were often the simple and unlettered, and that is why he speaks with them at times. But his diction, his imagery, and indeed his prose style generally have a versatility, a richness, and sometimes a grandeur that might equally well be described as "speaking with the noble." His writing, just as such, has polarities that "correspond" to the deep polarities of his thought.

## V

In his aesthetics as well as in his metaphysics and his ethics, Emerson was a part of that powerful swing away from the older attitudes, the older materialisms, that oc-

curred in Europe and then in this country in the generation before him and in his own. The most characteristic conception of Beauty in the earlier time was a thoroughly hedonistic and, as Emerson would say, "sensual" one; a conception that associated it inextricably with pleasure. "Pleasure and pain," Hume had said,". . . . are not only necessary attendants of beauty and deformity, but constitute their very essence." In his rejection of this certainly rather simplistic hedonism, Emerson turned back to an older set of insights—those of Plato and the Neoplatonists—and reaffirmed the transcendental conception of Beauty as pure Idea, as one of the eternal Forms on which all temporal things depend for what reality they have, or as one of the aspects, along with the True and the Good, of the Absolute itself. The Artist, in this view, is no mere craftsman but a servant, religious in his dedication, of the Idea; and the arts exist, not essentially to give pleasure ("As soon as beauty is sought, not from religion and love but for pleasure, it degrades the seeker"), but "to educate the perception of beauty" in this Platonic sense.

Poetry, like the other arts, according to this conception, quite loses its neoclassical character as Imitation of Nature, and becomes "creation"—the giving of form and verbal expression to intuitions into the reality that lies behind Nature and of which Nature is itself only an ephemeral vestment. A consequence of this is that one can no longer speak, as the neoclassical critics had done, in the light of imitational criteria—criteria of mere "verisimilitude," of propriety, of correctness, of "the rules," and the like. There are no "rules," and the test of genuinely poetic language and form is not its conformity to inherited standards of correctness, but its expressive truth to the ever-fresh and ever-unique themes with which the poet deals. No established forms or styles can possibly be prescribed to the poet; his subject itself must dictate the pattern. "Ask the fact for the form," says Emerson; and as for language, "Any word, every word in language, every circumstance, becomes poetic in the hands of a higher thought."

Such, very sketchily hinted at, were Emerson's poetics, and such were the criteria in the light of which his own poems were written. "I wish," he said, "to write such rhymes as shall not suggest a restraint, but contrariwise, the wildest freedom." To readers now, Emerson's verse is probably less likely to suggest ideas of wildness or extravagance than of, if not "restraint," at least lowness of pitch, sobriety, and even sedateness. Yet there is more of the untamed in Emerson than meets the careless eye, and from the older point of view the truth is that he had thrown off many of the inhibitions that were supposed to have been essential to poetic form.

He had thrown them off quite consciously. As a youth he had written a fair amount of verse, but always in the conventional modes—an undergraduate poem on Hindu superstition was composed in the starchiest of pentameter couplets—but he had found these modes less and less bearable with the passage of time, and just as his prose began to shed its conventional qualities and to take on its recognizably "Emersonian" character in the year or two that followed his resignation from the ministry, so in the same years, with "Each and All" and "The Snow-Storm," he began to find his own voice, his own individual accent, as a poet. During the period of the celebrated early addresses he was also writing "The Humble-Bee" and "The Problem" and demonstrating that, in the one medium as in the other, he had achieved both a wonderful freshness and a wonderful ripeness of utterance.

If, in the formal and linguistic sense, Emerson's verse is typically untraditional and unprecedented, it is because he had new and unhackneyed things to say. No doubt in a sense they were also very old things, but if so, they were old things that had the novelty which always characterizes restatement in a new hour. The themes of eighteenth-century poetry had been suggested by the life of society, or by a very rational kind of reflection, or by nature and the seasons contemplated in a highly reasonable and Newtonian spirit. Most of Emerson's themes came to him, not from society, but from solitude; as the fruits, not of rational reflection, but of rapt meditation; or from nature and the seasons contemplated, not so much in a reasonable, as in an

enthusiastic spirit. The mystery of the One and the Many, the falsity of "linear" thinking, the identity of the soul of nature and the individual soul, the vatic or prophetic character of poetry itself—such were a few of the subjects that Emerson typically treated in his verse; they need only to be "stated" in this prosaic manner to make it clear that they could not, without loss, have been treated in the older styles.

To be sure, it would be misleading to overstate the unconventionality of *all* Emerson's verse. Some of his most successful poems, both early and late, are composed in well-tried metrical and stanzaic forms, and their verbal texture by no means always represents an abrupt departure from tradition. The blank verse of "The Snow-Storm" or "Xenophanes," the quatrains of "Waldeinsamkeit," the octaves of "The World-Soul" or "The Sphinx"—these, in themselves, were familiar enough; and neither the language nor the imagery always suggests "the wildest freedom" from the practice of English poets in the late eighteenth century. The personal qualities here are subtler and more elusive than sweeping innovation would be likely to produce; but they are there, and it says much for Emerson's versatility as a poet that he could infuse with so much fresh life the blank verse he had inherited from Landor or Wordsworth, or the quatrains he had lifted out of the hymnals.

Meanwhile, it was on another track that he was moving toward a still more personal and idiosyncratic mode of expression in poetry. There had been a peculiar felicity for him, in so early a poem as "Each and All," in a pattern of freely-syllabled four-stress lines, where the rhymes might, but need not, fall in couplets; and during the next few years he revealed how congenial this pattern was to him in such poems as "The Problem," "Uriel," and parts of "Monadnoc," with their increasingly free gait and increasingly "anti-poetic" diction. The next step was to abandon any sort of syllable-counting or consistency of rhyming, and he took that step in other parts of "Monadnoc," in the "Ode Inscribed to W. H. Channing," in "Give All to Love." If it were not for the rhymes—and they are not only irregular but sometimes missing—this verse might well be described simply as free verse; at all events, the peculiarly Emersonian note can be heard nowhere so unmistakably as in the poems composed in these "logaoedic," anti-lyrical, uneuphonious lines, intermediate as they are between verse and prose, with their suggestion of half-conversational improvisation, rising at times to a spirited recitatif and even, as in parts of "Threnody," to something like a solemn chant, but avoiding both lyricism and the familiar eloquence of traditional blank verse. The transition from this to the free verse of Pound and Eliot would not be a difficult one.

The real originality of these poems is enhanced, too, by what might be called the quiet boldness of Emerson's language and imagery. "Some of my first thinking about my own language," Robert Frost has said, "was certainly Emersonian"; and one can easily see how this might have been. The filiation between the two poets is evident enough when one does not more than glance at the opening lines of Emerson's "journal" poem, "The Adirondacs":

We crossed Champlain to Keeseville with our
  friends,
Thence, in strong country carts, rode up the forks
Of the Ausable stream, intent to reach
The Adirondac lakes. At Martin's Beach
We chose our boats; each man a boat and
  guide,—
Ten men, ten guides, our company all told.

The speaking tones here, to be sure, the Yankee cadences, are exceptional in Emerson, though they are to be found elsewhere too, as in the opening lines of "Hamatreya," but it is not hard to see how they might have served as a model to the young Frost in his search for a verse-rhythm and a diction that should be true to the natural speech of his own people. Emerson knew that speech well: he had listened to it in the post office at Concord, in the intervales of New Hampshire, in the village taverns at the base of Monadnoc; and he had felt that he could spare "the learned lecture," "institutes and dictionaries," and the like, for "that hardy English root" which throve "unvalued, un-

derfoot" among the unlettered country people of New England.

He never attempted, in any literal way, to reproduce that speech in his verse—any more, indeed, than Frost did—but he delighted in trying to catch some of its tart savor. He delighted in enriching the strong local quality of some poems with the imagery of the New England farm or field or wood—with "every windward stake," "coop or kennel," "hay, corn, roots, hemp, flax, apples, wool and wood," "clay, lime, gravel, granite-ledge," "the black ducks mounting from the lake," or "blue-vetch and trillium, hawkweed, sassafras." Nor did he hesitate, well before *Leaves of Grass*, to introduce into verse the unromantic imagery of nineteenth-century city or industrial or civic life—the imagery of "hotels," "railways," "a factory," "time-and-space conquering steam," "the light-outspeeding telegraph," "the mountain tunnelled," "the steamer built," "politics," "votes," and "polls."

He pointed the way here for Whitman, for Emily Dickinson, and possibly for Melville. But, striking as Emerson's localism and modernism are, and useful as his example proved to later poets, these are not, in the end, the most important things to say about him as a poet. His own claims to the status of poet were over-modest, and all but two or three of his poems were little esteemed in his own time. Yet the truth is that Emerson left behind him a small but impressive body of verse that entitles him to be ranked, for freshness, intensity, and prophetic power, with the poets just alluded to and with few others in this country in his age. Small as the number of his successful poems is, his range within them is greater than any brief treatment can suggest: if the gnomic and unlyrical manner of certain poems seems to be his most idiosyncratic one, it should not be forgotten that he was also capable of the more excited strain of "The World-Soul," the "Ode to Beauty," and "Bacchus," the wail of "Threnody," the effortless lyricism of "Waldeinsamkeit," or the hymnic and public elevation of the "Concord Hymn," the "Boston Hymn," and the "Ode" sung in the town hall at Concord in 1857 ("O tenderly the haughty day/Fills his blue urn with fire"). His great authority as a writer generally derives, ultimately, from the wonderful reach of his polarity, from the length of the leap he could take in spirit from the atom to the All, from details to Unity, from the minute and even mean to the sublime. This holds for his verse as well as for his prose; the author of his best poems can justly be said to have done what he tells us his archetypal bard, Merlin, did: can be said to have reconciled "extremes of nature," to have comprehended and expressed the most polar opposites. Only two or three of our other writers approach him in this achievement.

FROM

# NATURE

◇

〔THE idea of a book on the grand subject of Nature seems to have been in Emerson's mind for some time before he got round to writing it; in the journal he kept on shipboard when returning from England in 1833 he wrote: "I like my book about Nature, and wish I knew where and how I ought to live" (*Journals,* III, 196). He seems not to have been able to begin the book, however, until after he had gone to live as a boarder with his step-grandfather, Dr. Ripley, at the Manse in Concord in 1834. It was not finished, short as it was, until late in the summer of 1836, and was published anonymously in Boston that September. The edition was a very small one—five hundred copies—but even so, a second edition was not needed for thirteen years: in 1849 the little book reappeared as the first piece in a volume entitled *Nature, Addresses, and Lectures (Works,* I).

The book represented a kind of shimmering synthesis of ideas that had been floating about in the European and American mind for a generation or two, and indeed, in one sense, for many centuries; but the synthesis had, nevertheless, a powerful effect of freshness and novelty. It expressed a view of nature and the relations of the human spirit to it that seemed incomparably truer, to

some men, than the views that had been dominant for a hundred years and more; and it became, for such men, a Prophetic Book. It is easy, even now, to see why this was true.

## I. NATURE

TO GO into solitude, a man needs to retire as much from his chamber as from society. I am not solitary whilst I read and write, though nobody is with me. But if a man would be alone, let him look at the stars. The rays that come from those heavenly worlds will separate between him and what he touches. One might think the atmosphere was made transparent with this design, to give man, in the heavenly bodies, the perpetual presence of the sublime. Seen in the streets of cities, how great they are! If the stars should appear one night in a thousand years, how would men believe and adore; and preserve for many generations the remembrance of the city of God which had been shown! But every night come out these envoys of beauty, and light the universe with their admonishing smile.

The stars awaken a certain reverence, because though always present, they are inaccessible; but all natural objects make a kindred impression, when the mind is open to their influence. Nature never wears a mean appearance. Neither does the wisest man extort her secret, and lose his curiosity by finding out all her perfection. Nature never became a toy to a wise spirit. The flowers, the animals, the mountains, reflected the wisdom of his best hour, as much as they had delighted the simplicity of his childhood.

When we speak of nature in this manner, we have a distinct but most poetical sense in the mind. We mean the integrity of impression made by manifold natural objects. It is this which distinguishes the stick of timber of the wood-cutter from the tree of the poet. The charming landscape which I saw this morning is indubitably made up of some twenty or thirty farms. Miller owns this field, Locke that, and Manning the woodland beyond. But none of them owns the landscape. There is a property in the horizon which no man has but he whose eye can integrate all the parts, that is, the poet. This is the best part of these men's farms, yet to this their warranty-deeds give no title.

To speak truly, few adult persons can see nature. Most persons do not see the sun. At least they have a very superficial seeing. The sun illuminates only the eye of the man, but shines into the eye and the heart of the child. The lover of nature is he whose inward and outward senses are still truly adjusted to each other; who has retained the spirit of infancy even into the era of manhood. His intercourse with heaven and earth becomes part of his daily food. In the presence of nature a wild delight runs through the man, in spite of real sorrows. Nature says;—he is my creature, and maugre all his impertinent griefs, he shall be glad with me. Not the sun or the summer alone, but every hour and season yields its tribute of delight; for every hour and change corresponds to and authorizes a different state of the mind, from breathless noon to grimmest midnight. Nature is a setting that fits equally well a comic or a mourning piece. In good health, the air is a cordial of incredible virtue. Crossing a bare common, in snow puddles, at twilight, under a clouded sky, without having in my thoughts any occurrence of special good fortune, I have enjoyed a perfect exhilaration. I am glad to the brink of fear. In the woods, too, a man casts off his years, as the snake his slough, and at what period soever of life, is always a child. In the woods is perpetual youth. Within these plantations of God, a decorum and sanctity reign, a perennial festival is dressed, and the guest sees not how he should tire of them in a thousand years. In the woods, we return to reason and faith. There I feel that nothing can befall me in life,—no disgrace, no calamity (leaving me my eyes), which nature cannot repair. Standing on the bare ground,—my head bathed by the blithe air, and uplifted into infinite space,—all mean egotism vanishes. I become a transparent eyeball; I am nothing; I see all; the currents of the Universal Being circulate through me; I am part or parcel of God. The name of the nearest friend sounds then foreign and accidental: to be brothers, to be acquaintances,—master or servant, is then a trifle and a disturbance. I am the lover of uncontained and immortal beauty. In the wilderness, I find something more dear and connate than in streets or villages. In the tranquil landscape, and especially in the distant line of the horizon, man beholds somewhat as beautiful as his own nature.

The greatest delight which the fields and woods minister is the suggestion of an occult relation between man and the vegetable. I am not alone and unacknowledged. They nod to me, and I to them. The waving of the boughs in the storm is new to me and old. It takes me by surprise, and yet is not unknown. Its effect is like that of a higher thought or a better emotion coming over me, when I deemed I was thinking justly or doing right.

Yet it is certain that the power to produce this delight does not reside in nature, but in man, or in a harmony of both. It is necessary to use these pleasures with great temperance. For nature is not always tricked in holiday attire, but the same scene which yesterday breathed perfume and glittered as for the frolic of the nymphs, is overspread with melancholy to-day. Nature always wears the colors of the spirit. To a man laboring under calamity, the heat of his own fire hath sadness in it. Then there is a kind of contempt of the landscape felt by him who has just lost by death a dear friend. The sky is less grand as it shuts down over less worth in the population.

## IV. LANGUAGE

LANGUAGE is a third use which Nature subserves to man. Nature is the vehicle of thought, and in a simple, double, and threefold degree.

*1.* Words are signs of natural facts.

*2.* Particular natural facts are symbols of particular spiritual facts.

*3.* Nature is the symbol of spirit.[1]

1. Words are signs of natural facts. The use of natural history is to give us aid in supernatural history; the use of the outer creation, to give us language for the beings and changes of the inward creation. Every word which is used to express a moral or intellectual fact, if traced to its root, is found to be borrowed from some material appearance. *Right* means *straight; wrong* means *twisted. Spirit* primarily means *wind; transgression,* the crossing of a *line; supercilious,* the *raising of the eyebrow.* We say the *heart* to express emotion, the *head* to denote thought; and *thought* and *emotion* are words borrowed from sensible things, and now appropriated to spiritual nature. Most of the process by which this transformation is made, is hidden from us in the remote time when language was framed; but the same tendency may be daily observed in children. Children and savages use only nouns or names of things, which they convert into verbs, and apply to analogous mental acts.

2. But this origin of all words that convey a spiritual import,—so conspicuous a fact in the history of language,—is our least debt to nature. It is not words only that are emblematic; it is things

---

1. **Words . . . spirit:** These ideas, as developed in this chapter, Emerson had made his own, but they had precedents in the work of earlier writers. One of Emerson's sources was the Swedish mystic and theologian, Emanuel Swedenborg (1688–1772), in whose thought he had been deeply interested for some years before and while writing *Nature.* In Swedenborg's great treatise, *Heaven and Its Wonders, the World of Spirit, and Hell,* for example, he would have come upon such passages as this: "The whole natural world corresponds to the spiritual world; and not only the natural world collectively, but also its individual parts. . . ."

which are emblematic. Every natural fact is a symbol of some spiritual fact. Every appearance in nature corresponds to some state of the mind, and that state of the mind can only be described by presenting that natural appearance as its picture. An enraged man is a lion, a cunning man is a fox, a firm man is a rock, a learned man is a torch. A lamb is innocence; a snake is subtle spite; flowers express to us the delicate affections. Light and darkness are our familiar expression for knowledge and ignorance; and heat for love. Visible distance behind and before us, is respectively our image of memory and hope.

Who looks upon a river in a meditative hour and is not reminded of the flux of all things? Throw a stone into the stream, and the circles that propagate themselves are the beautiful type of all influence. Man is conscious of a universal soul within or behind his individual life, wherein, as in a firmament, the natures of Justice, Truth, Love, Freedom, arise and shine. This universal soul he calls Reason: it is not mine, or thine, or his, but we are its; we are its property and men. And the blue sky in which the private earth is buried, the sky with its eternal calm, and full of everlasting orbs, is the type of Reason. That which intellectually considered we call Reason, considered in relation to nature, we call Spirit. Spirit is the Creator. Spirit hath life in itself. And man in all ages and countries embodies it in his language as the FATHER.

It is easily seen that there is nothing lucky or capricious in these analogies, but that they are constant, and pervade nature. These are not the dreams of a few poets, here and there, but man is an analogist, and studies relations in all objects. He is placed in the centre of beings, and a ray of relation passes from every other being to him. And neither can man be understood without these objects, nor these objects without man. All the facts in natural history taken by themselves, have no value, but are barren, like a single sex. But marry it to human history, and it is full of life. Whole floras, all Linnaeus' and Buffon's volumes,[2] are dry catalogues of facts; but the most trivial of these facts, the habit of a plant, the organs, or work, or noise of an insect, applied to the illustration of a fact in intellectual philosophy, or in any way associated to human nature, affects us in the most lively and agreeable manner. The seed of a plant,—to what affecting analogies in the nature

of man is that little fruit made use of, in all discourse, up to the voice of Paul, who calls the human corpse a seed,—"It is sown a natural body; it is raised a spiritual body."[3] The motion of the earth round its axis and round the sun, makes the day and the year. These are certain amounts of brute light and heat. But is there no intent of an analogy between man's life and the seasons? And do the seasons gain no grandeur or pathos from that analogy? The instincts of the ant are very unimportant considered as the ant's; but the moment a ray of relation is seen to extend from it to man, and the little drudge is seen to be a monitor, a little body with a mighty heart, then all its habits, even that said to be recently observed, that it never sleeps, become sublime.

Because of this radical correspondence between visible things and human thoughts, savages, who have only what is necessary, converse in figures. As we go back in history, language becomes more picturesque, until its infancy, when it is all poetry; or all spiritual facts are represented by natural symbols. The same symbols are found to make the original elements of all languages. It has moreover been observed, that the idioms of all languages approach each other in passages of the greatest eloquence and power. And as this is the first language, so is it the last. This immediate dependence of language upon nature, this conversion of an outward phenomenon into a type of somewhat in human life, never loses its power to affect us. It is this which gives that piquancy to the conversation of a strong-natured farmer or backwoodsman, which all men relish.

A man's power to connect his thought with its proper symbol, and so to utter it, depends on the simplicity of his character, that is, upon his love of truth and his desire to communicate it without loss. The corruption of man is followed by the corruption of language. When simplicity of character and the sovereignty of ideas is broken up by the prevalence of secondary desires,—the desire of riches, of pleasure, of power, and of praise,—and duplicity and falsehood take place of simplicity and truth, the power over nature as an interpreter of the will is in a degree lost; new imagery ceases to be created, and old words are perverted to stand for things which are not; a paper currency is employed, when there is no bullion in the vaults. In due time the fraud is manifest, and words lose all power to stimulate the understanding or the affections. Hundreds of writers may be found in every long-civilized nation who for a short time believe and make others believe that they see and utter

2. **all Linnaeus' and Buffon's volumes:** Carl von Linné, or Linnaeus (1707–78), author of the *Systema Naturae* and originator of the system of binomial nomenclature for plant and animal species. Comte de Buffon (1707–88), author of the immensely influential *Histoire Naturelle*.

3. **"It . . . body":** See I Cor. 15:44.

truths, who do not of themselves clothe one thought in its natural garment, but who feed unconsciously on the language created by the primary writers of the country, those, namely, who hold primarily on nature.

But wise men pierce this rotten diction and fasten words again to visible things; so that picturesque language is at once a commanding certificate that he who employs it is a man in alliance with truth and God. The moment our discourse rises above the ground line of familiar facts and is inflamed with passion or exalted by thought, it clothes itself in images. A man conversing in earnest, if he watch his intellectual processes, will find that a material image more or less luminous arises in his mind, contemporaneous with every thought, which furnishes the vestment of the thought. Hence, good writing and brilliant discourse are perpetual allegories. This imagery is spontaneous. It is the blending of experience with the present action of the mind. It is proper creation. It is the working of the Original Cause through the instruments he has already made.

These facts may suggest the advantage which the country-life possesses, for a powerful mind, over the artificial and curtailed life of cities. We know more from nature than we can at will communicate. Its light flows into the mind evermore, and we forget its presence. The poet, the orator, bred in the woods, whose senses have been nourished by their fair and appeasing changes, year after year, without design and without heed,—shall not lose their lesson altogether, in the roar of cities or the broil of politics. Long hereafter, amidst agitation and terror in national councils, —in the hour of revolution,—these solemn images shall reappear in their morning lustre, as fit symbols and words of the thoughts which the passing events shall awaken. At the call of a noble sentiment, again the woods wave, the pines murmur, the river rolls and shines, and the cattle low upon the mountains, as he saw and heard them in his infancy. And with these forms, the spells of persuasion, the keys of power are put into his hands.

3. We are thus assisted by natural objects in the expression of particular meanings. But how great a language to convey such pepper-corn informations! Did it need such noble races of creatures, this profusion of forms, this host of orbs in heaven, to furnish man with the dictionary and grammar of his municipal speech? Whilst we use this grand cipher to expedite the affairs of our pot and kettle, we feel that we have not yet put it to its use, neither are able. We are like travellers using the cinders of a volcano to roast their eggs. Whilst we see that it always stands ready to clothe what we would say, we cannot avoid the question whether

the characters are not significant of themselves. Have mountains, and waves, and skies, no significance but what we consciously give them when we employ them as emblems of our thoughts? The world is emblematic. Parts of speech are metaphors, because the whole of nature is a metaphor of the human mind. The laws of moral nature answer to those of matter as face to face in a glass. "The visible world and the relation of its parts, is the dial plate of the invisible." The axioms of physics translate the laws of ethics. Thus, "the whole is greater than its part;" "reaction is equal to action;" "the smallest weight may be made to lift the greatest, the difference of weight being compensated by time;" and many the like propositions, which have an ethical as well as physical sense. These propositions have a much more extensive and universal sense when applied to human life, than when confined to technical use.

In like manner, the memorable words of history and the proverbs of nations consist usually of a natural fact, selected as a picture or parable of a moral truth. Thus, A rolling stone gathers no moss; A bird in the hand is worth two in the bush; A cripple in the right way will beat a racer in the wrong; Make hay while the sun shines; 'Tis hard to carry a full cup even; Vinegar is the son of wine; The last ounce broke the camel's back; Long-lived trees make roots first;—and the like. In their primary sense these are trivial facts, but we repeat them for the value of their analogical import. What is true of proverbs, is true of all fables, parables, and allegories.

This relation between the mind and matter is not fancied by some poet, but stands in the will of God, and so is free to be known by all men. It appears to men, or it does not appear. When in fortunate hours we ponder this miracle, the wise man doubts if at all other times he is not blind and deaf;

> "Can such things be,
> And overcome us like a summer's cloud,
> Without our special wonder?"[4]

for the universe becomes transparent, and the light of higher laws than its own shines through it. It is the standing problem which has exercised the wonder and the study of every fine genius since the world began; from the era of the Egyptians and the Brahmins to that of Pythagoras, of Plato, of Bacon, of Leibnitz, of Swedenborg. There sits the Sphinx at the roadside, and from age to age, as each prophet comes by, he tries his fortune at reading her riddle. There seems to be a necessity in spirit to manifest itself in material forms; and day and night, river and storm, beast and bird,

4. "Can . . . wonder?": Somewhat inaccurately quoted from *Macbeth*, III. iv. 109–11.

acid and alkali, preëxist in necessary Ideas in the mind of God, and are what they are by virtue of preceding affections in the world of spirit. A Fact is the end or last issue of spirit. The visible creation is the terminus or the circumference of the invisible world. "Material objects," said a French philosopher,[5] "are necessarily kinds of *scoriæ*[6] of the substantial thoughts of the Creator, which must always preserve an exact relation to their first origin; in other words, visible nature must have a spiritual and moral side."

This doctrine is abstruse, and though the images of "garment," *"scoriæ,"* "mirror," etc., may stimulate the fancy, we must summon the aid of subtler and more vital expositors to make it plain. "Every scripture is to be interpreted by the same spirit which gave it forth,"—is the fundamental law of criticism. A life in harmony with Nature, the love of truth and of virtue, will purge the eyes to understand her text. By degrees we may come to know the primitive sense of the permanent objects of nature, so that the world shall be to us an open book, and every form significant of its hidden life and final cause.

A new interest surprises us, whilst, under the view now suggested, we contemplate the fearful extent and multitude of objects; since "every object rightly seen, unlocks a new faculty of the soul." That which was unconscious truth, becomes, when interpreted and defined in an object, a part of the domain of knowledge,—a new weapon in the magazine of power.

# THE AMERICAN SCHOLAR

## AN ORATION DELIVERED BEFORE THE PHI BETA KAPPA SOCIETY, AT CAMBRIDGE, AUGUST 31, 1837

❖

❪ "THIS grand oration," said Oliver Wendell Holmes, "was our intellectual Declaration of Independence . . . the young men went out from it as if a prophet had been proclaiming to them 'Thus saith the Lord.' "

5. **French philosopher:** J. G. E. Oegger (whose name appears in other forms and whose exact dates are uncertain), a French Swedenborgian writer, one of whose books, *Le Vrai Messie* (1829), was translated in part as *The True Messiah* by Elizabeth Peabody, a friend of Emerson's. Though her translation was not published until 1842, Emerson had read it in manuscript before he wrote *Nature.* 6. **scoriæ:** dross, slag.

Emerson had been invited, in 1834, to read a poem at the annual Phi Beta Kappa exercises at Harvard; he had done so, and now again, in 1837, he was asked, on short notice, when another person declined, to deliver the annual oration before the Society. He agreed, and "the most famous of all Phi Beta Kappa orations" was delivered to a large and expectant audience in the meetinghouse across from the Harvard Yard on August 31, shortly after noon. The impression it created was immense. Bronson Alcott remembered "the mixed confusion, consternation, surprise, and wonder" of some members of the audience, but Holmes was right at least about the young men, and Lowell describes the occasion as

> an event without any former parallel in our literary annals, a scene to be always treasured in the memory for its picturesqueness and its inspiration. What crowded and breathless aisles, what windows clustering with eager heads, what enthusiasm of approval, what grim silence of foregone dissent! It was our Yankee version of a lecture by Abelard, our Harvard parallel to the last public appearance of Schelling.

❖

MR. PRESIDENT AND GENTLEMEN:

I greet you on the recommencement of our literary year. Our anniversary is one of hope, and, perhaps, not enough of labor. We do not meet for games of strength or skill, for the recitation of histories, tragedies, and odes, like the ancient Greeks; for parliaments of love and poesy, like the Troubadours; nor for the advancement of science, like our contemporaries in the British and European capitals. Thus far, our holiday has been simply a friendly sign of the survival of the love of letters amongst a people too busy to give to letters any more. As such it is precious as the sign of an indestructible instinct. Perhaps the time is already come when it ought to be, and will be, something else; when the sluggard intellect of this continent will look from under its iron lids and fill the postponed expectation of the world with something better than the exertions of mechanical skill. Our day of dependence, our long apprenticeship to the learning of other lands, draws to a close. The millions that around us are rushing into life, cannot always be fed on the sere remains of foreign harvests. Events, actions arise, that must be sung, that will sing themselves. Who can doubt that poetry will revive and lead in a new age, as the star in the constellation Harp, which now flames in our zenith, astronomers announce, shall one day be the pole-star for a thousand years?

In this hope I accept the topic which not only usage but the nature of our association seem to prescribe to this day,—the AMERICAN SCHOLAR. Year by year we come up hither to read one more chapter of his biography. Let us inquire what light new days and events have thrown on his character and his hopes.

It is one of those fables which out of an unknown antiquity convey an unlooked-for wisdom, that the gods, in the beginning, divided Man into men,[1] that he might be more helpful to himself; just as the hand was divided into fingers, the better to answer its end.

The old fable covers a doctrine ever new and sublime; that there is One Man,—present to all particular men only partially, or through one faculty; and that you must take the whole society to find the whole man. Man is not a farmer, or a professor, or an engineer, but he is all. Man is priest, and scholar, and statesman, and producer, and soldier. In the *divided* or social state these functions are parcelled out to individuals, each of whom aims to do his stint of the joint work, whilst each other performs his. The fable implies that the individual, to possess himself, must sometimes return from his own labor to embrace all the other laborers. But, unfortunately, this original unit, this fountain of power, has been so distributed to multitudes, has been so minutely subdivided and peddled out, that it is spilled into drops, and cannot be gathered. The state of society is one in which the members have suffered amputation from the trunk, and strut about so many walking monsters, —a good finger, a neck, a stomach, an elbow, but never a man.

Man is thus metamorphosed into a thing, into many things. The planter, who is Man sent out into the field to gather food, is seldom cheered by any idea of the true dignity of his ministry. He sees his bushel and his cart, and nothing beyond, and sinks into the farmer, instead of Man on the farm. The tradesman scarcely ever gives an ideal worth to his work, but is ridden by the routine of his craft, and the soul is subject to dollars. The priest becomes a form; the attorney a statute-book; the mechanic a machine; the sailor a rope of the ship.

In this distribution of functions the scholar is the delegated intellect. In the right state he is *Man Thinking*. In the degenerate state, when the victim of society, he tends to become a mere thinker, or still worse, the parrot of other men's thinking.

In this view of him, as Man Thinking, the theory of his office is contained. Him Nature solicits with all her placid, all her monitory pic-

tures; him the past instructs; him the future invites. Is not indeed every man a student, and do not all things exist for the student's behoof? And, finally, is not the true scholar the only true master? But the old oracle said, "All things have two handles: beware of the wrong one." In life, too often, the scholar errs with mankind and forfeits his privilege. Let us see him in his school, and consider him in reference to the main influences he receives.

I. The first in time and the first in importance of the influences upon the mind is that of nature. Every day, the sun; and, after sunset, Night and her stars. Ever the winds blow; ever the grass grows. Every day, men and women, conversing— beholding and beholden. The scholar is he of all men whom this spectacle most engages. He must settle its value in his mind. What is nature to him? There is never a beginning, there is never an end, to the inexplicable continuity of this web of God, but always circular power returning into itself. Therein it resembles his own spirit, whose beginning, whose ending, he never can find,—so entire, so boundless. Far too as her splendors shine, system on system shooting like rays, upward, downward, without centre, without circumference,—in the mass and in the particle, Nature hastens to render account of herself to the mind. Classification begins. To the young mind every thing is individual, stands by itself. By and by, it finds how to join two things and see in them one nature; then three, then three thousand; and so, tyrannized over by its own unifying instinct, it goes on tying things together, diminishing anomalies, discovering roots running under ground whereby contrary and remote things cohere and flower out from one stem. It presently learns that since the dawn of history there has been a constant accumulation and classifying of facts. But what is classification but the perceiving that these objects are not chaotic, and are not foreign, but have a law which is also a law of the human mind? The astronomer discovers that geometry, a pure abstraction of the human mind, is the measure of planetary motion. The chemist finds proportions and intelligible method throughout matter; and science is nothing but the finding of analogy, identity, in the most remote parts. The ambitious soul sits down before each refractory fact; one after another reduces all strange constitutions, all new powers, to their class and their law, and goes on forever to animate the last fibre of organization, the outskirts of nature, by insight.

Thus to him, to this schoolboy under the bending dome of day, is suggested that he and it pro-

THE AMERICAN SCHOLAR. 1. divided Man into men: Emerson may be alluding here to the speech of Aristophanes in Plato's *Symposium* or perhaps to a passage in Plutarch's essay, "Of Brotherly Love": but in either case, his allusion is not pedantically precise.

ceed from one root; one is leaf and one is flower; relation, sympathy, stirring in every vein. And what is that root? Is not that the soul of his soul? A thought too bold; a dream too wild. Yet when this spiritual light shall have revealed the law of more earthly natures,—when he has learned to worship the soul, and to see that the natural philosophy that now is, is only the first gropings of its gigantic hand, he shall look forward to an ever expanding knowledge as to a becoming creator. He shall see that nature is the opposite of the soul, answering to it part for part. One is seal and one is print. Its beauty is the beauty of his own mind. Its laws are the laws of his own mind. Nature then becomes to him the measure of his attainments. So much of nature as he is ignorant of, so much of his own mind does he not yet possess. And, in fine, the ancient precept, "Know thyself," and the modern precept, "Study nature," become at last one maxim.

II. The next great influence into the spirit of the scholar is the mind of the Past,—in whatever form, whether of literature, of art, of institutions, that mind is inscribed. Books are the best type of the influence of the past, and perhaps we shall get at the truth,—learn the amount of this influence more conveniently,—by considering their value alone.

The theory of books is noble. The scholar of the first age received into him the world around; brooded thereon; gave it the new arrangement of his own mind, and uttered it again. It came into him life; it went out from him truth. It came to him short-lived actions; it went out from him immortal thoughts. It came to him business; it went from him poetry. It was dead fact; now, it is quick thought. It can stand, and it can go. It now endures, it now flies, it now inspires. Precisely in proportion to the depth of mind from which it issued, so high does it soar, so long does it sing.

Or, I might say, it depends on how far the process had gone, of transmuting life into truth. In proportion to the completeness of the distillation, so will the purity and imperishableness of the product be. But none is quite perfect. As no airpump can by any means make a perfect vacuum, so neither can any artist entirely exclude the conventional, the local, the perishable from his book, or write a book of pure thought, that shall be as efficient, in all respects, to a remote posterity, as to contemporaries, or rather to the second age. Each age, it is found, must write its own books; or rather, each generation for the next succeeding. The books of an older period will not fit this.

Yet hence arises a grave mischief. The sacredness which attaches to the act of creation, the act

of thought, is transferred to the record. The poet chanting was felt to be a divine man: henceforth the chant is divine also. The writer was a just and wise spirit: henceforward it is settled the book is perfect; as love of the hero corrupts into worship of his statue. Instantly the book becomes noxious: the guide is a tyrant. The sluggish and perverted mind of the multitude, slow to open to the incursions of Reason, having once so opened, having once received this book, stands upon it, and makes an outcry if it is disparaged. Colleges are built on it. Books are written on it by thinkers, not by Man Thinking; by men of talent, that is, who start wrong, who set out from accepted dogmas, not from their own sight of principles. Meek young men grow up in libraries, believing it their duty to accept the views which Cicero, which Locke, which Bacon, have given; forgetful that Cicero, Locke, and Bacon were only young men in libraries when they wrote these books.

Hence, instead of Man Thinking, we have the bookworm. Hence the book-learned class, who value books, as such; not as related to nature and the human constitution, but as making a sort of Third Estate with the world and the soul. Hence the restorers of readings, the emendators, the bibliomaniacs of all degrees.

Books are the best of things, well used; abused, among the worst. What is the right use? What is the one end which all means go to effect? They are for nothing but to inspire. I had better never see a book than to be warped by its attraction clean out of my own orbit, and made a satellite instead of a system. The one thing in the world, of value, is the active soul. This every man is entitled to; this every man contains within him, although in almost all men obstructed and as yet unborn. The soul active sees absolute truth and utters truth, or creates. In this action it is genius; not the privilege of here and there a favorite, but the sound estate of every man. In its essence it is progressive. The book, the college, the school of art, the institution of any kind, stop with some past utterance of genius. This is good, say they,—let us hold by this. They pin me down. They look backward and not forward. But genius looks forward: the eyes of man are set in his forehead, not in his hind-head: man hopes: genius creates. Whatever talents may be, if the man create not, the pure efflux of the Deity is not his;—cinders and smoke there may be, but not yet flame. There are creative manners, there are creative actions, and creative words; manners, actions, words, that is, indicative of no custom or authority, but springing spontaneous from the mind's own sense of good and fair.

On the other part, instead of being its own seer,

let it receive from another mind its truth, though it were in torrents of light, without periods of solitude, inquest, and self-recovery, and a fatal disservice is done. Genius is always sufficiently the enemy of genius by over-influence. The literature of every nation bears me witness. The English dramatic poets have Shakspearized now for two hundred years.

Undoubtedly there is a right way of reading, so it be sternly subordinated. Man Thinking must not be subdued by his instruments. Books are for the scholar's idle times. When he can read God directly, the hour is too precious to be wasted in other men's transcripts of their readings. But when the intervals of darkness come, as come they must,—when the sun is hid and the stars withdraw their shining,—we repair to the lamps which were kindled by their ray, to guide our steps to the East again, where the dawn is. We hear, that we may speak. The Arabian proverb says, "A fig tree, looking on a fig tree, becometh fruitful."

It is remarkable, the character of the pleasure we derive from the best books. They impress us with the conviction that one nature wrote and the same reads. We read the verses of one of the great English poets, of Chaucer, of Marvell, of Dryden, with the most modern joy,—with a pleasure, I mean, which is in great part caused by the abstraction of all *time* from their verses. There is some awe mixed with the joy of our surprise, when this poet, who lived in some past world, two or three hundred years ago, says that which lies close to my own soul, that which I also had well-nigh thought and said. But for the evidence thence afforded to the philosophical doctrine of the identity of all minds, we should suppose some preëstablished harmony, some foresight of souls that were to be, and some preparation of stores for their future wants, like the fact observed in insects, who lay up food before death for the young grub they shall never see.

I would not be hurried by any love of system, by any exaggeration of instincts, to underrate the Book. We all know, that as the human body can be nourished on any food, though it were boiled grass and the broth of shoes, so the human mind can be fed by any knowledge. And great and heroic men have existed who had almost no other information than by the printed page. I only would say that it needs a strong head to bear that diet. One must be an inventor to read well. As the proverb says, "He that would bring home the wealth of the Indies, must carry out the wealth of the Indies." There is then creative reading as well as creative writing. When the mind is braced by labor and invention, the page of whatever book we read becomes luminous with manifold allusion. Every sentence is doubly significant, and the sense of our author is as broad as the world. We then see, what is always true, that as the seer's hour of vision is short and rare among heavy days and months, so is its record, perchance, the least part of his volume. The discerning will read, in his Plato or Shakspeare, only that least part,—only the authentic utterances of the oracle;—all the rest he rejects, were it never so many times Plato's and Shakspeare's.

Of course there is a portion of reading quite indispensable to a wise man. History and exact science he must learn by laborious reading. Colleges, in like manner, have their indispensable office,—to teach elements. But they can only highly serve us when they aim not to drill, but to create; when they gather from far every ray of various genius to their hospitable halls, and by the concentrated fires, set the hearts of their youth on flame. Thought and knowledge are natures in which apparatus and pretension avail nothing. Gowns and pecuniary foundations, though of towns of gold, can never countervail the least sentence or syllable of wit. Forget this, and our American colleges will recede in their public importance, whilst they grow richer every year.

III. There goes in the world a notion that the scholar should be a recluse, a valetudinarian,—as unfit for any handiwork or public labor as a penknife for an axe. The so-called "practical men" sneer at speculative men, as if, because they speculate or *see,* they could do nothing. I have heard it said that the clergy,—who are always, more universally than any other class, the scholars of their day,—are addressed as women; that the rough, spontaneous conversation of men they do not hear, but only a mincing and diluted speech. They are often virtually disfranchised; and indeed there are advocates for their celibacy. As far as this is true of the studious classes, it is not just and wise. Action is with the scholar subordinate, but it is essential. Without it he is not yet man. Without it thought can never ripen into truth. Whilst the world hangs before the eye as a cloud of beauty, we cannot even see its beauty. Inaction is cowardice, but there can be no scholar without the heroic mind. The preamble of thought, the transition through which it passes from the unconscious to the conscious, is action. Only so much do I know, as I have lived. Instantly we know whose words are loaded with life, and whose not.

The world,—this shadow of the soul, or *other me,*—lies wide around. Its attractions are the keys which unlock my thoughts and make me acquainted with myself. I run eagerly into this resounding tumult. I grasp the hands of those next me, and take my place in the ring to suffer and to work, taught by an instinct that so shall the dumb abyss be vocal with speech. I pierce its order; I dissipate its fear; I dispose of it within the circuit of my expanding life. So much only of life as I know by experience, so much of the wilderness have I vanquished and planted, or so far have I extended my being, my dominion. I do not see how any man can afford, for the sake of his nerves and his nap, to spare any action in which he can partake. It is pearls and rubies to his discourse. Drudgery, calamity, exasperation, want, are instructors in eloquence and wisdom. The true scholar grudges every opportunity of action past by, as a loss of power. It is the raw material out of which the intellect moulds her splendid products. A strange process too, this by which experience is converted into thought, as a mulberry leaf is converted into satin. The manufacture goes forward at all hours.

The actions and events of our childhood and youth are now matters of calmest observation. They lie like fair pictures in the air. Not so with our recent actions,—with the business which we now have in hand. On this we are quite unable to speculate. Our affections as yet circulate through it. We no more feel or know it than we feel the feet, or the hand, or the brain of our body. The new deed is yet a part of life,—remains for a time immersed in our unconscious life. In some contemplative hour it detaches itself from the life like a ripe fruit, to become a thought of the mind. Instantly it is raised, transfigured; the corruptible has put on incorruption. Henceforth it is an object of beauty, however base its origin and neighborhood. Observe too the impossibility of antedating this act. In its grub state, it cannot fly, it cannot shine, it is a dull grub. But suddenly, without observation, the selfsame thing unfurls beautiful wings, and is an angel of wisdom. So is there no fact, no event, in our private history, which shall not, sooner or later, lose its adhesive, inert form, and astonish us by soaring from our body into the empyrean. Cradle and infancy, school and playground, the fear of boys, and dogs, and ferules, the love of little maids and berries, and many another fact that once filled the whole sky, are gone already; friend and relative, profession and party, town and country, nation and world, must also soar and sing.

Of course, he who has put forth his total strength in fit actions has the richest return of wisdom. I will not shut myself out of this globe of action, and transplant an oak into a flowerpot, there to hunger and pine; nor trust the revenue of some single faculty, and exhaust one vein of thought, much like those Savoyards, who, getting their live-

lihood by carving shepherds, shepherdesses, and smoking Dutchmen, for all Europe, went out one day to the mountain to find stock, and discovered that they had whittled up the last of their pine trees. Authors we have, in numbers, who have written out their vein, and who, moved by a commendable prudence, sail for Greece or Palestine, follow the trapper into the prairie, or ramble round Algiers, to replenish their merchantable stock.

If it were only for a vocabulary, the scholar would be covetous of action. Life is our dictionary. Years are well spent in country labors; in town; in the insight into trades and manufactures; in frank intercourse with many men and women; in science; in art; to the one end of mastering in all their facts a language by which to illustrate and embody our perceptions. I learn immediately from any speaker how much he has already lived, through the poverty or the splendor of his speech. Life lies behind us as the quarry from whence we get tiles and copestones for the masonry of to-day. This is the way to learn grammar. Colleges and books only copy the language which the field and the work-yard made.

But the final value of action, like that of books, and better than books, is that it is a resource. That great principle of Undulation in nature, that shows itself in the inspiring and expiring of the breath; in desire and satiety; in the ebb and flow of the sea; in day and night; in heat and cold; and, as yet more deeply ingrained in every atom and every fluid, is known to us under the name of Polarity,— these "fits of easy transmission and reflection," as Newton called them, are the law of nature because they are the law of spirit.

The mind now thinks, now acts, and each fit reproduces the other. When the artist has exhausted his materials, when the fancy no longer paints, when thoughts are no longer apprehended and books are a weariness,—he has always the resource *to live*. Character is higher than intellect. Thinking is the function. Living is the functionary. The stream retreats to its source. A great soul will be strong to live, as well as strong to think. Does he lack organ or medium to impart his truths? He can still fall back on this elemental force of living them. This is a total act. Thinking is a partial act. Let the grandeur of justice shine in his affairs. Let the beauty of affection cheer his lowly roof. Those "far from fame," who dwell and act with him, will feel the force of his constitution in the doings and passages of the day better than it can be measured by any public and designed display. Time shall teach him that the scholar loses no hour which the man lives. Herein he unfolds the sacred germ of his instinct, screened from influence. What is lost in seemliness is gained in strength. Not out of those on whom systems of education have exhausted their culture, comes the helpful giant to destroy the old or to build the new, but out of unhandselled [2] savage nature; out of terrible Druids and Berserkers come at last Alfred and Shakspeare.

I hear therefore with joy whatever is beginning to be said of the dignity and necessity of labor to every citizen. There is virtue yet in the hoe and the spade, for learned as well as for unlearned hands. And labor is everywhere welcome; always we are invited to work; only be this limitation observed, that a man shall not for the sake of wider activity sacrifice any opinion to the popular judgments and modes of action.

I have now spoken of the education of the scholar by nature, by books, and by action. It remains to say somewhat of his duties.

They are such as become Man Thinking. They may all be comprised in self-trust. The office of the scholar is to cheer, to raise, and to guide men by showing them facts amidst appearances. He plies the slow, unhonored, and unpaid task of observation. Flamsteed [3] and Herschel,[4] in their glazed observatories, may catalogue the stars with the praise of all men, and the results being splendid and useful, honor is sure. But he, in his private observatory, cataloguing obscure and nebulous stars of the human mind, which as yet no man has thought of as such,—watching days and months sometimes for a few facts; correcting still his old records;—must relinquish display and immediate fame. In the long period of his preparation he must betray often an ignorance and shiftlessness in popular arts, incurring the disdain of the able who shoulder him aside. Long he must stammer in his speech; often forego the living for the dead. Worse yet, he must accept—how often!—poverty and solitude. For the ease and pleasure of treading the old road, accepting the fashions, the education, the religion of society, he takes the cross of making his own, and, of course, the self-accusation, the faint heart, the frequent uncertainty and loss of time, which are the nettles and tangling vines in the way

of the self-relying and self-directed; and the state of virtual hostility in which he seems to stand to society, and especially to educated society. For all this loss and scorn, what offset? He is to find consolation in exercising the highest functions of human nature. He is one who raises himself from private considerations and breathes and lives on public and illustrious thoughts. He is the world's eye. He is the world's heart. He is to resist the vulgar prosperity that retrogrades ever to barbarism, by preserving and communicating heroic sentiments, noble biographies, melodious verse, and the conclusions of history. Whatsoever oracles the human heart, in all emergencies, in all solemn hours, has uttered as its commentary on the world of actions, —these he shall receive and impart. And whatsoever new verdict Reason from her inviolable seat pronounces on the passing men and events of to-day,—this he shall hear and promulgate.

These being his functions, it becomes him to feel all confidence in himself, and to defer never to the popular cry. He and he only knows the world. The world of any moment is the merest appearance. Some great decorum, some fetish of a government, some ephemeral trade, or war, or man, is cried up by half mankind and cried down by the other half, as if all depended on this particular up or down. The odds are that the whole question is not worth the poorest thought which the scholar has lost in listening to the controversy. Let him not quit his belief that a popgun is a popgun, though the ancient and honorable of the earth affirm it to be the crack of doom. In silence, in steadiness, in severe abstraction, let him hold by himself; add observation to observation, patient of neglect, patient of reproach, and bide his own time,—happy enough if he can satisfy himself alone that this day he has seen something truly. Success treads on every right step. For the instinct is sure, that prompts him to tell his brother what he thinks. He then learns that in going down into the secrets of his own mind he has descended into the secrets of all minds. He learns that he who has mastered any law in his private thoughts, is master to that extent of all men whose language he speaks, and of all into whose language his own can be translated. The poet, in utter solitude remembering his spontaneous thoughts and recording them, is found to have recorded that which men in crowded cities find true for them also. The orator distrusts at first the fitness of his frank confessions, his want of knowledge of the persons he addresses, until he finds that he is the complement of his hearers;— that they drink his words because he fulfils for them their own nature; the deeper he dives into his

---

2. **unhandselled:** a rare word (see *OED*), used by Emerson here, in a very unliteral sense, to mean something like "unequipped," "unfurnished," "unprovided for," with overtones of rawness, crudity, and primitiveness.   3. **Flamsteed:** John Flamsteed (1646–1719), English astronomer, author of *Historia Coelestis Britannica.*   4. **Herschel:** Emerson may be referring to either Sir Frederick William Herschel (1738–1822), German-born but English-adopted astronomer, discoverer of the planet Uranus, or to his son, Sir John Frederick William Herschel (1792–1871), English astronomer and chemist.

privatest, secretest presentiment, to his wonder he finds this is the most acceptable, most public, and universally true. The people delight in it; the better part of every man feels, This is my music; this is myself.

In self-trust all the virtues are comprehended. Free should the scholar be,—free and brave. Free even to the definition of freedom, "without any hindrance that does not arise out of his own constitution." [5] Brave; for fear is a thing which a scholar by his very function puts behind him. Fear always springs from ignorance. It is a shame to him if his tranquillity, amid dangerous times, arise from the presumption that like children and women his is a protected class; or if he seek a temporary peace by the diversion of his thoughts from politics or vexed questions, hiding his head like an ostrich in the flowering bushes, peeping into microscopes, and turning rhymes, as a boy whistles to keep his courage up. So is the danger a danger still; so is the fear worse. Manlike let him turn and face it. Let him look into its eye and search its nature, inspect its origin,—see the whelping of this lion,—which lies no great way back; he will then find in himself a perfect comprehension of its nature and extent; he will have made his hands meet on the other side, and can henceforth defy it and pass on superior. The world is his who can see through its pretension. What deafness, what stone-blind custom, what overgrown error you behold is there only by sufferance, —by your sufferance. See it to be a lie, and you have already dealt it its mortal blow.

Yes, we are the cowed,—we the trustless. It is a mischievous notion that we are come late into nature; that the world was finished a long time ago. As the world was plastic and fluid in the hands of God, so it is ever to so much of his attributes as we bring to it. To ignorance and sin, it is flint. They adapt themselves to it as they may; but in proportion as a man has any thing in him divine, the firmament flows before him and takes his signet and form. Not he is great who can alter matter, but he who can alter my state of mind. They are the kings of the world who give the color of their present thought to all nature and all art, and persuade men by the cheerful serenity of their carrying the matter, that this thing which they do is the apple which the ages have desired to pluck, now at last ripe, and inviting nations to the harvest. The great man makes the great thing. Wherever Macdonald sits, there is the head of the table. Linnaeus [6] makes botany the most alluring of studies, and

wins it from the farmer and the herb-woman; Davy,[7] chemistry; and Cuvier,[8] fossils. The day is always his who works in it with serenity and great aims. The unstable estimates of men crowd to him whose mind is filled with a truth, as the heaped waves of the Atlantic follow the moon.

For this self-trust, the reason is deeper than can be fathomed,—darker than can be enlightened. I might not carry with me the feeling of my audience in stating my own belief. But I have already shown the ground of my hope, in adverting to the doctrine that man is one. I believe man has been wronged; he has wronged himself. He has almost lost the light that can lead him back to his prerogatives. Men are become of no account. Men in history, men in the world of to-day, are bugs, are spawn, and are called "the mass" and "the herd." In a century, in a millennium, one or two men; that is to say, one or two approximations to the right state of every man. All the rest behold in the hero or the poet their own green and crude being,—ripened; yes, and are content to be less, so *that* may attain to its full stature. What a testimony, full of grandeur, full of pity, is borne to the demands of his own nature, by the poor clansman, the poor partisan, who rejoices in the glory of his chief. The poor and the low find some amends to their immense moral capacity, for their acquiescence in a political and social inferiority. They are content to be brushed like flies from the path of a great person, so that justice shall be done by him to that common nature which it is the dearest desire of all to see enlarged and glorified. They sun themselves in the great man's light, and feel it to be their own element. They cast the dignity of man from their downtrod selves upon the shoulders of a hero, and will perish to add one drop of blood to make that great heart beat, those giant sinews combat and conquer. He lives for us, and we live in him.

Men, such as they are, very naturally seek money or power; and power because it is as good as money,—the "spoils," so called, "of office." And why not? for they aspire to the highest, and this, in their sleep-walking, they dream is highest. Wake them and they shall quit the false good and leap to the true, and leave governments to clerks and desks. This revolution is to be wrought by the gradual domestication of the idea of Culture. The main enterprise of the world for splendor, for ex-

---

5. "without . . . constitution": freedom as defined by Immanuel Kant.   6. Linnaeus: See *Nature*, 2 n.

7. Davy: Sir Humphry Davy (1778–1829), English chemist, discoverer of potassium and sodium, professor of chemistry at the Royal Institution.   8. Cuvier: Baron Cuvier (1769–1832), French naturalist, palaeontologist, comparative anatomist, author of the *Règne Animal*.

tent, is the upbuilding of a man. Here are the materials strewn along the ground. The private life of one man shall be a more illustrious monarchy, more formidable to its enemy, more sweet and serene in its influence to its friend, than any kingdom in history. For a man, rightly viewed, comprehendeth the particular natures of all men. Each philosopher, each bard, each actor has only done for me, as by a delegate, what one day I can do for myself. The books which once we valued more than the apple of the eye, we have quite exhausted. What is that but saying that we have come up with the point of view which the universal mind took through the eyes of one scribe; we have been that man, and have passed on. First, one, then another, we drain all cisterns, and waxing greater by all these supplies, we crave a better and more abundant food. The man has never lived that can feed us ever. The human mind cannot be enshrined in a person who shall set a barrier on any one side to this unbounded, unboundable empire. It is one central fire, which, flaming now out of the lips of Etna, lightens the capes of Sicily, and now out of the throat of Vesuvius, illuminates the towers and vineyards of Naples. It is one light which beams out of a thousand stars. It is one soul which animates all men.

But I have dwelt perhaps tediously upon this abstraction of the Scholar. I ought not to delay longer to add what I have to say of nearer reference to the time and to this country.

Historically, there is thought to be a difference in the ideas which predominate over successive epochs, and there are data for marking the genius of the Classic, of the Romantic, and now of the Reflective or Philosophical age. With the views I have intimated of the oneness or the identity of the mind through all individuals, I do not much dwell on these differences. In fact, I believe each individual passes through all three. The boy is a Greek; the youth, romantic; the adult, reflective. I deny not, however, that a revolution in the leading idea may be distinctly enough traced.

Our age is bewailed as the age of Introversion. Must that needs be evil? We, it seems, are critical; we are embarrassed with second thoughts; we cannot enjoy any thing for hankering to know whereof the pleasures consists; we are lined with eyes; we see with our feet; the time is infected with Hamlet's unhappiness,—

"Sicklied o'er with the pale cast of thought." 9

9. "Sicklied . . . thought": *Hamlet*, III.i.85.

It is so bad then? Sight is the last thing to be pitied. Would we be blind? Do we fear lest we should outsee nature and God, and drink truth dry? I look upon the discontent of the literary class as a mere announcement of the fact that they find themselves not in the state of mind of their fathers, and regret the coming state as untried; as a boy dreads the water before he has learned that he can swim. If there is any period one would desire to be born in, is it not the age of Revolution; when the old and the new stand side by side and admit of being compared; when the energies of all men are searched by fear and by hope; when the historic glories of the old can be compensated by the rich possibilities of the new era? This time, like all times, is a very good one, if we but know what to do with it.

I read with some joy of the auspicious signs of the coming days, as they glimmer already through poetry and art, through philosophy and science, through church and state.

One of these signs is the fact that the same movement which effected the elevation of what was called the lowest class in the state, assumed in literature a very marked and as benign an aspect. Instead of the sublime and beautiful, the near, the low, the common, was explored and poetized. That which had been negligently trodden under foot by those who were harnessing and provisioning themselves for long journeys into far countries, is suddenly found to be richer than all foreign parts. The literature of the poor, the feelings of the child, the philosophy of the street, the meaning of the household life, are the topics of the time. It is a great stride. It is a sign—is it not?—of new vigor when the extremities are made active, when currents of warm life run into the hands and the feet. I ask not for the great, the remote, the romantic; what is doing in Italy or Arabia; what is Greek art, or Provençal minstrelsy; I embrace the common, I explore and sit at the feet of the familiar, the low. Give me insight into to-day, and you may have the antique and future worlds. What would we really know the meaning of? The meal in the firkin; the milk in the pan; the ballad in the street; the news of the boat; the glance of the eye; the form and the gait of the body;—show me the ultimate reason of these matters; show me the sublime presence of the highest spiritual cause lurking, as always it does lurk, in these suburbs and extremities of nature; let me see every trifle bristling with the polarity that ranges it instantly on an eternal law; and the shop, the plough, and the ledger referred to the like cause by which light undulates and poets sing;—and the world lies no longer a dull miscellany and lumber-room, but has form and order; there is no trifle, there is no puzzle, but one design unites and animates the farthest pinnacle and the lowest trench.

This idea has inspired the genius of Goldsmith, Burns, Cowper, and, in a newer time, of Goethe, Wordsworth, and Carlyle. This idea they have differently followed and with various success. In contrast with their writing, the style of Pope, of Johnson, of Gibbon, looks cold and pedantic. This writing is blood-warm. Man is surprised to find that things near are not less beautiful and wondrous than things remote. The near explains the far. The drop is a small ocean. A man is related to all nature. This perception of the worth of the vulgar is fruitful in discoveries. Goethe, in this very thing the most modern of the moderns, has shown us, as none ever did, the genius of the ancients.

There is one man of genius who has done much for this philosophy of life, whose literary value has never yet been rightly estimated;—I mean Emanuel Swedenborg.[10] The most imaginative of men, yet writing with the precision of a mathematician, he endeavored to engraft a purely philosophical Ethics on the popular Christianity of his time. Such an attempt of course must have difficulty which no genius could surmount. But he saw and showed the connection between nature and the affections of the soul. He pierced the emblematic or spiritual character of the visible, audible, tangible world. Especially did his shade-loving muse hover over and interpret the lower parts of nature; he showed the mysterious bond that allies moral evil to the foul material forms, and has given in epical parables a theory of insanity, of beasts, of unclean and fearful things.

Another sign of our times, also marked by an analogous political movement, is the new importance given to the single person. Every thing that tends to insulate the individual,—to surround him with barriers of natural respect, so that each man shall feel the world is his, and man shall treat with man as a sovereign state with a sovereign state,—tends to true union as well as greatness. "I learned," said the melancholy Pestalozzi,[11] "that no man in God's wide earth is either willing or able to help any other man." Help must come from the bosom alone. The scholar is that man who must take up into himself all the ability of the time, all the contributions of the past, all the hopes

of the future. He must be an university of knowledges. If there be one lesson more than another which should pierce his ear, it is, The world is nothing, the man is all; in yourself is the law of all nature, and you know not yet how a globule of sap ascends; in yourself slumbers the whole of Reason; it is for you to know all; it is for you to dare all. Mr. President and Gentlemen, this confidence in the unsearched might of man belongs, by all motives, by all prophecy, by all preparation, to the American Scholar. We have listened too long to the courtly muses of Europe. The spirit of the American freeman is already suspected to be timid, imitative, tame. Public and private avarice make the air we breathe thick and fat. The scholar is decent, indolent, complaisant. See already the tragic consequence. The mind of this country, taught to aim at low objects, eats upon itself. There is no work for any but the decorous and the complaisant. Young men of the fairest promise, who begin life upon our shores, inflated by the mountain winds, shined upon by all the stars of God, find the earth below not in unison with these, but are hindered from action by the disgust which the principles on which business is managed inspire, and turn drudges, or die of disgust, some of them suicides. What is the remedy? They did not yet see, and thousands of young men as hopeful now crowding to the barriers for the career do not yet see, that if the single man plant himself indomitably on his instincts, and there abide, the huge world will come round to him. Patience,—patience; with the shades of all the good and great for company; and for solace the perspective of your own infinite life; and for work the study and the communication of principles, the making those instincts prevalent, the conversion of the world. Is it not the chief disgrace in the world, not to be an unit;—not to be reckoned one character;—not to yield that peculiar fruit which each man was created to bear, but to be reckoned in the gross, in the hundred, or the thousand, of the party, the section, to which we belong; and our opinion predicted geographically, as the north, or the south? Not so, brothers and friends—please God, ours shall not be so. We will walk on our own feet; we will work with our own hands; we will speak our own minds. The study of letters shall be no longer a name for pity, for doubt, and for sensual indulgence. The dread of man and the love of man shall be a wall of defence and a wreath of joy around all. A nation of men will for the first time exist, because each believes himself inspired by the Divine Soul which also inspires all men.

---

10. **Emanuel Swedenborg:** See *Nature*, 1n.  11. **the melancholy Pestalozzi:** Johann Heinrich Pestalozzi (1746–1827), Swiss educational reformer, much admired by the Transcendentalists. Pestalozzi's influence is discernible in Emerson's own essay "Education," in *Lectures and Biographical Sketches* (*Works*, X).

# SELF-RELIANCE

◇

⟨[ THIS famous discourse was first published in *Essays: First Series* (1841) (*Works*, II). The theme of moral independence, of resistance to external pressures, of nonconformity had been a favorite one with Emerson for many years before this essay was written: it was the subject, for example, of one of his best sermons, "Trust Yourself," which he had preached as early as 1830, and it is of course one of the major strains in "The American Scholar." Emerson's journals for the thirties abound in admonitions to himself to preserve his status as a free individual at all costs, and in the lectures he delivered in Boston and elsewhere he returned to the subject again and again. An interesting summary of the sources of "Self-Reliance" in Emerson's own journals and lectures may be found in Stephen E. Whicher, *Selections from Ralph Waldo Emerson* (1957), pp. 481–82.

◇

*"Ne te quæsiveris extra."* [1]

"Man is his own star; and the soul that can
Render an honest and a perfect man
Commands all light, all influence, all fate;
Nothing to him falls early or too late.
Our acts our angels are, or good or ill,
Our fatal shadows that walk by us still." [2]
EPILOGUE TO BEAUMONT AND
FLETCHER'S *Honest Man's Fortune*

Cast the bantling on the rocks,
Suckle him with the she-wolf's teat,
Wintered with the hawk and fox,
Power and speed be hands and feet.

I READ the other day some verses written by an eminent painter which were original and not conventional.[3] The soul always hears an admonition

SELF-RELIANCE. **1.** *"Ne . . . extra":* "Do not seek yourself outside of yourself"; or perhaps, "ask for no man's opinion but your own" (Persius, *Satires*, I.7), a favorite quotation of Emerson. In a journal passage Emerson himself paraphrased the line thus: "Thou art sufficient unto thyself" (*Journals*, III, 337). (A more correct reading: "Nec te quaesiveris extra.") **2.** "Man . . . still": See Beaumont and Fletcher, *The Honest Man's Fortune*, Epilogue, ll. 33–38. **3. some . . . conventional:** These verses seem to have been some lines in a poem by Washington Allston (1779–1843), American painter and man of letters, with whom Emerson was acquainted. To judge from a journal entry of 1837 (*Journals*, IV, 295), he is referring here to a poem of Allston's entitled "To the Author of 'The Diary of an Ennuyée' [Mrs. Jameson], One of the Truest and Most Beautiful Books Ever Written on Italy" (Washington Allston, *Lectures on Art, and Poems*, 1850). The seventh and eighth stanzas of this poem, with their characterization of Nature as a loving ministrant to man, may have been particularly appealing to Emerson.

in such lines, let the subject be what it may. The sentiment they instil is of more value than any thought they may contain. To believe your own thought, to believe that what is true for you in your private heart is true for all men,—that is genius. Speak your latent conviction, and it shall be the universal sense; for the inmost in due time becomes the outmost, and our first thought is rendered back to us by the trumpets of the Last Judgment. Familiar as the voice of the mind is to each, the highest merit we ascribe to Moses, Plato and Milton is that they set at naught books and traditions, and spoke not what men, but what *they* thought. A man should learn to detect and watch that gleam of light which flashes across his mind from within, more than the lustre of the firmament of bards and sages. Yet he dismisses without notice his thought, because it is his. In every work of genius we recognize our own rejected thoughts; they come back to us with a certain alienated majesty. Great works of art have no more affecting lesson for us than this. They teach us to abide by our spontaneous impression with good-humored inflexibility then most when the whole cry of voices is on the other side. Else to-morrow a stranger will say with masterly good sense precisely what we have thought and felt all the time, and we shall be forced to take with shame our own opinion from another.

There is a time in every man's education when he arrives at the conviction that envy is ignorance; that imitation is suicide; that he must take himself for better or worse as his portion; that though the wide universe is full of good, no kernel of nourishing corn can come to him but through his toil bestowed on that plot of ground which is given to him to till. The power which resides in him is new in nature, and none but he knows what that is which he can do, nor does he know until he has tried. Not for nothing one face, one character, one fact, makes much impression on him, and another none. This sculpture in the memory is not without preëstablished harmony. The eye was placed where one ray should fall, that it might testify of that particular ray. We but half express ourselves, and are ashamed of that divine idea which each of us represents. It may be safely trusted as proportionate and of good issues, so it be faithfully imparted, but God will not have his work made manifest by cowards. A man is relieved and gay when he has put his heart into his work and done his best; but what he has said or done otherwise shall give him no peace. It is a deliverance which does not deliver. In the attempt his genius deserts him; no muse befriends; no invention, no hope.

Trust thyself: every heart vibrates to that iron

string. Accept the place the divine providence has found for you, the society of your contemporaries, the connection of events. Great men have always done so, and confided themselves childlike to the genius of their age, betraying their perception that the absolutely trustworthy was seated at their heart, working through their hands, predominating in all their being. And we are now men, and must accept in the highest mind the same transcendent destiny; and not minors and invalids in a protected corner, not cowards fleeing before a revolution, but guides, redeemers and benefactors, obeying the Almighty effort and advancing on Chaos and the Dark.

What pretty oracles nature yields us on this text in the face and behavior of children, babes, and even brutes! That divided and rebel mind, that distrust of a sentiment because our arithmetic has computed the strength and means opposed to our purpose, these have not. Their mind being whole, their eye is as yet unconquered, and when we look in their faces we are disconcerted. Infancy conforms to nobody; all conform to it; so that one babe commonly makes four or five out of the adults who prattle and play to it. So God has armed youth and puberty and manhood no less with its own piquancy and charm, and made it enviable and gracious and its claims not to be put by, if it will stand by itself. Do not think the youth has no force, because he cannot speak to you and me. Hark! in the next room his voice is sufficiently clear and emphatic. It seems he knows how to speak to his contemporaries. Bashful or bold then, he will know how to make us seniors very unnecessary.

The nonchalance of boys who are sure of a dinner, and would disdain as much as a lord or do or say aught to conciliate one, is the healthy attitude for human nature. A boy is in the parlor what the pit is in the playhouse; independent, irresponsible, looking out from his corner on such people and facts as pass by, he tries and sentences them on their merits, in the swift, summary way of boys, as good, bad, interesting, silly, eloquent, troublesome. He cumbers himself never about consequences, about interests; he gives an independent, genuine verdict. You must court him; he does not court you. But the man is as it were clapped into jail by his consciousness. As soon as he has once acted or spoken with *éclat* he is a committed person, watched by the sympathy or the hatred of hundreds, whose affections must now enter into his account. There is no Lethe [4] for this. Ah, that he could pass again into his neutrality! Who can thus

avoid all pledges and, having observed, observe again from the same unaffected, unbiased, unbribable, unaffrighted innocence,—must always be formidable. He would utter opinions on all passing affairs, which being seen to be not private but necessary, would sink like darts into the ear of men and put them in fear.

These are the voices which we hear in solitude, but they grow faint and inaudible as we enter into the world. Society everywhere is in conspiracy against the manhood of every one of its members. Society is a joint-stock company, in which the members agree, for the better securing of his bread to each shareholder, to surrender the liberty and culture of the eater. The virtue in most request is conformity. Self-reliance is its aversion. It loves not realities and creators, but names and customs.

Whoso would be a man, must be a nonconformist. He who would gather immortal palms must not be hindered by the name of goodness, but must explore if it be goodness. Nothing is at last sacred but the integrity of your own mind. Absolve you to yourself, and you shall have the suffrage of the world. I remember an answer which when quite young I was prompted to make to a valued adviser who was wont to importune me with the dear old doctrines of the church. On my saying, "What have I to do with the sacredness of traditions, if I live wholly from within?" my friend suggested,— "But these impulses may be from below, not from above." I replied, "They do not seem to me to be such; but if I am the Devil's child, I will live then from the Devil." No law can be sacred to me but that of my nature. Good and bad are but names very readily transferable to that or this; the only right is what is after my constitution; the only wrong what is against it. A man is to carry himself in the presence of all opposition as if every thing were titular and ephemeral but he. I am ashamed to think how easily we capitulate to badges and names, to large societies and dead institutions. Every decent and well-spoken individual affects and sways me more than is right. I ought to go upright and vital, and speak the rude truth in all ways. If malice and vanity were the coat of philanthropy, shall that pass? If an angry bigot assumes this bountiful cause of Abolition, and comes to me with his last news from Barbadoes, why should I not say to him, "Go love thy infant; love thy wood-chopper; be good-natured and modest; have that grace; and never varnish your hard, uncharitable ambition with this incredible tenderness for black folk a thousand miles off. Thy love afar is spite at home." Rough and graceless would be such greeting, but truth is handsomer than the affectation of love. Your goodness must have some

---

4. **Lethe:** in classical mythology, the river of forgetfulness.

edge to it,—else it is none. The doctrine of hatred must be preached, as the counteraction of the doctrine of love, when that pules and whines. I shun father and mother and wife and brother when my genius calls me. I would write on the lintels of the door-post, *Whim*. I hope it is somewhat better than whim at last, but we cannot spend the day in explanation. Expect me not to show cause why I seek or why I exclude company. Then again, do not tell me, as a good man did to-day, of my obligation to put all poor men in good situations. Are they *my* poor? I tell thee, thou foolish philanthropist, that I grudge the dollar, the dime, the cent I give to such men as do not belong to me and to whom I do not belong. There is a class of persons to whom by all spiritual affinity I am bought and sold; for them I will go to prison if need be; but your miscellaneous popular charities; the education at college of fools; the building of meetinghouses to the vain end to which many now stand; alms to sots, and the thousand-fold Relief Societies;—though I confess with shame I sometimes succumb and give the dollar, it is a wicked dollar, which by and by I shall have the manhood to withhold.

Virtues are, in the popular estimate, rather the exception than the rule. There is the man *and* his virtues. Men do what is called a good action, as some piece of courage or charity, much as they would pay a fine in expiation of daily non-appearance on parade. Their works are done as an apology or extenuation of their living in the world,—as invalids and the insane pay a high board. Their virtues are penances. I do not wish to expiate, but to live. My life is for itself and not for a spectacle. I much prefer that it should be of a lower strain, so it be genuine and equal, than that it should be glittering and unsteady. I wish it to be sound and sweet, and not to need diet and bleeding. I ask primary evidence that you are a man, and refuse this appeal from the man to his actions. I know that for myself it makes no difference whether I do or forbear those actions which are reckoned excellent. I cannot consent to pay for a privilege where I have intrinsic right. Few and mean as my gifts may be, I actually am, and do not need for my own assurance or the assurance of my fellows any secondary testimony.

What I must do is all that concerns me, not what the people think. This rule, equally arduous in actual and in intellectual life, may serve for the whole distinction between greatness and meanness. It is the harder because you will always find those who think they know what is your duty better than you know it. It is easy in the world to live after the world's opinion; it is easy in solitude to live after our own; but the great man is he who in the midst of the crowd keeps with perfect sweetness the independence of solitude.

The objection to conforming to usages that have become dead to you is that it scatters your force. It loses your time and blurs the impression of your character. If you maintain a dead church, contribute to a dead Bible-society, vote with a great party either for the government or against it, spread your table like base housekeepers,—under all these screens I have difficulty to detect the precise man you are: and of course so much force is withdrawn from your proper life. But do your work, and I shall know you. Do your work, and you shall reinforce yourself. A man must consider what a blind-man's-buff is this game of conformity. If I know your sect I anticipate your argument. I hear a preacher announce for his text and topic the expediency of one of the institutions of his church. Do I not know beforehand that not possibly can he say a new and spontaneous word? Do I not know that with all this ostentation of examining the grounds of the institution he will do no such thing? Do I not know that he is pledged to himself not to look but at one side, the permitted side, not as a man, but as a parish minister? He is a retained attorney, and these airs of the bench are the emptiest affectation. Well, most men have bound their eyes with one or another handkerchief, and attached themselves to some one of these communities of opinion. This conformity makes them not false in a few particulars, authors of a few lies, but false in all particulars. Their every truth is not quite true. Their two is not the real two, their four not the real four; so that every word they say chagrins us and we know not where to begin to set them right. Meantime nature is not slow to equip us in the prison-uniform of the party to which we adhere. We come to wear one cut of face and figure, and acquire by degrees the gentlest asinine expression. There is a mortifying experience in particular, which does not fail to wreak itself also in the general history; I mean "the foolish face of praise," [5] the forced smile which we put on in company where we do not feel at ease, in answer to conversation which does not interest us. The muscles, not spontaneously moved but moved by a low usurping wilfulness, grow tight about the outline of the face, with the most disagreeable sensation.

For nonconformity the world whips you with its displeasure. And therefore a man must know how to estimate a sour face. The by-standers look askance on him in the public street or in the

---

5. **"the foolish face of praise":** "And wonder with a foolish face of praise" (Pope, "Epistle to Dr. Arbuthnot," l. 212).

friend's parlor. If this aversion had its origin in contempt and resistance like his own he might well go home with a sad countenance; but the sour faces of the multitude, like their sweet faces, have no deep cause, but are put on and off as the wind blows and a newspaper directs. Yet is the discontent of the multitude more formidable than that of the senate and the college. It is easy enough for a firm man who knows the world to brook the rage of the cultivated classes. Their rage is decorous and prudent, for they are timid, as being very vulnerable themselves. But when to their feminine rage the indignation of the people is added, when the ignorant and the poor are aroused, when the unintelligent brute force that lies at the bottom of society is made to growl and mow, it needs the habit of magnanimity and religion to treat it godlike as a trifle of no concernment.

The other terror that scares us from self-trust is our consistency; a reverence for our past act or word because the eyes of others have no other data for computing our orbit than our past acts, and we are loth to disappoint them.

But why should you keep your head over your shoulder? Why drag about this corpse of your memory, lest you contradict somewhat you have stated in this or that public place? Suppose you should contradict yourself; what then? It seems to be a rule of wisdom never to rely on your memory alone, scarcely even in acts of pure memory, but to bring the past for judgment into the thousand-eyed present, and live ever in a new day. In your metaphysics you have denied personality to the Deity, yet when the devout motions of the soul come, yield to them heart and life, though they should clothe God with shape and color. Leave your theory, as Joseph his coat in the hand of the harlot, and flee.[6]

A foolish consistency is the hobgoblin of little minds, adored by little statesmen and philosophers and divines. With consistency a great soul has simply nothing to do. He may as well concern himself with his shadow on the wall. Speak what you think now in hard words and to-morrow speak what to-morrow thinks in hard words again, though it contradict every thing you said to-day.—"Ah, so you shall be sure to be misunderstood."—Is it so bad then to be misunderstood? Pythagoras was misunderstood, and Socrates, and Jesus, and Luther, and Copernicus, and Galileo, and Newton, and every pure and wise spirit that ever took flesh. To be great is to be misunderstood.

I suppose no man can violate his nature. All the sallies of his will are rounded in by the law of his being, as the inequalities of Andes and Himmaleh are insignificant in the curve of the sphere. Nor does it matter how you gauge and try him. A character is like an acrostic or Alexandrian stanza; —read it forward, backward, or across, it still spells the same thing. In this pleasing contrite wood-life which God allows me, let me record day by day my honest thought without prospect or retrospect, and, I cannot doubt, it will be found symmetrical, though I mean it not and see it not. My book should smell of pines and resound with the hum of insects. The swallow over my window should interweave that thread or straw he carries in his bill into my web also. We pass for what we are. Character teaches above our wills. Men imagine that they communicate their virtue or vice only by overt actions, and do not see that virtue or vice emit a breath every moment.

There will be an agreement in whatever variety of actions, so they be each honest and natural in their hour. For of one will, the actions will be harmonious, however unlike they seem. These varieties are lost sight of at a little distance, at a little height of thought. One tendency unites them all. The voyage of the best ship is a zigzag line of a hundred tacks. See the line from a sufficient distance, and it strengthens itself to the average tendency. Your genuine action will explain itself and will explain your other genuine actions. Your conformity explains nothing. Act singly, and what you have already done singly will justify you now. Greatness appeals to the future. If I can be firm enough to-day to do right and scorn eyes, I must have done so much right before as to defend me now. Be it how it will, do right now. Always scorn appearances and you always may. The force of character is cumulative. All the foregone days of virtue work their health into this. What makes the majesty of the heroes of the senate and the field, which so fills the imagination? The consciousness of a train of great days and victories behind. They shed a united light on the advancing actor. He is attended as by a visible escort of angels. That is it which throws thunder into Chatham's[7] voice, and dignity into Washington's port, and America into Adams's eye. Honor is venerable to us because it is no ephemera. It is always ancient virtue. We worship it to-day because it is not of to-day. We love it and pay it homage because it is not a trap for our love and homage, but is self-dependent, self-derived, and therefore of an old immaculate pedigree, even if shown in a young person.

I hope in these days we have heard the last of

---

6. **Joseph . . . flee:** See Gen. 39:12.

7. **Chatham's voice:** William Pitt, Earl of Chatham (1708–78), English statesman and orator.

conformity and consistency. Let the words be gazetted [8] and ridiculous henceforward. Instead of the gong for dinner, let us hear a whistle from the Spartan fife. Let us never bow and apologize more. A great man is coming to eat at my house. I do not wish to please him; I wish that he should wish to please me. I will stand here for humanity, and though I would make it kind, I would make it true. Let us affront and reprimand the smooth mediocrity and squalid contentment of the times, and hurl in the face of custom and trade and office, the fact which is the upshot of all history, that there is a great responsible Thinker and Actor working wherever a man works; that a true man belongs to no other time or place, but is the centre of things. Where he is, there is nature. He measures you and all men and all events. Ordinarily, every body in society reminds us of somewhat else, or of some other person. Character, reality, reminds you of nothing else; it takes place of the whole creation. The man must be so much that he must make all circumstances indifferent. Every true man is a cause, a country, and an age; requires infinite spaces and numbers and time fully to accomplish his design;—and posterity seem to follow his steps as a train of clients. A man Cæsar is born, and for ages after we have a Roman Empire. Christ is born, and millions of minds so grow and cleave to his genius that he is confounded with virtue and the possible of man. An institution is the lengthened shadow of one man; as, Monachism,[9] of the Hermit Antony; the Reformation, of Luther; Quakerism, of Fox; Methodism, of Wesley; Abolition, of Clarkson.[10] Scipio, Milton called "the height of Rome;" and all history resolves itself very easily into the biography of a few stout and earnest persons.

Let a man then know his worth, and keep things under his feet. Let him not peep or steal, or skulk up and down with the air of a charity-boy, a bastard, or an interloper in the world which exists for him. But the man in the street, finding no worth in himself which corresponds to the force which built a tower or sculptured a marble god, feels poor when he looks on these. To him a palace, a statue, or a costly book have an alien and forbidding air, much like a gay equipage, and seem to say like that, "Who are you, Sir?" Yet they all are his, suitors for his notice, petitioners to his faculties that they will come out and take possession. The picture waits for my verdict; it is not to command

me, but I am to settle its claims to praise. That popular fable of the sot who was picked up deaddrunk in the street, carried to the duke's house, washed and dressed and laid in the duke's bed, and, on his waking, treated with all obsequious ceremony like the duke, and assured that he had been insane,[11] owes its popularity to the fact that it symbolizes so well the state of man, who is in the world a sort of sot, but now and then wakes up, exercises his reason and finds himself a true prince.

Our reading is mendicant and sycophantic. In history our imagination plays us false. Kingdom and lordship, power and estate, are a gaudier vocabulary than private John and Edward in a small house and common day's work; but the things of life are the same to both; the sum total of both is the same. Why all this deference to Alfred and Scanderbeg [12] and Gustavus? [13] Suppose they were virtuous; did they wear out virtue? As great a stake depends on your private act to-day as followed their public and renowned steps. When private men shall act with original views, the lustre will be transferred from the actions of kings to those of gentlemen.

The world has been instructed by its kings, who have so magnetized the eyes of nations. It has been taught by this colossal symbol the mutual reverence that is due from man to man. The joyful loyalty with which men have everywhere suffered the king, the noble, or the great proprietor to walk among them by a law of his own, make his own scale of men and things and reverse theirs, pay for benefits not with money but with honor, and represent the law in his person, was the hieroglyphic by which they obscurely signified their consciousness of their own right and comeliness, the right of every man.

The magnetism which all original action exerts is explained when we inquire the reason of selftrust. Who is the Trustee? [14] What is the aboriginal Self, on which a universal reliance may be grounded? What is the nature and power of that science-baffling star, without parallax, without calculable elements, which shoots a ray of beauty even into trivial and impure actions, if the least

---

8. **gazetted:** retired from active service; tabooed; prohibited. Emerson's special use of the word is his own. 9. **Monachism:** monasticism, of which St. Anthony (c. 250–350 A.D.) was the founder. 10. **Clarkson:** Thomas Clarkson (1760–1846), English antislavery agitator.

11. **That . . . insane:** This is a very widespread folk tale, one version of which is Shakespeare's in the Induction to *The Taming of the Shrew*, sc. ii, in which Christopher Sly, a tinker, wakes up in a bedchamber in a Lord's house and is treated with great deference by the servants standing about. 12. **Scanderbeg:** alternative spelling of Skanderbeg, otherwise known as George Castriota (1403–68), the national hero of the Albanians, who fought for the independence of Albania from the Turks; the subject of the Spanish Jew's Second Tale in Part Third of Longfellow's *Tales of a Wayside Inn*. 13. **Gustavus:** Gustavus II, Adolphus (1594–1632), king of Sweden, one of the leaders of the Protestant cause in the Thirty Years' War. 14. **Trustee:** he who is to be trusted or relied upon.

mark of independence appear? The inquiry leads us to that source, at once the essence of genius, of virtue, and of life, which we call Spontaneity or Instinct.[15] We denote this primary wisdom as Intuition, whilst all later teachings are tuitions.[16] In that deep force, the last fact behind which analysis cannot go, all things find their common origin. For the sense of being which in calm hours arises, we know not how, in the soul, is not diverse from things, from space, from light, from time, from man, but one with them and proceeds obviously from the same source whence their life and being also proceed. We first share the life by which things exist and afterwards see them as appearances in nature and forget that we have shared their cause. Here is the fountain of action and of thought. Here are the lungs of that inspiration which giveth man wisdom and which cannot be denied without impiety and atheism. We lie in the lap of immense intelligence, which makes us receivers of its truth and organs of its activity. When we discern justice, when we discern truth, we do nothing of ourselves, but allow a passage to its beams. If we ask whence this comes, if we seek to pry into the soul that causes, all philosophy is at fault. Its presence or its absence is all we can affirm. Every man discriminates between the voluntary acts of his mind and his involuntary perceptions, and knows that to his involuntary perceptions a perfect faith is due. He may err in the expression of them, but he knows that these things are so, like day and night, not to be disputed. My wilful actions and acquisitions are but roving;—the idlest reverie, the faintest native emotion, command my curiosity and respect. Thoughtless people contradict as readily the statement of perception as of opinions, or rather much more readily; for they do not distinguish between perception and notion. They fancy that I choose to see this or that thing. But perception is not whimsical, but fatal. If I see a trait, my children will see it after me, and in course of time all mankind,—although it may chance that no one has seen it before me. For my perception of it is as much a fact as the sun.

The relations of the soul to the divine spirit are so pure that it is profane to seek to interpose helps. It must be that when God speaketh he should communicate, not one thing, but all things; should fill the world with his voice; should scatter forth light, nature, time, souls, from the centre of the present thought; and new date and new create the whole. Whenever a mind is simple and receives a divine wisdom, old things pass away,—means, teachers, texts, temples fall; it lives now, and absorbs past and future into the present hour. All things are made sacred by relation to it,—one as much as another. All things are dissolved to their centre by their cause, and in the universal miracle petty and particular miracles disappear. If therefore a man claims to know and speak of God and carries you backward to the phraseology of some old mouldered nation in another country, in another world, believe him not. Is the acorn better than the oak which is its fulness and completion? Is the parent better than the child into whom he has cast his ripened being? Whence then this worship of the past? The centuries are conspirators against the sanity and authority of the soul. Time and space are but physiological colors which the eye makes, but the soul is light: where it is, is day; where it was, is night; and history is an impertinence and an injury if it be any thing more than a cheerful apologue or parable of my being and becoming.

Man is timid and apologetic; he is no longer upright; he dares not say "I think," "I am," but quotes some saint or sage. He is ashamed before the blade of grass or the blowing rose. These roses under my window make no reference to former roses or to better ones; they are for what they are; they exist with God to-day. There is no time to them. There is simply the rose; it is perfect in every moment of its existence. Before a leaf-bud has burst, its whole life acts; in the full-blown flower there is no more; in the leafless root there is no less. Its nature is satisfied and it satisfies nature in all moments alike. But man postpones or remembers; he does not live in the present, but with reverted eye laments the past, or, heedless of the riches that surround him, stands on tiptoe to foresee the future. He cannot be happy and strong until he too lives with nature in the present, above time.

This should be plain enough. Yet see what strong intellects dare not yet hear God himself unless he speak the phraseology of I know not what David, or Jeremiah, or Paul. We shall not always set so great a price on a few texts, on a few lives. We are like children who repeat by rote the sentences of grandames and tutors, and, as they grow older, of the men of talents and character they chance to see,—painfully recollecting the exact words they spoke; afterwards, when they come into the point of view which those had who uttered these sayings, they understand them and are will-

---

15. **Instinct:** a misunderstood and perhaps infelicitous word here. Emerson means by it, however, not, as has been unintelligently maintained, mere biological or animal drive, but an innate power of spiritual insight which is not and cannot be the product of any teaching or tuition. 16. **Intuition . . . tuitions:** a distinction (verbally striking, though without any literal etymological basis) between innate wisdom and the kinds of wisdom or knowledge that can be instilled or communicated from without.

ing to let the words go; for at any time they can use words as good when occasion comes. If we live truly, we shall see truly. It is as easy for the strong man to be strong, as it is for the weak to be weak. When we have new perception, we shall gladly disburden the memory of its hoarded treasures as old rubbish. When a man lives with God, his voice shall be as sweet as the murmur of the brook and the rustle of the corn.

And now at last the highest truth on this subject remains unsaid; probably cannot be said; for all that we say is the far-off remembering of the intuition. That thought by what I can now nearest approach to say it, is this. When good is near you, when you have life in yourself, it is not by any known or accustomed way; you shall not discern the footprints of any other; you shall not see the face of man; you shall not hear any name;—the way, the thought, the good, shall be wholly strange and new. It shall exclude example and experience. You take the way from man, not to man. All persons that ever existed are its forgotten ministers. Fear and hope are alike beneath it. There is somewhat low even in hope. In the hour of vision there is nothing that can be called gratitude, nor properly joy. The soul raised over passion beholds identity and eternal causation, perceives the self-existence of Truth and Right, and calms itself with knowing that all things go well. Vast spaces of nature, the Atlantic Ocean, the South Sea; long intervals of time, years, centuries, are of no account. This which I think and feel underlay every former state of life and circumstances, as it does underlie my present, and what is called life and what is called death.

Life only avails, not the having lived. Power ceases in the instant of repose; it resides in the moment of transition from a past to a new state, in the shooting of the gulf, in the darting to an aim. This one fact the world hates; that the soul *becomes;* for that forever degrades the past, turns all riches to poverty, all reputation to a shame, confounds the saint with the rogue, shoves Jesus and Judas equally aside. Why then do we prate of self-reliance? Inasmuch as the soul is present there will be power not confident but agent.[17] To talk of reliance is a poor external way of speaking. Speak rather of that which relies because it works and is. Who has more obedience than I masters me, though he should not raise his finger. Round him I must revolve by the gravitation of spirits. We fancy it rhetoric when we speak of eminent virtue. We do not yet see that virtue is Height, and that a man or a company of men, plastic and permeable to principles, by the law of nature must overpower and ride all cities, nations, kings, rich men, poets, who are not.

This is the ultimate fact which we so quickly reach on this, as on every topic, the resolution of all into the ever-blessed ONE.[18] Self-existence is the attribute of the Supreme Cause, and it constitutes the measure of good by the degree in which it enters into all lower forms. All things real are so by so much virtue as they contain. Commerce, husbandry, hunting, whaling, war, eloquence, personal weight, are somewhat,[19] and engage my respect as examples of its presence and impure action. I see the same law working in nature for conservation and growth. Power is, in nature, the essential measure of right. Nature suffers nothing to remain in her kingdoms which cannot help itself. The genesis and maturation of a planet, its poise and orbit, the bended tree recovering itself from the strong wind, the vital resources of every animal and vegetable, are demonstrations of the self-sufficing and therefore self-relying soul.

Thus all concentrates: let us not rove; let us sit at home with the cause. Let us stun and astonish the intruding rabble of men and books and institutions by a simple declaration of the divine fact. Bid the invaders take the shoes from off their feet, for God is here within. Let our simplicity judge them, and our docility to our own law demonstrate the poverty of nature and fortune beside our native riches.

But now we are a mob. Man does not stand in awe of man, nor is his genius admonished to stay at home, to put itself in communication with the internal ocean, but it goes abroad to beg a cup of water of the urns of other men. We must go alone. I like the silent church before the service begins, better than any preaching. How far off, how cool, how chaste the persons look, begirt each one with a precinct or sanctuary! So let us always sit. Why should we assume the faults of our friend, or wife, or father, or child, because they sit around our hearth, or are said to have the same blood? All men have my blood and I all men's. Not for that will I adopt their petulance or folly, even to the extent of being ashamed of it. But your isolation must not be mechanical, but spiritual, that is, must be elevation. At times the whole world seems to be in conspiracy to importune you with emphatic trifles. Friend, client, child, sickness, fear, want, charity, all knock at once at thy closet door and

---

17. **not confident but agent:** the two adjectives here have the force of participles (not *confiding* but *acting*), a touch of Emerson's verbal Latinism.

18. **the ever-blessed One:** the Over-Soul or spiritual Unity which lies at the center of all existence.  19. **somewhat:** an older substantive use of the word, signifying "something," "not a negligible quantity."

say,—"Come out unto us." But keep thy state; come not into their confusion. The power men possess to annoy me I give them by a weak curiosity. No man can come near me but through my act. "What we love that we have, but by desire we bereave ourselves of the love."

If we cannot at once rise to the sanctities of obedience and faith, let us at least resist our temptations; let us enter into the state of war and wake Thor and Woden, courage and constancy, in our Saxon breasts. This is to be done in our smooth times by speaking the truth. Check this lying hospitality and lying affection. Live no longer to the expectation of these deceived and deceiving people with whom we converse. Say to them, "O father, O mother, O wife, O brother, O friend, I have lived with you after appearances hitherto. Henceforward I am the truth's. Be it known unto you that henceforward I obey no law less than the eternal law. I will have no covenants but proximities. I shall endeavor to nourish my parents, to support my family, to be the chaste husband of one wife,— but these relations I must fill after a new and unprecedented way. I appeal from your customs. I must be myself. I cannot break myself any longer for you, or you. If you can love me for what I am, we shall be the happier. If you cannot, I will still seek to deserve that you should. I will not hide my tastes or aversions. I will so trust that what is deep is holy, that I will do strongly before the sun and moon whatever inly rejoices me and the heart appoints. If you are noble, I will love you; if you are not, I will not hurt you and myself by hypocritical attentions. If you are true, but not in the same truth with me, cleave to your companions; I will seek my own. I do this not selfishly but humbly and truly. It is alike your interest, and mine, and all men's, however long we have dwelt in lies, to live in truth. Does this sound harsh to-day? You will soon love what is dictated by your nature as well as mine, and if we follow the truth it will bring us out safe at last."—But so may you give these friends pain. Yes, but I cannot sell my liberty and my power, to save their sensibility. Besides, all persons have their moments of reason, when they look out into the region of absolute truth; then will they justify me and do the same thing.

The populace think that your rejection of popular standards is a rejection of all standard, and mere antinomianism;[20] and the bold sensualist will use the name of philosophy to gild his crimes. But the law of consciousness abides. There

**20. antinomianism:** the doctrine of those who hold that the regenerate Christian, by the influx of divine grace, is set free from the moral law. See "New England Reformers," 3 n.

are two confessionals, in one or the other of which we must be shriven. You may fulfil your round of duties by clearing yourself in the *direct,* or in the *reflex* way. Consider whether you have satisfied your relations to father, mother, cousin, neighbor, town, cat and dog—whether any of these can upbraid you. But I may also neglect this reflex standard and absolve me to myself: I have my own stern claims and perfect circle. It denies the name of duty to many offices that are called duties. But if I can discharge its debts it enables me to dispense with the popular code. If any one imagines that this law is lax, let him keep its commandment one day.

And truly it demands something godlike in him who has cast off the common motives of humanity and has ventured to trust himself for a taskmaster. High be his heart, faithful his will, clear his sight, that he may in good earnest be doctrine, society, law, to himself, that a simple purpose may be to him as strong as iron necessity is to others!

If any man consider the present aspects of what is called by distinction *society,* he will see the need of these ethics. The sinew and heart of man seem to be drawn out, and we are become timorous, desponding whimperers. We are afraid of truth, afraid of fortune, afraid of death, and afraid of each other. Our age yields no great and perfect persons. We want men and women who shall renovate life and our social state, but we see that most natures are insolvent, cannot satisfy their own wants, have an ambition out of all proportion to their practical force and do lean and beg day and night continually. Our housekeeping is mendicant, our arts, our occupations, our marriages, our religion we have not chosen, but society has chosen for us. We are parlor soldiers. We shun the rugged battle of fate, where strength is born.

If our young men miscarry in their first enterprises they lose all heart. If the young merchant fails, men say he is *ruined.* If the finest genius studies at one of our colleges and is not installed in an office within one year afterwards in the cities or suburbs of Boston or New York, it seems to his friends and to himself that he is right in being disheartened and in complaining the rest of his life. A sturdy lad from New Hampshire or Vermont, who in turn tries all the professions, who *teams it, farms it, peddles,* keeps a school, preaches, edits a newspaper, goes to Congress, buys a township, and so forth, in successive years, and always like a cat falls on his feet, is worth a hundred of these city dolls. He walks abreast with his days and feels no shame in not "studying a profession," for he does not postpone his life, but lives already. He has not one chance, but a hundred chances. Let a Stoic open the resources of man and tell men they are not leaning willows, but can and must detach themselves; that with the exercise of self-trust, new powers shall appear; that a man is the word made flesh, born to shed healing to the nations; that he should be ashamed of our compassion, and that the moment he acts for himself, tossing the laws, the books, idolatries and customs out of the window, we pity him no more but thank and revere him;— and that teacher shall restore the life of man to splendor and make his name dear to all history.

It is easy to see that a greater self-reliance must work a revolution in all the offices and relations of men; in their religion; in their education; in their pursuits; their modes of living; their association; in their property; in their speculative views.

1. In what prayers do men allow themselves! That which they call a holy office is not so much as brave and manly. Prayer looks abroad and asks for some foreign addition to come through some foreign virtue, and loses itself in endless mazes of natural and supernatural, and mediatorial and miraculous. Prayer that craves a particular commodity, anything less than all good, is vicious. Prayer is the contemplation of the facts of life from the highest point of view. It is the soliloquy of a beholding and jubilant soul. It is the spirit of God pronouncing his works good. But prayer as a means to effect a private end is meanness and theft. It supposes dualism and not a unity in nature and consciousness. As soon as the man is at one with God, he will not beg. He will then see prayer in all action. The prayer of the farmer kneeling in his field to weed it, the prayer of the rower kneeling with the stroke of his oar, are true prayers heard throughout nature, though for cheap ends. Cartach, in Fletcher's *Bonduca,* when admonished to inquire the mind of the god Audate, replies,—

"His hidden meaning lies in our endeavors;
Our valors are our best gods." 21

Another sort of false prayers are our regrets. Discontent is the want of self-reliance: it is infirmity of will. Regret calamities if you can thereby help the sufferer; if not, attend your own work and already the evil begins to be repaired Our sympathy is just as base. We come to them who weep foolishly and sit down and cry for company, instead of imparting to them truth and health in rough electric shocks, putting them once more

in communication with their own reason. The secret of fortune is joy in our hands. Welcome evermore to gods and men is the self-helping man. For him all doors are flung wide; him all tongues greet, all honors crown, all eyes follow with desire. Our love goes out to him and embraces him because he did not need it. We solicitously and apologetically caress and celebrate him because he held on his way and scorned our disapprobation. The gods love him because men hated him. "To the persevering mortal," said Zoroaster, "the blessed Immortals are swift."

As men's prayers are a disease of the will, so are their creeds a disease of the intellect. They say with those foolish Israelites, "Let not God speak to us, lest we die. Speak thou, speak any man with us, and we will obey." 22 Everywhere I am hindered of meeting God in my brother, because he has shut his own temple doors and recites fables merely of his brother's, or his brother's brother's God. Every new mind is a new classification. If it prove a mind of uncommon activity and power, a Locke, a Lavoisier,23 a Hutton,24 a Bentham, a Fourier,25 it imposes its classification on other men, and lo! a new system. In proportion to the depth of the thought, and so to the number of the objects it touches and brings within reach of the pupil, is his complacency. But chiefly is this apparent in creeds and churches, which are also classifications of some powerful mind acting on the elemental thought of duty and man's relation to the Highest. Such is Calvanism, Quakerism, Swedenborgism. The pupil takes the same delight in subordinating everything to the new terminology as a girl who has just learned botany in seeing a new earth and new seasons thereby. It will happen for a time that the pupil will find his intellectual power has grown by the study of his master's mind. But in all unbalanced minds the classification is idolized, passes for the end and not for a speedily exhaustible means, so that the walls of the system blend to their eye in the remote horizon with the walls of the universe; the luminaries of heaven seem to them hung on the arch their master built. They cannot imagine how you aliens have any right to see,—how you can see; "It must be somehow that you stole the light from us." They do not yet perceive that light, unsystematic, indomitable, will break into any cabin, even into theirs. Let them chirp awhile and call it their own. If they are honest and do well, presently their neat new pin-

---

21. when . . . gods: See Beaumont and Fletcher, *Bonduca,* III.i. Emerson misquotes oddly here, perhaps from a bad text of the play. "The god Audate" should read "the goddess Andate," and the first line of the quotation should read, "Her hidden meaning dwels in our endeavors."

22. "Let . . . obey": freely quoted from Exod. 20:19.  23. Lavoisier: Antoine Laurent Lavoisier (1743–94), French chemist, discoverer of oxygen.  24. Hutton: James Hutton (1726–97), Scottish geologist, one of the founders of modern scientific geology.  25. Fourier: See "New England Reformers," 9 n.

fold will be too strait and low, will crack, will lean, will rot and vanish, and the immortal light, all young and joyful, million-orbed, million-colored, will beam over the universe as on the first morning.

2. It is for want of self-culture that the superstition of Travelling, whose idols are Italy, England, Egypt, retains its fascination for all educated Americans. They who made England, Italy, or Greece venerable in the imagination, did so by sticking fast where they were, like an axis of the earth. In manly hours we feel that duty is our place. The soul is no traveller; the wise man stays at home, and when his necessities, his duties, on any occasion call him from his house, or into foreign lands, he is at home still and shall make men sensible by the expression of his countenance that he goes, the missionary of wisdom and virtue, and visits cities and men like a sovereign and not like an interloper or a valet.

I have no churlish objection to the circumnavigation of the globe for the purposes of art, of study, and benevolence, so that the man is first domesticated, or does not go abroad with the hope of finding somewhat greater than he knows. He who travels to be amused, or get somewhat which he does not carry, travels away from himself, and grows old even in youth among old things. In Thebes, in Palmyra, his will and mind have become old and dilapidated as they. He carries ruins to ruins.

Travelling is a fool's paradise. Our first journeys discover to us the indifference of places. At home I dream that at Naples, at Rome, I can be intoxicated with beauty and lose my sadness. I pack my trunk, embrace my friends, embark on the sea and at last wake up in Naples, and there beside me is the stern fact, the sad self, unrelenting, identical, that I fled from. I seek the Vatican and the palaces. I affect to be intoxicated with sights and suggestions, but I am not intoxicated. My giant goes with me wherever I go.

3. But the rage of travelling is a symptom of a deeper unsoundness affecting the whole intellectual action. The intellect is vagabond, and our system of education fosters restlessness. Our minds travel when our bodies are forced to stay at home. We imitate; and what is imitation but the travelling of the mind? Our houses are built with foreign taste; our shelves are garnished with foreign ornaments; our opinions, our tastes, our faculties lean, and follow the Past and the Distant. The soul created the arts wherever they have flourished. It was in his own mind that the artist sought his model. It was an application of his own thought to the thing to be done and the conditions to be observed. And why need we copy the Doric or the Gothic model?

Beauty, convenience, grandeur of thought and quaint expression are as near to us as to any, and if the American artist will study with hope and love the precise thing to be done by him, considering the climate, the soil, the length of the day, the wants of the people, the habit and form of the government, he will create a house in which all these will find themselves fitted, and taste and sentiment will be satisfied also.

Insist on yourself; never imitate. Your own gift you can present every moment with the cumulative force of a whole life's cultivation; but of the adopted talent of another you have only an extemporaneous half possession. That which each can do best, none but his Maker can teach him. No man yet knows what it is, nor can, till that person has exhibited it. Where is the master who could have taught Shakspeare? Where is the master who could have instructed Franklin, or Washington, or Bacon, or Newton? Every great man is a unique. The Scipionism of Scipio is precisely that part he could not borrow. Shakspeare will never be made by the study of Shakspeare. Do that which is assigned to you, and you cannot hope too much or dare too much. There is at this moment for you an utterance brave and grand as that of the colossal chisel of Phidias, or trowel of the Egyptians, or the pen of Moses or Dante, but different from all these. Not possibly will the soul, all rich, all eloquent, with thousand-cloven tongue, deign to repeat itself; but if you can hear what these patriarchs say, surely you can reply to them in the same pitch of voice; for the ear and the tongue are two organs of one nature. Abide in the simple and noble regions of thy life, obey thy heart, and thou shalt reproduce the Foreworld again.

4. As our Religion, our Education, our Art look abroad, so does our spirit of society. All men plume themselves on the improvement of society, and no man improves.

Society never advances. It recedes as fast on one side as it gains on the other. It undergoes continual changes; it is barbarous, it is civilized, it is christianized, it is rich, it is scientific; but this change is not amelioration. For every thing that is given something is taken. Society acquires new arts and loses old instincts. What a contrast between the well-clad, reading, writing, thinking American, with a watch, a pencil and a bill of exchange in his pocket, and the naked New Zealander, whose property is a club, a spear, a mat and an undivided twentieth of a shed to sleep under! But compare the health of the two men and you shall see that the white man has lost his aboriginal strength. If the traveller tell us truly, strike the savage with a broad-axe and in a day or two the flesh will unite and heal as if you struck the blow into soft pitch, and the same blow shall send the white to his grave.

The civilized man has built a coach, but has lost the use of his feet. He is supported on crutches, but lacks so much support of muscle. He has a fine Geneva watch, but he fails of the skill to tell the hour by the sun. A Greenwich nautical almanac he has, and so being sure of the information when he wants it, the man in the street does not know a star in the sky. The solstice he does not observe; the equinox he knows as little; and the whole bright calendar of the year is without a dial in his mind. His note-books impair his memory; his libraries overload his wit; the insurance-office increases the number of accidents; and it may be a question whether machinery does not encumber; whether we have not lost by refinement some energy, by a Christianity, entrenched in establishments and forms, some vigor of wild virtue. For every Stoic was a Stoic; but in Christendom where is the Christian?

There is no more deviation in the moral standard than in the standard of height or bulk. No greater men are now than ever were. A singular equality may be observed between the great men of the first and of the last ages; nor can all the science, art, religion, and philosophy of the nineteenth century avail to educate greater men than Plutarch's heroes, three or four and twenty centuries ago. Not in time is the race progressive. Phocion,[26] Socrates, Anaxagoras, Diogenes, are great men, but they leave no class. He who is really of their class will not be called by their name, but will be his own man, and in his turn the founder of a sect. The arts and inventions of each period are only its costume and do not invigorate men. The harm of the improved machinery may compensate its good. Hudson and Behring [27] accomplished so much in their fishing-boats as to astonish Parry [28] and Franklin, whose equipment exhausted the resources of science and art. Galileo, with an opera-glass, discovered a more splendid series of celestial phenomena than any one since. Columbus found the New World in an undecked boat. It is curious to see the periodical disuse and perishing of means and machinery which were introduced with loud laudation a few years or centuries before. The great genius returns to essential

man. We reckoned the improvements of the art of war among the triumphs of science, and yet Napoleon conquered Europe by the bivouac, which consisted of falling back on naked valor and disencumbering it of all aids. The Emperor held it impossible to make a perfect army, says Las Cases,[29] "without abolishing our arms, magazines, commissaries and carriages, until, in imitation of the Roman custom, the soldier should receive his supply of corn, grind it in his hand-mill and bake his bread himself."

Society is a wave. The wave moves onward, but the water of which it is composed does not. The same particle does not rise from the valley to the ridge. Its unity is only phenomenal. The persons who make up a nation to-day, next year die, and their experience dies with them.

And so the reliance on Property, including the reliance on governments which protect it, is the want of self-reliance. Men have looked away from themselves and at things so long that they have come to esteem the religious, learned and civil institutions as guards of property, and they deprecate assaults on these, because they feel them to be assaults on property. They measure their esteem of each other by what each has, and not by what each is. But a cultivated man becomes ashamed of his property, out of new respect for his nature. Especially he hates what he has if he see that it is accidental,—came to him by inheritance, or gift, or crime; then he feels that it is not having; it does not belong to him, has no root in him and merely lies there because no revolution or no robber takes it away. But that which a man is, does always by necessity acquire; and what the man acquires, is living property, which does not wait the beck of rulers, or mobs, or revolutions, or fire, or storm, or bankruptcies, but perpetually renews itself wherever the man breathes. "Thy lot or portion of life," said the Caliph Ali, "is seeking after thee; therefore be at rest from seeking after it." Our dependence on these foreign goods leads us to our lavish respect for numbers. The political parties meet in numerous conventions; the greater the concourse and with each new uproar of announcement, The delegation from Essex! [30] The Democrats from New Hampshire! [31] The Whigs of Maine! the young patriot feels himself stronger

---

26. **Phocion:** Athenian general and statesman of the fourth century B.C., subject of one of Plutarch's *Lives.*     27. **Behring:** alternative spelling of the surname of Vitus Jonassen Bering (1681–1741), Danish navigator and explorer, after whom Bering Strait was named.     28. **Parry:** Sir William Edward Parry (1790–1855), English explorer, leader of a series of important voyages in the Arctic.

29. **Las Cases:** the Comte de Las Cases (1766–1842), a French official who became Napoleon's companion on St. Helena and wrote a famous book on Napoleon's last days, the *Mémorial de Ste-Hélène* (1822–23).     30. **The delegation from Essex!:** that is, from Essex County, Mass.     31. **The Democrats from New Hampshire!:** Emerson took a very dim view of the politicians of New Hampshire, perhaps particularly of the Democrats. See "Ode Inscribed to W. H. Channing," 24–26n.

than before by a new thousand of eyes and arms. In like manner the reformers summon conventions and vote and resolve in multitude. Not so, O friends! will the God deign to enter and inhabit you, but by a method precisely the reverse. It is only as a man puts off all foreign support and stands alone that I see him to be strong and to prevail. He is weaker by every recruit to his banner. Is not a man better than a town? Ask nothing of men, and, in the endless mutation, thou only firm column must presently appear the upholder of all that surrounds thee. He who knows what power is inborn, that he is weak because he has looked for good out of him and elsewhere, and, so perceiving, throws himself unhesitatingly on his thought, instantly rights himself, stands in the erect position, commands his limbs, works miracles; just as a man who stands on his feet is stronger than a man who stands on his head.

So use all that is called Fortune. Most men gamble with her, and gain all, and lose all, as her wheel rolls.[32] But do thou leave as unlawful these winnings, and deal with Cause and Effect, the chancellors of God. In the Will work and acquire, and thou hast chained the wheel of Chance, and shall sit hereafter out of fear from her rotations. A political victory, a rise of rents, the recovery of our sick or the return of your absent friend, or some other favorable event raises your spirits, and you think good days are preparing for you. Do not believe it. Nothing can bring you peace but yourself. Nothing can bring you peace but the triumph of principles.

# NEW ENGLAND REFORMERS

### A Lecture Read Before the Society in Amory Hall,[1] on Sunday, March 3, 1844

◇

❨ THE inarticulate dissatisfaction which many persons felt with the conventionalities, the inequities, and the vices of American life had already, in the thirties, begun to find articulate expression in such reformist movements as temperance agitation and abolitionism. By the early forties the zeal for reform had gathered such head as to resemble a gale at sea or a prairie fire, and there was scarcely an aspect of nineteenth-century society—from the wage system to the shaving of men's beards, from factory production to the wearing of skirts by women—that did not come in for the most vigorous criticism, some of it intelligent and high-minded, some of it hardly short of insanity. Emerson's relation to this many-sided and passionate movement was necessarily an ambiguous one: he was torn between a natural sympathy with the spirit of innovation and amelioration and a distrust of the violent one-sidedness, the intellectual narrowness, and the pervasive humorlessness of many, perhaps most, of the actual reformers. In 1841, in a lecture on "Man the Reformer," he had already given expression to this characteristically contradictory and thoughtful attitude as probably no other man in the country could have done; in the present lecture, of 1844, while the movement was at its hottest, he came back to the subject and treated it with a still more rippling humor, on the one hand, and, on the other, with an even greater seriousness of sympathy.

◇

In the suburb, in the town,
On the railway, in the square,
Came a beam of goodness down
Doubling daylight everywhere:
Peace now each for malice takes,
Beauty for his sinful weeds,
For the angel Hope aye makes
Him an angel whom she leads.

WHOEVER has had opportunity of acquaintance with society in New England during the last twenty-five years, with those middle and with those leading sections that may constitute any just representation of the character and aim of the community, will have been struck with the great activity of thought and experimenting. His attention must be commanded by the signs that the Church, or religious party, is falling from the Church nominal, and is appearing in temperance and non-resistance societies; in movements of abolitionists and of socialists; and in very significant assemblies called Sabbath and Bible Conventions;[2] composed of ultraists, of seekers, of all the soul of the soldiery of dissent, and meeting to call in question the authority of the Sabbath, of the priesthood, and of the Church. In these movements nothing was more remarkable than the discontent they begot in the movers. The spirit of protest and of detachment drove the members of these Conventions to bear

---

32. **as her wheel rolls:** Fortuna, the goddess of fortune, is usually represented in art as standing on a wheel, or resting her hand on one, to symbolize her fickleness. NEW ENGLAND REFORMERS. 1. **the Society in Amory Hall:** the liberal Church of the Disciples in Boston, of which Emerson's friend, James Freeman Clarke, was minister.

2. **very . . . Conventions:** Emerson has in mind such gatherings of radicals and "come-outers" as the famous, or notorious, Chardon Street Convention, called by the Friends of Universal Reform in Boston in 1840, and the later Bible Convention of 1842. For an amusing account of the former, see his essay "Chardon Street Convention," in *Lectures and Biographical Sketches* (*Works*, X, 371–77).

testimony against the Church, and immediately afterwards to declare their discontent with these Conventions, their independence of their colleagues, and their impatience of the methods whereby they were working. They defied each other, like a congress of kings, each of whom had a realm to rule, and a way of his own that made concert unprofitable. What a fertility of projects for the salvation of the world! One apostle thought all men should go to farming, and another that no man should buy or sell, that the use of money was the cardinal evil; another that the mischief was in our diet, that we eat and drink damnation. These made unleavened bread, and were foes to the death to fermentation. It was in vain urged by the housewife that God made yeast, as well as dough, and loves fermentation just as dearly as he loves vegetation; that fermentation develops the saccharine element in the grain, and makes it more palatable and more digestible. No; they wish the pure wheat, and will die but it shall not ferment. Stop, dear nature, these incessant advances of thine; let us scotch these ever-rolling wheels! Others attacked the system of agriculture, the use of animal manures in farming, and the tyranny of man over brute nature; these abuses polluted his food. The ox must be taken from the plough and the horse from the cart, the hundred acres of the farm must be spaded, and the man must walk, wherever boats and locomotives will not carry him. Even the insect world was to be defended—that had been too long neglected, and a society for the protection of ground-worms, slugs, and mosquitos was to be incorporated without delay. With these appeared the adepts of homœopathy, of hydropathy, of mesmerism, of phrenology, and their wonderful theories of the Christian miracles! Others assailed particular vocations, as that of the lawyer, that of the merchant, of the manufacturer, of the clergyman, of the scholar. Others attacked the institution of marriage as the fountain of social evils. Others devoted themselves to the worrying of churches and meetings for public worship; and the fertile forms of antinomianism [3] among the elder Puritans seemed to have their match in the plenty of the new harvest of reform.

With this din of opinion and debate there was a keener scrutiny of institutions and domestic life than any we had known; there was sincere protesting against existing evils, and there were changes of employment dictated by conscience. No doubt there was plentiful vaporing, and cases of backsliding might occur. But in each of these movements emerged a good result, a tendency to the adoption of simpler methods, and an assertion of the sufficiency of the private man. Thus it was directly in the spirit and genius of the age, what happened in one instance when a church censured and threatened to excommunicate one of its members on account of the somewhat hostile part to the church which his conscience led him to take in the antislavery business; the threatened individual immediately excommunicated the church, in a public and formal process. This has been several times repeated: it was excellent when it was done the first time, but of course loses all value when it is copied. Every project in the history of reform, no matter how violent and surprising, is good when it is the dictate of a man's genius and constitution, but very dull and suspicious when adopted from another. It is right and beautiful in any man to say, "I will take this coat, or this book, or this measure of corn of yours"—in whom we see the act to be original, and to flow from the whole spirit and faith of him; for then that taking will have a giving as free and divine; but we are very easily disposed to resist the same generosity of speech when we miss originality and truth to character in it.

There was in all the practical activities of New England for the last quarter of a century, a gradual withdrawal of tender consciences from the social organizations. There is observable throughout, the contest between mechanical and spiritual methods, but with a steady tendency of the thoughtful and virtuous to a deeper belief and reliance on spiritual facts.

In politics for example it is easy to see the progress of dissent. The country is full of rebellion; the country is full of kings. Hands off! let there be no control and no interference in the administration of the affairs of this kingdom of me. Hence the growth of the doctrine and of the party of Free Trade, and the willingness to try that experiment, in the face of what appear incontestable facts. I confess, the motto of the Globe newspaper [4] is so attractive to me that I can seldom find much appetite to read what is below it in its columns: "The world is governed too much." So the country is frequently affording solitary examples of resistance to the government, solitary nullifiers,[5] who throw themselves on their reserved rights; nay, who have

---

3. **antinomianism:** See "Self-Reliance," 20 n. Emerson is here alluding to Ann Hutchinson and other antinomian heretics in seventeenth-century Massachusetts Bay whose teachings proved a source of embarrassment and anxiety to the magistrates of the colony.

4. **the Globe newspaper:** the Washington *Daily Globe.*    5. **solitary nullifiers:** In 1843 Emerson's friend and neighbor, Bronson Alcott, had refused to pay his poll tax in Concord as a protest against government; he was arrested but not, to his chagrin, incarcerated. Thoreau's similar protest was made three years later, in 1846.

reserved all their rights; who reply to the assessor and to the clerk of court that they do not know the State, and embarrass the courts of law by non-juring and the commander-in-chief of the militia by non-resistance.[6]

The same disposition to scrutiny and dissent appeared in civil, festive, neighborly, and domestic society. A restless, prying, conscientious criticism broke out in unexpected quarters. Who gave me the money with which I bought my coat? Why should professional labor and that of the counting-house be paid so disproportionately to the labor of the porter and woodsawyer? This whole business of Trade gives me to pause and think, as it constitutes false relations between men; inasmuch as I am prone to count myself relieved of any responsibility to behave well and nobly to that person whom I pay with money; whereas if I had not that commodity, I should be put on my good behavior in all companies, and man would be a benefactor to man, as being himself his only certificate that he had a right to those aids and services which each asked of the other. Am I not too protected a person? is there not a wide disparity between the lot of me and the lot of thee, my poor brother, my poor sister? Am I not defrauded of my best culture in the loss of those gymnastics which manual labor and the emergencies of poverty constitute? I find nothing healthful or exalting in the smooth conventions of society; I do not like the close air of saloons.[7] I begin to suspect myself to be a prisoner, though treated with all this courtesy and luxury. I pay a destructive tax in my conformity.

The same insatiable criticism may be traced in the efforts for the reform of Education. The popular education has been taxed with a want of truth and nature. It was complained that an education to things was not given. We are students of words: we are shut up in schools, and colleges, and recitation-rooms, for ten or fifteen years, and come out at last with a bag of wind, a memory of words, and do not know a thing. We cannot use our hands, or our legs, or our eyes, or our arms. We do not know an edible root in the woods, we cannot tell our course by the stars, nor the hour of the day by the sun. It is well if we can swim and skate. We are afraid of a horse, of a cow, of a dog, of a snake, of a spider. The Roman rule was to teach a boy nothing that he could not learn standing. The old English rule was, "All summer in the field, and all winter in the study." And it seems as if a man should learn to plant, or to fish, or to hunt, that he might

secure his subsistence at all events, and not be painful to his friends and fellow men. The lessons of science should be experimental also. The sight of a planet through a telescope is worth all the course on astronomy; the shock of the electric spark in the elbow outvalues all the theories; the taste of the nitrous oxide, the firing of an artificial volcano, are better than volumes of chemistry.

One of the traits of the new spirit is the inquisition it fixed on our scholastic devotion to the dead languages. The ancient languages, with great beauty of structure, contain wonderful remains of genius, which draw, and always will draw, certain like-minded men—Greek men, and Roman men—in all countries, to their study; but by a wonderful drowsiness of usage they had exacted the study of *all* men. Once (say two centuries ago), Latin and Greek had a strict relation to all the science and culture there was in Europe, and the Mathematics had a momentary importance at some era of activity in physical science. These things became stereotyped as *education,* as the manner of men is. But the Good Spirit never cared for the colleges, and though all men and boys were now drilled in Latin, Greek, and Mathematics, it had quite left these shells high and dry on the beach, and was now creating and feeding other matters at other ends of the world. But in a hundred high schools and colleges this warfare against common sense still goes on. Four, or six, or ten years, the pupil is parsing Greek and Latin, and as soon as he leaves the University, as it is ludicrously styled, he shuts those books for the last time. Some thousands of young men are graduated at our colleges in this country every year, and the persons who, at forty years, still read Greek, can all be counted on your hand. I never met with ten. Four or five persons I have seen who read Plato.

But is not this absurd, that the whole liberal talent of this country should be directed in its best years on studies which lead to nothing? What was the consequence? Some intelligent persons said or thought, "Is that Greek and Latin some spell to conjure with, and not words of reason? If the physician, the lawyer, the divine, never use it to come at their ends, I need never learn it to come at mine. Conjuring is gone out of fashion, and I will omit this conjugating, and go straight to affairs." So they jumped the Greek and Latin, and read law, medicine, or sermons, without it. To the astonishment of all, the self-made men took even ground at once with the oldest of the regular graduates, and in a few months the most conservative circles of Boston and New York had quite forgotten who of their gownsmen was college-bred, and who was not.

---

6. **non-resistance:** In 1839 a New England Non-Resistance Society was founded in Boston by William Lloyd Garrison, Edmund Quincy, and others, to advocate the principles of pacifism.
7. **saloons:** salons, drawing rooms.

One tendency appears alike in the philosophical speculation and in the rudest democratical movements, through all the petulance and all the puerility, the wish, namely, to cast aside the superfluous and arrive at short methods; urged, as I suppose, by an intuition that the human spirit is equal to all emergencies, alone, and that man is more often injured than helped by the means he uses.

I conceive this gradual casting off of material aids, and the indication of growing trust in the private self-supplied powers of the individual, to be the affirmative principle of the recent philosophy, and that it is feeling its own profound truth and is reaching forward at this very hour to the happiest conclusions. I readily concede that in this, as in every period of intellectual activity, there has been a noise of denial and protest; much was to be resisted, much was to be got rid of by those who were reared in the old, before they could begin to affirm and to construct. Many a reformer perishes in his removal of rubbish; and that makes the offensiveness of the class. They are partial; they are not equal to the work they pretend. They lose their way; in the assault on the kingdom of darkness they expend all their energy on some accidental evil, and lose their sanity and power of benefit. It is of little moment that one or two or twenty errors of our social system be corrected, but of much that the man be in his senses.

The criticism and attack on institutions, which we have witnessed, has made one thing plain, that society gains nothing whilst a man, not himself renovated, attempts to renovate things around him: he has become tediously good in some particular but negligent or narrow in the rest; and hypocrisy and vanity are often the disgusting result.

It is handsomer to remain in the establishment better than the establishment, and conduct that in the best manner, than to make a sally against evil by some single improvement, without supporting it by a total regeneration. Do not be so vain of your one objection. Do you think there is only one? Alas! my good friend, there is no part of society or of life better than any other part. All our things are right and wrong together. The wave of evil washes all our institutions alike. Do you complain of our Marriage? Our marriage is no worse than our education, our diet, our trade, our social customs. Do you complain of the laws of Property? It is a pedantry to give such importance to them. Can we not play the game of life with these counters, as well as with those? in the institution of property, as well as out of it? Let into it the new and renewing principle of love, and property will be universality. No

one gives the impression of superiority to the institution, which he must give who will reform it. It makes no difference what you say, you must make me feel that you are aloof from it; by your natural and supernatural advantages do easily see to the end of it—do see how man can do without it. Now all men are on one side. No man deserves to be heard against property. Only Love, only an Idea, is against property as we hold it.

I cannot afford to be irritable and captious, nor to waste all my time in attacks. If I should go out of church whenever I hear a false sentiment I could never stay there five minutes. But why come out? the street is as false as the church, and when I get to my house, or to my manners, or to my speech, I have not got away from the lie. When we see an eager assailant of one of these wrongs, a special reformer, we feel like asking him, What right have you, sir, to your one virtue? Is virtue piecemeal? This is a jewel amidst the rags of a beggar.

In another way the right will be vindicated. In the midst of abuses, in the heart of cities, in the aisles of false churches, alike in one place and in another—wherever, namely, a just and heroic soul finds itself, there it will do what is next at hand, and by the new quality of character it shall put forth it shall abrogate that old condition, law or school in which it stands, before the law of its own mind.

If partiality was one fault of the movement party, the other defect was their reliance on Association.[8] Doubts such as those I have intimated drove many good persons to agitate the questions of social reform. But the revolt against the spirit of commerce, the spirit of aristocracy, and the inveterate abuses of cities, did not appear possible to individuals; and to do battle against numbers they armed themselves with numbers, and against concert they relied on new concert.

Following or advancing beyond the ideas of St. Simon, of Fourier, and of Owen,[9] three communities[10] have already been formed in Massachusetts on kindred plans, and many more in the country at large. They aim to give every member a share in the manual labor, to give an equal reward to labor and to talent, and to unite a liberal culture

8. **Association:** the name used by the Fourierist Socialists of the period to describe the form of cooperative or communitarian industry they advocated. 9. **St. Simon . . . Owen:** Comte de Saint-Simon (1760–1825), F. C. M. Fourier (1772–1837), and Robert Owen (1771–1858) were all pre-Marxist or "Utopian" Socialists who had a considerable influence on American radicals in the forties. 10. **three communities:** no doubt the communities at West Roxbury (Brook Farm, founded in 1841), at Milford (Hopedale, founded in 1842), and at Harvard (Fruitlands, founded also in 1842). When this lecture was written the two former were still in operation, but the community of Fruitlands, of which Bronson Alcott was one of the leaders, had come to grief, after a few months of very unstable existence, early in 1843.

with an education to labor. The scheme offers, by the economies of associated labor and expense, to make every member rich, on the same amount of property that, in separate families, would leave every member poor. These new associations are composed of men and women of superior talents and sentiments; yet it may easily be questioned whether such a community will draw, except in its beginnings, the able and the good; whether those who have energy will not prefer their chance of superiority and power in the world, to the humble certainties of the association; whether such a retreat does not promise to become an asylum to those who have tried and failed, rather than a field to the strong; and whether the members will not necessarily be fractions of men, because each finds that he cannot enter it without some compromise. Friendship and association are very fine things, and a grand phalanx [11] of the best of the human race, banded for some catholic object; yes, excellent; but remember that no society can ever be so large as one man. He, in his friendship, in his natural and momentary associations, doubles or multiplies himself; but in the hour in which he mortgages himself to two or ten or twenty, he dwarfs himself below the stature of one.

But the men of less faith could not thus believe, and to such, concert appears the sole specific of strength. I have failed, and you have failed, but perhaps together we shall not fail. Our housekeeping is not satisfactory to us, but perhaps a phalanx, a community, might be. Many of us have differed in opinion, and we could find no man who could make the truth plain, but possibly a college, or an ecclesiastical council, might. I have not been able either to persuade my brother or to prevail on myself to disuse the traffic or the potation of brandy, but perhaps a pledge of total abstinence might effectually restrain us. The candidate my party votes for is not to be trusted with a dollar, but he will be honest in the Senate, for we can bring public opinion to bear on him. Thus concert was the specific in all cases. But concert is neither better nor worse, neither more nor less potent, than individual force. All the men in the world cannot make a statue walk and speak, cannot make a drop of blood, or a blade of grass, any more than one man can. But let there be one man, let there be truth in two men, in ten men, then is concert for the first time possible; because the force which moves the world is a new

quality, and can never be furnished by adding whatever quantities of a different kind. What is the use of the concert of the false and the disunited? There can be no concert in two, where there is no concert in one. When the individual is not *individual*,[12] but is dual; when his thoughts look one way and his actions another; when his faith is traversed by his habits; when his will, enlightened by reason, is warped by his sense; when with one hand he rows and with the other backs water, what concert can be?

I do not wonder at the interest these projects inspire. The world is awaking to the idea of union, and these experiments show what it is thinking of. It is and will be magic. Men will live and communicate, and plough, and reap, and govern, as by added ethereal power, when once they are united; as in a celebrated experiment, by expiration and respiration exactly together, four persons lift a heavy man from the ground by the little finger only, and without sense of weight. But this union must be inward, and not one of covenants, and is to be reached by a reverse of the methods they use. The union is only perfect when all the uniters are isolated. It is the union of friends who live in different streets or towns. Each man, if he attempts to join himself to others, is on all sides cramped and diminished of his proportion; and the stricter the union the smaller and the more pitiful he is. But leave him alone, to recognize in every hour and place the secret soul; he will go up and down doing the works of a true member, and, to the astonishment of all, the work will be done with concert, though no man spoke. Government will be adamantine without any governor. The union must be ideal in actual individualism.

I pass to the indication in some particulars of that faith in man, which the heart is preaching to us in these days, and which engages the more regard, from the consideration that the speculations of one generation are the history of the next following.

In alluding just now to our system of education, I spoke of the deadness of its details. But it is open to graver criticism than the palsy of its members: it is a system of despair. The disease with which the human mind now labors is want of faith. Men do not believe in a power of education. We do not think we can speak to divine sentiments in man, and we do not try. We renounce all high aims. We believe that the defects of so many perverse and so many frivolous people who make up society, are organic, and society is a hospital of incurables. A

11. **a grand phalanx:** Fourier had used the word "phalanx" for the smallest unit, sixteen hundred persons, into which his ideal society was to be organizationally divided. After the Brook Farm community turned Fourierist under the influence of Albert Brisbane, it was known as the "Phalanx," and the members published a periodical under that name.

12. *individual:* The etymological meaning of the word is "indivisible," "undivided."

man of good sense but of little faith, whose compassion seemed to lead him to church as often as he went there, said to me that "he liked to have concerts, and fairs, and churches, and other public amusements go on." I am afraid the remark is too honest, and comes from the same origin as the maxim of the tyrant, "If you would rule the world quietly, you must keep it amused." I notice too that the ground on which eminent public servants urge the claims of popular education is fear; "This country is filling up with thousands and millions of voters, and you must educate them to keep them from our throats." We do not believe that any education, any system of philosophy, any influence of genius, will ever give depth of insight to a superficial mind. Having settled ourselves into this infidelity, our skill is expended to procure alleviations, diversion, opiates. We adorn the victim with manual skill, his tongue with languages, his body with inoffensive and comely manners. So have we cunningly hid the tragedy of limitation and inner death we cannot avert. Is it strange that society should be devoured by a secret melancholy which breaks through all its smiles and all its gayety and games?

But even one step farther our infidelity has gone. It appears that some doubt is felt by good and wise men whether really the happiness and probity of men is increased by the culture of the mind in those disciplines to which we give the name of education. Unhappily too the doubt comes from scholars, from persons who have tried these methods. In their experience the scholar was not raised by the sacred thoughts amongst which he dwelt, but used them to selfish ends. He was a profane person, and became a showman, turning his gifts to a marketable use, and not to his own sustenance and growth. It was found that the intellect could be independently developed, that is, in separation from the man, as any single organ can be invigorated, and the result was monstrous. A canine appetite for knowledge was generated, which must still be fed but was never satisfied, and this knowledge, not being directed on action, never took the character of substantial, humane truth, blessing those whom it entered. It gave the scholar certain powers of expression, the power of speech, the power of poetry, of literary art, but it did not bring him to peace or to beneficence.

When the literary class betray a destitution of faith, it is not strange that society should be disheartened and sensualized by unbelief. What remedy? Life must be lifed on a higher plane. We must go up to a higher platform, to which we are always invited to ascend; there, the whole aspect of things changes. I resist the skepticism of our education and of our educated men. I do not believe that the differences of opinion and character in men are or-

ganic. I do not recognize, beside the class of the good and the wise, a permanent class of skeptics, or a class of conservatives, or of malignants, or of materialists. I do not believe in two classes. You remember the story of the poor woman who importuned King Philip of Macedon to grant her justice, which Philip refused: the woman exclaimed, "I appeal": the king, astonished, asked to whom she appealed: the woman replied, "From Philip drunk to Philip sober." [13] The text will suit me very well. I believe not in two classes of men, but in man in two moods, in Philip drunk and Philip sober. I think, according to the good-hearted word of Plato, "Unwillingly the soul is deprived of truth." Iron conservative, miser, or thief, no man is but by a supposed necessity which he tolerates by shortness or torpidity of sight. The soul lets no man go without some visitations and holy days of a diviner presence. It would be easy to show, by a narrow scanning of any man's biography, that we are not so wedded to our paltry performances of every kind but that every man has at intervals the grace to scorn his performances, in comparing them with his belief of what he should do—that he puts himself on the side of his enemies, listening gladly to what they say of him, and accusing himself of the same things.

What is it men love in Genius, but its infinite hope, which degrades all it has done? Genius counts all its miracles poor and short. Its own idea it never executed. The *Iliad,* the *Hamlet,* the Doric column, the Roman arch, the Gothic minster, the German anthem, when they are ended, the master casts behind him. How sinks the song in the waves of melody which the universe pours over his soul! Before that gracious Infinite out of which he drew these few strokes, how mean they look, though the praises of the world attend them. From the triumphs of his art he turns with desire to this greater defeat. Let those admire who will. With silent joy he sees himself to be capable of a beauty that eclipses all which his hands have done; all which human hands have ever done.

Well, we are all the children of genius, the children of virtue—and feel their inspirations in our happier hours. Is not every man sometimes a radical in politics? Men are conservatives when they are least vigorous, or when they are most luxurious. They are conservatives after dinner, or before taking their rest; when they are sick, or aged: in the morning, or when their intellect or their conscience has been aroused; when they hear music, or when they read poetry, they are radicals. In the

13. You . . . sober: This famous anecdote is told by Valerius Maximus in his *De Factis Dictisque Memorabilibus,* but it has long been familiar in English literary allusion.

circle of the rankest Tories that could be collected in England, Old or New, let a powerful and stimulating intellect, a man of great heart and mind act on them, and very quickly these frozen conservators will yield to the friendly influence, these hopeless will begin to hope, these haters will begin to love, these immovable statues will begin to spin and revolve. I cannot help recalling the fine anecdote which Warton relates of Bishop Berkeley,[14] when he was preparing to leave England with his plan of planting the gospel among the American savages. "Lord Bathurst told me that the members of the Scriblerus club being met at his house at dinner, they agreed to rally Berkeley, who was also his guest, on his scheme at Bermudas. Berkeley, having listened to the many lively things they had to say, begged to be heard in his turn, and displayed his plan with such an astonishing and animating force of eloquence and enthusiasm that they were struck dumb, and, after some pause, rose up all together with earnestness, exclaiming, 'Let us set out with him immediately.' " Men in all ways are better than they seem. They like flattery for the moment, but they know the truth for their own. It is a foolish cowardice which keeps us from trusting them and speaking to them rude truth. They resent your honesty for an instant, they will thank you for it always. What is it we heartily wish of each other? Is it to be pleased and flattered? No, but to be convicted and exposed, to be shamed out of our nonsense of all kinds, and made men of, instead of ghosts and phantoms. We are weary of gliding ghostlike through the world, which is itself so slight and unreal. We crave a sense of reality, though it come in strokes of pain. I explain so—by this manlike love of truth—those excesses and errors into which souls of great vigor, but not equal insight, often fall. They feel the poverty at the bottom of all the seeming affluence of the world. They know the speed with which they come straight through the thin masquerade, and conceive a disgust at the indigence of nature: Rousseau, Mirabeau, Charles Fox, Napoleon, Byron—and I could easily add names nearer home, of raging riders, who drive their steeds so hard, in the violence of living to forget its illusion: they would know the worst, and tread the floors of hell.[15] The heroes of ancient and modern fame, Cimon, Themistocles, Alcibiades,

Alexander, Cæsar, have treated life and fortune as a game to be well and skilfully played, but the stake not to be so valued but that any time it could be held as a trifle light as air, and thrown up. Cæsar, just before the battle of Pharsalia, discourses with the Egyptian priest concerning the fountains of the Nile, and offers to quit the army, the empire, and Cleopatra, if he will show him those mysterious sources.[16]

The same magnanimity shows itself in our social relations, in the preference, namely, which each man gives to the society of superiors over that of his equals. All that a man has will he give for right relations with his mates. All that he has will he give for an erect demeanor in every company and on each occasion. He aims at such things as his neighbors prize, and gives his days and nights, his talents and his heart, to strike a good stroke, to acquit himself in all men's sight as a man. The consideration of an eminent citizen, of a noted merchant, of a man of mark in his profession; a naval and military honor, a general's commission, a marshal's baton, a ducal coronet, the laurel of poets, and, anyhow procured, the acknowledgment of eminent merit—have this lustre for each candidate that they enable him to walk erect and unashamed in the presence of some persons before whom he felt himself inferior. Having raised himself to this rank, having established his equality with class after class of those with whom he would live well, he still finds certain others before whom he cannot possess himself, because they have somewhat fairer, somewhat grander, somewhat purer, which extorts homage of him. Is his ambition pure? then will his laurels and his possessions seem worthless: instead of avoiding these men who make his fine gold dim, he will cast all behind him and seek their society only, woo and embrace this his humiliation and mortification, until he shall know why his eye sinks, his voice is husky, and his brilliant talents are paralyzed in this presence. He is sure that the soul which gives the lie to all things will tell none. His constitution will not mislead him. If it cannot carry itself as it ought, high and unmatchable in the presence of any man; if the secret oracles whose whisper makes the sweetness and dignity of his life do here withdraw and accompany him no longer—it is time to undervalue what he has valued, to dispossess himself of what he has acquired, and with Cæsar to take in his hand the army, the empire, and Cleopatra, and say, "All these will I relinquish, if you will show me the fountains of the Nile." [17] Dear to us are those who

14. the . . . Berkeley: Joseph Warton tells this story about Berkeley in his *Essay on the Genius and Writings of Pope*, II, 198 n. 15. they . . . hell: a fragment of Pindar preserved by Plutarch in his "Consolation to Apollonius." The sentence in Plutarch reads in English translation: "It is an expression of Pindar, that we are held to the dark bottom of hell by necessities as hard as iron" (*Essays and Miscellanies*, ed. by A. H. Clough and William W. Goodwin, I, 303).

16. Cæsar . . . sources: See Lucan, *De Bello Civili*, X.172–92. Emerson may have been familiar with Nicholas Rowe's translation of Lucan's poem as the *Pharsalia*. 17. "All . . . Nile": an allusion to the passage in Lucan drawn on above.

love us; the swift moments we spend with them are a compensation for a great deal of misery; they enlarge our life—but dearer are those who reject us as unworthy, for they add another life: they build a heaven before us whereof we had not dreamed, and thereby supply to us new powers out of the recesses of the spirit, and urge us to new and unattempted performances.

As every man at heart wishes the best and not inferior society, wishes to be convicted of his error and to come to himself—so he wishes that the same healing should not stop in his thought, but should penetrate his will or active power. The selfish man suffers more from his selfishness than he from whom that selfishness withholds some important benefit. What he most wishes is to be lifted to some higher platform, that he may see beyond his present fear the trans-Alpine good, so that his fear, his coldness, his custom may be broken up like fragments of ice, melted and carried away in the great stream of good will. Do you ask my aid? I also wish to be a benefactor. I wish more to be a benefactor and servant than you wish to be served by me; and surely the greatest good fortune that could befall me is precisely to be so moved by you that I should say, "Take me and all mine, and use me and mine freely to your ends!" for I could not say it otherwise than because a great enlargement had come to my heart and mind, which made me superior to my fortunes. Here we are paralyzed with fear; we hold on to our little properties, house and land, office and money, for the bread which they have in our experience yielded us, although we confess that our being does not flow through them. We desire to be made great; we desire to be touched with that fire which shall command this ice to stream, and make our existence a benefit. If therefore we start objections to your project, O friend of the slave, or friend of the poor or of the race, understand well that it is because we wish to drive you to drive us into your measures. We wish to hear ourselves confuted. We are haunted with a belief that you have a secret which it would highliest advantage us to learn, and we would force you to impart it to us, though it should bring us to prison or to worse extremity.

Nothing shall warp me from the belief that every man is a lover of truth. There is no pure lie, no pure malignity in nature. The entertainment of the proposition of depravity [18] is the last profligacy and profanation. There is no skepticism, no atheism but that. Could it be received into common belief, suicide would unpeople the planet. It has had a name to live in some dogmatic theology, but each

man's innocence and his real liking of his neighbor have kept it a dead letter. I remember standing at the polls one day when the anger of the political contest gave a certain grimness to the faces of the independent electors, and a good man at my side,[19] looking on the people, remarked, "I am satisfied that the largest part of these men, on either side, mean to vote right." I suppose considerate observers, looking at the masses of men in their blameless and in their equivocal actions, will assent, that in spite of selfishness and frivolity, the general purpose in the great number of persons is fidelity. The reason why anyone refuses his assent to your opinion, or his aid to your benevolent design, is in you: he refuses to accept you as a bringer of truth, because though you think you have it, he feels that you have it not. You have not given him the authentic sign.

If it were worth while to run into details this general doctrine of the latent but ever soliciting Spirit, it would be easy to adduce illustration in particulars of a man's equality to the Church, of his equality to the State, and of his equality to every other man. It is yet in all men's memory that, a few years ago, the liberal churches [20] complained that the Calvinistic Church denied to them the name of Christian. I think the complaint was confession: a religious church would not complain. A religious man, like Behmen,[21] Fox,[22] or Swedenborg is not irritated by wanting the sanction of the Church, but the Church feels the accusation of his presence and belief.

It only needs that a just man should walk in our streets to make it appear how pitiful and inartificial a contrivance is our legislation. The man whose part is taken and who does not wait for society in anything, has a power which society cannot choose but feel. The familiar experiment called the hydrostatic paradox, in which a capillary column of water balances the ocean, is a symbol of the relation of one man to the whole family of men. The wise Dandamis, on hearing the lives of Socrates, Pythagoras and Diogenes read, "judged them to be great men every way, excepting that they were too much subjected to the reverence of the laws, which to second and authorize, true virtue must abate very much of its original vigor."

And as a man is equal to the Church and equal

18. the proposition of depravity: the Calvinist dogma of Total Depravity.

19. a good man at my side: Edmund Hosmer, a sagacious Concord farmer and great friend of Emerson's.    20. the liberal churches: the Unitarian churches.    21. Behmen: alternative spelling of the surname of Jakob Boehme, a German mystical writer of the late sixteenth and early seventeenth centuries, whose *Aurora* Emerson had read with enthusiasm in 1835.    22. Fox: George Fox (1624–91), English religious leader, founder of the Society of Friends, the members of which very early came to be known as Quakers.

to the State, so he is equal to every other man. The disparities of power in men are superficial; and all frank and searching conversation, in which a man lays himself open to his brother, apprises each of their radical unity. When two persons sit and converse in a thoroughly good understanding, the remark is sure to be made, See how we have disputed about words! Let a clear, apprehensive mind, such as every man knows among his friends, converse with the most commanding poetic genius, I think it would appear that there was no inequality such as men fancy, between them; that a perfect understanding, a like receiving, a like perceiving, abolished differences; and the poet would confess that his creative imagination gave him no deep advantage, but only the superficial one that he could express himself and the other could not; that his advantage was a knack, which might impose on indolent men but could not impose on lovers of truth; for they know the tax of talent, or what a price of greatness the power of expression too often pays. I believe it is the conviction of the purest men that the net amount of man and man does not much vary. Each is incomparably superior to his companion in some faculty. His want of skill in other directions has added to his fitness for his own work. Each seems to have some compensation yielded to him by his infirmity, and every hindrance operates as a concentration of his force.

These and the like experiences intimate that man stands in strict connection with a higher fact never yet manifested. There is power over and behind us, and we are the channels of its communications. We seek to say thus and so, and over our head some spirit sits which contradicts what we say. We would persuade our fellow to this or that; another self within our eyes dissuades him. That which we keep back, this reveals. In vain we compose our faces and our words; it holds uncontrollable communication with the enemy, and he answers civilly to us, but believes the spirit. We exclaim, "There's a traitor in the house!" but at last it appears that he is the true man, and I am the traitor. This open channel to the highest life is the first and last reality, so subtle, so quiet, yet so tenacious, that although I have never expressed the truth, and although I have never heard the expression of it from any other, I know that the whole truth is here for me. What if I cannot answer your questions? I am not pained that I cannot frame a reply to the question. What is the operation we call Providence? There lies the unspoken thing, present, omnipresent. Every time we converse we seek to translate it into speech, but whether we hit or whether we miss, we have the fact. Every discourse is an approximate answer: but it is of small consequence that we do

not get it into verbs and nouns, whilst it abides for contemplation forever.

If the auguries of the prophesying heart shall make themselves good in time, the man who shall be born, whose advent men and events prepare and foreshow, is one who shall enjoy his connection with a higher life, with the man within man; shall destroy distrust by his trust, shall use his native but forgotten methods, shall not take counsel of flesh and blood, but shall rely on the Law alive and beautiful which works over our heads and under our feet. Pitiless, it avails itself of our success when we obey it, and of our ruin when we contravene it. Men are all secret believers in it, else the word justice would have no meaning: they believe that the best is the true; that right is done at last; or chaos would come. It rewards actions after their nature, and not after the design of the agent. "Work," it saith to man, "in every hour, paid or unpaid, see only that thou work, and thou canst not escape the reward: whether thy work be fine or coarse, planting corn or writing epics, so only it be honest work, done to thine own approbation, it shall earn a reward to the senses as well as to the thought: no matter how often defeated, you are born to victory. The reward of a thing well done, is to have done it."

As soon as a man is wonted to look beyond surfaces, and to see how this high will prevails without an exception or an interval, he settles himself into serenity. He can already rely on the laws of gravity, that every stone will fall where it is due; the good globe is faithful, and carries us securely through the celestial spaces, anxious or resigned, we need not interfere to help it on: and he will learn one day the mild lesson they teach, that our own orbit is all our task, and we need not assist the administration of the universe. Do not be so impatient to set the town right concerning the unfounded pretensions and the false reputation of certain men of standing. They are laboring harder to set the town right concerning themselves, and will certainly succeed. Suppress for a few days your criticism on the insufficiency of this or that teacher or experimenter, and he will have demonstrated his insufficiency to all men's eyes. In like manner, let a man fall into the divine circuits, and he is enlarged. Obedience to his genius is the only liberating influence. We wish to escape from subjection and a sense of inferiority, and we make self-denying ordinances, we drink water, we eat grass, we refuse the laws, we go to jail: it is all in vain; only by obedience to his genius, only by the freest activity in the way constitutional to him, does an angel seem to arise before a man and lead him by the hand out of all the wards of the prison.

That which befits us, embosomed in beauty and wonder as we are, is cheerfulness and courage, and the endeavor to realize our aspirations. The life of man is the true romance, which when it is valiantly conducted will yield the imagination a higher joy than any fiction. All around us what powers are wrapped up under the coarse mattings of custom, and all wonder prevented. It is so wonderful to our neurologists that a man can see without his eyes, that it does not occur to them that it is just as wonderful that he should see with them; and that is ever the difference between the wise and the unwise: the latter wonders at what is unusual, the wise man wonders at the usual. Shall not the heart which has received so much, trust the Power by which it lives? May it not quit other leadings, and listen to the Soul that has guided it so gently and taught it so much, secure that the future will be worthy of the past?

# ILLUSIONS

◇

⟨ THIS essay appeared first in *The Conduct of Life* in 1860. It is too short to have been, as it stands, a lecture in "The Conduct of Life" series which Emerson had been delivering off and on during the fifties, and its unity of form seems too complete to justify the assumption that it is a mere fragmentary version of one of them. In any case, it is the most poetic expression in his works of Emerson's quasi-Oriental doctrine of Máyá —the illusoriness, the merely phenomenal character, of the world of "experience," and the "central reality" of the Unity that lies behind it.

◇

Flow, flow the waves hated,
Accursed, adored,
The waves of mutation:
No anchorage is.
Sleep is not, death is not;
Who seem to die live.
House you were born in,
Friends of your spring-time,
Old man and young maid,
Day's toil and its guerdon,
They are all vanishing,
Fleeing to fables,
Cannot be moored.
See the stars through them,

Through treacherous marbles.
Know, the stars yonder,
The stars everlasting,
Are fugitive also,
And emulate, vaulted,
The lambent heat-lightning,
And fire-fly's flight.

When thou dost return
On the wave's circulation,
Beholding the shimmer,
The wild dissipation,
And, out of endeavor
To change and to flow,
The gas become solid,
And phantoms and nothings
Return to be things,
And endless imbroglio
Is law and the world,—
Then first shalt thou know,
That in the wild turmoil,
Horsed on the Proteus,[1]
Thou ridest to power,
And to endurance.

SOME YEARS ago, in company with an agreeable party, I spent a long summer day in exploring the Mammoth Cave in Kentucky.[2] We traversed, through spacious galleries affording a solid masonry foundation for the town and country overhead, the six or eight black miles from the mouth of the cavern to the innermost recess which tourists visit,—a niche or grotto made of one seamless stalactite, and called, I believe, Serena's Bower. I lost the light of one day. I saw high domes and bottomless pits; heard the voice of unseen waterfalls; paddled three quarters of a mile in the deep Echo River, whose waters are peopled with the blind fish; crossed the streams "Lethe" and "Styx;" plied with music and guns the echoes in these alarming galleries; saw every form of stalagmite and stalactite in the sculptured and fretted chambers;—icicle, orange-flower, acanthus, grapes and snowball. We shot Bengal lights into the vaults and groins of the sparry cathedrals and examined all the masterpieces which the four combined engineers, water, limestone, gravitation and time, could make in the dark.

ILLUSIONS. 1. Proteus: in Greek mythology, the old man of the sea, who had the power of assuming one shape after another in order to avoid the answering of questions put to him. 2. the Mammoth Cave in Kentucky: In June 1850, Emerson, on a lecture tour in the West, visited the Mammoth Cave, near Brownsville, Kentucky. His impressions at the time were recorded in a letter of June 16 to his wife (*Letters*, IV, 209–14). In September 1857, he observed in his journal: "Curious that the best thing I saw in Mammoth Cave was an illusion. But I have had many experiences like that and many men have" (*Journals*, IX,113).

The mysteries and scenery of the cave had the same dignity that belongs to all natural objects, and which shames the fine things to which we foppishly compare them. I remarked especially the mimetic habit with which nature, on new instruments, hums her old tunes, making night to mimic day, and chemistry to ape vegetation. But I then took notice and still chiefly remember that the best thing which the cave had to offer was an illusion. On arriving at what is called the "Star-Chamber," our lamps were taken from us by the guide and extinguished or put aside, and, on looking upwards, I saw or seemed to see the night heaven thick with stars glimmering more or less brightly over our heads, and even what seemed a comet flaming among them. All the party were touched with astonishment and pleasure. Our musical friends sung with much feeling a pretty song, "The stars are in the quiet sky," [3] etc., and I sat down on the rocky floor to enjoy the serene picture. Some crystal specks in the black ceiling high overhead, reflecting the light of a half-hid lamp, yielded this magnificent effect.

I own I did not like the cave so well for eking out its sublimities with this theatrical trick. But I have had many experiences like it, before and since; and we must be content to be pleased without too curiously analyzing the occasions. Our conversation with nature is not just what it seems. The cloudrack, the sunrise and sunset glories, rainbows and Northern Lights are not quite so spheral as our childhood thought them, and the part our organization plays in them is too large. The senses interfere everywhere and mix their own structure with all they report of. Once we fancied the earth a plane, and stationary. In admiring the sunset we do not yet deduct the rounding, coördinating, pictorial powers of the eye.

The same interference from our organization creates the most of our pleasure and pain. Our first mistake is the belief that the circumstance gives the joy which we give to the circumstance. Life is an ecstasy. Life is sweet as nitrous oxide; and the fisherman dripping all day over a cold pond, the switchman at the railway intersection, the farmer in the field, the Negro in the rice-swamp, the fop in the street, the hunter in the woods, the barrister with the jury, the belle at the ball, all ascribe a certain pleasure to their employment, which they themselves give it. Health and appetite impart the sweetness to sugar, bread, and meat. We fancy that our civilization has got on far, but we still come back to our primers.

We live by our imaginations, by our admirations, by our sentiments. The child walks amid heaps of illusions, which he does not like to have disturbed. The boy, how sweet to him in his fancy! how dear the story of barons and battles! What a hero he is, whilst he feeds on his heroes! What a debt is his to imaginative books! He has no better friend or influence than Scott, Shakspeare, Plutarch and Homer. The man lives to other objects, but who dare affirm that they are more real? Even the prose of the streets is full of refractions. In the life of the dreariest alderman, fancy enters into all details and colors them with rosy hue. He imitates the air and actions of people whom he admires, and is raised in his own eyes. He pays a debt quicker to a rich man than to a poor man. He wishes the bow and compliment of some leader in the state or in society; weighs what he says; perhaps he never comes nearer to him for that, but dies at last better contented for this amusement of his eyes and his fancy.

The world rolls, the din of life is never hushed. In London, in Paris, in Boston, in San Francisco, the carnival, the masquerade is at its height. Nobody drops his domino. The unities, the fictions of the piece it would be an impertinence to break. The chapter of fascinations is very long. Great is paint; nay, God is the painter; and we rightly accuse the critic who destroys too many illusions. Society does not love its unmaskers. It was wittily if somewhat bitterly said by D'Alembert,[4] *"qu'un état de vapeur était un état très fâcheux, parcequ'il nous faisait voir les choses comme elles sont."* [5] I find men victims of illusion in all parts of life. Children, youths, adults and old men, all are led by one bawble or another. Yoganidra, the goddess of illusion,[6] Proteus, or Momus,[7] or Gylfi's Mocking,[8]—for the Power has many names,—is stronger than the Titans, stronger than Apollo. Few have overheard the gods or surprised their secret. Life is a succession of lessons which must be lived to be understood. All is riddle, and the key to a riddle is another riddle. There are as many pillows of illusion as flakes in a snow-storm. We

---

3. **"The . . . sky":** the song, "Night and Love," beginning "When stars are in the quiet skies," from Bulwer-Lytton's *Ernest Maltravers*, Book III, Chap. 1.

4. **D'Alembert:** Jean le Rond d'Alembert (1717–83), French mathematician and philosopher, collaborator with Diderot on the *Encyclopaedia*. 5. **"qu'un . . . sont":** that a vaporous state is a very annoying one because it makes us see things as they are. 6. **Yoganidra:** the great illusory energy of Vishnu, by whom the whole world is beguiled. 7. **Momus:** in Greek mythology, the god of mockery or fault-finding. 8. **Gylfi's Mocking:** The word "mocking" here might also be translated "delusion." Emerson is referring to the first part of the *Prose Edda*. Gylfi is a wise king of Sweden who journeys to Asgard, the abode of the gods, to learn the secret of their knowledge and power. But the gods conjure up a series of "false shows" to beguile him, and in the end, when these have all vanished, Gylfi is presumably unsure of the reality of what he has heard and seen.

wake from one dream into another dream. The toys to be sure are various, and are graduated in refinement to the quality of the dupe. The intellectual man requires a fine bait; the sots are easily amused. But everybody is drugged with his own frenzy, and the pageant marches at all hours, with music and banner and badge.

Amid the joyous troop who give in to the charivari, comes now and then a sad-eyed boy whose eyes lack the requisite refractions to clothe the show in due glory, and who is afflicted with a tendency to trace home the glittering miscellany of fruits and flowers to one root. Science is a search after identity, and the scientific whim is lurking in all corners. At the State Fair a friend of mine complained that all the varieties of fancy pears in our orchards seem to have been selected by somebody who had a whim for a particular kind of pear, and only cultivated such as had that perfume; they were all alike. And I remember the quarrel of another youth [9] with the confectioners, that when he racked his wit to choose the best comfits in the shops, in all the endless varieties of sweetmeat he could find only three flavors, or two. What then? Pears and cakes are good for something; and because you unluckily have an eye or nose too keen, why need you spoil the comfort which the rest of us find in them? I knew a humorist who in a good deal of rattle had a grain or two of sense. He shocked the company by maintaining that the attributes of God were two,—power and risibility, and that it was the duty of every pious man to keep up the comedy. And I have known gentlemen of great stake in the community, but whose sympathies were cold,—presidents of colleges and governors and senators,—who held themselves bound to sign every temperance pledge, and act with Bible societies and missions and peace-makers, and cry *Hist-a-boy!* to every good dog. We must not carry comity too far, but we all have kind impulses in this direction. When the boys come into my yard for leave to gather horse-chestnuts, I own I enter into nature's game, and affect to grant the permission reluctantly, fearing that any moment they will find out the imposture of that showy chaff. But this tenderness is quite unnecessary; the enchantments are laid on very thick. Their young life is thatched with them. Bare and grim to tears is the lot of the children in the hovel I saw yesterday; yet not the less they hung it round with frippery romance, like the children

of the happiest fortune, and talked of "the dear cottage where so many joyful hours had flown." Well, this thatching of hovels is the custom of the country. Women, more than all, are the element and kingdom of illusion. Being fascinated, they fascinate. They see through Claude-Lorraines.[10] And how dare any one, if he could, pluck away the *coulisses*,[11] stage effects and ceremonies, by which they live? Too pathetic, too pitiable, is the region of affection, and its atmosphere always liable to *mirage*.

We are not very much to blame for our bad marriages. We live amid hallucinations; and this especial trap is laid to trip up our feet with, and all are tripped up first or last. But the mighty Mother who had been so sly with us, as if she felt that she owed us some indemnity, insinuates into the Pandora-box of marriage some deep and serious benefits and some great joys. We find a delight in the beauty and happiness of children that makes the heart too big for the body. In the worst-assorted connections there is ever some mixture of true marriage. Teague [12] and his jade get some just relations of mutual respect, kindly observation, and fostering of each other; learn something, and would carry themselves wiselier if they were now to begin.

'T is fine for us to point at one or another fine madman, as if there were any exempts. The scholar in his library is none. I, who have all my life heard any number of orations and debates, read poems and miscellaneous books, conversed with many geniuses, am still the victim of any new page; and if Marmaduke, or Hugh, or Moosehead, or any other, invent a new style or mythology, I fancy that the world will be all brave and right if dressed in these colors, which I had not thought of. Then at once I will daub with this new paint; but it will not stick. 'T is like the cement which the peddler sells at the door; he makes broken crockery hold with it, but you can never buy of him a bit of cement which will make it hold when he is gone.

Men who make themselves felt in the world avail themselves of a certain fate in their constitution which they know how to use. But they never deeply interest us unless they lift a corner of the curtain, or betray, never so slightly, their penetration of what is behind it. 'T is the charm of practical men that outside of their practicality are a certain poetry and play, as if they led the good horse Power by the bridle, and preferred to walk, though they can ride so fiercely. Bonaparte is intellectual,

---

9. **the quarrel of another youth:** This youth seems to have been Emerson's younger friend, Ellery Channing, who is said to have remarked that "whatever you asked for at a confectioner's, they brought you only one thing, *but there were two kinds of it*" (*Works*, VI, 429).

10. **Claude-Lorraines:** more properly, Claude Lorrain (1600-82), French landscape painter. 11. *coulisses:* spaces behind the scenes in a theater. 12. **Teague:** generic name for an immigrant Irish laborer.

as well as Cæsar; and the best soldiers, sea-captains and railway men have a gentleness when off duty, a good-natured admission that there are illusions, and who shall say that he is not their sport? We stigmatize the cast-iron fellows who cannot so detach themselves, as "dragon-ridden," "thunder-stricken," and fools of fate, with whatever powers endowed.

Since our tuition is through emblems and indirections, it is well to know that there is method in it, a fixed scale and rank above rank in the phantasms. We begin low with coarse masks and rise to the most subtle and beautiful. The red men told Columbus "they had an herb which took away fatigue;" but he found the illusion of "arriving from the east at the Indies" more composing to his lofty spirit than any tobacco. Is not our faith in the impenetrability of matter more sedative than narcotics? You play with jackstraws, balls, bowls, horse and gun, estates and politics; but there are finer games before you. Is not time a pretty toy? Life will show you masks that are worth all your carnivals. Yonder mountain must migrate into your mind. The fine star-dust and nebulous blur in Orion, "the portentous year of Mizar and Alcor," [13] must come down and be dealt with in your household thought. What if you shall come to discern that the play and playground of all this pompous history are radiations from yourself, and that the sun borrows his beams? What terrible questions we are learning to ask! The former men believed in magic, by which temples, cities, and men were swallowed up, and all trace of them gone. We are coming on the secret of a magic which sweeps out of men's minds all vestige of theism and beliefs which they and their fathers held and were framed upon.

There are deceptions of the senses, deceptions of the passions, and the structural, beneficent illusions of sentiment and of the intellect. There is the illusion of love, which attributes to the beloved person all which that person shares with his or her family, sex, age or condition, nay, with the human mind itself. 'T is these which the lover loves, and Anna Matilda gets the credit of them. As if one shut up always in a tower, with one window through which the face of heaven and earth could be seen, should fancy that all the marvels he beheld belonged to that window. There is the illusion of time, which is very deep; who has disposed of it?—or come to the conviction that what seems the *succession* of thought is only the distribution of

wholes into causal series? The intellect sees that every atom carries the whole of nature; that the mind opens to omnipotence; that, in the endless striving and ascents, the metamorphosis is entire, so that the soul doth not know itself in its own act when that act is perfected. There is illusion that shall deceive even the elect. There is illusion that shall deceive even the performer of the miracle. Though he makes his body, he denies that he makes it. Though the world exist from thought, thought is daunted in presence of the world. One after the other we accept the mental laws, still resisting those which follow, which however must be accepted. But all our concessions only compel us to new profusion. And what avails it that science has come to treat space and time as simply forms of thought, and the material world as hypothetical, and withal our pretension of *property* and even of self-hood are fading with the rest, if, at last, even our thoughts are not finalities, but the incessant flowing and ascension reach these also, and each thought which yesterday was a finality, to-day is yielding to a larger generalization?

With such volatile elements to work in, 't is no wonder if our estimates are loose and floating. We must work and affirm, but we have no guess of the value of what we say or do. The cloud is now as big as your hand, and now it covers a county. That story of Thor, who was set to drain the drinking-horn in Asgard and to wrestle with the old woman and to run with the runner Lok, and presently found that he had been drinking up the sea, and wrestling with Time, and racing with Thought, [14]—describes us, who are contending, amid these seeming trifles, with the supreme energies of nature. We fancy we have fallen into bad company and squalid condition, low debts, shoe-bills, broken glass to pay for, pots to buy, butcher's meat, sugar, milk and coal. "Set me some great task, ye gods! and I will show my spirit." "Not so," says the good Heaven; "plod and plough, vamp your old coats and hats, weave a shoestring; great affairs and the best wine by and by." Well, 't is all phantasm; and if we weave a yard of tape in all humility and as well as we can, long hereafter we shall see it was no cotton tape at all but some galaxy which we braided, and that the threads were Time and Nature.

We cannot write the order of the variable winds. How can we penetrate the law of our shifting moods and susceptibility? Yet they differ as all and nothing. Instead of the firmament of yesterday,

---

13. "the . . . Alcor": Mizar and Alcor, two stars in the "handle" of the Great Dipper, known together to the Arabs as "The Horse and Rider." Mizar is said to revolve around Alcor once every 190,000 years.

14. That . . . Thought: This tale is told in the *Prose Edda* (see 8 n.), "Gylfi's Mocking," 46–47, but it is not in Asgard that Thor is subjected to these tests, but in the "burg" of the giant, Utgard-Loke.

which our eyes require, it is to-day an egg-shell which coops us in; we cannot even see what or where our stars of destiny are. From day to day the capital facts of human life are hidden from our eyes. Suddenly the mist rolls up and reveals them, and we think how much good time is gone that might have been saved had any hint of these things been shown. A sudden rise in the road shows us the system of mountains, and all the summits, which have been just as near us all the year, but quite out of mind. But these alternations are not without their order, and we are parties to our various fortune. If life seem a succession of dreams, yet poetic justice is done in dreams also. The visions of good men are good; it is the undisciplined will that is whipped with bad thoughts and bad fortunes. When we break the laws, we lose our hold on the central reality. Like sick men in hospitals, we change only from bed to bed, from one folly to another; and it cannot signify much what becomes of such castaways, wailing, stupid, comatose creatures, lifted from bed to bed, from the nothing of life to the nothing of death.

In this kingdom of illusions we grope eagerly for stays and foundations. There is none but a strict and faithful dealing at home and a severe barring out of all duplicity or illusion there. Whatever games are played with us, we must play no games with ourselves, but deal in our privacy with the last honesty and truth. I look upon the simple and childish virtues of veracity and honesty as the root of all that is sublime in character. Speak as you think, be what you are, pay your debts of all kinds. I prefer to be owned as sound and solvent, and my word as good as my bond, and to be what cannot be skipped, or dissipated, or undermined, to all the *éclat* in the universe. This reality is the foundation of friendship, religion, poetry, and art. At the top or at the bottom of all illusions, I set the cheat which still leads us to work and live for appearances; in spite of our conviction, in all sane hours, that it is what we really are that avails with friends, with strangers, and with fate or fortune.

One would think from the talk of men that riches and poverty were a great matter; and our civilization mainly respects it. But the Indians say that they do not think the white man, with his brow of care, always toiling, afraid of heat and cold, and keeping within doors, has any advantage of them. The permanent interest of every man is never to be in a false position, but to have the weight of nature to back him in all that he does. Riches and poverty are a thick or thin costume; and our life—the life of all of us—identical. For we transcend the circumstance continually and taste the real quality of existence; as in our employments, which only differ in the manifestations but express the same laws; or in our thoughts, which wear no silks and taste no ice-creams. We see God face to face every hour, and know the savor of nature.

The early Greek philosophers Heraclitus and Xenophanes [15] measured their force on this problem of identity. Diogenes of Apollonia [16] said that unless the atoms were made of one stuff, they could never blend and act with one another. But the Hindoos, in their sacred writings, express the liveliest feeling, both of the essential identity and of that illusion which they conceive variety to be. "The notions, *'I am,'* and *'This is mine,'* which influence mankind, are but delusions of the mother of the world. Dispel, O Lord of all creatures! the conceit of knowledge which proceeds from ignorance." [17] And the beatitude of man they hold to lie in being freed from fascination.

The intellect is stimulated by the statement of truth in a trope, and the will by clothing the laws of life in illusions. But the unities of Truth and of Right are not broken by the disguise. There need never be any confusion in these. In a crowded life of many parts and performers, on a stage of nations, or in the obscurest hamlet in Maine or California, the same elements offer the same choices to each new comer, and, according to his election, he fixes his fortune in absolute Nature. It would be hard to put more mental and moral philosophy than the Persians have thrown into a sentence,—

"Fooled thou must be, though wisest of the wise:
Then be the fool of virtue, not of vice."

There is no chance and no anarchy in the universe. All is system and gradation. Every god is there sitting in his sphere. The young mortal enters the hall of the firmament; there is he alone with them alone, they pouring on him benedictions and gifts, and beckoning him up to their thrones. On the instant, and incessantly, fall snow-storms of illusions. He fancies himself in a vast crowd which sways this way and that and whose movement and doings he must obey: he fancies himself poor, orphaned, insignificant. The mad crowd drives hither and thither, now furiously commanding this thing to be done, now that. What is he that he should resist their will, and think or act for himself? Every moment new changes and new showers of deceptions to baffle and distract him. And when, by and by, for an instant, the air clears

---

15. **Xenophanes:** See the poem, "Xenophanes," p. 298.　16. **Diogenes of Apollonia:** Greek philosopher of the fifth century B.C. Emerson seems here to be summarizing Fragment 2 of Diogenes. 17. **"The . . . ignorance":** from Aditi's praise of Krishna in the Vishnú Puráña, Book V, Chap. 30.

and the cloud lifts a little, there are the gods still sitting around him on their thrones,—they alone with him alone.[18]

FROM

# POEMS [1847]

❖

❨ THOUGH he had written verse from a very early age, Emerson was singularly diffident about appearing publicly in the role of a poet; and with one or two exceptions, he published no poems until late in the thirties, when James Freeman Clarke, who had gone to Louisville as minister of the Unitarian Church there, persuaded him in 1839 to contribute "Each and All," "The Rhodora," and one or two other poems to the *Western Literary Messenger*, which Clarke was then editing in Kentucky. After the *Dial* was founded in 1840, with Emerson's blessing and cooperation, he naturally allowed still further poems ("The Problem," "Woodnotes," "The Snow-Storm," and others) to be published in its pages; and at last, in 1847, he made a collection of the verse he had written up to that point, and with considerable hesitation brought out his first volume of *Poems*. Not for twenty years did he publish another book of verse, but in 1867 appeared *May-Day and Other Pieces*, which contained most of the poems he had written in the interval (the title poem, "Brahma," "Boston Hymn," "Waldeinsamkeit," and others). In 1876 he published a third and final volume, *Selected Poems*, mostly made up of poems that had come out in the earlier volumes with the addition of five or six new but unimportant pieces. A scattering of other poems, unfinished or in Emerson's own view not worth publishing, were included posthumously by his editors in an Appendix.

❖

## EACH AND ALL

❨ THE theme of this poem—that composition is "more important than the beauty of individual forms to effect" —had been expressed by Emerson in his journal some months before it was written (*Journals*, III, 298); and he came back to the thought later that year (1834) in an entry which reads in part:

---

18. **they alone with him alone:** an echo of the famous and sublime passage in the *Enneads* of Plotinus (VI.ix), as translated by Thomas Taylor: "This, therefore, is the life of the Gods, and of divine and happy men, a liberation from all terrene concerns, a life unaccompanied with human pleasures, and a flight of the alone to the alone." The whole paragraph is reminiscent also of a passage in the *Phaedo* of Plato (79).

Everything, to be appreciated, must be seen from the point where its rays converge to a focus . . . The shepherd or the beggar in his red cloak little knows what a charm he gives to the wide landscape that charms you on the mountain-top and whereof he makes the most agreeable feature, and I no more [than he know] that part my individuality plays in the All. [*Ibid.*, p. 373]

The reminiscence of the seashells was set down in the former of these entries, and the shepherd or the beggar in his red cloak seems to have lingered in Emerson's memory from his Italian travels in 1833:

Italy is the country of beauty, but I think specially in the northern part. Everything is ornamented. A peasant wears a scarlet cloak. If he has no other ornament, he ties on a red garter or knee-band. [*Ibid.*, p. 140]

Little thinks, in the field, yon red-cloaked clown
Of thee from the hill-top looking down;
The heifer that lows in the upland farm,
Far-heard, lows not thine ear to charm;
The sexton, tolling his bell at noon,
Deems not that great Napoleon
Stops his horse, and lists with delight,
Whilst his files sweep round yon Alpine height;
Nor knowest thou what argument
Thy life to thy neighbor's creed has lent.       10
All are needed by each one;
Nothing is fair or good alone.
I thought the sparrow's note from heaven,
Singing at dawn on the alder bough;
I brought him home, in his nest, at even;
He sings the song, but it cheers not now,
For I did not bring home the river and sky;
He sang to my ear—they sang to my eye.
The delicate shells lay on the shore;
The bubbles of the latest wave       20
Fresh pearls to their enamel gave,
And the bellowing of the savage sea
Greeted their safe escape to me.
I wiped away the weeds and foam,
I fetched my sea-born treasures home;
But the poor, unsightly, noisome things
Had left their beauty on the shore
With the sun and the sand and the wild uproar.
The lover watched his graceful maid,
As 'mid the virgin train she strayed,       30
Nor knew her beauty's best attire
Was woven still by the snow-white choir.
At last she came to his hermitage,
Like the bird from the woodlands to the cage;
The gay enchantment was undone,
A gentle wife, but fairy none.
Then I said, "I covet truth;
Beauty is unripe childhood's cheat;

I leave it behind with the games of youth":
As I spoke, beneath my feet                              40
The ground-pine curled its pretty wreath,
Running over the club-moss burrs;
I inhaled the violet's breath;
Around me stood the oaks and firs;
Pine-cones and acorns lay on the ground;
Over me soared the eternal sky,
Full of light and of deity;
Again I saw, again I heard,
The rolling river, the morning bird;
Beauty through my senses stole;                          50
I yielded myself to the perfect whole.

## THE PROBLEM

❲ ORIGINALLY entitled "The Priest," this poem expresses
Emerson's preoccupation, during the late thirties, with
the problem of vocation. He had resigned from the ministry seven years before the poem was written, and by
this time he had ceased to preach even occasionally as
a substitute for other clergymen, but the beauty and
grandeur of the priestly vocation at its highest never
ceased to exercise their claim upon his veneration. He
came to believe, however, that the role of the priest
could be played by other men than the ordained cleric,
even by the lyceum lecturer, but especially by the artist.
He also came to believe that the artist receives his deepest suggestion from nature herself; the structural forms
the architect "creates," for example, owe their beauty
and authority to their derivation from the organic forms
in nature.

I like a church; I like a cowl;
I love a prophet of the soul;
And on my heart monastic aisles
Fall like sweet strains, or pensive smiles;
Yet not for all his faith can see
Would I that cowlèd churchman be.

Why should the vest on him allure,
Which I could not on me endure?
Not from a vain or shallow thought
His awful Jove young Phidias brought;                    10
Never from lips of cunning fell
The thrilling Delphic oracle;
Out from the heart of nature rolled
The burdens of the Bible old;
The litanies of nations came,
Like the volcano's tongue of flame,
Up from the burning core below,—
The canticles of love and woe:
The hand that rounded Peter's dome

And groined the aisles of Christian Rome               20
Wrought in a sad sincerity;
Himself from God he could not free;
He builded better than he knew;—
The conscious stone to beauty grew.

Know'st thou what wove yon woodbird's nest
Of leaves, and feathers from her breast?
Or how the fish outbuilt her shell,
Painting with morn each annual cell?
Or how the sacred pine-tree adds
To her old leaves new myriads?                          30
Such and so grew these holy piles,
Whilst love and terror laid the tiles.
Earth proudly wears the Parthenon,
As the best gem upon her zone,
And Morning opes with haste her lids
To gaze upon the Pyramids;
O'er England's abbeys bends the sky,
As on its friends, with kindred eye;
For out of Thought's interior sphere
These wonders rose to upper air;                        40
And Nature gladly gave them place,
Adopted them into her race,
And granted them an equal date
With Andes and with Ararat.

These temples grew as grows the grass;
Art might obey, but not surpass.
The passive Master lent his hand
To the vast soul that o'er him planned;
And the same power that reared the shrine
Bestrode the tribes that knelt within.                  50
Ever the fiery Pentecost
Girds with one flame the countless host,
Trances the heart through chanting choirs,
And through the priest the mind inspires.
The word unto the prophet spoken
Was writ on tables yet unbroken;
The word by seers or sibyls told,
In groves of oak, or fanes of gold,
Still floats upon the morning wind,
Still whispers to the willing mind.                     60
One accent of the Holy Ghost
The heedless world hath never lost.
I know what say the fathers wise,—
The Book itself before me lies,
Old *Chrysostom*, best Augustine,
And he who blent both in his line,
The younger *Golden Lips* or mines,
Taylor, the Shakespeare of divines.

55. the prophet: Moses; see Exod. 31:18.   65. Old *Chrysostom:* St. John Chrysostom, bishop of Antioch in the fourth century. The sobriquet "Chrysostom," meaning "golden lips," was
applied to him because of his eloquence as a preacher.
67–68. The . . . divines: Jeremy Taylor (1613–67), bishop of
Dromore, one of the greatest of Anglican pulpit orators. **mines:**
that is, of golden eloquence.

THE PROBLEM.   10. His awful Jove: the gold and ivory statue
of Zeus at Olympia, the work of one of the greatest of Greek
sculptors, the fifth-century artist Phidias.   19. The . . .
dome: The hand was Michelangelo's, the architect of St. Peter's
at Rome.

His words are music in my ear,
I see his cowlèd portrait dear;                                70
And yet, for all his faith could see,
I would not the good bishop be.

## HAMATREYA

❲ IN THE autumn of 1845 Emerson copied into his journal certain passages from the Vishńu Puráńa, one of
the Hindu scriptures he had been reading in translation
(*Works*, IX, 416–17). "Hamatreya" is a quietly humorous Yankee version of one of these—a passage from
Book IV, Chap. 24, of the Puráńa which had evidently
caught Emerson's fancy. The revered sage, Paráśara,
is there represented as giving his disciple, Maitreya, a
summary account—a kind of Book of the Kings—of the
sovereigns who have held sway in the world; at the end
of all this he remarks that these great monarchs, with
their delusory belief that the earth itself was a possession
of theirs and their dynasties' forever, have now all
passed away. "Earth laughs," continues Paráśara, "as if
smiling with autumnal flowers, to behold her kings unable to effect the subjugation of themselves." He then
goes on to repeat to Maitreya the stanzas chanted, as
he says, by Earth on the folly of princes, deluded as they
are by the conviction of their absolute ownership. See
*The Vishńu Puráńa*, translated by H. H. Wilson
(1840), pp. 487–89.

Bulkeley, Hunt, Willard, Hosmer, Meriam, Flint,
Possessed the land which rendered to their toil
Hay, corn, roots, hemp, flax, apples, wool and
    wood.
Each of these landlords walked amidst his farm,
Saying, " 'Tis mine, my children's and my
    name's.
How sweet the west wind sounds in my own trees!
How graceful climb those shadows on my hill!
I fancy these pure waters and the flags
Know me, as does my dog: we sympathize;
And, I affirm, my actions smack of the soil."    10

Where are these men? Asleep beneath their
    grounds:
And strangers, fond as they, their furrows plough.
Earth laughs in flowers, to see her boastful boys
Earth-proud, proud of the earth which is not
    theirs;
Who steer the plough, but cannot steer their
    feet

HAMATREYA.    Why Emerson changed the name Maitreya to
the form he uses here is not clear: perhaps he simply felt that
this latter name was more euphonious; perhaps there is some
echo in it of the word "hamadryad," though this would have
no literal appropriateness.    1. Bulkeley . . . Flint:   names
of some of the early settlers of Concord. One of them, Peter
Bulkeley, was an ancestor of Emerson, and in his own time one
of the people he most respected in Concord; Edmund Hosmer,
a simple and sagacious farmer, was descended from another.
(See "New England Reformers," 19 n.)

Clear of the grave.
They added ridge to valley, brook to pond,
And sighed for all that bounded their domain;
"This suits me for a pasture; that's my park;
We must have clay, lime, gravel, granite-ledge,    20
And misty lowland, where to go for peat.
The land is well—lies fairly to the south.
'Tis good, when you have crossed the sea and back,
To find the sitfast acres where you left them."
Ah! the hot owner sees not Death, who adds
Him to his land, a lump of mold the more.
Hear what the Earth says:

### EARTH-SONG

"Mine and yours;
    Mine, not yours.
Earth endures;                                30
    Stars abide—
Shine down in the old sea;
    Old are the shores;
But where are old men?
    I who have seen much,
Such have I never seen.

"The lawyer's deed
    Ran sure,
    In tail,
To them, and to their heirs        40
    Who shall succeed,
    Without fail,
    Forevermore.

"Here is the land,
    Shaggy with wood,
With its old valley,
    Mound and flood.
But the heritors?
Fled like the flood's foam.
The lawyer, and the laws,        50
    And the kingdom,
Clean swept herefrom.
"They called me theirs,
    Who so controlled me;
Yet every one
Wished to stay, and is gone,
    How am I theirs,
If they cannot hold me,
    But I hold them?"

When I heard the Earth-song,        60
I was no longer brave;
My avarice cooled
Like lust in the chill of the grave.

24. sitfast: sitting firmly, well-established, fixed; cf. steadfast.
39. In tail: intail, entail; legal term for perpetual ownership of
an estate by a succession of heirs.

## THE RHODORA

### ON BEING ASKED, WHENCE IS THE FLOWER?

In May, when sea-winds pierced our solitudes,
I found the fresh Rhodora in the woods,
Spreading its leafless blooms in a damp nook,
To please the desert and the sluggish brook.
The purple petals, fallen in the pool,
Made the black water with their beauty gay;
Here might the red-bird come his plumes to cool,
And court the flower that cheapens his array.
Rhodora! if the sages ask thee why
This charm is wasted on the earth and sky,    10
Tell them, dear, that if eyes were made for seeing,
Then Beauty is its own excuse for being:
Why thou wert there, O rival of the rose!
I never thought to ask, I never knew:
But, in my simple ignorance, suppose
The self-same Power that brought me there
   brought you.

                 *1839*

## THE SNOW-STORM

❰ ONE of Emerson's earliest successful poems, "The Snow-Storm," was probably written in 1835, commemorative of a great snowfall in Concord the preceding winter. The thought of the second part of the poem—the suggestiveness of natural forms to the artist, particularly (here) to the architect—is the thought that he also expressed in "The Problem," and it has an echo in his essay "History" in *Essays: First Series:* "I have seen a snow-drift along the sides of the stone wall which obviously gave the idea of the common architectural scroll to abut a tower" (*Works*, II, 19).

Announced by all the trumpets of the sky,
Arrives the snow, and, driving o'er the fields,
Seems nowhere to alight: the whited air
Hides hills and woods, the river, and the heaven,
And veils the farm-house at the garden's end.
The sled and traveler stopped, the courier's feet
Delayed, all friends shut out, the housemates sit
Around the radiant fireplace, enclosed
In a tumultuous privacy of storm.

Come see the north wind's masonry.      10
Out of an unseen quarry evermore
Furnished with tile, the fierce artificer
Curves his white bastions with projected roof

Round every windward stake, or tree, or door.
Speeding, the myriad-handed, his wild work
So fanciful, so savage, nought cares he
For number or proportion. Mockingly,
On coop or kennel he hangs Parian wreaths;
A swan-like form invests the hidden thorn;
Fills up the farmer's lane from wall to wall,   20
Maugre the farmer's sighs; and at the gate
A tapering turret overtops the work.
And when his hours are numbered, and the world
Is all his own, retiring, as he were not,
Leaves, when the sun appears, astonished Art
To mimic in slow structures, stone by stone,
Built in an age, the mad wind's night-work,
The frolic architecture of the snow.

## ODE INSCRIBED TO W. H. CHANNING

❰ THIS poem seems to have been written, some time after the declaration of war on Mexico, in the spring of 1846, as a result of some conversation or correspondence with Emerson's younger friend, W. H. Channing, a Unitarian minister and ardent abolitionist, who had spoken in Concord in the summer of 1845. Channing must have attempted to persuade Emerson to take a more vigorous and more public stand against the aggressions of the proslavery forces both in the South and in the North. At this period, though certainly not later, Emerson felt that active and absorbing participation in the public agitation of such questions was not his true role: "I have," he wrote, "quite other slaves to free than those negroes, to wit, imprisoned spirits, imprisoned thoughts" (*Works*, IX, 428).

Though loath to grieve
The evil time's sole patriot,
I cannot leave
My honied thought
For the priest's cant,
Or statesman's rant.

If I refuse
My study for their politique,
Which at the best is trick,
The angry Muse          10
Puts confusion in my brain.

But who is he that prates
Of the culture of mankind,
Of better arts and life?
Go, blindworm, go,

---

THE SNOW-STORM. **9. In . . . storm:** Emily Dickinson was so much pleased by this line that she copied it on a sheet of stationery and enclosed it in a letter of her sister's to a friend (*Letters*, Johnson, III, 928).

18. **Parian:** The finest marble used by Greek sculptors in antiquity was quarried on the Aegean island of Paros. ODE INSCRIBED TO W. H. CHANNING. **2. sole patriot:** Channing; a consciously hyperbolic description of a man for whom, however, Emerson did in fact have great respect.

Behold the famous States
Harrying Mexico
With rifle and with knife!

Or who, with accent bolder,
Dare praise the freedom-loving mountaineer?          20
I found by thee, O rushing Contoocook!
And in thy valleys, Agiochook!
The jackals of the negro-holder.

The God who made New Hampshire
Taunted the lofty land
With little men;—
Small bat and wren
House in the oak:—
If earth-fire cleave
The upheaved land, and bury the folk,          30
The southern crocodile would grieve.
Virtue palters; Right is hence;
Freedom praised, but hid;
Funeral eloquence
Rattles the coffin-lid.

What boots thy zeal,
O glowing friend,
That would indignant rend
The northland from the south?
Wherefore? to what good end?          40
Boston Bay and Bunker Hill
Would serve things still;
Things are of the snake.

The horseman serves the horse,
The neatherd serves the neat,
The merchant serves the purse,
The eater serves his meat;
'Tis the day of the chattel,
Web to weave, and corn to grind;
Things are in the saddle,          50
And ride mankind.

There are two laws discrete,
Not reconciled,—
Law for man, and law for thing;
The last builds town and fleet,
But it runs wild,
And doth the man unking.

'Tis fit the forest fall,
The steep be graded,
The mountain tunneled,          60
The sand shaded,
The orchard planted,
The glebe tilled,
The prairie granted,
The steamer built.

Let man serve law for man;
Live for friendship, live for love,
For truth's and harmony's behoof;
The state may follow how it can,
As Olympus follows Jove.          70

     Yet do not I implore
The wrinkled shopman to my sounding woods,
Nor bid the unwilling senator
Ask votes of thrushes in the solitudes.
Every one to his chosen work;—
Foolish hands may mix and mar;
Wise and sure the issues are.
Round they roll till dark is light,
Sex to sex, and even to odd;—
The over-god          80
Who marries Right to Might,
Who peoples, unpeoples,—
He who exterminates
Races by stronger races,
Black by white faces,—
Knows to bring honey
Out of the lion;
Grafts gentlest scion
On pirate and Turk.

The Cossack eats Poland,          90
Like stolen fruit;
Her last noble is ruined,
Her last poet mute:
Straight, into double band
The victors divide;
Half for freedom strike and stand;—
The astonished Muse finds thousands at her side.

---

21. **Contoocook:** a river in New Hampshire.      22. **Agiochook:** the Indian name for the White Mountains.      23. **The . . . negro-holder:** overseers, deputies, and the like sent in pursuit of fugitive slaves.      24–26. **The . . . men:** This half-humorously low estimate of the men of New Hampshire is an echo of passages in Emerson's journal written during a vacation trip into that state in the summer of 1839 (*Journals*, V, 245–47).      41–42. **Boston Bay . . . still:** that is, despite their associations with the heroic memories of the Revolution.      45. **neat:** cattle.      52. **discrete:** distinct; not to be confused with one another.

64. **granted:** disposed of by land grants.      86–87. **honey . . . lion:** See Judg. 14:5–9.      90–93. **The . . . mute:** an allusion to the "partitions" of Poland in the late eighteenth century, of which the lion's share went to Russia; and to the suppression of political and intellectual liberties there by the Russians.      94–97. **Straight . . . side:** There was a nationalist insurrection in Poland in 1830–31 which had been plotted for some years by men who had been in touch with the "Decembrist" revolutionaries in Russia. "The astonished Muse" may refer to the role played in the struggle for Polish freedom by the patriot-poet, Adam Mickiewicz.

## GIVE ALL TO LOVE

❮ IN THIS poem, Robert Frost has said, "Emerson supplies the emancipating formula for giving an attachment up for an attraction, one nationality for another nationality, one love for another love . . . Left to myself I have gradually come to see what Emerson was meaning in 'Give All to Love' was, Give all to Meaning. The freedom is ours to insist on meaning" (see *Daedalus*, LXXXVIII [Fall, 1959], 715–16). The same apparently irresponsible but essentially Platonic doctrine is expressed in the essay "Love" (*Essays: First Series*) and at the end of the essay "Compensation" (*Ibid.*).

Give all to love;
Obey thy heart;
Friends, kindred, days,
Estate, good-fame,
Plans, credit and the Muse,—
Nothing refuse.

'Tis a brave master;
Let it have scope:
Follow it utterly,
Hope beyond hope:        10
High and more high
It dives into noon,
With wing unspent,
Untold intent;
But it is a god,
Knows its own path
And the outlets of the sky.

It was never for the mean;
It requireth courage stout.
Souls above doubt,        20
Valor unbending,
It will reward,—
They shall return
More than they were,
And every ascending.

Leave all for love;
Yet, hear me, yet,
One word more thy heart behoved,
One pulse more of firm endeavor,
Keep thee today,        30
Tomorrow, forever,
Free as an Arab
Of thy beloved.

Cling with life to the maid;
But when the surprise,
First vague shadow of surmise
Flits across her bosom young,
Of a joy apart from thee,

Free be she, fancy-free;
Nor thou detain her vesture's hem,    40
Nor the palest rose she flung
From her summer diadem.

Though thou loved her as thyself,
As a self of purer clay,
Though her parting dims the day,
Stealing grace from all alive;
Heartily know,
When half-gods go,
The gods arrive.

## XENOPHANES

❮ XENOPHANES was a pre-Socratic philosopher and poet who asserted that "There is one God, greatest among gods and men, neither in shape nor in thought like unto mortals." He is said also to have held that "The All is One and the One is God." Somewhat unhistorically, in all probability, Emerson is using Xenophanes here as the type of the philosopher whose insight into Unity is so powerful that it blinds him to the antithetical fact of Plurality—a state of mind which the poet represents himself for the moment as sharing. In *Nature*, V, Emerson remarks that "Xenophanes complained in his old age, that, look where he would, all things hastened back to Unity" (*Works*, I, 43).

By fate, not option, frugal Nature gave
One scent to hyson and to wall-flower,
One sound to pine-groves and to waterfalls,
One aspect to the desert and the lake.
It was her stern necessity: all things
Are of one pattern made; bird, beast and flower,
Song, picture, form, space, thought and character
Deceive us, seeming to be many things,
And are but one. Beheld far off, they part
As God and devil; bring them to the mind,    10
They dull its edge with their monotony.
To know one element, explore another,
And in the second reappears the first.
The specious panorama of a year
But multiplies the image of a day,—
A belt of mirrors round a taper's flame;
And universal Nature, through her vast
And crowded whole, an infinite paroquet,
Repeats one note.

---

GIVE ALL TO LOVE.   **39. fancy-free:** an echo of Shakespeare's line, "In maiden meditation, fancy-free" (*A Midsummer Night's Dream*, II.i.164).   XENOPHANES.   **2. hyson:** a kind of China tea.

# THRENODY

❡ IN January 1842, Emerson's five-year-old son Waldo, a beautiful and gifted child, died after a few days' illness. The bereavement was a terrible one, and in the first part of "Threnody" (ll. 1–175), which Emerson seems to have written during the early spring, shortly after the boy's death, he gives vent to a bitterness of grief such as one finds nowhere else in his verse or indeed, outside of his journal and his private letters, in his prose. The second part of the poem (ll. 176–289), which was written some months later, in 1843, expresses Emerson's recovery from the first anguish of loss and his acceptance of a calmer view of death and bereavement. The language and imagery throughout owe nothing to the tradition of the classical pastoral elegy, as most of the great elegiac poems in English have done; the poem is wholly native and unconventional.

The South-wind brings
Life, sunshine and desire,
And on every mount and meadow
Breathes aromatic fire;
But over the dead he has no power,
The lost, the lost, he cannot restore;
And, looking over the hills, I mourn
The darling who shall not return.

I see my empty house,
I see my trees repair their boughs;    10
And he, the wondrous child,
Whose silver warble wild
Outvalued every pulsing sound
Within the air's cerulean round,—
The hyacinthine boy, for whom
Morn well might break and April bloom,
The gracious boy, who did adorn
The world whereinto he was born,
And by his countenance repay
The favor of the loving Day,—    20
Has disappeared from the Day's eye;
Far and wide she cannot find him;
My hopes pursue, they cannot bind him.
Returned this day, the South-wind searches,
And finds young pines and budding birches;
But finds not the budding man;
Nature, who lost, cannot remake him;
Fate let him fall, Fate can't retake him;
Nature, Fate, men, him seek in vain.

And whither now, my truant wise and sweet,    30
O, whither tend thy feet?
I had the right, few days ago,
Thy steps to watch, thy place to know:
How have I forfeited the right?
Hast thou forgot me in a new delight?

I hearken for thy household cheer,
O eloquent child!
Whose voice, an equal messenger,
Conveyed thy meaning mild.
What though the pains and joys    40
Whereof it spoke were toys
Fitting his age and ken,
Yet fairest dames and bearded men,
Who heard the sweet request,
So gentle, wise and grave,
Bended with joy to his behest
And let the world's affairs go by,
A while to share his cordial game,
Or mend his wicker wagon-frame,
Still plotting how their hungry ear    50
That winsome voice again might hear;
For his lips could well pronounce
Words that were persuasions.

Gentlest guardians marked serene
His early hope, his liberal mien;
Took counsel from his guiding eyes
To make this wisdom earthly wise.
Ah, vainly do these eyes recall
The school-march, each day's festival,
When every morn my bosom glowed    60
To watch the convoy on the road;
The babe in willow wagon closed,
With rolling eyes and face composed;
With children forward and behind,
Like Cupids studiously inclined;
And he the chieftain paced beside,
The center of the troop allied,
With sunny face of sweet repose,
To guard the babe from fancied foes.
The little captain innocent    70
Took the eye with him as he went;
Each village senior paused to scan
And speak the lovely caravan.
From the window I look out
To mark thy beautiful parade,
Stately marching in cap and coat
To some tune by fairies played;—
A music heard by thee alone
To works as noble led thee on.

Now Love and Pride, alas! in vain,    80
Up and down their glances strain.
The painted sled stands where it stood;
The kennel by the corded wood;
His gathered sticks to stanch the wall
Of the snow-tower, when snow should fall;

---

THRENODY.    15. hyacinthine: classically beautiful, like the Greek youth, Hyacinth, beloved by Apollo.

48. cordial: in the sense of hearty, cheerful, or gay.
84. stanch: to make stanch; to support; not, of course, to stop the flow of.

The ominous hole he dug in the sand,
And childhood's castles built or planned;
His daily haunts I well discern,—
The poultry-yard, the shed, the barn,—
And every inch of garden ground        90
Paced by the blessed feet around,
From the roadside to the brook
Whereinto he loved to look.
Step the meek fowls where erst they ranged;
The wintry garden lies unchanged;
The brook into the stream runs on;
But the deep-eyed boy is gone.

On that shaded day,
Dark with more clouds than tempests are,
When thou didst yield thy innocent breath    100
In birdlike heavings unto death,
Night came, and Nature had not thee;
I said, "We are mates in misery."
The morrow dawned with needless glow;
Each snowbird chirped, each fowl must crow;
Each tramper started; but the feet
Of the most beautiful and sweet
Of human youth had left the hill
And garden,—they were bound and still.
There's not a sparrow or a wren,        110
There's not a blade of autumn grain,
Which the four seasons do not tend
And tides of life and increase lend;
And every chick of every bird,
And weed and rock-moss is preferred.
O ostrich-like forgetfulness!
O loss of larger in the less!
Was there no star that could be sent,
No watcher in the firmament,
No angel from the countless host       120
That loiters round the crystal coast,
Could stoop to heal that only child,
Nature's sweet marvel undefiled,
And keep the blossom of the earth,
Which all her harvests were not worth?
Not mine,—I never called thee mine,
But Nature's heir,—if I repine,
And seeing rashly torn and moved
Not what I made, but what I loved,
Grow early old with grief that thou     130
Must to the wastes of Nature go,—
'Tis because a general hope
Was quenched, and all must doubt and grope.
For flattering planets seemed to say
This child should ills of ages stay,

By wondrous tongue, and guided pen,
Bring the flown Muses back to men.
Perchance not he but Nature ailed,
The world and not the infant failed.
It was not ripe yet to sustain        140
A genius of so fine a strain,
Who gazed upon the sun and moon
As if he came unto his own,
And, pregnant with his grander thought,
Brought the old order into doubt.
His beauty once their beauty tried;
They could not feed him, and he died,
And wandered backward as in scorn,
To wait an aeon to be born.

Ill day which made this beauty waste,    150
Plight broken, this high face defaced!
Some went and came about the dead;
And some in books of solace read;
Some to their friends the tidings say;
Some went to write, some went to pray;
One tarried here, there hurried one;
But their heart abode with none.
Covetous death bereaved us all,
To aggrandize one funeral.
The eager fate which carried thee     160
Took the largest part of me:
For this losing is true dying;
This is lordly man's down-lying,
This his slow but sure reclining,
Star by star his world resigning.

O child of paradise,
Boy who made dear his father's home,
In whose deep eyes
Men read the welfare of the times to come,
I am too much bereft.          170
The world dishonored thou hast left.
O truth's and nature's costly lie!
O trusted broken prophecy!
O richest fortune sourly crossed!
Born for the future, to the future lost!

The deep Heart answered, "Weepest thou?
Worthier cause for passion wild
If I had not taken the child.
And deemest thou as those who pore,
With aged eyes, short way before,—    180
Think'st Beauty vanished from the coast
Of matter, and thy darling lost?
Taught he not thee—the man of eld,
Whose eyes within his eyes beheld
Heaven's numerous hierarchy span

96–97. The . . . gone: "If," wrote Emerson in his journal, "I go down to the bottom of the garden it seems as if some one had fallen into the brook. Every place is handsome or tolerable where he has been" (*Journals*, VI, 154).

176. The deep Heart: the heart of Nature.    183. the man of eld: Emerson may have in mind the Plato of *Phaedo* (79–80).

The mystic gulf from God to man?
To be alone wilt thou begin
When worlds of lovers hem thee in?
Tomorrow, when the masks shall fall
That dizen Nature's carnival, 190
The pure shall see by their own will,
Which overflowing Love shall fill,
'Tis not within the force of fate
The fate-conjoined to separate.
But thou, my votary, weepest thou?
I gave thee sight—where is it now?
I taught thy heart beyond the reach
Of ritual, bible, or of speech;
Wrote in thy mind's transparent table,
As far as the incommunicable; 200
Taught thee each private sign to raise
Lit by the supersolar blaze.
Past utterance, and past belief,
And past the blasphemy of grief,
The mysteries of Nature's heart;
And though no Muse can these impart,
Throb thine with Nature's throbbing breast,
And all is clear from east to west.

"I came to thee as to a friend;
Dearest, to thee I did not send 210
Tutors, but a joyful eye,
Innocence that matched the sky,
Lovely locks, a form of wonder,
Laughter rich as woodland thunder,
That thou might'st entertain apart
The richest flowering of all art:
And, as the great all-loving Day
Through smallest chambers takes its way,
That thou might'st break thy daily bread
With prophet, savior and head; 220
That thou might'st cherish for thine own
The riches of sweet Mary's Son,
Boy-Rabbi, Israel's paragon.
And thoughtest thou such guest
Would in thy hall take up his rest?
Would rushing life forget her laws,
Fate's glowing revolution pause?
High omens ask diviner guess;
Not to be conned to tediousness
And know my higher gifts unbind 230
The zone that girds the incarnate mind.
When the scanty shores are full
With Thought's perilous, whirling pool;
When frail Nature can no more,
Then the Spirit strikes the hour:
My servant Death, with solving rite,
Pours finite into infinite.
Wilt thou freeze love's tidal flow,

**236. solving:** perhaps in the sense of "dissolving."

Whose streams through Nature circling go?
Nail the wild star to its track 240
On the half-climbed zodiac?
Light is light which radiates,
Blood is blood which circulates,
Life is life which generates,
And many-seeming life is one,—
Wilt thou transfix and make it none?
Its onward force too starkly pent
In figure, bone and lineament?
Wilt thou, uncalled, interrogate,
Talker! the unreplying Fate? 250
Nor see the genius of the whole
Ascendant in the private soul,
Beckon it when to go and come,
Self-announced its hour of doom?
Fair the soul's recess and shrine,
Magic-built to last a season;
Masterpiece of love benign;
Fairer that expansive reason
Whose omen 'tis, and sign.
Wilt thou not ope thy heart to know 260
What rainbows teach, and sunsets show?
Verdict which accumulates
From lengthening scroll of human fates,
Voice of earth to earth returned,
Prayers of saints that inly burned,—
Saying, *What is excellent,*
*As God lives, is permanent;*
*Hearts are dust, hearts' loves remain;*
*Heart's love will meet thee again.*
Revere the Maker; fetch thine eye 270
Up to his style, and manners of the sky.
Not of adamant and gold
Built he heaven stark and cold;
No, but a nest of bending reeds,
Flowering grass and scented weeds;
Or like a traveler's fleeing tent,
Or bow above the tempest bent;
Built of tears and sacred flames,
And virtue reaching to its aims;
Built of furtherance and pursuing, 280
Not of spent deeds, but of doing.
Silent rushes the swift Lord
Through ruined systems still restored,
Broadsowing, bleak and void to bless,
Plants with worlds the wilderness;
Waters with tears of ancient sorrow
Apples of Eden ripe tomorrow.
House and tenant go to ground,
Lost in God, in Godhead found."

**247. too starkly pent:** too rigidly confined.　**284. bleak . . . bless:** to bless that which is bleak and empty; the two adjectives seem to be used as nouns.

## CONCORD HYMN

*Sung at the Completion of the Battle
Monument, July 4, 1837*

❨ A MONUMENT to the Minute Men who had fought
the British troops at Concord in 1775 was set up, in
the middle thirties, on a piece of land which had been
presented to the town by Emerson's step-grandfather,
the Rev. Ezra Ripley, on whose property the skirmish
had been fought—in a meadow just across the Concord River from his parsonage, the Manse. Although
Emerson himself could not be present on the occasion of the dedication of the monument, the Fourth of
July, 1837, the hymn he had composed for the event
was sung by a choir to the tune of "Old Hundred."
Holmes described the poem as "compact, expressive, serene, solemn, musical"; and Robert Frost has spoken
of the first four lines as "surpassing any other ever written about soldiers" (*Daedalus*, LXXXVIII [Fall, 1959],
718).

By the rude bridge that arched the flood,
   Their flag to April's breeze unfurled,
Here once the embattled farmers stood
   And fired the shot heard round the world.

The foe long since in silence slept;
   Alike the conqueror silent sleeps;
And Time the ruined bridge has swept
   Down the dark stream which seaward creeps.

On this green bank, by this soft stream,
   We set today a votive stone;         10
That memory may their deed redeem,
   When, like our sires, our sons are gone.

Spirit, that made those heroes dare
   To die, and leave their children free,
Bid Time and Nature gently spare
   The shaft we raise to them and thee.

---

F R O M

# MAY-DAY
# AND OTHER PIECES

---

## BOSTON HYMN

*Read in Music Hall, January 1, 1863*

❨ AS THE subtitle indicates, Emerson read this poem at
a great meeting in Boston to celebrate Lincoln's signing
of the Emancipation Proclamation.

The word of the Lord by night
To the watching Pilgrims came,
As they sat by the seaside,
And filled their hearts with flame.

God said, I am tired of kings,
I suffer them no more;
Up to my ear the morning brings
The outrage of the poor.

Think ye I made this ball
A field of havoc and war,         10
Where tyrants great and tyrants small
Might harry the weak and poor?

My angel,—his name is Freedom,—
Choose him to be your king;
He shall cut pathways east and west
And fend you with his wing.

Lo! I uncover the land
Which I hid of old time in the West,
As the sculptor uncovers the statue
When he has wrought his best;      20

I show Columbia, of the rocks
Which dip their foot in the seas
And soar to the air-borne flocks
Of clouds and the boreal fleece.

I will divide my goods;
Call in the wretch and slave:
None shall rule but the humble,
And none but Toil shall have.

I will have never a noble,
No lineage counted great;         30
Fishers and choppers and ploughmen
Shall constitute a state.

Go, cut down trees in the forest
And trim the straightest boughs;
Cut down trees in the forest
And build me a wooden house.

Call the people together,
The young men and the sires,
The digger in the harvest field,
Hireling and him that hires;      40

And here in a pine state-house
They shall choose men to rule

BOSTON HYMN.    1–4. The . . . flame: "That night [at Delfts-
haven] was spent with little sleep by the most, but with friendly
entertainment and Christian discourse and other real expressions
of true Christian love" (William Bradford, *Of Plymouth Plantation*, Chap. 7).   16. fend: defend.

In every needful faculty,
In church and state and school.

Lo, now! if these poor men
Can govern the land and sea
And make just laws below the sun,
As planets faithful be.

And ye shall succor men; 
'T is nobleness to serve;                                  50
Help them who cannot help again:
Beware from right to swerve.

I break your bonds and masterships,
And I unchain the slave:
Free be his heart and hand henceforth
As wind and wandering wave.

I cause from every creature
His proper good to flow:
As much as he is and doeth,
So much he shall bestow.                                  60

But, laying hands on another
To coin his labor and sweat,
He goes in pawn to his victim
For eternal years in debt.

To-day unbind the captive,
So only are ye unbound;
Lift up a people from the dust,
Trump of their rescue, sound!

Pay ransom to the owner
And fill the bag to the brim.                             70
Who is the owner? The slave is owner,
And ever was. Pay him.

O North! give him beauty for rags,
And honor, O South! for his shame;
Nevada! coin thy golden crags
With Freedom's image and name.
Up! and the dusky race
That sat in darkness long,—
Be swift their feet as antelopes,
And as behemoth strong.                                   80

Come, East and West and North,
By races, as snow-flakes,

And carry my purpose forth,
Which neither halts nor shakes.

My will fulfilled shall be,
For, in daylight or in dark,
My thunderbolt has eyes to see
His way home to the mark.

# VOLUNTARIES

❡ THE poem of which this is the third section was written as a eulogy of Colonel Robert Gould Shaw, a young Harvard man who had taken command of the first regiment of Negro soldiers in the Union Army, and had been killed in action at Fort Wagner, South Carolina, in June 1863. "Voluntaries" appeared in the *Atlantic Monthly* in October.

### III

In an age of fops and toys,
Wanting wisdom, void of right,
Who shall nerve heroic boys
To hazard all in Freedom's fight,—
Break sharply off their jolly games,
Forsake their comrades gay
And quit proud homes and youthful dames
For famine, toil and fray?
Yet on the nimble air benign
Speed nimbler messages,                                   10
That waft the breath of grace divine
To hearts in sloth and ease.
So nigh is grandeur to our dust,
So near is God to man,
When Duty whispers low, *Thou must,*
The youth replies, *I can.*

# WALDEINSAMKEIT

I do not count the hours I spend
In wandering by the sea;
The forest is my loyal friend,
Like God it useth me.

In plains that room for shadows make
Of skirting hills to lie,
Bound in by streams which give and take
Their colors from the sky;

---

49–52. And . . . swerve: See motto of "Speech on Affairs in Kansas," *Miscellanies* (1884), (*Works*, XI, 254).  69–70. Pay . . . brim: See passage from an address by Emerson before the Anti-Slavery Society in New York in 1855 (*Works*, IX, 469).  80. behemoth: a huge and powerful beast; see Job 40:15.

WALDEINSAMKEIT. "solitude of the forest."  1–2. I . . . sea: "They [the English] think . . . with the Arabs, that the days spent in the chase are not counted in the length of life" (*English Traits*, Chap. 4 [*Works*, V, 70]).

Or on the mountain-crest sublime,
Or down the oaken glade,     10
O what have I to do with time?
For this the day was made.

Cities of mortals woe-begone
Fantastic care derides,
But in the serious landscape lone
Stern benefit abides.

Sheen will tarnish, honey cloy,
And merry is only a mask of sad,
But, sober on a fund of joy,
The woods at heart are glad.     20

There the great Planter plants
Of fruitful worlds the grain,
And with a million spells enchants
The souls that walk in pain.

Still on the seeds of all he made
The rose of beauty burns;
Through times that wear and forms that fade,
Immortal youth returns.

The black ducks mounting from the lake,
The pigeon in the pines,     30
The bittern's boom, a desert make
Which no false art refines.

Down in yon watery nook,
Where bearded mists divide,
The gray old gods whom Chaos knew,
The sires of Nature, hide.

Aloft, in secret veins of air,
Blows the sweet breath of song,
O, few to scale those uplands dare,
Though they to all belong!     40
See thou bring not to field or stone
The fancies found in books;
Leave authors' eyes, and fetch your own,
To brave the landscape's looks.

Oblivion here thy wisdom is,
Thy thrift, the sleep of cares;
For a proud idleness like this
Crowns all thy mean affairs.

KENNETH S. LYNN

*Editor*

# Henry David Thoreau

## 1817–1862

LIKE John Brown, whom he deeply admired, and whose raid on Harper's Ferry he defended with unforgettable eloquence, Thoreau was possessed by a vision of perfect freedom to which he gave his life. In everything he did and said, he tested what it was like to be one's own master; his writings both record his experiments and call on us to be experimental, too.

In the fall of 1837, shortly after his graduation from Harvard College, when he was living once more with his family in Concord, Thoreau wrote in the journal he had just begun to keep regularly, "The world is a fit theatre today in which any part may be acted. There is this moment proposed to me every kind of life that men lead anywhere, or that imagination can paint." South African planter, Greenland whaler, soldier in Florida, navigator of any sea were among the occupations he conjectured for himself. Yet when a friend proposed to him that they work their passage across the Atlantic and travel through Europe, the celebrator of perfect freedom turned him down. The decision was characteristic. For if all the world was a theater to Thoreau, it is important to note that he seldom went on the road. The only other book besides *Walden* which he published in his lifetime was a travel book, to be sure, but it only recorded *A Week on the Concord and Merrimack Rivers*. That many of his posthumous publications bear place names as titles—*The Maine Woods, Cape Cod, A Yankee in Canada*—is indicative of the fact that occasionally he *did* leave Concord, but his absences were not for long and did not take him far. Even when he was living at Walden Pond he often returned home for weekends.

Part of the explanation for his homebodiness is that Thoreau was very dependent, emotionally speaking, on his family. He lived a great part of his life under his parents' roof and he died in his mother's house. He never married. When he was twenty-six he wrote a letter to his mother in which he confessed, "Methinks I should be content to sit at the back-door in Concord, under the poplar-tree, henceforth forever." But perhaps the most poignant instance of his attachment occurred when he was a senior at Harvard. He asked his mother what occupation he should choose, and when she replied, "You can buckle on your knapsack, and roam abroad to seek your fortune," he wept until his sister Helen embraced him and said, comfortingly, "No, Henry, you shall not go; you shall stay at home and live with us."

The main reason, however, that he never went anywhere is that Thoreau deliberately lived a life of paradox. He insisted that there was society in solitude, that silence was a mode of communication, that idleness was productive, that one could go far by staying put. Freedom, he said repeatedly, was not what his neighbors construed it to be; he found it difficult, he confessed, to exaggerate their error. To force them to redefine their terms by making them acknowledge the truth of his outrageous paradoxes was his consistent strategy. Like the cow he spoke of in *Walden,* "which kicks over the pail, leaps the cowyard fence, and runs after her calf in milking time," he lived a life of adventure in native pastures.

Thoreau, then, never went in search of his fortune, and never, in a certain sense, amounted to anything. For a time he taught school; he worked for the Emersons as a gardener and general handyman, and helped to edit the *Dial;* off and on, he was a surveyor; and he made pencils in his father's pencil factory. For a Harvard graduate it was an extravagant performance, and some of those who were witness to his behavior were disgusted by it. James Russell Lowell, who lived for a year in Concord, found Thoreau difficult and unpleasant, thought there was no excuse for his unbounded egotism, and contemptuously dismissed him as a failure who was spending his life picking up the windfalls in Emerson's orchard.

The wisecrack was not only directed against the scandalous means of livelihood Thoreau had chosen, but against the independence of his mind as well; in Lowell's view, Thoreau lived off Emerson's intellect as well as his charity. There is no doubt, of course, that Emerson's essays, especially *Nature* (1836) — which was published in the fall of Thoreau's senior year at Harvard — had an enormous impact on the younger man, stirring him to the depths of his being. He imbibed so many of Emerson's ideas that Emerson himself believed that his mind was mirrored in Thoreau's, the one significant difference being that his own was more metaphysical and Thoreau's more concrete; it was right that Thoreau, not Emerson, should write the "Natural History of Massachusetts" (1842), because Thoreau knew the facts of the subject as well as its truth. Yet this difference hardly exhausted the contrast between the two men. Emerson proclaimed that "whoso would be a man, must be a nonconformist," but Emerson's nonconformity had its distinct limits. If the authorities of the Harvard Divinity School turned their backs on him for the heresy of his 1838 address, Emerson was still invited to Boston for

meetings of the Saturday Club, an organization which was as proper as it was literary, and he was both a respectable and respected citizen of the Concord community. Although he was prepared to acknowledge that "for nonconformity the world whips you with its displeasure," he was nevertheless distressed at the news that Thoreau had carried his disapproval of America's war with Mexico to the point where he had been put in jail for refusing to pay a tax. Emerson was generous to Thoreau in a hundred ways — he encouraged him in his writing by persuading the editors of the *Dial* to print one of his poems; he gave him permission to live on some property he owned at Walden Pond; and he habitually referred to his lesser-known friend as "*the* man of Concord." But Emerson also patronized Thoreau, and nowhere more so than in his fond assumption that Thoreau's intransigent radicalism and intensity of spirit were merely personal idiosyncrasies and that when all was said and done their ideas of life were the same. As the years passed, the relationship with Emerson became increasingly unbearable for Thoreau. The latter years of his journal do not present a flattering portrait of the man who first proposed that he keep it. "I doubt," runs a scornful entry of 1852, "if Emerson could trundle a wheelbarrow through the streets." In 1856 Thoreau wrote of their friendship that it had been "one long tragedy."

For his part, Emerson was finally somewhat disappointed in his protégé. He had taken up Thoreau when the younger man was unknown because he had recognized his rare combination of qualities. Thoreau, Emerson perceived, was steeped in English poetry, especially in the works of the seventeenth-century Metaphysicals in whom Emerson was also interested; he possessed a knowledge of languages, of Greek, Latin, French, Italian, Spanish, German, and Anglo-Saxon that was astonishing; his acquaintance with the writings of the Hindu mystics eventually rivaled Emerson's. In the woods, Thoreau was unsurpassed. He saw everything; he knew everything; he could ice skate thirty miles a day over the frozen rivers; he could sniff the smoke of a man's pipe a third of a mile away. In the oration which Emerson gave at Thoreau's funeral (subsequently enlarged for publication in the *Atlantic Monthly*), the list of his physical achievements makes him seem almost legendary, like a figure out of a *Davy Crockett Almanack.*

His senses were acute, his frame well-knit and hardy . . . and there was a wonderful fitness of body and mind. He could pace sixteen rods more accurately than another man could measure them with rod and chain. He could find his path in the woods at night . . . better by his feet than his eyes. He could estimate the measure of a tree very well by his eye; he could estimate the weight of a calf or a pig, like a dealer . . . He was a good swimmer, runner, skater, boatman, and would probably outwalk most countrymen in a day's journey.

Thoreau also was accomplished in a variety of mechanical skills and could do any kind of handyman's job. He was, in Emerson's eyes, the potentially perfect example of the American scholar whom he had envisaged in his 1837 address, the man of books who was also the man of action, the "helpful giant" who would build a new American culture. But Thoreau never turned his talents to great enterprise and command. "I so much regret the loss," wrote Emerson, "that I cannot help counting it a fault in him that he had no ambition. Wanting this, instead of engineering for all America, he was the captain of a huckleberry-party. Pounding beans is good to the end of pounding empires one of these days; but if, at the end of years, it is still only beans!"

## II

FOR YOUNG college graduates who would engineer for all America, the nation of the 1830's offered two great opportunities: religion and business. The trouble was, as Thoreau said, that "neither the New Testament nor Poor Richard speaks to our condition." The job problem as he saw it was "how to make the getting our living poetic! for if it is not poetic it is not life but death that we get." Christianity, he conceded, conceived of life poetically. "Seek first the kingdom of

heaven." "Lay not up for yourselves treasures on earth." "For what is a man profited, if he shall gain the whole world and lose his own soul?" Such statements were so challenging that Thoreau could not believe any Yankee had ever read them. But the hypocrisy of New England churchgoers aside, Thoreau felt that the New Testament did not speak to his generation because it was too exclusively concerned with man's spiritual affairs. Tough-minded and practical, a shrewd Yankee for all his hatred of the type, Thoreau was convinced that Christ's thoughts were all directed toward another world, and for Thoreau this was unsatisfactory. "There is another kind of success than his," he said. "Even here we have a sort of living to get, and must buffet it somewhat longer. There are various tough problems to solve, and we must make shift to live, betwixt spirit and matter, such a human life as we can."

As for business, Thoreau was graduated from college in the midst of the financial panic of 1837, a time hardly calculated to make Poor Richard's philosophy of life seem attractive. In a commencement debate on the virtues of the Commercial Spirit, Thoreau chose to speak on the negative side, and he continued to do so all his adult life, most notably in his journals and in *Walden.* Even as a small boy he had known how he felt about the American dream of success. For Thoreau's father, once a prosperous storekeeper, had gone bankrupt and been forced into the business of manufacturing pencils. Thereafter the family took in boarders in order to make ends meet. The son they sent to Harvard was always neatly dressed, but his classmates noted that his clothes were unfashionable and occasionally patched. The Thoreaus, in sum, were shabby genteel. Life in America has a way of driving such people into a corner, of draining them emotionally, of sniffing out their pathetic pretenses with cruel skill; their tragedy has been one of the major concerns of the American novel from Howells on, and it has furnished the theme of the two most important American plays of our time, *Death of a Salesman* by Arthur Miller and *The Glass*

*Menagerie* by Tennessee Williams. Yet the experience of failing in a success-mad society has sometimes proved to be a liberation. For one of the striking facts about American literature is the number of our writers who have emerged from shabby-genteel backgrounds. Irving, Poe, Hawthorne, Melville, Emerson—to take only writers of Thoreau's time—all came from families of declining status, and the triumph of their art is in a variety of ways related to this circumstance. In Thoreau's case, the experience of wearing patches helped him to understand that "wealth and the approbation of man" constituted a hollow definition of success. "The *terra firma* of my existence," he affirmed, "lies far beyond."

### III

IN ORDER to reach the firm ground that lay beyond, Thoreau struck upon the idea—the year was 1840—of going to live at Walden Pond. Not until 1845, however, was he sufficiently clear of debts to carry out his plan. By doing a little farming on some acres that Emerson owned near the Pond, and by cutting his personal needs to the bone, he was able—as he told Horace Greeley—to get a year's living for six weeks of work. There he remained for two and a half years. His move to Walden was for a brief season the scandal of Concord, but the real drama of his sojourn by the Pond consisted of an action the town gossips never saw: the play of his mind and imagination. What he proposed to do was to explore the "Farthest Indies," not by actually going there, but by "other routes and other methods of travel."

Thoreau's passage to India began with his intense awareness of himself, with his terrific concentration on the resources of his own personality. So self-conscious was Thoreau that all his life he was aware of a certain doubleness in himself. He could all but literally stand aside and watch himself in action and in thought. "However intense my experience," he said, "I am conscious of the presence and criticism of a part of me which, as it were, is not a part of me, but spectator, sharing no experience, but taking note of it, and that is no more I than you." Along with

his self-centeredness went a faith that everything he thought and did was important. As a Transcendentalist, he believed that every fact could flower into truth; therefore, each experience of Henry Thoreau could be made to yield up a more heroic significance. It is scarcely accidental that the lines from the Elizabethan poet Samuel Daniel that are quoted both in *A Week on the Concord and Merrimack* and "A Plea for Captain John Brown" were on Thoreau's lips, according to some of his friends, more often than any other poem—

> Unless above himself he can
> Erect himself, how poor a thing is man.

To Nature he paid as unremitting attention as he did to Self. The naturalist John Burroughs, among others, has not been impressed by Thoreau as an observer of plants and animals, and has berated him for his sloppy classifications; such criticisms, however, are almost totally irrelevant because they fail to take into account Thoreau's real aim in studying the natural world. If there was anyone whom Thoreau hated it was the scientific observer who carefully recorded and classified biological phenomena and did nothing more. He specifically attacked Humboldt and Darwin for their automatic habit of minutely careful observation, followed by notebook citation, followed by nothing. He urged those who loved Nature to avoid their example. "Do not tread upon the heels of your experience," he said. "Be impressed without making a minute of it. Poetry puts an interval between the impression and the expression,—waits till the seed germinates naturally." The germination of the seed was an event the naturalists failed to wait for. They had no sense of awe or delight in the out-of-doors, and Thoreau dismissed them with sweeping contempt: "Most of our modern authors have not imagined the actual beasts which they presume to describe."

Underlying the bitterness of Thoreau's attack on the naturalists was the fear that in his own investigations of Nature his imagination would someday fail him—that he, too, would be caught in a morass of facts which would refuse to surrender their ultimate meaning to him. As the later volumes of his journals reveal, this was in fact the tragedy that lay in wait for him. But in the years of full intellectual power, and especially in the Walden period, every walk in the woods became "a sort of crusade . . . .to go forth and reconquer this Holy Land from the hands of the Infidels." His favorite direction for walking was west, because the West meant Wildness, and Wildness was "the preservation of the world . . . From the forest and wilderness come the tonics and barks which brace mankind." Yet if he literally walked westward, he reached the Wild only by an act of imagination. Once, in the primeval Maine woods, Thoreau declared that "we have not seen pure Nature, unless we have seen her thus vast and drear and inhuman, though in the midst of cities, Nature was here something savage and awful, though beautiful." Concord woods, however, were not the forests of Maine, and Thoreau knew it. He was fully aware that there were no cougars or panthers or lynxes or wolverines in eastern Massachusetts in the 1840's. As he once admitted,

I cannot but feel as if I lived in a tamed, and, as it were, emasculated country . . . Is it not a maimed and imperfect nature that I am conversant with? . . . I take infinite pains to know all the phenomena of spring, for instance, thinking that I have here the entire poem, and then, to my chagrin, I hear that it is but an imperfect copy that I possess, and have read, that my ancestors have torn out many of the first leaves and grandest passages and mutilated it in many places.

But the tameness of Concord woods did not put bracing tonics and barks beyond mankind's reach. "I shall never find in the wilds of Labrador," Thoreau triumphantly proclaimed, "any greater wildness than in some recess in Concord, i.e., than I import into it." Even in a woods where the wolf and the lynx no longer roamed, a walker could penetrate to the anarchic, wild freedom that lay at the heart of Nature if only his imagination were sufficiently extravagant; one could apprehend it, for example, simply by listening, with all one's faculties intensely concentrated, to a blue jay:

The unrelenting steel cold scream of a jay, unmelted, that never flows into a song, a sort of wintry trumpet, screaming cold; hard, tense, frozen music, like the winter sky itself; in the blue livery of winter's bands.

Another route to the farthest Indies lay in reading. Like every other activity, reading for Thoreau involved an absolute self-consciousness. "Books," he said, "must be read as deliberately and reservedly as they were written." He disliked novels and was acquainted with few of them; he preferred travel books (Josselyn's *New England Rarities Discovered* was one of his favorites) and philosophy. If walking took him Westward, his reading often took him East, toward Greece, India, and China. Indeed, the classics of Hindu and Buddhist thought absorbed him so completely that they made him feel as if he were living in another world. Thus in May of 1841, after reading the book of the Hindu god Menu, Thoreau observed in his journal:

That title, "The Laws of Menu with the Gloss of Culluca," comes to me with such a volume of sound as if it had swept unobstructed over the plains of Hindostan; and when my eye rests on yonder birches, or the sun in the water, or the shadows of the trees, it seems to signify the laws of them all. They are the laws of you and me, a fragrance wafted down from those old times, and no more to be refuted than the wind. When my imagination travels eastward and backward to those remote years of the gods, I seem to draw near to the habitation of the morning, and the dawn at length has a place. I remember the book as an hour before sunrise.

Thoreau's study of a book was an action that involved his whole being.

### IV

VIVIDLY aware in the face of every experience, Thoreau was more self-conscious, which in his terms is to say more alive, when he was writing than at any other time. His poetry and his prose both reflect a careful, deliberate craftsman whose remarkable ability to detach himself from his work and judge its quality with dispassionate objectivity is best summarized in his remark that an artist's work primarily consists of performing "post-mortem examinations of himself before he is dead." Thoreau's writing can seem spontaneous, but it is not; it is highly wrought, cunningly contrived; it is the supreme expression of his doubleness. His journals, in which he recorded his daily crusades, are more artful than Emerson's, and like the latter's journals they served a larger artfulness. For Thoreau's private works were a great sourcebook, a mine, out of which he extracted ideas and expressions which were then carefully reset, often after an immense amount of lapidary effort, in the mosaic of the more ambitious and more intricate designs of his public essays.

The two full-length books that Thoreau published in his lifetime are the products of the most beautifully disciplined writing talent of the age in America. *A Week on the Concord and Merrimack* is, however, a more experimental, less finished design, inasmuch as it represents the trying-out of the method of presentation that Thoreau would follow in *Walden*. As this masterpiece would, the *Week* recalls an experience of the author's past. In the summer of 1839, Thoreau, in company with his brother John, had taken a canoe trip on the Concord and Merrimack. Two years later, his brother died horribly of lockjaw. Thereafter, Thoreau's recollections of their idyllic river journey had a special poignance. Four years after John's death, Thoreau went to live by Walden Pond and wrote the *Week*. He continued to work on the manuscript, revising and adding to it, after he left the Pond. When the book was finally published—at Thoreau's personal expense—in 1849, the *Week* represented ten years of meditation and work.

Purporting to be a simple record of the 1839 trip, the *Week* in fact contains poems which Thoreau had printed in the *Dial*, journal entries, fragments of essays, and whole lectures written in periods both before and long after the journey. Though the actual trip took a good deal longer, the artful trip lasts seven days, with one chapter for each day. The book seems casually organized and to a certain extent this is true. But if the thought wanders, there is a transcendental, an organic, rationale for digression in the meandering flow of the rivers. The use of a drifting rhythm as the matrix for the thought and action of a book would not be exploited as successfully again by an American author until *Huckleberry Finn* (1885). Besides its streamlike movement, the book is held together by a rising and falling movement, the cycle of sunrise and sunset, which is repeated each day. The subjects which Thoreau discusses en route are not fortuitous, but are organically related to the unfolding panorama of the journey and to the particular day of the week. (World mythologies, for example, are discussed on Sunday.) Beneath its seeming looseness, the *Week* has the tightness and the economy for which Thoreau always strove.

### V

*Walden* (1854) is even more artful, and more deceptive; the supreme creation of Thoreau's self-consciousness, it lauds simplicity by means of complexity. In substance as well as in mode of expression, the "humor" of the book is paradoxical.

Thus the author asserts that neither the New Testament nor Poor Richard speaks to our condition, but the opening of *Walden* sounds remarkably like Benjamin Franklin's *Autobiography*. There is, first of all, the same disarmingly candid explanation as to why the author happened to write this book; in Thoreau's case, he insists that he has been prompted to authorship partly because so many of his townsmen have asked him questions about his sojourn at the Pond, just as Franklin claims that one of the reasons he became an author was that he felt his son might be interested in learning something about his ancestors. And just as Franklin is charmingly frank about his egotistic desire to talk about himself, so Thoreau admits in a delightful phrase, "I should not talk so much about myself if there were anybody else whom I knew as well." The title of the first chapter would surely have been approved of by Poor Richard: "Economy."

What Thoreau is doing, however, is to destroy the enemy with the enemy's own weapons. He deliberately appropriates the language of the success ethic in order to expose it. In the immemorial manner of the businessman, he talks about "conditions," except that he does not judge them by the standard of economic prosperity. Prosperity, indeed, is ruining the country. The mass of men lead lives of quiet desperation. Their fingers tremble from the hard work they do. They are nothing but machines. They are gasping for breath; they must lie and flatter to get ahead. Published two years after Harriet Beecher Stowe had made Simon Legree a national byword, *Walden* asserts that "it is hard to have a Southern overseer; it is worse to have a Northern one, but worst of all when you are the slave-driver of yourself." The unluckiest of all are those who succeed, for farms, houses, barns, and cattle—in sum, possessions—make horrible demands upon their owners, and are more easily acquired than got rid of. As for luxuries and the so-called comforts of life, they have been throughout history positive hindrances to the elevation of mankind.

Against this appalling picture of the economy of his neighbors, Thoreau sets forth his own economy, his personal plan of living, in a series of elaborate financial metaphors which appear at first glance to be an attempt to justify his plan in terms of the Poor Richard civilization he has just been scorning. The decision to go to the woods is spoken of as the determination "to go into business at once." Over the years, he has "well-nigh sunk all his capital" into listening to the wind; therefore why should he not turn to this new "enterprise"? For a long time he had felt that Walden Pond "would be a good place for business, not solely on account of the railroad and the ice trade; it offers advantages which it may not be good policy to divulge; it is a good port and a good foundation." Having always endeavored "to acquire strict business habits," he of course keeps ledgers and accounts during his sojourn. *Walden* contains itemized lists which outdo anything in the collected works of Franklin. The cost of the things Thoreau buys is given in meticulous detail, down to the half penny—even the quarter penny. And if Franklin's economies, his ability to cut his

meals down to a glass of water and a handful of raisins, seem awesome, Thoreau's tall tale of economy reduces Ben Franklin to a spendthrift. On food for the first eight months of his stay Thoreau spent $8.74; on clothing, $8.40 3/4; on housing, $28.12 1/2. Once again, however, this ruthless application of the principles of Poor Richard to the practical problems of daily living is made with an anti-Poor Richard purpose.

Poor Richard believed that early to bed and early to rise makes a man healthy, wealthy, and wise. Poor Richard was ascetic in the present, kept his shop now, so that in the future his shop would keep him. But the "Yankee shrewdness" of which Thoreau speaks is directed toward avoiding, not attaining, "the splendid mausoleum" where Poor Richard dreamed of living. The asceticism of Thoreau is directed toward the goal of a greater awareness, a superior intensity, a more and more absolute self-consciousness.

It occurred to me when I awoke this morning, feeling regret of the day before in eating fruit, which had dulled my sensibilities, that man was to be treated as a musical instrument, and if any viol was to be made of sound timber and kept well-turned always, it was he, so that when the bow of events is drawn across him he may vibrate and resound in perfect harmony. A sensitive soul will be continually trying its strings to see if they are in tune. A man's body must be rasped down exactly to a shaving. It is of far more importance than the wood of a Cremona violin.

Thoreau accepts the frugality of Poor Richard, but to the end that he will achieve the sensitivity of a Cremona violin, not that he will make a fortune. Thoreau cuts down on costs because "the cost of a thing is the amount of what I will call life which is required to be exchanged for it, immediately or in the long run," and, therefore, a cost reduction is not money saved but a life saved. He gets up at sunrise not for the purpose of getting ahead, but because "poetry and art date from such an hour." In perhaps the clearest indication that Thoreau had Franklin in mind when he wrote *Walden*, he says that one of his prime motives for early rising was so that he could hear the crowing of the wild cocks in the woods—for to hear those birds "who would not be early to rise, and rise earlier and earlier every successive day of his life, till he became unspeakably healthy, wealthy, and wise?" In this juxtaposition of the wild chanticleer of the woods with the most famous of Poor Richard's aphorisms is contained the essence of Thoreau's defiance of Franklin's America.

The bulk of the chapter "Economy" is taken up with an elaboration of his objections to the way in which his neighbors feed, clothe, and house themselves, and of his alternative ideas. His critique is largely centered on the habits of the group which Thorstein Veblen would forty-five years later call the leisure class. The Poor Richard who has made his pile can think of nothing to do except eat more and richer food, build larger and more splendid houses, and wear more abundant clothing. The result is that the rich are not simply comfortably warm, but unnaturally hot; they are in fact cooked—"of course *à la mode.*" Thoreau's concern is to strip away all these superfluities. "Fanciful clothes are our epidermis, or false skin, which partakes not of our life, and may be stripped off here and there without fatal injury." As for housing, Thoreau maintained that "before we can adorn our houses with beautiful objects the walls must be stripped, and beautiful housekeeping and beautiful living laid for a foundation." He wants to get rid of all pretense and display, he wants to get to the heart of things and start growing outward from there. He comes to the Pond to confront experience directly, to make a fresh start, to shuck off the dead skin of a materialistic civilization. This is the "private business" he wishes to transact, and *Walden* is the story of his metamorphosis.

In this light, the practical details of economy can be seen to have a transcendental significance. The stripping away of the layers of clothing and housing in which modern man is cooking to death is the symbolic first step in the act of metamorphosis—as Nature herself witnesses.

Our moulting season, like that of the fowls, must be a crisis in our lives. The loon retires to solitary ponds to spend it. Thus also the snake casts its slough, and the caterpillar its wormy coat, by an internal industry and expansion; for clothes are but our outmost cuticle and coil.

Yet if the casting of the old coat and the creation of a new one are accomplished in solitude, this does not mean that the new coat has no significance for society. In one of the first paragraphs of the book, Thoreau remarks that he hopes his readers will accept such portions of his narrative as apply to them, and that he trusts "none will stretch the seams in putting on the coat, for it may do good service to him whom it fits." *Walden* itself is a new "garment" for mankind as well as for the man who made it, and by donning it mankind can accomplish collective rebirth and renewal. For "if there is not a new man, how can the new clothes be made to fit?"

With that question we reach the heart of the chapter on economy, the building of Thoreau's house. In the spring of 1845, Thoreau tells us, he had gone out to Walden and cut down some "tall, arrowy white pines, still in their youth, for timber." He bleached and purified the boards in the sun. He dug his cellar where a woodchuck had a hole. Thus his house had grown from the inside out, like an organism. If all men built their own houses, says Thoreau, they would perhaps be poets. But his self-conscious purification of the boards in the sun is not merely poetic —it is religious. While Poor Richard did not speak to Thoreau's condition, *Walden* nonetheless has a Yankee economy to it; the New Testament did not speak to his condition either, and yet *Walden* has a Christian economy too. Christ's forty days in the wilderness were a process of purification, and to Thoreau, who regarded Christ as "a sublime actor on the stage of the world," such a retreat from the world was an act of supreme self-consciousness which he self-consciously wished to repeat. The Christian parallel by no means exhausted Thoreau's awareness of the religious nature of his sojourn at the Pond. The fable of withdrawal and renewal was one which was common to all the great religions of the world. ("It is interesting to observe," he wrote in the *Week*, "with what singular unanimity the farthest sundered nations and generations consent to give completeness and roundness to an ancient fable.") Thus his retreat to the Pond had Hindu as well as Christian overtones. The doctrine of Yoga, to which Emerson had introduced Thoreau, urged a complete abstraction from all worldly objects. Work must be done without the hope of material reward; sacrifice, mortification of the flesh, and controlling the breath were the indispensable preliminaries to a higher state of being. "Depend upon it that, rude and careless as I am," Thoreau wrote, "I would fain practice the yoga faithfully . . . To some extent, and at rare intervals, even I am a yogi." On another occasion he said, "One may discover the root of a Hindoo religion in his own private history, when, in the silent intervals of the day or the night, he does sometimes inflict on himself like austerities with a stern satisfaction."

It would be a mistake to think that Thoreau carried these Christian and Hindu analogies beyond the point of general resemblance. Thoreau was not a Yogi, of course, if for no other reason than that the Hindu mystic wishes release from the unending cycle of rebirth, whereas *Walden* glorifies it. But he did act in conscious knowledge of the general similarity between Eastern religion and his own reenactment of a universal fable; his invocations of Christ and the gods of Greece had the same general analogical purpose. While many of the fabulous parallels are drawn in a spirit of self-deflationary humor which rescues the book from the dangers of both egotism and blasphemy, in a very real sense the author of *Walden* is always serious. The prosaic details of cutting down trees and hewing timbers and digging a cellar, of paying an Irishman named Collins $4.25 for the lumber in a shanty that Collins had occupied, are quite deliberately arranged in such a way as to reveal their religious meaning. Thoreau's ideal was—

Facts should only be as the frame to my pictures; they should be material to the mythology which I am writing; not facts to assist men to make money, farmers to farm profitably, in any common sense; facts to tell who I am and where I have

been or what I have thought . . . My facts shall be falsehoods to the common sense. I would so state facts that they shall be significant, shall be mythic or mythologic.

He cuts down young trees in the spring and he bleaches boards in the sun: these are preliminary steps in building a house. They are also a part of the religious ceremony of purification and renewal.

The fourth chapter of *Walden,* "Sounds," introduces another major aspect of the renewal theme: the seeding, planting, fertilizing, flowering, and harvesting of crops. The progress of his bean field is a conversational topic of which Thoreau never grows tired; it also furnishes him with a rhythm that finally imposes an order on the entire book. The structure of the *Week* is a sequence of seven days; in *Walden,* the action begins in early summer and ends the following spring; the twenty-six months which Thoreau actually spent at the Pond are compressed into the cycle of a year; his account of his life in the woods follows the elemental pattern of the flowering, death, and replanting of a bean crop. Throughout the book one is constantly being reminded of the continuing drama of vegetation. In the chapter "Visitors," for example, after he has talked at some length about the people who have come to see him—the most memorable visitor being the French woodchopper, and the most fascinating being the runaway slave, whom "I helped to forward toward the north star"—Thoreau suddenly breaks off the description, and the next chapter begins: "Meanwhile my beans . . . were impatient to be hoed." And in the second half of the book, in the chapters which follow the crucial chapter "The Ponds," the seasonal cycle comes more and more to dominate the action.

Yet, far down inside Thoreau's submission of his life to Nature, there is an ambiguity. The chapter "Higher Laws" begins with the famous sentence,

As I came home through the woods with my string of fish, trailing my pole, it being now quite dark, I caught a glimpse of a woodchuck, stealing across my path, and felt a strange thrill of savage delight, and was strongly tempted to seize and devour him raw; not that I was hungry then, except for that wildness which he represented.

Here, seemingly, is the statement of the natural man who likes to spend his days up to his chin in a swamp, of the primitivist who wants to tear apart a woodchuck as if he were an animal himself. But there was an invincible fastidiousness about Thoreau, an abhorrence of dirt and filth that was very deep in him. As the chapter "Higher Laws" makes clear, his adherence to a simple diet sprang as much from his loathing of the unclean as it did from any positive belief in the spiritual efficacy of moderation. Despite the fantasy about the woodchuck, Thoreau was a vegetarian; as he says in "Higher Laws," "the practical objection to animal food in my case was its uncleanness." Such food had no ill effect on his body, but it disagreed, as he says, with his imagination. In revulsion, Thoreau compared meat-eaters to the gluttonous maggot and the gross larva of the caterpillar. The same thing was true of his drinking habits. Thoreau found that water was the only drink worth stomaching, again because his imagination revolted at anything stronger.

Thoreau could be self-consciously earthy and announce that "the poet writes the history of his own body," but no description could be more inapplicable to the poet that Thoreau in fact was. As reported in Emerson's biography of Thoreau, one of Thoreau's friends once said, "I love Henry, but . . . as for taking his arm, I should as soon think of taking the arm of an elm tree." Thoreau wrote that "there is no remedy for love but to love more," but he never married.

Thoreau worshiped the sun, its life-giving powers; over and over again in *Walden* he contrasts the clear sunlight with the "smoke of opinion" of misguided men which obscures it from sight, or with the "smoke and steam and hissing" of the railroad train which threatens man's whole relation to the sun. He talks of pouring water on the floor of his unfinished house and letting the sun dry it. The sun in all these connections is a symbol of purification and light. But the sun is

also a corrupter, the agent of overripeness, taint, putrefaction. Therefore, the sun, the fundamental source of all transcendental correspondences between man and Nature, was for Thoreau an uneasy subject. Constantly in *Walden*, when Thoreau is talking about the sun, one has the feeling that he is about to break through Emerson's formulation that Nature is the present expositor of the divine mind and confront the fact that Nature is not always so reassuringly disposed. But in the end he does not. He is merely squeamish, and averts his eyes from the full import of the solar correspondence. Thoreau could triumphantly proclaim that he "dreamed of purity last night," but he said very little about his nightmares. Only a more audacious voyager like Melville would be willing to stare into the sun and then tell all that he saw there.

The closest Thoreau came to facing up to the possible existence of ambiguity within the virtues he celebrated was in his discussion of poverty. Throughout *Walden* he glorifies poverty. "By poverty, i.e., simplicity of life and fewness of incidents, I am solidified and crystallized, as a vapor or liquid by cold. It is a singular concentration of strength and energy and flavor." But on the Baker Farm near Walden he discovers John Field, an Irishman, and his family living in a miserable rented hut. Poverty has not crystallized the Fields, it has degraded them. The roof of the hut leaks, they are all cold and miserable. Field works hard and so does his wife, but to no avail; the family is starving and filthy. Yet for all his recognition of what poverty has done to them, Thoreau clings to the belief that defiance is the solution. He tells them they must build a simple house of their own, cut out tea, coffee, butter, and meat, and then they will all be as healthy, wealthy, and wise as he is.

In the dramatic structure of *Walden*, "The Ponds" is the central chapter. Coming in the exact center of the book, it looks back on the more worldly first half and looks forward to the more seasonal, more mythological second half. In rejecting both the New Testament and Poor Richard, Thoreau had said, "We must make shift to live, betwixt spirit and matter, such a human life as we can," and "The Ponds" maintains an exquisite balance between these two realms of existence. Walden Pond, Thoreau tells us here, has two colors. Viewed at a certain distance on a certain day, the Pond is "a clear and deep green well." At other times it is a "matchless and indescribable blue, such as watered or changeable silks and sword blades suggest." Blue and green, the color of the sky and the color of the earth of this world and the next, Walden Pond brings together the rejected values of the New Testament and Poor Richard in a new synthesis which transforms both.

Both the "earth's eye" and "sky water," the Pond is also the supreme object of correspondence between the mind and Nature, between the soul and God. So profound is the correspondence that, fishing in the Pond one dark night, Thoreau feels that he might almost cast his line upward into the air as downward into the Pond. Sounding the bottom of the Pond corresponds to sounding the soul, for the Pond is "God's Drop." "Heaven," says Thoreau, speaking of Walden, "is under our feet as well as over our heads." For a man to whom "Self-Reliance" was a Bible, there was profound meaning in the fact that the Pond has no visible inlet or outlet; it maintains itself by an inner energy, its own fresh springs. Unlike the ambiguous sun, the Pond is an unmitigated "vision of serenity and purity." It is a great crystal on the surface of the earth, a lake of light. It is very old, older than America; Thoreau remembers having heard that a potter lived on its banks before the Revolution; indeed, it is older than mankind:

Perhaps on that spring morning when Adam and Eve were driven out of Eden, Walden Pond was already in existence, and even then breaking up in a gentle spring rain accompanied by mist and a southerly wind, and covered with myriads of ducks and geese, which had not heard of the fall, when still such pure lakes sufficed them.

The clean, wild ducks still come to the Pond in the course of their migrations, and in the fall the loon comes as always to Walden "to moult and bathe in the pond, making the woods ring with his wild laughter." The loon, with whose moulting Thoreau had already identified himself, is the great embodiment of the spirit of the Pond. The loon can soar and swoop in the sky; it can also dive underwater all the way to the bottom and swim underwater for great distances. Quite the most extraordinary event in *Walden* is the game which Thoreau plays with the loon, watching to see where it will dive and then rowing madly to the place where he anticipates the bird will come up, a magnificent game of tag played through the elements of air and water, lasting for an hour or more, while the bird makes the woods ring with its demoniac laughter. As Thoreau once wrote in his journals, "Not by constraint or severity shall you have access to true wisdom, but by abandonment, and childlike mirthfulness. If you would know aught, be gay before it."

If the Pond is old, it is also "perennially young. It has not acquired one permanent wrinkle after all its ripples." The villagers think of piping its waters into Concord, but Walden's inexhaustibility is proof against such desecration. Although the Fitchburg Railway, that "devilish Iron Horse," muddies the waters with its foot, Walden can absorb the engine's soot, wash out State Street in the bargain, and still retain its purity. The woods around the lake may be cut down, but after a season another forest "is springing up by its shore as lustily as ever." Surely such a Pond could never die.

But the great drama of the book is that it does. On the night of December 22, 1845, Walden freezes over. To be sure, the ice looks alternately blue and green, just as the water had; and even in the depths of winter a fisherman can bring up on an anchor from the bottom of the pond a bright green weed, a symbol of life and an object of correspondence: "Methinks my own soul must be a bright invisible green." But the ice-locked Pond is dying, nonetheless, and the sequence of four chapters beginning with "House-Warming" records its progressive strangulation. As for Thoreau, he slowly retreats into himself as winter sets in. In "House-Warming" he builds a chimney and plasters his house. When the snow covers the ground, "I withdrew yet farther into my shell and endeavored to keep a bright fire within my house and within my breast." The book becomes more and more elemental. Thoreau's movements outdoors are constricted; fewer animals and birds are seen. The book has been full of sounds, but suddenly a silence falls over everything. "Even the hooting of the owl was hushed." There are fewer visitors than before.

But in his shut-in solitude, Thoreau has at last reached the vital center from which true outward growth can begin. He has cast off his wormy coat and woven for himself "a silken web or chrysalis, and nymph-like shall ere long burst forth a more perfect creature, fitted for a higher society." In the chapter called "Spring" the ritual of renewal reaches its climactic stage, and Thoreau's transmutation, his recovery of life, is completed. In the warm sun, the ice on the Pond rots; here, for once, rottenness does not run counter to the over-all symbolism of the book; rottenness here means not decay but fertility, a fertility out of which death flows back into life; soon the air is filled with the cheerful music of "a thousand tinkling rills and rivulets whose veins are filled with the blood of winter they are bearing off. The symbol of perpetual youth, the grassblade," is seen again, the sun shines bright and warm, "re-creating the world." In May, the loon returns to the Pond. "Walden," says Thoreau, "was dead and is alive again." With its rebirth, Thoreau changes "from the lumpish grub in the earth to the airy and fluttering butterfly." Gathering together all the metamorphic symbolism of the book, Thoreau concludes *Walden* with the triumphant fable of the bug.

Every one has heard the story which has gone the rounds of New England, of a strong and beautiful bug which came out of the dry leaf of an old table of apple-tree wood, which had stood in a farmer's kitchen for sixty years, first in Connecticut, and afterward in Massachusetts,—from an egg deposited in the living tree many years earlier still . . . Who does not feel his faith in a resurrection and an immortality strengthened by hearing of this?

By his refusal to hurry, by the heroism of his patience and his singleness of purpose and his resolution, Thoreau in *Walden* triumphs over the tyranny of time. A gasping, clock-watching, hurrying America is enslaved by time, but Thoreau, like the Hindu artist Kouroo to whom he compares himself, has made no compromise with time, and therefore time has kept out of his way. Kouroo's resolve had been to create one perfect work of art—a beautiful staff—though it take his entire lifetime, and that had been Thoreau's resolve, too. By the time that Kouroo had selected the stick on which to begin his carving, all his friends had grown old and died. Before he had given it proper shape, the dynasty of the Candahars was at an end; by the time he had smoothed and polished the staff, Kalpa was no longer the polestar; ere he had adorned the head with precious stones, Brahma had awakened and slumbered many times. But

when the finishing stroke was put to his work, it suddenly expanded before the eyes of the astonished artist into the fairest of all the creations of Brahma. He had made a new system in making a staff, a world with full and fair proportions; in which, though the old cities and dynasties had passed away, fairer and more glorious ones had taken their places. And now he saw by the heap of shavings still fresh at his feet, that, for him and his work, the former lapse of time had been an illusion, and that no more time had elapsed than is required for a single scintillation from the brain of Brahma to fall on and inflame the tinder of a mortal brain.

The revisions, the years of meditation and devotion which Thoreau had poured into his great book, made it a veritable staff of Kouroo. Of all the gods with whom Thoreau compared himself, he seems perhaps most like Narcissus. At Walden Pond, he gazed down into the deep green well of the water and stared at his own reflection. He stared long and hard; he looked at no one else. But by that intense concentration on himself, his refusal to write about anyone else but himself, Thoreau transcended himself and wrote about humanity and for other people. Unlike Narcissus, he did not die as a result of gazing overly long into the water of Walden. Instead, he created a book about the Pond which cheated time and death and became as immortal as Brahma.

# CIVIL DISOBEDIENCE

◇

❮ IN THE course of his odd-job career, Thoreau sometimes gave lectures. Although he was not an effective speaker, some of his most powerful pieces were first enunciated in the Concord Lyceum, including "Civil Disobedience," which he delivered in February 1848. The following year it was published in Elizabeth Peabody's *Aesthetic Papers*, a volume which also included Emerson's essay "War" and Hawthorne's "Main Street." Well-known throughout the nineteenth century, "Civil Disobedience" became world-famous in the twentieth century when Mahatma Gandhi acknowledged it as the chief inspiration of his doctrine of passive resistance. Liberal critics who view big government as the chief agent of social justice have been embarrassed by the essay's notoriety and have attempted to play down its importance in the Thoreau canon, just as they have tried to de-emphasize Thoreau's dramatic refusal to pay his tax by pointing out that Bronson Alcott had done the same thing four years previously. But in the era of Martin Luther King and the "sit-ins," the dynamic, revolutionary power of individual protest cannot be denied. "Civil Disobedience" is surely an essay for our times.

◇

I HEARTILY accept the motto, "That government is best which governs least"; and I should like to see it acted up to more rapidly and systematically. Carried out, it finally amounts to this, which also I believe—"That government is best which governs not at all"; and when men are prepared for it, that will be the kind of government which they will have. Government is at best but an expedient; but most governments are usually, and all governments are sometimes, inexpedient. The objections which have been brought against a standing army, and they are many and weighty, and deserve to prevail, may also at last be brought against a standing government. The standing army is only an arm of the standing government. The government itself, which is only the mode which the people have chosen to execute their will, is equally liable to be abused and perverted before the people can act through it. Witness the present Mexican war, the work of comparatively a few individuals using the standing government as their tool; for,

in the outset, the people would not have consented to this measure.

This American government—what is it but a tradition, though a recent one, endeavoring to transmit itself unimpaired to posterity, but each instant losing some of its integrity? It has not the vitality and force of a single living man; for a single man can bend it to his will. It is a sort of wooden gun to the people themselves. But it is not the less necessary for this; for the people must have some complicated machinery or other, and hear its din, to satisfy that idea of government which they have. Governments show thus how successfully men can be imposed on, even impose on themselves, for their own advantage. It is excellent, we must all allow. Yet this government never of itself furthered any enterprise, but by the alacrity with which it got out of its way. *It* does not keep the country free. *It* does not settle the West. *It* does not educate. The character inherent in the American people has done all that has been accomplished; and it would have done somewhat more, if the government had not sometimes got in its way. For government is an expedient by which men would fain succeed in letting one another alone; and, as has been said, when it is most expedient, the governed are most let alone by it. Trade and commerce, if they were not made of india-rubber, would never manage to bounce over the obstacles which legislators are continually putting in their way; and, if one were to judge these men wholly by the effects of their actions and not partly by their intentions, they would deserve to be classed and punished with those mischievous persons who put obstructions on the railroads.

But, to speak practically and as a citizen, unlike those who call themselves no-government men, I ask for, not at once no government, but *at once* a better government. Let every man make known what kind of government would command his respect, and that will be one step toward obtaining it.

After all, the practical reason why, when the power is once in the hands of the people, a majority are permitted, and for a long period continue, to rule is not because they are most likely to be in the right, nor because this seems fairest to the minority, but because they are physically the strongest. But a government in which the majority rule in all cases cannot be based on justice, even as far as men understand it. Can there not be a government in which majorities do not virtually decide right and wrong, but conscience?—in which majorities decide only those questions to which the rule of expediency is applicable? Must the citizen ever for a moment, or in the least degree, resign his conscience to the legislator? Why has every man a conscience, then? I think that we should be men first, and subjects afterward. It is not desirable to cultivate a respect for the law, so much as for the right. The only obligation which I have a right to assume is to do at any time what I think right. It is truly enough said that a corporation has no conscience; but a corporation of conscientious men is a corporation *with* a conscience. Law never made men a whit more just; and, by means of their respect for it, even the well-disposed are daily made the agents of injustice. A common and natural result of an undue respect for law is, that you may see a file of soldiers, colonel, captain, corporal, privates, powder-monkeys, and all, marching in admirable order over hill and dale to the wars, against their wills, ay, against their common sense and consciences, which makes it very steep marching indeed, and produces a palpitation of the heart. They have no doubt that it is a damnable business in which they are concerned; they are all peaceably inclined. Now, what are they? Men at all? or small movable forts and magazines, at the service of some unscrupulous man in power? Visit the Navy Yard, and behold a marine, such a man as an American government can make, or such as it can make a man with its black arts—a mere shadow and reminiscence of humanity, a man laid out alive and standing, and already, as one may say, buried under arms with funeral accompaniments, though it may be,

"Not a drum was heard, not a funeral note,
    As his corse to the rampart we hurried;
Not a soldier discharged his farewell shot
    O'er the grave where our hero we buried." [1]

The mass of men serve the state thus, not as men mainly, but as machines, with their bodies. They are the standing army, and the militia, jailers, constables, *posse comitatus,* etc. In most cases there is no free exercise whatever of the judgment or of the moral sense; but they put themselves on a level with wood and earth and stones; and wooden men can perhaps be manufactured that will serve the purpose as well. Such command no more respect than men of straw or a lump of dirt. They have the same sort of worth only as horses and dogs. Yet such as these even are commonly esteemed good citizens. Others—as most legislators, politicians, lawyers, ministers, and office-holders—serve the state chiefly with their heads; and, as they rarely make any moral distinctions, they are as likely to serve the devil, without *intending*

it, as God. A very few—as heroes, patriots, martyrs, reformers in the great sense, and *men*—serve the state with their consciences also, and so necessarily resist it for the most part; and they are commonly treated as enemies by it. A wise man will only be useful as a man, and will not submit to be "clay," and "stop a hole to keep the wind away," [2] but leave that office to his dust at least:

"I am too high-born to be propertied,
To be a secondary at control,
Or useful serving-man and instrument
To any sovereign state throughout the world." [3]

He who gives himself entirely to his fellow men appears to them useless and selfish; but he who gives himself partially to them is pronounced a benefactor and philanthropist.

How does it become a man to behave toward this American government today? I answer, that he cannot without disgrace be associated with it. I cannot for an instant recognize that political organization as *my* government which is the *slave's* government also.

All men recognize the right of revolution; that is, the right to refuse allegiance to, and to resist, the government, when its tyranny or its inefficiency are great and unendurable. But almost all say that such is not the case now. But such was the case, they think, in the Revolution of '75. If one were to tell me that this was a bad government because it taxed certain foreign commodities brought to its ports, it is most probable that I should not make an ado about it, for I can do without them. All machines have their friction; and possibly this does enough good to counterbalance the evil. At any rate, it is a great evil to make a stir about it. But when the friction comes to have its machine, and oppression and robbery are organized, I say, let us not have such a machine any longer. In other words, when a sixth of the population of a nation which has undertaken to be the refuge of liberty are slaves, and a whole country is unjustly overrun and conquered by a foreign army, and subjected to military law, I think that it is not too soon for honest men to rebel and revolutionize. What makes this duty the more urgent is the fact that the country so overrun is not our own, but ours is the invading army.

Paley, [4] a common authority with many on moral questions, in his chapter on the "Duty of Submission to Civil Government," resolves all

CIVIL DISOBEDIENCE.  **1. "Not . . . buried":** The opening lines of "Burial of Sir John Moore at Corunna," by the Irish clergyman-poet Charles Wolfe (1791–1823).

**2. A . . . away:** Cf. Shakespeare. *Hamlet*, V.i.236–37.  **3. "I . . . world":** Cf. Shakespeare, *King John*, V.ii.79–82.  **4. Paley:** William Paley (1743–1805), British philosopher, whose moral utilitarianism is exemplified by this quotation from his *Principles of Moral and Political Philosophy* (1785).

civil obligation into expediency; and he proceeds to say that "so long as the interest of the whole society requires it, that is, so long as the established government cannot be resisted or changed without public inconveniency, it is the will of God . . . that the established government be obeyed—and no longer. This principle being admitted, the justice of every particular case of resistance is reduced to a computation of the quantity of the danger and grievance on the one side, and of the probability and expense of redressing it on the other." Of this, he says, every man shall judge for himself. But Paley appears never to have contemplated those cases to which the rule of expediency does not apply, in which a people, as well as an individual, must do justice, cost what it may. If I have unjustly wrested a plank from a drowning man, I must restore it to him though I drown myself. This, according to Paley, would be inconvenient. But he that would save his life, in such a case, shall lose it. This people must cease to hold slaves, and to make war on Mexico, though it cost them their existence as a people.

In their practice, nations agree with Paley; but does anyone think that Massachusetts does exactly what is right at the present crisis?

"A drab of state, a cloth-o'-silver slut,
  To have her train borne up, and her soul trail in the
    dirt."

Practically speaking, the opponents to a reform in Massachusetts are not a hundred thousand politicians at the South, but a hundred thousand merchants and farmers here, who are more interested in commerce and agriculture than they are in humanity, and are not prepared to do justice to the slave and to Mexico, *cost what it may*. I quarrel not with far-off foes, but with those who, near at home, co-operate with, and do the bidding of, those far away, and without whom the latter would be harmless. We are accustomed to say, that the mass of men are unprepared; but improvement is slow, because the few are not materially wiser or better than the many. It is not so important that many should be as good as you, as that there be some absolute goodness somewhere; for that will leaven the whole lump. There are thousands who are *in opinion* opposed to slavery and to the war, who yet in effect do nothing to put an end to them; who, esteeming themselves children of Washington and Franklin, sit down with their hands in their pockets, and say that they know not what to do, and do nothing; who even postpone the question of freedom to the question of free trade, and quietly read the prices-current along with the latest advices from Mexico, after dinner, and, it

may be, fall asleep over them both. What is the price-current of an honest man and patriot today? They hesitate, and they regret, and sometimes they petition; but they do nothing in earnest and with effect. They will wait, well disposed, for others to remedy the evil, that they may no longer have it to regret. At most, they give only a cheap vote, and a feeble countenance and Godspeed, to the right, as it goes by them. There are nine hundred and ninety-nine patrons of virtue to one virtuous man. But it is easier to deal with the real possessor of a thing than with the temporary guardian of it.

All voting is a sort of gaming, like checkers or backgammon, with a slight moral tinge to it, a playing with right and wrong, with moral questions; and betting naturally accompanies it. The character of the voters is not staked. I cast my vote, perchance, as I think right; but I am not vitally concerned that that right should prevail. I am willing to leave it to the majority. Its obligation, therefore, never exceeds that of expediency. Even voting *for the right* is *doing* nothing for it. It is only expressing to men feebly your desire that it should prevail. A wise man will not leave the right to the mercy of chance, nor wish it to prevail through the power of the majority. There is but little virtue in the action of masses of men. When the majority shall at length vote for the abolition of slavery, it will be because they are indifferent to slavery, or because there is but little slavery left to be abolished by their vote. *They* will then be the only slaves. Only *his* vote can hasten the abolition of slavery who asserts his own freedom by his vote.

I hear of a convention to be held at Baltimore, or elsewhere, for the selection of a candidate for the Presidency, made up chiefly of editors, and men who are politicians by profession; but I think, what is it to any independent, intelligent, and respectable man what decision they may come to? Shall we not have the advantage of his wisdom and honesty, nevertheless? Can we not count upon some independent votes? Are there not many individuals in the country who do not attend conventions? But no: I find that the respectable man, so called, has immediately drifted from his position, and despairs of his country, when his country has more reason to despair of him. He forthwith adopts one of the candidates thus selected as the only *available* one, thus proving that he is himself *available* for any purposes of the demagogue. His vote is of no more worth than that of any unprincipled foreigner or hireling native, who may have been bought. O for a man who is a *man*, and, as my neighbor says, has a bone in his back which you cannot pass your hand through! Our statistics are at fault: the population has been returned too large. How many *men* are there to a square thousand miles in this country? Hardly one. Does not America offer any inducement for men to settle here? The American has dwindled into an Odd Fellow—one who may be known by the development of his organ of gregariousness, and a manifest lack of intellect and cheerful self-reliance; whose first and chief concern, on coming into the world, is to see that the almshouses are in good repair; and, before yet he has lawfully donned the virile garb, to collect a fund for the support of the widows and orphans that may be; who, in short, ventures to live only by the aid of the Mutual Insurance company, which has promised to bury him decently.

It is not a man's duty, as a matter of course, to devote himself to the eradication of any, even the most enormous, wrong; he may still properly have other concerns to engage him; but it is his duty, at least, to wash his hands of it, and, if he gives it no thought longer, not to give it practically his support. If I devote myself to other pursuits and contemplations, I must first see, at least, that I do not pursue them sitting upon another man's shoulders. I must get off him first, that he may pursue his contemplations too. See what gross inconsistency is tolerated. I have heard some of my townsmen say, "I should like to have them order me out to help put down an insurrection of the slaves, or to march to Mexico—see if I would go"; and yet these very men have each, directly by their allegiance, and so indirectly, at least, by their money, furnished a substitute. The soldier is applauded who refuses to serve in an unjust war by those who do not refuse to sustain the unjust government which makes the war; is applauded by those whose own act and authority he disregards and sets at naught; as if the state were penitent to that degree that it hired one to scourge it while it sinned, but not to that degree that it left off sinning for a moment. Thus, under the name of Order and Civil Government, we are all made at last to pay homage to and support our own meanness. After the first blush of sin comes its indifference; and from immoral it becomes, as it were, *unmoral,* and not quite unnecessary to that life which we have made.

The broadest and most prevalent error requires the most disinterested virtue to sustain it. The slight reproach to which the virtue of patriotism is commonly liable, the noble are most likely to incur. Those who, while they disapprove of the character and measures of a government, yield to it their allegiance and support are undoubtedly its most conscientious supporters, and so frequently the most serious obstacles to reform. Some are petitioning the State to dissolve the Union, to disregard the requisitions of the President. Why do they not dissolve it themselves—the union between themselves and the State—and refuse to pay their quota into its treasury? Do not they stand in the same relation to the State that the State does to the Union? And have not the same reasons prevented the State from resisting the Union which have prevented them from resisting the State?

How can a man be satisfied to entertain an opinion merely, and enjoy *it?* Is there any enjoyment in it, if his opinion is that he is aggrieved? If you are cheated out of a single dollar by your neighbor, you do not rest satisfied with knowing that you are cheated, or with saying that you are cheated, or even with petitioning him to pay you your due; but you take effectual steps at once to obtain the full amount, and see that you are never cheated again. Action from principle, the perception and the performance of right, changes things and relations; it is essentially revolutionary, and does not consist wholly with anything which was. It not only divides States and churches, it divides families; ay, it divides the *individual,* separating the diabolical in him from the divine.

Unjust laws exist: shall we be content to obey them, or shall we endeavor to amend them, and obey them until we have succeeded, or shall we transgress them at once? Men generally, under such a government as this, think that they ought to wait until they have persuaded the majority to alter them. They think that, if they should resist, the remedy would be worse than the evil. But it is the fault of the government itself that the remedy *is* worse than the evil. *It* makes it worse. Why is it not more apt to anticipate and provide for reform? Why does it not cherish its wise minority? Why does it cry and resist before it is hurt? Why does it not encourage its citizens to be on the alert to point out its faults, and *do* better than it would have them? Why does it always crucify Christ, and excommunicate Copernicus and Luther, and pronounce Washington and Franklin rebels?

One would think, that a deliberate and practical denial of its authority was the only offence never contemplated by government; else, why has it not assigned its definite, its suitable and proportionate, penalty? If a man who has no property refuses but once to earn nine shillings for the State, he is put in prison for a period unlimited by any law that I know, and determined only by the discretion of those who placed him there; but if he should steal ninety times nine shillings from the State, he is soon permitted to go at large again.

If the injustice is part of the necessary friction of

the machine of government, let it go, let it go: perchance it will wear smooth—certainly the machine will wear out. If the injustice has a spring, or a pulley, or a rope, or a crank, exclusively for itself, then perhaps you may consider whether the remedy will not be worse than the evil; but if it is of such a nature that it requires you to be the agent of injustice to another, then, I say, break the law. Let your life be a counter-friction to stop the machine. What I have to do is to see, at any rate, that I do not lend myself to the wrong which I condemn.

As for adopting the ways which the State has provided for remedying the evil, I know not of such ways. They take too much time, and a man's life will be gone. I have other affairs to attend to. I came into this world, not chiefly to make this a good place to live in, but to live in it, be it good or bad. A man has not everything to do, but something; and because he cannot do *everything*, it is not necessary that he should do *something* wrong. It is not my business to be petitioning the Governor or the Legislature any more than it is theirs to petition me; and if they should not hear my petition, what should I do then? But in this case the State has provided no way: its very Constitution is the evil. This may seem to be harsh and stubborn and unconciliatory; but it is to treat with the utmost kindness and consideration the only spirit that can appreciate or deserves it. So is all change for the better, like birth and death, which convulse the body.

I do not hesitate to say, that those who call themselves Abolitionists should at once effectually withdraw their support, both in person and property, from the government of Massachusetts, and not wait till they constitute a majority of one, before they suffer the right to prevail through them. I think that it is enough if they have God on their side, without waiting for that other one. Moreover, any man more right than his neighbors constitutes a majority of one already.

I meet this American government, or its representative, the State government, directly, and face to face, once a year—no more—in the person of its tax-gatherer; this is the only mode in which a man situated as I am necessarily meets it; and it then says distinctly, Recognize me; and the simplest, the most effectual, and, in the present posture of affairs, the indispensablest mode of treating with it on this head, of expressing your little satisfaction with and love for it, is to deny it then. My civil neighbor, the tax-gatherer, is the very man I have to deal with—for it is, after all, with men and not with parchment that I quarrel—and he has voluntarily chosen to be an agent of the government.

How shall he ever know well what he is and does as an officer of the government, or as a man, until he is obliged to consider whether he shall treat me, his neighbor, for whom he has respect, as a neighbor and well-disposed man, or as a maniac and disturber of the peace, and see if he can get over this obstruction to his neighborliness without a ruder and more impetuous thought or speech corresponding with his action. I know this well, that if one thousand, if one hundred, if ten men whom I could name—if ten *honest* men only—ay, if *one* HONEST man, in this State of Massachusetts, *ceasing to hold slaves,* were actually to withdraw from this copartnership, and be locked up in the county jail therefor, it would be the abolition of slavery in America. For it matters not how small the beginning may seem to be: what is once well done is done forever. But we love better to talk about it: that we say is our mission. Reform keeps many scores of newspapers in its service, but not one man. If my esteemed neighbor, the State's ambassador,[5] who will devote his days to the settlement of the question of human rights in the Council Chamber, instead of being threatened with the prisons of Carolina, were to sit down the prisoner of Massachusetts, that State which is so anxious to foist the sin of slavery upon her sister—though at present she can discover only an act of inhospitality to be the ground of a quarrel with her—the Legislature would not wholly waive the subject the following winter.

Under a government which imprisons any unjustly, the true place for a just man is also a prison. The proper place today, the only place which Massachusetts has provided for her freer and less desponding spirits, is in her prisons, to be put out and locked out of the State by her own act, as they have already put themselves out by their principles. It is there that the fugitive slave, and the Mexican prisoner on parole, and the Indian come to plead the wrongs of his race should find them; on that separate, but more free and honorable, ground, where the State places those who are not *with* her, but *against* her—the only house in a slave State in which a free man can abide with honor. If any think that their influence would be lost there, and their voices no longer afflict the ear of the State, that they would not be as an enemy within its walls, they do not know by how much truth is stronger than error, nor how much more eloquently and effectively he can combat injustice who has experienced a little in his own person.

5. **the State's ambassador:** Samuel Hoar (1778–1856), Concord lawyer and Congressman, was sent to Charleston, S.C., to represent Negro seamen from Massachusetts threatened with arrest and enslavement. Hoar was forcibly expelled from the port.

Cast your whole vote, not a strip of paper merely, but your whole influence. A minority is powerless while it conforms to the majority; it is not even a minority then; but it is irresistible when it clogs by its whole weight. If the alternative is to keep all just men in prison, or give up war and slavery, the State will not hesitate which to choose. If a thousand men were not to pay their tax bills this year, that would not be a violent and bloody measure, as it would be to pay them, and enable the State to commit violence and shed innocent blood. This is, in fact, the definition of a peaceable revolution, if any such is possible. If the tax-gatherer, or any other public officer, asks me, as one has done, "But what shall I do?" my answer is, "If you really wish to do anything, resign your office." When the subject has refused allegiance, and the officer has resigned his office, then the revolution is accomplished. But even suppose blood should flow. Is there not a sort of blood shed when the conscience is wounded? Through this wound a man's real manhood and immortality flow out, and he bleeds to an everlasting death. I see this blood flowing now.

I have contemplated the imprisonment of the offender, rather than the seizure of his goods—though both will serve the same purpose—because they who assert the purest right, and consequently are most dangerous to a corrupt State, commonly have not spent much time in accumulating property. To such the State renders comparatively small service, and a slight tax is wont to appear exorbitant, particularly if they are obliged to earn it by special labor with their hands. If there were one who lived wholly without the use of money, the State itself would hesitate to demand it of him. But the rich man—not to make any invidious comparison—is always sold to the institution which makes him rich. Absolutely speaking, the more money, the less virtue; for money comes between a man and his objects, and obtains them for him; and it was certainly no great virtue to obtain it. It puts to rest many questions which he would otherwise be taxed to answer; while the only new question which it puts is the hard but superfluous one, how to spend it. Thus his moral ground is taken from under his feet. The opportunities of living are diminished in proportion as what are called the "means" are increased. The best thing a man can do for his culture when he is rich is to endeavor to carry out those schemes which he entertained when he was poor. Christ answered the Herodians according to their condition. "Show me the tribute-money," said he—and one took a penny out of his pocket—if you use money which has the image of Caesar on it, and which he has made current and valuable, that is, *if you are men of the State,* and gladly enjoy the advantages of Caesar's government, then pay him back some of his own when he demands it. "Render therefore to Caesar that which is Caesar's, and to God those things which are God's"—leaving them no wiser than before as to which was which; for they did not wish to know.

When I converse with the freest of my neighbors, I perceive that, whatever they may say about the magnitude and seriousness of the question, and their regard for the public tranquillity, the long and the short of the matter is, that they cannot spare the protection of the existing government, and they dread the consequences to their property and families of disobedience to it. For my own part, I should not like to think that I ever rely on the protection of the State. But, if I deny the authority of the State when it presents its tax bill, it will soon take and waste all my property, and so harass me and my children without end. This is hard. This makes it impossible for a man to live honestly, and at the same time comfortably, in outward respects. It will not be worth the while to accumulate property; that would be sure to go again. You must hire or squat somewhere, and raise but a small crop, and eat that soon. You must live within yourself, and depend upon yourself always tucked up and ready for a start, and not have many affairs. A man may grow rich in Turkey even, if he will be in all respects a good subject of the Turkish government. Confucius said: "If a state is governed by the principles of reason, poverty and misery are subjects of shame; if a state is not governed by the principles of reason, riches and honors are the subjects of shame." No: until I want the protection of Massachusetts to be extended to me in some distant Southern port, where my liberty is endangered, or until I am bent solely on building up an estate at home by peaceful enterprise, I can afford to refuse allegiance to Massachusetts, and her right to my property and life. It costs me less in every sense to incur the penalty of disobedience to the State than it would to obey. I should feel as if I were worth less in that case.

Some years ago, the State met me in behalf of the Church, and commanded me to pay a certain sum toward the support of a clergyman whose preaching my father attended, but never I myself. "Pay," it said, "or be locked up in the jail." I declined to pay.[6] But, unfortunately, another man saw fit to pay it. I did not see why the schoolmaster should be taxed to support the priest, and

6. I . . . **pay:** Thoreau signed off from church taxes in 1838 and went to jail in July 1846, for refusing to pay his poll tax.

not the priest the schoolmaster; for I was not the State's schoolmaster, but I supported myself by voluntary subscription. I did not see why the lyceum should not present its tax bill, and have the State to back its demand, as well as the Church. However, at the request of the selectmen, I condescended to make some such statement as this in writing: "Know all men by these presents, that I, Henry Thoreau, do not wish to be regarded as a member of any incorporated society which I have not joined." This I gave to the town clerk; and he has it. The State, having thus learned that I did not wish to be regarded as a member of that church, has never made a like demand on me since; though it said that it must adhere to its original presumption that time. If I had known how to name them, I should then have signed off in detail from all the societies which I never signed on to; but I did not know where to find a complete list.

I have paid no poll tax for six years. I was put into a jail once on this account, for one night; and, as I stood considering the walls of solid stone, two or three feet thick, the door of wood and iron, a foot thick, and the iron grating which strained the light, I could not help being struck with the foolishness of that institution which treated me as if I were mere flesh and blood and bones, to be locked up. I wondered that it should have concluded at length that this was the best use it could put me to, and had never thought to avail itself of my services in some way. I saw that, if there was a wall of stone between me and my townsmen, there was a still more difficult one to climb or break through before they could get to be as free as I was. I did not for a moment feel confined, and the walls seemed a great waste of stone and mortar. I felt as if I alone of all my townsmen had paid my tax. They plainly did not know how to treat me, but behaved like persons who are underbred. In every threat and in every compliment there was a blunder; for they thought that my chief desire was to stand the other side of that stone wall. I could not but smile to see how industriously they locked the door on my meditations, which followed them out again without let or hindrance, and *they* were really all that was dangerous. As they could not reach me, they had resolved to punish my body; just as boys, if they cannot come at some person against whom they have a spite, will abuse his dog. I saw that the State was half-witted, that it was timid as a lone woman with her silver spoons, and that it did not know its friends from its foes, and I lost all my remaining respect for it, and pitied it.

Thus the State never intentionally confronts a man's sense, intellectual or moral, but only his body, his senses. It is not armed with superior wit or honesty, but with superior physical strength. I was not born to be forced. I will breathe after my own fashion. Let us see who is the strongest. What force has a multitude? They only can force me who obey a higher law than I. They force me to become like themselves. I do not hear of *men* being *forced* to live this way or that by masses of men. What sort of life were that to live? When I meet a government which says to me, "Your money or your life," why should I be in haste to give it my money? It may be in a great strait, and not know what to do: I cannot help that. It must help itself; do as I do. It is not worth the while to snivel about it. I am not responsible for the successful working of the machinery of society. I am not the son of the engineer. I perceive that, when an acorn and a chestnut fall side by side, the one does not remain inert to make way for the other, but both obey their own laws, and spring and grow and flourish as best they can, till one, perchance, overshadows and destroys the other. If a plant cannot live according to its nature, it dies; and so a man.

The night in prison was novel and interesting enough. The prisoners in their shirtsleeves were enjoying a chat and the evening air in the doorway, when I entered. But the jailer said, "Come, boys, it is time to lock up"; and so they dispersed, and I heard the sound of their steps returning into the hollow apartments. My room-mate was introduced to me by the jailer as "a first-rate fellow and a clever man." When the door was locked, he showed me where to hang my hat, and how he managed matters there. The rooms were whitewashed once a month; and this one, at least, was the whitest, most simply furnished, and probably the neatest apartment in the town. He naturally wanted to know where I came from, and what brought me there; and, when I had told him, I asked him in my turn how he came there, presuming him to be an honest man, of course; and, as the world goes, I believe he was. "Why," said he, "they accuse me of burning a barn; but I never did it." As near as I could discover, he had probably gone to bed in a barn when drunk, and smoked his pipe there; and so a barn was burnt. He had the reputation of being a clever man, had been there some three months waiting for his trial to come on, and would have to wait as much longer; but he was quite domesticated and contented, since he got his board for nothing, and thought that he was well treated.

He occupied one window, and I the other; and I saw that if one stayed there long, his principal business would be to look out the window. I had soon read all the tracts that were left there, and examined where former prisoners had broken out, and where a grate had been sawed off, and heard the history of the various occupants of that room; for I found that even here there was a history and a gossip which never circulated beyond the walls of the jail. Probably this is the only house in the town where verses are composed, which are afterward printed in a circular form, but not published. I was shown quite a long list of verses which were composed by some young men who had been detected in an attempt to escape, who avenged themselves by singing them.

I pumped my fellow-prisoner as dry as I could, for fear I should never see him again; but at length he showed me which was my bed, and left me to blow out the lamp.

It was like traveling into a far country, such as I had never expected to behold, to lie there for one night. It seemed to me that I never had heard the town clock strike before, nor the evening sounds of the village; for we slept with the windows open, which were inside the grating. It was to see my native village in the light of the Middle Ages, and our Concord was turned into a Rhine stream, and visions of knights and castles passed before me. They were the voices of old burghers that I heard in the streets. I was an involuntary spectator and auditor of whatever was done and said in the kitchen of the adjacent village inn— a wholly new and rare experience to me. It was a closer view of my native town. I was fairly inside of it. I never had seen its institutions before. This is one of its peculiar institutions; for it is a shire town. I began to comprehend what its inhabitants were about.

In the morning, our breakfasts were put through the hole in the door, in small oblong-square tin pans, made to fit, and holding a pint of chocolate, with brown bread, and an iron spoon. When they called for the vessels again, I was green enough to return what bread I had left; but my comrade seized it, and said that I should lay that up for lunch or dinner. Soon after he was let out to work at haying in a neighboring field, whither he went every day, and would not be back till noon; so he bade me good-day, saying that he doubted if he should see me again.

When I came out of prison—for some one interfered, and paid that tax—I did not perceive that great changes had taken place on the common, such as he observed who went in a youth and emerged a tottering and gray-headed man; and yet a change had to my eyes come over the scene— the town, and State, and country—greater than any that mere time could effect. I saw yet more distinctly the State in which I lived. I saw to what extent the people among whom I lived could be trusted as good neighbors and friends; that their friendship was for summer weather only; that they did not greatly propose to do right; that they were a distinct race from me by their prejudices and superstitions, as the Chinamen and Malays are; that in their sacrifices to humanity they ran no risks, not even to their property; that after all they were not so noble but they treated the thief as he had treated them, and hoped, by a certain outward observance and a few prayers, and by walking in a particular straight though useless path from time to time, to save their souls. This may be to judge my neighbors harshly; for I believe that many of them are not aware that they have such an institution as the jail in their village.

It was formerly the custom in our village, when a poor debtor came out of jail, for his acquaintances to salute him, looking through their fingers, which were crossed to represent the grating of a jail window, "How do ye do?" My neighbors did not thus salute me, but first looked at me, and then at one another, as if I had returned from a long journey. I was put into jail as I was going to the shoemaker's to get a shoe which was mended. When I was let out the next morning, I proceeded to finish my errand, and, having put on my mended shoe, joined a huckleberry party, who were impatient to put themselves under my conduct; and in half an hour—for the horse was soon tackled— was in the midst of a huckleberry field, on one of our highest hills, two miles off, and then the State was nowhere to be seen.

This is the whole history of "My Prisons." [7]

I have never declined paying the highway tax, because I am as desirous of being a good neighbor as I am of being a bad subject; and as for supporting schools, I am doing my part to educate my fellow-countrymen now. It is for no particular item in the tax bill that I refuse to pay it. I simply wish to refuse allegiance to the State, to withdraw and stand aloof from it effectually. I do not care to trace the course of my dollar, if I could, till it buys a man or a musket to shoot one with—the dollar is innocent—but I am concerned to trace the effects of my allegiance. In fact, I quietly declare war with the State, after my fashion, though I will still make what use and get what advantage of her I can, as is usual in such cases.

If others pay the tax which is demanded of me, from a sympathy with the State, they do but what they have already done in their own case, or rather they abet injustice to a greater ex-

7. **"My Prisons"**: English translation of the title *Le Mie Prigioni*, a record of his Austrian incarceration by the Italian patriot and poet Silvio Pellico (1789-1854).

tent than the State requires. If they pay the tax from a mistaken interest in the individual taxed, to save his property, or prevent his going to jail, it is because they have not considered wisely how far they let their private feelings interfere with the public good.

This, then, is my position at present. But one cannot be too much on his guard in such a case, lest his action be biased by obstinacy or an undue regard for the opinions of men. Let him see that he does only what belongs to himself and to the hour.

I think sometimes, Why, this people mean well, they are only ignorant; they would do better if they knew how: why give your neighbors this pain to treat you as they are not inclined to? But I think again, This is no reason why I should do as they do, or permit others to suffer much greater pain of a different kind. Again, I sometimes say to myself, When many millions of men, without heat, without ill will, without personal feeling of any kind, demand of you a few shillings only, without the possibility, such is their constitution, of retracting or altering their present demand, and without the possibility, on your side, of appeal to any other millions, why expose yourself to this overwhelming brute force? You do not resist cold and hunger, the winds and the waves, thus obstinately; you quietly submit to a thousand similar necessities. You do not put your head into the fire. But just in proportion as I regard this as not wholly a brute force, but partly a human force, and consider that I have relations to those millions as to so many millions of men, and not of mere brute or inanimate things, I see that appeal is possible, first and instantaneously, from them to the Maker of them, and, secondly, from them to themselves. But if I put my head deliberately into the fire, there is no appeal to fire or to the Maker of fire, and I have only myself to blame. If I could convince myself that I have any right to be satisfied with men as they are, and to treat them accordingly, and not according, in some respects, to my requisitions and expectations of what they and I ought to be, then, like a good Mussulman and fatalist, I should endeavor to be satisfied with things as they are, and say it is the will of God. And, above all, there is this difference between resisting this and a purely brute or natural force, that I can resist this with some effect; but I cannot expect, like Orpheus, to change the nature of the rocks and trees and beasts.

I do not wish to quarrel with any man or nation. I do not wish to split hairs, to make fine distinctions, or set myself up as better than my neighbors. I seek rather, I may say, even an excuse for conforming to the laws of the land. I am but too ready to conform to them. Indeed, I have reason to suspect myself on this head; and each year, as the tax-gatherer comes round, I find myself disposed to review the acts and position of the general and State governments, and the spirit of the people, to discover a pretext for conformity.

> "We must affect our country as our parents,
> And if at any time we alienate
> Our love or industry from doing it honor,
> We must respect effects and teach the soul
> Matter of conscience and religion,
> And not desire of rule or benefit."

I believe that the State will soon be able to take all my work of this sort out of my hands, and then I shall be no better a patriot than my fellow-countrymen. Seen from a lower point of view, the Constitution, with all its faults, is very good; the law and the courts are very respectable; even this State and this American government are, in many respects, very admirable, and rare things, to be thankful for, such as a great many have described them; but seen from a point of view a little higher, they are what I have described them; seen from a higher still, and the highest, who shall say what they are, or that they are worth looking at or thinking of at all?

However, the government does not concern me much, and I shall bestow the fewest possible thoughts on it. It is not many moments that I live under a government, even in this world. If a man is thought-free, fancy-free, imagination-free, that which *is not* never for a long time appearing *to be* to him, unwise rulers or reformers cannot fatally interrupt him.

I know that most men think differently from myself; but those whose lives are by profession devoted to the study of these or kindred subjects content me as little as any. Statesmen and legislators, standing so completely within the institution, never distinctly and nakedly behold it. They speak of moving society, but have no resting-place without it. They may be men of a certain experience and discrimination, and have no doubt invented ingenious and even useful systems, for which we sincerely thank them; but all their wit and usefulness lie within certain not very wide limits. They are wont to forget that the world is not governed by policy and expediency. Webster never goes behind government, and so cannot speak with authority about it. His words are wisdom to those legislators who contemplate no essential reform in the existing government; but for thinkers, and those who legislate for all time, he never once glances at the subject. I know of those whose serene and wise speculations on this theme would soon reveal the limits of his mind's range and hospitality. Yet, compared with the cheap professions of most reformers, and the still cheaper wisdom and eloquence of politicians in general, his are almost the only sensible and valuable words, and we thank Heaven for him. Comparatively, he is always strong, original, and, above all, practical. Still, his quality is not wisdom, but prudence. The lawyer's truth is not Truth, but consistency or a consistent expediency. Truth is always in harmony with herself, and is not concerned chiefly to reveal the justice that may consist with wrong-doing. He well deserves to be called, as he has been called, the Defender of the Constitution. There are really no blows to be given by him but defensive ones. He is not a leader, but a follower. His leaders are the men of '87. "I have never made an effort," he says, "and never propose to make an effort; I have never countenanced an effort, and never mean to countenance an effort, to disturb the arrangement as originally made, by which the various States came into the Union." Still thinking of the sanction which the Constitution gives to slavery, he says, "Because it was a part of the original compact—let it stand." Notwithstanding his special acuteness and ability, he is unable to take a fact out of its merely political relations, and behold it as it lies absolutely to be disposed of by the intellect—what, for instance, it behooves a man to do here in America today with regard to slavery—but ventures, or is driven, to make some such desperate answer as the following, while professing to speak absolutely, and as a private man—from which what new and singular code of social duties might be inferred? "The manner," says he, "in which the governments of those States where slavery exists are to regulate it is for their own consideration, under their responsibility to their constituents, to the general laws of propriety, humanity, and justice, and to God. Associations formed elsewhere, springing from a feeling of humanity, or any other cause, have nothing whatever to do with it. They have never received any encouragement from me, and they never will." [8]

They who know of no purer sources of truth, who have traced up its stream no higher, stand, and wisely stand, by the Bible and the Constitution, and drink at it there with reverence and humility; but they who behold where it comes trickling into this lake or that pool, gird up their loins once more, and continue their pilgrimage toward its fountainhead.

No man with a genius for legislation has ap-

peared in America. They are rare in the history of the world. There are orators, politicians, and eloquent men, by the thousand; but the speaker has not yet opened his mouth to speak who is capable of settling the much-vexed questions of the day. We love eloquence for its own sake, and not for any truth which it may utter, or any heroism it may inspire. Our legislators have not yet learned the comparative value of free trade and of freedom, of union, and of rectitude, to a nation. They have no genius or talent for comparatively humble questions of taxation and finance, commerce and manufactures and agriculture. If we were left solely to the wordy wit of legislators in Congress for our guidance, uncorrected by the seasonable experience and the effectual complaints of the people, America would not long retain her rank among the nations. For eighteen hundred years, though perchance I have no right to say it, the New Testament has been written; yet where is the legislator who has wisdom and practical talent enough to avail himself of the light which it sheds on the science of legislation?

The authority of government, even such as I am willing to submit to—for I will cheerfully obey those who know and can do better than I, and in many things even those who neither know nor can do so well—is still an impure one: to be strictly just, it must have the sanction and consent of the governed. It can have no pure right over my person and property but what I concede to it. The progress from an absolute to a limited monarchy, from a limited monarchy to a democracy, is a progress toward a true respect for the individual. Even the Chinese philosopher was wise enough to regard the individual as the basis of the empire. Is a democracy, such as we know it, the last improvement possible in government? Is it not possible to take a step further towards recognizing and organizing the rights of man? There will never be a really free and enlightened State until the State comes to recognize the individual as a higher and independent power, from which all its own power and authority are derived, and treats him accordingly. I please myself with imagining a State at last which can afford to be just to all men, and to treat the individual with respect as a neighbor; which even would not think it inconsistent with its own repose if a few were to live aloof from it, not meddling with it, nor embraced by it, who fulfilled all the duties of neighbors and fellow men. A State which bore this kind of fruit, and suffered it to drop off as fast as it ripened, would prepare the way for a still more perfect and glorious State, which also I have imagined, but not yet anywhere seen.

---

8. "These extracts have been inserted since the lecture was read" [Thoreau's note].

# WALKING

◊

❦ ORIGINALLY entitled "The Wild," and first delivered before the Concord Lyceum in 1851, "Walking" was somewhat revised during Thoreau's final illness. It was published posthumously in the *Atlantic Monthly* in 1862. To a nation that was completing a transcontinental expansion, Thoreau set forth in this essay a vision of another West which could forever replenish and rejuvenate American culture with its "absolute freedom and wildness." This mythological West could not be located geographically; it did not lie beyond the Alleghenies or across the wide Missouri; a state of mind, not a place, it was present wherever man was willing to trust the untrammeled responses of his own genius.

◊

I WISH to speak a word for Nature, for absolute freedom and wildness, as contrasted with a freedom and culture merely civil—to regard man as an inhabitant, or a part and parcel of Nature, rather than a member of society. I wish to make an extreme statement, if so I may make an emphatic one, for there are enough champions of civilization: the minister and the school committee and every one of you will take care of that.

I have met with but one or two persons in the course of my life who understood the art of Walking, that is, of taking walks—who had a genius, so to speak, for *sauntering,* which word is beautifully derived "from idle people who roved about the country, in the Middle Ages, and asked charity, under pretense of going *à la Sainte Terre,*" to the Holy Land, till the children exclaimed, "There goes a *Sainte-Terrer,*" a Saunterer, a Holy-Lander. They who never go to the Holy Land in their walks, as they pretend, are indeed mere idlers and vagabonds; but they who do go there are saunterers in the good sense, such as I mean. Some, however, would derive the word from *sans terre,* without land or a home, which, therefore, in the good sense, will mean, having no particular home, but equally at home everywhere. For this is the secret of successful sauntering. He who sits still in a house all the time may be the greatest vagrant of all; but the saunterer, in the good sense, is no more vagrant than the meandering river, which is all the while sedulously seeking the shortest course to the sea. But I prefer the first, which, indeed, is the most probable derivation. For every walk is a sort of crusade, preached by some Peter the Hermit in us, to go forth and reconquer this Holy Land from the hands of the Infidels.

It is true, we are but faint-hearted crusaders, even the walkers, nowadays, who undertake no persevering, never-ending enterprises. Our expeditions are but tours, and come round again at evening to the old hearthside from which we set out. Half the walk is but retracing our steps. We should go forth on the shortest walk, perchance, in the spirit of undying adventure, never to return, prepared to send back our embalmed hearts only as relics to our desolate kingdoms. If you are ready to leave father and mother, and brother and sister, and wife and child and friends, and never see them again—if you have paid your debts, and made your will, and settled all your affairs, and are a free man—then you are ready for a walk.

To come down to my own experience, my companion and I, for I sometimes have a companion, take pleasure in fancying ourselves knights of a new, or rather an old, order—not Equestrians or Chevaliers, not Ritters or Riders, but Walkers, a still more ancient and honorable class, I trust. The chivalric and heroic spirit which once belonged to the Rider seems now to reside in, or perchance to have subsided into, the Walker—not the Knight, but Walker, Errant. He is a sort of fourth estate, outside of Church and State and People.

We have felt that we almost alone hereabouts practiced this noble art; though, to tell the truth, at least if their own assertions are to be received, most of my townsmen would fain walk sometimes, as I do, but they cannot. No wealth can buy the requisite leisure, freedom, and independence which are the capital in this profession. It comes only by the grace of God. It requires a direct dispensation from Heaven to become a walker. You must be born into the family of the Walkers. *Ambulator nascitur, non fit.* Some of my townsmen, it is true, can remember and have described to me some walks which they took ten years ago, in which they were so blessed as to lose themselves for half an hour in the woods; but I know very well that they have confined themselves to the highway ever since, whatever pretensions they may make to belong to this select class. No doubt they were elevated for a moment as by the reminiscence of a previous state of existence, when even they were foresters and outlaws.

> "When he came to grene wode,
>  In a mery mornynge,
> There he herde the notes small
>  Of byrdes mery syngynge.

"It is ferre gone, sayd Robyn,
That I was last here;
Me lyste a lytell for to shote
At the donne dere." [1]

I think that I cannot preserve my health and spirits, unless I spend four hours a day at least— and it is commonly more than that—sauntering through the woods and over the hills and fields, absolutely free from all worldly engagements. You may safely say, A penny for your thoughts, or a thousand pounds. When sometimes I am reminded that the mechanics and shopkeepers stay in their shops not only all the forenoon, but all the afternoon too, sitting with crossed legs, so many of them—as if the legs were made to sit upon, and not to stand or walk upon—I think that they deserve some credit for not having all committed suicide long ago.

I, who cannot stay in my chamber for a single day without acquiring some rust, and when sometimes I have stolen forth for a walk at the eleventh hour, or four o'clock in the afternoon, too late to redeem the day, when the shades of night were already beginning to be mingled with the daylight, have felt as if I had committed some sin to be atoned for—I confess that I am astonished at the power of endurance, to say nothing of the moral insensibility, of my neighbors who confine themselves to shops and offices the whole day for weeks and months, aye, and years almost together. I know not what manner of stuff they are of, sitting there now at three o'clock in the afternoon, as if it were three o'clock in the morning. Bonaparte may talk of the three-o'clock-in-the-morning courage, but it is nothing to the courage which can sit down cheerfully at this hour in the afternoon over against one's self whom you have known all the morning, to starve out a garrison to whom you are bound by such strong ties of sympathy. I wonder that about this time, or say between four and five o'clock in the afternoon, too late for the morning papers and too early for the evening ones, there is not a general explosion heard up and down the street, scattering a legion of antiquated and housebred notions and whims to the four winds for an airing—and so the evil cure itself.

How womankind, who are confined to the house still more than men, stand it I do not know; but I have ground to suspect that most of them do not *stand* it at all. When, early in a summer afternoon, we have been shaking the dust of the village from the skirts of our garments, making haste past those houses with purely Doric or Gothic fronts, which have such an air of repose about them, my companion whispers that probably about these

times their occupants are all gone to bed. Then it is that I appreciate the beauty and the glory of architecture, which itself never turns in, but forever stands out and erect, keeping watch over the slumberers.

No doubt temperament, and, above all, age, have a good deal to do with it. As a man grows older, his ability to sit still and follow indoor occupations increases. He grows vespertinal in his habits as the evening of life approaches, till at last he comes forth only just before sundown, and gets all the walk that he requires in half an hour.

But the walking of which I speak has nothing in it akin to taking exercise, as it is called, as the sick take medicine at stated hours—as the swinging of dumbbells or chairs; but is itself the enterprise and adventure of the day. If you would get exercise, go in search of the springs of life. Think of a man's swinging dumbbells for his health, when those springs are bubbling up in far-off pastures unsought by him!

Moreover, you must walk like a camel, which is said to be the only beast which ruminates when walking. When a traveler asked Wordsworth's servant to show him her master's study, she answered, "Here is his library, but his study is out of doors."

Living much out of doors, in the sun and wind, will no doubt produce a certain roughness of character—will cause a thicker cuticle to grow over some of the finer qualities of our nature, as on the face and hands, or as severe manual labor robs the hands of some of their delicacy of touch. So staying in the house, on the other hand, may produce a softness and smoothness, not to say thinness of skin, accompanied by an increased sensibility to certain impressions. Perhaps we should be more susceptible to some influences important to our intellectual and moral growth, if the sun had shone and the wind blown on us a little less; and no doubt it is a nice matter to proportion rightly the thick and thin skin. But methinks that is a scurf that will fall off fast enough—that the natural remedy is to be found in the proportion which the night bears to the day, the winter to the summer, thought to experience. There will be so much the more air and sunshine in our thoughts. The callous palms of the laborer are conversant with finer tissues of self-respect and heroism, whose touch thrills the heart, than the languid fingers of idleness. That is mere sentimentality that lies abed by day and thinks itself white, far from the tan and callus of experience.

When we walk, we naturally go to the fields and woods: what would become of us, if we walked only in a garden or a mall? Even some sects of

WALKING.    1. **"When . . . dere"**: the Robin Hood Ballads.

philosophers have felt the necessity of importing the woods to themselves, since they did not go to the woods. "They planted groves and walks of Platanes," where they took *subdiales ambulationes* in porticos open to the air. Of course it is of no use to direct our steps to the woods, if they do not carry us thither. I am alarmed when it happens that I have walked a mile into the woods bodily, without getting there in spirit. In my afternoon walk I would fain forget all my morning occupations and my obligations to society. But it sometimes happens that I cannot easily shake off the village. The thought of some work will run in my head and I am not where my body is—I am out of my senses. In my walks I would fain return to my senses. What business have I in the woods, if I am thinking of something out of the woods? I suspect myself, and cannot help a shudder, when I find myself so implicated even in what are called good works—for this may sometimes happen.

My vicinity affords many good walks; and though for so many years I have walked almost every day, and sometimes for several days together, I have not yet exhausted them. An absolutely new prospect is a great happiness, and I can still get this any afternoon. Two or three hours' walking will carry me to as strange a country as I expect ever to see. A single farmhouse which I had not seen before is sometimes as good as the dominions of the King of Dahomey. There is in fact a sort of harmony discoverable between the capabilities of the landscape within a circle of ten miles' radius, or the limits of an afternoon walk, and the threescore years and ten of human life. It will never become quite familiar to you.

Nowadays almost all man's improvements, so called, as the building of houses and the cutting down of the forest and of all large trees, simply deform the landscape, and make it more and more tame and cheap. A people who would begin by burning the fences and let the forest stand! I saw the fences half consumed, their ends lost in the middle of the prairie, and some worldly miser with a surveyor looking after his bounds, while heaven had taken place around him, and he did not see the angels going to and fro, but was looking for an old post-hole in the midst of paradise. I looked again, and saw him standing in the middle of a boggy Stygian fen, surrounded by devils, and he had found his bounds without a doubt, three little stones, where a stake had been driven, and looking nearer, I saw that the Prince of Darkness was his surveyor.

I can easily walk ten, fifteen, twenty, any number of miles, commencing at my own door, without going by any house, without crossing a road except where the fox and the mink do: first along by the river, and then the brook, and then the meadow and the woodside. There are square miles in my vicinity which have no inhabitant. From many a hill I can see civilization and the abodes of man afar. The farmers and their works are scarcely more obvious than woodchucks and their burrows. Man and his affairs, church and state and school, trade and commerce, and manufactures and agriculture, even politics, the most alarming of them all—I am pleased to see how little space they occupy in the landscape. Politics is but a narrow field, and that still narrower highway yonder leads to it. I sometimes direct the traveler thither. If you would go to the political world, follow the great road, follow that market-man, keep his dust in your eyes, and it will lead you straight to it; for it, too, has its place merely, and does not occupy all space. I pass from it as from a bean field into the forest, and it is forgotten. In one half-hour I can walk off to some portion of the earth's surface where a man does not stand from one year's end to another, and there, consequently, politics are not, for they are but as the cigar-smoke of a man.

The village is the place to which the roads tend, a sort of expansion of the highway, as a lake of a river. It is the body of which roads are the arms and legs—a trivial or quadrivial place, the thoroughfare and ordinary of travelers. The word is from the Latin *villa*, which together with *via*, a way, or more anciently *ved* and *vella*, Varro derives from veho, to carry, because the villa is the place to and from which things are carried. They who got their living by teaming were said *vellaturam facere*. Hence, too, the Latin word *vilis* and our vile, also *villain*. This suggests what kind of degeneracy villagers are liable to. They are wayworn by the travel that goes by and over them, without traveling themselves.

Some do not walk at all; others walk in the highways; a few walk across lots. Roads are made for horses and men of business. I do not travel in them much, comparatively, because I am not in a hurry to get to any tavern or grocery or livery-stable or depot to which they lead. I am a good horse to travel, but not from choice a roadster. The landscape-painter uses the figures of men to mark a road. He would not make that use of my figure. I walk out into a nature such as the old prophets and poets, Menu, Moses, Homer, Chaucer, walked in. You may name it America, but it is not America; neither Americus Vespucius, nor Columbus, nor the rest were the discoverers of it. There is a truer account of it in mythology than in any history of America, so called, that I have seen.

However, there are a few old roads that may be trodden with profit, as if they led somewhere now that they are nearly discontinued. There is the Old Marlborough Road, which does not go to Marlborough now, methinks, unless that is Marlborough where it carries me. I am the bolder to speak of it here, because I presume that there are one or two such roads in every town.

### THE OLD MARLBOROUGH ROAD

> Where they once dug for money,
> But never found any;
> Where sometimes Martial Miles
> Singly files,
> And Elijah Wood,
> I fear for no good:
> No other man,
> Save Elisha Dugan—
> O man of wild habits,
> Partridges and rabbits,
> Who hast no cares
> Only to set snares,
> Who liv'st all alone,
> Close to the bone,
> And where life is sweetest
> Constantly eatest.
> When the spring stirs my blood
> With the instinct to travel,
> I can get enough gravel
> On the Old Marlborough Road.
> Nobody repairs it,
> For nobody wears it;
> It is a living way,
> As the Christians say.
> Not many there be
> Who enter therein,
> Only the guests of the
> Irishman Quin.
> What is it, what is it,
> But a direction out there,
> And the bare possibility
> Of going somewhere?
> Great guide-boards of stone,
> But travelers none;
> Cenotaphs of the towns
> Named on their crowns.
> It is worth going to see
> Where you *might* be.
> What king
> Did the thing,
> I am still wondering;
> Set up how or when,
> By what selectmen,
> Gourgas or Lee,
> Clark or Darby?
> They're a great endeavor
> To be something forever;
> Blank tablets of stone,
> Where a traveler might groan,
> And in one sentence
> Grave all that is known;

> Which another might read,
> In his extreme need.
> I know one or two
> Lines that would do,
> Literature that might stand
> All over the land,
> Which a man could remember
> Till next December,
> And read again in the spring,
> After the thawing.
> If with fancy unfurled
> You leave your abode,
> You may go round the world
> By the Old Marlborough Road.

At present, in this vicinity, the best part of the land is not private property; the landscape is not owned, and the walker enjoys comparative freedom. But possibly the day will come when it will be partitioned off into so-called pleasure-grounds, in which a few will take a narrow and exclusive pleasure only—when fences shall be multiplied, and man-traps and other engines invented to confine men to the *public* road, and walking over the surface of God's earth shall be construed to mean trespassing on some gentleman's grounds. To enjoy a thing exclusively is commonly to exclude yourself from the true enjoyment of it. Let us improve our opportunities, then, before the evil days come.

What is it that makes it so hard sometimes to determine whither we will walk? I believe that there is a subtle magnetism in Nature, which, if we unconsciously yield to it, will direct us aright. It is not indifferent to us which way we walk. There is a right way; but we are very liable from heedlessness and stupidity to take the wrong one. We would fain take that walk, never yet taken by us through this actual world, which is perfectly symbolical of the path which we love to travel in the interior and ideal world; and sometimes, no doubt, we find it difficult to choose our direction, because it does not yet exist distinctly in our idea.

When I go out of the house for a walk, uncertain as yet whither I will bend my steps, and submit myself to my instinct to decide for me, I find, strange and whimsical as it may seem, that I finally and inevitably settle southwest, toward some particular wood or meadow or deserted pasture or hill in that direction. My needle is slow to settle, varies a few degrees, and does not always point due southwest, it is true, and it has good authority for this variation, but it always settles between west and south-southwest. The future lies that way to me, and the earth seems more unexhausted and richer on that side. The outline which would bound my walks would be, not a circle, but a parabola, or rather like one of those cometary orbits which have been thought to be non-returning curves, in this case opening westward, in which my house occupies the place of the sun. I turn round and round irresolute sometimes for a quarter of an hour, until I decide, for a thousandth time, that I will walk into the southwest or west. Eastward I go only by force; but westward I go free. Thither no business leads me. It is hard for me to believe that I shall find fair landscapes or sufficient wildness and freedom behind the eastern horizon. I am not excited by the prospect of a walk thither; but I believe that the forest which I see in the western horizon stretches uninterruptedly toward the setting sun, and there are no towns nor cities in it of enough consequence to disturb me. Let me live where I will, on this side is the city, on that the wilderness, and ever I am leaving the city more and more, and withdrawing into the wilderness. I should not lay so much stress on this fact, if I did not believe that something like this is the prevailing tendency of my countrymen. I must walk toward Oregon, and not toward Europe. And that way the nation is moving, and I may say that mankind progress from east to west. Within a few years we have witnessed the phenomenon of a southeastward migration, in the settlement of Australia; but this affects us as a retrograde movement, and, judging from the moral and physical character of the first generation of Australians, has not yet proved a successful experiment. The eastern Tartars think that there is nothing west beyond Thibet. "The world ends there," say they; "beyond there is nothing but a shoreless sea." It is unmitigated East where they live.

We go eastward to realize history and study the works of art and literature, retracing the steps of the race; we go westward as into the future, with a spirit of enterprise and adventure. The Atlantic is a Lethean stream, in our passage over which we have had an opportunity to forget the Old World and its institutions. If we do not succeed this time, there is perhaps one more chance for the race left before it arrives on the banks of the Styx; and that is in the Lethe of the Pacific, which is three times as wide.

I know not how significant it is, or how far it is an evidence of singularity, that an individual should thus consent in his pettiest walk with the general movement of the race; but I know that something akin to the migratory instinct in birds and quadrupeds—which, in some instances, is known to have affected the squirrel tribe, impelling them to a general and mysterious movement, in which they were seen, say some, crossing the broadest rivers, each on its particular chip,

with its tail raised for a sail, and bridging narrower streams with their dead—that something like the *furor* which affects the domestic cattle in the spring, and which is referred to a worm in their tails, affects both nations and individuals, either perennially or from time to time. Not a flock of wild geese cackles over our town, but it to some extent unsettles the value of real estate here, and, if I were a broker, I should probably take that disturbance into account.

"Than longen folk to gon on pilgrimages,
And palmeres for to seken strange strondes." [2]

Every sunset which I witness inspires me with the desire to go to a West as distant and as fair as that into which the sun goes down. He appears to migrate westward daily, and tempt us to follow him. He is the Great Western Pioneer whom the nations follow. We dream all night of those mountain-ridges in the horizon, though they may be of vapor only, which were last gilded by his rays. The island of Atlantis, and the islands and gardens of the Hesperides, a sort of terrestrial paradise, appear to have been the Great West of the ancients, enveloped in mystery and poetry. Who has not seen in imagination, when looking into the sunset sky, the gardens of the Hesperides, and the foundation of all those fables?

Columbus felt the westward tendency more strongly than any before. He obeyed it, and found a New World for Castile and León. The herd of men in those days scented fresh pastures from afar.

"And now the sun had stretched out all the hills,
And now was dropped into the western bay;
At last *he* rose, and twitched his mantle blue;
Tomorrow to fresh woods and pastures new." [3]

Where on the globe can there be found an area of equal extent with that occupied by the bulk of our States, so fertile and so rich and varied in its productions, and at the same time so habitable by the European, as this is? Michaux, who knew but part of them, says that "the species of large trees are much more numerous in North America than in Europe; in the United States there are more than one hundred and forty species that exceed thirty feet in height; in France there are but thirty that attain this size." Later botanists more than confirm his observations. Humboldt came to America to realize his youthful dreams of a tropical vegetation, and he beheld it in its greatest perfection in the primitive forests of the Amazon, the most gigantic wilderness on the earth, which he has

---

2. "Than . . . strondes": Chaucer, Prologue to *Canterbury Tales*, ll. 12–13.   3. "And . . . new": John Milton, *Lycidas*, ll. 190–93.

so eloquently described. The geographer Guyot, himself a European, goes farther—farther than I am ready to follow him; yet not when he says: "As the plant is made for the animal, as the vegetable world is made for the animal world, America is made for the man of the Old World. . . . The man of the Old World sets out upon his way. Leaving the highlands of Asia, he descends from station to station towards Europe. Each of his steps is marked by a new civilization superior to the preceding, by a greater power of development. Arrived at the Atlantic, he pauses on the shore of this unknown ocean, the bounds of which he knows not, and turns upon his footprints for an instant." When he has exhausted the rich soil of Europe, and reinvigorated himself, "then recommences his adventurous career westward as in the earliest ages." So far Guyot.

From this western impulse coming in contact with the barrier of the Atlantic sprang the commerce and enterprise of modern times. The younger Michaux, in his *Travels West of the Alleghenies in 1802,* says that the common inquiry in the newly settled West was, " 'From what part of the world have you come?' As if these vast and fertile regions would naturally be the place of meeting and common country of all the inhabitants of the globe."

To use an obsolete Latin word, I might say, *Ex Oriente lux; ex Occidente* FRUX. From the East light; from the West fruit.

Sir Francis Head, an English traveler and a Governor-General of Canada, tells us that "in both the northern and southern hemispheres of the New World, Nature has not only outlined her works on a larger scale, but has painted the whole picture with brighter and more costly colors than she used in delineating and in beautifying the Old World. . . . The heavens of America appear infinitely higher, the sky is bluer, the air is fresher, the cold is intenser, the moon looks larger, the stars are brighter, the thunder is louder, the lightning is vivider, the wind is stronger, the rain is heavier, the mountains are higher, the rivers longer, the forests bigger, the plains broader." This statement will do at least to set against Buffon's account of this part of the world and its productions.

Linnaeus said long ago, "*Nescio quae facies* laeta, glabra *plantis Americanis*" (I know not what there is of joyous and smooth in the aspect of American plants); and I think that in this country there are no, or at most very few, *Africanae bestiae,* African beasts, as the Romans called them, and that in this respect also it is peculiarly fitted for the habitation of man. We are told that within

three miles of the center of the East-Indian city of Singapore, some of the inhabitants are annually carried off by tigers; but the traveler can lie down in the woods at night almost anywhere in North America without fear of wild beasts.

These are encouraging testimonies. If the moon looks larger here than in Europe, probably the sun looks larger also. If the heavens of America appear infinitely higher, and the stars brighter, I trust that these facts are symbolical of the height to which the philosophy and poetry and religion of her inhabitants may one day soar. At length, perchance, the immaterial heaven will appear as much higher to the American mind, and the intimations that star it as much brighter. For I believe that climate does thus react on man—as there is something in the mountain air that feeds the spirit and inspires. Will not man grow to greater perfection intellectually as well as physically under these influences? Or is it unimportant how many foggy days there are in his life? I trust that we shall be more imaginative, that our thoughts will be clearer, fresher, and more ethereal, as our sky—our understanding more comprehensive and broader, like our plains—our intellect generally on a grander scale, like our thunder and lightning, our rivers and mountains and forests—and our hearts shall even correspond in breadth and depth and grandeur to our inland seas. Perchance there will appear to the traveler something, he knows not what, of *laeta* and *glabra,* of joyous and serene, in our very faces. Else to what end does the world go on, and why was America discovered?

To Americans I hardly need to say,

"Westward the star of empire takes its way." [4]

As a true patriot, I should be ashamed to think that Adam in paradise was more favorably situated on the whole than the backwoodsman in this country.

Our sympathies in Massachusetts are not confined to New England; though we may be estranged from the South, we sympathize with the West. There is the home of the younger sons, as among the Scandinavians they took to the sea for their inheritance. It is too late to be studying Hebrew; it is more important to understand even the slang of today.

Some months ago I went to see a panorama of the Rhine. It was like a dream of the Middle Ages. I floated down its historic stream in something more than imagination, under bridges built

4. "Westward . . . way": from the sixth stanza of *Verses on the Prospect of Planting Arts and Learning in America,* by Bishop George Berkeley (1685–1753). Thoreau replaced Berkeley's "course" with "star."

by the Romans, and repaired by later heroes, past cities and castles whose very names were music to my ears, and each of which was the subject of a legend. There were Ehrenbreitstein and Roland-seck and Coblentz, which I knew only in history. They were ruins that interested me chiefly. There seemed to come up from its waters and its vine-clad hills and valleys a hushed music as of Crusaders departing for the Holy Land. I floated along under the spell of enchantment, as if I had been transported to an heroic age, and breathed an atmosphere of chivalry.

Soon after, I went to see a panorama of the Mississippi, and as I worked my way up the river in the light of today, and saw the steamboats wooding up, counted the rising cities, gazed on the fresh ruins of Nauvoo, beheld the Indians moving west across the stream, and, as before I had looked up the Moselle, now looked up the Ohio and the Missouri and heard the legends of Dubuque and of Wenona's Cliff—still thinking more of the future than of the past or present—I saw that this was a Rhine stream of a different kind; that the foundations of castles were yet to be laid, and the famous bridges were yet to be thrown over the river; and I felt that *this was the heroic age itself,* though we know it not, for the hero is commonly the simplest and obscurest of men.

The West of which I speak is but another name for the Wild; and what I have been preparing to say is, that in Wildness is the preservation of the World. Every tree sends its fibers forth in search of the Wild. The cities import it at any price. Men plow and sail for it. From the forest and wilderness come the tonics and barks which brace mankind. Our ancestors were savages. The story of Romulus and Remus being suckled by a wolf is not a meaningless fable. The founders of every state which has risen to eminence have drawn their nourishment and vigor from a similar wild source. It was because the children of the Empire were not suckled by the wolf that they were conquered and displaced by the children of the northern forests who were.

I believe in the forest, and in the meadow, and in the night in which the corn grows. We require an infusion of hemlock, spruce or arbor vitae in our tea. There is a difference between eating and drinking for strength and from mere gluttony. The Hottentots eagerly devour the marrow of the koodoo and other antelopes raw, as a matter of course. Some of our northern Indians eat raw the marrow of the Arctic reindeer, as well as various other parts, including the summits of the antlers, as long as they are soft. And herein, perchance, they have

stolen a march on the cooks of Paris. They get what usually goes to feed the fire. This is probably better than stall-fed beef and slaughterhouse pork to make a man of. Give me a wildness whose glance no civilization can endure—as if we lived on the marrow of koodoos devoured raw.

There are some intervals which border the strain of the wood thrush, to which I would migrate—wild lands where no settler has squatted; to which, methinks, I am already acclimated.

The African hunter Cumming tells us that the skin of the eland, as well as that of most other antelopes just killed, emits the most delicious perfume of trees and grass. I would have every man so much like a wild antelope, so much a part and parcel of nature, that his very person should thus sweetly advertise our senses of his presence, and remind us of those parts of nature which he most haunts. I feel no disposition to be satirical, when the trapper's coat emits the odor of musquash even; it is a sweeter scent to me than that which commonly exhales from the merchant's or the scholar's garments. When I go into their wardrobes and handle their vestments, I am reminded of no grassy plains and flowery meads which they have frequented, but of dusty merchants' exchanges and libraries rather.

A tanned skin is something more than respectable, and perhaps olive is a fitter color than white for a man—a denizen of the woods. "The pale white man!" I do not wonder that the African pitied him. Darwin the naturalist says, "A white man bathing by the side of a Tahitian was like a plant bleached by the gardener's art, compared with a fine, dark green one, growing vigorously in the open fields."

Ben Jonson exclaims,

"How near to the good is what is fair!"

So I would say,

How near to good is what is *wild!*

Life consists with wildness. The most alive is the wildest. Not yet subdued to man, its presence refreshes him. One who pressed forward incessantly and never rested from his labors, who grew fast and made infinite demands on life, would always find himself in a new country or wilderness, and surrounded by the raw material of life. He would be climbing over the prostrate stems of primitive forest-trees.

Hope and the future for me are not in lawns and cultivated fields, not in towns and cities, but in the impervious and quaking swamps. When, formerly, I have analyzed my partiality for some farm which I had contemplated purchasing, I have frequently found that I was attracted solely by a few square rods of impermeable and unfathomable bog—a natural sink in one corner of it. That was the jewel which dazzled me. I derive more of my subsistence from the swamps which surround my native town than from the cultivated gardens in the village. There are no richer parterres to my eyes than the dense beds of dwarf andromeda (*Cassandra calyculata*) which cover these tender places on the earth's surface. Botany cannot go farther than tell me the names of the shrubs which grow there—the high blueberry, panicled andromeda, lambkill, azalea, and rhodora—all standing in the quaking sphagnum. I often think that I should like to have my house front on this mass of dull red bushes, omitting other flower plots and borders, transplanted spruce and trim box, even graveled walks—to have this fertile spot under my windows, not a few imported barrowfuls of soil only to cover the sand which was thrown out in digging the cellar. Why not put my house, my parlor, behind this plot, instead of behind that meager assemblage of curiosities, that poor apology for a Nature and Art, which I call my front yard? It is an effort to clear up and make a decent appearance when the carpenter and mason have departed, though done as much for the passer-by as the dweller within. The most tasteful front-yard fence was never an agreeable object of study to me; the most elaborate ornaments, acorn tops, or what not, soon wearied and disgusted me. Bring your sills up to the very edge of the swamp, then (though it may not be the best place for a dry cellar), so that there be no access on that side to citizens. Front yards are not made to walk in, but, at most, through, and you could go in the back way.

Yes, though you may think me perverse, if it were proposed to me to dwell in the neighborhood of the most beautiful garden that ever human art contrived, or else of a Dismal Swamp, I should certainly decide for the swamp. How vain, then, have been all your labors, citizens, for me!

My spirits infallibly rise in proportion to the outward dreariness. Give me the ocean, the desert, or the wilderness! In the desert, pure air and solitude compensate for want of moisture and fertility. The traveler Burton says of it: "Your *morale* improves; you become frank and cordial, hospitable and single-minded. . . . In the desert, spirituous liquors excite only disgust. There is a keen enjoyment in a mere animal existence." They who have been traveling long on the steppes of Tartary say, "On re-entering cultivated lands, the agitation, perplexity, and turmoil of civilization oppressed and suffocated us; the air seemed to fail us, and we felt every moment as if about to die of asphyxia." When I would recreate myself, I seek the darkest

wood, the thickest and most interminable and, to the citizen, most dismal, swamp. I enter a swamp as a sacred place, a *sanctum sanctorum*. There is the strength, the marrow, of Nature. The wildwood covers the virgin mould, and the same soil is good for men and for trees. A man's health requires as many acres of meadow to his prospect as his farm does loads of muck. There are the strong meats on which he feeds. A town is saved, not more by the righteous men in it than by the woods and swamps that surround it. A township where one primitive forest waves above while another primitive forest rots below—such a town is fitted to raise not only corn and potatoes, but poets and philosophers for the coming ages. In such a soil grew Homer and Confucius and the rest, and out of such a wilderness comes the Reformer eating locusts and wild honey.

To preserve wild animals implies generally the creation of a forest for them to dwell in or resort to. So it is with man. A hundred years ago they sold bark in our streets peeled from our own woods. In the very aspect of those primitive and rugged trees there was, methinks, a tanning principle which hardened and consolidated the fibers of men's thoughts. Ah! already I shudder for these comparatively degenerate days of my native village, when you cannot collect a load of bark of good thickness, and we no longer produce tar and turpentine.

The civilized nations—Greece, Rome, England—have been sustained by the primitive forests which anciently rotted where they stand. They survive as long as the soil is not exhausted. Alas for human culture! little is to be expected of a nation, when the vegetable mould is exhausted, and it is compelled to make manure of the bones of its fathers. There the poet sustains himself merely by his own superfluous fat, and the philosopher comes down on his marrow-bones.

It is said to be the task of the American "to work the virgin soil," and that "agriculture here already assumes proportions unknown everywhere else." I think that the farmer displaces the Indian even because he redeems the meadow, and so makes himself stronger and in some respects more natural. I was surveying for a man the other day a single straight line one hundred and thirty-two rods long, through a swamp at whose entrance might have been written the words which Dante read over the entrance to the infernal regions, "Leave all hope, ye that enter"—that is, of ever getting out again; where at one time I saw my employer actually up to his neck and swimming for his life in his property, though it was still winter. He had another similar swamp which I could not survey at all, because it was completely under water, and nevertheless, with regard to a third swamp, which I did *survey* from a distance, he remarked to me, true to his instincts, that he would not part with it for any consideration, on account of the mud which it contained. And that man intends to put a girdling ditch round the whole in the course of forty months, and so redeem it by the magic of his spade. I refer to him only as the type of a class.

The weapons with which we have gained our most important victories, which should be handed down as heirlooms from father to son, are not the sword and the lance, but the bushwhack, the turf-cutter, the spade, and the bog hoe, rusted with the blood of many a meadow, and begrimed with the dust of many a hard-fought field. The very winds blew the Indian's cornfield into the meadow, and pointed out the way which he had not the skill to follow. He had no better implement with which to intrench himself in the land than a clam-shell. But the farmer is armed with plow and spade.

In literature it is only the wild that attracts us. Dullness is but another name for tameness. It is the uncivilized free and wild thinking in Hamlet and the Iliad, in all the scriptures and mythologies, not learned in the schools, that delights us. As the wild duck is more swift and beautiful than the tame, so is the wild—the mallard—thought, which 'mid falling dews wings its way above the fens. A truly good book is something as natural, and as unexpectedly and unaccountably fair and perfect, as a wild-flower discovered on the prairies of the West or in the jungles of the East. Genius is a light which makes the darkness visible, like the lightning's flash, which perchance shatters the temple of knowledge itself—and not a taper lighted at the hearthstone of the race, which pales before the light of common day.

English literature, from the days of the minstrels to the Lake Poets—Chaucer and Spenser and Milton, and even Shakespeare, included—breathes no quite fresh and, in this sense, wild strain. It is an essentially tame and civilized literature, reflecting Greece and Rome. Her wilderness is a greenwood, her wild man a Robin Hood. There is plenty of genial love of Nature, but not so much of Nature herself. Her chronicles inform us when her wild animals, but not when the wild man in her, became extinct.

The science of Humboldt is one thing, poetry is another thing. The poet today, notwithstanding all the discoveries of science, and the accumulated learning of mankind, enjoys no advantage over Homer.

Where is the literature which gives expression to Nature? He would be a poet who could impress the winds and streams into his service, to speak for him; who nailed words to their primitive senses, as farmers drive down stakes in the spring, which the frost has heaved; who derived his words as often as he used them—transplanted them to his page with earth adhering to their roots; whose words were so true and fresh and natural that they would appear to expand like the buds at the approach of spring, though they lay half smothered between two musty leaves in a library—aye, to bloom and bear fruit there, after their kind, annually, for the faithful reader, in sympathy with surrounding Nature.

I do not know of any poetry to quote which adequately expresses this yearning for the Wild. Approached from this side, the best poetry is tame. I do not know where to find in any literature, ancient or modern, any account which contents me of that Nature with which even I am acquainted. You will perceive that I demand something which no Augustan nor Elizabethan age, which no *culture,* in short, can give. Mythology comes nearer to it than anything. How much more fertile a Nature, at least, has Grecian mythology its root in than English literature! Mythology is the crop which the Old World bore before its soil was exhausted, before the fancy and imagination were affected with blight; and which it still bears, wherever its pristine vigor is unabated. All other literatures endure only as the elms which overshadow our houses; but this is like the great dragon-tree of the Western Isles, as old as mankind, and, whether that does or not, will endure as long; for the decay of other literatures makes the soil in which it thrives.

The West is preparing to add its fables to those of the East. The valleys of the Ganges, the Nile, and the Rhine having yielded their crop, it remains to be seen what the valleys of the Amazon, the Plate, the Orinoco, the St. Lawrence, and the Mississippi will produce. Perchance, when, in the course of ages, American liberty has become a fiction of the past—as it is to some extent a fiction of the present—the poets of the world will be inspired by American mythology.

The wildest dreams of wild men, even, are not the less true, though they may not recommend themselves to the sense which is most common among Englishmen and Americans today. It is not every truth that recommends itself to the common sense. Nature has a place for the wild clematis as well as for the cabbage. Some expressions of truth are reminiscent, others merely *sensible,* as the phrase is, others prophetic. Some forms of disease, even, may prophesy forms of health. The geologist has discovered that the figures of serpents, griffins, flying dragons, and other fanciful embellishments of heraldry, have their prototypes in the forms of fossil species which were extinct before man was created, and hence "indicate a faint and shadowy knowledge of a previous state of organic existence." The Hindus dreamed that the earth rested on an elephant, and the elephant on a tortoise, and the tortoise on a serpent; and though it may be an unimportant coincidence, it will not be out of place here to state, that a fossil tortoise has lately been discovered in Asia large enough to support an elephant. I confess that I am partial to these wild fancies, which transcend the order of time and development. They are the sublimest recreation of the intellect. The partridge loves peas, but not those that go with her into the pot.

In short, all good things are wild and free. There is something in a strain of music, whether produced by an instrument or by the human voice—take the sound of a bugle in a summer night, for instance—which by its wildness, to speak without satire, reminds me of the cries emitted by wild beasts in their native forests. It is so much of their wildness as I can understand. Give me for my friends and neighbors wild men, not tame ones. The wildness of the savage is but a faint symbol of the awful ferity with which good men and lovers meet.

I love even to see the domestic animals reassert their native rights—any evidence that they have not wholly lost their original wild habits and vigor; as when my neighbor's cow breaks out of her pasture early in the spring and boldly swims the river, a cold, gray tide, twenty-five or thirty rods wide, swollen by the melted snow. It is the buffalo crossing the Mississippi. This exploit confers some dignity on the herd in my eyes—already dignified. The seeds of instinct are preserved under the thick hides of cattle and horses, like seeds in the bowels of the earth, an indefinite period.

Any sportiveness in cattle is unexpected. I saw one day a herd of a dozen bullocks and cows running about and frisking in unwieldy sport, like huge rats, even like kittens. They shook their heads, raised their tails, and rushed up and down a hill, and I perceived by their horns, as well as by their activity, their relation to the deer tribe. But, alas! a sudden loud *Whoa!* would have damped their ardor at once, reduced them from venison to beef, and stiffened their sides and sinews like the locomotive. Who but the Evil One has cried "Whoa!" to mankind? Indeed, the life of cattle, like that of many men, is but a sort of locomotiveness; they move a side at a time, and man, by his

machinery, is meeting the horse and the ox halfway. Whatever part the whip has touched is thenceforth palsied. Who would ever think of a *side* of any of the supple cat tribe, as we speak of a *side* of beef?

I rejoice that horses and steers have to be broken before they can be made the slaves of men, and that men themselves have some wild oats still left to sow before they become submissive members of society. Undoubtedly, all men are not equally fit subjects for civilization; and because the majority, like dogs and sheep, are tame by inherited disposition, this is no reason why the others should have their natures broken that they may be reduced to the same level. Men are in the main alike, but they were made several in order that they might be various. If a low use is to be served, one man will do nearly or quite as well as another; if a high one, individual excellence is to be regarded. Any man can stop a hole to keep the wind away, but no other man could serve so rare a use as the author of this illustration did. Confucius says, "The skins of the tiger and the leopard, when they are tanned, are as the skins of the dog and the sheep tanned." But it is not the part of a true culture to tame tigers, any more than it is to make sheep ferocious; and tanning their skins for shoes is not the best use to which they can be put.

When looking over a list of men's names in a foreign language, as of military officers, or of authors who have written on a particular subject, I am reminded once more that there is nothing in a name. The name Menschikoff, for instance, has nothing in it to my ears more human than a whisker, and it may belong to a rat. As the names of the Poles and Russians are to us, so are ours to them. It is as if they had been named by the child's rigmarole, *Iery wiery ichery van, tittle-tol-tan.* I see in my mind a herd of wild creatures swarming over the earth, and to each the herdsman has affixed some barbarous sound in his own dialect. The names of men are, of course, as cheap and meaningless as *Bose* and *Tray,* the names of dogs.

Methinks it would be some advantage to philosophy if men were named merely in the gross, as they are known. It would be necessary only to know the genus and perhaps the race or variety, to know the individual. We are not prepared to believe that every private soldier in a Roman army had a name of his own—because we have not supposed that he had a character of his own.

At present our only true names are nicknames. I knew a boy who, from his peculiar energy, was called "Buster" by his playmates, and this rightly supplanted his Christian name. Some travelers tell us that an Indian had no name given him at first, but earned it, and his name was his fame; and among some tribes he acquired a new name with every new exploit. It is pitiful when a man bears a name for convenience merely, who has earned neither name nor fame.

I will not allow mere names to make distinctions for me, but still see men in herds for all them. A familiar name cannot make a man less strange to me. It may be given to a savage who retains in secret his own wild title earned in the woods. We have a wild savage in us, and a savage name is perchance somewhere recorded as ours. I see that my neighbor, who bears the familiar epithet William or Edwin, takes it off with his jacket. It does not adhere to him when asleep or in anger, or aroused by any passion or inspiration. I seem to hear pronounced by some of his kin at such a time his original wild name in some jaw-breaking or else melodious tongue.

Here is this vast, savage, howling mother of ours, Nature, lying all around, with such beauty, and such affection for her children, as the leopard; and yet we are so early weaned from her breast to society, to that culture which is exclusively an interaction of man on man—a sort of breeding in and in, which produces at most a merely English nobility, a civilization destined to have a speedy limit.

In society, in the best institutions of men, it is easy to detect a certain precocity. When we should still be growing children, we are already little men. Give me a culture which imports much muck from the meadows, and deepens the soil—not that which trusts to heating manures, and improved implements and modes of culture only!

Many a poor sore-eyed student that I have heard of would grow faster, both intellectually and physically, if, instead of sitting up so very late, he honestly slumbered a fool's allowance.

There may be an excess even of informing light. Niepce, a Frenchman, discovered "actinism," that power in the sun's rays which produces a chemical effect; that granite rocks, and stone structures, and statues of metal "are all alike destructively acted upon during the hours of sunshine, and, but for provisions of Nature no less wonderful, would soon perish under the delicate touch of the most subtile of the agencies of the universe." But he observed that "those bodies which underwent this change during the daylight possessed the power of restoring themselves to their original conditions during the hours of night, when this excitement was no longer influencing them." Hence it has been inferred that "the hours of darkness are as necessary to the inorganic creation as we know

night and sleep are to the organic kingdom." Not even does the moon shine every night, but gives place to darkness.

I would not have every man nor every part of a man cultivated, any more than I would have every acre of earth cultivated: part will be tillage, but the greater part will be meadow and forest, not only serving an immediate use, but preparing a mould against a distant future, by the annual decay of the vegetation which it supports.

There are other letters for the child to learn than those which Cadmus invented. The Spaniards have a good term to express this wild and dusky knowledge, *Gramática parda,* tawny grammar, a kind of mother-wit derived from that same leopard to which I have referred.

We have heard of a Society for the Diffusion of Useful Knowledge. It is said that knowledge is power, and the like. Methinks there is equal need of a Society for the Diffusion of Useful Ignorance, what we will call Beautiful Knowledge, a knowledge useful in a higher sense: for what is most of our boasted so-called knowledge but a conceit that we know something, which robs us of the advantage of our actual ignorance? What we call knowledge is often our positive ignorance; ignorance our negative knowledge. By long years of patient industry and reading of the newspapers—for what are the libraries of science but files of newspapers? —a man accumulates a myriad facts, lays them up in his memory, and then when in some spring of his life he saunters abroad into the Great Fields of thought, he, as it were, goes to grass like a horse and leaves all his harness behind in the stable. I would say to the Society for the Diffusion of Useful Knowledge, sometimes, Go to grass. You have eaten hay long enough. The spring has come with its green crop. The very cows are driven to their country pastures before the end of May; though I have heard of one unnatural farmer who kept his cow in the barn and fed her on hay all the year round. So, frequently, the Society for the Diffusion of Useful Knowledge treats its cattle.

A man's ignorance sometimes is not only useful, but beautiful—while his knowledge, so called, is oftentimes worse than useless, besides being ugly. Which is the best man to deal with—he who knows nothing about a subject, and, what is extremely rare, knows that he knows nothing, or he who really knows something about it, but thinks that he knows all?

My desire for knowledge is intermittent, but my desire to bathe my head in atmospheres unknown to my feet is perennial and constant. The highest that we can attain to is not Knowledge, but Sympathy with Intelligence. I do not know that this higher knowledge amounts to anything more definite than a novel and grand surprise on a sudden revelation of the insufficiency of all that we called Knowledge before—a discovery that there are more things in heaven and earth than are dreamed of in our philosophy. It is the lighting up of the mist by the sun. Man cannot *know* in any higher sense than this, any more than he can look serenely and with impunity in the face of the sun: Ὡς τὶ νοῶν, οὐ χεῖνον νοήσεις, "You will not perceive that, as perceiving a particular thing," say the Chaldean Oracles.

There is something servile in the habit of seeking after a law which we may obey. We may study the laws of matter at and for our convenience, but a successful life knows no law. It is an unfortunate discovery certainly, that of a law which binds us where we did not know before that we were bound. Live free, child of the mist—and with respect to knowledge we are all children of the mist. The man who takes the liberty to live is superior to all the laws, by virtue of his relation to the lawmaker. "That is active duty," says the Vishnu Purana, "which is not for our bondage; that is knowledge which is for our liberation: all other duty is good only unto weariness; all other knowledge is only the cleverness of an artist."

It is remarkable how few events or crises there are in our histories, how little exercised we have been in our minds, how few experiences we have had. I would fain be assured that I am growing apace and rankly, though my very growth disturb this dull equanimity—though it be with struggle through long, dark, muggy nights or seasons of gloom. It would be well if all our lives were a divine tragedy even, instead of this trivial comedy or farce. Dante, Bunyan, and others appear to have been exercised in their minds more than we: they were subjected to a kind of culture such as our district schools and colleges do not contemplate. Even Mahomet, though many may scream at his name, had a good deal more to live for, aye, and to die for, than they have commonly.

When, at rare intervals, some thought visits one, as perchance he is walking on a railroad, then, indeed, the cars go by without his hearing them. But soon, by some inexorable law, our life goes by and the cars return.

"Gentle breeze, that wanderest unseen,
  And bendest the thistles round Loira of storms,
  Traveler of the windy glens,
  Why hast thou left my ear so soon?"

While almost all men feel an attraction drawing them to society, few are attracted strongly to Nature. In their reaction to Nature men appear to me for the most part, notwithstanding their arts, lower than the animals. It is not often a beautiful relation, as in the case of the animals. How little appreciation of the beauty of the landscape there is among us! We have to be told that the Greeks called the world Κόσμος, Beauty, or Order, but we do not see clearly why they did so, and we esteem it at best only a curious philological fact.

For my part, I feel that with regard to Nature I live a sort of border life, on the confines of a world into which I make occasional and transient forays only, and my patriotism and allegiance to the state into whose territories I seem to retreat are those of a moss-trooper. Unto a life which I call natural I would gladly follow even a will-o'-the-wisp through bogs and sloughs unimaginable, but no moon nor firefly has shown me the causeway to it. Nature is a personality so vast and universal that we have never seen one of her features. The walker in the familiar fields which stretch around my native town sometimes finds himself in another land than is described in their owners' deeds, as it were in some faraway field on the confines of the actual Concord, where her jurisdiction ceases, and the idea which the word Concord suggests ceases to be suggested. These farms which I have myself surveyed, these bounds which I have set up, appear dimly still as through a mist; but they have no chemistry to fix them; they fade from the surface of the glass, and the picture which the painter painted stands out dimly from beneath. The world with which we are commonly acquainted leaves no trace, and it will have no anniversary.

I took a walk on Spaulding's Farm the other afternoon. I saw the setting sun lighting up the opposite side of a stately pine wood. Its golden rays straggled into the aisles of the wood as into some noble hall. I was impressed as if some ancient and altogether admirable and shining family had settled there in that part of the land called Concord, unknown to me—to whom the sun was servant—who had not gone into society in the village—who had not been called on. I saw their park, their pleasure-ground, beyond through the wood, in Spaulding's cranberry-meadow. The pines furnished them with gables as they grew. Their house was not obvious to vision; the trees grew through it. I do not know whether I heard the sounds of a suppressed hilarity or not. They seemed to recline on the sunbeams. They have sons and daughters. They are quite well. The farmer's cart-path, which leads directly through their hall, does not in the least put them out, as the muddy bottom of a pool is sometimes seen through the reflected skies. They never heard of Spaulding, and do not know that he is their neighbor—notwithstanding I heard him whistle as he drove his team through the house. Nothing can equal the serenity of their lives. Their coat-of-arms is simply a lichen. I saw it painted on the pines and oaks. Their attics were in the tops of the trees. They are of no politics. There was no noise of labor. I did not perceive that they were weaving or spinning. Yet I did detect, when the wind lulled and hearing was done away, the finest imaginable sweet musical hum—as of a distant hive in May— which perchance was the sound of their thinking. They had no idle thoughts, and no one without could see their work, for their industry was not as in knots and excrescences embayed.

But I find it difficult to remember them. They fade irrevocably out of my mind even now while I speak, and endeavor to recall them and recollect myself. It is only after a long and serious effort to recollect my best thoughts that I become again aware of their cohabitancy. If it were not for such families as this, I think I should move out of Concord.

We are accustomed to say in New England that few and fewer pigeons visit us every year. Our forests furnish no mast for them. So, it would seem, few and fewer thoughts visit each growing man from year to year, for the grove in our minds is laid waste—sold to feed unnecessary fires of ambition, or sent to mill—and there is scarcely a twig left for them to perch on. They no longer build nor breed with us. In some more genial season, perchance, a faint shadow flits across the landscape of the mind, cast by the *wings* of some thought in its vernal or autumnal migration, but, looking up, we are unable to detect the substance of the thought itself. Our winged thoughts are turned to poultry. They no longer soar, and they attain only to a Shanghai and Cochin-China grandeur. Those *gra-a-ate thoughts,* those *gra-a-ate men* you hear of!

We hug the earth—how rarely we mount! Methinks we might elevate ourselves a little more. We might climb a tree, at least. I found my account in climbing a tree once. It was a tall white pine, on the top of a hill; and though I got well pitched, I was well paid for it, for I discovered new mountains in the horizon which I had never seen before—so much more of the earth and the heavens. I might have walked about the foot of the tree for threescore years and ten, and yet I certainly should never have seen them. But, above all, I discovered around me—it was near the end of June—on the ends of the topmost branches only, a few minute and delicate red conelike blossoms, the fertile flower of the white pine looking heavenward. I carried straightway to the village the topmost spire, and

showed it to stranger jurymen who walked the streets—for it was court week—and to farmers and lumber-dealers and woodchoppers and hunters, and not one had ever seen the like before, but they wondered as at a star dropped down. Tell of ancient architects finishing their works on the tops of columns as perfectly as on the lower and more visible parts! Nature has from the first expanded the minute blossoms of the forest only toward the heavens, above men's heads and unobserved by them. We see only the flowers that are under our feet in the meadows. The pines have developed their delicate blossoms on the highest twigs of the wood every summer for ages, as well over the heads of Nature's red children as of her white ones; yet scarcely a farmer or hunter in the land has ever seen them.

Above all, we cannot afford not to live in the present. He is blessed over all mortals who loses no moment of the passing life in remembering the past. Unless our philosophy hears the cock crow in every barnyard within our horizon, it is belated. That sound commonly reminds us that we are growing rusty and antique in our employments and habits of thought. His philosophy comes down to a more recent time than ours. There is something suggested by it that is a newer testament—the gospel according to this moment. He has not fallen astern; he has got up early and kept up early, and to be where he is is to be in season, in the foremost rank of time. It is an expression of the health and soundness of Nature, a brag for all the world— healthiness as of a spring burst forth, a new fountain of the Muses, to celebrate this last instant of time. Where he lives no fugitive slave laws are passed. Who has not betrayed his master many times since last he heard that note?

The merit of this bird's strain is in its freedom from all plaintiveness. The singer can easily move us to tears or to laughter, but where is he who can excite in us a pure morning joy? When, in doleful dumps, breaking the awful stillness of our wooden sidewalk on a Sunday, or, perchance, a watcher in the house of mourning, I hear a cockerel crow far or near, I think to myself, "There is one of us well, at any rate," and with a sudden gush return to my senses.

We had a remarkable sunset one day last November. I was walking in a meadow, the source of a small brook, when the sun at last, just before setting, after a cold, gray day, reached a clear stratum in the horizon, and the softest, brightest morning sunlight fell on the dry grass and on the stems of the trees in the opposite horizon and on the leaves of the shrub oaks on the hillside, while our shadows stretched long over the meadow eastward, as if we were the only motes in its beams. It was such a light as we could not have imagined a moment before, and the air also was so warm and serene that nothing was wanting to make a paradise of that meadow. When we reflected that this was not a solitary phenomenon, never to happen again, but that it would happen forever and ever, an infinite number of evenings, and cheer and reassure the latest child that walked there, it was more glorious still.

The sun sets on some retired meadow, where no house is visible, with all the glory and splendor that it lavishes on cities, and perchance as it has never set before—where there is but a solitary marsh hawk to have his wings gilded by it, or only a musquash looks out from his cabin, and there is some little black-veined brook in the midst of the marsh, just beginning to meander, winding slowly round a decaying stump. We walked in so pure and bright a light, gilding the withered grass and leaves, so softly and serenely bright, I thought I had never bathed in such a golden flood, without a ripple or a murmur to it. The west side of every wood and rising ground gleamed like the boundary of Elysium, and the sun on our backs seemed like a gentle herdsman driving us home at evening.

So we saunter toward the Holy Land, till one day the sun shall shine more brightly than ever he has done, shall perchance shine into our minds and hearts, and light up our whole lives with a great awakening light, as warm and serene and golden as on a bankside in autumn.

F R O M

# WALDEN

❖

❖[ THE SECOND chapter of Thoreau's masterpiece— which was published in 1854—contrasts the serene fullness of life at the Pond with the frenetic dissatisfactions of town life he had described in the first chapter. "Where I Lived" also includes one of Thoreau's most eloquent assertions of the importance of leading a Transcendental life: "We are able to apprehend at all what is sublime and noble only by the perpetual instilling and drenching of the reality that surrounds us."

❖

## WHERE I LIVED AND WHAT I LIVED FOR

AT A CERTAIN season of our life we are accustomed to consider every spot as the possible site of a house. I have thus surveyed the country on every side within a dozen miles of where I live. In imagination I have bought all the farms in succession, for all were to be bought, and I knew their price. I walked over each farmer's premises, tasted his wild apples, discoursed on husbandry with him, took his farm at his price, at any price, mortgaging it to him in my mind; even put a higher price on it—took everything but a deed of it—took his word for his deed, for I dearly loved to talk—cultivated it, and him too to some extent, I trust, and withdrew when I had enjoyed it long enough, leaving him to carry it on. This experience entitled me to be regarded as a sort of real-estate broker by my friends. Wherever I sat, there I might live, and the landscape radiated from me accordingly. What is a house but a *sedes,* a seat?—better if a country seat. I discovered many a site for a house not likely to be soon improved, which some might have thought too far from the village, but to my eyes the village was too far from it. Well, there I might live, I said; and there I did live, for an hour, a summer and a winter life; saw how I could let the years run off, buffet the winter through, and see the spring come in. The future inhabitants of this region, wherever they may place their houses, may be sure that they have been anticipated. An afternoon sufficed to lay out the land into orchard, woodlot, and pasture, and to decide what fine oaks or pines should be left to stand before the door, and whence each blasted tree could be seen to the best advantage; and then I let it lie, fallow perchance, for a man is rich in proportion to the number of things which he can afford to let alone.

My imagination carried me so far that I even had the refusal of several farms—the refusal was all I wanted—but I never got my fingers burned by actual possession. The nearest that I came to actual possession was when I bought the Hollowell place, and had begun to sort my seeds, and collected materials with which to make a wheelbarrow to carry it on or off with; but before the owner gave me a deed of it, his wife—every man has such a wife— changed her mind and wished to keep it, and he offered me ten dollars to release him. Now, to speak the truth, I had but ten cents in the world, and it surpassed my arithmetic to tell, if I was that man who had ten cents, or who had a farm, or ten dollars, or all together. However, I let him keep the ten dollars and the farm too, for I had carried it far enough; or rather, to be generous, I sold him the farm for just what I gave for it, and, as he was not a rich man, made him a present of ten dollars, and still had my ten cents, and seeds, and materials for a wheelbarrow left. I found thus that I had been a rich man without any damage to my poverty. But I retained the landscape, and I have since annually carried off what it yielded without a wheelbarrow. With respect to landscapes,

> "I am monarch of all I *survey,*
> My right there is none to dispute." [1]

I have frequently seen a poet withdraw, having enjoyed the most valuable part of a farm, while the crusty farmer supposed that he had got a few wild apples only. Why, the owner does not know it for many years when a poet has put his farm in rhyme, the most admirable kind of invisible fence, has fairly impounded it, milked it, skimmed it, and got all the cream, and left the farmer only the skimmed milk.

The real attractions of the Hollowell farm, to me, were: its complete retirement, being about two miles from the village, half a mile from the nearest neighbor, and separated from the highway by a broad field; its bounding on the river, which the owner said protected it by its fogs from frosts in the spring, though that was nothing to me; the gray color and ruinous state of the house and barn, and the dilapidated fences, which put such an interval between me and the last occupant; the hollow and lichen-covered apple trees, gnawed by rabbits, showing what kind of neighbors I should have; but above all, the recollection I had of it from my earliest voyages up the river, when the house was concealed behind a dense grove of red maples, through which I heard the house-dog bark. I was in haste to buy it, before the proprietor finished getting out some rocks, cutting down the hollow apple trees, and grubbing up some young birches which had sprung up in the pasture, or, in short, had made any more of his improvements. To enjoy these advantages I was ready to carry it on; like Atlas, to take the world on my shoulders—I never heard what compensation he received for that—and do all those things which had no other motive or excuse but that I might pay for it and be unmolested in my possession of it; for I knew all the while that it would yield the most abundant crop of the kind I wanted if I could only afford to let it alone. But it turned out as I have said.

All that I could say, then, with respect to farm-

ing on a large scale (I have always cultivated a garden), was, that I had had my seeds ready. Many think that seeds improve with age. I have no doubt that time discriminates between the good and the bad; and when at last I shall plant, I shall be less likely to be disappointed. But I would say to my fellows, once for all, As long as possible live free and uncommitted. It makes but little difference whether you are committed to a farm or the county jail.

Old Cato, whose *De Re Rusticâ* is my "Cultivator," says, and the only translation I have seen makes sheer nonsense of the passage, "When you think of getting a farm turn it thus in your mind, not to buy greedily; nor spare your pains to look at it, and do not think it enough to go round it once. The oftener you go there the more it will please you, if it is good." I think I shall not buy greedily, but go round and round it as long as I live, and be buried in it first, that it may please me the more at last.

The present was my next experiment of this kind, which I purpose to describe more at length, for convenience, putting the experience of two years into one. As I have said, I do not propose to write an ode to dejection, but to brag as lustily as chanticleer in the morning, standing on his roost, if only to wake my neighbors up.

When first I took up my abode in the woods, that is, began to spend my nights as well as days there, which, by accident, was on Independence Day, or the Fourth of July, 1845, my house was not finished for winter, but was merely a defense against the rain, without plastering or chimney, the walls being of rough weather-stained boards, with wide chinks, which made it cool at night. The upright white hewn studs and freshly planed door and window casings gave it a clean and airy look, especially in the morning, when its timbers were saturated with dew, so that I fancied that by noon some sweet gum would exude from them. To my imagination it retained throughout the day more or less of this auroral character, reminding me of a certain house on a mountain which I had visited a year before. This was an airy and unplastered cabin, fit to entertain a traveling god, and where a goddess might trail her garments. The winds which passed over my dwelling were such as sweep over the ridges of mountains, bearing the broken strains, or celestial parts only, of terrestrial music. The morning wind forever blows, the poem of creation is uninterrupted; but few are the ears that hear it. Olympus is but the outside of the earth everywhere.

The only house I had been the owner of before,

WALDEN.    1. "I . . . dispute": from the first stanza of "Verses Supposed to be Written by Alexander Selkirk," by William Cowper (1731–1800). Selkirk was the prototype Defoe had in mind when he wrote *Robinson Crusoe.*

if I except a boat, was a tent, which I used occasionally when making excursions in the summer, and this is still rolled up in my garret; but the boat, after passing from hand to hand, has gone down the stream of time. With this more substantial shelter about me, I had made some progress toward settling in the world. This frame, so slightly clad, was a sort of crystallization around me, and reacted on the builder. It was suggestive somewhat as a picture in outlines. I did not need to go outdoors to take the air, for the atmosphere within had lost none of its freshness. It was not so much within doors as behind a door where I sat, even in the rainiest weather. The Harivansa says, "An abode without birds is like a meat without seasoning." Such was not my abode, for I found myself suddenly neighbor to the birds; not by having imprisoned one, but having caged myself near them. I was not only nearer to some of those which commonly frequent the garden and the orchard, but to those wilder and more thrilling songsters of the forest which never, or rarely, serenade a villager—the wood-thrush, the veery, the scarlet tanager, the field-sparrow, the whippoorwill, and many others.

I was seated by the shore of a small pond, about a mile and a half south of the village of Concord and somewhat higher than it, in the midst of an extensive wood between that town and Lincoln, and about two miles south of that our only field known to fame, Concord Battle Ground; but I was so low in the woods that the opposite shore, half a mile off, like the rest, covered with wood, was my most distant horizon. For the first week, whenever I looked out on the pond it impressed me like a tarn high up on the side of a mountain, its bottom far above the surface of other lakes, and, as the sun arose, I saw it throwing off its nightly clothing of mist, and here and there, by degrees, its soft ripples or its smooth reflecting surface was revealed, while the mists, like ghosts, were stealthily withdrawing in every direction into the woods, as at the breaking up of some nocturnal conventicle. The very dew seemed to hang upon the trees later into the day than usual, as on the sides of mountains.

This small lake was of most value as a neighbor in the intervals of a gentle rainstorm in August, when, both air and water being perfectly still, but the sky overcast, mid-afternoon had all the serenity of evening, and the wood-thrush sang around, and was heard from shore to shore. A lake like this is never smoother than at such a time; and the clear portion of the air above it being shallow and darkened by clouds, the water, full of light and reflections, becomes a lower heaven itself so much the more important. From a hilltop near by, where the wood had been recently cut off, there was a pleasing vista southward across the pond, through a wide indentation in the hills which form the shore there, where their opposite sides sloping toward each other suggested a stream flowing out in that direction through a wooded valley, but stream there was none. That way I looked between and over the near green hills to some distant and higher ones in the horizon, tinged with blue. Indeed, by standing on tiptoe I could catch a glimpse of some of the peaks of the still bluer and more distant mountain ranges in the northwest, those true-blue coins from heaven's own mint, and also of some portion of the village. But in other directions, even from this point, I could not see over or beyond the woods which surrounded me. It is well to have some water in your neighborhood, to give buoyancy to and float the earth. One value even of the smallest well is, that when you look into it you see that earth is not continent but insular. This is as important as that it keeps butter cool. When I looked across the pond from this peak toward the Sudbury meadows, which in time of flood I distinguished elevated perhaps by a mirage in their seething valley, like a coin in a basin, all the earth beyond the pond appeared like a thin crust insulated and floated even by this small sheet of intervening water, and I was reminded that this on which I dwelt was but *dry land*.

Though the view from my door was still more contracted, I did not feel crowded or confined in the least. There was pasture enough for my imagination. The low shrub-oak plateau to which the opposite shore arose, stretched away toward the prairies of the West and the steppes of Tartary, affording ample room for all the roving families of men. "There are none happy in the world but beings who enjoy freely a vast horizon," said Damodara, when his herds required new and larger pastures.

Both place and time were changed, and I dwelt nearer to those parts of the universe and to those eras in history which had most attracted me. Where I lived was as far off as many a region viewed nightly by astronomers. We are wont to imagine rare and delectable places in some remote and more celestial corner of the system, behind the constellation of Cassiopeia's Chair, far from noise and disturbance. I discovered that my house actually had its site in such a withdrawn, but forever new and unprofaned, part of the universe. If it were worth the while to settle in those parts near to the Pleiades or the Hyades, to Aldebaran or Altair, then I was really there, or at an equal remoteness from the life which I had left behind, dwindled and twinkling with as fine a ray to my nearest neighbor, and to be seen only in moonless nights by him. Such was that part of creation where I had squatted;

> "There was a shepherd that did live,
> And held his thoughts as high
> As were the mounts whereon his flocks
> Did hourly feed him by."

What should we think of the shepherd's life if his flocks always wandered to higher pastures than his thoughts?

Every morning was a cheerful invitation to make my life of equal simplicity, and I may say innocence, with Nature herself. I have been as sincere a worshiper of Aurora as the Greeks. I got up early and bathed in the pond; that was a religious exercise, and one of the best things which I did. They say that characters were engraven on the bathing tub of King Tching-thang to this effect: "Renew thyself completely each day; do it again, and again, and forever again." I can understand that. Morning brings back the heroic ages. I was as much affected by the faint hum of a mosquito making its invisible and unimaginable tour through my apartment at earliest dawn, when I was sitting with door and windows open, as I could be by any trumpet that ever sang of fame. It was Homer's requiem; itself an Iliad and Odyssey in the air, singing its own wrath and wanderings. There was something cosmical about it; a standing advertisement, till forbidden, of the everlasting vigor and fertility of the world. The morning, which is the most memorable season of the day, is the awakening hour. Then there is least somnolence in us; and for an hour, at least, some part of us awakes which slumbers all the rest of the day and night. Little is to be expected of that day, if it can be called a day, to which we are not awakened by our Genius, but by the mechanical nudgings of some servitor, are not awakened by our own newly acquired force and aspirations from within, accompanied by the undulations of celestial music, instead of factory bells, and a fragrance filling the air—to a higher life than we fell asleep from; and thus the darkness bear its fruit, and prove itself to be good, no less than the light. That man who does not believe that each day contains an earlier, more sacred and auroral hour than he has yet profaned, has despaired of life, and is pursuing a descending and darkening way. After a partial cessation of his sensuous life, the soul of man, or its organs rather, are reinvigorated each day, and his Genius tries again what noble life it can make. All memorable events, I should say, transpire in morning time and in a morning atmosphere. The Vedas say, "All intelligences awake with the morning." Poetry and art,

and the fairest and most memorable of the actions of men, date from such an hour. All poets and heroes, like Memnon, are the children of Aurora, and emit their music at sunrise. To him whose elastic and vigorous thought keeps pace with the sun, the day is a perpetual morning. It matters not what the clocks say or the attitudes and labors of men. Morning is when I am awake and there is a dawn in me. Moral reform is the effort to throw off sleep. Why is it that men give so poor an account of their day if they have not been slumbering? They are not such poor calculators. If they had not been overcome with drowsiness they would have performed something. The millions are awake enough for physical labor; but only one in a million is awake enough for effective intellectual exertion, only one in a hundred millions to a poetic or divine life. To be awake is to be alive. I have never yet met a man who was quite awake. How could I have looked him in the face?

We must learn to reawaken and keep ourselves awake, not by mechanical aids, but by an infinite expectation of the dawn, which does not forsake us in our soundest sleep. I know of no more encouraging fact than the unquestionable ability of man to elevate his life by a conscious endeavor. It is something to be able to paint a particular picture, or to carve a statue, and so to make a few objects beautiful; but it is far more glorious to carve and paint the very atmosphere and medium through which we look, which morally we can do. To affect the quality of the day, that is the highest of arts. Every man is tasked to make his life, even in its details, worthy of the contemplation of his most elevated and critical hour. If we refused, or rather used up, such paltry information as we get, the oracles would distinctly inform us how this might be done.

I went to the woods because I wished to live deliberately, to front only the essential facts of life, and see if I could not learn what it had to teach, and not, when I came to die, discover that I had not lived. I did not wish to live what was not life, living is so dear; nor did I wish to practice resignation, unless it was quite necessary. I wanted to live deep and suck out all the marrow of life, to live so sturdily and Spartan-like as to put to rout all that was not life, to cut a broad swath and shave close, to drive life into a corner, and reduce it to its lowest terms, and, if it proved to be mean, why then to get the whole and genuine meanness of it, and publish its meanness to the world; or if it were sublime, to know it by experience, and be able to give a true account of it in my next excursion. For most men, it appears to me, are in a strange uncertainty about it, whether it is of the devil or of God, and have *somewhat hastily* concluded that it is the chief end of man here to "glorify God and enjoy him forever."

Still we live meanly, like ants; though the fable tells us that we were long ago changed into men; like pygmies we fight with cranes; it is error upon error, and clout upon clout, and our best virtue has for its occasion a superfluous and evitable wretchedness. Our life is frittered away by detail. An honest man has hardly need to count more than his ten fingers, or in extreme cases he may add his ten toes, and lump the rest. Simplicity, simplicity, simplicity! I say, let your affairs be as two or three, and not a hundred or a thousand; instead of a million count half a dozen, and keep your accounts on your thumb nail. In the midst of this chopping sea of civilized life, such are the clouds and storms and quicksands and thousand-and-one items to be allowed for, that a man has to live, if he would not founder and go to the bottom and not make his port at all, by dead reckoning, and he must be a great calculator indeed who succeeds. Simplify, simplify. Instead of three meals a day, if it be necessary eat but one; instead of a hundred dishes, five; and reduce other things in proportion. Our life is like a German Confederacy, made up of petty states, with its boundary forever fluctuating, so that even a German cannot tell you how it is bounded at any moment. The nation itself, with all its so-called internal improvements, which, by the way are all external and superficial, is just such an unwieldy and overgrown establishment, cluttered with furniture and tripped up by its own traps, ruined by luxury and heedless expense, by want of calculation and a worthy aim, as the million households in the land; and the only cure for it as for them is in a rigid economy, a stern and more than Spartan simplicity of life and elevation of purpose. It lives too fast. Men think that it is essential that the *Nation* have commerce, and export ice, and talk through a telegraph, and ride thirty miles an hour, without a doubt, whether *they* do or not; but whether we should live like baboons or like men, is a little uncertain. If we do not get out sleepers, and forge rails, and devote days and nights to the work, but go to tinkering upon our *lives* to improve *them*, who will build railroads? And if railroads are not built, how shall we get to heaven in season? But if we stay at home and mind our business, who will want railroads? We do not ride on the railroad; it rides upon us. Did you ever think what those sleepers [2] are that underlie the railroad? Each one is a man, an Irishman, or a Yankee man. The rails are laid on them, and they are covered with sand, and the cars run smoothly over them. They are sound sleepers, I assure you. And every few years a new

lot is laid down and run over; so that, if some have the pleasure of riding on a rail, others have the misfortune to be ridden upon. And when they run over a man that is walking in his sleep, a supernumerary sleeper in the wrong position, and wake him up, they suddenly stop the cars, and make a hue and cry about it, as if this were an exception. I am glad to know that it takes a gang of men for every five miles to keep the sleepers down and level in their beds as it is, for this is a sign that they may sometime get up again.

Why should we live with such hurry and waste of life? We are determined to be starved before we are hungry. Men say that a stitch in time saves nine, and so they take a thousand stitches today to save nine tomorrow. As for *work*, we haven't any of any consequence. We have the Saint Vitus' dance, and cannot possibly keep our heads still. If I should only give a few pulls at the parish bell-rope, as for a fire, that is, without setting the bell, there is hardly a man on his farm in the outskirts of Concord, notwithstanding that press of engagements which was his excuse so many times this morning, nor a boy, nor a woman, I might almost say, but would forsake all and follow that sound, not mainly to save property from the flames, but, if we will confess the truth, much more to see it burn, since burn it must, and we, be it known, did not set it on fire—or to see it put out, and have a hand in it, if that is done as handsomely; yes, even if it were the parish church itself. Hardly a man takes a half hour's nap after dinner, but when he wakes he holds up his head and asks, "What's the news?" as if the rest of mankind had stood his sentinels. Some give directions to be waked every half hour, doubtless for no other purpose; and then, to pay for it, they tell what they have dreamed. After a night's sleep the news is as indispensable as the breakfast. "Pray tell me anything new that has happened to a man anywhere on this globe"—and he reads it over his coffee and rolls, that a man has had his eyes gouged out this morning on the Wachito River; never dreaming the while that he lives in the dark unfathomed mammoth cave of this world, and has but the rudiment of an eye himself.

For my part, I could easily do without the post-office. I think that there are very few important communications made through it. To speak critically, I never received more than one or two letters in my life—I wrote this some years ago—that were worth the postage. The penny-post is, commonly, an institution through which you seriously offer a man that penny for his thoughts which is so often safely offered in jest. And I am sure that I never read any memorable news in a newspaper. If we

2. sleepers: railroad ties.

read of one man robbed, or murdered, or killed by accident, or one house burned, or one vessel wrecked, or one steamboat blown up, or one cow run over on the Western Railroad, or one mad dog killed, or one lot of grasshoppers in the winter—we never need read of another. One is enough. If you are acquainted with the principle, what do you care for a myriad instances and applications? To a philosopher all *news,* as it is called, is gossip, and they who edit and read it are old women over their tea. Yet not a few are greedy after this gossip. There was such a rush, as I hear, the other day at one of the offices to learn the foreign news by the last arrival, that several large squares of plate glass belonging to the establishment were broken by the pressure— news which I seriously think a ready wit might write a twelvemonth or twelve years beforehand with sufficient accuracy. As for Spain, for instance, if you know how to throw in Don Carlos and the Infanta, and Don Pedro and Seville and Granada, from time to time in the right proportions—they may have changed the names a little since I saw the papers—and serve up a bull-fight when other entertainments fail, it will be true to the letter, and give us as good an idea of the exact state or ruin of things in Spain as the most succinct and lucid reports under this head in the newspapers: and as for England, almost the last significant scrap of news from that quarter was the revolution of 1649; and if you have learned the history of her crops for an average year, you never need attend to that thing again, unless your speculations are of a merely pecuniary character. If one may judge who rarely looks into the newspapers, nothing new does ever happen in foreign parts, a French revolution not excepted.

What news! how much more important to know what that is which was never old! "Kieou-he-yu (great dignitary of the state of Wei) sent a man to Khoung-tseu to know his news. Khoung-tseu caused the messenger to be seated near him, and questioned him in these terms: What is your master doing? The messenger answered with respect: My master desires to diminish the number of his faults, but he cannot come to the end of them. The messenger being gone, the philosopher remarked: What a worthy messenger! What a worthy messenger!" The preacher, instead of vexing the ears of drowsy farmers on their day of rest at the end of the week—for Sunday is the fit conclusion of an ill-spent week, and not the fresh and brave beginning of a new one—with this one other draggle-tail of a sermon, should shout with thundering voice— "Pause! Avast! Why so seeming fast, but deadly slow?"

Shams and delusions are esteemed for soundest truths, while reality is fabulous. If men would steadily observe realities only, and not allow themselves to be deluded, life, to compare it with such things as we know, would be like a fairy tale and the Arabian Nights' Entertainments. If we respected only what is inevitable and has a right to be, music and poetry would resound along the streets. When we are unhurried and wise, we perceive that only great and worthy things have any permanent and absolute existence—that petty fears and petty pleasures are but the shadow of the reality. This is always exhilarating and sublime. By closing the eyes and slumbering, and consenting to be deceived by shows, men establish and confirm their daily life of routine and habit everywhere, which still is built on purely illusory foundations. Children, who play life, discern its true law and relations more clearly than men, who fail to live it worthily, but who think that they are wiser by experience, that is, by failure. I have read in a Hindu book that "there was a king's son, who, being expelled in infancy from his native city, was brought up by a forester, and, growing up to maturity in that state, imagined himself to belong to the barbarous race with which he lived. One of his father's ministers, having discovered him, revealed to him what he was, and the misconception of his character was removed, and he knew himself to be a prince. So soul," continues the Hindu philosopher, "from the circumstances in which it is placed, mistakes its own character, until the truth is revealed to it by some holy teacher, and then it knows itself to be *Brahme."* I perceive that we inhabitants of New England live this mean life that we do because our vision does not penetrate the surface of things. We think that that *is* which *appears* to be. If a man should walk through this town and see only the reality, where, think you, would the "Milldam" go to? If he should give us an account of the realities he beheld there, we should not recognize the place in his description. Look at a meetinghouse, or a courthouse, or a jail, or a shop, or a dwelling-house, and say what that thing really is before a true gaze, and they would all go to pieces in your account of them. Men esteem truth remote, in the outskirts of the system, behind the farthest star, before Adam and after the last man. In eternity there is indeed something true and sublime. But all these times and places and occasions are now and here. God himself culminates in the present moment, and will never be more divine in the lapse of all the ages. And we are enabled to apprehend at all what is sublime and noble only by the perpetual instilling and drenching of the reality that surrounds us. The universe constantly and obediently answers to our conceptions; whether we travel fast or slow, the track is laid for us. Let us spend our lives in conceiving then. The poet or the artist never yet had so fair and noble a design but some of his posterity at least could accomplish it.

Let us spend one day as deliberately as Nature, and not be thrown off the track by every nutshell and mosquito's wing that falls on the rails. Let us rise early and fast, or break fast, gently and without perturbation; let company come and let company go, let the bells ring and the children cry— determined to make a day of it. Why should we knock under and go with the stream? Let us not be upset and overwhelmed in that terrible rapid and whirlpool called a dinner, situated in the meridian shallows. Weather this danger and you are safe, for the rest of the way is down hill. With unrelaxed nerves, with morning vigor, sail by it, looking another way, tied to the mast like Ulysses. If the engine whistles, let it whistle till it is hoarse for its pains. If the bell rings, why should we run? We will consider what kind of music they are like. Let us settle ourselves, and work and wedge our feet downward through the mud and slush of opinion, and prejudice, and tradition, and delusion, and appearance, that alluvion which covers the globe, through Paris and London, through New York and Boston and Concord, through church and state, through poetry and philosophy and religion, till we come to a hard bottom and rocks in place, which we can call *reality*, and say, This is, and no mistake; and then begin, having a *point d'appui*,[3] below freshet and frost and fire, a place where you might found a wall or a state, or set a lamppost safely, or perhaps a gauge, not a Nilometer,[4] but a Realometer, that future ages might know how deep a freshet of shams and appearances had gathered from time to time. If you stand right fronting and face to face to a fact, you will see the sun glimmer on both its surfaces, as if it were a cimeter, and feel its sweet edge dividing you through the heart and marrow, and so you will happily conclude your mortal career. Be it life or death, we crave only reality. If we are really dying, let us hear the rattle in our throats and feel cold in the extremities; if we are alive, let us go about our business.

Time is but the stream I go a-fishing in. I drink at it; but while I drink I see the sandy bottom and detect how shallow it is. Its thin current slides away, but eternity remains. I would drink deeper; fish in the sky, whose bottom is pebbly with stars. I cannot count one. I know not the first letter of the alphabet. I have always been regretting that I was not as wise as the day I was born. The intellect is a cleaver; it discerns and rifts its way into the secret of things. I do not wish to be any more busy with my hands than is necessary. My head is hands and feet. I feel all my best faculties concentrated in it. My instinct tells me that my head is an organ for burrowing, as some creatures use their snout and forepaws, and with it I would mine and burrow my way through these hills. I think that the richest vein is somewhere hereabouts; so by the divining rod and thin rising vapors I judge; and here I will begin to mine.

---

F R O M

# CAPE COD

◇

❨ *Cape Cod* was published posthumously in 1865. The first four chapters had already been printed by Thoreau in *Putnam's Magazine* in 1855; two other chapters, including this one, were printed during the autumn preceding publication of the book in the *Atlantic Monthly*. The book takes its outline from the first trip Thoreau made to Cape Cod, in 1849, accompanied by his friend William Ellery Channing; but it also includes elements from two later trips, one alone and one again with Channing.

Thoreau had a fondness for queer, quirky, eccentric New England characters; he enjoyed their vivid independence and spectacular self-reliance. "The Wellfleet Oysterman" sketches an old man whom he obviously relished.

◇

## THE WELLFLEET OYSTERMAN

HAVING walked about eight miles since we struck the beach, and passed the boundary between Wellfleet and Truro, a stone post in the sand—for even this sand comes under the jurisdiction of one town or another—we turned inland over barren hills and valleys, whither the sea, for some reason, did not follow us, and, tracing up a Hollow, discovered two or three sober-looking houses within half a mile, uncommonly near the eastern coast. Their garrets were apparently so full of chambers, that their roofs could hardly lie down straight, and we did not doubt that there was room for us there. Houses near the sea are generally low and broad. These were a story and a half high; but if you

---

3. *point d'appui:* foundation.    4. **Nilometer:** an ancient device used to record the rise and fall of the Nile.

merely counted the windows in their gable ends, you would think that there were many stories more, or, at any rate, that the half-story was the only one thought worthy of being illustrated. The great number of windows in the ends of the houses, and their irregularity in size and position, here and elsewhere on the Cape, struck us agreeably—as if each of the various occupants who had their *cunabula* behind had punched a hole where his necessities required it, and according to his size and stature, without regard to outside effect. There were windows for the grown folks, and windows for the children—three or four apiece; as a certain man had a large hole cut in his barn door for the cat, and another smaller one for the kitten. Sometimes they were so low under the eaves that I thought they must have perforated the plate beam for another apartment, and I noticed some which were triangular, to fit that part more exactly. The ends of the houses had thus as many muzzles as a revolver, and, if the inhabitants have the same habit of staring out the windows that some of our neighbors have, a traveler must stand a small chance with them.

Generally, the old-fashioned and unpainted houses on the Cape looked more comfortable, as well as picturesque, than the modern and more pretending ones, which were less in harmony with the scenery, and less firmly planted.

These houses were on the shores of a chain of ponds, seven in number, the source of a small stream called Herring River, which empties into the Bay. There are many Herring Rivers on the Cape; they will, perhaps, be more numerous than herrings soon. We knocked at the door of the first house, but its inhabitants were all gone away. In the meanwhile, we saw the occupants of the next one looking out the window at us, and before we reached it an old woman came out and fastened the door of her bulkhead, and went in again. Nevertheless, we did not hesitate to knock at her door, when a grizzly-looking man appeared, whom we took to be sixty or seventy years old. He asked us, at first, suspiciously, where we were from, and what our business was; to which we returned plain answers.

"How far is Concord from Boston?" he inquired.

"Twenty miles by railroad."

"Twenty miles by railroad," he repeated.

"Didn't you ever hear of Concord of Revolutionary fame?"

"Didn't I ever hear of Concord? Why, I heard guns fire at the battle of Bunker Hill. [They hear the sound of heavy cannon across the Bay.] I am almost ninety; I am eighty-eight year old. I was fourteen year old at the time of Concord Fight—and where were you then?"

We were obliged to confess that we were not in the fight.

"Well, walk in, we'll leave it to the women," said he.

So we walked in, surprised, and sat down, an old woman taking our hats and bundles, and the old man continued, drawing up to the large, old-fashioned fireplace:

"I am a poor, good-for-nothing crittur, as Isaiah says; I am all broken down this year. I am under petticoat government here."

The family consisted of the old man, his wife, and his daughter, who appeared nearly as old as her mother, a fool, her son (a brutish-looking, middle-aged man, with a prominent lower face, who was standing by the hearth when we entered, but immediately went out), and a little boy of ten.

While my companion talked with the women, I talked with the old man. They said that he was old and foolish, but he was evidently too knowing for them.

"These women," said he to me, "are both of them poor good-for-nothing critturs. This one is my wife. I married her sixty-four years ago. She is eighty-four years old, and as deaf as an adder, and the other is not much better."

He thought well of the Bible, or at least he *spoke* well, and did not *think* ill, of it, for that would not have been prudent for a man of his age. He said that he had read it attentively for many years, and he had much of it at his tongue's end. He seemed deeply impressed with a sense of his own nothingness, and would repeatedly exclaim:

"I am a nothing. What I gather from my Bible is just this; that man is a poor good-for-nothing crittur, and everything is just as God sees fit and disposes."

"May I ask your name?" I said.

"Yes," he answered, "I am not ashamed to tell my name. My name is ———. My great-grandfather came over from England and settled here."

He was an old Wellfleet oysterman, who had acquired a competency in that business, and had sons still engaged in it.

Nearly all the oyster shops and stands in Massachusetts, I am told, are supplied and kept by natives of Wellfleet, and a part of this town is still called Billingsgate from the oysters having been formerly planted there; but the native oysters are said to have died in 1770. Various causes are assigned for this, such as a ground frost, the carcasses of blackfish, kept to rot in the harbor, and the like, but the most common account of the matter is—and I find that a similar superstition with regard to the disappearance of fishes exists almost everywhere—that when Wellfleet began to quarrel with the neighboring towns about the right to gather them, yellow specks appeared in them, and Providence caused them to disappear. A few years ago sixty thousand bushels were annually brought from the South and planted in the harbor of Wellfleet till they attained "the proper relish of Billingsgate"; but now they are imported commonly full-grown, and laid down near their markets, at Boston and elsewhere, where the water, being a mixture of salt and fresh, suits them better. The business was said to be still good and improving.

The old man said that the oysters were liable to freeze in the winter, if planted too high; but if it were not "so cold as to strain their eyes" they were not injured. The inhabitants of New Brunswick have noticed that "ice will not form over an oyster-bed, unless the cold is very intense indeed, and when the bays are frozen over the oyster-beds are easily discovered by the water above them remaining unfrozen, or as the French residents say, *dége-lée.*" Our host said that they kept them in cellars all winter.

"Without anything to eat or drink?" I asked.

"Without anything to eat or drink," he answered.

"Can the oysters move?"

"Just as much as my shoe."

But when I caught him saying that they "bedded themselves down in the sand, flat side up, round side down," I told him that my shoe could not do that, without the aid of my foot in it; at which he said that they merely settled down as they grew; if put down in a square they would be found so; but the clam could move quite fast. I have since been told by oystermen of Long Island, where the oyster is still indigenous and abundant, that they are found in large masses attached to the parent in their midst, and are so taken up with their tongs; in which case, they say, the age of the young proves that there could have been no motion for five or six years at least. And Buckland in his *Curiosities of Natural History* (page 50) says: "An oyster, who has once taken up his position and fixed himself when quite young, can never make a change. Oysters, nevertheless, that have not fixed themselves, but remain loose at the bottom of the sea, have the power of locomotion; they open their shells to their fullest extent, and then suddenly contracting them, the expulsion of the water forwards gives a motion backwards. A fisherman at Guernsey told me that he had frequently seen oysters moving in this way."

Some still entertain the question "whether the oyster was indigenous in Massachusetts Bay," and whether Wellfleet Harbor was a "natural habitat" of this fish; but, to say nothing of the testimony of old oystermen, which, I think, is quite conclusive, though the native oyster may now be extinct there, I saw that their shells, opened by the Indians, were strewn all over the Cape. Indeed, the Cape was at first thickly settled by Indians on account of the abundance of these and other fish. We saw many traces of their occupancy after this, in Truro, near Great Hollow, and at High Head, near East Harbor River—oysters, clams, cockles, and other shells, mingled with ashes and the bones of deer and other quadrupeds. I picked up half a dozen arrow-heads, and in an hour or two could have filled my pockets with them. The Indians lived about the edges of the swamps, then probably in some instances ponds, for shelter and water. Moreover, Champlain, in the edition of his "Voyages" printed in 1613, says that in the year 1606 he and Poitrincourt explored a harbor (Barnstable Harbor?) in the southerly part of what is now called Massachusetts Bay, in latitude 42°, about five leagues south, one point west of *Cap Blanc* (Cape Cod), and there they found many good oysters, and they named it *"le Port aux Huistres"* [sic] (Oyster Harbor). In one edition of his map (1632), the *"R. aux Escailles"* is drawn emptying into the same part of the bay, and on the map *"Novi Belgii,"* in Ogilby's America (1670), the words *"Port aux Huistres"* are placed against the same place. Also William Wood, who left New England in 1633, speaks, in his *New England's Prospect,* published in 1634, of "a great oyster-bank" in Charles River, and of another in the Mistick, each of which obstructed the navigation of its river. "The oysters," says he, "be great ones in form of a shoe-horn; some be a foot long; these breed on certain banks that are bare every spring tide. This fish without the shell is so big, that it must admit of a division before you can well get it into your mouth." Oysters are still found there.

Our host told us that the sea-clam, or hen, was not easily obtained; it was raked up, but never on the Atlantic side, only cast ashore there in small quantities in storms. The fisherman sometimes wades in water several feet deep, and thrusts a pointed stick into the sand before him. When this enters between the valves of a clam, he closes them on it, and is drawn out. It has been known to catch and hold coot and teal which were preying on it. I chanced to be on the bank of the Acushnet at New Bedford one day since this, watching some ducks, when a man informed me that, having let out his young ducks to seek their food amid the samphire

(*Salicornia*) and other weeds along the riverside at low tide that morning, at length he noticed that one remained stationary, amid the weeds, something preventing it from following the others, and going to it he found its foot tightly shut in a quahog's shell. He took up both together, carried them to his home, and his wife opening the shell with a knife released the duck and cooked the quahog. The old man said that the great clams were good to eat, but that they always took out a certain part which was poisonous, before they cooked them. "People said it would kill a cat." I did not tell him that I had eaten a large one entire that afternoon, but began to think that I was tougher than a cat. He stated that peddlers came round there, and sometimes tried to sell the women folks a skimmer, but he told them that their women had got a better skimmer than *they* could make, in the shell of their clams; it was shaped just right for this purpose. They call them "skim-alls" in some places. He also said that the sun-squall was poisonous to handle, and when the sailors came across it, they did not meddle with it, but heaved it out of their way. I told him that I had handled it that afternoon, and had felt no ill effects as yet. But he said it made the hands itch, especially if they had previously been scratched, or if I put it into my bosom, I should find out what it was.

He informed us that no ice ever formed on the back side of the Cape, or not more than once in a century, and but little snow lay there, it being either absorbed or blown or washed away. Sometimes in winter, when the tide was down, the beach was frozen, and afforded a hard road up the back side for some thirty miles, as smooth as a floor. One winter when he was a boy, he and his father "took right out into the Back Side before daylight, and walked to Provincetown and back to dinner."

When I asked what they did with all that barren-looking land, where I saw so few cultivated fields—"Nothing," he said.

"Then why fence your fields?"

"To keep the sand from blowing and covering up the whole."

"The yellow sand," said he, "has some life in it, but the white little or none."

When, in answer to his questions, I told him that I was a surveyor, he said that they who surveyed his farm were accustomed, where the ground was uneven, to loop up each chain as high as their elbows; that was the allowance they made, and he wished to know if I could tell him why they did not come out according to his deed, or twice alike. He seemed to have more respect for surveyors of the old school, which I did not wonder at. "King George the Third," said he, "laid out a road four rods wide and straight, the whole length of the Cape," but where it was now he could not tell.

This story of the surveyors reminded me of a Long Islander, who once, when I had made ready to jump from the bow of his boat to the shore, and he thought that I underrated the distance and would fall short—though I found afterward that he judged of the elasticity of my joints by his own—told me that when he came to a brook which he wanted to get over, he held up one leg, and then, if his foot appeared to cover any part of the opposite bank, he knew that he could jump it. "Why," I told him, "to say nothing of the Mississippi, and other small watery streams, I could blot out a star with my foot, but I would not engage to jump that distance," and asked how he knew when he had got his leg at the right elevation. But he regarded his legs as no less accurate than a pair of screw dividers or an ordinary quadrant, and appeared to have a painful recollection of every degree and minute in the arc which they described; and he would have had me believe that there was a kind of hitch in his hip-joint which answered the purpose. I suggested that he should connect his two ankles by a string of the proper length, which should be the chord of an arc, measuring his jumping ability on horizontal surfaces—assuming one leg to be a perpendicular to the plane of the horizon, which, however, may have been too bold an assumption in this case. Nevertheless, this was a kind of geometry in the legs which it interested me to hear of.

Our host took pleasure in telling us the names of the ponds, most of which we could see from his windows, and making us repeat them after him, to see if we had got them right. They were Gull Pond, the largest and a very handsome one, clear and deep, and more than a mile in circumference, Newcomb's, Swett's, Slough, Horse-Leech, Round, and Herring Ponds, all connected at high water, if I do not mistake. The coast-surveyors had come to him for their names, and he told them of one which they had not detected. He said that they were not so high as formerly. There was an earthquake about four years before he was born, which cracked the pans of the ponds, which were of iron, and caused them to settle. I did not remember to have read of this. Innumerable gulls used to resort to them; but the large gulls were now very scarce, for, as he said, the English robbed their nests far in the north, where they breed. He remembered well when gulls were taken in the gull-house, and when small birds were killed by means of a frying-pan and fire at night. His father once lost a valuable horse from this cause. A party from Wellfleet having lighted their fire for this purpose, one dark night, on Billingsgate Island, twenty horses which were pastured there, and this colt among them, being frightened by it, and endeavoring in the dark to cross the passage which separated them from the neighboring beach, and which was then fordable at low tide, were all swept out to sea and drowned. I observed that many horses were still turned out to pasture all summer on the islands and beaches in Wellfleet, Eastham, and Orleans, as a kind of common. He also described the killing of what he called "wild hens," here, after they had gone to roost in the woods, when he was a boy. Perhaps they were "prairie hens" (pinnated grouse).

He liked the beach pea (*Lathyrus maritimus*), cooked green, as well as the cultivated. He had seen it growing very abundantly in Newfoundland, where also the inhabitants ate them, but he had never been able to obtain any ripe for seed. We read, under the head of Chatham, that "in 1555, during a time of great scarcity, the people about Orford, in Sussex [England] were preserved from perishing by eating the seeds of this plant, which grew there in great abundance upon the sea coast. Cows, horses, sheep, and goats eat it." But the writer who quoted this could not learn that they had been used in Barnstable County.

He had been a voyager, then? Oh, he had been about the world in his day. He once considered himself a pilot for all our coast; but now they had changed the names so he might be bothered.

He gave us to taste what he called the Summer Sweeting, a pleasant apple which he raised, and frequently grafted from, but had never seen growing elsewhere, except once—three trees on Newfoundland, or at the bay of Chaleur, I forget which, as he was sailing by. He was sure that he could tell the tree at a distance.

At length the fool, whom my companion called the wizard, came in, muttering between his teeth, "Damn book-peddlers—all the time talking about books. Better do something. Damn 'em. I'll shoot 'em. Got a doctor down here. Damn him, I'll get a gun and shoot him"; never once holding up his head. Whereat the old man stood up and said in a loud voice, as if he was accustomed to command, and this was not the first time he had been obliged to exert his authority there: "John, go sit down, mind your business—we've heard you talk before —precious little you'll do—your bark is worse than your bite." But, without minding, John muttered the same gibberish over again, and then sat down at the table which the old folks had left. He ate all there was on it, and then turned to the apples, which his aged mother was paring, that she might give her guests some applesauce for breakfast, but she drew them away and sent him off.

When I approached this house the next summer, over the desolate hills between it and the shore, which are worthy to have been the birthplace of Ossian, I saw the wizard in the midst of a corn field on the hillside, but, as usual, he loomed so strangely, that I mistook him for a scarecrow.

This was the merriest old man that we had ever seen, and one of the best preserved. His style of conversation was coarse and plain enough to have suited Rabelais. He would have made a good Panurge. Or rather he was a sober Silenus, and we were the boys Chromis and Mnasilus, who listened to his story.

> "Not by Haemonian hills the Thracian bard,
> Nor awful Phoebus was on Pindus heard
> With deeper silence or with more regard."

There was a strange mingling of past and present in his conversation, for he had lived under King George, and might have remembered when Napoleon and the moderns generally were born. He said that one day, when the troubles between the Colonies and the mother country first broke out, as he, a boy of fifteen, was pitching hay out of a cart, one Donne, an old Tory, who was talking with his father, a good Whig, said to him, "Why, Uncle Bill, you might as well undertake to pitch that pond into the ocean with a pitchfork, as for the Colonies to undertake to gain their independence." He remembered well General Washington, and how he rode his horse along the streets of Boston, and he stood up to show us how he looked.

"He was a r—a—ther large and portly-looking man, a manly and resolute-looking officer, with a pretty good leg as he sat on his horse."—"There, I'll tell you, this was the way with Washington." Then he jumped up again, and bowed gracefully to right and left, making show as if he were waving his hat. Said he, *That* was Washington."

He told us many anecdotes of the Revolution, and was much pleased when we told him that we had read the same in history, and that his account agreed with the written.

"Oh," he said, "I know, I know! I was a young fellow of sixteen, with my ears wide open; and a fellow of that age, you know, is pretty wide awake, and likes to know everything that's going on. Oh, I know!"

He told us the story of the wreck of the Franklin, which took place there the previous spring; how a boy came to his house early in the morning to know whose boat that was by the shore, for there was a vessel in distress, and he, being an old man, first ate his breakfast, and then walked over to the top of the hill by the shore, and sat down there, having found a comfortable seat, to see the ship wrecked. She was on the bar, only a quarter of a mile from him, and still nearer to the men on the beach, who had got a boat ready, but could render no assistance on account of the breakers, for there was a pretty high sea running. There were the passengers all crowded together in the forward part of the ship, and some were getting out of the cabin windows and were drawn on deck by the others.

"I saw the captain get out his boat," said he; "he had one little one; and then they jumped into it one after another, down as straight as an arrow. I counted them. There were nine. One was a woman, and she jumped as straight as any of them. Then they shoved off. The sea took them back, one wave went over them, and when they came up there were six still clinging to the boat; I counted them. The next wave turned the boat bottom upward, and emptied them all out. None of them ever came ashore alive. There were the rest of them all crowded together on the forecastle, the other parts of the ship being under water. They had seen all that happened to the boat. At length a heavy sea separated the forecastle from the rest of the wreck, and set it inside of the worst breaker, and the boat was able to reach them, and it saved all that were left, but one woman."

He also told us of the steamer Cambria's getting aground on this shore a few months before we were there, and of her English passengers who roamed over his grounds, and who, he said, thought the prospect from the high hill by the shore, "the most delightsome they had ever seen," and also of the pranks which the ladies played with his scoop-net in the ponds. He spoke of these travelers with their purses full of guineas, just as our provincial fathers used to speak of British bloods in the time of King George the Third.

*Quid loquar?* Why repeat what he told us?

> "*Aut Scyllam Nisi, quam fama secuta est,*
> *Candida succinctam latrantibus inguina monstris,*
> *Dulichias vexâsse rates, et gurgite in alto*
> *Ah! timidos nautas canibus lacerâsse marinis?*" [1]

In the course of the evening I began to feel the potency of the clam which I had eaten, and I was obliged to confess to our host that I was no tougher than the cat he told of; but he answered, that he was a plain-spoken man, and he could tell me that it was all imagination. At any rate, it proved an emetic in my case, and I was made quite sick

by it for a short time, while he laughed at my expense. I was pleased to read afterward, in Mourt's Relation of the landing of the Pilgrims in Provincetown Harbor, these words: "We found great muscles [the old editor says that they were undoubtedly sea-clams] and very fat and full of sea-pearl; but we could not eat them, for they made us all sick that did eat, as well sailors as passengers, . . . but they were soon well again." It brought me nearer to the Pilgrims to be thus reminded by a similar experience that I was so like them. Moreover, it was a valuable confirmation of their story, and I am prepared now to believe every word of Mourt's Relation. I was also pleased to find that man and the clam lay still at the same angle to one another. But I did not notice sea-pearl. Like Cleopatra, I must have swallowed it. I have since dug these clams on a flat in the Bay and observed them. They could squirt full ten feet before the wind, as appeared by the marks of the drops on the sand.

"Now I am going to ask you a question," said the old man, "and I don't know as you can tell me; but you are a learned man, and I never had any learning, only what I got by natur."—It was in vain that we reminded him that he could quote Josephus to our confusion.—"I've thought, if I ever met a learned man I should like to ask him this question. Can you tell me how *Axy* is spelt, and what it means? *Axy,*" says he; "there's a girl over here is named *Axy*. Now what is it? What does it mean? Is it Scripture? I've read my Bible twenty-five years over and over, and I never came across it."

"Did you read it twenty-five years for this object?" I asked.

"Well, *how* is it spelt? Wife, how is it spelt?"

She said, "It is in the Bible; I've seen it."

"Well, how do you spell it?"

"I don't know. A c h, ach, s e h, seh,—Achseh."

"Does that spell Axy? Well, do *you* know what it means?" asked he, turning to me.

"No," I replied, "I never heard the sound before."

"There was a schoolmaster down here once, and they asked him what it meant, and he said it had no more meaning than a bean-pole."

I told him that I held the same opinion with the schoolmaster. I had been a schoolmaster myself, and had had strange names to deal with. I also heard of such names as Zoheth, Beriah, Amaziah, Bethuel, and Shearjashub, hereabouts.

At length the little boy, who had a seat quite in the chimney-corner, took off his stockings and shoes, warmed his feet, and having had his sore leg freshly salved, went off to bed; then the fool

---

CAPE COD.    I. "**Aut . . . marinis?**": Virgil, *Eclogues*, VI.74–77:
"Or the tale of Scylla, daughter of Nisus, whom report
   has followed to the effect that
She girt as to her white loins with barking dogs
Did afflict the Dulichian ships and in the deep surge
Ah! did she mangle the fearful sailors with marine dogs."

made bare his knotty-looking feet and legs, and followed him; and finally the old man exposed his calves also to our gaze. We had never had the good fortune to see an old man's legs before, and were surprised to find them fair and plump as an infant's, and we thought that he took a pride in exhibiting them. He then proceeded to make preparations for retiring, discoursing meanwhile with Panurgic plainness of speech on the ills to which old humanity is subject. We were a rare haul for him. He could commonly get none but ministers to talk to, though sometimes ten of them at once, and he was glad to meet some of the laity at leisure. The evening was not long enough for him. As I had been sick, the old lady asked if I would not go to bed—it was getting late for old people; but the old man, who had not yet done his stories, said, "You ain't particular, are you?"

"Oh, no," said I, "I am in no hurry. I believe I have weathered the Clam cape."

"They are good," said he; "I wish I had some of them now."

"They never hurt me," said the old lady.

"But then you took out the part that killed a cat," said I.

At last we cut him short in the midst of his stories, which he promised to resume in the morning. Yet, after all, one of the old ladies who came into our room in the night to fasten the fire-board, which rattled, as she went out took the precaution to fasten us in. Old women are by nature more suspicious than old men. However, the winds howled around the house, and made the fire-boards as well as the casements rattle well that night. It was probably a windy night for any locality, but we could not distinguish the roar which was proper to the ocean from that which was due to the wind alone.

The sounds which the ocean makes must be very significant and interesting to those who live near it. When I was leaving the shore at this place the next summer, and had got a quarter of a mile distant, ascending a hill, I was startled by a sudden, loud sound from the sea, as if a large steamer were letting off steam by the shore, so that I caught my breath and felt my blood run cold for an instant, and I turned about, expecting to see one of the Atlantic steamers thus far out of her course, but there was nothing unusual to be seen. There was a low bank at the entrance of the Hollow, between me and the ocean, and suspecting that I might have risen into another stratum of air in ascending the hill—which had wafted to me only the ordinary roar of the sea—I immediately descended again, to see if I lost hearing of it; but, without regard to my ascending or descending, it died away in a minute or two, and yet there was

scarcely any wind all the while. The old man said that this was what they called the "rut," a peculiar roar of the sea before the wind changes, which, however, he could not account for. He thought that he could tell all about the weather from the sounds which the sea made.

Old Josselyn, who came to New England in 1638, has it among his weather-signs, that "the resounding of the sea from the shore, and murmuring of the winds in the woods, without apparent wind, sheweth wind to follow."

Being on another part of the coast one night since this, I heard the roar of the surf a mile distant, and the inhabitants said it was a sign that the wind would work round east, and we should have rainy weather. The ocean was heaped up somewhere at the eastward, and this roar was occasioned by its effort to preserve its equilibrium, the wave reaching the shore before the wind. Also the captain of a packet between this country and England told me that he sometimes met with a wave on the Atlantic coming against the wind, perhaps in a calm sea, which indicated that at a distance the wind was blowing from an opposite quarter, but the undulation had traveled faster than it. Sailors tell of "tide-rips" and "ground-swells," which they suppose to have been occasioned by hurricanes and earthquakes, and to have traveled many hundred, and sometimes even two or three thousand miles.

Before sunrise the next morning they let us out again, and I ran over to the beach to see the sun come out of the ocean. The old woman of eighty-four winters was already out in the cold morning wind, bareheaded, tripping about like a young girl, and driving up the cow to milk. She got the breakfast with dispatch, and without noise or bustle; and meanwhile the old man resumed his stories, standing before us, who were sitting, with his back to the chimney, and ejecting his tobacco-juice right and left into the fire behind him, without regard to the various dishes which were there preparing. At breakfast we had eels, buttermilk cake, cold bread, green beans, doughnuts, and tea. The old man talked a steady stream; and when his wife told him he had better eat his breakfast, he said, "Don't hurry me; I have lived too long to be hurried." I ate of the applesauce and the doughnuts, which I thought had sustained the least detriment from the old man's shots, but my companion refused the applesauce, and ate of the hot cake and green beans, which had appeared to him to occupy the safest part of the hearth. But on comparing notes afterward, I told him that the buttermilk cake was particularly exposed, and I saw how it suffered repeatedly, and therefore I avoided it; but he declared that, however that might be, he witnessed that the applesauce was seriously injured, and had therefore declined that. After breakfast we looked at his clock, which was out of order, and oiled it with some "hen's grease," for want of sweet oil, for he scarcely could believe that we were not tinkers or peddlers; meanwhile, he told a story about visions, which had reference to a crack in the clock-case made by frost one night. He was curious to know to what religious sect we belonged. He said that he had been to hear thirteen kinds of preaching in one month, when he was young, but he did not join any of them—he stuck to his Bible. There was nothing like any of them in his Bible. While I was shaving in the next room, I heard him ask my companion to what sect he belonged, to which he answered,—

"Oh, I belong to the Universal Brotherhood."

"What's that?" he asked, "Sons o' Temperance?"

Finally, filling our pockets with doughnuts, which he was pleased to find that we called by the same name that he did, and paying for our entertainment, we took our departure; but he followed us out of doors, and made us tell him the names of the vegetables which he had raised from seeds that came out of the Franklin. They were cabbage, broccoli, and parsley. As I had asked him the names of so many things, he tried me in turn with all the plants which grew in his garden, both wild and cultivated. It was about half an acre, which he cultivated wholly himself. Besides the common garden vegetables, there were yellow dock, lemon balm, hyssop, gill-go-over-the-ground, mouse-ear, chick-weed, Roman wormwood, elecampane, and other plants. As we stood there, I saw a fish hawk stoop to pick a fish out of his pond.

"There," said I, "he has got a fish."

"Well," said the old man, who was looking all the while, but could see nothing, "he didn't dive, he just wet his claws."

And, sure enough, he did not this time, though it is said that they often do, but he merely stooped low enough to pick him out with his talons; but as he bore his shining prey over the bushes, it fell to the ground, and we did not see that he recovered it. That is not their practice.

Thus, having had another crack with the old man, he standing bareheaded under the eaves, he directed us "athwart the fields," and we took to the beach again for another day, it being now late in the morning.

It was but a day or two after this that the safe of the Provincetown Bank was broken open and robbed by two men from the interior, and we learned that our hospitable entertainers did at least transiently harbor the suspicion that we were the men.

---

FROM

# LIFE WITHOUT PRINCIPLE

---

◇

⟨ THIS was published posthumously in the *Atlantic Monthly* in 1863.

◇

AT A LYCEUM, not long since, I felt that the lecturer had chosen a theme too foreign to himself, and so failed to interest me as much as he might have done. He described things not in or near to his heart, but toward his extremities and superficies. There was, in this sense, no truly central or centralizing thought in the lecture. I would have had him deal with privatest experience, as the poet does. The greatest compliment that was ever paid me was when one asked me what *I thought,* and attended to my answer. I am surprised, as well as delighted, when this happens, it is such a rare use he would make of me, as if he were acquainted with the tool. Commonly, if men want anything of me, it is only to know how many acres I make of their land—since I am a surveyor —or, at most, what trivial news I have burdened myself with. They never will go to law for my meat; they prefer the shell. A man once came a considerable distance to ask me to lecture on Slavery; but on conversing with him, I found that he and his clique expected seven eighths of the lecture to be theirs, and only one eighth mine; so I declined. I take it for granted, when I am invited to lecture anywhere—for I have had a little experience in that business—that there is a desire to hear what *I think* on some subject, though I may be the greatest fool in the country, and not that I should say pleasant things merely, or such as the audience will assent to; and I resolve, accordingly, that I will give them a strong dose of myself. They have sent for me, and engaged to pay for me, and I am determined that they shall have me, though I bore them beyond all precedent.

So now I would say something similar to you, my readers. Since *you* are my readers, and I have not been much of a traveler, I will not talk about people a thousand miles off, but come as near home as I can. As the time is short, I will leave out all the flattery, and retain all the criticism.

Let us consider the way in which we spend our lives.

This world is a place of business. What an infinite bustle! I am awaked almost every night by the panting of the locomotive. It interrupts my dreams. There is no sabbath. It would be glorious to see mankind at leisure for once. It is nothing but work, work, work. I cannot easily buy a blank-book to write thoughts in; they are commonly ruled for dollars and cents. An Irishman, seeing me making a minute in the fields, took it for granted that I was calculating my wages. If a man was tossed out of a window when an infant, and so made a cripple for life, or scared out of his wits by the Indians, it is regretted chiefly because he was thus incapacitated for—business! I think that there is nothing, not even crime, more opposed to poetry, to philosophy, ay, to life itself, than this incessant business.

There is a coarse and boisterous money-making fellow in the outskirts of our town, who is going to build a bank-wall under the hill along the edge of his meadow. The powers have put this into his head to keep him out of mischief, and he wishes me to spend three weeks digging there with him. The result will be that he will perhaps get some more money to hoard, and leave for his heirs to spend foolishly. If I do this, most will commend me as an industrious and hard-working man; but if I choose to devote myself to certain labors which yield more real profit, though but little money, they may be inclined to look on me as an idler. Nevertheless, as I do not need the police of meaningless labor to regulate me, and do not see anything absolutely praiseworthy in this fellow's undertaking any more than in many an enterprise of our own or foreign governments, however amusing it may be to him or them, I prefer to finish my education at a different school.

If a man walk in the woods for love of them half of each day, he is in danger of being regarded as a loafer; but if he spends his whole day as a speculator, shearing off those woods and making earth bald before her time, he is esteemed an industrious and enterprising citizen. As if a town had no interest in its forests but to cut them down!

Most men would feel insulted if it were proposed to employ them in throwing stones over a wall, and then in throwing them back, merely that they might earn their wages. But many are no more worthily employed now. For instance: just after sunrise, one summer morning, I noticed one

of my neighbors walking beside his team, which was slowly drawing a heavy hewn stone swung under the axle, surrounded by an atmosphere of industry—his day's work begun, his brow commenced to sweat—a reproach to all sluggards and idlers—pausing abreast the shoulders of his oxen, and half turning round with a flourish of his merciful whip, while they gained their length on him. And I thought, Such is the labor which the American Congress exists to protect—honest, manly toil —honest as the day is long—that makes his bread taste sweet, and keeps society sweet—which all men respect and have consecrated; one of the sacred band, doing the needful but irksome drudgery. Indeed, I felt a slight reproach, because I observed this from a window, and was not abroad and stirring about a similar business. The day went by, and at evening I passed the yard of another neighbor, who keeps many servants, and spends much money foolishly, while he adds nothing to the common stock, and there I saw the stone of the morning lying beside a whimsical structure intended to adorn this Lord Timothy Dexter's [1] premises, and the dignity forthwith departed from the teamster's labor, in my eyes. In my opinion, the sun was made to light worthier toil than this. I may add that his employer has since run off, in debt to a good part of the town, and, after passing through Chancery, has settled somewhere else, there to become once more a patron of the arts.

The ways by which you may get money almost without exception lead downward. To have done anything by which you earned money *merely* is to have been truly idle or worse. If the laborer gets no more than the wages which his employer pays him, he is cheated, he cheats himself. If you would get money as a writer or lecturer, you must be popular, which is to go down perpendicularly. Those services which the community will most readily pay for, it is most disagreeable to render. You are paid for being something less than a man. The state does not commonly reward a genius any more wisely. Even the poet laureate would rather not have to celebrate the accidents of royalty. He must be bribed with a pipe of wine; and perhaps another poet is called away from his muse to gauge that very pipe. As for my own business, even that kind of surveying which I could do with most satisfaction my employers do not want. They would

LIFE WITHOUT PRINCIPLE. 1. Lord Timothy Dexter's: "Lord" Timothy Dexter (1747-1806) was an eccentric merchant of Newburyport, Mass., who established himself in a splendid mansion, the front yard of which was decorated by more than forty life-sized statues of famous men.

prefer that I should do my work coarsely and not too well, ay, not well enough. When I observe that there are different ways of surveying, my employer commonly asks which will give him the most land, not which is most correct. I once invented a rule for measuring cordwood, and tried to introduce it in Boston; but the measurer there told me that the sellers did not wish to have their wood measured correctly—that he was already too accurate for them, and therefore they commonly got their wood measured in Charlestown before crossing the bridge.

The aim of the laborer should be, not to get his living, to get "a good job," but to perform well a certain work; and, even in a pecuniary sense, it would be economy for a town to pay its laborers so well that they would not feel that they were working for low ends, as for a livelihood merely, but for scientific, or even moral ends. Do not hire a man who does your work for money, but him who does it for love of it.

It is remarkable that there are few men so well employed, so much to their minds, but that a little money or fame would commonly buy them off from their present pursuit. I see advertisements for *active* young men, as if activity were the whole of a young man's capital. Yet I have been surprised when one has with confidence proposed to me, a grown man, to embark in some enterprise of his, as if I had absolutely nothing to do, my life having been a complete failure hitherto. What a doubtful compliment this to pay me! As if he had met me halfway across the ocean beating up against the wind, but bound nowhere, and proposed to me to go along with him! If I did, what do you think the underwriters would say? No, no! I am not without employment at this stage of the voyage. To tell the truth, I saw an advertisement for able-bodied seamen, when I was a boy, sauntering in my native port, and as soon as I came of age I embarked.

The community has no bribe that will tempt a wise man. You may raise money enough to tunnel a mountain, but you cannot raise money enough to hire a man who is minding *his own* business. An efficient and valuable man does what he can, whether the community pay him for it or not. The inefficient offer their inefficiency to the highest bidder, and are forever expecting to be put into office. One would suppose that they were rarely disappointed.

Perhaps I am more than usually jealous with respect to my freedom. I feel that my connection with and obligation to society are still very slight and transient. Those slight labors which afford me a livelihood, and by which it is allowed that I am to some extent serviceable to my contemporaries, are as yet commonly a pleasure to me, and I am not often reminded that they are a necessity. So far I am successful. But I foresee that if my wants should be much increased, the labor required to supply them would become a drudgery. If I should sell both my forenoons and afternoons to society, as most appear to do, I am sure that for me there would be nothing left worth living for. I trust that I shall never thus sell my birthright for a mess of pottage. I wish to suggest that a man may be very industrious, and yet not spend his time well. There is no more fatal blunderer than he who consumes the greater part of his life getting his living. All great enterprises are self-supporting. The poet, for instance, must sustain his body by his poetry, as a steam planing-mill feeds its boilers with the shavings it makes. You must get your living by loving. But as it is said of the merchants that ninety-seven in a hundred fail, so the life of men generally, tried by this standard, is a failure, and bankruptcy may be surely prophesied.

Pray, let us live without being drawn by dogs, Esquimaux-fashion, tearing over hill and dale, and biting each other's ears.

Not without a slight shudder at the danger, I often perceive how near I had come to admitting into my mind the details of some trivial affair—the news of the street; and I am astonished to observe how willing men are to lumber their minds with such rubbish—to permit idle rumors and incidents of the most insignificant kind to intrude on ground which should be sacred to thought. Shall the mind be a public arena, where the affairs of the street and the gossip of the tea-table chiefly are discussed? Or shall it be a quarter of heaven itself—an hypethral temple, consecrated to the service of the gods? I find it so difficult to dispose of the few facts which to me are significant, that I hesitate to burden my attention with those which are insignificant, which only a divine mind could illustrate. Such is, for the most part, the news in newspapers and conversation. It is important to preserve the mind's chastity in this respect. Think of admitting the details of a single case of the criminal court into our thoughts, to stalk profanely through their very *sanctum sanctorum* for an hour, ay, for many hours! to make a very barroom of the mind's inmost apartment, as if for so long the dust of the street had occupied us—the very street itself, with all its travel, its bustle, and filth, had passed through our thoughts' shrine! Would it not be an intellectual and moral suicide? When I have been compelled to sit spectator and auditor in a court-room for some hours, and have seen my neighbors, who were not compelled, stealing in from time to time, and tiptoeing about with washed hands and faces, it has appeared to my mind's eye, that, when they took off their hats, their ears suddenly expanded into vast hoppers for sound, between which even their narrow heads were crowded. Like the vanes of windmills, they caught the broad but shallow stream of sound, which, after a few titillating gyrations in their coggy brains, passed out the other side. I wondered if, when they got home, they were as careful to wash their ears as before their hands and faces. It has seemed to me, at such a time, that the auditors and the witnesses, the jury and the counsel, the judge and the criminal at the bar—if I may presume him guilty before he is convicted—were all equally criminal, and a thunderbolt might be expected to descend and consume them all together.

By all kinds of traps and signboards, threatening the extreme penalty of the divine law, exclude such trespassers from the only ground which can be sacred to you. It is so hard to forget what it is worse than useless to remember! If I am to be a thoroughfare, I prefer that it be of the mountain brooks, the Parnassian streams, and not the town sewers. There is inspiration, that gossip which comes to the ear of the attentive mind from the courts of heaven. There is the profane and stale revelation of the barroom and the police court. The same ear is fitted to receive both communications. Only the character of the hearer determines to which it shall be open, and to which closed. I believe that the mind can be permanently profaned by the habit of attending to trivial things, so that all our thoughts shall be tinged with triviality. Our very intellect shall be macadamized, as it were, its foundation broken into fragments for the wheels of travel to roll over; and if you would know what will make the most durable pavement, surpassing rolled stones, spruce blocks; and asphaltum, you have only to look into some of our minds which have been subjected to this treatment so long.

If we have thus desecrated ourselves—as who has not?—the remedy will be by wariness and devotion to reconsecrate ourselves, and make once more a fane of the mind. We should treat our minds, that is, ourselves, as innocent and ingenuous children, whose guardians we are, and be careful what objects and what subjects we thrust on their attention. Read not the Times. Read the Eternities. Conventionalities are at length as bad as impurities. Even the facts of science may dust the mind by their dryness, unless they are in a sense effaced each morning, or rather rendered fertile by the dews of fresh and living truth. Knowledge does not come to us by details, but in flashes of light from heaven. Yes, every thought that passes through the mind helps to wear and tear it, and to deepen the ruts, which, as in the streets of Pompeii, evince how much it has been used. How many things there are concerning which we might well deliberate whether we had better know them—had better let their peddling-carts be driven, even at the slowest trot or walk, over that bridge of glorious span by which we trust to pass at last from the farthest brink of time to the nearest shore of eternity! Have we no culture, no refinement—but skill only to live coarsely and serve the Devil?—to acquire a little worldly wealth, or fame, or liberty, and make a false show with it, as if we were all husk and shell, with no tender and living kernel to us? Shall our institutions be like those chestnut burs which contain abortive nuts, perfect only to prick the fingers?

America is said to be the arena on which the battle of freedom is to be fought; but surely it cannot be freedom in a merely political sense that is meant. Even if we grant that the American has freed himself from a political tyrant, he is still the slave of an economical and moral tyrant. Now that the republic—the *res-publica*—has been settled, it is time to look after the *res-privata*—the private state—to see, as the Roman senate charged its consuls, *"ne quid res-*PRIVATA *detrimenti caperet,"* that the *private* state receive no detriment.

Do we call this the land of the free? What is it to be free from King George and continue the slaves of King Prejudice? What is it to be born free and not to live free? What is the value of any political freedom, but as a means to moral freedom? Is it a freedom to be slaves, or a freedom to be free, of which we boast? We are a nation of politicians, concerned about the outmost defenses only of freedom. It is our children's children who may perchance be really free. We tax ourselves unjustly. There is a part of us which is not represented. It is taxation without representation. We quarter troops, we quarter fools and cattle of all sorts upon ourselves. We quarter our gross bodies on our poor souls, till the former eat up all the latter's substance.

With respect to a true culture and manhood, we are essentially provincial still, not metropolitan—mere Jonathans. We are provincial, because we do not find at home our standards; because we do not worship truth, but the reflection of truth; because we are warped and narrowed by an exclusive devotion to trade and commerce and manufactures and agriculture and the like, which are but means, and not the end.

# POEMS

◊

❬ SOME of Thoreau's poems were published in H. S. Salt's and F. B. Sanborn's *Poems of Nature* in 1895, and in 1943 Carl Bode brought out *Collected Poems of Henry Thoreau.* During Thoreau's lifetime, however, the only poems he managed to publish in book form were those which he included in the *Week* and *Walden.* While an undergraduate at Harvard, Thoreau had observed that the Greek poets had an "appetite for visible images," whereas the poetry of northern Europe tended toward the "dark and mysterious." In his poetic practice, he usually attempted to follow the Greek ideal, and his best poems are distinguished by the firm grounding of their thought in a Nature that one can see.

◊

## SIC VITA

❬ "SIC VITA" was published in the *Dial*, II (July 1841), 81–82 and reprinted in the *Week* (1849). Written while Thoreau was still a Harvard undergraduate, this poem was then thrown into the window of a friend wrapped round a bunch of violets and tied loosely with straw. The friend was Mrs. Lucy Jackson Brown, a sister of Emerson's second wife, Lidian. Compare the sentence in the *Week* which immediately precedes "Sic Vita": "I have seen a bunch of violets in a glass vase, tied loosely with a straw, which reminded me of myself."

I am a parcel of vain strivings tied
 By a chance bond together,
Dangling this way and that, their links
 Were made so loose and wide,
   Methinks,
 For milder weather.

A bunch of violets without their roots,
 And sorrel intermixed,
Encircled by a wisp of straw
 Once coiled about their shoots,     10
   The law
 By which I'm fixed.

A nosegay which Time clutched from out
 Those fair Elysian fields,
With weeds and broken stems, in haste,
 Doth make the rabble rout
   That waste
 The day he yields.

And here I bloom for a short hour unseen,
 Drinking my juices up,     20
 With no root in the land

To keep my branches green,
   But stand
 In a bare cup.

Some tender buds were left upon my stem
 In mimicry of life,
But ah! the children will not know,
 Till time has withered them,
   The woe
 With which they're rife.     30

But now I see I was not plucked for naught,
 And after in life's vase
Of glass set while I might survive,
 But by a kind hand brought
   Alive
 To a strange place.

That stock thus thinned will soon redeem its hours,
 And by another year,
Such as God knows, with freer air,
 More fruits and fairer flowers     40
   Will bear,
 While I droop here.

## THE INWARD MORNING

❬ "THE INWARD MORNING" was written as two separate lyrics in 1841, but published as one poem in the *Dial*, III (October 1842), 198–99.

Packed in my mind lie all the clothes
 Which outward nature wears,
And in its fashion's hourly change
 It all things else repairs.

In vain I look for change abroad,
 And can no difference find,
Till some new ray of peace uncalled
 Illumes my inmost mind.

What is it gilds the trees and clouds,
 And paints the heavens so gay,     10
But yonder fast-abiding light
 With its unchanging ray?

Lo, when the sun streams through the wood,
 Upon a winter's morn,
Where'er his silent beams intrude
 The murky night is gone.

How could the patient pine have known
 The morning breeze would come,
Or humble flowers anticipate
 The insect's noonday hum,—     20

Till the new light with morning cheer
    From far streamed through the aisles,
And nimbly told the forest trees
    For many stretching miles?

I've heard within my inmost soul
    Such cheerful morning news,
In the horizon of my mind
    Have seen such orient hues,

As in the twilight of the dawn,
    When the first birds awake,       30
Are heard within some silent wood,
    Where they the small twigs break,

Or in the eastern skies are seen,
    Before the sun appears,
The harbingers of summer heats
    Which from afar he bears.

## WINTER MEMORIES

⟦ "WINTER MEMORIES" was published in "Natural History of Massachusetts," the *Dial*, III (July 1842), 19. The first version of this poem appears as an entry in Thoreau's journal for December 30, 1841.

    Within the circuit of this plodding life
There enter moments of an azure hue,
Untarnished fair as is the violet
Or anemone, when the spring strews them
By some meandering rivulet, which make
The best philosophy untrue that aims
But to console man for his grievances.
I have remembered when the winter came,
High in my chamber in the frosty nights,
When in the still light of the cheerful moon,    10
On every twig and rail and jutting spout,
The icy spears were adding to their length
Against the arrows of the coming sun,
How in the shimmering noon of summer past
Some unrecorded beam slanted across
The upland pastures where the Johnswort grew;
Or heard, amid the verdure of my mind,
The bee's long smothered hum, on the blue flag
Loitering amidst the mead; or busy rill,
Which now through all its course stands still and
    dumb       20
Its own memorial,—purling at its play
Along the slopes, and through the meadows next,
Until its youthful sound was hushed at last
In the staid current of the lowland stream;
Or seen the furrows shine but late upturned,
And where the fieldfare followed in the rear,
When all the fields around lay bound and hoar

Beneath a thick integument of snow.
So by God's cheap economy made rich
To go upon my winter's task again.       30

## MIST

⟦ "MIST" was probably written in 1842 and was first published in the *Week* (1849).

    Low-anchored cloud,
Newfoundland air,
Fountain-head and source of rivers,
Dew-cloth, dream drapery,
And napkin spread by fays;
Drifting meadow of the air,
Where bloom the daisied banks and violets,
And in whose fenny labyrinth
The bittern booms and heron wades;
Spirit of lakes and seas and rivers,    10
Bear only perfumes and the scent
Of healing herbs to just men's fields!

## SMOKE

⟦ "SMOKE" was published in the *Dial*, III (April 1843), 505–06, and reprinted in *Walden* (1854). This was one of the poems which Thoreau called "Orphics," a name which calls attention to its Grecian form and content.

    Light-winged Smoke, Icarian bird,
Melting thy pinions in thy upward flight,
Lark without song, and messenger of dawn,
Circling above the hamlets at thy nest;
Or else, departing dream, and shadowy form
Of midnight vision, gathering up thy skirts;
By night star-veiling, and by day
Darkening the light and blotting out the sun;
Go thou my incense upward from this hearth,
And ask the gods to pardon this clear flame.    10

## MANHOOD

⟦ "MANHOOD" was first published in Carl Bode, *Collected Poems of Henry Thoreau* (1943), p. 225.

I love to see the man, a long-lived child,
As yet uninjured by all worldly taint
As the fresh infant whose whole life is play.
'Tis a serene spectacle for a serene day;
But better still I love to contemplate
The mature soul of lesser innocence,
Who hath traveled far on life's dusty road
Far from the starting point of infancy
And proudly bears his small degen'racy

Blazon'd on his memorial standard high          10
Who from the sad experience of his fate
Since his bark struck on that unlucky rock
Has proudly steered his life with his own hands.
Though his face harbors less of innocence
Yet there do chiefly lurk within its depths
Furrowed by care, but yet all over spread
With the ripe bloom of a self-wrought content

Noble resolves which do reprove the gods
And it doth more assert man's eminence
Above the happy level of the brute          20
And more doth advertise me of the heights
To which no natural path doth ever lead
No natural light can ever light our steps,
—But the far-piercing ray that shines
From the recesses of a brave man's eye.

EDWARD H. DAVIDSON
*Editor*

# Nathaniel Hawthorne

## 1804–1864

THAT a century after he lived he should be included in a collection of major writers of America would have baffled and amused Hawthorne. During his lifetime the profession of letters was so poorly rewarded, and Hawthorne himself had been so consistently ignored, that to be a subject for literary study and analysis, to be termed a "classic" among American writers, would have seemed nothing short of grotesque. Yet, aside from the poor pay and the lack of recognition—certainly he had far less to complain of than did Poe—Hawthorne has not suffered the slow or sudden loss of popularity which befell many of his contemporaries, nor has he been made into a fashionable mode, a literary cliché in our own time. Indeed, his literary reputation has maintained its high place more steadily than has that of any other major American writer: Poe has never earned from critics the plaudits he has received from the general reading public, and Whitman could not win the place he wanted in the minds and hearts of his countrymen. If Hawthorne never found the quick surge of acceptance, the extraordinarily favorable critical reception which Melville has gained during the past forty years, he has sustained his reputation as a classic American writer virtually unchanged since his *Scarlet Letter* was published in 1850.

It is difficult to account for a reputaton which has remained so well established amid the fluctuating moods of history and the quixotic shifts in literary taste. Some critics have charged that Hawthorne's genius was thin and narrow: one can count the distinguished novels on the fingers of one hand—and the memorable short stories on the fingers of two. Others have supposed that Hawthorne's art was deep, not broad, as no doubt it was; and in our day, when depth and ambiguity are much admired in writing, Hawthorne has continued to offer enough complexity and mystery to hold a wide variety of readers. His writings seem to be very simple. Yet the tales are most skillfully contrived: they offer problems and require intense critical analysis which, once it is performed, suggests that Hawthorne is not a mere tale-teller but a skilled artist who can take his place with the leading writers of the world. There is something deceptive about the writings and the man who produced them; they appear to be both simple and meaningful, cautious and yet intense, remote and still formidable, as indeed they are.

In the life history of Nathaniel Hawthorne are no high surges of drama and excitement, no flaming and sulfurous sins over which biographers can exercise their rhetoric and pseudo-psychologists ponder the inhibition, the trauma, the concealed loathing which might, if one looks far enough, color the writings. The story is quite otherwise: Hawthorne's life was commonplace, even dull. He had the distinction of being born on Independence Day in 1804 of a family which

[361]

could boast colorful ancestors. William Hathorne—the *w* was added by Hawthorne himself, apparently to make the spelling conform to the pronunciation of the name—was that "steeple-crowned progenitor" who had come to Massachusetts with Governor Winthrop in 1630 and had played a prominent role in the early colony. His son, John Hathorne, became a lawyer and a judge of the special court which heard the evidence and passed sentences of death on nineteen witches in the famous trials held in Salem in 1692. Thereafter, the family had declined from positions of importance; Hawthorne's father lingered in the boy's memory as the sea captain who had been lost off Surinam, leaving a widow with three children to rear and educate. Years afterward Hawthorne admitted that little remained of a once-proud family except a mere scribbler of tales who might be making better and more lucrative use of his time than sitting at a writing desk.

Young Hawthorne attended the Salem schools and then, from 1821 to 1825, Bowdoin College in the far-off woods of Brunswick, Maine. The college was new; it looked as if its several buildings had been placed intact in the endless wilderness where a river flowed nearby. Yet Bowdoin would never again have students who would become quite so famous: Longfellow was to be the distinguished professor of modern languages and the equally distinguished poet; Franklin Pierce rose to be President of the United States. And, of course, there was Hawthorne, who, when he graduated, was in the middle of his class; his only high marks were in the courses which, more often than not, are the bane of the undergraduate— rhetoric and composition. In every other respect he showed little promise: he had not prepared to study law; he seemed in no way destined for the ministry—the law and the ministry were then the two main paths of adventure for ambitious college graduates—and he had even less interest in teaching school than would, a few years later, his friend Henry Thoreau. He had only one thing he really wanted to do, and he did it: he returned to his mother's home on Charter Street, Salem, and became a writer.

To become a writer was no easier in 1825 than it is in a later time. Then as now the young writer would need more patience and endurance than most people have, and sacrifice months and years to producing what the outside world seldom reads or even hears of; the rewards may come, but they usually come late, as they did for Hawthorne. In the meantime, the youthful writer must do the best he can, constantly practice to perfect his craft and style, and gain a maturity of mind which may someday reveal to him his true self and his true subject. Hawthorne's years of practice and experimentation were spent on a novel, *Fanshawe* (1828), which presented some of his undergraduate life behind a rather opaque disguise, and on a great number of short stories, some of which were printed and many of which were undoubtedly destroyed.

If a writer ever becomes a craftsman of distinction, he must find his true, his special genius. If he never finds his way during his impressionable years, he had better abandon writing altogether. The period in Hawthorne's life between twenty-one and thirty-three was the crucial time: Hawthorne found his special voice and style and fashioned the particular lines and colors of his art.

These "twelve dark years," as he afterward called them, have attracted a great deal of critical attention—those years from his graduation in 1825 until his "emergence" in 1837. Hawthorne himself helped to create the legend of his solitary existence, his withdrawal from the world, his lonely night walks along the deserted streets of Salem or down to the dark shoreline. In some of his notebook entries and in the letters he wrote to his fiancée, Sophia Peabody, he called up those months of self-denial and dedication to a useless literary indulgence for which the outside world had scant use or reward. One should always be wary of the confessions a young man puts in a letter to the woman he loves, especially if he is a literary young man. A young man in love is not necessarily a liar, but, like Huck Finn, he "stretches the truth" a little. Actually, throughout those twelve years Hawthorne lived a quite active life; he visited his friends; he took extensive summer tours to the New England mountains and as far west as Niagara Falls; he watched with fascination long and sensational murder trials; he attended the local taverns, and, in general, he behaved much as a young man between the ages of twenty-one and thirty-three is likely to behave.

Yet there is enough truth in the legend of the "twelve dark years" to give it literary significance. That a young man is taking trips or visiting taverns and murder trials does not obviate the possibility that he is thinking and living quite differently within himself. It is not important that a writer sit in an upstairs room and practice his craft for twelve years: what is important is that he open a negotiation with a world—not the world of actuality in which he lives and moves, but that other world of his imagination, of his deepest sensibility, of what Hawthorne called "the interior of the heart." Hawthorne early discovered what was his world of the imagination, and he was wise to remain in it for the rest of his life. It was not within the boundaries of Salem, or of Massachusetts, or even anywhere in the western hemisphere, though it had recognizable place names. It was that region within the human heart and consciousness where sin and guilt reside, where dark secrets are hidden from the peering eyes of men, where the deep festerings of remorse and conscience work to destroy, and where the eternal questions of men never quite find the answers which comfort and satisfy. Whether or not "twelve dark years" were needed to form this world, Hawthorne had lived, and was thereafter to live, with a dimension of blackness lodged in his work, for he was especially gifted with the insight to perceive and the craft to disclose the drama of human suffering which forever exists as a rule of existence.

The year 1837 was important in Hawthorne's life. He collected a number of short stories he had published in magazines and issued them in a volume entitled *Twice-Told Tales*. The book had little sale and attracted only modest critical attention; its odd title suggested that the author was doing nothing more than retell the same weary narratives which men had long known. In that same year Hawthorne met and became engaged to Sophia Peabody of Salem and Boston. In days when young lovers did not think that they had to be married at once, Hawthorne and Sophia waited—waited from 1839 to 1841 while Hawthorne had a dull job in the Boston customhouse. They continued to wait through the seven months from April to November 1841, when Hawthorne was a member of the famous Brook Farm community: there a group of people with high literary and grandly reformist social aspirations—many of them Transcendentalists, but not Emerson or Thoreau—tried to prove that men need not grind their lives away at monotonous, senseless work. Unfortunately for Hawthorne, the work on the farm was monotonous and unrewarding, and he found little interest in turning a wicked world to rights. He left the farm wiser than he had been in the ways of men and women; later he would recast the adventure in his novel *The Blithedale Romance* (1852).

In the summer of 1842 Hawthorne and Sophia Peabody were married and moved into the Old Manse in Concord, already made famous by Emerson's residence and the writing of *Nature* (1836). For a time the sale of stories supported the husband and wife and the children as they arrived. Yet, quite evidently, a life devoted to literature became ever more precarious: Hawthorne could not earn a living from his writing. Accordingly, out of need rather than desire, he accepted a political appointment from the Massachusetts Democrats who had been victorious in the election of 1844 and became surveyor in the Salem customhouse. For three years he drew his salary and had very little to do: Salem was in a commercial decline; it was not even in competition with the whaling ports New Bedford and Nantucket which Melville would celebrate a few years later. Then, in one of those political upheavals which regularly marked the early Republic, the Whigs triumphed; the Democrats must go, and in June 1849, Hawthorne lost his place as surveyor.

Although Hawthorne tried to get back his job, he knew that his only hope was his writing. Between that summer of 1849 and the opening of 1850 he produced his master-work, *The Scarlet Letter*. The Preface, which he entitled "The Custom House," was a wry, backhanded atttempt to get even with the political enemies who had made him lose his place; it also tells us something of what was going on in that other self, the imagination, during the dull hours and years in the cus-tomhouse. The book was at once a striking success and made Hawthorne's name known in literary circles. Six months later, in the summer of 1850, he first met Melville, who found in Hawthorne a writer who dared to investigate the dark underside of human sin and suffering. Perhaps the meeting and sub-sequent friendship encouraged Melville to go his own extraordinary way in *Moby-Dick*.

Even though Hawthorne published *The House of the Seven Gables* (1851), compiled another collection of short stories, *The Snow-Image and Other Twice-Told Tales* (1851), and issued *The Blithedale Romance* (1852), he was still driven to earn more money. After his friend, Franklin Pierce, was elected President, Hawthorne in 1853 ac-cepted an appointment as consul at Liver-pool, one of the most lucrative positions in the State Department. Throughout four years he worked diligently in the grimy consulate by the waterfront; he also found time to travel up and down the English countryside, to gaze at quaint English villages and churches, to explore the byways of London, and to receive the honors due a visiting lit-erary man. In 1858, again with the change of a political administration, Hawthorne re-signed from the consulate and for a year re-sided in Italy before returning to England. The results of these travels were the note-books he kept and *The Marble Faun* (1860), which he published shortly before he re-turned to the United States.

Hawthorne's last years were clouded by a nagging worry over money: his savings from the consulate did not last as long as he had hoped. The Civil War threatened and then began; Hawthorne could only sit and watch the collapse of a world, both real and imagi-nary, that he had once known. As he worked desperately to complete one last novel, he seemed visibly to weaken and to waste away. His friends and family were deeply con-cerned. A short journey to Washington and even to the scene of the war in 1862 was to no avail. In May 1864, Hawthorne died in his sleep while staying in Plymouth, New Hampshire. Of his generation of distin-guished literary men, only Thoreau had gone before him; those who survived were at the funeral in Concord to pay him tribute.

## II

HAWTHORNE'S lifelong dedication to his art puts him in the company of other American writers who were similarly dedicated and who were deeply concerned with the ques-tion of the artist in America. One of the cu-riosities of any reading of Hawthorne is that he tended to raise this question as if it were a joke. His wry and mordant comments on the folly of dreaming dreams and writing stories only to fascinate children are among the most devastating in our literary history: they reveal the misplacement of a writer in a society which has scant use for him. Henry James cogently remarked on the thinness of American life in the time Hawthorne lived; the suggestion is true if we suppose that Hawthorne was less an artist than he might otherwise have been had he had a deep past and lived in a land with the storied enchant-ment of history as his daily imaginative fare.

If a writer does feel misplaced in his na-tive land, then perforce he must solve his private dilemma as best he can or renounce his vocation. One of Hawthorne's ways was to project an alter ego, as though he lived with "another Hawthorne." One side of Hawthorne lived comfortably and unspectac-ularly in the world; it wisely abandoned the daily submission to the paper on the writing desk and went to work at desks in the Bos-ton and Salem customhouses; it bought property, paid taxes, and lived a decorous and dignified life. This side showed to the world a bland, retiring, even shy gentleman. Holmes once remarked that Hawthorne was like a candle burning on a mantelpiece; it did not give off much heat, but its light was clear. This Hawthorne baffles any reader, as it baffled Henry James, who took too literally the jocularity, the transparent and not very funny jokes, the rather trite commonplaces on man's folly, and the nearly total absence of any interest in the burning issues of Hawthorne's own day. The mood of jest, of bantering indifference, even colors Hawthorne's remarks on what was most important to him—his writings. The Prefaces to *The Scarlet Letter* and to *The House of the Seven Gables* are expressions of that side of a man who presumes to think that the profession of letters in America is a ludicrous joke.

Then there was the "other Hawthorne" which the tales and novels portray—the intensely brooding mind, the inquiring imagination, the speculator on the dark ambiguity of man's being. None of Hawthorne's friends and associates could quite reconcile these two differing aspects of the same man; Emerson professed to be delighted with the raffish satire of "The Celestial Railroad" and preferred to let the darker nature of his friend remain unpenetrated. Melville saw more clearly than anyone else that Hawthorne was not simply a shy artist whose delicate tales masked a profound moral understanding; for Melville, Hawthorne was a grand "No-sayer" who undercut the deceptive illusions by which men live comfortably and dully.

Any answer to the question of a dual Hawthorne might solve one aspect and ignore the other. The man and the artist were two quite separate beings. To attempt to find Hawthorne, the man, in his writings is to misjudge Hawthorne, the writer; and to read the writings as a mirror of the man is to falsify both the man and the writer. The man and the artist lived and worked together, but they were two quite differing expressions not only of the man but of the literary situation in America.

The question of a writer's displacement, whether real or imagined, is different every time a writer lives. The America in which Hawthorne lived lacked a tragic heritage and a tragic vision. Even though there had been powerful and profound inquiries into man's suffering and tragic situation, the adventure into the depths of man's moral nature had been customarily undertaken by clergymen, who, if they were marvelously skilled in revealing the terror of existence, were not competent to deal with the single human life as itself tragic. For the Puritan, man was tragic because God had so willed the human destiny; for a Deist of the eighteenth century the question of tragedy was academic and even slightly absurd: man's reason could overcome the "tragic" circumstance. For the Unitarian and the religious idealist of the nineteenth century, tragedy had long ceased to have any meaning. The later Emerson faced the dark implications of human disenfranchisement from a universe which was not all good; but that teaching was concealed by that other, the smiling-faced Emerson whom everyone already knew.

Yet, however much Hawthorne lacked an imaginative and intellectual heritage of literary tragedy, he was aware of the extent of the world's moral tragedy. He early discovered almost as if it were his unique domain, a world inhabited by the sin-sick and guilty who may find peace, not in illumination or redemption, but in the awareness of their suffering. The very lack of a literary and an artistic heritage, and his admission that as a writer he lived ill at ease in his own homeland turned Hawthorne into an anatomist of "the interior of the heart." His consciousness of the isolation of man in the universe, of the ring of darkness which encircles all joy, and the need of men, at least a few men, to see into their own souls was for Hawthorne, as it was for Melville and Mark Twain, the ethical substitution for the tragic vision which the English literary tradition had possessed since the time of Shakespeare.

If America has seldom had a tradition of literary tragedy, it can boast of a heritage of moral inquiry in its literature which is still one of the surprises of the world of letters. Europeans are always entranced by the startling discrepancy between a country which appears to bend its energies wholly on practical, technical accomplishments and yet, by contrast, whose writers seek out and uncover the dark abysm of human evil and suffering. Hawthorne is representative of one half of our tradition of moral inquiry; Emerson and Thoreau may well represent another. *Nature* and *Walden* are masterworks of inquiry in the quest of human thought for self-understanding. Yet, at the same time that they present a profound moral search, they are effectively disclosing the autobiography of moral understanding; they skillfully unfold the vagaries of a single self and at every moment chart for us the "psychology" of individual moral existence. To read *Nature* and *Walden* we must come to terms with and intimately know the brooding introspection and the moral ideas of Emerson and Thoreau.

When we read Hawthorne, we are not dealing with the "autobiography" of Hawthorne; his tales and novels are not about the man Hawthorne slowly approaching an understanding of human experience. Like their creator, the writings present an elaborate masquerade; they have a double life. The protagonists of the tales—Robin Molineux, Goodman Brown, Parson Hooper, to name a few—are forced to live by introspection, by the most private self-consciousness, and by some vision of a moral destiny of the universe. Yet they are never allowed to know what is happening in their minds at the moments of crucial thought and action. They are driven, even destroyed—yet they are forbidden to know their own ideas. This masquerade of consciousness is one of the most haunting aspects of Hawthorne's art.

Not only are Hawthorne's protagonists denied the power of introspection, but the movement of the story is away from the man or the woman under investigation and toward what Hawthorne himself called the "moral universe." Robin, Brown, and Hooper are placed in some nebulous, even timeless moral comprehension or blindness and then go the way they must go, not because their minds will that direction, but because every thought they have is but part of an infinitely larger "thought," the timeless, moral understanding of the universe. The knowledge of sin becomes a vantage point from which to establish a most intimate relation with the world and to find the truest knowledge of this world, for the universe has been sinful and guilt-ridden long before man came to exist.

"The Maypole of Merry Mount" introduces us not merely to a strangely misplaced scene of jollity and dancing but rather to a comprehension that merrymaking is some vestige of ancient harmony which man lost in the long ages since he has had the power of thought. Man may once have been joyful, in ages past, but darkness and gloom have by now become the measures of historical time. Only by understanding how temporary and fleeting are the joys of this world can men come to know that sin and evil are not acts of mind or motions of the body or even the breaking of a Puritan law. Sin and evil are the moral constants which link all men in the continuity of time past, present, and future. The "strange feeling" which Edith feels in her heart the moment she asks a question is the bond she establishes with the suffering and evil of the ages. Similarly, in the tales on art and artists Hawthorne considers this theme: in "The Artist of the Beautiful" the moral element of art is not its relation to contemporary society. Art does not reflect the present and the actual; indeed, for Hawthorne, the artist is like every other morally comprehending man: he is continually engaged, in ways far beyond his knowing, in uncovering the "pastness" of any act in the present. A picture presents a question in human consciousness and is a revelation of the inscrutable ways by which any action, no matter how trivial, is related to all other actions in the past. The portraits of the husband and wife were "prophetic" because they unmasked the long-concealed evil which all men carry with them behind their comfortable masquerade of success.

In nearly all Hawthorne's stories something keeps us at a distance, prevents us from discovering at once what the stories are about, and teases us into reading them more deeply than we might otherwise do. The tales are ambiguous because they present a very considerable gap between what the characters in the stories know about themselves and, by contrast, what is required of us as readers to know. We must exercise the privilege of penetrating the mystery and unravelling the secret. Hawthorne's artistic excellence is nowhere better demonstrated than in his power of deepening the commonplace, simple truths of human life. Mystery is a part of understanding, for knowledge of his moral truths never comes easily and no matter how far it goes, knowledge is always incomplete.

### III

SOME have said that Hawthorne was not really interested in living human beings but in men and women only as types or moral objects. The charge is true if we recognize that the characters in the tales and novels are always in intimate association with the scene in which they live and move: the village, the church, the study, the forest, the hill—these are outward projections of inward states of being and perhaps are themselves, as objects in the world, not very "real" either. In "Young Goodman Brown" Hawthorne's method of bringing the "moral universe" into association with human figures has been deepened and refined. The farther Brown journeys into the forest, the more suggestive and even prophetic the scene becomes. The dusky forest, the withered branch on the tree, the gnarled figures, and the red-lit fire all suggest the guilty heart of Brown himself. At the climax of the story Brown screams, the scene instantly dissolves, and Brown is back in Salem once more. What Brown eventually realized was that he had undertaken a journey which was not real: everything he experienced and everything he saw was but an outward manifestation of his own inner state of mind.

When Hawthorne wrote "The Maypole of Merry Mount," this method of objectifying inner states of being had become a key to his craft. The forest, the shower of withering rose petals, and the groan of the falling tree are not so much actions in nature as they are signs of what is occurring in the minds and hearts of Edith and Edgar. Indeed, the world "becomes psychology" for the characters. They are incapable of expressing their own inner states and so must have much of their private thought expressed by means other than the direct dialogue and straightforward expository devices common to the novel when Hawthorne began to write fiction. Hawthorne's craft so deepened that by

the time he wrote "Ethan Brand" and *The Scarlet Letter*, both published in 1850, this gauzy, suggestive, "moral universe" would be one of our best ways of knowing what was truly happening to his men and women in their innermost hearts.

Hawthorne's men and women live in a strange, dark world; they are burdened with sin and guilt which they are incapable of expressing on their own. Yet Hawthorne did not reduce his characters to puppets in a highly colored scene. He was not trying, as was Poe, to bring human life and the natural world into some unified, or convulsive, relationship. Nor was he trying to illustrate profound moral truths by moving human beings through a carefully contrived moral allegory to reach a fitting moral conclusion. Otherwise, he would have been a sermonizer or, like Franklin, a propounder of moral axioms as in "The Way to Wealth." Rather, he was a symbolist and, if the definition can be made more precisely, a "Puritan symbolist."

A symbolist is different every time he occurs or every time he has a thought. Hawthorne was a symbolist different from Melville, Whitman, or Emily Dickinson. No one can say what makes a symbolist writer or what forms the special symbolic imagination a writer may have. Certain times are favorable to the appearance of symbolist thought: the Middle Ages, the early seventeenth century, the period of the Puritan migration to Massachusetts, and the first half of the nineteenth century in America were propitious to a symbolist method of feeling, thinking, and making meaning known. Hawthorne came, therefore, at a time in the artistic and imaginative life of America which encouraged a form of thinking which is symbolist. However much Hawthorne differed from Emerson, he nonetheless was not too far from the questions which Emerson asked and even some of the answers which Emerson—or Thoreau, Whitman, and Melville too—obtained.

Symbols are ways of making meaning known. A falling leaf, a ray of sunshine, a smile, a mark on a young woman's cheek, a fire, a veil over a face—these and the infinite variety of objects and motions in nature are what become symbols when men see in them meanings beyond their mere experience as objects or events. Artists and writers are symbolists when they seek to interpret the world of fact according to ideas and premises which are not implicit in those objects. A burning bush is ostensibly a bush on fire, but it "becomes meaning" when it is interpreted and is known to offer a sign to men.

We should also understand that symbols are not invented; writers do not make up objects and then conveniently assign meanings to them. If a writer does so, he is a faker and soon detected. Furthermore, a symbol does not exist alone or as a single object of meaning; rather, symbols are always in relationship, context, association; they organize a wide variety of ideas into single, and sometimes simple, acts of understanding. A country's flag is a host of memories, historical events, emotional complexities which a rectangular cloth in varying colors and designs may embody. Again: symbols are part of a culture; certain symbols are very meaningful to Frenchmen, Germans, and Americans; objects may assume symbolic importance in differing times and places. Indeed, every writer lives in a unique historical situation which has its own complex of symbols, and he may express himself in ways, and according to designs of meaning, of which he is himself unknowing. A writer is virtually in the grip of his time and the symbolic situation which he inherits: what he writes is an unconscious reflection of the moral tone, the principal desires, the underlying directions which his age gives him, and, quite unaware of what he is doing, he may be mirroring some of the most tenuous and profound ideas of his age. Chiefly because he reflected a long-ago Puritan way of thinking about and looking at the world, because, in a real sense, he made his fiction out of "cases of conscience," and because he reflected certain moral ideas of his own time, Hawthorne can rightly be regarded as a latter-day Puritan, a moral symbolist.

Hawthorne's best subjects and his clearest vision were derived from the New England Puritan past—that long and memorable roll-call of themes, historical events, and significant men who had lived their lives in the early colony and commonwealth. What that past gave Hawthorne was what his own times could not, namely, a valid artistic subject matter and a range of imaginative speculation. If the contemporary soil of nineteenth-century America was thin, as Henry James believed, the older Puritan earth was deep and rich enough for a thousand tales. In this special imaginative, symbolic spectrum Hawthorne found his best work, "The Minister's Black Veil," "Young Goodman Brown," "Ethan Brand," and *The Scarlet Letter*.

Hawthorne rediscovered what another Puritan, Jonathan Edwards, had long ago known: the world contains meaning. Men may know or be ignorant—in theological Puritanism the terms were "saved" or "condemned"—insofar as they are provided with the perception to read and understand that world of sign, symbol, and meaning all around them. Edwards, as he informs us in his "Personal Narrative," rode into the woods and saw Christ in a vision; Goodman Brown took his night journey into the woods and returned forever a changed man. The understanding of what took place in both events could be presented only as an imaginative speculation, with all its tenuous hints and its partial answers. The problem both for Edwards and for Goodman Brown is essentially the same: How does a man come to know what he truly is and what his place is in the world? Edwards had asked this question as a theologian; another Puritan, the poet Edward Taylor, had found his answers in the objects of everyday life wherein God reveals His ways to men: "Huswifery" is a model of immediately known images as signs of God's presence.

Hawthorne was neither a theologian nor a poet; his symbolism is, however, rightly called "Puritan," for the objects of this world must necessarily be read aright. One obvious difference between Hawthorne and his Puritan antecedents is that, for a seventeenth- or eighteenth-century mind, a symbol is an invitation, even a demand, to further deeper meaning and understanding. For Hawthorne a symbol is not so much an idea or a meaning which the human mind slowly comes to know; rather, a symbol is a dimension of nature. The symbol fulfills itself; it contains all that is to be known; it does not promise that farther vision in Edwards' search for understanding in this world or in Taylor's reverent privilege to glorify a spinning wheel. When we have completed one of Hawthorne's tales or novels, we know all that we shall ever know about the falling leaf, the hand over the heart, the veil over the face; these symbols have been our only way to understand the people who have sinned and who suffer and our only way whereby we have known the world in which they live.

Hawthorne's symbolism so encloses the action and so fully determines what the characters shall be that a symbol becomes "psychology"; it is our way of learning the motives and purposes of men and women who are denied the right to know themselves. In "The Maypole of Merry Mount" what the people feel and think is almost nothing; yet the physical objects—the gaudily decorated tree, the masks, the dark lowering forest all around —"think" for them: every mood and whim is contained in and mirrored by that scene. Edith does not really think when she wonders about the mystery of sadness in her heart; by contrast, the shower of withering rose petals thinks for her; it shows that, however sad she may be, the world itself exists on the principle of universal suffering. Parson Hooper does not come to a knowledge of secret sin until he sees that all other faces and even the earth have their black veils. And when Goodman Brown has left his youthful innocence and truly matured, he knows that the most pious people and the most serene earth are cankered by what he has discovered in himself.

Hawthorne's symbolism, even his ideas which are behind those symbols, creates a closed world. Men and women are not capable of thinking about or shaping their destiny; the world and its symbols do that shaping for them. They are in the control of a mysterious, active force which has existed long before they lived and will continue to be exerted long after they are gone. If Hawthorne accepted most of Puritan thought and its symbolism, he did not show life as moving toward a Puritan self-enlightenment and peace. The characters suffer from a Puritan's troubled conscience, the need for self-scrutiny and self-understanding, and from the loneliness which is all men's history; yet they are without any sense that the divine hand is at work for ill or good in their lives. They exist as if every law in the universe were as rigid and exacting as for a seventeenth-century Puritan; yet God long ago removed Himself from His world. Here, in brief, is the paradox of Hawthorne's writings: the perdurable laws and the timeless symbols still remain as remorselessly in force as in a time long past; but man alone has somehow lost all sense of a God of law or a God of understanding.

## IV

HAWTHORNE was a latter-day Puritan. He was also a citizen of the literary world of his own time. If his symbolism was framed in the thinking of Puritanism, it was also investigating the most cogent thought of his own day. "Young Goodman Brown" appeared in 1835, the year before the publication of Emerson's *Nature*. Hawthorne's short story might be read as a mildly prefiguring dramatization of Emerson's thesis. Brown walks from the ostensibly real world of Salem into the test or "discipline" of the night meeting; once there, he is in a shimmering world of fact fused with dream, of wisdom threatened by insanity, of certainty mingled with fear, until he finally emerges with a cry—not into the enlightenment of Emersonian "prospects" but into that dark "ambiguity of sin or sorrow," the unresolved doubt which never answers the question which Emerson answered so affirmatively. "Know then," Emerson said triumphantly, "that the world exists for you. For you is the phenomenon perfect. . . . Build therefore your own world." For Brown, not the world, but man's own knowledge of his deceptions and self-delusions is all that exists. To be sure, one builds his own world, but it is one fashioned only in the awareness that nothing, not even one's self, is certain. In his novels, Hawthorne raised the Emersonian, the major nineteenth-century questions: Is the world real, or is it merely what we want it to be? Is human life formed in accordance with a divine destiny which man may come to know if he seeks hard and far enough? Does man ever gain self-knowledge, or is he thrust ever deeper into the loneliness of his private speculation?

These and similar issues are the bases for the tales from the earliest, in the 1830's, to the last, in 1850. Like his friend Melville, Hawthorne wrote a testament of rejection. For both writers the world is an unquiet place, and most men live in it their lives of wonder, searching, and piecemeal despair. Yet, if the two men are alike in their themes, they were quite unlike in other ways. Hawthorne's "double mind" spared him: he lived somehow free, as a man, of the perils which a vision of darkness might bring; his imagination seldom seems to have impinged on his everyday, practical life. By contrast, Melville lived as a private man precisely what he thought and presented as a writer; his was the truer vocation of the man to his art, for what he saw in his imagination he believed in his daily life. When the two friends met in 1856, after a separation of several years, Hawthorne's journal entry (see p. 410) vividly shows the ravages which the imagination of Melville had produced in the author of *Moby-Dick* and *Pierre*, a man whose thinking and imagination were one. Hawthorne was, by contrast, forever distanced from his art; his double mind was his insurance against the crippling effects of hypersensitivity and morbidity of conscience.

Yet, for all that one may admire in Hawthorne's thought, it is his art which has survived and gained the greatest favor in our own time. Hawthorne as a man is, accordingly, less interesting than Hawthorne as a craftsman and symbolist who, almost in spite of himself, became a major writer. One says "in spite of himself" because Hawthorne was curiously unwilling to talk about his art or about the problems of writing. The long hours he spent with Melville were filled with Hawthorne's monosyllables and Melville's tireless sentences which wove around and through the questions of man as

a writer, as a thinker, as a citizen of the domain of art. Hawthorne's notebooks have been much admired for presenting his inner life. They do so only on those rare and unexpected occasions when Hawthorne is at ease or when he does not have any other writing to do. The jottings of ideas for tales—a representative group is presented in these selections—are so hesitatingly and even waggishly noted that one can be puzzled. Hawthorne was not an interesting keeper of a notebook because he kept his notebook as if he did not take it very seriously. He seems to have understood that he had only a scant amount of imaginative energy; he husbanded it with care and discretion. Even his Prefaces to the collections of short stories and to the novels were written in a mood of apology, as if the writer shrank from intruding upon the privacy of the reader.

Hawthorne was a major writer not because of what he was as a man, a social thinker, or a judge of his own writings, but because, from first to last, he saw each human life as a single unit, a separate, isolated case of conscience which—just as for a Puritan of the seventeenth century or for Jonathan Edwards—was faced with its own unique destiny and had to find its own unique way. Hawthorne's men and women are always undertaking a journey of consciousness—the walk of Goodman Brown through the darkening forest; the haunted steps of Parson Hooper to his death; the endless wandering of Ethan Brand until he comes home; the pilgrimage of Hester Prynne from the scaffold and back to it again. Along the route of these journeys there are no guides such as directed Bunyan's Christian to the Celestial City, and there are not even the inner promptings of conscience to distinguish between a safe and a dangerous step.

The route of these journeys was, as we have seen, not shaped by or known to the persons undertaking them; rather, the journeys were prescribed and determined by the iron ring which Fate sets against each human Will. Emerson's "Fate" and "Illusions" are a commentary on Hawthorne's vision of human life: to think is to press against the enclosing ring of destiny, for not an atom moves or a shadow flickers but in accordance with the unyielding fate. Human thinking can go only as far as it is privileged to thrust itself and then breaks against the overmastering Necessity which binds it. To think is to be free only at that instant of thinking: Parson Hooper was free on the moment of his assuming the black veil; the artist Aylmer was free when he decided that he would paint a perfect picture. But the free act of thought was itself the end of freedom, for that thought thereafter necessitated the inevitable destiny which came to Hooper, Aylmer, Hester Prynne, and the others. Man lives, therefore, in his freedom, but his freedom is, as Emerson showed, his fate: every act of willing is a narrowing of the ring of one's life until, as Goodman Brown discovered, one lives in silence.

Such a view of life puts Hawthorne near Emerson—the Emerson, not of *Nature* or "The American Scholar," but of the later writings and of the poems. It links him even more closely than friendship could to Melville, who subtitled one of his novels "or, The Ambiguities," and whose wanderings within his own dark mind brought Ahab to the tightened circle of the whale rope and Billy Budd to the noose at the end of the yardarm. It places Hawthorne within the tradition of American writing from Edwards to Emily Dickinson and to Faulkner and beyond. He was one among many who were gifted with "the power of blackness"—the search into and beyond the mysterious underside of human thought into that interior heart of man where secrets remain forever hidden and into the narrowing distance between what men hope they can do and what little they eventually accomplish. Hawthorne's world was, to be sure, not a "real" world: it was fashioned of the ephemeral dreams, the chiaroscuros of human thinking set against the rigidity of time and chance. Hawthorne's was a profoundly moral vision which, if it were denied the grandeur of tragedy, was nonetheless sensitive to those shapes of emotion and thought which his symbolism displayed and made memorable.

Thus the key to Hawthorne is his symbolic imagination and his moral insight. His writings have remained alive and his artistic reputation continues unassailed through more than a century of changing literary taste. He has been able to outshine names of apparently greater brilliance because his writings, however simple they may appear and however limited their themes may be, have continually demanded that they be read anew with a quickening response to discover what must be known if one is to understand them fully. Our journey of understanding is like that of a Puritan of another age or like that of one of Hawthorne's own men and women: we are given the signs, the symbols of human thought, and we are privileged to know them as best we can. Yet their final revelation will forever escape us, because men's deepest beliefs are themselves symbolic and, being so, are wrapped in mysteries.

# YOUNG GOODMAN BROWN

❖

❰ THIS tale first appeared in the *New England Magazine* (April 1835), and was reprinted in *Mosses from an Old Manse* (1846). The locale of Salem and the use of well-known persons who suffered in the witchcraft delusion of 1692 would seem to give the narrative a solid historical basis. Actually, however, the persons who appear from history are of less consequence than the ambiguous study of an inquiring Puritan who discovers the extent and depth of evil both in society and in himself.

❖

YOUNG Goodman [1] Brown came forth at sunset into the street at Salem village; but put his head back, after crossing the threshold, to exchange a parting kiss with his young wife. And Faith, as the wife was aptly named, thrust her own pretty head into the street, letting the wind play with the pink ribbons of her cap while she called to Goodman Brown.

"Dearest heart," whispered she, softly and rather sadly, when her lips were close to his ear, "prithee put off your journey until sunrise and

---

YOUNG GOODMAN BROWN.  1. **Goodman:** The term referred to a man of middle estate; "Mr." referred to a man of position.

sleep in your own bed to-night. A lone woman is troubled with such dreams and such thoughts that she's afeared of herself sometimes. Pray tarry with me this night, dear husband, of all nights in the year."

"My love and my Faith," replied young Goodman Brown, "of all nights in the year, this one night must I tarry away from thee. My journey, as thou callest it, forth and back again, must needs be done 'twixt now and sunrise. What, my sweet, pretty wife, dost thou doubt me already, and we but three months married?"

"Then God bless you!" said Faith, with the pink ribbons; "and may you find all well when you come back."

"Amen!" cried Goodman Brown. "Say thy prayers, dear Faith, and go to bed at dusk, and no harm will come to thee."

So they parted; and the young man pursued his way until, being about to turn the corner by the meeting-house, he looked back and saw the head of Faith still peeping after him with a melancholy air, in spite of her pink ribbons.

"Poor little Faith!" thought he, for his heart smote him. "What a wretch am I to leave her on such an errand! She talks of dreams, too. Methought as she spoke there was trouble in her face, as if a dream had warned her what work is to be done to-night. But no, no; 't would kill her to think it. Well, she's a blessed angel on earth; and after this one night I'll cling to her skirts and follow her to heaven."

With this excellent resolve for the future, Goodman Brown felt himself justified in making more haste on his present evil purpose. He had taken a dreary road, darkened by all the gloomiest trees of the forest, which barely stood aside to let the narrow path creep through, and closed immediately behind. It was all as lonely as could be; and there is this peculiarity in such a solitude, that the traveller knows not who may be concealed by the innumerable trunks and the thick boughs overhead; so that with lonely footsteps he may yet be passing through an unseen multitude.

"There may be a devilish Indian behind every tree," said Goodman Brown to himself; and he glanced fearfully behind him as he added, "What if the devil himself should be at my very elbow!"

His head being turned back, he passed a crook of the road, and, looking forward again, beheld the figure of a man, in grave and decent attire, seated at the foot of an old tree. He arose at Goodman Brown's approach and walked onward side by side with him.

"You are late, Goodman Brown," said he. "The clock of the Old South [2] was striking as I came through Boston, and that is full fifteen minutes agone."

"Faith kept me back a while," replied the young man, with a tremor in his voice, caused by the sudden appearance of his companion, though not wholly unexpected.

It was now deep dusk in the forest, and deepest in that part of it where these two were journeying. As nearly as could be discerned, the second traveller was about fifty years old, apparently in the same rank of life as Goodman Brown, and bearing a considerable resemblance to him, though perhaps more in expression than features. Still they might have been taken for father and son. And yet, though the elder person was as simply clad as the younger, and as simple in manner too, he had an indescribable air of one who knew the world, and who would not have felt abashed at the governor's dinner table or in King William's [3] court, were it possible that his affairs should call him thither. But the only thing about him that could be fixed upon as remarkable was his staff, which bore the likeness of a great black snake, so curiously wrought that it might almost be seen to twist and wriggle itself like a living serpent. This, of course, must have been an ocular deception, assisted by the uncertain light.

"Come, Goodman Brown," cried his fellow-traveller, "this is a dull pace for the beginning of a journey. Take my staff, if you are so soon weary."

"Friend," said the other, exchanging his slow pace for a full stop, "having kept covenant by meeting thee here, it is my purpose now to return whence I came. I have scruples touching the matter thou wot'st of."

"Sayest thou so?" replied he of the serpent, smiling apart. "Let us walk on, nevertheless, reasoning as we go; and if I convince thee not thou shalt turn back. We are but a little way in the forest yet."

"Too far! too far!" exclaimed the goodman, unconsciously resuming his walk. "My father never went into the woods on such an errand, nor his father before him. We have been a race of honest men and good Christians since the days of the martyrs; and shall I be the first of the name of Brown that ever took this path and kept"—

"Such company, thou wouldst say," observed the elder person, interpreting his pause. "Well

---

2. **Old South:** the Boston church organized in 1669. The "clock" is an anachronism: the bell tower and clock were not erected until the new church structure was built in 1730—some time after the events in the story take place. 3. **King William's:** William III, King of England, 1689–1702.

said, Goodman Brown! I have been as well acquainted with your family as with ever a one among the Puritans; and that's no trifle to say. I helped your grandfather, the constable, when he lashed the Quaker woman [4] so smartly through the streets of Salem; and it was I that brought your father a pitch-pine knot, kindled at my own hearth, to set fire to an Indian village, in King Philip's war.[5] They were my good friends, both; and many a pleasant walk have we had along this path, and returned merrily after midnight. I would fain be friends with you for their sake."

"If it be as thou sayest," replied Goodman Brown, "I marvel they never spoke of these matters; or, verily, I marvel not, seeing that the least rumor of the sort would have driven them from New England. We are a people of prayer, and good works to boot, and abide no such wickedness."

"Wickedness or not," said the traveller with the twisted staff, "I have a very general acquaintance here in New England. The deacons of many a church have drunk the communion wine with me; the selectmen of divers towns make me their chairman; and a majority of the Great and General Court [6] are firm supporters of my interest. The governor and I, too—But these are state secrets."

"Can this be so?" cried Goodman Brown, with a stare of amazement at his undisturbed companion. "Howbeit, I have nothing to do with the governor and council; they have their own ways, and are no rule for a simple husbandman like me. But, were I to go on with thee, how should I meet the eye of that good old man, our minister, at Salem village? Oh, his voice would make me tremble both Sabbath day and lecture day."

Thus far the elder traveller had listened with due gravity; but now burst into a fit of irrepressible mirth, shaking himself so violently that his snake-like staff actually seemed to wriggle in sympathy.

"Ha! ha! ha!" shouted he again and again; then composing himself, "Well, go on, Goodman Brown, go on; but, prithee, don't kill me with laughing."

"Well, then, to end the matter at once," said Goodman Brown, considerably nettled, "there is my wife, Faith. It would break her dear little heart; and I'd rather break my own."

"Nay, if that be the case," answered the other,

"e'en go thy ways, Goodman Brown. I would not for twenty old women like the one hobbling before us that Faith should come to any harm."

As he spoke he pointed his staff at a female figure on the path, in whom Goodman Brown recognized a very pious and exemplary dame, who had taught him his catechism in youth, and was still his moral and spiritual adviser, jointly with the minister and Deacon Gookin.[7]

"A marvel, truly, that Goody Cloyse [8] should be so far in the wilderness at nightfall," said he. "But with your leave, friend, I shall take a cut through the woods until we have left this Christian woman behind. Being a stranger to you, she might ask whom I was consorting with and whither I was going."

"Be it so," said his fellow-traveller. "Betake you to the woods, and let me keep the path."

Accordingly the young man turned aside, but took care to watch his companion, who advanced softly along the road until he had come within a staff's length of the old dame. She, meanwhile, was making the best of her way, with singular speed for so aged a woman, and mumbling some indistinct words—a prayer, doubtless—as she went. The traveller put forth his staff and touched her withered neck with what seemed the serpent's tail.

"The devil!" screamed the pious old lady.

"Then Goody Cloyse knows her old friend?" observed the traveller, confronting her and leaning on his writhing stick.

"Ah, forsooth, and is it your worship indeed?" cried the good dame. "Yea, truly is it, and in the very image of my old gossip, Goodman Brown, the grandfather of the silly fellow that now is. But —would your worship believe it?—my broomstick hath strangely disappeared, stolen, as I suspect, by that unhanged witch, Goody Cory, and that, too, when I was all anointed with the juice of smallage, and cinquefoil, and wolf's bane"—[9]

"Mingled with fine wheat and the fat of a new-born babe," said the shape of old Goodman Brown.

"Ah, your worship knows the recipe," cried the old lady, cackling aloud. "So, as I was saying, being all ready for the meeting, and no horse to ride on, I made up my mind to foot it; for they tell

---

4. **lashed . . . woman:** William Hathorne (1607?–81) was reputed to have driven Quaker women out of Salem.   **5. King Philip's war:** a desperate and futile stand by the Indians in 1676.   **6. Great and General Court:** the legislative body of colonial Massachusetts.

7. **Deacon Gookin:** Daniel Gookin (1612–87), who was superintendent of the Indians and author of the *Historical Collections of the Indians of Massachusetts* (1674).   **8. Goody Cloyse:** She was sentenced to death for witchcraft in 1692, as were Goody Cory and Martha Carrier.   **9. smallage . . . bane:** "smallage" is parsley; "cinquefoil" is a plant of the rose family; "wolf's bane" is aconite or monkshood.

me there is a nice young man to be taken into communion to-night. But now your good worship will lend me your arm, and we shall be there in a twinkling."

"That can hardly be," answered her friend. "I may not spare you my arm, Goody Cloyse; but here is my staff, if you will."

So saying, he threw it down at her feet, where, perhaps, it assumed life, being one of the rods which its owner had formerly lent to the Egyptian magi.[10] Of this fact, however, Goodman Brown could not take cognizance. He had cast up his eyes in astonishment, and, looking down again, beheld neither Goody Cloyse nor the serpentine staff, but this fellow-traveller alone, who waited for him as calmly as if nothing had happened.

"That old woman taught me my catechism," said the young man; and there was a world of meaning in this simple comment.

They continued to walk onward, while the elder traveller exhorted his companion to make good speed and persevere in the path, discoursing so aptly that his arguments seemed rather to spring up in the bosom of his auditor than to be suggested by himself. As they went, he plucked a branch of maple to serve for a walking stick, and began to strip it of the twigs and little boughs, which were wet with evening dew. The moment his fingers touched them they became strangely withered and dried up as with a week's sunshine. Thus the pair proceeded, at a good free pace, until suddenly, in a gloomy hollow of the road, Goodman Brown sat himself down on the stump of a tree and refused to go any farther.

"Friend," said he, stubbornly, "my mind is made up. Not another step will I budge on this errand. What if a wretched old woman do choose to go to the devil when I thought she was going to heaven: is that any reason why I should quit my dear Faith and go after her?"

"You will think better of this by and by," said his acquaintance, composedly. "Sit here and rest yourself a while; and when you feel like moving again, there is my staff to help you along."

Without more words, he threw his companion the maple stick, and was as speedily out of sight as if he had vanished into the deepening gloom. The young man sat a few moments by the roadside, applauding himself greatly, and thinking with how clear a conscience he should meet the minister in his morning walk, nor shrink from the eye of good old Deacon Gookin. And what calm sleep would be his that very night, which was to have been spent so wickedly, but so purely and sweetly now,

in the arms of Faith! Amidst these pleasant and praiseworthy meditations, Goodman Brown heard the tramp of horses along the road, and deemed it advisable to conceal himself within the verge of the forest, conscious of the guilty purpose that had brought him thither, though now so happily turned from it.

On came the hoof tramps and the voices of the riders, two grave old voices, conversing soberly as they drew near. These mingled sounds appeared to pass along the road, within a few yards of the young man's hiding-place; but, owing doubtless to the depth of the gloom at that particular spot, neither the travellers nor their steeds were visible. Though their figures brushed the small boughs by the wayside, it could not be seen that they intercepted, even for a moment, the faint gleam from the strip of bright sky athwart which they must have passed. Goodman Brown alternately crouched and stood on tiptoe, pulling aside the branches and thrusting forth his head as far as he durst without discerning so much as a shadow. It vexed him the more, because he could have sworn, were such a thing possible, that he recognized the voices of the minister and Deacon Gookin, jogging along quietly, as they were wont to do, when bound to some ordination or ecclesiastical council. While yet within hearing, one of the riders stopped to pluck a switch.

"Of the two, reverend sir," said the voice like the deacon's, "I had rather miss an ordination dinner than to-night's meeting. They tell me that some of our community are to be here from Falmouth and beyond, and others from Connecticut and Rhode Island, besides several of the Indian powwows, who, after their fashion, know almost as much deviltry as the best of us. Moreover, there is a goodly young woman to be taken into communion."

"Mighty well, Deacon Gookin!" replied the solemn old tones of the minister. "Spur up, or we shall be late. Nothing can be done, you know, until I get on the ground."

The hoofs clattered again; and the voices, talking so strangely in the empty air, passed on through the forest, where no church had ever been gathered or solitary Christian prayed. Whither, then, could these holy men be journeying so deep into the heathen wilderness? Young Goodman Brown caught hold of a tree for support, being ready to sink down on the ground, faint and overburdened with the heavy sickness of his heart. He looked up to the sky, doubting whether there really was a heaven above him. Yet there was the blue arch, and the stars brightening in it.

"With heaven above and Faith below, I will yet

10. Egyptian magi: See Exod. 7:8–12.

stand firm against the devil!" cried Goodman Brown.

While he still gazed upward into the deep arch of the firmament and had lifted his hands to pray, a cloud, though no wind was stirring, hurried across the zenith and hid the brightening stars. The blue sky was still visible, except directly overhead, where this black mass of cloud was sweeping swiftly northward. Aloft in the air, as if from the depths of the cloud, came a confused and doubtful sound of voices. Once the listener fancied that he could distinguish the accents of towns-people of his own, men and women, both pious and ungodly, many of whom he had met at the communion table, and had seen others rioting at the tavern. The next moment, so indistinct were the sounds, he doubted whether he had heard aught but the murmur of the old forest, whispering without a wind. Then came a stronger swell of those familiar tones, heard daily in the sunshine at Salem village, but never until now from a cloud of night. There was one voice, of a young woman, uttering lamentations, yet with an uncertain sorrow, and entreating for some favor, which, perhaps, it would grieve her to obtain; and all the unseen multitude, both saints and sinners, seemed to encourage her onward.

"Faith!" shouted Goodman Brown, in a voice of agony and desperation; and the echoes of the forest mocked him, crying, "Faith! Faith!" as if bewildered wretches were seeking her all through the wilderness.

The cry of grief, rage, and terror was yet piercing the night, when the unhappy husband held his breath for a response. There was a scream, drowned immediately in a louder murmur of voices, fading into far-off laughter, as the dark cloud swept away, leaving the clear and silent sky above Goodman Brown. But something fluttered lightly down through the air and caught on the branch of a tree. The young man seized it, and beheld a pink ribbon.

"My Faith is gone!" cried he, after one stupefied moment. "There is no good on earth; and sin is but a name. Come, devil; for to thee is this world given."

And, maddened with despair, so that he laughed loud and long, did Goodman Brown grasp his staff and set forth again, at such a rate that he seemed to fly along the forest path rather than to walk or run. The road grew wilder and drearier and more faintly traced, and vanished at length, leaving him in the heart of the dark wilderness, still rushing onward with the instinct that guides mortal man to evil. The whole forest was peopled with frightful sounds—the creaking of the trees, the howling of wild beasts, and the yell of Indians; while sometimes the wind tolled like a distant church bell, and sometimes gave a broad roar around the traveller, as if all Nature were laughing him to scorn. But he was himself the chief horror of the scene, and shrank not from its other horrors.

"Ha! ha! ha!" roared Goodman Brown when the wind laughed at him. "Let us hear which will laugh loudest. Think not to frighten me with your deviltry. Come witch, come wizard, come Indian powwow, come devil himself, and here comes Goodman Brown. You may as well fear him as he fear you."

In truth, all through the haunted forest there could be nothing more frightful than the figure of Goodman Brown. On he flew among the black pines, brandishing his staff with frenzied gestures, now giving vent to an inspiration of horrid blasphemy, and now shouting forth such laughter as set all the echoes of the forest laughing like demons around him. The fiend in his own shape is less hideous than when he rages in the breast of man. Thus sped the demoniac on his course, until, quivering among the trees, he saw a red light before him, as when the felled trunks and branches of a clearing have been set on fire, and throw up their lurid blaze against the sky, at the hour of midnight. He paused, in a lull of the tempest that had driven him onward, and heard the swell of what seemed a hymn, rolling solemnly from a distance with the weight of many voices. He knew the tune; it was a familiar one in the choir of the village meeting-house. The verse died heavily away, and was lengthened by a chorus, not of human voices, but of all the sounds of the benighted wilderness pealing in awful harmony together. Goodman Brown cried out, and his cry was lost to his own ear by its unison with the cry of the desert.

In the interval of silence he stole forward until the light glared full upon his eyes. At one extremity of an open space, hemmed in by the dark wall of the forest, arose a rock, bearing some rude, natural resemblance either to an altar or a pulpit, and surrounded by four blazing pines, their tops aflame, their stems untouched, like candles at an evening meeting. The mass of foliage that had overgrown the summit of the rock was all on fire, blazing high into the night and fitfully illuminating the whole field. Each pendent twig and leafy festoon was in a blaze. As the red light arose and fell, a numerous congregation alternately shone forth, then disappeared in shadow, and again grew, as it were, out of the darkness, peopling the heart of the solitary woods at once.

"A grave and dark-clad company," quoth Goodman Brown.

In truth they were such. Among them, quivering to and fro between gloom and splendor, appeared faces that would be seen next day at the council board of the province, and others which, Sabbath after Sabbath, looked devoutly heavenward, and benignantly over the crowded pews, from the holiest pulpits in the land. Some affirm that the lady of the governor was there. At least there were high dames well known to her, and wives of honored husbands, and widows, a great multitude, and ancient maidens, all of excellent repute, and fair young girls, who trembled lest their mothers should espy them. Either the sudden gleams of light flashing over the obscure field bedazzled Goodman Brown, or he recognized a score of the church members of Salem village famous for their especial sanctity. Good old Deacon Gookin had arrived, and waited at the skirts of that venerable saint, his revered pastor. But, irreverently consorting with these grave, reputable, and pious people, these elders of the church, these chaste dames and dewy virgins, there were men of dissolute lives and women of spotted fame, wretches given over to all mean and filthy vice, and suspected even of horrid crimes. It was strange to see that the good shrank not from the wicked, nor were the sinners abashed by the saints. Scattered also among their pale-faced enemies were the Indian priests, or pow-wows, who had often scared their native forest with more hideous incantations than any known to English witchcraft.

"But where is Faith?" thought Goodman Brown; and, as hope came into his heart, he trembled.

Another verse of the hymn arose, a slow and mournful strain, such as the pious love, but joined to words which expressed all that our nature can conceive of sin, and darkly hinted at far more. Unfathomable to mere mortals is the lore of fiends. Verse after verse was sung; and still the chorus of the desert swelled between like the deepest tone of a mighty organ; and with the final peal of that dreadful anthem there came a sound, as if the roaring wind, the rushing streams, the howling beasts, and every other voice of the unconcerted wilderness were mingling and according with the voice of guilty man in homage to the prince of all. The four blazing pines threw up a loftier flame, and obscurely discovered shapes and visages of horror on the smoke wreaths above the impious assembly. At the same moment the fire on the rock shot redly forth and formed a glowing arch above its base, where now appeared a figure. With reverence be it spoken, the figure bore no

slight similitude, both in garb and manner, to some grave divine of the New England churches.

"Bring forth the converts!" cried a voice that echoed through the field and rolled into the forest.

At the word, Goodman Brown stepped forth from the shadow of the trees and approached the congregation, with whom he felt a loathful brotherhood by the sympathy of all that was wicked in his heart. He could have well-nigh sworn that the shape of his own dead father beckoned him to advance, looking downward from a smoke wreath, while a woman, with dim features of despair, threw out her hand to warn him back. Was it his mother? But he had no power to retreat one step, nor to resist, even in thought, when the minister and good old Deacon Gookin seized his arms and led him to the blazing rock. Thither came also the slender form of a veiled female, led between Goody Cloyse, that pious teacher of the catechism, and Martha Carrier, who had received the devil's promise to be queen of hell. A rampant hag was she. And there stood the proselytes beneath the canopy of fire.

"Welcome, my children," said the dark figure, "to the communion of your race. Ye have found thus young your nature and your destiny. My children, look behind you!"

They turned; and flashing forth, as it were, in a sheet of flame, the fiend worshippers were seen; the smile of welcome gleamed darkly on every visage.

"There," resumed the sable form, "are all whom ye have reverenced from youth. Ye deemed them holier than yourselves, and shrank from your own sin, contrasting it with their lives of righteousness and prayerful aspirations heavenward. Yet here are they all in my worshipping assembly. This night it shall be granted you to know their secret deeds: how hoary-bearded elders of the church have whispered wanton words to the young maids of their households; how many a woman, eager for widows' weeds, has given her husband a drink at bedtime and let him sleep his last sleep in her bosom; how beardless youths have made haste to inherit their fathers' wealth; and how fair damsels—blush not, sweet ones—have dug little graves in the garden, and bidden me, the sole guest, to an infant's funeral. By the sympathy of your human hearts for sin ye shall scent out all the places—whether in church, bed-chamber, street, field, or forest—where crime has been committed, and shall exult to behold the whole earth one stain of guilt, one mighty blood spot. Far more than this. It shall be yours to penetrate, in every bosom, the deep mystery of sin, the fountain of all wicked arts, and which inexhaustibly supplies more evil impulses than human power—than my power at its utmost—can make manifest in deeds. And now, my children, look upon each other."

They did so; and, by the blaze of the hell-kindled torches, the wretched man beheld his Faith, and the wife her husband, trembling before that unhallowed altar.

"Lo, there ye stand, my children," said the figure, in a deep and solemn tone, almost sad with its despairing awfulness, as if his once angelic nature could yet mourn for our miserable race. "Depending upon one another's hearts, ye had still hoped that virtue were not all a dream. Now are ye undeceived. Evil is the nature of mankind. Evil must be your only happiness. Welcome again, my children, to the communion of your race."

"Welcome," repeated the fiend worshippers, in one cry of despair and triumph.

And there they stood, the only pair, as it seemed, who were yet hesitating on the verge of wickedness in this dark world. A basin was hollowed, naturally, in the rock. Did it contain water, reddened by the lurid light? or was it blood? or, perchance, a liquid flame? Herein did the shape of evil dip his hand and prepare to lay the mark of baptism upon their foreheads, that they might be partakers of the mystery of sin, more conscious of the secret guilt of others, both in deed and thought, than they could now be of their own. The husband cast one look at his pale wife, and Faith at him. What polluted wretches would the next glance show them to each other, shuddering alike at what they disclosed and what they saw!

"Faith! Faith!" cried the husband, "look up to heaven, and resist the wicked one."

Whether Faith obeyed he knew not. Hardly had he spoken when he found himself amid calm night and solitude, listening to a roar of the wind which died heavily away through the forest. He staggered against the rock, and felt it chill and damp; while a hanging twig, that had been all on fire, besprinkled his cheek with the coldest dew.

The next morning young Goodman Brown came slowly into the street of Salem village, staring around him like a bewildered man. The good old minister was taking a walk along the graveyard to get an appetite for breakfast and meditate his sermon, and bestowed a blessing, as he passed, on Goodman Brown. He shrank from the venerable saint as if to avoid an anathema. Old Deacon Gookin was at domestic worship, and the holy words of his prayer were heard through the open window. "What God doth the wizard pray to?" quoth Goodman Brown. Goody Cloyse, that excellent old Christian, stood in the early sunshine at her own lattice, catechizing a little girl who had brought her a pint of morning's milk. Goodman Brown snatched away the child as from the grasp of the fiend himself. Turning the corner by the meeting-house, he spied the head of Faith, with the pink ribbons, gazing anxiously forth, and bursting into such joy at sight of him that she skipped along the street and almost kissed her husband before the whole village. But Goodman Brown looked sternly and sadly into her face, and passed on without a greeting.

Had Goodman Brown fallen asleep in the forest and only dreamed a wild dream of a witch-meeting?

Be it so if you will; but, alas! it was a dream of evil omen for young Goodman Brown. A stern, a sad, a darkly meditative, a distrustful, if not a desperate man did he become from the night of that fearful dream. On the Sabbath day, when the congregation were singing a holy psalm, he could not listen because an anthem of sin rushed loudly upon his ear and drowned all the blessed strain. When the minister spoke from the pulpit with power and fervid eloquence, and, with his hand on the open Bible, of the sacred truths of our religion, and of saint-like lives and triumphant deaths, and of future bliss or misery unutterable, then did Goodman Brown turn pale, dreading lest the roof should thunder down upon the gray blasphemer and his hearers. Often, awaking suddenly at midnight, he shrank from the bosom of Faith; and at morning or eventide, when the family knelt down at prayer, he scowled and muttered to himself, and gazed sternly at his wife, and turned away. And when he had lived long, and was borne to his grave a hoary corpse, followed by Faith, an aged woman, and children and grandchildren, a goodly procession, besides neighbors not a few, they carved no hopeful verse upon his tombstone, for his dying hour was gloom.

# THE MAYPOLE OF MERRY MOUNT

◇

⟨ SUBTITLED "A Parable" and first published in *The Token* for 1836, this story was included in the *Twice-Told Tales* (1837). Thomas Morton, the presumed villain of the story, was a London lawyer who was charged with selling rum and firearms to the Indians. In 1628 Captain Miles Standish arrested Morton, jailed him for a time, and caused him to be deported. John

Endicott and a party of Pilgrims cut down the maypole and, according to Governor Bradford, rebuked the merrymakers "for their profaneness and admonished them to look there should be better walking." The name of the place was changed to Mount Dagon.

◇

*There is an admirable foundation for a philosophic romance in the curious history of the early settlement of Mount Wollaston, or Merry Mount. In the slight sketch here attempted, the facts, recorded on the grave pages of our New England annalists, have wrought themselves, almost spontaneously, into a sort of allegory. The masques, mummeries, and festive customs, described in the text, are in accordance with the manners of the age. Authority on these points may be found in Strutt's Book [1] of English Sports and Pastimes.*

BRIGHT were the days at Merry Mount, when the Maypole was the banner staff of that gay colony! They who reared it, should their banner be triumphant, were to pour sunshine over New England's rugged hills, and scatter flower seeds throughout the soil. Jollity and gloom were contending for an empire. Midsummer eve had come, bringing deep verdure to the forest, and roses in her lap, of a more vivid hue than the tender buds of Spring. But May, or her mirthful spirit, dwelt all the year round at Merry Mount, sporting with the Summer months, and revelling with Autumn, and basking in the glow of Winter's fireside. Through a world of toil and care she flitted with a dreamlike smile, and came hither to find a home among the lightsome hearts of Merry Mount.

Never had the Maypole been so gayly decked as at sunset on midsummer eve. This venerated emblem was a pine-tree, which had preserved the slender grace of youth, while it equalled the loftiest height of the old wood monarchs. From its top streamed a silken banner, colored like the rainbow. Down nearly to the ground the pole was dressed with birchen boughs, and others of the liveliest green, and some with silvery leaves, fastened by ribbons that fluttered in fantastic knots of twenty different colors, but no sad ones. Garden flowers, and blossoms of the wilderness, laughed gladly forth amid the verdure, so fresh and dewy that they must have grown by magic on that happy pine-tree. Where this green and flowery splendor terminated, the shaft of the Maypole was stained with the seven brilliant hues of the banner at its

top. On the lowest green bough hung an abundant wreath of roses, some that had been gathered in the sunniest spots of the forest, and others, of still richer blush, which the colonists had reared from English seed. O, people of the Golden Age,[2] the chief of your husbandry was to raise flowers!

But what was the wild throng that stood hand in hand about the Maypole? It could not be that the fauns and nymphs, when driven from their classic groves and homes of ancient fable, had sought refuge, as all the persecuted did, in the fresh woods of the West. These were Gothic monsters, though perhaps of Grecian ancestry. On the shoulders of a comely youth uprose the head and branching antlers of a stag; a second, human in all other points, had the grim visage of a wolf; a third, still with the trunk and limbs of a mortal man, showed the beard and horns of a venerable he-goat. There was the likeness of a bear erect, brute in all but his hind legs, which were adorned with pink silk stockings. And here again, almost as wondrous, stood a real bear of the dark forest, lending each of his fore paws to the grasp of a human hand, and as ready for the dance as any in that circle. His inferior nature rose half way, to meet his companions as they stooped. Other faces wore the similitude of man or woman, but distorted or extravagant, with red noses pendulous before their mouths, which seemed of awful depth, and stretched from ear to ear in an eternal fit of laughter. Here might be seen the Salvage Man, well known in heraldry, hairy as a baboon, and girdled with green leaves. By his side, a noble figure, but still a counterfeit, appeared an Indian hunter, with feathery crest and wampum belt. Many of this strange company wore foolscaps, and had little bells appended to their garments, tinkling with a silvery sound, responsive to the inaudible music of their gleesome spirits. Some youths and maidens were of soberer garb, yet well maintained their places in the irregular throng by the expression of wild revelry upon their features. Such were the colonists of Merry Mount, as they stood in the broad smile of sunset round their venerated Maypole.

Had a wanderer, bewildered in the melancholy forest, heard their mirth, and stolen a half-affrighted glance, he might have fancied them the crew of Comus,[3] some already transformed to brutes, some midway between man and beast, and the others rioting in the flow of tipsy jollity that foreran the change. But a band of Puritans, who

---

THE MAYPOLE OF MERRY MOUNT. 1. **Strutt's Book:** Joseph Strutt (1749–1802), author of *The Sports and Pastimes of the People of England* (1801).

2. **Golden Age:** in the mythical history of the world, that time of pure happiness, joy, and love which was, in the inevitable decay, followed by the silver, the brass, and finally the iron age.　3. **crew of Comus:** See Milton, *Comus*, 1. 92 ff.

watched the scene, invisible themselves, compared the masques to those devils and ruined souls with whom their superstition peopled the black wilderness.

Within the ring of monsters appeared the two airiest forms that had ever trodden on any more solid footing than a purple and golden cloud. One was a youth in glistening apparel, with a scarf of the rainbow pattern crosswise on his breast. His right hand held a gilded staff, the ensign of high dignity among the revellers, and his left grasped the slender fingers of a fair maiden, not less gayly decorated than himself. Bright roses glowed in contrast with the dark and glossy curls of each, and were scattered round their feet, or had sprung up spontaneously there. Behind this lightsome couple, so close to the Maypole that its boughs shaded his jovial face, stood the figure of an English priest, canonically dressed, yet decked with flowers, in heathen fashion, and wearing a chaplet of the native vine leaves. By the riot of his rolling eye, and the pagan decorations of his holy garb, he seemed the wildest monster here, and the very Comus of the crew.

"Votaries of the Maypole," cried the flower-decked priest, "merrily, all day long, have the woods echoed to your mirth. But be this your merriest hour, my hearts! Lo, here stand the Lord and Lady of the May, whom I, a clerk of Oxford, and high priest of Merry Mount, am presently to join in holy matrimony. Up with your nimble spirits, ye morris-dancers, green men, and glee maidens, bears and wolves, and horned gentlemen! Come; a chorus now, rich with the old mirth of Merry England, and the wilder glee of this fresh forest; and then a dance, to show the youthful pair what life is made of, and how airily they should go through it! All ye that love the Maypole, lend your voices to the nuptial song of the Lord and Lady of the May!"

This wedlock was more serious than most affairs of Merry Mount, where jest and delusion, trick and fantasy, kept up a continual carnival. The Lord and Lady of the May, though their titles must be laid down at sunset, were really and truly to be partners for the dance of life, beginning the measure that same bright eve. The wreath of roses, that hung from the lowest green bough of the Maypole, had been twined for them, and would be thrown over both their heads, in symbol of their flowery union. When the priest had spoken, therefore, a riotous uproar burst from the rout of monstrous figures.

"Begin you the stave, reverend Sir," cried they all; "and never did the woods ring to such a merry peal as we of the Maypole shall send up!"

Immediately a prelude of pipe, cithern, and viol, touched with practised minstrelsy, began to play from a neighboring thicket, in such a mirthful cadence that the boughs of the Maypole quivered to the sound. But the May Lord, he of the gilded staff, chancing to look into his Lady's eyes, was wonder struck at the almost pensive glance that met his own.

"Edith, sweet Lady of the May," whispered he reproachfully, "is yon wreath of roses a garland to hang above our graves, that you look so sad? O, Edith, this is our golden time! Tarnish it not by any pensive shadow of the mind; for it may be that nothing of futurity will be brighter than the mere remembrance of what is now passing."

"That was the very thought that saddened me! How came it in your mind too?" said Edith, in a still lower tone than he, for it was high treason to be sad at Merry Mount. "Therefore do I sigh amid this festive music. And besides, dear Edgar, I struggle as with a dream, and fancy that these shapes of our jovial friends are visionary, and their mirth unreal, and that we are no true Lord and Lady of the May. What is the mystery in my heart?"

Just then, as if a spell had loosened them, down came a little shower of withering rose leaves from the Maypole. Alas, for the young lovers! No sooner had their hearts glowed with real passion than they were sensible of something vague and unsubstantial in their former pleasures, and felt a dreary presentiment of inevitable change. From the moment that they truly loved, they had subjected themselves to earth's doom of care and sorrow, and troubled joy, and had no more a home at Merry Mount. That was Edith's mystery. Now leave we the priest to marry them, and the masquers to sport round the Maypole, till the last sunbeam be withdrawn from its summit, and the shadows of the forest mingle gloomily in the dance. Meanwhile, we may discover who these gay people were.

Two hundred years ago, and more, the old world and its inhabitants became mutually weary of each other. Men voyaged by thousands to the West: some to barter glass beads, and such like jewels, for the furs of the Indian hunter; some to conquer virgin empires; and one stern band to pray. But none of these motives had much weight with the colonists of Merry Mount. Their leaders were men who had sported so long with life, that when Thought and Wisdom came, even these unwelcome guests were led astray by the crowd of vanities which they should have put to flight. Erring Thought and perverted Wisdom were made to put on masques, and play the fool. The men of whom we speak, after losing the heart's fresh gayety, imagined a wild philosophy of pleasure, and came hither to act out their latest daydream. They gathered followers from all that giddy tribe whose whole life is like the festal days of soberer men. In their train were minstrels, not unknown in London streets: wandering players, whose theatres had been the halls of noblemen; mummers, rope-dancers, and mountebanks, who would long be missed at wakes, church-ales, and fairs; in a word, mirth makers of every sort, such as abounded in that age, but now began to be discountenanced by the rapid growth of Puritanism. Light had their footsteps been on land, and as lightly they came across the sea. Many had been maddened by their previous troubles into a gay despair; others were as madly gay in the flush of youth, like the May Lord and his Lady; but whatever might be the quality of their mirth, old and young were gay at Merry Mount. The young deemed themselves happy. The elder spirits, if they knew that mirth was but the counterfeit of happiness, yet followed the false shadow wilfully, because at least her garments glittered brightest. Sworn triflers of a lifetime, they would not venture among the sober truths of life not even to be truly blest.

All the hereditary pastimes of Old England were transplanted hither. The King of Christmas was duly crowned, and the Lord of Misrule bore potent sway. On the eve of St. John,[4] they felled whole acres of the forest to make bonfires, and danced by the blaze all night, crowned with garlands, and throwing flowers into the flame. At harvest time, though their crop was of the smallest, they made an image with the sheaves of Indian corn, and wreathed it with autumnal garlands, and bore it home triumphantly. But what chiefly characterized the colonists of Merry Mount was their veneration for the Maypole. It has made their true history a poet's tale. Spring decked the hallowed emblem with young blossoms and fresh green boughs; Summer brought roses of the deepest blush, and the perfected foliage of the forest; Autumn enriched it with that red and yellow gorgeousness which converts each wildwood leaf into a painted flower; and Winter silvered it with sleet, and hung it round with icicles, till it flashed in the cold sunshine, itself a frozen sunbeam. Thus each alternate season did homage to the Maypole, and paid it a tribute of its own richest splendor. Its votaries danced round it, once, at least, in every month; sometimes they called it their religion, or

4. **eve of St. John:** Midsummer's Eve, June 23, an occasion for celebration throughout centuries in Old England.

their altar; but always, it was the banner staff of Merry Mount.

Unfortunately, there were men in the new world of a sterner faith than these Maypole worshippers. Not far from Merry Mount was a settlement of Puritans, most dismal wretches, who said their prayers before daylight, and then wrought in the forest or the cornfield till evening made it prayer time again. Their weapons were always at hand to shoot down the straggling savage. When they met in conclave, it was never to keep up the old English mirth, but to hear sermons three hours long, or to proclaim bounties on the heads of wolves and the scalps of Indians. Their festivals were fast days, and their chief pastime the singing of psalms. Woe to the youth or maiden who did but dream of a dance! The selectman nodded to the constable; and there sat the light-heeled reprobate in the stocks; or if he danced, it was round the whipping-post, which might be termed the Puritan Maypole.

A party of these grim Puritans, toiling through the difficult woods, each with a horseload of iron armor to burden his footsteps, would sometimes draw near the sunny precincts of Merry Mount. There were the silken colonists, sporting round their Maypole; perhaps teaching a bear to dance, or striving to communicate their mirth to the grave Indian; or masquerading in the skins of deer and wolves, which they had hunted for that especial purpose. Often, the whole colony were playing at blindman's buff, magistrates and all, with their eyes bandaged, except a single scapegoat, whom the blinded sinners pursued by the tinkling of the bells at his garments. Once, it is said, they were seen following a flower-decked corpse, with merriment and festive music, to his grave. But did the dead man laugh? In their quietest times, they sang ballads and told tales, for the edification of their pious visitors; or perplexed them with juggling tricks; or grinned at them through horse collars; and when sport itself grew wearisome, they made game of their own stupidity, and began a yawning match. At the very least of these enormities, the men of iron shook their heads and frowned so darkly that the revellers looked up, imagining that a momentary cloud had overcast the sunshine, which was to be perpetual there. On the other hand, the Puritans affirmed that, when a psalm was pealing from their place of worship, the echo which the forest sent them back seemed often like the chorus of a jolly catch, closing with a roar of laughter. Who but the fiend, and his bond slaves, the crew of Merry Mount, had thus disturbed them? In due time, a feud arose, stern and bitter on one side, and as serious on the other as anything could be among such light spirits as had sworn allegiance to the Maypole. The future complexion of New England was involved in this important quarrel. Should the grizzly saints establish their jurisdiction over the gay sinners, then would their spirits darken all the clime, and make it a land of clouded visages, of hard toil, of sermon and psalm forever. But should the banner staff of Merry Mount be fortunate, sunshine would break upon the hills, and flowers would beautify the forest, and late posterity do homage to the Maypole.

After these authentic passages from history, we return to the nuptials of the Lord and Lady of the May. Alas! we have delayed too long, and must darken our tale too suddenly. As we glance again at the Maypole, a solitary sunbeam is fading from the summit, and leaves only a faint, golden tinge blended with the hues of the rainbow banner. Even that dim light is now withdrawn, relinquishing the whole domain of Merry Mount to the evening gloom, which has rushed so instantaneously from the black surrounding woods. But some of these black shadows have rushed forth in human shape.

Yes, with the setting sun, the last day of mirth had passed from Merry Mount. The ring of gay masquers was disordered and broken; the stag lowered his antlers in dismay; the wolf grew weaker than a lamb; the bells of the morris-dancers tinkled with tremulous affright. The Puritans had played a characteristic part in the Maypole mummeries. Their darksome figures were intermixed with the wild shapes of their foes, and made the scene a picture of the moment, when waking thoughts start up amid the scattered fantasies of a dream. The leader of the hostile party stood in the centre of the circle, while the rout of monsters cowered around him, like evil spirits in the presence of a dread magician. No fantastic foolery could look him in the face. So stern was the energy of his aspect, that the whole man, visage, frame, and soul, seemed wrought of iron, gifted with life and thought, yet all of one substance with his headpiece and breastplate. It was the Puritan of Puritans: it was Endicott [5] himself!

"Stand off, priest of Baal!" said he, with a grim frown, and laying no reverent hand upon the surplice. "I know thee, Blackstone! [6] Thou art the man who couldst not abide the rule even of thine own corrupted church, and hast come hither to preach iniquity, and to give example of it in thy life. But now shall it be seen that the Lord hath sanctified this wilderness for his peculiar people. Woe unto them that would defile it! And first, for this flower-decked abomination, the altar of thy worship!"

And with his keen sword Endicott assaulted the hallowed Maypole. Nor long did it resist his arm. It groaned with a dismal sound; it showered leaves and rosebuds upon the remorseless enthusiast; and finally, with all its green boughs and ribbons and flowers, symbolic of departed pleasures, down fell the banner staff of Merry Mount. As it sank, tradition says, the evening sky grew darker, and the woods threw forth a more sombre shadow.

"There," cried Endicott, looking triumphantly on his work, "there lies the only Maypole in New England! The thought is strong within me that, by its fall, is shadowed forth the fate of light and idle mirth makers, amongst us and our posterity. Amen, saith John Endicott."

"Amen!" echoed his followers.

But the votaries of the Maypole gave one groan for their idol. At the sound, the Puritan leader glanced at the crew of Comus, each a figure of broad mirth, yet, at this moment, strangely expressive of sorrow and dismay.

"Valiant captain," quoth Peter Palfrey,[7] the Ancient [8] of the band, "what order shall be taken with the prisoners?"

"I thought not to repent me of cutting down a Maypole," replied Endicott, "yet now I could find in my heart to plant it again, and give each of these bestial pagans one other dance round their idol. It would have served rarely for a whipping-post!"

"But there are pine-trees enow," suggested the lieutenant.

"True, good Ancient," said the leader. "Wherefore, bind the heathen crew, and bestow on them a small matter of stripes apiece, as earnest of our future justice. Set some of the rogues in the stocks to rest themselves, so soon as Providence shall bring us to one of our own well-ordered settlements, where such accommodations may be found. Further penalties, such as branding and cropping of ears, shall be thought of hereafter."

"How many stripes for the priest?" inquired Ancient Palfrey.

"None as yet," answered Endicott, bending his iron frown upon the culprit. "It must be for the Great and General Court to determine, whether stripes and long imprisonment, and other grievous

---

5. **Endicott:** John Endicott (1589?–1665), governor of the Massachusetts Bay Colony. 6. **Blackstone:** "Did Governor Endicott speak less positively, we should suspect a mistake here. The Rev. Mr. Blackstone, though an eccentric, is not known to have been an immoral man. We rather doubt his identity with the priest of Merry Mount" [Hawthorne's note]. Blackstone was an Anglican priest who remained on good terms with the Pilgrims.

7. **Peter Palfrey:** identified by Hawthorne in "Main Street" as one of the first settlers in Salem. 8. **Ancient:** the standard-bearer or ensign of the troop.

penalty, may atone for his transgressions. Let him look to himself! For such as violate our civil order, it may be permitted us to show mercy. But woe to the wretch that troubleth our religion!"

"And this dancing bear," resumed the officer. "Must he share the stripes of his fellows?"

"Shoot him through the head!" said the energetic Puritan. "I suspect witchcraft in the beast."

"Here be a couple of shining ones," continued Peter Palfrey, pointing his weapon at the Lord and Lady of the May. "They seem to be of high station among these misdoers. Methinks their dignity will not be fitted with less than a double share of stripes."

Endicott rested on his sword, and closely surveyed the dress and aspect of the hapless pair. There they stood, pale, downcast, and apprehensive. Yet there was an air of mutual support, and of pure affection, seeking aid and giving it, that showed them to be man and wife, with the sanction of a priest upon their love. The youth, in the peril of the moment, had dropped his gilded staff, and thrown his arm about the Lady of the May, who leaned against his breast, too lightly to burden him, but with weight enough to express that their destinies were linked together, for good or evil. They looked first at each other, and then into the grim captain's face. There they stood, in the first hour of wedlock, while the idle pleasures, of which their companions were the emblems, had given place to the sternest cares of life, personified by the dark Puritans. But never had their youthful beauty seemed so pure and high as when its glow was chastened by adversity.

"Youth," said Endicott, "ye stand in an evil case, thou and thy maiden wife. Make ready presently, for I am minded that ye shall both have a token to remember your wedding day!"

"Stern man," cried the May Lord, "how can I move thee? Were the means at hand, I would resist to the death. Being powerless, I entreat! Do with me as thou wilt, but let Edith go untouched!"

"Not so," replied the immitigable zealot. "We are not wont to show an idle courtesy to that sex, which requireth the stricter discipline. What sayest thou, maid? Shall thy silken bridegroom suffer thy share of the penalty, besides his own?"

"Be it death," said Edith, "and lay it all on me!"

Truly, as Endicott had said, the poor lovers stood in a woful case. Their foes were triumphant, their friends captive and abased, their home desolate, the benighted wilderness around them, and a rigorous destiny, in the shape of the Puritan leader, their only guide. Yet the deepening twilight could not altogether conceal that the iron man was softened; he smiled at the fair spectacle of early love; he almost sighed for the inevitable blight of early hopes.

"The troubles of life have come hastily on this young couple," observed Endicott. "We will see how they comport themselves under their present trials ere we burden them with greater. If, among the spoil, there be any garments of a more decent fashion, let them be put upon this May Lord and his Lady, instead of their glistening vanities. Look to it, some of you."

"And shall not the youth's hair be cut?" asked Peter Palfrey, looking with abhorrence at the lovelock and long glossy curls of the young man.

"Crop it forthwith, and that in the true pumpkin-shell fashion," answered the captain. "Then bring them along with us, but more gently than their fellows. There be qualities in the youth, which may make him valiant to fight, and sober to toil, and pious to pray; and in the maiden, that may fit her to become a mother in our Israel, bringing up babes in better nurture than her own hath been. Nor think ye, young ones, that they are the happiest, even in our lifetime of a moment, who misspend it in dancing round a Maypole!"

And Endicott, the severest Puritan of all who laid the rock foundation of New England, lifted the wreath of roses from the ruin of the Maypole, and threw it, with his own gauntleted hand, over the heads of the Lord and Lady of the May. It was a deed of prophecy. As the moral gloom of the world overpowers all systematic gayety, even so was their home of wild mirth made desolate amid the sad forest. They returned to it no more. But as their flowery garland was wreathed of the brightest roses that had grown there, so, in the tie that united them, were intertwined all the purest and best of their early joys. They went heavenward, supporting each other along the difficult path which it was their lot to tread, and never wasted one regretful thought on the vanities of Merry Mount.

# THE MINISTER'S BLACK VEIL
## A PARABLE [1]

◊

❨ THE STORY appeared first in *The Token* (1836) and was included in the *Twice-Told Tales* (1837). The interest and literary value of the tale may not be so much its inquiry into the depths of human conscience—we may well take for granted that Parson Hooper is guiltless of any real sin—but rather the continual unfolding of the narrative. Men sin, not according to law, but "within." The Rev. Mr. Dimmesdale would learn in *The Scarlet Letter*—for Parson Hooper is Dimmesdale in an earlier guise—that each man is all his life "loathsomely treasuring up the secret of his [own] sin."

◇

THE SEXTON stood in the porch of Milford meeting-house, pulling busily at the bell-rope. The old people of the village came stooping along the street. Children, with bright faces, tripped merrily beside their parents, or mimicked a graver gait, in the conscious dignity of their Sunday clothes. Spruce bachelors looked sidelong at the pretty maidens, and fancied that the Sabbath sunshine made them prettier than on week days. When the throng had mostly streamed into the porch, the sexton began to toll the bell, keeping his eye on the Reverend Mr. Hooper's door. The first glimpse of the clergyman's figure was the signal for the bell to cease its summons.

"But what has good Parson Hooper got upon his face?" cried the sexton in astonishment.

All within hearing immediately turned about, and beheld the semblance of Mr. Hooper, pacing slowly his meditative way towards the meeting-house. With one accord they started, expressing more wonder than if some strange minister were coming to dust the cushions of Mr. Hooper's pulpit.

"Are you sure it is our parson?" inquired Goodman Gray of the sexton.

"Of a certainty it is good Mr. Hooper," replied the sexton. "He was to have exchanged pulpits with Parson Shute, of Westbury; but Parson Shute sent to excuse himself yesterday, being to preach a funeral sermon."

The cause of so much amazement may appear sufficiently slight. Mr. Hooper, a gentlemanly person, of about thirty, though still a bachelor, was dressed with due clerical neatness, as if a careful wife had starched his band, and brushed the weekly dust from his Sunday's garb. There was but one thing remarkable in his appearance. Swathed about his forehead, and hanging down

THE MINISTER'S BLACK VEIL. 1. **A Parable:** "Another clergyman in New England, Mr. Joseph Moody, of York, Maine, who died about eighty years since, made himself remarkable by the same eccentricity that is here related of the Reverend Mr. Hooper. In his case, however, the symbol had a different import. In early life he had accidentally killed a beloved friend; and from that day till the hour of his death, he hid his face from men" [H]. The story of the Rev. Joseph Moody (1700–53) is told in William Sprague's *Annals of the American Pulpit* (1804).

over his face, so low as to be shaken by his breath, Mr. Hooper had on a black veil. On a nearer view it seemed to consist of two folds of crape, which entirely concealed his features, except the mouth and chin, but probably did not intercept his sight, further than to give a darkened aspect to all living and inanimate things. With this gloomy shade before him, good Mr. Hooper walked onward, at a slow and quiet pace, stooping somewhat, and looking on the ground, as is customary with abstracted men, yet nodding kindly to those of his parishioners who still waited on the meeting-house steps. But so wonder-struck were they that his greeting hardly met with a return.

"I can't really feel as if good Mr. Hooper's face was behind that piece of crape," said the sexton.

"I don't like it," muttered an old woman, as she hobbled into the meeting-house. "He has changed himself into something awful, only by hiding his face."

"Our parson has gone mad!" cried Goodman Gray, following him across the threshold.

A rumor of some unaccountable phenomenon had preceded Mr. Hooper into the meeting-house, and set all the congregation astir. Few could refrain from twisting their heads towards the door; many stood upright, and turned directly about; while several little boys clambered upon the seats, and came down again with a terrible racket. There was a general bustle, a rustling of the women's gowns and shuffling of the men's feet, greatly at variance with that hushed repose which should attend the entrance of the minister. But Mr. Hooper appeared not to notice the perturbation of his people. He entered with an almost noiseless step, bent his head mildly to the pews on each side, and bowed as he passed his oldest parishioner, a white-haired great-grandsire, who occupied an arm-chair in the centre of the aisle. It was strange to observe how slowly this venerable man became conscious of something singular in the appearance of his pastor. He seemed not fully to partake of the prevailing wonder, till Mr. Hooper had ascended the stairs, and showed himself in the pulpit, face to face with his congregation, except for the black veil. That mysterious emblem was never once withdrawn. It shook with his measured breath, as he gave out the psalm; it threw its obscurity between him and the holy page, as he read the Scriptures; and while he prayed, the veil lay heavily on his uplifted countenance. Did he seek to hide it from the dread Being whom he was addressing?

Such was the effect of this simple piece of crape, that more than one woman of delicate nerves was forced to leave the meeting-house. Yet perhaps the pale-faced congregation was almost as fearful a sight to the minister, as his black veil to them.

Mr. Hooper had the reputation of a good preacher, but not an energetic one: he strove to win his people heavenward by mild, persuasive influences, rather than to drive them thither by the thunders of the Word. The sermon which he now delivered was marked by the same characteristics of style and manner as the general series of his pulpit oratory. But there was something, either in the sentiment of the discourse itself, or in the imagination of the auditors, which made it greatly the most powerful effort that they had ever heard from their pastor's lips. It was tinged, rather more darkly than usual, with the gentle gloom of Mr. Hooper's temperament. The subject had reference to secret sin, and those sad mysteries which we hide from our nearest and dearest, and would fain conceal from our own consciousness, even forgetting that the Omniscient can detect them. A subtle power was breathed into his words. Each member of the congregation, the most innocent girl, and the man of hardened breast, felt as if the preacher had crept upon them, behind his awful veil, and discovered their hoarded iniquity of deed or thought. Many spread their clasped hands on their bosoms. There was nothing terrible in what Mr. Hooper said, at least, no violence; and yet, with every tremor of his melancholy voice, the hearers quaked. An unsought pathos came hand in hand with awe. So sensible were the audience of some unwonted attribute in their minister, that they longed for a breath of wind to blow aside the veil, almost believing that a stranger's visage would be discovered, though the form, gesture, and voice were those of Mr. Hooper.

At the close of the services, the people hurried out with indecorous confusion, eager to communicate their pent-up amazement, and conscious of lighter spirits the moment they lost sight of the black veil. Some gathered in little circles, huddled closely together, with their mouths all whispering in the centre; some went homeward alone, wrapt in silent meditation; some talked loudly, and profaned the Sabbath day with ostentatious laughter. A few shook their sagacious heads, intimating that they could penetrate the mystery; while one or two affirmed that there was no mystery at all, but only that Mr. Hooper's eyes were so weakened by the midnight lamp, as to require a shade. After a brief interval, forth came good Mr. Hooper also, in the rear of his flock. Turning his veiled face from one group to another, he paid due reverence to the hoary heads, saluted the middle aged with kind dignity as their friend and spiritual guide, greeted the young with mingled authority and love, and laid his hands on the little children's heads to bless them. Such was always his custom on the Sabbath day. Strange and bewildered looks repaid him for his courtesy. None, as on former occasions, aspired to the honor of walking by their pastor's side. Old Squire Saunders, doubtless by an accidental lapse of memory, neglected to invite Mr. Hooper to his table, where the good clergyman had been wont to bless the food, almost every Sunday since his settlement. He returned, therefore, to the parsonage, and, at the moment of closing the door, was observed to look back upon the people, all of whom had their eyes fixed upon the minister. A sad smile gleamed faintly from beneath the black veil, and flickered about his mouth, glimmering as he disappeared.

"How strange," said a lady, "that a simple black veil, such as any woman might wear on her bonnet should become such a terrible thing on Mr. Hooper's face!"

"Something must surely be amiss with Mr. Hooper's intellects," observed her husband, the physician of the village. "But the strangest part of the affair is the effect of this vagary, even on a sober-minded man like myself. The black veil, though it covers only our pastor's face, throws its influence over his whole person, and makes him ghostlike from head to foot. Do you not feel it so?"

"Truly do I," replied the lady; "and I would not be alone with him for the world. I wonder he is not afraid to be alone with himself!"

"Men sometimes are so," said her husband.

The afternoon service was attended with similar circumstances. At its conclusion, the bell tolled for the funeral of a young lady. The relatives and friends were assembled in the house, and the more distant acquaintances stood about the door, speaking of the good qualities of the deceased, when their talk was interrupted by the appearance of Mr. Hooper, still covered with his black veil. It was now an appropriate emblem. The clergyman stepped into the room where the corpse was laid, and bent over the coffin, to take a last farewell of his deceased parishioner. As he stooped, the veil hung straight down from his forehead, so that, if her eyelids had not been closed forever, the dead maiden might have seen his face. Could Mr. Hooper be fearful of her glance, that he so hastily caught back the black veil? A person who watched the interview between the dead and living, scrupled not to affirm, that, at the instant when the clergyman's features were disclosed, the corpse had slightly shuddered, rustling the shroud and muslin cap, though the countenance retained the composure of death.[2] A superstitious old woman was the only witness of this prodigy. From the coffin Mr. Hooper passed into the chamber of the mourners, and thence to the head of the staircase, to make the funeral prayer. It was a tender and heart-dissolving prayer, full of sorrow, yet so imbued with celestial hopes, that the music of a heavenly harp, swept by the fingers of the dead, seemed faintly to be heard among the saddest accents of the minister. The people trembled, though they but darkly understood him when he prayed that they, and himself, and all of mortal race, might be ready, as he trusted this young maiden had been, for the dreadful hour that should snatch the veil from their faces. The bearers went heavily forth, and the mourners followed, saddening all the street, with the dead before them, and Mr. Hooper in his black veil behind.

"Why do you look back?" said one in the procession to his partner.

"I had a fancy," replied she, "that the minister and the maiden's spirit were walking hand in hand."

"And so had I, at the same moment," said the other.

That night, the handsomest couple in Milford village were to be joined in wedlock. Though reckoned a melancholy man, Mr. Hooper had a placid cheerfulness for such occasions, which often excited a sympathetic smile where livelier merriment would have been thrown away. There was no quality of his disposition which made him more beloved than this. The company at the wedding awaited his arrival with impatience, trusting that the strange awe, which had gathered over him throughout the day, would now be dispelled. But such was not the result. When Mr. Hooper came, the first thing that their eyes rested on was the same horrible black veil, which had added deeper gloom to the funeral, and could portend nothing but evil to the wedding. Such was its immediate effect on the guests that a cloud seemed to have rolled duskily from beneath the black crape, and dimmed the light of the candles. The bridal pair stood up before the minister. But the bride's cold fingers quivered in the tremulous hand of the bridegroom, and her deathlike paleness caused a whisper that the maiden who had been buried a

few hours before was come from her grave to be married. If ever another wedding were so dismal, it was that famous one where they tolled the wedding knell. After performing the ceremony, Mr. Hooper raised a glass of wine to his lips, wishing happiness to the new-married couple in a strain of mild pleasantry that ought to have brightened the features of the guests, like a cheerful gleam from the hearth. At that instant, catching a glimpse of his figure in the looking-glass, the black veil involved his own spirit in the horror with which it overwhelmed all others. His frame shuddered, his lips grew white, he spilt the untasted wine upon the carpet, and rushed forth into the darkness. For the Earth, too, had on her Black Veil.

The next day, the whole village of Milford talked of little else than Parson Hooper's black veil. That, and the mystery concealed behind it, supplied a topic for discussion between acquaintances meeting in the street, and good women gossiping at their open windows. It was the first item of news that the tavern-keeper told to his guests. The children babbled of it on their way to school. One imitative little imp covered his face with an old black handkerchief, thereby so affrighting his playmates that the panic seized himself, and he well-nigh lost his wits by his own waggery.

It was remarkable that of all the busybodies and impertinent people in the parish, not one ventured to put the plain question to Mr. Hooper, wherefore he did this thing. Hitherto, whenever there appeared the slightest call for such interference, he had never lacked advisers, nor shown himself averse to be guided by their judgment. If he erred at all, it was by so painful a degree of self-distrust, that even the mildest censure would lead him to consider an indifferent action as a crime. Yet, though so well acquainted with this amiable weakness, no individual among his parishioners chose to make the black veil a subject of friendly remonstrance. There was a feeling of dread, neither plainly confessed nor carefully concealed, which caused each to shift the responsibility upon another, till at length it was found expedient to send a deputation of the church, in order to deal with Mr. Hooper about the mystery, before it should grow into a scandal. Never did an embassy so ill discharge its duties. The minister received them with friendly courtesy, but became silent, after they were seated, leaving to his visitors the whole burden of introducing their important business. The topic, it might be supposed, was obvious enough. There was the black veil swathed round Mr. Hooper's forehead, and concealing every feature above his placid mouth, on which, at times, they could perceive the glimmering of a melan-

2. composure of death: In his review of the *Twice-Told Tales* Poe suggested that Parson Hooper had assumed the black veil because of the wrong he had done this young woman: "The moral put into the mouth of the dying minister will be supposed to convey the true import of the narrative; and that a crime of dark dye (having reference to the 'young lady') has been committed, is a point which only minds congenial with that of the author will perceive." Poe's explanation may be plausible, but it does not solve the moral problem which the story raises.

choly smile. But that piece of crape, to their imagination, seemed to hang down before his heart, the symbol of a fearful secret between him and them. Were the veil but cast aside, they might speak freely of it, but not till then. Thus they sat a considerable time, speechless, confused, and shrinking uneasily from Mr. Hooper's eye, which they felt to be fixed upon them with an invisible glance. Finally, the deputies returned abashed to their constituents, pronouncing the matter too weighty to be handled, except by a council of the churches, if, indeed, it might not require a general synod.

But there was one person in the village unappalled by the awe with which the black veil had impressed all beside herself. When the deputies returned without an explanation, or even venturing to demand one, she, with the calm energy of her character, determined to chase away the strange cloud that appeared to be settling round Mr. Hooper, every moment more darkly than before. As his plighted wife, it should be her privilege to know what the black veil concealed. At the minister's first visit, therefore, she entered upon the subject with a direct simplicity, which made the task easier both for him and her. After he had seated himself, she fixed her eyes steadfastly upon the veil, but could discern nothing of the dreadful gloom that had so overawed the multitude: it was but a double fold of crape, hanging down from his forehead to his mouth, and slightly stirring with his breath.

"No," said she aloud, and smiling, "there is nothing terrible in this piece of crape, except that it hides a face which I am always glad to look upon. Come, good sir, let the sun shine from behind the cloud. First lay aside your black veil: then tell me why you put it on."

Mr. Hooper's smile glimmered faintly.

"There is an hour to come," said he, "when all of us shall cast aside our veils. Take it not amiss, beloved friend, if I wear this piece of crape till then."

"Your words are a mystery, too," returned the young lady. "Take away the veil from them, at least."

"Elizabeth, I will," said he, "so far as my vow may suffer me. Know, then, this veil is a type and a symbol, and I am bound to wear it ever, both in light and darkness, in solitude and before the gaze of multitudes, and as with strangers, so with my familiar friends. No mortal eye will see it withdrawn. This dismal shade must separate me from the world: even you, Elizabeth, can never come behind it!"

"What grievous affliction hath befallen you," she earnestly inquired, "that you should thus darken your eyes forever?"

"If it be a sign of mourning," replied Mr. Hooper, "I, perhaps, like most other mortals, have sorrows dark enough to be typified by a black veil."

"But what if the world will not believe that it is the type of an innocent sorrow?" urged Elizabeth. "Beloved and respected as you are, there may be whispers that you hide your face under the consciousness of secret sin. For the sake of your holy office, do away this scandal!"

The color rose into her cheeks as she intimated the nature of the rumors that were already abroad in the village. But Mr. Hooper's mildness did not forsake him. He even smiled again—that same sad smile, which always appeared like a faint glimmering of light, proceeding from the obscurity beneath the veil.

"If I hide my face for sorrow, there is cause enough," he merely replied; "and if I cover it for secret sin, what mortal might not do the same?"

And with this gentle, but unconquerable obstinacy did he resist all her entreaties. At length Elizabeth sat silent. For a few moments she appeared lost in thought, considering, probably, what new methods might be tried to withdraw her lover from so dark a fantasy, which, if it had no other meaning, was perhaps a symptom of mental disease. Though of a firmer character than his own, the tears rolled down her cheeks. But, in an instant, as it were, a new feeling took the place of sorrow: her eyes were fixed insensibly on the black veil, when, like a sudden twilight in the air, its terrors fell around her. She arose, and stood trembling before him.

"And do you feel it then, at last?" said he mournfully.

She made no reply, but covered her eyes with her hand, and turned to leave the room. He rushed forward and caught her arm.

"Have patience with me, Elizabeth!" cried he, passionately. "Do not desert me, though this veil must be between us here on earth. Be mine, and hereafter there shall be no veil over my face, no darkness between our souls! It is but a mortal veil —it is not for eternity! O! you know not how lonely I am, and how frightened, to be alone behind my black veil. Do not leave me in this miserable obscurity forever!"

"Lift the veil but once, and look me in the face," said she.

"Never! It cannot be!" replied Mr. Hooper.

"Then farewell!" said Elizabeth.

She withdrew her arm from his grasp, and slowly departed, pausing at the door, to give one long shuddering gaze, that seemed almost to penetrate the mystery of the black veil. But, even amid his grief, Mr. Hooper smiled to think that only a material emblem had separated him from happiness, though the horrors, which it shadowed forth, must be drawn darkly between the fondest of lovers.

From that time no attempts were made to remove Mr. Hooper's black veil, or, by a direct appeal, to discover the secret which it was supposed to hide. By persons who claimed a superiority to popular prejudice, it was reckoned merely an eccentric whim, such as often mingles with the sober actions of men otherwise rational, and tinges them all with its own semblance of insanity. But with the multitude, good Mr. Hooper was irreparably a bugbear. He could not walk the street with any peace of mind, so conscious was he that the gentle and timid would turn aside to avoid him, and that others would make it a point of hardihood to throw themselves in his way. The impertinence of the latter class compelled him to give up his customary walk at sunset to the burial ground; for when he leaned pensively over the gate, there would always be faces behind the gravestones, peeping at his black veil. A fable went the rounds that the stare of the dead people drove him thence. It grieved him, to the very depth of his kind heart, to observe how the children fled from his approach, breaking up their merriest sports, while his melancholy figure was yet afar off. Their instinctive dread caused him to feel more strongly than aught else, that a preternatural horror was interwoven with the threads of the black crape. In truth, his own antipathy to the veil was known to be so great, that he never willingly passed before a mirror, nor stooped to drink at a still fountain, lest, in its peaceful bosom, he should be affrighted by himself. This was what gave plausibility to the whispers, that Mr. Hooper's conscience tortured him for some great crime too horrible to be entirely concealed, or otherwise than so obscurely intimated. Thus, from beneath the black veil, there rolled a cloud into the sunshine, and ambiguity of sin or sorrow, which enveloped the poor minister, so that love or sympathy could never reach him. It was said that ghost and fiend consorted with him there. With self-shudderings and outward terrors, he walked continually in its shadow, groping darkly within his own soul, or gazing through a medium that saddened the whole world. Even the lawless wind, it was believed, respected his dreadful secret, and never blew aside the veil. But still good Mr. Hooper sadly smiled at the pale visages of the worldly throng as he passed by.

Among all its bad influences, the black veil had the one desirable effect, of making its wearer a very efficient clergyman. By the aid of his mysterious emblem—for there was no other apparent cause—he became a man of awful power over souls that were in agony for sin. His converts always regarded him with a dread peculiar to themselves, affirming, though but figuratively, that, before he brought them to celestial light, they had been with him behind the black veil. Its gloom, indeed, enabled him to sympathize with all dark affections. Dying sinners cried aloud for Mr. Hooper, and would not yield their breath till he appeared; though ever, as he stooped to whisper consolation, they shuddered at the veiled face so near their own. Such were the terrors of the black veil, even when Death had bared his visage! Strangers came long distances to attend service at his church, with the mere idle purpose of gazing at his figure, because it was forbidden them to behold his face. But many were made to quake ere they departed! Once, during Governor Belcher's [3] administration, Mr. Hooper was appointed to preach the election sermon.[4] Covered with his black veil, he stood before the chief magistrate, the council, and the representatives, and wrought so deep an impression, that the legislative measures of that year were characterized by all the gloom and piety of our earliest ancestral sway.

In this manner Mr. Hooper spent a long life, irreproachable in outward act, yet shrouded in dismal suspicions; kind and loving, though unloved, and dimly feared; a man apart from men, shunned in their health and joy, but ever summoned to their aid in mortal anguish. As years wore on, shedding their snows above his sable veil, he acquired a name throughout the New England churches, and they called him Father Hooper. Nearly all his parishioners, who were of mature age when he was settled, had been borne away by many a funeral: he had one congregation in the church, and a more crowded one in the church-yard; and having wrought so late into the evening, and done his work so well, it was now good Father Hooper's turn to rest.

Several persons were visible by the shaded candlelight, in the death chamber of the old clergyman. Natural connections he had none. But there was the decorously grave, though unmoved physician, seeking only to mitigate the last pangs of

3. **Governor Belcher's:** Jonathan Belcher (1682–1757), royal governor of the Massachusetts Bay Colony, 1730–41. 4. **election sermon:** a formal address by a clergyman who thereby earned one of the highest rewards the colony could bestow upon him. The climax of *The Scarlet Letter* is on the occasion of the Rev. Mr. Dimmesdale's preaching the election sermon before the officers and the assembled citizens of the colony.

the patient whom he could not save. There were the deacons, and other eminently pious members of his church. There, also, was the Reverend Mr. Clark, of Westbury, a young and zealous divine, who had ridden in haste to pray by the bedside of the expiring minister. There was the nurse, no hired handmaiden of death, but one whose calm affection had endured thus long in secrecy, in solitude, amid the chill of age, and would not perish, even at the dying hour. Who, but Elizabeth! And there lay the hoary head of good Father Hooper upon the death pillow, with the black veil still swathed about his brow, and reaching down over his face, so that each more difficult gasp of his faint breath caused it to stir. All through life that piece of crape had hung between him and the world: it had separated him from cheerful brotherhood and woman's love, and kept him in that saddest of all prisons, his own heart; and still it lay upon his face, as if to deepen the gloom of his darksome chamber, and shade him from the sunshine of eternity.

For some time previous, his mind had been confused, wavering doubtfully between the past and the present, and hovering forward, as it were, at intervals, into the indistinctness of the world to come. There had been feverish turns, which tossed him from side to side, and wore away what little strength he had. But in his most convulsive struggles, and in the wildest vagaries of his intellect, when no other thought retained its sober influence, he still showed an awful solicitude lest the black veil should slip aside. Even if his bewildered soul could have forgotten, there was a faithful woman at his pillow, who, with averted eyes, would have covered that aged face, which she had last beheld in the comeliness of manhood. At length the death-stricken old man lay quietly in the torpor of mental and bodily exhaustion, with an imperceptible pulse, and breath that grew fainter and fainter, except when a long, deep, and irregular inspiration seemed to prelude the flight of his spirit.

The minister of Westbury approached the bedside.

"Venerable Father Hooper," said he, "the moment of your release is at hand. Are you ready for the lifting of the veil that shuts in time from eternity?"

Father Hooper at first replied merely by a feeble motion of his head; then, apprehensive, perhaps, that his meaning might be doubtful, he exerted himself to speak.

"Yea," said he, in faint accents, "my soul hath a patient weariness until that veil be lifted."

"And is it fitting," resumed the Reverend Mr. Clark, "that a man so given to prayer, of such a blameless example, holy in deed and thought, so far as mortal judgment may pronounce; is it fitting that a father in the church should leave a shadow on his memory, that may seem to blacken a life so pure? I pray you, my venerable brother, let not this thing be! Suffer us to be gladdened by your triumphant aspect as you go to your reward. Before the veil of eternity be lifted, let me cast aside this black veil from your face!"

And thus speaking, the Reverend Mr. Clark bent forward to reveal the mystery of so many years. But, exerting a sudden energy, that made all the beholders stand aghast, Father Hooper snatched both his hands from beneath the bedclothes, and pressed them strongly on the black veil, resolute to struggle, if the minister of Westbury would contend with a dying man.

"Never!" cried the veiled clergyman. "On earth, never!"

"Dark old man!" exclaimed the affrighted minister, "with what horrible crime upon your soul are you now passing to the judgment?"

Father Hooper's breath heaved; it rattled in his throat; but, with a mighty effort, grasping forward with his hands, he caught hold of life, and held it back till he should speak. He even raised himself in bed; and there he sat, shivering with the arms of death around him, while the black veil hung down, awful, at that last moment, in the gathered terrors of a lifetime. And yet the faint, sad smile, so often there, now seemed to glimmer from its obscurity, and linger on Father Hooper's lips.

"Why do you tremble at me alone?" cried he, turning his veiled face round the circle of pale spectators. "Tremble also at each other! Have men avoided me, and women shown no pity, and children screamed and fled, only for my black veil? What, but the mystery which it obscurely typifies, has made this piece of crape so awful? When the friend shows his inmost heart to his friend; the lover to his best beloved; when man does not vainly shrink from the eye of his Creator, loathsomely treasuring up the secret of his sin; then deem me a monster, for the symbol beneath which I have lived, and die! I look around me, and, lo! on every visage a Black Veil!"

While his auditors shrank from one another, in mutual affright, Father Hooper fell back upon his pillow, a veiled corpse, with a faint smile lingering on the lips. Still veiled, they laid him in his coffin, and a veiled corpse they bore him to the grave. The grass of many years has sprung up and withered on that grave, the burial stone is mossgrown, and good Mr. Hooper's face is dust; but awful is still the thought that it mouldered beneath the Black Veil!

# THE BIRTHMARK

❖

⟨ THE TWO notebook entries for 1837 (see p. 409) were probably the beginnings for this story which was first published in the *Pioneer* (March 1843) and included in *Mosses from an Old Manse* (1846). The theme of the tale is suggested in the notebook entries: although man directs his energy toward the most lovely and perfect thing he can create, the very nature of beauty is its being flawed, and that which, in this life, is most pure and ethereal is so only in its imperfection. If our humanity loses its imperfection, it may cease to be human and become even subhuman. Man's dreams and the Ideal are the measure of a perfection which can never be attained.

❖

IN THE latter part of the last century there lived a man of science, an eminent proficient in every branch of natural philosophy, who not long before our story opens had made experience of a spiritual affinity more attractive than any chemical one. He had left his laboratory to the care of an assistant, cleared his fine countenance from the furnace smoke, washed the stain of acids from his fingers, and persuaded a beautiful woman to become his wife. In those days when the comparatively recent discovery of electricity and other kindred mysteries of Nature seemed to open paths into the region of miracle, it was not unusual for the love of science to rival the love of woman in its depth and absorbing energy. The higher intellect, the imagination, the spirit, and even the heart might all find their congenial aliment in pursuits which, as some of their ardent votaries believed, would ascend from one step of powerful intelligence to another, until the philosopher should lay his hand on the secret of creative force and perhaps make new worlds for himself. We know not whether Aylmer possessed this degree of faith in man's ultimate control over Nature. He had devoted himself, however, too unreservedly to scientific studies ever to be weaned from them by any second passion. His love for his young wife might prove the stronger of the two; but it could only be by intertwining itself with his love of science, and uniting the strength of the latter to his own.

Such a union accordingly took place, and was attended with truly remarkable consequences and a deeply impressive moral. One day, very soon after their marriage, Aylmer sat gazing at his wife with a trouble in his countenance that grew stronger until he spoke.

"Georgiana," said he, "has it never occurred to you that the mark upon your cheek might be removed?"

"No, indeed," said she, smiling; but perceiving the seriousness of his manner, she blushed deeply. "To tell the truth it has been so often called a charm that I was simple enough to imagine it might be so."

"Ah, upon another face perhaps it might," replied her husband; "but never on yours. No, dearest Georgiana, you came so nearly perfect from the hand of Nature that this slightest possible defect, which we hesitate whether to term a defect or a beauty, shocks me, as being the visible mark of earthly imperfection."

"Shocks you, my husband!" cried Georgiana, deeply hurt; at first reddening with momentary anger, but then bursting into tears. "Then why did you take me from my mother's side? You cannot love what shocks you!"

To explain this conversation it must be mentioned that in the centre of Georgiana's left cheek there was a singular mark, deeply interwoven, as it were, with the texture and substance of her face. In the usual state of her complexion—a healthy though delicate bloom—the mark wore a tint of deeper crimson, which imperfectly defined its shape amid the surrounding rosiness. When she blushed it gradually became more indistinct, and finally vanished amid the triumphant rush of blood that bathed the whole cheek with its brilliant glow. But if any shifting motion caused her to turn pale there was the mark again, a crimson stain upon the snow, in what Aylmer sometimes deemed an almost fearful distinctness. Its shape bore not a little similarity to the human hand, though of the smallest pygmy size. Georgiana's lovers were wont to say that some fairy at her birth hour had laid her tiny hand upon the infant's cheek, and left this impress there in token of the magic endowments that were to give her such sway over all hearts. Many a desperate swain would have risked life for the privilege of pressing his lips to the mysterious hand. It must not be concealed, however, that the impression wrought by this fairy sign manual varied exceedingly, according to the difference of temperament in the beholders. Some fastidious persons—but they were exclusively of her own sex—affirmed that the bloody hand, as they chose to call it, quite destroyed the effect of Georgiana's beauty, and rendered her countenance even hideous. But it would be as reasonable to say that one of those small blue stains which sometimes occur in the purest statuary marble would convert the Eve of Powers [1] to a monster. Masculine observers, if the birthmark did not heighten their admiration, contented themselves with wishing it away, that the world might possess one living specimen of ideal loveliness without the semblance of a flaw. After his marriage,—for he thought little or nothing of the matter before,—Aylmer discovered that this was the case with himself.

Had she been less beautiful,—if Envy's self could have found aught else to sneer at,—he might have felt his affection heightened by the prettiness of this mimic hand, now vaguely portrayed, now lost, now stealing forth again and glimmering to and fro with every pulse of emotion that throbbed within her heart; but seeing her otherwise so perfect, he found this one defect grow more and more intolerable with every moment of their united lives. It was the fatal flaw of humanity which Nature, in one shape or another, stamps ineffaceably on all her productions, either to imply that they are temporary and finite, or that their perfection must be wrought by toil and pain. The crimson hand expressed the ineludible gripe in which mortality clutches the highest and purest of earthly mould, degrading them into kindred with the lowest, and even with the very brutes, like whom their visible frames return to dust. In this manner, selecting it as the symbol of his wife's liability to sin, sorrow, decay, and death, Aylmer's sombre imagination was not long in rendering the birthmark a frightful object, causing him more trouble and horror than ever Georgiana's beauty, whether of soul or sense, had given him delight.

At all the seasons which should have been their happiest, he invariably and without intending it, nay, in spite of a purpose to the contrary, reverted to this one disastrous topic. Trifling as it at first appeared, it so connected itself with innumerable trains of thought and modes of feeling that it became the central point of all. With the morning twilight Aylmer opened his eyes upon his wife's face and recognized the symbol of imperfection; and when they sat together at the evening hearth his eyes wandered stealthily to her cheek, and beheld, flickering with the blaze of the wood fire, the spectral hand that wrote mortality where he would fain have worshipped. Georgiana soon learned to shudder at his gaze. It needed but a glance with the peculiar expression that his face often wore to change the roses of her cheek into a deathlike paleness, amid which the crimson hand

was brought strongly out, like a bas-relief of ruby on the whitest marble.

Late one night when the lights were growing dim, so as hardly to betray the stain on the poor wife's cheek, she herself, for the first time, voluntarily took up the subject.

"Do you remember, my dear Aylmer," said she, with a feeble attempt at a smile, "have you any recollection of a dream last night about this odious hand?"

"None! none whatever!" replied Aylmer, starting; but then he added, in a dry, cold tone, affected for the sake of concealing the real depth of his emotion, "I might well dream of it; for before I fell asleep it had taken a pretty firm hold of my fancy."

"And you did dream of it?" continued Georgiana, hastily; for she dreaded lest a gush of tears should interrupt what she had to say. "A terrible dream! I wonder that you can forget it. Is it possible to forget this one expression?—'It is in her heart now; we must have it out!' Reflect, my husband; for by all means I would have you recall that dream."

The mind is in a sad state when Sleep, the all-involving, cannot confine her spectres within the dim region of her sway, but suffers them to break forth, affrighting this actual life with secrets that perchance belong to a deeper one. Aylmer now remembered his dream. He had fancied himself with his servant Aminadab, attempting an operation for the removal of the birthmark; but the deeper went the knife, the deeper sank the hand, until at length its tiny grasp appeared to have caught hold of Georgiana's heart; whence, however, her husband was inexorably resolved to cut or wrench it away.

When the dream had shaped itself perfectly in his memory, Aylmer sat in his wife's presence with a guilty feeling. Truth often finds its way to the mind close muffled in robes of sleep, and then speaks with uncompromising directness of matters in regard to which we practise an unconscious self-deception during our waking moments. Until now he had not been aware of the tyrannizing influence acquired by one idea over his mind, and of the lengths which he might find in his heart to go for the sake of giving himself peace.

"Aylmer," resumed Georgiana, solemnly, "I know not what may be the cost to both of us to rid me of this fatal birthmark. Perhaps its removal may cause cureless deformity; or it may be the stain goes as deep as life itself. Again: do we know that there is a possibility, on any terms, of unclasping the firm gripe of this little hand which was laid upon me before I came into the world?"

"Dearest Georgiana, I have spent much thought

THE BIRTHMARK. 1. **Eve of Powers:** Hiram Powers (1805–73), the American sculptor, created a life-size figure, "Eve Before the Fall."

upon the subject," hastily interrupted Aylmer. "I am convinced of the perfect practicability of its removal."

"If there be the remotest possibility of it," continued Georgiana, "let the attempt be made at whatever risk. Danger is nothing to me; for life, while this hateful mark makes me the object of your horror and disgust,—life is a burden which I would fling down with joy. Either remove this dreadful hand, or take my wretched life! You have deep science. All the world bears witness of it. You have achieved great wonders. Cannot you remove this little, little mark, which I cover with the tips of two small fingers? Is this beyond your power, for the sake of your own peace, and to save your poor wife from madness?"

"Noblest, dearest, tenderest wife," cried Aylmer, rapturously, "doubt not my power. I have already given this matter the deepest thought—thought which might almost have enlightened me to create a being less perfect than yourself. Georgiana, you have led me deeper than ever into the heart of science. I feel myself fully competent to render this dear cheek as faultless as its fellow; and then, most beloved, what will be my triumph when I shall have corrected what Nature left imperfect in her fairest work! Even Pygmalion,[2] when his sculptured woman assumed life, felt not greater ecstasy than mine will be."

"It is resolved, then," said Georgiana, faintly smiling. "And, Aylmer, spare me not, though you should find the birthmark take refuge in my heart at last."

Her husband tenderly kissed her cheek—her right cheek—not that which bore the impress of the crimson hand.

The next day Aylmer apprised his wife of a plan that he had formed whereby he might have opportunity for the intense thought and constant watchfulness which the proposed operation would require; while Georgiana, likewise, would enjoy the perfect repose essential to its success. They were to seclude themselves in the extensive apartments occupied by Aylmer as a laboratory, and where, during his toilsome youth, he had made discoveries in the elemental powers of Nature that had roused the admiration of all the learned societies in Europe. Seated calmly in this laboratory, the pale philosopher had investigated the secrets of the highest cloud region and of the profoundest mines; he had satisfied himself of the causes that kindled and kept alive the fires of the volcano; and had explained the mystery of fountains, and

how it is that they gush forth, some so bright and pure, and others with such rich medicinal virtues, from the dark bosom of the earth. Here, too, at an earlier period, he had studied the wonders of the human frame, and attempted to fathom the very process by which Nature assimilates all her precious influences from earth and air, and from the spiritual world, to create and foster man, her masterpiece. The latter pursuit, however, Aylmer had long laid aside in unwilling recognition of the truth —against which all seekers sooner or later stumble —that our great creative Mother, while she amuses us with apparently working in the broadest sunshine, is yet severely careful to keep her own secrets, and, in spite of her pretended openness, shows us nothing but results. She permits us, indeed, to mar, but seldom to mend, and, like a jealous patentee, on no account to make. Now, however, Aylmer resumed these half-forgotten investigations; not, of course, with such hopes or wishes as first suggested them; but because they involved much physiological truth and lay in the path of his proposed scheme for the treatment of Georgiana.

As he led her over the threshold of the laboratory, Georgiana was cold and tremulous. Aylmer looked cheerfully into her face, with intent to reassure her, but was so startled with the intense glow of the birthmark upon the whiteness of her cheek that he could not restrain a strong convulsive shudder. His wife fainted.

"Aminadab! Aminadab!" shouted Aylmer, stamping violently on the floor.

Forthwith there issued from an inner apartment a man of low stature, but bulky frame, with shaggy hair hanging about his visage, which was grimed with the vapors of the furnace. This personage had been Aylmer's underworker during his whole scientific career, and was admirably fitted for that office by his great mechanical readiness, and the skill with which, while incapable of comprehending a single principle, he executed all the details of his master's experiments. With his vast strength, his shaggy hair, his smoky aspect, and the indescribable earthiness that incrusted him, he seemed to represent man's physical nature; while Aylmer's slender figure, and pale, intellectual face, were no less apt a type of the spiritual element.

"Throw open the door of the boudoir, Aminadab," said Aylmer, "and burn a pastil."

"Yes, master," answered Aminadab, looking intently at the lifeless form of Georgiana; and then he muttered to himself, "If she were my wife, I'd never part with that birthmark."

When Georgiana recovered consciousness she found herself breathing an atmosphere of pene-

2. **Pygmalion:** a mythical king of Cyprus who fell in love with the ivory statue of Galatea; his prayers to Aphrodite brought the statue to life.

trating fragrance, the gentle potency of which had recalled her from her deathlike faintness. The scene around her looked like enchantment. Aylmer had converted those smoky, dingy, sombre rooms, where he had spent his brightest years in recondite pursuits, into a series of beautiful apartments not unfit to be the secluded abode of a lovely woman. The walls were hung with gorgeous curtains, which imparted the combination of grandeur and grace that no other species of adornment can achieve; and as they fell from the ceiling to the floor, their rich and ponderous folds, concealing all angles and straight lines, appeared to shut in the scene from infinite space. For aught Georgiana knew, it might be a pavilion among the clouds. And Aylmer, excluding the sunshine, which would have interfered with his chemical processes, had supplied its place with perfumed lamps, emitting flames of various hue, but all uniting in a soft, impurpled radiance. He now knelt by his wife's side, watching her earnestly, but without alarm; for he was confident in his science, and felt that he could draw a magic circle round her within which no evil might intrude.

"Where am I? Ah, I remember," said Georgiana, faintly; and she placed her hand over her cheek to hide the terrible mark from her husband's eyes.

"Fear not, dearest!" exclaimed he. "Do not shrink from me! Believe me, Georgiana, I even rejoice in this single imperfection, since it will be such a rapture to remove it."

"Oh, spare me!" sadly replied his wife. "Pray do not look at it again. I never can forget that convulsive shudder."

In order to soothe Georgiana, and, as it were, to release her mind from the burden of actual things, Aylmer now put in practice some of the light and playful secrets which science had taught him among its profounder lore. Airy figures, absolutely bodiless ideas, and forms of unsubstantial beauty came and danced before her, imprinting their momentary footsteps on beams of light. Though she had some indistinct idea of the method of these optical phenomena, still the illusion was almost perfect enough to warrant the belief that her husband possessed sway over the spiritual world. Then again, when she felt a wish to look forth from her seclusion, immediately, as if her thoughts were answered, the procession of external existence flitted across a screen. The scenery and the figures of actual life were perfectly represented, but with that bewitching, yet indescribable difference which always makes a picture, an image, or a shadow so much more attractive than the original. When wearied of this, Aylmer bade

her cast her eyes upon a vessel containing a quantity of earth. She did so, with little interest at first; but was soon startled to perceive the germ of a plant shooting upward from the soil. Then came the slender stalk; the leaves gradually unfolded themselves; and amid them was a perfect and lovely flower.

"It is magical!" cried Georgiana. "I dare not touch it."

"Nay, pluck it," answered Aylmer,—"pluck it, and inhale its brief perfume while you may. The flower will wither in a few moments and leave nothing save its brown seed vessels; but thence may be perpetuated a race as ephemeral as itself."

But Georgiana had no sooner touched the flower than the whole plant suffered a blight, its leaves turning coal-black as if by the agency of fire.

"There was too powerful a stimulus," said Aylmer, thoughtfully.

To make up for this abortive experiment, he proposed to take her portrait by a scientific process of his own invention. It was to be effected by rays of light striking upon a polished plate of metal. Georgiana assented; but, on looking at the result, was affrighted to find the features of the portrait blurred and indefinable; while the minute figure of a hand appeared where the cheek should have been. Aylmer snatched the metallic plate and threw it into a jar of corrosive acid.

Soon, however, he forgot these mortifying failures. In the intervals of study and chemical experiment he came to her flushed and exhausted, but seemed invigorated by her presence, and spoke in glowing language of the resources of his art. He gave a history of the long dynasty of the alchemists,[3] who spent so many ages in quest of the universal solvent by which the golden principle might be elicited from all things vile and base. Aylmer appeared to believe that, by the plainest scientific logic, it was altogether within the limits of possibility to discover this long-sought medium; "but," he added, "a philosopher who should go deep enough to acquire the power would attain too lofty a wisdom to stoop to the exercise of it." Not less singular were his opinions in regard to the elixir vitae. He more than intimated that it was at his option to concoct a liquid that should prolong life for years, perhaps interminably; but that it

3. He . . . alchemists: Alchemy, the predecessor of modern medical science, was the medieval chemistry which sought to transmute base metals into gold and to discover the universal cure for diseases. The search for the "elixir Vitae" was to discover the magical nostrum which would indefinitely prolong life. Aylmer's experiments, however modern they may be, are mostly of the "black arts" associated with alchemy.

would produce a discord in Nature which all the world, and chiefly the quaffer of the immortal nostrum, would find cause to curse.

"Aylmer, are you in earnest?" asked Georgiana, looking at him with amazement and fear. "It is terrible to possess such power, or even to dream of possessing it."

"Oh, do not tremble, my love," said her husband. "I would not wrong either you or myself by working such inharmonious effects upon our lives; but I would have you consider how trifling, in comparison, is the skill requisite to remove this little hand."

At the mention of the birthmark, Georgiana, as usual, shrank as if a redhot iron had touched her cheek.

Again Aylmer applied himself to his labors. She could hear his voice in the distant furnace room giving directions to Aminadab, whose harsh, uncouth, misshapen tones were audible in response, more like the grunt or growl of a brute than human speech. After hours of absence, Aylmer reappeared and proposed that she should now examine his cabinet of chemical products and natural treasures of the earth. Among the former he showed her a small vial, in which, he remarked, was contained a gentle yet most powerful fragrance, capable of impregnating all the breezes that blow across a kingdom. They were of inestimable value, the contents of that little vial; and, as he said so, he threw some of the perfume into the air and filled the room with piercing and invigorating delight.

"And what is this?" asked Georgiana, pointing to a small crystal globe containing a gold-colored liquid. "It is so beautiful to the eye that I could imagine it the elixir of life."

"In one sense it is," replied Aylmer; "or, rather, the elixir of immortality. It is the most precious poison that ever was concocted in this world. By its aid I could apportion the lifetime of any mortal at whom you might point your finger. The strength of the dose would determine whether he were to linger out years, or drop dead in the midst of a breath. No king on his guarded throne could keep his life if I, in my private station, should deem that the welfare of millions justified me in depriving him of it."

"Why do you keep such a terrific drug?" inquired Georgiana in horror.

"Do not mistrust me, dearest," said her husband, smiling; "its virtuous potency is yet greater than its harmful one. But see! here is a powerful cosmetic. With a few drops of this in a vase of water, freckles may be washed away as easily as the hands are cleansed. A stronger infusion would

take the blood out of the cheek, and leave the rosiest beauty a pale ghost."

"Is it with this lotion that you intend to bathe my cheek?" asked Georgiana, anxiously.

"Oh, no," hastily replied her husband; "this is merely superficial. Your case demands a remedy that shall go deeper."

In his interviews with Georgiana, Aylmer generally made minute inquiries as to her sensations and whether the confinement of the rooms and the temperature of the atmosphere agreed with her. These questions had such a particular drift that Georgiana began to conjecture that she was already subjected to certain physical influences, either breathed in with the fragrant air or taken with her food. She fancied likewise, but it might be altogether fancy, that there was a stirring up of her system—a strange, indefinite sensation creeping through her veins, and tingling, half painfully, half pleasurably, at her heart. Still, whenever she dared to look into the mirror, there she beheld herself pale as a white rose and with the crimson birthmark stamped upon her cheek. Not even Aylmer now hated it so much as she.

To dispel the tedium of the hours which her husband found it necessary to devote to the processes of combination and analysis, Georgiana turned over the volumes of his scientific library. In many dark old tomes she met with chapters full of romance and poetry. They were the works of the philosophers of the middle ages, such as Albertus Magnus, Cornelius Agrippa, Paracelsus, and the famous friar who created the prophetic Brazen Head.[4] All these antique naturalists stood in advance of their centuries, yet were imbued with some of their credulity, and therefore were believed, and perhaps imagined themselves to have acquired from the investigation of Nature a power above Nature, and from physics a sway over the spiritual world. Hardly less curious and imaginative were the early volumes of the Transactions of the Royal Society,[5] in which the members, knowing little of the limits of natural possibility, were continually recording wonders or proposing methods whereby wonders might be wrought.

But to Georgiana the most engrossing volume was a large folio from her husband's own hand, in which he had recorded every experiment of

---

4. **Albertus . . . Head:** Albertus Magnus (1193?–1280), German saint, philosopher, and alchemist. Cornelius Agrippa (1486?–1535), German physician, theologian, and writer. Paracelsus (1493–1541), Swiss-born alchemist and physician. **Brazen Head:** the English philosopher and man of science, Roger Bacon (1214–94), was reputed to have made a head of brass.   5. **Transactions . . . Society:** the *Philosophical Transactions* of The Royal Society for Improving Natural Knowledge, the famous scientific body founded in 1660.

his scientific career, its original aim, the methods adopted for its development, and its final success or failure, with the circumstances to which either event was attributable. The book, in truth, was both the history and emblem of his ardent, ambitious, imaginative, yet practical and laborious life. He handled physical details as if there were nothing beyond them; yet spiritualized them all, and redeemed himself from materialism by his strong and eager aspiration towards the infinite. In his grasp the veriest clod of earth assumed a soul. Georgiana, as she read, reverenced Aylmer and loved him more profoundly than ever, but with a less entire dependence on his judgment than heretofore. Much as he had accomplished, she could not but observe that his most splendid successes were almost invariably failures, if compared with the ideal at which he aimed. His brightest diamonds were the merest pebbles, and felt to be so by himself, in comparison with the inestimable gems which lay hidden beyond his reach. The volume, rich with achievements that had won renown for its author, was yet as melancholy a record as ever mortal hand had penned. It was the sad confession and continual exemplification of the shortcomings of the composite man, the spirit burdened with clay and working in matter, and of the despair that assails the higher nature at finding itself so miserably thwarted by the earthly part. Perhaps every man of genius in whatever sphere might recognize the image of his own experience in Aylmer's journal.

So deeply did these reflections affect Georgiana that she laid her face upon the open volume and burst into tears. In this situation she was found by her husband.

"It is dangerous to read in a sorcerer's books," said he, with a smile, though his countenance was uneasy and displeased. "Georgiana, there are pages in that volume which I can scarcely glance over and keep my senses. Take heed lest it prove as detrimental to you."

"It has made me worship you more than ever," said she.

"Ah, wait for this one success," rejoined he, "then worship me if you will. I shall deem myself hardly unworthy of it. But come, I have sought you for the luxury of your voice. Sing to me, dearest."

So she poured out the liquid music of her voice to quench the thirst of his spirit. He then took his leave with a boyish exuberance of gayety, assuring her that her seclusion would endure but a little longer, and that the result was already certain. Scarcely had he departed when Georgiana felt ir-

resistibly impelled to follow him. She had forgotten to inform Aylmer of a symptom which for two or three hours past had begun to excite her attention. It was a sensation in the fatal birthmark, not painful, but which induced a restlessness throughout her system. Hastening after her husband, she intruded for the first time into the laboratory.

The first thing that struck her eye was the furnace, that hot and feverish worker, with the intense glow of its fire, which by the quantities of soot clustered above it seemed to have been burning for ages. There was a distilling apparatus in full operation. Around the room were retorts, tubes, cylinders, crucibles, and other apparatus of chemical research. An electrical machine stood ready for immediate use. The atmosphere felt oppressively close, and was tainted with gaseous odors which had been tormented forth by the processes of science. The severe and homely simplicity of the apartment, with its naked walls and brick pavement, looked strange, accustomed as Georgiana had become to the fantastic elegance of her boudoir. But what chiefly, indeed almost solely, drew her attention, was the aspect of Aylmer himself.

He was pale as death, anxious and absorbed, and hung over the furnace as if it depended upon his utmost watchfulness whether the liquid which it was distilling should be the draught of immortal happiness or misery. How different from the sanguine and joyous mien that he had assumed for Georgiana's encouragement!

"Carefully now, Aminadab; carefully, thou human machine; carefully, thou man of clay!" muttered Aylmer, more to himself than his assistant. "Now, if there be a thought too much or too little, it is all over."

"Ho! ho!" mumbled Aminadab. "Look, master! look!"

Aylmer raised his eyes hastily, and at first reddened, then grew paler than ever, on beholding Georgiana. He rushed towards her and seized her arm with a gripe that left the print of his fingers upon it.

"Why do you come hither? Have you no trust in your husband?" cried he, impetuously. "Would you throw the blight of that fatal birthmark over my labors? It is not well done. Go, prying woman, go!"

"Nay, Aylmer," said Georgiana with the firmness of which she possessed no stinted endowment, "it is not you that have a right to complain. You mistrust your wife; you have concealed the anxiety with which you watch the development of this experiment. Think not so unworthily of me, my husband. Tell me all the risk we run, and fear not that I shall shrink; for my share in it is far less than your own."

"No, no, Georgiana!" said Aylmer, impatiently; "it must not be."

"I submit," replied she calmly. "And, Aylmer, I shall quaff whatever draught you bring me; but it will be on the same principle that would induce me to take a dose of poison if offered by your hand."

"My noble wife," said Aylmer, deeply moved, "I knew not the height and depth of your nature until now. Nothing shall be concealed. Know, then, that this crimson hand, superficial as it seems, has clutched its grasp into your being with a strength of which I had no previous conception. I have already administered agents powerful enough to do aught except to change your entire physical system. Only one thing remains to be tried. If that fail us we are ruined."

"Why did you hesitate to tell me this?" asked she.

"Because, Georgiana," said Aylmer, in a low voice, "there is danger."

"Danger? There is but one danger—that this horrible stigma shall be left upon my cheek!" cried Georgiana. "Remove it, remove it, whatever be the cost, or we shall both go mad!"

"Heaven knows your words are too true," said Aylmer, sadly. "And now, dearest, return to your boudoir. In a little while all will be tested."

He conducted her back and took leave of her with a solemn tenderness which spoke far more than his words how much was now at stake. After his departure Georgiana became rapt in musings. She considered the character of Aylmer, and did it completer justice than at any previous moment. Her heart exulted, while it trembled, at his honorable love—so pure and lofty that it would accept nothing less than perfection nor miserably make itself contented with an earthlier nature than he had dreamed of. She felt how much more precious was such a sentiment than that meaner kind which would have borne with the imperfection for her sake, and have been guilty of treason to holy love by degrading its perfect idea to the level of the actual; and with her whole spirit she prayed that, for a single moment, she might satisfy his highest and deepest conception. Longer than one moment she well knew it could not be; for his spirit was ever on the march, ever ascending, and each instant required something that was beyond the scope of the instant before.

The sound of her husband's footsteps aroused her. He bore a crystal goblet containing a liquor colorless as water, but bright enough to be the draught of immortality. Aylmer was pale; but it seemed rather the consequence of a highly-wrought state of mind and tension of spirit than of fear or doubt.

"The concoction of the draught has been perfect," said he, in answer to Georgiana's look. "Unless all my science have deceived me, it cannot fail."

"Save on your account, my dearest Aylmer," observed his wife, "I might wish to put off this birthmark of mortality by relinquishing mortality itself in preference to any other mode. Life is but a sad possession to those who have attained precisely the degree of moral advancement at which I stand. Were I weaker and blinder it might be happiness. Were I stronger, it might be endured hopefully. But, being what I find myself, methinks I am of all mortals the most fit to die."

"You are fit for heaven without tasting death!" replied her husband. "But why do we speak of dying? The draught cannot fail. Behold its effect upon this plant."

On the window seat there stood a geranium diseased with yellow blotches, which had overspread all its leaves. Aylmer poured a small quantity of the liquid upon the soil in which it grew. In a little time, when the roots of the plant had taken up the moisture, the unsightly blotches began to be extinguished in a living verdure.

"There needed no proof," said Georgiana, quietly. "Give me the goblet. I joyfully stake all upon your word."

"Drink, then, thou lofty creature!" exclaimed Aylmer, with fervid admiration. "There is no taint of imperfection on thy spirit. Thy sensible frame, too, shall soon be all perfect."

She quaffed the liquid and returned the goblet to his hand.

"It is grateful," said she with a placid smile. "Methinks it is like water from a heavenly fountain; for it contains I know not what of unobtrusive fragrance and deliciousness. It allays a feverish thirst that had parched me for many days. Now, dearest, let me sleep. My earthly senses are closing over my spirit like the leaves around the heart of a rose at sunset."

She spoke the last words with a gentle reluctance, as if it required almost more energy than she could command to pronounce the faint and lingering syllables. Scarcely had they loitered through her lips ere she was lost in slumber. Aylmer sat by her side, watching her aspect with the emotions proper to a man the whole value of whose existence was involved in the process now to be tested.

Mingled with this mood, however, was the philosophic investigation characteristic of the man of science. Not the minutest symptom escaped him. A heightened flush of the cheek, a slight irregularity of breath, a quiver of the eyelid, a hardly perceptible tremor through the frame,—such were the details which, as the moments passed, he wrote down in his folio volume. Intense thought had set its stamp upon every previous page of that volume, but the thoughts of years were all concentrated upon the last.

While thus employed, he failed not to gaze often at the fatal hand, and not without a shudder. Yet once, by a strange and unaccountable impulse, he pressed it with his lips. His spirit recoiled, however, in the very act; and Georgiana, out of the midst of her deep sleep, moved uneasily and murmured as if in remonstrance. Again Aylmer resumed his watch. Nor was it without avail. The crimson hand, which at first had been strongly visible upon the marble paleness of Georgiana's cheek, now grew more faintly outlined. She remained not less pale than ever; but the birthmark, with every breath that came and went, lost somewhat of its former distinctness. Its presence had been awful; its departure was more awful still. Watch the stain of the rainbow fading out of the sky, and you will know how that mysterious symbol passed away.

"By Heaven! it is well-nigh gone!" said Aylmer to himself, in almost irrepressible ecstasy. "I can scarcely trace it now. Success! success! And now it is like the faintest rose color. The lightest flush of blood across her cheek would overcome it. But she is so pale!"

He drew aside the window curtain and suffered the light of natural day to fall into the room and rest upon her cheek. At the same time he heard a gross, hoarse chuckle, which he had long known as his servant Aminadab's expression of delight.

"Ah, clod! ah, earthly mass!" cried Aylmer, laughing in a sort of frenzy, "you have served me well! Matter and spirit—earth and heaven—have both done their part in this! Laugh, thing of the senses! You have earned the right to laugh."

These exclamations broke Georgiana's sleep. She slowly unclosed her eyes and gazed into the mirror which her husband had arranged for that purpose. A faint smile flitted over her lips when she recognized how barely perceptible was now that crimson hand which had once blazed forth with such disastrous brilliancy as to scare away all their happiness. But then her eyes sought Aylmer's face with a trouble and anxiety that he could by no means account for.

"My poor Aylmer!" murmured she.

"Poor? Nay, richest, happiest, most favored!" exclaimed he. "My peerless bride, it is successful! You are perfect!"

"My poor Aylmer," she repeated, with a more than human tenderness, "you have aimed loftily; you have done nobly. Do not repent that with so high and pure a feeling, you have rejected the best the earth could offer. Aylmer, dearest Aylmer, I am dying!"

Alas! it was too true! The fatal hand had grappled with the mystery of life, and was the bond by which an angelic spirit kept itself in union with a mortal frame. As the last crimson tint of the birthmark—that sole token of human imperfection—faded from her cheek, the parting breath of the now perfect woman passed into the atmosphere, and her soul, lingering a moment near her husband, took its heavenward flight. Then a hoarse, chuckling laugh was heard again! Thus ever does the gross fatality of earth exult in its invariable triumph over the immortal essence which, in this dim sphere of half development, demands the completeness of a higher state. Yet, had Aylmer reached a profounder wisdom, he need not thus have flung away the happiness which would have woven his mortal life of the selfsame texture with the celestial. The momentary circumstance was too strong for him; he failed to look beyond the shadowy scope of time, and, living once for all in eternity, to find the perfect future in the present.

# THE ARTIST OF THE BEAUTIFUL

◊

❨ THIS story first appeared in the *Democratic Review* (June, 1844) and was gathered in *Mosses from an Old Manse* (1846). The narrative may be taken as a commentary on the nature of the artist, who, by his devotion to the artistic ideal, isolates himself from the community of men. His creation of art, however ephemeral and even useless, is its own reward. Some have thought that the story is an allegory of Hawthorne's idea of his own art. Whatever the interpretation, the action of the narrative goes counter to generally accepted ideas of art: art is here not a representation of nature nor is it a Platonic transcending of the physical world wherein, as Emerson proposed, the realm of "essence" is apprehended or reached. Indeed, the story is of interest for its opposition to principles of art in Hawthorne's day and for its linkages with some of Melville's ideas.

❖

AN ELDERLY man, with his pretty daughter on his arm, was passing along the street, and emerged from the gloom of the cloudy evening into the light that fell across the pavement from the window of a small shop. It was a projecting window; and on the inside were suspended a variety of watches, pinchbeck,[1] silver, and one or two of gold, all with their faces turned from the streets, as if churlishly disinclined to inform the wayfarers what o'clock it was. Seated within the shop, sidelong to the window, with his pale face bent earnestly over some delicate piece of mechanism on which was thrown the concentrated lustre of a shade lamp, appeared a young man.

"What can Owen Warland be about?" muttered old Peter Hovenden, himself a retired watchmaker, and the former master of this same young man whose occupation he was now wondering at. "What can the fellow be about? These six months past I have never come by his shop without seeing him just as steadily at work as now. It would be a flight beyond his usual foolery to seek for the perpetual motion; and yet I know enough of my old business to be certain that what he is now so busy with is no part of the machinery of a watch."

"Perhaps, father," said Annie, without showing much interest in the question, "Owen is inventing a new kind of timekeeper. I am sure he has ingenuity enough."

"Poh, child! He has not the sort of ingenuity to invent anything better than a Dutch toy," answered her father, who had formerly been put to much vexation by Owen Warland's irregular genius. "A plague on such ingenuity! All the effect that ever I knew of it was to spoil the accuracy of some of the best watches in my shop. He would turn the sun out of its orbit and derange the whole course of time, if, as I said before, his ingenuity could grasp anything bigger than a child's toy!"

"Hush, father! He hears you!" whispered Annie, pressing the old man's arm. "His ears are as delicate as his feelings; and you know how easily disturbed they are. Do let us move on."

So Peter Hovenden and his daughter Annie plodded on without further conversation, until in a by-street of the town they found themselves passing the open door of a blacksmith's shop. Within was seen the forge, now blazing up and illuminating the high and dusky roof, and now confining its lustre to a narrow precinct of the coal-strewn floor, according as the breath of the bellows was puffed

forth or again inhaled into its vast leathern lungs. In the intervals of brightness it was easy to distinguish objects in remote corners of the shop and the horseshoes that hung upon the wall; in the momentary gloom the fire seemed to be glimmering amidst the vagueness of unenclosed space. Moving about in this red glare and alternate dusk was the figure of the blacksmith, well worthy to be viewed in so picturesque an aspect of light and shade, where the bright blaze struggled with the black night, as if each would have snatched his comely strength from the other. Anon he drew a white-hot bar of iron from the coals, laid it on the anvil, uplifted his arm of might, and was soon enveloped in the myriads of sparks which the strokes of his hammer scattered into the surrounding gloom.

"Now, that is a pleasant sight," said the old watchmaker. "I know what it is to work in gold; but give me the worker in iron after all is said and done. He spends his labor upon a reality. What say you, daughter Annie?"

"Pray don't speak so loud, father," whispered Annie, "Robert Danforth will hear you."

"And what if he should hear me?" said Peter Hovenden. "I say again, it is a good and a wholesome thing to depend upon main strength and reality, and to earn one's bread with the bare and brawny arm of a blacksmith. A watchmaker gets his brain puzzled by his wheels within a wheel, or loses his health or the nicety of his eyesight, as was my case, and finds himself at middle age, or a little after, past labor at his own trade and fit for nothing else, yet too poor to live at his ease. So I say once again, give me main strength for my money. And then, how it takes the nonsense out of a man! Did you ever hear of a blacksmith being such a fool as Owen Warland yonder?"

"Well said, uncle Hovenden!" shouted Robert Danforth from the forge, in a full, deep, merry voice, that made the roof reëcho. "And what says Miss Annie to that doctrine? She, I suppose, will think it a genteeler business to tinker up a lady's watch than to forge a horseshoe or make a gridiron."

Annie drew her father onward without giving him time for reply.

But we must return to Owen Warland's shop, and spend more meditation upon his history and character than either Peter Hovenden, or probably his daughter Annie, or Owen's old schoolfellow, Robert Danforth, would have thought due to so slight a subject. From the time that his little fingers could grasp a penknife, Owen had been remarkable for a delicate ingenuity, which sometimes produced pretty shapes in wood, principally

---

THE ARTIST OF THE BEAUTIFUL.    1. **pinchbeck:** an alloy of copper and zinc, used to imitate gold in cheap jewelry; hence, anything counterfeit or spurious.

figures of flowers and birds, and sometimes seemed to aim at the hidden mysteries of mechanism. But it was always for purposes of grace, and never with any mockery of the useful. He did not, like the crowd of school-boy artisans, construct little windmills on the angle of a barn or watermills across the neighboring brook. Those who discovered such peculiarity in the boy as to think it worth their while to observe him closely, sometimes saw reason to suppose that he was attempting to imitate the beautiful movements of Nature as exemplified in the flight of birds or the activity of little animals. It seemed, in fact, a new development of the love of the beautiful, such as might have made him a poet, a painter, or a sculptor, and which was as completely refined from all utilitarian coarseness as it could have been in either of the fine arts. He looked with singular distaste at the stiff and regular processes of ordinary machinery. Being once carried to see a steam-engine, in the expectation that his intuitive comprehension of mechanical principles would be gratified, he turned pale and grew sick, as if something monstrous and unnatural had been presented to him. This horror was partly owing to the size and terrible energy of the iron laborer; for the character of Owen's mind was microscopic, and tended naturally to the minute, in accordance with his diminutive frame and the marvellous smallness and delicate power of his fingers. Not that his sense of beauty was thereby diminished into a sense of prettiness. The beautiful idea has no relation to size, and may be as perfectly developed in a space too minute for any but microscopic investigation as within the ample verge that is measured by the arc of the rainbow. But, at all events, this characteristic minuteness in his objects and accomplishments made the world even more incapable than it might otherwise have been of appreciating Owen Warland's genius. The boy's relatives saw nothing better to be done—as perhaps there was not—than to bind him apprentice to a watchmaker, hoping that his strange ingenuity might thus be regulated and put to utilitarian purposes.

Peter Hovenden's opinion of his apprentice has already been expressed. He could make nothing of the lad. Owen's apprehension of the professional mysteries, it is true, was inconceivably quick; but he altogether forgot or despised the grand object of a watchmaker's business, and cared no more for the measurement of time than if it had been merged into eternity. So long, however, as he remained under his old master's care, Owen's lack of sturdiness made it possible, by strict injunctions and sharp oversight, to restrain his creative eccentricity within bounds; but when his apprenticeship was served out, and he had taken the little shop which Peter Hovenden's failing eyesight compelled him to relinquish, then did people recognize how unfit a person was Owen Warland to lead old blind Father Time along his daily course. One of his most rational projects was to connect a musical operation with the machinery of his watches, so that all the harsh dissonances of life might be rendered tuneful, and each flitting moment fall into the abyss of the past in golden drops of harmony. If a family clock was intrusted to him for repair,—one of those tall, ancient clocks that have grown nearly allied to human nature by measuring out the lifetime of many generations, —he would take upon himself to arrange a dance or funeral procession of figures across its venerable face, representing twelve mirthful or melancholy hours. Several freaks of this kind quite destroyed the young watchmaker's credit with that steady and matter-of-fact class of people who hold the opinion that time is not to be trifled with, whether considered as the medium of advancement and prosperity in this world or preparation for the next. His custom rapidly diminished—a misfortune, however, that was probably reckoned among his better accidents by Owen Warland, who was becoming more and more absorbed in a secret occupation which drew all his science and manual dexterity into itself, and likewise gave full employment to the characteristic tendencies of his genius. This pursuit had already consumed many months.

After the old watchmaker and his pretty daughter had gazed at him out of the obscurity of the street, Owen Warland was seized with a fluttering of the nerves, which made his hand tremble too violently to proceed with such delicate labor as he was now engaged upon.

"It was Annie herself!" murmured he. "I should have known it, by this throbbing of my heart, before I heard her father's voice. Ah, how it throbs! I shall scarcely be able to work again on this exquisite mechanism to-night. Annie! dearest Annie! thou shouldst give firmness to my heart and hand, and not shake them thus; for if I strive to put the very spirit of beauty into form and give it motion, it is for thy sake alone. O throbbing heart, be quiet! If my labor be thus thwarted, there will come vague and unsatisfied dreams which will leave me spiritless to-morrow."

As he was endeavoring to settle himself again to his task, the shop door opened and gave admittance to no other than the stalwart figure which Peter Hovenden had paused to admire, as seen amid the light and shadow of the blacksmith's shop. Robert Danforth had brought a little anvil of his own manufacture, and peculiarly constructed, which the young artist had recently bespoken. Owen examined the article and pronounced it fashioned according to his wish.

"Why, yes," said Robert Danforth, his strong voice filling the shop as with the sound of a bass viol, "I consider myself equal to anything in the way of my own trade; though I should have made but a poor figure at yours with such a fist as this," added he, laughing, as he laid his vast hand beside the delicate one of Owen. "But what then? I put more main strength into one blow of my sledge hammer than all that you have expended since you were a 'prentice. Is not that the truth?"

"Very probably," answered the low and slender voice of Owen. "Strength is an earthly monster. I make no pretensions to it. My force, whatever there may be of it, is altogether spiritual."

"Well, but, Owen, what are you about?" asked his old schoolfellow, still in such a hearty volume of tone that it made the artist shrink, especially as the question related to a subject so sacred as the absorbing dream of his imagination. "Folks do say that you are trying to discover the perpetual motion."

"The perpetual motion? Nonsense!" replied Owen Warland, with a movement of disgust; for he was full of little petulances. "It can never be discovered. It is a dream that may delude men whose brains are mystified with matter, but not me. Besides, if such a discovery were possible, it would not be worth my while to make it only to have the secret turned to such purposes as are now effected by steam and water power. I am not ambitious to be honored with the paternity of a new kind of cotton machine."

"That would be droll enough!" cried the blacksmith, breaking out into such an uproar of laughter that Owen himself and the bell glasses on his workboard quivered in unison. "No, no, Owen! No child of yours will have iron joints and sinews. Well, I won't hinder you any more. Good night, Owen, and success, and if you need any assistance, so far as a downright blow of hammer upon anvil will answer the purpose, I'm your man."

And with another laugh the man of main strength left the shop.

"How strange it is," whispered Owen Warland to himself, leaning his head upon his hand, "that all my musings, my purposes, my passion for the beautiful, my consciousness of power to create it, —a finer, more ethereal power, of which this earthly giant can have no conception,—all, all, look so vain and idle whenever my path is crossed by Robert Danforth! He would drive me mad were I to meet him often. His hard, brute force darkens and confuses the spiritual element within me; but I, too, will be strong in my own way. I will not yield to him."

He took from beneath a glass a piece of minute machinery, which he set in the condensed light of his lamp, and, looking intently at it through a magnifying glass, proceeded to operate with a delicate instrument of steel. In an instant, however, he fell back in his chair and clasped his hands, with a look of horror on his face that made its small features as impressive as those of a giant would have been.

"Heaven! What have I done?" exclaimed he. "The vapor, the influence of that brute force,— it has bewildered me and obscured my perception. I have made the very stroke—the fatal stroke —that I have dreaded from the first. It is all over —the toil of months, the object of my life. I am ruined!"

And there he sat, in strange despair, until his lamp flickered in the socket and left the Artist of the Beautiful in darkness.

Thus it is that ideas, which grow up within the imagination and appear so lovely to it and of a value beyond whatever men call valuable, are exposed to be shattered and annihilated by contact with the practical. It is requisite for the ideal artist to possess a force of character that seems hardly compatible with its delicacy; he must keep his faith in himself while the incredulous world assails him with its utter disbelief; he must stand up against mankind and be his own sole disciple, both as respects his genius and the objects to which it is directed.

For a time Owen Warland succumbed to this severe but inevitable test. He spent a few sluggish weeks with his head so continually resting in his hands that the towns-people had scarcely an opportunity to see his countenance. When at last it was again uplifted to the light of day, a cold, dull, nameless change was perceptible upon it. In the opinion of Peter Hovenden, however, and that order of sagacious understandings who think that life should be regulated, like clockwork, with leaden weights, the alteration was entirely for the better. Owen now, indeed, applied himself to business with dogged industry. It was marvellous to witness the obtuse gravity with which he would inspect the wheels of a great old silver watch; thereby delighting the owner, in whose fob it had been worn till he deemed it a portion of his own life, and was accordingly jealous of its treatment. In consequence of the good report thus acquired, Owen Warland was invited by the proper authorities to regulate the clock in the church steeple. He succeeded so admirably in this matter of public interest that the merchants gruffly acknowledged his merits on 'Change;[2] the nurse whispered his praises as she gave the potion in the sick-chamber; the lover blessed him at the hour of appointed interview; and the town in general thanked Owen for the punctuality of dinner time. In a word, the heavy weight upon his spirits kept everything in order, not merely within his own system, but wheresoever the iron accents of the church clock were audible. It was a circumstance, though minute, yet characteristic of his present state, that, when employed to engrave names or initials on silver spoons, he now wrote the requisite letters in the plainest possible style, omitting a variety of fanciful flourishes that had heretofore distinguished his work in this kind.

One day, during the era of this happy transformation, old Peter Hovenden came to visit his former apprentice.

"Well, Owen," said he, "I am glad to hear such good accounts of you from all quarters, and especially from the town clock yonder, which speaks in your commendation every hour of the twenty-four. Only get rid altogether of your nonsensical trash about the beautiful, which I nor nobody else, nor yourself to boot, could ever understand,—only free yourself of that, and your success in life is as sure as daylight. Why, if you go on in this way, I should even venture to let you doctor this precious old watch of mine; though, except my daughter Annie, I have nothing else so valuable in the world."

"I should hardly dare touch it, sir," replied Owen, in a depressed tone; for he was weighed down by his old master's presence.

"In time," said the latter,—"in time, you will be capable of it."

The old watchmaker, with the freedom naturally consequent on his former authority, went on inspecting the work which Owen had in hand at the moment, together with other matters that were in progress. The artist, meanwhile, could scarcely lift his head. There was nothing so antipodal to his nature as this man's cold, unimaginative sagacity, by contact with which everything was converted into a dream except the densest matter of the physical world. Owen groaned in spirit and prayed fervently to be delivered from him.

"But what is this?" cried Peter Hovenden abruptly, taking up a dusty bell glass, beneath which appeared a mechanical something, as delicate and minute as the system of a butterfly's anat-

omy. "What have we here? Owen! Owen! there is witchcraft in these little chains, and wheels, and paddles. See! with one pinch of my finger and thumb I am going to deliver you from all future peril."

"For Heaven's sake," screamed Owen Warland, springing up with wonderful energy, "as you would not drive me mad, do not touch it! The slightest pressure of your finger would ruin me forever."

"Aha, young man! And is it so?" said the old watchmaker, looking at him with just enough of penetration to torture Owen's soul with the bitterness of worldly criticism. "Well, take your own course; but I warn you again that in this small piece of mechanism lives your evil spirit. Shall I exorcise him?"

"You are my evil spirit," answered Owen, much excited,—"you and the hard, coarse world! The leaden thoughts and the despondency that you fling upon me are my clogs, else I should long ago have achieved the task that I was created for."

Peter Hovenden shook his head, with the mixture of contempt and indignation which mankind, of whom he was partly a representative, deem themselves entitled to feel towards all simpletons who seek other prizes than the dusty one along the highway. He then took his leave, with an uplifted finger and a sneer upon his face that haunted the artist's dreams for many a night afterwards. At the time of his old master's visit, Owen was probably on the point of taking up the relinquished task; but, by this sinister event, he was thrown back into the state whence he had been slowly emerging.

But the innate tendency of his soul had only been accumulating fresh vigor during its apparent sluggishness. As the summer advanced he almost totally relinquished his business, and permitted Father Time, so far as the old gentleman was represented by the clocks and watches under his control, to stray at random through human life, making infinite confusion among the train of bewildered hours. He wasted the sunshine, as people said, in wandering through the woods and fields and along the banks of streams. There, like a child, he found amusement in chasing butterflies or watching the motions of water insects. There was something truly mysterious in the intentness with which he contemplated these living playthings as they sported on the breeze or examined the structure of an imperial insect whom he had imprisoned. The chase of butterflies was an apt emblem of the ideal pursuit in which he had spent so many golden hours; but would the beautiful idea ever be yielded to his hand like the butterfly

---

2. **'Change:** a shortened form of "Exchange"; in England the place in a town or city where merchants, bankers, brokers, and citizens met to do business.

that symbolized it? Sweet, doubtless, were these days, and congenial to the artist's soul. They were full of bright conceptions, which gleamed through his intellectual world as the butterflies gleamed through the outward atmosphere, and were real to him, for the instant, without the toil, and perplexity, and many disappointments of attempting to make them visible to the sensual eye. Alas that the artist, whether in poetry, or whatever other material, may not content himself with the inward enjoyment of the beautiful, but must chase the flitting mystery beyond the verge of his ethereal domain, and crush its frail being in seizing it with a material grasp. Owen Warland felt the impulse to give external reality to his ideas as irresistibly as any of the poets or painters who have arrayed the world in a dimmer and fainter beauty, imperfectly copied from the richness of their visions.

The night was now his time for the slow progress of re-creating the one idea to which all his intellectual activity referred itself. Always at the approach of dusk he stole into the town, locked himself within his shop, and wrought with patient delicacy of touch for many hours. Sometimes he was startled by the rap of the watchman, who, when all the world should be asleep, had caught the gleam of lamplight through the crevices of Owen Warland's shutters. Daylight, to the morbid sensibility of his mind, seemed to have an intrusiveness that interfered with his pursuits. On cloudy and inclement days, therefore, he sat with his head upon his hands, muffling, as it were, his sensitive brain in a mist of indefinite musings; for it was a relief to escape from the sharp distinctness with which he was compelled to shape out his thoughts during his nightly toil.

From one of these fits of torpor he was aroused by the entrance of Annie Hovenden, who came into the shop with the freedom of a customer, and also with something of the familiarity of a childish friend. She had worn a hole through her silver thimble, and wanted Owen to repair it.

"But I don't know whether you will condescend to such a task," said she, laughing, "now that you are so taken up with the notion of putting spirit into machinery."

"Where did you get that idea, Annie?" said Owen, starting in surprise.

"Oh, out of my own head," answered she, "and from something that I heard you say, long ago, when you were but a boy and I a little child. But come; will you mend this poor thimble of mine?"

"Anything for your sake, Annie," said Owen Warland,—"anything, even were it to work at Robert Danforth's forge."

"And that would be a pretty sight!" retorted

Annie, glancing with imperceptible slightness at the artist's small and slender frame. "Well; here is the thimble."

"But that is a strange idea of yours," said Owen, "about the spiritualization of matter."

And then the thought stole into his mind that this young girl possessed the gift to comprehend him better than all the world besides. And what a help and strength would it be to him in his lonely toil if he could gain the sympathy of the only being whom he loved! To persons whose pursuits are insulated from the common business of life—who are either in advance of mankind or apart from it—there often comes a sensation of moral cold that makes the spirit shiver as if it had reached the frozen solitudes around the pole. What the prophet, the poet, the reformer, the criminal, or any other man with human yearnings, but separated from the multitude by a peculiar lot, might feel, poor Owen felt.

"Annie," cried he, growing pale as death at the thought, "how gladly would I tell you the secret of my pursuit! You, methinks, would estimate it rightly. You, I know, would hear it with a reverence that I must not expect from the harsh, material world."

"Would I not? to be sure I would!" replied Annie Hovenden, lightly laughing. "Come; explain to me quickly what is the meaning of this little whirligig, so delicately wrought, that it might be a plaything for Queen Mab.[3] See! I will put it in motion."

"Hold!" exclaimed Owen, "hold!"

Annie had but given the slightest possible touch, with the point of a needle, to the same minute portion of complicated machinery which has been more than once mentioned, when the artist seized her by the wrist with a force that made her scream aloud. She was affrighted at the convulsion of intense rage and anguish that writhed across his features. The next instant he let his head sink upon his hands.

"Go, Annie," murmured he; "I have deceived myself, and must suffer for it. I yearned for sympathy and thought, and fancied, and dreamed that you might give it me; but you lack the talisman, Annie, that should admit you into my secrets. That touch has undone the toil of months and the thought of a lifetime! It was not your fault, Annie; but you have ruined me!"

Poor Owen Warland! He had indeed erred, yet pardonably; for if any human spirit could have sufficiently reverenced the processes so sacred in

3. **Queen Mab:** "the fairies' midwife" who delivers men of their dreams; see *Romeo and Juliet*, I.iv.53–94.

his eyes, it must have been a woman's. Even Annie Hovenden, possibly, might not have disappointed him had she been enlightened by the deep intelligence of love.

The artist spent the ensuing winter in a way that satisfied any persons who had hitherto retained a hopeful opinion of him that he was, in truth, irrevocably doomed to inutility as regarded the world, and to an evil destiny on his own part. The decease of a relative had put him in possession of a small inheritance. Thus freed from the necessity of toil, and having lost the steadfast influence of a great purpose,—great, at least, to him,—he abandoned himself to habits from which it might have been supposed the mere delicacy of his organization would have availed to secure him. But when the ethereal portion of a man of genius is obscured, the earthly part assumes an influence the more uncontrollable, because the character is now thrown off the balance to which Providence had so nicely adjusted it, and which, in coarser natures, is adjusted by some other method. Owen Warland made proof of whatever show of bliss may be found in riot. He looked at the world through the golden medium of wine, and contemplated the visions that bubble up so gayly around the brim of the glass, and that people the air with shapes of pleasant madness, which so soon grow ghostly and forlorn. Even when this dismal and inevitable change had taken place, the young man might still have continued to quaff the cup of enchantments, though its vapor did but shroud life in gloom and fill the gloom with spectres that mocked at him. There was a certain irksomeness of spirit, which, being real, and the deepest sensation of which the artist was now conscious, was more intolerable than any fantastic miseries and horrors that the abuse of wine could summon up. In the latter case he could remember, even out of the midst of his trouble, that all was but a delusion; in the former, the heavy anguish was his actual life.

From this perilous state he was redeemed by an incident which more than one person witnessed, but of which the shrewdest could not explain or conjecture the operation on Owen Warland's mind. It was very simple. On a warm afternoon of spring, as the artist sat among his riotous companions with a glass of wine before him, a splendid butterfly flew in at the open window and fluttered about his head.

"Ah," exclaimed Owen, who had drank freely, "are you alive again, child of the sun and playmate of the summer breeze, after your dismal winter's nap? Then it is time for me to be at work!"

And, leaving his unemptied glass upon the ta-

ble, he departed and was never known to sip another drop of wine.

And now, again, he resumed his wanderings in the woods and fields. It might be fancied that the bright butterfly, which had come so spirit-like into the window as Owen sat with the rude revellers, was indeed a spirit commissioned to recall him to the pure, ideal life that had so etherealized him among men. It might be fancied that he went forth to seek this spirit in its sunny haunts; for still, as in the summer time gone by, he was seen to steal gently up wherever a butterfly had alighted, and lose himself in contemplation of it. When it took flight his eyes followed the winged vision, as if its airy track would show the path to heaven. But what could be the purpose of the unseasonable toil, which was again resumed, as the watchman knew by the lines of lamplight through the crevices of Owen Warland's shutters? The towns-people had one comprehensive explanation of all these singularities. Owen Warland had gone mad! How universally efficacious—how satisfactory, too, and soothing to the injured sensibility of narrowness and dulness—is this easy method of accounting for whatever lies beyond the world's most ordinary scope! From St. Paul's [4] days down to our poor little Artist of the Beautiful, the same talisman had been applied to the elucidation of all mysteries in the words or deeds of men who spoke or acted too wisely or too well. In Owen Warland's case the judgment of his towns-people may have been correct. Perhaps he was mad. The lack of sympathy—that contrast between himself and his neighbors which took away the restraint of example—was enough to make him so. Or possibly he had caught just so much of ethereal radiance as served to bewilder him, in an earthly sense, by its intermixture with the common daylight.

One evening, when the artist had returned from a customary ramble and had just thrown the lustre of his lamp on the delicate piece of work so often interrupted, but still taken up again, as if his fate were embodied in its mechanism, he was surprised by the entrance of old Peter Hovenden. Owen never met this man without a shrinking of the heart. Of all the world he was most terrible, by reason of a keen understanding which saw so distinctly what it did see, and disbelieved so uncompromisingly in what it could not see. On this occasion the old watchmaker had merely a gracious word or two to say.

"Owen, my lad," said he, "we must see you at my house to-morrow night."

4. St. Paul's: See Acts 26:24: "Festus said with a loud voice, Paul, thou art beside thyself; much learning doth make thee mad."

The artist began to mutter some excuse.

"Oh, but it must be so," quoth Peter Hovenden, "for the sake of the days when you were one of the household. What, my boy! don't you know that my daughter Annie is engaged to Robert Danforth? We are making an entertainment, in our humble way, to celebrate the event."

"Ah!" said Owen.

That little monosyllable was all he uttered; its tone seemed cold and unconcerned to an ear like Peter Hovenden's; and yet there was in it the stifled outcry of the poor artist's heart, which he compressed within him like a man holding down an evil spirit. One slight outbreak, however, imperceptible to the old watchmaker, he allowed himself. Raising the instrument with which he was about to begin his work, he let it fall upon the little system of machinery that had, anew, cost him months of thought and toil. It was shattered by the stroke!

Owen Warland's story would have been no tolerable representation of the troubled life of those who strive to create the beautiful, if, amid all other thwarting influences, love had not interposed to steal the cunning from his hand. Outwardly he had been no ardent or enterprising lover; the career of his passion had confined its tumults and vicissitudes so entirely within the artist's imagination that Annie herself had scarcely more than a woman's intuitive perception of it; but, in Owen's view, it covered the whole field of his life. Forgetful of the time when she had shown herself incapable of any deep response, he had persisted in connecting all his dreams of artistical success with Annie's image; she was the visible shape in which the spiritual power that he worshipped, and on whose altar he hoped to lay a not unworthy offering, was made manifest to him. Of course he had deceived himself; there were no such attributes in Annie Hovenden as his imagination had endowed her with. She, in the aspect which she wore to his inward vision, was as much a creature of his own as the mysterious piece of mechanism would be were it ever realized. Had he become convinced of his mistake through the medium of successful love,—had he won Annie to his bosom, and there beheld her fade from angel into ordinary woman,—the disappointment might have driven him back, with concentrated energy, upon his sole remaining object. On the other hand, had he found Annie what he fancied, his lot would have been so rich in beauty that out of its mere redundancy he might have wrought the beautiful into many a worthier type than he had toiled for; but the guise in which his sorrow came to him, the sense that the angel

of his life had been snatched away and given to a rude man of earth and iron, who could neither need nor appreciate her ministrations,—this was the very perversity of fate that makes human existence appear too absurd and contradictory to be the scene of one other hope or one other fear. There was nothing left for Owen Warland but to sit down like a man that had been stunned.

He went through a fit of illness. After his recovery his small and slender frame assumed an obtuser garniture of flesh than it had ever before worn. His thin cheeks became round; his delicate little hand, so spiritually fashioned to achieve fairy task-work, grew plumper than the hand of a thriving infant. His aspect had a childishness such as might have induced a stranger to pat him on the head—pausing, however, in the act, to wonder what manner of child was here. It was as if the spirit had gone out of him, leaving the body to flourish in a sort of vegetable existence. Not that Owen Warland was idiotic. He could talk, and not irrationally. Somewhat of a babbler, indeed, did people begin to think him; for he was apt to discourse at wearisome length of marvels of mechanism that he had read about in books, but which he had learned to consider as absolutely fabulous. Among them he enumerated the Man of Brass, constructed by Albertus Magnus, and the Brazen Head of Friar Bacon;[5] and, coming down to later times, the automata of a little coach and horses, which it was pretended had been manufactured for the Dauphin of France;[6] together with an insect that buzzed about the ear like a living fly, and yet was but a contrivance of minute steel springs. There was a story, too, of a duck that waddled, and quacked, and ate; though, had any honest citizen purchased it for dinner, he would have found himself cheated with the mere mechanical apparition of a duck.

"But all these accounts," said Owen Warland, "I am now satisfied are mere impositions."

Then, in a mysterious way, he would confess that he once thought differently. In his idle and dreamy days he had considered it possible, in a certain sense, to spiritualize machinery, and to combine with the new species of life and motion thus produced a beauty that should attain to the ideal which Nature has proposed to herself in all her creatures, but has never taken pains to realize. He seemed, however, to retain no very distinct perception either of the process of achieving this object or of the design itself.

"I have thrown it all aside now," he would

5. **Man . . . Bacon:** See "The Birthmark," 4 n.   6. **Dauphin of France:** the son of Louis XVI, known as Louis XVII (1785–95).

say. "It was a dream such as young men are always mystifying themselves with. Now that I have acquired a little common sense, it makes me laugh to think of it."

Poor, poor and fallen Owen Warland! These were the symptoms that he had ceased to be an inhabitant of the better sphere that lies unseen around us. He had lost his faith in the invisible, and now prided himself, as such unfortunates invariably do, in the wisdom which rejected much that even his eye could see, and trusted confidently in nothing but what his hand could touch. This is the calamity of men whose spiritual part dies out of them and leaves the grosser understanding to assimilate them more and more to the things of which alone it can take cognizance; but in Owen Warland the spirit was not dead nor passed away; it only slept.

How it awoke again is not recorded. Perhaps the torpid slumber was broken by a convulsive pain. Perhaps, as in a former instance, the butterfly came and hovered about his head and reinspired him,—as indeed this creature of the sunshine had always a mysterious mission for the artist,—reinspired him with the former purpose of his life. Whether it were pain or happiness that thrilled through his veins, his first impulse was to thank Heaven for rendering him again the being of thought, imagination, and keenest sensibility that he had long ceased to be.

"Now for my task," said he. "Never did I feel such strength for it as now."

Yet, strong as he felt himself, he was incited to toil the more diligently by an anxiety lest death should surprise him in the midst of his labors. This anxiety, perhaps, is common to all men who set their hearts upon anything so high, in their own view of it, that life becomes of importance only as conditional to its accomplishment. So long as we love life for itself, we seldom dread the losing it. When we desire life for the attainment of an object, we recognize the frailty of its texture. But, side by side with this sense of insecurity, there is a vital faith in our invulnerability to the shaft of death while engaged in any task that seems assigned by Providence as our proper thing to do, and which the world would have cause to mourn for should we leave it unaccomplished. Can the philosopher, big with the inspiration of an idea that is to reform mankind, believe that he is to be beckoned from this sensible existence at the very instant when he is mustering his breath to speak the word of light? Should he perish so, the weary ages may pass away—the world's, whose life sand may fall, drop by drop—before another intellect is prepared to develop the truth that might have

been uttered then. But history affords many an example where the most precious spirit, at any particular epoch manifested in human shape, has gone hence untimely, without space allowed him, so far as mortal judgment could discern, to perform his mission on the earth. The prophet dies, and the man of torpid heart and sluggish brain lives on. The poet leaves his song half sung, or finishes it, beyond the scope of mortal ears, in a celestial choir. The painter—as Allston [7] did—leaves half his conception on the canvas to sadden us with its imperfect beauty, and goes to picture forth the whole, if it be no irreverence to say so, in the hues of heaven. But rather such incomplete designs of this life will be perfected nowhere. This so frequent abortion of man's dearest projects must be taken as a proof that the deeds of earth, however etherealized by piety or genius, are without value, except as exercises and manifestations of the spirit. In heaven, all ordinary thought is higher and more melodious than Milton's song. Then, would he add another verse to any strain that he had left unfinished here?

But to return to Owen Warland. It was his fortune, good or ill, to achieve the purpose of his life. Pass we over a long space of intense thought, yearning effort, minute toil, and wasting anxiety, succeeded by an instant of solitary triumph: let all this be imagined; and then behold the artist, on a winter evening, seeking admittance to Robert Danforth's fireside circle. There he found the man of iron, with his massive substance thoroughly warmed and attempered by domestic influences. And there was Annie, too, now transformed into a matron, with much of her husband's plain and sturdy nature, but imbued, as Owen Warland still believed, with a finer grace, that might enable her to be the interpreter between strength and beauty. It happened, likewise, that old Peter Hovenden was a guest this evening at his daughter's fireside, and it was his well-remembered expression of keen, cold criticism that first encountered the artist's glance.

"My old friend Owen!" cried Robert Danforth, starting up, and compressing the artist's delicate fingers within a hand that was accustomed to gripe bars of iron. "This is kind and neighborly to come to us at last. I was afraid your perpetual motion had bewitched you out of the remembrance of old times."

"We are glad to see you," said Annie, while a blush reddened her matronly cheek. "It was not like a friend to stay from us so long."

7. **Allston:** Washington Allston (1779–1843), the American painter who left his picture "Belshazzar's Feast" unfinished at his death.

"Well, Owen," inquired the old watchmaker, as his first greeting, "how comes on the beautiful? Have you created it at last?"

The artist did not immediately reply, being startled by the apparition of a young child of strength that was tumbling about on the carpet,— a little personage who had come mysteriously out of the infinite but with something so sturdy and real in his composition that he seemed moulded out of the densest substance which earth could supply. This hopeful infant crawled towards the newcomer, and setting himself on end, as Robert Danforth expressed the posture, stared at Owen with a look of such sagacious observation that the mother could not help exchanging a proud glance with her husband. But the artist was disturbed by the child's look, as imagining a resemblance between it and Peter Hovenden's habitual expression. He could have fancied that the old watchmaker was compressed into this baby shape, and looking out of those baby eyes, and repeating, as he now did, the malicious question:—

"The beautiful, Owen! How comes on the beautiful? Have you succeeded in creating the beautiful?"

"I have succeeded," replied the artist, with a momentary light of triumph in his eyes and a smile of sunshine, yet steeped in such depth of thought that it was almost sadness. "Yes, my friends, it is the truth. I have succeeded."

"Indeed!" cried Annie, a look of maiden mirthfulness peeping out of her face again. "And is it lawful, now, to inquire what the secret is?"

"Surely; it is to disclose it that I have come," answered Owen Warland. "You shall know, and see, and touch, and possess the secret! For, Annie, —if by that name I may still address the friend of my boyish years,—Annie, it is for your bridal gift that I have wrought this spiritualized mechanism, this harmony of motion, this mystery of beauty. It comes late, indeed; but it is as we go onward in life, when objects begin to lose their freshness of hue and our souls their delicacy of perception, that the spirit of beauty is most needed. If,—forgive me, Annie,—if you know how to value this gift, it can never come too late."

He produced, as he spoke, what seemed a jewel box. It was carved richly out of ebony by his own hand, and inlaid with a fanciful tracery of pearl, representing a boy in pursuit of a butterfly, which, elsewhere, had become a winged spirit, and was flying heavenward; while the boy, or youth, had found such efficacy in his strong desire that he ascended from earth to cloud, and from cloud to celestial atmosphere, to win the beautiful. This case of ebony the artist opened, and bade Annie

place her finger on its edge. She did so, but almost screamed as a butterfly fluttered forth, and, alighting on her finger's tip, sat waving the ample magnificence of its purple and gold-speckled wings, as if in prelude to a flight. It is impossible to express by words the glory, the splendor, the delicate gorgeousness which were softened into the beauty of this object. Nature's ideal butterfly was here realized in all its perfection; not in the pattern of such faded insects as flit among earthly flowers, but of those which hover across the meads of paradise for child-angels and the spirits of departed infants to disport themselves with. The rich down was visible upon its wings; the lustre of its eyes seemed instinct with spirit. The firelight glimmered around this wonder—the candles gleamed upon it; but it glistened apparently by its own radiance, and illuminated the finger and outstretched hand on which it rested with a white gleam like that of precious stones. In its perfect beauty, the consideration of size was entirely lost. Had its wings overreached the firmament, the mind could not have been more filled or satisfied.

"Beautiful! beautiful!" exclaimed Annie. "Is it alive? Is it alive?"

"Alive? To be sure it is," answered her husband. "Do you suppose any mortal has skill enough to make a butterfly, or would put himself to the trouble of making one, when any child may catch a score of them in a summer's afternoon? Alive? Certainly! But this pretty box is undoubtedly of our friend Owen's manufacture; and really it does him credit."

At this moment the butterfly waved its wings anew, with a motion so absolutely lifelike that Annie was startled, and even awe-stricken; for, in spite of her husband's opinion, she could not satisfy herself whether it was indeed a living creature or a piece of wondrous mechanism.

"Is it alive?" she repeated, more earnestly than before.

"Judge for yourself," said Owen Warland, who stood gazing in her face with fixed attention.

The butterfly now flung itself upon the air, fluttered round Annie's head, and soared into a distant region of the parlor, still making itself perceptible to sight by the starry gleam in which the motion of its wings enveloped it. The infant on the floor followed its course with his sagacious little eyes. After flying about the room, it returned in a spiral curve and settled again on Annie's finger.

"But is it alive?" exclaimed she again; and the finger on which the gorgeous mystery had alighted was so tremulous that the butterfly was forced to balance himself with his wings. "Tell me if it be alive, or whether you created it."

"Wherefore ask who created it, so it be beautiful?" replied Owen Warland. "Alive? Yes, Annie; it may well be said to possess life, for it has absorbed my own being into itself; and in the secret of that butterfly, and in its beauty,—which is not merely outward, but deep as its whole system,—is represented the intellect, the imagination, the sensibility, the soul of an Artist of the Beautiful! Yes; I created it. But"—and here his countenance somewhat changed—"this butterfly is not now to me what it was when I beheld it afar off in the daydreams of my youth."

"Be it what it may, it is a pretty plaything," said the blacksmith, grinning with childlike delight. "I wonder whether it would condescend to alight on such a great clumsy finger as mine? Hold it hither, Annie."

By the artist's direction, Annie touched her finger's tip to that of her husband; and, after a momentary delay, the butterfly fluttered from one to the other. It preluded a second flight by a similar, yet not precisely the same, waving of wings as in the first experiment; then, ascending from the blacksmith's stalwart finger, it rose in a gradually enlarging curve to the ceiling, made one wide sweep around the room, and returned with an undulating movement to the point whence it had started.

"Well, that does beat all nature!" cried Robert Danforth, bestowing the heartiest praise that he could find expression for; and, indeed, had he paused there, a man of finer words and nicer perception could not easily have said more. "That goes beyond me, I confess. But what then? There is more real use in one downright blow of my sledge hammer than in the whole five years' labor that our friend Owen has wasted on this butterfly."

Here the child clapped his hands and made a great babble of indistinct utterance, apparently demanding that the butterfly should be given him for a plaything.

Owen Warland, meanwhile, glanced sidelong at Annie, to discover whether she sympathized in her husband's estimate of the comparative value of the beautiful and the practical. There was, amid all her kindness towards himself, amid all the wonder and admiration with which she contemplated the marvellous work of his hands and incarnation of his idea, a secret scorn—too secret, perhaps, for her own consciousness, and perceptible only to such intuitive discernment as that of the artist. But Owen, in the latter stages of his pursuit, had risen out of the region in which such a discovery might have been torture. He knew that

the world, and Annie as the representative of the world, whatever praise might be bestowed, could never say the fitting word nor feel the fitting sentiment which should be the perfect recompense of an artist who, symbolizing a lofty moral by a material trifle,—converting what was earthly to spiritual gold,—had won the beautiful into his handiwork. Not at this latest moment was he to learn that the reward of all high performance must be sought within itself, or sought in vain. There was, however, a view of the matter which Annie and her husband, and even Peter Hovenden, might fully have understood, and which would have satisfied them that the toil of years had here been worthily bestowed. Owen Warland might have told them that this butterfly, this plaything, this bridal gift of a poor watchmaker to a blacksmith's wife, was, in truth, a gem of art that a monarch would have purchased with honors and abundant wealth, and have treasured it among the jewels of his kingdom as the most unique and wondrous of them all. But the artist smiled and kept the secret to himself.

"Father," said Annie, thinking that a word of praise from the old watchmaker might gratify his former apprentice, "do come and admire this pretty butterfly."

"Let us see," said Peter Hovenden, rising from his chair, with a sneer upon his face that always made people doubt, as he himself did, in everything but a material existence. "Here is my finger for it to alight upon. I shall understand it better when once I have touched it."

But, to the increased astonishment of Annie, when the tip of her father's finger was pressed against that of her husband, on which the butterfly still rested, the insect drooped its wings and seemed on the point of falling to the floor. Even the bright spots of gold upon its wings and body, unless her eyes deceived her, grew dim, and the glowing purple took a dusky hue, and the starry lustre that gleamed around the blacksmith's hand became faint and vanished.

"It is dying! it is dying!" cried Annie, in alarm.

"It has been delicately wrought," said the artist, calmly. "As I told you, it has imbibed a spiritual essence—call it magnetism, or what you will. In an atmosphere of doubt and mockery its exquisite susceptibility suffers torture, as does the soul of him who instilled his own life into it. It has already lost its beauty; in a few moments more its mechanism would be irreparably injured."

"Take away your hand, father!" entreated Annie, turning pale. "Here is my child; let it rest on his innocent hand. There, perhaps, its life will revive and its colors grow brighter than ever."

Her father, with an acrid smile, withdrew his finger. The butterfly then appeared to recover the power of voluntary motion, while its hues assumed much of their original lustre, and the gleam of starlight, which was its most ethereal attribute, again formed a halo round about it. At first, when transferred from Robert Danforth's hand to the small finger of the child, this radiance grew so powerful that it positively threw the little fellow's shadow back against the wall. He, meanwhile, extended his plump hand as he had seen his father and mother do, and watched the waving of the insect's wings with infantine delight. Nevertheless, there was a certain odd expression of sagacity that made Owen Warland feel as if here were old Peter Hovenden, partially, and but partially, redeemed from his hard scepticism into childish faith.

"How wise the little monkey looks!" whispered Robert Danforth to his wife.

"I never saw such a look on a child's face," answered Annie, admiring her own infant, and with good reason, far more than the artistic butterfly. "The darling knows more of the mystery than we do."

As if the butterfly, like the artist, were conscious of something not entirely congenial in the child's nature, it alternately sparkled and grew dim. At length it arose from the small hand of the infant with an airy motion that seemed to bear it upward without an effort, as if the ethereal instincts with which its master's spirit had endowed it impelled this fair vision involuntarily to a higher sphere. Had there been no obstruction, it might have soared into the sky and grown immortal. But its lustre gleamed upon the ceiling; the exquisite texture of its wings brushed against that earthly medium; and a sparkle or two, as of stardust, floated downward and lay glimmering on the carpet. Then the butterfly came fluttering down, and, instead of returning to the infant, was apparently attracted towards the artist's hand.

"Not so! not so!" murmured Owen Warland, as if his handiwork could have understood him. "Thou hast gone forth out of thy master's heart. There is no return for thee."

With a wavering movement, and emitting a tremulous radiance, the butterfly struggled, as it were, towards the infant, and was about to alight upon his finger; but while it still hovered in the air, the little child of strength, with his grandsire's sharp and shrewd expression in his face, made a snatch at the marvellous insect and compressed it in his hand. Annie screamed. Old Peter Hovenden burst into a cold and scornful laugh. The blacksmith, by main force, unclosed the infant's hand, and found within the palm a small heap of glittering fragments, whence the mystery of beauty had fled forever. And as for Owen Warland, he looked placidly at what seemed the ruin of his life's labor, and which was yet no ruin. He had caught a far other butterfly than this. When the artist rose high enough to achieve the beautiful, the symbol by which he made it perceptible to mortal senses became of little value in his eyes while his spirit possessed itself in the enjoyment of the reality.

---

FROM

# THE AMERICAN AND ENGLISH NOTEBOOKS

---

◊

❲ HAWTHORNE's notebooks were a narrative of his life, a record of his friendships and his travels, and a collection of ideas for tales. A representative selection of entries offers many glimpses into a writer's workshop: we can see that Hawthorne's mind was continually playing with moral hypotheses—those nebulous themes of good and evil which, once they could be dramatized in the lives of men and women, would offer insights into man's place in the total moral universe. Hawthorne's portraits of his friends, Thoreau and Melville, are the most vivid that we have.

◊

## [1835]

A SKETCH to be given of a modern reformer,— a type of the extreme doctrines on the subject of slaves, cold water, and other such topics. He goes about the streets haranguing most eloquently, and is on the point of making many converts, when his labors are suddenly interrupted by the appearance of the keeper of a madhouse, whence he has escaped. Much may be made of this idea.

A STORY, the hero of which is to be represented as naturally capable of deep and strong passion, and looking forward to the time when he shall feel passionate love, which is to be the great event of his existence. But it so chances that he never falls in love, and although he gives up the expectation of so doing, and marries calmly, yet it is somewhat sadly, with sentiments merely of esteem for his bride. The lady might be one who had loved him early in life, but whom then, in his expectation of passionate love, he had scorned.

THE SCENE of a story or sketch to be laid within the light of a street-lantern; the time, when the lamp is near going out; and the catastrophe to be simultaneous with the last flickering gleam.

TO REPRESENT the process by which sober truth gradually strips off all the beautiful draperies with which imagination has enveloped a beloved object, till from an angel she turns out to be a merely ordinary woman. This to be done without caricature, perhaps with a quiet humor interfused, but the prevailing impression to be a sad one. The story might consist of the various alterations in the feelings of the absent lover, caused by successive events that display the true character of his mistress; and the catastrophe should take place at their meeting, when he finds himself equally disappointed in her person; or the whole spirit of the thing may here be reproduced.

TWO PERSONS might be bitter enemies through life, and mutually cause the ruin of one another, and of all that were dear to them. Finally, meeting at the funeral of a grandchild, the offspring of a son and daughter married without their consent, —and who, as well as the child, had been the victims of their hatred,—they might discover that the supposed ground of the quarrel was altogether a mistake, and then be woefully reconciled.

TWO PERSONS, by mutual agreement, to make their wills in each other's favor, then to wait impatiently for one another's death, and both to be informed of the desired event at the same time. Both, in most joyous sorrow, hasten to be present at the funeral, meet, and find themselves both hoaxed.

THE STORY of a man, cool and hard-hearted, and acknowledging no brotherhood with mankind. At his death they might try to dig him a grave, but, at a little space beneath the ground, strike upon a rock, as if the earth refused to receive the unnatural son into her bosom. Then they would put him into an old sepulchre, where the coffins and corpses were all turned to dust, and so he would be alone. Then the body would petrify; and he having died in some characteristic act and expression, he would seem, through endless ages of death, to repel society as in life, and no one would be buried in that tomb forever.

IN AN old house, a mysterious knocking might be heard on the wall, where had formerly been a doorway, now bricked up.

IT MIGHT be stated, as the closing circumstance of a tale, that the body of one of the characters had been petrified, and still existed in that state.

TWO LOVERS, or other persons, on the most private business, to appoint a meeting in what they supposed to be a place of the utmost solitude, and to find it thronged with people.

SOME treasure or other thing to be buried, and a tree planted directly over the spot, so as to embrace it with its roots.

A TREE, tall and venerable, to be said by tradition to have been the staff of some famous man, who happened to thrust it into the ground, where it took root.

A FELLOW without money, having a hundred and seventy miles to go, fastened a chain and padlock to his legs, and lay down to sleep in a field. He was apprehended, and carried gratis to a jail in the town whither he desired to go.

A PERSON to consider himself as the prime mover of certain remarkable events, but to discover that his actions have not contributed in the least thereto. Another person to be the cause, without suspecting it.

A PERSON or family long desires some particular good. At last it comes in such profusion as to be, the great pest of their lives.

[*1836*]

IN THIS dismal chamber FAME was won. (Salem, Union Street.)

THE RACE of mankind to be swept away, leaving all their cities and works. Then another human pair to be placed in the world, with native intelligence like Adam and Eve, but knowing nothing of their predecessors or of their own nature and destiny. They, perhaps, to be described as working out this knowledge by their sympathy with what they saw, and by their own feelings.

CURIOUS to imagine what murmurings and discontent would be excited, if any of the great so-called calamities of human beings were to be abolished,—as, for instance, death.

TRIFLES to one are matters of life and death to another. As, for instance, a farmer desires a brisk breeze to winnow his grain; and mariners, to blow them out of the reach of pirates.

A RECLUSE, like myself, or a prisoner, to measure time by the progress of sunshine through his chamber.

A GIRL'S lover to be slain and buried in her flower-garden, and the earth levelled over him. That particular spot, which she happens to plant with some peculiar variety of flowers, produces them of admirable splendor, beauty, and perfume; and she delights, with an indescribable impulse, to wear them in her bosom, and scent her chamber with them. Thus the classic fantasy would be realized, of dead people transformed to flowers.

OUR BODY to be possessed by two different spirits; so that half of the visage shall express one mood, and the other half another.

### [1837]

A PERSON to be in the possession of something as perfect as mortal man has a right to demand; he tries to make it better, and ruins it entirely.

A PERSON to spend all his life and splendid talents in trying to achieve something naturally impossible,—as to make a conquest over Nature.

### [1842]

SOME MAN of powerful character to command a person, morally subjected to him, to perform some act. The commanding person to suddenly die; and, for all the rest of his life, the subjected one continues to perform that act.

TO TRACE out the influence of a frightful and disgraceful crime, in debasing and destroying a character naturally high and noble—the guilty person being alone conscious of the crime.

THE HUMAN Heart to be allegorized as a cavern; at the entrance there is sunshine, and flowers growing about it. You step within, but a short distance, and begin to find yourself surrounded with a terrible gloom, and monsters of divers kinds; it seems like Hell itself. You are bewildered, and wander long without hope. At last a light strikes upon you. You peep towards it, and find yourself in a region that seems, in some sort, to reproduce the flowers and sunny beauty of the entrance, but all perfect. These are the depths of the heart, or of a human nature, bright and peaceful; the gloom and terror may lie deep; but deeper still is the eternal beauty.

PEARL—the English of Margaret—a pretty name for a girl in a story.

A MAN seeks for something excellent, and seeks it in the wrong way, and in a wrong spirit, and finds something horrible—as for instance, he seeks for treasure, and finds a dead body—for the gold that somebody has hidden, and brings to light his accumulated sins.

THE SEARCH of an investigator for the Unpardonable Sin;—he at last finds it in his own heart and practice.

THE UNPARDONABLE Sin might consist in a want of love and reverence for the Human Soul; in consequence of which, the investigator pried into its dark depths, not with a hope or purpose of making it better, but from a cold philosophical curiosity. . . . Would not this, in other words, be the separation of the intellect from the heart?

THE LIFE of a woman, who, by the old colony law, was condemned always to wear the letter A, sewed on her garment, in token of her having committed adultery.

MR. THOROW dined with us yesterday.[1] He is a singular character—a young man with much of wild original stuff still remaining in him; and so far as he is sophisticated, it is in a way and method of his own. He is as ugly as sin, long-nosed, queer-mouthed, and with uncouth and somewhat rustic, although courteous manners, corresponding very well with such an exterior. But his ugliness is of an honest and agreeable fashion, and becomes him much better than beauty. He was educated, I believe at Cambridge, and formerly kept school in this town; but for two or three years back, he has repudiated all regular modes of getting a living, and seems inclined to lead a sort of Indian life among civilized men—an Indian life, I mean, as respects the absence of any systematic effort for a livelihood. He has been for sometime an inmate of Mr. Emerson's family; and, in requital, he labors in the garden, and performs such other offices as may suit him—being entertained by Mr. Emerson for the sake of what true manhood there is in him. Mr. Thorow is a keen and delicate observer of nature—a genuine observer, which, I suspect, is almost as rare a character as even an original poet; and Nature, in return for his love, seems to adopt

NOTEBOOKS. 1. Mr. Thorow . . . yesterday: Hawthorne's phonetic spelling of Thoreau suggests that the name was pronounced with the accent on the first syllable. The occasion was August 30, 1842.

him as her special child, and shows him secrets which few others are allowed to witness. He is familiar with beast, fish, fowl, and reptile, and has strange stories to tell of his adventures, and friendly passages with these lower brethren of mortality. . . . With all this he has more than a tincture of literature—a deep and true taste for poetry, especially the elder poets. . . . On the whole I find him a healthy and wholesome man to know.

### October 9th [1854]

MY ANCESTOR left England in 1635. I return in 1853. I sometimes feel as if I myself had been absent these two hundred and eighteen years—leaving England just emerging from the feudal system, and finding it on the verge of Republicanism. It brings the two far separated points of time very closely together, to view the matter thus.

### December 28th [1854]

I THINK I have been happier, this Christmas, than ever before,—by our own fireside, and with my wife and children about me. More content to enjoy what I had; less anxious for anything beyond it, in this life. My early life was perhaps a good preparation for the declining half of life, it having been such a blank that any possible thereafter would compare favorably with it. For a long, long while, I have occasionally been visited with a singular dream; and I have an impression that I have dreamed it, even since I have been in England. It is, that I am still at college—or, sometimes, even at school—and there is a sense that I have been there unconscionably long, and have quite failed to make such progress in life as my contemporaries have; and I seem to meet some of them with a feeling of shame and depression that broods over me, when I think of it, even at this moment. This dream, recurring all through these twenty or thirty years, must be one of the effects of that heavy seclusion in which I shut myself up, for twelve years, after leaving college, when everybody moved onward and left me behind. How strange that it should come now, when I may call myself famous, and prosperous!—when I am happy, too!—still that same dream of life hopelessly a failure!

### September 14th [1855]

SPEAKING of Thackeray, I cannot but wonder at his coolness in respect to his own pathos, and compare it with my emotions when I read the last scene of the Scarlet Letter to my wife, just after writing it—tried to read it, rather, for my voice swelled and heaved, as if I were tossed up and down on an ocean, as it subsided after a storm.

But I was in a very nervous state, then, having gone through a great diversity and severity of emotion, for many months past. I think I have never overcome my own adamant in any other instance.

### November 20th [1856]

A WEEK ago last Monday, Herman Melville came to see me at the Consulate, looking much as he used to do (a little paler, and perhaps a little sadder), in a rough outside coat, and with his characteristic gravity and reserve of manner. He had crossed from New York to Glasgow in a screw steamer, about a fortnight before, and had since been seeing Edinburgh and other interesting places. I felt rather awkward at first; because this is the first time I have met him since my ineffectual attempt to get him a consular appointment from General Pierce. However, I failed only from real lack of power to serve him; so there was no reason to be ashamed, and we soon found ourselves on pretty much our former terms of sociability and confidence. Melville has not been well, of late; he has been affected with neuralgic complaints in his head and limbs, and no doubt has suffered from too constant literary occupation, pursued without much success, latterly; and his writings, for a long while past, have indicated a morbid state of mind. So he left his place at Pittsfield, and has established his wife and family, I believe, with his father-in-law in Boston, and is thus far on his way to Constantinople. I do not wonder that he found it necessary to take an airing through the world, after so many years of toilsome pen-labor and domestic life, following upon so wild and adventurous a youth as his was. I invited him to come and stay with us at Southport, as long as he might remain in this vicinity; and accordingly, he did come, the next day, taking with him, by way of baggage, the least little bit of a bundle, which, he told me, contained a night-shirt and a tooth-brush. He is a person of very gentlemanly instincts in every respect, save that he is a little heterodox in the matter of clean linen.

He stayed with us from Tuesday till Thursday; and, on the intervening day, we took a pretty long walk together, and sat down in a hollow among the sand hills (sheltering ourselves from the high, cool wind) and smoked a cigar. Melville, as he always does, began to reason of Providence and futurity, and of everything that lies beyond human ken, and informed me that he had "pretty much made up his mind to be annihilated"; but still he does not seem to rest in that anticipation; and, I think, will never rest until he gets hold of a definite belief. It is strange how he persists—and has persisted ever since I knew him, and probably long before—in wandering to-and-fro over these deserts, as dismal and monotonous as the sand hills amid which we were sitting. He can neither believe, nor be comfortable in his unbelief; and he is too honest and courageous not to try to do one or the other. If he were a religious man, he would be one of the most truly religious and reverential; he has a very high and noble nature, and better worth immortality than most of us.

FROM

# THE OLD MANSE

### The Author Makes The Reader Acquainted with His Abode

◇

❪ This introductory essay to *Mosses from an Old Manse* (1846) may have been written as a record of Hawthorne's first years of marriage to Sophia Peabody, from 1842 to 1846. It was also a series of comments on Hawthorne's contemporaries who formed the Concord group and who, particularly under the guidance of Emerson, were churning with the ideas which Hawthorne found either amusing or slightly absurd. The essay presents the problem of a writer in a situation which was inimical, if not dangerous: the very charm of the Manse, the slow-moving river nearby, the inducements to absent one's self from work and linger among the piles of musty books in the attic or with the squashes in the garden— these were, as they so often became for Hawthorne, the obstacles which seemed to block one's vision but which, in the end, were the means whereby the daily routine was made into the stuff of Romance. If Hawthorne was an indifferent keeper of a daily journal, he was a splendid memorialist of his own private life and of that other life which belongs to the writer alone.

◇

BETWEEN two tall gate-posts of rough-hewn stone (the gate itself having fallen from its hinges at some unknown epoch) we beheld the gray front of the old parsonage terminating the vista of an avenue of black ash-trees. It was now a twelve-month since the funeral procession of the venerable clergyman,[1] its last inhabitant, had turned

from that gateway towards the village burying-ground. The wheel-track leading to the door, as well as the whole breadth of the avenue, was almost overgrown with grass, affording dainty mouthfuls to two or three vagrant cows and an old white horse who had his own living to pick up along the roadside. The glimmering shadows that lay half asleep between the door of the house and the public highway were a kind of spiritual medium, seen through which the edifice had not quite the aspect of belonging to the material world. Certainly it had little in common with those ordinary abodes which stand so imminent upon the road that every passer-by can thrust his head, as it were, into the domestic circle. From these quiet windows the figures of passing travelers looked too remote and dim to disturb the sense of privacy. In its near retirement and accessible seclusion it was the very spot for the residence of a clergyman, —a man not estranged from human life, yet enveloped in the midst of it with a veil woven of intermingled gloom and brightness. It was worthy to have been one of the time-honored parsonages of England in which, through many generations, a succession of holy occupants pass from youth to age, and bequeath each an inheritance of sanctity to pervade the house and hover over it as with an atmosphere.

Nor, in truth, had the Old Manse ever been profaned by a lay occupant until that memorable summer afternoon when I entered it as my home. A priest[2] had built it; a priest had succeeded to it; other priestly men from time to time had dwelt in it; and children born in its chambers had grown up to assume the priestly character. It was awful to reflect how many sermons must have been written there. . . . The boughs over my head seemed shadowy with solemn thoughts as well as with rustling leaves. I took shame to myself for having been so long a writer of idle stories, and ventured to hope that wisdom would descend upon me with the falling leaves of the avenue, and that I should light upon an intellectual treasure in the Old Manse well worth those hoards of long-hidden gold which people seek for in moss-grown houses. . . . In the humblest event, I resolved at least to achieve a novel that should evolve some deep lesson, and should possess physical substance enough to stand alone.

In furtherance of my design, and as if to leave me no pretext for not fulfilling it, there was in the rear of the house the most delightful little nook of a study that ever afforded its snug seclusion to a

THE OLD MANSE. 1. **venerable clergyman:** the Rev. Ezra Ripley, who planted the apple trees and who died in 1841.

2. **A priest:** Emerson's grandfather, the Rev. William Emerson, who witnessed the battle of Concord Bridge and who had built the house in 1765.

scholar. It was here that Emerson wrote *Nature;* for he was then an inhabitant of the Manse, and used to watch the Assyrian dawn and Paphian sunset[3] and moonrise from the summit of our eastern hill. When I first saw the room its walls were blackened with the smoke of unnumbered years, and made still blacker by the grim prints of Puritan ministers that hung around. These worthies looked strangely like bad angels, or at least like men who had wrestled so continually and so sternly with the devil that somewhat of his sooty fierceness had been imparted to their own visages. They had all vanished now; a cheerful coat of paint and golden-tinted paper-hangings lighted up the small apartment; while the shadow of a willow-tree that swept against the overhanging eaves attempered the cheery western sunshine. In place of the grim prints there was the sweet and lovely head of one of Raphael's Madonnas and two pleasant little pictures of the Lake of Como. The only other decorations were a purple vase of flowers, always fresh, and a bronze one containing graceful ferns. My books (few, and by no means choice; for they were chiefly such waifs as chance had thrown in my way) stood in order about the room, seldom to be disturbed.

The study had three windows, set with little, old-fashioned panes of glass, each with a crack across it. The two on the western side looked, or rather peeped, between the willow branches down into the orchard, with glimpses of the river through the trees. The third, facing northward, commanded a broader view of the river at a spot where its hitherto obscure waters gleam forth into the light of history. It was at this window that the clergyman who then dwelt in the Manse stood watching the outbreak of a long and deadly struggle between two nations; he saw the irregular array of his parishioners on the farther side of the river and the glittering line of the British on the hither bank. He awaited in an agony of suspense the rattle of the musketry. It came, and there needed but a gentle wind to sweep the battle smoke around this quiet house.

Perhaps the reader, whom I cannot help considering as my guest in the Old Manse and entitled to all courtesy in the way of sight-showing, —perhaps he will choose to take a nearer view of the memorable spot. We stand now on the river's brink. It may well be called the Concord, the river of peace and quietness; for it is certainly the most unexcitable and sluggish stream that ever loitered imperceptibly towards its eternity—the sea. Positively I had lived three weeks beside it before it grew quite clear to my perception which way the current flowed. It never has a vivacious aspect except when a northwestern breeze is vexing its surface on a sunshiny day. From the incurable indolence of its nature, the stream is happily incapable of becoming the slave of human ingenuity, as is the fate of so many a wild, free mountain torrent. While all things else are compelled to subserve some useful purpose, it idles its sluggish life away in lazy liberty, without turning a solitary spindle or affording even water power enough to grind the corn that grows upon its banks. The torpor of its movement allows it nowhere a bright, pebbly shore, nor so much as a narrow strip of glistening sand, in any part of its course. It slumbers between broad prairies, kissing the long meadow grass, and bathes the overhanging boughs of elder bushes and willows, or the roots of elms and ash trees and clumps of maples. Flags and rushes grow along its plashy shore; the yellow water-lily spreads its broad, flat leaves on the margin; and the fragrant white pond-lily abounds, generally selecting a position just so far from the river's brink that it cannot be grasped save at the hazard of plunging in.

It is a marvel whence this perfect flower derives its loveliness and perfume, springing as it does from the black mud over which the river sleeps, and where lurk the slimy eel, and speckled frog, and the mud turtle, whom continual washing cannot cleanse. It is the very same black mud out of which the yellow lily sucks its obscene life and noisome odor. Thus we see too in the world, that some persons assimilate only what is ugly and evil from the same moral circumstances which supply good and beautiful results—the fragrance of celestial flowers—to the daily life of others. . . .

. . . On the hither side grow two or three elms, throwing a wide circumference of shade, but which must have been planted at some period within the three-score years and ten that have passed since the battle day. On the farther shore, overhung by a clump of elder bushes, we discern the stone abutment of the bridge. Looking down into the river, I once discovered some heavy fragments of the timbers, all green with half a century's growth of watermoss; for during that length of time the tramp of horses and human footsteps have ceased along this ancient highway. The stream has here about the breadth of twenty strokes of a swimmer's arm,—a space not too wide when the bullets were whistling across. Old people who dwell hereabouts will point out the very spots on the western bank where our countrymen fell down and died; and on this side of the

3. **Assyrian . . . sunset:** an allusion to a passage in Emerson's *Nature.*

river an obelisk of granite has grown up from the soil that was fertilized with British blood. The monument, not more than twenty feet in height, is such as it befitted the inhabitants of a village to erect in illustration of a matter of local interest rather than what was suitable to commemorate an epoch of national history. Still, by the fathers of the village this famous deed was done; and their descendants might rightfully claim the privilege of building a memorial.

A humbler token of the fight, yet a more interesting one than the granite obelisk, may be seen close under the stone-wall which separates the battle-ground from the precincts of the parsonage. It is the grave—marked by a small, moss-grown fragment of stone at the head and another at the foot—the grave of two British soldiers who were slain in the skirmish, and have ever since slept peacefully where Zechariah Brown and Thomas Davis buried them. Soon was their warfare ended; a weary night march from Boston, a rattling volley of musketry across the river, and then these many years of rest. In the long procession of slain invaders who passed into eternity from the battle-fields of the revolution, these two nameless soldiers led the way.

Lowell, the poet, as we were once standing over this grave, told me a tradition in reference to one of the inhabitants below. The story has something deeply impressive, though its circumstances cannot altogether be reconciled with probability. A youth in the service of the clergymen happened to be chopping wood, that April morning, at the back door of the Manse, and when the noise of battle rang from side to side of the bridge he hastened across the intervening field to see what might be going forward. It is rather strange, by the way, that this lad should have been so diligently at work when the whole population of town and country were startled out of their customary business by the advance of the British troops. Be that as it might, the tradition says that the lad now left his task and hurried to the battle-field with the axe still in his hand. The British had by this time retreated, the Americans were in pursuit; and the late scene of strife was thus deserted by both parties. Two soldiers lay on the ground—one was a corpse; but, as the young New Englander drew nigh, the other Briton raised himself painfully upon his hands and knees and gave a ghastly stare into his face. The boy,—it must have been a nervous impulse, without purpose, without thought, and betokening a sensitive and impressible nature rather than a hardened one,—the boy uplifted his axe and dealt the wounded soldier a fierce and fatal blow upon the head.

I could wish that the grave might be opened; for I would fain know whether either of the skeleton soldiers has the mark of an axe in his skull. The story comes home to me like truth. Oftentimes, as an intellectual and moral exercise, I have sought to follow that poor youth through his subsequent career, and observe how his soul was tortured by the blood stain, contracted as it had been before the long custom of war had robbed human life of its sanctity, and while it still seemed murderous to slay a brother man. This one circumstance has borne more fruit for me than all that history tells us of the fight. . . .

. . . The Old Manse! We had almost forgotten it, but will return thither through the orchard. This was set out by the last clergyman, in the decline of his life, when the neighbors laughed at the hoary-headed man for planting trees from which he could have no prospect of gathering fruit. Even had that been the case, there was only so much the better motive for planting them, in the pure and unselfish hope of benefiting his successors,—an end so seldom achieved by more ambitious efforts. But the old minister, before reaching his patriarchal age of ninety, ate the apples from this orchard during many years, and added silver and gold to his annual stipend by disposing of the superfluity. It is pleasant to think of him walking among the trees in the quiet afternoons of early autumn and picking up here and there a windfall, while he observes how heavily the branches are weighed down, and computes the number of empty flour barrels that will be filled by their burden. He loved each tree, doubtless, as if it had been his own child. An orchard has a relation to mankind, and readily connects itself with matters of the heart. The trees possess a domestic character; they have lost the wild nature of their forest kindred, and have grown humanized by receiving the care of man as well as by contributing to his wants. There is so much individuality of character, too, among apple trees that it gives them an additional claim to be the objects of human interest. One is harsh and crabbed in its manifestations; another gives us fruit as mild as charity. One is churlish and illiberal, evidently grudging the few apples that it bears; another exhausts itself in free-hearted benevolence. The variety of grotesque shapes into which apple trees contort themselves has its effect on those who get acquainted with them: they stretch out their crooked branches, and take such hold of the imagination that we remember them as humorists and odd-fellows. And what is more melancholy than the old apple trees that linger about the spot where once stood a homestead, but where there is now only a ruined chimney rising out of a grassy and weed-grown cellar? They offer their fruit to every wayfarer,— apples that are bitter sweet with the moral of Time's vicissitude.

I have met with no other such pleasant trouble in the world as that of finding myself, with only the two or three mouths which it was my privilege to feed, the sole inheritor of the old clergyman's wealth of fruits. Throughout the summer there were cherries and currants; and then came autumn, with his immense burden of apples, dropping them continually from his overladen shoulders as he trudged along. In the stillest afternoon, if I listened, the thump of a great apple was audible, falling without a breath of wind, from the mere necessity of perfect ripeness. And, besides, there were pear trees, that flung down bushels upon bushels of heavy pears; and peach trees, which, in a good year, tormented me with peaches, neither to be eaten nor kept, nor, without labor and perplexity, to be given away. The idea of an infinite generosity and exhaustless bounty on the part of our Mother Nature was well worth obtaining through such cares as these. . . .

Not that it can be disputed that the light toil requisite to cultivate a moderately-sized garden imparts such zest to kitchen vegetables as is never found in those of the market gardener. Childless men, if they would know something of the bliss of paternity, should plant a seed,—be it squash, bean, Indian corn, or perhaps a mere flower or worthless weed,—should plant it with their own hands, and nurse it from infancy to maturity altogether by their own care. If there be not too many of them, each individual plant becomes an object of separate interest. My garden, that skirted the avenue of the Manse, was of precisely the right extent. An hour or two of morning labor was all that it required. But I used to visit and revisit it a dozen times a day, and stand in deep contemplation over my vegetable progeny with a love that nobody could share or conceive of, who had never taken part in the process of creation. It was one of the most bewitching sights in the world to observe a hill of beans thrusting aside the soil, or a row of early peas just peeping forth sufficiently to trace a line of delicate green. Later in the season the humming-birds were attracted by the blossoms of a peculiar variety of bean; and they were a joy to me, those little spiritual visitants, for deigning to sip airy food out of my nectar cups. Multitudes of bees used to bury themselves in the yellow blossoms of the summer squashes. This, too, was a deep satisfaction; although, when they had laden themselves with sweets, they flew away to some unknown hive, which would give back nothing in requital of what my garden had contributed. But I was glad thus to fling a benefaction upon the passing breeze with the certainty that somebody must profit by it, and that there would be a little more honey in the world to allay the sourness and bitterness which mankind is always complaining of. Yes, indeed; my life was the sweeter for that honey. . . .

What with the river, the battle-field, the orchard and the garden, the reader begins to despair of finding his way back into the Old Manse. But in agreeable weather it is the truest hospitality to keep him out-of-doors. I never grew quite acquainted with my habitation till a long spell of sulky rain had confined me beneath its roof. There could not be a more sombre aspect of external Nature than as then seen from the windows of my study. The great willow tree had caught and retained among its leaves a whole cataract of water, to be shaken down at intervals by the frequent gusts of wind. All day long, and for a week together, the rain was drip-drip-dripping and splash-splash-splashing from the eaves, and bubbling and foaming into the tubs beneath the spouts. The old, unpainted shingles of the house and out-buildings were black with moisture; and the mosses of ancient growth upon the walls looked green and fresh, as if they were the newest things and afterthought of Time. The usually mirrored surface of the river was blurred by an infinity of raindrops; the whole landscape had a completely water-soaked appearance, conveying the impression that the earth was wet through like a sponge; while the summit of a wooded hill, about a mile distant, was enveloped in a dense mist, where the demon of the tempest seemed to have his abiding-place and to be plotting still direr inclemencies.

Nature has no kindness, no hospitality, during a rain. In the fiercest heat of sunny days she retains a secret mercy, and welcomes the wayfarer to shady nooks of the woods whither the sun cannot penetrate; but she provides no shelter against her storms. It makes us shiver to think of those deep, umbrageous recesses, those overshadowing banks, where we found such enjoyment during the sultry afternoons. Not a twig of foliage there but would dash a little shower into our faces. Looking reproachfully towards the impenetrable sky,—if sky there be above that dismal uniformity of cloud,—we are apt to murmur against the whole system of the universe, since it involves the extinction of so many summer days in so short a life by the hissing and spluttering rain. In such spells of weather—and it is to be supposed such weather came—Eve's bower in paradise must have been but a cheerless and aguish kind of shelter, nowise comparable to the old parsonage, which had resources of its own to beguile the week's imprisonment. The idea of sleeping on a couch of wet roses!

Happy the man who in a rainy day can betake himself to a huge garret, stored, like that of the Manse, with lumber that each generation has left behind it from a period before the revolution. Our garret was an arched hall, dimly illuminated through small and dusty windows; it was but a twilight at the best; and there were nooks, or rather caverns, of deep obscurity, the secrets of which I never learned, being too reverent of their dust and cobwebs. The beams and rafters, roughly hewn and with strips of bark still on them, and the rude masonry of the chimneys, made the garret look wild and uncivilized,—an aspect unlike what was seen elsewhere in the quiet and decorous old house. But on one side there was a little whitewashed apartment which bore the traditionary title of the Saint's Chamber, because holy men in their youth had slept and studied and prayed there. With its elevated retirement, its one window, its small fireplace, and its closet, convenient for an oratory, it was the very spot where a young man might inspire himself with solemn enthusiasm and cherish saintly dreams. The occupants, at various epochs, had left brief records and ejaculations inscribed upon the walls. There, too, hung a tattered and shrivelled roll of canvas, which on inspection proved to be the forcibly wrought picture of a clergyman, in wig, band, and gown, holding a Bible in his hand. As I turned his face towards the light he eyed me with an air of authority such as men of his profession seldom assume in our days. The original had been pastor of the parish more than a century ago, a friend of Whitefield,[4] and almost his equal in fervid eloquence. I bowed before the effigy of the dignified divine, and felt as if I had now met face to face with the ghost by whom, as there was reason to apprehend, the Manse was haunted. . . .

. . . A part of my predecessor's library was stored in the garret,—no unfit receptacle indeed for such dreary trash as comprised the greater number of volumes. The old books would have been worth nothing at an auction. In this venerable garret, however, they possessed an interest, quite apart from their literary value, as heirlooms, many of which had been transmitted down through a series of consecrated hands from the days of the mighty Puritan divines. Autographs of famous

names were to be seen in faded ink on some of their flyleaves; and there were marginal observations or interpolated pages closely covered with manuscript in illegible shorthand, perhaps concealing matter of profound truth and wisdom. The world will never be the better for it. A few of the books were Latin folios, written by Catholic authors; others demolished Papistry, as with a sledgehammer, in plain English. A dissertation on the book of Job—which only Job himself could have had patience to read—filled at least a score of small, thickset quartos, at the rate of two or three volumes to a chapter. Then there was a vast folio body of divinity—too corpulent a body, it might be feared, to comprehend the spiritual element of religion. Volumes of this form dated back two-hundred years or more, and were generally bound in black leather, exhibiting precisely such an appearance as we should attribute to books of enchantment. Others equally antique were of a size proper to be carried in the large waistcoat pockets of old times,—diminutive, but as black as their bulkier brethren, and abundantly interfused with Greek and Latin quotations. These little old volumes impressed me as if they had been intended for very large ones, but had been unfortunately blighted at an early stage of their growth.

The rain pattered upon the roof and the sky gloomed through the dusty garret windows, while I burrowed among these venerable books in search of any living thought which should burn like a coal of fire, or glow like an inextinguishable gem, beneath the dead trumpery that had long hidden it. But I found no such treasure; all was dead alike; and I could not but muse deeply and wonderingly upon the humiliating fact that the works of man's intellect decay like those of his hands. Thought grows mouldy. What was good and nourishing food for the spirits of one generation affords no sustenance for the next. . . .

Nothing, strange to say, retained any sap except what had been written for the passing day and year without the remotest pretension or idea of permanence. There were a few old newspapers, and still older almanacs, which reproduced to my mental eye the epochs when they had issued from the press with a distinctness that was altogether unaccountable. It was as if I had found bits of magic looking-glass among the books, with the images of a vanished century in them. I turned my eyes towards the tattered picture above mentioned, and asked of the austere divine wherefore it was that he and his brethren, after the most painful rummaging and groping into their minds, had been able to produce nothing half so real as these

4. **original . . . Whitefield:** George Whitefield (1714–70), the English evangelist and associate of John Wesley, twice preached at Concord at the invitation of the Rev. Daniel Bliss, an ancestor of Emerson and the "original" referred to.

newspaper scribblers and almanac makers had thrown off in the effervescence of a moment. The portrait responded not; so I sought an answer for myself. It is the age itself that writes newspapers and almanacs, which, therefore, have a distinct purpose and meaning at the time, and a kind of intelligible truth for all times; whereas most other works—being written by men who, in the very act, set themselves apart from their age—are likely to possess little significance when new, and none at all when old. Genius, indeed, melts many ages into one, and thus effects something permanent, yet still with a similarity of office to that of the more ephemeral writer. A work of genius is but the newspaper of a century, or perchance of a hundred centuries.

Lightly as I have spoken of these old books, there yet lingers with me a superstitious reverence for literature of all kinds. A bound volume has a charm in my eyes similar to what scraps of manuscript possess for the good Mussulman. He imagines that those wind-wafted records are perhaps hallowed by some sacred verse; and I, that every new book or antique one may contain the 'open sesame,'—the spell to disclose treasures hidden in some unsuspected cave of Truth. Thus it was not without sadness that I turned away from the library of the Old Manse.

Blessed was the sunshine when it came again at the close of another stormy day, beaming from the edge of the western horizon; while the massive firmament of clouds threw down all the gloom it could, but served only to kindle the golden light into a more brilliant glow by the strongly contrasted shadows. Heaven smiled at the earth, so long unseen, from beneath its heavy eyelid. Tomorrow for the hill-tops and the wood-paths.

Or it might be that Ellery Channing[5] came up the avenue to join me in a fishing excursion on the river. Strange and happy times were those when we cast aside all irksome forms and strait-laced habitudes, and delivered ourselves up to the free air, to live like the Indians or any less conventional race during one bright semicircle of the sun. Rowing our boat against the current, between wide meadows, we turned aside into the Assabeth.[6] A more lovely stream than this, for a mile above its junction with the Concord, has never flowed on earth,—nowhere, indeed, except to lave the interior regions of a poet's imagination. It is sheltered from the breeze by woods and a hillside; so that elsewhere there might be a hurricane, and

here scarcely a ripple across the shaded water. The current lingers along so gently that the mere force of the boatman's will seems sufficient to propel his craft against it. It comes flowing softly through the midmost privacy and deepest heart of a wood which whispers it to be quiet; while the stream whispers back again from its sedgy borders, as if river and wood were hushing one another to sleep. Yes; the river sleeps along its course and dreams of the sky and of the clustering foliage, amid which fall showers of broken sunlight, imparting specks of vivid cheerfulness, in contrast with the quiet depth of the prevailing tint. Of all this scene, the slumbering river has a dream picture in its bosom. Which, after all, was the most real—the picture, or the original?—the objects palpable to our grosser senses, or their apotheosis in the stream beneath? Surely the disembodied images stand in closer relation to the soul. But both the original and the reflection had here an ideal charm; and, had it been a thought more wild, I could have fancied that this river had strayed forth out of the rich scenery of my companion's inner world; only the vegetation along its banks should then have had an Oriental character.[7]

The winding course of the stream continually shut out the scene behind us, and revealed as calm and lovely a one before. We glided from depth to depth, and breathed new seclusion at every turn. The shy kingfisher flew from the withered branch close at hand to another at a distance, uttering a shrill cry of anger or alarm. Ducks that had been floating there since the preceding eve were startled at our approach, and skimmed along the glassy river, breaking its dark surface with a bright streak. The pickerel leaped from among the lily-pads. The turtle, sunning itself upon a rock or at the root of a tree, slid suddenly into the water with a plunge. The painted Indian who paddled his canoe along the Assabeth three hundred years ago could hardly have seen a wilder gentleness displayed upon its banks and reflected in its bosom than we did. Nor could the same Indian have prepared his noontide meal with more simplicity. We drew up our skiff at some point where the overarching shade formed a natural bower, and there kindled a fire with the pine cones and decayed branches that lay strewn plentifully around. Soon the smoke ascended among the trees, impregnated with a savory incense, not heavy, dull, and surfeiting, like the steam of cookery within doors, but sprightly and piquant. The smell of our feast was akin to the woodland odors with which it mingled: there was no sacrilege committed by our intrusion

---

5. **Ellery Channing:** William Ellery Channing, nephew of the distinguished Unitarian clergyman, friend of Thoreau, and one of the Transcendentalist poets of Concord.     6. **Assabeth:** the Assabeth River joins the Concord River at Concord.

7. **Oriental character:** the Concord Transcendentalists were reading the recently translated books of Oriental philosophy.

there: the sacred solitude was hospitable, and granted us free leave to cook and eat in the recess that was at once our kitchen and banqueting hall. It is strange what humble offices may be performed in a beautiful scene without destroying its poetry. Our fire, red gleaming among the trees, and we beside it, busied with culinary rites and spreading out our meal on a moss-grown log, all seemed in unison with the river gliding by and the foliage rustling over us. And, what was strangest, neither did our mirth seem to disturb the propriety of the solemn woods; although the hobgoblins of the old wilderness and the will-of-the-wisps that glimmered in the marshy places might have come trooping to share our table-talk, and have added their shrill laughter to our merriment. It was the very spot in which to utter the extremest nonsense or the profoundest wisdom, or that ethereal product of the mind which partakes of both, and may become one or the other, in correspondence with the faith and insight of the auditor.

So amid sunshine and shadow, rustling leaves and sighing waters, up gushed our talk like the babble of a fountain. The evanescent spray was Ellery's; and his, too, the lumps of golden thought that lay glimmering in the fountain's bed and brightened both our faces by the reflection. Could he have drawn out that virgin gold and stamped it with the mint mark that alone gives currency, the world might have had the profit, and he the fame. My mind was the richer merely by the knowledge that it was there. But the chief profit of those wild days to him and me lay, not in any definite idea, not in any angular or rounded truth, which we dug out of the shapeless mass of problematical stuff, but in the freedom which we thereby won from all custom and conventionalism and fettering influences of man on man. We were so free to-day that it was impossible to be slaves again to-morrow. When we crossed the threshold of the house or trod the thronged pavements of a city, still the leaves of the trees that overhang the Assabeth were whispering to us, "Be free! be free!" Therefore along that shady river-bank there are spots, marked with a heap of ashes and half-consumed brands, only less sacred in my remembrance than the hearth of a household fire.

And yet how sweet, as we floated homeward adown the golden river at sunset,—how sweet was it to return within the system of human society, not as to a dungeon and a chain, but as to a stately edifice, whence we could go forth at will into statelier simplicity! How gently, too, did the sight of the Old Manse, best seen from the river, overshadowed with its willow and all environed about with the foliage of its orchard and avenue,—

how gently did its gray, homely aspect rebuke the speculative extravagances of the day! It had grown sacred in connection with the artificial life against which we inveighed; it had been a home for many years in spite of all; it was my home too; and, with these thoughts, it seemed to me that all the artifice and conventionalism of life was but an impalpable thinness upon its surface, and that the depth below was none the worse for it. Once, as we turned our boat to the bank, there was a cloud, in the shape of an immensely gigantic figure of a hound, couched above the house, as if keeping guard over it. Gazing at this symbol, I prayed that the upper influences might long protect the institutions that had grown out of the heart of mankind.

If ever my readers should decide to give up civilized life, cities, houses, and whatever moral or material enormities in addition to these the perverted ingenuity of our race has contrived, let it be in the early autumn. Then Nature will love him better than at any other season, and will take him to her bosom with a more motherly tenderness. I could scarcely endure the roof of the old house above me in those first autumnal days. How early in the summer, too, the prophecy of autumn comes! Earlier in some years than in others; sometimes even in the first weeks of July. There is no other feeling like what is caused by this faint, doubtful, yet real perception—if it be not rather a foreboding—of the year's decay, so blessedly sweet and sad in the same breath.

Did I say that there was no feeling like it? Ah, but there is a half-acknowledged melancholy like to this when we stand in the perfected vigor of our life and feel that Time has now given us all his flowers, and that the next work of his never idle fingers must be to steal them one by one away.

I have forgotten whether the song of the cricket be not as early a token of autumn's approach as any other,—that song which may be called an audible stillness; for though very loud and heard afar, yet the mind does not take note of it as a sound, so completely is its individual existence merged among the accompanying characteristics of the season. Alas for the pleasant summer time! In August the grass is still verdant on the hills and in the valleys; the foliage of the trees is as dense as ever, and as green; the flowers gleam forth in richer abundance along the margin of the river, and by the stone walls, and deep among the woods; the days, too, are as fervid now as they were a month ago; and yet in every breath of wind and in every beam of sunshine we hear the whispered farewell and behold the parting smile of a dear friend. There is a coolness amid all the heat, a mildness in the blazing noon. Not a breeze can stir but it thrills us with the breath of autumn. A pensive glory is seen in the far golden gleams; among the shadows of the trees. The flowers—even the brightest of them, and they are the most gorgeous of the year —have this gentle sadness wedded to their pomp, and typify the character of the delicious time each within itself. The brilliant cardinal flower has never seemed gay to me. . . .

When summer was dead and buried the Old Manse became as lonely as a hermitage. Not that ever—in my time at least—it had been thronged with company; but, at no rare intervals, we welcomed some friend out of the dusty glare and tumult of the world, and rejoiced to share with him the transparent obscurity that was floating over us. In one respect our precincts were like the Enchanted Ground through which the pilgrim travelled on his way to the Celestial City![8] The guests, each and all, felt a slumberous influence upon them; they fell asleep in chairs, or took a more deliberate siesta on the sofa, or were seen stretched among the shadows of the orchard, looking up dreamily through the boughs. They could not have paid a more acceptable compliment to my abode, nor to my own qualities as a host. I held it as a proof that they left their cares behind them as they passed between the stone gateposts at the entrance of our avenue, and that the so powerful opiate was the abundance of peace and quiet within and all around us. Others could give them pleasure and amusement or instruction—these could be picked up anywhere; but it was for me to give them rest— rest in a life of trouble. What better could be done for those weary and world-worn spirits?—for him[9] whose career of perpetual action was impeded and harassed by the rarest of his powers and the richest of his acquirements?—for another[10] who had thrown his ardent heart from earliest youth into the strife of politics, and now, perchance, began to suspect that one lifetime is too brief for the accomplishment of any lofty aim?—for her[11] on whose feminine nature had been imposed the heavy gift of intellectual power, such as a strong man might have staggered under, and with it the necessity to act upon the world?—in a word, not to

multiply instances, what better could be done for anybody who came within our magic circle than to throw the spell of a tranquil spirit over him? And when it had wrought its full effect, then we dismissed him, with but misty reminiscences, as if he had been dreaming of us.

Were I to adopt a pet idea, as so many people do, and fondle it in my embraces to the exclusion of all others, it would be, that the great want which mankind labors under at this present period is sleep. The world should recline its vast head on the first convenient pillow and take an age-long nap. It has gone distracted through a morbid activity, and, while preternaturally wide awake, is nevertheless tormented by visions that seem real to it now, but would assume their true aspect and character were all things once set right by an interval of sound repose. This is the only method of getting rid of old delusions and avoiding new ones; of regenerating our race, so that it might in due time awake as an infant out of dewy slumber; of restoring to us the simple perception of what is right, and the single-hearted desire to achieve it, both of which have long been lost in consequence of this weary activity of brain and torpor or passion of the heart that now afflict the universe. Stimulants, the only mode of treatment hitherto attempted, cannot quell the disease; they do but heighten the delirium.

Let not the above paragraph ever be quoted against the author; for, though tinctured with its modicum of truth, it is the result and expression of what he knew, while he was writing, to be but a distorted survey of the state and prospects of mankind. There were circumstances around me which made it difficult to view the world precisely as it exists; for, severe and sober as was the Old Manse, it was necessary to go but a little way beyond its threshold before meeting with stranger moral shapes of men than might have been encountered elsewhere in a circuit of a thousand miles.

These hobgoblins of flesh and blood were attracted thither by the widespreading influence of a great original thinker, who had his earthly abode at the opposite extremity of our village. His mind acted upon other minds of a certain constitution with wonderful magnetism, and drew many men upon long pilgrimages to speak with him face to face. Young visionaries—to whom just so much of insight had been imparted as to make life all a labyrinth around them—came to seek the clew that should guide them out of their self-involved bewilderment. Gray-headed theorists—whose systems, at first air, had finally imprisoned them in an iron frame-work—travelled painfully to his door, not to ask deliverance, but to invite the free spirit into their own thraldom. People that had lighted on a

8. Enchanted . . . City: an allusion to the Delectable Mountains in John Bunyan's *Pilgrim's Progress* (1678). 9. him: Horatio Bridge (1806–93), a classmate of Hawthorne at Bowdoin and a lifelong friend. Just before moving into the Old Manse, Hawthorne had helped Bridge edit the *Journal of an African Cruiser* (1845), a narrative of a voyage. Bridge, it would appear, suffered the privations and difficulties of authorship, as did Hawthorne himself. 10. another: Franklin Pierce (1804–69), another collegemate of Hawthorne and a lifelong friend who became President of the United States (1853–57) and appointed Hawthorne consul at Liverpool. 11. her: Margaret Fuller (1810–50), a friend of Emerson, an important member of the Concord group, and, occasionally, a visitor in the Old Manse.

new thought, or a thought that they fancied new, came to Emerson, as the finder of a glittering gem hastens to a lapidary, to ascertain its quality and value. Uncertain, troubled, earnest wanderers through the midnight of the moral world beheld his intellectual fire as a beacon burning on a hill-top, and, climbing the difficult ascent, looked forth into the surrounding obscurity more hopefully than hitherto. The light revealed objects unseen before, —mountains, gleaming lakes, glimpses of a creation among the chaos; but also, as was unavoidable, it attracted bats and owls and the whole host of night birds, which flapped their dusky wings against the gazer's eyes, and sometimes were mistaken for fowls of angelic feather. Such delusions always hover nigh whenever a beacon fire of truth is kindled.

For myself, there had been epochs of my life when I, too, might have asked of this prophet the master word that should solve me the riddle of the universe; but now, being happy, I felt as if there were no question to be put, and therefore admired Emerson as a poet of deep beauty and austere tenderness, but sought nothing from him as a philosopher. It was good, nevertheless, to meet him in the wood-paths, or sometimes in our avenue, with that pure intellectual gleam diffused about his presence like the garment of a shining one; and he so quiet, so simple, so without pretension, encountering each man alive as if expecting to receive more than he could impart. And, in truth, the heart of many an ordinary man had, perchance, inscriptions which he could not read. But it was impossible to dwell in his vicinity without inhaling more or less the mountain atmosphere of his lofty thought, which, in the brains of some people, wrought a singular giddiness,—new truth being as heady as new wine. Never was a poor little country village infested with such a variety of queer, strangely-dressed, oddly-behaved mortals, most of whom took upon themselves to be important agents of the world's destiny, yet were simply bores of a very intense water. Such, I imagine, is the invariable character of persons who crowd so closely about an original thinker as to draw in his unuttered breath and thus become imbued with a false originality. This triteness of novelty is enough to make any man of common sense blaspheme at all ideas of less than a century's standing, and pray that the world may be petrified and rendered immovable in precisely the worst moral and physical state that it ever yet arrived at, rather than be benefited by such schemes of such philosophers. . . .

Glancing back over what I have written, it seems but the scattered reminiscences of a single summer. In fairyland there is no measurement of time; and, in a spot so sheltered from the turmoil of life's ocean, three years hastened away with a noiseless flight, as the breezy sunshine chases the cloud shadows across the depths of a still valley. Now came hints, growing more and more distinct, that the owner of the old house was pining for his native air. Carpenters next appeared, making a tremendous racket among the out-buildings, strewing the green grass with pine shavings and chips of chestnut joists, and vexing the whole antiquity of the place with their discordant renovations. Soon, moreover, they divested our abode of the veil of woodbine which had crept over a large portion of its southern face. All the aged mosses were cleared unsparingly away; and there were horrible whispers about brushing up the external walls with a coat of paint—a purpose as little to my taste as might be that of rouging the venerable cheeks of one's grandmother. But the hand that renovates is always more sacrilegious than that which destroys. In fine, we gathered up our household goods, drank a farewell cup of tea in our pleasant little breakfast-room,—delicately fragrant tea, an unpurchasable luxury, one of the many angel gifts that had fallen like dew upon us,—and passed forth between the tall stone gateposts as uncertain as the wandering Arabs where our tent might next be pitched. Providence took me by the hand, and —an oddity of dispensation which, I trust, there is no irreverence in smiling at—has led me, as the newspapers announce while I am writing, from the Old Manse into a custom house. As a story teller, I have often contrived strange vicissitudes for my imaginary personages, but none like this.

The treasure of intellectual good which I hoped to find in our secluded dwelling had never come to light. No profound treatise of ethics, no philosophic history, no novel even, that could stand unsupported on its edges. All that I had to show, as a man of letters, were these few tales and essays, which had blossomed out like flowers in the calm summer of my heart and mind. Save editing (an easy task) the journal of my friend of many years, the *African Cruiser,* I had done nothing else. With these idle weeds and withering blossoms I have intermixed some that were produced long ago,—old, faded things, reminding me of flowers pressed between the leaves of a book,—and now offer the bouquet, such as it is, to any whom it may please. These fitful sketches, with so little of external life about them, yet claiming no profundity of purpose,—so reserved, even while they sometimes seem so frank,—often but half in earnest, and never, even when most so, expressing satisfactorily the thoughts which they profess to image,—such trifles, I truly feel, afford no solid basis for a literary reputation. Nevertheless, the public—if my limited number of readers, whom I venture to regard rather as a circle of friends, may be termed a public—will receive them the more kindly, as the last offering, the last collection, of this nature which it is my purpose ever to put forth. Unless I could do better, I have done enough in this kind. For myself the book will always retain one charm—as reminding me of the river, with its delightful solitudes, and of the avenue, the garden, and the orchard, and especially the dear Old Manse, with the little study on its western side, and the sunshine glimmering through the willow branches while I wrote.

Let the reader, if he will do me so much honor, imagine himself my guest, and that, having seen whatever may be worthy of notice within and about the Old Manse, he has finally been ushered into my study. There, after seating him in an antique elbow chair, an heirloom of the house, I take forth a roll of manuscript and entreat his attention to the following tales—an act of personal inhospitality, however, which I never was guilty of, nor ever will be, even to my worst enemy.

# THE CUSTOM HOUSE

## INTRODUCTORY TO
### *The Scarlet Letter*

◇

❴ HAWTHORNE's Prefaces continue the theme of personal reminiscence which colors "The Old Manse." But the mood of recollection was deepened by Hawthorne's commitment to the life of art. In the Custom House Introduction to *The Scarlet Letter* Hawthorne was getting even with his political enemies who made him lose his position and, at the same time, offering an "apology" for writing a novel. In the legend of Surveyor Pue and of the red letter A, he may have been trying to fabricate history as a means of strengthening the historical structure of his moral tale; he may also have been proposing that a writer must find that strange and special place where the "Actual" and the "Imaginary" meet. If the real is too obtrusive, then the artistic expression is stifled; if the imaginary can slowly emerge and the theme of the novel become apparent, then the novel can virtually write itself.

◇

. . . IN MY native town of Salem, at the head of what, half a century ago, in the days of old King Derby,[1] was a bustling wharf,—but which is now burdened with decayed wooden warehouses, and exhibits few or no symptoms of commercial life; except, perhaps, a bark or brig, half-way down its melancholy length, discharging hides; or, nearer at hand, a Nova Scotia schooner, pitching out her cargo of fire-wood,—at the head, I say, of this dilapidated wharf, which the tide often overflows, and along which, at the base and in the rear of the row of buildings, the track of many languid years is seen in a border of unthrifty grass,—here, with a view from its front windows adown this not very enlivening prospect, and thence across the harbor, stands a spacious edifice of brick. From the loftiest point of its roof, during precisely three and a half hours of each forenoon, floats or droops, in breeze or calm, the banner of the republic; but with the thirteen stripes turned vertically, instead of horizontally, and thus indicating that a civil, and not a military post of Uncle Sam's government, is here established. Its front is ornamented with a portico of half a dozen wooden pillars, supporting a balcony, beneath which a flight of wide granite steps descends towards the street. Over the entrance hovers an enormous specimen of the American eagle, with outspread wings, a shield before her breast, and, if I recollect aright, a bunch of intermingled thunderbolts and barbed arrows in each claw. With the customary infirmity of temper that characterizes this unhappy fowl, she appears, by the fierceness of her beak and eye, and the general truculency of her attitude, to threaten mischief to the inoffensive community; and especially to warn all citizens, careful of their safety, against intruding on the premises which she overshadows with her wings. Nevertheless, vixenly as she looks, many people are seeking, at this very moment, to shelter themselves under the wing of the federal eagle; imagining, I presume, that her bosom has all the softness and snugness of an eider-down pillow. But she has no great tenderness, even in her best of moods, and, sooner or later,—oftener soon than late,—is apt to fling off her nestlings, with a scratch of her claw, a dab of her beak, or a rankling wound from her barbed arrows.

The pavement round about the above-described edifice—which we may as well name at once as the Custom House of the port—has grass enough growing in its chinks to show that it has not, of late days, been worn by any multitudinous resort of business. In some months of the year, however, there often chances a forenoon when affairs move

THE CUSTOM HOUSE. 1. old King Derby: Elias Hasket Derby (1739–99), a merchant and shipowner of Salem who helped raise arms for the Revolution and dispatched the first ships which opened trade with the Orient.

onward with a livelier tread. Such occasions might remind the elderly citizen of that period before the last war with England,[2] when Salem was a port by itself; not scorned, as she is now, by her own merchants and ship-owners, who permit her wharves to crumble to ruin, while their ventures go to swell, needlessly and imperceptibly, the mighty flood of commerce at New York or Boston. On some such morning, when three of four vessels happen to have arrived at once,—usually from Africa or South America,—or to be on the verge of their departure thitherward, there is a sound of frequent feet, passing briskly up and down the granite steps. Here, before his own wife has greeted him, you may greet the sea-flushed shipmaster, just in port, with his vessel's papers under his arm, in a tarnished tin box. Here, too, comes his owner, cheerful or sombre, gracious or in the sulks, accordingly as his scheme of the now accomplished voyage has been realized in merchandise that will readily be turned to gold, or has buried him under a bulk of incommodities, such as nobody will care to rid him of. Here, likewise,—the germ of the wrinkle-browed, grizzly-bearded, care-worn merchant,—we have the smart young clerk, who gets the taste of traffic as a wolf-cub does of blood, and already sends adventures in his master's ships, when he had better be sailing mimic-boats upon a mill-pond. Another figure in the scene is the outward-bound sailor, in quest of a protection; or the recently arrived one, pale and feeble, seeking a passport to the hospital. Nor must we forget the captains of the rusty little schooners that bring firewood from the British provinces; a rough-looking set of tarpaulins, without the alertness of the Yankee aspect, but contributing an item of no slight importance to our decaying trade. . . .

. . . This old town of Salem—my native place, though I have dwelt much away from it, both in boyhood and maturer years—possesses, or did possess, a hold on my affections, the force of which I have never realized during my seasons of actual residence here. Indeed, so far as its physical aspect is concerned, with its flat, unvaried surface, covered chiefly with wooden houses, few or none of which pretend to architectural beauty,—its irregularity, which is neither picturesque nor quaint, but only tame,—its long and lazy street lounging wearisomely through the whole extent of the peninsula, with Gallows Hill and New Guinea at one end, and a view of the almshouse at the other,—such being the features of my native town, it would be quite as reasonable to form a sentimental attachment to a disarranged checkerboard. And yet, though invariably happiest elsewhere, there is within me a feeling for old Salem, which, in lack of a better phrase, I must be content to call affection. The sentiment is probably assignable to the deep and aged roots which my family has struck into the soil. It is now nearly two centuries and a quarter since the original Briton, the earliest emigrant of my name,[3] made his appearance in the wild and forest-bordered settlement, which has since become a city. And here his descendants have been born and died, and have mingled their earthly substance with the soil, until no small portion of it must necessarily be akin to the mortal frame wherewith, for a little while, I walk the streets. In part, therefore, the attachment which I speak of is the mere sensuous sympathy of dust for dust. Few of my countrymen can know what it is; nor, as frequent transplantation is perhaps better for the stock, need they consider it desirable to know.

But the sentiment has likewise its moral quality. The figure of that first ancestor, invested by family tradition with a dim and dusky grandeur, was present to my boyish imagination, as far back as I can remember. It still haunts me, and induces a sort of home-feeling with the past, which I scarcely claim in reference to the present phase of the town. I seem to have a stronger claim to a residence here on account of this grave, bearded, sable-cloaked and steeple-crowned progenitor,—who came so early, with his Bible and his sword, and trode the unworn street with such a stately port, and made so large a figure, as a man of war and peace,—a stronger claim than for myself, whose name is seldom heard and my face hardly known. He was a soldier, legislator, judge; he was a ruler in the Church; he had all the Puritanic traits, both good and evil. He was likewise a better persecutor, as witness the Quakers, who have remembered him in their histories, and relate an incident of his hard severity towards a woman of their sect, which will last longer, it is to be feared, than any record of his better deeds, although these were many. His son,[4] too, inherited the persecuting spirit, and made himself so conspicuous in the martyrdom of the witches, that their blood may fairly be said to have left a stain upon him. So deep a stain, indeed, that his old dry bones, in the Charter-street burial-ground, must still retain it, if they have not crumbled utterly to dust! I know not whether these ancestors of mine bethought themselves to repent, and ask pardon of heaven for their cruelties; or

2. **war with England:** the War of 1812 (to 1815).

3. **earliest . . . my name:** William Hathorne (1607?–81), who emigrated to New England in 1630 and afterward took a prominent part in Massachusetts politics. 4. **His son:** John Hathorne (1641–1717), the great-great-grandfather of Nathaniel, was one of the judges in the Salem witchcraft trials of 1692.

whether they are now groaning under the heavy consequences of them, in another state of being. At all events, I, the present writer, as their representative, hereby take shame upon myself for their sakes, and pray that any curse incurred by them— as I have heard, and as the dreary and unprosperous condition of the race, for many a long year back, would argue to exist—may be now and henceforth removed.

Doubtless, however, either of these stern and black-browed Puritans would have thought it quite a sufficient retribution for his sins, that, after so long a lapse of years, the old trunk of the family tree, with so much venerable moss upon it, should have borne, as its topmost bough, an idler like myself. No aim, that I have ever cherished, would they recognize as laudable; no success of mine—if my life, beyond its domestic scope, had ever been brightened by success—would they deem otherwise than worthless, if not positively disgraceful. "What is he?" murmurs one gray shadow of my forefathers to the other. "A writer of story-books! What kind of a business in life,—what mode of glorifying God, or being serviceable to mankind in his day and generation,—may that be? Why, the degenerate fellow might as well have been a fiddler!" Such are the compliments bandied between my great-grandsires and myself, across the gulf of time! And yet, let them scorn me as they will, strong traits of their nature have intertwined themselves with mine.

Planted deep, in the town's earliest infancy and childhood, by these two earnest and energetic men, the race has ever since subsisted here; always, too, in respectability; never, so far as I have known, disgraced by a single unworthy member; but seldom or never, on the other hand, after the first two generations, performing any memorable deed, or so much as putting forward a claim to public notice. Gradually, they have sunk almost out of sight; as old houses, here and there about the streets, get covered half-way to the eaves by the accumulation of new soil. From father to son, for above a hundred years, they followed the sea; a gray-headed shipmaster, in each generation, retiring from the quarter-deck to the homestead, while a boy of fourteen took the hereditary place before the mast, confronting the salt spray and the gale, which had blustered against his sire and grandsire. The boy, also, in due time, passed from the forecastle to the cabin, spent a tempestuous manhood, and returned from his world-wanderings, to grow old, and die, and mingle his dust with the natal earth. This long connection of a family with one spot, as its place of birth and burial, creates a kindred between the human being and the locality,

quite independent of any charm in the scenery or moral circumstances that surround him. It is not love, but instinct. The new inhabitant—who came himself from a foreign land, or whose father or grandfather came—has little claim to be called a Salemite; he has no conception of the oyster-like tenacity with which an old settler, over whom his third century is creeping, clings to the spot where his successive generations have been imbedded. It is no matter that the place is joyless for him; that he is weary of the old wooden houses, the mud and dust, the dead level of site and sentiment, the chill east wind, and the chillest of social atmospheres; —all these, and whatever faults besides he may see or imagine, are nothing to the purpose. The spell survives, and just as powerfully as if the natal spot were an earthly paradise. So has it been in my case. I felt it almost as a destiny to make Salem my home; so that the mould of features and cast of character which had all along been familiar here —ever, as one representative of the race lay down in his grave, another assuming, as it were, his sentry-march along the main street — might still in my little day be seen and recognized in the old town. Nevertheless, this very sentiment is an evidence that the connection, which has become an unhealthy one, should at least be severed. Human nature will not flourish, any more than a potato, if it be planted and replanted, for too long a series of generations, in the same worn-out soil. My children have had other birthplaces, and, so far as their fortunes may be within my control, shall strike their roots into unaccustomed earth. . . .

. . . Literature, its exertions and objects, were now of little moment in my regard. I cared not, at this period, for books; they were apart from me. Nature,—except it were human nature,—the nature that is developed in earth and sky, was, in one sense, hidden from me; and all the imaginative delight, wherewith it had been spiritualized, passed away out of my mind. A gift, a faculty, if it had not departed, was suspended and inanimate within me. There would have been something sad, unutterably dreary, in all this, had I not been conscious that it lay at my own option to recall whatever was valuable in the past. It might be true, indeed, that this was a life which could not with impunity be lived too long; else, it might have made me permanently other than I had been without transforming me into any shape which it would be worth my while to take. But I never considered it as other than a transitory life. There was always a prophetic instinct, a low whisper in my ear, that, within no long period, and whenever a new change of custom should be essential to my good, a change would come.

Meanwhile, there I was, a Surveyor of the Revenue,[5] and, so far as I have been able to understand, as good a Surveyor as need be. A man of thought, fancy, and sensibility (had he ten times the Surveyor's proportion of those qualities) may, at any time, be a man of affairs, if he will only choose to give himself the trouble. My fellow-officers, and the merchants and sea-captains, with whom my official duties brought me into any manner of connection, viewed me in no other light, and probably knew me in no other character. None of them, I presume, had ever read a page of my inditing, or would have cared a fig the more for me if they had read them all; nor would it have mended the matter, in the least, had those same unprofitable pages been written with a pen like that of Burns or of Chaucer, each of whom was a Custom Officer in his day, as well as I. It is a good lesson—though it may often be a hard one—for a man who has dreamed of literary fame, and of making for himself a rank among the world's dignitaries by such means, to step aside out of the narrow circle in which his claims are recognized, and to find how utterly devoid of significance, beyond that circle, is all that he achieves, and all he aims at. I know not that I especially needed the lesson, either in the way of warning or rebuke; but, at any rate, I learned it thoroughly: nor, it gives me pleasure to reflect, did the truth, as it came home to my perception, ever cost me a pang, or require to be thrown off in a sigh. In the way of literary talk, it is true, the Naval Officer—an excellent fellow, who came into office with me and went out only a little later—would often engage me in a discussion about one or the other of his favorite topics, Napoleon or Shakespeare. The Collector's junior clerk, too,—a young gentleman who, it was whispered, occasionally covered a sheet of Uncle Sam's letter-paper with what (at the distance of a few yards) looked very much like poetry,—used now and then to speak to me of books, as matters with which I might possibly be conversant. This was my all of lettered intercourse; and it was quite sufficient for my necessities.

No longer seeking or caring that my name should be blazoned abroad on title-pages, I smiled to think that it had now another kind of vogue. The Custom House marker imprinted it, with a stencil and black paint, on pepper-bags, and baskets of anatto, and cigar-boxes, and bales of all kinds of dutiable merchandise, in testimony that these commodities had paid the impost, and gone regularly through the office. Borne on such queer vehicle of fame, a knowledge of my existence, so far as a name conveys it, was carried where it had never been before, and, I hope, will never go again.

But the past was not dead. Once in a great while, the thoughts, that had seemed so vital and so active, yet had been put to rest so quietly, revived again. One of the most remarkable occasions, when the habit of bygone days awoke in me, was that which brings it within the law of literary propriety to offer the public the sketch which I am now writing.

In the second story of the Custom House, there is a large room, in which the brick-work and naked rafters have never been covered with panelling and plaster. The edifice—originally projected on a scale adapted to the old commercial enterprise of the port, and with an idea of subsequent prosperity destined never to be realized—contains far more space than its occupants know what to do with. This airy hall, therefore, over the Collector's apartments, remains unfinished to this day, and, in spite of the aged cobwebs that festoon its dusky beams, appears still to await the labor of the carpenter and mason. At one end of the room, in a recess, were a number of barrels, piled one upon another, containing bundles of official documents. Large quantities of similar rubbish lay lumbering the floor. It was sorrowful to think how many days, and weeks, and months, and years of toil, had been wasted on these musty papers, which were now only an encumbrance on earth, and were hidden away in this forgotten corner, never more to be glanced at by human eyes. But, then, what reams of other manuscripts—filled not with the dulness of official formalities, but with the thought of inventive brains and the rich effusion of deep hearts—had gone equally to oblivion; and that, moreover, without serving a purpose in their day, as these heaped-up papers had, and—saddest of all—without purchasing for their writers the comfortable livelihood which the clerks of the Custom House had gained by these worthless scratchings of the pen! Yet not altogether worthless, perhaps, as materials of local history. Here, no doubt, statistics of the former commerce of Salem might be discovered, and memorials of her princely merchants,—old King Derby,—old Billy Gray,[6]—old Simon Forrester,[7] —and many another magnate in his day; whose powdered head, however, was scarcely in the tomb, before his mountain pile of wealth began to dwindle. The founders of the greater part of the families which now compose the aristocracy of Salem might here be traced, from the petty and ob-

5. **Surveyor . . . Revenue:** Hawthorne's position in the custom house, 1846–49.

6. **Billy Gray:** William Gray (1750–1825), a wealthy shipowner of Salem and lieutenant governor of Massachusetts. 7. **Simon Forrester:** another well-to-do shipowner (1776–1851) in Salem.

scure beginnings of their traffic, at periods generally much posterior to the Revolution, upward to what their children look upon as long-established rank.

Prior to the Revolution, there is a dearth of records; the earlier documents and archives of the Custom House having, probably, been carried off to Halifax, when all the King's officials accompanied the British army in its flight from Boston. It has often been a matter of regret with me; for, going back, perhaps, to the days of the Protectorate, those papers must have contained many references to forgotten or remembered men, and to antique customs, which would have affected me with the same pleasure as when I used to pick up Indian arrow-heads in the field near the Old Manse.

But one idle and rainy day, it was my fortune to make a discovery of some little interest. Poking and burrowing into the heaped-up rubbish in the corner; unfolding one and another document, and reading the names of vessels that had long ago foundered at sea or rotted at the wharves, and those of merchants never heard of now on 'Change, nor very readily decipherable on their mossy tombstones; glancing at such matters with the saddened, weary, half-reluctant interest which we bestow on the corpse of dead activity,—and exerting my fancy, sluggish with little use, to raise up from dry bones an image of the old town's brighter aspect, when India was a new region, and only Salem knew the way thither,—I chanced to lay my hand on a small package, carefully done up in a piece of ancient yellow parchment. This envelope had the air of an official record of some period long past, when clerks engrossed their stiff and formal chirography on more substantial materials than at present. There was something about it that quickened an instinctive curiosity, and made me undo the faded red tape, that tied up the package, with the sense that a treasure would here be brought to light. Unbending the rigid folds of the parchment cover, I found it to be a commission, under the hand and seal of Governor Shirley,[8] in favor of one Jonathan Pue, as Surveyor of his Majesty's Customs for the port of Salem, in the Province of Massachusetts Bay. I remembered to have read (probably in Felt's *Annals*[9]) a notice of the decease of Mr. Surveyor Pue, about fourscore years ago; and likewise, in a newspaper of recent times, an account of the digging up of his remains in the little grave-yard of St. Peter's Church, during the renewal of that edifice. Nothing, if I rightly call to mind, was left of my respected predecessor,

save an imperfect skeleton, and some fragments of apparel, and a wig of majestic frizzle; which, unlike the head that it once adorned, was in very satisfactory preservation. But, on examining the papers which the parchment commission served to envelop, I found more traces of Mr. Pue's mental part, and the internal operations of his head, than the frizzled wig had contained of the venerable skull itself.

They were documents, in short, not official, but of a private nature, or, at least, written in his private capacity, and apparently with his own hand. I could account for their being included in the heap of Custom House lumber only by the fact that Mr. Pue's death had happened suddenly; and that these papers, which he probably kept in his official desk, had never come to the knowledge of his heirs, or were supposed to relate to the business of the revenue. On the transfer of the archives to Halifax, this package proving to be of no public concern, was left behind and had remained ever since unopened.

The ancient Surveyor—being little molested, I suppose, at that early day, with business pertaining to his office—seems to have devoted some of his many leisure hours to researches as a local antiquarian, and other inquisitions of a similar nature. These supplied material for petty activity to a mind that would otherwise have been eaten up with rust. A portion of his facts, by the by, did me good service in the preparation of the article entitled "MAIN STREET,"[10] included in the third volume of this edition. The remainder may perhaps be applied to purposes equally valuable hereafter; or not impossibly may be worked up, so far as they go, into a regular history of Salem, should my veneration for the natal soil ever impel me to so pious a task. Meanwhile, they shall be at the command of any gentleman, inclined, and competent, to take the unprofitable labor off my hands. As a final disposition, I contemplate depositing them with the Essex Historical Society.

But the object that most drew my attention, in the mysterious package, was a certain affair of fine red cloth, much worn and faded. There were traces about it of gold embroidery, which, however, was greatly frayed and defaced; so that none, or very little, of the glitter was left. It had been wrought, as was easy to perceive, with wonderful skill of needlework; and the stitch (as I am assured by ladies conversant with such mysteries) gives evidence of a now forgotten art, not to be recovered even by the process of picking out the threads. This rag of scarlet cloth,—for time and wear and a sac-

---

8. **Governor Shirley:** William Shirley (1694–1771), colonial governor of Massachusetts, 1741–57.    9. **Felt's *Annals*:** Joseph Felt, *Annals of Salem from Its First Settlement* (1827). The death of Jonathan Pue is mentioned as occurring March 24, 1760.

10. **"Main Street":** a description of Old Salem published in 1849 and later included in *The Snow-Image and Other Twice-Told Tales* (1852).

rilegious moth had reduced it to little other than a rag,—on careful examination, assumed the shape of a letter. It was the capital letter A. By an accurate measurement, each limb proved to be precisely three inches and a quarter in length. It had been intended, there could be no doubt, as an ornamental article of dress; but how it was to be worn, or what rank, honor, and dignity, in by-past times, were signified by it, was a riddle which (so evanescent are the fashions of the world in these particulars) I saw little hope of solving. And yet it strangely interested me. My eyes fastened themselves upon the old scarlet letter, and would not be turned aside. Certainly, there was some deep meaning in it, most worthy of interpretation, and which, as it were, streamed forth from the mystic symbol, subtly communicating itself to my sensibilities, but evading the analysis of my mind.

While thus perplexed,—and cogitating, among other hypotheses, whether the letter might not have been one of those decorations which the white men used to contrive, in order to take the eyes of Indians,—I happened to place it on my breast. It seemed to me,—the reader may smile, but must not doubt my word,—it seemed to me, then, that I experienced a sensation not altogether physical, yet almost so, as of burning heat; and as if the letter were not of red cloth, but red-hot iron. I shuddered, and involuntarily let it fall upon the floor.

In the absorbing contemplation of the scarlet letter, I had hitherto neglected to examine a small roll of dingy paper, around which it had been twisted. This I now opened, and had the satisfaction to find, recorded by the old Surveyor's pen, a reasonably complete explanation of the whole affair. There were several foolscap sheets, containing many particulars respecting the life and conversation of one Hester Prynne, who appeared to have been rather a noteworthy personage in the view of our ancestors. She had flourished during the period between the early days of Massachusetts and the close of the seventeenth century. Aged persons, alive in the time of Mr. Surveyor Pue, and from whose oral testimony he had made up his narrative, remembered her, in their youth, as a very old, but not decrepit woman, of a stately and solemn aspect. It had been her habit, from an almost immemorial date, to go about the country as a kind of voluntary nurse, and doing whatever miscellaneous good she might; taking upon herself, likewise, to give advice in all matters, especially those of the heart; by which means, as a person of such propensities inevitably must, she gained from many people the reverence due to an angel, but I should imagine, was looked upon by others as an intruder and a nuisance. Prying further into the manu-

script, I found the record of other doings and sufferings of this singular woman, for most of which the reader is referred to the story entitled, "THE SCARLET LETTER"; and it should be borne carefully in mind, that the main facts of that story are authorized and authenticated by the document of Mr. Surveyor Pue. The original papers, together with the scarlet letter itself,—a most curious relic, —are still in my possession, and shall be freely exhibited to whomsoever, induced by the great interest of the narrative, may desire a sight of them. I must not be understood as affirming, that, in the dressing up of the tale, and imagining the motives and modes of passion that influenced the characters who figure in it, I have invariably confined myself within the limits of the old Surveyor's half a dozen sheets of foolscap. On the contrary, I have allowed myself, as to such points, nearly or altogether as much license as if the facts had been entirely of my own invention. What I contend for is the authenticity of the outline.

This incident recalled my mind, in some degree, to its old track. There seemed to be here the ground-work of a tale. It impressed me as if the ancient Surveyor, in his garb of a hundred years gone by, and wearing his immortal wig,—which was buried with him, but did not perish in the grave,—had met me in the deserted chamber of the Custom House. In his port was the dignity of one who had borne his Majesty's commission, and who was therefore illuminated by a ray of the splendor that shone so dazzlingly about the throne. How unlike, alas! the hang-dog look of a republican official, who, as the servant of the people, feels himself less than the least, and below the lowest, of his masters. With his own ghostly hand, the obscurely seen but majestic figure had imparted to me the scarlet symbol, and the little roll of explanatory manuscript. With his own ghostly voice, he had exhorted me, on the sacred consideration of my filial duty and reverence towards him,—who might reasonably regard himself as my official ancestor,—to bring his mouldy and moth-eaten lucubrations before the public. "Do this," said the ghost of Mr. Surveyor Pue, emphatically nodding the head that looked so imposing within its memorable wig, "do this, and the profit shall be all your own! You will shortly need it; for it is not in your days as it was in mine, when a man's office was a life-lease, and oftentimes an heirloom. But, I charge you, in this matter of old Mistress Prynne, give to your predecessor's memory the credit which will be rightfully due!" And I said to the ghost of Mr. Surveyor Pue, "I will!"

On Hester Prynne's story, therefore, I bestowed much thought. It was the subject of my meditations for many an hour, while pacing to and fro cross my room, or traversing with a hundred-fold repetition, the long extent from the front-door of the Custom House to the side-entrance, and back again. Great were the weariness and annoyance of the old Inspector and the Weighers and Gaugers, whose slumbers were disturbed by the unmercifully lengthened tramp of my passing and returning footsteps. Remembering their own former habits, they used to say that the Surveyor was walking the quarter-deck. They probably fancied that my sole object—and, indeed, the sole object for which a sane man could ever put himself into voluntary motion—was, to get an appetite for dinner. And to say the truth, an appetite, sharpened by the east wind that generally blew along the passage, was the only valuable result of so much indefatigable exercise. So little adapted is the atmosphere of a Custom House to the delicate harvest of fancy and sensibility, that, had I remained there through ten Presidencies yet to come, I doubt whether the tale of "The Scarlet Letter" would ever have been brought before the public eye. My imagination was a tarnished mirror. It would not reflect, or only with miserable dimness, the figures with which I did my best to people it. The characters of the narrative would not be warmed and rendered malleable by any heat that I could kindle at my intellectual forge. They would take neither the glow of passion nor the tenderness of sentiment, but retained all the rigidity of dead corpses, and stared me in the face with a fixed and ghastly grin of contemptuous defiance. "What have you to do with us?" that expression seemed to say. "The little power you might once have possessed over the tribe of unrealities is gone! You have bartered it for a pittance of the public gold. Go, then, and earn your wages!" In short, the almost torpid creatures of my own fancy twitted me with imbecility, and not without fair occasion.

It was not merely during the three hours and a half which Uncle Sam claimed as his share of my daily life, that this wretched numbness held possession of me. It went with me on my sea-shore walks, and rambles into the country, whenever—which was seldom and reluctantly—I bestirred myself to seek that invigorating charm of Nature, which used to give me such freshness and activity of thought, the moment that I stepped across the threshold of the Old Manse. The same torpor, as regarded the capacity for intellectual effort, accompanied me home, and weighed upon me in the chamber which I most absurdly termed my study. Nor did it quit me, when, late at night, I sat in the deserted parlor, lighted only by the glimmering coal-fire and the moon, striving to picture forth imaginary scenes, which, the next day, might flow out on the brightening page in many-hued description.

If the imaginative faculty refused to act at such an hour, it might well be deemed a hopeless case. Moonlight, in a familiar room, falling so white upon the carpet, and showing all its figures so distinctly,—making every object so minutely visible, yet so unlike a morning or noontide visibility,—is a medium the most suitable for a romance-writer to get acquainted with his illusive guests. There is the little domestic scenery of the well-known apartment; the chairs, with each its separate individuality; the centre-table, sustaining a work-basket, a volume or two, and an extinguished lamp; the sofa; the book-case; the picture on the wall;—all these details, so completely seen, are so spiritualized by the unusual light, that they seem to lose their actual substance, and become things of intellect. Nothing is too small or too trifling to undergo this change, and acquire dignity thereby. A child's shoe; the doll, seated in her little wicker carriage; the hobby-horse;—whatever, in a word, has been used or played with, during the day, is now invested with a quality of strangeness and remoteness, though still almost as vividly present as by daylight. Thus, therefore, the floor of our familiar room has become a neutral territory, somewhere between the real world and fairy-land, where the Actual and the Imaginary may meet, and each imbue itself with the nature of the other. Ghosts might enter here, without affrighting us. It would be too much in keeping with the scene to excite surprise, were we to look about us and discover a form beloved, but gone hence, now sitting quietly in a streak of this magic moonshine, with an aspect that would make us doubt whether it had returned from afar, or had never once stirred from our fireside.

The somewhat dim coal-fire has an essential influence in producing the effect which I would describe. It throws its unobtrusive tinge throughout the room, with a faint ruddiness upon the walls and ceiling, and a reflected gleam from the polish of the furniture. This warmer light mingles itself with the cold spirituality of the moonbeams, and communicates, as it were, a heart and sensibilities of human tenderness to the forms which fancy summons up. It converts them from snow-images into men and women. Glancing at the looking-glass, we behold—deep within its haunted verge—the smouldering glow of the half-extinguished anthracite, the white moonbeams on the floor, and a repetition of all the gleam and shadow of the picture, with one remove further from the actual, and nearer to the imaginative. Then, at such an hour, and with this scene before him, if a man, sitting all alone, cannot dream strange things, and make them look like truth, he need never try to write romances.

But, for myself, during the whole of my Custom House experience, moonlight and sunshine, and the glow of fire-light, were just alike in my regard; and neither of them was of one whit more avail than the twinkle of a tallow-candle. An entire class of susceptibilities, and a gift connected with them, —of no great richness or value, but the best I had, —was gone from me.

It is my belief, however, that, had I attempted a different order of composition, my faculties would not have been found so pointless and inefficacious. I might, for instance, have contented myself with writing out the narratives of a veteran shipmaster, one of the Inspectors, whom I should be most ungrateful not to mention, since scarcely a day passed that he did not stir me to laughter and admiration by his marvellous gifts as a story-teller. Could I have preserved the picturesque force of his style, and the humorous coloring which nature taught him how to throw over his descriptions, the result, I honestly believe, would have been something new in literature. Or I might readily have found a more serious task. It was a folly, with the materiality of this daily life pressing so intrusively upon me, to attempt to fling myself back into another age; or to insist on creating the semblance of a world out of airy matter, when, at every moment, the impalpable beauty of my soap-bubble was broken by the rude contact of some actual circumstance. The wiser effort would have been to diffuse thought and imagination through the opaque substance of to-day, and thus to make it a bright transparency; to spiritualize the burden that began to weigh so heavily; to seek, resolutely, the true and indestructible value that lay hidden in the petty and wearisome incidents, and ordinary characters, with which I was now conversant. The fault was mine. The page of life that was spread out before me seemed dull and commonplace, only because I had not fathomed its deeper import. A better book than I shall ever write was there; leaf after leaf presenting itself to me, just as it was written out by the reality of the flitting hour, and vanishing as fast as written, only because my brain wanted the insight and my hand the cunning to transcribe it. At some future day, it may be, I shall remember a few scattered fragments and broken paragraphs, and write them down, and find the letters turn to gold upon the page. . . .

. . . The life of the Custom House lies like a dream behind me. The old Inspector,—who, by the by, I regret to say, was overthrown and killed by a horse, some time ago; else he would certainly have lived forever,—he, and all those other venerable personages who sat with him at the receipt of custom, are but shadows in my view; white-headed and wrinkled images, which my fancy used to sport with, and has now flung aside forever. The merchants,—Pingree, Phillips, Shepard, Upton, Kimball, Bertram, Hunt,—these, and many other names, which had such a classic familiarity for my ear six months ago,—these men of traffic, who seemed to occupy so important a position in the world,—how little time has it required to disconnect me from them all, not merely in act, but recollection! It is with an effort that I recall the figures and appellations of these few. Soon, likewise, my old native town will loom upon me through the haze of memory, a mist brooding over and around it; as if it were no portion of the real earth, but an overgrown village in cloud-land, with only imaginary inhabitants to people its wooden houses, and walk its homely lanes, and the unpicturesque prolixity of its main street. Henceforth, it ceases to be a reality of my life. I am a citizen of somewhere else. My good townspeople will not much regret me; for—though it has been as dear an object as any, in my literary efforts, to be of some importance in their eyes, and to win myself a pleasant memory in this abode and burial-place of so many of my forefathers—there has never been, for me, the genial atmosphere which a literary man requires, in order to ripen the best harvest of his mind. I shall do better amongst other faces; and these familiar ones, it need hardly be said, will do just as well without me. . . .

*1850*

---

# PREFACE TO TWICE-TOLD TALES, 1851 EDITION

---

THE AUTHOR of "TWICE-TOLD TALES" has a claim to one distinction, which, as none of his literary brethren will care about disputing it with him, he need not be afraid to mention. He was, for a good many years, the obscurest man of letters in America.

These stories were published in magazines and annuals, extending over a period of ten or twelve years, and comprising the whole of the writer's young manhood, without making (so far as he has ever been aware) the slightest impression on the public. One or two among them, the "Rill from the Town Pump," in perhaps a greater degree than any other, had a pretty wide newspaper circulation; as for the rest, he had no grounds for supposing that, on their first appearance, they met with the good or evil fortune to be read by anybody. Throughout the time above specified, he had no incitement to literary effort in a reasonable prospect of reputation or profit, nothing but the pleasure itself of composition—an enjoyment not at all amiss in its way, and perhaps essential to the merit of the work in hand, but which, in the long run, will hardly keep the chill out of a writer's heart, or the numbness out of his fingers. To this total lack of sympathy, at the age when his mind would naturally have been most effervescent, the public owe it (and it is certainly an effect not to be regretted on either part) that the Author can show nothing for the thought and industry of that portion of his life, save the forty sketches, or thereabouts, included in these volumes.

Much more, indeed, he wrote; and some very small part of it might yet be rummaged out (but it would not be worth the trouble) among the dingy pages of fifteen-or-twenty-year-old periodicals, or within the shabby morocco covers of faded souvenirs. The remainder of the works alluded to had a very brief existence, but, on the score of brilliancy, enjoyed a fate vastly superior to that of their brotherhood, which succeeded in getting through the press. In a word, the Author burned them without mercy or remorse, and, moreover, without any subsequent regret, and had more than one occasion to marvel that such very dull stuff, as he knew his condemned manuscripts to be, should yet have possessed inflammability enough to set the chimney on fire!

After a long while the first collected volume of the "Tales" was published. By this time, if the Author had ever been greatly tormented by literary ambition (which he does not remember or believe to have been the case), it must have perished, beyond resuscitation, in the dearth of nutriment. This was fortunate; for the success of the volume was not such as would have gratified a craving desire for notoriety. A moderate edition was "got rid of" (to use the publisher's very significant phrase) within a reasonable time, but apparently without rendering the writer or his productions much more generally known than before. The great bulk of the reading public probably ignored the book altogether. A few persons read it, and liked it better than it deserved. At an interval of three or four years, the second volume was published, and encountered much the same sort of kindly, but calm, and very

limited reception. The circulation of the two volumes was chiefly confined to New England; nor was it until long after this period, if it even yet be the case, that the Author could regard himself as addressing the American public, or, indeed, any public at all. He was merely writing to his known or unknown friends.

As he glances over these long-forgotten pages, and considers his way of life while composing them, the Author can very clearly discern why all this was so. After so many sober years, he would have reason to be ashamed if he could not criticise his own work as fairly as another man's; and, though it is little his business, and perhaps still less his interest, he can hardly resist a temptation to achieve something of the sort. If writers were allowed to do so, and would perform the task with perfect sincerity and unreserve, their opinions of their own productions would often be more valuable and instructive than the works themselves.

At all events, there can be no harm in the Author's remarking, that he rather wonders how the "TWICE-TOLD TALES" should have gained what vogue they did, than that it was so little and so gradual. They have the pale tint of flowers that blossomed in too retired a shade—the coolness of a meditative habit, which diffuses itself through the feeling and observation of every sketch. Instead of passion, there is sentiment; and, even in what purport to be pictures of actual life, we have allegory, not always so warmly dressed in its habiliments of flesh and blood, as to be taken into the reader's mind without a shiver. Whether from lack of power, or an unconquerable reserve, the Author's touches have often an effect of tameness; the merriest man can hardly contrive to laugh at his broadest humor; the tenderest woman, one would suppose, will hardly shed warm tears at his deepest pathos. The book, if you would see any thing in it, requires to be read in the clear, brown, twilight atmosphere in which it was written; if opened in the sunshine, it is apt to look exceedingly like a volume of blank pages.

With the foregoing characteristics, proper to the productions of a person in retirement, (which happened to be the Author's category at the time,) the book is devoid of others that we should quite as naturally look for. The sketches are not, it is hardly necessary to say, profound; but it is rather more remarkable that they so seldom, if ever, show any design on the writer's part to make them so. They have none of the abstruseness of idea, or obscurity of expression, which mark the written communications of a solitary mind with itself. They never need translation. It is, in fact, the style of a man of society. Every sentence, so far as it embodies thought or sensibility, may be understood and felt by anybody, who will give himself the trouble to read it, and will take up the book in a proper mood.

This statement of apparently opposite peculiarities leads us to a perception of what the sketches truly are. They are not the talk of a secluded man with his own mind and heart (had it been so, they could hardly have failed to be more deeply and permanently valuable), but his attempts, and very imperfectly successful ones, to open an intercourse with the world.

The Author would regret to be understood as speaking sourly or querulously of the slight mark made by his earlier literary efforts on the Public at large. It is so far the contrary, that he has been moved to write this Preface chiefly as affording him an opportunity to express how much enjoyment he has owed to these volumes, both before and since their publication. They are the memorials of very tranquil and not unhappy years. They failed, it is true,—nor could it have been otherwise,—in winning an extensive popularity. Occasionally, however, when he deemed them entirely forgotten, a paragraph or an article, from a native or foreign critic, would gratify his instincts of authorship with unexpected praise,—too generous praise, indeed, and too little alloyed with censure, which, therefore, he learned the better to inflict upon himself. And, by the by, it is a very suspicious symptom of a deficiency of the popular element in a book when it calls forth no harsh criticism. This has been particularly the fortune of the "TWICE-TOLD TALES." They made no enemies, and were so little known and talked about that those who read, and chanced to like them, were apt to conceive the sort of kindness for the book which a person naturally feels for a discovery of his own.

This kindly feeling (in some cases, at least) extended to the Author, who, on the internal evidence of his sketches, came to be regarded as a mild, shy, gentle, melancholic, exceedingly sensitive, and not very forcible man, hiding his blushes under an assumed name, the quaintness of which was supposed, somehow or other, to symbolize his personal and literary traits. He is by no means certain that some of his subsequent productions have not been influenced and modified by a natural desire to fill up so amiable an outline, and to act in consonance with the character assigned to him; nor, even now, could he forfeit it without a few tears of tender sensibility. To conclude, however: these volumes have opened the way to most agreeable associations, and to the formation of imperishable friendships; and there are many golden threads interwoven with his present happiness,

which he can follow up more or less directly, until he finds their commencement here; so that his pleasant pathway among realities seems to proceed out of the Dreamland of his youth, and to be bordered with just enough of its shadowy foliage to shelter him from the heat of the day. He is therefore satisfied with what the "TWICE-TOLD TALES" have done for him, and feels it to be far better than fame.

# PREFACE TO THE HOUSE OF THE SEVEN GABLES

WHEN a writer calls his work a Romance, it need hardly be observed that he wishes to claim a certain latitude, both as to its fashion and material, which he would not have felt himself entitled to assume, had he professed to be writing a Novel. The latter form of composition is presumed to aim at a very minute fidelity, not merely to the possible, but to the probable and ordinary course of man's experience. The former—while, as a work of art, it must rigidly subject itself to laws, and while it sins unpardonably so far as it may swerve aside from the truth of the human heart—has fairly a right to present that truth under circumstances, to a great extent, of the writer's own choosing or creation. If he thinks fit, also, he may so manage his atmospherical medium as to bring out or mellow the lights, and deepen and enrich the shadows, of the picture. He will be wise, no doubt, to make a very moderate use of the privileges here stated, and, especially, to mingle the Marvelous rather as a slight, delicate, and evanescent flavor, than as any portion of the actual substance of the dish offered to the public. He can hardly be said, however, to commit a literary crime, even if he disregard this caution.

In the present work the author has proposed to himself—but with what success, fortunately, it is not for him to judge—to keep undeviatingly within his immunities. The point of view in which this tale comes under the Romantic definition lies in the attempt to connect a bygone time with the very present that is flitting away from us. It is a legend, prolonging itself, from an epoch now gray in the distance down into our own broad daylight, and bringing along with it some of its legendary mist, which the reader, according to his pleasure, may either disregard or allow it to float almost imperceptibly about the characters and events for the sake of a picturesque effect. The narrative, it may be, is woven of so humble a texture as to require this advantage, and, at the same time, to render it the more difficult of attainment.

Many writers lay very great stress upon some definite moral purpose, at which they profess to aim their works. Not to be deficient in this particular, the author has provided himself with a moral; —the truth, namely, that the wrongdoing of one generation lives into the successive ones, and, divesting itself of every temporary advantage, becomes a pure and uncontrollable mischief,—and he would feel it a singular gratification, if this romance might effectually convince mankind—or, indeed, any one man—of the folly of tumbling down an avalanche of ill-gotten gold, or real estate, on the heads of an unfortunate posterity, thereby to maim and crush them, until the accumulated mass shall be scattered abroad in its original atoms. In good faith, however, he is not sufficiently imaginative to flatter himself with the slightest hope of this kind. When romances do really teach anything, or produce any effective operation, it is usually through a far more subtle process than the ostensible one. The author has considered it hardly worth his while, therefore, relentlessly to impale the story with its moral, as with an iron rod,—or, rather, as by sticking a pin through a butterfly,—thus at once depriving it of life, and causing it to stiffen in an ungainly and unnatural attitude. A high truth, indeed, fairly, finely, and skilfully wrought out, brightening at every step, and crowning the final development of a work of fiction, may add an artistic glory, but is never any truer, and seldom any more evident, at the last page than at the first.

The reader may perhaps choose to assign an actual locality to the imaginary events of this narrative. If permitted by the historical connection, —which, though slight, was essential to his plan,— the author would very willingly have avoided anything of this nature. Not to speak of other objections, it exposes the romance to an inflexible and exceedingly dangerous species of criticism, by bringing his fancy-pictures almost into positive contact with the realities of the moment. It has been no part of his object, however, to describe local manners, nor in any way to meddle with the characteristics of a community for whom he cherishes a proper respect and a natural regard. He trusts not to be considered as unpardonably offending, by laying out a street that infringes upon nobody's private rights, and appropriating a lot of land which had no visible owner, and building a house, of materials long in use for constructing castles in the air. The personages of the tale— though they give themselves out to be of ancient stability and considerable prominence—are really of the author's own making, or, at all events, of his own mixing; their virtues can shed no luster, nor their defects redound, in the remotest degree, to the discredit of the venerable town of which they profess to be inhabitants. He would be glad, therefore, if—especially in the quarter to which he alludes—the book may be read strictly as a romance, having a great deal more to do with the clouds overhead than with any portion of the actual soil of the County of Essex.

*1851*

WILLIAM CHARVAT
*Editor*

# Henry Wadsworth Longfellow

1807–1882

# James Russell Lowell

1819–1891

## Henry Wadsworth Longfellow

THE TERM "Fireside Poets" accurately describes a group of writers who were well known in New England in the 1840's, acquired a national audience after 1850, and were of unrivaled popularity in the quarter-century before World War I. The best-known members of the group were Henry Wadsworth Longfellow, James Russell Lowell, Oliver Wendell Holmes, John Greenleaf Whittier, and William Cullen Bryant. All were native New Englanders; indeed, all except Bryant lived in the adjacent communities of Cambridge and Boston.

The word "fireside" indicates that they had a family audience—men, women, and children. It also implies that their verse was read aloud in the family circle. Their books were published in a variety of formats—from paperback to expensive, illustrated editions —at prices to suit every pocketbook. One or another of these editions was owned by most northern, western, and some southern Americans who bought and read books.

In our time, there is no equivalent to this group of poets. The verse-reading audience is now so stratified that there is no common bond between those who buy Eliot, Pound, and Stevens, and those who prefer Edgar Guest, James Whitcomb Riley, or the amateur verse which appears in the Sunday edition of the local newspaper. The Fireside Poets, by contrast, were read alike by the highly educated and by some of the merely literate, though much of their work was beyond the comprehension of the latter.

It is to be expected that, writing for an audience both culturally mixed and family-centered, these poets emphasized certain subjects and avoided others. Their favorite themes were home, family, and children; nature; idealized love; religion—Protestant, but usually nondenominational; love of country, but rarely partisan politics; and they versified much story from history, legend, and anecdote, both native and foreign.

Their view of life can be described superficially by the soft term—common in nineteenth-century popular literature—"sunshine and shadow," which implies a balance of good and bad in human experience. The emphasis, one way or the other, varies somewhat from poet to poet. All had been taught to believe, through their heritage of eighteenth-century rationalism, that in the divine plan, apparent evil was part of a total good. But Longfellow and Bryant, influenced by Puritanism or current Romantic attitudes, tended to put their fingers on the somber side of the scales. Balance is suggested in Longfellow's work by the recurrence of pairs of verbal opposites—sorrow-delight, toil-rest, soothe-affright.

> Our little lives are kept in equipoise
> By opposite attractions and desires

he wrote in "Haunted Houses." Yet a careful reading of even his supposedly optimistic—and worst—poems shows that though he believed in balance, he did not feel it. The village blacksmith at work looks picturesque to the children, and he begins and finishes something each day, but we get the impression that he toils and sorrows more than he rejoices. In "The Wreck of the Hesperus," the captain's will to act is favorably presented, but it leads to nothing but pointless sacrifice of life. "A Psalm of Life," in which we are told to "Trust no Future" and to "Learn to labor and to wait," is anything but a cheerful poem.

Longfellow's basic lessons, then, are austere ones. We are to work for work's own sake. We are to *accept* life's labors, deprivals, and sorrows. The reward is rest, and rest ultimately means death. The terror of death is mitigated by a serene but not very insistent assumption of immortality.

It is to be expected that, their audience being what it was, these poets should have certain forms and techniques in common. Their rhythms, though often skillfully varied, derive from traditional meters; their stanzas follow formal patterns; they favor either blank verse or conventional end-rhymes (rather than, for example, the elusive internal recurrences of sound one finds in Emily Dickinson and Walt Whitman); their language is traditional—their English, usually British. They use inversions, and archaisms like "Thou see'st." Their images and metaphors are simple and familiar. Their symbolism is explicit, and their meanings and "lessons" are on the surface. The experienced reader of verse rarely has to read one

of their poems twice to comprehend all that is in it.

All these writers used poetry as a vehicle for teaching. Most good poetry teaches in one way or another; the way the Fireside Poets had in common was that of explicit analogy. Some object or phenomenon in nature or some action is presented; an analogy with the human condition is then drawn; and usually—but not always—the meaning or moral of the analogy is explicitly stated.

This is not to say that all their verse is easy for the common reader of our own time. They were not "mass" poets in any sense of the word: the Edgar Guest fan would be puzzled by much of what they wrote, for they made demands on their audience as mass literature today does not. Their many allusions show that they expected readers to have some knowledge of classical myth, of European and American history and legend, of the story of Christianity and other religions, and of the Bible. They assumed, also, that readers had enough knowledge of formal grammar to be able to follow an extended syntactical structure, and to locate the remote antecedent of a pronoun. Some of them used foreign words and phrases without building in translations. And they were not afraid of what are now considered "big words." In short, the merely literate reader of today must use dictionaries, guides to mythology, gazetteers, and other tools in order to understand fully what the Fireside Poets are saying.

As "public" poets they had, of course, an advantage that has since diminished. Education in their time was relatively fixed and formalized. The very considerable number of readers who attended the academies, the denominational colleges, and even the better common schools were likely to get some training in rhetoric, in Latin or French, and in moral philosophy, and to read some of the famous British classics—the work of Shakespeare, Milton, Pope, and John Bunyan. In other words, the poets could assume a far more homogeneous experience in literature and language in their readers than can be expected now.

Finally, they shared a belief or hope held

by most serious American writers of the century that it was possible, in Poe's phrase, "to suit at once the popular and the critical taste." From Poe and Emerson to Howells and the early Henry James, there was a general faith, often shaken but rarely wholly abandoned, that in a democracy writers could offer their best with some hope that even the culturally unsophisticated would accept them and support them sufficiently to make the literary life possible in America. Believing that the common reader was willing to exert himself, they did not resign themselves completely to his limitations. Moreover, all serious writers were conscious of belonging to the tradition—to the institution—of great Western literature, and made their readers aware that that tradition was being continued in America. In this respect, the Fireside Poets made a significant contribution. Much of their verse and prose is *about* the great writers of the past, and reading the work of the Poets was for their readers a kind of instruction in the history of literature.

## II

ONE of the remarkable facts about this group is that though they appealed to literate people of every social class, they themselves—with one exception, Whittier—were members of the social elite—of what might be called the patrician level in the American social scale. None of them was independently wealthy, but they came from families whose names carried prestige, for whom a college education and membership in a respected profession were matters of course, and to whom public service of some sort—in the courts, churches, legislatures, and in the military during the Revolutionary War—was a source of pride. In a word, they "belonged"—had a sense of place in the social structure and in the American past. Perhaps partly for that reason they could attempt the risky profession of literature with a confidence that was denied to, say, an Edgar Allan Poe. In this democracy there was still a good deal of respect for the "high-born"—especially if the high-born earned their keep by achieving some sort of profes-

sional or public distinction. Everyone knew that Longfellow was a professor and a learned man, that he lived in a mansion, and that after his marriage to the daughter of Nathan Appleton he was increasingly well-to-do, but few readers resented his status. Though Holmes said that some people thought his verse writing impugned his ability as a physician, most of his readers were happy to think of him as Doctor Holmes of Boston. And Bryant lost no prestige as poet by being editor of a great New York newspaper and a translator of Greek classics.

Although Longfellow's immediate family was anything but rich, he was from the beginning exempt from the poverty and the galling sense of social inferiority which, long before Shakespeare's time, had exacerbated writers of humble origin who lived in cultures dominated by a hereditary or landed aristocracy. Longfellow's paternal grandfather was a state senator; his maternal grandfather was a Revolutionary general, a representative to Congress from Maine, and had a ten-thousand-acre estate which the boy often visited. His father was a Harvard graduate and a lawmaker for both his state and the nation. A boy from such a background knew that some sort of public service and leadership was expected of him, and although he had had literary ambitions even as a schoolchild, he dutifully considered entering the law or the ministry, the professions with which a literary career was usually combined. When he was seventeen (1824) his father wisely warned him that "there is not wealth enough in this country to afford encouragement to merely literary men. And as you have not had the fortune (I will not say whether good or ill) to be born rich, you must adopt a profession which will afford you subsistence as well as reputation. . . ." Here was the tough New England attitude which required that the ambition to *be* somebody in terms not primarily materialistic be based solidly on the ability to make one's own living by work. When Longfellow's alma mater, Bowdoin Coolege, offered him its first professorship in modern languages, he found his solution: at the age of twenty-two he became the first American poet who supported his craft for any considerable length of time by being a teacher and scholar. Since about 1945 this arrangement has been common: most of our poets get employment in the universities.

Longfellow took his teaching seriously and for many years he put his major energies into academic chores. Essential to the spirit of his writings is the fact that, with no expectation of eventually inheriting wealth, he early assumed that his place was with the vast majority of the human race who must work for a living. As a teacher of foreign languages at Bowdoin (1829–34) and Harvard (1836–54), where much of his time was devoted to irksome elementary drilling, he knew the salaried worker's frustrations and dissatisfactions. Yet after his marriage into the affluent Appleton family, he continued to teach for eleven years. He left Harvard only when his reputation as a poet had become so firmly established that he knew he could earn at least a subsistence for himself through the hard work of writing poetry. Financially, what his marriage meant to him chiefly was that he need not give in to the pressures—which intensified as the century advanced—of publishers and of popular taste.

Essential also to the impact of his verse in his time was his passion for European culture. After his first sojourn abroad (1826–29) he was competent to write the foreign language textbooks he needed at Bowdoin, but he also prepared materials for an imitation of Irving's *Sketch Book*. *Outre-Mer* (1833–35) was the first of three semifictional, essay-structured prose works, all set in Europe, which in their time were as popular as his verse. *Hyperion* (1839) was the disguised autobiographical statement of an American teacher traveling in Europe who was making up his mind to be a professional poet in a culture which had hitherto not supported its poets. Glowing accounts of Europe's historic shrines, and long dialogues about European literature and art suggest that, consciously or not, Longfellow was planning to make his literary life an extension of a long tradition.

For the rest of his career he was to find much of his poetic subject matter in European history, legend, art, and scenery. In the twentieth century he has been much criticized for not being more native, more contemporary in his interests. But there has been increasing recognition that in bringing to Americans the culture of Europe, in the form of translations and adaptations of its poetry, and in celebrating Old World history and story, he did much to mitigate the provincialism which, from the beginning to our own times, has narrowed and shallowed the American character. He softened much that he imported, but he made his readers aware not only of the grandeur and beauty but of some of the terror in their European heritage. If he sentimentalized Europe, as some critics have said, there are fewer quaint villages and carillons in his foreign settings than there are bloody battles, bigotry, wretched serfs, murders, and hovering menaces to life and liberty.

Longfellow has also been accused of being incapable of sympathy for the common man, yet he was deeply involved in a movement in the 1840's toward a literature about and for the common people. Orestes Brownson, a representative spokesman of the time, wrote that American "scholars"—there was a general assumption then that men of letters were also men of learning—must abandon their "lone reveries" and their "scholastic asceticism," and seek their inspiration in the "really living, moving, toiling and sweating, joying and sorrowing people around them." Longfellow had had his years of lonely reveries and scholastic asceticism, but from 1839 on, his writings were informed by an awareness of the people and he wished to reach the people as well as the cultured classes. In 1840 this scholarly gentleman of Cambridge wrote that he wanted to "work upon people's feelings" and that he contemplated printing "The Wreck of the Hesperus" on a broadside sheet "with a coarse picture on it." He did not do so, but for years thereafter some of his work was published in our earliest mass magazines, and his verse was available in paperback editions selling for twelve and a half and fifty cents. The poet who could write about the

> weight of care,
> That crushes into dumb despair,

> One half the human race . . .
> Steeped to the lips in misery,
> Longing, and yet afraid to die

knew quite as well as Thoreau that the "mass of men lead lives of quiet desperation." The emotional weights in his vocabulary become obvious to one who reads enough of him. The endlessly reiterated words are "care," "weariness," "sorrow," "burden," "fear," "toil," and "defeat" — often in description of a man's work and a man's family. If, along with such words, we find a recurrence of others like "comfort," "balm," "cheer," and "soothe," it is because he felt that the need for comfort was great. But the comfort he offered was not delusive.

In 1839 he had said that the American artist "must wait." By 1850, in the "Dedication" to *The Seaside and the Fireside*, he could with confidence address his audience as "friends" and hope

> as no unwelcome guest,
> At your warm fireside, when the lamps are
>     lighted.
> To have my place reserved among the rest,
> Nor stand as one unsought and uninvited!

This confidence was, in part, a result of the enthusiastic reception given to his first long poem, *Evangeline* (1847). Thereafter, long narratives in verse or dramatic form constituted the bulk of his writings. This fact brings up the problem of the long poem in modern literature. The epic had once been the poetic form in which the life of a whole nation or culture could be subsumed, but, after Milton, secular and religious cultures lost the homogeneity which made a *Paradise Lost* possible. Yet many nineteenth-century poets were not content to write lyrics only, and sought to create forms capable of carrying the weight of subjects of some magnitude. Increasingly, poets from Byron to Ezra Pound radically changed the tradition of the long poem by making it an exploration of the poet's self, Whitman's final version of *Leaves of Grass* being America's finest example. Longfellow and his imitators, however, attempted to continue the older tradition in poems about the lives of ethnic or religious

or regional groups. *Evangeline* is the story of exiled Canadian villagers, *Hiawatha* (1855) of the myths of a group of Indian tribes, *The Courtship of Miles Standish* (1858) of a New England community. In *Tales of a Wayside Inn* (1863) he used Chaucerian devices to put twenty-two shorter tales, mostly about ancient Europe, into a framework resembling that of the *Canterbury Tales*.

Most of these pieces, however short or long, are in the anecdotal rather than in the epic strain. When, in his magnum opus — the three part verse drama, *Christus: A Mystery* (1872) — he attempted epic magnitude and unity, he failed.

The *Christus* was a failure not only as a work of the intellect but as a work of art; yet its very weakness as art reveals the source of Longfellow's overall success as a popular poet. Longfellow thought and felt in terms of parts rather than organically unified wholes. In 1849 he recorded in his journal his hope that his "broken melodies" would "unite themselves into a symphony not all unworthy [of] the sublime theme" of the *Christus*. Equally suggestive is his often repeated image of the poet as a builder, surrounded by blocks and yearning to build a tower with them. In *Michael Angelo*, his last long dramatic narrative — and one with moments of greatness in it — he described what he had been doing all his life:

> Men build their houses from the masonry
>     Of ruined tombs;
> So from old chronicles, where sleep in dust
>     Names that once filled the world with trumpet
>     tones,
> I build this verse; and flowers of song have thrust
> Their roots among the loose disjointed stones,
>     Which to this end I fashion as I must.
> Quickened are those who touch the Prophet's
>     bones.

Of course, "loose disjointed stones" no more unite themselves into a house or tower than melodies unite themselves into a symphony. We need not accept too literally Longfellow's modest implication that all he had to offer, in spite of his aspirations, was stones and flowers and melodies, but it is likely that his world-wide audience admired these rather than his attempts at symphonies and towers.

The quoted passage bears an interesting resemblance to Eliot's line near the end of *The Waste Land*, "These fragments I have shored against my ruins." Longfellow sensed what subsequent history made much clearer for Eliot forty years later: that modern man must search among the ruins of the past for the order and meaning that were going out of life even before the older poet died. Rome, says his Michael Angelo, is a

> malaria of the mind,
> Out of this tomb of the majestic Past;
> The fever to accomplish some great work
> That will not let us sleep.

He repaid his debt to Europe by writing verse that was as eagerly read abroad as in America: there were at least seven hundred translations of his work into twenty-four languages. In England, where his poetry was as popular as Tennyson's, he was given honorary degrees by Oxford and Cambridge, and he was the first American whose bust was placed in the Poet's Corner of Westminster Abbey.

# James Russell Lowell

Among the Fireside Poets, Lowell was the most versatile, the most erudite, the least popular, and in the broad terms of literary statesmanship, the most influential. His claim to membership in the group was based on a very few well-known poems, and on the fact that the publishers of the group, Ticknor & Fields, bracketed him with the others and printed his work in editions uniform with theirs. This is not to say that he was not widely known and respected by people who never read him, or that he did not earn such reputation as he achieved; rather, that there was much in his work that could not attract a popular audience. His learning was too conspicuous, his approach to life was too bookish, and he spread his many talents so thin that he never became really famous for any of them, except for his mastery of Yankee

dialect in *The Biglow Papers* and for the charm, wit, and journalistic intimacy of his portraits of contemporaries in *A Fable for Critics*.

His background, and in some respects his career, were much like Longfellow's. His name was ancient and respected. His forebears went to Harvard, entered the law or ministry, and rendered public service. One branch of the family became rich in industry and commerce, but not the poet's. His father was a Harvard-educated Boston minister who bought a historic house, later called Elmwood; in this house Lowell was born and died. After Harvard ('38) from which he was once suspended for cutting classes, he studied law—because that was what was expected of him—but never practiced it. Instead he combined the literary life with humanitarian activities, mostly in the cause of abolition. But although he contributed much to antislavery periodicals in the 1840's, it is generally agreed that his interest in reform was inspired not by any deep-rooted radicalism of his own, but by the enthusiasms of the gentle bluestocking, Maria White, whom he met in 1839 and married in 1843. Even before she died in 1853, he had lost interest in radical politics, though not in liberal principles.

Yet it was during his years with her that he wrote his most popular and enduring works. In an extraordinary burst of creative energy, he published in a single year, 1848, *A Fable for Critics*, the First Series of *The Biglow Papers*, and *The Vision of Sir Launfal*, as well as the first large collection of his lyrics. Exhilarated by critical recognition of his ability and versatility, he began planning a series of linked verse tales ("The Nooning") in the tradition of the *Canterbury Tales* and similar to Longfellow's later and successful *Tales of a Wayside Inn*. A few parts of it, including "Fitz Adam's Story," were printed but he never got very far with the project, perhaps fortunately, for he had little talent for sustained narrative.

Once he had passed through his radical period, his intellectual kinship with Longfellow became evident. Geographically, their horizons were the same—at once narrow and broad. Both were villagers deeply attached to the small town of Cambridge and to their historic homes, Elmwood and Craigie House. Neither had any interest in or liking for the West or the great growing cities of the coast and of the Mississippi River basin. Like most of the American people in mid-century they were phychologically and intellectually agrarian—which is one reason why they became Household Poets.

On the other hand, both were dedicated to Harvard, the institution which was our greatest center for European studies. Both were enthusiastic European travelers: in 1851 Lowell made the first of his eight sojourns abroad, some of them prolonged. In his mind there was a vital similarity between the Cambridge of his boyhood and what survived of Old Europe. Cambridge had been "essentially an English village, quiet, unspeculative, without enterprise, sufficing to itself." Harvard had "in its intellectual atmosphere a repose which recalls that of grand old Oxford." Continuing in his nostalgic "Cambridge Thirty Years Ago"—written in 1854 and addressed to a friend in Italy—he sees his boyhood community almost as an English hamlet:

Thirty years ago, the town had indeed a character. Railways and omnibuses had not rolled flat all little social prominences and peculiarities, making every man as much a citizen everywhere as at home. . . . The penny newspaper had not yet silenced the tripod of the barber, oracle of news. Everybody knew everybody, and all about everybody, and village wit, whose high 'change was around the little market-house in the town square, had labelled every more marked individuality with nicknames that clung like burs. Things were established then, and men did not run through all the figures on the dial of society so swiftly as now, when hurry and competition seem to have quite unhung the modulating pendulum of steady thrift and competent training. Some slow-minded persons even followed their father's trade,—a humiliating spectacle, rarer every day. We had our established loafers, topers, proverb-mongers, barber, parson, nay, postmaster, whose tenure was for life. The great political machine did not then come down at regular quadrennial intervals, like a nail-cutting machine, to make all official lives of a standard length, and to generate lazy and intriguing expectancy. Life flowed in recognized channels—narrower, perhaps, but with all the more individuality and force.

No reader need be taken in by the obvious ironies in this passage. It celebrates the individual, but only as part of a community; it celebrates "the established," the "recognized channel"; and it deplores Jacksonian democracy, which was destroying the old order.

The death of his first wife in 1853, long and grievously anticipated, brought a hitherto lacking focus into his intellectual and professional life. He had had from college days a deep and personal interest in the history of English literature (in 1844 he had published a work entitled *Conversations on Some of the Old Poets*), and he now returned with relief to his earlier studies. His new career began when a cousin, who was a trustee of the Lowell Institute, asked him to make use of his knowledge in a series of twelve lectures, given in 1854–55. These, ranging from the Old English ballads to Wordsworth, so impressed his Boston audience that he was appointed Longfellow's successor as Smith Professor of French and Spanish Languages and Literatures and Professor of Belles Lettres at Harvard University. The contrast of the two careers from this point on is remarkable. Longfellow, having established himself as a popular poet, resigned from Harvard in 1854, and the next year published one of the most popular of all nineteenth-century poems, *Hiawatha*. Lowell, having enjoyed much critical acclaim, if not popular success, for his works of 1848, took Longfellow's job and never again wrote a poem that had wide appeal.

Lowell had an important part in consolidating the literary prestige of New England, Massachusetts, Boston, Cambridge, and Harvard (the order is reversible). Before 1850 New England's provincial literary culture had little influence on the rest of the country. The region had a high literacy rate and published more books and magazines in ratio to its population than any other section. But it published its writers' works for itself rather than for the country at large. Its readers accepted and respected cultural achievement and leadership; and just as today New England tolerates more eccentricity of character in the private citizen than is permitted elsewhere, so in that day it gave its writers more latitude and freedom than was allowed in other regions. Emerson is a classic case in point. The least comprehensible of all lyceum speakers, he gave two and one-half times as many lectures inside New England as outside, and large local audiences patronized his most difficult lectures even while admitting they did not understand him. In other words, New England early accepted literature as an institution.

By 1850 New England had developed the greatest group of writers in the country and had a publishing house which was eager to put its imprint on all their works, whether popular or not. When, about the same time, railroads made the West accessible, Ticknor & Fields gave its writers national circulation and publicity. Two years after the *Atlantic Monthly* was established (1857), the firm bought it. Lowell was its first editor and started it on its career as the greatest of all American literary magazines. The firm also bought the *North American Review* (1815–1940), our oldest magisterial review, which, when Lowell became its editor in 1864, had an authority out of all proportion to its tiny circulation.

Lowell was a professor at Harvard while he edited these magazines, and naturally looked to New England in general and Harvard in particular for his contributors. This fact opened the *Atlantic* to charges of provincialism, but these are hardly convincing, considering the fact that the New England writers had already been accepted by the country at large. Boston, Cambridge, and Concord had become the true literary if not the publishing center of the United States.

After his appointment at Harvard, Lowell put most of his writing energy into literary and political essays. The political pieces, which were of Republican persuasion and which called for educated, upper-class leadership to stay the downward leveling tendency in our democracy, led to his appointment as minister to Spain (1877–80) by Hayes and minister to England (1880–85) by

Garfield. Far from being mere rewards for services to a political party, these appointments were in harmony with an American tradition—the support of distinguished literary men in the form of federal jobs at home or abroad. And we must not forget those writings of Lowell in the 1850's and 1860's which made the *Atlantic Monthly* a force in the abolition of slavery or the fact that in his "Ode Recited at the Harvard Commemoration" (1865) Lowell was one of the first of our writers to discern the true greatness of Abraham Lincoln.

The critical essays and addresses, which were often by-products of his Harvard lectures, fill five volumes and parts of two others in the collected editions. Ranging from Dante and Chaucer to Wordsworth and Keats, they made him the most influential academic critic in the later nineteenth century. One indication of his influence is that his hostile review of Thoreau's *Letters* in 1865 helped to delay the general acceptance of Thoreau for a generation or more.

His critical work has been the subject of endless controversy, partly because of his innumerable and unresolved internal conflicts between the claims of head and heart, reason and imagination, aristocracy and democracy, classicism and romanticism, humanism and humanitarianism, religion and science. All agree that much of his work is brilliant, scintillating, often generously and persuasively appreciative. It is also evident that he tended to reject the literature of his own century and to seek his values and principles in Dante, Chaucer, and Shakespeare—in other words, that he was uneasy among the multiplying confusions of the nineteenth century, and that he found peace and delight in the literatures of those older European societies whose cultures reflected stable and slowly changing orders in which each individual had his accepted place. Certainly, one of his central convictions was that literature which celebrates the ego of the individual at the expense of the social values which civilize him is unhealthy. This belief is at the center of two essays which are, historically, among the most important he wrote—"Rousseau and the Sentimentalists" (1867) and "Thoreau's Letters" (1865).

Any modern reader who has a taste for good prose can get pleasure and profit from browsing through collections of Lowell's essays. Among the best of the critical are those on Dante, Chaucer, Shakespeare, Milton, and Wordsworth, and the familiar "Cambridge Thirty Years Ago" and "On a Certain Condescension in Foreigners" are still enjoyable. He need not read the whole of an essay to get the good of it, for Lowell, brilliant, witty, and engagingly erudite as he was at his best, lacked the self-discipline to write a condensed, tightly constructed essay every part of which is essential to the whole. He was incurably digressive and discursive, and had no gift for unity. The Introduction to *The Biglow Papers* is an exception, perhaps because its subject is self-controlled.

In part, his diffuseness was the result of his extraordinary facility and versatility. Like Holmes, he could rhyme a lecture or a letter almost as easily as he could prose it; he was a brilliant and spontaneous punster; he found it hard to control the fireworks of his wit; and he had his foreign languages at his fingertips. At the same time, he could rarely achieve the density and intensity which characterize great poetry. There are fine lyrical passages in his verse, but many of his best and most characteristic pieces are long, rambling, rhymed personal essays rather than poems. "The Cathedral," for example, is studded with brilliant lines, but structurally it is a meandering, meditative essay on religion, science, and democracy. Lowell could achieve something like organization only when he donned the strait jacket of a rigid, established form like the ode.

He knew his faults—most of them. Scattered among his letters, which are among the most readable in American literature, are candid and perceptive statements about his own limitations. As of 1848, he was capable of saying of himself in *A Fable for Critics*,

There is Lowell, who's striving Parnassus to climb
With a whole bale of *isms* tied together with rhyme,
He might get on alone, spite of brambles and
    boulders,
But he can't with that bundle he has on his
    shoulders,

The top of the hill he will ne'er come nigh reaching
Till he learns the distinction 'twixt singing and
    preaching;
His lyre has some chords that would ring pretty
    well,
But he'd rather by half make a drum of the shell,
And rattle away till he's old as Methusalem,
At the head of a march to the last new Jerusalem.

Naturally, he did not advertise his strengths, but in spite of his dislike for much of the literature of his time, he contributed to the changes that were taking place. He took an important part in the shift from sentimentalism to realism in the American short story through his editorship of the *Atlantic*. His *A Fable for Critics* helped to establish a sense that America had, at last, a community of writers, and that these writers were strong enough to be evaluated on their own merits rather than on nationalistic or chauvinistic grounds. Moreover, the *Fable* helped to reduce the critical cliquishness, the regional bickering, and the political partisanship which were so harmful to American literature in the 1840's. This book by a New Englander, issued by an influential New York publisher, offered witty, kindly, balanced commentary on our writers without regard for the factions to which they had been assigned in the squalid quarrels of New York's Grub Street.

Finally, Lowell lent strong support to a movement which has profoundly affected the tone of modern literature. Before American writers could free themselves from the wrong kind of English influence, they needed assurance that native vernaculars and native speech rhythms were respectable substitutes for British language and rhetoric. It had always been granted that common speech was acceptable for the purpose of low comedy, but it was assumed that serious discourse needed the prop of traditional literary English. Lowell proved in *The Biglow Papers* that Yankee dialect was an effective instrument for impassioned political satire; and his Introduction to the Second Series is the most important document in the whole movement. In providing sound scholarly evidence that many Americanisms were of ancient European origin, and in demonstrating that the common speech is full of wit and colorful imagery, Lowell gave American vernaculars the academic support that they needed. In the crucial shift from the language of James

Fenimore Cooper to that of Mark Twain, we find abundant evidence of the influence of James Russell Lowell.

# Henry Wadsworth Longfellow

## THE BELEAGUERED CITY

◊

❲ SAMUEL LONGFELLOW, the poet's brother, explains that the suggestion for the poem came from a note in one of the volumes of Scott's *Border Minstrelsy:* "Similar to this was the *Nacht Lager,* or midnight camp, which seemed nightly to beleaguer the walls of Prague but which disappeared upon the recitation of [certain] magical words."

◊

I have read, in some old, marvellous tale,
 Some legend strange and vague,
That a midnight host of spectres pale
 Beleaguered the walls of Prague.

Beside the Moldau's rushing stream,
 With the wan moon overhead,
There stood, as in an awful dream,
 The army of the dead.

White as a sea-fog, landward bound,
 The spectral camp was seen,   10
And, with a sorrowful, deep sound,
 The river flowed between.

No other voice nor sound was there,
 No drum, nor sentry's pace;
The mist-like banners clasped the air
 As clouds with clouds embrace.

But when the old cathedral bell
 Proclaimed the morning prayer,
The white pavilions rose and fell
 On the alarmèd air.   20

Down the broad valley fast and far
 The troubled army fled;
Up rose the glorious morning star,
 The ghastly host was dead.

I have read, in the marvellous heart of man,
 That strange and mystic scroll,

That an army of phantoms vast and wan
 Beleaguer the human soul.

Encamped beside Life's rushing stream,
 In Fancy's misty light,   30
Gigantic shapes and shadows gleam
 Portentous through the night.

Upon its midnight battle-ground
 The spectral camp is seen,
And, with a sorrowful, deep sound,
 Flows the River of Life between.

No other voice nor sound is there,
 In the army of the grave;
No other challenge breaks the air,
 But the rushing of Life's wave.  40

And when the solemn and deep church-bell
 Entreats the soul to pray,
The midnight phantoms feel the spell,
 The shadows sweep away.

Down the broad Vale of Tears afar
 The spectral camp is fled;
Faith shineth as a morning star,
 Our ghastly fears are dead.

*1839*              *1839*

## THE SKELETON IN ARMOR

◊

❲ LONGFELLOW supposed a skeleton in armor, uncovered near Fall River, to be the remains of one of the old Northern sea rovers, who came to the northern coast of the Western Hemisphere in the tenth century. "Of course I make the tradition myself," he wrote. The date and origin of the Newport tower (l. 134) are controversial. As originally published in the *Knickerbocker* for January 1841, the poem had marginal notes

like those in Coleridge's "The Rime of the Ancient
Mariner."

◊

"Speak! speak! thou fearful guest!
　Who, with thy hollow breast
　Still in rude armor drest,
　　Comest to daunt me!
　Wrapt not in Eastern balms,
　But with thy fleshless palms
　Stretched, as if asking alms,
　　Why dost thou haunt me?"

Then, from those cavernous eyes
　Pale flashes seemed to rise,　　　　10
　As when the Northern skies
　　Gleam in December;
　And, like the water's flow
　Under December's snow,
　Came a dull voice of woe
　　From the heart's chamber.

"I was a Viking old!
　My deeds, though manifold,
　No Skald in song has told,
　　No Saga taught thee!　　　　20
　Take heed, that in thy verse
　Thou dost the tale rehearse,
　Else dread a dead man's curse;
　　For this I sought thee.

"Far in the Northern Land,
　By the wild Baltic's strand,
　I, with my childish hand,
　　Tamed the gerfalcon;
　And, with my skates fast-bound,
　Skimmed the half-frozen Sound,　　30
　That the poor whimpering hound
　　Trembled to walk on.

"Oft to his frozen lair
　Tracked I the grisly bear,
　While from my path the hare
　　Fled like a shadow;
　Oft through the forest dark
　Followed the were-wolf's bark,
　Until the soaring lark
　　Sang from the meadow.　　　　40

"But when I older grew,
　Joining a corsair's crew,
　O'er the dark sea I flew
　　With the marauders.
　Wild was the life we led;
　Many the souls that sped,

Many the hearts that bled,
　　By our stern orders.

"Many a wassail-bout
　Wore the long Winter out;　　　　50
　Often our midnight shout
　　Set the cocks crowing,
　As we the Berserk's tale
　Measured in cups of ale,
　Draining the oaken pail,
　　Filled to o'erflowing.

"Once as I told in glee
　Tales of the stormy sea,
　Soft eyes did gaze on me,
　　Burning yet tender;　　　　60
　And as the white stars shine
　On the dark Norway pine,
　On that dark heart of mine
　　Fell their soft splendor.

"I wooed the blue-eyed maid,
　Yielding, yet half afraid,
　And in the forest's shade
　　Our vows were plighted.
　Under its loosened vest
　Fluttered her little breast,　　　70
　Like birds within their nest
　　By the hawk frighted.

"Bright in her father's hall
　Shields gleamed upon the wall,
　Loud sang the minstrels all,
　　Chanting his glory;
　When of old Hildebrand
　I asked his daughter's hand,
　Mute did the minstrels stand
　　To hear my story.　　　　80

"While the brown ale he quaffed,
　Loud then the champion laughed,
　And as the wind-gusts waft
　　The sea-foam brightly,
　So the loud laugh of scorn,
　Out of those lips unshorn,
　From the deep drinking-horn
　　Blew the foam lightly.

"She was a Prince's child,
　I but a Viking wild,　　　　90
　And though she blushed and smiled
　　I was discarded!
　Should not the dove so white
　Follow the sea-mew's flight,
　Why did they leave that night
　　Her nest unguarded?

"Scarce had I put to sea,
  Bearing the maid with me,
  Fairest of all was she
    Among the Norsemen! 100
  When on the white sea-strand,
  Waving his armèd hand,
  Saw we old Hildebrand,
    With twenty horsemen.

"Then launched they to the blast,
  Bent like a reed each mast,
  Yet we were gaining fast,
    When the wind failed us;
  And with a sudden flaw
  Came round the gusty Skaw, 110
  So that our foe we saw
    Laugh as he hailed us.

"And as to catch the gale
  Round veered the flapping sail,
  'Death!' was the helmsman's hail,
    'Death without quarter!'
  Mid-ships with iron keel
  Struck we her ribs of steel;
  Down her black hulk did reel
    Through the black water! 120

"As with his wings aslant,
  Sails the fierce cormorant,
  Seeking some rocky haunt,
    With his prey laden,—
  So toward the open main,
  Beating to sea again,
  Through the wild hurricane,
    Bore I the maiden.

"Three weeks we westward bore,
  And when the storm was o'er, 130
  Cloud-like we saw the shore
    Stretching to leeward;
  There for my lady's bower
  Built I the lofty tower,
  Which, to this very hour,
    Stands looking seaward.

"There lived we many years;
  Time dried the maiden's tears;
  She had forgot her fears,
    She was a mother; 140
  Death closed her mild blue eyes,
  Under that tower she lies;
  Ne'er shall the sun arise
    On such another!

"Still grew my bosom then,
  Still as a stagnant fen!
  Hateful to me were men,
    The sunlight hateful!
  In the vast forest here,
  Clad in my warlike gear, 150
  Fell I upon my spear,
    Oh, death was grateful!

"Thus, seamed with many scars,
  Bursting these prison bars,
  Up to its native stars
    My soul ascended!
  There from the flowing bowl
  Deep drinks the warrior's soul,
  *Skoal!* to the Northland! *skoal!"*
    Thus the tale ended. 160

*1841*                                    *1840*

---

# GOD'S-ACRE

---

I like that ancient Saxon phrase, which calls
  The burial-ground God's-Acre! It is just;
It consecrates each grave within its walls,
  And breathes a benison o'er the sleeping dust.

God's-Acre! Yes, that blessed name imparts
  Comfort to those who in the grave have sown
The seed that they had garnered in their hearts,
  Their bread of life, alas! no more their own.

Into its furrows shall we all be cast,
  In the sure faith, that we shall rise again 10
At the great harvest, when the archangel's blast
  Shall winnow like a fan, the chaff and grain.

Then shall the good stand in immortal bloom,
  In the fair gardens of that second birth;
And each bright blossom mingle its perfume
  With that of flowers, which never bloomed on
    earth.

With thy rude ploughshare, Death, turn up the sod,
  And spread the furrow for the seed we sow;
This is the field and Acre of our God,
  This is the place where human harvests
    grow. 20

*1841*                                    *1841*

THE SKELETON IN ARMOR. 110. **Skaw:** Cape Skagen, northern point of Jutland in Denmark.

# THE GOBLET OF LIFE

Filled is Life's goblet to the brim;
And though my eyes with tears are dim,
I see its sparkling bubbles swim,
And chant a melancholy hymn
    With solemn voice and slow.

No purple flowers,—no garlands green,
Conceal the goblet's shade or sheen,
Nor maddening draughts of Hippocrene,
Like gleams of sunshine, flash between
    Thick leaves of mistletoe.      10

This goblet, wrought with curious art,
Is filled with waters, that upstart,
When the deep fountains of the heart,
By strong convulsions rent apart,
    Are running all to waste.

And as it mantling passes round,
With fennel is it wreathed and crowned,
Whose seed and foliage sun-imbrowned
Are in its waters steeped and drowned,
    And give a bitter taste.      20

Above the lowly plants it towers,
The fennel, with its yellow flowers,
And in an earlier age than ours
Was gifted with the wondrous powers,
    Lost vision to restore.

It gave new strength, and fearless mood;
And gladiators, fierce and rude,
Mingled it in their daily food;
And he who battled and subdued,
    A wreath of fennel wore.      30

Then in Life's goblet freely press
The leaves that give it bitterness,
Nor prize the colored waters less,
For in thy darkness and distress
    New light and strength they give!

And he who has not learned to know
How false its sparkling bubbles show,
How bitter are the drops of woe,
With which its brim may overflow,
    He has not learned to live.      40

The prayer of Ajax was for light;
Through all that dark and desperate fight,

The blackness of that noonday night,
He asked but the return of sight,
    To see his foeman's face.

Let our unceasing, earnest prayer
Be, too, for light,—for strength to bear
Our portion of the weight of care,
That crushes into dumb despair
    One half the human race.      50

O suffering, sad humanity!
O ye afflicted ones, who lie
Steeped to the lips in misery,
Longing, and yet afraid to die,
    Patient, though sorely tried!

I pledge you in this cup of grief,
Where floats the fennel's bitter leaf!
The Battle of our Life is brief,
The alarm,—the struggle,—the relief,
    Then sleep we side by side.      60

*1842*                                    *1841*

# THE ARSENAL AT SPRINGFIELD

◇

❨ THIS poem is related to the antiwar movement of the 1840's. One of the leaders, Charles Sumner, accompanied Longfellow on a visit to the arsenal.

◇

This is the Arsenal. From floor to ceiling,
    Like a huge organ, rise the burnished arms;
But from their silent pipes no anthem pealing
    Startles the villages with strange alarms.

Ah! what a sound will rise, how wild and dreary,
    When the death-angel touches those swift keys!
What loud lament and dismal Miserere
    Will mingle with their awful symphonies!

I hear even now the infinite fierce chorus,
    The cries of agony, the endless groan,      10
Which, through the ages that have gone before us,
    In long reverberations reach our own.

On helm and harness rings the Saxon hammer,
    Through Cimbric forest roars the Norseman's
        song,
And loud, amid the universal clamor,
    O'er distant deserts sounds the Tartar gong.

I hear the Florentine, who from his palace
    Wheels out his battle-bell with dreadful din,
And Aztec priests upon their teocallis
    Beat the wild war-drums made of serpent's
       skin;                 20

The tumult of each sacked and burning village:
    The shout that every prayer for mercy drowns;
The soldiers' revels in the midst of pillage;
    The wail of famine in beleaguered towns;

The bursting shell, the gateway wrenched asunder,
    The rattling musketry, the clashing blade;
And ever and anon, in tones of thunder
    The diapason of the cannonade.

Is it, O man, with such discordant noises,
    With such accursed instruments as these,    30
Thou drownest Nature's sweet and kindly voices,
    And jarrest the celestial harmonies?

Were half the power that fills the world with ter-
    ror,
    Were half the wealth bestowed on camps and
       courts,
Given to redeem the human mind from error,
    There were no need of arsenals or forts:

The warrior's name would be a name abhorrèd!
    And every nation, that should lift again
Its hand against a brother, on its forehead    39
    Would wear forevermore the curse of Cain!

Down the dark future, through long generations,
    The echoing sounds grow fainter and then
       cease;
And like a bell, with solemn, sweet vibrations,
    I hear once more the voice of Christ say,
       "Peace!"

Peace! and no longer from its brazen portals
    The blast of War's great organ shakes the skies!
But beautiful as songs of the immortals,
    The holy melodies of love arise.

*1844*                                   *1844*

---

# SEAWEED

---

◇

❪ LONGFELLOW here uses his method of teaching by
analogy with mechanical precision. If one puts the eight
stanzas into two parallel columns of four stanzas each,
the analogies between the ocean and poetry become conspicuous.

◇

When descends on the Atlantic
    The gigantic
Storm-wind of the equinox,
Landward in his wrath he scourges
    The toiling surges,
Laden with seaweed from the rocks:

From Bermuda's reefs; from edges
    Of sunken ledges,
In some far-off, bright Azore;
From Bahama, and the dashing,         10
    Silver-flashing
Surges of San Salvador;

From the tumbling surf, that buries
    The Orkneyan skerries,
Answering the hoarse Hebrides;
And from wrecks of ships, and drifting
    Spars, uplifting
On the desolate, rainy seas;—

Ever drifting, drifting, drifting
    On the shifting              20
Currents of the restless main;
Till in sheltered coves, and reaches
    Of sandy beaches,
All have found repose again.

So when storms of wild emotion
    Strike the ocean
Of the poet's soul, erelong
From each cave and rocky fastness,
    In its vastness,
Floats some fragment of a song:       30

From the far-off isles enchanted,
    Heaven has planted
With the golden fruit of Truth;
From the flashing surf, whose vision
    Gleams Elysian
In the tropic clime of Youth;

From the strong Will, and the Endeavor
    That forever
Wrestle with the tides of Fate;
From the wreck of Hopes far-scattered,    40
    Tempest-shattered,
Floating waste and desolate;—

Ever drifting, drifting, drifting
    On the shifting
Currents of the restless heart;
Till at length in books recorded,

They, like hoarded
Household words, no more depart.

*1845*                                    *1845*

# TO THE DRIVING CLOUD

Gloomy and dark art thou, O chief of the mighty
    Omahas;
Gloomy and dark as the driving cloud, whose
    name thou hast taken!
Wrapped in thy scarlet blanket, I see thee stalk
    through the city's
Narrow and populous streets, as once by the mar-
    gin of rivers
Stalked those birds unknown, that have left us
    only their footprints.
What, in a few short years, will remain of thy race
    but the footprints?

How canst thou walk these streets, who hast trod
    the green turf of the prairies?
How canst thou breathe this air, who hast breathed
    the sweet air of the mountains?
Ah! 't is in vain that with lordly looks of disdain
    thou dost challenge
Looks of disdain in return, and question these
    walls and these pavements,                    10
Claiming the soil for thy hunting-grounds, while
    down-trodden millions
Starve in the garrets of Europe, and cry from its
    caverns that they, too,
Have been created heirs of the earth, and claim its
    division!

Back, then, back to thy woods in the regions west
    of the Wabash!
There as a monarch thou reignest. In autumn the
    leaves of the maple
Pave the floors of thy palace-halls with gold, and
    in summer
Pine-trees waft through its chambers the odorous
    breath of their branches.
There thou art strong and great, a hero, a tamer of
    horses!
There thou chasest the stately stag on the banks
    of the Elkhorn,
Or by the roar of the Running-Water, or where
    the Omaha                                      20
Calls thee, and leaps through the wild ravine like
    a brave of the Blackfeet!

Hark! what murmurs arise from the heart of those
    mountainous deserts?
Is it the cry of the Foxes and Crows, or the
    mighty Behemoth,
Who, unharmed, on his tusks once caught the
    bolts of the thunder,
And now lurks in his lair to destroy the race of
    the red man?
Far more fatal to thee and thy race than the
    Crows and the Foxes,
Far more fatal to thee and thy race than the tread
    of Behemoth,
Lo! the big thunder-canoe, that steadily breasts
    the Missouri's

Merciless current! and yonder, afar on the prairies,
    the camp-fires
Gleam through the night; and the cloud of dust in
    the gray of the daybreak                        30
Marks not the buffalo's track, nor the Mandan's
    dexterous horse-race;
It is a caravan, whitening the desert where dwell
    the Camanches!
Ha! how the breath of these Saxons and Celts,
    like the blast of the east-wind,
Drifts evermore to the west the scanty smokes of
    thy wigwams!

*1845*                                    *1845*

# THE FIRE OF
# DRIFT-WOOD

### DEVEREUX FARM, NEAR MARBLEHEAD

We sat within the farm-house old,
    Whose windows, looking o'er the bay,
Gave to the sea-breeze damp and cold
    An easy entrance, night and day.

Not far away we saw the port,
    The strange, old-fashioned, silent town,
The lighthouse, the dismantled fort,
    The wooden houses, quaint and brown.

We sat and talked until the night,
    Descending, filled the little room;        10
Our faces faded from the sight,
    Our voices only broke the gloom.

We spake of many a vanished scene,
Of what we once had thought and said,

Of what had been, and might have been,
   And who was changed, and who was dead;

And all that fills the hearts of friends,
   When first they feel, with secret pain,
Their lives thenceforth have separate ends,
   And never can be one again;      20

The first slight swerving of the heart,
   That words are powerless to express,
And leave it still unsaid in part,
   Or say it in too great excess.

The very tones in which we spake
   Had something strange, I could but mark;
The leaves of memory seemed to make
   A mournful rustling in the dark.

Oft died the words upon our lips,
   As suddenly, from out the fire      30
Built of the wreck of stranded ships,
   The flames would leap and then expire.

And, as their splendor flashed and failed,
   We thought of wrecks upon the main,
Of ships dismasted, that were hailed
   And sent no answer back again.

The windows, rattling in their frames,
   The ocean, roaring up the beach,
The gusty blast, the bickering flames,
   All mingled vaguely in our speech;      40

Until they made themselves a part
   Of fancies floating through the brain,
The long-lost ventures of the heart,
   That send no answers back again.

O flames that glowed! O hearts that yearned!
   They were indeed too much akin,
The drift-wood fire without that burned,
   The thoughts that burned and glowed within.

*1849*                                *1848*

---

# Prelude to
# EVANGELINE

---

◊

〔 LONGFELLOW undertook this subject after his friend
Hawthorne refused it. In history, the French colony
known as Acadia, in Nova Scotia, was distrusted by
the dominant British because of its neutrality and its
friendliness with the Indians. In 1755 the British seized
and deported most of the inhabitants. Longfellow built
his tale on the resulting separation of a young husband
and wife. The Prelude is presented here as a sample of
Longfellow's tone in his handling of the story.

◊

This is the forest primeval. The murmuring pines
   and the hemlocks,
Bearded with moss, and in garments green, indistinct in the twilight,
Stand like Druids of eld, with voices sad and
   prophetic,
Stand like harpers hoar, with beards that rest on
   their bosoms.

Loud from its rocky caverns, the deep-voiced
   neighboring ocean
Speaks, and in accents disconsolate answers the
   wail of the forest.

This is the forest primeval; but where are the
   hearts that beneath it
Leaped like the roe, when he hears in the woodland the voice of the huntsman?

Where is the thatch-roofed village, the home of
   Acadian farmers,—
Men whose lives glided on like rivers that water
   the woodlands,      10
Darkened by shadows of earth, but reflecting an
   image of heaven?
Waste are those pleasant farms, and the farmers
   forever departed!
Scattered like dust and leaves, when the mighty
   blasts of October
Seize them, and whirl them aloft, and sprinkle
   them far o'er the ocean.
Naught but tradition remains of the beautiful
   village of Grand-Pré.

Ye who believe in affection that hopes, and endures, and is patient,
Ye who believe in the beauty and strength of
   woman's devotion,
List to the mournful tradition, still sung by the
   pines of the forest;
List to a Tale of Love in Acadie, home of the
   happy.

*1847*                                *1847*

# DEDICATION

FROM *The Seaside
and the Fireside*

As one who, walking in the twilight gloom,
  Hears round about him voices as it darkens,
And seeing not the forms from which they come,
  Pauses from time to time, and turns and heark-
    ens;

So walking here in twilight, O my friends!
  I hear your voices, softened by the distance,
And pause, and turn to listen, as each sends
  His words of friendship, comfort, and assist-
    ance.

If any thought of mine, or sung or told,
  Has ever given delight or consolation,      10
Ye have repaid me back a thousand-fold,
  By every friendly sign and salutation.

Thanks for the sympathies that ye have shown!
  Thanks for each kindly word, each silent token,
That teaches me, when seeming most alone,
  Friends are around us, though no word be spo-
    ken.

Kind messages, that pass from land to land;
  Kind letters, that betray the heart's deep history,
In which we feel the pressure of a hand,—
  One touch of fire,—and all the rest is mys-
    tery!      20

The pleasant books, that silently among
  Our household treasures take familiar places,
And are to us as if a living tongue
  Spake from the printed leaves or pictured
    faces!

Perhaps on earth I shall never behold,
  With eye of sense, your outward form and sem-
    blance;
Therefore to me ye never will grow old,
  But live forever young in my remembrance!

Never grow old, nor change, nor pass away!
  Your gentle voices will flow on forever,      30
When life grows bare and tarnished with decay,
  As through a leafless landscape flows a river.      *1853*

Not chance of birth or place has made us friends,
  Being oftentimes of different tongues and na-
    tions,
But the endeavor for the selfsame ends,
  With the same hopes, and fears, and aspirations.

Therefore I hope to join your seaside walk,
  Saddened, and mostly silent, with emotion;
Not interrupting with intrusive talk
  The grand, majestic symphonies of ocean.      40

Therefore I hope, as no unwelcome guest,
  At your warm fireside, when the lamps are
    lighted,
To have my place reserved among the rest,
  Nor stand as one unsought and uninvited!

*1849*

# IN THE CHURCHYARD
# AT CAMBRIDGE

In the village churchyard she lies,
Dust is in her beautiful eyes,
  No more she breathes, nor feels, nor stirs;
At her feet and at her head
Lies a slave to attend the dead,
  But their dust is white as hers.

Was she, a lady of high degree,
So much in love with the vanity
  And foolish pomp of this world of ours?
Or was it Christian charity,      10
And lowliness and humility,
  The richest and rarest of all dowers?

Who shall tell us? No one speaks;
No color shoots into those cheeks,
  Either of anger or of pride,
At the rude question we have asked;
Nor will the mystery be unmasked
  By those who are sleeping at her side.

Hereafter?—And do you think to look
On the terrible pages of that Book      20
  To find her failings, faults, and errors?
Ah, you will then have other cares,
In your own shortcomings and despairs,
  In your own secret sins and terrors!

*1851*

# THE JEWISH CEMETERY AT NEWPORT

How strange it seems! These Hebrews in their
   graves,
   Close by the street of this fair seaport town,
Silent beside the never-silent waves,
   At rest in all this moving up and down!

The trees are white with dust, that o'er their sleep
   Wave their broad curtains in the south-wind's
     breath,
While underneath these leafy tents they keep
   The long, mysterious Exodus of Death.

And these sepulchral stones, so old and brown,
   That pave with level flags their burial-place, 10
Seem like the tablets of the Law, thrown down
   And broken by Moses at the mountain's base.

The very names recorded here are strange,
   Of foreign accent, and of different climes;
Alvares and Rivera interchange
   With Abraham and Jacob of old times.

"Blessed be God, for he created Death!"
   The mourners said, "and Death is rest and
     peace;"
Then added, in the certainty of faith,
   "And giveth Life that nevermore shall
     cease." 20

Closed are the portals of their Synagogue,
   No Psalms of David now the silence break,
No Rabbi reads the ancient Decalogue
   In the grand dialect the Prophets spake.

Gone are the living, but the dead remain,
   And not neglected; for a hand unseen,
Scattering its bounty, like a summer rain,
   Still keeps their graves and their remembrance
     green.

How came they here? What burst of Christian
   hate,
   What persecution, merciless and blind, 30
Drove o'er the sea—that desert desolate—
   These Ishmaels and Hagars of mankind?

They lived in narrow streets and lanes obscure,

Ghetto and Judenstrass, in mirk and mire;
Taught in the school of patience to endure
   The life of anguish and the death of fire.

All their lives long, with the unleavened bread
   And bitter herbs of exile and its fears,
The wasting famine of the heart they fed,
   And slaked its thirst with marah of their
     tears. 40

Anathema maranatha! was the cry
   That rang from town to town, from street to
     street:
At every gate the accursed Mordecai
   Was mocked and jeered, and spurned by Chris-
     tian feet.

Pride and humiliation hand in hand
   Walked with them through the world where'er
     they went;
Trampled and beaten were they as the sand,
   And yet unshaken as the continent.

For in the background figures vague and vast
   Of patriarchs and of prophets rose sublime, 50
And all the great traditions of the Past
   They saw reflected in the coming time.

And thus forever with reverted look
   The mystic volume of the world they read,
Spelling it backward, like a Hebrew book,
   Till life became a Legend of the Dead.

But ah! what once has been shall be no more!
   The groaning earth in travail and in pain
Brings forth its races, but does not restore,
   And the dead nations never rise again. 60

*1852*                                 *1852*

# MY LOST YOUTH

Often I think of the beautiful town
   That is seated by the sea;
Often in thought go up and down
The pleasant streets of that dear old town,
   And my youth comes back to me.
     And a verse of a Lapland song
     Is haunting my memory still:

THE JEWISH CEMETERY AT NEWPORT. **32. Ishmaels and Hagars:** See Gen. 16:21.

**34. Ghetto and Judenstrass:** sections in which the Jews were segregated in European cities. **41. Anathema maranatha!:** a curse. See I Cor. 16:22. **43. Mordecai:** See the Book of Esther.

"A boy's will is the wind's will,
And the thoughts of youth are long, long
thoughts."

I can see the shadowy lines of its trees,    10
  And catch, in sudden gleams,
The sheen of the far-surrounding seas,
And islands that were the Hesperides
  Of all my boyish dreams.
    And the burden of that old song,
    It murmurs and whispers still:
  "A boy's will is the wind's will,
And the thoughts of youth are long, long
thoughts."

I remember the black wharves and the slips,
  And the sea-tides tossing free;    20
And Spanish sailors with bearded lips,
And the beauty and mystery of the ships,
  And the magic of the sea.
    And the voice of that wayward song
    Is singing and saying still:
  "A boy's will is the wind's will,
And the thoughts of youth are long, long
thoughts."

I remember the bulwarks by the shore,
  And the fort upon the hill;
The sunrise gun, with its hollow roar,    30
The drum-beat repeated o'er and o'er,
  And the bugle wild and shrill.
    And the music of that old song
    Throbs in my memory still:
  "A boy's will is the wind's will,
And the thoughts of youth are long, long
thoughts."

I remember the sea-fight far away,
  How it thundered o'er the tide!
And the dead captains, as they lay
In their graves, o'erlooking the tranquil bay    40
  Where they in battle died.
    And the sound of that mournful song
    Goes through me with a thrill:
  "A boy's will is the wind's will,
And the thoughts of youth are long, long
thoughts."

I can see the breezy dome of groves,
  The shadows of Deering's Woods;
And the friendships old and the early loves
Come back with a Sabbath sound, as of doves
  In quiet neighborhoods.    50
    And the verse of that sweet old song,
    It flutters and murmurs still:
  "A boy's will is the wind's will,
And the thoughts of youth are long, long
thoughts."

I remember the gleams and glooms that dart
  Across the school-boy's brain;
The song and the silence in the heart,
That in part are prophecies, and in part
  Are longings wild and vain.
    And the voice of that fitful song    60
    Sings on, and is never still:
  "A boy's will is the wind's will,
And the thoughts of youth are long, long
thoughts."

There are things of which I may not speak;
  There are dreams that cannot die;
There are thoughts that make the strong heart
    weak,
And bring a pallor into the cheek,
  And a mist before the eye.
    And the words of that fatal song
    Come over me like a chill:    70
  "A boy's will is the wind's will,
And the thoughts of youth are long, long
thoughts."

Strange to me now are the forms I meet
  When I visit the dear old town;
But the native air is pure and sweet,
And the trees that o'ershadow each well-known
    street,
  As they balance up and down,
    Are singing the beautiful song,
    Are sighing and whispering still:
  "A boy's will is the wind's will,    80
And the thoughts of youth are long, long
thoughts."

And Deering's Woods are fresh and fair,
  And with joy that is almost pain
My heart goes back to wander there,
And among the dreams of the days that were,
  I find my lost youth again.
    And the strange and beautiful song,
    The groves are repeating it still:
  "A boy's will is the wind's will,
And the thoughts of youth are long, long
  thoughts."    90

*1855*

# THE SICILIAN'S TALE
### KING ROBERT OF SICILY

◇

❲ "THE SICILIAN'S TALE" is from Part I of *Tales of a
Wayside Inn* of 1863. The pattern of the work as
a whole—the relating of a succession of stories by a

group of congenial acquaintances—follows that of Chaucer's *Canterbury Tales.* "King Robert of Sicily," a story of a proud then penitent king, finds its plot in the *Gesta Romanorum.*

◊

Robert of Sicily, brother of Pope Urbane
And Valmond, Emperor of Allemaine,
Apparelled in magnificent attire,
With retinue of many a knight and squire,
On St. John's eve, at vespers, proudly sat
And heard the priests chant the Magnificat.
And as he listened, o'er and o'er again
Repeated, like a burden or refrain,
He caught the words, *"Deposuit potentes
De sede, et exaltavit humiles;"*                          10
And slowly lifting up his kingly head
He to a learned clerk beside him said,
"What mean these words?" The clerk made an-
    swer meet,
"He has put down the mighty from their seat,
And has exalted them of low degree."
Thereat King Robert muttered scornfully,
" 'T is well that such seditious words are sung
Only by priests and in the Latin tongue;
For unto priests and people be it known,
There is no power can push me from my throne!"
And leaning back, he yawned and fell asleep,   21
Lulled by the chant monotonous and deep.

When he awoke, it was already night;
The church was empty, and there was no light,
Save where the lamps, that glimmered few and
    faint,
Lighted a little space before some saint.
He started from his seat and gazed around,
But saw no living thing and heard no sound.
He groped towards the door, but it was locked;
He cried aloud, and listened, and then knocked,
And uttered awful threatenings and complaints,
And imprecations upon men and saints.          32
The sounds reëchoed from the roof and walls
As if dead priests were laughing in their stalls.

At length the sexton, hearing from without
The tumult of the knocking and the shout,
And thinking thieves were in the house of prayer,
Came with his lantern, asking, "Who is there?"
Half choked with rage, King Robert fiercely said,
"Open: 't is I, the King! Art thou afraid?"     40
The frightened sexton, muttering, with a curse,
"This is some drunken vagabond, or worse!"
Turned the great key and flung the portal wide;
A man rushed by him at a single stride,
Haggard, half naked, without hat or cloak,

Who neither turned, nor looked at him, nor spoke,
But leaped into the blackness of the night,
And vanished like a spectre from his sight.

Robert of Sicily, brother of Pope Urbane
And Valmond, Emperor of Allemaine,             50
Despoiled of his magnificent attire,
Bareheaded, breathless, and besprent with mire,
With sense of wrong and outrage desperate,
Strode on and thundered at the palace gate;
Rushed through the courtyard, thrusting in his
    rage
To right and left each seneschal and page,
And hurried up the broad and sounding stair,
His white face ghastly in the torches' glare.
From hall to hall he passed with breathless speed;
Voices and cries he heard, but did not heed,   60
Until at last he reached the banquet-room,
Blazing with light, and breathing with perfume.

There on the dais sat another king,
Wearing his robes, his crown, his signet-ring,
King Robert's self in features, form, and height,
But all transfigured with angelic light!
It was an Angel; and his presence there
With a divine effulgence filled the air,
An exaltation, piercing the disguise,
Though none the hidden Angel recognize.        70

A moment speechless, motionless, amazed,
The throneless monarch on the Angel gazed,
Who met his look of anger and surprise
With the divine compassion of his eyes;
Then said, "Who art thou? and why com'st thou
    here?"
To which King Robert answered with a sneer,
"I am the King, and come to claim my own
From an impostor, who usurps my throne!"
And suddenly, at these audacious words,
Up sprang the angry guests, and drew their
    swords;                                      80
The Angel answered, with unruffled brow,
"Nay, not the King, but the King's Jester, thou
Henceforth shalt wear the bells and scalloped cape,
And for thy counsellor shalt lead an ape;
Thou shalt obey my servants when they call,
And wait upon my henchmen in the hall!"

Deaf to King Robert's threats and cries and
    prayers,
They thrust him from the hall and down the stairs;
A group of tittering pages ran before,
And as they opened wide the folding-door,      90
His heart failed, for he heard, with strange alarms,
The boisterous laughter of the men-at-arms,
And all the vaulted chamber roar and ring

With the mock plaudits of "Long live the King!"
Next morning, waking with the day's first beam,
He said within himself, "It was a dream!"
But the straw rustled as he turned his head,
There were the cap and bells beside his bed,
Around him rose the bare, discolored walls,
Close by, the steeds were champing in their stalls,
And in the corner, a revolting shape,                101
Shivering and chattering sat the wretched ape.
It was no dream; the world he loved so much
Had turned to dust and ashes at his touch!

Days came and went; and now returned again
To Sicily the old Saturnian reign;
Under the Angel's governance benign
The happy island danced with corn and wine,
And deep within the mountain's burning breast
Enceladus, the giant, was at rest.                110

Meanwhile King Robert yielded to his fate,
Sullen and silent and disconsolate.
Dressed in the motley garb that Jesters wear,
With look bewildered and a vacant stare,
Close shaven above the ears, as monks are shorn,
By courtiers mocked, by pages laughed to scorn,
His only friend the ape, his only food
What others left,—he still was unsubdued.
And when the Angel met him on his way,
And half in earnest, half in jest, would say,                120
Sternly, though tenderly, that he might feel
The velvet scabbard held a sword of steel,
"Art thou the King?" the passion of his woe
Burst from him in resistless overflow,
And, lifting high his forehead, he would fling
The haughty answer back, "I am, I am the King!"

Almost three years were ended; when there came
Ambassadors of great repute and name
From Valmond, Emperor of Allemaine,
Unto King Robert, saying that Pope Urbane                130
By letter summoned them forthwith to come
On Holy Thursday to his city of Rome.
The Angel with great joy received his guests,
And gave them presents of embroidered vests,
And velvet mantles with rich ermine lined,
And rings and jewels of the rarest kind.
Then he departed with them o'er the sea
Into the lovely land of Italy,
Whose loveliness was more resplendent made
By the mere passing of that cavalcade,                140
With plumes, and cloaks, and housings, and the stir
Of jewelled bridle and of golden spur.
And lo! among the menials, in mock state,
Upon a piebald steed, with shambling gait,
His cloak of fox-tails flapping in the wind,
The solemn ape demurely perched behind,

King Robert rode, making huge merriment
In all the country towns through which they went.

The Pope received them with great pomp and blare
Of bannered trumpets, on Saint Peter's square,
Giving his benediction and embrace,                151
Fervent, and full of apostolic grace.
While with congratulations and with prayers
He entertained the Angel unawares,
Robert, the Jester, bursting through the crowd,
Into their presence rushed, and cried aloud,
"I am the King! Look, and behold in me
Robert, your brother, King of Sicily!
This man, who wears my semblance to your eyes,
Is an impostor in a king's disguise.                160
Do you not know me? does no voice within
Answer my cry, and say we are akin?"

The Pope in silence, but with troubled mien,
Gazed at the Angel's countenance serene;
The Emperor, laughing, said, "It is strange sport
To keep a madman for thy Fool at court!"
And the poor, baffled Jester in disgrace
Was hustled back among the populace.

In solemn state the Holy Week went by,
And Easter Sunday gleamed upon the sky;                170
The presence of the Angel, with its light,
Before the sun rose, made the city bright,
And with new fervor filled the hearts of men,
Who felt that Christ indeed had risen again.
Even the Jester, on his bed of straw,
With haggard eyes the unwonted splendor saw,
He felt within a power unfelt before,
And, kneeling humbly on his chamber floor,
He heard the rushing garments of the Lord
Sweep through the silent air, ascending heaven-
                ward.                180

And now the visit ending, and once more
Valmond returning to the Danube's shore,
Homeward the Angel journeyed, and again
The land was made resplendent with his train,
Flashing along the towns of Italy
Unto Salerno, and from thence by sea.
And when once more within Palermo's wall,
And, seated on the throne in his great hall,
He heard the Angelus from convent towers,
As if the better world conversed with ours,                190
He beckoned to King Robert to draw nigher,
And with a gesture bade the rest retire;
And when they were alone, the Angel said,
"Art thou the King?" Then, bowing down his
                head,
King Robert crossed both hands upon his breast,
And meekly answered him: "Thou knowest best!

My sins as scarlet are; let me go hence,
And in some cloister's school of penitence,
Across those stones, that pave the way to heaven,
Walk barefoot, till my guilty soul be shriven!"    200

The Angel smiled, and from his radiant face
A holy light illumined all the place,
And through the open window, loud and clear,
They heard the monks chant in the chapel near,
Above the stir and tumult of the street:
"He has put down the mighty from their seat,
And has exalted them of low degree!"
And through the chant a second melody
Rose like the throbbing of a single string:
"I am an Angel, and thou art the King!"    210

King Robert, who was standing near the throne,
Lifted his eyes, and lo! he was alone!
But all apparelled as in days of old,
With ermined mantle and with cloth of gold;
And when his courtiers came, they found him
    there
Kneeling upon the floor, absorbed in silent prayer.

*1863*                                        *1862*

---

# THE POET'S TALE
## CHARLEMAGNE
## FROM PART III OF
### *Tales of A Wayside Inn*

---

Olger the Dane and Desiderio,
King of the Lombards, on a lofty tower
Stood gazing northward o'er the rolling plains,
League after league of harvests, to the foot
Of the snow-crested Alps, and saw approach
A mighty army, thronging all the roads
That led into the city. And the King
Said unto Olger, who had passed his youth
As hostage at the court of France, and knew    9
The Emperor's form and face: "Is Charlemagne
Among that host?" And Olger answered: "No."

And still the innumerable multitude
Flowed onward and increased, until the King
Cried in amazement: "Surely Charlemagne
Is coming in the midst of all these knights!"

And Olger answered slowly: "No; not yet;
He will not come so soon." Then much disturbed
King Desiderio asked: "What shall we do,
If he approach with a still greater army?"
And Olger answered: "When he shall appear,    20
You will behold what manner of man he is;
But what will then befall us I know not."

Then came the guard that never knew repose,
The Paladins of France; and at the sight
The Lombard King o'ercome with terror cried:
"This must be Charlemagne!" and as before
Did Olger answer: "No; not yet, not yet."

And then appeared in panoply complete
The Bishops and the Abbots and the Priests
Of the imperial chapel, and the Counts;    30
And Desiderio could no more endure
The light of day, nor yet encounter death,
But sobbed aloud and said: "Let us go down
And hide us in the bosom of the earth,
Far from the sight and anger of a foe
So terrible as this!" And Olger said:
"When you behold the harvests in the fields
Shaking with fear, the Po and the Ticino
Lashing the city walls with iron waves,
Then may you know that Charlemagne is come."
And even as he spake, in the northwest,    41
Lo! there uprose a black and threatening cloud,
Out of whose bosom flashed the light of arms
Upon the people pent up in the city;
A light more terrible than any darkness,
And Charlemagne appeared;—a Man of Iron!

His helmet was of iron, and his gloves
Of iron, and his breastplate and his greaves
And tassets were of iron, and his shield.
In his left hand he held an iron spear,    50
In his right hand his sword invincible.
The horse he rode on had the strength of iron,
And color of iron. All who went before him,
Beside him and behind him, his whole host,
Were armed with iron, and their hearts within
    them
Were stronger than the armor that they wore.
The fields and all the roads were filled with iron,
And points of iron glistened in the sun
And shed a terror through the city streets.

This at a single glance Olger the Dane    60
Saw from the tower, and turning to the King
Exclaimed in haste: "Behold! this is the man
You looked for with such eagerness!" and then
Fell as one dead at Desiderio's feet.

*1873*                                        *1872*

# DIVINA COMMEDIA

◇

❡ SIX sonnets, of which we give four, first published in the *Atlantic Monthly* (1864–66), served as prefaces to the three parts of Longfellow's translation of Dante's work. The poems reflect something of Longfellow's state of mind in the years following the tragic death of his second wife in 1861, during the Civil War.

◇

I

Oft have I seen at some cathedral door
  A laborer, pausing in the dust and heat,
  Lay down his burden, and with reverent feet
  Enter, and cross himself, and on the floor
Kneel to repeat his paternoster o'er;
  Far off the noises of the world retreat;
  The loud vociferations of the street
  Become an undistinguishable roar.
So, as I enter here from day to day,
  And leave my burden at this minster gate,   10
  Kneeling in prayer, and not ashamed to pray,
The tumult of the time disconsolate
  To inarticulate murmurs dies away,
  While the eternal ages watch and wait.

*1864*

II

How strange the sculptures that adorn these tow-
    ers!
  This crowd of statues, in whose folded sleeves
  Birds build their nests; while canopied with
    leaves
Parvis and portal bloom like trellised bowers,
And the vast minster seems a cross of flowers!
  But fiends and dragons on the gargoyled eaves
  Watch the dead Christ between the living
    thieves,
  And, underneath, the traitor Judas lowers!
Ah! from what agonies of heart and brain,
  What exultations trampling on despair,   10
  What tenderness, what tears, what hate of
    wrong,
What passionate outcry of a soul in pain,
  Uprose this poem of the earth and air,
  This mediæval miracle of song!

*1866*

III

I enter, and I see thee in the gloom
  Of the long aisles, O poet saturnine!
And strive to make my steps keep pace with
    thine.
The air is filled with some unknown perfume;
The congregation of the dead make room
  For thee to pass; the votive tapers shine;
  Like rooks that haunt Ravenna's groves of pine
The hovering echoes fly from tomb to tomb.
From the confessionals I hear arise
  Rehearsals of forgotten tragedies,   10
  And lamentations from the crypts below;
And then a voice celestial that begins
  With the pathetic words, "Although your sins
  As scarlet be," and ends with "as the snow."

*1866*

IV

With snow-white veil and garments as of flame,
  She stands before thee, who so long ago
  Filled thy young heart with passion and the woe
  From which thy song and all its splendors came;
And while with stern rebuke she speaks thy name,
  The ice about thy heart melts as the snow
  On mountain heights, and in swift overflow
  Comes gushing from thy lips in sobs of shame.
Thou makest full confession; and a gleam,
  As of the dawn on some dark forest cast,   10
  Seems on thy lifted forehead to increase;
Lethe and Eunoë—the remembered dream
  And the forgotten sorrow—bring at last
  That perfect pardon which is perfect peace.

*1865*

# CHAUCER

An old man in a lodge within a park;
  The chamber walls depicted all around
  With portraitures of huntsman, hawk, and
    hound,
  And the hurt deer. He listeneth to the lark,
Whose song comes with the sunshine through the
    dark
  Of painted glass in leaden lattice bound;
  He listeneth and he laugheth at the sound,
  Then writeth in a book like any clerk.

DIVINA COMMEDIA.   IV. 2. She: Beatrice.   5. And . . . rebuke: Beatrice's rebuke to Dante appears in Cantos XXX and XXXI of the *Purgatorio*.   12. Lethe and Eunoë: In the *Purgatorio* Dante drinks of Lethe, the river of forgetfulness, and of Eunoë, the river of memory of the good.

He is the poet of the dawn, who wrote
   The Canterbury Tales, and his old age    10
   Made beautiful with song; and as I read
I hear the crowing cock, I hear the note
   Of lark and linnet, and from every page
   Rise odors of ploughed field or flowery mead.

*1875*                     *1873*

# SHAKESPEARE

A vision as of crowded city streets,
   With human life in endless overflow;
   Thunder of thoroughfares; trumpets that blow
   To battle; clamor, in obscure retreats,
Of sailors landed from their anchored fleets;
   Tolling of bells in turrets, and below
   Voices of children, and bright flowers that throw
   O'er garden-walls their intermingled sweets!
This vision comes to me when I unfold
   The volume of the Poet paramount,    10
   Whom all the Muses loved, not one alone;—
Into his hands they put the lyre of gold,
   And, crowned with sacred laurel at their fount,
   Placed him as Musagetes on their throne.

*1875*                     *1873*

# MILTON

I pace the sounding sea-beach and behold
   How the voluminous billows roll and run,
   Upheaving and subsiding, while the sun
   Shines through their sheeted emerald far un-
      rolled,
And the ninth wave, slow gathering fold by fold
   All its loose-flowing garments into one,
   Plunges upon the shore, and floods the dun
   Pale reach of sands, and changes them to gold.
So in majestic cadence rise and fall
   The mighty undulations of thy song,    10
   O sightless bard, England's Mæonides!
And ever and anon, high over all

SHAKESPEARE. **14. Musagetes:** the leader of the Muses, i.e.,
Apollo. MILTON. **11. Mæonides:** Homer. Like Homer,
Milton was blind.

Uplifted, a ninth wave superb and strong,
Floods all the soul with its melodious seas.

*1875*                     *1873*

# THE TIDE RISES,
# THE TIDE FALLS

The tide rises, the tide falls,
The twilight darkens, the curlew calls;
Along the sea-sands damp and brown
The traveller hastens toward the town,
   And the tide rises, the tide falls.

Darkness settles on roofs and walls,
But the sea, the sea in the darkness calls;
The little waves, with their soft, white hands,
Efface the footprints in the sand,
   And the tide rises, the tide falls.    10

The morning breaks; the steeds in their stalls
Stamp and neigh, as the hostler calls;
The day returns, but nevermore
Returns the traveller to the shore,
   And the tide rises, the tide falls.

*1880*                     *1879*

# THE CROSS OF SNOW

In the long, sleepless watches of the night,
   A gentle face—the face of one long dead—
   Looks at me from the wall, where round its
      head
   The night-lamp casts a halo of pale light.
Here in this room she died; and soul more white
   Never through martyrdom of fire was led
   To its repose; nor can in books be read
   The legend of a life more benedight.
There is a mountain in the distant West
   That, sun-defying, in its deep ravines    10
   Displays a cross of snow upon its side.
Such is the cross I wear upon my breast
   These eighteen years, through all the changing
      scenes
   And seasons, changeless since the day she died.

*1885–86*                 *1879*

## DEDICATION
#### FROM *Michael Angelo: A Fragment*

◇

⟨ SOME of Longfellow's finest poetry is in his unfinished verse drama, *Michael Angelo*, which was posthumously published in 1883. For further information, see Horace E. Scudder's Cambridge edition of the poems.

◇

Nothing that is shall perish utterly,
  But perish only to revive again
In other forms, as clouds restore in rain
  The exhalations of the land and sea.

Men build their houses from the masonry
  Of ruined tombs; the passion and the pain
  Of hearts, that long have ceased to beat, remain
To throb in hearts that are, or are to be.
So from old chronicles, where sleep in dust
  Names that once filled the world with trumpet
     tones,           10
  I build this verse; and flowers of song have
    thrust
Their roots among the loose disjointed stones,
  Which to this end I fashion as I must.
  Quickened are they that touch the Prophet's
    bones.

*1883*

# James Russell Lowell

FROM

## A FABLE FOR CRITICS

◇

⟨ DURING the 1840's Lowell knew many writers in New York and Philadelphia, and deplored the critical squabbles which stemmed from regional hostilities and political factionalism. Lowell surveyed the contemporary literary scene more effectively and sympathetically than Poe had done in his "Literati" papers several years earlier. The speaker in the poem is a critic who is giving an account of American writers to Apollo. In a Preface, Lowell wrote:

> This *jeu d'esprit* was extemporized, I may say, so rapidly was it written, purely for my own amusement and with no thought of publication. I sent daily instalments of it to a friend in New York, the late Charles F. Briggs. He urged me to let it be printed, and I at last consented to its anonymous publication. The secret was kept till after several persons laid claim to its authorship.

◇

. . . . . . . . . . . . . . . . . .
"There comes Emerson first, whose rich words,
  every one,
Are like gold nails in temples to hang trophies on,
Whose prose is grand verse, while his verse, the
  Lord knows,
Is some of it pr— No, 't is not even prose;
I 'm speaking of metres; some poems have welled

From those rare depths of soul that have ne'er
  been excelled;
They 're not epics, but that does n't matter a pin,
In creating, the only hard thing 's to begin;
A grass-blade 's no easier to make than an oak;
If you 've once found the way, you 've achieved
  the grand stroke;     10
In the worst of his poems are mines of rich matter,
But thrown in a heap with a crash and a clatter;
Now it is not one thing nor another alone
Makes a poem, but rather the general tone,
The something pervading, uniting the whole,
The before unconceived, unconceivable soul,
So that just in removing this trifle or that, you
Take away, as it were, a chief limb of the statue;
Roots, wood, bark, and leaves singly perfect
  may be,
But, clapt hodge-podge together, they don't make
  a tree.     20

  "But, to come back to Emerson (whom, by the
  way,
I believe we left waiting),—his is, we may say,
A Greek head on right Yankee shoulders, whose
  range
Has Olympus for one pole, for t' other the Ex-
  change;
He seems, to my thinking (although I 'm afraid
The comparison must, long ere this, have been
  made),
A Plotinus-Montaigne, where the Egyptian's gold
  mist

**27. Plotinus-Montaigne:** referring to the mixture of idealism and skepticism in Emerson.

A FABLE FOR CRITICS.   **2. gold nails:** See Eccles. 12:11.

And the Gascon's shrewd wit cheek-by-jowl co-
    exist;
All admire, and yet scarcely six converts he 's got
To I don't (nor they either) exactly know what;
For though he builds glorious temples, 't is odd
He leaves never a doorway to get in a god.   32
'T is refreshing to old-fashioned people like me
To meet such a primitive Pagan as he,
In whose mind all creation is duly respected
As parts of himself—just a little projected;
And who 's willing to worship the stars and the
    sun,
A convert to—nothing but Emerson.
So perfect a balance there is in his head,
That he talks of things sometimes as if they were
    dead;   40
Life, nature, love, God, and affairs of that sort,
He looks at as merely ideas; in short,
As if they were fossils stuck round in a cabinet,
Of such vast extent that our earth 's a mere dab
    in it;
Composed just as he is inclined to conjecture her,
Namely, one part pure earth, ninety-nine parts
    pure lecturer;
You are filled with delight at his clear demonstra-
    tion,
Each figure, word, gesture, just fits the occasion,
With the quiet precision of science he 'll sort 'em,
But you can't help suspecting the whole a *post
mortem*.   50


"There is Bryant, as quiet, as cool, and as digni-
    fied,
As a smooth, silent iceberg, that never is ignified,
Save when by reflection 't is kindled o' nights
With a semblance of flame by the chill Northern
    Lights.
He may rank (Griswold says so) first bard of your
    nation
(There's no doubt that he stands in supreme ice-
    olation),
Your topmost Parnassus he may set his heel on,
But no warm applauses come, peal following peal
    on,—
He 's too smooth and too polished to hang any
    zeal on:
Unqualified merits, I 'll grant, if you choose, he
    has 'em,   60
But he lacks the one merit of kindling enthusiasm;
If he stir you at all, it is just, on my soul,
Like being stirred up with the very North Pole.

"He is very nice reading in summer, but *inter
Nos,* we don't want *extra* freezing in winter;
Take him up in the depth of July, my advice is,
When you feel an Egyptian devotion to ices.
But, deduct all you can, there 's enough that 's
    right good in him,
He has a true soul for field, river, and wood in
    him;
And his heart, in the midst of brick walls, or
    where'er it is,   70
Glows, softens, and thrills with the tenderest
    charities—
To you mortals that delve in this trade-ridden
    planet?
No, to old Berkshire's hills, with their limestone
    and granite.
If you 're one who *in loco* (add *foco* here) *desipis,*
You will get of his outermost heart (as I guess) a
    piece;
But you 'd get deeper down if you came as a preci-
    pice,
And would break the last seal of its inwardest
    fountain,
If you only could palm yourself off for a moun-
    tain.

  .  .  .  .  .  .  .  .  .  .  .  .  .

"There is Hawthorne, with genius so shrinking
    and rare
That you hardly at first see the strength that is
    there;
A frame so robust, with a nature so sweet,
So earnest, so graceful, so lithe and so fleet,
Is worth a descent from Olympus to meet;
'T is as if a rough oak that for ages had stood,
With his gnarled bony branches like ribs of the
    wood,
Should bloom, after cycles of struggle and scathe,
With a single anemone trembly and rathe;   120
His strength is so tender, his wildness so meek,
That a suitable parallel sets one to seek,—
He 's a John Bunyan Fouqué, a Puritan Tieck;
When Nature was shaping him, clay was not
    granted
For making so full-sized a man as she wanted,
So, to fill out her model, a little she spared

<hr>

55. **Griswold:** Rufus W. Griswold was the foremost antholo-
gist, literary middleman, and critical logroller of the 1840's.

64-65. *inter Nos* . . . : literally, "among ourselves"; however, with
Lowell's addition of "*extra*," a mischief is begun which is com-
pounded by punning.   74. *in loco* . . . *desipis:* A complicated
pun. *Loco desipis* refers to the saying, "You can be foolish in a
particular place." "Locofoco" was the name applied to "liberal"
political thinkers of the time.   123. **John Bunyan** . . . **Tieck:**
Lowell is here pairing opposites to suggest the contradictions in
Hawthorne's temperament. The moral austerity of Bunyan and the
Puritans is linked with the lush romanticism of the Germans,
Baron de La Motte-Fouqué (1777–1843) and Ludwig Tieck (1773–
1853).

From some finer-grained stuff for a woman pre-
    pared,
And she could not have hit a more excellent plan
For making him fully and perfectly man.

. . . . . . . . . . . . . . . . . . . . . . . . .

"Here 's Cooper, who 's written six volumes to
    show
He 's as good as a lord: well, let 's grant that
    he 's so;
If a person prefer that description of praise,
Why, a coronet 's certainly cheaper than bays;
But he need take no pains to convince us he 's
    not       140
(As his enemies say) the American Scott.
Choose any twelve men, and let C. read aloud
That one of his novels of which he 's most proud,
And I 'd lay any bet that, without ever quitting
Their box, they 'd be all, to a man, for acquitting.
He has drawn you one character, though, that is
    new,
One wildflower he 's plucked that is wet with the
    dew
Of this fresh Western world, and, the thing not to
    mince,
He has done naught but copy it ill ever since;
His Indians, with proper respect be it said,   150
Are just Natty Bumppo, daubed over with red,
And his very Long Toms are the same useful Nat,
Rigged up in duck pants and a sou'wester hat
(Though once in a Coffin, a good chance was
    found
To have slipped the old fellow away under-
    ground).
All his other men-figures are clothes upon sticks,
The *dernière chemise* of a man in a fix
(As a captain besieged, when his garrison 's small,
Sets up caps upon poles to be seen o'er the wall);
And the women he draws from one model don't
    vary,       160
All sappy as maples and flat as a prairie.
When a character 's wanted, he goes to the task
As a cooper would do in composing a cask;
He picks out the staves, of their qualities heedful,
Just hoops them together as tight as is needful,
And, if the best fortune should crown the at-
    tempt, he
Has made at the most something wooden and
    empty.

"Don't suppose I would underrate Cooper's
    abilities;
If I thought you 'd do that, I should feel very ill at
    ease;
The men who have given to *one* character life  170

152. **Long Toms:** Long Tom Coffin, the American sailor in
Cooper's *The Pilot* (1823).    **157.** *dernière chemise:* last shirt.

And objective existence are not very rife;
You may number them all, both prose-writers and
    singers,
Without overrunning the bounds of your fingers,
And Natty won't go to oblivion quicker
Than Adams the parson or Primrose the vicar.

"There is one thing in Cooper I like, too, and
    that is
That on manners he lectures his countrymen
    gratis;
Not precisely so either, because, for a rarity,
He is paid for his tickets in unpopularity.
Now he may overcharge his American pic-
    tures.       180
But you 'll grant there 's a good deal of truth in his
    strictures;
And I honor the man who is willing to sink
Half his present repute for the freedom to think,
And, when he has thought, be his cause strong or
    weak,
Will risk t' other half for the freedom to speak,
Caring naught for what vengeance the mob has in
    store,
Let that mob be the upper ten thousand or lower.

"There are truths you Americans need to be
    told,
And it never 'll refute them to swagger and scold;
John Bull, looking o'er the Atlantic, in
    choler       190
At your aptness for trade, says you worship the
    dollar;
But to scorn such eye-dollar-try 's what very
    few do,
And John goes to that church as often as you do.
No matter what John says, don't try to out-
    crow him,
'T is enough to go quietly on and outgrow him;
Like most fathers, Bull hates to see Number One
Displacing himself in the mind of his son,
And detests the same faults in himself he 'd neg-
    lected
When he sees them again in his child's glass re-
    flected;
To love one another you 're too like by half;  200
If he is a bull, you 're a pretty stout calf,
And tear your own pasture for naught but to show
What a nice pair of horns you 're beginning to
    grow.

"There are one or two things I should just like
    to hint,

175. **Than . . . vicar: Adams:** Parson Adams in Henry Fielding's *Joseph Andrews* (1742). **Primrose:** Dr. Primrose in Oliver
Goldsmith's *The Vicar of Wakefield* (1766).

For you don't often get the truth told you in print;
The most of you (this is what strikes all behold-
    ers)
Have a mental and physical stoop in the shoul-
    ders;
Though you ought to be free as the winds and the
    waves,
You 've the gait and the manners of run-away
    slaves;
Though you brag of your New World, you don't
    half believe in it; 210
And as much of the Old as is possible weave in it;
Your goddess of freedom, a tight, buxom girl,
With lips like a cherry and teeth like a pearl,
With eyes bold as Herë's, and hair floating free,
And full of the sun as the spray of the sea,
Who can sing at a husking or romp at a shearing,
Who can trip through the forests alone without
    fearing,
Who can drive home the cows with a song through
    the grass,
Keeps glancing aside into Europe's cracked glass,
Hides her red hands in gloves, pinches up her lithe
    waist, 220
And makes herself wretched with transmarine
    taste;
She loses her fresh country charm when she takes
Any mirror except her own rivers and lakes.

    "You steal Englishmen's books and think Eng-
    lishmen's thoughts,
With their salt on her tail your wild eagle is
    caught;
Your literature suits its each whisper and motion
To what will be thought of it over the ocean;
The cast clothes of Europe your statesmanship
    tries
And mumbles again the old blarneys and lies;—
Forget Europe wholly, your veins throb with
    blood, 230
To which the dull current in hers is but mud:
Let her sneer, let her say your experiment fails,
In her voice there 's a tremble e'en now while
    she rails,
And your shore will soon be in the nature of things
Covered thick with gilt drift-wood of castaway
    kings,
Where alone, as it were in a Longfellow's Waif
Her fugitive pieces will find themselves safe.
O my friends, thank your god, if you have one,
    that he
'Twixt the Old World and you set the gulf of a sea;
Be strong-backed, brown-handed, upright as your
    pines, 240

By the scale of a hemisphere shape your designs,
Be true to yourselves and this new nineteenth age,
As a statue by Powers, or a picture by Page,
Plough, sail, forge, build, carve, paint, make all
    over new,
To your own New-World instincts contrive to be
    true,
Keep your ears open wide to the Future's first call,
Be whatever you will, but yourselves first of all,
Stand fronting the dawn on Toil's heaven-scaling
    peaks,
And become my new race of more practical
    Greeks.—
Hem! your likeness at present, I shudder to
    tell o't, 250
Is that you have your slaves, and the Greek had
    his helot."

    "There comes Poe, with his raven, like Barnaby
    Rudge,
Three fifths of him genius and two fifths sheer
    fudge,
Who talks like a book of iambs and pentameters,
In a way to make people of common sense damn
    metres,
Who has written some things quite the best of their
    kind,
But the heart somehow seems all squeezed out by
    the mind,
Who— But hey-day! What 's this? Messieurs
    Mathews and Poe,
You must n't fling mud-balls at Longfellow so,
Does it make a man worse that his character's
    such 260
As to make his friends love him (as you think) too
    much?
Why, there is not a bard at this moment alive
More willing than he that his fellows should
    thrive;
While you are abusing him thus, even now
He would help either one of you out of a slough;
You may say that he 's smooth and all that till
    you 're hoarse,
But remember that elegance also is force;
After polishing granite as much as you will,
The heart keeps its tough old persistency still;
Deduct all you can, *that* still keeps you at bay;
Why, he 'll live till men weary of Collins and
    Gray. 271

214. **Herë's:** Herë, or Hera, the goddess of women, the sister and
wife of Zeus.

243. **Powers:** Hiram Powers (1805–73), American sculptor.
**Page:** William Page (1811–85), American historical and portrait
painter. 252. **Barnaby Rudge:** In Dickens' novel *Barnaby
Rudge* (1841), as in Poe's poem, a raven is central to the action.
258. **Mathews:** Cornelius Mathews (1817–89), a New Yorker
who, like Poe, attacked Longfellow. 271. **Why . . . Gray:**
William Collins (1721–59) and Thomas Gray (1716–71) were representative pre-Romantic English poets.

I'm not over-fond of Greek metres in English,
To me rhyme 's a gain, so it be not too jinglish,
And your modern hexameter verses are no more
Like Greek ones than sleek Mr. Pope is like
　　Homer;
As the roar of the sea to the coo of a pigeon is,
So, compared to your moderns, sounds old Mele-
　　sigenes;
I may be too partial, the reason, perhaps, o't is
That I 've heard the old blind man recite his own
　　rhapsodies, 　　　　　　　　　　　279
And my ear with that music impregnate may be,
Like the poor exiled shell with the soul of the sea,
Or as one can't bear Strauss when his nature is
　　cloven
To its deeps within deeps by the stroke of Beetho-
　　ven;
But, set that aside, and 't is truth that I speak,
Had Theocritus written in English, not Greek,
I believe that his exquisite sense would scarce
　　change a line
In that rare, tender, virgin-like pastoral Evange-
　　line.
That 's not ancient nor modern, its place is apart
Where time has no sway, in the realm of pure
　　Art,
'T is a shrine of retreat from Earth's hubbub and
　　strife 　　　　　　　　　　　　　290
As quiet and chaste as the author's own life.

　　"What! Irving? thrice welcome, warm heart
　　　　and fine brain,
You bring back the happiest spirit from Spain,
And the gravest sweet humor, that ever were there
Since Cervantes met death in his gentle despair;
Nay, don't be embarrassed, nor look so beseech-
　　ing,
I sha'n't run directly against my own preaching,
And, having just laughed at their Raphaels and
　　Dantes,
Go to setting you up beside matchless Cer-
　　vantes; 　　　　　　　　　　　299
But allow me to speak what I honestly feel,—
To a true poet-heart add the fun of Dick Steele,
Throw in all of Addison, *minus* the chill,
With the whole of that partnership's stock and
　　good-will,
Mix well, and while stirring, hum o'er, as a spell,
The fine *old* English Gentleman, simmer it well,
Sweeten just to your own private liking, then
　　strain,
That only the finest and clearest remain,

Let it stand out of doors till a soul it receives
From the warm lazy sun loitering down through
　　green leaves, 　　　　　　　　　309
And you'll find a choice nature, not wholly de-
　　serving
A name either English or Yankee,—just Irving.

　　　　　　　　　　　　　　　*1848*

---

# EMERSON THE LECTURER

---

❖

⟪ THIS was first published in the *Atlantic Monthly*
(February 1861) and revised for the *Nation* (November 12, 1868).

❖

IT IS a singular fact that Mr. Emerson is the most
steadily attractive lecturer in America. Into that
somewhat cold-waterish region adventurers of the
sensational kind come down now and then with
a splash, to become disregarded King Logs [1] before the next season. But Mr. Emerson always
draws. A lecturer now for something like a third
of a century, one of the pioneers of the lecturing
system, the charm of his voice, his manner, and
his matter has never lost its power over his earlier
hearers, and continually winds new ones in its enchanting meshes. What they do not fully understand they take on trust, and listen, saying to
themselves, as the old poet of Sir Philip Sidney,—

　　　"A sweet, attractive, kind of grace,
　　　　A full assurance given by looks,
　　　Continual comfort in a face,
　　　　The lineaments of gospel books." [2]

We call it a singular fact, because we Yankees
are thought to be fond of the spread-eagle style,
and nothing can be more remote from that than
his. We are reckoned a practical folk, who would
rather hear about a new air-tight stove than about
Plato; yet our favorite teacher's practicality is not
in the least of the Poor Richard variety. If he have
any Buncombe constituency, it is that unrealized
commonwealth of philosophers which Plotinus

---

275. Like . . . Homer: Alexander Pope (1688–1744) published
translations of the *Iliad* and *Odyssey*, 1715–26. 　277. Mele-
sigenes: Homer. 　293. You . . . Spain: Washington Irving
returned from his ambassadorship to Spain in 1845.

EMERSON THE LECTURER. 　1. King Logs: In the Aesop fable,
the frogs ask Jupiter for a king. He sends them a log, which they
accept as a ruler until they realize what it is. 　2. "A . . .
books": The verse is from Matthew Roydon's elegy to Sidney,
published in *The Phoenix Nest* (1593).

proposed to establish; and if he were to make an almanac, his directions to farmers would be something like this: "OCTOBER: *Indian Summer; now is the time to get in your early Vedas.*" What, then, is his secret? Is it not that he out-Yankees us all? that his range includes us all? that he is equally at home with the potato-disease and original sin, with pegging shoes and the Over-Soul? that, as we try all trades, so has he tried all cultures? and above all, that his mysticism gives us a counterpoise to our super-practicality?

There is no man living to whom, as a writer, so many of us feel and thankfully acknowledge so great an indebtedness for ennobling impulses,—none whom so many cannot abide. What does he mean? ask these last. Where is his system? What is the use of it all? What the deuce have we to do with Brahma? I do not propose to write an essay on Emerson at this time. I will only say that one may find grandeur and consolation in a starlit night without caring to ask what it means, save grandeur and consolation; one may like Montaigne, as some ten generations before us have done, without thinking him so systematic as some more eminently tedious (or shall we say tediously eminent?) authors; one may think roses as good in their way as cabbages, though the latter would make a better show in the witness-box, if cross-examined as to their usefulness; and as for Brahma, why, he can take care of himself, and won't bite us at any rate.

The bother with Mr. Emerson is, that, though he writes in prose, he is essentially a poet. If you undertake to paraphrase what he says, and to reduce it to words of one syllable for infant minds, you will make as sad work of it as the good monk with his analysis of Homer in the *Epistolæ Obscurorum Virorum.*[3] We look upon him as one of the few men of genius whom our age has produced, and there needs no better proof of it than his masculine faculty of fecundating other minds. Search for his eloquence in his books and you will perchance miss it, but meanwhile you will find that it has kindled all your thoughts. For choice and pith of language he belongs to a better age than ours, and might rub shoulders with Fuller and Browne,—though he does use that abominable word *reliable.* His eye for a fine, telling phrase that will carry true is like that of a backwoodsman for a rifle; and he will dredge you up a choice word from the mud of Cotton Mather himself. A diction at once so rich and so homely as his I know not where to match in these days of writing by the page; it is like homespun cloth-of-gold.

The many cannot miss his meaning, and only the few can find it. It is the open secret of all true genius. It is wholesome to angle in those profound pools, though one be rewarded with nothing more than the leap of a fish that flashes his freckled side in the sun and as suddenly absconds in the dark and dreamy waters again. There is keen excitement, though there be no ponderable acquisition. If we carry nothing home in our baskets, there is ample gain in dilated lungs and stimulated blood. What does he mean, quotha? He means inspiring hints, a divining-rod to your deeper nature. No doubt, Emerson, like all original men, has his peculiar audience, and yet I know none that can hold a promiscuous crowd in pleased attention so long as he. As in all original men, there is something for every palate. "Would you know," says Goethe, "the ripest cherries? Ask the boys and the blackbirds."

The announcement that such a pleasure as a new course of lectures by him is coming, to people as old as I am, is something like those forebodings of spring that prepare us every year for a familiar novelty, none the less novel, when it arrives, because it is familiar. We know perfectly well what we are to expect from Mr. Emerson, and yet what he says always penetrates and stirs us, as is apt to be the case with genius, in a very unlooked-for fashion. Perhaps genius is one of the few things which we gladly allow to repeat itself, —one of the few that multiply rather than weaken the force of their impression by iteration? Perhaps some of us hear more than the mere words, are moved by something deeper than the thoughts? If it be so, we are quite right, for it is thirty years and more of "plain living and high thinking" that speak to us in this altogether unique lay-preacher. We have shared in the beneficence of this varied culture, this fearless impartiality in criticism and speculation, this masculine sincerity, this sweetness of nature which rather stimulates than cloys, for a generation long. If ever there was a standing testimonial to the cumulative power and value of Character (and we need it sadly in these days), we have it in this gracious and dignified presence. What an antiseptic is a pure life! At sixty-five (or two years beyond his grand climacteric, as he would prefer to call it) he has that privilege of soul which abolishes the calendar, and presents him to us always the unwasted contemporary of his own prime. I do not know if he seem old to his younger hearers, but we who have known him so long wonder at the tenacity with which he maintains himself even in the outposts of youth. I suppose it is not the Emerson of 1868 to whom we listen. For us the

3. *Epistolæ Obscurorum Virorum: "Letters of Obscure Men,"* a sixteenth-century work.

whole life of the man is distilled in the clear drop of every sentence, and behind each word we divine the force of a noble character, the weight of a large capital of thinking and being. We do not go to hear what Emerson says so much as to hear Emerson. Not that we perceive any falling-off in anything that ever was essential to the charm of Mr. Emerson's peculiar style of thought or phrase. The first lecture,[4] to be sure, was more disjointed even than common. It was as if, after vainly trying to get his paragraphs into sequence and order, he had at last tried the desperate expedient of *shuffling* them. It was chaos come again, but it was a chaos full of shooting-stars, a jumble of creative forces. The second lecture, on "Criticism and Poetry," was quite up to the level of old times, full of that power of strangely subtle association whose indirect approaches startle the mind into almost painful attention, of those flashes of mutual understanding between speaker and hearer that are gone ere one can say it lightens. The vice of Emerson's criticism seems to be, that while no man is so sensitive to what is poetical, few men are less sensible than he of what makes a poem. He values the solid meaning of thought above the subtler meaning of style. He would prefer Donne, I suspect, to Spenser, and sometimes mistakes the queer for the original.

To be young is surely the best, if the most precarious, gift of life; yet there are some of us who would hardly consent to be young again, if it were at the cost of our recollection of Mr. Emerson's first lectures during the consulate[5] of Van Buren. We used to walk in from the country to the Masonic Temple (I think it was), through the crisp winter night, and listen to that thrilling voice of his, so charged with subtle meaning and subtle music, as shipwrecked men on a raft to the hail of a ship that came with unhoped-for food and rescue. Cynics might say what they liked. Did our own imaginations transfigure dry remainder-biscuit[6] into ambrosia? At any rate, he brought us *life,* which, on the whole, is no bad thing. Was it all transcendentalism? magic-lantern pictures on mist? As you will. Those, then, were just what we wanted. But it was not so. The delight and the benefit were that he put us in communication with a larger style of thought, sharpened our wits with a more pungent phrase, gave us ravishing glimpses of an ideal under the dry husk of our New England; made us conscious of the supreme and everlasting originality of whatever bit of soul

might be in any of us; freed us, in short, from the stocks of prose in which we had sat so long that we had grown well-nigh contented in our cramps. And who that saw the audience will ever forget it, where every one still capable of fire, or longing to renew in himself the half-forgotten sense of it, was gathered? Those faces, young and old, agleam with pale intellectual light, eager with pleased attention, flash upon me once more from the deep recesses of the years with an exquisite pathos. Ah, beautiful young eyes, brimming with love and hope, wholly vanished now in that other world we call the Past, or peering doubtfully through the pensive gloaming of memory, your light impoverishes these cheaper days! I hear again that rustle of sensation, as they turned to exchange glances over some pithier thought, some keener flash of that humor which always played about the horizon of his mind like heat-lightning, and it seems now like the sad whisper of the autumn leaves that are whirling around me. But would my picture be complete if I forgot that ample and vegete[7] countenance of Mr. R—— of W——,—how, from its regular post at the corner of the front bench, it turned in ruddy triumph to the profaner audience as if he were the inexplicably appointed fugleman of appreciation? I was reminded of him by those hearty cherubs in Titian's *Assumption*[8] that look at you as who should say, "Did you ever see a Madonna like *that?* Did you ever behold one hundred and fifty pounds of womanhood mount heavenward before like a rocket?"

To some of us that long-past experience remains as the most marvellous and fruitful we have ever had. Emerson awakened us, saved us from the body of this death. It is the sound of the trumpet that the young soul longs for, careless what breath may fill it. Sidney heard it in the ballad of "Chevy Chase,"[9] and we in Emerson. Nor did it blow retreat, but called to us with assurance of victory. Did they say he was disconnected? So were the stars, that seemed larger to our eyes, still keen with that excitement, as we walked homeward with prouder stride over the creaking snow. And were *they* not knit together by a higher logic than our mere sense could master? Were we enthusiasts? I hope and believe we were, and am thankful to the man who made us worth something for once in our lives. If asked what was left?

---

4. **The first lecture:** Lowell refers here to Emerson's series of six Boston lectures beginning October 12, 1868. He revised and reprinted this essay before the series was completed.　**5. consulate:** i.e., presidency.　**6. Did . . . remainder-biscuit:** See Shakespeare's *As You Like It,* II.vii.39.

7. **vegete:** ruddy, healthy.　8. **Titian's** *Assumption:* In this painting the amazed apostles gaze upward at the ascending Virgin.　9. **Sidney . . . Chase:** Sidney wrote in his *Defence of Poesie* (1595): "Certainly I must confess mine own barbarousness; I never heard the old song of Percy and Douglas that I found not my heart moved more than by a trumpet."

what we carried home? we should not have been careful for an answer. It would have been enough if we had said that something beautiful had passed that way. Or we might have asked in return what one brought away from a symphony of Beethoven? Enough that he had set that ferment of wholesome discontent at work in us. There is one, at least, of those old hearers, so many of whom are now in the fruition of that intellectual beauty of which Emerson gave them both the desire and the foretaste, who will always love to repeat:—

> "Che in la mente m' ê fitta, ed or m' accuora
> La cara e buona immagine paterna
> Di voi, quando nel mondo ad ora ad ora
> M' insegnavaste come l' uom s' eterna." [10]

I am unconsciously thinking, as I write, of the third lecture of the present course, in which Mr. Emerson gave some delightful reminiscences of the intellectual influences in whose movement he had shared. It was like hearing Goethe read some passages of the *Wahrheit aus seinem Leben*.[11] Not that there was not a little *Dichtung*,[12] too, here and there, as the lecturer built up so lofty a pedestal under certain figures as to lift them into a prominence of obscurity, and seem to masthead them there. Everybody was asking his neighbor who this or that recondite great man was, in the faint hope that somebody might once have heard of him. There are those who call Mr. Emerson cold. Let them revise their judgment in presence of this loyalty of his that can keep warm for half a century, that never forgets a friendship, or fails to pay even a fancied obligation to the uttermost farthing. This substantiation of shadows was but incidental, and pleasantly characteristic of the man to those who know and love him. The greater part of the lecture was devoted to reminiscences of things substantial in themselves. He spoke of Everett, fresh from Greece and Germany; of Channing; of the translations of Margaret Fuller, Ripley, and Dwight; of the *Dial* and Brook Farm. To what he said of the latter an undertone of good-humored irony gave special zest. But what every one of his hearers felt was that the protagonist in the drama was left out. The lecturer was no Æneas to babble the *quorum magna*

pars fui,[13] and, as one of his listeners, I cannot help wishing to say how each of them was commenting the story as it went along, and filling up the necessary gaps in it from his own private store of memories. His younger hearers could not know how much they owed to the benign impersonality, the quiet scorn of everything ignoble, the never-sated hunger of self-culture, that were personified in the man before them. But the older knew how much the country's intellectual emancipation was due to the stimulus of his teaching and example, how constantly he had kept burning the beacon of an ideal life above our lower region of turmoil. To him more than to all other causes together did the young martyrs of our civil war owe the sustaining strength of thoughtful heroism that is so touching in every record of their lives. Those who are grateful to Mr. Emerson, as many of us are, for what they feel to be most valuable in their culture, or perhaps I should say their impulse, are grateful not so much for any direct teachings of his as for that inspiring lift which only genius can give, and without which all doctrine is chaff.

This was something like the *caret* which some of us older boys wished to fill up on the margin of the master's lecture. Few men have been so much to so many, and through so large a range of aptitudes and temperaments and this simply because all of us value manhood beyond any or all other qualities of character. We may suspect in him, here and there, a certain thinness and vagueness of quality, but let the waters go over him as they list, this masculine fibre of his will keep its lively color and its toughness of texture. I have heard some great speakers and some accomplished orators, but never any that so moved and persuaded men as he. There is a kind of undertow in that rich baritone of his that sweeps our minds from their foothold into deeper waters with a drift we cannot and would not resist. And how artfully (for Emerson is a long-studied artist in these things) does the deliberate utterance, that seems waiting for the fit word, appear to admit us partners in the labor of thought and make us feel as if the glance of humor were a sudden suggestion, as if the perfect phrase lying written there on the desk were as unexpected to him as to us! In that closely filed speech of his at the Burns centenary dinner,[14] every word seemed to have just dropped down to him from the clouds. He looked far away over the heads of his hearers, with a vague kind of expectation, as into some private heaven of invention, and the winged period came at last obedi-

---

10. "*Che . . . eterna*": Dante's *Inferno*, XV.82–85. Longfellow's translation reads:

> For in my mind is fixed, and touches now
> My heart, the dear and good paternal image
> Of you, when in the world from hour to hour
> You taught me how a man becomes eternal.

11. *Wahrheit aus seinem Leben:* "Truth Out of His Life." The full title of Goethe's autobiography is *Dichtung und Wahrheit aus meinem Leben*.    12. *Dichtung:* Poetry.

13. *quorum magna pars fui:* "Of which things I was a great part" (*Aeneid*, II. 6).    14. In . . . dinner: Emerson spoke at the Burns Festival, Boston, January 25, 1859.

ent to his spell. "My dainty Ariel!" [15] he seemed murmuring to himself as he cast down his eyes as if in deprecation of the frenzy of approval and caught another sentence from the Sibylline leaves that lay before him, ambushed behind a dish of fruit and seen only by nearest neighbors. Every sentence brought down the house, as I never saw one brought down before,—and it is not so easy to hit Scotsmen with a sentiment that has no hint of native brogue in it. I watched, for it was an interesting study, how the quick sympathy ran flashing from face to face down the long tables, like an electric spark thrilling as it went, and then exploded in a thunder of plaudits. I watched till tables and faces vanished, for I, too, found myself caught up in the common enthusiasm, and my excited fancy set me under the *bema* [16] listening to him who fulmined over Greece. I can never help applying to him what Ben Jonson said of Bacon: "There happened in my time one noble speaker, who was full of gravity in his speaking. His language was nobly censorious. No man ever spake more neatly, more pressly, more weightily, or suffered less emptiness, less idleness, in what he uttered. No member of his speech but consisted of his own graces. His hearers could not cough, or look aside from him, without loss. He commanded where he spoke." Those who heard him while their natures were yet plastic, and their mental nerves trembled under the slightest breath of divine air, will never cease to feel and say:—

"Was never eye did see that face,
   Was never ear did hear that tongue,
Was never mind did mind his grace,
   That ever thought the travail long;
But eyes, and ears, and every thought,
   Were with his sweet perfections caught." [17]

*1861*

---

# SUNTHIN' IN THE PASTORAL LINE

### FROM *The Biglow Papers,*
### SECOND SERIES

---

❖

❪ LOWELL began serializing the First Series of *The Biglow Papers* in a Boston newspaper in 1846. These dialect poems were a protest against the Mexican War,

concerning which he wrote ten years later, it was "essentially a war of false pretences [which] would result in widening the boundaries and so prolonging the life of slavery." In the *Papers*, his "voice"—not to be completely identified with that of Lowell himself—was Hosea Biglow, a country Yankee whose common sense is "heated by conscience." Hosea's poems are "edited" by his pastor, Parson Wilbur, who sometimes serves as another "voice" for Lowell.

A Second Series, most of which appeared in the *Atlantic Monthly* between January 1862 and May 1866, offered commentary on issues connected with the Civil War. The sixth number, here printed, is an exception. Its descriptions of the New England scene are less dated than some of Lowell's political opinions.

❖

TO THE EDITORS OF THE *Atlantic Monthly*
                   Jaalam, 17th May, 1862.
GENTLEMEN,—

At the special request of Mr. Biglow, I intended to inclose, together with his own contribution, (into which, at my suggestion, he has thrown a little more of pastoral sentiment than usual,) some passages from my sermon on the day of the National Fast, from the text, "Remember them that are in bonds, as bound with them," Heb. xiii. 3. But I have not leisure sufficient at present for the copying of them, even were I altogether satisfied with the production as it stands. I should prefer, I confess, to contribute the entire discourse to the pages of your respectable miscellany, if it should be found acceptable upon perusal, especially as I find the difficulty in selection of greater magnitude than I had anticipated. What passes without challenge in the fervour of oral delivery, cannot always stand the colder criticism of the closet. I am not so great an enemy of Eloquence as my friend Mr. Biglow would appear to be from some passages in his contribution for the current month. I would not, indeed, hastily suspect him of covertly glancing at myself in his somewhat caustick animadversions, albeit some of the phrases he girds at are not entire strangers to my lips. I am a more hearty admirer of the Puritans than seems now to be the fashion, and believe, that, if they Hebraized a little too much in their speech, they showed remarkable practical sagacity as statesmen and founders. But such phenomena as Puritanism are the results rather of great religious than of merely social convulsions, and do not long survive them. So soon as an earnest conviction has cooled into a phrase, its work is over, and the best that can be done with it is to bury it. *Ite, missa est.*[1] I am inclined to agree with Mr. Biglow

---

15. "My . . . Ariel!": Shakespeare's *Tempest*. V.i.95.   16. *bema:* rostrum.   17. "Was . . . caught": Lowell quotes a second time from Roydon's "Elegie."

SUNTHIN' IN THE PASTORAL LINE.   1. *Ite, missa est:* "Go, the mass is finished." These words come just before the final blessing in the mass.

that we cannot settle the great political questions which are now presenting themselves to the nation by the opinions of Jeremiah or Ezekiel as to the wants and duties of the Jews in their time, nor do I believe that an entire community with their feelings and views would be practicable or even agreeable at the present day. At the same time I could wish that their habit of subordinating the actual to the moral, the flesh to the spirit, and this world to the other, were more common. They had found out, at least, the great military secret that soul weighs more than body.—But I am suddenly called to a sick-bed in the household of a valued parishioner.

With esteem and respect,
Your obedient servant,
HOMER WILBUR.

Once git a smell o' musk into a draw,
An' it clings hold like precerdents in law:
Your gra'ma'am put it there,—when, goodness
    knows,—
To jes' this-worldify her Sunday-clo'es;
But the old chist wun't sarve her gran'son's wife,
(For, 'thout new funnitoor, wut good in life?)
An' so ole clawfoot, from the precinks dread
O' the spare chamber, slinks into the shed
Where, dim with dust, it fust or last subsides
To holdin' seeds an' fifty things besides;     10
But better days stick fast in heart an' husk,
An' all you keep in 't gits a scent o' musk.

Jes' so with poets: wut they've airly read
Gits kind o' worked into their heart an' head,
So 's 't they can't seem to write but jest on sheers
With furrin countries or played-out ideers,
Nor hev a feelin', ef it doos n't smack
O' wut some critter chose to feel 'way back:
This makes 'em talk o' daisies, larks, an' things,
Ez though we 'd nothin' here that blows an'
    sings,—      20
(Why, I 'd give more for one live bobolink
Than a square mile o' larks in printer's ink,)—
This makes 'em think our fust o' May is May,
Which 't ain't, for all the almanicks can say.

O little city-gals, don't never go it
Blind on the word o' noospaper or poet!
They 're apt to puff, an' May-day seldom looks
Up in the country ez it doos in books;
They 're no more like than hornets'-nests an'
    hives,
Or printed sarmons be to holy lives.      30
I, with my trouses perched on cowhide boots,
Tuggin' my foundered feet out by the roots,
Hev seen ye come to fling on April's hearse

Your muslin nosegays from the milliner's,
Puzzlin' to find dry ground your queen to choose,
An' dance your throats sore in morocker shoes:
I 've seen ye an' felt proud, thet, come wut would,
Our Pilgrim stock wuz pethed with hardihood.
Pleasure doos make us Yankees kind o' winch,
Ez though 't wuz sunthin' paid for by the inch;
But yit we du contrive to worry thru,      41
Ef Dooty tells us thet the thing 's to du,
An' kerry a hollerday, ef we set out,
Ez stiddily ez though 't wuz a redoubt.

I, country-born an' bred, know where to find
Some blooms thet make the season suit the mind,
An' seem to metch the doubtin' bluebird's
    notes,—
Half-vent'rin' liverworts in furry coats,
Bloodroots, whose rolled-up leaves ef you oncurl,
Each on 'em 's cradle to a baby-pearl,—      50
But these are jes' Spring's pickets; sure ez sin,
The rebble frosts 'll try to drive 'em in;
For half our May 's so awfully like May n't,
't would rile a Shaker or an evrige saint;
Though I own up I like our back'ard springs
Thet kind o' haggle with their greens an' things,
An' when you 'most give up, 'uthout more words
Toss the fields full o' blossoms, leaves, an' birds;
Thet's Northun natur', slow an' apt to doubt,
But when it *doos* git stirred, ther' 's no ginout!   60

Fust come the blackbirds clatt'rin' in tall trees,
An' settlin' things in windy Congresses,—
Queer politicians, though, for I 'll be skinned
Ef all on 'em don't head aginst the wind.
'fore long the trees begin to show belief,—
The maple crimsons to a coral-reef,
Then saffern swarms swing off from all the willers
So plump they look like yaller caterpillars,
Then gray hossches'nuts leetle hands unfold
Softer 'n a baby's be at three days old:      70
Thet 's robin-redbreast's almanick; he knows
Thet arter this ther' 's only blossom-snows;
So, choosin' out a handy crotch an' spouse,
He goes to plast'rin' his adobe house.

Then seems to come a hitch,—things lag behind,
Till some fine mornin' Spring makes up her mind,
An' ez, when snow-swelled rivers cresh their dams
Heaped-up with ice thet dovetails in an' jams,
A leak comes spirtin' thru some pin-hole cleft,
Grows stronger, fercer, tears out right an' left,   80
Then all the waters bow themselves an' come,
Suddin, in one gret slope o' shedderin' foam,
Jes' so our Spring gits everythin' in tune
An' gives one leap from Aperl into June:
Then all comes crowdin' in; afore you think,

Young oak-leaves mist the side-hill woods with
    pink;
The catbird in the laylock-bush is loud:
The orchards turn to heaps o' rosy cloud;
Red-cedars blossom tu, though few folks know it,
An' look all dipt in sunshine like a poet;     90
The lime-trees pile their solid stacks o' shade
An' drows'ly simmer with the bees' sweet trade;
In ellum-shrouds the flashin' hangbird clings
An' for the summer vy'ge his hammock slings;
All down the loose-walled lanes in archin' bowers
The barb'ry droops its strings o' golden flowers,
Whose shrinkin' hearts the school-gals love to try
With pins,—they'll worry yourn so, boys, bimeby!
But I don't love your cat'logue style,—do you?—
Ez ef to sell off Natur' by vendoo;    100
One word with blood in 't 's twice ez good ez two:
'nuff sed, June's bridesman, poet o' the year,
Gladness on wings, the bobolink, is here;
Half-hid in tip-top apple-blooms he swings,
Or climbs aginst the breeze with quiverin' wings,
Or, givin' way to 't in a mock despair,
Runs down, a brook o' laughter, thru the air.

I ollus feel the sap start in my veins
In Spring, with curus heats an' prickly pains,
Thet drive me, when I git a chance, to walk   110
Off by myself to hev a privit talk
With a queer critter thet can't seem to 'gree
Along o' me like most folks,—Mister Me.
Ther' 's times when I'm unsoshle ez a stone,
An' sort o' suffercate to be alone,—
I 'm crowded jes' to think thet folks are nigh,
An' can't bear nothin' closer than the sky;
Now the wind 's full ez shifty in the mind
Ez wut it is ou'-doors, ef I ain't blind,
An' sometimes, in the fairest sou'west weather
My innard vane pints east for weeks together, 121
My natur' gits all goose-flesh, an' my sins
Come drizzlin' on my conscience sharp ez pins:
Wal, et sech times I jes' slip out o' sight
An' take it out in a fair stan'-up fight
With the one cuss I can't lay on the shelf,
The crook'dest stick in all the heap,—Myself.

'T wuz so las' Sabbath arter meetin'-time:
Findin' my feelin's would n't noways rhyme
With nobody's, but off the hendle flew   130
An' took things from an east-wind pint o' view,
I started off to lose me in the hills
Where the pines be, up back o' 'Siah's Mills:
Pines, ef you 're blue, are the best friends I know,
They mope an' sigh an' sheer your feelin's so,—
They hesh the ground beneath so, tu, I swan,
You half-forgit you 've gut a body on.
Ther' 's a small school'us' there where four roads
    meet,

The door-steps hollered out by little feet,
An' side-posts carved with names whose owners
    grew    140
To gret men, some on 'em, an' deacons, tu;
't ain't used no longer, coz the town hez gut
A high-school, where they teach the Lord knows
    wut:
Three-story larnin' 's pop'lar now; I guess
We thriv' ez wal on jes' two stories less,
For it strikes me ther' 's sech a thing ez sinnin'
By overloadin' children's underpinnin':
Wal, here it wuz I larned my A B C,
An' it's a kind o' favorite spot with me.

We 're curus critters: Now ain't jes' the minute
Thet ever fits us easy while we're in it;   151
Long ez 't wuz futur', 't would be perfect bliss,—
Soon ez it's past, *thet* time's wuth ten o' this;
An' yit there ain't a man thet need be told
Thet Now's the only bird lays eggs o' gold.
A knee-high lad, I used to plot an' plan
An' think 't wuz life's cap-sheaf to be a man;
Now, gittin' gray, there's nothin' I enjoy
Like dreamin' back along into a boy:
So the ole school'us' is a place I choose   160
Afore all others, ef I want to muse;
I set down where I used to set, an' git
My boyhood back, an' better things with it,—
Faith, Hope, an' sunthin', ef it is n't Cherrity,
It's want o' guile, an' thet 's ez gret a rerrity,—
While Fancy's cushin', free to Prince and Clown,
Makes the hard bench ez soft ez milkweed-down.

Now, 'fore I knowed, thet Sabbath arternoon
When I sot out to tramp myself in tune,
I found me in the school'us' on my seat,   170
Drummin' the march to No-wheres with my feet.
Thinkin' o' nothin', I've heerd ole folks say
Is a hard kind o' dooty in its way:
It's thinkin' everythin' you ever knew,
Or ever hearn, to make your feelin's blue.
I sot there tryin' thet on for a spell:
I thought o' the Rebellion, then o' Hell,
Which some folks tell ye now is jest a metterfor
(A the'ry, p'raps, it wun't *feel* none the better
    for);
I thought o' Reconstruction, wut we'd win   180
Patchin' our patent self-blow-up agin:
I thought ef this 'ere milkin' o' the wits,
So much a month, warn't givin' Natur' fits,—
Ef folks warn't druv, findin' their own milk fail,
To work the cow thet hez an iron tail,
An' ef idees 'thout ripenin' in the pan
Would send up cream to humor ary man:
From this to thet I let my worryin' creep,
Till finally I must ha' fell asleep.

Our lives in sleep are some like streams thet glide
'twixt flesh an' sperrit boundin' on each side,   191
Where both shores' shadders kind o' mix an' min-
gle
In sunthin' thet ain't jes' like either single;
An' when you cast off moorin's from To-day,
An' down towards To-morrer drift away,
The imiges thet tengle on the stream
Make a new upside-down'ard world o' dream:
Sometimes they seem like sunrise-streaks an'
warnin's
O' wut 'll be in Heaven on Sabbath-mornin's,
An', mixed right in ez ef jest out o' spite,   200
Sunthin' thet says your supper ain't gone right.
I 'm gret on dreams, an' often when I wake,
I've lived so much it makes my mem'ry ache,
An' can't skurce take a cat-nap in my cheer
'thout hevin' 'em, some good, some bad, all queer.
Now I wuz settin' where I 'd ben, it seemed,
An' ain't sure yit whether I r'ally dreamed,
Nor, ef I did, how long I might ha' slep',
When I hearn some un stompin' up the step,
An' lookin' round, ef two an' two make four,   210
I see a Pilgrim Father in the door.
He wore a steeple-hat, tall boots, an' spurs
With rowels to 'em big ez ches'nut-burrs,
An' his gret sword behind him sloped away
Long 'z a man's speech thet dunno wut to say.—
"Ef your name 's Biglow, an' your given-name
Hosee," sez he, "it 's arter you I came;
I'm your gret-gran'ther multiplied by three."—
"My *wut?*" sez I.—"Your gret-gret-gret," sez he:
"You would n't ha' never ben here but for me.
Two hundred an' three year ago this May   221
The ship I come in sailed up Boston Bay;
I'd been a cunnle in our Civil War,—
But wut on airth hev *you* gut up one for?
Coz we du things in England, 't ain't for you
To git a notion you can du 'em tu:
I 'm told you write in public prints: ef true,
It's nateral you should know a thing or two."—
"Thet air 's an argymunt I can't endorse,—
't would prove, coz you wear spurs, you kep' a
horse:   230
For brains," sez I, "wutever you may think,
Ain't boun' to cash the drafs o' pen-an'-ink,—
Though mos' folks write ez ef they hoped jes'
quickenin'
The churn would argoo skim-milk into thickenin';
But skim-milk ain't a thing to change its view
O' wut it 's meant for more 'n a smoky flue.
But du pray tell me, 'fore we furder go,
How in all Natur' did you come to know
'bout our affairs," sez I, "in Kingdom-Come?"—
"Wal, I worked round at sperrit-rappin' some,
An' danced the tables till their legs wuz gone,   241

In hopes o' larnin' wut wuz goin' on,"
Sez he, "but mejums lie so like all-split
Thet I concluded it wuz best to quit.
But, come now, ef you wun't confess to knowin',
You've some conjectures how the thing's
a-goin'."—
"Gran'ther," sez I, "a vane warn't never known
Nor asked to hev a jedgment of its own;
An' yit, ef 't ain't gut rusty in the jints,
It's safe to trust its say on certin pints:   250
It knows the wind's opinions to a T,
An' the wind settles wut the weather'll be."
"I never thought a scion of our stock
Could grow the wood to make a weathercock;
When I wuz younger 'n you, skurce more 'n a
shaver,
No airthly wind," sez he, "could make me waver!"
(Ez he said this, he clinched his jaw an' forehead,
Hitchin' his belt to bring his sword-hilt for-
rard.)—
"Jes so it wuz with me," sez I, "I swow,   259
When *I* wuz younger 'n wut you see me now,—
Nothin' from Adam's fall to Huldy's bonnet,
Thet I warn't full-cocked with my jedgment on it;
But now I'm gittin' on in life, I find
It 's a sight harder to make up my mind,—
Nor I don't often try tu, when events
Will du it for me free of all expense.
The moral question 's ollus plain enough,—
It 's jes' the human-natur' side thet's tough;
Wut 's best to think may n't puzzle me nor you,—
The pinch comes in decidin' wut to *du;*   270
Ef you *read* History, all runs smooth ez grease,
Coz there the men ain't nothin' more 'n idees,—
But come to *make* it, ez we must to-day,
Th' idees hev arms an' legs an' stop the way:
It's easy fixin' things in facts an' figgers,—
They can't resist, nor warn't brought up with nig-
gers;
But come to try your the'ry on,—why then
Your facts an' figgers change to ign'ant men
Actin' ez ugly—" —"Smite 'em hip an' thigh!"
Sez gran'ther, "and let every man-child die!   280
Oh for three weeks o' Cromwle an' the Lord!
Up, Isr'el, to your tents an' grind the sword!"—
"Thet kind o' thing worked wal in ole Judee,
But you forgit how long it's ben A.D.;
You think thet 's ellerkence,—I call it shoddy,
A thing," sez I, "wun't cover soul nor body;
I like the plain all-wool o' common-sense,
Thet warms ye now, an' will a twelve-month
hence.
*You* took to follerin' where the Prophets beck-
oned,
An', fust you knowed on, back come Charles the
Second;   290

Now wut I want 's to hev all *we* gain stick,
An' not to start Millennium too quick;
We hain't to punish only, but to keep,
An' the cure 's gut to go a cent'ry deep."
"Wall, milk-an'-water ain't the best o' glue,"
Sez he, "an' so you'll find afore you're thru;
Ef reshness venters sunthin', shilly-shally
Loses ez often wut 's ten times the vally.
Thet exe of ourn, when Charles's neck gut split,
Opened a gap thet ain't bridged over yit:   300
Slav'ry 's your Charles, the Lord hez gin the
   exe"—
"Our Charles," sez I, "hez gut eight million
   necks.
The hardest question ain't the black man's right,
The trouble is to 'mancipate the white;
One 's chained in body an' can be sot free,
But t' other 's chaincd in soul to an idee:
It 's a long job, but we shall worry thru it;
Ef bagnets fail, the spellin'-book must du it."
"Hosee," sez he, "I think you 're goin' to fail:
The rettlesnake ain't dangerous in the tail;   310
This 'ere rebellion 's nothing but the rettle,—
You 'll stomp on thet an' think you've won the
   bettle;
It's Slavery thet 's the fangs an' thinkin' head,
An' ef you want selvation, cresh it dead,—
An' cresh it suddin, or you 'll larn by waitin'
Thet Chance wun't stop to listen to debatin'!"—
"God's truth!" sez I,—"an' ef *I* held the club,
An' knowed jes' where to strike,—but there 's the
   rub!"—
"Strike soon," sez he, "or you 'll be deadly
   ailin',—
Folks thet 's afeared to fail are sure o' failin';   320
God hates your sneakin' creturs thet believe
He'll settle things they run away an' leave!"
He brought his foot down fercely, ez he spoke,
An' give me sech a startle thet I woke.

*1862*

---

FROM

# INTRODUCTION TO THE BIGLOW PAPERS, SECOND SERIES

---

◇

⟮ WHEN Lowell collected the several *Atlantic Monthly* installments of the Second Series of *The Biglow Papers* for publication as a separate book (1866), he prefixed this essay. It gives an account of the origin of the whole scheme, and a scholarly discussion of the historical backgrounds of American words.

◇

THOUGH prefaces seem of late to have fallen under some reproach, they have at least this advantage, that they set us again on the feet of our personal consciousness and rescue us from the gregarious mock-modesty or cowardice of that *we* which shrills feebly throughout modern literature like the shrieking of mice in the walls of a house that has passed its prime. Having a few words to say to the many friends whom the "Biglow Papers" have won me, I shall accordingly take the freedom of the first person singular of the personal pronoun. Let each of the good-natured unknown who have cheered me by the written communication of their sympathy look upon this Introduction as a private letter to himself.

When, more than twenty years ago, I wrote the first of the series, I had no definite plan and no intention of ever writing another. Thinking the Mexican war, as I think it still, a national crime committed in behoof of Slavery, our common sin, and wishing to put the feeling of those who thought as I did in a way that would tell, I imagined to myself such an upcountry man as I had often seen at antislavery gatherings, capable of district-school English, but always instinctively falling back into the natural stronghold of his homely dialect when heated to the point of self-forgetfulness. When I began to carry out my conception and to write in my assumed character, I found myself in a strait between two perils. On the one hand, I was in danger of being carried beyond the limit of my own opinions, or at least of that temper with which every man should speak his mind in print, and on the other I feared the risk of seeming to vulgarize a deep and sacred conviction. I needed on occasion to rise above the level of mere *patois,* and for this purpose conceived the Rev. Mr. Wilbur, who should express the more cautious element of the New England character and its pedantry, as Mr. Biglow should serve for its homely common-sense vivified and heated by conscience. The parson was to be the complement rather than the antithesis of his parishioner, and I felt or fancied a certain humorous element in the real identity of the two under a seeming incongruity. Mr. Wilbur's fondness for scraps of Latin, though drawn from the life, I adopted deliberately to heighten the contrast. Finding soon after that I needed some one as a mouthpiece of the mere drollery, for I conceive that true humor is never divorced from moral conviction, I invented Mr.

Sawin for the clown of my little puppet-show. I meant to embody in him that half-conscious *un-morality* which I had noticed as the recoil in gross natures from a puritanism that still strove to keep in its creed the intense savor which had long gone out of its faith and life. In the three I thought I should find room enough to express, as it was my plan to do, the popular feeling and opinion of the time. For the names of two of my characters, since I have received some remonstrances from very worthy persons who happen to bear them, I would say that they were purely fortuitous, probably mere unconscious memories of signboards or directories. Mr. Sawin's sprang from the accident of a rhyme at the end of his first epistle, and I purposely christened him by the impossible surname of Birdofredum not more to stigmatize him as the incarnation of "Manifest Destiny," in other words, of national recklessness as to right and wrong, than to avoid the chance of wounding any private sensitiveness.

The success of my experiment soon began not only to astonish me, but to make me feel the responsibility of knowing that I held in my hand a weapon instead of the mere fencing-stick I had supposed. Very far from being a popular author under my own name, so far, indeed, as to be almost unread, I found the verses of my pseudonym copied everywhere; I saw them pinned up in workshops; I heard them quoted and their authorship debated; I once even, when rumor had at length caught up my name in one of its eddies, had the satisfaction of overhearing it demonstrated, in the pauses of a concert, that *I* was utterly incompetent to have written anything of the kind. I had read too much not to know the utter worthlessness of contemporary reputation, especially as regards satire, but I knew also that by giving a certain amount of influence it also had its worth, if that influence were used on the right side. I had learned, too, that the first requisite of good writing is to have an earnest and definite purpose, whether aesthetic or moral, and that even good writing, to please long, must have more than an average amount either of imagination or common-sense. The first of these falls to the lot of scarcely one in several generations; the last is within the reach of many in every one that passes; and of this an author may fairly hope to become in part the mouthpiece. If I put on the cap and bells and made myself one of the court-fools of King Demos, it was less to make his majesty laugh than to win a passage to his royal ears for certain serious things which I had deeply at heart. I say this because there is no imputation that could be more galling to any man's self-respect than that of being a mere

jester. I endeavored, by generalizing my satire, to give it what value I could beyond the passing moment and the immediate application. How far I have succeeded I cannot tell, but I have had better luck than I ever looked for in seeing my verses survive to pass beyond their nonage.

In choosing the Yankee dialect, I did not act without forethought. It had long seemed to me that the great vice of American writing and speaking was a studied want of simplicity, that we were in danger of coming to look on our mother-tongue as a dead language, to be sought in the grammar and dictionary rather than in the heart, and that our only chance of escape was by seeking it at its living sources among those who were, as Scottowe says of Major-General Gibbons, "divinely illiterate." President Lincoln, the only really great public man whom these latter days have seen, was great also in this, that he was master—witness his speech at Gettysburg—of a truly masculine English, classic because it was of no special period, and level at once to the highest and lowest of his countrymen. I learn from the highest authority that his favorite reading was in Shakespeare and Milton, to which, of course, the Bible should be added. But whoever should read the debates in Congress might fancy himself present at a meeting of the city council of some city of Southern Gaul in the decline of the Empire, where barbarians with a Latin varnish emulated each other in being more than Ciceronian. Whether it be want of culture, for the highest outcome of that is simplicity, or for whatever reason, it is certain that very few American writers or speakers wield their native language with the directness, precision, and force that are common as the day in the mother country. We use it like Scotsmen, not as if it belonged to us, but as if we wished to prove that we belonged to it, by showing our intimacy with its written rather than with its spoken dialect. And yet all the while our popular idiom is racy with life and vigor and originality, bucksome (as Milton used the word) to our new occasions, and proves itself no mere graft by sending up new suckers from the old root in spite of us. It is only from its roots in the living generations of men that a language can be reinforced with fresh vigor for its needs; what may be called a literate dialect grows ever more and more pedantic and foreign, till it becomes at last as unfitting a vehicle for living thought as monkish Latin. That we should all be made to talk like books is the danger with which we are threatened by the Universal Schoolmaster, who does his best to enslave the minds and memories of his victims to what he esteems the best models of English composition, that is to say, to the writers whose style is faultily correct and has no blood-warmth in it. No language after it has faded into *diction,* none that cannot suck up the feeding juices secreted for it in the rich mother-earth of common folk, can bring forth a sound and lusty book. True vigor and heartiness of phrase do not pass from page to page, but from man to man, where the brain is kindled and the lips suppled by downright living interests and by passion in its very throe. Language is the soil of thought, and our own especially is a rich leaf-mould, the slow deposit of ages, the shed foliage of feeling, fancy, and imagination, which has suffered an earth-change, that the vocal forest, as Howell called it, may clothe itself anew with living green. There is death in the dictionary; and, where language is too strictly limited by convention, the ground for expression to grow in is limited also; and we get a *potted* literature, Chinese dwarfs instead of healthy trees.

But while the schoolmaster has been busy starching our language and smoothing it flat with the mangle of a supposed classical authority, the newspaper reporter has been doing even more harm by stretching and swelling it to suit his occasions. A dozen years ago I began a list, which I have added to from time to time, of some of the changes which may be fairly laid at his door. I give a few of them as showing their tendency, all the more dangerous that their effect, like that of some poisons, is insensibly cumulative, and that they are sure at last of effect among a people whose chief reading is the daily paper. I give in two columns the old style and its modern equivalent.

| OLD STYLE. | NEW STYLE. |
|---|---|
| Was hanged. | Was launched into eternity. |
| When the halter was put around his neck. | When the fatal noose was adjusted about the neck of the unfortunate victim of his own unbridled passions. |
| A great crowd came to see. | A vast concourse was assembled to witness. |
| Great fire. | Disastrous conflagration. |
| The fire spread. | The conflagration extended its devastating career. |
| House burned. | Edifice consumed. |
| The fire was got under. | The progress of the devouring element was arrested. |
| Man fell. | Individual was precipitated. |
| A horse and wagon ran against. | A valuable horse attached to a vehicle driven by J. S., in the employment of J. B., collided with. |
| The frightened horse. | The infuriated animal. |
| Sent for the doctor. | Called into requisition the services of the family physician. |
| The mayor of the city in a short speech welcomed. | The chief magistrate of the metropolis, in well-chosen and eloquent language, frequently interrupted by the plaudits of the surging multitude, officially tendered the hospitalities. |
| I shall say a few words. | I shall, with your permission, beg leave to offer some brief observations. |
| Began his answer. | Commenced his rejoinder. |
| Asked him to dine. | Tendered him a banquet. |
| A bystander advised. | One of those omnipresent characters who, as if in pursuance of some previous arrangement, are certain to be encountered in the vicinity when an accident occurs, ventured the suggestion. |
| He died. | He deceased, he passed out of existence, his spirit quitted its earthly habitation, winged its way to eternity, shook off its burden, etc. |

. . . . . . . . . . . . . . . . .

The quality of exaggeration has often been remarked on as typical of American character, and especially of American humor. In Dr. Petri's *Gedrängtes Handbuch der Fremdwörter,* we are told that the word *humbug* is commonly used for the exaggerations of the North-Americans. To be sure, one would be tempted to think the dream of Columbus half fulfilled, and that Europe had found in the West a nearer way to Orientalism, at least in diction. But it seems to me that a great deal of what is set down as mere extravagance is more fitly to be called intensity and picturesqueness, symptoms of the imaginative faculty in full health and strength, though producing, as yet, only the raw and formless material in which poetry is to work. By and by, perhaps, the world will see it fashioned into poem and picture, and Europe, which will be hard pushed for originality erelong, may have to thank us for a new sensation. The French continue to find Shakespeare exaggerated because he treated English just as our country-folk do when they speak of a "steep price," or say that they "freeze to" a thing. The first postulate of an original literature is that a people should use their language instinctively and unconsciously, as if it were a lively part of their growth and personality, not as the mere torpid boon of education or inheritance. Even Burns contrived to write very poor verse and prose in English. Vulgarisms are often only poetry in the egg. The late Mr. Horace Mann, in one of his public addresses, commented at some length on the beauty and moral significance of the French phrase *s'orienter*, and called on his young friends to practise upon it in life. There was not a Yankee in his audience whose problem had not always been to find out what was *about east*, and to shape his course accordingly. This charm which a familiar expression gains by being commented, as it were, and set in a new light by a foreign language, is curious and instructive. . . .

But it is affirmed that there is something innately vulgar in the Yankee dialect. M. Sainte-Beuve says, with his usual neatness: *"Je définis un patois une ancienne langue qui a eu des malheurs, ou encore une langue toute jeune et qui n'a pas fait fortune."*[1] . . .

I am not speaking now of Americanisms properly so called, that is, of words or phrases which have grown into use here either through necessity, invention, or accident, such as a *carry*, a *one-horse affair*, a *prairie*, to *vamose*. Even these are fewer than is sometimes taken for granted. But I think some fair defence may be made against the charge of vulgarity. Properly speaking, vulgarity is in the thought, and not in the word or the way of pronouncing it. Modern French, the most polite of languages, is barbarously vulgar if compared with the Latin out of which it has been corrupted, or even with Italian. There is a wider gap, and one implying greater boorishness, between *ministerium* and *métier*, or *sapiens* and *sachant*, than between *druv* and *drove* or *agin* and *against*, which last is plainly an arrant superlative. Our rustic *coverlid* is nearer its French original than the diminutive cover*let*, into which it has been ignorantly cor-

rupted in politer speech. I obtained from three cultivated Englishmen at different times three diverse pronunciations of a single word,—*cowcumber*, *coocumber*, and *cucumber*. Of these the first, which is Yankee also, comes nearest to the nasality of *concombre*. Lord Ossory assures us that Voltaire saw the best society in England, and Voltaire tells his countrymen that *handkerchief* was pronounced *hankercher*. I find it so spelt in Hakluyt and elsewhere. This enormity the Yankee still persists in, and as there is always a reason for such deviations from the sound as represented by the spelling, may we not suspect two sources of derivation, and find an ancestor for *kercher* in *couverture* rather than in *couvrechef*? And what greater phonetic vagary (which Dryden, by the way, called *fegary*) in our *lingua rustica* than this *ker* for *couvre*? I copy from the fly-leaves of my books, where I have noted them from time to time, a few examples of pronunciation and phrase which will show that the Yankee often has antiquity and very respectable literary authority on his side. My list might be largely increased by referring to glossaries, but to them every one can go for himself, and I have gathered enough for my purpose.

I will take first those cases in which something like the French sound has been preserved in certain single letters and diphthongs. And this opens a curious question as to how long this Gallicism maintained itself in England. Sometimes a divergence in pronunciation has given us two words with different meanings, as in *genteel* and *jaunty*, which I find coming in toward the close of the seventeenth century, and wavering between *genteel* and *jantee*. It is usual in America to drop the *u* in words ending in *our*,—a very proper change recommended by Howell two centuries ago, and carried out by him so far as his printers would allow. This and the corresponding changes in *musique*, *musick*, and the like, which he also advocated, show that in his time the French accent indicated by the superfluous letters (for French had once nearly as strong an accent as Italian) had gone out of use. There is plenty of French accent down to the end of Elizabeth's reign. In Daniel we have *riches'* and *counsel'*, in Bishop Hall *comet'*, *chapëlain*, in Donne *pictures'*, *virtue'*, *presence'*, *mortal'*, *merit'*, *hainous'*, *giant'*, with many more, and Marston's satires are full of them. The two latter, however, are not to be relied on, as they may be suspected of Chaucerizing. Herrick writes *baptime*. The tendency to throw the accent backward began early. But the incongruities are perplexing, and perhaps mark the period of transi-

INTRODUCTION TO THE BIGLOW PAPERS.    1. *"Je . . . fortune"*: "I define a *patois* as an old language that has had bad luck, or as a young language that has not made its fortune" [L].

tion. In Warner's "Albion's England" we have *creator'* and *crëature'* side by side with the modern *creator* and *creature*. *E'nvy* and *e'nvying* occur in Campion (1602), and yet *envy'* survived Milton. In some cases we have gone back again nearer to the French, as in *rev'enue* for *reven'ue*. I had been so used to hearing *imbecile* pronounced with the accent on the first syllable, which is in accordance with the general tendency in such matters, that I was surprised to find *imbec'ile* in a verse of Wordsworth. The dictionaries all give it so. I asked a highly cultivated Englishman, and he declared for *imbeceel'*. In general it may be assumed that accent will finally settle on the syllable dictated by greater ease and therefore quickness of utterance. *Blas'phemous*, for example, is more rapidly pronounced than *blasphem'ous*, to which our Yankee clings, following in this the usage of many of the older poets. *Amer'ican* is easier than *Ameri'can,* and therefore the false quantity has carried the day, though the true one may be found in George Herbert, and even so late as Cowley.

To come back to the matter in hand. Our "uplandish man" retains the soft or thin sound of the *u* in some words, such as *rule, truth* (sometimes also pronounced *trŭth*, not *trooth*), while he says *noo* for *new,* and gives to *view* and *few* so indescribable a mixture of the two sounds with a slight nasal tincture that it may be called the Yankee shibboleth. Voltaire says that the English pronounce *true* as if it rhymed with *view,* and this is the sound our rustics give to it. Spenser writes *deow* (*dew*) which can only be pronounced with the Yankee nasality. In *rule* the least sound of *a* precedes the *u.* I find *reule* in Pecock's "Repressor." He probably pronounced it *rayoolë*, as the old French word from which it is derived was very likely to be sounded at first, with a reminiscence of its original *regula*. Tindal has *rueler*, and the Coventry Plays have *preudent*. In the "Parlyament of Byrdes" I find *reule*. As for *noo,* may it not claim some sanction in its derivation, whether from *nouveau* or *neuf,* the ancient sound of which may very well have been *noof,* as nearer *novus? Beef* would seem more like to have come from *buffe* than from *bœuf,* unless the two were mere varieties of spelling. The Saxon *few* may have caught enough from its French cousin *peu* to claim the benefit of the same doubt as to sound; and our slang phrase *a few* (as "I licked him a few") may well appeal to *un peu* for sense and authority. Nay, might not *lick* itself turn out to be the good old word *lam* in an English disguise, if the latter should claim descent as, perhaps, he fairly might, from the Latin *lambere?* The New Eng-

land *ferce* for *fierce,* and *perce* for *pierce* (sometimes heard as *fairce* and *pairce*), are also Norman. For its antiquity I cite the rhyme of *verse* and *pierce* in Chapman and Donne, and in some commendatory verses by a Mr. Berkenhead before the poems of Francis Beaumont. Our *pairlous* for *perilous* is of the same kind, and is nearer Shakespeare's *parlous* than the modern pronunciation. One other Gallicism survives in our pronunciation. Perhaps I should rather call it a semi-Gallicism, for it is the result of a futile effort to reproduce a French sound with English lips. Thus for *joint, employ, royal,* we have *jynt, emply, rȳle,* the last differing only from *rile* (*roil*) in a prolongation of the *y* sound. I find *royal* so pronounced in the "Mirror for Magistrates." In Walter de Biblesworth I find *solives* Englished by *gistes*. This, it is true, may have been pronounced *jeests,* but the pronunciation *jystes* must have preceded the present spelling, which was no doubt adopted after the radical meaning was forgotten, as analogical with other words in *oi*. In the same way after Norman-French influence had softened the *l* out of *would* (we already find *woud* for *veut* in N. F. poems), *should* followed the example, and then an *l* was foisted into *could,* where it does not belong, to satisfy the logic of the eye, which has affected the pronunciation and even the spelling of English more than is commonly supposed. I meet with *eyster* for *oyster* as early as the fourteenth century. I find *viage* in Bishop Hall and Middleton the dramatist, *bile* for *boil* in Donne and Chrononhotontholo-gos, *line* for *loin* in Hall, *ryall* and *chyse* (for *choice*), *dystrye* for *destroy,* in the Coventry Plays. In Chapman's "All Fools" is the misprint of *employ* for *imply,* fairly inferring an identity of sound in the last syllable. Indeed, this pronunciation was habitual till after Pope, and Rogers tells us that the elegant Gray said *naise* for *noise* just as our rustics still do. Our *cornish* (which I find also in Herrick) remembers the French better than *cornice* does. While, clinging more closely to the Anglo-Saxon in dropping the *g* from the end of the present participle, the Yankee now and then pleases himself with an experiment in French nasality in words ending in *n*. It is not, so far as my experience goes, very common, though it may formerly have been more so. *Capting,* for instance, I never heard save in jest, the habitual form being *kepp'n*. But at any rate it is no invention of ours. In that delightful old volume, "Ane Compendious Buke of Godly and Spirituall Songs," in which I know not whether the piety itself or the simplicity of its expression be more charming, I find *burding, garding,* and *cousing,* and in the State Trials *un-*

*certing* used by a gentleman. I confess that I like the *n* better than the *ng*.

. . . . . . . . . . . . .

The Yankee has retained something of the long sound of the *a* in such words as *axe, wax,* pronouncing them *exe, wex* (shortened from *aix, waix*). He also says *hev* and *hed* (*hāve, hād*) for *have* and *had*. In most cases he follows an Anglo-Saxon usage. In *aix* for *axle* he certainly does. I find *wex* and *aisches* (*ashes*) in Pecock, and *exe* in the Paston Letters. Golding rhymes *wax* with *wexe* and spells *challenge chelenge*. Chaucer wrote *hendy*. Dryden rhymes *can* with *men,* as Mr. Biglow would. Alexander Gill, Milton's teacher, in his "Logonomia" cites *hez* for *hath* as peculiar to Lincolnshire. I find *hayth* in Collier's "Bibliographical Account of Early English Literature" under the date 1584, and Lord Cromwell so wrote it. Sir Christopher Wren wrote *belcony.* Our *fect* is only the O. F. *faict. Thaim* for *them* was common in the sixteenth century. We have an example of the same thing in the double form of the verb *thrash, thresh.* While the New-Englander cannot be brought to say *instead* for *instid* (commonly *'stid* where not the last word in a sentence), he changes the *i* into *e* in *red* for *rid, tell* for *till, hender* for *hinder, rense* for *rinse.* I find *red* in the old interlude of "Thersytes," *tell* in a letter of Daborne to Henslowe, and also, I shudder to mention it, in a letter of the great Duchess of Marlborough, Atossa herself! It occurs twice in a single verse of the Chester Plays,

"*Tell* the day of dome, *tell* the beames blow."

From the word *blow* (in another sense) is formed *blowth,* which I heard again this summer after a long interval. Mr. Wright [2] explains it as meaning "a blossom." With us a single blossom is a *blow,* while *blowth* means the blossoming in general. A farmer would say that there was a good blowth on his fruit-trees. The word retreats farther inland and away from the railways, year by year. Wither rhymes *hinder* with *slender,* and Shakespeare and Lovelace have *renched* for *rinsed.* In "Gammer Gurton" and "Mirror for Magistrates" is *sence* for *since;* Marlborough's Duchess so writes it, and Donne rhymes *since* with *Amiens* and *patience,* Bishop Hall and Otway with *pretence,* Chapman with *citizens,* Dryden with *providence.* Indeed, why should not *sithence* take that form? Dryden's wife (an earl's daughter) has *tell* for *till,* Margaret, mother of Henry VII., writes *seche* for *such,* and our *ef* finds authority in the old form *yeffe.*

*E* sometimes takes the place of *u,* as *jedge,*

*tredge, bresh.* I find *tredge* in the interlude of "Jack Jugler," *bresh* in a citation by Collier from "London Cries" of the middle of the seventeenth century, and *resche* for *rush* (fifteenth century) in the very valuable "Volume of Vocabularies" edited by Mr. Wright. *Resce* is one of the Anglo-Saxon forms of the word in Bosworth's A.-S. Dictionary. Golding has *shet.* The Yankee always shortens the *u* in the ending *ture,* making *ventur, natur, pictur,* and so on. This was common, also, among the educated of the last generation. I am inclined to think it may have been once universal, and I certainly think it more elegant than the vile *vencher, naycher, pickcher,* that have taken its place, sounding like the invention of a lexicographer to mitigate a sneeze. Nash in his "Pierce Penniless" has *ventur,* and so spells it, and I meet it also in Spenser, Drayton, Ben Jonson, Herrick, and Prior. Spenser has *tort'rest,* which can be contracted only from *tortur* and not from *torcher.* Quarles rhymes *nature* with *creator,* and Dryden with *satire,* which he doubtless pronounced according to its older form of *satyr.* Quarles has also *torture* and *mortar.* Mary Boleyn writes *kreatur.* I find *pikter* in Izaak Walton's autograph will.

. . . . . . . . . . . . .

I will now leave pronunciation and turn to words or phrases which have been supposed peculiar to us, only pausing to pick up a single dropped stitch, in the pronunciation of the word *su'preme,* which I had thought native till I found it in the well-languaged Daniel. I will begin with a word of which I have never met with any example in any English writer of authority. We express the first stage of withering in a green plant suddenly cut down by the verb *to wilt.* It is, of course, own cousin of the German *welken,* but I have never come upon it in literary use, and my own books of reference give me faint help. Graff gives *welhèn, marcescere,* and refers to *weih* (*weak*), and conjecturally to A.-S. *hvelan.* The A.-S. *wealwian* (*to wither*) is nearer, but not so near as two words in the Icelandic, which perhaps put us on the track of its ancestry,—*velgi, tepefacere* (and *velki,* with the derivative) meaning *contaminare. Wilt,* at any rate, is a good word, filling, as it does, a sensible gap between drooping and withering, and the imaginative phrase "he wilted right down," like "he caved right in," is a true Americanism. *Wilt* occurs in English provincial glossaries, but is explained by *wither,* which with us it does not mean. We have a few words such as *cache, cohog, carry* (*portage*), *shoot* (*chute*), *timber* (*forest*), *bushwhack* (to pull a boat along by the bushes on the edge of a stream), *buckeye* (a picturesque word for the horse-chestnut); but how

2. **Mr. Wright:** *Dictionary of Obsolete and Provincial English* [L].

many can we be said to have fairly brought into the language, as Alexander Gill, who first mentions Americanisms, meant it when he said, *"Sed et ab Americanis nonnulla mutuamur ut* MAIZ *et* CANOA"? Very few, I suspect, and those mostly by borrowing from the French, German, Spanish, or Indian.[3] "The Dipper" for the "Great Bear" strikes me as having a native air. *Bogus*, in the sense of *worthless,* is undoubtedly ours, but is, I more than suspect, a corruption of the French *bagasse* (from low Latin *bagasea*), which travelled up the Mississippi from New Orleans, where it was used for the refuse of the sugar-cane. It is true, we have modified the meaning of some words. We use *freshet* in the sense of *flood,* for which I have not chanced upon any authority. Our New England cross between Ancient Pistol and Dugald Dalgetty, Captain Underhill, uses the word (1638) to mean a *current,* and I do not recollect it elsewhere in that sense. I therefore leave it with a *?* for future explorers. *Crick* for *creek* I find in Captain John Smith and in the dedication of Fuller's "Holy Warre," and *run,* meaning a *small stream,* in Waymouth's "Voyage" (1605). *Humans* for *men,* which Mr. Bartlett includes in his "Dictionary of Americanisms," is Chapman's habitual phrase in his translation of Homer. I find it also in the old play of "The Hog hath lost his Pearl." *Dogs* for *andirons* is still current in New England, and in Walter de Biblesworth I find *chiens* glossed in the margin by *andirons. Gunning* for *shooting* is in Drayton. We once got credit for the poetical word *fall* for *autumn,* but Mr. Bartlett and the last edition of Webster's Dictionary refer us to Dryden. It is even older, for I find it in Drayton, and Bishop Hall has *autumn fall.* Middleton plays upon the word: "May'st thou have a reasonable good *spring,* for thou art like to have many dangerous foul *falls."* Daniel does the same, and Coleridge uses it as we do. Gray uses the archaism *picked* for *peaked,* and the word *smudge* (as our backwoodsmen do) for a smothered fire. Lord Herbert of Cherbury (more properly perhaps than even Sidney, the last *preux chevalier*) has "the Emperor's folks" just as a Yankee would say it. *Loan* for *lend,* with which we have hitherto been blackened, I must retort upon the mother island, for it appears so long ago as in "Albion's England." *Fleshy,* in the sense of *stout,* may claim Ben Jonson's warrant, and I find it also so lately as in Francklin's "Lucian." *Chore* is also Jonson's word, and I am inclined to prefer it to *chare* and *char,* because I think that I see a more natural ori-

gin for it in the French *jour*—whence it might come to mean a day's work, and thence a job—than anywhere else.[4] *At onst* for *at once* I thought a corruption of our own, till I found it in the Chester Plays. I am now inclined to suspect it no corruption at all, but only an erratic and obsolete superlative *at onest. To progress'* was flung in our teeth till Mr. Pickering retorted with Shakespeare's "doth pro'gress down thy cheeks." I confess that I was never satisfied with this answer, because the accent was different, and because the word might here be reckoned a substantive quite as well as a verb. Mr. Bartlett (in his dictionary above cited) adds a surrebutter in a verse from Ford's "Broken Heart." Here the word is clearly a verb, but with the accent unhappily still on the first syllable. Mr. Bartlett says that he "cannot say whether the word was used in Bacon's time or not." It certainly was, and with the accent we give to it. Ben Jonson, in the "Alchemist," has this verse,

"Progress' so from extreme unto extreme,"

and Sir Philip Sidney,

"Progressing then from fair Turias' golden place."

Surely we may now sleep in peace, and our English cousins will forgive us, since we have cleared ourselves from any suspicion of originality in the matter! Even after I had convinced myself that the chances were desperately against our having invented any of the *Americanisms* with which we are *faulted* and which we are in the habit of *voicing,* there were one or two which had so prevailingly indigenous an accent as to stagger me a little. One of these was "the biggest *thing out."* Alas, even this slender comfort is denied me. Old Gower has

"So harde an herte was none *oute,"*

and

"That such merveile was none *oute."*

He also, by the way, says "a *sighte* of flowres" as naturally as our up-country folk would say it. *Poor* for *lean, thirds* for *dower,* and *dry* for *thirsty* I find in Middleton's plays. *Dry* is also in Skelton and in the "World" (1754). In a note on Middleton, Mr. Dyce thinks it needful to explain the phrase *I can't tell* (universal in America) by the gloss *I could not say.* Middleton also uses *snecked,* which I had believed an Americanism till I saw it there. It is, of course, only another form of *snatch,* analogous to *theek* and *thatch* (cf. the

---

3. **Very . . . Indian:** "This was written twenty years ago, and now (1890) I cannot open an English journal without coming upon an Americanism" [L].

4. ***Chore* . . . else:** "The Rev. A. L. Mayhew of Wadham College, Oxford, has convinced me that I was astray in this" [L].

proper names Dekker and Thacher), *break* (*brack*) and *breach, make* (still common with us) and *match. 'Long on* for *occasioned by* ("who is this 'long on?") occurs constantly in Gower and likewise in Middleton. *'Cause why* is in Chaucer. *Raising* (an English version of the French *leaven*) for *yeast* is employed by Gayton in his "Festivous Notes on Don Quixote." I have never seen an instance of our New England word *emptins* in the same sense, nor can I divine its original. Gayton has *limekill;* also *shuts* for *shutters,* and the latter is used by Mrs. Hutchinson in her "Life of Colonel Hutchinson." Bishop Hall, and Purchas in his "Pilgrims," have *chist* for *chest,* and it is certainly nearer *cista,* as well as to its form in the Teutonic languages, whence probably we got it. We retain the old sound from *cist,* but *chest* is as old as Chaucer. Lovelace says *wropt* for *wrapt.* "Musicianer" I had always associated with the militia-musters of my boyhood, and too hastily concluded it an abomination of our own, but Mr. Wright calls it a Norfolk word, and I find it to be as old as 1642 by an extract in Collier. "Not worth the time of day" had passed with me for native till I saw it in Shakespeare's "Pericles." For *slick* (which is only a shorter sound of *sleek,* like *crick* and the now universal *britches* for *breeches*) I will only call Chapman and Jonson. "That's a sure card!" and "That's a stinger!" both sound like modern slang, but you will find the one in the old interlude of "Thersytes" (1537), and the other in Middleton. "Right here," a favorite phrase with our orators and with a certain class of our editors, turns up *passim* in the Chester and Coventry plays. Mr. Dickens found something very ludicrous in what he considered our neologism *right away.* But I find a phrase very like it, and which I would gladly suspect to be a misprint for it, in "Gammer Gurton":—

"Lyght it and bring it *tite away."*

But *tite* is the true word in this case. After all, what is it but another form of *straightway? Cussedness,* meaning *wickedness, malignity,* and *cuss,* a sneaking, ill-natured fellow, in such phrases as "He done it out o' pure cussedness," and "He is a nateral cuss," have been commonly thought Yankeeisms. To vent certain contemptuously indignant moods they are admirable in their rough-and-ready way. But neither is our own. *Cursydnesse,* in the same sense of malignant wickedness, occurs in the Coventry Plays, and *cuss* may perhaps claim to have come in with the Conqueror. At least the term is also French. Saint Simon uses it and confesses its usefulness. Speaking of the Abbé Dubois, he says, "Qui étoit en plein ce qu'un mauvais françois appelle un *sacre,* mais qui ne se peut

guère exprimer autrement." "Not worth a cuss," though supported by "not worth a damn," may be a mere corruption, since "not worth a *cress*" is in "Piers Ploughman." "I don't see it" was the popular slang a year or two ago, and seemed to spring from the soil; but no, it is in Cibber's "Careless Husband." *Green sauce* for *vegetables* I meet in Beaumont and Fletcher, Gayton, and elsewhere. Our rustic pronunciation *sahce* (for either the dipthong *au* was anciently pronounced *ah,* or else we have followed abundant analogy in changing it to the latter sound, as we have in *chance, dance,* and so many more) may be the older one, and at least gives some hint at its ancestor *salsa. Warn,* in the sense of *notify,* is, I believe, now peculiar to us, but Pecock so employs it. I find *primmer* (*primer,* as we pronounce it) in Beaumont and Fletcher, and a "square eater" too (compare our *square* meal"), *heft* for *weight,* and "muchness" in the "Mirror for Magistrates," *bankbill* in Swift and Fielding, and *as* for *that* I might say *passim. To cotton to* is, I rather think, an Americanism. The nearest approach to it I have found is *cotton together,* in Congreve's "Love for Love." To *cotton* or *cotten,* in another sense, is old and common. Our word means to *cling,* and its origin, possibly, is to be sought in another direction, perhaps in A.-S. *cvead,* which means *mud, clay* (both proverbially clinging), or better yet, in the Icelandic *qvoda* (otherwise *kód*), meaning *resin* and *glue,* which are κατ' ἐξοχήν, sticky substances. To *spit cotton* is, I think, American, and also, perhaps, *to flax* for *to beat. To the halves* still survives among us, though apparently obsolete in England. It means either to let or to hire a piece of land, receiving half the profit in money or in kind (*partibus locare*). I mention it because in a note by some English editor, to which I have lost my reference, I have seen it wrongly explained. The editors of Nares cite Burton. *To put,* in the sense of *to go,* as *Put!* for *Begone!* would seem our own, and yet it is strictly analogous to the French *se mettre à la voie,* and the Italian *mettersi in via.* Indeed, Dante has a verse,

"*Io sarei* [for *mi sarei*] *già messo per lo sentiero,"*

which, but for the indignity, might be translated,

"I should, ere this, have *put* along the way."

. . . . . . . . . . . . . . . .

A locution prevails in the Southern and Middle States which is so curious that, though never heard in New England, I will give a few lines to its discussion, the more readily because it is extinct elsewhere. I mean the use of *allow* in the sense of *affirm,* as "I allow that's a good horse." I find the word so used in 1558 by Anthony Jenkinson in

Hakluyt: "Corne they sowe not, neither doe eate any bread, mocking the Christians for the same, and disabling our strengthe, saying we live by eating the toppe of a weede, and drinke a drinke made of the same, *allowing* theyr great devouring of flesh and drinking of milke to be the increase of theyr strength." That is, they undervalued our strength, and affirmed their own to be the result of a certain diet. In another passage of the same narrative the word has its more common meaning of approving or praising: "The said king, much *allowing* this declaration, said." Ducange quotes Bracton *sub voce* ADLOCARE for the meaning "to admit as proved," and the transition from this to "affirm" is by no means violent. Izaak Walton has "Lebault *allows* waterfrogs to be good meat," and here the word is equivalent to *affirms*. At the same time, when we consider some of the meanings of *allow* in old English, and of *allouer* in old French, and also remember that the verbs *prize* and *praise* are from one root, I think we must admit *allaudare* to a share in the paternity of *allow*. The sentence from Hakluyt would read equally well, "contemning our strengthe, . . . and praising (or valuing) their great eating of flesh as the cause of their increase in strength." After all, if we confine ourselves to *allocare*, it may turn out that the word was somewhere and somewhen used for *to bet*, analogously to *put up, put down, post* (cf. Spanish *apostar*), and the like. I hear boys in the street continually saying, "I bet that 's a good horse," or what not, meaning by no means to risk anything beyond their opinion in the matter.

The word *improve*, in the sense of "to occupy, make use of, employ," as Dr. Pickering defines it, he long ago proved to be no neologism. He would have done better, I think, had he substituted *profit by* for *employ*. He cites Dr. Franklin as saying that the word had never, so far as he knew, been used in New England before he left it in 1723, except in Dr. Mather's "Remarkable Providences," which he oddly calls a "very old book." Franklin, as Dr. Pickering goes on to show, was mistaken. Mr. Bartlett in his "Dictionary" merely abridges Pickering. Both of them should have confined the application of the word to material things, its extension to which is all that is peculiar in the supposed American use of it. For surely "Complete Letter-Writers" have been *"improving* this opportunity" time out of mind. I will illustrate the word a little further, because Pickering cites no English authorities. Skelton has a passage in his "Phyllyp Sparowe," which I quote the rather as it contains also the word *allowed,* and as it distinguishes *improve* from *employ:*—

"His [Chaucer's] Englysh well alowed,
So as it is *enprowed,*

For as it is enployd,
There is no English voyd."

Here the meaning is *to profit by*. In Fuller's "Holy Warre" (1647), we have "The Egyptians standing on the firm ground, were thereby enabled to *improve* and enforce their darts to the utmost." Here the word might certainly mean *to make use of*. Mrs. Hutchinson ("Life of Colonel H.") uses the word in the same way: "And therefore did not *emproove* his interest to engage the country in the quarrell." Swift in one of his letters says: "There is not an acre of land in Ireland turned to half its advantage; yet it is better *improved* than the people." I find it also in "Strength out of Weakness" (1652), and Plutarch's "Morals" (1714), but I know of only one example of its use in the purely American sense, and that is "a very good *improvement* for a mill" in the "State Trials" (Speech of the Attorney-General in the Lady Ivy's case, 1684). In the sense of *employ*, I could cite a dozen old English authorities.

In running over the fly-leaves of those delightful folios for this reference, I find a note which reminds me of another word, for our abuse of which we have been deservedly ridiculed. I mean *lady*. It is true I might cite the example of the Italian *donna*[5] (*domina*), which has been treated in the same way by a whole nation, and not, as *lady* among us, by the uncultivated only. It perhaps grew into use in the half-democratic republics of Italy in the same way and for the same reasons as with us. But I admit that our abuse of the word is villanous. I know of an orator who once said in a public meeting where bonnets preponderated, that "the ladies were last at the cross and first at the tomb"! But similar sins were committed before our day and in the mother country. In the "Harleian Miscellany" (vol. v. p. 455) I find "this *lady* is my servant; the hedger's daughter Ioan." In the "State Trials" I learn of "a *gentlewoman* that lives cook with" such a one, and I hear the Lord High Steward speaking of the wife of a waiter at a bagnio as a *gentlewoman!* From the same authority, by the way, I can state that our vile habit of chewing tobacco had the somewhat unsavory example of Titus Oates, and I know by tradition from an eye-witness that the elegant General Burgoyne partook of the same vice. Howell, in one of his letters (dated 26 August, 1623), speaks thus of another "institution" which many have thought American: "They speak much of that boisterous Bishop of Halverstadt (for so they term him here), that, having taken a place wher ther were two Monasteries of Nuns and Friers, he caus'd

5. *donna:* "*Dame,* in English as a decayed gentlewoman of the same family" [L].

divers feather-beds to be rip'd, and all the feathers to be thrown in a great Hall, whither the Nuns and Friers were thrust naked with their bodies oil'd and pitch'd, and to tumble among the feathers." Howell speaks as if the thing were new to him, and I know not if the "boisterous" Bishop was the inventor of it, but I find it practised in England before our Revolution.

. . . . . . . . . . . . . . .

It is always worth while to note down the erratic words or phrases which one meets with in any dialect. They may throw light on the meaning of other words, on the relationship of languages, or even on history itself. In so composite a language as ours they often supply a different form to express a different shade of meaning, as in *viol* and *fiddle, thrid* and *thread, smother* and *smoulder,* where the *l* has crept in by a false analogy with *would.* We have given back to England the excellent adjective *lengthy,* formed honestly like *earthy, drouthy,* and others, thus enabling their journalists to characterize our President's messages by a word civilly compromising between *long* and *tedious,* so as not to endanger the peace of the two countries by wounding our national sensitiveness to British criticism. Let me give two curious examples of the antiseptic property of dialects at which I have already glanced. Dante has *dindi* as a childish or low word for *danari* (money), and in Shropshire small Roman coins are still dug up which the peasants call *dinders.* This can hardly be a chance coincidence, but seems rather to carry the word back to the Roman soldiery. So our farmers say *chuk, chuk,* to their pigs, and *ciacco* is one of the Italian words for *hog.* When a countryman tells us that he "fell *all of a heap,*" I cannot help thinking that he unconsciously points to an affinity between our word *tumble,* and the Latin *tumulus,* that is older than most others. I believe that words, or even the mere intonation of them, have an astonishing vitality and power of propagation by the root, like the gardener's pest, quitch-grass,[6] while the application or combination of them may be new. It is in these last that my countrymen seem to me full of humor, invention, quickness of wit, and that sense of subtle analogy which needs only refining to become fancy and imagination. Prosaic as American life seems in many of its aspects to a European, bleak and bare as it is on the side of tradition, and utterly orphaned of the solemn inspiration of antiquity, I cannot help thinking that the ordinary talk of unlettered men among us is fuller

of metaphor and of phrases that suggest lively images than that of any other people I have seen. Very many such will be found in Mr. Bartlett's book, though his short list of proverbs at the end seem to me, with one or two exceptions, as un-American as possible. Most of them have no character at all but coarseness, and are quite too long-skirted for working proverbs, in which language always "takes off its coat to it," as a Yankee would say. There are plenty that have a more native and puckery flavor, seedlings from the old stock often, and yet new varieties. One hears such not seldom among us Easterners, and the West would yield many more. "Mean enough to steal acorns from a blind hog"; "Cold as the north side of a Jenooary gravestone by starlight"; "Hungry as a graven image"; "Pop'lar as a hen with one chicken"; "A hen's time ain't much"; "Quicker 'n greased lightnin' "; "Ther's sech a thing ez bein' *tu*" (our Yankee paraphrase of $\mu\eta\delta\grave{\epsilon}\nu\ \breve{\alpha}\gamma\alpha\nu$); hence the phrase *tooin' round,* meaning a supererogatory activity like that of flies; "Stingy enough to skim his milk at both eends"; "Hot as the Devil's kitchen"; "Handy as a pocket in a shirt"; "He's a whole team and the dog under the wagon"; "All deacons are good, but there's odds in deacons" (to *deacon* berries is to put the largest atop); "So thievish they hev to take in their stone walls nights";[7] may serve as specimens. "I take my tea *barfoot,*" said a backwoodsman when asked if he would have cream and sugar. (I find *barfoot,* by the way, in the Coventry Plays.) A man speaking to me once of a very rocky clearing said, "Stone's got a pretty heavy mortgage on that land," and I overheard a guide in the woods say to his companions who were urging him to sing, "Wal, I *did* sing once, but toons gut invented, an' thet spilt my trade." Whoever has driven over a stream by a bridge made of *slabs* will feel the picturesque force of the epithet *slab-bridged* applied to a fellow of shaky character. Almost every county has some good die-sinker in phrase, whose mintage passes into the currency of the whole neighborhood. Such a one described the county jail (the one stone building where all the dwellings are of wood) as "the house whose underpinnin' come up to the eaves," and called hell "the place where they did n't rake up their fires nights." I once asked a stage-driver if the other side of a hill were as steep as the one we were climbing: "Steep? chain lightnin' could n' go down it 'thout puttin' the shoe on!" And this brings me back to the exaggeration of which I spoke before. To me there is

---

6. **quitch-grass:** "Which whether in that form, or under its aliases *witch*-grass and *cooch*-grass, points us back to its original Saxon *quick*" [L].

7. "**So . . . nights**": "And, by the way, the Yankee never says 'o' nights, but uses the older adverbial form, analogous to the German *nachts*" [L].

something very taking in the Negro "so black that charcoal made a chalk-mark on him," and the wooden shingle "painted so like marble that it sank in water," as if its very consciousness or its vanity had been overpersuaded by the cunning of the painter. I heard a man, in order to give a notion of some very cold weather, say to another that a certain Joe, who had been taking mercury, found a lump of quicksilver in each boot, when he went home to dinner. This power of rapidly dramatizing a dry fact into flesh and blood and the vivid conception of Joe as a human thermometer strike me as showing a poetic sense that may be refined into faculty. At any rate there is humor here, and not mere quickness of wit,—the deeper and not the shallower quality. The *tendency* of humor is always towards overplus of expression, while the very essence of wit is its logical precision. Captain Basil Hall denied that our people had any humor, deceived, perhaps, by their gravity of manner. But this very seriousness is often the outward sign of that humorous quality of the mind which delights in finding an element of identity in things seemingly the most incongruous, and then again in forcing an incongruity upon things identical. Perhaps Captain Hall had no humor himself, and if so he would never find it. Did he always feel the point of what was said to himself? I doubt it, because I happen to know a chance he once had given him in vain. The Captain was walking up and down the veranda of a country tavern in Massachusetts while the coach changed horses. A thunder-storm was going on, and, with that pleasant European air of indirect self-compliment in condescending to be surprised by American merit, which we find so conciliating, he said to a countryman lounging against the door, "Pretty heavy thunder you have here." The other, who had divined at a glance his feeling of generous concession to a new country, drawled gravely, "Waal, we *du*, considerin' the number of inhabitants." This, the more I analyze it, the more humorous does it seem. The same man was capable of wit also, when he would. He was a cabinet-maker, and was once employed to make some commandment-tables for the parish meeting-house. The parson, a very old man, annoyed him by looking into his workshop every morning, and cautioning him to be very sure to pick out "clear mahogany without any *knots* in it." At last, wearied out, he retorted one day: "Wal, Dr. B., I guess ef I was to leave the *nots* out o' some o' the c'man'ments, 't 'ould soot you full ez wal!"

If I had taken the pains to write down the proverbial or pithy phrases I have heard, or if I had sooner thought of noting the Yankeeisms I met with in my reading, I might have been able to do more justice to my theme. But I have done all I wished in respect to pronunciation, if I have proved that where we are vulgar, we have the countenance of very good company. . . .

· · · · · · · · · · · · · · · · · · · · · · · · ·

Of course in what I have said I wish to be understood as keeping in mind the difference between provincialisms properly so called and *slang*. *Slang* is always vulgar, because it is not a natural but an affected way of talking, and all mere tricks of speech or writing are offensive. I do not think that Mr. Biglow can be fairly charged with vulgarity, and I should have entirely failed in my design, if I had not made it appear that high and even refined sentiment may coexist with the shrewder and more comic elements of the Yankee character. I believe that what is essentially vulgar and mean-spirited in politics seldom has its source in the body of the people, but much rather among those who are made timid by their wealth or selfish by their love of power. A democracy can *afford* much better than an aristocracy to follow out its convictions, and is perhaps better qualified to build those convictions on plain principles of right and wrong, rather than on the shifting sands of expediency. I had always thought "Sam Slick" a libel on the Yankee character, and a complete falsification of Yankee modes of speech, though, for aught I know, it may be true in both respects so far as the British provinces are concerned. To me the dialect was native, was spoken all about me when a boy, at a time when an Irish day-laborer was as rare as an American one now. Since then I have made a study of it so far as opportunity allowed. But when I write in it, it is as in a mother tongue, and I am carried back far beyond any studies of it to long-ago noonings in my father's hay-fields, and to the talk of Sam and Job over their jug of *black-strap* under the shadow of the ash-tree which still dapples the grass whence they have been gone so long.

But life is short, and prefaces should be. And so, my good friends, to whom this introductory epistle is addressed, farewell. Though some of you have remonstrated with me, I shall never write any more "Biglow Papers," however great the temptation,—great especially at the present time,—unless it be to complete the original plan of this Series by bringing out Mr. Sawin as an "original Union man." The very favor with which they have been received is a hindrance to me, by forcing on me a self-consciousness from which I was entirely free when I wrote the First Series. Moreover, I am no longer the same careless youth, with nothing to do but live to myself, my books, and my friends, that

I was then. I always hated politics, in the ordinary sense of the word, and I am not likely to grow fonder of them, now that I have learned how rare it is to find a man who can keep principle clear from party and personal prejudice, or can conceive the possibility of another's doing so. I feel as if I could in some sort claim to be an *emeritus,* and I am sure that political satire will have full justice done it by that genuine and delightful humorist, the Rev. Petroleum V. Nasby. I regret that I killed off Mr. Wilbur so soon, for he would have enabled me to bring into this preface a number of learned quotations, which must now go a-begging, and also enabled me to dispersonalize myself into a vicarious egotism. He would have helped me likewise in clearing myself from a charge which I shall briefly touch on, because my friend Mr. Hughes has found it needful to defend me in his preface to one of the English editions of "The Biglow Papers." I thank Mr. Hughes heartily for his friendly care of my good name, and were his Preface accessible to my readers here (as I am glad it is not, for its partiality makes me blush), I should leave the matter where he left it. The charge is of profanity, brought in by persons who proclaimed African slavery of Divine institution, and is based (so far as I have heard) on two passages in the First Series—

> "An' you 've gut to git up airly,
> Ef you want t) take in God,"

and,

> "God 'll send the bill to you,"

and on some Scriptural illustrations by Mr. Sawin.

Now, in the first place, I was writing under an assumed character, and must talk as the person would whose mouthpiece I made myself. Will any one familiar with the New England countryman venture to tell me that he does *not* speak of sacred things familiarly? that Biblical allusions (allusions, that is, to the single book with whose language, from his church-going habits, he is intimate) are *not* frequent on his lips? If so, he cannot have pursued his studies of the character on so many long-ago muster-fields and at so many cattle-shows as I. But I scorn any such line of defence, and will confess at once that one of the things I am proud of in my countrymen is (I am not speaking now of such persons as I have assumed Mr. Sawin to be) that they do not put their Maker away far from them, or interpret the fear of God into being afraid of Him. The Talmudists had conceived a deep truth when they said, that "all things were in the power of God, save the fear of God"; and when people stand in great dread of an invisible power, I suspect they mistake quite another personage for the

Deity. I might justify myself for the passages criticised by many parallel ones from Scripture, but I need not. The Reverend Homer Wilbur's notebooks supply me with three apposite quotations. The first is from a Father of the Roman Church, the second from a Father of the Anglican, and the third from a Father of Modern English poetry. The Puritan divines would furnish me with many more such. St. Bernard says, *Sapiens nummularius est Deus: nummum fictum non recipiet;* "A cunning money-changer is God: he will take in no base coin." Latimer says, "You shall perceive that God, by this example, shaketh us by the noses and taketh us by the ears." Familiar enough, both of them, one would say! But I should think Mr. Biglow had verily stolen the last of the two maligned passages from Dryden's "Don Sebastian," where I find

> "And beg of Heaven to charge the bill on me!"

And there I leave the matter, being willing to believe that the Saint, the Martyr, and even the Poet, were as careful of God's honor as my critics are ever likely to be.

# FITZ ADAM'S STORY

◊

❮ AS EARLY as 1849 Lowell projected a long verse narrative, to be called "The Nooning," made up of stories told ostensibly by a group of his friends and himself, the framework and design of the whole resembling that of the *Canterbury Tales*. Only fragments of the work survive (see Scudder's note in the Cambridge edition, pp. 411–12), and of these "Fitz Adam's Story" is the only complete tale. It belongs not only to the American local color movement, but to the tradition, best exemplified in frontier humor, of the vernacular tale recorded by a cultivated observer.

◊

The next whose fortune 't was a tale to tell
Was one whom men, before they thought, loved
    well,
And after thinking wondered why they did,
For half he seemed to let them, half forbid,
And wrapped him so in humors, sheath on sheath,
'T was hard to guess the mellow soul beneath;
But, once divined, you took him to your heart,
While he appeared to bear with you as part
Of life's impertinence, and once a year
Betrayed his true self by a smile or tear,    10

Or rather something sweetly-shy and loath,
Withdrawn ere fully shown, and mixed of both.
A cynic? Not precisely: one who thrust
Against a heart too prone to love and trust,
Who so despised false sentiment he knew
Scarce in himself to part the false and true,
And strove to hide, by roughening-o'er the skin,
Those cobweb nerves he could not dull within.
Gentle by birth, but of a stem decayed,
He shunned life's rivalries and hated trade;     20
On a small patrimony and larger pride,
He lived uneaseful on the Other Side
(So he called Europe), only coming West
To give his Old-World appetite new zest;
Yet still the New World spooked it in his veins,
A ghost he could not lay with all his pains;
For never Pilgrims' offshoot scapes control
Of those old instincts that have shaped his soul.
A radical in thought, he puffed away
With shrewd contempt the dust of usage gray,     30
Yet loathed democracy as one who saw,
In what he longed to love, some vulgar flaw,
And, shocked through all his delicate reserves,
Remained a Tory by his taste and nerves.
His fancy's thrall, he drew all ergoes thence,
And thought himself the type of common sense;
Misliking women, not from cross or whim,
But that his mother shared too much in him,
And he half felt that what in them was grace
Made the unlucky weakness of his race.     40
What powers he had he hardly cared to know,
But sauntered through the world as through a
    show;
A critic fine in his haphazard way,
A sort of mild La Bruyère on half-pay.
For comic weaknesses he had an eye
Keen as an acid for an alkali,
Yet you could feel, through his sardonic tone,
He loved them all, unless they were his own.
You might have called him, with his humorous
    twist,
A kind of human entomologist:     50
As these bring home, from every walk they take,
Their hat-crowns stuck with bugs of curious make,
So he filled all the lining of his head
With characters impaled and ticketed,
And had a cabinet behind his eyes
For all they caught of mortal oddities.
He might have been a poet—many worse—
But that he had, or feigned, contempt of verse;
Called it tattooing language, and held rhymes
The young world's lullaby of ruder times.     60
Bitter in words, too indolent for gall,
He satirized himself the first of all,
In men and their affairs could find no law,
And was the ill logic that he thought he saw.

Scratching a match to light his pipe anew,
With eyes half shut some musing whiffs he drew
And thus began: "I give you all my word,
I think this mock-Decameron absurd;
Boccaccio's garden! how bring that to pass
In our bleak clime save under double glass?     70
The moral east-wind of New England life
Would snip its gay luxuriance like a knife;
Mile-deep the glaciers brooded here, they say,
Through æons numb; we feel their chill to-day.
These foreign plants are but half-hardy still,
Die on a south, and on a north wall chill.
Had we stayed Puritans! *They* had some heat,
(Though whence derived I have my own conceit,)
But you have long ago raked up their fires;
Where they had faith, you 've ten sham-Gothic
    spires.     80
Why more exotics? Try your native vines,
And in some thousand years you *may* have wines;
Your present grapes are harsh, all pulps and skins,
And want traditions of ancestral bins
That saved for evenings round the polished board
Old lava-fires, the sun-steeped hillside's hoard.
Without a Past, you lack that southern wall
O'er which the vines of Poesy should crawl;
Still they 're your only hope; no midnight oil
Makes up for virtue wanting in the soil;     90
Manure them well and prune them; 't won't be
    France,
Nor Spain, nor Italy, but there 's your chance.
You have one story-teller worth a score
Of dead Boccaccios,—nay, add twenty more,—
A hawthorn asking spring's most dainty breath,
And him you 're freezing pretty well to death.
However, since you say so, I will tease
My memory to a story by degrees,
Though you will cry, 'Enough!' I'm well-nigh
    sure,     99
Ere I have dreamed through half my overture.
Stories were good for men who had no books,
(Fortunate race!) and built their nests like rooks
In lonely towers, to which the Jongleur brought
His pedler's-box of cheap and tawdry thought,
With here and there a fancy fit to see
Wrought in quaint grace in golden filigree,—
Some ring that with the Muse's finger yet
Is warm, like Aucassin and Nicolete;
The morning newspaper has spoilt his trade,
(For better or for worse, I leave unsaid,)     110
And stories now, to suit a public nice,
Must be half epigram, half pleasant vice.

"All tourists know Shebagog County: there
The summer idlers take their yearly stare,

FITZ ADAM'S STORY.     93–95. story-teller . . . hawthorn: The
reference is to Nathaniel Hawthorne.

Dress to see Nature in a well-bred way,
As 't were Italian opera, or play,
Encore the sunrise (if they 're out of bed),
And pat the Mighty Mother on the head:
These have I seen,—all things are good to see,—
And wondered much at their complacency.   120
This world's great show, that took in getting-up
Millions of years, they finish ere they sup;
Sights that God gleams through with soul-tingling
    force
They glance approvingly as things of course,
Say, 'That 's a grand rock,' 'This a pretty fall,'
Not thinking, 'Are we worthy?' What if all
The scornful landscape should turn round and say,
'This is a fool, and that a popinjay'?
I often wonder what the Mountain thinks
Of French boots creaking o'er his breathless
    brinks,   130
Or how the Sun would scare the chattering crowd,
If some fine day he chanced to think aloud.
I, who love Nature much as sinners can,
Love her where she most grandeur shows,—in
    man:
Here find I mountain, forest, cloud, and sun,
River and sea, and glows when day is done;
Nay, where she makes grotesques, and moulds in
    jest
The clown's cheap clay, I find unfading zest.
The natural instincts year by year retire,   139
As deer shrink northward from the settler's fire,
And he who loves the wild game-flavor more
Than city-feasts, where every man's a bore
To every other man, must seek it where
The steamer's throb and railway's iron blare
Have not yet startled with their punctual stir
The shy, wood-wandering brood of Character.

    "There is a village, once the county town,
Through which the weekly mail rolled dustily
    down,
Where the courts sat, it may be, twice a year,
And the one tavern reeked with rustic cheer;   150
Cheeshogquesumscot erst, now Jethro hight,
Red-man and pale-face bore it equal spite.
The railway ruined it, the natives say,
That passed unwisely fifteen miles away,
And made a drain to which, with steady ooze,
Filtered away law, stage-coach, trade, and news.
The railway saved it; so at least think those
Who love old ways, old houses, old repose.
Of course the Tavern stayed: its genial host   159
Thought not of flitting more than did the post
On which high-hung the fading signboard creaks,
Inscribed, 'The Eagle Inn, by Ezra Weeks.'

    "If in life's journey you should ever find
An inn medicinal for body and mind,

'T is sure to be some drowsy-looking house
Whose easy landlord has a bustling spouse:
He, if he like you, will not long forego
Some bottle deep in cobwebbed dust laid low,
That, since the War we used to call the 'Last,'
Has dozed and held its lang-syne memories fast:
From him exhales that Indian-summer air   171
Of hazy, lazy welcome everywhere,
While with her toil the napery is white,
The china dustless, the keen knife-blades bright,
Salt dry as sand, and bread that seems as though
'T were rather sea-foam baked than vulgar dough.

    "In our swift country, houses trim and white
Are pitched like tents, the lodging of a night;
Each on its bank of baked turf mounted high
Perches impatient o'er the roadside dry,   180
While the wronged landscape coldly stands aloof,
Refusing friendship with the upstart roof.
Not so the Eagle; on a grass-green swell
That toward the south with sweet concessions fell
It dwelt retired, and half had grown to be
As aboriginal as rock or tree.
It nestled close to earth, and seemed to brood
O'er homely thoughts in a half-conscious mood,
As by the peat that rather fades than burns
The smouldering grandam nods and knits by
    turns,   190
Happy, although her newest news were old
Ere the first hostile drum at Concord rolled.
If paint it e'er had known, it knew no more
Than yellow lichens spattered thickly o'er
That soft lead-gray, less dark beneath the eaves
Which the slow brush of wind and weather leaves.
The ample roof sloped backward to the ground,
And vassal lean-tos gathered thickly round,
Patched on, as sire or son had felt the need,
Like chance growths sprouting from the old roof's
    seed,   200
Just as about a yellow-pine-tree spring
Its rough-barked darlings in a filial ring.
But the great chimney was the central thought
Whose gravitation through the cluster wrought;
For 't is not styles far-fetched from Greece or
    Rome,
But just the Fireside, that can make a home;
None of your spindling things of modern style,
Like pins stuck through to stay the card-built pile,
It rose broad shouldered, kindly, debonair,
Its warm breath whitening in the October air,   210
While on its front a heart in outline showed
The place it filled in that serene abode.

    "When first I chanced the Eagle to explore,
Ezra sat listless by the open door;
One chair careened him at an angle meet,

Another nursed his hugely-slippered feet;
Upon a third reposed a shirt-sleeved arm,
And the whole man diffused tobacco's charm.
'Are you the landlord?' 'Wahl, I guess I be,'
Watching the smoke, he answered leisurely.    220
He was a stoutish man, and through the breast
Of his loose shirt there showed a brambly chest;
Streaked redly as a wind-foreboding morn,
His tanned cheeks curved to temples closely
    shorn;
Clean-shaved he was, save where a hedge of gray
Upon his brawny throat leaned every way
About an Adam's-apple, that beneath
Bulged like a boulder from a brambly heath.
The Western World's true child and nursling he,
Equipt with aptitudes enough for three:    230
No eye like his to value horse or cow,
Or gauge the contents of a stack or mow;
He could foretell the weather at a word,
He knew the haunt of every beast and bird,
Or where a two-pound trout was sure to lie,
Waiting the flutter of his home-made fly;
Nay, once in autumns five, he had the luck
To drop at fair-play range a ten-tined buck;
Of sportsmen true he favored every whim,
But never cockney found a guide in him;    240
A natural man, with all his instincts fresh,
Not buzzing helpless in Reflection's mesh,
Firm on its feet stood his broad-shouldered mind,
As bluffly honest as a northwest wind;
Hard-headed and soft-hearted, you 'd scarce meet
A kindlier mixture of the shrewd and sweet;
Generous by birth, and ill at saying 'No,'
Yet in a bargain he was all men's foe,
Would yield no inch of vantage in a trade,
And give away ere nightfall all he made.    250


" 'Can I have lodging here?' once more I said.
He blew a whiff, and, leaning back his head,
'You come a piece through Bailey's woods, I
    s'pose,
Acrost a bridge where a big swamp-oak grows?
It don't grow, neither; it 's ben dead ten year,
Nor th' ain't a livin' creetur, fur nor near,
Can tell wut killed it; but I some misdoubt
'T was borers, there 's sech heaps on 'em about.
You did n' chance to run ag'inst my son,
A long, slab-sided youngster with a gun?    260
He 'd oughto ben back more 'n an hour ago,
An' brought some birds to dress for supper—
    sho!
There he comes now. 'Say, Obed, wut ye got?
(He 'll hev some upland plover like as not.)
Wal, them 's real nice uns, an 'll eat A 1,
Ef I can stop their bein' over-done;
Nothin' riles *me* (I pledge my fastin' word)
Like cookin' out the natur' of a bird;

(Obed, you pick 'em out o' sight an' sound,
Your ma'am don't love no feathers cluttrin'
    round;)    270
Jes' scare 'em with the coals,—thet 's *my* idee.'
Then, turning suddenly about on me,
'Wal, Square, I guess so. Callilate to stay?
I'll ask Mis' Weeks; 'bout *thet* it's hern to say.'


    "Well, there I lingered all October through,
In that sweet atmosphere of hazy blue,
So leisurely, so soothing, so forgiving,
That sometimes makes New England fit for living.
I watched the landscape, erst so granite glum,
Bloom like the south side of a ripening plum,    280
And each rock-maple on the hillside make
His ten days' sunset doubled in the lake;
The very stone walls draggling up the hills
Seemed touched, and wavered in their roundhead
    wills.
Ah! there 's a deal of sugar in the sun!
Tap me in Indian summer, I should run
A juice to make rock-candy of,—but then
We get such weather scarce one year in ten.


    "There was a parlor in the house, a room
To make you shudder with its prudish gloom.    290
The furniture stood round with such an air,
There seemed an old maid's ghost in every chair,
Which looked as it had scuttled to its place
And pulled extempore a Sunday face,
Too smugly proper for a world of sin,
Like boys on whom the minister comes in.
The table, fronting you with icy stare,
Strove to look witless that its legs were bare,
While the black sofa with its horse-hair pall
Gloomed like a bier for Comfort's funeral.    300
Each piece appeared to do its chilly best
To seem an utter stranger to the rest,
As if acquaintanceship were deadly sin,
Like Britons meeting in a foreign inn.
Two portraits graced the wall in grimmest truth,
Mister and Mistress W. in their youth,—
New England youth, that seems a sort of pill,
Half wish-I-dared, half Edwards on the Will,
Bitter to swallow, and which leaves a trace
Of Calvinistic colic on the face.    310
Between them, o'er the mantel, hung in state
Solomon's temple, done in copperplate;
Invention pure, but meant, we may presume,
To give some Scripture sanction to the room.
Facing this last, two samplers you might see,
Each, with its urn and stiffly-weeping tree,
Devoted to some memory long ago
More faded than their lines of worsted woe;

308. the Will: the theologian Jonathan Edwards' famous
treatise, *Freedom of the Will* (1754).

Cut paper decked their frames against the flies,
Though none e'er dared an entrance who were
    wise,         320
And bushed asparagus in fading green
Added its shiver to the franklin clean.

"When first arrived, I chilled a half-hour there,
Nor dared deflower with use a single chair;
I caught no cold, yet flying pains could find
For weeks in me,—a rheumatism of mind.
One thing alone imprisoned there had power
To hold me in the place that long half-hour:
A scutcheon this, a helm-surmounted shield,
Three griffins argent on a sable field;     330
A relic of the shipwrecked past was here,
And Ezra held some Old-World lumber dear.
Nay, do not smile; I love this kind of thing,
These cooped traditions with a broken wing,
This freehold nook in Fancy's pipe-blown ball,
This less than nothing that is more than all!
Have I not seen sweet natures kept alive
Amid the humdrum of your business hive,
Undowered spinsters shielded from all harms,
By airy incomes from a coat of arms?"     340

He paused a moment, and his features took
The flitting sweetness of that inward look
I hinted at before; but, scarcely seen,
It shrank for shelter 'neath his harder mien,
And, rapping his black pipe of ashes clear,
He went on with a self-derisive sneer:
"No doubt we make a part of God's design,
And break the forest-path for feet divine;
To furnish foothold for this grand prevision
Is good, and yet—to be the mere transition,   350
That, you will say, is also good, though I
Scarce like to feed the ogre By-and-by.
Raw edges rasp my nerves; my taste is wooed
By things that are, not going to be, good,
Though were I what I dreamed two lustres gone,
I 'd stay to help the Consummation on,
Whether a new Rome than the old more fair,
Or a deadflat of rascal-ruled despair;
But *my* skull somehow never closed the suture
That seems to knit yours firmly with the future,
So you 'll excuse me if I 'm sometimes fain   361
To tie the Past's warm nightcap o'er my brain;
I 'm quite aware 't is not in fashion here,
But then your northeast winds are *so* severe!

"But to my story: though 't is truly naught
But a few hints in Memory's sketchbook caught,
And which may claim a value on the score
Of calling back some scenery now no more.

Shall I confess? The tavern's only Lar
Seemed (be not shocked!) its homely-featured
    bar         370
Here dozed a fire of beechen logs, that bred
Strange fancies in its embers golden-red,
And nursed the loggerhead whose hissing dip,
Timed by nice instinct, creamed the mug of flip
That made from mouth to mouth its genial round,
Nor left one nature wholly winter-bound;
Hence dropt the tinkling coal all mellow-ripe
For Uncle Reuben's talk-extinguished pipe;
Hence rayed the heat, as from an indoor sun,
That wooed forth many a shoot of rustic fun.
Here Ezra ruled as king by right divine;     381
No other face had such a wholesome shine,
No laugh like his so full of honest cheer;
Above the rest it crowed like Chanticleer.

"In this one room his dame you never saw,
Where reigned by custom old a Salic law;
Here coatless lolled he on his throne of oak,
And every tongue paused midway if he spoke.
Due mirth he loved, yet was his sway severe;
No blear-eyed driveller got his stagger here;
'Measure was happiness; who wanted more,
Must buy his ruin at the Deacon's store;'   392
None but his lodgers after ten could stay,
Nor after nine on eves of Sabbath-day.
He had his favorites and his pensioners,
The same that gypsy Nature owns for hers:
Loose-ended souls, whose skills bring scanty gold,
And whom the poor-house catches when they 're
    old;
Rude country-minstrels, men who doctor kine,
Or graft, and, out of scions ten, save nine;     400
Creatures of genius they, but never meant
To keep step with the civic regiment.
These Ezra welcomed, feeling in his mind
Perhaps some motions of the vagrant kind;
These paid no money, yet for them he drew
Special Jamaica from a tap they knew,
And, for their feelings, chalked behind the door
With solemn face a visionary score.
This thawed to life in Uncle Reuben's throat
A torpid shoal of jest and anecdote,     410
Like those queer fish that doze the droughts away,
And wait for moisture, wrapped in sun-baked
    clay;
This warmed the one-eyed fiddler to his task,
Perched in the corner on an empty cask,
By whose shrill art rapt suddenly, some boor
Rattled a double-shuffle on the floor;

---

322. **franklin:** an open iron stove invented by Benjamin Franklin.

369. **Lar:** singular of *lares*: in Roman religion, images of household gods. Originally, the *lar* was a youth carrying a cup and a drinking horn. **385–86. In . . . law:** The code of laws of the Salian Franks excluded women from inheriting land.

'Hull's Victory' was, indeed, the favorite air,
Though 'Yankee Doodle' claimed its proper share.

   " 'T was there I caught from Uncle Reuben's
      lips,
In dribbling monologue 'twixt whiffs and sips,
The story I so long have tried to tell;    421
The humor coarse, the persons common,—well,
From Nature only do I love to paint,
Whether she send a satyr or a saint;
To me Sincerity 's the one thing good,
Soiled though she be and lost to maidenhood.
Quompegan is a town some ten miles south
From Jethro, at Nagumscot river-mouth,
A seaport town, and makes its title good
With lumber and dried fish and eastern wood.
Here Deacon Bitters dwelt and kept the Store,
The richest man for many a mile of shore;   432
In little less than everything dealt he,
From meeting-houses to a chest of tea;
So dextrous therewithal a flint to skin,
He could make profit on a single pin;
In business strict, to bring the balance true
He had been known to bite a fig in two,
And change a board-nail for a shingle-nail.
All that he had he ready held for sale,    440
His house, his tomb, whate'er the law allows,
And he had gladly parted with his spouse.
His one ambition still to get and get,
He would arrest your very ghost for debt.
His store looked righteous, should the Parson
     come,
But in a dark back-room he peddled rum,
And eased Ma'am Conscience, if she e'er would
     scold,
By christening it with water ere he sold.
A small, dry man he was, who wore a queue,
And one white neckcloth all the week-days
     through,—    450
On Monday white, by Saturday as dun
As that worn homeward by the prodigal son.
His frosted earlocks, striped with foxy brown,
Were braided up to hide a desert crown;
His coat was brownish, black perhaps of yore;
In summer-time a banyan loose he wore;
His trousers short, through many a season true,
Made no pretence to hide his stockings blue;
A waistcoat buff his chief adornment was,
Its porcelain buttons rimmed with dusky brass.
A deacon he, you saw it in each limb,    461
And well he knew to deacon-off a hymn,
Or lead the choir through all its wandering woes
With voice that gathered unction in his nose,

---

462. **deacon-off**: Part of "the office of deacon was to read aloud
the hymns *given out* by the minister, one line at a time, the
congregation singing each line as soon as read" [L].

Wherein a constant snuffle you might hear,
As if with him 't were winter all the year.
At pew-head sat he with decorous pains,
In sermon-time could foot his weekly gains,
Or, with closed eyes and heaven-abstracted air,
Could plan a new investment in long-prayer.
A pious man, and thrifty too, he made    471
The psalms and prophets partners in his trade,
And in his orthodoxy straitened more
As it enlarged the business at his store;
He honored Moses, but, when gain he planned,
Had his own notion of the Promised Land.

   "Soon as the winter made the sledding good,
From far around the farmers hauled him wood,
For all the trade had gathered 'neath his thumb.
He paid in groceries and New England rum,   480
Making two profits with a conscience clear,—
Cheap all he bought, and all he paid with dear.
With his own mete-wand measuring every load,
Each somehow had diminished on the road;
An honest cord in Jethro still would fail
By a good foot upon the Deacon's scale,
And, more to abate the price, his gimlet eye
Would pierce to cat-sticks that none else could
     spy;
Yet none dared grumble, for no farmer yet
But New Year found him in the Deacon's debt.

   "While the first snow was mealy under feet,
A team drawled creaking down Quompegan
     street.    492
Two cords of oak weighed down the grinding sled,
And cornstalk fodder rustled overhead;
The oxen's muzzles, as they shouldered through,
Were silver-fringed; the driver's own was blue
As the coarse frock that swung below his knee.
Behind his load for shelter waded he;
His mittened hands now on his chest he beat,
Now stamped the stiffened cowhides of his feet,
Hushed as a ghost's; his armpit scarce could
     hold    501
The walnut whipstock slippery-bright with cold.
What wonder if, the tavern as he past,
He looked and longed, and stayed his beasts at
     last,
Who patient stood and veiled themselves in steam
While he explored the bar-room's ruddy gleam?

   "Before the fire, in want of thought profound,
There sat a brother-townsman weather-bound:
A sturdy churl, crisp-headed, bristly-eared,
Red as a pepper; 'twixt coarse brows and beard
His eyes lay ambushed, on the watch for fools,

---

488. **catsticks**: Crooked logs concealed in a load of wood took up
extra space and therefore prevented honest measure.

Clear, gray, and glittering like two bay-edged
    pools;         512
A shifty creature, with a turn for fun,
Could swap a poor horse for a better one,—
He 'd a high-stepper always in his stall;
Liked far and near, and dreaded therewithal.
To him the in-comer, 'Perez, how d' ye do?'
'Jest as I 'm mind to, Obed; how do you?'
Then, his eyes twinkling such swift gleams as run
Along the levelled barrel of a gun     520
Brought to his shoulder by a man you know
Will bring his game down, he continued, 'So,
I s'pose you're haulin' wood? But you 're too late;
The Deacon 's off; Old Splitfoot could n't wait;
He made a bee-line las' night in the storm
To where he won't need wood to keep him warm.
'Fore this he 's treasurer of a fund to train
Young imps as missionaries; hopes to gain
That way a contract that he has in view
For fireproof pitchforks of a pattern new.     530
It must have tickled him, all drawbacks
    weighed,
To think he stuck the Old One in a trade;
His soul, to start with, was n't worth a carrot,
And all he 'd left 'ould hardly serve to swear at.'

    "By this time Obed had his wits thawed out,
And, looking at the other half in doubt,
Took off his fox-skin cap to scratch his head,
Donned it again, and drawled forth, 'Mean he 's
    dead?'
'Jesso; he 's dead and t' other *d* that follers
With folks that never love a thing but dollars.
He pulled up stakes last evening, fair and
    square,       541
And ever since there 's been a row Down There.
The minute the old chap arrived, you see,
Comes the Boss-devil to him, and says he,
"What are you good at? Little enough, I fear;
We callilate to make folks useful here."
"Well," says old Bitters, "I expect I can
Scale a fair load of wood with e'er a man."
"Wood we don't deal in; but perhaps you 'll suit,
Because we buy our brimstone by the foot:   550
Here, take this measurin'-rod, as smooth as
    sin,
And keep a reckonin' of what loads comes in.
You 'll not want business, for we need a lot
To keep the Yankees that you send us hot;
At firin' up they 're barely half as spry
As Spaniards or Italians, though they 're dry;
At first we have to let the draught on stronger,
But, heat 'em through, they seem to hold it
    longer."

    " 'Bitters he took the rod, and pretty soon
A teamster comes, whistling an ex-psalm tune.

A likelier chap you would n't ask to see,   561
No different, but his limp, from you or me'—
'No different, Perez! Don't your memory fail?
Why, where in thunder was his horns and tail?'
'They 're only worn by some old-fashioned pokes;
They mostly aim at looking just like folks.
Sech things are scarce as queues and top-boots
    here;
'T would spoil their usefulness to look too queer.
Ef you could always know 'em when they come,
They 'd get no purchase on you: now be mum.
On come the teamster, smart as Davy Crock-
    ett,      571
Jinglin' the red-hot coppers in his pocket,
And clost behind, ('t was gold-dust, you 'd ha'
    sworn,)
A load of sulphur yallower 'n seed-corn;
To see it wasted as it is Down There
Would make a Friction-Match Co. tear its hair!
"Hold on!" says Bitters, "stop right where you
    be;
You can't go in athout a pass from me."
"All right," says t' other, "only step round smart;
I must be home by noon-time with the cart."   580
Bitters goes round it sharp-eyed as a rat,
Then with a scrap of paper on his hat
Pretends to cipher. "By the public staff,
That load scarce rises twelve foot and a half."
"There 's fourteen foot and over," says the driver,
"Worth twenty dollars, ef it 's worth a stiver;
Good fourth-proof brimstone, that 'll make 'em
    squirm,—
I leave it to the Headman of the Firm;
After we masure it, we always lay
Some on to allow for settlin' by the way.   590
Imp and full-grown, I 've carted sulphur here,
And gi'n fair satisfaction, thirty year."
With that they fell to quarrellin' so loud
That in five minutes they had drawed a crowd,
And afore long the Boss, who heard the row,
Comes elbowin' in with "What 's to pay here
    now?"
Both parties heard, the measurin'-rod he takes,
And of the load a careful survey makes.
"Sence I have bossed the business here," says he,
"No fairer load was ever seen by me."   600
Then, turnin' to the Deacon, "You mean cus,
None of your old Quompegan tricks with us!
They won't do here: we 're plain old-fashioned
    folks,
And don't quite understand that kind o' jokes.
I know this teamster, and his pa afore him,
And the hard-working Mrs. D. that bore him;
He would n't soil his conscience with a lie,
Though he might get the custom-house thereby.
Here, constable, take Bitters by the queue,
And clap him into furnace ninety-two,   610

And try this brimstone on him; if he 's bright,
He 'll find the masure honest afore night.
He is n't worth his fuel, and I 'll bet
The parish oven has to take him yet!" '

"This is my tale, heard twenty years ago
From Uncle Reuben, as the logs burned low,
Touching the walls and ceiling with that bloom
That makes a rose's calyx of a room.
I could not give his language, wherethrough ran
The gamy flavor of the bookless man          620
Who shapes a word before the fancy cools,

As lonely Crusoe improvised his tools.
I liked the tale,—'t was like so many told
By Rutebeuf and his brother Trouvères bold;
Nor were the hearers much unlike to theirs,
Men unsophisticate, rude-nerved as bears.
Ezra is gone and his large-hearted kind,
The landlords of the hospitable mind;
Good Warriner of Springfield was the last;
An inn is now a vision of the past;          630
One yet-surviving host my mind recalls,—
You 'll find him if you go to Trenton Falls."

*1867*

## RICHARD CHASE
*Editor*

# Herman Melville

## 1819–1891

Nowadays Melville is generally regarded as one of the greatest of American writers. We have no hesitation in placing him among, perhaps indeed at the head of, the "classic" American authors, as D. H. Lawrence called James Fenimore Cooper, Edgar Allan Poe, Nathaniel Hawthorne, and other tale-tellers, novelists, and poets who achieved their best work before the Civil War. Melville has found in recent decades a large number of American readers. He has exercised a strong influence on the minds of contemporary writers, as we see from such poems as Hart Crane's elegy "At Melville's Tomb" (1920); W. H. Auden's "Herman Melville" (1945); and Robert Lowell's "The Quaker Graveyard in Nantucket" (1946), in itself a great poem but deriving some of its most effective imagery from Melville's masterpiece, *Moby-Dick*. Many contemporary writers of fiction, looking for resources of the symbolic imagination, have turned to Melville, and many of them have found in his works the "allegories of moral consciousness" which William Faulkner tells us he has found there.

Melville's reputation is not only great; it seems also secure, for it is impossible to imagine an America of the future which will not honor and read this author. There is therefore much irony in the fact that when Melville died in 1891, he had long outlived the popularity and fame that he briefly enjoyed during the 1840's, when his South-Seas adventure tales—notably *Typee* (1846)—were in

vogue. Although his later tales, novels, and poems had had a scattering of readers, perhaps more consistently in England than in his own country, he was virtually unknown at the time of his death, either to his fellow writers or to the world at large. Melville, one might think, should have occupied an important place in such an ambitious and influential survey of the American literary past as Van Wyck Brooks's *America's Coming of Age*, published in 1915. Yet he is not mentioned at all, so far had he sunk into obscurity. Nor, with the exception of Hawthorne, did the writers of his own century know him much better. Henry James, well versed in Whitman, Hawthorne, and Emerson, seems to have known next to nothing about Melville, except that he retained in late years, as his essay of 1898 on American magazines shows, a dim memory of the author of *Typee*. James speaks in a rather uncomplimentary way of "the prose, as mild and easy as an Indian summer in the woods, of Herman Melville, of George William Curtis, and 'Ik Marvel.'" No one nowadays, surely, would put these three writers on a plane of equality or describe Melville's prose, even in *Typee*—let alone *Redburn* (1849), *Moby-Dick* (1851), "Bartleby the Scrivener" (1853), "Benito Cereno" (1855), *The Confidence-Man* (1857), or *Billy Budd* (1924)—as James describes it. For this is a prose that knows more seasons than Indian summer and penetrates woods more deep, mysterious, and dangerous than those James had in mind.

It was not until the 1920's that Melville began to be salvaged from oblivion, as a part of the general historical and critical effort that Brooks had called for in order to "rediscover America" and to seek out our "usable past." Raymond Weaver, who gained access to many of Melville's papers including the manuscript of the unpublished *Billy Budd*, published in 1921 the first full-scale biography. From this work the modern Melville scholarship flows, just as the criticism that sees Melville as a significant and representative figure in American culture flows from D. H. Lawrence's two chapters in his *Studies in Classic American Literature*, which appeared in 1923.

In his own lifetime Melville suffered much from the lack of a community of the literary life, a community, that is, of his peers, who might have given him encouragement and useful criticism. This kind of community he was to know only briefly in the 1840's. But he seems always to have felt the need of it and to have understood how it might foster the creative spirit. See, for example, his strong expostulation in "Hawthorne and His Mosses" (1850), urging Americans to acknowledge immediately Hawthorne's greatness:

Give not over to future generations the glad duty of acknowledging him for what he is. Take that joy to yourself, in your own generation; and so shall he feel those grateful impulses on him, that may possibly prompt him to the full flower of some still greater achievement in your eyes. And by confessing him you thereby confess others; you brace the whole brotherhood. For genius, all over the world, stands hand in hand, and one shock of recognition runs the whole circle round.

Few enough people were to acknowledge Melville in his own time. Yet now, whether we are geniuses or not, we experience the shock of recognition of which he spoke whenever we look into his works.

## II

WHEN Herman Melville was born in New York on August 1, 1819, one would not have suspected that his youth would be characterized by trouble, heartache, hard work, and restless voyaging to Europe and the South Seas as a common sailor. For both his father, Allan Melvill (as the name was then spelled), and his mother, Maria Gansevoort, came from well-to-do families that had some claim to aristocratic status. Allan Melvill's father and grandfather had been successful merchants and importers, and Maria Gansevoort's background was the Dutch landholding patriciate of the Hudson Valley. But the unsuspected destiny of Herman Melville began to unfold in 1830 when his father's business suffered severe financial reverses, and in 1832 when his father died. There is no doubt that the early death of Melville's father had a lifelong effect on his son's psychic constitution. There are good personal reasons why Melville calls himself Ishmael in *Moby-Dick*, for, like Abraham's son by Hagar (Gen. 16), Melville early learned to feel bereft both of patrimony and paternity; like the Biblical Ishmael, he could easily think of himself as a wanderer whose hand was turned against every man. And when we hear the Ishmael of *Moby-Dick* exclaim out of his loneliness: "Where is the foundling's father hidden?" we reflect that a part of the search for truth and certitude that makes the theme of many of Melville's books was a search for a father, or for those emotions of security and power associated with a boy's feelings for his father. Nor can there be any doubt that, democrat though he was, the loss of patrician status was not easy for Melville to take. The humiliations and sufferings of a youth brought up in genteel surroundings who suddenly finds himself among the callous and brutal sailors on a merchant ship are memorably described in *Redburn*, and in *Pierre* (1852) we observe the nostalgia and reverence with which the ill-fated hero regards his eminent ancestors.

In a sense it can be said that on the verge of his teens Melville lost not only a father but a mother, or at least the bonds of love and respect which he would have continued to form with his mother had the family destiny been a happier one. For Maria Melville seems, under the pressure of adversity, to have grown ever more harsh and morally overbearing. The imperious and frigid mother portrayed in *Pierre* is surely in some measure a portrait of Melville's own mother, and one suspects that the imperiousness and frigidity are more real than the fantasied idyl of affection between mother and son Melville describes in the opening chapters of this revealing novel. There are doubtless cultural as well as personal reasons why there are so few, indeed almost no, sympathetic or convincingly real women in Melville's books, but one may conjecture that an early failure of love between mother and son had something to do with it.

With Melville's mother must also be associated the influence of the Dutch Reformed Church, to which she belonged, on the youthful imagination of her son. Melville was early introduced, imaginatively and emotionally if not intellectually, to the strict Calvinism of this church, with its dark view of the human lot and its creed of predestination. As we shall see, Melville came later in life to believe that no deeply thinking mind, no matter what its specific doctrinal commitments, could ever be free of the profound sense of imperfection and fate which the Calvinist idea of original sin requires. This influence on Melville's imagination was certainly no less strong for the fact that he remained throughout his life an agnostic, though an unhappy one.

Melville's education was spotty; as he says in *Moby-Dick*, a whaling ship was his Yale and Harvard. He did, however, attend the Albany Academy for a time. Soon it was necessary for him to help the impoverished family by clerking in his elder brother's store, by working on his uncle's farm, and later by schoolteaching, which he did in Pittsfield, Massachusetts, and later in Greenbush, New York. But in the spring of 1839 he made a move that was to be decisive in the development of his character and genius: he embarked on the merchant ship *St. Lawrence*, bound for Liverpool. The literary result of this journey was *Redburn*, Melville's fourth book, published in 1849. There is undoubtedly much genuine autobiography in this book, although the hero is represented as being somewhat younger and more callow than Melville actually was at the time,

and although the hard-bitten realism of the book is obviously mixed with elements of romance and fancy. But more important than the fact that the Liverpool trip later found literary representation is the fact that it inaugurated for Melville a period of nearly five years of restless wandering about the world that provided him with the material for his first six books, including *Moby-Dick*, and did much to give a definitive shape to his mind in all of its characteristic strength and weakness.

In January of 1841 Melville sailed out of Fairhaven, Massachusetts, on the whaler *Acushnet*, bound for the South Seas. We must suppose that the whaling ship, the South Seas, and the Marquesas Islands, where Melville underwent the experiences more or less accurately chronicled in *Typee*, roused his passions to their mature development and stirred, even in a sense created, his imagination. The whaling ship and the South Seas had a decisive effect on Melville's mind and his art, just as Europe stirred the mind of the young Henry James, Hannibal, Missouri, the mind of the young Mark Twain, Salem, the mind of the young Hawthorne, and frontier New York State the mind of the young Fenimore Cooper. Melville had an affinity not shared in equal degree by these other writers for the exotic and the bizarre, for tumultuous passions, on the one hand, and erotic indolence on the other, for wild adventures, and for nature seen in its most spacious, magnificent, and mysterious aspects. Nowhere better than in the South Seas could these proclivities have been nurtured. There is no doubt, however, that Melville's experiences as a sailor, despite such idyllic friendships as may be mirrored in the stories of Ishmael and Queequeg in *Moby-Dick* or Tommo and Toby in *Typee*, confirmed in him as a kind of fate the loneliness he had learned to feel as a child. Despite his capacity for conviviality, despite his marriage and family, he was always to be what he calls in *Moby-Dick* an "isolato."

Melville was to make other journeys later in life, but none of course had the effect upon him of his years on whaling ships, although the trip of 1856–57 to England and the Near East furnished him with fresh material and inspiration for the poetry he was to write during the 1860's and seventies. He returned in 1844 from the South Seas as a sailor in an American warship—as described in *White-Jacket* (1850)—and settled down to arduous years of writing. As I have said, Melville achieved considerable success and not a little notoriety with the publication of *Typee* in 1846. Yet only five years later, by which time he had written four other books and was in the midst of writing *Moby-Dick*, we find him ruefully conjecturing in a letter to Hawthorne that he was destined to be known only as "a man who had lived among the cannibals." "Dollars damn me," he says in another letter, "and the malicious Devil is forever grinning in upon me, holding the door ajar. . . . What I feel most moved to write, that is banned—it will not pay. Yet, altogether, write the *other* way I cannot." And again he says, "Try to get a living by the Truth—and go to the Soup Societies."

Elsewhere Melville exclaims, "There is the grand truth about Nathaniel Hawthorne. He says No! in thunder; but the Devil himself cannot make him say *yes*. For all men who say *yes*, lie." Although Melville was not exclusively a nay-sayer, his experiences and his reflections upon the quality of American civilization had taught him to utter the powerful "no" he attributes to Hawthorne. He had learned to say "no" to the boundlessly optimistic commercialized creed of most Americans, with its superficial and mean conception of the possibilities of human life, its denial of all the genuinely creative or heroic capacities of man, and its fear and dislike of any but the mildest truths. Melville's "no" finds expression in the tragic-comic tale "Bartleby the Scrivener." This story is too richly imaginative to be read simply as autobiography, at however great a remove. Yet in Bartleby's stubbornly repeated phrase, "I would prefer not to," we hear a version of Melville's "no." The story is a subtle study of the mystery, perhaps the pathology, of the fate of the dissenter or nay-sayer in a yea-saying culture.

By 1851, when he was only thirty-two, Melville had already largely lost the au-dience he had won with *Typee*. This was an audience which, as his letter to Hawthorne implies, wanted not truth but superficial and pleasant romance of the sort they took *Typee* to be. This audience, well enough pleased with *Omoo* (1847), the sequel to *Typee*, was disconcerted by *Mardi* (1849), with its allegories, its intellectuality, and ruminativeness. *Moby-Dick* was not to fare well either; too many readers regarded it as a potentially interesting adventure story spoiled by murky metaphysical speculations. And Melville's fate as an unappreciated and misunderstood writer was sealed with the publication in 1852 of *Pierre*, a novel about incest and suicide which was damned as not only obscure but morally reprehensible.

By this time Melville had become, as we look back upon him, the very archetype of the neglected and isolated writer in nineteenth-century America. Whitman and Henry James too suffered neglect and isolation, but never so drastically as did Melville. If any great American writer suffered an "ordeal," to borrow a word from Van Wyck Brooks's celebrated biography, *The Ordeal of Mark Twain* (1920), it was Melville. It is probable that his disappointment and feeling of isolation were deepened in 1851 by his failure to establish a close and lasting friendship with Hawthorne.

In 1847 Melville had married Elizabeth Shaw, the daughter of the chief justice of Massachusetts, and had settled in New York City. But for whatever reasons, personal or financial, the family—there were finally four children—moved in 1850 to a farm near Pittsfield, Massachusetts. At this time Hawthorne was living in nearby Lenox, and Melville felt an immediate affinity with him not only as a writer—as we see in "Hawthorne and his Mosses"—but, once he had met him, with Hawthorne himself. Melville's letters to Hawthorne are notable from an intellectual and literary point of view and tell us much about what was going on in the mind of the man who was engaged in writing *Moby-Dick*. But they are notable too for the community of feeling and mind which they invite, at times almost demand. Hawthorne's letters to Melville have not survived, but it is easy to conjecture that Melville's impulsiveness seemed excessive and was probably embarrassing to the reticent and retiring author of *The Scarlet Letter* (1850); he was not the man to match the ebullience of Melville. And although the friendship ostensibly lasted for some time, it must soon have seemed abortive to Melville.

But it was not only public neglect and loneliness that Melville had to contend with in 1851. There was also his own premonition that even as he was completing *Moby-Dick* he had already exhausted his special material and, even worse, his genius. So we sense from this passage in a letter to Hawthorne:

Until I was twenty-five I had no development at all. From my twenty-fifth year I date my life. Three weeks have scarcely passed, at any time between then and now, that I have not unfolded within myself. But I feel that I am now come to the inmost leaf of the bulb, and that shortly the flower will fall to the mould.

A sad premonition, especially when we reflect that under happier circumstances Melville might well have been looking forward to decades of further development, to the unfolding of ever more inward leaves. In a general way Melville's career seems to bear out F. Scott Fitzgerald's famous dictum that there are "no second acts" in American lives.

Fortunately, however, Melville's premonition was rather too pessimistic, for although he was never again to write a work that approaches the greatness of *Moby-Dick*, he did continue to write and even to find genuinely new and valuable subject matters and styles. But except for the magazine publication of stories like "Bartleby" and "Benito Cereno" and the meager body of readers who appreciated volumes like *The Confidence-Man* (1857) and *Battle-Pieces* (1866), Melville was destined to write almost, one might say, in private. Certainly there was little money in it, and the image of Melville that haunts us from out of the past—the unsung author of *Moby-Dick* moving his family back to New York and working obscurely for almost twenty years as a customs inspector—has

become legendary in the annals of our culture. That the customs inspector should have resolutely turned to the writing of poetry and, after his retirement in 1885, to the writing of *Billy Budd,* was surely an act of quiet heroism. Much of the poetry was privately printed and found virtually no readers. *Billy Budd,* completed in the year of the author's death, was not published until 1924. Yet Melville's posterity has learned to think highly of his poetry and to rank *Billy Budd*—as I am sure most readers would agree—second to *Moby-Dick* among his works. No doubt it is useless to speculate as to what Melville's development would have been had he met with a more fortunate reception and lived in a literary culture more immediately aware of true genius. We must content ourselves with what he left us, and that is a very great deal.

### III

MELVILLE shares with Hawthorne an interest in the darker side of human nature and destiny, and like Hawthorne he is fascinated by the involutions of human psychology, by the ultimate alienation that may be the human lot—as in "Bartleby the Scrivener"—and by the distortions of the ego—as in the portrait of Captain Ahab in *Moby-Dick.* Hawthorne traced his own interest in the darker side of human nature to the background of New England Puritanism from which his family stemmed. Melville makes a similar association in "Hawthorne and His Mosses." Here he speaks of "the great power of blackness" in Hawthorne's imagination and speculates that it

derives its force from its appeals to that Calvinistic sense of Innate Depravity and Original Sin, from whose visitations, in some shape or other, no deeply thinking mind is always and wholly free. For, in certain moods, no man can weigh this world without throwing in something, somehow like Original Sin, to strike the uneven balance.

Clearly, the fertile resources of the Puritan imagination entered into the works of Melville as deeply as they did into Hawthorne's writings.

But of course there is much in Melville that is quite beyond the interest or capacity of Hawthorne. Especially there is the idyllic pastoral mood that permeates *Typee* and is invoked in many of the later tales and poems. Like Cooper's Leatherstocking tales—for example, *Deerslayer* (1841) and *The Last of the Mohicans* (1826)—*Typee* relies for its appeal, though in a very different setting, on the perennial romantic desire of modern man to escape from civilization with all of its complexities, injustices, and tensions and to recapture a lost state of innocence in a pastoral environment. It is a commonplace of criticism that this perennial impulse has had in America a special poignance and found expression in a special form because of the phenomenon of a rampant civilization driving west and a frontier forever retreating before it. The frontier has been written about in many different ways in American literature, and, as a symbol of human happiness and freedom, has been discovered in many different places. But the archetypal form of the story about the flight to the frontier is doubtless the one we see in the opening chapters of *Moby-Dick,* where Ishmael and his friend Queequeg are leaving civilization and setting sail, in a mood of perfect friendship and emotional release, for the far Pacific. The archetype, in other words, is of a white man or boy escaping to freedom with an Indian or Negro or Polynesian companion. The story has proven to be a rich resource of the American imagination, as we see if we recall, for example, Cooper's Natty Bumppo and Chingachgook, Mark Twain's Huckleberry Finn and Jim, and Faulkner's Ike McCaslin and Sam Fathers in "The Bear."

If, as there seems good reason for saying, the two forces that did most to shape the imagination of the classic writers were, first, the Calvinist sense of "blackness" and of moral and psychological complexity and, second, the pastoral idyl of the frontier, we see a major reason for Melville's greatness as a writer. Among the best writers older than himself, Cooper and Hawthorne were able to draw on only one of these forces, for there is no more Calvinism in Cooper than there is pastoral romance in Hawthorne.

Melville was the first great writer who was able to draw on both these forces and in a measure to synthesize them.

But there is more to be said about the inclusiveness of Melville's mind. For one thing he was the first writer to make full use of the traditions of American folklore and "American humor," in Constance Rourke's phrase, forecasting in this way such writers as Mark Twain and William Faulkner, who were also to draw upon the accumulating fund of tall tales, legend, and folk humor that had appeared in this country after the Revolution, mostly on the ever receding frontier, although Hawthorne had of course already found a source of materials in the more specialized and confined folklore of Puritan New England, just as Washington Irving had in the folklore of New York. One finds evidences of this influence throughout Melville, especially in *Moby-Dick* and the much neglected tale called *Israel Potter* (1855), with its semilegendary portraits of the hero himself and of Benjamin Franklin, Ethan Allen, and John Paul Jones. And *Moby-Dick* does what every epic does: it absorbs the native materials of the popular imagination—such as the tall tales about the white whale—into a work of art, conceived on a grand scale.

Finally, in considering the inclusiveness of Melville's mind, one should observe that both his tendency to draw on native materials and his view of art relate him to Whitman. Many critics, including D. H. Lawrence and Van Wyck Brooks, have said that Whitman's poetry is the first culmination of the American imagination because in this poetry the real and the ideal, or as Brooks put it, the lowbrow and the highbrow, were first brought into relationship and fused. Whitman, in other words, was able to endow the spiritual heritage of Puritanism and Transcendentalism with the body, as it were, of actual American life. He was able to bring into his poems not only spiritual aspiration and refinement but also the thriving realities of a vastly growing nation along with the American gusto for experience, experience of all facets of life without aristocratic scruple or moral inhibition. No doubt this is a true account of Whitman's poems. But it also applies to a certain extent to Melville. The passages in *Redburn* describing Liverpool certainly leave nothing to be desired on the score of realism. *White-Jacket* is full of realistic detail in its account of life aboard an American warship. And despite its metaphysical subtleties, transcendental flights, and symbolic poetry, *Moby-Dick* presents us with a panorama of richly thriving life, as well as meticulously detailed descriptions of the apparatus and techniques of the whaling industry. Without this panorama of real life, *Moby-Dick* would be a far different, and a far paler, book than it is.

Despite his admiration for Hawthorne's nicely limned tales, Melville's own idea of art resembles that of Whitman. Hawthorne, judging from his works themselves, thought of the well-wrought tale as having a strict inner economy and as aiming to create a rather static, pictorial effect that would be complete in itself. Melville's idea of art is much more Promethean; he thought of a work of art as something never finished, something that remained living, organic, and emergent. "I have created the creative!" is the triumphant cry of the fanciful poet in *Mardi*. And at one point in *Moby-Dick* Melville bursts out with: "God keep me from ever completing anything. This whole book is but a draught—nay, but the draught of a draught." An exaggeration, of course, but reminding us of Whitman's account in his 1855 Preface to *Leaves of Grass* of the "organic" nature of poetry, and of his idea that "a great poem is no finish to a man or woman but rather a beginning."

Melville's mind, then, was capable of accommodating widely divergent ranges of experience and of projecting divergent images in the form of art. But if this power of inclusiveness contributed to the richness of his imagination, it did not give him inner serenity. Melville was in fact throughout his mature life a deeply divided, doubting, and troubled man. So Hawthorne noticed when Melville visited him in Liverpool in 1856. Melville, Hawthorne reports, discoursed ardently and eloquently about ultimate problems of truth and belief but despaired of finding any solution that would satisfy him.

He could neither believe, Hawthorne writes, "nor be comfortable in his unbelief." Contradiction and alienation are of the essence in Melville's view of life and in his art. He saw human experience and the moral world man constructs for himself, indeed he saw nature itself, as riven by contradictions that could never be satisfactorily reconciled. Although his pessimism was modified in later years, he characteristically saw life as the quest of the individual for the truth and moral harmony that would always elude him, and he saw the quest as alienating the individual from the world, society, and himself.

The beginnings of this theme are to be seen in Melville's first book, *Typee*. *Typee* is not a great book, but in writing it Melville was performing a significant moral and psychological act which gives the story—on the surface so gay, romantic, and jocose—a deep undercurrent of meaning. It is characteristic of Melville's art that *Typee* should have a pronounced rhythm or inner dramatic action. The events do not occur in a succession of static scenes, as usually happens in a story by Hawthorne or Poe. The rhythm of *Typee* consists of a series of imprisonments and liberations, of withdrawals from reality and of returns. The hero and his friend Toby escape from the ship. They are imprisoned among the thickly growing reeds as they flee inland. They escape from these to the mountains. Repeatedly they gain the top of a ridge and then plunge into a valley of dark defile. Then there is the long enforced stay among the seemingly benevolent Typees, with what might be called subrhythms of incipient escape. Finally there is the escape from the island at the end of the book. Despite the light tone of *Typee*, the action gives the effect of being cumulative, organic, morally and psychologically significant.

From the moral point of view the valley of Typee and its apparently idyllic life represent a kind of Eden, a state of innocence and happiness, and Melville's romanticized version of his stay among the cannibals is certainly one of the notable Eden fantasies of literature. But notwithstanding its pleasures, this Eden is seen to be illusory, not only because Eden is by nature illusory but because this is a partly fallen Eden, in which the effects of crime and violence, not to mention cannibalism, are real and present although held by the Typees furtively in the background. Hence, it is a fraudulent Eden and must be escaped. From the psychological point of view the valley of Typee represents the regressive impulses of escape, of a full indulgence of what Freud calls the pleasure principle. But in an adult—even so gay a youth as the author portrays himself as being—who belongs to the nervous, competitive, complicated Western world this indulgence produces anxiety and guilt and the fear of being unmanned—hence the symbolic leg injury of the hero. In a modern adult man the personality, in other words, must be integrated at a higher level than is afforded in Typee. The pleasure principle must be in part foresworn in favor of the reality principle.

The same parable is told in a different way by Hawthorne in such stories as "The Maypole of Merrymount" (1837) and *The Blithedale Romance* (1852). Hawthorne, however, was content, when he had rejected the Edenic ideal, to accept society pretty much as he found it, and he was content with such truths and solutions of man's dilemmas as did not too heavily tax his relatively serene skepticism. Not so Melville. Having rejected Typee as false, though not without retaining considerable nostalgia for it, he was determined to discover those truths—moral, philosophic, religious, political, aesthetic—which would make sense of the civilized world and provide a means of feeling in harmony with it. This quest, sometimes inspiring, sometimes agonized and despairing, is a central theme, though not necessarily the only theme, of Melville's writings at least through the late poem *Clarel* (1876).

Melville's third novel, *Mardi*, is a curious book which begins as a conventional adventure tale and then abruptly shifts into the realm of fantasy and allegory and depicts the imaginary voyage of a company of boon companions in search of truth, happiness, and experience in the fantasy world of Mardi. The story is an odd and not entirely successful amalgam of Rabelesian extrava-

ganza, mildly Swiftian satire, and Melvillian jocosity. All the high spirits notwithstanding, there is no doubt that the book has a serious intent. This we see in the character of Taji, a distant prefiguration of the Ishmael of *Moby-Dick*, and his perplexed pursuit of certainty. At the end the world of Mardi seems to the hero to be characterized by unreason and ambiguity, and he sails off alone in an open boat over dangerous seas in search of other worlds.

It is not surprising, given his sense of the contradictoriness of things, that Melville should often employ symbolic oppositions as a part of his artistic technique. He noted interestedly that Hawthorne did the same—at least that seems to be what he is saying in "Hawthorne and His Mosses" when he writes: "For spite of all the Indian-summer sunlight on the hither side of Hawthorne's soul, the other side—like the dark half of the physical sphere—is shrouded in a blackness ten times black." Like the other classic writers, Melville often uses symbolic lights and darks, a striking example of this being the great story "Benito Cereno." In *Mardi* the light and the dark are symbolized by two women: the angelic wraith Yillah, who seems to stand for innocence and reason, and the sinister, engrossing Hautia, the dark woman who suggests the destructive and irrational human impulses. In *Billy Budd*, the blond Billy and the dark villain Claggart are distant analogues to the symbolic women of *Mardi*, although the two girls in *Pierre*, Lucy and Isabel, are closer descendants of Yillah and Hautia.

We should not expect Yillah and Hautia to be "real," since they are frankly presented as figures in an allegory. But it may not be amiss to observe at this point that Melville was like a good many other of the most characteristic American writers from Cooper to Faulkner in being unable to present, even when he tried, a fully portrayed woman in whose reality we can quite believe—with the possible exception of Fayaway in *Typee*. *Pierre* is, at least by intention, the most "novelistic" of Melville's works, for in this book Melville was attempting to draw real characters in real situations without the element of romance, myth, or epic which we find in most of his writings. Yet Pierre's mother is never made believably real or female; she remains a kind of presiding magisterial presence, rather than a character. Lucy, though appealing, is impossibly pure and angelic. And Isabel, whom Melville tries to endow with passion, is only a dim—sometimes, alas, almost a ludicrous—replica of a real *femme fatale*. The probability is that she was not intended to be a *femme fatale* at all but only an unfortunate and unhappy girl. Yet into Melville's portrait of her the element of melodrama and myth inevitably crept.

It was not in Melville's power to write the "novel of society" or the "novel of manners." In such novels the class to which the characters belong, and the actual day-to-day moral dilemmas and personal involvements in which they find themselves, are always at the center of the writer's attention. Melville does not write this kind of novel—nor do any of the other great American writers, with the exception of Henry James. Melville's finest achievement, *Moby-Dick*, is not really a novel in the sense in which we are at present using the term; it is a kind of epic romance. It does not matter on board the *Pequod* that Ahab is a middleclass entrepreneur, that Starbuck is of the lower middle class, or that Ishmael has an aristocratic background. In his survey of human nature Melville practices what he calls in one of the letters to Hawthorne a "ruthless democracy." People are what they are because of some inner personal quality or fate. Writing to Hawthorne while he was still composing *Moby-Dick*, he speaks of "the tragedies of human thought in its own unbiased, native, and profounder workings." The embodiment of these inner tragedies of thought he purports to find in Hawthorne's *The House of the Seven Gables*, but it is obvious that the inner tragedies of his own characters—of Ahab and Ishmael—must also have been in his mind. Melville goes on to speak of the "visible truth" into which Hawthorne has entered so deeply, and then explains that "by visible truth, we mean the apprehension of the absolute condition of present things as they

strike the eye of the man who fears them not." Melville's concern, be it noted, is not with the *circumstantial* condition of present things; that is the concern of the novelist, properly so called. Melville wants to plunge as directly as may be possible to the absolute. This, he suggests to us in "Hawthorne and His Mosses," he has come to do not only by temperament but by emulating Hawthorne and Shakespeare. As Melville sees him, Shakespeare is primarily a truthseeker: "It is those deep far-away things in him; those occasional flashings-forth of the intuitive truth in him; those short, quick probings at the very axis of reality;—these are the things that make Shakespeare, Shakespeare." Thus it is that Melville has given Captain Ahab a "Shakespearean" mind, as well as a good many Shakespearean words, particularly from *Macbeth* and *King Lear*. At the same time it is easy to see that Melville has endowed Ahab with some of the dire characteristics of vengefulness, thirst for the truth, and ultimate alienation which we find in Hawthorne's Chillingworth of *The Scarlet Letter*.

A part of the power of *Moby-Dick* is to be attributed to the whaling story which makes the narrative line. The whaling ships, the whalemen, and the hunt are fascinating phenomena in themselves, and despite his concern with the inner life of the mind and with the absolute, Melville does not, as I have noted before, stint himself in giving us the full cetological details. Perhaps more important is that in the unusual, indeed uncanny, phenomenon of the white whale Melville found a perfect unifying symbol for his various strands of meaning. The whale, with all of its ambiguity, its enormous power and its mildness, its horrendous violence and its beauty, is the perfect foil both for Ahab's tortured search for vengeance and truth and for Ishmael's reveries and speculations. Critics have argued at length about what the whale symbolizes. Obviously he is in one of his aspects a symbol, but it cannot be said with finality, though many people do, that Moby-Dick symbolizes Evil. Only Ahab in his growing madness sees him this way. To Starbuck, the whale is only a "dumb brute."

To Ishmael he is something very like nature itself: a thing of infinite inner contradiction, complexity, and paradox—the rich, endlessly protean but finally inscrutable object of human dream and thought. As the spectacle of the white whale and Ahab, Melville's most compelling portrait of the isolated man, is sifted through the musing mind of Ishmael, there unfolds before us a work of grandeur and beauty such as Melville was never to achieve again.

Despite the looseness, even the waywardness, of its composition, *Moby-Dick* brings the various strands of Melville's mind into an imaginative unity. The unity, however, is in the metaphors, the language, the symbols, the dramatic action, in other words, in the imaginative and aesthetic qualities of the book. It is not in its ideas. The conflicts between self and society, identity and nothingness, faith and doubt, free will and necessity are never resolved into a harmony or a solution. The Epilogue, in which Ishmael is saved from drowning by the coffin-lifebuoy, seems symbolically to affirm that a rebirth and a new life have been achieved. But the tone belies this, and at the very end, with its picture of the infinite mystery of the sea and the aloneness and helplessness of the hero, we cannot help seeing that Melville, in whom there is something both of Ahab and Ishmael, has not arrived at the certitude he sought.

There is no doubt that Melville, as the mildly skeptical Hawthorne seems to have thought, was *too* anxious to get at "the truth." He laid siege to the truth, one might say, and tried to take it by storm. Ideally, what Melville wanted was that at some point in the dialectic of his mind a synthesis should occur between the truths of the imagination, or the aesthetic sense, and the truths of reason. But this did not happen, even in *Moby-Dick*. He felt, perhaps, the same dilemma that Ahab felt, who realized that in himself the "high perception," or rational faculty, was divorced from and at odds with "the low, enjoying power," or the aesthetic sense. Indeed the story of Ahab is basically the gradual alienation of the high perception from the low enjoying power and

the mad, solipsistic view of the world that is the result of this alienation. Why aesthetic truth and rational truth *should* be expected to coincide perhaps does not strike us as a question that has to be immediately or even finally answered. Surely, it did not so strike other American writers less given to speculative thought than Melville—like Hawthorne and Henry James. But for Melville the dilemma, in addition no doubt to the sheer fatigue he felt after his labors on *Moby-Dick*—he had after all published five books in five years—was nearly disastrous. For he had been led to the pessimistic conclusion that the aesthetic sense is mere illusion and that human reason is an alienating activity, leading to monomania and nihilism.

IV

WITH the exception of the months during which he was writing *Moby-Dick*, the decade of the 1850's, as we have noticed, was a dark and unhappy period for Melville. But *The Confidence-Man* was to be the last of his overly ambitious attempts to confront his unhappiness. His writing in succeeding years was to be mostly verse—until he came in his last years to *Billy Budd*—and in his poetry we find, not serenity to be sure, but a new calmness and contemplativeness. Melville had scaled down his drastic Promethean efforts to storm the citadels of truth, and although he never learned to live at ease with his incurable skepticism about human affairs, neither did he react to them in later life with the fury displayed in *Pierre* and *The Confidence-Man*.

The general modern opinion is that Melville, as an American poet, is second only to Whitman and Emily Dickinson in their century. It is true that apart from some isolated passages, and apart from a few short lyrics like "The Portent," "The Maldive Shark," and "Shiloh," he is not a highly accomplished artificer or master of poetic technique. His poems are often rather awkward in their phrasing, and his determination to use only traditional stanzaic forms sometimes leads him into writing an infelicitous phrase in order to get the right rhyme. In all the superficial techniques of versification he is inferior to Longfellow or James Russell Lowell. But the fact remains that his mistakes are usually verbal and metrical; they are seldom mistakes or faults of the intelligence or of the imagination. At its characteristic best, Melville's verse is a body of serious poetry, deeply felt and courageously thought through by a mind that, if not entirely free of poetic cliché, turns naturally to the great problems of the time: the Civil War, the future of democracy, religion, history, politics, myth, nature, art, literature.

The Civil War elicited from Melville his first volume of poetry, *Battle-Pieces and Aspects of the War*, the only volume of verse in the meager body of distinguished writing about the war that may be favorably compared with Whitman's *Drum-Taps*. It is quite possible to say that the Civil War was a godsend to Melville, as it was to Whitman. Both poets had passed through a dark period of low spirits and self-doubt in the late 1850's, and the coming of the tragic national conflict gave both writers a new sense of purpose and dedication. Although he doubtless rightly suspected that *Battle-Pieces* would not be widely read, Melville nevertheless adopts a kind of public role as a poet of the war. "I muse upon my country's ills," he says in "Misgivings," and he thought it incumbent upon him to speak such words of compassion, admonition, and counsel as he could. Although against slavery and believing the South in the wrong, Melville does not write as a partisan. The war as he sees it is a catastrophe that has happened, not so much because of a Southern insurrection, but because of innate imperfections in man's very nature, because of historical forces no man or group could fully control, and because of certain weaknesses in American democracy that the war itself has made ominously apparent. The general tendency of the war poems, as of all Melville's poetry, is a somewhat skeptical yet gravely reassuring attitude toward the future of America and of mankind. "Let us pray," he writes in a prose Supplement to *Battle-Pieces*, "that the great historic tragedy of our time may not have been enacted without instructing our whole beloved country through terror and pity; and may fulfilment verify in the end those expectations which kindle the bards of Progress and Humanity."

The poem called "The Conflict of Conviction" contains in essence much of Melville's reaction to the war. It is a dialogue between an optimist and a pessimist—the "Yea" and "Nay" referred to at the end. On the optimistic side there is the enduring power of faith, the hope that the young—"The light is on the youthful brow"—will have more wisdom than their forebears, the assertion that God still exists, that nature is not governed by mere necessity but that there is a "purpose strong" that "spins against" nature's destructive forces, that even though ugliness and evil have been loosed in the world—laying bare the gulfs with their "slimed foundation"—this fact in itself should allow man to build a better world on a deeper foundation. In rebuttal the pessimist, who in this poem at least seems to win the argument, says that the war is "man's latter fall," that Christianity is of no avail, that God has abdicated from human ken, leaving only "strong Necessity," and that the new iron dome of the Capitol building in Washington may symbolize not the realization of the aims of the founders of the country but the advent of a new iron age of injustice and oppression; that, in other words, the war may force an irreparable breach between America and all that it once stood for in its noble and youthful time.

Similar doubts are expressed as Melville ponders, in "The House-Top," the draft riots that occurred in New York. Here he fears that in breaking the relatively mild laws of a democratic nation the rioters are inviting a Draconian repression. In other poems, the need for stable laws, not only in civil matters but in art and all of man's activities, is asserted. In "A Utilitarian View of the Monitor's Fight" Melville returns to the idea of the new iron age, this time dwelling on the fact that the Civil War is the first really modern war, in the sense that it has called into being mechanized weapons and that "warriors / Are now but operatives."

Yet even while lamenting the damage the war may have done to the continuity of civilization and of democratic institutions, Melville expresses a residual faith in the poem "Shiloh" that nature and time, with their restorative processes, will heal the breaches that have been made and reconcile man with man and the future with the past. In a later poem, "The Maldive Shark," Melville was to reflect upon nature much as he had in *Moby-Dick* and other prose works, stressing the precariousness of life and the presence in nature of sinister mysteries unknown to shallow philosophies.

## V

*Billy Budd,* Melville's last work, carries on some of the themes of his poetry: the destruction of blameless youth; the necessity for law; the superiority from a human point of view of the heroic mode of warfare, typified by Lord Nelson, as opposed to grimly mechanized modern wars: the power of time and legend to bring about a perpetual rebirth of what is humanly valuable. Written between 1888 and 1891, when Melville was in his seventies, *Billy Budd* is understandably reminiscent and nostalgic. It might be said to be a Conradian tale. Captain Vere might imaginably appear in one of Conrad's books, for Conrad too liked to write about the dilemmas of a man in a position of responsibility whose duty conflicts with his humane impulses.

In reading *Billy Budd* one should keep in mind its *political* content, along with its broader moral and mythic themes. The French Revolution is the background of the tale, as Melville states in his Preface. He is writing of a time when the politics of insurgent democracy are very much in the air— when a hardheaded Dundee shipowner names his vessel the *Rights-of-Man* because he is a "staunch admirer of Thomas Paine whose book in rejoinder to Burke's arraignment of the French Revolution had then been published for some time and had gone everywhere." The reference to Edmund Burke's *Reflections on the Revolution in France* (1790) is significant, for despite his undoubted sympathies with democratic libertarianism Melville is concerned, like Burke, with showing the necessity of law, the

value of continuity in civilization, and the need for compromising extremes, such as are represented by the innocence of Billy and the evil of Claggart. For the political structure of a humane society is such that it can neither be perfectly good nor perfectly bad.

Claggart is the "given" quantity, in the sense that he is an example of "Natural Depravity: a depravity according to nature." True, Billy Budd is at first a kind of Adam in his innocence and then a kind of Christ in his sacrificial death, but we do not have the feeling that he is good by nature, or if he is, this is not where the emphasis falls. We would be surprised, in the light of Melville's general view of things, if it did. Given Claggart, we must, Melville seems to have reflected, if we are to preserve society, have Billy Budd with his goodness, his boyish hope and strength, and we must have Captain Vere, the stern father and magistrate whose duty it is to preserve order and rationality.

The political theme is enriched by the mythic and religious overtones of the story. For not only is Billy a kind of Adam and a kind of Christ, we are also reminded of the story of Abraham and Isaac, of the father who must be prepared to sacrifice the son and of the atonement between father and son. And the pathos of the story is enhanced by Melville's hint that the orphan Billy may actually be the son—"a presumable bye-blow"—of Captain Vere. The satanic or demonic quality of Claggart—here Melville is obviously influenced by Milton's portrait of Satan in *Paradise Lost*—does much to lend him the necessary mythic dimension which is given to the other characters. Moreover, the emotional implications of Claggart's acts are given a psychological complexity because of the perverse attraction he obviously feels for Billy.

The view of nature in *Billy Budd,* as we see from the many metaphors of devouring and eating ("The fleece of low-hanging vapor had vanished, licked up by the sun that late had so glorified it"), is the dark and dubious one we are accustomed to in Melville. What he had called in *Moby-Dick* "the horrible vulturism" of the world still obtains in *Billy Budd.* The metaphor becomes applicable to society in the suggestion of Melville's parable that civilization sustains itself only by feeding on youthful innocence and goodness, by the ritualistic sacrifice of the Christlike man. In this dark view of nature, as in his sense of the pain and evil in the world, Melville carried over into his last work what had been life-long preoccupations. He also impresses us again with his powerful sense of the irreconcilable contradictions involved in life, and perhaps nowhere in his work did he find better or more vivid symbols for this sense of things than Billy and Claggart. In Melville's last work the light and the dark, good and evil, are still in dramatic and mortal conflict. But what we encounter in *Billy Budd* that we do not encounter in the other prose writings is the feeling of elegy and resignation, tinged with at least a minimal faith in the power of time and legend to right wrongs. For as we are told at the end, "the fresh young image of the Handsome Sailor" lives on in the minds and hearts of men.

Melville's story leaves us, as do such late Shakespearean plays as *The Winter's Tale*, with the faith that there is in the world a minimal principle of grace, redemption, and spiritual rebirth. It is possible, after all, that the terrible contradictions with which our experience confronts us may be absorbed in history, or assuaged by the beneficence and spiritual health of which human nature is capable. The tortured author of *Pierre* and *The Confidence-Man* had found, late in life, at least some small measure of consolation.

# HAWTHORNE AND HIS MOSSES

◊

❲ THE FOLLOWING essay was published in two installments in August of 1850 in the *Literary World*, a magazine edited by Melville's friend Evert A. Duyckinck. Melville, acquainted with Hawthorne at the time but not yet a close friend, chose to sign the article "By a Virginian Spending July in Vermont" rather than by his own name. Both Hawthorne and his wife were much struck by the article and were anxious to know the identity of the author. "Hawthorne and His Mosses" is a review of Hawthorne's *Mosses from an Old Manse.*

But it is interesting to us not only because of what Melville has to say about the book he is reviewing but because it reveals so much about the mind and imagination of the reviewer, who in the summer of 1850 was engaged in writing and rewriting *Moby-Dick*. One feels in Melville's review—in his comments on Hawthorne's tales, his remarks about the qualities of a great imagination, his hopes for a pre-eminent national literature and a fellowship of writers—some of the inner turmoil, ambition, and burgeoning creativity of the author at the time when his genius was flourishing most powerfully.

◊

A PAPERED chamber in a fine old farm-house— a mile from any other dwelling, and dipped to the eaves in foliage—surrounded by mountains, old woods, and Indian ponds—this, surely, is the place to write of Hawthorne. Some charm is in this northern air, for love and duty seem both impelling to the task. A man of a deep and noble nature has seized me in this seclusion. His wild, witch voice rings through me; or, in softer cadences, I seem to hear it in the songs of the hillside birds that sing in the larch trees at my window.

Would that all excellent books were foundlings, without father or mother, that so it might be, we could glorify them, without including their ostensible authors! Nor would any true man take exception to this—least of all, he who writes: "When the Artist rises high enough to achieve the Beautiful, the symbol by which he makes it perceptible to mortal senses becomes of little value in his eyes, while his spirit possesses itself in the enjoyment of the reality."

But more than this. I know not what would be the right name to put on the title page of an excellent book; but this I feel, that the names of all fine authors are fictitious ones, far more so than that of Junius—simply standing, as they do, for the mystical, ever-eluding Spirit of all Beauty, which ubiquitously possesses men of genius. . . .

It is curious, how a man may travel along a country road, and yet miss the grandest or sweetest of prospects, by reason of an intervening hedge so like all other hedges as in no way to hint of the wide landscape beyond. So has it been with me concerning the enchanting landscape in the soul of this Hawthorne, this most excellent Man of Mosses. His *Old Manse* has been written now four years, but I never read it till a day or two since. I had seen it in the bookstores—heard of it often— even had it recommended to me by a tasteful friend, as a rare, quiet book, perhaps too deserving of popularity to be popular. But there are so many books called "excellent," and so much unpopular merit, that amid the thick stir of other things, the hint of my tasteful friend was disregarded; and for four years the Mosses on the Old Manse never refreshed me with their perennial green. It may be, however, that all this while, the book, like wine, was only improving in flavor and body. At any rate, it so chanced that this long procrastination eventuated in a happy result. At breakfast the other day, a mountain girl, a cousin of mine, who for the last two weeks has every morning helped me to strawberries and raspberries —which, like the roses and pearls in the fairy-tale, seemed to fall into the saucer from those strawberry-beds, her cheeks—this delightful creature, this charming Cherry, says to me—"I see you spend your mornings in the haymow; and yesterday I found there Dwight's *Travels in New England.* Now I have something far better than that— something more congenial to our summer on these hills. Take these raspberries, and then I will give you some moss."—"Moss!" said I.—"Yes, and you must take it to the barn with you, and good-by to 'Dwight.' "

With that she left me, and soon returned with a volume, verdantly bound, and garnished with a curious frontispiece in green—nothing less than a fragment of real moss cunningly pressed to a flyleaf.—"Why this," said I, spilling my raspberries, "this is the *Mosses from an Old Manse.*" "Yes," said cousin Cherry, "yes, it is that flowering Hawthorne."—"Hawthorne and Mosses," said I, "no more: it is morning: it is July in the country: and I am off for the barn."

Stretched on that new-mown clover, the hillside breeze blowing over me through the wide barn door, and soothed by the hum of the bees in the meadows around, how magically stole over me this Mossy Man! And how amply, how bountifully, did he redeem that delicious promise to his guests in the Old Manse, of whom it is written: "Others could give them pleasure and amusement, or instruction—these could be picked up anywhere— but it was for me to give them rest. Rest, in a life of trouble! What better could be done for those weary and world-worn spirits? . . . what better could be done for anybody, who came within our magic circle, than to throw the spell of a magic spirit over him?"—So all that day, half-buried in the new clover, I watched this Hawthorne's "Assyrian dawn and Paphian sunset and moonrise, from the summit of our eastern hill."

The soft ravishments of the man spun me round about in a web of dreams, and when the book was closed, when the spell was over, this wizard "dismissed me, with but misty reminiscences, as if I had been dreaming of him."

What a wild moonlight of contemplative humor bathes that Old Manse!—the rich and rare distillment of a spicy and slowly oozing heart. No rollicking rudeness, no gross fun fed on fat dinners, and bred in the lees of wine—but a humor so spiritually gentle, so high, so deep, and yet so richly relishable, that it were hardly inappropriate in an angel. It is the very religion of mirth; for nothing so human but it may be advanced to that. The orchard of the Old Manse seems the visible type of the fine mind that has described it. Those twisted and contorted old trees that "stretch out their crooked branches, and take such hold of the imagination, that we remember them as humorists and odd fellows." And then, as surrounded by these grotesque forms, and hushed in the noonday repose of this Hawthorne's spell, how aptly might the still fall of his ruddy thoughts into your soul be symbolized by "the thump of a great apple, in the stillest afternoon, falling without a breath of wind, from the mere necessity of perfect ripeness!" For no less ripe than ruddy are the apples of the thoughts and fancies in this sweet Man of Mosses.

. . . . . . . . . . . . . . . . . . . .

But he has still other apples, not quite so ruddy, though full as ripe—apples that have been left to wither on the tree, after the pleasant autumn gathering is past. The sketch of "The Old Apple-Dealer" is conceived in the subtlest spirit of sadness; he whose "subdued and nerveless boyhood prefigured his abortive prime, which, likewise, contained within itself the prophecy and image of his lean and torpid age." Such touches as are in this piece cannot proceed from any common heart. They argue such a depth of tenderness, such a boundless sympathy with all forms of being, such an omnipresent love, that we must needs say that this Hawthorne is here almost alone—in his generation at least—in the artistic manifestation of these things. Still more. Such touches as these— and many, very many similar ones, all through his chapters—furnish clues, whereby we enter a little way into the intricate, profound heart where they originated. And we see that suffering, some time or other and in some shape or other—this only can enable any man to depict it in others. All over him, Hawthorne's melancholy rests like an Indian summer, which, though bathing a whole country in one softness, still reveals the distinctive hue of every towering hill, and each far-winding vale.

But it is the least part of genius that attracts admiration. Where Hawthorne is known, he seems to be deemed a pleasant writer, with a pleasant style —a sequestered, harmless man, from whom any deep and weighty thing would hardly be anticipated: a man who means no meanings. But there is no man, in whom humor and love, like mountain peaks, soar to such a rapt height, as to receive the irradiations of the upper skies; there is no man in whom humor and love are developed in that high form called genius—no such man can exist without also possessing, as the indispensable complement of these, a great, deep intellect, which drops down into the universe like a plummet. Or, love and humor are only the eyes, through which such an intellect views this world. The great beauty in such a mind is but the product of its strength. What, to all readers, can be more charming than the piece entitled "Monsieur du Miroir"; and to a reader at all capable of fully fathoming it, what, at the same time, can possess more mystical depth of meaning?—Yes, there he sits, and looks at me— this "shape of mystery," this "identical Monsieur du Miroir."—"Methinks I should tremble now, were his wizard power, of gliding through all impediments in search of me, to place him suddenly before my eyes."

How profound, nay, appalling, is the moral evolved by the "Earth's Holocaust," where—beginning with the hollow follies and affectations of the world—all vanities and empty theories and forms are, one after another, and by an admirably graduated, growing comprehensiveness, thrown into the allegorical fire, till, at length, nothing is left but the all-engendering heart of man; which remaining still unconsumed, the great conflagration is naught.

Of a piece with this is "The Intelligence Office," a wondrous symbolizing of the secret workings in men's souls. There are other sketches, still more charged with ponderous import.

"The Christmas Banquet" and "The Bosom Serpent" would be fine subjects for a curious and elaborate analysis, touching the conjectural parts of the mind that produced them. For spite of all the Indian-summer sunlight on the hither side of Hawthorne's soul, the other side—like the dark half of the physical sphere—is shrouded in a blackness, ten times black. But this darkness but gives more effect to the ever-moving dawn, that forever advances through it, and circumnavigates his world. Whether Hawthorne has simply availed himself of this mystical blackness as a means to the wondrous effects he makes it to produce in his lights and shades; or whether there really lurks in him, perhaps unknown to himself, a touch of Puritanic gloom—this, I cannot altogether tell. Cer-

tain it is, however, that this great power of blackness in him derives its force from its appeals to that Calvinistic sense of Innate Depravity and Original Sin, from whose visitations, in some shape or other, no deeply thinking mind is always and wholly free. For, in certain moods, no man can weigh this world, without throwing in something, somehow like Original Sin, to strike the uneven balance. At all events, perhaps no writer has ever wielded this terrific thought with greater terror than this same harmless Hawthorne. Still more: this black conceit pervades him, through and through. You may be witched by his sunlight, transported by the bright gildings in the skies he builds over you, but there is the blackness of darkness beyond; and even his bright gildings but fringe and play upon the edges of thunder-clouds. —In one word, the world is mistaken in this Nathaniel Hawthorne. He himself must often have smiled at its absurd misconception of him. He is immeasurably deeper than the plummet of the mere critic. For it is not the brain that can test such a man; it is only the heart. You cannot come to know greatness by inspecting it; there is no glimpse to be caught of it, except by intuition; you need not ring it, you but touch it, and you find it is gold.

. . . . . . . . . . . . . . . . .

. . . If few men have time, or patience, or palate, for the spiritual truth as it is in great genius — it is, then, no matter of surprise that in a contemporaneous age, Nathaniel Hawthorne is a man as yet almost utterly mistaken among men. Here and there, in some quiet armchair in the noisy town, or some deep nook among the noiseless mountains, he may be appreciated for something of what he is. But unlike Shakespeare, who was forced to the contrary course by circumstances, Hawthorne (either from simple disinclination, or else from inaptitude) refrains from all the popularizing noise and show of broad farce, and blood-besmeared tragedy, content with the still, rich utterances of a great intellect in repose, and which sends few thoughts into circulation, except they be arterialized at his large warm lungs, and expanded in his honest heart.

Nor need you fix upon that blackness in him, if it suit you not. Nor, indeed, will all readers discern it, for it is, mostly insinuated to those who may best understand it, and account for it; it is not obtruded upon every one alike.

. . . . . . . . . . . . . . . . .

Let America then prize and cherish her writers; yea, let her glorify them. They are not so many in number as to exhaust her good will. And while she has good kith and kin of her own, to take to her bosom, let her not lavish her embraces upon the household of an alien. For believe it or not, England, after all, is, in many things, an alien to us. China has more bowels of real love for us than she. But even were there no strong literary individualities among us, as there are some dozen at least, nevertheless, let America first praise mediocrity even, in her own children, before she praises (for everywhere, merit demands acknowledgment from every one) the best excellence in the children of any other land. Let her own authors, I say, have the priority of appreciation. I was much pleased with a hot-headed Carolina cousin of mine, who once said, "If there were no other American to stand by, in Literature—why, then, I would stand by Pop Emmons and his *Fredoniad*,[1] and till a better epic came along, swear it was not very far behind the *Iliad*." Take away the words, and in spirit he was sound.

Not that American genius needs patronage in order to expand. For that explosive sort of stuff will expand though screwed up in a vise, and burst it, though it were triple steel. It is for the nation's sake, and not for her authors' sake, that I would have America be heedful of the increasing greatness among her writers. For how great the shame, if other nations should be before her, in crowning her heroes of the pen! But this is almost the case now. American authors have received more just and discriminating praise (however loftily and ridiculously given, in certain cases) even from some Englishmen, than from their own countrymen. There are hardly five critics in America; and several of them are asleep. As for patronage, it is the American author who now patronizes his country, and not his country him. And if at times some among them appeal to the people for more recognition, it is not always with selfish motives, but patriotic ones.

It is true that but few of them as yet have evinced that decided originality which merits great praise. But that graceful writer,[2] who perhaps of all Americans has received the most plaudits from his own country for his productions—that very popular and amiable writer, however good, and self-reliant in many things, perhaps owes his chief reputation to the self-acknowledged imitation of a foreign model, and to the studied avoidance of all topics but smooth ones. But it is better to fail in originality than to succeed in imitation. He who has never failed somewhere, that man can not be

great. Failure is the true test of greatness. And if it be said that continual success is a proof that a man wisely knows his powers, it is only to be added that, in that case, he knows them to be small. Let us believe it, then, once for all, that there is no hope for us in these smooth, pleasing writers that know their powers. Without malice, but to speak the plain fact, they but furnish an appendix to Goldsmith, and other English authors. And we want no American Goldsmiths; nay, we want no American Miltons. It were the vilest thing you could say of a true American author, that he were an American Tompkins. Call him an American, and have done; for you cannot say a nobler thing of him.—But it is not meant that all American writers should studiously cleave to nationality in their writings; only this, no American writer should write like an Englishman, or a Frenchman; let him write like a man, for then he will be sure to write like an American. Let us away with this leaven of literary flunkyism towards England. If either must play the flunky in this thing, let England do it, not us. While we are rapidly preparing for that political supremacy among the nations, which prophetically awaits us at the close of the present century, in a literary point of view we are deplorably unprepared for it, and we seem studious to remain so. Hitherto, reasons might have existed why this should be; but no good reason exists now. And all that is requisite to amendment in this matter is simply this: that, while freely acknowledging all excellence, everywhere, we should refrain from unduly lauding foreign writers and, at the same time, duly recognize the meritorious writers that are our own; those writers who breathe that unshackled, democratic spirit of Christianity in all things, which now takes the practical lead in this world, though at the same time led by ourselves— us Americans. Let us boldly contemn all imitation, though it comes to us graceful and fragrant as the morning, and foster all originality, though, at first, it be crabbed and ugly as our own pine knots. And if any of our authors fail, or seem to fail, then, in the words of my enthusiastic Carolina cousin, let let us clap him on the shoulder, and back him against all Europe for his second round. The truth is that, in our point of view, this matter of a national literature has come to such a pass with us that in some sense we must turn bullies, else the day is lost, or superiority so far beyond us, that we can hardly say it will ever be ours.

And now, my countrymen, as an excellent author, of your own flesh and blood—an unimitating, and, perhaps, in his way, an inimitable man— whom better can I commend to you, in the first place, than Nathaniel Hawthorne. He is one of

HAWTHORNE AND HIS MOSSES. **1. *Fredoniad:*** Richard Emmons' poem was an abortive epic about the War of 1812. **2. graceful writer:** undoubtedly an allusion to Washington Irving.

the new and far better generation of your writers. The smell of your beeches and hemlocks is upon him; your own broad prairies are in his soul; and if you travel away inland into his deep and noble nature, you will hear the far roar of his Niagara. Give not over to future generations the glad duty of acknowledging him for what he is. Take that joy to yourself, in your own generation; and so shall he feel those grateful impulses in him that may possibly prompt him to the full flower of some still greater achievement in your eyes. And by confessing him, you thereby confess others; you brace the whole brotherhood. For genius, all over the world, stands hand in hand, and one shock of recognition runs the whole circle round.

In treating of Hawthorne, or rather of Hawthorne in his writings (for I never saw the man,[3] and in the chances of a quiet plantation life, remote from his haunts, perhaps never shall); in treating of his works, I say, I have thus far omitted all mention of his *Twice-Told Tales,* and *The Scarlet Letter.* Both are excellent, but full of such manifold, strange, and diffusive beauties, that time would all but fail me to point the half of them out. But there are things in those two books which, had they been written in England a century ago, Nathaniel Hawthorne had utterly displaced many of the bright names we now revere on authority. But I am content to leave Hawthorne to himself, and to the infallible finding of posterity; and however great may be the praise I have bestowed upon him, I feel, that in so doing, I have more served and honored myself than him. For, at bottom, great excellence is praise enough to itself; but the feeling of a sincere and appreciative love and admiration towards it—this is relieved by utterance; and warm, honest praise ever leaves a pleasant flavor in the mouth; and it is an honorable thing to confess to what is honorable in others.

But I cannot leave my subject yet. No man can read a fine author, and relish him to his very bones, while he reads, without subsequently fancying to himself some ideal image of the man and his mind. And if you rightly look for it, you will almost always find that the author himself has somewhere furnished you with his own picture. For poets (whether in prose or verse), being painters of Nature, are like their brethren of the pencil, the true portrait painters, who, in the multitude of likenesses to be sketched, do not invariably omit their own; and in all high instances, they paint

them without any vanity, though, at times, with a lurking something, that would take several pages to properly define.

I submit it, then, to those best acquainted with the man personally, whether the following is not Nathaniel Hawthorne; and to himself, whether something involved in it does not express the temper of his mind—that lasting temper of all true, candid men—a seeker, not a finder yet:

A man now entered, in neglected attire, with the aspect of a thinker, but somewhat too rough-hewn and brawny for a scholar. His face was full of sturdy vigor, with some finer and keener attribute beneath; though harsh at first, it was tempered with the glow of a large, warm heart, which had force enough to heat his powerful intellect through and through. He advanced to the Intelligencer, and looked at him with a glance of such stern sincerity, that perhaps few secrets were beyond its scope.
"I seek for Truth," said he.

Twenty-four hours have elapsed since writing the foregoing. I have just returned from the haymow, charged more and more with love and admiration of Hawthorne. For I have just been gleaning through the *Mosses,* picking up many things here and there that had previously escaped me. And I found that but to glean after this man is better than to be in at the harvest of others. To be frank (though, perhaps, rather foolish), notwithstanding what I wrote yesterday of these Mosses, I had not then culled them all; but had, nevertheless, been sufficiently sensible of the subtle essences in them as to write as I did. To what infinite height of loving wonder and admiration I may yet be borne, when by repeatedly banqueting on these Mosses, I shall have thoroughly incorporated their whole stuff into my being—that, I can not tell. But already I feel that this Hawthorne has dropped germinous seeds into my soul. He expands and deepens down, the more I contemplate him; and further, and further, shoots his strong New England roots into the hot soil of my Southern soul.

· · · · · · · · · · · ·

But with whatever motive, playful or profound, Nathaniel Hawthorne has chosen to entitle his pieces in the manner he has, it is certain that some of them are directly calculated to deceive—egregiously deceive—the superficial skimmer of pages. To be downright and candid once more, let me cheerfully say that two of these titles did dolefully dupe no less an eagle-eyed reader than myself; and that, too, after I had been impressed with a sense of the great depth and breadth of this American man. "Who in the name of thunder" (as the

---

3. **for . . . man:** not strictly true, since Melville had been on a mountain hike and picnic with Hawthorne and other literary people shortly before he began the composition of "Hawthorne and His Mosses."

country people say in this neighborhood), "who in the name of thunder," would anticipate any marvel in a piece entitled "Young Goodman Brown"? You would of course suppose that it was a simple little tale, intended as a supplement to "Goody Two-Shoes." Whereas it is deep as Dante; nor can you finish it, without addressing the author in his own words: "It is yours to penetrate, in every bosom, the deep mystery of sin." And with Young Goodman, too, in allegorical pursuit of his Puritan wife, you cry out in your anguish:

"Faith!" shouted Goodman Brown, in a voice of agony and desperation; and the echoes of the forest mocked him, crying—"Faith! Faith!" as if bewildered wretches were seeking her, all through the wilderness.

Now this same piece, entitled "Young Goodman Brown," is one that I had not at all read yesterday, and I allude to it now, because it is, in itself, such a strong positive illustration of that blackness in Hawthorne which I had assumed from the mere occasional shadows of it, as revealed in several of the other sketches. But had I previously perused "Young Goodman Brown," I should have been at no pains to draw the conclusion which I came to at a time when I was ignorant that the book contained one such direct and unqualified manifestation of it.

. . . . . . . . . . . . . . . .

. . . Gainsay it who will, as I now write, I am Posterity speaking by proxy—and after times will make it more than good, when I declare that the American, who up to the present day, has evinced, in Literature, the largest brain with the largest heart—that man is Nathaniel Hawthorne. Moreover, that whatever Nathaniel Hawthorne may hereafter write, the *Mosses from an Old Manse* will be ultimately accounted his masterpiece. For there is a sure though a secret sign in some works which proves the culmination of the powers (only the developable ones, however) that produced them. But I am by no means desirous of the glory of a prophet. I pray Heaven that Hawthorne may *yet* prove me an impostor in this prediction. Especially, as I somehow cling to the strange fancy that, in all men, hiddenly reside certain wondrous, occult properties—as in some plants and minerals—which by some happy but very rare accident (as bronze was discovered by the melting of the iron and brass in the burning of Corinth) may chance to be called forth here on earth, not entirely waiting for their better discovery in the more congenial, blessed atmosphere of heaven.

Once more—for it is hard to be finite upon an infinite subject, and all subjects are infinite. By some people, this entire scrawl of mine may be esteemed altogether unnecessary, inasmuch, "as years ago" (they may say) "we found out the rich and rare stuff in this Hawthorne, whom you now parade forth as if only *yourself* were the discoverer of this Portuguese diamond in our Literature."—But even granting all this—and adding to it, the assumption that the books of Hawthorne have sold by the five thousand—what does that signify? They should be sold by the hundred thousand, and read by the million, and admired by every one who is capable of admiration.

---

# LETTERS TO HAWTHORNE

---

❖

[AS THEIR dates indicate, the first two of the following letters were written to Hawthorne before *Moby-Dick* was finished. The third is Melville's eloquent and grateful response to the letter (unfortunately not preserved) Hawthorne wrote to him after reading *Moby-Dick*. Like "Hawthorne and His Mosses," these impulsive and spontaneous letters are of inestimable value in understanding Melville's thoughts and feelings at this crucial point in his life.

❖

I

[June, 1851]

MY DEAR HAWTHORNE—

I should have been rumbling down to you in my pine-board chariot a long time ago, were it not that for some weeks past I have been more busy than you can well imagine,—out of doors,—building and patching and tinkering away in all directions. Besides, I had my crops to get in,—corn and potatoes (I hope to show you some famous ones by and by),—and many other things to attend to, all accumulating upon this one particular season. I work myself; and at night my bodily sensations are akin to those I have so often felt before, when a hired man, doing my day's work from sun to sun. But I mean to continue visiting you until you tell me that my visits are both supererogatory and superfluous. With no son of man do I stand upon any etiquette or ceremony, except the Christian ones of charity and honesty. I am told, my fellow-man, that there is an aristocracy of the brain. Some men have boldly advocated and asserted it.

Schiller[1] seems to have done so, though I don't know much about him. At any rate, it is true that there have been those who, while earnest in behalf of political equality, still accept the intellectual estates. And I can well perceive, I think, how a man of superior mind can, by its intense cultivation, bring himself, as it were, into a certain spontaneous aristocracy of feeling,—exceedingly nice and fastidious,—similar to that which, in an English Howard,[2] conveys a torpedo-fish thrill at the slightest contact with a social plebeian. So, when you see or hear of my ruthless democracy on all sides, you may possibly feel a touch of a shrink, or something of that sort. It is but nature to be shy of a mortal who boldly declares that a thief in jail is as honorable a personage as Gen. George Washington. This is ludicrous. But Truth is the silliest thing under the sun. Try to get a living by the Truth—and go to the Soup Societies. Heavens! Let any clergyman try to preach the Truth from its very stronghold, the pulpit, and they would ride him out of his church on his own pulpit bannister. It can hardly be doubted that all Reformers are bottomed upon the truth, more or less; and to the world at large are not reformers almost universally laughing-stocks? Why so? Truth is ridiculous to men. Thus easily in my room here do I, conceited and garrulous, reverse the test of my Lord Shaftesbury.[3]

It seems an inconsistency to assert unconditional democracy in all things, and yet confess a dislike to all mankind—in the mass. But not so. But it's an endless sermon,—no more of it. I began by saying that the reason I have not been to Lenox is this,—in the evening I feel completely done up, as the phrase is, and incapable of the long jolting to get to your house and back. In a week or so, I go to New York, to bury myself in a third-story room, and work and slave on my "Whale"[4] while it is driving through the press. *That* is the only way I can finish it now,—I am so pulled hither and thither by circumstances. The calm, the coolness, the silent grass-growing mood in which a man *ought* always to compose,—that, I fear, can seldom be mine. Dollars damn me; and the malicious Devil is forever grinning in upon me,

holding the door ajar. My dear Sir, a presentiment is on me,—I shall at last be worn out and perish, like an old nutmeg-grater, grated to pieces by the constant attrition of the wood, that is, the nutmeg. What I feel most moved to write, that is banned,—it will not pay. Yet, altogether, write the *other* way I cannot. So the product is a final hash, and all my books are botches. I'm rather sore, perhaps, in this letter; but see my hand! four blisters on this palm, made by hoes and hammers within the last few days. It is a rainy morning; so I am indoors, and all work suspended. I feel cheerfully disposed, and therefore I write a little bluely. Would the Gin[5] were here! If ever, my dear Hawthorne, in the eternal times that are to come, you and I shall sit down in Paradise, in some little shady corner by ourselves; and if we shall by any means be able to smuggle a basket of champagne there (I won't believe in a Temperance Heaven), and if we shall then cross our celestial legs in the celestial grass that is forever tropical, and strike our glasses and our heads together, till both musically ring in concert,—then, O my dear fellow-mortal, how shall we pleasantly discourse of all the things manifold which now so distress us,—when all the earth shall be but a reminiscence, yea, its final dissolution an antiquity. Then shall songs be composed as when wars are over: humorous, comic songs,—"Oh, when I lived in that queer little hole called the world," or, "Oh, when I toiled and sweated below," or, "Oh, when I knocked and was knocked in the fight"— yes, let us look forward to such things. Let us swear that, though now we sweat, yet it is because of the dry heat which is indispensable to the nourishment of the vine which is to bear the grapes that are to give us the champagne hereafter.

But I was talking about the "Whale." As the fishermen say, "he's in his flurry" when I left him some three weeks ago. I'm going to take him by his jaw, however, before long, and finish him up in some fashion or other. What's the use of elaborating what, in its very essence, is so short-lived as a modern book? Though I wrote the Gospels in this century, I should die in the gutter.—I talk all about myself, and this is selfishness and egotism. Granted. But how help it? I am writing to you; I know little about you, but something about myself. So I write about myself,—at least to you. Don't trouble yourself, though, about writing; and don't trouble yourself about visiting; and when you *do* visit, don't trouble yourself about talking. I will do all the writing and visiting and talking myself.— By the way, in the last "Dollar Magazine" I read "The Unpardonable Sin." He was a sad fellow,

---

1. **Schiller:** J. C. F. von Schiller (1759–1805), the German poet and critic.    2. **Howard:** Melville uses the illustrious Howard family as a general symbol of aristocracy.    3. **Lord Shaftesbury:** In his *Characteristics* (1711) Shaftesbury proposes to test the truth by subjecting it to ridicule, rather than, as Melville somewhat perversely does, declaring it to *be* ridiculous. Melville, however, does not mean that truth is in itself ridiculous; he means that as compared with the conventional half-truths by which men live it must always seem so.    4. **"Whale":** While he was writing his book, Melville evidently thought of calling it *The Whale*, and it was in fact published in England under that title. The American edition, which soon followed, was called *Moby-Dick: or, The Whale*.

5. **Gin:** A jinni is a spirit in Mohammedan mythology capable of performing services for (or doing evil to) human beings.

that Ethan Brand.[6] I have no doubt you are by this time responsible for many a shake and tremor of the tribe of "general readers." It is a frightful poetical creed that the cultivation of the brain eats out the heart. But it's my *prose* opinion that in most cases, in those men who have fine brains and work them well, the heart extends down to hams. And though you smoke them with the fire of tribulation, yet, like veritable hams, the head only gives the richer and the better flavor. I stand for the heart. To the dogs with the head! I had rather be a fool with a heart, than Jupiter Olympus with his head. The reason the mass of men fear God, and *at bottom dislike* Him, is because they rather distrust His Heart, and fancy Him all brain like a watch. (You perceive I employ a capital initial in the pronoun referring to the Deity; don't you think there is a slight dash of flunkeyism in that usage?) Another thing. I was in New York for four-and-twenty hours the other day, and saw a portrait of N.H. And I have seen and heard many flattering (in a publisher's point of view) allusions to the "Seven Gables." And I have seen "Tales" and "A New Volume" announced, by N.H. So upon the whole, I say to myself, this N.H. is in the ascendant. My dear Sir, they begin to patronize. All Fame is patronage. Let me be infamous; there is no patronage in *that*. What "reputation" H.M. has is horrible. Think of it! To go down to posterity is bad enough, any way; but to go down as a "man who lived among the cannibals"! When I speak of posterity, in reference to myself, I only mean the babies who will probably be born in the moment immediately ensuing upon my giving up the ghost. I shall go down to some of them, in all likelihood. "Typee" will be given to them, perhaps, with their gingerbread. I have come to regard this matter of Fame as the most transparent of all vanities. I read Solomon[7] more and more, and every time see deeper and deeper and unspeakable meanings in him. I did not think of Fame, a year ago, as I do now. My development has been all within a few years past. I am like one of those seeds taken out of the Egyptian Pyramids, which, after being three thousand years a seed and nothing but a seed, being planted in English soil, it developed itself, grew to greenness, and then fell to mould. So I. Until I was twenty-five, I had no development at all. From my twenty-fifth year I date my life. Three weeks have scarcely passed, at any time between then and now, that I have not unfolded within myself. But I feel that I am now come to the inmost leaf of the bulb, and that shortly the flower must fall to the mould. It seems to me now that Solomon was the truest man who ever spoke, and yet that he a little *managed* the truth with a view to popular conservatism; or else there have been many corruptions and interpolations of the text.—In reading some of Goethe's sayings, so worshipped by his votaries, I came across this, *"Live in the all."* That is to say, your separate identity is but a wretched one, —good; but get out of yourself, spread and expand yourself, and bring to yourself the tinglings of life that are felt in the flowers and the woods, that are felt in the planets Saturn and Venus, and the Fixed Stars. What nonsense! Here is a fellow with a raging toothache. "My dear boy," Goethe says to him, "you are sorely afflicted with that tooth; but you must *live in the all,* and then you will be happy!" As with all great genius, there is an immense deal of flummery in Goethe, and in proportion to my own contact with him, a monstrous deal of it in me.

H. MELVILLE

P.S. "Amen!" saith Hawthorne.
N.B. This "all" feeling, though, there is some truth in. You must often have felt it, lying on the grass on a warm summer's day. Your legs seem to send out shoots into the earth. Your hair feels like leaves upon your head. This is the *all* feeling. But what plays the mischief with the truth is that men will insist upon the universal application of a temporary feeling or opinion.
P.S. You must not fail to admire my discretion in paying the postage on this letter.

2

Pittsfield, June 29, 1851.

MY DEAR HAWTHORNE—

The clear air and open window invite me to write to you. For some time past I have been so busy with a thousand things that I have almost forgotten when I wrote you last, and whether I received an answer. This most persuasive season has now for weeks recalled me from certain crotchety and over-doleful chimeras, the like of which men like you and me, and some others, forming a chain of God's posts round the world, must be content to encounter now and then, and fight them the best way we can. But come they will,—for, in the boundless, trackless, but still glorious wild wilderness through which these outposts run, the Indians do sorely abound, as well as the insignificant but still stinging mosquitoes. Since you have been here, I have been building some shanties of houses (connected with the old one) and likewise some shanties of chapters and

---

6. **Ethan Brand:** It is of interest that Melville was struck by Hawthorne's "Ethan Brand," for this is a tale of a restless truthseeker somewhat resembling Melville himself. It cannot be a portrait of Melville, however, for it was written before Hawthorne had met him.    7. **Solomon:** Ecclesiastes.

essays. I have been ploughing and sowing and raising and painting and printing and praying,—and now begin to come out upon a less bristling time, and to enjoy the calm prospect of things from a fair piazza at the north of the old farmhouse here.

Not entirely yet, tho', am I without something to be urgent with. The "Whale" is only half thro' the press; for, wearied with the long delays of the printers, and disgusted with the heat and dust of the Babylonish brick-kiln of New York, I came back to the country to feel the grass—and end the book reclining on it, if I may.—I am sure you will pardon this speaking all about myself; for if I *say* so much on that head, be sure all the rest of the world are thinking about themselves ten times as much. Let us speak, tho' we show all our faults and weaknesses,—for it is a sign of strength to be weak, to know it, and out with it,—not in set way and ostentatiously, tho', but incidentally and without premeditation.——But I am falling into my old foible,—preaching. I am busy, but shall not be very long. Come and spend a day here, if you can and want to; if not, stay in Lenox, and God give you long life. When I am quite free of my present engagements, I am going to treat myself to a ride and a visit to you. Have ready a bottle of brandy, because I always feel like drinking that heroic drink when we talk ontological heroics together. This is rather a crazy letter in some respects, I apprehend. If so, ascribe it to the intoxicating effects of the latter end of June operating upon a very susceptible and peradventure feeble temperament.

Shall I send you a fin of the "Whale" by way of a specimen mouthful? The tail is not yet cooked —tho' the hell-fire in which the whole book is broiled might not unreasonably have cooked it all ere this. This is the book's motto (the secret one), Ego non baptiso te in nomine—but make out the rest yourself.[8]                                    H.M.

### 3

Pittsfield, Monday afternoon [November, 1851]

MY DEAR HAWTHORNE—

People think that if a man has undergone any hardship, he should have a reward; but for my part, if I have done the hardest possible day's work, and then come to sit down in a corner and eat my supper comfortably—why, then I don't think I deserve any reward for my hard day's work—for am I not now at peace? Is not my supper good? My peace and my supper are my re-

ward, my dear Hawthorne. So your joy-giving and exultation-breeding letter is not my reward for my ditcher's work with that book, but is the good goddess's bonus over and above what was stipulated for—for not one man in five cycles, who is wise, will expect appreciative recognition from his fellows, or any one of them. Appreciation! Recognition! Is love appreciated? Why, ever since Adam, who has got to the meaning of his great allegory—the world? Then we pygmies must be content to have our paper allegories but ill comprehended. I say your appreciation is my glorious gratuity. In my proud, humble way,—a shepherd-king,—I was lord of a little vale in the solitary Crimea; but you have now given me the crown of India. But on trying it on my head, I found it fell down on my ears, notwithstanding their asinine length—for it's only such ears that sustain such crowns.

Your letter was handed me last night on the road going to Mr. Morewood's, and I read it there. Had I been at home, I would have sat down at once and answered it. In me divine magnanimities are spontaneous and instantaneous—catch them while you can. The world goes round, and the other side comes up. So now I can't write what I felt. But I felt pantheistic then—your heart beat in my ribs and mine in yours, and both in God's. A sense of unspeakable security is in me this moment, on account of your having understood the book. I have written a wicked book,[9] and feel spotless as the lamb. Ineffable socialities are in me. I would sit down and dine with you and all the gods in old Rome's Pantheon. It is a strange feeling—no hopefulness is in it, no despair. Content —that is it; and irresponsibility; but without licentious inclination. I speak now of my profoundest sense of being, not of an incidental feeling.

Whence come you, Hawthorne? By what right do you drink from my flagon of life? And when I put it to my lips—lo, they are yours and not mine. I feel that the Godhead is broken up like the bread at the Supper, and that we are the pieces. Hence this infinite fraternity of feeling. Now, sympathizing with the paper, my angel turns over another page. You did not care a penny for the book. But, now and then as you read, you understood the pervading thought that impelled the book—and that you praised. Was it not so? You were arch-

---

8. **Ego . . . yourself:** The sense of Melville's words is made clear by Chapter 113 of *Moby-Dick*, where Ahab declares: "*Ego non baptizo te in nomine patris, sed in nomine diaboli*" ("I do not baptize you in the name of the Father, but in the name of the Devil").

9. **wicked book:** This pronouncement has occasioned much argument among critics of Melville, some holding that in *Moby-Dick* he surrendered to a kind of Black Magic (as 18 n. on baptism might also suggest) and that covertly he was out to annihilate God and all moral values from a purely atheistic point of view. Perhaps he had that impulse, but the passage about having written a wicked book may simply mean that *Moby-Dick* releases passions and deals with subject matters certain to prove shocking to the conventional readers of Melville's time.

angel enough to despise the imperfect body, and embrace the soul. Once you hugged the ugly Socrates because you saw the flame in the mouth, and heard the rushing of the demon,—the familiar,—and recognized the sound; for you have heard it in your own solitudes.

My dear Hawthorne, the atmospheric skepticisms steal into me now, and make me doubtful of my sanity in writing you this. But, believe me, I am not mad, most noble Festus![10] But truth is ever incoherent, and when the big hearts strike together, the concussion is a little stunning. Farewell. Don't write a word about the book. That would be robbing me of my miserly delight. I am heartily sorry I ever wrote anything about you—it was paltry. Lord, when shall we be done growing? As long as we have anything more to do, we have done nothing. So, now, let us add Moby Dick to our blessing, and step from that. Leviathan is not the biggest fish;—I have heard of Krakens.[11]

This is a long letter, but you are not at all bound to answer it. Possibly, if you do answer it, and direct it to Herman Melville, you will missend it—for the very fingers that now guide this pen are not precisely the same that just took it up and put it on this paper. Lord, when shall we be done changing? Ah! it's a long stage, and no inn in sight, and night coming, and the body cold. But with you for a passenger, I am content and can be happy. I shall leave the world, I feel, with more satisfaction for having come to know you. Knowing you persuades me more than the Bible of our immortality.

What a pity, that, for your plain, bluff letter, you should get such gibberish! Mention me to Mrs. Hawthorne and to the children, and so, good-by to you, with my blessing.

HERMAN

P.S. I can't stop yet. If the world was entirely made up of Magians,[12] I'll tell you what I should do. I should have a paper-mill established at one end of the house, and so have an endless riband of foolscap rolling in upon my desk; and upon that endless riband I should write a thousand—a million—billion thoughts, all under the form of a letter to you. The divine magnet is on you, and my magnet responds. Which is the biggest? A foolish question—they are *One*.

P.P.S. Don't think that by writing me a letter, you shall always be bored with an immediate reply to it—and so keep both of us delving over a writing-

desk eternally. No such thing! I sha'n't always answer your letters, and you may do just as you please.

---

# BARTLEBY THE SCRIVENER
## A STORY OF WALL STREET

◊

❲ THIS short story was first published in two installments in November and December of 1853 in *Putnam's Monthly Magazine*. When it was republished in Melville's *Piazza Tales* (1856), it was called by one reviewer "the most original story in the volume" and another pronounced it a "portrait from life" and "one of the best bits of writing which ever came from the author's pen." Time has amply confirmed these high estimates of Melville's haunting tale. The extent to which "Bartleby" is a "portrait from life" is a matter of conjecture. But if, as I suggested in the Introduction above, Melville is projecting some of his own impulses and attitudes in the figure of Bartleby, it is of further interest that both Melville's brother Allan and his father-in-law Judge Shaw were lawyers, and that both had, at various times and in various ways, come to the aid of Herman Melville and his shakily financed family.

◊

I AM a rather elderly man. The nature of my avocations, for the last thirty years, has brought me into more than ordinary contact with what would seem an interesting and somewhat singular set of men, of whom, as yet, nothing, that I know of, has ever been written—I mean, the law-copyists, or scriveners. I have known very many of them, professionally and privately, and, if I pleased, could relate divers histories, at which good-natured gentlemen might smile, and sentimental souls might weep. But I waive the biographies of all other scriveners, for a few passages in the life of Bartleby, who was a scrivener, the strangest I ever saw, or heard of. While, of other law-copyists, I might write the complete life, of Bartleby nothing of that sort can be done. I believe that no materials exist for a full and satisfactory biography of this man. It is an irreparable loss to literature. Bartleby was one of those beings of whom nothing is ascertainable, except from the original sources, and, in his case, those are very small. What my own astonished eyes saw of Bartleby, *that* is all I know of him, except, indeed, one vague report, which will appear in the sequel.

---

10. I . . . Festus!: The words of the prisoner, St. Paul, before the magistrate. See Acts 26:25. 11. Krakens: sea monsters in Norwegian mythology. 12. Magians: Persian priests, but Melville uses the word to mean magicians or conjurors.

Ere introducing the scrivener, as he first appeared to me, it is fit I make some mention of myself, my *employés,* my business, my chambers, and general surroundings; because some such description is indispensable to an adequate understanding of the chief character about to be presented. Imprimis: I am a man who, from his youth upwards, has been filled with a profound conviction that the easiest way of life is the best. Hence, though I belong to a profession proverbially energetic and nervous, even to turbulence, at times, yet nothing of that sort have I ever suffered to invade my peace. I am one of those unambitious lawyers who never addresses a jury, or in any way draws down public applause; but, in the cool tranquillity of a snug retreat, do a snug business among rich men's bonds, and mortgages, and title-deeds. All who know me, consider me an eminently *safe* man. The late John Jacob Astor, a personage little given to poetic enthusiasm, had no hesitation in pronouncing my first grand point to be prudence; my next, method. I do not speak it in vanity, but simply record the fact, that I was not unemployed in my profession by the late John Jacob Astor; a name which, I admit, I love to repeat; for it hath a rounded and orbicular sound to it, and rings like unto bullion. I will freely add, that I was not insensible to the late John Jacob Astor's good opinion.

Some time prior to the period at which this little history begins, my avocations had been largely increased. The good old office, now extinct in the State of New York, of a Master in Chancery, had been conferred upon me. It was not a very arduous office, but very pleasantly remunerative. I seldom lose my temper; much more seldom indulge in dangerous indignation at wrongs and outrages; but, I must be permitted to be rash here, and declare, that I consider the sudden and violent abrogation of the office of Master in Chancery, by the new Constitution, as a —— premature act; inasmuch as I had counted upon a life-lease of the profits, whereas I only received those of a few short years. But this is by the way.

My chambers were up stairs, at No. —— Wall Street. At one end, they looked upon the white wall of the interior of a spacious sky-light shaft, penetrating the building from top to bottom.

This view might have been considered rather tame than otherwise, deficient in what landscape painters call "life." But, if so, the view from the other end of my chambers offered, at least, a contrast, if nothing more. In that direction, my windows commanded an unobstructed view of a lofty brick wall, black by age and everlasting shade; which wall required no spy-glass to bring out its lurking beauties, but, for the benefit of all near-sighted spectators, was pushed up to within ten feet of my window panes. Owing to the great height of the surrounding buildings, and my chambers being on the second floor, the interval between this wall and mine not a little resembled a huge square cistern.

At the period just preceding the advent of Bartleby, I had two persons as copyists in my employment, and a promising lad as an office-boy. First, Turkey; second, Nippers; third, Ginger Nut. These may seem names, the like of which are not usually found in the Directory. In truth, they were nicknames, mutually conferred upon each other by my three clerks, and were deemed expressive of their respective persons or characters. Turkey was a short, pursy Englishman, of about my own age —that is, somewhere not far from sixty. In the morning, one might say, his face was of a fine florid hue, but after twelve o'clock, meridian—his dinner hour—it blazed like a grate full of Christmas coals; and continued blazing—but, as it were, with a gradual wane—till six o'clock P.M., or thereabouts; after which, I saw no more of the proprietor of the face, which, gaining its meridian with the sun, seemed to set with it, to rise, culminate, and decline the following day, with the like regularity and undiminished glory. There are many singular coincidences I have known in the course of my life, not the least among which was the fact, that, exactly when Turkey displayed his fullest beams from his red and radiant countenance, just then, too, at that critical moment, began the daily period when I considered his business capacities as seriously disturbed for the remainder of the twenty-four hours. Not that he was absolutely idle, or averse to business, then; far from it. The difficulty was, he was apt to be altogether too energetic. There was a strange, inflamed, flurried, flighty recklessness of activity about him. He would be incautious in dipping his pen into his inkstand. All his blots upon my documents were dropped there after twelve o'clock meridian. Indeed, not only would he be reckless, and sadly given to making blots in the afternoon, but, some days, he went further, and was rather noisy. At such times, too, his face flamed with augmented blazonry, as if cannel coal had been heaped on anthracite. He made an unpleasant racket with his chair; spilled his sand-box; in mending his pens, impatiently split them all to pieces, and threw them on the floor in a sudden passion; stood up, and leaned over his table, boxing his papers about in a most indecorous manner, very sad to behold in an elderly man like him. Nevertheless, as he was in many ways a most valuable person to me, and all the time before twelve o'clock meridian, was the quickest, steadiest creature, too, accomplishing a great deal of work in a style not easily to be matched—for these reasons, I was willing to overlook his eccentricities, though, indeed, occasionally, I remonstrated with him. I did this very gently, however, because, though the civilest, nay, the blandest and most reverential of men in the morning, yet, in the afternoon, he was disposed, upon provocation, to be slightly rash with his tongue—in fact, insolent. Now, valuing his morning services as I did, and resolved not to lose them —yet, at the same time, made uncomfortable by his inflamed ways after twelve o'clock—and being a man of peace, unwilling by my admonitions to call forth unseemly retorts from him, I took upon me, one Saturday noon (he was always worse on Saturdays) to hint to him, very kindly, that, perhaps, now that he was growing old, it might be well to abridge his labors; in short, he need not come to my chambers after twelve o'clock, but, dinner over, had best go home to his lodgings, and rest himself till tea-time. But no; he insisted upon his afternoon devotions. His countenance became intolerably fervid, as he oratorically assured me— gesticulating with a long ruler at the other end of the room—that if his services in the morning were useful, how indispensable, then, in the afternoon?

"With submission, sir," said Turkey, on this occasion, "I consider myself your right-hand man. In the morning I but marshal and deploy my columns; but in the afternoon I put myself at their head and gallantly charge the foe, thus"—and he made a violent thrust with the ruler.

"But the blots, Turkey," intimated I.

"True; but, with submission, sir, behold these hairs! I am getting old. Surely, sir, a blot or two of a warm afternoon is not to be severely urged against gray hairs. Old age—even if it blot the page—is honorable. With submission, sir, we *both* are getting old."

This appeal to my fellow-feeling was hardly to be resisted. At all events, I saw that go he would not. So, I made up my mind to let him stay, resolving, nevertheless, to see to it that, during the afternoon, he had to do with my less important papers.

Nippers, the second on my list, was a whiskered, sallow, and, upon the whole, rather piratical-looking young man, of about five and twenty. I always deemed him the victim of two evil powers—ambition and indigestion. The ambition was evinced by a certain impatience of the duties of a mere copyist, an unwarrantable usurpation of strictly professional affairs, such as the original drawing up of legal documents. The indigestion seemed betokened in an occasional nervous testiness and grin-

ning irritability, causing the teeth to audibly grind together over mistakes committed in copying; unnecessary maledictions, hissed, rather than spoken, in the heat of business; and especially by a continual discontent with the height of the table where he worked. Though of a very ingenious, mechanical turn, Nippers could never get this table to suit him. He put chips under it, blocks of various sorts, bits of pasteboard, and at last went so far as to attempt an exquisite adjustment, by final pieces of folded blotting-paper. But no invention would answer. If, for the sake of easing his back, he brought the table lid at a sharp angle well up towards his chin, and wrote there like a man using the steep roof of a Dutch house for his desk, then he declared that it stopped the circulation in his arms If now he lowered the table to his waistbands, and stooped over it in writing, then there was a sore aching in his back. In short, the truth of the matter was, Nippers knew not what he wanted. Or, if he wanted anything, it was to be rid of a scrivener's table altogether. Among the manifestations of his diseased ambition was a fondness he had for receiving visits from certain ambiguous-looking fellows in seedy coats, whom he called his clients. Indeed, I was aware that not only was he, at times, considerable of a ward-politician, but he occasionally did a little business at the Justices' courts, and was not unknown on the steps of the Tombs. I have good reason to believe, however, that one individual who called upon him at my chambers, and who, with a grand air, he insisted was his client, was no other than a dun, and the alleged title-deed, a bill. But, with all his failings, and the annoyances he caused me, Nippers, like his compatriot Turkey, was a very useful man to me; wrote a neat, swift hand; and, when he chose, was not deficient in a gentlemanly sort of deportment. Added to this, he always dressed in a gentlemanly sort of way; and so, incidentally, reflected credit upon my chambers. Whereas, with respect to Turkey, I had much ado to keep him from being a reproach to me. His clothes were apt to look oily, and smell of eating-houses. He wore his pantaloons very loose and baggy in summer. His coats were execrable; his hat not to be handled. But while the hat was a thing of indifference to me, inasmuch as his natural civility and deference, as a dependent Englishman, always led him to doff it the moment he entered the room, yet his coat was another matter. Concerning his coats, I reasoned with him; but with no effect. The truth was, I suppose, that a man with so small an income could not afford to sport such a lustrous face and a lustrous coat at one and the same time. As Nippers once observed, Turkey's money went chiefly for red ink. One winter day, I presented

Turkey with a highly respectable-looking coat of my own—a padded gray coat, of a most comfortable warmth, and which buttoned straight up from the knee to the neck. I thought Turkey would appreciate the favor, and abate his rashness and obstreperousness of afternoons. But no; I verily believe that buttoning himself up in so downy and blanket-like a coat had a pernicious effect upon him—upon the same principle that too much oats are bad for horses. In fact, precisely as a rash, restive horse is said to feel his oats, so Turkey felt his coat. It made him insolent. He was a man whom prosperity harmed.

Though, concerning the self-indulgent habits of Turkey, I had my own private surmises, yet, touching Nippers, I was well persuaded that, whatever might be his faults in other respects, he was, at least, a temperate young man. But, indeed, nature herself seemed to have been his vintner, and, at his birth, charged him so thoroughly with an irritable, brandy-like disposition, that all subsequent potations were needless. When I consider how, amid the stillness of my chambers, Nippers would sometimes impatiently rise from his seat, and stooping over his table, spread his arms wide apart, seize the whole desk, and move it, and jerk it, with a grim, grinding motion on the floor, as if the table were a perverse voluntary agent and vexing him, I plainly perceive that, for Nippers, brandy-and-water were altogether superfluous.

It was fortunate for me that, owing to its peculiar cause—indigestion—the irritability and consequent nervousness of Nippers were mainly observable in the morning, while in the afternoon he was comparatively mild. So that, Turkey's paroxysms only coming on about twelve o'clock, I never had to do with their eccentricities at one time. Their fits relieved each other, like guards. When Nippers's was on, Turkey's was off; and *vice versa.* This was a good natural arrangement, under the circumstances.

Ginger Nut, the third on my list, was a lad, some twelve years old. His father was a car-man, ambitious of seeing his son on the bench instead of a cart, before he died. So he sent him to my office, as student at law, errand-boy, cleaner and sweeper, at the rate of one dollar a week. He had a little desk to himself; but he did not use it much. Upon inspection, the drawer exhibited a great array of the shells of various sorts of nuts. Indeed, to this quick-witted youth, the whole noble science of the law was contained in a nutshell. Not the least among the employments of Ginger Nut, as well as one which he discharged with the most alacrity, was his duty as cake and apple purveyor for Turkey and Nippers. Copying law-papers being proverbially a dry, husky sort of business, my two

scriveners were fain to moisten their mouths very often with Spitzenbergs,[1] to be had at the numerous stalls nigh the Custom House and Post Office. Also, they sent Ginger Nut very frequently for that peculiar cake—small, flat, round, and very spicy—after which he had been named by them. Of a cold morning, when business was but dull, Turkey would gobble up scores of these cakes, as if they were mere wafers—indeed, they sell them at the rate of six or eight for a penny—the scrape of his pen blending with the crunching of the crisp particles in his mouth. Rashest of all the fiery afternoon blunders and flurried rashnesses of Turkey, was his once moistening a ginger-cake between his lips, and clapping it on to a mortgage, for a seal. I came within an ace of dismissing him then. But he mollified me by making an oriental bow, and saying—

"With submission, sir, it was generous of me to find you in stationery on my own account."

Now my original business—that of a conveyancer and title hunter, and drawer-up of recondite documents of all sorts—was considerably increased by receiving the master's office. There was now great work for scriveners. Not only must I push the clerks already with me, but I must have additional help.

In answer to my advertisement, a motionless young man one morning stood upon my office threshold, the door being open, for it was summer. I can see that figure now—pallidly neat, pitiably respectable, incurably forlorn! It was Bartleby.

After a few words touching his qualifications, I engaged him, glad to have among my corps of copyists a man of so singularly sedate an aspect, which I thought might operate beneficially upon the flighty temper of Turkey, and the fiery one of Nippers.

I should have stated before that ground glass folding-doors divided my premises into two parts, one of which was occupied by my scriveners, the other by myself. According to my humor, I threw open these doors, or closed them. I resolved to assign Bartleby a corner by the folding-doors, but on my side of them, so as to have this quiet man within easy call, in case any trifling thing was to be done. I placed his desk close up to a small side-window in that part of the room, a window which originally had afforded a lateral view of certain grimy backyards and bricks, but which, owing to subsequent erections, commanded at present no view at all, though it gave some light. Within three feet of the panes was a wall, and the light came down from far above, between two lofty buildings,

BARTLEBY THE SCRIVENER.    1. **Spitzenbergs:** spitzenburgs; a variety of apple.

as from a very small opening in a dome. Still further to a satisfactory arrangement, I procured a high green folding screen, which might entirely isolate Bartleby from my sight, though not remove him from my voice. And thus, in a manner, privacy and society were conjoined.

At first, Bartleby did an extraordinary quantity of writing. As if long famishing for something to copy, he seemed to gorge himself on my documents. There was no pause for digestion. He ran a day and night line, copying by sun-light and by candle-light. I should have been quite delighted with his application, had he been cheerfully industrious. But he wrote on silently, palely, mechanically.

It is, of course, an indispensable part of a scrivener's business to verify the accuracy of his copy, word by word. Where there are two or more scriveners in an office, they assist each other in this examination, one reading from the copy, the other holding the original. It is a very dull, wearisome, and lethargic affair. I can readily imagine that, to some sanguine temperaments, it would be altogether intolerable. For example, I cannot credit that the mettlesome poet, Byron, would have contentedly sat down with Bartleby to examine a law document of, say five hundred pages, closely written in a crimpy hand.

Now and then, in the haste of business, it had been my habit to assist in comparing some brief document myself, calling Turkey or Nippers for this purpose. One object I had, in placing Bartleby so handy to me behind the screen, was to avail myself of his services on such trivial occasions. It was on the third day, I think, of his being with me, and before any necessity had arisen for having his own writing examined, that, being much hurried to complete a small affair I had in hand, I abruptly called to Bartleby. In my haste and natural expectancy of instant compliance, I sat with my head bent over the original on my desk, and my right hand sideways, and somewhat nervously extended with the copy, so that, immediately upon emerging from his retreat, Bartleby might snatch it and proceed to business without the least delay.

In this very attitude did I sit when I called to him, rapidly stating what it was I wanted him to do —namely, to examine a small paper with me. Imagine my surprise, nay, my consternation, when, without moving from his privacy, Bartleby, in a singularly mild, firm voice, replied, "I would prefer not to."

I sat awhile in perfect silence, rallying my stunned faculties. Immediately it occurred to me that my ears had deceived me, or Bartleby had entirely misunderstood my meaning. I repeated my request in the clearest tone I could assume; but in quite as clear a one came the previous reply, "I would prefer not to."

"Prefer not to," echoed I, rising in high excitement, and crossing the room with a stride. "What do you mean? Are you moon-struck? I want you to help me compare this sheet here—take it," and I thrust it towards him.

"I would prefer not to," said he.

I looked at him steadfastly. His face was leanly composed; his gray eye dimly calm. Not a wrinkle of agitation rippled him. Had there been the least uneasiness, anger, impatience, or impertinence in his manner; in other words, had there been any thing ordinarily human about him, doubtless I should have violently dismissed him from the premises. But as it was, I should have as soon thought of turning my pale plaster-of-paris bust of Cicero out of doors. I stood gazing at him awhile, as he went on with his own writing, and then reseated myself at my desk. This is very strange, thought I. What had one best do? But my business hurried me. I concluded to forget the matter for the present, reserving it for my future leisure. So calling Nippers from the other room, the paper was speedily examined.

A few days after this, Bartleby concluded four lengthy documents, being quadruplicates of a week's testimony taken before me in my High Court of Chancery. It became necessary to examine them. It was an important suit, and great accuracy was imperative. Having all things arranged, I called Turkey, Nippers, and Ginger Nut from the next room, meaning to place the four copies in the hands of my four clerks, while I should read from the original. Accordingly, Turkey, Nippers, and Ginger Nut had taken their seats in a row, each with his document in his hand, when I called to Bartleby to join this interesting group.

"Bartleby! quick, I am waiting."

I heard a slow scrape of his chair legs on the uncarpeted floor, and soon he appeared standing at the entrance of his hermitage.

"What is wanted?" said he, mildly.

"The copies, the copies," said I, hurriedly. "We are going to examine them. There—" and I held towards him the fourth quadruplicate.

"I would prefer not to," he said, and gently disappeared behind the screen.

For a few moments I was turned into a pillar of salt, standing at the head of my seated column of clerks. Recovering myself, I advanced towards the screen, and demanded the reason for such extraordinary conduct.

"*Why* do you refuse?"

"I would prefer not to."

With any other man I should have flown outright into a dreadful passion, scorned all further words, and thrust him ignominiously from my presence. But there was something about Bartleby that not only strangely disarmed me, but in a wonderful manner, touched and disconcerted me. I began to reason with him.

"These are your own copies we are about to examine. It is labor saving to you, because one examination will answer for your four papers. It is common usage. Every copyist is bound to help examine his copy. Is it not so? Will you not speak? Answer!"

"I prefer not to," he replied in a flutelike tone. It seemed to me that, while I had been addressing him, he carefully revolved every statement that I made; fully comprehended the meaning; could not gainsay the irresistible conclusion; but, at the same time, some paramount consideration prevailed with him to reply as he did.

"You are decided, then, not to comply with my request—a request made according to common usage and common sense?"

He briefly gave me to understand, that on that point my judgment was sound. Yes: his decision was irreversible.

It is not seldom the case that, when a man is browbeaten in some unprecedented and violently unreasonable way, he begins to stagger in his own plainest faith. He begins, as it were, vaguely to surmise that, wonderful as it may be, all the justice and all the reason is on the other side. Accordingly, if any disinterested persons are present, he turns to them for some reinforcement of his own faltering mind.

"Turkey," said I, "what do you think of this? Am I not right?"

"With submission, sir," said Turkey, in his blandest tone, "I think that you are."

"Nippers," said I, "what do *you* think of it?"

"I think I should kick him out of the office."

(The reader, of nice [2] perceptions, will here perceive that, it being morning, Turkey's answer is couched in polite and tranquil terms, but Nippers replies in ill-tempered ones. Or, to repeat a previous sentence, Nippers's ugly mood was on duty, and Turkey's off.)

"Ginger Nut," said I, willing to enlist the smallest suffrage in my behalf, "what do *you* think of it?"

"I think, sir, he's a little *luny*," replied Ginger Nut, with a grin.

"You hear what they say," said I, turning towards the screen, "come forth and do your duty."

But he vouchsafed no reply. I pondered a moment in sore perplexity. But once more business hurried me. I determined again to postpone the consideration of this dilemma to my future leisure. With a little trouble we made out to examine the papers without Bartleby, though at every page or two Turkey deferentially dropped his opinion, that this proceeding was quite out of the common; while Nippers, twitching in his chair with a dyspeptic nervousness, ground out, between his set teeth, occasional hissing maledictions against the stubborn oaf behind the screen. And for his (Nippers's) part, this was the first and the last time he would do another man's business without pay.

Meanwhile Bartleby sat in his hermitage, oblivious to everything but his own peculiar business there.

Some days passed, the scrivener being employed upon another lengthy work. His late remarkable conduct led me to regard his ways narrowly. I observed that he never went to dinner; indeed, that he never went anywhere. As yet I had never, of my personal knowledge, known him to be outside of my office. He was a perpetual sentry in the corner. At about eleven o'clock though, in the morning, I noticed that Ginger Nut would advance toward the opening in Bartleby's screen, as if silently beckoned thither by a gesture invisible to me where I sat. The boy would then leave the office, jingling a few pence, and reappear with a handful of ginger-nuts, which he delivered in the hermitage, receiving two of the cakes for his trouble.

He lives, then, on ginger-nuts, thought I; never eats a dinner, properly speaking; he must be a vegetarian, then; but no; he never eats even vegetables; he eats nothing but ginger-nuts. My mind then ran on in reveries concerning the probable effects upon the human constitution of living entirely on ginger-nuts. Ginger-nuts are so called, because they contain ginger as one of their peculiar constituents, and the final flavoring one. Now, what was ginger? A hot, spicy thing. Was Bartleby hot and spicy? Not at all. Ginger, then, had no effect upon Bartleby. Probably he preferred it should have none.

Nothing so aggravates an earnest person as a passive resistance. If the individual so resisted be of a not inhumane temper, and the resisting one perfectly harmless in his passivity, then, in the better moods of the former, he will endeavor charitably to construe to his imagination what proves impossible to be solved by his judgment. Even so, for the most part, I regarded Bartleby and his ways. Poor fellow! thought I, he means no mis-

---

2. **nice:** precise.

chief; it is plain he intends no insolence; his aspect sufficiently evinces that his eccentricities are involuntary. He is useful to me. I can get along with him. If I turn him away, the chances are he will fall in with some less-indulgent employer, and then he will be rudely treated, and perhaps driven forth miserably to starve. Yes. Here I can cheaply purchase a delicious self-approval. To befriend Bartleby; to humor him in his strange willfulness, will cost me little or nothing, while I lay up in my soul what will eventually prove a sweet morsel for my conscience. But this mood was not invariable with me. The passiveness of Bartleby sometimes irritated me. I felt strangely goaded on to encounter him in new opposition—to elicit some angry spark from him answerable to my own. But, indeed, I might as well have essayed to strike fire with my knuckles against a bit of Windsor soap. But one afternoon the evil impulse in me mastered me, and the following little scene ensued:

"Bartleby," said I, "when those papers are all copied, I will compare them with you."

"I would prefer not to."

"How? Surely you do not mean to persist in that mulish vagary?"

No answer.

I threw open the folding-doors near by, and, turning upon Turkey and Nippers, exclaimed:

"Bartleby a second time says, he won't examine his papers. What do you think of it, Turkey?"

It was afternoon, be it remembered. Turkey sat glowing like a brass boiler; his bald head steaming; his hands reeling among his blotted papers.

"Think of it?" roared Turkey; "I think I'll just step behind his screen, and black his eyes for him!"

So saying, Turkey rose to his feet and threw his arms into a pugilistic position. He was hurrying away to make good his promise, when I detained him, alarmed at the effect of incautiously rousing Turkey's combativeness after dinner.

"Sit down, Turkey," said I, "and hear what Nippers has to say. What do you think of it, Nippers? Would I not be justified in immediately dismissing Bartleby?"

"Excuse me, that is for you to decide, sir. I think his conduct quite unusual, and, indeed, unjust, as regards Turkey and myself. But it may only be a passing whim."

"Ah," exclaimed I, "you have strangely changed your mind, then—you speak very gently of him now."

"All beer," cried Turkey; "gentleness is effects of beer—Nippers and I dined together to-day. You see how gentle *I* am, sir. Shall I go and black his eyes?"

"You refer to Bartleby, I suppose. No, not to-day, Turkey," I replied; "pray, put up your fists."

I closed the doors, and again advanced towards Bartleby. I felt additional incentives tempting me to my fate. I burned to be rebelled against again. I remembered that Bartleby never left the office.

"Bartleby," said I, "Ginger Nut is away; just step around to the Post Office, won't you? (it was but a three minutes' walk), and see if there is anything for me."

"I would prefer not to."

"You *will* not?"

"I *prefer* not."

I staggered to my desk, and sat there in a deep study. My blind inveteracy returned. Was there any other thing in which I could procure myself to be ignominiously repulsed by this lean, penniless wight?—my hired clerk? What added thing is there, perfectly reasonable, that he will be sure to refuse to do?

"Bartleby!"

No answer.

"Bartleby," in a louder tone.

No answer.

"Bartleby," I roared.

Like a very ghost, agreeably to the laws of magical invocation, at the third summons, he appeared at the entrance of his hermitage.

"Go to the next room, and tell Nippers to come to me."

"I prefer not to," he respectfully and slowly said, and mildly disappeared.

"Very good, Bartleby," said I, in a quiet sort of serenely-severe, self-possessed tone, intimating the unalterable purpose of some terrible retribution very close at hand. At the moment I half intended something of the kind. But upon the whole, as it was drawing towards my dinner-hour, I thought it best to put on my hat and walk home for the day, suffering much from perplexity and distress of mind.

Shall I acknowledge it? The conclusion of this whole business was, that it soon became a fixed fact of my chambers, that a pale young scrivener, by the name of Bartleby, had a desk there; that he copied for me at the usual rate of four cents a folio (one hundred words); but he was permanently exempt from examining the work done by him, that duty being transferred to Turkey and Nippers, out of compliment, doubtless, to their superior acuteness; moreover, said Bartleby was never, on any account, to be dispatched on the most trivial errand of any sort; and that even if entreated to take upon him such a matter, it was generally understood that he would "prefer not to"—in other words, that he would refuse point-blank.

As days passed on, I became considerably reconciled to Bartleby. His steadiness, his freedom from all dissipation, his incessant industry (except when he chose to throw himself into a standing revery behind his screen), his great stillness, his unalterableness of demeanor under all circumstances, made him a valuable acquisition. One prime thing was this—*he was always there*—first in the morning, continually through the day, and the last at night. I had a singular confidence in his honesty. I felt my most precious papers perfectly safe in his hands. Sometimes, to be sure, I could not, for the very soul of me, avoid falling into sudden spasmodic passions with him. For it was exceeding difficult to bear in mind all the time those strange peculiarities, privileges, and unheard of exemptions, forming the tacit stipulations on Bartleby's part under which he remained in my office. Now and then, in the eagerness of dispatching pressing business, I would inadvertently summon Bartleby, in a short, rapid tone, to put his finger, say, on the incipient tie of a bit of red tape with which I was about compressing some papers. Of course, from behind the screen the usual answer, "I prefer not to," was sure to come; and then, how could a human creature, with the common infirmities of our nature, refrain from bitterly exclaiming upon such perverseness—such unreasonableness. However, every added repulse of this sort which I received only tended to lessen the probability of my repeating the inadvertence.

Here it must be said, that according to the custom of most legal gentlemen occupying chambers in densely-populated law buildings, there were several keys to my door. One was kept by a woman residing in the attic, which person weekly scrubbed and daily swept and dusted my apartments. Another was kept by Turkey for convenience sake. The third I sometimes carried in my own pocket. The fourth I knew not who had.

Now, one Sunday morning I happened to go to Trinity Church, to hear a celebrated preacher, and finding myself rather early on the ground I thought I would walk around to my chambers for a while. Luckily I had my key with me; but upon applying it to the lock, I found it resisted by something inserted from the inside. Quite surprised, I called out; when to my consternation a key was turned from within; and thrusting his lean visage at me, and holding the door ajar, the apparition of Bartleby appeared, in his shirt sleeves, and otherwise in a strangely tattered *déshabille,* saying quietly that he was sorry, but he was deeply engaged just then, and—preferred not admitting me at present. In a brief word or two, he moreover added, that perhaps I had better walk around the block two or three times, and by that time he would probably have concluded his affairs.

Now, the utterly unsurmised appearance of Bartleby, tenanting my law-chambers of a Sunday morning, with his cadaverously gentlemanly *nonchalance,* yet withal firm and self-possessed, had such a strange effect upon me, that incontinently I slunk away from my own door, and did as desired. But not without sundry twinges of impotent rebellion against the mild effrontery of this unaccountable scrivener. Indeed, it was his wonderful mildness chiefly, which not only disarmed me, but unmanned me as it were. For I consider that one, for the time, is somehow unmanned when he tranquilly permits his hired clerk to dictate to him, and order him away from his own premises. Furthermore, I was full of uneasiness as to what Bartleby could possibly be doing in my office in his shirt sleeves, and in an otherwise dismantled condition of a Sunday morning. Was anything amiss going on? Nay, that was out of the question. It was not to be thought of for a moment that Bartleby was an immoral person. But what could he be doing there?—copying? Nay again, whatever might be his eccentricities, Bartleby was an eminently decorous person. He would be the last man to sit down to his desk in any state approaching to nudity. Besides, it was Sunday; and there was something about Bartleby that forbade the supposition that he would by any secular occupation violate the proprieties of the day.

Nevertheless, my mind was not pacified; and full of a restless curiosity, at last I returned to the door. Without hindrance I inserted my key, opened it, and entered. Bartleby was not to be seen. I looked round anxiously, peeped behind his screen; but it was very plain that he was gone. Upon more closely examining the place, I surmised that for an indefinite period Bartleby must have eaten, dressed, and slept in my office, and that, too, without plate, mirror, or bed. The cushioned seat of a ricketty old sofa in one corner bore the faint impress of a lean, reclining form. Rolled away under his desk, I found a blanket; under the empty grate, a blacking box and brush; on a chair, a tin basin, with soap and a ragged towel; in a newspaper a few crumbs of ginger-nuts and a morsel of cheese. Yes, thought I, it is evident enough that Bartleby has been making his home here, keeping bachelor's hall all by himself. Immediately then the thought came sweeping across me, what miserable friendlessness and loneliness are here revealed! His poverty is great; but his solitude, how horrible! Think of it. Of a Sunday, Wall Street is deserted as Petra;[3] and every night of

3. **Petra:** the ruins of an ancient city in Palestine.

every day it is an emptiness. This building, too, which of weekdays hums with industry and life, at nightfall echoes with sheer vacancy, and all through Sunday is forlorn. And here Bartleby makes his home; sole spectator of a solitude which he has seen all populous—a sort of innocent and transformed Marius [4] brooding among the ruins of Carthage!

For the first time in my life a feeling of overpowering stinging melancholy seized me. Before, I had never experienced aught but a not unpleasing sadness. The bond of a common humanity now drew me irresistibly to gloom. A fraternal melancholy! For both I and Bartleby were sons of Adam. I remembered the bright silks and sparkling faces I had seen that day, in gala trim, swanlike sailing down the Mississippi of Broadway; and I contrasted them with the pallid copyist, and thought to myself, Ah, happiness courts the light, so we deem the world is gay; but misery hides aloof, so we deem that misery there is none. These sad fancyings—chimeras, doubtless, of a sick and silly brain—led on to other and more special thoughts, concerning the eccentricities of Bartleby. Presentiments of strange discoveries hovered round me. The scrivener's pale form appeared to me laid out, among uncaring strangers, in its shivering winding sheet.

Suddenly I was attracted by Bartleby's closed desk, the key in open sight left in the lock.

I mean no mischief, seek the gratification of no heartless curiosity, thought I; besides, the desk is mine, and its contents, too, so I will make bold to look within. Everything was methodically arranged, the papers smoothly placed. The pigeon holes were deep, and removing the files of documents, I groped into their recesses. Presently I felt something there, and dragged it out. It was an old bandanna handkerchief, heavy and knotted. I opened it, and saw it was a savings's bank.

I now recalled all the quiet mysteries which I had noted in the man. I remembered that he never spoke but to answer; that, though at intervals he had considerable time to himself, yet I had never seen him reading—no, not even a newspaper; that for long periods he would stand looking out, at his pale window behind the screen, upon the dead brick wall; I was quite sure he never visited any refectory or eating house; while his pale face clearly indicated that he never drank beer like Turkey, or tea and coffee even, like other men; that he never went anywhere in particular that I could learn; never went out for a walk, unless, indeed,

that was the case at present; that he had declined telling who he was, or whence he came, or whether he had any relatives in the world; that though so thin and pale, he never complained of ill health. And more than all, I remembered a certain unconscious air of pallid—how shall I call it?—of pallid haughtiness, say, or rather an austere reserve about him, which had positively awed me into my tame compliance with his eccentricities, when I had feared to ask him to do the slightest incidental thing for me, even though I might know, from his long-continued motionlessness, that behind his screen he must be standing in one of those dead-wall reveries of his.

Revolving all these things, and coupling them with the recently discovered fact, that he made my office his constant abiding place and home, and not forgetful of his morbid moodiness; revolving all these things, a prudential feeling began to steal over me. My first emotions had been those of pure melancholy and sincerest pity; but just in proportion as the forlornness of Bartleby grew and grew to my imagination, did that same melancholy merge into fear, that pity into repulsion. So true it is, and so terrible, too, that up to a certain point the thought or sight of misery enlists our best affections; but, in certain special cases, beyond that point it does not. They err who would assert that invariably this is owing to the inherent selfishness of the human heart. It rather proceeds from a certain hopelessness of remedying excessive and organic ill. To a sensitive being, pity is not seldom pain. And when at last it is perceived that such pity cannot lead to effectual succor, common sense bids the soul be rid of it. What I saw that morning persuaded me that the scrivener was the victim of innate and incurable disorder. I might give alms to his body; but his body did not pain him; it was his soul that suffered, and his soul I could not reach.

I did not accomplish the purpose of going to Trinity Church that morning. Somehow, the things I had seen disqualified me for the time from church-going. I walked homeward, thinking what I would do with Bartleby. Finally, I resolved upon this—I would put certain calm questions to him the next morning, touching his history, etc., and if he declined to answer them openly and unreservedly (and I supposed he would prefer not), then to give him a twenty dollar bill over and above whatever I might owe him, and tell him his services were no longer required; but that if in any other way I could assist him, I would be happy to do so, especially if he desired to return to his native place, wherever that might be, I would willingly help to defray the expenses. Moreover, if, after reaching

---

4. **Marius:** Gaius Marius (155?–186 B.C.), a Roman general. He is brooding because although he had won great victories in Africa, he had been banished from Rome as a result of political maneuvers.

home, he found himself at any time in want of aid, a letter from him would be sure of a reply.

The next morning came.

"Bartleby," said I, gently calling to him behind his screen.

No reply.

"Bartleby," said I, in a still gentler tone, "come here; I am not going to ask you to do anything you would prefer not to do—I simply wish to speak to you."

Upon this he noiselessly slid into view.

"Will you tell me, Bartleby, where you were born?"

"I would prefer not to."

"Will you tell me *anything* about yourself?"

"I would prefer not to."

"But what reasonable objection can you have to speak to me? I feel friendly towards you."

He did not look at me while I spoke, but kept his glance fixed upon my bust of Cicero, which, as I then sat, was directly behind me, some six inches above my head.

"What is your answer, Bartleby," said I, after waiting a considerable time for a reply, during which his countenance remained immovable, only there was the faintest conceivable tremor of the white attenuated mouth.

"At present I prefer to give no answer," he said, and retired into his hermitage.

It was rather weak in me I confess, but his manner, on this occasion, nettled me. Not only did there seem to lurk in it a certain calm disdain, but his perverseness seemed ungrateful, considering the undeniable good usage and indulgence he had received from me.

Again I sat ruminating what I should do. Mortified as I was at his behavior, and resolved as I had been to dismiss him when I entered my office, nevertheless I strangely felt something superstitious knocking at my heart, and forbidding me to carry out my purpose, and denouncing me for a villain if I dared to breathe one bitter word against this forlornest of mankind. At last, familiarly drawing my chair behind his screen, I sat down and said: "Bartleby, never mind, then, about revealing your history; but let me entreat you, as a friend, to comply as far as may be with the usages of this office. Say now, you will help to examine papers to-morrow or next day: in short, say now, that in a day or two you will begin to be a little reasonable: —say so, Bartleby."

"At present I would prefer not to be a little reasonable," was his mildly cadaverous reply.

Just then the folding-doors opened, and Nippers approached. He seemed suffering from an unusually bad night's rest, induced by severer indigestion than common. He overheard those final words of Bartleby.

"*Prefer not*, eh?" gritted Nippers—"I'd *prefer* him, if I were you, sir," addressing me—"I'd *prefer* him; I'd give him preferences, the stubborn mule! What is it, sir, pray, that he *prefers* not to do now?"

Bartleby moved not a limb.

"Mr. Nippers," said I, "I'd prefer that you would withdraw for the present."

Somehow, of late, I had got into the way of involuntarily using this word "prefer" upon all sorts of not exactly suitable occasions. And I trembled to think that my contact with the scrivener had already and seriously affected me in a mental way. And what further and deeper aberration might it not yet produce? This apprehension had not been without efficacy in determining me to summary measures.

As Nippers, looking very sour and sulky, was departing, Turkey blandly and deferentially approached.

"With submission, sir," said he, "yesterday I was thinking about Bartleby here, and I think that if he would but prefer to take a quart of good ale every day, it would do much towards mending him, and enabling him to assist in examining his papers."

"So you have got the word, too," said I, slightly excited.

"With submission, what word, sir," asked Turkey, respectfully crowding himself into the contracted space behind the screen, and by so doing, making me jostle the scrivener. "What word, sir?"

"I would prefer to be left alone here," said Bartleby, as if offended at being mobbed in his privacy.

"*That's* the word, Turkey," said I—"*that's* it."

"Oh, *prefer*? oh yes—queer word. I never use it myself. But, sir, as I was saying, if he would but prefer—"

"Turkey," interrupted I, "you will please withdraw."

"Oh certainly, sir, if you prefer that I should."

As he opened the folding-door to retire, Nippers at his desk caught a glimpse of me, and asked whether I would prefer to have a certain paper copied on blue paper or white. He did not in the least roguishly accent the word prefer. It was plain that it involuntarily rolled from his tongue. I thought to myself, surely I must get rid of a demented man, who already has in some degree turned the tongues, if not the heads of myself and clerks. But I thought it prudent not to break the dismission at once.

The next day I noticed that Bartleby did nothing but stand at his window in his dead-wall revery. Upon asking him why he did not write, he said that he had decided upon doing no more writing.

"Why, how now? what next?" exclaimed I, "do no more writing?"

"No more."

"And what is the reason?"

"Do you not see the reason for yourself," he indifferently replied.

I looked steadfastly at him, and perceived that his eyes looked dull and glazed. Instantly it occurred to me, that his unexampled diligence in copying by his dim window for the first few weeks of his stay with me might have temporarily impaired his vision.

I was touched. I said something in condolence with him. I hinted that of course he did wisely in abstaining from writing for a while; and urged him to embrace that opportunity of taking wholesome exercise in the open air. This, however, he did not do. A few days after this, my other clerks being absent, and being in a great hurry to dispatch certain letters by the mail, I thought that, having nothing else earthly to do, Bartleby would surely be less inflexible than usual, and carry these letters to the post-office. But he blankly declined. So, much to my inconvenience, I went myself.

Still added days went by. Whether Bartleby's eyes improved or not, I could not say. To all appearance I thought they did. But when I asked him if they did, he vouchsafed no answer. At all events, he would do no copying. At last, in reply to my urgings, he informed me that he had permanently given up copying.

"What!" exclaimed I; "suppose your eyes should get entirely well—better than ever before—would you not copy then?"

"I have given up copying," he answered, and slid aside.

He remained as ever, a fixture in my chamber. Nay—if that were possible—he became still more of a fixture than before. What was to be done? He would do nothing in the office; why should he stay there? In plain fact, he had now become a millstone to me, not only useless as a necklace, but afflictive to bear. Yet I was sorry for him. I speak less than truth when I say that, on his own account, he occasioned me uneasiness. If he would but have named a single relative or friend, I would instantly have written, and urged their taking the poor fellow away to some convenient retreat. But he seemed alone, absolutely alone in the universe. A bit of wreck in the mid-Atlantic. At length, necessities connected with my business tyrannized over all other considerations. Decently as I could, I told Bartleby that in six days time he must unconditionally leave the office. I warned him to take

measures, in the interval, for procuring some other abode. I offered to assist him in his endeavor, if he himself would but take the first step towards a removal. "And when you finally quit me, Bartleby," added I, "I shall see that you go not away entirely unprovided. Six days from this hour, remember."

At the expiration of that period, I peeped behind the screen, and lo! Bartleby was there.

I buttoned up my coat, balanced myself; advanced slowly towards him, touched his shoulder, and said, "The time has come; you must quit this place; I am sorry for you; here is money; but you must go."

"I would prefer not," he replied, with his back still towards me.

"You *must*."

He remained silent.

Now I had an unbounded confidence in this man's common honesty. He had frequently restored to me sixpences and shillings carelessly dropped upon the floor, for I am apt to be very reckless in such shirt-button affairs. The proceeding, then, which followed will not be deemed extraordinary.

"Bartleby," said I, "I owe you twelve dollars on account; here are thirty-two; the odd twenty are yours—Will you take it?" and I handed the bills towards him.

But he made no motion.

"I will leave them here, then," putting them under a weight on the table. Then taking my hat and cane and going to the door, I tranquilly turned and added—"After you have removed your things from these offices, Bartleby, you will of course lock the door—since every one is now gone for the day but you—and if you please, slip your key underneath the mat, so that I may have it in the morning. I shall not see you again; so good-by to you. If, hereafter, in your new place of abode, I can be of any service to you, do not fail to advise me by letter. Good-by, Bartleby, and fare you well.

But he answered not a word; like the last column of some ruined temple, he remained standing mute and solitary in the middle of the otherwise deserted room.

As I walked home in a pensive mood, my vanity got the better of my pity. I could not but highly plume myself on my masterly management in getting rid of Bartleby. Masterly I call it, and such it must appear to any dispassionate thinker. The beauty of my procedure seemed to consist in its perfect quietness. There was no vulgar bullying, no bravado of any sort, no choleric hectoring, and striding to and fro across the apartment, jerking out vehement commands for Bartleby to bundle himself off with his beggarly traps. Nothing of the kind. Without loudly bidding Bartleby depart—as an inferior genius might have done—I *assumed* the ground that depart he must; and upon that assumption built all I had to say. The more I thought over my procedure, the more I was charmed with it. Nevertheless, next morning, upon awakening, I had my doubts—I had somehow slept off the fumes of vanity. One of the coolest and wisest hours a man has, is just after he awakes in the morning. My procedure seemed as sagacious as ever—but only in theory. How it would prove in practice—there was the rub. It was truly a beautiful thought to have assumed Bartleby's departure; but, after all, that assumption was simply my own, and none of Bartleby's. The great point was, not whether I had assumed that he would quit me, but whether he would prefer so to do. He was more a man of preferences than assumptions.

After breakfast, I walked down town, arguing the probabilities *pro* and *con*. One moment I thought it would prove a miserable failure, and Bartleby would be found all alive at my office as usual; the next moment it seemed certain that I should find his chair empty. And so I kept veering about. At the corner of Broadway and Canal Street, I saw quite an excited group of people standing in earnest conversation.

"I'll take odds he doesn't," said a voice as I passed.

"Doesn't go?—done!" said I; "put up your money."

I was instinctively putting my hand in my pocket to produce my own, when I remembered that this was an election day. The words I had overheard bore no reference to Bartleby, but to the success or non-success of some candidate for the mayoralty. In my intent frame of mind, I had, as it were, imagined that all Broadway shared in my excitement, and were debating the same question with me. I passed on, very thankful that the uproar of the street screened my momentary absent-mindedness.

As I had intended, I was earlier than usual at my office door. I stood listening for a moment. All was still. He must be gone. I tried the knob. The door was locked. Yes, my procedure had worked to a charm; he indeed must be vanished. Yet a certain melancholy mixed with this: I was almost sorry for my brilliant success. I was fumbling under the door mat for the key, which Bartleby was to have left there for me, when accidentally my knee knocked against a panel, producing a summoning sound, and in response a voice came to me from within—"Not yet; I am occupied."

It was Bartleby.

I was thunderstruck. For an instant I stood like the man who, pipe in mouth, was killed one cloudless afternoon long ago in Virginia, by summer lightning; at his own warm open window he was killed, and remained leaning out there upon the dreamy afternoon, till some one touched him, when he fell.

"Not gone!" I murmured at last. But again obeying that wondrous ascendancy which the inscrutable scrivener had over me, and from which ascendancy, for all my chafing, I could not completely escape, I slowly went down stairs and out into the street, and while walking round the block, considered what I should next do in this unheard-of perplexity. Turn the man out by an actual thrusting I could not; to drive him away by calling him hard names would not do; calling in the police was an unpleasant idea; and yet, permit him to enjoy his cadaverous triumph over me—this, too, I could not think of. What was to be done? or, if nothing could be done, was there anything further that I could *assume* in the matter? Yes, as before I had prospectively assumed that Bartleby would depart, so now I might retrospectively assume that departed he was. In the legitimate carrying out of this assumption, I might enter my office in a great hurry, and pretending not to see Bartleby at all, walk straight against him as if he were air. Such a proceeding would in a singular degree have the appearance of a home-thrust. It was hardly possible that Bartleby could withstand such an application of the doctrine of assumptions. But upon second thoughts the success of the plan seemed rather dubious. I resolved to argue the matter over with him again.

"Bartleby," said I, entering the office, with a quietly severe expression, "I am seriously displeased. I am pained, Bartleby. I had thought better of you. I had imagined you of such a gentlemanly organization, that in any delicate dilemma a slight hint would suffice—in short, an assumption. But it appears I am deceived. Why," I added, unaffectedly starting, "you have not even touched that money yet," pointing to it, just where I had left it the evening previous.

He answered nothing.

"Will you, or will you not, quit me?" I now demanded in a sudden passion, advancing close to him.

"I would prefer *not* to quit you," he replied, gently emphasizing the *not*.

"What earthly right have you to stay here? Do you pay any rent? Do you pay my taxes? Or is this property yours?"

He answered nothing.

"Are you ready to go on and write now? Are your eyes recovered? Could you copy a small paper for me this morning? or help examine a few lines? or step round to the post-office? In a word, will you do anything at all, to give a coloring to your refusal to depart the premises?"

He silently retired into his hermitage.

I was now in such a state of nervous resentment that I thought it but prudent to check myself at present from further demonstrations. Bartleby and I were alone. I remembered the tragedy of the unfortunate Adams and the still more unfortunate Colt in the solitary office of the latter; and how poor Colt, being dreadfully incensed by Adams, and imprudently permitted himself to get wildy excited, was at unawares hurried into his fatal act—an act which certainly no man could possibly deplore more than the actor himself. Often it had occurred to me in my ponderings upon the subject, that had that altercation taken place in the public street, or at a private residence, it would not have terminated as it did. It was the circumstance of being alone in a solitary office, up stairs, of a building entirely unhallowed by humanizing domestic associations—an uncarpeted office, doubtless, of a dusty, haggard sort of appearance—this it must have been, which greatly helped to enhance the irritable desperation of the hapless Colt.

But when this old Adam of resentment rose in me and tempted me concerning Bartleby, I grappled him and threw him. How? Why, simply by recalling the divine injunction: "A new commandment give I unto you, that ye love one another." [5] Yes, this it was that saved me. Aside from higher considerations, charity often operates as a vastly wise and prudent principle—a great safeguard to its possessor. Men have committed murder for jealousy's sake, and anger's sake, and hatred's sake, and selfishness' sake, and spiritual pride's sake; but no man, that ever I heard of, ever committed a diabolical murder for sweet charity's sake. Mere self-interest, then, if no better motive can be enlisted, should, especially with high-tempered men, prompt all beings to charity and philanthropy. At any rate, upon the occasion in question, I strove to drown my exasperated feelings towards the scrivener by benevolently construing his conduct. Poor fellow, poor fellow! thought I, he don't mean anything; and besides, he has seen hard times, and ought to be indulged.

I endeavored, also, immediately to occupy myself, and at the same time to comfort my despondency. I tried to fancy, that in the course of the morning, at such time as might prove agreeable to him, Bartleby, of his own free accord, would emerge from his hermitage and take up

some decided line of march in the direction of the door. But no. Half-past twelve o'clock came; Turkey began to glow in the face, overturn his inkstand, and become generally obstreperous; Nippers abated down into quietude and courtesy; Ginger Nut munched his noon apple; and Bartleby remained standing at his window in one of his profoundest dead-wall reveries. Will it be credited? Ought I to acknowledge it? That afternoon I left the office without saying one further word to him.

Some days now passed, during which, at leisure intervals I looked a little into "Edwards [6] on the Will," and "Priestley [7] on Necessity." Under the circumstances, those books induced a salutary feeling. Gradually I slid into the persuasion that these troubles of mine, touching the scrivener, had been all predestined from eternity, and Bartleby was billeted upon me for some mysterious purpose of an allwise Providence, which it was not for a mere mortal like me to fathom. Yes, Bartleby, stay there behind your screen, thought I; I shall persecute you no more; you are harmless and noiseless as any of these old chairs; in short, I never feel so private as when I know you are here. At last I see it, I feel it; I penetrate to the predestinated purpose of my life. I am content. Others may have loftier parts to enact; but my mission in this world, Bartleby, is to furnish you with office-room for such period as you may see fit to remain.

I believe that this wise and blessed frame of mind would have continued with me, had it not been for the unsolicited and uncharitable remarks obtruded upon me by my professional friends who visited the rooms. But thus it often is, that the constant friction of illiberal minds wears out at last the best resolves of the more generous. Though to be sure, when I reflected upon it, it was not strange that people entering my office should be struck by the peculiar aspect of the unaccountable Bartleby, and so be tempted to throw out some sinister observations concerning him. Sometimes an attorney, having business with me, and calling at my office, and finding no one but the scrivener there, would undertake to obtain some sort of precise information from him touching my whereabouts; but without heeding his idle talk, Bartleby would remain standing immovable in the middle of the room. So after contemplating him in that position for a time, the attorney would depart, no wiser than he came.

Also, when a reference was going on, and the room full of lawyers and witnesses, and business

---

5. love one another: John 13:24.

6. **Edwards:** Jonathan Edwards, *The Freedom of the Will* (1754). 7. **Priestley:** Joseph Priestley (1733–1804). It is not clear to which of this author's voluminous writings Melville refers.

driving fast, some deeply-occupied legal gentleman present, seeing Bartleby wholly unemployed, would request him to run round to his (the legal gentleman's) office and fetch some papers for him. Thereupon, Bartleby would tranquilly decline, and yet remain idle as before. Then the lawyer would give a great stare, and turn to me. And what could I say? At last I was made aware that all through the circle of my professional acquaintance, a whisper of wonder was running round, having reference to the strange creature I kept at my office. This worried me very much. And as the idea came upon me of his possibly turning out a long-lived man, and keep occupying my chambers, and denying my authority; and perplexing my visitors; and scandalizing my professional reputation; and casting a general gloom over the premises; keeping soul and body together to the last upon his savings (for doubtless he spent but half a dime a day), and in the end perhaps outlive me, and claim possession of my office by right of his perpetual occupancy: as all these dark anticipations crowded upon me more and more, and my friends continually intruded their relentless remarks upon the apparition in my room; a great change was wrought in me. I resolved to gather all my faculties together, and forever rid me of this intolerable incubus.

Ere revolving any complicated project, however, adapted to this end, I first simply suggested to Bartleby the propriety of his permanent departure. In a calm and serious tone, I commended the idea to his careful and mature consideration. But, having taken three days to meditate upon it, he apprised me, that his original determination remained the same; in short, that he still preferred to abide with me.

What shall I do? I now said to myself, buttoning up my coat to the last button. What shall I do? what ought I to do? what does conscience say I *should* do with this man, or, rather, ghost. Rid myself of him, I must; go, he shall. But how? You will not thrust him, the poor, pale, passive mortal —you will not thrust such a helpless creature out of your door? you will not dishonor yourself by such cruelty? No, I will not, I cannot do that. Rather would I let him live and die here, and then mason up his remains in the wall. What, then, will you do? For all your coaxing, he will not budge. Bribes he leaves under your own paper-weight on your table; in short, it is quite plain that he prefers to cling to you.

Then something severe, something unusual must be done. What! surely you will not have him collared by a constable, and commit his innocent pallor to the common jail? And upon what ground

could you procure such a thing to be done?—a vagrant, is he? What! he a vagrant, a wanderer, who refuses to budge? It is because he will *not* be a vagrant, then, that you seek to count him *as* a vagrant. That is too absurd. No visible means of support: there I have him. Wrong again: for indubitably he *does* support himself, and that is the only unanswerable proof that any man can show of his possessing the means so to do. No more, then. Since he will not quit me, I must quit him. I will change my offices; I will move elsewhere, and give him fair notice, that if I find him on my new premises I will then proceed against him as a common trespasser.

Acting accordingly, next day I thus addressed him: "I find these chambers too far from the City Hall; the air is unwholesome. In a word, I propose to remove my offices next week, and shall no longer require your services. I tell you this now, in order that you may seek another place."

He made no reply; and nothing more was said.

On the appointed day I engaged carts and men, proceeded to my chambers, and, having but little furniture, everything was removed in a few hours. Throughout, the scrivener remained standing behind the screen, which I directed to be removed the last thing. It was withdrawn; and, being folded up like a huge folio, left him the motionless occupant of a naked room. I stood in the entry watching him a moment, while something from within me upbraided me.

I re-entered, with my hand in my pocket—and —and my heart in my mouth.

"Good-by, Bartleby; I am going—good-by, and God some way bless you; and take that," slipping something in his hand. But it dropped upon the floor, and then—strange to say—I tore myself from him whom I had so longed to be rid of.

Established in my new quarters, for a day or two I kept the door locked, and started at every footfall in the passages. When I returned to my rooms, after any little absence, I would pause at the threshold for an instant, and attentively listen, ere applying my key. But these fears were needless. Bartleby never came nigh me.

I thought all was going well, when a perturbed-looking stranger visited me, inquiring whether I was the person who had recently occupied rooms at No. — Wall Street.

Full of forebodings, I replied that I was.

"Then, sir," said the stranger, who proved a lawyer, "you are responsible for the man you left there. He refuses to do any copying; he refuses to do anything; he says he prefers not to; and he refuses to quit the premises."

"I am very sorry, sir," said I, with assumed tranquillity, but an inward tremor, "but, really, the man you allude to is nothing to me—he is no relation or apprentice of mine, that you should hold me responsible for him."

"In mercy's name, who is he?"

"I certainly cannot inform you. I know nothing about him. Formerly I employed him as a copyist; but he has done nothing for me now for some time past."

"I shall settle him, then—good morning, sir."

Several days passed, and I heard nothing more; and, though I often felt a charitable prompting to call at the place and see poor Bartleby, yet a certain squeamishness, of I know not what, withheld me.

All is over with him, by this time, thought I, at last, when, through another week, no further intelligence reached me. But, coming to my room the day after, I found several persons waiting at my door in a high state of nervous excitement.

"That's the man—here he comes," cried the foremost one, whom I recognized as the lawyer who had previously called upon me alone.

"You must take him away, sir, at once," cried a portly person among them, advancing upon me, and whom I knew to be the landlord of No. —— Wall Street. "These gentlemen, my tenants, cannot stand it any longer; Mr. B——," pointing to the lawyer, "has turned him out of his room, and he now persists in haunting the building generally, sitting upon the banisters of the stairs by day, and sleeping in the entry by night. Everybody is concerned; clients are leaving the offices; some fears are entertained of a mob; something you must do, and that without delay."

Aghast at this torrent, I fell back before it, and would fain have locked myself in my new quarters. In vain I persisted that Bartleby was nothing to me—no more than to any one else. In vain—I was the last person known to have anything to do with him, and they held me to the terrible account. Fearful, then, of being exposed in the papers (as one person present obscurely threatened), I considered the matter, and, at length, said, that if the lawyer would give me a confidential interview with the scrivener, in his (the lawyer's) own room, I would, that afternoon, strive my best to rid them of the nuisance they complained of.

Going up stairs to my old haunt, there was Bartleby silently sitting upon the banister at the landing.

"What are you doing here, Bartleby?" said I.

"Sitting upon the banister," he mildly replied.

I motioned him into the lawyer's room, who then left us.

"Bartleby," said I, "are you aware that you are the cause of great tribulation to me, by persisting in occupying the entry after being dismissed from the office?"

No answer.

"Now one of two things must take place. Either you must do something, or something must be done to you. Now what sort of business would you like to engage in? Would you like to re-engage in copying for some one?"

"No; I would prefer not to make any change."

"Would you like a clerkship in a dry-goods store?"

"There is too much confinement about that. No, I would not like a clerkship; but I am not particular."

"Too much confinement," I cried, "why you keep yourself confined all the time!"

"I would prefer not to take a clerkship," he rejoined, as if to settle that little item at once.

"How would a bar-tender's business suit you? There is no trying of the eye-sight in that."

"I would not like it at all; though, as I said before, I am not particular."

His unwonted wordiness inspirited me. I returned to the charge.

"Well, then, would you like to travel through the country collecting bills for the merchants? That would improve your health."

"No, I would prefer to be doing something else."

"How, then, would going as a companion to Europe, to entertain some young gentleman with your conversation—how would that suit you?"

"Not at all. It does not strike me that there is anything definite about that. I like to be stationary. But I am not particular."

"Stationary you shall be, then," I cried, now losing all patience, and, for the first time in all my exasperating connection with him, fairly flying into a passion. "If you do not go away from these premises before night, I shall feel bound—indeed, I *am* bound—to—to—to quit the premises myself!" I rather absurdly concluded, knowing not with what possible threat to try to frighten his immobility into compliance. Despairing of all further efforts, I was precipitately leaving him, when a final thought occurred to me—one which had not been wholly unindulged before.

"Bartleby," said I, in the kindest tone I could assume under such exciting circumstances, "will you go home with me now—not to my office, but my dwelling—and remain there till we can conclude upon some convenient arrangement for you at our leisure? Come, let us start now, right away."

"No: at present I would prefer not to make any change at all."

I answered nothing; but, effectually dodging every one by the suddenness and rapidity of my flight, rushed from the building, ran up Wall Street towards Broadway, and, jumping into the first omnibus, was soon removed from pursuit. As soon as tranquillity returned, I distinctly perceived that I had now done all that I possibly could, both in respect to the demands of the landlord and his tenants, and with regard to my own desire and sense of duty, to benefit Bartleby, and shield him from rude persecution. I now strove to be entirely care-free and quiescent; and my conscience justified me in the attempt; though, indeed, it was not so successful as I could have wished. So fearful was I of being again hunted out by the incensed landlord and his exasperated tenants, that, surrendering my business to Nippers, for a few days, I drove about the upper part of the town and through the suburbs, in my rockaway; crossed over to Jersey City and Hoboken, and paid fugitive visits to Manhattanville and Astoria. In fact, I almost lived in my rockaway for the time.

When again I entered my office, lo, a note from the landlord lay upon the desk. I opened it with trembling hands. It informed me that the writer had sent to the police, and had Bartleby removed to the Tombs as a vagrant. Moreover, since I knew more about him than any one else, he wished me to appear at that place, and make a suitable statement of the facts. These tidings had a conflicting effect upon me. At first I was indignant; but, at last, almost approved. The landlord's energetic, summary disposition, had led him to adopt a procedure which I do not think I would have decided upon myself; and yet, as a last resort, under such peculiar circumstances, it seemed the only plan.

As I afterwards learned, the poor scrivener, when told that he must be conducted to the Tombs, offered not the slightest obstacle, but, in his pale, unmoving way, silently acquiesced.

Some of the compassionate and curious bystanders joined the party; and headed by one of the constables arm in arm with Bartleby, the silent procession filed its way through all the noise, and heat, and joy of the roaring thoroughfares at noon.

The same day I received the note, I went to the Tombs, or, to speak more properly, the Halls of Justice. Seeking the right officer, I stated the purpose of my call, and was informed that the individual I described was, indeed, within. I then assured the functionary that Bartleby was a perfectly honest man, and greatly to be compassionated, however unaccountably eccentric. I narrated all I knew, and closed by suggesting the idea of letting him remain in as indulgent confinement as possible, till something less harsh might be done—though, indeed, I hardly knew what. At all events, if nothing else could be decided upon, the almshouse must receive him. I then begged to have an interview.

Being under no disgraceful charge, and quite serene and harmless in all his ways, they had permitted him freely to wander about the prison, and, especially, in the inclosed grass-platted yards thereof. And so I found him there, standing all alone in the quietest of the yards, his face towards a high wall, while all around, from the narrow slits of the jail windows, I thought I saw peering out upon him the eyes of murderers and thieves.

"Bartleby!"

"I know you," he said, without looking round—"and I want nothing to say to you."

"It was not I that brought you here, Bartleby," said I, keenly pained at his implied suspicion. "And to you, this should not be so vile a place. Nothing reproachful attaches to you by being here. And see, it is not so sad a place as one might think. Look, there is the sky, and here is the grass."

"I know where I am," he replied, but would say nothing more, and so I left him.

As I entered the corridor again, a broad meat-like man, in an apron, accosted me, and jerking his thumb over his shoulder, said—"Is that your friend?"

"Yes."

"Does he want to starve? If he does, let him live on the prison fare, that's all."

"Who are you?" asked I, not knowing what to make of such an unofficially speaking person in such a place.

"I am the grub-man. Such gentlemen as have friends here, hire me to provide them with something good to eat."

"Is this so?" said I, turning to the turnkey.

He said it was.

"Well, then," said I, slipping some silver into the grub-man's hands (for so they called him), "I want you to give particular attention to my friend there; let him have the best dinner you can get. And you must be as polite to him as possible."

"Introduce me, will you?" said the grub-man, looking at me with an expression which seemed to say he was all impatience for an opportunity to give a specimen of his breeding.

Thinking it would prove of benefit to the scrivener, I acquiesced; and, asking the grub-man his name, went up with him to Bartleby.

"Bartleby, this is a friend; you will find him very useful to you."

"Your sarvant, sir, your sarvant," said the grub-man, making a low salutation behind his apron. "Hope you find it pleasant here, sir; nice grounds —cool apartments—hope you'll stay with us sometime—try to make it agreeable. What will you have for dinner to-day?"

"I prefer not to dine to-day," said Bartleby, turning away. "It would disagree with me; I am unused to dinners." So saying, he slowly moved to the other side of the inclosure, and took up a position fronting the dead-wall.

"How's this?" said the grub-man, addressing me with a stare of astonishment. "He's odd, ain't he?"

"I think he is a little deranged," said I, sadly.

"Deranged? deranged is it? Well, now, upon my word, I thought that friend of yourn was a gentleman forger; they are always pale and genteel-like, them forgers. I can't help pity 'em—can't help it, sir. Did you know Monroe Edwards?" he added, touchingly, and paused. Then, laying his hand piteously on my shoulder, sighed, "he died of consumption at Sing-Sing. So you weren't acquainted with Monroe?"

"No, I was never socially acquainted with any forgers. But I cannot stop longer. Look to my friend yonder. You will not lose by it. I will see you again."

Some few days after this, I again obtained admission to the Tombs, and went through the corridors in quest of Bartleby; but without finding him.

"I saw him coming from his cell not long ago," said a turnkey, "may be he's gone to loiter in the yards."

So I went in that direction.

"Are you looking for the silent man?" said another turnkey, passing me. "Yonder he lies—sleeping in the yard there. 'Tis not twenty minutes since I saw him lie down."

The yard was entirely quiet. It was not accessible to the common prisoners. The surrounding walls, of amazing thickness, kept off all sounds behind them. The Egyptian character of the masonry weighed upon me with its gloom. But a soft imprisoned turf grew under foot. The heart of the eternal pyramids, it seemed, wherein, by some strange magic, through the clefts, grass-seed, dropped by birds, had sprung.

Strangely huddled at the base of the wall, his knees drawn up, and lying on his side, his head touching the cold stones, I saw the wasted Bartleby. But nothing stirred. I paused; then went close up to him; stooped over, and saw that his dim eyes were open; otherwise he seemed profoundly sleeping. Something prompted me to touch him. I felt his hand, when a tingling shiver ran up my arm and down my spine to my feet.

The round face of the grub-man peered upon me now. "His dinner is ready. Won't he dine to-day, either? Or does he live without dining?"

"Lives without dining," said I, and closed the eyes.

"Eh!—He's asleep, ain't he?"

"With kings and counselors," [8] murmured I.

*  *  *

There would seem little need for proceeding further in this history. Imagination will readily supply the meagre recital of poor Bartleby's interment. But, ere parting with the reader, let me say, that if this little narrative has sufficiently interested him, to awaken curiosity as to who Bartleby was, and what manner of life he led prior to the present narrator's making his acquaintance, I can only reply, that in such curiosity I fully share, but am wholly unable to gratify it. Yet here I hardly know whether I should divulge one little item of rumor, which came to my ear a few months after the scrivener's decease. Upon what basis it rested, I could never ascertain; and hence, how true it is I cannot now tell. But, inasmuch as this vague report has not been without a certain suggestive interest to me, however said, it may prove the same with some others; and so I will briefly mention it. The report was this: that Bartleby had been a subordinate clerk in the Dead Letter Office at Washington, from which he had been suddenly removed by a change in the administration. When I think over this rumor, hardly can I express the emotions which seize me. Dead letters! does it not sound like dead men? Conceive a man by nature and misfortune prone to a pallid hopelessness, can any business seem more fitted to heighten it than that of continually handling these dead letters, and assorting them for the flames? For by the cart-load they are annually burned. Sometimes from out the folded paper the pale clerk takes a ring—the finger it was meant for, perhaps, moulders in the grave; a bank-note sent in swiftest charity—he whom it would relieve, nor eats nor hungers any more; pardon for those who died despairing; hope for those who died unhoping; good tidings for those who died stifled by unrelieved calamities. On errands of life, these letters speed to death.

Ah, Bartleby! Ah, humanity!

8. **kings . . . counselors:** See Job 3:13–14.

# BILLY BUDD, FORETOPMAN

◊

◖ *Billy Budd*, found among Melville's effects in manuscript and not published until 1924, is in part inspired by the case of the American naval brig *Somers*, which in 1842 became for many interested persons a *cause célèbre*. A young midshipman, named Philip Spencer, was convicted of mutiny and hanged on board, along with a boatswain's mate and a common seaman. The executive officer who presided over the drumhead court which meted out the punishment was Guert Gansevoort, a cousin of Melville. There was much controversy at the time over the justice or injustice of the harsh sentence, and the case seems to have thrown a cloud over Gansevoort for the rest of his life. As we see from Melville's treatment of a similar case in *Billy Budd*, he had pondered long and deeply over its moral implications. The general subject of the story also stirred up in the aging Melville many memories and thoughts about his own days at sea, when, as he felt, sailing was still in its golden age. He had found a rich source of materials, and as he wrote and rewrote *Billy Budd* it grew from short story to novel, as we have it. F. Barron Freeman, in his *Melville's Billy Budd* (1948), has described the difficulty of establishing an accurate text, because of the chaotic condition of the manuscript and the frequent illegibility of Melville's handwriting. It is Mr. Freeman's version of the text, as amended by subsequent corrigenda, that is followed below. (Copyright by the President and Fellows of Harvard College.)

◊

DEDICATED
TO
JACK CHACE [1]
*Englishman*

Wherever that great heart may now be Here on earth or harbored in Paradise Captain of the main-top in the year 1843 in the U.S. Frigate "United States"

## PREFACE

THE YEAR 1797, the year of this narrative, belongs to a period which as every thinker now feels, involved a crisis for Christendom not exceeded in its undetermined momentousness at the time by any other era whereof there is record. The opening proposition made by the Spirit of that Age, in-

volved the rectification of the Old World's hereditary wrongs. In France to some extent this was bloodily effected. But what then? Straightway the Revolution itself became a wrongdoer, one more oppressive than the kings. Under Napoleon it enthroned upstart Kings, and initiated that prolonged agony of continual war whose final throe was Waterloo. During those years not the wisest could have foreseen that the outcome of all would be what to some thinkers apparently it has since turned out to be, a political advance along nearly the whole line for Europeans.

Now, as elsewhere hinted, it was something caught from the Revolutionary Spirit that at Spithead emboldened the man-of-war's men to rise against real abuses, long-standing ones, and afterwards at the Nore [2] to make inordinate and agressive demands, successful resistance to which was confirmed only when the ringleaders were hung for an admonitory spectacle to the anchored fleet. Yet in a way analogous to the operation of the Revolution at large the Great Mutiny, though by Englishmen naturally deemed monstrous at the time, doubtless gave the first latent prompting to most important reforms in the British Navy.

## BILLY BUDD, SAILOR

(*An inside narrative.*)

I

IN THE time before steamships, or then more frequently than now, a stroller along the docks of any considerable sea-port would occasionally have his attention arrested by a group of bronzed mariners, man-of-war's men or merchant-sailors in holiday attire ashore on liberty. In certain instances they would flank, or, like a body-guard quite surround some superior figure of their own class, moving along with them like Aldebaran among the lesser lights of his constellation. That signal object was the "Handsome Sailor" of the less prosaic time alike of the military and merchant navies. With no perceptible trace of the vainglorious about him, rather with the off-hand unaffectedness of natural regality, he seemed to accept the spontaneous homage of his shipmates. A somewhat remarkable instance recurs to me. In Liverpool, now half a century ago I saw under the shadow of the great dingy street-wall of Prince's Dock (an obstruction long since removed) a common sailor, so intensely

---

BILLY BUDD.     1. **Jack Chace:** Chace, to whom Melville dedicates his book, is described at length in *White-Jacket*.

2. **the Nore:** anchorage at the mouth of the Thames where the mutiny of 1797 in the British Navy took place.

black that he must needs have been a native African of the unadulterate blood of Ham. A symmetric figure much above the average height. The two ends of a gay silk handkerchief thrown loose about the neck danced upon the displayed ebony of his chest; in his ears were big hoops of gold, and a Scotch Highland bonnet with a tartan band set off his shapely head.

It was a hot noon in July; and his face, lustrous with perspiration, beamed with barbaric good humor. In jovial sallies right and left his white teeth flashing into view, he rollicked along, the centre of a company of his shipmates. These were made up of such an assortment of tribes and complexions as would have well fitted them to be marched up by Anacharsis Cloots [3] before the bar of the first French Assembly as Representatives of the Human Race. At each spontaneous tribute rendered by the wayfarers to this black pagod of a fellow—the tribute of a pause and stare, and less frequent an exclamation,—the motley retinue showed that they took that sort of pride in the evoker of it which the Assyrian priests doubtless showed for their grand sculptured Bull when the faithful prostrated themselves.

To return.

If in some cases a bit of a nautical Murat [4] in setting forth his person ashore, the handsome sailor of the period in question evinced nothing of the dandified Billy-be-Dam, an amusing character all but extinct now, but occasionally to be encountered, and in a form yet more amusing than the original, at the tiller of the boats on the tempestuous Erie Canal or, more likely, vaporing in the groggeries along the tow-path. Invariably a proficient in his perilous calling, he was also more or less of a mighty boxer or wrestler. It was strength and beauty. Tales of his prowess were recited. Ashore he was the champion; afloat the spokesman; on every suitable occasion always foremost. Close-reefing topsails in a gale, there he was, astride the weather yard-arm-end, foot in the Flemish horse as "stirrup," both hands tugging at the "earring" as at a bridle, in very much the attitude of young Alexander curbing the fiery Bucephalus.[5] A superb figure, tossed up as by the horns of Taurus against the thunderous sky, cheerily hallooing to the strenuous file along the spar.

The moral nature was seldom out of keeping with the physical make. Indeed, except as toned by the former, the comeliness and power, always attractive in masculine conjunction, hardly could have drawn the sort of honest homage the Handsome Sailor in some examples received from his less gifted associates.

Such a cynosure, at least in aspect, and something such too in nature, though with important variations made apparent as the story proceeds, was welkin-eyed Billy Budd, or Baby Budd as more familiarly under circumstances hereafter to be given he at last came to be called, aged twenty-one, a foretopman of the British fleet toward the close of the last decade of the eighteenth century. It was not very long prior to the time of the narration that follows that he had entered the King's Service, having been impressed on the Narrow Seas from a homeward-bound English merchantman into a seventy-four outward-bound, H.M.S. *Indomitable;* which ship, as was not unusual in those hurried days having been obliged to put to sea short of her proper complement of men. Plump upon Billy at first sight in the gangway the boarding officer Lieutenant Ratcliffe pounced, even before the merchantman's crew was formally mustered on the quarter-deck for his deliberate inspection. And him only he elected. For whether it was because the other men who ranged before him showed to ill advantage after Billy, or whether he had some scruples in view of the merchantman being rather short-handed, however it might be, the officer contented himself with his first spontaneous choice. To the surprise of the ship's company, though much to the Lieutenant's satisfaction Billy made no demur. But, indeed, any demur would have been as idle as the protest of a goldfinch popped into a cage.

Noting his uncomplaining acquiescence, all but cheerful one might say, the shipmates turned a surprised glance of silent reproach at the sailor. The shipmaster was one of those worthy mortals found in every vocation even the humbler ones—the sort of person whom everybody agrees in calling "a respectable man." And—nor so strange to report as it may appear to be—though a ploughman of the troubled waters, life-long contending with the intractable elements, there was nothing this honest soul at heart loved better than simple peace and quiet. For the rest, he was fifty or thereabouts, a little inclined to corpulence, a prepossessing face, unwhiskered, and of an agreeable color—a rather full face, humanely intelligent in expression. On a fair day with a fair wind and all going well, a certain musical chime in his voice seemed to be the veritable unobstructed outcome of the innermost man. He had much prudence, much conscientiousness, and there were occasions when these virtues

---

3. **Cloots:** the Baron de Cloots (1755–94), who made a declaration of the rights of man before the French Assembly.     4. **Murat:** Joachim Murat (1767–1815) was one of Napoleon's generals.
5. **Bucephalus:** the horse of Alexander the Great.

were the cause of overmuch disquietude in him. On a passage, so long as his craft was in any proximity to land, no sleep for Captain Graveling. He took to heart those serious responsibilities not so heavily borne by some shipmasters.

Now while Billy Budd was down in the forecastle getting his kit together, the *Indomitable's* lieutenant, burly and bluff, nowise disconcerted by Captain Graveling's omitting to proffer the customary hospitalities on an occasion so unwelcome to him, an omission simply caused by preoccupation of thought, unceremoniously invited himself into the cabin, and also to a flask from the spirit-locker, a receptacle which his experienced eye instantly discovered. In fact he was one of those sea-dogs in whom all the hardship and peril of naval life in the great prolonged wars of his time never impaired the natural instinct for sensuous enjoyment. His duty he always faithfully did; but duty is sometimes a dry obligation, and he was for irrigating its aridity, whensoever possible with a fertilizing decoction of strong waters. For the cabin's proprietor there was nothing left but to play the part of the enforced host with whatever grace and alacrity were practicable. As necessary adjuncts to the flask, he silently placed tumbler and water-jug before the irrepressible guest. But excusing himself from partaking just then, he dismally watched the unembarrassed officer deliberately diluting his grog a little, then tossing it off in three swallows, pushing the empty tumbler away, yet not so far as to be beyond easy reach, at the same time settling himself in his seat and smacking his lips with high satisfaction, looking straight at the host.

These proceedings over, the Master broke the silence; and there lurked a rueful reproach in the tone of his voice: "Lieutenant, you are going to take my best man from me, the jewel of 'em."

"Yes, I know" rejoined the other, immediately drawing back the tumbler preliminary to a replenishing; "Yes, I know. Sorry."

"Beg pardon, but you don't understand, Lieutenant. See here now. Before I shipped that young fellow, my forecastle was a rat-pit of quarrels. It was black times, I tell you, aboard the *'Rights'* here. I was worried to that degree my pipe had no comfort for me. But Billy came; and it was like a Catholic priest striking peace in an Irish shindy. Not that he preached to them or said or did anything in particular; but a virtue went out of him, sugaring the sour ones. They took to him like hornets to treacle; all but the buffer of the gang, the big shaggy chap with the fire-red whiskers. He indeed out of envy, perhaps, of the newcomer, and thinking such a 'sweet and pleasant fellow,' as he mockingly designated him to the others, could hardly have the spirit of a game-cock, must needs bestir himself in trying to get up an ugly row with him. Billy forebore with him and reasoned with him in a pleasant way—he is something like myself, Lieutenant, to whom aught like a quarrel is hateful—but nothing served. So, in the second dog-watch one day the Red Whiskers in presence of the others, under pretence of showing Billy just whence a sirloin steak was cut—for the fellow had once been a butcher—insultingly gave him a dig under the ribs. Quick as lightning Billy let fly his arm. I dare say he never meant to do quite as much as he did, but anyhow he gave the burly fool a terrible drubbing. It took about half a minute, I should think. And, lord bless you, the lubber was astonished at the celerity. And will you believe it, Lieutenant, the Red Whiskers now really loves Billy—loves him, or is the biggest hypocrite that ever I heard of. But they all love him. Some of 'em do his washing, darn his old trousers for him; the carpenter is at odd times making a pretty little chest of drawers for him. Anybody will do anything for Billy Budd; and it's the happy family here. But now Lieutenant, if that young fellow goes—I know how it will be aboard the *'Rights.'* Not again very soon shall I, coming up from dinner, lean over the capstan smoking a quiet pipe—no, not very soon again, I think. Ay, Lieutenant, you are going to take away the jewel of 'em; you are going to take away my peacemaker!" And with that the good soul had really some ado in checking a rising sob.

"Well," said the officer who had listened with amused interest to all this, and now waxing merry with his tipple; "Well, blessed are the peacemakers especially the fighting peacemakers! And such are the seventy-four beauties some of which you see poking their noses out at the port-holes of yonder war-ship lying-to for me" pointing through the cabin window of the *Indomitable.* "But courage! don't look so downhearted, man. Why, I pledge you in advance the royal approbation. Rest assured that His Majesty will be delighted to know that in a time when his hard tack is not sought for by sailors with such avidity as should be; a time also when some shipmasters privily resent the borrowing from them a tar or two for the service; His Majesty, I say, will be delighted to learn that *one* shipmaster at least cheerfully surrenders to the King, the flower of his flock, a sailor who with equal loyalty makes no dissent.—But where's my beauty? Ah," looking through the cabin's open door, "Here he comes; and, by Jove—lugging along his chest—Apollo with his portmanteau!—

My man," stepping out to him, "you can't take that big box aboard a war-ship. The boxes there are mostly shot-boxes. Put your duds in a bag, lad. Boot and saddle for the cavalryman, bag and hammock for the man-of-war's man."

The transfer from chest to bag was made. And, after seeing his man into the cutter and then following him down, the lieutenant pushed off from the *Rights-of-Man.* That was the merchant-ship's name; though by her master and crew abbreviated in sailor fashion into *The Rights.* The hard-headed Dundee owner was a staunch admirer of Thomas Paine whose book in rejoinder to Burke's arraignment of the French Revolution [6] had then been published for some time and had gone everywhere. In christening his vessel after the title of Paine's volume the man of Dundee was something like his contemporary shipowner, Stephen Girard of Philadelphia, whose sympathies, alike with his native land and its liberal philosophers, he evinced by naming his ships after Voltaire, Diderot, and so forth.

But now, when the boat swept under the merchant-man's stern, and officer and oarsmen were noting—some bitterly and others with a grin,—the name emblazoned there; just then it was that the new recruit jumped up from the bow where the coxswain had directed him to sit, and waving his hat to his silent shipmates sorrowfully looking over at him from the taffrail, bade the lads a genial good-bye. Then, making a salutation as to the ship herself, "And good-bye to you too, old *Rights-of-Man.*"

"Down, Sir!" roared the lieutenant, instantly assuming all the rigor of his rank, though with difficulty repressing a smile.

To be sure Billy's action was a terrible breach of naval decorum. But in that decorum he had never been instructed; in consideration of which the lieutenant would hardly have been so energetic in reproof but for the concluding farewell to the ship. This he rather took as meant to convey a covert sally on the new recruit's part, a sly slur at impressment in general, and that of himself in especial. And yet, more likely, if satire it was in effect, it was hardly so by intention, for Billy though happily endowed with the gayety of high health, youth, and a free heart, was yet by no means of a satirical turn. The will to it and the sinister dexterity were alike wanting. To deal in double meanings and insinuations of any sort was quite foreign to his nature.

As to his enforced enlistment, that he seemed to take pretty much as he was wont to take any vicissitude of weather. Like the animals, though no philosopher, he was, without knowing it, practically a

6. **Burke's . . . Revolution:** See Introduction, p. 498.

fatalist. And, it may be, that he rather liked this adventurous turn in his affairs, which promised an opening into novel scenes and martial excitements.

Aboard the *Indomitable* our merchant-sailor was forthwith rated as an able-seaman and assigned to the starboard watch of the fore-top. He was soon at home in the service, not at all disliked for his unpretentious good looks and a sort of genial happy-go-lucky air. No merrier man in his mess: in marked contrast to certain other individuals included like himself among the impressed portion of the ship's company; for these when not actively employed were sometimes, and more particularly in the last dog-watch when the drawing near of twilight induced revery, apt to fall into a saddish mood which in some partook of sullenness. But they were not so young as our foretopman, and no few of them must have known a hearth of some sort, others may have had wives and children left, too probably, in uncertain circumstances, and hardly any but must have had acknowledged kith and kin, while for Billy, as will shortly be seen, his entire family was practically invested in himself.

2

THOUGH our new-made foretopman was well received in the top and on the gun-decks, hardly here was he that cynosure he had previously been among those minor ship's companies of the merchant marine, with which companies only had he hitherto consorted.

He was young; and despite his all but fully developed frame in aspect looked even younger than he really was, owing to a lingering adolescent expression in the as yet smooth face all but feminine in purity of natural complexion but where, thanks to his seagoing, the lily was quite suppressed and the rose had some ado visibly to flush through the tan.

To one essentially such a novice in the complexities of factitious life, the abrupt transition from his former and simpler sphere to the ampler and more knowing world of a great war-ship; this might well have abashed him had there been any conceit or vanity in his composition. Among her miscellaneous multitude, the *Indomitable* mustered several individuals who however inferior in grade were of no common natural stamp, sailors more signally susceptive of that air which continuous martial discipline and repeated presence in battle can in some degree impart even to the average man. As the *handsome sailor* Billy Budd's position aboard the seventy-four was something analogous to that of a rustic beauty transplanted from the provinces and brought into competition with the high-born dames of the court. But this change of circumstances he scarce noted. As little did he observe that something about him provoked an ambiguous smile in one or two harder faces among the blue-jackets. Nor less unaware was he of the peculiar favorable effect of his person and demeanor had upon the more intelligent gentlemen of the quarter-deck. Nor could this well have been otherwise. Cast in a mould peculiar to the finest physical examples of those Englishmen in whom the Saxon strain would seem not at all to partake of any Norman or other admixture, he showed in face that humane look of reposeful good nature which the Greek sculptor in some instances gave to his heroic strong man, Hercules. But this again was subtly modified by another and pervasive quality. The ear, small and shapely, the arch of the foot, the curve in mouth and nostril, even the indurated hand dyed to the orange-tawny of the toucan's bill, a hand telling alike of the halyards and tar-bucket; but, above all, something in the mobile expression, and every chance attitude and movement, something suggestive of a mother eminently favored by Love and the Graces; all this strangely indicated a lineage in direct contradiction to his lot. The mysteriousness here, became less mysterious through a matter-of-fact elicited when Billy at the capstan was being formally mustered into the service. Asked by the officer, a small brisk little gentleman as it chanced among other questions, his place of birth, he replied, "Please, Sir, I don't know."

"Don't know where you were born?—Who was your father?"

"God knows, Sir."

Struck by the straightforward simplicity of these replies, the officer next asked, "Do you know anything about your beginning?"

"No, Sir. But I have heard that I was found in a pretty silk-lined basket hanging one morning from the knocker of a good man's door in Bristol."

"*Found* say you? Well," throwing back his head and looking up and down the new recruit; "Well it turns out to have been a pretty good find. Hope they'll find some more like you, my man; the fleet sadly needs them."

Yes, Billy Budd was a foundling, a presumable bye-blow, and, evidently, no ignoble one. Noble descent was as evident in him as in a blood horse.

For the rest, with little or no sharpness of faculty or any trace of the wisdom of the serpent, nor yet quite a dove, he possessed that kind and degree of intelligence going along with the unconventional rectitude of a sound human creature, one to whom not yet has been proffered the questionable apple of knowledge. He was illiterate; he could not read, but he could sing, and like the illiterate nightingale was sometimes the composer of his own song.

Of self-consciousness he seemed to have little or none, or about as much as we may reasonably impute to a dog of Saint Bernard's breed.

Habitually living with the elements and knowing little more of the land than as a beach, or, rather, that portion of the terraqueous globe providentially set apart for dance-houses doxies and tapsters, in short what sailors call a "fiddlers' green," his simple nature remained unsophisticated by those moral obliquities which are not in every case incompatible with that manufacturable thing known as respectability. But are sailors, frequenters of "fiddlers'-greens," without vices? No; but less often than with landsmen do their vices, so called, partake of crookedness of heart, seeming less to proceed from viciousness than exuberance of vitality after long constraint; frank manifestations in accordance with natural law. By his original constitution aided by the cooperating influences of his lot, Billy in many respects was little more than a sort of upright barbarian, much such perhaps as Adam presumably might have been ere the urbane Serpent wriggled himself into his company.

And here be it submitted that apparently going to corroborate the doctrine of man's fall, a doctrine now popularly ignored, it is observable that where certain virtues pristine and unadulterate peculiarly characterize anybody in the external uniform of civilization, they will upon scrutiny seem not to be derived from custom or convention, but rather to be out of keeping with these, as if indeed exceptionally transmitted from a period prior to Cain's city and citified man. The character marked by such qualities has to an unvitiated taste an untampered-with flavor like that of berries, while the man thoroughly civilized even in a fair specimen of the breed has to the same moral palate a questionable smack as of a compounded wine. To any stray inheritor of these primitive qualities found, like Caspar Hauser,[7] wandering dazed in any Christian capital of our time the good-natured poet's famous invocation, near two thousand years ago, of the good rustic out of his latitude in the Rome of the Caesars, still appropriately holds:—

"Honest and poor, Faithful in word and thought
What has thee, Fabian, to the city brought." [8]

---

7. **Caspar Hauser:** a youth discovered in Germany in 1828 who seemingly had been brought up without any exposure to society. His case caused much interest, raising the question: What is human nature like without any (as we would now say) acculturation? 8. "**Honest . . . brought**": Martial, *Epigrams*, IV.5.

Though our Handsome Sailor had as much of masculine beauty as one can expect anywhere to see; nevertheless, like the beautiful woman in one of Hawthorne's minor tales,[9] there was just one thing amiss in him. No visible blemish indeed, as with the lady; no, but an occasional liability to a vocal defect. Though in the hour of elemental uproar or peril, he was everything that a sailor should be, yet under sudden provocation of strong heart-feeling his voice otherwise singularly musical, as if expressive of the harmony within, was apt to develop an organic hesitancy, in fact more or less of a stutter or even worse. In this particular Billy was a striking instance that the arch interferer, the envious marplot of Eden still has more or less to do with every human consignment to this planet of earth. In every case, one way or another he is sure to slip in his little card as much as to remind us—I too have a hand here.

The avowal of such an imperfection in the Handsome Sailor should be evidence not alone that he is not presented as a conventional hero, but also that the story in which he is the main figure is no romance.

3

AT THE TIME of Billy Budd's arbitrary enlistment into the *Indomitable* that ship was on her way to join the Mediterranean fleet. No long time elapsed before the junction was effected. As one of that fleet the seventy-four participated in its movements, though at times on account of her superior sailing qualities, in the absence of frigates, despatched on separate duty as a scout and at times on less temporary service. But with all this the story has little concernment, restricted as it is to the inner life of one particular ship and the career of an individual sailor.

It was the summer of 1797. In the April of that year had occurred the commotion at Spithead followed in May by a second and yet more serious outbreak in the fleet at the Nore. The latter is known, and without exaggeration in the epithet, as the Great Mutiny. It was indeed a demonstration more menacing to England than the contemporary manifestoes and conquering and proselyting armies of the French Directory.

To the British Empire the Nore Mutiny was what a strike in the fire-brigade would be to London threatened by general arson. In a crisis when the kingdom might well have anticipated the famous signal that some years later published along the naval line of battle what it was that upon occa-

sion England expected of Englishmen; *that* was the time when at the mast-heads of the three-deckers and seventy-fours moored in her own roadstead—a fleet, the right arm of a Power then all but the sole free conservative one of the Old World, the blue-jackets, to be numbered by thousands ran up with huzzas the British colors with the union and cross wiped out; by that cancellation transmuting the flag of founded law and freedom defined, into the enemy's red meteor of unbridled and unbounded revolt. Reasonable discontent growing out of practical grievances in the fleet had been ignited into irrational combustion as by live cinders blown across the Channel from France in flames.

The event converted into irony for a time those spirited strains of Dibdin—as a song-writer no mean auxiliary to the English Government at the European conjuncture—strains celebrating, among other things, the patriotic devotion of the British tar:

*"And as for my life, 'tis the King's!"*

Such an episode in the Island's grand naval story her naval historians naturally abridge; one of them (G. P. R. James [10]) candidly acknowledging that fain would he pass it over did not "impartiality forbid fastidiousness." And yet his mention is less a narration than a reference, having to do hardly at all with details. Nor are these readily to be found in the libraries. Like some other events in every age befalling states everywhere including America the Great Mutiny was of such character that national pride along with views of policy would fain shade it off into the historical background. Such events can not be ignored, but there is a considerate way of historically treating them. If a well-constituted individual refrains from blazoning aught amiss or calamitous in his family; a nation in the like circumstance may without reproach be equally discreet.

Though after parleyings between Government and the ringleaders, and concessions by the former as to some glaring abuses, the first uprising—that at Spithead—with difficulty was put down, or matters for the time pacified; yet at the Nore the unforeseen renewal of insurrection on a yet larger scale, and emphasized in the conferences that ensued by demands deemed by the authorities not only inadmissible but aggressively insolent, indicated—if the Red Flag did not sufficiently do so, what was the spirit animating the men. Final suppression, however, there was; but only made pos-

---

9. **tales:** Melville is thinking of "The Birthmark."

10. **G. P. R. James:** apparently a mistake for William James, author of *The Naval History of Great Britain* (1860).

sible perhaps by the unswerving loyalty of the marine corps and a voluntary resumption of loyalty among influential sections of the crews.

To some extent the Nore Mutiny may be regarded as analogous to the distempering irruption of contagious fever in a frame constitutionally sound, and which anon throws it off.

At all events, of these thousands of mutineers were some of the tars who not so very long afterwards—whether wholly prompted thereto by patriotism, or pugnacious instinct, or by both,— helped to win a coronet for Nelson at the Nile, and the naval crown of crowns for him at Trafalgar. To the mutineers those battles and especially Trafalgar were a plenary absolution and a grand one: For all that goes to make up scenic naval display, heroic magnificence in arms, those battles especially Trafalgar stand unmatched in human annals.

4

*Concerning "The greatest sailor since the world began."* TENNYSON?

IN THIS MATTER of writing, resolve as one may to keep to the main road, some by-paths have an enticement not readily to be withstood. I am going to err into such a by-path. If the reader will keep me company I shall be glad. At the least we can promise ourselves that pleasure which is wickedly said to be in sinning, for a literary sin the divergence will be.

Very likely it is no new remark that the inventions of our time have at last brought about a change in sea-warfare in degree corresponding to the revolution in all warfare effected by the original introduction from China into Europe of gunpowder. The first European fire-arm, a clumsy contrivance, was, as is well known, scouted by no few of the knights as a base implement, good enough peradventure for weavers too craven to stand up crossing steel with steel in frank fight. But as ashore knightly valor though shorn of its blazonry did not cease with the knights, neither on the seas though nowadays in encounters there a certain kind of displayed gallantry be fallen out of date as hardly applicable under changed circumstances, did the nobler qualities of such naval magnates as Don John of Austria, Doria, Van Tromp, Jean Bart, the long line of British Admirals and the American Decaturs of 1812 become obsolete with their wooden walls.

Nevertheless, to anybody who can hold the Present at its worth without being inappreciative of the Past, it may be forgiven, if to such an one the solitary old hulk at Portsmouth, Nelson's *Victory*, seems to float there, not alone as the decaying

monument of a fame incorruptible, but also as a poetic reproach, softened by its picturesqueness, to the *Monitors* and yet mightier hulls of the European iron-clads. And this not altogether because such craft are unsightly, unavoidably lacking the symmetry and grand lines of the old battle-ships, but equally for other reasons.

There are some, perhaps, who while not altogether inaccessible to that poetic reproach just alluded to, may yet on behalf of the new order, be disposed to parry it; and this to the extent of iconoclasm, if need be. For example, prompted by the sight of the star inserted in the *Victory's* quarter-deck designating the spot where the Great Sailor fell, these martial utilitarians may suggest considerations implying that Nelson's ornate publication of his person in battle was not only unnecessary, but not military, nay savored of foolhardiness and vanity. They may add, too, that at Trafalgar it was in effect nothing less than a challenge to death; and death came; and that but for his bravado the victorious Admiral might possibly have survived the battle, and so, instead of having his sagacious dying injunctions overruled by his immediate successor in command he himself when the contest was decided might have brought his shattered fleet to anchor, a proceeding which might have averted the deplorable loss of life by shipwreck in the elemental tempest that followed the martial one.

Well, should we set aside the more disputable point whether for various reasons it was possible to anchor the fleet, then plausibly enough the Benthamites [11] of war may urge the above.

But the *might-have-been* is but boggy ground to build on. And, certainly, in foresight as to the larger issue of an encounter, and anxious preparations for it—buoying the deadly way and mapping it out, as at Copenhagen—few commanders have been so painstakingly circumspect as this same reckless declarer of his person in fight.

Personal prudence even when dictated by quite other than selfish considerations surely is no special virtue in a military man; while an excessive love of glory, impassioning a less burning impulse the honest sense of duty, is the first. If the name *Wellington* is not so much of a trumpet to the blood as the simpler name *Nelson,* the reason for this may perhaps be inferred from the above. Alfred in his funeral ode [12] on the victor of Waterloo ventures not to call him the greatest soldier of all time,

11. **Benthamites:** Jeremy Bentham (1748–1832), the philosopher of utilitarianism.  12. **ode:** Tennyson's "Ode on the Death of the Duke of Wellington." Tennyson's line reads, "The greatest sailor since our world began."

though in the same ode he invokes Nelson as "the greatest sailor since the world began."

At Trafalgar Nelson on the brink of opening the fight sat down and wrote his last brief will and testament. If under the presentiment of the most magnificent of all victories to be crowned by his own glorious death, a sort of priestly motive led him to dress his person in the jewelled vouchers of his own shining deeds; if thus to have adorned himself for the altar and the sacrifice were indeed vain-glory, then affectation and fustian is each more heroic line in the great epics and dramas, since in such lines the poet but embodies in verse those exaltations of sentiment that a nature like Nelson, the opportunity being given, vitalizes into acts.

### 5

YES, THE OUTBREAK at the Nore was put down. But not every grievance was redressed. If the contractors, for example, were no longer permitted to ply some practices peculiar to their tribe everywhere, such as providing shoddy cloth, rations not sound, or false in the measure; not the less impressment, for one thing, went on. By custom sanctioned for centuries, and judicially maintained by a Lord Chancellor as late as Mansfield, that mode of manning the fleet, a mode now fallen into a sort of abeyance but never formally renounced, it was not practicable to give up in those years. Its abrogation would have crippled the indispensable fleet, one wholly under canvas, no steam-power, its innumerable sails and thousands of cannon, everything in short, worked by muscle alone; a fleet the more insatiate in demand for men, because then multiplying its ships of all grades against contingencies present and to come of the convulsed Continent.

Discontent foreran the Two Mutinies, and more or less it lurkingly survived them. Hence it was not unreasonable to apprehend some return of trouble sporadic or general. One instance of such apprehensions: In the same year with this story, Nelson, then Vice Admiral Sir Horatio, being with the fleet off the Spanish coast, was directed by the Admiral in command to shift his pennant from the *Captain* to the *Theseus;* and for this reason: that the latter ship having newly arrived on the station from home where it had taken part in the Great Mutiny, danger was apprehended from the temper of the men; and it was thought that an officer like Nelson was the one, not indeed to terrorize the crew into base subjection, but to win them, by force of his mere presence back to an allegiance if not as enthusiastic as his own, yet as true. So it was that for a time on more than one quarter-deck anxiety did exist. At sea precautionary vigilance

was strained against relapse. At short notice an engagement might come on. When it did, the lieutenants assigned to batteries felt it uncumbent on them, in some instances to stand with drawn swords behind the men working the guns.

### 6

BUT ON BOARD the seventy-four in which Billy now swung his hammock, very little in the manner of the men and nothing obvious in the demeanor of the officers would have suggested to an ordinary observer that the Great Mutiny was a recent event. In their general bearing and conduct the commissioned officers of a war-ship naturally take their tone from the commander, that is if he have that ascendancy of character that ought to be his.

Captain the Honorable Edward Fairfax Vere, to give his full title, was a bachelor of forty or thereabouts, a sailor of distinction even in a time prolfic of renowned seamen. Though allied to the higher nobility his advancement had not been altogether owing to influences connected with that circumstance. He had seen much service, been in various engagements, always acquitting himself as an officer mindful of the welfare of his men, but never tolerating an infraction of discipline; thoroughly versed in the science of his profession, and intrepid to the verge of temerity, though never injudiciously so. For his gallantry in the West Indian waters as flag-lieutenant under Rodney [13] in that Admiral's crowning victory over De Grasse, he was made a post-captain.

Ashore in the garb of a civilian scarce anyone would have taken him for a sailor, more especially that he never garnished unprofessional talk with nautical terms, and grave in his bearing, evinced little appreciation of mere humor. It was not out of keeping with these traits that on a passage when nothing demanded his paramount action, he was the most undemonstrative of men. Any landsman observing this gentleman not conspicuous by his stature and wearing no pronounced insignia, emerging from his cabin retreat to the open deck, and noting the silent deference of the officers retiring to leeward, might have taken him for the King's guest, a civilian aboard the King's-ship, some highly honorable discreet envoy on his way to an important post. But in fact this unobtrusiveness of demeanor may have proceeded from a certain unaffected modesty of manhood sometimes accompanying a resolute nature, a modesty evinced at all times not calling for pronounced action, and

---

13. **Rodney:** Admiral George Brydges Rodney (1719-92) defeated the French Admiral de Grasse off Martinique in 1782.

which shown in any rank of life suggests a virtue aristocratic in kind.

As with some others engaged in various departments of the world's more heroic activities, Captain Vere though practical enough upon occasion would at times betray a certain dreaminess of mood. Standing alone on the weather-side of the quarter deck, one hand holding by the rigging he would absently gaze off at the blank sea. At the presentation to him then of some minor matter interrupting the current of his thoughts he would show more or less irascibility; but instantly he would control it.

In the navy he was popularly known by the appellation—Starry Vere. How such a designation happened to fall upon one who whatever his sterling qualities was without any brilliant ones was in this wise: A favorite kinsman, Lord Denton, a free-hearted fellow, had been the first to meet and congratulate him upon his return to England from his West Indian cruise; and but the day previous turning over a copy of Andrew Marvell's poems had lighted, not for the first time however, upon the lines entitled *Appleton House,* the name of one of the seats of their common ancestor, a hero in the German wars of the seventeenth century, in which poem occur the lines,

> "This 'tis to have been from the first
> In a domestic heaven nursed,
> Under the discipline severe
> Of Fairfax and the starry Vere."

And so, upon embracing his cousin fresh from Rodney's great victory wherein he had played so gallant a part, brimming over with just family pride in the sailor of their house, he exuberantly exclaimed, "Give ye joy, Ed; give ye joy, my starray Vere!" This got currency, and the novel prefix serving in familiar parlance readily to distinguish the *Indomitable's* Captain from another Vere his senior, a distant relative an officer of like rank in the navy, it remained permanently attached to the surname.

7

In view of the part that the commander of the *Indomitable* plays in scenes shortly to follow, it may be well to fill out that sketch of him outlined in the previous chapter.

Aside from his qualities as a sea-officer Captain Vere was an exceptional character. Unlike no few of England's renowned sailors, long and arduous service with signal devotion to it, had not resulted in absorbing and *salting* the entire man. He had a marked leaning toward everything intellectual. He

loved books, never going to sea without a newly replenished library, compact but of the best. The isolated leisure, in some cases so wearisome, falling at intervals to commanders even during a war-cruise, never was tedious to Captain Vere. With nothing of that literary taste which less heeds the thing conveyed than the vehicle, his bias was toward those books to which every serious mind of superior order occupying any active post of authority in the world, naturally inclines: books treating of actual men and events no matter of what era—history, biography and unconventional writers, who, free from cant and convention, like Montaigne, honestly and in the spirit of common sense philosophize upon realities.

In this love of reading he found confirmation of his own more reserved thoughts—confirmation which he had vainly sought in social converse, so that as touching most fundamental topics, there had got to be established in him some positive convictions, which he forefelt would abide in him essentially unmodified so long as his intelligent part remained unimpaired. In view of the troubled period in which his lot was cast this was well for him. His settled convictions were as a dyke against those invading waters of novel opinion social political and otherwise, which carried away as in a torrent no few minds in those days, minds by nature not inferior to his own. While other members of that aristocracy to which by birth he belonged were incensed at the innovators mainly because their theories were inimical to the privileged classes, not alone Captain Vere disinterestedly opposed them because they seemed to him incapable of embodiment in lasting institutions, but at war with the peace of the world and the true welfare of mankind.

With minds less stored than his and less earnest, some officers of his rank, with whom at times he would necessarily consort, found him lacking in the companionable quality, a dry and bookish gentleman, as they deemed. Upon any chance withdrawal from their company one would be apt to say to another, something like this: "Vere is a noble fellow, Starry Vere. Spite the gazettes, Sir Horatio" meaning him with the Lord title "is at bottom scarce a better seaman or fighter. But between you and me now don't you think there is a queer streak of the pedantic running through him? Yes, like the King's yarn in a coil of navy-rope?"

Some apparent ground there was for this sort of confidential criticism; since not only did the Captain's discourse never fall into the jocosely familiar, but in illustrating of any point touching the stirring personages and events of the time as that he would be as apt to cite some historic character or incident of antiquity as he would to cite from the moderns. He seemed unmindful of the circumstance that to his bluff company such remote allusions however pertinent they might really be were altogether alien to men whose reading was mainly confined to the journals. But considerateness in such matters is not easy to natures constituted like Captain Vere's. Their honesty prescribes to them directness, sometimes far-reaching like that of a migratory fowl that in its flight never heeds when it crosses a frontier.

8

THE LIEUTENANTS and other commissioned gentlemen forming Captain Vere's staff it is not necessary here to particularize, nor needs it to make any mention of any of the warrant-officers. But among the petty-officers was one who having much to do with the story, may as well be forthwith introduced. His portrait I essay, but shall never hit it. This was John Claggart, the Master-at-arms. But that sea-title may to landsmen seem somewhat equivocal. Originally doubtless that petty-officer's function was the instruction of the men in the use of arms, sword or cutlas. But very long ago, owing to the advance in gunnery making hand-to-hand encounters less frequent and giving to nitre and sulphur the preeminence over steel, that function ceased; the Master-at-arms of a great war-ship becoming a sort of Chief of Police charged among other matters with the duty of preserving order on the populous lower gun-decks.

Claggart was a man about five and thirty, somewhat spare and tall, yet of no ill figure upon the whole. His hand was too small and shapely to have been accustomed to hard toil. The face was a notable one; the features all except the chin cleanly cut as those on a Greek medallion; yet the chin, beardless as Tecumseh's,[14] had something of strange protuberant heaviness in its make that recalled the prints of the Rev. Dr. Titus Oates, the historic deponent with the clerical drawl in the time of Charles II and the fraud of the alleged Popish Plot.[15] It served Claggart in his office that his eye could cast a tutoring glance. His brow was of the sort phrenologically associated with more than average intellect; silken jet curls partly clustering over it, making a foil to the pallor below, a pallor tinged with a faint shade of amber akin to the hue of time-tinted marbles of old. This complexion, singularly contrasting with the red or

deeply bronzed visages of the sailors, and in part the result of his official seclusion from the sunlight, though it was not exactly displeasing, nevertheless seemed to hint of something defective or abnormal in the constitution and blood. But his general aspect and manner were so suggestive of an education and career incongruous with his naval function that when not actively engaged in it he looked like a man of high quality, social and moral, who for reasons of his own was keeping incog. Nothing was known of his former life. It might be that he was an Englishman; and yet there lurked a bit of accent in his speech suggesting that possibly he was not such by birth, but through naturalization in early childhood. Among certain grizzled sea-gossips of the gun-decks and forecastle went a rumor perdue that the master-at-arms was a *chevalier* who had volunteered into the King's navy by way of compounding for some mysterious swindle whereof he had been arraigned at the King's Bench. The fact that nobody could substantiate this report was, of course, nothing against its secret currency. Such a rumor once started on the gun-decks in reference to almost anyone below the rank of a commissioned officer would, during the period assigned to this narrative, have seemed not altogether wanting in credibility to the tarry old wiseacres of a man-of-war crew. And indeed a man of Claggart's accomplishments, without prior nautical experience entering the navy at mature life, as he did, and necessarily allotted at the start to the lowest grade in it; a man too who never made allusion to his previous life ashore; these were circumstances which in the dearth of exact knowledge as to his true antecedents opened to the invidious a vague field for unfavorable surmise.

But the sailors' dog-watch gossip concerning him derived a vague plausibility from the fact that now for some period the British Navy could so little afford to be squeamish in the matter of keeping up the muster-rolls, that not only were press-gangs notoriously abroad both afloat and ashore, but there was little or no secret about another matter, namely that the London police were at liberty to capture any able-bodied suspect, any questionable fellow at large and summarily ship him to the dock-yard or fleet. Furthermore, even among voluntary enlistments there were instances where the motive thereto partook neither of patriotic impulse nor yet of a random desire to experience a bit of sea-life and martial adventure. Insolvent debtors of minor grade, together with the promiscuous lame ducks of morality found in the Navy a convenient and secure refuge. Secure, because once enlisted aboard a King's-Ship, they were as much in sanc-

---

14. **Tecumseh:** American Indian chief (1768?–1813).   15. **Popish Plot:** In 1687 the Reverend Titus Oates caused a great stir in London by alleging that the Catholics were about to subvert England.

tuary, as the transgressor of the Middle Ages harboring himself under the shadow of the altar. Such sanctioned irregularities which for obvious reasons the Government would hardly think to parade at the time and which consequently, and as affecting the least influential class of mankind, have all but dropped into oblivion, lend color to something for the truth whereof I do not vouch, and hence have some scruple in stating; something I remember having seen in print though the book I can not recall; but the same thing was personally communicated to me now more than forty years ago by an old pensioner in a cocked hat with whom I had a most interesting talk on the terrace at Greenwich, a Baltimore Negro, a Trafalgar man. It was to this effect: In the case of a warship short of hands whose speedy sailing was imperative, the deficient quota in lack of any other way of making it good, would be eked out by draughts culled direct from the jails. For reasons previously suggested it would not perhaps be easy at the present day directly to prove or disprove the allegation. But allowed as a verity, how significant would it be of England's straits at the time confronted by those wars which like a flight of harpies rose shrieking from the din and dust of the fallen bastille. That era appears measurably clear to us who look back at it, and but read of it. But to the grandfathers of us graybeards, the more thoughtful of them, the genius of it presented an aspect like that of Camoen's [16] Spirit of the Cape, an eclipsing menace mysterious and prodigious. Not America was exempt from apprehension. At the height of Napoleon's unexampled conquests, there were Americans who had fought at Bunker Hill who looked forward to the possibility that the Atlantic might prove no barrier against the ultimate schemes of this French portentous upstart from the revolutionary chaos who seemed in act of fulfilling judgment prefigured in the Apocalypse.[17]

But the less credence was to be given to the gundeck talk touching Claggart, seeing that no man holding his office in a man-of-war can ever hope to be popular with the crew. Besides, in derogatory comments upon anyone against whom they have a grudge, or for any reason or no reason mislike, sailors are much like landsmen, they are apt to exaggerate or romance it.

About as much was really known to the *Indomitable's* tars of the master-at-arms' career before entering the service as an astronomer knows about a comet's travels prior to its first observable appearance in the sky. The verdict of the sea quid-

nuncs has been cited only by way of showing what sort of moral impression the man made upon rude uncultivated natures whose conceptions of human wickedness were necessarily of the narrowest, limited to ideas of vulgar rascality,—a thief among the swinging hammocks during a night-watch, or the man-brokers and land-sharks of the sea-ports.

It was no gossip, however, but fact, that though, as before hinted, Claggart upon his entrance into the navy was, as a novice, assigned to the least honorable section of a man-of-war's crew, embracing the drudgery, he did not long remain there.

The superior capacity he immediately evinced, his constitutional sobriety, ingratiating deference to superiors, together with a peculiar ferreting genius manifested on a singular occasion, all this capped by a certain austere patriotism abruptly advanced him to the position of master-at-arms.

Of this maritime Chief of Police the ship's-corporals, so called, were the immediate subordinates, and compliant ones; and this, as is to be noted in some business departments ashore, almost to a degree inconsistent with entire moral volition. His place put various converging wires of underground influence under the Chief's control, capable when astutely worked through his understrappers of operating to the mysterious discomfort if nothing worse, of any of the sea-commonalty.

### 9

LIFE in the fore-top well agreed with Billy Budd. There, when not actually engaged on the yards yet higher aloft, the topmen, who as such had been picked out for youth and activity, constituted an aerial club lounging at ease against the smaller stun'sails rolled up into cushions, spinning yarns like the lazy gods, and frequently amused with what was going on in the busy world of the decks below. No wonder then that a young fellow of Billy's disposition was well content in such society. Giving no cause of offence to anybody, he was always alert at a call. So in the merchant service it had been with him. But now such a punctiliousness in duty was shown that his topmates would sometimes good-naturedly laugh at him for it. This heightened alacrity had its cause, namely, the impression made upon him by the first formal gangway-punishment he had ever witnessed, which befell the day following his impressment. It had been incurred by a little fellow, young, a novice, an after-guardsman absent from his assigned post when the ship was being put about; a dereliction resulting in a rather serious hitch to that manœuvre, one demanding instantaneous promptitude in letting go and making fast. When Billy saw the culprit's

16. **Camoen's:** Melville was fond of the epic poem the *Lusiads* by Luis de Camoëns (1524–80).   17. **Apocalypse:** Revelation, the last book of the Bible.

naked back under the scourge gridironed with red welts, and worse; when he marked the dire expression on the liberated man's face as with his woolen shirt flung over him by the executioner he rushed forward from the spot to bury himself in the crowd, Billy was horrified. He resolved that never through remissness would he make himself liable to such a visitation or do or omit aught that might merit even verbal reproof. What then was his surprise and concern when ultimately he found himself getting into petty trouble occasionally about such matters as the stowage of his bag or something amiss in his hammock, matters under the police oversight of the ship's-corporals of the lower decks, and which brought down on him a vague threat from one of them.

So heedful in all things as he was, how could this be? He could not understand it, and it more than vexed him. When he spoke to his young topmates about it they were either lightly incredulous or found something comical in his unconcealed anxiety. "Is it your bag, Billy?" said one, "well, sew yourself up in it, bully boy, and then you'll be sure to know if anybody meddles with it."

Now there was a veteran aboard who because his years began to disqualify him for more active work had been recently assigned duty as mainmast-man in his watch, looking to the gear belayed at the rail roundabout that great spar near the deck. At off-times the foretopman had picked up some acquaintance with him, and now in his trouble it occurred to him that he might be the sort of person to go to for wise counsel. He was an old Dansker [18] long anglicized in the service, of few words, many wrinkles and some honorable scars. His wizened face, time-tinted and weather-stained to the complexion of an antique parchment, was here and there peppered blue by the chance explosion of a gun-cartridge in action. He was an *Agamemnon*-man; some two years prior to the time of this story having served under Nelson when but Sir Horatio in that ship immortal in naval memory, and which dismantled and in part broken up to her bare ribs is seen a grand skeleton in Haydon's etching. As one of a boarding-party from the *Agamemnon* he had received a cut slantwise along one temple and cheek leaving a long pale scar like a streak of dawn's light falling athwart the dark visage. It was on account of that scar and the affair in which it was known that he had received it, as well as from his blue-peppered complexion that the Dansker went among the *Indomitable's* crew by the name of "Board-her-in-the-smoke."

Now the first time that his small weazel-eyes happened to light on Billy Budd, a certain grim internal merriment set all his ancient wrinkles into antic play. Was it that his eccentric unsentimental old sapience primitive in its kind saw or thought it saw something which in contrast with the warship's environment looked oddly incongruous in the handsome sailor? But after slyly studying him at intervals, the old Merlin's [19] equivocal merriment was modified; for now when the twain would meet, it would start in his face a quizzing sort of look, but it would be but momentary and sometimes replaced by an expression of speculative query as to what might eventually befall a nature like that, dropped into a world not without some man-traps and against whose subtleties simple courage lacking experience and address and without any touch of defensive ugliness, is of little avail; and where such innocence as man is capable of does yet in a moral emergency not always sharpen the faculties or enlighten the will.

However it was the Dansker in his ascetic way rather took to Billy. Nor was this only because of a certain philosophic interest in such a character. There was another cause. While the old man's eccentricities, sometimes bordering on the ursine, repelled the juniors, Billy, undeterred thereby, revering him as a salt hero would make advances, never passing the old Agamemnon-man without a salutation marked by that respect which is seldom lost on the aged however crabbed at times or whatever their station in life.

There was a vein of dry humor, or what not, in the mastman; and, whether in freak of patriarchal irony touching Billy's youth and athletic frame, or for some other and more recondite reason, from the first in addressing him he always substituted Baby for Billy. The Dansker in fact being the originator of the name by which the foretopman eventually became known aboard ship.

Well then, in his mysterious little difficulty going in quest of the wrinkled one, Billy found him off duty in a dog-watch ruminating by himself seated on a shot-box of the upper gun-deck now and then surveying with a somewhat cynical regard certain of the more swaggering promenaders there. Billy recounted his trouble, again wondering how it all happened. The salt seer attentively listened, accompanying the foretopman's recital with queer twitchings of his wrinkles and problematical little sparkles of his small ferret eyes. Making an end of his story, the foretopman asked, "And now, Dansker, do tell me what you think of it."

The old man, shoving up the front of his tarpaulin and deliberately rubbing the long slant scar at the point where it entered the thin hair, laconically

---

18. **Dansker:** Dane.

19. **Merlin:** the magician who figures in the legends of King Arthur.

said, "Baby Budd, *Jimmy Legs*" (meaning the master-at-arms) "is down on you."

"*Jimmy Legs!*" ejaculated Billy, his welkin eyes expanding; "what for? Why he calls me *the sweet and pleasant young fellow,* they tell me."

"Does he so?" grinned the grizzled one; then said, "Ay, Baby Lad, a sweet voice has *Jimmy Legs.*"

"No, not always. But to me he has. I seldom pass him but there comes a pleasant word."

"And that's because he's down upon you, Baby Budd."

Such reiteration along with the manner of it, incomprehensible to a novice, disturbed Billy almost as much as the mystery for which he had sought explanation. Something less unpleasingly oracular he tried to extract; but the old sea-Chiron thinking perhaps that for the nonce he had sufficiently instructed his young Achilles, pursed his lips, gathered all his wrinkles together and would commit himself to nothing further.

Years, and those experiences which befall certain shrewder men subordinated life-long to the will of superiors, all this had developed in the Dansker the pithy guarded cynicism that was his leading characteristic.

10

THE NEXT DAY an incident served to confirm Billy Budd in his incredulity as to the Dansker's strange summing up of the case submitted. The ship at noon going large before the wind was rolling on her course, and he below at dinner and engaged in some sportful talk with the members of his mess, chanced in a sudden lurch to spill the entire contents of his soup-pan upon the new scrubbed deck. Claggart, the Master-at-arms, offical rattan in hand, happened to be passing along the battery in a bay of which the mess was lodged, and the greasy liquid streamed just across his path. Stepping over it, he was proceeding on his way without comment, since the matter was nothing to take notice of under the circumstances, when he happened to observe who it was that had done the spilling. His countenance changed. Pausing, he was about to ejaculate something hasty at the sailor, but checked himself, and pointing down to the streaming soup, playfully tapped him from behind with his rattan, saying in a low musical voice peculiar to him at times, "Handsomely done, my lad! And handsome is as handsome did it too!" And with that passed on. Not noted by Billy as not coming within his view was the involuntary smile, or rather grimace, that accompanied Claggart's equivocal words. Aridly it drew down the

thin corners of his shapely mouth. But everybody taking his remark as meant for humorous, and at which therefore as coming from a superior they were bound to laugh, "with counterfeited glee" acted accordingly; and Billy tickled, it may be, by the allusion to his being the handsome sailor, merrily joined in; then addressing his messmates exclaimed "There now, who says that Jimmy Legs is down on me!" "And who said he was, Beauty?" demanded one Donald with some surprise. Whereat the foretopman looked a little foolish recalling that it was only one person, Board-her-in-the-smoke, who had suggested what to him was the smoky idea that this master-at-arms was in any peculiar way hostile to him. Meantime that functionary resuming his path must have momentarily worn some expression less guarded than that of the bitter smile, and usurping the face from the heart, some distorting expression perhaps, for a drummer-boy heedlessly frolicking along from the opposite direction and chancing to come into light collision with his person was strangely disconcerted by his aspect. Nor was the impression lessened when the official impulsively giving him a sharp cut with the rattan, vehemently exclaimed, "Look where you go!"

11

WHAT was the matter with the master-at-arms? And, be the matter what it might, how could it have direct relation to Billy Budd with whom prior to the affair of the spilled soup he had never come into any special contact official or otherwise? What indeed could the trouble have to do with one so little inclined to give offence as the merchant-ship's *peacemaker,* even him who in Claggart's own phrase was "the sweet and pleasant young fellow"? Yes, why should *Jimmy Legs,* to borrow the Dansker's expression, be *down* on the Handsome Sailor? But, at heart and not for nothing, as the later chance encounter may indicate to the discerning, down on him, secretly down on him, he assuredly was.

Now to invent something touching the more private career of Claggart, something involving Billy Budd, of which something the latter should be wholly ignorant, some romantic incident implying that Claggart's knowledge of the young blue-jacket began at some period anterior to catching sight of him on board the seventy-four—all this, not so difficult to do, might avail in a way more or less interesting to account for whatever of enigma may appear to lurk in the case. But in fact there was nothing of the sort. And yet the cause, necessarily to be assumed as the sole one assignable, is in its very realism as much charged with that prime element of Radcliffian [20] romance, *the mysterious,* as any that the ingenuity of the author of the *Mysteries of Udolpho* could devise. For what can more partake of the mysterious than an antipathy spontaneous and profound such as is evoked in certain exceptional mortals by the mere aspect of some other mortal, however harmless he may be? if not called forth by this very harmlessness itself.

Now there can exist no irritating juxtaposition of dissimilar personalities comparable to that which is possible aboard a great war-ship fully manned and at sea. There, every day among all ranks almost every man comes into more or less of contact with almost every other man. Wholly there to avoid even the sight of an aggravating object one must needs give it Jonah's toss or jump overboard himself. Imagine how all this might eventually operate on some peculiar human creature the direct reverse of a saint?

But for the adequate comprehending of Claggart by a normal nature these hints are insufficient. To pass from a normal nature to him one must cross "the deadly space between." And this is best done by indirection.

Long ago an honest scholar my senior, said to me in reference to one who like himself is now no more, a man so unimpeachably respectable that against him nothing was ever openly said though among the few something was whispered, "Yes, X—— is a nut not to be cracked by the tap of a lady's fan. You are aware that I am the adherent of no organized religion much less of any philosophy built into a system. Well, for all that, I think that to try and get into X——, enter his labyrinth and get out again, without a clue derived from some source other than what is known as *knowledge of the world*—that were hardly possible, at least for me."

"Why," said I, "X—— however singular a study to some, is yet human, and knowledge of the world assuredly implies the knowledge of human nature, and in most of its varieties."

"Yes, but a superficial knowledge of it, serving ordinary purposes. But for anything deeper, I am not certain whether to know the world and to know human nature be not two distinct branches of knowledge, which while they may coexist in the same heart, yet either may exist with little or nothing of the other. Nay, in an average man of the world, his constant rubbing with it blunts that fine spiritual insight indispensable to the understanding of the essential in certain exceptional characters, whether evil ones or good. In a matter of some importance I have seen a girl wind an old lawyer

20. Radcliffian: Ann Radcliffe (1764–1823), author of *The Mysteries of Udolpho* and other Gothic romances.

about her little finger. Nor was it the dotage of senile love. Nothing of the sort. But he knew law better than he knew the girl's heart. Coke and Blackstone hardly shed so much light into obscure spiritual places as the Hebrew prophets. And who were they? Mostly recluses."

At the time my inexperience was such that I did not quite see the drift of all this. It may be that I see it now. And, indeed, if that lexicon which is based on Holy Writ were any longer popular, one might with less difficulty define and denominate certain phenomenal men. As it is, one must turn to some authority not liable to the charge of being tinctured with the Biblical element.

In a list of definitions included in the authentic translation of Plato, a list attributed to him, occurs this: "Natural Depravity: a depravity according to nature." A definition which though savoring of Calvinism, by no means involves Calvin's dogma as to total mankind. Evidently its intent makes it applicable but to individuals. Not many are the examples of this depravity which the gallows and jail supply. At any rate for notable instances, since these have no vulgar alloy of the brute in them, but invariably are dominated by intellectuality, one must go elsewhere. Civilization, especially if of the austerer sort, is auspicious to it. It folds itself in the mantle of respectability. It has its certain negative virtues serving as silent auxiliaries. It never allows wine to get within in its guard. It is not going too far to say that it is without vices or small sins. There is a phenomenal pride in it that excludes them from anything mercenary or avaricious. In short the depravity here meant partakes nothing of the sordid or sensual. It is serious, but free from acerbity. Though no flatterer of mankind it never speaks ill of it.

But the thing which in eminent instances signalizes so exceptional a nature is this: though the man's even temper and discreet bearing would seem to intimate a mind peculiarly subject to the law of reason, not the less in his heart he would seem to riot in complete exemption from that law having apparently little to do with reason further than to employ it as an ambidexter implement for effecting the irrational. That is to say: Toward the accomplishment of an aim which in wantonness of malignity would seem to partake of the insane, he will direct a cool judgement sagacious and sound.

These men are true madmen, and of the most dangerous sort, for their lunacy is not continuous but occasional evoked by some special object; it is probably secretive, which is as much to say it is self-contained, so that when moreover, most active it is to the average mind not distinguishable from sanity, and for the reason above suggested that whatever its aims may be, and the aim is never declared—the method and the outward proceeding are always perfectly rational.

Now something such an one was Claggart, in whom was the mania of an evil nature, not engendered by vicious training or corrupting books or licentious living, but born with him and innate, in short "a depravity according to nature."

## 12

### *Lawyers, Experts, Clergy*
#### AN EPISODE

BY THE WAY, can it be the phenomenon, disowned or at least concealed, that in some criminal cases puzzles the courts? For this cause have our juries at times not only to endure the prolonged contentions of lawyers with their fees, but also the yet more perplexing strife of the medical experts with theirs?—But why leave it to them? why not subpoena(?) as well the clerical proficients? Their vocation bringing them into peculiar contact with so many human beings, and sometimes in their least guarded hour, in interviews very much more confidential than those of physician and patient; this would seem to qualify them to know something about those intricacies involved in the question of moral responsibility; whether in a given case, say, the crime proceeded from mania in the brain or rabies of the heart. As to any differences among themselves these clerical proficients might develop on the stand, these could hardly be greater than the direct contradictions exchanged between the remunerated medical experts.

Dark sayings are these, some will say. But why? Is it because they somewhat savor of Holy Writ in its phrase "mysteries of iniquity"? If they do, such savor was far enough from being intended for little will it commend these pages to many a reader of to-day.

The point of the present story turning on the hidden nature of the master-at-arms has necessitated this chapter. With an added hint or two in connection with the incident at the mess, the resumed narrative must be left to vindicate, as it may, its own credibility.

## 13

### *Pale ire, envy and despair* [21]

THAT Claggart's figure was not amiss, and his face, save the chin, well moulded, has already been said. Of these favorable points he seemed

not insensible, for he was not only neat but careful in his dress. But the form of Billy Budd was heroic; and if his face was without the intellectual look of the pallid Claggart's, not the less was it lit, like his, from within, though from a different source. The bonfire in his heart made luminous the rose-tan in his cheek.

In view of the marked contrast between the persons of the twain, it is more than probable that when the master-at-arms in the scene last given applied to the sailor the proverb *Handsome is as handsome does;* he there let escape an ironic inkling, not caught by the young sailors who heard it, as to what it was that had first moved him against Billy, namely, his significant personal beauty.

Now envy and antipathy passions irreconcilable in reason, nevertheless in fact may spring conjoined like Chang and Eng [22] in one birth. Is Envy then such a monster? Well, though many an arraigned mortal has in hopes of mitigated penalty pleaded guilty to horrible actions, did ever anybody seriously confess to envy? Something there is in it universally felt to be more shameful than even felonious crime. And not only does everybody disown it but the better sort are inclined to incredulity when it is in earnest imputed to an intelligent man. But since its lodgement is in the heart not the brain, no degree of intellect supplies a guarantee against it. But Claggart's was no vulgar form of the passion. Nor, as directed toward Billy Budd did it partake of that streak of apprehensive jealousy that marred Saul's visage perturbedly brooding on the comely young David. [23] Claggart's envy struck deeper. If askance he eyed the good looks, cheery health and frank enjoyment of young life in Billy Budd, it was because these went along with a nature that as Claggart magnetically felt, had in its simplicity never willed malice or experienced the reactionary bite of that serpent. To him, the spirit lodged within Billy, and looking out from his welkin eyes as from windows, that ineffability it was which made the dimple in his dyed cheek, suppled his joints, and dancing in his yellow curls made him preeminently the Handsome Sailor. One person excepted the master-at-arms was perhaps the only man in the ship intellectually capable of adequately appreciating the moral phenomenon presented in Billy Budd. And the insight but intensified his passion, which assuming various secret forms within him, at times assumed that of cynic disdain—disdain of innocence—To be nothing more than innocent! Yet in an aesthetic way he saw the charm of it, the courageous free-and-easy temper of it, and fain would have shared it, but he despaired of it.

---

21. *Pale . . . despair:* description of Satan in Milton's *Paradise Lost*, IV.115.

22. **Chang and Eng:** Siamese twins famous in Melville's time.
23. **Saul's . . . David:** I Sam. 18:9 ff.

With no power to annul the elemental evil in him, though readily enough he could hide it; apprehending the good, but powerless to be it; a nature like Claggart's surcharged with energy as such natures almost invariably are, what recourse is left to it but to recoil upon itself and like the scorpion for which the Creator alone is responsible, act out to the end the part allotted it.

### 14

PASSION, and passion in its profoundest, is not a thing demanding a palatial stage whereon to play its part. Down among the groundlings, among the beggars and rakers of the garbage, profound passion is enacted. And the circumstances that provoke it, however trivial or mean, are no measure of its power. In the present instance the stage is a scrubbed gun-deck, and one of the external provocations a man-of-war's-man's spilled soup.

Now when the Master-at-arms noticed whence came that greasy fluid streaming before his feet, he must have taken it—to some extent wilfully, perhaps—not for the mere accident it assuredly was, but for the sly escape of a spontaneous feeling on Billy's part more or less answering to the antipathy on his own. In effect a foolish demonstration he must have thought, and very harmless, like the futile kick of a heifer, which yet were the heifer a shod stallion, would not be so harmless. Even so was it that into the gall of Claggart's envy he infused the vitriol of his contempt. But the incident confirmed to him certain tell-tale reports purveyed to his ear by *Squeak,* one of his more cunning Corporals, a grizzled little man, so nicknamed by the sailors on account of his squeaky voice, and sharp visage ferreting about the dark corners of the lower decks after interlopers, satirically suggesting to them the idea of a rat in a cellar.

From his Chief's employing him as an implicit tool in laying little traps for the worriment of the Foretopman—for it was from the Master-at-arms that the petty persecutions heretofore adverted to had proceeded—the corporal having naturally enough concluded that his master could have no love for the sailor, made it his business, faithful understrapper that he was, to foment the ill blood by perverting to his Chief certain innocent frolics of the good natured Foretopman, besides inventing for his mouth sundry contumelious epithets he claimed to have overheard him let fall. The Master-at-arms never suspected the veracity of these reports, more especially as to the epithets, for he well knew how secretly unpopular may become a master-at-arms at least a master-at-arms of those days zealous in his function, and how the blue-

jackets shoot at him in private their raillery and wit; the nickname by which he goes among them (*Jimmy Legs*) implying under the form of merriment their cherished disrespect and dislike.

But in view of the greediness of hate for patrolmen it hardly needed a purveyor to feed Claggart's passion. An uncommon prudence is habitual with the subtler depravity, for it has everything to hide. And in case of an injury but suspected, its secretiveness voluntarily cuts it off from enlightenment or disillusion; and, not unreluctantly, action is taken upon surmise as upon certainty. And the retaliation is apt to be in monstrous disproportion to the supposed offence; for when in anybody was revenge in its exactions aught else but an inordinate usurer. But how with Claggart's conscience? for though consciences are unlike as foreheads, every intelligence, not excluding the Scriptural devils who "believe and tremble," has one. But Claggart's conscience being but the lawyer to his will, made ogres of trifles, probably arguing that the motive imputed to Billy in spilling the soup just when he did, together with the epithets alleged, these, if nothing more, made a strong case against him; nay, justified animosity into a sort of retributive righteousness. The Pharisee is the Guy Fawkes [24] prowling in the hid chambers underlying the Claggarts. And they can really form no conception of an unreciprocated malice. Probably, the master-at-arms' clandestine persecution of Billy was started to try the temper of the man; but it had not developed any quality in him that enmity could make official use of or even pervert into even plausible self-justification; so that the occurrence at the mess, petty if it were, was a welcome one to that peculiar conscience assigned to be the private mentor of Claggart; and, for the rest, not improbably it put him upon new experiments.

### 15

NOT MANY DAYS after the last incident narrated something befell Billy Budd that more gravelled him than aught that had previously occurred.

It was a warm night for the latitude; and the Foretopman, whose watch at the time was properly below, was dozing on the uppermost deck whither he had ascended from his hot hammock one of hundreds suspended so closely wedged together over a lower gun-deck that there was little or no swing to them. He lay as in the shadow of a hill-side, stretched under the lee of the *booms,* a piled ridge of spare spars amidships between foremast and mainmast and among which the ship's

24. **Guy Fawkes:** Fawkes plotted to blow up the Houses of Parliament in 1605.

largest boat, the launch, was stowed. Alongside of three other slumberers from below, he lay near that end of the booms which approaches the foremast; his station aloft on duty as a foretopman being just over the deck-station of the forecastlemen, entitling him according to usage to make himself more or less at home in that neighborhood.

Presently he was stirred into semi-consciousness by somebody, who must have previously sounded the sleep of the others, touching his shoulder, and then as the Foretopman raised his head, breathing into his ear in a quick whisper, "Slip into the lee forechains, Billy; there is something in the wind. Don't speak. Quick, I will meet you there;" and disappeared.

Now Billy like sundry other essentially good natured ones had some of the weaknesses inseparable from essential good nature; and among these was a reluctance, almost an incapacity of plumply saying *no* to an abrupt proposition not obviously absurd, on the face of it, nor obviously unfriendly, nor iniquitous. And being of warm blood he had not the phlegm tacitly to negative any proposition by unresponsive inaction. Like his sense of fear, his apprehension as to aught outside of the honest and natural was seldom very quick. Besides, upon the present occasion, the drowse from his sleep still hung upon him.

However it was, he mechanically rose, and sleepily wondering what could be in the wind, betook himself to the designated place, a narrow platform, one of six, outside of the high bulwarks and screened by the great dead-eyes and multiple columned lanyards of the shrouds and backstays; and, in a great war-ship of that time, of dimensions commensurate to the hull's magnitude; a tarry balcony in short overhanging the sea, and so secluded that one mariner of the *Indomitable,* a non-conformist old tar of a serious turn, made it even in daytime his private oratory.

In this retired nook the stranger soon joined Billy Budd. There was no moon as yet; a haze obscured the star-light. He could not distinctly see the stranger's face. Yet from something in the outline and carriage, Billy took him to be, and correctly, for one of the afterguard.

"Hist! Billy," said the man in the same quick cautionary whisper as before. "You were impressed, weren't you? Well, so was I," and he paused, as to mark the effect. But Billy not knowing exactly what to make of this said nothing. Then the other: "We are not the only impressed ones, Billy. There's a gang of us.—Couldn't you—help—at a pinch?"

"What do you mean?" demanded Billy here shaking off his drowse.

"Hist, hist!" the hurried whisper now growing

husky, "see here;" and the man held up two small objects faintly twinkling in the nightlight; "see, they are yours, Billy, if you'll only——"

But Billy broke in, and in his resentful eagerness to deliver himself his vocal infirmity somewhat intruded: "D-D-Damme, I don't know what you are d-d-driving at, or what you mean, but you had better g-g-go where you belong!" For the moment the fellow, as confounded, did not stir; and Billy springing to his feet, said, "If you d-don't start I'll t-t-toss you back over the r-rail!" There was no mistaking this and the mysterious emissary decamped disappearing in the direction of the mainmast in the shadow of the booms.

"Hallo, what's the matter?" here came growling from a forecastleman awakened from his deck-doze by Billy's raised voice. And as the foretopman reappeared and was recognized by him; "Ah, *Beauty,* is it you? Well, something must have been the matter for you st-st-stuttered."

"O," rejoined Billy, now mastering the impediment; "I found an afterguardsman in our part of the ship here and I bid him be off where he belongs."

"And is that all you did about it, foretopman?" gruffly demanded another, an irascible old fellow of brick-colored visage and hair, and who was known to his associate forecastlemen as *Red Pepper;* "such sneaks I should like to marry to the gunner's daughter!" by that expression meaning that he would like to subject them to disciplinary castigation over a gun.

However, Billy's rendering of the matter satisfactorily accounted to these inquirers for the brief commotion, since of all the sections of a ship's company the forecastlemen, veterans for the most part and bigoted in their sea-prejudices, are the most jealous in resenting territorial encroachments, especially on the part of any of the afterguard, of whom they have but a sorry opinion, chiefly landsmen, never going aloft except to reef or furl the mainsail, and in no wise competent to handle a marline spike or turn in a *dead-eye,* say.

### 16

THIS INCIDENT sorely puzzled Billy Budd. It was an entirely new experience; the first time in his life that he had ever been personally approached in underhand intriguing fashion. Prior to this encounter he had known nothing of the afterguardsman, the two men being stationed wide apart, one forward and aloft during his watch, the other on deck and aft.

What could it mean? And could they really be guineas, those two glittering objects the interloper had held up to his (Billy's) eyes? Where could the fellow get guineas? Why even buttons, spare buttons are not so plentiful at sea. The more he turned the matter over, the more he was non-plussed, and made uneasy and discomforted. In his disgustful recoil from an overture which though he but ill comprehended he instinctively knew must involve evil of some sort, Billy Budd was like a young horse fresh from the pasture suddenly inhaling a vile whiff from some chemical factory and by repeated snortings tries to get it out of his nostrils and lungs. This frame of mind barred all desire of holding further parley with the fellow, even were it but for the purpose of gaining some enlightenment as to his design in approaching him. And yet he was not without natural curiosity to see how such a visitor in the dark would look in broad day.

He espied him the following afternoon in his first dog-watch below one of the smokers on that forward part of the upper gun deck allotted to the pipe. He recognized him by his general cut and build, more than by his round freckled face and glassy eyes of pale blue, veiled with lashes all but white. And yet Billy was a bit uncertain whether indeed it were he—yonder chap about his own age chatting and laughing in free-hearted way, leaning against a gun; a genial young fellow enough to look at, and something of a rattle-brain, to all appearance. Rather chubby too for a sailor even an afterguardsman. In short the last man in the world, one would think, to be overburthened with thoughts, especially those perilous thoughts that must needs belong to a conspirator in any serious project, or even to the underling of such a conspirator.

Although Billy was not aware of it, the fellow, with a sidelong watchful glance had perceived Billy first, and then noting that Billy was looking at him, thereupon nodded a familiar sort of friendly recognition as to an old acquaintance, without interrupting the talk he was engaged in with the group of smokers. A day or two afterwards chancing in the evening promenade on a gun deck, to pass Billy, he offered a flying word of good-fellowship as it were, which by its unexpectedness, and equivocalness under the circumstances so embarrassed Billy that he knew not how to respond to it, and let it go unnoticed.

Billy was now left more at a loss than before. The ineffectual speculations into which he was led were so disturbingly alien to him that he did his best to smother them. It never entered his mind that here was a matter which from its extreme questionableness, it was his duty as a loyal blue-jacket to report in the proper quarter. And, probably, had such a step been suggested to him, he would have been deterred from taking it by the thought, one of novice-magnanimity, that it would savor overmuch of the dirty work of a tell-tale. He kept the thing to himself. Yet upon one occasion, he could not forbear a little disburthening himself to the old Dansker, tempted thereto perhaps by the influence of a balmy night when the ship lay becalmed; the twain, silent for the most part, sitting together on deck, their heads propped against the bulwarks. But it was only a partial and anonymous account that Billy gave, the unfounded scruples above referred to preventing full disclosure to anybody. Upon hearing Billy's version, the sage Dansker seemed to divine more than he was told; and after a little meditation during which his wrinkles were pursed as into a point, quite effacing for the time that quizzing expression his face sometimes wore,—"Didn't I say so, Baby Budd?"

"Say what?" demanded Billy.

"Why, *Jimmy Legs* is *down* on you."

"And what," rejoined Billy in amazement, "has *Jimmy Legs* to do with that cracked afterguardsman?"

"Ho, it was an afterguardsman then. A cat's-paw, a cat's-paw!" And with that exclamation, which, whether it had reference to a light puff of air just then coming over the calm sea, or subtler relation to the afterguardsman, there is no telling, the old Merlin gave a twisting wrench with his black teeth at his plug of tobacco, vouchsafing no reply to Billy's impetuous question, though now repeated, for it was his wont to relapse into grim silence when interrogated in skeptical sort as to any of his sententious oracles, not always very clear ones, rather partaking of that obscurity which invests most Delphic deliverances from any quarter.

Long experience had very likely brought this old man to that bitter prudence which never interferes in aught and never gives advice.

### 17

YES, DESPITE the Dansker's pithy insistence as to the Master-at-arms being at the bottom of these strange experiences of Billy on board the *Indomitable,* the young sailor was ready to ascribe them to almost anybody but the man who, to use Billy's own expression, "always had a pleasant word for him." This is to be wondered at. Yet not so much to be wondered at. In certain matters, some sailors even in mature life remain unsophisticated enough. But a young seafarer of the disposition of our athletic Foretopman, is much of a child-man. And yet a child's utter innocence is but its blank ignorance, and the innocence more or less wanes as intelligence waxes. But in Billy Budd intelligence, such as it was, had advanced, while yet his simplemindedness remained for the most part unaffected. Experience is a teacher indeed; yet did Billy's years make his experience small. Besides, he had none of that intuitive knowledge of the bad which in natures not good or incompletely so foreruns experience, and therefore may pertain, as in some instances it too clearly does pertain, even to youth.

And what could Billy know of man except of man as a mere sailor? And the old-fashioned sailor, the veritable man-before-the-mast, the sailor from boyhood up, he, though indeed of the same species as a landsman is in some respects singularly distinct from him. The sailor is frankness, the landsman is finesse. Life is not a game with the sailor, demanding the long head; no intricate game of chess where few moves are made in straightforwardness, and ends are attained by indirection; an oblique, tedious, barren game hardly worth that poor candle burnt out in playing it.

Yes, as a class, sailors are in character a juvenile race. Even their deviations are marked by juvenility. And this more especially holding true with the sailors of Billy's time. Then, too, certain things which apply to all sailors, do more pointedly operate here and there, upon the junior one. Every sailor, too is accustomed to obey orders without debating them; his life afloat is externally ruled for him; he is not brought into that promiscuous commerce with mankind where unobstructed free agency on equal terms—equal superficially, at least—soon teaches one that unless upon occasion he exercise a distrust keen in proportion to the fairness of the appearance, some foul turn may be served him. A ruled undemonstrative distrustfulness is so habitual, not with business-men so much, as with men who know their kind in less shallow relations than business, namely, certain men-of-the-world, that they come at last to employ it all but unconsciously; and some of them would very likely feel real surprise at being charged with it as one of their general characteristics.

18

BUT AFTER the little matter at the mess Billy Budd no more found himself in strange trouble at times about his hammock or his clothes-bag or what not. While, as to that smile that occasionally sunned him, and the pleasant passing word, these were if not more frequent, yet if anything more pronounced than before.

But for all that, there were certain other demonstrations now. When Claggart's unobserved glance happened to light on belted Billy rolling along the upper gun-deck in the leisure of the second dog-watch exchanging passing broadsides of fun with other young promenaders in the crowd; that glance would follow the cheerful sea-Hyperion [25] with a settled meditative and melancholy expression, his eyes strangely suffused with incipient feverish tears. Then would Claggart look like the man of sorrows. Yes, and sometimes the melancholy expression would have in it a touch of soft yearning, as if Claggart could even have loved Billy but for fate and ban. But this was an evanescence, and quickly repented of, as it were, by an immitigable look, pinching and shrivelling the visage into the momentary semblance of a wrinkled walnut. But sometimes catching sight in advance of the foretopman coming in his direction, he would, upon their nearing, step aside a little to let him pass, dwelling upon Billy for the moment with the glittering dental satire of a Guise.[26] But upon any abrupt unforeseen encounter a red light would flash forth from his eye like a spark from an anvil in a dusk smithy. That quick fierce light was a strange one, darted from orbs which in repose were of a color nearest approaching a deeper violet, the softest of shades.

Though some of these caprices of the pit could not but be observed by their object, yet were they beyond the construing of such a nature. And the *thews* of Billy were hardly compatible with that sort of sensitive spiritual organisation which in some cases instinctively conveys to ignorant innocence an admonition of the proximity of the malign. He thought the master-at-arms acted in a manner rather queer at times. That was all. But the occasional frank air and pleasant word went for what they purported to be, the young sailor never having heard as yet of the "too fair-spoken man."

Had the foretopman been conscious of having done or said anything to provoke the ill will of the official, it would have been different with him, and his sight might have been purged if not sharpened. As it was innocence was his blinder.

So was it with him in yet another matter. Two minor officers—the Armorer and Captain of the Hold, with whom he had never exchanged a word, his position in the ship not bringing him into contact with them; these men now for the first began to cast upon Billy when they chanced to encounter him, that peculiar glance which evidences that the man from whom it comes has been some way tampered with and to the prejudice of him upon

25. **sea-Hyperion:** Melville may have in mind the hero of Keats's unfinished poem *Hyperion*, rather than the dim figure of Greek myth. 26. **Guise:** a French family of the sixteenth century, often embroiled in plots.

whom the glance lights. Never did it occur to Billy as a thing to be noted or a thing suspicious, though he well knew the fact, that the Armorer and Captain of the Hold, with the ship's-yeoman, apothecary, and others of that grade, were by naval usage, mess-mates of the master-at-arms, men with ears convenient to his confidential tongue.

But the general popularity that our *Handsome Sailor's* manly forwardness upon occasion, and irresistible good nature indicating no mental superiority tending to excite an invidious feeling; this good will on the part of most of his shipmates made him the less to concern himself about such mute aspects toward him as those whereto allusion has just been made.

As to the afterguardsman, though Billy for reasons already given necessarily saw little of him, yet when the two did happen to meet, invariably came the fellow's off-hand cheerful recognition, sometimes accompanied by a passing pleasant word or two. Whatever that equivocal young person's original design may really have been, or the design of which he might have been the deputy, certain it was from his manner upon these occasions, that he had wholly dropped it.

It was as if his precocity of crookedness (and every vulgar villain is precocious) had for once deceived him, and the man he had sought to entrap as a simpleton had, through his very simplicity ignominiously baffled him.

But shrewd ones may opine that it was hardly possible for Billy to refrain from going up to the afterguardsman and bluntly demanding to know his purpose in the initial interview, so abruptly closed in the fore-chains. Shrewd ones may also think it but natural in Billy to set about sounding some of the other impressed men of the ship in order to discover what basis, if any, there was for the emissary's obscure suggestions as to plotting disaffection aboard. Yes, the shrewd may so think. But something more, or rather, something else than mere shrewdness is perhaps needful for the due understanding of such a character as Billy Budd's.

As to Claggart, the monomania in the man—if that indeed it were—as involuntarily disclosed by starts in the manifestations detailed, yet in general covered over by his self-contained and rational demeanor; this, like a subterranean fire was eating its way deeper and deeper in him. Something decisive must come of it.

## 19

AFTER the mysterious interview in the fore-chains, the one so abruptly ended there by Billy, nothing especially germane to the story occurred until the events now about to be narrated.

Elsewhere it has been said that in the lack of frigates (of course better sailers than line-of-battle ships) in the English squadron up the Straits at that period, the *Indomitable* was occasionally employed not only as an available substitute for a scout, but at times on detached service of more important kind. This was not alone because of her sailing qualities, not common in a ship of her rate, but quite as much, probably, that the character of her commander, it was thought, specially adapted him for any duty where under unforeseen difficulties a prompt initiative might have to be taken in some matter demanding knowledge and ability in addition to those qualities implied in good seamanship. It was on an expedition of the latter sort, a somewhat distant one, and when the *Indomitable* was almost at her furthest remove from the fleet that in the latter part of an afternoon-watch she unexpectedly came in sight of a ship of the enemy. It proved to be a frigate. The latter perceiving through the glass that the weight of men and metal would be heavily against her, invoking her light heels crowded sail to get away. After a chase urged almost against hope and lasting until about the middle of the first dog-watch, she signally succeeded in effecting her escape.

Not long after the pursuit had been given up, and ere the excitement incident thereto had altogether waned away, the master-at-arms ascending from his cavernous sphere made his appearance cap in hand by the mainmast respectfully waiting the notice of Captain Vere then solitary walking the weatherside of the quarter-deck, doubtless somewhat chafed at the failure of the pursuit. The spot where Claggart stood was the place allotted to men of lesser grades seeking some more particular interview either with the officer-of-the-deck or the Captain himself. But from the latter it was not often that a sailor or petty-officer of those days would seek a hearing; only some exceptional cause, would, according to established custom, have warranted that.

Presently, just as the Commander absorbed in his reflections was on the point of turning aft in his promenade, he became sensible of Claggart's presence, and saw the doffed cap held in deferential expectancy. Here be it said that Captain Vere's personal knowledge of this petty-officer had only begun at the time of the ship's last sailing from home, Claggart then for the first, in transfer from a ship detained for repairs, supplying on board the *Indomitable* the place of a previous master-at-arms disabled and ashore.

No sooner did the Commander observe who it

was that now deferentially stood awaiting his notice, than a peculiar expression came over him. It was not unlike that which uncontrollably will flit across the countenance of one at unawares encountering a person who though known to him indeed has hardly been long enough known for thorough knowledge, but something in whose aspect nevertheless now for the first provokes a vaguely repellent distaste. But coming to a stand, and resuming much of his wonted official manner, save that a sort of impatience lurked in the intonation of the opening word, he said, "Well? what is it, Master-at-Arms?"

With the air of a subordinate grieved at the necessity of being a messenger of ill tidings, and while conscientiously determined to be frank, yet equally resolved upon shunning overstatement, Claggart at this invitation or rather summons to disburthen, spoke up. What he said, conveyed in the language of no uneducated man, was to the effect following if not altogether in these words, namely, that during the chase and preparations for the possible encounter he had seen enough to convince him that at least one sailor aboard was a dangerous character in a ship mustering some who not only had taken a guilty part in the late serious troubles, but others also who, like the man in question, had entered His Majesty's service under another form than enlistment.

At this point Captain Vere with some impatience interrupted him: "Be direct, man; say impressed men."

Claggart made a gesture of subservience, and proceeded.

Quite lately, he (Claggart) had begun to suspect that on the gun-decks some sort of movement prompted by the sailor in question was covertly going on, but he had not thought himself warranted in reporting the suspicion so long as it remained indistinct. But from what he had that afternoon observed in the man referred to the suspicion of something clandestine going on had advanced to a point less removed from certainty. He deeply felt, he added, the serious responsibility assumed in making a report involving such possible consequences to the individual mainly concerned, besides tending to augment those natural anxieties which every naval commander must feel in view of extraordinary outbreaks so recent as those which, he sorrowfully said it, it needed not to name.

Now at the first broaching of the matter Captain Vere taken by surprise could not wholly dissemble his disquietude. But as Claggart went on, the former's aspect changed into restiveness under something in the witness' manner in giving his testimony. However, he refrained from interrupting

him. And Claggart, continuing, concluded with this:

"God forbid, your honor, that the *Indomitable's* should be the experience of the——"

"Never mind that!" here peremptorily broke in the superior, his face altering with anger, instinctively divining the ship that the other was about to name, one in which the Nore Mutiny had assumed a singularly tragical character that for a time jeopardized the life of its commander. Under the circumstances he was indignant at the purposed allusion. When the commissioned officers themselves were on all occasions very heedful how they referred to the recent events, for a petty-officer unnecessarily to allude to them in the presence of his Captain, this struck him as a most immodest presumption. Besides, to his quick sense of self-respect, it even looked under the circumstances something like an attempt to alarm him. Nor at first was he without some surprise that one who so far as he had hitherto come under his notice had shown considerable tact in his function should in this particular evince such lack of it.

But these thoughts and kindred dubious ones flitting across his mind were suddenly replaced by an intuitional surmise which though as yet obscure in form served practically to affect his reception of the ill tidings. Certain it is, that long versed in everything pertaining to the complicated gun-deck life, which like every other form of life, has its secret mines and dubious side, the side popularly disclaimed, Captain Vere did not permit himself to be unduly disturbed by the general tenor of his subordinate's report. Furthermore, if in view of recent events prompt action should be taken at the first palpable sign of recurring insubordination, for all that, not judicious would it be, he thought, to keep the idea of lingering disaffection alive by undue forwardness in crediting an informer even if his own subordinate and charged among other things with police surveillance of the crew. This feeling would not perhaps have so prevailed with him were it not that upon a prior occasion the patriotic zeal officially evinced by Claggart had somewhat irritated him as appearing rather supersensible and strained. Furthermore something even in the official's self-possessed and somewhat ostentatious manner in making his specifications strangely reminded him of a bandsman, a perjurous witness in a capital case before a court-martial ashore of which when a lieutenant he Captain Vere had been a member.

Now the peremptory check given to Claggart in the matter of the arrested allusion was quickly followed up by this: "You say that there is at least one dangerous man aboard. Name him."

"William Budd. A foretopman, your honor—"

"William Budd," repeated Captain Vere with unfeigned astonishment; "and mean you the man that Lieutenant Ratcliffe took from the merchantman not very long ago—the young fellow who seems to be so popular with the men—Billy, the Handsome Sailor, as they call him?"

"The same, your honor; but for all his youth and good looks, a deep one. Not for nothing does he insinuate himself into the good will of his shipmates, since at the least all hands will at a pinch say a good word for him at all hazards. Did Lieutenant Ratcliffe happen to tell your honor of that adroit fling of Budd's, jumping up in the cutter's bow under the merchantman's stern when he was being taken off? It is even masqued by that sort of good humored air that at heart he resents his impressment. You have but noted his fair cheek. A man-trap may be under his ruddy-tipped daisies."

Now the *Handsome Sailor* as a signal figure among the crew had naturally enough attracted the Captain's attention from the first. Though in general not very demonstrative to his officers, he had congratulated Lieutenant Ratcliffe upon his good fortune in lighting on such a fine specimen of the genus homo, who in the nude might have posed for a statue of young Adam before the Fall. As to Billy's adieu to the ship *Rights-of-Man*, which the boarding lieutenant had indeed reported to him, but in a deferential way more as a good story than aught else, Captain Vere, though mistakenly understanding it as a satiric sally, had but thought so much the better of the impressed man for it; as a military sailor, admiring the spirit that could take an arbitrary enlistment so merrily and sensibly. The foretopman's conduct, too, so far as it had fallen under the Captain's notice had confirmed the first happy augury, while the new recruit's qualities as a *sailor-man* seemed to be such that he had thought of recommending him to the executive officer for promotion to a place that would more frequently bring him under his own observation, namely, the captaincy of the mizzen-top, replacing there in the starboard watch a man not so young whom partly for that reason he deemed less fitted for the post. Be it parenthesized here that since the mizzen-topmen having not to handle such breadths of heavy canvas as the lower sails on the main-mast and fore-mast, a young man if of the right stuff not only seems best adapted to duty there, but in fact is generally selected for the captaincy of that top, and the company under him are light hands and often but striplings. In sum, Captain Vere had from the beginning deemed Billy Budd to be what in the naval parlance of the time

was called a *"King's bargain"* that is to say, for His Britannic Majesty's navy a capital investment at small outlay or none at all.

After a brief pause during which the reminiscences above mentioned passed vividly through his mind and he weighed the import of Claggart's last suggestion conveyed in the phrase "pitfall under the clover," and the more he weighed it the less reliance he felt in the informer's good faith. Suddenly he turned upon him and in a low voice: "Do you come to me, master-at-arms, with so foggy a tale? As to Budd, cite me an act or spoken word of his confirmatory of what you in general charge against him. Stay," drawing nearer to him "heed what you speak. Just now, and in a case like this, there is a yard-arm-end for the false-witness."

"Ah, your honor!" sighed Claggart mildly shaking his shapely head as in sad deprecation of such unmerited severity of tone. Then, bridling—erecting himself as in virtuous self-assertion, he circumstantially alleged certain words and acts, which collectively, if credited, led to presumptions mortally inculpating Budd. And for some of these averments, he added, substantiating proof was not far.

With gray eyes impatient and distrustful essaying to fathom to the bottom Claggart's calm violet ones, Captain Vere again heard him out; then for the moment stood ruminating. The mood he evinced, Claggart—himself for the time liberated from the other's scrutiny—steadily regarded with a look difficult to render,—a look curious of the operation of his tactics, a look such as might have been that of the spokesman of the envious children of Jacob deceptively imposing upon the troubled patriarch the blood-dyed coat of young Joseph.[27]

Though something exceptional in the moral quality of Captain Vere made him, in earnest encounter with a fellow-man, a veritable touch-stone of that man's essential nature, yet now as to Claggart and what was really going on in him his feeling partook less of intuitional conviction than of strong suspicion clogged by strange dubieties. The perplexity he evinced proceeded less from aught touching the man informed against—as Claggart doubtless opined—than from considerations how best to act in regard to the informer. At first indeed he was naturally for summoning that substantiation of his allegations which Claggart said was at hand. But such a proceeding would result in the matter at once getting abroad, which in the present stage of it, he thought, might undesirably affect the ship's company. If Claggart was a

27. Joseph: Gen. 37:31-34.

false witness,—that closed the affair. And therefore before trying the accusation, he would first practically test the accuser; and he thought this could be done in a quiet undemonstrative way.

The measure he determined upon involved a shifting of the scene, a transfer to a place less exposed to observation than the broad quarter-deck. For although the few gun-room officers there at the time had, in due observance of naval etiquette, withdrawn to leeward the moment Captain Vere had begun his promenade on the deck's weatherside; and though during the colloquy with Claggart they of course ventured not to diminish the distance; and though throughout the interview Captain Vere's voice was far from high, and Claggart's silvery and low; and the wind in the cordage and the wash of the sea helped the more to put them beyond ear-shot; nevertheless, the interview's continuance already had attracted observation from some topmen aloft and other sailors in the waist or further forward.

Having determined upon his measures, Captain Vere forthwith took action. Abruptly turning to Claggart, he asked, "Master-at-arms, is it now Budd's watch aloft?"

"No, your honor." Whereupon, "Mr. Wilkes!" summoning the nearest midshipman, "tell Albert to come to me." Albert was the Captain's hammockboy, a sort of sea-valet in whose discretion and fidelity his master had much confidence. The lad appeared. "You know Budd the foretopman?"

"I do, Sir."

"Go find him. It is his watch off. Manage to tell him out of ear-shot that he is wanted aft. Contrive it that he speaks to nobody. Keep him in talk yourself. And not till you get well aft here, not till then let him know that the place where he is wanted is my cabin. You understand. Go. Master-at-arms, show yourself on the decks below, and when you think it time for Albert to be coming with his man, stand by quietly to follow the sailor in."

20

NOW WHEN the foretopman found himself closeted there, as it were, in the cabin with the Captain and Claggart, he was surprised enough. But it was a surprise unaccompanied by apprehension or distrust. To an immature nature essentially honest and humane, forewarning intimations of subtler danger from one's kind come tardily if at all. The only thing that took shape in the young sailor's mind was this: Yes, the Captain, I have always thought, looks kindly upon me. Wonder if he's going to make me his coxswain. I should like that. And maybe now he

is going to ask the master-at-arms about me.

"Shut the door there, sentry," said the commander; "stand without, and let nobody come in. —Now, master-at-arms, tell this man to his face what you told of him to me;" and stood prepared to scrutinize the mutually confronting visages.

With the measured step and calm collected air of an asylum-physician approaching in the public hall some patient beginning to show indications of a coming paroxysm, Claggart deliberately advanced within short range of Billy, and mesmerically looking him in the eye, briefly recapitulated the accusation.

Not at first did Billy take it in. When he did, the rose-tan of his cheek looked struck as by white leprosy. He stood like one impaled and gagged. Meanwhile the accuser's eyes removing not as yet from the blue dilated ones, underwent a phenomenal change, their wonted rich violet color blurring into a muddy purple. Those lights of human intelligence losing human expression, gelidly protruding like the alien eyes of certain uncatalogued creatures of the deep. The first mesmeric glance was one of serpent fascination; the last was as the hungry lurch of the torpedo-fish.

"Speak, man!" said Captain Vere to the transfixed one struck by his aspect even more than by Claggart's, "Speak! defend yourself." Which appeal caused but a strange dumb gesturing and gurgling in Billy; amazement at such an accusation so suddenly sprung on inexperienced nonage; this, and, it may be, horror of the accuser, serving to bring out his lurking defect and in this instance for the time intensifying it into a convulsed tonguetie; while the intent head and entire form straining forward in an agony of ineffectual eagerness to obey the injunction to speak and defend himself, gave an expression to the face like that of a condemned Vestal priestess in the moment of being buried alive, and in the first struggle against suffocation.

Though at the time Captain Vere was quite ignorant of Billy's liability to vocal impediment, he now immediately divined it, since vividly Billy's aspect recalled to him that of a bright young schoolmate of his whom he had once seen struck by much the same startling impotence in the act of eagerly rising in the class to be foremost in response to a testing question put to it by the master. Going close up to the young sailor, and laying a soothing hand on his shoulder, he said: "There is no hurry, my boy. Take your time, take your time." Contrary to the effect intended, these words so fatherly in tone, doubtless touching Billy's heart to the quick, prompted yet more violent efforts at utterance—efforts soon ending for the time in confirming the paralysis, and bringing to his face an expression which was as a crucifixion to behold. The next instant, quick as the flame from a discharged cannon at night, his right arm shot out, and Claggart dropped to the deck. Whether intentionally or but owing to the young athlete's superior height, the blow had taken effect full upon the forehead, so shapely and intellectual-looking a feature in the master-at-arms; so that the body fell over lengthwise, like a heavy plank tilted from erectness. A gasp or two, and he lay motionless.

"Fated boy," breathed Captain Vere in tone so low as to be almost a whisper, "what have you done! But here, help me."

The twain raised the felled one from the loins up into a sitting position. The spare form flexibly acquiesced, but inertly. It was like handling a dead snake. They lowered it back. Regaining erectness Captain Vere with one hand covering his face stood to all appearance as impassive as the object at his feet. Was he absorbed in taking in all the bearings of the event and what was best not only now at once to be done, but also in the sequel? Slowly he uncovered his face; and the effect was as if the moon emerging from eclipse should reappear with quite another aspect than that which had gone into hiding. The father in him, manifested towards Billy thus far in the scene, was replaced by the military disciplinarian. In his official tone he bade the foretopman retire to a state-room aft (pointing it out) and there remain till thence summoned. This order Billy in silence mechanically obeyed. Then going to the cabin-door where it opened on the quarter-deck, Captain Vere said to the sentry without, "Tell somebody to send Albert here." When the lad appeared his master so contrived it that he should not catch sight of the prone one. "Albert," he said to him, "tell the Surgeon I wish to see him. You need not come back till called." When the Surgeon entered—a self-poised character of that grave sense and experience that hardly anything could take him aback, —Captain Vere advanced to meet him, thus unconsciously intercepting his view of Claggart and interrupting the other's wonted ceremonious salutation, said, "Nay, tell me how it is with yonder man," directing his attention to the prostrate one.

The Surgeon looked, and for all his self-command, somewhat started at the abrupt revelation. On Claggart's always pallid complexion, thick black blood was now oozing from nostril and ear. To the gazer's professional eye it was unmistakably no living man that he saw.

"Is it so then?" said Captain Vere intently watching him. "I thought it. But verify it." Whereupon the customary tests confirmed the Sur-

geon's first glance, who now looking up in unfeigned concern, cast a look of intense inquisitiveness upon his superior. But Captain Vere, with one hand to his brow, was standing motionless. Suddenly, catching the Surgeon's arm convulsively, he exclaimed, pointing down to the body—"It is the divine judgement on Ananias! [28] Look!"

Disturbed by the excited manner he had never before observed in the *Indomitable's* Captain, and as yet wholly ignorant of the affair, the prudent Surgeon nevertheless held his peace, only again looking an earnest interrogation as to what it was that had resulted in such a tragedy.

But Captain Vere was now again motionless standing absorbed in thought. But again starting, he vehemently exclaimed—"Struck dead by an angel of God! Yet the angel must hang!"

At these passionate interjections, mere incoherences to the listener as yet unapprised of the antecedents, the Surgeon was profoundly discomposed. But now as recollecting himself, Captain Vere in less passionate tone briefly related the circumstances leading up to the event.

"But come; we must despatch," he added. "Help me to remove him (meaning the body) to yonder compartment," designating one opposite that where the foretopman remained immured. Anew disturbed by a request that as implying a desire for secrecy, seemed unaccountably strange to him, there was nothing for the subordinate to do but comply.

"Go now," said Captain Vere with something of his wonted manner—"Go now. I shall presently call a drum-head court. Tell the lieutenants what has happened, and tell Mr. Mordant," meaning the captain of marines, "and charge them to keep the matter to themselves."

21

FULL OF disquietude and misgiving the Surgeon left the cabin. Was Captain Vere suddenly affected in his mind, or was it but a transient excitement, brought about by so strange and extraordinary a happening? As to the drum-head court, it struck the Surgeon as impolitic, if nothing more. The thing to do, he thought, was to place Billy Budd in confinement and in a way dictated by usage, and postpone further action in so extraordinary a case, to such time as they should rejoin the squadron, and then refer it to the Admiral. He recalled the unwonted agitation of Captain Vere and his excited exclamations so at variance with his normal manner. Was he unhinged? But

28. Ananias: Acts 5:5.

assuming that he is, it is not so susceptible of proof. What then can he do? No more trying situation is conceivable than that of an officer subordinate under a Captain whom he suspects to be, not mad indeed, but yet not quite unaffected in his intellect. To argue his order to him would be insolence. To resist him would be mutiny.

In obedience to Captain Vere he communicated what had happened to the lieutenants and captain of marines; saying nothing as to the Captain's state. They fully shared his own surprise and concern. Like him too they seemed to think that such a matter should be referred to the Admiral.

## 22

WHO IN the rainbow can show the line where the violet tint ends and the orange tint begins? Distinctly we see the difference of the colors, but when exactly does the one first blendingly enter into the other? So with sanity and insanity. In pronounced cases there is no question about them. But in some supposed cases, in various degrees supposedly less pronounced, to draw the exact line of demarkation few will undertake though for a fee some professional experts will. There is nothing namable but that some men will undertake to do it for pay.

Whether Captain Vere, as the Surgeon professionally and privately surmised, was really the sudden victim of any degree of aberration, one must determine for himself by such light as this narrative may afford.

That the unhappy event which has been narrated could not have happened at a worse juncture was but too true. For it was close on the heel of the suppressed insurrections, an after-time very critical to naval authority, demanding from every English sea-commander two qualities not readily interfusable—prudence and rigor. Moreover there was something crucial in the case.

In the jugglery of circumstances preceding and attending the event on board the *Indomitable* and in the light of that martial code whereby it was formally to be judged, innocence and guilt personified in Claggart and Budd in effect changed places. In a legal view the apparent victim of the tragedy was he who had sought to victimize a man blameless; and the indisputable deed of the latter, navally regarded, constituted the most heinous of military crimes. Yet more. The essential right and wrong involved in the matter, the clearer that might be, so much the worse for the responsibility of a loyal sea-commander inasmuch as he was not authorized to determine the matter on that primitive basis.

Small wonder then that the *Indomitable's* Captain though in general a man of rapid decision, felt that circumspectness not less than promptitude was necessary. Until he could decide upon his course, and in each detail; and not only so, but until the concluding measure was upon the point of being enacted, he deemed it advisable, in view of all the circumstances to guard as much as possible against publicity. Here he may or may not have erred. Certain it is however that subsequently in the confidential talk of more than one or two gun-rooms and cabins he was not a little criticized by some officers, a fact imputed by his friends and vehemently by his cousin Jack Denton to professional jealousy of Starry Vere. Some *imaginative* ground for invidious comment there was. The maintenance of secrecy in the matter, the confining all knowledge of it for a time to the place where the homicide occurred, the quarter-deck cabin; in these particulars lurked some resemblance to the policy adopted in those tragedies of the palace which have occurred more than once in the capital founded by Peter the Barbarian.[29]

The case indeed was such that fain would the *Indomitable's* Captain have deferred taking any action whatever respecting it further than to keep the foretopman a close prisoner till the ship rejoined the squadron and then submitting the matter to the judgement of his Admiral.

But a true military officer is in one particular like a true monk. Not with more of self-abnegation will the latter keep his vows of monastic obedience than the former his vows of allegiance to martial duty.

Feeling that unless quick action was taken on it, the deed of the foretopman, so soon as it should be known on the gun-decks would tend to awaken any slumbering embers of the Nore among the crew, a sense of the urgency of the case overruled in Captain Vere every other consideration. But though a conscientious disciplinarian he was no lover of authority for mere authority's sake. Very far was he from embracing opportunities for monopolizing to himself the perils of moral responsibility none at least that could properly be referred to an official superior or shared with him by his official equals or even subordinates. So thinking he was glad it would not be at variance with usage to turn the matter over to a summary court of his own officers, reserving to himself as the one on whom the ultimate accountability would rest, the right of maintaining a supervision of it, or formally or informally interposing at need. Accordingly a drum-head court was summarily convened,

29. **Peter the Barbarian:** Peter the Great of Russia (1672–1725).

he electing the individuals composing it, the First Lieutenant, the Captain of marines, and the Sailing Master.

In associating an officer of marines with the sea-lieutenants in a case having to do with a sailor the Commander perhaps deviated from general custom. He was prompted thereto by the circumstance that he took that soldier to be a judicious person, thoughtful, and not altogether incapable of grappling with a difficult case unprecedented in his prior experience. Yet even as to him he was not without some latent misgiving, for withal he was an extremely good-natured man, an enjoyer of his dinner, a sound sleeper, and inclined to obesity. A man who though he would always maintain his manhood in battle might not prove altogether reliable in a moral dilemma involving aught of the tragic. As to the First Lieutenant and the Sailing Master Captain Vere could not but be aware that though honest natures, of approved gallantry upon occasion their intelligence was mostly confined to the matter of active seamanship and the fighting demands of their profession. The court was held in the same cabin where the unfortunate affair had taken place. This cabin, the Commander's, embraced the entire area under the poop-deck. Aft, and on either side was a small state-room the one room temporarily a jail and the other a dead-house and a yet smaller compartment leaving a space between, expanding forward into a goodly oblong of length coinciding with the ship's beam. A skylight of moderate dimension was overhead and at each end of the oblong space were two sashed port-hole windows easily convertible back into embrasures for short carronades.

All being quickly in readiness, Billy Budd was arraigned, Captain Vere necessarily appearing as the sole witness in the case, and as such temporarily sinking his rank, though singularly maintaining it in a matter apparently trivial, namely, that he testified from the ship's weather-side with that object having caused the court to sit on the leeside. Concisely he narrated all that had led up to the catastrophe, omitting nothing in Claggart's accusation and deposing as to the manner in which the prisoner had received it. At this testimony the three officers glanced with no little surprise at Billy Budd, the last man they would have suspected either of the mutinous design alleged by Claggart or the undeniable deed he himself had done.

The First Lieutenant taking judicial primacy and turning toward the prisoner, said, "Captain Vere has spoken. Is it or is it not as Captain Vere says?" In response came syllables not so much impeded in the utterance as might have been anticipated. They were these: "Captain Vere tells the truth. It is just as Captain Vere says, but it is not as the Master-at-Arms said. I have eaten the King's bread and I am true to the King."

"I believe you, my man," said the witness, his voice indicating a suppressed emotion not otherwise betrayed.

"God will bless you for that, Your Honor!" not without stammering said Billy, and all but broke down. But immediately was recalled to self-control by another question, to which with the same emotional difficulty of utterance he said, "No, there was no malice between us. I never bore malice against the Master-at-arms. I am sorry that he is dead. I did not mean to kill him. Could I have used my tongue I would not have struck him. But he foully lied to my face and in presence of my Captain, and I had to say something, and I could only say it with a blow, God help me!"

In the impulsive above-board manner of the frank one the court saw confirmed all that was implied in words that just previously had perplexed them coming as they did from the testifier to the tragedy and promptly following Billy's impassioned disclaimer of mutinous intent—Captain Vere's words, "I believe you, my man."

Next it was asked of him whether he knew of or suspected aught savoring of incipient trouble (meaning mutiny, though the explicit term was avoided) going on in any section of the ship's company.

The reply lingered. This was naturally imputed by the court to the same vocal embarrassment which had retarded or obstructed previous answers. But in main it was otherwise here; the question immediately recalling to Billy's mind the interview with the afterguardsman in the forechains. But an innate repugnance to playing a part at all approaching that of an informer against one's own shipmates—the same erring sense of uninstructed honor which had stood in the way of his reporting the matter at the time though as a loyal man-of-war-man it was incumbent on him and failure so to do if charged against him and proven, would have subjected him to the heaviest of penalties; this, with the blind feeling now his, that nothing really was being hatched, prevailed with him. When the answer came it was a negative.

"One question more," said the officer of marines now first speaking and with a troubled earnestness. "You tell us that what the master-at-arms said against you was a lie. Now why should he have so lied, so maliciously lied, since you declare there was no malice between you?"

At that question unintentionally touching on a spiritual sphere wholly obscure to Billy's thoughts, he was nonplussed, evincing a confusion indeed that some observers, such as can readily be imagined, would have construed into involuntary evidence of hidden guilt. Nevertheless he strove some way to answer, but all at once relinquished the vain endeavor, at the same time turning an appealing glance towards Captain Vere as deeming him his best helper and friend. Captain Vere who had been seated for a time rose to his feet, addressing the interrogator. "The question you put to him comes naturally enough. But how can he rightly answer it? or anybody else? unless indeed it be he who lies within there" designating the compartment where lay the corpse. "But the prone one there will not rise to our summons. In effect, though, as it seems to me, the point you make is hardly material. Quite aside from any conceivable motive actuating the master-at-arms, and irrespective of the provocation to the blow, a martial court must needs in the present case confine its attention to the blow's consequence, which consequence justly is to be deemed not otherwise than as the striker's deed."

This utterance the full significance of which it was not at all likely that Billy took in, nevertheless caused him to turn a wistful interrogative look toward the speaker, a look in its dumb expressiveness not unlike that which a dog of generous breed might turn upon his master seeking in his face some elucidation of a previous gesture ambiguous to the canine intelligence. Nor was the same utterance without marked effect upon the three officers, more especially the soldier. Couched in it seemed to them a meaning unanticipated, involving a prejudgement on the speaker's part. It served to augment a mental disturbance previously evident enough.

The soldier once more spoke; in a tone of suggestive dubiety addressing at once his associates and Captain Vere: "Nobody is present—none of the ship's company, I mean, who might shed lateral light, if any is to be had, upon what remains mysterious in this matter."

"That is thoughtfully put," said Captain Vere; "I see your drift. Ay, there is a mystery; but, to use a Scriptural phrase, it is 'a mystery of iniquity,'[30] a matter for psychologic theologians to discuss. But what has a military court to do with it? Not to add that for us any possible investigation of it is cut off by the lasting tongue-tie of—him—in yonder," again designating the mortuary state-room. "The prisoner's deed,—with that alone we have to do."

To this, and particularly the closing reiteration, the marine soldier knowing not how aptly to re-

ply, sadly abstained from saying aught. The First Lieutenant who at the outset had not unnaturally assumed primacy in the court, now overrulingly instructed by a glance from Captain Vere, a glance more effective than words, resumed that primacy. Turning to the prisoner, "Budd," he said, and scarce in equable tones, "Budd, if you have aught further to say for yourself, say it now."

Upon this the young sailor turned another quick glance toward Captain Vere; then, as taking a hint from that aspect, a hint confirming his own instinct that silence was now best, replied to the Lieutenant, "I have said all, Sir."

The marine—the same who had been the sentinel without the cabin-door at the time that the foretopman followed by the master-at-arms, entered it—he, standing by the sailor throughout these judicial proceedings, was now directed to take him back to the after compartment originally assigned to the prisoner and his custodian. As the twain disappeared from view, the three officers as partially liberated from some inward constraint associated with Billy's mere presence, simultaneously stirred in their seats. They exchanged looks of troubled indecision, yet feeling that decide they must and without long delay. For Captain Vere, he for the time stood unconsciously with his back toward them, apparently in one of his absent fits, gazing out from a sashed port-hole to windward upon the monotonous blank of the twilight sea. But the court's silence continuing, broken only at moments by brief consultations in low earnest tones, this seemed to assure him and encourage him. Turning, he to-and-fro paced the cabin athwart; in the returning ascent to windward, climbing the slant deck in the ship's lee roll; without knowing it symbolizing thus in his action a mind resolute to surmount difficulties even if against primitive instincts strong as the wind and the sea. Presently he came to a stand before the three. After scanning their faces he stood less as mustering his thoughts for expression, than as one inly deliberating how best to put them to well-meaning men not intellectually mature, men with whom it was necessary to demonstrate certain principles that were axioms to himself. Similar impatience as to talking is perhaps one reason that deters some minds from addressing any popular assemblies.

When speak he did, something both in the substance of what he said and his manner of saying it, showed the influence of unshared studies modifying and tempering the practical training of an active career. This, along with his phraseology now and then was suggestive of the grounds whereon rested that imputation of a certain pedantry so-

---

30. 'a . . . iniquity': II Thess. 2:7.

cially alleged against him by certain naval men of wholly practical cast, captains who nevertheless would frankly concede that His Majesty's navy mustered no more efficient officer of their grade than *Starry Vere.*

What he said was to this effect: "Hitherto I have been but the witness, little more; and I should hardly think now to take another tone, that of your coadjutor, for the time, did I not perceive in you,—at the crisis too—a troubled hesitancy, proceeding, I doubt not from the clash of military duty with moral scruple—scruple vitalized by compassion. For the compassion how can I otherwise than share it. But, mindful of paramount obligations I strive against scruples that may tend to enervate decision. Not, gentlemen, that I hide from myself that the case is an exceptional one. Speculatively regarded, it well might be referred to a jury of casuists. But for us here acting not as casuists or moralists, it is a case practical, and under martial law practically to be dealt with.

"But your scruples: do they move as in a dusk? Challenge them. Make them advance and declare themselves. Come now: do they import something like this: If, mindless of palliating circumstances, we are bound to regard the death of the Master-at-arms as the prisoner's deed, then does that deed constitute a capital crime whereof the penalty is a mortal one. But in natural justice is nothing but the prisoner's overt act to be considered? How can we adjudge to summary and shameful death a fellow-creature innocent before God, and whom we feel to be so?—Does that state it aright? You sign sad assent. Well, I too feel that, the full force of that. It is Nature. But do these buttons that we wear attest that our allegiance is to Nature? No, to the King. Though the ocean, which is inviolate Nature primeval, though this be the element where we move and have our being as sailors, yet as the King's officers lies our duty in a sphere correspondingly natural? So little is that true, that in receiving our commissions we in the most important regards ceased to be natural free-agents. When war is declared are we the commissioned fighters previously consulted? We fight at command. If our judgements approve the war, that is but coincidence. So in other particulars. So now. For suppose condemnation to follow these present proceedings. Would it be so much we ourselves that would condemn as it would be martial law operating through us? For that law and the rigor of it, we are not responsible. Our avowed responsibility is in this: That however pitilessly that law may operate, we nevertheless adhere to it and administer it.

"But the exceptional in the matter moves the hearts within you. Even so too is mine moved. But let not warm hearts betray heads that should be cool. Ashore in a criminal case will an upright judge allow himself off the bench to be waylaid by some tender kinswoman of the accused seeking to touch him with her tearful plea? Well the heart here denotes the feminine in man, is as that piteous woman, and hard though it be, she must here be ruled out."

He paused, earnestly studying them for a moment; then resumed.

"But something in your aspect seems to urge that it is not solely the heart that moves in you, but also the conscience, the private conscience. But tell me whether or not, occupying the position we do, private conscience should not yield to that imperial one formulated in the code under which alone we officially proceed?"

Here the three men moved in their seats, less convinced than agitated by the course of an argument troubling but the more the spontaneous conflict within.

Perceiving which, the speaker paused for a moment; then abruptly changing his tone, went on.

"To steady us a bit, let us recur to the facts.—In wartime at sea a man-of-war's-man strikes his superior in grade, and the blow kills. Apart from its effect the blow itself is, according to the Articles of War, a capital crime. Furthermore—"

"Ay, Sir," emotionally broke in the officer of marines, "in one sense it was. But surely Budd proposed neither mutiny nor homicide."

"Surely not, my good man. And before a court less arbitrary and more merciful than a martial one, that plea would largely extenuate. At the Last Assizes it shall acquit. But how here? We proceed under the law of the Mutiny Act. In feature no child can resemble his father more than that Act resembles in spirit the thing from which it derives—War. In His Majesty's service—in this ship indeed—there are Englishmen forced to fight for the King against their will. Against their conscience, for aught we know. Though as their fellow-creatures some of us may appreciate their position, yet as navy officers, what reck we of it? Still less recks the enemy. Our impressed men he would fain cut down in the same swath with our volunteers. As regards the enemy's naval conscripts, some of whom may even share our own abhorrence of the regicidal French Directory, it is the same on our side. War looks but to the frontage, the appearance. And the Mutiny Act, War's child, takes after the father. Budd's intent or nonintent is nothing to the purpose.

"But while, put to it by those anxieties in you which I can not but respect, I only repeat myself—

while thus strangely we prolong proceedings that should be summary—the enemy may be sighted and an engagement result. We must do; and one of two things must we do—condemn or let go."

"Can we not convict and yet mitigate the penalty?" asked the junior Lieutenant here speaking, and falteringly, for the first.

"Lieutenant, were that clearly lawful for us under the circumstances consider the consequences of such clemency. The people" (meaning the ship's company) "have native-sense; most of them are familiar with our naval usage and tradition; and how would they take it? Even could you explain to them—which our official position forbids—they, long moulded by arbitrary discipline have not that kind of intelligent responsiveness that might qualify them to comprehend and discriminate. No, to the people the foretopman's deed however it be worded in the announcement will be plain homicide committed in a flagrant act of mutiny. What penalty for that should follow, they know. But it does not follow. *Why?* they will ruminate. You know what sailors are. Will they not revert to the recent outbreak at the Nore? Ay. They know the well-founded alarm—the panic it struck throughout England. Your clement sentence they would account pusillanimous. They would think that we flinch, that we are afraid of them—afraid of practising a lawful rigor singularly demanded at this juncture lest it should provoke new troubles. What shame to us such a conjecture on their part, and how deadly to discipline. You see then, whither prompted by duty and the law I steadfastly drive. But I beseech you, my friends, do not take me amiss. I feel as you do for this unfortunate boy. But did he know our hearts, I take him to be of that generous nature that he would feel even for us on whom in this military necessity so heavy a compulsion is laid."

With that, crossing the deck he resumed his place by the sashed port-hole, tacitly leaving the three to come to a decision. On the cabin's opposite side the troubled court sat silent. Loyal lieges, plain and practical, though at bottom they dissented from some points Captain Vere had put to them, they were without the faculty, hardly had the inclination to gainsay one whom they felt to be an earnest man, one too not less their superior in mind than in naval rank. But it is not improbable that even such of his words as were not without influence over them, less came home to them than his closing appeal to their instinct as sea-officers in the forethought he threw out as to the practical consequences to discipline, considering the unconfirmed tone of the fleet at the time,

should a man-of-war's-man's violent killing at sea of a superior in grade be allowed to pass for aught else than a capital crime demanding prompt infliction of the penalty.

Not unlikely they were brought to something more or less akin to that harrassed frame of mind which in the year 1842 actuated the commander of the U.S. brig-of-war *Somers* [31] to resolve, under the so-called Articles of War, Articles modelled upon the English Mutiny Act, to resolve upon the execution at sea of a midshipman and two petty-officers as mutineers designing the seizure of the brig. Which resolution was carried out though in a time of peace and within not many days sail of home. An act vindicated by a naval court of inquiry subsequently convened ashore. History, and here cited without comment. True, the circumstances on board the *Somers* were different from those on board the *Indomitable*. But the urgency felt, well-warranted or otherwise, was much the same.

Says a writer whom few know, "Forty years after a battle it is easy for a non-combatant to reason about how it ought to have been fought. It is another thing personally and under fire to direct the fighting while involved in the obscuring smoke of it. Much so with respect to other emergencies involving considerations both practical and moral, and when it is imperative promptly to act. The greater the fog the more it imperils the steamer, and speed is put on though at the hazard of running somebody down. Little ween the snug card-players in the cabin of the responsibilities of the sleepless man on the bridge."

In brief, Billy Budd was formally convicted and sentenced to be hung at the yard-arm in the early morning-watch, it being now night. Otherwise, as is customary in such cases, the sentence would forthwith have been carried out. In war-time on the field or in the fleet, a mortal punishment decreed by a drum-head court—on the field sometimes decreed by but a nod from the General—follows without delay on the heel of conviction without appeal.

23

IT WAS Captain Vere himself who of his own motion communicated the finding of the court to the prisoner; for that purpose going to the compartment where he was in custody and bidding the marine there to withdraw for the time.

Beyond the communication of the sentence what took place at this interview was never

31. *Somers:* See headnote, p. 525.

known. But in view of the character of the twain briefly closeted in that state-room, each radically sharing in the rarer qualities of our nature—so rare indeed as to be all but incredible to average minds however much cultivated—some conjectures may be ventured.

It would have been in consonance with the spirit of Captain Vere should he on this occasion have concealed nothing from the condemned one —should he indeed have frankly disclosed to him the part he himself had played in bringing about the decision, at the same time revealing his actuating motives. On Billy's side it is not improbable that such a confession would have been received in much the same spirit that prompted it. Not without a sort of joy indeed he might have appreciated the brave opinion of him implied in his Captain making such a confidant of him. Nor, as to the sentence itself could he have been insensible that it was imparted to him as to one not afraid to die. Even more may have been. Captain Vere in the end may have developed the passion sometimes latent under an exterior stoical or indifferent. He was old enough to have been Billy's father. The austere devotee of military duty letting himself melt back into what remains primeval in our formalized humanity may in the end have caught Billy to his heart even as Abraham may have caught young Isaac on the brink of resolutely offering him up in obedience to the exacting behest. But there is no telling the sacrament, seldom if in any case revealed to the gadding world wherever under circumstances at all akin to those here attempted to be set forth two of great Nature's nobler order embrace. There is privacy at the time, inviolable to the survivor, and holy oblivion the sequel to each diviner magnanimity, providentially covers all at last.

The first to encounter Captain Vere in act of leaving the compartment was the senior Lieutenant. The fact he beheld, for the moment one expressive of the agony of the strong, was to that officer, though a man of fifty, a startling revelation. That the condemned one suffered less than he who mainly had effected the condemnation was apparently indicated by the former's exclamation in the scene soon perforce to be touched upon.

### 24

OF A SERIES of incidents within a brief term rapidly following each other, the adequate narration may take up a term less brief, especially if explanation or comment here and there seem requisite to the better understanding of such in-

cidents. Between the entrance into the cabin of him who never left it alive, and him who when he did leave it left it as one condemned to die; between this and the closeted interview just given less than an hour and a half had elapsed. It was an interval long enough however to awaken speculations among no few of the ship's company as to what it was that could be detaining in the cabin the master-at-arms and the sailor; for a rumor that both of them had been seen to enter it and neither of them had been seen to emerge, this rumor had got abroad upon the gun-decks and in the tops; the people of a great war-ship being in one respect like villagers taking microscopic note of every outward movement or non-movement going on. When therefore in weather not at all tempestuous all hands were called in the second dog-watch, a summons under such circumstances not usual in those hours, the crew were not wholly unprepared for some announcement extraordinary, one having connection too with the continued absence of the two men from their wonted haunts.

There was a moderate sea at the time; and the moon, newly risen and near to being at its full, silvered the white spar-deck wherever not blotted by the clear-cut shadows horizontally thrown of fixtures and moving men. On either side the quarter-deck the marine guard under arms was drawn up; and Captain Vere standing in his place surrounded by all the ward-room officers, addressed his men. In so doing his manner showed neither more nor less than that properly pertaining to his supreme position aboard his own ship. In clear terms and concise he told them what had taken place in the cabin; that the master-at-arms was dead; that he who had killed him had been already tried by a summary court and condemned to death; and that the execution would take place in the early morning watch. The word *mutiny* was not named in what he said. He refrained too from making the occasion an opportunity for any preachment as to the maintenance of discipline, thinking perhaps that under existing circumstances in the navy the consequence of violating discipline should be made to speak for itself.

Their captain's announcement was listened to by the throng of standing sailors in a dumbness like that of a seated congregation of believers in hell listening to the clergyman's announcement of his Calvinistic text.

At the close, however, a confused murmur went up. It began to wax. All but instantly, then, at a sign, it was pierced and suppressed by shrill whistles of the Boatswain and his Mates piping down one watch.

To be prepared for burial Claggart's body was delivered to certain petty-officers of his mess. And here, not to clog the sequel with lateral matters, it may be added that at a suitable hour, the master-at-arms was committed to the sea with every funeral honor properly belonging to his naval grade.

In this proceeding as in every public one growing out of the tragedy strict adherence to usage was observed. Nor in any point could it have been at all deviated from, either with respect to Claggart or Billy Budd without begetting undesirable speculations in the ship's company, sailors, and more particularly men-of-war's men, being of all men the greatest sticklers for usage.

For similar cause, all communication between Captain Vere and the condemned one ended with the closeted interview already given, the latter being now surrendered to the ordinary routine preliminary to the end. This transfer under guard from the Captain's quarters was effected without unusual precautions—at least no visible ones.

If possible not to let the men so much as surmise that their officers anticipate aught amiss from them is the tacit rule in a military ship. And the more that some sort of trouble should really be apprehended the more do the officers keep that apprehension to themselves; though not the less unostentatious vigilance may be augmented.

In the present instance the sentry placed over the prisoner had strict orders to let no one have communication with him but the Chaplain. And certain unobtrusive measures were taken absolutely to insure this point.

### 25

IN A seventy-four of the old order the deck known as the upper gun-deck was the one covered over by the spar-deck which last though not without its armament was for the most part exposed to the weather. In general it was at all hours free from hammocks; those of the crew swinging on the lower gun-deck, and berth-deck, the latter being not only a dormitory but also the place for the stowing of the sailors' bags, and on both sides lined with the large chests or movable pantries of the many messes of the men.

On the starboard side of the *Indomitable's* upper gun-deck, behold Billy Budd under sentry lying prone in irons in one of the bays formed by the regular spacing of the guns comprising the batteries on either side. All these pieces were of the heavier calibre of that period. Mounted on lumbering wooden carriages they were hampered with cumbersome harness of breechen and strong side-tackles for running them out. Guns and carriages, together with the long rammers and shorter lintstocks lodged in loops overhead—all these, as customary, were painted black; and the heavy hempen breechens tarred to the same tint, wore the like livery of the undertakers. In contrast with the funeral hue of these surroundings the prone sailor's exterior apparel, white *jumper* and white duck trousers, each more or less soiled, dimly glimmered in the obscure light of the bay like a patch of discolored snow in early April lingering at some upland cave's black mouth. In effect he is already in his shroud or the garments that shall serve him in lieu of one. Over him but scarce illuminating him, two battle-lanterns swing from two massive beams of the deck above. Fed with the oil supplied by the war-contractors (whose gains, honest or otherwise, are in every land an anticipated portion of the harvest of death) with flickering splashes of dirty yellow light they pollute the pale moonshine all but ineffectually struggling in obstructed flecks through the open ports from which the tompioned cannon protrude. Other lanterns at intervals serve but to bring out somewhat the obscurer bays which like small confessionals or side-chapels in a cathedral branch from the long dim-vistaed broad aisle between the two batteries of that covered tier.

Such was the deck where now lay the Handsome Sailor. Through the rose-tan of his complexion, no pallor could have shown. It would have taken days of sequestration from the winds and the sun to have brought about the effacement of that. But the skeleton in the cheek-bone at the point of its angle was just beginning delicately to be defined under the warm-tinted skin. In fervid hearts self-contained some brief experiences devour our human tissue as secret fire in a ship's hold consumes cotton in the bale.

But now lying between the two guns, as nipped in the vice of fate, Billy's agony, mainly proceeding from a generous young heart's virgin experience of the diabolical incarnate and effective in some men—the tension of that agony was over now. It survived not the something healing in the closeted interview with Captain Vere. Without movement, he lay as in a trance. That adolescent expression previously noted as his, taking on something akin to the look of a slumbering child in the cradle when the warm hearth-glow of the still chamber at night plays on the dimples that at whiles mysteriously form in the cheek, silently coming and going there. For now and then in the gyved one's trance a serene happy light born of some wandering reminiscence or dream would diffuse itself over his face, and then wane away only anew to return.

The Chaplain coming to see him and finding him thus, and perceiving no sign that he was conscious of his presence, attentively regarded him for a space, then slipping aside, withdrew for the time, peradventure feeling that even he the minister of Christ though receiving his stipend from Mars had no consolation to proffer which could result in a peace transcending that which he beheld. But in the small hours he came again. And the prisoner now awake to his surroundings noticed his approach and civilly, all but cheerfully, welcomed him. But it was to little purpose that in the interview following the good man sought to bring Billy Budd to some godly understanding that he must die, and at dawn. True, Billy himself freely referred to his death as a thing close at hand; but it was something in the way that children will refer to death in general, who yet among their other sports will play a funeral with hearse and mourners.

Not that like children Billy was incapable of conceiving what death really is. No, but he was wholly without irrational fear of it, a fear more prevalent in highly civilized communities than those so-called barbarous ones which in all respects stand nearer to unadulterate Nature. And, as elsewhere said, a barbarian Billy radically was; as much so, for all the costume, as his countrymen the British captives, living trophies, made to march in the Roman triumph of Germanicus.[32] Quite as much so as those later barbarians, young men probably, and picked specimens among the earlier British converts to Christianity, at least nominally such and taken to Rome (as today converts from lesser isles of the sea may be taken to London) of whom the Pope of that time, admiring the strangeness of their personal beauty so unlike the Italian stamp, their clear ruddy complexion and curled flaxen locks, exclaimed, "Angles" (meaning *English* the modern derivative) "Angles do you call them? And is it because they look so like angels?" Had it been later in time one would think that the Pope had in mind Fra Angelico's [33] seraphs some of whom, plucking apples in gardens of the Hesperides have the faint rose-bud complexion of the more beautiful English girls.

If in vain the good Chaplain sought to impress the young barbarian with ideas of death akin to those conveyed in the skull, dial, and cross-bones on old tombstones; equally futile to all appearance were his efforts to bring home to him the thought of salvation and a Saviour. Billy listened, but less out of awe or reverence perhaps than from a certain natural politeness; doubtless at bottom regarding all that in much the same way that most mariners of his class take any discourse abstract or out of the common tone of the work-a-day world. And this sailor-way of taking clerical discourse is not wholly unlike the way in which the pioneer of Christianity full of transcendent miracles was received long ago on tropic isles by any superior *savage* so called—a Tahitian say of Captain Cook's time or shortly after that time. Out of natural courtesy he received, but did not appropriate. It was like a gift placed in the palm of an outreached hand upon which the fingers do not close.

But the *Indomitable's* Chaplain was a discreet man possessing the good sense of a good heart. So he insisted not in his vocation here. At the instance of Captain Vere, a lieutenant had apprised him of pretty much everything as to Billy; and since he felt that innocence was even a better thing than religion wherewith to go to Judgement, he reluctantly withdrew; but in his emotion not without first performing an act strange enough in an Englishman, and under the circumstances yet more so in any regular priest. Stooping over, he kissed on the fair cheek his fellow-man, a felon in martial law, one who though on the confines of death he felt he could never convert to a dogma; nor for all that did he fear for his future.

Marvel not that having been made acquainted with the young sailor's essential innocence (an irruption of heretic thought hard to suppress) the worthy man lifted not a finger to avert the doom of such a martyr to martial discipline. So to do would not only have been as idle as invoking the desert, but would also have been an audacious transgression of the bounds of his function, one as exactly prescribed to him by military law as that of the boatswain or any other naval officer. Bluntly put, a chaplain is the minister of the Prince of Peace serving in the host of the God of War— Mars. As such, he is as incongruous as that musket of Blücher etc. at Christmas. Why then is he there? Because he indirectly subserves the purpose attested by the cannon; because too he lends the sanction of the religion of the meek to that which practically is the abrogation of everything but brute Force.

---

32. **Roman . . . Germanicus:** in 17 A.D. Nero Claudius Germanicus, nephew of Tiberius, was famous for his campaigns against the German tribes. (When he was adopted by his uncle he took the name of Germanicus Julius Caesar.)  33. **Fra Angelico:** Italian painter (1387–1455).

26

THE NIGHT so luminous on the spar-deck but otherwise on the cavernous ones below, levels so like the tiered galleries in a coal-mine—the luminous night passed away. But, like the prophet in the chariot disappearing in heaven and dropping his mantle to Elisha, the withdrawing night transferred its pale robe to the breaking day. A meek shy light appeared in the East, where stretched a diaphanous fleece of white furrowed vapor. That light slowly waxed. Suddenly *eight bells* was struck aft, responded to by one louder metallic stroke from forward. It was four o'clock in the morning. Instantly the silver whistles were heard summoning all hands to witness punishment. Up through the great hatchways rimmed with racks of heavy shot, the watch below came pouring, overspreading with the watch already on deck the space between the mainmast and foremast including that occupied by the capacious *launch* and the black booms tiered on either side of it, boat and booms making a summit of observation for the powder-boys and younger tars. A different group comprising one watch of topmen leaned over the rail of that sea-balcony, no small one in a seventy-four, looking down on the crowd below. Man or boy none spake but in whisper, and few spake at all. Captain Vere—as before, the central figure among the assembled commissioned officers —stood nigh the break of the poop-deck facing forward. Just below him on the quarter-deck the marines in full equipment were drawn up much as at the scene of the promulgated sentence.

At sea in the old time, the execution by halter of a military sailor was generally from the fore-yard. In the present instance, for special reasons the mainyard was assigned. Under an arm of that weather or lee yard the prisoner was presently brought up, the Chaplain attending him. It was noted at the time and remarked upon afterwards, that in this final scene the good man evinced little or nothing of the perfunctory. Brief speech indeed he had with the condemned one, but the genuine Gospel was less on his tongue than in his aspect and manner towards him. The final preparations personal to the latter being speedily brought to an end by two boatswain's-mates, the consummation impended. Billy stood facing aft. At the penultimate moment, his words, his only ones, words wholly unobstructed in the utterance were these—"God bless Captain Vere!" Syllables so unanticipated coming from one with the ignominious hemp about his neck—a conventional felon's benediction directed aft towards the quarters of honor; syllables too delivered in the clear melody of a singing-bird on the point of launching from the twig, had a phe-

nomenal effect, not unenhanced by the rare personal beauty of the young sailor spiritualized now through late experiences so poignantly profound.

Without volition as it were, as if indeed the ship's populace were but the vehicles of some vocal current electric, with one voice from alow and aloft came a resonant sympathetic echo—"God bless Captain Vere!" And yet at that instant Billy alone must have been in their hearts, even as he was in their eyes.

At the pronounced words and the spontaneous echo that voluminously rebounded them, Captain Vere, either through stoic self-control or a sort of momentary paralysis induced by emotional shock, stood erectly rigid as a musket in the ship-armorer's rack.

The hull deliberately recovering from the periodic roll to leeward was just regaining an even keel, when the last signal a preconcerted dumb one was given. At the same moment it chanced that the vapory fleece hanging low in the East, was shot through with a soft glory as of the fleece of the Lamb of God seen in mystical vision and simultaneously therewith, watched by the wedged mass of upturned faces, Billy ascended; and, ascending, took the full rose of the dawn.

In the pinioned figure, arrived at the yard-end, to the wonder of all no motion was apparent, none save that created by the ship's motion, in moderate weather so majestic in a great ship ponderously cannoned.

27

*A Digression*

WHEN some days afterward in reference to the singularity just mentioned, the Purser a rather ruddy rotund person more accurate as an accountant than profound as a philosopher, said at mess to the Surgeon, "What testimony to the force lodged in will-power" the latter, saturnine, spare and tall, one in whom a discreet causticity went along with a manner less genial than polite, replied, "Your pardon, Mr. Purser. In a hanging scientifically conducted—and under special orders I myself directed how Budd's was to be effected— any movement following the completed suspension and originating in the body suspended, such movement indicates mechanical spasm in the muscular system. Hence the absence of that is no more attributable to will-power as you call it than to horse-power—begging your pardon."

"But this muscular spasm you speak of, is not that in a degree more or less invariable in these cases?"

"Assuredly so, Mr. Purser."

"How then, my good sir, do you account for its absence in this instance?"

"Mr. Purser, it is clear that your sense of the singularity in this matter equals not mine. You account for it by what you call will-power a term not yet included in the lexicon of science. For me I do not, with my present knowledge pretend to account for it at all. Even should we assume the hypothesis that at the first touch of the halyards the action of Budd's heart, intensified by extraordinary emotion at its climax, abruptly stopt— much like a watch when in carelessly winding it up you strain at the finish, thus snapping the chain—even under that hypothesis how account for the phenomenon that followed?"

"You admit then that the absence of spasmodic movement was phenomenal."

"It was phenomenal, Mr. Purser, in the sense that it was an appearance the cause of which is not immediately to be assigned."

"But tell me, my dear sir," pertinaciously continued the other, "was the man's death effected by the halter, or was it a species of euthanasia?"

"*Euthanasia,* Mr. Purser, is something like your *will-power:* I doubt its authenticity as a scientific term—begging your pardon again. It is at once imaginative and metaphysical,—in short, Greek. But" abruptly changing his tone "there is a case in the sick-bay that I do not care to leave to my assistants. Beg your pardon, but excuse me." And rising from the mess he formally withdrew.

### 28

THE SILENCE at the moment of execution and for a moment or two continuing thereafter, a silence but emphasized by the regular wash of the sea against the hull or the flutter of a sail caused by the helmsman's eyes being tempted astray, this emphasized silence was gradually disturbed by a sound not easily to be verbally rendered. Whoever has heard the freshet-wave of a torrent suddenly swelled by pouring showers in tropical mountains, showers not shared by the plain; whoever has heard the first muffled murmur of its sloping advance through precipitous woods, may form some conception of the sound now heard. The seeming remoteness of its source was because of its murmurous indistinctness since it came from close-by, even from the men massed on the ship's open deck. Being inarticulate, it was dubious in significance further than it seemed to indicate some capricious revulsion of thought or feeling such as mobs ashore are liable to, in the present instance possibly implying a sullen revocation on the men's part of their involuntary echoing of Billy's benediction. But ere the murmur

had time to wax into clamor it was met by a strategic command, the more telling that it came with abrupt unexpectedness.

"Pipe down the starboard watch Boatswain, and see that they go."

Shrill as the shriek of the sea-hawk, the whistles of the Boatswain and his Mates pierced that ominous low sound, dissipating it; and yielding to the mechanism of discipline the throng was thinned by one half. For the remainder most of them were set to temporary employments connected with trimming the yards and so forth, business readily to be got up to serve occasion by any officer-of-the-deck.

Now each proceeding that follows a mortal sentence pronounced at sea by a drum-head court is characterised by promptitude not perceptibly merging into hurry, though bordering that. The hammock, the one which had been Billy's bed when alive, having already been ballasted with shot and otherwise prepared to serve for his canvas coffin, the last offices of the sea-undertakers, the Sail-Maker's Mates, were now speedily completed. When everything was in readiness a second call for all hands made necessary by the strategic movement before mentioned was sounded and now to witness burial.

The details of this closing formality it needs not to give. But when the tilted plank let slide its freight into the sea, a second strange human murmur was heard, blended now with another inarticulate sound proceeding from certain larger sea-fowl whose attention having been attracted by the peculiar commotion in the water resulting from the heavy sloped dive of the shotted hammock into the sea, flew screaming to the spot. So near the hull did they come, that the stridor or bony creak of their gaunt double-jointed pinions was audible. As the ship under light airs passed on, leaving the burial-spot astern, they still kept circling it low down with the moving shadow of their outstretched wings and the croaked requiem of their cries.

Upon sailors as superstitious as those of the age preceding ours, men-of-war's men too who had just beheld the prodigy of repose in the form suspended in air and now foundering in the deeps; to such mariners the action of the sea-fowl though dictated by mere animal greed for prey, was big with no prosaic significance. An uncertain movement began among them, in which some encroachment was made. It was tolerated but for a moment. For suddenly the drum beat to quarters, which familiar sound happening at least twice every day, had upon the present occasion a signal peremptoriness in it. True martial discipline long continued superinduces in average man a sort of impulse of docility whose operation at the official sound of command much resembles in its promptitude the effect of an instinct.

The drum-beat dissolved the multitude, distributing most of them along the batteries of the two covered gun-decks. There, as wont, the guns' crews stood by their respective cannon erect and silent. In due course the First Officer, sword under arm and standing in his place on the quarter-deck formally received the successive reports of the sworded Lieutenants commanding the sections of batteries below; the last of which reports being made the summed report he delivered with the customary salute to the Commander. All this occupied time, which in the present case, was the object of beating to quarters at an hour prior to the customary one. That such variance from usage was authorized by an officer like Captain Vere, a martinet as some deemed him, was evidence of the necessity for unusual action implied in what he deemed to be temporarily the mood of his men. "With mankind" he would say "forms, measured forms are everything; and that is the import couched in the story of Orpheus with his lyre spell-binding the wild denizens of the wood." And this he once applied to the disruption of forms going on across the Channel and the consequences thereof.

At this unwonted muster at quarters, all proceeded as at the regular hour. The band on the quarter-deck played a sacred air. After which the Chaplain went through the customary morning service. That done, the drum beat the retreat, and toned by music and religious rites subserving the discipline and purpose of war, the men in their wonted orderly manner, dispersed to the places allotted them when not at the guns.

And now it was full day. The fleece of low-hanging vapor had vanished, licked up by the sun that late had so glorified it. And the circumambient air in the clearness of its serenity was like smooth white marble in the polished block not yet removed from the marble-dealer's yard.

### 29

THE SYMMETRY of form attainable in pure fiction can not so readily be achieved in a narration essentially having less to do with fable than with fact. Truth uncompromisingly told will always have its ragged edges; hence the conclusion of such a narration is apt to be less finished than an architectural finial.

How it fared with the Handsome Sailor during the year of the Great Mutiny has been faithfully given. But though properly the story ends with

his life, something in way of sequel will not be amiss. Three brief chapters will suffice.

In the general re-christening under the Directory of the craft originally forming the navy of the French monarchy, the *St. Louis* line-of-battle ship was named the *Athéiste.* Such a name, like some other substituted ones in the Revolutionary fleet while proclaiming the infidel audacity of the ruling power was yet, though not so intended to be, the aptest name, if one consider it, ever given to a war-ship; far more so indeed than the *Devastation,* the *Erebus* (the *Hell*) and similar names bestowed upon fighting-ships.

On the return-passage to the English fleet from the detached cruise during which occurred the events already recorded, the *Indomitable* fell in with the *Athéiste.* An engagement ensued; during which Captain Vere in the act of putting his ship alongside the enemy with a view of throwing his boarders across her bulwarks, was hit by a musket-ball from a port-hole of the enemy's main cabin. More than disabled he dropped to the deck and was carried below to the same cock-pit where some of his men already lay. The senior Lieutenant took command. Under him the enemy was finally captured and though much crippled was by rare good fortune successfully taken into Gibraltar, an English port not very distant from the scene of the fight. There, Captain Vere with the rest of the wounded was put ashore. He lingered for some days, but the end came. Unhappily he was cut off too early for the Nile and Trafalgar. The spirit that spite its philosophic austerity may yet have indulged in the most secret of all passions, ambition, never attained to the fulness of fame.

Not long before death while lying under the influence of that magical drug which soothing the physical frame mysteriously operates on the subtler element in man, he was heard to murmur words inexplicable to his attendant—"Billy Budd, Billy Budd." That these were not the accents of remorse, would seem clear from what the attendant said to the *Indomitable's* senior officer of marines who as the most reluctant to condemn of the members of the drum-head court, too well knew though here he kept the knowledge to himself, who Billy Budd was.

### 30

SOME few weeks after the execution, among other matters under the head of *News from the Mediterranean,* there appeared in a naval chronicle of the time, an authorized weekly publication, an account of the affair. It was doubtless for the most part written in good faith, though the medium, partly rumor, through which the facts must have reached the writer, served to deflect and in part falsify them. The account was as follows—

"On the tenth of the last month a deplorable occurrence took place on board H.M.S. *Indomitable*. John Claggart, the ship's master-at-arms, discovering that some sort of plot was incipient among an inferior section of the ship's company, and that the ringleader was one William Budd; he, Claggart in the act of arraigning the man before the Captain was vindictively stabbed to the heart by the suddenly drawn sheath-knife of Budd.

"The deed and the implement employed, sufficiently suggest that though mustered into the service under an English name the assassin was no Englishman, but one of those aliens adopting English cognomens whom the present extraordinary necessities of the Service have caused to be admitted into it in considerable numbers.

"The enormity of the crime and the extreme depravity of the criminal, appear the greater in view of the character of the victim, a middle-aged man respectable and discreet, belonging to that minor official grade, the petty-officers, upon whom, as none know better than the commissioned gentlemen, the efficiency of His Majesty's navy so largely depends. His function was a responsible one; at once onerous and thankless and his fidelity in it the greater because of his strong patriotic impulse. In this instance as in so many other instances in these days, the character of this unfortunate man signally refutes, if refutation were needed, that peevish saying attributed to the late Dr. Johnson, that patriotism is the last refuge of a scoundrel.

"The criminal paid the penalty of his crime. The promptitude of the punishment has proved salutary. Nothing amiss is now apprehended aboard H.M.S. *Indomitable*."

The above appearing in a publication now long ago superannuated and forgotten is all that hitherto has stood in human record to attest what manner of men respectively were John Claggart and Billy Budd.

### 31

EVERYTHING is for a term remarkable in navies. Any tangible object associated with some striking incident of the service is converted into a monument. The spar from which the foretopman was suspended, was for some few years kept trace of by the blue-jackets. Their knowledge followed it from ship to dock-yard and again from dock-yard to ship, till pursuing it even when at last reduced to a mere dock-yard boom. To them a chip of it was as a piece of the Cross. Ignorant though they were of the secret facts of the tragedy, and not thinking but that the penalty was somehow unavoidably inflicted from the naval point of view, for all that they instinctively felt that Billy was a sort of man as incapable of mutiny as of wilful murder. They recalled the fresh young image of the Handsome Sailor, that face never deformed by a sneer or subtler vile freak of the heart within. Their impression of him was doubtless deepened by the fact that he was gone, and in a measure mysteriously gone. On the gun-decks of the *Indomitable* the general estimate of his nature and its unconscious simplicity eventually found rude utterance from another foretopman one of his own watch gifted, as some sailors are, with an artless poetic temperament. The tarry hands made some lines which after circulating among the shipboard crew for a while, finally got rudely printed at Portsmouth as a ballad. The title given to it was the sailor's.

#### BILLY IN THE DARBIES [34]

Good of the Chaplain to enter Lone Bay
And down on his marrow-bones here and pray
For the like just o' me, Billy Budd.—But look:
Through the port comes the moon-shine astray!
It tips the guard's cutlas and silvers this nook;
But 'twill die in the dawning of Billy's last day.
A jewel-block they'll make of me tomorrow,
Pendant pearl from the yard-arm-end
Like the ear-drop I gave to Bristol Molly—
O, 'tis me, not the sentence they'll suspend.
Ay, Ay, all is up; and I must up too
Early in the morning, aloft from alow.
On an empty stomach, now, never it would do.
They'll give me a nibble—bit o' biscuit ere I go.
Sure, a messmate will reach me the last parting cup;
But, turning heads away from the hoist and the belay,
Heaven knows who will have the running of me up!
No pipe to those halyards.—But aren't it all sham?
A blur's in my eyes; it is dreaming that I am.
A hatchet to my hawser? all adrift to go?
The drum roll to grog, and Billy never know?
But Donald he has promised to stand by the plank;
So I'll shake a friendly hand ere I sink.
But—no! It is dead then I'll be, come to think.—
I remember Taff the Welshman when he sank.
And his cheek it was like the budding pink.
But me they'll lash me in hammock, drop me deep.
Fathoms down, fathoms down, how I'll dream fast
  asleep.
I feel it stealing now. Sentry, are you there?
Just ease this darbies at the wrist,
And roll me over fair,
I am sleepy, and the oozy weeds about me twist.

#### END OF BOOK

*April 19th*
*1891*

34. **Darbies:** handcuffs.

FROM

# BATTLE-PIECES AND ASPECTS OF THE WAR

❖

⟨ THE FOLLOWING group of poems, up to and including "Shiloh," are from *Battle-Pieces*, published in 1866. There is little evidence bearing upon the precise date of composition of most of Melville's later poetry, but concerning the Civil War poems we are on firmer ground. In his prefatory note to *Battle-Pieces* Melville wrote that "with few exceptions, the Pieces in this volume originated in an impulse imparted by the fall of Richmond." The "few exceptions" are presumably those which Melville himself dated in parentheses placed under the titles. As the present representative selection suggests, many of the best poems are among the relative few he wrote before the fall of Richmond, which took place on April 3, 1865.

❖

## THE PORTENT
(1859)

Hanging from the beam,
    Slowly swaying (such the law),
Gaunt the shadow on your green,
    Shenandoah!
The cut is on the crown
    (Lo, John Brown),
And the stabs shall heal no more.

Hidden in the cap
    Is the anguish none can draw;
So your future veils its face,         10
    Shenandoah!
But the streaming beard is shown
    (Weird John Brown),
The meteor of the war.

## MISGIVINGS
(1860)

When ocean-clouds over inland hills
    Sweep storming in late autumn brown,
And horror the sodden valley fills,

And the spire falls crashing in the town,
    I muse upon my country's ills—
    The tempest bursting from the waste of Time
On the world's fairest hope linked with man's foulest crime.
Nature's dark side is heeded now—
    (Ah! optimist-cheer disheartened flown)—
A child may read the moody brow     10
    Of yon black mountain lone.
With shouts the torrents down the gorges go,
    And storms are formed behind the storm we feel:
The hemlock shakes in the rafter, the oak in the driving keel.

## THE CONFLICT OF CONVICTIONS
(1860–1861)

On starry heights
    A bugle wails the long recall;
Derision stirs the deep abyss,
    Heaven's ominous silence over all.
Return, return, O eager Hope,
    And face man's latter fall.
Events, they make the dreamers quail;
    Satan's old age is strong and hale,
A disciplined captain, gray in skill,
And Raphael a white enthusiast still;     10
Dashed aims, at which Christ's martyrs pale,
Shall Mammon's slaves fulfill?

    (*Dismantle the fort,*
    *Cut down the fleet—*
    *Battle no more shall be!*
    *While the fields for fight in aeons to come*
    *Congeal beneath the sea.*)

The terrors of truth and dart of death
    To faith alike are vain;
Though comets, gone a thousand years,     20
    Return again,
Patient she stands—she can no more—
And waits, nor heeds she waxes hoar.

    (*At a stony gate,*
    *A statue of stone,*
    *Weed overgrown—*
    *Long 'twill wait!*)

---

THE PORTENT. **6. John Brown:** John Brown (1800–59) was the leader of an abortive attempt to liberate the Southern Negroes. He briefly captured the Federal Arsenal at Harper's Ferry on the Shenandoah River, but was soon made prisoner and hanged.

THE CONFLICT OF CONVICTIONS. **10. Raphael:** in Hebrew religion, the archangel of healing. There is little doubt, however, that Melville is thinking of the Raphael of Milton's *Paradise Lost*, where he is the angel sent by God to Adam and Eve to admonish and counsel them and to explain to them His divine purpose. By calling him a "white enthusiast," Melville means that Raphael is now powerless to act. **12. Mammon:** a personified Aramaic word, meaning inordinate wealth and greed; see Luke 6:24.

But God his former mind retains,
    Confirms his old decree;
The generations are inured to pains,           30
    And strong Necessity
Surges, and heaps Time's strand with wrecks.
    The People spread like a weedy grass,
    The thing they will they bring to pass,
And prosper to the apoplex.
The rout it herds around the heart,
    The ghost is yielded in the gloom;
Kings wag their heads—Now save thyself
    Who wouldst rebuild the world in bloom.

        (*Tide-mark*           40
        *And top of the ages' strife,*
        *Verge where they called the world to come,*
        *The last advance of life—*
        *Ha ha, the rust on the Iron Dome!*)

Nay, but revere the hid event;
    In the cloud a sword is girded on,
I mark a twinkling in the tent
    Of Michael the warrior one.
Senior wisdom suits not now,
The light is on the youthful brow.           50

        (*Ay, in caves the miner see:*
        *His forehead bears, a blinking light;*
        *Darkness so he feebly braves,*
        *A meagre wight!*)

But He who rules is old—is old;
Ah! faith is warm, but heaven with age is cold.

        (*Ho ho, ho ho,*
        *The cloistered doubt*
        *Of olden times*
        *Is blurted out!*)           60

The Ancient of Days forever is young,
    Forever the scheme of Nature thrives;
I know a wind in purpose strong—
    It spins *against* the way it drives
What if the gulfs their slimed foundations bare?
So deep must the stones be hurled
 Whereon the throes of ages rear
The final empire and the happier world.

        (*The poor old Past,*
        *The Future's slave,*           70
        *She drudged through pain and crime*
        *To bring about the blissful Prime,*
        *Then—perished.* There's *a grave!*)

48. **Michael:** in Jewish religion the most powerful of the arch-angels, but here again Melville is taking his characterization of angels from *Paradise Lost.*   61. **The Ancient of Days:** Melville takes this apocalyptic name for God from Dan. 7:9.

Power unanointed may come—
Dominion (unsought by the free)
    And the Iron Dome,
Stronger for stress and strain,
Fling her huge shadow athwart the main;
But the Founders' dream shall flee.
Age after age shall be           80
As age after age has been,
(From man's changeless heart their way they win);
And death be busy with all who strive—
Death, with silent negative.

YEA AND NAY—
EACH HATH HIS SAY;
BUT GOD HE KEEPS THE MIDDLE WAY.
NONE WAS BY
WHEN HE SPREAD THE SKY;
WISDOM IS VAIN, AND PROPHESY.    90

NOTE: "The gloomy lull of the early part of the winter of 1860–1861, seeming big with final disaster to our institutions, affected some minds that believed them to constitute one of the great hopes of mankind, much as the eclipse which came over the promise of the first French Revolution affected kindred natures, throwing them for the time into doubts and misgivings universal" [Melville's note].

# THE MARCH INTO VIRGINIA

*Ending in the First Manassas*

(July, 1861)

Did all the lets and bars appear
    To every just or larger end,
Whence should come the trust and cheer?
    Youth must its ignorant impulse lend—
Age finds place in the rear.
    All wars are boyish, and are fought by boys,
The champions and enthusiasts of the state:
    Turbid ardors and vain joys
        Not barrenly abate—
Stimulants to the power mature,           10
    Preparatives of fate.

Who here forecasteth the event?
What heart but spurns at precedent
And warnings of the wise,
Contemned foreclosures of surprise?
The banners play, the bugles call,
The air is blue and prodigal.
    No berrying party, pleasure-wooed,
No picnic party in the May,

THE MARCH INTO VIRGINIA.     Melville refers to the Battle of Bull Run—a Federal disaster—which occurred in and around Manassas Junction, Va.

Ever went less loth than they                    20
 Into that leafy neighborhood.
In Bacchic glee they file toward Fate,
Moloch's uninitiate;
Expectancy, and glad surmise
Of battle's unknown mysteries.
All they feel is this: 'tis glory,
A rapture sharp, though transitory,
Yet lasting in belaureled story.
So they gayly go to fight,
Chatting left and laughing right.                30

But some who this blithe mood present,
 As on in lightsome files they fare,
Shall die experienced ere three days be spent—
 Perish, enlightened by the vollied glare;
Or shame survive, and like to adamant,
 The throe of Second Manassas share.

## A UTILITARIAN VIEW OF THE
## MONITOR'S FIGHT

Plain be the phrase, yet apt the verse,
 More ponderous than nimble;
For since grimed War here laid aside
His Orient pomp, 'twould ill befit
 Overmuch to ply
The rhyme's barbaric cymbal.

Hail to victory without the gaud
 Of glory; zeal that needs no fans
Of banners; plain mechanic power
Plied cogently in War now placed—              10
 Where War belongs—
Among the trades and artisans.

Yet this was battle, and intense—
 Beyond the strife of fleets heroic;
Deadlier, closer, calm 'mid storm;
No passion; all went on by crank,
 Pivot, and screw,
And calculations of caloric.

Needless to dwell; the story's known.
 The ringing of those plates on plates         20

Still ringeth round the world—
The clangor of that blacksmiths' fray.
 The anvil-din
Resounds this message from the Fates:

War shall yet be, and to the end;
 But war-paint shows the streaks of weather;
War yet shall be, but warriors
Are now but operatives; War's made
 Less grand than Peace,
And a singe runs through lace and feather.  30

## IN THE PRISON PEN
(1864)

Listless he eyes the palisades
 And sentries in the glare;
'Tis barren as a pelican-beach—
 But his world is ended there.

Nothing to do; and vacant hands
 Bring on the idiot-pain;
He tries to think—to recollect,
 But the blur is on his brain.

Around him swarm the plaining ghosts
 Like those on Virgil's shore—                  10
A wilderness of faces dim,
 And pale ones gashed and hoar.

A smiting sun. No shed, no tree;
 He totters to his lair—
A den that sick hands dug in earth
 Ere famine wasted there,

Or, dropping in his place, he swoons,
 Walled in by throngs that press,
Till forth from the throngs they bear him dead—
 Dead in his meagreness.                        20

## THE COLLEGE COLONEL

He rides at their head;
 A crutch by his saddle just slants in view,
One slung arm is in splints, you see,
 Yet he guides his strong steed—how coldly too.
He brings his regiment home—
 Not as they filed two years before,
But a remnant half-tattered, and battered, and
 worn,

22. **Bacchic:** adjective form of one of the names of Dionysus, the Greek God of wine. Melville uses the word to suggest a festive or holiday spirit.   23. **Moloch:** a Semitic deity (mentioned in Lev. 18:21 and Amos 5:26) to whom parents sacrificed their children by burning.   A UTILITARIAN VIEW OF THE MONITOR'S FIGHT.   On March 8–9, 1862, the Federal ship *Monitor* defeated the Confederate *Merrimack* off Hampton Roads, Va. Melville sees in this first battle of ironclad vessels the advent of new conceptions of both the tactics and the moral meaning of war.   4. **Orient:** colorful.   18. **caloric:** what would now be called thermodynamics, or the calculation of the relation of heat to energy.

IN THE PRISON PEN.   9. **plaining:** mourning or lamenting. 10. **Virgil's shore:** a reference to the *Aeneid*, VI.320 ff., where Aeneas, descending into Hades, encounters a multitude of restless and tormented ghosts of those who were not buried with proper rites.

Like castaway sailors, who—stunned
   By the surf's loud roar,
  Their mates dragged back and seen no more—
Again and again breast the surge,      11
  And at last crawl, spent, to shore.

A still rigidity and pale—
   An Indian aloofness lones his brow;
He has lived a thousand years
Compressed in battle's pains and prayers,
  Marches and watches slow.
There are welcoming shouts, and flags;
  Old men off hat to the Boy,
Wreaths from gay balconies fall at his feet,   20
  But to *him*—there comes alloy.

It is not that a leg is lost,
  It is not that an arm is maimed,
It is not that the fever has racked—
  Self he has long disclaimed.
But all through the Seven Days' Fight,
  And deep in the Wilderness grim,
And in the field-hospital tent,
  And Petersburg crater, and dim
Lean brooding in Libby, there came—    30
  Ah heaven!—what *truth* to him.

## THE HOUSE-TOP

### *A Night Piece*
(July, 1863)

No sleep. The sultriness pervades the air
And binds the brain—a dense oppression, such
As tawny tigers feel in matted shades,
Vexing their blood and making apt for ravage.
Beneath the stars the roofy desert spreads
Vacant as Libya. All is hushed near by.
Yet fitfully from far breaks a mixed surf
Of muffled sound, the Atheist roar of riot.
Yonder, where parching Sirius set in drought,
Balefully glares red Arson—there—and there.  10
The Town is taken by its rats—ship-rats
And rats of the wharves. All civil charms

And priestly spells which late held hearts in awe—
Fear-bound, subjected to a better sway
Than sway of self; these like a dream dissolve,
And man rebounds whole aeons back in nature.
Hail to the low dull rumble, dull and dead,
And ponderous drag that shakes the wall.
Wise Draco comes, deep in the midnight roll
Of black artillery; he comes, though late;   20
In code corroborating Calvin's creed
 And cynic tyrannies of honest kings;
He comes, nor parlies; and the Town, redeemed,
Give thanks devout; nor, being thankful, heeds
The grimy slur on the Republic's faith implied,
Which holds that Man is naturally good,
And—more—is Nature's Roman, never to be
  scourged.

NOTE: " 'I dare not write the horrible and inconceivable atrocities committed,' says Froissart, in alluding to the remarkable sedition in France during his time. The like may be hinted of some proceedings of the draft-rioters" [M].

## SHILOH

### *A Requiem*
(April, 1862)

Skimming lightly, wheeling still,
  The swallows fly low
Over the field in clouded days,
  The forest-field of Shiloh—
Over the field where April rain
Solaced the parched ones stretched in pain
Through the pause of night
That followed the Sunday fight
  Around the church of Shiloh—
The church so lone, the log-built one,   10
That echoed to many a parting groan
   And natural prayer
  Of dying foemen mingled there—
Foemen at morn, but friends at eve—
  Fame or country least their care:

---

THE COLLEGE COLONEL. **26. Seven Days' Fight:** refers to the battle preceding that of Malvern Hill, where, in his effort to defend Richmond, Lee won temporarily over McClellan. **27. Wilderness:** The Battle of the Wilderness took place between the forces of Generals Grant and Lee in May 1864, in an area north of Richmond between the Shenandoah and Rappahannock Rivers. **29. Petersburg crater:** a crater formed by a Federal mine that blew up the Confederate fortifications at Petersburg, Va., in July 1864. **30. Libby:** a prison in Richmond, a converted warehouse where Federal officers were incarcerated, often under conditions of great hardship. THE HOUSE-TOP. **9. Sirius:** the dog-star in the constellation Canis Major. **11–12. The Town . . . wharves:** Mobs of rioters, largely Irish born, terrorized the city.

**13. priestly spells:** The reference is to John Hughes, Roman Catholic bishop of New York, whose authority and blunt speech were unable to prevent the outbreak of rioting, but whose advice and courage later did much to end the four days of fire, looting, and the lynching of Negroes. **19. Draco:** an Athenian legislator of the seventh century B.C., whose codification of the laws of his time gave him the reputation of a harsh and relentless oppressor. **21. Calvin's creed:** Melville refers to the inexorable Calvinist idea of the predestination of the elect and the damned. **27. Nature's . . . scourged:** Roman citizens by law could not be whipped. SHILOH. Shiloh, Tenn., was the site of a costly but indecisive battle between the Federal armies under Grant and Buell and the Confederates under Johnston and Beauregard.

(What like a bullet can undeceive!)
But now they lie low,
While over them the swallows skim,
And all is hushed at Shiloh.

F R O M

# JOHN MARR AND OTHER SAILORS [1888]

## THE MALDIVE SHARK

About the Shark, phlegmatical one,
Pale sot of the Maldive sea,
The sleek little pilot-fish, azure and slim,
How alert in attendance be.
From his saw-pit of mouth, from his charnel of
    maw
They have nothing of harm to dread,
But liquidly glide on his ghastly flank
Or before his Gorgonian head;
Or lurk in the port of serrated teeth
In white triple tiers of glittering gates,     10
And there find a haven when peril's abroad,
An asylum in jaws of the Fates!
They are friends; and friendly they guide him to
    prey,
Yet never partake of the treat—
Eyes and brains to the dotard lethargic and dull,
Pale ravener of horrible meat.

## TO NED

Where is the world we roved, Ned Bunn?
  Hollows thereof lay rich in shade
By voyagers old inviolate thrown
  Ere Paul Pry cruised with Pelf and Trade.
To us old lads some thoughts come home
Who roamed a world young lads no more shall
    roam.

Nor less the satiate year impends
  When, wearying of routine-resorts,
The pleasure-hunter shall break loose,
  Ned, for our Pantheistic ports:—     10
Marquesas and glenned isles that be
Authentic Edens in a Pagan sea.

The charm of scenes untried shall lure,
  And, Ned, a legend urge the flight—
The Typee-truants under stars
  Unknown to Shakespeare's *Midsummer-Night;*
And man, if lost to Saturn's Age,
Yet feeling life no Syrian pilgrimage.

But, tell, shall he, the tourist, find
  Our isles the same in violet-glow     20
Enamoring us what years and years—
  Ah, Ned, what years and years ago!
Well, Adam advances, smart in pace,
But scarce by violets that advance you trace.

But we, in anchor-watches calm,
  The Indian Psyche's languor won,
And, musing, breathed primeval balm
  From Edens ere yet overrun;
Marvelling mild if mortal twice,
Here and hereafter, touch a Paradise.     30

F R O M

# TIMOLEON [1891]

## FRAGMENTS OF A LOST GNOSTIC POEM OF THE 12TH CENTURY

\* \* \*

Found a family, build a state,
The pledged event is still the same:
Matter in end will never abate
His ancient brutal claim.

\* \* \*

THE MALDIVE SHARK.   **2. Maldive sea:** a part of the Indian Ocean southwest of India.   **3. pilot-fish:** a small, bluish fish often found accompanying, if not "piloting," sharks.   **8. Gorgonian head:** The name Gorgon was given to three sisters in Greek myth whose heads were covered with snakes instead of hair and the mere sight of whom turned the beholder to stone.   TO NED.   **1. Ned Bunn:** Melville's fictitious name for Richard Tobias Greene, who had been his companion in the adventures related in *Typee*; he is called Toby in that book.   **4. Paul Pry:** a proverbial name for any meddlesome, petty-minded, inquisitive person. The name comes from the farce *Paul Pry* by John Poole, produced in 1825.

**10. Pantheistic:** Melville is not using this word in an exact theological sense; he is saying that the ports are suffused with a spirit of felicity, harmony, and pleasure.   **26. Indian Psyche's languor:** In Greek "psyche" means breath, soul, or mind. In Greek myth Psyche is a beautiful princess beloved by Eros (Cupid). Perhaps Melville's curious phrase is meant to suggest a languorous pleasure of the spirit, tinged with erotic feeling, which he associates with the East or Indies.   FRAGMENTS OF A LOST GNOSTIC POEM OF THE 12TH CENTURY.   Melville's title is rather fanciful, but the brief poems under it do state the Gnostic belief in the ineradicable evil of the material world.

Indolence is heaven's ally here,
And energy the child of hell:
The Good Man pouring from his pitcher clear,
But brims the poisoned well.

## MONODY

To have known him, to have loved him
    After loneness long;
And then to be estranged in life,
    And neither in the wrong;
And now for death to set his seal—
    Ease me, a little ease, my song!

By wintry hills his hermit-mound
    The sheeted snow-drifts drape,
And houseless there the snow-bird flits
    Beneath the fir-trees' crape:                    10
Glazed now with ice the cloistral vine
    That hid the shyest grape.

## ART

In placid hours well pleased we dream
Of many a brave unbodied scheme.
    But form to lend, pulsed life create,
    What unlike things must meet and mate:

MONODY.    An elegy on Hawthorne, who died May 19, 1864.

A flame to melt—a wind to freeze;
Sad patience—joyous energies;
Humility—yet pride and scorn;
Instinct and study; love and hate;
Audacity—reverence. These must mate,
And fuse with Jacob's mystic heart,       10
To wrestle with the angel—Art.

## GREEK ARCHITECTURE

Not magnitude, not lavishness,
But Form—the Site;
Not innovating wilfulness,
But reverence for the Archetype.

## THE RAVAGED VILLA

In shards the sylvan vases lie,
    Their links of dance undone,
And brambles wither by thy brim,
    Choked fountain of the sun!
The spider in the laurel spins,
    The weed exiles the flower:
And, flung to kiln, Apollo's bust
    Makes lime for Mammon's tower.

ART.    10. **Jacob's mystic heart:** Jacob wrestles all night with an angel until convinced that it is the Lord (Gen. 32:24–30).    THE RAVAGED VILLA.    7–8. **Apollo's . . . tower:** The meaning is that beauty and tradition have been sacrificed to the rapacious purposes of man (see 12 n. under "The Conflict of Convictions").

R. W. B. LEWIS

*Editor*

# Walt Whitman

## 1819–1892

WALT WHITMAN is the most blurred, even contradictory figure in the classical or mid-nineteenth-century period of American literature. Recent scholarship and criticism have been clearing things up a good deal; but both the poet and his work remain something of a jumble. For a number of decades, Whitman was the most misrepresented of our major poets: and the misrepresentation began with Whitman himself in the last twenty-five years of his life. It was during those years, from 1867 onwards, that Whitman—initially a very self-exposed and self-absorbed poet—became willfully self-concealing, while at the same time he asserted in various ways an entity, a being, a persona radically other than the being that lay at the heart of his best poetry.

The chief mode of such concealment and assertion was not creative; it was editorial. Whitman wrote little poetry of lasting value after "Passage to India" (1871); what he did do in those later years was constantly to reshuffle the contents of his expanding book: to disperse the poems out of their original and effective order, to arrange them in new and fundamentally misleading groups, to suppress some of the more telling and suggestive of the items, and to revise or delete a series of key passages. The result of this process was a serious shift of emphasis

whereby the authentic Whitman was gradually dismembered and replaced by a synthetic entity that was more posture than poet, more mere representative than sovereign person. It, or he, was the representative—in nearly the conventional political sense—of a rather shallowly and narrowly conceived democratic culture: a hearty voice at the center of a bustling and progressive republic, a voice that saluted the pioneers, echoed the sound of America singing, itself sang songs of joy that foretold the future union of the nation and the world and the cosmos, chanted the square deific, and wept over the country's captain lying cold and dead on the deck of the ship of state.

Other and truer aspects of Whitman continued to exert an appeal, especially in certain lively corners of Europe. But in the English-speaking world, it was primarily the bombastic, or, as his disciples sometimes said, the "cosmic" Whitman that was better known; and it was this Whitman that was either revered or—in most literary circles after the advent of T. S. Eliot—dismissed or simply disregarded.

So much needs to be said, for our first task, and the task this Introduction confronts, is to disentangle Whitman, to separate the real from the unpersuasive, to separate the poet from the posture. To do that, we have, first of all, to put Whitman's poems back into their original and chronological order. It might be argued that we have no right to tamper with the poet's own editorial judgment; that *Leaves of Grass* is, after all, Whitman's book and that we are bound to take it in the order and the form he eventually decided on. The answer to this proposition is that there is no satisfactory way around the critical necessity of discriminating among Whitman's successive revisions of his own work, of appealing from the Whitman of 1867 and 1871 and later to the earlier Whitman of 1855 and 1856 and 1860. The dates just named are all dates of various editions of *Leaves of Grass;* and the latter three, the ones we appeal to, are those of the editions in which most (not all) of the real Whitman is to be found.

This Whitman is a great and unique figure who is also the recognizable ancestor of many significant poetic developments since his creative prime—from *symboliste* poetry to imagism to more recent neo-romantic and, less interestingly, "beat" writing; a chief, though by no means the only, American begetter of Wallace Stevens and Hart Crane, to some extent of Ezra Pound (as he once reluctantly confessed), and to an obscure but genuine degree of T. S. Eliot.

The importance of chronology, in Whitman's case, cannot be exaggerated. Without it, we can have no clear sense of Whitman's development as a consciousness and as a craftsman, an affair of far graver concern with Whitman than with many other poets of his stature. For, as I shall propose, the development of his consciousness and his craft, from moment to moment and year to year, is the very root of his poetic subject matter. It is what his best poems are mainly about, or what they re-enact: the thrust and withdrawal, the heightening and declining, the flowing and ebbing of his psychic and creative energy.

Whitman's poetry has to do with the drama of the psyche or "self" in its mobile and complex relation *to* itself, to the world of natural and human objects, and to the creative act. What is attempted here, consequently, is a sort of chart of Whitman's de-

velopment—in the belief that such a chart is not simply a required preliminary for getting at Whitman, but rather that it is the proper way to identify the poetic achievement, and to evaluate it. The poems selected have been grouped chronologically, according to the edition of *Leaves of Grass* in which they first appeared, though not always in the precise *version* in which they were first written. And in a case like Whitman's, the chart of the development is not finally separable from the graph of the life, or biography; the biographical material, therefore, has likewise been distributed among the successive commentaries on the editions of Whitman's single lifelong book.

### I: 1855

WHEN *Leaves of Grass* was published on July 4, 1855, Walt Whitman, now thirty-six years old, was living in Brooklyn with his parents and brothers, earning an occasional dollar by carpentering. Both his family and his carpentry served as sources of allusion and metaphor in the poetry; but neither—that is, neither his heredity nor his temporary employment—help much to explain how a relatively indolent odd-jobber and sometime journalist named Walter Whitman developed into Walt Whitman the poet.

His mother, whom he salutes in "There Was a Child Went Forth" for having "conceiv'd him in her womb and birth'd him" (the birthday being the last day in May 1819; the place, rural Long Island), was of Dutch and Quaker descent, not especially cultivated, and remembered by her son, in the same poem of 1855, as quiet and mild and clean. His father was a farmer of deteriorating fortunes, temper, and health: "manly, mean, anger'd, unjust" in his son's account; and it is a psychological curiosity that the father died within a week of the son's first public appearance, or birth, as a poet. Other members of the family were sources of that compassionate intimacy with the wretched and the depraved reflected, for example, in "Song of Myself." Two of Whitman's brothers were diseased, one of them dying eventually in an insane asylum and the other (who was also a drunkard) married to a woman who became a prostitute. Yet another brother was a congenital idiot; and one of Whitman's sisters suffered from severe nervous melancholy. From these surroundings emerged the figure who, in the carpentering imagery of "Song of Myself," felt "sure as the most certain sure, plumb in the uprights, well entretied, braced in the beams": a figure who not only felt like that but could write like that.

So remarkable and indeed so sudden has the appearance of Whitman the poet seemed and out of so unlikely and artistically inhospitable a background, that literary historians have been driven to making spectacular guesses about the miraculous cause of it: an intense love affair, for instance, with a Creole lady of high degree; a mystical seizure; the explosive impact of Emerson or of Carlyle or of George Sand. The literary influences can be documented, though they can scarcely be measured; with the other guesses, evidence is inadequate either to support or to discount them. But perhaps the problem itself has not been quite properly shaped. Whitman's poetic emergence was remarkable enough; but it was not, in fact, particularly sudden. Nor was the career, seen retrospectively, as haphazard and aimless as one might suppose. Looked at from a sufficient distance, Whitman's life shows the same pattern of thrust and withdrawal, advance and retreat, that pulsates so regularly in the very metrics as well as the emotional attitudes of his verses; and to much the same effect.

Up to about 1850, when he was thirty-one, Whitman—like the child in the autobiographical poem already quoted—was always going forth, always brushing up against the numberless persons and things of his world, and always *becoming* the elements he touched, as they became part of him. After 1850, he withdrew for a while into the privacies not only of his family but, more importantly, of his own imagination, in touch now with what he called the "Me myself"—his genius, or muse. It was this latter union between man and muse that, by 1855, produced the most extraordinary first volume of poems this country has so far seen.

One of the things Whitman did not become was a scholar, or even a college graduate. His school days, all spent in the Brooklyn to which his family moved in 1823, ended when he was eleven. Thereafter he was apprenticed as a typesetter for a Long Island newspaper; and characteristically, the boy not only worked at the job, he *became* a typesetter, and typesetting became a part of his imagination. The look of a printed page and the rhetoric of punctuation were integral elements in his poetry—the printing of which he actually set with his own hands or carefully supervised. Between 1831 and 1836, Whitman occasionally wrote articles as well as set type for the paper; and he continued to compose fugitive little pieces from time to time during the five years following, from 1836 to 1841, while he was teaching in a variety of schools in a variety of Long Island villages. Writing, too, became part of him; and Whitman became a writer—at last by intention, announcing very firmly in a newspaper article of 1840 that he "would compose a wonderful and ponderous book. . . . [treating] the nature and peculiarities of men, the diversities of their characters. . . . Yes: I *would* write a book! And who shall say that it might not be a very pretty book?"

In 1841, Whitman moved into New York City, where he was absorbed especially by what he called "the fascinating chaos" of lower Broadway, and by the life of saloons and theaters, of opera and art museums. Operatic techniques and museum lore went into his later verses; but what Whitman became at this stage was that elegant stroller, or *boulevardier*, known as a dandy. This role persisted during the five years passed as reporter for a number of New York newspapers; and even after he returned to Brooklyn in 1846 and became editor of the *Eagle*, he came back by ferry to stroll Manhattan on most afternoons. But he was a dandy much caught up in public and political affairs. Among the personae he took on was that of the political activist, an ardent Freesoiler, in fact, arguing the exclusion of Negro slavery from the territories with such editorial vehemence that its owner fired him in February 1848. Within a matter of days, however,

Whitman left for what turned out to be a three-month stay in New Orleans, where he served as assistant editor to that city's *Crescent*. It was there that rumor once assigned him the affair with the Creole lady, that soul-turning initiation into love that is said to have made a poet of him. The legend is almost certainly baseless; but something did happen to Whitman nonetheless. During the long weeks of travel, passing over the vast stretches of land and along the great rivers and the lakes (all that "geography and natural life" he catalogues so lavishly in the 1855 Preface), Whitman had his first encounter with the national landscape, and became (it may be hazarded) another of the personalities announced in *Leaves of Grass:* an American.

Back in Brooklyn, Whitman accepted the post of editor-in-chief on the liberal *Freeman,* and stayed with it till he resigned in political outrage the following year. He had clearly "become" a journalist, an uncommonly able and effective one; his best poetry sprang in good part from a journalistic imagination—"I witness the corpse with its dabbled hair, I note where the pistol has fallen."

At the same time, the forth-going impulse was nearly—for this moment—exhausted. After expressing his sense of both national and personal betrayal by the Fugitive Slave Law in 1850, Whitman withdrew from the political arena, withdrew from active or regular journalism, and from the life of the city. He moved back to his family and commenced a leisurely existence in which, according to his brother George, "he would lie abed late, and after getting up would write a few hours if he took the notion" or work at "house-building" for a bit with his father and brothers, if he took that notion. Now he became a workman; and it was in the role of working-class artisan that he presented himself both in the verses of the 1855 *Leaves of Grass* and in the portrait which appeared as substitute for the author's name in the front of the volume.

For Whitman, I am suggesting, the act of becoming a poet was not a sudden or an unpredictable one. He had always been in process of becoming a poet, and the figures he successively became, from his school days onward, were not false starts or diversions, but moments in the major process. Typesetter, reporter, dandy, stroller in the city, political activist, surveyor of the national scenery, skilled editor, representative American workman: none of these was ever fully replaced by any other, nor were all at last replaced by the poet. They were absorbed into the poet; and if they do not explain the appearance of genius (nothing can explain that), they explain to some real degree the kind of writing—observant, ambulatory, varied, politically aware, job-conscious —in which *this* particular genius expressed itself.

Signs and symptoms of the poet proper, however, can also be isolated over a good many years. The determination to write a "wonderful" book, in 1840, has already been mentioned; but that was presumably to be a philosophical disquisition in prose. In the early 1840's, the writer-in-general became a writer of fiction, and Whitman contributed a number of moralistic short stories to different New York periodicals, all signed by "Walter Whitman" and none worth remembering.

Not much later than that, certainly not later than 1847, Whitman's aspiration turned toward poetry. He began to carry a pocket-size notebook about with him; in this he would jot down topics for poems as they occurred, experimental lines, and trial workings of new metrical techniques. The process was stepped up from 1850 onwards. In June 1850, the New York *Tribune* published two free-verse poems by Whitman, the second—later called *Europe: The 72d and 73d Year of These States*, on the uprisings of 1848—to be included as the eighth item in the 1855 *Leaves of Grass*. It was probably in 1852 that he composed, though did not publish, a fairly long poem called "Pictures" which had everything characteristic of his genuine poetry except its maritime movement. And in 1854, the repeal of the Missouri Compromise and the arrest in Boston of a runaway slave named Anthony Burns drew from Whitman a forty-line satiric exclamation that would comprise the ninth poem in the first edition—later called "A Boston Ballad."

These creative forays were increasingly stimulated by Whitman's reading, which was not only wide but, as evidence shows, surprisingly careful. He had reviewed works by Carlyle, George Sand, Emerson, Goethe, and others for the Brooklyn *Eagle*. He had known Greek and Roman literature, in translation, for years. "I have wonder'd since," he remarked in *A Backward Glance* (1888), "why I was not overwhelm'd by these mighty masters. Likely because I read them. . . . in the full presence of Nature, under the sun. . . . [with] the sea rolling in." (The comment suggests much of the quality of Whitman's poetry, wherein a natural atmosphere and sea-rhythms help provide fresh versions of ancient and traditional archetypes.)

It should be stressed that Whitman's literary education at this time, though by no means skimpy, was fairly conventional. It included the major English poets, Shakespeare and Milton especially; but it did not include Oriental writing nor the literature of the mystical tradition nor that of German idealism—except as those sources reached him faintly through his occasional readings in the essays of Emerson. This is probably to be reckoned fortunate: Whitman's mystical instinct during his best creative years was held effectively in check by a passion for the concrete, a commitment to the actual; and discussion of his "mysticism" is well advised to follow his example.

"Art and Artists," was the title of an essay which Whitman himself read to the Brooklyn Art Union in 1851. And it was here that he first developed his large notion of the artist as hero—of the artist, indeed, as savior or redeemer of the community to which he offers his whole being as champion (sacrificial, if necessary) of freedom and humanity and spiritual health. "Read well the death of Socrates," he said portentously, "and of greater than Socrates." The image of the modern poet as godlike—even Christlike ("greater than Socrates")—was to run through and beneath Whitman's poetry from "Song of Myself" to "Passage to India"; and often,

as here, it drew added intensity from Whitman's disillusion with other possible sources for that miraculous national transformation scene he seems to have waited for during most of his life. It was an extravagant notion; but it was one that anticipated several not much less extravagant images in the twentieth century of the artist as hero. It was this image, at any rate, that Whitman sought to bring into play in the whole body of the 1855 *Leaves of Grass* and particularly in "Song of Myself."

The first edition contained a long Preface introducing the poet-hero who is then imaginatively created in the poems that follow. There were twelve of the latter, unnumbered and untitled and of varying length, with unconventional but effective typography—for example:

The atmosphere is not a perfume. . . . it has no
    taste of the distillation. . . . it is odorless,
It is for my mouth forever. . . . I am in love with
    it.

The first and by far the longest entry was, of course, the poem that in 1881 was labeled "Song of Myself." It is in part genuine though highly original autobiography; in part, it is a form of wish projection. We may think of it, among many other things, as a freeflowing recapitulation of the two processes I have been describing—the process by which a man of many roles becomes a poet, and the process by which the poet becomes a sort of god.

There are as many significant aspects to "Song of Myself" as there are critical discussions and analyses of it; if the comment here is mainly limited to the enlargement of its central figure—that is, to the question of its structure—it is because the structure tends to confirm one's sense of Whitman's characteristic movement both in life and in poetry. For if, again, this strange, sometimes baffling, stream-of-consciousness poem does have a discernible structure, an "action" with a beginning, middle, and end, it is almost certainly one that involves the two events or processes just named.

More than one astute reader, while acknowledging a typical pulse or rhythm in the poem, a tidal ebb and flow, has nonetheless denied to it any sustained and completed design. But it may be ventured, perhaps, that "Song of Myself" has not so much a single structure as a number of provisional structures—partly because Whitman, like Melville, believed in a deliberate absence of finish in a work of art; more importantly because of what we may call Whitman's democratic aesthetic. Just as the political activist was absorbed into the poet at some time after 1850, so, and at the same moment, a practical concern with the workings of a democratic society was carried over into the aesthetic realm and applied to the workings of poetry, to the writing and the reading of it. The shape of "Song of Myself" depended, in Whitman's view, on the creative participation of each reader—"I round and finish little," he remarked in *A Backward Glance*, "the reader will always have his or her part to do, just as much as I have had mine." In a real sense, the poem was intended to have as many structures as there were readers; and the reason was this, that Whitman aimed not simply to create a poet and then a god, but to assist at the creation of the poetic and godlike in every reader.

Like Emerson, Whitman was here giving a democratic twist to the European Romantic notion of the poet as mankind's loftiest figure. By both Emerson and Whitman, that notion got democratized—the poet's superiority, for them, lay exactly in his representativeness. "The poet is representative," Emerson had said in his essay "The Poet." "He stands among partial men for the complete man, and apprises us not of his wealth, but of the common wealth." This is what Whitman meant when he spoke of "the great poet" as "the equable man"; and it is what he asserted in the opening lines of "Song of Myself":

> I celebrate myself and sing myself
> And what I assume you shall assume.

As one or two commentators—notably Roy Harvey Pearce—have rightly suggested, "Song of Myself" is the first recognizable American epic; but if so, it is an epic of this peculiar and modern sort. It does not celebrate a hero and an action of ancient days; it creates (and its action *is* creative) a hero of future days—trusting thereby to summon the heroism implicit in each individual.

Considered in these terms, as the epic consequence of a democratic aesthetic, "Song of Myself" shows a variable number of structural parts. This reader discovers but does not insist upon the following: the invocation leads, in Sections 1 and 2, into a transition from the artificial to the natural—from perfume in houses to the atmosphere of the woods; uncontaminated nature is the scene of the drama. Next comes the recollection of the union—mystical in kind—between the two dimensions of the poet's being: the limited, conditioned Whitman and the "Me myself," his creative genius, what Emerson might have called the Over-Soul. This was the union that was consummated somehow and sometime in the early 1850's, and out of which there issued the poem in which the union was itself re-enacted.

There follows a long portion, continuing at least through Section 17, where—as a result of union—the *man* becomes a *poet*, and by the very act of creation. What is created is a world, an abundant world of persons and places and things—all sprung into existence by the action of seeing and naming:

> The little one sleeps in its cradle,
> I lift the gauze and look a long time. . . .
> The suicide sprawls on the bloody floor of the
>     bedroom,
> I witness the corpse with its dabbled hair. . . .
> Where are you off to, lady? for I see you. . . .

The democratic aesthetic is most palpably at work here. What we take at first to be sheer disorder, what some early reviewers regarded as simple slovenliness and lack of form is in fact something rather different. It is the representation of moral and spiritual and aesthetic equality; of a world carefully devoid of rank or hierarchy.

In "Song of Myself," this principle of moral equivalence is not so much stated as "suggested" (one of Whitman's favorite words), and suggested by "indirection" (another favorite word)—by the artfully casual juxtaposition of normally unrelated and unrelatable elements, a controlled flow of associations.

In the 1855 Preface, Whitman was willing to make the case explicit: "Each precise object or condition or combination or process exhibits a beauty." And he there illustrated the idea in a succession of surprising incongruities: "the multiplication table. . . . old age. . . . the carpenter's trade. . . . the grand-opera."

When, therefore, toward the end of this phase of the poem, the speaker begins to claim for himself the gradually achieved role of poet, it is as the poet of every mode of equality that he particularly wishes to be acknowledged. The announcement runs through Section 25:

> I play not marches for accepted victors only, I play marches for conquer'd and slain persons. . . .
> I am the poet of the Body, and I am the poet of the Soul. . . .
> I am the poet of the woman the same as the man. . . .
> I am not the poet of goodness only, I do not decline to be the poet of wickedness also. . . .

The *poet* now makes ready for the second great adventure, the long journey, as we may say, toward *godhood*. By way of preparation, he undergoes a second ecstatic experience in Section 26 and following: an experience of an almost overpoweringly sensuous kind.

The poet survives, and in Section 33 he is "afoot with [his] vision." In the visionary flight across the universe that is then recounted, the poet enlarges into a divine being by *becoming* each and every element within the totality that he experiences, while the universe in turn is drawn together into a single and harmonious whole since each element in it is invested in common with a portion of the poet's emergent divinity. The "I" is itself no longer the individual man-poet; it is the very force or *élan vital* of all humanity.

The journey lasts through Section 33; and in its later moments, as it will be noticed, the traveler associates especially with the de-

feated, the wretched, the wicked, the slaughtered. Whitman's poetic pores were oddly open, as were Melville's, to the grand or archetypal patterns common to the human imagination—so psychologists like Carl Jung tell us—in all times and places; and the journey of "Song of Myself" requires, at this point, the familar descent into darkness and hell—until (Section 33) "corpses rise, gashes heal, fastenings roll from me," and an enormous resurrection is accomplished.

But what gets reborn, what "troop[s] forth" from the grave is not the poet simply; it is the poet "replenish'd with supreme power," the poet become a divine figure. Just as, by the poetic act of creating a world, the man had been previously grown into a poet; so now, by experiencing and, so to speak, melting into the world's totality to its furthest width and darkest depth, the poet expands into a divinity. He has approximated at last that "greater than Socrates" invoked by Whitman in 1851; he has become that saving force which Whitman had proposed was to be the true role of the American poet. It is the divinity who speaks through Sections 39 to 51, proclaiming his divine inheritance, performing as healer and comforter, exhorting every man to his supreme and unique effort. For it is a divinity who insists at every turn that he speaks but for the divine potential of all men. And, having done so, in Section 52 he departs.

"There Was a Child Went Forth" is Whitman's most unequivocal account of the thrust toward being. It is a poem about growth, about burgeoning and sprouting; and it grows itself, quite literally, in size and thickness. The difference in the sheer physical or typographical look of the first and last stanzas is an immediate clue to the poem's thematic development. Yet what the poet enacts on the technical side is not an altogether uninterrupted increase in substance and vitality. The process is rather one of alternation, of enlarging and retracting, of stretching and shrinking in which, however, the impulse toward growth is *always* dominant. The quantitatively shrunken fourth stanza, for example, is flanked by the longer eight-line stanza that precedes it and the longest or eighteen-line stanza that follows it and completes the poem's swelling motion, giving us a process in fact of stretching-shrinking-stretching.

The same process is present more artfully still within the first stanza, with its rhythmic shift from short line to longer line to still longer and back to shorter once again, but where the line that contains the quantitative shrink is nonetheless a line accentuated by the word "stretching": "Or for many years or stretching cycles of years." The psychic stretching is thus quietly affirmed at the instant of technical shrinking; and it is the stretching impulse that triumphs and defines the poem.

The same effect is accomplished metrically. "There Was a Child Went Forth" is what is now called free verse; and no doubt the word "free" in this context would have had, had Whitman known the whole term, a political aura, and become a part of his democratic aesthetic. Whitman was the first American poet to break free from the convention of iambic pentameter as the principal and most decorous meter for poetry in English; in so doing he added to the declaration of literary independence—from England, chiefly—that had been triumphantly proclaimed for his generation in Emerson's "The American Scholar" and was the predictable artistic consequence of the political fact. Whitman's was a major gesture of technical liberation, for which every American poet after him has reason to be grateful; every such poet, as William Carlos Williams (a manifest heir of Whitman) has said, must show cause why iambic pentameter is proper for him. But it was not an act of purely negative liberation; it was emancipation with a purpose. It freed Whitman to attempt a closer approximation of metrics and the kind of experience he naturally aimed to express; and it made possible an eventual and occasional return to older and more orderly metrics—to possess them, to use them freshly, to turn them to the poet's established poetic intentions. The long uneven alternations I have been describing could hardly have been conveyed by a recurring five-stress line, or iambic pentameter, or by a fixed and even

alternation, let us say, of five-stress line and four-stress line. Whitman instinctively depended not on the regular alternating current of the iambic, but on an irregular alternation of *rising* and of *falling* rhythms—something that corresponded happily with the rise and fall of the felt life, with the flowing and ebbing: and the rising rhythm, once again, is always in command.

In the poem's conclusion—when a world and a child have been brought fully to interdependent life—the rhythm settles back in a line that neither rises nor falls; a line that rests in a sort of permanent stillness; a subdued iambic of almost perfectly even stress—a convention repossessed in the last long slow series of monosyllables broken only and rightly by the key words "became," "always," and "every."

## II: 1856

THE SECOND edition of *Leaves of Grass* appeared in June, 1856, less than a year after the first. There had been several more *printings* of the latter; and indeed, during the intervening months Whitman was mainly occupied with the new printings and with reading—and writing—reviews of his work. He still lived with his family in Brooklyn, but he had virtually given up any practical employment. He had no "business," as his mother told a visitor from Concord (Bronson Alcott)—"no business but going out and coming in to eat, drink, write and sleep." The same visitor quoted Whitman himself as saying that he only "lived to make pomes." Over the months he had made twenty new ones, and included them all in the considerably expanded edition.

Conventional norms of printing crept back a little into this edition. All the poems, old and new, were now numbered and given titles, the new poems always including the word "poem"—a word that obviously had a charismatic power for Whitman at the time. Among the poems added were: "Poem of Wonder at the Resurrection of Wheat"—to be known more tamely as "This Compost"; "Bunch Poem"—later "Spontaneous Me"; and "Sundown Poem"—later "Crossing

Brooklyn Ferry." The physical appearance of the poems had also become a trifle more conventional, as the eccentric but effective use of multiple dots was abandoned in favor of semicolons and commas. The poetry lost thereby its vivid impression of sistole and diastole, of speech and silence, of utterance and pause, always so close to Whitman's psychic and artistic intention: for example, "I am the man. . . . I suffered. . . . I was there" gets crowded together by punctuation and contraction into "I am the man, I suffer'd, I was there." But the earlier mode of punctuation might well have become exceedingly tiresome; and Whitman, in any event, had arrived at that necessary combination of originality and convention by which the most vigorous of talents always perpetuates itself.

For the rest, the new poems dilate upon the determining theme and emotion of the first edition. There is still the awareness of evil, both general and personal. There is even a fleeting doubt of his own abilities: "The best I had done seem'd to me blank and suspicious," a note that would become primary in the 1860 edition. But by and large, the compelling emotion is one of unimpeded creative fertility, of irresistible forward-thrusting energy. It registers the enormous excitement of the discovered vocation and of its miracle-making nature: Whitman's response to the experience of having published his first volume and to the headiest of the reviews of the book. Contrary to some reports, including Whitman's forgetful old-age account, the first edition had a reasonably good sale; and among the many reviews in America and England, some were admiring, some were acutely perceptive, and one or two were downright reverential and spoke of Whitman as almost that "greater than Socrates" he had been hoping to become. Much the most stirring for Whitman, of course, was the famous letter from Emerson, which found *Leaves of Grass* "the most extraordinary piece of wit and wisdom that America has yet contributed," with "incomparable things said incomparably well in it." One sentence from this letter—and without Emerson's permission—adorned the back

cover of the 1856 edition: "I greet you at the beginning of a great career."

The tone of the new poems, consequently, was one of achieved and boundless fertility. This is the poetry of day and the poetry of unending flow. The feeling, indeed, is so large and intense as to produce a sense of profound awe: a sense, almost, of terror. That sense arises from Whitman's convinced and total association of his own fecundity with the fecundity of nature-at-large, an association itself enough to intoxicate one.

But the terror, needless to say, did not disempower but electrified him. The most far-ranging and beautiful of the new poems, "Crossing Brooklyn Ferry," shows Whitman writing under the full force of his assurance—of his assured identification with the *élan vital* of all things. The interplay of the self and the large world it thrusts forward into is on a scale not unlike that of "Song of Myself"; the flow of the consciousness merges with the flow of reality. Every item encountered is a "dumb beautiful minister" to Whitman's responsive spirit; all the items in the universe are "glories strung like beads on my smallest sights and hearings." The complex of natural and human and created objects now forms a sort of glowing totality that is always in movement, always frolicking on. "Crossing Brooklyn Ferry" presents a vision of an entirety moving forward: a vision that is mystical in its sense of oneness but that is rendered in the most palpable and concrete language—the actual picture of the harbor is astonishingly alive and visible. And the poem goes beyond its jubilant cry of the soul—"Flow on river!"—to reach a peace that really does pass any normal understanding. Whitman was to write poetry no less consummate; but he was never again to attain so final a peak of creative and visionary intoxication.

### III: 1860

WHITMAN, as we have heard his mother saying, was always "going out and coming in." She meant quite literally that her son would go out of the house in the morning, often to travel the ferry to Manhattan and to absorb the spectacle of life, and would come back into the household to eat and sleep, perhaps to write. But she unwittingly gave a nice maternal formula to the larger, recurring pattern in Whitman's career—the foray into the world and the retreat back into himself and into a creative communion with his genius. The poetry he came in to write—through the 1856 edition just examined—reflected that pattern in content and rhythm, and in a way to celebrate the commanding power of the outward and forward movement. The early poetry bore witness as well, to be sure, of the darker mode of withdrawal, the descent into the abysses of doubt, self-distrust, and the death-consciousness; but it was invariably overcome in a burst of visionary renewal. The poetry of 1855 and 1856 is the poetry of day, of flood tide.

The 1860 *Leaves of Grass*, however, gives voice to genuine desolation. In it, betimes, the self appears as shrunken, indeed as fragmented, the psyche as dying, the creative vigor as dissipated. The most striking of the new poems belong to the poetry not of day but of death. A suggestive and immediate verbal sign of the new atmosphere may be found in the difference of title between so characteristic a poem of 1855 as "There Was a Child *Went Forth*" and perhaps the key 1860 poem, "As I *Ebb'd* with the Ocean of Life." Yet the case must be put delicately and by appeal to paradox. For in a sense, the new death-poetry represents in fact Whitman's most remarkable triumph over his strongest feelings of personal and artistic defeat. What we have is poetry that expresses the sense of loss so sharply and vividly that substantive loss is converted into artistic gain.

During the almost four years since June 1856, Whitman had once again gone out and come back in; but this time the withdrawal was compelled by suffering and self-distrust. Whitman's foray into the open world, beginning in the fall of 1856, took the form, first, of a brief new interest in the political scene; and second, of a return to journalism, as editor-in-chief of the Brooklyn *Daily Times* from May 1857 until June 1859. In the

morning, he busied himself writing editorials and articles for the newspaper; in the afternoon, he traveled into New York to saunter along lower Broadway and to sit watchful and silent near or amidst the literati who gathered in Pfaff's popular Swiss restaurant in the same neighborhood. In the evening, he continued to write—prolifically: seventy poems, more or less, in the first year after the 1856 edition and probably a few more in the months immediately following. Then there occurred a hiatus: a blank in our knowledge of Whitman's life, and apparently a blank in his creative activity. We cannot say just when the hiatus began—sometime in 1858, one judges. It ended, anyhow, at some time before the publication in the December 1859 issue of the New York *Saturday Press* of a poem called "A Child's Reminiscence" —its familiar title being "Out of the Cradle Endlessly Rocking."

On the political side, Whitman's disenchantment was even swifter than usual. The choices offered the American public in the election of 1856—Buchanan, Frémont, and Fillmore—seemed to him false, debased, and meaningless; and he called—in an unpublished pamphlet—for a president who might play the part of "Redeemer." His disappointment with the actual, in short, led as before to an appeal for some "greater than Socrates" to arise in America; and, also as before, Whitman soon turned from the political figure to the *poet*, in fact to himself, to perform the sacred function, asserting in his journal that *Leaves of Grass* was to be "the New Bible." (Not until 1866 would the two aspirations fuse in a poem—"When Lilacs Last in the Dooryard Bloom'd"—that found a new idiom of almost Biblical sonority to celebrate death in the person of a Redeemer President, Abraham Lincoln.)

Meanwhile, however, Whitman's private and inner life was causing him far more grief and dismay than the public life he had been observing. A chief cause for Whitman's season of despair, according to most Whitman biographers, was a love affair during the silent months: an affair that undoubtedly took place, that was the source at once of profound joy and profound guilt, and that, when it ended, left Whitman with a desolating sense of loss. Poems like "A Hand-Mirror" and "Hours Continuing Long, Sore and Heavy-Hearted" testify with painful clarity both to the guilt and to the subsequent misery of loneliness. Poems like "As I Ebb'd with the Ocean of Life" and "So Long!" strike a different and perhaps deeper note of loss: a note, that is, of poetic decline, of the loss not so much of a human loved one but of creative energy—accompanied by a loss of confidence in everything that energy had previously brought into being. There had been a hint of this in "Crossing Brooklyn Ferry" in 1856— "The best I had done seem'd to me blank and suspicious"—but there self-doubt had been washed away in a flood of assurance. Now it had become central and almost resistant to hope. It may be that the fear of artistic sterility was due to a certain climacteric in Whitman's psychic career—what is called *la crise de quarantaine*, the psychological crisis some men pass through when they reach the age of forty.

Whitman was forty in May 1859; and it was in the month after his birthday that he wrote two aggressive and disturbed articles for the Brooklyn *Daily Times* that resulted in his dismissal from the paper. Characteristically dismissed, Whitman characteristically withdrew. But no doubt the safest guess is that it was a conjunction of these factors—*la quarantaine*, the temporary but fearful exhaustion of talent after so long a period of fertility, the unhappy love affair—that begot the new poems which, in the 1860 edition, gave "death and night" their prominence.

The edition of 1860 contained 154 poems, which is to say that 122 had been composed since 1856, and of these, as has been said, several by the summer of 1857. Most of the other 50, it can be hazarded, were written late in 1859 and in the first six months of 1860. In 1856, Whitman was seized with a wonder verging on terror at the capacity of nature and of man to produce the beautiful out of the foul or shameful; here, in 1860, he is smitten with the dreadful conviction of having, in his own being, produced the foul and the shameful out of the potentially beautiful. "Hours Continuing Long, Sore and

Heavy-Hearted" is a statement of pain so severe, so unmitigated, that Whitman deleted the poem from all subsequent editions of *Leaves of Grass*. These poems of pain are uncommonly painful to read; and yet, in the other major new poems of 1860, we find Whitman executing what might be called the grand Romantic strategy—the strategy of converting private devastation into artistic achievement; of composing poetry of high distinction out of a feeling of personal, spiritual, and almost metaphysical extinction. Keats's "Ode on a Grecian Urn" offers an example of the same, at one chronological extreme, as, at another, does Hart Crane's "The Broken Tower."

That strategy is, indeed, what the 1860 edition may be said to be about; for more than the other versions of *Leaves of Grass*, that of 1860 has a sort of plot buried in it. The plot—in a very reduced summary—consists in the discovery that "death" is the source and beginning of "poetry," with "death" here understood to involve several kinds and sensations of loss, of suffering, of disempowering guilt, of psychic fragmentation; and "poetry" as the awakening of the power to catch and to order reality in language. What had so fundamentally changed since 1855 and 1856 was Whitman's concept of reality. In 1855, as we have seen, the thought of death led to a flat denial of it: "I swear I think there is nothing but immortality." But in "Scented Herbage" of 1860 he arrives at an opposite conclusion: "For now," as he says, "it is convey'd to me that you [death] are . . . . the real reality." If Whitman's poetic faculty had formerly been quickened by his sense of the absolute life, it now finds its inspiration in the adventure of death. In "So Long!" Whitman confesses to the death of his talent: "It appears to me that I am dying. . . . My songs cease, I abandon them." But by 1860 Whitman had reached the perception of Wallace Stevens—in "Sunday Morning" (1923)—that "death is the mother of beauty."

Stevens' phrase might serve as motto for the 1860 edition; as it might also serve for another of the several titles for the poem that was first called "A Child's Reminiscence," then "A Word Out of the Sea," and finally (in 1871), "Out of the Cradle Endlessly Rocking." Whatever else occurs in this in every sense brilliant poem, there unmistakably occurs the discovery of poetic power, the magical power of the word, through the experience—here presented as vicarious —of the departure and loss, perhaps the death, of the loved one. It is one of the most handsomely *made* of Whitman's poems; the craft is relaxed, firm, and sure. Only an artist in virtuoso control of his technical resources would attempt a poem with such effortless alternation of narrative (or recitatif) and impassioned aria, such dazzling metrical shifts, such hypnotic exactitude of language, not to mention a narrative "point of view" of almost Jamesian complexity: the man of forty recalling the child of, say, twelve observing the calamitous love affair of two other beings, and the same man of forty projecting, one assumes, his own recent and adult bereavement into the experience of an empathic child. Whitman, by 1860, was very impressively the poet in that word's original meaning of "maker," in addition to being still the poet as inspired singer; and "Out of the Cradle Endlessly Rocking"—for all its supple play of shadows and glancing light— will bear the utmost weight of analysis. But it has perhaps been sufficiently probed elsewhere, and this Introduction will instead take a longer look at "As I Ebb'd with the Ocean of Life."

We will not be far wrong, and in any case it will illuminate the pattern of Whitman's career, if we take this poem as an almost systematic inversion of the 1855 poem "There Was a Child Went Forth," as well as an inversion of a key moment—Sections 4 and 5—in the 1855 "Song of Myself." As against that younger Whitman of morning and of spring, of the early lilacs and the red morning-glories, here is the Whitman of the decline of the day and of the year—a poet now found "musing late in the autumn day" (the phrase should be read slowly, as though the chief words were, in the older fashion, divided by dots). All the sprouts and blossoms and fruit of "There Was a Child Went

Forth" are here replaced, in the poetically stunning second stanza by:

Chaff, straw, splinters of wood, weeds, and the
    sea-gluten,
Scum, scales from shining rocks, leaves of salt
    lettuce, left by the tide;

to which are added, later, "A few sands and dead leaves," "trail of drift and debris," and finally:

            loose windrows, little corpses,
Froth snowy white, and bubbles,
(See from my dead lips the ooze exuding at
    last . . . .)

The poem's rhythm, instead of pulsating outward in constantly larger spirals (though it seems to try to do that occasionally), tends to fall back on itself, to fall away, almost to disintegrate—no poem of Whitman's shows a more cunning fusion of technique and content. It is here, quite properly, the falling rather than the rising rhythm that catches the ear. As against

    There was a child went forth,

we now hear:

  Where the fierce old mother endlessly
      cries for her castaways

—a dying fall that conveys the shrinking away, the psychological slide toward death, the slope into oblivion that the poem is otherwise concerned with.

The major turn in the action appears in the grammatical shift from the past tense of Section 1 ("As I ebb'd," etc.) to the present tense of Section 2 ("As I wend," and so on). It is a shift from the known to the unknown, a shift indeed not so much from one moment of time to another as from the temporal to the timeless, and a shift not so much accomplished as desired. For what produces in the poet his feeling of near-death is just his conviction that neither he nor his poetry has ever known or ever touched upon the true and timeless realm of reality. The essential reality from which he now feels he has forever been cut off is rendered as "the real Me." To get the full force of the despondent confession of failure, one should place the lines about "the real Me" next to those Sections 4 and 5 in "Song of Myself" where Whitman had exultantly recalled the exact opposite. There he had celebrated a perfect union between the actual Me and the real Me: between the here-and-now Whitman and that timeless being, that Over-Soul or genius that he addressed as the Me myself. *That*, I suggest, was Whitman's real love affair; that was the union that was consummated in 1855 and that ended—so Whitman temporarily felt—in disunion three or fours years later; "the real Me" was the loved one that departed. And now, divorced and disjoined from the real Me, the actual Me threatens to come apart, to collapse into a trail of drift and debris, with ooze exuding from dead lips. (So, by analogy, a Puritan might have felt when cut off, through sin, from the God that created him.)

Still, as Richard Chase has insisted, this poem is saved from any suggestion of whimpering self-pity by the astonishing and courageous tone of self-mockery—in the image of the real Me ridiculing the collapsing Me:

> . . . .before all my arrogant poems the real Me stands yet untouch'd, untold, altogether unreach'd,
> Withdrawn far, mocking me with mock-congratulatory signs and bows,
> With peals of distant ironical laughter at every word I have written,
> Pointing in silence to these songs, and then to the sand beneath.

It is an image of immeasurable effect. And it is, so to speak, a triumph over its own content. Anyone who could construct an image of the higher power—the one he aspires toward—standing far off and mocking him with little satiric bows and gestures, comparing and consigning his verses to the sandy debris under his feet: such a person has already conquered his sense of sterility, mastered his

fear of spiritual and artistic death, rediscovered his genius, and returned to the fullest poetic authority. Within the poem, Whitman identifies the land as his father and the fierce old sea as his mother; he sees himself as alienated no less from them than from the real Me, and he prays to both symbolic parents for a rejuvenation of his poetic force, a resumption of "the secret of the murmuring I love." But the prayer is already answered in the very language in which it is uttered; Whitman never murmured more beautifully; and this is why, at the depth of his ebbing, Whitman can say, parenthetically, that the flow will return.

### IV: 1867

IF WHITMAN, by the spring of 1860, had not been "rescued" by his own internal capacity for resurgence, he would, more than likely, have been rescued anyhow by the enormous public event that began the following April with the outbreak of a national civil war. During the war years, Whitman "went forth" more strenuously than in any other period of his life, and he immersed himself more thoroughly in the activities and sufferings of his fellows. The immediate poetic fruit of the experience was a small, separately published volume of fifty-three new poems, in 1865, called *Drum-Taps*, with a *Sequel to Drum-Taps*, containing "When Lilacs Last in the Dooryard Bloom'd," tacked on to the original in 1866. Both titles were added as an Appendix to the fourth edition of *Leaves of Grass* in 1867, which otherwise contained only a handful of new poems. Several of Whitman's war poems have a certain lyric strength, either of compassion or of sheer imagistic precision; and the meditation occasioned by the death of Lincoln is among his finest artistic achievements. Nonetheless—and however remarkable and admirable his human performance was during the war—it was in this same period that Whitman the poet began to yield to Whitman the prophet, and what had been most compelling in his poetry to give away to the misrepresentation and concealment that disfigured *Leaves of Grass* over the decades to follow.

Until the last days of 1862, Whitman remained in Brooklyn, formally unemployed, making what he could out of earnings from *Leaves of Grass* and—once the fighting had started—following the course of the war with the liveliest concern. He was initially very much on the side of the North, which he regarded as the side of freedom, justice, and human dignity. But as time went on, he came to be increasingly on the side of the nation as a whole, more anxious to heal wounds than to inflict them—and this, of course, is what he literally turned to doing in 1863. In December of the previous year, he learned that his younger brother Jeff had been wounded. Whitman journeyed south at once, found his brother recuperating satisfactorily near Falmouth, Virginia, and stayed for eight memorable days among the forward troops in the battle area. It was only eight days, but the spectacle of horror and gallantry of which he was the closest eye-witness had an enduring, almost a conversionary effect upon him. He came back north only as far as Washington; and from that moment until 1867, he spent every free moment in the military hospitals, ministering to the needs of the wounded. He became, in fact, a "wound-dresser," though a dresser primarily of spiritual wounds, bearing gifts, writing letters, comforting, sustaining, exhorting; he became, indeed, the physician-priest with whom, in "Song of Myself," he had associated the figure of the poet.

He made a living in Washington through a series of governmental jobs: as assistant to the deputy paymaster for a while; as clerk in the Indian Bureau—a position from which he was summarily dismissed when the bureau chief read *Leaves of Grass* and pronounced it unpardonably obscene; finally, in the office of the Department of Interior. Here he stayed, relatively prosperous and content, until he suffered a partly paralyzing stroke in 1873. It was in the same year that traveling north, ill and exhausted, he settled almost by accident in Camden, New Jersey, where he lived until his death in 1892.

In short, when Whitman went forth this time, or was drawn forth, into the American world of war, he was drawn not merely into New York City but into the center of the country's national life: to the actual battlefields, to the seat of the nation's political power, to the offices of government, to the hospitals, and into the presence of the men who carried on their bodies the burden of the nation's tragedy. It is not surprising that the outer and public life of the country absorbed most of his energy; it is only regrettable that, as a result and in the course of time, the solitary singer disappeared into the public bard, into the singer of democracy, of companionship, the singer not of "Myself" but of "these States." This was the figure celebrated by William Douglas O'Connor in a book written as an angry and rhapsodic defense of Whitman at the time of his dismissal from the Indian Bureau—a book which, in its title, provided the phrase which all but smothered the genuine Whitman for almost a century: *The Good Gray Poet* (1866).

There had been a faint but ominous foreshadowing of the good gray poet in the 1860 edition: in the frontispiece, where Whitman appeared for the first time as the brooding, far-gazing prophetic figure; in the first tinkerings with and slight revisions of the earlier poems; and in the group of poems called "Chants Democratic," the volume's major blemish. The 1867 edition had no frontispiece at all; but now the process of revising, deleting, and rearranging was fully at work.

In a general way, it was the intense and personal *self* of Whitman that got shaded over by the new editing—that self, in its always rhythmic and sometimes wild oscillations that was the true source and subject of the true poetry. The private self was reshaped into the public person, and the public stage on which this person chanted and intoned became the major subject of the would-be national bard. Whitman became less and less the original artist singing by indirection of his own psychic advances and retreats; he was becoming and wanted to become the Poet of Democracy. No longer the watchful solitary, he was changing into the Poet of Comradeship.

It should not be assumed that, because these were postures, they were necessarily false or worthless; they were simply uncongenial to Whitman's kind of poetry. The democratic element in the early poems was, as has been suggested, an aesthetic element. It was part of the very stress and rhythm of the verse, implicit in the poet's way of looking at persons and things, in the principle of equality in his catalogues and the freedom of his meters, in the dynamic of his relation to his readers. Tackling democracy head on in poetry, Whitman became unpersuasive, even boring.

In the same way, Whitman's poems about the actual war were least striking when they were least personal. There is critical disagreement on this point, but in one reader's opinion, Melville wrote far more authentic war-poetry. Melville could do so because he had what Whitman did not—a powerful sense of history as allegory, so that, in "The Conflict of Convictions," for example, he could suggest the thrust and scale of the struggle in a frame of grand tragedy and in a somberly prophetic mode that the aspiring prophet, Whitman, could never approach. Whitman, the man, had entered the public arena, but his muse did not follow him there; and the enduring poems culled from the war are rather of the intimate and lyrical variety —tender reminiscences or crisp little vignettes like "Cavalry Crossing a Ford," where the image is everything.

There appears among these poems, however, like an unexpected giant out of an earlier age, the work that is widely regarded as Whitman's supreme accomplishment: "When Lilacs Last in the Dooryard Bloom'd." This poem does not, in fact, have quite the artistic finality of "As I Ebb'd" or "Out of the Cradle"; or rather, its finality is more on the surface, where it is asserted, than in the interior and self-completing pulse of the verses. But like the other two poems just named, "When Lilacs Last in the Dooryard Bloom'd"—a string of words, D. H. Lawrence once said, that mysteriously makes the ear tingle—has to do with the relation between death and poetry.

The death of Lincoln provided the occasion, and the emergent grief of an entire nation served as large but distant background. What is enacted in the foreground, however, is what so often summoned up Whitman's most genuine power: the effort to come to terms with profound sorrow by converting that sorrow into poetry. By finding the language of mourning, Whitman found the answer to the challenge of death. By focusing not on the public event but rather on the vibrations *of* that event—vibrations converted into symbols within his private self—Whitman produced one of his masterpieces and perhaps his last unmistakable one.

## V: 1871 AND LATER

THE transformation that both Whitman's figure and his work had slowly undergone was acknowledged by Whitman himself in his Preface to the fifth edition of *Leaves of Grass*, which had two identical printings in 1871 and 1872 while Whitman was still in Washington. The earlier editions, he said, had dealt with the *Democratic Individual* (the italics are his); in the new edition, he is concerned instead with the "vast, composite, electric *Democratic Nationality*." It was never clear just what the latter entity amounted to; in any case, Whitman was not able to make it susceptible to satisfactory poetic expression. It became the subject not of poetry but of oratory and rant —elements that had always been present in Whitman's work but that, for the most part, had hitherto been sweetened by music and, as it were, liquefied by verbal sea-drift.

Whitman spent the last nineteen years of his life in Camden, New Jersey. He made a partial recovery from the stroke of 1873, but then suffered further seizures from time to time until the one that carried him off. In between these bouts, he continued to "go out" as much as he could: to nearby Philadelphia frequently, to Baltimore and Washington, to New York, and once—in 1879—to Kansas, Colorado, and Canada. Otherwise he remained in Camden, writing short and generally trivial poems, a great amount of prose, and countless letters to friends and admirers all over the world. His old age was punctuated by a series of controversies about him in the public press. In 1876, for example, a clamor from England to raise a subscription for Whitman was countered by a verbal assault upon him in the New York *Tribune* by Bayard Taylor. The charge was almost always obscenity. In the instance mentioned, the charge only aroused the English to greater efforts, and Whitman was so encouraged as to feel, in his own word, "saved" by the contributions—then and later—of Rossetti, Tennyson, Ruskin, Gosse, Saintsbury, and others. Longfellow and Oscar Wilde, old Dr. Holmes and Henry James, Sr. were among the visitors to his Camden home. He became the genius of the city; and his birthday became an annual celebration. It was amid such flurries of support and defamation, idolatry and contempt, that the old man—cheerful and garrulous to the end—succumbed at last to a horde of diseases that would have killed most men many years sooner.

Whitman *was*, as M. Asselineau says of him, a "heroic invalid." But it may be that his physical and psychological heroism as a man was what produced, by overcompensating for the terrible discomforts he felt, the relentless optimism of so much of his writing in his last two decades—optimism not only about himself and his condition, but about America and about history, for which and in which every disaster, every betrayal was seen by Whitman as a moment in the irresistible progress of things toward the better. The "word signs" of his poetry after 1867 became, as Whitman himself remarked in *A Backward Glance O'er Travel'd Roads* (1888), "Good Cheer, Content and Hope," along with "Comradeship for all lands." Those were also the words that fixed and froze the popular understanding of the poet.

Mention of *A Backward Glance*, however, reminds one that Whitman's most valuable work after 1867 tended to be in prose rather than in verse. The sixth edition of *Leaves of Grass*, printed in 1876 and called the "Centennial Edition" (America's centennial—America now being Whitman's subject), added almost no significant new poetry; but it did include the remarkable essay "Democratic Vistas." The latter poses a noble emphasis upon individual integrity against the moral squalor of a society that was already an impossible mixture of chaos and conformity; and in its plea for "national original archetypes in literature" that will truly "put the nation in form," it presents one of the great statements about the relation between art and culture. The next or seventh edition, that of 1881–82, was characterized by endless revisions and expurgations, and now, especially, of regroupings of earlier poems: the process whereby the old man steadily buried his youth. In the same year, though, Whitman also published a separate volume of prose: *Specimen Days and Collect*. In it, along with *Specimen Days* and the several indispensable Prefaces to *Leaves of Grass*, were "Democratic Vistas," Civil War reminiscences, and Whitman's annual lecture on Lincoln. *A Backward Glance* first appeared in 1888; the following year it served as the Preface to, and was the one memorable new piece of writing in, the *Leaves of Grass* of 1889.

Though it is indeed memorable and even beguiling, *A Backward Glance* is also somewhat misleading. In it, the real motivations and the actual achievement of *Leaves of Grass* lay half-forgotten behind the comradeship, good cheer, and democratic enthusiasm of the ailing elderly bard. Like F. Scott Fitzgerald, Whitman could have said, though one cannot imagine him doing so, that he had found his proper form at a certain moment in his career, but that he had then been diverted into other forms, other endeavors less appropriate to his talent. The fact that it was in these other forms that Whitman's reputation got established make the development more lamentable. At his best, Whitman was not really the bard of the democratic society at all; nor was he the prophet of the country's and the world's glorious future. He was, perhaps, the poet of an aesthetic and moral democracy. But he was above all the poet of the self and of the self's swaying motion—outward into a teeming world where objects were "strung like beads of glory" on his sight, backward into private communion with the "real Me." He was the poet of the self's motion downward into the abysses of darkness and guilt and pain and isolation, and upward to the creative act in which darkness was transmuted into beauty. When the self became lost to the world,

Whitman was lost for poetry. But before that happened, Whitman had, in his own example, made poetry possible in America.

# POEMS

## I: 1855

◇

❬ THE FOLLOWING poems appeared untitled—and their individual stanzas and sections unnumbered—as the first, third, fourth, and tenth of the twelve items that made up the first edition of *Leaves of Grass*. The book was published simultaneously in New York and Brooklyn, on or about July 4, 1855. The name of the author did not appear on the cover or title page, but facing the title page was a portrait of Whitman in canvas trousers and open shirt and with his hat on. On the following page, in small print, the work was copyrighted by "Walter Whitman." The poems selected are intended to represent, among other things, the profound and characteristic alternation in Whitman's poetry between the sense of burgeoning life, of the psyche's forward thrust—"Song of Myself" and "There Was a Child Went Forth"—and the sense of death and dying, of the night-side of experience—"To Think of Time." In the 1855 edition, the force of life is always absolutely victorious, and death, finally, is denied any reality. "Song of Myself," in addition, is Whitman's longest and most comprehensive poem, and it remains, perhaps, America's most authentic verse epic, though an epic of a very modern and indeed peculiar kind.

◇

## FROM SONG OF MYSELF

### 1

I celebrate myself, and sing myself,
And what I assume you shall assume,
For every atom belonging to me as good belongs to you.

I loafe and invite my soul,
I lean and loafe at my ease observing a spear of summer grass.

My tongue, every atom of my blood, form'd from this soil, this air,
Born here of parents born here from parents the same, and their parents the same,
I, now thirty-seven years old in perfect health begin,
Hoping to cease not till death.

Creeds and schools in abeyance, 10
Retiring back a while sufficed at what they are, but never forgotten,

SONG OF MYSELF. Untitled in 1855; "A Poem of Walt Whitman, an American," 1856; "Walt Whitman" in 1860 and 1867; not "Song of Myself" until 1881. **1. 8.** (Numbered references are to stanza and line.) **thirty-seven years old:** Whitman in fact was at most barely thirty-six, probably only thirty-five, when he "began" this poem. Lines 6–13 were written in 1860 as part of "Starting from Paumanok" and were transferred to "Song of Myself" in 1881.

I harbor for good or bad, I permit to speak at every hazard,
Nature without check with original energy.

2

Houses and rooms are full of perfumes, the shelves are crowded with perfumes,
I breathe the fragrance myself and know it and like it,
The distillation would intoxicate me also, but I shall not let it.

The atmosphere is not a perfume, it has no taste of the distillation, it is odorless,
It is for my mouth forever, I am in love with it,
I will go to the bank by the wood and become undisguised and naked,
I am mad for it to be in contact with me.

The smoke of my own breath,
Echoes, ripples, buzz'd whispers, love-root, silk-thread, crotch and vine,
My respiration and inspiration, the beating of my heart, the passing of blood and air
        through my lungs,        10
The sniff of green leaves and dry leaves, and of the shore and dark-color'd sea-rocks,
        and of hay in the barn,
The sound of the belch'd words of my voice loos'd to the eddies of the wind,
A few light kisses, a few embraces, a reaching around of arms,
The play of shine and shade on the trees as the supple boughs wag,
The delight alone or in the rush of the streets, or along the fields and hill-sides,
The feeling of health, the full-noon trill, the song of me rising from bed and meeting
        the sun.

Have you reckon'd a thousand acres much? have you reckon'd the earth much?
Have you practis'd so long to learn to read?
Have you felt so proud to get at the meaning of poems?

Stop this day and night with me and you shall possess the origin of all poems,    20
You shall possess the good of the earth and sun, (there are millions of suns left,)
You shall no longer take things at second or third hand, nor look through the eyes of
        the dead, nor feed on the spectres in books,
You shall not look through my eyes either, nor take things from me,
You shall listen to all sides and filter them from your self.

3

I have heard what the talkers were talking, the talk of the beginning and the end,
But I do not talk of the beginning or the end.

There was never any more inception than there is now,
Nor any more youth or age than there is now,
And will never be any more perfection than there is now,
Nor any more heaven or hell than there is now.

Urge and urge and urge,
Always the procreant urge of the world.
Out of the dimness opposite equals advance, always substance and increase, always sex,
Always a knit of identity, always distinction, always a breed of life.    10

To elaborate is no avail, learn'd and unlearn'd feel that it is so.

Sure as the most certain sure, plumb in the uprights, well entretied, braced in the beams,
Stout as a horse, affectionate, haughty, electrical,
I and this mystery here we stand.

Clear and sweet is my soul, and clear and sweet is all that is not my soul.

Lack one lacks both, and the unseen is proved by the seen,
Till that becomes unseen and receives proof in its turn.

Showing the best and dividing it from the worst age vexes age,
Knowing the perfect fitness and equanimity of things, while they discuss I am silent,
    and go bathe and admire myself.

Welcome is every organ and attribute of me, and of any man hearty and clean,    20
Not an inch nor a particle of an inch is vile, and none shall be less familiar than the
    rest.

I am satisfied—I see, dance, laugh, sing;
As the hugging and loving bed-fellow sleeps at my side through the night, and with-
    draws at the peep of the day with stealthy tread,
Leaving me baskets cover'd with white towels swelling the house with their plenty,
Shall I postpone my acceptation and realization and scream at my eyes,
That they turn from gazing after and down the road,
And forthwith cipher and show me to a cent,
Exactly the value of one and exactly the value of two, and which is ahead?

4

Trippers and askers surround me,
People I meet, the effect upon me of my early life or the ward and city I live in, or
    the nation,
The latest dates, discoveries, inventions, societies, authors old and new,
My dinner, dress, associates, looks, compliments, dues,
The real or fancied indifference of some man or woman I love,
The sickness of one of my folks or of myself, or ill-doing or loss or lack of money,
    or depressions or exaltations,
Battles, the horrors of fratricidal war, the fever of doubtful news, the fitful events;
These come to me days and nights and go from me again,
But they are not the Me myself.

Apart from the pulling and hauling stands what I am,    10
Stands amused, complacent, compassionating, idle, unitary,
Looks down, is erect, or bends an arm on an impalpable certain rest,
Looking with side-curved head curious what will come next,
Both in and out of the game and watching and wondering at it.

Backward I see in my own days where I sweated through fog with linguists and con-
    tenders,
I have no mockings or arguments, I witness and wait.

5

I believe in you my soul, the other I am must not abase itself to you,
And you must not be abased to the other.

. . . . . . . . . . . . . . . . . . . . . . . . . . . . . . .

. . . and spread around me the peace and knowledge that pass all the argument of the
    earth,    10

---

3. 23. **hugging and loving bed-fellow:** In 1855, the "bed-fellow" is identified as God, the source of the poet's spiritual abundance ("baskets cover'd with white towels").

And I know that the hand of God is the promise of my own,
And I know that the spirit of God is the brother of my own,
And that all the men ever born are also my brothers, and the women my sisters and
       lovers,
And that a kelson of the creation is love,
And limitless are leaves stiff or drooping in the fields,
And brown ants in the little wells beneath them,
And mossy scabs of the worn fence, heap'd stones, elder, mullein and poke-weed.

6

A child said *What is the grass?* fetching it to me with full hands,
How could I answer the child? I do not know what it is any more than he.

I guess it must be the flag of my disposition, out of hopeful green stuff woven.

Or I guess it is the handkerchief of the Lord,
A scented gift and remembrancer designedly dropt,
Bearing the owner's name someway in the corners, that we may see and remark, and
      say *Whose?*

Or I guess the grass is itself a child, the produced babe of the vegetation.

Or I guess it is a uniform hieroglyphic,
And it means, Sprouting alike in broad zones and narrow zones,
Growing among black folks as among white,           10
Kanuck, Tuckahoe, Congressman, Cuff, I give them the same, I receive them the same.

And now it seems to me the beautiful uncut hair of graves.

Tenderly will I use you curling grass,
It may be you transpire from the breasts of young men,
It may be if I had known them I would have loved them,
It may be you are from old people, or from offspring taken soon out of their moth-
      ers' laps,
And here you are the mothers' laps.

This grass is very dark to be from the white heads of old mothers,
Darker than the colorless beards of old men,
Dark to come from under the faint red roofs of mouths.        20
O I perceive after all so many uttering tongues,
And I perceive they do not come from the roofs of mouths for nothing.

I wish I could translate the hints about the dead young men and women,
And the hints about old men and mothers, and the offspring taken soon out of their
      laps.

What do you think has become of the young and old men?
And what do you think has become of the women and children?

They are alive and well somewhere,
The smallest sprout shows there is really no death,
And if ever there was it led forward life, and does not wait at the end to arrest it,
And ceas'd the moment life appear'd.          30

5. 14. kelson: a line of joined timbers, fastened by bolts.

All goes onward and outward, nothing collapses,
And to die is different from what any one supposed, and luckier.

8

The little one sleeps in its cradle,
I lift the gauze and look a long time, and silently brush away flies with my hand.

The youngster and the red-faced girl turn aside up the bushy hill,
I peeringly view them from the top.

The suicide sprawls on the bloody floor of the bedroom,
I witness the corpse with its dabbled hair, I note where the pistol has fallen.

The blab of the pave, tires of carts, sluff of boot-soles, talk of the promenaders,
The heavy omnibus, the driver with his interrogating thumb, the clank of the shod
        horses on the granite floor,
The snow-sleighs, clinking, shouted jokes, pelts of snow-balls,
The hurrahs for popular favorites, the fury of rous'd mobs,                     10
The flap of the curtain'd litter, a sick man inside borne to the hospital,
The meeting of enemies, the sudden oath, the blows and fall,
The excited crowd, the policeman with his star quickly working his passage to the
        centre of the crowd,
The impassive stones that receive and return so many echoes,
What groans of over-fed or half-starv'd who fall sunstruck or in fits,
What exclamations of women taken suddenly who hurry home and give birth to babes,
What living and buried speech is always vibrating here, what howls restrain'd by
        decorum,
Arrests of criminals, slights, adulterous offers made, acceptances, rejections with con-
        vex lips,
I mind them or the show or resonance of them—I come and I depart.

9

The big doors of the country barn stand open and ready,
The dried grass of the harvest-time loads the slow-drawn wagon,
The clear light plays on the brown gray and green intertinged,
The armfuls are pack'd to the sagging mow.

I am there, I help, I came stretch'd atop of the load,
I felt its soft jolts, one leg reclined on the other,
I jump from the cross-beams and seize the clover and timothy,
And roll head over heels and tangle my hair full of wisps.

10

Alone far in the wilds and mountains I hunt,
Wandering amazed at my own lightness and glee,
In the late afternoon choosing a safe spot to pass the night,
Kindling a fire and broiling the fresh-kill'd game,
Falling asleep on the gather'd leaves with my dog and gun by my side.

The Yankee clipper is under her sky-sails, she cuts the sparkle and scud,
My eyes settle the land, I bend at her prow or shout joyously from the deck.

The boatmen and clam-diggers arose early and stopt for me,

I tuck'd my trowser-ends in my boots and went and had a good time;
You should have been with us that day round the chowder-kettle.          10

I saw the marriage of the trapper in the open air in the far west, the bride was a
          red girl,
Her father and his friends sat near cross-legged and dumbly smoking, they had moc-
          casins to their feet and large thick blankets hanging from their shoulders,
On a bank lounged the trapper, he was drest mostly in skins, his luxuriant beard and
          curls protected his neck, he held his bride by the hand,
She had long eyelashes, her head was bare, her coarse straight locks descended upon
          her voluptuous limbs and reach'd to her feet.

The runaway slave came to my house and stopt outside,
I heard his motions crackling the twigs of the woodpile,
Through the swung half-door of the kitchen I saw him limpsy and weak,
And went where he sat on a log and led him in and assured him,
And brought water and fill'd a tub for his sweated body and bruis'd feet,
And gave him a room that enter'd from my own, and gave him some coarse clean
          clothes,          20
And remember perfectly well his revolving eyes and his awkwardness,
And remember putting plasters on the galls of his neck and ankles;
He staid with me a week before he was recuperated and pass'd north,
I had him sit next me at table, my fire-lock lean'd in the corner.

13

The Negro holds firmly the reins of his four horses, the block swags underneath on its
          tied-over chain,
The Negro that drives the long dray of the stone-yard, steady and tall he stands pois'd
          on one leg on the string-piece,
His blue shirt exposes his ample neck and breast and loosens over his hip-band,
His glance is calm and commanding, he tosses the slouch of his hat away from his
          forehead,
The sun falls on his crispy hair and mustache, falls on the black of his polish'd and
          perfect limbs.

I behold the picturesque giant and love him, and I do not stop there,
I go with the team also.

In me the caresser of life wherever moving, backward as well as forward sluing,
To niches aside and junior bending, not a person or object missing,
Absorbing all to myself and for this song.          10

Oxen that rattle the yoke and chain or halt in the leafy shade, what is that you ex-
          press in your eyes?
It seems to me more than all the print I have read in my life.

My tread scares the wood-drake and wood-duck on my distant and day-long ramble,
They rise together, they slowly circle around.

I believe in those wing'd purposes,
And acknowledge red, yellow, white, playing within me,
And consider green and violet and the tufted crown intentional,
And do not call the tortoise unworthy because she is not something else,
And the jay in the woods never studied the gamut, yet trills pretty well to me,
And the look of the bay mare shames silliness out of me.          20

13. 19. **gamut:** the whole musical scale.

14

The wild gander leads his flock through the cool night,
*Ya-honk* he says, and sounds it down to me like an invitation,
The pert may suppose it meaningless, but I listening close,
Find its purpose and place up there toward the wintry sky.

The sharp-hoof'd moose of the north, the cat on the house-sill, the chickadee, the
        prairie-dog,
The litter of the grunting sow as they tug at her teats,
The brood of the turkey-hen and she with her half-spread wings,
I see in them and myself the same old law.

The press of my foot to the earth springs a hundred affections,
They scorn the best I can do to relate them.          10

I am enamour'd of growing out-doors,
Of men that live among cattle or taste of the ocean or woods,
Of the builders and steerers of ships and the wielders of axes and mauls, and the drivers
        of horses,
I can eat and sleep with them week in and week out.

What is commonest, cheapest, nearest, easiest, is Me,
Me going in for my chances, spending for vast returns,
Adorning myself to bestow myself on the first that will take me,
Not asking the sky to come down to my good will,
Scattering it freely forever.

16

I am of old and young, of the foolish as much as the wise,
Regardless of others, ever regardful of others,
Maternal as well as paternal, a child as well as a man,
Stuff'd with the stuff that is coarse and stuff'd with the stuff that is fine,
One of the Nation of many nations, the smallest the same and the largest the same,
A Southerner soon as a Northerner, a planter nonchalant and hospitable down by the
        Oconee I live,
A Yankee bound my own way ready for trade, my joints the limberest joints on
        earth and the sternest joints on earth,
A Kentuckian walking the vale of the Elkhorn in my deer-skin leggings, a Louisianian
        or Georgian,
A boatman over lakes or bays or along coasts, a Hoosier, Badger, Buckeye;
At home on Kanadian snow-shoes or up in the bush, or with fishermen off Newfound-
        land,        10
At home in the fleet of ice-boats, sailing with the rest and tacking,
At home on the hills of Vermont or in the woods of Maine, or the Texan ranch,
Comrade of Californians, comrade of free North-Westerners, (loving their big propor-
        tions,)
Comrade of raftsmen and coalmen, comrade of all who shake hands and welcome to
        drink and meat,
A learner with the simplest, a teacher of the thoughtfullest,
A novice beginning yet experient of myriads of seasons,
Of every hue and caste am I, of every rank and religion,
A farmer, mechanic, artist, gentleman, sailor, quaker,
Prisoner, fancy-man, rowdy, lawyer, physician, priest.

I resist any thing better than my own diversity,        20

Breathe the air but leave plenty after me,
And am not stuck up, and am in my place.

(The moth and the fish-eggs are in their place,
The bright suns I see and the dark suns I cannot see are in their place,
The palpable is in its place and the impalpable is in its place.)

17

These are really the thoughts of all men in all ages and lands, they are not original
    with me,
If they are not yours as much as mine they are nothing, or next to nothing,
If they are not the riddle and the untying of the riddle they are nothing,
If they are not just as close as they are distant they are nothing.
This is the grass that grows wherever the land is and the water is,
This is the common air that bathes the globe.

21

I am the poet of the Body and I am the poet of the Soul,
The pleasures of heaven are with me and the pains of hell are with me,
The first I graft and increase upon myself, the latter I translate into a new tongue.

I am the poet of the woman the same as the man,
And I say it is as great to be a woman as to be a man,
And I say there is nothing greater than the mother of men.

I chant the chant of dilation or pride,
We have had ducking and deprecating about enough,
I show that size is only development.

Have you outstript the rest? are you the President?       10
It is a trifle, they will more than arrive there every one, and still pass on.

I am he that walks with the tender and growing night,
I call to the earth and sea half-held by the night.

Press close bare-bosom'd night—press close magnetic nourishing night!
Night of south winds—night of the large few stars!
Still nodding night—mad naked summer night.

Smile O voluptuous cool-breath'd earth!
Earth of the slumbering and liquid trees!
Earth of departed sunset—earth of the mountains misty-topt!
Earth of the vitreous pour of the full moon just tinged with blue!       20
Earth of shine and dark mottling the tide of the river!
Earth of the limpid gray of clouds brighter and clearer for my sake!
Far-swooping elbow'd earth—rich apple-blossom'd earth!
Smile, for your lover comes.

Prodigal, you have given me love—therefore I to you give love!
O unspeakable passionate love.

26

Now I will do nothing but listen,
To accrue what I hear into this song, to let sounds contribute toward it.

I hear bravuras of birds, bustle of growing wheat, gossip of flames, clack of sticks cook-
        ing my meals,
I hear the sound I love, the sound of the human voice,
I hear all sounds running together, combined, fused or following,
Sounds of the city and sounds out of the city, sounds of the day and night,
Talkative young ones to those that like them, the loud laugh of work-people at their
        meals,
The angry base of disjointed friendship, the faint tones of the sick,
The judge with hands tight to the desk, his pallid lips pronouncing a death-sentence,
The heave'e'yo of stevedores unlading ships by the wharves, the refrain of the anchor-
        lifters,              10
The ring of alarm-bells, the cry of fire, the whirr of swift-streaking engines and hose-
        carts with premonitory tinkles and color'd lights,
The steam-whistle, the solid roll of the train of approaching cars,
The slow march play'd at the head of the association marching two and two,
(They go to guard some corpse, the flag-tops are draped with black muslin.)
I hear the violoncello, ('tis the young man's heart's complaint,)
I hear the key'd cornet, it glides quickly in through my ears,
It shakes mad-sweet pangs through my belly and breast.

I hear the chorus, it is a grand opera,
Ah this indeed is music—this suits me.

A tenor large and fresh as the creation fills me,        20
The orbic flex of his mouth is pouring and filling me full.

I hear the train'd soprano (what work with hers is this?)
The orchestra whirls me wider than Uranus flies,
It wrenches such ardors from me I did not know I possess'd them,
It sails me, I dab with bare feet, they are lick'd by the indolent waves,
I am cut by bitter and angry hail, I lose my breath,
Steep'd amid honey'd morphine, my windpipe throttled in fakes of death,
At length let up again to feel the puzzle of puzzles,
And that we call Being.

31

I believe a leaf of grass is no less than the journey-work of the stars,
And the pismire is equally perfect, and a grain of sand, and the egg of the wren,
And the tree-toad is a chef-d'œuvre for the highest,
And the running blackberry would adorn the parlors of heaven,
And the narrowest hinge in my hand puts to scorn all machinery,
And the cow crunching with depress'd head surpasses any statue,
And a mouse is miracle enough to stagger sextillions of infidels.

I find I incorporate gneiss, coal, long-threaded moss, fruits, grains, esculent roots,
And am stucco'd with quadrupeds and birds all over,
And have distanced what is behind me for good reasons,        10
But call any thing back again when I desire it.

In vain the speeding or shyness,
In vain the plutonic rocks send their old heat against my approach,
In vain the mastodon retreats beneath its own powder'd bones,
In vain objects stand leagues off and assume manifold shapes,
In vain the ocean settling in hollows and the great monsters lying low,
In vain the buzzard houses herself with the sky,
In vain the snake slides through the creepers and logs,
In vain the elk takes to the inner passes of the woods,

In vain the razor-bill'd auk sails far north to Labrador,                                    20
I follow quickly, I ascend to the nest in the fissure of the cliff.


                                        33

Space and Time! now I see it is true, what I guess'd at,
What I guess'd when I loaf'd on the grass,
What I guess'd while I lay alone in my bed,
And again as I walk'd the beach under the paling stars of the morning.

My ties and ballasts leave me, my elbows rest in sea-gaps,
I skirt sierras, my palms cover continents,
I am afoot with my vision.

By the city's quadrangular houses—in log huts, camping with lumber-men,
Along the ruts of the turnpike, along the dry gulch and rivulet bed,
Weeding my onion-patch or hoeing rows of carrots and parsnips, crossing savannas,
        trailing in forests,                                                           10
Prospecting, gold-digging, girdling the trees of a new purchase,
Scorch'd ankle-deep by the hot sand, hauling my boat down the shallow river,
Where the panther walks to and fro on a limb overhead, where the buck turns furiously
        at the hunter,
Where the rattlesnake suns his flabby length on a rock, where the otter is feeding
        on fish,
Where the alligator in his tough pimples sleeps by the bayou,
Where the black bear is searching for roots or honey, where the beaver pats the mud
        with his paddle-shaped tail;
Over the growing sugar, over the yellow-flower'd cotton plant, over the rice in its
        low moist field,
Over the sharp-peak'd farmhouse, with its scallop'd scum and slender shoots from the
        gutters,
Over the western persimmon, over the long-leav'd corn, over the delicate blue-flower
        flax,
Over the white and brown buckwheat, a hummer and buzzer there with the rest,      20
Over the dusky green of the rye as it ripples and shades in the breeze;
Scaling mountains, pulling myself cautiously up, holding on by low scragged limbs,
Walking the path worn in the grass and beat through the leaves of the brush,
Where the quail is whistling betwixt the woods and the wheat-lot,
Where the bat flies in the Seventh-month eve, where the great gold-bug drops through
        the dark,
Where the brook puts out of the roots of the old tree and flows to the meadow,
Where cattle stand and shake away flies with the tremulous shuddering of their hides,
Where the cheese-cloth hangs in the kitchen, where andirons straddle the hearth-slab,
        where cobwebs fall in festoons from the rafters;
Where trip-hammers crash, where the press is whirling its cylinders,
Where the human heart beats with terrible throes under its ribs,                          30
Where the pear-shaped balloon is floating aloft, (floating in it myself and looking com-
        posedly down,)
Where the life-car is drawn on the slip-noose, where the heat hatches pale-green eggs in
        the dented sand,
Where the she-whale swims with her calf and never forsakes it,
Where the steam-ship trails hind-ways its long pennant of smoke,
Where the fin of the shark cuts like a black chip out of the water,
Where the half-burn'd brig is riding on unknown currents,
Where shells grow to her slimy deck, where the dead are corrupting below;
Where the dense-starr'd flag is borne at the head of the regiments,
Approaching Manhattan up by the long-stretching island,

Under Niagara, the cataract falling like a veil over my countenance, 40
Upon a door-step, upon the horse-block of hard wood outside,
Upon the race-course, or enjoying picnics or jigs or a good game of base-ball,
At he-festivals, with blackguard gibes, ironical license, bull-dances, drinking, laughter,
At the cider-mill tasting the sweets of the brown mash, sucking the juice through a straw,
At apple-peelings wanting kisses for all the red fruit I find,
At musters, beach-parties, friendly bees, huskings, house-raisings;
Where the mocking-bird sounds his delicious gurgles, cackles, screams, weeps,
Where the hay-rick stands in the barn-yard, where the dry-stalks are scatter'd, where
     the brood-cow waits in the hovel,

. . . . . . . . . . . . . . . . . . . . . . . . . . . . . .

Where the heifers browse, where geese nip their food with short jerks, 50
Where sun-down shadows lengthen over the limitless and lonesome prairie,
Where herds of buffalo make a crawling spread of the square miles far and near,
Where the humming-bird shimmers, where the neck of the long-lived swan is curving
     and winding,
Where the laughing-gull scoots by the shore, where she laughs her near-human laugh,
Where bee-hives range on a gray bench in the garden half hid by the high weeds,
Where band-neck'd partridges roost in a ring on the ground with their heads out,
Where burial coaches enter the arch'd gates of a cemetery,
Where winter wolves bark amid wastes of snow and icicled trees,
Where the yellow-crown'd heron comes to the edge of the marsh at night and feeds
     upon small crabs,
Where the splash of swimmers and divers cools the warm noon, 60
Where the katy-did works her chromatic reed on the walnut-tree over the well,
Through patches of citrons and cucumbers with silver-wired leaves,
Through the salt-lick or orange glade, or under conical firs,
Through the gymnasium, through the curtain'd saloon, through the office or public hall;
Pleas'd with the native and pleas'd with the foreign, pleas'd with the new and old,
Pleas'd with the homely woman as well as the handsome,
Pleas'd with the quakeress as she puts off her bonnet and talks melodiously,
Pleas'd with the tune of the choir of the whitewash'd church,
Pleas'd with the earnest words of the sweating Methodist preacher, impress'd seriously
     at the camp-meeting;
Looking in at the shop-windows of Broadway the whole forenoon, flatting the flesh of
     my nose on the thick plate glass, 70
Wandering the same afternoon with my face turn'd up to the clouds, or down a lane
     or along the beach,
My right and left arms round the sides of two friends, and I in the middle;
Coming home with the silent and dark-cheek'd bush-boy, (behind me he rides at the
     drape of the day,)
Far from the settlements studying the print of animals' feet, or the moccasin print,
By the cot in the hospital reaching lemonade to a feverish patient,
Nigh the coffin'd corpse when all is still, examining with a candle;
Voyaging to every port to dicker and adventure,
Hurrying with the modern crowd as eager and fickle as any,
Hot toward one I hate, ready in my madness to knife him,
Solitary at midnight in my back yard, my thoughts gone from me a long while, 80
Walking the old hills of Judæa with the beautiful gentle God by my side,
Speeding through space, speeding through heaven and the stars,
Speeding amid the seven satellites and the broad ring, and the diameter of eighty thou-
     sand miles,
Speeding with tail'd meteors, throwing fire-balls like the rest,
Carrying the crescent child that carries its own full mother in its belly,
Storming, enjoying, planning, loving, cautioning,

Backing and filling, appearing and disappearing,
I tread day and night such roads.

I visit the orchards of spheres and look at the product,
And look at quintillions ripen'd and look at quintillions green.                    90

I fly those flights of a fluid and swallowing soul,
My course runs below the soundings of plummets.

I help myself to material and immaterial,
No guard can shut me off, no law prevent me.

I anchor my ship for a little while only,
My messengers continually cruise away or bring their returns to me.

I go hunting polar furs and the seal, leaping chasms with a pike-pointed staff, clinging to
        topples of brittle and blue.

I ascend to the foretruck,
I take my place late at night in the crow's-nest,
We sail the arctic sea, it is plenty light enough,                    100
Through the clear atmosphere I stretch around on the wonderful beauty,
The enormous masses of ice pass me and I pass them, the scenery is plain in all direc-
        tions,
The white-topt mountains show in the distance, I fling out my fancies toward them,
We are approaching some great battle-field in which we are soon to be engaged,
We pass the colossal outposts of the encampment, we pass with still feet and caution,
Or we are entering by the suburbs some vast and ruin'd city,
The blocks and fallen architecture more than all the living cities of the globe.

.   .   .   .   .   .   .   .   .   .   .   .   .   .   .   .   .   .   .   .   . 110

I understand the large hearts of heroes,
The courage of present times and all times,
How the skipper saw the crowded and rudderless wreck of the steam-ship, and Death
        chasing it up and down the storm,
How he knuckled tight and gave not back an inch, and was faithful of days and
        faithful of nights,
And chalk'd in large letters on a board, *Be of good cheer, we will not desert you;*
How he follow'd with them and tack'd with them three days and would not give it up.
How he saved the drifting company at last,
How the lank loose-gown'd women look'd when boated from the side of their prepared
        graves,                    120
How the silent old-faced infants and the lifted sick, and the sharp-lipp'd unshaved men;
All this I swallow, it tastes good, I like it well, it becomes mine,
I am the man, I suffer'd, I was there.

The disdain and calmness of martyrs,
The mother of old, condemn'd for a witch, burnt with dry wood, her children gaz-
        ing on,
The hounded slave that flags in the race, leans by the fence, blowing, cover'd with
        sweat,
The twinges that sting like needles his legs and neck, the murderous buckshot and the
        bullets,
All these I feel or am.

I am the hounded slave, I wince at the bite of the dogs,

Hell and despair are upon me, crack and again crack the marksmen,      130
I clutch the rails of the fence, my gore dribs, thinn'd with the ooze of my skin,
I fall on the weeds and stones,
The riders spur their unwilling horses, haul close,
Taunt my dizzy ears and beat me violently over the head with whip-stocks.

Agonies are one of my changes of garments.
I do not ask the wounded person how he feels, I myself become the wounded person,
My hurts turn livid upon me as I lean on a cane and observe.

I am the mash'd fireman with breast-bone broken,
Tumbling walls buried me in their debris,
Heat and smoke I inspired, I heard the yelling shouts of my comrades,      140
I heard the distant click of their picks and shovels,
They have clear'd the beams away, they tenderly lift me forth.

I lie in the night air in my red shirt, the pervading hush is for my sake,
Painless after all I lie exhausted but not so unhappy,
White and beautiful are the faces around me, the heads are bared of their fire-caps,
The kneeling crowd fades with the light of the torches.

Distant and dead resuscitate,
They show as the dial or move as the hands of me, I am the clock myself.

I am an old artillerist, I tell of my fort's bombardment,
I am there again.      150

Again the long roll of the drummers,
Again the attacking cannon, mortars,
Again to my listening ears the cannon responsive.

I take part, I see and hear the whole,
The cries, curses, roar, the plaudits for well-aim'd shots,
The ambulanza slowly passing trailing its red drip,
Workmen searching after damages, making indispensable repairs,
The fall of grenades through the rent roof, the fan-shaped explosion,
The whizz of limbs, heads, stone, wood, iron, high in the air.

Again gurgles the mouth of my dying general, he furiously waves with his hand,   160
He gasps through the clot *Mind not me—mind—the entrenchments.*

34

Now I tell what I know in Texas in my early youth,
(I tell not the fall of Alamo,
Not one escaped to tell the fall of Alamo,
The hundred and fifty are dumb yet at Alamo,)
'Tis the tale of the murder in cold blood of four hundred and twelve young men.

Retreating they had form'd in a hollow square with their baggage for breastworks,
Nine hundred lives out of the surrounding enemy's, nine times their number, was the
          price they took in advance,
Their colonel was wounded and their ammunition gone,
They treated for an honorable capitulation, receiv'd writing and seal, gave up their arms
          and march'd back prisoners of war.

33. 131. **dribs:** i.e., dribbles.    34. 5. **the tale of the murder:** the shooting of several hundred American prisoners of war by order of the Mexican general Santa Anna, at Goliad, Texas, in March 1836.

They were the glory of the race of rangers, 10
Matchless with horse, rifle, song, supper, courtship,
Large, turbulent, generous, handsome, proud, and affectionate,
Bearded, sunburnt, drest in the free costume of hunters,
Not a single one over thirty years of age.

The second First-day morning they were brought out in squads and massacred, it was
          beautiful early summer,
The work commenced about five o'clock and was over by eight.

None obey'd the command to kneel,
Some made a mad and helpless rush, some stood stark and straight,
A few fell at once, shot in the temple or heart, the living and dead lay together,
The maim'd and mangled dug in the dirt, the new-comers saw them there, 20
Some half-kill'd attempted to crawl away,
These were despatch'd with bayonets or batter'd with the blunts of muskets.
A youth not seventeen years old seiz'd his assassin till two more came to release him,
The three were all torn and cover'd with the boy's blood.

At eleven o'clock began the burning of the bodies;
That is the tale of the murder of the four hundred and twelve young men.

35

Would you hear of an old-time sea-fight?
Would you learn who won by the light of the moon and stars?
List to the yarn, as my grandmother's father the sailor told it to me.

Our foe was no skulk in his ship I tell you, (said he,)
His was the surly English pluck, and there is no tougher or truer, and never was, and
          never will be;
Along the lower'd eve he came horribly raking us.

We closed with him, the yards entangled, the cannon touch'd,
My captain lash'd fast with his own hands.

We had receiv'd some eighteen pound shots under the water,
On our lower-gun-deck two large pieces had burst at the first fire, killing all around
          and blowing up overhead. 10

Fighting at sun-down, fighting at dark,
Ten o'clock at night, the full moon well up, our leaks on the gain, and five feet of
          water reported,
The master-at-arms loosing the prisoners confined in the after-hold to give them a
          chance for themselves.

The transit to and from the magazine is now stopt by the sentinels,
They see so many strange faces they do not know whom to trust.

Our frigate takes fire,
The other asks if we demand quarter?
If our colors are struck and the fighting done?

Now I laugh content, for I hear the voice of my little captain,
*We have not struck,* he composedly cries, *we have just begun our part of the fight-*
        *ing.* 20

Only three guns are in use,
One is directed by the captain himself against the enemy's main-mast,
Two well serv'd with grape and canister silence his musketry and clear his decks.

The tops alone second the fire of this little battery, especially the main-top,
They hold out bravely during the whole of the action.

Not a moment's cease,
The leaks gain fast on the pumps, the fire eats toward the powder-magazine.
One of the pumps has been shot away, it is generally thought we are sinking.

Serene stands the little captain,
He is not hurried, his voice is neither high nor low, 30
His eyes give more light to us than our battle-lanterns.

Toward twelve there in the beams of the moon they surrender to us.

36

Stretch'd and still lies the midnight,
Two great hulls motionless on the breast of the darkness,
Our vessel riddled and slowly sinking, preparations to pass to the one we nave conquer'd,
The captain on the quarter-deck coldly giving his orders through a countenance white as a sheet,
Near by the corpse of the child that serv'd in the cabin,
The dead face of an old salt with long white hair and carefully curl'd whiskers,
The flames spite of all that can be done flickering aloft and below,
The husky voices of the two or three officers yet fit for duty,
Formless stacks of bodies and bodies by themselves, dabs of flesh upon the masts and spars,
Cut of cordage, dangle of rigging, slight shock of the soothe of waves, 10
Black and impassive guns, litter of powder-parcels, strong scent,
A few large stars overhead, silent and mournful shining,
Delicate sniffs of sea-breeze, smells of sedgy grass and fields by the shore, death-messages given in charge to survivors,
The hiss of the surgeon's knife, the gnawing teeth of his saw,
Wheeze, cluck, swash of falling blood, short wild scream, and long, dull, tapering groan,
These so, these irretrievable.

43

I do not despise you priests, all time, the world over,
My faith is the greatest of faiths and the least of faiths,
Enclosing worship ancient and modern and all between ancient and modern,
Believing I shall come again upon the earth after five thousand years,
Waiting responses from oracles, honoring the gods, saluting the sun,
Making a fetich of the first rock or stump, powwowing with sticks in the circle of obis,
Helping the llama or brahmin as he trims the lamps of the idols,
Dancing yet through the streets in a phallic procession, rapt and austere in the woods a gymnosophist,
Drinking mead from the skull-cup, to Shastas and Vedas admirant, minding the Koran,
Walking the teokallis, spotted with gore from the stone and knife, beating the serpent-skin drum, 10

43. 6. **obis:** amulets with magical powers. 43. 8. **gymnosophist:** ancient Hindu philosopher, member of sect that went nearly naked and devoted itself to mystical contemplation. 43. 10. **teokallis:** Mexican temples.

Accepting the Gospels, accepting him that was crucified, knowing assuredly that he is
        divine,
To the mass kneeling or the puritan's prayer rising, or sitting patiently in a pew,
Ranting and frothing in my insane crisis, or waiting dead-like till my spirit arouses me,
Looking forth on pavement and land, or outside of pavement and land,
Belonging to the winders of the circuit of circuits.

One of that centripetal and centrifugal gang I turn and talk like a man leaving charges
        before a journey.
Down-hearted doubters, dull and excluded,
Frivolous, sullen, moping, angry, affected, dishearten'd, atheistical,
I know every one of you, I know the sea of torment, doubt, despair and unbelief.

How the flukes splash!                                          20
How they contort rapid as lightning, with spasms and spouts of blood!

Be at peace bloody flukes of doubters and sullen mopers,
I take my place among you as much as among any,
The past is the push of you, me, all, precisely the same,
And what is yet untried and afterward is for you, me, all precisely the same.

I do not know what is untried and afterward,
But I know it will in its turn prove sufficient, and cannot fail.

Each who passes is consider'd, each who stops is consider'd, not a single one can it fail.

It cannot fail the young man who died and was buried,
Nor the young woman who died and was put by his side,               30
Nor the little child that peep'd in at the door, and then drew back and was never seen
        again,
Nor the old man who has lived without purpose, and feels it with bitterness worse than
        gall,
Nor him in the poor house tubercled by rum and the bad disorder,
Nor the numberless slaughter'd and wreck'd, nor the brutish koboo call'd the ordure of
        humanity,
Nor the sacs merely floating with open mouths for food to slip in,
Nor any thing in the earth, or down in the oldest graves of the earth,
Nor any thing in the myriads of spheres, nor the myriads of myriads that inhabit them,
Nor the present, nor the least wisp that is known.

44

It is time to explain myself—let us stand up.

What is known I strip away,
I launch all men and women forward with me into the Unknown.

The clock indicates the moment—but what does eternity indicate?

We have thus far exhausted trillions of winters and summers,
There are trillions ahead, and trillions ahead of them.

Births have brought us richness and variety,
And other births will bring us richness and variety.

43. 34. koboo: wild men; brutish forms of humanity.

I do not call one greater and one smaller,
That which fills its period and place is equal to any.                          10

Were mankind murderous or jealous upon you, my brother, my sister?
I am sorry for you, they are not murderous or jealous upon me,
All has been gentle with me, I keep no account with lamentation,
(What have I to do with lamentation?)

I am an acme of things accomplish'd, and I an encloser of things to be.

My feet strike an apex of the apices of the stairs,
On every step bunches of ages, and larger bunches between the steps,
All below duly travel'd, and still I mount and mount.

Rise after rise bow the phantoms behind me,
Afar down I see the huge first Nothing, I know I was even there,              20
I waited unseen and always, and slept through the lethargic mist,
And took my time, and took no hurt from the fetid carbon.

Long I was hugg'd close—long and long.

Immense have been the preparations for me,
Faithful and friendly the arms that have help'd me.

Cycles ferried my cradle, rowing and rowing like cheerful boatmen,
For room to me stars kept aside in their own rings,
They sent influences to look after what was to hold me.

Before I was born out of my mother generations guided me,
My embryo has never been torpid, nothing could overlay it.                   30

For it the nebula cohered to an orb,
The long slow strata piled to rest it on,
Vast vegetables gave it sustenance,
Monstrous sauroids transported it in their mouths and deposited it with care.

All forces have been steadily employ'd to complete and delight me,
Now on this spot I stand with my robust soul.

### 46

I know I have the best of time and space, and was never measured and never will
          be measured.

I tramp a perpetual journey, (come listen all!)
My signs are a rain-proof coat, good shoes, and a staff cut from the woods,
No friend of mine takes his ease in my chair,
I have no chair, no church, no philosophy,
I lead no man to a dinner-table, library, exchange,
But each man and each woman of you I lead upon a knoll,
My left hand hooking you round the waist,
My right hand pointing to landscapes of continents and the public road.

Not I, not any one else can travel that road for you,                        10
You must travel it for yourself.

44. 34. **sauroids:** large fish with lizard-like jaws, now extinct.

It is not far, it is within reach,
Perhaps you have been on it since you were born and did not know,
Perhaps it is everywhere on water and on land.

Shoulder your duds dear son, and I will mine, and let us hasten forth,
Wonderful cities and free nations we shall fetch as we go.

If you tire, give me both burdens, and rest the chuff of your hand on my hip,
And in due time you shall repay the same service to me,
For after we start we never lie by again.

This day before dawn I ascended a hill and look'd at the crowded heaven,        20
And I said to my spirit *When we become the enfolders of those orbs, and the pleasure
        and knowledge of every thing in them, shall we be fill'd and satisfied then?*
And my spirit said *No, we but level that lift to pass and continue beyond.*

You are also asking me questions and I hear you,
I answer that I cannot answer, you must find out for yourself.

Sit a while dear son,
Here are biscuits to eat and here is milk to drink,
But as soon as you sleep and renew yourself in sweet clothes, I kiss you with a good-by
        kiss and open the gate for your egress hence.

Long enough have you dream'd contemptible dreams,
Now I wash the gum from your eyes,
You must habit yourself to the dazzle of the light and of every moment of your
        life.        30

Long have you timidly waded holding a plank by the shore,
Now I will you to be a bold swimmer,
To jump off in the midst of the sea, rise again, nod to me, shout, and laughingly dash
        with your hair.

### 50

There is that in me—I do not know what it is—but I know it is in me.

Wrench'd and sweaty—calm and cool then my body becomes,
I sleep—I sleep long.

I do not know it—it is without name—it is a word unsaid,
It is not in any dictionary, utterance, symbol.

Something it swings on more than the earth I swing on,
To it the creation is the friend whose embracing awakes me.

Perhaps I might tell more. Outlines! I plead for my brothers and sisters.

Do you see O my brothers and sisters?
It is not chaos or death—it is form, union, plan—it is eternal life—it is Happiness.        10

### 51

The past and present wilt—I have fill'd them, emptied them,
And proceed to fill my next fold of the future.

46. 16. fetch: fetch up at, reach.

Listener up there! what have you to confide to me?
Look in my face while I snuff the sidle of evening,
(Talk honestly, no one else hears you, and I stay only a minute longer.)

Do I contradict myself?
Very well then I contradict myself,
(I am large, I contain multitudes.)

I concentrate toward them that are nigh, I wait on the door-slab.

Who has done his day's work? who will soonest be through with his supper?          10
Who wishes to walk with me?

Will you speak before I am gone? will you prove already too late?

### 52

The spotted hawk swoops by and accuses me, he complains of my gab and my loitering.

I too am not a bit tamed, I too am untranslatable,
I sound my barbaric yawp over the roofs of the world.

The last scud of day holds back for me,
It flings my likeness after the rest and true as any on the shadow'd wilds,
It coaxes me to the vapor and the dusk.

I depart as air, I shake my white locks at the runaway sun,
I effuse my flesh in eddies, and drift it in lacy jags.

I bequeath myself to the dirt to grow from the grass I love,
If you want me again look for me under your boot-soles.          10

You will hardly know who I am or what I mean,
But I shall be good health to you nevertheless,
And filter and fibre your blood.

Failing to fetch me at first keep encouraged,
Missing me one place search another,
I stop somewhere waiting for you.


# TO THINK OF TIME

### I

To think of time—of all that retrospection,
To think of to-day, and the ages continued henceforward.

Have you guess'd you yourself would not continue?
Have you dreaded these earth-beetles?
Have you fear'd the future would be nothing to you?

Is to-day nothing? is the beginningless past nothing?
If the future is nothing they are just as surely nothing.

---

51. 4. **sidle:** edging-along movement (here the slipping-in of evening).     TO THINK OF TIME.     Untitled in 1855, "Burial Poem" in 1856, "To Think of Time" in 1871.

To think that the sun rose in the east—that men and women were flexible, real, alive
    —that every thing was alive,
To think that you and I did not see, feel, think, nor bear our part,
To think that we are now here and bear our part.      10

2

Not a day passes, not a minute or second without an accouchement,
Not a day passes, not a minute or second without a corpse.

The dull nights go over and the dull days also,
The soreness of lying so much in bed goes over,
The physician after long putting off gives the silent and terrible look for an answer,
The children come hurried and weeping, and the brothers and sisters are sent for,
Medicines stand unused on the shelf, (the camphor-smell has long pervaded the rooms,)
The faithful hand of the living does not desert the hand of the dying,
The twitching lips press lightly on the forehead of the dying,
The breath ceases and the pulse of the heart ceases,      10
The corpse stretches on the bed and the living look upon it,
It is palpable as the living are palpable.
The living look upon the corpse with their eyesight,
But without eyesight lingers a different living and looks curiously on the corpse.

3

To think the thought of death merged in the thought of materials,
To think of all these wonders of city and country, and others taking great interest in
    them, and we taking no interest in them.

To think how eager we are in building our houses,
To think others shall be just as eager, and we quite indifferent.

(I see one building the house that serves him a few years, or seventy or eighty years at
    most,
I see one building the house that serves him longer than that.)

Slow-moving and black lines creep over the whole earth—they never cease—they are
    the burial lines,
He that was President was buried, and he that is now President shall surely be buried.

4

A reminiscence of the vulgar fate,
A frequent sample of the life and death of workmen,
Each after his kind.

Cold dash of waves at the ferry-wharf, posh and ice in the river, half-frozen mud in
    the streets,
A gray discouraged sky overhead, the short last daylight of December,
A hearse and stages, the funeral of an old Broadway stage-driver, the cortege mostly
    drivers.

Steady the trot to the cemetery, duly rattles the death-bell,
The gate is pass'd, the new-dug grave is halted at, the living alight, the hearse un-
    closes,

**2. 1. accouchement:** childbirth.    **4. 4. posh:** slush.

The coffin is pass'd out, lower'd and settled, the whip it laid on the coffin, the earth is
      swiftly shovel'd in,
The mound above is flatted with the spades—silence,               10
A minute—no one moves or speaks—it is done,
He is decently put away—is there any thing more?

He was a good fellow, free-mouth'd, quick-temper'd, not bad-looking,
Ready with life or death for a friend, fond of women, gambled, ate hearty, drank
      hearty,
Had known what it was to be flush, grew low-spirited toward the last, sicken'd, was
      help'd by a contribution,
Died, aged forty-one years—and that was his funeral.

Thumb extended, finger uplifted, apron, cape, gloves, strap, wet-weather clothes, whip
      carefully chosen,
Boss, spotter, starter, hostler, somebody loafing on you, you loafing on somebody,
      headway, man before and man behind,
Good day's work, bad day's work, pet stock, mean stock, first out, last out, turning-in
      at night,
To think that these are so much and so nigh to other drivers, and he there takes no
      interest in them.               20

5

The markets, the government, the working-man's wages, to think what account they
      are through our nights and days,
To think that other working-men will make just as great account of them, yet we make
      little or no account.

The vulgar and the refined, what you call sin and what you call goodness, to think
      how wide a difference,
To think the difference will still continue to others, yet we lie beyond the difference.

To think how much pleasure there is,
Do you enjoy yourself in the city? or engaged in business? or planning a nomination
      and election? or with your wife and family?
Or with your mother and sisters? or in womanly housework? or the beautiful maternal
      cares?
These also flow onward to others, you and I flow onward,
But in due time you and I shall take less interest in them.

Your farm, profits, crops—to think how engross'd you are,           10
To think there will still be farms, profits, crops, yet for you of what avail?

6

What will be will be well, for what is is well,
To take interest is well, and not to take interest shall be well.

The domestic joys, the daily housework or business, the building of houses, are not
      phantasms, they have weight, form, location,
Farms, profits, crops, markets, wages, government, are none of them phantasms,
The difference between sin and goodness is no delusion,
The earth is not an echo, man and his life and all the things of his life are well-consider'd.

You are not thrown to the winds, you gather certainly and safely around yourself,
Yourself! yourself! yourself, for ever and ever!

7

It is not to diffuse you that you were born of your mother and father, it is to identify
    you,
It is not that you should be undecided, but that you should be decided,
Something long preparing and formless is arrived and form'd in you,
You are henceforth secure, whatever comes or goes.

The threads that were spun are gather'd, the weft crosses the warp, the pattern is
    systematic.

The preparations have every one been justified,
The orchestra have sufficiently tuned their instruments, the baton has given the signal.

The guest that was coming, he waited long, he is now housed,
He is one of those who are beautiful and happy, he is one of those that to look upon and
    be with is enough.

The law of the past cannot be eluded,          10
The law of the present and future cannot be eluded,
The law of the living cannot be eluded, it is eternal,
The law of promotion and transformation cannot be eluded,
The law of heroes and good-doers cannot be eluded,
The law of drunkards, informers, mean persons, not one iota thereof can be eluded.

8

Slow moving and black lines go ceaselessly over the earth,
Northerner goes carried and Southerner goes carried, and they on the Atlantic side
    and they on the Pacific,
And they between, and all through the Mississippi country, and all over the earth.

The great masters and kosmos are well as they go, the heroes and good-doers are
    well,
The known leaders and inventors and the rich owners and pious and distinguish'd may
    be well,
But there is more account than that, there is strict account of all.

The interminable hordes of the ignorant and wicked are not nothing,
The barbarians of Africa and Asia are not nothing,
The perpetual successions of shallow people are not nothing as they go.

Of and in all these things,          10
I have dream'd that we are not to be changed so much, nor the law of us changed,
I have dream'd that heroes and good-doers shall be under the present and past law,
And that murderers, drunkards, liars, shall be under the present and past law,
For I have dream'd that the law they are under now is enough.

And I have dream'd that the purpose and essence of the known life, the transient,
Is to form and decide identity for the unknown life, the permanent.

If all came but to ashes of dung,
If maggots and rats ended us, then Alarum! for we are betray'd,
Then indeed suspicion of death.

Do you suspect death? if I were to suspect death I should die now,     20
Do you think I could walk pleasantly and well-suited toward annihilation?

Pleasantly and well-suited I walk,
Whither I walk I cannot define, but I know it is good,
The whole universe indicates that it is good,
The past and the present indicate that it is good.

How beautiful and perfect are the animals!
How perfect the earth, and the minutest thing upon it!
What is called good is perfect, and what is called bad is just as perfect,
The vegetables and minerals are all perfect, and the imponderable fluids perfect;
Slowly and surely they have pass'd on to this, and slowly and surely they yet pass on.     30

9

I swear I think now that every thing without exception has an eternal soul!
The trees have, rooted in the ground! the weeds of the sea have! the animals!

I swear I think there is nothing but immortality!

That the exquisite scheme is for it, and the nebulous float is for it, and the cohering is
          for it!
And all preparation is for it—and identity is for it—and life and materials are alto-
          gether for it!

## THERE WAS A CHILD WENT FORTH

There was a child went forth every day,
And the first object he look'd upon, that object he became,
And that object became part of him for the day or a certain part of the day,
Or for many years or stretching cycles of years.

The early lilacs became part of this child,
And grass and white and red morning-glories, and white and red clover, and the song
          of the phœbe-bird,
And the Third-month lambs and the sow's pink-faint litter, and the mare's foal and
          the cow's calf,
And the noisy brood of the barnyard or by the mire of the pond-side,
And the fish suspending themselves so curiously below there, and the beautiful curious
          liquid,
And the water-plants with their graceful flat heads, all became part of him.               10

The field-sprouts of Fourth-month and Fifth-month became part of him,
Winter-grain sprouts and those of the light-yellow corn, and the esculent roots of the
          garden,
And the apple-trees cover'd with blossoms and the fruit afterward, and wood-berries,
          and the commonest weeds by the road,
And the old drunkard staggering home from the outhouse of the tavern whence he had
          lately risen,
And the schoolmistress that pass'd on her way to the school,
And the friendly boys that pass'd, and the quarrelsome boys,
And the tidy and fresh-cheek'd girls, and the barefoot Negro boy and girl,
And all the changes of city and country wherever he went.
His own parents, he that had father'd him and she that had conceiv'd him in her womb
          and birth'd him,

THERE WAS A CHILD WENT FORTH.     Untitled in 1855; "Poem of the Child That Went Forth, and Always Goes Forth, Forever
and Forever" in 1856; present title in 1867.

They gave this child more of themselves than that, 20
They gave him afterward every day, they became part of him.

The mother at home quietly placing the dishes on the supper-table,
The mother with mild words, clean her cap and gown, a wholesome odor falling off her
    person and clothes as she walks by,
The father, strong, self-sufficient, manly, mean, anger'd, unjust,
The blow, the quick loud word, the tight bargain, the crafty lure,
The family usages, the language, the company, the furniture, the yearning and swelling
    heart,
Affection that will not be gainsay'd, the sense of what is real, the thought if after all it
    should prove unreal,
The doubts of day-time and the doubts of night-time, the curious whether and how,
Whether that which appears so is so, or is it all flashes and specks?
Men and women crowding fast in the streets, if they are not flashes and specks what
    are they? 30
The streets themselves and the façades of houses, and goods in the windows,
Vehicles, teams, the heavy-plank'd wharves, the huge crossing at the ferries,
The village on the highland seen from afar at sunset, the river between,
Shadows, aureola and mist, the light falling on roofs and gables of white or brown two
    miles off,
The schooner near by sleepily dropping down the tide, the little boat slack-tow'd astern,
The hurrying tumbling waves, quick-broken crests, slapping,
The strata of color'd clouds, the long bar of maroon-tint away solitary by itself, the
    spread of purity it lies motionless in,
The horizon's edge, the flying sea-crow, the fragrance of salt marsh and shore mud,
These became part of that child who went forth every day, and who now goes, and
    will always go forth every day.

# II: 1856

◇

❲ THIS poem, along with nineteen others, were added to the second, or 1856, edition of *Leaves of Grass*. All thirty-two poems in this edition were titled, numbered, and classified. Earlier eccentricities of punctuation and spacing were much restrained. On the back cover of the edition, there was quoted—without permission—a line from the letter Emerson had written to Whitman on receipt of the first edition: "I greet you at the beginning of a great career." Many of the new poems reflect an excitement verging on intoxication: an emotion generated in part by responses like that of Emerson, and by Whitman's conviction that he had found his true vocation and that the vocation was a great one. The excitement takes the form of an identification of Whitman's own artistic and physical fecundity and the mysterious and paradoxical fecundity of nature. "Crossing Brooklyn Ferry" is perhaps Whitman's most satisfying and accomplished "visionary" poem.

◇

## CROSSING BROOKLYN FERRY

I

Flood-tide below me! I see you face to face!
Clouds of the west—sun there half an hour high—I see you also face to face.

Crowds of men and women attired in the usual costumes, how curious you are to me!
On the ferry-boats the hundreds and hundreds that cross, returning home, are more
    curious to me than you suppose,

CROSSING BROOKLYN FERRY. "Sun-down Poem" in 1856; present title in 1860.

And you that shall cross from shore to shore years hence are more to me, and more
    in my meditations, than you might suppose.


2

The impalpable sustenance of me from all things at all hours of the day,
The simple, compact, well-join'd scheme, myself disintegrated, every one disintegrated
    yet part of the scheme,
The similitudes of the past and those of the future,
The glories strung like beads on my smallest sights and hearings, on the walk in the
    street and the passage over the river,
The current rushing so swiftly and swimming with me far away,
The others that are to follow me, the ties between me and them,
The certainty of others, the life, love, sight, hearing of others.

Others will enter the gates of the ferry and cross from shore to shore,
Others will watch the run of the flood-tide,
Others will see the shipping of Manhattan north and west, and the heights of Brooklyn
    to the south and east,           10
Others will see the islands large and small;
Fifty years hence, others will see them as they cross, the sun half an hour high,
A hundred years hence, or ever so many hundred years hence, others will see them,
Will enjoy the sunset, the pouring-in of the flood-tide, the falling-back to the sea of the
    ebb-tide.


3

It avails not, time nor place—distance avails not,
I am with you, you men and women of a generation, or ever so many generations
    hence,
Just as you feel when you look on the river and sky, so I felt,
Just as any of you is one of a living crowd, I was one of a crowd,
Just as you are refresh'd by the gladness of the river and the bright flow, I was refresh'd,
Just as you stand and lean on the rail, yet hurry with the swift current, I stood yet was
    hurried,
Just as you look on the numberless masts of ships and the thick-stemm'd pipes of
    steamboats, I look'd.
I too many and many a time cross'd the river of old,
Watched the Twelfth-month sea-gulls, saw them high in the air floating with motionless
    wings, oscillating their bodies,
Saw how the glistening yellow lit up parts of their bodies and left the rest in strong
    shadow,           10
Saw the slow-wheeling circles and the gradual edging toward the south,
Saw the reflection of the summer sky in the water,
Had my eyes dazzled by the shimmering track of beams,
Look'd at the fine centrifugal spokes of light round the shape of my head in the sun-
    lit water,
Look'd on the haze on the hills southward and south-westward,
Look'd on the vapor as it flew in fleeces tinged with violet,
Look'd toward the lower bay to notice the vessels arriving,
Saw their approach, saw aboard those that were near me,
Saw the white sails of schooners and sloops, saw the ships at anchor,
The sailors at work in the rigging or out astride the spars,           20
The round masts, the swinging motion of the hulls, the slender serpentine pennants,
The large and small steamers in motion, the pilots in their pilot-houses,
The white wake left by the passage, the quick tremulous whirl of the wheels,
The flags of all nations, the falling of them at sunset,

The scallop-edged waves in the twilight, the ladled cups, the frolicsome crests and
       glistening,
The stretch afar growing dimmer and dimmer, the gray walls of the granite storehouses
       by the docks,
On the river the shadowy group, the big steam-tug closely flank'd on each side by the
       barges, the hay-boat, the belated lighter,
On the neighboring shore the fires from the foundry chimneys burning high and glaringly
       into the night,
Casting their flicker of black contrasted with wild red and yellow light over the tops of
       houses, and down into the clefts of streets.


4

These and all else were to me the same as they are to you,
I loved well those cities, loved well the stately and rapid river,
The men and women I saw were all near to me,
Others the same—others who look back on me because I look'd forward to them,
(The time will come, though I stop here to-day and to-night.)


5

What is it then between us?
What is the count of the scores or hundreds of years between us?

Whatever it is, it avails not—distance avails not, and place avails not,
I too lived, Brooklyn of ample hills was mine,
I too walk'd the streets of Manhattan island, and bathed in the waters around it,
I too felt the curious abrupt questionings stir within me.
In the day among crowds of people sometimes they came upon me,
In my walks home late at night or as I lay in my bed they came upon me,
I too had been struck from the float forever held in solution,
I too had receiv'd identity by my body,                 10
That I was I knew was of my body, and what I should be I knew I should be of my
       body.


6

It is not upon you alone the dark patches fall,
The dark threw its patches down upon me also,
The best I had done seem'd to me blank and suspicious,
My great thoughts as I supposed them, were they not in reality meagre?
Nor is it you alone who know what it is to be evil,
I am he who knew what it was to be evil,
I too knitted the old knot of contrariety,
Blabb'd, blush'd, resented, lied, stole, grudg'd,
Had guile, anger, lust, hot wishes I dared not speak,
Was wayward, vain, greedy, shallow, sly, cowardly, malignant,        10
The wolf, the snake, the hog, not wanting in me,
The cheating look, the frivolous word, the adulterous wish, not wanting,
Refusals, hates, postponements, meanness, laziness, none of these wanting,
Was one with the rest, the days and haps of the rest,
Was call'd by my nighest name by clear loud voices of young men as they saw me ap-
       proaching or passing,
Felt their arms on my neck as I stood, or the negligent leaning of their flesh against me
       as I sat,

---

5. 9. float: Both the word and the line are elusive, but "float" is probably used here in its obsolete sense of flux or flood.

Saw many I loved in the street or ferry-boat or public assembly, yet never told them a
        word,
Lived the same life with the rest, the same old laughing, gnawing, sleeping,
Play'd the part that still looks back on the actor or actress,
The same old role, the role that is what we make it, as great as we like,        20
Or as small as we like, or both great and small.


7

Closer yet I approach you,
What thought you have of me now, I had as much of you—I laid in my stores in ad-
        vance,
I consider'd long and seriously of you before you were born.

Who was to know what should come home to me?
Who knows but I am enjoying this?
Who knows, for all the distance, but I am as good as looking at you now, for all you
        cannot see me?


8

Ah, what can ever be more stately and admirable to me than masthemm'd Manhattan?
River and sunset and scallop-edg'd waves of flood-tide?
The sea-gulls oscillating their bodies, the hay-boat in the twilight, and the belated
        lighter?
What gods can exceed these that clasp me by the hand, and with voices I love call me
        promptly and loudly by my nighest name as I approach?

What is more subtle than this which ties me to the woman or man that looks in my face?
Which fuses me into you now, and pours my meaning into you?

We understand then do we not?
What I promis'd without mentioning it, have you not accepted?
What the study could not teach—what the preaching could not accomplish is accom-
        plish'd, is it not?


9

Flow on, river! flow with the flood-tide, and ebb with the ebb-tide!
Frolic on, crested and scallop-edg'd waves!
Gorgeous clouds of the sunset! drench with your splendor me, or the men and women
        generations after me!
Cross from shore to shore, countless crowds of passengers!
Stand up, tall masts of Mannahatta! stand up, beautiful hills of Brooklyn!
Throb, baffled and curious brain! throw out questions and answers!
Suspend here and everywhere, eternal float of solution!
Gaze, loving and thirsting eyes, in the house or street or public assembly!
Sound out, voices of young men! loudly and musically call me by my nighest name!
Live, old life! play the part that looks back on the actor or actress!       10
Play the old role, the role that is great or small according as one makes it!
Consider, you who peruse me, whether I may not in unknown ways be looking upon
        you;
Be firm, rail over the river, to support those who lean idly, yet haste with the hasting
        current;
Fly on, sea-birds! fly sideways, or wheel in large circles high in the air;

Receive the summer sky, you water, and faithfully hold it till all downcast eyes have
 time to take it from you!
Diverge, fine spokes of light, from the shape of my head, or any one's head, in the
 sunlit water!
Come on, ships from the lower bay! pass up or down, white-sail'd schooners, sloops,
 lighters!
Flaunt away, flags of all nations! be duly lower'd at sunset!
Burn high your fires, foundry chimneys! cast black shadows at nightfall! cast red and
 yellow light over the tops of the houses!
Appearances, now or henceforth, indicate what you are,        20
You necessary film, continue to envelop the soul,
About my body for me, and your body for you, be hung our divinest aromas,
Thrive, cities—bring your freight, bring your shows, ample and sufficient rivers,
Expand, being than which none else is perhaps more spiritual,
Keep your places, objects than which none else is more lasting.

You have waited, you always wait, you dumb, beautiful ministers,
We receive you with free sense at last, and are insatiate henceforward,
Not you any more shall be able to foil us, or withhold yourselves from us,
We use you, and do not cast you aside—we plant you permanently within us,
We fathom you not—we love you—there is perfection in you also,    30
You furnish your parts toward eternity,
Great or small, you furnish your parts toward the soul.

# III: 1860

◇

THE 1860 edition of *Leaves of Grass* contained the following new poems, along with over one hundred others. This was the most carefully and meaningfully organized of all the versions of *Leaves of Grass*. The arrangement is so artful as to suggest a story or plot being unfolded in it—the story, perhaps, of the poet discovering his creative powers through the experience of moral and psychological death. The note of suffering, of a sense of loss so intense as to approximate death, is what characterizes the best of the new poems. But in poems like "As I Ebb'd with the Ocean of Life" and "Out of the Cradle Endlessly Rocking"—two of Whitman's masterpieces—the private loss is transformed into immense artistic gain.

◇

## HOURS CONTINUING LONG, SORE AND HEAVY-HEARTED

Hours continuing long, sore and heavy-hearted,
Hours of the dusk, when I withdraw to a lonesome and unfrequented spot, seating
 myself, leaning my face in my hands;
Hours sleepless, deep in the night, when I go forth, speeding swiftly the country roads,
 or through the city streets, or pacing miles and miles, stifling plaintive
 cries;
Hours discouraged, distracted—for the one I cannot content myself without, soon I
 saw him content himself without me;
Hours when I am forgotten, (O weeks and months are passing, but I believe I am
 never to forget!)
Sullen and suffering hours! (I am ashamed—but it is useless—I am what I am;)
Hours of my torment—I wonder if other men ever have the like, out of the like feelings?

HOURS CONTINUING LONG, SORE AND HEAVY-HEARTED.  "Calamus, No. 9" in 1860; rejected in 1867.

Is there even one other like me—distracted—his friend, his lover, lost to him?
Is he too as I am now? Does he still rise in the morning, dejected, thinking who is lost
          to him? and at night, awaking, think who is lost?
Does he too harbor his friendship silent and endless? harbor his anguish and passion?    10
Does some stray reminder, or the casual mention of a name, bring the fit back upon
          him, taciturn and deprest?
Does he see himself reflected in me? In these hours, does he see the face of his hours
          reflected?


# I SAW IN LOUISIANA A LIVE-OAK GROWING

I saw in Louisiana a live-oak growing,
All alone stood it and the moss hung down from the branches,
Without any companion it grew there uttering joyous leaves of dark green.
And its look, rude, unbending, lusty, made me think of myself,
But I wonder'd how it could utter joyous leaves standing alone there without its friend
          near, for I knew I could not,
And I broke off a twig with a certain number of leaves upon it, and twined around it a
          little moss,
And brought it away, and I have placed it in sight in my room,
It is not needed to remind me as of my own dear friends,
(For I believe lately I think of little else than of them,)
Yet it remains to me a curious token, it makes me think of manly love;      10
For all that, and though the live-oak glistens there in Louisiana solitary in a wide flat
          space,
Uttering joyous leaves all its life without a friend a lover near,
I know very well I could not.


# SO LONG!

To conclude, I announce what comes after me.

I remember I said before my leaves sprang at all,
I would raise my voice jocund and strong with reference to consummations.

When America does what was promis'd,
When through these States walk a hundred millions of superb persons,
When the rest part away for superb persons and contribute to them,
When breeds of the most perfect mothers denote America,
Then to me and mine our due fruition.

I have press'd through in my own right,
I have sung the body and the soul, war and peace have I sung, and the songs of life and
          death,      10
And the songs of birth, and shown that there are many births.

I have offer'd my style to every one, I have journey'd with confident step;
While my pleasure is yet at the full I whisper *So long!*
And take the young woman's hand and the young man's hand for the last time.

I announce natural persons to arise,
I announce justice triumphant,

I SAW IN LOUISIANA A LIVE-OAK GROWING.    "Calamus, No. 20" in 1860; present title in 1867.    1. **live-oak:** evergreen oak of southern U.S.

I announce uncompromising liberty and equality,
I announce the justification of candor and the justification of pride.

I announce that the identity of these States is a single identity only,
I announce the Union more and more compact, indissoluble,                    20
I announce splendors and majesties to make all the previous politics of the earth insignifi-
    cant.

I announce adhesiveness, I say it shall be limitless, unloosen'd,
I say you shall yet find the friend you were looking for.

I announce a man or woman coming, perhaps you are the one, (*So long!*)
I announce the great individual, fluid as Nature, chaste, affectionate, compassionate,
    fully arm'd.

I announce a life that shall be copious, vehement, spiritual, bold,
I announce an end that shall lightly and joyfully meet its translation.

I announce myriads of youths, beautiful, gigantic, sweet-blooded,
I announce a race of splendid and savage old men.

O thicker and faster—(*So long!*)                                            30
O crowding too close upon me,
I foresee too much, it means more than I thought,
It appears to me I am dying.
Hasten throat and sound your last,
Salute me—salute the days once more. Peal the old cry once more.

Screaming electric, the atmosphere using,
At random glancing, each as I notice absorbing,
Swiftly on, but a little while alighting,
Curious envelop'd messages delivering,
Sparkles hot, seed ethereal down in the dirt dropping,                       40
Myself unknowing, my commission obeying, to question it never daring,
To ages and ages yet the growth of the seed leaving,
To troops out of the war arising, they the task I have set promulging,
To women certain whispers of myself bequeathing, their affection me more clearly ex-
    plaining,
To young men my problems offering—no dallier I—I the muscle of their brains crying,
So I pass, a little time vocal, visible, contrary,
Afterward a melodious echo, passionately bent for, (death making me really undying,)
The best of me then when no longer visible, for toward that I have been incessantly pre-
    paring.

What is there more, that I lag and pause and crouch extended with unshut mouth?
Is there a single final farewell?                                            50

My songs cease, I abandon them,
From behind the screen where I hid I advance personally solely to you.

Camerado, this is no book,
Who touches this touches a man,
(Is it night? are we here together alone?)
It is I you hold and who holds you,
I spring from the pages into your arms—decease calls me forth.

O how your fingers drowse me,
Your breath falls around me like dew, your pulse lulls the tympans of my ears,
I feel immerged from head to foot,                                        60
Delicious, enough.

Enough O deed impromptu and secret,
Enough O gliding present—enough O summ'd-up past.

Dear friend whoever you are take this kiss,
I give it especially to you, do not forget me,
I feel like one who has done work for the day to retire awhile,
I receive now again of my many translations, from my avatars ascending, while others
                 doubtless await me,
An unknown sphere more real than I dream'd, more direct, darts awakening rays about
                 me, *So long!*
Remember my words, I may again return,
I love you, I depart from materials,                                        70
I am as one disembodied, triumphant, dead.

## AS I EBB'D WITH THE OCEAN OF LIFE

1

As I ebb'd with the ocean of life,
As I wended the shores I know,
As I walk'd where the ripples continually wash you Paumanok,
Where they rustle up hoarse and sibilant,
Where the fierce old mother endlessly cries for her castaways,
I musing late in the autumn day, gazing off southward,
Held by this electric self out of the pride of which I utter poems,
Was seiz'd by the spirit that trails in the lines underfoot,
The rim, the sediment that stands for all the water and all the land of the globe.

Fascinated, my eyes reverting from the south, dropt, to follow those slender windrows,
Chaff, straw, splinters of wood, weeds, and the sea-gluten,                 11
Scum, scales from shining rocks, leaves of salt-lettuce, left by the tide,
Miles walking, the sound of breaking waves the other side of me,
Paumanok there and then as I thought the old thought of likenesses,
These you presented to me you fish-shaped island,
As I wended the shores I know,
As I walk'd with that electric self seeking types.

2

As I wend to the shores I know not,
As I list to the dirge, the voices of men and women wreck'd,
As I inhale the impalpable breezes that set in upon me,
As the ocean so mysterious rolls toward me closer and closer,
I too but signify at the utmost a little wash'd-up drift,
A few sands and dead leaves to gather,
Gather, and merge myself as part of the sands and drift.

O baffled, balk'd, bent to the very earth,
Oppress'd with myself that I have dared to open my mouth,

AS I EBB'D WITH THE OCEAN OF LIFE. Published as "Bardic Symbols" in the April 1860 *Atlantic Monthly;* "Leaves of Grass, No. 1" in the 1860 edition; "Elemental Drifts" in 1867; present title in 1881.   1. 3. **Paumanok:** Indian name for Long Island.

Aware now that amid all that blab whose echoes recoil upon me I have not once had the
     least idea who or what I am,     10
But that before all my arrogant poems the real Me stands yet untouch'd, untold, alto-
     gether unreach'd,
Withdrawn far, mocking me with mock-congratulatory signs and bows,
With peals of distant ironical laughter at every word I have written,
Pointing in silence to these songs, and then to the sand beneath.
I perceive I have not really understood any thing, not a single object, and that no man
     ever can,
Nature here in sight of the sea taking advantage of me to dart upon me and sting me,
Because I have dared to open my mouth to sing at all.

3

You oceans both, I close with you,
We murmur alike reproachfully rolling sands and drift, knowing not why,
These little shreds indeed standing for you and me and all.

You friable shore with trails of debris,
You fish-shaped island, I take what is underfoot,
What is yours is mine my father.

I too Paumanok,
I too have bubbled up, floated the measureless float, and been wash'd on your shores,
I too am but a trail of drift and debris,
I too leave little wrecks upon you, you fish-shaped island.     10

I throw myself upon your breast my father,
I cling to you so that you cannot unloose me,
I hold you so firm till you answer me something.

Kiss me my father,
Touch me with your lips as I touch those I love,
Breathe to me while I hold you close the secret of the murmuring I envy.

4

Ebb, ocean of life, (the flow will return,)
Cease not your moaning you fierce old mother,
Endlessly cry for your castaways, but fear not, deny not me,
Rustle not up so hoarse and angry against my feet as I touch you or gather from you.

I mean tenderly by you and all,
I gather for myself and for this phantom looking down where we lead, and following
     me and mine.

Me and mine, loose windrows, little corpses,
Froth, snowy white, and bubbles,
(See, from my dead lips the ooze exuding at last,
See, the prismatic colors glistening and rolling,)     10
Tufts of straw, sands, fragments,

---

**3. 4. friable:** easily crumbled.    **3. 16. Breathe . . . envy:** This line, in the 1860 edition, was followed by:

> For I fear I shall become crazed, if I cannot emulate
>    it, and utter myself as well as it.
> Sea-raff! Crook-tongued waves!
> O, I will yet sing, some day, what you have said to me.

Those lines were dropped in 1867.

Buoy'd hither from many moods, one contradicting another,
From the storm, the long calm, the darkness, the swell,
Musing, pondering, a breath, a briny tear, a dab of liquid or soil,
Up just as much out of fathomless workings fermented and thrown,
A limp blossom or two, torn, just as much over waves floating, drifted at random,
Just as much for us that sobbing dirge of Nature,
Just as much whence we come that blare of the cloud-trumpets,
We, capricious, brought hither we know not whence, spread out before you,
You up there walking or sitting,                                                      20
Whoever you are, we too lie in drifts at your feet.


## OUT OF THE CRADLE ENDLESSLY ROCKING

Out of the cradle endlessly rocking,
Out of the mocking-bird's throat, the musical shuttle,
Out of the Ninth-month midnight,
Over the sterile sands and the fields beyond, where the child leaving his bed wander'd
        alone, barcheaded, barefoot,
Down from the shower'd halo,
Up from the mystic play of shadows twining and twisting as if they were alive,
Out from the patches of briers and blackberries,
From the memories of the bird that chanted to me,
From your memories sad brother, from the fitful risings and fallings I heard,
From under that yellow half-moon late-risen and swollen as if with tears,          10
From those beginning notes of yearning and love there in the mist,
From the thousand responses of my heart never to cease,
From the myriad thence-arous'd words,
From the word stronger and more delicious than any,
From such as now they start the scene revisiting,
As a flock, twittering, rising, or overhead passing,
Borne hither, ere all eludes me, hurriedly,
A man, yet by these tears a little boy again,
Throwing myself on the sand, confronting the waves,
I, chanter of pains and joys, uniter of here and hereafter,                        20
Taking all hints to use them, but swiftly leaping beyond them,
A reminiscence sing.


Once Paumanok,
When the lilac-scent was in the air and Fifth-month grass was growing,
Up this seashore in some briers,
Two feather'd guests from Alabama, two together,
And their nest, and four light-green eggs spotted with brown,
And every day the he-bird to and fro near at hand,
And every day the she-bird crouch'd on her nest, silent, with bright eyes,
And every day I, a curious boy, never too close, never disturbing them,            30
Cautiously peering, absorbing, translating.


*Shine! shine! shine!*
*Pour down your warmth, great sun!*
*While we bask, we two together.*

OUT OF THE CRADLE ENDLESSLY ROCKING.     Published as "A Child's Reminiscence" in the December 1859 New York *Saturday Press*; "A
Word Out of the Sea" in the 1860 edition; present title in 1871.     1. Out . . . rocking: This line read: "Out of the rocked cradle" in 1860;
present version is that of 1871.     2. Out . . . shuttle: In 1860, this line was followed by: "Out of the boy's mother's womb, and from the nipples of her breasts"—dropped in 1867.

*Two together!*
*Winds blow south, or winds blow north,*
*Day come white, or night come black,*
*Home, or rivers and mountains from home,*
*Singing all time, minding no time,*
*While we two keep together.*                                        40

Till of a sudden,
May-be kill'd, unknown to her mate,
One forenoon the she-bird crouch'd not on the nest,
Nor return'd that afternoon, nor the next,
Nor ever appear'd again.

And thenceforward all summer in the sound of the sea,
And at night under the full of the moon in calmer weather,
Over the hoarse surging of the sea,
Or flitting from brier to brier by day,
I saw, I heard at intervals the remaining one, the he-bird,    50
The solitary guest from Alabama.

*Blow! blow! blow!*
*Blow up sea-winds along Paumanok's shore;*
*I wait and I wait till you blow my mate to me.*

Yes, when the stars glisten'd,
All night long on the prong of a moss-scallop'd stake,
Down almost amid the slapping waves,
Sat the lone singer wonderful causing tears.

He call'd on his mate,
He pour'd forth the meanings which I of all men know.          60
Yes my brother I know,
The rest might not, but I have treasur'd every note,
For more than once dimly down to the beach gliding,
Silent, avoiding the moonbeams, blending myself with the shadows,
Recalling now the obscure shapes, the echoes, the sounds and sights after their sorts,
The white arms out in the breakers tirelessly tossing,
I, with bare feet, a child, the wind wafting my hair,
Listen'd long and long.

Listen'd to keep, to sing, now translating the notes,
Following you my brother.                                      70

*Soothe! soothe! soothe!*
*Close on its wave soothes the wave behind,*
*And again another behind embracing and lapping, every one close,*
*But my love soothes not me, not me.*

*Low hangs the moon, it rose late,*
*It is lagging—O I think it is heavy with love, with love.*

*O madly the sea pushes upon the land,*
*With love, with love.*

*O night! do I not see my love fluttering out among the breakers?*
*What is that little black thing I see there in the white?*     80

*Loud! loud! loud!*
*Loud I call to you, my love!*
*High and clear I shoot my voice over the waves,*
*Surely you must know who is here, is here,*
*You must know who I am, my love.*

*Low-hanging moon!*
*What is that dusky spot in your brown yellow?*
*O it is the shape, the shape of my mate!*
*O moon do not keep her from me any longer.*

*Land! land! O land!*                                                          90
*Whichever way I turn, O I think you could give me my mate back again if you only*
*            would,*
*For I am almost sure I see her dimly whichever way I look.*

*O rising stars!*
*Perhaps the one I want so much will rise, will rise with some of you.*

*O throat! O trembling throat!*
*Sound clearer through the atmosphere!*
*Pierce the woods, the earth,*
*Somewhere listening to catch you must be the one I want.*

*Shake out carols!*
*Solitary here, the night's carols!*                                           100
*Carols of lonesome love! death's carols!*
*Carols under that lagging, yellow, waning moon!*
*O under that moon where she droops almost down into the sea!*
*O reckless despairing carols.*

*But soft! sink low!*
*Soft! let me just murmur,*
*And do you wait a moment you husky-nois'd sea,*
*For somewhere I believe I heard my mate responding to me,*
*So faint, I must be still, be still to listen,*
*But not altogether still, for then she might not come immediately to me.*       110

*Hither my love!*
*Here I am! here!*
*With this just-sustain'd note I announce myself to you,*
*This gentle call is for you my love, for you.*

*Do not be decoy'd elsewhere,*
*That is the whistle of the wind, it is not my voice,*
*That is the fluttering, the fluttering of the spray,*
*Those are the shadows of leaves.*

*O darkness! O in vain!*
*O I am very sick and sorrowful.*                                              120

*O brown halo in the sky near the moon, drooping upon the sea!*
*O troubled reflection in the sea!*
*O throat! O throbbing heart!*
*And I singing uselessly, uselessly all the night.*

*O past! O happy life! O songs of joy!*
*In the air, in the woods, over fields,*
*Loved! loved! loved! loved! loved!*
*But my mate no more, no more with me!*
*We two together no more.*

The aria sinking,          130
All else continuing, the stars shining,
The winds blowing, the notes of the bird continuous echoing,
With angry moans the fierce old mother incessantly moaning,
On the sands of Paumanok's shore gray and rustling,
The yellow half-moon enlarged, sagging down, drooping, the face of the sea almost
            touching,
The boy ecstatic, with his bare feet the waves, with his hair the atmosphere dallying,
The love in the heart long pent, now loose, now at last tumultuously bursting,
The aria's meaning, the ears, the soul, swiftly depositing,
The strange tears down the cheeks coursing,
The colloquy there, the trio, each uttering,          140
The undertone, the savage old mother incessantly crying,
To the boy's soul's questions sullenly timing, some drown'd secret hissing,
To the outsetting bard.

Demon or bird! (said the boy's soul,)
Is it indeed toward your mate you sing? or is it really to me?
For I, that was a child, my tongue's use sleeping, now I have heard you,
Now in a moment I know what I am for, I awake,
And already a thousand singers, a thousand songs, clearer, louder and more sorrowful
            than yours,
A thousand warbling echoes have started to life within me, never to die.
O you singer solitary, singing by yourself, projecting me,      150
O solitary me listening, never more shall I cease perpetuating you,
Never more shall I escape, never more the reverberations,
Never more the cries of unsatisfied love be absent from me,
Never again leave me to be the peaceful child I was before what there in the night,
By the sea under the yellow and sagging moon,
The messenger there arous'd, the fire, the sweet hell within,
The unknown want, the destiny of me.

O give me the clew! (it lurks in the night here somewhere,)
O if I am to have so much, let me have more!

A word then, (for I will conquer it,)          160
The word final, superior to all,
Subtle, sent up—what is it?—I listen;
Are you whispering it, and have been all the time, you sea waves?
Is that it from your liquid rims and wet sands?

Whereto answering, the sea,
Delaying not, hurrying not,
Whisper'd me through the night, and very plainly before daybreak,
Lisp'd to me the low and delicious word death,
And again death, death, death, death,
Hissing melodious, neither like the bird nor like my arous'd child's heart,     170
But edging near as privately for me rustling at my feet,
Creeping thence steadily up to my ears and laving me softly all over,
Death, death, death, death, death.

Which I do not forget,
But fuse the song of my dusky demon and brother,
That he sang to me in the moonlight on Paumanok's gray beach,
With the thousand responsive songs at random,
My own songs awaked from that hour,
And with them the key, the word up from the waves,
The word of the sweetest song and all songs,                    180
That strong and delicious word which, creeping to my feet,
(Or like some old crone rocking the cradle, swathed in sweet garments, bending aside,)
The sea whisper'd me.

# IV: 1867

◇

❨ IN 1865, Whitman published a separate little volume of war poems called *Drum-Taps*, to which, in the following year, he added a *Sequel to Drum-Taps*, including "When Lilacs Last in the Dooryard Bloom'd" and others. The poems contained were then attached as an Appendix to the fourth, or 1867, edition of *Leaves of Grass* and later still were incorporated into the main text. It was in the 1867 edition, too, that Whitman made the first of the extensive revisions, deletions, and rearrangements of the sequence of poems that so greatly changed—in fact, distorted—the character of *Leaves of Grass*. In the poem occasioned by the death of Lincoln, however, Whitman arrived at what many readers take to be his supreme accomplishment.

◇

## CAVALRY CROSSING A FORD

A line in long array where they wind betwixt green islands,
They take a serpentine course, their arms flash in the sun—hark to the musical clank,
Behold the silvery river, in it the splashing horses loitering stop to drink.
Behold the brown-faced men, each group, each person a picture, the negligent rest on the
        saddles,
Some emerge on the opposite bank, others are just entering the ford—while,
Scarlet and blue and snowy white,
The guidon flags flutter gayly in the wind.

## BIVOUAC ON A MOUNTAIN SIDE

I see before me now a traveling army halting,
Below a fertile valley spread, with barns and the orchards of summer,
Behind, the terraced sides of a mountain, abrupt, in places rising high,
Broken, with rocks, with clinging cedars, with tall shapes dingily seen,
The numerous camp-fires scatter'd near and far, some away up on the mountain,
The shadowy forms of men and horses, looming, large-sized, flickering,
And over all the sky—the sky! far, far out of reach, studded, breaking out, the eternal
        stars.

## THE WOUND-DRESSER

I

An old man bending I come among new faces,
Years looking backward resuming in answer to children,

THE WOUND-DRESSER.    "The Dresser" in 1867; present title in 1881.

Come tell us old man, as from young men and maidens that love me,
(Arous'd and angry, I'd thought to beat the alarum, and urge relentless war,
But soon my fingers fail'd me, my face droop'd and I resign'd myself,
To sit by the wounded and soothe them, or silently watch the dead;)
Years hence of these scenes, of these furious passions, these chances,
Of unsurpass'd heroes, (was one side so brave? the other was equally brave;)
Now be witness again, paint the mightiest armies of earth,
Of those armies so rapid so wondrous what saw you to tell us?                    10
What stays with you latest and deepest? of curious panics,
Of hard-fought engagements or sieges tremendous what deepest remains?


2

O maidens and young men I love and that love me,
What you ask of my days those the strangest and sudden your talking recalls,
Soldier alert I arrive after a long march cover'd with sweat and dust,
In the nick of time I come, plunge in the fight, loudly shout in the rush of successful
            charge,
Enter the captur'd works—yet lo, like a swift-running river they fade,
Pass and are gone they fade—I dwell not on soldiers' perils or soldiers' joys,
(Both I remember well—many of the hardships, few the joys, yet I was content.)

But in silence, in dreams' projections,
While the world of gain and appearance and mirth goes on,
So soon what is over forgotten, and waves wash the imprints off the sand,          10
With hinged knees returning I enter the doors, (while for you up there,
Whoever you are, follow without noise and be of strong heart.)

Bearing the bandages, water and sponge,
Straight and swift to my wounded I go,
Where they lie on the ground after the battle brought in,
Where their priceless blood reddens the grass the ground,
Or to the rows of the hospital tent, or under the roof'd hospital,
To the long rows of cots up and down each side I return,
To each and all one after another I draw near, not one do I miss,
An attendant follows holding a tray, he carries a refuse pail,                     20
Soon to be fill'd with clotted rags and blood, emptied, and fill'd again.

I onward go, I stop,
With hinged knees and steady hand to dress wounds,
I am firm with each, the pangs are sharp yet unavoidable,
One turns to me his appealing eyes—poor boy! I never knew you,
Yet I think I could not refuse this moment to die for you, if that would save you.


3

On, on I go, (open doors of time! open hospital doors!)
The crush'd head I dress, (poor crazed hand tear not the bandage away,)
The neck of the cavalry-man with the bullet through and through I examine,
Hard the breathing rattles, quite glazed already the eye, yet life struggles hard,
(Come sweet death! be persuaded O beautiful death!
In mercy come quickly.)

From the stump of the arm, the amputated hand,
I undo the clotted lint, remove the slough, wash off the matter and blood,
Back on his pillow the soldier bends with curv'd neck and side falling head,
His eyes are closed, his face is pale, he dares not look on the bloody stump,       10
And has not yet look'd on it.

I dress a wound in the side, deep, deep,
But a day or two more, for see the frame all wasted and sinking,
And the yellow-blue countenance see.

I dress the perforated shoulder, the foot with the bullet-wound,
Cleanse the one with a gnawing and putrid gangrene, so sickening, so offensive,
While the attendant stands behind aside me holding the tray and pail.

I am faithful, I do not give out,
The fractur'd thigh, the knee, the wound in the abdomen,
These and more I dress with impassive hand, (yet deep in my breast a fire, a burning
       flame.)                                    20

4

Thus in silence in dreams' projections,
Returning, resuming, I thread my way through the hospitals,
The hurt and wounded I pacify with soothing hand,
I sit by the restless all the dark night, some are so young,
Some suffer so much, I recall the experience sweet and sad,
(Many a soldier's loving arms about this neck have cross'd and rested,
Many a soldier's kiss dwells on these bearded lips.)

RECONCILIATION

Word over all, beautiful as the sky,
Beautiful that war and all its deeds of carnage must in time be utterly lost,
That the hands of the sisters Death and Night incessantly softly wash again, and ever
       again, this soil'd world;
For my enemy is dead, a man divine as myself is dead,
I look where he lies white-faced and still in the coffin—I draw near,
Bend down and touch lightly with my lips the white face in the coffin.

WHEN LILACS LAST IN THE DOORYARD BLOOM'D

1

When lilacs last in the dooryard bloom'd,
And the great star early droop'd in the western sky in the night,
I mourn'd, and yet shall mourn with ever-returning spring.

Ever-returning spring, trinity sure to me you bring,
Lilac blooming perennial and drooping star in the west,
And thought of him I love.

2

O powerful western fallen star!
O shades of night—O moody, tearful night!
O great star disappear'd—O the black murk that hides the star!
O cruel hands that hold me powerless—O helpless soul of me!
O harsh surrounding cloud that will not free my soul.

3

In the dooryard fronting an old farm-house near the white-wash'd palings,
Stands the lilac-bush tall-growing with heart-shaped leaves of rich green,

With many a pointed blossom rising delicate, with the perfume strong I love,
With every leaf a miracle—and from this bush in the dooryard,
With delicate-color'd blossoms and heart-shaped leaves of rich green,
A sprig with its flower I break.

4

In the swamp in secluded recesses,
A shy and hidden bird is warbling a song.

Solitary the thrush,
The hermit withdrawn to himself, avoiding the settlements,
Sings by himself a song.

Song of the bleeding throat,
Death's outlet song of life, (for well dear brother I know,
If thou wast not granted to sing thou would'st surely die.)

5

Over the breast of the spring, the land, amid cities,
Amid lanes and through old woods, where lately the violets peep'd from the ground, spot-
        ting the gray debris,
Amid the grass in the fields each side of the lanes, passing the endless grass,
Passing the yellow-spear'd wheat, every grain from its shroud in the dark-brown fields
        uprisen,
Passing the apple-tree blows of white and pink in the orchards,
Carrying a corpse to where it shall rest in the grave,
Night and day journeys a coffin.

6

Coffin that passes through lanes and streets,
Through day and night with the great cloud darkening the land,
With the pomp of the inloop'd flags with the cities draped in black,
With the show of the States themselves as of crape-veil'd women standing,
With processions long and winding and the flambeaus of the night,
With the countless torches lit, with the silent sea of faces and the unbared heads,
With the waiting depot, the arriving coffin, and the sombre faces,
With dirges through the night, with the thousand voices rising strong and solemn,
With all the mournful voices of the dirges pour'd around the coffin,
The dim-lit churches and the shuddering organs—where amid these you journey,    10
With the tolling tolling bells' perpetual clang,
Here, coffin that slowly passes,
I give you my sprig of lilac.

7

(Nor for you, for one alone,
Blossoms and branches green to coffins all I bring,
For fresh as the morning, thus would I chant a song for you O sane and sacred death.

All over bouquets of roses,
O death, I cover you over with roses and early lilies,
But mostly and now the lilac that blooms the first,
Copious I break, I break the sprigs from the bushes,
With loaded arms I come, pouring for you,
For you and the coffins all of you O death.)

8

O western orb sailing the heaven,
Now I know what you must have meant as a month since I walk'd,
As I walk'd in silence the transparent shadowy night,
As I saw you had something to tell as you bent to me night after night,
As you droop'd from the sky low down as if to my side, (while the other stars all look'd
   on,)
As we wander'd together the solemn night, (for something I know not what kept me
   from sleep,)
As the night advanced, and I saw on the rim of the west how full you were of woe,
As I stood on the rising ground in the breeze in the cool transparent night,
As I watch'd where you pass'd and was lost in the netherward black of the night,
As my soul in its trouble dissatisfied sank, as where you sad orb,      10
Concluded, dropt in the night, and was gone.

9

Sing on there in the swamp,
O singer bashful and tender, I hear your notes, I hear your call,
I hear, I come presently, I understand you,
But a moment I linger, for the lustrous star has detain'd me,
The star my departing comrade holds and detains me.

10

O how shall I warble myself for the dead one there I loved?
And how shall I deck my song for the large sweet soul that has gone?
And what shall my perfume be for the grave of him I love?

Sea-winds blown from east and west,
Blown from the Eastern sea and blown from the Western sea, till there on the prairies
   meeting,
These and with these and the breath of my chant,
I'll perfume the grave of him I love.

11

O what shall I hang on the chamber walls?
And what shall the pictures be that I hang on the walls,
To adorn the burial-house of him I love?

Pictures of growing spring and farms and homes,
With the Fourth-month eve at sundown, and the gray smoke lucid and bright,
With floods of the yellow gold of the gorgeous, indolent, sinking sun, burning, expanding
   the air,
With the fresh sweet herbage under foot, and the pale green leaves of the trees prolific,
In the distance the flowing glaze, the breast of the river, with a wind-dapple here and
   there,
With ranging hills on the banks, with many a line against the sky, and shadows,
And the city at hand with dwellings so dense, and stacks of chimneys,     10
And all the scenes of life and the workshops, and the workmen homeward returning.

12

Lo, body and soul—this land,
My own Manhattan with spires, and the sparkling and hurrying tides, and the ships,
The varied and ample land, the South and the North in the light, Ohio's shores and flash-
   ing Missouri,
And ever the far-spreading prairies cover'd with grass and corn.

Lo, the most excellent sun so calm and haughty,
The violet and purple morn with just-felt breezes,
The gentle soft-born measureless light,
The miracle spreading bathing all, the fulfill'd noon,
The coming eve delicious, the welcome night and the stars, 
Over my cities shining all, enveloping man and land.                    10

13

Sing on, sing on you gray-brown bird,
Sing from the swamps, the recesses, pour your chant from the bushes,
Limitless out of the dusk, out of the cedars and pines.

Sing on dearest brother, warble your reedy song,
Loud human song, with voice of uttermost woe.

O liquid and free and tender!
O wild and loose to my soul—O wondrous singer!
You only I hear—yet the star holds me, (but will soon depart,)
Yet the lilac with mastering odor holds me.

14

Now while I sat in the day and look'd forth,
In the close of the day with its light and the fields of spring, and the farmers preparing
          their crops,
In the large unconscious scenery of my land with its lakes and forests,
In the heavenly aerial beauty, (after the perturb'd winds and the storms,)
Under the arching heavens of the afternoon swift passing, and the voices of children and
          women,
The many-moving sea-tides, and I saw the ships how they sail'd,
And the summer approaching with richness, and the fields all busy with labor,
And the infinite separate houses, how they all went on, each with its meals and minutia of
          daily usages,
And the streets how their throbbings throbb'd, and the cities pent—lo, then and there,
Falling upon them all and among them all, enveloping me with the rest,            10
Appear'd the cloud, appear'd the long black trail,
And I knew death, its thought, and the sacred knowledge of death.

Then with the knowledge of death as walking one side of me,
And the thought of death close-walking the other side of me,
And I in the middle as with companions, and as holding the hands of companions,
I fled forth to the hiding receiving night that talks not,
Down to the shores of the water, the path by the swamp in the dimness,
To the solemn shadowy cedars and ghostly pines so still.

And the singer so shy to the rest receiv'd me,
The gray-brown bird I know receiv'd us comrades three,                    20
And he sang the carol of death, and a verse for him I love.

From deep secluded recesses,
From the fragrant cedars and the ghostly pines so still,
Came the carol of the bird.

And the charm of the carol rapt me,
As I held as if by their hands my comrades in the night,
And the voice of my spirit tallied the song of the bird.

WHEN LILACS LAST IN THE DOORYARD BLOOM'D.    14. 27. The italicized song bore a title, "Death Carol," in the 1871 edition.

*Come lovely and soothing death,*
*Undulate round the world, serenely arriving, arriving,*
*In the day, in the night, to all, to each,* 30
*Sooner or later delicate death.*

*Prais'd be the fathomless universe,*
*For life and joy, and for objects and knowledge curious,*
*And for love, sweet love—but praise! praise! praise!*
*For the sure-enwinding arms of cool-enfolding death.*

*Dark mother always gliding near with soft feet,*
*Have none chanted for thee a chant of fullest welcome?*
*Then I chant it for thee, I glorify thee above all,*
*I bring thee a song that when thou must indeed come, come unfalteringly.*

*Approach strong deliveress,* 40
*When it is so, when thou hast taken them I joyously sing the dead,*
*Lost in the loving floating ocean of thee,*
*Laved in the flood of thy bliss O death.*

*From me to thee glad serenades,*
*Dances for thee I propose saluting thee, adornments and feastings for thee,*
*And the sights of the open landscape and the high-spread sky are fitting,*
*And life and the fields, and the huge and thoughtful night.*

*The night in silence under many a star,*
*The ocean shore and the husky whispering wave whose voice I know,*
*And the soul turning to thee O vast and well-veil'd death,* 50
*And the body gratefully nestling close to thee.*

*Over the tree-tops I float thee a song,*
*Over the rising and sinking waves, over the myriad fields and the prairies wide,*
*Over the dense-pack'd cities all and the teeming wharves and ways,*
*I float this carol with joy, with joy to thee O Death.*


15

To the tally of my soul,
Loud and strong kept up the gray-brown bird,
With pure deliberate notes spreading filling the night.

Loud in the pines and cedars dim,
Clear in the freshness moist and the swamp-perfume,
And I with my comrades there in the night.

While my sight that was bound in my eyes unclosed,
As to long panoramas of visions.

And I saw askant the armies,
I saw as in noiseless dreams hundreds of battle-flags, 10
Borne through the smoke of the battles and pierc'd with missiles I saw them,
And carried hither and yon through the smoke, and torn and bloody,
And at last but a few shreds left on the staffs, (and all in silence,)
And the staffs all splinter'd and broken.

I saw battle-corpses, myriads of them,
And the white skeletons of young men, I saw them,
I saw the debris and debris of all the slain soldiers of the war,

But I saw they were not as was thought,
They themselves were fully at rest, they suffer'd not,
The living remain'd and suffer'd, the mother suffer'd,                    20
And the wife and the child and the musing comrade suffer'd,
And the armies that remain'd suffer'd.


16

Passing the visions, passing the night,
Passing, unloosing the hold of my comrades' hands,
Passing the song of the hermit bird and the tallying song of my soul,
Victorious song, death's outlet song, yet varying ever-altering song,
As low and wailing, yet clear the notes, rising and falling, flooding the night,
Sadly sinking and fainting, as warning and warning, and yet again bursting with joy,
Covering the earth and filling the spread of the heaven,
As that powerful psalm in the night I heard from recesses,
Passing, I leave thee lilac with heart-shaped leaves,
I leave thee there in the door-yard, blooming, returning with spring.        10

I cease from my song for thee,
From my gaze on thee in the west, fronting the west, communing with thee,
O comrade lustrous with silver face in the night.

Yet each to keep and all, retrievements out of the night,
The song, the wondrous chant of the gray-brown bird,
And the tallying chant, the echo arous'd in my soul,
With the lustrous and drooping star with the countenance full of woe,
With the holders holding my hand nearing the call of the bird,
Comrades mine and I in the midst, and their memory ever to keep, for the dead I loved
 so well,
For the sweetest, wisest soul of all my days and lands—and this for his dear sake,        20
Lilac and star and bird twined with the chant of my soul,
There in the fragrant pines and the cedars dusk and dim.


# PROSE


FROM
## Preface to the 1855 Edition of
## LEAVES OF GRASS

. . . . . . . . . . . . . . . . . . . . .

The Americans of all nations at any time upon the earth have probably the fullest poetical nature. The United States themselves are essentially the greatest poem. In the history of the earth hitherto the largest and most stirring appear tame and orderly to their ampler largeness and stir. Here at last is something in the doings of man that corresponds with the broadcast doings of the day and night. Here is not merely a nation but a teeming nation of nations. Here is action untied from strings necessarily blind to particulars and details magnificently moving in vast masses. Here is the hospitality which forever indicates heroes. . . . Here are the roughs and beards and space and ruggedness and nonchalance that the soul loves. Here the performance disdaining the trivial unapproached in the tremendous audacity of its crowds and groupings and the push of its perspective spreads with crampless and flowing breadth and showers its prolific and splendid extravagance. . . .

Other states indicate themselves in their deputies . . . but the genius of the United States is not best or most in its executives or legislatures, nor in its ambassadors or authors or colleges or churches or parlors, nor even in its newspapers or inventors . . . but always most in the common people. Their manners speech dress friendships— the freshness and candor of their physiognomy— the picturesque looseness of their carriage . . . their deathless attachment to freedom—their aversion to anything indecorous or soft or mean—the practical acknowledgment of the citizens of one state by the citizens of all other states—the fierceness of their roused resentment—their curiosity and welcome of novelty—their self-esteem and wonderful sympathy—their susceptibility to a slight—the air they have of persons who never knew how it felt to stand in the presence of superiors—the fluency of their speech—their delight in music, the sure symptom of manly tenderness and native elegance of soul . . . their good temper and openhandedness—the terrible significance of their elections—the President's taking off his hat to them not they to him—these too are unrhymed poetry. It awaits the gigantic and generous treatment worthy of it.

. . . . . . . . . . . . . . . . . . . . . . . . . . .

The American poets are to enclose old and new for America is the race of races. Of them a bard is to be commensurate with a people. To him the other continents arrive as contributions . . . he gives them reception for their sake and his own sake. His spirit responds to his country's spirit . . . he incarnates its geography and natural life and rivers and lakes. Mississippi with annual freshets and changing chutes, Missouri and Columbia and Ohio and Saint Lawrence with the falls and beautiful masculine Hudson, do not embouchure where they spend themselves more than they embouchure into him. The blue breadth over the inland sea of Virginia and Maryland and the sea off Massachusetts and Maine and over Manhattan bay and over Champlain and Erie and over Ontario and Huron and Michigan and Superior, and over the Texan and Mexican and Floridian and Cuban seas and over the seas of California and Oregon, is not tallied by the blue breadth of the waters below more than the breadth of above and below is tallied by him. When the long Atlantic coast stretches longer and the Pacific coast stretches longer he easily stretches with them north or south. He spans between them also from east to west and reflects what is between them. . . . For such the expression of the American poet is to be transcendent

and new. It is to be indirect and not direct or descriptive or epic. Its quality goes through these to much more. Let the age and wars of other nations be chanted and their eras and characters be illustrated and that finish the verse. Not so the great psalm of the republic. Here the theme is creative and has vista. Here comes one among the wellbeloved stonecutters and plans with decision and science and sees the solid and beautiful forms of the future where there are now no solid forms.

Of all nations the United States with veins full of poetical stuff most need poets and will doubtless have the greatest and use them the greatest. Their Presidents shall not be their common referee so much as their poets shall. Of all mankind the great poet is the equable man. Not in him but off from him things are grotesque or eccentric or fail of their sanity. Nothing out of its place is good and nothing in its place is bad. He bestows on every object or quality its fit proportions neither more nor less. He is the arbiter of the diverse and he is the key. He is the equalizer of his age and land . . . he supplies what wants supplying and checks what wants checking. If peace is the routine out of him speaks the spirit of peace, large, rich, thrifty, building vast and populous cities, encouraging agriculture and the arts and commerce—lighting the study of man, the soul, immortality—federal, state or municipal government, marriage, health, freetrade, intertravel by land and sea . . . nothing too close, nothing too far off . . . the stars not too far off. In war he is the most deadly force of the war. Who recruits him recruits horse and foot . . . he fetches parks of artillery the best that engineer ever knew. If the time becomes slothful and heavy he knows how to arouse it . . . he can make every word he speaks draw blood. Whatever stagnates in the flat of custom or obedience or legislation he never stagnates. Obedience does not master him, he masters it. . . . His thoughts are the hymns of the praise of things. In the talk on the soul and eternity and God off of his equal plane he is silent. He sees eternity less like a play with a prologue and denouement . . . he sees eternity in men and women . . . he does not see men and women as dreams or dots. Faith is the antiseptic of the soul . . . it pervades the common people and preserves them . . . they never give up believing and expecting and trusting. There is that indescribable freshness and unconsciousness about an illiterate person that humbles and mocks the power of the noblest expressive genius. The poet sees for a certainty how one not a great artist may be just as sacred as the greatest artist. . . .

. . . . . . . . . . . . . . . . . . . . . . . . . . .

The land and sea, the animals, fishes and birds, the sky of heaven and the orbs, the forests mountains and rivers, are not small themes . . . but folks expect of the poet to indicate more than the beauty and dignity which always attach to dumb real objects . . . they expect him to indicate the path between reality and their souls. Men and women perceive the beauty well enough . . . probably as well as he. The passionate tenacity of hunters, woodmen, early risers, cultivators of gardens and orchards and fields, the love of healthy women for the manly form, seafaring persons, drivers of horses, the passion for light and the open air, all is an old varied sign of the unfailing perception of beauty and of a residence of the poetic in outdoor people. They can never be assisted by poets to perceive . . . some may but they never can. The poetic quality is not marshalled in rhyme or uniformity or abstract addresses to things nor in melancholy complaints or good precepts, but is the life of these and much else and is in the soul. The profit of rhyme is that it drops seeds of a sweeter and more luxuriant rhyme, and of uniformity that it conveys itself into its own roots in the ground out of sight. The rhyme and uniformity of perfect poems show the free growth of metrical laws and bud from them as unerringly and loosely as lilacs or roses on a bush, and take shapes as compact as the shapes of chestnuts and oranges and melons and pears, and shed the perfume impalpable to form. The fluency and ornaments of the finest poems or music or orations or recitations are not independent but dependent. All beauty comes from beautiful blood and a beautiful brain. If the greatnesses are in conjunction in a man or woman it is enough . . . the fact will prevail through the universe . . . but the gaggery and gilt of a million years will not prevail. Who troubles himself about his ornaments or fluency is lost. This is what you shall do: Love the earth and sun and the animals, despise riches, give alms to every one that asks, stand up for the stupid and crazy, devote your income and labor to others, hate tyrants, argue not concerning God, have patience and indulgence toward the people, take off your hat to nothing known or unknown or to any man or number of men, go freely with powerful uneducated persons and with the young and with the mothers of families, read these leaves in the open air every season of every year of your life, re-examine all you have been told at school or church or in any book, dismiss whatever insults your own soul, and your very flesh shall be a great poem and have the richest fluency not only in its words but in the silent lines of its lips and face and between the lashes of your eyes and in every motion and joint of your body. . . .

The known universe has one complete lover and that is the greatest poet. He consumes an eternal passion and is indifferent which chance happens and which possible contingency of fortune or misfortune and persuades daily and hourly his delicious pay. What balks or breaks others is fuel for his burning progress to contact and amorous joy. Other proportions of the reception of pleasure dwindle to nothing to his proportions. All expected from heaven or from the highest he is rapport with in the sight of the daybreak or a scene of the winter-woods or the presence of children playing or with his arm round the neck of a man or woman. His love above all love has leisure and expanse . . . he leaves room ahead of himself. He is no irresolute or suspicious lover . . . he is sure . . . he scorns intervals. His experience and the showers and thrills are not for nothing. Nothing can jar him . . . suffering and darkness cannot—death and fear cannot. To him complaint and jealousy and envy are corpses buried and rotten in the earth . . . he saw them buried. The sea is not surer of the shore or the shore of the sea than he is of the fruition of his love and of all perfection and beauty.

. . . . . . . . . . . . . . . .

The art of art, the glory of expression and the sunshine of the light of letters is simplicity. Nothing is better than simplicity . . . nothing can make up for excess or for the lack of definiteness. To carry on the heave of impulse and pierce intellectual depths and give all subjects their articulations are powers neither common nor very uncommon. But to speak in literature with the perfect rectitude and insouciance of the movements of animals and the unimpeachableness of the sentiment of trees in the woods and grass by the roadside is the flawless triumph of art. If you have looked on him who has achieved it you have looked on one of the masters of the artists of all nations and times. You shall not contemplate the flight of the graygull over the bay or the mettlesome action of the blood horse or the tall leaning of sunflowers on their stalk or the appearance of the sun journeying through heaven or the appearance of the moon afterward with any more satisfaction than you shall contemplate him. The greatest poet has less a marked style and is more the channel of thoughts and things without increase or diminution, and is the free channel of himself. He swears to his art, I will not be meddlesome, I will not have in my writing any elegance or effect or originality to hang in the way between me and the rest like curtains. I will have nothing hang in the way, not the richest curtains. What I tell I tell for precisely what it is. Let who may exalt or startle or fascinate or sooth I will have purposes as health or heat or snow has and be as regardless of observation. What I experience or portray shall go from my composition without a shred of my composition. You shall stand by my side and look in the mirror with me.

The old red blood and stainless gentility of great poets will be proved by their unconstraint. A heroic person walks at his ease through and out of that custom or precedent or authority that suits him not. . . .

The messages of great poets to each man and woman are, Come to us on equal terms, Only then can you understand us, We are no better than you, What we enclose you enclose, What we enjoy you may enjoy. Did you suppose there could be only one Supreme? We affirm there can be unnumbered Supremes, and that one does not countervail another any more than one eyesight countervails another . . . and that men can be good or grand only of the consciousness of their supremacy within them. What do you think is the grandeur of storms and dismemberments and the deadliest battles and wrecks and the wildest fury of the elements and the power of the sea and the motion of nature and of the throes of human desires and dignity and hate and love? It is that something in the soul which says, Rage on, Whirl on, I tread master here and everywhere, Master of the spasms of the sky and of the shatter of the sea, Master of nature and passion and death, And of all terror and all pain.

The American bards shall be marked for generosity and affection and for encouraging competitors. . . . He shall delineate no class of persons nor one or two out of the strata of interests nor love most nor truth most nor the soul most nor the body most . . . and not be for the eastern states more than the western or the northern states more than the southern.

Exact science and its practical movements are no checks on the greatest poet but always his encouragement and support. The outset and remembrance are there . . . there are the arms that lifted him first and brace him best . . . there he returns after all his goings and comings. The sailor and traveler . . . the atomist chemist astronomer geologist phrenologist spiritualist mathematician historian and lexicographer are not poets, but they are the lawgivers of poets and their construction underlies the structure of every perfect poem. . . . In the beauty of poems are the tuft and final applause of science.

. . . . . . . . . . . . . . . . . . . . . . . . . . . .

In the make of the great masters the idea of political liberty is indispensable. Liberty takes the

adherence of heroes wherever men and women exist . . . but never takes any adherence or welcome from the rest more than from poets. They are the voice and exposition of liberty. They out of ages are worthy the grand idea . . . to them it is confided and they must sustain it. Nothing has precedence of it and nothing can warp or degrade it. The attitude of great poets is to cheer up slaves and horrify despots. The turn of their necks, the sound of their feet, the motions of their wrists, are full of hazard to the one and hope to the other. Come nigh them awhile and though they neither speak or advise you shall learn the faithful American lesson. Liberty is poorly served by men whose good intent is quelled from one failure or two failures or any number of failures, or from the casual indifference or ingratitude of the people, or from the sharp show of the tushes of power, or the bringing to bear soldiers and cannon or any penal statutes. Liberty relies upon itself, invites no one, promises nothing, sits in calmness and light, is positive and composed, and knows no discouragement. The battle rages with many a loud alarm and frequent advance and retreat . . . the enemy triumphs . . . the prison, the handcuffs, the iron necklace and anklet, the scaffold, garrote and leadballs do their work . . . the cause is asleep . . . the strong throats are choked with their own blood . . . the young men drop their eyelashes toward the ground when they pass each other . . . and is liberty gone out of that place? No never. When liberty goes it is not the first to go nor the second nor third to go . . . it waits for all the rest to go . . . it is the last. . . . When the memories of the old martyrs are faded utterly away . . . when the large names of patriots are laughed at in the public halls from the lips of the orators . . . when the boys are no more christened after the same but christened after tyrants and traitors instead . . . when the laws of the free are grudgingly permitted and laws for informers and bloodmoney are sweet to the taste of the people . . . when I and you walk abroad upon the earth stung with compassion at the sight of numberless brothers answering our equal friendship and calling no man master—and when we are elated with noble joy at the sight of slaves . . . when the soul retires in the cool communion of the night and surveys its experience and has much extasy over the word and deed that put back a helpless innocent person into the gripe of the gripers or into any cruel inferiority . . . when those in all parts of these states who could easier realize the true American character but do not yet—when the swarms of cringers, suckers, doughfaces, lice of politics, planners of sly involutions for their own preferment to city offices or state legislatures or the judiciary or congress or the presidency, obtain a response of love and natural deference from the people whether they get the offices or no . . . when it is better to be a bound booby and rogue in office at a high salary than the poorest free mechanic or farmer with his hat unmoved from his head and firm eyes and a candid and generous heart . . . and when servility by town or state or the federal government or any oppression on a large scale or small scale can be tried on without its own punishment following duly after in exact proportion against the smallest chance of escape . . . or rather when all life and all the souls of men and women are discharged from any part of the earth —then only shall the instinct of liberty be discharged from that part of the earth.

. . . The poets of the kosmos advance through all interpositions and coverings and turmoils and stratagems to first principles. They are of use . . . they dissolve poverty from its need and riches from its conceit. Your large proprietor they say shall not realize or perceive more than any one else. The owner of the library is not he who holds a legal title to it having bought it and paid for it. Any one and every one is owner of the library who can read the same through all the varieties of tongues and subjects and styles, and in whom they enter with ease and take residence and face toward paternity and maternity, and make supple and powerful and rich and large. . . . These American states strong and healthy and accomplished shall receive no pleasure from violations of natural models and must not permit them. In paintings or mouldings or carvings in mineral or wood, or in the illustrations of books or newspapers, or in any comic or tragic prints, or in the patterns of woven stuffs or anything to beautify rooms or furniture or costumes, or to put upon cornices of monuments or on the prows or sterns of ships, or to put anywhere before the human eye indoors or out, that which distorts honest shapes or which creates unearthly beings or places or contingencies is a nuisance and revolt. Of the human form especially it is so great it must never be made ridiculous. Of ornaments to a work nothing outré can be allowed . . . but those ornaments can be allowed that conform to the perfect facts of the open air and that flow out of the nature of the work and come irrepressibly from it and are necessary to the completion of the work. Most works are most beautiful without ornament. . . . Exaggerations will be revenged in human physiology. Clean and vigorous children are jetted and conceived only in those communities where the models of natural forms are public every day. . . . Great genius and the people of these states must

never be demeaned to romances. As soon as histories are properly told there is no more need of romances.

. . . . . . . . . . . . . . . . . . . . . . . . . .

The direct trial of him who would be the greatest poet is today. If he does not flood himself with the immediate age as with vast oceanic tides . . . The prescient poet projects himself centuries ahead and judges performer or performance after the changes of time. Does it live through them? Does it still hold on untired? Will the same style and the direction of genius to similar points be satisfactory now? Has no new discovery in science or arrival at superior planes of thought and judgment and behaviour fixed him or his so that either can be looked down upon? Have the marches of tens and hundreds and thousands of years made willing detours to the right hand and the left hand for his sake? Is he beloved long and long after he is buried? Does the young man think often of him? and the young woman think often of him? and do the middle-aged and the old think of him?

A great poem is for ages and ages in common and for all degrees and complexions and all departments and sects and for a woman as much as a man and a man as much as a woman. A great poem is no finish to a man or woman but rather a beginning. Has any one fancied he could sit at last under some due authority and rest satisfied with explanations and realize and be content and full? To no such terminus does the greatest poet bring . . . he brings neither cessation nor sheltered fatness and ease. The touch of him tells in action. Whom he takes he takes with firm sure grasp into live regions previously unattained . . . thenceforward is no rest . . . they see the space and ineffable sheen that turn the old spots and lights into dead vacuums. The companion of him beholds the birth and progress of stars and learns one of the meanings. Now there shall be a man cohered out of tumult and chaos . . . the elder encourages the younger and shows him how . . . they too shall launch off fearlessly together till the new world fits an orbit for itself and looks unabashed on the lesser orbits of the stars and sweeps through the ceaseless rings and shall never be quiet again.

There will soon be no more priests. Their work is done. They may wait awhile . . . perhaps a generation or two . . . dropping off by degrees. A superior breed shall take their place . . . the gangs of kosmos and prophets en masse shall take their place. A new order shall arise and they shall be the priests of man, and every man shall be his own priest. The churches built under their umbrage shall be the churches of men and women. Through the divinity of themselves shall the kosmos and the new breed of poets be interpreters of men and women and of all events and things. They shall find their inspiration in real objects today, symptoms of the past and future . . . They shall not deign to defend immortality or God or the perfection of things or liberty or the exquisite beauty and reality of the soul. They shall arise in America and be responded to from the remainder of the earth.

The English language befriends the grand American expression . . . it is brawny enough and limber and full enough. On the tough stock of a race who through all change of circumstances was never without the idea of political liberty, which is the animus of all liberty, it has attracted the terms of daintier and gayer and subtler and more elegant tongues. It is the powerful language of resistance . . . it is the dialect of common sense. It is the speech of the proud and melancholy races and of all who aspire. It is the chosen tongue to express growth faith self-esteem freedom justice equality friendliness amplitude prudence decision and courage. It is the medium that shall well nigh express the inexpressible.

No great literature nor any like style of behaviour or oratory or social intercourse or household arrangements or public institutions or the treatment by bosses of employed people, nor executive detail or detail of the army or navy, nor spirit of legislation or courts or police or tuition or architecture or songs or amusements or the costumes of young men, can long elude the jealous and passionate instinct of American standards. Whether or no the sign appears from the mouths of the people, it throbs a live interrogation in every freeman's and freewoman's heart after that which passes by or this built to remain. Is it uniform with my country? Are its disposals without ignominious distinctions? Is it for the evergrowing communes of brothers and lovers, large, well-united, proud beyond the old models, generous beyond all models? Is it something grown fresh out of the fields or drawn from the sea for use to me today here? I know that what answers for me an American must answer for any individual or nation that serves for a part of my materials. Does this answer? or is it without reference to universal needs? or sprung of the needs of the less developed society of special ranks? or old needs of pleasure overlaid by modern science and forms? Does this acknowledge liberty with audible and absolute acknowledgment, and set slavery at naught for life and death? Will it help breed one goodshaped and wellhung man, and a woman to

be his perfect and independent mate? Does it improve manners? Is it for the nursing of the young of the republic? Does it solve readily with the sweet milk of the nipples of the breasts of the mother of many children? Has it too the old ever-fresh forbearance and impartiality? Does it look with the same love on the last born and those hardening toward stature, and on the errant, and on those who disdain all strength of assault outside of their own?

The poems distilled from other poems will probably pass away. The coward will surely pass away. The expectation of the vital and great can only be satisfied by the demeanor of the vital and great. The swarms of the polished deprecating and reflectors and the polite float off and leave no remembrance. America prepares with composure and goodwill for the visitors that have sent word. It is not intellect that is to be their warrant and welcome. The talented, the artist, the ingenious, the editor, the statesman, the erudite . . . they are not unappreciated . . . they fall in their place and do their work. The soul of the nation also does it work. No disguise can pass on it . . . no disguise can conceal from it. It rejects none, it permits all. Only toward as good as itself and toward the like of itself will it advance half-way. An individual is as superb as a nation when he has the qualities which make a superb nation. The soul of the largest and wealthiest and proudest nation may well go half-way to meet that of its poets. The signs are effectual. There is no fear of mistake. If the one is true the other is true. The proof of a poet is that his country absorbs him as affectionately as he has absorbed it.

## A BACKWARD GLANCE O'ER TRAVEL'D ROADS

PERHAPS the best of songs heard, or of any and all true love, or life's fairest episodes, or sailors', soldiers' trying scenes on land or sea, is the *résumé* of them, or any of them, long afterwards, looking at the actualities away back past, with all their practical excitations gone. How the soul loves to float amid such reminiscences!

So here I sit gossiping in the early candle-light of old age—I and my book—casting backward glances over our travel'd road. After completing, as it were, the journey—(a varied jaunt of years, with many halts and gaps of intervals—or some lengthen'd ship-voyage, wherein more than once the last hour had apparently arrived, and we seem'd certainly going down—yet reaching port in a sufficient way through all discomfitures at last)

—After completing my poems, I am curious to review them in the light of their own (at the time unconscious, or mostly unconscious) intentions, with certain unfoldings of the thirty years they seek to embody. These lines, therefore, will probably blend the weft of first purposes and speculations, with the warp of that experience afterwards, always bringing strange developments.

Result of seven or eight stages and struggles extending through nearly thirty years, (as I nigh my three-score-and-ten I live largely on memory,) I look upon "Leaves of Grass," now finish'd to the end of its opportunities and powers, as my definitive *carte visite* to the coming generations of the New World,[1] if I may assume to say so. That I have not gain'd the acceptance of my own time, but have fallen back on fond dreams of the future —anticipations—("still lives the song, though Regnar dies")—That from a worldly and business point of view "Leaves of Grass" has been worse than a failure—that public criticism on the book and myself as author of it yet shows mark'd anger and contempt more than anything else—("I find a solid line of enemies to you everywhere,"—letter from W. S. K., Boston, May 28, 1884)—And that solely for publishing it I have been the object of two or three pretty serious special official buffetings—is all probably no more than I ought to have expected. I had my choice when I commenc'd. I bid neither for soft eulogies, big money returns, nor the approbation of existing schools and conventions. As fulfill'd, or partially fulfill'd, the best comfort of the whole business (after a small band of the dearest friends and upholders ever vouchsafed to man or cause—doubtless all the more faithful and uncompromising—this little phalanx!—for being so few) is that, unstopp'd and unwarp'd by any influence outside the soul within me, I have had my say entirely my own way, and put it unerringly on record—the value thereof to be decided by time.

In calculating that decision, William O'Connor and Dr. Bucke are far more peremptory than I am. Behind all else that can be said, I consider "Leaves of Grass" and its theory experimental— as, in the deepest sense, I consider our American republic itself to be, with its theory. (I think I have at least enough philosophy not to be too absolutely certain of any thing, or any results.) In the second place, the volume is a *sortie*—whether to prove triumphant, and conquer its field of aim and escape and construction, nothing less than a hun-

dred years from now can fully answer. I consider the point that I have positively gain'd a hearing, to far more than make up for any and all other lacks and withholdings. Essentially, *that* was from the first, and has remain'd throughout, the main object. Now it seems to be achiev'd, I am certainly contented to waive any otherwise momentous drawbacks, as of little account. Candidly and dispassionately reviewing all my intentions, I feel that they were creditable—and I accept the result, whatever it may be.

After continued personal ambition and effort, as a young fellow, to enter with the rest into competition for the usual rewards, business, political, literary, &c.—to take part in the great *mêlée*, both for victory's prize itself and to do some good —After years of those aims and pursuits, I found myself remaining possess'd, at the age of thirty-one to thirty-three, with a special desire and conviction. Or rather, to be quite exact, a desire that had been flitting through my previous life, or hovering on the flanks, mostly indefinite hitherto, had steadily advanced to the front, defined itself, and finally dominated everything else. This was a feeling or ambition to articulate and faithfully express in literary or poetic form, and uncompromisingly, my own physical, emotional, moral, intellectual, and æsthetic Personality, in the midst of, and tallying, the momentous spirit and facts of its immediate days, and of current America—and to exploit that Personality, identified with place and date, in a far more candid and comprehensive sense than any hitherto poem or book.

Perhaps this is in brief, or suggests, all I have sought to do. Given the Nineteenth Century, with the United States, and what they furnish as area and points of view, "Leaves of Grass" is, or seeks to be, simply a faithful and doubtless self-will'd record. In the midst of all, it gives one man's—the author's—identity, ardors, observations, faiths, and thoughts, color'd hardly at all with any decided coloring from other faiths or other identities. Plenty of songs had been sung—beautiful, matchless songs—adjusted to other lands than these—another spirit and stage of evolution; but I would sing, and leave out or put in, quite solely with reference to America and to-day. Modern science and democracy seem'd to be throwing out their challenge to poetry to put them in its statements in contradistinction to the songs and myths of the past. As I see it now (perhaps too late,) I have unwittingly taken up that challenge and made an attempt at such statements—which I certainly would not assume to do now, knowing more clearly what it means.

For grounds for "Leaves of Grass," as a poem,

A BACKWARD GLANCE O'ER TRAVEL'D ROADS. 1. "When Champollion, on his death-bed, handed to the printer the revised proof of his *Egyptian Grammar*, he said gayly, 'Be careful of this—it is my *carte de visite* to posterity '" [W].

I abandon'd the conventional themes, which do not appear in it: none of the stock ornamentation, or choice plots of love or war, or high, exceptional personages of Old-World song; nothing, as I may say, for beauty's sake—no legend, or myth, or romance, nor euphemism, nor rhyme. But the broadest average of humanity and its identities in the now ripening Nineteenth Century, and especially in each of their countless examples and practical occupations in the United States to-day.

One main contrast of the ideas behind every page of my verses, compared with establish'd poems, is their different relative attitude towards God, towards the objective universe, and still more (by reflection, confession, assumption, &c.) the quite changed attitude of the ego, the one chanting or talking, towards himself and towards his fellow-humanity. It is certainly time for America, above all, to begin this readjustment in the scope and basic point of view of verse; for everything else has changed. As I write, I see in an article on Wordsworth, in one of the current English magazines, the lines, "A few weeks ago an eminent French critic said that, owing to the special tendency to science and to its all-devouring force, poetry would cease to be read in fifty years." But I anticipate the very contrary. Only a firmer, vastly broader, new area begins to exist—nay, is already form'd—to which the poetic genius must emigrate. Whatever may have been the case in years gone by, the true use for the imaginative faculty of modern times is to give ultimate vivification to facts, to science, and to common lives, endowing them with the glows and glories and final illustriousness which belong to every real thing, and to real things only. Without that ultimate vivification—which the poet or other artist alone can give—reality would seem incomplete, and science, democracy, and life itself, finally in vain.

Few appreciate the moral revolutions, our age, which have been profounder far than the material or inventive or war-produced ones. The Nineteenth Century, now well towards its close (and ripening into fruit the seeds of the two preceding centuries [2])—the uprisings of national masses and shiftings of boundary-lines—the historical and other prominent facts of the United States—the war of attempted Secession—the stormy rush and haste of nebulous forces—never can future years witness more excitement and din of action—never

completer change of army front along the whole line, the whole civilized world. For all these new and evolutionary facts, meanings, purposes, new poetic messages, new forms and expressions, are inevitable.

My Book and I—what a period we have presumed to span! those thirty years from 1850 to '80—and America in them! Proud, proud indeed may we be, if we have cull'd enough of that period in its own spirit to worthily waft a few live breaths of it to the future!

Let me not dare, here or anywhere, for my own purposes, or any purposes, to attempt the definition of Poetry, nor answer the question what it is. Like Religion, Love, Nature, while those terms are indispensable, and we all give a sufficiently accurate meaning to them, in my opinion no definition that has ever been made sufficiently encloses the name Poetry; nor can any rule or convention ever so absolutely obtain but some great exception may arise and disregard and overturn it.

Also it must be carefully remember'd that first-class literature does not shine by any luminosity of its own; nor do its poems. They grow of circumstances, and are evolutionary. The actual living light is always curiously from elsewhere—follows unaccountable sources, and is lunar and relative at the best. There are, I know, certain controling themes that seem endlessly appropriated to the poets—as war, in the past—in the Bible, religious rapture and adoration—always love, beauty, some fine plot, or pensive or other emotion. But, strange as it may sound at first, I will say there is something striking far deeper and towering far higher than those themes for the best elements of modern song.

Just as all the old imaginative works rest, after their kind, on long trains of presuppositions, often entirely unmention'd by themselves, yet supplying the most important bases of them, and without which they could have had no reason for being, so "Leaves of Grass," before a line was written, presupposed something different from any other, and, as it stands, is the result of such presupposition. I should say, indeed, it were useless to attempt reading the book without first carefully tallying that preparatory background and quality in the mind. Think of the United States to-day—the fact of these thirty-eight or forty empires solder'd in one—sixty or seventy millions of equals, with their lives, their passions, their future—these incalculable, modern, American, seething multitudes around us, of which we are inseparable parts! Think, in comparison, of the petty environage and limited area of the poets of past or present Europe, no matter how great their genius. Think

---

2. "The ferment and germination even of the United States to-day, dating back to, and in my opinion mainly founded on, the Elizabethan age in English history, the age of Francis Bacon and Shakspere. Indeed, when we pursue it, what growth or advent is there that does not date back, until lost—perhaps its most tantalizing clues lost—in the receded horizons of the past?" [W].

of the absence and ignorance, in all cases hitherto, of the multitudinousness, vitality, and the unprecedented stimulants of to-day and here. It almost seems as if a poetry with cosmic and dynamic features of magnitude and limitlessness suitable to the human soul, were never possible before. It is certain that a poetry of absolute faith and equality for the use of the democratic masses never was.

In estimating first-class song, a sufficient Nationality, or, on the other hand, what may be call'd the negative and lack of it, (as in Goethe's case, it sometimes seems to me,) is often, if not always, the first element. One needs only a little penetration to see, at more or less removes, the material facts of their country and radius, with the coloring of the moods of humanity at the time, and its gloomy or hopeful prospects, behind all poets and each poet, and forming their birthmarks. I know very well that my "Leaves" could not possibly have emerged or been fashion'd or completed, from any other era than the latter half of the Nineteenth Century, nor any other land than democratic America, and from the absolute triumph of the National Union arms.

And whether my friends claim it for me or not, I know well enough, too, that in respect to pictorial talent, dramatic situations, and especially in verbal melody and all the conventional technique of poetry, not only the divine works that to-day stand ahead in the world's reading, but dozens more, transcend (some of them immeasurably transcend) all I have done, or could do. But it seem'd to me, as the objects in Nature, the themes of æstheticism, and all special exploitations of the mind and soul, involve not only their own inherent quality, but the quality, just as inherent and important, of *their point of view,*[3] the time had come to reflect all themes and things, old and new, in the lights thrown on them by the advent of America and democracy—to chant those themes through the utterance of one, not only the grateful and reverent legatee of the past, but the born child of the New World—to illustrate all through the genesis and ensemble of to-day; and that such illustration and ensemble are the chief demands of America's prospective imaginative literature. Not to carry out, in the approved style, some choice plot of fortune or misfortune, or fancy, or fine thoughts, or incidents, or courtesies—all of which has been done overwhelmingly and well, probably never to be excell'd—but that while in such æsthetic presentation of objects, passions,

plots, thoughts, &c., our lands and days do not want, and probably will never have, anything better than they already possess from the bequests of the past, it still remains to be said that there is even towards all those a subjective and contemporary point of view appropriate to ourselves alone, and to our new genius and environments, different from anything hitherto; and that such conception of current or gone-by life and art is for us the only means of their assimilation consistent with the Western world.

Indeed, and anyhow, to put it specifically, has not the time arrived when, (if it must be plainly said, for democratic America's sake, if for no other) there must imperatively come a readjustment of the whole theory and nature of Poetry? The question is important, and I may turn the argument over and repeat it: Does not the best thought of our day and Republic conceive of a birth and spirit of song superior to anything past or present? To the effectual and moral consolidation of our lands (already, as materially establish'd, the greatest factors in known history, and far, far greater through what they prelude and necessitate, and are to be in future)—to conform with and build on the concrete realities and theories of the universe furnish'd by science, and henceforth the only irrefragable basis for anything, verse included—to root both influences in the emotional and imaginative action of the modern time, and dominate all that precedes or opposes them—is not either a radical advance and step forward, or a new verteber of the best song indispensable?

The New World receives with joy the poems of the antique, with European feudalism's rich fund of epics, plays, ballads—seeks not in the least to deaden or displace those voices from our ear and area—holds them indeed as indispensable studies, influences, records, comparisons. But though the dawn-dazzle of the sun of literature is in those poems for us of to-day—though perhaps the best parts of current character in nations, social groups, or any man's or woman's individuality, Old World or New, are from them—and though if I were ask'd to name the most precious bequest to current American civilization from all the hitherto ages, I am not sure but I would name those old and less old songs ferried hither from east and west—some serious words and debits remain; some acrid considerations demand a hearing. Of the great poems receiv'd from abroad and from the ages, and to-day enveloping and penetrating America, is there one that is consistent with these United States, or essentially applicable to

3. "According to Immanuel Kant, the last essential reality, giving shape and significance to all the rest" [W].

them as they are and are to be? Is there one whose underlying basis is not a denial and insult to democracy? What a comment it forms, anyhow, on this era of literary fulfilment, with the splendid day-rise of science and resuscitation of history, that our chief religious and poetical works are not our own, nor adapted to our light, but have been furnish'd by far-back ages out of their arriere and darkness, or, at most, twilight dimness! What is there in those works that so imperiously and scornfully dominates all our advanced civilization, and culture?

Even Shakspere, who so suffuses current letters and art (which indeed have in most degrees grown out of him,) belongs essentially to the buried past. Only he holds the proud distinction for certain important phases of that past, of being the loftiest of the singers life has yet given voice to. All, however, relate to and rest upon conditions, standards, politics, sociologies, ranges of belief, that have been quite eliminated from the Eastern hemisphere, and never existed at all in the Western. As authoritative types of song they belong in America just about as much as the persons and institutes they depict. True, it may be said, the emotional, moral, and æsthetic natures of humanity have not radically changed—that in these the old poems apply to our times and all times, irrespective of date; and that they are of incalculable value as pictures of the past. I willingly make those admissions, and to their fullest extent; then advance the points herewith as of serious, even paramount importance.

I have indeed put on record elsewhere my reverence and eulogy for those never-to-be-excell'd poetic bequests, and their indescribable preciousness as heirlooms for America. Another and separate point must now be candidly stated. If I had not stood before those poems with uncover'd head, fully aware of their colossal grandeur and beauty of form and spirit, I could not have written "Leaves of Grass." My verdict and conclusions as illustrated in its pages are arrived at through the temper and inculcation of the old works as much as through anything else—perhaps more than through anything else. As America fully and fairly construed is the legitimate result and evolutionary outcome of the past, so I would dare to claim for my verse. Without stopping to qualify the averment, the Old World has had the poems of myths, fictions, feudalism, conquest, caste, dynastic wars, and splendid exceptional characters and affairs, which have been great; but the New World needs the poems of realities and science and of the democratic average and basic equality, which shall

be greater. In the centre of all, and object of all, stands the Human Being, towards whose heroic and spiritual evolution poems and everything directly or indirectly tend, Old World or New.

Continuing the subject, my friends have more than once suggested—or may be the garrulity of advancing age is possessing me—some further embryonic facts of "Leaves of Grass," and especially how I enter'd upon them. Dr. Bucke has, in his volume, already fully and fairly described the preparation of my poetic field, with the particular and general plowing, planting, seeding, and occupation of the ground, till everything was fertilized, rooted, and ready to start its own way for good or bad. Not till after all this, did I attempt any serious acquaintance with poetic literature. Along in my sixteenth year I had become possessor of a stout, well-cramm'd one thousand page octavo volume (I have it yet,) containing Walter Scott's poetry entire—an inexhaustible mine and treasury of poetic forage (especially the endless forests and jungles of notes)—has been so to me for fifty years, and remains so to this day.[4]

Later, at intervals, summers and falls, I used to go off, sometimes for a week at a stretch, down in the country, or to Long Island's seashores—there, in the presence of outdoor influences, I went over thoroughly the Old and New Testaments, and absorb'd (probably to better advantage for me than in any library or indoor room—it makes such difference *where* you read,) Shakspere, Ossian, the best translated versions I could get of Homer, Eschylus, Sophocles, the old German Nibelungen, the ancient Hindoo poems, and one or two other masterpieces, Dante's among them. As it happen'd, I read the latter mostly in an old wood. The Iliad (Buckley's prose version,) I read first thoroughly on the peninsula of Orient, northeast end of Long Island, in a shelter'd hollow of rocks and sand, with the sea on each side. (I have wonder'd since why I was not overwhelm'd by those mighty masters. Likely because I read them, as described, in the full presence of Nature, under the sun, with the far-spreading landscape and vistas, or the sea rolling in.)

4. "Sir Walter Scott's *Complete Poems;* especially including *Border Minstrelsy; then Sir Tristrem; Lay of the Last Minstrel; Ballads from the German; Marmion; Lady of the Lake; Vision of Don Roderick; Lord of the Isles; Rokeby; Bridal of Triermain; Field of Waterloo; Harold the Dauntless;* all the Dramas, various Introductions, endless interesting Notes, and Essays on Poetry, Romance, &c.

"Lockhart's 1833 (or '34) edition with Scott's latest and copious revisions and annotations. (All the poems were thoroughly read by me, but the ballads of the *Border Minstrelsy* over and over again)" [W].

Toward the last I had among much else look'd over Edgar Poe's poems—of which I was not an admirer, tho' I always saw that beyond their limited range of melody (like perpetual chimes of music bells, ringing from lower *b* flat up to *g*) they were melodious expressions, and perhaps never excell'd ones, of certain pronounc'd phases of human morbidity. (The Poetic area is very spacious—has room for all—has so many mansions!) But I was repaid in Poe's prose by the idea that (at any rate for our occasions, our day) there can be no such thing as a long poem. The same thought had been haunting my mind before, but Poe's argument, though short, work'd the sum out and proved it to me.

Another point had an early settlement, clearing the ground greatly. I saw, from the time my enterprise and questionings positively shaped themselves (how best can I express my own distinctive era and surroundings, America, Democracy?) that the trunk and centre whence the answer was to radiate, and to which all should return from straying however far a distance, must be an identical body and soul, a personality—which personality, after many considerations and ponderings I deliberately settled should be myself—indeed could not be any other. I also felt strongly (whether I have shown it or not) that to the true and full estimate of the Present both the Past and the Future are main considerations.

These, however, and much more might have gone on and come to naught (almost positively would have come to naught,) if a sudden, vast, terrible, direct and indirect stimulus for new and national declamatory expression had not been given to me. It is certain, I say, that, although I had made a start before, only from the occurrence of the Secession War, and what it show'd me as by flashes of lightning, with the emotional depths it sounded and arous'd (of course, I don't mean in my own heart only, I saw it just as plainly in others, in millions)—that only from the strong flare and provocation of that war's sights and scenes the final reasons-for-being of an autochthonic and passionate song definitely came forth.

I went down to the war fields in Virginia (end of 1862), lived thenceforward in camp—saw great battles and the days and nights afterward—partook of all the fluctuations, gloom, despair, hopes again arous'd, courage evoked—death readily risk'd—*the cause,* too—along and filling those agonistic and lurid following years, 1863–'64–'65 —the real parturition years (more than 1776–'83) of this henceforth homogeneous Union. Without those three or four years and the experiences they gave, "Leaves of Grass" would not now be existing.

But I set out with the intention also of indicating or hinting some point-characteristics which I since see (though I did not then, at least not definitely) were bases and object-urgings toward those "Leaves" from the first. The word I myself put primarily for the description of them as they stand at last, is the word Suggestiveness. I round and finish little, if anything; and could not, consistently with my scheme. The reader will always have his or her part to do, just as much as I have had mine. I seek less to state or display any theme or thought, and more to bring you, reader, into the atmosphere of the theme or thought—there to pursue your own flight. Another impetus-word is Comradeship as for all lands, and in a more commanding and acknowledg'd sense than hitherto. Other word-signs would be Good Cheer, Content, and Hope.

The chief trait of any given poet is always the spirit he brings to the observation of Humanity and Nature—the mood out of which he contemplates his subjects. What kind of temper and what amount of faith report these things? Up to how recent a date is the song carried? What the equipment, and special raciness of the singer—what his tinge of coloring? The last value of artistic expressers, past and present—Greek æsthetes, Shakspere —or in our own day Tennyson, Victor Hugo, Carlyle, Emerson—is certainly involv'd in such questions. I say the profoundest service that poems or any other writings can do for their reader is not merely to satisfy the intellect, or supply something polish'd and interesting, nor even to depict great passions, or persons or events, but to fill him with vigorous and clean manliness, religiousness, and give him *good heart* as a radical possession and habit. The educated world seems to have been growing more and more ennuyed for ages, leaving to our time the inheritance of it all. Fortunately there is the original inexhaustible fund of buoyancy, normally resident in the race, forever eligible to be appeal'd to and relied on.

As for native American individuality, though certain to come, and on a large scale, the distinctive and ideal type of Western character (as consistent with the operative political and even money-making features of United States' humanity in the Nineteenth Century as chosen knights, gentlemen and warriors were the ideals of the centuries of European feudalism) it has not yet appear'd. I have allow'd the stress of my poems from beginning to end to bear upon American individuality and to assist it—not only because that is a great lesson in Nature, amid all her generalizing laws, but as counterpoise to the leveling tendencies of Democracy—and for other reasons. Defiant of ostensible literary and other conventions, I avowedly chant "the great pride of man in himself," and permit it to be more or less a *motif* of nearly all my verse. I think this pride indispensable to an American. I think it not inconsistent with obedience, humility, deference, and self-questioning.

Democracy has been so retarded and jeopardized by powerful personalities, that its first instincts are fain to clip, conform, bring in stragglers, and reduce everything to a dead level. While the ambitious thought of my song is to help the forming of a great aggregate Nation, it is, perhaps, altogether through the forming of myriads of fully develop'd and enclosing individuals. Welcome as are equality's and fraternity's doctrines and popular education, a certain liability accompanies them all, as we see. That primal and interior something in man, in his soul's abysms, coloring all, and, by exceptional fruitions, giving the last majesty to him—something continually touch'd upon and attain'd by the old poems and ballads of feudalism, and often the principal foundation of them—modern science and democracy appear to be endangering, perhaps eliminating. But that forms an appearance only; the reality is quite different. The new influences, upon the whole, are surely preparing the way for grander individualities than ever. To-day and here personal force is behind everything, just the same. The times and depictions from the Iliad to Shakspere inclusive can happily never again be realized—but the elements of courageous and lofty manhood are unchanged.

Without yielding an inch the working-man and working-woman were to be in my pages from first to last. The ranges of heroism and loftiness with which Greek and feudal poets endow'd their godlike or lordly born characters—indeed prouder and better based and with fuller ranges than those—I was to endow the democratic averages of America. I was to show that we, here and to-day, are eligible to the grandest and the best—more eligible now than any times of old were. I will also want my utterances (I said to myself before beginning) to be in spirit the poems of the morning. (They have been founded and mainly written in the sunny forenoon and early midday of my life.) I will want them to be the poems of women entirely as much as men. I have wish'd to put the complete Union of the States in my songs without any preference or partiality whatever. Henceforth, if they live and are read, it must be just as much

South as North—just as much along the Pacific as Atlantic—in the valley of the Mississippi, in Canada, up in Maine, down in Texas, and on the shores of Puget Sound.

From another point of view "Leaves of Grass" is avowedly the song of Sex and Amativeness, and even Animality—though meanings that do not usually go along with those words are behind all, and will duly emerge; and all are sought to be lifted into a different light and atmosphere. Of this feature, intentionally palpable in a few lines, I shall only say the espousing principle of those lines so gives breath of life to my whole scheme that the bulk of the pieces might as well have been left unwritten were those lines omitted. Difficult as it will be, it has become, in my opinion, imperative to achieve a shifted attitude from superior men and women towards the thought and fact of sexuality, as an element in character, personality, the emotions, and a theme in literature. I am not going to argue the question by itself; it does not stand by itself. The vitality of it is altogether in its relations, bearings, significance—like the clef of a symphony. At last analogy the lines I allude to, and the spirit in which they are spoken, permeate all "Leaves of Grass," and the work must stand or fall with them, as the human body and soul must remain as an entirety.

Universal as are certain facts and symptoms of communities or individuals all times, there is nothing so rare in modern conventions and poetry as their normal recognizance. Literature is always calling in the doctor for consultation and confession, and always giving evasions and swathing suppressions in place of that "heroic nudity" [5] on which only a genuine diagnosis of serious cases can be built. And in respect to editions of "Leaves of Grass" in time to come (if there should be such) I take occasion now to confirm those lines with the settled convictions and deliberate renewals of thirty years, and to hereby prohibit, as far as word of mine can do so, any elision of them.

Then still a purpose enclosing all, and over and beneath all. Ever since what might be call'd thought, or the budding of thought, fairly began in my youthful mind, I had had a desire to attempt some worthy record of that entire faith and acceptance ("to justify the ways of God to man" is Milton's well-known and ambitious phrase) which is the foundation of moral America. I felt it all as positively then in my young days as I do now in my old ones; to formulate a poem whose every thought or fact should directly or indirectly be or connive at an implicit belief in the wisdom,

5. *"Nineteenth Century,* July 1883" [W].

health, mystery, beauty of every process, every concrete object, every human or other existence, not only consider'd from the point of view of all, but of each.

While I can not understand it or argue it out, I fully believe in a clue and purpose in Nature, entire and several; and that invisible spiritual results, just as real and definite as the visible, eventuate all concrete life and all materialism, through Time. My book ought to emanate buoyancy and gladness legitimately enough, for it was grown out of those elements, and has been the comfort of my life since it was originally commenced.

One main genesis-motive of the "Leaves" was my conviction (just as strong to-day as ever) that the crowning growth of the United States is to be spiritual and heroic. To help start and favor that growth—or even to call attention to it, or the need of it—is the beginning, middle and final purpose of the poems. (In fact, when really cipher'd out and summ'd to the last, plowing up in earnest the interminable average fallows of humanity—not "good government" merely, in the common sense —is the justification and main purpose of these United States.)

Isolated advantages in any rank or grace or fortune—the direct or indirect threads of all the poetry of the past—are in my opinion distasteful to the republican genius, and offer no foundation for its fitting verse. Establish'd poems, I know, have the very great advantage of chanting the already perform'd, so full of glories, reminiscences dear to the minds of men. But my volume is a candidate for the future. "All original art," says Taine, anyhow, "is self-regulated, and no original art can be regulated from without; it carries its own counterpoise, and does not receive it from elsewhere— lives on its own blood"—a solace to my frequent bruises and sulky vanity.

As the present is perhaps mainly an attempt at personal statement or illustration, I will allow myself as further help to extract the following anecdote from a book, *Annals of Old Painters,* conn'd by me in youth. Rubens, the Flemish painter, in one of his wanderings through the galleries of old convents, came across a singular work. After looking at it thoughtfully for a good while, and listening to the criticisms of his suite of students, he said to the latter, in answer to their questions (as to what school the work implied or belong'd,) "I do not believe the artist, unknown and perhaps no longer living, who has given the world this legacy, ever belong'd to any school, or ever painted anything but this one picture, which is a personal affair—a piece out of a man's life."

"Leaves of Grass" indeed (I cannot too often

reiterate) has mainly been the outcropping of my own emotional and other personal nature—an attempt, from first to last, to put *a Person,* a human being (myself, in the latter half of the Nineteenth Century, in America,) freely, fully and truly on record. I could not find any similar personal record in current literature that satisfied me. But it is not on "Leaves of Grass" distinctively *as literature,* or a specimen thereof, that I feel to dwell, or advance claims. No one will get at my verses who insists upon viewing them as a literary performance, or attempt at such performance, or as aiming mainly toward art or æstheticism.

I say no land or people or circumstances ever existed so needing a race of singers and poems differing from all others, rigidly their own, as the land and people and circumstances of our United States need such singers and poems to-day, and for the future. Still further, as long as the States continue to absorb and be dominated by the poetry of the Old World, and remain unsupplied with autochthonous song, to express, vitalize and give color to and define their material and political success, and minister to them distinctively, so long will they stop short of first-class Nationality and remain defective.

In the free evening of my day I give to you, reader, the foregoing garrulous talk, thoughts, reminiscences,

As idly drifting down the ebb,
Such ripples, half-caught voices, echo from the
  shore.

Concluding with two items for the imaginative genius of the West, when it worthily rises—First, what Herder taught to the young Goethe, that really great poetry is always (like the Homeric or Biblical canticles) the result of a national spirit, and not the privilege of a polish'd and select few; Second, that the strongest and sweetest songs yet remain to be sung.

*1888*

F R O M

# SPECIMEN DAYS

([ *Specimen Days* (1882), from which the following items are taken, is Whitman's kind of autobiography: random and lyrical reminiscences of his early years in Manhattan, literary encounters and opinions, diary-jottings on his day-to-day activities and predilections. One passage can be read as an illuminating, belated footnote to the poem "Crossing Brooklyn Ferry," another to "As I Ebb'd" and "Out of the Cradle," and still a third (the conversation with Emerson) to "Spontaneous Me." Included in *Specimen Days,* as well, was the body of Whitman's prose writing about the Civil War and Lincoln, previously published (1875) as *Memoranda During the War.* There is a good deal of literary interest in comparing Whitman's report on the Battle of Chancellorsville with Stephen Crane's wholly imaginative re-creation of the same battle in *The Red Badge of Courage* (1895).

#### MY PASSION FOR FERRIES

LIVING in Brooklyn or New York city from this time forward, my life, then, and still more the following years, was curiously identified with Fulton ferry, already becoming the greatest of its sort in the world for general importance, volume, variety, rapidity, and picturesqueness. Almost daily, later, ('50 to '60,) I cross'd on the boats, often up in the pilot-houses where I could get a full sweep, absorbing shows, accompaniments, surroundings. What oceanic currents, eddies, underneath—the great tides of humanity also, with ever-shifting movements. Indeed, I have always had a passion for ferries; to me they afford inimitable, streaming, never-failing, living poems. The river and bay scenery, all about New York island, any time of a fine day—the hurrying, splashing sea-tides—the changing panorama of steamers, all sizes, often a string of big ones outward bound to distant ports—the myriads of white-sail'd schooners, sloops, skiffs, and the marvellously beautiful yachts—the majestic sound boats as they rounded the Battery and came along towards 5, afternoon, eastward bound—the prospect off towards Staten island, or down the Narrows, or the other way up the Hudson—what refreshment of spirit such sights and experiences gave me years ago (and many a time since.) My old pilot friends, the Balsirs, Johnny Cole, Ira Smith, William White, and my young ferry friend, Tom Gere—how well I remember them all.

#### BROADWAY SIGHTS

BESIDES Fulton ferry, off and on for years, I knew and frequented Broadway—that noted avenue of New York's crowded and mixed humanity, and of so many notables. Here I saw, during those times, Andrew Jackson, Webster, Clay, Seward, Martin Van Buren, filibuster Walker, Kossuth, Fitz Greene Halleck, Bryant, the Prince of Wales, Charles Dickens, the first Japanese ambassadors, and lots of other celebrities of the time. Always something novel or inspiriting; yet mostly to me the hurrying and vast amplitude of those neverending human currents. I remember seeing James Fenimore Cooper in a court-room in Chambers

street, back of the city hall, where he was carrying on a law case—(I think it was a charge of libel he had brought against some one.) I also remember seeing Edgar A. Poe, and having a short interview with him, (it must have been in 1845 or '6,) in his office, second story of a corner building, (Duane or Pearl street.) He was editor and owner or part owner of "the Broadway Journal." The visit was about a piece of mine he had publish'd. Poe was very cordial, in a quiet way, appear'd well in person, dress, &c. I have a distinct and pleasing remembrance of his looks, voice, manner and matter; very kindly and human, but subdued, perhaps a little jaded. For another of my reminiscences, here on the west side, just below Houston street, I once saw (it must have been about 1832, of a sharp, bright January day) a bent, feeble but stout-built very old man, bearded, swathed in rich furs, with a great ermine cap on his head, led and assisted, almost carried, down the steps of his high front stoop (a dozen friends and servants, emulous, carefully holding, guiding him) and then lifted and tuck'd in a gorgeous sleigh, envelop'd in other furs, for a ride. The sleigh was drawn by as fine a team of horses as I ever saw. (You needn't think all the best animals are brought up nowadays; never was such horseflesh as fifty years ago on Long Island, or south, or in New York city; folks look'd for spirit and mettle in a nag, not tame speed merely.) Well, I, a boy of perhaps thirteen or fourteen, stopp'd and gazed long at the spectacle of that fur-swathed old man, surrounded by friends and servants, and the careful seating of him in the sleigh. I remember the spirited, champing horses, the driver with his whip, and a fellow-driver by his side, for extra prudence. The old man, the subject of so much attention, I can almost see now. It was John Jacob Astor.

The years 1846, '47, and there along, see me still in New York city, working as writer and printer, having my usual good health, and a good time generally.

#### OMNIBUS JAUNTS AND DRIVERS

ONE PHASE of those days must by no means go unrecorded—namely, the Broadway omnibuses, with their drivers. The vehicles still (I write this paragraph in 1881) give a portion of the character of Broadway—the Fifth avenue, Madison avenue, and Twenty-third street lines yet running. But the flush days of the old Broadway stages, characteristic and copious, are over. The Yellow-birds, the Red-birds, the original Broadway, the Fourth avenue, the Knickerbocker, and a dozen others of twenty or thirty years ago, are all gone. And the men specially identified with them, and giving vitality and meaning to them—the drivers —a strange, natural, quick-eyed and wondrous race—(not only Rabelais and Cervantes would have gloated upon them, but Homer and Shakspere would)—how well I remember them, and must here give a word about them. How many hours, forenoons and afternoons—how many exhilarating night-times I have had—perhaps June or July, in cooler air—riding the whole length of Broadway, listening to some yarn, (and the most vivid yarns ever spun, and the rarest mimicry)— or perhaps I declaiming some stormy passage from Julius Cæsar or Richard, (you could roar as loudly as you chose in that heavy, dense, uninterrupted street-bass.) Yes, I knew all the drivers then, Broadway Jack, Dressmaker, Balky Bill, George Storms, Old Elephant, his brother Young Elephant (who came afterward,) Tippy, Pop Rice, Big Frank, Yellow Joe, Pete Callahan, Patsy Dee, and dozens more; for there were hundreds. They had immense qualities, largely animal—eating, drinking, women—great personal pride, in their way—perhaps a few slouches here and there, but I should have trusted the general run of them, in their simple good-will and honor, under all circumstances. Not only for comradeship, and sometimes affection—great studies I found them also. (I suppose the critics will laugh heartily, but the influence of those Broadway omnibus jaunts and drivers and declamations and escapades undoubtedly enter'd into the gestation of "Leaves of Grass.")

### A NIGHT BATTLE, OVER A WEEK SINCE

MAY 12.—There was part of the late battle at Chancellorsville, (second Fredericksburgh,) a little over a week ago, Saturday, Saturday night and Sunday, under Gen. Joe Hooker, I would like to give just a glimpse of—(a moment's look in a terrible storm at sea—of which a few suggestions are enough, and full details impossible.) The fighting had been very hot during the day, and after an intermission the latter part, was resumed at night, and kept up with furious energy till 3 o'clock in the morning. That afternoon (Saturday) an attack sudden and strong by Stonewall Jackson had gain'd a great advantage to the southern army, and broken our lines, entering us like a wedge, and leaving things in that position at dark. But Hooker at 11 at night made a desperate push, drove the secesh forces back, restored his original lines, and resumed his plans. This

night scrimmage was very exciting, and afforded countless strange and fearful pictures. The fighting had been general both at Chancellorsville and northeast at Fredericksburgh. (We hear of some poor fighting, episodes, skedaddling on our part. I think not of it. I think of the fierce bravery, the general rule.) One corps, the 6th, Sedgwick's, fights four dashing and bloody battles in thirty-six hours, retreating in great jeopardy, losing largely but maintaining itself, fighting with the sternest desperation under all circumstances, getting over the Rappahannock only by the skin of its teeth, yet getting over. It lost many, many brave men, yet it took vengeance, ample vengeance.

But it was the tug of Saturday evening, and through the night and Sunday morning, I wanted to make a special note of. It was largely in the woods, and quite a general engagement. The night was very pleasant, at times the moon shining out full and clear, all Nature so calm in itself, the early summer grass so rich, and foliage of the trees—yet there the battle raging, and many good fellows lying helpless, with new accessions to them, and every minute amid the rattle of muskets and crash of cannon, (for there was an artillery contest too,) the red life-blood oozing out from heads or trunks or limbs upon that green and dew-cool grass. Patches of the woods take fire, and several of the wounded, unable to move, are consumed—quite large spaces are swept over, burning the dead also—some of the men have their hair and beards singed—some, burns on their faces and hands—others holes burnt in their clothing. The flashes of fire from the cannon, the quick flaring flames and smoke, and the immense roar—the musketry so general, the light nearly bright enough for each side to see the other—the crashing, tramping of men—the yelling—close quarters—we hear the secesh yells— our men cheer loudly back, especially if Hooker is in sight—hand to hand conflicts, each side stands up to it, brave, determin'd as demons, they often charge upon us—a thousand deeds are done worth to write newer greater poems on— and still the woods on fire—still many are not only scorch'd—too many, unable to move, are burn'd to death.

Then the camps of the wounded—O heavens, what scene is this?—is this indeed *humanity*— these butchers' shambles? There are several of them. There they lie, in the largest, in an open space in the woods, from 200 to 300 poor fellows —the groans and screams—the odor of blood, mixed with the fresh scent of the night, the grass, the trees—that slaughter-house! O well is it their mothers, their sisters cannot see them—cannot conceive, and never conceiv'd, these things. One man is shot by a shell, both in the arm and leg—both are amputated—there lie the rejected members. Some have their legs blown off—some bullets through the breast—some indescribably horrid wounds in the face or head, all mutilated, sickening, torn, gouged out—some in the abdomen—some mere boys—many rebels, badly hurt—they take their regular turns with the rest, just the same as any—the surgeons use them just the same. Such is the camp of the wounded—such a fragment, a reflection afar off of the bloody scene—while over all the clear, large moon comes out at times softly, quietly shining. Amid the woods, that scene of flitting souls—amid the crack and crash and yelling sounds—the impalpable perfume of the woods—and yet the pungent, stifling smoke—the radiance of the moon, looking from heaven at intervals so placid—the sky so heavenly—the clear-obscure up there, those buoyant upper oceans—a few large placid stars beyond, coming silently and languidly out, and then disappearing—the melancholy, draperied night above, around. And there, upon the roads, the fields, and in those woods, that contest, never one more desperate in any age or land—both parties now in force—masses—no fancy battle, no semi-play, but fierce and savage demons fighting there—courage and scorn of death the rule, exceptions almost none.

What history, I say, can ever give—for who can know—the mad, determin'd tussle of the armies, in all their separate large and little squads—as this—each stepp'd from crown to toe in desperate, mortal purports? Who know the conflict, hand-to-hand—the many conflicts in the dark, those shadowy-tangled, flashing-moon-beam'd woods—the writhing groups and squads—the cries, the din, the cracking guns and pistols—the distant cannon—the cheers and calls and threats and awful music of the oaths—the indescribable mix—the officers' orders, persuasions, encouragements—the devils fully rous'd in human hearts—the strong shout, *Charge, men, charge*—the flash of the naked sword, and rolling flame and smoke? And still the broken, clear and clouded heaven—and still again the moonlight pouring silvery soft its radiant patches over all. Who paint the scene, the sudden partial panic of the afternoon, at dusk? Who paint the irrepressible advance of the second division of the Third corps, under Hooker himself, suddenly order'd up—those rapid-filing phantoms through the woods? Who show what moves there in the shadows, fluid and firm—to save, (and it did save,) the

army's name, perhaps the nation? as there the veterans hold the field. (Brave Berry falls not yet—but death has mark'd him—soon he falls.)

### A CAVALRY CAMP

I AM writing this, nearly sundown, watching a cavalry company (acting Signal service,) just come in through a shower, making their night's camp ready on some broad, vacant ground, a sort of hill, in full view opposite my window. There are the men in their yellow-striped jackets. All are dismounted; the freed horses stand with drooping heads and wet sides; they are to be led off presently in groups, to water. The little wall-tents and shelter tents spring up quickly. I see the fires already blazing, and pots and kettles over them. Some among the men are driving in tent-poles, wielding their axes with strong, slow blows. I see great huddles of horses, bundles of hay, groups of men (some with unbuckled sabres yet on their sides,) a few officers, piles of wood, the flames of the fires, saddles, harness, &c. The smoke streams upward, additional men arrive and dismount—some drive in stakes, and tie their horses to them; some go with buckets for water, some are chopping wood, and so on.

*July 6th.*—A steady rain, dark and thick and warm. A train of six-mule wagons has just pass'd bearing pontoons, great square-end flat-boats, and the heavy planking for overlaying them. We hear that the Potomac above here is flooded, and are wondering whether Lee will be able to get back across again, or whether Meade will indeed break him to pieces. The cavalry camp on the hill is a ceaseless field of observation for me. This forenoon there stand the horses, tether'd together, dripping, steaming, chewing their hay. The men emerge from their tents, dripping also. The fires are half quench'd.

*July 10th.*—Still the camp opposite—perhaps fifty or sixty tents. Some of the men are cleaning their sabres (pleasant to-day,) some brushing boots, some laying off, reading, writing—some cooking, some sleeping. On long temporary cross-sticks back of the tents are cavalry accoutrements—blankets and overcoats are hung out to air—there are the squads of horses tether'd, feeding, continually stamping and whisking their tails to keep off flies. I sit long in my third story window and look at the scene—a hundred little things going on—peculiar objects connected with the camp that could not be described, any one of them justly, without much minute drawing and coloring in words.

### HOSPITALS ENSEMBLE

AUG., SEP., AND OCT., '63.—I am in the habit of going to all, and to Fairfax seminary, Alexandria, and over Long bridge to the great Convalescent camp. The journals publish a regular directory of them—a long list. As a specimen of almost any one of the larger of these hospitals, fancy to yourself a space of three to twenty acres of ground, on which are group'd ten or twelve very large wooden barracks, with, perhaps, a dozen or twenty, and sometimes more than that number, small buildings, capable altogether of accommodating from five hundred to a thousand or fifteen hundred persons. Sometimes these wooden barracks or wards, each of them perhaps from a hundred to a hundred and fifty feet long, are rang'd in a straight row, evenly fronting the street; others are plann'd so as to form an immense V; and others again are ranged around a hollow square. They make altogether a huge cluster, with the additional tents, extra wards for contagious diseases, guard-houses, sutler's stores, chaplain's house; in the middle will probably be an edifice devoted to the offices of the surgeon in charge and the ward surgeons, principal attachés, clerks, &c. The wards are either letter'd alphabetically, ward G, ward K, or else numerically, 1, 2, 3, &c. Each has its ward surgeon and corps of nurses. Of course, there is, in the aggregate, quite a muster of employés, and over all the surgeon in charge. Here in Washington, when these army hospitals are all fill'd, (as they have been already several times,) they contain a population more numerous in itself than the whole of the Washington of ten or fifteen years ago. Within sight of the capitol, as I write, are some thirty or forty such collections, at times holding from fifty to seventy thousand men. Looking from any eminence and studying the topography in my rambles, I use them as landmarks. Through the rich August verdure of the trees, see that white group of buildings off yonder in the outskirts; then another cluster half a mile to the left of the first; then another a mile to the right, and another a mile beyond, and still another between us and the first. Indeed, we can hardly look in any direction but these clusters are dotting the landscape and environs. That little town, as you might suppose it, off there on the brow of a hill, is indeed a town, but of wounds, sickness, and death. It is Finley hospital, northeast of the city, on Kendall green, as it used to be call'd. That other is Campbell hospital. Both are large establishments. I have known these two alone to have from two thousand to twenty-five hundred inmates. Then there is Carver hospital, larger still,

a wall'd and military city regularly laid out, and guarded by squads of sentries. Again, off east, Lincoln hospital, a still larger one; and half a mile further Emory hospital. Still sweeping the eye around down the river toward Alexandria, we see, to the right, the locality where the Convalescent camp stands, with its five, eight, or sometimes ten thousand inmates. Even all these are but a portion. The Harewood, Mount Pleasant, Armory-square, Judiciary hospitals, are some of the rest, and all large collections.

### THE INAUGURATION

MARCH 4.[1]—The President very quietly rode down to the capitol in his own carriage, by himself, on a sharp trot, about noon, either because he wish'd to be on hand to sign bills, or to get rid of marching in line with the absurd procession, the muslin temple of liberty, and pasteboard monitor. I saw him on his return, at three o'clock, after the performance was over. He was in his plain two-horse barouche, and look'd very much worn and tired; the lines, indeed, of vast responsibilities, intricate questions, and demands of life and death, cut deeper than ever upon his dark brown face; yet all the old goodness, tenderness, sadness, and canny shrewdness, underneath the furrows. (I never see that man without feeling that he is one to become personally attach'd to, for his combination of purest, heartiest tenderness, and native western form of manliness.) By his side sat his little boy, of ten years. There were no soldiers, only a lot of civilians on horseback, with huge yellow scarfs over their shoulders, riding around the carriage. (At the inauguration four years ago, he rode down and back again surrounded by a dense mass of arm'd cavalrymen eight deep, with drawn sabres; and there were sharpshooters station'd at every corner on the route.) I ought to make mention of the closing levee of Saturday night last. Never before was such a compact jam in front of the White House —all the grounds fill'd, and away out to the spacious sidewalks. I was there, as I took a notion to go—was in the rush inside with the crowd—surged along the passage-ways, the blue and other rooms, and through the great east room. Crowds of country people, some very funny. Fine music from the Marine band, off in a side place. I saw Mr. Lincoln, drest all in black, with white kid gloves and a claw-hammer coat, receiving, as in duty bound, shaking hands, looking very disconsolate, and as if he would give anything to be somewhere else.

THE INAUGURATION. 1. **March 4:** March 4, 1865.

## THE REAL WAR WILL NEVER GET IN THE BOOKS

AND SO good-bye to the war. I know not how it may have been, or may be, to others—to me the main interest I found, (and still, on recollection, find,) in the rank and file of the armies, both sides, and in those specimens amid the hospitals, and even the dead on the field. To me the points illustrating the latent personal character and eligibilities of these States, in the two or three millions of American young and middle-aged men, North and South, embodied in those armies —and especially the one-third or one-fourth of their number, stricken by wounds or disease at some time in the course of the contest—were of more significance even than the political interests involved. (As so much of a race depends on how it faces death, and how it stands personal anguish and sickness. As, in the glints of emotions under emergencies, and the indirect traits and asides in Plutarch, we get far profounder clues to the antique world than all its more formal history.)

Future years will never know the seething hell and the black infernal background of countless minor scenes and interiors, (not the official surface-courteousness of the Generals, not the few great battles) of the Secession war; and it is best they should not—the real war will never get in the books. In the mushy influences of current times, too, the fervid atmosphere and typical events of those years are in danger of being totally forgotten. I have at night watch'd by the side of a sick man in the hospital, one who could not live many hours. I have seen his eyes flash and burn as he raised himself and recurr'd to the cruelties on his surrender'd brother, and mutilations of the corpse afterward. (See, in the preceding pages, the incident at Upperville—the seventeen kill'd as in the description, were left there on the ground. After they dropt dead, no one touch'd them—all were made sure of, however. The carcasses were left for the citizens to bury or not, as they chose.)

Such was the war. It was not a quadrille in a ball-room. Its interior history will not only never be written—its practicality, minutiæ of deeds and passions, will never be even suggested. The actual soldier of 1862–'65, North and South, with all his ways, his incredible dauntlessness, habits, practices, tastes, language, his fierce friendship, his appetite, rankness, his superb strength and animality, lawless gait, and a hundred unnamed lights and shades of camp, I say, will never be written—perhaps must not and should not be.

The preceding notes may furnish a few stray glimpses into that life, and into those lurid interiors, never to be fully convey'd to the future.

The hospital part of the drama from '61 to '65, deserves indeed to be recorded. Of that many-threaded drama, with its sudden and strange surprises, its confounding of prophecies, its moments of despair, the dread of foreign interference, the interminable campaigns, the bloody battles, the mighty and cumbrous and green armies, the drafts and bounties—the immense money expenditure, like a heavy-pouring constant rain—with, over the whole land, the last three years of the struggle, an unending, universal mourning-wail of women, parents, orphans—the marrow of the tragedy concentrated in those Army Hospitals— (it seem'd sometimes as if the whole interest of the land, North and South, was one vast central hospital, and all the rest of the affair but flanges) —those forming the untold and unwritten history of the war—infinitely greater (like life's) than the few scraps and distortions that are ever told or written. Think how much, and of importance, will be—how much, civic and military, has already been—buried in the grave, in eternal darkness.

### SEA-SHORE FANCIES

EVEN as a boy, I had the fancy, the wish, to write a piece, perhaps a poem, about the sea-shore—that suggesting, dividing line, contact, junction, the solid marrying the liquid—that curious, lurking something, (as doubtless every objective form finally becomes to the subjective spirit,) which means far more than its mere first sight, grand as that is—blending the real and ideal, and each made portion of the other.[1] Hours, days, in my Long Island youth and early manhood, I haunted the shores of Rockaway or Coney island, or away east to the Hamptons or Montauk. Once, at the latter place, (by the old lighthouse, nothing but sea-tossings in sight in every direction as far as the eye could reach,) I remember well, I felt that I must one day write a book expressing this liquid, mystic theme. Afterward, I recollect, how it came to me that instead of any special lyrical or epical or literary attempt, the sea-shore should be an invisible *influence*, a pervading gauge and tally for me, in my composition. (Let me give a hint here to young writers. I am not sure but I have unwittingly follow'd out the same rule with other powers besides sea and shores—avoiding them, in the way of any dead set at poetizing them, as too big for formal handling—quite satisfied if I could indirectly show that we have met and fused, even if only once, but enough—that we have really absorb'd each other and understand each other.)

SEA-SHORE FANCIES.   1. December 1876.

There is a dream, a picture, that for years at intervals, (sometimes quite long ones, but surely again, in time,) has come noiselessly up before me, and I really believe, fiction as it is, has enter'd largely into my practical life—certainly into my writings, and shaped and color'd them. It is nothing more or less than a stretch of interminable white-brown sand, hard and smooth and broad, with the ocean perpetually, grandly, rolling in upon it, with slow-measured sweep, with rustle and hiss and foam, and many a thump as of low bass drums. This scene, this picture, I say, has risen before me at times for years. Sometimes I wake at night and can hear and see it plainly.

MY TRIBUTE TO FOUR POETS

APRIL 16.[1]—A short but pleasant visit to Longfellow. I am not one of the calling kind, but as the author of "Evangeline" kindly took the trouble to come and see me three years ago in Camden, where I was ill, I felt not only the impulse of my own pleasure on that occasion, but a duty. He was the only particular eminence I called on in Boston, and I shall not soon forget his lit-up face and glowing warmth and courtesy, in the modes of what is called the old school.

And now just here I feel the impulse to interpolate something about the mighty four who stamp this first American century with its birthmarks of poetic literature. In a late magazine one of my reviewers, who ought to know better, speaks of my "attitude of contempt and scorn and intolerance" toward the leading poets—of my "deriding" them, and preaching their "uselessness." If anybody cares to know what I think—and have long thought and avow'd—about them, I am entirely willing to propound. I can't imagine any better luck befalling these States for a poetical beginning and initiation than has come from Emerson, Longfellow, Bryant, and Whittier. Emerson, to me, stands unmistakably at the head, but for the others I am at a loss where to give any precedence. Each illustrious, each rounded, each distinctive. Emerson for his sweet, vital-tasting melody, rhym'd philosophy, and poems as amber-clear as the honey of the wild bee he loves to sing. Longfellow for rich color, graceful forms and incidents—all that makes life beautiful and love refined—competing with the singers of Europe on their own ground, and, with one exception, better and finer work than that of any of them. Bryant pulsing the first interior verse-throbs of a mighty world—bard of the river and

the wood, ever conveying a taste of open air, with scents as from hayfields, grapes, birch-borders—always lurkingly fond of threnodies—beginning and ending his long career with chants of death, with here and there through all, poems, or passages of poems, touching the highest universal truths, enthusiasms, duties—morals as grim and eternal, if not as stormy and fateful, as anything in Eschylus. While in Whittier, with his special themes—(his outcropping love of heroism and war, for all his Quakerdom, his verses at times like the measur'd step of Cromwell's old veterans) —in Whittier lives the zeal, the moral energy, that founded New England—the splendid rectitude and ardor of Luther, Milton, George Fox— I must not, dare not, say the wilfulness and narrowness—though doubtless the world needs now, and always will need, almost above all, just such narrowness and wilfulness.

BOSTON COMMON—MORE OF
EMERSON

OCT. 10–13.[1]—I spend a good deal of time on the Common, these delicious days and nights—every mid-day from 11:30 to about 1—and almost every sunset another hour. I know all the big trees, especially the old elms along Tremont and Beacon streets, and have come to a sociable-silent understanding with most of them, in the sunlit air, (yet crispy-cool enough,) as I saunter along the wide unpaved walks. Up and down this breadth by Beacon street, between these same old elms, I walk'd for two hours, of a bright sharp February mid-day twenty-one years ago,[2] with Emerson, then in his prime, keen, physically and morally magnetic, arm'd at every point, and when he chose, wielding the emotional just as well as the intellectual. During those two hours he was the talker and I the listener. It was an argument-statement, reconnoitring, review, attack, and pressing home, (like an army corps in order, artillery, cavalry, infantry,) of all that could be said against that part (and a main part) in the construction of my poems, "Children of Adam." More precious than gold to me that dissertation—it afforded me, ever after, this strange and paradoxical lesson; each point of E.'s statement was unanswerable, no judge's charge ever more complete or convincing, I could never hear the points better put—and then I felt down in my soul the clear and unmistakable conviction to disobey all, and pursue my own way. "What have

MY TRIBUTE TO FOUR POETS.     1. **April 16:** April 16, 1881.

BOSTON COMMON.     1. **Oct.  10–13:** October  10–13, 1881.
2. **bright . . . ago:** This meeting, in fact, took place in late March 1860.

you to say then to such things?" said E., pausing in conclusion. "Only that while I can't answer them at all, I feel more settled than ever to adhere to my own theory, and exemplify it," was my candid response. Whereupon we went and had a good dinner at the American House. And thenceforward I never waver'd or was touch'd with qualms, (as I confess I had been two or three times before).

## NORTHROP FRYE
*Editor*

# Emily Dickinson

## 1830–1886

EMILY DICKINSON was born in Amherst, Massachusetts, in the Connecticut River Valley in 1830. She died in the house she was born in, and her travels out of the region consisted of one trip to Washington and Philadelphia and two or three to Boston and Cambridge. Amherst had recently acquired, largely through the energy of her grandfather, an academy which she attended, and a college. Her father, Edward Dickinson, was a leading citizen of the town, a lawyer, active and successful in state politics, and treasurer of the college. Such a town illustrated more effectively than any Oneida or Brook Farm the Utopian pattern in nineteenth-century American society. It was a little world in itself, so well balanced economically as to be nearly self-sufficient, with a provincial but intense religious and intellectual culture, the latter growing as the college grew. Throughout her life Emily Dickinson was able to say what she had said at sixteen: "I dont know anything more about affairs in the world, than if I was in a trance," and her ability to shut all distractions out of her life owed much to the social coherence of her surroundings.

There was a strong family feeling among the Dickinsons, and neither Emily nor her younger sister Lavinia married or left home. The older brother, Austin, went to Harvard Law School, where Emily pelted him with affectionate letters telling him how much he was missed, then returned to Amherst to practice law. Gossip said that the father's possessiveness kept his daughters beside him ministering to his domestic comforts, but this may not be true. The image of awful integrity he inspired, which made his daughter say at his death: "His Heart was pure and terrible, and I think no other like it exists" may have grown on her gradually, as her youthful remarks in letters to Austin sound normally bratty. Thus: "Father and mother sit in state in the sitting room perusing such papers only, as they are well assured have nothing carnal in them." Her mother she was never close to until later years. Austin's wife, Susan Gilbert, was another person whom Emily Dickinson seems always to have loved passionately, in spite of a good deal of tension and occasional open ruptures. To Sue, across the fence, Emily sent nearly three hundred poems, besides messages, epigrams, gifts, and other symbols of affection.

At seventeen, Emily left the Amherst Academy and went to Mount Holyoke College, or Seminary, as it was then called, a few miles away in South Hadley. The discipline there was strict but humane, and she seems to have enjoyed herself in spite of the religious instruction, but her father withdrew her after a year. Emily thus had, for a poet, relatively little formal education. It is unlikely that she read any language except her own. She knew the Bible (involuntarily), she knew Shakespeare, she knew the classical myths, and she took a good deal of interest in contemporary women writers, especially Elizabeth Browning, George Eliot, and the Brontës. The Brontë references in earlier letters are to Charlotte, but "gigantic Emily Brontë" haunts the later ones. Dickens and Robert Browning appear in her rare literary allusions; there are one or two echoes of Tennyson; and, of the more serious American writers, she knew Emerson and something of Thoreau and Hawthorne. Her main literary instructors, however, were her dictionary and her hymnbook. She has a large vocabulary for a poet so limited in subject matter, and most of her stanzas, as has often been pointed out, are the ordinary hymn stanzas, the eight-six-eight-six "common meter" and the six-six-eight-six "short meter" being especially frequent.

Creative people often seem to need certain types of love or friendship that make manifest for them the human relations or conflicts with which their work is concerned. Emily Dickinson seemed to need in her life an older man to act as her "preceptor" or "master," to use her own terms, who could keep her in touch with qualities she did not profess to have: intellectual consistency, sociability, knowledge of the world, firm and settled convictions. Benjamin F. Newton, a lawyer who had articled with her father, was apparently her first "preceptor." Her letters to him have not been preserved, but he seems to have awakened her literary tastes, expanded her cultural horizons, and perhaps given her a more liberal idea of her religion — at any rate she refers to him as "a friend, who taught me Immortality." He died in 1853, before Emily had started to write poetry in earnest.

Then came Charles Wadsworth, a Presbyterian clergyman whom Emily may have heard on her trip to Philadelphia, and who, for all his married and middle-aged respectability, seems to have been the one great love of the poet's life. It is unlikely that the kind of love she offered him would have interfered with his marriage or social position, but some pathetic drafts of letters addressed to a "Master," if they were intended for Wadsworth, indicate something of the tumult of her feelings. In 1862 Wadsworth accepted a call to a church in San Francisco, a removal which seems to have been a profound shock to the poet, for reasons we can only guess at — again the correspondence has not survived. The name of the church he went to — Calvary — became the center of a drama of loss and renunciation in which the poet becomes "Empress of Calvary," and the bride of an invisible marriage followed immediately by separation instead of union.

But Wadsworth, whatever her feeling for him, could hardly have had more than a perfunctory interest in the poetry that was now becoming the central activity of her life. In her early years she seems to have written little except letters and occasional valentines, of which two most elaborate and ingenious efforts have been preserved. In the later 1850's she began writing poetry consistently, binding her completed poems up into packets, and sometimes sending copies to Sue or enclosing them in letters to other correspondents. In addition to her fair copies, there are many worksheet drafts scribbled on anything within reach — once on the back of an invitation to a "candy pulling" sent her twenty-six years earlier. Her impetus to write seems to have come on her in a flood, as the poems written or copied out in the year 1862 alone average one a day. With Wadsworth gone, another "preceptor" was urgently needed, this time a literary critic. Having liked an article by Thomas Wentworth Higginson she had read in the *Atlantic Monthly*, Emily sent the author a letter (No. 260, see p. 679), enclosing her card and four poems, and asking if in his opinion her poetry was "alive" and "breathed."

Higginson was an influential critic, and, as such, a natural target for amateur poets pretending that they wanted his frank opinion of their work when what they really wanted was advice on how to get published. He saw at once that Emily Dickinson was more serious business than this. She said explicitly that she wanted her work criticized by the literary standards that he knew about, and he was bound to be misled by that. But he realized, perhaps more quickly than she did, that she did not want specific criticisms of her poems, which she had no intention of altering for anyone's views. Nor was she interested in publication, as she made clear. All she wanted was contact with a sympathetic reader of informed taste and knowledge of the world of thought and action. Higginson had the sense to be flattered by her confidence, and seems to have responded with unfailing courtesy to her gentle but persistent nudgings to write her. She may have been exaggerating when she told him that he had saved her life, but she was not underestimating the service he did her, nor should we. At the same time, she was never in love with Higginson, and her attitude toward him was one of devotion tempered by an ironic detachment.

After 1862, the poet became increasingly a recluse, dressing in white, apparently with reference to her inner "Calvary" drama of renunciation. For the last decade of her life she did not leave her house and refused to see any strangers, her experience bounded by her house and garden, her social life completely absorbed in the brief letters she constantly sent to friends and neighbors, which sometimes contained poems and often accompanied small gifts of flowers or fruit. She expected her friends to be cultivated and tolerant people, and most of them were, prizing her enigmatic notes and respecting her privacy. There was no mistaking the good will and affection in her letters, however oblique in expression. One feels something Oriental in her manner of existence: the seclusion, the need for a "preceptor," the use of brief poems as a form of social communication would have seemed normal enough in the high cultures of the Far East, however unusual in her own. And even her culture was one in which the telephone had not yet destroyed the traditional balance between the spoken and the written word.

In the last decade of Emily Dickinson's life her father's friend Judge Otis P. Lord became a widower, and his friendship with the poet quickly ripened into love. Though, as usual, the letters themselves have disappeared, we do have a few drafts of letters to

him among her papers which put the fact beyond doubt. After living as she had, the adjustment needed for marriage would have been formidable, probably impossible. But she was deeply in love, which indicates that her retired life was the choice of her temperament, not a dedication. She was not a nun *manquée*, even if she does call herself a "Wayward Nun." Conscious human perception is, we are told, highly selective, and very efficient about excluding whatever threatens its balance. "Strong" people and men of action are those for whom such perception functions predictably: they are made strong by habit, by continually meeting the expected response. Creative abilities normally go with more delicate and mysterious nuances of awareness; hence they are often accompanied by some kind of physical or psychic weakness. Emily Dickinson's perceptions were so immediate that they absorbed her whole energy, or as she says, "The mere sense of living is joy enough":

> To be alive—is Power—
> Existence—in itself—
> Without a further function—

But she realized that there was danger as well as ecstasy in so sensitive a response. "Had we the first intimation of the Definition of Life," she says, "the calmest of us would be Lunatics!" To reverse a well-known phrase from Lewis Carroll, it took all the staying in the same place she could do to keep running. The intensity of her ordinary consciousness left her with few reserves to spend on a social life.

In a life so retired it was inevitable that the main events should be the deaths of friends, and Emily Dickinson became a prolific writer of notes of condolence. Her father, her mother, Sue's little boy Gilbert (struck down by typhoid fever at the age of eight), Bowles, Wadsworth, Lord, Helen Jackson all died in the last few years of her life. As early as 1883 she had a nervous collapse, and observed: "The Crisis of the sorrow of so many years is all that tires me." Two years later a more serious illness began.

In the second week of May 1886, she wrote to her cousins Louisa and Fanny Norcross:

> Little Cousins,
> Called back.
> Emily.

A few days later she was dead.

A life in which such things as the death of her dog or an unexpected call by Wadsworth are prominent incidents is not simply a quiet life but a carefully obliterated one. There are poets—and they include Shakespeare—who seem to have pursued a policy of keeping their lives away from their readers. Human nature being what it is, it is precisely such poets who are most eagerly read for biographical allusions. We shall find Emily Dickinson most rewarding if we look in her poems for what her imagination has created, not for what event may have suggested it. When, under the spell of Ik Marvel's *Reveries of a Bachelor* (1850), a favorite book of hers, she writes:

> Many cross the Rhine
> In this cup of mine.
> Sip old Frankfort air
> From my brown Cigar,

it would be a literal-minded reader who would infer that she had actually taken up cigar-smoking, yet this would be no more far-fetched than many other biographical inferences. A poet is entitled to speak in many voices, male, female, or childlike, to express many different moods and to develop an experience in reading or life into an imaginative form that has no resemblance whatever to the original experience. Just as she made the whole of her conception of nature out of the bees and bobolinks and roses of her garden, so she constructed her drama of life, death and immortality, of love and renunciation, ecstasy and suffering, out of tiny incidents in her life. But to read biographical allegory where we ought to be reading poetry is precisely the kind of vulgarity that made her dread publication and describe it as a foul thing.

It would be hard to name another poet in the history of the English language with so little interest in social or political events. The Civil War seemed to her "oblique," outside her orbit, and her only really peevish letter describes her reaction to a woman who told her that she ought to use her gifts for the good of humanity. There are one or two patriotic poems, but they show no freshness of insight. "My business is Circumference," she told Higginson. She concerned herself only with what she felt she could surround. It is characteristic of lyrical poetry to turn its back on the reader: the lyrical poet regularly pretends to be addressing his mistress or friend or God, or else he is soliloquizing or apostrophizing something in nature. But lyrical poetry also tends to create its own highly selected and intimate audience, like the sonnets and love poems of Shakespeare's day that circulated in manuscript among friends long before they reached print. For Emily Dickinson poetry was a form of private correspondence: "This is my letter to the World," is what she says of her poetry, and she describes the Gospel as "The Savior's . . . Letter he wrote to all mankind." Such a correspondence forms what, for Emily Dickinson, was the only genuine kind of human community, the small body of friends united in love and understanding. "Please to need me," as she wrote to Bowles.

> By a flower—By a letter—
> By a nimble love—
> If I weld the Rivet faster—
> Final fast—above—
>
> Never mind my breathless Anvil!
> Never mind Repose!
> Never mind the sooty faces
> Tugging at the Forge!

## II

AT HER death Emily Dickinson was the author of seven published poems, all anonymous, some issued without her authorization, six of them at least in what she would have considered garbled versions, altered by editors to make them more conventional. Her friends knew that she wrote poetry, but nobody, not even her sister Lavinia who had lived with her all her life, had any notion that she had written close to 1,800 poems. She left instructions to Lavinia that her "papers" were to be destroyed, as was customary at that time, but no instructions were given about the piled-up packets of verse that Lavinia, to her astonishment, discovered in her sister's room. Lavinia took the packets to Sue, with a demand that they be transcribed and published immediately, meeting all complaints about the length and difficulty of the task with: "But they are Emily's poems!" Sue proved to be indolent, and perhaps jealous, and after a long wait Lavinia took them to Mrs. Mabel Loomis Todd, wife of an Amherst professor of astronomy, an attractive and highly accomplished young woman, who knew Emily, so to speak, by ear, having played the piano in the Dickinson house while the poet sat invisibly in the dark hall outside and commented on the music.

Higginson's help was enlisted. At first he felt that it would be a mistake to publish Emily Dickinson. But he gradually became first interested, then fascinated, by what he found, and helped publicize her by writing articles about her. The two editors, Mrs. Todd and Higginson, produced *Poems by Emily Dickinson* in 1890, where a selection of her poems was distributed in various categories labeled "Life," "Love," "Nature," and the like, with titles for individual poems supplied by Higginson. A second and a third selection appeared in 1891 and 1896, respectively. Although Mrs. Todd's original transcripts were accurate, the poems were systematically smoothed out in punctuation, meter, grammar, and rhymes. Higginson took the lead in this at first, but as he went on he began to realize that the poet's liberties were not those of carelessness or incompetence. When the second selection was being prepared, he wrote to Mrs. Todd: "Let us alter as little as possible, now that the public ear is opened," including his own ear; but by that time Mrs. Todd had caught the improving fever. Mrs. Todd also went through the laborious task of collecting and publishing two volumes of Emily Dickinson's letters, where she had to engage in a long tactful struggle with the owners, and pre-

vented a good many of them from being irreparably lost. Through no fault of hers, some of them, notably those to the Norcross sisters, survive only in mutilated versions.

Some highly unedifying family squabbles stopped further publication. Sue had been alienated by the giving of the manuscripts to Mrs. Todd; then Lavinia, for reasons too complicated to go into here, turned against Mrs. Todd after Austin Dickinson's death and brought suit to recover a strip of land willed to Mrs. Todd by Austin. Nothing further was done until the next generation grew up, in the form of Sue's daughter, Martha Dickinson Bianchi, and Mrs. Todd's daughter, Millicent Todd Bingham, who produced a series of editions of both poems and letters between 1914 and 1950. Finally, the bulk of the manuscripts came into the possession of Harvard. With Thomas H. Johnson's definitive edition of the poems (1955) and letters (1958), Emily Dickinson achieved publication on her own uncompromising terms.

When Mrs. Todd's volumes appeared, there were, despite her editorial efforts, some hostile reviews and some complaints about the poet's lack of "technique," by which was meant smooth rhymes and meters. The complaints came mainly from such minor poets as Andrew Lang in England and Thomas Bailey Aldrich in America, who naturally ascribed the greatest importance and difficulty to the only poetic quality they themselves had. Against this, we may set the fact that the first volume alone went through sixteen editions in eight years, and was constantly reprinted thereafter. Mrs. Todd gave dozens of lectures on the poet, and could have given far more. It is inconceivable that the first volume of an unknown poet today could achieve such a success unless fortified by pornography. *Somebody* wanted Emily Dickinson's poetry, and we cannot avoid the inference that in the 1890's she was a genuinely popular poet who found her own public in spite of what the highbrows said. When she reappeared in the 1920's, her reputation was curiously reversed. Then the highbrows took her up, hailed her as a precursor of whatever happened to be fashionable at the time, such as imagism or free verse or metaphysical poetry, and emphasized everything in her work that was unconventional, difficult, or quaint. Both conceptions have some truth in them.

The good popular poet is usually one who does well what a great many have tried to do with less success. For the thousands of people, most of them women, who make verse out of a limited range of imaginative experience in life, love, nature, and religion, who live without fame and without much knowledge of literature beyond their schoolbooks, Emily Dickinson is the literary spokesman. She is popular too in her conceptual use of language, for popular expression tends to the proverbial, and the unsophisticated poet is usually one who tries to put prose statements into verse. Mrs. Todd often spoke of encountering poems in Emily Dickinson that took her breath away, but what surprises in her work is almost always some kind of direct statement, sharpened into wit or epigram. When she describes a hummingbird as "A route of evanescence," or says of the bluebird:

> Her conscientious Voice will soar unmoved
> Above ostensible Vicissitude,

she is using what medieval poets called "aureate diction," big soft bumbling abstract words that absorb images into categories and ideas. She does not—like, for example, D. H. Lawrence—try to get inside the bird's skin and identify herself with it; she identifies the bird with the human consciousness in herself. Many of her poems start out by making some kind of definition of an abstract noun:

> Presentiment—is that long Shadow—
> on the Lawn—
>
> Renunciation—is a piercing Virtue—
>
> Publication—is the Auction
> Of the Mind of Man—

and most of her best-loved poems are in one of the oldest and most primitive forms of poetry, the riddle or oblique description of some object. In "A route of evanescence" there is no explicit mention of a hummingbird

because the poem tries to catch the essence of the feeling of the bird without mentioning it. She does the same with the snow in "It sifts from leaden sieves," and with the railway train in "I like to see it lap the miles."

Such popular features in her work have their own difficulties, and there are others inherent in her peculiar style. She has for the most part no punctuation, except a point represented in the Johnson edition by a dash, which, as the editor points out, is really a rhythmical beat, and is of little use in unraveling the syntax. She also shows a curious preference for an indirect subjunctive form of expression that appears in such phrases as "Beauty be not caused," and she has what seems a most unreasonable dislike of adding the $s$ to the third person singular of verbs. The effect of such sidelong grammar is twofold: it increases the sense of epigrammatic wit, and it makes her poetry sound oracular, as though the explicit statements of which her poetry is so largely made up were coming to us shrouded in mystery. As she says:

> Tell all the Truth but tell it slant—
> Success in Circuit lies.

The result is not invariably success. Sometimes we may agree with enthusiasm:

> How powerful the Stimulus
> Of an Hermetic Mind.

At other times we can only say, with the captain in *H.M.S. Pinafore* confronted with a similar type of gnomic utterance: "I don't see at what you're driving, mystic lady":

> Endanger it, and the Demand
> Of tickets for a sigh
> Amazes the Humility
> Of Credibility—
>
> Recover it to Nature
> And that dejected Fleet
> Find Consternation's Carnival
> Divested of it's Meat.

Every age has its conventional notions of what poetry ought to be like, and the conventional notions of Emily Dickinson's day were that poetry should be close to prose in its grammar and syntax, and that its vocabulary should be more refined than that of ordinary speech. Thus Robert Louis Stevenson was outraged by the word *hatter* in a poem of Whitman's, and asserted that using such a word was not "literary tact." Emily Dickinson deliberately flouts both conventions. Her beat punctuation and offbeat syntax go with an abrupt and colloquial diction. The tang of her local speech comes out in such spellings as "Febuary" and "boquet," in such locutions as "it don't" and "it is him," and in such words as *heft* for *weight*. Speaking of heaven, she writes:

> Yet certain am I of the spot
> As if the Checks were given —

meaning railway checks, the guarantee the conductor gives that one is proceeding to the right destination. Her editors altered this to *chart*, which was a more conventionally poetic word, being slightly antique. Emily Dickinson could easily have provided such a word herself, but preferred to form her diction at a humorously twisted angle to the conventional expectations of the reader.

There is little in Emily Dickinson, then, of the feeling that a writer must come to terms with conventional language at all costs. When she meets an inadequacy in the English language she simply walks through it, as a child might do. If the dictionary does not provide an abstract noun for *giant*, the poet will coin *gianture;* if the ordinary *diminution* does not give her enough sense of movement, she will substitute *diminuet*. Similarly the fact that there is no singular form for *grass* or *hay* does not stop her from speaking of "every Grass," or from writing, to Higginson's horror:

> The Grass so little has to do
> I wish I were a Hay —

A similar teasing of the conventional reader's ear comes out in her slanting rhymes, which often have the effect of disappointing or letting down one's sense of an expected sound. At the same time even a conventional reader can see that her commonplace stanza forms

could hardly achieve any variety of nuance without some irregularities. This is particularly true of the sinewy rhythm that syncopates against her rigid hymnbook meters and keeps them so far out of reach of monotony or doggerel:

> Those not live yet
> Who doubt to live again —
> "Again" is of a twice
> But this — is one —
> The Ship beneath the Draw
> Aground — is he?
> Death — so — the Hyphen of the Sea —
> Deep is the Schedule
> Of the Disk to be —
> Costumeless Consciousness —
> That is he.

In sophisticated poetry close attention is paid to the sounds of words: vowels and consonants are carefully balanced for assonance and variety, and we feel, when such poetry is successful, that we have the inevitably right words in their inevitably right order. In popular poetry there is a clearly marked rhythm and the words chosen to fill it up give approximately the intended meaning, but there is no sense of any *mot juste* or uniquely appropriate word. In the ballad, for example, we may have a great number of verbal variants of the same poem. Here again Emily Dickinson's practice is the popular, not the sophisticated one. For a great many of her poems, she has provided alternative words, phrases, even whole lines, as though the rhythm, like a figured bass in music, allowed the editor or reader to establish his own text. Thus in the last line of one poem, "To meet so enabled a Man," we have *religious*, *accomplished*, *accoutred*, *established*, and *conclusive* all suggested as alternates for *enabled*. Another poem ends

> And Kinsmen as divulgeless
> As throngs of Down —

with "Kindred as responsive," "Clans of Down," "And Pageants as impassive As Porcelain" — or, presumably, any combination of these — as possible variants. It is rather more disconcerting to find *New* suggested as an alternate for *Old* in a poem ending with a reference to "Our Old Neighbor—God."

What we find in Emily Dickinson's poetry, then, is a diffused vitality in rhythm and the free play of a lively and exhilarating mind, crackling with wit and sharp perception. These were clearly the qualities that she herself knew were there and especially prized. She asked Higginson simply whether her verse was "alive." As a poet, she is popular in the sense of being able, like Burns or Kipling or the early Wordsworth, to introduce poetry to readers who have had no previous experience of it. She has, on the other hand, a withdrawn consciousness and an intense intellectual energy that makes her almost esoteric, certainly often difficult.

In any case she seems, after her early valentines, to have reached her mature style almost in a single bound. It is otherwise with her prose, no doubt because we have so much more of it from her early years. Her schoolgirl letters, with their engaging mixture of child's prattle and adolescent's self-consciousness, show a Lamblike gift for fantasy and a detached and humorous shrewdness. She speaks of other girls who "are perfect models of propriety," and remarks: "There 'most always are a few, whom the teachers look up to and regard as their satellites"—which is sharp observation for a fourteen-year-old. After her writing of poetry begins, her prose rhythm moves very close to verse. The first letter to Higginson is really a free verse poem; some of her earlier poems were originally written as prose, and she often falls into her favorite metrical rhythms, as in the opening of a letter to Bowles: "I am so far from Land—To offer *you* the cup—it might some Sabbath come *my* turn—Of wine how solemn—full!" which is a short meter stanza. Her later letters show a remarkable command of the techniques of discontinuous prose: they were most carefully composed, and the appearance of random jottings is highly deceptive. Continuous or expository prose assumes an equality between writer and reader: the writer is putting all he has in front of us. Discontinuous prose, with gaps in the sense

that only intuition can cross, assumes an aloofness on the writer's part, a sense of reserve of connection that we must make special efforts to reach. The aphoristic style of her later letters is, if slightly more frequent in Continental literatures, extremely rare in England or America, yet she seems to have developed it without models or influences.

> Her Grace is all she has—
> And that, so least displays—
> One Art to recognize, must be,
> Another Art, to praise.

### III

THE MOST cursory glance at Emily Dickinson will reveal that she is a deeply religious poet, preoccupied to the verge of obsession with the themes of death and immortality—the latter being, as she called it, the "Flood subject." Even in her use of the Bible, her most frequent references are to the passages in Corinthians and Revelation usually read at funeral services; and Paul's remark, that we now see in a riddle, translated as "through a glass darkly," is echoed in her recurrent use of the words "Riddle" and "Disc":

> Further than Guess can gallop
> Further than Riddle ride—
> Oh for a Disc to the Distance
> Between Ourselves and the Dead!

Yet another glance at her letters will also show that in her evangelical surroundings she steadily resisted all revivals, all spiritual exhortations, all the solicitous and charitable heat that at home, at school, and at church was steadily turned on the uncommitted. Like Huckleberry Finn, whom she resembles in more ways than one, Emily Dickinson had a great respect for orthodox religion and morality, did not question the sincerity of those who practiced it, and even turned to it for help. But she never felt that the path of social conformity and assent to doctrine was her path. Her resistance gave her no feeling of superiority: even her schoolgirl letters are full of a wistful regret that she could not feel what her friends all asserted that they felt.

As she recalled later: "When a Child and fleeing from Sacrament I could hear the Clergyman saying 'All who loved the Lord Jesus Christ—were asked to remain—.' My flight kept time to the Words." She belonged in the congregation but not in the Church.

Her elders referred her to the Bible: she read the Bible and took an immediate dislike to the deity that she calls "Burglar! Banker —Father!"—that is, the legal providential God who seems to ratify everything that is meaningless and cruel in life. She remarked to Higginson that her family were all religious except her, "and address an Eclipse, every morning—whom they call their 'Father'." She read with distaste the stories of Elisha and the bears ("I believe the love of God may be taught not to seem like bears"), of the sacrifice of Isaac, of the drowning of the world in a divine tantrum and the corresponding threat to burn it later:

> No vacillating God
> Created this Abode
> To put it out—

of Adam who was asserted to be alone responsible for his fall:

> Of Heaven above the firmest proof
> We fundamental know
> Except for it's marauding Hand
> It had been Heaven below.

The whole "punishing" aspect of religious doctrine struck her as "a doubtful solace finding tart response in the lower Mind," and she asks: "Why should we censure Othello, when the Criterion Lover says, 'Thou shalt have no other Gods before Me'?" That is, why blame Othello for being jealous when God tells us that he is himself? She concluded that "I do not respect 'doctrines.'"

It seems clear that her relation to the Nonconformist faith in which she was brought up was itself nonconformist, and that it would have violated her conscience ever to have made either a final acceptance or a final rejection of that faith. Her method, the reverse of Tennyson's in *In Memoriam*, was to prove where she could not believe. She did not want to repudiate her faith but to struggle with it. She was fascinated by the story of the "bewildered Gymnast" Jacob, wrestling with and finally defeating an angel who—according to a literal reading of the text which the poet promptly adopted— turned out to be God, and to this story she reverts more than once in her letters. When she compares the Bible unfavorably with Orpheus, whose sermon captivated and did not condemn; when she speaks of Cupid as an authentic deity and asks if God is Love's adversary, she is saying that there is another kind of religious experience that counterbalances, but does not necessarily contradict, the legal and doctrinal Christianity which she had been taught. As she says with a calculated ambivalence: "'We thank thee Oh Father' for these strange Minds, that enamor us against thee."

This other kind of religious experience is a state of heightened consciousness often called "Transport" and associated with the word "Circumference," when the poet feels directly in communion with nature and in a state of "identity"—another frequent term —with it. Nature is then surrounded by the circumference of human consciousness, and such a world is Paradise, the Biblical Eden, a nature with a human shape and meaning, a garden for man. "Home is the definition of God," and home is what is inside the circumference of one's being. In this state the mind feels immortal: "To include, is to be touchless, for Ourself cannot cease." It also enters into a condition of unity or oneness which is partly what the word identity means. "*One* is a dainty sum! One bird, one cage, one flight; one song in those far woods, as yet suspected by faith only!" Similarly the poet can speak, without any violation of grammar, of a "Myriad Daisy," and, with Emerson, of the single Man who is all men:

> What News will do when every Man
> Shall comprehend as one
> And not in all the Universe
> A thing to tell remain?

Such an experience is based, not on the compelling argument, but on the infinitely suggestive image, or "emblem," as she calls it.

"Emblem is immeasurable," she says, and speaks of human beings as the "trembling Emblems" of love. The language of emblems is as rational as the language of doctrine, but its logic is the poetic logic of metaphor, not the abstract logic of syllogism.

Circumference in its turn is the "Bride of Awe," and "Awe" is her most frequent name for the God that is reached by this experience. The human circumference is surrounded by a greater consciousness to which the poet is related as bride to bridegroom, as sea to moon, as daisy to sun, as brook to ocean—all recurring images. Sometimes the poet uses the word "peninsula" to describe an individual consciousness projecting into experience and attached to an invisible mainland. Invisible because "No man saw awe," any more than we can see our own backbones. Awe is a lover, incarnate in the bee who loves the rose and the harebell, and a divine lover for whom a feminine poet may make the response of a bacchante or of a vestal virgin with equal appropriateness. Awe is not a dogmatic God, and is tolerant enough to satisfy not only the poet's Christian longings but the paganism that makes her feel that there ought to be a god for every mood of the soul and every department of nature:

> If "All is possible" with him
> As he besides concedes
> He will refund us finally
> Our confiscated Gods.

In fact he may even be female, a sheltering mother. "I always ran Home to Awe when a child . . . He was an awful Mother, but I liked him better than none."

In Christian terms, this divine Awe, as she well understood, is the third person of the Trinity, the Holy Spirit, symbolized in the Bible by two of her favorite images, the bird and the wind, the giver of life to nature and of inspiration to humanity, the creative force that makes the poet's verses "breathe," and the "Conscious Ear" that imagination hears with. The conventional Biblical image for the Holy Spirit is the dove, and the poet, picturing herself as Noah sailing the flood of experience, associates the dove who brought him news of land with the fact that the name of another well-known navigator, Christopher Columbus, also means dove:

> Thrice to the floating casement
> The Patriarch's bird returned,
> Courage! My brave Columba!
> There may yet be *Land*!

To this person of God, Emily Dickinson continually turned when other things in Christianity puzzled her imagination or were rejected by her reason. She seems to associate him with the power which "stands in the Bible between the Kingdom and the Glory, because it is wilder than either of them." In the detached comment on the Atonement which she superimposes on the famous proverb, "God tempers the wind to the shorn lamb," the "Wind" is the power that escapes from the breakdown of doctrinal machinery:

> How ruthless are the gentle—
> How cruel are the kind—
> God broke his contract to his Lamb
> To qualify the Wind.

In a congratulatory message on the occasion of a wedding, the divine power of making one flesh out of two bodies is associated, not with the Father or the Son, but with the wind that bloweth where it listeth:

> The Clock strikes one that just struck two—
> Some schism in the Sum—
> A Vagabond from Genesis
> Has wrecked the Pendulum.

The confusion with a female principle, as when she says that "the Little Boy in the Trinity had no Grandmama, only a Holy Ghost," is at least as old as the apocryphal Gospels, where Jesus speaks of the Holy Spirit as his mother. When she says, "The Bible dealt with the Centre, not with the Circumference," she means apparently that the Bible considers man in his ordinary state of isolation, separated from God by a gulf that only God can cross. Such a God is thought of as coming from the outside; but while God is known "By his intrusion," his movement in the human soul is to be compared rather to the tides moving in the sea. "They say that God is everywhere, and yet we always think of Him as somewhat of a recluse." If so, it takes a recluse to find him, and to discover him as the inmost secret of consciousness.

The first fact of Emily Dickinson's experience, then, was that whatever the Bible may mean by Paradise or Eden, the world of lost innocence and happiness symbolized by the unfallen Adam and Eve, it is something that is already given in experience. It is attainable; the poet has attained it; it is not, therefore, a "superhuman site," nor could it survive the extinction of the human mind. Earth is heaven, whether heaven is heaven or not: the supernatural is only the natural disclosed: the charms of the heaven in the bush are superseded by the heaven in the hand—to paraphrase almost at random. To her the essence of the Gospel was the proclamation of the Paradisal vision in such passages as "consider the lilies." But the Bible also speaks of regaining this Paradise and living in it eternally after death. If so, then the experience of Paradise in life is identical with the experience of eternity.

The people we ordinarily call mystics are the people for whom this is true. Eternity to them is not endless time, but a real present, a "now" which absorbs all possible hereafters. Emily Dickinson also often speaks with the mystics of death as a rejoining of heaven, of "Forever" as "composed of Nows," of an eternal state of consciousness symbolized by a continuous summer and noon, of a coming "Aurora," a dawn that will have no night. But in her background there were two powerful antimystical tendencies at work. One was the rationalism of her generation; the other was the Puritanism in which she had been reared, with its insistence that the divine will was inscrutable, that it made sense only to itself, not to man, and that no human experience could transcend the limits of fallen humanity. For Emily Dickinson, therefore, the identity between the experience of circumference she had had and the postmortal eternity taught in the Bible remained a matter of "inference." It could be held by faith or hope but not by direct knowledge.

This "inference" became the central issue in her struggle with her faith, a fact which she expresses most poignantly when she says: "Consciousness is the only home of which we *now* know. That sunny adverb had been enough, were it not foreclosed."

Paradoxically, the experience of unity with God and nature also produces a sense of division, or "bisection," as the poet often calls it, in the mind. Part of oneself is certainly mortal; part may not be, though even it must also go through death. In a poem beginning "Conscious am I in my Chamber" she speaks of the indwelling Spirit as the immortal part of herself; sometimes the distinction is between the poet herself and her soul; sometimes, and more commonly, it is between the soul and the mind of consciousness. "We know that the mind of the Heart must live," she says, and a letter to her seems like immortality because "it is the mind alone without corporeal friend." She also speaks of the body as a "trinket" which is worn but not owned, and in one striking poem the soul is attended by a "single Hound" which is its own identity. But she never seemed to accept the Platonic view that the soul is immortal by nature. If the first fact of her experience is a vision of earth as heaven, the second fact is that this vision is "evanescent," comes and goes unpredictably, and, so far as experience itself goes, ceases entirely at death. It is significant, therefore, that Emily Dickinson should so often symbolize her vision as a temporary and abnormal state of intoxication:

> Inebriate of Air—am I—
> And Debauchee of Dew—
> Reeling—thro endless summer days—
> From inns of Molten Blue.

The liquor responsible for this state is usually called rum, or some synonym like "Domingo," "Manzanilla," or "Jamaica." When it is the more traditional wine, the word "sacrament," as in the poem "Exhilaration—is within," is seldom far away, for such imaginative intoxication is a genuine communion. Still, it can lead to hangovers "With a tomorrow knocking," and, whatever it is or means, it goes and is replaced by ordinary experience.

Ordinary experience is the sacramental or ecstatic experience turned inside-out. Here the mind is not a circumference at all, but a center, and the only circumference is an indifferent and unresponsive Nature—"Nature—in Her monstrous House." We may still realize that such "Vastness—is but the Shadow of the Brain which casts it," but in this state the brain cannot cast any other shadow. Where the mind is a center and nature the circumference, there is no place for any divinity: that has vanished somewhere beyond the sky or beyond life. This is the state of "Those Evenings of the Brain," in which the body, so far from being a circumference incorporating its experience, is a "magic Prison," sealed against all intimations of immortality:

> The Rumor's Gate was shut so tight
> Before my Mind was sown
> Not even a Prognostic's Push
> Could make a Dent thereon.

Like Blake, with whom she has been compared ever since Higginson's preface to the 1890 volume, Emily Dickinson shows us two contrary states of the human soul, a vision of innocence and a vision of "experience," or ordinary life. One is a vision of "Presence," the other of "Place"; in one the primary fact of life is partnership, in the other it is parting. Thus she may say, depending on the context, both "Were Departure Separation, there would be neither Nature nor Art, for there would be no World" and

> Parting is all we know of heaven,
> And all we need of hell.

But she has nothing of Blake's social vision, and the state that he associates with child labor, Negro slavery, and war she associates only with loneliness.

Her two states are often associated with summer and winter, or, less frequently, with day and night. Often, especially in poems addressed to Sue, she speaks of a "Summer—Sister—Seraph!" who inhabits the

paradisal world, in contrast to herself as a "dark sister," a "Druid" spirit of winter, frost, and the north, waiting for the birds to come back, like Noah's dove, to tell her of a sunnier world beyond. Hence the times of year that have the greatest significance for her are the equinoxes, the March when the birds return and the white dress of winter breaks into color, and the moment in late summer when the invisible presence of autumn enters the year and makes "a Druidic difference" in nature. The association of this latter period with the moment at which human life faces death makes it particularly the point at which the two lines of her imagination converge:

> God made a little Gentian—
> It tried—to be a Rose—
> And failed—and all the Summer laughed—
> But just before the Snows
>
> There rose a Purple Creature—
> That ravished all the Hill—
> And Summer hid her Forehead—
> And Mockery—was still—
>
> The Frosts were her conditon—
> The Tyrian would not come
> Until the North—invoke it—
> Creator—Shall I—bloom?

Emily Dickinson is an impressionist in the sense that she tends to organize her visual experience by color rather than outline, and purple, the color of mourning and of triumph, is the central symbol for her of the junction between life and death. Various synonyms of it such as "Iodine," "Amethyst," and the "Tyrian" above run through her writings.

At times the poet speaks of the paradisal vision as being, not only a "stimulant" given in cases of despair or stupor, but a light by which all the rest of life can be lived, as providing a final answer to the question raised by its passing:

> Why Bliss so scantily disburse—
> Why Paradise defer—
> Why Floods be served to Us—in Bowls—
> I speculate no more.

At other times, in such poems as those beginning "Why—do they shut Me out of Heaven?" and "If I'm lost—now," she laments over a lost vision that hints at a still greater loss. Such sudden changes of mood would be inconsistent if she were arguing a thesis, but, being a poet, what she is doing is expressing a variety of possible imaginative reactions to a central unsolved riddle. The fact that her vision is transient sharpens the intensity of her relation to it, for

> In Insecurity to lie
> Is Joy's insuring quality.

Two recurring words in her poems are *suspense* and *expanse.* The former refers to the shadow that falls between an experience and the realization that it has happened, the shadow that adumbrates death; the latter to the possession of the spiritual body which, for us, brings vision but not peace. "These sudden intimacies with Immortality, are expanse—not Peace—as Lightning at our feet, instills a foreign Landscape." She deals mainly with the virtues of faith, hope, and love, but her life had shown her that love, which normally tends to union, may incorporate a great deal of its opposite, which is renunciation. Similarly with faith and hope, "Faith is *Doubt*," she says, and hope is the thinnest crust of ice over despair:

> Could Hope inspect her Basis
> Her Craft were done —
> Has a fictitious Charter
> Or it has none.

Like the Puritans before her, who refused to believe that their own righteousness would necessarily impress God into recognizing them, Emily Dickinson refused to believe that her own vision of Paradise guaranteed the existence of Paradise, even though she had nothing else to go on. And—Puritan to the last—she even faced the possibility that the Spirit of life within her might turn out to be Death, hence the ambiguous tone of such poems as "Doubt Me! My Dim Companion!" and "Struck, was I, nor yet by Lightning." She told Sue that if Jesus did not recognize

her at the last day, "there is a darker spirit will not disown it's child." She means death, not the devil, though her pose recalls the demonic figures in Hawthorne. There are many poems about the physical experience of dying, some tranquil, some agonizing, some dealing with death by execution, by warfare, by drowning. In at least two poems the poet is an Andromeda swallowed by a sea monster. The region of death to be entered, or traversed, is usually a sea, sometimes a forest, or a "Maelstrom—in the Sky," or simply "a wild Night and a new Road," and in "I never told the buried gold," it is an underworld guarded by a dragon.

The world of death is not one that we have to die to explore: it is there all the time, the end and final cause of the vision of the center, just as Awe is the end and final cause of the vision of circumference. "I suppose there are depths in every Consciousness," she says, "from which we cannot rescue ourselves—to which none can go with us—which represent to us Mortally—the Adventure of Death." Some of her psychological poems take us into this buried jungle of the mind. There are a few about ghosts, but Emily Dickinson's sharp inquiring mind has little in common with the ectoplasmic, and these poems impress us as made rather than born. A more genuine fear comes out at the end of this:

> Remembrance has a Rear and Front —
> 'Tis something like a House —
> It has a Garret also
> For Refuse and the Mouse.
>
> Besides the deepest Cellar
> That ever Mason laid —
> Look to it by it's Fathoms
> Ourselves be not pursued.

This is as near to hell as she ever brings us, as the original version of the last two lines indicates:

> Leave me not ever there alone
> Oh thou Almighty God!

Yet even such a hell as this has a place and a function. Its presence is in an odd way the basis of vision itself, for "the unknown is the largest need of the intellect," and "could we see all we hope—there would be madness near." Emily Dickinson has a poem about Enoch and Elijah, the two Biblical prophets who were taken directly to heaven, but the figure she identifies herself with is Moses, standing on the mountaintop with the wilderness of death on one side and the Promised Land on the other, able to see his Paradise if not to enter it:

> Such are the inlets of the mind—
> His outlets—would you see
> Ascend with me the Table Land
> Of immortality.

Many, perhaps most, of Emily Dickinson's readers will simply take their favorite poems from her and leave the rest, with little curiosity about the larger structure of her imagination. For many, too, the whole bent of her mind will seem irresponsible or morbid. It is perhaps as well that this should be so. "It is essential to the sanity of mankind," the poet remarks, "that each one should think the other crazy." There are more serious reasons: a certain perversity, an instinct for looking in the opposite direction from the rest of society, is frequent among creative minds. When the United States was beginning to develop an entrepreneur capitalism on a scale unprecedented in history, Thoreau retired to Walden to discover the meaning of the word "property," and found that it meant only what was proper or essential to unfettered human life. When the Civil War was beginning to force on America the troubled vision of its revolutionary destiny, Emily Dickinson retired to her garden to remain, like Wordsworth's skylark, within the kindred points of heaven and home. She will always have readers who will know what she means when she says: "Each of us gives or takes heaven in corporeal person, for each of us has the skill of life." More restless minds will not relax from taking thought for the morrow to spend much time with her. But even some of them may still admire the energy and humor with which she fought her angel until she had forced out of him the crippling blessing of genius.

NOTE

The texts of the poems and letters that follow are taken from the Johnson edition, and the poems bear the numbers assigned to them in that edition, where they are arranged in chronological order. Poems in this selection range in date from No. 9, written about 1858, to No. 1631, written about 1885, the dates of those from No. 1651 to the end being unknown.

As explained in the Introduction, Emily Dickinson provided alternative words, phrases, or even whole lines, on the margins of her manuscripts of some of the poems, thus enabling the reader in a sense to construct his own text. In the following selection all the poems are printed in their original forms with her eccentric spelling and punctuation preserved. Except in one or two cases, all of her suggested alternatives are ignored. For full information about variant readings, as well as for the dates of the individual poems, the student is referred to the Johnson edition.

# POEMS

### 9

Through lane it lay – thro' bramble –
Through clearing and thro' wood –
Banditti often passed us
Upon the lonely road.

The wolf came peering curious –
The owl looked puzzled down –
The serpent's satin figure
Glid stealthily along –

The tempests touched our garments –
The lightning's poinards gleamed –
Fierce from the Crag above us
The hungry Vulture screamed –

The satyrs fingers beckoned –
The valley murmured "Come" –
*These* were the mates –
*This* was the road
These children fluttered home.

10

### 24

There is a morn by men unseen –
Whose maids upon remoter green
Keep their Seraphic May –
And all day long, with dance and game,
And gambol I may never name –
Employ their holiday.

Here to light measure, move the feet
Which walk no more the village street –
Nor by the wood are found –
Here are the birds that sought the sun     10
When last year's distaff idle hung
And summer's brows were bound.

Ne'er saw I such a wondrous scene –
Ne'er such a ring on such a green –
Nor so serene array –
As if the stars some summer night
Should swing their cups of Chrysolite –
And revel till the day –

Like thee to dance – like thee to sing –
People upon that mystic green –     20
I ask, each new May Morn.
I wait thy far, fantastic bells –
Announcing me in other dells –
Unto the different dawn!

### 30

Adrift! A little boat adrift!
And night is coming down!
Will *no* one guide a little boat
Unto the nearest town?

So Sailors say – on yesterday –
Just as the dusk was brown
One little boat gave up it's strife
And gurgled down and down.

So angels say – on yesterday –
Just as the dawn was red     10
One little boat – o'erspent with gales –
Retrimmed it's masts – redecked it's sails –
And shot – exultant on!

### 49

I never lost as much but twice,
And that was in the sod.
Twice have I stood a beggar
Before the door of God!

Angels – twice descending
Reimbursed my store –

Burglar! Banker – Father!
I am poor once more!

### 55

By Chivalries as tiny,
A Blossom, or a Book,
The seeds of smiles are planted –
Which blossom in the dark.

### 67

Success is counted sweetest
By those who ne'er succeed.
To comprehend a nectar
Requires sorest need.

Not one of all the purple Host
Who took the Flag today
Can tell the definition
So clear of Victory

As he defeated – dying –
On whose forbidden ear     10
The distant strains of triumph
Burst agonized and clear!

### 80

Our lives are Swiss –
So still – so Cool –
Till some odd afternoon
The Alps neglect their Curtains
And we look farther on!

*Italy* stands the other side!
While like a guard between –
The solemn Alps –
The siren Alps
Forever intervene!     10

### 81

We should not mind so small a flower –
Except it quiet bring
Our little garden that we lost
Back to the Lawn again.

So spicy her Carnations nod –
So drunken, reel her Bees –
So silver steal a hundred flutes
From out a hundred trees –

That whoso sees this little flower
By faith may clear behold     10

POEMS.   **67.** Published anonymously, with several alterations, in *A Masque of Poets* (1878), ed. by Thomas Niles (see Introduction).

The Bobolinks around the throne
And Dandelions gold.

### 119

Talk with prudence to a Beggar
Of "Potosi," and the mines!
Reverently, to the Hungry
Of your viands, and your wines!

Cautious, hint to any Captive
You have passed enfranchized feet!
Anecdotes of air in Dungeons
Have sometimes proved deadly sweet!

### 128

Bring me the sunset in a cup,
Reckon the morning's flagon's up
And say how many Dew,
Tell me how far the morning leaps –
Tell me what time the weaver sleeps
Who spun the breadths of blue!

Write me how many notes there be
In the new Robin's extasy
Among astonished boughs –
How many trips the Tortoise makes –     10
How many cups the Bee partakes,
The Debauchee of Dews!

Also, who laid the Rainbow's piers,
Also, who leads the docile spheres
By withes of supple blue?
Whose fingers string the stalactite –
Who counts the wampum of the night
To see that none is due?

Who built this little Alban House
And shut the windows down so close     20
My spirit cannot see?
Who'll let me out some gala day
With implements to fly away,
Passing Pomposity?

### 141

Some, too fragile for winter winds
The thoughtful grave encloses –
Tenderly tucking them in from frost
Before their feet are cold.

Never the treasures in her nest
The cautious grave exposes,
Building where schoolboy dare not look,
And sportsman is not bold.

This covert have all the children
Early aged, and often cold,                     10
Sparrows, unnoticed by the Father –
Lambs for whom time had not a fold.

### 160

Just lost, when I was saved!
Just felt the world go by!
Just girt me for the onset with Eternity,
When breath blew back,
And on the other side
I heard recede the disappointed tide!

Therefore, as One returned, I feel,
Odd secrets of the line to tell!
Some Sailor, skirting foreign shores –
Some pale Reporter, from the awful doors   10
Before the Seal!

Next time, to stay!
Next time, the things to see
By Ear unheard,
Unscrutinized by Eye –

Next time, to tarry,
While the Ages steal –
Slow tramp the Centuries,
And the Cycles wheel!

### 187

How many times these low feet staggered –
Only the soldered mouth can tell –
Try – can you stir the awful rivet –
Try – can you lift the hasps of steel!

Stroke the cool forehead – hot so often –
Lift – if you care – the listless hair –
Handle the adamantine fingers
Never a thimble – more – shall wear –

Buzz the dull flies – on the chamber window –   9
Brave – shines the sun through the freckled pane –
Fearless – the cobweb swings from the ceiling –
Indolent Housewife – in Daisies – lain!

---

119. 2. "Potosi": a town in Bolivia famous for its silver mines.
128. 19. Alban House: a house built of Alban stone, much used in ancient Rome.

141. 11. Sparrows: Cf. Luke 12:6.   160. 11. Seal: Cf. Matt. 27:66; cf. No. 322.   13–15. Next . . . Eye: Cf. I Cor. 2:9; II Cor. 12:3–4.

### 214

I taste a liquor never brewed –
From Tankards scooped in Pearl –
Not all the Frankfort Berries
Yield such an Alcohol!

Inebriate of Air – am I –
And Debauchee of Dew –
Reeling – thro endless summer days –
From inns of Molten Blue –

When "Landlords" turn the drunken Bee
Out of the Foxglove's door –                    10
When Butterflies – renounce their "drams" –
I shall but drink the more!

Till Seraphs swing their snowy Hats –
And Saints – to windows run –
To see the little Tippler
From Manzanilla come!

### 216

Safe in their Alabaster Chambers –
Untouched by Morning
And untouched by Noon –
Sleep the meek members of the Resurrection –
Rafter of satin,
And Roof of stone.

Light laughs the breeze
In her Castle above them –
Babbles the Bee in a stolid Ear,
Pipe the Sweet Birds in ignorant cadence –    10
Ah, what sagacity perished here!

*version of 1859*

Safe in their Alabaster Chambers –
Untouched by Morning –
And untouched by Noon –
Lie the meek members of the Resurrection –
Rafter of Satin – and Roof of Stone!

Grand go the Years – in the Crescent – above
    them –
Worlds scoop their Arcs –
And Firmaments – row –

214. 3. **Frankfort Berries**: explained by the alternative reading,
"Vats upon the Rhine." 16. **Manzanilla**: Manzanillo, a city
in Cuba, clearly associated here with rum. Most readers would
prefer the alternative reading, "Leaning against the – Sun –."
216. The revision of this poem appears to have been the result
of criticism by Sue. The earlier version was published anonymously in the Springfield *Daily Republican* in 1862.

Diadems – drop – and Doges – surrender –
Soundless as dots – on a Disc of Snow –        10

*version of 1861*

### 241

I like a look of Agony,
Because I know it's true –          *not baked*
Men do not sham Convulsion,
Nor simulate, a Throe –

The Eyes glaze once – and that is Death –
Impossible to feign
The Beads upon the Forehead
By homely Anguish strung.

### 249

Wild Nights – Wild Nights!
Were I with thee
Wild Nights should be
Our luxury!

Futile – the Winds –
To a Heart in port –
Done with the Compass –
Done with the Chart!

Rowing in Eden –
Ah, the Sea!                                    10
Might I but moor – Tonight –
In Thee!

### 258     *nature*

There's a certain Slant of light,
Winter Afternoons –
That oppresses, like the Heft
Of Cathedral Tunes –

Heavenly Hurt, it gives us –
We can find no scar,
But internal difference,
Where the Meanings, are –

None may teach it – Any –
'Tis the Seal Despair –                         10
An imperial affliction
Sent us of the Air –

When it comes, the Landscape listens –
Shadows – hold their breath –
When it goes, 'tis like the Distance
On the look of Death –

### 266

This – is the land – the Sunset washes –
These – are the Banks of the Yellow Sea –
Where it rose – or whither it rushes –
These – are the Western Mystery!

Night after Night
Her purple traffic
Strews the landing with Opal Bales –
Merchantmen – poise upon Horizons –
Dip – and vanish like Orioles!

### 274

The only Ghost I ever saw
Was dressed in Mechlin – so –
He had no sandal on his foot –
And stepped like flakes of snow –

His Mien, was soundless, like the Bird –
But rapid – like the Roe –
His fashions, quaint, Mosaic –
Or haply, Mistletoe –

His conversation – seldom –
His laughter, like the Breeze                    10
That dies away in Dimples
Among the pensive Trees –

Our interview – was transient –
Of me, himself was shy –
And God forbid I look behind –
Since that appalling Day!

### 280

I felt a Funeral, in my Brain,
And Mourners to and fro
Kept treading – treading – till it seemed
That Sense was breaking through –

And when they all were seated,
A Service, like a Drum –
Kept beating – beating – till I thought
My Mind was going numb –

And then I heard them lift a Box
And creak across my Soul                    10

With those same Boots of Lead, again,
Then Space – began to toll,

As all the Heavens were a Bell,
And Being, but an Ear,
And I, and Silence, some strange Race
Wrecked, solitary, here –

And then a Plank in Reason, broke,
And I dropped down, and down –
And hit a World, at every plunge,
And Finished knowing – then –                    20

### 281

'Tis so appalling – it exhilirates –
So over Horror, it half Captivates –
The Soul stares after it, secure –
To know the worst, leaves no dread more –

To scan a Ghost, is faint –
But grappling, conquers it –
How easy, Torment, now –
Suspense kept sawing so –

The Truth, is Bald, and Cold –
But that will hold –                    10
If any are not sure –
We show them – prayer –
But we, who know,
Stop hoping, now –

Looking at Death, is Dying –
Just let go the Breath –
And not the pillow at your Cheek
So Slumbereth –

Others, Can wrestle –
Your's, is done –                    20
And so of Wo, bleak dreaded – come,
It sets the Fright at liberty –
And Terror's free –
Gay, Ghastly, Holiday!

### 287

A Clock stopped –
Not the Mantel's –
Geneva's farthest skill
Cant put the puppet bowing –
That just now dangled still –

An awe came on the Trinket!
The Figures hunched, with pain –

---

266. 6. **purple traffic:** Cf. Tennyson, "Locksley Hall," 121–22.
274. 2. **Mechlin:** the English name for the town of Malines in France, famous for fine lace.    7–8. **His . . . Mistletoe:** He reminded one of the quaint, stylized figures in Byzantine mosaics, or, perhaps, of the rites of the Druids, connected with the mistletoe. Cf. No. 1068.

287. 3. **Geneva's:** Geneva, Switzerland, famous for clocks and watches.

Then quivered out of Decimals –
Into Degreeless Noon –

It will not stir for Doctor's – 10
This Pendulum of snow –
The Shopman importunes it –
While cool – concernless No –

Nods from the Gilded pointers –
Nods from the Seconds slim –
Decades of Arrogance between
The Dial life –
And Him –

292

If your Nerve, deny you –
Go above your Nerve –
He can lean against the Grave,
If he fear to swerve –

That's a steady posture –
Never any bend
Held of those Brass arms –
Best Giant made –

If your Soul seesaw –
Lift the Flesh door – 10
The Poltroon wants Oxygen –
Nothing more –

303

The Soul selects her own Society –
Then – shuts the Door –
To her divine Majority –
Present no more –

Unmoved – she notes the Chariots – pausing –
At her low Gate –
Unmoved – an Emperor be kneeling
Upon her Mat –

I've known her – from an ample nation –
Choose One – 10
Then – close the Valves of her attention –
Like Stone –

305

The difference between Despair
And Fear – is like the One
Between the instant of a Wreck –
And when the Wreck has been –

The Mind is smooth – no Motion –
Contented as the Eye

Upon the Forehead of a Bust –
That knows – it cannot see –

306

The Soul's Superior instants
Occur to Her – alone –
When friend – and Earth's occasion
Have infinite withdrawn –

Or She – Herself – ascended
To too remote a Hight
For lower Recognition
Than Her Omnipotent –

This Mortal Abolition
Is seldom – but as fair 10
As Apparition – subject
To Autocratic Air –

Eternity's disclosure
To favorites – a few –
Of the Colossal substance
Of Immortality.

311

It sifts from Leaden Sieves –
It powders all the Wood.
It fills with Alabaster Wool
The Wrinkles of the Road –

It makes an Even Face
Of Mountain, and of Plain –
Unbroken Forehead from the East
Unto the East again –

It reaches to the Fence –
It wraps it Rail by Rail 10
Till it is lost in Fleeces –
It deals Celestial Vail

To Stump, and Stack – and Stem –
A Summer's empty Room –
Acres of Joints, where Harvests were,
Recordless, but for them –

It Ruffles Wrists of Posts
As Ankles of a Queen –
Then stills it's Artisans – like Ghosts –
Denying they have been – 20

322

There came a Day at Summer's full,
Entirely for me –
I thought that such were for the Saints,
Where Resurrections – be –

The Sun, as common, went abroad,
The flowers, accustomed, blew,
As if no soul the solstice passed
That maketh all things new –

The time was scarce profaned, by speech –
The symbol of a word                              10
Was needless, as at Sacrament,
The Wardrobe – of our Lord –

Each was to each The Sealed Church,
Permitted to commune this – time –
Lest we too awkward show
At Supper of the Lamb.

The Hours slid fast – as Hours will,
Clutched tight, by greedy hands –
So faces on two Decks, look back,
Bound to opposing lands –                        20

And so when all the time had leaked,
Without external sound
Each bound the Other's Crucifix –
We gave no other Bond –

Sufficient troth, that we shall rise –
Deposed – at length, the Grave –
To that new Marriage,
Justified – through Calvaries of Love –

341

After great pain, a formal feeling comes –
The Nerves sit ceremonious, like Tombs –
The stiff Heart questions was it He, that bore,
And Yesterday, or Centuries before?

The Feet, mechanical, go round –
Of Ground, or Air, or Ought –
A Wooden way
Regardless grown,
A Quartz contentment, like a stone –

This is the Hour of Lead –                        10
Remembered, if outlived,
As Freezing persons, recollect the Snow –
First – Chill – then Stupor – then the letting go –

358

If any sink, assure that this, now standing –
Failed like Themselves – and conscious that it rose –

322. 8. new: Cf. Rev. 21:5.     11. needless: i.e., at Sacrament,
where the Word becomes Flesh, no conception of clothing is
needed; cf. John 20:5–7.     13. Sealed Church: Cf. Rev. 7:3.

Grew by the Fact, and not the Understanding
How Weakness passed – or Force – arose –

Tell that the Worst, is easy in a Moment –
Dread, but the Whizzing, before the Ball –
When the Ball enters, enters Silence –
Dying – annuls the power to kill.

378

I saw no Way – The Heavens were stitched –
I felt the Columns close –
The Earth reversed her Hemispheres –
I touched the Universe –

And back it slid – and I alone –
A Speck upon a Ball –
Went out upon Circumference –
Beyond the Dip of Bell –

410

The first Day's Night had come –
And grateful that a thing
So terrible – had been endured –
I told my Soul to sing –

She said her Strings were snapt –
Her Bow – to Atoms blown –
And so to mend her – gave me work
Until another Morn –

And then – a Day as huge
As Yesterdays in pairs,                           10
Unrolled it's horror in my face –
Until it blocked my eyes –

My Brain – begun to laugh –
I mumbled – like a fool –
And tho' 'tis Years ago – that Day –
My Brain keeps giggling – still.

And Something's odd – within –
That person that I was –
And this One – do not feel the same –
Could it be Madness – this?                       20

441

This is my letter to the World
That never wrote to Me –
The simple News that Nature told –
With tender Majesty.

Her Message is committed
To Hands I cannot see –
For love of Her – Sweet – countrymen –
Judge tenderly – of Me.

## 448

This was a Poet – It is That
Distills amazing sense
From ordinary Meanings –
And Attar so immense

From the familiar species
That perished by the Door –
We wonder it was not Ourselves
Arrested it – before –

Of Pictures, the Discloser –
The Poet – it is He –                                    10
Entitles Us – by Contrast –
To ceaseless Poverty –

Of Portion – so unconscious –
The Robbing – could not harm –
Himself – to Him – a Fortune –
Exterior – to Time –

## 465

I heard a Fly buzz – when I died –
The Stillness in the Room
Was like the Stillness in the Air –
Between the Heaves of Storm –

The Eyes around – had wrung them dry –
And Breaths were gathering firm
For that last Onset – when the King  *death*
Be witnessed – in the Room –

I willed my Keepsakes – Signed away
What portion of me be                                    10
Assignable – and then it was
There interposed a Fly –  *good for blip*

With Blue – uncertain stumbling Buzz –
Between the light – and me –
And then the Windows failed – and then
I could not see to see –

## 483

A Solemn thing within the Soul
To feel itself get ripe –
And golden hang – while farther up –
The Maker's Ladders stop –
And in the Orchard far below –
You hear a Being – drop –

A Wonderful – to feel the Sun
Still toiling at the Cheek
You thought was finished –
Cool of eye, and critical of Work –        10

He shifts the stem – a little –
To give your Core – a look –

But solemnest – to know
Your chance in Harvest moves
A little nearer – Every Sun
The Single – to some lives.

## 505

I would not paint – a picture –
I'd rather be the One
It's bright impossibility
To dwell – delicious – on –
And wonder how the fingers feel
Whose rare – celestial – stir –
Evokes so sweet a Torment –
Such sumptuous – Despair –

I would not talk, like Cornets –
I'd rather be the One                                    10
Raised softly to the Ceilings –
And out, and easy on –
Through Villages of Ether –
Myself endued Balloon
By but a lip of Metal –
The pier to my Pontoon –

Nor would I be a Poet –
It's finer – own the Ear –
Enamored – impotent – content –
The License to revere,                                    20
A privilege so awful
What would the Dower be,
Had I the Art to stun myself
With Bolts of Melody!

## 507

She sights a Bird – she chuckles –
She flattens – then she crawls –
She runs without the look of feet –
Her eyes increase to Balls –

Her Jaws stir – twitching – hungry –
Her Teeth can hardly stand –
She leaps, but Robin leaped the first –
Ah, Pussy, of the Sand,

The Hopes so juicy ripening –
You almost bathed your Tongue –           10
When Bliss disclosed a hundred Toes –
And fled with every one –

## 537

Me prove it now – Whoever doubt
Me stop to prove it – now –

Make haste – the Scruple! Death be scant
For Opportunity –

The River reaches to my feet –
As yet – My Heart be dry –
Oh Lover – Life could not convince –
Might Death – enable Thee –

The River reaches to My Breast –
Still – still – My Hands above      10
Proclaim with their remaining Might –
Dost recognize the Love?

The River reaches to my Mouth –
Remember – when the Sea
Swept by my searching eyes – the last –
Themselves were quick – with Thee!

### 540

I took my Power in my Hand –
And went against the World –
'Twas not so much as David – had –
But I – was twice as bold –

I aimed my Pebble – but Myself
Was all the one that fell –
Was it Goliath – was too large –
Or was myself – too small?

### 585

I like to see it lap the Miles –
And lick the Valleys up –
And stop to feed itself at Tanks –
And then – prodigious step

Around a Pile of Mountains –
And supercilious peer
In Shanties – by the sides of Roads –
And then a Quarry pare

To fit it's sides
And crawl between      10
Complaining all the while
In horrid – hooting stanza –
Then chase itself down Hill –

And neigh like Boanerges –
Then – prompter than a Star
Stop – docile and omnipotent
At it's own stable door –

### 590

Did you ever stand in a Cavern's Mouth –
Widths out of the Sun –
And look – and shudder, and block your breath –
And deem to be alone

In such a place, what horror,
How Goblin it would be –
And fly, as 'twere pursuing you?
Then Loneliness – looks so –

Did you ever look in a Cannon's face –
Between whose Yellow eye –      10
And your's – the Judgment intervened –
The Question of "To die" –

Extemporizing in your ear
As cool as Satyr's Drums –
If you remember, and were saved –
It's liker so – it seems –

### 619

Glee – The great storm is over –
Four – have recovered the Land –
Forty – gone down together –
Into the boiling Sand –

Ring – for the Scant Salvation –
Toll – for the bonnie Souls –
Neighbor – and friend – and Bridegroom –
Spinning upon the Shoals –

How they will tell the Story –
When Winter shake the Door –      10
Till the Children urge –
{But the Forty –
{Did they – come back no more?

Then a softness – suffuse the Story –
And a silence – the Teller's eye –
And the Children – no further question –
And only the Sea – reply –

### 652

A Prison gets to be a friend –
Between it's Ponderous face
And Our's – a Kinsmanship express –
And in it's narrow Eyes –

We come to look with gratitude
For the appointed Beam
It deal us – stated as our food –
And hungered for – the same –

---

537. 5. **River:** The image of the river of death may come from the conclusion of the second part of *Pilgrim's Progress.*   **540. 3. David:** For the story of David and Goliath, see I Sam. 17.   **585. 14. Boanerges:** "sons of thunder"; cf. Mark 3:17.

We learn to know the Planks —
That answer to Our feet —                    10
So miserable a sound — at first —
Nor even now — so sweet —

As plashing in the Pools —
When Memory was a Boy —
But a Demurer Circuit —
A Geometric Joy —

The Posture of the Key
That interrupt the Day
To Our Endeavor — Not so real
The Cheek of Liberty —                       20

As this Phantasm Steel —
Whose features — Day and Night —
Are present to us — as Our Own —
And as escapeless — quite —

The narrow Round — the Stint —
The slow exchange of Hope —
For something passiver — Content
Too steep for looking up —

The Liberty we knew
Avoided — like a Dream —                     30
Too wide for any Night but Heaven —
If That — indeed — redeem —

### 664

Of all the Souls that stand create —
I have elected — One —
When Sense from Spirit — files away —
And Subterfuge — is done —
When that which is — and that which was —
Apart — intrinsic — stand —
And this brief Tragedy of Flesh —
Is shifted — like a Sand —
When Figures show their royal Front —
And Mists — are carved away,                 10
Behold the Atom — I preferred —
To all the lists of Clay!

### 683

The Soul unto itself
Is an imperial friend —
Or the most agonizing Spy —
An Enemy — could send —

Secure against it's own —
No treason it can fear —
Itself — it's Sovreign — of itself
The Soul should stand in Awe —

### 712

Because I could not stop for Death —
He kindly stopped for me —
The Carriage held but just Ourselves —
And Immortality.

We slowly drove — He knew no haste
And I had put away
My labor and my leisure too,
For His Civility —

We passed the School, where Children strove
At Recess — in the Ring —                    10
We passed the Fields of Gazing Grain —
We passed the Setting Sun —

Or rather — He passed Us —
The Dews drew quivering and chill —
For only Gossamer, my Gown —
My Tippet    only Tulle —

We paused before a House that seemed
A Swelling of the Ground —
The Roof was scarcely visible —
The Cornice — in the Ground —                20

Since then — 'tis Centuries — and yet
Feels shorter than the Day
I first surmised the Horses Heads
Were toward Eternity —

### 756

One Blessing had I than the rest
So larger to my Eyes
That I stopped guaging — satisfied —
For this enchanted size —

It was the limit of my Dream —
The focus of my Prayer —
A perfect — paralyzing Bliss —
Contented as Despair —

I knew no more of Want — or Cold —
Phantasms both become                        10
For this new Value in the Soul —
Supremest Earthly Sum —

The Heaven below the Heaven above —
Obscured with ruddier Blue —
Life's Latitudes leant over — full —
The Judgment perished — too —

Why Bliss so scantily disburse –
Why Paradise defer –
Why Floods be served to Us – in Bowls –
I speculate no more –                    20

### 777

The Loneliness One dare not sound –
And would as soon surmise
As in it's Grave go plumbing
To ascertain the size –

The Loneliness whose worst alarm
Is lest itself should see –
And perish from before itself
For just a scrutiny –

The Horror not to be surveyed –
But skirted in the Dark –                    10
With Consciousness suspended –
And Being under Lock –

I fear me this – is Loneliness –
The Maker of the soul
It's Caverns and it's Corridors
Illuminate – or seal –

### 793

Grief is a Mouse –
And chooses Wainscot in the Breast
For His Shy House –
And baffles quest –

Grief is a Thief – quick startled –
Pricks His Ear – report to hear
Of that Vast Dark –
That swept His Being – back –

Grief is a Juggler – boldest at the Play –
Lest if He flinch – the eye that way          10
Pounce on His Bruises – One – say – or Three –
Grief is a Gourmand – spare His luxury –

Best Grief is Tongueless – before He'll tell –
Burn Him in the Public Square –
His Ashes – will
Possibly – if they refuse – How then know –
Since a Rack could'nt coax a syllable – now.

### 817

Given in Marriage unto Thee
Oh thou Celestial Host –
Bride of the Father and the Son
Bride of the Holy Ghost.
Other Betrothal shall dissolve –
Wedlock of Will, decay –

817. 3. **Bride:** Cf. Rev. 21:2.

Only the Keeper of this Ring
Conquer Mortality –

### 822

This Consciousness that is aware
Of Neighbors and the Sun
Will be the one aware of Death
And that itself alone

Is traversing the interval
Experience between
And most profound experiment
Appointed unto Men –

How adequate unto itself
It's properties shall be                    10
Itself unto itself and none
Shall make discovery.

Adventure most unto itself
The Soul condemned to be –
Attended by a single Hound
It's own identity.

### 842

Good to hide, and hear 'em hunt!
Better, to be found,
If one care to, that is,
The Fox fits the Hound –

Good to know, and not tell,
Best, to know and tell,
Can one find the rare Ear
Not too dull –

### 861

Split the Lark – and you'll find the Music –
Bulb after Bulb, in Silver rolled –
Scantily dealt to the Summer Morning
Saved for your Ear when Lutes be old.

Loose the Flood – you shall find it patent –
Gush after Gush, reserved for you –
Scarlet Experiment! Sceptic Thomas!
Now, do you doubt that your Bird was true?

### 870

Finding is the first Act
The second, loss,
Third, Expedition for
The "Golden Fleece"

861. 7. **Thomas:** Cf. John 20:24–25.    870. 3. **Expedition:** the quest of the Argonauts, under the command of Jason, to obtain the Golden Fleece on the east coast of the Black Sea.

Fourth, no Discovery –
Fifth, no Crew –
Finally, no Golden Fleece –
Jason – sham – too.

### 871

The Sun and Moon must make their haste –
The Stars express around
For in the Zones of Paradise
The Lord alone is burned –

His Eye, it is the East and West –
The North and South when He
Do concentrate His Countenance
Like Glow Worms, flee away –

Oh Poor and Far –
Oh Hindered Eye                                10
That hunted for the Day –
The Lord a Candle entertains
Entirely for Thee –

### 945

This is a Blossom of the Brain –
A small – italic Seed
Lodged by Design or Happening
The Spirit fructified –

Shy as the Wind of his Chambers
Swift as a Freshet's Tongue
So of the Flower of the Soul
It's process is unknown.

When it is found, a few rejoice
The Wise convey it Home                        10
Carefully cherishing the spot
If other Flower become.

When it is lost, that Day shall be
The Funeral of God,
Upon his Breast, a closing Soul
The Flower of our Lord.

### 956

What shall I do when the Summer troubles –
What, when the Rose is ripe –
What when the Eggs fly off in Music
From the Maple Keep?

What shall I do when the Skies a'chirrup
Drop a Tune on me –
When the Bee hangs all Noon in the Buttercup

What will become of me?

Oh, when the Squirrel fills His Pockets
And the Berries stare                          10
How can I bear their jocund Faces
Thou from Here, so far?

'Twould'nt afflict a Robin –
All His Goods have Wings –
I – do not fly, so wherefore
My Perennial Things?

### 959

A loss of something ever felt I –
The first that I could recollect
Bereft I was – of what I knew not
Too young that any should suspect

A Mourner walked among the children
I notwithstanding went about
As one bemoaning a Dominion
Itself the only Prince cast out –

Elder, Today, a session wiser
And fainter, too, as Wiseness is –             10
I find myself still softly searching
For my Delinquent Palaces –

And a Suspicion, like a Finger
Touches my Forehead now and then
That I am looking oppositely
For the site of the Kingdom of Heaven –

### 970

Color – Caste – Denomination –
These – are Times's Affair –
Death's diviner Classifying
Does not know they are –

As in sleep – All Hue forgotten –
Tenets – put behind –
Death's large – Democratic fingers
Rub away the Brand –

If Circassian – He is careless –
If He put away                                 10
Chrysalis of Blonde – or Umber –
Equal Butterfly –

They emerge from His Obscuring –
What Death – knows so well –
Our minuter intuitions –
Deem unplausible.

871. 4. burned: Cf. Rev. 22:5.    12. Candle: Cf. Ps. 18:28.    970. 9. Circassian:  i.e.,  white.

### 986

A narrow Fellow in the Grass
Occasionally rides –
You may have met Him – did you not
His notice sudden is –

The Grass divides as with a Comb –
A spotted shaft is seen –
And then it closes at your feet
And opens further on –

He likes a Boggy Acre
A Floor too cool for Corn –      10
Yet when a Boy, and Barefoot –
I more than once at Noon
Have passed, I thought, a Whip lash
Unbraiding in the Sun
When stooping to secure it
It wrinkled, and was gone –

Several of Nature's People
I know, and they know me –
I feel for them a transport
Of cordiality –      20

But never met this Fellow
Attended, or alone
Without a tighter breathing
And Zero at the Bone –

### 1000

The Fingers of the Light
Tapped soft upon the Town
With "I am great and cannot wait
So therefore let me in."

"You're soon," the Town replied,
"My Faces are asleep –
But swear, and I will let you by
You will not wake them up."

The easy Guest complied
But once within the Town      10
The transport of His Countenance
Awakened Maid and Man

The Neighbor in the Pool
Upon His Hip elate
Made loud obeisance and the Gnat
Held up His Cup for Light.

### 1017

To die – without the Dying
And live – without the Life
This is the hardest Miracle
Propounded to Belief.

### 1039

I heard, as if I had no Ear
Until a Vital Word
Came all the way from Life to me
And then I knew I heard.

I saw, as if my Eye were on
Another, till a Thing
And now I know 'twas Light, because
It fitted them, came in.

I dwelt, as if Myself were out,
My Body but within      10
Until a Might detected me
And set my kernel in.

And Spirit turned unto the Dust
"Old Friend, thou knowest me,"
And Time went out to tell the News
And met Eternity.

### 1046

I've dropped my Brain – My Soul is numb –
The Veins that used to run
Stop palsied – 'tis Paralysis
Done perfecter on stone.

Vitality is Carved and cool.
My nerve in Marble lies –
A Breathing Woman
Yesterday – Endowed with Paradise.

Not dumb – I had a sort that moved –
A Sense that smote and stirred –      10
Instincts for Dance – a caper part –
An Aptitude for Bird –

Who wrought Carrara in me
And chiselled all my tune
Were it a Witchcraft – were it Death –
I've still a chance to strain

To Being, somewhere – Motion – Breath –
Though Centuries beyond,
And every limit a Decade –
I'll shiver, satisfied.      20

---

986. 10. A . . . Corn: Samuel Bowles, editor of the Springfield *Daily Republican,* where this poem was published anonymously in 1866, is said to have commented on this line: "How did that girl ever know that a boggy field wasn't good for corn?"

1046. 13. Carrara: i.e., marble, for which Carrara in Italy is a source.

1052

I never saw a Moor –
I never saw the Sea –
Yet know I how the Heather looks
And what a Billow be.

I never spoke with God
Nor visited in Heaven –
Yet certain am I of the spot
As if the Checks were given –

1068

Further in Summer than the Birds
Pathetic from the Grass
A minor Nation celebrates
It's unobtrusive Mass.

No Ordinance be seen
So gradual the Grace
A pensive Custom it becomes
Enlarging Loneliness.

Antiquest felt at Noon
When August burning low                     10
Arise this spectral Canticle
Repose to typify.

Remit as yet no Grace
No Furrow on the Glow
Yet a Druidic Difference
Enhances Nature now.

1084

At Half past Three, a single Bird
Unto a silent Sky
Propounded but a single term
Of cautious melody.

At Half past Four, Experiment
Had subjugated test
And lo, Her silver Principle
Supplanted all the rest.

At Half past Seven, Element
Nor Implement, be seen –                     10
And Place was where the Presence was
Circumference between.

1090

I am afraid to own a Body –
I am afraid to own a Soul –

Profound – precarious Property –
Possession, not optional –

Double Estate – entailed at pleasure
Upon an unsuspecting Heir –
Duke in a moment of Deathlessness
And God, for a Frontier.

1126

Shall I take thee, the Poet said
To the propounded word?
Be stationed with the Candidates
Till I have finer tried –

The Poet searched Philology
And was about to ring
For the suspended Candidate
There came unsummoned in –

That portion of the Vision
The Word applied to fill                     10
Not unto nomination
The Cherubim reveal –

1129

Tell all the Truth but tell it slant –
Success in Circuit lies
Too bright for our infirm Delight
The Truth's superb surprise.

As Lightning to the Children eased
With explanation kind
The Truth must dazzle gradually
Or every man be blind –

1142

The Props assist the House
Until the House is built
And then the Props withdraw
And adequate, erect,
The House support itself
And cease to recollect
The Augur and the Carpenter –
Just such a retrospect
Hath the perfected Life –
A past of Plank and Nail                     10
And slowness – then the Scaffolds drop
Affirming it a Soul.

---

1068. 15. **Druidic:** This word associates the song of the crickets with a mysterious ritual (cf. "Mass," above) connected with the dying of the year into winter.

1126. 12. **Cherubim:** Cf. Ezek. 10:5; I Pet. 1:12. This is one of several poems in which Emily Dickinson associates the Christian conception of a divine Word with poetry.

### 1197

I should not dare to be so sad
So many Years again –
A Load is first impossible
When we have put it down –

The Superhuman then withdraws
And we who never saw
The Giant at the other side
Begin to perish now.

### 1226

The Popular Heart is a Cannon first –
Subsequent a Drum –
Bells for an Auxiliary
And an Afterward of Rum –

Not a Tomorrow to know it's name
Nor a Past to stare –
Ditches for Realms and a Trip to Jail
For a Souvenir.

### 1232

The Clover's simple Fame
Remembered of the Cow –
Is better than enameled Realms
Of notability.
Renown perceives itself
And that degrades the Flower –
The Daisy that has looked behind
Has compromised it's power –

### 1247

To pile like Thunder to it's close
Then crumble grand away
While Everything created hid
This – would be Poetry –

Or Love – the two coeval come –
We both and neither prove –
Experience either and consume –
For None see God and live –

### 1286

I thought that nature was enough
Till Human nature came
But that the other did absorb
As Parallax a Flame –

1247. 8. For . . . live: Cf. Exod. 33:20.

Of Human nature just aware
There added the Divine
Brief struggle for capacity
The power to contain

Is always as the contents
But give a Giant room                    10
And you will lodge a Giant
And not a smaller man.

### 1298

The Mushroom is the Elf of Plants –
At Evening, it is not –
At Morning, in a Truffled Hut
It stop upon a Spot

As if it tarried always
And yet it's whole Career
Is shorter than a Snake's Delay
And fleeter than a Tare –

'Tis Vegetation's Juggler –
The Germ of Alibi –                      10
Doth like a Bubble antedate
And like a Bubble, hie –

I feel as if the Grass was pleased
To have it intermit –
This surreptitious scion
Of Summer's circumspect.

Had Nature any supple Face
Or could she one contemn –
Had Nature an Apostate –
That Mushroom – it is Him!                20

### 1317

Abraham to kill him
Was distinctly told –
Isaac was an Urchin –
Abraham was old –

Not a hesitation –
Abraham complied –
Flattered by Obeisance
Tyranny demurred –

Isaac – to his children
Lived to tell the tale –                  10
Moral – with a Mastiff
Manners may prevail.

1317. 1–2. Abraham . . . told: The story alluded to is told in Gen. 22.

### 1339

A Bee his burnished Carriage
Drove boldly to a Rose –
Combinedly alighting –
Himself – his Carriage was –
The Rose received his visit
With frank tranquility
Withholding not a Crescent
To his Cupidity –

Their Moment consummated –
Remained for him – to flee –      10
Remained for her – of rapture
But the humility.

### 1377

Forbidden Fruit a flavor has
That lawful Orchards mocks –
How luscious lies within the Pod
The Pea that Duty locks –

### 1400

What mystery pervades a well!
The water lives so far –
A neighbor from another world
Residing in a jar

Whose limit none have ever seen,
But just his lid of glass –
Like looking every time you please
In an abyss's face!

The grass does not appear afraid,
I often wonder he      10
Can stand so close and look so bold
At what is awe to me.

Related somehow they may be,
The sedge stands next the sea –
Where he is floorless
And does no timidity betray

But nature is a stranger yet;
The ones that cite her most
Have never passed her haunted house,
Nor simplified her ghost.      20

To pity those that know her not
Is helped by the regret
That those who know her, know her less
The nearer her they get.

### 1405

Bees are Black, with Gilt Surcingles –
Bucaneers of Buzz.

Ride abroad in ostentation
And subsist on Fuzz.

Fuzz ordained – not Fuzz contingent –
Marrows of the Hill.
Jugs – a Universe's fracture
Could not jar or spill.

### 1428

Water makes many Beds
For those averse to sleep –
It's awful chamber open stands –
It's Curtains blandly sweep –
Abhorrent is the Rest
In undulating Rooms
Whose Amplitude no end invades –
Whose Axis never comes.

### 1434

Go not too near a House of Rose –
The depredation of a Breeze
Or inundation of a Dew
Alarm it's walls away –
Nor try to tie the Butterfly,
Nor climb the Bars of Ecstasy,
In insecurity to lie
Is Joy's insuring quality.

### 1462

We knew not that we were to live –
Nor when – we are to die –
Our ignorance – our cuirass is –
We wear Mortality
As lightly as an Option Gown
Till asked to take it off –
By his intrusion, God is known –
It is the same with Life –

### 1463

A Route of Evanescence
With a revolving Wheel –
A Resonance of Emerald –
A Rush of Cochineal –
And every Blossom on the Bush
Adjusts it's tumbled Head –
The mail from Tunis, probably,
An easy Morning's Ride –

1463. 7. **Tunis:** perhaps derived from Shakespeare's *Tempest*,
II.i.241.

### 1475

Fame is the one that does not stay –
It's occupant must die
Or out of sight of estimate
Ascend incessantly –
Or be that most insolvent thing
A Lightning in the Germ –
Electrical the embryo
But we demand the Flame.

### 1483

The Robin is a Gabriel
In humble circumstances –
His Dress denotes him socially,
Of Transport's Working Classes –
He has the punctuality
Of the New England Farmer –
The same oblique integrity,
A Vista vastly warmer –

A small but sturdy Residence,
A self denying Household,                              10
The Guests of Perspicacity
Are all that cross his Threshold –
As covert as a Fugitive,
Cajoling Consternation
By Ditties to the Enemy
And Sylvan Punctuation –

### 1487

The Savior must have been
A docile Gentleman –
To come so far so cold a Day
For little Fellowmen –

The Road to Bethlehem
Since He and I were Boys
Was leveled, but for that twould be
A rugged billion Miles –

### 1510

How happy is the little Stone
That rambles in the Road alone,
And does'nt care about Careers
And Exigencies never fears –
Whose Coat of elemental Brown
A passing Universe put on,
And independent as the Sun
Associates or glows alone,
Fulfilling absolute Decree
In casual simplicity –                              10

### 1553

Bliss is the plaything of the child –
The secret of the man
The sacred stealth of Boy and Girl
Rebuke it if we can—

### 1599

Though the great Waters sleep,
That they are still the Deep,
We cannot doubt –
No vacillating God
Ignited this Abode
To put it out –

### 1628

A Drunkard cannot meet a Cork
Without a Revery –
And so encountering a Fly
This January Day
Jamaicas of Remembrance stir
That send me reeling in –
The moderate drinker of Delight
Does not deserve the spring –
Of juleps, part are in the Jug
And more are in the joy –                              10
Your connoisseur in Liquors
Consults the Bumble Bee –

### 1631

Oh Future! thou secreted peace
Or subterranean wo –
Is there no wandering route of grace
That leads away from thee –
No circuit sage of all the course
Descried by cunning Men
To balk thee of thy sacred Prey –
Advancing to thy Den –

### 1651

A Word made Flesh is seldom
And tremblingly partook
Nor then perhaps reported
But have I not mistook
Each one of us has tasted
With ecstasies of stealth
The very food debated
To our specific strength –

1475. 3. Or: either.    1483. 1. Gabriel: the angel of the Annunciation; cf. Luke 1:26.

1651. 7. food debated: The reference is to the sacrament of the Eucharist, but the meaning of "debated" is obscure, as the context seems to demand some such word as "allotted."

A Word that breathes distinctly
Has not the power to die                                    10
Cohesive as the Spirit
It may expire if He –
"Made Flesh and dwelt among us"
Could condescension be
Like this consent of Language
This loved Philology.

### 1679

Rather arid delight
If Contentment accrue
Make an abstemious Ecstasy
Not so good as joy –

But Rapture's Expense
Must not be incurred
With a to-morrow knocking
And the Rent unpaid –

### 1695

There is a solitude of space
A solitude of sea
A solitude of death, but these
Society shall be
Compared with that profounder site
That polar privacy
A soul admitted to itself –
Finite Infinity.

### 1712

A Pit – but Heaven over it –
And Heaven beside, and Heaven abroad;
And yet a Pit –
With Heaven over it.

To stir would be to slip –
To look would be to drop –
To dream – to sap the Prop
That holds my chances up.
Ah! Pit! With Heaven over it!

The depth is all my thought –                              10
I dare not ask my feet –
'Twould start us where we sit
So straight you'd scarce suspect
It was a Pit – with fathoms under it
Its Circuit just the same
Seed – summer – tomb –
Whose Doom to whom –

1651. 13. "Made . . . us": Cf. John 1:14. Apparently, the meaning is
that if the analogy holds between the Christian and the poetic
meanings of "word" ("consent of Language"), then the poetic word
is also immortal, or can die only in the way in which Christ did, to
rise again.

### 1717

Did life's penurious length
Italicize its sweetness,
The men that daily live
Would stand so deep in joy
That it would clog the cogs
Of that revolving reason
Whose esoteric belt
Protects our sanity.

### 1731

Love can do all but raise the Dead
I doubt if even that
From such a giant were withheld
Were flesh equivalent

But love is tired and must sleep,
And hungry and must graze
And so abets the shining Fleet
Till it is out of gaze.

### 1732

My life closed twice before its close;
It yet remains to see
If Immortality unveil
A third event to me,

So huge, so hopeless to conceive
As these that twice befel.
Parting is all we know of heaven,
And all we need of hell.

### 1736

Proud of my broken heart, since thou didst break
    it,
Proud of the pain I did not feel till thee,
Proud of my night, since thou with moons dost
    slake it,
*Not* to partake thy passion, *my* humility.

Thou can'st not boast, like Jesus, drunken without
    companion
Was the strong cup of anguish brewed for the
    Nazarene

Thou can'st not pierce tradition with the peerless
    puncture,
See! I usurped *thy* crucifix to honor mine!

### 1741

That it will never come again
Is what makes life so sweet.

1736. 6. cup: Cf. Matt. 26:42.

Believing what we don't believe
Does not exhilarate.
That if it be, it be at best
An ablative estate –
This instigates an appetite
Precisely opposite.

### 1745

The mob within the heart
Police cannot suppress
The riot given at the first
Is authorized as peace

Uncertified of scene
Or signified of sound
But growing like a hurricane
In a congenial ground.

### 1749

The waters chased him as he fled,
Not daring look behind;
A billow whispered in his Ear,
"Come home with me, my friend;
My parlor is of shriven glass,
My pantry has a fish
For every palate in the Year," –
To this revolting bliss
The object floating at his side
Made no distinct reply.                    10

### 1764

The saddest noise, the sweetest noise,
   The maddest noise that grows, –
The birds, they make it in the spring,
   At night's delicious close.

Between the March and April line –
   That magical frontier
Beyond which summer hesitates,
   Almost too heavenly near.

It makes us think of all the dead
   That sauntered with us here,        10
By separation's sorcery
   Made cruelly more dear.

It makes us think of what we had,
   And what we now deplore.
We almost wish those siren throats
   Would go and sing no more.

An ear can break a human heart
   As quickly as a spear,
We wish the ear had not a heart
   So dangerously near.                    20

1741. 6. **ablative estate:** condition of removal or deprivation.

# LETTERS

### 193: TO SAMUEL BOWLES

late August 1858?

Dear Mr. Bowles.

I got the little pamphlet. I think you sent it to me, though unfamiliar with your hand – I may mistake.

Thank you if I am right. Thank you, if not, since here I find bright pretext to ask you how you are tonight, and for the health of four more, Elder and Minor "Mary," Sallie and Sam, tenderly to inquire. I hope your cups are full. I hope your vintage is untouched. In such a porcelain life, one likes to be *sure* that all is well, lest one stumble upon one's hopes in a pile of broken crockery.

My friends are my "estate." Forgive me then the avarice to hoard them! They tell me those were poor early, have different views of gold. I dont know how that is. God is not so wary as we, else he would give us no friends, lest we forget him! The Charms of the Heaven in the bush are superceded I fear, by the Heaven in the hand, occasionally. Summer stopped since you were here. Nobody noticed her – that is, no men and women. Doubtless, the fields are rent by petite anguish, and "mourners go about"[1] the Woods. But this is not for us. Business enough indeed, our stately Resurrection! A special Courtesy, I judge, from what the Clergy say! To the "natural man," Bumblebees would seem an improvement, and a spicing of Birds, but far be it from me, to impugn such majestic tastes. Our Pastor says we are a "Worm." How is that reconciled? "Vain – sinful Worm" is possibly of another species.

Do you think we shall "see God"? Think of "Abraham" strolling with him in genial promenade![2]

The men are mowing the second Hay. The cocks are smaller than the first, and spicier.

I would distill a cup, and bear to all my friends, drinking to her no more astir, by beck, or burn, or moor!

Good night, Mr Bowles! This is what they say who come back in the morning, also the closing paragraph on repealed lips. Confidence in Daybreak modifies Dusk.

Blessings for Mrs Bowles, and kisses for the

LETTERS.    **193.** 1. Cf. Eccles. 12:5.    2. "Abraham" . . .
promenade: The allusion appears to be to Gen. 18.

bairns' lips. We want to see you, Mr Bowles, but spare you the rehearsal of "familiar truths."

Good Night,

Emily.

## 260: TO T. W. HIGGINSON

15 April 1862

Mr Higginson,

Are you too deeply occupied to say if my Verse is alive?

The Mind is so near itself – it cannot see, distinctly – and I have none to ask –

Should you think it breathed – and had you the leisure to tell me, I should feel quick gratitude –

If I make the mistake – that you dared to tell me – would give me sincerer honor – toward you –

I enclose my name – asking you, if you please – Sir – to tell me what is true?

That you will not betray me – it is needless to ask – since Honor is it's own pawn –

## 261: TO T. W. HIGGINSON

25 April 1862

Mr. Higginson,

Your kindness claimed earlier gratitude – but I was ill – and write today from my pillow.

Thank you for the surgery [1] – it was not so painful as I supposed. I bring you others – as you ask – though they might not differ –

While my thought is undressed – I can make the distinction, but when I put them in the Gown – they look alike, and numb.

You asked how old I was? I made no verse – but one or two – until this winter – Sir –

I had a terror – since September – I could tell to none – and so I sing, as the Boy does by the Burying Ground – because I am afraid – You inquire my Books – For Poets – I have Keats – and Mr and Mrs Browning. For prose – Mr Ruskin – Sir Thomas Browne – and the Revelations. I went to school – but in your manner of the phrase – had no education. When a little Girl, I had a friend,[2] who taught me Immortality – but venturing too near, himself – he never returned – Soon after, my Tutor, died – and for several years, my Lexicon – was my only companion – Then I found one more [3] – but he was not contented I be his scholar – so he left the Land.

You ask of my Companions Hills – Sir – and the Sundown – and a Dog – large as myself, that my Father bought me – They are better than Beings – because they know – but do not tell – and the noise in the Pool, at Noon – excels my Piano. I have a Brother and Sister – My Mother does not care for thought – and Father, too busy with his Briefs – to notice what we do – He buys me many Books – but begs me not to read them – because he fears they joggle the Mind. They are religious – except me – and address an Eclipse, every morning – whom they call their "Father." But I fear my story fatigues you – I would like to learn – Could you tell me how to grow – or is it unconveyed – like Melody – or Witchcraft?

You speak of Mr Whitman – I never read his Book – but was told that he was disgraceful –

I read Miss Prescott's "Circumstance," [4] but it followed me, in the Dark – so I avoided her –

Two Editors of Journals [5] came to my Father's House, this winter – and asked me for my Mind – and when I asked them "Why," they said I was penurious – and they, would use it for the World –

I could not weigh myself – Myself –

My size felt small – to me – I read your Chapters in the Atlantic – and experienced honor for you – I was sure you would not reject a confiding question –

Is this – Sir – what you asked me to tell you?

Your friend,

E – Dickinson

## 265: TO T. W. HIGGINSON

7 June 1862

Dear friend.

Your letter gave no Drunkenness, because I tasted Rum before – Domingo comes but once – yet I have had few pleasures so deep as your opinion, and if I tried to thank you, my tears would block my tongue –

My dying Tutor told me that he would like to live till I had been a poet, but Death was much of Mob as I could master – then – And when far afterward – a sudden light on Orchards, or a new fashion in the wind troubled my attention – I felt a palsy, here – the Verses just relieve –

Your second letter surprised me, and for a moment, swung – I had not supposed it. Your first – gave no dishonor, because the True – are not ashamed – I thanked you for your justice – but could not drop the Bells whose jingling cooled

**261. 1.** The allusion is to the criticisms Higginson had made on the poems enclosed in the previous letter. **2.** Usually identified with Benjamin F. Newton. **3.** Probably Charles Wadsworth.

**4.** **"Circumstance":** a story recently (May 1860) published in the *Atlantic Monthly.* **5.** Perhaps Samuel Bowles and J. G. Holland.

my Tramp – Perhaps the Balm, seemed better, because you bled me, first.

I smile when you suggest that I delay "to publish" – that being foreign to my thought, as Firmament to Fin –

If fame belonged to me, I could not escape her – if she did not, the longest day would pass me on the chase – and the approbation of my Dog, would forsake me – then – My Barefoot-Rank is better –

You think my gait "spasmodic" – I am in danger – Sir –

You think me "uncontrolled" – I have no Tribunal.

Would you have time to be the "friend" you should think I need? I have a little shape – it would not crowd your Desk – nor make much Racket as the Mouse, that dents your Galleries –

If I might bring you what I do – not so frequent to trouble you – and ask you if I told it clear – 'twould be control, to me –

The Sailor cannot see the North – but knows the Needle can –

The "hand you stretch me in the Dark," I put mine in, and turn away – I have no Saxon, now –

> As if I asked a common Alms,
> And in my wondering hand
> A Stranger pressed a Kingdom,
> And I, bewildered, stand –
>
> As if I asked the Orient
> Had it for me a Morn –
> And it should lift it's purple Dikes,
> And shatter me with Dawn!

But, will you be my Preceptor, Mr Higginson?
Your friend
E Dickinson –

## 268: TO T. W. HIGGINSON

July 1862

Could you believe me – without? I had no portrait, now, but am small, like the Wren, and my Hair is bold, like the Chestnut Bur – and my eyes, like the Sherry in the Glass, that the Guest leaves – Would this do just as well?

It often alarms Father – He says Death might occur, and he has Molds [1] of all the rest – but has no Mold of me, but I noticed the Quick wore off those things, in a few days, and forestall the dishonor – You will think no caprice of me –

You said "Dark." I know the Butterfly – and the Lizard – and the Orchis –

Are not those *your* Countrymen?

268. 1. **Molds:** here meaning "pictures."

I am happy to be your scholar, and will deserve the kindness, I cannot repay.

If you truly consent, I recite, now –

Will you tell me my fault, frankly as to yourself, for I had rather wince, than die. Men do not call the surgeon, to commend – the Bone, but to set it, Sir, and fracture within, is more critical. And for this, Preceptor, I shall bring you – Obedience – the Blossom from my Garden, and every gratitude I know. Perhaps you smile at me. I could not stop for that – My Business is Circumference – An ignorance, not of Customs, but if caught with the Dawn – or the Sunset see me – Myself the only Kangaroo among the Beauty, Sir, if you please, it afflicts me, and I thought that instruction would take it away.

Because you have much business, beside the growth of me – you will appoint, yourself, how often I shall come – without your inconvenience. And if at any time – you regret you received me, or I prove a different fabric to that you supposed – you must banish me –

When I state myself, as the Representative of the Verse – it does not mean – me – but a supposed person. You are true, about the "perfection."

Today, makes Yesterday mean.

You spoke of Pippa Passes [2] – I never heard anybody speak of Pippa Passes – before.

You see my posture is benighted.

To thank you, baffles me. Are you perfectly powerful? Had I a pleasure you had not, I could delight to bring it.

Your Scholar

## 271: TO T. W. HIGGINSON

August 1862

Dear friend –

Are these more orderly? I thank you for the Truth –

I had no Monarch in my life, and cannot rule myself, and when I try to organize – my little Force explodes – and leaves me bare and charred –

I think you called me "Wayward." Will you help me improve?

I suppose the pride that stops the Breath, in the Core of Woods, is not of Ourself –

You say I confess the little mistake,[1] and omit the large – Because I can see Orthography – but

2. **Pippa Passes:** a dramatic poem by Robert Browning, published in 1841. **271.** 1. Emily Dickinson was always ready to correct spellings, but refused to alter the irregular syntax and meter which Higginson regarded as mistakes.

the Ignorance out of sight – is my Preceptor's charge –

Of "shunning Men and Women" – they talk of Hallowed things, aloud – and embarrass my Dog – He and I dont object to them, if they'll exist their side. I think Carl[o] would please you – He is dumb, and brave – I think you would like the Chestnut Tree, I met in my walk. It hit my notice suddenly – and I thought the Skies were in Blossom –

Then there's a noiseless noise in the Orchard – that I let persons hear – You told me in one letter, you could not come to see me, "now," and I made no answer, not because I had none, but did not think myself the price that you should come so far –

I do not ask so large a pleasure, lest you might deny me –

You say "Beyond your knowledge." You would not jest with me, because I believe you – but Preceptor – you cannot mean it? All men say "What" to me, but I thought it a fashion –

When much in the Woods as a little Girl, I was told that the Snake would bite me, that I might pick a poisonous flower, or Goblins kidnap me, but I went along and met no one but Angels, who were far shyer of me, than I could be of them, so I hav'nt that confidence in fraud which many exercise.

I shall observe your precept – though I dont understand it, always.

I marked a line in One Verse – because I met it after I made it – and never consciously touch a paint, mixed by another person –

I do not let go it, because it is mine.

Have you the portrait of Mrs Browning? Persons sent me three – If you had none, will you have mine?

Your Scholar –

## 318: TO MRS. J. G. HOLLAND

early May 1866

Dear Sister,

After you went, a low wind warbled through the house like a spacious bird, making it high but lonely. When you had gone the love came. I supposed it would. The supper of the heart is when the guest has gone.

Shame is so intrinsic in a strong affection we must all experience Adam's reticence.[1] I suppose the street that the lover travels is thenceforth divine, incapable of turnpike aims.

That you be with me annuls fear and I await Commencement with merry resignation. Smaller

than David you clothe me with extreme Goliath.

Friday I tasted life. It was a vast morsel. A circus passed the house – still I feel the red in my mind though the drums are out.

The book you mention, I have not met. Thank you for tenderness.

The lawn is full of south and the odors tangle, and I hear today for the first the river in the tree.

You mentioned spring's delaying – I blamed her for the opposite. I would eat evanescence slowly.

Vinnie [2] is deeply afflicted in the death of her dappled cat, though I convince her it is immortal which assists her some. Mother resumes lettuce, involving my transgression – suggestive of yourself, however, which endears disgrace.

"House" is being "cleaned." I prefer pestilence. That is more classic and less fell.

Yours was my first arbutus. It was a rosy boast. I will send you the first witch hazel.

A woman died last week, young and in hope but a little while – at the end of our garden. I thought since of the power of death, not upon affection, but its mortal signal. It is to us the Nile.[3]

You refer to the unpermitted delight to be with those we love. I suppose that to be the license not granted of God.

Count not that far that can be had,
Though sunset lie between –
Nor that adjacent, that beside,
Is further than the sun.

Love for your embodiment of it.

Emily.

## 330: TO T. W. HIGGINSON

June 1869

Dear friend

A Letter always feels to me like immortality because it is the mind alone without corporeal friend. Indebted in our talk to attitude and accent, there seems a spectral power in thought that walks alone – I would like to thank you for your great kindness but never try to lift the words which I cannot hold.

Should you come to Amherst, I might then succeed, though Gratitude is the timid wealth of those who have nothing. I am sure that you speak the truth, because the noble do, but your letters always surprise me. My life has been too simple and stern to embarrass any.

---

**318.** 1. Cf. Gen. 3:7.

2. **Vinnie:** her sister, Lavinia. 3. Perhaps an allusion to the fact that the rising of the Nile, on which the life of Egypt depended, was heralded by the rising of the Dog Star, its "signal."

"Seen of Angels" [1] scarcely my responsibility
It is difficult not to be fictitious in so fair a place, but test's severe repairs are permitted all.

When a little Girl I remember hearing that remarkable passage and preferring the "Power," not knowing at the time that "Kingdom" and "Glory" were included.

You noticed my dwelling alone – To an Emigrant, Country is idle except it be his own. You speak kindly of seeing me. Could it please your convenience to come so far as Amherst I should be very glad, but I do not cross my Father's ground to any House or town.

Of our greatest acts we are ignorant –

You were not aware that you saved my Life. To thank you in person has been since then one of my few requests. The child that asks my flower "Will you," he says – "Will you" – and so to ask for what I want I know no other way.

You will excuse each that I say, because no other taught me?

Dickinson

### 339: TO LOUISE AND FRANCES NORCROSS

*early spring 1870*

Dear Children,

I think the bluebirds do their work exactly like me. They dart around just so, with little dodging feet, and look so agitated. I really feel for them, they seem to be so tried.

The mud is very deep – up to the wagons' stomachs – arbutus making pink clothes, and everything alive.

Even the hens are touched with the things of Bourbon,[1] and make republicans like me feel strangely out of scene.

Mother went rambling, and came in with a burdock on her shawl, so we know that the snow has perished from the earth. Noah [2] would have liked mother.

I am glad you are with Eliza. It is next to shade to know that those we love are cool on a parched day.

Bring my love to —— and Mr. ——. You will not need a hod. C[lara] writes often, full of joy and liberty. I guess it is a case of peace. . . .

Pussy has a daughter in the shavings barrel.

Father steps like Cromwell when he gets the kindlings.

Mrs. S[weetser] gets bigger, and rolls down the lane to church like a reverend marble. Did you know little Mrs. Holland was in Berlin for her eyes? . . .

Did you know about Mrs. J——? She fledged her antique wings. 'Tis said that "nothing in her life became her like the leaving it." [8]

Great Streets of Silence led away
To Neighborhoods of Pause –
Here was no Notice – no Dissent,
No Universe – no Laws –

By Clocks – 'twas Morning, and for Night
The Bells at Distance called –
But Epoch had no basis here,
For Period exhaled.

Emily.

### 354: TO MRS. J. G. HOLLAND

*early October 1870*

I guess I wont send that note now, for the mind is such a new place, last night feels obsolete.

Perhaps you thought dear Sister, I wanted to elope with you and feared a vicious Father.

It was not quite that.

The Papers thought the Doctor was mostly in New York. Who then would read for you? Mr. Chapman, doubtless, or Mr. Buckingham! The Doctor's sweet reply makes me infamous.

Life is the finest secret.

So long as that remains, we must all whisper.

With that sublime exception I had no clandestineness.

It was lovely to see you and I hope it may happen again. These beloved accidents must become more frequent.

We are by September and yet my flowers are bold as June. Amherst has gone to Eden.

To shut our eyes is Travel.

The Seasons understand this.

How lonesome to be an Article! I mean – to have no soul.

An Apple fell in the night and a Wagon stopped.

I suppose the Wagon ate the Apple and resumed it's way.

How fine it is to talk.
What Miracles the News is!
Not Bismark [1] but ourselves.

The Life we have is very great.
The Life that we shall see
Surpasses it, we know, because
It is Infinity.
But when all Space has been beheld
And all Dominion shown

---

330. 1. Cf. I Tim. 3:16.   339. 1. **Bourbon:** i.e., with plumage like royalty.   2. Cf. Gen. 8:11.

3. "nothing . . . it": See *Macbeth*, I. iv. 7–8.   354. 1. Bismarck was at the time Chancellor of Prussia, and as the Franco-Prussian War had just begun he was the chief name in the news.

The smallest Human Heart's extent
Reduces it to none.

Love for the Doctor, and the Girls.
Ted might not acknowledge me.

                                        Emily.

## 432: TO MRS. J. G. HOLLAND

                            late January 1875
Sister.

This austere Afternoon is more becoming to a Patriot than to one whose Friend is it's sole Land.

No event of Wind or Bird breaks the Spell of Steel.

Nature squanders Rigor – now – where she squandered Love.

Chastening – it may be – the Lass that she receiveth.

My House is a House of Snow – true – sadly – of few.

Mother is asleep in the Library – Vinnie – in the Dining Room – Father – in the Masked Bed – in the Marl House.

How soft his Prison is –
How sweet those sullen Bars –
No Despot – but the King of Down
Invented that Repose!

When I think of his firm Light – quenched so causelessly, it fritters the worth of much that shines. "Dust unto the Dust" indeed – but the final clause of that marvelous sentence – who has rendered it?

"I say unto you," Father would read at Prayers, with a militant Accent that would startle one.

Forgive me if I linger on the first Mystery of the House.

It's specific Mystery – each Heart had before – but within this World. Father's was the first Act distinctly of the Spirit.

Austin's Family went to Geneva, and Austin lived with us four weeks. It seemed peculiar – pathetic – and Antediluvian. We missed him while he was with us and missed him when he was gone.

All is so very curious.

Thank you for that "New Year" – the first with a fracture. I trust it is whole and hale – to you.

"Kingsley" rejoins "Argemone" [1] –

Thank you for the Affection. It helps me up the Stairs at Night, where as I passed my Father's Door – I used to think was safety. The Hand that plucked the Clover – I seek, and am

                                        Emily.

## 459A: TO T. W. HIGGINSON

                                        1876

Nature is a Haunted House – but Art – a House that tries to be haunted.

## 580: TO SUSAN GILBERT DICKINSON

                                  about 1878

The Solaces of Theft are first – Theft – second – Superiority to Detection –

                                        Emily.

## 605: TO EDWARD (NED) DICKINSON [1]

                                  about 1879

Dear Ned—

Dennis [2] was happy yesterday, and it made him graceful – I saw him waltzing with the Cow – and suspected his status, but he afterward started for your House in a frame that was unmistakable –

You told me he had'nt tasted Liquor since his Wife's decease – then she must have been living at six o'clock last Evening –

I fear for the rectitude of the Barn –

Love for the Police –

## 868: TO SUSAN GILBERT DICKINSON

                              early October 1883

Dear Sue –

The Vision of Immortal Life has been fulfilled –

How simply at the last the Fathom comes! The Passenger and not the Sea, we find surprises us –

Gilbert rejoiced in Secrets –

His Life was panting with them – With what menace of Light he cried "Dont tell, Aunt Emily"! Now my ascended Playmate must instruct *me*. Show us, prattling Preceptor, but the way to thee!

He knew no niggard moment – His Life was full of Boon – The Playthings of the Dervish were not so wild as his –

No crescent was this Creature – He traveled from the Full –

Such soar, but never set –

I see him in the Star, and meet his sweet velocity in everything that flies – His Life was

---

432. 1. "Argemone": the heroine of Charles Kingsley's first novel, *Yeast*.

605. 1. Edward (Ned) Dickinson: Emily's nephew, the oldest son of Austin and Sue.    2. Dennis: Dennis Scannell, a handyman who worked for the Dickinsons and whose wife had recently died.

like the Bugle, which winds itself away, his Elegy
an echo – his Requiem ecstasy –
  Dawn and Meridian in one.
  Wherefore would he wait, wronged only of
Night, which he left for us –
  Without a speculation, our little Ajax [1] spans the
whole –

    Pass to thy Rendezvous of Light,
    Pangless except for us –
    Who slowly ford the Mystery
    Which thou hast leaped across!
                              Emily.

1024: TO SUSAN GILBERT DICKINSON
                                          late 1885
  The World hath not known her, but *I* have
known her, was the sweet Boast of Jesus – [1]
  The small Heart cannot break – The Ecstasy of
it's penalty solaces the large –
  Emerging from an Abyss, and reentering it –
that is Life, is it not, Dear?
  The tie between us is very fine, but a Hair never
dissolves.
                              Lovingly –
                                          Emily –

868. 1. **Ajax:** The name is used here as a symbol of defiant heroism.

1024. 1. **The . . . Jesus:** See John 17:25.

HENRY NASH SMITH
*Editor*

# Mark Twain

## 1835-1910

THE LIFE of Mark Twain is a part of our culture—even of our folklore, for it is clothed in an aura of legend that he himself created. His best books are all autobiographical; at first glance his imagination seems almost childishly self-centered. But the appearance is deceptive because he viewed his experience with detachment. He had the remarkable gift of seeing his own life as if it were a work of fiction composed by someone else.

This state of affairs poses a special problem for Mark Twain's biographers: they know at once too much and too little about their subject. He has exhibited himself at length in volume after volume, but he wore many different disguises. What was the man himself like behind the masks? The question is even more difficult than it might seem because the role of the "Mark Twain" who assumed the character of a boy to tell his greatest story, and signed it "Yours truly, Huck Finn," is itself a persona, a kind of mask that partially conceals the features of the actual Samuel L. Clemens. Yet only partially; for Clemens often thought of himself as Mark Twain, and signed himself "Mark" in letters to such friends as William Dean Howells and the Rev. Joseph H. Twichell, and to his manager James Redpath. On the other hand, in writing to members of his family he was more often "Sam" or

"Saml." It is not surprising that he was preoccupied with the problem of identity, and that his books are filled with characters who, like Huck Finn, assume a variety of names and roles.

Samuel Langhorne Clemens was born on November 30, 1835, in the backwoods settlement of Florida in northeastern Missouri, some thirty miles inland from the Mississippi. His parents had arrived from Tennessee only six months earlier, in response to the urging of relatives who had come west the previous year. John Marshall Clemens, Sam's father, was a Virginian—"a stern, unsmiling man," as the son remembered him, "of perfect probity and high principle." He was ambitious to practice law and held office as justice of the peace and county judge, but was condemned to farming and storekeeping in a never quite successful effort to support his family. Sam's mother, Jane Lampton of Adair County, Kentucky, was described by her granddaughter as "a great beauty, a fine dancer, and very witty." She came of a family of Indian fighters; Sam inherited from her his red hair and also, no doubt, his fiery temper. He was the sixth of seven children, of whom three died in childhood and a fourth, Henry, the youngest, was killed in a steamboat explosion in 1858 at the age of twenty.

When Sam was four years old his father,

[685]

having failed as a storekeeper in Florida, moved to Hannibal, a town on the river, in yet another effort to improve his fortunes. Although he was a prominent man in the community and served on various committees dedicated to civic projects, he continued on the edge of bankruptcy until death in 1847, when Sam was eleven years old. During this last phase of the father's frustrating life, Sam Clemens was passing through the archetypal[1] boyhood of America, storing up memories that were to become the basic vocabulary of the artist for the expression of his thought about the human condition.

It was only a brief period—six or seven years. Sam's real boyhood came to an end when he was eleven; for soon after his father's death he was apprenticed to a printer. He had no further formal education. In 1850, when his elder brother Orion started a weeky newspaper in Hannibal, Sam went to work for him as printer and editorial assistant. Together they undertook to support their mother and sister. But Sam grew more and more exasperated with Orion, who had his father's gift for high-minded failure, and in 1853 he struck out on his own. It took him more than fifteen years to decide on a vocation. In the course of that time he was a printer in St. Louis, New York, Philadelphia, Washington, Cincinnati, and a couple of towns in Iowa; a steamboat pilot on the Mississippi between St. Louis and New Orleans; a soldier, of sorts, for a couple of weeks in a vaguely Confederate militia company;[2] a prospector in various parts of Nevada; a local reporter for the *Territorial Enterprise* in Virginia City; a freelance journalist in San Francisco; a traveling newspaper correspondent in Hawaii, Europe, and the Near East; a newspaper editor in Buffalo; and a humorous lecturer.

The crucial period in his development began in June 1867, when he persuaded the San Francisco *Alta California* to send him as a correspondent with a company of tourists bound from New York to Europe and the Holy Land on board the steamer *Quaker City*. During the next three years both Mark Twain's conception of himself and the image he presented to the world underwent an extraordinary change. When he booked passage on the *Quaker City*, he was an irresponsible, Bohemian newspaper man, rejoicing in the sobriquet of "The Wild Humorist of the Pacific Slope." A New York publisher he called on to discuss publication of a volume of his sketches thought he looked too disreputable to bother with. The pose he affected—for it was a pose, closely related to the "moral paradox" Bret Harte was just beginning to make into a literary formula—is indicated in a letter to his mother written a few days before he sailed describing Dan Slote, with whom he was to share a cabin: "I have got a splendid, immoral, tobacco-smoking, wine-drinking, godless roommate who is as good and true and right-minded a man as ever lived. . . ."

This was in the spring of 1867. By the spring of 1870 Clemens was married to the delicate and fastidious Olivia Langdon of Elmira, New York, who would presently inherit a quarter of a million dollars from her father; the young couple were living in a handsome house in Buffalo, given them by the bride's parents as a wedding present; Mark Twain was editing the Buffalo *Express*, in which his father-in-law had helped him to buy an interest; and he had acquired many of the attitudes appropriate to Livy's social environment.

Neither the Bohemianism of 1867 nor the respectability of 1870 means quite what it seems to on the surface, because each image shows the histrionic exaggeration that was a part of Clemens' personal style. He was not so raffish as he made himself out to be before he met Livy nor so conventional, by far, as he seemed to be after they were married. Just here, perhaps, is where Van Wyck Brooks went astray in his famous contention that Mark Twain destroyed himself as an artist by surrendering to the philistinism[3] of Elmira and Hartford. A sounder interpretation would recognize that he was expressing some part of his true self all along by means

[1]archetypal: original pattern or model. [2]Mark Twain describes this experience with comic exaggeration in "The Private History of a Campaign That Failed," *Century* (December 1885).

[3] philistinism: priggishness guided by material values.

of the successive poses and disguises with which he experimented. Augustin Daly told him he could have been a great actor: to assume by turns a variety of roles was a part of his essential nature. But there was something solid underneath. In the end, when the marriage had attained its durable harmony, Livy had given up more of her habits and attitudes than he had of his.

The power of imagination that enabled Mark Twain to conceive of many different ways of life made it difficult for him to settle upon one. The arrangement for him to buy an interest in the Buffalo *Express* had rested on the assumption that his true vocation was journalism. But he could not endure for very long the relentless routine of getting a daily paper to press. Fortunately, an alternative vocation now came into view. *Innocents Abroad,* published in August 1869 on almost the very day he reported for work in the *Express* office, quickly became a best-seller: 12,000 copies were sold within a month and 67,000 during the first year. Elisha Bliss, president of the American Publishing Company of Hartford, was eager for a second book. When Mark Twain was convinced he could make a good income by writing books, he sold out his interest in the *Express* (at a loss of $10,000), and in October 1871, he moved his family to Hartford.

The success of *Roughing It,* published the following spring, and the acclaim with which Mark Twain was received when he lectured in England later that year, confirmed his decision to give up journalism. The Clemenses acquired an ample lot in the Nook Farm community on the western edge of Hartford, and in the spring of 1873 began building a house, which they moved into something more than a year later. It was three stories high and contained a score of rooms. On the outside were a half-dozen balconies, two towers, a portecochere, and a broad veranda. With the furnishings, it cost more than $120,000 at a time when the dollar had perhaps three times its present purchasing power. The house symbolized Clemens' new status; it was also the realization of the kind of dream he had ascribed to himself and Calvin Higbie in *Roughing It,* when for ten

days they thought they had struck it rich in the mines. At an even deeper level the house gave expression to what he called the "circus side" of his nature—the Tom Sawyer strain in him which reveled in theatrical display and believed with Hank Morgan, the Connecticut Yankee, that "you can't throw too much style into a miracle."

The Hartford house was also a monument to domesticity, to the idea of the family. It was built for Livy, for the eldest daughter (Susy) who had been born in 1872, and for the two other daughters (Clara and Jean) who would be born during the next ten years. Even by nineteenth-century standards, the Clemenses were a close-knit group. Although Mark Twain might disappear into his study for several hours a day, parents and children all gathered at meals, where he talked with unfailing energy and brilliance about whatever was on his mind; and the habitual evening program consisted of reading aloud in the family circle—often from the pages he had written during the day. The girls were taught at home by tutors. When Susy reached eighteen and it seemed inevitable she should receive some education outside the household, she entered Bryn Mawr. Both parents went down with her when she enrolled, stayed at a nearby hotel for two or three weeks, and returned for frequent visits. In February of her freshman year Clemens wrote to Howells:

Mrs. Clemens has been in Philadelphia a week at the Continental Hotel with Susy (who, to my private regret is beginning to love Bryn Mawr) & I've had to stay here alone. But this is the last time this brace of old fools, old indispensables-to-each-other, are going to separate themselves in this foolish fashion.

His regret was unfounded: Susy was so homesick she was ill much of the time, and she withdrew from college in April. This was the only effort the Clemenses made to send any of the daughters away from home to be educated. Later, when Clara was studying music in Europe, they often took up residence in the cities where her teachers were situated.

The other side of the coin was Mark Twain's gregariousness and love of excitement. There was much visiting back and forth in the Nook Farm community, and the Clemenses had frequent house guests. As one of the leading citizens of Hartford, Mark Twain was elected to the Monday Evening Club which met every two weeks to discuss papers read by members. He was invited to lecture for the benefit of various charities and to speak at Republican rallies—until he scandalized his friends by supporting Cleveland in 1884. By the middle of the 1870's, he was finding he could count on uninterrupted time for writing only during the summers, which the family usually spent at Quarry Farm near Elmira, the home of Livy's foster sister Susan Crane. The program of entertaining, added to the routine expense of maintaining the great house with its staff of six servants, became so burdensome that in 1878–79 and again in the early 1890's, the Clemenses made long visits to Europe in order to cut down their household expenses.

The most important literary influence on Mark Twain during his Hartford period was his friendship with Howells, novelist, editor of the *Atlantic Monthly* (until 1881), and the leading critic in the United States. From the time Howells singled out *Innocents Abroad* for review in 1869 until Mark Twain's death and after, he acclaimed his friend's extraordinary gifts as an artist. He urged him to contribute to the *Atlantic*, defended him in Brahmin circles that were inclined to look down on the unconventional Westerner, helped him to distinguish good work from bad in his own writing, and on occasion cheerfully read proof or performed any function, however menial, that would help Clemens get his books into print. In return, Clemens declared that Howells was his "only author." He often sent enthusiastic praise of Howells' novels as they came out serially in the magazines.

Except for Livy's semi-invalidism, the later 1870's and early 1880's were a period of golden prosperity and happiness for Clemens. He adored his wife and daughters; his fame and his income were constantly increasing. Yet his prickly disposition caused him to be continually dissatisfied with his publishers. Upon the death of Elisha Bliss in

1880, he turned from the American Publishing Company to James R. Osgood of Boston and then to his own publishing firm, which he established in New York in 1884 under the management of his nephew, Charles L. Webster. The company throve. Its first book, *The Adventures of Huckleberry Finn*, sold 51,000 copies within fourteen months, and its handling of the *Personal Memoirs of Ulysses S. Grant* was a landmark in mass publishing. But Clemens was involved in other business enterprises that were less profitable, especially the promotion of the Paige typesetter. This machine was ingenious and, within its limitations, successful, but it was too complicated for general service. In the later 1880's the construction of a pilot model in the Pratt & Whitney machine shops in Hartford was costing Clemens two or three thousand dollars a month. During these same years the Webster company needed capital to sustain a pioneer plan for selling the Stedman and Hutchinson ten-volume *Library of American Literature* on the installment plan. By 1894 the shortage of credit resulting from the panic of 1893 brought matters to a crisis. The Webster company faced bankruptcy. Clemens was forced to abandon his efforts to put the Paige machine into production, after he had sunk about $200,000 in it. His finances would have been hopeless had it not been for the intervention of Henry H. Rogers, Standard Oil executive and one of the powers of Wall Street, who generously took over direction of Clemens' business affairs, compounded with the creditors, and eventually made arrangement whereby Harper & Brothers became publishers of all his works and guaranteed him a substantial income. Although Mark Twain was not legally liable for the debts remaining after the Webster company was liquidated, he insisted, like Walter Scott before him, on paying all legitimate claims in full. Largely by means of a lecture tour around the world in 1895–96, he achieved this goal by 1898.

Bankruptcy was but one of the disasters in store for Clemens. Psychological disturbances in his daughter Jean were diagnosed in 1896 as symptoms of epilepsy. (She was never entirely well again, and in 1909 she died as the result of an epileptic seizure.) While he was still in England on his way home from his lecture tour, Susy died in Hartford of spinal meningitis. It was a shattering blow for both parents. Livy, never very strong, suffered in 1902 a violent attack of asthma. It left her in such a state of nervous exhaustion that for months on end her husband was allowed to see her only a few minutes each day. On the recommendation of the doctors, he established the family in a villa near Florence for the sake of the milder climate, but Livy did not really gain strength, and she died in 1904.

Mark Twain was growing old. He was inconsolably lonely, and some of his basic attitudes and beliefs had undergone a change that weakened his power of imagination. But his trip through the southern hemisphere had broadened his political horizon, and in the years before and after the turn of the century he published scathing attacks on the imperialistic ventures of Britain and Belgium in Africa, and of the United States in Asia. Howells shared his old friend's views; both men were heatedly denounced in the press as subversives for their protests against American occupation of the Philippines. Clemens also took a vigorous part in the New York municipal elections of 1901 which led to the defeat of Boss Richard Croker. As time went on, however, his disillusionment with the promises of democracy led him to a gloomy acquiescence in the trend toward what he called "monarchy."

In 1907 he made a triumphal trip to Oxford to receive the degree of Litt.D. This was his fourth honorary degree. The others had been an M.A. (1888) and Litt.D. (1901) from Yale, and an LL.D. (1902) from the University of Missouri. He was an international celebrity whose comings and goings and opinions on the affairs of the world were reported constantly in the press.

After the death of Livy, Clemens lived for a time in rented houses in New York, spending his summers in the White Mountains or the Adirondacks. He was much in demand as an after-dinner speaker at banquets, and the emptiness of his life led him to accept many invitations. As his energies slowly declined, however, he left New York to live in a handsome villa designed by Howells' son, John Mead Howells, which he built in 1906–07 near Redding, Connecticut. He called it "Stormfield" after one of his favorite characters, the hero of "Captain Stormfield's Visit to Heaven." Here he was delighted to be able to preside over the wedding of his daughter Clara to Ossip Gabrilowitsch, a brilliant pianist and conductor, and to welcome the guests who never ceased coming—Howells, the publisher George Harvey, Joe Twichell, Helen Keller, the actress Billie Burke. He dictated further chapters of his rambling memoirs, or struggled to revise and to complete the unfinished stories and novels into whose confused symbolism he poured the bitterness of his last years. He was heavily dependent psychologically on Albert Bigelow Paine, the young editor and free-lance writer who had been given permission in 1906 to write his biography, and who became an almost constant companion. It was Paine who went to Bermuda to bring Clemens back home when the angina pectoris that had been threatening him for some time grew suddenly worse. He died at Stormfield on April 21, 1910.

## II

JUST AS the man Samuel L. Clemens wore now one mask, now another, his writings also have had widely different meanings for different audiences. Most readers in his own day considered him simply a funny man, a literary comedian like Artemus Ward, Bill Arp, or Josh Billings; and amid the solemnities of twentieth-century criticism it is worth remembering that even after we discard much joking which no longer comes off, Mark Twain's work is often very funny indeed. It was his humor that made him a best-selling writer and a popular favorite on the lecture platform. This mass appeal brought him a handsome income and freed him from the necessity of turning out copy month in and month out, whether he felt like it or not, as Howells was compelled to do for half a century. But as both Mark Twain and Howells recognized, there was something ambiguous about his relation to his public. Howells observed that "no book of literary quality was made to go by subscription except Mr. Clemens' books, and I think these went because the subscription public never knew what good literature they were." After Mark Twain's death, Howells returned to this point, remarking that the "average practical American public . . . was his first tribunal, and must always be his court of final appeal." The word "practical" here means something like "lowbrow"; it alludes to the fact that, except for Howells, few critics took Mark Twain seriously enough during his lifetime to analyze and discuss his work as literature. This was the great disadvantage of his status as a writer for the mass audience: he was deprived of the benefit of discriminating criticism. It was not that he might have learned something about his craft from the critics—although Howells certainly helped him in this regard—but rather that serious critical attention might have spared him his lifelong struggle to justify to himself what he was doing, and might have helped him not to take himself at too low a valuation.

From the very first Howells called attention to the "pure human nature" in Mark Twain's work and its evocation of whole areas of American experience. He also noted with approval Mark Twain's function as a critic of society who attacked tyranny and superstition in the name of democracy and enlightenment. These emphases determined the prevalent view of Mark Twain until quite recently. But the cult of realism has given way to the cults of symbolism and of form in literature. For twenty years and more, a new Mark Twain has been coming into view, a Mark Twain who is an artist rather than a chronicler, a creator of symbols as well as an observer of society. And it has become clear that he was not an illiterate backwoodsman but a man of considerable if unsystematic reading. Walter Blair, for example, has called attention to echoes of a dozen writers—from Shakespeare and Cervantes to Saint-Simon, Taine, Carlyle, and Lecky—in *Huckleberry Finn* alone.

The student will get the most out of Mark Twain who does not commit himself exclusively to any one of these critical perspectives but tries to find what is valid in each of them; for Mark Twain is too rich a writer to be exhausted by any formula. Nevertheless, the inspired humorist and the incomparable chronicler in him still seem more accessible than the artist engaged in advanced technical experiments that laid the foundation for a native American literary prose.

The equipment with which he began, the tradition of native American humor and the insouciance of Nevada and California journalism, gave him what may be called for convenience a vernacular perspective and also a feeling for the poetic vividness of colloquial language. But these are matters involving primarily the texture of prose; they have little bearing on the problem of structure. When he undertook to be a writer of books rather than a journalist, and therefore faced the task of constructing a long narrative, he was at a frontier of literary innovation. This was his situation when he sat down in San Francisco in April 1868 to make over his dispatches from the *Quaker City* excursion into *Innocents Abroad*. He could not follow the example of Bayard Taylor and produce a travel book by merely stringing his newspaper pieces together because he was not just describing what he had seen, but writing what was in effect a work of fiction. Yet he could hardly use as a model the only large fictional form that lay at hand, that of the novel, because a novel was assumed to be a love story. He would have to contrive a new imaginative pattern to provide a structure for his book.

He adopted the only logical course: he undertook to expand the fictional elements in the newspaper dispatches into a larger narrative pattern. These fictional elements were implicit in the tradition of backwoods humor, which often involved a contrast or conflict between a "straight" and a vernacular character. Mark Twain had experimented with many variations on this pattern. In "The Celebrated Jumping Frog of Calaveras County," for example, which had brought him his first national recognition when it was published in the New York *Saturday Press* in 1865, the tall tale about filling a frog with shot is merely a pretext for bringing the straight narrator into contact with Simon Wheeler, whose simplicity and candor the writer finds admirable. It is a form of the pastoral pattern which European poets had used through the centuries.

The polarity of the two roles suggested the device of heightening the gentility of the straight character and the vulgarity of his vernacular companion or adversary. In the letters sent to the Sacramento *Union* from Hawaii in 1866, Mark Twain cast himself as straight man and for contrast created the violently antigenteel Mr. Brown. He continued using Mr. Brown in the *Quaker City* dispatches: Brown, for example, was confused by what he took to be the names of the railway stations in France because they were all the same: *Côte des hommes*. But the device was actually in conflict with the meanings Mark Twain had discovered in his materials during the journey. In proportion as he grew irritated with the representatives of the official culture who dominated the group of passengers, he realized that his basic sympathies lay with the subversives, the outsiders. The antagonism of Mark Twain and the cronies, whom he calls "Sinners," for the austere "Pilgrims" is depicted in the description of the Pilgrim Bird in the Marseilles zoo—a passage, incidentally, that was added in revision.

In this situation Mark Twain found himself gravitating toward the role of Mr. Brown rather than that of the straight character. When he revised the *Quaker City* dispatches, therefore, he abolished Brown and parceled out Brown's impertinencies among the Sinners. The transformation was not complete— Mark Twain was in a hurry, and he was always bored with the job of revision; he was so far from realizing the implications of his decision that he actually added a number of passages, such as the rhapsody about the Sphinx, exhibiting the narrator in the role of genteel tourist. But he had at least glimpsed the possibility of using the vernacular character as narrator, and this maneuver, developed in successive episodes, gives a rudimentary coherence to the narrative.

In *Roughing It,* at least in the first half of the book, Mark Twain uses the narrator more effectively. He is a tenderfoot being initiated into the community of men who have "seen the elephant" by undergoing the hardships of prospecting in Nevada. The pronoun "I" as used by the narrator refers simultaneously to this tenderfoot and to the seasoned Old Timer looking back on his own callowness as he tells the story. The subject matter of the narrative—the initiation of the tenderfoot—is thus assimilated into the narrative point of view. The crisis in the narrator's initiation comes in the snowstorm episode; the account of the Buncombe trial reveals him as an accepted member of the community. These chapters show how humorous anecdotes of the sort that had traditionally stood alone could take on new meaning when they were incorporated into a larger narrative pattern. The anecdote of the cayote illustrates the same phenomenon. Here the "town-bred" tenderfoot dog is exposed to the firmer and more durable values of the Far West. At the hands of the Old Timer cayote of unpretentious appearance but hidden power, the tenderfoot gains a fresh (and in this environment, indispensable) humility— although the educational process is painful and the tenderfoot must be humiliated before he can learn his lesson.

Mark Twain's next book after *Roughing It,* written in collaboration with his new neighbor, Charles Dudley Warner, was *The Gilded Age* (1873), a satire on the political corruption involved in Congressional pork-barrel appropriations.[4] Although the authors set out to undercut the sentimental clichés of the contemporary popular novel, they ended up using many novelistic stereotypes themselves, including a melodramatic subplot about a beautiful heroine who shoots her betrayer. Neither a skillful example of the conventional novel nor a successful burlesque of the genre, the book contributed nothing to the solution of Mark Twain's problem of narrative structure. It does, however, contain one unforgettable character, Colonel Sellers; and his creation marks a significant step toward Mark Twain's discovery of his prime literary

[4]**pork-barrel appropriations:** federal projects for local enterprise designed to gain local support for the politician.

resource in what may be called the Matter of Hannibal—the store of boyhood memories that was to provide the substance of his best work for the next thirty years. This material is used even more extensively in "Old Times on the Mississippi," the series of articles he wrote at the instance of Howells for the *Atlantic Monthly* (January—August 1875). These sketches resemble *Roughing It* in being the story of an initiation, and in exploiting the contrast between the callowness of the narrator as a cub pilot and the sophistication with which he looks back on his experiences. The chapters added later to make up the book published as *Life on the Mississippi* (1883) resemble the section on Hawaii in *Roughing It;* they fail to sustain the imaginative power achieved in the "Old Times" series by skillful management of point of view.

In the Preface to *The Adventures of Tom Sawyer* (1876) Mark Twain declares: "Most of the adventures recorded in this book really occurred; one or two were experiences of my own, the rest those of boys who were schoolmates of mine." But the story is told in the third person. It was perhaps a necessary choice for a narrative centering about Tom; his basic conformity makes him an unlikely spokesman for satire directed against the society of Hannibal, and his chronic viewing of experience through the lens of his reading in historical romances would have made it difficult to present either incidents or characters in Tom's words without distortion. But whatever may have been the cause, the management of the narrative is a good deal more awkward than it is in "Old Times on the Mississippi."

Nevertheless, the subject matter almost redeems the uncertainties of technique; the book is truly, as Mark Twain called it later, a prose hymn—to boyhood and to preindustrial America. And the writing of the story brought a priceless stroke of good fortune in the discovery of Huckleberry Finn. Even before *The Adventures of Tom Sawyer* was published, Mark Twain plunged into the writing of the story of "Tom Sawyer's Comrade." In his customary fashion, he put the manuscript aside more than once; it was seven years before he finished it. In the mean-

time he had written *A Tramp Abroad* (1880), a travel book about Europe in which he unfortunately cast himself again in the straight role of genteel traveler, and a carefully constructed children's story, *The Prince and the Pauper* (1882), which has a few echoes of the Matter of Hannibal—the pauper Tom Canty has been described as "an amalgam of the characteristics of Huck Finn and Tom Sawyer." But these books are much thinner in substance than *Tom Sawyer*, and neither represents an advance in narrative technique.

For that, we must turn to the momentous decision to tell Huck's story not only from his point of view but in his own words. The difference between this method of narration and the one used in *Tom Sawyer* can best be seen in a comparison of passages. Here is the description (in *Tom Sawyer*) of Tom's reaction to being unjustly scolded by Aunt Polly for a misdemeanor committed by his half-brother Sid:

He pictured himself lying sick unto death and his aunt bending over him beseeching one little forgiving word, but he would turn his face to the wall, and die with that word unsaid. . . . And he pictured himself brought home from the river, dead, with his curls all wet, and his sore heart at rest. How she would throw herself upon him, and how her tears would fall like rain . . . But he would lie there cold and white and make no sign—a poor little sufferer, whose griefs were at an end. He so worked upon his feelings with the pathos of these dreams, that he had to keep swallowing, he was so like to choke . . .

Mark Twain has in mind here a standard comic device, a form of burlesque that consists in using elevated diction for trivial subjects. He intends to exploit the discrepancy between the slight injury Tom has received and his false dramatization of it. But Mark Twain is not capable of managing the third-person point of view so as to achieve his effect consistently; the exalted language is not located firmly in either Tom's consciousness or the writer's, and the ironic contrast is therefore unstable. A further sign of confusion is the conspicuous colloquialism "he was . . . like to choke," which must be ascribed to the author.

The use of Huck as narrator for *The Adventures of Huckleberry Finn* helps keep things under control. In the following passage, Huck suffers a real injury and is threatened with worse. His Pap has taken him to a cabin on the Illinois shore:

But by-and-by Pap got too handy with his hick'ry, and I couldn't stand it. I was all over welts. He got to going away so much, too, and locking me in. Once he locked me in and was gone three days. It was dreadful lonesome. I judged he had got drowned and I wasn't ever going to get out any more. I was scared. I made up my mind I would fix up some way to leave there.

The elimination of the omniscient author has removed the temptation to comment directly on the action. This not only makes for economy, it prevents confusion about whose language is being used; the reader is not forced to concern himself with the sensibility of an unidentified observer who both is and is not in the story.

Other passages in *Huckleberry Finn* show even more remarkable consequences of the new method. The contrast between Huck's vernacular speech and the high-flown diction of false pathos leads to a discovery of new meanings in the material. When Huck is about to commit himself irrevocably to the awe-inspiring sin of helping Jim escape from slavery, he reports an inner debate in which he tries to defend himself against the accusations of his conscience. His conscience employs the inflated diction of the pulpit, tinged to be sure with Huck's colloquial grammar, but clearly a mode of speech not his own:

. . . it hit me all of a sudden that here was the plain hand of Providence slapping me in the face and letting me know my wickedness was being watched all the time from up there in heaven, whilst I was stealing a poor old woman's nigger that hadn't ever done me no harm, and now was showing me there's One that's always on the lookout, and ain't agoing to allow no such miserable doings to go on only just so fur and no further . . .

The contrast between elevated and vernacular diction becomes here a means of repre-

senting the conflict between what Mark Twain later called Huck's sound heart and his depraved conscience. Without resorting to an abstract technical vocabulary, Mark Twain shows how the mores of a corrupt society have been internalized as Huck's categorical imperatives, and thus come into conflict with his naturally humane impulses.

Unfortunately, the technical discoveries that Mark Twain made in writing *Huckleberry Finn* did not enable him to repeat his triumph. The power of that book depends on more than the use of his memories of the river and the choice of Huck as narrator; it depends also on the theme of freedom versus bondage, which is important in itself and of deep concern to the writer. The overt plot dealing with Jim's effort to escape is reinforced by the indirect statement of the theme of freedom in the contrast between the happiness and peace of Huck and Jim on the raft, and the degraded society of the towns along the shore, where actual slavery is only one aspect of the pervasive fraud, greed, meanness, and gullibility. Mark Twain tried several times to write a sequel to *Huckleberry Finn,* using Huck as narrator. These efforts are mediocre or worse, evidently because they are built around inconsequential themes. The Phelps plantation sequence at the end of *Huckleberry Finn* had already shown the disastrous consequences of substituting a trivial theme for a serious one. When Tom reappears in Chapter 33, the author has decided to abandon the story of how Huck helped his friend in spite of danger and inner suffering. In its place we have a farcical treatment of Jim's escape. Since Tom knows that Jim has been freed in Miss Watson's will, the elaborate ceremonies and paraphernalia that follow are but a prolonged boyish prank. Huck is pushed to the periphery of the narrative as a mere observer; Jim is transformed from a human being into a character from a blackface minstrel show; and in place of the significant action of the middle section of the book, we are given a burlesque of Tom's favorite cloak-and-sword fiction.

The real fable of *Huckleberry Finn* ends up in the air as Huck approaches the Phelps plantation in Chapter 32, helplessly seeking some way to release Jim from the cabin where he is locked up until he can be delivered to his owner. The boyhood Eden of St. Petersburg has been destroyed by Huck's discovery of the truth about the river towns; and although the decadence of these towns might be considered peculiar to the prewar South because it is the result of slavery, there has been a strong hint that Bricksville and its people are but a metaphor for the human condition in general. Colonel Sherburn of Bricksville is all too directly speaking for the author when he says to the mob in front of his house: "I know you clear through. I was born and raised in the South, and I've lived in the North, so I know the average all around. The average man's a coward."

Mark Twain's next book was an effort to test this dark generalization, to determine whether human society could be changed so that the possibility of happiness would not be confined to the dreamlike isolation of a raft. To state the problem more abstractly, Mark Twain now confronted the contradiction between his growing disillusionment concerning human nature and human society and his deeply rooted faith in the idea of progress. *A Connecticut Yankee in King Arthur's Court*, like *Huckleberry Finn*, passed through several stages in the course of its gestation, and the final result was perhaps not at all what the author had intended when he first began playing with the idea of a burlesque of Malory's *Morte d'Arthur*. As the book was finally published, sixth-century Britain is a magnified Bricksville, and Hank Morgan is a vernacular hero, an "ignoramus" devoid of culture but equipped with the whole arsenal of modern technical skills, who is launched upon the magnificent adventure of transforming a sty of filth and poverty and superstition and tyranny into its polar opposite—an enlightened republic where industrialization will provide the material basis for comfort and general happiness.

In the end Hank fails because he is unable to educate "the superstition out of those people." His proclamation of a republic has no effect because the Established Church is able to coerce the populace by an Interdict into supporting the "righteous cause" of monarchy. He is surprised by this outcome, and we must imagine that the author was to some extent surprised also. Mark Twain's career had been sustained by a basic confidence in the sanity, health, and sturdiness of the mass of mankind. He had also assumed that technology was the peculiar possession of the common people as contrasted with the upper classes. Thus democracy and progress—especially the general enlightenment of mankind as a result of industrialization—had seemed to him so closely related that one could not be imagined without the other. But in the course of writing *A Connecticut Yankee* he had become aware that his assumptions might not be valid. Whether we are to seek the cause in outer events of the 1880's or in his penetration to a deeper level of intuitive awareness within himself when he tried to imagine in detail a Utopia of progressive democracy, his loss of faith both in the soundness of the common people and in the benign effects of technology is unmistakable.

This disillusionment deprived Mark Twain's fictive universe of meaning and threatened to paralyze him as a writer. During the last twenty years of his life he produced thousands of pages of manuscript in the form of incomplete stories and novels, some of them running to book length. Recurrent, even obsessive images and situations in this material indicate that he felt enclosed with his family and a few other companions in a hermetically sealed universe. He had the sensation of being bound on an endless voyage to an unknown destination; he was haunted by the idea that he was experiencing a nightmare from which he might at any moment awaken. Most of this late fiction is so baldly symbolic that it fails to create the illusion of reality. But even during the years of financial strain in the early 1890's, Mark Twain was able, by prolonged labor, to bring one major novel to completion. *Pudd'nhead Wilson* (1894) is marred by vestiges of a pair of Siamese twins who originally figured in it and had to be almost surgically removed. Except for this blemish, however, it is an impressive work.

Once again, the setting is a town on the bank of the Mississippi. Pudd'nhead Wilson, isolated from the townspeople by his superior intelligence, belongs to a series of transcendent figures who appear with increasing frequency in Mark Twain's later works. In their developed form—represented by Satan in *The Mysterious Stranger*—these creatures of fantasy enjoy immunity from the constraints of determinism, the sense of guilt, and the limited intellectual horizons that are the bane of all merely human beings. Wilson's transcendence is only rudimentary, but it is perceptible. Through his independent discovery of the principle of identification by means of fingerprints, he solves a murder mystery and establishes the identity of two characters exchanged years before in the cradle. His extraordinary gift of analysis, that is, confers on him the power to intervene decisively in the affairs of the village. The fact that his secret is revealed dramatically in a courtroom scene gives him the air of a grown-up Tom Sawyer. A more serious link between Wilson and the author is the bitter maxims from "Pudd'nhead Wilson's Calendar" placed at the chapter headings: they seem to say that both author and hero have attained a superhuman perspective on mortal affairs. Although Mark Twain does not tell the story in the first person, the general point of view is Wilson's: the author no longer finds congenial the vernacular persona he had adopted in *Huckleberry Finn* and *A Connecticut Yankee*, but is identifying himself with a quite different character. For the transcendent figure has little in common with the vernacular hero.

The sardonic negations of "Puddn'head Wilson's Calendar" are belied by the immense vitality of Roxie, fair of complexion, beautiful of face, noble and stately of carriage, yet "a slave, and saleable as such" because she is one-sixteenth Negro. Her intelligence and force of character are the mainspring of the action. But these human qualities are of no avail against the organized injustice of the slave system. Pudd'nhead

Wilson's revelation of the true state of affairs beneath the deceptive surface of appearances benefits no one: Roxie's son, reared as the "white" heir to a leading citizen, but eventually revealed as a Negro, is sold down the river; the "white" boy who has been reared as a Negro has received the stamp of caste beyond the possibility of change even after his identity is revealed: "He could neither read nor write, and his speech was the basest dialect of the Negro quarter. His gait, his attitudes, his gestures, his bearing, his laugh—all were vulgar and uncouth; his manners were the manners of a slave." As for Roxie herself: ". . . the spirit in her eye was quenched, her martial bearing departed with it, and the voice of her laughter ceased in the land." The story seems to say that the penetration of the surface of society by analytical intelligence is as useless as was Hank Morgan's effort to transform it by means of technology. Since the author has closely identified himself with his principal character, we can hardly avoid finding one of the meanings of the book to be the futility of the artist's revelation of the hidden truth about man and society.

The other important work of fiction published during the last twenty years of Mark Twain's life is the sardonic fable called "The Man That Corrupted Hadleyburg" (1898). Hadleyburg is Hannibal—it is everybody's hometown. The characters are chosen for their commonplaceness, and nothing seems remarkable about the community except its self-righteous claim to be honest. The mysterious stranger who proves the townspeople to be dishonest merely by dropping a sum of money into their midst is another transcendent figure. His motive is said to be revenge, but the offense offered him by the town is never specified, and since his plan to corrupt all the leaders of the community merely provides an occasion for latent dishonesty to show itself, his function resembles Pudd'nhead Wilson's. The emphasis falls on the universality of guilt: the whole human race is tainted and damned.

The other writings of the 1890's now seem of minor importance, although Mark Twain and many of his contemporaries thought highly of the *Personal Recollections of Joan of Arc* (serialized, at first anonymously, to make sure no one would take it for a joke, in *Harper's Magazine* in 1895). Later readers, while recognizing the pathos of the author's fixation upon this story of doomed innocence, have found the characterization of Joan too idolatrous to be convincing. And the presence of a character of such absolute purity imposes on the story the pattern of melodrama: Joan's adversaries are necessarily villains of the deepest dye. *Following the Equator* (1897) is a travel diary produced by force of will in order to pay the author's debts. The short pieces of fiction published during these later years, such as the intensely sentimental "A Horse's Tale" and "A Dog's Tale," are negligible, or worse.

*The Mysterious Stranger*, left unfinished at Mark Twain's death and somewhat arbitrarily constructed by Albert B. Paine through the addition of a last chapter found separately among the author's papers, is of more consequence. It carries to their logical extremity the principal themes of the last period: the inexorable determinism of man's actions; the burdensomeness of life; man's inferiority in consequence of his being endowed with the "moral sense"—i.e., the capacity to feel guilt, which makes him cruel. The angel Satan, nephew of His Satanic Majesty, is the supreme transcendent figure. Like Tom Sawyer arranging Jim's "evasion" from the Phelps plantation, or Hank Morgan industrializing Arthur's Britain, or the stranger who corrupts Hadleyburg, or Pudd'nhead Wilson with his fingerprints, Satan comes from without to intervene in the lives of earth-bound mortals, but it makes no real difference because, as he eventually informs the narrator, "Life itself is only a vision, a dream. . . . Nothing exists save empty space—and you!" It is the only consolation Mark Twain can find for having to continue life as a member of "the damned human race" in a universe apparently presided over by the God preached from all the pulpits:

. . . a God who could make good children as easily as bad, yet preferred to make bad ones; who could have made every one of them happy, yet never made a single happy one; who made them prize their bitter life, yet stingily cut it short; who mouths justice and invented hell—mouths mercy and invented hell—mouths Golden Rules, and forgiveness multiplied by seventy times seven, and invented hell; who created man without invitation, then tries to shuffle the responsibility for man's acts upon man, instead of honorably placing it where it belongs, upon himself; and finally, with altogether divine obtuseness, invites this poor, abused slave to worship him!

The distance from *Huckleberry Finn* to this bleak epilogue is not so great as it might seem: the senseless violence of the Shepherdson-Grangerford feud made Huck sick, and he was ashamed of the human race when he watched the King and the Duke gulling the fellow townsmen of Peter Wilks. But the Mark Twain who is cherished all over the world in our day is the writer who could affirm life in spite of his recognition of the dark abysses in human nature. He continues to be read by many people who are quite indifferent to sophisticated critical opinion. They value him for his humor, which at its best provides some of the world's great comic moments, and for his unmatched depiction of American character and American society in the years of the nation's turbulent, expansive, formless youth. In recent decades he has also come to be recognized as a pioneer technician. The often-quoted, over-dogmatic assertion in Hemingway's *Green Hills of Africa* (1935) that "all modern American literature comes from one book by Mark Twain called *Huckleberry Finn*" has been echoed by Faulkner, who declared that "all of us . . . are his heirs," and by Eliot, who said that he "discovered a new way of writing" by creating "a literary language based on American colloquial speech." Although some critics have rightly pointed out the existence of a different American literary tradition represented by Melville, Hawthorne, and Henry James, Mark Twain's unique and continuing appeal to highbrows and lowbrows alike goes far toward justifying H. L. Mencken's claim that he is "the true father of our national literature."

# PART I:
# THE RIVER AND THE WEST

◊

❨ MARK TWAIN's autobiographical reminiscences consist of fact transformed by the refracting medium of his imagination—even when, as in his *Autobiography*, his conscious intention was to set down events just as they occurred. ". . . I am grown old and my memory is not as active as it used to be," he said on the day when he dictated his description of the Quarles farm. "When I was younger I could remember anything, whether it happened or not; but my faculties are decaying now, and soon I shall be so I cannot remember any but the things that never happened." Nevertheless, the reader who does not confuse imaginative truth with literal fact can find in Mark Twain's work an unmatched record of American experience in the nearer and farther Wests of the mid-nineteenth century.

◊

## FROM THE QUARLES FARM
### *Mark Twain's Autobiography* [1924]

❨ THIS passage was dictated in 1897 or 1898. John Adams Quarles, a genial, open-hearted native of Virginia, married Jane Lampton Clemens' younger sister Martha Ann (nicknamed "Patsy") in Kentucky in 1825. After living for a time in Tennessee, the Quarleses moved westward again in 1834 with Jane Clemens' father, Benjamin Lampton, and settled near the three-year-old village of Florida in Monroe County, Missouri. John Marshall Clemens was Quarles's partner in a general store for a couple of years after he arrived in Missouri, but Mark Twain's recollections of the Quarles farm refer to a period after 1839, when the Clemens family moved from Florida to Hannibal.

M Y U N C L E, John A. Quarles, was a farmer, and his place was in the country four miles from Florida. He had eight children and fifteen or twenty Negroes, and was also fortunate in other ways, particularly in his character. I have not come across a better man than he was. I was his guest for two or three months every year, from the fourth year after we removed to Hannibal till I was eleven or twelve years old. I have never consciously used him or his wife in a book, but his farm has come very handy to me in literature once or twice. In *Huck Finn* and in *Tom Sawyer, Detective* I moved it down to Arkansas. It was all of six hundred miles, but it was no trouble; it was not a very large farm—five hundred acres, perhaps—

but I could have done it if it had been twice as large. And as for the morality of it, I cared nothing for that; I would move a state if the exigencies of literature required it.

It was a heavenly place for a boy, that farm of my uncle John's. The house was a double log one, with a spacious floor (roofed in) connecting it with the kitchen. In the summer the table was set in the middle of that shady and breezy floor, and the sumptuous meals—well, it makes me cry to think of them. Fried chicken, roast pig; wild and tame turkeys, ducks, and geese; venison just killed; squirrels, rabbits, pheasants, partridges, prairie-chickens; biscuits, hot batter cakes, hot buckwheat cakes, hot "wheat bread," hot rolls, hot corn pone; fresh corn boiled on the ear, succotash, butter-beans, string-beans, tomatoes, peas, Irish potatoes, sweet potatoes; buttermilk, sweet milk, "clabber"; watermelons, muskmelons, cantaloupes—all fresh from the garden; apple pie, peach pie, pumpkin pie, apple dumplings, peach cobbler—I can't remember the rest. The way that the things were cooked was perhaps the main splendor—particularly a certain few of the dishes. For instance, the corn bread, the hot biscuits and wheat bread, and the fried chicken. These things have never been properly cooked in the North—in fact, no one there is able to learn the art, so far as my experience goes. The North thinks it knows how to make corn bread, but this is mere superstition. Perhaps no bread in the world is quite so good as Southern corn bread, and perhaps no bread in the world is quite so bad as the Northern imitation of it. The North seldom tries to fry chicken, and this is well; the art cannot be learned north of the line of Mason and Dixon, nor anywhere in Europe. This is not hearsay; it is experience that is speaking. In Europe it is imagined that the custom of serving various kinds of bread blazing hot is "American," but that is too broad a spread; it is custom in the South, but is much less than that in the North. In the North and in Europe hot bread is considered unhealthy. This is probably another fussy superstition, like the European superstition that ice-water is unhealthy. Europe does not need ice-water and does not drink it; and yet, notwithstanding this, its word for it is better than ours, because it describes it, whereas ours doesn't. Europe calls it "iced" water. Our word describes water made from melted ice—a drink which has a characterless taste and which we have but little acquaintance with.

It seems a pity that the world should throw away so many good things merely because they are unwholesome. I doubt if God has given us any refreshment which, taken in moderation, is unwholesome, except microbes. Yet there are people who strictly deprive themselves of each and every eatable, drinkable, and smokable which has in any way acquired a shady reputation. They pay this price for health. And health is all they get for it. How strange it is! It is like paying out your whole fortune for a cow that has gone dry.

The farmhouse stood in the middle of a very large yard, and the yard was fenced on three sides with rails and on the rear side with high palings; against these stood the smoke-house; beyond the palings was the orchard; beyond the orchard were the Negro quarters and the tobacco fields. The front yard was entered over a stile made of sawed-off logs of graduated heights; I do not remember any gate. In a corner of the front yard were a dozen lofty hickory trees and a dozen black walnuts, and in the nutting season riches were to be gathered there.

Down a piece, abreast the house, stood a little log cabin against the rail fence; and there the woody hill fell sharply away, past the barns, the corn-crib, the stables, and the tobacco-curing house, to a limpid brook which sang along over its gravelly bed and curved and frisked in and out and here and there and yonder in the deep shade of overhanging foliage and vines—a divine place for wading, and it had swimming pools, too, which were forbidden to us and therefore much frequented by us. For we were little Christian children and had early been taught the value of forbidden fruit.

In the little log cabin lived a bedridden white-headed slave woman whom we visited daily and looked upon with awe, for we believed she was upward of a thousand years old and had talked with Moses. The younger Negroes credited these statistics and had furnished them to us in good faith. We accommodated all the details which came to us about her; and so we believed that she had lost her health in the long desert trip coming out of Egypt, and had never been able to get it back again. She had a round bald place on the crown of her head, and we used to creep around and gaze at it in reverent silence, and reflect that it was caused by fright through seeing Pharaoh drowned. We called her "Aunt" Hannah, Southern fashion. . . .

All the Negroes were friends of ours, and with those of our own age we were in effect comrades. I say in effect, using the phrase as a modification. We were comrades, and yet not comrades; color and condition interposed a subtle line which both parties were conscious of and which rendered complete fusion impossible. We had a faithful and affectionate good friend, ally, and adviser in "Uncle Dan'l," a middle-aged slave whose head was the best one in the Negro quarter, whose sympathies were wide and warm, and whose heart was honest and simple and knew no guile. He has served me well these many, many years. I have not seen him for more than half a century, and yet spiritually I have had his welcome company a good part of that time, and have staged him in books under his own name and as "Jim," and carted him all around—to Hannibal, down the Mississippi on a raft, and even across the Desert of Sahara in a balloon [1]—and he has endured it all with the patience and friendliness and loyalty which were his birthright. It was on the farm that I got my strong liking for his race and my appreciation of certain of its fine qualities. This feeling and this estimate have stood the test of sixty years and more, and have suffered no impairment. . . .

In my schoolboy days I had no aversion to slavery. I was not aware that there was anything wrong about it. No one arraigned it in my hearing; the local papers said nothing against it; the local pulpit taught us that God approved it, that it was a holy thing, and that the doubter need only look in the Bible if he wished to settle his mind—and then the texts were read aloud to us to make the matter sure; if the slaves themselves had an aversion to slavery, they were wise and said nothing. In Hannibal we seldom saw a slave misused; on the farm, never.

There was, however, one small incident of my boyhood days which touched this matter, and it must have meant a good deal to me or it would not have stayed in my memory, clear and sharp, vivid and shadowless, all these slow-drifting years. We had a little slave boy whom we had hired from some one, there in Hannibal. He was from the eastern shore of Maryland, and had been brought away from his family and his friends, halfway across the American continent, and sold. He was a cheery spirit, innocent and gentle, and the noisiest creature that ever was, perhaps. All day long he was singing, whistling, yelling, whooping, laughing —it was maddening, devastating, unendurable. At last, one day, I lost all my temper, and went raging to my mother and said Sandy had been singing for an hour without a single break, and I couldn't stand it, and *wouldn't* she please shut him up. The tears came into her eyes and her lip trembled, and she said something like this:

THE QUARLES FARM.    1. across . . . balloon: in *Tom Sawyer Abroad.*

"Poor thing, when he sings it shows that he is not remembering, and that comforts me; but when he is still I am afraid he is thinking, and I cannot bear it. He will never see his mother again; if he can sing, I must not hinder it, but be thankful for it. If you were older, you would understand me; then that friendless child's noise would make you glad."

It was a simple speech and made up of small words, but it went home, and Sandy's noise was not a trouble to me any more. She never used large words, but she had a natural gift for making small ones do effective work. She lived to reach the neighborhood of ninety years and was capable with her tongue to the last—especially when a meanness or an injustice roused her spirit. She has come handy to me several times in my books, where she figures as Tom Sawyer's Aunt Polly. I fitted her out with a dialect and tried to think up other improvements for her, but did not find any. I used Sandy once, also; it was in *Tom Sawyer.* I tried to get him to whitewash the fence, but it did not work. I do not remember what name I called him by in the book.[2]

I can see the farm yet, with perfect clearness. I can see all its belongings, all its details; the family room of the house, with a "trundle" bed in one corner and a spinning-wheel in another—a wheel whose rising and falling wail, heard from a distance, was the mournfulest of all sounds to me, and made me homesick and low spirited, and filled my atmosphere with the wandering spirits of the dead; the vast fireplace, piled high, on winter nights, with flaming hickory logs from whose ends a sugary sap bubbled out, but did not go to waste, for we scraped it off and ate it; the lazy cat spread out on the rough hearthstones; the drowsy dogs braced against the jambs and blinking; my aunt in one chimney corner, knitting; my uncle in the other, smoking his corn-cob pipe; the slick and carpetless oak floor faintly mirroring the dancing flame tongues and freckled with black indentations where fire coals had popped out and died a leisurely death; half a dozen children romping in the background twilight; "split"-bottomed chairs here and there, some with rockers; a cradle—out of service, but waiting, with confidence; in the early cold mornings a snuggle of children, in shirts and chemises, occupying the hearthstone and procrastinating—they could not bear to leave that comfortable place and go out on the wind-swept floor space between the house and kitchen where the general tin basin stood, and wash.

2. **what . . . book:** He was also called Jim.

## THE BOYS' AMBITION
FROM *Life on the Mississippi* [1883]

[ THIS was first published in the *Atlantic Monthly,* (January 1875).

WHEN I was a boy, there was but one permanent ambition among my comrades in our village[1] on the west bank of the Mississippi River. That was, to be a steamboatman. We had transient ambitions of other sorts, but they were only transient. When a circus came and went, it left us all burning to become clowns; the first Negro minstrel show that came to our section left us all suffering to try that kind of life; now and then we had a hope that if we lived and were good, God would permit us to be pirates. These ambitions faded out, each in its turn; but the ambition to be a steamboatman always remained.

Once a day a cheap, gaudy packet arrived upward from St. Louis, and another downward from Keokuk. Before these events, the day was glorious with expectancy; after them, the day was a dead and empty thing. Not only the boys, but the whole village, felt this. After all these years I can picture that old time to myself now, just as it was then: the white town drowsing in the sunshine of a summer's morning; the streets empty, or pretty nearly so; one or two clerks sitting in front of the Water Street stores, with their splint-bottomed chairs tilted back against the wall, chins on breasts, hats slouched over their faces, asleep—with shingle-shavings enough around to show what broke them down; a sow and a litter of pigs loafing along the sidewalk, doing a good business in watermelon rinds and seeds; two or three lonely little freight piles scattered about the "levee;" a pile of "skids" on the slope of the stone-paved wharf, and the fragrant town drunkard asleep in the shadow of them; two or three wood flats at the head of the wharf, but nobody to listen to the peaceful lapping of the wavelets against them; the great Mississippi, the majestic, the magnificent Mississippi, rolling its mile-wide tide along, shining in the sun; the dense forest away on the other side; the "point" above the town, and the "point" below, bounding the river-glimpse and turning it into a sort of sea, and withal a very still and brilliant and lonely one. Presently a film of dark smoke appears above one of those remote "points;" instantly a negro drayman, famous for his quick eye and prodigious voice, lifts up the cry, "S-t-e-a-m-boat a-comin'!"

THE BOYS' AMBITION.    1. **our village:** "Hannibal, Missouri" [Mark Twain's note].

and the scene changes! The town drunkard stirs, the clerks wake up, a furious clatter of drays follows, every house and store pours out a human contribution, and all in a twinkling the dead town is alive and moving. Drays, carts, men, boys, all go hurrying from many quarters to a common centre, the wharf. Assembled there, the people fasten their eyes upon the coming boat as upon a wonder they are seeing for the first time. And the boat *is* rather a handsome sight, too. She is long and sharp and trim and pretty; she has two tall, fancy-topped chimneys, with a gilded device of some kind swung between them; a fanciful pilot-house, all glass and "gingerbread," perched on top of the "texas" deck behind them; the paddle-boxes are gorgeous with a picture or with gilded rays above the boat's name; the boiler deck, the hurricane deck, and the texas deck are fenced and ornamented with clean white railings; there is a flag gallantly flying from the jack-staff; the furnace doors are open and the fires glaring bravely; the upper decks are black with passengers; the captain stands by the big bell, calm, imposing, the envy of all; great volumes of the blackest smoke are rolling and tumbling out of the chimneys—a husbanded grandeur created with a bit of pitch pine just before arriving at a town; and the crew are grouped on the forecastle; the broad stage is run far out over the port bow, and an envied deck-hand stands picturesquely on the end of it with a coil of rope in his hand; the pent steam is screaming through the gauge-cocks; the captain lifts his hand, a bell rings, the wheels stop; then they turn back, churning the water to foam, and the steamer is at rest. Then such a scramble as there is to get aboard, and to get ashore, and to take in freight and to discharge freight, all at one and the same time; and such a yelling and cursing as the mates facilitate it all with! Ten minutes later the steamer is under way again, with no flag on the jack-staff and no black smoke issuing from the chimneys. After ten more minutes the town is dead again, and the town drunkard asleep by the skids once more.

My father was a justice of the peace, and I supposed he possessed the power of life and death over all men and could hang anybody that offended him. This was distinction enough for me as a general thing; but the desire to be a steamboatman kept intruding, nevertheless. I first wanted to be a cabin-boy, so that I could come out with a white apron on and shake a table-cloth over the side, where all my old comrades could see me; later I thought I would rather be the deck-hand who stood on the end of the stage-plank with the coil of rope in his hand, because he was particularly conspicuous. But these were only day-dreams,—they were too heavenly to be contemplated as real possibilities. By and by one of our boys went away. He was not heard of for a long time. At last he turned up as apprentice engineer or "striker" on a steamboat. This thing shook the bottom out of all my Sunday-school teachings. That boy had been notoriously worldly, and I just the reverse; yet he was exalted to this eminence, and I left in obscurity and misery. There was nothing generous about this fellow in his greatness. He would always manage to have a rusty bolt to scrub while his boat tarried at our town, and he would sit on the inside guard and scrub it, where we could all see him and envy him and loathe him. And whenever his boat was laid up he would come home and swell around the town in his blackest and greasiest clothes, so that nobody could help remembering that he was a steamboatman; and he used all sorts of steamboat technicalities in his talk, as if he were so used to them that he forgot common people could not understand them. He would speak of the "labboard" side of a horse in an easy, natural way that would make one wish he was dead. And he was always talking about "St. Looy" like an old citizen; he would refer casually to occasions when he "was coming down Fourth Street," or when he was "passing by the Planter's House," or when there was a fire and he took a turn on the brakes [2] of "the old Big Missouri;" and then he would go on and lie about how many towns the size of ours were burned down there that day. Two or three of the boys had long been persons of consideration among us because they had been to St. Louis once and had a vague general knowledge of its wonders, but the day of their glory was over now. They lapsed into a humble silence, and learned to disappear when the ruthless "cub"-engineer approached. This fellow had money, too, and hair oil. Also an ignorant silver watch and a showy brass watch chain. He wore a leather belt and used no suspenders. If ever a youth was cordially admired and hated by his comrades, this one was. No girl could withstand his charms. He "cut out" every boy in the village. When his boat blew up at last, it diffused a tranquil contentment among us such as we had not known for months. But when he came home the next week, alive, renowned, and appeared in church all battered up and bandaged, a shining hero, stared at and wondered over by everybody, it seemed to us that the partiality of Providence for an undeserving reptile had reached a point where it was open to criticism.

This creature's career could produce but one result, and it speedily followed. Boy after boy

2. **brakes:** handles of a pump.

managed to get on the river. The minister's son became an engineer. The doctor's and the post-master's sons became "mud clerks;" the whole-sale liquor dealer's son became a bar-keeper on a boat; four sons of the chief merchant, and two sons of the county judge, became pilots. Pilot was the grandest position of all. The pilot, even in those days of trivial wages, had a princely salary —from a hundred and fifty to two hundred and fifty dollars a month, and no board to pay. Two months of his wages would pay a preacher's sala-ry for a year. Now some of us were left discon-solate. We could not get on the river—at least our parents would not let us.

So by and by I ran away. I said I never would come home again till I was a pilot and could come in glory. But somehow I could not manage it. I went meekly aboard a few of the boats that lay packed together like sardines at the long St. Louis wharf, and very humbly inquired for the pilots, but got only a cold shoulder and short words from mates and clerks. I had to make the best of this sort of treatment for the time being, but I had comforting day-dreams of a future when I should be a great and honored pilot, with plenty of money, and could kill some of these mates and clerks and pay for them.

# LOST IN A SNOWSTORM
## FROM *Roughing It* [1872]

❡ THE narrator is returning with his two companions from Unionville, in the Humboldt mining region, to Carson City, Nevada Territory. Clemens made such a trip in January 1862, with an elderly blacksmith named Tillou and a German named Pfersdorff, but the account in *Roughing It* has evidently been elaborated in the au-thor's imagination.

THE NEXT morning it was still snowing furiously when we got away with our new stock of saddles and accoutrements. We mounted and started. The snow lay so deep on the ground that there was no sign of a road perceptible, and the snow-fall was so thick that we could not see more than a hundred yards ahead, else we could have guided our course by the mountain ranges. The case looked dubious, but Ollendorff said his instinct was as sensitive as any compass, and that he could "strike a bee-line" for Carson city and never diverge from it. He said that if he were to straggle a single point out of the true line his instinct would assail him like an out-raged conscience. Consequently we dropped into his wake happy and content. For half an hour we

poked along warily enough, but at the end of that time we came upon a fresh trail, and Ollendorff shouted proudly:

"I knew I was as dead certain as a compass, boys! Here we are, right in somebody's tracks that will hunt the way for us without any trouble. Let's hurry up and join company with the party."

So we put the horses into as much of a trot as the deep snow would allow, and before long it was evident that we were gaining on our predecessors, for the tracks grew more distinct. We hurried along, and at the end of an hour the tracks looked still newer and fresher—but what surprised us was, that the *number* of travelers in advance of us seemed to steadily increase. We wondered how so large a party came to be traveling at such a time and in such a solitude. Somebody suggested that it must be a company of soldiers from the fort, and so we accepted that solution and jogged along a little faster still, for they could not be far off now. But the tracks still multiplied, and we began to think the platoon of soldiers was miraculously expanding into a regiment—Ballou said they had already increased to five hundred! Presently he stopped his horse and said:

"Boys, these are our own tracks, and we've ac-tually been circussing round and round in a circle for more than two hours, out here in this blind desert! By George this is perfectly hydraulic!"

Then the old man waxed wroth and abusive. He called Ollendorff all manner of hard names—said he never saw such a lurid fool as he was, and ended with the peculiarly venomous opinion that he "did not know as much as a logarythm!"

We certainly had been following our own tracks. Ollendorff and his "mental compass" were in disgrace from that moment. After all our hard travel, here we were on the bank of the stream again, with the inn beyond dimly outlined through the driving snow-fall. While we were considering what to do, the young Swede landed from the canoe and took his pedestrian way Carson-wards, singing his same tiresome song about his "sister and his brother" and "the child in the grave with its mother," and in a short minute faded and dis-appeared in the white oblivion. He was never heard of again. He no doubt got bewildered and lost, and Fatigue delivered him over to Sleep and Sleep betrayed him to Death. Possibly he fol-lowed our treacherous tracks till he became ex-hausted and dropped.

Presently the Overland stage forded the now fast receding stream and started toward Carson on its first trip since the flood came. We hesitated no longer, now, but took up our march in its wake, and trotted merrily along, for we had good confidence in the driver's bump of locality. But our horses were no match for the fresh stage team. We were soon left out of sight; but it was no matter, for we had the deep ruts the wheels made for a guide. By this time it was three in the afternoon, and consequently it was not very long before night came—and not with a lingering twilight, but with a sudden shutting down like a cellar door, as is its habit in that country. The snow-fall was still as thick as ever, and of course we could not see fifteen steps before us; but all about us the white glare of the snow-bed enabled us to discern the smooth sugar-loaf mounds made by the covered sage-bushes, and just in front of us the two faint grooves which we knew were the steadily filling and slowly disappearing wheel-tracks.

Now those sage-bushes were all about the same height—three or four feet; they stood just about seven feet apart, all over the vast desert; each of them was a mere snow-mound, now; in *any* direction that you proceeded (the same as in a well laid out orchard) you would find yourself moving down a distinctly defined avenue, with a row of these snow-mounds on either side of it—an avenue the customary width of a road, nice and level in its breadth, and rising at the sides in the most natural way, by reason of the mounds. But we had not thought of this. Then imagine the chilly thrill that shot through us when it finally occurred to us, far in the night, that since the last faint trace of the wheel-tracks had long ago been buried from sight, we might now be wandering down a mere sage-brush avenue, miles away from the road and diverging further and further away from it all the time. Having a cake of ice slipped down one's back is placid comfort compared to it. There was a sudden leap and stir of blood that had been asleep for an hour, and as sudden a rousing of all the drowsing activities in our minds and bodies. We were alive and awake at once—and shaking and quaking with consternation, too. There was an instant halting and dismounting, a bending low and an anxious scanning of the road-bed. Useless, of course; for if a faint depression could not be discerned from an altitude of four or five feet above it, it certainly could not with one's nose nearly against it.

We seemed to be in a road, but that was no proof. We tested this by walking off in various directions—the regular snow-mounds and the regular avenues between them convinced each man that *he* had found the true road, and that the others had found only false ones. Plainly the situation was desperate. We were cold and stiff and the horses were tired. We decided to build a sage-brush fire and camp out till morning. This was wise, because if we were wandering from the right road and the snow-storm continued another day our case would be the next thing to hopeless if we kept on.

All agreed that a camp fire was what would come nearest to saving us, now, and so we set about building it. We could find no matches, and so we tried to make shift with the pistols. Not a man in the party had ever tried to do such a thing before, but not a man in the party doubted that it *could* be done, and without any trouble—because every man in the party had read about it in books many a time and had naturally come to believe it, with trusting simplicity, just as he had long ago accepted and believed *that other* common book-fraud about Indians and lost hunters making a fire by rubbing two dry sticks together.

We huddled together on our knees in the deep snow, and the horses put their noses together and bowed their patient heads over us; and while the feathery flakes eddied down and turned us into a group of white statuary, we proceeded with the momentous experiment. We broke twigs from a sage bush and piled them on a little cleared place in the shelter of our bodies. In the course of ten or fifteen minutes all was ready, and then, while conversation ceased and our pulses beat low with anxious suspense, Ollendorff applied his revolver, pulled the trigger and blew the pile clear out of the county! It was the flattest failure that ever was.

This was distressing, but it paled before a greater horror—the horses were gone! I had been appointed to hold the bridles, but in my absorbing anxiety over the pistol experiment I had unconsciously dropped them and the released animals had walked off in the storm. It was useless to try to follow them, for their footfalls could make no sound, and one could pass within two yards of the creatures and never see them. We gave them up without an effort at recovering them, and cursed the lying books that said horses would stay by their masters for protection and companionship in a distressful time like ours.

We were miserable enough, before; we felt still more forlorn, now. Patiently, but with blighted hope, we broke more sticks and piled them, and once more the Prussian shot them into annihilation. Plainly, to light a fire with a pistol was an art requiring practice and experience, and the middle of a desert at midnight in a snow-storm was not a good place or time for the acquiring of the accomplishment. We gave it up and tried the other. Each man took a couple of sticks and fell to chafing them together. At the end of half an hour we were thoroughly chilled, and so were the sticks. We bitterly execrated the Indians, the hunters and the books that had betrayed us with the silly device, and wondered dismally what was next to be done. At this critical moment Mr. Ballou fished out four matches from the rubbish of an overlooked pocket. To have found four gold bars would have seemed poor and cheap good luck compared to this. One cannot think how good a match looks under such circumstances—or how lovable and precious, and sacredly beautiful to the eye. This time we gathered sticks with high hopes; and when Mr. Ballou prepared to light the first match, there was an amount of interest centred upon him that pages of writing could not describe. The match burned hopefully a moment, and then went out. It could not have carried more regret with it if it had been a human life. The next match simply flashed and died. The wind puffed the third one out just as it was on the imminent verge of success. We gathered together closer than ever, and developed a solicitude that was rapt and painful, as Mr. Ballou scratched our last hope on his leg. It lit, burned blue and sickly, and then budded into a robust flame. Shading it with his hands, the old gentleman bent gradually down and every heart went with him—everybody, too, for that matter—and blood and breath stood still. The flame touched the sticks at last, took gradual hold upon them—hesitated—took a stronger hold —hesitated again—held its breath five heartbreaking seconds, then gave a sort of human gasp and went out.

Nobody said a word for several minutes. It was a solemn sort of silence; even the wind put on a stealthy, sinister quiet, and made no more noise than the falling flakes of snow. Finally a sad-voiced conversation began, and it was soon apparent that in each of our hearts lay the conviction that this was our last night with the living. I had so hoped that I was the only one who felt so. When the others calmly acknowledged their conviction, it sounded like the summons itself. Ollendorff said:

"Brothers, let us die together. And let us go without one hard feeling towards each other. Let us forget and forgive bygones. I know that you have felt hard towards me for turning over the canoe, and for knowing too much and leading you round and round in the snow—but I meant well; forgive me. I acknowledge freely that I have had hard feelings against Mr. Ballou for abusing me and calling me a logarythm, which is a thing I do not know what, but no doubt a thing considered

disgraceful and unbecoming in America, and it has scarcely been out of my mind and has hurt me a great deal—but let it go; I forgive Mr. Ballou with all my heart, and—"

Poor Ollendorff broke down and the tears came. He was not alone, for I was crying too, and so was Mr. Ballou. Ollendorff got his voice again and forgave me for things I had done and said. Then he got out his bottle of whisky and said that whether he lived or died he would never touch another drop. He said he had given up all hope of life, and although ill-prepared, was ready to submit humbly to his fate; that he wished he could be spared a little longer, not for any selfish reason, but to make a thorough reform in his character, and by devoting himself to helping the poor, nursing the sick, and pleading with the people to guard themselves against the evils of intemperance, make his life a beneficent example to the young, and lay it down at last with the precious reflection that it had not been lived in vain. He ended by saying that his reform should begin at this moment, even here in the presence of death, since no longer time was to be vouchsafed wherein to prosecute it to men's help and benefit—and with that he threw away the bottle of whisky.

Mr. Ballou made remarks of similar purport, and began the reform he could not live to continue, by throwing away the ancient pack of cards that had solaced our captivity during the flood and made it bearable. He said he never gambled, but still was satisfied that the meddling with cards in any way was immoral and injurious, and no man could be wholly pure and blemishless without eschewing them. "And therefore," continued he, "in doing this act I already feel more in sympathy with that spiritual saturnalia necessary to entire and obsolete reform." These rolling syllables touched him as no intelligible eloquence could have done, and the old man sobbed with a mournfulness not unmingled with satisfaction.

My own remarks were of the same tenor as those of my comrades, and I know that the feelings that prompted them were heartfelt and sincere. We were all sincere, and all deeply moved and earnest, for we were in the presence of death and without hope. I threw away my pipe, and in doing it felt that at last I was free of a hated vice and one that had ridden me like a tyrant all my days. While I yet talked, the thought of the good I might have done in the world and the still greater good I might *now* do, with these new incentives and higher and better aims to guide me if I could only be spared a few years longer, overcame me and the tears came again. We put our arms about each other's necks and awaited the warning drowsiness that precedes death by freezing.

It came stealing over us presently, and then we bade each other a last farewell. A delicious dreaminess wrought its web about my yielding senses, while the snow-flakes wove a winding sheet about my conquered body. Oblivion came. The battle of life was done.

I do not know how long I was in a state of forgetfulness, but it seemed an age. A vague consciousness grew upon me by degrees, and then came a gathering anguish of pain in my limbs and through all my body. I shuddered. The thought flitted through my brain, "this is death—this is the hereafter."

Then came a white upheaval at my side, and a voice said, with bitterness:

"Will some gentleman be so good as to kick me behind?"

It was Ballou—at least it was a towzled snow image in a sitting posture, with Ballou's voice.

I rose up, and there in the gray dawn, not fifteen steps from us, were the frame buildings of a stage station, and under a shed stood our still saddled and bridled horses!

An arched snow-drift broke up, now, and Ollendorff emerged from it, and the three of us sat and stared at the houses without speaking a word. We really had nothing to say. We were like the profane man who could not "do the subject justice," the whole situation was so painfully ridiculous and humiliating that words were tame and we did not know where to commence anyhow.

The joy in our hearts at our deliverance was poisoned; well-nigh dissipated, indeed. We presently began to grow pettish by degrees, and sullen; and then, angry at each other, angry at ourselves, angry at everything in general, we moodily dusted the snow from our clothing and in unsociable single file plowed our way to the horses, unsaddled them, and sought shelter in the station.

I have scarcely exaggerated a detail of this curious and absurd adventure. It occurred almost exactly as I have stated it. We actually went into camp in a snow-drift in a desert, at midnight in a storm, forlorn and hopeless, within fifteen steps of a comfortable inn.

For two hours we sat apart in the station and ruminated in disgust. The mystery was gone, now, and it was plain enough why the horses had deserted us. Without a doubt they were under that shed a quarter of a minute after they had left us, and they must have overheard and enjoyed all our confessions and lamentations.

After breakfast we felt better, and the zest of life soon came back. The world looked bright again, and existence was as dear to us as ever. Presently an uneasiness came over me—grew upon me—assailed me without ceasing. Alas, my regeneration was not complete—I wanted to smoke! I resisted with all my strength, but the flesh was weak. I wandered away alone and wrestled with myself an hour. I recalled my promises of reform and preached to myself persuasively, upbraidingly, exhaustively. But it was all vain, I shortly found myself sneaking among the snow-drifts hunting for my pipe. I discovered it after a considerable search, and crept away to hide myself and enjoy it. I remained behind the barn a good while, asking myself how I would feel if my braver, stronger, truer comrades should catch me in my degradation. At last I lit the pipe, and no human being can feel meaner and baser than I did then. I was ashamed of being in my own pitiful company. Still dreading discovery, I felt that perhaps the further side of the barn would be somewhat safer, and so I turned the corner. As I turned the one corner, smoking, Ollendorff turned the other with his bottle to his lips, and between us sat unconscious Ballou deep in a game of "solitaire" with the old greasy cards!

Absurdity could go no farther. We shook hands and agreed to say no more about "reform" and "examples to the rising generation."

# THE CASE OF HYDE VS. MORGAN

## FROM *Roughing It* [1872]

⟨ THERE actually was an Isaac N. Roop who had been first provisional governor of Nevada Territory, and other characters in the sketch bear names suggesting those of actual residents of Nevada: Attorney General Benjamin B. Bunker, for example, and Hal Clayton, a noted Confederate sympathizer.

THE MOUNTAINS are very high and steep about Carson, Eagle and Washoe Valleys—very high and very steep, and so when the snow gets to melting off fast in the Spring and the warm surface-earth begins to moisten and soften, the disastrous landslides commence. The reader cannot know what a land-slide is, unless he has lived in that country and seen the whole side of a mountain taken off some fine morning and deposited down in the valley, leaving a vast, treeless, unsightly scar upon the mountain's front to keep the circumstance fresh in his memory all the years that he may go on living within seventy miles of that place.

General Buncombe was shipped out to Nevada

in the invoice of Territorial officers, to be United States Attorney. He considered himself a lawyer of parts, and he very much wanted an opportunity to manifest it—partly for the pure gratification of it and partly because his salary was Territorially meagre (which is a strong expression). Now the older citizens of a new territory look down upon the rest of the world with a calm, benevolent compassion, as long as it keeps out of the way—when it gets in the way they snub it. Sometimes this latter takes the shape of a practical joke.

One morning Dick Hyde rode furiously up to General Buncombe's door in Carson city and rushed into his presence without stopping to tie his horse. He seemed much excited. He told the General that he wanted him to conduct a suit for him and would pay him five hundred dollars if he achieved a victory. And then, with violent gestures and a world of profanity, he poured out his griefs. He said it was pretty well known that for some years he had been farming (or ranching as the more customary term is) in Washoe District, and making a successful thing of it, and furthermore it was known that his ranch was situated just in the edge of the valley, and that Tom Morgan owned a ranch immediately above it on the mountain side. And now the trouble was, that one of those hated and dreaded land-slides had come and slid Morgan's ranch, fences, cabins, cattle, barns and everything down on top of *his* ranch and exactly covered up every single vestige of his property, to a depth of about thirty-eight feet. Morgan was in possession and refused to vacate the premises—said he was occupying his own cabin and not interfering with anybody else's—and said the cabin was standing on the same dirt and same ranch it had always stood on, and he would like to see anybody make him vacate.

"And when I reminded him," said Hyde, weeping, "that it was on top of my ranch and that he was trespassing, he had the infernal meanness to ask me why didn't I *stay* on my ranch and hold possession when I see him a-coming! Why didn't I *stay* on it, the blathering lunatic—by George, when I heard that racket and looked up that hill it was just like the whole world was a-ripping and a-tearing down that mountain side—splinters, and cord-wood, thunder and lightning, hail and snow, odds and ends of hay stacks, and awful clouds of dust!—trees going end over end in the air, rocks as big as a house jumping 'bout a thousand feet high and busting into ten million pieces, cattle turned inside out and a-coming head on with their tails hanging out between their teeth!—and in the midst of all that wrack and destruction sot that cussed Morgan on his gate-post, a-wondering why

I didn't *stay and hold possession!* Laws bless me, I just took one glimpse, General, and lit out'n the county in three jumps exactly.

"But what grinds me is that that Morgan hangs on there and won't move off'n that ranch—says it's his'n and he's going to keep it—likes it better'n he did when it was higher up the hill. Mad! Well, I've been so mad for two days I couldn't find my way to town—been wandering around in the brush in a starving condition—got anything here to drink, General? But I'm here *now,* and I'm a-going to law. You hear *me!*"

Never in all the world, perhaps, were a man's feelings so outraged as were the General's. He said he had never heard of such high-handed conduct in all his life as this Morgan's. And he said there was no use in going to law—Morgan had no shadow of right to remain where he was—nobody in the wide world would uphold him in it, and no lawyer would take his case and no judge listen to it. Hyde said that right there was where he was mistaken—everybody in town sustained Morgan; Hal Brayton, a very smart lawyer, had taken his case; the courts being in vacation, it was to be tried before a referee, and ex-Governor Roop had already been appointed to that office and would open his court in a large public hall near the hotel at two that afternoon.

The General was amazed. He said he had suspected before that the people of that Territory were fools, and now he knew it. But he said rest easy, rest easy and collect the witnesses, for the victory was just as certain as if the conflict were already over. Hyde wiped away his tears and left.

At two in the afternoon referee Roop's Court opened, and Roop appeared throned among his sheriffs, the witnesses, and spectators, and wearing upon his face a solemnity so awe-inspiring that some of his fellow-conspirators had misgivings that maybe he had not comprehended, after all, that this was merely a joke. An unearthly stillness prevailed, for at the slightest noise the judge uttered sternly the command:

"Order in the Court!"

And the sheriffs promptly echoed it. Presently the General elbowed his way through the crowd of spectators, with his arms full of law-books, and on his ears fell an order from the judge which was the first respectful recognition of his high official dignity that had ever saluted them, and it trickled pleasantly through his whole system:

"Way for the United States Attorney!"

The witnesses were called—legislators, high government officers, ranchmen, miners, Indians, Chinamen, negroes. Three fourths of them were called by the defendant Morgan, but no matter, their testimony invariably went in favor of the plaintiff Hyde. Each new witness only added new testimony to the absurdity of a man's claiming to own another man's property because his farm had slid down on top of it. Then the Morgan lawyers made their speeches, and seemed to make singularly weak ones—they did really nothing to help the Morgan cause. And now the General, with exultation in his face, got up and made an impassioned effort; he pounded the table, he banged the law-books, he shouted, and roared, and howled, he quoted from everything and everybody, poetry, sarcasm, statistics, history, pathos, bathos, blasphemy, and wound up with a grand war-whoop for free speech, freedom of the press, free schools, the Glorious Bird of America and the principles of eternal justice! [Applause.]

When the General sat down, he did it with the conviction that if there was anything in good strong testimony, a great speech and believing and admiring countenances all around, Mr. Morgan's case was killed. Ex-Governor Roop leant his head upon his hand for some minutes, thinking, and the still audience waited for his decision. Then he got up and stood erect, with bended head, and thought again. Then he walked the floor with long, deliberate strides, his chin in his hand, and still the audience waited. At last he returned to his throne, seated himself, and began, impressively:

"Gentlemen, I feel the great responsibility that rests upon me this day. This is no ordinary case. On the contrary it is plain that it is the most solemn and awful that ever man was called upon to decide. Gentlemen, I have listened attentively to the evidence, and have perceived that the weight of it, the overwhelming weight of it, is in favor of the plaintiff Hyde. I have listened also to the remarks of counsel, with high interest—and especially will I commend the masterly and irrefutable logic of the distinguished gentleman who represents the plaintiff. But gentlemen, let us beware how we allow mere human testimony, human ingenuity in argument and human ideas of equity, to influence us at a moment so solemn as this. Gentlemen, it ill becomes us, worms as we are, to meddle with the decrees of Heaven. It is plain to me that Heaven, in its inscrutable wisdom, has seen fit to move this defendant's ranch for a purpose. We are but creatures, and we must submit. If Heaven has chosen to favor the defendant Morgan in this marked and wonderful manner; and if Heaven, dissatisfied with the position of the Morgan ranch upon the mountain side, has chosen to remove it to a position more eligible and more advantageous for its owner, it ill becomes us, insects as we are, to question the legality of the act

or inquire into the reasons that prompted it. No —Heaven created the ranches and it is Heaven's prerogative to rearrange them, to experiment with them, to shift them around at its pleasure. It is for us to submit, without repining. I warn you that this thing which has happened is a thing with which the sacrilegious hands and brains and tongues of men must not meddle. Gentlemen, it is the verdict of this court that the plaintiff, Richard Hyde, has been deprived of his ranch by the visitation of God! And from this decision there is no appeal."

Buncombe seized his cargo of law-books and plunged out of the court-room frantic with indignation. He pronounced Roop to be a miraculous fool, an inspired idiot. In all good faith he returned at night and remonstrated with Roop upon his extravagant decision, and implored him to walk the floor and think for half an hour, and see if he could not figure out some sort of modification of the verdict. Roop yielded at last and got up to walk. He walked two hours and a half, and at last his face lit up happily and he told Buncombe it had occurred to him that the ranch underneath the new Morgan ranch still belonged to Hyde, that his title to the ground was just as good as it had ever been, and therefore he was of opinion that Hyde had a right to dig it out from under there and—

The General never waited to hear the end of it. He was always an impatient and irascible man, that way. At the end of two months the fact that he had been played upon with a joke had managed to bore itself, like another Hoosac Tunnel, through the solid adamant of his understanding.

## THE STORY OF THE OLD RAM

### FROM *Roughing It* [1872]

⟨ THE setting is Virginia City. This version of the story should be compared with the version revised for oral delivery contained in "Platform Readings" (see pp. 749 – 754).

EVERY now and then, in these days, the boys used to tell me I ought to get one Jim Blaine to tell me the stirring story of his grandfather's old ram—but they always added that I must not mention the matter unless Jim was drunk at the time—just comfortably and sociably drunk. They kept this up until my curiosity was on the rack to hear the story. I got to haunting Blaine; but it was of no use, the boys always found fault with his condition; he was often moderately but never satisfactorily drunk. I never watched a man's condition with such absorbing interest, such anxious solicitude; I never so pined to see a man uncompromisingly drunk before. At last, one evening I hurried to his cabin, for I learned that this time his situation was such that even the most fastidious could find no fault with it —he was tranquilly, serenely, symmetrically drunk —not a hiccup to mar his voice, not a cloud upon his brain thick enough to obscure his memory. As I entered, he was sitting upon an empty powder-keg, with a clay pipe in one hand and the other raised to command silence. His face was round, red, and very serious; his throat was bare and his hair tumbled; in general appearance and costume he was a stalwart miner of the period. On the pine table stood a candle, and its dim light revealed "the boys" sitting here and there on bunks, candle-boxes, powder-kegs, etc. They said:

"Sh—! Don't speak—he's going to commence."

### THE STORY OF THE OLD RAM

I found a seat at once, and Blaine said:

"I don't reckon them times will ever come again. There never was a more bullier old ram than what he was. Grand-father fetched him from Illinois—got him of a man by the name of Yates —Bill Yates—maybe you might have heard of him; his father was a deacon—Baptist—and he was a rustler, too; a man had to get up ruther early to get the start of old Thankful Yates; it was him that put the Greens up to jining teams with my grand-father when he moved west. Seth Green was prob'ly the pick of the flock; he married a Wilkerson—Sarah Wilkerson—good cretur, she was—one of the likeliest heifers that was ever raised in old Stoddard, everybody said that knowed her. She could heft a bar'l of flour as easy as I can flirt a flapjack. And spin? Don't mention it! Independent? Humph! When Sile Hawkins come a browsing around her, she let him know that for all his tin he couldn't trot in harness alongside of *her*. You see, Sile Hawkins was— no, it warn't Sile Hawkins, after all—it was a galoot by the name of Filkins—I disremember his first name; but he *was* a stump—come into pra'r meeting drunk, one night, hooraying for Nixon, becuz he thought it was a primary; and old deacon Ferguson up and scooted him through the window and he lit on old Miss Jefferson's head, poor old filly. She was a good soul—had a glass eye and used to lend it to old Miss Wagner, that hadn't any, to receive company in; it warn't big enough, and when Miss Wagner warn't noticing, it would get twisted around in the socket, and look up, maybe, or out to one side, and every which way,

while t' other one was looking as straight ahead as a spy-glass. Grown people didn't mind it, but it most always made the children cry, it was so sort of scary. She tried packing it in raw cotton, but it wouldn't work, somehow—the cotton would get loose and stick out and look so kind of awful that the children couldn't stand it no way. She was always dropping it out, and turning up her old dead-light on the company empty, and making them uncomfortable, becuz *she* never could tell when it hopped out, being blind on that side, you see. So somebody would have to hunch her and say, 'Your game eye has fetched loose, Miss Wagner dear'—and then all of them would have to sit and wait till she jammed it in again—wrong side before, as a general thing, and green as a bird's egg, being a bashful cretur and easy sot back before company. But being wrong side before warn't much difference, anyway, becuz her own eye was sky-blue and the glass one was yaller on the front side, so whichever way she turned it it didn't match nohow. Old Miss Wagner was considerable on the borrow, she was. When she had a quilting, or Dorcas S'iety at her house she gen'ally borrowed Miss Higgins's wooden leg to stump around on; it was considerable shorter than her other pin, but much *she* minded that. She said she couldn't abide crutches when she had company, becuz they were so slow; said when she had company and things had to be done, she wanted to get up and hump herself. She was as bald as a jug, and so she used to borrow Miss Jacops's wig—Miss Jacops was the coffin-peddler's wife—a ratty old buzzard, he was, that used to go roosting around where people was sick, waiting for 'em; and there that old rip would sit all day, in the shade, on a coffin that he judged would fit the can'idate; and if it was a slow customer and kind of uncertain, he'd fetch his rations and a blanket along and sleep in the coffin nights. He was anchored out that way, in frosty weather, for about three weeks, once, before old Robbins's place, waiting for him; and after that, for as much as two years, Jacops was not on speaking terms with the old man, on account of his disapp'inting him. He got one of his feet froze, and lost money, too, becuz old Robbins took a favorable turn and got well. The next time Robbins got sick, Jacops tried to make up with him, and varnished up the same old coffin and fetched it along; but old Robbins was too many for him; he had him in, and 'peared to be powerful weak; he bought the coffin for ten dollars and Jacops was to pay it back and twenty-five more besides if Robbins didn't like the coffin after he'd tried it. And then Robbins died, and at the funeral he bursted off the lid and riz up in his shroud and told the parson to let up on the performances, becuz he could *not* stand such a coffin as that. You see he had been in a trance once before, when he was young, and he took the chances on another, cal'lating that if he made the trip it was money in his pocket, and if he missed fire he couldn't lose a cent. And by George he sued Jacops for the rhino and got jedgment; and he set up the coffin in his back parlor and said he 'lowed to take his time, now. It was always an aggravation to Jacops, the way that miserable old thing acted. He moved back to Indiany pretty soon—went to Wellsville—Wellsville was the place the Hogadorns was from. Mighty fine family. Old Maryland stock. Old Squire Hogadorn could carry around more mixed licker, and cuss better than most any man I ever see. His second wife was the widder Billings—she that was Becky Martin; her dam was deacon Dunlap's first wife. Her oldest child, Maria, married a missionary and died in grace—et up by the savages. They et *him,* too, poor feller—biled him. It warn't the custom, so they say, but they explained to friends of his'n that went down there to bring away his things, that they'd tried missionaries every other way and never could get any good out of 'em—and so it annoyed all his relations to find out that that man's life was fooled away just out of a dern'd experiment, so to speak. But mind you, there ain't anything ever reely lost; everything that people can't understand and don't see the reason of does good if you only hold on and give it a fair shake; Prov'dence don't fire no blank ca'tridges, boys. That there missionary's substance, unbeknowns to himself, actu'ly converted every last one of them heathens that took a chance at the barbacue. Nothing ever fetched them but that. Don't tell *me* it was an accident that he was biled. There ain't no such a thing as an accident. When my uncle Lem was leaning up agin a scaffolding once, sick, or drunk, or suthin, an Irishman with a hod full of bricks fell on him out of the third story and broke the old man's back in two places. People said it was an accident. Much accident there was about that. He didn't know what he was there for, but he was there for a good object. If he hadn't been there the Irishman would have been killed. Nobody can ever make me believe anything different from that. Uncle Lem's dog was there. Why didn't the Irishman fall on the dog? Becuz the dog would a seen him a coming and stood from under. That's the reason the dog warn't appinted. A dog can't be depended on to carry out a special providence. Mark my words it was a put-up thing. Accidents don't happen, boys. Uncle Lem's dog—I wish you could a seen that dog. He

was a reglar shepherd—or ruther he was part bull and part shepherd—splendid animal; belonged to parson Hagar before Uncle Lem got him. Parson Hagar belonged to the Western Reserve Hagars; prime family; his mother was a Watson; one of his sisters married a Wheeler; they settled in Morgan county, and he got nipped by the machinery in a carpet factory and went through in less than a quarter of a minute; his widder bought the piece of carpet that had his remains wove in, and people came a hundred mile to 'tend the funeral. There was fourteen yards in the piece. She wouldn't let them roll him up, but planted him just so—full length. The church was middling small where they preached the funeral, and they had to let one end of the coffin stick out of the window. They didn't bury him—they planted one end, and let him stand up, same as a monument. And they nailed a sign on it and put—put on—put on it—sacred to—the m-e-m-o-r-y—of fourteen y-a-r-d-s—of three-ply—car - - - pet—containing all that was—m-o-r-t-a-l—of—of—W-i-l-l-i-a-m—W-h-e—"

Jim Blaine had been growing gradually drowsy and drowsier—his head nodded, once, twice, three times—dropped peacefully upon his breast, and he fell tranquilly asleep. The tears were running down the boys' cheeks—they were suffocating with suppressed laughter—and had been from the start, though I had never noticed it. I perceived that I was "sold." I learned then that Jim Blaine's peculiarity was that whenever he reached a certain stage of intoxication, no human power could keep him from setting out, with impressive unction, to tell about a wonderful adventure which he had once had with his grandfather's old ram—and the mention of the ram in the first sentence was as far as any man had ever heard him get, concerning it. He always maundered off, interminably, from one thing to another, till his whisky got the best of him and he fell asleep. What the thing was that happened to him and his grandfather's old ram is a dark mystery to this day, for nobody has ever yet found out.

## COLONEL SELLERS
### FROM *The Gilded Age* [1873]

〖 WASHINGTON HAWKINS, in his early twenties, arrives at Hawkeye, Missouri, from the even more remote village where his family has lived for ten years since emigrating from Tennessee. Financial distress has compelled Squire Hawkins to send his son out into the world to seek his fortune under the guidance of Colonel Sellers, an old friend and former business associate of the Squire. Mark Twain declared later that Colonel Sellers was an exact portrait of his mother's cousin, James Lampton. Biographers have seen in Squire Hawkins certain traits of John Marshall Clemens and in Washington Hawkins certain traits of Orion Clemens.

TOWARD evening, the stage-coach came thundering into Hawkeye with a perfectly triumphant ostentation—which was natural and proper, for Hawkeye was a pretty large town for interior Missouri. Washington, very stiff and tired and hungry, climbed out, and wondered how he was to proceed now. But his difficulty was quickly solved. Col. Sellers came down the street on a run and arrived panting for breath. He said:

"Lord bless you—I'm glad to see you, Washington—perfectly delighted to see you, my boy! I got your message. Been on the look-out for you. Heard the stage horn, but had a party I couldn't shake off—man that's got an enormous thing on hand—wants me to put some capital into it—and I tell you, my boy, I could do worse, I could do a deal worse. No, now, let that luggage alone; I'll fix that. Here, Jerry, got anything to do? All right —shoulder this plunder and follow me. Come along, Washington. Lord I'm glad to see you! Wife and the children are just perishing to look at you. Bless you, they won't know you, you've grown so. Folks all well, I suppose? That's good— glad to hear that. We're always going to run down and see them, but I'm into so many operations, and they're not things a man feels like trusting to other people, and so somehow we keep putting it off. Fortunes in them! Good gracious, it's the country to pile up wealth in! Here we are—here's where the Sellers dynasty hangs out. Dump it on the door-step, Jerry—mighty likely boy, is Jerry. That's all right when a man works for me—when a man—why, where the mischief *is* that portmonnaie!—when a—well now that's odd—Oh, now I remember, must have left it at the bank; and b'George I've left my check-book, too— Polly says I ought to have a nurse—well, no matter. Let me have a dime, Washington, if you've got—ah, thanks. Now clear out, Jerry. Here he is, Polly! Washington's come, children!—come now, don't eat him up—finish him in the house. Welcome, my boy, to a mansion that is proud to shelter the son of the best man that walks on the ground. Si Hawkins has been a good friend to me, and I believe I can say that whenever I've had a chance to put him into a good thing I've done it, and done it pretty cheerfully, too. I put him into that sugar speculation—what a grand thing that was, if we hadn't held on too long!"

True enough; but holding on too long had utterly ruined both of them; and the saddest part of it was, that they never had had so much money to lose before, for Sellers's sale of their mule crop that year in New Orleans had been a great financial success. If he had kept out of sugar and gone back home content to stick to mules it would have been a happy wisdom. As it was, he managed to kill two birds with one stone—that is to say, he killed the sugar speculation by holding for high rates till he had to sell at the bottom figure, and that calamity killed the mule that laid the golden egg—which is but a figurative expression and will be so understood. Sellers had returned home cheerful but empty-handed, and the mule business lapsed into other hands. The sale of the Hawkins property by the Sheriff had followed, and the Hawkins' hearts been torn to see Uncle Dan'l and his wife pass from the auction-block into the hands of a negro trader and depart for the remote South to be seen no more by the family. It had seemed like seeing their own flesh and blood sold into banishment.

Washington was greatly pleased with the Sellers mansion. It was a two-story-and-a-half brick, and much more stylish than any of its neighbors. He was borne to the family sitting room in triumph by the swarm of little Sellerses, the parents following with their arms about each other's waists.

The whole family were poorly and cheaply dressed; and the clothing, although neat and clean, showed many evidences of having seen long service. The Colonel's "stovepipe" hat was napless and shiny with much polishing, but nevertheless it had an almost convincing expression about it of having been just purchased new. The rest of his clothing was napless and shiny, too, but it had the air of being entirely satisfied with itself and blandly sorry for other people's clothes. It was growing rather dark in the house, and the evening air was chilly, too. Sellers said:

"Lay off your overcoat, Washington, and draw up to the stove and make yourself at home—just consider yourself under your own shingles my boy—I'll have a fire going, in a jiffy. Light the lamp, Polly, dear, and let's have things cheerful —just as glad to see you, Washington, as if you'd been lost a century and we'd found you again!"

By this time the Colonel was conveying a lighted match into a poor little stove. Then he propped the stove door to its place by leaning the poker against it, for the hinges had retired from business. This door framed a small square of isinglass, which now warmed up with a faint glow. Mrs. Sellers lit a cheap, showy lamp, which dissipated a good deal of the gloom, and then everybody gathered into the light and took the stove into close companionship.

The children climbed all over Sellers, fondled him, petted him, and were lavishly petted in return. Out from this tugging, laughing, chattering disguise of legs and arms and little faces, the Colonel's voice worked its way and his tireless tongue ran blithely on without interruption; and the purring little wife, diligent with her knitting, sat near at hand and looked happy and proud and grateful; and she listened as one who listens to oracles and gospels and whose grateful soul is being refreshed with the bread of life. Bye and bye the children quieted down to listen; clustered about their father, and resting their elbows on his legs, they hung upon his words as if he were uttering the music of the spheres.

A dreary old hair-cloth sofa against the wall; a few damaged chairs; the small table the lamp stood on; the crippled stove—these things constituted the furniture of the room. There was no carpet on the floor; on the wall were occasional square-shaped interruptions of the general tint of the plaster which betrayed that there used to be pictures in the house—but there were none now. There were no mantel ornaments, unless one might bring himself to regard as an ornament a clock which never came within fifteen strokes of striking the right time, and whose hands always hitched together at twenty-two minutes past anything and traveled in company the rest of the way home.

"Remarkable clock!" said Sellers, and got up and wound it. "I've been offered—well, I wouldn't expect you to believe what I've been offered for that clock. Old Gov. Hager never sees me but he says, 'Come, now, Colonel, name your price—I *must* have that clock!' But my goodness I'd as soon think of selling my wife. As I was saying to ———silence in the court, now, she's begun to strike! You can't talk against her—you have to just be patient and hold up till she's said her say. Ah—well, as I was saying, when—she's beginning again! Nineteen, twenty, twenty-one, twenty-two, twen———ah, that's all.—Yes, as I was saying to old Judge———go it, old girl, don't mind me.— Now how is that?—isn't that a good, spirited tone? She can wake the dead! Sleep? Why you might as well try to sleep in a thunder-factory. Now just listen at that. She'll strike a hundred and fifty, now, without stopping,—you'll see. There ain't another clock like that in Christendom."

Washington hoped that this might be true, for

the din was distracting—though the family, one and all, seemed filled with joy; and the more the clock "buckled down to her work" as the Colonel expressed it, and the more insupportable the clatter became, the more enchanted they all appeared to be. When there was silence, Mrs. Sellers lifted upon Washington a face that beamed with a childlike pride, and said:

"It belonged to his grandmother."

The look and the tone were a plain call for admiring surprise, and therefore Washington said— (it was the only thing that offered itself at the moment:)

"Indeed!"

"Yes, it did, didn't it, father!" exclaimed one of the twins. "She was my great-grandmother— and George's too; wasn't she, father! *You* never saw her, but Sis has seen her, when Sis was a baby—didn't you, Sis! Sis has seen her most a hundred times. She was awful deaf—she's dead, now. Ain't she, father!"

All the children chimed in, now, with one general Babel of information about deceased—nobody offering to read the riot act or seeming to discountenance the insurrection or disapprove of it in any way—but the head twin drowned all the turmoil and held his own against the field:

"It's our clock, now—and it's got wheels inside of it, and a thing that flutters every time she strikes —don't it, father! Great-grandmother died before hardly any of us was born—she was an Old-School Baptist and had warts all over her—you ask father if she didn't. She had an uncle once that was bald-headed and used to have fits; he wasn't *our* uncle, I don't know what he was to us —some kin or another I reckon—father's seen him a thousand times—hain't you, father! We used to have a calf that et apples and just chawed up dishrags like nothing, and if you stay here you'll see lots of funerals—won't he, Sis! Did you ever see a house afire? *I* have! Once me and Jim Terry———"

But Sellers began to speak now, and the storm ceased. He began to tell about an enormous speculation he was thinking of embarking some capital in—a speculation which some London bankers had been over to consult with him about—and soon he was building glittering pyramids of coin, and Washington was presently growing opulent under the magic of his eloquence. But at the same time Washington was not able to ignore the cold entirely. He was nearly as close to the stove as he could get, and yet he could not persuade himself that he felt the slightest heat, notwithstanding the isinglass door was still gently and serenely glowing. He tried to get a trifle closer to the stove, and the consequence was, he tripped the supporting poker and the stove-door tumbled to the floor. And then there was a revelation—there was nothing in the stove but a lighted tallow-candle!

The poor youth blushed and felt as if he must die with shame. But the Colonel was only disconcerted for a moment—he straightway found his voice again:

"A little idea of my own, Washington—one of the greatest things in the world! You must write and tell your father about it—don't forget that, now. I have been reading up some European Scientific reports—friend of mine, Count Fugier, sent them to me—sends me all sorts of things from Paris—he thinks the world of me, Fugier does. Well, I saw that the Academy of France had been testing the properties of heat, and they came to the conclusion that it was a non-conductor or something like that, and of course its influence must necessarily be deadly in nervous organizations with excitable temperaments, especially where there is any tendency toward rheumatic affections. Bless you I saw in a moment what was the matter with us, and says I, out goes your fires!—no more slow torture and certain death for me, sir. What you want is the *appearance* of heat, not the heat itself—that's the idea. Well how to do it was the next thing. I just put my head to work, pegged away a couple of days, and here you are! Rheumatism? Why a man can't any more start a case of rheumatism in this house than he can shake an opinion out of a mummy! Stove with a candle in it and a transparent door—that's it—it has been the salvation of this family. Don't you fail to write your father about it, Washington. And tell him the idea is mine—I'm no more conceited than most people, I reckon, but you know it is human nature for a man to want credit for a thing like that."

Washington said with his blue lips that he would, but he said in his secret heart that he would promote no such iniquity. He tried to believe in the healthfulness of the invention, and succeeded tolerably well; but after all he could not feel that good health in a frozen body was any real improvement on the rheumatism.

*[Two months later].*

The Sellers family were just starting to dinner when Washington burst upon them. . . . For an instant the Colonel looked nonplussed, and just a bit uncomfortable; and Mrs. Sellers looked actually distressed; but the next moment the head of the house was himself again, and exclaimed:

"All right, my boy, all right—always glad to see you—always glad to hear your voice and take you by the hand. Don't wait for special invitations—that's all nonsense among friends. Just come whenever you can, and come as often as you can—the oftener the better. You can't please us any better than that, Washington; the little woman will tell you so herself. We don't pretend to style. Plain folks, you know—plain folks. Just a plain family dinner, but such as it is, our friends are *always* welcome, I reckon you know that yourself, Washington. Run along, children, run along; Lafayette,[1] stand off the cat's tail, child, can't you see what you're doing?—Come, come, come, Roderick Dhu, it isn't nice for little boys to hang onto young gentlemen's coat tails—but never mind him, Washington, he's full of spirits and don't mean any harm. Children will be children, you know. Take the chair next to Mrs. Sellers, Washington—tut, tut, Marie Antoinette, let your brother have the fork if he wants it, you are bigger than he is."

Washington contemplated the banquet, and wondered if he were in his right mind. Was this the plain family dinner? And was it all present? It was soon apparent that this was indeed the dinner: it was all on the table: it consisted of abundance of clear, fresh water, and a basin of raw turnips—nothing more.

Washington stole a glance at Mrs. Sellers's face, and would have given the world, the next moment, if he could have spared her that. The poor woman's face was crimson, and the tears stood in her eyes. Washington did not know what to do. He wished he had never come there and spied out this cruel poverty and brought pain to that poor little lady's heart and shame to her cheek; but he was there, and there was no escape. Col. Sellers hitched back his coat sleeves airily from his wrists as who should say *"Now* for solid enjoyment!" seized a fork, flourished it and began to harpoon turnips and deposit them in the plates before him:

"Let me help you, Washington—Lafayette, pass this plate to Washington—ah, well, well, my boy, things are looking pretty bright, now, *I* tell

COLONEL SELLERS.   1. Lafayette: "In those old days the average man called his children after his most revered literary and historical idols; consequently there was hardly a family, at least in the West, but had a Washington in it—and also a Lafayette, a Franklin, and six or eight sounding names from Byron, Scott, and the Bible, if the offspring held out. To visit such a family, was to find one's self confronted by a congress made up of representatives of the imperial myths and the majestic dead of all the ages. There was something thrilling about it, to a stranger, not to say awe inspiring" [M T].

you. Speculation—my! the whole atmosphere's full of money. I wouldn't take three fortunes for one little operation I've got on hand now—have anything from the casters? No? Well, you're right, you're right. Some people like mustard with turnips, but—now there was Baron Poniatowski—Lord, but that man did know how to live!—true Russian you know, Russian to the back bone; I say to my wife, give me a Russian every time, for a table comrade. The Baron used to say, 'Take mustard, Sellers, try the mustard,—a man *can't* know what turnips are in perfection without mustard,' but I always said, 'No, Baron, I'm a plain man, and I want my food plain—none of your embellishments for Eschol Sellers—no made dishes for me!' And it's the best way – high living kills more than it cures in this world, you can rest assured of that.—Yes indeed, Washington, I've got one little operation on hand that—take some more water—help yourself, won't you?—help yourself, there's plenty of it.—You'll find it pretty good, I guess. How does that fruit strike you?"

Washington said he did not know that he had ever tasted better. He did not add that he detested turnips even when they were cooked—loathed them in their natural state. No, he kept this to himself, and praised the turnips to the peril of his soul.

"I thought you'd like them. Examine them—examine them—they'll bear it. See how perfectly firm and juicy they are—they can't start any like them in this part of the country, I can tell you. These are from New Jersey—I imported them myself. They cost like sin, too; but lord bless me, I go in for having the best of a thing, even if it does cost a little more—it's the best economy, in the long run. These are the Early Malcolm—it's a turnip that can't be produced except in just one orchard, and the supply never is up to the demand. Take some more water, Washington—you can't drink too much water with fruit—all the doctors say that. The plague can't come where this article is, my boy!"

"Plague? What plague?"

"What plague, indeed? Why the Asiatic plague that nearly depopulated London a couple of centuries ago."

"But how does that concern us? There is no plague here, I reckon."

"Sh! I've let it out! Well, never mind—just keep it to yourself. Perhaps I oughtn't said anything, but it's *bound* to come out sooner or later, so what is the odds? Old McDowells wouldn't like me to—to—bother it all, I'll just tell the whole thing and let it go. You see, I've been down to St. Louis, and I happened to run across old Dr.

McDowells—thinks the world of me, does the doctor. He's a man that keeps himself to himself, and well he may, for he knows that he's got a reputation that covers the whole earth—he won't condescend to open himself out to many people, but lord bless you, he and I are just like brothers; he won't let me go to a hotel when I'm in the city—says I'm the only man that's company to him, and I don't know but there's some truth in it, too, because although I never like to glorify myself and make a great to-do over what I am or what I can do or what I know, I don't mind saying here among friends that I *am* better read up in most sciences, maybe, than the general run of professional men in these days. Well, the other day he let me into a little secret, strictly on the quiet, about this matter of the plague.

"You see it's booming right along in our direction—follows the Gulf Stream, you know, just as all those epidemics do,—and within three months it will be just waltzing through this land like a whirlwind! And whoever it touches can make his will and contract for the funeral. Well you can't *cure* it, you know, but you can prevent it. How? Turnips! that's it! Turnips and water! Nothing like it in the world, old McDowells says, just fill yourself up two or three times a day, and you can snap your fingers at the plague. Sh!—keep mum, but just you confine yourself to that diet and you're all right. I wouldn't have old McDowells know that I told about it for anything—he never would speak to me again. Take some more water, Washington—the more water you drink, the better. Here, let me give you some more of the turnips. No, no, no, now, I insist. There, now. Absorb those. They're mighty sustaining —brim full of nutriment—all the medical books say so. Just eat from four to seven good-sized turnips at a meal, and drink from a pint and a half to a quart of water, and then just sit around a couple of hours and let them ferment. You'll feel like a fighting cock next day."

Fifteen or twenty minutes later the Colonel's tongue was still chattering away—he had piled up several future fortunes out of several incipient "operations" which he had blundered into within the past week, and was now soaring along through some brilliant expectations born of late promising experiments upon the lacking ingredient of the eye-water.[2] And at such a time Washington ought to have been a rapt and enthusiastic listener, but he was not, for two matters disturbed his mind and distracted his attention. One was,

2. eye-water: "Sellers's Infallible Imperial Oriental Optic Liniment and Salvation for Sore Eyes," which the Colonel is trying to perfect by discovering the one essential ingredient not yet identified.

that he discovered, to his confusion and shame, that in allowing himself to be helped a second time to the turnips, he had robbed those hungry children. He had not needed the dreadful "fruit," and had not wanted it; and when he saw the pathetic sorrow in their faces when they asked for more and there was no more to give them, he hated himself for his stupidity and pitied the famishing young things with all his heart. The other matter that disturbed him was the dire inflation that had begun in his stomach. It grew and grew, it became more and more insupportable. Evidently the turnips were "fermenting." He forced himself to sit still as long as he could, but his anguish conquered him at last.

He rose in the midst of the Colonel's talk and excused himself on the plea of a previous engagement. The Colonel followed him to the door, promising over and over again that he would use his influence to get some of the Early Malcolms for him, and insisting that he should not be such a stranger but come and take pot-luck with him every chance he got. Washington was glad enough to get away and feel free again. He immediately bent his steps toward home.

In bed he passed an hour that threatened to turn his hair gray, and then a blessed calm settled down upon him that filled his heart with gratitude. Weak and languid, he made shift to turn himself about and seek rest and sleep; and as his soul hovered upon the brink of unconsciousness, he heaved a long, deep sigh, and said to himself that in his heart he had cursed the Colonel's preventive of rheumatism, before, and now *let* the plague come if it must—he was done with preventives; if ever any man beguiled him with turnips and water again, let him die the death.

# PART II:
# SOME ANIMALS

◊

❨ MARK TWAIN's interest in animals is conspicuous from beginning to end of his career. It appears, for example, in the sympathetic attention to the "fiery untamed steed" in the production of *Mazeppa* and in the observation that the horses of the travelers lost in the Nevada snowstorm "were under that shed a quarter of a minute after they had left us, and. . . must have overheard and enjoyed all our confessions and lamentations" (above, p. 704). The passages about animals reprinted

in this section, covering a span of thirty years, are among the most amusing things Mark Twain ever wrote; limitation of space has made it necessary to omit others equally good, such as the description of the horse Oahu in his dispatches from the Sandwich Islands. Like the cayote in the selections here, Mark Twain's animals usually have a vernacular point of view, but not always: the camel who eats the narrator's overcoat in Chapter 3 of *Roughing It* is definitely one of the genteel, or would-be genteel, and so is the Pilgrim Bird described below.

◊

## CRUELTY TO ANIMALS:
## THE HISTRIONIC PIG

❨ FIRST published in the San Francisco *Alta California* under the date line New York, April 30, 1867, this text is from *Mark Twain's Travels with Mr. Brown*, ed. by Franklin Walker and G. Ezra Dane (1940).

ONE OF the most praiseworthy institutions in New York, and one which must plead eloquently for it when its wickedness shall call down the anger of the gods, is the Society for the Prevention of Cruelty to Animals. Its office is located on the corner of Twelfth street and Broadway, and its affairs are conducted by humane men who take a genuine interest in their work, and who have got worldly wealth enough to make it unnecessary for them to busy themselves about anything else. They have already put a potent check upon the brutality of draymen and others to their horses, and in future will draw a still tighter rein upon such abuses, a late law of the Legislature having quadrupled their powers, and distinctly marked and specified them. You seldom see a horse beaten or otherwise cruelly used in New York now, so much has the society made itself feared and respected. Its members promptly secure the arrest of guilty parties and relentlessly prosecute them.

The new law gives the Society power to designate an adequate number of agents in every county, and these are appointed by the Sheriff, but work independently of all other branches of the civil organization. They can make arrests of guilty persons on the spot, without calling upon the regular police, and what is better, they can compel a man to stop abusing his horse, his dog, or any other animal, at a moment's warning. The object of the Society, as its name implies, is to prevent cruelty to animals, rather than punish men for being guilty of it.

They are going to put up hydrants and water tanks at convenient distances all over the city, for drinking places for men, horses and dogs.

Mr. Bergh,[1] the President of the Society, is a sort of enthusiast on the subject of cruelty to animals—or perhaps it would do him better justice to say he is full of honest earnestness upon the subject. Nothing that concerns the happiness of a brute is a trifling matter with him—no brute of whatever position or standing, however plebeian or insignificant, is beneath the range of his merciful interest. I have in my mind an example of his kindly solicitude for his dumb and helpless friends.

He went to see the dramatic version of "Griffith Gaunt"[2] at Wallack's Theatre.[3] The next morning he entered the manager's office and the following conversation took place:

*Mr. Bergh*—"Are you the manager of this theatre?"

*Manager*—"I am, sir. What can I do for you?"

*Mr. B.*—"I am President of the Society for the Prevention of Cruelty to Animals, and I have come to remonstrate against your treatment of that pig in the last act of the play last night. It is cruel and wrong, and I beg that you will leave the pig out in future."

"That is impossible! The pig is necessary to the play."

"But it is cruel, and you could alter the play in some way so as to leave the pig out."

"It cannot possibly be done, and besides I do not see anything wrong about it at all. What is it you complain of?"

"Why, it is plain enough. They punch the pig with sticks, and chase him and harass him, and contrive all manner of means to make him unhappy. The poor thing runs about in its distress, and tries to escape, but is met at every turn by its tormentors and its hopes blighted. The pig does not understand it. If the pig understood it, it might be well enough, but the pig does not know it is a play, but takes it all as reality, and is frightened and bewildered by the crowd of people and the glare of the lights, and yet no time is given it for reflection—no time is given it to arrive at a just appreciation of its circumstances—but its persecutors constantly assail it and keep its mind in such a chaotic state that it can form no opinion upon any point in the case. And besides, the pig is cast in the play without its consent, is forced to conduct itself in a manner which cannot but be humiliating to it, and leaves that stage every night with a conviction that it would rather die than take a character in a theatrical performance again. Pigs

are not fitted for the stage; they have no dramatic talent; all their inclinations are toward a retired and unostentatious career in the humblest walks of life, and——"

*Manager*—"Say no more, sir. The pig is yours. I meant to have educated him for tragedy and made him a blessing to mankind and an ornament to his species, but I am convinced, now, that I ought not to do this in the face of his marked opposition to the stage, and so I present him to you, who will treat him well, I am amply satisfied. I am the more willing to part with him, since the play he performs in was taken off the stage last night, and I could not conveniently arrange a part for him in the one we shall run for the next three weeks, which is Richard III."

# THE CAYOTE

## FROM *Roughing It* [1872]

THE CAYOTE is a long, slim, sick and sorry-looking skeleton, with a gray wolf-skin stretched over it, a tolerably bushy tail that forever sags down with a despairing expression of forsakenness and misery, a furtive and evil eye, and a long, sharp face, with slightly lifted lip and exposed teeth. He has a general slinking expression all over. The cayote is a living, breathing allegory of Want. He is *always* hungry. He is always poor, out of luck and friendless. The meanest creatures despise him, and even the fleas would desert him for a velocipede. He is so spiritless and cowardly that even while his exposed teeth are pretending a threat, the rest of his face is apologizing for it. And he is *so* homely!—so scrawny, and ribby, and coarse-haired, and pitiful. When he sees you he lifts his lip and lets a flash of his teeth out, and then turns a little out of the course he was pursuing, depresses his head a bit, and strikes a long, soft-footed trot through the sage-brush, glancing over his shoulder at you, from time to time, till he is about out of easy pistol range, and then he stops and takes a deliberate survey of you; he will trot fifty yards and stop again—another fifty and stop again; and finally the gray of his gliding body blends with the gray of the sage-brush, and he disappears. All this is when you make no demonstration against him; but if you do, he develops a livelier interest in his journey, and instantly electrifies his heels and puts such a deal of real estate between himself and your weapon, that by the time you have raised the hammer you see that you need a minie rifle, and by the time you have got him in line you need a rifled can-

---

CRUELTY TO ANIMALS: THE HISTRIONIC PIG. 1. **Mr. Bergh:** Henry Bergh (1811–88), who had obtained the first charter for the American S.P.C.A. in 1866. 2. **"Griffith Gaunt":** Augustin Daly's dramatization of Charles Reade's novel, first produced on November 7, 1866. 3. **Wallack's Theatre:** on Broadway at 13th Street.

non, and by the time you have "drawn a bead" on him you see well enough that nothing but an unusually long-winded streak of lightning could reach him where he is now. But if you start a swift-footed dog after him, you will enjoy it ever so much—especially if it is a dog that has a good opinion of himself, and has been brought up to think he knows something about speed. The cayote will go swinging gently off on that deceitful trot of his, and every little while he will smile a fraudful smile over his shoulder that will fill that dog entirely full of encouragement and worldly ambition, and make him lay his head still lower to the ground, and stretch his neck further to the front, and pant more fiercely, and stick his tail out straighter behind, and move his furious legs with a yet wilder frenzy, and leave a broader and broader, and higher and denser cloud of desert sand smoking behind, and marking his long wake across the level plain! And all this time the dog is only a short twenty feet behind the cayote, and to save the soul of him he cannot understand why it is that he cannot get perceptibly closer; and he begins to get aggravated, and it makes him madder and madder to see how gently the cayote glides along and never pants or sweats or ceases to smile; and he grows still more and more incensed to see how shamefully he has been taken in by an entire stranger, and what an ignoble swindle that long, calm, soft-footed trot is; and next he notices that he is getting fagged, and that the cayote actually has to slacken speed a little to keep from running away from him—and *then* that town-dog is mad in earnest, and he begins to strain and weep and swear, and paw the sand higher than ever, and reach for the cayote with concentrated and desperate energy. This "spurt" finds him six feet behind the gliding enemy, and two miles from his friends. And then, in the instant that a wild new hope is lighting up his face, the cayote turns and smiles blandly upon him once more, and with a something about it which seems to say: "Well, I shall have to tear myself away from you, bub—business is business, and it will not do for me to be fooling along this way all day"—and forthwith there is a rushing sound, and the sudden splitting of a long crack through the atmosphere, and behold that dog is solitary and alone in the midst of a vast solitude!

It makes his head swim. He stops, and looks all around; climbs the nearest sand-mound, and gazes into the distance; shakes his head reflectively, and then, without a word, he turns and jogs along back to his train, and takes up a humble position under the hindmost wagon, and feels unspeakably mean, and looks ashamed, and hangs his tail at half-mast for a week. And for as much as a year after that, whenever there is a great hue and cry after a cayote, that dog will merely glance in that direction without emotion, and apparently observe to himself, "I believe I do not wish any of the pie."

## TOM QUARTZ, THE CAT
### FROM *Roughing It* [1872]

❲ DICK BAKER is a fictional name for Jim Gillis, the pocket-miner whom Mark Twain visited on Jackass Hill in the winter of 1864–65.

ONE OF my comrades there—another of those victims of eighteen years of unrequited toil and blighted hopes—was one of the gentlest spirits that ever bore its patient cross in a weary exile: grave and simple Dick Baker, pocket-miner of Dead-House Gulch.—He was forty-six, gray as a rat, earnest, thoughtful, slenderly educated, slouchily dressed and clay-soiled, but his heart was finer metal than any gold his shovel ever brought to light—than any, indeed, that ever was mined or minted.

Whenever he was out of luck and a little downhearted, he would fall to mourning over the loss of a wonderful cat he used to own (for where women and children are not, men of kindly impulses take up with pets, for they must love something). And he always spoke of the strange sagacity of that cat with the air of a man who believed in his secret heart that there was something human about it—maybe even supernatural.

I heard him talking about this animal once. He said:

"Gentlemen, I used to have a cat here, by the name of Tom Quartz, which you'd a took an interest in I reckon—most any body would. I had him here eight year—and he was the remarkablest cat *I* ever see. He was a large gray one of the Tom specie, an' he had more hard, natchral sense than any man in this camp—'n' a *power* of dignity—he wouldn't let the Gov'ner of Californy be familiar with him. He never ketched a rat in his life—'peared to be above it. He never cared for nothing but mining. He knowed more about mining, that cat did, than any man *I* ever, ever see. You couldn't tell *him* noth'n' 'bout placer diggin's—'n' as for pocket mining, why he was just born for it. He would dig out after me an' Jim when we went over the hills prospect'n', and he would trot along behind us for as much as five mile, if we went so fur. An' he had the best judgment about mining ground—why you never see anything like it. When we went to work, he'd scatter a glance around, 'n' if he didn't think much of the indications, he would give a look as much as to say, 'Well, I'll have to get you to excuse *me,*' 'n' without another word he'd hyste his nose into the air 'n' shove for home. But if the ground suited him, he would lay low 'n' keep dark till the first pan was washed, 'n' then he would sidle up 'n' take a look, an' if there was about six or seven grains of gold *he* was satisfied—he didn't want no better prospect 'n' that—'n' then he would lay down on our coats and snore like a steamboat till we'd struck the pocket, an' then get up 'n' superintend. He was nearly lightnin' on superintending.

"Well, bye an' bye, up comes this yer quartz excitement. Every body was into it—every body was pick'n' 'n' blast'n' instead of shovelin' dirt on the hill side—every body was put'n' down a shaft instead of scrapin' the surface. Noth'n' would do Jim, but *we* must tackle the ledges, too, 'n' so we did. We commenced put'n' down a shaft, 'n' Tom Quartz he begin to wonder what in the Dickens it was all about. *He* hadn't ever seen any mining like that before, 'n' he was all upset, as you may say—he couldn't come to a right understanding of it no way—it was too many for *him*. He was down on it, too, you bet you—he was down on it powerful—'n' always appeared to consider it the cussedest foolishness out. But that cat, you know, was *always* agin new fangled arrangements— somehow he never could abide 'em. *You* know how it is with old habits. But by an' by Tom Quartz begin to git sort of reconciled a little, though he never *could* altogether understand that eternal sinkin' of a shaft an' never pannin' out any thing. At last he got to comin' down in the shaft, hisself, to try to cipher it out. An' when he'd git the blues, 'n' feel kind o' scruffy, 'n' aggravated 'n' disgusted—knowin' as he did, that the bills was runnin' up all the time an' we warn't makin' a cent—he would curl up on a gunny sack in the corner an' go to sleep. Well, one day when the shaft was down about eight foot, the rock got so hard that we had to put in a blast—the first blast'n' we'd ever done since Tom Quartz was born. An' then we lit the fuse 'n' clumb out 'n' got off 'bout fifty yards—'n' forgot 'n' left Tom Quartz sound asleep on the gunny sack. In 'bout a minute we seen a puff of smoke bust up out of the hole, 'n' then everything let go with an awful crash, 'n' about four million ton of rocks 'n' dirt 'n' smoke 'n' splinters shot up 'bout a mile an' a half into the air, an' by George, right in the dead centre of it was old Tom Quartz a goin' end over end, an' a snortin' an' a sneez'n', an' a clawin' an' a reachin'

for things like all possessed. But it warn't no use, you know, it warn't no use. An' that was the last we see of *him* for about two minutes 'n' a half, an' then all of a sudden it begin to rain rocks and rubbage, an' directly he come down ker-whop about ten foot off f'm where we stood. Well, I reckon he was p'raps the orneriest lookin' beast you ever see. One ear was sot back on his neck, 'n' his tail was stove up, 'n' his eye-winkers was swinged off, 'n' he was all blacked up with powder an' smoke, an' all sloppy with mud 'n' slush f'm one end to the other. Well sir, it warn't no use to try to apologize—we couldn't say a word. He took a sort of a disgusted look at hisself, 'n' then he looked at us—an' it was just exactly the same as if he had said—'Gents, may be *you* think it's smart to take advantage of a cat that 'ain't had no experience of quartz minin', but *I* think *different'*—an' then he turned on his heel 'n' marched off home without ever saying another word.

"That was jest his style. An' may be you won't believe it, but after that you never see a cat so prejudiced agin quartz mining as what he was. An' by an' bye when he *did* get to goin' down in the shaft agin, you'd 'a been astonished at his sagacity. The minute we'd tetch off a blast 'n' the fuse'd begin to sizzle, he'd give a look as much as to say: 'Well, I'll have to git you to excuse *me,*' an' it was surpris'n' the way he'd shin out of that hole 'n' go f'r a tree. Sagacity? It ain't no name for it. 'Twas *inspiration!'*"

I said, "Well, Mr. Baker, his prejudice against quartz-mining *was* remarkable, considering how he came by it. Couldn't you ever cure him of it?"

*"Cure him!* No! When Tom Quartz was sot once, he was *always* sot—and you might a blowed him up as much as three million times 'n' you'd never a broken him of his cussed prejudice agin quartz mining."

The affection and the pride that lit up Baker's face when he delivered this tribute to the firmness of his humble friend of other days, will always be a vivid memory with me.


## JIM BAKER'S BLUEJAY YARN
### FROM *A Tramp Abroad* [1880]

⟨ JIM BAKER is another pseudonym for Jim Gillis.

ANIMALS talk to each other, of course. There can be no question about that; but I suppose there are very few people who can understand them. I never knew but one man who could. I knew he could, however, because he told me so himself. He was a middle-aged, simple-hearted miner who had lived in a lonely corner of California, among the woods and mountains, a good many years, and had studied the ways of his only neighbors, the beasts and the birds, until he believed he could accurately translate any remark which they made. This was Jim Baker. According to Jim Baker, some animals have only a limited education, and use only very simple words, and scarcely ever a comparison or a flowery figure; whereas, certain other animals have a large vocabulary, a fine command of language and a ready and fluent delivery; consequently these latter talk a great deal; they like it; they are conscious of their talent, and they enjoy "showing off." Baker said, that after long and careful observation, he had come to the conclusion that the blue-jays were the best talkers he had found among birds and beasts. Said he:—

"There's more *to* a blue-jay than any other creature. He has got more moods, and more different kinds of feelings than other creature; and mind you, whatever a blue-jay feels, he can put into language. And no mere commonplace language, either, but rattling, out-and-out book-talk —and bristling with metaphor, too—just bristling! And as for command of language—why *you* never see a blue-jay get stuck for a word. No man ever did. They just boil out of him! And another thing: I've noticed a good deal, and there's no bird, or cow, or anything that uses as good grammar as a blue-jay. You may say a cat uses good grammar. Well, a cat does—but you let a cat get excited, once; you let a cat get to pulling fur with another cat on a shed, nights, and you'll hear grammar that will give you the lockjaw. Ignorant people think it's the *noise* which fighting cats make that is so aggravating, but it ain't so; it's the sickening grammar they use. Now I've never heard a jay use bad grammar but very seldom; and when they do, they are as ashamed as a human; they shut right down and leave.

"You may call a jay a bird. Well, so he is, in a measure—because he's got feathers on him, and don't belong to no church, perhaps; but otherwise he is just as much a human as you be. And I'll tell you for why. A jay's gifts, and instincts, and feelings, and interests, cover the whole ground. A jay hasn't got any more principle than a Congressman. A jay will lie, a jay will steal, a jay will deceive, a jay will betray; and four times out of five, a jay will go back on his solemnest promise. The sacredness of an obligation is a thing which you can't cram into no blue-jay's head. Now on top of all this, there's another thing: a jay can out-swear any gentleman in the mines. You think a cat can

swear. Well, a cat can; but you give a blue-jay a subject that calls for his reserve-powers, and where is your cat? Don't talk to *me*—I know too much about this thing. And there's yet another thing: in the one little particular of scolding—just good, clean, out-and-out scolding—a blue-jay can lay over anything, human or divine. Yes, sir, a jay is everything that a man is. A jay can cry, a jay can laugh, a jay can feel shame, a jay can reason and plan and discuss, a jay likes gossip and scandal, a jay has got a sense of humor, a jay knows when he is an ass just as well as you do—maybe better. If a jay ain't human, he better take in his sign, that's all. Now I'm going to tell you a perfectly true fact about some blue-jays.

"When I first begun to understand jay language correctly, there was a little incident happened here. Seven years ago, the last man in this region but me, moved away. There stands his house,— been empty ever since; a log house, with a plank roof—just one big room, and no more; no ceiling —nothing between the rafters and the floor. Well, one Sunday morning I was sitting out here in front of my cabin, with my cat, taking the sun, and looking at the blue hills, and listening to the leaves rustling so lonely in the trees, and thinking of the home away yonder in the States, that I hadn't heard from in thirteen years, when a blue-jay lit on that house, with an acorn in his mouth, and says, 'Hello, I reckon I've struck something.' When he spoke, the acorn dropped out of his mouth and rolled down the roof, of course, but he didn't care; his mind was all on the thing he had struck. It was a knot-hole in the roof. He cocked his head to one side, shut one eye and put the other one to the hole, like a 'possum looking down a jug; then he glanced up with his bright eyes, gave a wink or two with his wings—which signifies gratification, you understand,—and says, 'It looks like a hole, it's located like a hole,— blamed if I don't believe it *is* a hole!'

"Then he cocked his head down and took another look; he glances up perfectly joyful, this time; winks his wings and his tail both, and says, 'O, no, this ain't no fat thing, I reckon! If I ain't in luck!—why it's a perfectly elegant hole!' So he flew down and got that acorn, and fetched it up and dropped it in, and was just tilting his head back, with the heavenliest smile on his face, when all of a sudden he was paralyzed into a listening attitude and that smile faded gradually out of his countenance like breath off'n a razor, and the queerest look of surprise took its place. Then he says, 'Why I didn't hear it fall!' He cocked his eye at the hole again, and took a long look; raised up and shook his head; stepped around to the other side of the hole and took another look from that side; shook his head again. He studied a while, then he just went into the *de*tails—walked round and round the hole and spied into it from every point of the compass. No use. Now he took a thinking attitude on the comb of the roof and scratched the back of his head with his right foot a minute, and finally says, 'Well, it's too many for *me,* that's certain; must be a mighty long hole; however, I ain't got no time to fool around here, I got to 'tend to business; I reckon it's all right—chance it, anyway.'

"So he flew off and fetched another acorn and dropped it in, and tried to flirt his eye to the hole quick enough to see what become of it, but he was too late. He held his eye there as much as a minute; then he raised up and sighed, and says, 'Consound it, I don't seem to understand this thing, no way; however, I'll tackle her again.' He fetched another acorn, and done his level best to see what become of it, but he couldn't. He says, 'Well, *I* never struck no such a hole as this, before; I'm of the opinion it's a totally new kind of a hole.' Then he begun to get mad. He held in for a spell, walking up and down the comb of the roof and shaking his head and muttering to himself; but his feelings got the upper hand of him, presently, and he broke loose and cussed himself black in the face. I never see a bird take on so about a little thing. When he got through he walks to the hole and looks in again for half a minute; then he says, 'Well, you're a long hole, and a deep hole, and a mighty singular hole altogether—but I've started in to fill you, and I'm d—d if I *don't* fill you, if it takes a hundred years!'

"And with that, away he went. You never see a bird work so since you was born. He laid into his work, and the way he hove acorns into that hole for about two hours and a half was one of the most exciting and astonishing spectacles I ever struck. He never stopped to take a look any more—he just hove 'em in and went for more. Well at last he could hardly flop his wings, he was so tuckered out. He comes a-drooping down, once more, sweating like an ice-pitcher, drops his acorn in and says, '*Now* I guess I've got the bulge on you by this time!' So he bent down for a look. If you'll believe me, when his head come up again he was just pale with rage. He says, 'I've shoveled acorns enough in there to keep the family thirty years, and if I can see a sign of one of 'em I wish I may land in a museum with a belly full of sawdust in two minutes!'

"He just had strength enough to crawl up on to the comb and lean his back agin the chimbly, and then he collected his impressions and begun to free his mind. I see in a second that what I had mistook for profanity in the mines was only just the rudiments, as you may say.

"Another jay was going by, and heard him doing his devotions, and stops to inquire what was up. The sufferer told him the whole circumstance, and says, 'Now yonder's the hole, and if you don't believe me, go and look for yourself.' So this fellow went and looked, and comes back and says, 'How many did you say you put in there?' 'Not any less than two tons,' says the sufferer. The other jay went and looked again. He couldn't seem to make it out, so he raised a yell, and three more jays come. They all examined the hole, they all made the sufferer tell it over again, then they all discussed it, and got off as many leather-headed opinions about it as an average crowd of humans could have done.

"They called in more jays; then more and more, till pretty soon this whole region 'peared to have a blue flush about it. There must have been five thousand of them; and such another jawing and disputing and ripping and cussing, you never heard. Every jay in the whole lot put his eye to the hole and delivered a more chuckle-headed opinion about the mystery than the jay that went there before him. They examined the house all over, too. The door was standing half open, and at last one old jay happened to go and light on it and look in. Of course that knocked the mystery galley west in a second. There lay the acorns, scattered all over the floor. He flopped his wings and raised a whoop. 'Come here!' he says, 'Come here, everybody; hang'd if this fool hasn't been trying to fill up a house with acorns!' They all came a-swooping down like a blue cloud, and as each fellow lit on the door and took a glance, the whole absurdity of the contract that that first jay had tackled hit him home and he fell over backwards suffocating with laughter, and the next jay took his place and done the same.

"Well, sir, they roosted around here on the house-top and the trees for an hour, and guffawed over that thing like human beings. It ain't any use to tell me a blue-jay hasn't got a sense of humor, because I know better. And memory, too. They brought jays here from all over the United States to look down that hole, every summer for three years. Other birds too. And they could all see the point, except an owl that come from Nova Scotia to visit the Yo Semite, and he took this thing in on his way back. He said he couldn't see anything funny in it. But then he was a good deal disappointed about Yo Semite, too."

# PART III:
# SOCIAL CRITICISM

◇

❲ IN San Francisco in the 1860's, Mark Twain was sometimes called "The Moralist of the Main" in joking acknowledgment of his concern with social abuses. He criticized speculators in mining stocks, volunteer fire departments, undertakers, and especially the police force, which he accused of brutality to Chinese and to all prisoners without money or influential friends. Many passages in *Innocents Abroad* are devoted to the poverty, filth, and disease which Mark Twain considered the result of corrupt or despotic government in Italy and the Near East. *The Gilded Age* satirizes graft in the Federal Congress; *Huckleberry Finn* is, among other things, a powerful attack on Negro slavery; and *The Prince and the Pauper* and *A Connecticut Yankee in King Arthur's Court* make frontal assaults on various forms of tyranny and inhumane punishments for crime. But his most powerful satire belongs to the last fifteen years of his life, when he had become convinced that accumulating wealth had caused a "moral rot" in American life and broadened the scope of his invective to denounce what he believed to be the universal and ineradicable cowardice, cruelty, and hypocrisy of mankind. The unfinished moral fable *The Mysterious Stranger* is the major work of this period. Its indictment of the human race was anticipated, however, in *Pudd'nhead Wilson* (1894) and *The Man That Corrupted Hadleyburg* (1899). *The Man That Corrupted Hadleyburg* is also remarkable for the hard symmetry of its plot and its severe economy of means.

◇

## THE MAN THAT CORRUPTED
## HADLEYBURG

❲ FIRST published in *Harper's Magazine* (December 1899), this tale was written at a time when Mark Twain was also working on *The Mysterious Stranger*. The outsider who decides to corrupt Hadleyburg belongs to the series of transcendent figures of which Satan in *The Mysterious Stranger* is the fully developed example; indeed, Richards in his delirium says that the checks given to him by the stranger "came from Satan."

### I

IT WAS many years ago. Hadleyburg was the most honest and upright town in all the region around about. It had kept that reputation unsmirched during three generations, and was prouder of it than of any other of its possessions. It was so proud of it, and so anxious to insure its perpetuation, that it began to teach the principles of honest dealing to its babies in the cradle, and made the like teachings the staple of their culture thenceforward through all the years devoted to their education. Also, throughout the formative years temptations were kept out of the way of the young people, so that their honesty could have every chance to harden and solidify, and become a part of their very bone. The neighboring towns were jealous of this honorable supremacy, and affected to sneer at Hadleyburg's pride in it and call it vanity; but all the same they were obliged to acknowledge that Hadleyburg was in reality an incorruptible town; and if pressed they would also acknowledge that the mere fact that a young man hailed from Hadleyburg was all the recommendation he needed when he went forth from his natal town to seek for responsible employment.

But at last, in the drift of time, Hadleyburg had the ill luck to offend a passing stranger—possibly without knowing it, certainly without caring, for Hadleyburg was sufficient unto itself, and cared not a rap for strangers or their opinions. Still, it would have been well to make an exception in this one's case, for he was a bitter man and revengeful. All through his wanderings during a whole year he kept his injury in mind, and gave all his leisure moments to trying to invent a compensating satisfaction for it. He contrived many plans, and all of them were good, but none of them was quite sweeping enough; the poorest of them would hurt a great many individuals, but what he wanted was a plan which would comprehend the entire town, and not let so much as one person escape unhurt. At last he had a fortunate idea, and when it fell into his brain it lit up his whole head with an evil joy. He began to form a plan at once, saying to himself, "That is the thing to do—I will corrupt the town."

Six months later he went to Hadleyburg, and arrived in a buggy at the house of the old cashier of the bank about ten at night. He got a sack out of the buggy, shouldered it, and staggered with it through the cottage yard, and knocked at the door. A woman's voice said "Come in," and he entered, and set his sack behind the stove in the parlor, saying politely to the old lady who sat reading the *Missionary Herald* by the lamp:

"Pray keep your seat, madam, I will not disturb you. There—now it is pretty well concealed; one would hardly know it was there. Can I see your husband a moment, madam?"

No, he was gone to Brixton, and might not return before morning.

"Very well, madam, it is no matter. I merely wanted to leave that sack in his care, to be delivered to the rightful owner when he shall be found. I am a stranger; he does not know me; I am merely passing through the town to-night to discharge a matter which has been long in my mind. My errand is now completed, and I go pleased and a little proud, and you will never see me again. There is a paper attached to the sack which will explain everything. Good night, madam."

The old lady was afraid of the mysterious big stranger, and was glad to see him go. But her curiosity was roused, and she went straight to the sack and brought away the paper. It began as follows:

*TO BE PUBLISHED; or, the right man sought out by private inquiry—either will answer. This sack contains gold coin weighing a hundred and sixty pounds four ounces—*

"Mercy on us, and the door not locked!"

Mrs. Richards flew to it all in a tremble and locked it, then pulled down the window-shades and stood frightened, worried, and wondering if there was anything else she could do toward making herself and the money more safe. She listened awhile for burglars, then surrendered to curiosity and went back to the lamp and finished reading the paper:

*I am a foreigner, and am presently going back to my own country, to remain there permanently. I am grateful to America for what I have received at her hands during my long stay under her flag; and to one of her citizens—a citizen of Hadleyburg—I am especially grateful for a great kindness done me a year or two ago. Two great kindnesses, in fact. I will explain. I was a gambler. I say I WAS. I was a ruined gambler. I arrived in this village at night, hungry and without a penny. I asked for help—in the dark; I was ashamed to beg in the light. I begged of the right man. He gave me twenty dollars—that is to say, he gave me life, as I considered it. He also gave me fortune; for out of that money I have made myself rich at the gaming-table. And finally, a remark which he made to me has remained with me to this day, and has at last conquered me; and in conquering has saved the remnant of my morals; I shall gamble no more. Now I have no idea who that man was, but I want him found, and I want him to have this money, to give away, throw away, or keep, as he pleases. It is merely my way of testifying my gratitude to him. If I could stay, I would find him myself; but no matter, he will be found. This is an honest town, an incorruptible town, and I know I can trust it without fear. This man can be identified by the remark which he made to me; I feel persuaded that he will remember it.*

*And now my plan is this: If you prefer to conduct the inquiry privately, do so. Tell the contents of this present writing to any one who is likely to be the right man. If he shall answer, 'I am the man; the remark I made was so-and-so,' apply the test—to wit: open the sack, and in it you will find a sealed envelope containing that remark. If the remark mentioned by the candidate tallies with it, give him the money, and ask no further questions, for he is certainly the right man.*

*But if you shall prefer a public inquiry, then publish this present writing in the local paper—with these instructions added, to wit: Thirty days from now, let the candidate appear at the town-hall at eight in the evening (Friday), and hand his remark, in a sealed envelope, to the Rev. Mr. Burgess (if he will be kind enough to act); and let Mr. Burgess there and then destroy the seals of the sack, open it, and see if the remark is correct; if correct, let the money be delivered, with my sincere gratitude, to my benefactor thus identified.*

Mrs. Richards sat down, gently quivering with excitement, and was soon lost in thinkings—after this pattern: "What a strange thing it is! . . . And what a fortune for that kind man who set his bread afloat upon the waters! . . . If it had only been my husband that did it!—for we are so poor, so old and poor! . . ." Then, with a sigh—"But it was not my Edward; no, it was not he that gave a stranger twenty dollars. It is a pity, too; I see it now. . . ." Then, with a shudder—"But it is *gambler's* money! the wages of sin: we couldn't take it; we couldn't touch it. I don't like to be near it; it seems a defilement." She moved to a farther chair. . . . "I wish Edward would come and take it to the bank; a burglar might come at any moment; it is dreadful to be here all alone with it."

At eleven Mr. Richards arrived, and while his wife was saying, "I am *so* glad you've come!" he was saying, "I'm so tired—tired clear out; it is dreadful to be poor, and have to make these dismal journeys at my time of life. Always at the grind, grind, grind, on a salary—another man's slave, and he sitting at home in his slippers, rich and comfortable."

"I am so sorry for you, Edward, you know that; but be comforted: we have our livelihood; we have our good name—"

"Yes, Mary, and that is everything. Don't mind my talk—it's just a moment's irritation and doesn't mean anything. Kiss me—there, it's all gone now, and I am not complaining any more. What have you been getting? What's in the sack?"

Then his wife told him the great secret. It dazed him for a moment; then he said:

"It weighs a hundred and sixty pounds? Why, Mary, it's for-ty thou-sand dollars—think of it—

a whole fortune! Not ten men in this village are worth that much. Give me the paper."

He skimmed through it and said:

"Isn't it an adventure! Why, it's a romance; it's like the impossible things one reads about in books, and never sees in life." He was well stirred up now; cheerful, even gleeful. He tapped his old wife on the cheek, and said, humorously, "Why, we're rich, Mary, rich; all we've got to do is to bury the money and burn the papers. If the gambler ever comes to inquire, we'll merely look coldly upon him and say: 'What is this nonsense you are talking? We have never heard of you and your sack of gold before'; and then he would look foolish, and——"

"And in the mean time, while you are running on with your jokes, the money is still here, and it is fast getting along toward burglar-time."

"True. Very well, what shall we do—make the inquiry private? No, not that: it would spoil the romance. The public method is better. Think what a noise it will make! And it will make all the other towns jealous; for no stranger would trust such a thing to any town but Hadleyburg, and they know it. It's a great card for us. I must get to the printing-office now, or I shall be too late."

"But stop—stop—don't leave me here alone with it, Edward!"

But he was gone. For only a little while, however. Not far from his own house he met the editor-proprietor of the paper, and gave him the document, and said, "Here is a good thing for you, Cox—put it in."

"It may be too late, Mr. Richards, but I'll see."

At home again he and his wife sat down to talk the charming mystery over; they were in no condition for sleep. The first question was, Who could the citizen have been who gave the stranger the twenty dollars? It seemed a simple one; both answered it in the same breath:

"Barclay Goodson."

"Yes," said Richards, "he could have done it, and it would have been like him, but there's not another in the town."

"Everybody will grant that, Edward—grant it privately, anyway. For six months, now, the village has been its own proper self once more—honest, narrow, self-righteous, and stingy."

"It is what he always called it, to the day of his death—said it right out publicly, too."

"Yes, and he was hated for it."

"Oh, of course; but he didn't care. I reckon he was the best-hated man among us, except the Reverend Burgess."

"Well, Burgess deserves it—he will never get another congregation here. Mean as the town is, it knows how to estimate *him*. Edward, doesn't it seem odd that the stranger should appoint Burgess to deliver the money?"

"Well, yes—it does. That is—that is—"

"Why so much that-*is*-ing? Would *you* select him?"

"Mary, maybe the stranger knows him better than this village does."

"Much *that* would help Burgess!"

The husband seemed perplexed for an answer; the wife kept a steady eye upon him, and waited. Finally Richards said, with the hesitancy of one who is making a statement which is likely to encounter doubt:

"Mary, Burgess is not a bad man."

His wife was certainly surprised.

"Nonsense!" she exclaimed.

"He is not a bad man. I know. The whole of his unpopularity had its foundation in that one thing —the thing that made so much noise."

"That 'one thing,' indeed! As if that 'one thing' wasn't enough, all by itself."

"Plenty. Plenty. Only he wasn't guilty of it."

"How you talk! Not guilty of it! Everybody knows he *was* guilty."

"Mary, I give you my word—he was innocent."

"I can't believe it, and I don't. How do you know?"

"It is a confession. I am ashamed, but I will make it. I was the only man who knew he was innocent. I could have saved him, and—and—well, you know how the town was wrought up—I hadn't the pluck to do it. It would have turned everybody against me. I felt mean, ever so mean; but I didn't dare; I hadn't the manliness to face that."

Mary looked troubled, and for a while was silent. Then she said, stammeringly:

"I—I don't think it would have done for you to—to— One mustn't—er—public opinion—one has to be so careful—so—" It was a difficult road, and she got mired; but after a little she got started again. "It was a great pity, but— Why, we couldn't afford it, Edward—we couldn't indeed. Oh, I wouldn't have had you do it for anything!"

"It would have lost us the good will of so many people, Mary; and then—and then——"

"What troubles me now is, what *he* thinks of us, Edward."

"He? *He* doesn't suspect that I could have saved him."

"Oh," exclaimed the wife, in a tone of relief, "I am glad of that! As long as he doesn't know that you could have saved him, he—he—well, that makes it a great deal better. Why, I might have known he didn't know, because he is always trying to be friendly with us, as little encouragement as we give him. More than once people have twitted me with it. There's the Wilsons, and the Wilcoxes, and the Harknesses, they take a mean pleasure in saying, 'Your friend Burgess,' because they know it pesters me. I wish he wouldn't persist in liking us so; I can't think why he keeps it up."

"I can explain it. It's another confession. When the thing was new and hot, and the town made a plan to ride him on a rail, my conscience hurt me so that I couldn't stand it, and I went privately and gave him notice, and he got out of the town and staid out till it was safe to come back."

"Edward! If the town had found it out—"

"*Don't!* It scares me yet, to think of it. I repented of it the minute it was done; and I was even afraid to tell you, lest your face might betray it to somebody. I didn't sleep any that night, for worrying. But after a few days I saw that no one was going to suspect me, and after that I got to feeling glad I did it. And I feel glad yet, Mary—glad through and through."

"So do I, now, for it would have been a dreadful way to treat him. Yes, I'm glad; for really you did owe him that, you know. But, Edward, suppose it should come out yet, some day!"

"It won't."

"Why?"

"Because everybody thinks it was Goodson."

"Of course they would!"

"Certainly. And of course *he* didn't care. They persuaded poor old Sawlsberry to go and charge it on him, and he went blustering over there and did it. Goodson looked him over, like as if he was hunting for a place on him that he could despise the most, then he says, 'So you are the Committee of Inquiry, are you?' Sawlsberry said that was about what he was. 'Hm. Do they require particulars, or do you reckon a kind of a *general* answer will do?' 'If they require particulars, I will come back, Mr. Goodson; I will take the general answer first.' 'Very well, then, tell them to go to hell—I reckon that's general enough. And I'll give you some advice, Sawlsberry; when you come back for the particulars, fetch a basket to carry the relics of yourself home in.' "

"Just like Goodson; it's got all the marks. He had only one vanity: he thought he could give advice better than any other person."

"It settled the business, and saved us, Mary. The subject was dropped."

"Bless you, I'm not doubting *that*."

Then they took up the gold-sack mystery again, with strong interest. Soon the conversation began to suffer breaks—interruptions caused by absorbed thinkings. The breaks grew more and more frequent. At last Richards lost himself wholly in thought. He sat long, gazing vacantly at the floor, and by and by he began to punctuate his thoughts with little nervous movements of his hands that seemed to indicate vexation. Meantime his wife too had relapsed into a thoughtful silence, and her movements were beginning to show a troubled discomfort. Finally Richards got up and strode aimlessly about the room, plowing his hands through his hair, much as a somnambulist might do who was having a bad dream. Then he seemed to arrive at a definite purpose; and without a word he put on his hat and passed quickly out of the house. His wife sat brooding, with a drawn face, and did not seem to be aware that she was alone. Now and then she murmured, "Lead us not into t— . . . but—but—we are so poor, so poor! . . . Lead us not into . . . Ah, who would be hurt by it?—and no one would ever know. . . . Lead us . . . ." The voice died out in mumblings. After a little she glanced up and muttered in a half-frightened, half-glad way:

"He is gone! But, oh dear, he may be too late —too late. . . . Maybe not—maybe there is still time." She rose and stood thinking, nervously clasping and unclasping her hands. A slight shudder shook her frame, and she said, out of a dry throat, "God forgive me—it's awful to think such things—but . . . Lord, how we are made—how strangely we are made!"

She turned the light low, and slipped stealthily over and kneeled down by the sack and felt of its ridgy sides with her hands, and fondled them lovingly; and there was a gloating light in her poor old eyes. She fell into fits of absence; and came half out of them at times to mutter, "If we had only waited!—oh, if we had only waited a little, and not been in such a hurry!"

Meantime Cox had gone home from his office and told his wife all about the strange thing that had happened, and they had talked it over eagerly, and guessed that the late Goodson was the only man in the town who could have helped a suffering stranger with so noble a sum as twenty dollars. Then there was a pause, and the two became thoughtful and silent. And by and by nervous and fidgety. At last the wife said, as if to herself:

"Nobody knows this secret but the Richardses . . . and us . . . nobody."

The husband came out of his thinkings with a slight start, and gazed wistfully at his wife, whose face was become very pale; then he hesitatingly rose, and glanced furtively at his hat, then at his wife—a sort of mute inquiry. Mrs. Cox swallowed once or twice, with her hand at her throat, then in place of speech she nodded her head. In a moment she was alone, and mumbling to herself.

And now Richards and Cox were hurrying through the deserted streets, from opposite directions. They met, panting, at the foot of the printing-office stairs; by the night light there they read each other's face. Cox whispered:

"Nobody knows about this but us?"

The whispered answer was,

"Not a soul—on honor, not a soul!"

"If it isn't too late to—"

The men were starting up-stairs; at this moment they were overtaken by a boy, and Cox asked:

"Is that you, Johnny?"

"Yes, sir."

"You needn't ship the early mail—nor *any* mail; wait till I tell you."

"It's already gone, sir."

"*Gone?*" It had the sound of an unspeakable disappointment in it.

"Yes, sir. Time-table for Bixton and all the towns beyond changed to-day, sir—had to get the papers in twenty minutes earlier than common. I had to rush; if I had been two minutes later—"

The men turned and walked slowly away, not waiting to hear the rest. Neither of them spoke during ten minutes; then Cox said, in a vexed tone:

"What possessed you to be in such a hurry, *I* can't make out."

The answer was humble enough:

"I see it now, but somehow I never thought, you know, until it was too late. But the next time—"

"Next time be hanged! It won't come in a thousand years."

Then the friends separated without a good night, and dragged themselves home with the gait of mortally stricken men. At their homes their wives sprang up with an eager "Well?"—then saw the answer with their eyes and sank down sorrowing, without waiting for it to come in words. In both houses a discussion followed of a heated sort—a new thing; there had been discussions before, but not heated ones, not ungentle ones. The discussions to-night were a sort of seeming plagiarisms of each other. Mrs. Richards said:

"If you had only waited, Edward—if you had only stopped to think; but no, you must run straight to the printing-office and spread it all over the world."

"It *said* publish it."

"That is nothing; it also said do it privately, if

you liked. There, now—is that true, or not?"

"Why, yes—yes, it is true; but when I thought what a stir it would make, and what a compliment it was to Hadleyburg that a stranger should trust it so—"

"Oh, certainly, I know all that; but if you had only stopped to think, you would have seen that you *couldn't* find the right man, because he is in his grave, and hasn't left chick nor child nor relation behind him; and as long as the money went to somebody that awfully needed it, and nobody would be hurt by it, and—and—"

She broke down, crying. Her husband tried to think of some comforting thing to say, and presently came out with this:

"But after all, Mary, it must be for the best—it *must* be; we know that. And we must remember that it was so ordered—"

"Ordered! Oh, everything's *ordered*, when a person has to find some way out when he has been stupid. Just the same, it was *ordered* that the money should come to us in this special way, and it was you that must take it on yourself to go meddling with the designs of Providence—and who gave you the right? It was wicked, that is what it was—just blasphemous presumption, and no more becoming to a meek and humble professor of—"

"But, Mary, you know how we have been trained all our lives long, like the whole village, till it is absolutely second nature to us to stop not a single moment to think when there's an honest thing to be done—"

"Oh, I know it, I know it—it's been one everlasting training and training and training in honesty—honesty shielded, from the very cradle, against every possible temptation, and so it's *artificial* honesty, and weak as water when temptation comes, as we have seen this night. God knows I never had shade nor shadow of a doubt of my petrified and indestructible honesty until now—and now, under the very first big and real temptation, I—Edward, it is my belief that this town's honesty is as rotten as mine is; as rotten as yours is. It is a mean town, a hard, stingy town, and hasn't a virtue in the world but this honesty it is so celebrated for and so conceited about; and so help me, I do believe that if ever the day comes that its honesty falls under great temptation, its grand reputation will go to ruin like a house of cards. There, now, I've made confession, and I feel better; I am a humbug, and I've been one all my life, without knowing it. Let no man call me honest again—I will not have it."

"I—well, Mary, I feel a good deal as you do; I certainly do. It seems strange, too, so strange. I never could have believed it—never."

A long silence followed; both were sunk in thought. At last the wife looked up and said:

"I know what you are thinking, Edward."

Richards had the embarrassed look of a person who is caught.

"I am ashamed to confess it, Mary, but—"

"It's no matter, Edward, I was thinking the same question myself."

"I hope so. State it."

"You were thinking, if a body could only guess out *what the remark was* that Goodson made to the stranger."

"It's perfectly true. I feel guilty and ashamed. And you?"

"I'm past it. Let us make a pallet here; we've got to stand watch till the bank vault opens in the morning and admits the sack. . . . Oh dear, oh dear—if we hadn't made the mistake!"

The pallet was made, and Mary said:

"The open sesame—what could it have been? I do wonder what that remark could have been? But come; we will get to bed now."

"And sleep?"

"No: think."

"Yes, think."

By this time the Coxes too had completed their spat and their reconciliation, and were turning in—to think, to think, and toss, and fret, and worry over what the remark could possibly have been which Goodson made to the stranded derelict; that golden remark; that remark worth forty thousand dollars, cash.

The reason that the village telegraph-office was open later than usual that night was this: The foreman of Cox's paper was the local representative of the Associated Press. One might say its honorary representative, for it wasn't four times a year that he could furnish thirty words that would be accepted. But this time it was different. His despatch stating what he had caught got an instant answer:

*Send the whole thing—all the details—twelve hundred words.*

A colossal order! The foreman filled the bill; and he was the proudest man in the State. By breakfast-time the next morning the name of Hadleyburg the Incorruptible was on every lip in America, from Montreal to the Gulf, from the glaciers of Alaska to the orange-groves of Florida; and millions and millions of people were discussing the stranger and his money-sack, and wondering if the right man would be found, and hoping some more news about the matter would come soon—right away.

## II

HADLEYBURG village woke up world-celebrated—astonished—happy—vain. Vain beyond imagination. Its nineteen principal citizens and their wives went about shaking hands with each other, and beaming, and smiling, and congratulating, and saying *this* thing adds a new word to the dictionary—*Hadleyburg,* synonym for *incorruptible*—destined to live in dictionaries forever! And the minor and unimportant citizens and their wives went around acting in much the same way. Everybody ran to the bank to see the gold-sack; and before noon grieved and envious crowds began to flock in from Brixton and all neighboring towns; and that afternoon and next day reporters began to arrive from everywhere to verify the sack and its history and write the whole thing up anew, and make dashing free-hand pictures of the sack, and of Richards's house, and the bank, and the Presbyterian church, and the Baptist church, and the public square, and the town-hall where the test would be applied and the money delivered; and damnable portraits of the Richardses, and Pinkerton the banker, and Cox, and the foreman, and Reverend Burgess, and the postmaster—and even of Jack Halliday, who was the loafing, good-natured, no-account, irreverent fisherman, hunter, boys' friend, stray-dogs' friend, typical "Sam Lawson" [1] of the town. The little mean, smirking, oily Pinkerton showed the sack to all comers, and rubbed his sleek palms together pleasantly, and enlarged upon the town's fine old reputation for honesty and upon this wonderful indorsement of it, and hoped and believed that the example would now spread far and wide over the American world, and be epoch-making in the matter of moral regeneration. And so on, and so on.

By the end of a week things had quieted down again; the wild intoxication of pride and joy had sobered to a soft, sweet, silent delight—a sort of deep, nameless, unutterable content. All faces bore a look of peaceful, holy happiness.

Then a change came. It was a gradual change: so gradual that its beginnings were hardly noticed; maybe were not noticed at all, except by Jack Halliday, who always noticed everything; and always made fun of it, too, no matter what it was. He began to throw out chaffing remarks about people not looking quite so happy as they did a day or two ago; and next he claimed that the new aspect was deepening to positive sadness; next, that it was taking on a sick look; and finally he said that

THE MAN THAT CORRUPTED HADLEYBURG. 1. "Sam Lawson": The homely philosopher who is used as narrator in Harriet Beecher Stowe's *Sam Lawson's Oldtown Fireside Stories* (1872).

everybody was become so moody, thoughtful, and absentminded that he could rob the meanest man in town of a cent out of the bottom of his breeches pocket and not disturb his revery.

At this stage—or at about this stage—a saying like this was dropped at bedtime—with a sigh, usually—by the head of each of the nineteen principal households: "Ah, what *could* have been the remark that Goodson made?"

And straightway—with a shudder—came this, from the man's wife:

"Oh, *don't!* What horrible thing are you mulling in your mind? Put it away from you, for God's sake!"

But that question was wrung from those men again the next night—and got the same retort. But weaker.

And the third night the men uttered the question yet again—with anguish, and absently. This time—and the following night—the wives fidgeted feebly, and tried to say something. But didn't.

And the night after that they found their tongues and responded—longingly:

"Oh, if we *could* only guess!"

Halliday's comments grew daily more and more sparklingly disagreeable and disparaging. He went diligently about, laughing at the town, individually and in mass. But his laugh was the only one left in the village: it fell upon a hollow and mournful vacancy and emptiness. Not even a smile was findable anywhere. Halliday carried a cigar-box around on a tripod, playing that it was a camera, and halted all passers and aimed the thing and said, "Ready!—now look pleasant, please," but not even this capital joke could surprise the dreary faces into any softening.

So three weeks passed—one week was left. It was Saturday evening—after supper. Instead of the aforetime Saturday-evening flutter and bustle and shopping and larking, the streets were empty and desolate. Richards and his old wife sat apart in their little parlor—miserable and thinking. This was become their evening habit now: the lifelong habit which had preceded it, of reading, knitting, and contented chat, or receiving or paying neighborly calls, was dead and gone and forgotten, ages ago—two or three weeks ago; nobody talked now, nobody read, nobody visited—the whole village sat at home, sighing, worrying, silent. Trying to guess out that remark.

The postman left a letter. Richards glanced listlessly at the superscription and the postmark—unfamiliar, both—and tossed the letter on the table and resumed his might-have-beens and his

hopeless dull miseries where he had left them off. Two or three hours later his wife got wearily up and was going away to bed without a good night—custom now—but she stopped near the letter and eyed it awhile with a dead interest, then broke it open, and began to skim it over. Richards, sitting there with his chair tilted back against the wall and his chin between his knees, heard something fall. It was his wife. He sprang to her side, but she cried out:

"Leave me alone, I am too happy. Read the letter—read it!"

He did. He devoured it, his brain reeling. The letter was from a distant state, and it said:

*I am a stranger to you, but no matter: I have something to tell. I have just arrived home from Mexico, and learned about that episode. Of course you do not know who made that remark, but I know, and I am the only person living who does know. It was* GOODSON. *I knew him well, many years ago. I passed through your village that very night, and was his guest till the midnight train came along. I overheard him make that remark to the stranger in the dark—it was in Hale Alley. He and I talked of it the rest of the way home, and while smoking in his house. He mentioned many of your villagers in the course of his talk—most of them in a very uncomplimentary way, but two or three favorably; among these latter yourself. I say "favorably"—nothing stronger. I remember his saying he did not actually* LIKE *any person in the town—not one; but that you—I* THINK *he said you—am almost sure—had done him a very great service once, possibly without knowing the full value of it, and he wished he had a fortune, he would leave it to you when he died, and a curse apiece for the rest of the citizens. Now, then, if it was you that did him that service, you are his legitimate heir, and entitled to the sack of gold. I know that I can trust to your honor and honesty, for in a citizen of Hadleyburg these virtues are an unfailing inheritance, and so I am going to reveal to you the remark, well satisfied that if you are not the right man you will seek and find the right one and see that poor Goodson's debt of gratitude for the service referred to is paid. This is the remark:* "YOU ARE FAR FROM BEING A BAD MAN: GO, AND REFORM."

HOWARD L. STEPHENSON.

"Oh, Edward, the money is ours, and I am so grateful, *oh,* so grateful—kiss me, dear, it's forever since we kissed—and we needed it so—the money—and now you are free of Pinkerton and his bank, and nobody's slave any more; it seems to me I could fly for joy."

It was a happy half-hour that the couple spent there on the settee caressing each other; it was the old days come again—days that had begun with their courtship and lasted without a break till the stranger brought the deadly money. By and by the wife said:

"Oh, Edward, how lucky it was you did him that grand service, poor Goodson! I never liked him, but I love him now. And it was fine and beautiful of you never to mention it or brag about it." Then, with a touch of reproach, "But you ought to have told *me,* Edward, you ought to have told your wife, you know."

"Well, I—er—well, Mary, you see—"

"Now stop hemming and hawing, and tell me about it, Edward. I always loved you, and now I'm proud of you. Everybody believes there was only one good generous soul in this village, and now it turns out that you—Edward, why don't you tell me?"

"Well—er—er—Why, Mary, I can't!"

"You *can't? Why* can't you?"

"You see, he—well, he—he made me promise I wouldn't."

The wife looked him over, and said, very slowly:

"Made—you—promise? Edward, what do you tell me that for?"

"Mary, do you think I would lie?"

She was troubled and silent for a moment, then she laid her hand within his and said:

"No . . . no. We have wandered far enough from our bearings—God spare us that! In all your life you have never uttered a lie. But now—now that the foundations of things seem to be crumbling from under us, we—we—" She lost her voice for a moment, then said, brokenly, "Lead us not into temptation. . . . I think you made the promise, Edward. Let it rest so. Let us keep away from that ground. Now—that is all gone by; let us be happy again; it is no time for clouds."

Edward found it something of an effort to comply, for his mind kept wandering—trying to remember what the service was that he had done Goodson.

The couple lay awake the most of the night, Mary happy and busy, Edward busy but not so happy. Mary was planning what she would do with the money. Edward was trying to recall that service. At first his conscience was sore on account of the lie he had told Mary—if it was a lie. After much reflection—suppose it *was* a lie? What then? Was it such a great matter? Aren't we always *acting* lies? Then why not *tell* them? Look at Mary—look what she had done. While he was hurrying off on his honest errand, what was she doing? Lamenting because the papers hadn't been destroyed and the money kept! Is theft better than lying?

*That* point lost its sting—the lie dropped into the background and left comfort behind it. The next point came to the front: *Had* he rendered that service? Well, here was Goodson's own evidence as reported in Stephenson's letter; there could be no better evidence than that—it was even *proof* that he had rendered it. Of course. So that point was settled. . . . No, not quite. He recalled with a wince that this unknown Mr. Stephenson was just a trifle unsure as to whether the performer of it was Richards or some other—and, oh dear, he had put Richards on his honor! He must himself decide whither that money must go—and Mr. Stephenson was not doubting that if he was the wrong man he would go honorably and find the right one. Oh, it was odious to put a man in such a situation—ah, why couldn't Stephenson have left out that doubt! What did he want to intrude that for?

Further reflection. How did it happen that *Richards's* name remained in Stephenson's mind as indicating the right man, and not some other man's name? That looked good. Yes, that looked very good. In fact, it went on looking better and better, straight along—until by and by it grew into positive *proof.* And then Richards put the matter at once out of his mind, for he had a private instinct that a proof once established is better left so.

He was feeling reasonably comfortable now, but there was still one other detail that kept pushing itself on his notice: of course he had done that service—that was settled; but what *was* that service? He must recall it—he would not go to sleep till he had recalled it; it would make his peace of mind perfect. And so he thought and thought. He thought of a dozen things—possible services, even probable services—but none of them seemed adequate, none of them seemed large enough, none of them seemed worth the money—worth the fortune Goodson had wished he could leave in his will. And besides, he couldn't remember having done them, anyway. Now, then —now, then—what *kind* of a service would it be that would make a man so inordinately grateful? Ah—the saving of his soul! That must be it. Yes, he could remember, now, how he once set himself the task of converting Goodson, and labored at it as much as—he was going to say three months; but upon closer examination it shrunk to a month, then to a week, then to a day, then to nothing. Yes, he remembered now, and with unwelcome vividness, that Goodson had told him to go to thunder and mind his own business—*he* wasn't hankering to follow Hadleyburg to heaven!

So that solution was a failure—he hadn't saved Goodson's soul. Richards was discouraged. Then after a little came another idea: had he saved Goodson's property? No, that wouldn't do—he hadn't any. His life? That is it! Of course. Why, he might have thought of it before. This time he was on the right track, sure. His imagination-mill was hard at work in a minute, now.

Thereafter during a stretch of two exhausting hours he was busy saving Goodson's life. He saved it in all kinds of difficult and perilous ways. In every case he got it saved satisfactorily up to a certain point; then, just as he was beginning to get well persuaded that it had really happened, a troublesome detail would turn up which made the whole thing impossible. As in the matter of drowning, for instance. In that case he had swum out and tugged Goodson ashore in an unconscious state with a great crowd looking on and applauding, but when he had got it all thought out and was just beginning to remember all about it, a whole swarm of disqualifying details arrived on the ground: the town would have known of the circumstance, Mary would have known of it, it would glare like a limelight in his own memory instead of being an inconspicuous service which he had possibly rendered "without knowing its full value." And at this point he remembered that he couldn't swim, anyway.

Ah—*there* was a point which he had been overlooking from the start: it had to be a service which he had rendered "possibly without knowing the full value of it." Why, really, that ought to be an easy hunt—much easier than those others. And sure enough, by and by he found it. Goodson, years and years ago, came near marrying a very sweet and pretty girl, named Nancy Hewitt, but in some way or other the match had been broken off; the girl died, Goodson remained a bachelor, and by and by became a soured one and a frank despiser of the human species. Soon after the girl's death the village found out, or thought it had found out, that she carried a spoonful of Negro blood in her veins. Richards worked at these details a good while, and in the end he thought he remembered things concerning them which must have gotten mislaid in his memory through long neglect. He seemed to dimly remember that it was *he* that found out about the Negro blood; that it was he that told the village; that the village told Goodson where they got it; that he thus saved Goodson from marrying the tainted girl; that he had done him this great service "without knowing the full value of it," in fact without knowing that he *was* doing it; but that Goodson knew the value of it, and what a narrow escape he had had, and so went to his grave grateful to his benefactor and wishing he had a fortune to leave him. It was all clear and simple now, and the more he went over it the more luminous and certain it grew; and at

last, when he nestled to sleep satisfied and happy, he remembered the whole thing just as if it had been yesterday. In fact, he dimly remembered Goodson's *telling* him his gratitude once. Meantime Mary had spent six thousand dollars on a new house for herself and a pair of slippers for her pastor, and then had fallen peacefully to rest.

That same Saturday evening the postman had delivered a letter to each of the other principal citizens—nineteen letters in all. No two of the envelopes were alike, and no two of the superscriptions were in the same hand, but the letters inside were just like each other in every detail but one. They were exact copies of the letter received by Richards—handwriting and all—and were all signed by Stephenson, but in place of Richards's name each receiver's own name appeared.

All night long eighteen principal citizens did what their caste-brother Richards was doing at the same time—they put in their energies trying to remember what notable service it was that they had unconsciously done Barclay Goodson. In no case was it a holiday job; still they succeeded.

And while they were at this work, which was difficult, their wives put in the night spending the money, which was easy. During that one night the nineteen wives spent an average of seven thousand dollars each out of the forty thousand in the sack—a hundred and thirty-three thousand altogether.

Next day there was a surprise for Jack Halliday. He noticed that the faces of the nineteen chief citizens and their wives bore that expression of peaceful and holy happiness again. He could not understand it, neither was he able to invent any remarks about it that could damage it or disturb it. And so it was his turn to be dissatisfied with life. His private guesses at the reasons for the happiness failed in all instances, upon examination. When he met Mrs. Wilcox and noticed the placid ecstasy in her face, he said to himself, "Her cat has had kittens"—and went and asked the cook: it was not so; the cook had detected the happiness, but did not know the cause. When Halliday found the duplicate ecstasy in the face of "Shadbelly" Billson (village nickname), he was sure some neighbor of Billson's had broken his leg, but inquiry showed that this had not happened. The subdued ecstasy in Gregory Yates's face could mean but one thing—he was a mother-in-law short: it was another mistake. "And Pinkerton—Pinkerton—he has collected ten cents that he thought he was going to lose." And so on, and so on. In some cases the guesses had to remain in doubt, in the others they proved distinct errors. In the end Halliday said to himself, "Anyway it foots up that there's nineteen Hadleyburg families temporarily in heaven: I don't know how it happened; I only know Providence is off duty today."

An architect and builder from the next state had lately ventured to set up a small business in this unpromising village, and his sign had now been hanging out a week. Not a customer yet; he was a discouraged man, and sorry he had come. But his weather changed suddenly now. First one and then another chief citizen's wife said to him privately:

"Come to my house Monday week—but say nothing about it for the present. We think of building."

He got eleven invitations that day. That night he wrote his daughter and broke off her match with her student. He said she could marry a mile higher than that.

Pinkerton the banker and two or three other well-to-do men planned country-seats—but waited. That kind don't count their chickens until they are hatched.

The Wilsons devised a grand new thing—a fancy-dress ball. They made no actual promises, but told all their acquaintanceship in confidence that they were thinking the matter over and thought they should give it—"and if we do, you will be invited, of course." People were surprised, and said, one to another, "Why, they are crazy, those poor Wilsons, they can't afford it." Several among the nineteen said privately to their husbands, "It is a good idea: we will keep still till their cheap thing is over, then *we* will give one that will make it sick."

The days drifted along, and the bill of future squanderings rose higher and higher, wilder and wilder, more and more foolish and reckless. It began to look as if every member of the nineteen would not only spend his whole forty thousand dollars before receiving-day, but be actually in debt by the time he got the money. In some cases light-headed people did not stop with planning to spend, they really spent—on credit. They bought land, mortgages, farms, speculative stocks, fine clothes, horses, and various other things, paid down the bonus, and made themselves liable for the rest—at ten days. Presently the sober second thought came, and Halliday noticed that a ghastly anxiety was beginning to show up in a good many faces. Again he was puzzled, and didn't know what to make of it. "The Wilcox kittens aren't dead, for they weren't born; nobody's broken a leg; there's no shrinkage in mother-in-laws; *nothing* has happened—it is an unsolvable mystery."

There was another puzzled man, too—the Rev. Mr. Burgess. For days, wherever he went, people seemed to follow him or to be watching out for him; and if he ever found himself in a retired spot, a member of the nineteen would be sure to appear, thrust an envelope privately into his hand, whisper "To be opened at the town-hall Friday evening," then vanish away like a guilty thing. He was expecting that there might be one claimant for the sack—doubtful, however, Goodson being dead—but it never occurred to him that all this crowd might be claimants. When the great Friday came at last, he found that he had nineteen envelopes.

### III

THE TOWN hall had never looked finer. The platform at the end of it was backed by a showy draping of flags; at intervals along the walls were festoons of flags; the gallery fronts were clothed in flags; the supporting columns were swathed in flags; all this was to impress the stranger, for he would be there in considerable force, and in a large degree he would be connected with the press. The house was full. The 412 fixed seats were occupied; also the 68 extra chairs which had been packed into the aisles; the steps of the platform were occupied; some distinguished strangers were given seats on the platform; at the horseshoe of tables which fenced the front and sides of the platform sat a strong force of special correspondents who had come from everywhere. It was the best-dressed house the town had ever produced. There were some tolerably expensive toilets there, and in several cases the ladies who wore them had the look of being unfamiliar with that kind of clothes. At least the town thought they had that look, but the notion could have arisen from the town's knowledge of the fact that these ladies had never inhabited such clothes before.

The gold-sack stood on a little table at the front of the platform where all the house could see it. The bulk of the house gazed at it with a burning interest, a mouth-watering interest, a wistful and pathetic interest; a minority of nineteen couples gazed at it tenderly, lovingly, proprietarily, and the male half of this minority kept saying over to themselves the moving little impromptu speeches of thankfulness for the audience's applause and congratulations which they were presently going to get up and deliver. Every now and then one of these got a piece of paper out of his vest pocket and privately glanced at it to refresh his memory.

Of course there was a buzz of conversation going on—there always is; but at last when the Rev. Mr. Burgess rose and laid his hand on the sack he could hear his microbes gnaw, the place was so still. He related the curious history of the sack, then went on to speak in warm terms of Hadleyburg's old and well-earned reputation for spotless honesty, and of the town's just pride in this reputation. He said that this reputation was a treasure of priceless value; that under Providence its value had now become inestimably enhanced, for the recent episode had spread this fame far and wide, and thus had focused the eyes of the American world upon this village, and made its name for all time, as he hoped and believed, a synonym for commercial incorruptibility. [*Applause.*] "And who is to be the guardian of this noble treasure—the community as a whole? No! The responsibility is individual, not communal. From this day forth each and every one of you is in his own person its special guardian, and individually responsible that no harm shall come to it. Do you—does each of you—accept this great trust? [*Tumultuous assent.*] Then all is well. Transmit it to your children and to your children's children. To-day your purity is beyond reproach—see to it that it shall remain so. To-day there is not a person in your community who could be beguiled to touch a penny not his own—see to it that you abide in this grace. [*"We will! we will!"*] This is not the place to make comparisons between ourselves and other communities—some of them ungracious toward us; they have their ways, we have ours; let us be content. [*Applause.*] I am done. Under my hand, my friends, rests a stranger's eloquent recognition of what we are; through him the world will always henceforth know what we are. We do not know who he is, but in your name I utter your gratitude, and ask you to raise your voices in indorsement."

The house rose in a body and made the walls quake with the thunders of its thankfulness for the space of a long minute. Then it sat down, and Mr. Burgess took an envelope out of his pocket. The house held its breath while he slit the envelope open and took from it a slip of paper. He read its contents—slowly and impressively—the audience listening with tranced attention to this magic document, each of whose words stood for an ingot of gold:

"*The remark which I made to the distressed stranger was this: "You are very far from being a bad man: go, and reform.'* " Then he continued:

"We shall know in a moment now whether the remark here quoted corresponds with the one concealed in the sack; and if that shall prove to be so—and it undoubtedly will—this sack of gold belongs to a fellow-citizen who will henceforth stand before the nation as the symbol of the special virtue which has made our town famous throughout the land—Mr. Billson!"

The house had gotten itself all ready to burst into the proper tornado of applause; but instead of doing it, it seemed stricken with a paralysis; there was a deep hush for a moment or two, then a wave of whispered murmurs swept the place—of about this tenor: "*Billson!* oh, come, this is *too* thin! Twenty dollars to a stranger—or *anybody*—*Billson!* tell it to the marines!" And now at this point the house caught its breath all of a sudden in a new access of astonishment, for it discovered that whereas in one part of the hall Deacon Billson was standing up with his head meekly bowed, in another part of it Lawyer Wilson was doing the same. There was a wondering silence now for a while.

Everybody was puzzled, and nineteen couples were surprised and indignant.

Billson and Wilson turned and stared at each other. Billson asked, bitingly:

"Why do *you* rise, Mr. Wilson?"

"Because I have a right to. Perhaps you will be good enough to explain to the house why *you* rise?"

"With great pleasure. Because I wrote that paper."

"It is an impudent falsity! I wrote it myself."

It was Burgess's turn to be paralyzed. He stood looking vacantly at first one of the men and then the other, and did not seem to know what to do. The house was stupefied. Lawyer Wilson spoke up, now, and said,

"I ask the Chair to read the name signed to that paper.

That brought the Chair to itself, and it read out the name:

" 'John Wharton *Billson*.' "

"There!" shouted Billson, "what have you got to say for yourself, now? And what kind of apology are you going to make to me and to this insulted house for the imposture which you have attempted to play here?"

"No apologies are due, sir; and as for the rest of it, I publicly charge you with pilfering my note from Mr. Burgess and substituting a copy of it signed with your own name. There is no other way by which you could have gotten hold of the test-remark; I alone, of living men, possessed the secret of its wording."

There was likely to be a scandalous state of things if this went on; everybody noticed with distress that the short-hand scribes were scribbling like mad; many people were crying "Chair, Chair! Order! order!" Burgess rapped with his gavel, and said:

"Let us not forget the proprieties due. There has evidently been a mistake somewhere, but surely that is all. If Mr. Wilson gave me an envelope—and I remember now that he did—I still have it."

He took one out of his pocket, opened it, glanced at it, looked surprised and worried, and stood silent a few moments. Then he waved his hand in a wandering and mechanical way, and made an effort or two to say something, then gave it up, despondently. Several voices cried out:

"Read it! read it! What is it?"

So he began in a dazed and sleep-walker fashion:

" *'The remark which I made to the unhappy stranger was this: "You are far from being a bad man.* [The house gazed at him, marveling.] *Go, and reform.'* " [*Murmurs:* "Amazing! what can this mean?"] This one," said the Chair, "is signed Thurlow G. Wilson."

"There!" cried Wilson. "I reckon that settles it! I know perfectly well my note was purloined."

"Purloined!" retorted Billson. "I'll let you know that neither you nor any man of your kidney must venture to—"

*The Chair.* "Order, gentlemen, order! Take your seats, both of you, please."

They obeyed, shaking their heads and grumbling angrily. The house was profoundly puzzled; it did not know what to do with this curious emergency. Presently Thompson got up. Thompson was the hatter. He would have liked to be a Nineteener; but such was not for him: his stock of hats was not considerable enough for the position. He said:

"Mr. Chairman, if I may be permitted to make a suggestion, can both of these gentlemen be right? I put it to you, sir, can both have happened to say the very same words to the stranger? It seems to me—"

The tanner got up and interrupted him. The tanner was a disgruntled man; he believed himself entitled to be a Nineteener, but he couldn't get recognition. It made him a little unpleasant in his ways and speech. Said he:

"Sho, *that's* not the point! *That* could happen—twice in a hundred years—but not the other thing. *Neither* of them gave the twenty dollars!"

[*A ripple of applause.*]

*Billson.* "*I* did!"

*Wilson.* "*I* did!"

Then each accused the other of pilfering.

*The Chair.* "Order! Sit down, if you please—both of you. Neither of the notes has been out of my possession at any moment."

*A Voice.* "Good—that settles *that!*"

*The Tanner.* "Mr. Chairman, one thing is now plain: one of these men has been eavesdropping under the other one's bed, and filching family secrets. If it is not unparliamentary to suggest it, I will remark that both are equal to it. [*The Chair.* "Order! order!"] I withdraw the remark, sir, and will confine myself to suggesting that *if* one of them has overheard the other reveal the test-remark to his wife, we shall catch him now."

*A Voice.* "How?"

*The Tanner.* "Easily. The two have not quoted the remark in exactly the same words. You would have noticed that, if there hadn't been a considerable stretch of time and an exciting quarrel inserted between the two readings."

*A Voice.* "Name the difference."

*The Tanner.* "The word *very* is in Billson's note, and not in the other."

*Many Voices.* "That's so—he's right!"

*The Tanner.* "And so, if the Chair will examine the test-remark in the sack, we shall know which of these two frauds—[*The Chair.* "Order!"]—which of these two adventurers—[*The Chair.* "Order! order!"]—which of these two gentlemen—[*laughter and applause*]—is entitled to wear the belt as being the first dishonest blatherskite ever bred in this town—which he has dishonored, and which will be a sultry place for him from now out!" [*Vigorous applause.*]

*Many Voices.* "Open it!—open the sack!"

Mr. Burgess made a slit in the sack, slid his hand in and brought out an envelope. In it were a couple of folded notes. He said:

"One of these is marked, 'Not to be examined until all written communications which have been addressed to the Chair—if any—shall have been read.' The other is marked '*The Test.*' Allow me. It is worded—to wit:

" 'I do not require that the first half of the remark which was made to me by my benefactor shall be quoted with exactness, for it was not striking, and could be forgotten; but its closing fifteen words are quite striking, and I think easily rememberable; unless *these* shall be accurately reproduced, let the applicant be regarded as an impostor. My benefactor began by saying he seldom gave advice to any one, but that it always bore the hall-mark of high value when he did give it. Then he said this—and it has never faded from my memory: *"You are far from being a bad man—"* ' "

*Fifty Voices.* "That settles it—the money's Wilson's! Wilson! Wilson! Speech! Speech!"

People jumped up and crowded around Wilson, wringing his hand and congratulating fervently—meantime the Chair was hammering with the gavel and shouting:

"Order, gentlemen! Order! Order! Let me finish

reading, please." When quiet was restored, the reading was resumed—as follows:

" ' "*Go, and reform—or, mark my words— some day, for your sins, you will die and go to hell or Hadleyburg*—TRY AND MAKE IT THE FORMER." ' "

A ghastly silence followed. First an angry cloud began to settle darkly upon the faces of the citizenship; after a pause the cloud began to rise, and a tickled expression tried to take its place; tried so hard that it was only kept under with great and painful difficulty; the reporters, the Brixtonites, and other strangers bent their heads down and shielded their faces with their hands, and managed to hold in by main strength and heroic courtesy. At this most inopportune time burst upon the stillness the roar of a solitary voice—Jack Halliday's:

*"That's got the hall-mark on it!"*

Then the house let go, strangers and all. Even Mr. Burgess's gravity broke down presently, then the audience considered itself officially absolved from all restraint, and it made the most of its privilege. It was a good long laugh, and a tempestuously whole-hearted one, but it ceased at last—long enough for Mr. Burgess to try to resume, and for the people to get their eyes partially wiped; then it broke out again; and afterward yet again; then at last Burgess was able to get out these serious words:

"It is useless to try to disguise the fact—we find ourselves in the presence of a matter of grave import. It involves the honor of your town, it strikes at the town's good name. The difference of a single word between the test-remarks offered by Mr. Wilson and Mr. Billson was itself a serious thing, since it indicated that one or the other of these gentlemen had committed a theft—"

The two men were sitting limp, nerveless, crushed; but at these words both were electrified into movement, and started to get up—

"Sit down!" said the Chair, sharply, and they obeyed. "That, as I have said, was a serious thing. And it was—but for only one of them. But the matter has become graver; for the honor of *both* is now in formidable peril. Shall I go even further, and say in inextricable peril? *Both* left out the crucial fifteen words." He paused. During several moments he allowed the pervading stillness to gather and deepen its impressive effects, then added: "There would seem to be but one way whereby this could happen. I ask these gentlemen —Was there *collusion?—agreement?*"

A low murmur sifted through the house; its import was, "He's got them both."

Billson was not used to emergencies; he sat in a helpless collapse. But Wilson was a lawyer. He struggled to his feet, pale and worried, and said:

"I ask the indulgence of the house while I explain this most painful matter. I am sorry to say what I am about to say, since it must inflict irreparable injury upon Mr. Billson, whom I have always esteemed and respected until now, and in whose invulnerability to temptation I entirely believed—as did you all. But for the preservation of my own honor I must speak—and with frankness. I confess with shame—and I now beseech your pardon for it—that I said to the ruined stranger all of the words contained in the test-remark, including the disparaging fifteen. [*Sensation.*] When the late publication was made I recalled them, and I resolved to claim the sack of coin, for by every right I was entitled to it. Now I will ask you to consider this point, and weigh it well: that stranger's gratitude to me that night knew no bounds; he said himself that he could find no words for it that were adequate, and that if he should ever be able he would repay me a thousandfold. Now, then, I ask you this: Could I expect—could I believe—could I even remotely imagine—that, feeling as he did, he would do so ungrateful a thing as to add those quite unnecessary fifteen words to his test?—set a trap for me? —expose me as a slanderer of my own town before my own people assembled in a public hall? It was preposterous; it was impossible. His test would contain only the kindly opening clause of my remark. Of that I had no shadow of doubt. You would have thought as I did. You would not have expected a base betrayal from one whom you had befriended and against whom you had committed no offense. And so, with perfect confidence, perfect trust, I wrote on a piece of paper the opening words—ending with 'Go, and reform,'— and signed it. When I was about to put it in an envelope I was called into my back office, and without thinking I left the paper lying open on my desk." He stopped, turned his head slowly toward Billson, waited a moment, then added: "I ask you to note this: when I returned, a little later, Mr. Billson was retiring by my street door." [*Sensation.*]

In a moment Billson was on his feet and shouting:

"It's a lie! It's an infamous lie!"

*The Chair.* "Be seated, sir! Mr. Wilson has the floor."

Billson's friends pulled him into his seat and quieted him, and Wilson went on:

"Those are the simple facts. My note was now lying in a different place on the table from where I had left it. I noticed that, but attached no importance to it, thinking a draught had blown it there. That Mr. Billson would read a private paper was a thing which could not occur to me; he was an honorable man, and he would be above that. If you will allow me to say it, I think his extra word *'very'* stands explained; it is attributable to a defect of memory. I was the only man in the world who could furnish here any detail of the test-remark—by *honorable* means. I have finished."

There is nothing in the world like a persuasive speech to fuddle the mental apparatus and upset the convictions and debauch the emotions of an audience not practised in the tricks and delusions of oratory. Wilson sat down victorious. The house submerged him in tides of approving applause; friends swarmed to him and shook him by the hand and congratulated him, and Billson was shouted down and not allowed to say a word. The Chair hammered and hammered with its gavel, and kept shouting:

"But let us proceed, gentlemen, let us proceed!"

At last there was a measurable degree of quiet, and the hatter said:

"But what is there to proceed with, sir, but to deliver the money?"

*Voices.* "That's it! That's it! Come forward, Wilson!"

*The Hatter.* "I move three cheers for Mr. Wilson, Symbol of the special virtue which—"

The cheers burst forth before he could finish; and in the midst of them—and in the midst of the clamor of the gavel also—some enthusiasts mounted Wilson on a big friend's shoulder and were going to fetch him in triumph to the platform. The Chair's voice now rose above the noise—

"Order! To your places! You forget that there is still a document to be read." When quiet had been restored he took up a document, and was going to read it, but laid it down again, saying, "I forgot; this is not to be read until all written communications received by me have first been read." He took an envelope out of his pocket, removed its inclosure, glanced at it—seemed astonished—held it out and gazed at it—stared at it.

Twenty or thirty voices cried out:

"What is it? Read it! read it!"

And he did—slowly, and wondering:

" 'The remark which I made to the stranger—[*Voices.* "Hello! how's this?"]—was this: "You are far from being a bad man. [*Voices.* "Great Scott!"] Go, and reform.' " [*Voice.* "Oh, saw my leg off!"] Signed by Mr. Pinkerton, the banker."

The pandemonium of delight which turned itself loose now was of a sort to make the judicious weep. Those whose withers were unwrung laughed till the tears ran down; the reporters, in throes of

laughter, set down disordered pot-hooks, which would never in the world be decipherable; and a sleeping dog jumped up, scared out of its wits, and barked itself crazy at the turmoil. All manner of cries were scattered through the din: "We're getting rich—*two* Symbols of Incorruptibility!—without counting Billson!" *"Three!*—count Shadbelly in—we can't have too many!" "All right—Billson's elected!" "Alas, poor Wilson—victim of *two* thieves!"

*A Powerful Voice.* "Silence! The Chair's fished up something more out of its pocket."

*Voices.* "Hurrah! Is it something fresh? Read it! read! read!"

*The Chair* [*reading*]. " 'The remark which I made,' etc.: ' "You are far from being a bad man. Go," ' etc. Signed, 'Gregory Yates.' "

*Tornado of Voices.* "Four Symbols!" " 'Rah for Yates!" "Fish again!"

The house was in a roaring humor now, and ready to get all the fun out of the occasion that might be in it. Several Nineteeners, looking pale and distressed, got up and began to work their way toward the aisles, but a score of shouts went up:

"The doors, the doors—close the doors; no Incorruptible shall leave this place! Sit down, everybody!"

The mandate was obeyed.

"Fish again! Read! read!"

The Chair fished again, and once more the familiar words began to fall from its lips—" 'You are far from being a bad man.' "

"Name! name! What's his name?"

" 'L. Ingoldsby Sargent.' "

"Five elected! Pile up the Symbols! Go on, go on!"

" 'You are far from being a bad—' "

"Name! name!"

" 'Nicholas Whitworth.' "

"Hooray! hooray! it's a symbolical day!"

Somebody wailed in, and began to sing this rhyme (leaving out "it's") to the lovely "Mikado" tune of "When a man's afraid, a beautiful maid—"; the audience joined in, with joy; then, just in time, somebody contributed another line—

And don't you this forget—

The house roared it out. A third line was at once furnished—

Corruptibles far from Hadleyburg are—

The house roared that one too. As the last note died, Jack Halliday's voice rose high and clear, freighted with a fine line—

But the Symbols are here, you bet!

That was sung, with booming enthusiasm. Then the happy house started in at the beginning and sang the four lines through twice, with immense swing and dash, and finished up with a crashing three-times-three and a tiger for "Hadleyburg the Incorruptible and all Symbols of it which we shall find worthy to receive the hall-mark to-night."

Then the shoutings at the Chair began again, all over the place:

"Go on! go on! Read! read some more! Read all you've got!"

"That's it—go on! We are winning eternal celebrity!"

A dozen men got up now and began to protest. They said that this farce was the work of some abandoned joker, and was an insult to the whole community. Without a doubt these signatures were all forgeries—

"Sit down! sit down! Shut up! You are confessing. We'll find *your* names in the lot."

"Mr. Chairman, how many of those envelopes have you got?"

The Chair counted.

"Together with those that have been already examined, there are nineteen."

A storm of derisive applause broke out.

"Perhaps they all contain the secret. I move that you open them all and read every signature that is attached to a note of that sort—and read also the first eight words of the note."

"Second the motion!"

It was put and carried—uproariously. Then poor old Richards got up, and his wife rose and stood at his side. Her head was bent down, so that none might see that she was crying. Her husband gave her his arm, and so supporting her, he began to speak in a quavering voice:

"My friends, you have known us two—Mary and me—all our lives, and I think you have liked us and respected us—"

The Chair interrupted him:

"Allow me. It is quite true—that which you are saying, Mr. Richards: this town *does* know you two; it *does* like you; it *does* respect you; more— it honors you and *loves* you—"

Halliday's voice rang out:

"That's the hall-marked truth, too! If the Chair is right, let the house speak up and say it. Rise! Now, then—hip! hip! hip!—all together!"

The house rose in mass, faced toward the old couple eagerly, filled the air with a snow-storm of waving handkerchiefs, and delivered the cheers with all its affectionate heart.

The Chair then continued:

"What I was going to say is this: We know your good heart, Mr. Richards, but this is not a time for the exercise of charity toward offenders. [*Shouts of "Right! right!"*] I see your generous purpose in your face, but I cannot allow you to plead for these men—"

"But I was going to—"

"Please take your seat, Mr. Richards. We must examine the rest of these notes—simple fairness to the men who have already been exposed requires this. As soon as that has been done—I give you my word for this—you shall be heard."

*Many Voices.* "Right!—the Chair is right—no interruption can be permitted at this stage! Go on!—the names! the names!—according to the terms of the motion!"

The old couple sat reluctantly down, and the husband whispered to the wife, "It is pitifully hard to have to wait; the shame will be greater than ever when they find we were only going to plead for *ourselves.*"

Straightway the jollity broke loose again with the reading of the names.

" 'You are far from being a bad man—' Signature, 'Robert J. Titmarsh.'

" 'You are far from being a bad man—' Signature, 'Eliphalet Weeks.'

" 'You are far from being a bad man—' Signature, 'Oscar B. Wilder.' "

At this point the house lit upon the idea of taking the eight words out of the Chairman's hands. He was not unthankful for that. Thenceforward he held up each note in its turn, and waited. The house droned out the eight words in a massed and measured and musical deep volume of sound (with a daringly close resemblance to a well known church chant)—" 'You are f-a-r from being a b-a-a-a-d man.' " Then the Chair said, "Signature, 'Archibald Wilcox.' " And so on, and so on, name after name, and everybody had an increasingly and gloriously good time except the wretched Nineteen. Now and then, when a particularly shining name was called, the house made the Chair wait while it chanted the whole of the test-remark from the beginning to the closing words, "And go to hell or Hadleyburg—try and make it the for-or-m-e-r!" and in these special cases they added a grand and agonized and imposing "A-a-a-a-*men!*"

The list dwindled, dwindled, dwindled, poor old Richards keeping tally of the count, wincing when a name resembling his own was pronounced, and waiting in miserable suspense for the time to come when it would be his humiliating privilege to rise with Mary and finish his plea, which he was intending to word thus: ". . . for until now we have never done any wrong thing, but have gone our humble way unreproached. We are very poor, we are old, and have no chick nor child to help us; we were sorely tempted, and we fell. It was my purpose when I got up before to make confession and beg that my name might not be read out in this public place, for it seemed to us that we could not bear it; but I was prevented. It was just; it was our place to suffer with the rest. It has been hard for us. It is the first time we have ever heard our name fall from any one's lips—sullied. Be merciful—for the sake of the better days; make our shame as light to bear as in your charity you can." At this point in his revery Mary nudged him, perceiving that his mind was absent. The house was chanting, "You are f-a-r," etc.

"Be ready," Mary whispered. "Your name comes now; he has read eighteen."

The chant ended.

"Next! next! next!" came volleying from all over the house.

Burgess put his hand into his pocket. The old couple, trembling, began to rise. Burgess fumbled a moment, then said, "I find I have read them all."

Faint with joy and surprise, the couple sank into their seats, and Mary whispered:

"Oh, bless God, we are saved!—he has lost ours —I wouldn't give this for a hundred of those sacks!"

The house burst out with its "Mikado" travesty, and sang it three times with ever-increasing enthusiasm, rising to its feet when it reached for the third time the closing line—

But the Symbols are here, you bet!

and finishing up with cheers and a tiger for "Hadleyburg purity and our eighteen immortal representatives of it."

Then Wingate, the saddler, got up and proposed cheers "for the cleanest man in town, the one solitary important citizen in it who didn't try to steal that money—Edward Richards."

They were given with great and moving heartiness; then somebody proposed that Richards be elected sole guardian and Symbol of the now Sacred Hadleyburg Tradition, with power and right to stand up and look the whole sarcastic world in the face.

Passed, by acclamation; then they sang the "Mikado" again, and ended it with:

And there's *one* Symbol left, you bet!

There was a pause; then—

*A Voice.* "Now, then, who's to get the sack?"

*The Tanner* [*with bitter sarcasm*]. "That's easy. The money has to be divided among the eighteen Incorruptibles. They gave the suffering stranger twenty dollars apiece—and that remark —each in his turn—it took twenty-two minutes for the procession to move past. Staked the stranger—total contribution, $360. All they want is just the loan back—and interest—forty thousand dollars altogether."

*Many Voices* [*derisively*]. "That's it! Divvy! divvy! Be kind to the poor—don't keep them waiting!"

*The Chair.* "Order! I now offer the stranger's remaining document. It says: 'If no claimant shall appear [*grand chorus of groans*] I desire that you open the sack and count out the money to the principal citizens of your town, they to take it in trust [*cries of "Oh! Oh! Oh!"*], and use it in such ways as to them shall seem best for the propagation and preservation of your community's noble reputation for incorruptible honesty [*more cries*]—a reputation to which their names and their efforts will add a new and far-reaching luster.' [*Enthusiastic outburst of sarcastic applause.*] That seems to be all. No—here is a postscript:

" 'P. S.—CITIZENS OF HADLEYBURG: There *is* no test-remark—nobody made one. [*Great sensation.*] There wasn't any pauper stranger, nor any twenty-dollar contribution, nor any accompanying benediction and compliment—these are all inventions. [*General buzz and hum of astonishment and delight.*] Allow me to tell my story—it will take but a word or two. I passed through your town at a certain time, and received a deep offense which I had not earned. Any other man would have been content to kill one or two of you and call it square, but to me that would have been a trivial revenge, and inadequate; for the dead do not *suffer*. Besides, I could not kill you all—and, anyway, made as I am, even that would not have satisfied me. I wanted to damage every man in the place, and every woman—and not in their bodies or in their estate, but in their vanity—the place where feeble and foolish people are most vulnerable. So I disguised myself and came back and studied you. You were easy game. You had an old and lofty reputation for honesty, and naturally you were proud of it—it was your treasure of treasures, the very apple of your eye. As soon as I found out that you carefully and vigilantly kept yourselves and your children *out of temptation,* I knew how to proceed. Why, you simple creatures, the weakest of all weak things is a virtue which has not been tested in the fire. I laid a plan, and gathered a list of names. My project was to corrupt Hadleyburg the Incorruptible. My idea was to make liars and thieves of nearly half a hundred smirchless men and women who had never in their lives uttered a lie or stolen a penny. I was afraid of Goodson. He was neither born nor reared in Hadleyburg. I was afraid that if I started to operate my scheme by getting my letter laid before you, you would say to yourselves, "Goodson is the only man among us who would give away twenty dollars to a poor devil"—and then you might not bite at my bait. But Heaven took Goodson; then I knew I was safe, and I set my trap and baited it. It may be that I shall not catch all the men to whom I mailed the pretended test secret, but I shall catch the most of them, if I know Hadleyburg nature. [*Voices.* "Right—he got every last one of them."] I believe they will even steal ostensible *gamble*-money, rather than miss, poor, tempted, and mistrained fellows. I am hoping to eternally and everlastingly squelch your vanity and give Hadleyburg a new renown—one that will *stick*—and spread far. If I have succeeded, open the sack and summon the Committee on Propagation and Preservation of the Hadleyburg Reputation.' "

*A Cyclone of Voices.* "Open it! Open it! The Eighteen to the front! Committee on Propagation of the Tradition! Forward—the Incorruptibles!"

The Chair ripped the sack wide, and gathered up a handful of bright, broad, yellow coins, shook them together, then examined them—

"Friends, they are only gilded disks of lead!"

There was a crashing outbreak of delight over this news, and when the noise had subsided, the tanner called out:

"By right of apparent seniority in this business, Mr. Wilson is Chairman of the Committee on Propagation of the Tradition. I suggest that he step forward on behalf of his pals, and receive in trust the money."

*A Hundred Voices.* "Wilson! Wilson! Wilson! Speech! Speech!"

*Wilson* [*in a voice trembling with anger*]. "You will allow me to say, and without apologies for my language, *damn* the money!"

*A Voice.* "Oh, and him a Baptist!"

*A Voice.* "Seventeen Symbols left! Step up, gentlemen, and assume your trust!"

There was a pause—no response.

*The Saddler.* "Mr. Chairman, we've got *one* clean man left, anyway, out of the late aristocracy; and he needs money, and deserves it. I move that you appoint Jack Halliday to get up there and auction off that sack of gilt twenty-dollar pieces, and give the result to the right man—the man whom Hadleyburg delights to honor—Edward Richards."

This was received with great enthusiasm, the dog taking a hand again; the saddler started the

bids at a dollar, the Brixton folk and Barnum's representative fought hard for it, the people cheered every jump that the bids made, the excitement climbed moment by moment higher and higher, the bidders got on their mettle and grew steadily more and more daring, more and more determined, the jumps went from a dollar up to five, then to ten, then to twenty, then fifty, then to a hundred, then—

At the beginning of the auction Richards whispered in distress to his wife: "O Mary, can we allow it? It—it—you see, it is an honor-reward, a testimonial to purity of character, and—and—can we allow it? Hadn't I better get up and—O Mary, what ought we to do?—what do you think we—" [*Halliday's voice. "Fifteen I'm bid!—fifteen for the sack!—twenty!—ah, thanks!—thirty—thanks again! Thirty, thirty, thirty!—do I hear forty?— forty it is! Keep the ball rolling, gentlemen, keep it rolling!—fifty! thanks, noble Roman! going at fifty, fifty, fifty!—seventy!—ninety!—splendid!— a hundred!—pile it up, pile it up!—hundred and twenty—forty!—just in time!—hundred and fifty! —*TWO hundred!—superb! Do I hear two h— thanks!—two hundred and fifty!—*"]

"It is another temptation, Edward—I'm all in a tremble—but, oh, we've escaped *one* temptation, and that ought to warn us to—[*"Six did I hear? —thanks!—six-fifty, six-f—*SEVEN *hundred!"*] And yet, Edward, when you think—nobody susp— [*"Eight hundred dollars!—hurrah!— make it nine!—Mr. Parsons, did I hear you say— thanks—nine!—this noble sack of virgin lead going at only nine hundred dollars, gilding and all— come! do I hear—a thousand!—gratefully yours! —did some one say eleven?—a sack which is going to be the most celebrated in the whole Uni—* "] O Edward" (beginning to sob), "we are *so* poor!—but—but—do as you think best—do as you think best."

Edward fell—that is, he sat still; sat with a conscience which was not satisfied, but which was overpowered by circumstances.

Meantime a stranger, who looked like an amateur detective gotten up as an impossible English earl, had been watching the evening's proceedings with manifest interest, and with a contented expression in his face; and he had been privately commenting to himself. He was now soliloquizing somewhat like this: "None of the Eighteen are bidding; that is not satisfactory; I must change that—the dramatic unities require it; they must buy the sack they tried to steal; they must pay a heavy price, too—some of them are rich. And another thing, when I make a mistake in Hadleyburg nature the man that puts that error upon me is entitled to a high honorarium, and some one must pay it. This poor old Richards has brought my judgment to shame; he is an honest man:—I don't understand it, but I acknowledge it. Yes, he saw my deuces *and* with a straight flush, and by rights the pot is his. And it shall be a jack-pot, too, if I can manage it. He disappointed me, but let that pass."

He was watching the bidding. At a thousand, the market broke; the prices tumbled swiftly. He waited—and still watched. One competitor dropped out; then another, and another. He put in a bid or two, now. When the bids had sunk to ten dollars, he added a five; some one raised him a three; he waited a moment, then flung in a fifty-dollar jump, and the sack was his—at $1,282. The house broke out in cheers—then stopped; for he was on his feet, and had lifted his hand. He began to speak.

"I desire to say a word, and ask a favor. I am a speculator in rarities, and I have dealings with persons interested in numismatics all over the world. I can make a profit on this purchase, just as it stands; but there is a way, if I can get your approval, whereby I can make every one of these leaden twenty-dollar pieces worth its face in gold, and perhaps more. Grant me that approval, and I will give part of my gains to your Mr. Richards, whose invulnerable probity you have so justly and so cordially recognized to-night; his share shall be ten thousand dollars, and I will hand him the money to-morrow. [*Great applause from the house.* But the "invulnerable probity" made the Richardses blush prettily; however, it went for modesty, and did no harm.] If you will pass my proposition by a good majority—I would like a two-thirds vote—I will regard that as the town's consent, and that is all I ask. Rarities are always helped by any device which will rouse curiosity and compel remark. Now if I may have your permission to stamp upon the faces of each of these ostensible coins the names of the eighteen gentlemen who—"

Nine-tenths of the audience were on their feet in a moment—dog and all—and the proposition was carried with a whirlwind of approving applause and laughter.

They sat down, and all the Symbols except "Dr." Clay Harkness got up, violently protesting against the proposed outrage, and threatening to—

"I beg you not to threaten me," said the stranger, calmly. "I know my legal rights, and am not accustomed to being frightened at bluster." [*Applause.*] He sat down. "Dr." Harkness saw an opportunity here. He was one of the two very rich men of the place, and Pinkerton was the other. Harkness was proprietor of a mint; that is to say, a popular patent medicine. He was running for the legislature on one ticket, and Pinkerton on the other. It was a close race and a hot one, and getting hotter every day. Both had strong appetites for money; each had bought a great tract of land, with a purpose; there was going to be a new railway, and each wanted to be in the legislature and help locate the route to his own advantage; a single vote might make the decision, and with it two or three fortunes. The stake was large, and Harkness was a daring speculator. He was sitting close to the stranger. He leaned over while one or another of the other Symbols was entertaining the house with protests and appeals, and asked, in a whisper.

"What is your price for the sack?"

"Forty thousand dollars."

"I'll give you twenty."

"No."

"Twenty-five."

"No."

"Say thirty."

"The price is forty thousand dollars; not a penny less."

"All right, I'll give it. I will come to the hotel at ten in the morning. I don't want it known: will see you privately."

"Very good." Then the stranger got up and said to the house:

"I find it late. The speeches of these gentlemen are not without merit, not without interest, not without grace; yet if I may be excused I will take my leave. I thank you for the great favor which you have shown me in granting my petition. I ask the Chair to keep the sack for me until to-morrow, and to hand these three five-hundred-dollar notes to Mr. Richards." They were passed up to the Chair. "At nine I will call for the sack, and at eleven will deliver the rest of the ten thousand to Mr. Richards in person, at his home. Good night."

Then he slipped out, and left the audience making a vast noise, which was composed of a mixture of cheers, the "Mikado" song, dog-disapproval, and the chant, "You are f-a-r from being a b-a-a-d man—a-a-a-a-men!"

IV

AT HOME the Richardses had to endure congratulations and compliments until midnight. Then they were left to themselves. They looked a little sad, and they sat silent and thinking. Finally Mary sighed and said,

"Do you think we are to blame, Edward—

*much* to blame?" and her eyes wandered to the accusing triplet of big bank-notes lying on the table, where the congratulators had been gloating over them and reverently fingering them. Edward did not answer at once; then he brought out a sigh and said, hesitatingly:

"We—we couldn't help it, Mary. It—well, it was ordered. *All* things are."

Mary glanced up and looked at him steadily, but he didn't return the look. Presently she said:

"I thought congratulations and praises always tasted good. But—it seems to me, now—Edward?"

"Well?"

"Are you going to stay in the bank?"

"N-no."

"Resign?"

"In the morning—by note."

"It does seem best."

Richards bowed his head in his hands and muttered:

"Before, I was not afraid to let oceans of people's money pour through my hands, but— Mary, I am so tired, so tired—"

"We will go to bed."

At nine in the morning the stranger called for the sack and took it to the hotel in a cab. At ten Harkness had a talk with him privately. The stranger asked for and got five checks on a metropolitan bank—drawn to "Bearer"—four for $1,500 each, and one for $34,000. He put one of the former in his pocketbook, and the remainder, representing $38,500, he put in an envelope, and with these he added a note, which he wrote after Harkness was gone. At eleven he called at the Richards house and knocked. Mrs. Richards peeped through the shutters, then went and received the envelope, and the stranger disappeared without a word. She came back flushed and a little unsteady on her legs, and gasped out:

"I am sure I recognized him! Last night it seemed to me that maybe I had seen him somewhere before."

"He is the man that brought the sack here?"

"I am almost sure of it."

"Then he is the ostensible Stephenson, too, and sold every important citizen in this town with his bogus secret. Now if he has sent checks instead of money, we are sold, too, after we thought we had escaped. I was beginning to feel fairly comfortable once more, after my night's rest, but the look of that envelope makes me sick. It isn't fat enough; $8,500 in even the largest bank-notes makes more bulk than that."

"Edward, why do you object to checks?"

"Checks signed by Stephenson! I am resigned to take the $8,500 if it could come in bank-notes —for it does seem that it was so ordered, Mary— but I have never had much courage, and I have not the pluck to try to market a check signed with that disastrous name. It would be a trap. That man tried to catch me; we escaped somehow or other; and now he is trying a new way. If it is checks—"

"Oh, Edward, it is *too* bad!" and she held up the checks and began to cry.

"Put them in the fire! quick! we mustn't be tempted. It is a trick to make the world laugh at *us,* along with the rest, and— Give them to *me,* since you can't do it!" He snatched them and tried to hold his grip till he could get to the stove; but he was human, he was a cashier, and he stopped a moment to make sure of the signature. Then he came near to fainting.

"Fan me, Mary, fan me! They are the same as gold!"

"Oh, how lovely, Edward! Why?"

"Signed by Harkness. What can the mystery of that be, Mary?"

"Edward, do you think—"

"Look here—look at this! Fifteen—fifteen— fifteen—thirty-four. Thirty-eight thousand five hundred! Mary, the sack isn't worth twelve dollars, and Harkness—apparently—has paid about par for it."

"And does it all come to us, do you think—instead of the ten thousand?"

"Why, it looks like it. And the checks are made to 'Bearer,' too."

"Is that good, Edward? What is it for?"

"A hint to collect them at some distant bank, I reckon. Perhaps Harkness doesn't want the matter known. What is that—a note?"

"Yes. It was with the checks."

It was in the "Stephenson" handwriting, but there was no signature. It said:

*"I am a disappointed man. Your honesty is beyond the reach of temptation. I had a different idea about it, but I wronged you in that, and I beg pardon, and do it sincerely. I honor you—and that is sincere too. This town is not worthy to kiss the hem of your garment. Dear sir, I made a square bet with myself that there were nineteen debauchable men in your self-righteous community. I have lost. Take the whole pot, you are entitled to it."*

Richards drew a deep sigh, and said:

"It seems written with fire—it burns so. Mary —I am miserable again."

"I, too. Ah, dear, I wish—"

"To think, Mary—he *believes* in me."

"Oh, don't, Edward—I can't bear it."

"If those beautiful words were deserved, Mary —and God knows I believed I deserved them once

—I think I could give the forty thousand dollars for them. And I would put that paper away, as representing more than gold and jewels, and keep it always. But now— We could not live in the shadow of its accusing presence, Mary."

He put it in the fire.

A messenger arrived and delivered an envelope.

Richards took from it a note and read it; it was from Burgess.

*"You saved me, in a difficult time. I saved you last night. It was at cost of a lie, but I made the sacrifice freely, and out of a grateful heart. None in this village knows so well as I know how brave and good and noble you are. At bottom you cannot respect me, knowing as you do of that matter of which I am accused, and by the general voice condemned; but I beg that you will at least believe that I am a grateful man; it will help me to bear my burden.*

[*Signed*]          "BURGESS."

"Saved, once more. And on such terms!" He put the note in the fire. "I—I wish I were dead, Mary, I wish I were out of it all."

"Oh, these are bitter, bitter days, Edward. The stabs, through their very generosity, are so deep— and they come so fast!"

Three days before the election each of two thousand voters suddenly found himself in possession of a prized memento—one of the renowned bogus double-eagles. Around one of its faces was stamped these words: "THE REMARK I MADE TO THE POOR STRANGER WAS—" Around the other face was stamped these: "GO, AND REFORM. [SIGNED] PINKERTON." Thus the entire remaining refuse of the renowned joke was emptied upon a single head, and with calamitous effect. It revived the recent vast laugh and concentrated it upon Pinkerton; and Harkness's election was a walkover.

Within twenty-four hours after the Richardses had received their checks their consciences were quieting down, discouraged; the old couple were learning to reconcile themselves to the sin which they had committed. But they were to learn, now, that a sin takes on new and real terrors when there seems a chance that it is going to be found out. This gives it a fresh and most substantial and important aspect. At church the morning sermon was of the usual pattern; it was the same old things said in the same old way; they had heard them a thousand times and found them innocuous, next to meaningless, and easy to sleep under; but now it was different: the sermon seemed to bristle with accusations; it seemed aimed straight and specially at people who were concealing deadly sins. After church they got away from the mob of congratulators as soon as they could, and hurried homeward, chilled to the bone at they did not

know what—vague, shadowy, indefinite fears. And by chance they caught a glimpse of Mr. Burgess as he turned a corner. He paid no attention to their nod of recognition! He hadn't seen it; but they did not know that. What could his conduct mean? It might mean—it might mean—oh, a dozen dreadful things. Was it possible that he knew that Richards could have cleared him of guilt in that bygone time, and had been silently waiting for a chance to even up accounts? At home, in their distress they got to imagining that their servant might have been in the next room listening when Richards revealed the secret to his wife that he knew of Burgess's innocence; next, Richards began to imagine that he had heard the swish of a gown in there at that time; next, he was sure he *had* heard it. They would call Sarah in, on a pretext, and watch her face: if she had been betraying them to Mr. Burgess, it would show in her manner. They asked her some questions—questions which were so random and incoherent and seemingly purposeless that the girl felt sure that the old people's minds had been affected by their sudden good fortune; the sharp and watchful gaze which they bent upon her frightened her, and that completed the business. She blushed, she became nervous and confused, and to the old people these were plain signs of guilt—guilt of some fearful sort or other—without doubt she was a spy and a traitor. When they were alone again they began to piece many unrelated things together and get horrible results out of the combination. When things had got about to the worst, Richards was delivered of a sudden gasp, and his wife asked:

"Oh, what is it?—what is it?"

"The note—Burgess's note! Its language was sarcastic, I see it now." He quoted: " 'At bottom you cannot respect me, *knowing,* as you do, of *that matter* of which I am accused'—oh, it is perfectly plain, now, God help me! He knows that I know! You see the ingenuity of the phrasing. It was a trap—and like a fool, I walked into it. And Mary—?"

"Oh, it is dreadful—I know what you are going to say—he didn't return your transcript of the pretended test-remark."

"No—kept it to destroy us with. Mary, he has exposed us to some already. I know it—I know it well. I saw it in a dozen faces after church. Ah, he wouldn't answer our nod of recognition—*he* knew what he had been doing!"

In the night the doctor was called. The news went around in the morning that the old couple were rather seriously ill—prostrated by the exhausting excitement growing out of their great windfall, the congratulations, and the late hours, the doctor said. The town was sincerely distressed; for these old people were about all it had left to be proud of, now.

Two days later the news was worse. The old couple were delirious, and were doing strange things. By witness of the nurses, Richards had exhibited checks—for $8,500? No—for an amazing sum—$38,500! What could be the explanation of this gigantic piece of luck?

The following day the nurses had more news—and wonderful. They had concluded to hide the checks, lest harm come to them; but when they searched they were gone from under the patient's pillow—vanished away. The patient said:

"Let the pillow alone; what do you want?"

"We thought it best that the checks—"

"You will never see them again—they are destroyed. They came from Satan. I saw the hell-brand on them, and I knew they were sent to betray me to sin." Then he fell to gabbling strange and dreadful things which were not clearly understandable, and which the doctor admonished them to keep to themselves.

Richards was right; the checks were never seen again.

A nurse must have talked in her sleep, for within two days the forbidden gabblings were the property of the town; and they were of a surprising sort. They seemed to indicate that Richards had been a claimant for the sack himself, and that Burgess had concealed that fact and then maliciously betrayed it.

Burgess was taxed with this and stoutly denied it. And he said it was not fair to attach weight to the chatter of a sick old man who was out of his mind. Still, suspicion was in the air, and there was much talk.

After a day or two it was reported that Mrs. Richards's delirious deliveries were getting to be duplicates of her husband's. Suspicion flamed up into conviction, now, and the town's pride in the purity of its one undiscredited important citizen began to dim down and flicker toward extinction.

Six days passed, then came more news. The old couple were dying. Richards's mind cleared in his latest hour, and he sent for Burgess. Burgess said:

"Let the room be cleared. I think he wishes to say something in privacy."

"No!" said Richards: "I want witnesses. I want you all to hear my confession, so that I may die a man, and not a dog. I was clean—artificially—like the rest; and like the rest I fell when temptation came. I signed a lie, and claimed the miserable sack. Mr. Burgess remembered that I had done him a service, and in gratitude (and ignorance) he suppressed my claim and saved me. You know

the thing that was charged against Burgess years ago. My testimony, and mine alone, could have cleared him, and I was a coward, and left him to suffer disgrace—"

"No—no—Mr. Richards, you—"

"My servant betrayed my secret to him—"

"No one has betrayed anything to me—"

—"and then he did a natural and justifiable thing, he repented of the saving kindness which he had done me, and he *exposed* me—as I deserved—"

"Never!—I make oath—"

"Out of my heart I forgive him."

Burgess's impassioned protestations fell upon deaf ears; the dying man passed away without knowing that once more he had done poor Burgess a wrong. The old wife died that night.

The last of the sacred Nineteen had fallen a prey to the fiendish sack; the town was stripped of the last rag of its ancient glory. Its mourning was not showy, but it was deep.

By act of the Legislature—upon prayer and petition—Hadleyburg was allowed to change its name to (never mind what—I will not give it away), and leave one word out of the motto that for many generations had graced the town's official seal.

It is an honest town once more, and the man will have to rise early that catches it napping again.

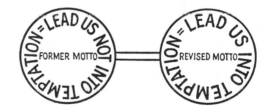

## THE WAR PRAYER

❨ DICTATED in 1904 or 1905 but first published posthumously in 1923, "The War Prayer" is reprinted from the Definitive Edition, Vol. XXIX. Mark Twain had followed with rapt attention the various wars, declared and undeclared, of the years just before and after the turn of the twentieth century: the Spanish-American War and its aftermath—the campaign against Aguinaldo in the Philippines; the Boer War; the European invasion of China during the Boxer uprising of 1900; and the Russo-Japanese War. This prayer concentrates in brief space his repudiation of the nationalist and imperialist enthusiasms of his day.

IT WAS a time of great and exalting excitement. The country was up in arms, the war was on, in every breast burned the holy fire of patriotism; the drums were beating, the bands playing, the toy pistols popping, the bunched firecrackers hissing and spluttering; on every hand and far down the receding and fading spread of roofs and balconies a fluttering wilderness of flags flashed in the sun; daily the young volunteers marched down the wide avenue gay and fine in their new uniforms, the proud fathers and mothers and sisters and sweethearts cheering them with voices choked with happy emotion as they swung by; nightly the packed mass meetings listened, panting, to patriot oratory which stirred the deepest deeps of their hearts, and which they interrupted at briefest intervals with cyclones of applause, the tears running down their cheeks the while; in the churches the pastors preached devotion to flag and country, and invoked the God of Battles, beseeching His aid in our good cause in outpouring of fervid eloquence which moved every listener. It was indeed a glad and gracious time, and the half dozen rash spirits that ventured to disapprove of the war and cast a doubt upon its righteousness straightway got such a stern and angry warning that for their personal safety's sake they quickly shrank out of sight and offended no more in that way.

Sunday morning came—next day the battalions would leave for the front; the church was filled; the volunteers were there, their young faces alight with martial dreams—visions of the stern advance, the gathering momentum, the rushing charge, the flashing sabers, the flight of the foe, the tumult, the enveloping smoke, the fierce pursuit, the surrender!—them home from the war, bronzed heroes, welcomed, adored, submerged in golden seas of glory! With the volunteers sat their dear ones, proud, happy, and envied by the neighbors and friends who had no sons and brothers to send forth to the field of honor, there to win for the flag, or, failing, die the noblest of noble deaths. The service proceeded; a war chapter from the Old Testament was read; the first prayer was said; it was followed by an organ burst that shook the building, and with one impulse the house rose, with glowing eyes and beating hearts, and poured out that tremendous invocation—

"God the all-terrible! Thou who ordainest,
    Thunder thy clarion and lightning thy sword!"

Then came the "long" prayer. None could remember the like of it for passionate pleading and moving and beautiful language. The burden of its supplication was, that an ever-merciful and benignant Father of us all would watch over our noble young soldiers, and aid, comfort, and encourage them in their patriotic work; bless them,

shield them in the day of battle and the hour of peril, bear them in His mighty hand, make them strong and confident, invincible in the bloody onset; help them to crush the foe, grant to them and to their flag and country imperishable honor and glory—

An aged stranger entered and moved with slow and noiseless step up the main aisle, his eyes fixed upon the minister, his long body clothed in a robe that reached to his feet, his head bare, his white hair descending in a frothy cataract to his shoulders, his seamy face unnaturally pale, pale even to ghastliness. With all eyes following him and wondering, he made his silent way; without pausing, he ascended to the preacher's side and stood there, waiting. With shut lids the preacher, unconscious of his presence, continued his moving prayer, and at last finished it with the words, uttered in fervent appeal, "Bless our arms, grant us the victory, O Lord our God, Father and Protector of our land and flag!"

The stranger touched his arm, motioned him to step aside—which the startled minister did—and took his place. During some moments he surveyed the spellbound audience with solemn eyes, in which burned an uncanny light; then in a deep voice he said:

"I come from the Throne—bearing a message from Almighty God!" The words smote the house with a shock; if the stranger perceived it he gave no attention. "He has heard the prayer of His servant your shepherd, and will grant it if such shall be your desire after I, His messenger, shall have explained to you its import—that is to say, its full import. For it is like unto many of the prayers of men, in that it asks for more than he who utters it is aware of—except he pause and think.

"God's servant and yours has prayed his prayer. Has he paused and taken thought? Is it one prayer? No, it is two—one uttered, the other not. Both have reached the ear of Him Who heareth all supplications, the spoken and the unspoken. Ponder this—keep it in mind. If you would beseech a blessing upon yourself, beware! lest without intent you invoke a curse upon a neighbor at the same time. If you pray for the blessing of rain upon your crop which needs it, by that act you are possibly praying for a curse upon some neighbor's crop which may not need rain and can be injured by it.

"You have heard your servant's prayer—the uttered part of it. I am commissioned of God to put into words the other part of it—that part which the pastor—and also you in your hearts—fervently prayed silently. And ignorantly and unthinkingly? God grant that it was so! You heard these words: 'Grant us the victory, O Lord our God!' That is sufficient. The *whole* of the uttered prayer is compact into those pregnant words Elaborations were not necessary. When you have prayed for victory you have prayed for many unmentioned results which follow victory—*must* follow it, cannot help but follow it. Upon the listening spirit of God the Father fell also the unspoken part of the prayer. He commandeth me to put it into words. Listen!

"O Lord our Father, our young patriots, idols of our hearts, go forth to battle—be Thou near them! With them—in spirit—we also go forth from the sweet peace of our beloved firesides to smite the foe. O Lord our God, help us to tear their soldiers to bloody shreds with our shells; help us to cover their smiling fields with the pale forms of their patriot dead; help us to drown the thunder of the guns with the shrieks of their wounded, writhing in pain; help us to lay waste their humble homes with a hurricane of fire; help us to wring the hearts of their unoffending widows with unavailing grief; help us to turn them out roofless with their little children to wander unfriended the wastes of their desolated land in rags and hunger and thirst, sports of the sun flames of summer and the icy winds of winter, broken in spirit, worn with travail, imploring Thee for the refuge of the grave and denied it—for our sakes who adore Thee, Lord, blast their hopes, blight their lives, protract their bitter pilgrimage, make heavy their steps, water their way with their tears, stain the white snow with the blood of their wounded feet! We ask it, in the spirit of love, of Him Who is the Source of Love, and Who is the ever-faithful refuge and friend of all that are sore beset and seek His aid with humble and contrite hearts. Amen."

(*After a pause.*) "Ye have prayed it; if ye still desire it, speak! The messenger of the Most High waits."

It was believed afterward that the man was a lunatic, because there was no sense in what he said.

# PART IV: DRAMATIC & LITERARY CRITICISM

❖

❪ Mark Twain seldom dealt in general principles or the systematic analysis of works of art. Yet the small amount of criticism he published is nearer the taste of our own

day than is the work of such professional critics as James Russell Lowell or even Howells. Whereas they tended to be vague and moralistic, Mark Twain was usually specific and technical. Both in his rejection of ornate rhetoric—as in the essay on Cooper—and in his preference for direct, colloquial language—as in the essays on the art of oral storytelling—he anticipates the revolution in taste that would occur during the two decades following his death.

❖

# WHITTIER BIRTHDAY DINNER SPEECH

❪ THIS speech (which was delivered on December 17, 1877) is reprinted here from the text of the original manuscript reproduced in the *Harvard Library Bulletin* (Spring, 1955). Mark Twain wrote the speech out and memorized it for the program of a dinner given by H. O. Houghton & Co., publishers of the *Atlantic Monthly*, in honor of John G. Whittier's seventieth birthday. After a number of conventional laudatory addresses and poems had been read, Mark Twain was introduced to provide comic relief. Some of his auditors, however, felt that his little burlesque was in bad taste, and both Clemens and Howells, who was presiding, came away suffering under the conviction that the speech had been a serious affront to Longfellow, Emerson, and Holmes, all of whom were present. Mark Twain wrote an abject letter of apology to these men and received polite reassurances in return, but he continued to brood over the incident for many years, unable to make up his mind whether or not he had been at fault. The sources of the verse quotations, in the order of their appearance in the text, are as follows:

1. Holmes, "The Chambered Nautilus"
2. Emerson, "Mithridates"
3. Longfellow, "Hiawatha"
4. Holmes, "Mare Rebrum 1858"
5. Longfellow, "Evangeline"
6. Emerson, "Concord Hymn"
7. Emerson, "Brahma"
8. Emerson, "Song of Nature"
9. Longfellow, "The Village Blacksmith"
10. Holmes, "A Voice of the Loyal North 1861 (January Third)"
11. Longfellow, "A Psalm of Life"

MR. CHAIRMAN—This is an occasion peculiarly meet for the digging up of pleasant reminiscences concerning literary folk; therefore I will drop lightly into history myself. Standing here on the shore of the Atlantic & contemplating certain of its biggest literary billows, I am reminded of a thing which happened to me fifteen years ago, when I had just succeeded in stirring up a little Nevadian literary ocean-puddle myself, whose spume-flakes were beginning to blow thinly California-wards. I started on an inspection-tramp through the Southern mines of California. I was callow & conceited, & I resolved to try the virtue of my nom de plume. I very soon had an opportunity. I knocked at a miner's lonely log cabin in the foot-hills of the Sierras just at nightfall. It was snowing at the time. A jaded, melancholy man of fifty, barefooted, opened to me. When he heard my nom de plume, he looked more dejected than before. He let me in—pretty reluctantly, I thought —& after the customary bacon & beans, black coffee & a hot whisky, I took a pipe. This sorrowful man had not said three words up to this time. Now he spoke up & said in the voice of one who is secretly suffering, "You're the fourth—I'm a-going to move." "The fourth what?" said I. "The fourth littery man that's been here in twenty-four hours—I'm a-going to move." "You don't tell me!" said I; "Who were the others?" "Mr. Longfellow, Mr. Emerson, & Mr. Oliver Wendell Holmes—dad fetch the lot!"

### THE MINER'S STORY

You can easily believe I was interested.—I supplicated—three hot whiskies did the rest—& finally the melancholy miner began. Said he—

They came here just at dark yesterday evening, & I let them in, of course. Said they were going to Yo Semite. They were a rough lot—but that's nothing—everybody looks rough that travels afoot. Mr. Emerson was a seedy little bit of a chap —red headed. Mr. Holmes was as fat as a balloon —he weighed as much as three hundred, & had double chins all the way down to his stomach. Mr. Longfellow was built like a prize fighter. His head was cropped & bristly—like as if he had a wig made of hair-brushes. His nose lay straight down his face, like a finger, with the end-joint tilted up. They had been drinking—I could see that. And what queer talk they used! Mr. Holmes inspected this cabin, then he took me by the button-hole, & says he—

> "Through the deep caves of thought
> I hear a voice that sings:
> Build thee more stately mansions,
> O my Soul!"

Says I, "I can't afford it, Mr. Holmes, & moreover I don't want to." Blamed if I liked it pretty well, either, coming from a stranger, that way! However, I started to get out my bacon & beans, when Mr. Emerson came & looked on a while, & then *he* takes me aside by the button-hole & says—

> "Give me agates for my meat;
> Give me cantharids to eat;
> From air & ocean bring me foods,
> From all zones & altitudes."

Says I, "Mr. Emerson, if you'll excuse me, this ain't no hotel." You see it sort of riled me—I warn't used to the ways of littery swells. But I went on a-sweating over my work, & next comes Mr. Longfellow & button-holes me, & interrupts me. Says he—

> "Honor be to Mudjekeewis!
> You shall hear how Pau-Puk-Kee-wis—"

But I broke in, & says I, "Begging your pardon, Mr. Longfellow, if you'll be so kind as to hold your yawp for about five minutes, & let me get this grub ready, you'll do me proud." Well, sir, after they'd filled up, I set out the jug. Mr. Holmes looks at it, & then he fires up all of a sudden & yells—

> "Flash out a stream of blood-red wine!—
> For I would drink to other days."

By George, I was getting kind of worked up. I don't deny it, I was getting kind of worked up. I turns to Mr. Holmes, & says I, "Looky-here, my fat friend, I'm a-running this shanty, & if the court knows herself, you'll take whisky-straight or you'll go dry!" Them's the very words I said to him. Now I didn't want to sass such famous littery people, but you see they kind of forced me. There ain't nothing onreasonable 'bout me; I don't mind a passel of guests a-tread'n on my tail three or four times, but when it comes to *standing* on it, it's different, & if the court knows herself, you'll take whisky-straight or you'll go dry!" Well, between drinks they'd swell around the cabin & strike attitudes & spout. Says Mr. Longfellow—

> "This is the forest primeval."

Says Mr. Emerson—

> "Here once the embattled farmers stood,
> And fired the shot heard round the world."

Says I, "O, blackguard the premises as much as you want to—it don't cost you a cent." Well, they went on drinking, & pretty soon they got out a greasy old deck & went to playing cut-throat euchre at ten cents a corner—on trust. I begun to notice some pretty suspicious things. Mr. Emerson dealt, looked at his hand, shook his head, says—

> "I am the doubter & the doubt—"

—& calmly bunched the hands & went to shuffling for a new lay-out. Says he—

> "They reckon ill who leave me out;
> They know not well the subtle ways
> I keep. [*pause*] I pass, & deal *again!*"

Hang'd if he didn't go ahead & do it, too! O, he was a cool one! Well, in about a minute, things were running pretty tight, but all of a sudden I see by Mr. Emerson's eye that he judged he had 'em. He had already coralled two tricks, & each of the others one. So now he kinds of lifts a little, in his chair, & says—

"I tire of globes & aces!— Too long the game is played!"

—and down he fetches a right bower. Mr. Longfellow smiles as sweet as pie, & says—:

"Thanks, thanks to thee, my worthy friend, For the lesson thou hast taught!"

—and dog my cats if he didn't down with *another* right bower! Well, sir, up jumps Holmes, a-war-whooping, as usual, & says—

"God help them if the tempest swings The pine against the palm!"

—and I wish I may go to grass if he didn't swoop down with *another* right bower! Emerson claps his hand on his bowie, Longfellow claps his on his revolver, & I went under a bunk. There was going to be trouble; but that monstrous Holmes rose up, wobbling his double chins, & says he, "Order, gentlemen; the first man that draws, I'll lay down on him & smother him!" All quiet on the Potomac, you bet you! They were pretty how-come-you-so, now, & they begun to blow. Emerson says, "The bulliest thing I ever wrote, was Barbara Frietchie." Says Longfellow, "It don't begin with my Biglow Papers." Says Holmes, "My Thanatopsis lays over 'em both." They mighty near ended in a fight. Then they wished they had some more company—& Mr. Emerson pointed at me & says—

"Is yonder squalid peasant all That this proud nursery could breed?"

He was a-whetting his bowie on his boot—so I let it pass. Well, sir, next they took it into their heads that they would like some music; so they made me stand up & sing "When Johnny Comes Marching Home" till I dropped—at thirteen minutes past four this morning. That's what I've been through, my friend. When I woke at seven, they were leaving, thank goodness, & Mr. Longfellow had my only boots on, & his own under his arm. Says I, "Hold on, there, Evangeline, what you going to do with *them?*"—He says: "Going to make tracks with 'em; because—

"Lives of great men all remind us We can make our lives sublime; And departing, leave behind us Footprints on the sands of Time."

[As I said, Mr. Twain, you are the fourth in twenty-four hours—and I'm going to move; I ain't suited to a'] littery atmosphere." [1]

I said to the miner, "Why my dear sir, *these* were not the gracious singers to whom we & the world pay loving reverence & homage: these were impostors." The miner investigated me with a calm eye for a while, then said he, "Ah—impostors, were they? are *you?*" I did not pursue the subject; and since then I haven't traveled on my nom de plume enough to hurt. Such is the reminiscence I was moved to contribute, Mr. Chairman. In my enthusiasm I may have exaggerated the details a little, but you will easily forgive me that fault since I believe it is the first time I have ever deflected from perpendicular fact on an occasion like this.

## HOW TO TELL A STORY

❲ REPRINTED here from Definitive Edition, Vol. XXIV, "How to Tell a Story" was first published in *Youth's Companion* (1895). This discussion of the technique of oral storytelling should be compared with the discussion in "Platform Readings" (see pp. 749–754). The simulated laughter which James Whitcomb Riley used in his role of "a dull-witted old farmer" might be described as a reverse dead-pan: it seems to violate Mark Twain's prescription that the teller of a humorous story "does his best to conceal the fact that he even dimly suspects there is anything funny about it," but is actually an illustration of the same underlying principle of the use of a mask or persona by the artist.

I DO NOT claim that I can tell a story as it ought to be told. I only claim to know how a story ought to be told, for I have been almost daily in the company of the most expert story-tellers for many years.

There are several kinds of stories, but only one difficult kind—the humorous. I will talk mainly about that one. The humorous story is American, the comic story is English, the witty story is French. The humorous story depends for its effect upon the *manner* of the telling; the comic story and the witty story upon the *matter*.

The humorous story may be spun out to great length, and may wander around as much as it pleases, and arrive nowhere in particular; but the comic and witty stories must be brief and end with a point. The humorous story bubbles gently along, the others burst.

The humorous story is strictly a work of art— high and delicate art—and only an artist can tell

WHITTIER BIRTHDAY DINNER SPEECH.   1. Mark Twain's manuscript has been mutilated here. The omitted words are supplied from the version of the speech he inclosed in his Autobiographical Dictation.

it; but no art is necessary in telling the comic and the witty story; anybody can do it. The art of telling a humorous story—understand, I mean by word of mouth, not print—was created in America, and has remained at home.

The humorous story is told gravely; the teller does his best to conceal the fact that he even dimly suspects that there is anything funny about it; but the teller of the comic story tells you beforehand that it is one of the funniest things he has ever heard, then tells it with eager delight, and is the first person to laugh when he gets through. And sometimes, if he has had good success, he is so glad and happy that he will repeat the "nub" of it and glance around from face to face, collecting applause, and then repeat it again. It is a pathetic thing to see.

Very often, of course, the rambling and disjointed humorous story finishes with a nub, point, snapper, or whatever you like to call it. Then the listener must be alert, for in many cases the teller will divert attention from that nub by dropping it in a carefully casual and indifferent way, with the pretense that he does not know it is a nub.

Artemus Ward [1] used that trick a good deal; then when the belated audience presently caught the joke he would look up with innocent surprise, as if wondering what they had found to laugh at. Dan Setchell [2] used it before him, Nye [3] and Riley [4] and others use it to-day.

But the teller of the comic story does not slur the nub; he shouts it at you—every time. And when he prints it, in England, France, Germany, and Italy, he italicizes it, puts some whooping exclamation-points after it, and sometimes explains it in a parenthesis. All of which is very depressing, and makes one want to renounce joking and lead a better life.

Let me set down an instance of the comic method, using an anecdote which has been popular all over the world for twelve or fifteen hundred years. The teller tells it in this way:

#### THE WOUNDED SOLDIER

In the course of a certain battle a soldier whose leg had been shot off appealed to another soldier who was hurrying by to carry him to the rear, informing him at the same time of the loss which he had sustained; whereupon the generous son of

Mars, shouldering the unfortunate, proceeded to carry out his desire. The bullets and cannon-balls were flying in all directions, and presently one of the latter took the wounded man's head off—without, however, his deliverer being aware of it. In no long time he was hailed by an officer, who said:

"Where are you going with that carcass?"

"To the rear, sir—he's lost his leg!"

"His leg, forsooth?" responded the astonished officer; "you mean his head, you booby."

Whereupon the soldier dispossessed himself of his burden, and stood looking down upon it in great perplexity. At length he said:

"It is true, sir, just as you have said." Then after a pause he added, *"But he* TOLD *me* IT WAS HIS LEG! ! ! ! !"

Here the narrator bursts into explosion after explosion of thunderous horse-laughter, repeating that nub from time to time through his gaspings and shriekings and suffocatings.

It takes only a minute and a half to tell that in its comic-story form; and isn't worth the telling, after all. Put into the humorous-story form it takes ten minutes, and is about the funniest thing I have ever listened to—as James Whitcomb Riley tells it.

He tells it in the character of a dull-witted old farmer who has just heard it for the first time, thinks it is unspeakably funny, and is trying to repeat it to a neighbor. But he can't remember it; so he gets all mixed up and wanders helplessly round and round, putting in tedious details that don't belong in the tale and only retard it; taking them out conscientiously and putting in others that are just as useless; making minor mistakes now and then and stopping to correct them and explain how he came to make them; remembering things which he forgot to put in in their proper place and going back to put them in there; stopping his narrative a good while in order to try to recall the name of the soldier that was hurt, and finally remembering that the soldier's name was not mentioned, and remarking placidly that the name is of no real importance, anyway—better, of course, if one knew it, but not essential, after all—and so on, and so on, and so on.

The teller is innocent and happy and pleased with himself, and has to stop every little while to hold himself in and keep from laughing outright; and does hold in, but his body quakes in a jelly-like way with interior chuckles; and at the end of the ten minutes the audience have laughed until they are exhausted, and the tears are running down their faces.

The simplicity and innocence and sincerity and unconsciousness of the old farmer are perfectly simulated, and the result is a performance which is thoroughly charming and delicious. This is art—

HOW TO TELL A STORY.   1. Artemus Ward: pseudonym of Charles Farrar Browne (1834–67), newspaper humorist and lecturer.   2. Dan Setchell: a famous comic actor on the New York and Boston stages in the 1850's and 1860's.   3. Nye: Edgar W. Nye (1850–96), a popular literary comedian in the tradition of Artemus Ward.   4. Riley: James Whitcomb Riley (1849–1916), best known for his dialect poems about Indiana, such as "The Old Swimmin' Hole," but also a gifted platform artist with whom Mark Twain once contemplated making a tour in a joint program of readings.

and fine and beautiful, and only a master can compass it; but a machine could tell the other story.

To string incongruities and absurdities together in a wandering and sometimes purposeless way, and seem innocently unaware that they are absurdities, is the basis of the American art, if my position is correct. Another feature is the slurring of the point. A third is the dropping of a studied remark apparently without knowing it, as if one were thinking aloud. The fourth and last is the pause.

Artemus Ward dealt in numbers three and four a good deal. He would begin to tell with great animation something which he seemed to think was wonderful; then lose confidence, and after an apparently absent-minded pause add an incongruous remark in a soliloquizing way; and that was the remark intended to explode the mine—and it did.

For instance, he would say eagerly, excitedly, "I once knew a man in New Zealand who hadn't a tooth in his head"—here his animation would die out; a silent, reflective pause would follow, then he would say dreamily, and as if to himself, "and yet that man could beat a drum better than any man I ever saw."

The pause is an exceedingly important feature in any kind of story, and a frequently recurring feature, too. It is a dainty thing, and delicate, and also uncertain and treacherous; for it must be exactly the right length—no more and no less—or it fails of its purpose and makes trouble. If the pause is too short [long?] the impressive point is passed, and the audience have had time to divine that a surprise is intended—and then you can't surprise them, of course.

On the platform I used to tell a negro ghost story that had a pause in front of the snapper on the end, and that pause was the most important thing in the whole story. If I got it the right length precisely, I could spring the finishing ejaculation with effect enough to make some impressible girl deliver a startled little yelp and jump out of her seat—and that was what I was after. This story was called "The Golden Arm," [5] and was told in this fashion. You can practise with it yourself—and mind you look out for the pause and get it right.

### THE GOLDEN ARM

Once 'pon a time dey wuz a monsus mean man, en he live 'way out in de prairie all 'lone by hisself, 'cep'n he had a wife. En bimeby she died, en he tuck en toted her way out dah in de prairie en bur-

5. "The Golden Arm": Mark Twain had learned this story from his father's slave, Uncle Ned, when he was a child in Florida, Mo. The story is mentioned again in "Platform Readings" (see p. 749).

ied her. Well, she had a golden arm—all solid gold, fum de shoulder down. He wuz pow'ful mean—pow'ful; en dat night he couldn't sleep, caze he want dat golden arm so bad.

When it come midnight he couldn't stan' it no mo'; so he git up, he did, en tuck his lantern en shoved out thoo de storm en dug her up en got de golden arm; en he bent his head down 'gin de win', en plowed en plowed en plowed thoo de snow. Den all on a sudden he stop (make a considerable pause here, and look startled, and take a listening attitude) en say: "My *lan'*, what's dat?"

En he listen—en listen—en de win' say (set your teeth together and imitate the wailing and wheezing singsong of the wind), "Bzzz-z-zzz"—en den, way back yonder whah de grave is, he hear a *voice!*—he hear a voice all mix' up in de win'—can't hardly tell 'em 'part—"Bzzz—zzz—W-h-o—g-o-t—m-y—g-o-l-d-e-n *arm?*" (You must begin to shiver violently now.)

En he begin to shiver en shake, en say, "Oh, my! *Oh,* my lan'!" en de win' blow de lantern out, en de snow en sleet blow in his face en mos' choke him, en he start a-plowin' knee-deep towards home mos' dead, he so sk'yerd—en pooty soon he hear de voice agin, en (pause) it 'us comin' *after* him! "Bzzz—zzz—zzz—W-h-o—g-o-t—m-y—g-o-l-d-e-n—*arm?*"

When he git to de pasture he hear it agin—closter now, en a-*comin'!*—a-comin' back dah in de dark en de storm—(repeat the wind and the voice). When he git to de house he rush up-stairs en jump in de bed en kiver up, head and years, en lay dah shiverin' en shakin'—en den way out dah he hear it *agin!*—en a-*comin'!* En bimeby he hear (pause—awed, listening attitude)—pat—pat—pat—*hit's a-comin' up-stairs!* Den he hear de latch, en he *know* it's in de room!

Den pooty soon he know it's a-*stannin' by de bed!* (Pause.) Den—he know it's a-*bendin' down over him*—en he cain't skasely git his breath! Den—den—he seem to feel someth'n' *c-o-l-d,* right down 'most agin his head! (Pause.)

Den de voice say, *right at his year*—"W-h-o—g-o-t—m-y—g-o-l-d-e-n *arm?*" (You must wail it out very plaintively and accusingly; then you stare steadily and impressively into the face of the farthest-gone auditor—a girl, preferably—and let that awe-inspiring pause begin to build itself in the deep hush. When it has reached exactly the right length, jump suddenly at that girl and yell, *"You've* got it!")

If you've got the *pause* right, she'll fetch a dear little yelp and spring right out of her shoes. But you *must* get the pause right; and you will find it the most troublesome and aggravating and uncertain thing you ever undertook.

## FENIMORE COOPER'S FURTHER LITERARY OFFENSES

❲ WRITTEN in 1894 or 1895, this essay is the second of two which purport to be lectures by "Mark Twain, M.A., Professor of Belles Lettres in the Veterinary College of Arizona." The first was published in the *North American Review* in July 1895. At the head of it Mark Twain placed quotations from Thomas R. Lounsbury, Brander Matthews, and Wilkie Collins praising Cooper as a literary artist. He then listed nineteen "rules governing literary art in the domain of romantic fiction" and demonstrated that in *The Deerslayer* and *The Pathfinder* Cooper violated almost all of them. The second lecture was not published until 1946, when Bernard DeVoto edited it with a commentary. The following text is from the *New England Quarterly* (September 1946).

YOUNG GENTLEMEN: In studying Cooper you will find it profitable to study him in detail—word by word, sentence by sentence. For every sentence of his is interesting. Interesting because of its make-up; its peculiar make-up, its original make-up. Let us examine a sentence or two, and see. Here is a passage from Chapter XI of *The Last of the Mohicans,* one of the most famous and most admired of Cooper's books:

Notwithstanding the swiftness of their flight, one of the Indians had found an opportunity to strike a straggling fawn with an arrow, and had borne the more preferable fragments of the victim, patiently on his shoulders, to the stopping-place. Without any aid from the science of cookery, he was immediately employed, in common with his fellows, in gorging himself with this digestible sustenance. Magua alone sat apart, without participating in the revolting meal, and apparently buried in the deepest thought.

This little paragraph is full of matter for reflection and inquiry. The remark about the swiftness of the flight was unnecessary, as it was merely put in to forestall the possible objection of some over-particular reader that the Indian couldn't have found the needed "opportunity" while fleeing swiftly. The reader would not have made that objection. He would care nothing about having that small matter explained and justified. But that is Cooper's way; frequently he will explain and justify little things that do not need it and then make up for this by as frequently failing to explain important ones that do need it. For instance he allowed that astute and cautious person, Deerslayer-Hawkeye, to throw his rifle heedlessly down and leave it lying on the ground where some hostile Indians would presently be sure to find it—a rifle prized by that person above all things else in the earth—and the reader gets no word of explanation of that strange act. There was a reason, but it wouldn't bear exposure. Cooper meant to get a fine dramatic effect out of the finding of the rifle by the Indians, and he accomplished this at the happy time; but all the same, Hawkeye could have hidden the rifle in a quarter of a minute where the Indians could not have found it. Cooper couldn't think of any way to explain why Hawkeye didn't do that, so he just shirked the difficulty and did not explain at all. In another place Cooper allowed Heyward to shoot at an Indian with a pistol that wasn't loaded—and grants us not a word of explanation as to how the man did it.

No, the remark about the swiftness of their flight was not necessary; neither was the one which said that the Indian found an opportunity; neither was the one which said he *struck* the fawn; neither was the one which explained that it was a "straggling" fawn; neither was the one which said the striking was done with an arrow; neither was the one which said the Indian bore the "fragments;" nor the remark that they were preferable fragments; nor the remark that they were *more* preferable fragments; nor the explanation that they were fragments of the "victim;" nor the over-particular explanation that specifies the Indian's "shoulders" as the part of him that supported the fragments; nor the statement that the Indian bore the fragments patiently. None of those details has any value. We don't care what the Indian struck the fawn with; we don't care whether it was a straggling fawn or an unstraggling one; we don't care which fragments the Indian saved; we don't care why he saved the "more" preferable ones when the merely preferable ones would have amounted to just the same thing and couldn't have been told from the more preferable ones by anybody, dead or alive; we don't care whether the Indian carried them on his shoulders or in his handkerchief; and finally, we don't care whether he carried them patiently or struck for higher pay and shorter hours. We are indifferent to that Indian and all his affairs.

There was only one fact in that long sentence that was worth stating, and it could have been squeezed into these few words—and with advantage to the narrative, too:

"During the flight one of the Indians had killed a fawn, and he brought it into camp." You will notice that "During the flight one of the Indians had killed a fawn and he brought it into camp," is more straightforward and businesslike, and less mincing and smirky, than it is to say "Notwithstanding the swiftness of their flight, one of the Indians had found an opportunity to strike a straggling fawn with an arrow, and had borne the more preferable fragments of the victim, patiently on his shoulders, to the stopping-place." You will notice that the form "During the flight one of the Indians had killed a fawn and he brought it into camp" holds up its chin and moves to the front with the steady stride of a grenadier, whereas the form "Notwithstanding the swiftness of their flight, one of the Indians had found an opportunity to strike a straggling fawn with an arrow, and had borne the more preferable fragments of the victim, patiently on his shoulders, to the stopping-place," simpers along with an airy, complacent, monkey-with-a-parasol gait which is not suited to the transportation of raw meat.

I beg to remind you that an author's way of setting forth a matter is called his Style, and that an author's style is a main part of his equipment for business. The style of some authors has variety in it, but Cooper's style is remarkable for the absence of this feature. Cooper's style is always grand and stately and noble. Style may be likened to an army, the author to its general, the book to the campaign. Some authors proportion an attacking force to the strength or weakness, the importance or unimportance, of the object to be attacked; but Cooper doesn't. It doesn't make any difference to Cooper whether the object of attack is a hundred thousand men or a cow; he hurls his entire force against it. He comes thundering down with all his battalions at his back, cavalry in the van, artillery on the flanks, infantry massed in the middle, forty bands braying, a thousand banners streaming in the wind; and whether the object be an army or a cow you will see him come marching sublimely in, at the end of the engagement, bearing the more preferable fragments of the victim patiently on his shoulders, to the stopping-place. Cooper's style is grand, awful, beautiful; but it is sacred to Cooper, it is his very own, and no student of the Veterinary College of Arizona will be allowed to filch it from him.

In one of his chapters Cooper throws an ungentle slur at one Gamut because he is not exact enough in his choice of words. But Cooper has that failing himself, as was remarked in our first Lecture. If the Indian had "struck" the fawn with a brick, or with a club, or with his fist, no one could find fault with the word used. And one cannot find much fault when he strikes it with an arrow; still it sounds affected, and it might have been a little better to lean to simplicity and say he shot it with an arrow.

"Fragments" is well enough, perhaps, when one is speaking of the parts of a dismembered deer, yet it hasn't just exactly the right sound— and sound is something; in fact sound is a good

deal. It makes the difference between good music and poor music, and it can sometimes make the difference between good literature and indifferent literature. "Fragments" sounds all right when we are talking about the wreckage of a breakable thing that has been smashed; it also sounds all right when applied to cat's-meat; but when we use it to describe large hunks and chunks like the fore- and hind-quarters of a fawn, it grates upon the fastidious ear.

"Without any aid from the science of cookery, he was immediately employed, in common with his fellows, in gorging himself with this digestible sustenance."

This was a mere statistic; just a mere cold, colorless statistic; yet you see Cooper has made a chromo out of it. To use another figure, he has clothed a humble statistic in flowing, voluminous and costly raiment, whereas both good taste and economy suggest that he ought to have saved these splendors for a king, and dressed the humble statistic in a simple breech-clout. Cooper spent twenty-four words here on a thing not really worth more than eight. We will reduce the statistic to its proper proportions and state it in this way:

"He and the others ate the meat raw."

"Digestible sustenance" is a handsome phrase, but it was out of place there, because we do not know these Indians or care for them; and so it cannot interest us to know whether the meat was going to agree with them or not. Details which do not assist a story are better left out.

"Magua alone sat apart, without participating in the revolting meal," is a statement which we understand, but that is our merit, not Cooper's. Cooper is not clear. He does not say who it is that is revolted by the meal. It is really Cooper himself, but there is nothing in the statement to indicate that it isn't Magua. Magua is an Indian and likes raw meat.

The word "alone" could have been left out and space saved. It has no value where it is.

I must come back with some frequency, in the course of these Lectures, to the matter of Cooper's inaccuracy as an Observer. In this way I shall hope to persuade you that it is well to look at a thing carefully before you try to describe it; but I shall rest you between times with other matters and thus try to avoid over fatiguing you with that detail of our theme. In *The Last of the Mohicans* Cooper gets up a stirring "situation" on an island flanked by great cataracts—a lofty island with steep sides—a sort of tongue which projects downstream from the midst of the divided waterfall. There are caverns in this mass of rock, and a party of Cooper people hide themselves in one of these to get away from some hostile Indians. There is a small exit at each end of this cavern. These exits are closed with blankets and the light excluded. The exploring hostiles back themselves up against the blankets and rave and rage in a blood-curdling way, but they are Cooper Indians and of course fail to discover the blankets; so they presently go away baffled and disappointed. Alice, in her gratitude for this deliverance, flings herself on her knees to return thanks. The darkness in there must have been pretty solid; yet if we may believe Cooper, it was a darkness which could not have been told from daylight; for here are some nice details which were visible in it:

"Both Heyward and the more tempered Cora witnessed the act of involuntary emotion with powerful sympathy, the former secretly believing that piety had never worn a form so lovely as it had now assumed in the youthful person of Alice. Her eyes were radiant with the glow of grateful feelings; the flush of her beauty was again seated on her cheeks, and her whole soul seemed ready and anxious to pour out its thanksgivings, through the medium of her eloquent features. But when her lips moved, the words they should have uttered appeared frozen by some new and sudden chill. Her bloom gave place to the paleness of death; her soft and melting eyes grew hard, and seemed contracting with horror; while those hands which she had raised, clasped in each other, towards heaven, dropped in horizontal lines before her, the fingers pointed forward in convulsed motion."

It is a case of strikingly inexact observation. Heyward and the more tempered Cora could not have seen the half of it in the dark that way.

I must call your attention to certain details of this work of art which invite particular examination. "Involuntary" is surplusage, and violates Rule 14.[1] All emotion is involuntary when genuine, and then the qualifying term is not needed; a qualifying term is needed only when the emotion is pumped-up and ungenuine. "Secretly" is surplusage, too; because Heyward was not believing out loud, but all to himself; and a person cannot believe a thing all to himself without doing it privately. I do not approve of the word "seated," to describe the process of locating a flush. No one can seat a flush. A flush is not a deposit on an exterior surface, it is a something which squashes out from within.

I cannot approve of the word "new." If Alice had had an old chill, formerly, it would be all right to distinguish this one from that one by calling

this one the new chill; but she had not had any old chill, this one was the only chill she had had, up till now, and so the tacit reference to an old anterior chill is unwarranted and misleading. And I do not altogether like the phrase "while those hands which she had raised." It seems to imply that she had some other hands—some other ones which she had put on the shelf a minute so as to give her a better chance to raise those ones; but it is not true; she had only the one pair. The phrase is in the last degree misleading. But I like to see her extend these ones in front of her and work the fingers. I think that that is a very good effect. And it would have almost doubled the effect if the more tempered Cora had done it some, too.

A Cooper Indian who has been washed is a poor thing, and commonplace; it is the Cooper Indian in his paint that thrills. Cooper's extra words are Cooper's paint—his paint, his feathers, his tomahawk, his warwhoop.

In the two-thirds of a page elsewhere referred to, wherein Cooper scored 114 literary transgressions out of a possible 115, he appears before us with all his things on. As follows, the italics are mine—they indicate violations of Rule 14:

In a minute he was once more fastened to the tree, *a helpless object of any insult or wrong that might be offered. So eagerly did every one now act, that nothing was said.* The fire was immediately lighted *in the pile, and the end of all was anxiously expected.*

It was not the intention of the Hurons *absolutely* to destroy *the life of* their victim by *means of* fire. They designed merely to put his *physical fortitude* to the severest proofs it could endure, short of that extremity. In the end, they fully intended to carry his scalp into their village, but it was their wish first to break down his resolution, and to reduce him to *the level of* a complaining sufferer. With this view, the pile of brush *and branches* had been placed at a *proper* distance, *or one* at which it was thought the heat would soon become intolerable, though *it might* not *be* immediately dangerous. *As often happened, however, on these occasions,* this distance had been miscalculated, and the flames *began to wave their forked tongues in a proximity to the face of the victim that* would have proved fatal in another instant had not Hetty rushed through the crowd, armed with a stick, and scattered the blazing pile *in a dozen directions.* More than one hand was raised to strike the *presumptuous* intruder to the earth; but the chiefs prevented the blows by reminding their *irritated* followers of the state of her mind. Hetty, herself, was insensible to the risk she ran; but, *as soon as she had performed this bold act, she* stood looking about her in frowning resentment, as if to rebuke the *crowd of attentive* savages *for their cruelty.*

'God bless you, dear*est sister,* for that brave and ready act,' murmured Judith, *herself unnerved so much* *as to be incapable of exertion;* 'Heaven itself has sent you on its holy errand.'

Number of words, 320; necessary ones, 220; words wasted by the generous spendthrift, 100.

In our day those 100 unnecessary words would have to come out. We will take them out presently and make the episode approximate the modern requirement in the matter of compression.

If we may consider each unnecessary word in Cooper's report of that barbecue a separate and individual violation of Rule 14, then that rule is violated 100 times in that report. Other rules are violated in it. Rule 12,[2] two instances; Rule 13,[3] three instances; Rule 15,[4] one instance; Rule 16,[5] two instances; Rule 17,[6] one or two little instances; the Report in its entirety is an offense against Rule 18[7]—also against Rule 16. Total score, about 114 violations of the laws of literary art out of a possible 115.

Let us now bring forward the Report again, with the most of the unnecessary words knocked out. By departing from Cooper's style and manner, all the facts could be put into 150 words, and the effects heightened at the same time—this is manifest, of course—but that would not be desirable. We must stick to Cooper's language as closely as we can:

In a minute he was once more fastened to the tree. The fire was immediately lighted. It was not the intention of the Hurons to destroy Deerslayer's life by fire; they designed merely to put his fortitude to the severest proofs it could endure short of that extremity. In the end, they fully intended to take his life, but it was their wish first to break down his resolution and reduce him to a complaining sufferer. With this view the pile of brush had been placed at a distance at which it was thought the heat would soon become intolerable, without being immediately dangerous. But this distance had been miscalculated; the fire was so close to the victim that he would have been fatally burned in another instant if Hetty had not rushed through the crowd and scattered the brands with a stick. More than one Indian raised his hand to strike her down but the chiefs saved her by reminding them of the state of her mind. Hetty herself was insensible to the risk she ran; she stood looking about her in frowning resentment, as if to rebuke the savages for their cruelty.

'God bless you, dear!' cried Judith, 'for that brave and ready act. Heaven itself has sent you on its holy errand, and you shall have a chromo.'

Number of words, 220—and the facts are all in.

2. **Rule 12:** "*Say* what he is proposing to say, not merely come near it." 3. **Rule 13:** "Use the right word, not its second cousin." 4. **Rule 15:** "Not omit necessary details." 5. **Rule 16:** "Avoid slovenliness of form." 6. **Rule 17:** "Use good grammar." 7. **Rule 18:** "Employ a simple and straightforward style."

## PLATFORM READINGS

❨ FROM the Autobiographical Dictation of October 10, 1907, first published in *Mark Twain in Eruption*, edited by Bernard DeVoto (1940), these comments on "reading" in public are the observations of one of the great masters of the art. They have a direct bearing on Mark Twain's writing; for he created a written style cunningly designed to simulate oral speech. And this style has been one of the major influences on American prose in the twentieth century.

WHAT is called a "reading," as a public platform entertainment, was first essayed by Charles Dickens, I think. He brought the idea with him from England in 1867. He had made it very popular at home and he made it so acceptable and so popular in America that his houses were crowded everywhere, and in a single season he earned two hundred thousand dollars. I heard him once during that season; it was in Steinway Hall, in December,[1] and it made the fortune of my life—not in dollars, I am not thinking of dollars; it made the real fortune of my life in that it made the happiness of my life; on that day I called at the St. Nicholas Hotel to see my *Quaker City* Excursion shipmate, Charley Langdon, and was introduced to a sweet and timid and lovely young girl, his sister. The family went to the Dickens reading, and I accompanied them. It was forty years ago; from that day to this the sister has never been out of my mind nor heart.

Mr. Dickens read scenes from his printed books. From my distance, he was a small and slender figure, rather fancifully dressed, and striking and picturesque in appearance. He wore a black velvet coat with a large and glaring red flower in the button-hole. He stood under a red upholstered shed behind whose slant was a row of strong lights—just such an arrangement as artists use to concentrate a strong light upon a great picture. Dickens's audience sat in a pleasant twilight, while he performed in the powerful light cast upon him from the concealed lamps. He read with great force and animation, in the lively passages, and with stirring effect. It will be understood that he did not merely read but also acted. His reading of the storm scene in which Steerforth lost his life was so vivid, and so full of energetic action, that his house was carried off its feet, so to speak.

Dickens had set a fashion which others tried to follow, but I do not remember that anyone was any more than temporarily successful in it. The

PLATFORM READINGS.   1. **in December:** actually, January 2 or 3, 1868. Clemens had first met Olivia Langdon on December 27, 1867.

public reading was discarded after a time and was not resumed until something more than twenty years after Dickens had introduced it; then it rose and struggled along for a while in that curious and artless industry called Authors' Readings. When Providence had had enough of that kind of crime the Authors' Readings ceased from troubling and left the world at peace.

Lecturing and reading were quite different things; the lecturer didn't use notes or manuscript or book, but got his lecture by heart and delivered it night after night in the same words during the whole lecture season of four winter months. The lecture field had been a popular one all over the country for many years when I entered it in 1868;[2] it was then at the top of its popularity; in every town there was an organization of citizens who occupied themselves in the off season, every year, in arranging for a course of lectures for the coming winter; they chose their platform people from the Boston Lecture Agency list and they chose according to the town's size and ability to pay the prices. The course usually consisted of eight or ten lectures. All that was wanted was that it should pay expenses; that it should come out with a money balance at the end of the season was not required. Very small towns had to put up with fifty-dollar men and women, with one or two second-class stars at a hundred dollars each as an attraction; big towns employed hundred-dollar men and women altogether, and added John B. Gough, or Henry Ward Beecher, or Anna Dickinson, or Wendell Phillips, as a compelling attraction;[3] large cities employed this whole battery of stars. Anna Dickinson's price was four hundred dollars a night; so was Henry Ward Beecher's; so was Gough's, when he didn't charge five or six hundred. I don't remember Wendell Phillips's price but it was high.

I remained in the lecture field three seasons— long enough to learn the trade; then domesticated myself in my new married estate after a weary life of wandering, and remained under shelter at home for fourteen or fifteen years. Meantime, specula-

tors and money-makers had taken up the business of hiring lecturers, with the idea of getting rich at it. In about five years they killed that industry dead and when I returned to the platform for a season, in 1884, there had been a happy and holy silence for ten years, and a generation had come to the front who knew nothing about lectures and readings and didn't know how to take them nor what to make of them. They were difficult audiences, those untrained squads, and Cable[4] and I had a hard time with them sometimes.

Cable had been scouting the country alone for three years with readings from his novels, and he had been a good reader in the beginning for he had been born with a natural talent for it, but unhappily he prepared himself for his public work by taking lessons from a teacher of elocution, and so by the time he was ready to begin his platform work he was so well and thoroughly educated that he was merely theatrical and artificial and not half as pleasing and entertaining to a house as he had been in the splendid days of his ignorance. I had never tried reading as a trade and I wanted to try it. I hired Major Pond[5] on a percentage to conduct me over the country, and I hired Cable as a helper at six hundred dollars a week and expenses, and we started out on our venture.

It was ghastly! At least in the beginning. I had selected my readings well enough, but had not studied them. I supposed it would only be necessary to do like Dickens—get out on the platform and read from the book. I did that and made a botch of it. Written things are not for speech; their form is literary; they are stiff, inflexible, and will not lend themselves to happy and effective delivery with the tongue—where their purpose is to merely entertain, not instruct; they have to be limbered up, broken up, colloquialized, and turned into the common forms of unpremeditated talk— otherwise they will bore the house, not entertain it. After a week's experience with the book I laid it aside and never carried it to the platform again; but meantime I had memorized those pieces, and in delivering them from the platform they soon transformed themselves into flexible talk, with all their obstructing precisenesses and formalities gone out of them for good.

One of the readings which I used was a part of

---

2. in 1868: Mark Twain means that he first set out on a lecture tour in 1868 under the management of James Redpath's Boston Lyceum Bureau (not "Lecture Agency"). He had first appeared on a public platform for pay in San Francisco in 1866 with a lecture on the Sandwich Islands and then had toured the Mother Lode country and Nevada with it. 3. John B. Gough . . . attraction: Gough (1817–86) was a famous temperance lecturer. Beecher (1813–87) had made his reputation by antislavery discourses in this country and in England. Later he spoke often on evolution and religion, and on many other topics. Miss Dickinson (1842–1932) specialized in slavery and women's rights. Phillips (1811–84), also a noted antislavery orator before the Civil War, subsequently lectured on historical, literary, and humanitarian subjects.

4. Cable: George Washington Cable (1844–1925), a native of New Orleans and a Confederate veteran, aroused such hostility in the South with articles and speeches on the rights of the Negro that he was forced to move with his family to Massachusetts. The tour he made with Mark Twain lasted four months in the winter of 1884–85. 5. Major Pond: James B. Pond (1838–1903) had bought out Redpath's interest in the Boston Lyceum Bureau in 1875 and had opened his own lecture agency in New York in 1879.

an extravagant chapter in dialect from *Roughing It* which I entitled "His Grandfather's Old Ram." After I had memorized it it began to undergo changes on the platform and it continued to edit and revise itself, night after night, until by and by, from dreading to begin on it before an audience I came to like it and enjoy it. I never knew how considerable the changes had been when I finished the season's work; I never knew until ten or eleven years later, when I took up that book in a parlor in New York one night to read that chapter to a dozen friends of the two sexes who had asked for it. It *wouldn't read*—that is, it wouldn't read aloud. I struggled along with it for five minutes and then gave it up and said I should have to tell the tale as best I might from memory. It turned out that my memory was equal to the emergency; it reproduced the platform form of the story pretty faithfully, after that interval of years. I still remember that form of it, I think, and I wish to recite it here, so that the reader may compare it with the story as told in *Roughing It,*[6] if he pleases, and note how different the spoken version is from the written and printed version.

The idea of the tale is to exhibit certain bad effects of a good memory: the sort of memory which is too good, which remembers everything and forgets nothing, which has no sense of proportion and can't tell an important event from an unimportant one but preserves them all, states them all, and thus retards the progress of a narrative, at the same time making a tangled, inextricable confusion of it and intolerably wearisome to the listener. The historian of "His Grandfather's Old Ram" had that kind of a memory. He often tried to communicate that history to his comrades, the other surface miners, but he could never complete it because his memory defeated his every attempt to march a straight course; it persistently threw remembered details in his way that had nothing to do with the tale; these unrelated details would interest him and sidetrack him; if he came across a name or a family or any other thing that had nothing to do with his tale, he would diverge from his course to tell about the person who owned that name or explain all about that family —with the result that as he plodded on he always got further and further from his grandfather's memorable adventure with the ram, and finally went to sleep before he got to the end of the story, and so did his comrades. Once he did manage to approach so nearly to the end, apparently, that the boys were filled with an eager hope; they believed that at last they were going to find out all about the

grandfather's adventure and what it was that had happened. After the usual preliminaries, the historian said:

"Well, as I was a-sayin', he bought that old ram from a feller up in Siskiyou County and fetched him home and turned him loose in the medder, and next morning he went down to have a look at him, and accident'ly dropped a ten-cent piece in the grass and stooped down—so—and was a-fumblin' around in the grass to git it, and the ram he was a-standin' up the slope taking notice; but my grandfather wasn't taking notice, because he had his back to the ram and was int'rested about the dime. Well, there he was, as I was a-sayin', down at the foot of the slope a-bendin' over—so—fumblin' in the grass, and the ram he was up there at the top of the slope, and Smith—Smith was a-standin' there—no, not jest there, a little further away—fifteen foot perhaps—well, my grandfather was a-stoopin' way down—so—and the ram was up there observing, you know, and Smith he . . . (musing) . . . the ram he bent his head down, so . . . Smith of Calaveras . . . no, no it couldn't ben Smith of Calaveras—I remember now that he—b'George it was Smith of Tulare County—course it was, I remember it now perfectly plain.

"Well, Smith he stood just there, and my grandfather he stood just here, you know, and he was a-bendin' down just so, fumblin' in the grass, and when the old ram see him in that attitude he took it fur an invitation—and here he come! down the slope thirty mile an hour and his eye full of business. You see my grandfather's back being to him, and him stooping down like that, of course he—why sho! it *warn't* Smith of Tulare at all, it was Smith of Sacramento—my goodness, how did I ever come to get them Smiths mixed like that—why, Smith of Tulare was jest a nobody, but Smith of Sacramento—why the Smiths of Sacramento come of the best Southern blood in the United States; there warn't ever any better blood south of the line than the Sacramento Smiths. Why look here, one of them married a Whitaker! I reckon that gives you an idea of the kind of society the Sacramento Smiths could 'sociate around in; there ain't no better blood than that Whitaker blood; I reckon anybody'll tell you that.

"Look at Mariar Whitaker—there was a girl for you! Little? Why yes, she was little, but what of that? Look at the heart of her—had a heart like a bullock—just as good and sweet and lovely and generous as the day is long; if she had a thing and you wanted it, you could have it—have it and welcome; why Mariar Whitaker couldn't have a thing

6. **as told in *Roughing It*:** The version from *Roughing It* is reprinted above, pp. 706–708.

and another person need it and not get it—get it and welcome. She had a glass eye, and she used to lend it to Flora Ann Baxter that hadn't any, to receive company with; well, she was pretty large, and it didn't fit; it was a number seven, and she was excavated for a fourteen, and so that eye wouldn't lay still; every time she winked it would turn over. It was a beautiful eye and set her off admirable, because it was a lovely pale blue on the front side—the side you look out of—and it was gilded on the back side; didn't match the other eye, which was one of them browny-yellery eyes and tranquil and quiet, you know, the way that kind of eyes are; but that warn't any matter—they worked together all right and plenty picturesque. When Flora Ann winked, that blue and gilt eye would whirl over, and the other one stand still, and as soon as she begun to get excited that handmade eye would give a whirl and then go on a-whirlin' and a-whirlin' faster and faster, and a-flashin' first blue and then yaller and then blue and then yaller, and when it got to whizzing and flashing like that, the oldest man in the world couldn't keep up with the expression on that side of her face. Flora Ann Baxter married a Hogadorn. I reckon that lets you understand what kind of blood she was—old Maryland Eastern Shore blood; not a better family in the United States than the Hogadorns.

"Sally—that's Sally Hogadorn—Sally married a missionary, and they went off carrying the good news to the cannibals out in one of them way-off islands round the world in the middle of the ocean somers, and they et her; et him too, which was irregular; it warn't the custom to eat the missionary, but only the family, and when they see what they had done they was dreadful sorry about it, and when the relations sent down there to fetch away the things they said so—said so right out—said they was sorry, and 'pologized, and said it shouldn't happen again; said 'twas an accident.

"Accident! now that's foolishness; there ain't no such thing as an accident; there ain't nothing happens in the world but what's ordered just so by a wiser Power than us, and it's always fur a good purpose; we don't know what the good purpose was, sometimes—and it was the same with the families that was short a missionary and his wife. But that ain't no matter, and it ain't any of our business; all that concerns us is that it was a special providence and it had a good intention. No, sir, there ain't no such thing as an accident. Whenever a thing happens that you think is an accident you make up your mind it ain't no accident at all —it's a special providence.

"You look at my Uncle Lem—what do you say

to that? That's all I ask you—you just look at my Uncle Lem and talk to me about accidents! It was like this: one day my Uncle Lem and his dog was downtown, and he was a-leanin' up against a scaffolding—sick, or drunk, or somethin'—and there was an Irishman with a hod of bricks up the ladder along about the third story, and his foot slipped and down he come, bricks and all, and hit a stranger fair and square and knocked the everlasting aspirations out of him; he was ready for the coroner in two minutes. Now then people said it was an accident.

"Accident! there warn't no accident about it; 'twas a special providence, and had a mysterious, noble intention back of it. The idea was to save that Irishman. If the stranger hadn't been there that Irishman would have been killed. The people said 'special providence—sho! the dog was there —why didn't the Irishman fall on the dog? Why warn't the dog app'inted?' Fer a mighty good reason—the dog would 'a' seen him a-coming; you can't depend on no dog to carry out a special providence. You couldn't hit a dog with an Irishman because—lemme see, what was that dog's name . . . (musing) . . . oh, yes, Jasper—and a mighty good dog too; he wa'n't no common dog, he wa'n't no mongrel; he was a composite. A composite dog is a dog that's made up of all the valuable qualities that's in the dog breed—kind of a syndicate; and a mongrel is made up of the riffraff that's left over. That Jasper was one of the most wonderful dogs you ever see. Uncle Lem got him of the Wheelers. I reckon you've heard of the Wheelers; ain't no better blood south of the line than the Wheelers.

"Well, one day Wheeler was a-meditating and dreaming around in the carpet factory and the machinery made a snatch at him and first you know he was a-meandering all over that factory, from the garret to the cellar, and everywhere, at such another gait as—why, you couldn't even see him; you could only hear him whiz when he went by. Well, you know a person can't go through an experience like that and arrive back home the way he was when he went. No, Wheeler got wove up into thirty-nine yards of best three-ply carpeting. The widder was sorry, she was uncommon sorry, and loved him and done the best she could fur him in the circumstances, which was unusual. She took the whole piece—thirty-nine yards—and she wanted to give him proper and honorable burial, but she couldn't bear to roll him up; she took and spread him out full length, and said she wouldn't have it any other way. She wanted a buy a tunnel for him but there wasn't any tunnel for sale, so she boxed him in a beautiful box and stood it on the hill on a pedestal twenty-one foot high, and so it was monument and grave together, and economical—sixty foot high—you could see it from everywhere—and she painted on it 'To the loving memory of thirty-nine yards best three-ply carpeting containing the mortal remainders of Millington G. Wheeler go thou and do likewise.' "

At this point the historian's voice began to wobble and his eyelids to droop with weariness, and he fell asleep; and so from that day to this we are still in ignorance; we don't know whether the old grandfather ever got the ten-cent piece out of the grass; we haven't any idea what it was that happened, or whether anything happened at all.

Upon comparing the above with the original in *Roughing It,* I find myself unable to clearly and definitely explain why the one can be effectively *recited* before an audience and the other can't; there is a reason but it is too subtle for adequate conveyance by the lumbering vehicle of words; I sense it but cannot express it; it is as elusive as an odor, pungent, pervasive, but defying analysis. I give it up. I merely know that the one version will recite, and the other won't.

By reciting I mean, of course, delivery from memory; neither version can be read effectively from the book. There are plenty of good reasons why this should be so, but there is one reason which is sufficient by itself, perhaps; in reading from the book you are telling another person's tale at secondhand; you are a mimic, and not the person involved; you are an artificiality, not a reality; whereas in telling the tale without the book you absorb the character and presently become the man himself, just as is the case with the actor.

The greatest actor would not be able to carry his audience by storm with a book in his hand; reading from the book renders the nicest shadings of delivery impossible. I mean those studied fictions which seem to be the impulse of the moment and which are so effective: such as, for instance, fictitious hesitancies for the right word, fictitious unconscious pauses, fictitious unconscious side remarks, fictitious unconscious embarrassments, fictitious unconscious emphases placed upon the wrong word with a deep intention back of it— these and all the other artful fictive shades which give to a recited tale the captivating naturalness of an impromptu narration can be attempted by a book reader and are attempted, but they are easily detectable as artifice, and although the audience may admire their cleverness and their ingenuity as artifice, they only get at the intellect of the house, they don't get at its heart; and so the reader's success lacks a good deal of being complete.

When a man is reading from a book on the plat-

form, he soon realizes that there is one powerful gun in his battery of artifice that he can't work with an effect proportionate to its caliber: that is the *pause*—that impressive silence, that eloquent silence, that geometrically progressive silence which often achieves a desired effect where no combination of words howsoever felicitous could accomplish it. The pause is not of much use to the man who is reading from a book because he cannot know what the exact length of it ought to be; he is not the one to determine the measurement— the audience must do that for him. He must perceive by their faces when the pause has reached the proper length, but his eyes are not on the faces, they are on the book; therefore he must determine the proper length of the pause by guess; he cannot guess with exactness and nothing but exactness, absolute exactness, will answer.

The man who recites without the book has all the advantage; when he comes to an old familiar remark in his tale which he has uttered nightly for a hundred nights—a remark preceded or followed by a pause—the faces of the audience tell him when to end the pause. For one audience the pause will be short, for another a little longer, for another a shade longer still; the performer must vary the length of the pause to suit the shades of difference between audiences. These variations of measurement are so slight, so delicate, that they may almost be compared with the shadings achieved by Pratt and Whitney's ingenious machine which measures the five-millionth part of an inch. An audience is that machine's twin; it can measure a pause down to that vanishing fraction.

I used to play with the pause as other children play with a toy. In my recitals, when I went reading around the world for the benefit of Mr. Webster's creditors,[7] I had three or four pieces in which the pauses performed an important part, and I used to lengthen them or shorten them according to the requirements of the case, and I got much pleasure out of the pause when it was accurately measured, and a certain discomfort when it wasn't. In the negro ghost story of "The Golden Arm"[8] one of these pauses occurs just in front of the closing remark. Whenever I got the pause the right length, the remark that followed it was sure of a satisfactorily startling effect, but if the length

7. **Mr. Webster's creditors:** It was a fixed idea of Clemens in his last years that his financial disaster in 1894 had been caused by Charles L. Webster's mismanagement of the publishing company that bore his name. This notion was erroneous, as is evident from the correspondence published by Webster's son, Samuel C. Webster, in *Mark Twain, Business Man* (1946). When Charles L. Webster retired from the company because of ill health in 1888, its affairs were in a sound condition. 8. **"The Golden Arm":** The story is reprinted above, p. 745.

of the pause was wrong by the five-millionth of an inch, the audience had had time in that infinitesimal fraction of a moment to wake up from its deep concentration in the grisly tale and foresee the climax, and be prepared for it befóre it burst upon them—and so it fell flat.

In Susy's little biography of me she tells about my proceeding to tell this ghost tale to the multitude of young lady students at Vassar College [9]— a tale which poor Susy always dreaded—and she tells how this time she gathered her fortitude together and was resolved that she wouldn't be startled, and how all her preparations were of no avail, and how when the climax fell that multitude of girls "jumped as one man"—which is an indication that I had the pause rightly measured that time.

In "His Grandfather's Old Ram" a pause has place; it follows a certain remark, and Mrs. Clemens and Clara, when we were on our way around the world, would afflict themselves with my whole performance every night when there was no sort of necessity for it, in order that they might watch the house when that pause came; they believed that by the effect they could accurately measure the high or low intelligence of the audience. I

9. **at Vassar College:** on May 15, 1885.

knew better but it was not in my interest to say so. When the pause was right, the effect was sure; when the pause was wrong in length, by the five-millionth of an inch, the laughter was only mild, never a crash. That passage occurs in "His Grandfather's Old Ram" where the question under discussion is whether the falling of the Irishman on the stranger was an accident, or was a special providence. If it was a special providence, and if the sole purpose of it was to save the Irishman, why was it necessary to sacrifice the stranger? "The dog was there. Why didn't he fall on the dog? Why wa'n't the dog app'inted? Becuz *the dog would 'a' seen him a-comin'.*" That last remark was the one the family waited for. A pause *after* the remark was absolutely necessary with any and all audiences because no man, howsoever intelligent he may be, can instantly adjust his mind to a new and unfamiliar, and yet for a moment or two apparently plausible, logic which recognizes in a dog an instrument too indifferent to pious restraints and too alert in looking out for his own personal interest to be safely depended upon in an emergency requiring self-sacrifice for the benefit of another, even when the command comes from on high.

F. W. DUPEE
*Editor*

# Henry James

## 1 8 4 3 – 1 9 1 6

HENRY JAMES tried as hard as any writer ever has to make his stories and novels self-contained and self-explanatory. Ideally, they require no special knowledge of his life and times, no research into his literary sources, no analysis of his ideas as such. One need ask questions of them as little as one does of some good play in lively progress before one's eyes in a theater.

But James's ideal was not always realized in his fiction. And when it was, which was more often than not, the very means he employed to realize it can prove puzzling to some readers on their first encounter with his work. His scenes are highly allusive and concentrated. His style is exceptionally rich in implication. His judgment as to what materials are relevant, and what irrelevant, to a given story is strict. Inevitably, such judgments are more than matters of literary technique; they suggest what to James was more important and less important in life itself. And inevitably, some readers are less impressed by what he puts into his work than they are depressed by what he leaves out.

Doesn't he appear to make life center in the drawing room and other settings of polite intercourse among human beings: the formal garden, the terrace, the museum, the restaurant, the public square? Where in his work are the bedroom, the factory, the business office, the farm, the forest, the sea, and those other backgrounds against which men and women experience the elemental hardships, animal pleasures, and sheer accidents of life? If such experiences are implied in his work, as in fact they often are, why are they *merely* implied rather than being dealt with openly and fully? Why are they not at the heart of things, as they are apt to be in the fiction of Cooper, Melville, Mark Twain, Dreiser, Hemingway, and Faulkner, to name only novelists of America? What is Henry James doing in such company?

Self-contained though they are, James's stories and novels have always given rise to questions of this kind. They still do today, although he was long ago recognized as a major writer and given a high place in American literature. He remains a very exceptional writer by the standards of our literature. Indeed, certain modern British critics claim him for British literature. And we should probably not try to situate him too firmly in *any* national tradition. Yet he is too great a writer to be described as a mere "sport."[1] If he belongs exclusively to no single national tradition, he belongs very definitely to the modern literature of what we now call the West, that is, Western Europe and America. No writer has ever cultivated more passionately his intellectual and emotional ties (his "relations," as he called them) to family and friends, to other writers, to

[1] **sport:** in biology, a marked variation from the normal type.

[755]

cities and countries, and to the cultural manifestations of the various modern nations—in particular the United States, England, France, and Italy. It was out of his intimate responses to the forms of literature and life in these countries that he shaped his special variety of "humanism," his idea of what was highest in human culture and character. His very conception of the art of the novel was a blend of influences stemming from the American Hawthorne, the English George Eliot, the French Balzac and Flaubert, the Russian Turgenev. The essays he wrote on these and other novelists are not merely examples of good literary criticism; they are also implied testimonials to his relations, literary and sometimes personal, with these novelists. The same is true of his travel essays (*Italian Hours*, 1909; *A Little Tour of France*, 1885; *The American Scene*, 1907; etc.); his biographies (Hawthorne, 1879; *William Wetmore Story*, 1903); and his autobiographical writings (*A Small Boy and Others*, 1913; *Notes of a Son and Brother*, 1914; and the posthumously published fragment *The Middle Years*, 1917). All these writings are made lively and often profound by his peculiar genius for relating himself to the most far-flung persons, places, and things. He was himself what he believed Americans generally were by reason of the newness and greatness of their country, "the heir of all the ages."

In a sense, therefore, no great writer was ever more thoroughly involved in tradition or committed to a profession and a way of life than James was. The old belief that he was a "rootless cosmopolitan" is no longer widely held. On the other hand, his idea of tradition was so complex, his way of life so unusual, and his work so selective in its values and methods, that he is not easily defined and classified. It is a part of the interest he has for us that he *is* exceptional and that every reader has to come to his own terms with him.

## II

JAMES was born in New York City on April 15, 1843. His parents, Henry and Mary Walsh James, were descended from pros-

perous Hudson Valley families of largely Irish ancestry. His paternal grandfather was the prime mover in the extremely animated history of the James family. A youth from County Cavan in Ireland, the first American James, William, settled in Albany in 1793, bore numerous children by three successive wives, and accumulated an enormous fortune. Improbably enough, this successful Irishman was also a doctrinaire Calvinist; and when he died, his son Henry, father of the novelist, fell heir not only to a good deal of money but to recollections of grim Sundays, hell-fire sermons, and other strictly imposed disciplines as well.

Similar memories did not prevent many of his brothers and sisters from frankly enjoying their legacies. In most cases they left their native Albany and austere childhood background far behind. Marrying into other rich families, settling in New York City or Rome or Paris, many of them joined that small band of newly rich Americans who, in the mid-nineteenth century, traveled extensively, cultivated their minds a little and their pleasures a lot, and sometimes thought of themselves as composing a new American aristocracy. Gay, talkative, affectionate, impulsive, they suffered in some instances from the very excess of these qualities and led troubled or empty lives which made a mild mockery of their aristocratic claims. As a child, the future novelist was surrounded by the members of this populous "cousinage," as he was to call it; and he later drew from its members much of his knowledge of American society—its individual types, its problems and promises. One cousin, Mary ("Minny") Temple, was to become an especially engaging and tragic figure in the family annals. Pretty, intelligent, spirited, she was exceptionally attractive to Henry and other young men of his circle. But, expectant of life though she was, she died young. Minny Temple lived on, however, in Henry's affections and literary work, representing for him a type of the American girl to which he was to return again and again throughout his long career.

As it happened, young Henry James knew the "cousinage" not only from the inside, so to speak, but also from the outside. His own branch of the James family was always a little apart from the rest of it, more serious and purposive. His father, Henry James, Sr., combined the family gaiety with unusual gifts of mind and character. Having lost a leg in an accident during his Albany boyhood, he experienced a long and painful convalescence in the course of which he acquired the habit of reflection and a passion for ideas and literature. Eventually, his share in the family fortune made a life of leisure possible for him and he resolved to devote it to two main pursuits. One of these was the effort to replace his father's Calvinism with a religious faith which would be more "spiritual" (a favorite word of his) and would allow the individual believer a greater freedom to develop his peculiar mind and talents. Such a faith Henry James, Sr., finally found, partly through his own mystical experiences, partly through his readings in Emmanuel Swedenborg, the Swedish philosopher. The second pursuit to which he gave himself was the raising of a family whose members would be allowed to develop their individualities with a minimum of imposed discipline. He married Mary Walsh and their devotion to one another became legendary; it was equaled only by their devotion to their five children: Henry, the future novelist; an older son, William, the future philosopher and psychologist; a younger daughter; and two younger sons.

On their tragic side, the elder James's views resembled Hawthorne's rather than those of the Transcendentalist school, with which, in other respects, he was to some extent associated. He admired Hawthorne's work; one of Henry, Jr.'s, earliest memories was of a new novel lying on the library table with the somewhat scary title of *The Scarlet Letter.* But the elder James was Emerson's friend and longtime correspondent, despite all their differences. Emerson sometimes visited the Jameses in their New York house; young Henry was always to recall his kindly but somewhat dim presence by the fireside. He had memories of visitors from other lands as well, including Thackeray, who stayed with the family in the course of a

tour of America; and in his early manhood Henry was to be presented to Dickens, whose novels he had devoured as they came out during his childhood and youth.

From these and other such experiences the young Jameses learned more than they ever learned by the usual routines of the classroom. Their father wanted it that way, giving them a peculiar kind of education which greatly affected their minds and future lives. He distrusted education of the formal variety. The average schoolroom of the time seemed to him a place where children were made to conform to rules and conventions rather than encouraged to develop their own natures. So the young Jameses received their principal education in the family circle. Reading, games and travel, and, above all, conversation made up their "routines." Their father urged them to talk, dispute, examine everything, declare their minds, articulate their least feelings. All this was done informally, amid shouts and laughter, with Henry James, Sr., playing his part in the proceedings as a near equal. To be sure, the children had some training of the formal kind, although this tended to be chaotic. They went from institution to institution, tutor to tutor, governess to governess, while their father vainly sought the ideal school or teacher. Meanwhile, they attended no church as other children did. Their father's Christian mysticism was passionately superior to Christian institutions and rituals. Nor did he have any recognized profession or job which could give the family a point of reference in society. It was his profession to be, in the broadest sense, simply a man.

This way of life was stimulating and in the long run rewarding for some of the James children. But it put a severe strain on their minds and nerves, throwing the family as a whole very much on its own, and each small member of the family very much on his or her own. At first, young Henry seems to have been more the victim than the beneficiary of his father's liberality. By his own account, in *A Small Boy and Others,* he was on his own to the point of feeling somewhat helpless. His childhood years were largely spent in the Washington Square neighborhood of New

York, a quiet and distinguished quarter of what was already a large and busy metropolis. His central experience in those years was of the "otherness" of things and people. The world seemed to be oddly estranged from him. The James family was very unlike other families and he was not only very unlike other children, he was very unlike his own brothers and boy cousins, especially his energetic, brilliant, probably rather bossy, older brother William. By contrast with these "others," Henry tended to think himself uncommonly passive, incompetent, dreamy, and slow of speech—something of a silent partner in the enterprise of education by conversation. But if this was his fate, he did not rebel against it in any of the usual ways. Then, as later on, he was devoted to most members of his immediate family, solicitous of their welfare, solicitous of their good opinion of himself.

When Henry James, Sr., died in 1881 a few months after his wife's death, William saluted him as "sacred old Father." To Henry, Jr., he was scarcely less sacred. Father and son were, however, quite different in temperament and Henry, Jr., in his memoirs, was to gently criticize his father's radical mysticism and experimental mode of life. Toward his mother he cherished emotions, as he said simply, "too deep for any words." He seems to have had a great deal in common with her. Like him, she was quiet, gentle, moderate in her opinions. Amid the excitement of their lives she seems to have embodied stability, order, and a capacity for self-sacrifice when it was necessary. Her affectionate presence evidently fortified young Henry in his possession of similar qualities. Her example probably helped to give him confidence in himself, however different he was from "others."

*Confidence* is the title of one of his early novels; confidence in the self is a recurring theme in all his work; and the search for confidence in his own self seems to have occupied him deeply during his youth. He quietly cultivated his peculiar attitudes and powers; if he "accepted his fate," he *made* it acceptable by converting it into something good and promising. How this came about is

told with modesty and humor, though with much complication of language, in *A Small Boy and Others* and its sequels, *Notes of a Son and Brother* and *The Middle Years*. He read endlessly and wrote quantities of juvenile stories and plays. He observed the sights of New York with rare intentness: the people, the streets, the houses, above all the stage plays, to which he was frequently taken by his parents, and the paintings that were sometimes on exhibit in commercial galleries (there was no Metropolitan Museum of Art, or anything like it, in those days). Thus he made the "otherness" of things more familiar and understandable, and thus he developed fantastic powers of memory and observation.

Such powers are part of the standard equipment of major novelists; and James's youthful habit of "gaping," as he called it, and of brooding on what he gaped at, became the basis of his literary vocation, indeed of his very methods as a storyteller. For "observation" was to have a more specialized meaning for him than for many of the literary realists and naturalists of the nineteenth century. His idea of it tended to be less scientific, more visionary, than theirs. To "observe" was to accumulate, not facts and appearances but images, or in the more technical term often employed by James, "impressions." A fully developed Jamesian impression of a phenomenon combines a glimpse of its external appearance with a hint as to its moral significance. Thus he writes of one of his characters, a New York hostess, that her home was a "wedge of brownstone violently driven into 53rd Street." From this, we get a peculiarly vivid picture of a New York brownstone house, narrow, solid, fiercely holding its own against the narrow, solid houses on both sides. We also get a possible suggestion that the occupant of the house is a socially ambitious woman, intent on thrusting her way into society.

Thus, in the course of time, James's childish sense of "otherness" was converted into a working quality of his imagination and art. Two major strains of experience contributed to this development. One, more or less negative, was his rather consistent feeling of powerlessness, a feeling that received concentrated expression when, during his adolescent years, he suffered a spinal injury while fighting a fire. A severe illness followed. He was unable to take part in the Civil War as his younger brothers did, and he continued to feel the effects of the injury at intervals throughout his life.

Meanwhile the other and more positive strain of experience had begun to play its part in his growth as an artist. Between his twelfth and seventeenth years he lived for the most part in Europe with his family. Leaving New York, the Jameses settled by turns in London, Paris, and Boulogne; and Henry continued to receive schooling, partly in the family circle, partly at institutions in Switzerland and elsewhere. Europe seemed very far away from America in those days. Ocean travel in primitive steamships was still a prolonged and hazardous affair. Europe was still the "Old World," the very antithesis of the "New World" of America. Indeed, Europe, with England at its head, then ruled the earth; whereas the United States was as yet only the land of promise—young, isolated, relatively unformed in its institutions, manners, and art. To the eye of the young American visitor, Europe's greatness was fully and richly formed. It was embodied in the splendid cities; in the wealth of magnificent buildings, museums, theaters, paintings; in the long-established social customs which gave definition and color to the daily life of people of all classes. All this fed young Henry's habitual fascination with whatever was "other"; it also gratified his desire for stability, order, and beauty. Later on, when he visited Europe on his own, and even more when he made Europe his residence, he came to view its civilization in a highly critical spirit. His mature novels mirror sharply the corrupting effects of excessive power and outworn institutions. What was fully "formed" could also be oppressive. Yet the Old World continued to haunt James's imagination, much as memories of the sea haunted Melville's, though with quite different implications. If he became a realistic social critic, he remained primarily an artist, that is, a

man of imagination; and to the artist in him, Europe remained, as he remarked himself, "vast, vague, and dazzling—an irradiation of light from objects undefined."

Henry James became one of the most thoroughly reasonable and self-controlled figures in all of literature. He nevertheless continued to consult his dreams and desires, however wayward, intangible, and contradictory. The "inward romantic principle," as he called it, was never to be denied. He obeyed his artist's instinct to remain open to the solicitations of experience, whether rational or irrational, conscious or unconscious. His mind, beneath its composed and purposeful surface, seethed with powerful associations. At this depth "Europe" (he himself eventually put the word in quotation marks) ceased to be a place and became a symbol. It was associated not only with historic cities and beautiful works of art but with the human values he felt to be embodied in those spectacles. As he makes clear in *Notes of a Son and Brother*, "Europe" at its best symbolized "the general sense of glory."

Yet it was in the United States, more particularly in New England, that he came of age as a man and embarked on his career as a writer. Returning from Europe in 1860, the James family settled eventually in Cambridge, Massachusetts. New England had been the dominant force in American literature throughout James's childhood and youth. He had first felt its impact through his father's connections and he now came to know it at first hand. Harvard College was across the street from the family residence; Boston was a short ride by horsecar or carriage; Concord was only some seven miles distant. Many of the writers associated with these places were his father's acquaintances; several of their sons and daughters were youthful companions of Henry and William. William Dean Howells, another young immigrant to New England, became Henry's closest literary friend. William James entered Harvard as a student of science, finished his studies there, and, after travel and study abroad, stayed on till the end of his life as a famous lecturer in psychology and philosophy. Henry himself was briefly enrolled in the

Harvard Law School. When he turned to literature, it was the *Atlantic Monthly* and the *North American Review* (then edited in New England) that printed many of his early stories and articles and thus helped to give him an audience.

But Henry James could not become an adoptive son of New England to the extent that William James was to do or that Howells did for many years. After all, he had been born in New York City, a fact which he always recalled with pride, and he had spent several formative years in Europe. He was cosmopolitan almost by nature. He admired large, complex, pleasure-loving societies—societies in which good and evil, and the freedom to choose between them, existed in abundance. On the whole, the New England society was the opposite of cosmopolitan. It was proudly pastoral, self-contained, exclusive. Could not the whole meaning of the universe be read in the annals of its history and the character of its people? Were not the very hills, fields, woods, ponds, and coasts of the region images of eternity? As it happened, the New England culture was not timeless and universal, much as its original greatness depended on the heroic fiction that it was. In time the genius of the region declined, and with its decline the New England pride gave way to a sort of self-protective complacency. Boston claimed to be "the hub of the universe" in proportion as Boston became a city of the past.

It was James's partial awareness of these historical considerations, together with his New York background, that made him a diffident citizen of literary New England. He came of age there during the years of the Civil War, when the literary consciousness of Americans was becoming more and more national, less and less regional and local. This development contributed to the decline of the New England culture, making it seem what James in his youth liked to call "provincial." But if the New England order was passing, a new intellectual and literary order was coming into existence in America. It is a fact of some historical interest that James published his first story in 1864, the same year during which Hawthorne died

after a protracted and fruitless struggle to recover his creative powers.

Thus, in relation to New England, James was in an advantageous position. He could profit from the energies originally set flowing by that culture and at the same time escape the worst effects of their dwindling. He could become, as T. S. Eliot has said, "positively a continuator of the New England genius." In this much-quoted remark the word *positively* should be stressed. Whatever James perpetuated of the New England genius, he transformed thoroughly, often beyond easy recognition.

### III

AMONG New England writers, Hawthorne was James's chief inspiration, in fact his only important one. For Hawthorne had been an artist of fiction, as James hoped to be. Moreover his art was based on a deep awareness of the human past, a feeling for human continuity, a recognition of human fallibility, all of which were congenial to James. In an essay on Emerson published in 1888, he was to declare (with some exaggeration) that Hawthorne's "vision was all for the evil and sin of the world; a side of life as to which Emerson's eyes were thickly bandaged." James had meanwhile acknowledged his relation to Hawthorne by frankly imitating him in certain youthful stories. And he was to publish in his thirty-sixth year, during the first flush of his international fame as a novelist, a searching and delightful biography of Hawthorne. The small book, published in 1879, was a sort of affectionate hail and farewell to the author of *The Scarlet Letter*. On the subject of Emerson, as we have seen, James's writings amounted to a respectful farewell with a very muted hail. He could not forgive Emerson his hyperbolic confidence in the universe. He could feel little literary sympathy for a man who confessed to seeing nothing in *Don Quixote* or the novels of Dickens and Jane Austen—or, for that matter, in Hawthorne's novels. (Emerson said that his Concord neighbor's books were "not worthy of him.") If we consider what the writing and reading of novels imply about the importance of worldly adventure, realistic social experience, and the here and now in the scheme of things, and if we compare Emerson's dismissal of the novel with James's devotion to it, we shall have a succinct idea of the differences between the two men and—Hawthorne excepted—their two generations.

James stated the differences clearly in the Hawthorne biography. The meaning of Hawthorne's career, with its fine achievements and partial failures, was that "the flower of art blooms only where the soil is deep, that it takes a great deal of history to produce a little literature, that it needs a complex social machinery to set a writer in motion." Much history had been made in the course of the Civil War and a new "era in the history of the American mind" had arrived. Americans would find the world "a more complicated place than it had hitherto seemed, the future more treacherous, success more difficult . . . The good American, in days to come, will be a more critical person than his complacent and confident grandfather. He has eaten of the tree of knowledge." As James presents them here, the advantages afforded him by the "new era" look somewhat grim. Whereas Thoreau, following Emerson, had confidently cried, "Simplify, simplify!" James now talks about "complication" and "difficulty" and a general failure of confidence. Americans are left in the position of Adam and Eve when the apple has been eaten and the newly acquired knowledge of good and evil hangs over them like a curse. What then? In *The American Scene*, a book published late in his life (1907), James could answer, with all confidence, the "what then?" The post-Civil War years had seen Americans embarked on the "great adventure" of "reaching out into the apparent void for the amenities, the consummations, after having earnestly gathered in so many of the preparations and necessities." In other words, the practical work of settling the continent and securing the political unity of the nation was complete enough to allow Americans to reach out for the relatively refined pleasures of conversation, travel, and art.

Conversation, travel, and art were pursuits of the cultivated life as James conceived it.

The "great adventure" thus consisted in the search for a broader American culture. In this, as in any genuine adventure, however, there were possibilities not only of pleasure and instruction but also of danger and frustration. By exchanging one's own poor culture for another, a person could lose his own rich, necessary identity. It thus became James's affair as a novelist to record the adventure of culture in its double aspect; so he compounded the pleasures he saw in it and added the frustrations and dangers he perceived to the sum. And he tried to see the whole adventure as it affected men and women engaged in the common routines of loving, marrying, and making their way in the world. What literary form was better suited to these purposes than the novel? For the novel, considered as a fully developed instrument of realistic social representation, was as new to American literature as the adventure of culture was.

Such were some of the literary opportunities present to James in post-Civil War America. But peculiarities of temperament and social position made it hard for him and others of his generation to take full and immediate advantage of them. James was an exceptionally reticent youth; marked feelings of powerlessness still mingled in him with strong feelings of pride and ambition. By belonging to a rich and cultivated family he belonged in some degree to a social class and literary generation which included—to take a notable example—Henry Adams. Many members of this class and generation tended to believe that they were in some important ways excluded from American life in the years following the Civil War. Their patrician birthright seemed to be threatened by the growing corruption of American politics, the rise of industrialism, the intrusion into the social picture of families newly rich and immigrants newly arrived in masses. In this situation, how could they exercise the duties and responsibilities, as well as enjoy the privileges, of their patrician heritage? James often speaks of "possessing oneself" of something, making something "one's own." Such phrases are a clue to his whole performance as an artist and moralist; they also make clear his affinity with this half-disinherited class and generation.

In time he did create a world of experience which was supremely his own. And thus he overcame in himself the worst distortions of character experienced by certain of the others: the nostalgia for Europe and the past, the snobbishness, the feeling of uselessness. He sank his roots into the firm ground of a profession, that of novelist, and made the ground still firmer by taking his profession with immense seriousness. Partly for professional, partly for temperamental reasons, he eventually took up residence in Europe. This step was grave but it was better than hovering between worlds and feeling a perpetual conflict between duty and nostalgia. In England, his eventual residence, he could attach himself to a society in which the aristocratic standard was still stoutly planted. There, too, he could find the "complex social machinery" to set him in motion as a writer.

Whether or not that machinery could have been found in America is probably an academic question, so far as James is concerned. For him, with his temperament and his youthful experience of Europe, the machinery was over there; and he had, as we have noted, the artist's instinct to trust to his experience and temperament rather than to socially imposed duties and hypothetical alternatives. The result was not, of course, an unqualified triumph. James's work is not the wholly self-contained and self-sufficient creation of a supremely free spirit. His work has a negative, or at least a problematical, aspect and has been rejected by certain generations and types of readers and critics. In their minds James is connected with the "genteel tradition" which Adams, Mark Twain, and Howells had also to cope with in their various ways, even when they did not belong to the patriciate. And it is probably true that there is a strain of unresolved personal gentility in James and his work. He makes, at times, an excessive evaluation of refinement, consciousness, and polite manners for their own sake. He tends generally to view the sexual life of man as a lurid mystery. Even his profound dedication to art can look negative when, as in certain off his Prefaces and his tales of writers and painters, he associates art too exclusively with difficulty, complexity, obliquity, sickness, and death. Yet he once wrote to Henry Adams that the practice of art is "an act of life," and this belief is strongly impressed on all the greater aspects of his work. For the body of his work is vast and various; it changes in mode and matter from period to period throughout his long career; and in the scale of the whole work the "genteel" or sentimental part of it looks increasingly small. It is the temerity and originality of James, rather than his refinements and inhibitions, which more and more command the interest of readers.

He published his first story, "A Tragedy of Error," in the *Continental Monthly* in February 1864. This was followed by many other stories and by numerous book reviews and travel essays. His early critical writings are still readable; they show a rather self-consciously classical intelligence working to absorb, besides Hawthorne, the gentle realism of George Eliot, the fierce realism of Balzac, Flaubert, and other Europeans whose work was still new to America, still touched with scandal. His early stories were a little dim and derivative. Certain of them have the biographical interest, however, of reflecting some of his own youthful problems and of anticipating his later themes. The heroes of several of them are young men suffering from wounds, illnesses, or simply lack of animal spirits; they have a difficult time living, loving, and becoming mature men. The theme of the young or otherwise inexperienced person's initiation into "maturity" —the word means many things in James—is to be a persistent theme in his major work. But the drama of self-discovery was not treated memorably until it was combined with his other great source of drama, the discovery of Europe.

IV

AS A YOUNG man James had made two trips to Europe on his own, and in 1876, at age thirty-three, he came to his momentous decision to try living abroad permanently. The decision cost him much anxious thought at the time and was to have incalculable consequences for his mind, work, and reputation. As he became more famous through his books, he also became more notorious: he was that queer monster of perversity, frivolity, or near-treason, an "expatriate." His notoriety had its peculiar disadvantages: people tended to read and review his books with the queer monster, rather than the books' actual contents, in mind. On the other hand his embattled state probably strengthened his character, fortified his resolve to be a great writer, and clarified his general point of view. On the whole he acquitted himself magnificently as the accused in the long expatriation trial which was his life. Throughout the ordeal he kept his American sympathies very much alive, his sense of humor intact. But it is hard to judge, pro or con, the deeper effects of his self-exile, for the evidence is intricately strewn through a long complex life and work. Speculation on the subject used to be rife among his critics but has now generally been abandoned as idle.

After a year spent in Paris, where he met Flaubert, Turgenev, and other novelists of the realist school, he moved to England; and there he remained, except for frequent journeys to the Continent and very occasional visits to America. His English life was centered in London until in his fifty-fifth year, he acquired a small estate in the country town of Rye and went into semi-retirement. In general, his life was devoid of dramatic incident or variety. He remained unmarried and, so far as we positively know, otherwise unattached except by way of friendship, a form of communion for which he had a genius and to which we owe his large legacy of extraordinary letters. Solitary work and social intercourse, both pursued on a grand scale, were the stable poles of his existence. They also helped to determine the character of his novels, in which conversation alternates with intimate private reflection, and the advantages and evils of life in society are paralleled by the advantages and dangers of the private life. If the dangers of society involve a loss of individual integrity, those of the private life consist of loneliness, egotism,

and a tendency toward self-delusion. James's twin existences nourished him as long as his work went well and he got reasonable recognition from a discerning public. This he did get during his early London years, when he enjoyed considerable fame as the inventor of that charming novelty, the "international" subject, as he was the first to call it.

This subject consisted of the bringing together, in intimate situations, of persons of various nationalities. There were precedents for the subject in such writers as Stendhal, Mérimée, and Dickens. But James made more of the element of conflicting manners, less of the element of physical adventure, than others before him had done; and his ability to depict national traits in the form of individual characters was, and has remained, unsurpassed. Besides, his characters belong to one or the other of two "worlds," the American and the European, the new and the old, the democratic and the aristocratic, which then figured as intense opposites and rivals, not only in the casual journalism of the day but in the serious social studies of, for example, Tocqueville, Mrs. Trollope, and Dickens. As James treated the subject, say in *Daisy Miller*, contrasting systems of manners imply contrasting systems of morality, and the contrasts can prove by turns comic and fatal. Moreover, James's American characters are themselves far from being all of a piece. The general drama of differences is intensified by his eye for the differences observable among persons of American nationality. He gives us Yankee Puritans, newly rich New Yorkers, Southerners, cosmopolitan types long habituated to Europe. He gives us people for whom "culture" implies the lighter pleasures, and people for whom it is synonymous with the perfection of the self. He gives us people who claim a certain innocence as part of their American birthright, and people whose innocence is more intrinsic, complex, and durable.

The international subject proved moderately popular and James treated it in a variety of moods, bringing all aspects of the subject to a high state of development in *The*

*Portrait of a Lady* (1881). In the later eighties he devoted his major efforts to the writing of three lengthy novels (*The Bostonians*, 1886; *The Princess Cassamassima*, 1886; *The Tragic Muse*, 1890), all of which deal with the more general problems of humanity. The action of these novels takes place not in the fairly enchanted world of the tourist but in a thoroughly disenchanted Boston or New York, Paris or London. These books failed with the public, however, and James, hoping to recover his audience and market, attempted a career in the theater (1890–95). (Despite his family's onetime wealth, he was a self-supporting writer.) This theatrical venture failed too, but for altogether different reasons. The three long novels were too rich and strange for the public taste of the time. The plays were dull from any point of view. In writing them James emptied himself of everything except his skill in mechanical contrivance. They suggest large ornate houses from which the owners have decamped with all their belongings. After he was booed from the stage while taking a curtain call at the first-night performance of *Guy Domville* in 1895, he gave up playwriting altogether.

This half-tragic, half-ridiculous period in James's career was to have extraordinary consequences. He recovered his mastery of himself and his art—recovered it all the more firmly perhaps for having briefly, and in part, lost it. Instead of expecting a large popular audience, such as Dickens and Balzac had enjoyed, he began to write for a small advanced audience, and gradually he acquired one. Meanwhile, out of his experience of loss and isolation came a series of tales based on relatively new situations and human types. Obsessed men and women, forlorn children, even ghosts fill his shorter narratives, from "The Pupil" (1890) to *The Turn of the Screw* (1898) to "The Beast in the Jungle" (1903) and beyond. Meanwhile, returning to the full-length novel, he went through two quite distinct phases of fiction writing. The first, extending from 1897 to 1900, gave rise to *What Maisie Knew* (1897), *The Spoils of Poynton* (1897), and *The Awk-*

*ward Age* (1899). In these novels, "the moral sense" is austerely affirmed by the principal characters, living as they do in a social milieu corrupt beyond any James had yet imagined.

In *The Awkward Age*, however, the comic sense wins at least a partial victory over the moral sense. In *The Ambassadors*, which ushered in his last great period, the comic sense is omnipresent, and James's powers of plot-making, scene-writing, and character-creating reach a supreme height. *The Ambassadors* (completed 1901, published 1903), *The Wings of the Dove* (1902), and *The Golden Bowl* (1904) are the principal achievements of his final phase as a novelist. The three novels have in common the fact that they return to the international subject of James's earlier days. Again American characters of relative inexperience travel to Europe, form intimacies there, and are conspired against by their more experienced intimates. But there are striking differences between the new uses and the old uses of the international subject, differences which obviously reflect James's own long habituation to Europe. The two "worlds," the American and the European, now seem less incompatible than formerly. The comedy and tragedy of comparative manners are somewhat in abeyance; there are no villains. The American characters are more positively "innocent," the Europeans less secure in their possession of "experience." The former win victories only through an intricate process of collaboration with the latter. It follows that the moral question, so prominent in the novels of the nineties, is, in these last novels, merged with the question of culture considered in a broad historical light. There is a growing recognition of what culture costs, almost necessarily, in terms of unregenerate passion, intrigue, and violence. With all their "sins," Mme. de Vionnet of *The Ambassadors* and Prince Amerigo of *The Golden Bowl* remain magnificent embodiments of their respective civilizations, the French and the Italian, as opposed to the thinner civilization of the Americans, which is still in the making. In these last novels, especially *The Golden Bowl*, the sometimes conflicting claims of morality and culture give rise to ambiguities which are the delight of some readers, the torment of others. And the settings of the novels loom prodigiously with symbolic import. When the guilt-stricken hero of *The Wings of the Dove* wanders disconsolately around Venice in an autumn storm he sees his own state of soul reflected in the appearance of the storm-bound Piazza San Marco: that famous public square is "more than ever like a great drawing-room, the drawing-room of Europe, profaned and bewildered by some reverse of fortune." The drawing room, once the scene of more or less polite intercourse in James's novels, has here become the setting of a great international tragedy.

## V

THE LAST novels bring several aspects of James's art of fiction to their fullest development. What are the most important of these aspects and how do they unite to form that peculiar phenomenon which we call Henry James's "world"? His world is peculiar in that it rests on an ideal abundance of money, beauty, intelligence, and informed good will. By contrast, the world of *Huckleberry Finn* — and those of other representative American novels — rests on something more like an ideal destitution: life is happiest and most "real" for Huck when he and Jim are together on the raft with a minimum of worldly goods, a maximum of instinctive daring, endurance, know-how, and fellowship. Where Mark Twain and so many others seek the authentic America by reconstituting in an idealized form the conditions of the frontier, even of the wilderness, Henry James seeks it in the contrary impulse toward a high civilization. His America is, quite literally, what the old slogan says it is: "the land of plenty." Its great problem is what to do with this plenty, this wealth of space, energy, good will, and money. For the abundance that prevails in James's world can itself be a cause of weakness and failure. In theory, it promises freedom of moral choice to all and makes it at least possible that all will choose the good. In fact, it often promotes egotism, greed, and

other negative distortions of character. These impair or subvert the good in some characters, while others can retain their hold on the good only by strenuous moral exertions and practical sacrifices.

Indeed, the failure of good will in James's world is the more appalling because the conditions for its success seem so favorable. This contrast between the possible and the actual, appearance and reality, makes for the Jamesian irony. Implicit in all his major work, the irony is greatly magnified in his late novels. With it, there is a further development of his characteristic forms and methods of storytelling. His style grows ever denser in images, implications, and subtle humor. The style suggests not the aloof impersonal speech of an omniscient author but the living voice of one deeply committed to his creations, thoroughly intent on suffusing them with mind and sensibility. More particularly, the story has always been told in such a way that the narrator seems to be an intimate observer of the action, usually a direct participant in it. Moreover, in order to enhance the appearance of free will and personal power on the part of his characters, James has always made them reveal themselves as much as possible through pointed dialogue and small but decisive actions. "Dramatize, dramatize!" was his slogan, and his narratives consequently tend to fall into long, highly developed "scenes" like those in stage plays. All such Jamesian elements — the style, the irony, the role of the observer-narrator, the scenic arrangement — undergo intensive development in his later work. They help to account for its triumphs as well as its occasional excesses of subtlety and complication.

With the publication of *The Golden Bowl* James's work as a novelist was substantially complete. In his remaining years he wrote some excellent shorter narratives and worked at two long novels (*The Sense of the Past* and *The Ivory Tower*) which were published as fragments after his death. He visited the United States in 1904−05 and wrote *The American Scene* on the basis of his impressions. In 1910 James fell seriously ill from the combined effects of fatigue and disappointment. Following his brother William's death in that year, he recovered sufficiently to undertake the writing of the autobiographical volumes we have referred to above. He was able to respond intensely to the tragedy of World War I, to take an active part in war work, and in 1915, the year before his death, to make his bold gesture of sympathy toward England in her historic crisis — he became a British subject.

Meanwhile, amid all his sufferings and disappointments, James had availed himself of the traditionally English privilege of becoming a "character." The character he assumed was that of a gentleman fallen among roaring democrats, a master craftsman of literature fallen among slipshod performers. He played the dual role with a dignity which nevertheless permitted him displays of delicate humor and pathos at his own expense. A portly figure, formal in dress, exquisite in manners, he had a head which one observer described as "majestic" and large eyes which were capable, another observer said, of an "intolerable scrutiny." Adored by some, scorned by others, constantly quoted and misquoted in the press, formally painted in oils by Sargent and other famous portraitists, caricatured by Max Beerbohm, subjected to the dubious flattery of having his literary style and personal conversation parodied again and again, he was perhaps the most conspicuously unread author in the Anglo-American world of the time. Only the widely read Mark Twain, among American writers, surpassed him as an international figure.

He died on February 28, 1916, after a series of strokes. In her recollections of James, Edith Wharton, a friend of his old age, reports a rumor which, whether true or apocryphal, is entirely "in character." "He is said to have told his friend Lady Prothero, when she saw him after his first stroke, that in the very act of falling, he heard in the room a voice which was distinctly, it seemed, not his own, saying: 'So here it is at last, the distinguished thing!'" This gentlemanly salute to death was the end for Henry James of his great life and work, and of the great adventure of culture they exemplified.

# DAISY MILLER:
## A STUDY

❖

❲ James gave the subtitle of "A Study" to *Daisy Miller* because he feared that his picture of the heroine was more of a sketch than a full-fledged portrait. Nevertheless, the work came as close to being a popular success as any other book he wrote. First published in England in the *Cornhill Magazine* (1878), it was reprinted in the United States later in the same year and has since reappeared in numerous collections and anthologies, including the New York Edition. Two "pirated," or unauthorized, publications of the book in 1878 testified to its contemporary fame, a part of which arose from a mild scandal provoked by the heroine's unconventional behavior.

Through the years *Daisy Miller* has been read with ever increasing pleasure in its mastery of the *nouvelle* form, the precision and wit of its characterizations, the meaningful use made of its Swiss and Roman settings, the subtlety with which a comedy of manners is joined to something bordering on a tragedy, the delicacy with which the claims of Roman manners are balanced against the claims of American manners (or the lack of them). Indeed *Daisy Miller* is now generally called the small masterpiece, as *The Portrait of a Lady* is called the large masterpiece, of James's early concern with the "international subject."

❖

### I

AT THE little town of Vevey, in Switzerland, there is a particularly comfortable hotel. There are, indeed, many hotels; for the entertainment of tourists is the business of the place, which, as many travellers will remember, is seated upon the edge of a remarkably blue lake—a lake that it behooves every tourist to visit. The shore of the lake presents an unbroken array of establishments of this order, of every category, from the "grand hotel" of the newest fashion, with a chalk-white front, a hundred balconies, and a dozen flags flying from its roof, to the little Swiss *pension* of an elder day, with its name inscribed in German-looking lettering upon a pink or yellow wall, and an awkward summer-house in the angle of the garden. One of the hotels at Vevey, however, is famous, even classical, being distinguished from many of its upstart neighbors by an air both of luxury and of maturity. In this region, in the month of June, American travellers are extremely numerous; it may be said, indeed, that Vevey assumes at this period some of the characteristics of an American watering-place. There are sights and sounds which evoke a vision, an echo, of Newport and Saratoga. There is a flitting hither and thither of "stylish" young girls, a rustling of muslin flounces, a rattle of dance-music in the morning hours, a sound of high-pitched voices at all times. You receive an impression of these things at the excellent inn of the "Trois Couronnes," and are transported in fancy to the Ocean House or to Congress Hall. But at the "Trois Couronnes," it must be added, there are other features that are much at variance with these suggestions: neat German waiters, who look like secretaries of legation; Russian princesses sitting in the garden; little Polish boys walking about, held by the hand, with their governors; a view of the sunny crest of the Dent du Midi and the picturesque towers of the Castle of Chillon.

I hardly know whether it was the analogies or the differences that were uppermost in the mind of a young American, who, two or three years ago, sat in the garden of the "Trois Couronnes," looking about him, rather idly, at some of the graceful objects I have mentioned. It was a beautiful summer morning, and in whatever fashion the young American looked at things, they must have seemed to him charming. He had come from Geneva the day before, by the little steamer, to see his aunt, who was staying at the hotel — Geneva having been for a long time his place of residence. But his aunt had a headache—his aunt had almost always a headache—and now she was shut up in her room, smelling camphor, so that he was at liberty to wander about. He was some seven-and-twenty years of age; when his friends spoke of him, they usually said that he was at Geneva, "studying." When his enemies spoke of him, they said—but, after all, he had no enemies; he was an extremely amiable fellow, and universally liked. What I should say is, simply, that when certain persons spoke of him they affirmed that the reason of his spending so much time at Geneva was that he was extremely devoted to a lady who lived there—a foreign lady—a person older than himself. Very few Americans—indeed I think none—had ever seen this lady, about whom there were some singular stories. But Winterbourne had an old attachment for the little metropolis of Calvinism; he had been put to school there as a boy, and he had afterwards gone to college there—circumstances which had led to his forming a great many youthful friendships. Many of these he had kept, and they were a source of great satisfaction to him.

After knocking at his aunt's door and learning that she was indisposed, he had taken a walk about the town, and then he had come in to his breakfast. He had now finished his breakfast; but he was drinking a small cup of coffee, which had been served to him on a little table in the garden by one of the waiters who looked like an *attaché*. At last he finished his coffee and lit a cigarette. Presently a small boy came walking along the path—an urchin of nine or ten. The child, who was diminutive for his years, had an aged expression of countenance, a pale complexion, and sharp little features. He was dressed in knickerbockers, with red stockings, which displayed his poor little spindleshanks; he also wore a brilliant red cravat. He carried in his hand a long alpenstock, the sharp point of which he thrust into everything that he approached—the flower-beds, the garden-benches, the trains of the ladies' dresses. In front of Winterbourne he paused, looking at him with a pair of bright, penetrating little eyes.

"Will you give me a lump of sugar?" he asked, in a sharp, hard little voice—a voice immature, and yet, somehow, not young.

Winterbourne glanced at the small table near him, on which his coffee-service rested, and saw that several morsels of sugar remained. "Yes, you may take one," he answered; "but I don't think sugar is good for little boys."

This little boy stepped forward and carefully selected three of the coveted fragments, two of which he buried in the pocket of his knickerbockers, depositing the other as promptly in another place. He poked his alpenstock, lance-fashion, into Winterbourne's bench, and tried to crack the lump of sugar with his teeth.

"Oh, blazes; it's har-r-d!" he exclaimed, pronouncing the adjective in a peculiar manner.

Winterbourne had immediately perceived that he might have the honour of claiming him as a fellow-countryman. "Take care you don't hurt your teeth," he said, paternally.

"I haven't got any teeth to hurt. They have all come out. I have only got seven teeth. My mother counted them last night, and one came out right afterwards. She said she'd slap me if any more came out. I can't help it. It's this old Europe. It's the climate that makes them come out. In America they didn't come out. It's these hotels."

Winterbourne was much amused. "If you eat three lumps of sugar, your mother will certainly slap you," he said.

"She's got to give me some candy, then," rejoined his young interlocutor. "I can't get any candy here—any American candy. American candy's the best candy."

"And are American little boys the best little boys?" asked Winterbourne.

"I don't know. I'm an American boy," said the child.

"I see you are one of the best!" laughed Winterbourne.

"Are you an American man?" pursued this vivacious infant. And then, on Winterbourne's affirmative reply—"American men are the best," he declared.

His companion thanked him for the compliment; and the child, who had now got astride of his alpenstock, stood looking about him, while he attacked a second lump of sugar. Winterbourne wondered if he himself had been like this in his infancy, for he had been brought to Europe at about this age.

"Here comes my sister!" cried the child, in a moment. "She's an American girl."

Winterbourne looked along the path and saw a beautiful young lady advancing. "American girls are the best girls," he said, cheerfully, to his young companion.

"My sister ain't the best!" the child declared. "She's always blowing at me."

"I imagine that is your fault, not hers," said Winterbourne. The young lady meanwhile had drawn near. She was dressed in white muslin, with a hundred frills and flounces, and knots of pale-colored ribbon. She was bare-headed; but she balanced in her hand a large parasol, with a deep border of embroidery; and she was strikingly, admirably pretty. "How pretty they are!" thought Winterbourne, straightening himself in his seat, as if he were prepared to rise.

The young lady paused in front of his bench, near the parapet of the garden, which overlooked the lake. The little boy had now converted his alpenstock into a vaulting-pole, by the aid of which he was springing about in the gravel, and kicking it up not a little.

"Randolph," said the young lady, "what *are* you doing?"

"I'm going up the Alps," replied Randolph. "This is the way!" And he gave another little jump, scattering the pebbles about Winterbourne's ears.

"That's the way they come down," said Winterbourne.

"He's an American man!" cried Randolph, in his little hard voice.

The young lady gave no heed to this announcement, but looked straight at her brother. "Well, I guess you had better be quiet," she simply observed.

It seemed to Winterbourne that he had been in a manner presented. He got up and stepped slowly towards the young girl, throwing away his cigarette. "This little boy and I have made acquaintance," he said, with great civility. In Geneva, as he had been perfectly aware, a young man was not at liberty to speak to a young unmarried lady except under certain rarely-occurring conditions; but here at Vevey, what conditions could be better than these?—a pretty American girl coming and standing in front of you in a garden. This pretty American girl, however, on hearing Winterbourne's observation, simply glanced at him; she then turned her head and looked over the parapet, at the lake and the opposite mountains. He wondered whether he had gone too far; but he decided that he must advance farther, rather than retreat. While he was thinking of something else to say, the young lady turned to the little boy again.

"I should like to know where you got that pole," she said.

"I bought it!" responded Randolph.

"You don't mean to say you're going to take it to Italy."

"Yes, I am going to take it to Italy!" the child declared.

The young girl glanced over the front of her dress, and smoothed out a knot or two of ribbon. Then she rested her eyes upon the prospect again. "Well, I guess you had better leave it somewhere," she said, after a moment.

"Are you going to Italy?" Winterbourne inquired, in a tone of great respect.

The young lady glanced at him again. "Yes, sir," she replied. And she said nothing more.

"Are you—a—going over the Simplon?"[1] Winterbourne pursued, a little embarrassed.

"I don't know," she said. "I suppose it's some mountain. Randolph, what mountain are we going over?"

"Going where?" the child demanded.

"To Italy," Winterbourne explained.

"I don't know," said Randolph. "I don't want to go to Italy. I want to go to America."

"Oh, Italy is a beautiful place!" rejoined the young man.

"Can you get candy there?" Randolph loudly inquired.

"I hope not," said his sister. "I guess you have had enough candy, and mother thinks so too."

"I haven't had any for ever so long—for a hundred weeks!" cried the boy, still jumping about.

The young lady inspected her flounces and smoothed her ribbons again; and Winterbourne

DAISY MILLER. 1. **Simplon:** one of the two passes through the Alps from Switzerland into Italy.

presently risked an observation upon the beauty of the view. He was ceasing to be embarrassed, for he had begun to perceive that she was not in the least embarrassed herself. There had not been the slightest alteration in her charming complexion; she was evidently neither offended nor fluttered. If she looked another way when he spoke to her, and seemed not particularly to hear him, this was simply her habit, her manner. Yet, as he talked a little more, and pointed out some of the objects of interest in the view, with which she appeared quite unacquainted, she gradually gave him more of the benefit of her glance; and then he saw that this glance was perfectly direct and unshrinking. It was not, however, what would have been called an immodest glance, for the young girl's eyes were singularly honest and fresh. They were wonderfully pretty eyes; and, indeed, Winterbourne had not seen for a long time anything prettier than his fair countrywoman's various features—her complexion, her nose, her ears, her teeth. He had a great relish for feminine beauty; he was addicted to observing and analyzing it; and as regards this young lady's face he made several observations. It was not at all insipid, but it was not exactly expressive; and though it was eminently delicate Winterbourne mentally accused it—very forgivingly—of a want of finish. He thought it very possible that Master Randolph's sister was a coquette; he was sure she had a spirit of her own; but in her bright, sweet, superficial little visage there was no mockery, no irony. Before long it became obvious that she was much disposed towards conversation. She told him that they were going to Rome for the winter—she and her mother and Randolph. She asked him if he was a "real American"; she shouldn't have taken him for one; he seemed more like a German—this was said after a little hesitation, especially when he spoke. Winterbourne, laughing, answered that he had met Germans who spoke like Americans; but that he had not, so far as he remembered, met an American who spoke like a German. Then he asked her if she should not be more comfortable in sitting upon the bench which he had just quitted. She answered that she liked standing up and walking about; but she presently sat down. She told him she was from New York State—"if you know where that is." Winterbourne learned more about her by catching hold of her small, slippery brother and making him stand a few minutes by his side.

"Tell me your name, my boy," he said.

"Randolph C. Miller," said the boy, sharply. "And I'll tell you her name;" and he levelled his alpenstock at his sister.

"You had better wait till you are asked!" said this young lady, calmly.

"I should like very much to know your name," said Winterbourne.

"Her name is Daisy Miller!" cried the child. "But that isn't her real name; that isn't her name on her cards."

"It's a pity you haven't got one of my cards!" said Miss Miller.

"Her real name is Annie P. Miller," the boy went on.

"Ask him *his* name," said his sister, indicating Winterbourne.

But on this point Randolph seemed perfectly indifferent; he continued to supply information in regard to his own family. "My father's name is Ezra B. Miller," he announced. "My father ain't in Europe; my father's in a better place than Europe."

Winterbourne imagined for a moment that this was the manner in which the child had been taught to intimate that Mr. Miller had been removed to the sphere of celestial rewards. But Randolph immediately added, "My father's in Schenectady. He's got a big business. My father's rich, you bet."

"Well!" ejaculated Miss Miller, lowering her parasol and looking at the embroidered border. Winterbourne presently released the child, who departed, dragging his alpenstock along the path. "He doesn't like Europe," said the young girl. "He wants to go back."

"To Schenectady, you mean?"

"Yes; he wants to go right home. He hasn't got any boys here. There is one boy here, but he always goes round with a teacher; they won't let him play."

"And your brother hasn't any teacher?" Winterbourne inquired.

"Mother thought of getting him one to travel round with us. There was a lady told her of a very good teacher; an American lady—perhaps you know her—Mrs. Sanders. I think she came from Boston. She told her of this teacher, and we thought of getting him to travel round with us. But Randolph said he didn't want a teacher travelling round with us. He said he wouldn't have lessons when he was in the cars. And we *are* in the cars about half the time. There was an English lady we met in the cars—I think her name was Miss Featherstone; perhaps you know her. She wanted to know why I didn't give Randolph lessons—give him 'instructions,' she called it. I guess he could give me more instruction than I could give him. He's very smart."

"Yes," said Winterbourne; "he seems very smart."

"Mother's going to get a teacher for him as soon as we get to Italy. Can you get good teachers in Italy?"

"Very good, I should think," said Winterbourne.

"Or else she's going to find some school. He ought to learn some more. He's only nine. He's going to college." And in this way Miss Miller continued to converse upon the affairs of her family, and upon other topics. She sat there with her extremely pretty hands, ornamented with very brilliant rings, folded in her lap, and with her pretty eyes now resting upon those of Winterbourne, now wandering over the garden, the people who passed by, and the beautiful view. She talked to Winterbourne as if she had known him a long time. He found it very pleasant. It was many years since he had heard a young girl talk so much. It might have been said of this unknown young lady, who had come and sat down beside him upon a bench, that she chattered. She was very quiet; she sat in a charming tranquil attitude, but her lips and her eyes were constantly moving. She had a soft, slender, agreeable voice, and her tone was decidedly sociable. She gave Winterbourne a history of her movements and intentions, and those of her mother and brother, in Europe, and enumerated, in particular, the various hotels at which they had stopped. "That English lady, in the cars," she said—"Miss Featherstone—asked me if we didn't all live in hotels in America. I told her I had never been in so many hotels in my life as since I came to Europe. I have never seen so many—it's nothing but hotels." But Miss Miller did not make this remark with a querulous accent; she appeared to be in the best humor with everything. She declared that the hotels were very good, when once you got used to their ways, and that Europe was perfectly sweet. She was not disappointed—not a bit. Perhaps it was because she had heard so much about it before. She had ever so many intimate friends that had been there ever so many times. And then she had had ever so many dresses and things from Paris. Whenever she put on a Paris dress she felt as if she were in Europe.

"It was a kind of a wishing-cap," said Winterbourne.

"Yes," said Miss Miller, without examining this analogy; "it always made me wish I was here. But I needn't have done that for dresses. I am sure they send all the pretty ones to America; you see the most frightful things here. The only thing I don't like," she proceeded, "is the society. There isn't any society; or, if there is, I don't know where it keeps itself. Do you? I suppose there is some society somewhere, but I haven't seen anything of it. I'm very fond of society, and I have always had a great deal of it. I don't mean only in Schenectady, but in New York. I used to go to New York every winter. In New York I had lots of society. Last winter I had seventeen dinners given me; and three of them were by gentlemen," added Daisy Miller. "I have more friends in New York than in Schenectady—more gentlemen friends; and more young lady friends too," she resumed in a moment. She paused again for an instant; she was looking at Winterbourne with all her prettiness in her lively eyes and in her light, slightly monotonous smile. "I have always had," she said, "a great deal of gentlemen's society."

Poor Winterbourne was amused, perplexed, and decidedly charmed. He had never yet heard a young girl express herself in just this fashion; never, at least, save in cases where to say such things seemed a kind of demonstrative evidence of a certain laxity of deportment. And yet was he to accuse Miss Daisy Miller of actual or potential *inconduite*,[2] as they said at Geneva? He felt that he had lived at Geneva so long that he had lost a good deal; he had become dishabituated to the American tone. Never, indeed, since he had grown old enough to appreciate things, had he encountered a young American girl of so pronounced a type as this. Certainly she was very charming, but how deucedly sociable! Was she simply a pretty girl from New York State—were they all like that, the pretty girls who had a good deal of gentlemen's society? Or was she also a designing, an audacious, an unscrupulous young person? Winterbourne had lost his instinct in this matter, and his reason could not help him. Miss Daisy Miller looked extremely innocent. Some people had told him that, after all, American girls were exceedingly innocent; and others had told him that, after all, they were not. He was inclined to think Miss Daisy Miller was a flirt—a pretty American flirt. He had never, as yet, had any relations with young ladies of this category. He had known, here in Europe, two or three women—persons older than Miss Daisy Miller, and provided, for respectability's sake, with husbands—who were great coquettes—dangerous, terrible women, with whom one's relations were liable to take a serious turn. But this young girl was not a coquette in that sense; she was very unsophisticated; she was only a pretty American flirt. Winterbourne was almost grateful for having found the formula that applied to Miss Daisy Miller. He leaned back in his seat; he remarked to himself that she had the

2. *inconduite:* indiscretion. Unless otherwise noted, foreign expressions are French throughout the selections from James.

most charming nose he had ever seen; he wondered what were the regular conditions and limitations of one's intercourse with a pretty American flirt. It presently became apparent that he was on the way to learn.

"Have you been to that old castle?" asked the young girl, pointing with her parasol to the far-gleaming walls of the Château de Chillon.[3]

"Yes, formerly, more than once," said Winterbourne. "You too, I suppose, have seen it?"

"No; we haven't been there. I want to go there dreadfully. Of course I mean to go there. I wouldn't go away from here without having seen that old castle."

"It's a very pretty excursion," said Winterbourne, "and very easy to make. You can drive, you know, or you can go by the little steamer."

"You can go in the cars," said Miss Miller.

"Yes; you can go in the cars," Winterbourne assented.

"Our courier says they take you right up to the castle," the young girl continued. "We were going last week; but my mother gave out. She suffers dreadfully from dyspepsia. She said she couldn't go. Randolph wouldn't go either; he says he doesn't think much of old castles. But I guess we'll go this week, if we can get Randolph."

"Your brother is not interested in ancient monuments?" Winterbourne inquired, smiling.

"He says he don't care much about old castles. He's only nine. He wants to stay at the hotel. Mother's afraid to leave him alone, and the courier won't stay with him; so we haven't been to many places. But it will be too bad if we don't go up there." And Miss Miller pointed again at the Château de Chillon.

"I should think it might be arranged," said Winterbourne. "Couldn't you get some one to stay—for the afternoon—with Randolph?"

Miss Miller looked at him a moment; and then, very placidly, "I wish *you* would stay with him!" she said.

Winterbourne hesitated a moment. "I should much rather go to Chillon with you."

"With me?" asked the young girl, with the same placidity.

She didn't rise, blushing, as a young girl at Geneva would have done; and yet Winterbourne, conscious that he had been very bold, thought it possible she was offended. "With your mother," he answered, very respectfully.

But it seemed that both his audacity and his respect were lost upon Miss Daisy Miller. "I guess

my mother won't go after all," she said. "She don't like to ride round in the afternoon. But did you really mean what you said just now; that you would like to go up there?"

"Most earnestly," Winterbourne declared.

"Then we may arrange it. If mother will stay with Randolph, I guess Eugenio will."

"Eugenio?" the young man inquired.

"Eugenio's our courier. He doesn't like to stay with Randolph; he's the most fastidious man I ever saw. But he's a splendid courier. I guess he'll stay at home with Randolph if mother does, and then we can go to the castle."

Winterbourne reflected for an instant as lucidly as possible—"we" could only mean Miss Daisy Miller and himself. This programme seemed almost too agreeable for credence; he felt as if he ought to kiss the young lady's hand. Possibly he would have done so—and quite spoiled the project; but at this moment another person—presumably Eugenio—appeared. A tall, handsome man, with superb whiskers, wearing a velvet morning-coat and a brilliant watch-chain, approached Miss Miller, looking sharply at her companion. "Oh, Eugenio!" said Miss Miller, with the friendliest accent.

Eugenio had looked at Winterbourne from head to foot; he now bowed gravely to the young lady. "I have the honour to inform mademoiselle that luncheon is upon the table."

Miss Miller slowly rose. "See here, Eugenio," she said. "I'm going to that old castle, anyway."

"To the Château de Chillon, mademoiselle?" the courier inquired. "Mademoiselle has made arrangements?" he added, in a tone which struck Winterbourne as very impertinent.

Eugenio's tone apparently threw, even to Miss Miller's own apprehension, a slightly ironical light upon the young girl's situation. She turned to Winterbourne, blushing a little—a very little. "You won't back out?" she said.

"I shall not be happy till we go!" he protested.

"And you are staying in this hotel?" she went on. "And you are really an American?"

The courier stood looking at Winterbourne, offensively. The young man, at least, thought his manner of looking an offence to Miss Miller; it conveyed an imputation that she "picked up" acquaintances. "I shall have the honour of presenting to you a person who will tell you all about me," he said, smiling, and referring to his aunt.

"Oh, well, we'll go some day," said Miss Miller. And she gave him a smile and turned away. She put up her parasol and walked back to the inn beside Eugenio. Winterbourne stood looking after her; and as she moved away, drawing her muslin

3. **Château de Chillon:** See Byron's poem "The Prisoner of Chillon." See also p. 777n.

furbelows over the gravel, said to himself that she had the *tournure* [4] of a princess.

He had, however, engaged to do more than proved feasible, in promising to present his aunt, Mrs. Costello, to Miss Daisy Miller. As soon as the former lady had got better of her headache he waited upon her in her apartment; and, after the proper inquiries in regard to her health, he asked her if she had observed, in the hotel, an American family—a mamma, a daughter, and a little boy.

"And a courier?" said Mrs. Costello. "Oh, yes, I have observed them. Seen them—heard them—and kept out of their way." Mrs. Costello was a widow with a fortune; a person of much distinction, who frequently intimated that, if she were not so dreadfully liable to sick-headaches, she would probably have left a deeper impress upon her time. She had a long pale face, a high nose, and a great deal of very striking white hair, which she wore in large puffs and *rouleaux* [5] over the top of her head. She had two sons married in New York, and another who was now in Europe. This young man was amusing himself at Hombourg, [6] and, though he was on his travels, was rarely perceived to visit any particular city at the moment selected by his mother for her own appearance there. Her nephew, who had come up to Vevey expressly to see her, was therefore more attentive than those who, as she said, were nearer to her. He had imbibed at Geneva the idea that one must always be attentive to one's aunt. Mrs. Costello had not seen him for many years, and she was greatly pleased with him, manifesting her approbation by initiating him into many of the secrets of that social sway which, as she gave him to understand, she exerted in the American capital. She admitted that she was very exclusive; but, if he were acquainted with New York, he would see that one had to be. And her picture of the minutely hierarchical constitution of the society of that city, which she presented to him in many different lights, was, to Winterbourne's imagination, almost oppressively striking.

He immediately perceived, from her tone, that Miss Daisy Miller's place in the social scale was low. "I am afraid you don't approve of them," he said.

"They are very common," Mrs. Costello declared. "They are the sort of Americans that one does one's duty by not—not accepting."

"Ah, you don't accept them?" said the young man.

"I can't, my dear Frederick. I would if I could, but I can't."

"The young girl is very pretty," said Winterbourne, in a moment.

"Of course she's pretty. But she is very common."

"I see what you mean, of course," said Winterbourne, after another pause.

"She has that charming look that they all have," his aunt resumed. "I can't think where they pick it up; and she dresses in perfection—no, you don't know how well she dresses. I can't think where they get their taste."

"But, my dear aunt, she is not, after all, a Comanche savage."

"She is a young lady," said Mrs. Costello, "who has an intimacy with her mamma's courier."

"An intimacy with the courier?" the young man demanded.

"Oh, the mother is just as bad! They treat the courier like a familiar friend—like a gentleman. I shouldn't wonder if he dines with them. Very likely they have never seen a man with such good manners, such fine clothes, so like a gentleman. He probably corresponds to the young lady's idea of a count. He sits with them in the garden, in the evening. I think he smokes."

Winterbourne listened with interest to these disclosures; they helped him to make up his mind about Miss Daisy. Evidently she was rather wild.

"Well," he said, "I am not a courier, and yet she was very charming to me."

"You had better have said at first," said Mrs. Costello with dignity, "that you had made her acquaintance."

"We simply met in the garden, and we talked a bit."

"*Tout bonnement!* [7] And pray what did you say?"

"I said I should take the liberty of introducing her to my admirable aunt."

"I am much obliged to you."

"It was to guarantee my respectability," said Winterbourne.

"And pray who is to guarantee hers?"

"Ah, you are cruel!" said the young man. "She's a very nice young girl."

"You don't say that as if you believed it," Mrs. Costello observed.

"She is completely uncultivated," Winterbourne went on. "But she is wonderfully pretty, and, in short, she is very nice. To prove that I believe it, I am going to take her to the Château de Chillon."

---

4. *tournure:* carriage.   5. *rouleaux:* rolls or coils.   6. Hombourg: a health resort, not to be confused with the northwest-German metropolis, Hamburg.

7. *"Tout bonnement!":* "Oh, really!" spoken with an ironic edge, would approximate it in American English.

"You two are going off there together? I should say it proved just the contrary. How long had you known her, may I ask, when this interesting project was formed? You haven't been twenty-four hours in the house."

"I had known her half an hour!" said Winterbourne, smiling.

"Dear me!" cried Mrs. Costello. "What a dreadful girl!"

Her nephew was silent for some moments. "You really think, then," he began, earnestly, and with a desire for trustworthy information—"you really think that—" But he paused again.

"Think what, sir?" said his aunt.

"That she is the sort of young lady who expects a man—sooner or later—to carry her off?"

"I haven't the least idea what such young ladies expect a man to do. But I really think that you had better not meddle with little American girls that are uncultivated, as you call them. You have lived too long out of the country. You will be sure to make some great mistake. You are too innocent."

"My dear aunt, I am not so innocent," said Winterbourne, smiling and curling his moustache.

"You are too guilty, then!"

Winterbourne continued to curl his moustache, meditatively. "You won't let the poor girl know you, then?" he asked at last.

"Is it literally true that she is going to the Château de Chillon with you?"

"I think that she fully intends it."

"Then, my dear Frederick," said Mrs. Costello, "I must decline the honour of her acquaintance. I am an old woman, but I am not too old—thank Heaven—to be shocked!"

"But don't they all do these things—the young girls in America?" Winterbourne inquired.

Mrs. Costello stared a moment. "I should like to see my granddaughters do them!" she declared, grimly.

This seemed to throw some light upon the matter, for Winterbourne remembered to have heard that his pretty cousins in New York were "tremendous flirts." If, therefore, Miss Daisy Miller exceeded the liberal margin allowed to these young ladies, it was probable that anything might be expected of her. Winterbourne was impatient to see her again, and he was vexed with himself that, by instinct, he should not appreciate her justly.

Though he was impatient to see her, he hardly knew what he should say to her about his aunt's refusal to become acquainted with her; but he discovered, promptly enough, that with Miss Daisy Miller there was no great need of walking on tiptoe. He found her that evening in the garden, wandering about in the warm starlight, like an indolent sylph, and swinging to and fro the largest fan he had ever beheld. It was ten o'clock. He had dined with his aunt, had been sitting with her since dinner, and had just taken leave of her till the morrow. Miss Daisy Miller seemed very glad to see him; she declared it was the longest evening she had ever passed.

"Have you been all alone?" he asked.

"I have been walking round with mother. But mother gets tired walking round," she answered.

"Has she gone to bed?"

"No; she doesn't like to go to bed," said the young girl. "She doesn't sleep—not three hours. She says she doesn't know how she lives. She's dreadfully nervous. I guess she sleeps more than she thinks. She's gone somewhere after Randolph; she wants to try to get him to go to bed. He doesn't like to go to bed."

"Let us hope she will persuade him," observed Winterbourne.

"She will talk to him all she can; but he doesn't like her to talk to him," said Miss Daisy, opening her fan. "She's going to try to get Eugenio to talk to him. But he isn't afraid of Eugenio. Eugenio's a splendid courier, but he can't make much impression on Randolph! I don't believe he'll go to bed before eleven." It appeared that Randolph's vigil was in fact triumphantly prolonged, for Winterbourne strolled about with the young girl for some time without meeting her mother. "I have been looking round for that lady you want to introduce me to," his companion resumed. "She's your aunt." Then, on Winterbourne's admitting the fact, and expressing some curiosity as to how she had learned it, she said she had heard all about Mrs. Costello from the chambermaid. She was very quiet, and very *comme il faut;* [8] she wore white puffs; she spoke to no one, and she never dined at the *table d'hôte.* Every two days she had a headache. "I think that's a lovely description, headache and all!" said Miss Daisy, chattering along in her thin, gay voice. "I want to know her ever so much. I know just what *your* aunt would be; I know I should like her. She would be very exclusive. I like a lady to be exclusive; I'm dying to be exclusive myself. Well, we *are* exclusive, mother and I. We don't speak to every one—or they don't speak to us. I suppose it's about the same thing. Anyway, I shall be ever so glad to know your aunt."

Winterbourne was embarrassed. "She would be most happy," he said; "but I am afraid those headaches will interfere."

8. *comme il faut:* mannerly.

The young girl looked at him through the dusk. "But I suppose she doesn't have a headache every day," she said, sympathetically.

Winterbourne was silent a moment. "She tells me she does," he answered at last—not knowing what to say.

Miss Daisy Miller stopped, and stood looking at him. Her prettiness was still visible in the darkness; she was opening and closing her enormous fan. "She doesn't want to know me!" she said, suddenly. "Why don't you say so? You needn't be afraid. I'm not afraid!" And she gave a little laugh.

Winterbourne fancied there was a tremor in her voice; he was touched, shocked, mortified by it. "My dear young lady," he protested, "she knows no one. It's her wretched health."

The young girl walked on a few steps, laughing still. "You needn't be afraid," she repeated. "Why should she want to know me?" Then she paused again; she was close to the parapet of the garden, and in front of her was the starlit lake. There was a vague sheen upon its surface, and in the distance were dimly-seen mountain forms. Daisy Miller looked out upon the mysterious prospect, and then she gave another little laugh. "Gracious! she *is* exclusive!" she said. Winterbourne wondered whether she was seriously wounded, and for a moment almost wished that her sense of injury might be such as to make it becoming in him to attempt to reassure and comfort her. He had a pleasant sense that she would be very approachable for consolatory purposes. He felt then, for the instant, quite ready to sacrifice his aunt, conversationally; to admit that she was a proud, rude woman, and to declare that they needn't mind her. But before he had time to commit himself to this perilous mixture of gallantry and impiety, the young lady, resuming her walk, gave an exclamation in quite another tone. "Well; here's mother! I guess she hasn't got Randolph to go to bed." The figure of a lady appeared, at a distance, very indistinct in the darkness, and advancing with a slow and wavering movement. Suddenly it seemed to pause.

"Are you sure it is your mother? Can you distinguish her in this thick dusk?" Winterbourne asked.

"Well!" cried Miss Daisy Miller, with a laugh, "I guess I know my own mother. And then she has got on my shawl, too! She is always wearing my things."

The lady in question, ceasing to advance, hovered vaguely about the spot at which she had checked her steps.

"I am afraid your mother doesn't see you," said Winterbourne. "Or perhaps," he added—thinking, with Miss Miller, the joke permissible—"perhaps she feels guilty about your shawl."

"Oh, it's a fearful old thing!" the young girl replied, serenely. "I told her she could wear it. She won't come here, because she sees you."

"Ah, then," said Winterbourne, "I had better leave you."

"Oh, no; come on!" urged Miss Daisy Miller.

"I'm afraid your mother doesn't approve of my walking with you."

Miss Miller gave him a serious glance. "It isn't for me; it's for you—that is, it's for *her*. Well, I don't know who it's for! But mother doesn't like any of my gentlemen friends. She's right down timid. She always makes a fuss if I introduce a gentleman. But I *do* introduce them—almost always. If I didn't introduce my gentlemen friends to mother," the young girl added, in her little soft, flat monotone, "I shouldn't think I was natural."

"To introduce me," said Winterbourne, "you must know my name." And he proceeded to pronounce it.

"Oh, dear, I can't say all that!" said his companion, with a laugh. But by this time they had come up to Mrs. Miller, who, as they drew near, walked to the parapet of the garden and leaned upon it, looking intently at the lake, and turning her back to them. "Mother!" said the young girl, in a tone of decision. Upon this the elder lady turned round. "Mr. Winterbourne," said Miss Daisy Miller, introducing the young man very frankly and prettily. "Common" she was, as Mrs. Costello had pronounced her; yet it was a wonder to Winterbourne that, with her commonness, she had a singularly delicate grace.

Her mother was a small, spare, light person, with a wandering eye, a very exiguous nose, and a large forehead, decorated with a certain amount of thin, much-frizzled hair. Like her daughter, Mrs. Miller was dressed with extreme elegance; she had enormous diamonds in her ears. So far as Winterbourne could observe, she gave him no greeting—she certainly was not looking at him. Daisy was near her, pulling her shawl straight. "What are you doing, poking round here?" this young lady inquired; but by no means with that harshness of accent which her choice of words may imply.

"I don't know," said her mother, turning towards the lake again.

"I shouldn't think you'd want that shawl!" Daisy exclaimed.

"Well—I do!" her mother answered, with a little laugh.

"Did you get Randolph to go to bed?" asked the young girl.

"No; I couldn't induce him," said Mrs. Miller, very gently. "He wants to talk to the waiter. He likes to talk to that waiter."

"I was telling Mr. Winterbourne," the young girl went on; and to the young man's ear her tone might have indicated that she had been uttering his name all her life.

"Oh, yes!" said Winterbourne; "I have the pleasure of knowing your son."

Randolph's mamma was silent; she turned her attention to the lake. But at last she spoke. "Well, I don't see how he lives!"

"Anyhow, it isn't so bad as it was at Dover," said Daisy Miller.

"And what occurred at Dover?" Winterbourne asked.

"He wouldn't go to bed at all. I guess he sat up all night—in the public parlour. He wasn't in bed at twelve o'clock; I know that."

"It was half-past twelve," declared Mrs. Miller, with mild emphasis.

"Does he sleep much during the day?" Winterbourne demanded.

"I guess he doesn't sleep much," Daisy rejoined.

"I wish he would!" said her mother. "It seems as if he couldn't."

"I think he's real tiresome," Daisy pursued.

Then, for some moments, there was silence. "Well, Daisy Miller," said the elder lady, presently, "I shouldn't think you'd want to talk against your own brother!"

"Well, he *is* tiresome, mother," said Daisy, quite without the asperity of a retort.

"He's only nine," urged Mrs. Miller.

"Well, he wouldn't go to that castle," said the young girl. "I'm going there with Mr. Winterbourne."

To this announcement, very placidly made, Daisy's mamma offered no response. Winterbourne took for granted that she deeply disapproved of the projected excursion; but he said to himself that she was a simple, easily-managed person, and that a few deferential protestations would take the edge from her displeasure. "Yes," he began; "your daughter has kindly allowed me the honour of being her guide."

Mrs. Miller's wandering eyes attached themselves, with a sort of appealing air, to Daisy, who, however, strolled a few steps farther, gently humming to herself. "I presume you will go in the cars," said her mother.

"Yes; or in the boat," said Winterbourne.

"Well, of course, I don't know," Mrs. Miller rejoined. "I have never been to that castle."

"It is a pity you shouldn't go," said Winterbourne, beginning to feel reassured as to her opposition. And yet he was quite prepared to find that, as a matter of course, she meant to accompany her daughter.

"We've been thinking ever so much about going," she pursued; "but it seems as if we couldn't. Of course Daisy—she wants to go round. But there's a lady here—I don't know her name—she says she shouldn't think we'd want to go to see castles *here;* she should think we'd want to wait till we got to Italy. It seems as if there would be so many there," continued Mrs. Miller, with an air of increasing confidence. "Of course, we only want to see the principal ones. We visited several in England," she presently added.

"Ah, yes! in England there are beautiful castles," said Winterbourne. "But Chillon, here, is very well worth seeing."

"Well, if Daisy feels up to it—," said Mrs. Miller, in a tone impregnated with a sense of the magnitude of the enterprise. "It seems as if there was nothing she wouldn't undertake."

"Oh, I think she'll enjoy it!" Winterbourne declared. And he desired more and more to make it a certainty that he was to have the privilege of a *tête-à-tête* with the young lady, who was still strolling along in front of them, softly vocalizing. "You are not disposed, madam," he inquired, "to undertake it yourself?"

Daisy's mother looked at him, an instant, askance, and then walked forward in silence. Then — "I guess she had better go alone," she said, simply. Winterbourne observed to himself that this was a very different type of maternity from that of the vigilant matrons who massed themselves in the forefront of social intercourse in the dark old city at the other end of the lake. But his meditations were interrupted by hearing his name very distinctly pronounced by Mrs. Miller's unprotected daughter.

"Mr. Winterbourne!" murmured Daisy.

"Mademoiselle!" said the young man.

"Don't you want to take me out in a boat?"

"At present?" he asked.

"Of course!" said Daisy.

"Well, Annie Miller!" exclaimed her mother.

"I beg you, madam, to let her go," said Winterbourne, ardently; for he had never yet enjoyed the sensation of guiding through the summer starlight a skiff freighted with a fresh and beautiful young girl.

"I shouldn't think she'd want to," said her mother. "I should think she'd rather go indoors."

"I'm sure Mr. Winterbourne wants to take me," Daisy declared. "He's so awfully devoted!"

"I will row you over to Chillon, in the starlight."

"I don't believe it!" said Daisy.

"Well!" ejaculated the elder lady again.

"You haven't spoken to me for half an hour," her daughter went on.

"I have been having some very pleasant conversation with your mother," said Winterbourne.

"Well, I want you to take me out in a boat!" Daisy repeated. They had all stopped, and she had turned round and was looking at Winterbourne. Her face wore a charming smile, her pretty eyes were gleaming, she was swinging her great fan about. No; it's impossible to be prettier than that, thought Winterbourne.

"There are half a dozen boats moored at that landing-place," he said, pointing to certain steps which descended from the garden to the lake. "If you will do me the honour to accept my arm, we will go and select one of them."

Daisy stood there smiling; she threw back her head and gave a little, light laugh. "I like a gentleman to be formal!" she declared.

"I assure you it's a formal offer."

"I was bound I would make you say something," Daisy went on.

"You see it's not very difficult," said Winterbourne. "But I am afraid you are chaffing me."

"I think not, sir," remarked Mrs. Miller, very gently.

"Do, then, let me give you a row," he said to the young girl.

"It's quite lovely, the way you say that!" cried Daisy.

"It will be still more lovely to do it."

"Yes, it would be lovely!" said Daisy. But she made no movement to accompany him; she only stood there laughing.

"I should think you had better find out what time it is," interposed her mother.

"It is eleven o'clock, madam," said a voice, with a foreign accent, out of the neighbouring darkness; and Winterbourne, turning, perceived the florid personage who was in attendance upon the two ladies. He had apparently just approached.

"Oh, Eugenio," said Daisy, "I am going out in a boat!"

Eugenio bowed. "At eleven o'clock, mademoiselle?"

"I am going with Mr. Winterbourne. This very minute."

"Do tell her she can't," said Mrs. Miller to the courier.

"I think you had better not go out in a boat, mademoiselle," Eugenio declared.

Winterbourne wished to Heaven this pretty girl were not so familiar with her courier; but he said nothing.

"I suppose you don't think it's proper!" Daisy exclaimed. "Eugenio doesn't think anything's proper."

"I am at your service," said Winterbourne.

"Does mademoiselle propose to go alone?" asked Eugenio of Mrs. Miller.

"Oh, no; with this gentleman!" answered Daisy's mamma.

The courier looked for a moment at Winterbourne—the latter thought he was smiling—and then, solemnly, with a bow, "As mademoiselle pleases!" he said.

"Oh, I hoped you would make a fuss!" said Daisy. "I don't care to go now."

"I myself shall make a fuss if you don't go," said Winterbourne.

"That's all I want—a little fuss!" And the young girl began to laugh again.

"Mr. Randolph has gone to bed!" the courier announced, frigidly.

"Oh, Daisy; now we can go!" said Mrs. Miller.

Daisy turned away from Winterbourne, looking at him, smiling, and fanning herself. "Goodnight," she said; "I hope you are disappointed, or disgusted, or something!"

He looked at her, taking the hand she offered him. "I am puzzled," he answered.

"Well, I hope it won't keep you awake!" she said, very smartly; and, under the escort of the privileged Eugenio, the two ladies passed towards the house.

Winterbourne stood looking after them; he was indeed puzzled. He lingered beside the lake for a quarter of an hour, turning over the mystery of the young girl's sudden familiarities and caprices. But the only very definite conclusion he came to was that he should enjoy deucedly "going off" with her somewhere.

Two days afterwards he went off with her to the Castle of Chillon. He waited for her in the large hall of the hotel, where the couriers, the servants, the foreign tourists were lounging about and staring. It was not the place he should have chosen, but she had appointed it. She came tripping downstairs, buttoning her long gloves, squeezing her folded parasol against her pretty figure, dressed in the perfection of a soberly elegant travelling-costume. Winterbourne was a man of imagination and, as our ancestors used to say, sensibility; as he looked at her dress and, on the great staircase, her little rapid, confiding step, he felt as if there were something romantic going forward. He could have believed he was going to elope with her. He passed out with her among all the idle people that were assembled there; they were all looking at her very hard; she had begun to chatter as soon as she joined him. Winterbourne's preference had been that they should be conveyed to Chillon in a carriage; but she expressed a lively wish to go in the little steamer; she declared that she had a passion for steamboats. There was always such a lovely breeze upon the water, and you saw such lots of people. The sail was not long, but Winterbourne's companion found time to say a great many things. To the young man himself their little excursion was so much of an escapade—an adventure—that, even allowing for her habitual sense of freedom, he had some expectation of seeing her regard it in the same way. But it must be confessed that, in this particular, he was disappointed. Daisy Miller was extremely animated, she was in charming spirits; but she was apparently not at all excited; she was not fluttered; she avoided neither his eyes nor those of any one else; she blushed neither when she looked at him nor when she felt that people were looking at her. People continued to look at her a great deal, and Winterbourne took much satisfaction in his pretty companion's distinguished air. He had been a little afraid that she would talk loud, laugh overmuch, and even, perhaps, desire to move about the boat a good deal. But he quite forgot his fears; he sat smiling, with his eyes upon her face, while, without moving from her place, she delivered herself of a great number of original reflections. It was the most charming garrulity he had ever heard. He had assented to the idea that she was "common"; but was she so, after all, or was he simply getting used to her commonness? Her conversation was chiefly of what metaphysicians term the objective cast; but every now and then it took a subjective turn.

"What on *earth* are you so grave about?" she suddenly demanded, fixing her agreeable eyes upon Winterbourne's.

"Am I grave?" he asked. "I had an idea I was grinning from ear to ear."

"You look as if you were taking me to a funeral. If that's a grin, your ears are very near together."

"Should you like me to dance a hornpipe on the deck?"

"Pray do, and I'll carry round your hat. It will pay the expenses of our journey."

"I never was better pleased in my life," murmured Winterbourne.

She looked at him a moment, and then burst into a little laugh. "I like to make you say those things! You're a queer mixture!"

In the castle, after they had landed, the subjective element decidedly prevailed. Daisy tripped about the vaulted chambers, rustled her skirts in the corkscrew staircases, flirted back with a pretty little cry and a shudder from the edge of the *oubliettes,* and turned a singularly well-shaped ear to everything that Winterbourne told her about the place. But he saw that she cared very little for feudal antiquities, and that the dusky traditions of Chillon made but a slight impression upon her. They had the good fortune to have been able to walk without other companionship than that of the custodian; and Winterbourne arranged with this functionary that they should not be hurried—that they should linger and pause wherever they chose. The custodian interpreted the bargain generously—Winterbourne, on his side, had been generous—and ended by leaving them quite to themselves. Miss Miller's observations were not remarkable for logical consistency; for anything she wanted to say she was sure to find a pretext. She found a great many pretexts in the rugged embrasures of Chillon for asking Winterbourne sudden questions about himself—his family, his previous history, his tastes, his habits, his intentions—and for supplying information upon corresponding points in her own personality. Of her own tastes, habits, and intentions Miss Miller was prepared to give the most definite, and, indeed, the most favourable, account.

"Well, I hope you know enough!" she said to her companion, after he had told her the history of the unhappy Bonnivard.[9] "I never saw a man that knew so much!" The history of Bonnivard had evidently, as they say, gone into one ear and out of the other. But Daisy went on to say that she wished Winterbourne would travel with them, and "go round" with them; they might know something, in that case. "Don't you want to come and teach Randolph?" she asked. Winterbourne said that nothing could possibly please him so much; but that he had unfortunately other occupations. "Other occupations? I don't believe it!" said Miss Daisy. "What do you mean? You are not in business." The young man admitted that he was not in business; but he had engagements which, even within a day or two, would force him to go back to Geneva. "Oh, bother!" she said; "I don't believe it!" and she began to talk about something else. But a few moments later, when he was pointing out to her the pretty design of an antique fireplace, she broke out irrelevantly,

9. **Bonnivard:** François Bonivard (or Bonnivard) (1496–1570), Swiss patriot, religious and political martyr, who was confined for seven years by the Duke of Savoy in the Castle of Chillon. See Byron's poem "The Prisoner of Chillon."

"You don't mean to say you are going back to Geneva?"

"It is a melancholy fact that I shall have to return to-morrow."

"Well, Mr. Winterbourne," said Daisy, "I think you're horrid!"

"Oh, don't say such dreadful things!" said Winterbourne—"just at the last!"

"The last!" cried the young girl; "I call it the first. I have half a mind to leave you here and go straight back to the hotel alone." And for the next ten minutes she did nothing but call him horrid. Poor Winterbourne was fairly bewildered; no young lady had as yet done him the honour to be so agitated by the announcement of his movements. His companion, after this, ceased to pay any attention to the curiosities of Chillon or the beauties of the lake; she opened fire upon the mysterious charmer in Geneva, whom she appeared to have instantly taken for granted that he was hurrying back to see. How did Miss Daisy Miller know that there was a charmer in Geneva? Winterbourne, who denied the existence of such a person, was quite unable to discover; and he was divided between amazement at the rapidity of her induction and amusement at the frankness of her *persiflage*. She seemed to him, in all this, an extraordinary mixture of innocence and crudity. "Does she never allow you more than three days at a time?" asked Daisy, ironically. "Doesn't she give you a vacation in summer? There is no one so hard worked but they can get leave to go off somewhere at this season. I suppose, if you stay another day, she'll come after you in the boat. Do wait over till Friday, and I will go down to the landing to see her arrive!" Winterbourne began to think he had been wrong to feel disappointed in the temper in which the young lady had embarked. If he had missed the personal accent, the personal accent was now making its appearance. It sounded very distinctly, at last, in her telling him she would stop "teasing" him if he would promise her solemnly to come down to Rome in the winter.

"That's not a difficult promise to make," said Winterbourne. "My aunt has taken an apartment in Rome for the winter, and has already asked me to come and see her."

"I don't want you to come for your aunt," said Daisy; "I want you to come for me." And this was the only allusion that the young man was ever to hear her make to his invidious kinswoman. He declared that, at any rate, he would certainly come. After this Daisy stopped teasing. Winterbourne took a carriage, and they drove back to Vevey in the dusk; the young girl was very quiet.

In the evening Winterbourne mentioned to Mrs. Costello that he had spent the afternoon at Chillon with Miss Daisy Miller.

"The Americans—of the courier?" asked this lady.

"Ah, happily," said Winterbourne, "the courier stayed at home."

"She went with you all alone?"

"All alone."

Mrs. Costello sniffed a little at her smelling-bottle. "And that," she exclaimed, "is the young person whom you wanted me to know!"

## II

WINTERBOURNE, who had returned to Geneva the day after his excursion to Chillon, went to Rome towards the end of January. His aunt had been established there for several weeks, and he had received a couple of letters from her. "Those people you were so devoted to last summer at Vevey have turned up here, courier and all," she wrote. "They seem to have made several acquaintances, but the courier continues to be the most *intime*. The young lady, however, is also very intimate with some third-rate Italians, with whom she rackets about in a way that makes much talk. Bring me that pretty novel of Cherbuliez's [10]— 'Paule Méré'—and don't come later than the 23rd."

In the natural course of events, Winterbourne, on arriving in Rome, would presently have ascertained Mrs. Miller's address at the American banker's, and have gone to pay his compliments to Miss Daisy. "After what happened at Vevey I think I may certainly call upon them," he said to Mrs. Costello.

"If, after what happens—at Vevey and everywhere—you desire to keep up the acquaintance, you are very welcome. Of course a man may know every one. Men are welcome to the privilege!"

"Pray what is it that happens—here, for instance?" Winterbourne demanded.

"The girl goes about alone with her foreigners. As to what happens further, you must apply elsewhere for information. She has picked up half-a-dozen of the regular Roman fortune-hunters, and she takes them about to people's houses. When she comes to a party she brings with her a gentleman with a good deal of manner and a wonderful moustache."

"And where is the mother?"

"I haven't the least idea. They are very dreadful people."

10. **Cherbuliez's:** Victor Cherbuliez (1829–99), minor French novelist of Swiss origin.

Winterbourne meditated a moment. "They are very ignorant—very innocent only. Depend upon it they are not bad."

"They are hopelessly vulgar," said Mrs. Costello. "Whether or no being hopelessly vulgar is being 'bad' is a question for the metaphysicians. They are bad enough to dislike, at any rate; and for this short life that is quite enough."

The news that Daisy Miller was surrounded by half-a-dozen wonderful moustaches checked Winterbourne's impulse to go straightway to see her. He had perhaps not definitely flattered himself that he had made an ineffaceable impression upon her heart, but he was annoyed at hearing of a state of affairs so little in harmony with an image that had lately flitted in and out of his own meditations; the image of a very pretty girl looking out of an old Roman window and asking herself urgently when Mr. Winterbourne would arrive. If, however, he determined to wait a little before reminding Miss Miller of his claims to her consideration, he went very soon to call upon two or three other friends. One of these friends was an American lady who had spent several winters at Geneva, where she had placed her children at school. She was a very accomplished woman, and she lived in the Via Gregoriana. Winterbourne found her in a little crimson drawing-room, on a third floor; the room was filled with southern sunshine. He had not been there ten minutes when the servant came in, announcing "Madame Mila!" This announcement was presently followed by the entrance of little Randolph Miller, who stopped in the middle of the room and stood staring at Winterbourne. An instant later his pretty sister crossed the threshold; and then, after a considerable interval, Mrs. Miller slowly advanced.

"I know you!" said Randolph.

"I'm sure you know a great many things," exclaimed Winterbourne, taking him by the hand. "How is your education coming on?"

Daisy was exchanging greetings very prettily with her hostess; but when she heard Winterbourne's voice she quickly turned her head. "Well, I declare!" she said.

"I told you I should come, you know," Winterbourne rejoined, smiling.

"Well—I didn't believe it," said Miss Daisy.

"I am much obliged to you," laughed the young man.

"You might have come to see me!" said Daisy.

"I arrived only yesterday."

"I don't believe that!" the young girl declared.

Winterbourne turned with a protesting smile to her mother; but this lady evaded his glance, and, seating herself, fixed her eyes upon her son. "We've got a bigger place than this," said Randolph. "It's all gold on the walls."

Mrs. Miller turned uneasily in her chair. "I told you if I were going to bring you, you would say something!" she murmured.

"I told *you!*" Randolph exclaimed. "I tell *you,* sir!" he added, jocosely, giving Winterbourne a thump on the knee. "It *is* bigger, too!"

Daisy had entered upon a lively conversation with her hostess; and Winterbourne judged it becoming to address a few words to her mother. "I hope you have been well since we parted at Vevey," he said.

Mrs. Miller now certainly looked at him—at his chin. "Not very well, sir," she answered.

"She's got the dyspepsia," said Randolph. "I've got it, too. Father's got it. I've got it most!"

This announcement, instead of embarrassing Mrs. Miller, seemed to relieve her. "I suffer from the liver," she said. "I think it's this climate; it's less bracing than Schenectady, especially in the winter season. I don't know whether you know we reside at Schenectady. I was saying to Daisy that I certainly hadn't found any one like Dr. Davis, and I didn't believe I should. Oh, at Schenectady he stands first; they think everything of him. He has so much to do, and yet there was nothing he wouldn't do for me. He said he never saw anything like my dyspepsia, but he was bound to cure it. I'm sure there was nothing he wouldn't try. He was just going to try something new when we came off. Mr. Miller wanted Daisy to see Europe for herself. But I wrote to Mr. Miller that it seems as if I couldn't get on without Dr. Davis. At Schenectady he stands at the very top; and there's a great deal of sickness there, too. It affects my sleep."

Winterbourne had a good deal of pathological gossip with Dr. Davis's patient, during which Daisy chattered unremittingly to her own companion. The young man asked Mrs. Miller how she was pleased with Rome. "Well, I must say I am disappointed," she answered. "We had heard so much about it; I suppose we had heard too much. But we couldn't help that. We had been led to expect something different."

"Ah, wait a little, and you will become very fond of it," said Winterbourne.

"I hate it worse and worse every day!" cried Randolph.

"You are like the infant Hannibal," [11] said Winterbourne.

11. **infant Hannibal:** Carthaginian general (247–183 B.C.), sworn by his father, Hamilcar Barca, to an eternal hatred of Rome.

"No, I ain't!" Randolph declared, at a venture.

"You are not much like an infant," said his mother. "But we have seen places," she resumed, "that I should put a long way before Rome." And in reply to Winterbourne's interrogation, "There's Zürich," she concluded; "I think Zürich is lovely; and we hadn't heard half so much about it."

"The best place we've seen is the City of Richmond!" said Randolph.

"He means the ship," his mother explained. "We crossed in that ship. Randolph had a good time on the *City of Richmond*."

"It's the best place I've seen," the child repeated. "Only it was turned the wrong way."

"Well, we've got to turn the right way some time," said Mrs. Miller, with a little laugh. Winterbourne expressed the hope that her daughter at least found some gratification in Rome, and she declared that Daisy was quite carried away. "It's on account of the society—the society's splendid. She goes round everywhere; she has made a great number of acquaintances. Of course she goes round more than I do. I must say they have been very sociable; they have taken her right in. And then she knows a great many gentlemen. Oh, she thinks there's nothing like Rome. Of course, it's a great deal pleasanter for a young lady if she knows plenty of gentlemen."

By this time Daisy had turned her attention again to Winterbourne. "I've been telling Mrs. Walker how mean you were!" the young girl announced.

"And what is the evidence you have offered?" asked Winterbourne, rather annoyed at Miss Miller's want of appreciation of the zeal of an admirer who on his way down to Rome had stopped neither at Bologna nor at Florence, simply because of a certain sentimental impatience. He remembered that a cynical compatriot had once told him that American women—the pretty ones, and this gave a largeness to the axiom— were at once the most exacting in the world and the least endowed with a sense of indebtedness.

"Why, you were awfully mean at Vevey," said Daisy. "You wouldn't do anything. You wouldn't stay there when I asked you."

"My dearest young lady," cried Winterbourne, with eloquence, "have I come all the way to Rome to encounter your reproaches?"

"Just hear him say that!" said Daisy to her hostess, giving a twist to a bow on this lady's dress. "Did you ever hear anything so quaint?"

"So quaint, my dear?" murmured Mrs. Walker, in a tone of a partisan of Winterbourne.

"Well, I don't know," said Daisy, fingering Mrs. Walker's ribbons. "Mrs. Walker, I want to tell you something."

"Mother-r," interposed Randolph, with his rough ends to his words, "I tell you you've got to go. Eugenio'll raise—something!"

"I'm not afraid of Eugenio," said Daisy, with a toss of her head. "Look here, Mrs. Walker," she went on, "you know I'm coming to your party."

"I am delighted to hear it."

"I've got a lovely dress!"

"I am very sure of that."

"But I want to ask a favour—permission to bring a friend."

"I shall be happy to see any of your friends," said Mrs. Walker, turning with a smile to Mrs. Miller.

"Oh, they are not my friends," answered Daisy's mamma, smiling shyly, in her own fashion. "I never spoke to them."

"It's an intimate friend of mine—Mr. Giovanelli," said Daisy, without a tremor in her clear little voice, or a shadow on her brilliant little face.

Mrs. Walker was silent a moment; she gave a rapid glance at Winterbourne. "I shall be glad to see Mr. Giovanelli," she then said.

"He's an Italian," Daisy pursued, with the prettiest serenity. "He's a great friend of mine—he's the handsomest man in the world—except Mr. Winterbourne! He knows plenty of Italians, but he wants to know some Americans. He thinks ever so much of Americans. He's tremendously clever. He's perfectly lovely!"

It was settled that this brilliant personage should be brought to Mrs. Walker's party, and then Mrs. Miller prepared to take her leave. "I guess we'll go back to the hotel," she said.

"You may go back to the hotel, mother, but I'm going to take a walk," said Daisy.

"She's going to walk with Mr. Giovanelli," Randolph proclaimed.

"I am going to the Pincio," said Daisy, smiling.

"Alone, my dear—at this hour?" Mrs. Walker asked. The afternoon was drawing to a close— it was the hour for the throng of carriages and of contemplative pedestrians. "I don't think it's safe, my dear," said Mrs. Walker.

"Neither do I," subjoined Mrs. Miller. "You'll get the fever, as sure as you live. Remember what Dr. Davis told you!"

"Give her some medicine before she goes," said Randolph.

The company had risen to its feet; Daisy, still showing her pretty teeth, bent over and kissed her hostess. "Mrs. Walker, you are too perfect," she said. "I'm not going alone; I am going to meet a friend."

"Your friend won't keep you from getting the fever," Mrs. Miller observed.

"Is it Mr. Giovanelli?" asked the hostess.

Winterbourne was watching the young girl; at this question his attention quickened. She stood there smiling and smoothing her bonnet ribbons; she glanced at Winterbourne. Then, while she glanced and smiled, she answered, without a shade of hesitation, "Mr. Giovanelli—the beautiful Giovanelli."

"My dear young friend," said Mrs. Walker, taking her hand, pleadingly, "don't walk off to the Pincio at this hour to meet a beautiful Italian."

"Well, he speaks English," said Mrs. Miller.

"Gracious me!" Daisy exclaimed, "I don't want to do anything improper. There's an easy way to settle it." She continued to glance at Winterbourne. "The Pincio is only a hundred yards distant, and if Mr. Winterbourne were as polite as he pretends, he would offer to walk with me!"

Winterbourne's politeness hastened to affirm itself, and the young girl gave him gracious leave to accompany her. They passed down stairs before her mother, and at the door Winterbourne perceived Mrs. Miller's carriage drawn up, with the ornamental courier whose acquaintance he had made at Vevey seated within. "Good-bye, Eugenio!" cried Daisy, "I'm going to take a walk." The distance from the Via Gregoriana to the beautiful garden at the other end of the Pincian Hill is, in fact, rapidly traversed. As the day was splendid, however, and the concourse of vehicles, walkers, and loungers numerous, the young Americans found their progress much delayed. This fact was highly agreeable to Winterbourne, in spite of his consciousness of his singular situation. The slow-moving, idly-gazing Roman crowd bestowed much attention upon the extremely pretty young foreign lady who was passing through it upon his arm; and he wondered what on earth had been in Daisy's mind when she proposed to expose herself, unattended, to its appreciation. His own mission, to her sense, apparently, was to consign her to the hands of Mr. Giovanelli; but Winterbourne, at once annoyed and gratified, resolved that he would do no such thing.

"Why haven't you been to see me?" asked Daisy. "You can't get out of that."

"I have had the honour of telling you that I have only just stepped out of the train."

"You must have stayed in the train a good while after it stopped!" cried the young girl, with her little laugh. "I suppose you were asleep. You have had time to go to see Mrs. Walker."

"I knew Mrs. Walker—" Winterbourne began to explain.

"I know where you knew her. You knew her at Geneva. She told me so. Well, you knew me at Vevey. That's just as good. So you ought to have come." She asked him no other question than this; she began to prattle about her own affairs. "We've got splendid rooms at the hotel; Eugenio says they're the best rooms in Rome. We are going to stay all winter, if we don't die of the fever; and I guess we'll stay then. It's a great deal nicer than I thought; I thought it would be fearfully quiet; I was sure it would be awfully poky. I was sure we should be going round all the time with one of those dreadful old men that explain about the pictures and things. But we only had about a week of that, and now I'm enjoying myself. I know ever so many people, and they are all so charming. The society's extremely select. There are all kinds—English, and Germans, and Italians. I think I like the English best. I like their style of conversation. But there are some lovely Americans. I never saw anything so hospitable. There's something or other every day. There's not much dancing; but I must say I never thought dancing was everything. I was always fond of conversation. I guess I shall have plenty at Mrs. Walker's—her rooms are so small." When they had passed the gate of the Pincian Gardens, Miss Miller began to wonder where Mr. Giovanelli might be. "We had better go straight to that place in front," she said, "where you look at the view."

"I certainly shall not help you to find him," Winterbourne declared.

"Then I shall find him without you," said Miss Daisy.

"You certainly won't leave me!" cried Winterbourne.

She burst into her little laugh. "Are you afraid you'll get lost—or run over? But there's Giovanelli, leaning against that tree. He's staring at the women in the carriages; did you ever see anything so cool?"

Winterbourne perceived at some distance a little man standing with folded arms, nursing his cane. He had a handsome face, an artfully poised hat, a glass in one eye, and a nosegay in his button-hole. Winterbourne looked at him a moment, and then said, "Do you mean to speak to that man?"

"Do I mean to speak to him? Why, you don't suppose I mean to communicate by signs?"

"Pray understand, then," said Winterbourne, "that I intend to remain with you."

Daisy stopped and looked at him, without a

sign of troubled consciousness in her face; with nothing but the presence of her charming eyes and her happy dimples. "Well, she's a cool one!" thought the young man.

"I don't like the way you say that," said Daisy. "It's too imperious."

"I beg your pardon if I say it wrong. The main point is to give you an idea of my meaning."

The young girl looked at him more gravely, but with eyes that were prettier than ever. "I have never allowed a gentleman to dictate to me, or to interfere with anything I do."

"I think you have made a mistake," said Winterbourne. "You should sometimes listen to a gentleman—the right one."

Daisy began to laugh again. "I do nothing but listen to gentlemen!" she exclaimed. "Tell me if Mr. Giovanelli is the right one."

The gentleman with the nosegay in his bosom had now perceived our two friends, and was approaching the young girl with obsequious rapidity. He bowed to Winterbourne as well as to the latter's companion; he had a brilliant smile, an intelligent eye; Winterbourne thought him not a bad-looking fellow. But he nevertheless said to Daisy, "No, he's not the right one."

Daisy evidently had a natural talent for performing introductions; she mentioned the name of each of her companions to the other. She strolled along with one of them on each side of her; Mr. Giovanelli, who spoke English very cleverly—Winterbourne afterwards learned that he had practised the idiom upon a great many American heiresses—addressed to her a great deal of very polite nonsense; he was extremely urbane, and the young American, who said nothing, reflected upon that profundity of Italian cleverness which enables people to appear more gracious in proportion as they are more acutely disappointed. Giovanelli, of course, had counted upon something more intimate; he had not bargained for a party of three. But he kept his temper in a manner which suggested far-stretching intentions. Winterbourne flattered himself that he had taken his measure. "He is not a gentleman," said the young American; "he is only a clever imitation of one. He is a music-master, or a penny-a-liner, or a third-rate artist. Damn his good looks!" Mr. Giovanelli had certainly a very pretty face; but Winterbourne felt a superior indignation at his own lovely fellow-country woman's not knowing the difference between a spurious gentleman and a real one. Giovanelli chattered and jested, and made himself wonderfully agreeable. It was true that, if he was an imitation, the imitation

was brilliant. "Nevertheless," Winterbourne said to himself, "a nice girl ought to know!" And then he came back to the question whether this was, in fact, a nice girl. Would a nice girl—even allowing for her being a little American flirt—make a rendezvous with a presumably low-lived foreigner? The rendezvous in this case, indeed, had been in broad daylight, and in the most crowded corner of Rome; but was it not impossible to regard the choice of these circumstances as a proof of extreme cynicism? Singular though it may seem, Winterbourne was vexed that the young girl, in joining her *amoroso*,[12] should not appear more impatient of his own company, and he was vexed because of his inclination. It was impossible to regard her as a perfectly well-conducted young lady; she was wanting in a certain indispensable delicacy. It would therefore simplify matters greatly to be able to treat her as the object of one of those sentiments which are called by romancers "lawless passions." That she should seem to wish to get rid of him would help him to think more lightly of her, and to be able to think more lightly of her would make her much less perplexing. But Daisy, on this occasion, continued to present herself as an inscrutable combination of audacity and innocence.

She had been walking some quarter of an hour, attended by her two cavaliers, and responding in a tone of very childish gaiety, as it seemed to Winterbourne, to the pretty speeches of Mr. Giovanelli, when a carriage that had detached itself from the revolving train drew up beside the path. At the same moment Winterbourne perceived that his friend Mrs. Walker—the lady whose house he had lately left—was seated in the vehicle, and was beckoning to him. Leaving Miss Miller's side, he hastened to obey her summons. Mrs. Walker was flushed; she wore an excited air. "It is really too dreadful," she said. "That girl must not do this sort of thing. She must not walk here with you two men. Fifty people have noticed her."

Winterbourne raised his eyebrows. "I think it's a pity to make too much fuss about it."

"It's a pity to let the girl ruin herself!"

"She is very innocent," said Winterbourne.

"She's very crazy!" cried Mrs. Walker. "Did you ever see anything so imbecile as her mother? After you had all left me, just now, I could not sit still for thinking of it. It seemed too pitiful not even to attempt to save her. I ordered the carriage and put on my bonnet, and came here

12. *amoroso:* Italian for lover.

as quickly as possible. Thank Heaven I have found you!"

"What do you propose to do with us?" asked Winterbourne, smiling.

"To ask her to get in, to drive her about here for half-an-hour, so that the world may see that she is not running absolutely wild, and then to take her safely home."

"I don't think it's a very happy thought," said Winterbourne; "but you can try."

Mrs. Walker tried. The young man went in pursuit of Miss Miller, who had simply nodded and smiled at his interlocutor in the carriage, and had gone her way with her companion. Daisy, on learning that Mrs. Walker wished to speak to her, retraced her steps with a perfect good grace and with Mr. Giovanelli at her side. She declared that she was delighted to have a chance to present this gentleman to Mrs. Walker. She immediately achieved the introduction, and declared that she had never in her life seen anything so lovely as Mrs. Walker's carriage-rug.

"I am glad you admire it," said this lady, smiling sweetly. "Will you get in and let me put it over you?"

"Oh no, thank you," said Daisy. "I shall admire it much more as I see you driving round with it."

"Do get in and drive with me!" said Mrs. Walker.

"That would be charming, but it's so enchanting just as I am!" and Daisy gave a brilliant glance at the gentlemen on either side of her.

"It may be enchanting, dear child, but it is not the custom here," urged Mrs. Walker, leaning forward in her victoria, with her hands devoutly clasped.

"Well, it ought to be, then!" said Daisy. "If I didn't walk I should expire."

"You should walk with your mother, dear," cried the lady from Geneva, losing patience.

"With my mother, dear!" exclaimed the young girl. Winterbourne saw that she scented interference. "My mother never walked ten steps in her life. And then, you know," she added, with a laugh, "I am more than five years old."

"You are old enough to be more reasonable. You are old enough, dear Miss Miller, to be talked about."

Daisy looked at Mrs. Walker, smiling intensely. "Talked about? What do you mean?"

"Come into my carriage, and I will tell you."

Daisy turned her quickened glance again from one of the gentlemen beside her to the other. Mr. Giovanelli was bowing to and fro, rubbing down his gloves and laughing very agreeably; Winterbourne thought it a most unpleasant scene.

"I don't think I want to know what you mean," said Daisy, presently. "I don't think I should like it."

Winterbourne wished that Mrs. Walker would tuck in her carriage-rug and drive away; but this lady did not enjoy being defied, as she afterwards told him. "Should you prefer being thought a very reckless girl?" she demanded.

"Gracious!" exclaimed Daisy. She looked again at Mr. Giovanelli, then she turned to Winterbourne. There was a little pink flush in her cheek; she was tremendously pretty. "Does Mr. Winterbourne think," she asked slowly, smiling, throwing back her head and glancing at him from head to foot, "that—to save my reputation—I ought to get into the carriage?"

Winterbourne coloured; for an instant he hesitated greatly. It seemed so strange to hear her speak that way of her "reputation." But he himself, in fact, must speak in accordance with gallantry. The finest gallantry here was simply to tell her the truth; and the truth for Winterbourne—as the few indications I have been able to give have made him known to the reader— was that Daisy Miller should take Mrs. Walker's advice. He looked at her exquisite prettiness; and then said, very gently, "I think you should get into the carriage."

Daisy gave a violent laugh. "I never heard anything so stiff! If this is improper, Mrs. Walker," she pursued, "then I am all improper, and you must give me up. Good-bye; I hope you'll have a lovely ride!" and, with Mr. Giovanelli, who made a triumphantly obsequious salute, she turned away.

Mrs. Walker sat looking after her, and there were tears in Mrs. Walker's eyes. "Get in here, sir," she said to Winterbourne, indicating the place beside her. The young man answered that he felt bound to accompany Miss Miller; whereupon Mrs. Walker declared that if he refused her this favour she would never speak to him again. She was evidently in earnest. Winterbourne overtook Daisy and her companion, and, offering the young girl his hand, told her that Mrs. Walker had made an imperious claim upon his society. He expected that in answer she would say something rather free, something to commit herself still further to that "recklessness" from which Mrs. Walker had so charitably endeavoured to dissuade her. But she only shook his hand, hardly looking at him; while Mr. Giovanelli bade him farewell with a too emphatic flourish of the hat.

Winterbourne was not in the best possible humour as he took his seat in Mrs. Walker's victoria. "That was not clever of you," he said, candidly, while the vehicle mingled again with the throng of carriages.

"In such a case," his companion answered, "I don't wish to be clever; I wish to be *earnest!*"

"Well, you earnestness has only offended her and put her off."

"It has happened very well," said Mrs. Walker. "If she is so perfectly determined to compromise herself, the sooner one knows it the better; one can act accordingly."

"I suspect she meant no harm," Winterbourne rejoined.

"So I thought a month ago. But she has been going too far."

"What has she been doing?"

"Everything that is not done here. Flirting with any man she could pick up; sitting in corners with mysterious Italians; dancing all the evening with the same partners; receiving visits at eleven o'clock at night. Her mother goes away when visitors come."

"But her brother," said Winterbourne, laughing, "sits up till midnight."

"He must be edified by what he sees. I'm told that at their hotel every one is talking about her, and that a smile goes round among all the servants when a gentleman comes and asks for Miss Miller."

"The servants be hanged!" said Winterbourne, angrily. "The poor girl's only fault," he presently added, "is that she is very uncultivated."

"She is naturally indelicate," Mrs. Walker declared. "Take that example this morning. How long had you known her at Vevey?"

"A couple of days."

"Fancy, then, her making it a personal matter that you should have left the place!"

Winterbourne was silent for some moments; then he said, "I suspect, Mrs. Walker, that you and I have lived too long at Geneva!" And he added a request that she should inform him with what particular design she had made him enter her carriage.

"I wished to beg you to cease your relations with Miss Miller—not to flirt with her—to give her no further opportunity to expose herself—to let her alone, in short."

"I'm afraid I can't do that," said Winterbourne. "I like her extremely."

"All the more reason that you shouldn't help her to make a scandal."

"There shall be nothing scandalous in my attentions to her."

"There certainly will be in the way she takes them. But I have said what I had on my conscience," Mrs. Walker pursued. "If you wish to rejoin the young lady I will put you down. Here, by-the-way, you have a chance."

The carriage was traversing that part of the Pincian Garden that overhangs the wall of Rome and overlooks the beautiful Villa Borghese. It is bordered by a large parapet, near which there are several seats. One of the seats, at a distance, was occupied by a gentleman and a lady, towards whom Mrs. Walker gave a toss of her head. At the same moment these persons rose and walked towards the parapet. Winterbourne had asked the coachman to stop; he now descended from the carriage. His companion looked at him a moment in silence; then, while he raised his hat, she drove majestically away. Winterbourne stood there: he had turned his eyes towards Daisy and her cavalier. They evidently saw no one; they were too deeply occupied with each other. When they reached the low garden-wall they stood a moment looking off at the great flat-topped pine-clusters of the Villa Borghese; then Giovanelli seated himself familiarly upon the broad ledge of the wall. The western sun in the opposite sky sent out a brilliant shaft through a couple of cloud-bars, whereupon Daisy's companion took her parasol out of her hands and opened it. She came a little nearer, and he held the parasol over her; then, still holding it, he let it rest upon her shoulder, so that both of their heads were hidden from Winterbourne. This young man lingered a moment, then he began to walk. But he walked—not towards the couple with the parasol—towards the residence of his aunt, Mrs. Costello.

He flattered himself on the following day that there was no smiling among the servants when he, at least, asked for Mrs. Miller at her hotel. This lady and her daughter, however, were not at home; and on the next day after, repeating his visit, Winterbourne again had the misfortune not to find them. Mrs. Walker's party took place on the evening of the third day, and, in spite of the frigidity of his last interview with the hostess, Winterbourne was among the guests. Mrs. Walker was one of those American ladies who, while residing abroad, make a point, in their own phrase, of studying European society; and she had on this occasion collected several specimens of her diversely-born fellow-mortals to serve, as it were, as text-books. When Winterbourne arrived, Daisy Miller was not there, but in a few moments he saw her mother come in alone, very shyly and ruefully. Mrs. Miller's hair above her exposed-looking temples was more frizzled than ever. As she approached Mrs. Walker, Winterbourne also drew near.

"You see I've come all alone," said poor Mrs.

Miller. "I'm so frightened I don't know what to do. It's the first time I've ever been to a party alone, especially in this country. I wanted to bring Randolph, or Eugenio, or some one, but Daisy just pushed me off by myself. I ain't used to going round alone."

"And does not your daughter intend to favour us with her society?" demanded Mrs. Walker, impressively.

"Well, Daisy's all dressed," said Mrs. Miller, with that accent of the dispassionate, if not of the philosophic, historian with which she always recorded the current incidents of her daughter's career. "She got dressed on purpose before dinner. But she's got a friend of hers there; that gentleman—the Italian—that she wanted to bring. They've got going at the piano; it seems as if they couldn't leave off. Mr. Giovanelli sings splendidly. But I guess they'll come before very long," concluded Mrs. Miller, hopefully.

"I'm sorry she should come—in that way," said Mrs. Walker.

"Well, I told her that there was no use in her getting dressed before dinner if she was going to wait three hours," responded Daisy's mamma. "I didn't see the use of her putting on such a dress as that to sit round with Mr. Giovanelli."

"This is most horrible!" said Mrs. Walker, turning away and addressing herself to Winterbourne. "*Elle s'affiche.*[13] It's her revenge for my having ventured to remonstrate with her. When she comes I shall not speak to her."

Daisy came after eleven o'clock; but she was not, on such an occasion, a young lady to wait to be spoken to. She rustled forward in radiant loveliness, smiling and chattering, carrying a large bouquet, and attended by Mr. Giovanelli. Every one stopped talking, and turned and looked at her. She came straight to Mrs. Walker. "I'm afraid you thought I never was coming, so I sent mother off to tell you. I wanted to make Mr. Giovanelli practise some things before he came; you know he sings beautifully, and I want you to ask him to sing. This is Mr. Giovanelli; you know I introduced him to you; he's got the most lovely voice, and he knows the most charming set of songs. I made him go over them this evening on purpose; we had the greatest time at the hotel." Of all this Daisy delivered herself with the sweetest, brightest audibleness, looking now at her hostess and now round the room, while she gave a series of little pats round her shoulders to the edges of her dress. "Is there any one I know?" she asked.

"I think every one knows you!" said Mrs.

13. *Elle s'affiche:* "She's making a public spectacle of herself."

Walker, pregnantly, and she gave a very cursory greeting to Mr. Giovanelli. This gentleman bore himself gallantly. He smiled and bowed, and showed his white teeth; he curled his moustaches and rolled his eyes, and performed all the proper functions of a handsome Italian at an evening party. He sang very prettily half-a-dozen songs, though Mrs. Walker afterwards declared that she had been quite unable to find out who asked him. It was apparently not Daisy who had given him his orders. Daisy sat at a distance from the piano; and though she had publicly, as it were, professed a high admiration for his singing, talked, not inaudibly, while it was going on.

"It's a pity these rooms are so small; we can't dance," she said to Winterbourne, as if she had seen him five minutes before.

"I am not sorry we can't dance," Winterbourne answered; "I don't dance."

"Of course you don't dance; you're too stiff," said Miss Daisy. "I hope you enjoyed your drive with Mrs. Walker!"

"No, I didn't enjoy it; I preferred walking with you."

"We paired off; that was much better," said Daisy. "But did you ever hear anything so cool as Mrs. Walker's wanting me to get into her carriage and drop poor Mr. Giovanelli, and under the pretext that it was proper? People have different ideas! It would have been most unkind; he had been talking about that walk for ten days."

"He should not have talked about it at all," said Winterbourne; "he would never have proposed to a young lady of this country to walk about the streets with him."

"About the streets?" cried Daisy, with her pretty stare. "Where, then, would he have proposed to her to walk? The Pincio is not the streets, either; and I, thank goodness, am not a young lady of this country. The young ladies of this country have a dreadfully poky time of it, so far as I can learn; I don't see why I should change my habits for *them.*"

"I am afraid your habits are those of a flirt," said Winterbourne, gravely.

"Of course they are," she cried, giving him her little smiling stare again. "I'm a fearful, frightful flirt! Did you ever hear of a nice girl that was not? But I suppose you will tell me now that I am not a nice girl."

"You're a very nice girl; but I wish you would flirt with me, and me only," said Winterbourne.

"Ah! thank you—thank you very much; you are the last man I should think of flirting with. As I have had the pleasure of informing you, you are too stiff."

"You say that too often," said Winterbourne.

Daisy gave a delighted laugh. "If I could have the sweet hope of making you angry, I should say it again."

"Don't do that; when I am angry I'm stiffer than ever. But if you won't flirt with me, do cease, at least, to flirt with your friend at the piano; they don't understand that sort of thing here."

"I thought they understood nothing else!" exclaimed Daisy.

"Not in young unmarried women."

"It seems to me much more proper in young unmarried women than in old married ones," Daisy declared.

"Well," said Winterbourne, "when you deal with natives you must go by the custom of the place. Flirting is a purely American custom; it doesn't exist here. So when you show yourself in public with Mr. Giovanelli, and without your mother—"

"Gracious! poor mother!" interposed Daisy.

"Though you may be flirting, Mr. Giovanelli is not; he means something else."

"He isn't preaching, at any rate," said Daisy with vivacity. "And if you want very much to know, we are neither of us flirting; we are too good friends for that; we are very intimate friends."

"Ah!" rejoined Winterbourne, "if you are in love with each other it is another affair."

She had allowed him up to this point to talk so frankly that he had no expectation of shocking her by this ejaculation; but she immediately got up, blushing visibly, and leaving him to exclaim mentally that little American flirts were the queerest creatures in the world. "Mr. Giovanelli, at least," she said, giving her interlocutor a single glance, "never says such very disagreeable things to me."

Winterbourne was bewildered; he stood staring. Mr. Giovanelli had finished singing; he left the piano and came over to Daisy. "Won't you come into the other room and have some tea?" he asked, bending before her with his ornamental smile.

Daisy turned to Winterbourne, beginning to smile again. He was still more perplexed, for this inconsequent smile made nothing clear, though it seemed to prove, indeed, that she had a sweetness and softness that reverted instinctively to the pardon of offences. "It has never occurred to Mr. Winterbourne to offer me any tea," she said, with her little tormenting manner.

"I have offered you advice," Winterbourne rejoined.

"I prefer weak tea!" cried Daisy, and she went off with the brilliant Giovanelli. She sat with him in the adjoining room, in the embrasure of the window, for the rest of the evening. There was an interesting performance at the piano, but neither of these young people gave heed to it. When Daisy came to take leave of Mrs. Walker, this lady conscientiously repaired the weakness of which she had been guilty at the moment of the young girl's arrival. She turned her back straight upon Miss Miller and left her to depart with what grace she might. Winterbourne was standing near the door; he saw it all. Daisy turned very pale and looked at her mother, but Mrs. Miller was humbly unconscious of any violation of the usual social forms. She appeared, indeed, to have felt an incongruous impulse to draw attention to her own striking observance of them. "Good-night, Mrs. Walker," she said; "we've had a beautiful evening. You see, if I let Daisy come to parties without me, I don't want her to go away without me." Daisy turned away, looking with a pale, grave face at the circle near the door; Winterbourne saw that, for the first moment, she was too much shocked and puzzled even for indignation. He on his side was greatly touched.

"That was very cruel," he said to Mrs. Walker.

"She never enters my drawing-room again!" replied his hostess.

Since Winterbourne was not to meet her in Mrs. Walker's drawing-room, he went as often as possible to Mrs. Miller's hotel. The ladies were rarely at home; but when he found them the devoted Giovanelli was always present. Very often the brilliant little Roman was in the drawing-room with Daisy alone, Mrs. Miller being apparently constantly of the opinion that discretion is the better part of surveillance. Winterbourne noted, at first with surprise, that Daisy on these occasions was never embarrassed or annoyed by his own entrance; but he very presently began to feel that she had no more surprises for him; the unexpected in her behaviour was the only thing to expect. She showed no displeasure at her *tête-à-tête* with Giovanelli being interrupted; she could chatter as freshly and freely with two gentlemen as with one; there was always, in her conversation, the same odd mixture of audacity and puerility. Winterbourne remarked to himself that if she was seriously interested in Giovanelli, it was very singular that she should not take more trouble to preserve the sanctity of their interviews; and he liked her the more for her innocent-looking indifference and her apparently inexhaustible good humour. He could hardly have said why, but she seemed to him a girl who would never be jealous. At the risk of exciting a somewhat derisive smile on the reader's part, I may affirm that with regard to the women who had hitherto interested him, it very often seemed to Winterbourne among the possibilities that, given certain contingencies, he should be afraid—literally afraid—of these ladies; he had a pleasant sense that he should never be afraid of Daisy Miller. It must be added that this sentiment was not altogether flattering to Daisy; it was part of his conviction, or rather of his apprehension, that she would prove a very light young person.

But she was evidently very much interested in Giovanelli. She looked at him whenever he spoke; she was perpetually telling him to do this and to do that; she was constantly "chaffing" and abusing him. She appeared completely to have forgotten that Winterbourne had said anything to displease her at Mrs. Walker's little party. One Sunday afternoon, having gone to St. Peter's with his aunt, Winterbourne perceived Daisy strolling about the great church in company with the inevitable Giovanelli. Presently he pointed out the young girl and her cavalier to Mrs. Costello. This lady looked at them a moment through her eyeglass, and then she said,

"That's what makes you so pensive in these days, eh?"

"I had not the least idea I was pensive," said the young man.

"You are very much pre-occupied; you are thinking of something."

"And what is it," he asked, "that you accuse me of thinking of?"

"Of that young lady's—Miss Baker's, Miss Chandler's—what's her name?—Miss Miller's intrigue with that little barber's block."

"Do you call it an intrigue," Winterbourne asked—"an affair that goes on with such peculiar publicity?"

"That's their folly," said Mrs. Costello, "it's not their merit."

"No," rejoined Winterbourne, with something of that pensiveness to which his aunt had alluded. "I don't believe that there is anything to be called an intrigue."

"I have heard a dozen people speak of it; they say she is quite carried away by him."

"They are certainly very intimate," said Winterbourne.

Mrs. Costello inspected the young couple again with her optical instrument. "He is very handsome. One easily sees how it is. She thinks him the most elegant man in the world, the finest gentleman. She has never seen anything like him; he is better even than the courier. It was the

courier, probably, who introduced him; and if he succeeds in marrying the young lady, the courier will come in for a magnificent commission."

"I don't believe she thinks of marrying him," said Winterbourne, "and I don't believe he hopes to marry her."

"You may be very sure she thinks of nothing. She goes on from day to day, from hour to hour, as they did in the Golden Age. I can imagine nothing more vulgar. And at the same time," added Mrs. Costello, "depend upon it that she may tell you any moment that she is 'engaged.' "

"I think that is more than Giovanelli expects," said Winterbourne.

"Who is Giovanelli?"

"The little Italian. I have asked questions about him and learned something. He is apparently a perfectly respectable little man. I believe he is, in a small way, a *cavaliere avvocato*.[14] But he doesn't move in what are called the first circles. I think it is really not absolutely impossible that the courier introduced him. He is evidently immensely charmed with Miss Miller. If she thinks him the finest gentleman in the world, he, on his side, has never found himself in personal contact with such splendour, such opulence, such expensiveness, as this young lady's. And then she must seem to him wonderfully pretty and interesting. I rather doubt that he dreams of marrying her. That must appear to him too impossible a piece of luck. He has nothing but his handsome face to offer, and there is a substantial Mr. Miller in that mysterious land of dollars. Giovanelli knows that he hasn't a title to offer. If he were only a count or a *marchese!* He must wonder at his luck, at the way they have taken him up."

"He accounts for it by his handsome face, and thinks Miss Miller a young lady *qui se passe ses fantaisies!*"[15] said Mrs. Costello.

"It is very true," Winterbourne pursued, "that Daisy and her mamma have not yet risen to that stage of—what shall I call it?—of culture, at which the idea of catching a count or a *marchese* begins. I believe that they are intellectually incapable of that conception."

"Ah! but the *avvocato* can't believe it," said Mrs. Costello.

Of the observation excited by Daisy's "intrigue," Winterbourne gathered that day at St. Peter's sufficient evidence. A dozen of the American colonists in Rome came to talk with Mrs. Costello, who sat on a little portable stool at the

14. *cavaliere avvocato:* Italian for lawyer; *cavaliere* is an honorific designation.    15. *qui . . . fantaisies!:* "who is indulging her whims."

base of one of the great pilasters. The vesper service was going forward in splendid chants and organ-tones in the adjacent choir, and meanwhile, between Mrs. Costello and her friends, there was a great deal said about poor little Miss Miller's going really "too far." Winterbourne was not pleased with what he heard; but when, coming out upon the great steps of the church, he saw Daisy, who had emerged before him, get into an open cab with her accomplice and roll away through the cynical streets of Rome, he could not deny to himself that she was going very far indeed. He felt very sorry for her—not exactly that he believed that she had completely lost her head, but because it was painful to hear so much that was pretty, and undefended, and natural, assigned to a vulgar place among the categories of disorder. He made an attempt after this to give a hint to Mrs. Miller. He met one day in the Corso [16] a friend—a tourist like himself, who had just come out of the Doria Palace, where he had been walking through the beautiful gallery. His friend talked for a moment about the superb portrait of Innocent X., by Velasquez [17] which hangs in one of the cabinets of the palace, and then said, "And in the same cabinet, by-the-way, I had the pleasure of contemplating a picture of a different kind—that pretty American girl whom you pointed out to me last week." In answer to Winterbourne's inquiries, his friend narrated that the pretty American girl—prettier than ever—was seated with a companion in the secluded nook in which the great papal portrait was enshrined.

"Who was her companion?" asked Winterbourne.

"A little Italian with a bouquet in his buttonhole. The girl is delightfully pretty; but I thought I understood from you the other day that she was a young lady *du meilleur monde.*" [18]

"So she is!" answered Winterbourne; and having assured himself that his informant had seen Daisy and her companion but five minutes before, he jumped into a cab and went to call on Mrs. Miller. She was at home; but she apologized to him for receiving him in Daisy's absence.

"She's gone out somewhere with Mr. Giovanelli," said Mrs. Miller. "She's always going round with Mr. Giovanelli."

"I have noticed that they are very intimate," Winterbourne observed.

"Oh, it seems as if they couldn't live without

each other!" said Mrs. Miller. "Well, he's a real gentleman, anyhow. I keep telling Daisy she's engaged!"

"And what does Daisy say?"

"Oh, she says she isn't engaged. But she might as well be!" this impartial parent resumed. "She goes on as if she was. But I've made Mr. Giovanelli promise to tell me, if *she* doesn't. I should want to write to Mr. Miller about it—shouldn't you?"

Winterbourne replied that he certainly should; and the state of mind of Daisy's mamma struck him as so unprecedented in the annals of parental vigilance that he gave up as utterly irrelevant the attempt to place her upon her guard.

After this Daisy was never at home, and Winterbourne ceased to meet her at the houses of their common acquaintances because, as he perceived, these shrewd people had quite made up their minds that she was going too far. They ceased to invite her, and they intimated that they desired to express to observant Europeans the great truth that, though Miss Daisy Miller was a young American lady, her behaviour was not representative—was regarded by her compatriots as abnormal. Winterbourne wondered how she felt about all the cold shoulders that were turned towards her, and sometimes it annoyed him to suspect that she did not feel at all. He said to himself that she was too light and childish, too uncultivated and unreasoning, too provincial, to have reflected upon her ostracism, or even to have perceived it. Then at other moments he believed that she carried about in her elegant and irresponsible little organism a defiant, passionate, perfectly observant consciousness of the impression she produced. He asked himself whether Daisy's defiance came from the consciousness of innocence, or from her being, essentially, a young person of the reckless class. It must be admitted that holding one's self to a belief in Daisy's "innocence" came to seem to Winterbourne more and more a matter of fine-spun gallantry. As I have already had occasion to relate, he was angry at finding himself reduced to chopping logic about this young lady; he was vexed at his want of instinctive certitude as to how far her eccentricities were generic, national, and how far they were personal. From either view of them he had somehow missed her, and now it was too late. She was "carried away" by Mr. Giovanelli.

A few days after his brief interview with her mother, he encountered her in that beautiful abode of flowering desolation known as the Palace of the Caesars. The early Roman spring had filled the air with bloom and perfume, and

16. *Corso:* principal Roman avenue.    17. *Velasquez:* Diego Rodríquez de Silva y Velázquez (1599–1660), Spanish painter. 18. *du meilleur monde:* "of the best society."

the rugged surface of the Palatine was muffled with tender verdure. Daisy was strolling along the top of one of those great mounds of ruin that are embanked with mossy marble and paved with monumental inscriptions. It seemed to him that Rome had never been so lovely as just then. He stood looking off at the enchanting harmony of line and colour that remotely encircles the city, inhaling the softly humid odours, and feeling the freshness of the year and the antiquity of the place reaffirm themselves in mysterious interfusion. It seemed to him, also, that Daisy had never looked so pretty; but this had been an observation of his whenever he met her. Giovanelli was at her side, and Giovanelli, too, wore an aspect of even unwonted brilliancy.

"Well," said Daisy, "I should think you would be lonesome!"

"Lonesome?" asked Winterbourne.

"You are always going round by yourself. Can't you get any one to walk with you?"

"I am not so fortunate," said Winterbourne, "as your companion."

Giovanelli, from the first, had treated Winterbourne with distinguished politeness; he listened with a deferential air to his remarks; he laughed, punctiliously, at his pleasantries; he seemed disposed to testify to his belief that Winterbourne was a superior young man. He carried himself in no degree like a jealous wooer; he had obviously a great deal of tact; he had no objection to your expecting a little humility of him. It even seemed to Winterbourne at times that Giovanelli would find a certain mental relief in being able to have a private understanding with him—to say to him, as an intelligent man, that, bless you, *he* knew how extraordinary was this young lady, and didn't flatter himself with delusive—or, at least, *too* delusive—hopes of matrimony and dollars. On this occasion he strolled away from his companion to pluck a sprig of almond-blossom, which he carefully arranged in his button-hole.

"I know why you say that," said Daisy, watching Giovanelli. "Because you think I go round too much with *him*." And she nodded at her attendant.

"Every one thinks so—if you care to know," said Winterbourne.

"Of course I care to know!" Daisy exclaimed, seriously. "But I don't believe it. They are only pretending to be shocked. They don't really care a straw what I do. Besides, I don't go round so much."

"I think you will find they do care. They will show it—disagreeably."

Daisy looked at him a moment. "How—disagreeably?"

"Haven't you noticed anything?" Winterbourne asked.

"I have noticed you. But I noticed you were as stiff as an umbrella the first time I saw you."

"You will find I am not so stiff as several others," said Winterbourne, smiling.

"How shall I find it?"

"By going to see the others."

"What will they do to me?"

"They will give you the cold shoulder. Do you know what that means?"

Daisy was looking at him intently; she began to colour.

"Do you mean as Mrs. Walker did the other night?"

"Exactly!" said Winterbourne.

She looked away at Giovanelli, who was decorating himself with his almond-blossom. Then, looking back at Winterbourne, "I shouldn't think you would let people be so unkind!" she said.

"How can I help it?" he asked.

"I should think you would say something."

"I did say something;" and he paused a moment. "I say that your mother tells me that she believes you are engaged."

"Well, she does," said Daisy very simply.

Winterbourne began to laugh. "And does Randolph believe it?" he asked.

"I guess Randolph doesn't believe anything," said Daisy. Randolph's scepticism excited Winterbourne to further hilarity, and he observed that Giovanelli was coming back to them. Daisy, observing it too, addressed herself again to her countryman. "Since you have mentioned it," she said, "I *am* engaged.". . . Winterbourne looked at her; he had stopped laughing. "You don't believe it!" she added.

He was silent a moment; and then, "Yes, I believe it," he said.

"Oh, no, you don't!" she answered. "Well, then—I am not!"

The young girl and her cicerone were on their way to the gate of the enclosure, so that Winterbourne, who had but lately entered, presently took leave of them. A week afterwards he went to dine at a beautiful villa on the Caelian Hill, and, on arriving, dismissed his hired vehicle. The evening was charming, and he promised himself the satisfaction of walking home beneath the Arch of Constantine and past the vaguely-lighted monuments of the Forum. There was a waning moon in the sky, and her radiance was not brilliant, but she was veiled in a thin cloud-curtain which seemed to diffuse and equalize it. When, on his return from the villa (it was eleven o'clock), Winterbourne approached the dusky circle of the Colosseum, it occurred to him, as a lover of the picturesque, that the interior, in the pale moonshine, would be well worth a glance. He turned aside and walked to one of the empty arches, near which, as he observed, an open carriage—one of the little Roman street-cabs—was stationed. Then he passed in, among the cavernous shadows of the great structure, and emerged upon the clear and silent arena. The place had never seemed to him more impressive. One-half of the gigantic circus was in deep shade; the other was sleeping in the luminous dusk. As he stood there he began to murmur Byron's famous lines, out of "Manfred" [19]; but before he had finished his quotation he remembered that if nocturnal meditations in the Colosseum are recommended by the poets, they are deprecated by the doctors. The historic atmosphere was there, certainly; but the historic atmosphere, scientifically considered, was no better than a villainous miasma. Winterbourne walked to the middle of the arena, to take a more general glance, intending thereafter to make a hasty retreat. The great cross in the centre was covered with shadow; it was only as he drew near it that he made it out distinctly. Then he saw that two persons were stationed upon the low steps which formed its base. One of these was a woman, seated; her companion was standing in front of her.

Presently the sound of the woman's voice came to him distinctly in the warm night-air. "Well, he looks at us as one of the old lions or tigers may have looked at the Christian martyrs!" These were the words he heard, in the familiar accent of Miss Daisy Miller.

"Let us hope he is not very hungry," responded the ingenious Giovanelli. "He will have to take me first; you will serve for dessert!"

Winterbourne stopped, with a sort of horror; and, it must be added, with a sort of relief. It was as if a sudden illumination had been flashed upon the ambiguity of Daisy's behaviour, and the riddle had become easy to read. She was a young lady whom a gentleman need no longer be at pains to respect. He stood there looking at her —looking at her companion, and not reflecting that though he saw them vaguely, he himself must have been more brightly visible. He felt angry with himself that he had bothered so much about the right way of regarding Miss Daisy Miller. Then, as he was going to advance again, he checked himself; not from the fear that he was doing her injustice, but from the sense of the danger of appearing unbecomingly exhilarated by this sudden revulsion from cautious criticism. He turned away towards the entrance of the place; but, as he did so, he heard Daisy speak again.

"Why, it was Mr. Winterbourne! He saw me— and he cuts me!"

What a clever little reprobate she was, and how smartly she played at injured innocence! But he wouldn't cut her. Winterbourne came forward again, and went towards the great cross. Daisy had got up; Giovanelli lifted his hat. Winterbourne had now begun to think simply of the craziness, from a sanitary point of view, of a delicate young girl lounging away the evening in this nest of malaria. What if she *were* a clever little reprobate? that was no reason for her dying of the *perniciosa*.[20] "How long have you been here?" he asked, almost brutally.

Daisy, lovely in the flattering moonlight, looked at him a moment. Then—"All the evening," she answered, gently. . . . "I never saw anything so pretty."

"I am afraid," said Winterbourne, "that you will not think Roman fever very pretty. This is the way people catch it. I wonder," he added, turning to Giovanelli, "that you, a native Roman, should countenance such a terrible indiscretion."

"Ah," said the handsome native, "for myself I am not afraid."

"Neither am I—for you! I am speaking for this young lady."

Giovanelli lifted his well-shaped eyebrows and showed his brilliant teeth. But he took Winterbourne's rebuke with docility. "I told the signorina it was a grave indiscretion; but when was the signorina ever prudent?"

"I never was sick, and I don't mean to be!" the signorina declared. "I don't look like much, but I'm healthy! I was bound to see the Colosseum by moonlight; I shouldn't have wanted to go home without that; and we have had the most beautiful time, haven't we, Mr. Giovanelli? If there has been any danger, Eugenio can give me some pills. He has got some splendid pills."

"I should advise you," said Winterbourne, "to drive home as fast as possible and take one!"

"What you say is very wise," Giovanelli rejoined. "I will go and make sure the carriage is at hand." And he went forward rapidly.

Daisy followed with Winterbourne. He kept looking at her; she seemed not in the least embar-

19. "Manfred": The lines are from Manfred's soliloquy in Act III, sc. iv, and begin: "The stars are forth, the moon above the tops . . ."

20. *perniciosa*: Italian for malaria.

rassed. Winterbourne said nothing; Daisy chattered about the beauty of the place. "Well, I *have* seen the Colosseum by moonlight!" she exclaimed. "That's one good thing." Then, noticing Winterbourne's silence, she asked him why he didn't speak. He made no answer; he only began to laugh. They passed under one of the dark archways; Giovanelli was in front with the carriage. Here Daisy stopped a moment, looking at the young American. *"Did* you believe I was engaged the other day?" she asked.

"It doesn't matter what I believed the other day," said Winterbourne, still laughing.

"Well, what do you believe now?"

"I believe that it makes very little difference whether you are engaged or not!"

He felt the young girl's pretty eyes fixed upon him through the thick gloom of the archway; she was apparently going to answer. But Giovanelli hurried her forward. "Quick! quick!" he said; "if we get in by midnight we are quite safe."

Daisy took her seat in the carriage, and the fortunate Italian placed himself beside her. "Don't forget Eugenio's pills!" said Winterbourne, as he lifted his hat.

"I don't care," said Daisy, in a little strange tone, "whether I have Roman fever or not!" Upon this the cab-driver cracked his whip, and they rolled away over the desultory patches of the antique pavement.

Winterbourne—to do him justice, as it were —mentioned to no one that he had encountered Miss Miller, at midnight, in the Colosseum with a gentleman; but, nevertheless, a couple of days later, the fact of her having been there under these circumstances was known to every member of the little American circle, and commented accordingly. Winterbourne reflected that they had of course known it at the hotel, and that, after Daisy's return, there had been an exchange of remarks between the porter and the cab-driver. But the young man was conscious, at the same moment, that it had ceased to be a matter of serious regret to him that the little American flirt should be "talked about" by low-minded menials. These people, a day or two later, had serious information to give: the little American flirt was alarmingly ill. Winterbourne, when the rumour came to him, immediately went to the hotel for more news. He found that two or three charitable friends had preceded him, and that they were being entertained in Mrs. Miller's salon by Randolph.

"It's going round at night," said Randolph— "that's what made her sick. She's always going round at night. I shouldn't think she'd want to—

it's so plaguy dark. You can't see anything here at night, except when there's a moon! In America there's always a moon!" Mrs. Miller was invisible; she was now, at least, giving her daughter the advantage of her society. It was evident that Daisy was dangerously ill.

Winterbourne went often to ask for news of her, and once he saw Mrs. Miller, who, though deeply alarmed, was—rather to his surprise— perfectly composed, and, as it appeared, a most efficient and judicious nurse. She talked a good deal about Dr. Davis, but Winterbourne paid her the compliment of saying to himself that she was not, after all, such a monstrous goose. "Daisy spoke of you the other day," she said to him. "Half the time she doesn't know what she's saying, but that time I think she did. She gave me a message; she told me to tell you—she told me to tell you that she never was engaged to that handsome Italian. I am sure I am very glad; Mr. Giovanelli hasn't been near us since she was taken ill. I thought he was so much of a gentleman; but I don't call that very polite! A lady told me that he was afraid I was angry with him for taking Daisy round at night. Well, so I am; but I suppose he knows I'm a lady. I would scorn to scold him. Anyway, she says she's not engaged. I don't know why she wanted you to know; but she said to me three times, 'Mind you tell Mr. Winterbourne.' And then she told me to ask if you remembered the time you went to that castle in Switzerland. But I said I wouldn't give any such messages as that. Only, if she is not engaged, I'm sure I'm glad to know it."

But, as Winterbourne had said, it mattered very little. A week after this the poor girl died; it had been a terrible case of the fever. Daisy's grave was in the little Protestant cemetery, in an angle of the wall of imperial Rome, beneath the cypresses and the thick spring-flowers. Winterbourne stood there beside it, with a number of other mourners—a number larger than the scandal excited by the young lady's career would have led you to expect. Near him stood Giovanelli, who came nearer still before Winterbourne turned away. Giovanelli was very pale; on this occasion he had no flower in his buttonhole; he seemed to wish to say something. At last he said, "She was the most beautiful young lady I ever saw, and the most amiable." And then he added in a moment, "and she was the most innocent."

Winterbourne looked at him, and presently repeated his words, "And the most innocent?"

"The most innocent!"

Winterbourne felt sore and angry. "Why the

devil," he asked, "did you take her to that fatal place?"

Mr. Giovanelli's urbanity was apparently imperturbable. He looked on the gound a moment, and then he said, "For myself, I had no fear; and she wanted to go."

"That was no reason!" Winterbourne declared.

The subtle Roman again dropped his eyes. "If she had lived, I should have got nothing. She would never have married me, I am sure."

"She would never have married you?"

"For a moment I hoped so. But no, I am sure."

Winterbourne listened to him; he stood staring at the raw protuberance among the April daisies. When he turned away again, Mr. Giovanelli with his light, slow step, had retired.

Winterbourne almost immediately left Rome; but the following summer he again met his aunt, Mrs. Costello, at Vevey. Mrs. Costello was fond of Vevey. In the interval Winterbourne had often thought of Daisy Miller and her mystifying manners. One day he spoke of her to his aunt— said it was on his conscience that he had done her injustice.

"I am sure I don't know," said Mrs. Costello. "How did your injustice affect her?"

"She sent me a message before her death which I didn't understand at the time. But I have understood it since. She would have appreciated one's esteem."

"Is that a modest way," asked Mrs. Costello, "of saying that she would have reciprocated one's affection?"

Winterbourne offered no answer to this question; but he presently said, "You were right in that remark that you made last summer. I was booked to make a mistake. I have lived too long in foreign parts."

Nevertheless, he went back to live at Geneva, whence there continue to come the most contradictory accounts of his motives of sojourn: a report that he is "studying" hard—an intimation that he is much interested in a very clever foreign lady.

# THE REAL THING

◇

❦ "The Real Thing" is one of James's many tales about the conflicts between illusion and reality, art and life, as they affect the lives and works of artists and writers (and here of models). The setting, as in most of his artist tales, is contemporary London. For James's account of the genesis and development of "The Real Thing" see the passage from his notebooks.

◇

## I

WHEN the porter's wife (she used to answer the house-bell) announced, "A gentleman—with a lady, sir," I had, as I often had in those days, for the wish was father to the thought, an immediate vision of sitters. Sitters my visitors in this case proved to be; but not in the sense I should have preferred. However, there was nothing at first to indicate that they might not have come for a portrait. The gentleman, a man of fifty, very high and very straight, with a moustache slightly grizzled and a dark grey walking-coat admirably fitted, both of which I noted professionally—I don't mean as a barber or yet as a tailor—would have struck me as a celebrity if celebrities often were striking. It was a truth of which I had for some time been conscious that a figure with a good deal of frontage was, as one might say, almost never a public institution. A glance at the lady helped to remind me of this paradoxical law: she also looked too distinguished to be a "personality." Moreover one would scarcely come across two variations together.

Neither of the pair spoke immediately—they only prolonged the preliminary gaze which suggested that each wished to give the other a chance. They were visibly shy; they stood there letting me take them in—which, as I afterwards perceived, was the most practical thing they could have done. In this way their embarrassment served their cause. I had seen people painfully reluctant to mention that they desired anything so gross as to be represented on canvas; but the scruples of my new friends appeared almost insurmountable. Yet the gentleman might have said "I should like a portrait of my wife," and the lady might have said "I should like a portrait of my husband." Perhaps they were not husband and wife—this naturally would make the matter more delicate. Perhaps they wished to be done together—in which case they ought to have brought a third person to break the news.

"We come from Mr. Rivet," the lady said at last, with a dim smile which had the effect of a moist sponge passed over a "sunk" piece of painting, as well as of a vague allusion to vanished beauty. She was as tall and straight, in her degree, as her companion, and with ten years less to carry. She looked as sad as a woman could look whose face was not charged with expression; that is her tinted oval mask showed friction as an exposed surface shows it. The hand of time had played over her freely, but only to simplify. She was slim and stiff, and so well-dressed, in dark blue cloth, with lappets and pockets and buttons, that it was clear she employed the same tailor as her husband. The couple had an indefinable air of prosperous thrift—they evidently got a good deal of luxury for their money. If I was to be one of their luxuries it would behove me to consider my terms.

"Ah, Claude Rivet recommended me?" I inquired; and I added that it was very kind of him, though I could reflect that, as he only painted landscape, this was not a sacrifice.

The lady looked very hard at the gentleman, and the gentleman looked round the room. Then staring at the floor a moment and stroking his moustache, he rested his pleasant eyes on me with the remark: "He said you were the right one."

"I try to be, when people want to sit."

"Yes, we should like to," said the lady anxiously.

"Do you mean together?"

My visitors exchanged a glance. "If you could do anything with *me,* I suppose it would be double," the gentleman stammered.

"Oh yes, there's naturally a higher charge for two figures than for one."

"We should like to make it pay," the husband confessed.

"That's very good of you," I returned, appreciating so unwonted a sympathy—for I supposed he meant pay the artist.

A sense of strangeness seemed to dawn on the lady. "We mean for the illustrations—Mr. Rivet said you might put one in."

"Put one in—an illustration?" I was equally confused.

"Sketch her off, you know," said the gentleman, colouring.

It was only then that I understood the service Claude Rivet had rendered me; he had told them that I worked in black and white, for magazines, for story-books, for sketches of contemporary life, and consequently had frequent employment for models. These things were true, but it was not less true (I may confess it now—whether because the aspiration was to lead to everything or to nothing I leave the reader to guess), that I couldn't get the honours, to say nothing of the emoluments, of a great painter of portraits out of my head. My "illustrations" were my pot-boilers; I looked to a different branch of art (far and away the most in-

teresting it had always seemed to me), to perpetuate my fame. There was no shame in looking to it also to make my fortune; but that fortune was by so much further from being made from the moment my visitors wished to be "done" for nothing. I was disappointed; for in the pictorial sense I had immediately *seen* them. I had seized their type—I had already settled what I would do with it. Something that wouldn't absolutely have pleased them, I afterwards reflected.

"Ah, you're—you're—a—?" I began, as soon as I had mastered my surprise. I couldn't bring out the dingy word "models"; it seemed to fit the case so little.

"We haven't had much practice," said the lady.

"We've got to *do* something, and we've thought that an artist in your line might perhaps make something of us," her husband threw off. He further mentioned that they didn't know many artists and that they had gone first, on the off-chance (he painted views of course, but sometimes put in figures—perhaps I remembered), to Mr. Rivet, whom they had met a few years before at a place in Norfolk where he was sketching.

"We used to sketch a little ourselves," the lady hinted.

"It's very awkward, but we absolutely *must* do something," her husband went on.

"Of course, we're not so *very* young," she admitted, with a wan smile.

With the remark that I might as well know something more about them, the husband had handed me a card extracted from a neat new pocket-book (their appurtenances were all of the freshest) and inscribed with the words "Major Monarch." Impressive as these words were they didn't carry my knowledge much further; but my visitor presently added: "I've left the army, and we've had the misfortune to lose our money. In fact our means are dreadfully small."

"It's an awful bore," said Mrs. Monarch.

They evidently wished to be discreet—to take care not to swagger because they were gentlefolks. I perceived they would have been willing to recognise this as something of a drawback, at the same time that I guessed at an underlying sense—their consolation in adversity—that they *had* their points. They certainly had; but these advantages struck me as preponderantly social; such for instance as would help to make a drawing-room look well. However, a drawing-room was always, or ought to be, a picture.

In consequence of his wife's allusion to their age Major Monarch observed: "Naturally, it's more for the figure that we thought of going in. We can still hold ourselves up." On the instant I saw that the figure was indeed their strong point. His "naturally" didn't sound vain, but it lighted up the question. *"She* has got the best," he continued, nodding at his wife, with a pleasant after-dinner absence of circumlocution. I could only reply, as if we were in fact sitting over our wine, that this didn't prevent his own from being very good; which led him in turn to rejoin: "We thought that if you ever have to do people like us, we might be something like it. *She,* particularly—for a lady in a book, you know."

I was so amused by them that, to get more of it, I did my best to take their point of view; and though it was an embarrassment to find myself appraising physically, as if they were animals on hire or useful blacks, a pair whom I should have expected to meet only in one of the relations in which criticism is tacit, I looked at Mrs. Monarch judicially enough to be able to exclaim, after a moment, with conviction: "Oh yes, a lady in a book!" She was singularly like a bad illustration.

"We'll stand up, if you like," said the Major; and he raised himself before me with a really grand air.

I could take his measure at a glance—he was six feet two and a perfect gentleman. It would have paid any club in process of formation and in want of a stamp to engage him at a salary to stand in the principle window. What struck me immediately was that in coming to me they had rather missed their vocation; they could surely have been turned to better account for advertising purposes. I couldn't of course see the thing in detail, but I could see them make someone's fortune—I don't mean their own. There was something in them for a waistcoat-maker, an hotel-keeper or a soap-vendor. I could imagine "We always use it" pinned on their bosoms with the greatest effect; I had a vision of the promptitude with which they would launch a table d'hôte.

Mrs. Monarch sat still, not from pride but from shyness, and presently her husband said to her: "Get up my dear and show how smart you are." She obeyed, but she had no need to get up to show it. She walked to the end of the studio, and then she came back blushing, with her fluttered eyes on her husband. I was reminded of an incident I had accidentally had a glimpse of in Paris—being with a friend there, a dramatist about to produce a play—when an actress came to him to ask to be intrusted with a part. She went through her paces before him, walked up and down as Mrs. Monarch was doing. Mrs. Monarch did it quite as well, but I abstained from applauding. It was very odd to see such people apply for such poor pay. She looked as if she had ten thousand a year. Her husband had used the word that de-

scribed her: she was, in the London current jargon, essentially and typically "smart." Her figure was, in the same order of ideas, conspicuously and irreproachably "good." For a woman of her age her waist was surprisingly small; her elbow moreover had the orthodox crook. She held her head at the conventional angle; but why did she come to *me?* She ought to have tried on jackets at a big shop. I feared my visitors were not only destitute, but "artistic"—which would be a great complication. When she sat down again I thanked her, observing that what a draughtsman most valued in his model was the faculty of keeping quiet.

"Oh, *she* can keep quiet," said Major Monarch. Then he added, jocosely: "I've always kept her quiet."

"I'm not a nasty fidget, am I?" Mrs. Monarch appealed to her husband.

He addressed his answer to me. "Perhaps it isn't out of place to mention—because we ought to be quite business-like, oughtn't we?—that when I married her she was known as the Beautiful Statue."

"Oh dear!" said Mrs. Monarch, ruefully.

"Of course I should want a certain amount of expression," I rejoined.

"Of *course!"* they both exclaimed.

"And then I suppose you know that you'll get awfully tired."

"Oh, we *never* get tired!" they eagerly cried.

"Have you had any kind of practice?"

They hesitated—they looked at each other. "We've been photographed, *immensely,"* said Mrs. Monarch.

"She means the fellows have asked us," added the Major.

"I see—because you're so good-looking."

"I don't know what they thought, but they were always after us."

"We always got our photographs for nothing," smiled Mrs. Monarch.

"We might have brought some, my dear," her husband remarked.

"I'm not sure we have any left. We've given quantities away," she explained to me.

"With our autographs and that sort of thing," said the Major.

"Are they to be got in the shops?" I inquired, as a harmless pleasantry.

"Oh, yes; *hers*—they used to be."

"Not now," said Mrs. Monarch, with her eyes on the floor.

II

I COULD fancy the "sort of thing" they put on the presentation-copies of their photographs, and I was sure they wrote a beautiful hand. It was odd how quickly I was sure of everything that concerned them. If they were now so poor as to have to earn shillings and pence, they never had had much of a margin. Their good looks had been their capital, and they had good-humouredly made the most of the career that this resource marked out for them. It was in their faces, the blankness, the deep intellectual repose of the twenty years of country-house visiting which had given them pleasant intonations. I could see the sunny drawing-rooms, sprinkled with periodicals she didn't read, in which Mrs. Monarch had continuously sat; I could see the wet shrubberies in which she had walked, equipped to admiration for either exercise. I could see the rich covers the Major had helped to shoot and the wonderful garments in which, late at night, he repaired to the smoking-room to talk about them. I could imagine their leggings and waterproofs, their knowing tweeds and rugs, their rolls of sticks and cases of tackle and neat umbrellas; and I could evoke the exact appearance of their servants and the compact variety of their luggage on the platforms of country stations.

They gave small tips, but they were liked; they didn't do anything themselves, but they were welcome. They looked so well everywhere; they gratified the general relish for stature, complexion and "form." They knew it without fatuity or vulgarity, and they respected themselves in consequence. They were not superficial; they were thorough and kept themselves up—it had been their line. People with such a taste for activity had to have some line. I could feel how, even in a dull house, they could have been counted upon for cheerfulness. At present something had happened —it didn't matter what, their little income had grown less, it had grown least—and they had to do something for pocket-money. Their friends liked them, but didn't like to support them. There was something about them that represented credit —their clothes, their manners, their type; but if credit is a large empty pocket in which an occasional chink reverberates, the chink at least must be audible. What they wanted of me was to help to make it so. Fortunately they had no children— I soon divined that. They would also perhaps wish our relations to be kept secret: this was why it was "for the figure"—the reproduction of the face would betray them.

I liked them—they were so simple; and I had no objection to them if they would suit. But, somehow, with all their perfections I didn't easily believe in them. After all they were amateurs, and the ruling passion of my life was the detestation of the amateur. Combined with this was another perversity—an innate preference for the represented subject over the real one: the defect of the real one was so apt to be a lack of representation. I liked things that appeared; then one was sure. Whether they *were* or not was a subordinate and almost always a profitless question. There were other considerations, the first of which was that I already had two or three people in use, notably a young person with big feet, in alpaca, from Kilburn, who for a couple of years had come to me regularly for my illustrations and with whom I was still—perhaps ignobly—satisfied. I frankly explained to my visitors how the case stood; but they had taken more precautions than I supposed. They had reasoned out their opportunity, for Claude Rivet had told them of the projected *édition de luxe* of one of the writers of our day— the rarest of the novelists—who, long neglected by the multitudinous vulgar and dearly prized by the attentive (need I mention Philip Vincent?) had had the happy fortune of seeing, late in life, the dawn and then the full light of a higher criticism—an estimate in which, on the part of the public, there was something really of expiation. The edition in question, planned by a publisher of taste, was practically an act of high reparation; the wood-cuts with which it was to be enriched were the homage of English art to one of the most independent representatives of English letters. Major and Mrs. Monarch confessed to me that they had hoped I might be able to work *them* into my share of the enterprise. They knew I was to do the first of the books, "Rutland Ramsay," but I had to make clear to them that my participation in the rest of the affair—this first book was to be a test —was to depend on the satisfaction I should give. If this should be limited my employers would drop me without a scruple. It was therefore a crisis for me, and naturally I was making special preparations, looking about for new people, if they should be necessary, and securing the best types. I admitted however that I should like to settle down to two or three good models who would do for everything.

"Should we have often to—a—put on special clothes?" Mrs. Monarch timidly demanded.

"Dear, yes—that's half the business."

"And should we be expected to supply our own costumes?"

"Oh, no; I've got a lot of things. A painter's models put on—or put off—anything he likes."

"And do you mean—a—the same?"

"The same?"

Mrs. Monarch looked at her husband again.

"Oh, she was just wondering," he explained, "if the costumes are in *general* use." I had to confess that they were, and I mentioned further that some of them (I had a lot of genuine, greasy last-century things), had served their time, a hundred years'ago, on living, world-stained men and women. "We'll put on anything that *fits*," said the Major.

"Oh, I arrange that—they fit in the pictures."

"I'm afraid I should do better for the modern books. I would come as you like," said Mrs. Monarch.

"She has got a lot of clothes at home: they might do for contemporary life," her husband continued.

"Oh, I can fancy scenes in which you'd be quite natural." And indeed I could see the slipshod rearrangements of stale properties—the stories I tried to produce pictures for without the exasperation of reading them—whose sandy tracts the good lady might help to people. But I had to return to the fact that for this sort of work—the daily mechanical grind—I was already equipped; the people I was working with were fully adequate.

"We only thought we might be more like *some* characters," said Mrs. Monarch mildly, getting up.

Her husband also rose; he stood looking at me with a dim wistfulness that was touching in so fine a man. "Wouldn't it be rather a pull sometimes to have—a—to have—?" He hung fire; he wanted me to help him by phrasing what he meant. But I couldn't—I didn't know. So he brought it out, awkwardly: "The *real* thing; a gentleman, you know, or a lady." I was quite ready to give a general assent—I admitted that there was a great deal in that. This encouraged Major Monarch to say, following up his appeal with an unacted gulp: "It's awfully hard—we've tried everything." The gulp was communicative; it proved too much for his wife. Before I knew it Mrs. Monarch had dropped again upon a divan and burst into tears. Her husband sat down beside her, holding one of her hands; whereupon she quickly dried her eyes with the other, while I felt embarrassed as she looked up at me. "There isn't a confounded job I haven't applied for—waited for—prayed for. You can fancy we'd be pretty bad first. Secretaryships and that sort of thing? You might as well ask for a peerage. I'd be *anything*—I'm strong; a messenger or a coalheaver. I'd put on a gold-laced cap and open carriage-doors in front of the haberdasher's; I'd hang about a station, to carry portmanteaus; I'd be a postman. But they won't *look* at you; there are thousands, as good as yourself, already on the ground. *Gentlemen,* poor beggars, who have drunk their wine, who have kept their hunters!"

I was as reassuring as I knew how to be, and my visitors were presently on their feet again while, for the experiment, we agreed on an hour. We were discussing it when the door opened and Miss Churm came in with a wet umbrella. Miss Churm had to take the omnibus to Maida Vale [1] and then walk half-a-mile. She looked a trifle blowsy and slightly splashed. I scarcely ever saw her come in without thinking afresh how odd it was that, being so little in herself, she should yet be so much in others. She was a meagre little Miss Churm, but she was an ample heroine of romance. She was only a freckled cockney, but she could represent everything, from a fine lady to a shepherdess; she had the faculty, as she might have had a fine voice or long hair. She couldn't spell, and she loved beer, but she had two or three "points," and practice, and a knack, and mother-wit, and a kind of whimsical sensibility, and a love of the theatre, and seven sisters, and not an ounce of respect, especially for the *h.* The first thing my visitors saw was that her umbrella was wet, and in their spotless perfection they visibly winced at it. The rain had come on since their arrival.

"I'm all in a soak; there *was* a mess of people in the 'bus. I wish you lived near a stytion," said Miss Churm. I requested her to get ready as quickly as possible, and she passed into the room in which she always changed her dress. But before going out she asked me what she was to get into this time.

"It's the Russian princess, don't you know?" I answered; "the one with the 'golden eyes,' in black velvet, for the long thing in the *Cheapside.*" [2]

"Golden eyes? I *say!*" cried Miss Churm, while my companions watched her with intensity as she withdrew. She always arranged herself, when she was late, before I could turn round; and I kept my visitors a little, on purpose, so that they might get an idea, from seeing her, what would be expected of themselves. I mentioned that she was quite my notion of an excellent model —she was really very clever.

"Do you think she looks like a Russian princess?" Major Monarch asked, with lurking alarm.

"When I make her, yes."

"Oh, if you have to *make* her—!" he reasoned, acutely.

"That's the most you can ask. There are so many that are not makeable."

"Well now, *here's* a lady"—and with a persuasive smile he passed his arm into his wife's— "who's already made!"

THE REAL THING.    1. **Maida Vale:** unfashionable residential quarter of London.    2. *Cheapside:* imaginary magazine named after London's famous commercial thoroughfare.

"Oh, I'm not a Russian princess," Mrs. Monarch protested, a little coldly. I could see that she had known some and didn't like them. There, immediately, was a complication of a kind that I never had to fear with Miss Churm.

This young lady came back in black velvet—the gown was rather rusty and very low on her lean shoulders—and with a Japanese fan in her red hands. I reminded her that in the scene I was doing she had to look over someone's head. "I forget whose it is; but it doesn't matter. Just look over a head."

"I'd rather look over a stove," said Miss Churm; and she took her station near the fire. She fell into position, settled herself into a tall attitude, gave a certain backward inclination to her head and a certain forward droop to her fan, and looked, at least to my prejudiced sense, distinguished and charming, foreign and dangerous. We left her looking so, while I went down-stairs with Major and Mrs. Monarch.

"I think I could come about as near it as that," said Mrs. Monarch.

"Oh, you think she's shabby, but you must allow for the alchemy of art."

However, they went off with an evident increase of comfort, founded on their demonstrable advantage in being the real thing. I could fancy them shuddering over Miss Churm. She was very droll about them when I went back, for I told her what they wanted.

"Well, if *she* can sit I'll tyke to bookkeeping," said my model.

"She's very lady-like," I replied, as an innocent form of aggravation.

"So much the worse for *you*. That means she can't turn round."

"She'll do for the fashionable novels."

"Oh yes, she'll *do* for them!" my model humorously declared. "Ain't they bad enough without her?" I had often sociably denounced them to Miss Churm.

### III

IT WAS for the elucidation of a mystery in one of these works that I first tried Mrs. Monarch. Her husband came with her, to be useful if necessary —it was sufficiently clear that as a general thing he would prefer to come with her. At first I wondered if this were for "propriety's" sake—if he were going to be jealous and meddling. The idea was too tiresome, and if it had been confirmed it would speedily have brought our acquaintance to a close. But I soon saw there was nothing in it and that if he accompanied Mrs. Monarch it was (in addition to the chance of being wanted), simply

because he had nothing else to do. When she was away from him his occupation was gone—she never *had* been away from him. I judged, rightly, that in their awkward situation their close union was their main comfort and that this union had no weak spot. It was a real marriage, an encouragement to the hesitating, a nut for pessimists to crack. Their address was humble (I remember afterwards thinking it had been the only thing about them that was really professional), and I could fancy the lamentable lodgings in which the Major would have been left alone. He could bear them with his wife—he couldn't bear them without her.

He had too much tact to try and make himself agreeable when he couldn't be useful; so he simply sat and waited, when I was too absorbed in my work to talk. But I liked to make him talk—it made my work, when it didn't interrupt it, less sordid, less special. To listen to him was to combine the excitement of going out with the economy of staying at home. There was only one hindrance: that I seemed not to know any of the people he and his wife had known. I think he wondered extremely, during the term of our intercourse, whom the deuce I *did* know. He hadn't a stray sixpence of an idea to fumble for; so we didn't spin it very fine—we confined ourselves to questions of leather and even of liquor (saddlers and breeches-makers and how to get good claret cheap), and matters like "good trains" and the habits of small game. His lore on these last subjects was astonishing, he managed to interweave the station-master with the ornithologist. When he couldn't talk about greater things he could talk cheerfully about smaller, and since I couldn't accompany him into reminiscences of the fashionable world he could lower the conversation without a visible effort to my level.

So earnest a desire to please was touching in a man who could so easily have knocked one down. He looked after the fire and had an opinion on the draught of the stove, without my asking him, and I could see that he thought many of my arrangements not half clever enough. I remember telling him that if I were only rich I would offer him a salary to come and teach me how to live. Sometimes he gave a random sigh, of which the essence was: "Give me even such a bare old barrack as *this*, and I'd do something with it!" When I wanted to use him he came alone; which was an illustration of the superior courage of women. His wife could bear her solitary second floor, and she was in general more discreet; showing by various small reserves that she was alive to the propriety of keeping our relations markedly professional—not letting them slide into sociability. She wished it to remain clear that she and the Major were employed, not cultivated, and if she approved of me as a superior, who could be kept in his place, she never thought me quite good enough for an equal.

She sat with great intensity, giving the whole of her mind to it, and was capable of remaining for an hour almost as motionless as if she were before a photographer's lens. I could see she had been photographed often, but somehow the very habit that made her good for that purpose unfitted her for mine. At first I was extremely pleased with her lady-like air, and it was a satisfaction, on coming to follow her lines, to see how good they were and how far they could lead the pencil. But after a few times I began to find her too insurmountably stiff; do what I would with it my drawing looked like a photograph or a copy of a photograph. Her figure had no variety of expression—she herself had no sense of variety. You may say that this was my business, was only a question of placing her. I placed her in every conceivable position, but she managed to obliterate their differences. She was always a lady certainly, and into the bargain was always the same lady. She was the real thing, but always the same thing. There were moments when I was oppressed by the serenity of her confidence that she *was* the real thing. All her dealings with me and all her husband's were an implication that this was lucky for *me*. Meanwhile I found myself trying to invent types that approached her own, instead of making her own transform itself—in the clever way that was not impossible, for instance, to poor Miss Churm. Arrange as I would and take the precautions I would, she always, in my pictures, came out too tall—landing me in the dilemma of having represented a fascinating woman as seven feet high, which, out of respect perhaps to my own very much scantier inches, was far from my idea of such a personage.

The case was worse with the Major—nothing I could do would keep *him* down, so that he became useful only for the representation of brawny giants. I adored variety and range, I cherished human accidents, the illustrative note; I wanted to characterise closely, and the thing in the world I most hated was the danger of being ridden by a type. I had quarrelled with some of my friends about it—I had parted company with them for maintaining that one *had* to be, and that if the type was beautiful (witness Raphael and Leonardo), the servitude was only a gain. I was neither Leonardo nor Raphael; I might only be a presumptuous young modern searcher, but I held that

everything was to be sacrificed sooner than character. When they averred that the haunting type in question could easily *be* character, I retorted, perhaps superficially: "Whose?" It couldn't be everybody's—it might end in being nobody's.

After I had drawn Mrs. Monarch a dozen times I perceived more clearly than before that the value of such a model as Miss Churm resided precisely in the fact that she had no positive stamp, combined of course with the other fact that what she did have, was a curious and inexplicable talent for imitation. Her usual appearance was like a curtain which she could draw up at request for a capital performance. This performance was simply suggestive; but it was a word to the wise—it was vivid and pretty. Sometimes, even, I thought it, though she was plain herself, too insipidly pretty; I made it a reproach to her that the figures drawn from her were monotonously (*bêtement*,[3] as we used to say) graceful. Nothing made her more angry: it was so much her pride to feel that she could sit for characters that had nothing in common with each other. She would accuse me at such moments of taking away her "reputytion."

It suffered a certain shrinkage, this queer quantity, from the repeated visits of my new friends. Miss Churm was greatly in demand, never in want of employment, so I had no scruple in putting her off occasionally, to try them more at my ease. It was certainly amusing at first to do the real thing—it was amusing to do Major Monarch's trousers. They *were* the real thing, even if he did come out colossal. It was amusing to do his wife's back hair (it was so mathematically neat) and the particular "smart" tension of her tight stays. She lent herself especially to positions in which the face was somewhat averted or blurred; she abounded in lady-like back views and *profils perdus*.[4] When she stood erect she took naturally one of the attitudes in which court-painters represent queens and princesses; so that I found myself wondering whether, to draw out this accomplishment, I couldn't get the editor of the *Cheapside* to publish a really royal romance, "A Tale of Buckingham Palace." Sometimes, however, the real thing and the make-believe came into contact; by which I mean that Miss Churm, keeping an appointment or coming to make one on days when I had much work in hand, encountered her invidious rivals. The encounter was not on their part, for they noticed her no more than if she had been the housemaid; not from intentional lofti-

---

3. *bêtement:* beastly.  4. *profils perdus:* averted glances.

ness, but simply because, as yet, professionally, they didn't know how to fraternise, as I could guess that they would have liked—or at least that the Major would. They couldn't talk about the omnibus—they always walked; and they didn't know what else to try—she wasn't interested in good trains or cheap claret. Besides, they must have felt—in the air—that she was amused at them, secretly derisive of their ever knowing how. She was not a person to conceal her scepticism if she had had a chance to show it. On the other hand Mrs. Monarch didn't think her tidy; for why else did she take pains to say to me (it was going out of the way, for Mrs. Monarch), that she didn't like dirty women?

One day when my young lady happened to be present with my other sitters (she even dropped in, when it was convenient, for a chat), I asked her to be so good as to lend a hand in getting tea —a service with which she was familiar and which was one of a class that, living as I did in a small way, with slender domestic resources, I often appealed to my models to render. They liked to lay hands on my property, to break the sitting, and sometimes the china—I made them feel Bohemian. The next time I saw Miss Churm after this incident she surprised me greatly by making a scene about it—she accused me of having wished to humiliate her. She had not resented the outrage at the time, but had seemed obliging and amused, enjoying the comedy of asking Mrs. Monarch, who sat vague and silent, whether she would have cream and sugar, and putting an exaggerated simper into the question. She had tried intonations—as if she too wished to pass for the real thing; till I was afraid my other visitors would take offence.

Oh, *they* were determined not to do this; and their touching patience was the measure of their great need. They would sit by the hour, uncomplaining, till I was ready to use them; they would come back on the chance of being wanted and would walk away cheerfully if they were not. I used to go to the door with them to see in what magnificent order they retreated. I tried to find other employment for them—I introduced them to several artists. But they didn't "take," for reasons I could appreciate, and I became conscious, rather anxiously, that after such disappointments they fell back upon me with a heavier weight. They did me the honour to think that it was I who was most *their* form. They were not picturesque enough for the painters, and in those days there were not so many serious workers in black and white. Besides, they had an eye to the great job I

had mentioned to them—they had secretly set their hearts on supplying the right essence for my pictorial vindication of our fine novelist. They knew that for this undertaking I should want no costume-effects, none of the frippery of past ages —that it was a case in which everything would be contemporary and satirical and, presumably, genteel. If I could work them into it their future would be assured, for the labour would of course be long and the occupation steady.

One day Mrs. Monarch came without her husband—she explained his absence by his having had to go to the City.[5] While she sat there in her usual anxious stiffness there came, at the door, a knock which I immediately recognised as the subdued appeal of a model out of work. It was followed by the entrance of a young man whom I easily perceived to be a foreigner and who proved in fact an Italian acquainted with no English word but my name, which he uttered in a way that made it seem to include all others. I had not then visited his country, nor was I proficient in his tongue; but as he was not so meanly constituted—what Italian is?—as to depend only on that member for expression he conveyed to me, in familiar but graceful mimicry, that he was in search of exactly the employment in which the lady before me was engaged. I was not struck with him at first, and while I continued to draw I emitted rough sounds of discouragement and dismissal. He stood his ground, however, not importunately, but with a dumb, dog-like fidelity in his eyes which amounted to innocent impudence—the manner of a devoted servant (he might have been in the house for years), unjustly suspected. Suddenly I saw that this very attitude and expression made a picture, whereupon I told him to sit down and wait till I should be free. There was another picture in the way he obeyed me, and I observed as I worked that there were others still in the way he looked wonderingly, with his head thrown back, about the high studio. He might have been crossing himself in St. Peter's. Before I finished I said to myself: "The fellow's a bankrupt orange-monger, but he's a treasure."

When Mrs. Monarch withdrew he passed across the room like a flash to open the door for her, standing there with the rapt, pure gaze of the young Dante spellbound by the young Beatrice.[6] As I never insisted, in such situations, on the blankness of the British domestic, I reflected that

---

5. the City: London's banking and commercial center.
6. Beatrice: Dante's youthful love for Beatrice Portinari is told in his *La Vita Nuova*.

he had the making of a servant (and I needed one, but couldn't pay him to be only that), as well as of a model; in short I made up my mind to adopt my bright adventurer if he would agree to officiate in the double capacity. He jumped at my offer, and in the event my rashness (for I had known nothing about him), was not brought home to me. He proved a sympathetic though a desultory ministrant, and had in a wonderful degree the *sentiment de la pose*.[7] It was uncultivated, instinctive; a part of the happy instinct which had guided him to my door and helped him to spell out my name on the card nailed to it. He had had no other introduction to me than a guess, from the shape of my high north window, seen outside, that my place was a studio and that as a studio it would contain an artist. He had wandered to England in search of fortune, like other itinerants, and had embarked, with a partner and a small green hand-cart, on the sale of penny ices. The ices had melted away and the partner had dissolved in their train. My young man wore tight yellow trousers with reddish stripes and his name was Oronte. He was sallow but fair, and when I put him into some old clothes of my own he looked like an Englishman. He was as good as Miss Churm, who could look, when required, like an Italian.

### IV

I THOUGHT Mrs. Monarch's face slightly convulsed when, on her coming back with her husband, she found Oronte installed. It was strange to have to recognise in a scrap of a *lazzarone*[8] a competitor to her magnificent Major. It was she who scented danger first, for the Major was anecdotically unconscious. But Oronte gave us tea, with a hundred eager confusions (he had never seen such a queer process), and I think she thought better of me for having at last an "establishment." They saw a couple of drawings that I had made of the establishment, and Mrs. Monarch hinted that it never would have struck her that he had sat for them. "Now the drawings you make from *us,* they look exactly like us," she reminded me, smiling in triumph; and I recognised that this was indeed just their defect. When I drew the Monarchs I couldn't, somehow, get away from them—get into the character I wanted to represent; and I had not the least desire my model should be discoverable in my picture. Miss Churm never was, and Mrs. Monarch thought I hid her, very properly, because she was vulgar; whereas if

she was lost it was only as the dead who go to heaven are lost—in the gain of an angel the more.

By this time I had got a certain start with "Rutland Ramsay," the first novel in the great projected series; that is I had produced a dozen drawings, several with the help of the Major and his wife, and I had sent them in for approval. My understanding with the publishers, as I have already hinted, had been that I was to be left to do my work, in this particular case, as I liked, with the whole book committed to me; but my connection with the rest of the series was only contingent. There were moments when, frankly, it *was* a comfort to have the real thing under one's hand; for there were characters in "Rutland Ramsay" that were very much like it. There were people presumably as straight as the Major and women of as good a fashion as Mrs. Monarch. There was a great deal of country-house life—treated, it is true, in a fine, fanciful, ironical, generalised way— and there was a considerable implication of knickerbockers and kilts. There were certain things I had to settle at the outset; such things for instance as the exact appearance of the hero, the particular bloom of the heroine. The author of course gave me a lead, but there was a margin for interpretation. I took the Monarchs into my confidence, I told them frankly what I was about, I mentioned my embarrassments and alternatives. "Oh, take *him!*" Mrs. Monarch murmured sweetly, looking at her husband; and "What could you want better than my wife?" the Major inquired, with the comfortable candour that now prevailed between us.

I was not obliged to answer these remarks—I was only obliged to place my sitters. I was not easy in mind, and I postponed, a little timidly perhaps, the solution of the question. The book was a large canvas, the other figures were numerous, and I worked off at first some of the episodes in which the hero and the heroine were not concerned. When once I had set *them* up I should have to stick to them—I couldn't make my young man seven feet high in one place and five feet nine in another. I inclined on the whole to the latter measurement, though the Major more than once reminded me that *he* looked about as young as anyone. It was indeed quite possible to arrange him, for the figure, so that it would have been difficult to detect his age. After the spontaneous Oronte had been with me a month, and after I had given him to understand several different times that his native exuberance would presently constitute an insurmountable barrier to our further intercourse, I waked to a sense of his heroic capacity. He was only five feet seven, but the remain-

---

7. *sentiment de la pose:* "the instinct for striking poses."    8. *lazzarone:* Italian for beggar.

ing inches were latent. I tried him almost secretly at first, for I was really rather afraid of the judgment my other models would pass on such a choice. If they regarded Miss Churm as little better than a snare, what would they think of the representation by a person so little the real thing as an Italian street-vendor of a protagonist formed by a public school?

If I went a little in fear of them it was not because they bullied me, because they had got an oppressive foothold, but because in their really pathetic decorum and mysteriously permanent newness they counted on me so intensely. I was therefore very glad when Jack Hawley came home: he was always of such good counsel. He painted badly himself, but there was no one like him for putting his finger on the place. He had been absent from England for a year; he had been somewhere—I don't remember where—to get a fresh eye. I was in a good deal of dread of any such organ, but we were old friends; he had been away for months and a sense of emptiness was creeping into my life. I hadn't dodged a missile for a year.

He came back with a fresh eye, but with the same old black velvet blouse, and the first evening he spent in my studio we smoked cigarettes till the small hours. He had done no work himself, he had only got the eye; so the field was clear for the production of my little things. He wanted to see what I had done for the *Cheapside,* but he was disappointed in the exhibition. That at least seemed the meaning of two or three comprehensive groans which, as he lounged on my big divan, on a folded leg, looking at my latest drawings, issued from his lips with the smoke of the cigarette.

"What's the matter with you?" I asked.

"What's the matter with *you?"*

"Nothing save that I'm mystified."

"You are indeed. You're quite off the hinge. What's the meaning of this new fad?" And he tossed me, with visible irreverence, a drawing in which I happened to have depicted both my majestic models. I asked if he didn't think it good, and he replied that it struck him as execrable, given the sort of thing I had always represented myself to him as wishing to arrive at; but I let that pass, I was so anxious to see exactly what he meant. The two figures in the picture looked colossal, but I supposed this was *not* what he meant, inasmuch as, for aught he knew to the contrary, I might have been trying for that. I maintained that I was working exactly in the same way as when he last had done me the honour to commend me. "Well, there's a big hole somewhere," he answered; "wait a bit and I'll discover it." I depended upon him to do so: where else was the

fresh eye? But he produced at last nothing more luminous than "I don't know—I don't like your types." This was lame, for a critic who had never consented to discuss with me anything but the question of execution, the direction of strokes and the mystery of values.

"In the drawings you've been looking at I think my types are very handsome."

"Oh, they won't do!"

"I've had a couple of new models."

"I see you have. *They* won't do."

"Are you very sure of that?"

"Absolutely—they're stupid."

"You mean *I* am—for I ought to get round that."

"You *can't*—with such people. Who are they?"

I told him, as far as was necessary, and he declared, heartlessly: *"Ce sont des gens qu'il faut mettre à la porte."* [9]

"You've never seen them; they're awfully good," I compassionately objected.

"Not seen them? Why, all this recent work of yours drops to pieces with them. It's all I want to see of them."

"No one else has said anything against it—the *Cheapside* people are pleased."

"Everyone else is an ass, and the *Cheapside* people the biggest asses of all. Come, don't pretend, at this time of day, to have pretty illusions about the public, especially about publishers and editors. It's not for *such* animals you work—it's for those who know, *coloro che sanno;* [10] so keep straight for *me* if you can't keep straight for yourself. There's a certain sort of thing you tried for from the first—and a very good thing it is. But this twaddle isn't *in* it." When I talked with Hawley later about "Rutland Ramsay" and its possible successors he declared that I must get back into my boat again or I would go to the bottom. His voice in short was the voice of warning.

I noted the warning, but I didn't turn my friends out of doors. They bored me a good deal; but the very fact that they bored me admonished me not to sacrifice them—if there was anything to be done with them—simply to irritation. As I look back at this phase they seem to me to have pervaded my life not a little. I have a vision of them as most of the time in my studio, seated, against the wall, on an old velvet bench to be out of the way, and looking like a pair of patient courtiers in a royal ante-chamber. I am convinced that during the coldest weeks of the winter they held their

9. *"Ce sont . . . porte":* "Such people ought to be shown the door."     10. *coloro che sanno:* Hawley is misquoting a famous phrase, *il maestro di color che sanno,* "the master of those who know," which Dante applies to Aristotle (*Inferno,* IV.131).

ground because it saved them fire. Their newness was losing its gloss, and it was impossible not to feel that they were objects of charity. Whenever Miss Churm arrived they went away, and after I was fairly launched in "Rutland Ramsay" Miss Churm arrived pretty often. They managed to express to me tacitly that they supposed I wanted her for the low life of the book, and I let them suppose it, since they had attempted to study the work—it was lying about the studio—without discovering that it dealt only with the highest circles. They had dipped into the most brilliant of our novelists without deciphering many passages. I still took an hour from them, now and again, in spite of Jack Hawley's warning: it would be time enough to dismiss them, if dismissal should be necessary, when the rigour of the season was over. Hawley had made their acquaintance—he had met them at my fireside—and thought them a ridiculous pair. Learning that he was a painter they tried to approach him, to show him too that they were the real thing; but he looked at them, across the big room, as if they were miles away: they were a compendium of everything that he most objected to in the social system of his country. Such people as that, all convention and patent-leather, with ejaculations that stopped conversation, had no business in a studio. A studio was a place to learn to see, and how could you see through a pair of feather beds?

The main inconvenience I suffered at their hands was that, at first, I was shy of letting them discover how my artful little servant had begun to sit to me for "Rutland Ramsay." They knew that I had been odd enough (they were prepared by this time to allow oddity to artists) to pick a foreign vagabond out of the streets, when I might have had a person with whiskers and credentials; but it was some time before they learned how high I rated his accomplishments. They found him in an attitude more than once, but they never doubted I was doing him as an organ-grinder. There were several things they never guessed, and one of them was that for a striking scene in the novel, in which a footman briefly figured, it occurred to me to make use of Major Monarch as the menial. I kept putting this off, I didn't like to ask him to don the livery—besides the difficulty of finding a livery to fit him. At last, one day late in the winter, when I was at work on the despised Oronte (he caught one's idea in an instant), and was in the glow of feeling that I was going very straight, they came in, the Major and his wife, with their society laugh about nothing (there was less and less to laugh at), like country-callers—they al-

ways reminded me of that—who have walked across the park after church and are presently persuaded to stay to luncheon. Luncheon was over, but they could stay to tea—I knew they wanted it. The fit was on me, however, and I couldn't let my ardour cool and my work wait, with the fading daylight, while my model prepared it. So I asked Mrs. Monarch if she would mind laying it out—a request which, for an instant, brought all the blood to her face. Her eyes were on her husband's for a second, and some mute telegraphy passed between them. Their folly was over the next instant; his cheerful shrewdness put an end to it. So far from pitying their wounded pride, I must add, I was moved to give it as complete a lesson as I could. They bustled about together and got out the cups and saucers and made the kettle boil. I know they felt as if they were waiting on my servant, and when the tea was prepared I said: "He'll have a cup, please—he's tired." Mrs. Monarch brought him one where he stood, and he took it from her as if he had been a gentleman at a party, squeezing a crush-hat with an elbow.

Then it came over me that she had made a great effort for me—made it with a kind of nobleness —and that I owed her a compensation. Each time I saw her after this I wondered what the compensation could be. I couldn't go on doing the wrong thing to oblige them. Oh, it *was* the wrong thing, the stamp of the work for which they sat—Hawley was not the only person to say it now. I sent in a large number of the drawings I had made for "Rutland Ramsay," and I received a warning that was more to the point that Hawley's. The artistic adviser of the house for which I was working was of opinion that many of my illustrations were not what had been looked for. Most of these illustrations were the subjects in which the Monarchs had figured. Without going into the question of what *had* been looked for, I saw at this rate I shouldn't get the other books to do. I hurled myself in despair upon Miss Churm, I put her through all her paces. I not only adopted Oronte publicly as my hero, but one morning when the Major looked in to see if I didn't require him to finish a figure for the *Cheapside,* for which he had begun to sit the week before, I told him that I had changed my mind—I would do the drawing from my man. At this my visitor turned pale and stood looking at me. "Is *he* your idea of an English gentleman?" he asked.

I was disappointed, I was nervous, I wanted to get on with my work; so I replied with irritation: "Oh, my dear Major—I can't be ruined for *you!*"

He stood another moment; then, without a word, he quitted the studio. I drew a long breath when he was gone, for I said to myself that I shouldn't see him again. I had not told him definitely that I was in danger of having my work rejected, but I was vexed at his not having felt the catastrophe in the air, read with me the moral of our fruitless collaboration, the lesson that, in the deceptive atmosphere of art, even the highest respectability may fail of being plastic.

I didn't owe my friends money, but I did see them again. They re-appeared together, three days later, and under the circumstances there was something tragic in the fact. It was a proof to me that they could find nothing else in life to do. They had threshed the matter out in a dismal conference—they had digested the bad news that they were not in for the series. If they were not useful to me even for the *Cheapside* their function seemed difficult to determine, and I could only judge at first that they had come, forgivingly, decorously, to take a last leave. This made me rejoice in secret that I had little leisure for a scene; for I had placed both my other models in position together and I was pegging away at a drawing from which I hoped to derive glory. It had been suggested by the passage in which Rutland Ramsay, drawing up a chair to Artemisia's piano-stool, says extraordinary things to her while she ostensibly fingers out a difficult piece of music. I had done Miss Churm at the piano before—it was an attitude in which she knew how to take on an absolutely poetic grace. I wished the two figures to "compose" together, intensely, and my little Italian had entered perfectly into my conception. The pair were vividly before me, the piano had been pulled out; it was a charming picture of blended youth and murmured love, which I had only to catch and keep. My visitors stood and looked at it, and I was friendly to them over my shoulder.

They made no response, but I was used to silent company and went on with my work, only a little disconcerted (even though exhilarated by the sense that *this* was at least the ideal thing), at not having got rid of them after all. Presently I heard Mrs. Monarch's sweet voice beside, or rather above me: "I wish her hair was a little better done." I looked up and she was staring with a strange fixedness at Miss Churm, whose back was turned to her. "Do you mind my just touching it?" she went on—a question which made me spring up for an instant, as with the instinctive fear that she might do the young lady a harm. But she quieted me with a glance I shall never forget— I confess I should like to have been able to paint

*that*—and went for a moment to my model. She spoke to her softly, laying a hand upon her shoulder and bending over her; and as the girl, understanding, gratefully assented, she disposed her rough curls, with a few quick passes, in such a way as to make Miss Churm's head twice as charming. It was one of the most heroic personal services I have ever seen rendered. Then Mrs. Monarch turned away with a low sigh and, looking about her as if for something to do, stooped to the floor with a noble humility and picked up a dirty rag that had dropped out of my paint-box.

The Major meanwhile had also been looking for something to do and, wandering to the other end of the studio, saw before him my breakfast things, neglected, unremoved. "I say, can't I be useful *here?*" he called out to me with an irrepressible quaver. I assented with a laugh that I fear was awkward and for the next ten minutes, while I worked, I heard the light clatter of china and the tinkle of spoons and glass. Mrs. Monarch assisted her husband—they washed up my crockery, they put it away. They wandered off into my little scullery, and I afterwards found that they had cleaned my knives and that my slender stock of plate had an unprecedented surface. When it came over me, the latent eloquence of what they were doing, I confess that my drawing was blurred for a moment—the picture swam. They had accepted their failure, but they couldn't accept their fate. They had bowed their heads in bewilderment to the perverse and cruel law in virtue of which the real thing could be so much less precious than the unreal; but they didn't want to starve. If my servants were my models, my models might be my servants. They would reverse the parts—the others would sit for the ladies and gentlemen, and *they* would do the work. They would still be in the studio—it was an intense dumb appeal to me not to turn them out. "Take us on," they wanted to say—"we'll do *anything*."

When all this hung before me the *afflatus* vanished—my pencil dropped from my hand. My sitting was spoiled and I got rid of my sitters, who were also evidently rather mystified and awestruck. Then, alone with the Major and his wife, I had a most uncomfortable moment. He put their prayer into a single sentence: "I say, you know—just let *us* do for you, can't you?" I couldn't—it was dreadful to see them emptying my slops; but I pretended I could, to oblige them, for about a week. Then I gave them a sum of money to go away; and I never saw them again. I obtained the remaining books, but my friend Hawley repeats that Major and Mrs. Monarch did me a permanent harm, got me into a second-rate trick. If it be true I am content to have paid the price—for the memory.

# 'EUROPE'

◇

[ " 'Europe' " recalls certain of James's early stories about the frustration, in an American setting, of the desire for experience, especially the desire for travel in the Old World. But it reflects the later James in its more concentrated form and more severely ironic spirit. 'Europe,' in quotation marks, has become a kind of cliché. First published in *Scribner's Monthly* (June 1899), the story was reprinted in the collection *The Soft Side* (1900) and reprinted again in the New York Edition.

◇

I

'OUR feeling is, you know, that Becky *should* go.' That earnest little remark comes back to me, even after long years, as the first note of something that began, for my observation, the day I went with my sister-in-law to take leave of her good friends. It is a memory of the American time, which revives so at present—under some touch that doesn't signify—that it rounds itself off as an anecdote. That walk to say good-bye was the beginning; and the end, so far as I was concerned with it, was not till long after; yet even the end also appears to me now as of the old days. I went, in those days, on occasion, to see my sister-in-law, in whose affairs, on my brother's death, I had had to take a helpful hand. I continued to go, indeed, after these little matters were straightened out, for the pleasure, periodically, of the impression—the change to the almost pastoral sweetness of the good Boston suburb from the loud, longitudinal New York. It was another world, with other manners, a different tone, a different taste; a savour nowhere so mild, yet so distinct, as in the square white house—with a pair of elms, like gigantic wheat-sheaves in front, the rustic orchard not far behind, the old-fashioned door-lights, the big blue and white jars in the porch, the straight, bricked walk from the high gate—that enshrined the extraordinary merit of Mrs. Rimmle and her three daughters.

These ladies were so much of the place and the place so much of themselves that, from the first of their being revealed to me, I felt that nothing else at Brookbridge much mattered. They were what, for me, at any rate, Brookbridge had most to give: I mean in the way of what it was naturally strongest in, the thing that we called in New York the New England expression, the air of Puritanism reclaimed and refined. The Rimmles had brought it down to a wonderful delicacy. They struck me even then—all four almost equally—as very ancient and very earnest, and I think theirs must have been the house, in all the world, in which 'culture' first came to the aid of morning calls. The head of the family was the widow of a great public character—as public characters were understood at Brookbridge—whose speeches on anniversaries formed a part of the body of national eloquence spouted in the New England schools by little boys covetous of the most marked, though perhaps the easiest, distinction. He was reported to have been celebrated, and in such fine declamatory connections that he seemed to gesticulate even from the tomb. He was understood to have made, in his wife's company, the tour of Europe at a date not immensely removed from that of the battle of Waterloo. What was the age, then, of the bland, firm, antique Mrs. Rimmle at the period of her being first revealed to me? That is a point I am not in a position to determine—I remember mainly that I was young enough to regard her as having reached the limit. And yet the limit for Mrs. Rimmle must have been prodigiously extended; the scale of its extension is, in fact, the very moral of this reminiscence. She was old, and her daughters were old, but I was destined to know them all as older. It was only by comparison and habit that—however much I recede—Rebecca, Maria, and Jane were the 'young ladies.'

I think it was felt that, though their mother's life, after thirty years of widowhood, had had a grand backward stretch, her blandness and firmness—and this in spite of her extreme physical frailty—would be proof against any surrender not overwhelmingly justified by time. It had appeared, years before, at a crisis of which the waves had not even yet quite subsided, a surrender not justified by anything, that she should go, with her daughters, to Europe for her health. Her health was supposed to require constant support; but when it had at that period tried conclusions with the idea of Europe, it was not the idea of Europe that had been insidious enough to prevail. She had not gone, and Becky, Maria, and Jane had not gone, and this was long ago. They still merely floated in the air of the visit achieved, with such introductions and such acclamations, in the early part of the century; they still, with fond glances at the sunny parlour-walls, only referred, in conversation, to divers pictorial and other reminders of it. The Miss Rimmles had quite been brought up on it, but Becky, as the most literary, had most mastered the subject. There were framed letters— tributes to their eminent father—suspended among the mementos, and of two or three of these, the most foreign and complimentary, Becky had executed translations that figured beside the text. She knew already, through this and other illumination, so much about Europe that it was hard to believe, for her, in that limit of adventure which consisted only of her having been twice to Philadelphia. The others had not been to Philadelphia, but there was a legend that Jane had been to Saratoga. Becky was a short, stout, fair person with round, serious eyes, a high forehead, the sweetest, neatest enunciation, and a miniature of her father—'done in Rome'—worn as a breast-pin. She had written the life, she had edited the speeches, of the original of this ornament, and now at last, beyond the seas, she was really to tread in his footsteps.

Fine old Mrs. Rimmle, in the sunny parlour and with a certain austerity of cap and chair— though with a gay new 'front' that looked like rusty brown plush—had had so unusually good a winter that the question of her sparing two members of her family for an absence had been threshed as fine, I could feel, as even under that Puritan roof any case of conscience had ever been threshed. They were to make their dash while the coast, as it were, was clear, and each of the daughters had tried—heroically, angelically, and for the sake of each of her sisters—not to be one of the two. What I encountered that first time was an opportunity to concur with enthusiasm in the general idea that Becky's wonderful preparation would be wasted if she were the one to stay with their mother. They talked of Becky's preparation —they had a sly, old-maidish humour that was as mild as milk—as if it were some mixture, for application somewhere, that she kept in a precious bottle. It had been settled, at all events, that, armed with this concoction and borne aloft by their introductions, she and Jane were to start. They were wonderful on their introductions, which proceeded naturally from their mother and were addressed to the charming families that, in vague generations, had so admired vague Mr. Rimmle. Jane, I found at Brookbridge, had to be described, for want of other description, as the pretty one, but it would not have served to identify her unless you had seen the others. *Her* preparation was only this figment of her prettiness—only,

that is, unless one took into account something that, on the spot, I silently divined: the lifelong, secret, passionate ache of her little rebellious desire. They were all growing old in the yearning to go, but Jane's yearning was the sharpest. She struggled with it as people at Brookbridge mostly struggled with what they liked, but fate, by threatening to prevent what she *dis*liked, and what was therefore duty—which was to stay at home instead of Maria—had bewildered her, I judged, not a little. It was she who, in the words I have quoted, mentioned to me Becky's case and Becky's affinity as the clearest of all. Her mother, moreover, on the general subject, had still more to say.

'I positively desire, I really quite insist that they shall go,' the old lady explained to us from her still chair. 'We've talked about it so often, and they've had from me so clear an account—I've amused them again and again with it—of what is to be seen and enjoyed. If they've had hitherto too many duties to leave, the time seems to have come to recognise that there are also many duties to *seek*. Wherever we go we find them—I always remind the girls of that. There's a duty that calls them to those wonderful countries, just as it called, at the right time, their father and myself—if it be only that of laying up for the years to come the same store of remarkable impressions, the same wealth of knowledge and food for conversation as, since my return, I have found myself so happy to possess.' Mrs. Rimmle spoke of her return as of something of the year before last, but the future of her daughters was, somehow, by a different law, to be on the scale of great vistas, of endless after-tastes. I think that, without my being quite ready to say it, even this first impression of her was somewhat upsetting; there was a large, placid perversity, a grim secrecy of intention, in her estimate of the ages.

'Well, I'm so glad you don't delay it longer,' I said to Miss Becky before we withdrew. 'And whoever should go,' I continued in the spirit of the sympathy with which the good sisters had already inspired me, 'I quite feel, with your family, you know, that *you* should. But of course I hold that every one should.' I suppose I wished to attenuate my solemnity; there was something in it, however, that I couldn't help. It must have been a faint foreknowledge.

'Have you been a great deal yourself?' Miss Jane, I remember, inquired.

'Not so much but that I hope to go a good deal more. So perhaps we shall meet,' I encouragingly suggested.

I recall something—something in the nature of

susceptibility to encouragement—that this brought into the more expressive brown eyes to which Miss Jane mainly owed it that she was the pretty one. 'Where, do you think?'

I tried to think. 'Well, on the Italian lakes—Como, Bellagio, Lugano.' I liked to say the names to them.

' "Sublime, but neither bleak nor bare—nor misty are the mountains there!" ' Miss Jane softly breathed, while her sister looked at her as if her familiarity with the poetry of the subject made her the most interesting feature of the scene she evoked.

But Miss Becky presently turned to me. 'Do you know everything——?'

'Everything?'

'In Europe.'

'Oh, yes,' I laughed, 'and one or two things even in America.'

The sisters seemed to me furtively to look at each other. 'Well, you'll have to be quick—to meet *us*,' Miss Jane resumed.

'But surely when you're once there you'll stay on.'

'Stay on?'—they murmured it simultaneously and with the oddest vibration of dread as well as of desire. It was as if they had been in the presence of a danger and yet wished me, who 'knew everything,' to torment them with still more of it.

Well, I did my best. 'I mean it will never do to cut it short.'

'No, that's just what I keep saying,' said brilliant Jane. 'It would be better, in that case, not to go.'

'Oh, don't talk about not going—at this time!' It was none of my business, but I felt shocked and impatient.

'No, not at *this* time!' broke in Miss Maria, who, very red in the face, had joined us. Poor Miss Maria was known as the flushed one; but she was not flushed—she only had an unfortunate surface. The third day after this was to see them embark.

Miss Becky, however, desired as little as any one to be in any way extravagant. 'It's only the thought of our mother,' she explained.

I looked a moment at the old lady, with whom my sister-in-law was engaged. 'Well—your mother's magnificent.'

'*Isn't* she magnificent?'—they eagerly took it up.

She *was*—I could reiterate it with sincerity, though I perhaps mentally drew the line when Miss Maria again risked, as a fresh ejaculation: 'I think she's better than Europe!'

'Maria!' they both, at this, exclaimed with a strange emphasis; it was as if they feared she had

suddenly turned cynical over the deep domestic drama of their casting of lots. The innocent laugh with which she answered them gave the measure of her cynicism.

We separated at last, and my eyes met Mrs. Rimmle's as I held for an instant her aged hand. It was doubtless only my fancy that her calm, cold look quietly accused me of something. Of what *could* it accuse me? Only, I thought, of thinking.

## II

I LEFT Brookbridge the next day, and for some time after that had no occasion to hear from my kinswoman; but when she finally wrote there was a passage in her letter that affected me more than all the rest. 'Do you know the poor Rimmles never, after all, "went"? The old lady, at the eleventh hour, broke down; everything broke down, and all of *them* on top of it, so that the dear things are with us still. Mrs. Rimmle, the night after our call, had, in the most unexpected manner, a turn for the worse—something in the nature (though they're rather mysterious about it) of a seizure; Becky and Jane felt it—dear, devoted, stupid angels that they are—heartless to leave her at such a moment, and Europe's indefinitely postponed. However, they think they're still going—or *think* they think it—when she's better. They also think—or think they think—that she *will* be better. I certainly pray she may.' So did I—quite fervently. I was conscious of a real pang—I didn't know how much they had made me care.

Late that winter my sister-in-law spent a week in New York; when almost my first inquiry on meeting her was about the health of Mrs. Rimmle.

'Oh, she's rather bad—she really is, you know. It's not surprising that at her age she should be infirm.'

'Then what the deuce *is* her age?'

'I can't tell you to a year—but she's immensely old.'

'That of course I saw,' I replied—'unless you literally mean so old that the records have been lost.'

My sister-in-law thought. 'Well, I believe she wasn't positively young when she married. She lost three or four children before these women were born.'

We surveyed together a little, on this, the 'dark backward.' 'And they were born, I gather, *after* the famous tour? Well, then, as the famous tour was in a manner to celebrate—wasn't it?—the restoration of the Bourbons [1]—' I considered, I

'EUROPE.'    1. the . . . Bourbons: The return of the Bourbon dynasty to the French throne after the Revolution occurred in 1814.

gasped. 'My dear child, what on earth do you make her out?'

My relative, with her Brookbridge habit, transferred her share of the question to the moral plane —turned it forth to wander, by implication at least, in the sandy desert of responsibility. 'Well, you know, we all immensely admire her.'

'You can't admire her more than I do. She's awful.'

My interlocutress looked at me with a certain fear. 'She's *really* ill.'

'Too ill to get better?'

'Oh, no—we hope not. Because then they'll be able to go.'

'And *will* they go, if she should?'

'Oh, the moment they should be quite satisfied. I mean *really*,' she added.

I'm afraid I laughed at her—the Brookbridge 'really' was a thing so by itself. 'But if she shouldn't get better?' I went on.

'Oh, don't speak of it! They want so to go.'

'It's a pity they're so infernally good,' I mused.

'No—don't say that. It's what keeps them up.'

'Yes, but isn't it what keeps *her* up too?'

My visitor looked grave. 'Would you like them to kill her?'

I don't know that I was then prepared to say I should—though I believe I came very near it. But later on I burst all bounds, for the subject grew and grew. I went again before the good sisters ever did—I mean I went to Europe. I think I went twice, with a brief interval, before my fate again brought round for me a couple of days at Brookbridge. I had been there repeatedly, in the previous time, without making the acquaintance of the Rimmles; but now that I had had the revelation I couldn't have it too much, and the first request I preferred was to be taken again to see them. I remember well indeed the scruple I felt—the real delicacy—about betraying that *I* had, in the pride of my power, since our other meeting, stood, as their phrase went, among romantic scenes; but they were themselves the first to speak of it, and what, moreover, came home to me was that the coming and going of their friends in general— Brookbridge itself having even at that period one foot in Europe—was such as to place constantly before them the pleasure that was only postponed. They were thrown back, after all, on what the situation, under a final analysis, had most to give —the sense that, as every one kindly said to them and they kindly said to every one, Europe would keep. Every one felt for them so deeply that their own kindness in alleviating every one's feeling was really what came out most. Mrs. Rimmle was still in her stiff chair and in the sunny parlour, but if *she* made no scruple of introducing the Italian

lakes my heart sank to observe that she dealt with them, as a topic, not in the least in the leave-taking manner in which Falstaff babbled of green fields.

I am not sure that, after this, my pretexts for a day or two with my sister-in-law were not apt to be a mere cover for another glimpse of these particulars: I at any rate never went to Brookbridge without an irrepressible eagerness for our customary call. A long time seems to me thus to have passed, with glimpses and lapses, considerable impatience and still more pity. Our visits indeed grew shorter, for, as my companion said, they were more and more of a strain. It finally struck me that the good sisters even shrank from me a little, as from one who penetrated their consciousness in spite of himself. It was as if they knew where I thought they ought to be, and were moved to deprecate at last, by a systematic silence on the subject of that hemisphere, the criminality I fain would fix on them. They were full instead—as with the instinct of throwing dust in my eyes—of little pathetic hypocrisies about Brookbridge interests and delights. I dare say that as time went on my deeper sense of their situation came practically to rest on my companion's report of it. I think I recollect, at all events, every word we ever exchanged about them, even if I have lost the thread of the special occasions. The impression they made on me after each interval always broke out with extravagance as I walked away with her.

'*She* may be as old as she likes—I don't care. It's the fearful age the "girls" are reaching that constitutes the scandal. One shouldn't pry into such matters, I know; but the years and the chances are really going. They're all growing old together—it will presently be too late; and their mother meanwhile perches over them like a vulture—what shall I call it?—calculating. Is she waiting for them successively to drop off? She'll survive them each and all. There's something too remorseless in it.'

'Yes; but what do you want her to do? If the poor thing *can't* die, she can't. Do you want her to take poison or to open a blood-vessel? I dare say she would prefer to go.'

'I beg your pardon,' I must have replied; 'you daren't say anything of the sort. If she would prefer to go she *would* go. She would feel the propriety, the decency, the necessity of going. She just prefers *not* to go. She prefers to stay and keep up the tension, and her calling them "girls" and talking of the good time they'll still have is the mere conscious mischief of a subtle old witch. They won't have *any* time—there isn't any time to have! I mean there's, on her own part, no real loss of measure or of perspective in it. She *knows* she's a hundred and ten, and takes a cruel pride in it.'

My sister-in-law differed with me about this; she held that the old woman's attitude was an honest one and that her magnificent vitality, so great in spite of her infirmities, made it inevitable that she should attribute youth to persons who had come into the world so much later. 'Then suppose she should die?'—so my fellow-student of the case always put it to me.

'Do you mean while her daughters are away? There's not the least fear of that—not even if at the very moment of their departure she should be *in extremis*. They would find her all right on their return.'

'But think how they would feel not to have been with her!'

'That's only, I repeat, on the unsound assumption. If they would only go to-morrow—literally make a good rush for it—they'll be with her when they come back. That will give them plenty of time.' I'm afraid I even heartlessly added that if she *should,* against every probability, pass away in their absence, they wouldn't have to come back at all—which would be just the compensation proper to their long privation. And then Maria would come out to join the two others, and they would be—though but for the too scanty remnant of their career—as merry as the day is long.

I remained ready, somehow, pending the fulfilment of that vision, to sacrifice Maria; it was only over the urgency of the case for the others respectively that I found myself balancing. Sometimes it was for Becky I thought the tragedy deepest—sometimes, and in quite a different manner, I thought it most dire for Jane. It was Jane, after all, who had most sense of life. I seemed in fact dimly to descry in Jane a sense—as yet undescried by herself or by any one—of all sorts of queer things. Why didn't *she* go? I used desperately to ask; why didn't she make a bold personal dash for it, strike up a partnership with some one or other of the travelling spinsters in whom Brookbridge more and more abounded? Well, there came a flash for me at a particular point of the grey middle desert: my correspondent was able to let me know that poor Jane at last *had* sailed. She had gone of a sudden—I liked my sister-in-law's view of suddenness—with the kind Hathaways, who had made an irresistible grab at her and lifted her off her feet. They were going for the summer and for Mr. Hathaway's health, so that the opportunity was perfect, and it was impossible not to be glad that something very like physical force had finally prevailed. This was the general feeling at Brookbridge, and I might imagine what Brookbridge had

been brought to from the fact that, at the very moment she was hustled off, the doctor, called to her mother at the peep of dawn, had considered that *he* at least must stay. There had been real alarm—greater than ever before; it actually did seem as if this time the end had come. But it was Becky, strange to say, who, though fully recognising the nature of the crisis, had kept the situation in hand and insisted upon action. This, I remember, brought back to me a discomfort with which I had been familiar from the first. One of the two had sailed, and I was sorry it was not the other. But if it had been the other I should have been equally sorry.

I saw with my eyes, that very autumn, what a fool Jane would have been if she had again backed out. Her mother had of course survived the peril of which I had heard, profiting by it indeed as she had profited by every other; she was sufficiently better again to have come down stairs. It was there that, as usual, I found her, but with a difference of effect produced somehow by the absence of one of the girls. It was as if, for the others, though they had not gone to Europe, Europe had come to them: Jane's letters had been so frequent and so beyond even what could have been hoped. It was the first time, however, that I perceived on the old woman's part a certain failure of lucidity. Jane's flight was, clearly, the great fact with her, but she spoke of it as if the fruit had now been plucked and the parenthesis closed. I don't know what sinking sense of still further physical duration I gathered, as a menace, from this first hint of her confusion of mind.

'My daughter has been; my daughter has been ——' She kept saying it, but didn't say where; that seemed unnecessary, and she only repeated the words to her visitors with a face that was all puckers and yet now, save in so far as it expressed an ineffaceable complacency, all blankness. I think she wanted us a little to know that she had not stood in the way. It added to something—I scarce knew what—that I found myself desiring to extract privately from Becky. As our visit was to be of the shortest my opportunity—for one of the young ladies always came to the door with us—was at hand. Mrs. Rimmle, as we took leave, again sounded her phrase, but she added this time: 'I'm so glad she's going to have always——'

I knew so well what she meant that, as she again dropped, looking at me queerly and becoming momentarily dim, I could help her out. 'Going to have what *you* have?'

'Yes, yes—my privilege. Wonderful experience,' she mumbled. She bowed to me a little as if I would understand. 'She has things to tell.'

I turned, slightly at a loss, to Becky. 'She has then already arrived?'

Becky was at that moment looking a little strangely at her mother, who answered my question. 'She reached New York this morning—she comes on to-day.'

'Oh, then——!' But I let the matter pass as I met Becky's eye—I saw there was a hitch somewhere. It was not she but Maria who came out with us; on which I cleared up the question of their sister's reappearance.

'Oh, no, not to-night,' Maria smiled; 'that's only the way mother puts it. We shall see her about the end of November—the Hathaways are so indulgent. They kindly extend their tour.'

'For *her* sake? How sweet of them!' my sister-in-law exclaimed.

I can see our friend's plain, mild old face take on a deeper mildness, even though a higher colour, in the light of the open door. 'Yes, it's for Jane they prolong it. And do you know what they write?' She gave us time, but it was too great a responsibility to guess. 'Why, that it has brought her out.'

'Oh, I knew it *would!*' my companion sympathetically sighed.

Maria put it more strongly still. 'They say we wouldn't know her.'

This sounded a little awful, but it was, after all, what I had expected.

### III

MY correspondent in Brookbridge came to me that Christmas, with my niece, to spend a week; and the arrangement had of course been prefaced by an exchange of letters, the first of which from my sister-in-law scarce took space for acceptance of my invitation before going on to say: 'The Hathaways are back—but without Miss Jane!' She presented in a few words the situation thus created at Brookbridge, but was not yet, I gathered, fully in possession of the other one—the situation created in 'Europe' by the presence there of that lady. The two together, at any rate, demanded, I quickly felt, all my attention, and perhaps my impatience to receive my relative was a little sharpened by my desire for the whole story. I had it at last, by the Christmas fire, and I may say without reserve that it gave me all I could have hoped for. I listened eagerly, after which I produced the comment: 'Then she simply refused——'

'To budge from Florence? Simply. She had it out there with the poor Hathaways, who felt responsible for her safety, pledged to restore her to her mother's, to her sisters' hands, and showed

herself in a light, they mention under their breath, that made their dear old hair stand on end. Do you know what, when they first got back, they said of her—at least it was *his* phrase—to two or three people?'

I thought a moment. 'That she had "tasted blood"?'

My visitor fairly admired me. 'How clever of you to guess! It's exactly what he did say. She appeared—she continues to appear, it seems—in a new character.'

I wondered a little. 'But that's exactly—don't you remember?—what Miss Maria reported to us from them; that we "wouldn't know her." '

My sister-in-law perfectly remembered. 'Oh, yes —she broke out from the first. But when they left her she was worse.'

'Worse?'

'Well, different—different from anything she ever *had* been, or—for that matter—had had a chance to be.' My interlocutress hung fire a moment, but presently faced me. 'Rather strange and free and obstreperous.'

'Obstreperous?' I wondered again.

'Peculiarly so, I inferred, on the question of not coming away. She wouldn't hear of it, and, when they spoke of her mother, said she had given her mother up. She had thought she should like Europe, but didn't know she should like it so much. They had been fools to bring her if they expected to take her away. She was going to see what she could—she hadn't yet seen half. The end of it was, at any rate, that they had to leave her alone.'

I seemed to see it all—to see even the scared Hathaways. 'So she *is* alone?'

'She told them, poor thing, it appears, and in a tone they'll never forget, that she was, at all events, quite old enough to be. She cried—she quite went on—over not having come sooner. That's why the only way for her,' my companion mused, '*is*, I suppose, to stay. They wanted to put her with some people or other—to find some American family. But she says she's on her own feet.'

'And she's still in Florence?'

'No—I believe she was to travel. She's bent on the East.'

I burst out laughing. 'Magnificent Jane! It's most interesting. Only I feel that I distinctly *should* "know" her. To my sense, always, I must tell you, she had it in her.'

My relative was silent a little. 'So it now appears Becky always felt.'

'And yet pushed her off? Magnificent Becky!'

My companion met my eyes a moment. 'You

don't know the queerest part. I mean the way it has *most* brought her out.'

I turned it over; I felt I should like to know—to that degree indeed that, oddly enough, I jocosely disguised my eagerness. 'You don't mean she has taken to drink?'

My visitor hesitated. 'She has taken to flirting.'

I expressed disappointment. 'Oh, she took to *that* long ago. Yes,' I declared at my kinswoman's stare, 'she positively flirted—with *me!*'

The stare perhaps sharpened. 'Then you flirted with *her?*'

'How else could I have been as sure as I wanted to be? But has she means?'

'Means to flirt?'—my friend looked an instant as if she spoke literally. 'I don't understand about the means—though of course they have something. But I have my impression,' she went on. 'I think that Becky——' It seemed almost too grave to say.

But *I* had no doubts. 'That Becky's backing her?'

She brought it out. 'Financing her.'

'Stupendous Becky! So that morally then——'

'Becky's quite in sympathy. But isn't it too odd?' my sister-in-law asked.

'Not in the least. Didn't we know, as regards Jane, that Europe was to bring her out? Well, it has also brought out Rebecca.'

'It has indeed!' my companion indulgently sighed. 'So what would it do if she were there?'

'I should like immensely to see. And we *shall* see.'

'Why, do you believe she'll still go?'

'Certainly. She *must.*'

But my friend shook it off. 'She won't.'

'She shall!' I retorted with a laugh. But the next moment I said: 'And what does the old woman say?'

'To Jane's behaviour? Not a word—never speaks of it. She talks now much less than she used—only seems to wait. But it's my belief she thinks.'

'And—do you mean—knows?'

'Yes, knows that she's abandoned. In her silence there she takes it in.'

'It's her way of making Jane pay?' At this, somehow, I felt more serious. 'Oh, dear, dear—she'll disinherit her!'

When, in the following June, I went on to return my sister-in-law's visit the first object that met my eyes in her little white parlour was a figure that, to my stupefaction, presented itself for the moment as that of Mrs. Rimmle. I had gone to my room after arriving, and, on dressing, had come

down: the apparition I speak of had arisen in the interval. Its ambiguous character lasted, however, but a second or two—I had taken Becky for her mother because I knew no one but her mother of that extreme age. Becky's age was quite startling; it had made a great stride, though, strangely enough, irrecoverably seated as she now was in it, she had a wizened brightness that I had scarcely yet seen in her. I remember indulging on this occasion in two silent observations: one to the effect that I had not hitherto been conscious of her full resemblance to the old lady, and the other to the effect that, as I had said to my sister-in-law at Christmas, 'Europe,' even as reaching her only through Jane's sensibilities, had really at last brought her out. She was in fact 'out' in a manner of which this encounter offered to my eyes a unique example: it was the single hour, often as I had been at Brookbridge, of my meeting her elsewhere than in her mother's drawing-room. I surmise that, besides being adjusted to her more marked time of life, the garments she wore abroad, and in particular her little plain bonnet, presented points of resemblance to the close sable sheath and the quaint old headgear that, in the white house behind the elms, I had from far back associated with the eternal image in the stiff chair. Of course I immediately spoke of Jane, showing an interest and asking for news; on which she answered me with a smile, but not at all as I had expected.

'*Those* are not really the things you want to know—where she is, whom she's with, how she manages and where she's going next—oh, no!' And the admirable woman gave a laugh that was somehow both light and sad—sad, in particular, with a strange, long weariness. 'What you do want to know is when she's coming back.'

I shook my head very kindly, but out of a wealth of experience that, I flattered myself, was equal to Miss Becky's. 'I do know it. Never.'

Miss Becky, at this, exchanged with me a long, deep look. 'Never.'

We had, in silence, a little luminous talk about it, in the course of which she seemed to tell me the most interesting things. 'And how's your mother?' I then inquired.

She hesitated, but finally spoke with the same serenity. 'My mother's all right. You see, she's not alive.'

'Oh, Becky!' my sister-in-law pleadingly interjected.

But Becky only addressed herself to me. 'Come and see if she is. *I* think she isn't—but Maria perhaps isn't so clear. Come, at all events, and judge and tell me.'

It was a new note, and I was a little bewildered. 'Ah, but I'm not a doctor!'

'No, thank God—you're not. That's why I ask you.' And now she said good-bye.

I kept her hand a moment. '*You're* more alive than ever!'

'I'm very tired.' She took it with the same smile, but for Becky it was much to say.

## IV

'NOT alive,' the next day, was certainly what Mrs. Rimmle looked when, coming in according to my promise, I found her, with Miss Maria, in her usual place. Though shrunken and diminished she still occupied her high-backed chair with a visible theory of erectness, and her intensely aged face—combined with something dauntless that belonged to her very presence and that was effective even in this extremity—might have been that of some centenarian sovereign, of indistinguishable sex, brought forth to be shown to the people as a disproof of the rumour of extinction. Mummified and open-eyed she looked at me, but I had no impression that she made me out. I had come this time without my sister-in-law, who had frankly pleaded to me—which also, for a daughter of Brookbridge, was saying much—that the house had grown too painful. Poor Miss Maria excused Miss Becky on the score of her not being well—and that, it struck me, was saying most of all. The absence of the others gave the occasion a different note; but I talked with Miss Maria for five minutes and perceived that—save for her saying, of her own movement, anything about Jane—she now spoke as if her mother had lost hearing or sense, or both, alluding freely and distinctly, though indeed favourably, to her condition. 'She has expected your visit and she much enjoys it,' my interlocutress said, while the old woman, soundless and motionless, simply fixed me without expression. Of course there was little to keep me; but I became aware, as I rose to go, that there was more than I had supposed. On my approaching her to take leave Mrs. Rimmle gave signs of consciousness.

'Have you heard about Jane?'

I hesitated, feeling a responsibility, and appealed for direction to Maria's face. But Maria's face was troubled, was turned altogether to her mother's. 'About her life in Europe?' I then rather helplessly asked.

The old woman fronted me, on this, in a manner that made me feel silly. 'Her life?'—and her voice, with this second effort, came out stronger. 'Her death, if you please.'

'Her death?' I echoed, before I could stop myself, with the accent of deprecation.

Miss Maria uttered a vague sound of pain, and I felt her turn away, but the marvel of her mother's little unquenched spark still held me. 'Jane's dead. We've heard,' said Mrs. Rimmle. 'We've heard from—where is it we've heard from?' She had quite revived—she appealed to her daughter.

The poor old girl, crimson, rallied to her duty. 'From Europe.'

Mrs. Rimmle made at us both a little grim inclination of the head. 'From Europe.' I responded, in silence, with a deflection from every rigour, and, still holding me, she went on: 'And now Rebecca's going.'

She had gathered by this time such emphasis to say it that again, before I could help myself, I vibrated in reply. 'To Europe—now?' It was as if for an instant she had made me believe it.

She only stared at me, however, from her wizened mask; then her eyes followed my companion. 'Has she gone?'

'Not yet, mother.' Maria tried to treat it as a joke, but her smile was embarrassed and dim.

'Then where is she?'

'She's lying down.'

The old woman kept up her hard, queer gaze, but directing it, after a minute, to me. 'She's going.'

'Oh, some day!' I foolishly laughed; and on this I got to the door, where I separated from my younger hostess, who came no further. Only, as I held the door open, she said to me under cover of it and very quietly:

'It's poor mother's idea.'

I saw—it was her idea. Mine was—for some time after this, even after I had returned to New York and to my usual occupations—that I should never again see Becky. I had seen her for the last time, I believed, under my sister-in-law's roof, and in the autumn it was given to me to hear from that fellow-admirer that she had succumbed at last to the situation. The day of the call I have just described had been a date in the process of her slow shrinkage—it was literally the first time she had, as they said at Brookbridge, given up. She had been ill for years, but the other state of health in the contemplation of which she had spent so much of her life had left her, till too late, no margin for meeting it. The encounter, at last, came simply in the form of the discovery that it *was* too late; on which, naturally, she had given up more and more. I had heard indeed, all summer, by letter, how Brookbridge had watched her do so; whereby the end found me in a manner prepared. Yet in spite of my preparation there remained with me a soreness, and when I was next —it was some six months later—on the scene of her martyrdom I replied, I fear, with an almost rabid negative to the question put to me in due course by my kinswoman. 'Call on them? Never again!'

I went, none the less, the very next day. Everything was the same in the sunny parlour—everything that most mattered, I mean: the immemorial mummy in the high chair and the tributes, in the little frames on the walls, to the celebrity of its late husband. Only Maria Rimmle was different: if Becky, on my last seeing her, had looked as old as her mother, Maria—save that she moved about—looked older. I remember that she moved about, but I scarce remember what she said; and indeed what was there to say? When I risked a question, however, she had a reply.

'But *now* at least——?' I tried to put it to her suggestively.

At first she was vague. ' "Now?" '

'Won't Miss Jane come back?'

Oh, the headshake she gave me! 'Never.' It positively pictured to me, for the instant, a well-preserved woman, a sort of rich, ripe *seconde jeunesse* [2] by the Arno.

'Then that's only to make more sure of your finally joining her.'

Maria Rimmle repeated her headshake. 'Never.'

We stood so, a moment, bleakly face to face; I could think of no attenuation that would be particularly happy. But while I tried I heard a hoarse gasp that, fortunately, relieved me—a signal strange and at first formless from the occupant of the high-backed chair. 'Mother wants to speak to you,' Maria then said.

So it appeared from the drop of the old woman's jaw, the expression of her mouth opened as if for the emission of sound. It was difficult to me, somehow, to seem to sympathise without hypocrisy, but, so far as a step nearer could do so, I invited communication. 'Have you heard where Becky's gone?' the wonderful witch's white lips then extraordinarily asked.

It drew from Maria, as on my previous visit, an uncontrollable groan, and this, in turn, made me take time to consider. As I considered, however, I had an inspiration. 'To Europe?'

I must have adorned it with a strange grimace, but my inspiration had been right. 'To Europe,' said Mrs. Rimmle.

2. *seconde jeunesse:* second youth.

F R O M

# HAWTHORNE

❪ IN 1879, James published *Hawthorne*, a brief critical biography of the author whose work had meant so much to him in his youth and to which he was to return in a centenary essay in 1904. For further comment on *Hawthorne*, see the Introduction.

## THE SCARLET LETTER

HIS PUBLISHER, Mr. Fields,[1] in a volume entitled *Yesterdays with Authors,* has related the circumstances in which Hawthorne's masterpiece came into the world. "In the winter of 1849, after he had been ejected from the Custom-house, I went down to Salem to see him and inquire after his health, for we heard he had been suffering from illness. He was then living in a modest wooden house. . . . I found him alone in a chamber over the sitting-room of the dwelling, and as the day was cold he was hovering near a stove. We fell into talk about his future prospects, and he was, as I feared I should find him, in a very desponding mood." His visitor urged him to bethink himself of publishing something, and Hawthorne replied by calling his attention to the small popularity his published productions had yet acquired, and declaring he had done nothing and had no spirit for doing anything. The narrator of the incident urged upon him the necessity of a more hopeful view of his situation, and proceeded to take leave. He had not reached the street, however, when Hawthorne hurried to overtake him, and, placing a roll of MS. in his hand, bade him take it to Boston, read it, and pronounce upon it. "It is either very good or very bad," said the author; "I don't know which." "On my way back to Boston," says Mr. Fields, "I read the germ of *The Scarlet Letter;* before I slept that night I wrote him a note all aglow with admiration of the marvellous story he had put into my hands, and told him that I would come again to Salem the next day and arrange for its publication. I went on in such an amazing state of excitement, when we met again in the little house, that he would not believe I was really in earnest. He seemed to think I was beside myself, and laughed sadly at my enthusiasm." Haw-

HAWTHORNE.     1. **Mr. Fields:** James Thomas Fields (1817–81), a leading American publisher of the mid-nineteenth century, author of *Yesterdays with Authors* (1872).

thorne, however, went on with the book and finished it, but it appeared only a year later. His biographer quotes a passage from a letter which he wrote in February, 1850, to his friend Horatio Bridge. "I finished my book only yesterday; one end being in the press at Boston, while the other was in my head here at Salem, so that, as you see, my story is at least fourteen miles long. . . . My book, the publisher tells me, will not be out before April. He speaks of it in tremendous terms of approbation; so does Mrs. Hawthorne, to whom I read the conclusion last night. It broke her heart, and sent her to bed with a grievous headache—which I look upon as a triumphant success. Judging from the effect upon her and the publisher, I may calculate on what bowlers call a ten-strike. But I don't make any such calculation." And Mr. Lathrop [2] calls attention, in regard to this passage, to an allusion in the *English Note-Books* (September 14, 1855). "Speaking of Thackeray, I cannot but wonder at his coolness in respect to his own pathos, and compare it to my emotions when I read the last scene of *The Scarlet Letter* to my wife, just after writing it—tried to read it rather, for my voice swelled and heaved as if I were tossed up and down on an ocean as it subsides after a storm. But I was in a very nervous state then, having gone through a great diversity of emotion while writing it, for many months."

The work has the tone of the circumstances in which it was produced. If Hawthorne was in a sombre mood, and if his future was painfully vague, *The Scarlet Letter* contains little enough of gaiety or of hopefulness. It is densely dark, with a single spot of vivid colour in it; and it will probably long remain the most consistently gloomy of English novels of the first order. But I just now called it the author's masterpiece, and I imagine it will continue to be, for other generations than ours, his most substantial title to fame. The subject had probably lain a long time in his mind, as his subjects were apt to do; so that he appears completely to possess it, to know it and feel it. It is simpler and more complete than his other novels; it achieves more perfectly what it attempts, and it has about it that charm, very hard to express, which we find in an artist's work the first time he has touched his highest mark—a sort of straightness and naturalness of execution, an unconsciousness of his public, and freshness of interest in his theme. It was a great success, and he immediately found himself famous. The writer of these lines, who was a child at the time, remembers

2. **Mr. Lathrop:** George Parsons Lathrop (1851–98), Hawthorne's son-in-law, author of *A Study of Hawthorne* (1876).

dimly the sensation the book produced, and the little shudder with which people alluded to it, as if a peculiar horror were mixed with its attractions. He was too young to read it himself, but its title, upon which he fixed his eyes as the book lay upon the table, had a mysterious charm. He had a vague belief, indeed, that the "letter" in question was one of the documents that come by the post, and it was a source of perpetual wonderment to him that it should be of such an unaccustomed hue. Of course it was difficult to explain to a child the significance of poor Hester Prynne's blood-coloured *A*. But the mystery was at last partly dispelled by his being taken to see a collection of pictures (the annual exhibition of the National Academy), where he encountered a representation of a pale, handsome woman, in a quaint black dress and a white coif, holding between her knees an elfish-looking little girl, fantastically dressed, and crowned with flowers. Embroidered on the woman's breast was a great crimson *A*, over which the child's fingers, as she glanced strangely out of the picture, were maliciously playing. I was told that this was Hester Prynne and little Pearl, and that when I grew older I might read their interesting history. But the picture remained vividly imprinted on my mind; I had been vaguely frightened and made uneasy by it; and when, years afterwards, I first read the novel, I seemed to myself to have read it before, and to be familiar with its two strange heroines. I mention this incident simply as an indication of the degree to which the success of *The Scarlet Letter* had made the book what is called an actuality. Hawthorne himself was very modest about it; he wrote to his publisher, when there was a question of his undertaking another novel, that what had given the history of Hester Prynne its "vogue" was simply the introductory chapter. In fact, the publication of *The Scarlet Letter* was in the United States a literary event of the first importance. The book was the finest piece of imaginative writing yet put forth in the country. There was a consciousness of this in the welcome that was given it—a satisfaction in the idea of America having produced a novel that belonged to literature, and to the forefront of it. Something might at last be sent to Europe as exquisite in quality as anything that had been received, and the best of it was that the thing was absolutely American; it belonged to the soil, to the air; it came out of the very heart of New England.

It is beautiful, admirable, extraordinary; it has in the highest degree that merit which I have spoken of as the mark of Hawthorne's best things—

an indefinable purity and lightness of conception, a quality which in a work of art affects one in the same way as the absence of grossness does in a human being. His fancy, as I just now said, had evidently brooded over the subject for a long time; the situation to be represented had disclosed itself to him in all its phases. When I say in all its phases, the sentence demands modification; for it is to be remembered that if Hawthorne laid his hand upon the well-worn theme, upon the familiar combination of the wife, the lover, and the husband, it was after all but to one period of the history of these three persons that he attached himself. The situation is the situation after the woman's fault has been committed, and the current of expiation and repentance has set in. In spite of the relation between Hester Prynne and Arthur Dimmesdale, no story of love was surely ever less of a "love story." To Hawthorne's imagination the fact that these two persons had loved each other too well was of an interest comparatively vulgar; what appealed to him was the idea of their moral situation in the long years that were to follow. The story, indeed, is in a secondary degree that of Hester Prynne; she becomes, really, after the first scene, an accessory figure; it is not upon her the *dénoûment* depends. It is upon her guilty lover that the author projects most frequently the cold, thin rays of his fitfully-moving lantern, which makes here and there a little luminous circle, on the edge of which hovers the livid and sinister figure of the injured and retributive husband. The story goes on, for the most part, between the lover and the husband—the tormented young Puritan minister, who carries the secret of his own lapse from pastoral purity locked up beneath an exterior that commends itself to the reverence of his flock, while he sees the softer partner of his guilt standing in the full glare of exposure and humbling herself to the misery of atonement—between this more wretched and pitiable culprit, to whom dishonour would come as a comfort and the pillory as a relief, and the older, keener, wiser man, who, to obtain satisfaction for the wrong he has suffered, devises the infernally ingenious plan of conjoining himself with his wronger, living with him, living upon him, and while he pretends to minister to his hidden ailment and to sympathise with his pain, revels in his unsuspected knowledge of these things and stimulates them by malignant arts. The attitude of Roger Chillingworth, and the means he takes to compensate himself—these are the highly original elements in the situation that Hawthorne so ingeniously treats. None of his works are so impreg-

nated with that after-sense of the old Puritan consciousness of life to which allusion has so often been made. If, as M. Montégut[3] says, the qualities of his ancestors *filtered* down through generations into his composition, *The Scarlet Letter* was, as it were, the vessel that gathered up the last of the precious drops. And I say this not because the story happens to be of so-called historical cast, to be told of the early days of Massachusetts and of people in steeple-crowned hats and sad-coloured garments. The historical colouring is rather weak than otherwise; there is little elaboration of detail, of the modern realism of research; and the author has made no great point of causing his figures to speak the English of their period. Nevertheless, the book is full of the moral presence of the race that invented Hester's penance—diluted and complicated with other things, but still perfectly recognisable. Puritanism, in a word, is there, not only objectively, as Hawthorne tried to place it there, but subjectively as well. Not, I mean, in his judgment of his characters, in any harshness of prejudice, or in the obtrusion of a moral lesson; but in the very quality of his own vision, in the tone of the picture, in a certain coldness and exclusiveness of treatment.

The faults of the book are, to my sense, a want of reality and an abuse of the fanciful element—of a certain superficial symbolism. The people strike me not as characters, but as representatives, very picturesquely arranged, of a single state of mind; and the interest of the story lies, not in them, but in the situation, which is insistently kept before us, with little progression, though with a great deal, as I have said, of a certain stable variation; and to which they, out of their reality, contribute little that helps it to live and move. I was made to feel this want of reality, this over-ingenuity, of *The Scarlet Letter*, by chancing not long since upon a novel which was read fifty years ago much more than to-day, but which is still worth reading—the story of *Adam Blair*, by John Gibson Lockhart.[4] This interesting and powerful little tale has a great deal of analogy with Hawthorne's novel—quite enough, at least, to suggest a comparison between them; and the comparison is a very interesting one to make, for it speedily leads us to larger considerations than simple resemblances and divergences of plot.

Adam Blair, like Arthur Dimmesdale, is a Cal-

3. **M. Montégut:** Émile Montégut (1825–95), French critic, author of *Un Romancier Pessimiste* (*Revue des Deux Mondes*, 1860) and other studies of American writers. 4. **John Gibson Lockhart:** Scottish writer and editor (1794–1854), author of *Adam Blair* (1822), son-in-law and biographer of Sir Walter Scott.

vinistic minister who becomes the lover of a married woman, is overwhelmed with remorse at his misdeed, and makes a public confession of it; then expiates it by resigning his pastoral office and becoming the humble tiller of the soil, as his father had been. The two stories are of about the same length, and each is the masterpiece (putting aside of course, as far as Lockhart is concerned, the *Life of Scott*) of the author. They deal alike with the manners of a rigidly theological society, and even in certain details they correspond. In each of them, between the guilty pair, there is a charming little girl; though I hasten to say that Sarah Blair (who is not the daughter of the heroine, but the legitimate offspring of the hero, a widower) is far from being as brilliant and graceful an apparition as the admirable little Pearl of *The Scarlet Letter*. The main difference between the two tales is the fact that in the American story the husband plays an all-important part, and in the Scottish plays almost none at all. *Adam Blair* is the history of the passion, and *The Scarlet Letter* the history of its sequel; but nevertheless, if one has read the two books at a short interval, it is impossible to avoid confronting them. I confess that a large portion of the interest of *Adam Blair*, to my mind, when once I had perceived that it would repeat in a great measure the situation of *The Scarlet Letter*, lay in noting its difference of tone. It threw into relief the passionless quality of Hawthorne's novel, its element of cold and ingenious fantasy, its elaborate imaginative delicacy. These things do not precisely constitute a weakness in *The Scarlet Letter*; indeed, in a certain way they constitute a great strength; but the absence of a certain something warm and straightforward, a trifle more grossly human and vulgarly natural, which one finds in *Adam Blair*, will always make Hawthorne's tale less touching to a large number of even very intelligent readers, than a love-story told with the robust, synthetic pathos which served Lockhart so well. His novel is not of the first rank (I should call it an excellent second-rate one), but it borrows a charm from the fact that his vigorous, but not strongly imaginative, mind was impregnated with the reality of his subject. He did not always succeed in rendering this reality; the expression is sometimes awkward and poor. But the reader feels that his vision was clear, and his feeling about the matter very strong and rich. Hawthorne's imagination, on the other hand, plays with his theme so incessantly, leads it such a dance through the moon-lighted air of his intellect, that the thing cools off, as it were, hardens and stiffens, and, producing effects much more exquisite, leaves the reader with a sense of having handled a splendid piece of silversmith's work. Lockhart, by means much more vulgar, produces at moments a greater illusion, and satifies our inevitable desire for something, in the people in whom it is sought to interest us, that should be of the same pitch and the same continuity with ourselves. Above all, it is interesting to see how the same subject appears to two men of a thoroughly different cast of mind and of a different race. Lockhart was struck with the warmth of the subject that offered itself to him, and Hawthorne with its coldness; the one with its glow, its sentimental interest—the other with its shadow, its moral interest. Lockhart's story is as decent, as severely draped, as *The Scarlet Letter;* but the author has a more vivid sense than appears to have imposed itself upon Hawthorne, of some of the incidents of the situation he describes; his tempted man and tempting woman are more actual and personal; his heroine in especial, though not in the least a delicate or a subtle conception, has a sort of credible, visible, palpable property, a vulgar roundness and relief, which are lacking to the dim and chastened image of Hester Prynne. But I am going too far; I am comparing simplicity with subtlety, the usual with the refined. Each man wrote as his turn of mind impelled him, but each expressed something more than himself. Lockhart was a dense, substantial Briton, with a taste for the concrete, and Hawthorne was a thin New Englander, with a miasmatic conscience.

In *The Scarlet Letter* there is a great deal of symbolism; there is, I think, too much. It is overdone at times, and becomes mechanical; it ceases to be impressive, and grazes triviality. The idea of the mystic *A* which the young minister finds imprinted upon his breast and eating into his flesh, in sympathy with the embroidered badge that Hester is condemned to wear, appears to me to be a case in point. This suggestion should, I think, have been just made and dropped; to insist upon it and return to it, is to exaggerate the weak side of the subject. Hawthorne returns to it constantly, plays with it, and seems charmed by it; until at last the reader feels tempted to declare that his enjoyment of it is puerile. In the admirable scene, so superbly conceived and beautifully executed, in which Mr. Dimmesdale, in the stillness of the night, in the middle of the sleeping town, feels impelled to go and stand upon the scaffold where his mistress had formerly enacted her dreadful penance, and then, seeing Hester pass along the street, from watching at a sick-bed, with little Pearl at her side, calls them both to come and stand there beside him—in this masterly episode the effect is almost spoiled by the introduction of one of these superficial conceits. What leads up to it is very fine—so fine that I cannot do better than quote it as a specimen of one of the striking pages of the book.

But before Mr. Dimmesdale had done speaking, a light gleamed far and wide over all the muffled sky. It was doubtless caused by one of those meteors which the night-watcher may so often observe burning out to waste in the vacant regions of the atmosphere. So powerful was its radiance that it thoroughly illuminated the dense medium of cloud, betwixt the sky and earth. The great vault brightened, like the dome of an immense lamp. It showed the familiar scene of the street with the distinctness of mid-day, but also with the awfulness that is always imparted to familiar objects by an unaccustomed light. The wooden houses, with their jutting stories and quaint gable-peaks; the door-steps and thresholds, with the early grass springing up about them; the garden-plots, black with freshly-turned earth; the wheel-track, little worn, and, even in the market-place, margined with green on either side;—all were visible, but with a singularity of aspect that seemed to give another moral interpretation to the things of this world than they had ever borne before. And there stood the minister, with his hand over his heart; and Hester Prynne, with the embroidered letter glimmering on her bosom; and little Pearl, herself a symbol, and the connecting-link between these two. They stood in the noon of that strange and solemn splendour, as if it were the light that is to reveal all secrets, and the daybreak that shall unite all that belong to one another.

That is imaginative, impressive, poetic; but when, almost immediately afterwards, the author goes on to say that "the minister looking upward to the zenith, beheld there the appearance of an immense letter—the letter *A*—marked out in lines of dull red light," we feel that he goes too far and is in danger of crossing the line that separates the sublime from its intimate neighbour. We are tempted to say that this is not moral tragedy, but physical comedy. In the same way, too much is made of the intimation that Hester's badge had a scorching property, and that if one touched it one would immediately withdraw one's hand. Hawthorne is perpetually looking for images which shall place themselves in picturesque correspondence with the spiritual facts with which he is concerned, and of course the search is of the very essence of poetry. But in such a process discretion is everything, and when the image becomes importunate it is in danger of seeming to stand for nothing more serious than itself. When

Hester meets the minister by appointment in the forest, and sits talking with him while little Pearl wanders away and plays by the edge of the brook, the child is represented as at last making her way over to the other side of the woodland stream, and disporting herself there in a manner which makes her mother feel herself "in some indistinct and tantalising manner, estranged from Pearl; as if the child, in her lonely ramble through the forest, had strayed out of the sphere in which she and her mother dwelt together, and was now vainly seeking to return to it." And Hawthorne devotes a chapter to this idea of the child's having, by putting the brook between Hester and herself, established a kind of spiritual gulf, on the verge of which her little fantastic person innocently mocks at her mother's sense of bereavement. This conception belongs, one would say, quite to the lighter order of a story-teller's devices, and the reader hardly goes with Hawthorne in the large development he gives to it. He hardly goes with him either, I think, in his extreme predilection for a small number of vague ideas which are represented by such terms as "sphere" and "sympathies." Hawthorne makes too liberal a use of these two substantives; it is the solitary defect of his style; and it counts as a defect partly because the words in question are a sort of specialty with certain writers immeasurably inferior to himself.

I had not meant, however, to expatiate upon his defects, which are of the slenderest and most venial kind. *The Scarlet Letter* has the beauty and harmony of all original and complete conceptions, and its weaker spots, whatever they are, are not of its essence; they are mere light flaws and inequalities of surface. One can often return to it; it supports familiarity and has the inexhaustible charm and mystery of great works of art. It is admirably written. Hawthorne afterwards polished his style to a still higher degree, but in his later productions—it is almost always the case in a writer's later productions—there is a touch of mannerism. In *The Scarlet Letter* there is a high degree of polish, and at the same time a charming freshness; his phrase is less conscious of itself. His biographer very justly calls attention to the fact that his style was excellent from the beginning; that he appeared to have passed through no phase of learning how to write, but was in possession of his means from the first of his handling a pen. His early tales, perhaps, were not of a character to subject his faculty of expression to a very severe test, but a man who had not Hawthorne's natural sense of language would certainly have contrived to write them less well. This natural sense of language—this turn for saying things lightly and yet touchingly, picturesquely yet simply, and for infusing a gently colloquial tone into matter of the most unfamiliar import, he had evidently cultivated with great assiduity. I have spoken of the anomalous character of his Note-Books—of his going to such pains often to make a record of incidents which either were not worth remembering or could be easily remembered without its aid. But it helps us to understand the Note-Books if we regard them as a literary exercise. They were compositions, as school-boys say, in which the subject was only the pretext, and the main point was to write a certain amount of excellent English. Hawthorne must at least have written a great many of these things for practice, and he must often have said to himself that it was better practice to write about trifles, because it was a greater tax upon one's skill to make them interesting. And his theory was just, for he has almost always made his trifles interesting. In his novels his art of saying things well is very positively tested, for here he treats of those matters among which it is very easy for a blundering writer to go wrong—the subtleties and mysteries of life, the moral and spiritual maze. In such a passage as one I have marked for quotation from *The Scarlet Letter,* there is the stamp of the genius of style.

Hester Prynne, gazing steadfastly at the clergyman, felt a dreary influence come over her, but wherefore or whence she knew not, unless that he seemed so remote from her own sphere and utterly beyond her reach. One glance of recognition she had imagined must needs pass between them. She thought of the dim forest with its little dell of solitude, and love, and anguish, and the mossy tree-trunk, where, sitting hand in hand, they had mingled their sad and passionate talk with the melancholy murmur of the brook. How deeply had they known each other then! And was this the man? She hardly knew him now! He, moving proudly past, enveloped as it were in the rich music, with the procession of majestic and venerable fathers; he, so unattainable in his worldly position, and still more so in that far vista in his unsympathising thoughts, through which she now beheld him! Her spirit sank with the idea that all must have been a delusion, and that vividly as she had dreamed it, there could be no real bond betwixt the clergyman and herself. And thus much of woman there was in Hester, that she could scarcely forgive him—least of all now, when the heavy footstep of their approaching fate might be heard, nearer, nearer, nearer!—for being able to withdraw himself so completely from their mutual world, while she groped darkly, and stretched forth her cold hands, and found him not!

# THE ART OF FICTION

◇

⟨ PUBLISHED in *Longman's Magazine* (September 1884) and reprinted in *Partial Portraits* (1888), "The Art of Fiction" was James's answer to a lecture on the art and morality of the novel delivered before the Royal Institution of London by Walter Besant (1826–1901), an English novelist and man of letters. Robert Louis Stevenson disagreed with both James and Besant in an essay, "A Humble Remonstrance," published in *Longman's* (December 1884).

◇

I SHOULD not have affixed so comprehensive a title to these few remarks, necessarily wanting in any completeness upon a subject the full consideration of which would carry us far, did I not seem to discover a pretext for my temerity in the interesting pamphlet lately published under this name by Mr. Walter Besant. Mr. Besant's lecture at the Royal Institution—the original form of his pamphlet—appears to indicate that many persons are interested in the art of fiction, and are not indifferent to such remarks, as those who practise it may attempt to make about it. I am therefore anxious not to lose the benefit of this favourable association, and to edge in a few words under cover of the attention which Mr. Besant is sure to have excited. There is something very encouraging in his having put into form certain of his ideas on the mystery of story-telling.

It is a proof of life and curiosity—curiosity on the part of the brotherhood of novelists as well as on the part of their readers. Only a short time ago it might have been supposed that the English novel was not what the French call *discutable.*[1] It had no air of having a theory, a conviction, a consciousness of itself behind it—of being the expression of an artistic faith, the result of choice and comparison. I do not say it was necessarily the worse for that: it would take much more courage than I possess to intimate that the form of the novel as Dickens and Thackeray (for instance) saw it had any taint of incompleteness. It was, however, *naïf* (if I may help myself out with another French word); and evidently if it be destined to suffer in any way for having lost its *naïveté* it has now an idea of making sure of the corresponding advantages. During the period I have

THE ART OF FICTION.    1. *discutable:* discussable.

alluded to there was a comfortable, good-humoured feeling abroad that a novel is a novel, as a pudding is a pudding, and that our only business with it could be to swallow it. But within a year or two, for some reason or other, there have been signs of returning animation—the era of discussion would appear to have been to a certain extent opened. Art lives upon discussion, upon experiment, upon curiosity, upon variety of attempt, upon the exchange of views and the comparison of standpoints; and there is a presumption that those times when no one has anything particular to say about it, and has no reason to give for practice or preference, though they may be times of honour, are not times of development—are times, possibly even, a little of dulness. The successful application of any art is a delightful spectacle, but the theory too is interesting; and though there is a great deal of the latter without the former I suspect there has never been a genuine success that has not had a latent core of conviction. Discussion, suggestion, formulation, these things are fertilizing when they are frank and sincere. Mr. Besant has set an excellent example in saying what he thinks, for his part, about the way in which fiction should be written, as well as about the way in which it should be published; for his view of the "art," carried on into an appendix, covers that too. Other labourers in the same field will doubtless take up the argument, they will give it the light of their experience, and the effect will surely be to make our interest in the novel a little more what it had for some time threatened to fail to be—a serious, active, inquiring interest, under protection of which this delightful study may, in moments of confidence, venture to say a little more what it thinks of itself.

It must take itself seriously for the public to take it so. The old superstition about fiction being "wicked" has doubtless died out in England; but the spirit of it lingers in a certain oblique regard directed toward any story which does not more or less admit that it is only a joke. Even the most jocular novel feels in some degree the weight of the proscription that was formerly directed against literary levity: the jocularity does not always succeed in passing for orthodoxy. It is still expected, though perhaps people are ashamed to say it, that a production which is after all only a "make-believe" (for what else is a "story"?) shall be in some degree apologetic—shall renounce the pretension of attempting really to represent life. This, of course, any sensible, wide-awake story declines to do, for it quickly perceives that the tolerance granted to it on such a condition is only an attempt to stifle it disguised in the form of generosity. The old evangelical hostility to the novel, which was as

explicit as it was narrow, and which regarded it as little less favourable to our immortal part than a stage-play, was in reality far less insulting. The only reason for the existence of a novel is that it does attempt to represent life. When it relinquishes this attempt, the same attempt that we see on the canvas of the painter, it will have arrived at a very strange pass. It is not expected of the picture that it will make itself humble in order to be forgiven; and the analogy between the art of the painter and the art of the novelist is, so far as I am able to see, complete. Their inspiration is the same, their process (allowing for the different quality of the vehicle) is the same, their success is the same. They may learn from each other, they may explain and sustain each other. Their cause is the same, and the honour of one is the honour of another. The Mahometans think a picture an unholy thing, but it is a long time since any Christian did, and it is therefore the more odd that in the Christian mind the traces (dissimulated though they may be) of a suspicion of the sister art should linger to this day. The only effectual way to lay it to rest is to emphasize the analogy to which I just alluded—to insist on the fact that as the picture is reality, so the novel is history. That is the only general description (which does it justice) that we may give of the novel. But history also is allowed to represent life; it is not, any more than painting, expected to apologize. The subject-matter of fiction is stored up likewise in documents and records, and if it will not give itself away, as they say in California, it must speak with assurance, with the tone of the historian. Certain accomplished novelists have a habit of giving themselves away which must often bring tears to the eyes of people who take their fiction seriously. I was lately struck, in reading over many pages of Anthony Trollope, with his want of discretion in this particular. In a digression, a parenthesis or an aside, he concedes to the reader that he and this trusting friend are only "making believe." He admits that the events he narrates have not really happened, and that he can give his narrative any turn the reader may like best. Such a betrayal of a sacred office seems to me, I confess, a terrible crime; it is what I mean by the attitude of apology, and it shocks me every whit as much in Trollope as it would have shocked me in Gibbon or Macaulay. It implies that the novelist is less occupied in looking for the truth (the truth, of course I mean, that he assumes, the premises that we must grant him, whatever they may be) than the historian, and in doing so it deprives him at a stroke of all his standing-room. To represent and illustrate the past, the actions of men, is the task of either writer, and the only difference that I can see is, in proportion as he succeeds, to the honour of the novelist, consisting as it does in his having more difficulty in collecting his evidence, which is so far from being purely literary. It seems to me to give him a great character, the fact that he has at once so much in common with the philosopher and the painter; this double analogy is a magnificent heritage.

It is of all this evidently that Mr. Besant is full when he insists upon the fact that fiction is one of the *fine* arts, deserving in its turn of all the honours and emoluments that have hitherto been reserved for the successful profession of music, poetry, painting, architecture. It is impossible to insist too much on so important a truth, and the place that Mr. Besant demands for the work of the novelist may be represented, a trifle less abstractly, by saying that he demands not only that it shall be reputed artistic, but that it shall be reputed very artistic indeed. It is excellent that he should have struck this note, for his doing so indicates that there was need of it, that his proposition may be to many people a novelty. One rubs one's eyes at the thought; but the rest of Mr. Besant's essay confirms the revelation. I suspect in truth that it would be possible to confirm it still further, and that one would not be far wrong in saying that in addition to the people to whom it has never occurred that a novel ought to be artistic, there are a great many others who, if this principle were urged upon them, would be filled with an indefinable mistrust. They would find it difficult to explain their repugnance, but it would operate strongly to put them on their guard. "Art," in our Protestant communities, where so many things have got so strangely twisted about, is supposed in certain circles to have some vaguely injurious effect upon those who make it an important consideration, who let it weigh in the balance. It is assumed to be opposed in some mysterious manner to morality, to amusement, to instruction. When it is embodied in the work of the painter (the sculptor is another affair!) you know what it is: it stands there before you, in the honesty of pink and green and a gilt frame; you can see the worst of it at a glance, and you can be on your guard. But when it is introduced into literature it becomes more insidious —there is danger of its hurting you before you know it. Literature should be either instructive or amusing, and there is in many minds an impression that these artistic preoccupations, the search for form, contribute to neither end, interfere indeed with both. They are too frivolous to be edifying, and too serious to be diverting; and they are moreover priggish and paradoxical and superfluous. That, I think, represents the manner in which

the latent thought of many people who read novels as an exercise in skipping would explain itself if it were to become articulate. They would argue, of course, that a novel ought to be "good," but they would interpret this term in a fashion of their own, which indeed would vary considerably from one critic to another. One would say that being good means representing virtuous and aspiring characters, placed in prominent positions; another would say that it depends on a "happy ending," on a distribution at the last of prizes, pensions, husbands, wives, babies, millions, appended paragraphs, and cheerful remarks. Another still would say that it means being full of incident and movement, so that we shall wish to jump ahead, to see who was the mysterious stranger, and if the stolen will was ever found, and shall not be distracted from this pleasure by any tiresome analysis or "description." But they would all agree that the "artistic" idea would spoil some of their fun. One would hold it accountable for all the description, another would see it revealed in the absence of sympathy. Its hostility to a happy ending would be evident, and it might even in some cases render any ending at all impossible. The "ending" of a novel is, for many persons, like that of a good dinner, a course of dessert and ices, and the artist in fiction is regarded as a sort of meddlesome doctor who forbids agreeable aftertastes. It is therefore true that this conception of Mr. Besant's of the novel as a superior form encounters not only a negative but a positive indifference. It matters little that as a work of art it should really be as little or as much of its essence to supply happy endings, sympathetic characters, and an objective tone, as if it were a work of mechanics: the association of ideas, however incongruous, might easily be too much for it if an eloquent voice were not sometimes raised to call attention to the fact that it is at once as free and as serious a branch of literature as any other.

Certainly this might sometimes be doubted in presence of the enormous number of works of fiction that appeal to the credulity of our generation, for it might easily seem that there could be no great character in a commodity so quickly and easily produced. It must be admitted that good novels are much compromised by bad ones, and that the field at large suffers discredit from overcrowding. I think, however, that this injury is only superficial, and that the superabundance of written fiction proves nothing against the principle itself. It has been vulgarized, like all other kinds of literature, like everything else to-day, and it has proved more than some kinds accessible to vulgarization. But there is as much difference as there ever was between a good novel and a bad one: the bad is swept with all the daubed canvases and spoiled marble into some unvisited limbo, or infinite rubbish-yard beneath the back-windows of the world, and the good subsists and emits its light and stimulates our desire for perfection. As I shall take the liberty of making but a single criticism of Mr. Besant, whose tone is so full of the love of his art, I may as well have done with it at once. He seems to me to mistake in attempting to say so definitely beforehand what sort of an affair the good novel will be. To indicate the danger of such an error as that has been the purpose of these few pages; to suggest that certain traditions on the subject, applied *a priori,* have already had much to answer for, and that the good health of an art which undertakes so immediately to reproduce life must demand that it be perfectly free. It lives upon exercise, and the very meaning of exercise is freedom. The only obligation to which in advance we may hold a novel, without incurring the accusation of being arbitrary, is that it be interesting. That general responsibility rests upon it, but it is the only one I can think of. The ways in which it is at liberty to accomplish this result (of interesting us) strike me as innumerable, and such as can only suffer from being marked out or fenced in by prescription. They are as various as the temperament of man, and they are successful in proportion as they reveal a particular mind, different from others. A novel is in its broadest definition a personal, a direct impression of life: that, to begin with, constitutes its value, which is greater or less according to the intensity of the impression. But there will be no intensity at all, and therefore no value, unless there is freedom to feel and say. The tracing of a line to be followed, of a tone to be taken, of a form to be filled out, is a limitation of that freedom and a suppression of the very thing that we are most curious about. The form, it seems to me, is to be appreciated after the fact: then the author's choice has been made, his standard has been indicated; then we can follow lines and directions and compare tones and resemblances. Then in a word we can enjoy one of the most charming of pleasures, we can estimate quality, we can apply the test of execution. The execution belongs to the author alone; it is what is most personal to him, and we measure him by that. The advantage, the luxury, as well as the torment and responsibility of the novelist, is that there is no limit to what he may attempt as an executant—no limit to his possible experiments, efforts, discoveries, successes. Here it is especially that he works, step by step, like his brother of the brush, of whom we may always say that he has painted his picture in a manner best known to himself. His manner is his secret, not necessarily a jealous one. He cannot

disclose it as a general thing if he would; he would be at a loss to teach it to others. I say this with a due recollection of having insisted on the community of method of the artist who paints a picture and the artist who writes a novel. The painter *is* able to teach the rudiments of his practice, and it is possible, from the study of good work (granted the aptitude), both to learn how to paint and to learn how to write. Yet it remains true, without injury to the *rapprochement,* that the literary artist would be obliged to say to his pupil much more than the other, "Ah, well, you must do it as you can!" It is a question of degree, a matter of delicacy. If there are exact sciences, there are also exact arts, and the grammar of painting is so much more definite that it makes the difference.

I ought to add, however, that if Mr. Besant says at the beginning of his essay that the "laws of fiction may be laid down and taught with as much precision and exactness as the laws of harmony, perspective, and proportion," he mitigates what might appear to be an extravagance by applying his remark to "general" laws, and by expressing most of these rules in a manner with which it would certainly be unaccommodating to disagree. That the novelist must write from his experience, that his "characters must be real and such as might be met with in actual life"; that "a young lady brought up in a quiet country village should avoid descriptions of garrison life," and "a writer whose friends and personal experiences belong to the lower middle-class should carefully avoid introducing his characters into society"; that one should enter one's notes in a common-place book; that one's figures should be clear in outline; that making them clear by some trick of speech or of carriage is a bad method, and "describing them at length" is a worse one; that English Fiction should have a "conscious moral purpose"; that "it is almost impossible to estimate too highly the value of careful workmanship—that is, of style"; that "the most important point of all is the story," that "the story is everything": these are principles with most of which it is surely impossible not to sympathize. That remark about the lower middle-class writer and his knowing his place is perhaps rather chilling; but for the rest I should find it difficult to dissent from any one of these recommendations. At the same time, I should find it difficult positively to assent to them, with the exception, perhaps, of the injunction as to entering one's notes in a common-place book. They scarcely seem to me to have the quality that Mr. Besant attributes to the rules of the novelist—the "precision and exactness" of "the laws of harmony, perspective, and proportion." They are suggestive, they are even inspiring, but they are not exact, though they are doubtless as much so as the case admits of: which is a proof of that liberty of interpretation for which I just contended. For the value of these different injunctions—so beautiful and so vague—is wholly in the meaning one attaches to them. The characters, the situation, which strike one as real will be those that touch and interest one most, but the measure of reality is very difficult to fix. The reality of Don Quixote or of Mr. Micawber is a very delicate shade; it is a reality so coloured by the author's vision that, vivid as it may be, one would hesitate to propose it as a model: one would expose one's self to some very embarrassing questions on the part of a pupil. It goes without saying that you will not write a good novel unless you possess the sense of reality; but it will be difficult to give you a recipe for calling that sense into being. Humanity is immense, and reality has a myriad forms; the most one can affirm is that some of the flowers of fiction have the odour of it, and others have not; as for telling you in advance how your nosegay should be composed, that is another affair. It is equally excellent and inconclusive to say that one must write from experience; to our supposititious aspirant such a declaration might savour of mockery. What kind of experience is intended, and where does it begin and end? Experience is never limited, and it is never complete; it is an immense sensibility, a kind of huge spider-web of the finest silken threads suspended in the chamber of consciousness, and catching every air-borne particle in its tissue. It is the very atmosphere of the mind; and when the mind is imaginative—much more when it happens to be that of a man of genius—it takes to itself the faintest hints of life, it converts the very pulses of the air into revelations. The young lady living in a village has only to be a damsel upon whom nothing is lost to make it quite unfair (as it seems to me) to declare to her that she shall have nothing to say about the military. Greater miracles have been seen than that, imagination assisting, she should speak the truth about some of these gentlemen. I remember an English novelist, a woman of genius, telling me that she was much commended for the impression she had managed to give in one of her tales of the nature and way of life of the French Protestant youth. She had been asked where she learned so much about this recondite being, she had been congratulated on her peculiar opportunities. These opportunities consisted in her having once, in Paris, as she ascended a staircase, passed an open door where, in the household of a *pasteur*,[2] some of the young Protestants were seated at table round a finished meal. The glimpse

made a picture; it lasted only a moment, but that moment was experience. She had got her direct personal impression, and she turned out her type. She knew what youth was, and what Protestantism; she also had the advantage of having seen what it was to be French, so that she converted these ideas into a concrete image and produced a reality. Above all, however, she was blessed with the faculty which when you give it an inch takes an ell, and which for the artist is a much greater source of strength than any accident of residence or of place in the social scale. The power to guess the unseen from the seen, to trace the implication of things, to judge the whole piece by the pattern, the condition of feeling life in general so completely that you are well on your way to knowing any particular corner of it—this cluster of gifts may almost be said to constitute experience, and they occur in country and in town, and in the most differing stages of education. If experience consists of impressions, it may be said that impressions *are* experience, just as (have we not seen it?) they are the very air we breathe. Therefore, if I should certainly say to a novice, "Write from experience and experience only," I should feel that this was rather a tantalizing monition if I were not careful immediately to add, "Try to be one of the people on whom nothing is lost!"

I am far from intending by this to minimize the importance of exactness—of truth of detail. One can speak best from one's own taste, and I may therefore venture to say that the air of reality (solidity of specification) seems to me to be the supreme virtue of a novel—the merit on which all its other merits (including that conscious moral purpose of which Mr. Besant speaks) helplessly and submissively depend. If it be not there they are all as nothing, and if these be there, they owe their effect to the success with which the author has produced the illusion of life. The cultivation of this success, the study of this exquisite process, form, to my taste, the beginning and the end of the art of the novelist. They are his inspiration, his despair, his reward, his torment, his delight. It is here in very truth that he competes with life; it is here that he competes with his brother the painter in *his* attempt to render the look of things, the look that conveys their meaning, to catch the colour, the relief, the expression, the surface, the substance of the human spectacle. It is in regard to this that Mr. Besant is well inspired when he bids him take notes. He cannot possibly take too many, he cannot possibly take enough. All life solicits him, and to "render" the simplest surface, to produce the most momentary illusion, is a very complicated business. His case would be easier, and the rule would be more exact, if Mr. Besant had been able

2. *pasteur:* pastor, clergyman.

to tell him what notes to take. But this, I fear, he can never learn in any manual; it is the business of his life. He has to take a great many in order to select a few, he has to work them up as he can, and even the guides and philosophers who might have most to say to him must leave him alone when it comes to the application of precepts, as we leave the painter in communion with his palette. That his characters "must be clear in outline," as Mr. Besant says—he feels that down to his boots; but how he shall make them so is a secret between his good angel and himself. It would be absurdly simple if he could be taught that a great deal of "description" would make them so, or that on the contrary the absence of description and the cultivation of dialogue, or the absence of dialogue and the multiplication of "incident," would rescue him from his difficulties. Nothing, for instance, is more possible than that he be of a turn of mind for which this odd, literal opposition of description and dialogue, incident and description, has little meaning and light. People often talk of these things as if they had a kind of internecine distinctness, instead of melting into each other at every breath, and being intimately associated parts of one general effort of expression. I cannot imagine composition existing in a series of blocks, nor conceive, in any novel worth discussing at all, of a passage of description that is not in its intention narrative, a passage of dialogue that is not in its intention descriptive, a touch of truth of any sort that does not partake of the nature of incident, or an incident that derives its interest from any other source than the general and only source of the success of a work of art—that of being illustrative. A novel is a living thing, all one and continuous, like any other organism, and in proportion as it lives will it be found, I think, that in each of the parts there is something of each of the other parts. The critic who over the close texture of a finished work shall pretend to trace a geography of items will mark some frontiers as artificial, I fear, as any that have been known to history. There is an old-fashioned distinction between the novel of character and the novel of incident which must have cost many a smile to the intending fabulist who was keen about his work. It appears to me as little to the point as the equally celebrated distinction between the novel and the romance—to answer as little to any reality. There are bad novels and good novels, as there are bad pictures and good pictures; but that is the only distinction in which I see any meaning, and I can as little imagine speaking of a novel of character as I can imagine speaking of a picture of character. When one says picture one says of character, when one says novel one says of incident, and the terms may be transposed at will. What is character but the determination of incident? What is incident but the illustration of character? What is either a picture or a novel that is *not* of character? What else do we seek in it and find in it? It is an incident for a woman to stand up with her hand resting on a table and look out at you in a certain way; or if it be not an incident I think it will be hard to say what it is. At the same time it is an expression of character. If you say you don't see it (character in *that*—*allons donc!*),[3] this is exactly what the artist who has reasons of his own for thinking he *does* see it undertakes to show you. When a young man makes up his mind that he has not faith enough after all to enter the church as he intended, that is an incident, though you may not hurry to the end of the chapter to see whether perhaps he doesn't change once more. I do not say that these are extraordinary or startling incidents. I do not pretend to estimate the degree of interest proceeding from them, for this will depend upon the skill of the painter. It sounds almost puerile to say that some incidents are intrinsically much more important than others, and I need not take this precaution after having professed my sympathy for the major ones in remarking that the only classification of the novel that I can understand is into that which has life and that which has it not.

The novel and the romance, the novel of incident and that of character—these clumsy separations appear to me to have been made by critics and readers for their own convenience, and to help them out of some of their occasional queer predicaments, but to have little reality or interest for the producer, from whose point of view it is of course that we are attempting to consider the art of fiction. The case is the same with another shadowy category which Mr. Besant apparently is disposed to set up—that of the "modern English novel"; unless indeed it be that in this matter he has fallen into an accidental confusion of standpoints. It is not quite clear whether he intends the remarks in which he alludes to it to be didactic or historical. It is as difficult to suppose a person intending to write a modern English as to suppose him writing an ancient English novel: that is a label which begs the question. One writes the novel, one paints the picture, of one's language and of one's time, and calling it modern English will not, alas! make the difficult task any easier. No more, unfortunately, will calling this or that work of one's fellow-artist a romance—unless it be, of course, simply for the pleasantness of the thing, as for instance when

3. *allons donc!:* "go on!"

Hawthorne gave this heading to his story of *Blithedale*. The French, who have brought the theory of fiction to remarkable completeness, have but one name for the novel, and have not attempted smaller things in it, that I can see, for that. I can think of no obligation to which the "romancer" would not be held equally with the novelist; the standard of execution is equally high for each. Of course it is of execution that we are talking—that being the only point of a novel that is open to contention. This is perhaps too often lost sight of, only to produce interminable confusions and cross-purposes. We must grant the artist his subject, his idea, his *donnée:* [4] our criticism is applied only to what he makes of it. Naturally I do not mean that we are bound to like it or find it interesting: in case we do not our course is perfectly simple—to let it alone. We may believe that of a certain idea even the most sincere novelist can make nothing at all, and the event may perfectly justify our belief; but the failure will have been a failure to execute, and it is in the execution that the fatal weakness is recorded. If we pretend to respect the artist at all, we must allow him his freedom of choice, in the face, in particular cases, of innumerable presumptions that the choice will not fructify. Art derives a considerable part of its beneficial exercise from flying in the face of presumptions, and some of the most interesting experiments of which it is capable are hidden in the bosom of common things. Gustave Flaubert [5] has written a story about the devotion of a servant-girl to a parrot, and the production, highly-finished as it is, cannot on the whole be called a success. We are perfectly free to find it flat, but I think it might have been interesting; and I, for my part, am extremely glad he should have written it; it is a contribution to our knowledge of what can be done—or what cannot. Ivan Turgénieff [6] has written a tale about a deaf and dumb serf and a lap-dog, and the thing is touching, loving, a little masterpiece. He struck the note of life where Gustave Flaubert missed it—he flew in the face of a presumption and achieved a victory.

Nothing, of course, will ever take the place of the good old fashion of "liking" a work of art or not liking it: the most improved criticism will not abolish that primitive, that ultimate test. I mention this to guard myself from the accusation of inti-

mating that the idea, the subject, of a novel or a picture, does not matter. It matters, to my sense, in the highest degree, and if I might put up a prayer it would be that artists should select none but the richest. Some, as I have already hastened to admit, are much more remunerative than others, and it would be a world happily arranged in which persons intending to treat them should be exempt from confusions and mistakes. This fortunate condition will arrive only, I fear, on the same day that critics become purged from error. Meanwhile, I repeat, we do not judge the artist with fairness unless we say to him, "Oh, I grant you your starting-point, because if I did not I should seem to prescribe to you, and heaven forbid I should take that responsibility. If I pretend to tell you what you must not take, you will call upon me to tell you then what you must take; in which case I shall be prettily caught. Moreover, it isn't till I have accepted your data that I can begin to measure you. I have the standard, the pitch; I have no right to tamper with your flute and then criticize your music. Of course I may not care for your idea at all; I may think it silly, or stale, or unclean; in which case I wash my hands of you altogether. I may content myself with believing that you will not have succeeded in being interesting, but I shall, of course, not attempt to demonstrate it, and you will be as indifferent to me as I am to you. I needn't remind you that there are all sorts of tastes: who can know it better? Some people, for excellent reasons, don't like to read about carpenters; others, for reasons even better, don't like to read about courtesans. Many object to Americans. Others (I believe they are mainly editors and publishers) won't look at Italians. Some readers don't like quiet subjects; others don't like bustling ones. Some enjoy a complete illusion, others the consciousness of large concessions. They choose their novels accordingly, and if they don't care about your idea they won't, *a fortiori,* care about your treatment."

So that it comes back very quickly, as I have said, to the liking: in spite of M. Zola, who reasons less powerfully than he represents, and who will not reconcile himself to this absoluteness of taste, thinking that there are certain things that people ought to like, and that they can be made to like. I am quite at a loss to imagine anything (at any rate in this matter of fiction) that people *ought* to like or to dislike. Selection will be sure to take care of itself, for it has a constant motive behind it. That motive is simply experience. As people feel life, so they will feel the art that is most closely related to it. This closeness of relation is what we should never forget in talking of the effort of the novel. Many people speak of it as a factitious, artificial

---

4. *donnée:* what is given, the subject as distinguished from the final or entire treatment of a novel or story. A standard term in James's criticism.  5. **Gustave Flaubert:** French novelist (1821–80). His *Un Coeur Simple (A Simple Heart)* (1877), one of his *Trois Contes*, is "about" something much less simple than James's account here suggests.  6. **Turgénieff:** The story by Ivan Turgenev (1818–83), as the Russian novelist's name is now commonly spelled, is "Mumu" (1854).

form, a product of ingenuity, the business of which is to alter and arrange the things that surround us, to translate them into conventional, traditional moulds. This, however, is a view of the matter which carries us but a very short way, condemns the art to an eternal repetition of a few familiar *clichés,* cuts short its development, and leads us straight up to a dead wall. Catching the very note and trick, the strange irregular rhythm of life, that is the attempt whose strenuous force keeps Fiction upon her feet. In proportion as in what she offers us we see life *without* rearrangement do we feel that we are touching the truth; in proportion as we see it *with* rearrangement do we feel that we are being put off with a substitute, a compromise and convention. It is not uncommon to hear an extraordinary assurance of remark in regard to this matter of rearranging, which is often spoken of as if it were the last word of art. Mr. Besant seems to me in danger of falling into the great error with his rather unguarded talk about "selection." Art is essentially selection, but it is a selection whose main care is to be typical, to be inclusive. For many people art means rose-coloured window-panes, and selection means picking a bouquet for Mrs. Grundy. They will tell you glibly that artistic considerations have nothing to do with the disagreeable, with the ugly; they will rattle off shallow commonplaces about the province of art and the limits of art till you are moved to some wonder in return as to the province and the limits of ignorance. It appears to me that no one can ever have made a seriously artistic attempt without becoming conscious of an immense increase—a kind of revelation—of freedom. One perceives in that case—by the light of a heavenly ray—that the province of art is all life, all feeling, all observation, all vision. As Mr. Besant so justly intimates, it is all experience. That is a sufficient answer to those who maintain that it must not touch the sad things of life, who stick into its divine unconscious bosom little prohibitory inscriptions on the end of sticks, such as we see in public gardens—"It is forbidden to walk on the grass; it is forbidden to touch the flowers; it is not allowed to introduce dogs or to remain after dark; it is requested to keep to the right." The young aspirant in the line of fiction whom we continue to imagine will do nothing without taste, for in that case his freedom would be of little use to him; but the first advantage of his taste will be to reveal to him the absurdity of the little sticks and tickets. If he have taste, I must add, of course he will have ingenuity, and my disrespectful reference to that quality just now was not meant to imply that it is useless in fiction. But it is only a secondary aid; the first is a capacity for receiving straight impressions.

Mr. Besant has some remarks on the question of "the story" which I shall not attempt to criticize, though they seem to me to contain a singular ambiguity, because I do not think I understand them. I cannot see what is meant by talking as if there were a part of a novel which is the story and part of it which for mystical reasons is not—unless indeed the distinction be made in a sense in which it is difficult to suppose that any one should attempt to convey anything. "The story," if it represents anything, represents the subject, the idea, the *donnée* of the novel; and there is surely no "school"— Mr. Besant speaks of a school—which urges that a novel should be all treatment and no subject. There must assuredly be something to treat; every school is intimately conscious of that. This sense of the story being the idea, the starting-point, of the novel, is the only one that I see in which it can be spoken of as something different from its organic whole; and since in proportion as the work is successful the idea permeates and penetrates it, informs and animates it, so that every word and every punctuation-point contribute directly to the expression, in that proportion do we lose our sense of the story being a blade which may be drawn more or less out of its sheath. The story and the novel, the idea and the form, are the needle and thread, and I never heard of a guild of tailors who recommended the use of the thread without the needle, or the needle without the thread. Mr. Besant is not the only critic who may be observed to have spoken as if there were certain things in life which constitute stories, and certain others which do not. I find the same odd implication in an entertaining article in the *Pall Mall Gazette,* devoted, as it happens, to Mr. Besant's lecture. "The story is the thing!" says this graceful writer, as if with a tone of opposition to some other idea. I should think it was, as every painter who, as the time for "sending in" his picture looms in the distance, finds himself still in quest of a subject—as every belated artist not fixed about his theme will heartily agree. There are some subjects which speak to us and others which do not, but he would be a clever man who should undertake to give a rule— an *index expurgatorius*—by which the story and the no-story should be known apart. It is impossible (to me at least) to imagine any such rule which shall not be altogether arbitrary. The writer in the *Pall Mall* opposes the delightful (as I suppose) novel of *Margot la Balafrée* to certain tales in which "Bostonian nymphs" appear to have "rejected English dukes for psychological reasons." [7] I am not acquainted with the romance just desig-

7. **psychological reasons:** In Henry James's story "An International Episode" (1878) a girl of Boston origins refuses an English duke for various reasons.

nated, and can scarcely forgive the *Pall Mall* critic for not mentioning the name of the author, but the title appears to refer to a lady who may have received a scar in some heroic adventure. I am inconsolable at not being acquainted with this episode, but am utterly at a loss to see why it is a story when the rejection (or acceptance) of a duke is not, and why a reason, psychological or other, is not a subject when a cicatrix is. They are all particles of the multitudinous life with which the novel deals, and surely no dogma which pretends to make it lawful to touch the one and unlawful to touch the other will stand for a moment on its feet. It is the special picture that must stand or fall, according as it seem to possess truth or to lack it. Mr. Besant does not, to my sense, light up the subject by intimating that a story must, under penalty of not being a story, consist of "adventures." Why of adventures more than of green spectacles? He mentions a category of impossible things, and among them he places "fiction without adventure." Why without adventure, more than without matrimony, or celibacy, or parturition, or cholera, or hydropathy, or Jansenism? This seems to me to bring the novel back to the hapless little *rôle* of being an artificial, ingenious thing—bring it down from its large, free character of an immense and exquisite correspondence with life. And what *is* adventure, when it comes to that, and by what sign is the listening pupil to recognize it? It is an adventure—an immense one—for me to write this little article; and for a Bostonian nymph to reject an English duke is an adventure only less stirring, I should say, than for an English duke to be rejected by a Bostonian nymph. I see dramas within dramas in that, and innumerable points of view. A psychological reason is, to my imagination, an object adorably pictorial; to catch the tint of its complexion—I feel as if that idea might inspire one to Titianesque efforts. There are few things more exciting to me, in short, than a psychological reason, and yet, I protest, the novel seems to me the most magnificent form of art. I have just been reading, at the same time, the delightful story of *Treasure Island,* by Mr. Robert Louis Stevenson and, in a manner less consecutive, the last tale from M. Edmond de Goncourt, which is entitled *Chérie.* One of these works treats of murders, mysteries, islands of dreadful renown, hair-breadth escapes, miraculous coincidences and buried doubloons. The other treats of a little French girl who lived in a fine house in Paris, and died of wounded sensibility because no one would marry her. I call *Treasure Island* delightful, because it appears to me to have succeeded wonderfully in what it attempts; and I venture to bestow no epithet upon *Chérie,* which strikes me as having failed deplor-

ably in what it attempts—that is in tracing the development of the moral consciousness of a child. But one of these productions strikes me as exactly as much of a novel as the other, and as having a "story" quite as much. The moral consciousness of a child is as much a part of life as the islands of the Spanish Main, and the one sort of geography seems to me to have those "surprises" of which Mr. Besant speaks quite as much as the other. For myself (since it comes back in the last resort, as I say, to the preference of the individual), the picture of the child's experience has the advantage that I can at successive steps (an immense luxury, near to the "sensual pleasure" of which Mr. Besant's critic in the *Pall Mall* speaks) say Yes or No, as it may be, to what the artist puts before me. I have been a child in fact, but I have been on a quest for a buried treasure only in supposition, and it is a simple accident that with M. de Goncourt I should have for the most part to say No. With George Eliot, when she painted that country with a far other intelligence, I always said Yes.

The most interesting part of Mr. Besant's lecture is unfortunately the briefest passage—his very cursory allusion to the "conscious moral purpose" of the novel. Here again it is not very clear whether he be recording a fact or laying down a principle; it is a great pity that in the latter case he should not have developed his idea. This branch of the subject is of immense importance, and Mr. Besant's few words point to considerations of the widest reach, not to be lightly disposed of. He will have treated the art of fiction but superficially who is not prepared to go every inch of the way that these considerations will carry him. It is for this reason that at the beginning of these remarks I was careful to notify the reader that my reflections on so large a theme have no pretension to be exhaustive. Like Mr. Besant, I have left the question of the morality of the novel till the last, and at the last I find I have used up my space. It is a question surrounded with difficulties, as witness the very first that meets us, in the form of a definite question, on the threshold. Vagueness, in such a discussion, is fatal, and what is the meaning of your morality and your conscious moral purpose? Will you not define your terms and explain how (a novel being a picture) a picture can be either moral or immoral? You wish to paint a moral picture or carve a moral statue: will you not tell us how you would set about it? We are discussing the Art of Fiction; questions of art are questions (in the widest sense) of execution; questions of morality are quite another affair, and will you not let us see how it is that you find it so easy to mix them up? These things are so clear to Mr. Besant that he has deduced from them a law which he sees embodied in English Fiction, and which is "a truly admirable thing and a great cause for congratulation." It is a great cause for congratulation indeed when such thorny problems become as smooth as silk. I may add that in so far as Mr. Besant perceives that in point of fact English fiction has addressed itself preponderantly to these delicate questions he will appear to many people to have made a vain discovery. They will have been positively struck, on the contrary, with the moral timidity of the usual English novelist; with his (or with her) aversion to face the difficulties with which on every side the treatment of reality bristles. He is apt to be extremely shy (whereas the picture that Mr. Besant draws is a picture of boldness), and the sign of his work, for the most part, is a cautious silence on certain subjects. In the English novel (by which of course I mean the American as well), more than in any other, there is a traditional difference between that which people know and that which they agree to admit that they know, that which they see and that which they speak of, that which they feel to be a part of life and that which they allow to enter into literature. There is the great difference, in short, between what they talk of in conversation and what they talk of in print. The essence of moral energy is to survey the whole field, and I should directly reverse Mr. Besant's remark and say not that the English novel has a purpose, but that it has a diffidence. To what degree a purpose in a work of art is a source of corruption I shall not attempt to inquire; the one that seems to me least dangerous is the purpose of making a perfect work. As for our novel, I may say lastly on this score that as we find it in England to-day it strikes me as addressed in a large degree to "young people," and that this in itself constitutes a presumption that it will be rather shy. There are certain things which it is generally agreed not to discuss, not even to mention, before young people. That is very well, but the absence of discussion is not a symptom of the moral passion. The purpose of the English novel—"a truly admirable thing, and a great cause for congratulation"—strikes me therefore as rather negative.

There is one point at which the moral sense and the artistic sense lie very near together; that is in the light of the very obvious truth that the deepest quality of a work of art will always be the quality of the mind of the producer. In proportion as that intelligence is fine will the novel, the picture, the statue partake of the substance of beauty and truth. To be constituted of such elements is, to my vision, to have purpose enough. No good novel will ever proceed from a superficial mind; that seems to me an axiom which, for the artist in fic-

tion, will cover all needful moral ground: if the youthful aspirant take it to heart it will illuminate for him many of the mysteries of "purpose." There are many other useful things that might be said to him, but I have come to the end of my article, and can only touch them as I pass. The critic in the *Pall Mall Gazette,* whom I have already quoted, draws attention to the danger, in speaking of the art of fiction, of generalizing. The danger that he has in mind is rather, I imagine, that of particularizing, for there are some comprehensive remarks which, in addition to those embodied in Mr. Besant's suggestive lecture, might without fear of misleading him be addressed to the ingenuous student. I should remind him first of the magnificence of the form that is open to him, which offers to sight so few restrictions and such innumerable opportunities. The other arts, in comparison, appear confined and hampered; the various conditions under which they are exercised are so rigid and definite. But the only condition that I can think of attaching to the composition of the novel is, as I have already said, that it be sincere. This freedom is a splendid privilege, and the first lesson of the young novelist is to learn to be worthy of it.

"Enjoy it as it deserves [I should say to him]; take possession of it, explore it to its utmost extent, publish it, rejoice in it. All life belongs to you, and do not listen either to those who would shut you up into corners of it and tell you that it is only here and there that art inhabits, or to those who would persuade you that this heavenly messenger wings her way outside of life altogether, breathing a superfine air, and turning away her head from the truth of things. There is no impression of life, no manner of seeing it and feeling it, to which the plan of the novelist may not offer a place; you have only to remember that talents so dissimilar as those of Alexandre Dumas and Jane Austen, Charles Dickens and Gustave Flaubert have worked in this field with equal glory. Do not think too much about optimism and pessimism; try and catch the colour of life itself. In France to-day we see a prodigious effort (that of Émile Zola, to whose solid and serious work no explorer of the capacity of the novel can allude without respect), we see an extraordinary effort vitiated by a spirit of pessimism on a narrow basis. M. Zola is magnificent, but he strikes an English reader as ignorant; he has an air of working in the dark; if he had as much light as energy, his results would be of the highest value. As for the aberrations of a shallow optimism, the ground (of English fiction especially) is strewn with their brittle particles as with broken glass. If you must indulge in conclusions, let them have the taste of a wide knowledge. Remember that your first duty is to be as complete as possible—to make as perfect a work. Be generous and delicate and pursue the prize.''

---

F R O M

# THE NOTEBOOKS

---

◇

⟨ JAMES kept a series of notebooks, of which those dating from 1878 to 1910 have survived. They were collected by F. O. Matthiessen and Kenneth B. Murdock in *The Notebooks of Henry James* (1947). For the most part he used them to record ideas for stories and novels, often to outline their development, to list possible names for his characters, and, in a few important instances, to meditate on his personal experiences and his general problems as an artist. The notebooks were not intended for publication.

◇

### THE REAL THING
*Paris, Hotel Westminster, February 22d, 1891.*

IN PURSUANCE of my plan of writing some very short tales—things of from 7000 to 10,000 words, the easiest length to 'place,' I began yesterday the little story that was suggested to me some time ago by an incident related to me by George du Maurier [1]—the lady and gentleman who called upon him with a word from Frith, an oldish, faded, ruined pair—he an officer in the army—who unable to turn a penny in any other way, were trying to find employment as models. I was struck with the pathos, the oddity and typicalness of the situation—the little tragedy of good-looking gentlefolk, who had been all their life stupid and well-dressed, living, on a fixed income, at country-houses, watering places and clubs, like so many others of their class in England, and were now utterly unable to *do* anything, had no cleverness, no art nor craft to make use of as a *gagne-pain* [2]—could only *show* themselves, clumsily, for the fine, clean, well-groomed animals that they were, only hope to make a little money by—in this manner—just simply *being*. I thought I saw a subject for very brief treatment in this *donnée* [3]—and I think I do still; but to do anything worth while with it I must (as

always, great Heavens!) be very clear as to what is in it and what I wish to get out of it. I tried a beginning yesterday, but I instantly became conscious that I must straighten out the little idea. It must be an idea—it can't be a 'story' in the vulgar sense of the word. It must be a picture; it must illustrate something. God knows that's enough—if the thing *does* illustrate. To make little anecdotes of this kind real *morceaux de vie* [4] is a plan quite inspiring enough. *Voyons un peu,* therefore, what one can put into this one—I mean how much of life. One must put a little action—not a stupid, mechanical, arbitrary action, but something that is of the real essence of the subject. I thought of representing the husband as jealous of the wife— that is, jealous of the artist employing her, from the moment that, in point of fact, she begins to sit. But this is vulgar and obvious—worth nothing. What I wish to represent is the baffled, ineffectual, incompetent character of their attempt, and how it illustrates once again the everlasting English amateurishness—the way superficial, untrained, unprofessional effort goes to the wall when confronted with trained, competitive, intelligent, *qualified* art—in whatever line it may be a question of. It is out of *that* element that my little action and movement must come; and now I begin to see just how—as one always *does*—Glory be to the Highest—when one begins to look at a thing hard and straight and seriously—to fix it—as I am so sadly lax and desultory about doing. What subjects I should find—for *everything*—if I could only achieve this more as a habit! Let my contrast and complication here come from the opposition —to my melancholy Major and his wife—of a couple of little vulgar professional people *who know,* with the consequent bewilderment, vagueness, depression of the former—their failure to understand how such people can be better than *they* —their failure, disappointment, disappearance— going forth into the vague again. *Il y a bien quelque chose à tirer de ça.* [5] They have no pictorial sense. They are only clean and stiff and stupid. The others are dirty, even—the melancholy Major and his wife remark on it, wondering. The artist is beginning a big illustrated book, a new edition of a famous novel—say *Tom Jones*—and he is willing to try to work them in—for he takes an interest in their predicament, and feels—sceptically, but, with his flexible artistic sympathy—the appeal of their type. He is willing to give them a trial. Make it out that *he* himself is on trial—he is young and 'rising,' but he has still his golden spurs to win. He can't afford, *en somme,* to make many mistakes.

---

NOTEBOOKS.    **1. George du Maurier:** English artist and writer of French birth (1834–96), illustrator of certain of James's works.    **2. *gagne-pain:*** means of livelihood.    **3. *donnée:*** See note above, page 823.

**4. *morceaux de vie:*** morsels of life.    **5. *Il y a . . . ça:*** "there's certainly something to be got out of that."

He has regular work in drawing every week for a serial novel in an illustrated paper; but the great project—that of a big house—of issuing an illustrated Fielding promises him a big lift. He has been intrusted with (say) *Joseph Andrews*,[6] experimentally; he will have to do this brilliantly in order to have the engagement for the rest confirmed. He has already 2 models in his service—the 'complication' must come from *them*. One is a common, clever, London girl, of the smallest origin and without conventional beauty, but of aptitude, of perceptions—knowing thoroughly *how*. She says 'lydy' and 'plice,' but she has the pictorial sense; and can look like anything he wants her to look like. She poses, in short, in perfection. So does her colleague, a professional Italian, a little fellow—ill dressed, smelling of garlic, but admirably serviceable, quite universal. They must be contrasted, confronted, *juxtaposed* with the others; whom they take for people who *pay*, themselves, till they learn the truth when they are overwhelmed with derisive amazement. The denouement simply that the melancholy Major and his wife won't do—they're not 'in it.' Their surprise—their helpless, proud assent—without other prospects: yet at the same time *their* degree of more silent amazement at the success of the two inferior people—who are so much less nice-looking than themselves. Frankly, however, is this contrast enough of a *story*, by itself? It seems to me Yes—for it's an IDEA—and how the deuce should I get

*more* into 7000 words? It must be simply 50 pp. of my manuscript. The little tale of *The Servant* (*Brooksmith*) [7] which I did the other day for *Black and White* and which I thought of at the same time as this, proved a very tight squeeze into the same tiny number of words, and I probably shall find that there is much more to be done with this than the compass will admit of. Make it tremendously succinct—with a very short pulse or rhythm —and the closest selection of detail—in other words *summarize* intensely and keep down the lateral development. It *should* be a little gem of bright, quick, vivid form. I shall get every grain of 'action' that the space admits of if I make something, for the artist, hang in the balance—depend on the way he does this particular work. It's when he finds that he shall lose his great opportunity if he keeps on with them, that he has to tell the gentlemanly couple, that, frankly, they won't serve his turn—and make them wander forth into the cold world again. I must keep them the age I've made them—50 and 40—because it's more touching; but I must bring up the age of the 2 real models to almost the same thing. That increases the incomprehensibility (to the amateurs) of their usefulness. Picture the immanence, in the latter, of the idle, provided-for, country-house habit—the blankness of their *manière d'être*.[8] But in how tremendously few words I must do it. This is a lesson—a *magnificent* lesson—if I'm to do a good many. Something as admirably compact and *selected* as a Maupassant.

6. *Joseph Andrews:* novel (1742) by Henry Fielding (1707–54), author also of *Tom Jones* (1749).

7. *Brooksmith:* "Brooksmith" was published in *Black and White* (May 1891).    8. *manière d'etre:* way of life.

# J. C. LEVENSON
*Editor*

# Stephen Crane

## 1871–1900

IN THE last three decades of the nineteenth century, it was a wise American who knew his own country: the era was one of rapid, confused, and basic change, when the United States was neither still an agrarian nor yet an industrialized nation, neither the old-fashioned antebellum democracy nor the massive mechanized urban society of the present. And Stephen Crane was peculiarly the child of this age—if only because the brevity of his life kept him from knowing any other. He almost completely lacked the sense of the past that his older contemporaries, Henry James and Henry Adams, had in uncommon measure. They knew full well that the Civil War had riven them from the America they were brought up to understand; Crane, born in 1871 into the thoroughly disrupted postwar era, had no such memory of order to help him comprehend the disorder around him: *The Red Badge of Courage* and the Civil War represent very nearly the limit of his reach into the past. On the other hand, his chance to accumulate experience was cut off early. He died of tuberculosis in 1900, when Theodore Dreiser—also born in 1871—had not yet published a novel. But the circumstances which made him so much the creature of his time also projected him into the timelessness of a classic American legend. He was a kind of innocent in a fallen world. Free from the burdens of the past, he went unarmed by its

lessons. Confronting strange and perilous situations, he had to rely almost entirely on his own gifts and character and vision. Certain that true victory was different from worldly success, he struggled toward a goal he could not name.

Being a legendary figure was a doubtful advantage for Crane. His extraordinary gifts and youthful intensity were enviable assets, of course. Thanks to them, his life and writing moved in a world which, though sometimes thin, was vivid, immediate, and momentous. Though he was hardly aware that he faced historic problems of American and human life, he instinctively knew that he was beset by cosmic issues. But his handicaps should not be understated. While his short life partly accounted for his being a man without a historical shadow, his peculiar innocence must be attributed partly to failure of mind. Too much the legendary innocent, he was slow to learn that culture is man's substitute for experience, and that without it a young man is prey to deceptions that arise as much from his own ignorance as from the falsity of the world.

Crane's knowledge from books and men was negligible compared to James's or Adams', and he could not make up for it with an education like Mark Twain's in the lore and customs of a traditional community. He belonged to the middle class, whose literary situation Yeats defined as having lost

[829]

the culture of the folk without having yet reached the level of high culture. But when folk and high culture are missing, a third kind fills the vacuum. The conventions of popular literature, with all their sensationalism and sentimentality, dominated Crane's experience, so that even when he consciously rejected them, he did so without any idea of what next step to take. While his lively eye for contrasts between popular illusion and the way things happen might have freed him from the conventions he scorned, he neglected other ways of overcoming the limitations of his milieu. Having early and rightly concluded that direct observation was much more valuable than a fraudulent literary version of reality, he erroneously decided that books were only for the scholar's idle time. He lived hard and observed much, but read little. Within the circumscribed range of his experience, he was undoubtedly one of James's "people on whom nothing is lost"; but his famous irony was the necessary instrument of an intelligence which had so little material on which to work.

Crane's limitations are evident in his best work as well as his failures, as a passage from his greatest story makes clear. "The Open Boat" is based on his first-hand experience as a correspondent shipwrecked on a filibustering expedition to the Cuban revolutionaries of 1897. The bare facts of four men in a dinghy fighting the sea for twenty-seven hours and reaching land with three safe, one dead, convey neither the suffering of the men nor the meaning of the experience. But once a writer gets past externals and tries to render an event as it has been felt, he has to fall back on the resources of his personal culture. In this case, Crane presented actual heroism by reference to the banality of a schoolboy's poem:

To chime the notes of his emotion, a verse mysteriously entered the correspondent's head. He had even forgotten that he had forgotten this verse, but it suddenly was in his mind.

*A soldier of the Legion lay dying in Algiers;*
*There was lack of woman's nursing, there was*
*   dearth of woman's tears;*

*But a comrade stood beside him, and he took that*
*   comrade's hand,*
*And he said, "I never more shall see my own, my*
*   native land."*

In his childhood the correspondent had been made acquainted with the fact that a soldier of the Legion lay dying in Algiers, but he had never regarded the fact as important. Myriads of his schoolfellows had informed him of the soldier's plight, but the dinning had naturally ended by making him perfectly indifferent. He had never considered it his affair that a soldier of the Legion lay dying in Algiers, nor had it appeared to him as a matter for sorrow. It was less to him than the breaking of a pencil's point.

Now, however, it quaintly came to him as a human, living thing. It was no longer merely a picture of a few throes in the breast of a poet, meanwhile drinking tea and warming his feet at the grate: it was an actuality—stern, mournful, and fine.

The passage is full of Crane's strongest qualities. The realism has a center of consciousness and a style which can dramatize that consciousness. The argument implies some complicated and interesting ideas on the relation of literature to life, especially when we remember that it occurs in a story for readers who will be warming their feet at the grate. Readers, like poets, must get away from the comforts and platitudes of conventional existence if they are to get at the actualities which count most in human life. Although Crane seems to be tethered to the mawkish poem which he quotes, he manages to suggest that such foolish triteness characterizes the culture which is of, by, and for the comfortable classes. A subversive irony is his most striking means of transcending the historic situation into which he was born.

Crane's attack on popular culture is the most consistent and varied theme in all his work, but not the only one. After all, "The Open Boat" is not only a vivid, wryly presented story, but also a considered expression of Crane's disbeliefs and his residual faith. The same thing may be said of all his best work, that it passes the test of high seriousness as well as technical virtuosity. Despite his limited background, he attained this twofold qualification of the genuine artist. The great social and moral questions which are traditionally the substance of literature enter his work also, even though they come in indirectly and without the usual signs. If he scorned to preach like the moralizing authors of popular fiction, he nevertheless learned to shape the significance of the unsaid. If he lacked the recognizable techniques of the acknowledged masters, he developed literary methods of his own. The list of his surprising achievements could be lengthened, provided we not allow ourselves to suggest that sheer genius is explanation enough of how Crane made up for his cultural deficiencies. We would do better to turn to the sources from which he supplied his imagination: firsthand experience, a religious upbringing, and the American literary situation of the nineties.

## II

CONSIDERING Crane's ironic relation to popular culture—both dependent and profoundly antagonistic—there is rather too much poetic justice in the fact that his life tended to the pattern of a bad novel: we are forced to remind ourselves that he actually lived what his average countrymen collectively dreamed. He was the youngest child in a happy parsonage; his father died when he was nine; his mother, with a kind of Louisa May Alcott resolution and resourcefulness, kept the household together by writing for the Methodist papers. The boy, whose frail health had been a leading reason for his family's removal from Newark to upstate New York, grew up to be a baseball star—first at military school and then at college. Indeed he might have become a professional athlete had his older brother not persuaded him at least to try college first. He tried two colleges in fact, but it took him less than a year to decide that "humanity was a more interesting study" than the curriculum.

In the spring of 1891, he quit Syracuse University and became a full-time reporter. He had worked for his brother Townley's Asbury Park news agency during his summers and had been a college correspondent for a New York paper. Now he resumed his apprenticeship under his brother, until in August 1892, he seemed to wreck his career—and did wreck Townley's—by writing too candidly and too well about a workingmen's parade in the New Jersey resort. His ironic coverage of the marchers caused an inch-high political scandal and, though the newspaper's editor later denied any connection, he himself suddenly became a freelance journalist in New York. Thus began what Crane was to call his "artistic education on the Bowery." There he not only sketched the life of poverty, he endured it.

Through these years of hardship he worked at his first novel, then at his second. Publishers would not touch his *Maggie, A Girl of the Streets*; when he printed it himself in 1892, booksellers would not handle it. If it had not been for the encouragement of Hamlin Garland (a young literary prophet whom Crane had met as a newspaperman) and of William Dean Howells, he might have given up. The reversal, when it came at last, was sudden: at twenty-four, the neglected and almost starving writer found himself a best-selling novelist. He was shortly to disparage as "a mere episode" *The Red Badge of Courage* (1895) which made him famous, and to prefer to it the poetry which gave his "ideas of life as a whole." But *The Black Riders*, also published in 1895, went into six printings within a year, despite the critical attacks. On whatever terms he chose, Stephen Crane had won through.

The sequel to the boy's success story was melodramatic too. His fame helped him become one of the outstanding newspaper correspondents in the heyday of yellow journalism. Traveling to the West and Mexico, enduring shipwreck off the Florida coast, covering wars in Greece and Cuba, he filed his dispatches to Pulitzer and Hearst and often made news himself. He never knew the public, almost official responsibilities of journalism as they had existed for Franklin and Whitman, Sam Clemens, and Henry Adams; nor could he, within the newspaper conventions, entertain the public by his *writing* as Franklin and Mark Twain had done. A Mr. Dooley might still exist, but Crane was never a humorist in that broad sense. In those days before film and television shared the market of mass entertainment, Crane was a star reporter who was indeed a star. Though a reporter rather than an actor, he performed for the public: his sensational vehicle was news of famine and war rather than manufactured drama, but his social function was clear. The age of publicity was at hand, and the customers responded gratefully when Crane underwent dangers which made their image of the reporter seem real. The shy and modest Crane did not glory in his part as did Richard Harding Davis (1864–1916), the Rudolph Valentino of newspaperdom. But he was the prisoner of his role, economically at least, and to some degree psychologically: his journalistic career abetted in him the fascination of violence—of seeing it and testing his courage in it—that wore him out so young.

Domesticity settled upon Crane at twenty-five—in a luridly appropriate manner. Waiting for the filibuster's ship to sail from Jacksonville, he spent the last weeks of 1896 in regular attendance at a favorite night spot of newspapermen and miscellaneous adventurers, the Hotel de Dream, and struck up an alliance with its proprietress. Cora Taylor was a rare woman, even though it may sound as if a script-writer had invented her. She had a shadowed and unhappy past—two failed marriages and only one divorce. She was intelligent, charming, patient, and loyal. After Crane's ordeal at sea, she took him in and cared for him. Thereafter, she followed him to Greece as the "first woman war correspondent," and when the Greek-Turkish War ended in May 1897, she and Crane established themselves in England as man and wife. There, in the interval before the Spanish-American War, Crane wrote some of his most remarkable stories, and there he struck up the literary friendships which put him in touch at last with the main international stream of letters. But his career was virtually over. The exposure to which the war correspondent willfully submitted himself and the unremitting frenzy of trying to write his way out of debt took their toll, and by the end of 1899 his tuberculosis entered the final fatal stage. In the spring, Cora arranged, with the financial help of friends, to take Stephen to a sanatorium in the Black Forest, but the stretcher patient was too far gone. He died at Badenweiler, June 5, 1900, hardly more than a week after their arrival.

### III

LATE IN 1895 *The Red Badge of Courage* and his book of verse were published and the English reviews which made the success of the novel were just beginning to cross the Atlantic. Two years after his war novel appeared, when he saw actual combat in Greece, he said with evident relief, "*The Red Badge* is all right." With his imagination thus proved trustworthy, he was confirmed in his method of drawing on personal history for literary material. The method sounds like everyone else's, but Crane practiced it with unusual simplicity. He personally knew hunger, exposure, mortal danger, lonely resistance to convention, and self-doubt worse than all, and he could infer from experience his reactions to imaginary ordeals. Hence his candid reply, when he heard that readers took him for a veteran of the Civil War, had been that he learned the emotions of *The Red Badge* on the football field. The transfer of feelings became the main resource of his story-telling, to the exclusion of other techniques that he might have learned from the masters of fiction.

Perhaps his imagination worked this way for psychological as well as intellectual reasons: while he could vividly imagine his own response to almost any crucial situation, he was not strong at imagining other kinds of people. The figures in his tales seem to be individuated mainly by circumstances, and their character defined by a few primary emotions like fear and courage. Just as the author stands apart from traditional culture, they stand apart from traditional characters, for the nineteenth-century novel presented people as the rich compound of personal and social history, ideals and knowledge, as well as circumstances and temperament. Crane's bent for *short* fiction can be inferred from his being interested less in the structure of society than in the rendering of situation, less in the sum of character than in the response to a particular crisis. The archetypal event for him, whether experienced or imagined, is intense and isolated, the undergoing of an ultimate trial.

While circumstance and temperament help explain Crane's affinity for this pattern, the concern for physical tests of character was hardly a peculiarity with him. He had distinguished company in his strenuous reaction against the comfortable life: restiveness under uneventful middle-class prosperity affected some of the most sophisticated minds on both sides of the Atlantic—and affected them in a way which must be distinguished from the popular cult of sensationalism. For them all, the trials which allowed a man to rise above himself conformed in a thoroughly naturalistic way with the psychology of conversion, as if physical ordeals filled the unconscious need of men who could no longer practice the introspective spiritual exercises of Protestantism. Conversely, we may say that their religious heritage, even when it was apparently out of mind, lent form and intensity to their response to natural events. So, in turning from the general view of Crane's life and art to the development of his work in the early Bowery fiction and then the tales of war, we may expect to find that his religious history is at least as important as his individual experience.

### IV

SUPERFICIALLY, Crane's religious upbringing as a Methodist had a light hold upon him. The comfort of religion seemed unnecessary to the comfortable life of a prosperous society, and the discipline of religion appeared superfluous to a life which proceeded happily and decently without the restraints that more coercive societies imposed. The case was not unusual: like Mark Twain, Henry James, and Henry Adams in the older generation, Crane slipped from religion *before* he had intellectual reasons to offer for his defection. Having already become a naturalist in belief, he was not much disturbed by the metaphysical problems that might have been raised for him by Darwinian biology and modern science. He gathered the new knowledge more

or less from the air, and he absorbed it easily. His sardonic poem on social Darwinism is of a piece with his poems on newspaper half-truth, churchgoing, or success, all of them alike rebellious against the prevailing culture. What little he knew of the scientific revolution did not cause his disbelief; it merely confirmed it.

Other kinds of religious problems did come to disturb Crane—for example, the irrelevance of the church's questions to the actual choices most people have to make. He thought that conventional religious moralism evaded urgent questions that were religious and moral in a deeper sense. The inscription he wrote in a gift copy of *Maggie* shows one way in which he faced such questions:

It is inevitable that you will be greatly shocked by this book but continue please with all possible courage to the end. For it tries to show that environment is a tremendous thing in the world and frequently shapes lives regardless. If one proves that theory one makes room in Heaven for all sorts of souls (notably an occasional street girl) who are not confidently expected to be there by many excellent people. . . .

And an inscription he wrote three years later, when *Maggie* was re-issued, shows how he had by 1896 begun to think that Biblical religion missed the problem in the book:

"And the wealth of the few shall be built upon the patience of the poor"
Prophecy not made B.C. 1090

This ironic inscription reveals the starting point of his thought as surely as his citing the dying soldier at Algiers reveals his roots in popular culture. He had thrown off religion, but his religious inheritance survived.

What he lacked in intellectual subtlety was made up for by the complexity of his personal involvement with the classic problems of religion. The influences which worked upon him, taken separately, were simple, but their combined effect was not. His father, Jonathan Townley Crane, had left the stern Presbyterianism of his boyhood and committed himself to a gentler piety that emphasized redemption more than sin.

Against the doctrine of total depravity, he held to a belief in the enduring innocence of created beings and the accessibility to perfect holiness of all God's children. His mild theology corresponded to an equally mild view of what constituted depravity: from his Methodist pulpit and in his writings, he preached against drink, tobacco, baseball, and novels, recommending total abstinence from them all. The vices he denounced could not seem essential to the son who indulged in every one of them and still did not find that they touched upon ultimate evil. And the gentleness of the man who "never drove a horse faster than two yards an hour even if some Christian was dying elsewhere" seemed ineffectual to the son who early guessed—and saw—the cruelty, violence, and Christian and unchristian dyings which were always just beyond the vision of respectable society.

Crane's mother was an even stronger influence than his father. The daughter and niece of ministers, she came of a Methodist line which expressed its evangelism in brimstone exhortation. Mrs. Crane fervidly opposed, as her husband gently did, the evident vices, but she had a strong sense also of the sins which unloving piety might commit. Able to discriminate respectability from goodness, she could, if need be, defy social convention in her own way.

Crane began the novel *Maggie* when he was in college, that is, before he knew the Bowery as a reporter. Even when he put the book into final form, writing with more accurate knowledge and greater skill, he left signs of its origin in his reaction against the women of Asbury. The book has more in common with nineteenth-century religious tracts on the vices of cities than with reportorial investigations like Jacob Riis's *How the Other Half Lives* (1890) or *The Children of the Poor* (1892). Crane's child of the slums, seeing a local saloon hero as the lover "under the trees in her dream garden," is seduced young and deserted early: instead of returning to the sweatshops from which she was rescued by vice, she becomes a prostitute and thus begins a quick downhill journey which leads to the river and suicide. The melancholy which descends on Maggie is caused not by guilt, but by helplessness and physical deterioration. Crane rules out sentimentality as well as priggishness. He keeps fuzzy emotions at an ironic distance by having Maggie's slatternly mother, who had cursed her fall and turned her out, end the novel with a drunken gush of sentiment, screaming "Oh, yes, I'll fergive her! I'll fergive her!"

Insofar as environment accounts for the destiny of Maggie Johnson, Crane recognized that socialism and the changing of environment provided a solution; but having shaken one ideology, he did not care to take on another. In the same tone he used for religion, he once remarked that he "was a Socialist once for two weeks but when a couple of Socialists assured me I had no right to think differently from any other Socialist and then quarreled with each other about what Socialism meant, I ran away." Instead, he became a radical without a program who distinguished the spirit from the letter. To those who hastily fixed the damnable responsibility for vice on the Maggies of the world, he declared that environment was a "tremendous thing"; he did not say it was all.

What Crane believed in was not doctrinaire reformism, but heart-conviction based on a converting knowledge of ultimate social reality. The weakness of his Bowery novels is the thinness of characterization, but the rendering of character is less important to his novels than the vision of horror. The mission preacher's threat of hell in *Maggie* conveys nothing to hearers already in torment from hunger. While hellfire preaching is held up for contempt, the characters play their part in a brimstone fable.

If a brimstone fable is to be effective, the reader should be caught up in it. But apart from Crane's difficulties of sympathy, his ironic technique detaches the reader from the characters of his novels and from the horrifying events. "An Experiment in Misery" solves the problem of ethical distance by shifting the point of view to a consciousness within the story. The dramatic concentration invites the reader to share the protagonist's experience and to sense that the struggle is not only with the world but with oneself. Indeed, Crane later recalled the story as if this were its main point: "In a story of mine called 'An Experiment in Misery' I tried to make plain that the root of Bowery life is a sort of cowardice. Perhaps I mean a lack of ambition or to willingly be knocked flat and accept the licking." But there is more to "An Experiment" than this, for Crane here discovered the most dramatic form for his theme, the story of initiation into a terrible knowledge. The young man, who sees his night in a flophouse in images of the graveyard or the lower world, comes back from his journey into hell with a new sense of reality. After the event, he wears the guilty look "that comes with certain convictions." Having learned the meaning of despair and felt what it is to be cut off from "social position, comfort, the pleasures of living," he implicitly rejects these "unconquerable kingdoms" because they are founded on human wretchedness. Unlike Maggie Johnson, he has the capacity not only to feel but to understand. Whether he can also resist the moral undertow of experienced misery we cannot tell, for vision, like environment, is a tremendous thing: he will never again be as he was.

V

WAR, the second great subject Crane turned to, gave him material he could better mold to his conception of outward *and* inner struggle. In his tales of battle, he could so intensify the event and hold attention to ultimate questions that ordinary problems of character and society were excluded. Given his limitations, war was simpler for him to handle than poverty. The circumstances of battle did not imply an environmental determinism; the weaknesses of soldiers did not blur over into degeneracy; the violence of war could be taken as the absolutely given condition of an action, since men caught up in that ultimate violence do not have occasion to consider causes.

War provided a self-enclosing context within which Crane could work out his narratives of spiritual ordeal. The pattern did not change: storybook illusions of glory are the starting point, and yielding to the pres-

sure of battle is an alternative as false as yielding to the moral numbness of misery, whether it be by giving in to fear and turning coward or by submitting to the frenzy of the kill and turning madman. Popular illusion is the characteristic of the once-born; but Crane, the unconscious heir of Jonathan Edwards on religious affections, also showed the delusive states that might pass as evidence of being twice-born. Henry Fleming, in *The Red Badge of Courage* (1895), proves the need for discrimination: little need be said of his fear and panic, but his moment of physical courage, it should be noted, is a travesty of true virtue, "a temporary but sublime absence of selfishness"; his genuine manhood comes with the unassertive knowledge that "he had been to touch the great death, and found that, after all, it was but the great death."

True heroism for Crane cannot be judged by externals, and as the title of "A Mystery of Heroism" makes clear, that story gives a definitive illustration of his argument. The circumstantially induced courage which prompts Collins to cross under enemy fire to the well, and the panic with which he speeds back to his platoon with the filled bucket, explain away the apparent heroism of his act, while the spilled and empty bucket at the end proves the exploit worthless. But beneath the ironies of heroism which have been generally noticed lies the mystery. For the young soldier, crazed by the terrors of no man's land, runs past a dying artillery officer who asks him for a drink. "I can't" is his screamed answer, and yet, a moment later, he wheels back as if under a power stronger than his own will. There is no conscious goodness in the act—nor tenderness either: "Collins tried to hold the bucket steadily, but his shaking hands caused the water to splash all over the face of the dying man. Then he jerked it away and ran on." Yet every detail of the incident helps the reader to penetrate the mystery of heroism. Inarticulate, awkward, acting on an impulse which transcends the logical course of events, Collins passes the great test by giving water to a dying man. Though his deed is unrecognized by the world or even by himself, it is the secret glory which no irony can reduce.

The dying artilleryman to whom Collins gives water has the non-functional role of victim. In many of Crane's narratives, the victim's sacrifice is a pre-condition to the initiation into truth. Here, too, the logic of the naturalistic world which his fiction presents resembles the logic of Crane's inherited religion. The pattern is made clearer by the fact that after writing *The Red Badge*, the storyteller turned to poetry: Crane's verse gives his religious opinions with direct emotional expression.[1] The God of wrath and the God of sacrificial redemption both appear literally in the poetry rather than by suggestion as in the prose. Of the two conceptions of divinity, Crane believes in the latter, in the sense of affirming his loyalty, but he also believes that the former presides over the world and he affirms his moral defiance. His fiction runs on the lines of his belief. The casting out of fear and the finding of brotherly love are touchstones of his naturalistic parables.

## VI

EXCEPT for the Bible, Crane's literary background all too quickly came down to his contemporaries and in particular to William Dean Howells. In literature as in life, he was virtually without a knowledge of the past. He did read Emerson early and, with more telling effect, Whitman, Flaubert, and Tolstoy. Whitman's universal sympathy gave direction to the young man's eager observation, confirming the desire to record people and emotions beyond the pale of respectability. Flaubert taught a meticulous care for significant detail. Tolstoy, with what one critic has called his "ironic pacifism," supplied ideas of war as an institution, with its pretended control of chaos. But the influence of all these writers remained dormant until Howells'

realism helped Crane to find himself. What Howells saw was that in the name of respectability and fine ideals a hollow literature was falsifying the serious issues of life. To be sure, he wanted—for the sake of honesty—a middle-class literature that would represent the life of prudence, prosperity, and pleasantness; and he is condescendingly remembered for having said that "the more smiling aspects of life . . . are the more American." What is commonly overlooked is that that phrase states only an observation, and not a convention by which he encouraged in his readers a blindness to their environment and their fellow men. Not Howells, but his opponents—then and since—lulled men into thinking that the poor are no longer with us.

Realism was still very recent when Crane and his generation began to write. For the defenders of ideality, the symbolic battleground was "Boston": in the seventies, Mark Twain had jolted the keepers of the sacred fire by his innocent miscalculation of the Whittier fête. But soon the ruling class of American culture and respectability sustained the greater shock of apparent betrayal from within by Howells and James. The gentility of these novelists now seems so unquestionable that it is hard to conceive that their work of the eighties was denounced as scandalous; yet *The Rise of Silas Lapham* (1885) led to Howells' being regarded as a vulgarizer of literature, and *The Bostonians* (1886) lost James a large American audience for the rest of his life. Boston, as the holy city of the muses, proved to be a taboo subject for realism: the novelists knew how to distinguish between genuine values and sham ideals, but for the reading public, sanctity was indivisible. These writers, who seem so little dangerous today, fully recognized the implications of the critical wars. James had declared the artist's absolute freedom in the choice of subject. Howells, though he was personally as prudish as his opponents, roundly declared that "the worst French naturalism" was better than the best "unnaturalism" and fought for Zola as well as himself. Once the issues were thus clarified, writers could break through conventionality.

Howells had other principles of fiction be-

---

[1] Like all poems, Crane's cannot be taken as perfectly reliable biographical documents. But the literary explanation of the language of his verse points just as surely to his religious background: his verse often took the form of parable, a fact which is largely explained by his immersion in the Bible at home and in school; and the succinctness of the form virtually required the shorthand of religious terminology.

sides truthfulness. Since a democratic literature should be of the people, he called for openness to subjects generally called common and low. He believed that literary language ought to copy the language spoken by the people in the particular locale of a story. He insisted that a narrative could convey its true meaning to the people without the author's intruding his own rhetoric or analysis on the representation of life. His democratic realism—emphasizing the moral discovery of new material, the renewal of written language from living speech, and the exclusion of comment for the sake of dramatic construction—served the novel well, and it accounts for the taste behind Howells' welcoming the author of *Maggie* to the front rank of American fiction.

Crane's departures from the Howellsian theory, which he thought "identical" with his own, may be understood from the way he first encountered it. In August 1891, he covered for his brother's agency a literary lecture at a nearby New Jersey resort. Hamlin Garland, a second-generation realist, was then publishing somber stories of Middle Western rural life which violated the conventions of the American agrarian myth. In his zeal as a lecturer and prophet, Garland added something to the received doctrine of simple truthfulness. "The secret of every lasting success in art and literature lies," he later wrote, "in a powerful, sincere, emotional concept of life first, and, second, in the acquired power to convey that concept to others." His "veritism" differed from his master's realism in its stress on individuality and on skill, and it was precisely here that he pointed the way to the young reporter who heard him at Avon-by-the-Sea. When Crane covered the workingmen's parade at Asbury Park a year later, he was accurate, but he was being true first of all to himself and his way of seeing the event. The young author was a reporter of what he himself was sensitive to rather than a historian of things as they actually were.

The same may be said even more forcefully of *The Red Badge of Courage*, the subjectivity of which kept Howells from ever admiring it as much as he did *Maggie*. Crane had taken unconsciously the course which Henry James so thoroughly charted: what he saw depended not only on the objects seen, but on the point of view of the observer. As he put it, ". . . I understand that a man is born into the world with his own pair of eyes, and he is not at all responsible for his vision—he is merely responsible for his personal honesty. To keep close to this personal honesty is my supreme ambition."

Crane's artistic achievement was to fuse his particular vision and personal honesty. Little more need be said of his fertility of ironic reference, but the pictorial quality of his work, a matter of both style and method, repays a closer look: it is the signature of Crane's imagination. His earliest work shows the knack for vivid phrase which he gradually disciplined into a style best described by analogy to painting: Hamlin Garland's enthusiasm for Monet and the Impressionists and Crane's own life with artist friends (whose studios he haunted and often camped in during his luckless New York years) both help account for the visual effects in his writing. Impressionism in painting developed from the realistic tradition. The new practice avoided a literalist rendering of the parts for the sake of catching a true impression of the whole. But Crane's own understanding of the painters went deeper than that: he watched his friends record color and light more truthfully as they freed themselves from realistic conventions of seeing. Once, while with his brother in the country, he is reported to have said: "Will, isn't that cloud green? . . . But they wouldn't believe it if I put it in a book." Further, Crane went beyond the paintings he knew and mixed realistic impressionism with expressive color and imagery. The columns of troops "like two serpents crawling out of the cavern of the night," the "crimson roar" of battle, and even the red sun "pasted in the sky like a wafer" are Henry Fleming's personal vision. The expressionist technique seems less bizarre because the subjective coloring is not the only vividness in the objectively brilliant scene. And in the ending, when the young soldier has become a man, emotional vision and objective appearance come together in a final harmony—"Over the river a golden ray of sun came through the hosts of leaden rain clouds."

In his mastery of language Crane left Garland and even Howells far behind. The style of *The Red Badge*—impressionist and objective on the one hand, expressionist and subjective on the other—may have been an almost instinctive discovery, but its adaptation and use were a matter of conscious skill. Crane had worked out the proper medium for his irony. Because his characters commonly see more or less than is there to be seen, we depend on the author as well as the character for our picture of events. To use James's terms, the center of consciousness does not have, strictly speaking, a monopoly on our point of view. A remarkable tact preserves the illusion of unity. The author sees more than his characters without ever asserting that he knows more than they do. He lets their feelings and their vision conduct our responses along one line, while his own darting images may be reminding us of ironic perspectives and critical doubts. The man who could do this was no longer merely the precocious writer dependent on slim resources: he was becoming the mature artist who could rely on a supple craftsmanship.

## VII

TECHNICAL mastery freed Crane's imagination. At twenty-five, he had grown to the point where his imagination could embrace a larger world. His war dispatches from Greece, for example, showed a new recognition that battles are not the only events of war, nor soldiers the only sufferers. And as his view of personal experience broadened, so did his professional sense. When he went from Greece to England in 1897, he was welcomed into friendship by such writers as Joseph Conrad and Henry James. The older novelists helped give him a conception of their common craft. As a consequence, the mature art of Stephen Crane, along with its greater social depth, also has a richer literary context.

In "The Bride Comes to Yellow Sky," the writer works with conventions as well as against them. That Jack Potter, the town marshal, and Scratchy Wilson, the ferocious outlaw, should be realistically portrayed within a stale convention is the first sur-prise. More interesting, however, is their failure to fight it out to the death, for in the denouement Crane has crossed his Wild West story with that anticlimactic Western-humor tradition which also keeps Mark Twain's roaring raftsmen from actual combat. While the ordeal is still central to the plot, we see something more than courage at work: the outlaw cannot face the lonely stoical marshal because the code of melodrama doesn't cover the case of bridegrooms. The stylized villain is helplessly a type, unable to break free, and in the ancient comic manner, he is the ridiculous victim of his own routinized mind. Crane's irony is recognizably his own, but here it exists in the same world with Mark Twain.

The other side of the easy mastery of "The Bride" is a new humility—which can submit to the discipline of using a model. Tolstoy had always been the writer he admired most, but the young Crane had boyishly mocked at *War and Peace* with the comment that he "could have done the whole business in one-third the time." Without brashness now, he proceeded to make "Death and the Child" his own variation on themes by the older master. Crane's Peza, like Pierre Bezuhov at Borodino, wanders through a battle where nothing looks like the official version of what goes on and he can never quite mesh with organized reality. He is like Tolstoy's Prince Andrey, too, in his sense that the overarching natural scene diminishes the human event. In his encounter with death and panic, neither the blue sky nor the golden sun offers reassurance to his spirit. But the generations of men provide a great fact outside oneself which may help a man back to life. The lost man and the abandoned child are frightening images of human isolation in a violent world, but together they stand for the irreducible minimum of faith in the continuity of the race.

The year's work at the height of his artistic powers came to a sudden end: at the outbreak of the Spanish-American War, Crane responded as if he were personally summoned. One reason for his flight to adventure must certainly have been his often-expressed sense of not being able to sustain his best performances very long. He was also in constant anxiety over money since, even at the peak of creativity, he was getting more and more hopelessly into debt. Leaving England, he left behind the absurd and pressing question: Would his imagination or his credit be the first to crack? But he was running headlong into something grimmer still. When he tried to enlist in the navy, he learned from the medical examiner that he had tuberculosis. In Cuba as a correspondent, he played his role well, but fever and exhaustion gave him good cause for the lassitude of spirit that settled on him. Perhaps his stoical indifference had its roots in depression as well as courage. Clearly, when the correspondent in the white raincoat stood up before the firing Spaniards as if he were in a dream, he was giving himself to death. And although he failed to die in Cuba, he also failed for months to muster the will to go home.

When he did return to England, he was solicited by life. Cora's love, the warm friendship of Conrad and James, and recognition by the literary community might be said to have offered the perfect situation for a young writer. What he kept to himself as much as he could was the overwork and harassment, the falling off of his talent and the giving out of his body. After so often testing literature by experience, he was learning to measure life by imagined possibilities of grace. He could not always meet the standards he set forth in his writing, but he redeemed a portion of dignity from the enveloping chaos.

---

# REPORTAGE

---

## DARK SIDE OF WAR

❴ JOURNALISM became Crane's substitute for keeping a journal: though he kept working notebooks for his fiction, his record of experience was in his dispatches, like this one from the Greek-Turkish War. Despite his obviously having had to write this piece hastily in snatched moments between the episodes reported, he still maintained the control over selection which Willa Cather admired:

> He simply knew from the beginning how to handle detail. He estimated it at its true worth—made it serve his purpose and felt no further responsibility about it. . . . If he saw one thing that engaged him in a room, he mentioned it. If he saw one thing in a landscape that thrilled him, he put it on paper, but he never tried to make a faithful report of everything else within his field of vision, as if he were a conscientious salesman making out his expense-account.

This war report appeared in the New York *Journal* (May 23, 1897), under a bold headline announcing that Hearst's star reporters were performing: "STEPHEN CRANE AND JULIAN RALPH TELL OF WAR'S HORRORS AND TURKEY'S BOLD PLAN." Further down the same page, a reader would find the further article: "How Novelist Crane Acts on the Battlefield—Journal's War Correspondent's Sangfroid Under Fire at Velestino Described by a Fellow Worker," by John Bass. Hearst exploited the star-system to the fullest, and Crane was the star. ❵

ATHENS, May 22 (On Board the St. Marina, Which Left Chalkis, Greece, May 18.)—We are carrying the wounded away from Domokos. There are eight hundred bullet-torn men aboard, some of them dead. This steamer was formerly used for transporting sheep, but it was taken by the Government for ambulance purposes. It is not a nice place for a well man, but war takes the finical quality out of its victims, and the soldiers do not complain. The ship is not large enough for its dreadful freight. But the men must be moved, and so 800 bleeding soldiers are jammed together in an insufferably hot hole, the light in which is so faint that we cannot distinguish the living from the dead.

Near the hatch where I can see him is a man shot through the mouth. The bullet passed through both cheeks. He is asleep, with his head pillowed on the bosom of a dead comrade. He had been awake for days, doubtless, marching on bread and water, to be finally wounded at Domokos and taken aboard this steamer. He is too weary to mind either his wound or his awful pillow. There is a breeze on the gulf and the ship is rolling, heaving one wounded man against the other.

Some of the wounded were taken off at Chalkis; the others will be taken to Athens, because there is not room for them in the Chalkis hospitals. Already we have travelled a night and a day under these cheerful circumstances that war brings to some of those that engage in it.

When we with our suffering freight arrived at Piraeus they were selling the newspaper extra, and people were shouting, "Hurrah! Hurrah for war!"

And while they shouted a seemingly endless procession of stretchers proceeded from the ship, the still figures upon them.

There is just enough moaning and wailing to make a distinct chorus above the creaking of the deck timbers over that low hole where the lamps are smoking.

This is Wednesday, I think. We are at Stylidia. All day there have been clouds of dust upon the highroad over which Smolenski's division is retreating toward Thermopylae. The movement completely uncovers this place, and the Turks are advancing from Halmyros.

One long line of dust marked the road across the green plain where Smolenski marched away. And the people stared at this and then at the great mountains in back of the town, whence the Turks were coming. All the household goods of the city were piled on the pier. The town was completely empty, except for two battalions of Smolenski's rear guard, who slept in the streets, worn out, after a twenty hours' march. We loaded the steamer and schooner with women and children, and household goods. The anchor was raised by two man-of-war's men, three fugitives, and one Greek Red Cross nurse.

The refugees seemed dazed. The old women particularly, uprooted from the spot they had lived so long, kept their red eyes turned toward the shore as they sat on their rough bundles of clothes and blankets.

Our deck looked like an emigrant quarter of an Atlantic liner, except for the sick soldiers. The Journal steamer then went to St. Marina and landed the hospital stores.

Lieutenant-Colonel Caracolas came aboard there, much disturbed because some bread had been left at Stylidia. He was at the head of the commissary department of Smolenski's division. He asked us if we would try to get the bread. We agreed and found another schooner. We told the captain we were going to take him to Stylidia and he flatly refused to go. There was no time for argument; our extra bluejackets, seven in number, promptly stormed the schooner and took it by assault. I guess the captain of the schooner is talking of the outrage yet. The bluejackets got us a hawser, raised the anchor, and we towed the protesting schooner back to Stylidia, with the captain on the bow, gesticulating violently throughout the voyage. Incidentally we never found the bread.

We steamed back to St. Marina and found Dr. Belline, chief surgeon of the Greek army. He was worried about the safety of the hospital at St. Marina, but no orders had been issued for its removal. The obvious thing to do was to get orders from Thermopylae headquarters, and we carried the doctor across the gulf. He got the orders promptly and we took him back to St. Marina and took aboard the wounded men and Red Cross nurses of the hospital. The last boat had left the shore when a soldier came and said something to the interpreter, who shook his head negatively. The soldier turned quietly away.

On board the steamer your correspondent idly asked the interpreter what the soldier had said, and he answered that the soldier had asked for transportation to Chalkis on the ground that he was sick. The interpreter thought the man too well to go on a boat containing wounded men.

We sent ashore and after some trouble found the soldier. He was ill with fever, was shot through the calf of the leg and his knees were raw from kneeling in the trenches.

There is more of this sort of thing in war than glory and heroic death, flags, banners, shouting and victory.

---

# STORIES

---

## AN EXPERIMENT IN MISERY

⟮ THIS story is in many ways the best of Crane's Bowery fiction. The quality of personal vision is partly defined by the way the character who first appears to the youth "like an assassin" is known thereafter by his epithet, "the assassin." Concentrating on the subjective experience, Crane cut from the book version the beginning and end which the story originally carried in the New York *Press* (April 22, 1894):

Two men stood regarding a tramp.

"I wonder how he feels," said one, reflectively. "I suppose he is homeless, friendless, and has, at the most, only a few cents in his pocket. And if this is so, I wonder how he feels."

The other, being the elder, spoke with an air of authoritative wisdom. "You can tell nothing of it unless you are in that condition yourself. It is idle to speculate about it from this distance."

"I suppose so," said the younger man, and then he added as from an inspiration: "I think I'll try it. Rags and tatters, you know, a couple of dimes, and hungry, too, if possible. Perhaps I could discover his point of view or something near it."

"Well, you might," said the other, and from those words begins this veracious narrative of an experiment in misery.

The youth went to the studio of an artist friend, who, from his store, rigged him out in an aged suit and a brown derby hat that had been made long years before. And then the youth went forth to try to eat as the tramp may eat, and sleep as the wanderers sleep.

. . . . . . . . . . . . . . . . . . . . . . . . . .

"Well," said the friend, "did you discover his point of view?"

"I don't know that I did," replied the young man; "but at any rate I think my own has undergone a considerable alteration."

IT WAS late at night, and a fine rain was swirling softly down, causing the pavements to glisten with hue of steel and blue and yellow in the rays of the innumerable lights. A youth was trudging slowly, without enthusiasm, with his hands buried deep in his trousers pockets, toward the downtown places where beds can be hired for coppers. He was clothed in an aged and tattered suit, and his derby was a marvel of dust-covered crown and torn rim. He was going forth to eat as the wanderer may eat, and sleep as the homeless sleep. By the time he had reached City Hall Park he was so completely plastered with yells of "bum" and "hobo," and with various unholy epithets that small boys had applied to him at intervals, that he was in a state of the most profound dejection. The sifting rain saturated the old velvet collar of his overcoat, and as the wet cloth pressed against his neck, he felt that there no longer could be pleasure in life. He looked about him searching for an outcast of highest degree that they two might share miseries, but the lights threw a quivering glare over rows and circles of deserted benches that glistened damply, showing patches of wet sod behind them. It seemed that their usual freights had fled on this night to better things. There were only squads of well-dressed Brooklyn people who swarmed toward the bridge.

The young man loitered about for a time and then went shuffling off down Park Row. In the sudden descent in style of the dress of the crowd he felt relief, and as if he were at last in his own country. He began to see tatters that matched his tatters. In Chatham Square there were aimless men strewn in front of saloons and lodging-houses, standing sadly, patiently, reminding one vaguely of the attitudes of chickens in a storm. He aligned himself with these men, and turned slowly to occupy himself with the flowing life of the great street.

Through the mists of the cold and storming night, the cable cars went in silent procession, great affairs shining with red and brass, moving with formidable power, calm and irresistible, dangerful and gloomy, breaking silence only by the loud fierce cry of the gong. Two rivers of people swarmed along the sidewalks, spattered with black mud which made each shoe leave a scarlike impression. Overhead, elevated trains with a shrill grinding of the wheels stopped at the station, which upon its leg-like pillars seemed to resemble some monstrous kind of crab squatting over the street. The quick fat puffings of the engines could be heard. Down an alley there were somber curtains of purple and black, on which street lamps dully glittered like embroidered flowers.

A saloon stood with a voracious air on a corner. A sign leaning against the front of the doorpost announced "Free hot soup to-night!" The swing doors, snapping to and fro like ravenous lips, made gratified smacks as the saloon gorged itself with plump men, eating with astounding and endless appetite, smiling in some indescribable manner as the men came from all directions like sacrifices to a heathenish superstition.

Caught by the delectable sign, the young man allowed himself to be swallowed. A bartender placed a schooner of dark and portentous beer on the bar. Its monumental form upreared until the froth atop was above the crown of the young man's brown derby.

"Soup over there, gents," said the bartender affably. A little yellow man in rags and the youth grasped their schooners and went with speed toward a lunch-counter, where a man with oily but imposing whiskers ladled genially from a kettle until he had furnished his two mendicants with a soup that was steaming hot, and in which there were little floating suggestions of chicken. The young man, sipping his broth, felt the cordiality expressed by the warmth of the mixture, and he beamed at the man with oily but imposing whiskers, who was presiding like a priest behind an altar. "Have some more, gents?" he inquired of the two sorry figures before him. The little yellow man accepted with a swift gesture, but the youth shook his head and went out, following a man whose wondrous seediness promised that he would have a knowledge of cheap lodging-houses.

On the sidewalk he accosted the seedy man. "Say, do you know a cheap place to sleep?"

The other hesitated for a time, gazing sideways. Finally he nodded in the direction of the street. "I sleep up there," he said, "when I've got the price."

"How much?"

"Ten cents."

The young man shook his head dolefully. "That's too rich for me."

At that moment there approached the two a reeling man in strange garments. His head was a fuddle of bushy hair and whiskers, from which his eyes peered with a guilty slant. In a close scrutiny it was possible to distinguish the cruel lines of a mouth which looked as if its lips had just closed with satisfaction over some tender and piteous morsel. He appeared like an assassin steeped in crimes performed awkwardly.

But at this time his voice was tuned to the coaxing key of an affectionate puppy. He looked at the men with wheedling eyes, and began to sing a little melody for charity. "Say, gents, can't yeh give a poor feller a couple of cents t' git a bed? I got five, an' I gits anudder two I gits me a bed. Now, on th' square, gents, can't yeh jest gimme two cents t' git a bed? Now, yeh know how a respecterble gentlem'n feels when he's down on his luck, an' I—"

The seedy man, staring with imperturbable countenance at a train which clattered overhead, interrupted in an expressionless voice: "Ah, go t' hell!"

But the youth spoke to the prayerful assassin in tones of astonishment and inquiry. "Say, you must be crazy! Why don't yeh strike somebody that looks as if they had money?"

The assassin, tottering about on his uncertain legs, and at intervals brushing imaginary obstacles from before his nose, entered into a long explanation of the psychology of the situation. It was so profound that it was unintelligible.

When he had exhausted the subject, the young man said to him: "Let's see th' five cents."

The assassin wore an expression of drunken woe at this sentence, filled with suspicion of him. With a deeply pained air he began to fumble in his clothing, his red hands trembling. Presently he announced in a voice of bitter grief, as if he had been betrayed: "There's on'y four."

"Four," said the young man thoughtfully. "Well, look-a here, I'm a stranger here, an' if ye'll steer me to your cheap joint I'll find the other three."

The assassin's countenance became instantly radiant with joy. His whiskers quivered with the wealth of his alleged emotions. He seized the young man's hand in a transport of delight and friendliness.

"B' Gawd," he cried, "if ye'll do that, b' Gawd, I'd say yeh was a damned good fellow, I would, an' I'd remember yeh all m' life, I would, b' Gawd, an' if I ever got a chance I'd return the compliment"—he spoke with drunken dignity— "b' Gawd, I'd treat yeh white, I would, an' I'd allus remember yeh."

The young man drew back, looking at the assassin coldly. "Oh, that's all right," he said. "You show me th' joint—that's all you've got t' do."

The assassin, gesticulating gratitude, led the young man along a dark street. Finally he stopped before a little dusty door. He raised his hand impressively. "Look-a here," he said, and there was a thrill of deep and ancient wisdom upon his face, "I've brought yeh here, an' that's my part, ain't it? If th' place don't suit yeh, yeh needn't git mad at me, need yeh? There won't be no bad feelin', will there?"

"No," said the young man.

The assassin waved his arm tragically, and led the march up the steep stairway. On the way the young man furnished the assassin with three pennies. At the top a man with benevolent spectacles looked at them through a hole in a board. He collected their money, wrote some names on a register, and speedily was leading the two men along a gloom-shrouded corridor.

Shortly after the beginning of this journey the young man felt his liver turn white, for from the dark and secret places of the building there suddenly came to his nostrils strange and unspeakable odors, that assailed him like malignant diseases with wings. They seemed to be from human bodies closely packed in dens; the exhalations from a hundred pairs of reeking lips; the fumes from a thousand bygone debauches; the expression of a thousand present miseries.

A man, naked save for a little snuff-colored undershirt, was parading sleepily along the corridor. He rubbed his eyes and, giving vent to a prodigious yawn, demanded to be told the time.

"Half-past one."

The man yawned again. He opened a door, and for a moment his form was outlined against a black, opaque interior. To this door came the three men, and as it was again opened the unholy odors rushed out like fiends, so that the young man was obliged to struggle as against an overpowering wind.

It was some time before the youth's eyes were good in the intense gloom within, but the man with benevolent spectacles led him skilfully, pausing but a moment to deposit the limp assassin upon a cot. He took the youth to a cot that lay tranquilly by the window, and showing him a tall locker for clothes that stood near the head with the ominous air of a tombstone, left him.

The youth sat on his cot and peered about him. There was a gas-jet in a distant part of the room, that burned a small flickering orange-hued flame. It caused vast masses of tumbled shadows in all parts of the place; save where, immediately about it, there was a little gray haze. As the young man's eyes became used to the darkness, he could see upon the cots that thickly littered the floor the forms of men sprawled out, lying in death-like silence, or heaving and snoring with tremendous effort, like stabbed fish.

The youth locked his derby and his shoes in the mummy-case near him, and then lay down with an old and familiar coat around his shoulders. A blanket he handled gingerly, drawing it over part of the coat. The cot was covered with leather, and as cold as melting snow. The youth was obliged to shiver for some time on this affair, which was like a slab. Presently, however, his chill gave him peace, and during this period of leisure from it he turned his head to stare at his friend the assassin, whom he could dimly discern where he lay sprawled on a cot in the abandon of a man filled with drink. He was snoring with incredible vigor. His wet hair and beard dimly glistened, and his inflamed nose shone with subdued luster like a red light in a fog.

Within reach of the youth's hand was one who lay with yellow breast and shoulders bare to the cold draughts. One arm hung over the side of the cot, and the fingers lay full length upon the wet cement floor of the room. Beneath the inky brows could be seen the eyes of the man, exposed by the partly opened lids. To the youth it seemed that he and this corpse-like being were exchanging a prolonged stare, and that the other threatened with his eyes. He drew back, watching his neighbor from the shadows of his blanket-edge. The man did not move once through the night, but lay in this stillness as of death like a body stretched out expectant of the surgeon's knife.

And all through the room could be seen the tawny hues of naked flesh, limbs thrust into the darkness, projecting beyond the cots; upreared knees, arms hanging long and thin over the cot-edges. For the most part they were statuesque, carven, dead. With the curious lockers standing all about like tombstones, there was a strange effect of a graveyard where bodies were merely flung.

Yet occasionally could be seen limbs wildly tossing in fantastic nightmare gestures, accompanied by guttural cries, grunts, oaths. And there was one fellow off in a gloomy corner, who in his dreams was oppressed by some frightful calamity, for of a sudden he began to utter long wails that went almost like yells from a hound, echoing wailfully and weird through this chill place of tombstones where men lay like the dead.

The sound, in its high piercing beginnings that dwindled to final melancholy moans, expressed a red and grim tragedy of the unfathomable possibilities of the man's dreams. But to the youth these were not merely the shrieks of a vision-pierced man: they were an utterance of the meaning of the room and its occupants. It was to him the protest of the wretch who feels the touch of the imperturbable granite wheels, and who then cries with an impersonal eloquence, with a strength not from him, giving voice to the wail of a whole section, a class, a people. This, weaving into the young man's brain, and mingling with his views of the vast and somber shadows that, like mighty black fingers, curled around the naked bodies, made the young man so that he did not sleep, but lay carving the biographies for these men from his meager experience. At times the fellow in the corner howled in a writhing agony of his imaginations.

Finally a long lance-point of gray light shot through the dusty panes of the window. Without, the young man could see roofs drearily white in the dawning. The point of light yellowed and grew brighter, until the golden rays of the morning sun came in bravely and strong. They touched with radiant color the form of a small fat man who snored in stuttering fashion. His round and shiny bald head glowed suddenly with the valor of a decoration. He sat up, blinked at the sun, swore fretfully, and pulled his blanket over the ornamental splendors of his head.

The youth contentedly watched this rout of the shadows before the bright spears of the sun, and presently he slumbered. When he awoke he heard the voice of the assassin raised in valiant curses. Putting up his head, he perceived his comrade seated on the side of the cot engaged in scratching his neck with long fingernails that rasped like files.

"Hully Jee, dis is a new breed. They've got can-openers on their feet." He continued in a violent tirade.

The young man hastily unlocked his closet and took out his shoes and hat. As he sat on the side of the cot lacing his shoes, he glanced about and saw that daylight had made the room comparatively commonplace and uninteresting. The men, whose faces seemed stolid, serene, or absent, were engaged in dressing, while a great crackle of bantering conversation arose.

A few were parading in unconcerned nakedness. Here and there were men of brawn, whose skins shone clear and ruddy. They took splendid poses, standing massively like chiefs. When they had dressed in their ungainly garments there was an extraordinary change. They then showed bumps and deficiencies of all kinds.

There were others who exhibited many deformities. Shoulders were slanting, humped, pulled this way and pulled that way. And notable among these latter men was the little fat man who had refused to allow his head to be glorified. His pudgy form, builded like a pear, bustled to and fro, while he swore in fishwife fashion. It appeared that some article of his apparel had vanished.

The young man attired himself speedily, and went to his friend the assassin. At first the latter looked dazed at the sight of the youth. This face seemed to be appealing to him through the cloud-wastes of his memory. He scratched his neck and reflected. At last he grinned, a broad smile gradually spreading until his countenance was a round illumination. "Hello, Willie," he cried cheerily.

"Hello," said the young man. "Are yeh ready t' fly?"

"Sure." The assassin tied his shoe carefully with some twine and came ambling.

When he reached the street the young man experienced no sudden relief from unholy atmospheres. He had forgotten all about them, and had been breathing naturally, and with no sensation of discomfort or distress.

He was thinking of these things as he walked along the street, when he was suddenly startled by feeling the assassin's hand, trembling with excitement, clutching his arm, and when the assassin spoke, his voice went into quavers from a supreme agitation.

"I'll be hully, bloomin' blowed if there wasn't a feller with a nightshirt on up there in that joint."

The youth was bewildered for a moment, but presently he turned to smile indulgently at the assassin's humor. "Oh, you're a damned liar," he merely said.

Whereupon the assassin began to gesture extravagantly and take oath by strange gods. He frantically placed himself at the mercy of remarkable fates if his tale were not true. "Yes, he did! I cross m' heart thousan' times!" he protested, and at the moment his eyes were large with amazement, his mouth wrinkled in unnatural glee. "Yessir! A nightshirt! A hully white nightshirt!"

"You lie!"

"No, sir! I hope ter die b'fore I kin git anudder ball if there wasn't a jay wid a hully, bloomin' white nightshirt!"

His face was filled with the infinite wonder of it. "A hully white nightshirt," he continually repeated.

The young man saw the dark entrance to a basement restaurant. There was a sign which read "No mystery about our hash!" and there were other age-stained and world-battered legends which told him that the place was within his means. He stopped before it and spoke to the assassin. "I guess I'll git somethin' t' eat."

At this the assassin, for some reason, appeared to be quite embarrassed. He gazed at the seductive front of the eating-place for a moment. Then he started slowly up the street. "Well, good-bye, Willie," he said bravely.

For an instant the youth studied the departing figure. Then he called out, "Hol' on a minnet." As they came together he spoke in a certain fierce way, as if he feared that the other would think him to be charitable. "Look-a here, if yeh wanta git some breakfas' I'll lend yeh three cents t' do it with. But say, look-a here, you've gotta git out an' hustle. I ain't goin' t' support yeh, or I'll go broke b'fore night. I ain't no millionaire."

"I take me oath, Willie," said the assassin earnestly, "th' on'y thing I really needs is a ball.[1] Me t'roat feels like a fryin'-pan. But as I can't get a ball, why, th' next bes' thing is breakfast, an' if yeh do that for me, b' Gawd, I say yeh was th' whitest lad I ever see."

They spent a few moments in dexterous exchanges of phrases, in which they each protested that the other was, as the assassin had originally said, "a respecterble gentlem'n." And they concluded with mutual assurances that they were the souls of intelligence and virtue. Then they went into the restaurant.

There was a long counter, dimly lighted from hidden sources. Two or three men in soiled white aprons rushed here and there.

The youth bought a bowl of coffee for two cents and a roll for one cent. The assassin purchased the same. The bowls were webbed with brown seams, and the tin spoons wore an air of having emerged from the first pyramid. Upon them were black moss-like encrustations of age, and they were bent and scarred from the attacks of long-forgotten teeth. But over their repast the wanderers waxed warm and mellow. The assassin grew affable as the hot mixture went soothingly down his parched throat, and the young man felt courage flow in his veins.

Memories began to throng in on the assassin, and he brought forth long tales, intricate, incoherent, delivered with a chattering swiftness as from an old woman. "—great job out 'n Orange. Boss keep yeh hustlin', though, all time. I was there three days, and then I went an ask 'im t' lend me a dollar. 'G-g-go ter the devil,' he says, an' I lose me job.

"South no good. Damn niggers work for

AN EXPERIMENT IN MISERY.    1. **ball:** an alcoholic drink.

twenty-five an' thirty cents a day. Run white man out. Good grub, though. Easy livin'.

"Yas; useter work little in Toledo, raftin' logs. Make two or three dollars er day in the spring. Lived high. Cold as ice, though, in the winter.

"I was raised in northern N' York. O-o-oh, yeh jest oughto live there. No beer ner whisky, though, 'way off in the woods. But all th' good hot grub yeh can eat. B' Gawd, I hung around there long as I could till th' ol' man fired me. 'Git t' hell outa here, yeh wuthless skunk, git t' hell outa here, an' go die,' he says. 'You're a hell of a father,' I says, 'you are,' an' I quit 'im."

As they were passing from the dim eating-place, they encountered an old man who was trying to steal forth with a tiny package of food, but a tall man with an indomitable moustache stood dragon-fashion, barring the way of escape. They heard the old man raise a plaintive protest. "Ah, you always want to know what I take out, and you never see that I usually bring a package in here from my place of business."

As the wanderers trudged slowly along Park Row, the assassin began to expand and grow blithe. "B' Gawd, we've been livin' like kings," he said, smacking appreciative lips.

"Look out, or we'll have t' pay fer it t'-night," said the youth with gloomy warning.

But the assassin refused to turn his gaze toward the future. He went with a limping step, into which he injected a suggestion of lamb-like gambols. His mouth was wreathed in a red grin.

In City Hall Park the two wanderers sat down in the little circle of benches sanctified by traditions of their class. They huddled in their old garments, slumbrously conscious of the march of the hours which for them had no meaning.

The people of the street hurrying hither and thither made a blend of black figures, changing, yet frieze-like. They walked in their good clothes as upon important missions, giving no gaze to the two wanderers seated upon the benches. They expressed to the young man his infinite distance from all that he valued. Social position, comfort, the pleasures of living were unconquerable kingdoms. He felt a sudden awe.

And in the background a multitude of buildings, of pitiless hues and sternly high, were to him emblematic of a nation forcing its regal head into the clouds, throwing no downward glances; in the sublimity of its aspirations ignoring the wretches who may flounder at its feet. The roar of the city in his ear was to him the confusion of strange tongues, babbling heedlessly; it was the clink of coin, the voice of the city's hopes, which were to him no hopes.

He confessed himself an outcast, and his eyes from under the lowered rim of his hat began to glance guiltily, wearing the criminal expression that comes with certain convictions.

## A MYSTERY OF HEROISM

❲ THIS story is truly a companion-piece to *The Red Badge of Courage*, for it first appeared August 1 and 2, 1895, in the Philadelphia *Press*, the newspaper that had serialized the novel eight months before and then brought Crane down to be personally congratulated by the whole enthusiastic staff. The first object of irony in both tales is the popular attitude he was satirizing in verse at about the same time:

> A youth in apparel that glittered
> Went to walk in a grim forest.
> There he met an assassin
> Attired all in garb of old days;
> He, scowling through the thickets,
> And dagger poised quivering,
> Rushed upon the youth.
> "Sir," said this latter,
> "I am enchanted, believe me,
> To die, thus,
> In this medieval fashion,
> According to the best legends;
> Ah, what joy!"
> Then took he the wound, smiling,
> And died, content.

THE DARK uniforms of the men were so coated with dust from the incessant wrestling of the two armies that the regiment almost seemed a part of the clay bank which shielded them from the shells. On the top of the hill a battery was arguing in tremendous roars with some other guns, and to the eye of the infantry the artillerymen, the guns, the caissons, the horses, were distinctly outlined upon the blue sky. When a piece was fired, a red streak as round as a log flashed low in the heavens, like a monstrous bolt of lightning. The men of the battery wore white duck trousers, which somehow emphasized their legs; and when they ran and crowded in little groups at the bidding of the shouting officers, it was more impressive than usual to the infantry.

Fred Collins, of A Company, was saying: "Thunder! I wisht I had a drink. Ain't there any water round here?" Then somebody yelled: "There goes th' bugler!"

As the eyes of half the regiment swept in one machine-like movement, there was an instant's picture of a horse in a great convulsive leap of a death-wound and a rider leaning back with a crooked arm and spread fingers before his face. On the ground was the crimson terror of an exploding shell, with fibers of flame that seemed like lances. A glittering bugle swung clear of the rider's back as fell headlong the horse and the man. In the air was an odor as from a conflagration.

Sometimes they of the infantry looked down at a fair little meadow which spread at their feet. Its long green grass was rippling gently in a breeze. Beyond it was the gray form of a house half torn to pieces by shells and by the busy axes of soldiers who had pursued firewood. The line of an old fence was now dimly marked by long weeds and by an occasional post. A shell had blown the wellhouse to fragments. Little lines of gray smoke ribboning upward from some embers indicated the place where had stood the barn.

From beyond a curtain of green woods there came the sound of some stupendous scuffle, as if two animals of the size of islands were fighting. At a distance there were occasional appearances of swift-moving men, horses, batteries, flags, and with the crashing of infantry volleys were heard, often, wild and frenzied cheers. In the midst of it all Smith and Ferguson, two privates of A Company, were engaged in a heated discussion which involved the greatest questions of the national existence.

The battery on the hill presently engaged in a frightful duel. The white legs of the gunners scampered this way and that way, and the officers redoubled their shouts. The guns, with their demeanors of stolidity and courage, were typical of something infinitely self-possessed in this clamor of death that swirled around the hill.

One of a "swing" team was suddenly smitten quivering to the ground, and his maddened brethren dragged his torn body in their struggle to escape from this turmoil and danger. A young soldier astride one of the leaders swore and fumed in his saddle and furiously jerked at the bridle. An officer screamed out an order so violently that his voice broke and ended the sentence in a falsetto shriek.

The leading company of infantry regiment was somewhat exposed, and the colonel ordered it moved more fully under the shelter of the hill. There was the clank of steel against steel.

A lieutenant of the battery rode down and passed them, holding his right arm carefully in his left hand. And it was as if this arm was not at all a part of him, but belonged to another man. His sober and reflective charger went slowly. The officer's face was grimy and perspiring, and his uniform was tousled as if he had been in direct grapple with an enemy. He smiled grimly when the men stared at him. He turned his horse toward the meadow.

Collins, of A Company, said: "I wisht I had a drink. I bet there's water in that there ol' well yonder!"

"Yes; but how you goin' to git it?"

For the little meadow which intervened was now suffering a terrible onslaught of shells. Its green and beautiful calm had vanished utterly. Brown earth was being flung in monstrous handfuls. And there was a massacre of the young blades of grass. They were being torn, burned, obliterated. Some curious fortune of the battle had made this gentle little meadow the object of the red hate of the shells, and each one as it exploded seemed like an imprecation in the face of a maiden.

The wounded officer who was riding across this expanse said to himself: "Why, they couldn't shoot any harder if the whole army was massed here!"

A shell struck the gray ruins of the house, and as, after the roar, the shattered wall fell in fragments, there was a noise which resembled the flapping of shutters during a wild gale of winter. Indeed, the infantry paused in the shelter of the bank appeared as men standing upon a shore contemplating a madness of the sea. The angel of calamity had under its glance the battery upon the hill. Fewer white-legged men labored about the guns. A shell had smitten one of the pieces, and after the flare, the smoke, the dust, the wrath of this blow were gone, it was possible to see white legs stretched horizontally upon the ground. And at that interval to the rear where it is the business of battery horses to stand with their noses to the fight, awaiting the command to drag their guns out of the destruction, or into it, or wheresoever these incomprehensible humans demanded with whip and spur—in this line of passive and dumb spectators, whose fluttering hearts yet would not let them forget the iron laws of man's control of them—in this rank of brute-soldiers there had been relentless and hideous carnage. From the ruck of bleeding and prostrate horses, the men of the infantry could see one animal raising its stricken body with its forelegs and turning its nose with mystic and profound eloquence toward the sky.

Some comrades joked Collins about his thirst. "Well, if yeh want a drink so bad, why don't yeh go git it?"

"Well, I will in a minnet, if yeh don't shut up!"

A lieutenant of artillery floundered his horse straight down the hill with as little concern as if it were level ground. As he galloped past the colonel of the infantry, he threw up his hand in swift salute. "We've got to get out of that," he roared angrily. He was a black-bearded officer, and his eyes, which resembled beads, sparkled like those of an insane man. His jumping horse sped along the column of infantry.

The fat major, standing carelessly with his sword held horizontally behind him and with his legs far apart, looked after the receding horseman and laughed. "He wants to get back with orders pretty quick, or there'll be no batt'ry left," he observed.

The wise young captain of the second company hazarded to the lieutenant-colonel that the enemy's infantry would probably soon attack the hill, and the lieutenant-colonel snubbed him.

A private in one of the rear companies looked out over the meadow, and then turned to a companion and said, "Look there, Jim!" It was the wounded officer from the battery, who some time before had started to ride across the meadow, supporting his right arm carefully with his left hand. This man had encountered a shell, apparently, at a time when no one perceived him, and he could now be seen lying face downward with a stirruped foot stretched across the body of his dead horse. A leg of the charger extended slantingly upward, precisely as stiff as a stake. Around this motionless pair the shells still howled.

There was a quarrel in A Company. Collins was shaking his fist in the faces of some laughing comrades. "Dern yeh! I ain't afraid t' go. If yeh say much, I will go!"

"Of course, yeh will! You'll run through that there medder, won't yeh?"

Collins said, in a terrible voice: "You see now!"

At this ominous threat his comrades broke into renewed jeers.

Collins gave them a dark scowl, and went to find his captain. The latter was conversing with the colonel of the regiment.

"Captain," said Collins, saluting and standing at attention—in those days all trousers bagged at the knees—"Captain, I want t' get permission to go git some water from that there well over yonder!"

The colonel and the captain swung about simultaneously and stared across the meadow. The captain laughed. "You must be pretty thirsty, Collins?"

"Yes, sir, I am."

"Well—ah," said the captain. After a moment, he asked, "Can't you wait?"

"No, sir."

The colonel was watching Collins's face. "Look here, my lad," he said, in a pious sort of voice— "Look here, my lad"—Collins was not a lad— "don't you think that's taking pretty big risks for a little drink of water?"

"I dunno," said Collins uncomfortably. Some of the resentment toward his companions, which perhaps had forced him into this affair, was beginning to fade. "I dunno w'ether 'tis."

The colonel and the captain contemplated him for a time.

"Well," said the captain finally.

"Well," said the colonel, "if you want to go, why, go."

Collins saluted. "Much obliged t' yeh."

As he moved away the colonel called after him. "Take some of the other boys' canteens with you, an' hurry back, now."

"Yes, sir, I will."

The colonel and the captain looked at each other then, for it had suddenly occurred that they could not for the life of them tell whether Collins wanted to go or whether he did not.

They turned to regard Collins, and as they perceived him surrounded by gesticulating comrades, the colonel said: "Well, by thunder! I guess he's going."

Collins appeared as a man dreaming. In the midst of the questions, the advice, the warnings, all the excited talk of his company mates, he maintained a curious silence.

They were very busy in preparing him for his ordeal. When they inspected him carefully, it was somewhat like the examination that grooms give a horse before a race; and they were amazed, staggered, by the whole affair. Their astonishment found vent in strange repetitions.

"Are yeh sure a-goin'?" they demanded again and again.

"Certainly I am," cried Collins at last, furiously.

He strode sullenly away from them. He was swinging five or six canteens by their cords. It seemed that his cap would not remain firmly on his head, and often he reached and pulled it down over his brow.

There was a general movement in the compact column. The long animal-like thing moved slightly. Its four hundred eyes were turned upon the figure of Collins.

"Well, sir, if that ain't th' derndest thing! I never thought Fred Collins had the blood in him for that kind of business."

"What's he goin' to do, anyhow?"

"He's goin' to that well there after water."

"We ain't dyin' of thirst, are we? That's foolishness."

"Well, somebody put him up to it, an' he's doin' it."

"Say, he must be a desperate cuss."

When Collins faced the meadow and walked away from the regiment, he was vaguely conscious that a chasm, the deep valley of all prides, was suddenly between him and his comrades. It was provisional, but the provision was that he return as a victor. He had blindly been led by quaint emotions, and laid himself under an obligation to walk squarely up to the face of death.

But he was not sure that he wished to make a retraction, even if he could do so without shame. As a matter of truth, he was sure of very little. He was mainly surprised.

It seemed to him supernaturally strange that he had allowed his mind to manœuvre his body into such a situation. He understood that it might be called dramatically great.

However, he had no full appreciation of anything, excepting that he was actually conscious of being dazed. He could feel his dulled mind groping after the form and color of this incident. He wondered why he did not feel some keen agony of fear cutting his sense like a knife. He wondered at this, because human expression had said loudly for centuries that men should feel afraid of certain things, and that all men who did not feel this fear were phenomena—heroes.

He was, then, a hero. He suffered that disappointment which we would all have if we discovered that we were ourselves capable of those deeds which we most admire in history and legend. This, then, was a hero. After all, heroes were not much.

No, it could not be true. He was not a hero. Heroes had no shames in their lives, and, as for him, he remembered borrowing fifteen dollars from a friend and promising to pay it back the next day, and then avoiding that friend for ten months. When, at home, his mother had aroused him for the early labor of his life on the farm, it had often been his fashion to be irritable, childish, diabolical; and his mother had died since he had come to the war.

He saw that, in this matter of the well, the canteens, the shells, he was an intruder in the land of fine deeds.

He was now about thirty paces from his comrades. The regiment had just turned its many faces toward him.

From the forest of terrific noises there suddenly emerged a little uneven line of men. They fired fiercely and rapidly at distant foliage on which appeared little puffs of white smoke. The spatter of skirmish firing was added to the thunder of the guns on the hill. The little line of men ran forward. A color-sergeant fell flat with his flag as if he had slipped on ice. There was hoarse cheering from this distant field.

Collins suddenly felt that two demon fingers were pressed into his ears. He could see nothing but flying arrows, flaming red. He lurched from the shock of this explosion, but he made a mad rush for the house, which he viewed as a man submerged to the neck in a boiling surf might view the shore. In the air little pieces of shell howled, and the earthquake explosions drove him insane with the menace of their roar. As he ran the canteens knocked together with a rhythmical tinkling.

As he neared the house, each detail of the scene became vivid to him. He was aware of some bricks of the vanished chimney lying on the sod. There was a door which hung by one hinge.

Rifle bullets called forth by the insistent skirmishers came from the far-off bank of foliage. They mingled with the shells and the pieces of shells until the air was torn in all directions by hootings, yells, howls. The sky was full of fiends who directed all their wild rage at his head.

When he came to the well, he flung himself face downward and peered into its darkness. There were furtive silver glintings some feet from the surface. He grabbed one of the canteens and, unfastening its cap, swung it down by the cord. The water flowed slowly in with an indolent gurgle.

And now, as he lay with his face turned away, he was suddenly smitten with the terror. It came upon his heart like the grasp of claws. All the power faded from his muscles. For an instant he was no more than a dead man.

The canteen filled with a maddening slowness, in the manner of all bottles. Presently he recovered his strength and addressed a screaming oath to it. He leaned over until it seemed as if he intended to try to push water into it with his hands. His eyes as he gazed down into the well shone like two pieces of metal, and in their expression was a great appeal and a great curse. The stupid water derided him.

There was the blaring thunder of a shell. Crimson light shone through the swift-boiling smoke and made a pink reflection on part of the wall of the well. Collins jerked out his arm and canteen with the same motion that a man would use in withdrawing his head from a furnace.

He scrambled erect and glared and hesitated. On the ground near him lay the old well bucket, with a length of rusty chain. He lowered it swiftly into the well. The bucket struck the water and then, turning lazily over, sank. When, with hand reaching tremblingly over hand, he hauled it out, it knocked often against the walls of the well and spilled some of its contents.

In running with a filled bucket, a man can adopt but one kind of gait. So, through this terrible field over which screamed practical angels of death, Collins ran in the manner of a farmer chased out of a dairy by a bull.

His face went staring white with anticipation —anticipation of a blow that would whirl him around and down. He would fall as he had seen other men fall, the life knocked out of them so suddenly that their knees were no more quick to touch the ground than their heads. He saw the long blue line of the regiment, but his comrades were standing looking at him from the edge of an impossible star. He was aware of some deep wheel-ruts and hoofprints in the sod beneath his feet.

The artillery officer who had fallen in this meadow had been making groans in the teeth of the tempest of sound. These futile cries, wrenched from him by his agony, were heard only by shells, bullets. When wild-eyed Collins came running, this officer raised himself. His face contorted and blanched from pain, he was about to utter some great beseeching cry. But suddenly his face straightened, and he called: "Say, young man, give me a drink of water, will you?"

Collins had no room amid his emotions for surprise. He was mad from the threats of destruction.

"I can't!" he screamed, and in his reply was a full description of his quaking apprehension. His cap was gone and his hair was riotous. His clothes made it appear that he had been dragged over the ground by the heels. He ran on.

The officer's head sank down, and one elbow crooked. His foot in its brass-bound stirrup still stretched over the body of his horse, and the other leg was under the steed.

But Collins turned. He came dashing back. His face had now turned gray, and in his eyes was all terror. "Here it is! here it is!"

The officer was as a man gone in drink. His arm bent like a twig. His head drooped as if his neck were of willow. He was sinking to the ground, to lie face downward.

Collins grabbed him by the shoulder. "Here it is. Here's your drink. Turn over. Turn over, man, for God's sake!"

With Collins hauling at his shoulder, the officer twisted his body and fell with his face turned toward that region where lived the unspeakable noises of the swirling missiles. There was the faintest shadow of a smile on his lips as he looked at Collins. He gave a sigh, a little primitive breath like that from a child.

Collins tried to hold the bucket steadily, but his shaking hands caused the water to splash all over the face of the dying man. Then he jerked it away and ran on.

The regiment gave him a welcoming roar. The grimed faces were wrinkled in laughter.

His captain waved the bucket away. "Give it to the men!"

The two genial, skylarking young lieutenants were the first to gain possession of it. They played over it in their fashion.

When one tried to drink, the other teasingly knocked his elbow. "Don't Billie! You'll make me spill it," said the one. The other laughed.

Suddenly there was an oath, the thud of wood on the ground, and a swift murmur of astonishment among the ranks. The two lieutenants glared at each other. The bucket lay on the ground, empty.

## THE OPEN BOAT

*A Tale Intended to be after the Fact: Being the Experience of Four Men from the Sunk Steamer* COMMODORE

❑ ON January 1, 1897, the *Commodore* under Captain Edward Murphy left Jacksonville, Florida, with munitions and men for the Cuban rebels. That night she began to founder—sabotage was suspected—and before dawn she had to be abandoned. Among the last to leave the ship was Crane, who with four others got back to Daytona Beach in the ten-foot dinghy. The change in the number of occupants from five to four is one of the ways by which he simplified the story for the sake of fictional truth. But while he simplified the story, he complicated the telling. The dancing point of view of the style implies a fundamental irony of perspective which Crane had worked out in a poem published nine months *before* the event:

> To the maiden
> The sea was blue meadow,
> Alive with little froth-people
> Singing.
>
> To the sailor, wrecked,
> The sea was dead gray walls
> Superlative in vacancy,
> Upon which nevertheless at fateful time
> Was written
> The grim hatred of nature.

The story first appeared in *Scribner's Magazine* (June 1897). Newspaper accounts, including Crane's own, are reprinted by R. W. Stallman in *Stephen Crane: An Omnibus.*

## I

NONE of them knew the color of the sky. Their eyes glanced level, and were fastened upon the waves that swept toward them. These waves were of the hue of slate, save for the tops, which were of foaming white, and all of the men knew the colors of the sea. The horizon narrowed and widened, and dipped and rose, and at all times its edge was jagged with waves that seemed thrust up in points like rocks.

Many a man ought to have a bathtub larger than the boat which here rode upon the sea. These waves were most wrongfully and barbarously abrupt and tall, and each froth-top was a problem in small-boat navigation.

The cook squatted in the bottom, and looked with both eyes at the six inches of gunwale which separated him from the ocean. His sleeves were rolled over his fat forearms, and the two flaps of his unbuttoned vest dangled as he bent to bail out the boat. Often he said, "Gawd! that was a narrow clip." As he remarked it he invariably gazed eastward over the broken sea.

The oiler, steering with one of the two oars in the boat, sometimes raised himself suddenly to keep clear of water that swirled in over the stern. It was a thin little oar, and it seemed often ready to snap.

The correspondent, pulling at the other oar, watched the waves and wondered why he was there.

The injured captain, lying in the bow, was at this time buried in that profound dejection and indifference which comes, temporarily at least, to even the bravest and most enduring when, willy-nilly, the firm fails, the army loses, the ship goes down. The mind of the master of a vessel is rooted deep in the timbers of her, though he command for a day or a decade; and this captain had on him the stern impression of a scene in the grays of dawn of seven turned faces, and later a stump of a topmast with a white ball on it, that slashed to and fro at the waves, went low and lower, and down. Thereafter there was something strange in his voice. Although steady, it was deep with mourning, and of a quality beyond oration or tears.

"Keep 'er a little more south, Billie," said he.

"A little more south, sir," said the oiler in the stern.

A seat in his boat was not unlike a seat upon a bucking broncho, and by the same token a broncho is not much smaller. The craft pranced and reared and plunged like an animal. As each wave came, and she rose for it, she seemed like a horse making at a fence outrageously high. The manner of her scramble over these walls of water is a mystic thing, and, moreover, at the top of them were ordinarily these problems in white water, the foam racing down from the summit of each wave requiring a new leap, and a leap from the air. Then, after scornfully bumping a crest, she would slide and race and splash down a long incline, and arrive bobbing and nodding in front of the next menace.

A singular disadvantage of the sea lies in the fact that after successfully surmounting one wave you discover that there is another behind it just as important and just as nervously anxious to do something effective in the way of swamping boats. In a ten-foot dinghy one can get an idea of the resources of the sea in the line of waves that is not probable to the average experience which is never at sea in a dinghy. As each slaty wall of water approached, it shut all else from the view of the men in the boat, and it was not difficult to imagine that this particular wave was the final outburst of the ocean, the last effort of the grim water. There was a terrible grace in the move of the waves, and they came in silence, save for the snarling of the crests.

In the wan light the faces of the men must have been gray. Their eyes must have glinted in strange ways as they gazed steadily astern. Viewed from a balcony, the whole thing would doubtless have been weirdly picturesque. But the men in the boat had no time to see it, and if they had had leisure, there were other things to occupy their minds. The sun swung steadily up the sky, and they knew it was broad day because the color of the sea changed from slate to emerald green streaked with amber lights, and the foam was like tumbling snow. The process of the breaking day was unknown to them. They were aware only of this effect upon the color of the waves that rolled toward them.

In disjointed sentences the cook and the correspondent argued as to the difference between a life-saving station and a house of refuge. The cook had said: "There's a house of refuge just north of the Mosquito Inlet Light, and as soon as they see us they'll come off in their boat and pick us up."

"As soon as who see us?" said the correspondent.

"The crew," said the cook.

"Houses of refuge don't have crews," said the correspondent. "As I understand them, they are only places where clothes and grub are stored for the benefit of shipwrecked people. They don't carry crews."

"Oh, yes, they do," said the cook.

"No, they don't," said the correspondent.

"Well, we're not there yet, anyhow," said the oiler, in the stern.

"Well," said the cook, "perhaps it's not a house of refuge that I'm thinking of as being near Mosquito Inlet Light; perhaps it's a life-saving station."

"We're not there yet," said the oiler in the stern.

## II

AS THE boat bounced from the top of each wave the wind tore through the hair of the hatless men, and as the craft plopped her stern down again the spray slashed past them. The crest of each of these waves was a hill, from the top of which the men surveyed for a moment a broad tumultuous expanse, shining and wind-riven. It was probably splendid, it was probably glorious, this play of the free sea, wild with lights of emerald and white and amber.

"Bully good thing it's an on-shore wind," said the cook. "If not, where would we be? Wouldn't have a show."

"That's right," said the correspondent.

The busy oiler nodded his assent.

Then the captain, in the bow, chuckled in a way that expressed humor, contempt, tragedy, all in one. "Do you think we've got much of a show now, boys?" said he.

Whereupon the three were silent, save for a trifle of hemming and hawing. To express any particular optimism at this time they felt to be childish and stupid, but they all doubtless possessed this sense of the situation in their minds. A young man thinks doggedly at such times. On the other hand, the ethics of their condition was decidedly against any open suggestion of hopelessness. So they were silent.

"Oh, well," said the captain, soothing his children, "we'll get ashore all right."

But there was that in his tone which made them think; so the oiler quoth, "Yes! if this wind holds."

The cook was bailing. "Yes! if we don't catch hell in the surf."

Canton-flannel gulls flew near and far. Sometimes they sat down on the sea, near patches of brown seaweed that rolled over the waves with a movement like carpets on a line in a gale. The birds sat comfortably in groups, and they were envied by some in the dinghy, for the wrath of the sea was no more to them than it was to a covey of prairie chickens a thousand miles inland. Often they came very close and stared at the men with black bead-like eyes. At these times they were uncanny and sinister in their unblinking scrutiny,

and the men hooted angrily at them, telling them to be gone. One came, and evidently decided to alight on the top of the captain's head. The bird flew parallel to the boat and did not circle, but made short sidelong jumps in the air in chicken-fashion. His black eyes were wistfully fixed upon the captain's head. "Ugly brute," said the oiler to the bird. "You look as if you were made with a jackknife." The cook and the correspondent swore darkly at the creature. The captain naturally wished to knock it away with the end of the heavy painter, but he did not dare do it, because anything resembling an emphatic gesture would have capsized this freighted boat; and so, with his open hand, the captain gently and carefully waved the gull away. After it had been discouraged from the pursuit the captain breathed easier on account of his hair, and others breathed easier because the bird struck their minds at this time as being somehow gruesome and ominous.

In the meantime the oiler and the correspondent rowed. And also they rowed. They sat together in the same seat, and each rowed an oar. Then the oiler took both oars; then the correspondent took both oars; then the oiler; then the correspondent. They rowed and they rowed. The very ticklish part of the business was when the time came for the reclining one in the stern to take his turn at the oars. By the very last star of truth, it is easier to steal eggs from under a hen than it was to change seats in the dinghy. First the man in the stern slid his hand along the thwart and moved with care, as if he were of Sèvres. Then the man in the rowing-seat slid his hand along the other thwart. It was all done with the most extraordinary care. As the two sidled past each other, the whole party kept watchful eyes on the coming wave, and the captain cried: "Look out, now! Steady, there!"

The brown mats of seaweed that appeared from time to time were like islands, bits of earth. They were traveling, apparently, neither one way nor the other. They were, to all intents, stationary. They informed the men in the boat that it was making progress slowly toward the land.

The captain, rearing cautiously in the bow after the dinghy soared on a great swell, said that he had seen the lighthouse at Mosquito Inlet. Presently the cook remarked that he had seen it. The correspondent was at the oars then, and for some reason he too wished to look at the lighthouse; but his back was toward the far shore, and the waves were important, and for some time he could not seize an opportunity to turn his head. But at last there came a wave more gentle than the others, and when at the crest of it he swiftly scoured the western horizon.

"See it?" said the captain.

"No," said the correspondent, slowly; "I didn't see anything."

"Look again," said the captain. He pointed. "It's exactly in that direction."

At the top of another wave the correspondent did as he was bid, and this time his eyes chanced on a small, still thing on the edge of the swaying horizon. It was precisely like the point of a pin. It took an anxious eye to find a lighthouse so tiny.

"Think we'll make it, Captain?"

"If this wind holds and the boat don't swamp, we can't do much else," said the captain.

The little boat, lifted by each towering sea and splashed viciously by the crests, made progress that in the absence of seaweed was not apparent to those in her. She semed just a wee thing wallowing, miraculously top up, at the mercy of five oceans. Occasionally a great spread of water, like white flames, swarmed into her.

"Bail her, cook," said the captain, serenely.

"All right, Captain," said the cheerful cook.

### III

IT WOULD be difficult to describe the subtle brotherhood of men that was here established on the seas. No one said that it was so. No one mentioned it. But it dwelt in the boat, and each man felt it warm him. They were a captain, an oiler, a cook, and a correspondent, and they were friends— friends in a more curiously iron-bound degree than may be common. The hurt captain, lying against the water-jar in the bow, spoke always in a low voice and calmly; but he could never command a more ready and swiftly obedient crew than the motley three of the dinghy. It was more than a mere recognition of what was best for the common safety. There was surely in it a quality that was personal and heart-felt. And after this devotion to the commander of the boat, there was this comradeship, that the correspondent, for instance, who had been taught to be cynical of men, knew even at the time was the best experience of his life. But no one said that it was so. No one mentioned it.

"I wish we had a sail," remarked the captain. "We might try my overcoat on the end of an oar, and give you two boys a chance to rest." So the cook and the correspondent held the mast and spread wide the overcoat; the oiler steered; and the little boat made good way with her new rig. Sometimes the oiler had to scull sharply to keep a sea from breaking into the boat, but otherwise sailing was a success.

Meanwhile the lighthouse had been growing slowly larger. It had now almost assumed color, and appeared like a little gray shadow on the sky. The man at the oars could not be prevented from turning his head rather often to try for a glimpse of this little gray shadow.

At last, from the top of each wave, the men in the tossing boat could see land. Even as the lighthouse was an upright shadow on the sky, this land seemed but a long black shadow on the sea. It certainly was thinner than paper. "We must be about opposite New Smyrna," said the cook, who had coasted this shore often in schooners. "Captain, by the way, I believe they abandoned that lifesaving station there about a year ago."

"Did they?" said the captain.

The wind slowly died away. The cook and the correspondent were not now obliged to slave in order to hold high the oar. But the waves continued their old impetuous swooping at the dinghy, and the little craft, no longer under way, struggled woundily over them. The oiler or the correspondent took the oars again.

Shipwrecks are apropos of nothing. If men could only train for them and have them occur when the men had reached pink condition, there would be less drowning at sea. Of the four in the dinghy none had slept any time worth mentioning for two days and two nights previous to embarking in the dinghy, and in the excitement of clambering about the deck of a foundering ship they had also forgotten to eat heartily.

For these reasons, and for others, neither the oiler nor the correspondent was fond of rowing at this time. The correspondent wondered ingenuously how in the name of all that was sane could there be people who thought it amusing to row a boat. It was not an amusement; it was a diabolical punishment, and even a genius of mental aberrations could never conclude that it was anything but a horror to the muscles and a crime against the back. He mentioned to the boat in general how the amusement of rowing struck him, and the wearyfaced oiler smiled in full sympathy. Previously to the foundering, by the way, the oiler had worked a double watch in the engine-room of the ship.

"Take her easy now, boys," said the captain. "Don't spend yourselves. If we have to run a surf you'll need all your strength, because we'll sure have to swim for it. Take your time."

Slowly the land arose from the sea. From a black line it became a line of black and a line of white—trees and sand. Finally the captain said that he could make out a house on the shore. "That's the house of refuge, sure," said the cook. "They'll see us before long, and come out after us."

The distant lighthouse reared high. "The

keeper ought to be able to make us out now, if he's looking through a glass," said the captain. "He'll notify the life-saving people."

"None of those other boats could have got ashore to give word of this wreck," said the oiler, in a low voice, "else the life-boat would be out hunting us."

Slowly and beautifully the land loomed out of the sea. The wind came again. It had veered from the north-east to the south-east. Finally a new sound struck the ears of the men in the boat. It was the low thunder of the surf on the shore. "We'll never be able to make the lighthouse now," said the captain. "Swing her head a little more north, Billie."

"A little more north, sir," said the oiler.

Whereupon the little boat turned her nose once more down the wind, and all but the oarsman watched the shore grow. Under the influence of this expansion doubt and direful apprehension were leaving the minds of the men. The management of the boat was still most absorbing, but it could not prevent a quiet cheerfulness. In an hour, perhaps, they would be ashore.

Their backbones had become thoroughly used to balancing in the boat, and they now rode this wild colt of a dinghy like circus men. The correspondent thought that he had been drenched to the skin, but happening to feel in the top pocket of his coat, he found therein eight cigars. Four of them were soaked with sea-water; four were perfectly scatheless. After a search, somebody produced three dry matches; and thereupon the four waifs rode impudently in their little boat and, with an assurance of an impending rescue shining in their eyes, puffed at the big cigars, and judged well and ill of all men. Everybody took a drink of water.

### IV

"COOK," remarked the captain, "there don't seem to be any signs of life about your house of refuge."

"No," replied the cook. "Funny they don't see us!"

A broad stretch of lowly coast lay before the eyes of the men. It was of low dunes topped with dark vegetation. The roar of the surf was plain, and sometimes they could see the white lip of a wave as it spun up the beach. A tiny house was blocked out black upon the sky. Southward, the slim lighthouse lifted its little gray length.

Tide, wind, and waves were swinging the dinghy northward. "Funny they don't see us," said the men.

The surf's roar was here dulled, but its tone was nevertheless thunderous and mighty. As the boat swam over the great rollers the men sat listening to this roar. "We'll swamp sure," said everybody.

It is fair to say here that there was not a life-saving station within twenty miles in either direction; but the men did not know this fact, and in consequence they made dark and opprobrious remarks concerning the eyesight of the nation's lifesavers. Four scowling men sat in the dinghy and surpassed records in the invention of epithets.

"Funny they don't see us."

The light-heartedness of a former time had completely faded. To their sharpened minds it was easy to conjure pictures of all kinds of incompetency and blindness and, indeed, cowardice. There was the shore of the populous land, and it was bitter and bitter to them that from it came no sign.

"Well," said the captain, ultimately, "I suppose we'll have to make a try for ourselves. If we stay out here too long, we'll none of us have strength left to swim after the boat swamps."

And so the oiler, who was at the oars, turned the boat straight for the shore. There was a sudden tightening of muscles. There was some thinking.

"If we don't all get ashore," said the captain— "if we don't all get ashore, I suppose you fellows know where to send news of my finish?"

They then briefly exchanged some addresses and admonitions. As for the reflections of the men, there was a great deal of rage in them. Perchance they might be formulated thus: "If I am going to be drowned—if I am going to be drowned—if I am going to be drowned, why, in the name of the seven mad gods who rule the sea, was I allowed to come thus far and contemplate sand and trees? Was I brought here merely to have my nose dragged away as I was about to nibble the sacred cheese of life? It is preposterous. If this old ninny-woman, Fate, cannot do better than this, she should be deprived of the management of men's fortunes. She is an old hen who knows not her intention. If she has decided to drown me, why did she not do it in the beginning and save me all this trouble? The whole affair is absurd.—But no; she cannot mean to drown me. She dare not drown me. She cannot drown me. Not after all this work." Afterward the man might have had an impulse to shake his fist at the clouds. "Just you drown me, now, and then hear what I call you!"

The billows that came at this time were more formidable. They seemed always just about to break and roll over the little boat in a turmoil of foam. There was a preparatory and long growl in the speech of them. No mind unused to the sea would have concluded that the dinhgy could ascend these sheer heights in time. The shore was still afar. The oiler was a wily surfman. "Boys," he said swiftly, "she won't live three minutes more, and we're too far out to swim. Shall I take her to sea again, Captain?"

"Yes; go ahead!" said the captain.

This oiler, by a series of quick miracles and fast and steady oarsmanship, turned the boat in the middle of the surf and took her safely to sea again.

There was a considerable silence as the boat bumped over the furrowed sea to deeper water. Then somebody in gloom spoke: "Well, anyhow, they must have seen us from the shore by now."

The gulls went in slanting flight up the wind toward the gray, desolate east. A squall, marked by dingy clouds and clouds brick-red like smoke from a burning building, appeared from the south-east.

"What do you think of those life-saving people? Ain't they peaches?"

"Funny they haven't seen us."

"Maybe they think we're out here for sport! Maybe they think we're fishin'. Maybe they think we're damned fools."

It was a long afternoon. A changed tide tried to force them southward, but wind and wave said northward. Far ahead, where coast-line, sea, and sky formed their mighty angle, there were little dots which seemed to indicate a city on the shore.

"St. Augustine?"

The captain shook his head. "Too near Mosquito Inlet."

And the oiler rowed, and then the correspondent rowed; then the oiler rowed. It was a weary business. The human back can become the seat of more aches and pains than are registered in books for the composite anatomy of a regiment. It is a limited area, but it can become the theater of innumerable muscular conflicts, tangles, wrenches, knots, and other comforts.

"Did you ever like to row, Billie?" asked the correspondent.

"No," said the oiler; "hang it!"

When one exchanged the rowing-seat for a place in the bottom of the boat, he suffered a bodily depression that caused him to be careless of everything save an obligation to wiggle one finger. There was cold sea-water swashing to and fro in the boat, and he lay in it. His head, pillowed on a thwart, was within an inch of the swirl of a wave-crest, and sometimes a particularly obstreperous sea came inboard and drenched him once more. But these matters did not annoy him. It is almost certain that if the boat had capsized he would

have tumbled comfortably out upon the ocean as if he felt sure that it was a great soft mattress.

"Look! There's a man on the shore!"

"Where?"

"There! See 'im? See 'im?"

"Yes, sure! He's walking along."

"Now he's stopped. Look! He's facing us!"

"He's waving at us!"

"So he is! By thunder!"

"Ah, now we're all right! Now we're all right! There'll be a boat out here for us in half an hour."

"He's going on. He's running. He's going up to that house there."

The remote beach seemed lower than the sea, and it required a searching glance to discern the little black figure. The captain saw a floating stick, and they rowed to it. A bath towel was by some weird chance in the boat, and, tying this on the stick, the captain waved it. The oarsman did not dare turn his head, so he was obliged to ask questions.

"What's he doing now?"

"He's standing still again. He's looking, I think. —There he goes again—toward the house.—Now he's stopped again."

"Is he waving at us?"

"No, not now; he was, though."

"Look! There comes another man!"

"He's running."

"Look at him go, would you!"

"Why, he's on a bicycle. Now he's met the other man. They're both waving at us. Look!"

"There comes something up the beach."

"What the devil is that thing?"

"Why, it looks like a boat."

"Why, certainly, it's a boat."

"No; it's on wheels."

"Yes, so it is. Well, that must be the life-boat. They drag them along shore on a wagon."

"That's the life-boat, sure."

"No, by God, it's—it's an omnibus."

"I tell you it's a life-boat."

"It is not! It's an omnibus. I can see it plain. See? One of these big hotel omnibuses."

"By thunder, you're right. It's an omnibus, sure as fate. What do you suppose they are doing with an omnibus? Maybe they are going around collecting the life-crew, hey?"

"That's it, likely. Look! There's a fellow waving a little black flag. He's standing on the steps of the omnibus. There come those other two fellows. Now they're all talking together. Look at the fellow with the flag. Maybe he ain't waving it!"

"That ain't a flag, is it? That's his coat. Why, certainly, that's his coat."

"So it is; it's his coat. He's taken it off and is

waving it around his head. But would you look at him swing it!"

"Oh, say, there isn't any life-saving station there. That's just a winter-resort hotel omnibus that has brought over some of the boarders to see us drown."

"What's that idiot with the coat mean? What's he signalling, anyhow?"

"It looks as if he were trying to tell us to go north. There must be a life-saving station up there."

"No; he thinks we're fishing. Just giving us a merry hand. See? Ah, there, Willie!"

"Well, I wish I could make something out of those signals. What do you suppose he means?"

"He don't mean anything; he's just playing."

"Well, if he'd just signal us to try the surf again, or to go to sea and wait, or go north, or go south, or go to hell, there would be some reason in it. But look at him! He just stands there and keeps his coat revolving like a wheel. The ass!"

"There come more people."

"Now there's quite a mob. Look! Isn't that a boat?"

"Where? Oh, I see where you mean. No, that's no boat."

"That fellow is still waving his coat."

"He must think we like to see him do that. Why don't he quit it? It don't mean anything."

"I don't know. I think he is trying to make us go north. It must be that there's a life-saving station there somewhere."

"Say, he ain't tired yet. Look at 'im wave!"

"Wonder how long he can keep that up. He's been revolving his coat ever since he caught sight of us. He's an idiot. Why aren't they getting men to bring a boat out? A fishing-boat—one of those big yawls—could come out here all right. Why don't he do something?"

"Oh, it's all right now."

"They'll have a boat out here for us in less than no time, now that they've seen us."

A faint yellow tone came into the sky over the low land. The shadows on the sea slowly deepened. The wind bore coldness with it, and the men began to shiver.

"Holy smoke!" said one, allowing his voice to express his impious mood, "if we keep on monkeying out here! If we've got to flounder out here all night!"

"Oh, we'll never have to stay here all night! Don't you worry. They've seen us now, and it won't be long before they'll come chasing out after us."

The shore grew dusky. The man waving a coat blended gradually into this gloom, and it swallowed in the same manner the omnibus and the group of people. The spray, when it dashed uproariously over the side, made the voyagers shrink and swear like men who were being branded.

"I'd like to catch the chump who waved the coat. I feel like socking him one, just for luck."

"Why? What did he do?"

"Oh, nothing, but then he seemed so damned cheerful."

In the meantime the oiler rowed, and then the correspondent rowed, and then the oiler rowed. Gray-faced and bowed forward, they mechanically, turn by turn, plied the leaden oars. The form of the lighthouse had vanished from the southern horizon, but finally a pale star appeared, just lifting from the sea. The streaked saffron in the west passed before the all-merging darkness, and the sea to the east was black. The land had vanished, and was expressed only by the low and drear thunder of the surf.

"If I am going to be drowned—if I am going to be drowned—if I am going to be drowned, why, in the name of the seven mad gods who rule the sea, was I allowed to come thus far and contemplate sand and trees? Was I brought here merely to have my nose dragged away as I was about to nibble the sacred cheese of life?"

The patient captain, drooped over the water-jar, was sometimes obliged to speak to the oarsman

"Keep her head up! Keep her head up!"

"Keep her head up, sir." The voices were weary and low.

This was surely a quiet evening. All save the oarsman lay heavily and listlessly in the boat's bottom. As for him, his eyes were just capable of noting the tall black waves that swept forward in a most sinister silence, save for an occasional subdued growl of a crest.

The cook's head was on a thwart, and he looked without interest at the water under his nose. He was deep in other scenes. Finally he spoke. "Billie," he murmured dreamfully, "what kind of pie do you like best?"

### V

"PIE!" said the oiler and the correspondent, agitatedly. "Don't talk about those things, blast you!"

"Well," said the cook, "I was just thinking about ham sandwiches and—"

A night on the sea in an open boat is a long night. As darkness settled finally, the shine of the light, lifting from the sea in the south, changed to full gold. On the northern horizon a new light appeared, a small bluish gleam on the edge of the waters. These two lights were the furniture of the world. Otherwise there was nothing but waves.

Two men huddled in the stern, and distances were so magnificent in the dinghy that the rower was enabled to keep his feet partly warm by thrusting them under his companions. Their legs indeed extended far under the rowing-seat until they touched the feet of the captain forward. Sometimes, despite the efforts of the tired oarsman, a wave came piling into the boat, an icy wave of the night, and the chilling water soaked them anew. They would twist their bodies for a moment and groan, and sleep the dead sleep once more, while the water in the boat gurgled about them as the craft rocked.

The plan of the oiler and the correspondent was for one to row until he lost the ability, and then arouse the other from his sea-water couch in the bottom of the boat.

The oiler plied the oars until his head drooped forward and the overpowering sleep blinded him; and he rowed yet afterward. Then he touched a man in the bottom of the boat, and called his name. "Will you spell me for a little while?" he said, meekly.

"Sure, Billie," said the correspondent, awaking and dragging himself to a sitting position. They exchanged places carefully, and the oiler, cuddling down in the sea-water at the cook's side, seemed to go to sleep instantly.

The particular violence of the sea had ceased. The waves came without snarling. The obligation of the man at the oars was to keep the boat headed so that the tilt of the rollers would not capsize her, and to preserve her from filling when the crests rushed past. The black waves were silent and hard to be seen in the darkness. Often one was almost upon the boat before the oarsman was aware.

In a low voice the correspondent addressed the captain. He was not sure that the captain was awake, although this iron man seemed to be always awake. "Captain, shall I keep her making for that light north, sir?"

The same steady voice answered him. "Yes. Keep it about two points off the port bow."

The cook had tied a life-belt around himself in order to get even the warmth which this clumsy cork contrivance could donate, and he seemed almost stove-like when a rower, whose teeth invariably chattered wildly as soon as he ceased his labour, dropped down to sleep.

The correspondent, as he rowed, looked down at the two men sleeping underfoot. The cook's arm was around the oiler's shoulders, and, with their fragmentary clothing and haggard faces, they were the babes of the sea—a grotesque rendering of the old babes in the wood.

Later he must have grown stupid at his work, for suddenly there was a growling of water, and a crest came with a roar and a swash into the boat, and it was a wonder that it did not set the cook afloat in his life-belt. The cook continued to sleep, but the oiler sat up, blinking his eyes and shaking with the new cold.

"Oh, I'm awful sorry, Billie," said the correspondent, contritely.

"That's all right, old boy," said the oiler, and lay down again and was asleep.

Presently it seemed that even the captain dozed, and the correspondent thought that he was the one man afloat on all the oceans. The wind had a voice as it came over the waves, and it was sadder than the end.

There was a long, loud swishing astern of the boat, and a gleaming trail of phosphorescence, like blue flame, was furrowed on the black waters. It might have been made by a monstrous knife.

Then there came a stillness, while the correspondent breathed with open mouth and looked at the sea.

Suddenly there was another swish and another long flash of bluish light, and this time it was alongside the boat, and might almost been reached with an oar. The correspondent saw an enormous fin speed like a shadow through the water, hurling the crystalline spray and leaving the long glowing trail.

The correspondent looked over his shoulder at the captain. His face was hidden, and he seemed to be asleep. He looked at the babes of the sea. They certainly were asleep. So, being bereft of sympathy, he leaned a little way to one side and swore softly into the sea.

But the thing did not then leave the vicinity of the boat. Ahead or astern, on one side or the other, at intervals long or short, fled the long sparkling streak, and there was to be heard the *whirroo* of the dark fin. The speed and power of the thing was greatly to be admired. It cut the water like a gigantic and keen projectile.

The presence of this biding thing did not affect the man with the same horror that it would if he had been a picnicker. He simply looked at the sea dully and swore in an undertone.

Nevertheless, it is true that he did not wish to be alone with the thing. He wished one of his companions to awake by chance and keep him company with it. But the captain hung motionless over the water-jar, and the oiler and the cook in the bottom of the boat were plunged in slumber.

## VI

"IF I AM going to be drowned—if I am going to be drowned, why, in the name of the seven mad gods who rule the sea, was I allowed to come thus far and contemplate sand and trees?"

During this dismal night, it may be remarked that a man would conclude that it was really the intention of the seven mad gods to drown him, despite the abominable injustice of it. For it was certainly an abominable injustice to drown a man who had worked so hard, so hard. The man felt it would be a crime most unnatural. Other people had drowned at sea since galleys swarmed with painted sails, but still—

When it occurs to a man that nature does not regard him as important, and that she feels she would not maim the universe by disposing of him, he at first wishes to throw bricks at the temple, and he hates deeply the fact that there are no bricks and no temples. Any visible expression of nature would surely be pelleted with his jeers.

Then, if there be no tangible thing to hoot, he feels, perhaps, the desire to confront a personification and indulge in pleas, bowed to one knee, and with hands supplicant, saying, "Yes, but I love myself."

A high cold star on a winter's night is the word he feels that she says to him. Thereafter he knows the pathos of his situation.

The men in the dinghy had not discussed these matters, but each had, no doubt, reflected upon them in silence and according to his mind. There was seldom any expression upon their faces save the general one of complete weariness. Speech was devoted to the business of the boat.

To chime the notes of his emotion, a verse mysteriously entered the correspondent's head. He had even forgotten that he had forgotten this verse, but it suddenly was in his mind.

A soldier of the Legion lay dying in Algiers;
There was lack of woman's nursing, there was dearth
    of woman's tears;
But a comrade stood beside him, and he took that
    comrade's hand,
And he said, "I never more shall see my own, my na-
    tive land."

In his childhood the correspondent had been made acquainted with the fact that a soldier of the Legion lay dying in Algiers, but he had never regarded the fact as important. Myriads of his school-fellows had informed him of the soldier's plight, but the dinning had naturally ended by making him perfectly indifferent. He had never considered it his affair that a soldier of the Legion lay dying in Algiers, nor had it appeared to him as a matter for sorrow. It was less to him than the breaking of a pencil's point.

Now, however, it quaintly came to him as a human, living thing. It was no longer merely a picture of a few throes in the breast of a poet, meanwhile drinking tea and warming his feet at the grate; it was an actuality—stern, mournful, and fine.

The correspondent plainly saw the soldier. He lay on the sand with his feet out straight and still. While his pale left hand was upon his chest in an attempt to thwart the going of his life, the blood came between his fingers. In the far Algerian distance, a city of low square forms was set against a sky that was faint with the last sunset hues. The correspondent, plying the oars and dreaming of the slow and slower movements of the lips of the soldier, was moved by a profound and perfectly impersonal comprehension. He was sorry for the soldier of the Legion who lay dying in Algiers.

The thing which had followed the boat and waited had evidently grown bored at the delay. There was no longer to be heard the slash of the cutwater, and there was no longer the flame of the long trail. The light in the north still glimmered, but it was apparently no nearer to the boat. Sometimes the boom of the surf rang in the correspondent's ears, and he turned the craft seaward then and rowed harder. Southward, some one had evidently built a watch-fire on the beach. It was too low and too far to be seen, but it made a shimmering, roseate reflection upon the bluff in back of it, and this could be discerned from the boat. The wind came stronger, and sometimes a wave suddenly raged out like a mountain cat, and there was to be seen the sheen and sparkle of a broken crest.

The captain, in the bow, moved on his water-jar and sat erect. "Pretty long night," he observed to the correspondent. He looked at the shore. "Those life-saving people take their time."

"Did you see that shark playing around?"

"Yes, I saw him. He was a big fellow, all right."

"Wish I had known you were awake."

Later the correspondent spoke into the bottom of the boat. "Billie!" There was a slow and gradual disentanglement. "Billie, will you spell me?"

"Sure," said the oiler.

As soon as the correspondent touched the cold, comfortable sea-water in the bottom of the boat and had huddled close to the cook's life-belt he was deep in sleep, despite the fact that his teeth played all the popular airs. This sleep was so good to him that it was but a moment before he heard a voice call his name in a tone that demonstrated the last stages of exhaustion. "Will you spell me?"

"Sure, Billie."

The light in the north had mysteriously vanished, but the correspondent took his course from the wide-awake captain.

Later in the night they took the boat farther out to sea, and the captain directed the cook to take one oar at the stern and keep the boat facing the seas. He was to call out if he should hear the thunder of the surf. This plan enabled the oiler and the correspondent to get respite together. "We'll give those boys a chance to get into shape again," said the captain. They curled down and, after a few preliminary chatterings and trembles, slept once more the dead sleep. Neither knew they had bequeathed to the cook the company of another shark, or perhaps the same shark.

As the boat caroused on the waves, spray occasionally bumped over the side and gave them a fresh soaking, but this had no power to break their repose. The ominous slash of the wind and the water affected them as it would have affected mummies.

"Boys," said the cook, with the notes of every reluctance in his voice, "she's drifted in pretty close. I guess one of you had better take her to sea again." The correspondent, aroused, heard the crash of the toppled crests.

As he was rowing, the captain gave him some whisky-and-water, and this steadied the chills out of him. "If I ever get ashore and anybody shows me even a photograph of an oar—"

At last there was a short conversation.

"—Billie!—Billie, will you spell me?"

"Sure," said the oiler.

## VII

WHEN the correspondent again opened his eyes, the sea and the sky were each of the gray hue of the dawning. Later, carmine and gold was painted upon the waters. The morning appeared finally, in its splendor, with a sky of pure blue, and the sunlight flamed on the tips of the waves.

On the distant dunes were set many little black cottages, and a tall white windmill reared above them. No man, nor dog, nor bicycle appeared on the beach. The cottages might have formed a deserted village.

The voyagers scanned the shore. A conference was held in the boat. "Well," said the captain, "if no help is coming, we might better try a run through the surf right away. If we stay out here much longer we will be too weak to do anything for ourselves at all." The others silently acquiesced in this reasoning. The boat was headed for the beach. The correspondent wondered if none ever ascended the tall windtower, and if then they never looked seaward. This tower was a giant, standing with its back to the plight of the ants. It represented in a degree, to the correspondent, the serenity of nature amid the struggles of the individual—nature in the wind, and nature in the vision of men. She did not seem cruel to him then, nor beneficent, nor treacherous, nor wise. But she was indifferent, flatly indifferent. It is, perhaps, plausible that a man in this situation, impressed with the unconcern of the universe, should see the innumerable flaws of his life, and have them taste wickedly in his mind, and wish for another chance. A distinction between right and wrong seems absurdly clear to him, then, in this new ignorance of the grave-edge, and he understands that if he were given another opportunity he would mend his conduct and his words, and be better and brighter during an introduction or at a tea.

"Now, boys," said the captain, "she is going to swamp sure. All we can do is to work her in as far as possible, and then when she swamps, pile out and scramble for the beech. Keep cool now, and don't jump until she swamps sure."

The oiler took the oars. Over his shoulders he scanned the surf. "Captain," he said, "I think I'd better bring her about and keep her head-on to the seas and back her in."

"All right, Billie," said the captain. "Back her in." The oiler swung the boat then, and, seated in the stern, the cook and the correspondent were obliged to look over their shoulders to contemplate the lonely and indifferent shore.

The monstrous inshore rollers heaved the boat high until the men were again enabled to see the white sheets of water scudding up the slanted beach. "We won't get in very close," said the captain. Each time a man could wrest his attention from the rollers, he turned his glance toward the shore, and in the expression of the eyes during this contemplation there was a singular quality. The correspondent, observing the others, knew that they were not afraid, but the full meaning of their glances was shrouded.

As for himself, he was too tired to grapple fundamentally with the fact. He tried to coerce his mind into thinking of it, but the mind was dominated at this time by the muscles, and the muscles said they did not care. It merely occurred to him that if he should drown it would be a shame.

There were no hurried words, no pallor, no plain agitation. The men simply looked at the shore. "Now, remember to get well clear of the boat when you jump," said the captain.

Seaward the crest of a roller suddenly fell with a thunderous crash, and the long white comber came roaring down upon the boat.

"Steady now," said the captain. The men were silent. They turned their eyes from the shore to the comber and waited. The boat slid up the incline, leaped at the furious top, bounced over it, and swung down the long back of the wave. Some water had been shipped, and the cook bailed it out.

But the next crest crashed also. The tumbling, boiling flood of white water caught the boat and whirled it almost perpendicular. Water swarmed in from all sides. The correspondent had his hands on the gunwale at this time, and when the water entered at that place he swiftly withdrew his fingers, as if he objected to wetting them.

The little boat, drunken with this weight of water, reeled and snuggled deeper into the sea.

"Bail her out, cook! Bail her out!" said the captain.

"All right, Captain," said the cook.

"Now, boys, the next one will do for us sure," said the oiler. "Mind to jump clear of the boat."

The third wave moved forward, huge, furious, implacable. It fairly swallowed the dinghy, and almost simultaneously the men tumbled into the sea. A piece of life-belt had lain in the bottom of the boat, and as the correspondent went overboard he held this to his chest with his left hand.

The January water was icy, and he reflected immediately that it was colder than he had expected to find it off the coast of Florida. This appeared to his dazed mind as a fact important enough to be noted at the time. The coldness of the water was sad; it was tragic. This fact was somehow mixed and confused with his opinion of his own situation, so that it seemed almost a proper reason for tears. The water was cold.

When he came to the surface he was conscious of little but the noisy water. Afterward he saw his companions in the sea. The oiler was ahead in the race. He was swimming strongly and rapidly. Off to the correspondent's left, the cook's great white and corked back bulged out of the water; and in the rear the captain was hanging with his one good hand to the keel of the overturned dinghy.

There is a certain immovable quality to a shore, and the correspondent wondered at it amid the confusion of the sea.

It seemed also very attractive; but the correspondent knew that it was a long journey, and he paddled leisurely. The piece of life-preserver lay under him, and sometimes he whirled down the incline of a wave as if he were on a hand-sled.

But finally he arrived at a place in the sea where travel was beset with difficulty. He did not pause swimming to inquire what manner of current had caught him, but there his progress ceased. The shore was set before him like a bit of scenery on a stage, and he looked at it and understood with his eyes each detail of it.

As the cook passed, much farther to the left, the captain was calling to him, "Turn over on your back, cook! Turn over on your back and use the oar."

"All right, sir." The cook turned on his back, and, paddling with an oar, went ahead as if he were a canoe.

Presently the boat also passed to the left of the correspondent, with the captain clinging with one hand to the keel. He would have appeared like a man raising himself to look over a board fence if it were not for the extraordinary gymnastics of the boat. The correspondent marveled that the captain could still hold to it.

They passed on nearer to shore—the oiler, the cook, the captain—and following them went the water-jar, bouncing gaily over the seas.

The correspondent remained in the grip of this strange new enemy—a current. The shore, with its white slope of sand and its green bluff topped with little silent cottages, was spread like a picture before him. It was very near to him then, but he was impressed as one who, in a gallery, looks at a scene from Brittany or Algiers.

He thought: "I am going to drown? Can it be possible? Can it be possible? Can it be possible?" Perhaps an individual must consider his own death to be the final phenomenon of nature.

But later a wave perhaps whirled him out of this small deadly current, for he found suddenly that he could again make progress toward the shore. Later still he was aware that the captain, clinging with one hand to the keel of the dinghy, had his face turned away from the shore and toward him, and was calling his name. "Come to the boat! Come to the boat!"

In his struggle to reach the captain and the boat, he reflected that when one gets properly wearied drowning must really be a comfortable arrangement—a cessation of hostilities accompanied by a large degree of relief; and he was glad of it, for the main thing in his mind for some moments had been horror of the temporary agony. He did not wish to be hurt.

Presently he saw a man running along the shore. He was undressing with most remarkable speed. Coat, trousers, shirt, everything flew magically off him.

"Come to the boat!" called the captain.

"All right, Captain." As the correspondent paddled, he saw the captain let himself down to bottom and leave the boat. Then the correspondent performed his one little marvel of the voyage. A large wave caught him and flung him with ease and supreme speed completely over the boat and far beyond it. It struck him even then as an event in gymnastics and a true miracle of the sea. An overturned boat in the surf is not a plaything to a swimming man.

The correspondent arrived in water that reached only to his waist, but his condition did not enable him to stand for more than a moment. Each wave knocked him into a heap, and the undertow pulled at him.

Then he saw the man who had been running and undressing, and undressing and running, come bounding into the water. He dragged ashore the cook, and then waded toward the captain; but the captain waved him away and sent him to the correspondent. He was naked—naked as a tree in winter; but a halo was about his head, and he shone like a saint. He gave a strong pull, and a long drag, and a bully heave at the correspondent's hand. The correspondent, schooled in the minor formulæ, said, "Thanks, old man." But suddenly the man cried, "What's that?" He pointed a swift finger. The correspondent said, "Go."

In the shallows, face downward, lay the oiler. His forehead touched sand that was periodically, between each wave, clear of the sea.

The correspondent did not know all that transpired afterward. When he achieved safe ground he fell, striking the sand with each particular part of his body. It was as if he had dropped from a roof, but the thud was grateful to him.

It seemed that instantly the beach was populated with men with blankets, clothes, and flasks, and women with coffee-pots and all the remedies sacred to their minds. The welcome of the land to the men from the sea was warm and generous; but a still and dripping shape was carried slowly up the beach, and the land's welcome for it could only be the different and sinister hospitality of the grave.

When it came night, the white waves paced to and fro in the moonlight, and the wind brought the sound of the great sea's voice to the men on the shore, and they felt that they could then be interpreters.

# THE BRIDE COMES TO YELLOW SKY

◖ CRANE'S easy handling of Wild West melodrama and Western humor stemmed from a knowing detachment. Neither literary tradition possessed him as did evangelical preaching or heroic legend, and writing in England in the autumn of 1897, he was almost three years and nearly five thousand miles from any direct experience of the subject. Though he liked the West heartily, he was immune to the prevalent cultural image of it that he once spoofed in inscribing a copy of *George's Mother*: "To Hamlin Garland of the great honest West, from Stephen Crane of the false East."

I

THE GREAT Pullman was whirling onward with such dignity of motion that a glance from the window seemed simply to prove that the plains of Texas were pouring eastward. Vast flats of green grass, dull-hued spaces of mesquit and cactus, little groups of frame houses, woods of light and tender trees, all were sweeping into the east, sweeping over the horizon, a precipice.

A newly married pair had boarded this coach at San Antonio. The man's face was reddened from many days in the wind and sun, and a direct result of his new black clothes was that his brick-colored hands were constantly performing in a most conscious fashion. From time to time he looked down respectfully at his attire. He sat with a hand on each knee, like a man waiting in a barber's shop. The glances he devoted to other passengers were furtive and shy.

The bride was not pretty, nor was she very young. She wore a dress of blue cashmere, with small reservations of velvet here and there, and with steel buttons abounding. She continually twisted her head to regard her puff sleeves, very stiff, straight, and high. They embarrassed her. It was quite apparent that she had cooked, and that she expected to cook, dutifully. The blushes caused by the careless scrutiny of some passengers as she had entered the car were strange to see upon this plain, under-class countenance, which was drawn in placid, almost emotionless lines.

They were evidently very happy. "Ever been in a parlor-car before?" he asked, smiling with delight.

"No," she answered; "I never was. It's fine, ain't it?"

"Great! And then after a while we'll go forward to the diner, and get a big lay-out. Finest meal in the world. Charge a dollar."

"Oh, do they?" cried the bride. "Charge a dollar? Why, that's too much—for us—ain't it, Jack?"

"Not this trip, anyhow," he answered bravely. "We're going to go the whole thing."

Later he explained to her about the trains. "You see, it's a thousand miles from one end of Texas to the other; and this train runs right across it, and never stops but four times." He had the pride of an owner. He pointed out to her the dazzling fittings of the coach; and in truth her eyes opened wider as she contemplated the sea-green figured velvet, the shining brass, silver, and glass, the wood that gleamed as darkly brilliant as the surface of a pool of oil. At one end a bronze figure sturdily held a support for a separated chamber, and at convenient places on the ceiling were frescoes in olive and silver.

To the minds of the pair, their surroundings reflected the glory of their marriage that morning in San Antonio; this was the environment of their new estate; and the man's face in particular beamed with an elation that made him appear ridiculous to the negro porter. This individual at times surveyed them from afar with an amused and superior grin. On other occasions he bullied them with skill in ways that did not make it exactly plain to them that they were being bullied. He subtly used all the manners of the most unconquerable kind of snobbery. He oppressed them; but of this oppression they had small knowledge, and they speedily forgot that infrequently a number of travelers covered them with stares of derisive enjoyment. Historically there was supposed to be something infinitely humorous in their situation.

"We are due in Yellow Sky at 3:42," he said, looking tenderly into her eyes.

"Oh, are we?" she said, as if she had not been aware of it. To evince surprise at her husband's statement was part of her wifely amiability. She took from a pocket a little silver watch; and as she held it before her, and stared at it with a frown of attention, the new husband's face shone.

"I bought it in San Anton' from a friend of mine," he told her gleefully.

"It's seventeen minutes past twelve," she said, looking up at him with a kind of shy and clumsy coquetry. A passenger, noting this play, grew excessively sardonic, and winked at himself in one of the numerous mirrors.

At last they went to the dining-car. Two rows of negro waiters, in glowing white suits, surveyed their entrance with the interest, and also the equanimity, of men who had been forewarned. The pair fell to the lot of a waiter who happened to feel pleasure in steering them through their meal. He viewed them with the manner of a fatherly pilot, his countenance radiant with benevolence. The patronage, entwined with the ordinary deference, was not plain to them. And yet, as they returned to their coach, they showed in their faces a sense of escape.

To the left, miles down a long purple slope, was a little ribbon of mist where moved the keening Rio Grande. The train was approaching it at an angle, and the apex was Yellow Sky. Presently it was apparent that, as the distance from Yellow Sky grew shorter, the husband became commensurately restless. His brick-red hands were more insistent in their prominence. Occasionally he was even rather absent-minded and far-away when the bride leaned forward and addressed him.

As a matter of truth, Jack Potter was beginning to find the shadow of a deed weigh upon him like a leaden slab. He, the town marshal of Yellow Sky, a man known, liked, and feared in his corner, a prominent person, had gone to San Antonio to meet a girl he believed he loved, and there, after the usual prayers, had actually induced her to marry him, without consulting Yellow Sky for any part of the transaction. He was now bringing his bride before an innocent and unsuspecting community.

Of course people in Yellow Sky married as it pleased them, in accordance with a general custom; but such was Potter's thought of his duty to his friends, or of their idea of his duty, or of an unspoken form which does not control men in these matters, that he felt he was heinous. He had committed an extraordinary crime. Face to face with this girl in San Antonio, and spurred by his sharp impulse, he had gone headlong over all the social hedges. At San Antonio he was like a man hidden in the dark. A knife to sever any friendly duty, any form, was easy to his hand in that remote city. But the hour of Yellow Sky—the hour of daylight—was approaching.

He knew full well that his marriage was an important thing to his town. It could only be exceeded by the burning of the new hotel. His friends could not forgive him. Frequently he had reflected on the advisability of telling them by telegraph, but a new cowardice had been upon him. He feared to do it. And now the train was hurrying him toward a scene of amazement, glee, and reproach. He glanced out of the window at the line of haze swinging slowly in toward the train.

Yellow Sky had a kind of brass band, which played painfully, to the delight of the populace. He laughed without heart as he thought of it. If the citizens could dream of his prospective arrival with his bride, they would parade the band at the station and escort them, amid cheers and laughing congratulations, to his adobe home.

He resolved that he would use all the devices of speed and plainscraft in making the journey from the station to his house. Once within that safe citadel, he could issue some sort of vocal bulletin, and then not go among the citizens until they had time to wear off a little of their enthusiasm.

The bride looked anxiously at him. "What's worrying you, Jack?"

He laughed again. "I'm not worrying, girl; I'm only thinking of Yellow Sky."

She flushed in comprehension.

A sense of mutual guilt invaded their minds and developed a finer tenderness. They looked at each other with eyes softly aglow. But Potter often laughed the same nervous laugh; the flush upon the bride's face seemed quite permanent.

The traitor to the feelings of Yellow Sky narrowly watched the speeding landscape. "We're nearly there," he said.

Presently the porter came and announced the proximity of Potter's home. He held a brush in his hand, and, with all his airy superiority gone, he brushed Potter's new clothes as the latter slowly turned this way and that way. Potter fumbled out a coin and gave it to the porter, as he had seen others do. It was a heavy and muscle-bound business, as that of a man shoeing his first horse.

The porter took their bag, and as the train began to slow they moved forward to the hooded platform of the car. Presently the two engines and their long string of coaches rushed into the station of Yellow Sky.

"They have to take water here," said Potter, from a constricted throat and in mournful cadence, as one announcing death. Before the train stopped his eye had swept the length of the platform, and he was glad and astonished to see there was none upon it but the station-agent, who, with a slightly hurried and anxious air, was walking toward the water-tanks. When the train had halted, the porter alighted first, and placed in position a little temporary step.

"Come on, girl," said Potter, hoarsely. As he helped her down they each laughed on a false note. He took the bag from the negro, and bade his wife cling to his arm. As they slunk rapidly away, his hang-dog glance perceived that they were unloading the two trunks, and also that the station-agent, far ahead near the baggage-car, had turned and was running toward him, making gestures. He laughed, and groaned as he laughed, when he noted the first effect of his marital bliss

upon Yellow Sky. He gripped his wife's arm firmly to his side, and they fled. Behind them the porter stood, chuckling fatuously.

## II

THE California express on the Southern Railway was due at Yellow Sky in twenty-one minutes. There were six men at the bar of the Weary Gentleman saloon. One was a drummer who talked a great deal and rapidly; three were Texans who did not care to talk at that time; and two were Mexican sheep-herders, who did not talk as a general practice in the Weary Gentleman saloon. The barkeeper's dog lay on the board walk that crossed in front of the door. His head was on his paws, and he glanced drowsily here and there with the constant vigilance of a dog that is kicked on occasion. Across the sandy street were some vivid green grass-plots, so wonderful in appearance, amid the sands that burned near them in a blazing sun, that they caused a doubt in the mind. They exactly resembled the grass mats used to represent lawns on the stage. At the cooler end of the railway station, a man without a coat sat in a tilted chair and smoked his pipe. The fresh-cut bank of the Rio Grande circled near the town, and there could be seen beyond it a great plum-colored plain of mesquit.

Save for the busy drummer and his companions in the saloon, Yellow Sky was dozing. The newcomer leaned gracefully upon the bar, and recited many tales with the confidence of a bard who has come upon a new field.

"—and at the moment that the old man fell downstairs with the bureau in his arms, the old woman was coming up with two scuttles of coal, and of course—"

The drummer's tale was interrupted by a young man who suddenly appeared in the open door. He cried: "Scratchy Wilson's drunk, and has turned loose with both hands." The two Mexicans at once set down their glasses and faded out of the rear entrance of the saloon.

The drummer, innocent and jocular, answered: "All right, old man. S'pose he has? Come in and have a drink, anyhow."

But the information had made such an obvious cleft in every skull in the room that the drummer was obliged to see its importance. All had become instantly solemn. "Say," said he, mystified, "what is this?" His three companions made the introductory gesture of eloquent speech; but the young man at the door forestalled them.

"It means, my friend," he answered, as he

came into the saloon, "that for the next two hours this town won't be a health resort."

The barkeeper went to the door, and locked and barred it; reaching out of the window, he pulled in heavy wooden shutters, and barred them. Immediately a solemn, chapel-like gloom was upon the place. The drummer was looking from one to another.

"But say," he cried, "what is this, anyhow? You don't mean there is going to be a gun-fight?"

"Don't know whether there'll be a fight or not," answered one man, grimly; "but there'll be some shootin'—some good shootin'."

The young man who had warned them waved his hand. "Oh, there'll be a fight fast enough, if any one wants it. Anybody can get a fight out there in the street. There's a fight just waiting."

The drummer seemed to be swayed between the interest of a foreigner and a perception of personal danger.

"What did you say his name was?" he asked.

"Scratchy Wilson," they answered in chorus.

"And will he kill anybody? What are you going to do? Does this happen often? Does he rampage around like this once a week or so? Can he break in that door?"

"No; he can't break down that door," replied the barkeeper. "He's tried it three times. But when he comes you'd better lay down on the floor, stranger. He's dead sure to shoot at it, and a bullet may come through."

Thereafter the drummer kept a strict eye upon the door. The time had not yet been called for him to hug the floor, but, as a minor precaution, he sidled near to the wall. "Will he kill anybody?" he said again.

The men laughed low and scornfully at the question.

"He's out to shoot, and he's out for trouble. Don't see any good in experimentin' with him."

"But what do you do in a case like this? What do you do?"

A man responded: "Why, he and Jack Potter—"

"But," in chorus the other men interrupted, "Jack Potter's in San Anton'."

"Well, who is he? What's he got to do with it?"

"Oh, he's the town marshal. He goes out and fights Scratchy when he gets on one of these tears."

"Wow!" said the drummer, mopping his brow. "Nice job he's got."

The voices had toned away to mere whisperings. The drummer wished to ask further questions, which were born of an increasing anxiety and bewilderment; but when he attempted them, the men merely looked at him in irritation and motioned him to remain silent. A tense waiting hush was upon them. In the deep shadows of the room their eyes shone as they listened for sounds from the street. One man made three gestures at the barkeeper; and the latter, moving like a ghost, handed him a glass and a bottle. The man poured a full glass of whisky, and set down the bottle noiselessly. He gulped the whisky in a swallow, and turned again toward the door in immovable silence. The drummer saw that the barkeeper, without a sound, had taken a Winchester from beneath the bar. Later he saw this individual beckoning to him, so he tiptoed across the room.

"You better come with me back of the bar."

"No, thanks," said the drummer, perspiring; "I'd rather be where I can make a break for the back door."

Whereupon the man of bottles made a kindly but peremptory gesture. The drummer obeyed it, and, finding himself seated on a box with his head below the level of the bar, balm was laid upon his soul at sight of various zinc and copper fittings that bore a resemblance to armor-plate. The barkeeper took a seat comfortably upon an adjacent box.

"You see," he whispered, "this here Scratchy Wilson is a wonder with a gun—a perfect wonder; and when he goes on the war-trail, we hunt our holes—naturally. He's about the last one of the old gang that used to hang out along the river here. He's a terror when he's drunk. When he's sober he's all right—kind of simple—wouldn't hurt a fly—nicest fellow in town. But when he's drunk—whoo!"

There were periods of stillness. "I wish Jack Potter was back from San Anton'," said the barkeeper. "He shot Wilson up once—in the leg—and he would sail in and pull out the kinks in this thing."

Presently they heard from a distance the sound of a shot, followed by three wild yowls. It instantly removed a bond from the men in the darkened saloon. There was a shuffling of feet. They looked at each other. "Here he comes," they said.

### III

A MAN in a maroon-colored flannel shirt, which had been purchased for purposes of decoration, and made principally by some Jewish women on the East Side of New York, rounded a corner and walked into the middle of the main street of Yellow Sky. In either hand the man held a long, heavy, blue-black revolver. Often he yelled, and these cries rang through a semblance of a deserted village, shrilly flying over the roofs in a volume that seemed to have no relation to the ordinary vocal strength of a man. It was as if the surrounding stillness formed the arch of a tomb over him. These cries of ferocious challenge rang against walls of silence. And his boots had red tops with gilded imprints, of the kind beloved in winter by little sledding boys on the hillsides of New England.

The man's face flamed in a rage begot of whisky. His eyes, rolling, and yet keen for ambush, hunted the still doorways and windows. He walked with the creeping movement of the midnight cat. As it occurred to him, he roared menacing information. The long revolvers in his hands were as easy as straws; they were moved with an electric swiftness. The little fingers of each hand played sometimes in a musician's way. Plain from the low collar of the shirt, the cords of his neck straightened and sank, straightened and sank, as passion moved him. The only sounds were his terrible invitations. The calm adobes preserved their demeanor at the passing of this small thing in the middle of the street.

There was no offer of fight—no offer of fight. The man called to the sky. There were no attractions. He bellowed and fumed and swayed his revolvers here and everywhere.

The dog of the barkeeper of the Weary Gentleman saloon had not appreciated the advance of events. He yet lay dozing in front of his master's door. At sight of the dog, the man paused and raised his revolver humorously. At sight of the man, the dog sprang up and walked diagonally away, with a sullen head, and growling. The man yelled, and the dog broke into a gallop. As it was about to enter an alley, there was a loud noise, a whistling, and something spat the ground directly before it. The dog screamed, and, wheeling in terror, galloped headlong in a new direction. Again there was a noise, a whistling, and sand was kicked viciously before it. Fear-stricken, the dog turned and flurried like an animal in a pen. The man stood laughing, his weapons at his hips.

Ultimately the man was attracted by the closed door of the Weary Gentleman saloon. He went to it and, hammering with a revolver, demanded drink.

The door remaining imperturbable, he picked a bit of paper from the walk, and nailed it to the framework with a knife. He then turned his back contemptuously upon this popular resort and, walking to the opposite side of the street and spinning there on his heel quickly and lithely, fired at the bit of paper. He missed it by a half-inch. He swore at himself, and went away. Later he comfortably fusilladed the windows of his most intimate friend. The man was playing with this town; it was a toy for him.

But still there was no offer of fight. The name of Jack Potter, his ancient antagonist, entered his mind, and he concluded that it would be a glad thing if he should go to Potter's house, and by bombardment induce him to come out and fight. He moved in the direction of his desire, chanting Apache scalp-music.

When he arrived at it, Potter's house presented the same still front as had the other adobes. Taking up a strategic position, the man howled a challenge. But this house regarded him as might a great stone god. It gave no sign. After a decent wait, the man howled further challenges, mingling with them wonderful epithets.

Presently there came the spectacle of a man churning himself into deepest rage over the immobility of a house. He fumed at it as the winter wind attacks a prairie cabin in the North. To the distance there should have gone the sound of a tumult like the fighting of two hundred Mexicans. As necessity bade him, he paused for breath or to reload his revolvers.

## IV

POTTER and his bride walked sheepishly and with speed. Sometimes they laughed together shamefacedly and low.

"Next corner, dear," he said finally.

They put forth the efforts of a pair walking bowed against a strong wind. Potter was about to raise a finger to point the first appearance of the new home when, as they circled the corner, they came face to face with a man in a maroon-colored shirt, who was feverishly pushing cartridges into a large revolver. Upon the instant the man dropped his revolver to the ground and, like lightning, whipped another from its holster. The second weapon was aimed at the bridegroom's chest.

There was a silence. Potter's mouth seemed to be merely a grave for his tongue. He exhibited an instinct to at once loosen his arm from the woman's grip, and he dropped the bag to the sand. As for the bride, her face had gone as yellow as old cloth. She was a slave to hideous rites, gazing at the apparitional snake.

The two men faced each other at a distance of three paces. He of the revolver smiled with a new and quiet ferocity.

"Tried to sneak up on me," he said. "Tried to sneak up on me!" His eyes grew more baleful. As Potter made a slight movement, the man thrust his revolver venomously forward. "No; don't you do it, Jack Potter. Don't you move a finger toward a gun just yet. Don't you move an eyelash. The time has come for me to settle with you, and I'm goin' to do it my own way, and loaf along with no interferin'. So if you don't want a gun bent on you, just mind what I tell you."

Potter looked at his enemy. "I ain't got a gun on me Scratchy," he said. "Honest, I ain't." He was stiffening and steadying, but yet somewhere at the back of his mind a vision of the Pullman floated: the sea-green figured velvet, the shining brass, silver, and grass, the wood that gleamed as darkly brilliant as the surface of a pool of oil—all the glory of the marriage, the environment of the new estate. "You know I fight when it comes to fighting, Scratchy Wilson; but I ain't got a gun on me. You'll have to do all the shootin' yourself."

His enemy's face went livid. He stepped forward, and lashed his weapon to and fro before Potter's chest. "Don't you tell me you ain't got no gun on you, you whelp. Don't tell me no lie like that. There ain't a man in Texas ever seen you without no gun. Don't take me for no kid." His eyes blazed with light, and his throat worked like a pump.

"I ain't takin' you for no kid," answered Potter. His heels had not moved an inch backward. "I'm takin' you for a damn fool. I tell you I ain't got a gun, and I ain't. If you're goin' to shoot me up, you better begin now; you'll never get a chance like this again."

So much enforced reasoning had told on Wilson's rage; he was calmer. "If you ain't got a gun, why ain't you got a gun?" he sneered. "Been to Sunday-school?"

"I ain't got a gun because I've just come from San Anton' with my wife. I'm married," said Potter. "And if I'd thought there was going to be any galoots like you prowling around when I brought my wife home, I'd had a gun, and don't you forget it."

"Married!" said Scratchy, not at all comprehending.

"Yes, married. I'm married," said Potter, distinctly.

"Married?" said Scratchy. Seemingly for the first time, he saw the drooping, drowning woman at the other man's side. "No!" he said. He was like a creature allowed a glimpse of another world. He moved a pace backward, and his arm, with the revolver, dropped to his side. "Is this the lady?" he asked.

"Yes; this is the lady," answered Potter.

There was another period of silence.

"Well," said Wilson at last, slowly, "I s'pose it's all off now."

"It's all off if you say so, Scratchy. You know I didn't make the trouble." Potter lifted his valise.

"Well, I 'low it's off, Jack," said Wilson. He was looking at the ground. "Married!" He was not a student of chivalry; it was merely that in the presence of this foreign condition he was a simple child of the earlier plains. He picked up his starboard revolver, and, placing both weapons in their holsters, he went away. His feet made funnel-shaped tracks in the heavy sand.

## DEATH AND THE CHILD

❮ INTERVIEWED by a fellow correspondent in Greece, Crane casually lit a cigarette while sitting on an ammunition box and said: "Between two great armies battling against each other, the interesting thing is the mental attitude of the men. The Greeks I can see and understand, but the Turks seem unreal. They are shadows on the plain—vague figures in black, indications of a mysterious force." How Crane handled this force in the story based on his Greek experience has been discussed in the Introduction, p. 838.

Crane wrote while self-invited guests were swarming upon his privacy at Ravensbrook, and at the beginning of December 1897, he even had to go up to London and take a hotel room in order to have a quiet place to finish the story. *Harper's Weekly* published the story the following March, and with "The Bride" it came out in *The Open Boat and Other Stories* in April, in both New York and London.

### I

THE PEASANTS who were streaming down the mountain trail had, in their sharp terror, evidently lost their ability to count. The cattle and the huge round bundles seemed to suffice to the minds of the crowd if there were now two in each case where there had been three. This brown stream poured on with a constant wastage of goods and beasts. A goat fell behind to scout the dried grass, and its owner, howling, flogging his donkeys, passed far ahead. A colt, suddenly frightened, made a stumbling charge up the hillside. The expenditure was always profligate, and always unnamed, unnoted. It was as if fear was a river, and this horde had simply been caught in the torrent, man tumbling over beast, beast over man, as helpless in it as the logs that fall and shoulder grindingly through the gorges of a lumber country. It was a freshet that might sear the face of the tall, quiet mountain; it might draw a livid line across the land, this downpour of fear with a thousand homes adrift in the current—men, women, babes, animals. From it there arose a constant babble of tongues, shrill, broken, and sometimes choking, as from men drowning. Many made gestures, painting their agonies on the air with fingers that twirled swiftly.

The blue bay, with its pointed ships, and the white town lay below them, distant, flat, serene. There was upon this vista a peace that a bird knows when, high in air, it surveys the world, a great, calm thing rolling noiselessly toward the end of the mystery. Here on the height one felt the existence of the universe scornfully defining the pain in ten thousand minds. The sky was an arch of stolid sapphire. Even to the mountains, raising their mighty shapes from the valley, this headlong rush of the fugitives was too minute. The sea, the sky, and the hills combined in their grandeur to term this misery inconsequent. Then, too, it sometimes happened that a face seen as it passed on the flood reflected curiously the spirit of them all, and still more. One saw then a woman of the opinion of the vaults above the clouds. When a child cried, it cried always because of some adjacent misfortune—some discomfort of a pack-saddle or rudeness of an encircling arm. In the dismal melody of this flight there were often sounding chords of apathy. Into these preoccupied countenances one felt that needles could be thrust without purchasing a scream. The trail wound here and there, as the sheep had willed in the making of it.

Although this throng seemed to prove that the whole of humanity was fleeing in one direction— with every tie severed that binds us to the soil—a young man was walking rapidly up the mountain, hastening to a side of the path from time to time to avoid some particularly wide rush of people and cattle. He looked at everything in agitation and pity. Frequently he called admonitions to maniacal fugitives, and at other times he exchanged strange stares with the imperturbable ones. They seemed to him to wear merely the expressions of so many boulders rolling down the hill. He exhibited wonder and awe with his pitying glances.

Turning once toward the rear, he saw a man in the uniform of a lieutenant of infantry marching the same way. He waited then, subconsciously elated at a prospect of being able to make into words the emotion which heretofore had been expressed only in the flash of eyes and sensitive movements of his flexible mouth. He spoke to the officer in rapid French, waving his arms wildly, and often pointing with a dramatic finger. "Ah, this is too cruel, too cruel, too cruel! is it not? I did not think it would be as bad as this. I did not think—God's mercy!—I did not think at all. And yet, I am a Greek; or, at least, my father was a Greek. I did not come here to fight; I am really a correspondent; you see? I was to write for an Italian paper. I have been educated in Italy; I have spent nearly all my life in Italy—at the schools and universities. I knew nothing of war! I was a student—a student. I came here merely because my father was a Greek, and for his sake I thought of Greece. I loved Greece; but I did not dream—"

He paused, breathing heavily. His eyes glistened from that soft overflow which comes on occasion to the glance of a young woman. Eager, passionate, profoundly moved, his first words while facing the procession of fugitives had been an active definition of his own dimension, his personal relation to men, geography, life. Throughout he had preserved the fiery dignity of a tragedian.

The officer's manner at once deferred to this outburst. "Yes," he said, polite, but mournful; "these poor people—these poor people! I do not know what is to become of these poor people."

The young man declaimed again: "I had no dream—I had no dream that it would be like this! This is too cruel—too cruel! Now I want to be a soldier. Now I want to fight. Now I want to do battle for the land of my father." He made a sweeping gesture into the north-west.

The officer was also a young man, but he was bronzed and steady. Above his high military collar of crimson cloth with one silver star upon it appeared a profile stern, quiet, and confident, respecting fate, fearing only opinion. His clothes were covered with dust; the only bright spot was the flame of the crimson collar. At the violent cries of his companion he smiled as if to himself, meanwhile keeping his eyes fixed in a glance ahead.

From a land toward which their faces were bent came a continuous boom of artillery fire. It was sounding in regular measures, like the beating of a colossal clock—a clock that was counting the seconds in the lives of the stars, and men had time to die between the ticks. Solemn, oracular, inexorable, the great seconds tolled over the hills as if God fronted this dial rimmed by the horizon. The soldier and the correspondent found themselves silent. The latter in particular was sunk in a great mournfulness, as if he had resolved willynilly to swing to the bottom of the abyss where dwelt secrets of this kind, and had learned beforehand that all to be met there was cruelty and hopelessness. A strap of his bright new leather leggings came unfastened, and he bowed over it slowly, impressively, as one bending over the grave of a child.

Then, suddenly, the reverberations mingled until one could not separate one explosion from another, and into the hubbub came the drawling sound of a leisurely musketry fire. Instantly, for some reason of cadence, the noise was irritating, silly, infantile. This uproar was childish. It forced the nerves to object, to protest against this racket, which was as idle as the din of a lad with a drum.

The lieutenant lifted his finger and pointed. He spoke in vexed tones, as if he held the other man personally responsible for the noise. "Well, there!" he said. "If you wish for war, you now have an opportunity magnificent."

The correspondent raised himself upon his toes. He tapped his chest with gloomy pride. "Yes! There is war! There is the war I wish to enter. I fling myself in. I am a Greek—a Greek, you understand. I wish to fight for my country. You know the way. Lead me! I offer myself." Struck with a sudden thought, he brought a case from his pocket, and, extracting a card, handed it to the officer with a bow. "My name is Peza," he said simply.

A strange smile passed over the soldier's face. There was pity and pride—the vanity of experience—and contempt in it. "Very well," he said, returning the bow. "If my company is in the middle of the fight, I shall be glad for the honor of your companionship. If my company is not in the middle of the fight, I will make other arrangements for you."

Peza bowed once more, very stiffly, and correctly spoke his thanks. On the edge of what he took to be a great venture toward death, he discovered that he was annoyed at something in the lieutenant's tone. Things immediately assumed new and extraordinary proportions. The battle, the great carnival of woe, was sunk at once to an equation with a vexation by a stranger. He wanted to ask the lieutenant what was his meaning. He bowed again majestically. The lieutenant bowed. They flung a shadow of manners, of capering tinsel ceremony, across a land that groaned, and it satisfied something within themselves completely.

In the meantime the river of fleeing villagers was changed to simply a last dropping of belated creatures who fled past stammering and flinging their hands high. The two men had come to the top of the great hill. Before them was a green plain as level as an inland sea. It swept northward, and merged finally into a length of silvery mist. Upon the near part of this plain, and upon two gray, treeless mountains at the sides of it, were little black lines from which floated slanting sheets of smoke. It was not a battle, to the nerves; one could survey it with equanimity, as if it were a tea-table. But upon Peza's mind it struck a loud, clang-

ing blow. It was war. Edified, aghast, triumphant, he paused suddenly, his lips apart. He remembered the pageants of carnage that had marched through the dreams of his childhood. Love he knew; that he had confronted alone, isolated, wondering, an individual, an atom taking the hand of a titanic principle. Like the faintest breeze on his forehead, he felt here the vibration from the hearts of forty thousand men.

The lieutenant's nostrils were moving. "I must go at once," he said. "I must go at once."

"I will go with you, wherever you go," shouted Peza, loudly.

A primitive track wound down the side of the mountain, and in their rush they bounded from here to there, choosing risks which in the ordinary caution of man would surely have seemed of remarkable danger. The ardor of the correspondent surpassed the full energy of the soldier. Several times he turned and shouted: "Come on! Come on!"

At the foot of the path they came to a wide road which extended toward the battle in a yellow and straight line. Some men were trudging wearily to the rear. They were without rifles; their clumsy uniforms were dirty and all awry. They turned eyes dully aglow with fever upon the pair striding toward the battle. Others were bandaged with the triangular kerchief, upon which one could still see, through blood-stains, the little explanatory pictures illustrating the ways to bind various wounds—"Fig. 1," "Fig. 2," "Fig. 7." Mingled with the pacing soldiers were peasants, indifferent, capable of smiling, gibbering about the battle, which was to them an ulterior drama. A man was leading a string of three donkeys to the rear, and at intervals he was accosted by wounded or fevered soldiers, from whom he defended his animals with ape-like cries and mad gesticulations. After much chattering they usually subsided gloomily, and allowed him to go with his sleek little beasts unburdened. Finally he encountered a soldier who walked slowly, with the assistance of a staff. His head was bound with a wide bandage, grimy from blood and mud. He made application to the peasant, and immediately they were involved in a hideous Levantine discussion. The peasant whined and clamored, sometimes spitting like a kitten. The wounded soldier jawed on thunderously, his great hands stretched in claw-like graspings over the peasant's head. Once he raised his staff and made threat with it. Then suddenly the row was at an end. The other sick men saw their comrade mount the leading donkey, and at once begin to drum with his heels. None attempted to gain the backs of the remaining animals. They gazed after him dully. Finally they saw the caravan outlined for a moment against the sky. The soldier was still waving his arms passionately, having it out with the peasant.

Peza was alive with despair for these men who looked at him with such doleful, quiet eyes. "Ah, my God!" he cried to the lieutenant, "these poor souls!—these poor souls!"

The officer faced about angrily. "If you are coming with me, there is no time for this." Peza obeyed instantly and with a sudden meekness. In the moment some portion of egotism left him, and he modestly wondered if the universe took cognizance of him to an important degree. This theater for slaughter, built by the inscrutable needs of the earth, was an enormous affair, and he reflected that the accidental destruction of an individual, Peza by name, would perhaps be nothing at all.

With the lieutenant, he was soon walking along behind a series of little crescent-shaped trenches, in which were soldiers tranquilly interested, gossiping with the hum of a tea-party. Although these men were not at this time under fire, he concluded that they were fabulously brave, else they would not be so comfortable, so at home, in their sticky brown trenches. They were certain to be heavily attacked before the day was old. The universities had not taught him to understand this attitude. At the passing of the young man in very nice tweed, with his new leggings, his new white helmet, his new field-glass case, his new revolver holster, the soiled soldiers turned with the same curiosity which a being in strange garb meets at the corners of streets. He might as well have been promenading a populous avenue. The soldiers volubly discussed his identity.

To Peza there was something awful in the absolute familiarity of each tone, expression, gesture. These men, menaced with battle, displayed the curiosity of the café. Then, on the verge of his great encounter toward death, he found himself extremely embarrassed, composing his face with difficulty, wondering what to do with his hands, like a gawk at a levee.

He felt ridiculous, and also he felt awed, aghast at these men who could turn their faces from the ominous front and debate his clothes, his business. There was an element which was new-born into his theory of war.

He was not averse to the brisk pace at which the lieutenant moved along the line. The roar of fighting was always in Peza's ears. It came from some short hills ahead and to the left. The road curved suddenly and entered a wood. The trees stretched their luxuriant and graceful branches over grassy slopes. A breeze made all this verdure gently rustle

and speak in long silken sighs. Absorbed in listening to the hurricane racket from the front, he still remembered that these trees were growing, the grass-blades were extending, according to their process. He inhaled a deep breath of moisture and fragrance from the grove, a wet odor which expressed the opulent fecundity of unmoved nature, marching on with her million plans for multiple life, multiple death.

Farther on, they came to a place where the Turkish shells were landing. There was a long, hurtling sound in the air, and then one had sight of a shell. To Peza it was of the conical missiles which friendly officers had displayed to him on board warships. Curiously enough, too, this first shell smacked of the foundry—of men with smudged faces, of the blare of furnace fires. It brought machinery immediately into his mind. He thought that if he was killed there at that time, it would be as romantic to the old standards as death by a bit of falling iron in a factory.

## II

A CHILD was playing on a mountain, and disregarding a battle that was waging on the plain. Behind him was the little cobbled hut of his fled parents. It was now occupied by a pearl-colored cow, that stared out from the darkness, thoughtful and tender-eyed. The child ran to and fro, fumbling with sticks, and making great machinations with pebbles. By a striking exercise of artistic license, the sticks were ponies, cows, and dogs, and the pebbles were sheep. He was managing large agricultural and herding affairs. He was too intent on them to pay much heed to the fight four miles away, which at that distance resembled in sound the beating of surf upon rocks. However, there were occasions when some louder outbreak of that thunder stirred him from his serious occupation, and he turned then a questioning eye upon the battle, a small stick poised in his hand, interrupted in the act of sending his dog after his sheep. His tranquillity in regard to the death on the plain was as invincible as that of the mountain on which he stood.

It was evident that fear had swept the parents away from their home in a manner that could make them forget this child, the first-born. Nevertheless, the hut was cleaned bare. The cow had committed no impropriety in billeting herself at the domicile of her masters. This smoke-colored and odorous interior contained nothing as large as a humming-bird. Terror had operated on these runaway people in its sinister fashion—elevating details to enormous heights, causing a man to remember a button while he forgot a coat, overpowering every one with recollections of a broken coffee-cup, deluging them with fears for the safety of an old pipe, and causing them to forget their first-born. Meanwhile the child played soberly with his trinkets.

He was solitary. Engrossed in his own pursuits, it was seldom that he lifted his head to inquire of the world why it made so much noise. The stick in his hand was much larger to him than was an army corps of the distance. It was too childish for the mind of the child. He was dealing with sticks.

The battle-lines writhed at times in the agony of a sea-creature on the sands. These tentacles flung and waved in a supreme excitement of pain, and the struggles of the great outlined body brought it near and nearer to the child. Once he looked at the plain, and saw some men running wildly across a field. He had seen people chasing obdurate beasts in such fashion, and it struck him immediately that it was a manly thing, which he would incorporate in his game. Consequently he raced furiously at his stone sheep, flourishing a cudgel, crying the shepherd calls. He paused frequently to get a cue of manner from the soldiers fighting on the plain. He reproduced, to a degree, any movements which he accounted rational to his theory of sheep-herding, the business of men, the traditional and exalted living of his father.

### III

IT WAS as if Peza was a corpse walking on the bottom of the sea, and finding there fields of grain, groves, weeds, the faces of men, voices. War, a strange employment of the race, presented to him a scene crowded with familiar objects which wore the livery of their commonness placidly, undauntedly. He was smitten with keen astonishment; a spread of green grass, lit with the flames of poppies, was too old for the company of this new ogre. If he had been devoting the full lens of his mind to this phase, he would have known that he was amazed that the trees, the flowers, the grass, all tender and peaceful nature, had not taken to heels at once upon the outbreak of battle. He venerated the immovable poppies.

The road seemed to lead into the apex of an angle formed by the two defensive lines of the Greeks. There was a struggle of wounded men, and of gunless and jaded men. These latter did not seem to be frightened. They remained very cool, walking with unhurried steps, and busy in gossip. Peza tried to define them. Perhaps during the fight they had reached the limit of their mental storage, their capacity for excitement, for tragedy, and had then simply come away. Peza remembered his visit to a certain place of pictures, where he had found

himself amid heavenly skies and diabolic midnights—the sunshine beating red upon desert sands, nude bodies flung to the shore in the green moonglow, ghastly and starving men clawing at a wall in darkness, a girl at her bath, with screened rays falling upon her pearly shoulders, a dance, a funeral, a review, an execution—all the strength of argus-eyed art; and he had whirled and whirled amid this universe, with cries of woe and joy, sin and beauty, piercing his ears until he had been obliged to simply come away. He remembered that as he had emerged he had lit a cigarette with unction, and advanced promptly to a café. A great hollow quiet seemed to be upon the earth.

This was a different case, but in his thoughts he conceded the same causes to many of these gunless wanderers. They, too, may have dreamed at lightning speed, until the capacity for it was overwhelmed. As he watched them, he again saw himself walking toward the café, puffing upon his cigarette. As if to reinforce his theory, a soldier stopped him with an eager but polite inquiry for a match. He watched the man light his little roll of tobacco and paper and begin to smoke ravenously.

Peza no longer was torn with sorrow at the sight of wounded men. Evidently he found that pity had a numerical limit, and when this was passed the emotion became another thing. Now, as he viewed them, he merely felt himself very lucky, and beseeched the continuance of his superior fortune. At the passing of these slouched and stained figures he now heard a reiteration of warning. A part of himself was appealing through the medium of these grim shapes. It was plucking at his sleeve and pointing, telling him to beware of these soldiers only as he would have cared for the harms of broken dolls. His whole vision was focused upon his own chance.

The lieutenant suddenly halted. "Look," he said; "I find that my duty is in another direction; I must go another way. But if you wish to fight, you have only to go forward, and any officer of the fighting line will give you opportunity." He raised his cap ceremoniously. Peza raised his new white helmet. The stranger to battles uttered thanks to his chaperon, the one who had presented him. They bowed punctiliously, staring at each other with civil eyes.

The lieutenant moved quietly away through a field. In an instant it flashed upon Peza's mind that this desertion was perfidious. He had been subjected to a criminal discourtesy. The officer had fetched him into the middle of the thing, and then left him to wander helplessly toward death. At one time he was upon the point of shouting at the officer.

In the vale there was an effect as if one was then beneath the battle. It was going on above, somewhere. Alone, unguided, Peza felt like a man groping in a cellar. He reflected, too, that one should always see the beginning of a fight. It was too difficult to thus approach it when the affair was in full swing. The trees hid all the movements of troops from him, and he thought he might be walking out to the very spot which chance had provided for the reception of a fool. He asked eager questions of passing soldiers. Some paid no heed to him; others shook their heads mournfully. They knew nothing, save that war was hard work. If they talked at all, it was in testimony of having fought well, savagely. They did not know if the army was going to advance, hold its ground, or retreat. They were weary.

A long, pointed shell flashed through the air, and struck near the base of a tree with a fierce upheaval, compounded of earth and flames. Looking back, Peza could see the shattered tree quivering from head to foot. Its whole being underwent a convulsive tremor which was an exhibition of pain and, furthermore, deep amazement. As he advanced through the vale, the shells continued to hiss and hurtle in long, low flights, and the bullets purred in the air. The missiles were flying into the breast of an astounded nature. The landscape, bewildered, agonized, was suffering a rain of infamous shots, and Peza imagined a million eyes gazing at him with the gaze of startled antelopes.

There was a resolute crashing of musketry from the tall hill on the left, and from directly in front there was a mingled din of artillery and musketry firing. Peza felt that his pride was playing a great trick in forcing him forward in this manner under conditions of strangeness, isolation, and ignorance; but he recalled the manner of the lieutenant, the smile on the hilltop among the flying peasants. Peza blushed, and pulled the peak of his helmet down on his forehead. He strode on firmly. Nevertheless, he hated the lieutenant, and he resolved that on some future occasion he would take much trouble to arrange a stinging social revenge upon that grinning jackanapes. It did not occur to him, until later, that he was now going to battle mainly because at a previous time a certain man had smiled.

### IV

THE ROAD moved around the base of a little hill, and on this hill a battery of mountain guns was leisurely shelling something unseen. In the lee of the height, the mules, contented under their heavy saddles, were quietly browsing the long grass. Peza ascended the hill by a slanting path. He felt his heart beat swiftly. Once at the top of the hill, he would be obliged to look this phenomenon in the face. He hurried with a mysterious idea of preventing by this strategy the battle from making his appearance a signal for some tremendous renewal. This vague thought seemed logical at the time. Certainly this living thing had knowledge of his coming. He endowed it with the intelligence of a barbaric deity. And so he hurried. He wished to surprise war, this terrible emperor, when it was only growling on its throne. The ferocious and horrible sovereign was not to be allowed to make the arrival a pretext for some fit of smoky rage and blood. In this half-lull, Peza had distinctly the sense of stealing upon the battle unawares.

The soldiers watching the mules did not seem to be impressed by anything august. Two of them sat side by side and talked comfortably; another lay flat upon his back, staring dreamily at the sky; another cursed a mule for certain refractions. Despite their uniforms, their bandoleers and rifles, they were dwelling in the peace of hostlers. However, the long shells were whooping from time to time over the brow of the hill, and swirling in almost straight lines toward the vale of trees, flowers, and grass. Peza, hearing and seeing the shells, and seeing the pensive guardians of the mules, felt reassured. They were accepting the conditions of war as easily as an old sailor accepts the chair behind the counter of a tobacco-shop. Or it was merely that the farm boy had gone to sea, and he had adjusted himself to the circumstances immediately, and with only the usual first misadventures in conduct. Peza was proud and ashamed that he was not of them—these stupid peasants who, throughout the world, hold potentates on their thrones, make statesmen illustrious, provide generals with lasting victories, all with ignorance, indifference, or half-witted hatred, moving the world with the strength of their arms, and getting their heads knocked together, in the name of God, the king, or the stock exchange—immortal, dreaming, hopeless asses who surrender their reason to the care of a shining puppet, and persuade some toy to carry their lives in his purse. Peza mentally abased himself before them, and wished to stir them with furious kicks.

As his eyes ranged above the rim of the plateau, he saw a group of artillery officers talking busily. They turned at once, and regarded his ascent. A moment later a row of infantry soldiers, in a trench beyond the little guns, all faced him. Peza bowed to the officers. He understood at the time that he had made a good and cool bow, and he wondered at it; for his breath was coming in gasps—he was stifling from sheer excitement. He felt like a tipsy man trying to conceal his muscular uncertainty from the people in the street. But the officers did not display any knowledge. They bowed. Behind them Peza saw the plain, glittering green, with three lines of black marked upon it heavily. The front of the first of these lines was frothy with smoke. To the left of this hill was a craggy mountain, from which came a continual dull rattle of musketry. Its summit was ringed with the white smoke. The black lines on the plain slowly moved. The shells that came from there passed overhead, with the sound of great birds frantically flapping their wings. Peza thought of the first sight of the sea during a storm. He seemed to feel against his face the wind that races over the tops of cold and tumultuous billows.

He heard a voice afar off: "Sir, what would you?" He turned, and saw the dapper captain of the battery standing beside him. Only a moment had elapsed.

"Pardon me, sir," said Peza, bowing again.

The officer was evidently reserving his bows. He scanned the new-comer attentively. "Are you a correspondent?" he asked.

Peza produced a card. "Yes; I came as a correspondent," he replied. "But now, sir, I have other thoughts. I wish to help. You see? I wish to help."

"What do you mean?" said the captain. "Are you a Greek? Do you wish to fight?"

"Yes; I am a Greek; I wish to fight." Peza's voice surprised him by coming from his lips in even and deliberate tones. He thought with gratification that he was behaving rather well. Another shell, traveling from some unknown point on the plain, whirled close and furiously in the air, pursuing an apparently horizontal course, as if it were never going to touch the earth. The dark shape swished across the sky.

"Ah," cried the captain, now smiling, "I am not sure that we will be able to accommodate you with a fierce affair here just at this time, but—" He walked gaily to and fro behind the guns with Peza, pointing out to him the lines of the Greeks, and describing his opinion of the general plan of defense. He wore the air of an amiable host. Other officers questioned Peza in regard to the politics of the war. The king, the ministry, Germany, England, Russia—all these huge words were continually upon their tongues. "And the people in Athens, were they—?" Amid this vivacious babble, Peza, seated upon an ammunition-box, kept his glance high, watching the appearance of shell after shell. These officers were like men who had been lost for days in the forest. They were thirsty for any scrap of news. Nevertheless, one of them would occasionally dispute their in-

formant courteously. What would Servia have to say to that? No, no; France and Russia could never allow it. Peza was elated. The shells killed no one. War was not so bad! He was simply having coffee in the smoking-room of some embassy where reverberate the names of nations.

A rumor had passed along the motley line of privates in the trench. The new arrival with the clean white helmet was a famous English cavalry officer, come to assist the army with his counsel. They stared at the figure of him, surrounded by officers. Peza, gaining sense of the glances and whispers, felt that his coming was an event.

Later, he resolved that he could, with temerity, do something finer. He contemplated the mountain where the Greek infantry was engaged, and announced leisurely to the captain of the battery that he thought presently of going in that direction and getting into the fight. He reaffirmed the sentiments of a patriot. The captain seemed surprised. "Oh, there will be fighting here at this knoll in a few minutes," he said orientally. "That will be sufficient. You had better stay with us. Besides, I have been ordered to resume fire." The officers all tried to dissuade him from departing. It was really not worth the trouble. The battery would begin again directly; then it would be amusing for him.

Peza felt that he was wandering, with his protestations of high patriotism, through a desert of sensible men. These officers gave no heed to his exalted declarations. They seemed too jaded. They were fighting the men who were fighting them. Palaver of the particular kind had subsided before their intense preoccupation in war as a craft. Moreover, many men had talked in that manner, and only talked.

Peza believed at first that they were treating him delicately; they were considerate of his inexperience. War had turned out to be such a gentle business that Peza concluded that he could scorn this idea. He bade them an heroic farewell, despite their objections.

However, when he reflected upon their ways afterward, he saw dimly that they were actuated principally by some universal childish desire for a spectator of their fine things. They were going into action, and they wished to be seen at war, precise and fearless.

## V

CLIMBING slowly to the high infantry position, Peza was amazed to meet a soldier whose jaw had been half shot away, and who was being helped down the steep track by two tearful comrades. The man's breast was drenched with blood, and from a cloth which he held to the wound drops were splashing wildly upon the stones of the path. He gazed at Peza for a moment. It was a mystic gaze, which Peza withstood with difficulty. He was exchanging looks with a specter; all aspect of the man was somehow gone from this victim. As Peza went on, one of the unwounded soldiers loudly shouted to him to return and assist in this tragic march. But even Peza's fingers revolted. He was afraid of the specter; he would not have dared to touch it. He was surely craven in the movement of refusal he made to them. He scrambled hastily on up the path. He was running away!

At the top of the hill he came immediately upon a part of the line that was in action. Another battery of mountain guns was here, firing at the streaks of black on the plain. There were trenches filled with men lining parts of the crest, and near the base were other trenches, all crashing away mightily. The plain stretched as far as the eye could see, and from where silver mist ended this emerald ocean of grass, a great ridge of snow-topped mountains poised against a fleckless blue sky. Two knolls, green and yellow with grain, sat on the prairie, confronting the dark hills of the Greek position. Between them were the lines of the enemy. A row of trees, a village, a stretch of road showed faintly on this great canvas, this tremendous picture; but men, the Turkish battalions, were emphasized startlingly upon it. The ranks of troops between the knolls and the Greek position were as black as ink. The first line, of course, was muffled in smoke; but at the rear of it, battalions crawled up, and to and fro, plainer than beetles on a plate. Peza had never understood that masses of men were so declarative, so unmistakable, as if nature makes every arrangement to give information of the coming and the presence of destruction, the end, oblivion. The firing was full, complete, a roar of cataracts, and this pealing of concerted volleys was adjusted to the grandeur of the far-off range of snowy mountains. Peza, breathless, pale, felt that he had been set upon a pillar, and was surveying mankind, the world. In the meantime dust had got in his eye. He took his handkerchief and mechanically administered to it.

An officer with a double stripe of purple on his trousers paced in the rear of the battery of howitzers. He waved a little cane. Sometimes he paused in his promenade to study the field through his glasses. "A fine scene, sir," he cried airily, upon the approach of Peza. It was like a blow in the chest to the wide-eyed volunteer. It revealed to him a point of view.

"Yes, sir; it is a fine scene," he answered.

They spoke in French. "I am happy to be able to entertain monsieur with a little fine practice," continued the officer. "I am firing upon that mass of troops you see there, a little to the right. They are probably forming for another attack."

Peza smiled. Here again appeared manners—manners erect by the side of death.

The right-flank gun of the battery thundered; there was a belch of fire and smoke; the shell, flung swiftly and afar, was known only to the ear, in which rang a broadening, hooting wake of sound. The howitzer had thrown itself backward convulsively, and lay with its wheels moving in the air as a squad of men rushed toward it; and later, it seemed as if each little gun had made the supreme effort of its being in each particular shot. They roared with voices far too loud, and the thunderous effort caused a gun to bound as in a dying convulsion. And then occasionally one was hurled with wheels in air. These shuddering howitzers presented an appearance of so many cowards, always longing to bolt to the rear, but being implacably held up to their business by this throng of soldiers who ran in squads to drag them up again to their obligation. The guns were herded and cajoled and bullied interminably. One by one, in relentless program, they were dragged forward to contribute a profound vibration of steel and wood, a flash and a roar, to the important happiness of men.

The adjacent infantry celebrated a good shot with smiles and an outburst of gleeful talk.

"Look, sir," cried an officer once to Peza. Thin smoke was drifting lazily before Peza, and, dodging impatiently, he brought his eyes to bear upon that part of the plain indicated by the officer's finger. The enemy's infantry was advancing to attack. From the black lines had come forth an inky mass which was shaped much like a human tongue. It advanced slowly, casually, without apparent spirit, but with an insolent confidence that was like a proclamation of the inevitable.

The impetuous part was all played by the defensive side.

Officers called; men plucked each other by the sleeve. There were shouts—motion. All eyes were turned upon the inky mass which was flowing toward the base of the hills, heavily, languorously, as oily and thick as one of the streams that ooze through a swamp.

Peza was chattering a question at every one. In the way, pushed aside, or in the way again, he continued to repeat it: "Can they take the position? Can they take the position? Can they take the position?" He was apparently addressing an assemblage of deaf men. Every eye was busy watching every hand. The soldiers did not even seem to see the interesting stranger in the white helmet, who was crying out so feverishly.

Finally, however, the hurried captain of the battery espied him, and heeded his question. "No, sir! No, sir! It is impossible!" he shouted angrily. His manner seemed to denote that if he had had sufficient time he would have completely insulted Peza. The latter swallowed the crumb of news without regard to the coating of scorn, and, waving his hand in adieu, he began to run along the crest of the hill toward the part of the Greek line against which the attack was directed.

## VI

PEZA, as he ran along the crest of the mountain, believed that his action was receiving the wrathful attention of the hosts of the foe. To him, then, it was incredible foolhardiness thus to call to himself the stares of thousands of hateful eyes. He was like a lad induced by playmates to commit some indiscretion in a cathedral. He was abashed; perhaps he even blushed as he ran. It seemed to him that the whole solemn ceremony of war had paused during this commission. So he scrambled wildly over the rocks in his haste to end the embarrassing ordeal. When he came among the crowning rifle-pits, filled with eager soldiers, he wanted to yell with joy. None noticed him, save a young officer of infantry, who said: "Sir, what do you want?" It was obvious that people had devoted some attention to their own affairs.

Peza asserted, in Greek, that he wished above everything to battle for the fatherland. The officer nodded. With a smile he pointed to some dead men, covered with blankets, from which were thrust upturned dusty shoes.

"Yes; I know, I know," cried Peza. He thought the officer was poetically alluding to the danger.

"No," said the officer, at once. "I mean cartridges—a bandoleer. Take a bandoleer from one of them."

Peza went cautiously toward a body. He moved a hand toward a corner of a blanket. There he hesitated, stuck, as if his arm had turned to plaster. Hearing a rustle behind him, he spun quickly. Three soldiers of the close rank in the trench were regarding him. The officer came again, and tapped him on the shoulder. "Have you any tobacco?" Peza looked at him in bewilderment. His hand was still extended toward the blanket which covered the dead soldier.

"Yes," he said; "I have some tobacco." He gave the officer his pouch. As if in compensation, the other directed a soldier to strip the bandoleer from the corpse. Peza, having crossed the long cartridge-belt on his breast, felt that the dead man had flung his two arms around him.

A soldier, with a polite nod and smile, gave Peza a rifle—a relic of another dead man. Thus he felt, besides the clutch of a corpse about his neck, that the rifle was as unhumanly horrible as a snake that lives in a tomb. He heard at his ear something that was in effect like the voices of those two dead men, their low voices speaking to him of bloody death, mutilation. The bandoleer gripped him tighter; he wished to raise his hands to his throat, like a man who is choking. The rifle was clumsy; upon his palms he felt the movement of the sluggish currents of a serpent's life; it was crawling and frightful.

All about him were these peasants, with their interested countenances, gibbering of the fight. From time to time a soldier cried out in semi-humorous lamentations descriptive of his thirst. One bearded man sat munching a great bit of hard bread. Fat, greasy, squat, he was like an idol made of tallow. Peza felt dimly that there was a distinction between this man and a young student who could write sonnets and play the piano quite well. This old blockhead was coolly gnawing at the bread, while he—Peza—was being throttled by a dead man's arms.

He looked behind him, and saw that a head, by some chance, had been uncovered from its blanket. Two liquid-like eyes were staring into his face. The head was turned a little sideways, as if to get better opportunity for the scrutiny. Peza could feel himself blanch. He was being drawn and drawn by these dead men, slowly, firmly down, as to some mystic chamber under the earth, where they could walk, dreadful figures, swollen and blood-marked. He was bidden; they had commanded him; he was going, going, going.

When the man in the new white helmet bolted for the rear, many of the soldiers in the trench thought that he had been struck. But those who had been nearest to him knew better. Otherwise they would have heard the silken, sliding, tender noise of the bullet, and the thud of its impact. They bawled after him curses, and also outbursts of self-congratulation and vanity. Despite the prominence of the cowardly part, they were enabled to see in this exhibition a fine comment upon their own fortitude. The other soldiers thought that Peza had been wounded somewhere in the neck, because, as he ran, he was tearing madly at the bandoleer—the dead man's arms. The soldier with the bread paused in his eating, and cynically remarked upon the speed of the runaway.

An officer's voice was suddenly heard calling out the calculation of the distance to the enemy, the readjustment of the sights. There was a stirring rattle along the line. The men turned their eyes to the front. Other trenches, beneath them, to the right, were already heavily in action. The smoke was lifting toward the blue sky. The soldier with the bread placed it carefully on a bit of paper beside him as he turned to kneel in the trench.

### VII

IN THE late afternoon the child ceased his play on the mountain with his flocks and his dogs. Part of the battle had whirled very near to the base of his hill, and the noise was great. Sometimes he could see fantastic, smoky shapes, which resembled the curious figures in foam which one sees on the slant of a rough sea. The plain, indeed, was etched in white circles and whirligigs, like the slope of a colossal wave. The child took seat on a stone, and contemplated the fight. He was beginning to be astonished. He had never before seen cattle herded with such uproar. Lines of flame flashed out here and there. It was mystery.

Finally, without any preliminary indication, he began to weep. If the men struggling on the plain had had time, and greater vision, they could have seen this strange, tiny figure seated on a boulder, surveying them while the tears streamed. It was as simple as some powerful symbol.

As the magic clear light of day amid the mountains dimmed the distances, and the plain shone as a pallid blue cloth marked by the red threads of the firing, the child arose and moved off to the unwelcoming door of his home. He called softly for his mother, and complained of his hunger in the familiar formulæ. The pearl-colored cow, grinding her jaws thoughtfully, stared at him with her large eyes. The peaceful gloom of evening was slowly draping the hills.

The child heard a rattle of loose stones on the hillside, and, facing the sound, saw, a moment later, a man drag himself up to the crest of the hill and fall panting. Forgetting his mother and his hunger, filled with calm interest, the child walked forward, and stood over the heaving form. His eyes, too, were now large and inscrutably wise and sad, like those of the animal in the house.

After a silence, he spoke inquiringly: "Are you a man?"

Peza rolled over quickly, and gazed up into the fearless and cherubic countenance. He did not attempt to reply. He breathed as if life was about to leave his body. He was covered with dust; his face had been cut in some way, and his cheek was ribboned with blood. All the spick of his former appearance had vanished in a general dishevelment, in which he resembled a creature that had been flung to and fro, up and down, by cliffs and prairies during an earthquake. He rolled his eye glassily at the child.

They remained thus until the child repeated his words: "Are you a man?"

Peza gasped in the manner of a fish. Palsied, windless, and abject, he confronted the primitive courage, the sovereign child, the brother of the mountains, the sky, and the sea, and he knew that the definition of his misery could be written on a wee grass-blade.

---

# POEMS

---

◊

❡ CRANE called his poems "lines" and disliked being called a poet. His grudge against conventional verse is perhaps sufficiently explained by his parody of Longfellow's "A Psalm of Life" with its theme of uplift; the quatrain, first printed in 1957 from an undated manuscript, need not be an early piece in order to qualify as a logical starting point of Crane's poetic practice. His impulse to write "lines" apparently dates from the evening in 1893 when Howells read aloud to him from the then newly published poems of Emily Dickinson. He construed her departures from strict rhyme and meter as abandonment of them, and in the epigrammatic statements among her dramatic and lyric lines, he noticed the statement more than the wit. She seemed to reaffirm for his time the precedent of Whitman in breaking from meter and "speaking the truth" unadorned. His own unadorned truths often turned out to be rhetorical gestures and obvious ironies, but his best parables asked questions instead of giving away answers: is the simplicity of "Once there came a man," below, the simplicity of death or of order? is the wisdom of "A man feared that he might find an assassin" the fear of death or the fear of killing? Occasionally he used his visual style to fix his argument in a presented image.

Lack of literary training created two problems for Crane. His unsuccessful poems show how hard it was for him to develop a poetic idea without serious lapses of taste. A more positive difficulty, on the other hand, was that of sustaining a poetic idea at all: just as in his fiction he often had to reinvent Jamesian techniques, in his poetry he seemed to reinvent poetic form. He had the terseness of a newspaperman who knows how to summarize the essentials of his story, but not many ideas can be adequately treated in three lines. So Crane got back to the stanza and the refrain and regularity of cadence. The patterned meditative progression of his finest verse results from a self-imposed discipline of thought and form. Moreover, in "War is kind" and "A man adrift on a slim spar," his subtle use of rhyme and rhythm gives the proper answer to the Longfellowism he deplored: he did not give up the sensuous resources of language, he controlled them and made them serve his serious poetic aims.

◇

1

Tell me not in joyous numbers
We can make our lives sublime
By—well, at least, not by
Dabbling much in rhyme.

*1957*

2

Once there came a man
Who said,
"Range me all men of the world in rows."
And instantly
There was terrific clamor among the people
Against being ranged in rows.
There was a loud quarrel, world-wide.
It endured for ages;
And blood was shed
By those who would not stand in rows,     10
And by those who pined to stand in rows.
Eventually, the man went to death, weeping.
And those who stayed in bloody scuffle
Knew not the great simplicity.

*1895*

3

The ocean said to me once,
"Look!
Yonder on the shore
Is a woman, weeping.
I have watched her.
Go you and tell her this—
Her lover I have laid
In cool green hall.
There is wealth of golden sand
And pillars, coral-red;     10
Two white fish stand guard at his bier.

"Tell her this
And more—
That the king of the seas
Weeps too, old, helpless man.

The bustling fates
Heap his hands with corpses
Until he stands like a child
With surplus of toys."

*1895*

4

A man feared that he might find an assassin;
Another that he might find a victim.
One was more wise than the other.

*1895*

5

Do not weep, maiden, for war is kind.
Because your lover threw wild hands toward the
    sky
And the affrighted steed ran on alone,
Do not weep.
War is kind.

Hoarse, booming drums of the regiment,
Little souls who thirst for fight,
These men were born to drill and die.
The unexplained glory flies above them,
Great is the battle-god, great, and his king-
    dom—     10
A field where a thousand corpses lie.

Do not weep, babe, for war is kind.
Because your father tumbled in the yellow
    trenches,
Raged at his breast, gulped and died,
Do not weep.
War is kind.

Swift blazing flag of the regiment,
Eagle with crest of red and gold,
These men were born to drill and die.
Point for them the virtue of slaughter,     20
Make plain to them the excellence of killing
And a field where a thousand corpses lie.

Mother whose heart hung humble as a button
On the bright splendid shroud of your son,
Do not weep.
War is kind.

*1896, 1899*

6

"I have heard the sunset song of the birches,
"A white melody in the silence,

POEMS.   1. Manuscript in Columbia University Library, Stephen Crane Collection; published by Daniel G. Hoffman in *The Poetry of Stephen Crane* (1957), p. 41.   2. This and the two succeeding poems appeared in Crane's first book of lines, *The Black Riders* (1895); poems for that volume were written in 1893 and early 1894.

5. This and the two succeeding poems appeared in *War Is Kind* (1899); the first date given on the left after each poem is that of magazine publication.

"I have seen a quarrel of the pines.
"At nightfall
"The little grasses have rushed by me
"With the wind men.
"These things have I lived," quoth the maniac,
"Possessing only eyes and ears.
"But you—
"You don green spectacles before you look at
    roses."         10

*1895, 1899*


### 7

In the night
Gray heavy clouds muffled the valleys,
And the peaks looked toward God alone.
    "O Master that movest the wind with a fin-
      ger,
    "Humble, idle, futile peaks are we.
    "Grant that we may run swiftly across the
      world
    "To huddle in worship at Thy feet."

In the morning
A noise of men at work came the clear blue miles,
And the little black cities were apparent.     10
    "O Master that knowest the meaning of rain-
      drops,
    "Humble, idle, futile peaks are we.
    "Give voice to us, we pray, O Lord,
    "That we may sing Thy goodness to the sun."

In the evening
The far valleys were sprinkled with tiny lights.
    "O Master,
    "Thou that knowest the value of kings and
      birds,
    "Thou hast made us humble, idle, futile
      peaks.
  "Thou only needest eternal patience;     20
    "We bow to Thy wisdom, O Lord—
    "Humble, idle, futile peaks."

In the night
Gray heavy clouds muffled the valleys,
And the peaks looked toward God alone.

*1896, 1899*


### 8

A man adrift on a slim spar
A horizon smaller than the rim of a bottle.
Tented waves rearing lashy dark points
The near whine of froth in circles.
        God is cold.

The incessant raise and swing of the sea
And the growl after growl of crest
The sinkings, green, seething, endless
The upheaval half-completed.
        God is cold.     10

The seas are in the hollow of Thy Hand;
Oceans may be turned to a spray
Raining down through the stars
Because of a gesture of pity toward a babe.
Oceans may become gray ashes
Die with a long moan and a roar
Amid the tumult of the fishes
And the cries of the ships,
Because The Hand beckons the mice.
A horizon smaller than a doomed assassin's cap,
Inky, surging tumults     21
A reeling, drunken sky and no sky
A pale hand sliding from a polished spar.
        God is cold.

The puff of a coat imprisoning air:
A face kissing the water-death
A weary slow sway of a lost hand
And the sea, the moving sea, the sea.
        God is cold.

*1929, 1930*


### 9

Unwind my riddle.
Cruel as hawks the hours fly;
Wounded men seldom come home to die;
The hard waves see an arm flung high;
Scorn hits strong because of a lie;
Yet there exists a mystic tie.
Unwind my riddle.

*1900*

---

8. This poem, not printed in Crane's lifetime but probably written in 1897 or 1898, is to be found in *The Collected Poems of Stephen Crane* (1930), Wilson Follett, editor.   9. Crane used this poem as the epigraph to his story "The Clan of No-Name" (published posthumously in *Wounds in the Rain*, 1900). He wrote it in late 1899 or early 1900. The "clan of No-Name" is the company of true heroes whose reward has been the obliteration of death.

ALVIN B. KERNAN
*Editor*

# Eugene O'Neill

## 1888-1953

BY AND large, the theater has been a place of entertainment, which means that its staples have always been strong emotion, spectacle, and rhetoric. The custard pie in the face and the pratfall, in variant forms, were as common in the cruder modes of Greek and Roman comedy as they are in the popular comedy today. The tear-jerking scene and the outsize heroic gesture too have had equally long and useful careers leading to, but not ending in, such plays as William Inge's *Come Back, Little Sheba* and such television shows as *Gunsmoke*. The life of this popular drama has been continuous, and from its beginnings to the present it has taken such strange and various forms as fertility rites, mimes, circuses, itinerant jugglers and singers, medieval church dramas, Italian street comedy, opera, stand-up comics, puppet shows, musical comedy, and movies.

Only at great intervals, and then for reasons which no one quite understands, are all of the diverse theatrical techniques and forms developed in the popular drama used for some purpose other than amusement. When this occurs, as it did in Athens in the fifth century B.C., in London between 1588 and 1620, in Paris in the middle years of the seventeenth century, and in Europe after 1875, a great theater comes into being. Such theaters, which always involve the work of

more than one playwright, usually endure for only a relatively short time, fifty to seventy-five years at the most. But during their brief life, they reveal the full possibility of the theater as a focus of the community's intellectual life, as a place where the full nature of man as the people of the time understand it is put before our eyes. An Oedipus dragging his wounded foot behind him on the way to Thebes only to discover that he is at once the saviour of the city and its polluter; a Hamlet staring at the skull of Yorick and remembering that only a few years ago this grisly object could speak words of comfort, humor, and kindness to him; a Phaedra who is at once passionately and hopelessly in love with her stepson, and at the same time icily logical and moral about her situation; and a Mrs. Alving, who comes at last to face the fact of a hopelessly insane son whom no truth can cure—are all images, caught and held for a moment on stage, which reveal man face-to-face with the essential paradox of his nature.

Such theaters are understandably rare, if for no other reason than that the insight and honesty about self which they manifest are uncommon. Nevertheless such a theater appeared in Europe about 1870, first in the work of Ibsen, and then later in the plays of such writers as Strindberg, Chekhov, and Shaw. This was the theater of realism, which for a time revivified the European theater by the honesty of its craftsmanship and the social significance of its subject matter. In the United States, however, which until recently followed rather than led European movements in literature, the theater up to about the end of World War I remained primarily a place of entertainment. To be sure there were productions of the new European plays, and Shakespeare was always popular. But there was no native drama of any real importance. Farce and melodrama, always the stocks in trade of a busy and prosperous theater, produced a number of excellent actors, but no great playwrights. The names of such plays as *Lord Chumley, The Two Orphans, The Millionaire's Daughter* and *The Mother's Secret* convey perfectly the nature of this theater. It was, in fact, the equivalent of the movies in the thirties and forties of this century. The emphasis was on "stars"—stars who had their fans and whose lives were minutely reported by the newspapers. Nevertheless, there was little or no interest in the actual quality of the plays. So long as they provided strong sentiment, emotional charge, and the triumph of good over villainy, everyone was happy and prosperous.

Most of these plays are easily and mercifully forgotten. One of them however is of peculiar interest, not because it has any intrinsic value, but because of the effect it had on the life of the O'Neill family, and particularly on the son Eugene. James O'Neill, the father, came to this country from Ireland as a young boy. After a childhood of painful poverty, he managed to become one of the star actors of the day. He was already well on his way to success when, in the early 1880's, as a result of the accidental death of another actor, he took the part of Edmund Dantès in adaptation by Charles Schecter of Dumas' novel *The Count of Monte Cristo*. The play was a hit at once and continued to fill theaters on the circuit for over twenty-five years. The senior O'Neill bought the play two years after he first appeared in it and, forming his own company, toured the country year after year, playing one night here and one night there, and only occasionally

spending as long as a week in some large city. The play made the O'Neill fortune—it has been estimated that he made close to a million dollars from it—but it destroyed what apparently were genuine acting talents in James O'Neill. Many years later in *A Long Day's Journey Into Night*, James Tyrone, who represents the father, remarks resentfully:

That . . . play I bought for a song and made such a great success in—a great money success —it ruined me with its promise of an easy fortune. I didn't want to do anything else, and by the time I woke up to the fact I'd become a slave to the damned thing and did try other plays, it was too late. They had identified me with that one part, and didn't want me in anything else. They were right too; I'd lost the great talent I once had through years of easy repetition, never learning a new part, never really working hard.

*The Count of Monte Cristo* itself was the usual romantic tale of derring-do, beautiful maidens in difficulty, and swaggering heroes. The hero, Edmund Dantès, is torn from the arms of his beautiful young wife Mercedes, who is carrying his child, and imprisoned in Chateau d'If by three of his enemies, who bear the appropriately villainous names —at least to American ears—Fernand, Danglars, and de Villefort. After eighteen years Dantès manages to escape in a spectacular manner. He assumes the name and wealth of Monte Cristo and carries out his revenge on the three villains. As he dispatches each one of them in exciting duels, he holds his fingers above his head and counts in turn, "One! Two! Three!" While he is achieving his revenge, Dantès is unknown to his now-grown son, Albert, and upon one mistaken occasion nearly kills him; but in the curtain lines of the play, Albert comes to know his father, and the family is reunited.

The attitude of the young Eugene O'Neill toward this kind of harmless entertainment was one of uncontrolled scorn. Once in a derisive gesture he carved the initials "M.C." in the newelpost of the family home in New London, Connecticut. On another occasion he poured a can of green paint into a box filled with statues of the older O'Neill cast in the part of Monte Cristo. Later, he was more outspoken:

My early experience with the theater through my father really made my revolt against it. As a boy I saw so much of the old, ranting, artificial romantic stuff that I always had a sort of contempt for the theater.

This contempt later took a more practical form, for instead of turning away from the American theater, Eugene O'Neill transformed it. In a succession of plays, beginning in 1916, the younger O'Neill made the American stage for the first time a place where truly serious issues were explored, where man was not bathed in the colors of romance but illuminated by the stark light of truth. Whatever the final judgment on O'Neill as a dramatist—and the value of his plays is still very much debated—there can be no question that he was the first to transform the American stage from a place of illusion and amusement into a true theater. Thereby, he prepared the way for the few other dramatists of the first order who have written for the American theater—Thornton Wilder, Arthur Miller, and Tennessee Williams.

It would be inaccurate, however, to leave the impression that *The Count of Monte Cristo* was the exact opposite of the kind of plays Eugene O'Neill wrote. A number of critics have pointed out that, crude as the old melodrama may have been, O'Neill in his association with it learned the fundamental lesson of the practicing dramatist: the necessity of translating ideas into the terms of action, for constructing "strong scenes," and for moving the plot along at a rapid pace. Indeed, other critics have remarked that throughout O'Neill's plays one can still see the ghost of that old swaggerer Monte Cristo and hear at the crucial points of the action his fateful "One! Two! Three!" But even beyond this, there is a curious relationship between the old play and those of O'Neill. The old melodrama was undoubtedly put together for no grander purpose than to make money, which it did in large amounts. The details—characters, situations, story,

and language—were chosen for their sensational qualities and arranged to create a maximum of suspense. But, contrived or not, the forms and shapes given to life in *The Count of Monte Cristo* were still the products of the imagination; and the human imagination tends to be conservative in that it creates again and again in new forms the old symbols and stories that express our basic longings and fears. Take *Monte Cristo*, for example. Behind the swordplay and the swaggering, the bombast and the posing, we can still perceive certain primal fears: the sudden attack by powerful, unknown enemies; hopeless imprisonment in a dungeon below the sea; the interruption of life, the destruction of marriage, and the alienation of wife and husband, son and father. But here, as in the many fairy stories which *Monte Cristo* resembles, the hero ultimately triumphs over all obstacles.

Except for the happy resolution at the end, this basic story is very much like the situation which O'Neill dramatized again and again. The characteristic state of his heroes is some dungeon-like containment. In the old melodrama the containment takes the form of a romantic dungeon in the fabulous Chateau d'If. In O'Neill's plays, on the other hand, the imprisonment is rendered in such realistic terms as the forecastle on the fogbound *S.S. Glencairn*, where the sailor Yank is dying in *Bound East for Cardiff*; or the farm in *Beyond the Horizon* where the young poet, Robert Mayo, is trapped in a life from which he can never escape; or Harry Hope's saloon where everyone has hit rock-bottom in *The Iceman Cometh*. In psychological terms, containment takes the form of the mask of the socially assigned personality which the characters are condemned to wear in *The Great God Brown*, for example. The other elements in the *Monte Cristo* story, the separation of family and the unknown son, are equally prominent in O'Neill's plays, but once again they take realistic forms such as the alienation of his heroes from parents, wives, and children, or the isolation of his characters from society, or the ultimate psychological separation—the division within the self.

O'Neill seems, unconsciously, to have taken the basic symbols, imprisonment and separation—rendered in the melodrama by dungeon and castle—and transformed them into the farm, stokehold, or bar. At the same time, of course, he lopped off the happy ending. But the pattern of *Monte Cristo* extended beyond O'Neill's plays, and in a most curious way came to be in a sense the model for the way the O'Neill family saw themselves personally in relation to one another. Thus for O'Neill, biography and plays flow strangely together in such a way that all of his life he was moved to write the history of his family as if it were a reenactment of *The Count of Monte Cristo*.

## II

EUGENE GLADSTONE O'Neill was born in New York City on October 16, 1888, in a hotel on what is now Times Square. His father was, as we have said, a distinguished and prosperous actor, and his mother Ella Quinlan O'Neill, the daughter of a well-to-do Cleveland merchant. The first son, James Jr., was born in 1878. Eugene was the third son of the family. The second son, Edmund, had died of measles while quite young. Since the elder O'Neill made his living as an actor on tour, the family spent a great deal of time on the road. Consequently, many of the children's earliest memories were of trains, hotels, and theaters. In an attempt to provide some kind of settled life for his family and himself, James O'Neill purchased a home in New London, Connecticut, where the family lived in the rare periods when the father was not on tour or when it was deemed advisable for the children and the mother not to accompany him. Apparently, however, the older O'Neill missed his wife greatly and persuaded her to accompany him on many occasions when she would have been happier to remain at home. It was during one of these absences—a time when the first two children had been left in New York alone— that Edmund contracted measles and died.

In 1895, Eugene was sent to a boarding school, St. Aloysious Academy for Boys, in what is now the Bronx. In 1900, when he was twelve, he became a day student at De La Salle Institute in Manhattan. In 1902 he entered Betts Academy in Stamford, Connecticut, where he remained for four years until his entrance into Princeton in the fall of 1906. During these years he seems to have been a good though not distinguished student. He was always a voracious reader. His reading however seemed to lead him away from formal study rather than toward it. This tendency toward rebellion became most pronounced in his freshman year at Princeton, from which after a year of extended absences from the campus and sundry troubles, he left with the consent of all parties involved.

The next six years of O'Neill's life were restless and difficult for his biographers to follow. He lived a bohemian life in New York for a time, spent some time at the house in New London, worked for his father in his touring company, married, begot a child, was divorced, searched for gold in Honduras, and went to sea. The last experience seems to have been by far the most crucial for him, for at sea he apparently found at least intimations of a meaningful way of life, a way which contrasted with his hitherto aimless, uncertain, and unsatisfactory existence.

Throughout his plays, the sea and life on the sea signify for his characters a simple, direct contact with healing nature. It is this yearning for freedom, and nostalgia for lost simplicity which is expressed, for example, by an old sailor in *The Hairy Ape:*

Oh, there was fine beautiful ships them days— clippers wid tall masts touching the sky—fine strong men in them—men that was sons of the sea as if 'twas the mother that bore them. . . . We'd be sailing out, bound down round the Horn maybe. We'd be making sail in the dawn, with a fair breeze, singing a chanty song wid no care to it. And astern the land would be sinking low and dying out, but we'd give it no heed but a laugh, and never a look behind. For the day that was, was enough, for we was free men. . . . Oh, to be scudding south again wid the power of the Trade Wind driving her on steady through the nights and the days! Full sail on her! Nights and Days! Nights when the foam of the wake would be flaming wid fire, when the sky'd be blazing and winking wid stars.

Whatever the sea spoke of to O'Neill in private, the actual events of his travels, however, seem as drab and aimless as his life at home at the time. He shipped out on a Norwegian barque in 1910 and left her at Buenos Aires, where he spent a long time on the beach drinking and idly drifting from one small job to another. Later he went to South Africa with a cargo of mules, then came back to New York and served as an able-bodied seaman for one round-trip on a passenger liner across the Atlantic. All the time he seemed to be sinking lower and lower into a depression which reached its nadir in a flophouse in New York run by a man named Jimmie the Priest. Here, in the most squalid of circumstances, he tried to take his own life.

This may have been the bottom for O'Neill. There was, however, no sharp upward turn in his fortunes. In 1912 he was back in New London working as a reporter for the *New London Telegraph*. In the latter part of the year he was told that he had tuberculosis, and he eventually was sent to the Gaylord Sanatorium in Wallingford, Connecticut. As it turned out, however, his case was not an extremely serious one, and he left the sanatorium in less than six months. During his convalescence he made the basic decision of his life. He had written a good deal of poetry before this—most of it an awkward imitation of such English poets as Wilde and Dowson—but at Gaylord he began to think of himself as a playwright and wrote one play, *A Wife for a Life*, which he later destroyed. When he returned to New London he continued to write plays, completing eleven one-act and two full length plays during 1912–13. Five of these plays were printed in 1914 under the title *Thirst*. The cost of printing was paid for by his father. The older man considered his son hopeless but still continued to help him in odd ways. (At one time when O'Neill was drifting aimlessly about New York, his father left a dollar each day for him with the cashier of a hotel where Eugene and his brother drank.)

O'Neill's determination to be a dramatist, however, endured. In an attempt to learn his trade more thoroughly, he enrolled—again with the aid of his father—in a post-graduate class in playwrighting at Harvard, taught by George Pierce Baker. In later years when O'Neill had become famous, both he and Baker assumed and stated publicly on a number of occasions that the course had been of great value to the young playwright. The fact of the matter, however, is that while O'Neill stuck the year out, his views and Baker's on the drama were at odds, and Baker had little understanding of O'Neill's ideas and talents. When, for example, the time came for Baker to select a play written in his class for production, he chose not an O'Neill play, but one titled *Plots and Playwrights* by a forgotten dramatist named Edward Massey.

O'Neill's real entrance into the theater came in the summer of 1916 in Provincetown, where he had gone with a group of intellectuals from New York. His friends were greatly interested in bringing new life and honesty to the American theater and making it comparable to the theater of Europe. They lacked, however, the crucial element necessary to bring about such a transformation, a playwright. One evening while they were trying to decide which of their own rather feeble efforts to produce, O'Neill appeared with a copy of his one-acter, *Bound East for Cardiff*, written in the previous year. His friends at once recognized its virtues and produced the play that summer in an old fish-house made over into a theater. To the American theater the event was epochal; to the little audience, who had no such foresight, the production was merely powerful. The back wall of the stage opened to reveal the moon and the waters of the bay, and the lapping of the waves under the floor of the building provided just the right sound effects for a play about the sea.

The American theater really began with this production. With some sense of this fact, the group formed the Provincetown Players and set up shop during the winter in New York, determined to remain amateurs and to insure that theirs was a theater of art, not money. O'Neill's plays were their mainstay, and despite a good deal of theatrical crudeness and endless difficulties about production, they provided him with an honestly experimental theater in which to deal with subjects unpresentable at that time in a Broadway theater. Despite the usual difficulties, the Provincetown Players managed to hang together until 1924. During this eight-year period O'Neill gave them some of his finest plays: *In the Zone, The Long Voyage Home, The Emperor Jones, The Hairy Ape,* and *Desire Under the Elms.*

During this time, O'Neill was prolific. He wrote a great many other plays, some of which were staged by the Provincetown group in their small theater on Macdougal Street. What is more, he emerged finally from obscurity. Recognition of his qualities as a playwright was almost immediate by such critics as Alexander Woolcott, Heywood Broun, and George Nathan. From 1920, when *Beyond the Horizon,* his first full-length play to be staged, was produced at a Broadway theater, O'Neill plays could be seen both uptown and downtown. *Beyond the Horizon* won the Pulitzer Prize in 1920 and *Anna Christie,* in 1922. O'Neill's position in the American theater was now assured, and he wrote steadily and successfully until 1934 when *Days Without End* was produced by the Theater Guild. In 1936 he won the Nobel Prize for Literature. Now, however, even though he had not stopped writing, his plays were no longer produced. It was not until 1946, twelve years after, that a new O'Neill play was seen in New York, *The Iceman Cometh.* In the following year *A Moon for the Misbegotten* tried out in Columbus, Ohio, but was withdrawn before it reached New York.

In 1918 O'Neill married Agnes Boulton, a short-story writer who was part of the group around the Provincetown Players. They had two children, Shane and Oona, now Mrs. Charles Chaplin. The marriage ended in divorce in 1929, and in that year O'Neill married Carlotta Monterey, an actress who had played the part of Mildred in *The Hairy Ape.* This third marriage, despite stormy moments, lasted until the end of O'Neill's life. In 1947 O'Neill was found to have some variety of Parkinson's disease, a malady desperately serious for anyone but absolutely catastrophic for him since the attendant loss

of muscular control made it nearly impossible for him to write, and he could not compose by dictation. Palsy, an early symptom of the disease, had affected him as early as 1939, when he began to write *A Long Day's Journey Into Night.* The illness progressed, and he was able to complete only one more play, *Moon for the Misbegotten.* He died in Boston in 1953.

Nevertheless, as John Gassner has remarked, O'Neill won *two* reputations in his lifetime—one in the 1920's and another after his death when *Long Day's Journey* was presented. Following upon this success, two previously unknown plays, *A Touch of the Poet* and *More Stately Mansions,* came to light. They appear to be part of a long cycle of plays written in the late 1930's but probably never finished.

These are the vital statistics of O'Neill's life. Reported in this way, they rehearse the American success story in its most classic form. There are uncomfortable facts here—attempted suicide, drink, an abandoned wife and son—but the overall pattern is an Horatio Algerish rise of the poor son of an immigrant father to the "pinnacles of fame," international recognition, and monetary success. For most men it would be only fairness to leave it at this and to refrain from tarnishing the splendid public image by prying into private matters. Such matters, however, distinguish life from myth. And O'Neill himself was unable or unwilling to leave it at this. Throughout his life he was driven to write his private life into his plays, turning and examining his emotional agonies from a variety of angles. In *Long Day's Journey,* which he did not want published until twenty-five years after his death, he wrote almost the full story of the family which created him. I say *almost* the full story because even here he left out a few facts which perhaps he could still not face. In other words, he himself invites us to view the darker side of his public image and suggests that his life illuminates his plays.

O'Neill has himself provided us with an interpretative scheme in *Long Day's Journey Into Night.* While the scheme offered there does not account for all the facts, it does ring remarkably true. The central figure in the story seems to be the father, James O'Neill. Emigrating to this country when quite young, he and his mother were abandoned here by his father who returned to Ireland when he was taken by a strange, but accurate premonition that he was going to die. The result for the mother and children was a dreadful, grinding poverty. James was forced into brutal work at an early age. Worse, it bred deep into his bones a fear of poverty from which he was never able to escape, even much later after he made a great deal of money. This fear, engendered by the old misery, created new miseries in turn, for James gave up his native and quite genuine acting talent in order to appear over and over again in *Monte Cristo* — a play he hated but could never bring himself to abandon because he feared the poorhouse even more. It also bred in him a penury with his family and prevented him, first of all, from giving his wife Ella the house and the established respectability she had been brought up to expect and, as it happened, needed so desperately for her self-respect. It even appeared that James's fear of poverty persuaded him to engage a cheap doctor to attend his wife when she was sick after the birth of Eugene. To relieve the pain, this doctor prescribed a medicine with morphine in it. Ella continued on the medicine so long that she became an addict, condemning herself thereafter to use the drug throughout most of her life, not only to dull physical pain but mental anguish as well.

The children were gradually estranged from the parents. What they considered their father's miserliness isolated them from him throughout all his life. Even more terribly, they were driven from the mother as well. Ella apparently believed that her son Jamie, who had been warned to stay away from his infant brother Edmund because he had measles, had purposely wandered into the younger child's room and thus brought about his death. She was long in forgiving him this transgression, if she ever did. Thus burdened, Jamie developed an antagonism toward his younger brother Eugene, natural enough in some ways but intensified by his

feeling that the birth of Eugene had caused his mother, not only to turn away from him, but to begin taking morphine as well. As Jamie grew older, he turned into a hopeless drunk; and Eugene, butting vainly against the wall of indifference raised by his mother's morphine and his father's stinginess, followed his older brother almost deliberately into despair.

It would be easy enough to moralize — to view the family disasters as the result of self-indulgence and a failure of will, but O'Neill was never tempted to do so. He came to know that Ella O'Neill's need for a settled home — perhaps a trivial value in itself which she should have abandoned when she saw that it could not be achieved — was in fact a fundamental, ineradicable part of her character. It was bred into her by her middle class home and education. Men and women do not give up such values willingly, and if they are forced to do so, as Ella was, some central support of their character is sapped and weakened. What O'Neill saw at work in his own family, at least as he looked back on them from 1941, was a process wherein a group of people, each with his own peculiar fears and needs which must be expressed, inevitably thwarted one another, thereby setting in motion an iron chain of irreversible events which could never be broken, only lived out to its grim end. This is tragedy in its fullest sense. In such ill-starred households, agony intensifies. The actors become more desperate, turning inward upon themselves and upon the people they love, seeking to destroy what they cannot control. Perhaps one of the saddest illustrations of the whole vicious round is the figure of Jamie, Eugene's older brother, touring in his father's company. Bewildered and thwarted, hating and loving his father at the same time, Jamie could never do anything on his own, and so was forced to work for his father in the play they both loathed. Each time, moreover, as he was forced to turn to his father for whiskey money, his sense of inadequacy deepened. The self-loathing was further exacerbated by the plain truth that his father was the only man who would hire him. And so the disease, instead of working itself out, tended to compound itself. Had the audience sensed the whole truth, what an unbelievable scene lay before them on the stage when *Monte Cristo* was presented! Each time the swaggering Count broke free from the dungeon of the Chateau d'If and rose through waves of the sea, the O'Neill family sank deeper into despair; and each time after long separation, the Count and Albert knew themselves as father and son, James and his father were driven further apart.

By 1923 all the members of the family except Eugene were dead. Death, however, does not end such histories as this. In one way it was perpetuated in O'Neill's relations with his own children and his wives. In *Long Day's Journey* the fictional O'Neill brings himself to understand and accept his father. The real O'Neill, however, could not bring himself to accept his own son. Haunted thus by old and unassuageable guilt, the past lived on in the mind of Eugene O'Neill; and each play, under always different guises, seeks to exorcise the ghosts of the past by dramatizing it over and over again. In *Beyond the Horizon*, for example, we can still hear private angers and miseries, their smart undiminished, in such scenes as the turning away of the elder son by the angry father. We can sense also the wandering of Eugene in the profitless sea voyages, and we can see the general hopelessness of the O'Neill family in the plight of Robert Mayo and his wife caught on a farm which poisons their love as it deteriorates.

It is likely that in rewriting the family history so many times, O'Neill sought to purge himself by re-enacting the old pains and guilts until they were at last understood and accepted. At least a number of psychologists have assured us that this was what he was doing. It must not be forgotten, however, that O'Neill brought art to bear upon this re-enacted family history. Crude experience is transfigured and given form and meaning. He made the dumb miseries speak; gave pain a shape; and so intensified the flat, shapeless facts of day-to-day life that they were transformed into a symbolic representation of the tragic experience of modern man.

## III

BECAUSE AT various times, O'Neill destroyed a good many of his plays, it is impossible to tell exactly how many he wrote. To date, forty-five have been published. The most important of his plays, with the dates of writing, are listed below in three groups.

| | |
|---|---|
| *Bound East for Cardiff* | *1913–14* |
| *In the Zone* | *1916–17* |
| *The Long Voyage Home* | *1916–17* |
| *Beyond the Horizon* | *1918* |
| *Anna Christie* | *1920* |
| | |
| *The Emperor Jones* | *1920* |
| *The Hairy Ape* | *1921* |
| *Desire Under the Elms* | *1924* |
| *The Great God Brown* | *1925* |
| *Strange Interlude* | *1926–27* |
| *Mourning Becomes Electra* | *1929–31* |
| *Ah, Wilderness!* | *1932* |
| | |
| *The Iceman Cometh* | *1939* |
| *A Long Day's Journey Into Night* | *1939–41* |
| *A Moon for the Misbegotten* | *1943* |

In the first period O'Neill wrote fairly conventional realistic plays, which do not impose much strain on our credulity. The deck of a ship, a farmhouse, or a barge tied to a dock are ordinary enough, and the people who inhabit these places are as believable as the settings. About 1920, however, he began to seek ways to reveal more directly the workings of the mind and to open up farther ranges of experience. In order to do so he was forced to find new modes of expression. While he did not abandon realism completely—returning to it altogether in a play like *Ah, Wilderness!*—he began to experiment with theatrical devices. In *The Emperor Jones*, for example, a continuing drum-beat, which gradually increases in tempo, accompanies the action of a lost and solitary man from whom the veneer of civilization drops away as he becomes more and more frightened and prey to old irrational fears. In *The Hairy Ape*, the stoker Yank, rejected by a society which he had previously thought he controlled, is knocked about Fifth Avenue by weird marionettes all dressed alike in the clothes of wealthy men and women. Some of these devices O'Neill borrowed from the European Expressionistic theater, notably from the works of Strindberg, but he searched even further afield and restored to the stage such older dramatic devices as masks, choruses, asides, and soliloquies—all of which helped him to reveal the depths of his characters' minds. At the same time, he began to experiment with the length of his plays, writing ever longer and longer works in the effort to portray the *full* history of a man or a family. This line of development reached its climax in *Mourning Becomes Electra*, a trilogy written in imitation of the three plays of the *Oresteia* (457 B.C.) by the Greek dramatist Aeschylus. *Electra*, which recounts the history of a New England family, the Mannons, at about the time of the Civil War, took a full seven hours to perform.

These latter experiments were not, however, enthusiastically received. By the end of the thirties O'Neill had returned to a strict variety of naturalism. The life he reveals in such plays as *The Iceman Cometh* and *Long Day's Journey* is bizarre enough, but it transpires in realistic places such as a bar or a middle-class home. Much of the power of these later plays is generated by the contrast between the shabby everydayness of the places and the extravagant human emotions revealed within them.

Despite O'Neill's restless search for new theatrical devices, his basic subject remained the same. During his long career, O'Neill dealt with a great many ideas and themes—American materialism, Freudian psychology, the power of the sea, the struggle of the individual with society, and others besides. But behind all of these lay a continuing concern with fate:

I'm always acutely conscious of the Force behind —Fate, God, our biological past creating our present, whatever one calls it—Mystery certainly —and of the one eternal tragedy of Man in his glorious, self-destructive struggle to make the Force express him instead of being, as an animal is, an infinitesimal incident in its expression.

Fate is perhaps an un-American concept, for throughout our brief history Americans have assumed that they are free rather than fated—free to make of the land and themselves what they wish. Even today, when historical forces seem more than ever to be closing in on us we still assume that each individual operates in an atmosphere of boundless possibility where he need only make the right choice to ensure himself peace, prosperity, and happiness. In the past, however, few people have thought of themselves in this romantic and democratic fashion. Certainly the Greeks did not, and it was in the Greek tragedy of the fifth century B.C. that O'Neill found a sense of fate as remorseless as his own. In the *Oresteia* of Aeschylus, which O'Neill imitated, the blood-stained history of the House of Atreus is chronicled. The main events of the play take place in the city of Argos. Its ruler Agamemnon has been for ten years at war with Troy to revenge the theft of Helen. Upon his departure from Greece, he has sacrificed his daughter Iphigenia in order to cajole favorable winds from the goddess Artemis. This sacrifice makes an implacable enemy of his wife Clytemnestra. In revenge she takes as a lover Aegisthus, whose brothers had earlier been killed by Agamemnon's father. The guilty lovers murder Agamemnon when he returns from Troy. This murder however necessitates another in turn when the son of Agamemnon, Orestes, returns from exile. Fate is inexorable. Prince Orestes must murder his mother and her lover.

What we have here is a net of crimes binding the House of Atreus and the City of Argos. Each murder is a kind of rough justice, but each murder becomes in turn a new crime requiring still another murder to execute justice on its predecessor. Man in pursuit of the ideal has trapped himself in a fatal net. Each executioner seeks only justice but is forced thereby to become in turn a criminal and be executed.

Aeschylus actually arrests the terrible cycle with the establishment of a court of justice in Athens, The Areopagus, which punishes murder but relieves the individual of the necessity of being himself the executioner. In the *Oresteia* man is forced to think even while he suffers and is driven to question the fates even while the mesh of circumstances tightens around him. "Wisdom comes alone through suffering," says Aeschylus, and he treats suffering as the tragic but necessary condition through which the human spirit must pass on its way to the establishment of law.

This view of man's fate profoundly influenced O'Neill. He modernized the House of Atreus by translating its historical circumstances into psychological, social, biological, and environmental forces. Where Aeschylus showed men entangled in the historical past, O'Neill shows them entangled by such powers as heredity, psychology, natural environment, and social condition—all of which limit their freedom of choice as precisely as did the Greek nemesis. His heroes are no longer bound by such heroic necessities as avenging the murder of a father and a king, but rather by such "trivialities" as the unlucky chance of being born on a farm when they have no aptitude for farming, or by falling in love with the wrong girl at the wrong moment, or by inheriting a taste for drink, or by having suffered some deep psychological wound in childhood. Whatever its genesis, fate traps all his heroes, preventing them from achieving the goals which their humanity requires. In the settings of the plays, this condition of servitude is reflected in dingy farmhouse rooms, a fogbound ship, or a cage in the zoo. It is also the realistic equivalent of the imprisonment of Monte Cristo in the dungeon of the Chateau d'If.

But where Monte Cristo breaks free from his dungeon, and the characters of Aeschylus find their way through suffering to wisdom, O'Neill's characters seldom escape their fatal prisons. To be sure, they protest violently against their fate, but it continues to hold them in an iron grasp until they die—death being the ultimate form of biological fate.

This pessimism in O'Neill's plays has often disaffected his critics. It has also had a good deal to do with the unwillingness of Americans to accept O'Neill wholeheartedly as their first great dramatist. But O'Neill felt that the charges of pessimism were unfounded.

I have been accused of unmitigated gloom. Is this a pessimistic view of life? I do not think so. There is a skin deep optimism and another higher optimism, not skin deep, which is usually confounded with pessimism. To me, the tragic alone had that significant beauty which is truth. It is the meaning of life—and the hope. The noblest is eternally the most tragic. The people who succeed and do not push on to a greater failure are the spiritual middle classers. . . . Only through the unattainable does man achieve a hope worth living and dying for—and so attain himself. He with the spiritual guerdon of a hope in hopelessness, is nearest to the stars and the rainbow's root.

It must be said that this sense of triumph gleams faintly, if at all, in the general gloom of his plays, but what he says here is worth serious consideration. Most of us would take the death of Robert Mayo in *Beyond the Horizon* as an unrelieved disaster. All that he wanted has been denied him by a combination of circumstances over which he has no control. And he wanted so little! His death from tuberculosis in a roadside ditch, his love gone and his child dead, seems like the grimmest end a man can imagine—made all the grimmer by the absence of any heroic circumstances. But O'Neill invites us to see grandeur in this tale of suffering. Of course it is sad; it is more than sad, it is tragic. There is solace however in this fact: in the face of an unbeatable combination of fates, Robert Mayo has continued to believe and to struggle for some shining thing beyond the horizon. A lesser man, O'Neill is saying, would have either lapsed into cynicism or would have accepted his lot wryly and forgot his dreams. Both would have avoided tragedy. Mayo reaches tragedy in his refusal to relinquish his one claim to greatness: his vision of a broader, deeper, more significant life lying just beyond the horizons of ordinary life.

### IV

O'Neill once reported to his friends that the idea for *Beyond the Horizon* came from a brief conversation with a boy on the beach.

The Boy. What's out there?
O'Neill. The horizon.
The Boy. And what's beyond the horizon?

But whatever the source of the title, O'Neill poured much of his personal experience and family history into the play. The antagonism between Eugene and Jamie smoulders again in the struggle between Andrew and Robert Mayo. The disappointment of James O'Neill, Sr., with his older son becomes the angry quarrel between the older Mayo and the son Andrew when the latter decides to leave the farm. The Mayo farm itself is modeled on a lonely farm near Truro—on the Atkins-Mayo Road—where even today the incessant roar of the sea brings in the romance of far places. The lure of the sea which Robert Mayo feels so strongly is surely an expression of what O'Neill himself felt about the sea and travel. Personal experience however is merely the raw material of the play; for as O'Neill worked on it through 1917 and later, the fragments of life gradually were transmuted into art.

At first he intended to dramatize the life of a wanderer—a peculiarly American figure who pursues his dreams over all the world without "success or a completed deed in his life" but one who at last achieves "a real accretion from his wandering and dreaming, a thing intangible but real and precious beyond compare." Then, however, the plan changed. He

. . . started to think of a more intellectual, civilized type—a weaker type. . . —a man who would have [an] inborn craving for the sea's unrest, only in him it would be conscious, too conscious, intellectually diluted into a vague, intangible, romantic wanderlust. His powers of resistance, both moral and physical, would. . . be . . . watered. He would throw away his instinctive dream and accept the thralldom of the farm for, why for almost any nice little poetical craving—the romance of sex, say. And so Robert Mayo was born, and developed from that beginning, and Ruth and the others, and finally the complete play.

*Beyond the Horizon* has been compared to the novels of Thomas Hardy, and the comparison is apt, for in both, fate closes all avenues of escape with the precise clicks of a machine. In the play's first scene, life seems so simple and filled with hope. We see a prospering farm, a son who loves it and works it efficiently; another son who, although something of a dreamer, is nevertheless about to undertake the way of life most suited for him. Then with the arrival of Ruth the first and fatal click occurs. All the lives are thereafter redirected into paths which narrow toward disaster. Andrew's dream is corroded. He finds only dirt and discomfort in foreign places and ends as a speculator in grain rather than a producer of it. This fate is as much a perversion of his nature as the life of a farmer is for Robert. Crossed and thwarted, all life drains away like blood; and the alternation of indoor and outdoor scenes serves only to remind us of the narrowness of the cramped farmhouse room where freedom is ever denied the prisoners.

In the face of this unrelieved gloom, O'Neill insisted nevertheless that his tragedy inspired "exultance."

The tragedy of man is perhaps the only significant thing about him. What I am after is to get an audience to leave the theatre with an exultant feeling from seeing somebody on the stage facing life, fighting against the eternal odds, not conquering but perhaps inevitably being conquered. The individual life is made significant just by the struggle.

*Beyond the Horizon* was first performed on the afternoon of February 3, 1920. It was put on because of the interest of an actor, Richard Bennett, the father of two famous movie actresses, who having read the play and admired it, persuaded several other actors to join him in playing it in the afternoon before their regular show at night. James O'Neill was there at the opening night. After the play he remarked to his son—in that mixture of antagonism and pride so characteristic of the O'Neills—"Are you trying to send the audience home to commit suicide?" Most of the critics in attendance had similar mixed feelings, and none of them, it must be said, recognized the production as a great turning point in the American theater. On the whole, however, they were favorable.

Alexander Woolcott went even further: "The only reason for not calling *Beyond the Horizon* a great play is the natural gingerliness with which a reviewer uses that word—particularly in the flush of the first hour after the fall of the final curtain."

Forty-five years have passed since that afternoon, but Woolcott's doubt about the word "great" has lingered on to haunt this and O'Neill's other plays. On this matter the reader must make up his own mind, but he should not forget that this was the first American play about which the question of greatness could be seriously asked.

# BEYOND THE HORIZON

## A PLAY IN THREE ACTS

### CHARACTERS

JAMES MAYO, *a farmer*
KATE MAYO, *his wife*
CAPTAIN DICK SCOTT, *of the bark "Sunda," her brother*
ANDREW MAYO ⎱ *sons of* JAMES MAYO
ROBERT MAYO ⎰
RUTH ATKINS
MRS. ATKINS, *her widowed mother*
MARY
BEN, *a farm hand*
DOCTOR FAWCETT

### SCENES

#### ACT ONE

*Scene 1:* The Road. Sunset of a day in Spring.
*Scene 2:* The Farm House. The same night.

#### ACT TWO

(*Three years later*)
*Scene 1:* The Farm House. Noon of a Summer day.
*Scene 2:* The top of a hill on the farm overlooking the sea. The following day.

#### ACT THREE

(*Five years later*)
*Scene 1:* The Farm House. Dawn of a day in late Fall.
*Scene 2:* The Road. Sunrise.

## ACT ONE

### SCENE I

A SECTION *of country highway. The road runs diagonally from the left, forward, to the right, rear, and can be seen in the distance winding toward the horizon like a pale ribbon between the low, rolling hills with their freshly plowed fields clearly divided from each other, checkerboard fashion, by the lines of stone walls and rough snakefences.*

*The forward triangle cut off by the road is a section of a field from the dark earth of which myriad bright-green blades of fall-sown rye are sprouting. A straggling line of piled rocks, too low to be called a wall, separates this field from the road.*

*To the rear of the road is a ditch with a sloping, grassy bank on the far side. From the center of this an old, gnarled apple tree, just budding into leaf, strains its twisted branches heavenwards, black against the pallor of distance. A snake-fence sidles from left to right along the top of the bank, passing beneath the apple tree.*

*The hushed twilight of a day in May is just beginning. The horizon hills are still rimmed by a faint line of flame, and the sky above them glows with the crimson flush of the sunset. This fades gradually as the action of the scene progresses.*

*At the rise of the curtain,* ROBERT MAYO *is discovered sitting on the fence. He is a tall, slender young man of twenty-three. There is a touch of the poet about him expressed in his high forehead and wide, dark eyes. His features are delicate and refined, leaning to weakness in the mouth and chin. He is dressed in gray corduroy trousers pushed into high laced boots, and a blue flannel shirt with a bright colored tie. He is reading a book by the fading sunset light. He shuts this, keeping a finger in to mark the place, and turns his head toward the horizon, gazing out over the fields and hills. His lips move as if he were reciting something to himself.*

*His brother* ANDREW *comes along the road from the right, returning from his work in the fields. He is twenty-seven years old, an opposite type to* ROBERT—*husky, sunbronzed, handsome in a large-featured, manly fashion—a son of the soil, intelligent in a shrewd way, but with nothing of the intellectual about him. He wears overalls, leather boots, a gray flannel shirt open at the neck, and a soft, mud-stained hat pushed back on his head. He stops to talk to* ROBERT, *leaning on the hoe he carries.*

ANDREW (*seeing* ROBERT *has not noticed his presence—in a loud shout*). Hey there! (ROBERT *turns with a start. Seeing who it is, he smiles.*) Gosh, you do take the prize for day-dreaming! And I see you've toted one of the old books along with you. (*He crosses the ditch and sits on the fence near his brother.*) What is it this time—poetry, I'll bet. (*He reaches for the book.*) Let me see.

ROBERT (*handing it to him rather reluctantly*). Look out you don't get it full of dirt.

ANDREW (*glancing at his hands*). That isn't dirt—it's good clean earth. (*He turns over the pages. His eyes read something and he gives an exclamation of disgust.*) Humph! (*With a provoking grin at his brother he reads aloud in a doleful, sing-song voice.*) "I have loved wind and light and the bright sea. But Holy and most sacred night, not as I love and have loved thee." (*He hands the book back.*) Here! Take it and bury it. I suppose it's that year in college gave you a liking for that kind of stuff. I'm darn glad I stopped at High School, or maybe I'd been crazy too. (*He grins and slaps* ROBERT *on the back affectionately.*) Imagine me reading poetry and plowing at the same time. The team'd run away, I'll bet.

ROBERT (*laughing*). Or picture me plowing.

ANDREW. You should have gone back to college last fall, like I know you wanted to. You're fitted for that sort of thing—just as I ain't.

ROBERT. You know why I didn't go back, Andy. Pa didn't like the idea, even if he didn't say so; and I know he wanted the money to use improving the farm. And besides, I'm not keen on being a student, just because you see me reading books all the time. What I want to do now is keep on moving so that I won't take root in any one place.

ANDREW. Well, the trip you're leaving on tomorrow will keep you moving all right. (*At this mention of the trip they both fall silent. There is a pause. Finally* ANDREW *goes on, awkwardly, attempting to speak casually.*) Uncle says you'll be gone three years.

ROBERT. About that, he figures.

ANDREW (*moodily*). That's a long time.

ROBERT. Not so long when you come to consider it. You know the "Sunda" sails around the Horn for Yokohama first, and that's a long voyage on a sailing ship; and if we go to any of the other places Uncle Dick mentions—India, or Australia, or South Africa, or South America —they'll be long voyages, too.

ANDREW. You can have all those foreign parts for all of me. (*After a pause*) Ma's going to miss you a lot, Rob.

ROBERT. Yes—and I'll miss her.

ANDREW. And Pa ain't feeling none too happy to have you go—though he's been trying not to show it.

ROBERT. I can see how he feels.

ANDREW. And you can bet that I'm not giving any cheers about it. (*He puts one hand on the fence near* ROBERT.)

ROBERT (*putting one hand on top of* ANDREW'S *with a gesture almost of shyness*). I know that, too, Andy.

ANDREW. I'll miss you as much as anybody, I guess. You see, you and I ain't like most brothers—always fighting and separated a lot of the time, while we've always been together—just the two of us. It's different with us. That's why it hits so hard, I guess.

ROBERT (*with feeling*). It's just as hard for me, Andy—believe that! I hate to leave you and the old folks—but—I feel I've got to. There's something calling me—(*He points to the horizon.*) Oh, I can't just explain it to you, Andy.

ANDREW. No need to, Rob. (*Angry at himself*) Hell! You want to go—that's all there is to it; and I wouldn't have you miss this chance for the world.

ROBERT. It's fine of you to feel that way, Andy.

ANDREW. Huh! I'd be a nice sun-of-a-gun if I didn't, wouldn't I? When I know how you need this sea trip to make a new man of you—in the body, I mean—and give you your full health back.

ROBERT (*a trifle impatiently*). All of you seem to keep harping on my health. You were so used to seeing me lying around the house in the old days that you never will get over the notion that I'm a chronic invalid. You don't realize how I've bucked up in the past few years. If I had no other excuse for going on Uncle Dick's ship but just my health, I'd stay right here and start in plowing.

ANDREW. Can't be done. Farming ain't your nature. There's all the difference shown in just the way us two feel about the farm. You—well, you like the home part of it, I expect; but as a place to work and grow things, you hate it. Ain't that right?

ROBERT. Yes, I suppose it is. For you it's different. You're a Mayo through and through.

You're wedded to the soil. You're as much a product of it as an ear of corn is, or a tree. Father is the same. This farm is his life-work, and he's happy in knowing that another Mayo, inspired by the same love, will take up the work where he leaves off. I can understand your attitude, and Pa's; and I think it's wonderful and sincere. But I—well, I'm not made that way.

ANDREW. No, you ain't; but when it comes to understanding, I guess I realize that you've got your own angle of looking at things.

ROBERT (*musingly*). I wonder if you do, really.

ANDREW (*confidently*). Sure I do. You've seen a bit of the world, enough to make the farm seem small, and you've got the itch to see it all.

ROBERT. It's more than that, Andy.

ANDREW. Oh, of course. I know you're going to learn navigation, and all about a ship, so's you can be an officer. That's natural, too. There's fair pay in it, I expect, when you consider that you've always got a home and grub thrown in; and if you're set on traveling, you can go anywhere you're a mind to without paying fare.

ROBERT (*with a smile that is half sad*). It's more than that, Andy.

ANDREW. Sure it is. There's always a chance of a good thing coming your way in some of those foreign ports or other. I've heard there are great opportunities for a young fellow with his eyes open in some of those new countries that are just being opened up. (*Jovially*) I'll bet that's what you've been turning over in your mind under all your quietness! (*He slaps his brother on the back with a laugh.*) Well, if you get to be a millionaire all of a sudden, call 'round once in a while and I'll pass the plate to you. We could use a lot of money right here on the farm without hurting it any.

ROBERT (*forced to laugh*). I've never considered that practical side of it for a minute, Andy.

ANDREW. Well, you ought to.

ROBERT. No, I oughtn't. (*Pointing to the horizon—dreamily*) Supposing I was to tell you that it's just Beauty that's calling me, the beauty of the far off and unknown, the mystery and spell of the East which lures me in the books I've read, the need of the freedom of great wide spaces, the joy of wandering on and on—in quest of the secret which is hidden over there, beyond the horizon? Suppose I told you that was the one and only reason for my going?

ANDREW. I should say you were nutty.

ROBERT (*frowning*). Don't, Andy. I'm serious.

ANDREW. Then you might as well stay here, because we've got all you're looking for right on this farm. There's wide space enough, Lord knows; and you can have all the sea you want by walking a mile down to the beach; and there's plenty of horizon to look at, and beauty enough for anyone, except in the winter. (*He grins.*) As for the mystery and spell, I haven't met 'em yet, but they're probably lying around somewheres. I'll have you understand this is a first class farm with all the fixings. (*He laughs.*)

ROBERT (*joining in the laughter in spite of himself*). It's no use talking to you, you chump!

ANDREW. You'd better not say anything to Uncle Dick about spells and things when you're on the ship. He'll likely chuck you overboard for a Jonah. (*He jumps down from the fence.*) I'd better run along. I've got to wash up some as long as Ruth's Ma is coming over for supper.

ROBERT (*pointedly—almost bitterly*). And Ruth.

ANDREW (*confused—looking everywhere except at* ROBERT—*trying to appear unconcerned*). Yes, Ruth'll be staying too. Well, I better hustle, I guess, and— (*He steps over the ditch to the road while he is talking.*)

ROBERT (*who appears to be fighting some strong inward emotion—impulsively*). Wait a minute, Andy! (*He jumps down from the fence.*) There is something I want to— (*He stops abruptly, biting his lips, his face coloring.*)

ANDREW (*facing him; half-defiantly*). Yes?

ROBERT (*confusedly*). No—never mind—it doesn't matter, it was nothing.

ANDREW (*after a pause, during which he stares fixedly at* ROBERT's *averted face*). Maybe I can guess what—you were going to say—but I guess you're right not to talk about it. (*He pulls* ROBERT's *hand from his side and grips it tensely; the two brothers stand looking into each other's eyes for a minute.*) We can't help those things, Rob. (*He turns away, suddenly releasing* ROBERT's *hand.*) You'll be coming along shortly, won't you?

ROBERT (*dully*). Yes.

ANDREW. See you later, then. (*He walks off down the road to the left.* ROBERT *stares after him for a moment; then climbs to the fence rail again, and looks out over the hills, an expression of deep grief on his face. After a moment or so,* RUTH *enters hurriedly from the left. She is a healthy, blonde, out-of-door girl of twenty, with a graceful, slender figure. Her face, though inclined to roundness, is undeniably pretty, its large eyes of a deep blue set off strikingly by the sun-bronzed complexion. Her small, regular features are marked by a certain strength—an underlying, stubborn fixity of purpose hidden in the frankly-appealing charm of her fresh youthfulness. She wears a simple white dress but no hat.*)

RUTH (*seeing him*). Hello, Rob!

ROBERT (*startled*). Hello, Ruth!

RUTH (*jumps the ditch and perches on the fence beside him*). I was looking for you.

ROBERT (*pointedly*). Andy just left here.

RUTH. I know. I met him on the road a second ago. He told me you were here. (*Tenderly playful*) I wasn't looking for Andy, Smarty, if that's what you mean. I was looking for *you*.

ROBERT. Because I'm going away tomorrow?

RUTH. Because your mother was anxious to have you come home and asked me to look for you. I just wheeled Ma over to your house.

ROBERT (*perfunctorily*). How is your mother?

RUTH (*a shadow coming over her face*). She's about the same. She never seems to get any better or any worse. Oh, Rob, I do wish she'd try to make the best of things that can't be helped.

ROBERT. Has she been nagging at you again?

RUTH (*nods her head, and then breaks forth rebelliously*). She never stops nagging. No matter what I do for her she finds fault. If only Pa was still living— (*She stops as if ashamed of her outburst.*) I suppose I shouldn't complain this way. (*She sighs.*) Poor Ma, Lord knows it's hard enough for her. I suppose it's natural to be cross when you're not able ever to walk a step. Oh, I'd like to be going away some place—like you!

ROBERT. It's hard to stay—and equally hard to go, sometimes.

RUTH. There! If I'm not the stupid body! I swore I wasn't going to speak about your trip —until after you'd gone; and there I go, first thing!

ROBERT. Why didn't you want to speak of it?

RUTH. Because I didn't want to spoil this last night you're here. Oh, Rob, I'm going to—we're all going to miss you so awfully. Your mother is going around looking as if she'd burst out crying any minute. You ought to know how I feel. Andy and you and I—why it seems as if we'd always been together.

ROBERT (*with a wry attempt at a smile*). You and Andy will still have each other. It'll be harder for me without anyone.

RUTH. But you'll have new sights and new people to take you mind off; while we'll be here with the old, familiar place to remind us every minute of the day. It's a shame you're going—just at this time, in spring, when everything is getting so nice. (*With a sigh*) I oughtn't to talk that way when I know going's the best thing for you. You're bound to find all sorts of opportunities to get on, your father says.

ROBERT (*heatedly*). I don't give a damn about that! I wouldn't take a voyage across the road for the best opportunity in the world of the kind Pa

thinks of. (*He smiles at his own irritation.*) Excuse me, Ruth, for getting worked up over it; but Andy gave me an overdose of the practical considerations.

RUTH (*slowly, puzzled*). Well, then, if it isn't— (*with sudden intensity*) Oh, Rob, why *do* you want to go?

ROBERT (*turning to her quickly, in surprise —slowly*). Why do you ask that, Ruth?

RUTH (*dropping her eyes before his searching glance*). Because— (*lamely*) It seems such a shame.

ROBERT (*insistently*). Why?

RUTH. Oh, because—everything.

ROBERT. I could hardly back out now, even if I wanted to. And I'll be forgotten before you know it.

RUTH (*indignantly*). You won't! I'll never forget— (*She stops and turns away to hide her confusion.*)

ROBERT (*softly*). Will you promise me that?

RUTH (*evasively*). Of course. It's mean of you to think that any of us would forget so easily.

ROBERT (*disappointedly*). Oh!

RUTH (*with an attempt at lightness*). But you haven't told me your reason for leaving yet.

ROBERT (*moodily*). I doubt if you'll understand. It's difficult to explain, even to myself. Either you feel it, or you don't. I can remember being conscious of it first when I was only a kid—you haven't forgotten what a sickly specimen I was then, in those days, have you?

RUTH (*with a shudder*). Let's not think about them.

ROBERT. You'll have to, to understand. Well, in those days, when Ma was fixing meals, she used to get me out of the way by pushing my chair to the west window and telling me to look out and be quiet. That wasn't hard. I guess I was always quiet.

RUTH (*compassionately*). Yes, you always were—and you suffering so much, too!

ROBERT (*musingly*). So I used to stare out over the fields to the hills, out there—(*he points to the horizon*) and somehow after a time I'd forget any pain I was in, and start dreaming. I knew the sea was over beyond those hills —the folks had told me—and I used to wonder what the sea was like, and try to form a picture of it in my mind. (*With a smile*) There was all the mystery in the world to me then about that —far-off sea—and there still is! It called to me then just as it does now. (*After a slight pause*) And other times my eyes would follow this road, winding off into the distance, toward the hills, as if it, too, was searching for the sea.

And I'd promise myself that when I grew up and was strong, I'd follow that road, and it and I would find the sea together. (*With a smile*) You see, my making this trip is only keeping that promise of long ago.

RUTH (*charmed by his low, musical voice telling the dreams of his childhood*). Yes, I see.

ROBERT. Those were the only happy moments of my life then, dreaming there at the window. I liked to be all alone—those times. I got to know all the different kinds of sunsets by heart. And all those sunsets took place over there—(*he points*) beyond the horizon. So gradually I came to believe that all the wonders of the world happened on the other side of those hills. There was the home of the good fairies who performed beautiful miracles. I believed in fairies then. (*With a smile*) Perhaps I still do believe in them. Anyway, in those days they were real enough, and sometimes I could actually hear them calling to me to come out and play with them, dance with them down the road in the dusk in a game of hide-and-seek to find out where the sun was hiding himself. They sang their little songs to me, songs that told of all the wonderful things they had in their home on the other side of the hills; and they promised to show me all of them, if I'd only come, come! But I couldn't come then, and I used to cry sometimes and Ma would think I was in pain. (*He breaks off suddenly with a laugh.*) That's why I'm going now, I suppose. For I can still hear them calling. But the horizon is as far away and as luring as ever. (*He turns to her—softly*) Do you understand now, Ruth?

RUTH (*spellbound, in a whisper*). Yes.

ROBERT. You feel it then?

RUTH. Yes, yes, I do! (*Unconsciously she snuggles close against his side. His arm steals about her as if he were not aware of the action.*) Oh, Rob, how could I help feeling it? You tell things so beautifully!

ROBERT (*suddenly realizing that his arm is around her, and that her head is resting on his shoulder, gently takes his arm away. RUTH, brought back to herself, is overcome with confusion.*) So now you know why I'm going. It's for that reason—that and one other.

RUTH. You've another? Then you must tell me that, too.

ROBERT (*looking at her searchingly. She drops her eyes before his gaze.*) I wonder if I ought to! You'll promise not to be angry—whatever it is?

RUTH (*softly, her face still averted*). Yes, I promise.

ROBERT (*simply*). I love you. That's the other reason.

RUTH (*hiding her face in her hands*). Oh, Rob!

ROBERT. I wasn't going to tell you, but I feel I have to. It can't matter now that I'm going so far away, and for so long—perhaps forever. I've loved you all these years, but the realization never came 'til I agreed to go away with Uncle Dick. Then I thought of leaving you, and the pain of that thought revealed to me in a flash—that I loved you, had loved you as long as I could remember. (*He gently pulls one of* RUTH's *hands away from her face.*) You mustn't mind my telling you this, Ruth. I realize how impossible it all is—and I understand; for the revelation of my own love seemed to open my eyes to the love of others. I saw Andy's love for you—and I knew that you must love him.

RUTH (*breaking out stormily*). I don't! I don't love Andy! I don't! (ROBERT *stares at her in stupid astonishment.* RUTH *weeps hysterically.*) Whatever—put such a fool notion into— into your head? (*She suddenly throws her arms about his neck and hides her head on his shoulder.*) Oh, Rob! Don't go away! Please! You mustn't now! You can't! I won't let you! It'd break my—my heart!

ROBERT (*the expression of stupid bewilderment giving way to one of overwhelming joy. He presses her close to him—slowly and tenderly.*) Do you mean that—that you love me?

RUTH (*sobbing*). Yes, yes—of course I do —what d'you s'pose? (*She lifts up her head and looks into his eyes with a tremulous smile.*) You stupid thing! (*He kisses her.*) I've loved you right along.

ROBERT (*mystified*). But you and Andy were always together!

RUTH. Because you never seemed to want to go any place with me. You were always reading an old book, and not paying any attention to me. I was too proud to let you see I cared because I thought the year you were away to college had made you stuck-up, and you thought yourself too educated to waste any time on me.

ROBERT (*kissing her*). And I was thinking—(*with a laugh*) What fools we've both been!

RUTH (*overcome by a sudden fear*). You won't go away on the trip, will you, Rob? You'll tell them you can't go on account of me, won't you? You can't go now! You can't!

ROBERT (*bewildered*). Perhaps—you can come too.

RUTH. Oh, Rob, don't be so foolish. You know I can't. Who'd take care of Ma? Don't you see I couldn't go—on her account? (*She clings to him imploringly.*) Please don't go—not now. Tell them you've decided not to. They won't mind. I know your mother and father'll be glad. They'll all be. They don't want you to go so far away from them. Please, Rob! We'll be so happy here together where it's natural and we know things. Please tell me you won't go!

ROBERT (*face to face with a definite, final decision, betrays the conflict going on within him*). But—Ruth—I—Uncle Dick—

RUTH. He won't mind when he knows it's for your happiness to stay. How could he? (*As* ROBERT *remains silent she bursts into sobs again.*) Oh, Rob! And you said—you loved me!

ROBERT (*conquered by this appeal—an irrevocable decision in his voice*). I won't go, Ruth. I promise you. There! Don't cry! (*He presses her to him, stroking her hair tenderly. After a pause he speaks with happy hopefulness.*) Perhaps after all Andy was right—righter than he knew—when he said I could find all the things I was seeking for here, at home on the farm. I think love must have been the secret—the secret that called to me from over the world's rim—the secret beyond every horizon; and when I did not come, it came to me. (*He clasps* RUTH *to him fiercely.*) Oh, Ruth, our love is sweeter than any distant dream! (*He kisses her passionately and steps to the ground, lifting* RUTH *in his arms and carrying her to the road where he puts her down.*)

RUTH (*with a happy laugh*). My, but you're strong!

ROBERT. Come! We'll go and tell them at once.

RUTH (*dismayed*). Oh, no, don't, Rob, not 'til after I've gone. There'd be bound to be such a scene with them all together.

ROBERT (*kissing her—gayly*). As you like—little Miss Common Sense!

RUTH. Let's go, then. (*She takes his hand, and they start to go off left.* ROBERT *suddenly stops and turns as though for a last look at the hills and the dying sunset flush.*)

ROBERT (*looking upward and pointing*). See! The first star. (*He bends down and kisses her tenderly.*) Our star!

RUTH (*in a soft murmur*). Yes. Our very own star. (*They stand for a moment looking up at it, their arms around each other. Then* RUTH *takes his hand again and starts to lead him away.*) Come, Rob, let's go. (*His eyes are fixed again on the horizon as he half turns to follow her.* RUTH *urges.*) We'll be late for supper, Rob.

ROBERT (*shakes his head impatiently, as though he were throwing off some disturbing thought —with a laugh*). All right. We'll run then. Come on! (*They run off laughing as the curtain falls.*)

# ACT ONE

## SCENE II

THE *small sitting room of the Mayo farmhouse about nine o'clock same night. On the left, two windows looking out on the fields. Against the wall between the windows, an old-fashioned walnut desk. In the left corner, rear, a sideboard with a mirror. In the rear wall to the right of the sideboard, a window looking out on the road. Next to the window a door leading out into the yard. Farther right, a black horsehair sofa, and another door opening on a bedroom. In the corner, a straight-backed chair. In the right wall, near the middle, an open doorway leading to the kitchen. Farther forward a double-heater stove with coal scuttle, etc. In the center of the newly-carpeted floor, an oak dining-room table with a red cover. In the center of the table, a large oil reading lamp. Four chairs, three rockers with crocheted tidies on their backs, and one straight-backed, are placed about the table. The walls are papered a dark red with a scrolly-figured pattern.*

*Everything in the room is clean, well-kept, and in its exact place, yet there is no suggestion of primness about the whole. Rather, the atmosphere is one of the orderly comfort of a simple, hard-earned prosperity, enjoyed and maintained by the family as a unit.*

JAMES MAYO, *his wife, her brother,* CAPTAIN DICK SCOTT, *and* ANDREW *are discovered.* MAYO *is his son* ANDREW *over again in body and face—an* ANDREW *sixty-five years old with a short, square, white beard.* MRS. MAYO *is a slight, round-faced, rather prim-looking woman of fifty-five who had once been a school teacher. The labors of a farmer's wife have bent but not broken her, and she retains a certain refinement of movement and expression foreign to the* MAYO *part of the family. Whatever resemblance* ROBERT *has to his parents may be traced to her. Her brother, the* CAPTAIN, *is short and stocky, with a weatherbeaten, jovial face and a white mustache—a typical old salt, loud of voice and given to gesture. He is fifty-eight years old.*

JAMES MAYO *sits in front of the table. He wears spectacles, and a farm journal which he has been reading lies in his lap. The* CAPTAIN *leans forward from a chair in the rear, his hands on the table in front of him.* ANDREW *is tilted back on the straight-backed chair to the left, his chin sunk forward on his chest, staring at the carpet, preoccupied and frowning.*

*As the curtain rises the* CAPTAIN *is just finishing the relation of some sea episode. The others are pretending an interest which is belied by the absent-minded expressions on their faces.*

THE CAPTAIN (*chuckling*). And that mission woman, she hails me on the dock as I was acomin' shore, and she says—with her silly face all screwed up serious as judgment—"Captain," she says, "would you be so kind as to tell me where the sea-gulls sleeps at nights?" Blow me if them warn't her exact words! (*He slaps the table with the palms of his hands and laughs loudly. The others force smiles.*) Ain't that just like a fool woman's question? And I looks at her serious as I could. "Ma'm," says I, "I couldn't rightly answer that question. I ain't never seed a sea-gull in his bunk yet. The next time I hears one snorin'," I says, "I'll make a note of where he's turned in, and write you a letter 'bout it." And then she calls me a fool real spiteful and tacks away from me quick. (*He laughs again uproariously.*) So I got rid of her that way. (*The others smile but immediately relapse into expressions of gloom again.*)

MRS. MAYO (*absent-mindedly—feeling that she has to say something*). But when it comes to that, where *do* sea-gulls sleep, Dick?

SCOTT (*slapping the table*). Ho! Ho! Listen to her, James. 'Nother one! Well, if that don't beat all hell—'scuse me for cussin', Kate.

MAYO (*with a twinkle in his eyes*). They unhitch their wings, Katey, and spreads 'em out on a wave for a bed.

SCOTT. And then they tells the fish to whistle to 'em when it's time to turn out. Ho! Ho!

MRS. MAYO (*with a forced smile*). You men folks are too smart to live, aren't you? (*She resumes her knitting.* MAYO *pretends to read his paper;* ANDREW *stares at the floor.*)

SCOTT (*looks from one to the other of them with a puzzled air. Finally he is unable to bear the thick silence a minute longer, and blurts out*) You folks look as if you was settin' up with a corpse. (*With exaggerated concern*) God A'mighty, there ain't anyone dead, be there?

MAYO (*sharply*). Don't play the dunce, Dick! You know as well as we do there ain't no great cause to be feelin' chipper.

SCOTT (*argumentatively*). And there ain't no cause to be wearin' mourning, either, I can make out.

MRS. MAYO (*indignantly*). How can you talk that way, Dick Scott, when you're taking our Robbie away from us, in the middle of the night, you might say, just to get on that old boat of yours on time! I think you might wait until morning when he's had his breakfast.

SCOTT (*appealing to the others hopelessly*).

Ain't that a woman's way o' seein' things for you? God A'mighty, Kate I can't give orders to the tide that it's got to be high just when it suits me to have it. I ain't gettin' no fun out o' missing sleep and leavin' here at six bells myself. (*Protestingly*) And the "Sunda" ain't an old ship —leastways, not very old—and she's good's she ever was.

MRS. MAYO (*her lips trembling*). I wish Robbie weren't going.

MAYO (*looking at her over his glasses—consolingly*). There, Katey!

MRS. MAYO (*rebelliously*). Well, I *do* wish he wasn't!

SCOTT. You shouldn't be taking it so hard, 's far as I kin see. This vige'll make a man of him. I'll see to it he learns how to navigate, 'n' study for a mate's c'tificate right off—and it'll give him a trade for the rest of his life, if he wants to travel.

MRS. MAYO. But I don't want him to travel all his life. You've got to see he comes home when this trip is over. Then he'll be all well, and he'll want to—to marry—(ANDREW *sits forward in his chair with an abrupt movement.*)—and settle down right here. (*She stares down at the knitting in her lap after a pause.*) I never realized how hard it was going to be for me to have Robbie go—or I wouldn't have considered it a minute.

SCOTT. It ain't no good goin' on that way, Kate, now it's all settled.

MRS. MAYO (*on the verge of tears*). It's all right for *you* to talk. You've never had any children. You don't know what it means to be parted from them—and Robbie my youngest, too. (ANDREW *frowns and fidgets in his chair.*)

ANDREW (*suddenly turning to them*). There's one thing none of you seem to take into consideration—that Rob wants to go. He's dead set on it. He's been dreaming over this trip ever since it was first talked about. It wouldn't be fair to him not to have him go. (*A sudden uneasiness seems to strike him.*) At least, not if he still feels the same way about it he did when he was talking to me this evening.

MAYO (*with an air of decision*). Andy's right, Katey. That ends all argyment, you can see that. (*Looking at his big silver watch*) Wonder what's happened to Robert? He's been gone long enough to wheel the widder to home, certain. He can't be out dreamin' at the stars his last night.

MRS. MAYO (*a bit reproachfully*). Why didn't you wheel Mrs. Atkins back tonight, Andy? You usually do when she and Ruth come over.

ANDREW (*avoiding her eyes*). I thought maybe Robert wanted to tonight. He offered to go right away when they were leaving.

MRS. MAYO. He only wanted to be polite.

ANDREW (*gets to his feet*). Well, he'll be right back, I guess. (*He turns to his father.*) Guess I'll go take a look at the black cow, Pa—see if she's ailing any.

MAYO. Yes—better had, son. (ANDREW *goes into the kitchen on the right.*)

SCOTT (*as he goes out—in a low tone*). There's the boy that would make a good, strong sea-farin' man—if he'd a mind to.

MAYO (*sharply*). Don't you put no such fool notions in Andy's head, Dick—or you'n' me's goin' to fall out. (*Then he smiles.*) You couldn't tempt him, no ways. Andy's a Mayo bred in the bone and he's a born farmer, and a damn good one, too. He'll live and die right here on this farm, like I expect to. (*With proud confidence*) And he'll make this one of the slickest, best-payin' farms in the state, too, afore he gits through!

SCOTT. Seems to me it's a pretty slick place right now.

MAYO (*shaking his head*). It's too small. We need more land to make it amount to much, and we ain't got the capital to buy it. (ANDREW *enters from the kitchen. His hat is on, and he carries a lighted lantern in his hand. He goes to the door in the rear leading out.*)

ANDREW (*opens the door and pauses*). Anything else you can think of to be done, Pa?

MAYO. No, nothin' I know of. (ANDREW *goes out, shutting the door.*)

MRS. MAYO (*after a pause*). What's come over Andy tonight, I wonder? He acts so strange.

MAYO. He does seem sort o' glum and out of sorts. It's 'count o' Robert leavin,' I s'pose. (*To* SCOTT) Dick, you wouldn't believe how them boys o'mine sticks together. They ain't like most brothers. They've been thick as thieves all their lives, with nary a quarrel I kin remember.

SCOTT. No need to tell me that. I can see how they take to each other.

MRS. MAYO (*pursuing her train of thought*). Did you notice, James, how queer everyone was at supper? Robert seemed stirred up about something; and Ruth was so flustered and giggly; and Andy sat there dumb, looking as if he'd lost his best friend; and all of them only nibbled at their food.

MAYO. Guess they was all thinkin' about tomorrow, same as us.

MRS. MAYO (*shaking her head*). No. I'm afraid somethin's happened—somethin' else.

MAYO. You mean—'bout Ruth?

MRS. MAYO. Yes.

MAYO (*after a pause—frowning*). I hope her and Andy ain't had a serious fallin'-out. I always

sorter hoped they'd hitch up together sooner or later. What d'you say, Dick? Don't you think them two'd pair up well?

SCOTT (*nodding his head approvingly*). A sweet wholesome couple they'd make.

MAYO. It'd be a good thing for Andy in more ways than one. I ain't what you'd call calculatin' generally, and I b'lieve in lettin' young folks run their affairs to suit themselves; but there's advantages for both o' them in this match you can't overlook in reason. The Atkins farm is right next to ourn. Jined together they'd make a jim-dandy of a place, with plenty o' room to work in. And bein' a widder with only a daughter, and laid up all the time to boot, Mrs. Atkins can't do nothin' with the place as it ought to be done. She needs a man, a first-class farmer, to take hold o' things; and Andy's just the one.

MRS. MAYO (*abruptly*). I don't think Ruth loves Andy.

MAYO. You don't? Well, maybe a woman's eyes is sharper in such things, but—they're always together. And if she don't love him now, she'll likely come around to it in time. (*As* MRS. MAYO *shakes her head*) You seem mighty fixed in your opinion, Katey. How d'you know?

MRS. MAYO. It's just what I feel.

MAYO (*a light breaking over him*). You don't mean to say—(MRS. MAYO *nods.* MAYO *chuckles scornfully.*) Shucks! I'm losin' my respect for your eyesight, Katey. Why, Robert ain't got no time for Ruth, 'cept as a friend!

MRS. MAYO (*warningly*). Sss-h-h! (*The door from the yard opens, and* ROBERT *enters. He is smiling happily, and humming a song to himself, but as he comes into the room an undercurrent of nervous uneasiness manifests itself in his bearing.*)

MAYO. So here you be at last! (ROBERT *comes forward and sits on* ANDY'S *chair.* MAYO *smiles slyly at his wife.*) What have you been doin' all this time—countin' the stars to see if they all come out right and proper?

ROBERT. There's only one I'll ever look for any more, Pa.

MAYO (*reproachfully*). You might've even not wasted time lookin' for that one—your last night.

MRS. MAYO (*as if she were speaking to a child*). You ought to have worn your coat a sharp night like this, Robbie.

SCOTT (*disgustedly*). God A'mighty, Kate, you treat Robert as if he was one year old!

MRS. MAYO (*notices* ROBERT'S *nervous uneasiness*). You look all worked up over something, Robbie. What is it?

ROBERT (*swallowing hard, looks quickly from*

*one to the other of them—then begins determinedly*). Yes, there is something—something I must tell you—all of you. (*As he begins to talk* ANDREW *enters quietly from the rear, closing the door behind him, and setting the lighted lantern on the floor. He remains standing by the door, his arms folded, listening to* ROBERT *with a repressed expression of pain on his face.* ROBERT *is so much taken up with what he is going to say that he does not notice* ANDREW'S *presence.*) Something I discovered only this evening—very beautiful and wonderful—something I did not take into consideration previously because I hadn't dared to hope that such happiness could ever come to me. (*Appealingly*) You must all remember that fact, won't you?

MAYO (*frowning*). Let's get to the point, son.

ROBERT (*with a trace of defiance*). Well, the point is this, Pa: I'm not going—I mean—I can't go tomorrow with Uncle Dick—or at any future time, either.

MRS. MAYO (*with a sharp sigh of joyful relief*). Oh, Robbie, I'm so glad!

MAYO (*astounded*). You ain't serious, be you, Robert? (*Severely*) Seems to me it's pretty late hour in the day for you to be upsettin' all your plans so sudden!

ROBERT. I asked you to remember that until this evening I didn't know myself. I had never dared to dream—

MAYO (*irritably*). What is this foolishness you're talkin' of?

ROBERT (*flushing*). Ruth told me this evening that—she loved me. It was after I'd confessed I loved her. I told her I hadn't been conscious of my love until after the trip had been arranged, and I realized it would mean—leaving her. That was the truth. I *didn't* know until then. (*As if justifying himself to the others*) I hadn't intended telling her anything but—suddenly—I felt I must. I didn't think it would matter, because I was going away. And I thought she loved—someone else. (*Slowly—his eyes shining*) And then she cried and said it was I she'd loved all the time, but I hadn't seen it.

MRS. MAYO (*rushes over and throws her arms about him*). I knew it! I was just telling your father when you came in—and, oh, Robbie, I'm so happy you're not going!

ROBERT (*kissing her*). I knew you'd be glad, Ma.

MAYO (*bewilderedly*). Well, I'll be damned! You do beat all for gettin' folks' minds all tangled up, Robert. And Ruth too! Whatever got into her of a sudden? Why, I was thinkin'—

MRS. MAYO (*hurriedly—in a tone of warning*). Never mind what you were thinking, James. It wouldn't be any use telling us that now. (*Meaningly*) And what you were hoping for turns out just the same almost, doesn't it?

MAYO (*thoughtfully—beginning to see this side of the argument*). Yes; I suppose you're right, Katey. (*Scratching his head in puzzlement*) But how it ever come about! It do beat anything ever I heard. (*Finally he gets up with a sheepish grin and walks over to* ROBERT.) We're glad you ain't goin', your Ma and I, for we'd have missed you terrible, that's certain and sure; and we're glad you've found happiness. Ruth's a fine girl and'll make a good wife to you.

ROBERT (*much moved*). Thank you, Pa. (*He grips his father's hand in his.*)

ANDREW (*his face tense and drawn comes forward and holds out his hand, forcing a smile*). I guess it's my turn to offer congratulations, isn't it?

ROBERT (*with a startled cry when his brother appears before him so suddenly*). Andy! (*Confused*) Why—I—I didn't see you. Were you here when—

ANDREW. I heard everything you said; and here's wishing you every happiness, you and Ruth. You both deserve the best there is.

ROBERT (*taking his hand*). Thanks, Andy, it's fine of you to—(*His voice dies away as he sees the pain in* ANDREW'S *eyes.*)

ANDREW (*giving his brother's hand a final grip*). Good luck to you both! (*He turns away and goes back to the rear where he bends over the lantern, fumbling with it to hide his emotion from the others.*)

MRS. MAYO (*to the* CAPTAIN, *who has been too flabbergasted by* ROBERT'S *decision to say a word*). What's the matter, Dick? Aren't you going to congratulate Robbie?

SCOTT (*embarrassed*). Of course I be! (*He gets to his feet and shakes* ROBERT'S *hand, muttering a vague*) Luck to you, boy. (*He stands beside* ROBERT *as if he wanted to say something more but doesn't know how to go about it.*)

ROBERT. Thanks, Uncle Dick.

SCOTT. So you're not acomin' on the "Sunda" with me? (*His voice indicates disbelief.*)

ROBERT. I can't, Uncle—not now. I wouldn't miss it for anything in the world under any other circumstances. (*He sighs unconsciously.*) But you see I've found—a bigger dream. (*Then with joyous high spirits*) I want you all to understand one thing—I'm not going to be a loafer on your hands any longer. This means the beginning of a new life for me in every way. I'm going to settle right down and take a real interest in the farm, and do my share. I'll prove to you, Pa, that I'm as good a Mayo as you are—or Andy, when I want to be.

MAYO (*kindly but skeptically*). That's the right spirit, Robert. Ain't none of us doubts your willin'ness, but you ain't never learned—

ROBERT. Then I'm going to start learning right away, and you'll teach me, won't you?

MAYO (*mollifyingly*). Of course I will, boy, and be glad to, only you'd best go easy at first.

SCOTT (*who has listened to this conversation in mingled consternation and amazement*). You don't mean to tell me you're going to let him stay, do you, James?

MAYO. Why, things bein' as they be, Robert's free to do as he's a mind to.

MRS. MAYO. *Let him!* The very idea!

SCOTT (*more and more ruffled*). Then all I got to say is, you're a soft, weak-willed critter to be permittin' a boy—and women, too—to be layin' your course for you wherever they damn pleases.

MAYO (*slyly amused*). It's just the same with me as 'twas with you, Dick. You can't order the tides on the seas to suit you, and I ain't pretendin' I can reg'late love for young folks.

SCOTT (*scornfully*). Love! They ain't old enough to know love when they sight it! Love! I'm ashamed of you, Robert, to go lettin' a little huggin' and kissin' in the dark spile your chances to make a man out o' yourself. It ain't common sense—no siree, it ain't—not by a hell of a sight! (*He pounds the table with his fists in exasperation.*)

MRS. MAYO (*laughing provokingly at her brother*). A fine one you are to be talking about love, Dick—an old cranky bachelor like you. Goodness sakes!

SCOTT (*exasperated by their joking*). I've never been a damn fool like most, if that's what you're steerin' at.

MRS. MAYO (*tauntingly*). Sour grapes, aren't they, Dick? (*She laughs.* ROBERT *and his father chuckle.* SCOTT *sputters with annoyance.*) Good gracious, Dick, you do act silly, flying into a temper over nothing.

SCOTT (*indignantly*). Nothin'! You talk as if I wasn't concerned nohow in this here business. Seems to me I've got a right to have my say. Ain't I made all arrangements with the owners and stocked up with some special grub all on Robert's account?

ROBERT. You've been fine, Uncle Dick; and I appreciate it. Truly.

MAYO. 'Course; we all does, Dick.

SCOTT (*unplacated*). I've been countin' sure on

havin' Robert for company on this vige—to sorta talk to and show things to, and teach, kinda, and I got my mind so set on havin' him I'm goin' to be double lonesome this vige. (*He pounds on the table, attempting to cover up this confession of weakness.*) Darn all this silly lovin' business, anyway. (*Irritably*) But all this talk ain't tellin' me what I'm to do with that sta'b'd cabin I fixed up. It's all painted white, an' a bran' new mattress on the bunk, 'n' new sheets 'n' blankets 'n' things. And Chips built in a book-case so's Robert could take his books along—with a slidin' bar fixed across't it, mind, so's they couldn't fall out no matter how she rolled. (*With excited consternation*) What d'you suppose my officers is goin' to think when there's no one comes aboard to occupy that sta'b'd cabin? And the men what did the work on it—what'll *they* think? (*He shakes his finger indignantly.*) They're liable as not to suspicion it was a *woman* I'd planned to ship along, and that she gave me the go-by at the last moment! (*He wipes his perspiring brow in anguish at this thought.*) Gawd A'mighty! They're only lookin' to have the laugh on me for something like that. They're liable to b'lieve anything, those fellers is!

MAYO (*with a wink*). Then there's nothing to it but for you to get right out and hunt up a wife somewheres for that spick 'n' span cabin. She'll have to be a pretty one, too, to match it. (*He looks at his watch with exaggerated concern.*) You ain't got much time to find her, Dick.

SCOTT (*as the others smile—sulkily*). You kin go to thunder, Jim Mayo!

ANDREW (*comes forward from where he has been standing by the door, rear, brooding. His face is set in a look of grim determination.*) You needn't worry about that spare cabin, Uncle Dick, if you've a mind to take me in Robert's place.

ROBERT (*turning to him quickly*). Andy! (*He sees at once the fixed resolve in his brother's eyes, and realizes immediately the reason for it—in consternation*) Andy, you mustn't!

ANDREW. You've made your decision, Rob, and now I've made mine. You're out of this, remember.

ROBERT (*hurt by his brother's tone*). But Andy—

ANDREW. Don't interfere, Rob—that's all I ask. (*Turning to his uncle*) You haven't answered my question, Uncle Dick.

SCOTT (*clearing his throat, with an uneasy side glance at* JAMES MAYO *who is staring at his elder son as if he thought he had suddenly gone mad*). O' course, I'd be glad to have you, Andy.

ANDREW. It's settled then. I can pack the little I want to take in a few minutes.

MRS. MAYO. Don't be a fool, Dick. Andy's only joking you.

SCOTT (*disgruntledly*). It's hard to tell who's jokin' and who's not in this house.

ANDREW (*firmly*). I'm not joking, Uncle Dick. (*As* SCOTT *looks at him uncertainly*) You needn't be afraid I'll go back on my word.

ROBERT (*hurt by the insinuation he feels in* AN-DREW's *tone*). Andy! That isn't fair!

MAYO (*frowning*). Seems to me this ain't no subject to joke over—not for Andy.

ANDREW (*facing his father*). I agree with you, Pa, and I tell you again, once and for all, that I've made up my mind to go.

MAYO (*dumbfounded—unable to doubt the determination in* ANDREW's *voice—helplessly*). But why, son? Why?

ANDREW (*evasively*). I've always wanted to go.

ROBERT. Andy!

ANDREW (*half angrily*). You shut up, Rob! (*Turning to his father again*) I didn't ever mention it because as long as Rob was going I knew it was no use; but now Rob's staying on here, there isn't any reason for me not to go.

MAYO (*breathing hard*). No reason? Can you stand there and say that to me, Andrew?

MRS. MAYO (*hastily—seeing the gathering storm*). He doesn't mean a word of it, James.

MAYO (*making a gesture to her to keep silence*). Let me talk, Katey. (*In a more kindly tone*) What's come over you so sudden, Andy? You know's well as I do that it wouldn't be fair o' you to run off at a moment's notice right now when we're up to our necks in hard work.

ANDREW (*avoiding his eyes*). Rob'll hold his end up as soon as he learns.

MAYO. Robert was never cut out for a farmer, and you was.

ANDREW. You can easily get a man to do my work.

MAYO (*restraining his anger with an effort*). It sounds strange to hear you, Andy, that I always thought had good sense, talkin' crazy like that. (*Scornfully*) Get a man to take your place! You ain't been workin' here for no hire, Andy, that you kin give me your notice to quit like you've done. The farm is your'n as well as mine. You've always worked on it with that understanding; and what you're sayin' you intend doin' is just skulkin' out o' your rightful responsibility.

ANDREW (*looking at the floor—simply*). I'm

sorry, Pa. (*After a slight pause*) It's no use talking any more about it.

MRS. MAYO (*in relief*). There! I knew Andy'd come to his senses!

ANDREW. Don't get the wrong idea, Ma. I'm not backing out.

MAYO. You mean you're goin' in spite of—everythin'?

ANDREW. Yes. I'm going. I've got to. (*He looks at his father defiantly*.) I feel I oughtn't to miss this chance to go out into the world and see things, and—I want to go.

MAYO (*with bitter scorn*). So—you want to go out into the world and see thin's? (*His voice raised and quivering with anger*) I never thought I'd live to see the day when a son o' mine'd look me in the face and tell a bare-faced lie! (*Bursting out*) You're a liar, Andy Mayo, and a mean one to boot!

MRS. MAYO. James!

ROBERT. Pa!

SCOTT. Steady there, Jim!

MAYO (*waving their protests aside*). He is and he knows it.

ANDREW (*his face flushed*). I won't argue with you, Pa. You can think as badly of me as you like.

MAYO (*shaking his finger at* ANDY, *in a colder rage*). You know I'm speakin' truth—that's why you're afraid to argy! You lie when you say you want to go 'way—and see thin's! You ain't got no likin' in the world to go. I've watched you grow up, and I know your ways, and they're my ways. You're runnin' against your own nature, and you're goin' to be a'mighty sorry for it if you do. 'S if I didn't know your real reason for runnin' away! And runnin' away's the only words to fit it. You're runnin' away 'cause you're put out and riled 'cause your own brother's got Ruth 'stead o' you, and—

ANDREW (*his face crimson—tensely*). Stop, Pa! I won't stand hearing that—not even from you!

MRS. MAYO (*rushing to* ANDY *and putting her arms about him protectingly*). Don't mind him, Andy dear. He don't mean a word he's saying! (*ROBERT stands rigidly, his hands clenched, his face contracted by pain.* SCOTT *sits dumbfounded and open-mouthed.* ANDREW *soothes his mother who is on the verge of tears.*)

MAYO (*in angry triumph*). It's the truth, Andy Mayo! And you ought to be bowed in shame to think of it!

ROBERT (*protestingly*). Pa!

MRS. MAYO (*coming from* ANDREW *to his father; puts her hands on his shoulders as though to try to push him back in the chair from which he has risen*). Won't you be still, James? Please won't you?

MAYO (*looking at* ANDREW *over his wife's shoulder—stubbornly*). The truth—God's truth!

MRS. MAYO. Sh-h-h! (*She tries to put a finger across his lips, but he twists his head away.*)

ANDREW (*who has regained control over himself*). You're wrong, Pa, it isn't truth. (*With defiant assertiveness*) I don't love Ruth. I never loved her, and the thought of such a thing never entered my head.

MAYO (*with an angry snort of disbelief*). Hump! You're pilin' lie on lie.

ANDREW (*losing his temper—bitterly*). I suppose it'd be hard for you to explain anyone's wanting to leave this blessed farm except for some outside reason like that. But I'm sick and tired of it—whether you want to believe me or not—and that's why I'm glad to get a chance to move on.

ROBERT. Andy! Don't! Youre only making it worse.

ANDREW (*sulkily*). I don't care. I've done my share of work here. I've earned my right to quit when I want to. (*Suddenly overcome with anger and grief; with rising intensity*) I'm sick and tired of the whole damn business. I hate the farm and every inch of ground in it. I'm sick of digging in the dirt and sweating in the sun like a slave without getting a word of thanks for it. (*Tears of rage starting to his eyes—hoarsely*) I'm through, through for good and all; and if Uncle Dick won't take me on his ship, I'll find another. I'll get away somewhere, somehow.

MRS. MAYO (*in a frightened voice*). Don't you answer him, James, He doesn't know what he's saying. Don't say a word to him 'til he's in his right senses again. Please James, don't—

MAYO (*pushes her away from him; his face is drawn and pale with the violence of his passion. He glares at* ANDREW *as if he hated him.*) You dare to—you dare to speak like that to me? You talk like that 'bout this farm—the Mayo farm—where you was born—you—you—(*He clenches his fist above his head and advances threateningly on* ANDREW.) You damned whelp!

MRS. MAYO (*with a shriek*). James! (*She covers her face with her hands and sinks weakly into* MAYO's *chair.* ANDREW *remains standing motionless, his face pale and set.*)

SCOTT (*starting to his feet and stretching his arms across the table toward* MAYO). Easy there, Jim!

ROBERT (*throwing himself between father and brother*). Stop! Are you mad?

MAYO (*grabs* ROBERT's *arm and pushes him aside—then stands for a moment gasping for breath before* ANDREW. *He points to the door with a shaking finger*). Yes—go—go!— You're no son o' mine—no son o' mine! You can go to hell if you want to! Don't let me find you here—in the mornin'—or—or—I'll *throw* you out!

ROBERT. Pa! For God's sake! (MRS. MAYO *bursts into noisy sobbing.*)

MAYO (*He gulps convulsively and glares at* ANDREW.) You go—tomorrow mornin'—and by God—don't come back—don't dare come back —by God, not while I'm livin'—or I'll—I'll (*He shakes over his muttered threat and strides toward the door rear, right.*)

MRS. MAYO (*rising and throwing her arms around him—hysterically*). James! James! Where are you going?

MAYO (*incoherently*). I'm goin'—to bed, Katey. It's late, Katey—it's late. (*He goes out.*)

MRS. MAYO (*following him, pleading hysterically*). James! Take back what you've said to Andy. James! (*She follows him out.* ROBERT *and the* CAPTAIN *stare after them with horrified eyes.* ANDREW *stands rigidly looking straight in front of him, his fists clenched at his sides.*

SCOTT (*the first to find his voice—with an explosive sigh*). Well, if he ain't the devil himself when he's roused! You oughtn't to have talked to him that way, Andy, 'bout the damn farm, knowin' how touchy he is about it. (*With another sigh*) Well, you won't mind what he's said in anger. He'll be sorry for it when he's calmed down a bit.

ANDREW (*in a dead voice*). You don't know him. (*Defiantly*) What's said is said and can't be unsaid; and I've chosen.

ROBERT (*with violent protest*). Andy! You can't go! This is all so stupid—and terrible!

ANDREW (*coldly*). I'll talk to you in a minute, Rob. (*Crushed by his brother's attitude* ROBERT *sinks down into a chair, holding his head in his hands.*)

SCOTT (*comes and slaps* ANDREW *on the back*). I am damned glad you're shippin' on, Andy. I like your spirit, and the way you spoke to him. (*Lowering his voice to a cautious whisper*) The sea's the place for a young feller like you that isn't half dead 'n' alive. (*He gives* ANDY *a final approving slap.*) You 'n' me'll get along like twins, see if we don't. I am goin' aloft to turn in. Don't forget to pack your dunnage. And git some sleep, if you kin. We'll want to sneak out extra early b'fore they're up. It'll do away with more argyments. Robert can drive us down to the town, and bring back the team. (*He goes to the door in the rear, left.*) Well, good night.

ANDREW. Good night. (SCOTT *goes out. The two brothers remain silent for a moment. Then* AN-DREW *comes over to his brother and puts a hand on his back. He speaks in a low voice, full of feeling.*) Buck up, Rob. It ain't any use crying over spilt milk; and it'll all turn out for the best—let's hope. It couldn't be helped—what's happened.

ROBERT (*wildly*). But it's a lie, Andy, a lie!

ANDREW. Of course it's a lie. You know it and I know it,—but that's all ought to know it.

ROBERT. Pa'll never forgive you. Oh, the whole affair is so senseless—and tragic. Why did you think you must go away?

ANDREW. You know better than to ask that. You know why. (*Fiercely*) I can wish you and Ruth all the good luck in the world, and I do, and I mean it; but you can't expect me to stay around here and watch you two together, day after day—and me alone. I couldn't stand it—not after all the plans I'd made to happen on this place thinking—(*his voice breaks*) thinking she cared for me.

ROBERT (*putting a hand on his brother's arm*). God! It's horrible! I feel so guilty—to think that I should be the cause of your suffering, after we've been such pals all our lives. If I could have forseen what'd happen, I swear to you I'd have never said a word to Ruth. I swear I wouldn't have, Andy!

ANDREW. I know you wouldn't; and that would've been worse, for Ruth would've suffered then. (*He pats his brother's shoulder.*) It's best as it is. It had to be, and I've got to stand the gaff, that's all. Pa'll see how I felt—after a time. (*As* ROBERT *shakes his head*)—and if he don't—well, it can't be helped.

ROBERT. But think of Ma! God, Andy, you can't go! You can't!

ANDREW (*fiercely*). I've got to go—to get away! I've got to, I tell you. I'd go crazy here, bein' reminded every second of the day what a fool I'd made of myself. I've got to get away and try and forget, if I can. And I'd hate the farm if I stayed, hate it for bringin' things back. I couldn't take interest in the work any more, work with no purpose in sight. Can't you see what a hell it'd be? You love her too, Rob. Put yourself in my place, and remember I haven't stopped loving her, and couldn't if I was to stay. Would that be fair to you or to her? Put yourself in my place. (*He shakes his brother fiercely by the shoulder.*) What'd you do then? Tell me the truth! You love her. What'd you do?

ROBERT (*chokingly*). I'd—I'd go, Andy! (*He buries his face in his hands with a shuddering sob.*) God!

ANDREW (*seeming to relax suddenly all over his body—in a low, steady voice*). Then you know why I got to go; and there's nothing more to be said.

ROBERT (*in a frenzy of rebellion*). Why did this have to happen to us? It's damnable! (*He looks about him wildly, as if his vengeance were seeking the responsible fate.*)

ANDREW (*soothingly—again putting his hands on his brother's shoulder*). It's no use fussing any more, Rob. It's done. (*Forcing a smile*) I guess Ruth's got a right to have who she likes. She made a good choice—and God bless her for it!

ROBERT. Andy! Oh, I wish I could tell you half I feel of how fine you are!

ANDREW (*interrupting him quickly*). Shut up! Let's go to bed. I've got to be up long before sun-up. You, too, if you're going to drive us down.

ROBERT. Yes. Yes.

ANDREW (*turning down the lamp*). And I've got to pack yet. (*He yawns with utter weariness.*) I'm as tired as if I'd been plowing twenty-four hours at a stretch. (*Dully*) I feel—dead. (ROBERT *covers his face again with his hands.* ANDREW *shakes his head as if to get rid of his thoughts, and continues with a poor attempt at cheery briskness.*) I'm going to douse the light. Come on. (*He slaps his brother on the back.* ROBERT *does not move.* ANDREW *bends over and blows out the lamp. His voice comes from the darkness.*) Don't sit there mourning, Rob. It'll all come out in the wash. Come and get some sleep. Everything'll turn out all right in the end. (ROBERT *can be heard stumbling to his feet, and the dark figures of the two brothers can be seen groping their way toward the doorway in the rear as the curtain falls.*)

# ACT TWO
## SCENE I

SAME *as Act One, Scene 2. Sitting room of the farmhouse about half past twelve in the afternoon of a hot, sun-baked day in mid-summer, three years later. All the windows are open but no breeze stirs the soiled white curtains. A patched screen door is in the rear. Through it the yard can be seen, its small stretch of lawn divided by the dirt path leading to the door from the gate in the white picket fence which borders the road.*

*The room has changed, not so much in its outward appearance as in its general atmosphere. Little significant details give evidence of carelessness, of inefficiency, of an industry gone to seed. The chairs appear shabby from lack of paint; the table cover is spotted and askew; holes show in the curtains; a child's doll, with one arm gone, lies under the table; a hoe stands in a corner; a man's coat is flung on the couch in the rear; the desk is cluttered with odds and ends; a number of books are piled carelessly on the sideboard. The noon enervation of the sultry, scorching day seems to have penetrated indoors, causing even inanimate objects to wear an aspect of despondent exhaustion.*

*A place is set at the end of the table, left, for someone's dinner. Through the open door to the kitchen comes the clatter of dishes being washed, interrupted at intervals by a woman's irritated voice and the peevish whining of a child.*

*At the rise of the curtain* MRS. MAYO *and* MRS. ATKINS *are discovered sitting facing each other,* MRS. MAYO *to the rear,* MRS. ATKINS *to the right of the table.* MRS. MAYO'S *face has lost all character, disintegrated, become a weak mask wearing a helpless, doleful expression of being constantly on the verge of comfortless tears. She speaks in an uncertain voice, without assertiveness, as if all power of willing had deserted her.* MRS. ATKINS *is in her wheelchair. She is a thin, pale-faced, unintelligent-looking woman of about forty-eight, with hard, bright eyes. A victim of partial paralysis for many years, condemned to be pushed from day to day of her life in a wheelchair, she has developed the selfish, irritable nature of the chronic invalid. Both women are dressed in black.* MRS. ATKINS *knits nervously as she talks. A ball of unused yarn, with needles stuck through it, lies on the table before* MRS. MAYO.

MRS. ATKINS (*with a disapproving glance at the place set on the table*). Robert's late for his dinner again, as usual. I don't see why Ruth puts up with it, and I've told her so. Many's the time I've said to her, "It's about time you put a stop to his nonsense. Does he suppose you're runnin' a hotel—with no one to help with things?" But she don't pay no attention. She's as bad as he is, a'most—thinks she knows better than an old, sick body like me.

MRS. MAYO (*dully*). Robbie's always late for things. He can't help it, Sarah.

MRS. ATKINS (*with a snort*). Can't help it! How you do go on, Kate, findin' excuses for him! Anybody can help anything they've a mind to—as long as they've got health, and ain't rendered helpless like me—(*She adds as a pious afterthought*)—through the will of God.

MRS. MAYO. Robbie can't.

MRS. ATKINS. Can't! It do make me mad, Kate Mayo, to see folks that God gave all the use of their limbs to potterin' round and wastin' time doin' everything the wrong way—and me powerless to help and at their mercy, you might say. And it ain't that I haven't pointed the right way to 'em. I've talked to Robert thousands of times and told him how things ought to be done. You know that, Kate Mayo. But d'you s'pose he takes any notice of what I say? Or Ruth, either—my own daughter? No, they think I'm a crazy, cranky old woman, half dead a'ready, and the sooner I'm in the grave and out o' their way the better it'd suit them.

MRS. MAYO. You musn't talk that way, Sarah. They're not as wicked as that. And you've got years and years before you.

MRS. ATKINS. You're like the rest, Kate. You don't know how near the end I am. Well, at least I can go to my eternal rest with a clear conscience. I've done all a body could do to avert ruin from this house. On their heads be it!

MRS. MAYO (*with hopeless indifference*). Things might be worse. Robert never had any experience in farming. You can't expect him to learn in a day.

MRS. ATKINS (*snappily*). He's had three years to learn, and he's gettin worse 'stead of better. Not on'y your place but mine too is driftin' to rack and ruin, and I can't do nothin' to prevent.

MRS. MAYO (*with a spark of assertiveness*). You can't say but Robbie works hard, Sarah.

MRS. ATKINS. What good's workin' hard if it don't accomplish anythin', I'd like to know?

MRS. MAYO. Robbie's had bad luck against him.

MRS. ATKINS. Say what you've a mind to, Kate, the proof of the puddin's in the eatin'; and you can't deny that things have been goin' from bad to worse ever since your husband died two years back.

MRS. MAYO (*wiping tears from her eyes with her handkerchief*). It was God's will that he should be taken.

MRS. ATKINS (*triumphantly*). It was God's punishment on James Mayo for the blasphemin' and denyin' of God he done all his sinful life! (MRS. MAYO *begins to weep softly.*) There, Kate, I shouldn't be remindin' you, I know. He's at peace, poor man, and forgiven, let's pray.

MRS. MAYO (*wiping her eyes—simply*). James was a good man.

MRS. ATKINS (*ignoring this remark*). What I was sayin' was that since Robert's been in charge things've been goin' down hill steady. You don't know *how* bad they are. Robert don't let on to you what's happenin'; and you'd never see it yourself if 'twas under your nose. But, thank the Lord, Ruth still comes to me once in a while for advice when she's worried near out of her senses by his goin's on. Do you know what she told me last night? But I forgot, she said not to tell you —still I think you've got a right to know, and it's my duty not to let such things go on behind your back.

MRS. MAYO (*wearily*). You can tell me if you want to.

MRS. ATKINS (*bending over toward her—in a low voice*). Ruth was almost crazy about it. Robert told her he'd have to mortgage the farm—said he didn't know how he'd pull through 'til harvest without it, and he can't get money any other way. (*She straightens up—indignantly*) Now what do you think of your Robert?

MRS. MAYO (*resignedly*). If it has to be—

MRS. ATKINS. You don't mean to say you're goin' to sign away your farm, Kate Mayo—after me warnin' you?

MRS. MAYO. I'll do what Robbie says is needful.

MRS. ATKINS (*holding up her hands*). Well, of all the foolishness!—well, it's your farm, not mine, and I've nothin' more to say.

MRS. MAYO. Maybe Robbie'll manage till Andy gets back and sees to things. It can't be long now.

MRS. ATKINS (*with keen interest*). Ruth says Andy ought to turn up any day. When does Robert figger he'll get here?

MRS. MAYO. He says he can't calculate exactly on account o' the "Sunda" being a sail boat. Last letter he got was from England, the day they were sailing for home. That was over a month ago, and Robbie thinks they're overdue now.

MRS. ATKINS. We can praise to God then that he'll be back in the nick o' time. He ought to be tired of travelin' and anxious to get home and settle down to work again.

MRS. MAYO. Andy *has* been working. He's head officer on Dick's boat, he wrote Robbie. You know that.

MRS. ATKINS. That foolin' on ships is all right for a spell, but he must be right sick of it by this.

MRS. MAYO (*musingly*). I wonder if he's changed much. He used to be so fine-looking and strong. (*With a sigh*) Three years! It seems more

like three hundred. (*Her eyes filling—piteously*) Oh, if James could only have lived 'til he came back—and forgiven him!

MRS. ATKINS. He never would have—not James Mayo! Didn't he keep his heart hardened against him till the last in spite of all you and Robert did to soften him?

MRS. MAYO (*with a feeble flash of anger*). Don't you dare say that! (*Brokenly*) Oh, I know deep down in his heart he forgave Andy, though he was too stubborn ever to own up to it. It was that brought on his death—breaking his heart just on account of his stubborn pride. (*She wipes her eyes with her handkerchief and sobs.*)

MRS. ATKINS (*piously*). It was the will of God. (*The whining crying of the child sounds from the kitchen.* MRS. ATKINS *frowns irritably.*) Drat that young one! Seems as if she cries all the time on purpose to set a body's nerves on edge.

MRS. MAYO (*wiping her eyes*). It's the heat upsets her. Mary doesn't feel any too well these days, poor little child!

MRS. ATKINS. She gets it right from her Pa —being sickly all the time. You can't deny Robert was always ailin' as a child. (*She sighs heavily.*) It was a crazy mistake for them two to get married. I argued against it at the time, but Ruth was so spelled with Robert's wild poetry notions she wouldn't listen to sense. Andy was the one would have been the match for her.

MRS. MAYO. I've often thought since it might have been better the other way. But Ruth and Robbie seem happy enough together.

MRS. ATKINS. At any rate it was God's work —and His will be done. (*The two women sit in silence for a moment.* RUTH *enters from the kitchen, carrying in her arms her two-year-old daughter,* MARY, *a pretty but sickly and anemic-looking child with a tear-stained face.* RUTH *has aged appreciably. Her face has lost its youth and freshness. There is a trace in her expression of something hard and spiteful. She sits in the rocker in front of the table and sighs wearily. She wears a gingham dress with a soiled apron tied around her waist.*)

RUTH. Land sakes, if this isn't a scorcher! That kitchen's like a furnace. Phew! (*She pushes the damp hair back from her forehead.*)

MRS. MAYO. Why didn't you call me to help with the dishes?

RUTH (*shortly*). No. The heat in there'd kill you.

MARY (*sees the doll under the table and struggles on her mother's lap*). Dolly, Mama! Dolly!

RUTH (*pulling her back*). It's time for your nap. You can't play with Dolly now.

MARY (*commencing to cry whiningly*). Dolly!

MRS. ATKINS (*irritably*). Can't you keep that child still? Her racket's enough to split a body's ears. Put her down and let her play with the doll if it'll quiet her.

RUTH (*lifting* MARY *to the floor*). There! I hope you'll be satisfied and keep still. (MARY *sits down on the floor before the table and plays with the doll in silence.* RUTH *glances at the place set on the table.*) It's a wonder Rob wouldn't try to get to meals on time once in a while.

MRS. MAYO (*dully*). Something must have gone wrong again.

RUTH (*wearily*). I s'pose so. Something's always going wrong these days, it looks like.

MRS. ATKINS (*snappily*). It wouldn't if you possessed a bit of spunk. The idea of you permittin' him to come in to meals at all hours—and you doin' the work! I never heard of such a thin'. You're too easy goin', that's the trouble.

RUTH. Do stop your nagging at me, Ma! I'm sick of hearing you. I'll do as I please about it; and thank you for not interfering. (*She wipes her moist forehead—wearily*) Phew! It's too hot to argue. Let's talk of something pleasant. (*Curiously*) Didn't I hear you speaking about Andy a while ago?

MRS. MAYO. We were wondering when he'd get home.

RUTH (*brightening*). Rob says any day now he's liable to drop in and surprise us—him and the Captain. It'll certainly look natural to see him around the farm again.

MRS. ATKINS. Let's hope the farm'll look more natural, too, when he's had a hand at it. The way thin's are now!

RUTH (*irritably*). Will you stop harping on that, Ma? We all know things aren't as they might be. What's the good of your complaining all the time?

MRS. ATKINS. There, Kate Mayo! Ain't that just what I told you? I can't say a word of advice to my own daughter even, she's that stubborn and self-willed.

RUTH (*putting her hands over her ears—in exasperation*). For goodness sakes, Ma!

MRS. MAYO (*dully*). Never mind. Andy'll fix everything when he comes.

RUTH (*hopefully*). Oh, yes, I know he will. He always did know just the right thing ought to be done. (*With weary vexation*) It's a shame for him to come home and have to start in with things in such a topsy-turvy.

MRS. MAYO. Andy'll manage.

RUTH (*sighing*). I s'pose it isn't Rob's fault things go wrong with him.

MRS. ATKINS (*scornfully*). Humph! (*She fans herself nervously.*) Land o' Goshen, but it's bakin'

in here! Let's go out in under the trees where there's a breath of fresh air. Come, Kate. (MRS. MAYO *gets up obediently and starts to wheel the invalid's chair toward the screen door.*) You better come too, Ruth. It'll do you good. Learn him a lesson and let him get his own dinner. Don't be such a fool.

RUTH (*going and holding the screen door open for them—listlessly*). He wouldn't mind. He doesn't eat much. But I can't go anyway. I've got to put baby to bed.

MRS. ATKINS. Let's go, Kate. I'm boilin' in here. (MRS. MAYO *wheels her out and off left.* RUTH *comes back and sits down in her chair.*)

RUTH (*mechanically*). Come and let me take off your shoes and stockings, Mary, that's a good girl. You've got to take your nap now. (*The child continues to play as if she hadn't heard, absorbed in her doll. An eager expression comes over* RUTH's *tired face. She glances toward the door furtively—then gets up and goes to the desk. Her movements indicate a guilty fear of discovery. She takes a letter from a pigeon-hole and retreats swiftly to her chair with it. She opens the envelope and reads the letter with great interest, a flush of excitement coming to her cheeks.* ROBERT *walks up the path and opens the screen door quietly and comes into the room. He, too, has aged. His shoulders are stooped as if under too great a burden. His eyes are dull and lifeless, his face burned by the sun and unshaven for days. Streaks of sweat have smudged the layer of dust on his cheeks. His lips drawn down at the corners give him a hopeless, resigned expression. The three years have accentuated the weakness of his mouth and chin. He is dressed in overalls, laced boots, and a flannel shirt open at the neck.*)

ROBERT (*throwing his hat over on the sofa —with a great sigh of exhaustion*). Phew! The sun's hot today! (RUTH *is startled. At first she makes an instinctive motion as if to hide the letter in her bosom. She immediately thinks better of this and sits with the letter in her hands looking at him with defiant eyes. He bends down and kisses her.*)

RUTH (*feeling of her cheek—irritably*). Why don't you shave? You look awful.

ROBERT (*indifferently*). I forgot—and it's too much trouble this weather.

MARY (*throwing aside her doll, runs to him with a happy cry*). Dada! Dada!

ROBERT (*swinging her up above his head—lovingly*). And how's this little girl of mine this hot day, eh?

MARY (*screeching happily*). Dada! Dada!

RUTH (*in annoyance*). Don't do that to her!

You know it's time for her nap and you'll get her all waked up; then I'll be the one that'll have to sit beside her till she falls asleep.

ROBERT (*sitting down in the chair on the left of table and cuddling* MARY *on his lap*). You needn't bother. I'll put her to bed.

RUTH (*shortly*). You've got to get back to your work, I s'pose.

ROBERT (*with a sigh*). Yes, I was forgetting. (*He glances at the open letter on* RUTH's *lap.*) Reading Andy's letter again? I should think you'd know it by heart by this time.

RUTH (*coloring as if she'd been accused of something—defiantly*). I've got a right to read it, haven't I? He says it's meant for all of us.

ROBERT (*with a trace of irritation*). Right? Don't be so silly. There's no question of right. I was only saying that you must know all that's in it after so many readings.

RUTH. Well, I don't. (*She puts the letter on the table and gets wearily to her feet.*) I s'pose you'll be wanting your dinner now.

ROBERT (*listlessly*). I don't care. I'm not hungry.

RUTH. And here I been keeping it hot for you!

ROBERT (*irritably*). Oh, all right then. Bring it in and I'll try to eat.

RUTH. I've got to get her to bed first. (*She goes to lift* MARY *off his lap.*) Come, dear. It's after time and you can hardly keep your eyes open now.

MARY (*crying*). No, no! (*Appealing to her father*) Dada! No!

RUTH (*accusingly to* ROBERT). There! Now see what you've done! I told you not to—

ROBERT (*shortly*). Let her alone, then. She's all right where she is. She'll fall asleep on my lap in a minute if you'll stop bothering her.

RUTH (*hotly*). She'll not do any such thing! She's got to learn to mind me! (*Shaking her finger at* MARY) You naughty child! Will you come with Mama when she tells you for your own good?

MARY (*clinging to her father*). No, Dada!

RUTH (*losing her temper*). A good spanking's what you need, my young lady—and you'll get one from me if you don't mind better, d'you hear? (MARY *starts to whimper frightenedly.*)

ROBERT (*with sudden anger*). Leave her alone! How often have I told you not to threaten her with whipping? I won't have it. (*Soothing the wailing* MARY) There! There, little girl! Baby mustn't cry. Dada won't like you if you do. Dada'll hold you and you must promise to go to sleep like a good little girl. Will you when Dada asks you?

MARY (*cuddling up to him*). Yes, Dada.

RUTH (*looking at them, her pale face set and drawn*). A fine one you are to be telling folks how to do things! (*She bites her lips. Husband and wife look into each other's eyes with something akin to hatred in their expressions; then* RUTH *turns away with a shrug of affected indifference.*) All right, take care of her then, if you think it's so easy. (*She walks away into the kitchen.*)

ROBERT (*smoothing* MARY's *hair—tenderly*). We'll show Mama you're a good little girl, won't we?

MARY (*crooning drowsily*). Dada, Dada.

ROBERT. Let's see: Does your mother take off your shoes and stockings before your nap?

MARY (*nodding with half-shut eyes*). Yes, Dada.

ROBERT (*taking off her shoes and stockings*). We'll show Mama we know how to do these things, won't we? There's one old shoe off—and there's the other old shoe—and here's one old stocking—and there's the other old stocking. There we are, all nice and cool and comfy. (*He bends down and kisses her.*) And now will you promise to go right to sleep if Dada takes you to bed? (MARY *nods sleepily.*) That's the good little girl. (*He gathers her up in his arms carefully and carries her into the bedroom. His voice can be heard faintly as he lulls the child to sleep.* RUTH *comes out of the kitchen and gets the plate from the table. She hears the voice from the room and tiptoes to the door to look in. Then she starts for the kitchen but stands for a moment thinking, a look of ill-concealed jealousy on her face. At a noise from inside she hurriedly disappears into the kitchen. A moment later* ROBERT *re-enters. He comes forward and picks up the shoes and stockings which he shoves carelessly under the table. Then, seeing no one about, he goes to the sideboard and selects a book. Coming back to his chair, he sits down and immediately becomes absorbed in reading.* RUTH *returns from the kitchen bringing his plate heaped with food, and a cup of tea. She sets those before him and sits down in her former place.* ROBERT *continues to read, oblivious to the food on the table.*)

RUTH (*after watching him irritably for a moment*). For heaven's sakes, put down that old book! Don't you see your dinner's getting cold?

ROBERT (*closing his book*) Excuse me, Ruth. I didn't notice. (*He picks up his knife and fork and begins to eat gingerly, without appetite.*)

RUTH. I should think you might have some feeling for me, Rob, and not always be late for meals. If you think it's fun sweltering in that oven of a kitchen to keep things warm for you, you're mistaken.

ROBERT. I'm sorry, Ruth, really I am. Something crops up every day to delay me. I mean to be here on time.

RUTH (*with a sigh*). Mean-to's don't count.

ROBERT (*with a conciliating smile*). Then punish me, Ruth. Let the food get cold and don't bother about me.

RUTH. I'd have to wait just the same to wash up after you.

ROBERT. But I can wash up.

RUTH. A nice mess there'd be then!

ROBERT (*with an attempt at lightness*). The food is lucky to be able to get cold this weather. (*As* RUTH *doesn't answer or smile he opens his book and resumes his reading, forcing himself to take a mouthful of food every now and then.* RUTH *stares at him in annoyance.*)

RUTH. And besides, you've got your own work that's got to be done.

ROBERT (*absent-mindedly, without taking his eyes from the book*). Yes, of course.

RUTH (*spitefully*). Work you'll never get done by reading books all the time.

ROBERT (*shutting the book with a snap*). Why do you persist in nagging at me for getting pleasure out of reading? Is it because—(*He checks himself abruptly.*)

RUTH (*coloring*). Because I'm too stupid to understand them, I s'pose you were going to say.

ROBERT (*shame-facedly*). No—no. (*In exasperation*) Why do you goad me into saying things I don't mean? Haven't I got my share of troubles trying to work this cursed farm without your adding to them? You know how hard I've tried to keep things going in spite of bad luck—

RUTH (*scornfully*). Bad luck!

ROBERT. And my own very apparent unfitness for the job, I was going to add; but you can't deny there's been bad luck to it, too. Why don't you take things into consideration? Why can't we pull together? We used to. I know it's hard on you also. Then why can't we help each other instead of hindering?

RUTH (*sullenly*). I do the best I know how.

ROBERT (*gets up and puts his hand on her shoulder*). I know you do. But let's both of us try to do better. We can improve. Say a word of encouragement once in a while when things go wrong, even if it is my fault. You know the odds I've been up against since Pa died. I'm not a farmer. I've never claimed to be one. But there's nothing else I can do under the circumstances, and I've got to pull things through somehow. With your help, I can do it. With you against me—(*He shrugs his shoulders. There is a pause. Then he bends down and kisses her hair—with*

*an attempt at cheerfulness*) So you promise that; and I'll promise to be here when the clock strikes—and anytime else you tell me to. Is it a bargain?

RUTH (*dully*). I s'pose so. (*They are interrupted by the sound of a loud knock at the kitchen door.*) There's someone at the kitchen door. (*She hurries out. A moment later she reappears.*) It's Ben.

ROBERT (*frowning*). What's the trouble now, I wonder? (*In a loud voice*) Come on in here, Ben. (BEN *slouches in from the kitchen. He is a hulking, awkward young fellow with a heavy, stupid face and shifty, cunning eyes. He is dressed in overalls, boots, etc., and wears a broad-brimmed hat of coarse straw pushed back on his head.*) Well, Ben, what's the matter?

BEN (*drawlingly*). The mowin' machine's bust.

ROBERT. Why, that can't be. The man fixed it only last week.

BEN. It's bust just the same.

ROBERT. And can't you fix it?

BEN. No. Don't know what's the matter with the goll-darned thing. 'Twon't work, anyhow.

ROBERT (*getting up and going for his hat*). Wait a minute and I'll go look it over. There can't be much the matter with it.

BEN (*impudently*). Don't make no diff'rence t' me whether there be or not. I'm quittin'.

ROBERT (*anxiously*). You don't mean you're throwing up your job here?

BEN. That's what! My month's up today and I want what's owin' t' me.

ROBERT. But why are you quitting now, Ben, when you know I've so much work on hand? I'll have a hard time getting another man at such short notice.

BEN. That's for you to figger. I'm quittin'.

ROBERT. But what's your reason? You haven't any complaint to make about the way you've been treated, have you?

BEN. No. 'Tain't that. (*Shaking his finger*) Look-a-here. I'm sick o' being made fun at, that's what; an' I got a job up to Timms' place; an' I'm quittin' here.

ROBERT. Being made fun of? I don't understand you. Who's making fun of you?

BEN. They all do. When I drive down with the milk in the mornin' they all laughs and jokes at me—that boy up to Harris' and the new feller up to Slocum's, and Bill Evans down to Meade's, and all the rest on 'em.

ROBERT. That's a queer reason for leaving me flat. Won't they laugh at you just the same when you're working for Timms?

BEN. They wouldn't dare to. Timms is the best farm hereabouts. They was laughin' at me for workin' for *you*, that's what! "How're things up to the Mayo place?" they hollers every mornin'. "What's Robert doin' now—pasturin' the cattle in the cornlot? Is he seasonin' his hay with rain this year, same as last?" they shouts. "Or is he inventin' some 'lectrical milkin' engine to fool them dry cows o' his into givin' hard cider?" (*Very much ruffled*) That's like they talks; and I ain't goin' to put up with it no longer. Everyone's always knowed me as a first-class hand hereabouts, and I ain't wantin' 'em to get no different notion. So I'm quittin' you. And I wants what's comin' to me.

ROBERT (*coldly*). Oh, if that's the case, you can go to the devil. You'll get your money tomorrow when I get back from town—not before!

BEN (*turning to doorway to kitchen*). That suits me. (*As he goes out he speaks back over his shoulder.*) And see that I do get it, or there'll be trouble. (*He disappears and the slamming of the kitchen door is heard.*)

ROBERT (*as* RUTH *comes from where she has been standing by the doorway and sits down dejectedly in her old place*). The stupid damn fool! And now what about the haying? That's an example of what I'm up against. No one can say I'm responsible for that.

RUTH. He wouldn't dare act that way with anyone else! (*Spitefully, with a glance at* ANDREW's *letter on the table*) It's lucky Andy's coming back.

ROBERT (*without resentment*). Yes, Andy'll see the right thing to do in a jiffy. (*With an affectionate smile*) I wonder if the old chump's changed much? He doesn't seem to from his letters, does he? (*Shaking his head*) But just the same I doubt if he'll want to settle down to a humdrum farm life, after all he's been through.

RUTH (*resentfully*). Andy's not like you. He likes the farm.

ROBERT (*immersed in his own thoughts—enthusiastically*). Gad, the things he's seen and experienced! Think of the places he's been! All the wonderful far places I used to dream about! God, how I envy him! What a trip! (*He springs to his feet and instinctively goes to the window and stares out at the horizon.*)

RUTH (*bitterly*). I s'pose you're sorry now you didn't go?

ROBERT (*too occupied with his own thoughts to hear her—vindictively*). Oh, those cursed hills out there that I used to think promised me so much! How I've grown to hate the sight of them! They're like the walls of a narrow prison yard shutting me in from all the freedom and wonder of life! (*He turns back to the room with a gesture of loathing.*) Sometimes I think if it wasn't for you, Ruth, and—(*his voice softening*)—little Mary,

I'd chuck everything up and walk down the road with just one desire in my heart—to put the whole rim of the world between me and those hills, and be able to breathe freely once more! (*He sinks down into his chair and smiles with bitter self-scorn.*) There I go dreaming again—my old fool dreams.

RUTH (*in a low, repressed voice—her eyes smoldering*). You're not the only one!

ROBERT (*buried in his own thoughts—bitterly*). And Andy, who's had the chance—what has he got out of it? His letters read like the diary of a—of a farmer! "We're in Singapore now. It's a dirty hole of a place and hotter than hell. Two of the crew are down with fever and we're shorthanded on the work. I'll be damn glad when we sail again, although tacking back and forth in these blistering seas is a rotten job too!" (*Scornfully*) That's about the way he summed up his impressions of the East.

RUTH (*her repressed voice trembling*). You needn't make fun of Andy.

ROBERT. When I think—but what's the use? You know I wasn't making fun of Andy personally, but his attitude toward things is—

RUTH (*her eyes flashing—bursting into uncontrollable rage*). You was too making fun of him! And I ain't going to stand for it! You ought to be ashamed of yourself! (ROBERT *stares at her in amazement. She continues furiously*) A fine one to talk about anyone else—after the way you've ruined everything with your lazy loafing!—and the stupid way you do things!

ROBERT (*angrily*). Stop that kind of talk, do you hear?

RUTH. You findin' fault—with your own brother who's ten times the man you ever was or ever will be! You're jealous, that's what! Jealous because he's made a man of himself, while you're nothing but a—but a—(*She stutters incoherently, overcome by rage.*)

ROBERT. Ruth! Ruth! You'll be sorry for talking like that.

RUTH. I won't! I won't never be sorry! I'm only saying what I've been thinking for years.

ROBERT (*aghast*). Ruth! You can't mean that!

RUTH. What do you think—living with a man like you—having to suffer all the time because you've never been man enough to work and do things like other people. But no! You never own up to that. You think you're so much better than other folks, with your college education, where you never learned a thing, and always reading your stupid books instead of working. I s'pose you think I ought to be *proud* to be your wife—a poor, ignorant thing like me! (*Fiercely*) But I'm not. I hate it! I hate the sight of you. Oh, if I'd only known! If I hadn't been such a fool to listen to your cheap, silly, poetry talk that you learned out of books! If I could have seen how you were in your true self—like you are now—I'd have killed myself before I'd have married you! I was sorry for it before we'd been together a month. I knew what you were really like—when it was too late.

ROBERT (*his voice raised loudly*). And now— I'm finding out what you're really like—what a— a creature I've been living with. (*With a harsh laugh*) God! It wasn't that I haven't guessed how mean and small you are—but I've kept on telling myself that I must be wrong—like a fool!—like a damned fool!

RUTH. You were saying you'd go out on the road if it wasn't for me. Well, you can go, and the sooner the better! I don't care! I'll be glad to get rid of you! The farm'll be better off too. There's been a curse on it ever since you took hold. So go! Go and be a tramp like you've always wanted. It's all you're good for. I can get along without you, don't you worry. (*Exulting fiercely*) Andy's coming back, don't forget that! He'll attend to things like they should be. He'll show what a man can do! I don't need you. Andy's coming!

ROBERT (*They are both standing. ROBERT grabs her by the shoulders and glares into her eyes.*) What do you mean? (*He shakes her violently.*) What are you thinking of? What's in your evil mind, you—you— (*His voice is a harsh shout.*)

RUTH (*in a defiant scream*). Yes, I do mean it! I'd say it if you was to kill me! I do love Andy! I do! I do! I always loved him. (*Exultantly*) And he loves me! He loves me! I know he does. He always did! And you know he did, too! So go! Go if you want to!

ROBERT (*throwing her away from him. She staggers back against the table—thickly*) You —you slut! (*He stands glaring at her as she leans back, supporting herself by the table, gasping for breath. A loud frightened whimper sounds from the awakened child in the bedroom. It continues. The man and woman stand looking at one another in horror, the extent of their terrible quarrel suddenly brought home to them. A pause. The noise of a horse and carriage comes from the road before the house. The two, suddenly struck by the same premonition, listen to it breathlessly, as to a sound heard in a dream. It stops. They hear* ANDY'S *voice from the road shouting a long hail—"Ahoy there!"*)

RUTH (*with a strangled cry of joy*). Andy! Andy! (*She rushes and grabs the knob of the screen door, about to fling it open.*)

ROBERT (*in a voice of command that forces obedience*). Stop! (*He goes to the door and gent-*

ly *pushes the trembling* RUTH *away from it. The child's crying rises to a louder pitch.*) I'll meet Andy. You better go in to Mary, Ruth. (*She looks at him defiantly for a moment, but there is something in his eyes that makes her turn and walk slowly into the bedroom.*)

ANDY'S VOICE (*in a louder shout*). Ahoy there, Rob!

ROBERT (*in an answering shout of forced cheeriness*). Hello, Andy! (*He opens the door and walks out as the curtain falls.*)

## ACT TWO
### SCENE II

THE *top of a hill on the farm. It is about eleven o'clock the next morning. The day is hot and cloudless. In the distance the sea can be seen.*

*The top of the hill slopes downward slightly toward the left. A big boulder stands in the center toward the rear. Further right is a large oak tree. The faint trace of a path leading upward to it from the left foreground can be detected through the bleached, sun-scorched grass.*

ROBERT *is discovered sitting on the boulder, his chin resting on his hands, staring out toward the horizon seaward. His face is pale and haggard, his expression one of utter despondency.* MARY *is sitting on the grass near him in the shade, playing with her doll, singing happily to herself. Presently she casts a curious glance at her father, and, propping her doll up against the tree, comes over and clambers to his side.*

MARY (*pulling at his hand—solicitously*). Dada sick?

ROBERT (*looking at her with a forced smile*). No, dear. Why?

MARY. Play wif Mary.

ROBERT (*gently*). No, dear, not today. Dada doesn't feel like playing today.

MARY (*protestingly*). Yes, Dada!

ROBERT. No, dear. Dada does feel sick—a little. He's got a bad headache.

MARY. Mary see. (*He bends his head. She pats his hair.*) Bad head.

ROBERT (*kissing her—with a smile*). There! It's better now, dear, thank you. (*She cuddles up close against him. There is a pause during which each of them looks out seaward. Finally ROBERT turns to her tenderly.*) Would you like Dada to go away?—far, far away?

MARY (*tearfully*). No! No! No, Dada, no!

ROBERT. Don't you like Uncle Andy—the man that came yesterday—not the old man with the white mustache—the other?

MARY. Mary loves Dada.

ROBERT (*with fierce determination*). He won't go away, baby. He was only joking. He couldn't leave his little Mary. (*He presses the child in his arms.*)

MARY (*with an exclamation of pain*). Oh! Hurt!

ROBERT. I'm sorry, little girl. (*He lifts her down to the grass.*) Go play with Dolly, that's a good girl; and be careful to keep in the shade. (*She reluctantly leaves him and takes up her doll again. A moment later she points down the hill to the left.*)

MARY. Mans, Dada.

ROBERT (*looking that way*). It's your Uncle Andy. (*A moment later* ANDREW *comes up from the left, whistling cheerfully. He has changed but little in appearance, except for the fact that his face has been deeply bronzed by his years in the tropics; but there is a decided change in his manner. The old easy-going good nature seems to have been partly lost in a breezy, business-like briskness of voice and gesture. There is an authoritative note in his speech as though he were accustomed to give orders and have them obeyed as a matter of course. He is dressed in the simple blue uniform and cap of a merchant ship's officer.*)

ANDREW. Here you are, eh?

ROBERT. Hello, Andy.

ANDREW (*going over to* MARY). And who's this young lady I find you all alone with, eh? Who's this pretty young lady? (*He tickles the laughing, squirming* MARY, *then lifts her up arm's length over his head.*) And there you are! (*He walks over and sits down on the boulder beside* ROBERT *who moves to one side to make room for him.*) Ruth told me I'd probably find you up top-side here; but I'd have guessed it, anyway. (*He digs his brother in the ribs affectionately.*) Still up to your old tricks, you old beggar! I can remember how you used to come up here to mope and dream in the old days.

ROBERT (*with a smile*). I come up here now because it's the coolest place on the farm. I've given up dreaming.

ANDREW (*grinning*). I don't believe it. You can't have changed that much. (*After a pause —with boyish enthusiasm*) Say, it sure brings back old times to be up here with you having a chin all by our lonesomes again. I feel great being back home.

ROBERT. It's great for us to have you back.

ANDREW (*after a pause—meaningly*). I've been looking over the old place with Ruth. Things don't seem to be—

ROBERT (*his face flushing—interrupts his brother shortly*). Never mind the damn farm!

Let's talk about something interesting. This is the first chance I've had to have a word with you alone. Tell me about your trip.

ANDREW. Why, I thought I told you everything in my letters.

ROBERT (*smiling*). Your letters were—sketchy, to say the least.

ANDREW. Oh, I know I'm no author. You needn't be afraid of hurting my feelings. I'd rather go through a typhoon again than write a letter.

ROBERT (*with eager interest*). Then you were through a typhoon?

ANDREW. Yes—in the China sea. Had to run before it under bare poles for two days. I thought we were bound down for Davy Jones, sure. Never dreamed waves could get so big or the wind blow so hard. If it hadn't been for Uncle Dick being such a good skipper we'd have gone to the sharks, all of us. As it was we came out minus a main topmast and had to beat back to Hong-Kong for repairs. But I must have written you all this.

ROBERT. You never mentioned it.

ANDREW. Well, there was so much dirty work getting things ship-shape again I must have forgotten about it.

ROBERT (*looking at* ANDREW—*marveling*). Forget a typhoon? (*With a trace of scorn*) You're a strange combination, Andy. And is what you've told me all you remember about it?

ANDREW. Oh, I could give you your bellyful of details if I wanted to turn loose on you. It was all-wool-and-a-yard-wide-Hell, I'll tell you. You ought to have been there. I remember thinking about you at the worst of it, and saying to myself: "This'd cure Rob of them ideas of his about the beautiful sea, if he could see it." And it would have too, you bet! (*He nods emphatically.*)

ROBERT (*dryly*). The sea doesn't seem to have impressed you very favorably.

ANDREW. I should say it didn't! I'll never set foot on a ship again if I can help it—except to carry me some place I can't get to by train.

ROBERT. But you studied to become an officer!

ANDREW. Had to do something or I'd gone mad. The days were like years. (*He laughs.*) And as for the East you used to rave about—well, you ought to see it, and *smell* it! One walk down one of their filthy narrow streets with the tropic sun beating on it would sicken you for life with the "wonder and mystery" you used to dream of.

ROBERT (*shrinking from his brother with a glance of aversion*). So all you found in the East was a stench?

ANDREW. *A* stench! Ten thousand of them!

ROBERT. But you did like some of the places,

judging from your letters—Sydney, Buenos Aires—

ANDREW. Yes, Sydney's a good town. (*Enthusiastically*) But Buenos Aires—there's the place for you. Argentine's a country where a fellow has a chance to make good. You're right I like it. And I'll tell you, Rob, that's right where I'm going just as soon as I've seen you folks a while and can get a ship. I can get a berth as second officer, and I'll jump the ship when I get there. I'll need every cent of the wages Uncle's paid me to get a start at something in B.A.

ROBERT (*staring at his brother—slowly*). So you're not going to stay on the farm?

ANDREW. Why sure not! Did you think I was? There wouldn't be any sense. One of us is enough to run this little place.

ROBERT. I suppose it does seem small to you now.

ANDREW (*not noticing the sarcasm in* ROBERT's *tone*). You've no idea, Rob, what a splendid place Argentine is. I had a letter from a marine insurance chap that I'd made friends with in Hong Kong to his brother, who's in the grain business in Buenos Aires. He took quite a fancy to me, and what's more important, he offered me a job if I'd come back there. I'd have taken it on the spot, only I couldn't leave Uncle Dick in the lurch, and I'd promised you folks to come home. But I'm going back there, you bet, and then you watch me get on! (*He slaps* ROBERT *on the back.*) But don't you think it's a big chance, Rob?

ROBERT. It's fine—for you, Andy.

ANDREW. We call this a farm—but you ought to hear about the farms down there—ten square miles where we've got an acre. It's a new country where big things are opening up—and I want to get in on something big before I die. I'm no fool when it comes to farming, and I know something about grain. I've been reading up a lot on it, too, lately. (*He notices* ROBERT's *absentminded expression and laughs.*) Wake up, you old poetry bookworm, you! I know my talking about business makes you want to choke me, doesn't it?

ROBERT (*with an embarrassed smile*). No, Andy, I—I just happened to think of something else. (*Frowning*) There've been lots of times lately that I wished I had some of your faculty for business.

ANDREW (*soberly*). There's something I want to talk about, Rob—the farm. You don't mind, do you?

ROBERT. No.

ANDREW. I walked over it this morning with Ruth—and she told me about things—(*evasively*) I could see the place had run down; but you

mustn't blame yourself. When luck's against anyone—

ROBERT. Don't, Andy! It *is* my fault. You know it as well as I do. The best I've ever done was to make ends meet.

ANDREW (*after a pause*). I've got over a thousand saved, and you can have that.

ROBERT (*firmly*). No. You need that for your start in Buenos Aires.

ANDREW. I don't. I can—

ROBERT (*determinedly*). No, Andy! Once and for all, no! I won't hear of it!

ANDREW (*protestingly*). You obstinate old son of a gun!

ROBERT. Oh, everything'll be on a sound footing after harvest. Don't worry about it.

ANDREW (*doubtfully*). Maybe. (*After a pause*) It's too bad Pa couldn't have lived to see things through. (*With feeling*) It cut me up a lot—hearing he was dead. He never—softened up, did he—about me, I mean?

ROBERT. He never understood, that's a kinder way of putting it. He does now.

ANDREW (*after a pause*). You've forgotten all about what—caused me to go, haven't you, Rob? (ROBERT *nods but keeps his face averted.*) I was a slushier damn fool in those days than you were. But it was an act of Providence I did go. It opened my eyes to how I'd been fooling myself. Why, I'd forgotten all about—that—before I'd been at sea six months.

ROBERT (*turns and looks into* ANDREW's *eyes searchingly*). You're speaking of—Ruth?

ANDREW (*confused*). Yes. I didn't want you to get false notions in your head, or I wouldn't say anything. (*Looking* ROBERT *squarely in the eyes*) I'm telling you the truth when I say I'd forgotten long ago. It don't sound well for me, getting over things so easy, but I guess it never really amounted to more than a kid idea I was letting rule me. I'm certain now I never was in love—I was getting fun out of thinking I was—and being a hero to myself. (*He heaves a great sigh of relief.*) There! Gosh, I'm glad that's off my chest. I've been feeling sort of awkward ever since I've been home, thinking of what you two might think. (*A trace of appeal in his voice*) You've got it all straight now, haven't you, Rob?

ROBERT (*in a low voice*). Yes, Andy.

ANDREW. And I'll tell Ruth, too, if I can get up the nerve. She must feel kind of funny having me round—after what used to be—and not knowing how I feel about it.

ROBERT (*slowly*). Perhaps—for her sake—you'd better not tell her.

ANDREW. For her sake? Oh, you mean she

wouldn't want to be reminded of my foolishness? Still, I think it'd be worse if—

ROBERT (*breaking out—in an agonized voice*). Do as you please, Andy; but for God's sake, let's not talk about it! (*There is a pause.* ANDREW *stares at* ROBERT *in hurt stupefaction.* ROBERT *continues after a moment in a voice which he vainly attempts to keep calm.*) Excuse me, Andy. This rotten headache has my nerves shot to pieces.

ANDREW (*mumbling*). It's all right, Rob—long as you're not sore at me.

ROBERT. Where did Uncle Dick disappear to this morning?

ANDREW. He went down to the port to see to things on the "Sunda." He said he didn't know exactly when he'd be back. I'll have to go down and tend to the ship when he comes. That's why I dressed up in these togs.

MARY (*pointing down to the hill to the left*). See! Mama! Mama! (*She struggles to her feet.* RUTH *appears at left. She is dressed in white, shows she has been fixing up. She looks pretty, flushed and full of life.*)

MARY (*running to her mother*). Mama!

RUTH (*kissing her*). Hello, dear! (*She walks toward the rock and addresses* ROBERT *coldly.*) Jake wants to see you about something. He finished working where he was. He's waiting for you at the road.

ROBERT (*getting up—wearily*). I'll go down right away. (*As he looks at* RUTH, *noting her changed appearance, his face darkens with pain.*)

RUTH. And take Mary with you, please. (*To* MARY) Go with Dada, that's a good girl. Grandma has your dinner 'most ready for you.

ROBERT (*shortly*). Come, Mary!

MARY (*taking his hand and dancing happily beside him*). Dada! Dada! (*They go down the hill to the left.* RUTH *looks after them for a moment, frowning—then turns to* ANDY *with a smile.*) I'm going to sit down. Come on, Andy. It'll be like old times. (*She jumps lightly to the top of the rock and sits down.*) It's so fine and cool up here after the house.

ANDREW (*half-sitting on the side of the boulder*). Yes. It's great.

RUTH. I've taken a holiday in honor of your arrival. (*Laughing excitedly*) I feel so free I'd like to have wings and fly over the sea. You're a man. You can't know how awful and stupid it is —cooking and washing dishes all the time.

ANDREW (*making a wry face*). I can guess.

RUTH. Besides, your mother just insisted on getting your first dinner to home, she's that happy at having you back. You'd think I was planning to poison you the flurried way she shooed me out of the kitchen.

ANDREW. That's just like Ma, bless her!

RUTH. She's missed you terrible. We all have. And you can't deny the farm has, after what I showed you and told you when we was looking over the place this morning.

ANDREW (*with a frown*). Things are run down, that's a fact! It's too darn hard on poor old Rob.

RUTH (*scornfully*). It's his own fault. He never takes any interest in things.

ANDREW (*reprovingly*). You can't blame him. He wasn't born for it; but I know he's done his best for your sake and the old folks and the little girl.

RUTH (*indifferently*). Yes, I suppose he has. (*Gaily*) But thank the Lord, all those days are over now. The "hard luck" Rob's always blaming won't last long when you take hold, Andy. All the farm's ever needed was someone with the knack of looking ahead and preparing for what's going to happen.

ANDREW. Yes, Rob hasn't got that. He's frank to own up to that himself. I'm going to try and hire a good man for him—an experienced farmer—to work the place on a salary and percentage. That'll take it off of Rob's hands, and he needn't be worrying himself to death any more. He looks all worn out, Ruth. He ought to be careful.

RUTH (*absent-mindedly*). Yes, I s'pose. (*Her mind is filled with premonitions by the first part of his statement.*) Why do you want to hire a man to oversee things? Seems as if now that you're back it wouldn't be needful.

ANDREW. Oh, of course I'll attend to everything while I'm here. I mean after I'm gone.

RUTH (*as if she couldn't believe her ears*). Gone!

ANDREW. Yes. When I leave for the Argentine again.

RUTH (*aghast*). You're going away to sea!

ANDREW. Not to sea, no; I'm through with the sea for good as a job. I'm going down to Buenos Aires to get in the grain business.

RUTH. But—that's far off—isn't it?

ANDREW (*easily*). Six thousand miles more or less. It's quite a trip. (*With enthusiasm*) I've got a peach of a chance down there, Ruth. Ask Rob if I haven't. I've just been telling him all about it.

RUTH (*a flush of anger coming over her face*). And didn't he try to stop you from going?

ANDREW (*in surprise*). No, of course not. Why?

RUTH (*slowly and vindictively*). That's just like him—not to.

ANDREW (*resentfully*). Rob's too good a chum to try and stop me when he knows I'm set on a thing. And he could see just as soon's I told him what a good chance it was.

RUTH (*dazedly*). And you're bound on going?

ANDREW. Sure thing. Oh, I don't mean right off. I'll have to wait for a ship sailing there for quite a while, likely. Anyway, I want to stay to home and visit with your folks a spell before I go.

RUTH (*dumbly*). I s'pose. (*With sudden anguish*) Oh, Andy, you can't go! You can't. Why we've all thought—we've all been hoping and praying you was coming home to stay, to settle down on the farm and see to things. You mustn't go! Think of how your Ma'll take on if you go —and how the farm'll be ruined if you leave it to Rob to look after. You can see that.

ANDREW (*frowning*). Rob hasn't done so bad. When I get a man to direct things the farm'll be safe enough.

RUTH (*insistently*). But your Ma—think of her.

ANDREW. She's used to me being away. She won't object when she knows it's best for her and all of us for me to go. You ask Rob. In a couple of years down there, I'll make my pile, see if I don't; and then I'll come back and settle down and turn this farm into the crackiest place in the whole state. In the meantime, I can help you both from down there. (*Earnestly*) I tell you, Ruth, I'm going to make good right from the minute I land, if working hard and a determination to get on can do it; and I *know* they can! (*Excitedly—in a rather boastful tone*) I tell you, I feel ripe for bigger things than settling down here. The trip did that for me, anyway. It showed me the world is a larger proposition than ever I thought it was in the old days. I couldn't be content any more stuck here like a fly in molasses. It all seems trifling, somehow. You ought to be able to understand what I feel.

RUTH (*dully*). Yes—I s'pose I ought. (*After a pause—a sudden suspicion forming in her mind*) What did Rob tell you—about me?

ANDREW. Tell? About you? Why, nothing.

RUTH (*staring at him intensely*). Are you telling me the truth, Andy Mayo? Didn't he say—I— (*She stops confusedly.*)

ANDREW (*surprised*). No, he didn't mention you, I can remember. Why? What made you think he did?

RUTH (*wringing her hands*). Oh, I wish I could tell if you're lying or not!

ANDREW (*indignantly*). What're you talking about? I didn't used to lie to you, did I? And what in the name of God is there to lie for?

RUTH (*still unconvinced*). Are you sure—will you swear—it isn't the reason— (*She lowers her eyes and half turns away from him.*) The same

reason that made you go last time that's driving you away again? 'Cause if it is—I was going to say—you mustn't go—on that account. (*Her voice sinks to a tremulous, tender whisper as she finishes.*)

ANDREW (*confused—forces a laugh*). Oh, is *that* what you're driving at? Well, you needn't worry about that no more—(*soberly*) I don't blame you, Ruth, feeling embarrassed having me round again, after the way I played the dumb fool about going away last time.

RUTH (*her hope crushed—with a gasp of pain*). Oh, Andy!

ANDREW (*misunderstanding*). I know I oughtn't to talk about such foolishness to you. Still I figure it's better to get it out of my system so's we three can be together same's years ago, and not be worried thinking one of us might have the wrong notion.

RUTH. Andy! Please! Don't!

ANDREW. Let me finish now that I've started. It'll help clear things up. I don't want you to think once a fool always a fool, and be upset all the time I'm here on my fool account. I want you to believe I put all that silly nonsense back of me a long time ago—and now—it seems—well—as if you'd always been my sister, that's what, Ruth.

RUTH (*at the end of her endurance—laughing hysterically*). For God's sake, Andy—won't you please stop talking! (*She again hides her face in her hands, her bowed shoulders trembling.*)

ANDREW (*ruefully*). Seems if I put my foot in it whenever I open my mouth today. Rob shut me up with almost the same words when I tried speaking to him about it.

RUTH (*fiercely*). You told him—what you've told me?

ANDREW (*astounded*). Why sure! Why not?

RUTH (*shuddering*). Oh, my God!

ANDREW (*alarmed*). Why? Shouldn't I have?

RUTH (*hysterically*). Oh, I don't care what you do! I don't care! Leave me alone! (ANDREW *gets up and walks down the hill to the left, embarrassed, hurt, and greatly puzzled by her behavior.*)

ANDREW (*after a pause—pointing down the hill*). Hello! Here they come back—and the Captain's with them. How'd he come to get back so soon, I wonder? That means I've got to hustle down to the port and get on board. Rob's got the baby with him. (*He comes back to the boulder.*) RUTH *keeps her face averted from him.*) Gosh, I never saw a father so tied up in a kid as Rob is! He just watches every move she makes. And I don't blame him. You both got a right to feel proud of her. She's surely a little winner. (*He glances at* RUTH *to see if this very obvious attempt to get back in her good graces is having any effect.*) I can see the likeness to Rob standing out all over her, can't you? But there's no denying she's your young one, either. There's something about her eyes—

RUTH (*piteously*). Oh, Andy, I've a headache! I don't want to talk! Leave me alone, won't you please?

ANDREW (*stands staring at her for a moment—then walks away saying in a hurt tone*) Everybody hereabouts seems to be on edge today. I begin to feel as if I'm not wanted around. (*He stands near the path, left, kicking at the grass with the toe of his shoe. A moment later* CAPTAIN DICK SCOTT *enters, followed by* ROBERT *carrying* MARY. *The* CAPTAIN *seems scarcely to have changed at all from the jovial, booming person he was three years before. He wears a uniform similar to* ANDREW'S. *He is puffing and breathless from his climb and mops wildly at his perspiring countenance.* ROBERT *casts a quick glance at* ANDREW, *noticing the latter's discomfited look, and then turns his eyes on* RUTH *who, at their approach, has moved so her back is toward them, her chin resting on her hands as she stares out seaward.*)

MARY. Mama! Mama! (ROBERT *puts her down and she runs to her mother.* RUTH *turns and grabs her up in her arms with a sudden fierce tenderness, quickly turning away again from the others. During the following scene she keeps* MARY *in her arms.*)

SCOTT (*wheezily*). Phew! I got great news for you, Andy. Let me get my wind first. Phew! God A'mighty, mountin' this damned hill is worser'n goin' aloft to the skys'l yard in a blow. I got to lay to a while. (*He sits down on the grass, mopping his face.*)

ANDREW. I didn't look for you this soon, Uncle.

SCOTT. I didn't figger it, neither; but I run across a bit o' news down to the Seamen's Home made me 'bout ship and set all sail back here to find you.

ANDREW (*eagerly*). What is it, Uncle?

SCOTT. Passin' by the Home I thought I'd drop in an' let 'em know I'd be lackin' a mate next trip count o' your leavin'. Their man in charge o' the shippin' asked after you 'special curious. "Do you think he'd consider a berth as Second on a steamer, Captain?" he asks. I was going to say no when I thinks o' you wantin' to get back down south to the Plate agen; so I asked him: "What is she and where's she bound?" "She's the 'El Paso,'

a brand new tramp," he says, "and she's bound for Buenos Aires."

ANDREW (*his eyes lighting up—excitedly*). Gosh, that is luck! When does she sail?

SCOTT. Tomorrow mornin'. I didn't know if you'd want to ship away agen so quick an' I told him so. "Tell him I'll hold the berth open for him until late this afternoon," he says. So there you be, an' you can make your own choice.

ANDREW. I'd like to take it. There may not be another ship for Buenos Aires with a vacancy in months. (*His eyes roving from* ROBERT *to* RUTH *and back again—uncertainly*) Still—damn it all —tomorrow morning *is* soon. I wish she wasn't leaving for a week or so. That'd give me a chance—it seems hard to go right away again when I've just got home. And yet it's a chance in a thousand— (*Appealing to* ROBERT) What do you think, Rob? What would you do?

ROBERT (*forcing a smile*). He who hesitates, you know. (*Frowning*) It's a piece of good luck thrown in your way—and—I think you owe it to yourself to jump at it. But don't ask me to decide for you.

RUTH (*turning to look at* ANDREW *—in a tone of fierce resentment*). Yes, go, Andy! (*She turns quickly away again. There is a moment of embarrassed silence.*)

ANDREW (*thoughtfully*). Yes, I guess I will. It'll be the best thing for all of us in the end, don't you think so, Rob? (ROBERT *nods but remains silent.*)

SCOTT (*getting to his feet*). Then, that's settled.

ANDREW (*now that he has definitely made a decision his voice rings with hopeful strength and energy*). Yes, I'll take the berth. The sooner I go the sooner I'll be back, that's a certainty; and I won't come back with empty hands next time. You bet I won't!

SCOTT. You ain't got so much time, Andy. To make sure you'd best leave here soon's you kin. I got to get right back aboard. You'd best come with me.

ANDREW. I'll go to the house and repack my bag right away.

ROBERT (*quietly*). You'll both be here for dinner, won't you?

ANDREW (*worriedly*). I don't know. Will there be time? What time is it now, I wonder?

ROBERT (*reproachfully*). Ma's been getting dinner especially for you, Andy.

ANDREW (*flushing—shamefacedly*). Hell! And I was forgetting! Of course I'll stay for dinner if I missed every damned ship in the world. (*He turns to the* CAPTAIN*—briskly*) Come on, Uncle. Walk down with me to the house and you can tell me more about this berth on the way. I've got to pack before dinner. (*He and the* CAPTAIN *start down to the left.* ANDREW *calls back over his shoulder.*) You're coming soon, aren't you, Rob?

ROBERT. Yes. I'll be right down. (ANDREW *and the* CAPTAIN *leave.* RUTH *puts* MARY *on the ground and hides her face in her hands. Her shoulders shake as if she were sobbing.* ROBERT *stares at her with a grim, somber expression.* MARY *walks backward toward* ROBERT, *her wondering eyes fixed on her mother.*)

MARY (*her voice vaguely frightened, taking her father's hand*). Dada, Mama's cryin', Dada.

ROBERT (*bending down and stroking her hair—in a voice he endeavors to keep from being harsh*). No, she isn't, little girl. The sun hurts her eyes, that's all. Aren't you beginning to feel hungry, Mary?

MARY (*decidedly*). Yes, Dada.

ROBERT (*meaningly*). It must be your dinner time now.

RUTH (*in a muffled voice*). I'm coming, Mary. (*She wipes her eyes quickly and, without looking at* ROBERT, *comes and takes* MARY's *hand—in a dead voice*) Come on and I'll get your dinner for you. (*She walks out left, her eyes fixed on the ground, the skipping* MARY *tugging at her hand.* ROBERT *waits a moment for them to get ahead and then slowly follows as the curtain falls.*)

# ACT THREE
## SCENE I

SAME *as Act Two, Scene I—The sitting room of the farmhouse about six o'clock in the morning of a day toward the end of October five years later. It is not yet dawn, but as the action progresses the darkness outside the windows gradually fades to gray.*

*The room, seen by the light of the shadeless oil lamp with a smoky chimney which stands on the table, presents an appearance of decay, of dissolution. The curtains at the windows are torn and dirty and one of them is missing. The closed desk is gray with accumulated dust as if it had not been used in years. Blotches of dampness disfigure the wallpaper. Threadbare trails, leading to the kitchen and outer doors, show in the faded carpet. The top of the coverless table is stained with the imprints of hot dishes and spilt food. The rung of one rocker has been clumsily mended with a piece of plain board. A brown coating of*

*rust covers the unblacked stove. A pile of wood is stacked up carelessly against the wall by the stove.*

*The whole atmosphere of the room, contrasted with that of former years, is one of an habitual poverty too hopelessly resigned to be any longer ashamed or even conscious of itself.*

*At the rise of the curtain* RUTH *is discovered sitting by the stove, with hands outstretched to the warmth as if the air in the room were damp and cold. A heavy shawl is wrapped about her shoulders, half-concealing her dress of deep mourning. She has aged horribly. Her pale, deeply-lined face has the stony lack of expression of one to whom nothing more can ever happen, whose capacity for emotion has been exhausted. When she speaks, her voice is without timbre, low and monotonous. The negligent disorder of her dress, the slovenly arrangement of her hair, now streaked with gray, her muddied shoes run down at the heel, give full evidence of the apathy in which she lives.*

*Her mother is asleep in her wheelchair beside the stove toward the rear, wrapped up in a blanket.*

*There is a sound from the open bedroom door in the rear as if someone were getting out of bed.* RUTH *turns in that direction with a look of dull annoyance. A moment later* ROBERT *appears in the doorway, leaning weakly against it for support. His hair is long and unkempt, his face and body emaciated. There are bright patches of crimson over his cheekbones and his eyes are burning with fever. He is dressed in corduroy pants, a flannel shirt, and wears worn carpet slippers on his bare feet.*

RUTH (*dully*). Sh-s-s-h! Ma's asleep.

ROBERT (*speaking with an effort*). I won't wake her. (*He walks weakly to a rocker by the side of the table and sinks down in it, exhausted.*)

RUTH (*staring at the stove*). You better come near the fire where it's warm.

ROBERT. No. I'm burning up now.

RUTH. That's the fever. You know the doctor told you not to get up and move around.

ROBERT (*irritably*). That old fossil! He doesn't know anything. Go to bed and stay there—that's his only prescription.

RUTH (*indifferently*). How are you feeling now?

ROBERT (*buoyantly*). Better! Much better than I've felt in ages. Really I'm fine now—only very weak. It's the turning point, I guess. From now on I'll pick up so quick I'll surprise you—and no thanks to that old fool of a country quack, either.

RUTH. He's always tended to us.

ROBERT. Always helped us to die, you mean! He "tended" to Pa and Ma and—(*his voice breaks*) and to—Mary.

RUTH (*dully*). He did the best he knew, I s'pose. (*After a pause*) Well, Andy's bringing a specialist with him when he comes. That ought to suit you.

ROBERT (*bitterly*). Is that why you're waiting up all night?

RUTH. Yes.

ROBERT. For Andy?

RUTH (*without a trace of feeling*). Somebody had got to. It's only right for someone to meet him after he's been gone five years.

ROBERT (*with bitter mockery*). Five years! It's a long time.

RUTH. Yes.

ROBERT (*meaningly*). To *wait!*

RUTH (*indifferently*). It's past now.

ROBERT. Yes, it's past. (*After a pause*) Have you got his two telegrams with you? (RUTH *nods.*) Let me see them, will you? My head was so full of fever when they came I couldn't make head or tail of them. (*Hastily*) But I'm feeling fine now. Let me read them again. (RUTH *takes them from the bosom of her dress and hands them to him.*)

RUTH. Here. The first one's on top.

ROBERT (*opening it*). New York. "Just landed from steamer. Have important business to wind up here. Will be home as soon as deal is completed." (*He smiles bitterly.*) Business first was always Andy's motto. (*He reads*) "Hope you are all well. Andy." (*He repeats ironically*) "Hope you are all well!"

RUTH (*dully*). He couldn't know you'd been took sick till I answered that and told him.

ROBERT (*contritely*). Of course he couldn't. I'm a fool. I'm touchy about nothing lately. Just what did you say in your reply?

RUTH (*inconsequentially*). I had to send it collect.

ROBERT (*irritably*). What did you say was the matter with me?

RUTH. I wrote you had lung trouble.

ROBERT (*flying into a petty temper*). You *are* a fool! How often have I explained to you that it's *pleurisy* is the matter with me. You can't seem to get it in your head that the pleura is outside the lungs, not in them!

RUTH (*callously*). I only wrote what Doctor Smith told me.

ROBERT (*angrily*). He's a damned ignoramus!

RUTH (*dully*). Makes no difference. I had to tell Andy something, didn't I?

ROBERT (*after a pause, opening the other telegram*). He sent this last evening. Let's see. (*He reads*) "Leave for home on midnight train. Just

received your wire. Am bringing specialist to see Rob. Will motor to farm from Port." (*He calculates*) What time is it now?

RUTH. Round six, must be.

ROBERT. He ought to be here soon. I'm glad he's bringing a doctor who knows something. A specialist will tell you in a second that there's nothing the matter with my lungs.

RUTH (*stolidly*). You've been coughing an awful lot lately.

ROBERT (*irritably*). What nonsense! For God's sake, haven't you ever had a bad cold yourself? (RUTH *stares at the stove in silence.* ROBERT *fidgets in his chair. There is a pause. Finally* ROBERT'S *eyes are fixed on the sleeping* MRS. ATKINS.) Your mother is lucky to be able to sleep so soundly.

RUTH. Ma's tired. She's been sitting up with me most of the night.

ROBERT (*mockingly*). Is she waiting for Andy, too? (*There is a pause.* ROBERT *sighs.*) I couldn't get to sleep to save my soul. I counted ten million sheep if I counted one. No use! I gave up trying finally and just laid there in the dark thinking. (*He pauses, then continues in a tone of tender sympathy.*) I was thinking about you, Ruth—of how hard these last years must have been for you. (*Appealingly*) I'm sorry, Ruth.

RUTH (*in a dead voice*). I don't know. They're past now. They were hard on all of us.

ROBERT. Yes; on all of us but Andy. (*With a flash of sick jealousy*) Andy's made a big success of himself—the kind he wanted. (*Mockingly*) And now he's coming home to let us admire his greatness. (*Frowning—irritably*) What am I talking about? My brain must be sick, too. (*After a pause*) Yes, these years have been terrible for both of us. (*His voice is lowered to a trembling whisper.*) Especially the last eight months since Mary—died. (*He forces back a sob with a convulsive shudder—then breaks out in a passionate agony.*) Our last hope of happiness! I could curse God from the bottom of my soul—if there was a God! (*He is racked by a violent fit of coughing and hurriedly puts his handkerchief to his lips.*)

RUTH (*without looking at him*). Mary's better off—being dead.

ROBERT (*gloomily*). We'd all be better off for that matter. (*With a sudden exasperation*) You tell that mother of yours she's got to stop saying that Mary's death was due to a weak constitution inherited from me. (*On the verge of tears of weakness*) It's got to stop, I tell you!

RUTH (*sharply*). Sh-h-h! You'll wake her; and then she'll nag at me—not you.

ROBERT (*coughs and lies back in his chair*

*weakly—a pause*). It's all because your mother's down on me for not begging Andy for help.

RUTH (*resentfully*). You might have. He's got plenty.

ROBERT. How can *you* of all people think of taking money from *him?*

RUTH (*dully*). I don't see the harm. He's your own brother.

ROBERT (*shrugging his shoulders*). What's the use of talking to you? Well, I couldn't. (*Proudly*) And I've managed to keep things going, thank God. You can't deny that without help I've succeeded in—(*he breaks off with a bitter laugh*) My God, what am I boasting of? Debts to this one and that, taxes, interest unpaid! I'm a fool! (*He lies back in his chair closing his eyes for a moment, then speaks in a low voice*) I'll be frank, Ruth. I've been an utter failure, and I've dragged you with me. I couldn't blame you in all justice, —for hating me.

RUTH (*without feeling*). I don't hate you. It's been my fault too, I s'pose.

ROBERT. No. You couldn't help loving—Andy.

RUTH (*dully*). I don't love anyone.

ROBERT (*waving her remark aside*). You needn't deny it. It doesn't matter. (*After a pause—with a tender smile*) Do you know, Ruth, what I've been dreaming back there in the dark? (*With a short laugh*) I was planning our future when I get well. (*He looks at her with appealing eyes as if afraid she will sneer at him. Her expression does not change. She stares at the stove. His voice takes on a note of eagerness.*) After all, why shouldn't we have a future? We're young yet. If we can only shake off the curse of this farm! It's the farm that's ruined our lives, damn it! And now that Andy's coming back—I'm going to sink my foolish pride, Ruth! I'll borrow the money from him to give us a good start in the city. We'll go where people live instead of stagnating, and start all over again. (*Confidently*) I won't be the failure there that I've been here, Ruth. You won't need to be ashamed of me there. I'll prove to you the reading I've done can be put to some use. (*Vaguely*) I'll write, or something of that sort. I've always wanted to write. (*Pleadingly*) You'll want to do that, won't you, Ruth?

RUTH (*dully*). There's Ma.

ROBERT. She can come with us.

RUTH. She wouldn't.

ROBERT (*angrily*). So that's your answer! (*He trembles with violent passion. His voice is so strange that* RUTH *turns to look at him in alarm.*) You're lying, Ruth! Your mother's just an excuse. You want to stay here. You think that be-

cause Andy's coming back that—(*He chokes and has an attack of coughing.*)

RUTH (*getting up—in a frightened voice*). What's the matter? (*She goes to him.*) I'll go with you, Rob. Stop that coughing for goodness' sake! It's awful bad for you. (*She soothes him in dull tones.*) I'll go with you to the city—soon's you're well again. Honest I will, Rob, I promise! (ROBERT *lies back and closes his eyes. She stands looking down at him anxiously.*) Do you feel better now?

ROBERT. Yes. (RUTH *goes back to her chair. After a pause he opens his eyes and sits up in his chair. His face is flushed and happy.*) Then you *will* go, Ruth?

RUTH. Yes.

ROBERT (*excitedly*). We'll make a new start, Ruth—just you and I. Life owes us some happiness after what we've been through. (*Vehemently*) It must! Otherwise our suffering would be meaningless—and that is unthinkable.

RUTH (*worried by his excitement*). Yes, yes, of course, Rob, but you mustn't—

ROBERT. Oh, don't be afraid. I feel completely well, really I do—now that I can hope again. Oh if you knew how glorious it feels to have something to look forward to! Can't you feel the thrill of it, too—the vision of a new life opening up after all the horrible years?

RUTH. Yes, yes, but do be—

ROBERT. Nonsense! I won't be careful. I'm getting back all my strength. (*He gets lightly to his feet.*) See! I feel light as a feather. (*He walks to her chair and bends down to kiss her smilingly.*) One kiss—the first in years, isn't it?—to greet the dawn of a new life together.

RUTH (*submitting to his kiss—worriedly*). Sit down, Rob, for goodness' sake!

ROBERT (*with tender obstinacy—stroking her hair*). I won't sit down. You're silly to worry. (*He rests one hand on the back of her chair.*) Listen. All our suffering has been a test through which we had to pass to prove ourselves worthy of a finer realization. (*Exultingly*) And we did pass through it! It hasn't broken us! And now the dream is to come true! Don't you see?

RUTH (*looking at him with frightened eyes as if she thought he had gone mad*). Yes, Rob, I see; but won't you go back to bed now and rest?

ROBERT. No. I'm going to see the sun rise. It's an augury of good fortune. (*He goes quickly to the window in the rear left, and pushing the curtains aside, stands looking out.* RUTH *springs to her feet and comes quickly to the table, left, where she remains watching* ROBERT *in a tense, expectant attitude. As he peers out his body seems gradually to sag, to grow limp and tired.*

*His voice is mournful as he speaks.*) No sun yet. It isn't time. All I can see is the black rim of the damned hills outlined against a creeping grayness. (*He turns around, letting the curtains fall back, stretching a hand out to the wall to support himself. His false strength of a moment has evaporated leaving his face drawn and hollow-eyed. He makes a pitiful attempt to smile.*) That's not a very happy augury, is it? But the sun'll come —soon. (*He sways weakly.*)

RUTH (*hurrying to his side and supporting him*). Please go to bed, won't you, Rob? You don't want to be all wore out when the specialist comes, do you?

ROBERT (*quickly*). No. That's right. He mustn't think I'm sicker than I am. And I feel as if I could sleep now—(*cheerfully*) a good, sound, restful sleep.

RUTH (*helping him to the bedroom door*). That's what you need most. (*They go inside. A moment later she reappears calling back*) I'll shut this door so's you'll be quiet. (*She closes the door and goes quickly to her mother and shakes her by the shoulder.*) Ma! Ma! Wake up!

MRS. ATKINS (*coming out of her sleep with a start*). Glory be! What's the matter with you?

RUTH. It was Rob. He's just been talking to me out here. I put him back to bed. (*Now that she is sure her mother is awake her fear passes and she relapses into dull indifference. She sits down in her chair and stares at the stove—dully.*) He acted—funny; and his eyes looked so—so wild like.

MRS. ATKINS (*with asperity*). And is that all you woke me out of a sound sleep for, and scared me near out of my wits?

RUTH. I was afraid. He talked so crazy. I couldn't quiet him. I didn't want to be alone with him that way. Lord knows what he might do.

MRS. ATKINS (*scornfully*). Humph! A help I'd be to you and me not able to move a step! Why didn't you run and get Jake?

RUTH (*dully*). Jake isn't here. He quit last night. He hasn't been paid in three months.

MRS. ATKINS (*indignantly*). I can't blame him. What decent person'd want to work on a place like this? (*With sudden exasperation*) Oh, I wish you'd never married that man!

RUTH (*wearily*). You oughtn't to talk about him now when he's sick in his bed.

MRS. ATKINS (*working herself into a fit of rage*). You know very well, Ruth Mayo, if it wasn't for me helpin' you on the sly out of my savin's, you'd both been in the poor house—and all 'count of his pigheaded pride in not lettin' Andy know the state thin's were in. A nice thin' for me to have to support him out of what I'd saved for my last days—and me an invalid with no one to look to!

RUTH. Andy'll pay you back, Ma. I can tell him so's Rob'll never know.

MRS. ATKINS (*with a snort*). What'd Rob think you and him was livin' on, I'd like to know?

RUTH (*dully*). He didn't think about it, I s'pose. (*After a slight pause*) He said he'd made up his mind to ask Andy for help when he comes. (*As a clock in the kitchen strikes six*) Six o'clock. Andy ought to get here directly.

MRS. ATKINS. D'you think this special doctor'll do Rob any good?

RUTH (*hopelessly*). I don't know. (*The two women remain silent for a time staring dejectedly at the stove.*)

MRS. ATKINS (*shivering irritably.*) For goodness' sake put some wood on that fire. I'm 'most freezin'!

RUTH (*pointing to the door in the rear*). Don't talk so loud. Let him sleep if he can. (*She gets wearily from the chair and puts a few pieces of wood in the stove.*) This is the last of the wood. I don't know who'll cut more now that Jake's left. (*She sighs and walks to the window in the rear, left, pulls the curtains aside, and looks out.*) It's getting gray out. (*She comes back to the stove.*) Looks like it'd be a nice day. (*She stretches out her hands to warm them.*) Must've been a heavy frost last night. We're paying for the spell of warm weather we've been having. (*The throbbing whine of a motor sounds from the distance outside.*)

MRS. ATKINS (*sharply*). Sh-h-h! Listen! Ain't that an auto I hear?

RUTH (*without interest*). Yes. It's Andy, I s'pose.

MRS. ATKINS (*with nervous irritation*). Don't sit there like a silly goose. Look at the state of this room! What'll this strange doctor think of us? Look at that lamp chimney all smoke! Gracious sakes, Ruth—

RUTH (*indifferently*). I've got a lamp all cleaned up in the kitchen.

MRS. ATKINS (*peremptorily*). Wheel me in there this minute. I don't want him to see me looking a sight. I'll lay down in the room the other side. You don't need me now and I'm dead for sleep. (RUTH *wheels her mother off right. The noise of the motor grows louder and finally ceases as the car stops on the road before the farmhouse.* RUTH *returns from the kitchen with a lighted lamp in her hand which she sets on the table beside the other. The sound of footsteps on the path is heard—then a sharp rap on the door.* RUTH *goes and opens it.* ANDREW *enters, followed by* DOCTOR FAWCETT *carrying a small black bag.* ANDREW *has changed greatly. His face seems to have grown highstrung, hardened by the look of decisiveness which comes from being constantly un-*

*der a strain where judgments on the spur of the moment are compelled to be accurate. His eyes are keener and more alert. There is even a suggestion of ruthless cunning about them. At present, however, his expression is one of tense anxiety.* DOCTOR FAWCETT *is a short, dark, middle-aged man with a Vandyke beard. He wears glasses.)*

RUTH. Hello, Andy! I've been waiting—

ANDREW (*kissing her hastily*). I got here as soon as I could. (*He throws off his cap and heavy overcoat on the table, introducing* RUTH *and the* DOCTOR *as he does so. He is dressed in an expensive business suit and appears stouter.*) My sister-in-law, Mrs. Mayo—Doctor Fawcett. (*They bow to each other silently.* ANDREW *casts a quick glance about the room.*) Where's Rob?

RUTH (*pointing*). In there.

ANDREW. I'll take your coat and hat, Doctor. (*As he helps the* DOCTOR *with his things*) Is he very bad, Ruth?

RUTH (*dully*). He's been getting weaker.

ANDREW. Damn! This way, Doctor. Bring the lamp, Ruth. (*He goes into the bedroom, followed by the* DOCTOR *and* RUTH *carrying the clean lamp.* RUTH *reappears almost immediately, closing the door behind her, and goes slowly to the outside door, which she opens, and stands in the doorway looking out. The sound of* ANDREW's *and* ROBERT's *voices comes from the bedroom. A moment later* ANDREW *re-enters, closing the door softly. He comes forward and sinks down in the rocker on the right of table, leaning his head on his hand. His face is drawn in a shocked expression of great grief. He sighs heavily, staring mournfully in front of him.* RUTH *turns and stands watching him. Then she shuts the door and returns to her chair by the stove, turning it so she can face him.*)

ANDREW (*glancing up quickly—in a harsh voice*). How long has this been going on?

RUTH. You mean—how long has he been sick?

ANDREW (*shortly*). Of course! What else?

RUTH. It was last summer he had a bad spell first, but he's been ailin' ever since Mary died—eight months ago.

ANDREW (*harshly*). Why didn't you let me know—cable me? Do you want him to die, all of you? I'm damned if it doesn't look that way! (*His voice breaking*) Poor old chap! To be sick in this out-of-the-way hole without anyone to attend to him but a country quack! It's a damned shame!

RUTH (*dully*). I wanted to send you word once, but he only got mad when I told him. He was too proud to ask anything, he said.

ANDREW. Proud? To ask *me*? (*He jumps to his feet and paces nervously back and forth.*) I can't

understand the way you've acted. Didn't you see how sick he was getting? Couldn't you realize —why, I nearly dropped in my tracks when I saw him! He looks— (*he shudders*) terrible! (*With fierce scorn*) I suppose you're so used to the idea of his being delicate that you took his sickness as a matter of course. God, if I'd only known!

RUTH (*without emotion*). A letter takes some time to get where you were—and we couldn't afford to telegraph. We owed everyone already, and I couldn't ask Ma. She'd been giving me money out of her savings till she hadn't much left. Don't say anything to Rob about it. I never told him. He'd only be mad at me if he knew. But I had to, because—God knows how we'd have got on if I hadn't.

ANDREW. You mean to say— (*His eyes seemed to take in the poverty-stricken appearance of the room for the first time.*) You sent that telegram to me collect. Was it because— (RUTH *nods silently.* ANDREW *pounds on the table with his fist.*) Good God! And all this time I've been—why I've had everything! (*He sits down in his chair and pulls it close to* RUTH's *impulsively.*) But—I can't get it through my head. Why? Why? What has happened? How did it ever come about? Tell me!

RUTH (*dully*). There's nothing much to tell. Things kept getting worse, that's all—and Rob didn't seem to care. He never took any interest since way back when your Ma died. After that he got men to take charge, and they nearly all cheated him—he couldn't tell—and left one after another. Then after Mary died he didn't pay no heed to anything any more—just stayed indoors and took to reading books again. So I had to ask Ma if she wouldn't help us some.

ANDREW (*surprised and horrified*). Why, damn it, this is frightful! Rob must be mad not to have let me know. Too proud to ask help of *me!* What's the matter with him in God's name? (*A sudden, horrible suspicion entering his mind*) Ruth! Tell me the truth. His mind hasn't gone back on him, has it?

RUTH (*dully*). I don't know. Mary's dying broke him up terrible—but he's used to her being gone by this time, I s'pose.

ANDREW (*looking at her queerly*). Do you mean to say *you're* used to it?

RUTH (*in a dead tone*). There's a time comes —when you don't mind any more—anything.

ANDREW (*looks at her fixedly for a moment —with great pity*). I'm sorry, Ruth—if I seemed to blame you. I didn't realize—the sight of Rob lying in bed there, so gone to pieces—it made me furious at everyone. Forgive me, Ruth.

RUTH. There's nothing to forgive. It doesn't matter.

ANDREW (*springing to his feet again and pacing up and down*). Thank God I came back before it was too late. This doctor will know exactly what to do. That's the first thing to think of. When Rob's on his feet again we can get the farm working on a sound basis once more. I'll see to that—before I leave.

RUTH. You're going away again?

ANDREW. I've got to.

RUTH. You wrote Rob you was coming back to stay this time.

ANDREW. I expected to—until I got to New York. Then I learned certain facts that make it necessary. (*With a short laugh*) To be candid, Ruth, I'm not the rich man you've probably been led to believe by my letters—not now. I was when I wrote them. I made money hand over fist as long as I stuck to legitimate trading; but I wasn't content with that. I wanted it to come easier, so like all the rest of the idiots, I tried speculation. Oh, I won all right! Several times I've been almost a millionaire—on paper—and then come down to earth again with a bump. Finally the strain was too much. I got disgusted with myself and made up my mind to get out and come home and forget it and really live again. (*He gives a harsh laugh.*) And now comes the funny part. The day before the steamer sailed I saw what I thought was a chance to become a millionaire again. (*He snaps his fingers.*) That easy! I plunged. Then, before things broke, I left—I was so confident I couldn't be wrong. But when I landed in New York—I wired you I had business to wind up, didn't I? Well, it was the business that wound me up! (*He smiles grimly, pacing up and down, his hands in his pockets.*)

RUTH (*dully*). You found—you'd lost everything?

ANDREW (*sitting down again*). Practically. (*He takes a cigar from his pocket, bites the end off, and lights it.*) Oh, I don't mean I'm dead broke. I've saved ten thousand from the wreckage, maybe twenty. But that's a poor showing for five years' hard work. That's why I'll have to go back. (*Confidently*) I can make it up in a year or so down there—and I don't need but a shoestring to start with. (*A weary expression comes over his face and he sighs heavily.*) I wish I didn't have to. I'm sick of it all.

RUTH. It's too bad—things seem to go wrong so.

ANDREW (*shaking off his depression—briskly*). They might be much worse. There's enough left to fix the farm O.K. before I go. I won't leave 'til Rob's on his feet again. In the meantime I'll make

things fly around here. (*With satisfaction*) I need a rest, and the kind of rest I need is hard work in the open—just like I used to do in the old days. (*Stopping abruptly and lowering his voice cautiously*) Not a word to Rob about my losing money! Remember that, Ruth! You can see why. If he's grown so touchy he'd never accept a cent if he thought I was hard up; see?

RUTH. Yes, Andy. (*After a pause, during which* ANDREW *puffs at his cigar abstractedly, his mind evidently busy with plans for the future, the bedroom door is opened and* DR. FAWCETT *enters, carrying a bag. He closes the door quietly behind him and comes forward, a grave expression on his face.* ANDREW *springs out of his chair.*)

ANDREW. Ah, Doctor! (*He pushes a chair between his own and* RUTH's.) Won't you have a chair?

FAWCETT (*glancing at his watch*). I must catch the nine o'clock back to the city. It's imperative. I have only a moment. (*Sitting down and clearing his throat—in a perfunctory, impersonal voice*) The case of your brother, Mr. Mayo, is— (*he stops and glances at* RUTH *and says meaningly to* ANDREW) Perhaps it would be better if you and I—

RUTH (*with dogged resentment*). I know what you mean, Doctor. (*Dully*) Don't be afraid I can't stand it. I'm used to bearing trouble by this time; and I can guess what you've found out. (*She hesitates for a moment—then continues in a monotonous voice*) Rob's going to die.

ANDREW (*angrily*). Ruth!

FAWCETT (*raising his hand as if to command silence*). I am afraid my diagnosis of your brother's condition forces me to the same conclusion as Mrs. Mayo's.

ANDREW (*groaning*). But, Doctor, surely—

FAWCETT (*calmly*). Your brother hasn't long to live—perhaps a few days, perhaps only a few hours. It's a marvel that he's alive at this moment. My examination revealed that both of his lungs are terribly affected.

ANDREW (*brokenly*). Good God! (RUTH *keeps her eyes fixed on her lap in a trance-like stare.*)

FAWCETT. I am sorry I have to tell you this. If there was anything that could be done—

ANDREW. There isn't anything?

FAWCETT (*shaking his head*). It's too late. Six months ago there might have—

ANDREW (*in anguish*). But if we were to take him to the mountains—or to Arizona—or—

FAWCETT. That might have prolonged his life six months ago. (ANDREW *groans.*) But now— (*He shrugs his shoulders significantly.*)

ANDREW (*appalled by a sudden thought*). Good heavens, you haven't told him this, have you, Doctor?

FAWCETT. No. I lied to him. I said a change of climate— (*He looks at his watch again nervously.*) I must leave you. (*He gets up.*)

ANDREW (*getting to his feet—insistently*). But there must still be some chance—

FAWCETT (*as if he were reassuring a child*). There is always that last chance—the miracle. (*He puts on his hat and coat—bowing to* RUTH) Good-by, Mrs. Mayo.

RUTH (*without raising her eyes—dully*). Good-by.

ANDREW (*mechanically*). I'll walk to the car with you, Doctor. (*They go out the door.* RUTH *sits motionless. The motor is heard starting and the noise gradually recedes into the distance.* ANDREW *re-enters and sits down in his chair, holding his head in his hands.*) Ruth! (*She lifts her eyes to his.*) Hadn't we better go in and see him? God! I'm afraid to! I know he'll read it in my face. (*The bedroom door is noiselessly opened and* ROBERT *appears in the doorway. His cheeks are flushed with fever, and his eyes appear unusually large and brilliant.* ANDREW *continues with a groan*) It can't be, Ruth. It can't be as hopeless as he said. There's always a fighting chance. We'll take Rob to Arizona. He's got to get well. There *must* be a chance!

ROBERT (*in a gentle tone*). Why must there, Andy? (RUTH *turns and stares at him with terrified eyes.*)

ANDREW (*whirling around*). Rob! (*Scoldingly*) What are you doing out of bed? (*He gets up and goes to him.*) Get right back now and obey the Doc, or you're going to get a licking from me!

ROBERT (*ignoring these remarks*). Help me over to the chair, please, Andy.

ANDREW. Like hell I will! You're going right back to bed, that's where you're going, and stay there! (*He takes hold of* ROBERT's *arm.*)

ROBERT (*mockingly*). Stay there 'til I die, eh, Andy? (*Coldly*) Don't behave like a child. I'm sick of lying down. I'll be more rested sitting up. (*As* ANDREW *hesitates—violently*) I swear I'll get out of bed every time you put me there. You'll have to sit on my chest, and that wouldn't help my health any. Come on, Andy. Don't play the fool. I want to talk to you, and I'm going to. (*With a grim smile*) A dying man has some rights, hasn't he?

ANDREW (*with a shudder*). Don't talk that way, for God's sake! I'll only let you sit down if you'll promise that. Remember. (*He helps* ROBERT *to*

the chair between his own and RUTH's.) Easy now! There you are! Wait, and I'll get a pillow for you. (*He goes into the bedroom.* ROBERT *looks at* RUTH, *who shrinks away from him in terror.* ROBERT *smiles bitterly.* ANDREW *comes back with the pillow which he places behind* ROBERT's *back.*) How's that?

ROBERT (*with an affectionate smile*). Fine! Thank you! (*As* ANDREW *sits down*) Listen, Andy. You've asked me not to talk—and I won't after I've made my position clear. (*Slowly*) In the first place I know I'm dying. (RUTH *bows her head and covers her face with her hands. She remains like this all during the scene between the two brothers.*)

ANDREW. Rob! That isn't so!

ROBERT (*wearily*). It *is* so! Don't lie to me. After Ruth put me to bed before you came, I saw it clearly for the first time. (*Bitterly*) I'd been making plans for our future—Ruth's and mine—so it came hard at first—the realization. Then when the doctor examined me, I knew—although he tried to lie about it. And then to make sure I listened at the door to what he told you. So don't mock me with fairy tales about Arizona, or any such rot as that. Because I'm dying is no reason you should treat me as an imbecile or a coward. Now that I'm sure what's happening I can say Kismet to it with all my heart. It was only the silly uncertainty that hurt. (*There is a pause.* ANDREW *looks around in impotent anguish, not knowing what to say.* ROBERT *regards him with an affectionate smile.*)

ANDREW (*finally blurts out*). It isn't foolish. You *have* got a chance. If you heard all the Doctor said that ought to prove it to you.

ROBERT. Oh, you mean when he spoke of the miracle? (*Dryly*) I don't believe in miracles—in my case. Besides, I know more than any doctor on earth *could* know—because I *feel* what's coming. (*Dismissing the subject*) But we've agreed not to talk of it. Tell me about yourself, Andy. That's what I'm interested in. Your letters were too brief and far apart to be illuminating.

ANDREW. I meant to write oftener.

ROBERT (*with a faint trace of irony*). I judge from them you've accomplished all you set out to do five years ago?

ANDREW. That isn't much to boast of.

ROBERT (*surprised*). Have you really, honestly reached that conclusion?

ANDREW. Well, it doesn't seem to amount to much now.

ROBERT. But you're rich, aren't you?

ANDREW (*with a quick glance at* RUTH). Yes, I s'pose so.

ROBERT. I'm glad. You can do to the farm all I've undone. But what did you do down there? Tell me. You went in the grain business with that friend of yours?

ANDREW. Yes. After two years I had a share in it. I sold out last year. (*He is answering* ROBERT'S *questions with great reluctance.*)

ROBERT. And then?

ANDREW. I went in on my own.

ROBERT. Still in grain?

ANDREW. Yes.

ROBERT. What's the matter? You look as if I were accusing you of something.

ANDREW. I'm proud enough of the first four years. It's after that I'm not boasting of. I took to speculating.

ROBERT. In wheat?

ANDREW. Yes.

ROBERT. And you made money—gambling?

ANDREW. Yes.

ROBERT (*thoughtfully*). I've been wondering what the great change was in you. (*After a pause*) You—a farmer—to gamble in a wheat pit with scraps of paper. There's a spiritual significance in that picture, Andy. (*He smiles bitterly*) I'm a failure, and Ruth's another—but we can both justly lay some of the blame for our stumbling on God. But you're the deepest-dyed failure of the three, Andy. You've spent eight years running away from yourself. Do you see what I mean? You used to be a creator when you loved the farm. You and life were in harmonious partnership. And now— (*He stops as if seeking vainly for words.*) My brain is muddled. But part of what I mean is that your gambling with the thing you used to love to create proves how far astray— So you'll be punished. You'll have to suffer to win back— (*His voice grows weaker and he sighs wearily.*) It's no use. I can't say it. (*He lies back and closes his eyes, breathing pantingly.*)

ANDREW (*slowly*). I think I know what you're driving at, Rob—and it's true, I guess. (ROBERT *smiles gratefully and stretches out his hand, which* ANDREW *takes in his.*)

ROBERT. I want you to promise me to do one thing, Andy, after—

ANDREW. I'll promise anything, as God is my Judge!

ROBERT. Remember, Andy, Ruth has suffered double her share. (*His voice faltering with weakness*) Only through contact with suffering, Andy, will you—awaken. Listen. You must marry Ruth—afterwards.

RUTH (*with a cry*). Rob! (ROBERT *lies back, his eyes closed, gasping heavily for breath.*)

ANDREW (*making signs to her to humor him —gently*). You're tired out, Rob. You better lie down and rest a while, don't you think? We can talk later on.

ROBERT (*with a mocking smile*). Later on! You always were an optimist, Andy! (*He sighs with exhaustion.*) Yes, I'll go and rest a while. (*As* ANDREW *comes to help him*) It must be near sunrise, isn't it?

ANDREW. It's after six.

ROBERT (*as* ANDREW *helps him into the bedroom*). Shut the door, Andy. I want to be alone. (ANDREW *reappears and shuts the door softly. He comes and sits down on his chair again, supporting his head on his hands, his face drawn with the intensity of his dry-eyed anguish.*)

RUTH (*glancing at him—fearfully*). He's out of his mind now, isn't he?

ANDREW. He may be a little delirious. The fever would do that. (*With impotent rage*) God, what a shame! And there's nothing we can do but sit and—wait! (*He springs from his chair and walks to the stove.*)

RUTH (*dully*). He was talking—wild—like he used to—only this time it sounded—unnatural, don't you think?

ANDREW. I don't know. The things he said to me had truth in them—even if he did talk them way up in the air, like he always sees things. Still—(*He glances down at* RUTH *keenly.*) Why do you suppose he wanted us to promise we'd— (confusedly) You know what he said.

RUTH (*dully*). His mind was wandering, I s'pose.

ANDREW (*with conviction*). No—there was something back of it.

RUTH. He wanted to make sure I'd be all right —after he'd gone, I expect.

ANDREW. No, it wasn't that. He knows very well I'd naturally look after you without—anything like that.

RUTH. He might be thinking of—something happened five years back, the time you came home from the trip.

ANDREW. What happened? What do you mean?

RUTH (*dully*). We had a fight.

ANDREW. A fight? What has that to do with me?

RUTH. It was about you—in a way.

ANDREW. (*amazed*). About me?

RUTH. Yes, mostly. You see I'd found out I'd made a mistake about Rob soon after we were married—when it was too late.

ANDREW. Mistake? (*Slowly*) You mean—you found out you didn't love Rob?

RUTH. Yes.

ANDREW. Good God!

RUTH. And then I thought that when Mary came it'd be different, and I'd love him; but it didn't happen that way. And I couldn't bear with his blundering and bookreading—and I grew to hate him, almost.

ANDREW. Ruth!

RUTH. I couldn't help it. No woman could. It had to be because I loved someone else, I'd found out. (*She sighs wearily*) It can't do no harm to tell you now—when it's all past and gone—and dead. *You* were the one I really loved—only I didn't come to the knowledge of it 'til too late.

ANDREW (*stunned*). Ruth! Do you know what you're saying?

RUTH. It was true—then. (*With sudden fierceness*) How could I help it? No woman could.

ANDREW. Then—you loved me—that time I came home?

RUTH (*doggedly*). I'd known your real reason for leaving home the first time—everybody knew it—and for three years I'd been thinking—

ANDREW. That I loved you?

RUTH. Yes. Then that day on the hill you laughed about what a fool you'd been for loving me once—and I knew it was all over.

ANDREW. Good God, but I never thought —(*he stops, shuddering at his remembrance*) And did Rob—

RUTH. That was what I'd started to tell. We'd had a fight just before you came and I got crazy mad—and I told him all I've told you.

ANDREW (*gaping at her speechlessly for a moment*). You told Rob—you loved me?

RUTH. Yes.

ANDREW (*shrinking away from her in horror*). You—you—you mad fool, you! How could you do such a thing?

RUTH. I couldn't help it. I'd got to the end of bearing things—without talking.

ANDREW. Then Rob must have known every moment I stayed here! And yet he never said or showed—God, how he must have suffered! Didn't you know how much he loved you?

RUTH (*dully*). Yes, I knew he liked me.

ANDREW. Liked you! What kind of a woman are you? Couldn't you have kept silent? Did you have to torture him? No wonder he's dying! And you've lived together for five years with this between you?

RUTH. We've lived in the same house.

ANDREW. Does he still think—

RUTH. I don't know. We've never spoke a word about it since that day. Maybe, from the way he went on, he s'poses I care for you yet.

ANDREW. But you don't. It's outrageous. It's stupid! You don't love me!

RUTH (*slowly*). I wouldn't know how to feel love, even if I tried, any more.

ANDREW (*brutally*). And I don't love you, that's sure! (*He sinks into his chair, his head between his hands.*) It's damnable such a thing should be between Rob and me. Why, I love Rob better'n anybody in the world and always did. There isn't a thing on God's green earth I wouldn't have done to keep trouble away from him. And I have to be the very one—it's damnable! How am I going to face him again? What can I say to him now? (*He groans with anguished rage. After a pause*) He asked me to promise—what am I going to do?

RUTH. You can promise—so's it'll ease his mind—and not mean anything.

ANDREW. What? Lie to him now—when he's dying? (*Determinedly*). No! It's *you* who'll have to do the lying, since it must be done. You've got a chance now to undo some of all the suffering you've brought on Rob. Go in to him! Tell him you never loved me—it was all a mistake. Tell him you only said so because you were mad and didn't know what you were saying! Tell him something, anything, that'll bring him peace!

RUTH (*dully*). He wouldn't believe me.

ANDREW (*furiously*). You've got to make him believe you, do you hear? You've got to—now —hurry—you never know when it may be too late. (*As she hesitates—imploringly*) For God's sake, Ruth! Don't you see you owe it to him? You'll never forgive yourself if you don't.

RUTH (*dully*). I'll go. (*She gets wearily to her feet and walks slowly toward the bedroom.*) But it won't do any good. (ANDREW's *eyes are fixed on her anxiously. She opens the door and steps inside the room. She remains standing there for a minute. Then she calls in a frightened voice*) Rob! Where are you? (*Then she hurries back, trembling with fright.*) Andy! Andy! He's gone!

ANDREW (*misunderstanding her—her face pale with dread*). He's not—

RUTH (*interrupting him—hysterically*). He's gone! The bed's empty. The window's wide open. He must have crawled out into the yard!

ANDREW (*springing to his feet. He rushes into the bedroom and returns immediately with an expression of alarmed amazement on his face.*) Come! He can't have gone far! (*Grabbing his hat he takes* RUTH's *arm and shoves her toward the door.*) Come on! (*Opening the door*) Let's hope to God—(*The door closes behind them, cutting off his words as the curtain falls.*)

# ACT THREE

## SCENE II

SAME *as Act One, Scene I—A section of country highway. The sky to the east is already alight with bright color and a thin, quivering line of flame is spreading slowly along the horizon rim of the dark hills. The roadside, however, is still steeped in the grayness of the dawn, shadowy and vague. The field in the foreground has a wild, uncultivated appearance as if it had been allowed to remain fallow the preceding summer. Parts of the snakefence in the rear have been broken down. The apple tree is leafless and seems dead.*

ROBERT *staggers weakly in from the left. He stumbles into the ditch and lies there for a moment, then crawls with a great effort to the top of the bank where he can see the sun rise, and collapses weakly.* RUTH *and* ANDREW *come hurriedly along the road from the left.*

ANDREW (*stopping and looking about him*). There he is! I knew it! I knew we'd find him here.

ROBERT (*trying to raise himself to a sitting position as they hasten to his side—with a wan smile*). I thought I'd given you the slip.

ANDREW (*with kindly bullying*). Well you didn't, you old scoundrel, and we're going to take you right back where you belong—in bed. (*He makes a motion to lift* ROBERT.)

ROBERT. Don't, Andy. Don't, I tell you!

ANDREW. You're in pain?

ROBERT (*simply*). No. I'm dying. (*He falls back weakly.* RUTH *sinks down beside him with a sob and pillows his head on her lap.* ANDREW *stands looking down at him helplessly.* ROBERT *moves his head restlessly on* RUTH's *lap.*) I couldn't stand it back there in the room. It seemed as if all my life—I'd been cooped in a room. So I thought I'd try to end as I might have—if I'd had the courage—alone—in a ditch by the open road—watching the run rise.

ANDREW. Rob! Don't talk. You're wasting your strength. Rest a while and then we'll carry you—

ROBERT. Still hoping, Andy? Don't. I know. (*There is a pause during which he breathes heavily, straining his eyes toward the horizon.*) The sun comes so slowly. (*With an ironical smile*) The doctor told me to go to the far-off places—and I'd be cured. He was right. That was always the cure for me. It's too late—for this life—but— (*He has a fit of coughing which racks his body.*)

ANDREW (*with a hoarse sob*). Rob! (*He clenches his fists in an impotent rage against Fate.*) God! God! (RUTH *sobs brokenly and wipes* ROBERT's *lips with her handkerchief.*)

ROBERT (*in a voice which is suddenly ringing with the happiness of hope*). You mustn't feel sorry for me. Don't you see I'm happy at last—free—free!—freed from the farm—free to wander on and on—eternally! (*He raises himself on his elbow, his face radiant, and points to the horizon.*) Look! Isn't it beautiful beyond the hills? I can hear the old voices calling me to come —(*exultantly*) And this time I'm going! It isn't the end. It's a free beginning—the start of my voyage! I've won to my trip—the right of release—beyond the horizon! Oh, you ought to be glad—glad—for my sake! (*He collapses weakly.*) Andy! (ANDREW *bends down to him.*) Remember Ruth—

ANDREW. I'll take care of her, I swear to you, Rob!

ROBERT. Ruth has suffered—remember, Andy—only through sacrifice—the secret beyond there— (*He suddenly raises himself with his last remaining strength and points to the horizon where the edge of the sun's disc is rising from the rim of the hills.*) The sun! (*He remains with his eyes fixed on it for a moment. A rattling noise throbs from his throat. He mumbles*) Remember! (*and falls back and is still.* RUTH *gives a cry of horror and springs to her feet, shuddering, her hands over her eyes.* ANDREW *bends on one knee beside the body, placing a hand over* ROBERT's *heart, then he kisses his brother reverentially on the forehead and stands up.*)

ANDREW (*facing* RUTH, *the body between them—in a dead voice*). He's dead. (*With a sudden burst of fury*) God damn you, you never told him!

RUTH (*piteously*). He was so happy without my lying to him.

ANDREW (*pointing to the body—trembling with the violence of his rage*). This is your doing, you damn woman, you coward, you murderess!

RUTH (*sobbing*). Don't, Andy! I couldn't help it—and he knew how I'd suffered, too. He told you—to remember.

ANDREW (*stares at her for a moment, his rage ebbing away, an expression of deep pity gradually coming over his face. Then he glances down at his brother and speaks brokenly in a compassionate voice*). Forgive me, Ruth—for his sake—and I'll remember—(RUTH *lets her hands fall from her face and looks at him uncomprehendingly. He lifts his eyes to hers and forces out falteringly*) I—you—we've both made a mess of things! We must try to help each other—and—in time—we'll come to know what's right— (*Desperately*) And perhaps we— (*But* RUTH, *if she is aware of his words, gives no sign. She remains silent, gazing at him dully with the sad humility of* exhaustion, *her mind already sinking back into that spent calm beyond the further troubling of any hope.*)

CURTAIN

## LOUISE BOGAN
*Editor*

# Robert Frost

## 1874–1963

THE CAREER of Robert [Lee] Frost, the American poet whose popularity, in his seventies and eighties, came to exceed that of any of his contemporaries, presents a number of paradoxes. For most of his life his reputation came to be based on the figure he presented to his audience: that of a New England poet who lived close to the land, and whose principal interests, apart from writing and teaching, were rural ones. Yet he spent his formative years—until the age of eleven—in San Francisco, where he was born in 1874, and his years of adolescence and young manhood in industrial New England towns and cities—chiefly Lawrence, Massachusetts. His direct forebears, moreover, on his father's side, were town-dwellers. His paternal grandfather was an overseer of a cotton mill in Lawrence, and his father, William Prescott Frost, Jr., after graduating from Harvard, moved west to become a newspaperman and politician in the growing city of San Francisco. His mother, Isabelle Moodie Frost, had come to America from Scotland as a girl of fifteen. She met Frost's father at Bucknell Academy in Lewistown, Pennsylvania, where the young Easterner on his way west had taken a teaching position, and where she herself taught mathematics. She, too, was city bred (in Edinburgh) and it is apparent that many of the poet's charac-

teristics—his intuition and imagination, as well as his belief in the importance of positive aims and values—were derived from her.

But there is no doubt that Frost's lifelong affection for the land was central and genuine. He possessed from the beginning the individualistic and independent nature which was, at one time, common not only in New England—where the Frost family had long been established—but in the rural areas of America as a whole. The elder Frost's streak of Yankee intransigence expressed itself in his youthful espousal of the theory of States' rights and the cause of the South: and he proved himself a member of the post-Civil War generation by his restless move toward the new opportunities lying westward. Frost's own temperament, as W. H. Auden—a knowledgeable admirer—has pointed out, was that of the "small-holder," of the farmer who owns and works his land. In Frost, the inheritance of the Yankee countryman and of the Scottish crofter met, and reinforced each other.

In his later years, Frost described to biographers the difficulties of his childhood in some detail. They were difficulties which contributed to many of the tensions of his adolescence and young manhood, as well as to his choice, at an early age, of a responsible pattern of behavior. His father's character, it would appear, had more of Yankee gregariousness than Yankee reserve, and as a newspaperman and a dabbler in politics, the elder Frost's free and untrammeled participation in San Francisco's ebullient frontier atmosphere was frequently shared by his son, who went along as his companion—missing school and catching glimpses of the growing city's rougher side. Frost's mother exhibited courage by keeping the family and the household together during the San Francisco years, and by persisting in her independent attitude toward Frost's rather grim and hard-fisted grandfather when, after Frost's father's death at thirty-four in 1885, she returned with Robert and his younger sister to Lawrence. Her Scottish inheritance included a respect for learning and an aptitude for teaching, and she soon took charge of a district school in nearby Salem, New Hampshire. Here she put into practice her teaching methods—original for the time—seating her pupils according to their grades of excellence, giving them individual instruction, and getting them to commit to memory passages of poetry or prose which she read aloud. This harking back to an oral tradition—usual in a society where books are scarce—made a strong impression upon Frost, whose ear, as it turned out, was unusually true and accurate. Her dealings with her pupils were easy and natural; she was remembered singing children's ballads to the youngest, as she held them on her knee. Her religious interests were also marked; once a Unitarian, she later became interested in the mystical doctrines of Swedenborg.

Frost's devotion to his mother was complete; he willingly took on any small job that would "help out." He entered Lawrence High School—having been his mother's pupil up to that time—in the fall of 1888, at the age of fourteen. Here he acquired the rudiments of the old-fashioned classical education then prevalent in the New England public high schools. Latin, Greek, and ancient history were subjects in the curriculum, and he made good marks. It was now that he met Elinor Miriam White, the charming and tal-

ented daughter of a former Universalist minister, who was to share with young Frost the honor of being valedictorian on their graduation in June of 1892. By this time Frost had published poems in the school paper, and had made plans to go to Dartmouth on funds contributed by his grandmother.

From this point on, the progress of young Frost toward what he began to sense as his true interests—the interests of a poet and perhaps, on his own terms, an instructor of the young—ran into a series of obstacles. His stay at Dartmouth was brief. His interest in poetry was becoming more definitely centered as his reading broadened, and he was writing verse. But his creative enthusiasm was baffled, rather than aided, by academic routine. Moreover, he felt that his mother—who had opened a small school in Methuen, Massachusetts—needed him. He left Dartmouth without giving official notice, and spent the winter of 1893 giving his mother the help she needed in managing her sometimes recalcitrant pupils. Mill work claimed him during the following summer and winter. It was at this period that he sold his first poem—"My Butterfly"—to the *Independent*, then a leading weekly, and attracted the attention not only of its editor, William Hayes Ward, but of the editor's sister, Miss Susan Ward. Part of the correspondence between the youthful poet of twenty and this learned spinster has been preserved at the Huntington Library, and Frost's positive belief in his talent comes through clearly (". . . I have but recently discovered my powers"). Frost now turned his back on the mills, for good.

Meanwhile, the relationship between himself and Elinor White was undergoing rapid changes, not always fortunate ones from Frost's point of view. Miss White had become a student at St. Lawrence, a Universalist college in upper New York State. She was, therefore, except for summer visits home, out of direct communication with her young friend, whose devotion to her was constant. Moreover, Frost's inability to attach himself to any conventional way of making a living did not appeal to her family and her academic mentors. Frost, on a visit to St. Lawrence in the autumn of 1894, with a sheaf of privately printed poems in hand, felt himself to be severely rebuffed, and he reacted to this crucial disappointment by flight—to Maryland, Virginia, and North Carolina. His feeling of desperation at this time was to be recorded in a poem of his late maturity ("Kittyhawk 1894"), and he speaks of the "desperately absorbing experiences" of this journey in a letter to Miss Ward. This is the only break with a pattern of strict accountability to demands made upon him that the hard-pressed young poet allowed himself in these transitional years.

Matters then took a better turn. The *Independent* gave "My Butterfly" a prominent place in its issue of November 8, 1894, and he became engaged to Elinor White at the Christmas season. Elinor returned to college for her final year, and Frost occupied himself with tutoring, teaching, and a short spell of reporting for the Lawrence *Sentinel*. The young couple, after their marriage in December 1895, together took up teaching duties, again in Frost's mother's school, now situated in Lawrence.

The next five years were crowded ones. Frost's friendly relations with the Wards continued, and two other poems were published in the *Independent* in 1896 and 1897. The Frosts' first child, Eliot, was born in September 1896. And it was now that Frost made his second effort to enter college. The advantages of a college degree to a man whose talents and background seemed to fit him for a career as instructor to the young were evident; and Frost, after correspondence with Dean Briggs, entered Harvard in the fall of 1897. His grandfather paid his tuition, and Elinor Frost's mother took a house in Boston in order to make matters somewhat easier for the young family. As a freshman he "was too mature for [the required] English A and hated it." And, although he received high marks in the classics, in his sophomore year "nothing went well." In addition, his duties as a son, a husband, and a father proved to be overwhelming. "Harvard," he later wrote in the *Harvard Alumni Bulletin*, "had taken me away

from the question whether I could write or not." He resigned from the sophomore class at the end of March 1899. The next month his daughter Lesley was born.

A way of life which was to prove over a long period of time a background for some of his most remarkable work was about to become possible, but a double tragedy was to intervene: Frost's mother was stricken with cancer, and in July 1900, his little son Eliot died. Elinor Frost, in spite of her grief, made the sensible request of Frost's grandfather that he buy them a farm, which the young husband and wife had "found for themselves" in West Derry, New Hampshire— "thirty acres, rather run down and poor, but with orchard, fields, pasture, woodland and spring." "Shall I give you a year? Will you settle down if I give you a year to try this out?" his grandfather asked. "Give me twenty!" Frost replied, and, as he said later, "that is just what it took. . . ."

Frost's mother died in November 1900, soon after their move to the farm. She was fifty-six years old.

In 1900, when Frost and his family first settled in West Derry, it was not so difficult for a man to leave an industrial environment to seek out a subsistence living on a "one man, one horse" farm, as it would be today. But it was difficult enough, especially in New England, where the land was poor and where the native Yankee stock had lost much of its vigor through the losses of the Civil War, the trek to the West, and the flight to the cities of many of its more adventuresome sons. For Frost, the step was drastic. He was going, it is true, toward a way of life he believed, instinctively, to be his: toward true, old-fashioned values, outside— and opposed to—the period's ethos of competition and "success." And he was saving that poet's part of himself which he had believed in from earliest adolescence. He and his wife were putting a touching trust in what they must have sensed was ultimately an impossible way of making a living. To persist in their desires for a world of their own in which they could bring up children beyond the reach of mill-town blight and the interference of hard-fisted relatives took courage. This courage, and the idealism which existed at its center, proved to be the source of the most original, moving, and sincere poems of Frost's early work — very nearly all the poems in *A Boy's Will* and *North of Boston*, as well as much of *Mountain Interval*.

The farm, as it turned out, could not produce even a subsistence living for the Frosts. After six years, and the birth of four more children, one of whom died in earliest infancy, Frost turned once more to teaching, this time as a part-time teacher of English at the nearby Pinkerton Academy — "a good two-mile walk from the farm." His teaching methods were somewhat unorthodox, but his pupils remembered his genial informality, his "admirable" direction of certain Shakespeare plays, and his interest in botany and baseball. The family now began to spend their summers in Bethlehem, in the White Mountains, for reasons of Frost's health — "a high, free mountain world." In 1910, they moved from the farm nearer to the academy, and in the fall of 1911, to Plymouth, where Frost began to teach psychology and education at the state normal school.

The lyric poems later to be collected in Frost's first volume, *A Boy's Will* (1913), continued to be written; and Frost has said that as early as 1905 he had discovered a new dramatic vein which was to result in the blank-verse poems in *North of Boston* (1914). Early in 1912, the impulse to break away from teaching — at which he was having a good deal of success — and to prove or disprove his faith in himself as a writer, took hold. The farm was now his to sell, and he sold it. With its price in hand, along with a small allowance from his grandfather's estate, he bought steamer passage for himself, his wife, and his four small children — destination, England — and sailed, in the early autumn of 1912, at the age of thirty-eight, from Boston to a country where he knew no one.

Frost's departure for England coincided with two major publishing ventures, which heralded the beginnings of a new serious attitude toward poetry written in English. In October, Harriet Monroe, in Chicago, published the first number of *Poetry: A Magazine of Verse*, and in England in December, under the generous patronage of Edward Marsh, the first *Georgian Anthology* appeared. The Georgian group, whose admiration for the poetry of Thomas Hardy and Robert Bridges was marked, included, at the time, Walter de la Mare, John Masefield, W. H. Davies, and Rupert Brooke. And in London, The Poetry Bookshop, which was to become a center for poetic activity, had recently been opened by Harold Monro. Frost knew nothing of any of these developments upon his arrival in England. His first preoccupation was to find a country place where he and his family could settle and farm. On the advice of a writer of a country column in a newspaper, he found a first home in Beaconsfield, Bucks. He then set about finding a publisher, and here good luck played into his hands.[1] Late in 1912, he was able to arrange for the publication of *A Boy's Will* with the firm of David Nutt.

*A Boy's Will*, published in his thirty-ninth year, made an immediate impression upon those critics to whom it was sent for review, and Frost began to meet, and to know, many members of the Georgian circle. Among them was Edward Thomas, who at the time was struggling with the pressures of a journalist's career. Thomas, like Frost, was a lover of the countryside and an amateur botanist. At the beginning of their close friendship Thomas had never written a line of verse. Frost advised him to begin, telling him that he had been a poet all his life. Thomas, who had undergone periods of depression for many years, found in poetry a tremendous release, and he was a frequent visitor of the Frosts throughout their English stay.

Soon after *A Boy's Will* appeared, Frost met Ezra Pound. Pound's own career was beginning to expand into many areas. Already for some years established in London, with several books to his credit, the young

[1] Frost's publication in American magazines, through 1912, had been severely limited: several poems in the *Independent*, two in the *Youth's Companion*, and one in the *Forum*.

Pound was beginning to take on his role of instigator and innovator, and in 1913 was actively engaged in formulating rules for the Imagists — a "school" with more experimental aims and interests than those of the Georgians, and he had already appointed himself foreign advisor to Harriet Monroe. Pound's review of *A Boy's Will* appeared in *Poetry* in May 1913. Pound discovered, in Frost, a salutary attention paid to the truth, as well as compression and clarity of expression. "This man has the good sense to speak naturally and to paint the thing, the thing as he sees it." Another American poet was helping to clear away the falsity and fustian of Victorian verse.

Pound's friendship with Frost was short-lived; the young enthusiast soon found that his older compatriot was intent on going his own way. But Pound expressed his admiration for Frost's rendering of "the natural speech of New England" in a review of *North of Boston*, published in *Poetry* late in 1914 under the title "Modern Georgics." "Mr. Frost's work is the work of a man who will make neither concessions or pretenses . . . His book is a contribution to American literature."

*North of Boston*, published by David Nutt in April 1914, again impressed English reviewers. Edward Thomas, who was soon to die in the war, wrote of this collection of New England "eclogues":[2]

This is one of the most exciting books of modern times, but one of the quietest and least aggressive . . . These poems are revolutionary because they lack the exaggeration of rhetoric . . . Many, if not most, of the separate lines and separate sentences are plain, and, in themselves, nothing. But they are bound together and made elements of beauty by a calm eagerness of emotion . . . [The best poems in the book] are masterpieces of deep and mysterious tenderness.[3]

IT IS interesting to come upon a portrait of this man of thirty-eight in the reminiscences of his English friends, just as he is emerging from his years of obscurity and isolation. Frost had evidently reached a point of spiritual equilibrium by the time of the English journey. Eleanor Farjeon, a close friend of the Thomases, speaks in Book I of her memoirs[4] of Frost and his family after they had settled near Little Iddens, in Herefordshire, in beautiful orchard country. Here the Frosts were poor, and indifferent to the conditions of poverty. Frost had [evidently] always taken life as it came where he found it . . . Whatever he did he made worth doing . . . His manner was friendly and undemonstrative. He looked at you directly; his talk was shrewd and speculative, withholding nothing and derived from nobody but himself. His New England speech came readily and leisurely, and of all the writers of worth I had met, he spoke with the least sophistication. [He was] unhurried in all he said and did. The Frosts did not live by the clock . . . their center was out-of-doors. Meals were taken at odd hours. And when there were visitors, talk and the reading of poetry went on far into the night, by candlelight, in the home the poet and his wife had made of "a labourer's cottage standing in a rough plot of ground planted chiefly with potatoes."

The difficulties brought on by the outbreak of the war in August 1914, proved insuperable, and the Frosts returned to America in February 1915. An American publisher, Henry Holt & Company, had already brought out a small edition (150 copies) of *North of Boston* from imported English sheets; the first "strictly American" edition of it and of *A Boy's Will* appeared in March 1915. Frost now experienced his first taste of success. At forty-one, he emerged from almost total obscurity into best-seller status, thus receiving from his new audience the kind of encouragement which proved, in his case, to be the source of fresh energy. The scars of his difficult youth and young manhood were still there, but, as it turned out, these were not irremediable. They became, in fact, impor-

---

[2]eclogue: a short pastoral poem, usually a dialogue.
[3]The London *Daily News* and the *English Review* (August 1914, unsigned review).

[4]Eleanor Farjeon, *Edward Thomas: The Last Years* (Oxford, 1958).

tant and available parts of his richly creative nature, which was to remain vigorous for many decades to come.

And Frost did not disappoint his audience. He began to publish regularly and at length. *Mountain Interval* appeared in 1916, and *New Hampshire* in 1923. Both volumes were filled with a variety of interesting and original work, although neither approached *North of Boston* in power of dramatic concept or depth of tragic implication. *New Hampshire* marked a revival, and even extension, of the poet's early lyricism. And the long title poem signaled the beginning of a new Frostian manner: the direct and open assumption of the role of shrewd Yankee sage; the translation of aphoristic Yankee wit and the charm of the born talker into poetic terms. This role, this manner, was to become, over the years, a perhaps too insistent one, but on its first appearance it was delightful.

Frost did not alter his way of living; he kept to the simple pattern of his early days. Having bought a farm near Franconia, he continued to live, if not as a farmer, at least as a thoroughly non-urban citizen. Soon he began to lecture and to teach; his connection with Amherst College dates back to 1917. He remained faithful to his native bent and worked, as far as possible, on his own terms. As the years drew him more and more into the circle of academic life, he continued to talk more than he wrote, and kept his published prose to a minimum. He left it to his listeners — some of whom were his warmest disciples — to take notes on his discourses, formal and informal; even the Charles Eliot Norton lectures which he delivered at Harvard in 1936 were never published. In this way, with an instinctive regard for both his gifts and his limitations, he recreated, in fairly unfavorable circumstances, the ancient oral tradition of the bard, as well as the refreshing legend of the "dry" Yankee sage.

Close critical examination of Frost's work has been slow to appear; only during the last decade do we find any sustained attempts at detached appraisal in appreciable quantity, as distinguished from the fulsome praise which certain colleagues and fellow poets have lavished on Frost, the man and the poet, since his work began to be known. Several factors explain this critical lag. In the first place, Frost, in a period of extreme experimentation with form, continued to write conventionally, and in a manner which presented to the reader no prosodic difficulty of any kind. Again, Frost's poetry, at a time when symbol and myth had become important carriers of meaning, was allusive only in a restricted way; it offered few leads into elaborate subtlety; it did not encourage "close" reading or fine-drawn explication. It stood outside those currents of avantgarde poetic theory which restlessly absorbed diverse ideas from many adjacent fields — those of anthropology, medical psychology, history, and religion. Finally, Frost's popularity with a large audience — a popularity, it is true, based on a very limited selection of his work — rendered the quality of his appeal suspect to those who believed with Edwin Muir "that the imaginative writer today can be widely popular only by writing falsely."

Frost's diction has none of the "richness and virtuosity" characteristic of modern writing at large. But Frost's very limitation of means often leads the reader into the poet's most striking effects, and an inspection of his general poetic practice brings to light a very real power and control over language which is one basis of his incontestable originality. His mastery of formal poetics is remarkable from first to last; he is a trained and meticulous craftsman. His lyric style is flexible, musical, and completely natural. His form, moreover, is remarkably varied and never seems in any way to have been cut to fit the emotion. Each poem, from short lyric to longer dramatic blank verse, has its own "given" form, and the authenticity of the poet's gift is everywhere apparent.

Frost has put down, in "The Figure a Poem Makes," one of the most interesting and intelligible summations ever made by a poet of the genesis and progress of poetic composition. He describes the poet's ready passivity, open to the initial subconscious impulse, which must be undeviatingly followed and only lightly controlled at the outset by conscious ways and means. It is clear that Frost served a long technical apprenticeship. Actual influences, however, even in his early work, are difficult to trace. He had read and admired Edward Arlington Robinson's *The Town Down the River* (1908), and his Introduction to Robinson's *King Jasper* (1935) clearly shows his admiration for the work of the older man. Robinson, born in Maine in 1869, belonged to the cultivated New England town tradition (which had produced Emily Dickinson)—a tradition which had begun to dissolve and decay during his youth. His attitude toward this dissolution—of standards and manners as well as material prosperity—was not entirely nostalgic. Robinson possessed an honest and unerring eye, and a talent for the "simple accuracy" that he admired in George Crabbe. He described his townsmen—particularly the failures, misfits, and outcasts produced by a society in transition—in sharp and tragic detail, and with insight, and he everywhere avoided the soft blur of outworn poetic terms. He turned toward the rhythm of the spoken idiom of his time and place— "Mr. Flood's Party," a favorite poem of Frost's, keeps closely to the turns of native speech.

But there is a great difference between Robinson's occasional approximation of the colloquial and Frost's final success in fitting the "cadences" of common speech to a regular verse pattern, perhaps his central contribution to modern poetic procedures. Poets contemporary with, or slightly older than Frost—among them Swinburne, Kipling, and Robert Bridges—had tried to vary the rhythms of English verse,[5] finding "the old, dull iambic Wordsworthian measures" tedious. Masefield, reviving the Chaucerian couplet with much success, had dealt boldly with the rough diction of the English working class.[6] Frost had evidently tried out one method after another (he has said that he tried to write "The Black Cottage" in rhymed couplets while at Dartmouth). "We must write with the ear on the speaking voice," he later remarked. To that end he

had worked in complete separation from the feeble and genteel American literary tendencies of his time, in the ten years from 1902 to 1912. His choice of blank verse proved to be exactly right for his special purposes. Through this unrhymed five-beat iambic line—which, since the sixteenth century, had been established as the most workable long carrying-line in English—the American poet was given a measure of freedom. The New England manner of speech—at once laconic and meandering—could be caught into this pattern without distortion and with completely natural emphasis. Frost had, indeed, instinctively put into practice an Imagist tenet ("the natural words in the natural order") before that tenet was formulated (around 1913) by the Imagists themselves.

Certainly, at the time, a new, direct, and truth-telling attitude toward reality, as well as a complete refreshment of poetic diction and use of form in poetry was in order. The Romantic tradition, which had begun with Blake and ended with Keats, had become threadbare. The Romantic poets had made a conscious effort toward simplicity and clarity of expression; at the same time, their belief in the power of the imagination had enabled them successfully to describe strong and complex emotions. The Victorian era was one of uneasy compromise. The Victorian audience—largely unenlightened aesthetically and unsure of its moral values—began to demand from poets, and from artists in general, reassurance and consolation; and even Tennyson and Browning partially acceded to this demand. By the end of the nineteenth century, English poetry had become feeble and monotonously minor. The opening stanza of "By the Statue of King Charles at Charing Cross" by Lionel Johnson (1867–1902) illustrates one prevalent style:

> Sombre and rich, the skies,
> Great glooms, and starry plains;
> Gently the nightwind sighs;
> Else a vast silence reigns.

Here, the inflated emotion has drawn to itself language equally false. It was against such

[5]See Swinburne's "A Forsaken Garden," Kipling's "The Law of the Jungle," and Bridges' "London Snow."    [6]In *The Everlasting Mercy* (1911) and *The Widow in the Bye Street* (1912).

falsity that the best of the Georgians, together with the small but highly intelligent and articulate group of Imagists—with several Americans in their number—had begun their revolt. Frost, working in America in provincial isolation with little but his instinct for sincerity and a sensitive eye and ear to guide him, had already succeeded in clarifying language and intensifying form.

It is difficult to speak of Frost's first two books with detachment. The harshness, bafflements, loneliness, and grief of his childhood and adolescence here have been made to surrender their meaning at the same time that the tragic aspects of a neglected countryside have been absorbed and recreated by an eager young sensibility. The tone, though often tender, is never romantic. C. Day Lewis speaks of Frost's preoccupation with "hard fact": "no working farmer is romantic—not about nature, at any rate."[7] And W. H. Auden has written: "[Frost's] qualities of irony and understatement, his distrust of fine writing, are those of the practical man. His poems on natural objects . . . are always concerned with them not as *foci* for mystical meditation, but as things with which and on which man acts in the course of his daily gaining of a livelihood."[8] And both Day Lewis and Auden speak of the quality of "good gossip" which the blank-verse poems often take on. "[These] anecdotes," says Day Lewis, "are told in a discursive, racy, countryfied way, which may cause us to overlook their psychological penetration, the technical skill of their verse . . . and the economy of means behind their apparent ranginess." And he then singles out for special praise the poems "where Frost broods and comments on familiar country things, imperceptibly weaving a pattern, catching a truth in it almost absent-mindedly, like a conjurer reaching down a penny out of the air."

The dramatic monologue of Browning—which was to undergo a vigorous rehandling in the work of more than one of Frost's contemporaries, notably Pound and T. S. Eliot—reappears in this most unpretentious of

settings; and Frost's dialogues and monologues often resolve into talk so disarmingly natural that it seems to be overheard. This simplicity is by no means naïve; it involves a highly trained ear as well as the utmost probity of choice. "The Pasture," the lyric which served as an epigraph to *North of Boston*, written with a controlled and distilled simplicity, is a love song, among other things—surely one of the loveliest in the language.

As has been pointed out, Frost's power of close and accurate description in which all the senses are involved at times approaches clairvoyance. The early books, like many of the later ones, are scattered through with details from the natural scene: things seen, heard, caught in motion, breathed in, touched. "The slow wheel that pours the sand"; the blue berries of the woodbine and its "littered leaves"; the leaves of the hardwood grove that "fit the earth like a leather glove"; the brook's "slender tinkling fall"; the "tattered and swift" line-storm clouds; the "thawing wind" that invades the house —these are things brought into focus by flashes of piercing vision.

In the West Derry years Frost came to take pleasure in—and derive courage from—the varied patterns of character in people whose circumscribed way of life was becoming increasingly difficult to maintain. This isolation was often burdensome to a crippling degree, but they were on their own, and managing in some way to survive. Far from being "an isolated, brutish and taciturn peasantry," these New England farmers were, on the whole, gentle, high-minded, and articulate. Frost presents a range of their emotions, often in first-person narratives, from the normal, sympathetic, and humane— "The Black Cottage," "The Death of the Hired Man"—through degrees of comedy —"A Hundred Collars," "Blueberries"—to hatred, terror, and incipient madness—"The Housekeeper," "The Fear," "A Servant to Servants." Both "The Fear" and "Home Burial" describe extreme states of panic, guilt, and obsessive grief with clinical exactness.

Frost continued to explore, through several books, the possibilities of his blank

---

[7]C. Day Lewis, Introduction to *Selected Poems of Robert Frost* Penguin, 1955).   [8]*Recognition of Robert Frost*, ed. by Richard Thornton (1937).

verse, although the later short dramatic vignettes are less grim in subject and tone than those in *North of Boston*. Two narratives, "The Witch of Coös" and "The Pauper Witch of Grafton" (which appeared in *New Hampshire* in 1923 under the covering title of "Two Witches") mark a high point in Frost's use of the form. In both, the mania of extreme old age is described with the utmost insight into, and sympathy with, woman's nature and character beset by time. As Day Lewis points out, "The Witch of Coös," "all the more sinister for the homeliness and disturbing visual precision of its similes" (the skeleton mounts the stairs "like a pile of dishes"), is projected—in spite of its grisly detail—in a delicately established tone of high comedy. "The Pauper Witch of Grafton," a recreation of a love story in the most fantastic terms, ends upon a note of true pathos, with a passage which is one of the most memorable in Frost.

Frost's early relations with the machine and with man as a machine-tender left an indelible mark on his character, and understandably so. The relation of young people to the New England textile mills was a difficult and crucial one. Children went into the mills and, very often, remained in them throughout their lifetimes. Sarah Cleghorn's famous quatrain (1919),

> The golf links lie so near the mill
>     That almost every day
> The laboring children can look out
>     And see the men at play,

records a fact that Frost, who was later to write the Preface to Miss Cleghorn's *Threescore: An Autobiography* (1936), could verify in his own experience. The adult uneducated artisan, too, was trapped into long hours at a mechanical round, under the crudest of labor conditions. Not until the Lawrence strike of 1909 were these conditions brought into general notice.

Frost's experience implanted in him not only a dislike of supervised mechanical tasks, but a nightmare image of the machine as menace—an object to be viewed with fear and dread. The locomotive, the buzz saw, even the stones of the primitive grist mill, be-

come, as it were, centers of evil force which override, kill, and maim ("Out, Out—," "The Self-Seeker," "The Vanishing Red"). "The Lone Striker" is the single poem which brings a textile mill into sight (with certain of its processes meticulously described)—but then only as a trap which the young man in the poem must escape from at all costs. Frost is never concerned (as many poets and men of letters have shown themselves to be since the beginning of the industrial revolution) with the blighting results of industry upon human beings in general. His is a personal feud, with the machine as adversary. "The Egg and the Machine," for example, which presents a singularly inept one-to-one encounter between a man and a locomotive headlight, occurs fairly late—in *West-Running Brook* (1928). And the long poem "New Hampshire," while it lists many of that state's charming and diversified features, omits all mention of its mills and factories, which had flourished in numbers along its principal rivers for decades.

A central criticism brought to bear on Frost's middle and later work is pointed toward such omissions of ugly fact from the New England scene. Do these omissions constitute actual evasions; is Frost, at times, involved in the propagation of a kind of false pastoral? The scene to which he had become emotionally committed from youth on—the background of small town, village, and isolated farms beyond the village—was, in fact, changing with great rapidity during his mature years. The railroads and the telegraph poles had already penetrated deeply into rural areas in the time of Thoreau, whose attitude toward both was not completely hostile. But with the appearance of the automobile and the telephone, the older concepts of speed and communication were drastically altered. Certain features of the countryside and of local custom were gone for good; the tractor was soon to supersede the plow. And certain appurtenances and tools of the older way of living suddenly became completely obsolete. At the same time, a deeply felt nostalgia for a vanished way of rural existence began to manifest itself in a generation that had experienced the transition. It cannot truly be said of Frost that he catered to this nostalgia. His material was his by virtue of hard-won experience. His meticulous attention to his own craft was closely linked with the handcraftsman's love of method and material, so tellingly described in "The Axe-Helve." If a large proportion of his readers preferred to separate out from his work those poems which satisfied their yearning for some version of a lost American Golden Age, the fault was theirs.

It is true that Frost's conservatism—a natural trait in those who live on the land "closely bound to the wheel of the seasons"—became more marked with the passage of the years. Although many of his admirers wished to think of him as "ordinary" to the core, Frost's nature, of course, was complicated in the extreme. As a poet, he was a man of strong feelings, and strong feelings are bound to include resentments. A relapse into small-mindedness is, however, a danger lying in wait for any artist of a conservative cast of mind. Statements come to be built not only on emotional conviction, but on hidden prejudice as well. Ill-tempered disputation is then in order, together with a wrong-headed pleasure in holding "notions." The detachment of the artist disappears; the work begins to be in favor of this or that small conception or opinion; the thought becomes whimsical; ideas are no longer large and centered. Emerson and Thoreau, local exemplars from whom Frost learned much, do not coerce the reader. They express themselves with deliberate casualness. This is the philosopher's, and the poet's, way—a way which rises above pettiness and irritability. Any other must lead toward constriction of vision and asperity of tone.

The fact that Frost's more sharply edged comments on national affairs and the state of the world began to appear in years of economic depression brought against him the charge of callousness. Many of the poems written in these crucial years are bitterly opposed to the main tenets of the liberal thought of the time—particularly to collective action, of which even the extreme individualist, Thoreau, approved. Frost's confidence that the terrors of his time could be adequately dealt with by processes of will and determination alone, his lack of flexibility toward the shifts and changes of modern life and society were certainly limiting, especially in view of the efforts made by many of his contemporaries—Yeats, Pound, Eliot and, later, Auden—not only to understand but to remedy, restore, and repair. The fact that Frost was able to hold to his convictions in a period of great confusion of values testifies to a central force of character that he was never in any danger of losing. But now for the first time in Frost's work, nature appears as a refuge to which man must retreat, rather than as a natural environment which man may freely choose as his own. Frost begins to repeat injunctions to stand fast, ward off, dig in, take care.

The three later books, *A Further Range* (1936), *A Witness Tree* (1942), and *Steeplebush* (1947), were not, however, consistently given over to preachments concerning the paths mankind should follow or the policies the nation should adopt. Quick wit, apt comment and true lyricism are present in all three, together with a continuing insight into human motives. There are traces, too, of a new melancholy—"The Wind and the Rain" and "Come In"—as well as a new tenderness—"The Silken Tent." Frost had undergone tragedy and loss in these years (Mrs. Frost had died in 1938 and his son Carol in 1940); and they marked his passage into old age. His limitations and self-limitations were now fixed and, in all probability, were to remain unchanged: his tendency, when forced into a tight corner, to lapse into the ambiguous parable; his occasional narrowing of perspective; his inability to establish "a hierarchy of values." In Frost's late career, the evidence increasingly showed there would be no shocking confrontations, as in the later Yeats, and no profound spiritual insights, as in the case of Eliot. On the other hand, with his own weapons, the old poet was still capable not only of standing his ground, but of dealing some wicked blows. His will remained indomitable. If he consistently clung to the middle regions of mild faith and to a middle tone—which ruled out the noble, "lofty," and transcendent manner—he did not slip back into any false romanticism of style or attitude; and he continued to avoid the plaintive, the inflated, and the confused.

The tensions, dark conflicts, and passionate involvements which must inform poetry at any level—and had been evident in Frost's from the beginning—in the later Frost were by no means entirely suppressed. When allowed to come through, they pervade certain poems with almost nightmare intensity. The strangely projected pathos of "The Lovely Shall be Choosers" (a poem in memory of his mother); the suggestions of planned evil in "Design"; the thwarted and maimed human passions described with the utmost compression and subtlety in "The Subverted Flower" and "The Discovery of the Madeiras"—these are unforgettable examples of the imagination working in deep psychic regions. Recurrent moments of anguish and spiritual doubt and alienation in the later work, as in the earlier, are indicative, as one of Frost's more perceptive critics has pointed out, of "Frost's capacity for a kind of power frequently ignored or underestimated by his admirers." It is a power springing from the poet's close relation to the untouched, the wild and the primordial: to nature's pure but terrifying springs; to unobstructed height and depth; to snow, stars, darkness, and storm. And Frost has often been able to describe in unflinching terms the precarious balance in man, as in nature—the always imperfect resolution of conflicts in the human heart and mind. That this power and insight have persisted proves Frost extraordinary, in spite of his basic countryman's caution and his frequent shrewd assumption of the mask of "the ordinary man."

But, although Frost in age maintained his creative energy past the crucial point where many poets decline into repetition or subside into silence, he failed to achieve that last extension and renovation of thought and emotion—that masterful ordering of ex-

perience—which we constantly find in the later poems of Yeats, up to the time of his death in 1939, and in Eliot's *Four Quartets* (1935–43). Frost's *A Masque of Reason* (1945) and *A Masque of Mercy* (1947) seem extremely light in weight compared to these.

Frost's apotheosis in his middle eighties—his final emergence as an ideal manifestation of American character as well as American poetic genius—resulted, on the whole, in a happy and beneficent relation between the poet and the population at large. His honors—literary, academic, and, finally, national—were evidently a source of pleasurable satisfaction to the man who had experienced obscurity over a singularly extended period of time. The honorary degrees conferred by Oxford and Cambridge Universities in 1957 brought him back to England, where he had first met positive encouragement and warm literary friendships. Resolutions of the United States Senate on his seventy-sixth (1950)[9] and eighty-fifth (1959) birthdays, conferred on him a kind of unofficial poet-laureateship, and this standing was accented and reinforced by the invitation extended by John F. Kennedy when newly elected to the presidency in 1960, that Frost read one of his poems at the inaugural ceremony. Frost responded by writing "Dedication: For John F. Kennedy His Inauguration," which, on the occasion itself, merciless winter sunlight prevented him from reading. He then, quite unperturbed, proceeded to recite "The Gift Outright" (from *A Witness Tree*) by heart.

*A Witness Tree* (1942) takes its title from trees "blazed" by early surveyors of the American wilderness to mark the corner of each square mile. As Edwin Way Teale explains, "When the bark that has grown over these scars is pried off, its inner side reveals, in a perfect negative, the scratches of the code-marks put there a century before." It is understandable why this symbol was chosen by an elder Frost—poet by gift, countryman by nature, and frequent explorer of the wilderness by choice.

[9]The year 1874 was established as his correct birth date after this time.

# THE PASTURE

◊

⟨[ "The Pasture" first appeared as a kind of invitation, or foreword, to Frost's second book, *North of Boston* (London, 1914; New York, 1915). In *Collected Poems*, 1939, and in *Complete Poems of Robert Frost*, 1949, the poem assumes this function for all of Frost's verse.

◊

I'm going out to clean the pasture spring;
I'll only stop to rake the leaves away
(And wait to watch the water clear, I may):
I sha'n't be gone long.—You come too.

I'm going out to fetch the little calf
That's standing by the mother. It's so young
It totters when she licks it with her tongue.
I sha'n't be gone long.—You come too.

## OCTOBER

O hushed October morning mild,
Thy leaves have ripened to the fall;
Tomorrow's wind, if it be wild,
Should waste them all.
The crows above the forest call;
Tomorrow they may form and go.
O hushed October morning mild,
Begin the hours of this day slow.
Make the day seem to us less brief.
Hearts not averse to being beguiled,          10
Beguile us in the way you know.
Release one leaf at break of day;
At noon release another leaf;
One from our trees, one far away.
Retard the sun with gentle mist;
Enchant the land with amethyst.
Slow, slow!
For the grapes' sake, if they were all,
Whose leaves already are burnt with frost,
Whose clustered fruit must else be lost—      20
For the grapes' sake along the wall.

FROM

# A BOY'S WILL [1913]

## IN HARDWOOD GROVES

The same leaves over and over again!
They fall from giving shade above
To make one texture of faded brown
And fit the earth like a leather glove.

Before the leaves can mount again
To fill the trees with another shade,
They must go down past things coming up.
They must go down into the dark decayed.

They *must* be pierced by flowers and put
Beneath the feet of dancing flowers.          10
However it is in some other world
I know that this is the way in ours.

FROM

# NORTH OF BOSTON [1914]

## THE BLACK COTTAGE

We chanced in passing by that afternoon
To catch it in a sort of special picture
Among tar-banded ancient cherry trees,
Set well back from the road in rank lodged grass,
The little cottage we were speaking of,
A front with just a door between two windows,
Fresh painted by the shower a velvet black.
We paused, the minister and I, to look.
He made as if to hold it at arm's length
Or put the leaves aside that framed it in.      10
'Pretty,' he said. 'Come in. No one will care.'
The path was a vague parting in the grass
That led us to a weathered window-sill.
We pressed our faces to the pane. 'You see,' he said,
'Everything's as she left it when she died.
Her sons won't sell the house or the things in it.

They say they mean to come and summer here
Where they were boys. They haven't come this
    year.
They live so far away—one is out west—
It will be hard for them to keep their word.    20
Anyway they won't have the place disturbed.'
A buttoned hair-cloth lounge spread scrolling
    arms
Under a crayon portrait on the wall,
Done sadly from an old daguerreotype.
'That was the father as he went to war.
She always, when she talked about the war,
Sooner or later came and leaned, half knelt
Against the lounge beside it, though I doubt
If such unlifelike lines kept power to stir
Anything in her after all the years.    30
He fell at Gettysburg or Fredericksburg,
I ought to know—it makes a difference which:
Fredericksburg wasn't Gettysburg, of course.
But what I'm getting to is how forsaken
A little cottage this has always seemed;
Since she went more than ever, but before—
I don't mean altogether by the lives
That had gone out of it, the father first,
Then the two sons, till she was left alone.
(Nothing could draw her after those two sons.  40
She valued the considerate neglect
She had at some cost taught them after years.)
I mean by the world's having passed it by—
As we almost got by this afternoon.
It always seems to me a sort of mark
To measure how far fifty years have brought us.
Why not sit down if you are in no haste?
These doorsteps seldom have a visitor.
The warping boards pull out their own old nails
With none to tread and put them in their
    place.    50
She had her own idea of things, the old lady.
And she liked talk. She had seen Garrison
And Whittier, and had her story of them.
One wasn't long in learning that she thought
Whatever else the Civil War was for,
It wasn't just to keep the States together,
Nor just to free the slaves, though it did both.
She wouldn't have believed those ends enough
To have given outright for them all she gave.
Her giving somehow touched the principle    60
That all men are created free and equal.
And to hear her quaint phrases—so removed
From the world's view today of all those things.
That's a hard mystery of Jefferson's.
What did he mean? Of course the easy way
Is to decide it simply isn't true.
It may not be. I heard a fellow say so.
But never mind, the Welshman got it planted
Where it will trouble us a thousand years.

Each age will have to reconsider it.    70
You couldn't tell her what the West was saying,
And what the South to her serene belief.
She had some art of hearing and yet not
Hearing the latter wisdom of the world.
White was the only race she ever knew.
Black she had scarcely seen, and yellow never.
But how could they be made so very unlike
By the same hand working in the same stuff?
She had supposed the war decided that.
What are you going to do with such a person?  80
Strange how such innocence gets its own way.
I shouldn't be surprised if in this world
It were the force that would at last prevail.
Do you know but for her there was a time
When to please younger members of the church,
Or rather say non-members in the church,
Whom we all have to think of nowadays,
I would have changed the Creed a very little?
Not that she ever had to ask me not to;
It never got so far as that; but the bare
    thought    90
Of her old tremulous bonnet in the pew,
And of her half asleep was too much for me.
Why, I might wake her up and startle her.
It was the words "descended into Hades"
That seemed too pagan to our liberal youth.
You know they suffered from a general onslaught.
And well, if they weren't true why keep right on
Saying them like the heathen? We could drop
    them.
Only—there was the bonnet in the pew.
Such a phrase couldn't have meant much to
    her.    100
But suppose she had missed it from the Creed
As a child misses the unsaid Good-night,
And falls asleep with heartache—how should *I*
    feel?
I'm just as glad she made me keep hands off,
For, dear me, why abandon a belief
Merely because it ceases to be true.
Cling to it long enough, and not a doubt
It will turn true again, for so it goes.
Most of the change we think we see in life
Is due to truths being in and out of favor.    110
As I sit here, and oftentimes, I wish
I could be monarch of a desert land
I could devote and dedicate forever
To the truths we keep coming back and back to.
So desert it would have to be, so walled
By mountain ranges half in summer snow,
No one would covet it or think it worth
The pains of conquering to force change on.
Scattered oases where men dwelt, but mostly
Sand dunes held loosely in tamarisk    120
Blown over and over themselves in idleness.

Sand grains should sugar in the natal dew
The babe born to the desert, the sand storm
Retard mid-waste my cowering caravans—
There are bees in this wall.' He struck the clap-
    boards,
Fierce heads looked out; small bodies pivoted.
We rose to go. Sunset blazed on the windows.

### AFTER APPLE-PICKING

My long two-pointed ladder's sticking through a
    tree
Toward heaven still,
And there's a barrel that I didn't fill
Beside it, and there may be two or three
Apples I didn't pick upon some bough.
But I am done with apple-picking now.
Essence of winter sleep is on the night,
The scent of apples: I am drowsing off.
I cannot rub the strangeness from my sight
I got from looking through a pane of glass          10
I skimmed this morning from the drinking trough
And held against the world of hoary grass.
It melted, and I let it fall and break.
But I was well
Upon my way to sleep before it fell,
And I could tell
What form my dreaming was about to take.
Magnified apples appear and disappear,
Stem end and blossom end,
And every fleck of russet showing clear.          20
My instep arch not only keeps the ache,
It keeps the pressure of a ladder-round.
I feel the ladder sway as the boughs bend.
And I keep hearing from the cellar bin
The rumbling sound
Of load on load of apples coming in.
For I have had too much
Of apple-picking: I am overtired
Of the great harvest I myself desired.
There were ten thousand thousand fruit to
    touch,                                         30
Cherish in hand, lift down, and not let fall.
For all
That struck the earth,
No matter if not bruised or spiked with stubble,
Went surely to the cider-apple heap
As of no worth.
One can see what will trouble
This sleep of mine, whatever sleep it is.
Were he not gone,
The woodchuck could say whether it's like his   40
Long sleep, as I describe its coming on,
Or just some human sleep.

# MOUNTAIN INTERVAL
## [1916]

### AN OLD MAN'S WINTER NIGHT

All out-of-doors looked darkly in at him
Through the thin frost, almost in separate stars,
That gathers on the pane in empty rooms.
What kept his eyes from giving back the gaze
Was the lamp tilted near them in his hand.
What kept him from remembering what it was
That brought him to that creaking room was age.
He stood with barrels round him—at a loss.
And having scared the cellar under him
In clomping here, he scared it once again          10
In clomping off;—and scared the outer night,
Which has its sounds, familiar, like the roar
Of trees and crack of branches, common things,
But nothing so like beating on a box.
A light he was to no one but himself
Where now he sat, concerned with he knew what,
A quiet light, and then not even that.
He consigned to the moon, such as she was,
So late-arising, to the broken moon
As better than the sun in any case                 20
For such a charge, his snow upon the roof,
His icicles along the wall to keep;
And slept. The log that shifted with a jolt
Once in the stove, disturbed him and he shifted,
And eased his heavy breathing, but still slept.
One aged man—one man—can't keep a house,
A farm, a countryside, or if he can,
It's thus he does it of a winter night.

### THE GUM-GATHERER

There overtook me and drew me in
To his down-hill, early-morning stride,
And set me five miles on my road
Better than if he had had me ride,
A man with a swinging bag for load
And half the bag wound round his hand.
We talked like barking above the din
Of water we walked along beside.
And for my telling him where I'd been
And where I lived in mountain land                 10
To be coming home the way I was,
He told me a little about himself.
He came from higher up in the pass

Where the grist of the new-beginning brooks
Is blocks split off the mountain mass—
And hopeless grist enough it looks
Ever to grind to soil for grass.
(The way it is will do for moss.)
There he had built his stolen shack.
It had to be a stolen shack          20
Because of the fears of fire and loss
That trouble the sleep of lumber folk:
Visions of half the world burned black
And the sun shrunken yellow in smoke.
We know who when they come to town
Bring berries under the wagon seat,
Or a basket of eggs between their feet;
What this man brought in a cotton sack
Was gum, the gum of the mountain spruce.
He showed me lumps of the scented stuff    30
Like uncut jewels, dull and rough.
It comes to market golden brown;
But turns to pink between the teeth.

I told him this is a pleasant life
To set your breast to the bark of trees
That all your days are dim beneath,
And reaching up with a little knife,
To loose the resin and take it down
And bring it to market when you please.


## THE SOUND OF TREES

I wonder about the trees.
Why do we wish to bear
Forever the noise of these
More than another noise
So close to our dwelling place?
We suffer them by the day
Till we lose all measure of pace,
And fixity in our joys,
And acquire a listening air.
They are that that talks of going      10
But never gets away;
And that talks no less for knowing,
As it grows wiser and older,
That now it means to stay.
My feet tug at the floor
And my head sways to my shoulder
Sometimes when I watch trees sway,
From the window or the door.
I shall set forth for somewhere,
I shall make the reckless choice      20
Some day when they are in voice
And tossing so as to scare
The white clouds over them on.
I shall have less to say,
But I shall be gone.

FROM

# NEW HAMPSHIRE [1923]

## TWO WITCHES

## II

THE PAUPER WITCH OF GRAFTON

Now that they've got it settled whose I be,
I'm going to tell them something they won't like:
They've got it settled wrong, and I can prove it.
Flattered I must be to have two towns fighting
To make a present of me to each other.
They don't dispose me, either one of them,
To spare them any trouble. Double trouble's
Always the witch's motto anyway.
I'll double theirs for both of them—you watch me.
They'll find they've got the whole thing to do
    over,                      10
That is, if facts is what they want to go by.
They set a lot (now don't they?) by a record
Of Arthur Amy's having once been up
For Hog Reeve in March Meeting here in Warren.
I could have told them any time this twelvemonth
The Arthur Amy I was married to
Couldn't have been the one they say was up
In Warren at March Meeting for the reason
He wa'n't but fifteen at the time they say.
The Arthur Amy I was married to       20
Voted the only times he ever voted,
Which wasn't many, in the town of Wentworth.
One of the times was when 'twas in the warrant
To see if the town wanted to take over
The tote road to our clearing where we lived.
I'll tell you who'd remember—Heman Lapish.
Their Arthur Amy was the father of mine.
So now they've dragged it through the law courts
    once
I guess they'd better drag it through again.
Wentworth and Warren's both good towns to
    live in,                  30
Only I happen to prefer to live
In Wentworth from now on; and when all's said,
Right's right, and the temptation to do right
When I can hurt someone by doing it
Has always been too much for me, it has.
I know of some folks that'd be set up
At having in their town a noted witch:
But most would have to think of the expense
That even I would be. They ought to know
That as a witch I'd often milk a bat      40
And that'd be enough to last for days.
It'd make my position stronger, think,

If I was to consent to give some sign
To make it surer that I was a witch?
It wa'n't no sign, I s'pose, when Mallice Huse
Said that I took him out in his old age
And rode all over everything on him
Until I'd had him worn to skin and bones,
And if I'd left him hitched and unblanketed
In front of one Town Hall, I'd left him hitched  50
In front of every one in Grafton County.
Some cried shame on me not to blanket him,
The poor old man. It would have been all right
If someone hadn't said to gnaw the posts
He stood beside and leave his trade mark on them,
So they could recognize them. Not a post
That they could hear tell of was scarified.
They made him keep on gnawing till he whined.
Then that same smarty someone said to look—
He'd bet Huse was a cribber and had gnawed  60
The crib he slept in—and as sure's you're born
They found he'd gnawed the four posts of his bed,
All four of them to splinters. What did that prove?
Not that he hadn't gnawed the hitching posts
He said he had besides. Because a horse
Gnaws in the stable ain't no proof to me
He don't gnaw trees and posts and fences too.
But everybody took it for a proof.
I was a strapping girl of twenty then.
The smarty someone who spoiled everything  70
Was Arthur Amy. You know who he was.
That was the way he started courting me.
He never said much after we were married,
But I mistrusted he was none too proud
Of having interfered in the Huse business.
I guess he found he got more out of me
By having me a witch. Or something happened
To turn him round. He got to saying things
To undo what he'd done and make it right,
Like, 'No, she ain't come back from kiting yet.  80
Last night was one of her nights out. She's kiting.
She thinks when the wind makes a night of it
She might as well herself.' But he liked best
To let on he was plagued to death with me:
If anyone had seen me coming home
Over the ridgepole, 'stride of a broomstick,
As often as he had in the tail of the night,
He guessed they'd know what he had to put up
    with.
Well, I showed Arthur Amy signs enough
Off from the house as far as we could keep  90
And from barn smells you can't wash out of
    plowed ground
With all the rain and snow of seven years;
And I don't mean just skulls of Rogers' Rangers
On Moosilauke, but woman signs to man,
Only bewitched so I would last him longer.
Up where the trees grow short, the mosses tall,

I made him gather me wet snow berries
On slippery rocks beside a waterfall.
I made him do it for me in the dark.
And he liked everything I made him do.  100
I hope if he is where he sees me now
He's so far off he can't see what I've come to.
You *can* come down from everything to nothing.
All is, if I'd a-known when I was young
And full of it, that this would be the end,
It doesn't seem as if I'd had the courage
To make so free and kick up in folks' faces.
I might have, but it doesn't seem as if.

## STOPPING BY WOODS ON A SNOWY EVENING

Whose woods these are I think I know.
His house is in the village though;
He will not see me stopping here
To watch his woods fill up with snow.

My little horse must think it queer
To stop without a farmhouse near
Between the woods and frozen lake
The darkest evening of the year.

He gives his harness bells a shake
To ask if there is some mistake.  10
The only other sound's the sweep
Of easy wind and downy flake.

The woods are lovely, dark and deep,
But I have promises to keep,
And miles to go before I sleep,
And miles to go before I sleep.

## TO EARTHWARD

Love at the lips was touch
As sweet as I could bear;
And once that seemed too much;
I lived on air

That crossed me from sweet things
The flow of—was it musk
From hidden grapevine springs
Down hill at dusk?

I had the swirl and ache
From sprays of honeysuckle          10
That when they're gathered shake
Dew on the knuckle.

I craved strong sweets, but those
Seemed strong when I was young;
The petal of the rose
It was that stung.

Now no joy but lacks salt
That is not dashed with pain
And weariness and fault;
I crave the stain          20

Of tears, the aftermark
Of almost too much love,
The sweet of bitter bark
And burning clove.

When stiff and sore and scarred
I take away my hand
From leaning on it hard
In grass and sand,

The hurt is not enough:
I long for weight and strength          30
To feel the earth as rough
To all my length.

## ON A TREE
## FALLEN ACROSS THE ROAD

### ( T O   H E A R   U S   T A L K )

The tree the tempest with a crash of wood
Throws down in front of us is not to bar
Our passage to our journey's end for good,
But just to ask us who we think we are

Insisting always on our own way so.
She likes to halt us in our runner tracks,
And make us get down in a foot of snow
Debating what to do without an ax.

And yet she knows obstruction is in vain:
We will not be put off the final goal          10
We have it hidden in us to attain,
Not though we have to seize earth by the pole

And, tired of aimless circling in one place,
Steer straight off after something into space.

FROM

# WEST-RUNNING BROOK
## [1928]

## THE COCOON

As far as I can see this autumn haze
That spreading in the evening air both ways,
Makes the new moon look anything but new,
And pours the elm-tree meadow full of blue,
Is all the smoke from one poor house alone
With but one chimney it can call its own;
So close it will not light an early light,
Keeping its life so close and out of sight
No one for hours has set a foot outdoors
So much as to take care of evening chores.          10
The inmates may be lonely women-folk.
I want to tell them that with all this smoke
They prudently are spinning their cocoon
And anchoring it to an earth and moon
From which no winter gale can hope to blow it,—
Spinning their own cocoon did they but know it.

## ACQUAINTED WITH THE NIGHT

I have been one acquainted with the night.
I have walked out in rain—and back in rain.
I have outwalked the furthest city light.

I have looked down the saddest city lane.
I have passed by the watchman on his beat
And dropped my eyes, unwilling to explain.

I have stood still and stopped the sound of feet
When far away an interrupted cry
Came over houses from another street,

But not to call me back or say good-by;          10
And further still at an unearthly height,
One luminary clock against the sky

Proclaimed the time was neither wrong nor right.
I have been one acquainted with the night.

## THE EGG AND THE MACHINE

He gave the solid rail a hateful kick.
From far away there came an answering tick

And then another tick. He knew the code:
His hate had roused an engine up the road.
He wished when he had had the track alone
He had attacked it with a club or stone
And bent some rail wide open like a switch
So as to wreck the engine in the ditch.
Too late though, now, he had himself to thank.
Its click was rising to a nearer clank.          10
Here it came breasting like a horse in skirts.
(He stood well back for fear of scalding squirts.)
Then for a moment all there was was size
Confusion and a roar that drowned the cries
He raised against the gods in the machine.
Then once again the sandbank lay serene.
The traveler's eye picked up a turtle trail,
Between the dotted feet a streak of tail,
And followed it to where he made out vague
But certain signs of buried turtle's egg;          20
And probing with one finger not too rough,
He found suspicious sand, and sure enough,
The pocket of a little turtle mine.
If there was one egg in it there were nine,
Torpedo-like, with shell of gritty leather
All packed in sand to wait the trump together.
'You'd better not disturb me any more,'
He told the distance, 'I am armed for war.
The next machine that has the power to pass
Will get this plasm in its goggle glass.'          30

FROM

# A FURTHER RANGE [1936]

## DESERT PLACES

Snow falling and night falling fast, oh, fast
In a field I looked into going past,
And the ground almost covered smooth in snow,
But a few weeds and stubble showing last.

The woods around it have it—it is theirs.
All animals are smothered in their lairs.
I am too absent-spirited to count;
The loneliness includes me unawares.

And lonely as it is that loneliness
Will be more lonely ere it will be less—          10
A blanker whiteness of benighted snow
With no expression, nothing to express.

They cannot scare me with their empty spaces
Between stars—on stars where no human race is.
I have it in me so much nearer home
To scare myself with my own desert places.

## LEAVES COMPARED WITH FLOWERS

A tree's leaves may be ever so good,
So may its bark, so may its wood;
But unless you put the right thing to its root
It never will show much flower or fruit.

But I may be one who does not care
Ever to have tree bloom or bear.
Leaves for smooth and bark for rough,
Leaves and bark may be tree enough.

Some giant trees have bloom so small
They might as well have none at all.          10
Late in life I have come on fern.
Now lichens are due to have their turn.

I bade men tell me which in brief,
Which is fairer, flower or leaf.
They did not have the wit to say,
Leaves by night and flowers by day.

Leaves and bark, leaves and bark,
To lean against and hear in the dark.
Petals I may have once pursued.
Leaves are all my darker mood.          20

## NEITHER OUT FAR NOR IN DEEP

The people along the sand
All turn and look one way.
They turn their back on the land.
They look at the sea all day.

As long as it takes to pass
A ship keeps raising its hull;
The wetter ground like glass
Reflects a standing gull.

The land may vary more;
But wherever the truth may be—          10
The water comes ashore,
And the people look at the sea.

They cannot look out far.
They cannot look in deep.
But when was that ever a bar
To any watch they keep?

## PROVIDE, PROVIDE

The witch that came (the withered hag)
To wash the steps with pail and rag,
Was once the beauty Abishag,

The picture pride of Hollywood.
Too many fall from great and good
For you to doubt the likelihood.

Die early and avoid the fate.
Or if predestined to die late,
Make up your mind to die in state.

Make the whole stock exchange your own!    10
If need be occupy a throne,
Where nobody can call *you* crone.

Some have relied on what they knew;
Others on being simply true.
What worked for them might work for you.

No memory of having starred
Atones for later disregard,
Or keeps the end from being hard.

Better to go down dignified
With boughten friendship at your side    20
Than none at all. Provide, provide!

F R O M

# A WITNESS TREE [1942]

## THE SILKEN TENT

She is as in a field a silken tent
At midday when a sunny summer breeze
Has dried the dew and all its ropes relent,
So that in guys it gently sways at ease,
And its supporting central cedar pole,
That is its pinnacle to heavenward
And signifies the sureness of the soul,
Seems to owe naught to any single cord,
But strictly held by none, is loosely bound
By countless silken ties of love and thought    10
To everything on earth the compass round,
And only by one's going slightly taut
In the capriciousness of summer air
Is of the slightest bondage made aware.

## THE GIFT OUTRIGHT

⟨ THIS poem was read before the Phi Beta Kappa Society at William and Mary College, December 5, 1941, and recited from memory at President Kennedy's inauguration, January 20, 1961.

The land was ours before we were the land's.
She was our land more than a hundred years
Before we were her people. She was ours
In Massachusetts, in Virginia,
But we were England's, still colonials,
Possessing what we still were unpossessed by,
Possessed by what we now no more possessed.
Something we were withholding made us weak
Until we found out that it was ourselves
We were withholding from our land of living,    10
And forthwith found salvation in surrender.
Such as we were we gave ourselves outright
(The deed of gift was many deeds of war)
To the land vaguely realizing westward,
But still unstoried, artless, unenhanced,
Such as she was, such as she would become.

F R O M

# STEEPLE BUSH [1947]

## ONE STEP BACKWARD TAKEN

Not only sands and gravels
Were once more on their travels,
But gulping muddy gallons
Great boulders off their balance
Bumped heads together dully
And started down the gully.
Whole capes caked off in slices.
I felt my standpoint shaken
In the universal crisis.
But with one step backward taken    10
I saved myself from going.
A world torn loose went by me.
Then the rain stopped and the blowing
And the sun came out to dry me.

## DIRECTIVE

Back out of all this now too much for us,
Back in a time made simple by the loss
Of detail, burned, dissolved, and broken off
Like graveyard marble sculpture in the weather,

There is a house that is no more a house
Upon a farm that is no more a farm
And in a town that is no more a town.
The road there, if you'll let a guide direct you
Who only has at heart your getting lost,
May seem as if it should have been a quarry— 10
Great monolithic knees the former town
Long since gave up pretense of keeping covered.
And there's a story in a book about it:
Besides the wear of iron wagon wheels
The ledges show lines ruled southeast northwest,
The chisel work of an enormous Glacier
That braced his feet against the Arctic Pole.
You must not mind a certain coolness from him
Still said to haunt this side of Panther Mountain.
Nor need you mind the serial ordeal 20
Of being watched from forty cellar holes
As if by eye pairs out of forty firkins.
As for the woods' excitement over you
That sends light rustle rushes to their leaves,
Charge that to upstart inexperience.
Where were they all not twenty years ago?
They think too much of having shaded out
A few old pecker-fretted apple trees.
Make yourself up a cheering song of how
Someone's road home from work this once
   was, 30
Who may be just ahead of you on foot
Or creaking with a buggy load of grain.
The height of the adventure is the height
Of country where two village cultures faded
Into each other. Both of them are lost.
And if you're lost enough to find yourself
By now, pull in your ladder road behind you
And put a sign up CLOSED to all but me.
Then make yourself at home. The only field
Now left's no bigger than a harness gall. 40
First there's the children's house of make believe,
Some shattered dishes underneath a pine,
The playthings in the playhouse of the children.
Weep for what little things could make them glad.
Then for the house that is no more a house,
But only a belilaced cellar hole,
Now slowly closing like a dent in dough.
This was no playhouse but a house in earnest.
Your destination and your destiny's
A brook that was the water of the house, 50
Cold as a spring as yet so near its source,
Too lofty and original to rage.
(We know the valley streams that when aroused
Will leave their tatters hung on barb and thorn.)
I have kept hidden in the instep arch
Of an old cedar at the waterside
A broken drinking goblet like the Grail
Under a spell so the wrong ones can't find it,
So can't get saved, as Saint Mark says they
   mustn't.

(I stole the goblet from the children's playhouse.) 60
Here are your waters and your watering
   place.
Drink and be whole again beyond confusion.

# PROSE

## THE WATERSPOUT

⟨ THESE few words were written by Frost as the Introduction to *The Arts Anthology: Dartmouth Verse
1925*, a collection of undergraduate verse.

NO ONE given to looking under-ground in spring
can have failed to notice how a bean starts its
growth from the seed. Now the manner of a poet's
germination is less like that of a bean in the ground
than of a waterspout at sea. He has to begin as a
cloud of all the other poets he ever read. That
can't be helped. And first the cloud reaches down
toward the water from above and then the water
reaches up toward the cloud from below and finally cloud and water join together to roll as one
pillar between heaven and earth. The base of water he picks up from below is of course all the life
he ever lived outside of books.

These, then, are the three figures of the waterspout and the first is about as far as the poet doomed to die young in everyone of us usually gets. He
brings something down from Dowson, Yeats, Morris, Masefield, or the Imagists (often a long way
down), but lifts little or nothing up. If he were
absolutely certain to do as doomed and die young,
he would hardly be worth getting excited over in
college or elsewhere. But you can't be too careful
about whom you will ignore in this world. Cases
have been known of his refusing at the last minute
to abdicate the breast in favor of the practical and
living on to write lyric like Landor till ninety.

Right in this book he will be found surviving
into the second figure of the waterspout, and,
by several poems and many scattered lines, even
into the third figure. [Certain poems], good as
they are of their kind—accomplished and all that
—are of the first figure and frankly derivative.
They are meant to do credit to anyone's reading.
But [certain others] . . . at least get up the salt
water. Their realism represents an advance. They

show acceptance of the fact that the way to better is often through worse. In [at least one poem] the pillar revolves pretty much unbroken.

We are here getting a long way with poetry, considering all there is against it in school and college. The poet, as everyone knows, must strike his individual note sometime between the ages of fifteen and twenty-five. He may hold it a long time, or a short time, but it is then he must strike it or never. School and college have been conducted with the almost express purpose of keeping him busy with something else till the danger of his ever creating anything is past. Their motto has been, the muses find some mischief still for idle hands to do. No one is asking to see poetry regularized in courses and directed by coaches like sociology and football. It must remain a theft to retain its savor. But it does seem as if it could be a little more connived at than it is. I for one should be in favor of the colleges setting the expectation of poetry forward a few years (the way the clocks are set forward in May), so as to get the young poets started earlier in the morning before the freshness dries off. Just setting the expectation of poetry forward might be all that was needed to give us our proportioned number of poets to Congressmen.

## THE FIGURE A POEM MAKES

❡ WRITTEN as a Preface to the 1939 *Collected Poems*, this celebrated statement was retained in the *Complete Poems* published ten years later.

ABSTRACTION is an old story with the philosophers, but it has been like a new toy in the hands of the artists of our day. Why can't we have any one quality of poetry we choose by itself? We can have in thought. Then it will go hard if we can't in practice. Our lives for it.

Granted no one but a humanist much cares how sound a poem is if it is only *a* sound. The sound is the gold in the ore. Then we will have the sound out alone and dispense with the inessential. We do till we make the discovery that the object in writing poetry is to make all poems sound as different as possible from each other, and the resources for that of vowels, consonants, punctuation, syntax, words, sentences, meter are not enough. We need the help of context—meaning—subject matter. That is the greatest help towards variety. All that can be done with words is soon told. So also with meters—particularly in our language where there are virtually but two, strict iambic and loose iambic. The ancients with many were still poor if they depended on meters for all tune. It is painful to watch our sprung-rhythmists straining at the point of omitting one short from a foot for relief from monotony. The possibilities for tune from the dramatic tones of meaning struck across the rigidity of a limited meter are endless. And we are back in poetry as merely one more art of having something to say, sound or unsound. Probably better if sound, because deeper and from wider experience.

Then there is this wildness whereof it is spoken. Granted again that it has an equal claim with sound to being a poem's better half. If it is a wild tune, it is a poem. Our problem then is, as modern abstractionists, to have the wildness pure —to be wild with nothing to be wild about. We bring up as aberrationists, giving way to undirected associations and kicking ourselves from one chance suggestion to another in all directions as of a hot afternoon in the life of a grasshopper. Theme alone can steady us down. Just as the first mystery was how a poem could have a tune in such a straightness as meter, so the second mystery is how a poem can have wildness and at the same time a subject that shall be fulfilled.

It should be of the pleasure of a poem itself to tell how it can. The figure a poem makes. It begins in delight and ends in wisdom. The figure is the same as for love. No one can really hold that the ecstasy should be static and stand still in one place. It begins in delight, it inclines to the impulse, it assumes direction with the first line laid down, it runs a course of lucky events, and ends in a clarification of life—not necessarily a great clarification, such as sects and cults are founded on, but in a momentary stay against confusion. It has denouement. It has an outcome that though unforeseen was predestined from the first image of the original mood—and indeed from the very mood. It is but a trick poem and no poem at all if the best of it was thought of first and saved for the last. It finds its own name as it goes and discovers the best waiting for it in some final phrase at once wise and sad—the happy-sad blend of the drinking song.

No tears in the writer, no tears in the reader. No surprise for the writer, no surprise for the reader. For me the initial delight is in the surprise of remembering something I didn't know I knew. I am in a place, in a situation, as if I had materialized from cloud or risen out of the ground. There is a glad recognition of the long lost and the rest follows. Step by step the wonder of unexpected supply keeps growing. The impressions most useful to my purpose seem always those I was unaware of and so made no note of at the time when taken, and the conclusion is come to that like giants we are always hurling experience ahead of us to pave the future with against the day when we may want to strike a line of purpose across it for somewhere. The line will have the more charm for not being mechanically straight. We enjoy the straight crookedness of a good walking stick. Modern instruments of precision are being used to make things crooked as if by eye and hand in the old days.

I tell how there may be a better wildness of logic than of inconsequence. But the logic is backward, in retrospect, after the act. It must be more felt than seen ahead like prophecy. It must be a revelation, or a series of revelations, as much for the poet as for the reader. For it to be that there must have been the greatest freedom of the material to move about in it and to establish relations in it regardless of time and space, previous relation, and everything but affinity. We prate of freedom. We call our schools free because we are not free to stay away from them till we are sixteen years of age. I have given up my democratic prejudices and now willingly set the lower classes free to be completely taken care of by the upper classes. Political freedom is nothing to me. I bestow it right and left. All I would keep for myself is the freedom of my material—the condition of body and mind now and then to summons aptly from the vast chaos of all I have lived through.

Scholars and artists thrown together are often annoyed at the puzzle of where they differ. Both work from knowledge; but I suspect they differ most importantly in the way their knowledge is come by. Scholars get theirs with conscientious thoroughness along projected lines of logic; poets theirs cavalierly and as it happens in and out of books. They stick to nothing deliberately, but let what will stick to them like burrs where they walk in the fields. No acquirement is on assignment, or even self-assignment. Knowledge of the second kind is much more available in the wild free ways of wit and art. A schoolboy may be defined as one who can tell you what he knows in the order in which he learned it. The artist must value himself as he snatches a thing from some previous order in time and space into a new order with not so much as a ligature clinging to it of the old place where it was organic.

More than once I should have lost my soul to radicalism if it had been the originality it was mistaken for by its young converts. Originality and initiative are what I ask for my country. For myself the originality need be no more than the freshness of a poem run in the way I have described: from delight to wisdom. The figure is the same as for love. Like a piece of ice on a hot stove the poem must ride on its own melting. A poem may be worked over once it is in being, but may not be worried into being. Its most precious quality will remain its having run itself and carried away the poet with it. Read it a hundred times: it will forever keep its freshness as a metal keeps its fragrance. It can never lose its sense of a meaning that once unfolded by surprise as it went.

## MARK SCHORER
*Editor*

# Sherwood Anderson

### 1876–1941

# F. Scott Fitzgerald

### 1896–1940

# Ernest Hemingway

### 1898–1961

## SHERWOOD ANDERSON

OF HIS life Sherwood Anderson always wished to construct a parable, even a myth. It had various forms, but they all sprang from a central action. That action he recounted with varying details throughout his work, fiction and nonfiction, and that is why his fiction is never without autobiography just as his autobiographies are never without fiction. The central action is this: on November 27, 1912, a successful manufacturer in the town of Elyria, Ohio, dreaming sometimes of becoming a great benevolent tycoon, chafing more often at the stultifying routines of promotion and salesmanship, Sherwood Anderson, aged thirty-six, walked out of his office and away from his wife and family into the freedom of a wandering literary life, never to return to business. "'For the rest of my life I will be a servant to [words] alone,' I whispered to myself as I went along a spur of railroad track, over a

bridge, out of a town and out of that phase of my life."

It is a pretty fable that has considerable psychological relevance to the lives of many modern American writers even when its literal relevance is as slight as it was to the facts of Anderson's life.

Sherwood Anderson was born on September 13, 1876, the third child of a harness maker whose handicraft could not long compete with a rapidly developing mechanization throughout American enterprise. Forced out of business, he took to drink, spun endless tales for anyone who would listen, and became an itinerant sign and house painter. The family moved to Clyde, Ohio. Sherwood Anderson's education was always irregular and it ceased after one year of high school. His real education had come to him through the endless variety of odd jobs that filled his youth, through the wisdom of laborers and

[947]

Negroes and livery stable hands and hangers-on, through race track touts and trainers, through tramps. When he was nineteen, his mother died, the father wandered off, the family broke up.

Sherwood Anderson went to Chicago to become a laborer in a cold-storage warehouse until, in desperation with that dogged work, he enlisted in the United States Army to fight in the Spanish-American War. His company did not reach Cuba until four months after the armistice had been signed, and he was released from the army in less than a year after his enlistment. Back in Clyde, he worked on a farm, and in September of 1899, enrolled in the Wittenberg Academy in Springfield, Ohio, preparatory to enrolling in Wittenberg College when he would have been twenty-four years old. Before he reached that age, he gave up the brief academic dream and returned to Chicago.

In the opening year of the twentieth century, significantly enough, Sherwood Anderson became an advertising man, and soon he was writing copy in which, very much in keeping with the times, he glorified the adventure of business. Always attractive to women, he married a girl above him in social station, moved to Cleveland where he became the president of a mail-order firm, and from there to Elyria, Ohio—an enterprising family man who presently bought a paint factory that produced something called "Roof-Fix." Wanting to "ennoble" that business activity which he had chosen as his own, he was at the same time writing "lies" in his copy; a conflict developed between his wish to succeed in the ordinary commercial world and his wish to escape into the imaginative world and into real writing. More and more he brooded about the character of the artist and about his situation in an industrial society. In about 1910 he began to write short fiction, and by 1912 he had written drafts of what would become his first two novels. At the same time, torn by conflict, he had taken to drink, turned from his wife, and was neglecting his business, which suffered accordingly. If, in his later recollections, he was to say that he let people think he was a little mad so that his creditors would forgive

him when he deserted his business, the fact is that he was a little mad. On November 27, that famous day of liberation, his nerves collapsed. Four days later, haggard, disheveled, and suffering from aphasia, he was found wandering around Cleveland in a daze and was hospitalized by the police. Late in December his wife brought him back to Elyria. In February he disposed of his business and left alone for Chicago, to return to the servitude of advertising. He was now thirty-six years old, his marriage would last another two years—when he would marry a sculptress named Tennessee Mitchell—but he would continue in advertising for another ten years.

When he was not in his office writing copy, still trying to make something good of a competitive life that he hated, he was working at his novels and at his queer, untutored short sketches. He began to meet writers. Through his brother Karl, a painter, he met Floyd Dell, and chiefly through him, a whole circle of garrulous literary people including Ben Hecht, Burton Rascoe, Harry Hansen, Eunice Tietjens, Carl Sandburg, sometimes Theodore Dreiser, and, presently, Margaret Anderson, who was to found the *Little Review* in Chicago in 1914. When Floyd Dell read the manuscript of Anderson's first novel, *Windy McPherson's Son*, he was enthusiastic and took it upon himself to find a publisher. After many rejections, it found a publisher at last in the American branch of the English house of John Lane. It was published in 1916, and, having given Lane an option on his second novel, Anderson immediately produced the manuscript of that work, *Marching Men*, which was published in 1917.

These novels, although they caused considerable critical excitement as marking the appearance of an original genius, had small sales and were, in fact, poor novels. They are loose and sprawling works, without unity of theme or action, with comically unreal dialogue, and with narrative and analytical passages written in long, straggling sentences that bear no relation to the style that Anderson presently would make his remarkable own. His major preoccupations are evident in the themes: the brooding boyhood in a drab Iowa town; the eccentric character of Windy, drawn, Anderson said, after his own father; and above all, the criticism of the myth of business idealism and the assertion at the end of the novel of his own myth—the break with manufacturing into freedom, to "find truth." In *Marching Men,* a curious story about a mindless and militant brotherhood formed by workers under the leadership of Beaut McGregor, intent on violence to free themselves from the routine of industrial slavery, both the inarticulate, somewhat Whitmanesque yearning for a bond between man and man and the aspiration to freedom, however ill-defined, suggest characteristic future themes. It is less easy to see the future Anderson at his best in the volume of inchoate poems called *Mid-American Chants,* published in 1918.

All the time, from 1913 on, Anderson was working toward something quite different from these books—his masterpiece, *Winesburg, Ohio,* published in 1919. A number of separate pieces from this work appeared in the *Little Review* and elsewhere between 1916 and the year of book publication, and these seemed to be autonomous if rather amorphous narrative entities. Only when the book as a whole was published was its overall design and significance to appear.

The book comes directly out of the life of Anderson's boyhood in Clyde, and the central figure, who appears in most of the separate parts, George Willard, is drawn after Anderson in his late adolescence. Without explication of any sort, the book somehow evokes the dying end of an agrarian culture as it slips over into industrial culture. It evokes, too, the intellectual climate of that late nineteenth-century mid-America in which Anderson grew up: the world that fostered the heroic individualism of men like Abraham Lincoln and Mark Twain; the atmosphere that encouraged the atheism of a man like Robert Ingersoll, the rhetoric of William Jennings Bryan, the "grass roots" stir of such a movement as the Populist party; the era that brought to an end gas-lit streets, wooden sidewalks and the cracker barrel, the flourishing village saloon, thriving village eccentrics.

All this is the inheritance of Sherwood Anderson, and within all this he had ob-

served, and was still observing in Chicago, the character of individuals. How to use it? He was not happy with the more or less conventional novel form that he had already twice attempted. He was no more happy with the prevailing fashions in the short story, either in the formal sense—the slick machinery of O. Henry, for example—or in the conventional interpretation of village life—the sentimental romanticism of the Hoosier school. He had observed the pathos, the suffocation of hope and dream in small town characters, the cruelty no less than the comedy. And in form he wanted something loose and impressionistic and without the contrivances of "plot" that would permit him to get under the surface of manners and character, into the secret life, and into what he felt was the soft, warm flow that, taken together, all the secret lives made into life itself. "A man keeps thinking of his own life," he was later to write, in a note probably intended for his *Memoirs,* ". . . life itself is a loose, flowing thing. There are no plot stories in life."

What is wanted is a new looseness. Do we not live in a great, loose land, of many states and yet all of these states together do make something, a land, a country. I submit that the form of my Winesburg tales and all of the tales on which I am at work, even now, as I write . . . may offer a suggestion to other writers.

A new looseness, lives flowing past each other, the whole however to leave a definite impression, this as a form that fits one way of life. I submit it as something for our younger writers to be thinking about.

He had heard talk of Sigmund Freud in bohemian Chicago, and this helped him. He was reading, or was about to read, the fiction of D. H. Lawrence, and this would help him, too. Gertrude Stein's *Three Lives* (1909) had helped him to discover the language that he now knew he wanted to use—the colloquial language of Mark Twain, of everyday America, of country roads and village streets. Yet his problem was not solved until 1915, when he read Edgar Lee Masters' long poem, *The Spoon River Anthology.* As Masters had done in verse, so he could do in prose!

Like Masters, he would give a certain unification to the separate stories of his twenty-two characters through the background of a single community. As the stories progressed, characters would keep reappearing: someone who had been a minor figure in one story would presently emerge as the major figure in another, and so on, until a whole sense of the community would emerge. He would supplement Masters' unification with another means: in most of the stories George Willard would appear, and while the other characters would come to George in the dumb expectation that he could somehow tell their story, their stories would also be like gifts to him, gifts that would help him grow until, at the end, he was mature and made the characteristic gesture of flight into freedom. And he would have a third means of unification—a theory embodied in the opening section, a prelude called "The Book of the Grotesque."

A "grotesque" is formed, Anderson tells us, when an individual seizes on some single truth from the whole body of truths and tries to live by that alone. A single truth, a single wish, a single memory, a single obsessive ambition that distorts the self even as it compels it—these are the motivations of Sherwood Anderson's grotesques. But what is probably a further consequence of these motivations is perhaps more important than the grotesques themselves: in their single pursuits, the characters isolate themselves from one another, and in their isolation, they are at once lonely and mute. Everyone in this world seems to grope helplessly toward everyone else, but no one can communicate with anyone else—or only with the artist-reporter, George Willard. And that, as Anderson came to understand it, is the function of the artist: to absorb the lives of others into himself, and himself to become those others and their lives.

As a totality, as a book, that is, *Winesburg, Ohio* is the height of Anderson's achievement. Taken singly, however, none of its separate pieces is as good as any of a half-dozen or more truly separate short stories that he was to write then and later—stories like "The Egg" and "I Want to Know Why" from *The Triumph of the Egg* (1921), "I'm

a Fool" and "The Man Who Became a Woman" from *Horses and Men* (1923), and "A Meeting South" and "Death in the Woods" from the volume called *Death in the Woods and Other Stories* (1933). Grotesques still appear in all of them; perhaps Anderson's masterpiece of grotesquery is the father in "The Egg." Loneliness and isolation continue to be the condition of the characters whether grotesques or adolescent boys—drawn again after Anderson himself. The style continues much the same—the slightly hesitant, slightly repetitious, and considerably rhythmical prose that bases itself so clearly on the spoken American language, sometimes, indeed, as in "I'm a Fool" and "I Want to Know Why," becoming the dialect itself, as it had been earlier used by Mark Twain in *Huckleberry Finn* and elsewhere.

Whatever similarities these later stories may bear to the slighter sketches of *Winesburg, Ohio*, it is nevertheless in their fuller embodiment that we can best see why Sherwood Anderson was nothing less than a revolutionary force in the American short story, and why the short story was the form most suited to the full expression of his talent. These stories, like the Winesburg pieces, seemed to contemporary readers to be a new victory for realism, and in a sense they were. They closed their eyes to nothing, glossed over nothing, neither the brutalities of men nor the beauty of animals. Their implied criticism of a society that frustrates individuality and of an individualism that creates a society of hermits, their accurate report of physical detail and of a certain range in the speaking voice—all this and more made Anderson seem to be the liberating champion of realism both in subject matter and in method. Yet when we put a story like "The Egg" beside the work of such a realist as Stephen Crane or such a naturalist as Theodore Dreiser, we see readily enough that, with their impressionistic method, the first story is more nearly a fable and the second more nearly a poetic lamentation than either is a conventionally realistic or a naturalistic report, that Anderson's important observations are at once under the surface of manners and transcendent of the surface of society.

The short story was perfectly calculated to articulate those glimpses—James Joyce's word, "epiphany," is not inappropriate to Anderson's gift—into the secret, inarticulate life that was his special province. Yet over and over he would attempt the longer form of the novel where, over and over, he would lose his imaginative grip on his materials. Even before *Winesburg, Ohio* was published, Anderson began his next novel, *Poor White.* Finished and published in 1920, it is his best attempt in the form, but still much less satisfactory than the best of the stories.

By the time that *Poor White* was published, Anderson had several times attempted to escape Chicago—and his second wife—by trips to New York and to various parts of the South; in the East he made new and important literary friends—Van Wyck Brooks, Waldo Frank, Paul Rosenfeld, Alfred Stieglitz—all of whom were enthusiastically responsive to his writing; but his books did not yet bring him an income adequate to free him from advertising once and for all, and in the winter of 1920–21, he was still writing copy in Chicago. In the summer of 1921, he escaped once more—but with his wife—when his friend, Paul Rosenfeld, invited them to come to Europe with him. Europe, and especially Paris—where he met Gertrude Stein, probably his most important contemporary literary "influence"—were to make Chicago forever impossible thereafter. Even those Chicago writers who were his friends and who were to have brought about that literary renaissance that had somehow fizzled, now seemed less than glamorous. In the summer of 1922, Anderson at last broke for good with advertising, with Chicago, and with his second wife. In the meantime, he had become acquainted with one younger Chicago writer, not of that older group nor of any group, who had impressed him more than any of his friends and who, in turn, had been impressed by the Anderson short stories. On December 3, 1921, Anderson wrote a letter of introduction to his new friend Gertrude Stein for the unknown young writer on his way to Paris—Ernest Hemingway.

## II

# ERNEST HEMINGWAY

ERNEST HEMINGWAY, although a Midwesterner too, came, nevertheless, from a very different background. He was born into the respectable Chicago suburb of Oak Park on July 21, 1899, the son of a doctor who loved the out-of-doors, and of a polite, rather pious mother. His father was more important to the boy than his mother, and the most important experiences of his boyhood were not to take place in genteel Oak Park but in the northern Michigan woods where the Hemingways spent their summers and where the father and son enjoyed hunting and fishing. The boy was an athlete, but in high school he also became interested in writing. He published stories in the high school literary magazine and imitated Ring Lardner in the school newspaper—Lardner was important to each of the three writers represented in these selections. He was graduated in 1917 and his ambition now was to enlist and get into the war in Europe, but his father forbade that, and Hemingway chafed through his last summer in Michigan. In the fall of 1917 he went to Kansas City to become a reporter on the Kansas City *Star.* He was eighteen and his formal education was over.

Many of the qualities of Hemingway's early prose style—among them, the short sentences, the sparse use of adjectives, the clarity of statement—were developed through his writing for the *Star* during the seven months of his employment. In April 1918, he managed at last to get into the war as an honorary lieutenant in the Red Cross ambulance corps serving on the Italian front. His service was short: on July 8 he was severely wounded by the explosion of a mortar shell and the next three months he spent in a hospital in Milan. Nothing more important than this wounding was ever to happen to him. A wound was to become the central symbol of nearly everything he was to write, and the consequences of a wound his persistent thematic preoccupation.

He returned to Oak Park and to Chicago,

spent the summer and autumn in northern Michigan trying to write, went to Canada to write for the Toronto *Star Weekly* for the first half of 1920, and then, back in Chicago, went to work for an advertising firm. His spare time he spent in loitering about gymnasiums, boxing and watching boxers, and trying to write short stories and poems. Already familiar with the stories of Sherwood Anderson, some of whose material was drawn from the same areas of life as Hemingway's would be, he now met Anderson. The older man knew at once that he had met a young man who was going to become an important writer, and whether or not he influenced him profoundly—but surely Hemingway's early story, "My Old Man," is simply his version of Anderson's "I Want to Know Why"—the example of his success was a powerful incentive to the still unpublished but seriously struggling Hemingway. His style was to develop into something tighter, more concentrated, and more lucid than Anderson's and would achieve a character quite its own, but in diction and in rhythm it looks back to Anderson. Interestingly enough, both men thought of Mark Twain as the great model—in a moment of exaggeration Hemingway said that *all* American literature came from *Huckleberry Finn*—and both men accepted the tutelage of the same contemporary, Gertrude Stein.

The famous remark that she would presently make to him—"You are all a lost generation"—marks the important difference between Hemingway and Anderson. In a long letter to his son Robert, written in November 1929, Anderson tried to explain the difference between their generations, the difference between men who were formed before the World War and men who were largely formed by it. The rebellion of the older generation, of men like Anderson, was against the repressive conventions of American life, but they still believed in American life and they still sought their values in its promises. The war ended those conventions at a blow, and the younger generation, men like Hemingway, had nothing to rebel against and found little in American life that they

could believe in. Hemingway, Alfred Kazin has written, "had no basic relation to any prewar culture." In Chicago, he grew increasingly cynical about America and about his employment in particular—with reason, he soon discovered, for his employer was in fact committing an enormous fraud in his enterprise. In 1921 he married, obtained the promise of employment as roving correspondent for the Toronto *Star*, and left for Europe. The expatriation of Ernest Hemingway is as symbolic of his career as the hypothetical break with business is symbolic of Anderson's.

From Gertrude Stein, Hemingway learned his major lessons in style—learned about effective repetition of words, the most rigorous economy, and that degree of concentration on diction and rhythm that alone will evoke for the reader the essential physical quality of the object or experience that is under observation. In Paris, in the years before 1925, he was her attentive pupil. At the same time, as a newspaper correspondent, he was traveling all over Europe and the Near East, and thus broadening the scope of his subject matter. Nearly all of the brief vignettes that form the interchapters of his second book, *In Our Time*, are derived directly from his newspaper experience. These sketches were written in August 1923, before his first published book, *Three Stories and Ten Poems*. The poems are negligible, but the stories—"My Old Man," "Out of Season," and "Up in Michigan"—announced the appearance of a brilliant and original talent. Two years later, with the publication of *In Our Time*, the future of that talent was assured.

It was Sherwood Anderson who urged the publication of this book on his publisher in New York, Horace Liveright. Like *Winesburg, Ohio*, it is a group of related short stories which must be read as a whole if the total impact of the book is to be felt. Like *Winesburg*, too, it has a central character, Nick Adams, modeled after the author in his youth and young manhood, who appears, if not in all the stories, at least throughout, and who, like George Willard, comes into his maturity in the course of the book. The stories in which he does not actually appear are, one must assume, observations made by Nick Adams as he advances into his maturity. Unlike *Winesburg,* the stories in *In Our Time* are interspersed with brief vignettes about war, bullfighting, or journalism. Each of these recounts in the sparsest prose, without any commentary, events of brutal violence, and they include one which recounts the wounding of Nick Adams in the war. Brutal violence, they assert, is the characteristic of our time; and a mute, apparent indifference, grim and tight-lipped, they seem to assert, is the only possible attitude that one can take toward the brutal violence of our time. This is the Hemingway attitude, and the attitude of Hemingway's hero.

In the stories proper, we begin with Nick Adams as a small boy in Michigan, introduced to violence, to death, to the multiple pains and perplexities of his initiation into life. All this violence is brought to its climax in his battle wounds. At the end of the book, in "Big Two-Hearted River," he returns to Michigan, about twenty years old, and in this remarkable story that seems to be little more than an almost monotonously detailed report of two days in which Nick, alone, makes his camp on the river and fishes for trout, we are given the man he has become.

He is not a well man. He is a man who has suffered not only physically but deeply in his spirit. He must occupy himself in physical acts so that his mind does not revert to the climax of his suffering or to the steps of lesser suffering that led to it. He must exhaust himself or he cannot sleep, and when he does sleep, he often has bad dreams. After he was wounded, "no patriot," he made "a separate peace" with the enemy and went a little insane. Now, symbolically, he makes his tent and gets into it. "He was there, in the good place" where he could keep his separate peace. And next day, again symbolically, he will not fish in the fearsome swamp into which the river flows, as he keeps his mind above that swamplike state into which it had fallen in his wartime trauma. Physically active, solitary, cut off from society, without either self-pity or hope,

forever wounded, he will *endure* life, and only that.

This is the Hemingway hero and his famous "code," living by his "guts" alone, which is to say with "grace under pressure." He will appear in various guises throughout the rest of Hemingway's work except for his next book, *The Torrents of Spring* (1926), which is a sport, a parody of a successful book by his mentor, Sherwood Anderson.

III

# F. SCOTT FITZGERALD

IN 1922 Sherwood Anderson did at last flee business and Chicago, more or less on the heels of Hemingway. His major work was finished when finally he won his freedom. He left his second wife and presently married a third, Elizabeth Prall, and there was to be one more wife after her, Eleanor Copenhaver. Now, in 1922, he was quite appropriately working on a novel called *Many Marriages.* He wandered about in the South and in and out of literary New York. At the height of his fame, he was meeting many other writers, among them a phenomenal young success from Minnesota named F. Scott Fitzgerald. Fitzgerald thought Anderson's a "brilliant and almost inimitable prose style," but these two men, temperamentally so different, were never to have the kind of close association that, briefly, Anderson and Hemingway had enjoyed in Chicago, or that, later, Hemingway and Fitzgerald would enjoy in France.

Francis Scott Key Fitzgerald was born on September 24, 1896, in Saint Paul, Minnesota. His father was the somewhat shiftless descendant of an old American line; his mother was the daughter of an Irish immigrant. On one side was "breeding" and failure, on the other, money but not enough of it. To this situation Fitzgerald later attributed his inferiority complex, and to it he should have attributed his fascination with the very rich and with social success. Still, a good looking boy of charm and social grace, he got along well enough with the young people he admired, even though his family always lived on the periphery of the best neighborhoods, and in rather shabby circumstances. He began to write in the St. Paul Academy and continued to write at the Newman Academy, near New York City, where he finished his secondary school education. He was admitted to Princeton, with the dream of being a football player, in 1913. This ambition he was unable to realize, but he threw himself into other activities, literary and theatrical, and was elected to a top social club. A romantic young man, he found the social world of Princeton to be vastly glamorous and all-important. His academic work was undistinguished and it was not made better by his outside activities. In his junior year, when illness further retarded his already limping studies, he dropped out of Princeton for the rest of the year and was put on probation. When he returned, his interests were more serious and so were his friends—T. K. Whipple, John Peale Bishop, and Edmund Wilson were among them. All through that winter and spring, students were going off to war. Fitzgerald applied for a commission in the army, received it, and left Princeton for Fort Leavenworth, Kansas, in November of 1917. He did not get abroad but was transferred from training camp to training camp while he worked at a novel. Called *The Romantic Egotist*, it was declined by Charles Scribner's Sons in August of 1918. In the next month, at an officers' dance at Camp Sheridan, he met Zelda Sayre, a Montgomery, Alabama belle, with whom he fell hopelessly in love.

Discharged from the Army early in 1919, he went to New York to earn enough money to persuade Zelda Sayre to marry him; the third of our trio, he entered an advertising agency at a miserable salary. When, by the summer of 1919, it was clear that this work could not make marriage possible, he left his job, returned to St. Paul, and rewrote *The Romantic Egotist*. It became his first novel, *This Side of Paradise*. Scribner's accepted it, and when it was published in March of 1920, it was a sensation. The "jazz age" had found its definition.

Before its publication, Fitzgerald, who, half the time, was behaving like one of his own characters in crazy, drunken carousing, was, the other half, writing stories with abandon, good and bad, and selling them to magazines, chiefly the *Saturday Evening Post*, at about a thousand dollars each, often more. His success was sudden and spectacular. *This Side of Paradise*, a kind of autobiography, made him famous and gave Princeton a new reputation as a frenzied pleasure dome. Miss Sayre married him in April. A spectacular, champagne-drenched marriage and an extraordinary literary career were simultaneously launched, everything about both, for the moment, glittering and golden. Neither Anderson nor Hemingway had yet escaped from Chicago.

In New York, with money now, very popular, the dazzling young Fitzgeralds tried to realize their romantic dream of success and happiness through endless parties and debauchery, and for a time it was, indeed, fun. This life, with its night club glitter, its atmosphere of great, beautiful ballrooms, its irrepressible and irresponsible youthfulness, is evoked in story after story that Fitzgerald was writing in his sober hours and which he collected in two books—*Flappers and Philosophers* (1920) and *Tales of the Jazz Age* (1922). But where was it to lead them? The answer is contained in his next novel, the title of which in itself contains it; *The Beautiful and Damned* of 1922 is not so much an autobiographical novel as it is a prophecy of autobiography.

That work finished, they had a brief and frantic fling in Europe and then, disappointed and depressed, returned to the United States. They took a house in St. Paul and Fitzgerald wrote his publisher to say:

Loafing puts me in this particularly obnoxious and abominable gloom. My 3rd novel, if I ever write another, will I am sure be black as death with gloom. I should like to sit down with ½ a dozen chosen companions and drink myself to death but I am sick alike of life, liquor and literature. If it wasn't for Zelda I think I'd disappear out of sight . . .

Zelda presently gave birth to their only child, a girl named Frances. And Fitzgerald did, in fact, work very hard.

He wrote a play, *The Vegetable*, which, when it finally found a producer in 1923, was unsuccessful. And they moved East again, now to Long Island, and gave great parties and drove recklessly in and out of Manhattan even as Fitzgerald was writing that novel about great parties and reckless drives that would be *The Great Gatsby*. This work was interrupted by a burst of story writing, necessary to clear them of their debts, and that accomplished, they went to Europe again with the partially completed novel. In November of 1924 he sent his first finished version of it to his publishers.

*The Great Gatsby* was published in 1925. Probably Fitzgerald's most flawless novel, it is certainly the point at which his talent was most fully consolidated and the point, too, at which all his themes and interests achieved their fullest synthesis. Here is the romantic dream of an impossibly glamorous existence, the frenetic, even orgiastic attempt to make it real, the corruption that underlies its approximation, the sense of disaster that pervades it, and the disaster in which it ends. Here, too, is that constant concern of Fitzgerald's with "the very rich," who "are different from you and me." When Fitzgerald made that observation to Hemingway, it is said, Hemingway replied, "Yes, they have more money." But for Fitzgerald, as for Jay Gatsby, the poor boy who has been made rich by bootlegging and crime but who has not been able to enter the world of those who were born to riches, there is a greater difference.

"She's got an indiscreet voice," I remarked. "It's full of—" I hesitated.

"Her voice is full of money," [Gatsby] said suddenly.

That was it. I'd never understood before. It was full of money—that was the inexhaustible charm that rose and fell in it, the jingle of it, the cymbals' song of it . . . High in a white palace the king's daughter, the golden girl . . ."

The romance of money! But there is also the reality of it:

I couldn't forgive him or like him, but I saw that what he had done was, to him, entirely justified. It was all very careless and confused. They were careless people, Tom and Daisy—they smashed up things and creatures and then retreated back into their money or their vast carelessness, or whatever it was that kept them together, and let other people clean up the mess they had made . . .

I shook hands with him; it seemed silly not to, for I felt suddenly as though I were talking to a child. Then he went into the jewelry store to buy a pearl necklace—or perhaps only a pair of cuff buttons—rid of my provincial squeamishness forever.

The narrator is a young man named Nick Carroway who has come from the Middle West to be an Easterner, and for him, finally, the Middle West comes to represent simplicity and innocence, and the East, complexity and corruption. Fitzgerald's use of Carroway is an act of technical brilliance, for it enables him to put a certain objective distance between himself and the subject matter that was in itself so fascinating for him. At his best—and certainly here in *The Great Gatsby*—Fitzgerald manages to do two things simultaneously: to make us feel, along with him, the Circean charm and glamour and romance of the careless world of the very rich, and at the same time to judge it. When his stories fail, it is because the second element is missing, and when it is, the first is somehow shoddy and unreal. When they succeed, when these two elements are held in balance, he is among our greatest novelists of manners.

At just about the point at which *The Great Gatsby* was published, Fitzgerald began work on one of his finest short stories, "The Rich Boy," which occupied him for most of the summer of 1925. In this story he addressed himself directly to the matter of "the very rich," and the subtle revelation that the story makes through the character of Anson Hunter is that not only does their "carelessness" serve to be brutally destructive of others, but that their ease and pride and self-sufficiency prevent their own fulfillment in human relationships, numb the capacity for love, make personal commitment impossible. Once again, Fitzgerald managed—as he repeatedly would—the double imaginative act of making us feel, with his peculiar eloquence of style, the charged charm of a certain way of life, and demonstrating to us its rather terrible fatality. Many other fine stories in *All the Sad Young Men*, the volume in which "The Rich Boy" appeared in the next year, 1926, perform the same feat. This is all the more remarkable in that now in the mid-twenties, Fitzgerald himself more and more succumbed to the gaudy pleasures of that world which would at last destoy him.

He was seeing a good deal of Ernest Hemingway in Paris, and Hemingway gives us a metaphorical glimpse of him:

It was at this point in the story, reader, that Mr. F. Scott Fitzgerald came to our home one afternoon, and after remaining for quite a while suddenly sat down in the fireplace and would not (or was it could not, reader?) get up and let the fire burn something else so as to keep the room warm.

## IV

THE LAST quotation comes from Hemingway's book called *The Torrents of Spring*, published in 1926. Sherwood Anderson in 1925 had at last written a commercially successful novel in *Dark Laughter*, an unfortunate work that rests on a supposed contrast between the rich sensuality of Negroes and the anemic sterility of whites. At just this time, Fitzgerald was working to obtain a wider audience for Hemingway, and had urged his work upon his own publisher, Scribner's. Hemingway, however, was under option to Liveright, Anderson's publisher. *The Torrents of Spring*, which he said he wrote in ten days, was a professed and not very funny parody of *Dark Laughter*. When it was submitted to Liveright, that unhappy man could only decline to publish it since it treated his stellar author so outrageously. The refusal released Hemingway from his contract and Scribner's published the book. Anderson was hurt and bewildered, and his friendship with Hemingway came to an end. For Hemingway, the writing of that book was an act by which he exorcised an influence, and his next book would show that he was now nearly his own man.

Although Anderson had finally written a successful book, his work continued to de-

cline. He became a country newspaper editor in Virginia and he turned his interest to the influence of machines on American life and to the situation of the American worker in the industrial South. Writing still an occasional good short story, his major efforts went into a number of works of semi-autobiography such as *A Story Teller's Story*, into impressionistic essays, and into two more novels, *Beyond Desire* and *Kit Brandon*, which reveal no significant extension of his thematic interests, even when labor became his subject matter. Like many another writer, he flirted with leftwing politics during the depression years in the 1930's, but Anderson was no man to commit himself to the disciplines of party politics. Even after he had his farm in Virginia, he continued to be a wanderer, yearning always for some freedom that his individuality was never quite satisfied that it had found. During the last twenty years of his life, when he was more or less free to serve words alone at last, he became in many ways his own legend. Yet that legend was suitable, somehow, only to an older, more expansive America. Symbolically enough, his death, in 1941, occurred on a journey. No less symbolic was the cause of his death: peritonitis brought about by a fragment of colored toothpick that he had swallowed at a cocktail party.

## V

IN THE mid-twenties, Anderson's lost friend, Ernest Hemingway, began to create his own legend. The devil-may-care, somehow bittersweet expatriate who fought bulls and studied the ritual of bullfighting, the athlete who boxed and sometimes brawled, the big game hunter and the deep-sea fisherman, the war-lover who turned up on every front in every war, the lover of women—he too had four wives—whose heroines are always the same submissive dream figure in different guises, the adventurer miraculously rescued from various physical catastrophes, and finally that "Papa" whose best friend was Marlene Dietrich. The legend is in large part true but it is partial, and, omitting Hemingway, the fine writer, it omits the most important fact about him and the fact that the legend tends to obscure.

If 1925 saw the appearance of one great American novel in *Gatsby*, 1926 saw another in *The Sun Also Rises*. This novel of the lost generation in Paris and Spain, with its wounded hero, Jake Barnes, and its bitterly gallant, unobtainable heroine, Brett Ashley, is not only Hemingway at his purest but perhaps the classic of postwar American fiction. Here Hemingway's prose has been distilled to its essence; here the code of endurance amidst fatality achieves its clearest definition; here the flicker of satire plays most effectively over the pathos; and here the style is the perfect expression of the subject, the attitude, the man himself.

Like Fitzgerald, Hemingway alternated his novels with books of short stories, and his short stories became more and more impressive, reaching their climax, perhaps, in those two of 1936, "The Short Happy Life of Francis Macomber" and "The Snows of Kilimanjaro," and in that extended short story of 1952, *The Old Man and the Sea*, which is said to be only a portion of a very big novel on which Hemingway had long been engaged. The short stories, with their technically brilliant finish and with their strangely reverberating depths, are all variations on the central pattern of Hemingway's fiction, which Philip Young has described as "the pattern of violence, psychological wounding, escape and death."

*A Farewell to Arms* (1929), the novel that followed *The Sun Also Rises*, is a war novel that gives us the background of the earlier novel. Lieutenant Henry, disastrously wounded in the war, makes his "separate peace" and flees with his lovely nurse, Catharine Barkley, who dies in childbirth. He is left with nothing at all, like Jake Barnes, and can only, like the Hemingway hero always, enact the ritual of endurance as a kind of living demonstration of A. E. Housman's lines—

> Could man be drunk for ever
> With liquor, love, or fights,
> Lief should I rouse at morning
> And lief lie down of nights.

> But men at whiles are sober
> And think by fits and starts,
> And if they think, they fasten
> Their hands upon their hearts.

Physical activity, whether to keep from thinking or not, was as important to Hemingway as to his heroes, and in two works of nonfiction he gave extended treatment to two of the forms of physical activity that interested him most. *Death in the Afternoon* (1932) is about bullfighting and death; *The Green Hills of Africa* (1935) is about big game hunting, literary matters, and death. These are among Hemingway's lesser works, but, revealing as they do a man of bias and prejudice as well as of courage and daring, they are important to an understanding of a not entirely engaging literary personality. In the 1930's, the Hemingways moved from France to Key West, Florida, and out of the Florida experience came the novel *To Have and Have Not* in 1937. Like Anderson, Hemingway, observing the America of the depression years, was briefly pushed toward the left, and this novel is an attempt to vindicate the "outlaw" hero, Harry Morgan, for whom society makes an honest living impossible, and to denounce the decadent rich.

The final wisdom of Harry Morgan, as he lies dying, is that no man can go it alone, that no man is an island. It is this wisdom— which may be taken as an ambiguous retraction of the code implicit in *The Sun Also Rises* and *A Farewell to Arms*—that provides the theme for Hemingway's next novel, *For Whom the Bell Tolls*, published in 1940. A novel about the Spanish Civil War, in which Hemingway was deeply involved both personally and professionally (it impelled him to write his single play, *The Fifth Column*, of 1938), it is different from his other fiction in that his hero, although he must die for it, is committed to a cause. The novel attempts an epic scale unlike any other book that Hemingway published, and while it has many memorable scenes and some magnificently realized Spanish characters, the whole does not sustain the heroic intention.

The same problem plagues his first novel to be published after World War II, *Across the River and Into the Trees*, of 1950. It is possible that the old pattern of the wounded hero who returns to the scene of his wounding for a kind of ritualistic exorcism is worn rather thin. It is possible that the lovely young heroine is too much an old man's fancy to be real. It is possible that Colonel Cantwell is too much like Hemingway himself, or too directly a transcription of his dream of himself, his legend. Yet there are those who argue that the true Hemingway *aficionado* can be tested by his response to this book, that if he does not think it great, his entire judgment of Hemingway is suspect. In his review of this novel, John O'Hara—only one of the scores and scores of younger writers who have been influenced by Hemingway in style, in attitude, in the conception of fictional form—began by saying that Hemingway was "the most important, the outstanding author out of the millions of writers who have lived since 1616," since, that is, the death of William Shakespeare.

Many other readers, less certain in their judgment, were reassured by Hemingway's next book, the novelette called *The Old Man and the Sea*. It contained, for example, no women—only an old man, a small boy, and a large fish. And the athletic performance of the heroic old man was precisely as gratifying as the aesthetic performance of the heroically aging novelist. The point was the same as ever: winner take nothing.

## VI

F. SCOTT FITZGERALD was no longer present, in these later years, to judge the performance of his friend, whom he had named once, together with Edmund Wilson, as his "conscience." But he felt, toward the end of his life, that he lived in Hemingway's shadow. "I don't write any more," he said to Thornton Wilder in the middle thirties. "Ernest has made all my writing unnecessary." In April of 1934 he had started—and he worked at this project off and on for the rest of his life—a fantastically ill-conceived novel to be called *The Count of Darkness*. Set in the ninth and tenth centuries, this novel was

to have as its hero a daring young man named Phillipe who would play a part in the founding of France and in the consolidation of feudalism. Fitzgerald's plan was that "it shall be the story of Ernest" and his hope that "just as Stendahl's portrait of a Byronic man made *Le Rouge et Noir* so couldn't *my* portrait of Ernest as Phillipe make the real modern man." It is not surprising that those portions of this work that he finished are among the least satisfactory pieces of writing he ever did.

He managed, through a deteriorating life, still to achieve work that was equal to and perhaps greater than the old magnificence. The dizzy pace of the Fitzgeralds' life accelerated in the mid-twenties, in Paris and on the Riviera, until, with Zelda nervously ill and Fitzgerald himself nearly a physical ruin, they returned to the United States at the end of 1926 and went to Hollywood. There things were hardly quieter. They bought a large, serene house outside Wilmington, Delaware, and hoped for peace. He was working at a novel to be called *The World's Fair*, never to be finished. As their marriage had grown older, Zelda Fitzgerald had developed stronger and stronger competitive feelings about her husband, and now she decided that she must study ballet dancing, and chiefly for that purpose they returned to Paris in the summer of 1928. In 1929 he abandoned *The World's Fair*, and living much of the time on the Riviera, began to work on material that would lead to *Tender Is the Night*. In April of 1930, Mrs. Fitzgerald suffered a complete nervous collapse and spent nearly a year in a Swiss sanatorium. The diagnosis was schizophrenia, and the possibilty of her recovery was slight. But there were brief recoveries. They returned to the United States. Hollywood again. Another breakdown. Another sanatorium. Another house, now near Baltimore, inappropriately called *La Paix*. Working on *Tender Is the Night*, Fitzgerald's life had nevertheless become a nightmare, with liquor necessary to work, and work necessary if he was to live. The novel was finished late in 1933 and published in the next April.

Much more complex than *The Great*

*Gatsby*, the new novel, in spite of the circumstances of its composition, is probably Fitzgerald's greatest achievement. A story of "emotional bankruptcy," it depicts not only the dissolution of a life but of a way of life. It is the elegy of the 1920's, the allegory of the dream that Fitzgerald himself tried to make of reality and the dissipation of that dream. It is, quite simply, one of the most moving novels in all American fiction. And the reviews were lukewarm, obtuse, the sales trivial. It was Fitzgerald's greatest defeat.

His wife was now incurably insane, even though she managed to write a novel, *Save Me the Waltz* (1932), in one period of hospitalization. Fitzgerald managed one more collection of short stories (*Taps at Reveille*, 1935), but really, the remaining years of his life were all downhill. Early in 1936 he published his extraordinary self-diagnosis in the three pieces that make "The Crack-Up" and was again in Hollywood, looking for work. Treated like a hack writer by producers, nearly forgotten by the public, a dim figure lost in the now legendary twenties, he was rescued by the columnist Sheilah Graham, and had, at the end of his life, at least his love for her, and hers. The story of his disastrous attempt to write a scenario with Budd Schulberg about Dartmouth College and its Winter Carnival is told in fictional form in Schulberg's novel, *The Disenchanted* (1950), and again in the play of that name, written by Schulberg and Harvey Breit. He managed to write a series of stories about a character named Pat Hobby ("he is what Fitzgerald in his worst moments saw himself becoming"),[1] and he began to make notes for and write fragments of another novel that, after his death, Edmund Wilson was to put together as *The Last Tycoon*. Had he lived to finish it, it would almost certainly have been the one great novel about Hollywood.

In November of 1940, he had a serious heart attack. He stopped drinking. But on December 21 he had a second attack, and that was fatal.

Sherwood Anderson, who had always brooded about the situation of the artist in America, felt sad, and in his *Memoirs*, which he at this time was straining to finish, he tried once more to define the problem for himself. What was it, in America, that destroyed its writers, or drove them to destroy themselves? "Did you ever hear of an artist who had an easy road to travel in life?" he exclaimed, rather than asked, in 1938. Ernest Hemingway, three years before, had given the world his speculations on the subject.

"We do not have great writers," I said. "Something happens to our good writers at a certain age. I can explain but it is quite long and may bore you."

"Please explain," he said. . . .

"We destroy them in many ways. First, economically. . . ."

"Tell me . . . what are the things, the actual, concrete things that harm a writer?"

I was tired of the conversation which was becoming an interview. So I would make it an interview and finish it. The necessity to put a thousand intangibles into a sentence, now, before lunch, was too bloody.

"Politics, women, drink, money, ambition. And the lack of politics, women, drink, money and ambition," I said profoundly. . . .

"But drink. I do not understand about that. That has always seemed silly to me. I understand it as a weakness."

"It is a way of ending a day. . . ."

What happened to Hemingway himself remains something of a mystery, but his violent death in 1961 reminds us that there are other and more final ways of ending a day.

While he was apparently sympathetic to the Castro regime, he nevertheless left Cuba in 1960 for his ranch in Idaho. He was ill, sick with who knows what besides depression, and he spent a long time under observation in the Mayo Clinic, where he twice underwent shock therapy that did not help him. Then early one morning the silence of the Idaho ranch house was shattered by the blast of a double-barreled shotgun. The entire world was shaken, and not alone by the death of the man but by the very force of the drama. With the end of this man, a legend had also been rounded out, brought to its end with a stunning symmetry.

[1] Arthur Mizener, *The Far Side of Paradise* (1951), p. 285.

# Sherwood Anderson

FROM

## A STORY TELLER'S STORY

❖

⟨[ THIS book, the earliest of Sherwood Anderson's semi-autobiographical efforts, was written in 1923. Fictionalizing the facts of his life, he described it quite properly as a "tale of an American writer's journey through his own imaginative world and through the world of facts." The characteristic departure from the facts is nowhere more evident than in the following selection, which is one of Anderson's literary accounts of the supposed climax in his life when, at thirty-seven years of age, he broke with business and strode into the freedom of the literary life.

❖

### NOTE II

ON AN evening of the late summer I got off a train at a growing Ohio industrial town where I had once lived. I was rapidly becoming a middle-aged man. Two years before I had left the place in disgrace. There I had tried to be a manufacturer, a money-maker, and had failed, and I had been trying and failing ever since. In the town some thousands of dollars had been lost for others. An effort to conform to the standard dreams of the men of my times had failed and in the midst of my disgrace and generally hopeless outlook, as regards making a living, I had been filled with joy at coming to the end of it all. One morning I had left the place afoot, leaving my poor little factory, like an illegitimate child, on another man's doorstep. I had left, merely taking what money was in my pocket, some eight or ten dollars.

What a moment that leaving had been! To one of the European artists I afterward came to know the situation would have been unbelievably grotesque. Such a man could not have believed in my earnestness about it all and would have thought my feelings of the moment a worked-up thing. I can in fancy hear one of the Frenchmen, Italians or Russians I later knew laughing at me. "Well, but why get so worked up? A factory is a factory, is it not? Why may not one break it like an empty bottle? You have lost some money for others? See the light on that field over there. These others, for whom you lost money, were they compelled to beg in the streets, were their children torn by wolves? What is it you Americans get so excited about when a little money is lost?"

A European artist may not understand but an American will understand. The devil! It is not a question of money. No men are so careless and free with money as the Americans. There is another matter involved.

It strikes rather deeply at the roots of our beings. Childish as it all may have seemed to an older and more sophisticated world, we Americans, from the beginning, have been up to something, or we have wanted to think we were up to something. We came here, or our fathers or grandfathers came here, from a hundred diverse places—and you may be sure it was not the artists who came. Artists do not want to cut down trees, root stumps out of the ground, build towns and railroads. The artist wants to sit with a strip of canvas before him, face an open space on a wall, carve a bit of wood, make combinations of words and sentences, as I am doing now—trying to express to others some thought or feeling of his own. He wants to dream of color, to lay hold of form, free the sensual in himself, live more fully and freely in his contact with the materials before him than he can possibly live in life. He seeks a kind of controlled ecstasy and is a man with a passion, a "nut," as we love to say in America. And very often, when he is not in actual contact with his materials, he is a much more vain and disagreeable ass than any man, not an artist, could possibly be. As a living man he is almost always a pest. It is only when dead he begins to have value.

The simple truth is that in a European country the artist is more freely accepted than he is among us, and only because he has been longer about. They know how harmless he really is—or rather do not know how subtly dangerous he can be—and accept him only as one might accept a hybrid cross between a dog and a cat that went growling mewing barking and spitting about the house. One might want to kill the first of such strange beasts one sees but after one has seen a dozen and has realized that, like the mule, they cannot breed their own kind one laughs and lets them live, paying no more attention to them than modern France for example pays to its artists.

But in America things are somewhat different. Here something went wrong in the beginning. We pretended to so much and were going to do such great things here. This vast land was to be a refuge for all the outlawed brave foolish folk of the world. The declaration of the rights of man was to have a new hearing in a new place. The devil! We did get ourselves into a bad hole. We were going to be superhuman and it turned out we were sons of men who were not such devilish fellows after all. You cannot blame us that we are somewhat reluctant about finding out the very human things concerning ourselves. One does so hate to come down off the perch.

We are now losing our former feeling of inherent virtue, are permitting ourselves occasionally to laugh at ourselves for our pretensions, but there was a time here when we were sincerely in earnest about all this American business, "the land of the free and the home of the brave." We actually meant it and no one will ever understand present-day America or Americans who does not concede that we meant it and that while we were building all of our big ugly hurriedly thrown-together towns, creating our great industrial system, growing always more huge and prosperous, we were as much in earnest about what we thought we were up to as were the French of the thirteenth century when they built the cathedral of Chartres to the glory of God.

They built the cathedral of Chartres to the glory of God and we really intended building here a land to the glory of Man, and thought we were doing it too. That was our intention and the affair only blew up in the process, or got perverted, because Man, even the brave and the free Man, is somewhat a less worthy object of glorification than God. This we might have found out long ago but that we did not know each other. We came from too many different places to know each other well, had been promised too much, wanted too much. We were afraid to know each other.

Oh, how Americans have wanted heroes, wanted brave simple fine men! And how sincerely and deeply we Americans have been afraid to understand and love one another, fearing to find ourselves at the end no more brave heroic and fine than the people of almost any other part of the world.

I however digress. What I am trying to do is to give the processes of my own mind at two distinct moments of my own life. First, the moment when after many years of effort to conform to an unstated and but dimly understood American dream by making myself a successful man in the material world I threw all overboard and then at another moment when, having come back to the same spot where I passed through the first moment, I attempted to confront myself with myself with a somewhat changed point of view.

As for the first of these moments, it was melodramatic and even silly enough. The struggle centered itself at the last within the walls of a particular moment and within the walls of a particular room.

I sat in the room with a woman who was my secretary. For several years I had been sitting there, dictating to her regarding the goods I had made in my factory and that I was attempting to sell. The attempt to sell the goods had become a sort of madness in me. There were certain thousands or perhaps hundreds of thousands of men living in towns or on farms in many states of my country who might possibly buy the goods I had made rather than the goods made in another factory by another man. How I had wheedled! How I had schemed! In some years I gave myself quite fully to the matter in hand and the dollars trickled in. Well, I was about to become rich. It was a possibility. After a good day or week, when many dollars had come, I went to walk and when I had got into a quiet place where I was unobserved I threw back my shoulders and strutted. During the year I had made for myself so many dollars. Next year I would make so many more, and the next year so many more. But my thoughts of the matter did not express themselves in the dollars. It never does to the American man. Who calls the American a dollar-lover is foolish. My factory was of a certain size—it was really a poor haphazardly enough run place—but after a time I would build a great factory and after that a greater and greater. Like a true American, I thought in size.

My fancy played with the matter of factories as a child would play with a toy. There would be a great factory with walls going up and up and a little open place for a lawn at the front, shower baths for the workers with perhaps a fountain playing on a lawn, and up before the door of this place I would drive in a large automobile.

Oh, how I would be respected by all, how I would be looked up to by all! I walked in a little dark street, throwing back my shoulders. How grand and glorious I felt!

The houses along the street in which I walked were small and ugly and dirty-faced children played in the yards. I wondered. Having walked, dreaming my dream for a long time I returned to the neighborhood of my factory and opening my office went in to sit at my desk smoking a cigarette. The night watchman came in. He was an old man who had once been a school-teacher but, as he said, his eyes had gone back on him.

When I had walked alone I had been able to make myself feel somewhat as I fancied a prince might have felt but when anyone came near me something exploded inside. I was a deflated balloon. Well, in fancy, I had a thousand workmen under me. They were children and I was their father and would look out for them. Perhaps I would build them model houses to live in, a town of model houses built about my great factory, eh? The workmen would be my children and I would look out for my children. "Land of the free— home of the brave."

But I was back in my factory now and the night watchman sat smoking with me. Sometimes we talked far into the night. The devil! He was a fellow like myself, having the same problems as myself. How could I be his father? The thought was absurd. Once, when he was a younger man, he had dreamed of being a scholar but his eyes had gone back on him. What had he wanted to do? He spoke of it for a time. He had wanted to be a scholar and I had myself spent those earlier years eagerly reading books. "I would really like to have been a learned monk, one of those fellows such as appeared in the Middle Ages, one of the fellows who went off and lived by himself and gave himself up wholly to learning, one who believed in learning, who spent his life humbly seeking new truths—but I got married and my wife had kids, and then, you see, my eyes went back on me." He spoke of the matter philosophically. One did not let oneself get too much excited. After a time one got over any feeling of bitterness. The night watchman had a boy, a lad of fifteen, who also loved books. "He is pretty lucky, can get all the books he wants at the public library. In the afternoon after school is out and before I come down here to my job he reads aloud to me."

\* \* \*

Men and women, many men and many women! There were men and women working in my factory, men and women walking in streets with me, many men and women scattered far and wide over the country to whom I wanted to sell my goods. I sent men, salesmen, to see them—I wrote letters; how many thousands of letters, all to the same purpose! "Will you buy my goods?" And again, "Will you buy my goods?"

What were the other men thinking about? What was I myself thinking about? Suppose it were possible to know something of the men and women, to know something of oneself, too. The devil! These were not thoughts that would help me to sell my goods to all the others. What were all the others like? What was I myself like? Did I want a large factory with a little lawn and a fountain in front and with a model town built about it?

Days of endlessly writing letters to men, nights of walking in strange quiet streets. What had happened to me? "I shall go get drunk," I said to myself and I did go and get drunk. Taking a train to a near-by city I drank until a kind of joy came to me and with some man I had found and who had joined in my carousal I walked in streets, shouting at other men, singing songs, going sometimes into strange houses to laugh with people, to talk with people I found there.

Here was something I liked and something the others liked too. When I had come to people in strange houses, half drunk, released, they were not afraid of me. "Well, he wants to talk," they seemed to be saying to themselves. "That's fine!" There was something broken down between us, a wall broken down. We talked of outlandish things for Anglo-Saxon trained people to speak of, of love between men and women, of what children's coming meant. Food was brought forth. Often in a single evening of this sort I got more from people than I could get from weeks of ordinary intercourse. The people were a little excited by the strangeness of two unknown men in their houses. With my companion I went boldly to the door and knocked. Laughter. "Hello, the house!" It might be the house of a laborer or that of a well-to-do merchant. I had hold of my new-found friend's arm and explained our presence as well as I could. "We are a little drunk and we are travelers. We just want to sit and visit with you a while."

There was a kind of terror in people's eyes, and a kind of gladness too. An old workman showed us a relic he had brought home with him from the Civil War while his wife ran into a bedroom and changed her dress. Then a child awoke in a near-by room and began to cry and was permitted to come in in her nightgown and lie in my arms or in the arms of the new-found friend who had got drunk with me. The talk swept over strange intimate subjects. What were men up to? What were women up to? There was a kind of deep taking of breath, as though we had all been holding something back from one another and had suddenly decided to let go. Once or twice we stayed all night in the house to which we had gone.

What thoughts in the mind! There was a note due and payable at the bank. "Now here, you man, attend to your affairs. You have induced others to put money into your enterprises. If you are to build a great enterprise here you must be up and at it."

How often in after years I have laughed at myself for the thoughts and emotions of that time. There is a thought I have had that is very delicious. It is this, and I dare say it will be an unwelcome thought to many, "I am the American man. I think there is no doubt of it. I am just the mixture, the cold, moral man of the North into whose body has come the warm pagan blood of the South. I love and am afraid to love. Behold in me the American man striving to become an artist, to become conscious of himself, filled with wonder concerning himself and others, trying to have a good time and not fake a good time. I am not English Italian Jew German Frenchman Russian. What am I? I am tremendously serious about it all but at the same time I laugh constantly at myself for my own seriousness. Like all real American men of our day I wander constantly from place to place striving to put down roots into the American soil and not quite doing it. If you say the real American man is not yet born, you lie. I am the type of the fellow."

This is somewhat of a joke on me but it is a greater joke on the reader. As respectable and conventional a man as Calvin Coolidge has me in him—and I have him in myself? Do not doubt it. I have him in me and Eugene Debs in me and the crazy political idealists of the Western States and Mr. Gary of the Steel Trust and the whole crew. I accept them all as part of myself. Would to God they would thus accept me!

* * *

And being this thing I have tried to describe I return now to myself sitting between the walls of a certain room and between the walls of a certain moment too. Just why was that moment so pregnant? I will never quite know.

It came with a rush, the feeling that I must quit buying and selling, the overwhelming feeling of uncleanliness. I was in my whole nature a taleteller. My father had been one and his not knowing had destroyed him. The tale-teller cannot bother with buying and selling. To do so will destroy him. No class of men I have ever known are so dull and cheerless as the writers of glad sentimental romances, the painters of glad pretty pictures. The corrupt unspeakable thing that had happened to tale-telling in America was all concerned with this matter of buying and selling. The horse cannot sing like a canary bird nor the canary bird pull a plow like a horse and either of them attempting it becomes something ridiculous.

NOTE III

THERE was a door leading out from my office to the street. How many steps to the door? I counted them, "five, six, seven." "Suppose," I asked myself, "I could take those five, six, seven steps to the door, pass out at the door, go along that railroad track out there, disappear into the far horizon beyond. Where was I to go? In the town where my factory was located I had still the reputation of being a bright young business man. In my first years there I had been filled with shrewd vast schemes. I had been admired, looked up to. Since that time I had gone down and down as a bright young man but no one yet knew how far I had gone. I was still respected in the town, my word was still good at the bank. I was a respectable man.

Did I want to do something not respectable, not decent? I am trying to give you the history of a moment and as a tale-teller I have come to think that the true history of life is but a history of moments. It is only at rare moments we live. I wanted to walk out at a door and go away into the distance. The American is still a wanderer, a migrating bird not yet ready to build a nest. All our cities are built temporarily as are the houses in which we live. We are on the way—toward what? There have been other times in the history of the world when many strange peoples came together in a new strange land. To assume that we have made an America, even materially, seems to me now but telling ourselves fairy tales in the night. We have not even made it materially yet and the American man has only gone in for money-making on a large scale to quiet his own restlessness, as the monk of old days was given the Regula of Augustine to quiet him and still the lusts in himself. For the monk, kept occupied with the saying of prayers and the doing of many little sacred offices, there was no time for the lusts of the world to enter in and for the American to be perpetually busy with his affairs, with his automobiles, with his movies, there is no time for unquiet thoughts.

On that day in the office at my factory I looked at myself and laughed. The whole struggle I am trying to describe and that I am confident will be closer to the understanding of most Americans than anything else I have ever written was accompanied by a kind of mocking laughter at myself and my own seriousness about it all.

Very well, then, I wanted to go out of the door and never come back. How many Americans want to go—but where do they want to go? I wanted to accept for myself all the little restless thoughts of which myself and the others had been so afraid and you, who are Americans, will understand the necessity of my continually laughing at myself and at all things dear to me. I must laugh at the thing I love the more intensely because of my love. Any American will understand that.

It was a trying moment for me. There was the woman, my secretary, now looking at me. What did she represent? What did she not represent? Would I dare be honest with her? It was quite apparent to me I would not. I had got to my feet and we stood looking at each other. "It is now or never," I said to myself, and I remember that I kept smiling. I had stopped dictating to her in the midst of a sentence. "The goods about which you have inquired are the best of their kind made in the—"

I stood and she sat and we were looking at each other intently. "What's the matter?" she asked. She was an intelligent woman, more intelligent I am sure than myself, just because she was a woman and good, while I have never been good, do not know how to be good. Could I explain all to her? The words of a fancied explanation marched through my mind: "My dear young woman, it is all very silly but I have decided to no longer concern myself with this buying and selling. It may be all right for others but for me it is poison. There is this factory. You may have it if it please you. It is of little value I dare say. Perhaps it is money ahead and then again it may well be it is money behind. I am uncertain about it all and now I am going away. Now, at this moment, with the letter I have been dictating, with the very sentence you have been writing left unfinished, I am going out that door and never come back. What am I going to do? Well now, that I don't know. I am going to wander about. I am going to sit with people, listen to words, tell tales of people, what they are thinking, what they are feeling. The devil! It may even be I am going forth in search of myself."

The woman was looking into my eyes the while I looked into hers. Perhaps I had grown a little pale and now she grew pale. "You're sick," she said and her words gave me an idea. There was wanted a justification of myself, not to myself but to the others. A crafty thought came. Was the thought crafty or was I, at the moment, a little insane, a "nut," as every American so loves to say of every man who does something a little out of the groove.

I had grown pale and it may be I was ill but nevertheless I was laughing—the American laugh. Had I suddenly become a little insane? What a comfort that thought would be, not to myself but to the others. My leaving the place I was then in

would tear up roots that had gone down a little into the ground. The ground I did not think would support the tree that was myself and that I thought wanted to grow.

My mind dwelt on the matter of roots and I looked at my feet. The whole question with which I was at the moment concerned became a matter of feet. I had two feet that could take me out of the life I was then in and that, to do so, would need but take three or four steps to a door. When I had reached the door and had stepped out of my little factory office everything would be quite simplified, I was sure. I had to lift myself out. Others would have to tackle the job of getting me back, once I had stepped over that threshold.

Whether at the moment I merely became shrewd and crafty or whether I really became temporarily insane I shall never quite know. What I did was to step very close to the woman and looking directly into her eyes I laughed gayly. Others besides herself would, I knew, hear the words I was now speaking. I looked at my feet. "I have been wading in a long river and my feet are wet," I said.

Again I laughed as I walked lightly toward the door and out of a long and tangled phase of my life, out of the door of buying and selling, out of the door of affairs.

"They want me to be a 'nut,' will love to think of me as a 'nut,' and why not? It may just be that's what I am," I thought gayly and at the same time turned and said a final confusing sentence to the woman who now stared at me in speechless amazement. "My feet are cold wet and heavy from long wading in a river. Now I shall go walk on dry land," I said, and as I passed out at the door a delicious thought came. "Oh, you little tricky words, you are my brothers. It is you, not myself, have lifted me over this threshold. It is you who have dared give me a hand. For the rest of my life I will be a servant to you," I whispered to myself as I went along a spur of railroad track, over a bridge, out of a town and out of that phase of my life.

*1924*

# THE EGG

◇

⟨ THIS story, written in 1918, was first published in the *Dial* for March 1919 under the title "The Triumph of the Egg." Anderson then took that title for a whole collection of short stories of which "The Egg" was to prove the keystone. "The Egg," his great success in the exploration of grotesques, is a very funny story. It is also very sad. In a letter of October 10, 1932, to The Dramatic Publishing Company, discussing a dramatized version of the story and his interest in maintaining a balance between comedy and pathos, he makes the intention of his story clear.

◇

MY FATHER was, I am sure, intended by nature to be a cheerful, kindly man. Until he was thirty-four years old he worked as a farm-hand for a man named Thomas Butterworth whose place lay near the town of Bidwell, Ohio. He had then a horse of his own and on Saturday evenings drove into town to spend a few hours in social intercourse with other farm-hands. In town he drank several glasses of beer and stood about in Ben Head's saloon—crowded on Saturday evenings with visiting farm-hands. Songs were sung and glasses thumped on the bar. At ten o'clock father drove home along a lonely country road, made his horse comfortable for the night and himself went to bed, quite happy in his position in life. He had at that time no notion of trying to rise in the world.

It was in the spring of his thirty-fifth year that father married my mother, then a country school-teacher, and in the following spring I came wriggling and crying into the world. Something happened to the two people. They became ambitious. The American passion for getting up in the world took possession of them.

It may have been that mother was responsible. Being a school-teacher she had no doubt read books and magazines. She had, I presume, read of how Garfield, Lincoln, and other Americans rose from poverty to fame and greatness and as I lay beside her—in the days of her lying-in—she may have dreamed that I would some day rule men and cities. At any rate she induced father to give up his place as a farm-hand, sell his horse and embark on an independent enterprise of his own. She was a tall silent woman with a long nose and troubled grey eyes. For herself she wanted nothing. For father and myself she was incurably ambitious.

The first venture into which the two people went turned out badly. They rented ten acres of poor stony land on Griggs's Road, eight miles from Bidwell, and launched into chicken raising. I grew into boyhood on the place and got my first impressions of life there. From the beginning they were impressions of disaster and if, in my turn, I am a gloomy man inclined to see the darker side of life, I attribute it to the fact that what should have been

for me the happy joyous days of childhood were spent on a chicken farm.

One unversed in such matters can have no notion of the many and tragic things that can happen to a chicken. It is born out of an egg, lives for a few weeks as a tiny fluffy thing such as you will see pictured on Easter cards, then becomes hideously naked, eats quantities of corn and meal bought by the sweat of your father's brow, gets diseases called pip, cholera, and other names, stands looking with stupid eyes at the sun, becomes sick and dies. A few hens and now and then a rooster, intended to serve God's mysterious ends, struggle through to maturity. The hens lay eggs out of which come other chickens and the dreadful cycle is thus made complete. It is all unbelievably complex. Most philosophers must have been raised on chicken farms. One hopes for so much from a chicken and is so dreadfully disillusioned. Small chickens, just setting out on the journey of life, look so bright and alert and they are in fact so dreadfully stupid. They are so much like people they mix one up in one's judgments of life. If disease does not kill them they wait until your expectations are thoroughly aroused and then walk under the wheels of a wagon—to go squashed and dead back to their maker. Vermin infest their youth, and fortunes must be spent for curative powders. In later life I have seen how a literature has been built up on the subject of fortunes to be made out of the raising of chickens. It is intended to be read by the gods who have just eaten of the tree of the knowledge of good and evil. It is a hopeful literature and declares that much may be done by simple ambitious people who own a few hens. Do not be led astray by it. It was not written for you. Go hunt for gold on the frozen hills of Alaska, put your faith in the honesty of a politician, believe if you will that the world is daily growing better and that good will triumph over evil, but do not read and believe the literature that is written concerning the hen. It was not written for you.

I, however, digress. My tale does not primarily concern itself with the hen. If correctly told it will centre on the egg. For ten years my father and mother struggled to make our chicken farm pay and then they gave up that struggle and began another. They moved into the town of Bidwell, Ohio, and embarked in the restaurant business. After ten years of worry with incubators that did not hatch, and with tiny—and in their own way lovely—balls of fluff that passed on into semi-naked pullethood and from that into dead henhood, we threw all aside and packing our belongings on a wagon drove down Griggs's Road toward Bidwell, a tiny caravan of hope looking for a new place from which to start on our upward journey through life.

We must have been a sad looking lot, not, I fancy, unlike refugees fleeing from a battlefield. Mother and I walked in the road. The wagon that contained our goods had been borrowed for the day from Mr. Albert Griggs, a neighbor. Out of its sides stuck the legs of cheap chairs and at the back of the pile of beds, tables, and boxes filled with kitchen utensils was a crate of live chickens, and on top of that the baby carriage in which I had been wheeled about in my infancy. Why we stuck to the baby carriage I don't know. It was unlikely other children would be born and the wheels were broken. People who have few possessions cling tightly to those they have. That is one of the facts that make life so discouraging.

Father rode on top of the wagon. He was then a bald-headed man of forty-five, a little fat and from long association with mother and the chickens he had become habitually silent and discouraged. All during our ten years on the chicken farm he had worked as a laborer on neighboring farms and most of the money he had earned had been spent for remedies to cure chicken diseases, on Wilmer's White Wonder Cholera Cure or Professor Bidlow's Egg Producer or some other preparations that mother found advertised in the poultry papers. There were two little patches of hair on father's head just above his ears. I remember that as a child I used to sit looking at him when he had gone to sleep in a chair before the stove on Sunday afternoons in the winter. I had at that time already begun to read books and have notions of my own and the bald path that led over the top of his head was, I fancied, something like a broad road, such a road as Caesar might have made on which to lead his legions out of Rome and into the wonders of an unknown world. The tufts of hair that grew above father's ears were, I thought, like forests. I fell into a half-sleeping, half-waking state and dreamed I was a tiny thing going along the road into a far beautiful place where there were no chicken farms and where life was a happy eggless affair.

One might write a book concerning our flight from the chicken farm into town. Mother and I walked the entire eight miles—she to be sure that nothing fell from the wagon and I to see the wonders of the world. On the seat of the wagon beside father was his greatest treasure. I will tell you of that.

On a chicken farm where hundreds and even thousands of chickens come out of eggs surprising things sometimes happen. Grotesques are born out of eggs as out of people. The accident does not often occur—perhaps once in a thousand births. A chicken is, you see, born that has four legs, two pairs of wings, two heads or what not. The things do not live. They go quickly back to the hand of their maker that has for a moment trembled. The fact that the poor little things could not live was one of the tragedies of life to father. He had some sort of notion that if he could but bring into henhood or roosterhood a five-legged hen or a two-headed rooster his fortune would be made. He dreamed of taking the wonder about to county fairs and of growing rich by exhibiting it to other farm-hands.

At any rate he saved all the little monstrous things that had been born on our chicken farm. They were preserved in alcohol and put each in its own glass bottle. These he had carefully put into a box and on our journey into town it was carried on the wagon seat beside him. He drove the horses with one hand and with the other clung to the box. When we got to our destination the box was taken down at once and the bottles removed. All during our days as keepers of a restaurant in the town of Bidwell, Ohio, the grotesques in their little glass bottles sat on a shelf back of the counter. Mother sometimes protested but father was a rock on the subject of his treasure. The grotesques were, he declared, valuable. People, he said, liked to look at strange and wonderful things.

Did I say that we embarked in the restaurant business in the town of Bidwell, Ohio? I exaggerated a little. The town itself lay at the foot of a low hill and on the shore of a small river. The railroad did not run through the town and the station was a mile away to the north at a place called Pickleville. There had been a cider mill and pickle factory at the station, but before the time of our coming they had both gone out of business. In the morning and in the evening busses came down to the station along a road called Turner's Pike from the hotel on the main street of Bidwell. Our going to the out of the way place to embark in the restaurant business was mother's idea. She talked of it for a year and then one day went off and rented an empty store building opposite the railroad station. It was her idea that the restaurant would be profitable. Travelling men, she said, would be always waiting around to take trains out of town and town people would come to the station to await incoming trains. They would come to the restaurant to buy pieces of pie and drink coffee. Now that I am older I know that she had another motive in going. She was ambitious for me. She wanted me to rise in the world, to get into a town school and become a man of the towns.

At Pickleville father and mother worked hard

as they always had done. At first there was the necessity of putting our place into shape to be a restaurant. That took a month. Father built a shelf on which he put tins of vegetables. He painted a sign on which he put his name in large red letters. Below his name was the sharp command—"EAT HERE"—that was so seldom obeyed. A show case was bought and filled with cigars and tobacco. Mother scrubbed the floor and the walls of the room. I went to school in the town and was glad to be away from the farm and from the presence of the discouraged, sad-looking chickens. Still I was not very joyous. In the evening I walked home from school along Turner's Pike and remembered the children I had seen playing in the town school yard. A troop of little girls had gone hopping about and singing. I tried that. Down along the frozen road I went hopping solemnly on one leg. "Hippity Hop To The Barber Shop," I sang shrilly. Then I stopped and looked doubtfully about. I was afraid of being seen in my gay mood. It must have seemed to me that I was doing a thing that should not be done by one who, like myself, had been raised on a chicken farm where death was a daily visitor.

Mother decided that our restaurant should remain open at night. At ten in the evening a passenger train went north past our door followed by a local freight. The freight crew had switching to do in Pickleville and when the work was done they came to our restaurant for hot coffee and food. Sometimes one of them ordered a fried egg. In the morning at four they returned north-bound and again visited us. A little trade began to grow up. Mother slept at night and during the day tended the restaurant and fed our boarders while father slept. He slept in the same bed mother had occupied during the night and I went off to the town of Bidwell and to school. During the long nights, while mother and I slept, father cooked meats that were to go into sandwiches for the lunch baskets of our boarders. Then an idea in regard to getting up in the world came into his head. The American spirit took hold of him. He also became ambitious.

In the long nights when there was little to do father had time to think. That was his undoing. He decided that he had in the past been an unsuccessful man because he had not been cheerful enough and that in the future he would adopt a cheerful outlook on life. In the early morning he came upstairs and got into bed with mother. She woke and the two talked. From my bed in the corner I listened.

It was father's idea that both he and mother should try to entertain the people who came to eat at our restaurant. I cannot now remember his words, but he gave the impression of one about to become in some obscure way a kind of public entertainer. When people, particularly young people from the town of Bidwell, came into our place, as on very rare occasions they did, bright entertaining conversation was to be made. From father's words I gathered that something of the jolly innkeeper effect was to be sought. Mother must have been doubtful from the first, but she said nothing discouraging. It was father's notion that a passion for the company of himself and mother would spring up in the breasts of the younger people of the town of Bidwell. In the evening bright happy groups would come singing down Turner's Pike. They would troop shouting with joy and laughter into our place. There would be song and festivity. I do not mean to give the impression that father spoke so elaborately of the matter. He was as I have said an uncommunicative man. "They want some place to go. I tell you they want some place to go," he said over and over. That was as far as he got. My own imagination has filled in the blanks.

For two or three weeks this notion of father's invaded our house. We did not talk much, but in our daily lives tried earnestly to make smiles take the place of glum looks. Mother smiled at the boarders and I, catching the infection, smiled at our cat. Father became a little feverish in his anxiety to please. There was no doubt, lurking somewhere in him, a touch of the spirit of the showman. He did not waste much of his ammunition on the railroad men he served at night but seemed to be waiting for a young man or woman from Bidwell to come in to show what he could do. On the counter in the restaurant there was a wire basket kept always filled with eggs, and it must have been before his eyes when the idea of being entertaining was born in his brain. There was something pre-natal about the way eggs kept themselves connected with the development of his idea. At any rate an egg ruined his new impulse in life. Late one night I was awakened by a roar of anger coming from father's throat. Both mother and I sat upright in our beds. With trembling hands she lighted a lamp that stood on a table by her head. Downstairs the front door of our restaurant went shut with a bang and in a few minutes father tramped up the stairs. He held an egg in his hand and his hand trembled as though he were having a chill. There was a half insane light in his eyes. As he stood glaring at us I was sure he intended throwing the egg at either mother or me. Then he laid it gently on the table beside the lamp and dropped on his knees beside mother's bed. He began to cry like a boy and I, carried away by his grief, cried with him. The two of us filled the little upstairs room with our wailing voices. It is ridiculous, but of the picture we made I can remember only the fact that mother's hand continually stroked the bald path that ran across the top of his head. I have forgotten what mother said to him and how she induced him to tell her of what had happened downstairs. His explanation also has gone out of my mind. I remember only my own grief and fright and the shiny path over father's head glowing in the lamp light as he knelt by the bed.

As to what happened downstairs. For some unexplainable reason I know the story as well as though I had been a witness to my father's discomfiture. One in time gets to know many unexplainable things. On that evening young Joe Kane, son of a merchant of Bidwell, came to Pickleville to meet his father, who was expected on the ten o'clock evening train from the South. The train was three hours late and Joe came into our place to loaf about and to wait for its arrival. The local freight train came in and the freight crew were fed. Joe was left alone in the restaurant with father.

From the moment he came into our place the Bidwell young man must have been puzzled by my father's actions. It was his notion that father was angry at him for hanging around. He noticed that the restaurant keeper was apparently disturbed by his presence and he thought of going out. However, it began to rain and he did not fancy the long walk to town and back. He bought a five-cent cigar and ordered a cup of coffee. He had a newspaper in his pocket and took it out and began to read. "I'm waiting for the evening train. It's late," he said apologetically.

For a long time father, whom Joe Kane had never seen before, remained silently gazing at his visitor. He was no doubt suffering from an attack of stage fright. As so often happens in life he had thought so much and so often of the situation that now confronted him that he was somewhat nervous in its presence.

For one thing, he did not know what to do with his hands. He thrust one of them nervously over the counter and shook hands with Joe Kane. "How-de-do," he said. Joe Kane put his newspaper down and stared at him. Father's eye lighted on the basket of eggs that sat on the counter and he began to talk. "Well," he began hesitatingly, "well, you have heard of Christopher Columbus, eh?" He seemed to be angry. "That Christopher Columbus was a cheat," he declared emphatically. "He talked of making an egg stand on its end.

He talked, he did, and then he went and broke the end of the egg."

My father seemed to his visitor to be beside himself at the duplicity of Christopher Columbus. He muttered and swore. He declared it was wrong to teach children that Christopher Columbus was a great man when, after all, he cheated at the critical moment. He had declared he would make an egg stand on end and then when his bluff had been called he had done a trick. Still grumbling at Columbus, father took an egg from the basket on the counter and began to walk up and down. He rolled the egg between the palms of his hands. He smiled genially. He began to mumble words regarding the effect to be produced on an egg by the electricity that comes out of the human body. He declared that without breaking its shell and by virtue of rolling it back and forth in his hands he could stand the egg on its end. He explained that the warmth of his hands and the gentle rolling movement he gave the egg created a new centre of gravity, and Joe Kane was mildly interested. "I have handled thousands of eggs," father said. "No one knows more about eggs than I do."

He stood the egg on the counter and it fell on its side. He tried the trick again and again, each time rolling the egg between the palms of his hands and saying the words regarding the wonders of electricity and the laws of gravity. When after a half hour's effort he did succeed in making the egg stand for a moment he looked up to find that his visitor was no longer watching. By the time he had succeeded in calling Joe Kane's attention to the success of his effort the egg had again rolled over and lay on its side.

Afire with the showman's passion and at the same time a good deal disconcerted by the failure of his first effort, father now took the bottles containing the poultry monstrosities down from their place on the shelf and began to show them to his visitor. "How would you like to have seven legs and two heads like this fellow?" he asked, exhibiting the most remarkable of his treasures. A cheerful smile played over his face. He reached over the counter and tried to slap Joe Kane on the shoulder as he had seen men do in Ben Head's saloon when he was a young farm-hand and drove to town on Saturday evenings. His visitor was made a little ill by the sight of the body of the terribly deformed bird floating in the alcohol in the bottle and got up to go. Coming from behind the counter father took hold of the young man's arm and led him back to his seat. He grew a little angry and for a moment had to turn his face away and force himself to smile. Then he put the bottles back on the shelf. In an outburst of generosity he fairly compelled Joe Kane to have a fresh cup of coffee and another cigar at his expense. Then he took a pan and filling it with vinegar, taken from a jug that sat beneath the counter, he declared himself about to do a new trick. "I will heat this egg in this pan of vinegar," he said. "Then I will put it through the neck of a bottle without breaking the shell. When the egg is inside the bottle it will resume its normal shape and the shell will become hard again. Then I will give the bottle with the egg in it to you. You can take it about with you wherever you go. People will want to know how you got the egg in the bottle. Don't tell them. Keep them guessing. That is the way to have fun with this trick."

Father grinned and winked at his visitor. Joe Kane decided that the man who confronted him was mildly insane but harmless. He drank the cup of coffee that had been given him and began to read his paper again. When the egg had been heated in vinegar father carried it on a spoon to the counter and going into a back room got an empty bottle. He was angry because his visitor did not watch him as he began to do his trick, but nevertheless went cheerfully to work. For a long time he struggled, trying to get the egg to go through the neck of the bottle. He put the pan of vinegar back on the stove, intending to reheat the egg, then picked it up and burned his fingers. After a second bath in the hot vinegar the shell of the egg had been softened a little but not enough for his purpose. He worked and worked and a spirit of desperate determination took possession of him. When he thought that at last the trick was about to be consummated the delayed train came in at the station and Joe Kane started to go nonchalantly out at the door. Father made a last desperate effort to conquer the egg and make it do the thing that would establish his reputation as one who knew how to entertain guests who came into his restaurant. He worried the egg. He attempted to be somewhat rough with it. He swore and the sweat stood out on his forehead. The egg broke under his hand. When the contents spurted over his clothes, Joe Kane, who had stopped at the door, turned and laughed.

A roar of anger rose from my father's throat. He danced and shouted a string of inarticulate words. Grabbing another egg from the basket on the counter, he threw it, just missing the head of the young man as he dodged through the door and escaped.

Father came upstairs to mother and me with an egg in his hand. I do not know what he intended to do. I imagine he had some idea of destroying it, of destroying all eggs, and that he intended to let

mother and me see him begin. When, however, he got into the presence of mother something happened to him. He laid the egg gently on the table and dropped on his knees by the bed as I have already explained. He later decided to close the restaurant for the night and to come upstairs and get into bed. When he did so he blew out the light and after much muttered conversation both he and mother went to sleep. I suppose I went to sleep also, but my sleep was troubled. I awoke at dawn and for a long time looked at the egg that lay on the table. I wondered why eggs had to be and why from the egg came the hen who again laid the egg. The question got into my blood. It has stayed there, I imagine, because I am the son of my father. At any rate, the problem remains unsolved in my mind. And that, I conclude, is but another evidence of the complete and final triumph of the egg —at least as far as my family is concerned.

*1919*

# THE CORN-PLANTING

◇

❨ THIS story was first published in the *American Magazine* in 1934. It is notable among Anderson's stories in its oddly pathetic last scene in which the old people, despite their crushing loss, make a brave gesture of affirmation.

◇

THE FARMERS who come to our town to trade are a part of the town life. Saturday is the big day. Often the children come to the high school in town.

It is so with Hatch Hutchenson. Although his farm, some three miles from town, is small, it is known to be one of the best-kept and best-worked places in all our section. Hatch is a little gnarled old figure of a man. His place is on the Scratch Gravel Road and there are plenty of poorly kept places out that way.

Hatch's place stands out. The little frame house is always kept painted, the trees in his orchard are whitened with lime halfway up the trunks, and the barn and sheds are in repair, and his fields are always clean-looking.

Hatch is nearly seventy. He got a rather late start in life. His father, who owned the same farm, was a Civil War man and came home badly wounded, so that, although he lived a long time after the war, he couldn't work much. Hatch was the only son and stayed at home, working the place until his father died. Then, when he was nearing fifty, he married a school-teacher of forty, and they had a son. The schoolteacher was a small one like Hatch. After they married, they both stuck close to the land. They seemed to fit into their farm life as certain people fit into the clothes they wear. I have noticed something about people who make a go of marriage. They grow more and more alike. They even grow to look alike.

Their one son, Will Hutchenson, was a small but remarkably strong boy. He came to our high school in town and pitched on our town baseball team. He was a fellow always cheerful, bright and alert, and a great favorite with all of us.

For one thing, he began as a young boy to make amusing little drawings. It was a talent. He made drawings of fish and pigs and cows and they looked like people you knew. I never did know before that people could look so much like cows and horses and pigs and fish.

When he had finished in the town high school, Will went to Chicago, where his mother had a cousin living, and he became a student in the Art Institute out there. Another young fellow from our town was also in Chicago. He really went two years before Will did. His name is Hal Weyman, and he was a student at the University of Chicago. After he graduated, he came home and got a job as principal of our high school.

Hal and Will Hutchenson hadn't been close friends before, Hal being several years older than Will, but in Chicago they got together, went together to see plays, and, as Hal later told me, they had a good many long talks.

I got it from Hal that, in Chicago, as at home here, when he was a young boy, Will was immediately popular. He was good-looking, so the girls in the art school liked him, and he had a straightforwardness that made him popular with all the young fellows.

Hal told me that Will was out to some party nearly every night, and right away he began to sell some of his amusing little drawings and to make money. The drawings were used in advertisements, and he was well paid.

He even began to send some money home. You see, after Hal came back here, he used to go quite often out to the Hutchenson place to see Will's father and mother. He would walk or drive out there in the afternoon or on summer evenings and sit with them. The talk was always of Will.

Hal said it was touching how much the father and mother depended on their one son, how much they talked about him and dreamed of his future. They had never been people who went about much with the town folks or even with their neighbors. They were of the sort who work all the time, from early morning till late in the evenings, and on moonlight nights, Hal said, and after the little old wife had got the supper, they often went out into the fields and worked again.

You see, by this time old Hatch was nearing seventy and his wife would have been ten years younger. Hal said that whenever he went out to the farm they quit work and came to sit with him. They might be in one of the fields, working together, but when they saw him in the road, they came running. They had got a letter from Will. He wrote every week.

The little old mother would come running following the father. 'We got another letter, Mr. Weyman,' Hatch would cry, and then his wife, quite breathless, would say the same thing, 'Mr. Weyman, we got a letter.'

The letter would be brought out at once and read aloud. Hal said the letters were always delicious. Will larded them with little sketches. There were humorous drawings of people he had seen or been with, rivers of automobiles on Michigan Avenue in Chicago, a policeman at a street crossing, young stenographers hurrying into office buildings. Neither of the old people had ever been to the city and they were curious and eager. They wanted the drawings explained, and Hal said they were like two children wanting to know every little detail Hal could remember about their son's life in the big city. He was always at them to come there on a visit and they would spend hours talking of that.

'Of course,' Hatch said, 'we couldn't go.'

'How could we?' he said. He had been on that one little farm since he was a boy. When he was a young fellow, his father was an invalid and so Hatch had to run things. A farm, if you run it right, is very exacting. You have to fight weeds all the time. There are the farm animals to take care of. 'Who would milk our cows?' Hatch said. The idea of anyone but him or his wife touching one of the Hutchenson cows seemed to hurt him. While he was alive, he didn't want anyone else plowing one of his fields, tending his corn, looking after things about the barn. He felt that way about his farm. It was a thing you couldn't explain, Hal said. He seemed to understand the two old people.

It was spring night, past midnight, when Hal came to my house and told me the news. In our town we have a night telegraph operator at the railroad station and Hal got a wire. It was really addressed to Hatch Hutchenson, but the operator brought it to Hal. Will Hutchenson was dead, had been killed. It turned out later that he was at a party with some other young fellows and there might have been some drinking. Anyway, the car was wrecked, and Will Hutchenson was killed. The operator wanted Hal to go out and take the message to Hatch and his wife, and Hal wanted me to go along.

I offered to take my car, but Hal said no. 'Let's walk out,' he said. He wanted to put off the moment, I could see that. So we did walk. It was early spring, and I remember every moment of the silent walk we took, the little leaves just coming on the trees, the little streams we crossed, how the moonlight made the water seem alive. We loitered and loitered, not talking, hating to go on.

Then we got out there, and Hal went to the front door of the farmhouse while I stayed in the road. I heard a dog bark, away off somewhere. I heard a child crying in some distant house. I think that Hal, after he got to the front door of the house, must have stood there for ten minutes, hating to knock.

Then he did knock, and the sound his fist made on the door seemed terrible. It seemed like guns going off. Old Hatch came to the door, and I heard Hal tell him. I know what happened. Hal had been trying, all the way out from town, to think up words to tell the old couple in some gentle way, but when it came to the scratch, he couldn't. He blurted everything right out, right into old Hatch's face.

That was all. Old Hatch didn't say a word. The door was opened, he stood there in the moonlight, wearing a funny long white nightgown, Hal told him, and the door went shut again with a bang, and Hal was left standing there.

He stood for a time, and then came back out into the road to me. 'Well,' he said, and 'Well,' I said. We stood in the road looking and listening. There wasn't a sound from the house.

And then—it might have been ten minutes or it might have been a half-hour—we stood silently, listening and watching, not knowing what to do —we couldn't go away—'I guess they are trying to get so they can believe it,' Hal whispered to me. I got his notion all right. The two old people must have thought of their son Will always only in terms of life, never of death.

We stood watching and listening, and then, suddenly, after a long time, Hal touched me on the arm. 'Look,' he whispered. There were two white-clad figures going from the house to the barn. It turned out, you see, that old Hatch had been plowing that day. He had finished plowing and harrowing a field near the barn.

The two figures went into the barn and presently came out. They went into the field, and Hal and I crept across the farmyard to the barn and got to where we could see what was going on without being seen.

It was an incredible thing. The old man had got a hand corn-planter out of the barn and his wife had got a bag of seed corn, and there, in the moonlight, that night, after they got that news, they were planting corn.

It was a thing to curl your hair—it was so ghostly. They were both in their nightgowns. They would do a row across the field, coming quite close to us as we stood in the shadow of the barn, and then, at the end of each row, they would kneel side by side by the fence and stay silent for a time. The whole thing went on in silence. It was the first time in my life I ever understood something, and I am far from sure now that I can put down what I understood and felt that night—I mean something about the connection between certain people and the earth—a kind of silent cry, down into the earth, of these two old people, putting corn down into the earth. It was as though they were putting death down into the ground that life might grow again—something like that.

They must have been asking something of the earth, too. But what's the use? What they were up to in connection with the life in their field and the lost life in their son is something you can't very well make clear in words. All I know is that Hal and I stood the sight as long as we could, and then we crept away and went back to town, but Hatch Hutchenson and his wife must have got what they were after that night, because Hal told me that when he went out in the morning to see them and to make the arrangements for bringing their dead son home, they were both curiously quiet and Hal thought in command of themselves. Hal said he thought they had got something. 'They have their farm and they have still got Will's letters to read,' Hal said.

---

FROM

# LETTERS, 1918–1938

◇

❨ WE ARE fortunate in having the *Letters of Sherwood Anderson,* selected and edited by Howard Mumford Jones in association with Walter B. Rideout, published in 1953. Anderson was so much a "talking" writer that it is not surprising to find him at his greatest ease when he is "talking" to his friends through his nearly illegible pen. In his letters he could really be that spontaneous, uncalculating person that he pretended to be in his art. The selection here runs from 1918 to 1938.

❖

## 29: TO VAN WYCK BROOKS [1]

[Chicago, early April, 1918]

MY DEAR BROOKS:

Your letter has stirred up a world of thought in me. It isn't Twain I'm thinking of, but the profound truth of some of your own observations.

As far as Twain is concerned, we have to remember the influences about him. Remember how he came into literature—the crude buffoon of the early days in the mining camp, the terrible cheap and second-rate humor of much of *Innocents Abroad*. It seems to me that when he began he addressed an audience that gets a big laugh out of the braying of a jackass, and without a doubt Mark often brayed at them. He knew that later. There was tenderness and subtlety in Mark when he grew older.

You get the picture of him, Brooks—the river man who could write going East and getting in with that New England crowd, the fellows from barren hills and barren towns. The best he got out of the bunch was Howells, and Howells did Twain no good.

There's another point, Brooks. I can't help wishing Twain hadn't married such a good woman. There was such a universal inclination to tame the man—to save his soul, as it were. Left alone, I fancy Mark might have been willing to throw his soul overboard and then—ye gods, what a fellow he might have been, what poetry might have come from him.

The big point is: it seems to me that this salvation of the soul business gets under everybody's skin. With artists it takes the form of being concerned with their reputation as writers. A struggle constantly goes on. Call the poet a poet and he is no longer the poet. You see what I mean.

There is a fellow like Waldo,[2] for example. He writes me long letters. His days are often made happy or miserable according to whether or not he is writing well.

Is it so important? What stardust we are. What does it matter?

The point is that I catch Waldo so often striving to say things in an unusual way. It makes me cringe. I want to beat him with my fists.

I pick on Waldo as an example because I love him and I know he feels deeply. He should write with a swing—weeping, praying, and crying to the gods on paper instead of making sentences as he so often does.

Well, now, you see I'm coming around. The cultural fellows got hold of Mark. They couldn't hold him. He was too big and too strong. He brushed their hands aside.

But their words got into his mind. In the effort to get out beyond that he became a pessimist.

Now, Brooks, you know a man cannot be a pessimist who lives near a brook or a cornfield. When the brook chatters or at night when the moon comes up and the wind plays in the corn, a man hears the whispering of the gods.

Mark got to that once—when he wrote *Huck Finn*. He forgot Howells and the good wife and everyone. Again he was the half-savage, tender, god-worshiping, believing boy. He had proud, conscious innocence.

I believe he wrote that book in a little hut on a hill on his farm. It poured out of him. I fancy that at night he came down from his hill stepping like a king, a splendid playboy playing with rivers and men, riding on the Mississippi, on the broad river that is the great artery flowing out of the heart of the land.

Well, Brooks, I'm alone in a boat on that stream sometimes. The rhythm and swing of it is in some of my songs that are to be published next month. It sometimes gets into some of the Winesburg things. I'll ride it some more, perhaps. It depends on whether or not I can avoid taking myself serious[ly]. Whom the gods wish to destroy they first make drunk with the notion of being a writer.

Waldo is coming out to spend a month with me.

Wish I could see you sometime this summer. I'll be in the East for a month or more in June or July. Why couldn't you come to the mountains and have a few days' walk with me?

## 63: TO PAUL ROSENFELD

Palos Park, Illinois [after October 24, 1921]

DEAR PAUL:

It was good to hear from you. I have been in the country almost continuously since I got home, and whenever I have gone to town or whenever Tennessee has come out here, the greeting has

LETTERS. 1. **Van Wyck Brooks:** Brooks, the distinguished American critic (b. 1886) published *The Ordeal of Mark Twain* in 1920 [Ed.]. (Footnotes to the Anderson letters, save those followed by [Ed.], are from the *Letters of Sherwood Anderson*, ed. by Howard Mumford Jones and Walter Rideout.) 2. **Waldo:** Waldo Frank, novelist and editor of *The Seven Arts*, which published some early Anderson stories [Ed.].

been the same. "Have you heard from Paul?" It threatened to become one of those annoying family sayings that no one else understands, but that always makes the members of the family smile.

I'm glad you reminded me of *Windy*. I'll send it Monday from town. Also I'll have what there is of the *Testament* copied and send it at once. There should be more than the one copy anyway.

You understand, of course, Paul, that the *Testament* is a purely experimental thing with me. Many of the things you will now find in it will no doubt eventually be cast out altogether. However, I'm going to send it to you just as it is. In this book I am trying to get at something that I think was very beautifully done in some parts of the Old Testament by the Hebrew poets. That is to say, I want to achieve in it rhythm of words with rhythm of thought. Do I make myself clear? The thing if achieved will be felt rather tha[n] seen or heard, perhaps. You see, as the things are, many of them violate my own conception of what I am after. In making this book I have felt no call to responsibility to anything but my own inner sense of what is beautiful in the arrangement of words and ideas. It is in a way my own Bible. I think in a way you and Brooks and Waldo have always a little misunderstood something in me. Have you ever known well an old priest of the Catholic faith? He will make almost ribald remarks about Mother Church sometimes, but if you take that to mean he hasn't real love and devotion to her, you make a great mistake.

You see, after all I was raised in a different atmosphere than most of you fellows. Among workers, farmers, etc., here in the Middle West it used to be thought almost unwholesome to be outwardly serious about anything. After all, you see, I am a product of the same thing Brooks talks so much about in his Mark Twain.

There was, you see, an outward technique. If a man say anything seriously to another, he must immediately turn it about and make a kind of half joke of it. The serious, not the half-joking thing, was meant. The half-joking thing did, however, answer a purpose. "We must laugh or die" was at bottom the thing felt.

I emphasize this phase of myself to you, Paul, because you, Brooks, and Waldo were all brought up in a different atmosphere. I think your atmosphere was as difficult as my own to penetrate, but it was different. The New Englanders and the Jews have always at least had the privilege of being serious. You see, I put Brooks among the New Englanders. He may not have been born there,[3] but

spiritually he belongs there and has in his make-up the beauty and the inner cold fright of the New Englander. That's what makes it so difficult for me to feel warm and close to him, as I so often do to you and Waldo, although I respect him sometimes more than any other living man. Is all this stupid? However, I will go on and try to get off my chest what I am trying to say. I have in my inner consciousness conceived of what we roughly speak of as the Middle West, and what I have so often called Mid-America, as an empire with its capital in Chicago. When I started writing, my conception wasn't so clear. Then I went only so far as to want health for myself. I was a money-getter, a schemer, a chronic liar. One day I found out that when I sat down to write, it was more difficult to lie. The lie lay before one on the paper. It haunted one at night.

Then, you see, I knew no writers, no artists. Everything was very much mixed up. When I began to know writers and painters, I couldn't abide the way most of them talked. They were also doing the American trick. They were putting it over.

You see, I had by this time got up out of the ranks of laborers and lived among businessmen, had them for my friends. I went to conferences, lunched with these men. They were always talking so earnestly and seriously about nothing. . . .

Let me go on. You will see in *Windy* and in *Marching Men* the effects of a reaction from businessmen back to my former associates, the workers. I believe now it was a false reaction and carried with it something else. It is the thing Mencken calls "sentimental liberalism." For a time I did dream of a new world to come out of some revolutionary movement that would spring up out of the mass of people.

That went. A break came. You will see it in *Mid-American Chants*. What happened was something like this. A new conception came. Will you read now the first of the New Testaments. "In a purely subconscious way I am a patriot. I live in a wide valley of cornfields and men and towns and strange, jangling sounds, and in spite of the curious perversion of life here, I have a feeling that the great basin of the Mississippi River, where I have always lived and moved about, is one day to be the seat of the culture of the universe."

Now you understand, Paul, something in me. There is acceptance in that. I take these little, ugly factory towns, these big, sprawling cities into something. I wish it would not sound to[o] silly to say I pour a dream over it, consciously, intentionally, for a purpose. I want to write beautifully, create beautifully, not outside but in this thing in which I am born, in this place where, in the midst

---

3. Brooks was born in Plainfield, N.J.

of ugly towns, cities, Fords, moving pictures, I have always lived, must always live. I do not want, Paul, even those old monks at Chartres, building their cathedral, to be at bottom any purer than myself.

There are infinite difficulties. You with your quick, warm nature will perhaps never quite understand my slowness or the slowness of men like Sandburg. I am stupid. You will never believe how stupid. . . .

This leads to misunderstandings, too. There are men, like Jones[4] of the Chicago *Post,* who, having no doubt at some time heard me say something derogatory to smart men and smartness, have got the idea fixed in their heads that I am without respect for old things, old beauty. Jones, for example, is always harping on the idea that I do not believe in reading the work of the old masters of my craft and that I am no respecter of words, am afraid of words. I do not blame Jones. If he has such a notion, it is because of something I have myself said.

I have had a great fear of phrase-making. Words, as you know, Paul, are very tricky things. Look, for example, how that man Mencken can rattle words like dice in a box. Our Ben Hecht, here in Chicago, has naturally the same talent, but I happen to know he isn't particularly proud of it, not at bottom.

Being, as I have said, slow in my nature, I do have to come to words slowly. I do not want to make them rattle. And well enough I know that you, Waldo, Brooks might do in a flash what I will never be able to do. You may get to heights I can never reach. That isn't quite the point. I'm not competitive. I want, if I can to save myself.

And now, you see, this brings me to the point of all this. Granted I am slow and stupid. Now, at this time, in America, culture is not a part of our lives out here in Mid-America. We are all, businessmen, workers, farmers, town, city and country dwellers, a little ashamed of trying for beauty. We are imprisoned. There is a wall about us. You will see, as you get into the spirit of the *New Testament,* how that wall has become a symbol of life to me. More men than you and I will ever know have become embittered and ugly in America, Paul. The flush-looking, hearty, go-with-a-slam-bang businessmen and others, what we have come to think of as the up-and-going American, are not so up-and-going. They are little children. Immaturity is the note of the age, and immaturity is a wall too.

And so in my inner self I have accepted my own Mid-America as a walled-in place. There are walls everywhere, about individuals, about groups. The houses are mussy. People die inside the walls without ever having seen the light. I want the houses cleaned, the doorsteps washed, the walls broken away. That can't happen in my time. Culture is a slow growth. How silly to think you won't understand all this, that you haven't understood from the first. Sometimes, however, you, Brooks, Waldo, all the men I love and respect seem so far away. I say stupid things, act stupidly. I grow afraid too.

You see, all I want is to have such men as you know at bottom that I love what you love—that is enough. Artists have to be strangers to the body of the people now in Chicago, in Ohio, in all this empire of Mid-America. I just don't want any of you fellows who are real, who love beauty and who understand more than I ever will, to be fooled by my crudeness or to be led to believe that I am not, in my own way, trying to live in the old tradition of artists. And that's all of that. "Thank God," you'll probably say. . . .

260: TO ROY JANSEN[5]

[Marion, Virginia, late April, 1935]

DEAR ROY JANSEN:

I think the most absorbingly interesting and exciting moment in any writer's life must come at the moment when he, for the first time, knows that he is a real writer. Any professional writer, any Hemingway, Wolfe, Faulkner, Stein, Dreiser, Lewis—I could name a dozen others, prosemen, I mean—will know what I mean. You begin, of course, being not yourself. We all do. There have been so many great ones. "If I could write as that man does." There is, more than likely, some one man you follow slavishly. How magnificently his sentences march. It is like a field being plowed. You are thinking of the man's style, his way of handling words and sentences.

You read everything the man has written, go from him to others. You read, read, read. You live in the world of books. It is only after a long time that you know that this is a special world, fed out of the world of reality, but not of the world of reality.

.You have yourself not yet brought anything up out of the real world into this special world, to make it live there.

And then, if you are ever to be a real writer,

<hr/>

4. **Jones:** Llewellyn Jones (1884– ), literary editor of the Chicago *Evening Post,* 1914–32.

5. **Roy Jansen:** author and proprietor of a bookstore in Pittsburgh.

your moment comes. I remember mine. I walked along a city street in the snow. I was working at work I hated. Already I had written several long novels. They were not really mine. I was ill, discouraged, broke. I was living in a cheap rooming house. I remember that I went upstairs and into the room. It was very shabby. I had no relatives in the city and few enough friends. I remember how cold the room was. On that afternoon I had heard that I was to lose my job.

I grew desperate, went and threw up a window. I sat by the open window. It began to snow. "I'll catch cold sitting here."

"What do I care?" There was some paper on a small kitchen table I had bought and had brought up into the room. I turned on a light and began to write. I wrote, without looking up—I never changed a word of it afterwards—a story called "Hands." It was and is a very beautiful story.

I wrote the story and then got up from the table at which I had been sitting, I do not know how long, and went down into the city street. I thought that the snow had suddenly made the city very beautiful. There were people in the street, all sorts of people, shabby ones, brisk young ones, old discouraged ones. I went along wanting to hug people, to shout.

"I've done it. At last, after all these years I've done something." How did I know I had? I did know. I was drunk with a new drunkenness. I cannot remember all of the absurd, foolish things I did that evening. I had a little money in my pocket and went into saloons. I called men up to the bar. "Drink. Drink to me, men." I remember that a prostitute accosted me and that I threw some money toward her and ran away laughing. It must have been several hours before I got the courage to return to my room and read my own story.

It was all right. It was sound. It was real. I went to sit by my desk. A great many others have had such moments. I wonder what they did. I sat there and cried. For the moment I thought the world very wonderful, and I thought also that there was a great deal of wonder in me.

[P.S.] If you use this, will you see that I get copy?

## 342: TO GEORGE FREITAG[6]

[Troutdale, Virginia] August 27, 1938

DEAR GEORGE FREITAG:

It sometimes seems to me that I should prepare a book designed to be read by other and younger

writers. This not because of accomplishment on my own part, but because of the experiences, the particular experiences, I have had.

It is so difficult for most of us to realize how fully and completely commercialism enters into the arts. For example, how are you to know that really the opinion of the publisher or the magazine editor in regard to your work, what is a story and what isn't, means nothing? Some of my own stories, for example, that have now become almost American classics, that are put before students in our schools and colleges as examples of good storytelling, were, when first written, when submitted to editors, and when seen by some of the so-called outstanding American critics, declared not stories at all.

It is true they were not nice little packages, wrapped and labeled in the O. Henry manner. They were obviously written by one who did not know the answers. They were simple little tales of happenings, things observed and felt. There were no cowboys or daring wild game hunters. None of the people in the tales got lost in burning deserts or went seeking the North Pole. In my stories I simply stayed at home, among my own people, wherever I happened to be, people in my own street. I think I must, very early, have realized that this was my milieu, that is to say, common everyday American lives. The ordinary beliefs of the people about me, that love lasted indefinitely, that success meant happiness, simply did not seem true to me.

Things were always happening. My eyes began to see, my ears to hear. Most of our American storytelling at that time had concerned only the rich and the well-to-do. I was a storyteller but not yet a writer of stories. As I came of a poor family, older men were always repeating to me the old saying.

"Get money. Money makes the mare go."

For a time I was a laborer. As I had a passion for fast trotting and pacing horses, I worked about race tracks. I became a soldier, I got into business.

I knew, often quite intensively, Negro swipes about race tracks, small gamblers, prize fighters, common laboring men and women. There was a violent, dangerous man, said to be a killer. One night he walked and talked to me and became suddenly tender. I was forced to realize that all sorts of emotions went on in all sorts of people. A young man who seemed outwardly a very clod suddenly began to run wildly in the moonlight. Once I was walking in a wood and heard the sound of a man weeping. I stopped, looked, and listened. There was a farmer who, because of ill luck, bad weather, and perhaps even poor management, had lost his farm. He had gone to work in a fac-

---

6. **George Freitag:** George Freitag of Canton, Ohio, entered into correspondence with Anderson in the summer of 1938 on problems of the young writer. He published "The Transaction" in the *Atlantic* for August 1938.

tory in town, but, having a day off, had returned secretly to the fields he loved. He was on his knees by a low fence, looking across the fields in which he had worked from boyhood. He and I were employed at the time in the same factory, and in the factory he was a quiet, smiling man, seemingly satisfied with his lot.

I began to gather these impressions. There was a thing called happiness toward which men were striving. They never got to it. All of life was amazingly accidental. Love, moments of tenderness and despair, came to the poor and the miserable as to the rich and successful.

It began to seem to me that what was most wanted by all people was love, understanding. Our writers, our storytellers, in wrapping life up into neat little packages were only betraying life. It began to seem to me that what I wanted for myself most of all, rather than so-called success, acclaim, to be praised by publishers and editors, was to try to develop, to the top of my bent, my own capacity to feel, see, taste, smell, hear. I wanted, as all men must want, to be a free man, proud of my own manhood, always more and more aware of earth, people, streets, houses, towns, cities. I wanted to take all into myself, digest what I could.

I could not give the answers, and so for a long time when my stories began to appear, at first only in little highbrow magazines, I was almost universally condemned by the critics. My stories, it seemed, had no definite ends. They were not conclusive and did not give the answers, and so I was called vague. "Groping" was a favorite term. It seems I could not get a formula and stick to it. I could not be smart about life. When I wrote my Winesburg stories—for the whole series I got eighty-five dollars—such critics as Mr. Floyd Dell and Henry Mencken, having read them, declared they were not stories. They were merely, it seemed, sketches. They were too vague, too groping. Some ten or fifteen years after Mr. Mencken told me they were not stories, he wrote, telling of how, when he first saw them, he realized their strength and beauty. An imagined conversation between us, that never took place, was spoken about.

And for this I did not blame Mr. Mencken. He thought he had said what he now thinks he said.

There was a time when Mr. Dell was, in a way, my literary father. He and Mr. Waldo Frank had been the first critics to praise some of my earlier work. He was generous and warm. He, with Mr. Theodore Dreiser, was instrumental in getting my first book published. When he saw the Winesburg stories, he, however, condemned them heartily. He was at that time, I believe, deeply under the in-

fluence of Maupassant. He advised me to throw the Winesburg stories away. They had no form. They were not stories. A story, he said, must be sharply definite. There must be a beginning and an end. I remember very clearly our conversation. "If you plan to go somewhere on a train and start for the station, but loiter along the way, so that the train comes into the station, stops to discharge and take on passengers, and then goes on its way, and you miss it, don't blame the locomotive engineer," I said. I daresay it was an arrogant saying, but arrogance is also needed.

And so I had written, let us say, the Winesburg stories. The publisher who had already published two of my early novels refused them, but at last I found a publisher. The stories were called unclean, dirty, filthy, but they did grow into the American consciousness, and presently the same critic who had condemned them began asking why I did not write more Winesburg stories.

I am telling you all of this, I assure you, not out of bitterness. I have had a good life, a full, rich life. I am still having a full, rich life. I tell it only to point out to you, a young writer, filled as I am made aware by your letter to me, of tenderness for life, I tell it simply to suggest to you plainly what you are up against. For ten or fifteen years after I had written and published the Winesburg stories, I was compelled to make my living outside of the field of writing. You will find none of my stories even yet in the great popular magazines that pay high prices to writers.

I do not blame the publishers or the editors. Once I was in the editorial rooms of a great magazine. They had asked me in for an editorial conference.

Would it not be possible for them to begin publishing my stories?

I advised against it. "If I were you, I would let Sherwood Anderson alone."

I had been for a long time an employee of a big advertising agency. I wrote the kind of advertisements on which great magazines live.

But I had no illusions about advertising, could have none. I was an advertising writer too long. The men employed with me, the businessmen, many of them successful and even rich, were like the laborers, gamblers, soldiers, race track swipes I had formerly known. Their guards down, often over drinks, they told me the same stories of tangled, thwarted lives.

How could I throw a glamour over such lives? I couldn't.

The Winesburg stories, when first published, were bitterly condemned. They were thrown out of libraries. In one New England town, where three copies of the book had been bought, they were publicly burned in the public square of the town. I remember a letter I once received from a woman. She had been seated beside me at the table of a friend. "Having sat beside you and having read your stories, I feel that I shall never be clean again," she wrote. I got many such letters.

Then a change came. The book found its way into schools and colleges. Critics who had ignored or condemned the book now praised it.

"It's Anderson's best work. It is the height of his genius. He will never again do such work."

People constantly came to me, all saying the same thing.

"But what else of mine have you read since?"

A blank look upon faces.

They had read nothing else of mine. For the most part they were simply repeating, over and over, an old phrase picked up.

Now, I do not think all of this matters. I am one of the fortunate ones. In years when I have been unable to make a living with my pen, there have always been friends ready and willing to help me. There was one man who came to me in a year when I felt, when I knew, that I had done some of my best and truest work, but when, no money coming in, I was trying to sell my house to get money to live.

He wanted, he said, one of my manuscripts. "I will lend you five thousand dollars." He did lend it, knowing I could never return his money, but he did not deceive me. He had an affection for me as I had for him. He wanted me to continue to live in freedom. I have found this sort of thing among the rich as well as the poor. My house where I live is filled with beautiful things, all given to me. I live well enough. I have no quarrel with life.

And I am only writing all of this to you to prepare you. In a world controlled by business why should we not expect businessmen to think first of business?

And do bear in mind that publishers of books, of magazines, of newspapers are, first of all, businessmen. They are compelled to be.

And do not blame them when they do not buy your stories. Do not be romantic. There is no golden key that unlocks all doors. There is only the joy of living as richly as you can, always feeling more, absorbing more, and, if you are by nature a teller of tales, the realization that by faking, trying to give people what they think they want, you are in danger of dulling and in the end quite destroying what may be your own road into life.

There will remain for you, to be sure, the matter of making a living, and I am sorry to say to you that in the solution of that problem, for you and other young writers, I am not interested. That, alas, is your own problem. I am interested only in what you may be able to contribute to the advancement of our mutual craft.

But why not call it an art? That is what it is.

Did you ever hear of an artist who had an easy road to travel in life?

# F. Scott Fitzgerald

## THE ICE PALACE

◇

❨ INCLUDED among the short stories bound into *Flappers and Philosophers* (1920), this story reflects Fitzgerald's youthful high spirits. Its heroine, Sally Carrol, is patterned at least in some respects upon Zelda Sayre, his bride and a former Montgomery belle.

◇

THE SUNLIGHT dripped over the house like golden paint over an art jar, and the freckling shadows here and there only intensified the rigor of the bath of light. The Butterworth and Larkin houses flanking were intrenched behind great stodgy trees; only the Happer house took the full sun, and all day long faced the dusty road-street with a tolerant kindly patience. This was the city of Tarleton in southernmost Georgia, September afternoon.

Up in her bedroom window Sally Carrol Happer rested her nineteen-year-old chin on a fifty-two-year-old sill and watched Clark Darrow's ancient Ford turn the corner. The car was hot —being partly metallic it retained all the heat it absorbed or evolved—and Clark Darrow sitting bolt upright at the wheel wore a pained, strained expression as though he considered himself a spare part, and rather likely to break. He laboriously crossed two dust ruts, the wheels squeeking indignantly at the encounter, and then with a terrifying expression he gave the steering-gear a final wrench and desposited self and car approximately in front of the Happer steps. There was a plaintive heaving sound, a death-rattle, followed by a short silence; and then the air was rent by a startling whistle.

Sally Carrol gazed down sleepily. She started to yawn, but finding this quite impossible unless she raised her chin from the window-sill, changed her mind and continued silently to regard the car, whose owner sat brilliantly if perfunctorily at attention as he waited for an answer to his signal. After a moment the whistle once more split the dusty air.

"Good mawnin'."

With difficulty Clark twisted his tall body round and bent a distorted glance on the window.

"'Tain't mawnin', Sally Carrol."

"Isn't it, sure enough?"

"What you doin'?"

"Eatin' 'n apple."

"Come on go swimmin'—want to?"

"Reckon so."

"How 'bout hurryin' up?"

"Sure enough."

Sally Carrol sighed voluminously and raised herself with profound inertia from the floor, where she had been occupied in alternately destroying parts of a green apple and painting paper dolls for her younger sister. She approached a mirror, regarded her expression with a pleased and pleasant languor, dabbed two spots of rouge on her lips and a grain of powder on her nose, and covered her bobbed corn-colored hair with a rose-littered sunbonnet. Then she kicked over the painting water, said, "Oh, damn!"—but let it lay—and left the room.

"How you, Clark?" she inquired a minute later as she slipped nimbly over the side of the car.

"Mighty fine, Sally Carrol."

"Where we go swimmin'?"

"Out to Walley's Pool. Told Marylyn we'd call by an' get her an' Joe Ewing."

Clark was dark and lean, and when on foot was rather inclined to stoop. His eyes were ominous and his expression somewhat petulant except when startlingly illuminated by one of his frequent smiles. Clark had "a income"—just enough to keep himself in ease and his car in gasoline —and he had spent the two years since he graduated from Georgia Tech in dozing round the lazy streets of his home town, discussing how he could best invest his capital for an immediate fortune.

Hanging round he found not at all difficult; a crowd of little girls had grown up beautifully, the amazing Sally Carrol foremost among them; and they enjoyed being swum with and danced with and made love to in the flower-filled summery evenings—and they all liked Clark immensely. When feminine company palled there were half a dozen other youths who were always just about to do something, and meanwhile were quite willing to join him in a few holes of golf, or a game of billiards, or the consumption of a quart of "hard yella licker." Every once in a while one of these contemporaries made a farewell round of calls before going up to New York or Philadelphia or Pittsburgh to go into business, but mostly they just stayed round in this languid paradise of dreamy skies and firefly evenings and noisy niggery street fairs—and especially of gracious, soft-voiced girls, who were brought up on memories instead of money.

The Ford having been excited into a sort of restless resentful life, Clark and Sally Carrol rolled and rattled down Valley Avenue into Jefferson Street, where the dust road became a pavement; along opiate Millicent Place, where there were half a dozen prosperous, substantial mansions; and on into the down-town section. Driving was perilous here, for it was shopping time; the population idled casually across the streets and a drove of low-moaning oxen were being urged along in front of a placid street-car; even the shops seemed only yawning their doors and blinking their windows in the sunshine before retiring into a state of utter and finite coma.

"Sally Carrol," said Clark suddenly, "is it a fact that you're engaged?"

She looked at him quickly.

"Where'd you hear that?"

"Sure enough, you engaged?"

"'At's a nice question!"

"Girl told me you were engaged to a Yankee you met up in Asheville last summer."

Sally Carrol sighed.

"Never saw such an old town for rumors."

"Don't marry a Yankee, Sally Carrol. We need you round here." Sally Carrol was silent a moment.

"Clark," she demanded suddenly, "who on earth shall I marry?"

"I offer my services."

"Honey, you couldn't support a wife," she answered cheerfully. "Anyway, I know you too well to fall in love with you."

"'At doesn't mean you ought to marry a Yankee," he persisted.

"S'pose I love him?"

He shook his head.

"You couldn't. He'd be a lot different from us, every way."

He broke off as he halted the car in front of a rambling, dilapidated house. Marylyn Wade and Joe Ewing appeared in the doorway.

"'Lo, Sally Carrol."

"Hi!"

"How you-all?"

"Sally Carrol," demanded Marylyn as they started off again, "you engaged?"

"Lawdy, where'd all this start? Can't I look at a man 'thout everybody in town engagin' me to him?"

Clark stared straight in front of him at a bolt on the clattering windshield.

"Sally Carrol," he said with a curious intensity, "don't you like us?"

"What?"

"Us down here?"

"Why, Clark, you know I do. I adore all you boys."

"Then why you gettin' engaged to a Yankee?"

"Clark, I don't know. I'm not sure what I'll do, but—well, I want to go places and see people. I want my mind to grow. I want to live where things happen on a big scale."

"What you mean?"

"Oh, Clark, I love you, and I love Joe here, and Ben Arrot, and you-all, but you'll—you'll—"

"We'll all be failures?"

"Yes. I don't mean only money failures, but just sort of—of ineffectual and sad, and—oh, how can I tell you?"

"You mean because we stay here in Tarleton?"

"Yes, Clark; and because you like it and never want to change things or think or go ahead."

He nodded and she reached over and pressed his hand.

"Clark," she said softly, "I wouldn't change you for the world. You're sweet the way you are. The things that'll make you fail I'll love always—the living in the past, the lazy days and nights you have, and all your carelessness and generosity."

"But you're goin' away?"

"Yes—because I couldn't ever marry you. You've a place in my heart no one else ever could have, but tied down here I'd get restless. I'd feel I was—wastin' myself. There's two sides to me, you see. There's the sleepy old side you love; an' there's a sort of energy—the feelin' that makes me do wild things. That's the part of me that may be useful somewhere, that'll last when I'm not beautiful any more."

She broke off with characteristic suddenness and sighed, "Oh, sweet cooky!" as her mood changed.

Half closing her eyes and tipping back her head till it rested on the seat-back she let the savory breeze fan her eyes and ripple the fluffy curls of her bobbed hair. They were in the country now, hurrying between tangled growths of bright-green coppice and grass and tall trees that sent sprays of foliage to hang a cool welcome over the road. Here and there they passed a battered Negro cabin, its oldest white-haired inhabitant smoking a corncob pipe beside the door, and half a dozen scantily clothed pickaninnies parading tattered dolls on the wild-grown grass in front. Farther out were lazy cotton-fields, where even the workers seemed intangible shadows lent by the sun to the earth, not for toil, but to while away some age-old tradition in the golden September fields. And round the drowsy picturesqueness, over the trees and shacks and muddy rivers, flowed the heat, never hostile, only comforting, like a great warm nourishing bosom for the infant earth.

"Sally Carrol, we're here!"

"Poor chile's soun' asleep."

"Honey, you dead at last outa sheer laziness?"

"Water, Sally Carrol! Cool water waitin' for you!"

Her eyes opened sleepily.

"Hi!" she murmured, smiling.

II

IN NOVEMBER Harry Bellamy, tall, broad, and brisk, came down from his Northern city to spend four days. His intention was to settle a matter that had been hanging fire since he and Sally Carrol had met in Asheville, North Carolina, in midsummer. The settlement took only a quiet afternoon and an evening in front of a glowing open fire, for Harry Bellamy had everything she wanted; and besides, she loved him—loved him with that side of her she kept especially for loving. Sally Carrol had several rather clearly defined sides.

On his last afternoon they walked, and she found their steps tending half-unconsciously toward one of her favorite haunts, the cemetery. When it came in sight, gray-white and golden-green under the cheerful late sun, she paused, irresolute, by the iron gate.

"Are you mournful by nature, Harry?" she asked with a faint smile.

"Mournful? Not I."

"Then let's go in here. It depresses some folks, but I like it."

They passed through the gateway and followed a path that led through a wavy valley of graves—dusty-gray and mouldy for the fifties; quaintly carved with flowers and jars for the seventies; ornate and hideous for the nineties, with fat marble cherubs lying in sodden sleep on stone pillows, and great impossible growths of nameless granite flowers. Occasionally they saw a kneeling figure with tributary flowers, but over most of the graves lay silence and withered leaves with only the fragrance that their own shadowy memories could waken in living minds.

They reached the top of a hill where they were fronted by a tall, round head-stone, freckled with dark spots of damp and half grown over with vines.

"Margery Lee," she read; "1844–1873. Wasn't she nice? She died when she was twenty-nine. Dear Margery Lee," she added softly. "Can't you see her, Harry?"

"Yes, Sally Carrol."

He felt a little hand insert itself into his.

"She was dark, I think; and she always wore her hair with a ribbon in it, and gorgeous hoop-skirts of alice blue and old rose."

"Yes."

"Oh, she was sweet, Harry! And she was the sort of girl born to stand on a wide, pillared porch and welcome folks in. I think perhaps a lot of men went away to war meanin' to come back to her; but maybe none of 'em ever did."

He stooped down close to the stone, hunting for any record of marriage.

"There's nothing here to show."

"Of course not. How could there be anything there better than just 'Margery Lee,' and that eloquent date?"

She drew close to him and an unexpected lump came into his throat as her yellow hair brushed his cheek.

"You see how she was, don't you, Harry?"

"I see," he agreed gently. "I see through your precious eyes. You're beautiful now, so I know she must have been."

Silent and close they stood, and he could feel her shoulders trembling a little. An ambling breeze swept up the hill and stirred the brim of her floppidy hat.

"Let's go down there!"

She was pointing to a flat stretch on the other side of the hill where along the green turf were a thousand grayish-white crosses stretching in endless, ordered rows like the stacked arms of a battalion.

"Those are the Confederate dead," said Sally Carrol simply.

They walked along and read the inscriptions, always only a name and a date, sometimes quite indecipherable.

"The last row is the saddest—see, 'way over

there. Every cross has just a date on it, and the word 'Unknown.'"

She looked at him and her eyes brimmed with tears.

"I can't tell you how real it is to me, darling—if you don't know."

"How you feel about it is beautiful to me."

"No, no, it's not me, it's them—that old time that I've tried to have live in me. These were just men, unimportant evidently or they wouldn't have been 'unknown'; but they died for the most beautiful thing in the world—the dead South. You see," she continued, her voice still husky, her eyes glistening with tears, "people have these dreams they fasten onto things, and I've always grown up with that dream. It was so easy because it was all dead and there weren't any disillusions comin' to me. I've tried in a way to live up to those past standards of noblesse oblige—there's just the last remnants of it, you know, like the roses of an old garden dying all round us—streaks of strange courtliness and chivalry in some of these boys an' stories I used to hear from a Confederate soldier who lived next door, and a few old darkies. Oh, Harry, there was something, there was something! I couldn't ever make you understand, but it was there."

"I understand," he assured her again quietly.

Sally Carrol smiled and dried her eyes on the tip of a handkerchief protruding from his breast pocket.

"You don't feel depressed, do you, lover? Even when I cry I'm happy here, and I get a sort of strength from it."

Hand in hand they turned and walked slowly away. Finding soft grass she drew him down to a seat beside her with their backs against the remnants of a low broken wall.

"Wish those three old women would clear out," he complained. "I want to kiss you, Sally Carrol."

"Me, too."

They waited impatiently for the three bent figures to move off, and then she kissed him until the sky seemed to fade out and all her smiles and tears to vanish in an ecstasy of eternal seconds.

Afterward they walked slowly back together, while on the corners twilight played at somnolent black-and-white checkers with the end of day.

"You'll be up about mid-January," he said, "and you've got to stay a month at least. It'll be slick. There's a winter carnival on, and if you've never really seen snow it'll be like fairy-land to you. There'll be skating and skiing and tobogganing and sleigh-riding, and all sorts of torchlight parades on snow-shoes. They haven't had one for years, so they're going to make it a knock-out."

"Will I be cold, Harry?" she asked suddenly.

"You certainly won't. You may freeze your nose, but you won't be shivery cold. It's hard and dry, you know."

"I guess I'm a summer child. I don't like any cold I've ever seen."

She broke off and they were both silent for a minute.

"Sally Carrol," he said very slowly, "what do you say to—March?"

"I say I love you."

"March?"

"March, Harry."

### III

ALL NIGHT in the Pullman it was very cold. She rang for the porter to ask for another blanket, and when he couldn't give her one she tried vainly, by squeezing down into the bottom of her berth and doubling back the bedclothes, to snatch a few hours' sleep. She wanted to look her best in the morning.

She rose at six and sliding uncomfortably into her clothes stumbled up to the diner for a cup of coffee. The snow had filtered into the vestibules and covered the floor with a slippery coating. It was intriguing, this cold, it crept in everywhere. Her breath was quite visible and she blew into the air with a naïve enjoyment. Seated in the diner she stared out the window at white hills and valleys and scattered pines whose every branch was a green platter for a cold feast of snow. Sometimes a solitary farmhouse would fly by, ugly and bleak and lone on the white waste; and with each one she had an instant of chill compassion for the souls shut in there waiting for spring.

As she left the diner and swayed back into the Pullman she experienced a surging rush of energy and wondered if she was feeling the bracing air of which Harry had spoken. This was the North, the North—her land now!

> Then blow, ye winds, heigho!
> A-roving I will go,

she chanted exultantly to herself.

"What's 'at?" inquired the porter politely.

"I said: 'Brush me off.'"

The long wires of the telegraph-poles doubled; two tracks ran up beside the train—three—four; came a succession of white-roofed houses, a glimpse of a trolley-car with frosted windows, streets—more streets—the city.

She stood for a dazed moment in the frosty station before she saw three fur-bundled figures descending upon her.

"There she is!"

"Oh, Sally Carrol!"

Sally Carrol dropped her bag.

"Hi!"

A faintly familiar icy-cold face kissed her, and then she was in a group of faces all apparently emitting great clouds of heavy smoke; she was shaking hands. There were Gordon, a short, eager man of thirty who looked like an amateur knocked-about model for Harry, and his wife, Myra, a listless lady with flaxen hair under a fur automobile cap. Almost immediately Sally Carrol thought of her as vaguely Scandinavian. A cheerful chauffeur adopted her bag, and amid ricochets of half-phrases, exclamations, and perfunctory listless "my dears" from Myra, they swept each other from the station.

Then they were in a sedan bound through a crooked succession of snowy streets where dozens of little boys were hitching sleds behind grocery wagons and automobiles.

"Oh," cried Sally Carrol, "I want to do that! Can we, Harry?"

"That's for kids. But we might—"

"It looks like such a circus!" she said regretfully.

Home was a rambling frame house set on a white lap of snow, and there she met a big, gray-haired man of whom she approved, and a lady who was like an egg, and who kissed her—these were Harry's parents. There was a breathless indescribable hour crammed full of half-sentences, hot water, bacon and eggs and confusion; and after that she was alone with Harry in the library, asking him if she dared smoke.

It was a large room with a Madonna over the fireplace and rows upon rows of books in covers of light gold and dark gold and shiny red. All the chairs had little lace squares where one's head should rest, the couch was just comfortable, the books looked as if they had been read—some—and Sally Carrol had an instantaneous vision of the battered old library at home, with her father's huge medical books, and the oil-paintings of her three great-uncles, and the old couch that had been mended up for forty-five years and was still luxurious to dream in. This room struck her as being neither attractive nor particularly otherwise. It was simply a room with a lot of fairly expensive things in it that all looked about fifteen years old.

"What do you think of it up here?" demanded Harry eagerly. "Does it surprise you? Is it what you expected, I mean?"

"You are, Harry," she said quietly, and reached out her arms to him.

But after a brief kiss he seemed anxious to extort enthusiasm from her.

"The town, I mean. Do you like it? Can you feel the pep in the air?"

"Oh, Harry," she laughed, "you'll have to give me time. You can't just fling questions at me."

She puffed at her cigarette with a sigh of contentment.

"One thing I want to ask you," he began rather apologetically; "you Southerners put quite an emphasis on family, and all that—not that it isn't quite all right, but you'll find it a little different here. I mean—you'll notice a lot of things that'll seem to you sort of vulgar display at first, Sally Carrol; but just remember that this is a three-generation town. Everybody has a father, and about half of us have grandfathers. Back of that we don't go."

"Of course," she murmured.

"Our grandfathers, you see, founded the place, and a lot of them had to take some pretty queer jobs while they were doing the founding. For instance, there's one woman who at present is about the social model for the town; well, her father was the first public ash man—things like that."

"Why," said Sally Carrol, puzzled, "did you s'pose I was goin' to make remarks about people?"

"Not at all," interrupted Harry; "and I'm not apologizing for any one either. It's just that—well, a Southern girl came up here last summer and said some unfortunate things, and—oh, I just thought I'd tell you."

Sally Carrol felt suddenly indignant—as though she had been unjustly spanked—but Harry evidently considered the subject closed, for he went on with a great surge of enthusiasm.

"It's carnival time, you know. First in ten years. And there's an ice palace they're building now that's the first they've had since eighty-five. Built out of blocks of the clearest ice they could find—on a tremedous scale."

She rose and walking to the window pushed aside the heavy Turkish portières and looked out.

"Oh!" she cried suddenly. There's two little boys makin' a snow man! Harry do you reckon I can go out an' help 'em?"

"You dream! Come here and kiss me."

She left the window rather reluctantly.

"I don't guess this is a very kissable climate, is it? I mean, it makes you so you don't want to sit round, doesn't it?"

"We're not going to. I've got a vacation for the first week you're here, and there's a dinner-dance to-night."

"Oh, Harry," she confessed, subsiding in a heap, half in his lap, half in the pillows, "I sure do feel confused. I haven't got an idea whether I'll

like it or not, an' I don't know what people expect, or anythin'. You'll have to tell me, honey."

"I'll tell you," he said softly, "if you'll just tell me you're glad to be here."

"Glad—just awful glad!" she whispered, insinuating herself into his arms in her own peculiar way. "Where you are is home for me, Harry."

And as she said this she had the feeling for almost the first time in her life that she was acting a part.

That night, amid the gleaming candles of a dinner-party, where the men seemed to do most of the talking while the girls sat in a haughty and expensive aloofness, even Harry's presence on her left failed to make her feel at home.

"They're a good-looking crowd, don't you think?" he demanded. "Just look round. There's Spud Hubbard, tackle at Princeton last year, and Junie Morton—he and the red-haired fellow next to him were both Yale hockey captains; Junie was in my class. Why, the best athletes in the world come from these States round here. This is a man's country, I tell you. Look at John J. Fishburn!"

"Who's he?" asked Sally Carrol innocently.

"Don't you know?"

"I've heard the name."

"Greatest wheat man in the Northwest, and one of the greatest financiers in the country."

She turned suddenly to a voice on her right.

"I guess they forgot to introduce us. My name's Roger Patton."

"My name is Sally Carrol Happer," she said graciously.

"Yes, I know. Harry told me you were coming."

"You a relative?"

"No, I'm a professor."

"Oh," she laughed.

"At the university. You're from the South, aren't you?"

"Yes; Tarleton, Georgia."

She liked him immediately—a reddish-brown mustache under watery blue eyes that had something in them that these other eyes lacked, some quality of appreciation. They exchanged stray sentences through dinner, and she made up her mind to see him again.

After coffee she was introduced to numerous good-looking young men who danced with conscious precision and seemed to take it for granted that she wanted to talk about nothing except Harry.

"Heavens," she thought, "they talk as if my being engaged made me older than they are—as if I'd tell their mothers on them!"

In the South an engaged girl, even a young

married woman, expected the same amount of half-affectionate badinage and flattery that would be accorded a débutante, but here all that seemed banned. One young man, after getting well started on the subject of Sally Carrol's eyes, and how they had allured him ever since she entered the room, went into a violent confusion when he found she was visiting the Bellamys—was Harry's fiancée. He seemed to feel as though he had made some risqué and inexcusable blunder, became immediately formal, and left her at the first opportunity.

She was rather glad when Roger Patton cut in on her and suggested that they sit out a while.

"Well," he inquired, blinking cheerily, "how's Carmen from the South?"

"Mighty fine. How's—how's Dangerous Dan McGrew? Sorry, but he's the only Northerner I know much about."

He seemed to enjoy that.

"Of course," he confessed, "as a professor of literature I'm not supposed to have read Dangerous Dan McGrew."

"Are you a native?"

"No, I'm a Philadelphian. Imported from Harvard to teach French. But I've been here ten years."

"Nine years, three hundred an' sixty-four days longer than me."

"Like it here?"

"Uh-huh. Sure do!"

"Really?"

"Well, why not? Don't I look as if I were havin' a good time?"

"I saw you look out the window a minute ago—and shiver."

"Just my imagination," laughed Sally Carrol. "I'm used to havin' everythin' quiet outside, an' sometimes I look out an' see a flurry of snow, an' it's just as if somethin' dead was movin'."

He nodded appreciatively.

"Ever been North before?"

"Spent two Julys in Asheville, North Carolina."

"Nice-looking crowd, aren't they?" suggested Patton, indicating the swirling floor.

Sally Carrol started. This had been Harry's remark.

"Sure are! They're—canine."

"What?"

She flushed.

"I'm sorry; that sounded worse than I meant it. You see I always think of people as feline or canine, irrespective of sex."

"Which are you?"

"I'm feline. So are you. So are most Southern men an' most of these girls here."

"What's Harry?"

"Harry's canine distinctly. All the men I've met to-night seem to be canine."

"What does 'canine' imply? A certain conscious masculinity as opposed to subtlety?"

"Reckon so. I never analyzed it—only I just look at people an' say 'canine' or 'feline' right off. It's right absurd, I guess."

"Not at all. I'm interested. I used to have a theory about these people. I think they're freezing up."

"What?"

"I think they're growing like Swedes—Ibsenesque, you know. Very gradually getting gloomy and melancholy. It's these long winters. Ever read any Ibsen?"

She shook her head.

"Well, you find in his characters a certain brooding rigidity. They're righteous, narrow, and cheerless, without infinite possibilities for great sorrow or joy."

"Without smiles or tears?"

"Exactly. That's my theory. You see there are thousands of Swedes up here. They come, I imagine, because the climate is very much like their own, and there's been a gradual mingling. There're probably not half a dozen here to-night, but—we've had four Swedish governors. Am I boring you?"

"I'm mighty interested."

"Your future sister-in-law is half Swedish. Personally I like her, but my theory is that Swedes react rather badly on us as a whole. Scandinavians, you know, have the largest suicide rate in the world."

"Why do you live here if it's so depressing?"

"Oh, it doesn't get me. I'm pretty well cloistered, and I suppose books mean more than people to me anyway."

"But writers all speak about the South being tragic. You know—Spanish señoritas, black hair and daggers an' haunting music."

He shook his head.

"No, the Northern races are the tragic races —they don't indulge in the cheering luxury of tears."

Sally Carrol thought of her graveyard. She supposed that that was vaguely what she had meant when she said it didn't depress her.

"The Italians are about the gayest people in the world—but it's a dull subject," he broke off. "Anyway, I want to tell you you're marrying a pretty fine man."

Sally Carrol was moved by an impulse of confidence.

"I know. I'm the sort of person who wants to be taken care of after a certain point, and I feel sure I will be."

"Shall we dance? You know," he continued as they rose, "it's encouraging to find a girl who knows what she's marrying for. Nine-tenths of them think of it as a sort of walking into a moving-picture sunset."

She laughed, and liked him immensely.

Two hours later on the way home she nestled near Harry in the back seat.

"Oh, Harry," she whispered, "it's so co-old!"

"But it's warm in here, darling girl."

"But outside it's cold; and oh, that howling wind!"

She buried her face deep in his fur coat and trembled involuntarily as his cold lips kissed the tip of her ear.

### IV

THE FIRST week of her visit passed in a whirl. She had her promised toboggan-ride at the back of an automobile through a chill January twilight. Swathed in furs she put in a morning toboganing on the country-club hill; even tried skiing, to sail through the air for a glorious moment and then land in a tangled laughing bundle on a soft snow-drift. She liked all the winter sports, except an afternoon spent snow-shoeing over a glaring plain under pale yellow sunshine, but she soon realized that these things were for children—that she was being humored and that the enjoyment round her was only a reflection of her own.

At first the Bellamy family puzzled her. The men were reliable and she liked them; to Mr. Bellamy especially, with his iron-gray hair and energetic dignity, she took an immediate fancy, once she found that he was born in Kentucky; this made of him a link between the old life and the new. But toward the women she felt a definite hostility. Myra, her future sister-in-law, seemed the essence of spiritless conventionality. Her conversation was so utterly devoid of personality that Sally Carrol, who came from a country where a certain amount of charm and assurance could be taken for granted in the women, was inclined to despise her.

"If those women aren't beautiful," she thought, "they're nothing. They just fade out when you look at them. They're glorified domestics. Men are the center of every mixed group."

Lastly there was Mrs. Bellamy, whom Sally Carrol detested. The first day's impression of an egg had been confirmed—an egg with a cracked, veiny voice and such an ungracious dumpiness of carriage that Sally Carrol felt that if she once fell she would surely scramble. In addition, Mrs. Bellamy seemed to typify the town in being innately hostile to strangers. She called Sally Carrol

"Sally," and could not be persuaded that the double name was anything more than a tedious ridiculous nickname. To Sally Carrol this shortening of her name was like presenting her to the public half clothed. She loved "Sally Carrol"; she loathed "Sally." She knew also that Harry's mother disapproved of her bobbed hair; and she had never dared smoke down-stairs after that first day when Mrs. Bellamy had come into the library sniffing violently.

Of all the men she met she preferred Roger Patton, who was a frequent visitor at the house. He never again alluded to the Ibsenesque tendency of the populace, but when he came in one day and found her curled upon the sofa bent over "Peer Gynt" he laughed and told her to forget what he'd said—that it was all rot.

And then one afternoon in her second week she and Harry hovered on the edge of a dangerously steep quarrel. She considered that he precipitated it entirely, though the Serbia in the case was an unknown man who had not had his trousers pressed.

They had been walking homeward between mounds of high-piled snow and under a sun which Sally Carrol scarcely recognized. They passed a little girl done up in gray wool until she resembled a small Teddy bear, and Sally Carrol could not resist a gasp of maternal appreciation.

"Look ! Harry!"

"What?"

"That little girl—did you see her face?"

"Yes, why?"

"It was red as a little strawberry. Oh, she was cute!"

"Why, your own face is almost as red as that already! Everybody's healthy here. We're out in the cold as soon as we're old enough to walk. Wonderful climate!"

She looked at him and had to agree. He was mighty healthy-looking; so was his brother. And she had noticed the new red in her own cheeks that very morning.

Suddenly their glances were caught and held, and they stared for a moment at the street-corner ahead of them. A man was standing there, his knees bent, his eyes gazing upward with a tense expression as though he were about to make a leap toward the chilly sky. And then they both exploded into a shout of laughter, for coming closer they discovered it had been a ludicrous momentary illusion produced by the extreme bagginess of the man's trousers.

"Reckon that's one on us," she laughed.

"He must be a Southerner, judging by those trousers," suggested Harry mischievously.

"Why, Harry!"

Her surprised look must have irritated him.

"Those damn Southerners!"

Sally Carrol's eyes flashed.

"Don't call 'em that!"

"I'm sorry, dear," said Harry, malignantly apologetic, "but you know what I think of them. They're sort of—sort of degenerates—not at all like the old Southerners. They've lived so long down there that they've gotten lazy and shiftless."

"Hush your mouth, Harry!" she cried angrily. "They're not! They may be lazy—anybody would be in that climate—but they're my best friends, an' I don't want to hear 'em criticized in any such sweepin' way. Some of 'em are the finest men in the world."

"Oh, I know. They're all right when they come North to college, but of all the hangdog, ill-dressed, slovenly lot I ever saw, a bunch of small-town Southerners are the worst!"

Sally Carrol was clinching her gloved hands and biting her lip furiously.

"Why," continued Harry, "there was one in my class at New Haven, and we all thought that at last we'd found the true type of Southern aristocrat, but it turned out that he wasn't an aristocrat at all—just the son of a Northern carpetbagger, who owned about all the cotton round Mobile."

"A Southerner wouldn't talk the way you're talking now," she said evenly.

"They haven't the energy!"

"Or the somethin' else."

"I'm sorry, Sally Carrol, but I've heard you say yourself that you'd never marry—"

"That's quite different. I told you I wouldn't want to tie my life to any of the boys that are round Tarleton now, but I never made any sweepin' generalities."

They walked along in silence.

"I probably spread it on a bit thick, Sally Carrol. I'm sorry."

She nodded but made no answer. Five minutes later as they stood in the hallway she suddenly threw her arms round him.

"Oh, Harry," she cried, her eyes brimming with tears, "let's get married next week. I'm afraid of having fusses like that. I'm afraid, Harry. It wouldn't be that way if we were married."

But Harry, being in the wrong, was still irritated.

"That'd be idiotic. We decided on March."

The tears in Sally Carrol's eyes faded; her expression hardened slightly.

"Very well—I suppose I shouldn't have said that."

Harry melted.

"Dear little nut!" he cried. "Come and kiss me and let's forget."

That very night at the end of a vaudeville performance the orchestra played "Dixie" and Sally Carrol felt something stronger and more enduring than her tears and smiles of the day brim up inside her. She leaned forward gripping the arms of her chair until her face grew crimson.

"Sort of get you, dear?" whispered Harry.

But she did not hear him. To the spirited throb of the violins and the inspiring beat of the kettle-drums her own old ghosts were marching by and on into the darkness, and as fifes whistled and sighed in the low encore they seemed so nearly out of sight that she could have waved good-by.

> Away, away,
> Away down South in Dixie!
> Away, away,
> Away down South in Dixie!

### V

IT WAS a particularly cold night. A sudden thaw had nearly cleared the streets the day before, but now they were traversed again with a powdery wraith of loose snow that travelled in wavy lines before the feet of the wind, and filled the lower air with a fine-particled mist. There was no sky—only a dark, ominous tent that draped in the tops of the streets and was in reality a vast approaching army of snowflakes—while over it all, chilling away the comfort from the brown-and-green glow of lighted windows and muffling the steady trot of the horse pulling their sleigh, interminably washed the north wind. It was a dismal town after all, she thought—dismal.

Sometimes at night it had seemed to her as though no one lived here—they had all gone long ago—leaving lighted houses to be covered in time by tombing heaps of sleet. Oh, if there should be snow on her grave! To be beneath great piles of it all winter long, where even her headstone would be a light shadow against light shadows. Her grave—a grave that should be flower-strewn and washed with sun and rain.

She thought again of those isolated country houses that her train had passed, and of the life there the long winter through—the ceaseless glare through the windows, the crust forming on the soft drifts of snow, finally the slow, cheerless melting, and the harsh spring of which Roger Patton had told her. Her spring—to lose it forever—with its lilacs and the lazy sweetness it stirred in her heart. She was laying away that spring—afterward she would lay away that sweetness.

With a gradual insistence the storm broke. Sally Carrol felt a film of flakes melt quickly on her eyelashes, and Harry reached over a furry arm and drew down her complicated flannel cap. Then the small flakes came in skirmish-line, and the horse bent his neck patiently as a transparency of white appeared momentarily on his coat.

"Oh, he's cold, Harry," she said quickly.

"Who? The horse? Oh, no, he isn't. He likes it!"

After another ten minutes they turned a corner and came in sight of their destination. On a tall hill outlined in vivid glaring green against the wintry sky stood the ice palace. It was three stories in the air, with battlements and embrasures and narrow icicled windows, and the innumerable electric lights inside made a gorgeous transparency of the great central hall. Sally Carrol clutched Harry's hand under the fur robe.

"It's beautiful!" he cried excitedly. "My golly, it's beautiful, isn't it! They haven't had one here since eighty-five!"

Somehow the notion of there not having been one since eighty-five oppressed her. Ice was a ghost, and this mansion of it was surely peopled by those shades of the eighties, with pale faces and blurred snowfilled hair.

"Come on, dear," said Harry.

She followed him out of the sleigh and waited while he hitched the horse. A party of four —Gordon, Myra, Roger Patton, and another girl —drew up beside them with a mighty jingle of bells. There were quite a crowd already, bundled in fur or sheepskin, shouting and calling to each other as they moved through the snow, which was now so thick that people could scarcely be distinguished a few yards away.

"It's a hundred and seventy feet tall," Harry was saying to a muffled figure beside him as they trudged toward the entrance; "covers six thousand square yards."

She caught snatches of conversation: "One main hall"—"walls twenty to forty inches thick" —"and the ice cave has almost a mile of —" —"this Canuck who built it—"

They found their way inside, and dazed by the magic of the great crystal walls Sally Carrol found herself repeating over and over two lines from "Kubla Khan":

> It was a miracle of rare device,
> A sunny pleasure-dome with caves of ice!

In the great glittering cavern with the dark shut out she took a seat on a wooden bench, and the evening's oppression lifted. Harry was right—it was beautiful; and her gaze travelled the smooth surface of the walls, the blocks for which had been selected for their purity and clearness to obtain this opalescent, translucent effect.

"Look! Here we go—oh, boy!" cried Harry.

A band in a far corner struck up "Hail Hail, the Gang's All Here!" which echoed over to them in wild muddled acoustics, and then the lights suddenly went out; silence seemed to flow down the icy sides and sweep over them. Sally Carrol could still see her white breath in the darkness, and a dim row of pale faces over on the other side.

The music eased to a sighing complaint, and from outside drifted in the full-throated resonant chant of the marching clubs. It grew louder like some paean of a viking tribe traversing an ancient wild; it swelled—they were coming nearer; then a row of torches appeared, and another and another, and keeping time with their moccasined feet a long column of gray-mackinawed figures swept in, snowshoes slung at their shoulders, torches soaring and flickering as their voices rose along the great walls.

The gray column ended and another followed, the light streaming luridly this time over red toboggan caps and flaming crimson mackinaws, and as they entered they took up the refrain; then came a long platoon of blue and white, of green, of white, of brown and yellow.

"Those white ones are the Wacouta Club," whispered Harry eagerly. "Those are the men you've met round at dances."

The volume of the voices grew; the great cavern was a phantasmagoria of torches waving in great banks of fire, of colors and the rhythm of soft-leather steps. The leading column turned and halted, platoon deployed in front of platoon until the whole procession made a solid flag of flame, and then from thousands of voices burst a mighty shout that filled the air like a crash of thunder, and sent the torches wavering. It was magnificent, it was tremendous! To Sally Carrol it was the North offering sacrifice on some mighty altar to the gray pagan God of Snow. As the shout died the band struck up again and there came more singing, and then long reverberating cheers by each club. She sat very quiet listening while the staccato cries rent the stillness; and then she started, for there was a volley of explosion, and great clouds of smoke went up here and there through the cavern—the flash-light photographers at work—and the council was over. With the band at their head the clubs formed in column once more, took up their chant, and began to march out.

"Come on!" shouted Harry. "We want to see the labyrinths downstairs before they turn the lights off!"

They all rose and started toward the chute —Harry and Sally Carrol in the lead, her little mitten buried in his big fur gantlet. At the bottom of the chute was a long empty room of ice, with the ceiling so low that they had to stoop—and their hands were parted. Before she realized what he intended Harry had darted down one of the half-dozen glittering passages that opened into the room and was only a vague receding blot against the green shimmer.

"Harry!" she called.

"Come on!" he cried back.

She looked round the empty chamber; the rest of the party had evidently decided to go home, were already outside somewhere in the blundering snow. She hesitated and then darted in after Harry.

"Harry!" she shouted.

She had reached a turning-point thirty feet down; she heard a faint muffled answer far to the left, and with a touch of panic fled toward it. She passed another turning, two more yawning alleys.

"Harry!"

No answer. She started to run straight forward, and then turned like lightning and sped back the way she had come, enveloped in a sudden icy terror.

She reached a turn—was it here?—took the left and came to what should have been the outlet into the long, low room, but it was only another glittering passage with darkness at the end. She called again but the walls gave back a flat, lifeless echo with no reverberations. Retracing her steps she turned another corner, this time following a wide passage. It was like the green lane between the parted waters of the Red Sea, like a damp vault connecting empty tombs.

She slipped a little now as she walked, for ice had formed on the bottom of her overshoes; she had to run her gloves along the half-slippery, half-sticky walls to keep her balance.

"Harry!"

Still no answer. The sound she made bounced mockingly down to the end of the passage.

Then on an instant the lights went out, and she was in complete darkness. She gave a small, frightened cry, and sank down into a cold little heap on the ice. She felt her left knee do something as she fell, but she scarcely noticed it as some deep terror far greater than any fear of being lost settled upon her. She was alone with this presence that came out of the North, the dreary loneliness that rose from ice-bound whal-ers in the Arctic seas, from smokeless, trackless wastes where were strewn the whitened bones of adventure. It was an icy breath of death; it was rolling down low across the land to clutch at her.

With a furious, despairing energy she rose again and started blindly down the darkness. She must get out. She might be lost in here for days, freeze to death and lie embedded in the ice like corpses she had read of, kept perfectly preserved until the melting of a glacier. Harry probably thought she had left with the others—he had gone by now; no one would know until late next day. She reached pitifully for the wall. Forty inches thick, they had said—forty inches thick!

"Oh!"

On both sides of her along the walls she felt things creeping, damp souls that haunted this palace, this town, this North.

"Oh, send somebody—send somebody!" she cried aloud.

Clark Darrow—he would understand; or Joe Ewing; she couldn't be left here to wander forever—to be frozen, heart, body, and soul. This her—this Sally Carrol! Why, she was a happy thing. She was a happy little girl. She liked warmth and summer and Dixie. These things were foreign—foreign.

"You're not crying," something said aloud. "You'll never cry any more. Your tears would just freeze; all tears freeze up here!"

She sprawled full length on the ice.

"Oh, God!" she faltered.

A long single file of minutes went by, and with a great weariness she felt her eyes closing. Then some one seemed to sit down near her and take her face in warm, soft hands. She looked up gratefully.

"Why, it's Margery Lee," she crooned softly to herself. "I knew you'd come." It really was Margery Lee, and she was just as Sally Carrol had known she would be, with a young, white brow, and wide, welcoming eyes, and a hoop-skirt of some soft material that was quite comforting to rest on.

"Margery Lee."

It was getting darker now and darker—all those tombstones ought to be repainted, sure enough, only that would spoil 'em, of course. Still, you ought to be able to see 'em.

Then after a succession of moments that went fast and then slow, but seemed to be ultimately resolving themselves into a multitude of blurred rays converging toward a pale-yellow sun, she heard a great cracking noise break her new-found stillness.

It was the sun, it was a light; a torch, and a

torch beyond that, and another one, and voices; a face took flesh below the torch, heavy arms raised her, and she felt something on her cheek —it felt wet. Some one had seized her and was rubbing her face with snow. How ridiculous —with snow!

"Sally Carrol! Sally Carrol!"

It was Dangerous Dan McGrew; and two other faces she didn't know.

"Child, child! We've been looking for you two hours! Harry's half-crazy!"

Things came rushing back into place—the singing, the torches, the great shout of the marching clubs. She squirmed in Patton's arms and gave a long low cry.

"Oh, I want to get out of here! I'm going back home. Take me home"—her voice rose to a scream that sent a chill to Harry's heart as he came racing down the next passage—"To-morrow!" she cried with delirious, unrestrained passion—"To-morrow! To-morrow! To-morrow!"

### VI

THE WEALTH of golden sunlight poured a quite enervating yet oddly comforting heat over the house where day long it faced the dusty stretch of road. Two birds were making a great to-do in a cool spot found among the branches of a tree next door, and down the street a colored woman was announcing herself melodiously as a purveyor of strawberries. It was April afternoon.

Sally Carrol Happer, resting her chin on her arm, and her arm on an old window-seat gazed sleepily down over the spangled dust whence the heat waves were rising for the first time this spring. She was watching a very ancient Ford turn a perilous corner and rattle and groan to a jolting stop at the end of the walk. She made no sound, and in a minute a strident familiar whistle rent the air. Sally Carrol smiled and blinked.

"Good mawnin'."

A head appeared tortuously from under the car-top below.

"'Tain't mawnin', Sally Carrol."

"Sure enough!" she said in affected surprise. "I guess maybe not."

"What you doin'?"

"Eatin' green peach. 'Spect to die any minute."

Clark twisted himself a last impossible notch to get a view of her face.

"Water's warm as a kettla steam, Sally Carrol. Wanta go swimmin'?"

"Hate to move," sighed Sally Carrol lazily, "but I reckon so."

*1920*

# THE CRACK-UP

◇

⟨ THE THREE sketches that make up this autobiographical account of a psychic collapse were first published in February, March, and April of 1936 in *Esquire*, which then carried the subtitle "The Magazine for Young Men." Fitzgerald was old beyond his years, and old enough to write what is certainly one of the most extraordinarily candid pieces of self-examination in the history of literature. The pieces were published more permanently in Edmund Wilson's posthumous collection of Fitzgerald prose, called *The Crack-Up* (1945). It is appropriate that Wilson, perhaps the best critic in the United States, should have put together the fugitive pieces of his old friend, for it is in the second part of "The Crack-Up" that Fitzgerald named Wilson as his "intellectual conscience."

◇

February, 1936

OF COURSE all life is a process of breaking down, but the blows that do the dramatic side of the work —the big sudden blows that come, or seem to come, from outside—the ones you remember and blame things on and, in moments of weakness, tell your friends about, don't show their effect all at once. There is another sort of blow that comes from within—that you don't feel until it's too late to do anything about it, until you realize with finality that in some regard you will never be as good a man again. The first sort of breakage seems to happen quick—the second kind happens almost without your knowing it but is realized suddenly indeed.

Before I go on with this short history, let me make a general observation—the test of a first-rate intelligence is the ability to hold two opposed ideas in the mind at the same time, and still retain the ability to function. One should, for example, be able to see that things are hopeless and yet be determined to make them otherwise. This philosophy fitted on to my early adult life, when I saw the improbable, the implausible, often the "impossible," come true. Life was something you dominated if you were any good. Life yielded easily to intelligence and effort, or to what proportion could be mustered of both. It seemed a romantic business to be a successful literary man—you were not ever going to be as famous as a movie star but what note you had was probably longer-lived—you were never going to have the power of a man of strong political or religious convictions but you were certainly more independent. Of course within the practice of your trade you were forever unsatisfied —but I, for one, would not have chosen any other.

As the twenties passed, with my own twenties marching a little ahead of them, my two juvenile regrets—at not being big enough (or good enough) to play football in college, and at not getting overseas during the war—resolved themselves into childish waking dreams of imaginary heroism that were good enough to go to sleep on in restless nights. The big problems of life seemed to solve themselves, and if the business of fixing them was difficult, it made one too tired to think of more general problems.

Life, ten years ago, was largely a personal matter. I must hold in balance the sense of the futility of effort and the sense of the necessity to struggle; the conviction of the inevitability of failure and still the determination to "succeed"—and, more than these, the contradiction between the dead hand of the past and the high intentions of the future. If I could do this through the common ills—domestic, professional and personal—then the ego would continue as an arrow shot from nothingness to nothingness with such force that only gravity would bring it to earth at last.

For seventeen years, with a year of deliberate loafing and resting out in the center—things went on like that, with a new chore only a nice prospect for the next day. I was living hard, too, but: "Up to forty-nine it'll be all right," I said. "I can count on that. For a man who's lived as I have, that's all you could ask."

—And then, ten years this side of forty-nine, I suddenly realized that I had prematurely cracked.

## II

NOW a man can crack in many ways—can crack in the head—in which case the power of decision is taken from you by others! or in the body, when one can but submit to the white hospital world; or in the nerves. William Seabrook [1] in an unsympathetic book tells, with some pride and a movie ending, of how he became a public charge. What led to his alcoholism or was bound up with it, was a collapse of his nervous system. Though the present writer was not so entangled—having at the time not tasted so much as a glass of beer for six months—it was his nervous reflexes that were giving way—too much anger and too many tears.

Moreover, to go back to my thesis that life has a varying offensive, the realization of having cracked was not simultaneous with a blow, but with a reprieve.

THE CRACK-UP.   1. **William Seabrook:** William Buehler Seabrook (1886–1945), American adventure and travel writer.

Not long before, I had sat in the office of a great doctor and listened to a grave sentence. With what, in retrospect, seems some equanimity, I had gone on about my affairs in the city where I was then living, not caring much, not thinking how much had been left undone, or what would become of this and that responsibility, like people do in books; I was well insured and anyhow I had been only a mediocre caretaker of most of the things left in my hands, even of my talent.

But I had a strong sudden instinct that I must be alone. I didn't want to see any people at all. I had seen so many people all my life—I was an average mixer, but more than average in a tendency to identify myself, my ideas, my destiny, with those of all classes that I came in contact with. I was always saving or being saved—in a single morning I would go through the emotions ascribable to Wellington at Waterloo. I lived in a world of inscrutable hostiles and inalienable friends and supporters.

But now I wanted to be absolutely alone and so arranged a certain insulation from ordinary cares.

It was not an unhappy time. I went away and there were fewer people. I found I was good-and-tired. I could lie around and was glad to, sleeping or dozing sometimes twenty hours a day and in the intervals trying resolutely not to think—instead I made lists—made lists and tore them up, hundreds of lists: of cavalry leaders and football players and cities, and popular tunes and pitchers, and happy times, and hobbies and houses lived in and how many suits since I left the army and how many pairs of shoes (I didn't count the suit I bought in Sorrento that shrunk, nor the pumps and dress shirt and collar that I carried around for years and never wore, because the pumps got damp and grainy and the shirt and collar got yellow and starch-rotted). And lists of women I'd liked, and of the times I had let myself be snubbed by people who had not been my betters in character or ability.

—And then suddenly, surprisingly, I got better.

—And cracked like an old plate as soon as I heard the news.

That is the real end of this story. What was to be done about it will have to rest in what used to be called the "womb of time." Suffice it to say that after about an hour of solitary pillow-hugging, I began to realize that for two years my life had been a drawing on resources that I did not possess, that I had been mortgaging myself physically and spiritually up to the hilt. What was the small gift of life given back in comparison to that?—when there had once been a pride of direction and a confidence in enduring independence.

I realized that in those two years, in order to

preserve something—an inner hush maybe, maybe not—I had weaned myself from all the things I used to love—that every act of life from the morning tooth-brush to the friend at dinner had become an effort. I saw that for a long time I had not liked people and things, but only followed the rickety old pretense of liking. I saw that even my love for those closest to me was become only an attempt to love, that my casual relations—with an editor, a tobacco seller, the child of a friend, were only what I remembered I *should* do, from other days. All in the same month I became bitter about such things as the sound of the radio, the advertisements in the magazines, the screech of tracks, the dead silence of the country—contemptuous at human softness, immediately (if secretively) quarrelsome toward hardness—hating the night when I couldn't sleep and hating the day because it went toward night. I slept on the heart side now because I knew that the sooner I could tire that out, even a little, the sooner would come that blessed hour of nightmare which, like a catharsis, would enable me to better meet the new day.

There were certain spots, certain faces I could look at. Like most Middle Westerners, I have never had any but the vaguest race prejudices—I always had a secret yen for the lovely Scandinavian blondes who sat on porches in St. Paul but hadn't emerged enough economically to be part of what was then society. They were too nice to be "chickens" and too quickly off the farmlands to seize a place in the sun, but I remember going round blocks to catch a single glimpse of shining hair—the bright shock of a girl I'd never know. This is urban, unpopular talk. It strays afield from the fact that in these latter days I couldn't stand the sight of Celts, English, Politicians, Strangers, Virginians, Negroes (light or dark), Hunting People, or retail clerks, and middlemen in general, all writers (I avoided writers very carefully because they can perpetuate trouble as no one else can)—and all the classes as classes and most of them as members of their class . . .

Trying to cling to something, I liked doctors and girl children up to the age of about thirteen and well-brought-up boy children from about eight years old on. I could have peace and happiness with these few categories of people. I forgot to add that I liked old men—men over seventy, sometimes over sixty if their faces looked seasoned. I liked Katharine Hepburn's face on the screen, no matter what was said about her pretentiousness, and Miriam Hopkins' face, and old friends if I only saw them once a year and could remember their ghosts.

All rather inhuman and undernourished, isn't it? Well, that, children, is the true sign of cracking up.

It is not a pretty picture. Inevitably it was carted here and there within its frame and exposed to various critics. One of them can only be described as a person whose life makes other people's lives seem like death—even this time when she was cast in the usually unappealing role of Job's comforter. In spite of the fact that this story is over, let me append our conversation as a sort of postscript:

"Instead of being so sorry for yourself, listen—" she said. (She always says "Listen," because she thinks while she talks—*really* thinks.) So she said: "Listen. Suppose this wasn't a crack in you —suppose it was a crack in the Grand Canyon."

"The crack's in me," I said heroically.

"Listen! The world only exists in your eyes— your conception of it. You can make it as big or as small as you want to. And you're trying to be a little puny individual. By God, if I ever cracked, I'd try to make the world crack with me. Listen! The world only exists through your apprehension of it, and so it's much better to say that it's not you that's cracked—it's the Grand Canyon."

"Baby et up all her Spinoza?" [2]

"I don't know anything about Spinoza. I know––" She spoke, then, of old woes of her own, that seemed, in the telling, to have been more dolorous than mine, and how she had met them, over-ridden them, beaten them.

I felt a certain reaction to what she said, but I am a slow-thinking man, and it occurred to me simultaneously that of all natural forces, vitality is the incommunicable one. In days when juice came into one as an article without duty, one tried to distribute it—but always without success; to further mix metaphors, vitality never "takes." You have it or you haven't it, like health or brown eyes or honor or a baritone voice. I might have asked some of it from her, neatly wrapped and ready for home cooking and digestion, but I could never have got it—not if I'd waited around for a thousand hours with the tin cup of self-pity. I could walk from her door, holding myself very carefully like cracked crockery, and go away into the world of bitterness, where I was making a home with such materials as are found there—and quote to myself after I left her door:

*"Ye are the salt of the earth. But if the salt hath lost its savour, wherewith shall it be salted?"*
*Matthew 5–13.*

---

2. **Spinoza:** Benedictus de Spinoza (1632–77), Dutch philosopher.

### HANDLE WITH CARE

March, 1936

IN A previous article this writer told about his realization that what he had before him was not the dish that he had ordered for his forties. In fact—since he and the dish were one, he described himself as a cracked plate, the kind that one wonders whether it is worth preserving. Your editor thought that the article suggested too many aspects without regarding them closely, and probably many readers felt the same way—and there are always those to whom all self-revelation is contemptible, unless it ends with a noble thanks to the gods for the Unconquerable Soul.[3]

But I had been thanking the gods too long, and thanking them for nothing. I wanted to put a lament into my record, without even the background of the Euganean Hills[4] to give it color. There weren't any Euganean hills that I could see.

Sometimes, though, the cracked plate has to be retained in the pantry, has to be kept in service as a household necessity. It can never again be warmed on the stove nor shuffled with the other plates in the dishpan; it will not be brought out for company, but it will do to hold crackers late at night or to go into the ice box under leftovers . . .

Hence this sequel—a cracked plate's further history.

Now the standard cure for one who is sunk is to consider those in actual destitution or physical suffering—this is an all-weather beatitude for gloom in general and fairly salutory day-time advice for everyone. But at three o'clock in the morning, a forgotten package has the same tragic importance as a death sentence, and the cure doesn't work—and in a real dark night of the soul it is always three o'clock in the morning, day after day. At that hour the tendency is to refuse to face things as long as possible by retiring into an infantile dream—but one is continually startled out of this by various contacts with the world. One meets these occasions as quickly and carelessly as possible and retires once more back into the dream, hoping that things will adjust themselves by some great material or spiritual bonanza. But as the withdrawal persists there is less and less chance of the bonanza—one is not waiting for the fade-out of a single sorrow, but rather being an unwilling witness of an execution, the disintegration of one's own personality . . .

Unless madness or drugs or drink come into it, this phase comes to a dead-end, eventually, and is succeeded by a vacuous quiet. In this you can try to estimate what has been sheared away and what is left. Only when this quiet came to me, did I realize that I had gone through two parallel experiences.

The first time was twenty years ago, when I left Princeton in junior year with a complaint diagnosed as malaria. It transpired, through an X-ray taken a dozen years later, that it had been tuberculosis—a mild case, and after a few months of rest I went back to college. But I had lost certain offices, the chief one was the presidency of the Triangle Club, a musical comedy idea, and also I dropped back a class. To me college would never be the same. There were to be no badges of pride, no medals, after all. It seemed on one March afternoon that I had lost every single thing I wanted—and that night was the first time that I hunted down the spectre of womanhood that, for a little while, makes everything else seem unimportant.

Years later I realized that my failure as a big shot in college was all right—instead of serving on committees, I took a beating on English poetry; when I got the idea of what it was all about, I set about learning how to write. On Shaw's principle that "If you don't get what you like, you better like what you get," it was a lucky break—at the moment it was a harsh and bitter business to know that my career as a leader of men was over.

Since that day I have not been able to fire a bad servant, and I am astonished and impressed by people who can. Some old desire for personal dominance was broken and gone. Life around me was a solemn dream, and I lived on the letters I wrote to a girl in another city. A man does not recover from such jolts—he becomes a different person and, eventually, the new person finds new things to care about.

The other episode parallel to my current situation took place after the war, when I had again over-extended my flank. It was one of those tragic loves doomed for lack of money, and one day the girl closed it out on the basis of common sense. During a long summer of despair I wrote a novel instead of letters, so it came out all right, but it came out all right for a different person. The man with the jingle of money in his pocket who married the girl a year later would always cherish an abiding distrust, an animosity, toward the leisure class—not the conviction of a revolutionist but

---

3. **Unconquerable Soul:** a reference to "Invictus" by William Ernest Henley (1849–1903), British poet, self-avowed "master of my fate; . . . captain of my soul." 4. **Euganean Hills:** Shelley's poem, "Lines Written Among the Euganean Hills" (1818), attempts to transcend his deep despair.

the smouldering hatred of a peasant. In the years since then I have never been able to stop wondering where my friends' money came from, nor to stop thinking that at one time a sort of *droit de seigneur*[5] might have been exercised to give one of them my girl.

For sixteen years I lived pretty much as this latter person, distrusting the rich, yet working for money with which to share their mobility and the grace that some of them brought into their lives. During this time I had plenty of the usual horses shot from under me—I remember some of their names—*Punctured Pride, Thwarted Expectation, Faithless, Show-off, Hard Hit, Never Again.* And after awhile I wasn't twenty-five, then not even thirty-five, and nothing was quite as good. But in all these years I don't remember a moment of discouragement. I saw honest men through moods of suicidal gloom—some of them gave up and died; others adjusted themselves and went on to a larger success than mine; but my morale never sank below the level of self-disgust when I had put on some unsightly personal show. Trouble has no necessary connection with discouragement—discouragement has a germ of its own, as different from trouble as arthritis is different from a stiff joint.

When a new sky cut off the sun last spring, I didn't at first relate it to what had happened fifteen or twenty years ago. Only gradually did a certain family resemblance come through—an over-extension of the flank, a burning of the candle at both ends; a call upon physical resources that I did not command, like a man over-drawing at his bank. In its impact this blow was more violent than the other two but it was the same in kind—a feeling that I was standing at twilight on a deserted range, with an empty rifle in my hands and the targets down. No problem set—simply a silence with only the sound of my own breathing.

In this silence there was a vast irresponsibility toward every obligation, a deflation of all my values. A passionate belief in order, a disregard of motives or consequences in favor of guess work and prophecy, a feeling that craft and industry would have a place in any world—one by one, these and other convictions were swept away. I saw that the novel, which at my maturity was the strongest and supplest medium for conveying thought and emotion from one human being to another, was becoming subordinated to a mechanical and communal art that, whether in the hands of Hollywood merchants or Russian idealists, was capable of reflecting only the tritest

thought, the most obvious emotion. It was an art in which words were subordinate to images, where personality was worn down to the inevitable low gear of collaboration. As long past as 1930, I had a hunch that the talkies would make even the best selling novelist as archaic as silent pictures. People still read, if only Professor Canby's book of the month[6]—curious children nosed at the slime of Mr. Tiffany Thayer in the drugstore libraries—but there was a rankling indignity, that to me had become almost an obsession, in seeing the power of the written word subordinated to another power, a more glittering, a grosser power . . .

I set that down as an example of what haunted me during the long night—this was something I could neither accept nor struggle against, something which tended to make my efforts obsolescent, as the chain stores have crippled the small merchant, an exterior force, unbeatable—

(I have the sense of lecturing now, looking at a watch on the desk before me and seeing how many more minutes—).

Well, when I had reached this period of silence, I was forced into a measure that no one ever adopts voluntarily: I was impelled to think. God, was it difficult! The moving about of great secret trunks. In the first exhausted halt, I wondered whether I had ever thought. After a long time I came to these conclusions, just as I write them here:

(1) That I had done very little thinking, save within the problems of my craft. For twenty years a certain man had been my intellectual conscience. That was Edmund Wilson.

(2) That another man represented my sense of the "good life," though I saw him once in a decade, and since then he might have been hung. He is in the fur business in the Northwest and wouldn't like his name set down here. But in difficult situations I had tried to think what *he* would have thought, how *he* would have acted.

(3) That a third contemporary had been an artistic conscience to me—I had not imitated his infectious style, because my own style, such as it is, was formed before he published anything, but there was an awful pull toward him when I was on a spot.[7]

(4) That a fourth man[8] had come to dictate my relations with other people when these relations were successful: how to do, what to say. How to make people at least momentarily happy (in

---

5. *droit de seigneur: droit du seigneur,* "master's right."

6. **Professor Canby's book of the month:** Henry Seidel Canby (1878–1961), once a professor at Yale, served for many years on the board of the Book of the Month Club.    7. The reference is to Ernest Hemingway.    8. **a fourth man:** Gerald Murphy, a wealthy American friend in France.

opposition to Mrs. Post's [9] theories of how to make everyone thoroughly uncomfortable with a sort of systematized vulgarity). This always confused me and made me want to go out and get drunk, but this man had seen the game, analyzed it and beaten it, and his word was good enough for me.

(5) That my political conscience had scarcely existed for ten years save as an element of irony in my stuff. When I became again concerned with the system I should function under, it was a man much younger than myself who brought it to me, with a mixture of passion and fresh air.[10]

So there was not an "I" any more—not a basis on which I could organize my self-respect—save my limitless capacity for toil that it seemed I possessed no more. It was strange to have no self—to be like a little boy left alone in a big house, who knew that now he could do anything he wanted to do, but found that there was nothing that he wanted to do—

(The watch is past the hour and I have barely reached my thesis. I have some doubts as to whether this is of general interest, but if anyone wants more, there is plenty left, and your editor will tell me. If you've had enough, say so—but not too loud, because I have the feeling that someone, I'm not sure who, is sound asleep—someone who could have helped me to keep my shop open. It wasn't Lenin, and it wasn't God.)

### PASTING IT TOGETHER

April, 1936

I HAVE spoken in these pages of how an exceptionally optimistic young man experienced a crack-up of all values, a crack-up that he scarcely knew of until long after it occurred. I told of the succeeding period of desolation and of the necessity of going on, but without benefit of Henley's familiar heroics,[11] "my head is bloody but unbowed." For a check-up of my spiritual liabilities indicated that I had no particular head to be bowed or unbowed. Once I had had a heart but that was about all I was sure of.

This was at least a starting place out of the morass in which I floundered: "I felt—therefore I was." At one time or another there had been many people who had leaned on me, come to me in difficulties or written me from afar, believed implicitly in my advice and my attitude toward life. The dullest platitude monger or the most unscrupulous Rasputin who can influence the destinies of many people must have some individuality, so the question became one of finding why and where I had changed, where was the leak through which, unknown to myself, my enthusiasm and my vitality had been steadily and prematurely trickling away.

One harassed and despairing night I packed a brief case and went off a thousand miles to think it over. I took a dollar room in a drab little town where I knew no one and sunk all the money I had with me in a stock of potted meat, crackers and apples. But don't let me suggest that the change from a rather overstuffed world to a comparative asceticism was any Research Magnificent [12]—I only wanted absolute quiet to think out why I had developed a sad attitude toward sadness, a melancholy attitude toward melancholy and a tragic attitude toward tragedy—*why I had become identified with the objects of my horror or compassion.*

Does this seem a fine distinction? It isn't: identification such as this spells the death of accomplishment. It is something like this that keeps insane people from working. Lenin did not willingly endure the sufferings of his proletariat, nor Washington of his troops, nor Dickens of his London poor. And when Tolstoy tried some such merging of himself with the objects of his attention, it was a fake and a failure. I mention these because they are the men best known to us all.

It was dangerous mist. When Wordsworth decided that "there had passed away a glory from the earth," he felt no compulsion to pass away with it, and the Fiery Particle Keats never ceased his struggle against t. b. nor in his last moments relinquished his hope of being among the English poets.

My self-immolation was something sodden-dark. It was very distinctly not modern—yet I saw it in others, saw it in a dozen men of honor and industry since the war. (I heard you, but that's too easy—there were Marxians among these men.) I had stood by while one famous contemporary of mine played with the idea of the Big Out for half a year; I had watched when another, equally eminent, spent months in an asylum unable to endure any contact with his fellow men. And of those who had given up and passed on I could list a score.

This led me to the idea that the ones who had survived had made some sort of clean break. This is a big word and is no parallel to a jail-break when one is probably headed for a new jail or will be forced back to the old one. The famous "Escape" or "run away from it all" is an excursion in a trap even if the trap includes the south seas, which are

---

9. **Mrs. Post:** Emily Post, commercial authority on etiquette.
10. Probably Budd Schulberg, the American novelist (1914–  ).
11. **Henley's familiar heroics:** See above, 3 n.

12. **Research Magnificent:** title of a novel by H. G. Wells about a search for a fulfilling way of life.

only for those who want to paint them or sail them. A clean break is something you cannot come back from; that is irretrievable because it makes the past cease to exist. So, since I could no longer fulfill the obligations that life had set for me or that I had set for myself, why not slay the empty shell who had been posturing as it for four years? I must continue to be a writer because that was my only way of life, but I would cease any attempts to be a person—to be kind, just or generous. There were plenty of counterfeit coins around that would pass instead of these and I knew where I could get them at a nickel on the dollar. In thirty-nine years an observant eye has learned to detect where the milk is watered and the sugar is sanded, the rhinestone passed for diamond and the stucco for stone. There was to be no more giving of myself—all giving was to be outlawed henceforth under a new name, and that name was Waste.

The decision made me rather exuberant, like anything that is both real and new. As a sort of beginning there was a whole shaft of letters to be tipped into the waste basket when I went home, letters that wanted something for nothing—to read this man's manuscript, market this man's poem, speak free on the radio, indite notes of introduction, give this interview, help with the plot of this play, with this domestic situation, perform this act of thoughtfulness or charity.

The conjuror's hat was empty. To draw things out of it had long been a sort of sleight of hand, and now, to change the metaphor, I was off the dispensing end of the relief roll forever.

The heady villainous feeling continued.

I felt like the beady-eyed men I used to see on the commuting train from Great Neck fifteen years back—men who didn't care whether the world tumbled into chaos tomorrow if it spared their houses. I was one with them now, one with the smooth articles who said:

"I'm sorry but business is business." Or:

"You ought to have thought of that before you got into this trouble." Or:

"I'm not the person to see about that."

And a smile—ah, I would get me a smile. I'm still working on that smile. It is to combine the best qualities of a hotel manager, an experienced old social weasel, a headmaster on visitors' day, a colored elevator man, a pansy pulling a profile, a producer getting stuff at half its market value, a trained nurse coming on a new job, a body-vender in her first rotogravure, a hopeful extra swept near the camera, a ballet dancer with an infected toe, and of course the great beam of loving kindness common to all those from Washington to Beverly Hills who must exist by virtue of the contorted pan.

The voice too—I am working with a teacher on the voice. When I have perfected it the larynx will show no ring of conviction except the conviction of the person I am talking to. Since it will be largely called upon for the elicitation of the word "yes," my teacher (a lawyer) and I are concentrating on that, but in extra hours, I am learning to bring into it that polite acerbity that makes people feel that far from being welcome they are not even tolerated and are under continual and scathing analysis at every moment. These times will of course not coincide with the smile. This will be reserved exclusively for those from whom I have nothing to gain, old worn-out people or young struggling people. They won't mind—what the hell, they get it most of the time anyhow.

But enough. It is not a matter of levity. If you are young and you should write asking to see me and learn how to be a sombre literary man writing pieces upon the state of emotional exhaustion that often overtakes writers in their prime—if you should be so young and so fatuous as to do this, I would not do so much as acknowledge your letter, unless you were related to someone very rich and important indeed. And if you were dying of starvation outside my window, I would go out quickly and give you the smile and the voice (if no longer the hand) and stick around till somebody raised a nickel to phone for the ambulance, that is if I thought there would be any copy in it for me.

I have now at last become a writer only. The man I had persistently tried to be became such a burden that I have "cut him loose" with as little compunction as a Negro lady cuts loose a rival on Saturday night. Let the good people function as such—let the overworked doctors die in harness, with one week's "vacation" a year that they can devote to straightening out their family affairs, and let the underworked doctors scramble for cases at one dollar a throw; let the soldiers be killed and enter immediately into the Valhalla of their profession. That is their contract with the gods. A writer need have no such ideals unless he makes them for himself, and this one has quit. The old dream of being an entire man in the Goethe-Byron-Shaw tradition, with an opulent American touch, a sort of combination of J. P. Morgan, Topham Beauclerk and St. Francis of Assisi, has been relegated to the junk heap of the shoulder pads worn for one day on the Princeton freshman football field and the overseas cap never worn overseas.

So what? This is what I think now: that the natural state of the sentient adult is a qualified unhappiness. I think also that in an adult the desire to be finer in grain than you are, "a constant striving" (as those people say who gain their bread by saying it) only adds to this unhappiness in the end —that end that comes to our youth and hope. My own happiness in the past often approached such an ecstasy that I could not share it even with the person dearest to me but had to walk it away in quiet streets and lanes with only fragments of it to distil into little lines in books—and I think that my happiness, or talent for self-delusion or what you will, was an exception. It was not the natural thing but the unnatural—unnatural as the Boom; and my recent experience parallels the wave of despair that swept the nation when the Boom was over.

I shall manage to live with the new dispensation, though it has taken some months to be certain of

the fact. And just as the laughing stoicism which has enabled the American Negro to endure the intolerable conditions of his existence has cost him his sense of the truth—so in my case there is a price to pay. I do not any longer like the postman, nor the grocer, nor the editor, nor the cousin's husband, and he in turn will come to dislike me, so that life will never be very pleasant again, and the sign *Cave Canem* [13] is hung permanently just above my door. I will try to be a correct animal though, and if you throw me a bone with enough meat on it I may even lick your hand.

*1936*

# Ernest Hemingway

## BIG TWO-HEARTED RIVER

◊

❲ THIS story, which first appeared in the Parisian avant-garde review *This Quarter* in May of 1925, is also the climactic story in the volume *In Our Time*, which appeared in October of that year. This presentation of Nick Adams in his maturity may derive, in some ways, from a story by one of Hemingway's favorite authors —*Heart of Darkness* by Joseph Conrad. As that story rests on contrasts of light and darkness, so Hemingway's story opposes two stretches of the river—the river that Nick fishes, where all is bright, clear sunlight and pellucid water, and the swamp into which it flows, the threatening place of corruption, darkness, chaos, and disarray that, for the time being, Nick cannot contemplate. He has already been in the heart of darkness and for the present will remain in the better part of the two-hearted river.

◊

### PART I

THE TRAIN went on up the track out of sight, around one of the hills of burnt timber. Nick sat down on the bundle of canvas and bedding the baggage man had pitched out of the door of the baggage car. There was no town, nothing but the rails and the burned-over country. The thirteen saloons that had lined the one street of Seney had not left a trace. The foundations of the Mansion House hotel stuck up above the ground. The stone

was chipped and split by the fire. It was all that was left of the town of Seney. Even the surface had been burned off the ground.

Nick looked at the burned-over stretch of hillside, where he had expected to find the scattered houses of the town and then walked down the railroad track to the bridge over the river. The river was there. It swirled against the log spiles of the bridge. Nick looked down into the clear, brown water, colored from the pebbly bottom, and watched the trout keeping themselves steady in the current with wavering fins. As he watched them they changed their positions by quick angles, only to hold steady in the fast water again. Nick watched them a long time.

He watched them holding themselves with their noses into the current, many trout in deep, fast moving water, slightly distorted as he watched far down through the glassy convex surface of the pool, its surface pushing and swelling smooth against the resistance of the log-driven piles of the bridge. At the bottom of the pool were the big trout. Nick did not see them at first. Then he saw them at the bottom of the pool, big trout looking to hold themselves on the gravel bottom in a varying mist of gravel and sand, raised in spurts by the current.

Nick looked down into the pool from the bridge. It was a hot day. A kingfisher flew up the stream. It was a long time since Nick had looked into a stream and seen trout. They were very satisfactory. As the shadow of the kingfisher moved up the stream, a big trout shot upstream in a long angle, only his shadow marking the angle, then lost his shadow as he came through the surface of the

13. *Cave Canem:* "Beware of the dog."

water, caught the sun, and then, as he went back into the stream under the surface, his shadow seemed to float down the stream with the current, unresisting, to his post under the bridge where he tightened facing up into the current.

Nick's heart tightened as the trout moved. He felt all the old feeling.

He turned and looked down the stream. It stretched away, pebbly-bottomed with shallows and big boulders and a deep pool as it curved away around the foot of a bluff.

Nick walked back up the ties to where his pack lay in the cinders beside the railway track. He was happy. He adjusted the pack harness around the bundle, pulling straps tight, slung the pack on his back, got his arms through the shoulder straps and took some of the pull off his shoulders by leaning his forehead against the wide band of the tump-line. Still, it was too heavy. It was much too heavy. He had his leather rod-case in his hand and leaning forward to keep the weight of the pack high on his shoulders he walked along the road that paralleled the railway track, leaving the burned town behind in the heat, and then turned off around a hill with a high, fire-scarred hill on either side onto a road that went back into the country. He walked along the road feeling the ache from the pull of the heavy pack. The road climbed steadily. It was hard work walking up-hill. His muscles ached and the day was hot, but Nick felt happy. He felt he had left everything behind, the need for thinking, the need to write, other needs. It was all back of him.

From the time he had gotten down off the train and the baggage man had thrown his pack out of the open car door things had been different. Seney was burned, the country was burned over and changed, but it did not matter. It could not all be burned. He knew that. He hiked along the road, sweating in the sun, climbing to cross the range of hills that separated the railway from the pine plains.

The road ran on, dipping occasionally, but always climbing. Nick went on up. Finally the road after going parallel to the burnt hillside reached the top. Nick leaned back against a stump and slipped out of the pack harness. Ahead of him, as far as he could see, was the pine plain. The burned country stopped off at the left with the range of hills. On ahead islands of dark pine trees rose out of the plain. Far off to the left was the line of the river. Nick followed it with his eye and caught glints of the water in the sun.

There was nothing but the pine plain ahead of him, until the far blue hills that marked the Lake Superior height of land. He could hardly see them, faint and far away in the heat-light over the plain. If he looked too steadily they were gone. But if he only half-looked they were there, the far off hills of the height of land.

Nick sat down against the charred stump and smoked a cigarette. His pack balanced on the top of the stump, harness holding ready, a hollow molded in it from his back. Nick sat smoking, looking out over the country. He did not need to get his map out. He knew where he was from the position of the river.

As he smoked, his legs stretched out in front of him, he noticed a grasshopper walk along the ground and up onto his woolen sock. The grasshopper was black. As he had walked along the road, climbing, he had started many grasshoppers from the dust. They were all black. They were not the big grasshoppers with yellow and black or red and black wings whirring out from their black wing sheathing as they fly up. These were just ordinary hoppers, but all a sooty black in color. Nick had wondered about them as he walked, without really thinking about them. Now, as he watched the black hopper that was nibbling at the wool of his sock with its fourway lip, he realized that they had all turned black from living in the burned-over land. He realized that the fire must have come the year before, but the grasshoppers were all black now. He wondered how long they would stay that way.

Carefully he reached his hand down and took hold of the hopper by the wings. He turned him up, all his legs walking in the air, and looked at his jointed belly. Yes, it was black too, iridescent where the back and head were dusty.

"Go on, hopper," Nick said, speaking out loud for the first time, "Fly away somewhere."

He tossed the grasshopper up into the air and watched him sail away to a charcoal stump across the road.

Nick stood up. He leaned his back against the weight of his pack where it rested upright on the stump and got his arms through the shoulder straps. He stood with the pack on his back on the brow of the hill looking out across the country, toward the distant river and then struck down the hillside away from the road. Underfoot the ground was good walking. Two hundred yards down the hillside the fire line stopped. Then it was sweet fern, growing ankle high, to walk through, and clumps of jack pines; a long undulating country with frequent rises ane descents, sandy underfoot and the country alive again.

Nick kept his direction by the sun. He knew where he wanted to strike the river and he kept on through the pine plain, mounting small rises to see other rises ahead of him and sometimes from the top of a rise a great solid island of pines off to his right or his left. He broke off some sprigs of the heathery sweet fern, and put them under his pack straps. The chafing crushed it and he smelled it as he walked.

He was tired and very hot, walking across the uneven, shadeless pine plain. At any time he knew he could strike the river by turning off to his left. It could not be more than a mile away. But he kept on toward the north to hit the river as far upstream as he could go in one day's walking.

For some time as he walked Nick had been in sight of one of the big islands of pine standing out above the rolling high ground he was crossing. He dipped down and then as he came slowly up to the crest of the ridge he turned and made toward the pine trees.

There was no underbrush in the island of pine trees. The trunks of the trees went straight up or slanted toward each other. The trunks were straight and brown without branches. The branches were high above. Some interlocked to make a solid shadow on the brown forest floor. Around the grove of trees was a bare space. It was brown and soft underfoot as Nick walked on it. This was the over-lapping of the pine needle floor, extending out beyond the width of the high branches. The trees had grown tall and the branches moved high, leaving in the sun this bare space they had once covered with shadow. Sharp at the edge of this extension of the forest floor commenced the sweet fern.

Nick slipped off his pack and lay down in the shade. He lay on his back and looked up into the pine trees. His neck and back and the small of his back rested as he stretched. The earth felt good against his back. He looked up at the sky, through the branches, and then shut his eyes. He opened them and looked up again. There was a wind high up in the branches. He shut his eyes again and went to sleep.

Nick woke stiff and cramped. The sun was nearly down. His pack was heavy and the straps painful as he lifted it on. He leaned over with the pack on and picked up the leather rod-case and started out from the pine trees across the sweet fern swale, toward the river. He knew it could not be more than a mile.

He came down a hillside covered with stumps into a meadow. At the edge of the meadow flowed the river. Nick was glad to get to the river. He walked upstream through the meadow. His trousers were soaked with the dew as he walked. After the hot day, the dew had come quickly and heavily. The river made no sound. It was too fast and smooth. At the edge of the meadow, before he mounted to a piece of high ground to make camp, Nick looked down the river at the trout rising. They were rising to insects come from the swamp on the other side of the stream when the sun went down. The trout jumped out of water to take them. While Nick walked through the little stretch of meadow alongside the stream, trout had jumped high out of water. Now as he looked down the river, the insects must be settling on the surface, for the trout were feeding steadily all down the stream. As far down the long stretch as he could see, the trout were rising, making circles all down the surface of the water, as though it were starting to rain.

The ground rose, wooded and sandy, to overlook the meadow, the stretch of river and the swamp. Nick dropped his pack and rod-case and looked for a level piece of ground. He was very hungry and he wanted to make his camp before he cooked. Between two jack pines, the ground was quite level. He took the ax out of the pack and chopped out two projecting roots. That leveled a piece of ground large enough to sleep on. He smoothed out the sandy soil with his hand and pulled all the sweet fern bushes by their roots. His hands smelled good from the sweet fern. He smoothed the uprooted earth. He did not want anything making lumps under the blankets. When he had the ground smooth, he spread his three blankets. One he folded double, next to the ground. The other two he spread on top.

With the ax he slit off a bright slab of pine from one of the stumps and split it into pegs for the tent. He wanted them long and solid to hold in the ground. With the tent unpacked and spread on the ground, the pack, leaning against a jackpine, looked much smaller. Nick tied the rope that served the tent for a ridge-pole to the trunk of one of the pine trees and pulled the tent up off the ground with the other end of the rope and tied it to the other pine. The tent hung on the rope like a canvas blanket on a clothes line. Nick poked a pole he had cut up under the back peak of the canvas and then made it a tent by pegging out the sides. He pegged the sides out taut and drove the pegs deep, hitting them down into the ground with the flat of the ax until the rope loops were buried and the canvas was drum tight.

Across the open mouth of the tent Nick fixed cheese cloth to keep out mosquitoes. He crawled inside under the mosquito bar with various things from the pack to put at the head of the bed under the slant of the canvas. Inside the tent the light came through the brown canvas. It smelled pleasantly of canvas. Already there was something mysterious and homelike. Nick was happy as he crawled inside the tent. He had not been unhappy all day. This was different though. Now things were done. There had been this to do. Now it was done. It had been a hard trip. He was very tired. That was done. He had made his camp. He was settled. Nothing could touch him. It was a good place to camp. He was there, in the good place. He was in his home where he had made it. Now he was hungry.

He came out, crawling under the cheese cloth. It was quite dark outside. It was lighter in the tent.

Nick went over to the pack and found, with his fingers, a long nail in a paper sack of nails, in the bottom of the pack. He drove it into the pine tree, holding it close and hitting it gently with the flat of the ax. He hung the pack up on the nail. All his supplies were in the pack. They were off the ground and sheltered now.

Nick was hungry. He did not believe he had ever been hungrier. He opened and emptied a can of pork and beans and a can of spaghetti into the frying pan.

"I've got a right to eat this kind of stuff, if I'm willing to carry it," Nick said. His voice sounded strange in the darkening woods. He did not speak again.

He started a fire with some chunks of pine he got with the ax from a stump. Over the fire he stuck a wire grill, pushing the four legs down into the ground with his boot. Nick put the frying pan on the grill over the flames. He was hungrier. The beans and spaghetti warmed. Nick stirred them and mixed them together. They began to bubble, making little bubbles that rose with difficulty to the surface. There was a good smell. Nick got out a bottle of tomato catchup and cut four slices of bread. The little bubbles were coming faster now. Nick sat down beside the fire and lifted the frying pan off. He poured about half the contents out into the tin plate. It spread slowly on the plate. Nick knew it was too hot. He poured on some tomato catchup. He knew the beans and spaghetti were still too hot. He looked at the fire, then at the tent, he was not going to spoil it all by burning his tongue. For years he had never enjoyed fried bananas because he had never been able to wait for them to cool. His tongue was very sensitive. He was very hungry. Across the river in the swamp, in the almost dark, he saw a mist rising. He looked at the tent once more. All right. He took a full spoonful from the plate.

"Chrise," Nick said, "Geezus Chrise," he said happily.

He ate the whole plateful before he remem-

bered the bread. Nick finished the second plateful with the bread, mopping the plate shiny. He had not eaten since a cup of coffee and a ham sandwich in the station restaurant at St. Ignace. It had been a very fine experience. He had been that hungry before, but had not been able to satisfy it. He could have made camp hours before if he had wanted to. There were plenty of good places to camp on the river. But this was good.

Nick tucked two big chips of pine under the grill. The fire flared up. He had forgotten to get water for the coffee. Out of the pack he got a folding canvas bucket and walked down the hill, across the edge of the meadow, to the stream. The other bank was in the white mist. The grass was wet and cold as he knelt on the bank and dipped the canvas bucket into the stream. It bellied and pulled hard in the current. The water was ice cold. Nick rinsed the bucket and carried it full up to the camp. Up away from the stream it was not so cold.

Nick drove another big nail and hung up the bucket full of water. He dipped the coffee pot half full, put some more chips under the grill onto the fire and put the pot on. He could not remember which way he made coffee. He could remember an argument about it with Hopkins, but not which side he had taken. He decided to bring it to a boil. He remembered now that was Hopkins's way. He had once argued about everything with Hopkins. While he waited for the coffee to boil, he opened a small can of apricots. He liked to open cans. He emptied the can of apricots out into a tin cup. While he watched the coffee on the fire, he drank the juice syrup of the apricots, carefully at first to keep from spilling, then meditatively, sucking the apricots down. They were better than fresh apricots.

The coffee boiled as he watched. The lid came up and coffee and grounds ran down the side of the pot. Nick took it off the grill. It was a triumph for Hopkins. He put sugar in the empty apricot cup and poured some of the coffee out to cool. It was too hot to pour and he used his hat to hold the handle of the coffee pot. He would not let it steep in the pot at all. Not the first cup. It should be straight Hopkins all the way. Hop deserved that. He was a very serious coffee maker. He was the most serious man Nick had ever known. Not heavy, serious. That was a long time ago. Hopkins spoke without moving his lips. He had played polo. He made millions of dollars in Texas. He had borrowed carfare to go to Chicago, when the wire came that his first big well had come in. He could have wired for money. That would have been too slow. They called Hop's girl the Blonde Venus. Hop did not mind because she was not his real girl. Hopkins said very confidently that none of them would make fun of his real girl. He was right. Hopkins went away when the telegram came. That was on the Black River. It took eight days for the telegram to reach him. Hopkins gave away his .22 caliber Colt automatic pistol to Nick. He gave his camera to Bill. It was to remember him always by. They were all going fishing again next summer. The Hop Head was rich. He would get a yacht and they would all cruise along the north shore of Lake Superior. He was excited but serious. They said good-bye and all felt bad. It broke up the trip. They never saw Hopkins again. That was a long time ago on the Black River.

Nick drank the coffee, the coffee, according to Hopkins. The coffee was bitter. Nick laughed. It made a good ending to the story. His mind was starting to work. He knew he could choke it because he was tired enough. He spilled the coffee out of the pot and shook the grounds loose into the fire. He lit a cigarette and went inside the tent. He took off his shoes and trousers, sitting on the blankets, rolled the shoes up inside the trousers for a pillow and got in between the blankets.

Out through the front of the tent he watched the glow of the fire, when the night wind blew on it. It was a quiet night. The swamp was perfectly quiet. Nick stretched under the blanket comfortably. A mosquito hummed close to his ear. Nick sat up and lit a match. The mosquito was on the canvas, over his head. Nick moved the match quickly up to it. The mosquito made a satisfactory hiss in the flame. The match went out. Nick lay down again under the blankets. He turned on his side and shut his eyes. He was sleepy. He felt sleep coming. He curled up under the blanket and went to sleep.

### PART II

IN THE morning the sun was up and the tent was starting to get hot. Nick crawled out under the mosquito netting stretched across the mouth of the tent, to look at the morning. The grass was wet on his hands as he came out. He held his trousers and his shoes in his hands. The sun was just up over the hill. There was the meadow, the river and the swamp. There were birch trees in the green of the swamp on the other side of the river.

The river was clear and smoothly fast in the early morning. Down about two hundred yards were three logs all the way across the stream. They made the water smooth and deep above them. As Nick watched, a mink crossed the river on the logs and went into the swamp. Nick was excited. He was excited by the early morning and the river. He was really too hurried to eat breakfast, but he knew he must. He built a little fire and put on the coffee pot. While the water was heating in the pot he took an empty bottle and went down over the edge of the high ground to the meadow. The meadow was wet with dew and Nick wanted to catch grasshoppers for bait before the sun dried the grass. He found plenty of good grasshoppers. They were at the base of the grass stems. Sometimes they clung to a grass stem. They were cold and wet with the dew, and could not jump until the sun warmed them. Nick picked them up, taking only the medium sized brown ones, and put them into the bottle. He turned over a log and just under the shelter of the edge were several hundred hoppers. It was a grasshopper lodging house. Nick put about fifty of the medium browns into the bottle. While he was picking up the hoppers the others warmed in the sun and commenced to hop away. They flew when they hopped. At first they made one flight and stayed stiff when they landed, as though they were dead.

Nick knew that by the time he was through with breakfast they would be as lively as ever. Without dew in the grass it would take him all day to catch a bottle full of good grasshoppers and he would have to crush many of them, slamming at them with his hat. He washed his hands at the stream. He was excited to be near it. Then he walked up to the tent. The hoppers were already jumping stiffly in the grass. In the bottle, warmed by the sun, they were jumping in a mass. Nick put in a pine stick as a cork. It plugged the mouth of the bottle enough, so the hoppers could not get out and left plenty of air passage.

He had rolled the log back and knew he could get grasshoppers there every morning.

Nick laid the bottle full of jumping grasshoppers against a pine trunk. Rapidly he mixed some buckwheat flour with water and stirred it smooth, one cup of flour, one cup of water. He put a handful of coffee in the pot and dipped a lump of grease out of a can and slid it sputtering across the hot skillet. On the smoking skillet he poured smoothly the buckwheat batter. It spread like lava, the grease spitting sharply. Around the edges the buckwheat cake began to firm, then brown, then crisp. The surface was bubbling slowly to porousness. Nick pushed under the browned under surface with a fresh pine chip. He shook the skillet sideways and the cake was loose on the surface. I won't try and flop it, he thought. He slid the chip of clean wood all the way under the cake, and flopped it over onto its face. It sputtered in the pan.

When it was cooked Nick regreased the skillet. He used all the batter. It made another big flapjack and one smaller one.

Nick ate a big flapjack and a smaller one, covered with apple butter. He put apple butter on the third cake, folded it over twice, wrapped it in oiled paper and put it in his shirt pocket. He put the apple butter jar back in the pack and cut bread for two sandwiches.

In the pack he found a big onion. He sliced it in two and peeled the silky outer skin. Then he cut one half into slices and made onion sandwiches. He wrapped them in oiled paper and buttoned them in the other pocket of his khaki shirt. He turned the skillet upside down on the grill, drank the coffee, sweetened and yellow brown with the condensed milk in it, and tidied up the camp. It was a nice little camp.

Nick took his fly rod out of the leather rod-case, jointed it, and shoved the rod-case back into the tent. He put on the reel and threaded the line through the guides. He had to hold it from hand to hand, as he threaded it, or it would slip back through its own weight. It was a heavy, double tapered fly line. Nick had paid eight dollars for it a long time ago. It was made heavy to lift back in the air and come forward flat and heavy and straight to make it possible to cast a fly which has no weight. Nick opened the aluminum leader box. The leaders were coiled between the damp flannel pads. Nick had wet the pads at the water cooler on the train up to St. Ignace. In the damp pads the gut leaders had softened and Nick unrolled one and tied it by a loop at the end to the heavy fly line. He fastened a hook on the end of the leader. It was a small hook; very thin and springy.

Nick took it from his hook book, sitting with the rod across his lap. He tested the knot and the spring of the rod by pulling the line taut. It was a good feeling. He was careful not to let the hook bite into his finger.

He started down to the stream, holding his rod, the bottle of grasshoppers hung from his neck by a thong tied in half hitches around the neck of the bottle. His landing net hung by a hook from his belt. Over his shoulder was a long flour sack tied at each corner into an ear. The cord went over his shoulder. The sack flapped against his legs.

Nick felt awkward and professionally happy with all his equipment hanging from him. The grasshopper bottle swung against his chest. In his shirt the breast pockets bulged against him with the lunch and his fly book.

He stepped into the stream. It was a shock. His trousers clung tight to his legs. His shoes felt the gravel. The water was a rising cold shock.

Rushing, the current sucked against his legs. Where he stepped in, the water was over his knees. He waded with the current. The gravel slid under his shoes. He looked down at the swirl of water below each leg and tipped up the bottle to get a grasshopper.

The first grasshopper gave a jump in the neck of the bottle and went out into the water. He was sucked under in the whirl by Nick's right leg and came to the surface a little way down stream. He floated rapidly, kicking. In a quick circle, breaking the smooth surface of the water, he disappeared. A trout had taken him.

Another hopper poked his head out of the bottle. His antennæ wavered. He was getting his front legs out of the bottle to jump. Nick took him by the head and held him while he threaded the slim hook under his chin, down through his thorax and into the last segments of his abdomen. The grasshopper took hold of the hook with his front feet, spitting tobacco juice on it. Nick dropped him into the water.

Holding the rod in his right hand he let out line against the pull of the grasshopper in the current. He stripped off line from the reel with his left hand and let it run free. He could see the hopper in the little waves of the current. It went out of sight.

There was a tug on the line. Nick pulled against the taut line. It was his first strike. Holding the now living rod across the current, he brought in the line with his left hand. The rod bent in jerks, the trout pumping against the current. Nick knew it was a small one. He lifted the rod straight up in the air. It bowed with the pull.

He saw the trout in the water jerking with his head and body against the shifting tangent of the line in the stream.

Nick took the line in his left hand and pulled the trout, thumping tiredly against the current, to the surface. His back was mottled the clear, water-over-gravel color, his side flashing in the sun. The rod under his right arm, Nick stooped, dipping his right hand into the current. He held the trout, never still, with his moist right hand, while he unhooked the barb from his mouth, then dropped him back into the stream.

He hung unsteadily in the current, then settled to the bottom beside a stone. Nick reached down his hand to touch him, his arm to the elbow under water. The trout was steady in the moving stream, resting on the gravel, beside a stone. As Nick's fingers touched him, touched his smooth, cool, underwater feeling he was gone, gone in a shadow across the bottom of the stream.

He's all right, Nick thought. He was only tired.

He had wet his hand before he touched the trout, so he would not disturb the delicate mucus that covered him. If a trout was touched with a dry hand, a white fungus attacked the unprotected spot. Years before when he had fished crowded streams, with fly fishermen ahead of him and behind him, Nick had again and again come on dead trout, furry with white fungus, drifted against a rock, or floating belly up in some pool. Nick did not like to fish with other men on the river. Unless they were of your party, they spoiled it.

He wallowed down the stream, above his knees in the current, through the fifty yards of shallow water above the pile of logs that crossed the stream. He did not rebait his hook and held it in his hand as he waded. He was certain he could catch small trout in the shallows, but he did not want them. There would be no big trout in the shallows this time of day.

Now the water deepened up his thighs sharply and coldly. Ahead was the smooth dammed-back flood of water above the logs. The water was smooth and dark; on the left, the lower edge of the meadow; on the right the swamp.

Nick leaned back against the current and took a hopper from the bottle. He threaded the hopper on the hook and spat on him for good luck. Then he pulled several yards of line from the reel and tossed the hopper out ahead onto the fast, dark water. It floated down towards the logs, then the weight of the line pulled the bait under the surface. Nick held the rod in his right hand, letting the line run out through his fingers.

There was a long tug. Nick struck and the rod came alive and dangerous, bent double, the line tightening, coming out of water, tightening, all in a heavy, dangerous, steady pull. Nick felt the moment when the leader would break if the strain increased and let the line go.

The reel ratcheted into a mechanical shriek as the line went out in a rush. Too fast. Nick could not check it, the line rushing out, the reel note rising as the line ran out.

With the core of the reel showing, his heart feeling stopped with the excitement, leaning back against the current that mounted icily his thighs, Nick thumbed the reel hard with his left hand. It was awkward getting his thumb inside the fly reel frame.

As he put on pressure the line tightened into sudden hardness and beyond the logs a huge trout went high out of water. As he jumped, Nick lowered the tip of the rod. But he felt, as he dropped the tip to ease the strain, the moment when the strain was too great; the hardness too tight. Of course, the leader had broken. There was no

mistaking the feeling when all spring left the line and it became dry and hard. Then it went slack.

His mouth dry, his heart down, Nick reeled in. He had never seen so big a trout. There was a heaviness, a power not to be held, and then the bulk of him, as he jumped. He looked as broad as a salmon.

Nick's hand was shaky. He reeled in slowly. The thrill had been too much. He felt, vaguely, a little sick, as though it would be better to sit down.

The leader had broken where the hook was tied to it. Nick took it in his hand. He thought of the trout somewhere on the bottom, holding himself steady over the gravel, far down below the light, under the logs, with the hook in his jaw. Nick knew the trout's teeth would cut through the snell of the hook. The hook would imbed itself in his jaw. He'd bet the trout was angry. Anything that size would be angry. That was a trout. He had been solidly hooked. Solid as a rock. He felt like a rock, too, before he started off. By God, he was a big one. By God, he was the biggest one I ever heard of.

Nick climbed out onto the meadow and stood, water running down his trousers and out of his shoes, his shoes squelchy. He went over and sat on the logs. He did not want to rush his sensations any.

He wriggled his toes in the water, in his shoes, and got out a cigarette from his breast pocket. He lit it and tossed the match into the fast water below the logs. A tiny trout rose at the match, as it swung around in the fast current. Nick laughed. He would finish the cigarette.

He sat on the logs, smoking, drying in the sun, the sun warm on his back, the river shallow ahead entering the woods, curving into the woods, shallows, light glittering, big water-smooth rocks, cedars along the bank and white birches, the logs warm in the sun, smooth to sit on, without bark, gray to the touch; slowly the feeling of disappointment left him. It went away slowly, the feeling of disappointment that came sharply after the thrill that made his shoulders ache. It was all right now. His rod lying out on the logs, Nick tied a new hook on the leader, pulling the gut tight until it grimped into itself in a hard knot.

He baited up, then picked up the rod and walked to the far end of the logs to get into the water, where it was not too deep. Under and beyond the logs was a deep pool. Nick walked around the shallow shelf near the swamp shore until he came out on the shallow bed of the stream.

On the left, where the meadow ended and the woods began, a great elm tree was uprooted. Gone over in a storm, it lay back into the woods, its roots clotted with dirt, grass growing in them, rising a solid bank beside the stream. The river cut to the edge of the uprooted tree. From where Nick stood he could see deep channels, like ruts, cut in the shallow bed of the stream by the flow of the current. Pebbly where he stood and pebbly and full of boulders beyond; where it curved near the tree roots, the bed of the stream was marly and between the ruts of deep water green weed fronds swung in the current.

Nick swung the rod back over his shoulder and forward, and the line, curving forward, laid the grasshopper down on one of the deep channels in the weeds. A trout struck and Nick hooked him.

Holding the rod far out toward the uprooted tree and sloshing backward in the current, Nick worked the trout, plunging, the rod bending alive, out of the danger of the weeds into the open river. Holding the rod, pumping alive against the current, Nick brought the trout in. He rushed, but always came, the spring of the rod yielding to the rushes, sometimes jerking under water, but always bringing him in. Nick eased downstream with the rushes. The rod above his head he led the trout over the net, then lifted.

The trout hung heavy in the net, mottled trout back and silver sides in the meshes. Nick unhooked him; heavy sides, good to hold, big undershot jaw, and slipped him, heaving and big sliding, into the long sack that hung from his shoulders in the water.

Nick spread the mouth of the sack against the current and it filled, heavy with water. He held it up, the bottom in the stream, and the water poured out through the sides. Inside at the bottom was the big trout, alive in the water.

Nick moved downstream. The sack out ahead of him, sunk, heavy in the water, pulling from his shoulders.

It was getting hot, the sun hot on the back of his neck.

Nick had one good trout. He did not care about getting many trout. Now the stream was shallow and wide. There were trees along both banks. The trees of the left bank made short shadows on the current in the forenoon sun. Nick knew there were trout in each shadow. In the afternoon, after the sun had crossed toward the hills, the trout would be in the cool shadows on the other side of the stream.

The very biggest ones would lie up close to the bank. You could always pick them up there on the Black. When the sun was down they all moved out into the current. Just when the sun made the water blinding in the glare before it went down, you were liable to strike a big trout anywhere in the current. It was almost impossible

to fish then, the surface of the water was blinding as a mirror in the sun. Of course, you could fish upstream, but in a stream like the Black, or this, you had to wallow against the current and in a deep place, the water piled up on you. It was no fun to fish upstream with this much current.

Nick moved along through the shallow stretch watching the banks for deep holes. A beech tree grew close beside the river, so that the branches hung down into the water. The stream went back in under the leaves. There were always trout in a place like that.

Nick did not care about fishing that hole. He was sure he would get hooked in the branches.

It looked deep though. He dropped the grasshopper so the current took it under water, back in under the overhanging branch. The line pulled hard and Nick struck. The trout threshed heavily, half out of water in the leaves and branches. The line was caught. Nick pulled hard and the trout was off. He reeled in and holding the hook in his hand, walked down the stream.

Ahead, close to the left bank, was a big log. Nick saw it was hollow; pointing up river the current entered it smoothly, only a little ripple spread each side of the log. The water was deepening. The top of the hollow log was gray and dry. It was partly in the shadow.

Nick took the cork out of the grasshopper bottle and a hopper clung to it. He picked him off, hooked him and tossed him out. He held the rod far out so that the hopper on the water moved into the current flowing into the hollow log. Nick lowered the rod and the hopper floated in. There was a heavy strike. Nick swung the rod against the pull. It felt as though he were hooked into the log itself, except for the live feeling.

He tried to force the fish out into the current. It came, heavily.

The line went slack and Nick thought the trout was gone. Then he saw him, very near, in the current, shaking his head, trying to get the hook out. His mouth was clamped shut. He was fighting the hook in the clear flowing current.

Looping in the line with his left hand, Nick swung the rod to make the line taut and tried to lead the trout toward the net, but he was gone, out of sight, the line pumping. Nick fought him against the current, letting him thump in the water against the spring of the rod. He shifted the rod to his left hand, worked the trout upstream, holding his weight, fighting on the rod, and then let him down into the net. He lifted him clear of the water, a heavy half circle in the net, the net dripping, unhooked him and slid him into the sack.

He spread the mouth of the sack and looked

down in at the two big trout alive in the water.

Through the deepening water, Nick waded over to the hollow log. He took the sack off, over his head, the trout flopping as it came out of water, and hung it so the trout were deep in the water. Then he pulled himself up on the log and sat, the water from his trousers and boots running down into the stream. He laid his rod down, moved along to the shady end of the log and took the sandwiches out of his pocket. He dipped the sandwiches in the cold water. The current carried away the crumbs. He ate the sandwiches and dipped his hat full of water to drink, the water running out through his hat just ahead of his drinking.

It was cool in the shade, sitting on the log. He took a cigarette out and struck a match to light it. The match sunk into the gray wood, making a tiny furrow. Nick leaned over the side of the log, found a hard place and lit the match. He sat smoking and watching the river.

Ahead the river narrowed and went into a swamp. The river became smooth and deep and the swamp looked solid with cedar trees, their trunks close together, their branches solid. It would not be possible to walk through a swamp like that. The branches grew so low. You would have to keep almost level with the ground to move at all. You could not crash through the branches. That must be why the animals that lived in swamps were built the way they were, Nick thought.

He wished he had brought something to read. He felt like reading. He did not feel like going on into the swamp. He looked down the river. A big cedar slanted all the way across the stream. Beyond that the river went into the swamp.

Nick did not want to go in there now. He felt a reaction against deep wading with the water deepening up under his armpits, to hook big trout in places impossible to land them. In the swamp the banks were bare, the big cedars came together overhead, the sun did not come through, except in patches; in the fast deep water, in the half light, the fishing would be tragic. In the swamp fishing was a tragic adventure. Nick did not want it. He did not want to go down the stream any further today.

He took out his knife, opened it and stuck it in the log. Then he pulled up the sack, reached into it and brought out one of the trout. Holding him near the tail, hard to hold, alive, in his hand, he whacked him against the log. The trout quivered, rigid. Nick laid him on the log in the shade and broke the neck of the other fish the same way. He laid them side by side on the log. They were fine trout.

Nick cleaned them, slitting them from the vent to the tip of the jaw. All the insides and the gills and tongue came out in one piece. They were both males; long gray-white strips of milt, smooth and clean. All the insides clean and compact, coming out all together. Nick tossed the offal ashore for the minks to find.

He washed the trout in the stream. When he held them back up in the water they looked like live fish. Their color was not gone yet. He washed his hands and dried them on the log. Then he laid the trout on the sack spread out on the log, rolled them up in it, tied the bundle and put it in the landing net. His knife was still standing, blade stuck in the log. He cleaned it on the wood and put it in his pocket.

Nick stood up on the log, holding his rod, the landing net hanging heavy, then stepped into the water and splashed ashore. He climbed the bank and cut up into the woods, toward the high ground. He was going back to camp. He looked back. The river just showed through the trees. There were plenty of days coming when he could fish the swamp.

*1925*

---

F R O M

# THE GREEN HILLS OF AFRICA

---

❖

⟨ THESE selections, taken from the opening pages of one of Hemingway's two books of nonfictional prose published in his lifetime, are interesting in that they provide the background in personal experience of such important short stories as "The Snows of Kilimanjaro," but more especially because they reveal some of Hemingway's literary attitudes and prejudices. Since he was not much given to talk about writing, these opinions about American literature and the situation of the American writer are all the more interesting.

❖

WE WERE sitting in the blind that Wanderobo hunters had built of twigs and branches at the edge of the salt-lick when we heard the truck coming. At first it was far away and no one could tell what the noise was. Then it was stopped and we hoped it had been nothing or perhaps only the wind. Then it moved slowly nearer, unmistakable now, louder and louder until, agonizing in a clank of loud irregular explosions, it passed close behind us to go on up the road. The theatrical one of the two trackers stood up.

"It is finished," he said.

I put my hand to my mouth and motioned him down.

"It is finished," he said again and spread his arms wide. I had never liked him and I liked him less now.

"After," I whispered. M'Cola shook his head. I looked at his bald black skull and he turned his face a little so that I saw the thin Chinese hairs at the corners of his mouth.

"No good," he said. *"Hapana m'uzuri."*

"Wait a little," I told him. He bent his head down again so that it would not show above the dead branches and we sat there in the dust of the hole until it was too dark to see the front sight on my rifle; but nothing more came. The theatrical tracker was impatient and restless. A little before the last of the light was gone he whispered to M'Cola that it was now too dark to shoot.

"Shut up, you," M'Cola told him. "The Bwana can shoot after you cannot see."

The other tracker, the educated one, gave another demonstration of his education by scratching his name, Abdullah, on the black skin of his leg with a sharp twig. I watched without admiration and M'Cola looked at the word without a shadow of expression on his face. After a while the tracker scratched it out.

Finally I made a last sight against what was left of the light and saw it was no use, even with the large aperture.

M'Cola was watching.

"No good," I said.

"Yes," he agreed, in Swahili. "Go to camp?"

"Yes."

We stood up and made our way out of the blind and out through the trees, walking on the sandy loam, feeling our way between trees and under branches, back to the road. A mile along the road was the car. As we came alongside, Kamau, the driver, put the lights on.

The truck had spoiled it. That afternoon we had left the car up the road and approached the salt-lick very carefully. There had been a little rain, the day before, though not enough to flood the lick, which was simply an opening in the trees with a patch of earth worn into deep circles and grooved at the edges with hollows where the animals had licked the dirt for salt, and we had seen long, heart-shaped, fresh tracks of four greater kudu bulls that had been on the salt the night before, as well as many newly pressed tracks of lesser kudu. There was also a rhino who, from the tracks and the kicked-up mound of strawy dung, came there each night. The blind had been built at close arrow-shot of the lick and sitting, leaning back, knees high, heads low, in a hollow half full of ashes and dust, watching through the dried leaves and thin branches I had seen a lesser kudu bull come out of the brush to the edge of the opening where the salt was and stand there, heavy-necked, gray, and handsome, the horns spiralled against the sun while I sighted on his chest and then refused the shot, wanting not to frighten the greater kudu that should surely come at dusk. But before we ever heard the truck the bull had heard it and run off into the trees and everything else that had been moving, in the bush on the flats, or coming down from the small hills through the trees, coming toward the salt, had halted at that exploding, clanking sound. They would come, later, in the dark; but then it would be too late.

So now, going along the sandy track of the road in the car, the lights picking out the eyes of night birds that squatted close on the sand until the bulk of the car was on them and they rose in soft panic; passing the fires of the travellers that all moved to the westward by day along this road, abandoning the famine country that was ahead of us; me sitting, the butt of my rifle on my foot, the barrel in the crook of my left arm, a flask of whiskey between my knees, pouring the whiskey into a tin cup and passing it over my shoulder in the dark for M'Cola to pour water into it from the canteen, drinking this, the first one of the day, the finest one there is, and looking at the thick bush we passed in the dark, feeling the cool wind of the night and smelling the good smell of Africa, I was altogether happy.

Then ahead we saw a big fire and as we came up and passed, I made out a truck beside the road. I told Kamau to stop and go back and as we backed into the firelight there was a short, bandy-legged man with a Tyroler hat, leather shorts, and an open shirt standing before an un-hooded engine in a crowd of natives.

"Can we help?" I asked him.

"No," he said. "Unless you are a mechanic. It has taken a dislike to me. All engines dislike me."

"Do you think it could be the timer? It sounded as though it might be a timing knock when you went past us."

"I think it is much worse than that. It sounds to be something very bad."

"If you can get to our camp we have a mechanic."

"How far is it?"

"About twenty miles."

"In the morning I will try it. Now I am afraid to make it go farther with that noise of death inside. It is trying to die because it dislikes me. Well,

I dislike it too. But if I die it would not annoy it."

"Will you have a drink?" I held out the flask. "Hemingway is my name."

"Kandisky," he said and bowed. "Hemingway is a name I have heard. Where? Where have I heard it? Oh, yes. The *dichter*.[1] You know Hemingway the poet?"

"Where did you read him?"

"In the *Querschnitt*." [2]

"That is me," I said, very pleased. The *Querschnitt* was a German magazine I had written some rather obscene poems for, and published a long story in, years before I could sell anything in America.

"This is very strange," the man in the Tyroler hat said. "Tell me, what do you think of Ringelnatz?" [3]

"He is splendid."

"So. You like Ringelnatz. Good. What do you think of Heinrich Mann?' [4]

"He is no good."

"You believe it?"

"All I know is that I cannot read him."

"He is no good at all. I see we have things in common. What are you doing here?"

"Shooting."

"Not ivory, I hope."

"No. For kudu."

"Why should any man shoot a kudu? You, an intelligent man, a poet, to shoot kudu."

"I haven't shot any yet," I said. "But we've been hunting them hard now for ten days. We would have got one tonight if it hadn't been for your lorry."

"That poor lorry. But you should hunt for a year. At the end of that time you have shot everything and you are sorry for it. To hunt for one special animal is nonsense. Why do you do it?"

"I like to do it."

"Of course, if you *like* to do it. Tell me, what do you really think of Rilke?" [5]

"I have read only the one thing."

"Which?"

"The Cornet." [6]

"You liked it?"

"Yes."

"I have no patience with it. It is snobbery.

Valery,[7] yes. I see the point of Valery; although there is much snobbery too. Well at least you do not kill elephants."

"I'd kill a big enough one."

"How big?"

"A seventy pounder. Maybe smaller."

"I see there are things we do not agree on. But it is a pleasure to meet one of the great old *Querschnitt* group. Tell me what is Joyce like? I have not the money to buy it.[8] Sinclair Lewis [9] is nothing. I bought it. No. No. Tell me tomorrow. You do not mind if I am camped near? You are with friends? You have a white hunter?"

"With my wife. We would be delighted. Yes, a white hunter."

"Why is he not out with you?"

"He believes you should hunt kudu alone."

"It is better not to hunt them at all. What is he? English?"

"Yes."

"Bloody English?"

"No. Very nice. You will like him."

"You must go. I must not keep you. Perhaps I will see you tomorrow. It was very strange that we should meet."

"Yes," I said. "Have them look at the truck tomorrow. Anything we can do."

"Good night," he said. "Good trip."

"Good night," I said. . . .

. . . The people one would see if one saw whom one wished to see. You know all of those people? You must know them."

"Some of them," I said. "Some in Paris. Some in Berlin."

I did not wish to destroy anything this man had, and so I did not go into those brilliant people in detail.

"They're marvellous," I said, lying.

"I envy you to know them," he said. "And tell me who is the greatest writer in America?"

"My husband," said my wife.

"No. I do not mean for you to speak from family pride. I mean who really? Certainly not Upton Sinclair.[10] Certainly not Sinclair Lewis. Who is your Thomas Mann? [11] Who is your Valery?"

"We do not have great writers," I said. "Some-

THE GREEN HILLS OF AFRICA.   1. *dichter:* poet.   2. *Querschnitt:* a periodical published in Berlin by Propyläen-Verlag from 1921 to 1936. Typical of the literally scores of similar journals which flourished in Germany in the 1920's and thirties.   3. **Ringelnatz:** Joachim Ringelnatz was the pseudonym of Hans Bötticher (1883–1934), a German writer rather well known for his slightly scurrilous satiric verse.   4. **Heinrich Mann:** German writer (1871–1950), brother of Thomas.   5. **Rilke:** Rainer Maria Rilke (1875–1926), German poet.   6. **The Cornet:** *The Tale of the Love and Death of Cornet Christopher Rilke.*

7. **Valery:** Paul Valéry (1871–1945), influential French poet. 8. **it:** *Ulysses.*   9. **Sinclair Lewis:** Sinclair Lewis (1885–1951), first American novelist to win the Nobel prize in literature. The "it" may refer to any one of his many novels, but probably refers to *Babbitt*, his best-known novel in Europe.   10. **Upton Sinclair:** Upton Sinclair (1878–     ), American propagandistic novelist. Author of more than thirty-five novels, among them *The Jungle* (1906), *Oil* (1927), and the Lanny Budd series.   11. **Thomas Mann:** Thomas Mann (1875–1955), German novelist.

thing happens to our good writers at a certain age. I can explain but it is quite long and may bore you."

"Please explain," he said. "This is what I enjoy. This is the best part of life. The life of the mind. This is not killing kudu."

"You haven't heard it yet," I said.

"Ah, but I can see it coming. You must take more beer to loosen your tongue."

"It's loose," I told him. "It's always too bloody loose. But *you* don't drink anything."

"No, I never drink. It is not good for the mind. It is unnecessary. But tell me. Please tell me."

"Well," I said, "we have had, in America, skillful writers. Poe is a skillful writer. It is skillful, marvellously constructed, and it is dead. We have had writers of rhetoric who had the good fortune to find a little, in a chronicle of another man and from voyaging, of how things, actual things, can be, whales for instance, and this knowledge is wrapped in the rhetoric like plums in a pudding. Occasionally it is there, alone, unwrapped in pudding, and it is good. This is Melville. But the people who praise it, praise it for the rhetoric which is not important. They put a mystery in which is not there."

"Yes," he said. "I see. But it is the mind working, its ability to work, which makes the rhetoric. Rhetoric is the blue sparks from the dynamo."

"Sometimes. And sometimes it is only blue sparks and what is the dynamo driving?"

"So. Go on."

"I've forgotten."

"No. Go on. Do not pretend to be stupid."

"Did you ever get up before daylight——"

"Every morning," he said. "Go on."

"All right. There were others who wrote like exiled English colonials from an England of which they were never a part to a newer England that they were making. Very good men with the small, dried, and excellent wisdom of Unitarians; men of letters; Quakers with a sense of humor."

"Who were these?"

"Emerson, Hawthorne, Whittier, and Company. All our early classics who did not know that a new classic does not bear any resemblance to the classics that have preceded it. It can steal from anything that it is better than, anything that is not a classic, all classics do that. Some writers are only born to help another writer to write one sentence. But it cannot derive from or resemble a previous classic. Also all these men were gentlemen, or wished to be. They were all very respectable. They did not use the words that people always have used in speech, the words that survive in language. Nor would you gather that they had

bodies. They had minds, yes. Nice, dry, clean minds. This is all very dull, I would not state it except that you ask for it."

"Go on."

"There is one at that time that is supposed to be really good, Thoreau. I cannot tell you about it because I have not yet been able to read it. But that means nothing because I cannot read other naturalists unless they are being extremely accurate and not literary. Naturalists should all work alone and some one else should correlate their findings for them. Writers should work alone. They should see each other only after their work is done, and not too often then. Otherwise they become like writers in New York. All angleworms in a bottle, trying to derive knowledge and nourishment from their own contact and from the bottle. Sometimes the bottle is shaped art, sometimes economics, sometimes economic-religion. But once they are in the bottle they stay there. They are lonesome outside of the bottle. They do not want to be lonesome. They are afraid to be alone in their beliefs and no woman would love any of them enough so that they could kill their lonesomeness in that woman, or pool it with hers, or make something with her that makes the rest unimportant."

"But what about Thoreau?"

"You'll have to read him. Maybe I'll be able to later. I can do nearly everything later."

"Better have some more beer, Papa."

"All right."

"What about the good writers?"

"The good writers are Henry James, Stephen Crane, and Mark Twain. That's not the order they're good in. There is no order for good writers."

"Mark Twain is a humorist. The others I do not know."

"All modern American literature comes from one book by Mark Twain called *Huckleberry Finn*. If you read it you must stop where the Nigger Jim is stolen from the boys. That is the real end. The rest is just cheating. But it's the best book we've had. All American writing comes from that. There was nothing before. There has been nothing as good since."

"What about the others?"

"Crane wrote two fine stories. *The Open Boat* and *The Blue Hotel*. The last one is the best."

"And what happened to him?"

"He died. That's simple. He was dying from the start."

"But the other two?"

"They both lived to be old men but they did not get any wiser as they got older. I don't know what they really wanted. You see we make our writers into something very strange."

"I do not understand."

"We destroy them in many ways. First, economically. They make money. It is only by hazard a writer makes money although good books always make money eventually. Then our writers when they have made some money increase their standard of living and they are caught. They have to write to keep up their establishments, their wives, and so on, and they write slop. It is slop not on purpose but because it is hurried. Because they write when there is nothing to say or no water in the well. Because they are ambitious. Then, once they have betrayed themselves, they justify it and you get more slop. Or else they read the critics. If they believe the critics when they say they are great then they must believe them when they say they are rotten and they lose confidence. At present we have two good writers who cannot write because they have lost confidence through reading critics. If they wrote, sometimes it would be good and sometimes not so good and sometimes it would be quite bad, but the good would get out. But they have read the critics and they must write masterpieces. The masterpieces the critics said they wrote. They weren't masterpieces, of course. They were just quite good books. So now they cannot write at all. The critics have made them impotent."

"Who are these writers?"

"Their names would mean nothing to you and by now they may have written, become frightened, and be impotent again."

"But what is it that happens to American writers? Be definite."

"I was not here in the old days so I cannot tell you about them, but now there are various things. At a certain age the men writers change into Old Mother Hubbard. The women writers become Joan of Arc without the fighting. They become leaders. It doesn't matter who they lead. If they do not have followers they invent them. It is useless for those selected as followers to protest. They are accused of disloyalty. Oh, hell. There are too many things happen to them. That is one thing. The others try to save their souls with what they write. That is an easy way out. Others are ruined by the first money, the first praise, the first attack, the first time they find they cannot write, or the first time they cannot do anything else, or else they get frightened and join organizations that do their thinking for them. Or they do not know what they want. Henry James wanted to make money. He never did, of course."

"And you?"

"I am interested in other things. I have a good life but I must write because if I do not write a certain amount I do not enjoy the rest of my life."

"And what do you want?"

"To write as well as I can and learn as I go along. At the same time I have my life which I enjoy and which is a damned good life."

"Hunting kudu?"

"Yes. Hunting kudu and many other things."

"What other things?"

"Plenty of other things."

"And you know what you want?"

"Yes."

"You really like to do this, what you do now, this silliness of kudu?"

"Just as much as I like to be in the Prado."

"One is not better than the other?"

"One is as necessary as the other. There are other things, too."

"Naturally. There must be. But this sort of thing means something to you, really?"

"Truly."

"And you know what you want?"

"Absolutely, and I get it all the time."

"But it takes money."

"I could always make money and besides I have been very lucky."

"Then you are happy?"

"Except when I think of other people."

"Then you think of other people?"

"Oh, yes."

"But you do nothing for them?"

"No."

"Nothing?"

"Maybe a little."

"Do you think your writing is worth doing— as an end in itself?"

"Oh, yes."

"You are sure?"

"Very sure."

"That must be very pleasant."

"It is," I said. "It is the one altogether pleasant thing about it."

"This is getting awfully serious," my wife said.

"It's a damned serious subject."

"You see, he is really serious about something," Kandisky said. "I knew he must be serious on something besides kudu."

"The reason every one now tries to avoid it, to deny that it is important, to make it seem vain to try to do it, is because it is so difficult. Too many factors must combine to make it possible."

"What is this now?"

"The kind of writing that can be done. How far prose can be carried if any one is serious enough and has luck. There is a fourth and fifth dimension that can be gotten."

"You believe it?"

"I know it."

"And if a writer can get this?"

"Then nothing else matters. It is more important than anything he can do. The chances are, of course, that he will fail. But there is a chance that he succeeds."

"But that is poetry you are talking about."

"No. It is much more difficult than poetry. It is a prose that has never been written. But it can be written, without tricks and without cheating. With nothing that will go bad afterwards."

"And why has it not been written?"

"Because there are too many factors. First, there must be talent, much talent. Talent such as Kipling had. Then there must be discipline. The discipline of Flaubert.[12] Then there must be the conception of what it can be and an absolute conscience as unchanging as the standard meter in Paris, to prevent faking. Then the writer must be intelligent and disinterested and above all he must survive. Try to get all these in one person and have him come through all the influences that

done. But I would like us to have such a writer and to read what he would write. What do you say? Should we talk about something else?"

"It is interesting what you say. Naturally I do not agree with everything."

"Naturally."

"What about a gimlet?" Pop asked. "Don't you think a gimlet might help?"

"Tell me first what are the things, the actual, concrete things that harm a writer?"

I was tired of the conversation which was becoming an interview. So I would make it an interview and finish it. The necessity to put a thousand intangibles into a sentence, now, before lunch, was too bloody.

"Politics, women, drink, money, ambition. And the lack of politics, women, drink, money and ambition," I said profoundly.

"He's getting much too easy now," Pop said.

"But drink. I do not understand about that. That has always seemed silly to me. I understand it as a weakness."

"It is a way of ending a day. . . ."

*1935*

---

12. **Flaubert:** Gustave Flaubert (1821–80), French novelist and master stylist, the author of *Madame Bovary*.

IRVING HOWE
*Editor*

# William Faulkner

## 1897–1962

No TWENTIETH-CENTURY American novelist, with the possible exception of Hemingway, has been so greatly admired, discussed, and emulated as William Faulkner. During the thirties, when he was publishing one remarkable book after another, he suffered shameful neglect from the literary public; as late as 1945 all of his books were out of print; then, in the years since World War II, there occurred a major shift of critical opinion, and Faulkner has become one of the most celebrated American novelists. We have learned to see that his series of novels centered on Yoknapatawpha County—his imaginary locale in northern Mississippi—not only provides a brilliant portrait of life in the deep South but also dramatizes some of the most insistent problems of human consciousness in our time.

Faulkner's work can be difficult: it abounds in jumbled time sequences, involuted narrative structures, mangled syntax, and tortuous diction. It demands from the reader that he take psychic and intellectual risks. One must bring to his novels a capacity for concentration, a readiness to abandon set notions about life and literature, and above all, a willingness to expose oneself to a gamut of feelings. At a time when men in a mass society often believe that their possibilities for significant experience are shrinking, Faulkner insisted upon the largeness of human possibility. He returned to traditional dramatic gestures, he reasserted the claims of uncompromising tragedy, extreme melodrama, wild comedy. The force of human desire breaks through in his novels with a grandeur and terror that are almost unequaled in our time. Indeed, it is this readiness for confronting the largest ranges of experience which helps explain the hold Faulkner has won upon modern readers, both those who admire his work and even some who do not.

Faulkner was a prodigious talent, sweeping and erratic, inventive and wasteful, utterly caught up in the demands of his imaginative vision. He followed in the American tradition of the "natural genius"—the untutored or self-tutored writer whose impulse is to strive for relaxed and open forms rather than for tidiness of presentation, the writer who appropriates myths and legends from the collective memory of his homeland rather than inventing neatly compressed plots, the writer who offers encompassing statements and images of the human condition rather than resting content with self-sufficient dramatizations.

The world in which Faulkner grew up was laden with memories of the regional past—and to the South, it should be remembered, the region was actually a nation, a *lost* nation. At the center of these memories stood a figure who, with time, had acquired a legendary stature. William C. Falkner,[1] the novelist's great-grandfather, had come to Mississippi in 1839 as a poor fourteen-year-old boy. Energetic, willful, and hot-tempered, he had worked his way up to economic and political prominence, so much so that by the time of the Civil War he took command as colonel of the Second Mississippi Regiment. But as the novelist indicates in his fictional portrait of the great-grandfather—who appears as Colonel Bayard Sartoris in the novel *Sartoris*—Colonel Falkner was not quite a conventional Southerner. By temperament and conviction somewhat apart from the plantation aristocracy, he also showed recurrent signs of impatience with the grandiose self-delusion and moral falseness of "the Southern way of life." Colonel Falkner was one of those rising "new men," strong and independent figures who by the force of circumstance became defenders of a society they did not entirely accept. And it may not be too farfetched to suppose that this mixture of attitudes toward the South was partly inherited by the novelist William Faulkner, in whose work ambivalent feelings toward the homeland would become a major element.

The Second Mississippi Regiment saw a good deal of action in the Civil War, but when it replaced Falkner as its colonel, he simply packed up, went home, and formed a guerrilla band which harassed the Northern armies that were slicing into Mississippi. Once the war was over, Falkner refused to sink into lethargy or compensating daydreams; instead, he became an active figure in Mississippi politics, built a local railroad, and wrote a best-selling novel called *The White Rose of Memphis*. His life came to an end, characteristically, through a stroke of violence: he was murdered on the street by a business associate in 1889. Colonel Falkner's son, who also appears as a character in *Sartoris*, was a colorful man, and his grandson, the father of the novelist, a decent one; but they clearly represent a decline in personal forcefulness, a decline that parallels the fate of the homeland itself.

During his childhood William Faulkner, born in 1897, heard an endless number of stories about his great-grandfather and other heroes of the South, stories about gallantry, courage, and honor, told with all the greater emphasis as the past seemed less and less retrievable. As a boy, Faulkner did not need to study the history of the South— he lived in its shadow and suffered its decay. It was inevitable that the figure of the great-grandfather—a figure, one supposes, who became inseparable from the archetypal Southern hero—should come to seem splendid in his mind and that, like other Southern boys, he should saturate himself in legends of a past which if not more virtuous certainly seemed more vigorous than the present.

Most of Faulkner's childhood and youth were spent in Oxford, Mississippi, a university town which figures in his novels as Jefferson. His education was erratic. He did not formally complete high school, but in his late teens he read widely, especially in Romantic poetry which, as he would remember, "completely satisfied me and filled my inner life." He formed a lasting friendship with Phil Stone, a young Mississippian studying to be a lawyer (and later to serve as a model for Gavin Stevens, the spokesman-character who appears in several Faulkner novels). Caught up in a passion for literature, Stone helped introduce the young Faulkner to the world of culture and to a somewhat more critical, or at least ironic, view of the South than was common at the time.

Back in Mississippi, after having served for a time in the Canadian Air Force during World War I, Faulkner took some courses at the state university—it is amusing, perhaps encouraging, that he did poorly in English—but remained a student for only a year. He then became something of a town "character," affecting eccentricities and supporting himself by doing odd jobs. He held a brief appointment as university postmaster, but a disinclination to distribute the mail regularly cut short his career.

Like many young men home from the war and uncertain as to what to make of themselves, Faulkner was now badly adrift. It can even be said that he had entered a period of crisis which would serve as a necessary pre-

---

[1]The novelist himself would add the *u* to the family name.

lude to his career as a writer. He had no skill, no training, no visible prospects; he showed a marked distaste for regular employment, and he shared some of the vague discontents that were afflicting young men in the postwar years. The usual kinds of release which the more sensitive members of Faulkner's generation found for their restlessness—the Left Bank in Paris, the New York literary world, political radicalism—did not interest him. Mississippi itself was not an entirely satisfying place for a young man with literary tastes, even though it contained the only stretch of earth he knew well and loved entirely. At times, the land to which he returned was like an old battlefield, and its people seemed to be living in a dream world of the past, lost to a willed and romantic nostalgia. The evidence of his early novels —*Soldiers' Pay* (1926) and *Mosquitoes* (1927), both unsuccessful apprentice work—suggests that to Faulkner the two wars, the 1914 one in Europe and the old war of his homeland, had a way of melting into one desolation. And at least as disturbing was the fact that slowly the South *was* beginning to change. The traditional society was starting to break up; new and unattractive figures—later to be immortalized in Faulkner's Snopes clan— were coming to the forefront.

In 1924 Faulkner published a little book of verse called *The Marble Faun*, most of which showed little more than an indulgence in provincial romanticism. That Faulkner commanded a major gift for poetic evocation, his fiction makes clear; but it is not a gift that can be contained within the strict limits of verse. The book won neither attention nor sales, and perhaps in order to find a more sympathetic environment, perhaps simply out of boredom, Faulkner left Oxford in 1924 and settled for a time in New Orleans. There he fell in with a group of literary intellectuals who were publishing a little magazine, *The Double Dealer*, and more importantly, met Sherwood Anderson, the author of *Winesburg, Ohio*, who was then at the peak of his success. The two men became friends, meeting in the afternoons to talk, drink, and tell each other tall tales. Years later Faulkner would recall that when he saw how attractive Anderson's life as a writer

was, he decided to become one too. He then—so Faulkner's story continues—sat down to write a novel and six weeks later brought *Soldiers' Pay* to Anderson, who agreed to recommend it to his publisher on the condition that he would not have to read it first. Faulkner's is a story which satisfies the need of so many American writers to feel that their writing is something casually undertaken—years later, at the climax of a productive career, Faulkner would describe himself as "a farmer!"—and that they do not share the veneration for the "creative" which is to be found among some literary people. Such stories may be taken with grains of salt. Faulkner, from this time on, devoted himself with a ferocious energy to writing novels and stories; indeed, for our present purposes, his biography becomes almost indistinguishable from the record of his literary production.

Faulkner's first two novels were of minor consequence. *Soldiers' Pay*, the story of a mangled war veteran, is a book that quivers with intense emotions; it records Faulkner's feeling, so similar to that of many other writers in the 1920's, that the war generation was "lost"; but in the book itself he did not succeed in sufficiently dramatizing the problem. *Mosquitoes* was an effort to write a satiric comedy in the manner of Aldous Huxley, a genre[2] for which Faulkner had no particular gifts. Still, both novels offer plenty of evidence that their young author had a considerable flair for language—indeed, the writing tends to go soft and purple—but that he had not yet found his true subject.

Faulkner never felt entirely at ease in the cosmopolitan environment of New Orleans, and soon he returned to Oxford, where he was to make his permanent home. Outwardly his life was quiet. He had little to do with other novelists or literary intellectuals; he preserved a manner of taciturn solitariness; and until the 1950's, when he suddenly began to make public pronouncements on everything from segregation to the future of man, he kept himself steadily apart from cultural and intellectual disputes. Except for brief engagements as a Hollywood script-

---

[2]**genre:** a certain form or style.

writer, undertaken to support his family, Faulkner spent most of his mature life in the place he knew with an intimacy deeper than love or hate; and there he wrote the books that made him an international figure and for which in 1950 he won the Nobel prize. In 1962, honored by his countrymen and the literate world, he died in Oxford.

The early Faulkner, as he moved beyond his apprentice novels, was a writer in quest, both of some organizing principle in experience and a subject by which to release it in his writing. Once he discovered this subject, he stayed with it in almost all his books, for the truth is that the subject really discovered him, gripped and controlled him with the power of an intolerable but inescapable memory. As André Gide has remarked, a writer needs "a special world of which he alone has the key."

## II

FAULKNER'S "special world," his great subject, was the South: the Southern memory, the Southern reality, the Southern myth.

Perhaps because it had so little else to give its people, the post-Civil War South nurtured in them a generous and often obsessive sense of the past. The rest of the country might be committed to commercial expansion or addicted to the notion of progressive optimism, but the South was unable to accept these dominant American values. It had been left behind, broken in defeat; it was living on the margin of history, a position that often provides the keenest perspective on history itself. It was this advantage of distance, this perspective from the social rear, that was the major dispensation the South could offer its writers.

The Southern writer did not have to cast about for his materials; he hardly enjoyed a spontaneous choice in his use of them, for they welled within him like a recurrent dream. Faulkner has given a vivid if somewhat idealized description of this subject in *Intruder in the Dust:*

For every Southern boy fourteen years old, not once but whenever he wants it, there is the instance when it's still not two o'clock on that July afternoon in 1863, the brigades are in position behind the rail fence, the guns are laid and ready in the woods and the furled flags are already loosened to break out and Pickett himself with his long oiled ringlets and his hat in one hand probably and his sword in the other looking up the hill waiting for Longstreet to give the word and it's all in the balance, it hasn't happened yet, it hasn't even begun . . .

But of course it has happened, it must begin. The basic Southern subject is the defeat of the homeland, though its presentation in Faulkner's work can vary from the romancing in parts of *Sartoris* to the despairing portrait of social loss in *The Sound and the Fury.* Nor, for the moment, does it much matter whether one defines this subject as the humiliation of the homeland through superior force and its later degradation by carpetbaggers and scalawags, or as the defeat of a decadent slave-owning class followed by its partial recapture of power through corrupt and unscrupulous means. Regardless of which interpretation one accepts, the important point is that for a writer like Faulkner the subject was implacably *there.* Not long before the Civil War Nathaniel Hawthorne had remarked on "the difficulty of writing a romance about a country where there is no shadow, no antiquity, no picturesque and gloomy wrong, nor anything but a commonplace prosperity." But now the war and Reconstruction gave the Southern writers all that Hawthorne had found lacking—all but antiquity. And there were ruins to take its place.

It was not until World War I, however, that most serious Southern writing began to appear; that is, not until Southern regional consciousness had begun to break down. For it was the reality of twentieth-century life, in all its provocation, which drove so many Southern writers to a regional past that in happier circumstances they might have learned peaceably to forget.

Before the Southern writers could make imaginative statements about their own past, they had to be exposed to intellectual drafts from beyond their regional horizon. Southern literature at its best—the work of Faulkner, the early Caldwell, Allen Tate—was conceived in an explosive mixture of provincialism and cosmopolitanism, tradition and modernity. To measure the stature of their ancestor Poe, the Southern writers had first to understand what he meant to Baudelaire, and for that they had to gain a sophisticated awareness of the European literary past. For the Southern imagination to burst into high flame it had to be stimulated, or irritated, by the pressures of European and Northern ideas and literary modes. Left to itself, a regional consciousness is seldom likely to result in anything but a tiresome romanticizing of the past. Once, however, the South reached the point at which it still remained a distinct region but was already cracking under alien influences, it could begin to yield serious works of art.

It is therefore insufficient to say, as some critics do, that Faulkner was a Southern traditionalist or conservative moralist drawing his creative strength from his attachment to the past of the homeland. The truth is that he wrote in opposition to his received pieties as well as in acceptance, that he struggled against the conventional vision of the South even as he continued to acknowledge its power and charm. As he moved from book to book, turning a more critical and mature eye upon his material, the rejection of an inherited tradition took on a much greater intellectual and emotional force than its defense. At no point, either in his early romanticizing or his later moral realism, was Faulkner's attitude toward the Southern tradition a simple or fixed one. His relation to his own beliefs was characteristically "modern," full of instability, self-consciousness, and ambivalence. He worked with the decayed fragments of a myth, the soured pieties of regional memory—which is one reason his language is so often tortured, forced, and even incoherent—but the mind he brought to bear upon this subject was a mind deeply committed to the idea of life as *problematic*. He offered queries, not certainties, anxieties, not assurances. One reads him, to borrow a phrase from the novelist Franz Kafka, "in order to ask questions."

We have been using the word "myth," a tricky word which in popular terms often signifies little more than a lie and in literary discussion takes on an astonishing range of meanings. But as we use it here, the Southern myth refers to a story or cluster of stories that expresses the deepest attitudes and reflects the most fundamental experiences of a people. The homeland—so the story goes—had proudly insisted that it alone should determine its destiny; provoked into a war impossible to win, it had nevertheless fought to its last strength, and had fought this war with a reckless gallantry and superb heroism. Yet the homeland fell, and from this fall came misery and squalor: the ravaging by the conquerors, the loss of faith among the descendants of the defeated, and the rise of a new breed of faceless men who would batten on their neighbors' troubles. From such stories there follows that pride in ancestral glory and that mourning over the decline of the homeland which constitute the psychology of "the lost cause"—a sentiment often expressed in Faulkner's earlier novels.

The Southern myth, like any other, is less an attempt at historical description than a voicing of the collective imagination, perhaps of the collective will. The Old South over which it chants in threnody is an ideal image—a buried city, as Allen Tate has called it. And perhaps also a buried city that can never be found.

Such myths form the raw material of literature. The writer often comes to a myth eager to acquiesce, but after absorbing its assumptions into his work he may begin to wonder about its meaning, its value. In his novels and stories Faulkner set his pride in the past against his despair over the present, and from this counterpoint came much of the tension in his work. He investigated the myth itself insofar as it pretends to historical description; wondered about the relation between the Southern tradition he partly admired and that memory of Southern slavery to which he was compelled to return; tested not only the present by the past but also the past by the myth, and finally the myth by that morality which has slowly emerged from this entire process of exploration. This testing of the myth, though by no means the only important activity in Faulkner's work, is basic to the Yoknapatawpha novels and stories.

## III

YOKNAPATAWPHA COUNTY—Faulkner slyly remarked that he was its sole owner and proprietor—bears some rough similarities to Lafayette County, Mississippi. It is 2,400 square miles in area, bounded by the Talahatchie and Yoknapatawpha rivers, and comprises mainly farm lands and pine hills. After a private census, which by now may be somewhat dated, Faulkner announced that of 15,611 people living in Yoknapatawpha County, 6,298 are white and 9,313 Negro. The preciseness of these figures is whimsy, the proportion not. For they indicate how closely the imaginary world of Yoknapatawpha County is related to the patch of the deep South in which Faulkner spent his life. If we are able to feel that in some sense the implications of Faulkner's work are "universal," that is because he was so thoroughly a master at describing a particular time and place—he knew exactly how a farm girl sits in a wagon when she goes to town, or how the members of a decaying aristocratic family talk to one another, or how Negroes will set up social masks in order to get by in a hostile world. One of Faulkner's major subjects is human rootlessness, but it is a subject made possible by the rootedness of his own experience.

Like Mississippi itself, Yoknapatawpha is a land blighted by poverty, and while it does have social classes, they are either remnants of the Old South or embryos of the New South. Most of Yoknapatawpha is kept from splitting into distinct social classes by the flattening pressures of poverty and the scarcity of industrialization—indeed, it is important to bear in mind that the bulk of Faulkner's work, and the best part of it too, is set roughly between the 1890's and the late 1930's, that is, at a time when social change was beginning to break the crust of traditional Southern customs. This was a time when the ideology of regional separateness and its attendant Confederate rhetoric were

being threatened by new ideas and new commerce, but when there was still some reason for saying that the deep South possessed a style of life notably different from that of the rest of the country. It is Faulkner's particular strength as a writer to have been the most faithful—which is to say, most loving and critical—recorder of that style of life, while still managing to "transcend" mere local idiosyncracies. In his best work, as in all serious literature, universal implications are entirely imbedded in and inseparable from the depiction of particular human events.

Clan rather than class forms the basic social unit in the world of Yoknapatawpha. Pride in family and reverence for ancestors are central motives in behavior—which is to be expected in a society where the past clings to the present like a habitual lover neither relinquished nor enjoyed. Each of the major families in Faulkner's world comes to signify a distinct mode of conduct based upon a moral code, and the breakup of traditional Southern patterns of life is depicted through the breakup of the clans. Such families as the Compsons, Sartorises, and McCaslins not only provide the narrative matter of Faulkner's chronicle—they respond to the invasion of modernity in Yoknapatawpha with a range of styles that reveals a spectrum of moral valuations. Thus, the Sartorises come to stand for chivalric recklessness and self-destruction, the Compsons for a more extreme and tragic disintegration, and the McCaslins for a profound expiation of the evil of the past. The Snopes clan, on a lower social level, represents the amoralism of the "sourceless" flotsam (the adjective is Faulkner's) which takes over once a society starts falling apart.

Now there is always a danger of exaggerating the degree of coherence and conscious planning in the Yoknapatawpha books. The events of Faulkner's world are hardly meant to illustrate social tendencies, nor do they stem from a methodical scheme for the representation of Southern history. They may be reduced to such a scheme by the critic and perhaps they have to be, but in doing so he risks overestimating the extent to which they have been explicitly designed and underestimating the extent to which they have been imaginatively summoned. Despite the virtuosity that goes into much of Faulkner's work, his fundamental source was less the artificer's plan than the chronicler's vision, less a conscious worked-out scheme than a sudden "seeing" of the past of the homeland.

Though neither social photography nor historical record, the Yoknapatawpha chronicle is intimately related to the milieu from which it derives; it is an appropriation from a communal memory, some great store of half-forgotten legends of which Faulkner was the last grieving recorder. It is as if the whole thing, no longer available to public experience, lived fresh and imperious in his mind: a tragic charade of the past. And as Faulkner told these stories, there was always a desperate search for order, not merely as a strategy in narrative but also as a motive for composition. Incidents reappear from book to book, their meanings changed and tone modified; characters trivial in one book reach major dimension in another; narrative bits left fallow for years are suddenly worked over with great energy.

Faulkner's vision of life is hardly to be formulated in simple terms, nor is it at all the same as the resolution or sum of his attitudes toward the South. But for the moment let us agree to consider mainly the latter. Malcolm Cowley has described Faulkner's social view as that of an "antislavery Southern nationalist," while George Marion O'Donnell finds him a "traditional moralist" defending the "Southern socio-economic-ethical tradition." Perhaps if Faulkner's responses to the South were kneaded into a tight ideological ball it would resemble antislavery nationalism, but actually his work contains a wide range of attitudes toward the South, from sentimentality to denunciation, from identification to rejection. While in his earlier books he may be seen as a "traditional moralist" defending—though even then, only in part—the Old South, his work shows a gradual recognition that his values can now be realized only in new and untested social groups. The Southern myth

appears in its simplest version in Faulkner's collection of Civil War stories called *The Unvanquished,* a few of which are barely distinguishable from the romancing of popular fiction. The Southern myth appears in its most tortuous version in *Absalom, Absalom!,* a novel written out of sheer pain, in which Faulkner forced himself to see how the will to domination had corrupted the white community. Between these two extremes lies the bulk of his major fiction.

Faulkner did his best work during a span of twelve or thirteen years, from 1929 to 1942. And during those years there was a shorter period of truly astonishing creativity, between 1928 and 1932, when he wrote *The Sound and the Fury, As I Lay Dying, Sanctuary,* and *Light in August.* Fine things came from his pen during the 1940's and 1950's, usually bits and sections of novels, but nothing to compare with the outpouring of these inspired early years.

The novels written between 1929 and 1932 form a profound criticism of Southern society—but far more important, a profound criticism of modern life. Many of the dominant and recurrent themes of contemporary literature—the disintegration of moral values under the pressures of commercialism, the loss of the capacity for making close human connections, the costs and terrors of isolation in an impersonal world, the bewilderment of sensitive men and the powerlessness of good ones before the onslaughts of rapacity and vulgarity—all these are dramatized in Faulkner's earlier novels with a marvelous concreteness of detail and pictorial imagery. It is hard to think of another twentieth-century novelist who has given us so many living characters: the idiot Benjy Compson and his money-chasing brother Jason in *The Sound and the Fury;* the whole Bundren clan in *As I Lay Dying;* the criminal Popeye and the flapper Temple Drake in *Sanctuary;* the crucified mulatto Joe Christmas and the bovine madonna Lena Grove in *Light in August;* and many more, companions of our imagination who survive in memory long after one has put away the books in which they appear.

Surely the greatest of these novels is *The*

*Sound and the Fury*, a book recording the fall of a family and the death of a world. As it penetrates the life of the Compsons—the neurasthenic mother who evades reality with her claims to gentility; Benjy, the idiot son, whose chaotic burden of memory holds the family's past in a purity of suspension; Jason, the superbly comic son, who has made his peace with and embodies the amorality of commercialism—*The Sound and the Fury* exudes the smell of death, the death of the traditional South but of much more as well. The plot line is rigidly confined to a single family, moving from the consciousness of one member to another, and seeming almost claustrophobic in its concentration on a narrow sequence of events; yet its effect is to suggest a full awareness of human trouble, for we see that the moral death of the Compsons, and behind them of Yoknapatawpha, is an acting-out of the disorder of our time.

A contrast and companion-piece to *The Sound and the Fury* is *As I Lay Dying*, a tragicomic story, at once grotesque and tender, about the blundering efforts of the poorwhite Bundrens to bring the body of their dead mother back to Jefferson for burial. The book explores in subtle detail the inner workings and relationships of the family, and as such—but this is true of all Faulkner's books—it has values and implications that cannot be apprehended merely by placing it in the context of the Yoknapatawpha saga. To the extent, however, that it may be so limited, *As I Lay Dying* seems to be saying that even the Bundrens can come together for a brief act of humanity in a way the once proud and aristocratic Compsons no longer can.

*Light in August*, a novel which shows some signs of the social concerns of the 1930's, plunges directly into the life of modern Yoknapatawpha, as this life is shaped by hatred, alienation, martyrdom, isolation, and social division. Full of brilliant scenes and sharply evoked characters, *Light in August* renders not only Faulkner's immediate sense of the injustice so often at the heart of twentieth-century life, but also, and more "timelessly," his sense of the crushing weight of all human experience. The book is organized about

three major figures: Joe Christmas, who believes he has mixed blood, cannot bear the guilt or pain that being categorized as white or Negro would cause him, and after vainly seeking some mode of personal independence climaxes his life as a martyr to both the vindictiveness of society and his own buried striving toward human dignity; the Reverend Hightower, a sensitive man lost to delusional memories of the past and therefore unable to help, even as he sympathizes with, Joe Christmas; and Lena Grove, pregnant and serene, who breezes through the turmoil of the book as if she represented the very principle of life survival. Between the fate of Joe Christmas and the fate of Lena Grove—he all anxious striving, she benign passivity—there is a discrepancy so radical that nothing can justify it; as Faulkner would say, this discrepancy reflects the very outrage of existence. The arrangement of the book thus comes to resemble an early Renaissance painting: in the foreground a bleeding martyr, far to the rear a scene of bucolic peacefulness, with women working quietly in the fields. *Light in August* is a book which touches on a theme profoundly significant for the American imagination: the theme of human lostness and loneliness.

In the three major works that follow—*Absalom, Absalom!*, *The Hamlet*, and *Go Down, Moses*—Faulkner turned again to the Southern past, as if to re-examine the historical sources of the human debacle he portrayed in his novels of the present. *Absalom, Absalom!*, written in a highly rhetorical style that sometimes approaches grandeur and sometimes hysteria, focuses on Thomas Sutpen, a plantation owner in the mid-nineteenth century whose amoral willfulness summarizes a whole side of Southern experience. In *The Hamlet*, a racy comic extravaganza which borrows from the American tradition of the tall tale, Faulkner concentrated on the Snopeses, that verminlike clan which spreads its corruption and nihilism over the entire surface of Yoknapatawpha. And in *Go Down, Moses* he returned to one of his major themes: the relations between Negro and white. The central figure of this book is also the moral hero of the Yoknapatawpha saga: Isaac

McCaslin emerges as a saintly man who decides that his heritage has been fouled by the sins of the past—slavery, above all—and who therefore refuses that heritage in order to live as a poor and simple carpenter. The centerpiece of *Go Down, Moses*—and, in some ways, the centerpiece of Faulkner's entire work—is a novelette called "The Bear," both a beautiful account of a hunt and a symbolic fable concerning the moral growth of Isaac McCaslin.

Like many of Faulkner's stories, "The Bear" turns to the past. It turns to a vision of American life not yet soiled by greed or commerce, nor tainted by the anxieties of social existence and the sordidness of urban life. When the men of Yoknapatawpha, taking with them young Isaac McCaslin, go off on their annual visit to the forest, "not to hunt bear and deer but to keep the yearly rendezvous with the bear which they did not even intend to kill," their expedition soon takes on the tone of a religious retreat: away from money, away from the town, away from women, away from social distinctions. This yearly hunting trip becomes, as Faulkner said, "a pageant-rite"—and not only for the adult figures who lead it but still more so for sixteen-year-old Isaac and for Sam Fathers, the "taintless and incorruptible" old man of mixed Negro and Indian blood who is the boy's mentor in the hunt and the acknowledged priest of the ceremony that can be held only in the forest.

This "pageant-rite" stirs a rich association of memories for anyone acquainted with American literature. For the idea of a pastoral retreat to the Eden of the wilderness where men can again find the rhythmic harmonies of the natural world, in contrast to the frenzy and corruption of social life, is a recurrent and profoundly-embraced theme in American fiction. It can be found in the Leatherstocking tales of Cooper, the picaresque narratives of Mark Twain, the novels of Melville—where the sea replaces the forest—and some of Hemingway's stories. All of these American writers posit a radical disjunction between man and nature. The wilderness is primal, the source and scene of mobility, of freedom, of innocence; society,

soon after it appears in the New World, begins to suffocate these values.

The myth of a natural return is a myth of space, possible only to a people for whom the land once seemed to stretch out endlessly, as an invitation for men to accept with love and a temptation for men to violate with greed. It is a myth of space, recalling a time when men could measure their independence by their distance from each other, and when, as Faulkner wrote, "personal liberty and freedom were almost physical conditions like fire and flood." In magnified volume but steady pitch, it records the secret voice of a society yearning for its innocent past and regretting its very existence.

Meanwhile, however, it knows there is no choice—indeed, the power and poignancy of the myth reside largely in the sense that the past cannot be recaptured. Each year, as the forest line recedes, the men of Yoknapatawpha go back for two weeks, to find rest and pleasure, forgiveness and cleansing, but above all, those energies of renewal that only the natural world can yield them and with which they may find it possible to survive until their next return.

In "The Bear" the hunt becomes a ceremony of initiation and maturing, a test of proper conduct through which Isaac McCaslin ceases to be a boy; yet truly to become a man he must retain something of that awe before truth characteristic of boyhood. When he meets the great bear Ben, it is only after having stripped himself of such material objects—and social possessions—as his watch and compass. Seeing the bear, the boy experiences an ecstasy of communion which results in his refusal to kill the animal. For to destroy the bear would mean to violate the mute bond with nature that the "pageant-rite" is intended to establish, and thereby to disrupt the fraternity of the men in the hunting camp; yet as they all know, such a violation is sooner or later inevitable, a part of the historic transformation of their lives. At the end it will be given to Isaac—even as the Biblical Isaac, the son blessed by the father—to lead in the killing of the bear, the destruction of the totem. He alone will keep true the memory of the totem and the tribe, not so much the rites themselves or the men who performed them but the meaning of the rites and the value of the men. And he will do this by the mode of life he will adopt in the town, where his refusal to accept his heritage and his decision to live in simple poverty will perhaps break the chain of guilt binding him to the communal past.

Faulkner's later books, both those set in Yoknapatawpha—like *Intruder in the Dust, Requiem for a Nun, The Town,* and *The Mansion*—and those set elsewhere—like *The Fable*, a grandiose story about a Second Coming during World War I—represent a decline in creative energy and achievement. These books were all written during the 1940's and 1950's, years that brought Faulkner many honors but also a slowly mounting crisis in his work. Despite some excellent parts, these novels are forced, anxious, and often shrill, the work of a man, no longer driven, who was obliged now to drive himself. *Intruder in the Dust* is marred by stretches of dead Southern oratory, *The Fable* by intellectual pretentiousness and a mechanically whipped-up style, *The Town* and *The Mansion* by efforts to deal with subject matter for which Faulkner was not entirely equipped.

What went wrong in these last years? It is too early to say and at most we can only speculate, but a few symptoms of the trouble can be noted. In all these works there is a reliance on a high-powered rhetoric which bears the outer marks of Faulkner's earlier style, but is really a kind of willful self-imitation. The very abandon with which Faulkner later used language seems itself calculated, a device in the repertoire of a writer who sensed the dangers of relaxation even as he approached the dangers of exhaustion.

There is also in these later novels a tendency to fall back upon high jinks of plot, a flaunting arbitrariness of invention—as if Faulkner, having examined and brooded upon human life for so long and with such pain, felt finally that *anything* is possible to man and that our desire for realism in fiction is little more than a reluctance to confront the strangeness of reality; or as if Faulkner,

wearied of telling stories and creating characters, were at last ready to betray his impatience with his own skill. In the ripeness of his honor, he was in many ways as baffled and perplexed as when he first published his melancholy poems. But perhaps that is in the nature of the human journey.

Still, Faulkner remains one of the most brilliant writers America has ever produced.

### IV

THROUGHOUT Faulkner's novels one can detect a steady though uneven and painful growth of moral vision, and perhaps the most dramatic evidence of this growth lies in his changing attitudes toward the Negroes. For all Southern writers the Negroes form a particularly difficult challenge in moral terms, for here they must try to grapple with and overcome inherited pieties, and in literary terms, for here they must try to break past the stereotypes of conventional perception.

Faulkner's early treatment of Negro characters is indulgent, mild, and occasionally condescending. When one of them, like Caspey in *Sartoris*, is shown as rebellious, it is not with any acute sense of either the power of feeling behind that rebelliousness or the power of resistance among the whites. What is damaging in these early portraits is not so much Faulkner's laziness of treatment as the assumption, which he then shared with so many Southerners, that Negroes are *easily knowable:* an assumption that is, of course, at the heart of benevolent paternalism. But even in the early books, overtones of doubt creep in. And in *The Sound and the Fury* the Negro cook, though conceived within the boundaries of benevolent paternalism, is a figure remarkable for her poise, her dignity, and her hard realism. Dilsey is the last of Faulkner's Negroes who can still believe that the South is a "natural" community to which they totally belong. After Dilsey, there is only estrangement and oblique rebellion; and after her, Faulkner broke away from the received notions of the South.

The Faulkner to whom Negro characters had seemed so accessible at the end began to stress that for the whites the Negro often exists not as a distinct person but as a specter or phantasm. In *Light in August* he wrote brilliantly of what might be called the fetishism of false perception, the kind of false perception that has become systematic and acquired a pseudo-religious sanction. Joanna Burden, daughter of abolitionists but raised in the South, confesses:

I had seen and known Negroes since I could remember. I just looked at them as I did at rain, or furniture, or food or sleep. But after that I seemed to see them for the first time not as people, but as a thing, a shadow in which I lived, we lived, all white people, all other people . . . And I seemed to see the black shadow in the shape of a cross.

What is so remarkable about this passage is that here the false perception comes from a mixture of fright and humaneness, the two no longer separable, but bound together in an apocalyptic image of martyrdom and violation.

In Faulkner's treatment of Negroes there is, then, a quick and steep ascent: from benevolence to recognition of injustice, from amusement over idiosyncrasies to a principled concern with human status, from cozy familiarity to a discovery of the profound estrangement of the races. And as Faulkner discovered the difficulties of approaching Negroes, he also developed an admirable sense of reserve, a blend of shyness and respect.

Faulkner began to see the Negro as victim and to write a good deal about mulattoes. Trapped between the demarcated races, the mulatto is an unavoidable candidate for the role of victim. Velery Bon in *Absalom, Absalom!* is a man adrift. The Negroes "thought he was a white man and believed it only the more strongly when he denied it," while the whites "when he said he was a Negro, believed that he lied in order to save his skin." Joe Christmas in *Light in August* is cursed by "that stain on his white blood or his black blood, whichever you will." Surely the most affecting of Faulkner's Negro characters, Christmas becomes a summation of the predicament of Yoknapatawpha, his existence torn by the conflict of color as violently and

wastefully as the land itself. He is one of the most extreme instances in all modern literature of man as victim, man estranged from awareness and friendship — a figure in whom neither good nor evil counts nearly so much as the sheer fact of his suffering. He is entirely vulnerable, and if he were able to articulate a creed, he might say that the condition of his humanity is that he remain vulnerable.

Not only are the mulattoes important in Faulkner's novels because they underscore the inhumanity and irrationality of the racial scheme; they also figure as living agents of the "threat" of miscegenation, a threat which seemed most to disturb Faulkner whenever he was most sympathetic to the Negro. All rationalizations for prejudice having crumbled, there remained only a fierce emotional resistance to an idea that was both immediately frightening and distantly attractive. For even as the thought of blood mixture triggers the fears of the white unconscious, it also suggests, as Faulkner hinted in the story "Delta Autumn" (a self-sufficient part of *Go Down, Moses*, 1942), a vision of a distant time when barriers of caste and color will be removed.

The last major Negro figure in Faulkner's world is Lucas Beauchamp, neither at home in the South, like Dilsey, nor homeless, like Joe Christmas. Lucas is well enough aware of white society and he knows exactly what it is. But as he strides into full sight in *Intruder in the Dust*, a man powerful and complete, he is entirely on his own: he has put society behind him. Too proud to acquiesce in submission, too self-contained to be either outcast or rebel, Lucas has transformed the stigma of alienation into a mark of assurance. Apparently meant by Faulkner as a tribute to the strength and endurance of the Negroes, Lucas is something better still: a member of an oppressed group who appears not as a catalogue of disabilities or even virtues, but as a human being in his own right.

Ultimately, Faulkner's greatest tribute to the Negroes was a novelist's tribute: a body of dramatic actions, a group of realized characters. No other American novelist watched them so carefully and patiently;

none other listened with such fidelity to the nuances of their speech; none other exposed his imagination so freely to discover their meaning for American life.

And in doing this Faulkner returned again and again to a sort of primal vision: a buried memory of boyhood friendship, unaffected by social grade and resting on that intuitive sense of scruple, that belief in *fairness* available to boys. It is a vision, a memory that runs through much of American literature, though seldom with such persistence and poignancy as in Faulkner, and it is a vision that is daily stultified in the South.

Forever and forever—the terribleness of estrangement recurs in Faulkner's work as a cry of bafflement and loss. It is as if his novels keep saying that ultimately the whole apparatus of separation must seem too wearisome in its call to alertness, too costly in its tax on the emotions, and simply tedious as a brake on spontaneous life.

What finally concerned him most, as it concerns every significant writer, was to release a vision of human life that is serious and mature: a vision that can include both moral criticism and pleasure in sensuous experience, a vision that accepts both the power of fate, all that binds and breaks us, and the possibility of freedom, all that permits us to shape our being.

When Faulkner stepped forth to "talk philosophy," he was somewhat less than impressive. In explicit statement he showed an alarming fondness for platitude, a fondness that lured him into portentous abstractions. But at his best Faulkner was a writer deeply concerned with the moral qualities of—as distinct from mere moral formulas about—human existence.

As might be expected from a writer bred in the South, Faulkner was much occupied with the notion of honor. Frequently invoked in his books, particularly the earlier ones, it is a notion that proves strangely elusive—more a cry than a substance—and increasingly cut off from moral issues. It allows some of Faulkner's characters a gamut of theatrical display, as also, at times, a release of more substantial values, such as their readiness to stake everything on a personal act defined not so much through its intrinsic value as through the fullness of passion that is brought to it. But the concept of honor remains hard to define, and the code of honor hard to embody and justify in actual conduct.

As Faulkner's work developed, there was a gradual shift in emphasis from honor to integrity, a shift that revealed his deepening humaneness and thoughtfulness. Honor points to what one is in the world, integrity to what one is in oneself. Honor involves a standard of pride and dignity, a level of status and reputation; integrity an ease of being and a security of conscience. Honor depends upon an assertion of one's worth, integrity upon a readiness to face the full burden of one's existence. Many of the whites in Faulkner's novels are eager to preserve their honor; the more impressive among the Negroes, though not they alone, exemplify the life of integrity. As Faulkner developed and deepened his sense of human life and human trouble, he placed a greater and greater stress upon the way a man turns inward, living out a dialogue with his own needs and conscience, confronting his own defeats and acknowledging his own value.

Some attempts have been made to see Faulkner as a Christian traditionalist. There can be no doubt that one of the more important sources of his moral outlook is an imperiled version of Christianity. The South in which Faulkner grew up was perhaps more concerned with Christian belief than most other sections of the country, but the quality of that concern was hardly such as to win the adherence of a sensitive young writer. For him the idea of Christianity could survive only when wrenched from its institutional and perhaps historical context: it survived, that is, as an extreme possibility of personal saintliness.

Like the Southern past, Christianity is felt mainly and most poignantly through its absence. Easter week forms a backdrop for the Compson tragedy in *The Sound and the Fury*. the crucifixion of Christ, for the murder of Joe Christmas in *Light in August*. Christianity appears as an occasional standard of judgment, a force to resist, a memory that troubles, a principle of contrast, but not as a secure inheritance. Faulkner struggled to define his moral outlook against the background of a dissolution of traditional beliefs, and usually the struggle matters more than the background.

His work, to be sure, is full of symbols, references, and echoes drawn from Christian drama, theology, and tradition. The recurrent figures of simple virtue—Dilsey, Byron Bunch, Isaac McCaslin—may be seen as embodiments of primitive Christian virtues, and Faulkner's commitment to these virtues as rooted in a sympathy for the uncontaminated Christianity which has sometimes flourished among rural Negroes in the South. At the other extreme in Faulkner's imagination there are figures and emblems of crucifixion which show how deeply the story of Jesus and the stern doctrines of Protestantism have left their mark. None of these, however, is enough to warrant our speaking of Faulkner as a traditional Christian writer, for they constitute fragments of belief and memory rather than an integrated outlook. In moral outlook Faulkner was a writer who moved between the far extremes of simplicity and sophistication, and he did this as a man thoroughly caught up in the "modern"—that is, an uncertain and problematic—view of life.

Given the fact that he shared at least part of the "modern" outlook, it becomes understandable why Faulkner, like other contemporary writers, should have placed so heavy a stress upon integrity, the virtue which flows from within and does not depend upon the presence of a set belief. As Faulkner saw it, integrity is accessible to people of every social grade and is to be found in a wide variety of situations—though in his novels he favored the use of extreme situations because he wished to submit all that is "intractable" and "indomitable" in human character to the most urgent pressures. Dramatically, this test occurs in the clash of antithetical forces of freedom and necessity in the Yoknapatawpha world. Cursed by the tragic need to compromise their freedom, men can still redeem themselves through a gesture which, if it does not mitigate their defeat, can at least declare their humanity in defeat.

A curse hangs over all those Faulkner characters who reach into the depths of experience or struggle to extend the range of their consciousness. It is the curse of whatever in life cannot be escaped, whatever is *conditioned:* Joe Christmas battling his whiteness and his blackness; the Reverend Hightower unable to mediate between dream and reality; Bayard Sartoris wondering whether his existence has any purpose; Thomas Sutpen compelled to die in a squalor of exploitation; Quentin Compson driven to suicide by the sheer pain of consciousness. Whatever is burden in life—be it the consequence of society or character, economics or sin, injustice or evil—constitutes the curse. A key work in most of Faulkner's books is *outrage,* a word which for him signified both the workings of this curse and the violence with which men act it out.

But there also remains available to each man the gesture, striking or subdued, by which he can declare himself. This gesture can be one of rebellion or submission; it can signify adherence to ritual or the need to accept defeat in total loneliness; it can be, as with Ab Snopes in the short story "Barn Burning," an arbitrary sign of selfhood or, as with Popeye's request that his hair be fixed just before he is to be executed, a final assertion of indifference. But always it is the mark of distinct being, the way a man defines himself.

The opposition between curse and gesture forms the dramatic and moral pattern of Faulkner's work, and within that opposition he declared the items of his bias: his respect before suffering, his contempt for deceit, his belief in the rightness of self-trust, his enlarging compassion for the defeated. At its greatest, the gesture showed that for Faulkner, heroism signified exposure, the taking and enduring and resisting of everything that comes to man between birth and death. And thereby it brings a kind of freedom.

### V

FAULKNER was a constant and restless experimenter in his use of the novel. He was quite capable of putting together a well-made piece of fiction in which every incident and (almost) every word is "functionally" justified, in which there is a neat pattern of events moving from a precise beginning to a precise end, and in which the language serves as a clear glass enabling the reader to get immediately to the matter of the story. But only seldom did he choose to abide with the familiar conventions of the novel. He preferred, instead, to break up and jumble his time sequences; to divide his narrative into fragments told by a variety of participants and observers; to weight his prose with lyric intensities, baroque displays, and philosophic speculations; to lure the reader from difficulty to difficulty, so that the very effort to read a Faulkner novel forces one into an act of esthetic and moral discovery, parallel to those discoveries his narrators make in the course of telling their stories. In *Absalom, Absalom!*, for example, the main action of the novel is not a line of events traced by the author and followed by the reader, but the struggle of the narrator, Quentin Compson, to piece together the facts concerning the life of Thomas Sutpen, a ruthless figure in the Southern past, and to make out what these facts really meant. The story is unfolded not in the orderly sequence of the traditional novel, which assumes that an omniscient author has everything under control, but rather in a temporarily bewildering series of intuitions, false starts, gasps, and corrections.

There are, to be sure, times when some of Faulkner's technical experiments seem wanton or trivial; but whenever he is at or near his best, they always have a serious purpose. That purpose is usually to draw the reader into a more direct and perilous relation to the happenings of the story, to saturate him in the atmospheres of an imagined world, to force him to abandon the posture of a passive listener and become an active participant struggling, like some of Faulkner's characters themselves, to discover meaning in the represented events. Faulkner wanted the reader to share with his characters the full weight of human experience, so that, in a sense, the reader becomes "part of" the novel. All of Faulkner's devices—such as his use of stream of consciousness, multiple narrators, interior monologues and a convo-

luted style—are put to the service of making us active collaborators in the working out of the Yoknapatawpha saga.

From book to book Faulkner employed different methods. In *The Sound and the Fury* he penetrated the private consciousness of several members of the Compson family: with the idiot Benjy, through a flow of language resembling what psychoanalysts call "free association," and with the villainous Jason, through an interior monologue which bears outer signs of rational structure. The effect Faulkner created is like a spiraling back and forth over the same stretch of human history, but each time in terms of radically different moral perceptions and each time with a further dissolution of the boundary between past and present, so that the past becomes part of the present, a memory imprisoned in consciousness.

In most of his novels Faulkner continued to experiment. *As I Lay Dying*, his most astonishing piece of virtuosity, is composed somewhat like a cantata in which a theme is pursued through a succession of voices: fifteen characters speak through sixty narrative and reflective fragments. Nothing being explained, everything must be shown. The danger is that the frequent breaks in point of view will impede the flow of narrative—a danger Faulkner overcame with great skill. In *Light in August* Faulkner moved closer to the naturalistic novel, with its accumulation of social detail, its sense of human fatality, and its readiness to face the grimness of modern existence. *Absalom, Absalom!* employed some of the mildewed properties of the Gothic romance—Faulknerian versions of the haunted house, the demon lover, the passively suffering heroine—but endowed these with a seriousness that lifts the book far above the mechanical diabolism and shrillness one usually associates with the Gothic. Structurally, there was a relaxation in both *The Hamlet* and *Go Down, Moses*, both books being organized through a succession of loosely connected and rather sprawling tales. In *The Hamlet* Faulkner borrowed from the tradition of the American tall tale, with its slyness of understatement and extravagance of action. In *The*

*Wild Palms* Faulkner wove together alternating sections of two distinct narratives, so that the meaning of one becomes involved with the meaning of the other. And in *Requiem for a Nun* he shuttled between the acts of a play and elegiac prose rhapsodies about the Yoknapatawpha past.

Faulkner was especially gifted at a certain kind of narrative which we may call the tale, and which is somewhere between the short story and the novel in length and approach. "The Bear," "Spotted Horses," and parts of some of his novels can be read as long tales, which by their nature forgo the strict requirements of the short story and the somewhat less strict requirements of the novel. "That Evening Sun" shows that, when he cared to be, Faulkner was a master of the short story: it is a work all compact, economical, and terse. In the tale, by contrast, there is no inescapable need for either that economy of effect which is essential to the short story or those complications of social behavior which are often depicted in the novel. Sharing some of the qualities of fable and myth, the tale inclines toward simplicity of action, spaciousness and freedom of invention, and the elaboration of folk materials. It can spin or wander off on its own, in a flexible style that allows for a wide variety of effects, ranging (in parts of "The Bear") from bardic eloquence to (in "Spotted Horses") native humor.

As Faulkner's work developed, there occurred an interesting, though sometimes troublesome, shift in his strategy of narration. The earlier books employed one of two methods: either the objective, impersonal narration that is found in *Sanctuary* and *Light in August* or the subjective revelation of character through inner voices and reflections, as in *The Sound and the Fury* and *As I Lay Dying*. But beginning with *Light in August*, and becoming increasingly evident in many of the later novels, there was a new voice, not really that of any of the characters and finally not that of Faulkner himself. It was, so to say, an "over-voice" speaking for the memories and conscience of a people: a voice which carried some of the impassioned rhetoric of traditional Southern oratory, as

well as some of its unfortunate fondness for pasteboard flashiness and grandiloquent rhythms. In *Intruder in the Dust* this oratory is "official," groaning with echoes of addresses to Southern state legislatures and Fourth of July orations; but in *Absalom, Absalom!* it is private—private to Faulkner's vision of the South—in both source and quality. The voice we hear at last in the best of the late novels speaks for an afflicted imagination, a grieved mind familiar with the springs of evil; it evokes an image of a man rasping from the heart, perhaps to no one but himself: a man who cries out with the burden of human history. Its effect is somewhat like that which Morris Croll, in a fine study, "The Baroque Style," attributes to sixteenth-century rhetoricians: "Their purpose was to portray, not a thought, but a mind thinking, or in Pascal's words, *la peinture de la pensée*.[3] They knew that an idea separated from the act of experiencing it is not the idea that was experienced."

This description holds for most of Faulkner's writing, no matter what pitch he struck in his prose or what shape he gave it at a particular moment: it is true for his writing no matter which of his several styles he employed. His mimetic capacities—his gift for rendering the precise nuances of speech, for differentiating among a variety of accents and stresses—were granted even by his most hostile critics. But Faulkner was also capable of writing the sort of clean, simple, efficient prose which is so much favored in our time: the prose of unadorned evocation, of the pure picture. The following passage from *The Sound and the Fury*, for example, in which the Negro cook Dilsey is seen working in the kitchen while Mrs. Compson keeps whimpering after her, is a strong and exact rendering of person and place:

Dilsey prepared to make biscuit. As she ground the sifter steadily above the breadboard, she sang, to herself at first, something without particular tune or words, repetitive, mournful and plaintive, austere, as she ground a faint, steady snowing of flour onto the breadboard. The stove had begun to heat the room and to fill it with

[3]*la peinture de la pensée:* painter of the mind.

murmurous minors of the fire, and presently she was singing louder, as if her voice too had been thawed out by the growing warmth, and then Mrs. Compson called her name again from within the house. Dilsey raised her face as if her eyes could and did penetrate the walls and ceiling and saw the old woman in her quilted dressing gown at the head of the stairs, calling her name with machine-like regularity.

"Oh Lawd," Dilsey said . . .

Faulkner's novels and stories are full of realisitc evocations done in strong outline and primary colors. But if Faulkner could, upon need, write a severely disciplined prose—he was also quite capable of moving toward other styles. In parts of "The Bear" he achieved a style of quiet gravity; in *Absalom, Absalom!* a fierce grinding rhetoric which makes that book so difficult and memorable to read; and in *The Hamlet* a wildly exuberant prose, full of juice and bounce.

It would be pointless to deny, of course, that in some of Faulkner's books, especially the later ones, the language tends to cascade wildly, noun upon noun, adjective upon adjective, breathless phrase upon phrase. The syntax can become hopelessly entangled in its own convolutions: a thickly matted jungle of clauses and phrases defying, by clear intention, the schoolbook rules of grammar. Such prose is clearly vulnerable to criticism and even sneering; it involves greater risks than the taut style of a Hemingway, but at least on occasion it also brings greater rewards. In fiction there is no single "good" or "accepted" style. The clumsy, leaden prose of a Dreiser can be remarkably moving and powerful. The artful simplicities of Sherwood Anderson's style can help evoke moods of loneliness and sadness. The tough restraints of Hemingway's prose can give one the exact "feel" of an object. There are many possibilities in the use of language in fiction, and none can be prejudged, all depend upon the specific context in which they appear and the particular skill with which they are employed. When Faulkner seems to be torturing some of his sentences and wrenching some of his words, crowding into a unit of language more than seems possible for it to bear, this is not because he was indifferent

to the need for clarity or the value of communication. His more rhetorical style is the result of his desire not merely to pack into a sentence or paragraph a description of a present state of being or a continuing action, but also to communicate something of its half-buried causes, its complicating consequences, its ironic contraries, its continuous muddle and possible magnificence. It is as if he were trying to pack into a sentence or a paragraph the sense of simultaneity which is so characteristic of human consciousness, the sense of the palpitating complexity of felt experience. This means that he sometimes strained, sometimes drove too hard, sometimes fell into obscurity. But when he succeeds—and that was often enough—the result is marvelously rich, a full impression of the way an experience feels, the way a relationship moves, the way a human being responds at one and the same time to the pressures of his outer life and the needs of his inner life.

These remarks are the merest beginning of a discussion of Faulkner's style, but then the selection that follows is the merest beginning of a display of his gifts. The reader who enjoys it should turn both to Faulkner's stories and, more important, to that sequence of remarkable novels which forms the achievement of his great period in the 1930's. It is not, to be sure, an easy journey and no one can take it who would read while he runs. Faulkner demands attention and offers difficulties, but in literature, as elsewhere, the confrontation of difficulties can bring large and unexpected rewards.

# THE BEAR

◊

⟨[ "THE BEAR" is a self-contained short novel which appears as a major part of Faulkner's volume *Go Down, Moses* (1942). In the following version, only the hunt section is included. The last part of the tale, Section 4, recounts Isaac McCaslin's efforts to construe for himself and for other Southerners the significance of the ritual hunt and the death of the bear.

I

THERE was a man and a dog too this time. Two beasts, counting Old Ben, the bear, and two men, counting Boon Hogganbeck, in whom some of the same blood ran which ran in Sam Fathers, even though Boon's was a plebeian strain of it and only Sam and Old Ben and the mongrel Lion were taintless and incorruptible.

He was sixteen. For six years now he had been a man's hunter. For six years now he had heard the best of all talking. It was of the wilderness, the big woods, bigger and older than any recorded document:—of white man fatuous enough to believe he had bought any fragment of it, of Indian ruthless enough to pretend that any fragment of it had been his to convey; bigger than Major de Spain and the scrap he pretended to, knowing better; older than old Thomas Sutpen of whom Major de Spain had had it and who knew better; older even than old Ikkemotubbe, the Chickasaw chief, of whom old Sutpen had had it and who knew better in his turn. It was of the men, not white nor black nor red but men, hunters, with the will and hardihood to endure and the humility and skill to survive, and the dogs and the bear and deer juxtaposed and reliefed against it, ordered and compelled by and within the wilderness in the ancient and unremitting contest according to the ancient and immitigable rules which voided all regrets and brooked no quarter;—the best game of all, the best of all breathing and forever the best of all listening, the voices quiet and weighty and deliberate for retrospection and recollection and exactitude among the concrete trophies—the racked guns and the heads and skins—in the libraries of town houses or the offices of plantation houses or (and best of all) in the camps themselves where the intact and still-warm meat yet hung, the men who had slain it sitting before the burning logs on hearths when there were houses and hearths or about the smoky blazing of piled wood in front of stretched tarpaulins when there were not. There was always a bottle present, so that it would seem to him that those fine fierce instants of heart and brain and courage and wiliness and speed were concentrated and distilled into that brown liquor which not women, not boys and children, but only hunters drank, drinking not of the blood they spilled but some condensation of the wild immortal spirit, drinking it moderately, humbly even, not with the pagan's base and baseless hope of acquiring thereby the virtues of cunning and strength and speed but in salute to them. Thus it seemed to him on this December morning not only natural but actually fitting that this should have begun with whisky.

He realized later that it had begun long before that. It had already begun on that day when he first wrote his age in two ciphers and his cousin McCaslin brought him for the first time to the camp, the big woods, to earn for himself from the wilderness the name and state of hunter provided he in his turn were humble and enduring enough. He had already inherited them, without ever having seen it, the big old bear with one trap-ruined foot that in an area almost a hundred miles square had earned for himself a name, a definite designation like a living man:—the long legend of corn-cribs broken down and rifled, of shoats and grown pigs and even calves carried bodily into the woods and devoured and traps and deadfalls overthrown and dogs mangled and slain and shotgun and even rifle shots delivered at point-blank range yet with no more effect than so many peas blown through a tube by a child—a corridor of wreckage and destruction beginning back before the boy was born, through which sped, not fast but rather with the ruthless and irresistible deliberation of a locomotive, the shaggy tremendous shape. It ran in his knowledge before he ever saw it. It loomed and towered in his dreams before he even saw the unaxed woods where it left its crooked print, shaggy, tremendous, red-eyed, not malevolent but just big, too big for the dogs which tried to bay it, for the horses which tried to ride it down, for the men and the bullets they fired into it; too big for the very country which was its constricting scope. It was as if the boy had already divined what his senses and intellect had not encompassed yet: that doomed wilderness whose edges were being constantly and punily gnawed at by men with plows and axes who feared it because it was wilderness, men myriad and nameless even to one another in the land where the old bear had earned a name, and through which ran not even a mortal beast but an anachronism indomitable and invincible out of an old dead time, a phantom, epitome and apotheosis of the old wild life which the little puny humans swarmed and hacked at in a fury of abhorrence and fear like pygmies about the ankles of a drowsing elephant;—the old bear, solitary, indomitable, and alone; widowered childless and absolved of mortality—old Priam reft of his old wife and outlived all his sons.

Still a child, with three years then two years then one year yet before he too could make one of them, each November he would watch the wagon containing the dogs and the bedding and food and guns and his cousin McCaslin and Tennie's Jim and Sam Fathers too until Sam moved to the camp to live, depart for the Big Bottom, the big woods. To him, they were going not to hunt bear and deer but to keep yearly rendezvous with the bear which they did not even intend to kill. Two weeks later they would' return, with no trophy, no skin. He had not expected it. He had not even feared that it might be in the wagon this time with the other skins and heads. He did not even tell himself that in three years or two years or one year more he would be present and that it might even be his gun. He believed that only after he had served his apprenticeship in the woods which would prove him worthy to be a hunter, would he even be permitted to distinguish the crooked print, and that even then for two November weeks he would merely make another minor one, along with his cousin and Major de Spain and General Compson and Walter Ewell and Boon and the dogs which feared to bay it and the shotguns and rifles which failed even to bleed it, in the yearly pageant-rite of the old bear's furious immortality.

His day came at last. In the surrey with his cousin and Major de Spain and General Compson he saw the wilderness through a slow drizzle of November rain just above the ice point as it seemed to him later he always saw it or at least always remembered it—the tall and endless wall of dense November woods under the dissolving afternoon and the year's death, sombre, impenetrable (he could not even discern yet how, at what point they could possibly hope to enter it even though he knew that Sam Fathers was waiting there with the wagon), the surrey moving through the skeleton stalks of cotton and corn in the last of open country, the last trace of man's puny gnawing at the immemorial flank, until, dwarfed by that perspective into an almost ridiculous diminishment, the surrey itself seemed to have ceased to move (this too to be completed later, years later, after he had grown to a man and had seen the sea) as a solitary small boat hangs in lonely immobility, merely tossing up and down, in the infinite waste of the ocean while the water and then the apparently impenetrable land which it nears without appreciable progress, swings slowly and opens the widening inlet which is the anchorage. He entered it. Sam was waiting, wrapped in a quilt on the wagon seat behind the patient and steaming mules. He entered his novitiate to the true wilderness with Sam beside him as he had begun his apprenticeship in miniature to manhood after the rabbits and such with Sam beside him, the two of them wrapped in the damp, warm, Negro-rank quilt while the wilderness closed behind his entrance as it had opened momentarily to accept him, opening before his advancement as it closed behind his progress, no fixed path the wagon fol-lowed but a channel nonexistent ten yards ahead of it and ceasing to exist ten yards after it had passed, the wagon progressing not by its own volition but by attrition of their intact yet fluid circumambience, drowsing, earless, almost light-less.

It seemed to him that at the age of ten he was witnessing his own birth. It was not even strange to him. He had experienced it all before, and not merely in dreams. He saw the camp—a paintless six-room bungalow set on piles above the spring high-water—and he knew already how it was going to look. He helped in the rapid orderly disorder of their establishment in it and even his motions were familiar to him, foreknown. Then for two weeks he ate the coarse, rapid food—the shapeless sour bread, the wild strange meat, venison and bear and turkey and coon which he had never tasted before—which men ate, cooked by men who were hunters first and cooks afterward; he slept in harsh sheetless blankets as hunters slept. Each morning the gray of dawn found him and Sam Fathers on the stand, the crossing, which had been allotted him. It was the poorest one, the most barren. He had expected that; he had not dared yet to hope even to himself that he would even hear the running dogs this first time. But he did hear them. It was on the third morning—a murmur, sourceless, almost indistinguishable, yet he knew what it was although he had never before heard that many dogs running at once, the murmur swelling into separate and distinct voices until he could call the five dogs which his cousin owned from among the others. "Now," Sam said, "slant your gun up a little and draw back the hammers and then stand still."

But it was not for him, not yet. The humility was there; he had learned that. And he could learn the patience. He was only ten, only one week. The instant had passed. It seemed to him that he could actually see the deer, the buck, smoke-colored, elongated with speed, vanished, the woods, the gray solitude still ringing even when the voices of the dogs had died away; from far away across the sombre woods and the gray half-liquid morning there came two shots. "Now let your hammers down," Sam said.

He did so. "You knew it too," he said.

"Yes," Sam said. "I want you to learn how to do when you didn't shoot. It's after the chance for the bear or the deer has done already come and gone that men and dogs get killed."

"Anyway, it wasn't him," the boy said. "It wasn't even a bear. It was just a deer."

"Yes," Sam said, "it was just a deer."

Then one morning, it was in the second week,

he heard the dogs again. This time before Sam even spoke he readied the too-long, too-heavy, man-size gun as Sam had taught him, even though this time he knew the dogs and the deer were coming less close than ever, hardly within hearing even. They didn't sound like any running dogs he had ever heard before even. Then he found that Sam, who had taught him first of all to cock the gun and take position where he could see best in all directions and then never to move again, had himself moved up beside him. "There," he said. "Listen." The boy listened, to no ringing chorus strong and fast on a free scent but a moiling yapping an octave too high and with something more than indecision and even abjectness in it which he could not yet recognize, reluctant, not even moving very fast, taking a long time to pass out of hearing, leaving even then in the air that echo of thin and almost human hysteria, abject, almost humanly grieving, with this time nothing ahead of it, no sense of a fleeing unseen smoke-colored shape. He could hear Sam breathing at his shoulder. He saw the arched curve of the old man's inhaling nostrils.

"It's Old Ben!" he cried, whispering.

Sam didn't move save for the slow gradual turning of his head as the voices faded on and the faint steady rapid arch and collapse of his nostrils. "Hah," he said. "Not even running. Walking."

"But up here!" the boy cried. "Way up here!"

"He do it every year," Sam said. "Once. Ash and Boon say he comes up here to run the other little bears away. Tell them to get to hell out of here and stay out until the hunters are gone. Maybe." The boy no longer heard anything at all, yet still Sam's head continued to turn gradually and steadily until the back of it was toward him. Then it turned back and looked down at him—the same face, grave, familiar, expressionless until it smiled, the same old man's eyes from which as he watched there faded slowly a quality darkly and fiercely lambent, passionate and proud. "He dont care no more for bears than he does for dogs or men neither. He come to see who's here, who's new in camp this year, whether he can shoot or not, can stay or not. Whether we got the dog yet that can bay and hold him until a man gets there with a gun. Because he's the head bear. He's the man." It faded, was gone; again they were the eyes as he had known them all his life. "He'll let them follow him to the river. Then he'll send them home. We might as well go too; see how they look when they get back to camp."

The dogs were there first, ten of them huddled back under the kitchen, himself and Sam squatting to peer back into the obscurity where they crouched, quiet, the eyes rolling and luminous, vanishing, and no sound, only that effluvium which the boy could not quite place yet, of something more than dog, stronger than dog and not just animal, just beast even. Because there had been nothing in front of the abject and painful yapping except the solitude, the wilderness, so that when the eleventh hound got back about mid-afternoon and he and Tennie's Jim held the passive and still trembling bitch while Sam daubed her tattered ear and raked shoulder with turpentine and axle-grease, it was still no living creature but only the wilderness which, leaning for a moment, had patted lightly once her temerity. "Just like a man," Sam said. "Just like folks. Put off as long as she could having to be brave, knowing all the time that sooner or later she would have to be brave once so she could keep on calling herself a dog, and knowing beforehand what was going to happen when she done it."

He did not know just when Sam left. He only knew that he was gone. For the next three mornings he rose and ate breakfast and Sam was not waiting for him. He went to his stand alone; he found it without help now and stood on it as Sam had taught him. On the third morning he heard the dogs again, running strong and free on a true scent again, and he readied the gun as he had learned to do and heard the hunt sweep past on since he was not ready yet, had not deserved other yet in just one short period of two weeks as compared to all the long life which he had already dedicated to the wilderness with patience and humility; he heard the shot again, one shot, the single clapping report of Walter Ewell's rifle. By now he could not only find his stand and then return to camp without guidance, by using the compass his cousin had given him he reached Walter waiting beside the buck and the moiling of dogs over the cast entrails before any of the others except Major de Spain and Tennie's Jim on the horses, even before Uncle Ash arrived with the one-eyed wagon-mule which did not mind the smell of blood or even, so they said, of bear.

It was not Uncle Ash on the mule. It was Sam, returned. And Sam was waiting when he finished his dinner and, himself on the one-eyed mule and Sam on the other one of the wagon team, they rode for more than three hours through the rapid shortening sunless afternoon, following no path, no trail even that he could discern, into a section of country he had never seen before. Then he understood why Sam had made him ride the one-eyed mule which would not spook at the smell of blood, of wild animals. The other one, the sound one, stopped short and tried to whirl and bolt even as Sam got down, jerking and wrenching at the rein while Sam held it, coaxing it forward with his voice since he did not dare risk hitching it, drawing it forward while the boy dismounted from the marred one which would stand. Then, standing beside Sam in the thick great gloom of ancient woods and the winter's dying afternoon, he looked quietly down at the rotted log scored and gutted with claw-marks and, in the wet earth beside it, the print of the enormous warped two-toed foot. Now he knew what he had heard in the hounds' voices in the woods that morning and what he had smelled when he peered under the kitchen where they huddled. It was in him too, a little different because they were brute beasts and he was not, but only a little different—an eagerness, passive; an abjectness, a sense of his own fragility and impotence against the timeless woods, yet without doubt or dread; a flavor like brass in the sudden run of saliva in his mouth, a hard sharp constriction either in his brain or his stomach, he could not tell which and it did not matter; he knew only that for the first time he realized that the bear which had run in his listening and loomed in his dreams since before he could remember and which therefore must have existed in the listening and the dreams of his cousin and Major de Spain and even old General Compson before they began to remember in their turn, was a mortal animal and that they had departed for the camp each November with no actual intention of slaying it, not because it could not be slain but because so far they had no actual hope of being able to. "It will be tomorrow," he said.

"You mean we will try tomorrow," Sam said. "We aint got the dog yet."

"We've got eleven," he said. "They ran him Monday."

"And you heard them," Sam said. "Saw them too. We aint got the dog yet. It wont take but one. But he aint there. Maybe he aint nowhere. The only other way will be for him to run by accident over somebody that had a gun and knowed how to shoot it."

"That wouldn't be me," the boy said. "It would be Walter or Major or——"

"It might," Sam said. "You watch close tomorrow. Because he's smart. That's how come he has lived this long. If he gets hemmed up and has got to pick out somebody to run over, he will pick out you."

"How?" he said. "How will he know. . . ." He ceased. "You mean he already knows me, that I aint never been to the big bottom before, aint had time to find out yet whether I . . ." He ceased again, staring at Sam; he said humbly, not even amazed: "It was me he was watching. I dont reckon he did need to come but once."

"You watch tomorrow," Sam said. "I reckon we better start back. It'll be long after dark now before we get to camp."

The next morning they started three hours earlier than they had ever done. Even Uncle Ash went, the cook, who called himself by profession a camp cook and who did little else save cook for Major de Spain's hunting and camping parties, yet who had been marked by the wilderness from simple juxtaposition to it until he responded as they all did, even the boy who until two weeks ago had never even seen the wilderness, to a hound's ripped ear and shoulder and the print of a crooked foot in a patch of wet earth. They rode. It was too far to walk: the boy and Sam and Uncle Ash in the wagon with the dogs, his cousin and Major de Spain and General Compson and Boon and Walter and Tennie's Jim riding double on the horses; again the first gray light found him, as on that first morning two weeks ago, on the stand where Sam had placed and left him. With the gun which was too big for him, the breech-loader which did not even belong to him but to Major de Spain and which he had fired only once, at a stump on the first day to learn the recoil and how to reload it with the paper shells, he stood against a big gum tree beside a little bayou whose black still water crept without motion out of a cane-brake, across a small clearing and into the cane again, where, invisible, a bird, the big woodpecker called Lord-to-God by Negroes, clattered at a dead trunk. It was a stand like any other stand, dissimilar only in incidentals to the one where he had stood each morning for two weeks; a territory new to him yet no less familiar than that other one which after two weeks he had come to believe he knew a little—the same solitude, the same loneliness through which frail and timorous man had merely passed without altering it, leaving no mark nor scar, which looked exactly as it must have looked when the first ancestor of Sam Fathers' Chickasaw predecessors crept into it and looked about him, club or stone axe or bone arrow drawn and ready, different only because, squatting at the edge of the kitchen, he had smelled the dogs huddled and cringing beneath it and saw the raked ear and side of the bitch that, as Sam had said, had to be brave once in order to keep on calling herself a dog, and saw yesterday in the earth beside the gutted log, the print of the living foot. He heard no dogs at all. He never did certainly hear them. He only heard the drumming of the woodpecker stop short off, and knew that the bear was looking at him. He never saw it. He did not know whether it was facing him from the cane or behind him. He did not move, holding the useless gun which he knew now he would never fire at it, now or ever, tasting in his saliva that taint of brass which he had smelled in the huddled dogs when he peered under the kitchen.

Then it was gone. As abruptly as it had stopped, the woodpecker's dry hammering set up again, and after a while he believed he even heard the dogs —a murmur, scarce a sound even, which he had probably been hearing for a time, perhaps a minute or two, before he remarked it, drifting into hearing and then out again, dying away. They came nowhere near him. If it was dogs he heard, he could not have sworn to it; if it was a bear they ran, it was another bear. It was Sam himself who emerged from the cane and crossed the bayou, the injured bitch following at heel as a bird dog is taught to walk. She came and crouched against his leg, trembling. "I didn't see him," he said. "I didn't, Sam."

"I know it," Sam said. "He done the looking. You didn't hear him neither, did you?"

"No," the boy said. "I——"

"He's smart," Sam said. "Too smart." Again the boy saw in his eyes that quality of dark and brooding lambence as Sam looked down at the bitch trembling faintly and steadily against the boy's leg. From her raked shoulder a few drops of fresh blood clung like bright berries. "Too big. We aint got the dog yet. But maybe some day."

Because there would be a next time, after and after. He was only ten. It seemed to him that he could see them, the two of them, shadowy in the limbo from which time emerged and became time: the old bear absolved of mortality and himself who shared a little of it. Because he recognized now what he had smelled in the huddled dogs and tasted in his own saliva, recognized fear as a boy, a youth, recognizes the existence of love and passion and experience which is his heritage but not yet his patrimony, from entering by chance the presence or perhaps even merely the bedroom of a woman who has loved and been loved by many men. *So I will have to see him,* he thought, without dread or even hope. *I will have to look at him.* So it was in June of the next summer. They were at the camp again, celebrating Major de Spain's and General Compson's birthdays. Although the one had been born in September and the other in the depth of winter and almost thirty years earlier, each June the two of them and McCaslin and Boon and Walter Ewell (and the boy too from now on) spent two weeks at the camp, fishing and shooting squirrels and turkey and running coons and wildcats with the dogs at night. That is, Boon

and the Negroes (and the boy too now) fished and shot squirrels and ran the coons and cats, because the proven hunters, not only Major de Spain and old General Compson (who spent those two weeks sitting in a rocking chair before a tremendous iron pot of Brunswick stew, stirring and tasting, with Uncle Ash to quarrel with about how he was making it and Tennie's Jim to pour whisky into the tin dipper from which he drank it) but even McCaslin and Walter Ewell who were still young enough, scorned such other than shooting the wild gobblers with pistols for wagers or to test their marksmanship.

That is, his cousin McCaslin and the others thought he was hunting squirrels. Until the third evening he believed that Sam Fathers thought so too. Each morning he would leave the camp right after breakfast. He had his own gun now, a new breech-loader, a Christmas gift; he would own and shoot it for almost seventy years, through two new pairs of barrels and locks and one new stock, until all that remained of the original gun was the silver-inlaid trigger-guard with his and McCaslin's engraved names and the date in 1878. He found the tree beside the little bayou where he had stood that morning. Using the compass he ranged from that point; he was teaching himself to be better than a fair woodsman without even knowing he was doing it. On the third day he even found the gutted log where he had first seen the print. It was almost completely crumbled now, healing with unbelievable speed, a passionate and almost visible relinquishment, back into the earth from which the tree had grown. He ranged the summer woods now, green with gloom, if anything actually dimmer than they had been in November's gray dissolution, where even at noon the sun fell only in windless dappling upon the earth which never completely dried and which crawled with snakes —moccasins and watersnakes and rattlers, themselves the color of the dappled gloom so that he would not always see them until they moved; returning to camp later and later and later, first day, second day, passing in the twilight of the third evening the little log pen enclosing the log barn where Sam was putting up the stock for the night. "You aint looked right yet," Sam said.

He stopped. For a moment he didn't answer. Then he said peacefully, in a peaceful rushing burst, as when a boy's miniature dam in a little brook gives way: "All right. Yes. But how? I went to the bayou. I even found that log again. I——"

"I reckon that was all right. Likely he's been watching you. You never saw his foot?"

"I . . ." the boy said. "I didn't . . . I never thought . . ."

"It's the gun," Sam said. He stood beside the fence, motionless, the old man, son of a Negro slave and a Chickasaw chief, in the battered and faded overalls and the frayed five-cent straw hat which had been the badge of the Negro's slavery and was now the regalia of his freedom. The camp—the clearing, the house, the barn and its tiny lot with which Major de Spain in his turn had scratched punily and evanescently at the wilderness—faded in the dusk, back into the immemorial darkness of the woods. *The gun,* the boy thought. *The gun.* "You will have to choose," Sam said.

He left the next norning before light, without breakfast, long before Uncle Ash would wake in his quilts on the kitchen floor and start the fire. He had only the compass and a stick for the snakes. He could go almost a mile before he would need to see the compass. He sat on a log, the invisible compass in his hand, while the secret night-sounds which had ceased at his movements, scurried again and then fell still for good and the owls ceased and gave over to the waking day birds and there was light in the gray wet woods and he could see the compass. He went fast yet still quietly, becoming steadily better and better as a woodsman without yet having time to realise it; he jumped a doe and a fawn, walked them out of the bed, close enough to see them—the crash of undergrowth, the white scut, the fawn scudding along behind her, faster than he had known it could have run. He was hunting right, upwind, as Sam had taught him, but that didn't matter now. He had left the gun; by his own will and relinquishment he had accepted not a gambit, not a choice, but a condition in which not only the bear's heretofore inviolable anonymity but all the ancient rules and balances of hunter and hunted had been abrogated. He would not even be afraid, not even in the moment when the fear would take him completely: blood, skin, bowels, bones, memory from the long time before it even became his memory—all save that thin clear quenchless lucidity which alone differed him from this bear and from all the other bears and bucks he would follow during almost seventy years, to which Sam had said: "Be scared. You cant help that. But dont be afraid. Aint nothing in the woods going to hurt you if you dont corner it or it dont smell that you are afraid. A bear or a deer has got to be scared of a coward the same as a brave man has got to be."

By noon he was far beyond the crossing on the little bayou, farther into the new and alien country than he had ever been, travelling now not only by the compass but by the old, heavy, biscuit-thick silver watch which had been his father's.

He had left the camp nine hours ago; nine hours from now, dark would already have been an hour old. He stopped, for the first time since he had risen from the log when he could see the compass face at last, and looked about, mopping his sweating face on his sleeve. He had already relinquished, of his will, because of his need, in humility and peace and without regret, yet apparently that had not been enough, the leaving of the gun was not enough. He stood for a moment—a child, alien and lost in the green and soaring gloom of the markless wilderness. Then he relinquished completely to it. It was the watch and the compass. He was still tainted. He removed the linked chain of the one and the looped thong of the other from his overalls and hung them on a bush and leaned the stick beside them and entered it.

When he realized he was lost, he did as Sam had coached and drilled him: made a cast to cross his backtrack. He had not been going very fast for the last two or three hours, and he had gone even less fast since he left the compass and watch on the bush. So he went slower still now, since the tree could not be very far; in fact, he found it before he really expected to and turned and went to it. But there was no bush beneath it, no compass nor watch, so he did next as Sam had coached and drilled him: made this next circle in the opposite direction and much larger, so that the pattern of the two of them would bisect his track somewhere, but crossing no trace nor mark anywhere of his feet or any feet, and now he was going faster though still not panicked, his heart beating a little more rapidly but strong and steady enough, and this time it was not even the tree because there was a down log beside it which he had never seen before and beyond the log a little swamp, a seepage of moisture somewhere between earth and water, and he did what Sam had coached and drilled him as the next and the last, seeing as he sat down on the log the crooked print, the warped indentation in the wet ground which while he looked at it continued to fill with water until it was level full and the water began to overflow and the sides of the print began to dissolve away. Even as he looked up he saw the next one, and, moving, the one beyond it; moving, not hurrying, running, but merely keeping pace with them as they appeared before him as though they were being shaped out of thin air just one constant pace short of where he would lose them forever and be lost forever himself, tireless, eager, without doubt or dread, panting a little above the strong rapid little hammer of his heart, emerging suddenly into a little glade and the wilderness coalesced. It rushed, soundless, and solidified—the tree, the bush, the compass and the watch glinting where a ray of sunlight touched them. Then he saw the bear. It did not emerge, appear: it was just there, immobile, fixed in the green and windless noon's hot dappling, not as big as he had dreamed it but as big as he had expected, bigger, dimensionless against the dappled obscurity, looking at him. Then it moved. It crossed the glade without haste, walking for an instant into the sun's full glare and out of it, and stopped again and looked back at him across one shoulder. Then it was gone. It didn't walk into the woods. It faded, sank back into the wilderness without motion as he had watched a fish, a huge old bass, sink back into the dark depths of its pool and vanish without even any movement of its fins.

### 2

SO HE should have hated and feared Lion. He was thirteen then. He had killed his buck and Sam Fathers had marked his face with the hot blood, and in the next November he killed a bear. But before that accolade he had become as competent in the woods as many grown men with the same experience. By now he was a better woodsman than most grown men with more. There was no territory within twenty-five miles of the camp that he did not know—bayou, ridge, landmark trees and path; he could have led anyone direct to any spot in it and brought him back. He knew game trails that even Sam Fathers had never seen; in the third fall he found a buck's bedding-place by himself and unbeknown to his cousin he borrowed Walter Ewell's rifle and lay in wait for the buck at dawn and killed it when it walked back to the bed as Sam had told him how the old Chickasaw fathers did.

By now he knew the old bear's footprint better than he did his own, and not only the crooked one. He could see any one of the three sound prints and distinguish it at once from any other, and not only because of its size. There were other bears within that fifty miles which left tracks almost as large, or at least so near that the one would have appeared larger only by juxtaposition. It was more than that. If Sam Fathers had been his mentor and the backyard rabbits and squirrels his kindergarten, then the wilderness the old bear ran was his college and the old male bear itself, so long unwifed and childless as to have become its own ungendered progenitor, was his alma mater.

He could find the crooked print now whenever he wished, ten miles or five miles or sometimes closer than that, to the camp. Twice while on stand during the next three years he heard the dogs strike its trail and once even jump it by chance, the voices high, abject, almost human in their hysteria. Once, still-hunting with Walter Ewell's rifle, he saw it cross a long corridor of down timber where a tornado had passed. It rushed through rather than across the tangle of trunks and branches as a locomotive would, faster than he had ever believed it could have moved, almost as fast as a deer even because the deer would have spent most of that distance in the air; he realized then why it would take a dog not only of abnormal courage but size and speed too ever to bring it to bay. He had a little dog at home, a mongrel, of the sort called fyce by Negroes, a ratter, itself not much bigger than a rat and possessing that sort of courage which had long since stopped being bravery and had become foolhardiness. He brought it with him one June and, timing them as if they were meeting an appointment with another human being, himself carrying the fyce with a sack over its head and Sam Fathers with a brace of the hounds on a rope leash, they lay downwind of the trail and actually ambushed the bear. They were so close that it turned at bay although he realized later this might have been from surprise and amazement at the shrill and frantic uproar of the fyce. It turned at bay against the trunk of a big cypress, on its hind feet; it seemed to the boy that it would never stop rising, taller and taller, and even the two hounds seemed to have taken a kind of desperate and despairing courage from the fyce. Then he realized that the fyce was actually not going to stop. He flung the gun down and ran. When he overtook and grasped the shrill, frantically pinwheeling little dog, it seemed to him that he was directly under the bear. He could smell it, strong and hot and rank. Sprawling, he looked up where it loomed and towered over him like a thunderclap. It was quite familiar, until he remembered: this was the way he had used to dream about it.

Then it was gone. He didn't see it go. He knelt, holding the frantic fyce with both hands, hearing the abased wailing of the two hounds drawing further and further away, until Sam came up, carrying the gun. He laid it quietly down beside the boy and stood looking down at him. "You've done seed him twice now, with a gun in your hands," he said. "This time you couldn't have missed him."

The boy rose. He still held the fyce. Even in his arms it continued to yap frantically, surging and straining toward the fading sound of the hounds like a collection of live-wire springs. The boy was panting a little. "Neither could you," he said. "You had the gun. Why didn't you shoot him?"

Sam didn't seem to have heard. He put out his hand and touched the little dog in the boy's arms which still yapped and strained even though the two hounds were out of hearing now. "He's done gone," Sam said. "You can slack off and rest now, until next time." He stroked the little dog until it began to grow quiet under his hand. "You's almost the one we wants," he said. "You just aint big enough. We aint got that one yet. He will need to be just a little bigger than smart, and a little braver than either." He withdrew his hand from the fyce's head and stood looking into the woods where the bear and the hounds had vanished. "Somebody is going to, some day."

"I know it," the boy said. "That's why it must be one of us. So it wont be until the last day. When even he dont want it to last any longer."

So he should have hated and feared Lion. It was in the fourth summer, the fourth time he had made one in the celebration of Major de Spain's and General Compson's birthday. In the early spring Major de Spain's mare had foaled a horse colt. One evening when Sam brought the horses and mules up to stable them for the night, the colt was missing and it was all he could do to get the frantic mare into the lot. He had thought at first to let the mare lead him back to where she had become separated from the foal. But she would not do it. She would not even feint toward any particular part of the woods or even in any particular direction. She merely ran, as if she couldn't see, still frantic with terror. She whirled and ran at Sam once, as if to attack him in some ultimate desperation, as if she could not for the moment realise that he was a man and a long-familiar one. He got her into the lot at last. It was too dark by that time to back-track her, to unravel the erratic course she had doubtless pursued.

He came to the house and told Major de Spain. It was an animal, of course, a big one, and the colt was dead now, wherever it was. They all knew that. "It's a panther," General Compson said at once. "The same one. That doe and fawn last March." Sam had sent Major de Spain word of it when Boon Hogganbeck came to the camp on a routine visit to see how the stock had wintered —the doe's throat torn out, and the beast had run down the helpless fawn and killed it too.

"Sam never did say that was a panther," Major de Spain said. Sam said nothing now, standing behind Major de Spain where they sat at supper, inscrutable, as if he were just waiting for them to stop talking so he could go home. He didn't even seem to be looking at anything. "A panther might jump a doe, and he wouldn't have much trouble catching the fawn afterward. But no panther would have jumped that colt with the dam right there with it. It was Old Ben," Major de Spain said. "I'm disappointed in him. He has broken the rules. I didn't think he would have done that. He has killed mine and McCaslin's dogs, but that was all right. We gambled the dogs against him; we gave each other warning. But now he has come into my house and destroyed my property, out of season too. He broke the rules. It was Old Ben, Sam." Still Sam said nothing, standing there until Major de Spain should stop talking. "We'll back-track her tomorrow and see," Major de Spain said.

Sam departed. He would not live in the camp; he had built himself a little hut something like Joe Baker's, only stouter, tighter, on the bayou a quarter-mile away, and a stout log crib where he stored a little corn for the shoat he raised each year. The next morning he was waiting when they waked. He had already found the colt. They did not even wait for breakfast. It was not far, not five hundred yards from the stable—the three-months' colt lying on its side, its throat torn out and the entrails and one ham partly eaten. It lay not as if it had been dropped but as if it had been struck and hurled, and no cat-mark, no claw-mark where a panther would have gripped it while finding its throat. They read the tracks where the frantic mare had circled and at last rushed in with that same ultimate desperation with which she had whirled on Sam Fathers yesterday evening, and the long tracks of dead and terrified running and those of the beast which had not even rushed at her when she advanced but had merely walked three or four paces toward her until she broke, and General Compson said, "Good God, what a wolf!"

Still Sam said nothing. The boy watched him while the men knelt, measuring the tracks. There was something in Sam's face now. It was neither exultation nor joy nor hope. Later, a man, the boy realized what it had been, and that Sam had known all the time what had made the tracks and what had torn the throat out of the doe in the spring and killed the fawn. It had been foreknowledge in Sam's face that morning. *And he was glad*, he told himself. *He was old. He had no children, no people, none of his blood anywhere above earth that he would ever meet again. And even if he were to, he could not have touched it, spoken to it, because for seventy years now he had had to be a Negro. It was almost over now and he was glad.*

They returned to camp and had breakfast and came back with guns and the hounds. Afterward the boy realized that they also should have known then what killed the colt as well as Sam Fathers did. But that was neither the first nor the last time he had seen men rationalize from and even act upon their misconceptions. After Boon, standing astride the colt, had whipped the dogs away from it with his belt, they snuffed at the tracks. One of them, a young dog hound without judgment yet, bayed once, and they ran for a few feet on what seemed to be a trail. Then they stopped, looking back at the men, eager enough, not baffled, merely questioning, as if they were asking "Now what?" Then they rushed back to the colt, where Boon, still astride it, slashed at them with the belt.

"I never knew a trail to get cold that quick," General Compson said.

"Maybe a single wolf big enough to kill a colt with the dam right there beside it dont leave scent," Major de Spain said.

"Maybe it was a hant," Walter Ewell said. He looked at Tennie's Jim. "Hah, Jim?"

Because the hounds would not run it, Major de Spain had Sam hunt out and find the tracks a hundred yards farther on and they put the dogs on it again and again the young one bayed and not one of them realised then that the hound was not baying like a dog striking game but was merely bellowing like a country dog whose yard has been invaded. General Compson spoke to the boy and Boon and Tennie's Jim: to the squirrel hunters. "You boys keep the dogs with you this morning. He's probably hanging around somewhere, waiting to get his breakfast off the colt. You might strike him."

But they did not. The boy remembered how Sam stood watching them as they went into the woods with the leashed hounds—the Indian face in which he had never seen anything until it smiled, except that faint arching of the nostrils on that first morning when the hounds had found Old Ben. They took the hounds with them on the next day, though when they reached the place where they hoped to strike a fresh trail, the carcass of the colt was gone. Then on the third morning Sam was waiting again, this time until they had finished breakfast. He said, "Come." He led them to his house, his little hut, to the corn-crib beyond it. He had removed the corn and had made a dead-fall of the door, baiting it with the colt's carcass; peering between the logs, they saw an animal almost the color of a gun or pistol barrel, what little time they had to examine its color or shape. It was not crouched nor even standing. It was in motion, in the air, coming toward them—a heavy body crashing with tremendous force against the door so that the thick door jumped and clattered in its frame, the animal, whatever it was, hurling

itself against the door again seemingly before it could have touched the floor and got a new purchase to spring from. "Come away," Sam said, "fore he break his neck." Even when they retreated the heavy and measured crashes continued, the stout door jumping and clattering each time, and still no sound from the beast itself—no snarl, no cry.

"What in hell's name is it?" Major de Spain said.

"It's a dog," Sam said, his nostrils arching and collapsing faintly and steadily and that faint, fierce milkiness in his eyes again as on that first morning when the hounds had struck the old bear. "It's the dog."

"*The* dog?" Major de Spain said.

"That's gonter hold Old Ben."

"Dog the devil," Major de Spain said. "I'd rather have Old Ben himself in my pack than that brute. Shoot him."

"No," Sam said.

"You'll never tame him. How do you ever expect to make an animal like that afraid of you?"

"I dont want him tame," Sam said; again the boy watched his nostrils and the fierce milky light in his eyes. "But I almost rather he be tame than scared, of me or any man or any thing. But he wont be neither, of nothing."

"Then what are you going to do with it?"

"You can watch," Sam said.

Each morning through the second week they would go to Sam's crib. He had removed a few shingles from the roof and had put a rope on the colt's carcass and had drawn it out when the trap fell. Each morning they would watch him lower a pail of water into the crib while the dog hurled itself tirelessly against the door and dropped back and leaped again. It never made any sound and there was nothing frenzied in the act but only a cold and grim indomitable determination. Toward the end of the week it stopped jumping at the door. Yet it had not weakened appreciably and it was not as if it had rationalized the fact that the door was not going to give. It was as if for that time it simply disdained to jump any longer. It was not down. None of them had ever seen it down. It stood, and they could see it now—part mastiff, something of Airedale and something of a dozen other strains probably, better than thirty inches at the shoulders and weighing as they guessed almost ninety pounds, with cold yellow eyes and a tremendous chest and over all that strange color like a blued gun-barrel.

Then the two weeks were up. They prepared to break camp. The boy begged to remain and his cousin let him. He moved into the little hut with

Sam Fathers. Each morning he watched Sam lower the pail of water into the crib. By the end of that week the dog was down. It would rise and half stagger, half crawl to the water and drink and collapse again. One morning it could not even reach the water, could not raise its forequarters even from the floor. Sam took a short stick and prepared to enter the crib. "Wait," the boy said. "Let me get the gun——"

"No," Sam said. "He cant move now." Nor could it. It lay on its side while Sam touched it, its head and the gaunted body, the dog lying motionless, the yellow eyes open. They were not fierce and there was nothing of petty malevolence in them, but a cold and almost impersonal malignance like some natural force. It was not even looking at Sam nor at the boy peering at it between the logs.

Sam began to feed it again. The first time he had to raise its head so it could lap the broth. That night he left a bowl of broth containing lumps of meat where the dog could reach it. The next morning the bowl was empty and the dog was lying on its belly, its head up, the cold yellow eyes watching the door as Sam entered, no change whatever in the cold yellow eyes and still no sound from it even when it sprang, its aim and coordination still bad from weakness so that Sam had time to strike it down with the stick and leap from the crib and slam the door as the dog, still without having had time to get its feet under it to jump again seemingly, hurled itself against the door as if the two weeks of starving had never been.

At noon that day someone came whooping through the woods from the direction of the camp. It was Boon. He came and looked for a while between the logs, at the tremendous dog lying again on its belly, its head up, the yellow eyes blinking sleepily at nothing: the indomitable and unbroken spirit. "What we better do," Boon said, "is to let that son of a bitch go and catch Old Ben and run him on the dog." He turned to the boy his weather-reddened and beetling face. "Get your traps together. Cass says for you to come on home. You been in here fooling with that horse-eating varmint long enough."

Boon had a borrowed mule at the camp; the buggy was waiting at the edge of the bottom. He was at home that night. He told McCaslin about it. "Sam's going to starve him again until he can go in and touch him. Then he will feed him again. Then he will starve him again, if he has to."

"But why?" McCaslin said. "What for? Even Sam will never tame that brute."

"We dont want him tame. We want him like he is. We just want him to find out at last that the only way he can get out of that crib and stay out of it is to do what Sam or somebody tells him to do. He's the dog that's going to stop Old Ben and hold him. We've already named him. His name is Lion."

Then November came at last. They returned to the camp. With General Compson and Major de Spain and his cousin and Walter and Boon he stood in the yard among the guns and bedding and boxes of food and watched Sam Fathers and Lion come up the lane from the lot—the Indian, the old man in battered overalls and rubber boots and a worn sheepskin coat and a hat which had belonged to the boy's father; the tremendous dog pacing gravely beside him. The hounds rushed out to meet them and stopped, except the young one which still had but little of judgment. It ran up to Lion, fawning. Lion didn't snap at it. He didn't even pause. He struck it rolling and yelping for five or six feet with a blow of one paw as a bear would have done and came on into the yard and stood, blinking sleepily at nothing, looking at no one, while Boon said, "Jesus. Jesus.—Will he let me touch him?"

"You can touch him," Sam said. "He dont care. He dont care about nothing or nobody."

The boy watched that too. He watched it for the next two years from that moment when Boon touched Lion's head and then knelt beside him, feeling the bones and muscles, the power. It was as if Lion were a woman—or perhaps Boon was the woman. That was more like it—the big, grave, sleepy-seeming dog which, as Sam Fathers said, cared about no man and no thing; and the violent, insensitive, hard-faced man with his touch of remote Indian blood and the mind almost of a child. He watched Boon take over Lion's feeding from Sam and Uncle Ash both. He would see Boon squatting in the cold rain beside the kitchen while Lion ate. Because Lion neither slept nor ate with the other dogs though none of them knew where he did sleep until in the second November, thinking until then that Lion slept in his kennel beside Sam Fathers' hut, when the boy's cousin McCaslin said something about it to Sam by sheer chance and Sam told him. And that night the boy and Major de Spain and McCaslin with a lamp entered the back room where Boon slept—the little, tight, airless room rank with the smell of Boon's unwashed body and his wet hunting-clothes—where Boon, snoring on his back, choked and waked and Lion raised his head beside him and looked back at them from his cold, slumbrous yellow eyes.

"Damn it, Boon," McCaslin said. "Get that dog out of here. He's got to run Old Ben tomorrow morning. How in hell do you expect him to smell anything fainter than a skunk after breathing you all night?"

"The way I smell aint hurt my nose none that I ever noticed," Boon said.

"It wouldn't matter if it had," Major de Spain said. "We're not depending on you to trail a bear. Put him outside. Put him under the house with the other dogs."

Boon began to get up. "He'll kill the first one that happens to yawn or sneeze in his face or touches him."

"I reckon not," Major de Spain said. "None of them are going to risk yawning in his face or touching him either, even asleep. Put him outside. I want his nose right tomorrow. Old Ben fooled him last year. I dont think he will do it again."

Boon put on his shoes without lacing them; in his long soiled underwear, his hair still tousled from sleep, he and Lion went out. The others returned to the front room and the poker game where McCaslin's and Major de Spain's hands waited for them on the table. After a while McCaslin said, "Do you want me to go back and look again?"

"No," Major de Spain said. "I call," he said to Walter Ewell. He spoke to McCaslin again. "If you do, dont tell me. I am beginning to see the first sign of my increasing age: I dont like to know that my orders have been disobeyed, even when I knew when I gave them that they would be.—A small pair," he said to Walter Ewell.

"How small?" Walter said.

"Very small," Major de Spain said.

And the boy, lying beneath his piled quilts and blankets waiting for sleep, knew likewise that Lion was already back in Boon's bed, for the rest of that night and the next one and during all the nights of the next November and the next one. He thought then: *I wonder what Sam thinks. He could have Lion with him, even if Boon is a white man. He could ask Major or McCaslin either. And more than that. It was Sam's hand that touched Lion first and Lion knows it.* Then he became a man and he knew that too. It had been all right. That was the way it should have been. Sam was the chief, the prince; Boon, the plebeian, was his huntsman. Boon should have nursed the dogs.

On the first morning that Lion led the pack after Old Ben, seven strangers appeared in the camp. They were swampers: gaunt, malaria-ridden men appearing from nowhere, who ran trap-lines for coons or perhaps farmed little patches of cotton and corn along the edge of the bottom, in clothes but little better than Sam Fathers' and nowhere near as good as Tennie's Jim's, with worn shotguns

and rifles, already squatting patiently in the cold drizzle in the side yard when day broke. They had a spokesman; afterward Sam Fathers told Major de Spain how all during the past summer and fall they had drifted into the camp singly or in pairs and threes, to look quietly at Lion for a while and then go away: "Mawnin, Major. We heerd you was aimin to put that ere blue dawg on that old two-toed bear this mawnin. We figgered we'd come up and watch, if you dont mind. We wont do no shooting, lessen he runs over us."

"You are welcome," Major de Spain said. "You are welcome to shoot. He's more your bear than ours."

"I reckon that aint no lie. I done fed him enough cawn to have a sheer in him. Not to mention a shoat three years ago."

"I reckon I got a sheer too," another said. "Only it aint in the bear." Major de Spain looked at him. He was chewing tobacco. He spat. "Hit was a heifer calf. Nice un too. Last year. When I finally found her, I reckon she looked about like that colt of yourn looked last June."

"Oh," Major de Spain said. "Be welcome. If you see game in front of my dogs, shoot it."

Nobody shot Old Ben that day. No man saw him. The dogs jumped him within a hundred yards of the glade where the boy had seen him that day in the summer of his eleventh year. The boy was less than a quarter-mile away. He heard the jump but he could distinguish no voice among the dogs that he did not know and therefore would be Lion's, and he thought, believed, that Lion was not among them. Even the fact that they were going much faster than he had ever heard them run behind Old Ben before and that the high thin note of hysteria was missing now from their voices was not enough to disabuse him. He didn't comprehend until that night, when Sam told him that Lion would never cry on a trail. "He gonter growl when he catches Old Ben's throat," Sam said. "But he aint gonter never holler, no more than he ever done when he was jumping at that two-inch door. It's that blue dog in him. What you call it?"

"Airedale," the boy said.

Lion was there; the jump was just too close to the river. When Boon returned with Lion about eleven that night, he swore that Lion had stopped Old Ben once but that the hounds would not go in and Old Ben broke away and took to the river and swam for miles down it and he and Lion went down one bank for about ten miles and crossed and came up the other but it had begun to get dark before they struck any trail where Old Ben had come up out of the water, unless he was still in the water when he passed the ford where they crossed. Then he fell to cursing the hounds and ate the supper Uncle Ash had saved for him and went off to bed and after a while the boy opened the door of the little stale room thunderous with snoring and the great grave dog raised its head from Boon's pillow and blinked at him for a moment and lowered its head again.

When the next November came and the last day, the day on which it was now becoming traditional to save for Old Ben, there were more than a dozen strangers waiting. They were not all swampers this time. Some of them were townsmen, from other county seats like Jefferson, who had heard about Lion and Old Ben and had come to watch the great blue dog keep his yearly rendezvous with the old two-toed bear. Some of them didn't even have guns and the hunting-clothes and boots they wore had been on a store shelf yesterday.

This time Lion jumped Old Ben more than five miles from the river and bayed and held him and this time the hounds went in, in a sort of desperate emulation. The boy heard them; he was that near. He heard Boon whooping; he heard the two shots when General Compson delivered both barrels, one containing five buckshot, the other a single ball, into the bear from as close as he could force his almost unmanageable horse. He heard the dogs when the bear broke free again. He was running now; panting, stumbling, his lungs bursting, he reached the place where General Compson had fired and where Old Ben had killed two of the hounds. He saw the blood from General Compson's shots, but he could go no further. He stopped, leaning against a tree for his breathing to ease and his heart to slow, hearing the sound of the dogs as it faded on and died away.

In camp that night—they had as guests five of the still terrified strangers in new hunting coats and boots who had been lost all day until Sam Fathers went out and got them—he heard the rest of it: how Lion had stopped and held the bear again but only the one-eyed mule which did not mind the smell of wild blood would approach and Boon was riding the mule and Boon had never been known to hit anything. He shot at the bear five times with his pump gun, touching nothing, and Old Ben killed another hound and broke free once more and reached the river and was gone. Again Boon and Lion hunted as far down one bank as they dared. Too far; they crossed in the first of dusk and dark overtook them within a mile. And this time Lion found the broken trail, the blood perhaps, in the darkness where Old Ben had come up out of the water, but Boon had him on a rope,

luckily, and he got down from the mule and fought Lion hand-to-hand until he got him back to camp. This time Boon didn't even curse. He stood in the door, muddy, spent, his huge gargoyle's face tragic and still amazed. "I missed him," he said. "I was in twenty-five feet of him and I missed him five times."

"But we have drawn blood," Major de Spain said. "General Compson drew blood. We have never done that before."

"But I missed him," Boon said. "I missed him five times. With Lion looking right at me."

"Never mind," Major de Spain said. "It was a damned fine race. And we drew blood. Next year we'll let General Compson or Walter ride Katie, and we'll get him."

Then McCaslin said, "Where is Lion, Boon?"

"I left him at Sam's," Boon said. He was already turning away. "I aint fit to sleep with him."

So he should have hated and feared Lion. Yet he did not. It seemed to him that there was a fatality in it. It seemed to him that something, he didn't know what, was beginning; had already begun. It was like the last act on a set stage. It was the beginning of the end of something, he didn't know what except that he would not grieve. He would be humble and proud that he had been found worthy to be a part of it too or even just to see it too.

3

IT WAS December. It was the coldest December he had ever remembered. They had been in camp four days over two weeks, waiting for the weather to soften so that Lion and Old Ben could run their yearly race. Then they would break camp and go home. Because of these unforeseen additional days which they had had to pass waiting on the weather, with nothing to do but play poker, the whisky had given out and he and Boon were being sent to Memphis with a suitcase and a note from Major de Spain to Mr Semmes, the distiller, to get more. That is, Major de Spain and McCaslin were sending Boon to get the whisky and sending him to see that Boon got back with it or most of it or at least some of it.

Tennie's Jim waked him at three. He dressed rapidly, shivering, not so much from the cold because a fresh fire already boomed and roared on the hearth, but in that dead winter hour when the blood and the heart are slow and sleep is incomplete. He crossed the gap between house and kitchen, the gap of iron earth beneath the brilliant and rigid night where dawn would not begin for three hours yet, tasting, tongue palate and to the very bottom of his lungs the searing dark, and entered the kitchen, the lamplit warmth where the stove glowed, fogging the windows, and where Boon already sat at the table at breakfast, hunched over his plate, almost in his plate, his working jaws blue with stubble and his face innocent of water and his coarse, horse-mane hair innocent of comb—the quarter Indian, grandson of a Chickasaw squaw, who on occasion resented with his hard and furious fists the intimation of one single drop of alien blood and on others, usually after whisky, affirmed with the same fists and the same fury that his father had been the full-blood Chickasaw and even a chief and that even his mother had been only half white. He was four inches over six feet; he had the mind of a child, the heart of a horse, and little hard shoe-button eyes without depth or meanness or generosity or viciousness or gentleness or anything else, in the ugliest face the boy had ever seen. It looked like somebody had found a walnut a little larger than a football and with a machinist's hammer had shaped features into it and then painted it, mostly red; not Indian red but a fine bright ruddy color which whisky might have had something to do with but which was mostly just happy and violent out-of-doors, the wrinkles in it not the residue of the forty years it had survived but from squinting into the sun or into the gloom of cane-brakes where game had run, baked into it by the camp fires before which he had lain trying to sleep on the cold November or December ground while waiting for daylight so he could rise and hunt again, as though time were merely something he walked through as he did through air, aging him no more than air did. He was brave, faithful, improvident and unreliable; he had neither profession job nor trade and owned one vice and one virtue: whisky, and that absolute and unquestioning fidelity to Major de Spain and the boy's cousin McCaslin. "Sometimes I'd call them both virtues," Major de Spain said once. "Or both vices," McCaslin said.

He ate his breakfast, hearing the dogs under the kitchen, wakened by the smell of frying meat or perhaps by the feet overhead. He heard Lion once, short and peremptory, as the best hunter in any camp has only to speak once to all save the fools, and none other of Major de Spain's and McCaslin's dogs were Lion's equal in size and strength and perhaps even in courage, but they were not fools; Old Ben had killed the last fool among them last year.

Tennie's Jim came in as they finished. The wagon was outside. Ash decided he would drive them over to the log-line where they would flag the outbound log-train and let Tennie's Jim wash the dishes. The boy knew why. It would not be the first time he had listened to old Ash badgering Boon.

It was cold. The wagon wheels banged and clattered on the frozen ground; the sky was fixed and brilliant. He was not shivering, he was shaking, slow and steady and hard, the food he had just eaten still warm and solid inside him while his outside shook slow and steady around it as though his stomach floated loose. "They wont run this morning," he said. "No dog will have any nose today."

"Cep Lion," Ash said. "Lion dont need no nose. All he need is a bear." He had wrapped his feet in towsacks and he had a quilt from his pallet bed on the kitchen floor drawn over his head and wrapped around him until in the thin brilliant starlight he looked like nothing at all that the boy had ever seen before. "He run a bear through a thousand-acre ice-house. Catch him too. Them other dogs dont matter because they aint going to keep up with Lion nohow, long as he got a bear in front of him."

"What's wrong with the other dogs?" Boon said. "What the hell do you know about it anyway? This is the first time you've had your tail out of that kitchen since we got here except to chop a little wood."

"Aint nothing wrong with them," Ash said. "And long as it's left up to them, aint nothing going to be. I just wish I had knowed all my life how to take care of my health good as them hounds knows."

"Well, they aint going to run this morning," Boon said. His voice was harsh and positive. "Major promised they wouldn't until me and Ike get back."

"Weather gonter break today. Gonter soft up. Rain by night." Then Ash laughed, chuckled, somewhere inside the quilt which concealed even his face. "Hum up here, mules!" he said, jerking the reins so that the mules leaped forward and snatched the lurching and banging wagon for several feet before they slowed again into their quick, short-paced, rapid plodding. "Sides, I like to know why Major need to wait on you. It's Lion he aiming to use. I aint never heard tell of you bringing no bear nor no other kind of meat into this camp."

*Now Boon's going to curse Ash or maybe even hit him,* the boy thought. But Boon never did, never had; the boy knew he never would even though four years ago Boon had shot five times with a borrowed pistol at a negro on the street in Jefferson, with the same result as when he had shot five times at Old Ben last fall. "By God," Boon said, "he aint going to put Lion or no other dog on nothing until I get back tonight. Because he promised me. Whip up them mules and keep them whipped up. Do you want me to freeze to death?"

They reached the log-line and built a fire. After a while the log-train came up out of the woods under the paling east and Boon flagged it. Then in the warm caboose the boy slept again while Boon and the conductor and brakeman talked about Lion and Old Ben as people later would talk about Sullivan and Kilrain and, later still, about Dempsey and Tunney. Dozing, swaying as the springless caboose lurched and clattered, he would hear them still talking, about the shoats and calves Old Ben had killed and the cribs he had rifled and the traps and deadfalls he had wrecked and the lead he probably carried under his hide—Old Ben, the two-toed bear in a land where bears with trap-ruined feet had been called Two-Toe or Three-Toe or Cripple-Foot for fifty years, only Old Ben was an extra bear (the head bear, General Compson called him) and so had earned a name such as a human man could have worn and not been sorry.

They reached Hoke's at sunup. They emerged from the warm caboose in their hunting clothes, the muddy boots and stained khaki and Boon's blue unshaven jowls. But that was all right. Hoke's was a sawmill and commissary and two stores and a loading-chute on a sidetrack from the main line, and all the men in it wore boots and khaki too. Presently the Memphis train came. Boon bought three packages of popcorn-and-molasses and a bottle of beer from the news butch and the boy went to sleep again to the sound of his chewing.

But in Memphis it was not all right. It was as if the high buildings and the hard pavements, the fine carriages and the horse cars and the men in starched collars and neckties made their boots and khaki look a little rougher and a little muddier and made Boon's beard look worse and more unshaven and his face look more and more like he should never have brought it out of the woods at all or at least out of reach of Major de Spain or McCaslin or someone who knew it and could have said, "Dont be afraid. He wont hurt you." He walked through the station, on the slick floor, his face moving as he worked the popcorn out of his teeth with his tongue, his legs spraddled and stiff in the hips as if he were walking on buttered glass, and that blue stubble on his face like the filings from a new gun-barrel. They passed the first saloon. Even through the closed doors the boy could seem to smell the sawdust and the reek of old drink. Boon began to cough. He coughed for something less than a minute. "Damn this cold," he said. "I'd sure like to know where I got it."

"Back there in the station," the boy said.

Boon had started to cough again. He stopped. He looked at the boy. "What?" he said.

"You never had it when we left camp nor on the train either." Boon looked at him, blinking. Then he stopped blinking. He didn't cough again. He said quietly:

"Lend me a dollar. Come on. You've got it. If you ever had one, you've still got it. I dont mean you are tight with your money because you aint. You just dont never seem to ever think of nothing you want. When I was sixteen a dollar bill melted off of me before I even had time to read the name of the bank that issued it." He said quietly: "Let me have a dollar, Ike."

"You promised Major. You promised McCaslin. Not till we get back to camp."

"All right," Boon said in that quiet and patient voice. "What can I do on just one dollar? You aint going to lend me another."

"You're damn right I aint," the boy said, his voice quiet too, cold with rage which was not at Boon, remembering: Boon snoring in a hard chair in the kitchen so he could watch the clock and wake him and McCaslin and drive them the seventeen miles in to Jefferson to catch the train to Memphis; the wild, never-bridled Texas paint pony which he had persuaded McCaslin to let him buy and which he and Boon had bought at auction for four dollars and seventy-five cents and fetched home wired between two gentle old mares with pieces of barbed wire and which had never even seen shelled corn before and didn't even know what it was unless the grains were bugs maybe and at last (he was ten and Boon had been ten all his life) Boon said the pony was gentled and with a towsack over its head and four negroes to hold it they backed it into an old two-wheeled cart and hooked up the gear and he and Boon got up and Boon said, "All right, boys. Let him go" and one of the Negroes—it was Tennie's Jim—snatched the towsack off and leaped for his life and they lost the first wheel against a post of the open gate only at that moment Boon caught him by the scruff of the neck and flung him into the roadside ditch so he only saw the rest of it in fragments: the other wheel as it slammed through the side gate and crossed the back yard and leaped up onto the gallery and scraps of the cart here and there along the road and Boon vanishing rapidly on his stomach in the leaping and spurting dust and still holding the reins until they broke too and two days later they finally caught the pony seven miles away still wearing the hames and the headstall of the bridle around its neck like a duchess with two necklaces at one time. He gave Boon the dollar.

"All right," Boon said. "Come on in out of the cold."

"I aint cold," he said.

"You can have some lemonade."

"I dont want any lemonade."

The door closed behind him. The sun was well up now. It was a brilliant day, though Ash had said it would rain before night. Already it was warmer; they could run tomorrow. He felt the old lift of the heart, as pristine as ever, as on the first day; he would never lose it, no matter how old in hunting and pursuit: the best, the best of all breathing, the humility and the pride. He must stop thinking about it. Already it seemed to him that he was running, back to the station, to the tracks themselves: the first train going south; he must stop thinking about it. The street was busy. He watched the big Norman draft horses, the Percherons; the trim carriages from which the men in the fine overcoats and the ladies rosy in furs descended and entered the station. (They were still next door to it but one.) Twenty years ago his father had ridden into Memphis as a member of Colonel Sartoris' horse in Forrest's command, up Main street and (the tale told) into the lobby of the Gayoso Hotel where the Yankee officers sat in the leather chairs spitting into the tall bright cuspidors and then out again, scot-free——

The door opened behind him. Boon was wiping his mouth on the back of his hand. "All right," he said. "Let's go tend to it and get the hell out of here."

They went and had the suitcase packed. He never knew where or when Boon got the other bottle. Doubtless Mr Semmes gave it to him. When they reached Hoke's again at sundown, it was empty. They could get a return train to Hoke's in two hours; they went straight back to the station as Major de Spain and then McCaslin had told Boon to do and then ordered him to do and had sent the boy along to see that he did. Boon took the first drink from his bottle in the wash room. A man in a uniform cap came to tell him he couldn't drink there and looked at Boon's face once and said nothing. The next time he was pouring into his water glass beneath the edge of a table in the restaurant when the manager (she was a woman) did tell him he couldn't drink there and he went back to the wash room. He had been telling the Negro waiter and all the other people in the restaurant who couldn't help but hear him and who had never heard of Lion and didn't want to, about Lion and Old Ben. Then he happened to think of the zoo. He had found out that there was another

train to Hoke's at three oclock and so they would spend the time at the zoo and take the three oclock train until he came back from the wash room for the third time. Then they would take the first train back to camp, get Lion and come back to the zoo where, he said, the bears were fed on ice cream and lady fingers and he would match Lion against them all.

So they missed the first train, the one they were supposed to take, but he got Boon onto the three oclock train and they were all right again, with Boon not even going to the wash room now but drinking in the aisle and talking about Lion and the men he buttonholed no more daring to tell Boon he couldn't drink there than the man in the station had dared.

When they reached Hoke's at sundown, Boon was asleep. The boy waked him at last and got him and the suitcase off the train and he even persuaded him to eat some supper at the sawmill commissary. So he was all right when they got in the caboose of the log-train to go back into the woods, with the sun going down red and the sky already overcast and the ground would not freeze tonight. It was the boy who slept now, sitting behind the ruby stove while the springless caboose jumped and clattered and Boon and the brakeman and the conductor talked about Lion and Old Ben because they knew what Boon was talking about because this was home. "Overcast and already thawing," Boon said. "Lion will get him tomorrow."

It would have to be Lion, or somebody. It would not be Boon. He had never hit anything bigger than a squirrel that anybody ever knew, except the Negro woman that day when he was shooting at the Negro man. He was a big Negro and not ten feet away but Boon shot five times with the pistol he had borrowed from Major de Spain's Negro coachman and the Negro he was shooting at outed with a dollar-and-a-half mail-order pistol and would have burned Boon down with it only it never went off, it just went snick-snicksnicksnicksnick five times and Boon still blasting away and he broke a plate-glass window that cost McCaslin forty-five dollars and hit a Negro woman who happened to be passing in the leg only Major de Spain paid for that; he and McCaslin cut cards, the plate-glass window against the Negro woman's leg. And the first day on stand this year, the first morning in camp, the buck ran right over Boon; he heard Boon's old pump gun go whow. whow. whow. whow. whow. and then his voice: "God damn, here he comes! Head him! Head him!" and when he got there the buck's tracks and the five exploded shells were not twenty paces apart.

There were five guests in camp that night, from Jefferson: Mr. Bayard Sartoris and his son and General Compson's son and two others. And the next morning he looked out the window, into the gray thin drizzle of daybreak which Ash had predicted, and there they were, standing and squatting beneath the thin rain, almost two dozen of them who had fed Old Ben corn and shoats and even calves for ten years, in their worn hats and hunting coats and overalls which any town Negro would have thrown away or burned and only the rubber boots strong and sound, and the worn and blueless guns and some even without guns. While they ate breakfast a dozen more arrived, mounted and on foot: loggers from the camp thirteen miles below and sawmill men from Hoke's and the only gun among them that one which the log-train conductor carried: so that when they went into the woods this morning Major de Spain led a party almost as strong, excepting that some of them were not armed, as some he had led in the last darkening days of '64 and '65. The little yard would not hold them. They overflowed it, into the lane where Major de Spain sat his mare while Ash in his dirty apron thrust the greasy cartridges into his carbine and passed it up to him and the great grave blue dog stood at his stirrup not as a dog stands but as a horse stands, blinking his sleepy topaz eyes at nothing, deaf even to the yelling of the hounds which Boon and Tennie's Jim held on leash.

"We'll put General Compson on Katie this morning," Major de Spain said. "He drew blood last year; if he'd had a mule then that would have stood, he would have——"

"No," General Compson said. "I'm too old to go helling through the woods on a mule or a horse or anything else any more. Besides, I had my chance last year and missed it. I'm going on a stand this morning. I'm going to let that boy ride Katie."

"No, wait," McCaslin said. "Ike's got the rest of his life to hunt bears in. Let somebody else——"

"No," General Compson said. "I want Ike to ride Katie. He's already a better woodsman than you or me either and in another ten years he'll be as good as Walter."

At first he couldn't believe it, not until Major de Spain spoke to him. Then he was up, on the one-eyed mule which would not spook at wild blood, looking down at the dog motionless at Major de Spain's stirrup, looking in the gray streaming light bigger than a calf, bigger than he knew it actually was—the big head, the chest almost as big as his own, the blue hide beneath which the muscles

flinched or quivered to no touch since the heart which drove blood to them loved no man and no thing, standing as a horse stands yet different from a horse which infers only weight and speed while Lion inferred not only courage and all else that went to make up the will and desire to pursue and kill, but endurance, the will and desire to endure beyond all imaginable limits of flesh in order to overtake and slay. Then the dog looked at him. It moved its head and looked at him across the trivial uproar of the hounds, out of the yellow eyes as depthless as Boon's, as free as Boon's of meanness or generosity or gentleness or viciousness. They were just cold and sleepy. Then it blinked, and he knew it was not looking at him and never had been, without even bothering to turn its head away.

That morning he heard the first cry. Lion had already vanished while Sam and Tennie's Jim were putting saddles on the mule and horse which had drawn the wagon and he watched the hounds as they crossed and cast, snuffing and whimpering, until they too disappeared. Then he and Major de Spain and Sam and Tennie's Jim rode after them and heard the first cry out of the wet and thawing woods not two hundred yards ahead, high, with that abject, almost human quality he had come to know, and the other hounds joining in until the gloomed woods rang and clamored. They rode then. It seemed to him that he could actually see the big blue dog boring on, silent, and the bear too: the thick, locomotive-like shape which he had seen that day four years ago crossing the blow-down, crashing on ahead of the dogs faster than he had believed it could have moved, drawing away even from the running mules. He heard a shotgun, once. The woods had opened, they were going fast, the clamor faint and fading on ahead; they passed the man who had fired—a swamper, a pointing arm, a gaunt face, the small black orifice of his yelling studded with rotten teeth.

He heard the changed note in the hounds' uproar and two hundred yards ahead he saw them. The bear had turned. He saw Lion drive in without pausing and saw the bear strike him aside and lunge into the yelling hounds and kill one of them almost in its tracks and whirl and run again. Then they were in a streaming tide of dogs. He heard Major de Spain and Tennie's Jim shouting and the pistol sound of Tennie's Jim's leather thong as he tried to turn them. Then he and Sam Fathers were riding alone. One of the hounds had kept on with Lion though. He recognized its voice. It was the young hound which even a year ago had had no judgment and which, by the lights of the other hounds anyway, still had none. *Maybe that's what courage is,* he thought. "Right," Sam said behind him. "Right. We got to turn him from the river if we can."

Now they were in cane: a brake. He knew the path through it as well as Sam did. They came out of the undergrowth and struck the entrance almost exactly. It would traverse the brake and come out onto a high open ridge above the river. He heard the flat clap of Walter Ewell's rifle, then two more. "No," Sam said. "I can hear the hound. Go on."

They emerged from the narrow roofless tunnel of snapping and hissing cane, still galloping, onto the open ridge below which the thick yellow river, reflectionless in the gray and streaming light, seemed not to move. Now he could hear the hound too. It was not running. The cry was a high frantic yapping and Boon was running along the edge of the bluff, his old gun leaping and jouncing against his back on its sling made of a piece of cotton plowline. He whirled and ran up to them, wild-faced, and flung himself onto the mule behind the boy. "That damn boat!" he cried. "It's on the other side! He went straight across! Lion was too close to him! That little hound too! Lion was so close I couldn't shoot! Go on!" he cried, beating his heels into the mule's flanks. "Go on!"

They plunged down the bank, slipping and sliding in the thawed earth, crashing through the willows and into the water. He felt no shock, no cold, he on one side of the swimming mule, grasping the pommel with one hand and holding his gun above the water with the other, Boon opposite him. Sam was behind them somewhere, and then the river, the water about them, was full of dogs. They swam faster than the mules; they were scrabbling up the bank before the mules touched bottom. Major de Spain was whooping from the bank they had just left and, looking back, he saw Tennie's Jim and the horse as they went into the water.

Now the woods ahead of them and the rain-heavy air were one uproar. It rang and clamored; it echoed and broke against the bank behind them and reformed and clamored and rang until it seemed to the boy that all the hounds which had ever bayed game in this land were yelling down at him. He got his leg over the mule as it came up out of the water. Boon didn't try to mount again. He grasped one stirrup as they went up the bank and crashed through the undergrowth which fringed the bluff and saw the bear, on its hind feet, its back against a tree while the bellowing hounds swirled around it and once more Lion drove in, leaping clear of the ground.

This time the bear didn't strike him down. It caught the dog in both arms, almost loverlike, and they both went down. He was off the mule now. He drew back both hammers of the gun but he could see nothing but moiling spotted hound-bodies until the bear surged up again. Boon was yelling something, he could not tell what; he could see Lion still clinging to the bear's throat and he saw the bear, half erect, strike one of the hounds with one paw and hurl it five or six feet and then, rising and rising as though it would never stop, stand erect again and begin to rake at Lion's belly with its forepaws. Then Boon was running. The boy saw the gleam of the blade in his hand and watched him leap among the hounds, hurdling them, kicking them aside as he ran, and fling himself astride the bear as he had hurled himself onto the mule, his legs locked around the bear's belly, his left arm under the bear's throat where Lion clung, and the glint of the knife as it rose and fell.

It fell just once. For an instant they almost resembled a piece of statuary: the clinging dog, the bear, the man stride its back, working and probing the buried blade. Then they went down, pulled over backward by Boon's weight, Boon underneath. It was the bear's back which reappeared first but at once Boon was astride it again. He had never released the knife and again the boy saw the almost infinitesimal movement of his arm and shoulder as he probed and sought; then the bear surged erect, raising with it the man and the dog too, and turned and still carrying the man and the dog it took two or three steps toward the woods on its hind feet as a man would have walked and crashed down. It didn't collapse, crumple. It fell all of a piece, as a tree falls, so that all three of them, man dog and bear, seemed to bounce once.

He and Tennie's Jim ran forward. Boon was kneeling at the bear's head. His left ear was shredded, his left coat sleeve was completely gone, his right boot had been ripped from knee to instep; the bright blood thinned in the thin rain down his leg and hand and arm and down the side of his face which was no longer wild but was quite calm. Together they prized Lion's jaws from the bear's throat. "Easy, goddamn it," Boon said. "Cant you see his guts are all out of him?" He began to remove his coat. He spoke to Tennie's Jim in that calm voice: "Bring the boat up. It's about a hundred yards down the bank there. I saw it." Tennie's Jim rose and went away. Then, and he could not remember if it had been a call or an exclamation from Tennie's Jim or if he had glanced up by chance, he saw Tennie's Jim stooping and saw Sam Fathers lying motionless on his face in the trampled mud.

The mule had not thrown him. He remembered that Sam was down too even before Boon began to run. There was no mark on him whatever and when he and Boon turned him over, his eyes were open and he said something in that tongue which he and Joe Baker had used to speak together. But he couldn't move. Tennie's Jim brought the skiff up; they could hear him shouting to Major de Spain across the river. Boon wrapped Lion in his hunting coat and carried him down to the skiff and they carried Sam down and returned and hitched the bear to the one-eyed mule's saddle-bow with Tennie's Jim's leash-thong and dragged him down to the skiff and got him into it and left Tennie's Jim to swim the horse and the two mules back across. Major de Spain caught the bow of the skiff as Boon jumped out and past him before it touched the bank. He looked at Old Ben and said quietly: "Well." Then he walked into the water and leaned down and touched Sam and Sam looked up at him and said something in that old tongue he and Joe Baker spoke. "You dont know what happened?" Major de Spain said.

"No, sir," the boy said. "It wasn't the mule. It wasn't anything. He was off the mule when Boon ran in on the bear. Then we looked up and he was lying on the ground." Boon was shouting at Tennie's Jim, still in the middle of the river.

"Come on, goddamn it!" he said. "Bring me that mule!"

"What do you want with a mule?" Major de Spain said.

Boon didn't even look at him. "I'm going to Hoke's to get the doctor," he said in that calm voice, his face quite calm beneath the steady thinning of the bright blood.

"You need a doctor yourself," Major de Spain said. "Tennie's Jim——"

"Damn that," Boon said. He turned on Major de Spain. His face was still calm, only his voice was a pitch higher. "Cant you see his goddamn guts are all out of him?"

"Boon!" Major de Spain said. They looked at one another. Boon was a good head taller than Major de Spain; even the boy was taller now than Major de Spain.

"I've got to get the doctor," Boon said. "His goddamn guts——"

"All right," Major de Spain said. Tennie's Jim came up out of the water. The horse and the sound mule had already scented Old Ben; they surged and plunged all the way up to the top of the bluff, dragging Tennie's Jim with them, before he could stop them and tie them and come back. Major de Spain unlooped the leather thong of his compass from his buttonhole and gave it to Tennie's Jim. "Go straight to Hoke's," he said. "Bring Doctor Crawford back with you. Tell him there are two men to be looked at. Take my mare. Can you find the road from here?"

"Yes, sir," Tennie's Jim said.

"All right," Major de Spain said. "Go on." He turned to the boy. "Take the mules and the horse and go back and get the wagon. We'll go on down the river in the boat to Coon bridge. Meet us there. Can you find it again?"

"Yes, sir," the boy said.

"All right. Get started."

He went back to the wagon. He realized then how far they had run. It was already afternoon when he put the mules into the traces and tied the horse's lead-rope to the tail-gate. He reached Coon bridge at dusk. The skiff was already there. Before he could see it and almost before he could see the water he had to leap from the tilting wagon, still holding the reins, and work around to where he could grasp the bit and then the ear of the plunging sound mule and dig his heels and hold it until Boon came up the bank. The rope of the led horse had already snapped and it had already disappeared up the road toward camp. They turned the wagon around and took the mules out and he led the sound mule a hundred yards up the road and tied it. Boon had already brought Lion up to the wagon and Sam was sitting up in the skiff now and when they raised him he tried to walk, up the bank and to the wagon and he tried to climb into the wagon but Boon did not wait; he picked Sam up bodily and set him on the seat. Then they hitched Old Ben to the one-eyed mule's saddle again and dragged him up the bank and set two skid-poles into the open tail-gate and got him into the wagon and he went and got the sound mule and Boon fought it into the traces, striking it across its hard hollow-sounding face until it came into position and stood trembling. Then the rain came down, as though it had held off all day waiting on them.

They returned to camp through it, through the streaming and sightless dark, hearing long before they saw any light the horn and the spaced shots to guide them. When they came to Sam's dark little hut he tried to stand up. He spoke again in the tongue of the old fathers; then he said clearly: "Let me out. Let me out."

"He hasn't got any fire," Major said. "Go on!" he said sharply.

But Sam was struggling now, trying to stand up. "Let me out, master," he said. "Let me go home."

So he stopped the wagon and Boon got down and lifted Sam out. He did not wait to let Sam try to walk this time. He carried him into the hut and Major de Spain got light on a paper spill from the buried embers on the hearth and lit the lamp and Boon put Sam on his bunk and drew off his boots and Major de Spain covered him and the boy was not there, he was holding the mules, the sound one which was trying again to bolt since when the wagon stopped Old Ben's scent drifted forward again along the streaming blackness of air, but Sam's eyes were probably open again on that profound look which saw further than them or the hut, further than the death of a bear and the dying of a dog. Then they went on, toward the long wailing of the horn and the shots which seemed each to linger intact somewhere in the thick streaming air until the next spaced report joined and blended with it, to the lighted house, the bright streaming windows, the quiet faces as Boon entered, bloody and quite calm, carrying the bundled coat. He laid Lion, blood coat and all, on his stale sheetless pallet bed which not even Ash, as deft in the house as a woman, could ever make smooth.

The sawmill doctor from Hoke's was already there. Boon would not let the doctor touch him until he had seen to Lion. He wouldn't risk giving Lion chloroform. He put the entrails back and sewed him up without it while Major de Spain held his head and Boon his feet. But he never tried to move. He lay there, the yellow eyes open upon nothing while the quiet men in the new hunting clothes and in the old ones crowded into the little airless room rank with the smell of Boon's body and garments, and watched. Then the doctor cleaned and disinfected Boon's face and arm and leg and bandaged them and, the boy in front with a lantern and the doctor and McCaslin and Major de Spain and General Compson following, they went to Sam Fathers' hut. Tennie's Jim had built up the fire; he squatted before it, dozing. Sam had not moved since Boon had put him in the bunk and Major de Spain had covered him with the blankets, yet he opened his eyes and looked from one to another of the faces and when McCaslin touched his shoulder and said, "Sam. The doctor wants to look at you," he even drew his hands out of the blanket and began to fumble at his shirt buttons until McCaslin said, "Wait. We'll do it." They undressed him. He lay there—the copper-brown, almost hairless body, the old man's body, the old man, the wild man not even one generation from the woods, childless, kinless, peopleless —motionless, his eyes open but no longer looking at any of them, while the doctor examined him and drew the blankets up and put the stethoscope back into his bag and snapped the bag and only the boy knew that Sam too was going to die.

"Exhaustion," the doctor said. "Shock maybe. A man his age swimming rivers in December. He'll be all right. Just make him stay in bed for a day or two. Will there be somebody here with him?"

"There will be somebody here," Major de Spain said.

They went back to the house, to the rank little room where Boon still sat on the pallet bed with Lion's head under his hand while the men, the ones who had hunted behind Lion and the ones who had never seen him before today, came quietly in to look at him and went away. Then it was dawn and they all went out into the yard to look at Old Ben, with his eyes open too and his lips snarled back from his worn teeth and his mutilated foot and the little hard lumps under his skin which were the old bullets (there were fifty-two of them, buckshot rifle and ball) and the single almost invisible slit under his left shoulder where Boon's blade had finally found his life. Then Ash began to beat on the bottom of the dishpan with a heavy spoon to call them to breakfast and it was the first time he could remember hearing no sound from the dogs under the kitchen while they were eating. It was as if the old bear, even dead there in the yard, was a more potent terror still than they could face without Lion between them.

The rain had stopped during the night. By midmorning the thin sun appeared, rapidly burning away mist and cloud, warming the air and the earth; it would be one of those windless Mississippi December days which are a sort of Indian summer's Indian summer. They moved Lion out to the front gallery, into the sun. It was Boon's idea. "Goddamn it," he said, "he never did want to stay in the house until I made him. You know that." He took a crowbar and loosened the floor boards under his pallet bed so it could be raised, mattress and all, without disturbing Lion's position, and they carried him out to the gallery and put him down facing the woods.

Then he and the doctor and McCaslin and Major de Spain went to Sam's hut. This time Sam didn't open his eyes and his breathing was so quiet, so peaceful that they could hardly see that he breathed. The doctor didn't even take out his stethoscope nor even touch him. "He's all right," the doctor said. "He didn't even catch cold. He just quit."

"Quit?" McCaslin said.

"Yes. Old people do that sometimes. Then they get a good night's sleep or maybe it's just a drink of whisky, and they change their minds."

They returned to the house. And then they began to arrive—the swamp-dwellers, the gaunt men who ran trap-lines and lived on quinine and coons and river water, the farmers of little corn- and cotton-patches along the bottom's edge whose fields and cribs and pig-pens the old bear had rifled, the loggers from the camp and the sawmill men from Hoke's and the town men from further away than that, whose hounds the old bear had slain and traps and deadfalls he had wrecked and whose lead he carried. They came up mounted and on foot and in wagons, to enter the yard and look at him and then go on to the front where Lion lay, filling the little yard and overflowing it until there were almost a hundred of them squatting and standing in the warm and drowsing sunlight, talking quietly of hunting, of the game and the dogs which ran it, of hounds and bear and deer and men of yesterday vanished from the earth, while from time to time the great blue dog would open his eyes, not as if he were listening to them but as though to look at the woods for a moment before closing his eyes again, to remember the woods or to see that they were still there. He died at sundown.

Major de Spain broke camp that night. They carried Lion into the woods, or Boon carried him that is, wrapped in a quilt from his bed, just as he had refused to let anyone else touch Lion yesterday until the doctor got there; Boon carrying Lion, and the boy and General Compson and Walter and still almost fifty of them following with lanterns and lighted pine-knots—men from Hoke's and even further, who would have to ride out of the bottom in the dark, and swampers and trappers who would have to walk even, scattering toward the little hidden huts where they lived. And Boon would let nobody else dig the grave either and lay Lion in it and cover him and then General Compson stood at the head of it while the blaze and smoke of the pine-knots streamed away among the winter branches and spoke as he would have spoken over a man. Then they returned to camp. Major de Spain and McCaslin and Ash had rolled and tied all the bedding. The mules were hitched to the wagon and pointed out of the bottom and the wagon was already loaded and the stove in the kitchen was cold and the table was set with scraps of cold food and bread and only the coffee was hot when the boy ran into the kitchen where Major de Spain and McCaslin had already eaten. "What?" he cried. "What? I'm not going."

"Yes," McCaslin said, "we're going out tonight. Major wants to get on back home."

"No!" he said. "I'm going to stay."

"You've got to be back in school Monday. You've already missed a week more than I intended. It will take you from now until Monday to catch up. Sam's all right. You heard Doctor Crawford. I'm going to leave Boon and Tennie's Jim both to stay with him until he feels like getting up."

He was panting. The others had come in. He looked rapidly and almost frantically around at the other faces. Boon had a fresh bottle. He upended it and started the cork by striking the bottom of the bottle with the heel of his hand and drew the cork with his teeth and spat it out and drank. "You're damn right you're going back to school," Boon said. "Or I'll burn the tail off of you myself if Cass dont, whether you are sixteen or sixty. Where in hell do you expect to get without education? Where would Cass be? Where in hell would I be if I hadn't never went to school?"

He looked at McCaslin again. He could feel his breath coming shorter and shorter and shallower and shallower, as if there were not enough air in the kitchen for that many to breathe. "This is just Thursday. I'll come home Sunday night on one of the horses. I'll come home Sunday, then. I'll make up the time I lost studying Sunday night, McCaslin," he said, without even despair.

"No, I tell you," McCaslin said. "Sit down here and eat your supper. We're going out to——"

"Hold up, Cass," General Compson said. The boy did not know General Compson had moved until he put his hand on his shoulder. "What is it, bud?" he said.

"I've got to stay," he said. "I've got to."

"All right," General Compson said. "You can stay. If missing an extra week of school is going to throw you so far behind you'll have to sweat to find out what some hired pedagogue put between the covers of a book, you better quit altogether.— And you shut up, Cass," he said, though McCaslin had not spoken. "You've got one foot straddled into a farm and the other foot straddled into a bank; you aint even got a good hand-hold where this boy was already an old man long before you damned Sartorises and Edmondses invented farms and banks to keep yourselves from having to find out what this boy was born knowing and fearing too maybe but without being afraid, that could go ten miles on a compass because he wanted to look at a bear none of us had ever got near enough to put a bullet in and looked at the bear and came the ten miles back on the compass in the dark; maybe by God that's the why and the wherefore of farms and banks.—I reckon you still aint going to tell what it is?"

But still he could not. "I've got to stay," he said.

"All right," General Compson said. "There's plenty of grub left. And you'll come home Sunday, like you promised McCaslin? Not Sunday night: Sunday."

"Yes, sir," he said.

"All right," General Compson said. "Sit down and eat, boys," he said. "Let's get started. It's going to be cold before we get home."

They ate. The wagon was already loaded and ready to depart; all they had to do was to get into it. Boon would drive them out to the road, to the farmer's stable where the surrey had been left. He stood beside the wagon, in silhouette on the sky, turbaned like a Paythan and taller than any there, the bottle tilted. Then he flung the bottle from his lips without even lowering it, spinning and glinting in the faint starlight empty. "Them that's going," he said, "get in the goddamn wagon. Them that aint, get out of the goddamn way." The others got in. Boon mounted to the seat beside General Compson and the wagon moved, on into the obscurity until the boy could no longer see it, even the moving density of it amid the greater night. But he could still hear it, for a long while: the slow, deliberate banging of the wooden frame as it lurched from rut to rut. And he could hear Boon even when he could no longer hear the wagon. He was singing, harsh, tuneless, loud.

That was Thursday. On Saturday morning Tennie's Jim left on McCaslin's woods-horse which had not been out of the bottom one time now in six years, and late that afternoon rode through the gate on the spent horse and on to the commissary where McCaslin was rationing the tenants and the wage-hands for the coming week, and this time McCaslin forestalled any necessity or risk of having to wait while Major de Spain's surrey was being horsed and harnessed. He took their own, and with Tennie's Jim already asleep in the back seat he drove in to Jefferson and waited while Major de Spain changed to boots and put on his overcoat, and they drove the thirty miles in the dark of that night and at daybreak on Sunday morning they swapped to the waiting mare and mule and as the sun rose they rode out of the jungle and onto the low ridge where they had buried Lion: the low mound of unannealed earth where Boon's spade-marks still showed and beyond the grave the platform of freshly cut saplings bound between four posts and the blanket-wrapped bundle upon the platform and Boon and the boy squatting between the platform and the grave until Boon, the bandage removed, ripped, from his head so that the long scoriations of Old Ben's claws resembled crusted tar in the sunlight, sprang up and threw down upon them with the old gun with which he had never been known to hit anything although McCaslin was already off the mule, kicked both feet free of the irons and vaulted down before the mule had stopped, walking toward Boon.

"Stand back," Boon said. "By God, you wont touch him. Stand back, McCaslin." Still McCaslin came on, fast yet without haste.

"Cass!" Major de Spain said. Then he said "Boon! You, Boon!" and he was down too and the boy rose too, quickly, and still McCaslin came on not fast but steady and walked up to the grave and reached his hand steadily out, quickly yet still not fast, and took hold the gun by the middle so that he and Boon faced one another across Lion's grave, both holding the gun, Boon's spent indomitable amazed and frantic face almost a head higher than McCaslin's beneath the black scoriations of beast's claws and then Boon's chest began to heave as though there were not enough air in all the woods, in all the wilderness, for all of them, for him and anyone else, even for him alone.

"Turn it loose, Boon," McCaslin said.

"You damn little spindling—" Boon said. "Dont you know I can take it away from you? Dont you know I can tie it around your neck like a damn cravat?"

"Yes," McCaslin said. "Turn it loose, Boon."

"This is the way he wanted it. He told us. He told us exactly how to do it. And by God you aint going to move him. So we did it like he said, and I been sitting here ever since to keep the damn wildcats and varmints away from him and by God—" Then McCaslin had the gun, downslanted while he pumped the slide, the five shells snicking out of it so fast that the last one was almost out before the first one touched the ground and McCaslin dropped the gun behind him without once having taken his eyes from Boon's.

"Did you kill him, Boon?" he said. Then Boon moved. He turned, he moved like he was still drunk and then for a moment blind too, one hand out as he blundered toward the big tree and seemed to stop walking before he reached the tree so that he plunged, fell toward it, flinging up both hands and catching himself against the tree and turning until his back was against it, backing with the tree's trunk his wild spent scoriated face and the tremendous heave and collapse of his chest, McCaslin following, facing him again, never once having moved his eyes from Boon's eyes. "Did you kill him, Boon?"

"No!" Boon said. "No!"

"Tell the truth," McCaslin said. "I would have done it if he had asked me to." Then the boy moved. He was between them, facing McCaslin; the water felt as if it had burst and sprung not from his eyes alone but from his whole face, like sweat.

"Leave him alone!" he cried. "Goddamn it! Leave him alone!"

# AUTHOR-TITLE INDEX

Authors' names are in **boldface type,** and the page numbers of the introductions to their works are in *italics*.

# INDEX OF FIRST LINES OF POEMS

D 9
E 0
F 1
G 2
H 3
I 4
J 5